200 SEASONS
— OF —
AUSTRALIAN
Cricket

200 SEASONS
– OF –
AUSTRALIAN
Cricket

The Ashes won, 1989.

IRONBARK

Clarrie Grimmett.

First published 1997 in Ironbark by Pan Macmillan Australia Pty Limited.
St Martins Tower, 31 Market Street, Sydney

Copyright © Pan Macmillan Australia Limited 1997
Published in association with the Australian Cricket Board.

National Library of Australia
cataloguing-in-publication data:

200 Seasons of Australian Cricket

ISBN 0 330 36034 5

1. Cricket - Australia - History. 2. Cricket players - Australia - Biography. I Hutchinson,
Garrie, 1949-. II Ross, John, 1938 -. III Title Two hundred seasons of Australian cricket.

796.358650994

Printed in Australia by McPherson's Printing Group.

Contents

Allan Border, 200, fourth Test, Leeds, 1993.

200 Seasons of Australian Cricket was produced by Ross, Hutchinson & Associates for Pan Macmillan Australia.

Conceived and edited by Garrie Hutchinson and John Ross

Writers: David Austin, Damien Cash, Russell Holmesby, Garrie Hutchinson, John Ross

Editorial Services: Peter Ascot, Damien Cash

Production Services: Ken Yendell

Design Services: David Constable

Research: Lynda Carroll

Index: Fay Donlevy

Statistics: Ross Dundas

Photographic Services: Sporting Pix Australia

Cover: David Lancashire Design.

Acknowledgements

A book project the size and duration of *200 Seasons of Australian Cricket* has necessarily involved a large number of people over a long period of time. We began thinking seriously about the book just after Mark Taylor won the 1995 series in the West Indies. We have finished it 13 Tests and two summers later - just as Australia is about to take on England in 1997.

At the New South Wales Cricket Association, Heather Kelly, John Wood and Stephen Gibbs Honorary Librarian; Queensland Cricket Association, Warwick Torrens and Ian Sturgess; Victorian Cricket Association, Ken Jacobs; the Oxley Library, Diane Burn.

At the State Library of Victoria: Kim Wilson, Graham Barnett, Deirdre Wilmott, Phillip Carr, Annemarie Carnell, Don Baker, Michael Koch, Sandra Sindici,

bible, this is it. We were privileged to be able to consult a good deal of Vol 2, to 1977 as well, before publication.

In addition Alf Batchelder, Kate Ryan, Pauline Maloney, John Carroll, Gordon Carroll, Rosemary Carroll, Vivian Carroll, Brenda Jackson, Arthur Jackson and cricket bookseller extraordinaire Roger Page helped in a variety of ways.

Every endeavour has been made to trace and acknowledge copy-

Heroes all: (front) Fred Spofforth, Tom Horan, Jack Blackham, Harry Boyle.

We are most grateful to the Australian Cricket Board and in particular David Fouvy, Narelle Finch and Ian McDonald for their co-operation; to Bob Parish for his devotion to the facts, in correcting our errors; and to chairman Dennis Rogers for his foreword, and board members Colin Egar and Des Rundle for conversation at the cricket. Any remaining errors of fact or interpretation are ours alone.

We acknowledge the support of Ansett Australia, through Andrew Geils and Wendi Pearce, for this project.

The illustrations could not have been inspected, collected, collated and donated without the co-operation of many people.

At the Melbourne Cricket Club Museum: Jenna Pullman, Kristin Thornton and Graeme Atkinson, and in the MCC Library, Ross Peacock and David Studham.

Steve Shannon, Mario Frattin, Boris Bojovski, Neil Munro, Jula Ryder, Laurie Ferdinands.

At *The Age* Sally Dugan; in the *Age* Picture Library, Paul Rovere, Catherine Ryan, Jacqui Cheng, and Kylie Moss.

At Sporting Pix, Kerryn Feder and Stuart Milligan; Sport - The Library Geoff Crowe; at the Australian Picture Library, John Mikalcic. And Delly Carr at Sportshoot

Special thanks are due to Peter Nicholson, John Spooner and Ron Tandberg for their illustrations, to Alex Hutchinson, Sarah Ross and Margeth Heliosz for additional editorial services, to Robert Rozetsky for renting us his Mac.

Sources for this book are listed in the bibliography, but special mention must be made of Ray Webster's *First Class Cricket in Australia Vol 1 1850-51 to 1941-42* (Ray Webster, 1991). If there is an Australian cricket statistical

right holders, as listed in the picture credits. The publishers apologise for any accidental infringement and welcome information that would rectify any error or omission in subsequent editions.

'There is only one team sport that crosses the boundaries ...'

There is only one team sport that crosses the boundaries of all states and territories in Australia and still maintains a cherished place in the hearts of all those who play and watch it. Only one team sport in Australia can provoke a discussion on the merits of a player or a performance, be it East or West, North or South.

That is, of course, cricket.

While Australians argue over their favourite football code, cricket is the summer sport that all can play and offer an opinion upon.

Australia's cricket history is as rich and diverse as the country itself, making *200 Seasons of Australian Cricket* a compelling work.

This book is not an official history of the sport but is an unashamedly Australian view of the game in this country, season-by-season, over the past 200 years.

Here are the highs, and lows, of our game and all the heroes who have written their name into history – from Bannerman and Spofforth, through Trumper, Bradman and O'Reilly, to the stars of today.

Australian cricket has a proud history and the Australian Cricket Board, together with the players, looks forward to a similarly successful future.

Denis W Rogers
Chairman
Australian Cricket Board.

'The game has certainly travelled well'

Cricket was one of Australia's earliest imports and the game has certainly travelled well.

It is played by Australians at countless locations the length and breadth of our land. And 200 seasons have given the game a strongly Australian ingredient to add to the cosmopolitan flavour which cricket now enjoys around the globe.

We at Ansett Australia are proud that Australian Test and Sheffield Shield cricket chooses to travel with us. We wish players at all levels the best of luck for this summer's cricket, we congratulate the contributors to this collection and are sure that lovers of the noble game will have their affection for the sport increased by this book.

Rod Eddington
Executive Chairman
Ansett Australia

Glen McGrath takes the wicket of Shivnarine Chanderpaul, 3rd Test 1996/97.

Cricket in Old Sydney Town

A view of Hyde Park, Sydney in the summer of 1842. A cricket match is in progress, probably involving the Australian Club – and some heavy betting.

The first newspaper published in the colony of New South Wales was the official government paper the *Sydney Gazette & New South Wales Advertiser,* which first appeared on 5 March 1803. A printing press had come out from England with the First Fleet in 1788, but there was no one skilled to operate it until the task was given to convict George Howe.

On 8 January 1804 he published the first account of a cricket match – which is also the first account of any sporting event in Australia.

'The late intense weather has been very favourable to the amateurs of cricket who scarce have lost a day for the past month. The frequent immoderate weather might have been considered inimical to the amusement, but was productive of the very opposite consequences, as the state of the atmosphere might always regulate the portions of exercise necessary to the ends that this laborious diversion was originally intended to answer.'

It appears that cricketers in the season 1803–04 had been hard at it, and despite the hot weather sending them indoors had continued to play.

Some cricket scholars think that the first players were from the ship *Calcutta,* but it seems clear from the way that this match was report-

ed that cricket had been played in that summer at least, and possibly for one or two summers before. The celebrated diary of Watkin Tench does not record any cricket, but that is not positive evidence that it had not been played.

There are few references to cricket in the *Gazette* from 1803–24, when press restrictions were removed and other newspapers commenced publication in Sydney such as William Charles Wentworth's *Australian* (1824), the *Sydney Monitor* (1826), and the *Sydney Herald* (1831 – later the *Sydney Morning Herald*) and Horatio Wills' *The Currency Lad,* 1832–33.

Cricket would feature more prominently in newspapers concerned more with the news than with government pronouncements, which was the function of the *Gazette.*

However the *Gazette* mentions an Easter Monday fair at the 'Cricket Ground' on 28 April 1810.

Governor Lachlan Macquarie ordered cricket gear for his son, also named Lachlan, who was then at Reddall's School. 12 cricket bats and 6 cricket balls were delivered on 22 August 1821 from His Majesty's Timber Yard. Macquarie noted, 'The above articles are to be considered as belonging to Lachlan so long as he remains at Rev'd Mr

Reddall's school and afterwards to be left for the use of the school.'

Cricket players were prominent early editors and journalists – the *Australian* was edited by player John Hardy in December 1834 and George Cavenagh was editor of the *Gazette* in 1836–39. Hardy introduced semi round–arm bowling to NSW in 1832, that is the bowler could raise his arm to level with his elbow, a kind of under arm bowling, in fact. Hardy taught it to Robert and brother William Still.

Clubs were formed, though not all lasted very long. The Australian Cricket Club dates from 1826 and was founded by cornstalk emancipists. It survived through the 1830s unlike the Amateur, Union and Victoria clubs.

The *Australian* of 9 August 1826 records a match of the Australian Club where the players 'exerted all their most active faculties during the continuance of this manly and healthful diversion.' They used bats made of cedar. Matches were sporadic over the next few years, often having more to do with betting (wagers were as high as £300) than with the pursuit of cricket for its own sake.

Visiting regiments provided other games. A match between the 57th Regiment and XI from 'all Sydney' was played in February 1830. Eight currency lads and three 'sterling'

batsmen made up the Civilians, who made 76 and 136 and defeated the 57th Regiment, 101 and 87. These were the first results published in the *Sydney Monitor.* The game was watched by 'several hundred' spectators and played for a £20 purse.

The first 'match report' was published in the *Australian* on 6 July 1832. It was written by 'Etonian' about a game between Civilians and Military played on 18 June 1832 at Hyde Park before a crowd of 2000 including 'many respectable females'.

The *Sydney Morning Herald's* brief report detailed the scores: Military 57 and 4/81 defeating Civilians 43 and 86, whereupon 'the air was darkened with caps'. The *Australian* initially had not covered the game, a situation rectified by a disappointed Etonian.

He wrote: 'The game of Cricket is peculiarly English, and possesses a fascination to those who have been players ... that no time eradicates; old as I am, I never see wickets pitched, without longing, as in the days of yore, to have a bat in hand, and to make the ball whistle along the ground, topping the daisies, and forming that elegant curve ... is considered the perfection of pretty hitting ... It was evident that the Military had all along the advantage, not however from

The 4th or King's Own Regiment play a cricket match on Barrack Square, Wynyard, in 1845. A lithograph by C. Hutchins, from a sketch by Captain Hext.

superior batting, but from the inferior fielding of their adversaries; were I indeed required to decide upon the batting, I should award the palm to the Currency lads, who in the second innings made 85 off some very good bowling, and in the face of at least six as good fielders as are not often seen in one eleven.'

(One D Conn who took two catches was 'beautiful' at position three yards from the bat called 'pointing of the bat', now point.)

Civilians lost because of a 'fatal' 'want of match-playing' when they seemed 'confused at the quick notching of their opponents' and played with less method than before. There was also a 'deterioration' in the quality of the bowling largely because a great wind sprang up and the Civilians were playing when the sun sank low.

'It was said, too, that some of the losing party had been too long in their tents … I did not perceive this to be the case … but suggest a plan – very little beer is allowed 'til the match is over…'

Etonian understood that there would be another match and suggested '1st – To practise frequently the eleven who are to play, and not to vary their stations. 2ndly – To discipline a third bowler by way of a change, and if possible one who bowls differently from their pre-

sent hands. 3rdly – To have a fixed wicket keeper. 4thly not to be cowed.

'In my opinion the native youth shew qualities of cricket playing I never saw surpassed. Quickness of eye and foot, strength of arm in throwing, confidence in themselves, an ardent desire to win, and good temper under defeat.'

Those qualities of the native 'currency' Australian cricketers of 1832 have continued down the seasons.

The *Sydney Gazette* wrote in that year: 'Cricket is now the prevailing amusement of the day. Let no man henceforth set up for a sporting character whose name is not enrolled among the gentleman cricketers of Sydney. Let no ador-

ing swain hereafter think to "dangle at a lady's apron string" or "feast upon smiles from partial beauty won" unless he can boast of excellence at handling a bat, or sending up ball – the former will reject his company, the latter his addresses. Hyde Park is now almost daily graced by the aspiring youth of Sydney practising their favourite recreation, and respected females looking on to enliven the scene … We expect that New South Wales will soon be able to boast players that might bear away the palm of victory even at Lord's.'

Hyde Park was the main ground used in 1830s. There were constant complaints over its legal and illegal use. A two-horse roller was used in

1836. Complaints as late as 1851 said Hyde Park was 'rough and uneven' and 'in parts with alternate hillocks of earth and pebbles, long grass and ridges, holes, and drains innumerable which render it anything but a fit place for cricketing skill.' It was a public place, or common, used by the military and the public, and although the north-west corner was reserved for cricket, there was inadequate fencing to prevent the public wandering over it.

In 1844 'STMPS' wrote to the *Sydney Morning Herald* asking that 'a small area of forty by twenty yards be fenced off and used by clubs for matches, not by small boys in the city incessantly playing on it and cutting it up to dust.'

Melbourne took to cricket from the beginning. This view of the young city in 1838 shows a cricket ground already in place.

Cricket expands from 'splendid isolation'

A picnic cricket match in the Australian bush: the spectators are surprisingly well dressed. Picnic cricket matches were a popular diversion in the 'lungs of the city'.

Despite the exigencies of colonial life recreations of various kinds, including cricket, were soon taken up by the military and the growing number of free and emancipated settlers.

In **Van Diemen's Land,** as Tasmania was still named until 1856, cricket made its first appearance in Australia outside NSW.

The proprietor of the Lamb Inn in Hobart Town organised a match in 1825 between soldiers and free settlers, which was won by the more practised military.

The next year an even more successful game was played between the free colonists from Kent and Sussex who were 'impregnated with cricket lore' against an all-comer's side from the rest of the colony.

Governor Arthur granted land for the Hobart Town Cricket Club in October 1832, and the first match was played there In January 1833.

Quite a deal of cricket was played in Van Diemen's Land in the 1830s and 1840s, both in Hobart and Launceston.

One notable match was between the Hobart Town Club and the officers of the just-arrived HMS *Hyacinth* – in which no betting was allowed, the 'honour' of playing was enough, said the officers.

They were joined in the United Services team by officers of the 21st Regiment. Two bands played while four innings were completed, and John Marshall of Hobart displayed the prowess that made him the Champion Cricketer of Hobart Town for 20 years.

He still captained Tasmania in the 1854, aged 58, and was long concerned that cricket remained the province of the gentry rather than any lower-class personages. He made 13 of 83 and 10 of 84, then took eight wickets as bowler or 'stumper' (There were also five United Services men out 'hit wicket') Hobart Town won by 107 runs.

The Launceston Cricket Club was founded in 1843.

Cricket in Van Diemen's Land produced many top-class players, but also an intense rivalry between North and South.

Coupled with the disinclination of the leading clubs to improve standards generally by employing professional player– coaches in the 1850s and 1860s, this parochialism held the game back, especially after the initial first class matches in Australia were played by Tasmania in 1851.

In **Western Australia**, Perth was founded in 1829, and the first recorded cricket match was played between builders of Government House and those at the Commissariat site in April 1835.

No scores remain, but the *Perth Gazette* wrote 'the revival of the sports of our native country in a distant land forms a connection which it should be our pride to encourage.'

The newspaper refers to a number of clubs as having been formed including the Perth and Guildford Clubs.

The first match for which scores have been kept was one between the Perth Cricket Club and the Tradesmen of Perth in May 1846.

The *Perth Gazette* noted 'We have seldom seen any of our public amusements so well attended. In fact, everyone was there … Throughout the innings, the bowling was admirable, chiefly being of the 'slow school', but not less dangerous than the rapid play of some modern artists.

'As the scores show the hasty or incautious player had no chance, but so wary were the strikers in most cases that sometimes three overs were called without a notch.'

Clubs were soon formed in nearby areas such as Bunbury and York, and in Fremantle by 1852.

A series of matches between Perth and Fremantle was held in 1852–53. It was one match each in the deciding encounter, on a wet day in Perth.

Perth won this but it was agreed that conditions had prevented a good day's play so another decider was played in March, also won by Perth, whose 'crack' at batting and bowling was one Dr Jones.

These matches continued into the 1860s, by which time Fremantle came to predominate.

In nineteenth-century Australia horse riding was both a popular recreation as well as a mode of conveyance to a cricket match.

In **South Australia**, proclaimed a colony in 1836, the first games seem to have been played in 1838–39. An advertisement appeared in the *South Australian Register* on 3 November 1838 calling for gentleman players to form an Adelaide cricket club. Single wicket games were played, and in October 1839 a match for 22 guineas a side was scheduled between the gentlemen of the Adelaide Club and those of the Royal Victoria Independent Club at the Thebarton Cricket Ground.

John Collard Cocker was the first outstanding SA player. He had played in England with Alfred Mynn and was a devastating underarm bowler. He arrived in Adelaide in 1846. Cocker was publican of the Kentish Arms and had a club called Kent and Sussex, for whom Tom Botten bowled round-arm – the first in SA.

Dominant club in the 1850s was the Union Club, while the SA Cricket Club was on top in the 1860s mainly because it had the lease on the land where the

Adelaide Oval was to be built.

Queensland, founded as a penal colony in 1824, did not become separate colony until 1859. In 1842 free settlement was permitted at Moreton Bay. The *Sydney Morning Herald's* correspondent there reported in 1844 that 'The lovers of the manly and exhilarating game of cricket will soon have an opportunity of displaying their prowess, a club having been formed at South Brisbane, designated the 'Albion' cricket club …'

In 1846 the *Moreton Bay Courier* reported a match between eleven working men and eleven gentlemen for a stake of £5 10s. 0d. The gents won.

A club was formed at Ipswich in 1848 and challenged the cricketers of Brisbane.

A prominent early Queensland cricketer was William Gilbert Rees who was invited to play for NSW in an intercolonial match against Victoria in 1857. Rees was a cousin of W. G. Grace, his mother being sister to Grace's wife and 21 years older than W. G. He had played for

Gloucestershire and was well known as a 'crack' by former Middlesex player and NSW captain at the time George Gilbert. Rees gave W. G. his first cane-handled bat on a visit to England.

Ipswich, also known as the North Australian Cricket Club, regularly beat Brisbane's Moreton Bay Club and other clubs, until two games in 1859 when Brisbane obtained revenge.

In the first match Brisbane won by 51 runs in a game played over three days, despite one James Bolger making a century for Ipswich, the first recorded in Queensland.

The second game was played just before Queensland gained separation. Brisbane won by 33 runs.

After the settlement of the **Port Phillip District** began in earnest in 1834, and just four years later the Melbourne Cricket Club, Australia's oldest and most influential club still in existence was formed, on 15 November 1838. Fred Powlett, Port Phillip's first centurion was among the initial

group of paid up members (cost one guinea). The next week MCC played its first game against the Military at a ground now occupied by the Old Mint building in William Street.

The *Port Phillip Gazette* said it was a 'heart-enlivening sight'.

Shortly afterwards the Melbourne Union Cricket Club was founded and two matches between the clubs were played in January 1839. They won one match each.

The Melbourne Club moved to the south bank of the Yarra in 1848, where one of the town's founders, John Pascoe Fawkner, had planted wheat. Superintendent LaTrobe granted the MCC ten acres, and the club spent £24/13/6 on turfing the wicket and £20/13/4 on a four-rail pig-proof fence.

In 1853 now Governor La Trobe offered the MCC land in the Richmond Paddock. On 15 August 1853 the club wrote requesting permission to remove trees to establish a cricket ground, which La Trobe granted on September 23, – thus establishing the MCG.

Tom Wills and early Victorian cricket

Thomas Wentworth Wills, profesional sportsman in the colours of the MCC. A portrait by W. Handcock, painted in 1870.

Among mid-nineteenth century Australian sportsmen, a highly individual and even eccentric bunch, Tom Wills had the most influence in both cricket and Australian football.

Thomas Wentworth Wills was born on 19 December 1835 at Molonglo, in what is now the Australian Capital Territory, between Canberra and Queanbeyan. He was named for William Charles Wentworth, by his father Horatio Spencer Wills, who was a fellow believer in the emancipist cause – that is, he believed in a certain amount of political freedom for free settlers and 'emancipated' convicts.

Horatio was also Australian-born, and had already led an adventurous life, running away to sea at 15, and working for the *Sydney Gazette*, whose editor George Howe his mother had taken as her second husband. The *Gazette* was where the first cricket report had appeared in 1803, and when Horatio edited the short-lived emancipist paper the *Currency Lad* in 1832 and 1833 it also gave prominent coverage to cricket matches – notably those of the Australian Club.

Horatio overlanded his sheep and cattle from Molonglo in 1839 and squatted with his wife Elizabeth and young Tom in the Western District of Victoria near Ararat (which had a small mountain Horatio named) on a property called Lexington.

Cricket was widely played by the stations of the district in the 1840s and 1850s, and young Tom grew up playing cricket locally with European and Aboriginal cricketers. He is said to have learned the local Aboriginal language, and may also have played a version of football with a possum skin.

In 1852, when he was 17, Tom was sent to Rugby School in England, where they played cricket and a version of football. In his four-year stay he came to captain both teams. He did not go on to university as Horatio had hoped, but did play (for Cambridge) in the 1856 intervarsity match. James Lillywhite said of his cricket in England 'He uses a three-pound bat and hits terrific.'

Returning to Australia at the end of that year, Wills is said to have written a letter that caused the Melbourne Cricket Club to issue the challenge to 'all comers' which saw the first match between Victoria and NSW in March 1856.

He did not play in that game, but played in the second encounter at the Domain in Sydney on 14 January 1857, making a duck and one run, but taking 6/25 and 4/40 with his round-arm deliveries in Victoria's second loss. The Victoria team was captained by W. J. Hammersley, later editor of, and as 'Longstop', cricket writer for, the influential weekly the *Australasian*.

He had been a cricketer and friend in England at the same time as Wills. In season 1856–57 Wills played for Melbourne and topped the batting with 104 runs at an average of 34. He was Secretary of the MCC in 1857–58, and captain of Victoria in their first win over NSW in January, taking 5/25 and 3/34.

In 1858 he wrote his famous letter to a sporting paper which talks about forming a football club for the purpose of keeping cricketers fit in winter, and umpired what is ceremonially regarded as the first game of Australian football. It took place over several afternoons outside the MCG in August 1858.

He worked for a Melbourne solicitor in 1859, as an articled clerk, but soon gave this up. In May 1899, Wills and Hammersley (and 'Football' Smith of Scotch College among others) devised the rules of the Melbourne Football Club, the earliest known code of Australian football.

Tom Wills might lay claim to being the first professional sportsman in Australia, certainly at the age of 24 as captain of Victoria, and captain of the Melbourne Football Club he was the most influential sportsman of his time.

Two games were played against Tasmania in February and March, both won by Victoria. Wills took 6/25 and 6/10 in the second match in Hobart. In the next season 1858–59, he had another eleven wicket haul in the Victoria v NSW game which was the only first class encounter for the season, and took nine in the only game of 1859–60.

In the meantime the discovery of gold and the severe shortage of labour had affected Horatio's pastoral interests. In 1852 he had moved to Geelong, was elected a member of parliament for South Grant, and developed a model farm at Point Henry.

In 1860, sometime after the Victoria NSW game, Horatio moved to a property in Queensland, and Tom was persuaded to move there to help in establishing the new station. On 17 October 1861 at Cullinlaringo on

the Nogoa River, Horatio and 18 others were massacred by the Aborigines. Tom, however was two days down the track and survived. He remained with his family in Queensland until his younger brothers Cedric and Edgar returned from school in Germany in 1863, missing the first tour of Australia by an English team in 1861–62. In truth he wasn't much cut out to manage a sheep station.

He captained Victoria in a controversial match at the Domain on 5 February 1863. The controversy was over the running-out of a NSW batsman after 'over' had, or perhaps had not, been called.

After an overnight meeting the Victorians decided to allow the batsman to resume next day, and were boycotted by two of their own. Victoria lost, but Wills played well, taking eight wickets and being 25 not out and 17 not out.

In the 1863–64 season the second touring team led by George Parr played matches at odds, but also played one 'exhibition match' on even terms. In this match the tourists were divided between two teams with the additions of some locals, including Wills. The match,

between George Anderson's XI and George Parr's XI was played on 5–8 March 1864. Wills made 4 for Anderson's winning team, and took three wickets in four balls in the second innings.

The bad feeling engendered by the 1863 match meant that NSW and Victoria did not play each other until December 1865 – when Victoria gained a measure of revenge, winning by an innings and 20 runs. Wills made 58, the first half-century in Australian first class cricket, as well as taking six wickets for the match.

In 1866–67 Wills was involved in coaching at Edenhope in western Victoria and then in taking the first Aboriginal Australian team around Victoria and NSW.

There was more controversy in the 1869 intercolonial match which Hammersley said Wills refused to play in unless he was captain. He eventually played and took 7/44 to win the game for Victoria.

Wills was assailed in the media, especially by former mate W. J. Hammersley in the *Australasian*.

Wills riposted in the *Leader* of 18 January 1873: 'Allow me to inform him [Hammersley] that it was not

bad generalship that lost the match, but the bad batting, the worse fielding and the miserable bowling. What could anyone do in such a state of things?'

To which Hammersley blustered in the *Australasian* of January 25 – accusing him of being a 'middling bat', of 'throwing', of not being a gentleman, of being shallow-brained, and of assuming that Victoria's success was due to him alone.

Wills was told 'to take the pledge'. He would never captain Victoria again, but he played one more game at the age of 41 in February 1876, against NSW.

1876 was also when he played the last of his over 210 games of 'first class' Australian football.

Alcoholism, remorse over his father, and perhaps also the realisation that his life as a professional cricketer and footballer was over, saw him commit suicide, by stabbing himself with a pair of scissors, in Heidelberg Victoria on 2 May 1880.

In 32 first class matches Wills took 121 wickets at 10.08, with 15 five-wicket bags and 3 ten-wicket games. He made 602 runs at 12.28.

Melbourne Cricket Ground on 1 January 1864. XXII of Victoria play a controversial draw against George Parr's English XI.

The first 'first class' games are played

In March 1850, the Melbourne Cricket Club issued a challenge to the Launceston Cricket Club for a match between the representative cricketers of Port Phillip and Van Diemen's Land. Launceston, from where the first European settlers of Melbourne had come in 1834, accepted the challenge and asked that the match be played in Launceston the next month, April.

Unfortunately the reply did not arrive in time for this to take place, so the challenge was reissued, and taken up, in the following season, that of 1850–51.

In the meantime, legislation had been passed in England for the long awaited 'separation' of the Port Phillip District, afterwards Victoria, from NSW. When the news reached Melbourne, a fortnight's celebrations were declared from 11 November 1850 as Victorians observed their freedom from NSW with fireworks and the opening of a new Prince's Bridge.

The match against Tasmania, scheduled for February 1851 would be part of the general cheerfulness of the newly independent colony of Victoria.

The Victorian team selected by the MCC wore red, white and blue colours, and sailed to Launceston aboard the SS *Shamrock*.

The first ball in Australian first class cricket was bowled at the Launceston Racecourse (later the NTCA ground) at 11 a.m., on 11 February 1851. The ground was of the roughest description and only with difficulty were the umpires Lyon and Weedon able to select a place to play.

That ball was bowled, underarm, by William Henty to Duncan Cooper of Victoria. Cooper made four of Victoria's disappointing total of 82. Captain William Philpott and James Brodie top-scored with 17 each.

Tasmania was not expected to be able to withstand the fast overarm Victorian attack, and Thomas Antill was indeed effective, bowling just 12 overs, 7/33 including three wickets in four balls. However a large total of 24 extras, 11 byes and 8 no-balls helped the Tasmanians to 104.

In Victoria's second innings, 35 of the 57 total was made by Thomas Hamilton. Tasmania, despite Antill's 6/19 chased the 37 for the loss of just seven wickets in 13 overs.

About 2500 people had watched the locals win the inaugural first class game in Australia by three wickets.

Preparations immediately commenced for a return match in Melbourne in the following summer. A party of nine Tasmanians sailed over Bass Strait in February 1852. Three Melbourne-based Launcestonians completed the team.

The game was played on the then MCC ground on the south bank of the Yarra.

Records do not disclose who captained Victoria in this initial first class game played in Melbourne – it was probably either Thomas Hamilton or Fred Powlett.

This time Victoria made 80 and Tasmania 65 in the first innings. Victoria won the game when Hamilton added a second innings of 42 and Victoria made 127 in the second dig. Hamilton completed an excellent game, taking 5/27 in dismissing Tasmania for 81. The Victorian team featured two young brothers a'Beckett – Edward who was a fortnight short of his 16th birthday, and Malwyn who was 17. Edward took a wicket in each innings.

A third match, the decider or 'Conqueror' game, took place two years later in Launceston. In the interim the discovery of gold in Victoria had upset all arrangements in the colony.

This match was somewhat less well organised, the Victorians turning up three players short, and having to co-opt their scorer and a couple of locals. Tasmania won this match easily, by eight wickets. The Tasmanian captain John Marshall played his third and last first class game at the age of 58.

First class cricket was not played by Tasmania again until two matches against Victoria in 1858, which Victoria won easily. In the interim, battle had commenced

Victoria defeated NSW by two wickets on the Domain, Sydney in January 1859. 26,000 people watched as Victorian captain Tom Wills took 5/24 and 6/25 to secure victory.

The Grand National Cricket Match of 1857 between Elevens of Victoria and NSW, played on the Domain in Sydney. NSW won by 65 runs. George Gilbert top-scored, 31.

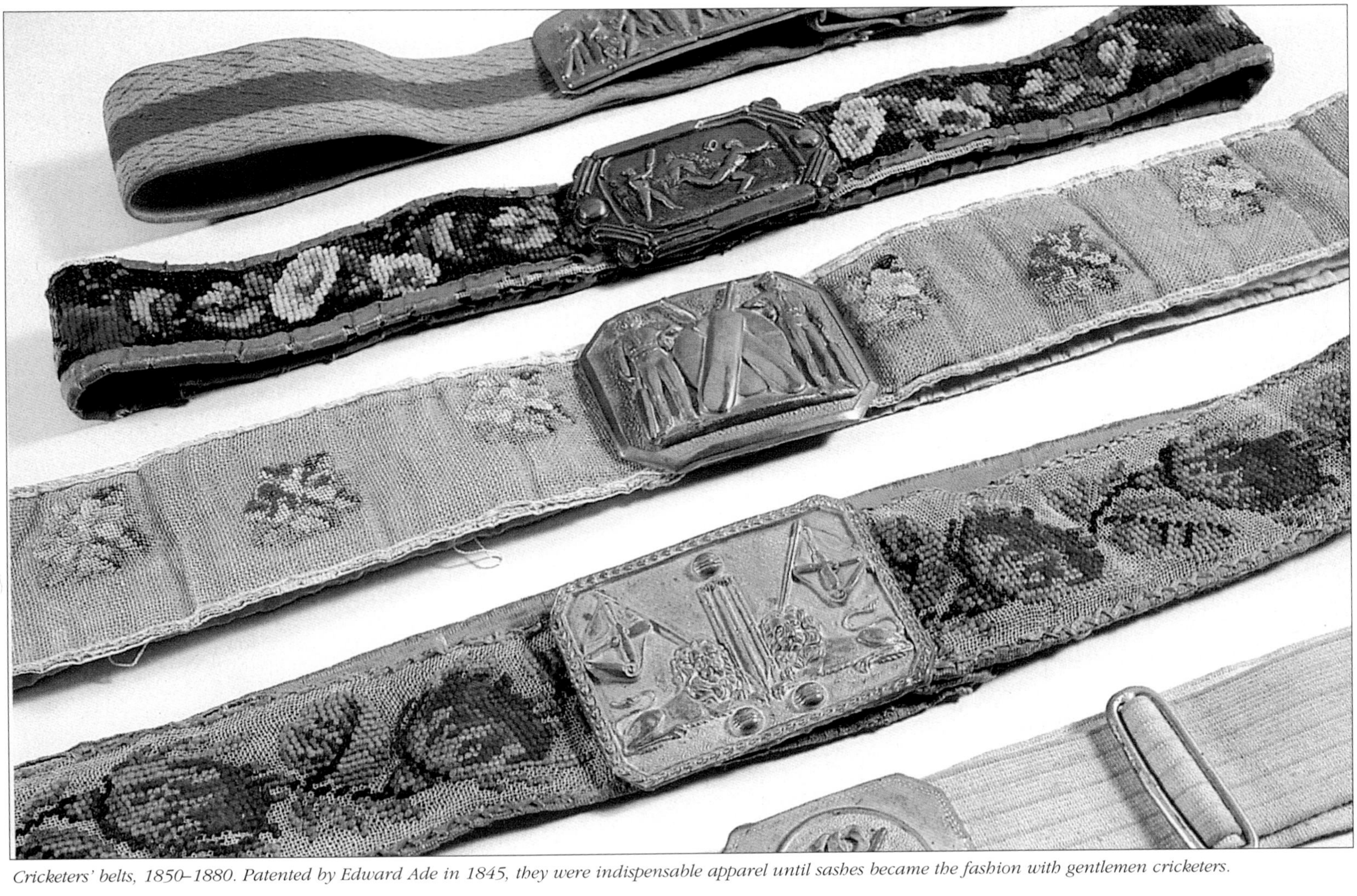

Cricketers' belts, 1850–1880. Patented by Edward Ade in 1845, they were indispensable apparel until sashes became the fashion with gentlemen cricketers.

The big matches – before Tests begin

NSW wins first game at the MCG

The first big game at the MCG was the initial first class encounter between Victoria and NSW. Some 5000 people turned up on 26 March 1856 as a result of the Melbourne Cricket Club challenging 'all-comers' late in 1855.

Initially there was to be £500 at stake, but NSW declined to play for money, in addition they could not raise the cash, and agreed to pay their own expenses. They only made it to the match it seems, because Richard Driver, politician and scorer, put in £60 himself to pay for the trip on the SS *Telegraph*. It took 48 hours.

A prominent NSW bowler named Joseph Rutter missed the boat, and Driver had to bat at eleven. But this occurred only after the match had been delayed for several days because of rain. Then the state of the pitch that had been marked out was found to be unsuitable, and the track next to it was used.

Victoria made 63, falling to the fast round-arm of NSW captain George Gilbert and the fast underarm of J. J. McKone. J. H Mather topscored with 16 and he was run out going for the fifth run – there being no boundaries marked.

NSW made 76, Driver 18, Elliott outstanding with 7/25. Victoria collapsed sensationally in the second innings making just 28, McKone 5/11. NSW scored the required 16 runs - for the loss of seven wickets, Elliott 3/7, Lowe 4/9.

Thus ended a match with the lowest aggregate, 183, and the lowest innings score, 28, by Victoria in all intercolonial matches.

NSW win again at Sydney Domain

NSW also won the next season's intercolonial match, played at the Domain in Sydney between NSW and Victoria on 14 January 1857. Highlight of this game was the bowling of Australian-born Tom Wills, in his first class debut in Australia, for Victoria. He had previously played for Kent and Cambridge University. His friend and later editor of the *Australasian,* William Hammersley, had also played for Cambridge and Surrey. Wills took 6/25 in NSW's first innings of 80, and 4/40 in their sec-

ond innings of 86. Unfortunately, he contributed a 'pair' with the bat, in Victoria's 63 and 38. NSW attracted opprobrium for not playing a specialist wicketkeeper. However there was a total of just three byes in both Victorian innings. NSW won by 65 runs.

Hat-trick, but Victoria wins

At the MCG on 11 January 1858 the right-arm, round-arm medium pacer and NSW captain George Gilbert took the first hat-trick in Australian first class cricket. His 5/23 helped bundle Victoria out for 59. This bowling was just about matched by Tom Wills in his first game as captain of Victoria, in taking 5/25 in NSW's innings of 57. Wills made 49 not out, the highest first class score to that date, in Victoria's second innings of 238, also the highest thus far. NSW managed a meagre 69 in the second innings, Wills taking 3/34 and George Elliott 5/17.

Tasmania trounced

A Victorian team led by Tom Wills was invited by the Launceston Cricket Club to play in Launceston on 25 February 1858. Another match was organised for Hobart after this one.

Gideon Elliott made a complete mess of Tasmania in Launceston, bowling 19 overs, 17 maidens, nine wickets for two runs, an extraordinary analysis in any form of cricket.

Elliott bowled fast round-arm – a form of bowling banned in Tasmania in the four years since Victoria had last played there. They were unable to cope.

Wills mercifully perhaps did not ask Elliott to bowl in the second innings (Elliott top scored with 38 in Victoria's 115). Victoria won by an innings and 20 runs.

The second match in Hobart was won by Victoria by 69 runs, and was notable for the fact that no Tasmanian batsman got into double figures in either innings – a unique first class achievement. Wills was the destroyer – 6/25 and 6/10.

For Tasmania, the captain William Brown, in his sole first class match, took 15/73 – the best match figures on debut for more than 150 years.

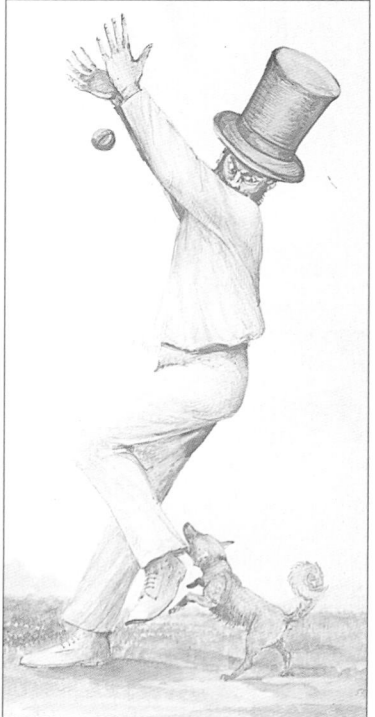

A problem in colonial cricket.

Victoria wins low-scoring games

In the Victoria v NSW games played in 1859, 1860 and 1861, only one innings exceeded 100, which was Victoria's 8/103 chasing a win at the Sydney Domain in 1859. Tom Wills took 5/24 and 6/25 in this match, and 6/23 and 3/16 in the 1860 match which Victoria won by 69 runs

Edward Ward, the round-arm fast bowler from NSW, confirmed the domination of ball over bat in the 1859 match, taking 6/24 and 4/33, and 5/31 and 3/18 in 1861. Wills was in Queensland on the ill-fated trip with his father Horatio during this game.

In this earliest period of first class cricket in Australia between 1850–51 and 1860–61, 11 games were played. Wills played in six of them, and was clearly the best bowler in the colonies taking 56 wickets at 5.17. He was second in the batting aggregates, making 142 runs at 14.2 just four runs behind another football team-mate Jerry Bryant, who played seven matches and made 146 runs at 11.23.

After the tour

The 1861–62 season was occupied by Stephenson's touring English side. One of these players, Charles Lawrence, remained in Australia.

In the next season, the sole first class match played was between Victoria and NSW. Tom Wills was captain of Victoria and Charles Lawrence captain of NSW. A bizarre contretemps over the rules and an umpiring decision saw two Victorian batsmen absent in Victoria's second innings, and NSW won by 84 runs.

What happened was, on the second day NSW batsman Sam Jones left his crease at the end of an over, whereupon Victorian wicketkeeper George Marshall removed the bails and appealed. The Victorian square leg umpire gave him out. The NSW umpire Richard Driver said he'd called 'over'. After 20 minutes animated discussion on the ground, the players left for the afternoon. There were disturbances in the crowd and Wills was hit in the head by a stone.

That night a Victorian team meeting agreed to recall the batsman the next day, which two players took to be an aspersion on their cricketing honour and absented themselves, as did the two umpires. One Warwick Fairfax umpired the remainder of the game, which was given in by Wills when Victoria was 8/45, and he was 17 not out. The repercussions of this dispute lingered for two years. No further NSW v Victoria game was played until 1865, though annual matches were held between Sydney's Albert Club and the Melbourne Cricket Club.

Antill scores the first century

NSW won the return match on Boxing Day 1866 against an understrength Victorian team. Dave Gregory, the future Australian captain, made his debut in this match, ripping the heart out of the Victorian batting with 3/36 and 4/31, bowling unchanged in both innings. NSW 145, defeated Victoria 74 and 58, by an innings and 13 runs.

On Boxing Day 1867, NSW captain Charles Lawrence sent Victoria in on an MCG pitch that the *Age* described as looking like a 'first-class billiard table'. Dick Wardill made the most of the conditions, making the first century in first class cricket, 110 in about 260 minutes with nine fours. He made 45 not out in the second innings. Tom Wills bowled 58 overs, 5/55 and Francis Allan, a fast medium left-

NSW lost to Victoria on the Albert Ground in Sydney by 24 runs on 8 March 1873, after Victorian bowler Sam Cosstick took 6/15 and 5/36. George Gibson made 32

arm round-armer, 62.3 overs 5/59 in NSW's first innings of 158. Wills bowled 44 overs 4/94, and Allan 40.3 very accurate overs for 3/43 in the NSW second innings. Victoria won by seven wickets.

The next first class century was scored by Victorian Joseph Phillips in the match against Tasmania at the MCG on 12 February 1869. This was the first game since 1858 against Tasmania on even terms. Victoria's total of 409, and the innings and 260 run win, was an indication of the deterioration in Tasmanian cricket standards.

The first Boxing Day match

The 'tradition' of Boxing Day cricket matches at the MCG began with the 1865 Victoria v NSW game. Ned Gregory, one of the famed NSW dynasty of Gregory brothers made 43 in the NSW first innings and helped his team to 122 in the

face of hostile bowling from Tom Wills and John Conway. Wills then made 58 batting at number ten in one of his best innings for years, and Victoria totalled an impressive 285. Conway and Wills bowled tightly and NSW were dismissed for 143. Conway bowled 36 overs, 6/68, and Wills 34 overs (2/25). Murmurings about Wills' action were heard in this match. He was regarded by some as 'shying' or chucking.

Test men: debuts

The players who formed Australia's first Test teams began their first class careers in the 1860s and 1870s. Dave Gregory took seven wickets for NSW in 1866. Charles Bannerman was bowled Tom Wills for 32 in the 1871 Victoria NSW match – the first to be played at the Albert Ground in Sydney. Fast bowler Harry Boyle made his debut in the 1872 game at the MCG, but was not called upon to bowl. (Tom Wills was no-balled

three times for throwing by NSW umpire A. Sellars. Wills' arm was above shoulder level – known as a 'high delivery'. Dave Gregory was not called – and in fact this type of bowling had been legalised by the Marylebone Cricket Club in 1864.)

Jack Blackham stumped one and caught three in his 'keeping debut in 1874. Tom Horan made 3 and 22 for Victoria in the same match – and Fred, later 'the Demon' Spofforth helped NSW to victory with 3/56 and 3/67.

Billy Midwinter made an all-round debut for Victoria in the 1874–75 match – equal top score in the first innings (15) and taking 6/61 and 2/61 – NSW won by 77 runs.

Billy Murdoch made a quiet entrance to Australian cricket with six runs in NSW's innings-and-one-run win in the 27 December 1875 match against Victoria.

And Tom Wills played his last game for Victoria, as captain, in February 1876, ending with four runs and 0/65 from 49 overs. The

first Test was played in the next season, 1876–77.

Mullagh's match

One other, post-first Test game deserves mention, because it was the sole first class game played by Johnny Mullagh, the best player of the 1868 Aboriginal tour of England.

Mullagh played for Victoria against Lord Harris's England XI at the MCG on 7 March 1879. He made 4 runs in the first innings, and top-scored with 36 in the second. This innings made a real impression on the crowd, who raised a subscription of £50 – equal to the sum he had not been paid for his tour of England.

Test fast bowler George Palmer also made his debut in this match, as a replacement for Francis Allan, who had missed his train.

Palmer was the sixth bowler used and had an immediate effect – taking 6/64 and 3/30 in Victoria's six-wicket loss.

Stephenson and the first English tour

The first intercolonial cricket match: H. H. Stephenson's XI versus a Victorian XVIII, played at the MCG on 1 January 1862. From a watercolour by Henry Burn.

H. H. Stephenson's first touring team. William Stephenson is seated, with pads on. William Caffyn is standing at his right shoulder.

The first match between a team from England and one from Australia took place at the MCG on New Year's Day, 1862. Somewhere between 15 and 25 thousand enthusiastic Melburnians turned out on a very hot day to watch the historic encounter. The teams, of 11 Englishmen and 18 Victorians (reduced by the promoters from 22), were given individually coloured ribbons for their sun-hats and similarly coloured sashes for their waists. Scorecards were printed with each player's colour and name, so they could be identified by the crowd thronging the refreshment tents or seated in the new MCG grandstand.

Some of these games were referred to as 'Test' matches by W. J. Hammersley in his *Victorian Cricketer's Guide* for 1861–62, the first time matches were so described – even though all were played against the odds.

The Englishmen were captained by H. H. (Heathfield Harman) Stephenson, captain of Surrey. The others were among the best English professional players of their day, mostly veterans of the famed All England and United England XIs – professional teams which did so much to improve and popularise the game in England before the rise of the county system.

Players who had come to Australia included William 'Terrible Billy' Caffyn and Charles Lawrence, who after this tour remained in Australia and had a profound influence on raising the standard of cricket in Australia, particularly in NSW. Lawrence was to captain NSW six times and play and coach at the Albert Club and take the 1868 Aboriginal Australians to England. Caffyn, who toured again with Parr's side in 1863–64 and then spent a year as ground bowler/coach for the Melbourne Cricket Club at £300 a year, went to Sydney where he played seven games for NSW and coached at the Warwick Club for six years.

The English tour had been sponsored by Melbourne hoteliers Felix Spiers and Christopher Pond. They had originally tried to bring the novelist Charles Dickens to Australia for £10,000 on one of his popular lecture tours, but the great man failed to reply to their overtures.

Instead, on the advice of the greatest entrepreneur (among many other things) of the day, George Coppin they turned their minds and budgets to a cricket tour. Spiers and Ponds' Royal Hotel and Cafe de Paris were located in front of Coppin's Theatre Royal in

The triumphant parade of the All England XI through Melbourne. Their coach stops outside Spiers & Ponds' Cafe de Paris.

Bourke Street, Melbourne.

A prior attempt to organise a tour had foundered on the question of how much the players wanted to be paid for the long tour.

Spiers and Pond budgeted on paying the required £150 per player plus expenses at around £7000, and despatched a Mr Mallam to do the negotiations in England. At that price Mallam could not secure 12 of the very best players, but he did sign up a dozen very good professionals.

They left Liverpool for Australia aboard the steamship *Great Britain,* and arrived in Melbourne on Christmas Eve 1861, and were taken on a coach-top parade from the dock up Bourke Street to Spiers and Pond's hotel for a reception.

Two days before the first match Stephenson requested that as his players were tired from their 67-day sea voyage that the number of opponents be reduced from XXII to XV. This was regarded as showing the 'white feather' by some of the more excitable local papers – who thought it a sign that the Englishmen weren't quite good enough to defeat twice as many Victorians. Spiers and Pond compromised – and so Victoria turned out a team of XVIII.

After some practice at a secret

location to avoid being mobbed by fans, the game between XVIII of Victoria and H. H Stephenson's XI commenced. Billy Caffyn bowled the first ball in England–Australia cricket to Jerry Bryant, publican and footballer of Melbourne, who went on to make 11. George Marshall made 27 and top-scored for Victoria which made 118 on the first innings, playing 18 batsmen. 'England' made 305 (Caffyn 79), and then bowled the Victorians out for 92. A total of 45,000 paid to see the match, which extended over four days, and included other entertainment such as a balloon ascent – the first in Australia. The takings for this one match in Melbourne covered Spiers and Ponds costs for the whole tour.

Other matches around the country followed – against XXII of the Ovens district, XXII of Victoria (a heartening draw), XXII of Geelong then XXII of Sydney, Bathurst (a draw) and then a Combined XXII of Victoria and NSW where George Moore, NSW cricket legend, (grandfather of Charlie Macartney) took 4/22 in the 'England' innings of 60. The Combination made 101, England 75, and lost the match when the Combination made 8/35. Great crowds greeted Stephenson's team wherever it went, which

including Tasmania.

There followed, on 1 March 1862, the only first class match of the tour at the MCG, between sides representing Surrey and The World, being the English touring party plus some Victorian players including George Marshall, Sam Coststick, Jerry Bryant and Jerry Conway. The World won by six wickets despite a typically hard hitting 75 not out from Caffyn.

About 8000 people watched this international match in Australia.

George Bennett from Kent played for the World and made 72, and then took 7/30 and 7/85.

Three more matches against odds took place in Victoria, against XXIIs of Ballarat, Bendigo and Victoria – the last of which Spiers and Ponds gave half the receipts to the English players. They could afford it. The tour made a profit of £11,000, which was invested in railway refreshment rooms in England and the Criterion Hotel in London. The English players were given a bonus of 100 sovereigns, and Australian cricket an enormous boost.

The feelings generated by the tour might be summarised by Roger Iddison who said 'Well I don't think much of their play, but they're a fine lot of drinkin' men.'

The second tour: George Parr in 1864

George Parr captained the second English tour of Australia in the season 1863–64. Parr was known in England as the 'Lion of the North' and his team included William Caffyn, back again; E.M. Grace older brother of W. G.; the Surrey veteran Julius Caesar, Robert Carpenter, Tom Hayward, George Tarrant, and Tom Lockyer. A formidable outfit.

They were managed and sponsored in Australia by publican and former Victorian captain George Marshall, who had once been a county team-mate of Parr's at Nottinghamshire. The invitation for the tour came from the Melbourne Cricket Club. Marshall had been involved in the umpiring furore in a Victoria v NSW match in the 1862–63 season (he had played well in the Surrey v the World match in 1861–62) which resulted in there being no first class matched played between Victoria and NSW in the season of Parr's tour. Could there have been a commercial reason behind Marshall's activity in perpetuating the 'intercolonial dispute'?

Parr agreed with Marshall as to the terms of the tour in a letter dated 21 February 1863, responding to one of Marshall's dated 24 December. The Victoria v NSW match took place on February 5.

In a further bit of intercolonial rivalry Charles Lawrence, who had remained in NSW after Stephenson's tour, and who captained NSW in the disputed match, also wrote to Parr requesting terms for a tour of NSW – but after Marshall had already done so.

Parr wrote to Lawrence: 'Perhaps in a few months the feeling of displeasure against Mr. Marshall in NSW may abate, or if not, you may be able to arrange terms with him as to our playing against you'. For his part the current Victorian captain Tom Wills (struck in the head by a rock during the Sydney match) thought Lawrence's action somewhat underhanded and suggested that the English party bypass NSW altogether and go to New Zealand after Victoria.

The tourists' first match was against a Victorian XXII on New Year's Day, 1864, at the MCG. Victoria scored 145 and England 176, Tom Hayward making 61 and Robert Carpenter 59. Victoria made 143 in the second innings leaving England 114 to win – but with England nine runs short at precisely six o'clock, the umpires drew stumps – ending the match in a controversial draw.

The English team toured New Zealand in early February, and then played a series of three

Sam Cosstick played 18 first class games for Victoria between 1861 and 1876.

George Parr's English XI. From left, G. Marshall, G. Parr, E. M. Grace, T. Lockyer, W. Caffyn, G. Tarrant, A. Clarke, G. Anderson, J. Caesar, T. Hayward, R. Carpenter.

A grand cricket match played at the Sydney Domain in 1864, featuring an All England XI and attracting a large and fashionable crowd.

matches against XXII of NSW organised in the end by Charles Lawrence. The third resulted in a close and exciting win by England, and was watched by a young Fred Spofforth. On the voyage back to Melbourne the steamer *Wonga Wonga* collided with the yacht *Viceroy*, causing some damage and much trepidation in the English team. The *Viceroy* sank, but its passengers were saved.

William Caffyn wrote of the behaviour of the Englishmen in this incident: 'Poor George Parr was utterly dazed and paralysed with alarm. Tarrant quite lost his head. The first thing he did was rush below to get a collection of curios given to him on the trip … Julius Caesar on the other hand, behaved in a manner worthy of his name, keeping very cool and collected, and doing all he could to assist the crew.'

On March 5, local cricket followers expressed through the sporting magazine *Bell's Life in Victoria*:

'That no opportunity had yet been offered of thoroughly testing the skill of the English champions'. As a result the tourists were divided into two teams, and leading Victorian players were added for the only first class match of the tour, at the MCG on 5 March 1864.

The match was delayed because five Victorians (including Jerry Bryant and Sam Cosstick) demanded higher match payments than the three guineas allowed. After argument they agreed to play – but then Parr said the Englishmen would not, if the five recalcitrants did. In the event they were substituted, and the standard of the match was lowered somewhat.

Tom Wills took 4/34 for George Anderson's XI which won the match by four wickets. E. M. Grace was the star with the ball, taking 5/33 and 4/36. Tom Lockyer with the bat, making 44 and 40 not out. About 13,000 people watched the game.

The tour proceeded by coach

around Victoria. E. M. Grace wrote: 'Driven by the coolest and ablest drivers that ever held the ribbons, the coaches dashed all night in and out of ruts and holes, over stones and mounds, round trees and logs, through creeks and gullies and waters that flow a foot deep in the coach itself.' The perils of touring!

In Ballarat on March 18, Tom Carpenter, the back-foot stylist, made the first century by an English batsman in Australia, 121 in a partnership of 166 with George Parr who made 65. The match was drawn after England scored 310, their highest total of the tour.

The last game, against XXII of Victoria, was affected by rain. Victoria made 150 and 17/83, England 131. In all matches against the odds, England won ten and drew six.

Carpenter topped the batting averages with 399 runs at 22.11 – mainly due to his century in the second-last match.

Of the English bowlers, the one who made the difference was Robert Tinley, the Nottinghamshire slow bowler whose teasing flight deceived a total of 171 batsmen at a cost of just 3.71 runs.

The team, minus E. M. Grace who remained to visit friends, and William Caffyn who took up his job coaching in Melbourne, sailed for Bombay on 26 April 1864, £250 richer.

Even Grace, the only amateur in the team of professional cricketers, could look to a change in their attitude: 'My position with the Eleven has been somewhat difficult. It required no great perception to see that any little occurrence might raise bad feeling. At first one or two had almost looked for chances to try and quarrel, but this had entirely passed. The Eleven had been attentive and kind to me, and now, when they were leaving me behind, two or three shook hands with me with tears glistening in their eyes.'

Aboriginal team is formed: the Australian

After the stimulation of the English tour of 1861–62 many cricket clubs were formed in Australia, including in the pastoral 'squatting' lands in the Western District of Victoria. No town or station could be complete without a cricket team: cricket became perhaps the most popular pastime in Australia.

Among the cattle stations around Edenhope and Harrow were Pine Hill and Mullagh, where a groom named Unaarrimin worked, on land which was probably his own country. By 1865 Unaarrimin was calling himself Johnny Mullagh after the station, and he was to become the most celebrated Aboriginal cricketer of his time.

James Edgar of Pine Hill (and Scotch College, Melbourne) taught Mullagh how to bowl round-arm, and the combined Aboriginal team defeated the station team in a match played on 24 January 1866. The team played some other matches, continued to do well and enjoyed a spreading fame. The Melbourne Cricket Club permitted an invitation to the Aboriginal team to play at the MCG, a match sponsored by the concessionaire of the MCG refreshment booths. The

game was to take place on Boxing Day.

Tom Wills, the celebrated cricketer and footballer who was appointed coach at Edenhope in August 1866, was also appointed coach of the Aboriginal team. He played and practised with them in December, when they chalked up some good wins over local sides.

8000 spectators turned out on Boxing Day, sufficient to make the team seemingly dubbed the 'Australian Aboriginal Cricketers' nervous, for there were seven ducks in the first innings of 39. Mullagh made 16. The MCC scored 101, Wills and Mullagh two wickets each, and the AAC made 87 in its second innings.

The team included seven of the players to make the first Australian tour of England in 1868. It comprised Mullagh, Officer, Bullocky, Tarpot, Cuzens, Dick-a-Dick, Peter, Officer and Sundown.

The MCC, which had several of its best players in Sydney for the intercolonial match, used some of the Aboriginal team in a club game, and then four of the team including the Australian-born Wills in a match between Australian

Natives and The World, and finally in the non-first class match, Victoria v Tasmania, Bullocky and Cuzens played for Victoria – the first Aboriginal sportsmen to represent their colony or state (Mullagh was unavailable through injury).

In January a somewhat suspect Sydney entrepreneur named W. E. B. Gurnett contracted with Wills and William Hayman, the manager of the Western District Aboriginal team, to tour them to NSW and England, promising bonuses for all on return.

They played a series of matches in Victoria, including one in Bendigo against a team that boasted the future Test players Billy Midwinter and Harry Boyle.

Illness, difficulties with Mr Gurnett's bouncing cheques and a smaller interest by spectators haunted the team. The return match against the MCC was not a success, although the Aboriginal team won.

And just before the team left for Sydney, on February 12, the Central Board for the Protection of Aborigines unsuccessfully requested the Governor demand a bond from Gurnett against the team

being left high and dry in England. The Governor declined to intervene.

A legal imbroglio developed where Wills and Hayman were arrested on the suit of Gurnett for alleged breach of contract; they were released on the security of Charles Lawrence, English-born NSW captain and former teammate of Wills in England. It seems that Gurnett for some now obscure reason wanted to get out of the contracts with Wills and Hayman.

Lawrence now joined the team for a series of matches in NSW, and the tour of England supposedly being organised by Gurnett was abandoned. Wills and Hayman, at some considerable cost, managed to get the team back to Melbourne by the beginning of May 1867, possibly aided by money from Lawrence, who, as a cricketer, saw the possibility of a future tour of England. Wills' association with the team ended in Melbourne.

Lawrence would later that year coach the surviving Aborigines in Edenhope. Four had died and three more were seriously ill by the time they reached home. None had been paid a penny.

The Aboriginal Australian team playing at the MCG on Boxing Day, 1866. The old Pavilion is seen, left. NSW beat Victoria at the same time in Sydney by an innings.

tour of 1866–67

Nannultera, painted by John Michael Crossland as Boy Playing Cricket *in 1854.*

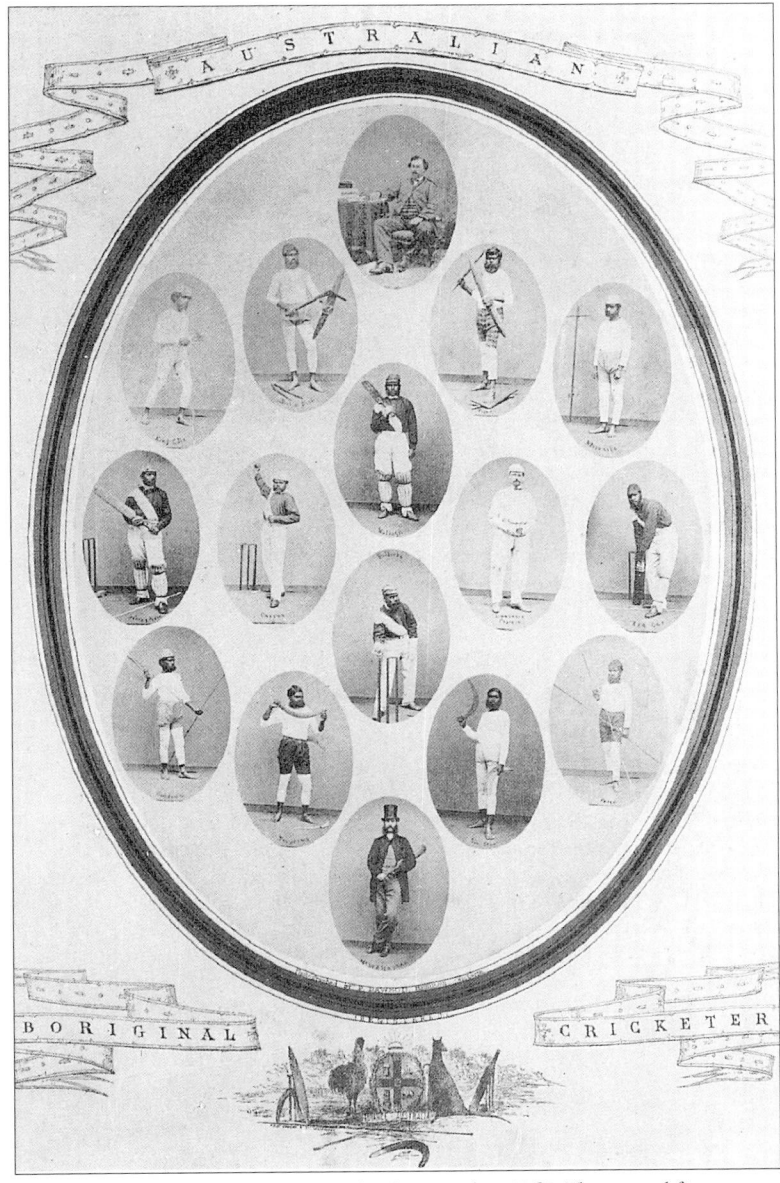

The team photographed in Warrnambool in October 1867. The central figures are Mullagh, top, and Bullocky, below. Lawrence is centre left.

The Aboriginal team, December 1866. From left: Tarpot, Tom Wills, Mullagh. Front: King Cole, Jellico, Peter, Red Cap, Harry Rose, Bullocky, Cuzens, Dick-a-Dick (standing).

The 1868 Australian Aboriginal team's tou

The four European backers of the 1868 Australian Aboriginal Tour of England were former English cricketer and NSW captain Charles Lawrence; George Smith, a Sydney alderman; George Graham, a solicitor; as well as manager of the 1866–67 tour, William Hayman.

After the debacle of the first attempt to get an Aboriginal team to England, these men proved remarkably fair and sincere (for the times) in their attitudes to the Aboriginal cricketers trained and selected around Edenhope in 1867.

They undoubtedly undertook organisation of the tour to make a profit for themselves (there is no evidence of any offer to pay the players) but in doing so they exhibited a high degree of organisation and concern for the welfare of their players.

Most of the team came from the Western District of Victoria, and one or two may have been brought by Lawrence from NSW.

The team chosen was Mullagh, Cuzens, Bullocky, Peter, Tarpot, Dick-a-Dick, Mosquito, Neddy (Jim Crow), S. Harry, Twopenny, King Cole, Sundown, Harry Rose and Red Cap.

Before setting out on an adventurous covered-wagon tour of Victoria, Lawrence equipped each player with a warm and distinctive uniform comprising white flannel trousers, a red Garibaldi shirt, diagonal blue sashes, hat bands, belts and neckties – and individually coloured peaked caps. Red Cap had a black cap, Mullagh a red cap.

Lawrence also had the team practise other skills, such as ball dodging, spear throwing, and a game using a shield as defence against thrown cricket balls as useful adjuncts to the cricket entertainment in England.

The covered wagon covered a lot of territory after it set off on 16 September, including playing one match at Corio where Tom Wills was playing. Wills was unhappy at not being included in the touring party, considering his work the previous season. Wills took four wickets but was out for 6, lbw to Lawrence. Wills was ground bowler and coach at the MCG, and deeply involved in Australian football, but was described as being 'hurt' at not being further involved.

The Protection Board had been making another attempt to stop the tour, but Lawrence, with the public on his side, circumvented any action in Victoria by leaving the colony not from Melbourne, but from Queenscliff, near Geelong, late in October.

In and around Sydney they played a number of games including one against the Army and Navy team which included William Caffyn, in front of the visiting Duke of Edinburgh and 4000 other spectators. This match ended in a draw. Next day 9000 turned up for an athletic entertainment.

The team sailed for England on February 8. Tarpot and Harry Rose did not sail with them. The team arrived on 13 May 1868.

They played their first match at the Oval on 25 May, and their last and 47th, also at the Oval on October 17.

King Cole died of TB on 24 June, and Sundown and Jim Crow were sent home ill in August. The remaining eleven players had to see out the tour.

They lost the first match against Surrey by an innings and seven runs after Surrey made 222 (Lawrence seven wickets, Mullagh three) and the Aboriginal team 83 and 132, Mullagh 33 and 73.

It was a great success financially and socially, attracting over 20,000 people to two days of cricket and one day of athletic sports. The tourists' profit was £309/9/1.

The historians of the 1868 tour, John Mulvaney and Rex Harcourt, spent some time working out the standard of opposition that the Aboriginal team met while on tour. (Considering the difficulties the first 'European' Australian tourists had in obtaining any matches at all ten years later, this first tour was better organised.)

None of the 47 matches is counted as first class, but ten matches were played against teams representing counties of which four were drawn and six lost. None of the counties fielded full teams. 16 matches were played against 'mid grade' for five wins, eight draws and three losses. 21 matches were played against minor teams, for nine wins, six draws and five losses.

W. G. Grace praised Mullagh and Cuzens for their good all-round form, but had less time for the rest of the team: 'very poor players, being boomerangers and spear throwers rather than cricketers.' In all 47 matches, 14 wins, 19 draws and 14 losses. (Dave Gregory's 1878 team played 41, won 19, lost seven and drew 15 – but 17 of these matches were rated first class.) They bowled better than they batted.

The players were regarded as 'quite civilised' by the English. They were an ebullient and charming bunch of cricketers, with fine

The Aboriginal Australian team at Trent Bridge, Nottingham, August 1868. From left, standing, Dick-a-Dick, Tiger, Mullagh, Lawrence, Cuzens, Red Cap, Bullocky, Twopenny. Seated Mosquito, Petyer, W. Shepherd, Dumas. The team gained in respect for its personality as well as its cricket as the tour progressed around England.

# of England

sense of fun, interested in what was happening, and quite up to the social graces when required. 'Their general behaviour, either at meals or in conversation, is quite equal to many beings who consider themselves highly civilised.'

The Rochdale *Observer* said they were 'stalwart men'. Compared to the behaviour of later touring Australian sides, this first team was genteel in the extreme.

Cricket was said to have had a 'humanising and civilising influence' on the muscular Christian tradition in sport – which had the same effect on other Australian natives.

The *Ballarat Star* wrote in 1867: 'The order of civilisation in the Christian sense seems to be first to make savages men, and then to make them Christians … To convert the savage into sheep shearer was something, but it seems more to make him into a smart cricketer … the savage rises to quite a higher social level.'

Such was the case when a team billed as The Australians played an MCC team at Lord's on June 12. The MCC included the Earl of Coventry, Viscount Downe, Lieutenant Colonel Bathurst – a team of high social standing if not supreme cricketing ability. No MCC professional played.

The MCC made 164 and 120 (Cuzens ten wickets, Mullagh eight for 101 off 62 four-ball overs). The Australians scored 185 (Mullagh 75), but collapsed for 45 in the second innings. W. G. Grace said they had acquitted themselves very well; as much praise as he allowed other Australian teams until much later in cricket history.

Mullagh was the outstanding player of the tour, and as later events in Australia demonstrated, he was one of the outstanding cricketers of the age in England or Australia.

The team arrived back in Sydney on 4 February 1869. They seem not to have been paid wages or the promised bonus of £50. Graham, the main backer, made a profit of about £1000 after expenses. Hayman and Lawrence had their expenses paid.

The Aborigines enjoyed themselves, and could not be said to be 'unduly' exploited as Harcourt and Mulvaney delicately put it. It was certainly more fun and possibly less dangerous to tour England as an Australian cricket team than to work as a drover on a Western District station.

Sports at the Trent Bridge ground, featuring some unusual events. These included throwing boomerangs and spears, and cricket-ball dodging.

A game evolves – early cricket rules and

Bats

The major highlights in the development of the cricket bat are the years 1773, 1835 and the 1855. Around 1773 the modern shape of the cricket bat with straight sides, shoulders and a bulge at the back was made by John Small in Hampshire in 1773. Before bats generally had a curve and were more like hockey sticks.

In 1835 the maximum dimensions of the bat were agreed – that it should be no more than four and a half inches wide (this was laid down by the Hambledon Club in 1771), and 38 inches long. And in the 1850s, by 1853, a professional at Lord's, Thomas Nixon, made a bat with a cane handle spliced into the blade. Until the development of these 'springy' bats, they had been made of a variety of different sorts of bone-jarring solid wood, depending on what was at hand for the bat maker. In Australia solid bats were frequently carved of cedar, but other wood including red gum was used. Many bats used after the development of the springy bat in 1850s were still made from solid wood. However, the willow (Salix alba caerulea) and the Sarawak cane came to be the standard materials for bats. Other material came to be used in the handle, between the sections of cane – such as whalebone, gutta-percha, cork and rubber.

Balls

Cricket balls have been made in much the same way from much the same materials of leather and cork for hundreds of years. Joseph Farrington wrote in his diary in 1811 that his company, Duke & Son had been making cricket balls for 250 years, which may or may not be true.

Balls were originally white, but in the past 100 years have been dyed red. In 1744 cricket balls were to weigh between five and six ounces – but in that year the weight was narrowed to between 5½ and 5¾ ounces. In 1838 the circumference of the ball was defined at between 9 and 9¼ inches. Traditionally the best cricket balls are made by making covers from cow hide, fashioning two 'quarters' into a hemispherical half with a ridge for stitching two together. They are placed around a 'quilt', a cube of cork wrapped in alternate layers of

The Victorian team which first played NSW, in 1859. The captains were Tom Wills (Victoria) and George Gilbert (NSW).

wet worsted and strips of cork which shrink when dry, tightening around the cork.

In Australia such balls were rare and expensive except in first class cricket and Test matches in the second half of the nineteenth century. Before and after this time much cricket was played with a 'composition' ball. A 'compo' ball was moulded from small pieces of rubber and cork.

The Over

Most matches played in Australia during the nineteenth century used a four-ball over. The exceptions were six-ball overs used in ten intercolonial matches between 1870–71 and 1888–89.

From that season six ball overs were used exclusively until World War I, except for two matches of NSW v Lord Sheffield's XI in 1891–92, and two matches in 1898–99 when five-ball overs were employed.

Bowlers were only permitted to change ends twice during an innings until 1889. A bowler was allowed to bowl consecutive overs – but no more than two. After 1889 a bowler could change ends as frequently as he wished, but could not bowl consecutive overs.

The Toss: using a bat has been standard practice in the absence of a coin.

equipment

The follow-on

Until 1897 Australia followed the law as laid down by the Marylebone Cricket Club. Until 1854 this provided that the team batting second would 'follow on' immediately if they were 100 runs or more behind. This did not occur in Australia. In 1854 the margin was reduced to 80 runs, and in 1894 extended to 120 runs. In Australia the margin was increased to 200 runs after an incident in 1896–97 when a fielding team conceded runs to avoid the follow-on. The follow-on was compulsory until about 1907–08 in Australia.

Bowling

All bowling was once underarm bowling though this did not necessarily mean that all were 'grubbers' or shooters. In fact many early nineteenth century bowlers, extending their arm to about the level of the elbow (legal in 1828), could achieve surprising pace, bounce and cut-in from the off side.

The slow version was 'lob' bowling which meant high balls aimed at dropping on or just in front of the stumps. Gradually, however, the underarm bowler's hand crept higher until it was close to the level of the armpit. 'Round-arm' bowling where the hand could go no higher than the shoulder was allowed in 1835. In England after a controversial series of no-balls being called in 1862, the law was amended in 1864 to allow over-arm bowling. In Australia all these changes took some time to catch on, with umpires no-balling bowlers and bowlers being accused of throwing when their deliveries were legitimate in England. In Tasmania, round-arm bowling was banned in the 1860s, and players such as Tom Wills was accused of throwing 'high deliveries', that is raising his hand above the shoulder, in the same period.

Pitches

When first class cricket began in Australia the laws allowed a new pitch to be used during a match if rain had fallen and both captains agreed. In addition, in some Sydney matches, pitches were changed for no obvious reason. In Melbourne, matches were generally played on the same pitch.

Gentlemen clad for cricket in the 1840s. Caps and bow ties are de rigeur and padded gloves are part of the equippage.

Prominent Victorian cricketers of 1859: Gideon Elliot, Barton Grindrod, George Marshall, Jerry Bryant and Tom Wills.

W. G. Grace in Australia, 1873–74

Grace was just 25 when he accepted an invitation from a consortium of the Melbourne, South Melbourne and East Melbourne cricket clubs to form a team to tour Australia in the summer of 1873–74. 'Can you, will you, bring a team at the end of the year?' read the telegram. Grace also accepted a fee of £1500, and all expenses paid for himself and his new wife. Aside from the cricket, he could look upon the tour as a kind of Antipodean honeymoon.

The professionals among the twelve chosen received £170, and included the seemingly ageless slow round-armer James Southerton, and another very effective bowler, James Lillywhite, W. G.'s younger brother G. F. and cousin Walter Gilbert, the Surrey batting pair Richard Humphrey and Henry Jupp, and the Nottinghamshire all-rounder William Oscroft.

The team left England on 23 October 1873 aboard the P&O steamer *Mirzapore*, and after the ship became stuck in the mud in the Suez Canal, completed the voy-age on the *Nubia*, arriving in Melbourne on December 13.

After a little practice before enthusiastic crowds, the All-England team took field at the MCG to play XVIII of Victoria, the odds having shortened from the XXII of a decade before. A vast assemblage witnessed the game: more than 16,000 people were there at the start of play.

Victoria batted on a pitch 'not to be surpassed in England' said James Southerton. This was per-haps because W. G. had, as he wrote later, 'shown the Australians how to prepare a pitch, and dis-abused their minds of the idea that a good pitch can be obtained with-out special attention.'

Some of the names in the Victorian side were destined for bigger things – Tom Horan, Billy Midwinter, Harry Boyle, and the fast bowler and entrepreneur of the first Test tour in 1976–77 John Conway, but the star of the show was Indian-born, former Middlesex and MCC batsman Bransby Beauchamp Cooper. B. B. had in partnership with W. G. put on a record 283 for Gentlemen v Players in 1869, when he made his only first class century. In this innings he made a splendid 84, Boyle 30 and Conway 32 in Victoria's 266.

The Victorians disposed of All England for 110, Boyle bowling W. G. with a 'shooter' for 33, and following on they were out for 135, W. G. not out 51.

Victoria won by an innings and 21 runs, to the great delight of the 40,000 who had paid 2/6 to see the match.

England's second match was at Ballarat against a XXII which included Sam Cosstick, Tom Wills, and Francis Allan – players who it was said were ready to represent any town or district on the Australian continent.

W. G. made 126 and G. F. 112 in All England's 470. The match was drawn.

In the next match in Stawell W. G. complained that 'the ground was in deplorable condition. Here and there were small patches of grass, but the greater part was utterly devoid of herbage … How bad the ground really was may be judged from the fact that one slow ball actually stuck in the dust and never reached the batsman.'

XXII of Stawell won the match because there were twice as many of them – 71 and 11/54, All England 43 and 91. W. G. noted that bad wickets reduced all play-ers to the same primitive level, which is not what the spectators paid to see – which was him.

The Englishmen did hard travel-ling to Warrnambool, before sail-ing to Sydney and the match against a NSW XVIII. This side boasted some of the rising stars of Australian cricket – Charles Bannerman, Fred Spofforth and Dave Gregory. The game was played at the Albert Ground on January 24. Once again the locals won, scoring 127 and 9/57 to All England's 92 and 90, thanks to some excellent bowling by Joseph Coates. Gregory made 32, the highest score of the match, and Spofforth took two wickets in the second innings.

A young and stylish W. G. Grace takes a net. Practice made him as close to perfect as any cricketer of his era. He was the greatest drawcard for good measure.

The *Evening News*, defending the English cricketers from scorn from Victoria that they weren't all that good, made the comment that 'cricket is so well known and vigorously practised here that the odds 18/11 are too great.' Soon, equality would have to prevail.

The Englishmen's match against Maitland was cancelled because of the floods. They travelled the switchback railway to Bathurst, with W. G. riding the engine, and defeated XXII by eight wickets.

They returned to Sydney for what was hoped to be a very testing match against a Combined Victorian and NSW XV at the Albert Ground.

It was quite a strong side, but was comprehensively outplayed by W. G.'s men. All England made 170 (Sam Costick 5/67), W. G. 9, G. F. 26, but the Combined could only manage 98, with Lillywhite 9/39, Southerton 4/56.

The second innings of All England was marked by some controversy. In making 236 and himself a hard-hitting 73, W. G. had seemed to urge some of his players to 'hit out or get out', so that they would have time to bowl out the XV. The crowd objected to this, just as W. G.

objected to some umpiring decisions in the Combined innings. The result however was salutary for Australian cricket – All England won by 218 runs, Combined all out for 90, Lillywhite taking another 9 for 33.

Back in Victoria, XXIIs of Bendigo and Castlemaine were easily defeated, as was another XV of Victoria on February 21 in a match at the MCG, by seven wickets. Southerton and Lillywhite were once again virtually unplayable.

Trips to Tasmania and South Australia, where the first important match at the Adelaide Oval was played, rounded out the tour. Sam Cosstick said 'Bar W. G. we're as good as they are, and some day we'll lick 'em with eleven.' In the meantime a way to play the wily English bowling would need to be found.

There was some unpleasantness on the trip, especially concerning the second-class treatment of the English professionals by the organisers, but the tourists played under all kinds of conditions, always against the odds and mostly with good humour.

They played 15 games, won ten and lost three.

Australian grounds and grandstands

In his definitive work *Some Grounds To Appeal*, Richard Christen notes that 39 venues have been used for first class cricket in Australia since 1850–51 Only seven have been used for Test matches since the first was played at the MCG in 1876–77.

Melbourne – MCG

The Melbourne Cricket Club, established in 1838, played its first match on a site in William Street now occupied by the Old Mint, and had its first ground on a flat area below Batman's Hill now occupied by the Spencer Street Station. In 1848 the MCC was granted occupancy of an area south of the Yarra in a swampy area of Emerald Hill, which was also taken over by the railways.

In September 1853 the MCC received approval to enclose 10 acres of Yarra Park, and the first first class match was played at the Metropolitan Cricket Ground, soon known as the Melbourne Cricket Ground, on 26 March 1856.

A temporary canvas and timber grandstand was built on the rough ground for H. H. Stephenson's tour in 1861–62, seating 6000.

The 1871–72 Victoria v NSW game seems to have been the first played on a remodelled oval playing area inside a circular ground plan. W. G. Grace's 1873–74 team played in front of a temporary grandstand, with a mound around the northern side. In 1876–77 a Public Stand with reversible seating enabled the watching of the cricket inside the ground, and the football outside it. (The Melbourne Football Club played all home games inside the MCG from 1879.)

The Pavilion was built in 1882 and extended in 1889. The Public Stand was rebuilt in 1884 after it was destroyed by fire.

The Grey Smith Stand was constructed west of the Pavilion in 1906, the Harrison Stand in 1908 and the Wardill Stand in 1912.

The Member's Stand replaced the old brick Pavilion in 1928.

The (old) two-tiered Southern Stand was completed in 1937.

The Public Stand was demolished in 1954 and replaced by the Olympic Stand in 1956. The MCG's east–west slope of over seven feet was removed in 1955. The Grey Smith Stand was replaced by the Western or Ponsford Stand in 1967.

An electronic scoreboard replaced the old one in 1982 and lighting towers were installed in 1984.

The Melbourne Cricket Ground in January 1858 during the Victoria v NSW Grand Intercolonial Match, by Harry Glover.

The Albert Ground, Redfern. Five first class matches were played here between 1870 and 1877.

The Great Southern Stand was completed for the 1991–92 season.

Sydney – SCG

First class cricket was played on the Domain on 14 January 1857. This was the northern part of the Domain, used as a parade ground, below Parliament House and the Sydney Hospital, marked out by W. Tunks and H. Hilliard. The Domain was picturesque but suffered from being a public place, used by pedestrians, soldiers and horses.

The Albert Ground in Redfern was used for five matches between 1871–72 and 1876–77.

NSW cricket authorities were granted use of the former Military ground at Moore Park in 1875, and in 1876 the NSW government appointed the first trustees to control the ground.

Some acrimony ensued in the 1880s about different sports' use of this, the Association ground, and in the activities of trustee Phillip Sheridan, a rival to the NSWCA in control of major cricket in NSW.

There was a pavilion and grandstand in place in 1877–78; in 1883 a Ladies Stand; and in 1886 the Member's Stand replaced the pavilion.

In March 1894 a red flag with the initials SCG flew over the ground, with the NSWCA the preferential lessee from the SCG Trustees. The argument over which sport had primary use of the SCG continued until World War One.

In 1895 the Hill Stand opened on the eastern side – and because it cost a shilling to get in it was soon renamed the Bob Stand. In 1896, the cycle track was constructed and the Hill and Paddington Hill were enlarged, and SCG No. 2 oval and The Northern Stand opened in 1897. The Brewongle Stand received a new roof with turrets in 1901. The Smokers Stand was removed to the SCG No. 2 in 1909 and a new stand constructed which became the Sheridan Stand in 1910. The cycle track was removed in 1920, and the scoreboard erected in 1924. The M. A. Noble Stand was built in 1936.

In 1973 the Bradman stand was built on the Paddington Hill.

Light towers were erected for World Series Cricket in 1978–79 and the Brewongle Stand was rebuilt into its present three-tiered structure in 1980. A stand named for Bill O'Reilly (1985) replaced the Bob Stand. Another was named after the rugby league champion Clive Churchill (1987), and new seating on the Hill became the Doug Walters stand (1990).

Adelaide

The Adelaide Oval was used for the initial first class match in SA v Tasmania on 10 November 1877, and was the venue for its first Test match in 1884–85. SACA had taken over the ground, used by the South Australian club in 1871. It was then improved and fenced and opened in December 1873. The first small grandstand was built in 1882. In 1897 the large banks were constructed as well as the tennis courts behind the ground.

The George Giffen stand replaced the 1882 grandstand, and was first known as the Members or Central Stand. The Sir Edwin Smith Stand was originally an open stand roofed in the 1890s. The Mostyn Evan Stand was built in 1924 as an extension of the Central Stand. The Sir Donald Bradman stand replaced the John Creswell Stand (1923) in 1989. The Victor Richardson Gates were constructed in 1967.

Perth

First class cricket commenced at the WACA ground in 1898–99, and the first Test against England, was played in 1970–71. The WACA obtained a 999 year lease in 1889, and built a modest grandstand in 1895. The Public Stand opened in 1922 and the Members or Farley Stand opened in 1931. WA entered the Sheffield Shield in 1947–48. the Player's Stand (1970) was originally dressing rooms erected in 1960.

The John Inverarity Stand was built in 1970 for the first Test, replacing the original 1897 Pavilion.

The Prindiville Stand was built in 1984 replacing the 1922 stand.

The Lillee–Marsh stand was opened in 1988. Light towers were erected for the 1986–87 season.

Hobart

Bellerive Oval had its first first class game when Tasmania played Sri Lanka in 1987–88, and staged its first Test, also against Sri Lanka, in 1989–90. Cricket was first played here in 1885, but major improvements did not occur until 1947. Turf pitches were laid for the 1956–57 season. Shield cricket has been played at Bellerive since 1990–91.

Brisbane

Exhibition Ground

This was the venue of the initial first class game in Queensland, against NSW on 1 April 1893.

The Ernest Baynes Stand was opened by the operator the RNA in 1922. Merri Creek soil was imported from Melbourne to improve the wicket in 1924, and games against England were played in 1924–25, leading to Queensland playing in the Sheffield Shield in 1926–27, and staging the first Test in Brisbane in 1928–29, and against the West Indies in 1930–31.

The 'Gabba

The ground at Woolloongabba opened in 1896, and staged a first class game in 1897–98 against the touring England team, and its first Test in 1931–32 against South Africa.

Facilities were modest through the 1930s and 1940s, but in 1959 legislation ws passed and the QCA formed the Queensland Cricketers' Club. New spectator facilities soon followed.

In 1971 the ground was also redeveloped for greyhound racing, and the Clem Jones Stand and the Gordon Chalk building were opened. Dog racing began in 1972. The Sir Leslie Wilson Stand was opened in 1974.

The Brisbane Bears, later the Brisbane Lions AFL team, agreed to play at the 'Gabba in 1993, resulting in dog racing moving out, and a major redevelopment of the oval. By the 1995–96 season new stands and lights were erected.

The Melbourne Cricket Ground in 1873, The stand was reversible, so that football in Richmond Paddock could be watched.

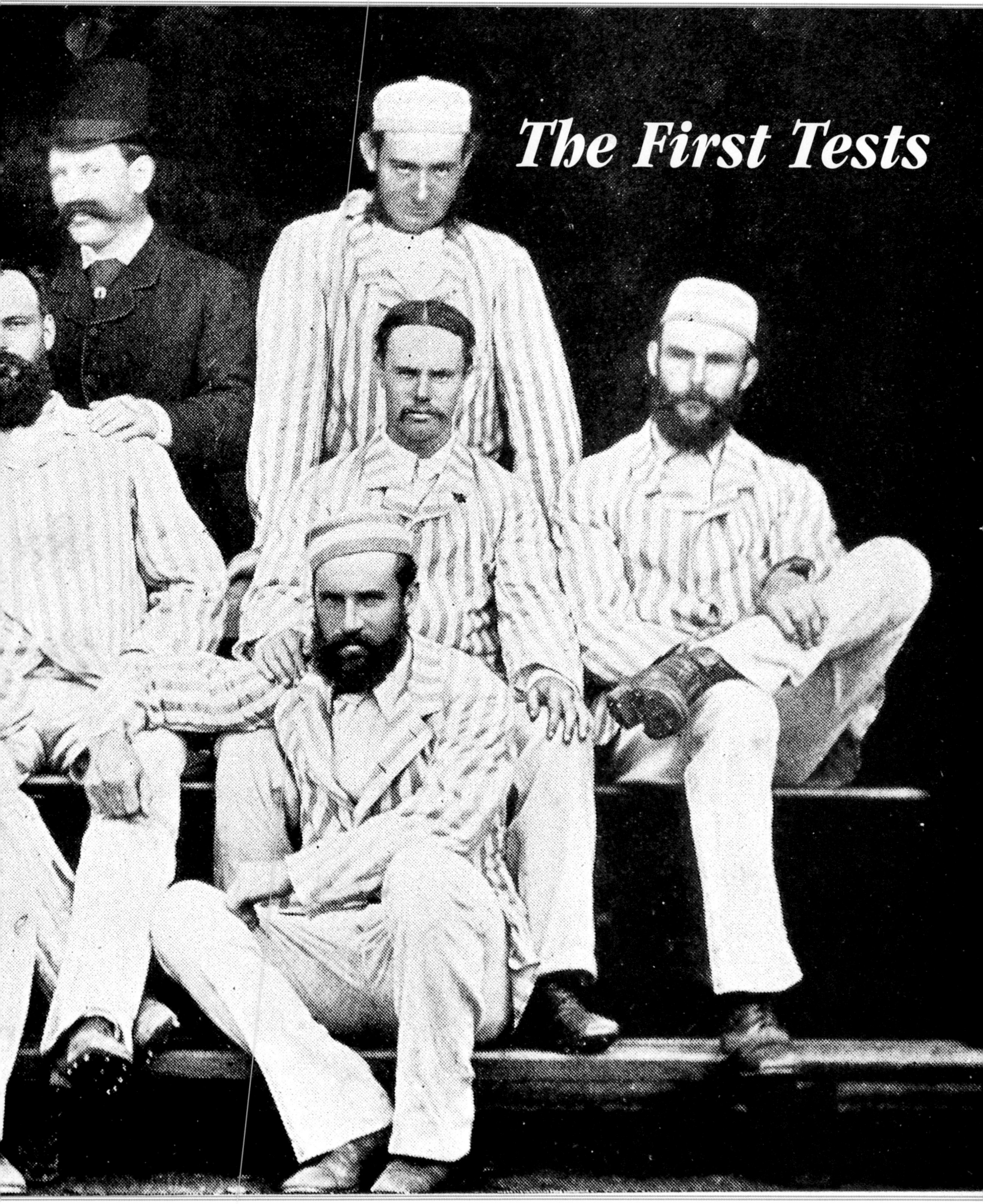

Colonial 15's on terms with 'All-England'

The English team on arrival after the long voyage, ready for six months of contests with the Australians.

Melbourne, Jan. 12. The 'All-England' team of James Lillywhite has had mixed success since its arrival in South Australia on November 6, losing to the colonial teams several times. The South Australian, Victorian and NSW teams have had superior numbers, but the conviction is growing that they are beginning to play cricket at the same sort of level as the Englishmen.

Admittedly the England team is not necessarily the best that the Old Country can muster, but the best that could be persuaded to make the tour, with a guarantee of £200 per player. Nor is the team from the length and breadth of England, but a party of professionals from four Counties – Sussex and Surrey in the south and Nottinghamshire and Yorkshire in the north.

Nevertheless, there are some very fine players. The best batsman is Yorkshireman George Ulyett, the youngest player at 25. In Adelaide he scored 58 against the South Australian 22.

Others from Yorkshire are Thomas Armitage and Andrew Greenwood (batsmen), and Tom Emmett and Alan Hill (bowlers). The oldest man in the side is bowler James Southerton of Surrey, at 49, while the other Surrey men are 'Stonewall' Henry Jupp and wicketkeeper Ted Pooley, who holds the record of 12 victims in a match.

The team's finest bowler Alfred Shaw is from Nottingham, as is batsman John Selby. Lillywhite bats down the order and bowls a bit, while his Sussex compatriot is the dashing batsman Henry Charlwood.

Shaw lands the ball so consistently that, after practice on a softish pitch, it was noticed a patch about the size of a saucer where the ball had landed. He is a man of ample girth and not a speedster, but can move the ball off the pitch both ways.

The English team's matches have been well attended, with many people coming in from the country.

England started with a win and a draw against the South Australian teams of 22, but teams of 15 have beaten the tourists, twice in Sydney and once in Melbourne. Now, in a two-day match at the Redfern Oval, in Sydney, a NSW team of 11 has drawn with the tourists.

While the England team is away in New Zealand for seven weeks, playing a series of matches against Provincial teams, a 'Test' match between a representative Australian XI and England is being arranged.

Bowler Spofforth refuses to play

Melbourne, March 13. The Australian side to play England won't field the two NSW fast bowlers Frederick Spofforth and Edwin Evans. The selection has been odd, in that half of the team was selected in Sydney and the other in Melbourne.

From Sydney are Nat Thomson, Charles Bannerman, Dave Gregory and Ned Gregory. Victorians are Tom Kendall, Jack Hodges, Tom Horan, Tom Garrett, Bransby Cooper, William Midwinter and wicketkeeper Jack Blackham.

Spofforth would not play because wicketkeeper William Murdoch, originally selected by NSW, was not accepted by the Victorian organisers, who proposed the local hero Jack Blackham in his place. Edwin Evans decided that he did not want to travel 600 miles.

The Victorian fast bowler Frank Allan has declared two days before the match that he is unable to play because of an agricultural show at his home town of Warrnambool. His replacement, Jack Hodges, and spinner Tom Kendall are making their first-class debuts. Dave Gregory has been named as the Australian captain, and he looks the part with his full beard and imposing physique.

QUICK SINGLES

A great view. A fine grandstand has been built at the Melbourne Cricket Ground, with five seating bays. The seating is reversible for winter, so that spectators can look into Yarra Park for the football.

Show of class. Victorian bowler Frank Allan takes 8/60 in a match between James Lillywhite's England XI and a Victorian 22, ending on Feb 20.

All not well. After a rough passage from New Zealand, the English team seemed generally unwell as they arrived in Melbourne on March 9 to play the Australian XI. Wicketkeeper Ted Pooley was left behind to face charges in New Zealand.

Late start. The opening day's play of the Test match on March 15 started at 1.05 p.m., and lunch was taken at 2 p.m. Three and-a-half-hours play was possible.

Up country cricket. Following its first Test loss in Melbourne, James Lillywhite's team has had a busy country schedule, with matches in Bendigo, Ballarat and Ararat. All were drawn.

Young Colonials. The Australian XI for the 'Test' match has an average age seven years younger than England, whose average is boosted by James Shaw at 45 and James Southerton at 49.

Homeward bound. At Canterbury on April 6, the Supreme Court in Christchurch, New Zealand, found England wicket-keeper Ted Pooley not guilty on a charge of assault and maliciously damaging the property of Ralph Donkin, following an argument over a cricket bet. Donkin said he would predict the scores of each batsman, and got most right – 0.

New cricket ground. A 12 acre site at Centennial Park was approved by the New South Wales Government on August 3 as the site for a cricket ground.

First-up win. South Australia played its first eleven-a-side match and the first first-class match on South Australian soil, at the Adelaide Oval on November 20. It beat Tasmania by an innings and 13 runs.

December 26, 27. Understrength Victorian and NSW teams met at the Melbourne Cricket Ground, as the players chosen to tour England were playing around the country to raise funds. New South Wales won by an innings and six runs, thanks to the efforts of Edwin Evans (9/92) and Joseph Coates (9/71).

Fred Spofforth: not available.

Australia wins the Melbourne Test match

Melbourne, March 20. The Australian XI has won the Test match against the English team by 45 runs. The hero was Charles Bannerman, the opening batsman, who made 165 in Australia's first innings.

The match revolved around that superb innings by Bannerman. He was 126 not out at stumps on the opening day, in a total of 6/166. The tragedy for England was the dropping of Bannerman, early in his innings. He was deceived into hitting a 'dolly' shot off Shaw, but the ball hit Armitage in the stomach and dropped to the turf.

The crowd had risen to 4500 as word of Bannerman's stand got around, and there were 3500 there at the start of the second day. The Australians went to lunch at 7/232, with Bannerman on 159.

Soon after lunch a ball from Ulyett struck Bannerman's right hand and split the finger to the bone. He retired hurt for 165 and the Australian innings soon folded at 245, with Tommy Garrett 18 not out. Shaw took 3/51 and off-spinner Southerton 3/61.

In Australia's first over Jupp seemed to dislodge the bails with his foot when attempting a leg glance. But the umpires appeared not to see the incident and 'not out' was the call, to hoots from the crowd.

Overall the England first innings had more quality and consistency than the Australian, but it lacked a big score. Jupp held the top of the innings together.

The Australian bowling was creditable, but there was quite a contrast in the fielding. The tourists had been safe while the Australians were reckless, diving around and sending wild returns.

At the end of the day England was 4/109, with Midwinter having gained two wickets with his off-spin. Jupp was 54 not out.

A crowd of around 12,000 turned out on Saturday. Billy Midwinter soon had Armitage out for 9, caught Blackham, and bowled his successor Shaw for 10.

Then the big blow was struck when Jupp fell leg-before to Garrett for 63, England soon tumbled to 196. Midwinter had taken 5/78, a bowling hero to match Bannerman.

Australia's second innings was a disaster, reminding everyone of the usual rout of Australian teams inflicted by England. Bannerman was cheered to the crease, but there was a deadly silence when he was bowled by Ulyett for four.

Horan looked good in making 20 before being caught off Hill, but the rest of the batsmen surrendered to Shaw and Australia was in a terrible state at 5/37. Midwinter and Ned Gregory dug in for a stand of 25, but at stumps Australia was 9/83.

At the start of play the next day, an England win looked inevitable. Kendall and Hodges carried the score to 104 before Hodges was bowled. England had only a moderate 153 to get.

But a new hero was to emerge for Australia, and Tom Kendall's 7/55 must rank almost as high as Bannerman's innings. The young Victorian slow bowler had the Englishmen in complete turmoil with his flight and ability to turn the ball both ways.

England had changed its order, opening with the Yorkshire pair of Hill and Greenwood. Hill started the rot when he skied Kendall's second ball of the innings to Thomson at mid-on. Greenwood, Jupp and Charlwood followed quickly and England was reeling at 4/22, with Kendall having 3/22. Midwinter had the stonewalling Jupp lbw for 4.

Selby and Ulyett set about retrieving the English position. These two raised the score to 62, and the free-scoring Ulyett looked the hope of the side until Kendall bowled him for 24. Shaw already had the fine bowling figures of 8/98 and looked formidable with the bat, but Kendall tempted him from the crease and he was brilliantly stumped by Blackham. England was 6/68.

Selby was now carrying the English batting. Gregory brought on the young Jack Hodges and the move paid off as Selby attempted to hit him over the long-on boundary and was caught for 31. The score was 7/92 and still 60 to win.

It was slow stuff, but the tension was acute. Hodges bowled yet another maiden, then Blackham took a beautiful catch to dismiss Armitage off Kendall: 8/93. Emmett and Lillywhite opted for attack, but Hodges clean bowled the England captain, leaving only Southerton to come in.

But when Emmett pulled Kendall on to his stumps for 9, England was all out for 108 – losers by 45 runs.

Hats went in the air and Kendall was cheered from the ground, while Hodges was well praised for having taking 2/7 off seven overs.

The new grandstand at the Melbourne Cricket Ground, all ready for the 'Test'.

Charles Bannerman, hero of Australia with his 165 not out in the first innings.

Heroes taste the fruits of victory

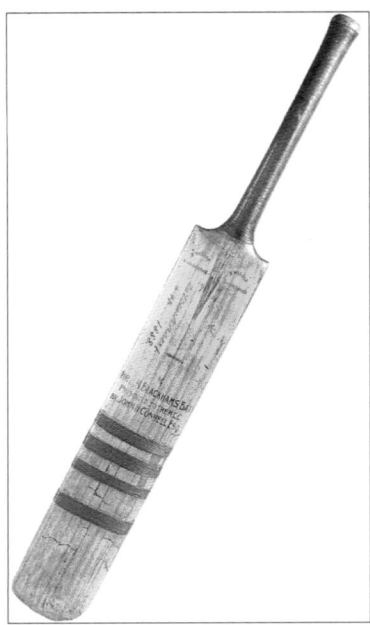

A bat presented to John Blackham.

Melbourne, June 30. The players who won the first Test match against England in March have received a commemorative gold medal from the Victorian Cricketers' Association. The Australian captain Dave Gregory was given a slightly larger version of the medal.

A subscription of funds from spectators and well wishers has raised £83 for the batting hero Charles Bannerman and £23 each for bowler Tom Kendall and the wicketkeeper John Blackham.

Australians have been gripped by cricketing euphoria since that first victory, and the pleasure has diminished little over the past few months. The newspapers have been full of it, with the *Argus* setting the tone on the morning after the win. It stated: 'For the time being we all – New South Wales and Victorians – must forget our geographical distinctions and only remember that we are of one nation, Australia.'

The *Australasian* warned against too much bragging, but then went on to say that Bannerman was the best batsman of the two sides, Kendall a better spinner and Blackham a better wicketkeeper than the absent Ted Pooley, detained in New Zealand on an assault charge.

The victory also brought back the words of former Surrey professional Sam Cosstick, now teaching in Australia, who made this prediction during W. G. Grace's tour of 1873–74: 'Bar W. G. we are as good as they are, and one day we'll lick 'em with 11.'

England squares the Test match ledger

Melbourne, April 4. The England team has restored its pride by beating Australia in the return Test match played at the Melbourne Cricket Ground, winning by four wickets. There was a harrowing time in its second innings when it seemed the tourists might be beaten again, but they rallied through the brilliant work of their finest batsman, George Ulyett.

The Australian team was strengthened by the inclusion of the New South Welshman Fred Spofforth, who announced himself available when his wicketkeeper/batsman friend Billy Murdoch was included. Victorian batsman Thomas Kelly was also brought in, while Cooper, Horan and Ned Gregory did not play. Tom Horan was in Adelaide on business, but Gregory was on hand and fielded as substitute early on the second day when Kelly missed his train.

Murdoch was brought in as a batsman, as John Blackham was retained as the wicketkeeper for Australia, although Murdoch did take over the gloves on the last day when Blackham was indisposed with sunstroke.

The match seemed virtually over on the first day as the Australians could amass only 122. English fast bowler Allen Hill of Yorkshire had the first four Australian wickets, but Bannerman (10), Thomson (18), Garrett (12) and Kelly (18) had all made a start. At 5/96 and with Billy Midwinter hitting out, the innings seemed to be building reasonably but the last five bats managed only 13 between them.

England lost its openers, Jupp and Shaw, cheaply to Kendall and Spofforth to be 2/4 but the innings then gained momentum. Solid contributions by the Yorkshiremen – Ulyett 52, Greenwood 49, Hill 49 and Emmett 48 – helped to take the total to 261. Tom Kendall was again the best bowler for Australia with 4/82.

Spofforth showed himself as a very fast bowler, and his suspicions of Blackham's ability to take him were no doubt allayed by the fact that Blackham stood up to the stumps for him, and brought off the brilliant stumping of Shaw.

The match started to veer Australia's way as Nat Thomson and Dave Gregory made a strong opening stand of 88, as a foundation for an accumulation of 259.

Bannerman scored the first five in the two Tests, with an off-drive off Lillywhite over the fence.

Two bowlers who had done little in the first Test, the veteran off-spinner James Southerton and the captain James Lillywhite, redeemed themselves as they bowled steadily to claim four wickets each.

With 120 to get, England began disastrously losing 3/9, and it seemed that Australia was poised for a momentous second victory. The game was still in the balance with England at 5/76 but George Ulyett showed the quality and fight in his batting to hold the Australian bowlers up, and he was well assisted by Hill (49) whose efforts in the two matches give rise to claims that he is an all-round player.

Ulyett went on to make 63 before losing his wicket.

The game was then beyond doubt and England coasted to victory.

Tom Kendall – first-Test hero.

Alfred Shaw: first ball in Tests.

Australia team to make tour of England

Sydney, Nov. 2. The organiser of the first two Test matches, John Conway, has an Australian team together for a tour of England next year. Conway, a journalist by profession, was born in Geelong. Each member of the touring party will have to find £50 to help with the expense of the trip.

The players are all from New South Wales and Victoria. One 'outsider', the veteran Tasmanian opening batsman John Arthur, was invited to join the team, but dropped dead two days after receiving the invitation.

He was replaced by George Bailey. Charles Bannerman's younger brother Alick has also been a late inclusion.

The team is: D. Gregory (Capt.), C. Bannerman, A. Bannerman, F. Spofforth, H. Boyle, T. Horan, G. Bailey, F. Allan, W. Midwinter, T. Kendall, J. Blackham, W. Murdoch, T. Garrett.

The team has assembled in Sydney to play some warm-up games for fund-raising purposes. Charles Bannerman has been outstanding among the batsman while the hope of the bowling is paceman Fred Spofforth, who recently took 19 wickets for 108 runs against a Sydney XV.

The team leaves in January for a seven-match tour of New Zealand provinces. Tom Kendall was omitted after the pre-tour games for over-indulgence in drink.

Dave Gregory, ready for England.

Bannerman – doughty professional

The last person to make a fuss over the first Australian Test century against England was the man who scored it – Charles Bannerman. He was a professional cricketer through and through and was there to do a job for his country.

Bannerman has the added distinction of being the man to receive the first ball ever bowled in a Test, and being the first man to score a Test five for hitting the ball over the fence.

However, his heroic status might have been denied him had Tom Armitage managed to hold the simple catch that lobbed from Bannerman's bat early in his innings.

Bannerman, born in Kent in 1851, came to Australia with his parents at the age of three and grew up in the working-class area of Paddington. His strength as a cricketer showed out in junior club games for the Warwick Cricket Club, and before long he was a member of the club side and a professional player. Bannerman was coached by Englishman William Caffyn, formerly of Surrey. He made his debut for New South Wales at the age of 20, when he was in the team which played Victoria in 1871, making 32 in his first outing.

His club cricket scores were high in this period, but it was not until his 81 against Victoria in 1874 that he began to score prodigiously in first class cricket. At the end of the decade he had the best Australian first class averages of any at 25.83 from 34 innings (ahead of Tom Horan of Victoria and Dave Gregory of New South Wales). He then retired to concentrate on a new position as coach of the Melbourne Cricket Club, which at that time had aspirations to be the premier cricket club in Australia, wielding a similar influence to the Marylebone Cricket Club in England. His Test average for a meagre three Tests is 59.75, extremely high for the period. (his great contemporary William Murdoch had an average of 32).

Bannerman was tall, well built and patrician-looking, with a steady, brown-eyed gaze and a fine moustache. He wore an air of confidence as he strode to the wicket. His batting was characterised by powerful hitting in front of the wicket and strong leg-side

An aged Charles Bannerman meets the young Don Bradman after Bradman had scored a record 452 not out in Sydney in 1930.

play. He was not a good cutter and so was more vulnerable on the off side. He was not an elegant stroke maker, applying power rather than finesse.

After his century in the first Test of 1877, he retained his form to be the best Australian batsman on the 1878 tour of England, scoring 723 runs at 24.10, twice as many runs as the next highest scorer, Tom Horan with 377. His century against Leicestershire was the first century by an Australian in England.

His brother Alick, at 5ft. 5in., was in marked contrast, both in height and style, as he became a renowned stonewaller and was known as 'Barndoor' Bannerman. The two enjoyed the 1878 tour together, and Alick went on to make six tours of England and play in 28 Tests.

Charles Bannerman continued to coach in Melbourne, Sydney and New Zealand until well into the twentieth century, and also stood as a first class umpire. He was given a Testimonial match in 1922, in a trial match between NSW teams. The match yielded £90. This was the first match in cricket history that was given a radio commentary.

A few months before he died in 1930 Charles Bannerman was at the Sydney Cricket Ground to see Don Bradman score 452 not out, then a record first class score. The two men were photographed together. The dignified Bannerman has his hand on the Don's shoulder almost as if he is seeking to pass on the mantle of greatness.

AUSTRALIA v ENGLAND 1877 (First Test)
At Melbourne Cricket Ground, March 15, 16 17, 19.
Toss: Australia. Australia won by 45 runs.

AUSTRALIA

C Bannerman retired hurt	165		b Ulyett	4
NFD Thomson b Hill	1		c Emmett b Shaw	7
TP Horan c Hill b Shaw	12		c Selby b Hill	20
DW Gregory* run out	1	(9)	b Shaw	3
BB Cooper b Southerton	15		b Shaw	3
WE Midwinter c Ulyett b Southerton	5		c Southerton b Ulyett	17
EJ Gregory c Greenwood b Lillywhite	0		c Emmett b Ulyett	11
JM Blackman† b Southerton b Shaw	17		lbw b Shaw	6
TW Garrett not out	18	(4)	c Emmett b Shaw	0
T Kendall c Southerton b Shaw	3		not out	17
JR Hodges b Shaw	0		b Lillywhite	8
EXTRAS (B 4, LB 2, W 2)	8		(B 5, LB 3,)	8
TOTAL	245			104

FOW *1st Inns*: 2 40 41 118 142 143 197 243 245
FOW *2nd Inns*: 7 27 31 31 35 58 71 75 75 104

Bowling: First Innings: Shaw 55.3-34-51-3; Hill 23-10-42-1; Ulyett 25-12-36-0; Southerton 37-17-61-3, Armitage 3-0-15-0, Lillywhite 14-5-19-1, Emmett 12-7-13-0 Second Innings: Shaw 34-16-38-5; Hill 14-6-18-1; Ulyett 19-7-39-3; Lillywhite 1-0-1-1

ENGLAND

H Jupp lbw b Garrett	63	(3)	lbw b Midwinter	4
J Selby† c Cooper b Hodges	7	(5)	c Horan b Hodges	38
HRJ Chatswood c Balckman b Midwinter	36	(4)	b Kendall	13
G Ulyett lbw b Thomson	10	(6)	b Kendall	24
A Greenwood c E.J.Gregory b Midwinter	1	(2)	c Midwinter b Kendall	5
T Armitage c Blackman b Midwinter	9	(8)	c Blackman b Kendall	3
A Shaw b Midwinter	10		st Blackman b Kendall	2
T Emmett b Midwinter	8	(9)	b Kendall	9
A Hill not out	35	(1)	c Thomson b Kendall	0
J Lillywhite* c and b Kendall	10		b Hodges	4
J Southerton c Cooper b Garrett	6		not out	1
EXTRAS (LB 1)	1		(B 4, LB 1)	5
TOTAL	196			108

FOW *1st Inns*: 23 79 98 109 121 135 145 145 168 196
FOW *2nd Inns*: 0 7 20 22 62 68 92 93 100 108

Bowling: First Innings: Hodges 9-0-27-1; Garrett 18.1-10-22-2; Kendall 38-16-54-1; Midwinter 54-23-78-5; Thomson 17-10-14-1; Second Innings: Hodges 7-5-7-2; Garrett 2-0-9-0; Kendall 33.1-12-55-7; Midwinter 19-7-23-1; D.W.Gregory 5-1-9-0

Umpires: CA Reid and RB Terry

AUSTRALIA v ENGLAND 1877 (Second Test)
At Melbourne Cricket Ground, March 31, April 2, 3, 4.
Toss: Australia. England won by 4 wickets.

AUSTRALIA

NFD Thomson lbw Hill	18		b Lillywhite	41
C Bannerman b Hill	10	(3)	c Jupp b Ulyett	30
JM Blackham (+) c Lillywhite b Hill	5	(10)	lbw Southerton	26
TW Garrett b Hill	12	(7)	c Jupp b Lillywhite	18
TJD Kelly b Ulyett	19	(4)	b Southerton	35
WE Midwinter c Emmett b Lillywhite	31		c Greenwood b Lillywhite	12
FR Spofforth b Ulyett	0	(8)	b Hill	17
WL Murdoch run out	3	(5)	c Shaw b Southerton	8
TK Kendall b Lillywhite	7		b Southerton	12
DW Gregory (c) not out	1	(2)	c Ulyett b Lillywhite	43
JH Hodges run out	2		not out	0
EXTRAS (B 8, LB 5, W 1)	14		(B 10, LB 7)	17
TOTAL	122			259

FOW *1st Inns*: 29 30 50 60 96 104 108 114 119 122
FOW *2nd Inns*: 88 112 135 164 169 196 203 221 259 259

Bowling: First Innings: Shaw 42-27-30-0, Lillywhite 29-17-36-2, Hill 27-12-27-4, Ulyett 14.1-6-15-2. Second Innings: Hill 21-9-43-1, Ulyett 19-9-33-1, Lillywhite 41-15-70-4, Shaw 32-19-27-0, Emmett 13-6-23-0, Southerton 28.3-13-46-4.

ENGLAND

H Jupp b Kendall	0		b Kendall	1
A Shaw st Blackham b Spofforth	1	(8)	not out	0
A Greenwood b Hodges	49		c Murdoch b Hodges	22
HRJ Charlwood c Kelly b Kendall	14		b Kendall	0
J Selby (+) b Kendall	7	(2)	b Spofforth	2
G Ulyett b Spofforth	52	(5)	c Spofforth b Hodges	63
T Emmett c Kendall b Spofforth	48	(6)	b Midwinter	8
A Hill run out	49	(7)	not out	17
T Armitage c Thomson b Midwinter	21			
J Lillywhite jr (c) not out	2			
J Southerton c Thomson b Kendall	0			
EXTRAS (B 5, LB 12, NB 1)	18		(B 8, LB 1)	9
TOTAL	261			6 for 122

FOW *1st Inns*: 0 4 55 72 88 162 196 255 259 261
FOW *2nd Inns*: 2 8 9 54 76 112

Bow3ling: First Innings: Kendall 52.2-21-82-4, Spofforth 29-6-67-3, Midwinter 21-8-30-1, Hodges 12-2-37-1, Garrett 5-2-10-0, Thomson 11-6-17-0. Second Innings: Kendall 17-7-24-2, Spofforth 15-3-44-1, Garrett 1-0-7-0, Hodges 6-2-13-2, Midwinter 13.1-6-25-1.

Umpires: S Cosstick & RB Terry

Australia's first wicketkeeper. John Blackham got the job ahead of Sydney favourite William Murdoch. His efforts secured a place in the first touring party.

Australians' long journey for tour of England

SA plays opening first class match

Adelaide, Nov. 12. South Australia has soundly beaten a team from Launceston in its first 11-a-side match, and the first match in SA of first class status.

A match had been arranged by the Queen and Albert Association of Port Adelaide to inaugurate its new ground at Alberton, and after this the South Australian Cricket Association issued a challenge for a match at the Adelaide Oval.

South Australia had a resounding win, scoring 182 and then dismissing Tasmania twice for 72 and 97. Its star player was John Bevan, who will soon be going to Melbourne to take up a position with the East Melbourne Cricket Club. Bevan took 6/23 and 8/36.

There has been a little dissension in the SA camp, resulting in their playing 12 men. James Ferguson was late as he had stopped over in Melbourne, and captain William Walker was so incensed he dropped him. But when William Birch injured his hand after bowling Ferguson was allowed to take his place in the side and to bat twice. He made 0 and 8.

Liverpool, May 13. The Australian team which has just arrived on English soil has lived a nomadic life of cricket since it was first assembled in Melbourne on November 2 last year. Their aim has been more to accumulate money to finance their journey than to gain cricket experience.

The first journey was to Brisbane, where the long train trip was rewarded by a procession through the streets and a lavish banquet. They played at Eagle Farm before a crowd of 4000 and, having despatched the Colonial side, went to Toowoomba to put paid to a side of twenty-two.

They then went to Sydney, Newcastle and Maitland. The main match in NSW was against a Sydney 15, but the expected contest was ended by Spofforth's dominant bowling, which netted him 19/108.

The poor crowds in NSW were contrasted by a big show of support in South Australia and Victoria, but most matches were one-sided.

In Melbourne, however, a combination side of 15 leading Sydney and Melbourne players produced a tie. Wanting one run to win, Tom Kendall went to the crease and was bowled by Edwin Evans.

In January the team went across to New Zealand and played seven matches, winning most of

Tour organiser John Conway.

them easily but managing to lose by three wickets to a 15 of Canterbury.

Back in Australia there was a big crowd in Sydney for the match against another Combined 15, with interest fuelled by supposed derogatory comments by the touring XI about their opponents.

The Australians won a close match, but it was obvious that the crowd was on the side of the Combine. After three more matches in Victoria it was time for embarkation for San Francisco. After the train journey across America they left New York for Liverpool, with their first match immediately scheduled at Nottingham.

A cricket match at Coranderrk Aboriginal Station, Healesville, about 1877. A visitor to the station, H. N. Mosely, had noted the Aborigines' keenness on cricket.

Australians thrash the MCC

Indifference greets the touring party

Liverpool, May 13. The Australian cricket team, managed by Jack Conway and captained by Dave Gregory, stepped ashore in England today.

The players, hardened by a preliminary tour in the antipodes, are reputed to be a hard drinking, hard playing and rough-mannered bunch, sure to give even the tough professionals of England a run for their money. Their routine of shipboard callisthenics has kept them in trim for what promises to be a long northern summer in England and the USA.

Their arrival, however, has not yet excited much interest in the press, and the forthcoming matches against Nottinghamshire and the MCC have not been widely advertised.

As the Australians have invested £50 each, they are hoping to more than recoup their costs, but the lack of interest by the press is slightly worrisome. More galling is the fact that the English authorities are not offering the Australians an official Test match, despite their success in Melbourne last year.

A thrashing from Nottinghamshire

Nottingham, May 13. The Australians were unprepared for freezing weather and a slippery outfield in their opening match against Nottinghamshire. They wore silk shirts when they needed fur coats.

The great English medium pace bowler Alfred Shaw took 5 for 20 and Australia made just 63 in their first innings.

Next day saw Notts make 153, leaving Australia 90 to avoid an innings defeat. There was a big crowd on hand to watch the Australian second innings.

They saw nothing to make them fear for English cricket. Only William Midwinter reached double figures in an innings of 76, and a defeat by an innings and 14 runs in less than two days was not a good start to the tour.

Spofforth in attack. An artist's impression of the match between the Australian XI and the New Orleans Club at Twickenham.

Lord's, May 27. Dave Gregory's Australians cut down the flower of English cricket at Lord's today, by defeating the Marylebone Cricket Club team in a single damp day.

'The Demon Bowler' Fred Spofforth and 'The Very Devil' Harry Boyle destroyed a team which one newspaper had stated was 'as good as could be found to represent London and England, and probably nearly as good as the Club has turned out.'

The MCC side included W. G. Grace, and bowlers Alfred Shaw, who played in the first Test in Australia and Fred Morley, who last year took 100 wickets touring America for just 354 runs. The bowlers did well enough, but the English bats were cut down by the withering firepower and accuracy of the Australian strike bowlers.

Grace hit the first ball for four, and was out off the second, the victim of a canny catch by Billy Midwinter who knew that the great man liked to help himself to early runs when square leg was vacant. Midwinter moved unobtrusively around and took a smart catch, to the Doctor's amazement and fury.

The MCC made just 33 in its first innings. Spofforth took 6 for 4, including a hat-trick. The Australian fielding was superlatively quick, with long throws from the outfield, and Boyle making a specialty of 'Boyley's mid-on' – a short 'silly' position.

The Australians opened with Charles Bannerman and William Midwinter, and controversy has raged whether Midwinter should be playing for Gloucestershire instead. He was the only player into double figures in the total of 41. Shaw took 5 for 10 and Morley 5 for 31.

The MCC second innings was even shorter – totalling 19, with Spofforth 4 for 16 and Boyle 6 for 3. The Australians needed just 12 to win and scored them with the loss of one wicket.

There were 4742 witnesses to this devastation, including 400 Australians, and both sides were very vocal in their support.

Punch was quick to rhyme:

'The Australians came down like a wolf on the fold,
The Marylebone cracks for a trifle were bowled;
Our Grace before dinner was very soon done,
And our Grace after dinner did not get a run.'

The Australian team presents itself for inspection by a curious English public. Standing: H. F. Boyle, C. Bannerman, W. L. Murdoch, T. Garrett, D. W. Gregory (captain), T. Horan, F. Allen, G. H. Bailey. Seated: F. R. Spofforth, J. Conway (manager), A. C. Bannerman, J. M. Blackham.

Big crowds for matches

The no-nonsense Australian team is attracting big crowds to its English games.

London, Sep. 20. In a lengthy editorial comment today, the London *Times* said that the 'visitors from the Antipodes, like other birds of passage, have taken their flight. They may be congratulated on the complete success of their visit.' After a shaky start, vast crowds are now attending the matches, apparently in tribute to the tourists' entertaining and competitive play.

The *Times* continued that if the Australians occasionally lost a match, 'they have at any rate shown that the national game is as well understood and as diligently practised in Australia as it is at home, and that the mysteries of batting, bowling, and fielding are not the exclusive privilege of a small island in the northern hemisphere.

'As far as cricket is concerned Englishmen in Australia are as good as Englishmen at home. They have produced an eleven very hard to beat and impossible to despise.

'They have accrued the habit of working together, of seconding each other's play'.

Not so many years ago it was England which played teams of 22 in Australia, now Australia plays the 15's and 16's of England.

'W.G.' kidnaps Billy Midwinter

London, June 20. Amazing scenes were witnessed today as Billy Midwinter's playing status was resolved – after a fashion.

W. G. Grace 'kidnapped' the young batsman as he was practising in the nets for Australia in preparation for the game against Middlesex at Lord's, and took him off to play for Gloucestershire against Surrey.

William Evans Midwinter was born in Gloucestershire, England in 1851 but brought up by his father, a butcher on the Bendigo goldfields, where as a lad he and erstwhile team-mate Harry Boyle once cleared a cricket pitch in the scrub.

A batting and billiards prodigy, he was known as 'the Bendigo Infant' and in fact played for Australia in the very first Test.

Midwinter later played some games for Gloucestershire, commuting several times between country and county.

W. G. Grace, county captain, was determined to have him in his team in 1878, and believed that Midwinter had committed himself. However, after playing 10 matches

Billy Midwinter: ours or theirs?

with his Australian friends, he changed his mind. On this day, manager Jack Conway went to tell Grace, who was playing at the Oval. Grace lost his temper and accused Conway and the Australians of being a lot of sneaks conniving at Midwinter and denying the county of his birth.

Conway left by hansom cab, and was followed by Grace to Lord's. After more argument, Midwinter was removed to the Oval by Grace, chased by Conway, Dave Gregory and Boyle. He will now play for Gloucestershire.

QUICK SINGLES

Not cricket. Fred Spofforth earned the ire of New Zealand spectators in attempting to run out a batsman at the bowler's end in the touring Australians' loss by six wickets to a Canterbury 15 in January. This is regarded as 'sharp practice' and was hissed by spectators.

Gentlemen win. On June 17 and 18 at Prince's Ground, Australia lost to the Gentlemen of England XI. Australia 75 and 63, Gentlemen 139. Allan Steel, of the 'golden' Cambridge University side which also defeated Australia, took 7/35 in the second innings.

An apology. W.G. Grace has grudgingly apologised for his use of 'unparliamentary language' to all Australian cricketers, including Jack Conway in the Midwinter affair. This means Australia will now play against Gloucestershire.

Champions down. Australia has inflicted the first defeat of current County champions, W.G. Grace's Gloucestershire, on their home turf. Spofforth's 7/49 and 5/41 were instrumental in the 10 wicket win in July.

First century. Charles Bannerman makes the first century by an Australian in England, hitting 133 in the Australians' win over Leicestershire on July 15–17.

Win over pro's. In September Australia defeated a Professional XI at the Oval in a thrilling match. This was not the first picked team as the initial selection wanted £20, not the standard £10 match fee. Edward Barratt took all 10 wickets in the Australian first innings of 77. Professionals needing 19 to win, lost 5/11, Australia winning.

Fund for tragedy. On September 3, two boats collided on the Thames with the loss of 700 lives. A match for the Thames Calamity Fund was proposed and agreed to, between Australia and The Players of England – but in the end could not be scheduled. Australians subscribed £100 to the Fund.

Garrett's haul. Back at Princes on September 11, Australia defeated The Players of England in a one-innings match 236 runs to 160, Tom Garrett taking 7/41 for Australia.

Australian climate approved. The victory of the Australians over the MCC has disproved the idea that Australians are a degenerate lot of ex-convicts. As the *Illustrated Sydney News* put it in October, 'the climate of Australia had no enervating influence on the Anglo-Saxon race'.

American Capers

Niceton, USA, Oct. 5. Australia walked off the field in a match against a Philadelphia XI after a number of 'home town' decisions in the not-so-nice town of Niceton.

'Keeper Blackham was incensed at a stumping not being given when the batsman was half way down the pitch. On being informed that their cheque would be dishonoured if they didn't resume, captain Dave Gregory took the team back on the ground – playing a draw in front of 10,000 enthusiastic spectators.

This was one of six matches played in the United States and Canada on the way home from the tour of England. Charles Bannerman scored a hundred in Canada, the first player to do so.

A big welcome

Sydney, Nov. 30. The Australian cricket team was given a great Sydney welcome on return from their arduous tour.

Boats greeted them in the harbour, a band waited on the wharf, and the team paraded through the streets en route to the Sydney Town Hall, banners with the old motto 'Advance Australia' spanning every corner.

From a cricket perspective the England tour had been an outstanding success – playing 39 matches, 17 against elevens, and 22 against odds, winning 18, losing seven with 4 draws.

Charles Bannerman made 726 runs at 24.6, and Fred Spofforth took 107 wickets at 11.6.

Financially it was an even greater success. Each player received more than £750.

Premier says 'no'

Sydney, Dec. 10. Public servants Dave Gregory, Tom Garrett and Charles Bannerman wrote to the Premier of NSW, Henry Parkes, asking for their full salaries for the 15 months of their recent tour. Gregory's salary was £320 per annum in the NSW Audit Office. Their application was supported by the President of the New South Wales Cricket Association, Richard Driver MP, in a speech of welcome at Sydney Town Hall and a petition signed by 32 fellow MP's.

The Premier refused the request, 'on principles which ought to be impartially applied', while allowing Gregory's grant of half pay to stand. Garrett and Bannerman will receive no wages, although they have the fruits of the tour to comfort them.

Bad umpiring and bad tempers

Adelaide, Dec. 28. There has been a sad contrast in recent weeks between the pleasure of the refined match played between Lord Harris' team against an Adelaide 15, and the surly behaviour of the Australian team in the match which followed.

Both matches were warm-ups before the engagement in Melbourne between the two teams, and some South Australians might be excused for now having a leaning towards the English.

The Lord Harris visit sent Adelaide into a spin, and people came from far and wide in the Colony to see the match.

The stands were packed with society in its finery, and the cricket was sometimes forgotten in the hum of conversation and greetings among visiting friends.

Lord Harris fielded a team of 12 so that they could get some practice on the first match of their tour. The South Australians fielded 18, and lost by four wickets, but the match ended in goodwill and congratulations all-round.

The South Australian team's performance seems to have been helped by the coaching of Jesse Hide, who arrived with Lord Harris to take over the coaching of South Australian teams, at a salary of £200 a year.

He immediately called players together for practice sessions and

Lord Harris and J. E. Gooden, captain of South Australia, prepare for battle.

selected the team to play the visitors.

Hide, 21, comes with the recommendation of James Lillywhite, captain of the 1877 visiting team. He is a fast round-arm bowler and forceful right handed bat with sound County experience.

The Australian match was a moody affair, and the Australian team collectively displayed a surly bad temper at losing. They blamed the local umpire, although the *South Australian Register* claimed the next day that: 'Mr Kennedy, the Australians' umpire, made three bad mistakes in one day – all in favour of his own side – and two of them so palpable as to be condemned by nine-tenths of the spectators.'

The Australian team's roughness of behaviour came under notice in England, and to a head in Canada.

High society swells the cricket crowds

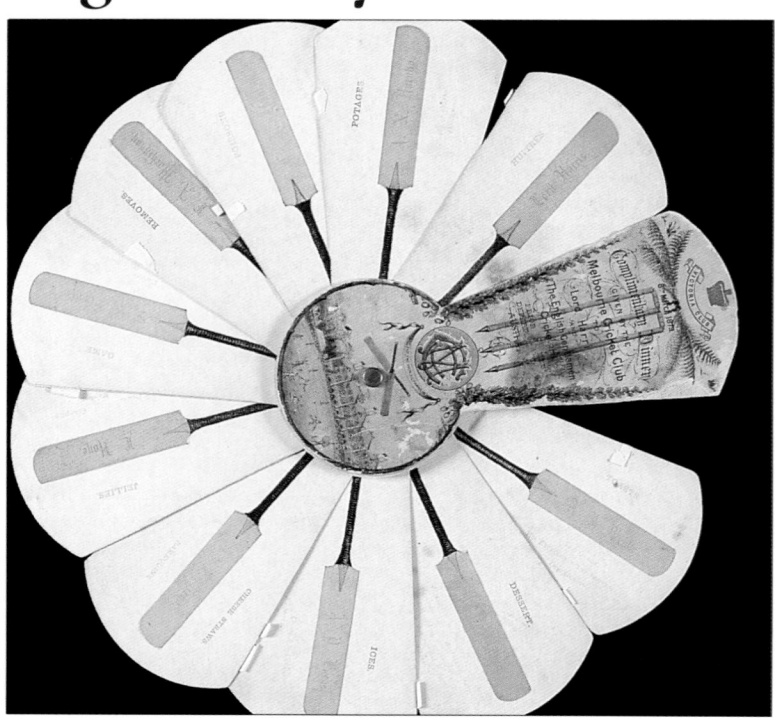

The menu for the MCC banquet in honour of Lord Harris and his team.

Melbourne, March 15. The progression of Lord Harris' team through the colonies has been marked by big attendances, with 10,000 on Saturdays, and an enthusiastic response on the social side.

Well-dressed women have been more than usually present in the crowd, enjoying the social occasion and often seeming oblivious to the cricket.

While there has been vocal support for the Australians from the the boundary, there has been enthusiasm for the English in the grandstands, where the society ladies and people not long out from the 'home country' have tended to gather in refined groups.

The English team has wined and dined well in the best houses and clubs in the land, and a magnificent dinner, with many exotic courses and many speeches, was held on March 8 by the Melbourne Cricket Club to mark the end of the tour.

Spofforth's hat-trick sets up Test win

Melbourne, March 10. Fred Spofforth, with seven wickets in the first innings and six in the next, was the dominant figure in the Test match which ended with a 10 wicket win to Australia. Spofforth finished with the match figures of of 13/110.

The match began after a violent rain-squall on the first morning, and Lord Harris probably made a big mistake in choosing to bat. George Ulyett was out to Spofforth's second ball and this began a procession which had England on 6/26.

Only stout defence by Lord Harris (33) and Charles Absolom (52) allowed England to struggle to 113.

Spofforth got a hat-trick, the first in Test cricket, when he had Vernon Royle, Francis Mackinnon and Tom Emmett in successive balls.

The match was virtually all over when the Australian batsmen settled in to make 256. Alick Bannerman made 73 on debut, although his innings lasted a painfully slow 245 minutes. He blocked nearly everything and looked impassable, taking the odd run with deflections.

English bowler Tom Emmett's

An English lady watches the play.

motto 'first a wide and then a wicket' proved true, as he bowled 7 wides and took 7/68 as he and George Ulyett carried the bowling.

Lord Harris (36) was the best batsman in the second England innings, but a total of 160 made the conclusion only a formality. Lord Harris said after the game that his team's defeat had to do with bad light and the conditions.

ONLY TEST 1878–79 AUSTRALIA v ENGLAND
Melbourne Cricket Ground, Melbourne. January 2, 3, 4, 1879.
Toss: England. Australia won by 10 wkts.

ENGLAND

G Ulyett b Spofforth	0	b Spofforth	14
AP Lucas b Allan	6	c Boyle b Allan	13
AJ Webbe b Allan	4	lbw Allan	0
AN Hornby b Spofforth	2	b Spofforth	4
Lord Harris (c) b Garrett	33	c Horan b Spofforth	36
VPFA Royle b Spofforth	3	c Spofforth b Boyle	18
FA MacKinnon b Spofforth	0	b Spofforth	5
T Emmett c Horan b Spofforth	0 (9)	not out	24
CA Absolom c AC Bannerman b Boyle	52 (8)	c & b Spofforth	6
L Hone (+) c Blackham b Spofforth	7	b Spofforth	6
SS Schultz not out	0	c & b Spofforth	20
EXTRAS (B 4, LB 2)	6	(B 10, LB 4)	14
TOTAL	113		160

FOW 1st Inns: 0 7 10 14 26 26 26 89 113 113
FOW 2nd Inns: 26 28 28 34 78 103 103 118 128 160

Bowling: *First Innings*: Spofforth 25-9-48-6, Allan 17-4-30-2, Garrett 5-0-18-1, Boyle 7-1-11-1. *Second Innings*: Spofforth 35-16-62-7, Allan 28-11-50-2, Garrett 10-6-18-0, Boyle 10-4-16-1.

AUSTRALIA

C Bannerman b Emmett	15	not out	15
WL Murdoch c Webbe b Ulyett	4	not out	4
TP Horan c Hone b Emmett	10		
AC Bannerman b Schultz	73		
FR Spofforth c Royle b Emmett	39		
TW Garrett c Hone b Emmett	26		
FE Allan b Hornby	5		
HF Boyle c Royle b Emmett	28		
JM Blackham (+) b Emmett	6		
TJD Kelly c Webbe b Emmett	10		
DW Gregory (c) not out	12		
EXTRAS (B 19, LB 2, W 7)	28		0
TOTAL	256		0 for 19

FOW 1st Inns: 16 30 37 101 131 158 215 224 234 256
FOW 2nd Inns:

Bowling: *First Innings*: Emmett 59-31-68-7, Ulyett 62-24-93-1, Lucas 18-6-31-0, Schultz 6.3-3-16-1, Hornby 7-7-0-1, Royle 4-1-6-0, Lord 3-0-14-0. *Second Innings*: Schultz 1.3-0-10-0, Ulyett 1-0-9-0.

Umpires: P Coady & G Coulthard

Sydney match riot

Sydney, Feb. 11. With spectators invading the pitch and assaults on the umpire and English players yesterday, the future of cricket relations between Australia and England are now in jeopardy.

The scenes occurred on the last day of the match between the England XI and NSW and arose out of William Murdoch (the hero of Australia's first innings with 82 not out) being adjudged run-out by umpire George Coulthard.

Coulthard was brought up from Melbourne as the English team's nominated umpire. His decision inflamed the crowd, many of whom had been illegally wagering on the outcome of the match.

Australian captain Dave Gregory compounded the crowd discontent when, in protest at the dismissal, he refused to send another man in. Lord Harris went towards the pavilion to plead for the match to continue, and at this stage hundreds of spectators jumped the fence and milled around him and other English cricketers. Lord Harris is reported to have been struck with a whip and umpire Coulthard also attacked. Albert Hornby took a blow, but he collared his assailant and delivered him to the police.

Some of the rioters are reported to have been of the 'larrikin' variety, flash young men with a reputation for trouble, but there were also members on the ground.

The last 90 minutes of play were abandoned, as the crowd could not be controlled, but the second umpire, Edmund Barton, had

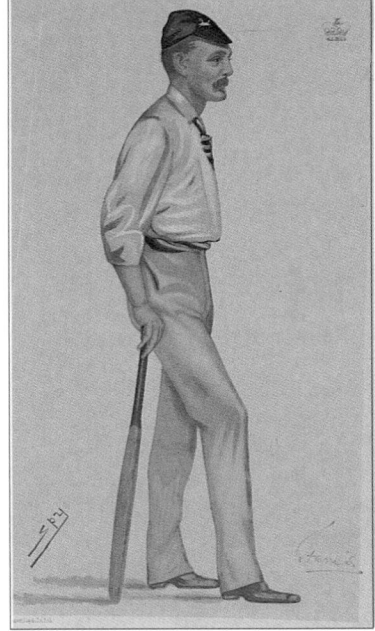

Lord Harris: centre of the riot.

secured a pledge from Gregory that the NSW would resume. At that stage NSW was 177 and 2/19 in response to 267.

Yesterday the *Sydney Morning Herald* described the events as 'a national humiliation', and an overnight thunderstorm had created impossible conditions. They were bundled out for 49, resulting in defeat by an innings and 41 runs.

Today a NSW Cricket Association deputation apologised to Lord Harris over the riot. He accepted, but could 'not say that the events would be easily forgotten.'

Harris' account

Lord Harris states (in part) in a letter reproduced in the London *Daily Telegraph*: 'I implored Gregory as a friend, and for the sake of the NSW Cricket Association ... not to raise the objection, but he refused to take my view.

Looking back I found the ground had been rushed ...

I at once returned to the ground, and in defending Coulthard from being attacked, was struck by some larrikin with a stick. I was surrounded by a howling mob ... I determined to obey the laws of cricket, and may add that for an hour and a half I never left the ground.

The NSW letter

The NSW Cricket Association has stated, in a letter sent to the *Daily Telegraph* in London that the Australian press and public had been loud in their condemnation of the riot. It said that betting was prohibited at the ground.

'Our English readers will be glad to learn that steps have been taken to wipe out the disgrace of the discreditable attack on Lord Harris and his cricketers.

'Two men have been charged ... inmates of the pavilion ... including a bookmaker from Victoria ... will never again be admitted to the ground.'

All even in a pitched Colonial battle

The scene at the Albert Ground, Sydney, where the match was played.

Sydney, Dec. 27. The cricketing rivalry between Victoria and New South Wales goes unabated, and honors are even this year. NSW won by 32 runs at the SCG in November, but Victoria had a big win in the game just completed at the MCG.

The teams are well matched, with names like Spofforth, Murdoch and the Bannerman brothers playing for NSW and Boyle, McDonnell, Horan and Allen for Victoria.

On the wet Sydney wicket the leg-breaks of Bill Cooper shot out the NSW second innings for 117. Spofforth, however, had the last say on the wearing pitch, taking 5/28 and clinching victory. In the end it was the first innings batting of brothers Alick Bannerman (54) and Charles (36) that won the day. They had a second wicket partnership of 82.

In Melbourne, Victoria's batting was supreme, with George Alexander (75) top-scoring in a total of 338. NSW failed in both innings. The attendance over the two days in Melbourne was 19,000.

Kendall's sad story

Sydney, Dec. 27. NSW cricketers were surprised over the omission of Tom Kendall from the Victorian team in November. Kendall bowled so impressively in the 1877 Test matches that his destiny seemed assured, but he was left out of the 1878 touring team 'for reasons other than cricket' – i.e. drink. He had been travelling with the touring team in their warm up matches, but only got as far as the embarkation point in Perth.

He has struggled since, but was in the return match this year. He made 43, but got only one wicket.

MCC swells coffers

Melbourne, Sep. 13. The Melbourne Cricket Club has been able to add £912 to its debenture account due to the visit last summer of the English cricket team led by Lord Harris, allowing for the 'heavy fees' of £443 'demanded' by the Australian players.

The annual report shows that the membership has also increased to 534 members, and attributes the increase of 134 members largely to the English visit.

The MCC – with its home ground the preferred venue for the big matches, has more to offer prospective members and is now the premier Victorian club.

The East Melbourne Cricket Ground pavilion was packed when the Australian XI of 1887 turned out for a 'welcome home' match against a Victorian XV.

The Australians are snubbed in England

Billy Murdoch is the big improver

Tom Garrett: missing the tour.

Melbourne, March 27. 'Felix' in the *Australasian* compares the averages of this year's team to tour England with those of the 1878 side, after completing the warm-up matches in Australia.

Murdoch is far ahead of his comrades with 383 runs from 14 innings at 27.3.

In 1878 he played 30 innings for 334 runs at 12.23 – and has plainly made great strides in scientific batsmanship. 'Felix' expects bigger things of him on this tour.

Harry Boyle has hit 225 runs in 15 innings for an average of 16. Last time he was very low down on the list with an average of 9.9.

The Prince of Wicketkeepers, Jack Blackham, has improved his batting with 14.6. Alick Bannerman is just as good as he was in 1878, batting at around 13 per innings.

In terms of bowling, Fred Spofforth averages 6 runs per wicket as against 4.81 with the pioneer team. Boyle averages 6.4 runs as against 5.6 with the first team, and newcomer George Palmer, replacing Tom Garrett, averages 6.1 with his right-arm medium-pace spinners.

The first touring team played 22 matches and lost one on the way to England. This second team has played nine and lost four.

Despite the statistics, Felix is confident that this year's tourists will prove the stronger team.

London, Aug. 20. The aftermath of the disturbances in Sydney in 1879 that prevented the playing of a second Test on that tour were felt as the 1880 team prepared to leave Australia.

A telegram was received from Lord Harris saying that he would not help to arrange matches unless the Australians agreed to play only for expenses.

As the whole tour was organized on a 'professional' basis, designed to make a profit for the players, this was not acceptable to them.

On arrival the Australians discovered that the leading county sides had already filled their fixture lists.

Lord's was unavailable for any matches; the two games arranged against Yorkshire were to be played against teams not approved by their committee.

Manager George Alexander wrote to the newspaper *Sporting Life*, challenging both Gentlemen and Players to play benefit matches for the Cricketer's Fund – but had no replies.

Alexander had already talked to the players on the ship to England, urging them to behave in a gentlemanly fashion.

He said: 'We will have to live down a bad name.'

The snub became even more apparent and galling when a Canadian team, which had arrived later than the Australians, was offered matches by counties who had 'full books' and 'could not' play the Australians.

Things, however, have recently begun to 'look up' under the sunny

The second Australian team. Standing: Palmer, Moule, Bonnor, George Alexander (manager), Groube. Seated: Spofforth, Boyle, Murdoch (captain), McDonnell, Bannerman. Front: Jarvis, Slight and Blackham.

and equable disposition of captain Billy Murdoch – largely because of his friendship with the great man of English cricket, W. G. Grace.

W. G. Grace had tried unsuccessfully to arrange a Test match at Lord's, but the growing popularity of the Australians as they played around the country indicated that a compromise was necessary – Grace used his good offices with Lord Harris, as did Surrey secretary Charles Alcock.

And the affable Billy Murdoch was a different man and captain than the somewhat belligerent Dave Gregory.

At the meeting between Murdoch and Alexander on the Australian side, and W. G. Grace, Lord Harris and Surrey Secretary Alcock, it was finally agreed to play a Test match at the Oval in London.

Bygones were agreed to be bygones.

Sussex agreed to postpone its fixture at Hove. Lord Harris relented on his demand that the Australians play solely for pleasure, and assented not only to choose an England team but to play himself.

The first match to be played in England, between teams of equal strengths from each country, was finally 'on'.

Croweater rejoicing. On March 4, the *Adelaide Advertiser* 'rejoiced' in the selection of the first South Australian in an Australian cricket team – Arthur 'Affie' Jarvis, as second wicketkeeper.

Cricket financed. Finance for the 1880 tour has been partly provided by the East Melbourne Cricket Club, and the Melbourne Cricket Club which made big profits from the 1879 Australian football season – £708 and £802 respectively.

Revenge on Kiwis. On the pre-England tour of New Zealand, Australia avenged their loss to Canterbury in 1878, winning by an innings and 100 runs. Billy Murdoch won a bet that he would score more than the entire Canterbury team.

Not for England. As the team gathered for the England tour, three candidates removed themselves from the list. Charles Bannerman was unwell and Frank Allan and Tom Garrett unavailable.

Captain deposed. In April aboard the SS *Garonne*, in the Suez Canal, a team meeting was held which replaced warehouseman Harry Boyle, originally selected as captain, with the affable lawyer William 'Billy' Murdoch.

Bendigo boys. The new captain of Australia was born in Bendigo, Victoria, as were Test players Harry Boyle and Bill Midwinter. But Murdoch moved to Sydney, each. studied law and learned his cricket at the Albert Club.

MCC financial dispute. A dispute over the financial state of the Melbourne Cricket Club burst into print in the *Australasian* in August. The secretary Mr. Ben Wardill claims the club is 'flush', yet at a general meeting the club's treasurer Mr. Pinnock said he would resign if

'sixpence' was voted to the retiring long time servant of the club, Mr. Rowland Newbury, because 'it would render the MCC insolvent'. Newbury was curator at the time of the first Test.

Grace dies. Fred Grace, brother of the great W. G., who played in a Test match a fortnight earlier, died on September 22, apparently from complications from a cold caught while playing in a club match. He is said to have gone to sleep in his wet clothes and caught a fever.

Spofforth the key. After the demon fast bowler Fred Spofforth was injured, Australia lost the only four matches on tour. In all Australia won 21 and drew 12 matches.

Murdoch on top. Billy Murdoch headed the batting averages in eleven-a-side matches with 25.15. The bowling was headed by Fred Spofforth whose 46 wickets cost 8 runs each.

The scene at Kennington Oval, packed with spectators who are vocal in their support for England. Lord Harris races to cut off a boundary in the Test match.

Murdoch beats Grace, but England wins Test at home

The Oval, Sep. 8. Three Graces, rain, and a bowler called Frank proved Australia's undoing in the first Test played on English soil.

Australia went into the match without the Demon, Fred Spofforth, who had had a finger broken by a bowler named Joseph Frank, a notorious thrower of the ball, in a minor game at Scarborough.

After the Test match Harry Boyle had this to say in a letter:

'I would not have cared at the result if Spofforth had not had his finger broken. [The umpire] did not no-ball Frank and, when we went on to the field in the second innings Spofforth asked the Scarborough umpire if he would no-ball Spofforth for bowling like Frank. The umpire said 'Yes, you try it,' and then Spofforth asked why Frank was not no-balled.

The umpire answered: 'That's my business.'

A total of 20,758 people paid to enter on the first day of the Test, 19,863 on the second day, and 3751 on the wrap-up final day – the first two being records for a cricket match in England.

Spectators unable to gain entrance were hanging from the trees, demonstrating the popularity of Billy Murdoch's Australians. Lord Harris overcame his anger at the Sydney riot, and played for England.

The three Graces in question were W. G., E. M. and G. F., and the rain came on the night of the first day after England, lead by W. G., who imperturbably scored 152 out of 8 for 410. E. M. made a solid 36 and Lord Harris a noble 52.

Grace's was the first Test century made in England, and his partnership with Alfred Lucas, who made 55, was the first century partnership in Test cricket.

England were quickly all out for 420 on the second day and Australia batted on a wet pitch, slumping to 9/126 by lunch.

The Australians, except for the stonewalling Alick Bannerman, were as yet not adapting to batting on wet and drying wickets.

Highlight of this innings was the catch by the third Grace, G. F., off the huge hitter George Bonnor. Bonnor had turned for his third run with the ball still in the air, before G. F. made the catch.

The hit was later measured at an astonishing 115 yards.

Alick Bannerman made a stout 32, and Harry Boyle hit out for 36 not out in the miserable Australian total of 149.

Following on, Australia were soon in trouble at 3/14, losing the early batsmen sent in to protect the good'uns while the pitch dried. However, by stumps Australia had

captain Billy Murdoch in fine form, on 79 not out in two and a half hours, in a score of 6/170.

Next day, George Alexander put on 52 for the ninth wicket with Murdoch, and then Bill Moule joined his captain for a last wicket 88, making a total of 327.

England had to bat again.

Murdoch was not out 153, one more than Grace with whom he had wagered a sovereign as to who would score the most runs.

It was the first century by a captain, and Murdoch's maiden first class century as well.

England needed 57 to win but took 33.3 overs to get them and lost five wickets in the process.

W. G. was not out 9 at the end. G. F. made a second duck, E. M. his first. Lord Harris did not bat.

The Australians shared a dividend of £1100 from the Test match.

An England victory. The crowd hails the victory and the players are greeted as they come off the ground, having atoned for the loss in Melbourne in 1877.

Murdoch is the best

George Giffen, no slouch himself with the bat, asked a rhetorical question in 1898 – 'Who is the greatest batsman Australia has produced?' Giffen wrote that a consensus of voices would reply that 'W. L. Murdoch has an undisputed claim to the title of champion.'

Murdoch produced two of the most famous innings of his time – 153 not out in the first Test played in England in 1880, and his 211 in eight hours at The Oval in 1884 was the first double century in Test cricket.

Murdoch was of medium build and his photographs show him somewhat exaggerated in his stance. He was a sportsman of the old world, a keen shot, a keeper of convivial company, a natural leader of men and a dressing room wit. He did not shun his players' company, and did not spare his big appetites at the bar and at the table. But he kept them in order, so much so that he was a fence-mending diplomat and gained favour for Australian cricket when he was in charge.

C.B. Fry, who knew him in later years when he was captain of Sussex, wrote that he was simply, genuinely and unaffectedly amusing.

Fry wrote: 'But mark him! A square-round – the double term applies – powerful, well knit figure, as active as most men half his age and every bit as keen; a man who would enjoy a Klondike or a Mansion House dinner … his spirit would refuse to be unfortunate; his body scorns incapacity for meat and drink. No wonder he led Australia well in the old days – a fine Odysseus to meet our mighty bearded Ajax.'

A favoured shot of the right hander was the famous Murdoch 'dog shot'. This involved lifting the front, or left leg, giving room to pat the ball away to the on-side, in front of his back leg.

In assessing the champion batsman, A.G. 'Johnnie' Moyes says: 'Until the arrival to maturity of Murdoch, Australia had no one who was considered overseas as being in the very top flight. Murdoch reigned as king during the eighties, had a brilliant career, was accepted as Australia's star, and ranked with the best in England. W. G. Grace alone was regarded as his superior.

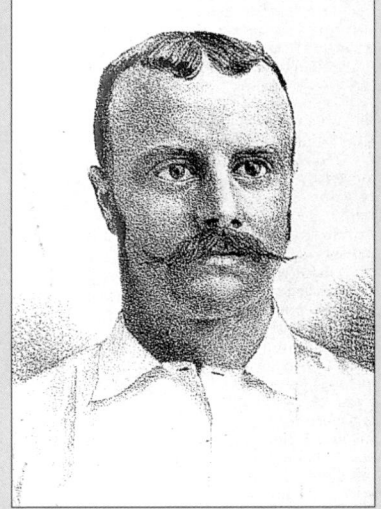

Billy Murdoch: brilliant career.

'Murdoch was clearly a cultured stroke-maker … both patient and scientific … and he could bat skilfully on difficult pitches.'

Born in the goldfields city of Bendigo, Victoria, on 18 October 1854, William Lloyd Murdoch moved as a lad to Sydney.

His early cricket was as a wicket-keeper with the Albert Cricket Club in Sydney, standing up to teammate Fred Spofforth. He first played for NSW in 1875.

Murdoch was not chosen as 'keeper for the first winning Test team in 1877, and as a consequence Australia won this first game without him and Spofforth, who stood out because Murdoch was not picked.

Both played in the second losing Test at the MCG in 1877, Murdoch's contribution being 3 and 8, with one catch in Australia's four-wicket loss. He then made 4 and 4 not out in Australia's 10-wicket win in the MCG Test played in January 1879.

Murdoch played a total 18 Test matches for Australia, his last in 1890. Though a lawyer by profession, Murdoch was a better cricketer. His firm Murdoch and Murdoch was dissolved in June 1879, Murdoch being declared bankrupt in December to the tune of £775. His only asset was £10 in clothes – and cricketing ability.

His first Test in England was as captain of the 1880 touring side, his affable and engaging manner being thought a better bet for a trouble free tour than the taciturn bowler Harry Boyle. The team made the switch while passing through the Suez Canal, and it was justified through Murdoch becoming fast friends with W. G. Grace and healing the rift caused by the 1879 Sydney riot with Lord Harris.

Murdoch had wagered Grace a sovereign that he would outscore

him in the 1880 Test – and did by a single.

He wore the gold sovereign he won on his watch chain for the rest of his life.

When Murdoch was discharged from bankruptcy it appeared that his share of the £110 Test profit and large tour dividend had been paid to his brother.

He was Captain in the 1881–82 series which Australia won 2–0, and in England in 1882 for the 'Ashes' Test his batting was crucial in the low scoring affair, dominated by his mate Fred Spofforth's legendary bowling.

Murdoch played in the drawn series in Australia in 1882–83, and the 1–0 loss in 1884, despite his 211 in Australia's only innings in the drawn third Test.

After this tour, Murdoch and the team refused to play against Shaw's touring England professionals in a dispute over player fees.

An arrangement was reached for the first Adelaide Test, which Murdoch played in a jolly mood a few days after he married Jemima Watson, a Bendigo mining heiress.

This looked like Murdoch's last test after a completely new team was chosen for the remaining matches. He was forgiven and chosen for two tests in 1890.

Murdoch found England much to his liking, settling there in 1893 and playing 137 matches for Sussex, most of them as captain. His liking for the place was exacerbated by not being chosen for the 1893 Australian tour. He made several centuries, including 105 for Sussex against Cambridge in 1897.

Murdoch toured South Africa – for England in 1891–92, playing as wicket keeper in the Cape Town Test match, thus joining that small, interesting band of players who played for two countries.

His last season in first class cricket was in 1904 for W. G. Grace's London County side.

Back in Australia for the 1910–11 South African tour, Murdoch watched the fourth Test at the MCG. After the Australian innings of 328 on the morning of the second day, 18 February, he predicted the South Africans would lose five wickets before lunch.

They did, 5/38, and lunching in the committee room he said: 'I'll never make another prophecy again. I've brought bad luck on those boys'.

He then said he felt ill, and slumped unconscious onto the table. He had suffered a stroke – and died two hours later.

ONLY TEST 1880 ENGLAND v AUSTRALIA
Kennington Oval, London. September 6, 7, 8, 1880.
Toss: England. England won by 5 wkts.

ENGLAND

EM Grace c Alexander b Bannerman	.36 (6)	b Boyle 0
WG Grace b Palmer	.152 (7)	not out 9
AP Lucas b Bannerman	.55	c Blackham b Palmer 2
W Barnes b Alexander	.28 (5)	c Moule b Boyle 5
Lord Harris (c) c Bonnor b Alexander	.52	
F Penn b Bannerman	.23 (4)	not out 27
AG Steel c Boyle b Moule	.42	
A Lyttelton (+) not out	.11 (1)	b Palmer 13
GF Grace c Bannerman b Moule	.0 (2)	b Palmer 0
A Shaw b Moule	.0	
F Morley run out	.2	
EXTRAS (B 8, LB 11)	.19	(NB 1) 1
TOTAL	.420	...........5 for 57

FOW 1st Inns: 91 211 269 281 322 404 410 410 413 420
FOW 2nd Inns: 2 10 22 31 31

Bowling: *First Innings*: Boyle 44-17-71-0, Palmer 70-27-116-1, Alexander 32-10-69-2, Bannerman 50-12-111-3, McDonnell 2-0-11-0, Moule 12.3-4-23-3. *Second Innings*: Boyle 17-7-21-2, Palmer 16.3-5-35-3.

AUSTRALIA

AC Bannerman b Morley	.32	c Lucas b Shaw 8
WL Murdoch (c) c Barnes b Steel	.0 (3)	not out 153
TU Groube b Steel	.11 (4)	c Shaw b Morley 0
PS McDonnell c Barnes b Morley	.27 (5)	lbw WG Grace 43
J Slight c GF Grace b Morley	.11 (6)	c Lord b WG Grace 0
JM Blackham (+) c & b Morley	.0 (7)	c EM Grace b Morley 19
GJ Bonnor c GF Grace b Shaw	.2 (8)	b Steel 16
HF Boyle not out	.36 (2)	run out 3
GE Palmer b Morley	.6	c & b Steel 4
G Alexander c WG Grace b Steel	.6	c Shaw b Morley 33
WH Moule c Morley b WG Grace	.6	b Barnes 34
EXTRAS (B 9, LB 3)	.12	(B 7, LB 7) 14
TOTAL	.149	327

FOW 1st Inns: 28 39 59 84 84 89 97 113 126 149
FOW 2nd Inns: 8 13 14 97 101 143 181 187 239 327

Bowling: *First Innings*: Morley 32-9-56-5, Steel 29-9-58-3, Shaw 13-5-21-1, WG Grace 1.1-0-2-1. *Second Innings*: Morley 61-30-90-3, Steel 31-6-73-2, Shaw 33-18-42-1, WG Grace 28-10-66-2, Barnes 8.3-3-17-1, Lucas 12-7-23-0, Penn 3-1-2-0.

Umpires: HH Stephenson & R Thoms

Steamer trip is a cricketers' ordeal

George Giffen: SA voyager.

Melbourne, Nov. 15. The East Melbourne Cricket Ground was the scene of the first match between Victoria and South Australia on even terms.

Even terms, that is, excluding the facts that five Victorians were still away with the Australian touring side, and that the South Australians had endured an uncomfortable 500 mile trip on a small steamer from Adelaide, followed by a Melbourne Town Hall reception.

The steamer trip can be a breezy delight or a howling hell, and unfortunately this time all the players suffered.

That it was a first class match seemed lost on Robert Pateman of Victoria, who made four runs on the first evening dressed in street clothes.

Tom Horan's 113 anchored the Victorian innings of 329.

George Coulthard, the champion Carlton footballer, made his first class debut for Victoria with 31 runs. Coulthard already had Test experience – as an umpire in the notorious Sydney match last season with the decision against Murdoch that caused the riot.

South Australia's first innings was a collapse against the puzzling leg-breaks of William Cooper (5/44), and the sharpish straight'uns of Coulthard (3/29).

The Croweaters' second innings, after following on, was a lot better, and they reached a total of 314. George Giffen made a smart 63, Jim Slight a patient 70 and S.A. coach Jesse Hide 48.

Victoria made the 63 required for the loss of three wickets.

A Combined XI beats the Test team

Sydney, Feb. 10. New Zealand faced and lost the match against a Combined NSW/Victoria XI at the SCG.

The Australian XI easily beat the Combined team at the MCG in January by 178 runs with Fred Spofforth in full cry for the Australians – 7/55 and 5/50 in Combined totals of 94 and 85 – opposed to 172 and 185.

The return match, with each innings played on a new wicket, was interrupted on the first and last of the three days by rain and hail – with the Australians batting in the worst of it.

Hugh Massie and the hero of the first Test, Charles Bannerman, put on 118 for the first wicket in the Combined total of 197. Combined bowlers 'Paddy' McShane (2/11) and right arm quick Edwin Evans (5/44) then dismissed Australia for 155. Billy Murdoch showed his usual stout form as he made 65.

The Combined XI's second innings was an excellent all-round performance against Spofforth (0/92), Joey Palmer (1/52) and Co. Hugh Massie made 50, Tom Horan 49 and Billy Midwinter 45.

The Australian XI was caught on a sticky in the second innings and left-armer McShane turned in the best bowling analysis since Gideon Elliott's 9/2 in Launceston in 1857–58. McShane took 9/45 from 29.1 overs.

The Australians were all out for 85 and lost by 246 runs. Again it was captain Billy Murdoch (31 not out and Percy McDonnell (19) who tried to retrieve the innings, but no other batsman reached double figures.

Billy Midwinter: a solid knock.

Edwin Evans: a damaging bowler.

A cricketing school. The XI of St Peter's College, Adelaide, are a part of the drive for schools to bring the sporting principles of the game to youngsters.

Bribery, betting and the wrong result

Melbourne, Dec. 20. Following allegations made at Cootamundra about three Englishmen being offered bribes to be 'non-triers' in the match against Victoria, the result was certainly curious.

The trouble was that it was Victoria which collapsed in the second innings – giving England a win, the first by a team forced to follow-on in Australian cricket.

It was alleged that George Ulyett and John Selby were to receive £500 each if Victoria won, and William Scotton £250. When Selby made a remark about the bribery matter to a team-mate, Ulyett is said to have threatened to 'jowl' your heads together.

Ulyett and Selby also beat up Billy Midwinter, who had refused to take part in the betting and bribery scheme and reported it.

The story of the match is that the players who weren't in on it played well, in particular Arthur Shrewsbury's 80 in England's second innings, and the bowler Ted Peate, who took 6/30 in Victoria's run chase of 94.

Peate said: 'The bookmakers were standing up doing business as if they were in Tattersall's ring. They were very badly hit by the result of the match. Certain of their schemes failed – much to the satisfaction of most of us.'

Captain Alfred Shaw said of the scheme that he gave 'no credence' to it when he first heard of it. However, on the field, as he was watching certain cases of misfielding, he 'came to the conclusion that the rumours were not without foundation.'

A grand poster to promote and commemorate the English tour.

NSW claims tours ruin local cricket

Sydney, April 1. Club cricket seems to be in decline in Sydney, and intercolonial cricket also is threatened, according to the NSW Cricket Association. Where once thousands would attend club games this past season saw them reduced to hundreds.

The NSWCA stated in its annual report, 'The refusal of members of returned teams to take part in the intercolonial contests has shorn these matches of much of their wanted interest.'

The NSW claim seems at odds with the actual attendances of the matches:

MCG. Victoria v NSW 27,000; first Test 50,000, fourth Test 13,000.

SCG. NSW v Victoria 30,600, second Test 34,000 , third Test 15,000.

Professional men keep long hours

Melbourne, Dec. 20. The behaviour of the English cricketers, with allegations of bribery relating to the match against Victoria, can be set against a background of generally wild behaviour which has been prevalent among some members of the team.

The *Australasian* has this to say: 'Professional cricketers who keep late hours, make bets to some amount, and are seen drinking champagne at a late hour with members of the betting ring when they ought to be in bed, must not be surprised if people put a wrong construction on their conduct. They have only themselves to blame.'

It is known that the English have split into several camps.

Colonial Rivals are all even again

Sydney, Feb. 15. NSW and Billy Murdoch massively restored the balance in matches against Victoria with a win by an innings and 138 runs at the SCG.

Victoria won the first match at the MCG in December mainly because of Tom Horan's 95 and George Palmers 5/64 in NSW's first innings.

Things were quite the opposite in the return match. Murdoch knocked up 321, the highest Australian first class score, and Tom Garrett made 163 out of a huge total of 775. Victoria used 10 bowlers in 398 overs.

Spofforth took 6/122 from 68 overs in Victoria's reply of 315. Horan made 102 and Jack Blackham 96 in Victoria's follow-on second innings of 322.

Australia wins twice

The second Melbourne Cricket Ground Pavilion, with its spacious roof balcony.

Sydney, March 7. Australia took an unbeatable two-up lead in the four-Test series, when it defeated England by six wickets in the third Test at Sydney.

Highlight of the match was Percy McDonnell's 147 in Australia's 262. He came in with Australia a shaky 3/16, chasing England's 188 but with Alick Bannerman solid as a rock at the other end, proceeded to put on 199 before Bannerman was bowled by erstwhile team-mate, the peripatetic Billy Midwinter, for 70.

McDonnell hit one 'fiver' out of the SCG, over the pavilion, landing near the caretaker's cottage. He was out with the score on 235 – caught Midwinter.

Except for McDonnell the game was dominated by the bowlers none more than Joey Palmer, the medium-paced right-arm spinner, who took 5/46 and 4/44 to go with his 7/87 and 4/97 in the second Test. Palmer was partnered by Tom Garrett, who took 3/75, then a career best 6/78 as he bowled in tandam with Palmer.

The second Test, played from February 17 to 21, and which Australia won by five wickets, was a relatively low-scoring affair, but was notable as being recognised as the first Test match played in Sydney. It was initially advertised as All England v Combined NSW and Victoria, but has quickly acquired Test status.

'Timeless Test' runs out of time

Melbourne, March 14. Tom Horan, writing as Felix in the *Australasian* noted that 'it would be well if the public was not mislead by advertisements to the effect that such and such a match will be positively played out', after the fourth Test ended in a draw after a washed-out fourth day.

Advertised to be played to a finish, the exigencies of the England tour always meant that this would be a four-day affair – and with even this day not available, the match was essentially a waste of time.

In his more familiar guise as a player, Horan knocked up 20 as Australia made 300 chasing England's first innings of 309, in which George Ulyett's 149 was the domi-

nant contribution.

Of the Australian bowlers Tom Garrett took 5/80 and Fred Spofforth an unusually modest return of 1/92.

England was 2/234 (with Ulyett 64) when rain stopped play. Tomorrow England is booked to play in Dunolly, Victoria, then in Ballarat on the 17th and 18th before boarding the *Chimborazo*.

The Australians leave aboard the *Assam* for England on the 17th. Their form, especially that of Horan, Billy Murdoch and Percy McDonnell with the bat should give England cause to think.

And the fact that Australia's two wins in Tests here were without Fred Spofforth should have them thinking even harder.

Percy McDonnell best in the wet

Percy 'Greatheart' McDonnell, was given that sobriquet by George Giffen because he was at his best when things were worst.

McDonnell wanted to play for Australia so much that he was taken aboard the *Assam* for the 1882 tour of England on a stretcher, suffering severe sunstroke.

Giffen wrote in 1898 that 'if I live to be a hundred I shall not see more elegant, graceful and effective batting. If "hit" was the game, he would blaze away like fury, but if he were not under orders and the wicket were good, he would settle down and bat as pretty as a Pailaret.'

McDonnell was born in London on 13 November 1858, but came to Victoria as a boy, playing for Melbourne at the age of 15, and making his first class debut against NSW at the SCG in February 1878, making 0 and 0 not out at no. 9.

Medical studies sometimes interfered with his availability, but he played for Victoria, NSW and Queensland until 1895, dying, ironically enough of a heart attack on 24 September 1896, aged 36.

His highest score was a majestic 239 for NSW against Victoria in December 1886 at the MCG. He made seven first class centuries.

McDonnell led Australia six times from 1886 to 1888 for one win and five losses, when England's batting was strong.

In Tests he made 147 in Sydney in 1881–82, 103 at the Oval in 1884 and 124 and 83 in Adelaide in 1884–85. He made 302 runs for 50.33 in 1881–81, 230 runs at 57.5 in 1884–5 and 159 at 39.8 in four innings in 1884.

Australian Averages

1881–82 AUSTRALIA v ENGLAND												
AUSTRALIA	M	Inn	NO	Runs	H.S	Avrge	Ct	St	Overs	Mds	Runs	Wkt	Avrge
Bannerman, AC	3	5	-	167	70	33.40	3	-	12.0	3	35	-	-
Blackham, JM	4	6	-	81	40	13.50	6	4	-	-	-	-	-
Boyle, HF	4	4	1	13	6	4.33	5	-	107.0	47	135	6	22.50
Cooper, WH	1	1	-	7	7	7.00	1	-	98.2	27	200	9	22.22
Couthard, G	1	1	1	6	6*	-	-	-	-	-	-	-	-
Evans, E	2	2	-	14	11	7.00	1	-	243.3	131	257	7	36.71
Garrett, TW	3	4	1	45	31*	15.00	2	-	213.3	76	367	18	20.39
Giffen, G	3	3	-	46	30	15.33	2	-	24.3	7	54	2	27.00
Horan, TP	4	7	1	212	124	35.33	-	-	-	-	-	-	-
Jones, SP	2	4	3	63	37	63.00	1	-	19.0	9	30	1	30.00
Massie, HH	4	6	-	101	49	16.83	3	-	-	-	-	-	-
McDonnell, PS	4	7	1	299	147	49.83	3	-	4.0	1	15	-	-
Murdoch, WL	4	7	1	215	85	35.83	3	-	-	-	-	-	-
Palmer, GE	4	4	-	88	34	22.00	3	-	365.2	145	522	24	21.75
Spofforth, FR	1	1	1	3	3*	-	-	-	66.0	17	128	1	128.00

(* not out)

English Averages

1881–82 AUSTRALIA v ENGLAND												
ENGLAND	M	Inn	NO	Runs	H.S	Avrge	Ct	St	Overs	Mds	Runs	Wkt	Avrge
Barlow, RG	4	8	-	210	62	26.25	2	-	50.0	24	61	-	-
Bates, W	4	8	1	192	58	27.43	2	-	241.0	121	334	16	20.88
Emmett, T	4	7	-	63	27	9.00	5	-	98.0	48	180	2	90.00
Midwinter, WE	4	7	-	95	36	13.57	5	-	194.0	79	272	10	27.20
Peate, E	4	7	5	40	13	20.00	1	-	232.0	117	257	11	23.36
Pilling, R	4	7	1	61	23	10.17	5	2	-	-	-	-	-
Scotton, WH	4	7	1	158	50*	26.33	1	-	-	-	-	-	-
Selby, J	4	8	1	202	70	28.86	-	-	-	-	-	-	-
Shaw, A	4	7	-	98	40	14.00	1	-	64.1	36	76	2	38.00
Shrewsbury, A	4	7	-	186	82	26.57	4	-	-	-	-	-	-
Ulyett, G	4	8	-	438	149	54.75	3	-	99.2	37	180	8	22.50

(* not out)

FIRST TEST 1881–82 AUSTRALIA v ENGLAND
Melbourne Cricket Ground, Melbourne. December 31, 1881, January 2, 3, 4, 1882.
Toss: England. Match Drawn.

ENGLAND

RG Barlow c Bannerman b Palmer	0	st Blackham b Palmer	33
G Ulyett c McDonnell b Cooper	87	st Blackham b Cooper	23
J Selby run out	55	c Boyle b Cooper	70
W Bates c Giffen b Boyle	58	c Bannerman b Cooper	47
A Shrewsbury c Blackham b Evans	11	b Cooper	16
WE Midwinter b Evans	36	c Massie b Cooper	4
T Emmett b Evans	5	b Cooper	6
WH Scotton run out	21	not out	50
A Shaw (c) c Boyle b Evans	5	c Cooper b Boyle	40
R Pilling (+) c Giffen b Cooper	5	b Palmer	3
E Peate not out	4	run out	2
EXTRAS (LB 6, NB 1)	7	(B 7, LB 2, NB 5)	14
TOTAL	294		308

FOW 1st Inns: 5 142 151 187 227 232 277 284 289 294
FOW 2nd Inns: 37 96 179 183 188 197 217 300 305 308

Bowling :*First Innings*: Palmer 36-9-73-1, Evans 71-35-81-3, Cooper 32.2-8-80-3, Boyle 18-9-18-1, Giffen 3-0-12-0, Bannerman 10-3-23-0. *Second Innings*: Palmer 77-19-77-2, Evans 75.2-45-63-0, Cooper 66-19-120-6, Boyle 15-6-19-1, McDonnell 4-1-15-0.

AUSTRALIA

HH Massie st Pilling b Midwinter	2		
AC Bannerman b Ulyett	38	b Ulyett	8
WL Murdoch (c) b Ulyett	39 (4)	not out	22
PS McDonnell b Midwinter	19 (5)	not out	33
TP Horan run out	124 (3)	c Emmett b Bates	26
G Giffen b Emmett	30		
JM Blackham (+) b Emmett	2 (1)	b Bates	25
GE Palmer c Pilling b Bates	34		
E Evans b Bates	3		
HF Boyle not out	4		
WH Cooper st Pilling b Peate	7		
EXTRAS (B 4, LB 11, W 3)	18	(B 9, LB 3, W 1)	13
TOTAL	320		3 for 127

FOW 1st Inns: 9 82 97 113 220 226 305 309 309 320
FOW 2nd Inns: 35 70 72

Bowling: *First Innings*: Peate 59-24-64-1, Midwinter 39-21-50-2, Bates 41-20-43-2, Emmett 35-12-61-2, Ulyett 20-5-41-2, Barlow 23-13-22-0, Shaw 20-11-21-0. *Second Innings*: Ulyett 15-3-30-1, Emmett 16-11-19-0, Bates 13-3-43-2, Peate 11-5-22-0.

Umpires: J Lillywhite jr & J Swift

SECOND TEST 1881–82 AUSTRALIA v ENGLAND
Sydney Cricket Ground, Sydney. February 17, 18, 20, 21, 1882.
Toss: England. Australia won by 5 wkts.

ENGLAND

G Ulyett c Murdoch b Evans	25	lbw Palmer	67
RG Barlow b Palmer	31	c Boyle b Garrett	62
J Selby c & b Evans	6	c Blackham b Palmer	2
W Bates c Murdoch b Palmer	4	b Palmer	5
A Shrewsbury b Palmer	7	c McDonnell b Garrett	22
WE Midwinter c Blackham b Palmer	4	b Palmer	8
WH Scotton b Palmer	30	lbw Garrett	12
T Emmett b Evans	10	c McDonnell b Garrett	9
A Shaw (c) c Massie b Palmer	11	b Evans	30
R Pilling (+) b Palmer	3	b Jones	9
E Peate not out	1	not out	1
EXTRAS (LB 1)	1	(B 3, LB 2)	5
TOTAL	133		232

FOW 1st Inns: 39 47 64 73 77 90 115 123 132 133
FOW 2nd Inns: 122 124 130 156 165 175 183 204 230 232

Bowling: *First Innings*: Palmer 58-36-68-7, Evans 57-32-64-3. *Second Innings*: Palmer 66-29-97-4, Garrett 36-12-62-4, Evans 40.1-19-49-1, Jones 11-4-19-1.

AUSTRALIA

HH Massie c Shrewsbury b Bates	49	b Ulyett	22
JM Blackham (+) c Shaw b Midwinter	40	c & b Bates	4
E Evans run out	11		
WL Murdoch (c) c Emmett b Bates	10 (3)	c Barlow b Midwinter	49
TP Horan run out	4 (4)	b Ulyett	21
PS McDonnell b Bates	14 (5)	b Shaw	25
SP Jones c Emmett b Ulyett	37 (6)	not out	13
TW Garrett c Shrewsbury b Peate	4 (7)	not out	31
GE Palmer b Bates	16		
HF Boyle c Shrewsbury b Ulyett	0		
G Couthard not out	6		
EXTRAS (B 1, LB 2, W 2, NB 1)	6	(B 3, LB 1)	4
TOTAL	197		5 for 169

FOW 1st Inns: 78 102 103 111 132 133 140 167 168 197
FOW 2nd Inns: 10 28 67 113 127

Bowling: *First Innings*: Peate 52-28-53-1, Midwinter 34-16-43-1, Emmett 6-2-24-0, Ulyett 22.2-16-11-2, Bates 72-43-52-4, Barlow 8-4-8-0. *Second Innings*: Bates 24-11-37-1, Ulyett 15-4-48-2, Peate 20-12-22-0, Emmett 6-3-17-0, Midwinter 18-8-23-1, Shaw 20.1-15-12-1, Barlow 4-1-6-0.

Umpires: J Lillywhite jr & J Swift

THIRD TEST 1881–82 AUSTRALIA v ENGLAND
Sydney Cricket Ground, Sydney. March 3, 4, 6, 7, 1882.
Toss: England. Australia won by 6 wkts.

ENGLAND

G Ulyett b Palmer	0	b Garrett	23
RG Barlow c Blackham b Garrett	4	c & b Garrett	8
J Selby c Massie b Palmer	13	b Palmer	1
W Bates c & b Palmer	1	c Bannerman b Garrett	2
A Shrewsbury c & b Boyle	82	c Boyle b Garrett	47
WE Midwinter b Palmer	12	b Palmer	10
WH Scotton c Jones b Garrett	18	b Palmer	1
T Emmett b Garrett	4	b Garrett	2
A Shaw (c) b Boyle	3	b Garrett	6
R Pilling (+) b Palmer	12	b Palmer	23
E Peate not out	11	not out	8
EXTRAS (B 22, LB 6)	28	(B 2, NB 1)	3
TOTAL	188		134

FOW 1st Inns: 2 8 17 35 56 148 154 159 164 188
FOW 2nd Inns: 28 29 32 42 60 70 73 79 113 134

Bowling: *First Innings*: Palmer 45.2-23-46-5, Garrett 60-25-85-3, Jones 8-5-11-0, Boyle 27-18-18-2. *Second Innings*: Palmer 40-19-44-4, Garrett 36.1-10-78-6, Boyle 4-1-9-0.

AUSTRALIA

AC Bannerman b Midwinter	70	c Pilling b Peate	14
HH Massie b Bates	0	c Midwinter b Peate	9
WL Murdoch (c) c Ulyett b Bates	6	c Midwinter b Bates	4
TP Horan c & b Bates	1	not out	16
PS McDonnell c Midwinter b Peate	147	c Emmett b Peate	9
G Giffen c Pilling b Peate	2		
JM Blackham (+) b Peate	4		
SP Jones not out	7 (6)	not out	6
TW Garrett b Peate	0		
GE Palmer b Midwinter	6		
HF Boyle c Pilling b Peate	3		
EXTRAS (B 6, LB 8, W 2)	16	(B 2, LB 3, W 1)	6
TOTAL	262		4 for 64

FOW 1st Inns: 0 10 16 215 228 235 244 245 252 262
FOW 2nd Inns: 14 21 39 49

Bowling: *First Innings*: Peate 45-24-43-5, Bates 38-17-67-3, Ulyett 3-1-10-0, Midwinter 62-25-75-2, Shaw 8-4-14-0, Emmett 16-6-37-0. *Second Innings*: Peate 25-18-15-3, Bates 24.3-13-43-1.

Umpires: J Lillywhite jr & J Swift

FOURTH TEST 1881–82 AUSTRALIA v ENGLAND
Melbourne Cricket Ground, Melbourne. March 10, 11, 13, 14 (no play), 1882.
Toss: England. Match Drawn.

ENGLAND

G Ulyett c Blackham b Garrett	149	c Palmer b Boyle	64
RG Barlow c Blackham b Garrett	16	run out	56
J Selby b Spofforth	7	not out	48
W Bates st Blackham b Garrett	23	not out	52
A Shrewsbury lbw Palmer	1		
WE Midwinter c Palmer b Boyle	21		
WH Scotton st Blackham b Giffen	26		
T Emmett b Giffen	27		
A Shaw (c) c Murdoch b Garrett	1		
R Pilling (+) not out	6		
E Peate c & b Garrett	13		
EXTRAS (B 10, LB 7)	17	(B 12, LB 2)	14
TOTAL	309		2 for 234

FOW 1st Inns: 32 49 98 109 177 239 281 284 288 309
FOW 2nd Inns: 98 152

Bowling: *First Innings*: Spofforth 51-14-92-1, Garrett 54.2-23-80-5, Palmer 23-5-70-1, Boyle 18-4-33-1, Giffen 13-6-17-2. *Second Innings*: Palmer 20-5-47-0, Garrett 27-6-62-0, Boyle 25-9-38-1, Spofforth 15-3-36-0, Giffen 8.3-1-25-0, Bannerman 2-0-12-0.

AUSTRALIA

WL Murdoch (c) b Midwinter	85
AC Bannerman c & b Midwinter	37
TP Horan c & b Midwinter	20
PS McDonnell c Barlow b Ulyett	52
HH Massie c Emmett b Shaw	19
G Giffen c Scotton b Peate	14
JM Blackham (+) c Pilling b Midwinter	6
TW Garrett c Ulyett b Bates	10
GE Palmer c Ulyett b Bates	32
HF Boyle c Shrewsbury b Bates	6
FR Spofforth not out	3
EXTRAS (B 2, LB 7, W 6, NB 1)	16
TOTAL	300

FOW 1st Inns: 110 149 153 189 228 247 247 280 297 300

Bowling: *First Innings*: Bates 28.1-14-49-3, Peate 20-6-38-1, Emmett 19-14-22-0, Ulyett 24-8-40-1, Midwinter 41-9-81-4, Barlow 15-6-25-0, Shaw 16-6-29-1.

Umpires: G Coulthard & J Lillywhite jr

Fit touring team looks the best yet

The Australian team: Sam Jones, Alick Bannerman, George Bonnor, Fred Spofforth, Jack Blackham, Billy Murdoch, George Palmer, George Giffen, Harry Boyle, Tom Garrett, Hugh Massie, Percy McDonnell and Tom Horan.

Fun and games for the boys at sea

At sea, April. The sea voyage to England, even after the opening of the Suez Canal in November 1869, still takes eight weeks, giving a cricket team such as the 1882 Australians aboard the SS *Assam* time for plenty of amusement.

The first stage of the trip across the Great Australian Bight had the ship rolling and a number of sea sick cricketers, including Alick Bannerman and Tom Horan, who took to eating apples as their only reliable form of sustenance.

The trip was interrupted by receptions in Melbourne and Adelaide, fishing in King George's Sound (Harry Boyle the best with five dozen) – and a visit to Ceylon.

Evenings were enlivened by concerts and a black-and-white minstrel show, worthy of the Christy Minstrels. Captain Billy Murdoch and 27-year-old manager Claude 'Charlie' Beal played Bones and Tambo in comic renditions, jokes, conundrums and puns which had the audience in tears of laughter.

Nearly as amusing was Jack Blackham's singing of 'See My Grave's Kept Clean', and Fred Spofforth's appearance as Mephistopheles.

Bonnor wins 100 sovereigns on bet

Plymouth, May 3. Luckiest man of the Australian team at this stage has proved to be George Bonnor, who wagered two or three of his fellow passengers on the SS *Assam* one hundred sovereigns that he could throw a cricket ball more than 100 yards.

Most of his team mates thought, despite his physique and his known prowess at both throwing and hitting a ball, he would be fortunate to make the distance because of his long spell of comparitive idleness aboard the ship.

Upon landing at Plymouth, however, the party gathered at a nearby barracks, where the blonde giant threw the ball 104 yards and some inches – starting the tour with a century!

Oxford, May 5. During the first Test at the MCG in January 1882, Billy Murdoch asked George Giffen, who had made a nervous 30 supporting Tom Horan's splendid 124, whether he would accompany the Australian Xl to England if the selectors chose him.

Would he!

'Had a thunderbolt struck me I would not have been more astonished, although I had so often built castles in the air about a trip to the Old Country …

'I found my tongue at last, and it was of course, to signify assent.'

Murdoch and Giffen are part of what is regarded as the finest team Australia have yet sent to England, men who have learned a lot from their encounters with the finest players from the old country.

Billy Murdoch, Australia's best batsman, is fresh from his 321 against Victoria and is likely to give a brilliant account of himself. Giffen is the talented tyro, with bowling skills to back him his growing reputation as a batsman.

Alick Bannerman is a steady and proven opener. Hugh Massie, George Bonnor and Sam Jones are splendid hitters, while Percy McDonnell has the style and will to forge some scores. Tom Horan is as adept with the bat as with the pen, with which he writes for the *Australasian*.

As for the bowlers – Fred Spofforth, Harry Boyle, Joey Palmer and Tom Garrett are a powerful combination of guile and speed. On his day Spofforth can run through a team of the best batsmen. And Jack Blackham is acknowledged the best 'keeper in cricket.

The Australians are a fit and disciplined team, primed to do well.

QUICK SINGLES

Chilly weather. The early part of the Australian tour has been plagued by rain and wind, causing the abandonment of games and misery for a team generally used to playing in the sun.

Umpire tells. George Giffen says that it is an education bowling when England umpire Robert Thoms was umpiring – giving as a reason the fact that Thoms explains his decisions and did not leave the batsman in the dark as he made his journey to the pavilion..

Good maxim. George Bonnor remarks: 'If I could only remember that balls hit on the ground can't be caught, and make it my pet proverb, I'd have those English bowlers looking both ways for Sunday in every match I played.'

Dashing Bonnor. In June in the match against Yorkshire, Bonnor twice rushed out to the bowler Peate and belted him clean out of the ground – six each time. Against I Zingari he made 122 not out in 105 minutes – with four sixers.

Booking agent. MCC secretary Henry Perkins has been making arrangements for the touring Australians in 1882, ensuring a full fixture book against the counties and a good profit. The general understanding is that the Australians will take half the gate.

Good manager. Despite his youth, the manager of the Australian team, Charles Beal has earned a reputation for efficiency and good humour and for fair dealings with the English players and managers.

No lunch at Notts. At Nottingham the notorious secretary Jack 'Hellfire' Holden refused the Australians lunch on the ground that they were professionals. He suggested they try the refreshment tent for a beer and a sandwich. The Australians left with a win, £238 profit and an apology from the Committee.

Winning record. The 1882 Australians won 23 matches, drew 11 and lost only four in a wet summer.

Best bats. Four Australian batsmen topped 1000 runs on the tour – Murdoch averaged 30.31, Bannerman 22.8, Massie 24.35 and Horan 25. Three bowlers took more than 100 wickets, Spofforth 188 wickets at 12.13, Boyle 144 at 11.68 and Garrett 128 at 13.74.

Grace Revived. W. G. Grace has revealed that he planned to retire from cricket after the visit of the Australian team, and concentrate on his medical practice., which has often taken second place to cricket over the years. The loss to Australia has fired his ambition, and he will remain in big cricket.

A great start against Counties

The Oval, July 15. The Australians have completed a magnificent win over the Gentlemen of England, by an innings and one run – as a lead up to the Test match this couldn't be bettered.

Giffen had the great satisfaction of bowling the doyen of English cricket W. G. Grace in his 8/49; George Bonnor made 74 in a lightning innings that included 10 huge hits for four, and Sam Jones ended the game with a one-handed catch on the long-on boundary.

Charles Pardon said of Giffen's bowling: 'Taking 8 wickets for just over 6 runs each against such a batting side is a performance which has seldom been excelled on a good wicket.'

This game confirmed the good early form of the Australians – evidence that began accruing from the first game after the team stepped off the boat, against Oxford University – when Hugh Massie made 206 in one of the finest innings by an Australian.

Oxford had four men stationed on the off side boundary about 25 yards apart to see whether they could stop Massie – but despite most athletic fielding, they could not. Giffen took 7/78 in the Oxford second innings.

Billy Murdoch later made 286 against Sussex, when Australia made 643, the highest total so far in cricket between the countries.

The team had its first loss against Cambridge, when the brothers Charles, George and Kynaston Studd scored between them 297 of Cambridge's 393 runs in the match.

Cambridge's three Studd brothers, matchwinners against tourists.

Irresistible as an avalanche

Kennington Oval in London is packed with tense spectators as the high drama of the Test match reaches its climax.

The Oval, Aug. 29. Australia has recorded its first Test win on English soil in an extraordinary game of cricket.

The game began with Billy Murdoch winning the toss and deciding to bat on a wet pitch he thought would not improve. Australia was all out for a miserable 63.

Spofforth took 7/46 in England's innings, but they finished with 101 at the end of the first day.

More rain fell overnight, and the English bowlers had trouble maintaining footholds.

Hugh Massie realised that the pitch would play best for half an hour or so, before it dried sufficiently to take spin. He hit out, Alick Bannerman defended in his usual fashion – before Massie was out at 66.

Murdoch made a careful 29, and was not out until the score reached 122, Australia's total.

While he was batting with Sam Jones, Murdoch turned a ball, and the players ran through for one. Then Jones wandered out of his crease thinking the ball was dead, and W.G. promptly took off the bails and appealed. Umpire Thoms said: 'As you claim it, Sir! Out!' Murdoch protested – but to no avail. The Australian dressing room was incensed at this bit of 'sport', and it fired their will to win.

At the change of innings with England needing just 85, the question was, could they? Spofforth made his declaration: 'This thing can be done'.

He had them at 2/15 early, but at 2/51 with W. G. and George Ulyett hitting strongly things looked less than promising.

Spofforth got Ulyett and then Harry Boyle bowled Grace – and it was 4/53.

Then it seems England lost confidence – Spofforth and Boyle bowled 12 successive maidens, until a bit of gamesmanship let Lyttleton score a run, changing the

bowler's targets. Spofforth then bowled 11 overs for 2 runs and four wickets.

Tom Horan said, 'I observed the incoming batsmen. They had ashen faces and parched lips.' Spofforth's off-cutters on a seaming pitch were all but unplayable. Giffen said every one of them would have hit the stumps had a bat not intervened.

Boyle got the last two wickets, and the stunned crowd – 38,194 watched over the two days – paused, then burst into a roar of cheering. Spofforth was carried from the ground.

Ted Peate: England's last man.

Hugh Harmon Massie: a valuable 55.

British humour surfaces after defeat

London, Sep. 27. After the Test match the remaining tour of England was a cake-walk for the Australians, wishing there could be more Tests just like it and playing cricket with an abandon that was a reminder of the great deed just done.

George Bonnor took a delight in whacking 'sixers', Fred Spofforth walked on air and Billy Murdoch never stopped smiling.

The English seemed equally

> **In Affectionate**
> **Remembrance**
> **of**
> **ENGLISH CRICKET**
> **which died at The Oval**
> **on**
> **29th. August, 1882**
> **Deeply lamented by a large**
> **circle of Sorrowing Friends**
> **and Acquaintances**
> **R.I.P.**
> **N.B. – The body will be**
> **cremated and the ashes**
> **taken to Australia**

bemused, though appreciative of the scale of the great event. Stiff upper lips all round seemed to be the approach from the nation's cricket lovers, and a determination that the colonials would not win the next country-to-country encounter.

The magazine *Bell's Life* said, 'Though England for the first time had to lower her colours to Australia at home, we were beaten

by a magnificent eleven, before whose prowess it was no disgrace to fall.'

The good humour provoked by a magnificent game of cricket was presaged by such incidents at the Oval, where an Epsom stockbroker by the name of Arthur Courcy was so tense during Spofforth and Boyle's succession of maidens that he chewed the handle off his brother-in-law's umbrella.

Some spectators fainted with the tension and one died of a heart attack in what is a new factor in our society – concern over the result of a sporting event, perhaps one in which there was not even any money wagered. Something new had emerged on to the cricket field, the sense of national pride that plunged the ordinary Englishman into the depths with such a loss, and would presumably elevate him with satisfaction if victory were to be gained.

English spectators were not the only ones affected. The mother of Charlie Beal, the Australian manager, was with the small crowd of Australians and ran down the steps on to the ground as soon as the game was over to give a hug and a big kiss to the first astonished Australian she encountered, which happened to be George Giffen.

Punch versified the whole matter and the important questions, at least those from an English point of view: 'Well done Cornstalks! whipt us fair and square. Was it luck that tript us? Or was it scare? Kangaroo land's Demon or our own want of devil, coolness, nerve, backbone.'

Then on September 2, the *Sporting Times* printed a mock obituary, written by Reginald

Brooks, the son of the editor of *Punch*.

This seemed to answer the *Punch* questions in the negative. 'In affectionate remembrance of English cricket which died at The Oval … deeply lamented by a large circle of sorrowing friends … RIP … the body will be cremated and the ashes taken to Australia.

One unintended effect of the victory at the Oval was that 35-year-old Dr W. G. Grace, who had

> **From *Punch* magazine**
>
> **Well done, Cornstalks, whipt**
> **us fair and square.**
> **Was it luck that tripped us?**
> **was it scare?**
> **Kangaroo land's 'Demon'**
> **or our own**
> **Want of devil, coolness,**
> **nerve, backbone.**

planned to retire to his rural medical practice was so annoyed at losing that he declared he had a renewed his interest in the game.

He said he looked forward to straightening out the record with some England victories.

Australia had won this Test battle, but the cricket war will surely continue as England seek to gain the upper hand over the colonial 'cornstalks'.

Murdoch aglow with national pride

London, Sep. 28. At a banquet at the Crichton Hotel in honour of the 1882 Australian team, captain Billy Murdoch responded to the toast 'The Australian Cricket team' by Sir Henry Barkly. It was clear from his demeanour that he had something significant to say: 'When we quitted Australia we did so as a band of cricketers, determined to do our best to uphold the reputation of the land of our birth, to leave no stone unturned to gain laurels so dear to every true sportsman.

'In this spirit we started on our daring enterprise to beard the English lion in his den. The result you know.

'Since landing here in May we have been constantly engaged in playing matches. On all occasions we simply did our best to play up to the true letter and spirit of the game. I can assure you that on the few occasions we lost there were not fourteen more grieved men in the world. We knew very well that the eyes of Australia were on us …

'If I may be permitted to say so, I feel at present something like your very able General Wolseley must feel when he contemplated the result of the Egyptian campaign. He was sent out to do a certain thing – to crush Araby – and he has done it. I was sent home as captain of an Australian cricket team to beat England and I am proud of having done it.

'Personally I have attained the height of my ambition, having captained a team which has beaten a representative eleven of England. Having done this, I do not wish to any more play cricket. [Cries of No! No!]

'But if I am called upon to occupy the position of commanding such a team again, I shall only be too proud to do so, and shall do my very best to win.

'If we have attained any position as cricketers, you in England have yourselves to thank for it, for you have been our instructors.

'We have been very ready and willing to learn, for the cricketing spirit is strong in Australia as in England. It is the national game of the colonies. We shall always be ready to take up the willow and do battle with any who desire to meet us in the field.

'Before resuming my seat I desire to propose the toast, 'The English cricketers, and success to Cricket.'

Grand American tour and triumphant homecoming

Sydney, Nov. 18. The 1882 Australian XI has arrived home after its triumphant tour of England, which was followed by an adventurous tour of the United States.

Leaving Liverpool on September 30, the tourists sailed aboard the SS *Alaska* for New York, via Ireland, enduring the sort of great storm that brings dark foreboding for the fate of the ship and life and limb.

Many concerts were held on board, with the cricketers showing their usual good spirits and performing songs and recitations. After one such concert, in aid of the Shipwrecked Mariners Fund, an old American gentleman proposed a toast 'To the Australian Colonies' expressing his firm conviction that a grand future was in

store for the nation that was slowly but surely rising in the sunny south.

Berthing on the Hudson in New York on the 8th, the team proceeded next day by ferry to the St George's ground in Hoboken

Spofforth and Boyle found the wicket a nicety – a sticky – and despatched the New York XVIII for 27 and 102, the Australians making 116 and 3/14. The cricket was not up to much but the team was said to have 'Waterlooed' the 'NY18' by the *New York Herald,* one of whom 'made a wild swipe for the horizon and was bowled for a duck by the demon'.

In Philadelphia at the ground of the Germantown club in Nicetown, the first day's play was

foreshortened by a Scotch mist, but completed over the next two, for an easy Australian victory. After Philadelphia, the team travelled to San Francisco via Chicago, leaving that fair city on October 22, arriving in Honolulu a week later, where the team drank to Australian success in bumpers at the leading hotel.

November 13 saw the team in Auckland, where George Bonnor nearly missed the boat to Sydney.

Back home, the 1882 Australian XI is to be banqueted and feted like no other team before it. The players' stamina will now be tested by a succession of dinners, receptions, processions, and benefits, along with some more cricket matches.

The Demon bowler, Fred Spofforth

Neville Cardus imagined himself dozing off at the cricket in 1921 waiting for Armstrong's Australians to practice, and finding in his day-dream that he had been transported back to that day on 29 August 1882 when Fred 'The Demon' Spofforth made a flame in history in the ashes of English cricket.

'Now I was behind his arm; I could see his superb break-back. And he bowled mainly medium pace at this time. With each off-break I could see his right hand, at the end of the swing over, finish near the left side, 'cutting' under the ball.

'Sometimes his arm went straight over and continued straight down in the follow-through – and then the batsman had to tackle fierce topspin. There was the sense of the inimical in his aspect now. He seemed taller than he was half an hour ago, the right arm more sinuous. 'There was no excitement in him he was … cold-blooded.'

In person, Spofforth was far from cold-blooded. He was a yarner, and a convivial host. He was also regarded as the best, the most lethal bowler of his day.

Spofforth had moved to England in 1888, at the same time as his boyhood friend and Australian captain Billy Murdoch. His career in Australian cricket was over. He played his last Test on the SCG in 1887, taking just 1/17 and finishing with 94 Test wickets – a record at the time. His last intercolonial match was for Victoria in 1887.

Spofforth was born in Balmain on 9 September 1853, spent some time in New Zealand when very young, but was living in Sydney in 1864 when he watched the second English touring team at the Domain.

'At once my great ambition was to bowl fast like [George] Tarrant, who always sent the stumps flying when he bowled a batsman out.'

Young Fred first played for Newtown and made a name for himself against the premier club of the day, Alberts when the captain tossed the ball to him for the first time. 'I had been gazing at him during the match, hoping to be asked.' Spofforth took five-for, saving the game and the papers next day said 'a wonderful boy bowler had been discovered.'

His Dad realised that he could never really succeed without playing for a club with the best ground and pitches – and paid his way into the Alberts for 1872–73 where he learned his craft in the seconds.

Spofforth was picked for a NSW XVIII which beat W. G. Grace's XI in January 1874.

On 26 December 1874 Spofforth made his first class debut for NSW, taking a wicket in his first over, and finishing with 3/56 and 3/67 and hitting 21 in a winning side.

In the 1875–76 season just two first class matches were played – between Victoria and NSW. Spofforth was outstanding in the game played at the Albert ground. Bowling in tandem with Edwin Evans and in both innings, Spofforth took 4/22 and 5/50. The *Sydney Mail* said his 'pace was something not likely to be forgotten by those who had to stand up against it.'

Spofforth refused to play in the first-ever Test in March 1877 because his mate Billy Murdoch wasn't chosen as 'keeper. One newspaper said without Billy, Spoff 'would have been shorn of his lustre.' But he played in the second Test and, when Jack Blackham stumped England's captain Alfred Shaw, standing up, Spofforth was professional enough to appreciate the better stumper. Murdoch had other qualities.

Spofforth toured with the first European Australian side to England in 1878, and played in the celebrated match against the MCC in May 1878 where he earned his name with 6/4, including a hat trick, and 4/16, Australia winning by an innings and one run.

In the only Test played on England's 1878–79 tour, Spofforth won the match with 6/48 and 7/62.

Highlight of his 1880 tour was a broken finger, due to a 'chucker' causing him to miss the first Test

played in England. On the 1882 tour he won the Ashes Test .

George Giffen said of him, 'The Demon who had made a deep study of the art of bowling, had a wonderful control over his pitch, and he seldom turned the ball, unless, if it were allowed to pass the bat, it would hit the wicket. What a sight it was to see Spofforth bowling when a game had to be pulled like a brand from the burning! He looked the Demon, every inch of him, and I verily believe he has frightened more batsmen out than many bowlers have fairly and squarely beaten. When the Demon meant business, the batsmen had to look out for squalls.'

In 1885 Spofforth, a bank officer like his father, took up a position in Melbourne as manager of the Moonee Ponds branch of the National Bank of Australasia, and the next year he married Phillis Cadman, the daughter of a wealthy tea merchant.

He played for Victoria in 1885–86, and 1886–87. In his first match he destroyed NSW, taking 10 wickets in the match.

His last matches in Australia were less successful – in the game against NSW and the first Test at the SCG in January. He was not selected for the other Test match, but was invited to tour in 1888. He declined the offer.

The *Bulletin* put it this way: 'Spoff the erstwhile Demon bowler, having come in for money, leaves next month to take up residence in England. If Turner keeps up his present form with bat and ball, the Britishers will forget about Spoff who at his best was only one part demon.'

Unfair, but Spofforth did move in to the tea business in England, saying at one point that it 'would be an honour to play for England against Australia.'

In 1896 he did play for an English XI against the Australians at Wembley Park, and took 6/49 and 5/51.

In 1897 the issue of 'throwing' was in the air, and, remembering perhaps what happened to him in 1880, Spofforth wrote to the *Sporting Times* complaining of it, naming two players who later had selection trouble, and suggesting that a committee be set up to oversee players actions with the power to suspend them.

Spoff died in England a wealthy man, cultivating gum trees, at his home in Surrey, on 4 June 1926.

ONLY TEST 1882 ENGLAND v AUSTRALIA
Kennington Oval, London. August 28, 29, 1882.
Toss: Australia. Australia won by 7 runs.

AUSTRALIA

Batsman	1st Innings		2nd Innings	
AC Bannerman c Grace b Peate	9		c Studd b Barnes	13
HH Massie b Ulyett	1		b Steel	55
WL Murdoch (c) b Peate	13	(4)	run out	29
GJ Bonnor b Barlow	1	(3)	b Ulyett	2
TP Horan b Barlow	3		c Grace b Peate	2
G Giffen b Peate	2		c Grace b Peate	0
JM Blackham (+) c Grace b Barlow	17		c Lyttelton b Peate	7
TW Garrett c Read b Peate	10	(10)	not out	2
HF Boyle b Barlow	2	(11)	b Steel	0
SP Jones c Barnes b Barlow	0	(8)	run out	6
FR Spofforth not out	4	(9)	b Peate	0
EXTRAS (B 1)	1		(B 6)	6
TOTAL	63			122

FOW 1st Inns: 6 21 22 26 30 30 48 53 59 63
FOW 2nd Inns: 66 70 70 79 79 99 114 117 122 122

Bowling: *First Innings*: Peate 38-24-31-4, Ulyett 9-5-11-1, Barlow 31-22-19-5, Steel 2-1-1-0. *Second Innings*: Peate 21-9-40-4, Ulyett 6-2-10-1, Barlow 13-5-27-0, Steel 7-0-15-2, Barnes 12-5-15-1, Studd 4-1-9-0.

ENGLAND

Batsman	1st Innings		2nd Innings	
RG Barlow c Bannerman b Spofforth	11	(3)	b Spofforth	0
WG Grace b Spofforth	4	(1)	c Bannerman b Boyle	32
G Ulyett st Blackham b Spofforth	26	(4)	c Blackham b Spofforth	11
AP Lucas c Blackham b Boyle	9	(5)	b Spofforth	5
A Lyttelton (+) c Blackham b Spofforth	2	(6)	b Spofforth	12
CT Studd b Spofforth	0	(10)	not out	0
JM Read not out	19	(8)	b Spofforth	0
W Barnes b Boyle	5	(9)	c Murdoch b Boyle	2
AG Steel b Garrett	14	(7)	c & b Spofforth	0
AN Hornby (c) b Spofforth	2	(2)	b Spofforth	9
E Peate c Boyle b Spofforth	0		b Boyle	2
EXTRAS (B 6, LB 2, NB 1)	9		(B 3, NB 1)	4
TOTAL	101			77

FOW 1st Inns: 13 18 57 59 60 63 70 96 101 101
FOW 2nd Inns: 15 15 51 53 66 70 70 75 75 77

Bowling: *First Innings*: Spofforth 36.3-18-46-7, Garrett 16-7-22-1, Boyle 19-7-24-2. *Second Innings*: Spofforth 28-15-44-7, Garrett 7-2-10-0, Boyle 20-11-19-3.

Umpires: L Greenwood & R Thoms

Ivo Bligh vows to take back the Ashes

Shipboard romance. The English captain, the Honourable Ivo Bligh, has been paying special attention to Florence Rose Morphy while travelling to Australia on the SS *Peshawur*. She is the Australian governess to the party of Sir William 'Big' Clarke, the millionaire squatter and philanthropist.

Tips from the top. The cricket publication *Boyle and Scott's Australian Guide*, published this year, includes Hints on Batting by W. L. Murdoch and Hints to Junior Bowlers by H. F. Boyle.

Top quarters. During the short stay of the English team in Adelaide in November, the gentlemen of the team were made honorary members of the South Australian Club. They stayed at the South Australian Club Hotel, while the professionals were quartered at the Duke of Kent.

Byes the winner. No batsman scored in England's second innings against Victoria on November 21. The four winning runs came from a bouncer that cleared the batsman and the wicketkeeper.

Extra hand. Mr George Alexander, the Australian cricketer nominated as manager of the English touring party by the Melbourne Cricket Club, has occasionally done duty for them as a substitute on the cricket field. Against Victoria he threw down the wicket and took a fine catch.

Heroes welcome. The returning 1882 team has been honored in Sydney, Melbourne and Adelaide during December. In Melbourne a torchlight procession to the MCG was followed by the presentation of a Victorian Cricketers' Association medal.

Reverse order. The intercolonial matches between NSW and Victoria again resulted in one game each this season, but this time NSW won in Melbourne (by seven wickets) and Victoria won in Sydney (by an innings and 66 runs).

Keen cricketer. Mr Charles Manion rode his bike to Ballarat in May to play for Emerald Hill against Ballarat. He left Melbourne at 1.30 p.m. on Friday, arrived at 11.15 on Saturday, and then made 68 not out.

The Victorian team, assembled to battle with the English team under the captaincy of the Honourable Ivo Bligh.

Melbourne, Nov. 15. The captain of the visiting England team, The Honourable Ivo Bligh, has declared his mission in Australia is to win back 'The Ashes', the mythical 'body' of English cricket which was created by the *Sporting Times* in London in August.

Bligh told a dinner in Melbourne last night that he and his team have 'come to beard the kangaroo in his den and try to recover those Ashes.'

Bligh, the eldest son of Lord Darnley, is a tall and dashing figure with his handlebar moustache and lordly bearing.

He is only 23, but seems to have command of his team, which has had only five rushed days in Australia. He played in the England side that beat Australia in 1878 and has had the classical cricketing path of the English gentleman, playing for Eton, Cambridge and Surrey.

He has come to be known as 'St. Ivo' as this tour has been likened to a pilgrimage, the cricketing equivalent of the search for the Holy Grail.

The portents, however, have not been good.

The team suffered a setback on the way out when their ship, the *Peshawur*, collided with another vessel near Colombo.

The only fast bowler, Fred Morley, suffered chest injuries and it seems his fitness is still in doubt.

Morley's form might be the key to the forthcoming Tests as he is a proven bowler and showed his mettle with the figures of 8/146 at the Oval two years ago.

Ivo Bligh: a tall and dashing captain.

Faces missing in this England team include Dr W. G. Grace, George Ulyett, Edmund Peate, Arthur Shrewsbury and Alfred Shaw, but they have chosen not to come.

Almost a University team, it includes the brothers Charles and George Studd and A. G. Steel from Bligh's university, Cambridge, and the batsman/wicketkeeper Edmund Tylecote and Charles Leslie, both from Oxford.

The amateur contingent will assist in making it a convivial tour in relation to banquets and receptions, and ensure good turnouts in the members stands and from ladies who are attracted to matches that carry some social cachet.

Fred Morley: injured en route.

There are, however, some strong professionals in Morley, and the all-rounders Dick Barlow of Lancashire, Billy Barnes of Notts, Billy Bates of Yorkshire and Walter Read of Surrey.

Barlow is likely to be the key player as he is a correct and skilled batsman and a left arm medium pacer.

The England team is in Australia ahead of the returning cricketers, still travelling across the Pacific.

The team, tried and tested and the bearers of the fruits of victory, is expected to remain largely unchanged, under the direction of William Murdoch, to take up the fight against the avenging English.

Depleted Colonial teams are thrashed

Sydney, Dec. 4. The England XI has had a flying start to its Australian campaign, with huge wins over Victoria and NSW, the first by 10 wickets and the latter by an innings and 144 runs. The Colonial teams were weakened by the absence of their English tour representatives, who are still returning.

Victoria was without nine regulars, six tourists and three unavailable, while NSW had six missing.

Ivo Bligh was missing for England with a hand injury, while Fred Morley was forced to make up the numbers without being fit.

The highlight of England's strong batting was 144 by Charles Leslie in the total of 461 against NSW.

Victoria's only consolation was the leg-spin of Bransby Cooper, which yielded five wickets. For NSW, Edwin Evans toiled manfully for 6/146.

H.J.H. Scott: Victorian hope.

Captain of the XI: a romantic view of the character-building game.

Huge crowds see first Test

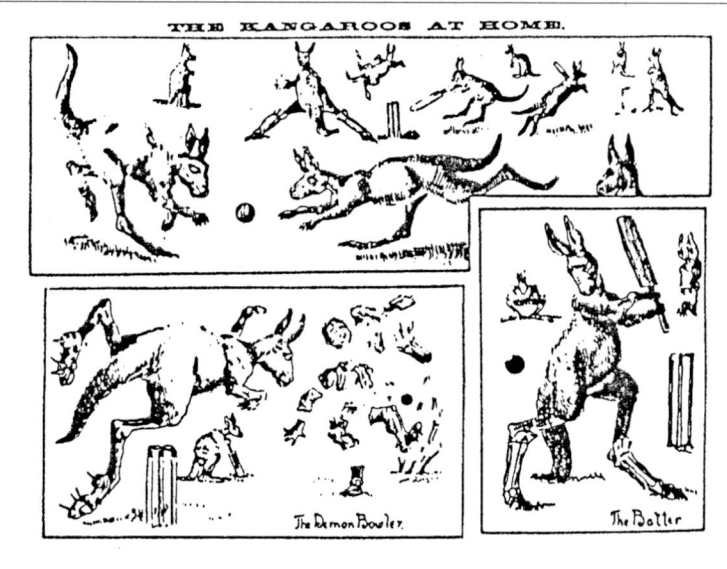

The conquering Australians, as seen in Queenland's Figaro *journal.*

Australia the winner by nine wickets

Melbourne, Jan. 3. Now that Australia's seasoned Test heroes are back on the arena the English team has been set back on its heels in its quest for a series win.

Australia has won the first Test by nine wickets. Its bowlers, particularly George Palmer, with a match return of 10/126, brought the English batsmen back to earth as they chased Australia's solid first innings of 291.

The Test has attracted huge crowds and has been been the dominant point of interest in Melbourne in recent weeks. There were attendances at the Melbourne Cricket Ground of 15,000, 23,000 and 16, 000 – crowds only rivalled in Melbourne by football match attendances.

The main excitement on the first day was over the batting of George Bonnor, who came in after Bannerman (30), Murdoch (48), McDonnell (43) and Giffen (36) had given Australia a steady start. The giant smashed the ball around for 85 runs, four times hitting the ball into the Ladies Reserve and silencing criticisms of his selection ahead of Boyle.

England's chances were affected by overnight rain, and it turned out that they had little answer for the medium-paced spin of George Palmer. They made 177, and lost one wicket in a run out in which Blackham ran the full length of the pitch, while Studd and Tylecote huddled at one end. They made 169 in the second innings.

Cricket missionaries to Queensland

Brisbane, Feb. 30. The England team has brought the 'gospel of cricket' to virtually untapped territory on its mission to Brisbane this month.

After three days of rough travel in a coastal steamer to Brisbane, the Englishmen played against two eighteens of Queensland. They found the standard of cricket low, and won both matches by an innings, but enjoyed both the hospitality and a glimpse of the sub-tropical areas of the country.

The enthusiastic crowds which attended the matches contributed to the touring party's coffers, and to the purse of the Queensland Cricket Association. It is to buy the Albert Sports Ground at Breakfast Creek from its profit of £400.

Queensland conquerers: England spans the cricket world.

SA fight for a Test that was promised

Adelaide, April 30. A breach of contract action, brought by the South Australian Cricket Association over a missing Test match, has been settled by the England tour organisers, the Melbourne Cricket Club.

The South Australians have been hounding the MCC secretary, Benjamin Wardill, over the Test match after the Australian captain William Murdoch told committee members in December that arrangements had been made in London for three Tests to take place – in Melbourne, Adelaide and Sydney.

Wardill had, indeed, written to the SACA in November, offering the possibility of a Test match, and suggesting five per cent of the gate takings as the fee to the local body. The SACA replied that it would not accept less than 10 per cent.

The matter rested there until the officials realised that they had been by-passed without notice and would not be having a Test. This

MCC Secretary, Major Ben Wardill.

was especially galling, given the reception that the England players received when they played South Australia. The SACA asked John Creswell, who is now the SACA secretary, to go to Melbourne and negotiate with both the players and Wardill.

Creswell returned empty-handed, and then the South Australians were further upset by Wardill's announcement that there would be a fourth Test, and it would be in Melbourne.

They bombarded Wardill, and other associations, with telegrams to press their case, but without any success, or even a reply from Wardill. Now their legal satisfaction may give rise to their pleasure of seeing future Tests in Adelaide.

England shines, Ashes claimed

A cartoon depiction of the Australian procession in the third Test.

Billy Bates: a 14-wicket haul.

Black day for SA – all out for 23

Melbourne, March 27. The pride of South Australia is in tatters following the ignominious showing of its cricketers against Victoria.

South Australia went to the crease on day one sure in the knowledge that they had advanced to full intercolonial status under the auspices of the coach Jesse Hide. They had a Test representative in George Giffen. They had had a good year, and well remembered that they had won the corresponding fixture last year by 31 runs.

Only 85 minutes later they were all back in the pavilion for the 23 runs. Seven batsmen (including their mentor Jesse Hide) had made ducks and only John Noel, with 18 runs, could hold his head up. The next best score was 2.

The damage on the damp pitch was done by George Palmer (5/16) and Harry Boyle (4/6). Victoria won the rain-interrupted match by an innings and 98 runs. Palmer bowled unchanged throughout both SA innings, having match figures of 10/44. He took three wickets in four balls in SA's first innings.

Sydney, Jan. 1. England has had the crowning moment of its tour tonight, with captain Ivo Bligh claiming a series win after two stunning victories over Australia.

England humbled Australia in the second Test, and showed grit in a tight and dramatic game to win the third by 69 runs. Australia won the hastily arranged fourth Test by four wickets.

The second Test in Melbourne started promisingly for England, with their batsman playing steadily to make 291.

Australia made some bad mistakes in the field, particularly in missing Barnes on 0 before he went on to 55.

Australia started well with Massie (43) and looked reasonably placed at 2/72. But then the roof fell in as Billy Bates' round-arm spinners carved through the Australians.

As the wickets tumbled Bates dismissed McDonnell, Giffen and Bonnor to be the first Englishman to take a Test hat-trick. He cleaned up the tail and captured 7/28 off 26.2 overs with 14 maidens. He went on to take 7/74 in Australia's second innings, and the result of his efforts was the first innings-win in Test matches.

In Sydney it was a tense affair with England getting 247, and Australia being beset by rain in its innings. Only a painstaking 94 by Alick 'Barndoor' Bannerman kept Australia alive as it reached 218.

The rain-affected pitch made it a bowlers paradise in the second innings, and Fred Spofforth lifted Australia's hopes as he took 7/44 and England crumbled for 123 – a lead of a mere 152.

This time it was the nagging accuracy and length of Dick Barlow's medium pacers that brought Australia down for 83. Barlow took 7/40.

Ashes go from bag to urn

Melbourne, March 12. Having claimed 'the Ashes' at a dinner after the third Test in Sydney, the Hon. Ivo Bligh has found the fancied remains of English cricket are something of a reality.

At the dinner Mrs Annie Fletcher, wife of the Paddington Cricket Club secretary, with whom Bligh is staying, presented him with an embroidered bag in which to place the Ashes. He accepted the offer in good part, full of good spirits after his team's success.

Now in Melbourne his lady friend, Florence Morphy and some of her friends have presented him with an urn filled with the Ashes. It is believed the Ashes in the engraved urn have been derived from the burning of some cricket bails or a stump.

There is some dissent over Bligh claiming a series win, and therefore the Ashes. He says that there were only three Tests in the original schedule, and England has won two of them. There has been no official argument against this, even though Australia won the fourth Test in Sydney by four wickets. The fourth Test was not on the original schedule, and the Australian desire for a fifth Test

'The Ashes': urned for England.

was thwarted by the schedule of the English team.

The fourth Test was remarkable for the fact that Billy Midwinter played for Australia. He has played for Australia twice and England four times, and has now reverted to Australia. The Test also yielded the first and only century of the series to England's Allan Steel, who showed his driving talents as he compiled 135 not out.

George Bonnor gave the crowd some thrills with his big-hitting 87 in the first innings, particularly as he gave many chances – five to Allan Steel alone.

Australian Averages													
1882–83 AUSTRALIA v ENGLAND													
AUSTRALIA	M	Inn	NO	Runs	H.S	Avrge	Ct	St	Overs	Mds	Runs	Wkt	Avrge
Bannerman, AC	4	8	1	255	94	36.43	1	-	11.0	2	17	1	17.00
Blackham, JM	4	7	1	204	58*	34.00	3	1	-	-	-	-	-
Bonnor, GJ	4	7	-	217	87	31.00	5	-	-	-	-	-	-
Boyle, HF	1	1	-	29	29	29.00	1	-	63.0	25	87	5	17.40
Evans, E	1	2	1	22	22*	22.00	-	-	11.0	3	15	-	-
Garrett, TW	3	5	-	16	10	3.20	2	-	103.0	34	168	3	56.00
Giffen, G	4	7	-	162	41	23.14	-	-	81.0	23	164	8	20.50
Horan, TP	4	7	-	49	19	7.00	1	-	38.0	16	63	5	12.60
Massie, HH	3	6	-	69	43	11.50	2	-	-	-	-	-	-
McDonnell, PS	3	5	-	59	43	11.80	2	-	4.0	-	16	-	-
Midwinter, WE	1	2	1	18	10	18.00	-	-	70.0	37	71	4	17.75
Murdoch, WL	4	8	2	153	48	25.50	6	-	-	-	-	-	-
Palmer, GE	4	6	2	20	7	5.00	3	-	270.1	113	397	21	18.90
Spofforth, FR	4	6	2	31	14*	7.75	-	-	244.1	93	408	18	22.67

English Averages													
1882–83 AUSTRALIA v ENGLAND													
ENGLAND	M	Inn	NO	Runs	H.S	Avrge	Ct	St	Overs	Mds	Runs	Wkt	Avrge
Barlow, RG	4	7	-	126	28	18.00	6	-	244.0	124	343	15	22.87
Barnes, W	4	7	1	87	32	14.50	3	-	108.0	40	170	6	28.33
Bates, W	4	7	1	172	55	28.67	4	-	192.3	87	286	19	15.05
Bligh, IFW	4	7	-	62	19	10.33	7	-	-	-	-	-	-
Leslie, CFH	4	7	-	106	54	15.14	1	-	24.0	10	44	4	11.00
Morley, F	3	5	2	4	2*	1.33	2	-	150.0	85	150	8	18.75
Read, WW	4	7	-	228	75	32.57	1	-	8.0	2	27	-	-
Steel, AG	4	7	1	274	135*	45.67	3	-	129.0	49	195	11	17.73
Studd, CT	4	7	-	160	48	22.86	4	-	92.0	59	89	3	29.67
Studd, GB	4	7	-	31	9	4.43	8	-	-	-	-	-	-
Tylecote, EFS	4	7	-	142	66	20.29	1	4	-	-	-	-	-
Vernon, GF	1	2	1	14	11*	14.00	-	-	-	-	-	-	-

FIRST TEST 1882–83 AUSTRALIA v ENGLAND
Melbourne Cricket Ground, Melbourne. December 30, 1882, January 1, 2, 1883.
Toss: Australia. Australia won by 9 wkts.

AUSTRALIA

AC Bannerman st Tylecote b Leslie	30	not out	25
HH Massie c & b CT Studd	4	c & b Barnes	0
WL Murdoch (c) b Leslie	48	not out	33
TP Horan c Barlow b Leslie	0		
PS McDonnell b Bates	43		
G Giffen st Tylecote b Steel	36		
GJ Bonnor c Barlow b Barnes	85		
JM Blackham (+) c Tylecote b CT Studd	25		
FR Spofforth c Steel b Barnes	9		
TW Garrett c CT Studd b Steel	0		
GE Palmer not out	0		
EXTRAS (B 4, LB 2, W 2, NB 3)	11		0
TOTAL	291		1 for 58

FOW *1st Inns:* 5 81 81 96 162 190 251 287 287 291
FOW *2nd Inns:* 0

Bowling: *First Innings:* CT Studd 46-30-35-2, Barnes 30-11-51-2, Steel 33-16-68-2, Barlow 20-6-37-0, Read 8-2-27-0, Bates 21-7-31-1, Leslie 11-1-31-3. *Second Innings:* CT Studd 14-11-7-0, Barnes 13-8-6-1, Steel 9-4-17-0, Bates 13.1-7-22-0, Barlow 4-2-6-0.

ENGLAND

RG Barlow st Blackham b Palmer	10	b Spofforth	28
IFW Bligh (c) b Palmer	0 (5)	b Spofforth	3
CFH Leslie c Garrett b Palmer	4 (7)	b Giffen	4
CT Studd b Spofforth	0 (3)	b Palmer	21
AG Steel b Palmer	27 (4)	lbw Giffen	29
WW Read b Palmer	19	b Giffen	29
W Bates c Bannerman b Garrett	28 (8)	c Massie b Palmer	11
EFS Tylecote (+) b Palmer	33 (2)	c Morley b Palmer	38
GB Studd run out	7	c Palmer b Giffen	0
W Barnes b Palmer	26	not out	2
GF Vernon not out	11	lbw Palmer	3
EXTRAS (B 8, LB 1, NB 3)	12	(LB 1)	1
TOTAL	177		169

FOW *1st Inns:* 2 7 8 36 45 96 96 117 156 177
FOW *2nd Inns:* 64 75 105 108 132 150 164 164 164 169

Bowling: *First Innings:* Spofforth 28-11-56-1, Palmer 52.2-25-65-7, Garrett 27-6-44-1. *Second Innings:* Palmer 36.1-11-61-3, Garrett 2-1-4-0, Spofforth 41-15-65-3, Giffen 20-7-38-4.

Umpires: EH Elliott & J Swift

SECOND TEST 1882–83 AUSTRALIA v ENGLAND
Melbourne Cricket Ground, Melbourne. January 19, 20, 22, 1883.
Toss: England. England won by an innings & 27 runs.

ENGLAND

RG Barlow b Palmer	14
CT Studd b Palmer	14
CFH Leslie run out	54
AG Steel c McDonnell b Giffen	39
WW Read c & b Palmer	75
W Barnes b Giffen	32
EFS Tylecote (+) b Giffen	0
IFW Bligh (c) b Giffen	0
W Bates c Horan b Palmer	55
GB Studd b Palmer	1
F Morley not out	0
EXTRAS (B 3, LB 3, NB 4)	10
TOTAL	294

FOW *1st Inns:* 28 35 106 131 193 199 199 287 293 294

Bowling: *First Innings:* Spofforth 34-11-57-0, Palmer 66.3-25-103-5, Giffen 49-13-89-4, Garrett 34-16-35-0.

AUSTRALIA

HH Massie b Barlow	43 (7)	c CT Studd b Barlow	10
AC Bannerman b Bates	14	c Bligh b Bates	14
WL Murdoch (c) not out	19 (1)	b Bates	17
TP Horan c & b Barnes	3 (5)	c Morley b Bates	15
PS McDonnell b Bates	3 (6)	b Bates	13
G Giffen c & b Bates	0 (8)	c Bligh b Bates	19
GJ Bonnor c Read b Bates	0 (4)	c Morley b Barlow	34
JM Blackham (+) b Barnes	5 (3)	b Barlow	6
TW Garrett b Bates	10	c Barnes b Bates	6
GE Palmer b Bates	7	c GB Studd b Bates	4
FR Spofforth b Bates	0	not out	14
EXTRAS (B 6, LB 3, NB 1)	10	(B 1)	1
TOTAL	114		153

FOW *1st Inns:* 56 72 75 78 78 78 85 104 114 114
FOW *2nd Inns:* 21 28 66 72 93 104 113 132 139 153

Bowling: *First Innings:* Studd 4-1-22-0, Morley 23-16-13-0, Barnes 23-7-32-2, Barlow 22-18-9-1, Bates 26.2-14-28-7. *Second Innings:* Bates 33-14-74-7, Barlow 31-6-67-3, Barnes 3-1-4-0, Morley 2-0-7-0.

Umpires: EH Elliott & J Swift

THIRD TEST 1882–83 AUSTRALIA v ENGLAND
Sydney Cricket Ground, Sydney. January 26, 27, 29, 30, 1883.
Toss: England. England won by 69 runs.

ENGLAND

RG Barlow c Murdoch b Spofforth	28 (3)	c Palmer b Horan	24
CT Studd c Blackham b Garrett	21	b Spofforth	25
CFH Leslie b Spofforth	0 (1)	b Spofforth	8
AG Steel b Garrett	17	lbw Spofforth	6
WW Read c Massie b Bannerman	66	b Horan	21
W Barnes c Blackham b Spofforth	2	lbw Spofforth	3
EFS Tylecote (+) run out	66	c Bonnor b Spofforth	0
W Bates c McDonnell b Spofforth	17	c Murdoch b Horan	4
GB Studd b Palmer	3 (10)	c Garrett b Spofforth	8
IFW Bligh (c) b Palmer	13 (9)	not out	17
F Morley not out	2	b Spofforth	0
EXTRAS (B 8, LB 3, NB 1)	12	(B 5, LB 2)	7
TOTAL	247		123

FOW *1st Inns:* 41 44 67 69 75 191 223 224 244 247
FOW *2nd Inns:* 13 45 55 87 92 94 97 98 115 123

Bowling: *First Innings:* Giffen 12-3-37-0, Palmer 38-21-38-2, Spofforth 51-19-73-4, Garrett 27-8-54-2, Bannerman 11-2-17-1, McDonnell 4-0-16-0. *Second Innings:* Spofforth 41.1-23-44-7, Garrett 13-3-31-0, Palmer 9-3-19-0, Horan 17-10-22-3.

AUSTRALIA

AC Bannerman c Bates b Morley	94	c Bligh b Barlow	5
G Giffen st Tylecote b Bates	41	b Barlow	7
WL Murdoch (c) lbw Steel	19	c GB Studd b Morley	0
PS McDonnell b Steel	0 (5)	c Bligh b Morley	0
TP Horan c Steel b Morley	19 (4)	run out	8
HH Massie c Bligh b Steel	1	c CT Studd b Barlow	11
GJ Bonnor c GB Studd b Morley	0	b Barlow	8
JM Blackham (+) b Barlow	27	b Barlow	26
TW Garrett c Barlow b Morley	0 (11)	b Barlow	0
GE Palmer c GB Studd b Barnes	7	b Barlow	7
FR Spofforth not out	0 (9)	c Steel b Barlow	7
EXTRAS (B 6, LB 2, W 1, NB 1)	10	(B 6, LB 2, W 1)	9
TOTAL	218		83

FOW *1st Inns:* 76 140 140 176 177 178 196 196 218 218
FOW *2nd Inns:* 11 12 18 18 30 33 56 72 80 83

Bowling: *First Innings:* Bates 45-20-55-1, Morley 34-16-47-4, Steel 26-14-27-3, Barlow 47.1-31-52-1, Barnes 13-6-22-1, Studd 14-11-5-0. *Second Innings:* Morley 35-19-34-2, Barlow 34.2-20-40-7.

Umpires: EH Elliott & J Swift

FOURTH TEST 1882–83 AUSTRALIA v ENGLAND
Sydney Cricket Ground, Sydney. February 17, 19, 20, 21, 1883.
Toss: England. Australia won by 4 wkts.

ENGLAND

RG Barlow c Murdoch b Midwinter	2	c Bonnor b Midwinter	20
CT Studd run out	48	c Murdoch b Midwinter	31
CFH Leslie c Bonnor b Boyle	17	b Horan	19
AG Steel not out	135	b Spofforth	21
WW Read c Bonnor b Boyle	11	b Spofforth	7
EFS Tylecote (+) b Boyle	5	b Palmer	0
W Barnes b Spofforth	2 (9)	c & b Boyle	20
W Bates c Bonnor b Midwinter	9 (7)	not out	48
IFW Bligh (c) b Palmer	19 (8)	c Murdoch b Horan	10
GB Studd run out	3	c Murdoch b Boyle	9
F Morley b Palmer	0	c Blackham b Palmer	2
EXTRAS (B 4, LB 7, NB 1)	12	(B 8, LB 1, NB 1)	10
TOTAL	263		197

FOW *1st Inns:* 13 37 110 150 156 159 199 236 263 263
FOW *2nd Inns:* 54 55 77 99 100 112 137 178 192 197

Bowling: *First Innings:* Palmer 24-9-52-2, Midwinter 47-24-50-2, Spofforth 21-8-56-1, Boyle 40-19-52-3, Horan 12-4-26-0, Evans 11-3-15-0. *Second Innings:* Spofforth 28-6-57-2, Boyle 23-6-35-2, Palmer 43.3-19-59-2, Midwinter 23-13-21-2, Horan 9-2-15-2.

AUSTRALIA

AC Bannerman c Barlow b Morley	10	c Bligh b CT Studd	63
GJ Bonnor c Barlow b Steel	87 (3)	c GB Studd b Steel	3
WL Murdoch (c) b Barlow	0 (2)	c Barlow b Bates	17
TP Horan c GB Studd b Morley	4	c & b Bates	0
G Giffen c GB Studd b Leslie	27	st Tylecote b Steel	32
WE Midwinter b Barlow	10 (8)	not out	8
JM Blackham (+) b Bates	57 (6)	not out	58
GE Palmer c Bligh b Steel	0		
E Evans not out	22 (7)	c Leslie b Steel	0
FR Spofforth c Bates b Steel	1		
HF Boyle c GB Studd b Barlow	29		
EXTRAS (B 10, LB 3, W 2)	15	(B 10, LB 4, W 4)	18
TOTAL	262		6 for 199

FOW *1st Inns:* 31 34 39 113 128 160 164 220 221 262
FOW *2nd Inns:* 44 51 51 107 162 164

Bowling: *First Innings:* Barlow 48-21-88-3, Morley 44-25-45-2, Barnes 10-2-33-0, Bates 15-6-24-1, Leslie 5-2-11-1, Steel 18-6-34-3, Studd 6-2-12-0. *Second Innings:* Bates 39-19-52-2, Barlow 37.1-20-44-0, Morley 12-9-4-0, Leslie 8-7-2-0, Steel 43-9-49-3, Studd 8-4-8-1, Barnes 16-5-22-0.

Umpires: EH Elliott & J Swift

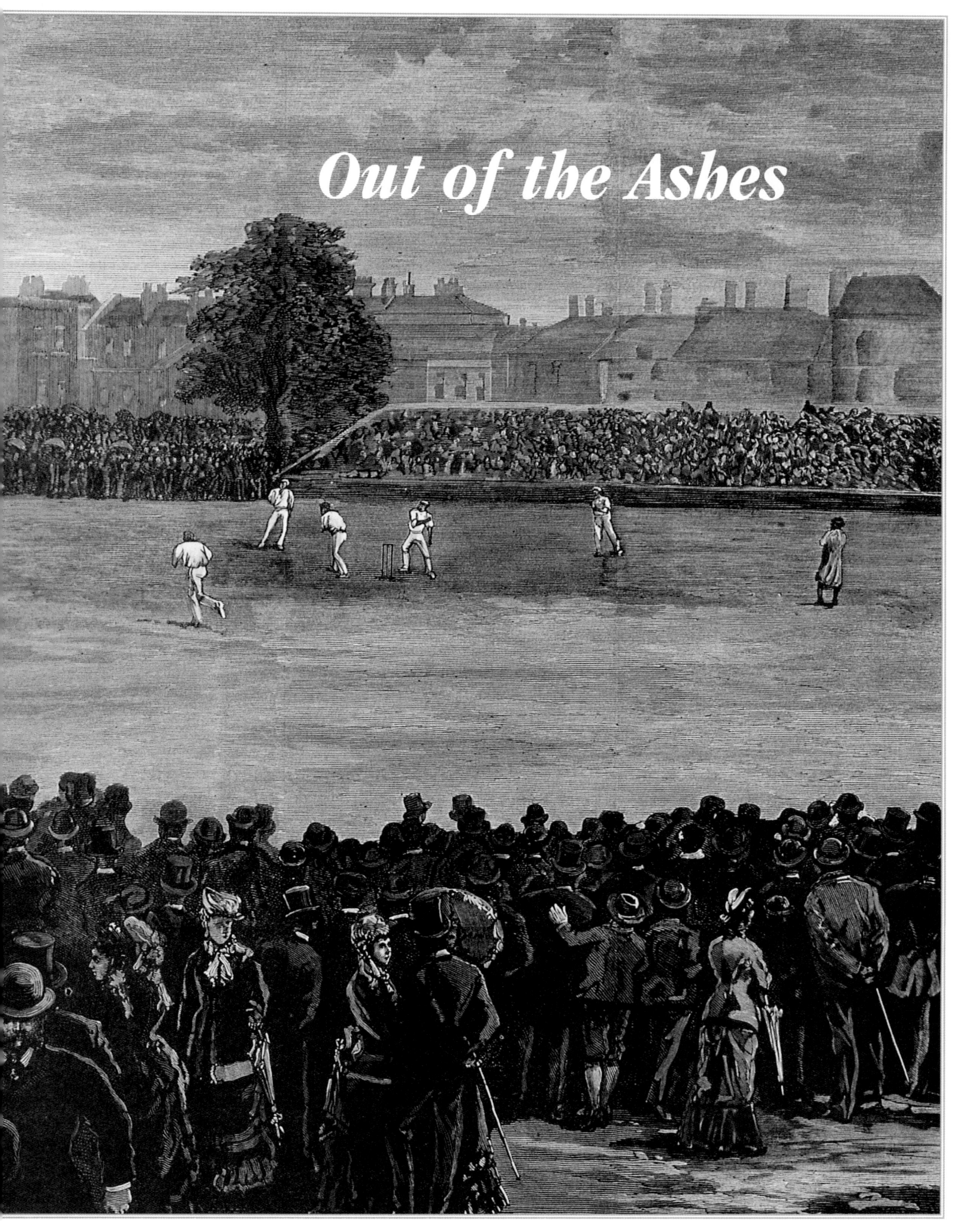

Out of the Ashes

Victoria wins MCG thriller

Horan: chanceless century.

Fred Walters: Victorian bat.

Melbourne, Jan. 1. There have been very big crowds at the Melbourne Cricket Ground since Boxing Day to watch the thrilling battle between Victoria and New South Wales.

It has been a big-hitting affair, with the result in the balance over the five days. In the end Victoria can thank its four most senior batsmen – George Bonnor, Tom Horan, Henry Scott and Percy McDonnell – for its three wicket victory. McDonnell made only 15 in the first innings, but it was he who held together the shaky second innings for long enough to set up the win.

The biggest attendance was 12,000 on Boxing day, and 31,000 people are recorded as having seen the game.

New South Wales opened, and their master batsman Billy Murdoch held sway over the Victorian bowlers. He made 158 and was well supported by Sam Jones (52), Edwin Evans (33) and Tom Garrett (64) as NSW got to 412. George Palmer took 5/130 among the toiling Victorian bowlers.

It was a similar story when Victoria batted, with Horan (126) and Scott (115) making the centuries, and Bonnor getting a quick 41 as an opener. Victoria led by eight runs on the first innings.

But the wicket had crumbled by the third day, and it was the bowlers' turn to dominate. Palmer and Billy Midwinter ripped through the NSW side for 143, after they had broken the opening resistance of Alick Bannerman (34) and Murdoch (22). Midwinter got 7/53 with his off-breaks.

Garrett and Evans (who had taken the third day off because of the death of his brother) were intent on doing the same for New South Wales, but Victoria grafted slowly to get to 136 and victory.

School cricket lift

Sydney, Feb. 20. Cricket is seen as a character building sport of such importance it might be regarded as the backbone of the British Empire. It is no wonder that the Australian headmasters have embraced the sport. Very big crowds are reported to turn out for the Public Schools contests.

But not all can afford the immaculate pitches of the wealthy schools, and matting wickets are now bringing cricket to the city parks, and taking it to the country.

The first wicket was laid down at Moore Park, Sydney, by F. J. Ironside, who ordered strips of coconut fibre matting, which is made by the prisoners in Darlinghurst gaol.

Tasmania makes progress; new cricket ground

Hobart, Feb. 28. Tasmania is doing its best to lift its cricket to the level of the mainland states, and a team of the best cricketers has just completed a five-week tour of New Zealand, playing four first class matches against the Provinces, drawing one and losing three.

The move follows the celebrations of the opening of a cricket ground at Hobart, in a picturesque setting near the Derwent Estuary.

This puts the aspiring cricketers of Hobart on an equal footing with those of Launceston, which has had a cricket ground since the 1850s. The annual tussles between the teams of Launceston and Hobart have the same intense character as the intercolonial matches on the mainland.

Cricket is still spreading out into the country, providing a day of sport and fellowship after a week of work. The new matting wickets, which can be quickly laid, are a boon to the small townships and country schools.

The Honourable Ivo Bligh is back in the Colony, announcing his engagement to Florence Morphy, Governess to Sir William Clarke.

Press anger as Australians scoop money

Cooper hurt as tour gets started

London, June 30. The Australian team has been labouring under a disadvantage since its arrival in England, as its leg spin bowler William Cooper is injured.

Cooper tore ligaments in his bowling hand in a shipboard game of shinty, a vigorous Irish game best played in the paddocks. His only Test in 1882 yielded 9/200 and the Australians had high hopes for him.

The injury has raised again the question of whether there should

William Cooper: wrong finger.

be at least 14 players chosen for these arduous tours.

The other question is whether there is enough variety in successive Australian teams. Five of the present team – Murdoch, Bannerman, Blackham, Boyle and Spofforth – are on their fourth tour. The only newcomers are the Victorians, Dr H. J. 'Tup' Scott and the luckless Cooper,

The tourists have only 11 fit men, and manager George Alexander is on call to fill in from time to time. In addition Billy Murdoch is not as agile as he used to be and Blackham has to do all the wicket-keeping.

So far the tourists have played 16 matches, with ten wins, two draws and four losses, so they have a mediocre record on the eve of the first Test.

Football kicks cricket out for the Australian winter, but the game goes on with the Australian team in England.

Lord's, July 23. The jubilation of England over its win in the exciting second Test at Lord's has given way to anger with news that the Australian team is making all the money.

The Australians have taken the entire proceeds from the match, £1334, while the England professionals were paid £10 per man.

Some sections of the English press have pointed to the Australians as cricket mercenaries, interested only in 'filthy lucre'. But the Australians have say they are neither amateur or professional players, merely cricketers on a tour that requires funding.

The arrangements for Lord's were made by the Australian manager, George Alexander, and Lord Harris, the England captain. Alexander made it clear that the tourists depended on the money to cover costs, as the Australians shared the gate at the county grounds and boosted the county clubs' funds.

During this unpleasantness the teams came together at Lord's after a rain affected draw at Manchester. The Lord's match was the first at that particular London ground and drew daily crowds around 15,000. Australia started creditably with 229, and might have made more

had 'Tup' Scott not been caught at 75 by his own Captain, Murdoch, fielding in place of his injured counterpart, W.G. Grace. It was the first Test catch by a substitute.

Australia had England in check at 5/135, when Allan Steel came to the wicket. The Cambridge captain, reckoned to be a batsman of the calibre of W.G. Grace took the match over, thrashing the Australian bowling for 148 in around four hours. The England total was 391.

George Ulyett completed the rout of the Australians on the third day, taking 7/36, and England had won by an innings and 5 runs.

Quick passage. The Australian team left Melbourne on March 11 on the P & O steamer *Sutlej*, and arrived in Plymouth on April 29.

A captain's check. The English captain of Lord Sheffield's XI demanded a check of the width of the Australians' bats, in front of the crowd, before the match, on May 12, proceeded. The Australians won by an innings.

A bad start. The star batsman of the Australian team, Billy Murdoch, has made 20 in his first four innings in England. In his last two hands he has been out first ball.

Umpire dismissed. The Australians objected to the appointment of Walter Price as an umpire in the Australian v

Gentlemen's fixture at Lord's on June 5. They claim they had been the victim of bad decisions in earlier matches. Mr Price stood aside, but *Cricket* says: 'his honesty and itegrity can in no way be called in question.'

Crowd displeased. A demonstraton by spectators occurred at the Oval on August 1 when, with the game against the Players nearly over, Australian captain Billy Murdoch requested a lunch interval in the hope that the drying ground might improve his team's flagging fortunes.

Spoff a dragger. *Cricket* of September 4 writes of Fred Spofforth's 'occasional habit' of scraping along the pitch at the end of his delivery so as to provide the bowler at the other end with a 'spot', and suggests it should be prohibited by the 'unwritten law of fair play.'

'Chucker' protest. Lord Harris refused to play in the first Test at Old Trafford, Manchester, on July 10, because the selectors had included a known 'chucker' John Crossland in the team. Crossland was omitted.

Puff paragraph. The Australian tour has ended lightheartedly in September with a Smokers v Non-Smokers match for the 'old cricketers fund', with Australians and English in both teams. George Bonnor revelled in the fray as he made 124 with 14 fours and a six.

Bad riddance. The *Illustrated Sporting and Dramatic News* said of the departing Australians in September: 'each player returning to the vast colonial regions of Australia took away £900 in his pocket. Their intrusion into the mother country will henceforth be regarded as a veritable nuisance.'

Murdoch gets 211

The Oval, Aug. 13. The English practice of completing Test matches within three days may have robbed Australia of victory in the third Test at Kennington Oval.

Australia scored a massive 551 in its first innings, and its captain William Murdoch made 211 to record the first double century in Test cricket. He took eight hours over the innings, showing his usual all-round range of strokes and sound defence. He was accompanied by two centurions in Percy MacDonnell (103) and 'Tup' Scott (102).

At one stage Australia was 4/432 and it seemed the England bowlers would never get them out. All eleven England bowlers had a bowl, including the wicketkeeper, Alfred Lyttleton, who wrapped up the innings with his lob bowling, taking 4/19.

On the even Oval pitch England was also able to produce two fine innings, from William Scotton (90) and Walter Read (117). The pair put on 151 for the ninth wicket to carry England to 346 after it had been 8/181. Read, furious at being sent in number 10, hit his runs in two hours. For Australia, Palmer took 4/90 and Spofforth 2/81.

William Murdoch: a record maker.

With England following-on and 2/85 on the third day the Test was over. What a day or two might have done for Australia.

So England now holds the Ashes, born two summers ago, having won the only Test in the series in which there was a result – the one at Lord's.

Generous praise from Australian press

The Australian team on tour. A losing fight for the Ashes, but they drew crowds.

Melbourne, Nov. 27. The Australian team has been well praised in the Australian press, despite its lack of Test success and controversy over gate takings.

'Observer' in the *Argus* says: 'The attitude of the English Press has not been at all generous … Australia is a working community, and young men with their own future to mould cannot afford the time and expense of an English tour without some return.' He had

not heard that the 'Australians, in a single instance, had conducted themselves otherwise than as gentlemen should.' 'Felix' in the *Australasian* takes umbrage at the 'narrow-minded' and insulting abuse of the English press.

One pundit suggested that England should enjoy its tenure of the Ashes rather than pour scorn on the Australians for trying to make ends meet and helping county finances.

Boyle – the 'very devil'

In 1873 the great Dr W. G. Grace faced a young Victorian round-arm bowler named Harry Boyle. Rumour had it that the Doctor had backed himself heavily that he would not be bowled during the England tour.

But he was soon looking back at his stumps, much to the joy of the crowd who watched the Victorian Eighteen beat the Englishmen by an innings. His conqueror was a tall and dark young man, from the gold mining town of Bendigo.

In his farewell speech at the end of the tour Grace averred: 'If you Australians ever come to England, and your bowlers are as good there as they are here, you will make a name for yourself.'

Five years later he was to face Boyle again, this time as part of a fearsome bowling duo – Fred 'The Demon' Spofforth and Harry 'The Devil' Boyle. And they were making a name for themselves.

Boyle did not play in the two Test matches of the previous year in Melbourne, while Spofforth was introduced, with modest success in the second Test.

They were virtually unknown quantities on their arrival in England with the 1878 Australian team. The Australians were somewhat shunned by the English administrators, who failed to arrange a Test match.

But the bowlers cut a swathe through the various teams they met, losing only four of the 11-a-side matches.

On one indelible day in cricket's history they humbled the best that England could muster, dismissing them for 41 and 33. Boyle's figures of 3/14 off 14 overs in the first innings and 6/3 off 8.1 overs in the second stand high among the best ever for Australia, and only a little behind Spofforth's 6/4 of 5.3 overs and 4/16.

Boyle took 64 wickets in the 19 evenly weighted matches that year. He was a model of accuracy, attacking the stumps and employing some subtlety of flight and spin. His consistency gave the England batsmen no relief from the menace of Spofforth.

He produced similar feats in 1880 and 1882, and his partnership with Spofforth brought the rivalry and intensity between English and Australian sides to a pitch of excitement previously not visited on English cricket.

The Old Country was staving off the upstart Colonial, and the

Harry Boyle: Conquered Grace

tradition was established even before the advent of the Ashes.

Boyle was the less flamboyant of the two bowlers, and his results were not quite as spectacular. He was tall and upright, bushy bearded and reticent by comparison to his fiery bowling partner. As with many famous bowling combinations, it can be assumed that his nagging accuracy at one end did a lot to contribute to Spofforth's success at the other. Boyle was well respected by his team-mates and was chosen as captain for the 1880 tour of England. However, a shipboard team meeting voted to replace him with the more gregarious William Murdoch.

He accepted the decision with good grace, and maintained good relations with Murdoch and his teammates. He was a man at ease with himself, unperturbed by such setbacks and able to enjoy his cricket at any level.

He made six tours to England, the last as player/manager in 1890, when he was aged 41. Despite his longevity he played at a time when Test matches were rare events and he played only 12 Tests, taking 32 wickets at 20.03.

His 370 first class wickets at 15.38 are more an indication of his contribution to Victoria and to the Australians on tour. He was a fine close fielder and had 10 Test catches to his credit.

Boyle made good business out of his cricket connections and opened a Melbourne 'sporting goods' emporium selling cricket goods and other equipment, and worked in the importing business.

He also wrote a book for young bowlers, and was active in cricket affairs throughout his life.

FIRST TEST 1884 ENGLAND v AUSTRALIA
Old Trafford, Manchester. July 10 (no play), 11, 12, 1884.
Toss: Australia. Match Drawn.

ENGLAND

WG Grace c Palmer b Boyle	8	b Palmer	31
AN Hornby (c) st Blackham b Boyle	0 (9)	st Blackham b Palmer	4
G Ulyett b Spofforth	5	c Bannerman b Boyle	1
A Shrewsbury b Boyle	43	b Palmer	25
AG Steel c Midwinter b Spofforth	15	c Blackham b Bonnor	18
AP Lucas not out	15 (2)	b Giffen	24
W Barnes c & b Boyle	0 (6)	b Palmer	8
TC O'Brien b Spofforth	0	c Bannerman b Spofforth	20
RG Barlow c Bonnor b Boyle	6 (7)	not out	14
R Pilling (+) c Scott b Boyle	0	b Spofforth	3
E Peate b Spofforth	2	not out	8
EXTRAS (LB 1)	1	(B 18, LB 5, NB 1)	24
TOTAL	95		9 for 180

FOW 1st Inns: 6 13 13 45 83 83 84 93 93 95
FOW 2nd Inns: 41 44 70 106 108 114 139 145 154

Bowling: *First Innings*: Spofforth 32-10-42-4, Boyle 25-9-42-6, Palmer 6-2-10-0. *Second Innings*: Spofforth 41-17-52-2, Boyle 20-8-27-1, Palmer 36-17-47-4, Giffen 29-15-25-1, Bonnor 4-1-5-1.

AUSTRALIA

PS McDonnell c Pilling b Steel	36
AC Bannerman lbw Ulyett	6
WL Murdoch (c) c Grace b Peate	28
G Giffen c & b Barnes	16
WE Midwinter c Grace b Ulyett	37
GJ Bonnor hit wicket b Peate	6
JM Blackham (+) lbw Steel	8
HJH Scott b Grace	12
GE Palmer not out	14
FR Spofforth c Shrewsbury b Peate	13
HF Boyle b Ulyett	4
EXTRAS (LB 2)	2
TOTAL	182

FOW 1st Inns: 10 56 86 90 97 118 141 157 172 182

Bowling: *First Innings*: Peate 49-25-62-3, Ulyett 30-17-41-3, Barlow 8-3-18-0, Steel 13-5-32-2, Barnes 19-10-25-1, Grace 11-10-2-1.

Umpires: CK Pullin & J Rowbotham

SECOND TEST 1884 ENGLAND v AUSTRALIA
Lord's Cricket Ground, London. July 21, 22, 23, 1884.
Toss: Australia. England won by an innings & 5 runs.

AUSTRALIA

PS McDonnell b Peate	0	b Steel	20
AC Bannerman b Peate	12	c & b Ulyett	27
WL Murdoch (c) lbw Peate	10	c Shrewsbury b Ulyett	17
G Giffen b Peate	63	c Peate b Ulyett	5
WE Midwinter b Peate	3 (7)	b Ulyett	6
GJ Bonnor c Grace b Christopherson	25 (5)	c & b Ulyett	4
JM Blackham (+) run out	0 (8)	retired hurt	0
HJH Scott c(S)WL Murdoch b Steel	75 (6)	not out	31
GE Palmer c Grace b Peate	7	b Ulyett	13
FR Spofforth c Barlow b Grace	4	c Shrewsbury b Barlow	11
HF Boyle not out	26	b Ulyett	10
EXTRAS (B 5, LB 3)	8	(B 1)	1
TOTAL	229		9 for 145

FOW 1st Inns: 0 25 32 46 88 93 132 155 160 229
FOW 2nd Inns: 23 60 65 73 84 90 118 133 145

Bowling: *First Innings*: Peate 40-14-85-6, Barlow 20-6-44-0, Ulyett 11-3-21-0, Christopherson 26-10-52-1, Grace 7-4-13-1, Steel 1.2-0-6-1. *Second Innings*: Peate 16-4-34-0, Barlow 21-8-31-1, Ulyett 39.1-23-36-7, Christopherson 8-3-17-0, Steel 10-2-26-1.

ENGLAND

WG Grace c Bonnor b Palmer	14
AP Lucas c Bonnor b Palmer	28
A Shrewsbury st Blackham b Giffen	27
G Ulyett b Palmer	32
AG Steel b Palmer	148
Lord Harris (c) b Spofforth	4
RG Barlow c Palmer b Bonnor	38
WW Read b Palmer	12
A Lyttelton (+) b Palmer	31
E Peate not out	8
S Christopherson c Bonnor b Spofforth	17
EXTRAS (B 15, LB 5)	20
TOTAL	379

FOW 1st Inns: 37 56 90 120 135 233 272 348 351 379

Bowling: *First Innings*: Spofforth 55.1-19-112-2, Palmer 75-26-111-6, Giffen 22-4-68-1, Boyle 11-3-16-0, Bonnor 8-1-23-1, Midwinter 13-2-29-0.

Umpires: FH Farrands & CK Pullin

THIRD TEST 1884 ENGLAND v AUSTRALIA
Kennington Oval, London. August 11, 12, 13, 1884.
Toss: Australia. Match Drawn.

AUSTRALIA

AC Bannerman c Read b Peate	4
PS McDonnell c Ulyett b Peate	103
WL Murdoch (c) c Peate b Barnes	211
HJH Scott c Lyttelton b Barnes	102
G Giffen c Steel b Ulyett	32
GJ Bonnor c Read b Grace	8
WE Midwinter c Grace b Lyttelton	30
JM Blackham (+) lbw Lyttelton	31
GE Palmer not out	8
FR Spofforth b Lyttelton	4
HF Boyle c Lord b Lyttelton	1
EXTRAS (B 7, LB 10)	17
TOTAL	551

FOW 1st Inns: 15 158 365 432 454 494 532 545 549 551

Bowling: *First Innings*: Peate 63-25-99-2, Ulyett 56-24-96-1, Steel 34-7-71-0, Barnes 52-25-81-2, Barlow 50-22-72-0, Grace 24-14-23-1, Read 7-0-36-0, Scotton 5-1-20-0, Lord 5-1-15-0, Lyttelton 12-5-19-4, Shrewsbury 3-2-2-0.

ENGLAND

WG Grace run out	19		
WH Scotton c Scott b Giffen	90		
W Barnes c Midwinter b Spofforth	19		
A Shrewsbury c Blackham b Midwinter	10 (3)	c Scott b Giffen	37
AG Steel lbw Palmer	31		
G Ulyett c Bannerman b Palmer	10		
RG Barlow c Murdoch b Palmer	0 (1)	not out	21
Lord Harris (c) lbw Palmer	14 (4)	not out	6
A Lyttelton (+) b Spofforth	8 (2)	b Boyle	17
WW Read b Boyle	117		
E Peate not out	4		
EXTRAS (B 8, LB 7, W 6, NB 3)	24	(B 3, LB 1)	4
TOTAL	346		2 for 85

FOW 1st Inns: 32 60 75 120 136 136 160 181 332 346
FOW 2nd Inns: 22 73

Bowling: *First Innings*: Bonnor 13-4-33-0, Palmer 54-19-90-4, Spofforth 58-31-81-2, Boyle 13-7-24-1, Midwinter 31-16-41-1, Giffen 26-13-36-1, Scott 3-0-17-0. *Second Innings*: Palmer 2-1-2-0, Spofforth 6-2-14-0, Boyle 8-1-32-1, Midwinter 3-0-15-0, Giffen 7-1-18-1.

Umpires: FH Farrands & CK Pullin

Australian Averages

1884 ENGLAND v AUSTRALIA

AUSTRALIA	M	Inn	NO	Runs	H.S	Avrge	Ct	St	Overs	Mds	Runs	Wkt	Avrge
Bannerman, AC	3	4	-	49	27	12.25	3	-					
Blackham, JM	3	4	1	39	31	13.00	2	3					
Bonnor, GJ	3	4	-	43	25	10.75	4	-	25.0	6	61	2	30.50
Boyle, HF	3	4	1	41	26*	13.67	1	-	77.0	28	141	9	15.67
Giffen, G	3	4	-	116	63	29.00	-	-	84.0	33	147	4	36.75
McDonnell, PS	3	4	-	159	103	39.75	-	-					
Midwinter, WE	3	4	-	76	37	19.00	2	-	47.0	18	85	1	85.00
Murdoch, WL	3	4	-	266	211	66.50	1	-					
Palmer, GE	3	4	2	42	14*	21.00	2	-	173.0	65	260	14	18.57
Scott, HJH	3	4	1	220	102	73.33	3	-	3.0	-	17	-	-
Spofforth, FR	3	4	-	28	13	7.00	-	-	192.1	79	301	10	30.10

English Averages

1884 ENGLAND v AUSTRALIA

ENGLAND	M	Inn	NO	Runs	H.S	Avrge	Ct	St	Overs	Mds	Runs	Wkt	Avrge
Barlow, RG	3	5	2	79	38	26.33	1	-	99.0	39	165	1	165.00
Barnes, W	2	3	-	27	19	9.00	1	-	71.0	35	106	3	35.33
Christopherson, S	1	1	-	17	17	17.00	-	-	34.0	13	69	1	69.00
Grace, WG	3	4	-	72	31	18.00	5	-	42.0	28	38	3	12.67
Hornby, AN	1	2	-	4	4	2.00	-	-	-	-	-	-	-
Lord Harris	2	3	1	24	14	12.00	1	-	5.0	1	15	-	-
Lucas, AP	2	3	1	67	28	33.50	-	-	12.0	5	19	4	4.75
Lyttelton, A	2	3	-	56	31	18.67	1	-	-	-	-	-	-
O'Brien, TC	1	2	-	20	20	10.00	-	-	-	-	-	-	-
Peate, E	3	4	3	22	8*	22.00	2	-	168.0	68	280	11	25.45
Pilling, R	1	2	1	3	3	1.50	1	-	-	-	-	-	-
Read, WW	2	2	-	129	117	64.50	2	-	7.0	-	36	-	-
Scotton, WH	1	1	-	90	90	90.00	-	-	5.0	1	20	-	-
Shrewsbury, A	3	5	-	142	43	28.40	3	-	3.0	2	2	-	-
Steel, AG	3	4	-	212	148	53.00	1	-	58.2	14	135	4	33.75
Ulyett, G	3	4	-	48	32	12.00	3	-	136.1	67	194	11	17.64

Adelaide Test is a bit of everything

A century to Billy Barnes.

Adelaide, Dec. 16. The South Australian Cricket Association secretary John Creswell is being congratulated roundly for, at last, having contrived to stage a Test match in Adelaide.

Creswell worked hard to get the Test, signing contracts with the England team before they left their ship in Adelaide, and taking himself to Melbourne to get the arriving Australian team on the dotted line.

He will, however, have cause to reflect on the anxieties of the whole occasion. For a start, wrangling over player payments almost threatened to halt the match – until the teams finally agreed on £450 each. Then there were arguments over the umpires. Murdoch's Australians (not yet disbanded and the Test team to a man) objected to England's James Lillywhite standing as an umpire.

The attendance of only 5000 on the first day of this long awaited match caused Creswell to halve the admission money to 1/-. The attendance picked up to 10,000 on the second day, but a dust storm ruined the day. Heavy rain left the Australians to struggle on a sticky wicket on the final day. England won by eight wickets, but at least Percy McDonnell of Australia almost made a century in each innings.

Despite all this excitement the SACA's gate receipts were £108 less than the cost required to stage the match.

Money wrangles issue in ugly Test scene

Sydney, Feb. 17. Ill-feeling which has arisen between the two national teams has led to the disruption of both colonial and Test cricket.

It is all about money. The returning 1884 Australians have objected strenuously to the payment arrangements for the visitors. They have demanded that they receive the excess gate receipts after the Englishmen have been paid, rather than allowing the revenue to go to the Colony Associations.

Matters were difficult from the start. The Australian manager George Alexander was referred by John Conway, the English team agent, to its manager, James Lillywhite, who told him he could make no arrangements.

The *Age* said on November 22 that the Australians 'were amazed at statements being made to the effect that public opinion could and would be aroused to force them to play on the English manager's terms.'

Their NSW players refused to play against the England XI in Sydney, and again refused to play in the second Test in Melbourne, when their demand for an equal share of gate receipts was denied by the Victorian Cricketers' Association.

All this has occurred against a background of English hostility, on their home soil last season, over the perceived rapaciousness of the touring Australian cricketers.

Matters came to a head for the Melbourne Test and the Victorian Cricket Association chose a new side, under Tom Horan as captain, with nine Test debutants, including Sam Morris, of West Indian parentage. It disqualified Blackham,

From Melbourne Punch*: John Blackham puts the blame on the negotiator for England, John Conway, as the money wrangles sour the cricket scene.*

Boyle, Bonnor, McDonnell, Palmer and Scott. England won by ten wickets.

In Sydney, Murdoch, Alex Bannerman and George Bonnor (who moved to NSW because of his suspension) stood out of the England v NSW match.

Matters have now eased between the teams, as the Englishmen have dispensed with John Conway as their representative. Murdoch and Conway have been at loggerheads, particularly as Conway appeared to have defected to the enemy camp and to have taken their side in the money arguments.

Australia looks likely now to select its best team, but it will be without experienced players in Murdoch, who has retired in disgust to his law practice in Cootamundra, and also Giffen, Palmer, Boyle and Cooper and Blackham.

Australia fights back to two Tests all

'Snow' in Sydney

Sydney, Feb. 24. Hail Fred Spofforth, the architect of Australia's tight second Test win. And hail, too, to hail which coated the cricket ground on the first day to the point that it was reported that 'the ground had the appearance of being wrapped in a coating of snow'.

After this the bowlers were on top, although a stubborn 10th-wicket stand of 80 between Garrett (51) and Evans (33) took the Australian first innings score to 181.

Spofforth took three English wickets in his first two overs, and they never recovered to be all out for 133. Spofforth took 4/54 as he bowled unchanged, and the other, unlikely, destroyer was Victoria's Tom Horan, with his best-ever Test figures of 6/40.

Australia made a meagre 165 (Bates 5/24) in its second dig, but England could not catch them in a tense finish. Spofforth was again the hero with 6/90 as England made 207 – and failed by six runs in a nail-biting finish that had the crowd hushed with tension. This is the closest Test result since they began in 1877.

The Kangaroo reminds the doleful British lion that it still has a bit of kick left.

Bonnor's big hit

Sydney, March 17. George Bonnor has broken his self-imposed shackles to score a truly remarkable century and establish Australia's win in the fourth Test. The five-match series now stands at two–all.

Bonnor has at times tried to emulate his recondite friend Alick Bannerman with 'batsmanship' instead of hitting, but he abandoned all this during his 154 run stand with Sam Jones (40) for the seventh wicket. He hit 120 of the stand and made his 100 in 100 minutes and 128 in 115 minutes, with four fives and 14 fours.

When the whirlwind was over Australia was 309 in reply to England's 269.

Rain on the morning of the third day caused England's demise for 77 as they were given a difficult task sparring at balls on the drying pitch, and Australia cruised to an eight-wicket win.

Palmer, Spofforth and Giffen all bowled well, but Giffen must take the palm for his 7/117 in England's first innings.

Six of his victims were bowled outright, as his off-breaks speared past their defences.

Bat sizes are set

Melbourne, Jan. 20. There has been an agreement on bats between the Australian cricket associations, following the practice of England county associations.

Players may no longer go to the wicket with bats of any width, but must comply with a standard of 4 1/2 to 5 inches.

Australian batsman of the barn-door variety may now find that the edges of the willow are far too close to the middle.

Tape measure test for barndoors.

Country crowds

Sydney, Jan. 22. The English team have had a pleasant respite from the money-grubbing politics of big cricket, and have been exceptionally well received as they have travelled the country.

They have played odds matches against country 22's or an 18 (in Bendigo), enjoying country hospitality and getting a good share of the big gates, without any rancour from the country clubs, which are also benefiting.

They are also enjoying the wholehearted appreciation of the crowds that have turned out to see them.

Matches have been staged at places like Bendigo, Benalla and Maryborough in Victoria, at Wagga Wagga and in the Hawkesbury and the Clarence River districts of NSW.

So keen are some towns that they will stretch their resources to see the visitors.

The NSW town of Candello, with a population of 200, guaranteed £300 for a match against its 22, and got a big turnout from the district to justify their extravagance.

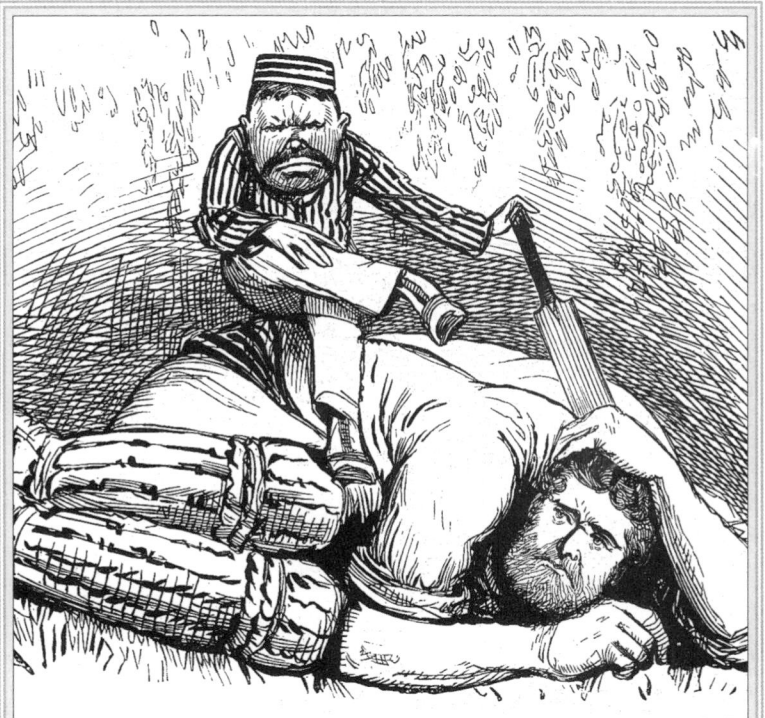

George Bonnor's breakout in the fourth Test, and his propensity for big hitting, is in marked contrast to the stalwart opener of the Australian team Alick 'Barndoor' Bannerman, whose slow innings have become commonplace. The pair opened together two years ago and Bonnor has vowed never to repeat the enervating experience.

England too professional

The infernal urn need not be stirred after England's win in the fifth Test.

Melbourne, March 25. The English team has displayed its experience and professionalism in crushing Australia in the fifth Test to retain the Ashes.

The game was virtually decided on the first day when Australia, winning the toss, opted to bat on a pitch still damp from the curator's watering. They were shot out for 163, with only Fred Spofforth's last-wicket 50 giving any respectibility.

The consistency of the Australian effort cannot have been helped by having had four captains in the series – Murdoch, Horan, Massie, Blackham and Horan again – and by the comings and goings over money and disqualification.

But the English were all discipline and work. Ulyett, Peel and Barnes shared the bowling honors, and then the batting went well, forcing the Australians to use eight bowlers in their efforts to break through. Arthur Shrewsbury's 105 crowned solid efforts by Barnes (74), Bates (61) and Briggs (43) as the total rose to 386.

Australia was dismissed cheaply in the second innings, a disappointing end after the series was squared at two Tests all.

The game had virtually seven umpires, as the two appointees did not stand, one through death and the other by disinclination. Of the replacements George Hodges walked off after insulting remarks by the Englishmen, and the other was taken ill. Three stand-ins were found to fill the vacancies at various times during the match.

Another umpiring oddity was that 'Paddie' McShane played in this Test after umpiring in the previous one in Sydney.

Residential laws

Sydney, May 2. There has been widespread concern, voiced in the press, over the rapid movement of Colonial cricketers from Melbourne to Sydney, and vice versa, to escape the effects of disqualification. The NSW Cricket Association has now resolved that a player must have four months of residence in either Colony before a player is eligible to play for that colony.

George Bonnor has been one to cross to Victoria, and there has been talk that Fred Spofforth is likely to travel south.

The short-term gains of such moves are obviously outweighed by the unsavoriness of bargaining for players, and by disruption to cricket associations and to the stability of teams.

The Cricketer *magazine publishes the following parody:*

All the world's a field, and all the men and women cricket players.

They have their innings and their fielding out,

And one man in his time plays many games, his life being seven matches.

First, the infant, mowing and poking at his nurses' lows;

And then the schoolboy, boundless in ambition,

But green in judging lengths, slogging like fun,

And bowled by yorkers; then the undergrad,

Smoking strange weeds, and Blazer'd like the Turk ... etc.

FIRST TEST 1884–85 AUSTRALIA v ENGLAND
Adelaide Oval, Adelaide. December 12, 13, 15, 16, 1884.
Toss: Australia. England won by 8 wkts.

AUSTRALIA

AC Bannerman lbw Peel	2	run out	83
PS McDonnell b Attewell	124	b Peel	7
WL Murdoch (c) c Hunter b Peel	5	lbw Peel	1
HJH Scott b Peel	19 (5)	b Peel	11
JM Blackham (+) c Attewell b Bates	66 (1)	c Shrewsbury b Peel	47
G Giffen b Bates	4 (4)	c Peel b Barnes	19
GJ Bonnor c Read b Bates	4	b Barnes	0
GE Palmer c Shrewsbury b Bates	6	not out	0
HF Boyle c Hunter b Bates	1 (10)	st Hunter b Peel	10
G Alexander run out	3 (9)	c Shrewsbury b Barnes	6
WH Cooper not out	0 (6)	(B 7)	7
EXTRAS (B 7, W 2)	9		
TOTAL	243		9 for 191

FOW 1st Inns: 33 47 95 190 224 227 233 239 242 243
FOW 2nd Inns: 28 56 125 139 160 160 171 182 191

Bowling: *First Innings:* Attewell 50-23-48-1, Peel 41-15-68-3, Ulyett 10-3-23-0, Flowers 10-1-27-0, Barnes 14-2-37-0, Bates 24.1-10-31-5. *Second Innings:* Peel 40.1-15-51-5, Bates 9-3-26-0, Barnes 31-10-51-3, Attewell 18-10-26-0, Flowers 16-4-27-0, Ulyett 2-1-3-0.

ENGLAND

WH Scotton st Blackham b Giffen	82 (2)	c Scott b Boyle	2
A Shrewsbury (c) b Boyle	0 (3)	not out	26
G Ulyett c Alexander b Boyle	68		
W Barnes b Palmer	134	not out	28
W Bates c Giffen b Palmer	18		
W Flowers lbw Palmer	15 (1)	c Scott b Palmer	7
JM Read c & b Giffen	14		
J Briggs c Blackham b Palmer	1		
W Attewell not out	12		
R Peel b Palmer	4		
J Hunter (+) run out	1		
EXTRAS (B 18, LB 1, NB 1)	20	(B 4)	4
TOTAL	369		2 for 67

FOW 1st Inns: 11 107 282 306 325 344 349 349 361 369
FOW 2nd Inns: 8 14

Bowling: *First Innings:* Boyle 63-25-95-2, Giffen 56.2-26-80-2, Cooper 18-4-26-0, Bonnor 16-10-23-0, Palmer 73-37-81-5, McDonnell 3-0-11-0, Scott 4-1-9-0, Alexander 10-3-24-0. *Second Innings:* Palmer 16-5-23-1, Boyle 9-3-21-1, Giffen 6-0-19-0.

Umpires: N Cole & IA Fisher

SECOND TEST 1884–85 AUSTRALIA v ENGLAND
Melbourne Cricket Ground, Melbourne. January 1, 2, 3, 5, 1885.
Toss: England. England won by 10 wkts.

ENGLAND

A Shrewsbury (c) c Worrall b Morris	72	not out	0
WH Scotton b Bruce	13	not out	7
W Barnes b Morris	58		
W Bates b Bruce	35		
W Flowers c Worrall b Bruce	5		
JM Read b Jones	3		
J Briggs c Horan b Jones	121		
G Ulyett b Jones	0		
W Attewell c Jones b Worrall	30		
R Peel b Jones	5		
J Hunter (+) not out	39		
EXTRAS (B 7, LB 12, NB 1)	20		0
TOTAL	401		0 for 7

FOW 1st Inns: 28 144 161 191 194 204 204 254 303 401
FOW 2nd Inns:

Bowling: *First Innings:* Bruce 55-22-88-3, Worrall 56-28-97-1, Marr 11-6-11-0, Trumble 23-9-41-0, Robertson 11-3-24-0, Morris 34-14-73-2, Jones 25.2-9-47-4, Horan 1-1-0-0. *Second Innings:* Marr 1-0-3-0, Bruce 0.1-0-4-0.

AUSTRALIA

SP Jones lbw Peel	19	b Ulyett	9
S Morris lbw Attewell	4 (10)	not out	10
TP Horan (c) c Shrewsbury b Peel	63	c Hunter b Barnes	16
JW Trumble c & b Barnes	59	c & b Barnes	11
AH Jarvis (+) c Briggs b Flowers	82	lbw Peel	9
RJ Pope c Flowers b Attewell	0	b Peel	3
AP Marr b Barnes	0	c & b Barnes	5
H Musgrove c Read b Barnes	4	c Bates b Peel	9
J Worrall b Flowers	34	c & b Barnes	6
W Bruce not out	3 (2)	c Hunter b Barnes	45
WR Robertson c Barnes b Peel	0	b Barnes	2
EXTRAS (B 3, LB 4, W 2, NB 2)	11		0
TOTAL	279		126

FOW 1st Inns: 4 46 124 190 193 193 203 276 278 279
FOW 2nd Inns: 29 66 80 83 86 95 99 108 116 126

Bowling: *First Innings:* Peel 102.1-56-78-3, Attewell 61-35-54-2, Barnes 50-27-50-3, Flowers 29-12-46-2, Ulyett 15-7-23-0, Bates 17-11-17-0. *Second Innings:* Flowers 11-6-11-0, Peel 44-26-45-3, Ulyett 8-3-19-1, Briggs 8-3-13-0, Attewell 5-2-7-0, Barnes 38.3-26-31-6.

Umpires: EH Elliott & J Lillywhite jr

THIRD TEST 1884–85 AUSTRALIA v ENGLAND
Sydney Cricket Ground, Sydney. February 20, 21, 23, 24, 1885.
Toss: Australia. Australia won by 6 runs.

AUSTRALIA
AC Bannerman c Peel b Flowers	13		c Shrewsbury b Ulyett	16
SP Jones st Hunter b Flowers	28 (4)		b Attewell	22
TP Horan c Hunter b Attewell	7		b Bates	36
HJH Scott c Ulyett b Attewell	5 (5)		c Barnes b Attewell	4
GJ Bonnor c Barnes b Flowers	18 (2)		b Ulyett	29
JW Trumble c Read b Attewell	13		c Ulyett b Bates	32
HH Massie (c) c Scotton b Flowers	2		b Bates	21
AH Jarvis (+) b Attewell	0		c & b Peel	2
FR Spofforth st Hunter b Flowers	3 (11)		c Barnes b Bates	0
TW Garrett not out	51		not out	0
E Evans c Hunter b Ulyett	33 (9)		b Bates	1
EXTRAS (B 3, LB 5)	8		(B 1, LB 1)	2
TOTAL	181			165

FOW 1st Inns: 45 46 56 73 77 83 83 94 101 181
FOW 2nd Inns: 37 56 91 95 119 151 161 165 165 165

Bowling: *First Innings*: Peel 32-13-51-0, Attewell 71-47-53-4, Ulyett 12.2-8-17-1, Flowers 46-24-46-5, Bates 6-2-6-0. *Second Innings*: Ulyett 39-25-42-2, Peel 20-10-24-1, Attewell 58-36-54-2, Flowers 20-14-19-0, Bates 20-10-24-5.

ENGLAND
WH Scotton c Jarvis b Horan	22		b Spofforth	2
A Shrewsbury (c) c & b Spofforth	18		b Spofforth	24
G Ulyett b Spofforth	2		run out	4
W Barnes st Jarvis b Spofforth	0		c Jarvis b Trumble	5
W Bates c Evans b Horan	12		c Jarvis b Spofforth	31
J Briggs c Scott b Horan	3		b Spofforth	1
W Flowers c Jarvis b Spofforth	24		c Evans b Spofforth	56
JM Read c Evans b Horan	4		b Spofforth	56
W Attewell b Horan	14		run out	0
R Peel not out	8		c Jarvis b Trumble	3
J Hunter (+) b Horan	13		not out	5
EXTRAS (B 8, LB 3, NB 2)	13		(B 7, LB 9, W 3, NB 1)	20
TOTAL	133			207

FOW 1st Inns: 31 33 33 46 56 70 82 111 111 133
FOW 2nd Inns: 14 18 29 59 61 92 194 194 199 207

Bowling: *First Innings*: Spofforth 48-23-54-4, Garrett 6-2-17-0, Horan 37.1-22-40-6, Evans 4-1-9-0. *Second Innings*: Spofforth 48.1-22-90-6, Garrett 21-8-31-0, Trumble 26-13-26-2, Horan 9-4-23-0, Evans 4-1-8-0, Jones 3-0-9-0.

Umpires: EH Elliott & JW Payne

FOURTH TEST 1884–85 AUSTRALIA v ENGLAND
Sydney Cricket Ground, Sydney. March 14, 16, 17, 1885.
Toss: England. Australia won by 8 wkts.

ENGLAND
G Ulyett b Giffen	10		c Garrett b Palmer	2
A Shrewsbury (c) b Giffen	40		c Bonnor b Spofforth	16
WH Scotton c Blackham b Giffen	4		c Jones b Spofforth	0
W Barnes b Giffen	50		c Bannerman b Spofforth	20
W Bates c & b Jones	64		c Blackham b Palmer	1
JM Read b Giffen	47		c Bannerman b Spofforth	6
W Flowers b Giffen	14		c Jones b Palmer	7
J Briggs c Palmer b Spofforth	3		run out	5
W Attewell b Giffen	1		not out	1
R Peel not out	17		c & b Spofforth	0
J Hunter (+) b Spofforth	13		b Palmer	4
EXTRAS (B 5, NB 1)	6		(B 14, NB 1)	15
TOTAL	269			77

FOW 1st Inns: 19 52 76 159 186 219 222 229 252 269
FOW 2nd Inns: 5 16 19 20 27 42 63 69 69 77

Bowling: *First Innings*: Giffen 52-14-117-7, Palmer 16-5-35-0, Spofforth 29-10-61-2, Garrett 2-1-5-0, Trumble 12-5-16-0, Horan 5-2-12-0, Jones 10-5-17-1. *Second Innings*: Spofforth 20-8-30-5, Palmer 19.1-7-32-4.

AUSTRALIA
GE Palmer b Ulyett	0			
TW Garrett b Barnes	32			
JW Trumble b Peel	5			
PS McDonnell c Attewell b Ulyett	20 (1)		c Ulyett b Peel	3
AC Bannerman c Shrewsbury b Flowers	51 (2)		b Barnes	8
G Giffen c Attewell b Barnes	1			
TP Horan c Barnes b Ulyett	9 (3)		not out	12
GJ Bonnor c Bates b Barnes	128			
SP Jones run out	40 (4)		not out	15
JM Blackham (c+) not out	11			
FR Spofforth c Read b Barnes	1			
EXTRAS (B 5, LB 1, W 2, NB 3)	11			0
TOTAL	309			2 for 38

FOW 1st Inns: 0 16 40 98 108 119 134 288 308 309
FOW 2nd Inns: 7 16

Bowling: *First Innings*: Ulyett 54-25-91-3, Peel 31-12-53-1, Attewell 18-13-22-0, Bates 17-5-44-0, Barnes 35.3-17-61-4, Flowers 14-5-27-1. *Second Innings*: Barnes 9-3-15-1, Peel 9-4-16-1, Attewell 3-1-4-0, Flowers 3.3-2-3-0.

Umpires: EH Elliott & PG McShane

FIFTH TEST 1884–85 AUSTRALIA v ENGLAND
Melbourne Cricket Ground, Melbourne. March 21, 23, 24, 25, 1885.
Toss: Australia. England won by an innings & 98 runs.

AUSTRALIA
AC Bannerman c Peel b Ulyett	5		c (S)GF Vernon b Ulyett	2
W Bruce c Briggs b Peel	15 (6)		c Bates b Attewell	35
G Giffen b Ulyett	13		c Peel b Ulyett	12
TP Horan (c) lbw Ulyett	0 (5)		b Attewell	20
SP Jones lbw Peel	0 (4)		b Peel	17
FH Walters b Ulyett	7 (8)		c Attewell b Flowers	5
AH Jarvis (+) c Hunter b Peel	15 (9)		c Peel b Flowers	1
JW Trumble not out	34 (7)		lbw Attewell	10
PG McShane c Hunter b Barnes	9 (11)		not out	12
TW Garrett c Briggs b Barnes	6 (2)		b Ulyett	5
FR Spofforth b Attewell	50 (10)		c (S)AH Jarvis b Flowers	1
EXTRAS (B 5, LB 1, NB 3)	9		(B 5)	5
TOTAL	163			125

FOW 1st Inns: 21 21 21 34 34 45 67 89 99 163
FOW 2nd Inns: 4 17 26 60 60 91 100 106 108 125

Bowling: *First Innings*: Peel 41-26-28-3, Ulyett 23-7-52-4, Barnes 28-12-47-2, Flowers 9-6-9-0, Attewell 5-1-18-1. *Second Innings*: Ulyett 15-7-25-3, Peel 30-16-37-1, Attewell 36.1-22-24-3, Flowers 21-7-34-3.

ENGLAND
WH Scotton b Bruce	27	
W Barnes c Horan b Bruce	74	
JM Read b Giffen	13	
G Ulyett b Spofforth	1	
A Shrewsbury (c) not out	105	
W Bates c Walters b Bruce	61	
W Flowers b Spofforth	16	
J Briggs c Walters b Trumble	43	
W Attewell c Bannerman b Trumble	0	
R Peel b Trumble	0	
J Hunter (+) b Giffen	18	
EXTRAS (B 10, LB 14, NB 4)	28	
TOTAL	386	

FOW 1st Inns: 61 96 97 141 256 324 324 335 337 386

Bowling: *First Innings*: Giffen 74.3-31-132-2, Bruce 51-13-99-3, Spofforth 49-21-71-2, Trumble 28-14-29-3, Garrett 8-6-12-0, McShane 3-2-3-0, Jones 5-2-7-0, Horan 3-0-5-0.

Umpires: GJ Hodges & J Phillips

Australian Averages

1884–85 AUSTRALIA v ENGLAND

AUSTRALIA	M	Inn	NO	Runs	H.S	Avrge	Ct	St	Overs	Mds	Runs	Wkt	Avrge
Alexander, G	1	2	-	13	10	6.50	1	-	10.0	3	24	-	-
Bannerman, AC	4	7	-	97	51	13.86	3	-	-	-	-	-	-
Blackham, JM	2	3	1	88	66	44.00	3	1	-	-	-	-	-
Bonnor, GJ	3	5	-	198	128	39.60	1	-	16.0	10	23	-	-
Boyle, HF	1	2	1	1	1	1.00	-	-	72.0	28	116	3	38.67
Bruce, W	2	4	1	98	45	32.67	-	-	106.1	35	191	6	31.83
Cooper, WH	1	2	1	6	6	6.00	-	-	18.0	4	26	-	-
Evans, E	1	2	-	34	33	17.00	3	-	8.0	2	17	-	-
Garrett, TW	3	5	2	94	51*	31.33	1	-	37.0	17	65	-	-
Giffen, G	3	5	-	77	47	15.40	2	-	189.1	71	348	11	31.64
Horan, TP	4	8	1	163	63	23.29	2	-	55.1	29	80	6	13.33
Jarvis, AH	3	6	-	110	82	18.33	5	1	-	-	-	-	-
Jones, SP	4	8	1	150	40	21.43	4	-	43.2	16	80	5	16.00
Marr, AP	1	2	-	5	5	2.50	-	-	12.0	6	14	-	-
Massie, HH	1	2	-	23	21	11.50	-	-	-	-	-	-	-
McDonnell, PS	2	4	-	230	124	57.50	-	-	3.0	-	11	-	-
McShane, PG	1	2	1	21	12*	21.00	-	-	3.0	2	3	-	-
Morris, S	1	2	1	14	10*	14.00	-	-	34.0	14	73	2	36.50
Murdoch, WL	1	2	-	12	7	6.00	-	-	-	-	-	-	-
Musgrove, H	1	2	-	13	9	6.50	-	-	-	-	-	-	-
Palmer, GE	2	3	-	6	6	2.00	1	-	124.1	54	171	10	17.10
Pope, RJ	1	2	-	3	3	1.50	-	-	-	-	-	-	-
Robertson, WR	1	2	-	2	2	1.00	-	-	11.0	3	24	-	-
Scott, HJH	2	4	-	29	19	7.25	3	-	4.0	1	9	-	-
Spofforth, FR	3	5	-	55	50	11.00	2	-	194.1	84	306	19	16.11
Trumble, JW	4	7	1	164	59	27.33	-	-	89.0	41	112	5	22.40
Walters, FH	1	2	-	12	7	6.00	2	-	-	-	-	-	-
Worrall, J	1	2	-	40	34	20.00	-	-	56.0	28	97	1	97.00

English Averages

1884–85 AUSTRALIA v ENGLAND

ENGLAND	M	Inn	NO	Runs	H.S	Avrge	Ct	St	Overs	Mds	Runs	Wkt	Avrge
Attewell, W	5	7	2	58	30	11.60	5	-	325.1	190	310	13	23.85
Barnes, W	5	8	1	369	134	52.71	8	-	206.2	97	292	19	15.37
Bates, W	5	7	-	222	64	31.71	3	-	93.1	41	148	10	14.80
Briggs, J	5	7	-	177	121	25.29	3	-	8.0	3	13	-	-
Flowers, W	5	8	-	144	56	18.00	1	-	179.3	81	249	11	22.64
Hunter, J	5	7	2	93	39*	18.60	8	3	-	-	-	-	-
Peel, R	5	7	2	37	17*	7.40	4	-	390.2	193	451	21	21.48
Read, JM	5	7	-	143	56	20.43	4	-	-	-	-	-	-
Scotton, WH	5	9	1	159	82	19.88	1	-	-	-	-	-	-
Shrewsbury, A	5	9	3	301	105*	50.17	6	-	-	-	-	-	-
Ulyett, G	5	7	-	87	68	12.43	3	-	178.2	86	295	14	21.07

MCC emerges as senior cricket body in Australia

Melbourne, Dec. 12. Tom Horan has written in the *Australasian* that the Melbourne Cricket Club 'is the leading cricket club of Australia and stands alone in influence, wealth, power and position.'

Despite the turmoil and financial losses of the 1884–5 tour of England, or perhaps because of them, the MCC has decided that it should organise the 1886 tour of England. A wealthy club with a strong membership, it has a balance of £1000 in an 'All England Eleven account.'

Originally South Australian secretary John Creswell suggested to the MCC secretary Major Ben Wardill that a combined committee from SA, New South Wales and Victoria choose the team.

The NSWCA declined to become involved. The Victorian Cricketers' Association asked its constituent clubs for approval to be involved in the venture, and received it at the annual general meeting in September. However, this was on the proviso that NSW eventually agreed to the idea.

Melbourne therefore felt able to assume the mantle of organiser of Australian cricket. This seems to be a milestone in the history of Australian cricket and the MCC, but the immediate future of both depends on the success of the upcoming tour.

A Bulletin cartoon plumbs the murky depths of cricket, with player payments blotting out the noble sprit of amateurism on which the game was founded.

Fred Spofforth leads Victorian charge

King Spofforth, the champion bowler now in Victoria, with his retinue of admirers.

Melbourne, Dec. 30. Victoria, spearheaded by the Demon, Fred Spofforth, recently transferred south, has proved too strong for his old side, the weakened NSW.

Percy McDonnell had travelled in the other direction – and played his first game for NSW.

In what has become a common occurrence in recent times Alick Bannerman refused to play for NSW for less than £15. Charles Bannerman and Hugh Massie were not picked – the latter for 'lack of practice'.

Victoria made 471 on a good pitch, with Dr. Henry Scott contributing 111 and John McIlwraith his highest score to date of 133.

But it was Spofforth, bowling with his old fire, who destroyed NSW with 5/43 and 5/95.

George Giffen's great game for SA

Adelaide, March 15. South Australia won the postponed game against Victoria because of the Herculean efforts of all-rounder George Giffen – who opened both batting and bowling.

Giffen became the first player to make 100 runs and take more than ten wickets in a first class match – probably any match – in Australia.

Victoria could not include over a dozen regular players, including Spofforth, Scott, Boyle, Worrall, Horan and Palmer but that should take nothing away from Giffen.

One Adelaide newspaper said 'Giffen's performance stands out as one of the best ever accomplished by any man.'

Giffen made 20 and 82 runs, but his full bowling figures are extraordinary.

First innings: 69.2 overs (four ball) 29 maidens, 9 wickets for 91. Second innings 47 overs, 12 maidens, eight wickets for 110.

South Australian captain Affie Jarvis had requested that the game be played with six-ball overs, but this was refused by Jack Blackham.

Match scores were South Australia 172 and 274, Victoria 187 and 219, South Australia winning by 40 runs.

Giffen is now one of Australia's leading all-rounders – an attacking right-hand batsman, and a very accurate slow-medium right-arm bowler with a surprise weapon – a slow lob which traps many victims caught and bowled. He has the stamina, and the will, to bowl all day.

Giffen's expenses. George Giffen corrected a misapprehension about his expenses last season. The £31.2s he charged was not for a single game but for three matches in Adelaide, Sydney and Melbourne involving travel of 2,200 miles by railway and steamboat, hotels and expenses – and the loss of five weeks salary.

VCA lifts ban. The Victorian Cricketers' Association has lifted the ban that was imposed on November 10 on its players in the Australian team, after Mr Justice Williams' campaign for them to revert to amateur status failed.

Australian practise. No NSW players were available for the planned Combined XI v MCC 1886 Australian XI at the MCG. John McIlwraith made 125 for the Australians in their 10 wicket win.

WACA formed. The Western Australian Cricket Association was formed in November. It hopes to organise first class matches against the other colonies in the next few years.

Turfed out. 'Censor' in the *Sydney Mail* reports that only the Association Ground in Sydney has practicable turf wickets. Elsewhere fibre matting must be used. The Doman turf is hazardous. 'Owing to the scarcity of water, combined with the frolicsome cricket of the small boy element, and the grazing of the cows, the sward of the Domain is terribly cut up.'

NSW revenge. NSW has defeated Victoria in the January return match at the SCG. Poor batting by Victoria was caused by excellent bowling by Tom Garrett, 6/55 and 6/56.

A likely tale. George Bonnor is not modest, and now claims to be the fastest bowler in the land. 'So great is my pace that in a match at Orange, after sending down one of my fastest deliveries, I ran down the pitch, chased the ball after it had been played, and caught it at deep first slip.'

No trial matches. Attempts to arrange a trial match between an Australian XI and a Combined XI, to assist in the selection of the 1886 touring party, have failed. New South Wales players were unavailable for the first, and the MCC objected to the SCG's ground-rental charges for the second match.

To tour. The 13 players to tour England in 1886 are: T. P. Horan, J. M. Blackham, W. Bruce, F. R. Spofforth, G. R. Palmer, G. J. Bonnor, J McIlwraith, H. J. H. Scott, A. H. Jarvis, G. Giffen, E. Evans, T. W. Garrett, S. P. Jones and J. W. Trumble. The fast bowler Edwin Evans has refused two previous invitations to tour, in 1882 and 1884.

Sullen tour is falling apart

Tom Garrett wearing his Melbourne Cricket Club cap fields a ball in an imaginary reconstruction of the 1886 Lord's Test.

Sheffield Park, May 7. The Fifth Australians, the first organized by the Melbourne Cricket Club and captained by Dr Harry Scott, have slumped to a loss in the tour opener against Lord Sheffield's XI.

The team was chosen on an amateur basis and therefore lacks the talents of Billy Murdoch, Percy McDonnell and Alick Bannerman, who were not chosen for this reason. Tom Horan, Harry Boyle and Hugh Massie were unavailable. These players were the heart of the earlier successful tours.

It was remarked in *Cricket* in February that the 1886 Australian team would have been 'coldly received' if it had contained professional players, particularly after the 'unwise and unsportsmanlike action of the leading spirits of Murdoch's combination' last Australian summer.

Yet Fred Spofforth, Jack Blackham, Joey Palmer and George Bonnor are part of the team. With the undoubted quality of George Giffen and captain Scott added they should be expected to do well.

One of the notable factors in earlier successes was team spirit, but this team seems to lack it. They left Australia in two parties, and did not get together until Naples.

The captain, Harry Scott, has been called on to adjudicate in altercations between players, and it has even been reported that 'bloodstained carriages' have borne witness that some of these disputes have come to blows.

Fred Spofforth back in business

London, June 26. Fred Spofforth, who injured his hand stopping a Lord Harris drive earlier this month, has made a good recovery, and will play in the first Test in Manchester on July 5.

Spofforth's mere presence as well as his prowess has been sorely missed over the past month, because injuries have laid other players low as well. Both manager Major Wardill and supporter Dr Rowley Pope have had to take the field, and the new bowlers such as Edwin Evans and Hugh Trumble have taken some punishment.

Sam Jones was the victim of W. G. Grace's run-out in the 1882 Ashes Test, but showed his batting class when he made 151 against W. G. and the Gentlemen of England at the Oval, Kennington, on this tour.

North of England still unconquered

Manchester, July 13. After a welcome win against Oxford University the Australians travelled to Manchester to play the North of England, a team never beaten by Australia.

Wet weather had provided a treacherous pitch, though that could not excuse a day's play which saw 31 wickets fall for 137 runs, Fred Spofforth taking 7/19 following his sensational 9/18 against Oxford. Rain interfered the next day, and the match could not be concluded. Australia have still not beaten the North of England.

No match for might of England

The Oval, Aug. 14. The 1886 Test series concluded with another capitulation by the Australian batsmen, this time to the bowling of George Lohmann, who took 7/36 and 5/68 in England's biggest win in Test cricket thus far – by an innings and 217 runs.

Only George Giffen's defiant 47 in the second innings prevented a worse drubbing. Giffen, however made just 13 runs in five previous innings. Captain Henry Scott, and Sam Jones were better in aggregate, but only once managed to 'go on with it'.

The Australian total of 68 in the first innings was the lowest since the 1882 Ashes innings of 62. This match was marked by a superb 170 by W. G. Grace and a typically pugnacious 94 by W.W. Read.

In the second Test at Lord's it had been Lohmann's partner Johnny Briggs who took 11 wickets, and Arthur Shrewsbury who made an elegant 164 in England's only innings. That match was lost by an innings and 106 runs.

In the more evenly contested first Test at Old Trafford, which Australia lost by 'only' four wickets, Dick Barlow's 7/44 in the second innings, as well as a patient 30 on a drying pitch, did the trick for England.

In the series Spofforth could not weave his demonic magic for

The adversaries: teams of Australia and England surround the field of play.

Australia in sufficient quantity to bowl England out twice.

His figures in these Tests – 14 wickets for 260 at 18 runs – are not a great return by the Demon's measure.

He was not helped by the Australian fielding which was uncharacteristically deplorable. Grace was dropped four times before he reached his century at the Oval.

It is notable that of the recent century scorers for Australia two are not here, Billy Murdoch and Percy McDonnell, and the other two, Scott and Bonnor, contributed

110 and 9 runs in total between them.

Wisden noted that 'Scott led the team with the best of intentions and greatest sincerity, but he was no Murdoch. It is exceedingly doubtful whether even an ideal captain would have pulled the team through its engagements unless, indeed, he had been backed by that confidence and energy which we so seldom see in any teams'.

Australia will have to find something extra in the next few seasons if it is to regain its reputation – let alone the Ashes.

Dr Harry Scott – an honourable end to cricket

'Overweighted' by the cares of captaincy, said George Giffen, Harry Scott retired from international cricket after the 1886 tour. He remained in London to further his studies in medicine.

Although not a model batsman in style, he combined abundant confidence with a stout defence, and could hit very hard. On the 1886 tour, in Sheffield, he hit 22 runs from a four-ball over, a record total.

Scott was born in Toorak, Victoria, on 26 December 1858, went to Wesley College and

Henry Scott: dual honors.

Melbourne University, and played for St Kilda then East Melbourne, always combining his medical duties and study with his love of playing cricket.

He made his first class debut for Victoria on 22 February 1878 at the age of 19 and took 6/33. With the Australian players back he did not get another chance for Victoria until March 1882. Scott made two centuries for Victoria, 114 in 1883–84 and 111 in 1885–86.

His finest hour was on the 1884 tour of England. He made 12, 75 and 31, then 102, his only Test century, at the Oval.

On this tour his habit of seeing London on bus tours costing tuppence earned him the nickname 'Tup'.

He became a respected country doctor, Mayor and Chief Magistrate of Scone, NSW – and was given to saying when provoked about 1886 – 'I have captained Australia and hit a Test century. Many would have liked two such honours as these.'

'Tup' Scott died of typhoid on 23 September 1910.

As the Bulletin *saw it; the broken and battered Australian team limps on to the docks on its return to Sydney.*

FIRST TEST 1886 ENGLAND v AUSTRALIA
Old Trafford, Manchester. July 5, 6, 7, 1886.
Toss: Australia. England won by 4 wkts.

AUSTRALIA

SP Jones lbw Grace	87	c Ulyett b Steel	12
HJH Scott (c) c Barlow b Ulyett	21	b Barlow	47
G Giffen b Steel	3	c Shrewsbury b Barlow	1
AH Jarvis (+) c Scotton b Ulyett	45	c Lohmann b Barlow	2
GJ Bonnor c Lohmann b Barlow	4	c Barlow b Peate	2
JW Trumble c Scotton b Steel	24	c Ulyett b Barlow	4
W Bruce run out	2 (8)	c Grace b Barlow	0
TW Garrett c Pilling b Lohmann	5 (9)	c Grace b Ulyett	22
JM Blackham not out	7 (7)	lbw Barlow	8
GE Palmer c Lohmann b Ulyett	4	c Pilling b Barlow	8
FR Spofforth c Barlow b Ulyett	2	not out	20
EXTRAS (W 1)	1	(B 3)	3
TOTAL	205		123

FOW 1st Inns: 58 71 134 141 181 187 188 192 201 205
FOW 2nd Inns: 37 42 44 53 68 70 70 73 103 123

Bowling: *First Innings*: Peate 19-7-30-0, Lohmann 23-9-41-1, Steel 27-5-47-2, Ulyett 36.1-20-46-4, Barlow 23-15-19-1, Grace 9-3-21-1. *Second Innings*: Peate 46-25-45-1, Barlow 52-34-44-7, Lohmann 5-3-14-0, Steel 8-3-9-1, Ulyett 6.3-3-7-1, Grace 1-0-1-0.

ENGLAND

WH Scotton c Trumble b Garrett	21	b Palmer	20
WG Grace c Bonnor b Spofforth	8	c Palmer b Giffen	4
A Shrewsbury b Spofforth	31	c & b Giffen	4
WW Read c Scott b Garrett	51	c Jones b Spofforth	9
AG Steel (c) c Jarvis b Palmer	12 (6)	not out	19
RG Barlow not out	38 (5)	c Palmer b Spofforth	30
G Ulyett b Spofforth	17	c Scott b Garrett	8
J Briggs c Garrett b Spofforth	1	not out	2
GA Lohmann b Giffen	32		
E Peate st Jarvis b Palmer	6		
R Pilling (+) c Bruce b Palmer	2		
EXTRAS (B 2, LB 2)	4	(B 10, LB 1)	11
TOTAL	223		6 for 107

FOW 1st Inns: 9 51 80 109 131 156 160 206 219 223
FOW 2nd Inns: 7 15 24 62 90 105

Bowling: *First Innings*: Spofforth 53-22-82-4, Giffen 32-15-44-1, Garrett 45-23-43-2, Bruce 10-7-9-0, Palmer 17.2-4-41-3. *Second Innings*: Spofforth 29.2-13-40-2, Giffen 24-9-31-2, Garrett 17-9-14-1, Palmer 7-3-11-1.

Umpires: CK Pullin & JE West

SECOND TEST 1886 ENGLAND v AUSTRALIA
Lord's Cricket Ground, London. July 19, 20, 21, 1886.
Toss: England. England won by an innings & 106 runs.

ENGLAND

WG Grace c Jarvis b Palmer	18
WH Scotton b Garrett	19
A Shrewsbury c Bonnor b Trumble	164
WW Read c Spofforth b Giffen	22
AG Steel (c) lbw Spofforth	5
W Barnes c Palmer b Garrett	58
RG Barlow c Palmer b Spofforth	12
G Ulyett b Spofforth	19
EFS Tylecote (+) b Spofforth	0
J Briggs c Jones b Trumble	0
GA Lohmann not out	7
EXTRAS (B 24, LB 4, NB 1)	29
TOTAL	353

FOW 1st Inns: 27 77 112 119 280 303 333 333 340 353

Bowling: *First Innings*: Garrett 72-40-77-2, Evans 36-20-37-0, Palmer 38-15-45-1, Spofforth 56-26-73-4, Trumble 14-4-27-2, Giffen 40-18-63-1, Jones 3-1-2-0.

AUSTRALIA

SP Jones c Grace b Briggs	25 (4)	b Briggs	17
HJH Scott (c) lbw Briggs	30 (5)	b Briggs	2
G Giffen b Steel	3 (6)	b Briggs	1
AH Jarvis (+) b Briggs	3 (7)	not out	13
GJ Bonnor c Grace b Steel	0 (8)	b Briggs	3
JW Trumble c Tylecote b Briggs	0 (3)	c Tylecote b Barnes	20
GE Palmer c Shrewsbury b Barnes	20 (1)	c Lohmann b Barlow	48
JM Blackham b Briggs	23 (9)	b Briggs	5
TW Garrett not out	7 (2)	b Briggs	4
FR Spofforth b Barnes	5 (11)	c & b Briggs	0
E Evans c Ulyett b Barnes	0 (10)	run out	0
EXTRAS (B 4, LB 1)	5	(B 13)	13
TOTAL	121		126

FOW 1st Inns: 45 52 59 60 62 67 99 109 121 121
FOW 2nd Inns: 6 56 91 95 98 105 120 126 126 126

Bowling: *First Innings*: Barnes 14.3-7-25-3, Lohmann 7-3-21-0, Briggs 34-22-29-5, Steel 21-8-34-2, Barlow 6-3-7-0. *Second Innings*: Barnes 10.5-5-18-1, Lohmann 14-9-11-0, Briggs 38.1-17-45-6, Steel 16-9-14-0, Barlow 25-20-12-2, Ulyett 8-3-13-0.

Umpires: FH Farrands & CK Pullin

THIRD TEST 1886 ENGLAND v AUSTRALIA
Kennington Oval, London. August 12, 13, 14, 1886.
Toss: England. England won by an innings & 217 runs.

ENGLAND

WG Grace c Blackham b Spofforth	170
WH Scotton b Garrett	34
A Shrewsbury c Jones b Trumble	44
WW Read c Jones b Spofforth	94
W Barnes c Evans b Trumble	3
AG Steel (c) st Blackham b Trumble	9
RG Barlow c Trumble b Garrett	3
G Ulyett c McIlwraith b Garrett	0
J Briggs c Trumble b Spofforth	53
EFS Tylecote (+) not out	10
GA Lohmann b Spofforth	7
EXTRAS (B 3, LB 2, NB 2)	7
TOTAL	434

FOW 1st Inns: 170 216 287 293 305 314 320 410 418 434

Bowling: *First Innings*: Giffen 62-32-96-0, Garrett 99-55-88-3, Palmer 47-21-80-0, Bruce 6-2-9-0, Spofforth 30.1-12-65-4, Evans 13-10-6-0, Trumble 47-14-83-3.

AUSTRALIA

SP Jones c Grace b Lohmann	2 (3)	c Read b Lohmann	2
GE Palmer c Barlow b Briggs	15 (6)	st Tylecote b Steel	35
G Giffen c Shrewsbury b Briggs	5 (4)	c & b Lohmann	47
HJH Scott (c) c Tylecote b Lohmann	6 (5)	c Grace b Lohmann	4
JW Trumble c Read b Lohmann	13 (7)	c Read b Briggs	18
J McIlwraith b Lohmann	2 (1)	c Tylecote b Briggs	7
JM Blackham (+) c & b Briggs	0 (8)	c Grace b Briggs	5
TW Garrett c Grace b Lohmann	2 (10)	c Shrewsbury b Lohmann	4
W Bruce c Ulyett b Lohmann	9	b Lohmann	11
E Evans not out	9 (2)	run out	3
FR Spofforth b Lohmann	1	not out	5
EXTRAS (B 4)	4	(B 7, LB 1)	8
TOTAL	68		149

FOW 1st Inns: 2 11 22 34 35 35 44 49 67 68
FOW 2nd Inns: 11 14 26 30 84 120 129 131 137 149

Bowling: *First Innings*: Lohmann 30.2-17-36-7, Briggs 30-17-28-3. *Second Innings*: Lohmann 37-14-68-5, Briggs 32-19-30-3, Barlow 14-8-13-0, Barnes 7-4-10-0, Steel 7-1-20-1.

Umpires: RP Carpenter & FH Farrands

Australian Averages

1886 ENGLAND v AUSTRALIA

AUSTRALIA	M	Inn	NO	Runs	H.S	Avrge	Ct	St	Overs	Mds	Runs	Wkt	Avrge
Blackham, JM	3	6	1	42	23	8.40	1	1	-	-	-	-	-
Bonnor, GJ	2	4	-	9	4	2.25	2	-	-	-	-	-	-
Bruce, W	2	4	-	22	11	5.50	1	-	16.0	9	18	-	-
Evans, E	2	4	1	12	9*	4.00	1	-	49.0	30	43	-	-
Garrett, TW	3	6	1	44	22	8.80	1	-	233.0	127	222	8	27.75
Giffen, G	3	6	-	60	47	10.00	4	-	158.0	74	234	4	58.50
Jarvis, AH	2	4	1	63	45	21.00	2	1	-	-	-	-	-
Jones, SP	3	6	-	145	87	24.17	4	-	3.0	1	2	-	-
McIlwraith, J	1	2	-	9	7	4.50	1	-	-	-	-	-	-
Palmer, GE	3	6	-	130	48	21.67	4	-	109.2	43	177	5	35.40
Scott, HJH	3	6	-	110	47	18.33	2	-	-	-	-	-	-
Spofforth, FR	3	6	2	33	20*	8.25	1	-	168.3	73	260	14	18.57
Trumble, JW	3	6	-	79	24	13.17	3	-	61.0	18	110	5	22.00

English Averages

1886 ENGLAND v AUSTRALIA

ENGLAND	M	Inn	NO	Runs	H.S	Avrge	Ct	St	Overs	Mds	Runs	Wkt	Avrge
Barlow, RG	3	4	1	83	38*	27.67	4	-	120.0	80	95	10	9.50
Barnes, W	2	2	-	61	58	30.50	-	-	31.3	16	53	4	13.25
Briggs, J	3	4	1	56	53	18.67	2	-	134.1	75	132	17	7.76
Grace, WG	3	4	-	200	170	50.00	8	-	10.0	3	22	1	22.00
Lohmann, GA	3	3	1	46	32	23.00	5	-	116.2	55	191	13	14.69
Peate, E	1	1	-	6	6	6.00	-	-	65.0	32	75	1	75.00
Pilling, R	1	1	-	2	2	2.00	2	-	-	-	-	-	-
Read, WW	3	4	-	176	94	44.00	3	-	-	-	-	-	-
Scotton, WH	3	4	-	94	34	23.50	2	-	-	-	-	-	-
Shrewsbury, A	3	4	-	243	164	60.75	4	-	-	-	-	-	-
Steel, AG	3	4	1	45	19*	15.00	-	-	79.0	26	124	6	20.67
Tylecote, EFS	2	2	1	10	10*	10.00	4	1	-	-	-	-	-
Ulyett, G	3	4	-	44	19	11.00	4	-	51.0	26	66	5	13.20

Season of fists and callow grumpiness

New star bowler, Jack Ferris.

The churlish mood of the season.

England captain Arthur Shrewsbury.

Sydney, March 1. The failure of the 1886 Australian tour of England, which was organized by the Melbourne Cricket Club, has affected the negotiations of Secretary Ben Wardill for an English tour under its auspices in 1886–87.

English professionals James Lillywhite, Arthur Shrewsbury and Alfred Shaw declined £10 a match per man and organized their own tour to include two Tests among 29 matches.

Perhaps some of the lack of interest by the public had to do with the unpleasantness betwixt and between Australians and the

English professionals, and the lack of support by the MCC.

In any event the tour lost money, fisticuffs between Australians were common, and amateur pugilistics between English and Australian players occurred on at least one occasion.

The first Test at the SCG on January 28 was remarkable for the fact that Australian captain Percy McDonnell, for the first time in Test history, won the toss and sent the opposition in. England made just 45, facing John 'J. J.' Ferris and 'Terror' Turner for the first time, but batted badly to lose by 13 runs.

A dispute over payment for time lost at work saw five new Australian players chosen for the second Test, also at the SCG. With Barnes injured by hitting a brick wall instead of Percy McDonnell in an off-field incident, England brought in an Australian resident Reginald Wood, who had already played against them for Victoria.

It was a bowler's match with Ferris and Turner collecting nine wickets each, and the Englishman George Lohmann 10. The English batting was 71 runs better. Ferris has made a remarkable start, taking 18 wickets in his first two Tests, with Turner taking 17.

Smokers and non-smokers turn on a carnival contest

Melbourne, March 21. The remarkable match between the Non-Smokers and the Smokers at the East Melbourne Cricket Ground ended with a thunderstorm, a unique umpiring decision by an umpire, and a draw.

This game between sides combining English and Australian players was supposed to be recompense for the switching of the tourists' other Melbourne matches to the MCG from the EMCG. However, characteristic disorganisation in this weird season and lack of interest in the English tour saw just a few hundred spectators at each day's play.

Billy Midwinter was unavailable for the match most suited to his multinational background.

Harry Boyle lead the Smokers on to the field 'each blowing a cloud from a cigar of colonial manufacture; but immediately play commenced "butts" were thrown away' reported the *Age*. They should have kept the cigars because the Non-Smokers went about compiling a record first class score in Australia of 803. Arthur

The teams ready for the rollicking Smokers v Non-smokers match.

Shrewsbury made 236, Victoria's William Bruce 131, England's William Gunn 150, and the local from Carlton, Jack Worrall made 78.

In reply, Smokers were 3/302 at the end of the third day, with Joey Palmer making an excellent 113. A thunderstorm the next morning changed the complexion of the wicket.

The Smokers tumbled to 356 all out, then 4/135 following on, with

one ball to play. This was defended by William Scotton in characteristic fashion.

He then picked it up as a souvenir – and was promptly given out by umpire Reg Wood, an ideal choice for the role as he had already played for both Victoria and England this season. With a draw the result, the happy teams trooped off for some fine ale and cigars to savour the most convivial match of the tour.

FIRST TEST 1886-87 AUSTRALIA v ENGLAND
Sydney Cricket Ground, Sydney. January 28, 29, 31, 1887.
Toss: Australia. England won by 13 runs.

ENGLAND

W Bates c Midwinter b Ferris	8	b Ferris	24
A Shrewsbury (c) c McShane b Ferris	2	b Ferris	29
W Barnes c Spofforth b Turner	0	c Moses b Garrett	32
RG Barlow b Turner	2	c Jones b Ferris	4
JM Read c Spofforth b Ferris	5	b Ferris	0
W Gunn b Turner	0	b Turner	4
WH Scotton c Jones b Turner	1 (9)	c Spofforth b Garrett	6
J Briggs c Midwinter b Turner	5	b Spofforth	33
GA Lohmann c Garrett b Ferris	17 (7)	lbw Ferris	3
W Flowers b Turner	2	c McDonnell b Turner	14
M Sherwin (+) not out	0	not out	21
EXTRAS (B 2, LB 1)	3	(B 9, LB 5)	14
TOTAL	45		184

FOW 1st Inns: 11 11 13 13 13 17 21 29 41 45
FOW 2nd Inns: 31 80 92 92 98 99 103 128 153 184

Bowling: First Innings: Turner 18-11-15-6, Ferris 17.3-7-27-4. *Second Innings:* Turner 44.2-22-53-2, Ferris 61-30-76-5, Spofforth 12-3-17-1, Midwinter 4-1-10-0, Garrett 12-7-8-2, McShane 3-0-6-0.

AUSTRALIA

JM Blackham (+) c Sherwin b Lohmann	4	b Barnes	5
PS McDonnell (c) b Barnes	14	lbw Barnes	0
H Moses b Barlow	31	c Shrewsbury b Barnes	24
SP Jones c Shrewsbury b Bates	31	c Read b Barnes	18
CTB Turner b Barlow	3	c & b Barnes	7
AC Bannerman not out	15	b Lohmann	4
PG McShane lbw Briggs	5	b Briggs	0
WE Midwinter c Shrewsbury b Barlow	12	lbw Barnes	10
TW Garrett b Lohmann	12	c Gunn b Lohmann	10
FR Spofforth b Lohmann	2	b Lohmann	5
JJ Ferris c Barlow b Barnes	1	not out	0
EXTRAS (B 1)	1	(B 12, LB 2)	14
TOTAL	119		97

FOW 1st Inns: 2 11 22 34 35 35 44 49 67 68
FOW 2nd Inns: 4 5 29 38 58 61 80 83 95 97

Bowling: First Innings: Barnes 22.1-16-19-2, Lohmann 21-12-30-3, Briggs 14-5-25-1, Barlow 35-23-25-3, Bates 21-9-19-1. *Second Innings:* Barlow 13-6-20-0, Barnes 46-29-28-6, Bates 17-11-8-0, Lohmann 24-11-20-3, Briggs 7-5-7-1.

Umpires: C Bannerman & H Rawlinson

After two Test wins, the British Lion is entitled to roar its defiance.

SECOND TEST 1886-87 AUSTRALIA v ENGLAND
Sydney Cricket Ground, Sydney. February 25, 26, 28, March 1, 1887.
Toss: England. England won by 71 runs.

ENGLAND

A Shrewsbury (c) b Turner	9	b Turner	6
W Bates c Ferris b Turner	8	b Turner	30
JM Read b Turner	11 (4)	st Burton b Ferris	2
W Gunn b Turner	9 (5)	c Cottam b Ferris	10
GA Lohmann b Ferris	2 (6)	b Ferris	2
WH Scotton b Turner	0 (7)	b Ferris	2
J Briggs b Ferris	17 (8)	b Garrett	16
RG Barlow c Allen b Ferris	34 (3)	not out	42
W Flowers c Allen b Ferris	37	b Turner	18
R Wood lbw Ferris	6	hit wicket b Midwinter	0
M Sherwin (+) not out	4	b Turner	5
EXTRAS (B 9, LB 3, NB 2)	14	(B 12, LB 5)	17
TOTAL	151		154

FOW 1st Inns: 14 19 35 38 43 50 73 130 145 151
FOW 2nd Inns: 21 42 47 59 73 77 98 136 137 154

Bowling: First Innings: Ferris 45-16-71-5, Turner 53-29-41-5, Garrett 6-2-12-0, Midwinter 3-1-2-0, Lyons 2-0-11-0. *Second Innings:* Turner 64.1-33-52-4, Ferris 60-33-69-4, Garrett 10-6-7-1, Midwinter 6-3-9-1.

AUSTRALIA

WF Giffen b Lohmann	2 (6)	b Briggs	0
JJ Lyons b Lohmann	11 (4)	c Gunn b Bates	0
H Moses b Flowers	28 (2)	st Sherwin b Bates	33
RC Allen b Lohmann	14 (3)	c (S)CTB Turner b Bates	30
PS McDonnell (c) c Gunn b Lohmann	10 (1)	c Gunn b Lohmann	35
WE Midwinter b Lohmann	1 (7)	c Sherwin b Lohmann	4
JT Cottam hit wicket b Lohmann	1 (5)	st Sherwin b Briggs	3
CTB Turner c & b Flowers	9	c Briggs b Bates	9
TW Garrett b Lohmann	1	c Sherwin b Briggs	20
JJ Ferris b Lohmann	1	run out	2
FJ Burton (+) not out	0	not out	2
EXTRAS (B 5, LB 1)	6	(B 9, LB 3)	12
TOTAL	84		150

FOW 1st Inns: 12 15 40 56 59 65 82 83 83 84
FOW 2nd Inns: 51 86 86 95 95 106 121 129 135 150

Bowling: First Innings: Briggs 20-6-34-0, Lohmann 27.1-12-35-8, Flowers 8-3-9-2. *Second Innings:* Lohmann 40-16-52-2, Briggs 22-9-31-3, Flowers 13-5-17-0, Barlow 9-2-12-0, Bates 26-13-26-4.

Umpires: C Bannerman & J Swift

Australian Averages

1886-87 AUSTRALIA v ENGLAND

AUSTRALIA	M	Inn	NO	Runs	H.S	Avrge	Ct	St	Overs	Mds	Runs	Wkt	Avrge
Allen, RC	1	2	-	44	30	22.00	2	-	-	-	-	-	-
Bannerman, AC	1	2	1	19	15*	19.00	-	-	-	-	-	-	-
Blackham, JM	1	2	-	9	5	4.50	-	-	-	-	-	-	-
Burton, FJ	1	2	2	2	2*	-	-	1	-	-	-	-	-
Cottam, JT	1	2	-	4	3	2.00	1	-	-	-	-	-	-
Ferris, JJ	2	4	1	4	2	1.33	-	-	183.3	86	243	18	13.50
Garrett, TW	2	4	-	43	20	10.75	1	-	28.0	15	27	3	9.00
Giffen, WF	1	2	-	2	2	1.00	-	-	-	-	-	-	-
Jones, SP	1	2	-	49	31	24.50	2	-	-	-	-	-	-
Lyons, JJ	1	2	-	11	11	5.50	-	-	2.0	-	11	-	-
McDonnell, PS	2	4	-	59	35	14.75	1	-	-	-	-	-	-
McShane, PG	1	2	-	5	5	2.50	1	-	3.0	-	6	-	-
Midwinter, WE	2	4	-	15	10	3.75	2	-	13.0	5	21	1	21.00
Moses, H	2	4	-	116	33	29.00	1	-	-	-	-	-	-
Spofforth, FR	1	2	-	7	5	3.50	3	-	12.0	3	17	1	17.00
Turner, CTB	2	4	-	28	9	7.00	-	-	179.3	95	161	17	9.47

English Averages

1886-87 AUSTRALIA v ENGLAND

ENGLAND	M	Inn	NO	Runs	H.S	Avrge	Ct	St	Overs	Mds	Runs	Wkt	Avrge
Barlow, RG	2	4	1	82	42*	27.33	1	-	57.0	31	57	3	19.00
Barnes, W	1	2	-	32	32	16.00	1	-	68.1	45	47	8	5.88
Bates, W	2	4	-	70	30	17.50	-	-	64.0	33	53	5	10.60
Briggs, J	2	4	-	71	33	17.75	1	-	63.0	25	97	5	19.40
Flowers, W	2	4	-	71	37	17.75	1	-	21.0	8	26	2	13.00
Gunn, W	2	4	-	23	10	5.75	4	-	-	-	-	-	-
Lohmann, GA	2	4	-	28	17	7.00	-	-	112.1	51	137	16	8.56
Read, JM	2	4	-	18	11	4.50	1	-	-	-	-	-	-
Scotton, WH	2	4	-	9	6	2.25	-	-	-	-	-	-	-
Sherwin, M	2	4	3	30	21*	30.00	3	2	-	-	-	-	-
Shrewsbury, A	2	4	-	46	29	11.50	3	-	-	-	-	-	-
Wood, R	1	2	-	6	6	3.00	-	-	-	-	-	-	-

Two tours and one Test in silly season

Sydney, Feb. 15. It seems Australian cricket has sunk to a nadir in organisation and ability in the Test match just concluded.

Despite the great efforts of 'Terror' Turner and J. J. Ferris in dismissing the England side combined from the two touring parties for 113 and 137, Australian batsmen could only manage 42 and 82.

Turner's 5/44 and 7/43, with Ferris' 4/60 and 2/43, were not quite good enough when compared to George Lohmann's' 5/17 and 4/35, and Bobby Peel's 5/18 and 4/40. The damp pitch certainly favoured the bowlers, perhaps Australia's batting was simply worse than that of the English.

The cause of the locals was not aided by the refusal to take part of players George Giffen, Tom Horan, Billy Bruce and Affie Jarvis – who wanted more money.

Giffen might have been useful. He hit the first double century, 203, by an Australian against a touring team in the match for SA against Vernon's XI.

Fewer than 2000 people attended the rain-marred match.

This Test match combined the two English teams for the first time since both stepped off the same boat, the *Iberia*, in Adelaide on October 25.

The amateur team tour, G. F. Vernon's England XI, was sponsored by the Melbourne Cricket Club, whose secretary Major Ben Wardill roamed the country organising matches for them.

The gentlemen tourists. George Vernon and his team, mostly of amateur players.

The MCC feel aggrieved with the NSWCA over this, believing that their tour was organised first and that the professionals should withdraw.

They were not persuaded. It appears that the NSWCA has been well aware of the amateur tour, first agreed in January 1887, but in an atmosphere of pique arranged its own tour without giving any advice as to its intentions.

The resulting confusion has made a mockery of inter-country Test matches.

The second professional team is A. Shrewsbury's England XI, looking for profitable matches under the old banner of Lillywhite, Shaw and Shrewsbury, sponsored by the NSW Cricket Association.

Vernon's amateurs have beaten an Australian XI, South Australia, Victoria and lost to NSW, and played a draw with SA.

Shrewsbury's professionals have lost to NSW twice, beaten NSW, Victoria, and a Combined XI. The Victorian win was huge – the biggest innings defeat in Australian first class cricket. Shrewsbury made 232 of his team's 624. Victoria managed 68 and 100, losing by an innings and 456 runs.

Crowds have been sparse for all matches, with heavy losses sustained by both tours.

Lord Hawke, who has returned early from Vernon's side on the death of his father, wrote of this season, 'There was never such a prominent case of folly.'

The Adelaide Oval, with its elegant grandstands, has developed a reputation for perfect wickets – for batsmen, that is.

Colonial matches draw biggest crowds

Sydney, Jan. 31. Colonial cricket lovers much prefer to see their own colony in action against another colony than any combined side, or the choice of English touring parties.

This was amply demonstrated in the return match between the Victorian gumsuckers and the NSW cornstalks. NSW, even with Turner (1/79 and 5/102) less terrifying than usual, got home by an innings and 35 runs.

This result is due in large measure to the calm and patient 297 not out from Harry Moses – widely regarded as the best left hand batsman in the world. Moses survived a difficult chance before he scored. Victoria used 10 bowlers, all of them in vain.

NSW 576, Victoria 267 and 274. The first match at the MCG over Christmas saw a slightly closer NSW win – by two wickets.

Harry Moses: topped averages.

Colonies vote to stop English visits

Melbourne, Dec. 21. A conference of delegates from the cricket associations of Victoria, NSW and South Australia and West Australia met at the Oriental Hotel in Collins Street Melbourne to discuss the future of intercolonial cricket.

Among the recommendations agreed to were that no English team visit the colonies for three seasons after 1887–88, and that no Australian team visit England for four years from this date.

The delegates agreed that six-ball overs should be used in Australia.

They also agreed to the suggestion that the authorities in England be asked to make an alteration to the leg-before-wicket rule, so that the bowler should get the benefit of his skill.

Further, each of the colonies of NSW, SA and Victoria should meet twice a season, home and away. This will bring some balance to South Australia's position. It will play only one intercolonial game this season, against Victoria, despite playing against both of the visiting teams from England.

The meeting was held to stem the tide of disillusionment with cricket in Australia where top players are often not available for their colony's sides, and attendances and receipts from intercolonial games were suffering.

While cricket associations might like more control over players, the players, especially the more 'professional' seem unlikely to give up potentially lucrative tours.

Once a swamp and a common sewer, the elegantly presented Brisbane Cricket Ground is now the centre of Queensland's cricket aspirations.

Turner's season of 100

Sydney, March 13. The brightest light in this dismal season of Australian cricket shines in the sparkling deliveries of Charles Thomas Biass 'Terror' Turner.

Turner's performance in taking 106 wickets at 13.59 this season is unique in the annals of Australian cricket.

His performance in the match between the Australian XI, and Arthur Shrewsbury's England XI, was a demonstration of his prowess.

Turner took 7/72 in the first innings and 4/135 in the second, finally dismissing Shrewsbury. But only after the master batsman had made 206.

He has played 12 first class matches this season for NSW, Australia and an Australian XI. It is the most anyone has played in a season in Australia.

He was just as enthusiastic at the end of the season as he was at the beginning – indeed his appetite for cricket is as undiminished this year as it was as a 19-year-old in Bathurst when he took 10 wickets in an innings for a XXII of that town, against Alfred Shaw's England team in 1881.

Charles Turner: ready for England.

Turner's front-on fast medium straight-at-the-stumps bowling, with a fast off-cutter that owes something to the Demon, are naggingly accurate and force the batsman to take risks. He is lethal on a helpful pitch.

He is an adept at reading the conditions of a pitch, and in knowing where to find a 'soft spot'. He is a bowler very suitable to English conditions.

ONLY TEST 1887–88 AUSTRALIA v ENGLAND
Sydney Cricket Ground, Sydney. February 10, 11–13 (no play), 14, 15, 1888.
Toss: Australia. England won by 126 runs.

ENGLAND

AE Stoddart c McShane b Turner	16	c Blackham b Turner	17
A Shrewsbury c Turner b Ferris	44	b Ferris	1
G Ulyett c Burton b Turner	5	b Ferris	5
WW Read (c) b Turner	10	b Turner	8
JM Read c & b Turner	0	c Bannerman b Turner	39
R Peel hit wicket b Ferris	3	st Blackham b Turner	9
W Newham c Worrall b Ferris	9 (8)	lbw Turner	17
GA Lohmann c Jones b Ferris	12 (7)	c Blackham b Turner	0
J Briggs b Turner	0	c Worrall b McShane	14
W Attewell not out	7	not out	10
R Pilling (+) run out	3	b Turner	5
EXTRAS (B 4)	4	(B 7, LB 5)	12
TOTAL	113		137

FOW 1st Inns: 27 36 54 54 57 88 102 103 103 113
FOW 2nd Inns: 9 15 27 54 82 82 84 111 131 137

Bowling: *First Innings*: Turner 50-27-44-5, Ferris 47-25-60-4, Garrett 3-1-5-0. *Second Innings*: Turner 38-23-43-7, Ferris 16-4-43-2, McShane 21-7-39-1.

AUSTRALIA

AC Bannerman c Ulyett b Lohmann	2	c Attewell b Lohmann	2
SP Jones c Shrewsbury b Peel	0 (4)	c Shrewsbury b Lohmann	15
H Moses c WW Read b Lohmann	3	c Briggs b Lohmann	11
FJ Burton c Stoddart b Lohmann	1 (5)	c Pilling b Peel	1
J Worrall st Pilling b Peel	6 (10)	b Lohmann	1
PG McShane c Shrewsbury b Peel	0 (8)	b Peel	0
PS McDonnell (c) b Lohmann	3 (2)	b Peel	6
JM Blackham (+) c Shrewsbury b Peel	2 (9)	not out	25
TW Garrett c Pilling b Lohmann	10 (7)	c Shrewsbury b Peel	1
CTB Turner not out	8 (6)	lbw Attewell	12
JJ Ferris c WW Read b Peel	0	c Shrewsbury b Attewell	5
EXTRAS (B 6, W 1)	7	(B 2, LB 1)	3
TOTAL	42		82

FOW 1st Inns: 2 2 10 16 18 21 23 26 37 42
FOW 2nd Inns: 8 8 20 21 44 47 53 60 61 82

Bowling: *First Innings*: Lohmann 19-13-17-5, Peel 18.3-9-18-5. *Second Innings*: Lohmann 32-18-35-4, Peel 33-14-40-4, Attewell 4.2-2-4-2.

Umpires: C Bannerman & J Phillips

New faces in a makeshift team

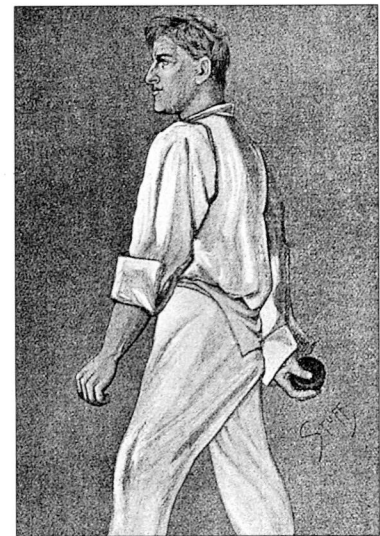

Sammy Woods: local recruit.

Sydney, April 4. Some of the most renowned Australian cricketers of the past few seasons were unavailable or not selected by Mr Charles Beal for the 1888 tour of England.

The resultant touring party is regarded as the weakest ever to leave Australia.

George Giffen won't play as his brother was not picked, and Harry Moses felt obliged to stay to look after his banking interests, although he topped the averages last season and seems a natural batting successor to Billy Murdoch.

Beal could not persuade left-hander Bill Bruce or the young off-spinner Hugh Trumble to tour, and Billy Murdoch and Fred Spofforth have retired.

The *Bulletin* wrote, half in jest, that 'If Turner keeps up his present form with bat and ball, the Britishers will forget about Spofforth, who at his best was only one part demon.'

C. T. B. 'Terror' Turner and his partner J. J. Ferris seem to be what stands in the way of another Australian drubbing at the hands of the English.

But without Giffen there is no bowling all-rounder to back them up, and Harry Boyle's best days are past him.

Captain Percy McDonnell and the stalwart Alick Bannerman are excellent batsmen on wet wickets, but others in the touring party, such as Jack Worrall and Jack Lyons, have little experience on the sort of mud heaps that will be found in England.

Big-hitting George Bonnor, with the ounce of fortune his style requires, may be a help.

A good and friendly start

The scene at the opening match at Norbury Park, Surrey.

Stoke, July 13. The deeds of 'Terror' Turner and J. J. Ferris on this tour have given the lie to the idea that this Australian team is not up to standard.

The batting has been much better than expected whilst the performances of the two bowlers have been extraordinary.

Turner himself hit a free scoring 103 against Surrey at the Oval in May. His 6/44 and Ferris' 6/45 brought about a decisive win.

In Birmingham against W. G. Grace's XI of England, it was Percy McDonnell, George Bonnor and Jack Worrall who knocked up 297 before Turner and Ferris demolished the English team for 99 in the second innings.

Against Leicestershire the heroic deeds by Turner and Ferris could not make up for Australia's poor batting when caught on a 'sticky'.

The Leicester side, more used to batting on soft pitches and in dull light, made 119 and 87, while the Australians were completely bemused by the pitch that made the ball rear and bounce, or slide and shoot, move either way of the seam, and break prodigiously with a bit of spin. They made 62 and 50.

Against another XI of England at Stoke, the Australians scored a modest 242 before Turner and Ferris went to work. Turner's 9/15 (the other was run out) was a sensation. The English team made 28 and 79.

Jack Worrall: disappointing tour.

Joe Lyons: a hard hitter.

Tests losses a damp disaster

Manchester, Aug. 31. The promising start to the England tour, and the great deeds of Turner and Ferris are distant memories after the capitulation in the third Test at Old Trafford in Manchester.

W. G. Grace won the toss and batted on a soft but playable wicket, and made a modest 172, W. G. top scoring with 38 and Turner taking 5/86.

But then the 'dreaded cypher' made its presence felt as a row of ducks' eggs became the most conspicuous feature of the Australian innings. Four 'ducks' in the woeful first innings of 81 were followed by six in the second knock of 70 – the worst Australian batting effort in memory.

It was all over in six and a half hours, before lunch on the second day. Bobby Peel was the destroyer on 'a bowler's wicket' with 11/68 for the match.

Before this match the second Test at the Oval was the worst performance with Australia managing just 80 batting first, England replying with 317 despite W. G. making just one (Turner 6/112) and Australia stumbling to 100. A loss by an innings and 137 runs on a good batting wicket.

These failures have all but eliminated the memory of Australia's win in the first Test at Lord's on another bowler's wicket. Turner took 5/27 and 5/36, and Ferris 3/19 and 5/26.

The batting at Lord's, by both sides, was nothing to write home about either. On the second day 27 wickets fell in just three hours of batting time on a mud pitch – the

1888.

The Australians of 1888 fell away in the third Test, after a good start to the tour.

highest number of wickets to fall in any day of Test cricket. Many players looked as if they were going to the gallows as they strode off into the gloom.

With plenty of moisture in the air Turney and Ferris routed England. Only W. G. offered any resistance, scoring 10 and 24, the highest score in the match.

Australia managed 116 in the first innings as it had the best of the first day conditions. There was even a semblance of batting from Percy McDonnell (22), Jack Blackham (22), Sammy Woods (18) and Jack Edwards (21). Then came the

capitulations of England (53), Australia (60), and England (62). Ferris completed a fine double with 14 and 20, modest scores but Australia's best.

Observers noted that the Australian side had 'gone to pieces' since that first Test win. The inevitable rain in England has demonstrated that our boys have not yet the batting ability for such wickets as the weather has created. Jack Edwards (26 and 36), Percy MacDonnell (32) and Charles Turner (26) are the only batsmen to exceed 20 in the last four Test match innings.

Turner and Ferris bowling heroes in poor season

London, Sep. 1. The first-rate bowling partnership between right-arm fast man C. B. T. Turner and left-arm fast-medium J. J. Ferris has been the most notable feature of the otherwise disappointing 1888 Australian tour.

With very little back-up from other bowlers, they bowled a gigantic number of balls on tour, and took an enormous number of wickets.

Turner bowled 10,359 balls for 314 wickets at 11.38, and Ferris 8890 balls for 220 wickets at 14.23. By comparison, George Lohmann, England's best bowler took 209 wickets at 10.9.

Turner is deceptively fast. He was taken to Woolwich Arsenal to have the speed of his bowling measured at 55 miles per hour, not a hurricane, but very brisk and generally a terror. He also has great variation of flight and spin to outwit the batsman, and a nagging control of length which tantalises the batsman into making a rash shot in trying to unsettle the rhythm.

The *Town and Country Journal*, in reviewing the tour stated, 'In bowling our Sydney men have had it all their own way; Turner and Ferris having accomplished feats with the ball which stamp them as equal, and we are inclined to think superior, to any of the bowlers of the present day.'

While they are to be credited with a full share of the glory of Australian victories, they are not responsible for the failures.

Affie Jarvis: affable by nature.

Harry Trott: quiet achiever.

Alick Bannerman: the stonewaller.

Jack Blackham: veteran stumper.

'The Terror' on bowling

'You ask me how I bowl,' he commenced. 'I look upon it as a pure gift – or knack, you can call it if you like – that some men possess. It is no good saying that any man can be a bowler, as some people do.

'He must be specially constituted for it; be strong, robust, healthy, have all his nerves about him, and a perfectly true eye. Lots of men have all these qualifications but still they are not bowlers, and would not be no matter how much they tried.

'There is a gift that I cannot explain, but it is still there all the time.

'No, I did not commence young. Indeed until I was 18 or so I never cared a straw about the game, and though our school played matches every week throughout the season, I only took part in two of them when I was there. This was at Bathurst, and later on I was induced to join the club there, and found out that I had the knack, or gift.

'In our club matches my average was the best, so when Shaw's team went up there in 1884 I was chosen against them, and my performance really made my name as a bowler.

'They put me on at the third wicket and I took 17 wickets in succession, taking the remaining seven in the first innings and the whole 10 in the second innings; and when I came down to Sydney I had no difficulty in getting into a good club.

'I go more for the wickets than for the catches. In bowling I have always made it a point to commence to a new man with a view of finding his weak points, and then go for him with a "break". With the wickets we have now on our best grounds it is a nonsense to suppose you can get a man out by straight or fast bowling. 'If you send them dead for the wicket you are knocked about all over the place.

'There is the "off theory" that everybody talks so much about just now. For myself I don't believe in it, for a good batsman may let every ball pass. The object, of course, is to induce him to try and hit them, and give someone an easy catch. In breaking a ball your eye must be very true; you must pitch it exactly in the right spot, and keep it up time after time, and to do this you must have energy and endurance.

'As a bowler I must be as good

C. T. B. Turner: 'the knack, the gift'.

at the finish as at the start and, so that I can keep all my strength, I never bowl in practice. You do not want it if you are in form and take care of yourself.

'I first of all find out the weak points of the batsman, and then look out for the soft spots of the ground.

'I do not make an examination of the ground before I start bowling in order to find the soft places. No; I let the ball do it all. It doesn't take very long … in an over or so you can find out all you want to.

'A great many people believe that we put the twist on the ball with our hands. I once thought there was something in that, and for a long time I tried in every way that was possible, and the result of this work was only to convince me that it could not be done. The break must be got after the ball touches the ground.

'Six balls an over? I like it, and wish they would adopt it here. Men who tell you it wearies the bowler don't know what they are talking about. I suppose I ought to know, for I do as much as anyone at it, and I am no more tired of a match with six balls to the over than with four.

'It has a wonderful tendency to shorten the game; and as one who believes that cricket is the best sport, I am naturally anxious to see it go ahead again, and this shortening I find increases interest tenfold.'

Bonnor: colonial Hercules

George Giffen wrote of George Bonnor that he was not only 'one of the most interesting figures which have strutted the cricket stage' but one of the finest specimens of manhood I have met.

'When, exerting all the strength of that Herculean frame, he smote the bowling, it was a sight for the gods … He was born to be a hitter; he had a distinct mission as a demoraliser of bowlers and fielders, and if he had adhered to the strict terms of his unwritten commission he would have made a great many more runs.'

As it was, Bonnor, all 6 ft 6 in and 16 stone of him, played 17 Tests, made 512 runs at a mediocre average for a top batsman of the day, of 17. By comparison Billy Murdoch averaged 32 in 18 Tests, and Percy McDonnell 36 in 19.

He was born in Bathurst, and his reputation from his big hits in country cricket matches brought him to the city and on to London in the Australian team in 1880, at the age of 25. He did not distinguish himself in the only Test at the Oval, scoring only 2 and 16 but he went out to the famous catch of Fred Grace.

With his big blond beard he became known as the 'Australian Giant' and the 'Colonial Hercules'.

On the 1882 tour he cracked 66 in half an hour against the Cambridge Players Past and Present, and against I Zingari he got 122 not out, including 20 in one over.

But he had a weakness – he wanted to be a batsman in the correct mould.

George Giffen wrote: 'We often wished that Bonnor would not get the idea into his head that he could, if he chose, bat as scientifically as anyone.

'This was generally after he had heard someone say: "Oh, Bonnor is nothing but a slogger." It was almost painful to watch a giant of six feet and a half playing the barndoor game when we knew that if he chose and got going, he could pulverise the bowling and disorganise the field.'

His major problem, which he shared with many Australian batsmen, was that he couldn't 'hit' on wet English wickets. On his four tours he averaged about four in Tests. By contrast in the 1882–83 series in Australia he averaged 31, and in the 1884–85 series he averaged 39.

Bonnor: 'sight for the gods'.

He made his debut in intercolonial first class cricket for Victoria in December 1881 and transferred to NSW in February 1885 after the controversy over the 1884 Australian side in the dispute over payment.

Bonnor's career for NSW stuttered to a conclusion. After 1886, he played just two games – in 1889, and 1891. He made five first class hundreds.

Bonnor was something of a humorist. In a team photo in 1884 the rest of the players are in cricket attire, but the handsome Bonnor is resplendent in a morning suit and a top hat, gazing at the camera with calm disdain.

Bonnor could throw the ball enormous distances. He bet a passenger 100 sovereigns he could throw a ball 100 yards on the day of team's arrival in England in 1882. He managed 104 yards.

Other feats included a hit at the Oval in 1884 that cleared the pavilion and went through the club secretary's window; a blow in Melbourne in 1881 that cleared the fence and the skittle alley and went into the Richmond paddock.

Bonnor's only Test century came in Sydney, when he made 128 in the fourth Test in 1884–85 and was the architect of a win that kept the series alive. He was still clouting the bowlers around the backblocks for many years after he retired from Test and first class cricket, making 267 for his home town Bathurst 'in a couple of hours' in a match against the Oriental Cricket Club in April 1890.

FIRST TEST 1888 ENGLAND v AUSTRALIA
Lord's Cricket Ground, London. July 16, 17, 1888.
Toss: Australia. Australia won by 61 runs.

AUSTRALIA
AC Bannerman c Grace b Lohmann	.0	b Peel	.0
PS McDonnell (c) c O'Brien b Peel	.22	b Lohmann	.1
GHS Trott c Lohmann b Peel	.0	b Lohmann	.3
GJ Bonnor b Lohmann	.6	c Lohmann b Peel	.8
JM Blackham (+) b Briggs	.22	run out	.1
SMJ Woods c Gunn b Briggs	.18	c Grace b Peel	.3
CTB Turner c Lohmann b Peel	.3	c Grace b Briggs	.12
JD Edwards not out	.21	c Sherwin b Lohmann	.0
AH Jarvis c Lohmann b Peel	.3 (11)	c Barnes b Peel	.4
J Worrall c Abel b Briggs	.2	b Lohmann	.4
JJ Ferris c Sherwin b Steel	.14 (9)	not out	.20
EXTRAS (B 5)	.5	(B 3, LB 1)	.4
TOTAL	.116		.60

FOW 1st Inns: 0 3 28 32 65 76 76 79 82 116
FOW 2nd Inns: 1 1 13 15 18 18 18 42 49 60

Bowling: *First Innings*: Lohmann 20-9-28-2, Peel 21-7-36-4, Briggs 21-8-26-3, Barnes 6-0-17-0, Steel 3.2-2-4-1. *Second Innings*: Lohmann 14-4-33-4, Peel 10.2-3-14-4, Briggs 4-1-9-1, Steel 1-1-0-0.

ENGLAND
WG Grace c Woods b Ferris	.10	c Bannerman b Ferris	.24
R Abel b Ferris	.3	c Bonnor b Ferris	.8
W Barnes c Jarvis b Turner	.3 (9)	st Blackham b Ferris	.1
GA Lohmann lbw Turner	.2 (10)	st Blackham b Ferris	.0
WW Read st Blackham b Turner	.4 (4)	b Turner	.3
TC O'Brien b Turner	.0 (5)	b Turner	.4
R Peel run out	.8 (3)	b Turner	.4
AG Steel (c) st Blackham b Turner	.3 (6)	not out	.10
W Gunn c Blackham b Ferris	.2 (7)	b Ferris	.8
J Briggs b Woods	.17 (8)	b Turner	.0
M Sherwin (+) not out	.0	c Ferris b Turner	.0
EXTRAS (LB 1)	.1		.0
TOTAL	.53		.62

FOW 1st Inns: 5 14 18 22 22 22 26 35 49 53
FOW 2nd Inns: 29 34 38 39 44 55 56 57 57 62

Bowling: *First Innings*: Turner 25-9-27-5, Ferris 21-13-19-3, Woods 4-2-6-1. *Second Innings*: Turner 24-8-36-5, Ferris 23-11-26-5.

Umpires: FH Farrands & CK Pullin

SECOND TEST 1888 ENGLAND v AUSTRALIA
Kennington Oval, London. August 13, 14, 1888.
Toss: Australia. England won by an innings & 117 runs.

AUSTRALIA
AC Bannerman c Lohmann b Barnes	.13	b Barnes	.5
PS McDonnell (c) c Lohmann b Peel	.0	b Peel	.32
GHS Trott b Briggs	.13	st Wood b Peel	.4
GJ Bonnor b Briggs	.0	c Wood b Barnes	.5
JD Edwards b Lohmann	.26	c Read b Barnes	.0
AH Jarvis b Briggs	.5 (9)	b Peel	.8
SMJ Woods run out	.0	c Abel b Barnes	.7
CTB Turner b Briggs	.0	b Peel	.18
JM Blackham (+) b Briggs	.0 (10)	c Lohmann b Barnes	.4
J Worrall c Grace b Barnes	.8 (11)	not out	.0
JJ Ferris not out	.13 (6)	run out	.16
EXTRAS (B 1, LB 1)	.2	(LB 1)	.1
TOTAL	.80		.100

FOW 1st Inns: 0 22 22 40 49 49 50 50 63 80
FOW 2nd Inns: 34 38 43 45 62 62 72 89 98 100

Bowling: *First Innings*: Lohmann 29.3-21-21-1, Peel 8-4-14-1, Briggs 37-24-25-5, Barnes 16-9-18-2. *Second Innings*: Lohmann 6-4-11-0, Peel 28.2-13-49-4, Briggs 6-3-7-0, Barnes 29-16-32-5.

ENGLAND
WG Grace (c) c Edwards b Turner	.1
J Shuter b Turner	.28
G Ulyett c Blackham b Turner	.0
WW Read b Turner	.18
R Abel run out	.70
W Barnes c Worrall b Turner	.62
FH Sugg b Turner	.31
R Peel b Woods	.25
J Briggs b Woods	.0
GA Lohmann not out	.62
H Wood (+) c Bannerman b Ferris	.8
EXTRAS (B 6, LB 4, W 2)	.12
TOTAL	.317

FOW 1st Inns: 2 6 46 53 165 191 241 242 259 317

Bowling: *First Innings*: Turner 60-24-112-6, Ferris 35.2-15-73-1, Trott 7-2-25-0, Woods 32-10-80-2, Worrall 4-1-15-0.

Umpires: RP Carpenter & FH Farrands

THIRD TEST 1888 ENGLAND v AUSTRALIA
Old Trafford, Manchester. August 30, 31, 1888.
Toss: England. England won by an innings & 21 runs.

ENGLAND
WG Grace (c) c Bonnor b Turner	.38
R Abel b Turner	.0
G Ulyett b Turner	.0
WW Read b Turner	.19
W Barnes b Ferris	.24
FH Sugg b Woods	.24
W Gunn lbw Turner	.15
R Peel lbw Ferris	.11
J Briggs not out	.22
GA Lohmann run out	.0
R Pilling (+) c Bonnor b Woods	.17
EXTRAS (B 2)	.2
TOTAL	.172

FOW 1st Inns: 0 6 58 59 96 115 127 135 136 172

Bowling: *First Innings*: Ferris 40-20-49-2, Turner 55-21-86-5, Woods 18.1-6-35-2.

AUSTRALIA
PS McDonnell (c) c Grace b Peel	.15	b Lohmann	.0
AC Bannerman b Peel	.1	c Grace b Peel	.0
GHS Trott st Pilling b Peel	.17	run out	.0
GJ Bonnor run out	.5	c Grace b Peel	.0
JD Edwards b Peel	.0 (9)	c Grace b Peel	.1
CTB Turner b Peel	.0 (8)	b Briggs	.26
SMJ Woods c Read b Briggs	.4	b Lohmann	.0
JM Blackham (+) c Read b Lohmann	.15 (5)	b Lohmann	.5
JJ Lyons c Lohmann b Peel	.22 (6)	b Briggs	.32
J Worrall not out	.0 (11)	not out	.0
JJ Ferris not out	.0 (10)	c Abel b Peel	.3
EXTRAS (B 2)	.2	(B 2, LB 1)	.3
TOTAL	.81		.70

FOW 1st Inns: 16 32 35 39 39 43 45 81 81 81
FOW 2nd Inns: 0 0 1 7 7 7 55 56 70 70

Bowling: *First Innings*: Peel 26.2-17-31-7, Lohmann 17-9-31-1, Briggs 9-4-17-1. *Second Innings*: Peel 16-4-37-4, Lohmann 8-3-20-3, Briggs 7.1-2-10-2.

Umpires: FH Farrands & CK Pullin

Australian Averages

1888 ENGLAND v AUSTRALIA

AUSTRALIA	M	Inn	NO	Runs	H.S	Avrge	Ct	St	Overs	Mds	Runs	Wkt	Avrge
Bannerman, AC	3	6	-	19	13	3.17	2	-	-	-	-	-	-
Blackham, JM	3	6	-	47	22	7.83	2	4	-	-	-	-	-
Bonnor, GJ	3	6	-	24	8	4.00	3	-	-	-	-	-	-
Edwards, JD	3	6	1	48	26	9.60	1	-	-	-	-	-	-
Ferris, JJ	3	6	3	66	20*	22.00	1	-	119.2	59	167	11	15.18
Jarvis, AH	2	4	-	20	8	5.00	1	-	-	-	-	-	-
Lyons, JJ	1	2	-	54	32	27.00	-	-	-	-	-	-	-
McDonnell, PS	3	6	-	70	32	11.67	-	-	-	-	-	-	-
Trott, GHS	3	6	-	37	17	6.17	-	-	7.0	2	25	-	-
Turner, CTB	3	6	-	59	26	9.83	-	-	164.0	62	261	21	12.43
Woods, SMJ	3	6	-	32	18	5.33	1	-	54.1	18	121	5	24.20
Worrall, J	3	6	2	14	8	3.50	1	-	4.0	1	15	-	-

English Averages

1888 ENGLAND v AUSTRALIA

ENGLAND	M	Inn	NO	Runs	H.S	Avrge	Ct	St	Overs	Mds	Runs	Wkt	Avrge
Abel, R	3	4	-	81	70	20.25	3	-	-	-	-	-	-
Barnes, W	3	4	-	90	62	22.50	1	-	51.0	25	67	7	9.57
Briggs, J	3	4	1	39	22*	13.00	-	-	84.1	42	94	12	7.83
Grace, WG	3	4	-	73	38	18.25	8	-	-	-	-	-	-
Gunn, W	2	3	-	25	15	8.33	1	-	-	-	-	-	-
Lohmann, GA	3	4	1	64	62*	21.33	8	-	94.3	50	144	11	13.09
O'Brien, TC	1	2	-	4	4	2.00	1	-	-	-	-	-	-
Peel, R	3	4	-	48	25	12.00	-	-	110.2	48	181	24	7.54
Pilling, R	1	1	-	17	17	17.00	-	1	-	-	-	-	-
Read, WW	3	4	-	44	19	11.00	3	-	-	-	-	-	-
Sherwin, M	1	2	1	0	0*	0.00	2	-	-	-	-	-	-
Shuter, J	1	1	-	28	28	28.00	-	-	-	-	-	-	-
Steel, AG	1	2	1	13	10*	13.00	-	-	4.2	3	4	1	4.00
Sugg, FH	2	2	-	55	31	27.50	-	-	-	-	-	-	-
Ulyett, G	2	2	-	0	0	0.00	-	-	-	-	-	-	-
Wood, H	1	1	-	8	8	8.00	1	1	-	-	-	-	-

Official bodies wrestle for supremacy

The Melbourne Cricket Ground, resplendent with its new grandstand, with an additional storey added at the cost of £15,000.

Melbourne, Jan. 8. The Victorian Cricketers' Association has passed a motion condemning the Melbourne Cricket Club for arranging matches with the NSWCA this season, despite the agreement supposedly reached last season that the Cricketers' Association would organise the home and away games.

This is despite the Association having just £168 in funds after last season, and as a consequence an inability to organize the matches.

The Association has requested matches with South Australia and NSW, and SA agreed to play one match rather than two, the NSWCA secretary Dave Gregory would only agree to the agreed two matches.

This is the latest quarrel in the long-running dispute over which body – the Association or the MCC – would control Victorian inter-colonial matches.

The Association has banned member clubs from playing with the MCC, and the MCC has set down two matches against NSW for later this month, making an agreement with the NSWCA to organise a five-year program of matches. In Melbourne, the MCC has managed to arrange matches against a number of city and country clubs, including Association members Carlton, South Melbourne and St Kilda in defiance of the 'invidious lead put out to them' by the Association.

It was clear to observers in Melbourne that on both the inter-colonial and local level, this dispute over control of cricket is having a deleterious effect.

For cricket to progress in Victoria, and indeed in Australia, many observers feel that there will need to be the formation of bodies working in harmony under the umbrella of a body responsible for Australian cricket.

1888 Australian XI woes continue

Adelaide, Nov. 26. The dismal recent form of the 1888 Australians continued when they played a match against South Australia on their return from England. They showed little spirit as they lost by eight wickets.

The pitch was somewhat damp, which must have been disheartening for the Australians who would have liked something hard and dry for a change.

For South Australia, George Giffen left no doubts that he would have been a very useful tourist, taking 5/54 and 4/72 and himself knocking up 35 of the 49 runs required to win the match.

'Terror' Turner showed some form with the bat, but was lethargic with the ball.

Throwing the ball is a minor sport

Melbourne, April 13. News that a Norman Warden threw a cricket ball 116 yards at Newington College has brought a number of deeds out of the woodwork.

Mr Warden's throw is good, but not the best.

One of Spalding's American base-ballers, Ed Crane, threw a cricket ball 128 yards 10 1/2 inches at the MCG in January.

More remarkable still is a report, verified by David Scott, of Boyle and Scott in Melbourne, that 16 years ago an Aboriginal cricketer named Billy threw the ball a measured 140 yards at the town of Clermont.

Billy is recalled as an astounding fieldsman with an astonishing throwing arm.

Vics break drought against NSW

Sydney, Jan. 30. After six straight losses to NSW, Victoria won a remarkable victory after having been forced to follow on.

The first match had been postponed from Boxing Day because of the 'muddling policy' of the Victorian Cricketers' Association and was organised by the MCC.

Victoria lost this match largely because of the bowling of J. J. Ferris. who took 3/46 and 6/62 and – and, some would say, a couple of rough decisions from NSW umpire Charles Bannerman.

The return match was a somewhat different story.

After following-on, Victoria finished just 75 runs ahead, but John Trumble took 6/33 to rout the New South Welshmen for 63.

Giffen refuses to leave crease

Adelaide, Dec. 17. In the SA v Victoria match of sensations, George Giffen's refusal to leave the crease after he was given out takes the cake.

On 9, facing Hugh Trumble's off-breaks, he survived an appeal for lbw when the Victorian players noticed that a bail was lying on the ground. They then appealed for hit wicket, which the umpire at the bowler's end upheld.

Giffen stayed put, saying that the ball was dead when the appeal was made.

Arguments ensued, the laws were produced, and Victorian captain Jack Blackham threatened a walk-off when it was decided to continue the match under protest to avoid friction and for the sake of the public.

Giffen added another 76 runs before being bowled by Trumble. SA made 282, Trumble 7/89, in reply to Victoria's 320. Victoria then made 221, Giffen 7/104.

South Australia, needing 259 to win on a wearing wicket, nearly got there thanks to a brilliant 134 from Jack Lyons. But Trumble's 8/110 was the decisive factor. Victoria won the match, a thriller, by 12 runs.

NSW team tours New Zealand

A cricket Christmas postcard.

Sydney, Jan. 31. J. Corbett Davis sought the permission of the NSWCA to take a team to New Zealand for five weeks but was told that his team 'could not be recognised as a representative team of the colony'.

However, under the captaincy of Joe Davis, no relation, the team played seven matches, winning six with the other a draw.

The only disturbance was at the Basin Reserve where Wellington captain Billy McGirr took exception to the umpiring of J. Corbett Davis. Joe asked Davis to leave his post when he was informed by McGirr that if the game was abandoned, the NSW side would not get paid.

Tour selection difficulties

Dr Jack Barrett: for England.

Sydney, March 27. Persuading Billy Murdoch to captain the 1890 Australian tour was the least of sole selector Harry Boyle's problems.

He thought he had George Giffen's agreement that he would tour if 'Terror' Turner and J.J. Ferris were going, but despite their selection, Giffen has pulled out, as has Alick Bannnerman. Harry Moses declined because of employment problems.

However, some of the new batsmen show promise to go with Turner's and Ferris' guile and experience.

In particular, left-hander Jack Barrett, young Syd Gregory and Percie Charlton show promise, as does John Trumble's younger brother Hugh.

SA loses its first Sydney encounter

Sydney, Feb. 18. On a damp pitch made even trickier for South Australia by some sunshine, George Giffen won the toss and put NSW in to bat in the inaugural first class match between the two colonies.

Sam Jones made an excellent 68 against the moving ball and NSW totalled 240.

With the exception of Giffen's 52 in the first innings and Jack Lyons 63 in the second, SA were not able to handle the penetration and variety of the NSW bowling.

They were all out for 155 and 148, NSW knocking the 66 needed in two hours after the fourth day was lost to rain.

Kenny Burn in selection blunder

Kenny Burn: the wrong man.

Sydney, April 24. In a tremendous selection muddle, Sydney Deane, the young NSW stumper, travelled with the Australian party aboard the *Liguria* from Sydney to Melbourne in the expectation that he would be among the 1890 Australians to England.

On arrival, the hapless Deane found that the Tasmanian batsman Kenny Burn was to fill the last place in the squad, even though he had never kept wickets in his life.

Apparently selector Harry Boyle was told by the great gloveman Jack Blackham that he had heard good things about Burn of Tasmania, but the Burn who is a 'keeper is a different person to lucky Kenny.

Kenny Burn, however, is by no means a complete unknown. He has a great variety of strokes. In the field – if not behind the stumps – he is above the average.

QUICK SINGLES

Hatchet buried. The Victorian Cricketers' Association rescinded its motion to expel the Melbourne Cricket Club on October 10, and the MCC has in return 'transferred engagements with the NSWCA to the VCA with the consent of all concerned.'

MCC breaks new ground. The MCC has taken over the Warehouseman's Ground in St Kilda Rd Melbourne to use when the Melbourne Cricket Ground was required for first class games.

Croweaters invited. NSWCA secretary Dave Gregory writes to SACA secretary John Creswell on November 12 with South Australia's first invitation to play NSW. Terms are agreed on December 3.

Tasmania trounced. Tasmania staged its first first class match since 1872–73 and

was humbled by Victoria by an innings and 147 runs. Tasmania's cause was not helped by two batsmen arriving too late to bat on the second day. Trott took 6/10 in Tasmania's 39 all out, and 6/81 in their 152.

NSW squares series. After Victoria 'Trumbled' to an 8 wicket win in December, Victoria were 'Terrored' in the return match in January by four wickets. Hugh Trumble's 10/107 was matched by 'Terror' Turner's 11/168 . Sam Jones hit an even 100 before he was 'Trotted'.

Suspensions mooted. The Victorian Cricketer's Association passed a motion at its February meeting, which had a direct relation to the George Giffen affair. It decided that 'if any cricketer refuses to obey the rules, and to concede to the judgement of the umpire, he might be disqualified for a particular term.'

Cashed-up. Receipts from the 1887 NSW

v Victoria match at the MCG were just £464 and the state of cricket was bewailed; this year's fixture amounted to a splendid £977. *Cricket* says: 'The whirligig of time has speedily brought its revenges.'

Queensland caned. The XV of Queensland played NSW in March and were beaten by an innings and 111 runs, but are showing improvement. They then played the MCC and lost on the first innings. Arthur Coningham stands out for Queensland.

Junior cricket. The *Age* reports that Mr N. Batchelor of the Capulet Club, and the cornerstone of junior cricket as organiser of Boyle and Scott's Cup in Victoria, is expected to throw down the gauntlet to the juniors of England when he arrives with the 1890 Australian team. Boyle and Scott juniors fought a creditable draw with Shrewsbury's English team at North Fitzroy in 1888–89.

Easy for England as standard rises

Scenes at the Lord's Test, with final cheers for England's victory, and for Dr W. G. Grace, who was England's top scorer.

Manchester, Aug. 27. The scheduled third Test match has been abandoned without a ball being bowled after incessant rain in Manchester.

This is perhaps just as well for the out-of-form and out-of-sorts Australian team, which has been well beaten in the two previous Tests at Lord's and the Oval, and was the first Australian team to play for the month of June without winning a single match.

Again the Australians have shown themselves to be unable to handle the softer, damper pitches of a wet English summer.

The first Test at Lord's did have its remarkable features – Jack Lyons, opening with Charlie Turner, terrorised the English bowlers with the quickest 50 on record – in 36 minutes, Turner caught and bowled W. G. Grace for a duck and then John Barrett, opening the

Australian second innings, 'carried his bat' for 67 – the first time a Test opener has done so.

In addition, there were no byes conceded in the whole match – another first at Test level.

England won a decisive victory by seven wickets, thanks to Grace's 75 not out.

The second Test played at the Oval produced a slightly better performance – by the bowlers at least – despite the fact that it was all over in two days on a wet pitch.

Ulyett and Peel, two prominent players in the first Test, were required to play for their county, Yorkshire, rather than for England, but 'Nutty' Martin, called up for his first match, destroyed Australia with six wickets in each innings, finishing with 12/102, a record on debut.

The medium-paced left-arm bowler is on the ground staff at

Kent, and his work indicated the depth of English cricket.

Only Harry Trott looked likely to make runs on the difficult wicket, with 39 and 25 out of totals of 92 and 102. England's batting against Jack Ferris, Charlie Turner and surprise packet Percie Charlton's target was small after Australia's two low scores.

However, the match retained its tension to the end. England lost 8/95 on the way to winning – and John Barrett had a slim chance to win the game when he fielded the ball close to the stumps.

His wild return missed everything and resulted in two overthrows rather than a run-out, when scores were level.

Harry Trott also dropped a chance from Grace, which would have given the great man a 'pair'. Grace made 16. Australia still has several matches to play.

Drinking men enjoy tour

A humiliating procession. The returning batsman's view of the Lord's pavilion.

Sydney, Nov. 11. The 1890 Australian team returned home to a less than enthusiastic welcome, having lost the series 2–0.

The cool reception, by press and public alike, is a marked contrast with the triumphant returns of past seasons, when our cricketers were seen as invincible, and there has been boastful talk of 'bearding the Englishman in his den'.

The team left captain Billy Murdoch behind, together with his reputation for tolerating an easy living, but hard drinking, tour. Murdoch had a good tour, but a miserable time with the bat when he was wanted, scoring only 36 runs in four Test innings.

Together with reports of fighting between team members – manager Harry Boyle and the powerfully built Jack Lyons have been particularly mentioned in dispatches – are other factors which may have resulted in some of the dismal batting performances.

As the *Bulletin* put it – 'The Australian cricketer in England, batting the day after a banquet, sees at least two balls approaching. One is dead on the wicket. He smites at the other and sees four bails flying about, two wicketkeepers looking the other way, two prostrate and two erect stumps.

'Then he retires to two pavilions, makes 22 excuses, and another cable about bad luck and wet wickets is dispatched.

'The Australians always bat on a wet wicket after a banquet.'

Perhaps it was at one of these convivial banquets that discussion over the forthcoming English tour took place between Harry Boyle and Lord Sheffield.

Much will depend on W. G. Grace's availability, and concentration by the Australians on cricket and team-play, rather than the social aspects that accompany tours 'home'.

Ceylonese stopover

Colombo, Oct. 15. After a tour of seven weeks and 10 or 11 matches proposed to the 1890 Australians by the Johannesburg Wanderers Club 'fell through', the weary tourists chose to stop over in Ceylon rather than Bombay for a cricket match.

The 1884 Australian team had played a Ceylon XVIII, and won quite easily. But cricket on the beautiful island has come on apace, and the Australian XI, this time against a Ceylon XI, only managed a draw. This was despite leading by 92 on the first innings and seeming comfortably in charge of affairs.

Harry Trott made 52 and Syd Gregory 41. Tom Kelaart took 3/42 for Ceylon.

An early highlight of the season: at the Earl of Sheffield's home.

Blackham – Prince of wicketkeepers

John McCarthy 'Jack' Blackham was born on 11 May 1854 in the inner Melbourne suburb of North Fitzroy.

He played his early cricket with Carlton, where he made an accidental debut as a wicketkeeper in the seconds in the early 1870s. Small and dark-bearded, with intense, hawk-like eyes, he was a quiet and good humoured man off the field, working as a bank clerk, but living for the cut and thrust of the cricket field.

He was quickly noticed by South Melbourne captain and Victorian player (and writer for the *Australasian* under the name Censor) John Conway, and lured South with the expectation of playing regularly in the firsts.

Blackham made his debut for Victoria on 26 December 1874 against NSW at the MCG, taking a catch and making a stumping in the first innings and two catches in the second innings, and hitting 32 and 5 in a losing cause. Fred Spofforth made his debut for NSW in this match.

Blackham eventually played 45 matches for Victoria, taking 51 catches and making 39 stumpings.

In addition, he played 35 Test matches for Australia, beginning with the very first one in March 1877.

His participation in this match caused Spofforth to make himself unavailable, because he wanted teammate Billy Murdoch to keep to him.

The selection of Blackham as wicketkeeper, and in the next match, of Murdoch as a batsman, and Spofforth as the demon bowler was proved correct.

Blackham was described in an English magazine before his sixth tour in 1890 as 'the greatest wicketkeeper the world has seen'.

It was Blackham who elevated wicketkeeping to a higher plane of skill. It was he who was first good enough to dispense with the then traditional fielding position of long stop, and who also 'stood up' close to the stumps to fast bowling – even Fred Spofforth's.

The weekly magazine *Cricket* in 1882 wrote 'he stands up without the slightest fear, no matter how fast the bowling.

'There is no pretense or show about his keeping, but he takes every kind of ball with the greatest ease, and on the leg side he is surer than anyone we have ever seen.'

In his book *With Bat and Ball* the South Australian all-rounder

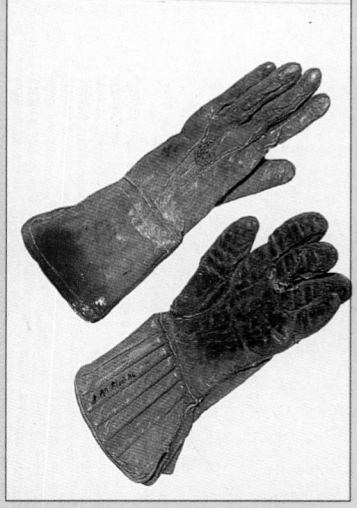

John McCarthy Blackham's gloves, now on display with a fine collection of cricket memorabilia at the MCC Museum, Melbourne.

George Giffen said: 'One could not help admiring him as he stood behind the stumps at a critical period of a game. With eyes keen as a hawk, and regardless of knocks, he would take the fastest bowling with marvellous dexterity, and woe betide the batsman who even so much as lifted the heel of his back foot as he played forward.'

Blackham captained Australia in six Tests, in 1891–92 and 1893, for two wins, two draws and two losses. He captained Victoria up until 1895, showing efficiency behind the stumps, marshalling his forces well and hitting many a saving innings with his swashbuckling style.

In his last Test, the first of 1894–95, Blackham's thumb was split, when as captain made he made his highest Test score of 74, from Australia's 586. His old teammate from the very first Test, Charles Bannerman, was umpire.

In all, Blackham played 35 Test matches – then a record – for 37 caught and 24 stumped, made 800 runs at 15.69 and conceded 389 byes.

Blackham's last Shield game was a week later against NSW when his thumb was struck again, and it became apparent that the injury was not going to heal while he continued to keep.

He never played first class cricket again. Victor Trumper, the golden future of Australian cricket, was 12th man for NSW.

Blackham died on 28 December 1932, just two days before the Bodyline Test at the MCG in Melbourne, aged 78.

Billy Murdoch tops tour averages again

London, Sep. 30. Despite failing in the two Tests played, Billy Murdoch headed the Australian touring averages (as against the Test averages recorded below) with 1459 runs in all matches at 23.53, highest score 158. This was the fourth time in five tours that he had achieved this feat – surely Murdoch is the best Australian batsman of his generation. Murdoch's departure from the Australian scene is regarded as a calamity.

Of the other batsmen only Dr John Barrett averaged above 20. Harry Trott, a good Test performer, was the only other century scorer with 186 and averaged 19.89.

Both Charles Turner and Jack Ferris took 215 wickets in all matches – Turner's were slightly cheaper at 12.67, Ferris 13.2.

Turner was a hundred wickets down on his return during the 1888 tour, and Ferris has decided to stay in England, following a similar 220 wicket haul to 1888.

Once again the lack of a back up bowler to Turner and Ferris proved costly on a long tour – next best was Hugh Trumble with 53 wickets at 21.47.

Kenny Burn, the accidental tourist, had 39 innings for 402 runs at 10.05. Like most of the other new selections he might be better for the experience, but he was not outstanding on tour.

Billy Murdoch: best four times.

In the Tests Jack Lyons of South Australia headed the averages on 30.50, with John Barrett on 26.67. Jack Ferris was easily the top wicket-taker with 13, well ahead of the six for his bowling partner Charles Turner.

For England the ageing but still able W. G. Grace headed the batting at 30.33, while one match was enough for Frank Martin to be the top wicket-taker with 12.

Australian Averages

1890 ENGLAND v AUSTRALIA

AUSTRALIA	M	Inn	NO	Runs	H.S	Avrge	Ct	St	Overs	Mds	Runs	Wkt	Avrge
Barrett, JE	2	4	1	80	67*	26.67	1	-	-	-	-	-	-
Blackham, JM	2	4	-	17	10	4.25	1	2	-	-	-	-	-
Burn, EJK	2	4	-	41	19	10.25	-	-	-	-	-	-	-
Charlton, PC	2	4	-	29	11	7.25	-	-	9.0	1	24	3	8.00
Ferris, JJ	2	4	-	23	8	5.75	2	-	113.0	50	171	13	13.15
Gregory, ES	2	4	1	15	9	5.00	1	-	-	-	-	-	-
Lyons, JJ	2	4	-	122	55	30.50	-	-	40.1	13	73	5	14.60
Murdoch, WL	2	4	-	36	19	9.00	2	-	-	-	-	-	-
Trott, GHS	2	4	-	76	39	19.00	1	-	3.0	-	16	-	-
Trumble, H	2	4	2	12	6	6.00	4	-	22.0	8	45	2	22.50
Turner, CTB	2	4	-	38	24	9.50	3	-	104.0	50	159	6	26.50

English Averages

1890 ENGLAND v AUSTRALIA

ENGLAND	M	Inn	NO	Runs	H.S	Avrge	Ct	St	Overs	Mds	Runs	Wkt	Avrge
Attewell, W	1	1	1	0	0*	-	2	-	74.2	37	96	5	19.20
Barnes, W	2	3	-	19	9	6.33	4	-	12.0	5	26	2	13.00
Cranston, J	1	2	-	31	16	15.50	1	-	-	-	-	-	-
Grace, WG	2	4	1	91	75*	30.33	1	-	14.0	10	12	2	6.00
Gunn, W	2	4	-	81	34	20.25	-	-	-	-	-	-	-
Lohmann, GA	2	3	-	24	19	8.00	3	-	103.2	56	137	9	15.22
MacGregor, G	2	3	1	3	2*	1.50	3	2	-	-	-	-	-
Martin, F	1	1	-	1	1	1.00	-	-	57.2	21	102	12	8.50
Peel, R	1	1	-	16	16	16.00	-	-	67.0	34	87	6	14.50
Read, JM	2	4	1	90	35	30.00	-	-	-	-	-	-	-
Read, WW	2	4	-	21	13	5.25	-	-	-	-	-	-	-
Sharpe, JW	1	2	2	7	5*	-	1	-	15.0	8	18	2	9.00
Shrewsbury, A	2	4	-	30	13	7.50	-	-	-	-	-	-	-
Ulyett, G	1	1	-	74	74	74.00	-	-	9.0	5	11	1	11.00

FIRST TEST 1890 ENGLAND v AUSTRALIA
Lord's Cricket Ground, London. July 21, 22, 23, 1890.
Toss: Australia. England won by 7 wkts.

AUSTRALIA

JJ Lyons b Barnes	55 (4)	c Attewell b Peel ... 33
CTB Turner b Attewell	24	lbw Peel ... 2
WL Murdoch (c) c & b Attewell	9 (5)	b Lohmann ... 19
JE Barrett c Grace b Ulyett	9 (1)	not out ... 67
GHS Trott run out	12 (3)	b Peel ... 0
ES Gregory b Attewell	0	c Lohmann b Barnes ... 9
PC Charlton st MacGregor b Peel	6	lbw Grace ... 2
JM Blackham (+) b Peel	5	c Barnes b Grace ... 10
JJ Ferris b Attewell	8	lbw Lohmann ... 8
EJK Burn st MacGregor b Peel	0 (11)	c MacGregor b Attewell ... 19
H Trumble not out	1 (10)	c Barnes b Lohmann ... 5
EXTRAS (LB 3)	3	(LB 2) ... 2
TOTAL	132	176

FOW 1st Inns: 66 82 93 109 111 113 120 131 131 132
FOW 2nd Inns: 6 8 48 84 106 109 119 136 142 176

Bowling: *First Innings*: Lohmann 21-10-43-0, Peel 24-11-28-3, Attewell 32-15-42-4, Barnes 6-2-16-1, Ulyett 3-3-0-1. *Second Innings*: Lohmann 29-19-28-3, Peel 43-23-59-3, Attewell 42.2-22-54-1, Barnes 6-3-10-1, Ulyett 6-2-11-0, Grace 14-10-12-2.

ENGLAND

WG Grace (c) c & b Turner	0	not out ... 75
A Shrewsbury st Blackham b Ferris	4	lbw Ferris ... 13
W Gunn run out	14	c & b Ferris ... 34
WW Read c & b Ferris	1	b Trumble ... 13
JM Read b Lyons	34	not out ... 2
G Ulyett b Lyons	74	
R Peel c & b Trumble	16	
W Barnes b Lyons	9	
GA Lohmann c & b Lyons	19	
G MacGregor (+) b Lyons	0	
W Attewell not out	0	
EXTRAS (LB 2)	2	... 0
TOTAL	173	3 for 137

FOW 1st Inns: 0 14 20 20 92 133 147 162 166 173
FOW 2nd Inns: 27 101 135

Bowling: *First Innings*: Turner 35-17-53-1, Ferris 40-17-55-2, Trott 3-0-16-0, Lyons 20.1-7-30-5, Trumble 12-7-17-1. *Second Innings*: Turner 22-12-31-0, Ferris 25-11-42-2, Lyons 20-6-43-0, Trumble 8-1-21-1.

Umpires: A Hill & CK Pullin

SECOND TEST 1890 ENGLAND v AUSTRALIA
Kennington Oval, London. August 11, 12, 1890.
Toss: Australia. England won by 2 wkts.

AUSTRALIA

JJ Lyons c WW Read b Martin	13 (4)	b Martin ... 21
CTB Turner c Sharpe b Lohmann	12 (7)	b Martin ... 0
WL Murdoch (c) b Martin	2 (5)	b Lohmann ... 6
JE Barrett c Lohmann b Martin	0 (1)	b Martin ... 4
GHS Trott c MacGregor b Martin	39 (6)	c Cranston b Martin ... 25
EJK Burn c MacGregor b Lohmann	7 (2)	b Martin ... 15
JM Blackham (+) b Martin	1 (8)	b Lohmann ... 1
JJ Ferris c Lohmann b Sharpe	6 (3)	b Martin ... 1
PC Charlton b Martin	10	b Sharpe ... 11
ES Gregory b Lohmann	2 (11)	not out ... 4
H Trumble not out	0 (10)	b Martin ... 6
EXTRAS	0	(B 7, LB 1) ... 8
TOTAL	92	102

FOW 1st Inns: 16 27 27 32 39 46 70 85 92 92
FOW 2nd Inns: 4 5 36 43 49 53 54 90 92 102

Bowling: *First Innings*: Martin 27-9-50-6, Lohmann 32.2-19-34-3, Sharpe 6-3-8-1. *Second Innings*: Martin 30.2-12-52-6, Lohmann 21-8-32-3, Sharpe 9-5-10-1.

ENGLAND

A Shrewsbury c Trott b Turner	4	lbw Ferris ... 9
WG Grace (c) c Trumble b Ferris	0	c Trumble b Ferris ... 16
W Gunn b Ferris	32	st Blackham b Ferris ... 1
WW Read b Turner	1	b Turner ... 6
J Cranston run out	16 (6)	c Trumble b Ferris ... 15
JM Read c Murdoch b Charlton	19 (5)	c Barrett b Turner ... 35
W Barnes c Murdoch b Charlton	5 (8)	lbw Ferris ... 5
GA Lohmann c Gregory b Ferris	3 (7)	c Blackham b Ferris ... 2
G MacGregor (+) c Turner b Ferris	1	not out ... 2
JW Sharpe not out	5	not out ... 2
F Martin c Turner b Charlton	1	
EXTRAS (B 9, LB 3, NB 1)	13	(LB 1, NB 1) ... 2
TOTAL	100	8 for 95

FOW 1st Inns: 0 10 16 55 79 90 91 93 94 100
FOW 2nd Inns: 24 25 28 32 83 83 86 93

Bowling: *First Innings*: Turner 22-12-37-2, Ferris 25-14-25-4, Trumble 2-0-7-0, Charlton 6-0-18-3. *Second Innings*: Turner 25-9-38-3, Ferris 23-8-49-5, Charlton 3-1-6-0.

Umpires: CK Pullin & J Street

SA scores mighty win over Victoria

Melbourne, Jan. 3. George Giffen has taken South Australia to a huge win over Victoria at the MCG, and put in another of those performances in which he completely dominates a match.

Giffen scored more runs and took more wickets than his team-mates combined, making 237 out of 472 and then taking 5/89 and 7/103.

He is, incidentally, the first man in Australia to take 10 wickets and make 200 runs in a match.

His innings was quite steady, taking 445 minutes and including one five and 23 fours, and he had good assistance from Jack Lyons (53), Harry Blinman (50) and Jack Noel (49).

Giffen bowled unchanged, working his slow-medium off-breaks and cutters and varying his flight and pace.

He was held up by the Victorian openers, Dick Houston (54) and William Bruce (58) in Victoria's first innings, but after that he had Victoria on the ropes.

Turner routs Vics with 15 wickets

Sydney, Jan. 29. The annual jousting between Victoria and New South Wales has brought no more spectacular effort that that of Charles 'Terror' Turner this week. He took 15 wickets in the match, as NSW won by an innings and 94 runs. The win allowed the usual 'one match all' result that keeps the pride of the Colonies intact.

Victoria had the worst of the sultry and sometimes wet weather. Its first innings started promisingly with Walters (106) going strongly. But when the rains came in mid-morning Turner showed his mastery of the sticky wicket and ran through the batsman, taking 8/74.

NSW batted with fine weather throughout and amassed 465, with Turner throwing in 70 runs to assist Harry Moses' brilliant 147.

Victorian captain John Blackham promoted himself seven places up the order to try and inspire his side and started aggressively in the second innings. He made a quick 50, but then the rains came again and Turner turned it on with 7/100.

The match in Melbourne was a more even affair, but again low scoring because of the conditions. Victoria won by 36 runs, thanks to Jim Phillips, who took 7/70 and 3/36, and Hugh Trumble, who had 6/33 in NSW second innings.

Kersosene-tin cricket rules the parks

In the parks and streets, the styles of the great players are seen in miniature.

The popularity of cricket goes well beyond the playing field. It goes out into the paddocks and streets, according to a report in the *Argus*.

'Given a bat, a ball and a tree stump, and three Victorian boys, you have a cricket match in full swing, with all rules reserved, and the styles of eminent players taken off in miniature.

'These youthful enthusiasts may always be found in their accustomed haunts, cherishing dearly the principle that to play in a small match is incomparably better than to be an inactive spectator in a great one.'

The favorite place is the reserve at Jolimont near the Melbourne Cricket Ground. Here the ground slopes in many places and is dotted with trees, but these often serve as boundary marks for miniature playing fields. Other favorite boundary marks are bicycles, coats, caps and bags placed along the imaginary boundary. Beyond that is an imaginary grandstand, packed with fancied supporters ready to cheer and whistle the heroics of the young players.

These scenes are also out in the suburban parks, and even in the streets and lanes of Melbourne. They are in country recreations reserves and may be duplicated in Hyde Park, Sydney, and beyond, around the Adelaide Oval and the cricket grounds of Brisbane and Perth, Launceston and Hobart.

But, back to Jolimont. The *Argus* reporter observes: 'Proceeding to where some 15 or 16 boys are congregated, it is ascertained that one great event of the day – Jolimonters versus Eastern Crescents – has fallen through.

'The Crescents are ... afraid, according to the Jolimonters, to come up to scratch, so the Jolimonters are going to play a match among themselves.

'From the lanky youth ... struggling bravely to look happy, in spite of his stand-up collar, to the infant just taken out of his mother's's arms and dropped into knickerbockers, you have them in all sizes.

'But what shall be done with little Slogger, who hasn't been selected for either team. 'Oh,' says the Slogger, 'I'm going to stand umpire and, taking a bat, he is as good as his word. 'Play,' he calls out in a piping treble ...'.

In another part of the reserve two rival clubs are playing. 'This is a very serious match between two rival clubs, and the cricket is high toned, boasting two umpires, four bats, sundry pads and a good deal of mystifying slang.

'As each wicket falls a yell of triumph celebrates the event. A knot of players, waiting their turn to bat, are sitting under a tree – smoking, applauding and offering remarks which are sometimes more pointed than delicate.

'The game comes to its climax, with "Wheezer" at the wicket and only one run wanted for a tie. "Play steady," shout his confederates.

'Wheezer advances to the first ball with glaring eye, raises his bat aloft, cuts a nimble caper, and strikes with such force that were he to hit the ball it would certainly be lost for ever.

'But unfortunately he does not hit it; and, sad blow to his hopes, is stumped. ... Illegally stumped, as he avers, and he loudly complains of the "hankey-doodleum" tricks of the umpire.

'The match is over, wickets are drawn, and the players go away in groups with their bats and pads tied in bundles on their shoulders.'

Lord Sheffield's trophy; and Ashes back

Lord Sheffield on tour in Australia.

W. G. Grace at the Adelaide Oval, with team-mates and umpires Carpenter and Thoms. The grand cricketer's presence attracted enormous crowds to the matches.

Sydney, Feb. 3. Australian cricket fortunes have been doubly restored – with the victory in the Sydney Test match giving Australia a 2–0 lead in the three-match series, and with the news that Lord Sheffield has donated £150 toward the advancement of colonial cricket.

At this time it is not known what form the 'advancement' will take.

Lord Sheffield's team, memorably captained by the 43-year-old colossus of cricket W. G. Grace, have swept all before them against the colonial teams before the first Test and it seemed the rather raw Australian team would be out-matched.

The opposite was the case and, paradoxically, Lord Sheffield's interest in strengthening Australian cricket, and giving the Federation movement a push, saw those particular chickens come home to roost when Australia won the exciting first Test at the MCG.

The game was played before an enormous crowd – easily the biggest seen in the colonies – with 63,352 attending over five days, the first Test match of this duration.

There was another 'first' in that this was the first Test match to use a six-ball over in Australia.

The game was evenly matched with England leading by 24 runs on the first innings.

The match turned on the last innings, when England, needing 211, succumbed to Charles Turner (5/51) and Harry Trott (3/52) to be all out for 158, giving Australia victory by 54 runs.

The second Test at the SCG proved to be one of the most exciting ever, again before a bumper crowd of 52,978 over five days.

England's George Lohmann despatched Australia's first innings with his deceptive medium pacers, taking 8/58 as Australia struggled to a meagre total of 144.

Bobby Abel carried his bat for 132 not out in England's reply of 307 and, when Australia lost Harry Trott for one, and with Harry Moses still injured it looked a foregone conclusion.

However, with a terrific innings of 134 by Jack Lyons and another barnacle by Alick Bannerman (91), Australia reached 391. Lyons did his work in 185 minutes, while Bannerman took an excruciating 451 minutes.

Then, in the last 20 minutes, Charles Turner and George Giffen despatched three Englishmen, leaving them at 3/11, and with 218 to get.

The next day only Stoddart (69), the England number four, offered any stout resistance and the tourists were out for 156 – a 72 run win for Australia. Turner (4/46) and Giffen (6/72) took all the wickets with a sustained attack of medium-pace bowling.

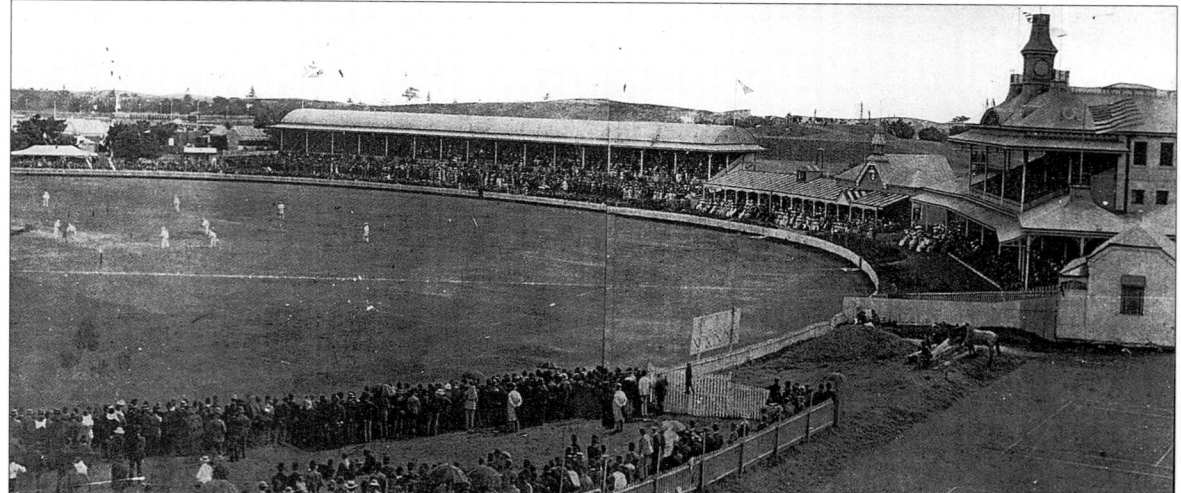

A large Saturday crowd of 20,169 gathered at Sydney Cricket Ground to watch play in the second Test match.

Grace's gamesmanship

W. G. Grace at the wicket against Victoria at the Melbourne Cricket Ground.

Adelaide, March 28. For his £3000 plus expenses for himself and family, W. G. Grace has contributed more to this tour than his 58 in the third Test.

His displays of 'unsporting' behaviour, such as in approving or not of a runner for Harry Moses, and a substitute for Robert McLeod in the second Test were not really the best kind of 'cricket'. Moses hurt his leg again early in the match, and Grace had him hobbling in the field before relenting on the second day. McLeod had to leave on news of his brother's death. When Grace was told that his replacement was a better fielder than McLeod, he demanded someone else.

Grace's attitude perhaps inspired the dredging up of an embarrassingly odious letter insulting to Australians, purportedly by Grace and printed in the *Daily Telegraph*. It was originally framed in 1874 on his first visit, and talked of 'greasy butchers' and 'scum'.

But this really did not excuse his behaviour before the third Test – not letting Jack Blackham toss with his 'lucky' penny, not attending the official lunch, grizzling about the pitch and the length of the ground.

Luckily, Grace won the toss, batted first in excellent conditions – England making 499. Then it rained from tea on the second day, all night – stopping just in time for a 'sticky' on which Australia could make just 100 and 169. It was Australia's heaviest loss against England – an innings and 230 runs.

Cricket Council meeting a success

Adelaide, March 25. A meeting at the Adelaide Town Hall of delegates from the cricket associations of South Australia, Victoria and NSW has decided to form the Australasian Cricket Council.

It was hoped that Queensland and Tasmania would soon join, and perhaps New Zealand one day as well, hence the name Australasian.

While unable to agree on a program of intercolonial matches, it was agreed that the ACC would regulate visits of overseas teams, and Australian teams to England, and oversee the Laws of Cricket in Australasia.

It would also appoint umpires for first class matches in Australia, and settle any disputes referred to it by colonial associations.

South Australia and Giffen on top

Sydney, Jan. 13. South Australia defeated NSW for the first time on a wet, then drying, wicket showing that it is the leading colonial side this season.

George Giffen made a century and took 10 wickets for the fourth time in Australia with 120 of SA's 330 and 7/122 in NSW's 215 and 5/28 in their 62.

His batting partner was another stalwart Joe Lyons, who made a hard hitting 145.

The remarkable cricketer had in SA's other match against an undermanned Victoria, made an even more extraordinary 271 of 562 and taken 9/96 in Victoria's 235 and 7/70 in the 163 second innings. Victoria defeated NSW twice in the other intercolonial games.

A fearsome duo: Terror and J.J.

Charles Thomas Biass Turner and John James Ferris formed the first great right and left-arm bowling combination in Australian cricket.

They played eight Tests together between 1886–87 and 1890, including two tours of England in 1888 and 1890.

In these matches they took 104 wickets and the other bowlers just 21. Ferris took 48 wickets at 14, and Turner 56 at 11.

Turner was born at Bathurst on 16 November 1862, and made his first class debut for NSW against Ivo Bligh's English XI on 1 December 1882, with an unpromising 1/76.

Not until Ferris played his first game against another Alfred Shaw English XI in November 1886 did Turner strike bowling form. He took 6/20 and 7/34 and was virtually unplayable. Ferris at the other end was more than useful: 4/50 and 3/49.

Both men made their Test debuts in the first Test at the SCG on 28 January 1887, bowling England out for 45 – Turner 6/15 and Ferris 4/27. Australia lost this match with seven of the eight they played. They could bowl, but the rest could not bat.

Johnnie Moyes wrote of Turner, a 'bowling immortal' that 'maybe he lacked the devilish intensity of the 'Demon' but he had all the virtues of Boyle and Palmer, with something else besides – that indefinable attribute which the gifted possess, something which cannot be explained in words, but which exists, and brings results … The art of bowling was born in Turner.'

English batsman Archie MacLaren described him as 'all life as he walked back, when with a sudden swing around, he would come trippingly to the wicket in the most cheery and, at the same time, graceful manner imaginable. His action was perfect, likewise his length, and he put heart and soul into every ball he bowled.'

Turner's was a chest-on action that allowed him to give his off-cutters some remarkable zip.

Giffen said he was a 'nasty bowler when the wicket was off-colour' and that 'the devil with which the ball, delivered at fast pace, seemed to rise from the pitch, and at the same time break from the off.'

Ferris was born in Sydney on 21 May 1867. Moyes wrote of him that 'he was left-hand, slowish, a master of length, full of courage,

J. J. Ferris: played for England, Australia and two colonies.

and under punishment had the priceless gift of being able to keep the ball right up to the batsman. He had a faster one which he hid cleverly.'

After the 1890 tour of England in which Ferris and Turner took 215 wickets each from more than 1650 overs (each!), Ferris stayed in England and played three relatively quiet seasons for Gloucestershire.

He toured South Africa for England in 1891–92, and took 235 wickets including 13 in the only Test played, said by W. G. Grace to be a performance 'remarkable, even for Ferris'.

Ferris then lost form, played for Gloucestershire and, on his return to Australia, played one game for SA in February 1896 making a duck and taking 0/3, and then two games for NSW in December 1897 and January 1898. He enlisted, and died in Durban, South Africa, during the Boer War.

Turner went on to play a total of 17 Tests, the last in 1894–95 at the SCG when he took 3/18 and 4/33 in an Australian win. Surprisingly he was dropped for the fifth Test in favour of Tom McKibbin who failed to perform and Australia lost the match.

Turner declined a belated invitation to tour in 1896, and played his second-last game for NSW in January 1897. McKibbin took 13 wickets, and Turner one.

He was actively involved in coaching in NSW after his retirement and played one last first class match – a NSW v The Rest benefit for the Terror himself at the SCG in January 1910. 10,000 people watched and raised £331 for Turner.

He died on 1 January 1944, at Manly.

FIRST TEST 1891-92 AUSTRALIA v ENGLAND
Melbourne Cricket Ground, Melbourne. January 1, 2, 4, 5, 6, 1892.
Toss: Australia. Australia won by 54 runs.

AUSTRALIA

AC Bannerman c Read b Sharpe	45	c Grace b Sharpe	41
JJ Lyons c Grace b Peel	19	c Abel b Briggs	51
G Giffen lbw Peel	2	b Attewell	1
W Bruce b Sharpe	57	c Lohmann b Sharpe	40
H Donnan b Sharpe	9 (9)	c & b Lohmann	2
H Moses c Lohmann b Sharpe	23	run out	15
GHS Trott c MacGregor b Sharpe	6	lbw Attewell	23
RW McLeod b Sharpe	14	b Peel	31
ST Callaway b Attewell	21 (10)	not out	13
CTB Turner b Peel	29 (5)	c Peel b Lohmann	19
JM Blackham (c+) not out	4	c MacGregor b Peel	0
EXTRAS (B 5, LB 6)	11		0
TOTAL	240		236

FOW 1st Inns: 32 36 123 136 136 148 164 191 232 240
FOW 2nd Inns: 66 67 120 152 152 182 197 210 236 236

Bowling: *First Innings*: Sharpe 51-20-84-6, Peel 43-23-54-3, Attewell 21.1-11-28-1, Lohmann 28-14-40-0, Briggs 3-1-13-0, Stoddart 5-2-10-0. *Second Innings*: Sharpe 54-25-81-2, Peel 16.5-7-25-2, Lohmann 39-15-53-2, Attewell 61-32-51-2, Briggs 21-9-26-1.

ENGLAND

WG Grace (c) b McLeod	50	c Bannerman b Turner	25
R Abel b McLeod	32 (5)	c Blackham b Turner	28
AE Stoddart c Giffen b McLeod	0 (2)	b Callaway	35
G Bean c Bruce b Giffen	50 (3)	c McLeod b Trott	3
JM Read c & b Giffen	36 (4)	b Trott	11
R Peel b McLeod	19	b Turner	6
GA Lohmann lbw Giffen	3	c Bannerman b Turner	0
J Briggs c Bruce b Turner	41	c Trott b McLeod	4
W Attewell c Bannerman b Turner	8 (10)	c Donnan b Turner	24
JW Sharpe c Blackham b McLeod	2 (11)	not out	5
G MacGregor (+) not out	9 (9)	c (S)ES Gregory b Trott	16
EXTRAS (B 9, LB 2, NB 3)	14	(B 1)	1
TOTAL	264		158

FOW 1st Inns: 84 85 85 171 179 187 232 249 256 264
FOW 2nd Inns: 60 60 71 75 93 93 98 125 139 158

Bowling: *First Innings*: Trott 10-2-25-0, Giffen 20-3-75-3, Turner 16-3-40-2, McLeod 28.4-12-53-5, Callaway 14-2-39-0, Bruce 3-0-18-0. *Second Innings*: McLeod 23-8-39-1, Turner 33.2-14-51-5, Trott 19-2-52-3, Callaway 4-1-7-1, Giffen 3-0-8-0.

Umpires: T Flynn & J Phillips

SECOND TEST 1891-92 AUSTRALIA v ENGLAND
Sydney Cricket Ground, Sydney. January 29, 30, February 1, 2, 3, 1892.
Toss: Australia. Australia won by 72 runs.

AUSTRALIA

AC Bannerman c Abel b Lohmann	12	c Grace b Briggs	91
JJ Lyons c Grace b Lohmann	41 (3)	c Grace b Lohmann	134
G Giffen c Abel b Lohmann	6 (4)	lbw Attewell	49
H Moses c Grace b Lohmann	29		
CTB Turner c MacGregor b Lohmann	15 (7)	not out	14
W Bruce c Bean b Attewell	15 (5)	c Briggs b Sharpe	72
GHS Trott b Lohmann	2 (2)	c Sharpe b Lohmann	1
RW McLeod c Attewell b Lohmann	13 (6)	c Read b Peel	18
WF Giffen c & b Lohmann	1 (8)	b Briggs	3
ST Callaway run out	1	c Grace b Briggs	0
JM Blackham (c+) not out	3 (9)	lbw Briggs	0
EXTRAS (B 3, LB 3)	6	(B 6, LB 2, W 1)	9
TOTAL	144		9 for 391

FOW 1st Inns: 31 57 62 90 117 123 126 132 141 144
FOW 2nd Inns: 1 175 254 347 364 376 391 391 391

Bowling: *First Innings*: Briggs 10-2-24-0, Sharpe 10-1-31-0, Lohmann 43.2-18-58-8, Attewell 31-20-25-1. *Second Innings*: Lohmann 51-14-84-2, Briggs 32.4-8-69-4, Attewell 46-24-43-1, Sharpe 35-7-91-1, Peel 35-13-49-1, Grace 16-2-34-0, Stoddart 4-1-12-0.

ENGLAND

R Abel not out	132	c G Giffen b G Giffen	1
WG Grace (c) b Turner	26	c Blackham b Turner	5
G Bean b G Giffen	19	c Lyons b Turner	4
AE Stoddart c Blackham b McLeod	27	b Turner	69
JM Read c Turner b G Giffen	3	c & b G Giffen	22
R Peel c G Giffen b Turner	20	st Blackham b G Giffen	6
GA Lohmann b G Giffen	10	c Bruce b G Giffen	15
G MacGregor (+) lbw McLeod	3	c & b G Giffen	12
J Briggs lbw Trott	28	c Trott b Turner	12
W Attewell b Trott	0	c & b G Giffen	0
JW Sharpe c Bannerman b G Giffen	26	not out	4
EXTRAS (B 10, LB 2, W 1)	13	(B 4, LB 2)	6
TOTAL	307		156

FOW 1st Inns: 50 79 123 127 152 167 178 235 235 307
FOW 2nd Inns: 2 6 11 64 83 117 133 140 140 156

Bowling: *First Innings*: Turner 37-11-90-2, McLeod 18-6-55-2, G Giffen 28.2-5-88-4, Trott 14-3-42-2, Callaway 17-10-19-0. *Second Innings*: Turner 23.2-7-46-4, G Giffen 28-10-72-6, Trott 5-0-11-0, Callaway 10-6-21-0.

Umpires: T Flynn & JA Tooher

THIRD TEST 1891-92 AUSTRALIA v ENGLAND
Adelaide Oval, Adelaide. March 24, 25, 26, 28, 1892.
Toss: England. England won by an innings & 230 runs.

ENGLAND

WG Grace (c) b McLeod	58
R Abel st Blackham b Trott	24
AE Stoddart lbw G Giffen	134
JM Read c Gregory b Turner	57
G Bean c McLeod b Lyons	16
R Peel c G Giffen b Turner	83
GA Lohmann lbw G Giffen	0
J Briggs b Turner	39
H Philipson (+) c Blackham b McLeod	1
G MacGregor run out	31
W Attewell not out	43
EXTRAS (B 5, LB 7, W 1)	13
TOTAL	499

FOW 1st Inns: 47 121 218 272 327 333 412 425 425 499

Bowling: *First Innings*: G Giffen 51.1-17-154-2, McLeod 41-11-78-2, Trott 12-0-80-1, Turner 46-17-111-3, Donnan 9-2-22-0, Lyons 5-0-22-1, Bruce 9-3-19-0.

AUSTRALIA

AC Bannerman c Bean b Lohmann	12	b Briggs	1
JJ Lyons c Peel b Briggs	23	c Stoddart b Briggs	19
G Giffen run out	5	c Bean b Attewell	27
W Bruce lbw Lohmann	5	lbw Attewell	37
CTB Turner c Lohmann b Briggs	10	c Grace b Briggs	5
ES Gregory c McLeod b Briggs	4	c Peel b Briggs	7
RW McLeod b Briggs	20	c Grace b Lohmann	30
GHS Trott b Briggs	0	st Philipson b Briggs	16
WF Giffen b Lohmann	3	c Peel b Briggs	2
H Donnan c Bean b Briggs	7	not out	11
JM Blackham (c+) not out	7	b Attewell	9
EXTRAS (B 5)	5	(B 3, LB 2)	5
TOTAL	100		169

FOW 1st Inns: 30 38 48 48 51 66 66 73 90 100
FOW 2nd Inns: 1 42 51 85 91 99 120 124 157 169

Bowling: *First Innings*: Briggs 21.5-4-49-6, Lohmann 21-8-46-3. Second Innings: Briggs 28-7-87-6, Attewell 34-10-69-3, Lohmann 6-2-8-1.

Umpires: GE Downs & WO Whitridge

Australian Averages

1891-92 AUSTRALIA v ENGLAND

AUSTRALIA	M	Inn	NO	Runs	H.S	Avrge	Ct	St	Overs	Mds	Runs	Wkt	Avrge
Bannerman, AC	3	6	–	202	91	33.67	4	–	–	–	–	–	–
Blackham, JM	3	6	3	23	9	7.67	5	2	–	–	–	–	–
Bruce, W	3	6	–	226	72	37.67	3	–	12.0	3	37	–	–
Callaway, ST	2	4	1	35	21	11.67	–	–	45.0	19	86	1	86.00
Donnan, H	2	4	1	29	11*	9.67	1	–	9.0	2	22	–	–
Giffen, G	3	6	–	90	49	15.00	8	–	130.3	35	397	15	26.47
Giffen, WF	2	4	–	9	3	2.25	–	–	–	–	–	–	–
Gregory, ES	1	2	–	10	7	5.00	1	–	–	–	–	–	–
Lyons, JJ	3	6	–	287	134	47.83	1	–	5.0	–	22	1	22.00
McLeod, RW	3	6	–	126	31	21.00	2	–	110.4	37	225	10	22.50
Moses, H	2	3	–	67	29	22.33	–	–	–	–	–	–	–
Trott, GHS	3	6	–	48	23	8.00	2	–	60.0	7	210	6	35.00
Turner, CTB	3	6	1	92	29	18.40	1	–	155.4	52	338	16	21.13

English Averages

1891-92 AUSTRALIA v ENGLAND

ENGLAND	M	Inn	NO	Runs	H.S	Avrge	Ct	St	Overs	Mds	Runs	Wkt	Avrge
Abel, R	3	5	1	217	132*	54.25	4	–	–	–	–	–	–
Attewell, W	3	5	1	75	43*	18.75	1	–	193.1	97	216	8	27.00
Bean, G	3	5	–	92	50	18.40	1	–	–	–	–	–	–
Briggs, J	3	5	–	124	41	24.80	1	–	116.3	31	268	17	15.76
Grace, WG	3	5	–	164	58	32.80	9	–	16.0	2	34	–	–
Lohmann, GA	3	5	–	28	15	5.60	5	–	188.2	71	289	16	18.06
MacGregor, G	3	5	1	71	31	17.75	3	–	–	–	–	–	–
Peel, R	3	5	–	134	83	26.80	4	–	94.5	43	128	6	21.33
Philipson, H	1	1	–	1	1	1.00	–	1	–	–	–	–	–
Read, JM	3	5	–	129	57	25.80	2	–	–	–	–	–	–
Sharpe, JW	2	4	2	37	26	18.50	1	–	150.0	53	287	9	31.89
Stoddart, AE	3	5	–	265	134	53.00	1	–	9.0	3	22	–	–

Cricket Council meets

All for cricket. Delegates to an Australasian Cricket Council get-together.

Sydney, Sep. 13. The Australasian Cricket Council held its first official meeting at the Oxford Hotel, Darlinghurst, yesterday.

It was the culmination of the meeting of colonial delegates and the agreement of aims for a national cricket body, held between SA, Victoria and NSW in Adelaide on 25 March 1892.

The most important business was discussion about the selection of the 1893 team to tour England, and the naming of the six ACC selectors to choose the team.

Following this, the meeting agenda moved to Lord Sheffield's gift of a trophy sum of £150 and how it might be used for the betterment of Australian cricket.

The Victorian delegate moved that, rather than create a trophy, the money be divided equally between the three Associations, and used by them as they saw fit. This was thrown out as being directly contrary to the wishes of Lord Sheffield to create something that would unify colonial cricket.

A South Australian delegate (Augustus Robinson) counter-proposed that the money be devoted to the purchase of a premiership shield, to be held by the premier colony for the year. The vote was a bare majority – 6/5.

It was further agreed that the Shield be won by the first colony to win a match against one of the other two, and held by the winning colony until it lost a match – a kind of 'challenge' shield.

The ACC agreed, at least in principle, that each colony should play the other two twice if arrangements could be made.

Triple centurion shows his skills at higher level

Melbourne, March 21. Frank Laver, East Melbourne Cricket Club's outstanding all-rounder, has 'struck oil' at last for Victoria with a punishing 104, in a partnership of 198 with Robert McLeod, in a meritorious win over SA in Adelaide.

The victory came despite George Giffen's almost obligatory dominance of the match, with 43 and 181, 9/147 and 2/88.

Tall and powerfully built, the 23-year-old Laver has topped 1000 runs at 65.3 for his club, and knocked up the Victorian record score of 352 not out against St Kilda earlier in the season.

His stooped over stance, his grip and style are ungainly, but he stays at the crease and hits the ball with great power.

He is also a penetrating medium-pace bowler, with a high action giving him bounce and a good off-cutter. He has been among the club wickets and looks a good all-round prospect for Australia.

Frank Laver: all-round prospect.

Victoria's clean sweep to win the first Sheffield Shield season

Sydney, Jan. 31. Victoria won the inaugural Sheffield Shield under the adjusted rules, by defeating South Australia and NSW twice.

The last win over NSW was a triumph for Victorian captain Jack Blackham, who made 64 batting at number 11, helping the Victorians to a commanding 331.

He then sportingly allowed stumps to be drawn early on the fourth day to let Charlie Turner have more time to recover from a blow to the hand, and a chance at getting the 232 runs to win.

Turner was dismissed after three balls next day – and Victoria won by 232.

This followed wins in Melbourne, by eight wickets over NSW and six wickets over SA.

The Victorian team, with Jack Worrall captain, before the first NSW match.

Debut century for Little Dasher

Prankster is 14th man in ACC team

Sheffield Park, May 8. In his first two first class matches for NSW, both against Victoria in the 1892–93 season, ex-Queenslander Arthur Coningham, aged 30, made 0 and 17, took 2/62 and 0/14, then 30 and 8, 4/90 and 5/79. Good figures but not the greatest. Perhaps not even the 14th best among Australian cricketers.

Yet Coningham was 14th man chosen for the England tour, upon the insistence of the Australasian Cricket Council. This was, presumably, a gesture to Queensland, which is now accorded first class status, if not elevation to rank among the colonies vying for the Sheffield Shield.

But such figures do not allow for some of the giddy pranks Coningham has got up to on the field in England – such as walking the length of the pitch after he had W.G. Grace caught for 63 in the match against Lord Sheffield's XI.

He is said to be unpopular with the rest of the tour party because of such antics as these, and because he has occasionally absented himself from the team without notice. His swashbuckling manner appears to have brought about dalliance beyond the cricket field.

But at least he has more form than Walter Giffen, who is an ordinary batsman and only on the tour at the insistence of brother George.

A gentleman saves the day with a fine one-handed catch in the grandstand at Lord's.

Lord's, July 19. Australia escaped with a draw in the first Test at Lord's, but had much to be pleased with over the debut Test century by young and diminutive Victorian Harry Graham.

Graham showed plenty of dash as he raced to 107 to score the first debut century since that of Charles Bannerman, in the very first Test in Melbourne.

England had made 334, thanks to 106 by Arthur Shrewsbury (who became the first batsman to score 1000 runs in Tests) and 91 by England's new boy, Francis Jackson.

Australia was perilously placed at 5/75 when Graham joined Syd Gregory. The new Test men then proceeded to smite the English bowling round the park. Gregory was out for 57, with the score on 6/217, and Graham, joined by Billy Bruce, took the score to 293 with his hard driving 107. He was always on the attack.

'The Little Dasher', as he is known, is not, as one commentator put it 'always strictly moral as regards the straightness of his bat, but he has the dash, audacity, vigour and love of adventure of a D'Artagnan.'

Graham had his first class debut only in the last Australian season.

He was the sixth-highest run scorer and had an average of 52.40. Others may have had higher claims, but no doubt it was Graham's spirit, rather than his technique, that influenced the selectors.

Billy Bruce, another Victorian, is slightly better credentialled having played for three seasons at home and made big scores. He contributed 23 at Lord's and had a stand of 47 with Graham

Graham's innings, and some rain, allowed Australia to escape and to remain on even terms. Charles Turner, who took 6/76 and 2/64, was Australia's top bowler.

Arthur Coningham: left-arm pace.

Experience. The selectors of the Australian team have only voluntarily included one new player, Harry Graham of Victoria, in the 14 to tour. Arthur Coningham was foist upon them. Jack Blackham, after a long apprenticeship, has been chosen by the players to captain the team.

Absent friends. The book of cricket record, *Wisden*, lamented the absence of Billy Murdoch in the 1893 party saying, as well as his batting that his 'judgement, tact, and strong will would have been invaluable in the management of the team despite, or perhaps because of, his residence in England.'

Giffen glorious. George Giffen gave Gloucestershire a taste of his ability with 180 and then 7/11. W. G. Grace held on to be 4 not out.

Brilliant hitting. Following on against the strong MCC side in May, Jack Lyons gave a great display of hitting, making his hundred in 50 minutes and proceeding to 149. In the end MCC had to fight for a draw.

Players Trumbled. Against the Players of England, at Lord's on June 19 and 20, Hugh Trumble takes 7/31 and 7/85.

Coningham cold caper. Fielding on a cold day in a match against a Blackpool XVIII Arthur Coningham gathered sticks and lit a fire in the outfield to keep warm. A spectator then offered to get some hot potatoes to put in his pocket.

Good byes Blackham. Jack Blackham, still standing up to the stumps, let in 72 byes in England's four completed Test innings. 28 leg byes also were scored.

An average tour. The 1893 Australians played 36 matches for 18 wins 10 losses and eight draws.

Little Dasher tops. Harry Graham, the 'Little Dasher' topped the averages with 1435 runs in 53 innings, highest score 219 and an average of 28.7, just ahead of Jack Lyons with 1527 at 28.27.

Turner, again. Charlie Turner may not be the 'Terror' of old, but he is still the best Australian bowler on tour – 149 wickets at 14.25, ahead of George Giffen 142 at 18.16.

Fist fights, blood and tensions mar tour's progress

Sussex, Aug. 20. A train pleasure-trip, taking the Australian team to Sussex after the innings defeat in the second Test, ended in fisticuffs. The violence was such that the train compartment was spattered with blood.

The names of the combatants are unknown, and the Australians are unwilling to discuss their affairs with either the English press or Australian scribes and well-wishers. But it seems that the animosities follow colonial boundaries.

This factional brawl is one example of the tension and lack of control by team manager Victor Cohen, or captain Jack Blackham.

Cohen is regarded as an agent of the Australasian Cricket Council, rather than a player's man, while Blackham is given to mood swings and anxieties.

Matters are perhaps not helped by the fact that, although the ACC chose the team, it is the players who control the money side of the tour.

George Giffen noted that Blackham lost a stone in weight between the first and third Tests with worry. During matches he is often filled with gloom in the dressing room, hiding his head in a towel and not watching, or else riding around the ground in a hansom cab.

Blackham seems unable to manage the colonial factions or the eccentricities of someone like Arthur Coningham. It is not helping matters that he does not appear to have the greatest tactical mind – especially in the matter of using all bowlers in measured spells and in the conditions that best suit them.

Australian press on the attack

Sydney, Aug. 17. Australia's dismal performance in the second Test was unmercifully attacked in the local press.

Aspersions were freely cast on the ability of the team to consume alcohol and play cricket.

One *Bulletin* wag maintained that the team's problem was that they were unable to find an effective pick-me-up after a night's celebration.

A correspondent to the *Sydney Mail* said that the teetotallers in the team were worn out from doing the heavy work for their drunken team-mates

W. G. leads England to victory

The Oval, Aug. 16. The Australians brought some good form into the second Test, played at the Oval. Somerset were beaten by six wickets after Australia had trailed on the first innings in very bad weather. Expatriate Australian Sammy Woods, called up again to help the team out, took 6/26.

Against Middlesex at Lord's they lost 9/56 before Hugh Trumble and Jack Blackham put on 91 for the last wicket. Then Trumble and Charlie Turner dispatched the opposition for 78. Harry Trott made a brilliant 145 and Syd Gregory a free-scoring 112 as they amassed 457 against Middlesex. The county team crumbled for 136 as Harry Trott captured 5/33.

This big score was eclipsed by the largest total by an Australian team in England, a world's record for a first class match – 843 against Oxford and Cambridge Past and Present at Portsmouth on July 31.

Alick Bannerman 133, William Bruce 191 and Hugh Trumble 105 led the picnic in grand style. Five other players got over 50. The students had a second-rate side, but it did include Ranjitsinhji, about whom high expectations are held.

Batting form declined somewhat in the other matches before the second Test – with a wet draw against Essex, a loss to Kent and a win over Liverpool and District, with Arthur Coningham taking 9/100 and Bob McLeod 10/56 in rare appearances.

But against the best of England in the Test, in 'tropical heat', England made 483, despite George Giffen's 7/128.

W. G. Grace was back as captain, and made 68, but it was F. S.

W.G. Grace is again the centre of attention as he comes in for lunch.

Jackson's elegant 103 that caught the eye. He was 98 when the ninth wicket fell and was the first player to complete a Test century with a 'fiver' over the boundary.

Australia made just 91 against Bill Lockwood (4/37) and Johnny Briggs (5/34), with only three batsman reaching double figures.

There was no apparent problem with the pitch and, following on, the Australians made a respectable but forlorn 349, to be beaten by an innings. The only consolation in this was that Harry Trott made 92 and Alick Bannerman became the first Australian to pass 1000 runs in Test cricket.

Third Test agony

Manchester, Aug. 26. Australia's fluky form continued after the second Test debacle.

In the first innings of 204 only Billy Bruce passed 50 with 68, and in the second only Alick Bannerman's 60 helped.

The match was saved by a time-consuming last-wicket partnership between Charlie Turner and Jack Blackham, which left England out of time for a run-chase.

And this was only effected after the good Doctor W. G. Grace helped end Turner's agonising dislocated finger by pulling it back into its socket.

There was no such quick end for the agony of the Australian tour.

Cricket in Western Australia. The Aboriginal team from the New Norcia district.

Australia suffers a shock loss to Philadelphia

Belmont Park, Oct. 2. Although kind words were said in Australia's defence, the truth of the matter is that an Australian XI was given a hiding by the Philadelphian team by the colossal margin of an innings and 68 runs.

Said one observer, 'Any cricketer picked up from the deck of an ocean liner after a long voyage, slipped into a railroad car in New York, rushed into cricket flannels at Belmont, stepping out to play on turf lurching and heaving beneath him will completely exonerate the Australians.'

Be that as it may, the Philadelphians made 525 and the Australians 199 and 238, with Bannerman retiring.

However, once they had regained their sea-legs, the Australians defeated XVIII's from New York and Philadelphia, and then the Philadelphia XI by six wickets, Hugh Trumble with match figures of 13/96. They won a final match against a Boston XVIII.

But questions will be asked back in Australia. Losing to Americans? That's not cricket.

Vic Cohen's books are all at sea

Sydney, Nov. 20. The Manager of the 1893 Australian team, Victor Cohen, had been appointed by the Australasian Cricket Council, but the players on the tour retained final control of the finances and distribution of profits.

However, Cohen, treasurer of the NSWCA and a man accustomed to the cheque book, ledger and journal, kept meticulous accounts of the incomes and outgoings of the long tour.

Despite this diligence, he has been a quiet figure, keeping largely apart from the players.

Before docking in Sydney he announced to the players that the dividend would only be £50 to £80 each per man. They weren't having that and they entered his cabin and took charge of his books, to make their own reckoning of affairs.

After the seizure and some heated discussion, Cohen agreed to pay the players £190 each, which meant that the penurious ACC lost a major share of the profits.

This was the fractious ending to a disappointing tour, marked more by monetary concerns and selfishness than good team play.

Giffen – spirit of South Australia

George Giffen, a big wicket-taker, surveys his own, destroyed by England's Tom Richardson at Lord's.

George Giffen was the very spirit of cricket in South Australia for 15 years, from 1880 to 1895, and laid claims to being Australia's greatest all-rounder – even to the point that he was known in his day as 'Australia's W. G. Grace'.

At 5ft 10in. and around 12 stone he was a big and fit man, with large hands that assisted his slow-medium bowling and made him an outstanding fielder in any position. He was a solid batsman, sound in technique, but capable of sustained hard hitting.

He was the outstanding player for South Australia from his debut in 1880 to his retirement in 1903, so much so that the fortunes of his team usually turned on his performances and his captaincy. At the age of 44 he made 81 and 97 not out and took 15/185 for South Australia against Victoria. His highest score for South Australia, amid seven centuries and four double centuries, was 271.

He is still the only Australian player to have the double of more than 10,000 runs (11,757) and 1000 wickets (1022) wickets.

His quality was soon evident to the Australian selectors and he made five tours to England. In 1882 he had only modest results, but played in the Ashes match, where he made 2 and a duck and did not bowl.

From 1884 onwards he was a much more important figure in touring teams, appearing in 31 Tests (14 in Australia) up to 1896. But he was not always available to tour, sometimes being obliged to opt for the security of his job with the South Australian postal service, at other times declining because his brother Walter was not chosen.

Having missed two Tests in Australia in 1884–85 he came into the side and skittled England in the fourth Test in Sydney, taking 7/117. In 1891–92 he took 4/88 in the first innings and 6/72 in the second, setting up a series win. In a match against Victoria that summer he took 16/166 for South Australia, then scored 271.

Giffen enjoyed the wider world that cricket brought, and he reminisced about it all cheerfully in his book *With Bat and Ball*, published in 1898. The book reflects the man, straightforward, modestly proud of his achievements, a good observer and story teller.

He loved going to England and the fellowship of the team. He writes of the voyage on the *Assam* in 1882 'sailing on the bosom of the mighty deep' and the rollicking fun, feasting, high jinks and practicing 'the art of elocution'.

On return from that Ashes win Giffen recalls: 'We were heroes. Everyone joined in honouring us. Personally, when I reached Adelaide again, I was made the recipient of a chronograph watch and chain valued at 100 guineas.'

By 1886 Giffen was the mainstay of the Australian team in England and he topped both batting and bowling averages.

In 1894–85 he had the honour of captaining Australia in four Tests, taking over from John Blackham after Australia lost the first Test, despite Giffen making 161 and Sid Gregory 201 in a first innings 587. Giffen also took eight wickets, but his second-innings tally of 4/164 was costly, as England made 437 to win by 10 runs.

Here both his weaknesses and strengths were revealed. As was well known in South Australia Giffen was a captain who could not take himself off. In the second Test England went two–up as Giffen laboured through 78 overs (for 6/155) as England made 475 in the second innings.

He performed brilliantly with bat and ball thereafter, winning two of the three remaining matches, but not snatching back the series.

His penchant for bowling came, it seems, not from selfishness, but from his love of playing. In his later years he enjoyed coaching schoolboys, but kept himself poor with visits to the racetracks.

There may be a Bradman stand at the Adelaide Oval, but there is also one named after the home-grown hero, George Giffen.

FIRST TEST 1893 ENGLAND v AUSTRALIA
Lord's Cricket Ground, London. July 17, 18, 19, 1893.
Toss: England. Match Drawn.

ENGLAND

A Shrewsbury c Blackham b Turner	106	b Giffen	81
AE Stoddart (c) b Turner	24	b Turner	13
W Gunn c Lyons b Turner	2	c Graham b Giffen	77
FS Jackson c Blackham b Turner	91	c Bruce b Giffen	5
JM Read b Bruce	6	c McLeod b Bruce	1
R Peel c Bruce b Trumble	12 (9)	not out	0
W Flowers b McLeod	35 (6)	b Turner	4
E Wainwright c Giffen b Turner	1	b Giffen	26
WH Lockwood b Bruce	22 (7)	b Giffen	0
G MacGregor (+) not out	5		
AW Mold b Turner	0		
EXTRAS (B 19, LB 9, NB 2)	30	(B 16, LB 9, W 1, NB 1)	27
TOTAL	334	8 dec	234

FOW 1st Inns: 29 31 168 189 213 293 298 313 333 334
FOW 2nd Inns: 27 179 195 198 198 198 234 234

Bowling: *First Innings*: Turner 36-16-67-6, Bruce 22-4-58-2, Trumble 19-7-42-1, Trott 9-2-38-0, McLeod 21-6-51-1, Giffen 18-3-48-0. *Second Innings*: Turner 32-15-64-2, Bruce 20-10-34-1, Trumble 11-2-33-0, Trott 2-0-5-0, McLeod 25-11-28-0, Giffen 26.4-6-43-5.

AUSTRALIA

JJ Lyons b Lockwood	7
AC Bannerman c Shrewsbury b Lockwood	17
G Giffen b Lockwood	0
GHS Trott c MacGregor b Lockwood	33
RW McLeod b Lockwood	5
ES Gregory c MacGregor b Lockwood	57
H Graham c MacGregor b Mold	107
W Bruce c Peel b Mold	23
CTB Turner b Flowers	0
H Trumble not out	2
JM Blackham (c+) lbw Mold	2
EXTRAS (B 15, LB 1)	16
TOTAL	269

FOW 1st Inns: 7 7 50 60 75 217 264 265 265 269

Bowling: *First Innings*: Peel 22-12-36-0, Lockwood 45-11-101-6, Mold 20.1-7-44-3, Jackson 5-1-10-0, Wainwright 11-3-41-0, Flowers 11-3-21-1.

Umpires: W Hearn & J Phillips

THIRD TEST 1893 ENGLAND v AUSTRALIA
Old Trafford, Manchester. August 24, 25, 26, 1893.
Toss: Australia. Match Drawn.

AUSTRALIA

AC Bannerman c MacGregor b Briggs	19	b Richardson	60
JJ Lyons c MacGregor b Briggs	27	b Mold	33
G Giffen b Richardson	17	c Brockwell b Richardson	17
GHS Trott c Grace b Richardson	9	b Mold	12
W Bruce c Read b Richardson	68 (6)	c Shrewsbury b Richardson	36
H Graham lbw Mold	18 (7)	st MacGregor b Briggs	3
ES Gregory b Briggs	0 (8)	lbw Richardson	3
H Trumble b Richardson	35 (9)	run out	8
RW McLeod b Briggs	2 (5)	c Read b Richardson	6
CTB Turner b Richardson	0	c Mold b Briggs	27
JM Blackham (c+) not out	0	not out	23
EXTRAS (B 5, LB 4)	9	(B 4, LB 4)	8
TOTAL	204		236

FOW 1st Inns: 32 59 69 73 129 130 194 198 201 204
FOW 2nd Inns: 56 79 92 99 153 170 173 182 200 236

Bowling: *First Innings*: Mold 28-11-48-1, Richardson 23.4-5-49-5, Briggs 42-18-81-4, Brockwell 3-0-17-0. *Second Innings*: Mold 23-6-57-2, Briggs 28.3-11-64-2, Richardson 44-15-107-5.

ENGLAND

AE Stoddart run out	0	c Gregory b Trumble	42
WG Grace (c) b Bruce	40	c Trott b McLeod	45
A Shrewsbury c Bruce b Giffen	12	not out	19
W Gunn not out	102	b Trumble	11
A Ward c Blackham b Turner	13	b Trumble	0
WW Read b Giffen	12	not out	0
W Brockwell c Gregory b Giffen	11		
J Briggs b Giffen	2		
G MacGregor (+) st Blackham b Turner	12		
T Richardson b Bruce	16		
AW Mold b Trumble	0		
EXTRAS (B 17, LB 6)	23	(B 1)	1
TOTAL	243	4 for	118

FOW 1st Inns: 4 43 73 93 112 136 165 196 238 243
FOW 2nd Inns: 78 100 117 117

Bowling: *First Innings*: Giffen 67-30-113-4, Turner 53-22-72-2, Bruce 17-5-26-2, Trumble 3.2-1-9-1. *Second Innings*: Giffen 6-3-10-0, Turner 7-1-18-0, Bruce 9-4-19-0, Trumble 25-4-49-3, McLeod 16-7-21-1.

Umpires: C Clements & J Phillips

SECOND TEST 1893 ENGLAND v AUSTRALIA
Kennington Oval, London. August 14, 15, 16, 1893.
Toss: England. England won by an innings & 43 runs.

ENGLAND

WG Grace (c) c Giffen b Trumble	68
AE Stoddart b Turner	83
A Shrewsbury c Graham b Giffen	66
W Gunn b Giffen	16
A Ward c & b Giffen	55
WW Read b Giffen	52
FS Jackson run out	103
J Briggs b Giffen	0
WH Lockwood c & b Giffen	10
G MacGregor (+) lbw Giffen	5
AW Mold not out	0
EXTRAS (B 19, LB 4, W 2)	25
TOTAL	483

FOW 1st Inns: 151 151 200 303 311 442 442 456 478 483

Bowling: *First Innings*: Turner 47-18-94-1, Trumble 47-16-101-1, McLeod 23-6-57-0, Giffen 54-17-128-7, Trott 6-1-33-0, Bruce 3-0-19-0, Lyons 7-1-26-0.

AUSTRALIA

AC Bannerman c MacGregor b Lockwood	10	c Read b Lockwood	55
JJ Lyons b Briggs	19 (7)	c Grace b Lockwood	31
GHS Trott b Lockwood	0 (4)	c Read b Lockwood	92
ES Gregory lbw Briggs	9 (5)	c Shrewsbury b Briggs	6
H Graham c MacGregor b Lockwood	0 (6)	b Briggs	42
G Giffen c MacGregor b Lockwood	4 (3)	b Lockwood	53
W Bruce not out	10 (2)	c Jackson b Mold	22
H Trumble b Briggs	5	b Briggs	8
RW McLeod c Lockwood b Briggs	2	c Jackson b Briggs	5
CTB Turner b Briggs	7	b Briggs	0
JM Blackham (c+) run out	17	not out	2
EXTRAS (B 5, LB 3)	8	(B 18, LB 15)	33
TOTAL	91		349

FOW 1st Inns: 30 31 32 40 48 57 59 69 91
FOW 2nd Inns: 54 126 165 189 295 311 340 342 342 349

Bowling: *First Innings*: Lockwood 19-9-37-4, Mold 4-0-12-0, Briggs 14.3-5-34-5. *Second Innings*: Lockwood 29-7-96-4, Mold 23.8-73-1, Briggs 35-6-114-5, Jackson 11-3-33-0.

Umpires: H Drapper & CK Pullin

Australian Averages

1893 ENGLAND v AUSTRALIA

AUSTRALIA	M	Inn	NO	Runs	H.S	Avrge	Ct	St	Overs	Mds	Runs	Wkt	Avrge
Bannerman, AC	3	5	-	161	60	32.20	-	-	-	-	-	-	-
Blackham, JM	3	5	3	44	23*	22.00	3	1	-	-	-	-	-
Bruce, W	3	5	1	159	68	39.75	3	-	71.0	23	156	5	31.20
Giffen, G	3	5	-	91	53	18.20	4	-	171.4	59	342	16	21.38
Graham, H	3	5	-	170	107	34.00	2	-	-	-	-	-	-
Gregory, ES	3	5	-	75	57	15.00	2	-	-	-	-	-	-
Lyons, JJ	3	5	-	117	33	23.40	1	-	7.0	1	26	-	-
McLeod, RW	3	5	-	20	6	4.00	1	-	85.0	30	157	2	78.50
Trott, GHS	3	5	-	146	92	29.20	1	-	17.0	3	76	-	-
Trumble, H	3	5	1	58	35	14.50	-	-	105.2	30	234	6	39.00
Turner, CTB	3	5	-	34	27	6.80	-	-	175.0	72	315	11	28.64

English Averages

1893 ENGLAND v AUSTRALIA

ENGLAND	M	Inn	NO	Runs	H.S	Avrge	Ct	St	Overs	Mds	Runs	Wkt	Avrge
Briggs, J	2	2	-	2	2	1.00	-	-	120.1	40	293	16	18.31
Brockwell, W	1	1	-	11	11	11.00	1	-	3.0	-	17	-	-
Flowers, W	1	2	-	39	35	19.50	-	-	11.0	3	21	1	21.00
Grace, WG	2	3	-	153	68	51.00	2	-	-	-	-	-	-
Gunn, W	3	5	1	208	102*	52.00	-	-	-	-	-	-	-
Jackson, FS	2	3	-	199	103	66.33	2	-	16.0	4	43	-	-
Lockwood, WH	2	3	-	32	22	10.67	1	-	93.0	27	234	14	16.71
MacGregor, G	3	3	1	22	12	11.00	8	1	-	-	-	-	-
Mold, AW	3	3	1	0	0*	0.00	1	-	98.1	32	234	7	33.43
Peel, R	1	2	1	12	12	12.00	1	-	22.0	12	36	-	-
Read, JM	1	2	-	7	6	3.50	-	-	-	-	-	-	-
Read, WW	2	3	1	64	52	32.00	4	-	-	-	-	-	-
Richardson, T	1	1	-	16	16	16.00	-	-	67.4	20	156	10	15.60
Shrewsbury, A	3	5	-	284	106	71.00	3	-	-	-	-	-	-
Stoddart, AE	3	5	-	162	83	32.40	-	-	-	-	-	-	-
Wainwright, E	1	2	-	27	26	13.50	-	-	11.0	3	41	-	-
Ward, A	2	3	-	68	55	22.67	-	-	-	-	-	-	-

The WACA oval is a jewel in the West

Perth, Feb. 3. Curator of the Western Australian Cricket Association ground, William Duffy, pronounced his new wickets 'ready for play' and the cricket lovers of Perth were there to watch.

To celebrate the opening of the ground, six short matches took place between Perth sides and teams from Kalgoorlie and Coolgardie.

Governor Sir Frederick Broome had granted the WACA 28 acres in 1889, and it has taken five years to develop the first turf pitches in WA. The WACA has received great encouragement for its endeavours to gain public support which has raised the colony to first class, and with hope of becoming part of the Sheffield Shield. The tour to the east last year, when six matches were played in South Australia and Victoria, two of them at first class level, were followed with great enthusiasm through the Western Australian newspapers. Plans to play in NSW went awry, but hopes are high for a further tour in the near future. The WACA secretary Frederick North has already cabled Edward Heather of Victoria on the subject.

Sheffield Shield win to SA

The Adelaide Oval scoreboard tells the story of a great year for South Australia.

Adelaide, July 14. The actual Sheffield Shield was formally handed over to the winners, South Australia, at half-time in the Norwood v Port Adelaide Australian football match at Norwood Oval.

In the presence of the Premier of the Colony, Charles Kingston, the Shield has been entrusted to the safekeeping of the popular vice-president, brewer, politician and mayor of Adelaide, Sir Edwin Smith.

The victory this season came down to the last match, played between SA and Victoria at the Adelaide Oval on March 2–7. Jack Reedman and Jack Lyons' hundreds, George Giffen, Affie Jarvis and the bowling of paceman Ernie Jones' gave SA the victory by 58 runs, 316 and 276 to 222 and 312.

Until this game was decided either of the other teams might

have won – Victoria a remote chance , but NSW would have won if Victoria had made the target.

Fittingly, George Giffen made the run out that won the match for SA. It was fitting not just because Giffen had had another outstanding season, but because as captain he had had to carry the burden of the mistake that lost SA the game in Sydney.

Giffen won the toss and decided to bat on a damp pitch, SA making just 119. SA was out of luck in the second innings, again batting after it had rained, and was dismissed for 118. NSW made 393 between showers. It was SA's only loss for the season.

The pattern was set from the first match in Adelaide in December, when Giffen made 205 out of 483 second innings runs to take SA to a 237-run win over NSW.

Queensland gives NSW a fright

Sydney, March 24. Queensland's second first class match, also against NSW, was very nearly a repetition of the first, a low-scoring affair which Queensland won.

This time, even with Arthur Coningham playing, they lost, but only by two wickets in a rain-affected match. Coningham, who played for NSW earlier in the year, took seven wickets, but made only 14 runs as an opener.

Sniffy NSW papers remarked that the action of Queensland fast bowler Ramsay, who took 1/18 and 4/64, 'was open to suspicion', but umpires Charles Bannerman and Jack Tooher did not call him for throwing.

Bulli soil brings perfect pitches

Sydney, Aug. 1. Ned Gregory, curator of the Sydney Cricket Ground, announced that he was very pleased with the pitch he had made with soil from the Bulli Creek, and that henceforward all Sydney Cricket Ground pitches would be made from it, rather than Victorian Merri Creek mud.

The NSWCA will offer a pound for pound subsidy for district clubs to change over to Bulli soil.

The SACA sent curator Charley Checkett to Sydney to look at the Bulli result, and also to Victoria to see the Victorian pitches. He was not impressed and will continue to use material from pockets of the Adelaide Hills.

Blackham causes national incident

Sydney, Jan. 30. Australian and Victorian captain Jack Blackham, known to all as 'Old Jack', can be a moody and curmudgeonly cricketer, especially when he feels his team is hard-done-by.

This was the case in the game against NSW where Old Jack felt that umpire Jack Tooher was aiding NSW by delaying the start of play by nearly an hour on the fourth day, allowing the pitch to become 'stickier' for Victoria, who were then batting.

Victoria lost by just 19 runs.

Umpire Tooher objected to Blackham's insinuations after the match and threatened not to umpire in a match Blackham played in – until he apologised. The stand-off is threatening the competition.

It's two–all in enthralling Test series

Bobby Peel bowls for England before the packed crowd at the Melbourne Cricket Ground in the second Test.

Sydney, Feb. 4. After four Tests in this splendid season, the Ashes score stands at two wins each with both new-look teams playing entertaining cricket.

In the fourth Test, Australia squared the series thanks to a century, 105, on his first Test appearance in Australia by the 'Little Dasher' Harry Graham and a solid 85 from 'Alberto' Trott.

The bowlers made short work of England in both innings – George Giffen, Charlie Turner and Harry Trott sharing the spoils.

Australia's other win was in Adelaide, where 'Alberto' Trott made his debut with an unbeaten 38 in the first innings and 72 in the second, as well as taking 8/43 in the England second innings.

Even Australia's losses have had their satisfactions.

Syd Gregory's great 201 in the first Test with George Giffen's 161, had England following on 261 behind Australia's 586. Though they made 437 in their second innings, and Giffen had added 4/164 to his 4/75 in the first innings, Australia was well placed at 2/113 overnight – with just 64 to get. But it rained overnight, then the sun shone on the wet pitch and Australia were out on a classic sticky for 166. They lost by 10 runs. It was the first time a team had won a Test match after following on.

And then in the second Test in Melbourne, George Giffen, taking over the captaincy from injured Jack Blackham, put England in on a damp pitch.

The tourists were bundled out for 75, with Archie MacLaren out first ball to Arthur Coningham's first delivery in a Test, but Australia managed only 123, and on the improved pitch England knocked up 475. Australia, needing 429, was bowled out for 333, losing by 94.

Worrall departs after the 'Fitzroy imbroglio'

Melbourne Feb. 23. Jack Worrall has left the Fitzroy club for Carlton after an imbroglio in January. The club refused leave for its caretaker and respected intercolonial umpire, Tom Flynn, to officiate at the Victoria – NSW match in Sydney.

'Mid On' in the magazine the *Leader* said the Fitzroy committee should 'feel somewhat ashamed' at sacking someone who had served the club so loyally and well.

Worrall had led the nine-player strike by the Fitzroy players, which resulted in his dismissal as Fitzroy delegate to the Victorian Cricketers' Association, and the sacking of Flynn from his job.

The Fitzroy committee was adjudged to have 'gone beyond the bounds of common sense' when it might have accepted the cantankerous Worrall's view that Flynn's original appointment as umpire 'honoured' the club.

Syd Gregory, 201 in the opening Test in Sydney, and Frank Iredale, 140 in Adelaide, are leading the Australian batting averages.

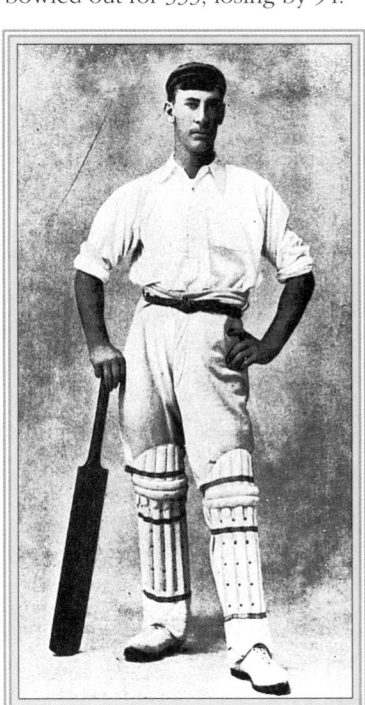

Albert Trott has made an all-round magnificent start for Australia in Adelaide, scoring 38 not out and 72 not out, and taking 8/35.

'Match of century' blunder

Melbourne, March 6. In what proved to be an embarrassing selection blunder for the fifth and deciding Test, Australia dropped the great 'Terror' Turner even after his fourth Test match figures of 7/51 in a winning side and brought in the promising but unproved Tom McKibbin after just five first class matches.

McKibbin's match figures, in a six-wicket loss, were 2/120.

The cricket did not quite live up to the expectation of it being dubbed the 'match of the century' but record crowds attended, and special trains were laid on.

The *Argus* noted: 'There appears to be an idea somewhere that there is a Depression here. To the spectator on Saturday (crowd 29,123) at the MCG that word had no meaning.'

A total of 103,636 people attended the five days of the match, a record for a game in Australia, or indeed anywhere else.

Giffen won the toss and batted, and thanks to a all-round solid effort Australia reached 414, Giffen making 57, Syd Gregory 70, Joe Darling 74, Jack Lyons 55, but no one getting a really big score.

England replied with 385, MacLaren making 120. Harry Trott and Giffen also lacked penetration as bowlers.

Then Australia scored a lacklustre 267 (Giffen consistent with 51 and Darling 50) leaving England an achievable total of 297.

They were in a bit of bother at 2/28 but John Brown of Yorkshire strode to the wicket and smote the bowling all over the MCG – making 50 in 28 minutes, 100 in 95 minutes and 140 in 145 minutes – the fastest scoring in Test matches, in what was described as an 'immortal' innings. He was ably assisted by opener Albert Ward, who made 93. England made the 298 with the loss of four wickets.

A. E. Stoddart: England captain.

George Giffen: took the reins.

Observers wondered whether the same result would have been achieved with the experience of 'Terror' Turner in the team.

As it stands he now seems lost to Australian cricket.

Giffen finished the series with the prodigious figures of 475 runs and 34 wickets. 'Alberto' Trott played three Tests for 205 runs and twice out – average 102.5, as well as taking nine wickets at 21.

MCC in debt

Melbourne, Oct. 1. Melbourne Cricket Club President Frank Grey-Smith had to use some of his influence to obtain a £500 overdraft at the National Bank of Australasia (where he was chief manager), after teh club's usual bank, the City of Melbourne Bank, crashed.

The MCC was overdrawn by £2336 at the time. Despite such financial upheavals, the MCC still underwrote the England tour, and was able to discharge its debt with the half share of the tour profit, a sum of £3599.

Vics shield win

Melbourne, March 25. Victoria won the Sheffield Shield with two wins against NSW and one against South Australia , while SA lost both 'away' games.

Victoria was once defeated by the titan of Australian cricket George Giffen in Adelaide with 12 wickets and 94 not out – but overall had a more balanced and talented side. The brothers Trott and the brothers McLeod were among Victoria's best. Victoria also defeated the English tourists by seven wickets, thanks to Harry Trott's 10 wickets.

FIRST TEST 1894–95 AUSTRALIA v ENGLAND
Sydney Cricket Ground, Sydney. December 14, 15, 17, 18, 19 ,20, 1894.
Toss: Australia. England won by 10 runs.

AUSTRALIA

Batsman	1st		2nd	
JJ Lyons b Richardson	1		b Richardson	25
GHS Trott b Richardson	12		c Gay b Peel	8
G Giffen c Ford b Brockwell	161		lbw Briggs	41
J Darling b Richardson	0		c Brockwell b Peel	53
FA Iredale c Stoddart b Ford	81	(6)	c & b Briggs	5
ES Gregory c Peel b Stoddart	201	(5)	c Gay b Peel	16
JC Reedman c Ford b Peel	17		st Gay b Peel	4
CE McLeod b Richardson	15		not out	2
CTB Turner c Gay b Peel	1		c Briggs b Peel	2
JM Blackham (c+) b Richardson	74	(11)	c & b Peel	2
E Jones not out	11	(10)	c MacLaren b Briggs	1
EXTRAS (B 8, LB 3, W 1)	12		(B 2, LB 1, NB 4)	7
TOTAL	586			166

FOW 1st Inns: 10 21 21 192 331 379 400 409 563 586
FOW 2nd Inns: 26 45 130 135 147 158 159 161 162 166

Bowling: *First Innings:* Richardson 55.3-13-181-5, Peel 53-14-140-2, Briggs 25-4-96-0, Brockwell 22-7-78-1, Ford 11-2-47-1, Stoddart 3-0-31-1, Lockwood 3-2-1-0. *Second Innings:* Richardson 11-3-27-1, Peel 30-9-67-6, Lockwood 16-3-40-0, Briggs 11-2-25-3.

ENGLAND

Batsman	1st		2nd	
AC MacLaren c Reedman b Turner	4		b Giffen	20
A Ward c Iredale b Turner	75		b Giffen	117
AE Stoddart (c) c Jones b Giffen	12		c Giffen b Turner	36
JT Brown run out	22		c Jones b Giffen	53
W Brockwell c Blackham b Jones	49		b Jones	37
R Peel c Gregory b Giffen	4		b Giffen	17
FGJ Ford st Blackham b Giffen	30		c & b McLeod	48
J Briggs b Giffen	57		b McLeod	42
WH Lockwood c Giffen b Trott	18		b Trott	29
LH Gay (+) c Gregory b Reedman	33		b Trott	4
T Richardson not out	0		not out	12
EXTRAS (B 17, LB 3, W 1)	21		(B 14, LB 8)	22
TOTAL	325			437

FOW 1st Inns: 14 43 78 149 155 211 211 252 325 325
FOW 2nd Inns: 44 115 217 245 290 296 385 398 420 437

Bowling: *First Innings:* Jones 19-7-44-1, Turner 44-16-89-2, Giffen 43-17-75-4, Trott 15-4-59-1, McLeod 14-2-25-0, Reedman 3.3-1-12-1, Lyons 2-2-0-0. *Second Innings:* Jones 19-0-57-1, Turner 35-14-78-1, Giffen 75-25-164-4, Trott 12.4-3-22-2, McLeod 30-6-67-2, Reedman 6-1-12-0, Lyons 2-0-12-0, Iredale 2-1-3-0.

Umpires: C Bannerman & J Phillips

SECOND TEST 1894–95 AUSTRALIA v ENGLAND
Melbourne Cricket Ground, Melbourne. December 29, 31, 1894, January 1, 2, 3, 1895.
Toss: Australia. England won by 94 runs.

ENGLAND

Batsman	1st		2nd	
AC MacLaren c Trott b Coningham	0		b Turner	15
A Ward c Darling b Trumble	30		b Turner	41
AE Stoddart (c) b Turner	10		b Giffen	173
JT Brown c Trumble b Turner	0		c Jarvis b Bruce	37
W Brockwell c Iredale b Coningham	0		b Turner	21
R Peel c Trumble b Turner	6		st Jarvis b Giffen	53
FGJ Ford c Giffen b Trumble	9		c Trott b Giffen	24
WH Lockwood not out	3	(9)	not out	33
J Briggs c Bruce b Turner	5	(8)	lbw Giffen	31
H Philipson (+) c Darling b Turner	1		b Giffen	30
T Richardson c Iredale b Trumble	0		c Gregory b Giffen	11
EXTRAS (LB 9, NB 2)	11		(B 1, LB 2, NB 3)	6
TOTAL	75			475

FOW 1st Inns: 0 19 23 26 44 58 60 70 71 75
FOW 2nd Inns: 24 101 191 222 320 362 385 402 455 475

Bowling: *First Innings:* Coningham 11-5-17-2, Turner 20-9-32-5, Trumble 9.1-4-15-3. *Second Innings:* Coningham 20-4-59-0, Giffen 78.2-21-155-6, Turner 55-21-99-3, Trott 17-0-60-0, Trumble 26-6-72-0, Bruce 4-0-21-1, Lyons 2-1-3-0.

AUSTRALIA

Batsman	1st		2nd	
JJ Lyons b Richardson	2	(7)	b Peel	14
W Bruce c Ford b Peel	4		c Stoddart b Peel	54
G Giffen (c) c Philipson b Briggs	32		c Brown b Brockwell	43
ES Gregory c Ward b Richardson	2		b Richardson	12
J Darling b Lockwood	32		b Brockwell	5
FA Iredale b Richardson	10		b Peel	68
GHS Trott run out	16	(1)	c & b Brockwell	95
A Coningham c Philipson b Richardson	10	(9)	b Peel	3
H Trumble b Richardson	1	(10)	run out	2
AH Jarvis (+) c Brown b Briggs	11	(8)	b Richardson	4
CTB Turner not out	1		not out	26
EXTRAS (W 2)	2		(B 5, LB 1, NB 1)	7
TOTAL	123			333

FOW 1st Inns: 4 12 14 53 80 96 108 110 116 123
FOW 2nd Inns: 26 45 130 135 147 158 159 161 162 166

Bowling: *FIRST INNINGS:* Richardson 23-6-57-5, Peel 14-4-21-1, Lockwood 5-0-17-1, Briggs 13.5-2-26-2. *Second Innings:* Richardson 40-10-100-2, Peel 40.1-9-77-4, Lockwood 25-5-60-0, Briggs 12-0-49-0, Ford 5-2-7-0, Brockwell 14-3-33-3.

Umpires: T Flynn & J Phillips

THIRD TEST 1894-95 AUSTRALIA v ENGLAND
Adelaide Oval, Adelaide. January 11, 12, 14, 15, 1895.
Toss: Australia. Australia won by 382 runs.

AUSTRALIA

W Bruce b Richardson	11	c Brockwell b Briggs 80
GHS Trott run out	48	b Peel 0
G Giffen (c) c Lockwood b Brockwell	58	c Ford b Peel 24
FA Iredale b Richardson	7	c & b Peel 140
J Darling c Philipson b Briggs	10	c Philipson b Lockwood 3
ES Gregory c Brown b Richardson	6	b Richardson 20
J Harry b Richardson	2	b Richardson 6
J Worrall run out	0	c Peel b Briggs 11
AH Jarvis (+) c & b Lockwood	13	c Brown b Peel 29
AE Trott not out	38	not out 72
ST Callaway b Richardson	41	b Richardson 11
EXTRAS (B 2, W 1, NB 1)	4	(B 7, LB 7, NB 1) 15
TOTAL	238	 411

FOW 1st Inns: 31 69 84 103 120 124 137 157 157 238
FOW 2nd Inns: 0 44 142 145 197 215 238 283 347 411

Bowling: *First Innings*: Richardson 21.1-4-75-5, Peel 16-1-43-0, Brockwell 20-13-30-1, Ford 8-2-19-0, Briggs 8-2-34-1, Lockwood 8-2-33-1. *Second Innings*: Peel 34-6-96-4, Richardson 31.2-8-89-3, Lockwood 15-2-70-1, Brockwell 10-1-50-0, Briggs 19-3-58-2, Ford 6-0-33-0.

ENGLAND

J Briggs b Callaway	12 (9)	b AE Trott 0
AC MacLaren c Callaway	25	c Iredale b AE Trott 35
W Brockwell c Harry b Callaway	12 (6)	c & b AE Trott 24
A Ward c Bruce b Giffen	5 (1)	b AE Trott 13
AE Stoddart (c) c b Giffen	1 (3)	not out 34
JT Brown not out	39 (5)	b AE Trott 2
R Peel b Callaway	0	c & b AE Trott 0
FGJ Ford c Worrall b Giffen	21	c GHS Trott b AE Trott 14
WH Lockwood c Worrall b Giffen	0 (10)	c Iredale b AE Trott 1
H Philipson (+) c Gregory b Giffen	7 (4)	b Giffen 1
T Richardson c Worrall b Callaway	0	c AE Trott b Giffen 12
EXTRAS (B 2)	2	(B 5, LB 2) 7
TOTAL	124	 143

FOW 1st Inns: 14 30 49 50 56 64 111 111 124 124
FOW 2nd Inns: 52 52 53 64 102 102 128 128 130 143

Bowling: *First Innings*: AE Trott 3-1-9-0, Giffen 28-11-76-5, Callaway 26.3-13-37-5. *Second Innings*: Callaway 7-1-19-0, Giffen 33.1-12-74-2, AE Trott 27-10-43-8.

Umpires: J Phillips & GHG Searcy

FOURTH TEST 1894-95 AUSTRALIA v ENGLAND
Sydney Cricket Ground, Sydney. February 1, 2 (no play), 4, 1895.
Toss: England. Australia won by an innings & 147 runs.

AUSTRALIA

GHS Trott c Brown b Peel	1
W Bruce c Brockwell b Peel	15
G Giffen (c) b Peel	8
H Moses b Richardson	1
H Graham st Philipson b Briggs	105
ES Gregory st Philipson b Briggs	5
FA Iredale c & b Briggs	0
J Darling b Richardson	31
AE Trott not out	85
AH Jarvis (+) c Philipson b Briggs	5
CTB Turner c Richardson b Lockwood	22
EXTRAS (B 3, LB 1, W 1, NB 1)	6
TOTAL	284

FOW 1st Inns: 2 20 26 26 51 51 119 231 239 284

Bowling: *First Innings*: Peel 24-5-74-3, Richardson 22-5-78-2, Briggs 22-4-65-4, Brockwell 5-1-25-0, Ford 2-0-14-0, Lockwood 8.5-3-22-1.

ENGLAND

AC MacLaren st Jarvis b GHS Trott	1 (4)	c Bruce b Giffen 0
A Ward c & b Turner	7	c Darling b Giffen 6
J Briggs b GHS Trott	11 (8)	c Bruce b Giffen 6
AE Stoddart (c) st Jarvis b GHS Trott	7 (3)	c Iredale b Turner 0
JT Brown not out	20 (1)	b Giffen 0
W Brockwell c Darling b Turner	1 (5)	c Bruce b Turner 17
FGJ Ford c GHS Trott b Giffen	0	c Darling b Giffen 11
R Peel st Jarvis b Turner	0 (6)	st Jarvis b Turner 0
H Philipson (+) c Graham b Giffen	4	c & b Turner 9
T Richardson c & b Giffen	2	not out 10
WH Lockwood		
EXTRAS (B 7, LB 3, NB 2)	12	(B 5, LB 7, NB 1) 13
TOTAL	9 for 65	.... 9 for 72

FOW 1st Inns: 2 20 24 31 40 43 56 63 65
FOW 2nd Inns: 0 5 5 12 14 29 47 52 72

Bowling: *First Innings*: Trott 14-5-21-3, Turner 19-10-18-3, Giffen 5.5-1-14-3. *Second Innings*: Giffen 15-7-26-5, Turner 14.1-6-33-4.

Umpires: C Bannerman & J Phillips

FIFTH TEST 1894-95 AUSTRALIA v ENGLAND
Melbourne Cricket Ground, Melbourne. March 1, 2 4, 5, 6, 1895.
Toss: Australia. England won by 6 wkts.

AUSTRALIA

GHS Trott b Briggs	42	b Peel 42
W Bruce c MacLaren b Peel	22	c & b Peel 11
G Giffen (c) b Peel	57	b Richardson 51
FA Iredale b Richardson	8	b Richardson 18
ES Gregory c Philipson b Richardson	70	b Richardson 30
J Darling c Ford b Peel	74	b Peel 50
JJ Lyons c Philipson b Lockwood	55	b Briggs 15
H Graham b Richardson	6	lbw Richardson 10
AE Trott c Lockwood b Peel	10	b Richardson 0
AH Jarvis (+) not out	34	not out 14
TR McKibbin c Peel b Briggs	23	c Philipson b Richardson 13
EXTRAS (B 3, LB 10)	13	(B 5, LB 6, NB 2) 13
TOTAL	414	 267

FOW 1st Inns: 40 101 126 142 284 286 304 335 367 414
FOW 2nd Inns: 32 75 125 148 179 200 219 219 248 267

Bowling: *First Innings*: Richardson 42-7-138-3, Peel 48-13-114-4, Lockwood 27-7-72-1, Briggs 23.4-5-46-2, Brockwell 6-1-22-0, Ford 2-0-9-0. *Second Innings*: Richardson 45.2-7-104-6, Peel 46-16-89-3, Lockwood 16-7-24-0, Briggs 16-3-37-1.

ENGLAND

A Ward b McKibbin	32	b GHS Trott 93
W Brockwell st Jarvis b GHS Trott	5	c & b Giffen 5
AE Stoddart (c) st Jarvis b GHS Trott	68	lbw GHS Trott 11
JT Brown b AE Trott	30	c Giffen b McKibbin 140
AC MacLaren hit wicket b GHS Trott	120	not out 20
R Peel c Gregory b Giffen	73	not out 15
WH Lockwood c GHS Trott b Giffen	5	
FGJ Ford c AE Trott b Giffen	11	
J Briggs c GHS Trott b Giffen	0	
H Philipson (+) not out	10	
T Richardson lbw GHS Trott	11	
EXTRAS (B 8, LB 8, W 4)	20	(B 6, LB 5, W 2, NB 1) 14
TOTAL	385	.... 4 for 298

FOW 1st Inns: 6 110 112 166 328 342 364 364 366 385
FOW 2nd Inns: 5 28 238 278

Bowling: *First Innings*: Giffen 45-13-130-4, GHS Trott 24-5-71-4, AE Trott 30-4-84-1, McKibbin 29-6-73-1, Bruce 5-1-7-0. *Second Innings*: GHS Trott 20.1-1-63-2, Giffen 31-4-106-1, AE Trott 19-2-56-0, McKibbin 14-2-47-1, Bruce 3-1-10-0, Lyons 1-0-2-0.

Umpires: T Flynn & J Phillips

Australian Averages

1894-95 AUSTRALIA v ENGLAND

AUSTRALIA	M	Inn	NO	Runs	H.S	Avrge	Ct	St	Overs	Mds	Runs	Wkt	Avrge
Blackham, JM	1	2	-	76	74	38.00	1	1					
Bruce, W	4	7	-	197	80	28.14	5	-	12.0	2	38	1	38.00
Callaway, ST	1	2	-	52	41	26.00	-	-	33.3	14	56	5	11.20
Coningham, A	1	2	-	13	10	6.50	-	-	31.0	9	76	2	38.00
Darling, J	5	9	-	258	74	28.67	5	-					
Giffen, G	5	9	-	475	161	52.78	6	-	354.2	111	820	34	24.12
Graham, H	2	3	-	121	105	40.33	1	-					
Gregory, ES	5	9	-	362	201	40.22	5	-					
Harry, J	1	2	-	8	6	4.00	1	-					
Iredale, FA	5	9	-	337	140	37.44	6	-	2.0	1	3	-	-
Jarvis, AH	4	7	2	110	34*	22.00	1	7					
Jones, E	1	2	1	12	11*	12.00	2	-	38.0	7	101	2	50.50
Lyons, JJ	3	6	-	112	55	18.67	-	-	7.0	3	17	-	-
McKibbin, TR	1	2	-	36	23	18.00	-	-	43.0	8	120	2	60.00
McLeod, CE	1	2	1	17	15	17.00	1	-	44.0	8	92	2	46.00
Moses, H	1	1	-	1	1	1.00	-	-					
Reedman, JC	1	2	-	21	17	10.50	1	-	9.3	2	24	1	24.00
Trott, AE	3	5	3	205	85*	102.50	4	-	79.0	17	192	9	21.33

English Averages

1894-95 AUSTRALIA v ENGLAND

ENGLAND	M	Inn	NO	Runs	H.S	Avrge	Ct	St	Overs	Mds	Runs	Wkt	Avrge
Briggs, J	5	9	-	164	57	18.22	3	-	150.3	25	436	15	29.07
Brockwell, W	5	10	-	171	49	17.10	4	-	77.0	26	238	5	47.60
Brown, JT	5	10	2	343	140	42.88	5	-					
Ford, FGJ	5	9	-	168	48	18.67	5	-	34.0	6	129	1	129.00
Gay, LH	1	2	-	37	33	18.50	3	1					
Lockwood, WH	5	7	2	89	33*	17.80	3	-	123.5	31	339	5	67.80
MacLaren, AC	5	10	-	240	120	26.67	2	-					
Peel, R	5	10	-	168	73	18.67	6	-	305.1	77	721	27	26.70
Philipson, H	4	7	1	62	30	10.33	8	2					
Richardson, T	5	9	3	58	12*	9.67	1	-	291.2	63	849	32	26.53
Stoddart, AE	5	10	-	352	173	39.11	2	-	3.0	-	31	1	31.00
Ward, A	5	10	1	419	117	41.90	1	-					

Hat-trick Hugh Trumble

'That great camel' said Pelham Warner; 'This Giant' said George Giffen; 'His proper place is up trees in the bush' said J. H. W. T. Douglas of England. 'Now the best bowler Australia has sent us,' said W. G. Grace in 1899.

Hugh Trumble was a tall, gangling man with a long jaw, big nose and big ears, a high leaping action, an awkward length and great variety who bowled well enough, often enough to get right up the nose of his opponents, especially the English.

He was born in Melbourne in 1867, played for Victoria in 1887 against England, and made his modest Test debut in 1890.

Monty Noble liked his run up – 'sidelong and insinuating, with his neck craned like a gigantic bird.'

Others admired his hard-to-pick slower ball, and the way he thought about how to exploit a batsman's weaknesses.

The majestic C. B. Fry wrote in 1904: 'I would prefer not to see Hughie Trumble against me in flannels for the simple reason that he is the most long-headed observant and acute judge of the game, a perfect master of the whole art of placing fieldsmen and changing

bowlers. It is his head – that long solemn head – I should fear in England this summer ... not his bowling arm, spinning finger, deft as they are. It is the head, best in the side, that makes the difference for the Australians.'

He bowled occasionally zippy medium-paced off-breaks with an immaculate length and surprising bounce, as well as in-swingers and a very deceptive late-dipping slower ball.

He took 141 wickets in 32 Test matches between 1890 and 1902, and he made three first class centuries. Perhaps his best match for Victoria was in December 1889 when he took 7/89 and 8/110 against George Giffen's SA.

For Australia – take your pick – from the 1901–02 series, 28 wickets at 20, 26 at 14 in 1902 or 24 at 16 in 1903–04.

Trumble captained Australia in two winning Test matches in 1901–02. He took eight wickets in the first of these and eight in the second. In this series Trumble wrapped up the second Test at the MCG with a hat-trick. His second hat-trick occurred in his last match in 1903–04, again at the MCG, when he took 7/28.

'Then he donned his sweater, walked off the field and out of international cricket. No man ever made such a dramatic exit as this, but then Trumble was an unusual

Hugh Trumble: bowling immortal.

man, one of the men who really mattered,' wrote Johnnie Moyes.

Trumble was secretary of the Melbourne Cricket Club between 1911 and his death in 1938.

Johnnie Moyes again: 'Trumble was one of the great bowlers of history ... imperturbable, resourceful, this giant ranks with the immortals of the bowling art.'

Unflappable Harry Trott

George Giffen said he remembered George Henry Stevens Trott, Harry, or Trotty to his team-mates, because he 'plunked him over the chains' in his opening first class innings against Giffen in 1885–86. Trott made 54 not out in this match – but it wasn't his first first class encounter.

That occurred earlier the same season, a Victorian XI v Australian XI match at the MCG and George Giffen couldn't make it because of work commitments in Adelaide. He didn't miss much, Trott made 4 and 18 not out, and bowled 18 overs for 0/39.

Regarded as 'the best all round player Victoria had sent to England in his time', Trott was a complete batsman, especially when under the whip. As Giffen wrote: 'Then the bowler finds out that he wields a very wide bat, and no matter how much he may stonewall, he never loses his elegance of style. The greater the match the better he plays.'

His 143 at Lord's in 1896 with Sid Gregory at the other end very nearly saved the match after

Australia had made just 53 in the first inings.

Trott was a more than useful slow leg spin bowler, taking 29 Test wickets and 386 in total in first class matches.

Fielding at what Giffen calls 'strong' or closer-in-than-usual point he took some great catches.

Trott went on to play 84 first class matches in Australia, his last for Victoria in February 1908 when he took five wickets against the touring MCC including Jack Hobbs, aged 41.

Between these games he participated in some other famous matches – including top scoring in Victoria's notorious innings of 15 against the MCC. Trott made 9 in the lowest ever first class innings total.

He played 24 Tests, in seven series, touring England four times. Trott is another player from South Melbourne Cricket Club who captained Australia, leading his country in 1896 in England, losing 2–1 and in Australia 1896–97 winning 4–1. Contemporaries regarded him as one of the best

captains Australia had had – genial, strong, tactically astute and a great friend of team-mates and opponents.

Harry Trott: tactically astute.

He had a kind of mental breakdown after the 1897–98 season and was confined to the asylum at Kew. A testimonial was held, which the MCC opened with £100. He made a miraculous recovery, and played a handful more games for Victoria from 1900–01.

Harry, the younger brother of Albert 'Alberto' Trott, died in 1917.

Hugh Trumble on playing 'stickies'

In May 1927, Hugh Trumble wrote in the *Sun News Pictorial*: 'There is a lack of knowledge among recognised players concerning the various conditions of pitches affected by rain. It is quite a common occurrence after inspection of a pitch to find half the side wanting to put the opposition in if they won the toss and the other half wanting to bat.

'In Australia it would be impossible to get a pitch to play at all for any great length of time after rain, whether it was affected by the sun or not. [But] on some wickets in England it is possible for a wicket to dry naturally and slowly after a good soaking and never really get difficult. Of course, the sticky pitch gives the bowler his day out, but it is not every bowler who can take advantage of it.

'Bowlers, as a rule, do not keep the ball up enough on these wickets, and what may be a fair length ball on a fast pitch is much too short on a slow-paced one and may be easily pulled to leg.

'A bowler cannot afford to bowl any bad length balls on a sticky pitch when forcing batsmen are about and looking for runs.

'It does not always follow if a pitch is wet it is going to be difficult, especially in England, where the soil is not of that sticky nature so common in Australia.

'In Australia the grass, mostly couch, is shaved right down to the roots; but this practice is not adopted in England. The grass there is not so closely cut and seldom loses its natural colour. The pitches there receive nothing like the preparation they get in Australia, and play a good deal slower ...

'It is no uncommon thing to see thousands of spectators at a Test ... squatting around in the rain. They naturally think that if they can brave the rain the players can too.

'A batsman of intelligence and resource should very soon adapt himself to the altered conditions of English pitches, quite able to hold his own even if the season is wet. The trouble with most batsmen is that they seem to lose heart when the pitch is affected by rain.'

Cricket's bureaucracy takes command

From the early days of cricket the fundamental point that had to be settled was: Who is in charge of the game, the administrators or the players?

The unseemly events of 1912, in which a boardroom brawl was followed by the refusal of six senior players to go on a Test tour to England, was the culmination of decades of unrest.

The administration side was slow in settling down. The dominant early organisations were the New South Wales Cricket Association, the South Australian Cricket Association and the Melbourne Cricket Club, which carried far more weight than the Victorian Cricketers' Association (as the first incarnation of the Victorian Cricket Association was known).

So strong was the MCC's grip on the game that it stepped into the breach during a rift between the VCA and the NSWCA in 1888–89 and arranged to control Victorian return matches with NSW for a period of five years.

In retaliation to this slight to its prestige, the VCA's constituent clubs – of which Melbourne was a member – decided not to play matches again in the local competition. Melbourne resigned from the VCA, but was later readmitted in a general smoothing of the waters, and the VCA then took over the arrangement of intercolonial matches.

But, relieved of this intercolonial task, the MCC still saw itself as the body controlling and organising the tours to and from England. At the time it had only an organising and managerial role. The game, including the selection of the team, captain and manager, still very much belonged to the players.

But it was an advance on the 'mates' system, in which the players to tour England banded together, financed themselves and agreed to share all profits and expenses. These early tours were about money, and some early teams were criticised for their mercenary approach to the game.

In Australia the MCC held sway, set in its ambitions to control cricket in much the same way as the Marylebone Cricket Club did in England. Its secretary Major Ben Wardill organised and managed the tours of 1886, 1899 and 1902, and it largely negotiated the itineraries and payments for the visiting teams from England. The SACA's active secretary John Creswell had a running battle with Wardill as he tried to get a Test match in Adelaide, and finally succeeded in 1884–5.

The need for a national controlling organisation was felt by the administrators, if not the players, and in 1891–92 the Australasian Cricket Council was formed by delegates from the SACA, NSWCA and VCA. But the MCC remained outside its influence, and it failed to gain financial independence or the support of the players. It disbanded after eight years, leaving the field again to the MCC or whoever would fill the power vacuum.

The VCA saw it was destined to be a figurehead organisation unless it took some decisive action. Its secretary Ernie Bean and the legal

The cherished symbol of Australian Test cricket: the coat of arms.

adviser to the NSWCA, E. L. McElhone, joined forces in pushing for a national body, and their efforts saw the formation of the Australian Board of Control for International Cricket in 1906. Its founding members were the VCA and the NSWCA, but gradually the other State associations sought and gained membership.

The Board, controlled by the fiercely outspoken McElhone, was despised by the players. Joe Darling used his influence with the Marylebone Cricket Club on his last tour of England in 1905 to prevent a Board-sponsored 1906–7 tour of an English team.

But by the 1909 tour of England the Board had sufficient control to vote itself a share of the tour receipts and to appoint Peter McAlister as treasurer, a Board man who was to work alongside the player-elected manager, Frank Laver. The two were playing partners, but such acrimony developed that Laver refused to hand his account books to McAlister.

This enmity was sparked again in the boardroom clash between McAlister and Clem Hill in 1911–12, ostensibly over team selection, but no doubt fuelled by years of antagonism between Board and players.

The brawl was headline news and so was the defection of the six leading players. But the Board stood firm, recognising that any capitulation now would put the game out of national and official hands and back with another body, probably the MCC, and the players. But in establishing this control they alienated many top players of the time, including Monty Noble.

The cricketer's bible is Cricket – a Weekly Record of the Game. *It is full of fascinating English and Australian gossip.*

NSW wins its first Shield

Frank Iredale: topped averages.

Sydney, March 15. NSW has won the Sheffield Shield, after four rather humiliating years for the colony that sees itself as the natural home of cricket in Australia.

Victoria, and the upstart South Australia, who had to field 22 men against NSW XI's not so long ago, have got in the way of NSW ambitions for the last three years.

The tide turned at the start of the year when NSW beat SA in Adelaide for the first time in Shield competition. It then won all but its Sydney match against Victoria, a hard-fought affair which went over five days. NSW beat SA by nine wickets at the SCG, despite a fine 206 from SA batsman Clem Hill. 'Terror' Turner cleaned SA up with 6/35 in the second innings.

NSW batsman Henry Donnan (626 at 69.55) and Frank Iredale (528 at 58.66) have headed the batting averages, while Tom McKibbin has dominated the bowling with 46 wickets from six matches.

Jack Worrall cracks up 417 not out

Jack Worrall: record breaker.

CRICKET. A REFRESHER.

Melbourne, Feb. 20. Australian Test batsman Jack Worrall has written himself into the record books with 417 not out, the highest score in Australian club cricket. Worrall has not played Tests for some years and is unavailable for Victoria this season, but he is making the most of his club games and is clearly still among the front rank of Australian batsmen.

Batting for Carlton against the University his score contributed to the mammoth total of 922, a world record cricket score.

After a spell of fine weather the hard and true wickets have made it a nightmare round for bowlers, as East Melbourne made 876 against Richmond and Melbourne 683 against St Kilda.

Official NZ tour

Christchurch, Jan. 5. The first official NSW Cricket Association team to visit New Zealand, has been beaten by a representative New Zealand XI by 142 runs.

The NSW side is a virtual seconds team, as the Shield players have remained in Australia for the all-important intercolonial contests.

The NZ team won despite the bowling efforts of Syd Callaway, who in a fine performance took 7/77 and 8/98.

The NSW team had previously beaten teams representing Canterbury, Otago and Wellington.

Postie Harry Trott to lead the tour

Harry Trott: the new captain.

Adelaide, March 19. The genial South Melbourne postman George 'Harry' Trott has been chosen as captain of the Australian XI to tour England this northern summer.

Selector George Giffen is also from the Postal Service in South Australia. He has captained Trott, played with Trott in many Tests, and has now elected to play under him. Despite his humble job, Trott is regarded a shrewd leader with a steady temperament.

A surprise is the omission of Trott's brother Albert, who did well against the Englishmen last summer. 'Felix' in the *Australasian* describes Albert as 'one of the finest young cricketers that Australia has ever produced.'

Wicketkeeper Jack Harry was chosen, but is now left out because a knee injury prevented him from playing in the Australian XI v The Rest match three weeks ago. J. J. 'Stumper' Kelly of NSW had been chosen in his place, to share the keeping duties with Victoria's Alfred Johns. Harry is protesting his dumping, and claiming compensation.

Another late inclusion in the team is 19-year-old Clem Hill, who recently scored 206 for SA against NSW.

The team is: Harry Donnan, Syd Gregory, Frank Iredale and Tom McKibbin, James Kelly (NSW), George 'Harry' Trott, Harry Graham, Hugh Trumble, Alfred Johns (Victoria), Joe Darling, George Giffen, Ernie Jones (South Australia) and Charles Eady (Tasmania).

Ernie Jones sends Dr's fur flying

Ernie Jones: fearsome speed.

Lord's, June 13. Dr W. G. Grace has seen some fast bowling, but he seemed truly straggered by the efforts of Ernie Jones.

In the opening match against Lord Sheffield's Xl 'Jonah's' first few balls hit Dr Grace on the body and his fourth went through his beard and on to the boundary.

Grace is said to have stepped up to Jones with a glare and demanded: 'Whatever are ye at?' Jones is thought to have replied: 'Sorry, Doctor, she slipped.'

An extraordinary crowd of 24,930 watched the first day of this drawn match against a near-Test strength English side. The Australian team had been going along quite happily until they met up with the MCC at Lord's this week.

The match seemed to be going well, with the MCC all out for 219 and Trumble taking 6/84. Then, to the shock of the crowd Australia were all out for 18. Dick Pougher took 5/0 from 15 balls, including a hat-trick. He came on when Australia was 3/18. John Hearne took 4/4 and then rubbed it in by taking 9/73 in Australia's second innings of 183.

Australia batted one short (Giffen was ill) and on a sticky wicket, but they have been staggered by the debacle.

Gregory, Trott hundreds can't save Test

Lord's, June 24. The Australians have shown the huge first-Test crowds that came to Lord's, which looks like a newly tilled sheep paddock, that they can play cricket.

Syd Gregory (103) and Harry Trott (143) both made centuries in the second innings, and scored a record partnership of 221 as well, but their efforts were all too late.

The team never recovered from their humiliation on the first day, when they were bundled out for 53. There were five ducks in that score. Men with big reputations, Giffen, Trott and Eady, had that figure against their names. Harry Donnan and Clem Hill scored one each.

The destruction came from the big, black moustached fast bowler Tom Richardson, who crashed through to take 6/39, and from George Lohmann, 3/13.

The Australians were soon in the field and the crowd of 30,000 saw Dr W. G. Grace complete his 1000 runs in Test cricket as, with 66, he anchored the England score of 292.

The Australians made a bad start in the second innings to be 2/3 and then 3/63. But Trott and Gregory suddenly seemed untroubled and in command of the bowlers. They scored quickly, driving strongly, with Gregory, particularly, sneaking quick singles with his speed between the wickets. Trott was the more majestic of the two, and had the satisfaction of a century on his debut as Australian captain.

The score rose to 3/283, and Australian hopes rose with it. But when the partnership was broken the later batsmen conceded their wickets far too easily. They were all out for 347, leaving England an easy 111. The home side scored the runs for the loss of eight wickets, despite losing its trump card in W. G. Grace for seven.

Australia must now consider its failures from the first Test. The much-vaunted Ernie Jones, thought to be the equal of Richardson, took only three wickets, and the softer pitches are not suiting him. None of the other bowlers made great inroads on the English team. New tourists Harry Donnan, Clem Hill, Charles Eady and Joe Darling all failed, and George Giffen and Harry Graham were little better.

Perhaps the Australian bowlers need to take a leaf from Richardson's book – he is reputed to drink a pint of stout for every hour he bowls.

A happy band of tourists. Harry Trott's team photographed in England.

A win, despite Ranji

'Ranji': sinuous batting skills.

Tom McKibbin: added some bite.

Manchester, July 18. The sporting Australians might almost have been rueing the day they allowed the inclusion of the Indian Prince, 'Ranji', in the England team.

His Highness Kumar Sri Ranjitsinhji, Jam Saheb of Nawanagar, known to his friends and team-mates as 'Smith', almost stole the show and the match as he scored 154 in the second innings, including 100 before lunch as he took his overnight score from 41 to 154. His sinuous grace and power brought a touch of eastern magic to the Anglo-Saxon game.

Until then the revitalised Australians seemed to have the game in their keeping, scoring 412 (Iredale 108, Giffen 80) in the first innings, despite Tom Richardson's herculean spell of 68 overs to take 7/168.

England was then out for 231. The difference to the Australian bowling was the off-spinner Tom McKibbin. He took only three wickets in each innings, but he gave the Australian attack the extra bite it needed.

Then came Ranji, who was a controversial selection and only allowed to play with Australian approval. Harry Trott and manager Harry Musgrove thought it would be unfair to exclude him as India did not have Test cricket. Some English authorities, including Lord Harris, opposed his selection.

Australia needed 125 in its second innings. Richardson sent down another 42 overs (which meant four more pints of stout) and had 6/76 as Australia stumbled to 7/125 and victory.

Another trojan, George Giffen, became the first Test player to complete the double of 1000 runs and 100 wickets.

Anglo-Australian relations saved

London, Oct. 10. The good will that has surrounded the tour of the ninth Australian touring team to England seems to overcome the sour relations that have affected cricket between the two countries for many years.

The Australian team has been disciplined, good humoured, well behaved and has carried a sporting demeanour on the field.

A lot of the credit can go to captain Harry Trott and manager Harry Musgrove.

Trott, a jovial man, has proved to be a bluff and entertaining speaker at cricket functions. He has led his team well and displayed shrewd captaincy. He might easily have won the series, which England took 2–1 after Australian lost the decider on a stinker of a wicket.

Trott ensured that young SA batsman Clem Hill was placed on the same financial terms as the other tourists, engendering the sense of team loyalty and discipline observed of his team.

A couple of acts of fair play come to mind. Trott and Musgrove allowed Ranjitsinhji to play for England, when he posed a threat only to Australia. And they responded to a call from the Australasian Cricket Council that they cancel a trip to NZ on their way home, with a firm message that they intended to fulfill their obligations.

Trumble shines, bats fail

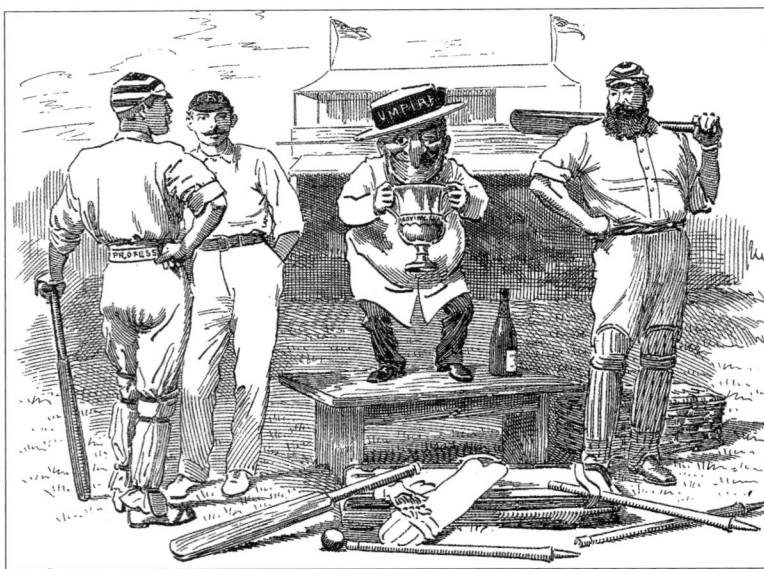

Punch magazine appeals for fair play as English professionals strike.

The Oval, Aug. 12. How close an Australian series victory looked at Kennington Oval today. A mere 110 runs stood in the path of the Australians as they went in for their second innings.

The result? They were bundled out for a miserable 44, the lowest Australian Test score so far. Only the last man in, Tom McKibbin (16) managed to reach double figures.

The pitch was difficult, with rain preventing play on the first day, but it conspired equally against both teams.

Australia was helped, particularly, by the disruption of a professionals' strike before the match. Five players threatened the action, seeking higher fees for working at the top of the scale in a notoriously precarious profession. Two men eventually did not play, George Lohmann and William Gunn, while Bobby Abel, Tom Hayward and Tom Richardson were cajoled back into the fold.

The tall, lanky big-handed and big-hearted Hugh Trumble emerged in this match as an off-spinner of great quality, taking 6/59 in the first innings and 6/30 in the second. Trumble's brisk pace and well controlled spin from his formidable height make him a tough proposition at any time. On a damp wicket, or a dusty one, he becomes a lethal force. His 'slower' ball was especially difficult for batsmen to pick – Stanley Jackson falling to it twice.

But the spinner who counted in the end was England left armer Bobby Peel, who took 6/23 as the Australian second innings fell apart.

An incident in New Zealand. Syd Gregory and Hugh Trumble 'shape up', and seem set for a dust-up. But all is well, and it ends in a handshake and laughter.

FIRST TEST 1896 ENGLAND v AUSTRALIA
Lord's Cricket Ground, London. June 22, 23, 24, 1896.
Toss: Australia. England won by 6 wkts.

AUSTRALIA

H Donnan run out	.1 (11)	b Hearne	.8
J Darling b Richardson	.22	b Richardson	.0
G Giffen c Lilley b Lohmann	.0	b Richardson	.32
GHS Trott (c) b Richardson	.0	c Hayward b Richardson	.143
ES Gregory b Richardson	.14	c Lohmann b Hearne	.103
H Graham b Richardson	.0	b Richardson	.10
C Hill b Lohmann	.1	b Hearne	.5
CJ Eady not out	.10 (1)	c Lilley b Richardson	.2
H Trumble b Richardson	.0 (8)	c Lilley b Hearne	.4
JJ Kelly (+) c Lilley b Lohmann	.0 (9)	not out	.24
E Jones b Richardson	.4 (10)	c Lilley b Hearne	.4
EXTRAS (B 1)	.1	(B 7, LB 4, W 1)	.12
TOTAL	.53		.347

FOW 1st Inns: 3 3 4 26 26 31 41 45 46 53
FOW 2nd Inns: 0 3 62 283 289 300 304 308 318 347

Bowling: *First Innings*: Richardson 11.3-3-39-6, Lohmann 11-6-13-3. *Second Innings*: Richardson 47-15-134-5, Lohmann 22-6-39-0, Hayward 11-3-44-0, Hearne 36-14-76-5, Jackson 11-5-28-0, Grace 6-1-14-0.

ENGLAND

WG Grace (c) c Trumble b Giffen	.66	c Hill b Trumble	.7
AE Stoddart b Eady	.17 (5)	not out	.30
R Abel b Eady	.94 (2)	c (S)FA Iredale b Jones	.4
JT Brown b Jones	.9	c Kelly b Eady	.36
W Gunn c Kelly b Trumble	.25 (6)	not out	.13
FS Jackson c Darling b Giffen	.44		
TW Hayward not out	.12 (3)	b Jones	.13
AFA Lilley (+) b Eady	.0		
GA Lohmann c(S)FA Iredale b Giffen	.1		
JT Hearne c Giffen b Trott	.11		
T Richardson c Hill b Trott	.6		
EXTRAS (B 5, LB 2)	.7	(B 3, LB 4, W 1)	.8
TOTAL	.292		.4 for 111

FOW 1st Inns: 38 143 152 197 256 266 266 267 286 292
FOW 2nd Inns: 16 20 42 82

Bowling: *First Innings*: Jones 26-6-64-1, Giffen 26-5-95-3, Eady 29-12-58-3, Trott 7.4-2-13-2, Trumble 19-3-55-1. *Second Innings*: Jones 23-10-42-2, Trumble 20-10-37-1, Giffen 1-0-9-0, Eady 3-0-11-1, Trott 0.1-0-14-0.

Umpires: J Phillips & WAJ West

SECOND TEST 1896 ENGLAND v AUSTRALIA
Old Trafford, Manchester. July 16, 17, 18, 1896.
Toss: Australia. Australia won by 3 wkts.

AUSTRALIA

FA Iredale b Briggs	.108	b Richardson	.11
J Darling c Lilley b Richardson	.27	c Lilley b Richardson	.16
G Giffen c & b Richardson	.80	c Ranjitsinhji b Richardson	.6
GHS Trott (c) c Brown b Lilley	.53	c Lilley b Richardson	.2
ES Gregory c Stoddart b Briggs	.25	c Ranjitsinhji b Briggs	.33
H Donnan b Richardson	.12	c Jackson b Richardson	.15
C Hill c Jackson b Richardson	.9	c Lilley b Richardson	.14
H Trumble b Richardson	.24	not out	.17
JJ Kelly (+) c Lilley b Richardson	.27	not out	.8
TR McKibbin not out	.28		
E Jones b Richardson	.4		
EXTRAS (B 6, LB 8, W 1)	.15	(LB 3)	.3
TOTAL	.412		.7 for 125

FOW 1st Inns: 41 172 242 294 294 314 325 362 403 412
FOW 2nd Inns: 20 26 28 45 79 95 100

Bowling: *First Innings*: Richardson 68-23-168-7, Briggs 40-18-99-2, Jackson 16-6-34-0, Hearne 28-11-53-0, Grace 7-3-11-0, Stoddart 6-2-9-0, Lilley 5-1-23-1. *Second Innings*: Richardson 42.3-16-76-6, Briggs 18-8-24-1, Hearne 24-13-22-0.

ENGLAND

AE Stoddart st Kelly b Trott	.15	b McKibbin	.41
WG Grace (c) st Kelly b Trott	.2	c Trott b Jones	.11
KS Ranjitsinhji c Trott b McKibbin	.62	not out	.154
R Abel c Trumble b McKibbin	.26	c McKibbin b Giffen	.13
FS Jackson run out	.18	c McKibbin b Giffen	.1
JT Brown c Kelly b Trumble	.22	c Iredale b Jones	.19
AC MacLaren c Trumble b McKibbin	.0	c Jones b Trumble	.15
AFA Lilley (+) not out	.65	c Trott b Giffen	.19
J Briggs b Trumble	.0	st Kelly b McKibbin	.16
JT Hearne c Trumble b Giffen	.18	c Kelly b McKibbin	.9
T Richardson run out	.2	c Jones b Trumble	.1
EXTRAS (B 1)	.1	(B 2, LB 3, W 1)	.6
TOTAL	.231		.305

FOW 1st Inns: 2 23 104 111 140 140 154 166 219 231
FOW 2nd Inns: 33 76 97 109 132 179 232 268 304 305

Bowling: *First Innings*: Jones 5-2-11-0, Trott 10-0-46-2, Giffen 19-3-48-1, Trumble 37-14-80-2, McKibbin 19-8-45-3. *Second Innings*: Jones 17-0-78-2, Trott 7-1-17-0, Giffen 16-1-65-3, Trumble 29.1-12-78-2, McKibbin 21-4-61-3.

Umpires: A Chester & J Phillips

THIRD TEST 1896 ENGLAND v AUSTRALIA
Kennington Oval, London. August 10, 11, 12, 1896.
Toss: England. England won by 66 runs.

ENGLAND

WG Grace (c) c Trott b Giffen	.24	b Trumble	.9
FS Jackson c McKibbin b Trumble	.45	b Trumble	.2
KS Ranjitsinhji b Giffen	.8	st Kelly b McKibbin	.11
R Abel c & b Trumble	.26	c Giffen b Trumble	.21
AC MacLaren b Trumble	.20	b Jones	.6
TW Hayward b Trumble	.0	c Trott b Trumble	.13
EG Wynyard c Darling b McKibbin	.10	c Kelly b McKibbin	.3
R Peel b Trumble	.0	b Trumble	.0
AFA Lilley (+) c Iredale b Trumble	.2	c McKibbin b Trumble	.6
JT Hearne b McKibbin	.8	b McKibbin	.1
T Richardson not out	.2	not out	.10
EXTRAS (LB 1)	.1	(LB 2)	.2
TOTAL	.145		.84

FOW 1st Inns: 54 78 78 114 114 131 132 135 138 145
FOW 2nd Inns: 11 12 24 50 56 67 67 67 68 84

Bowling: *First Innings*: Giffen 32-12-64-2, Trumble 40-10-59-6, McKibbin 9.3-0-21-2. *Second Innings*: Giffen 1-0-4-0, Trumble 25-9-30-6, McKibbin 20-8-35-3, Jones 3-0-13-1.

AUSTRALIA

J Darling c MacLaren b Hearne	.47	b Hearne	.0
FA Iredale run out	.30	c Jackson b Hearne	.3
G Giffen b Hearne	.0 (4)	b Hearne	.1
GHS Trott (c) b Peel	.5 (3)	c (S)W Brockwell b Peel	.3
ES Gregory b Hearne	.1	c Richardson b Peel	.6
C Hill run out	.1	b Peel	.0
H Donnan b Hearne	.10	c Hayward b Peel	.0
JJ Kelly (+) not out	.10	ibw Peel	.3
H Trumble b Hearne	.3	not out	.7
E Jones c MacLaren b Peel	.3	b Peel	.3
TR McKibbin b Hearne	.0	c Abel b Hearne	.16
EXTRAS (B 8, LB 1)	.9	(B 2)	.2
TOTAL	.119		.44

FOW 1st Inns: 75 77 82 83 84 85 112 116 119 119
FOW 2nd Inns: 0 3 7 7 11 11 14 19 25 44

Bowling: *First Innings*: Peel 20-9-30-2, Hearne 26.1-10-41-6, Richardson 5-0-22-0, Hayward 2-0-17-0. *Second Innings*: Peel 12-5-23-6, Hearne 13-8-19-4, Richardson 1-1-0-0.

Umpires: W Hearn & J Phillips

Australian Averages

1896 ENGLAND v AUSTRALIA

AUSTRALIA	M	Inn	NO	Runs	H.S	Avrge	Ct	St	Overs	Mds	Runs	Wkt	Avrge
Darling, J	3	6	-	112	47	18.67	2	-	-	-	-	-	-
Donnan, H	3	6	-	46	15	7.67	-	-	-	-	-	-	-
Eady, CJ	1	2	1	12	10*	12.00	-	-	32.0	12	69	4	17.25
Giffen, G	3	6	-	119	80	19.83	2	-	95.0	21	285	9	31.67
Graham, H	1	2	-	10	10	5.00	-	-	-	-	-	-	-
Gregory, ES	3	6	-	182	103	30.33	-	-	-	-	-	-	-
Hill, C	3	6	-	30	14	5.00	2	-	-	-	-	-	-
Iredale, FA	2	4	-	152	108	38.00	2	-	-	-	-	-	-
Jones, E	3	5	-	18	4	3.60	2	-	74.0	18	208	6	34.67
Kelly, JJ	3	6	3	72	27	24.00	5	4	-	-	-	-	-
McKibbin, TR	2	3	1	44	28*	22.00	-	-	69.3	20	162	11	14.73
Trott, GHS	3	6	-	206	143	34.33	5	-	25.0	3	80	4	20.00
Trumble, H	3	6	2	55	24	13.75	5	-	170.1	58	339	18	18.83

English Averages

1896 ENGLAND v AUSTRALIA

ENGLAND	M	Inn	NO	Runs	H.S	Avrge	Ct	St	Overs	Mds	Runs	Wkt	Avrge
Abel, R	3	6	-	184	94	30.67	1	-	-	-	-	-	-
Briggs, J	1	2	-	16	16	8.00	-	-	58.0	26	123	3	41.00
Brown, JT	2	4	-	86	36	21.50	1	-	-	-	-	-	-
Grace, WG	3	6	-	119	66	19.83	-	-	13.0	4	25	-	-
Gunn, W	1	2	1	38	25	38.00	-	-	-	-	-	-	-
Hayward, TW	2	4	1	38	13	12.67	2	-	13.0	3	61	-	-
Hearne, JT	3	5	-	47	18	9.40	-	-	127.1	56	211	15	14.07
Jackson, FS	3	5	-	110	45	22.00	4	-	27.0	11	62	-	-
Lilley, AFA	3	5	1	92	65*	23.00	9	-	5.0	1	23	1	23.00
Lohmann, GA	1	1	-	1	1	1.00	1	-	33.0	12	52	3	17.33
MacLaren, AC	2	4	-	41	20	10.25	-	-	-	-	-	-	-
Peel, R	1	2	-	0	0	0.00	-	-	32.0	14	53	8	6.63
Ranjitsinhji, KS	2	4	-	235	154*	78.33	2	-	-	-	-	-	-
Richardson, T	3	5	2	20	10*	6.67	2	-	175.1	58	439	24	18.29
Stoddart, AE	2	4	1	103	41	34.33	1	-	6.0	2	9	-	-
Wynyard, EG	1	2	-	13	10	6.50	-	-	-	-	-	-	-

NSW win Shield

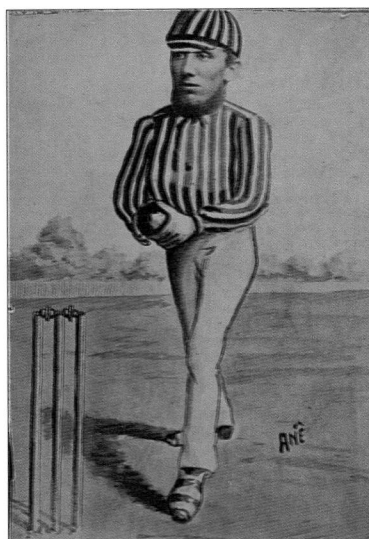

Tom Garrett: A late century.

Sydney, March 1. NSW has put practically a Test team in the field this season, and has won all its Sheffield Shield matches.

Tom Garrett, the captain and an old Test campaigner, had the added delight of scoring his maiden first class century in the twilight of his career, against South Australia in January.

The only non-capped players in NSW have been handy, with Monty Noble scoring a memorable 71 and 153 in the SCG match against Victoria and Bill Howell the third best wicket taker in the season. Tom McKibbin has been top with 44 wickets at just 14.88.

Year of Chuckers

London, Jan. 25. There is growing concern about the practice of 'throwing' or 'chucking' among bowlers, and it is now the subject of a letter to *Sporting Life* by the Australian bowler, Fred Spofforth.

Spofforth said in his article that there was scarcely a first class county that did not include a 'thrower' among its cricketers. He says: 'Australia has now taken it up, and with the last eleven there was one who hardly ever delivered a "fair" ball, and although I am quite aware I may raise a "hornet's nest" about my head by mentioning names I allude to Tom McKibbin who, I shall always maintain, should never be allowed to play under the existing rule.'

Spofforth describes throwing: 'They put the ball, which is they throw only from one point, mostly the elbow.'

He says the remedy is hard to find, as there is scarcely an umpire in England who would dare no-ball a cricketer for throwing.

But his solution is to form a committee of county captains with the power to suspend players for a week for a first offence, for a week with a fine for the second and for a season for a third instance.

Meanwhile in Australia Tom McKibbin is having a great season of wicket taking. Ernie 'Jonah' Jones' action has also been questioned, especially when he puts in his fast one.

Wisden Trumbled

Hugh Trumble: Wisden's anointed.

London, Feb. 15. *Wisden*, the 'bible' of cricket, in its annual edition, has named Hugh Trumble one of the 1897 Cricketers of the Year. Trumble's gifts have been on display in England for three tours, and he seemed to come of age on the last tour, particularly when he has displayed his skills on a soft or sticky wicket.

Trumble's height gives his flight a most deceptive flavour, and, with his slower ball, he uses it to deceive. After Stanley Jackson fell twice to him in the third Test last year he exclaimed: 'You devil, Hughie. But I'll pick that slower one sooner or later.'

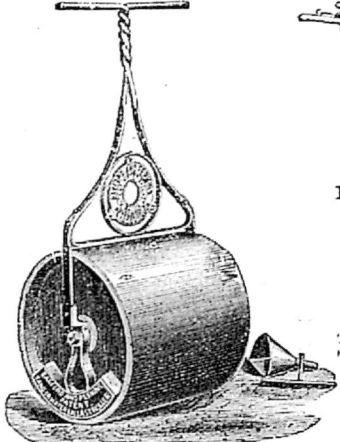
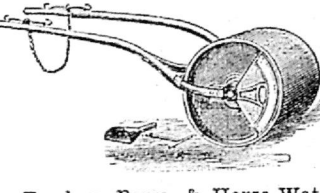

England crushed 4–1

The scene during the second Test in Melbourne, with Charles McLeod facing and Clem Hill backing up.

Sydney, March 3. Australia and England may well have entered a new phase of their cricketing relationship, following the 4–1 thrashing of the masters from the Old Country in this Test series.

It started out in a somewhat expected fashion as England, with Ranjitsinhji (175) rampant, made 551 in the first innings and won the first Test easily.

There was a hint of change in Australia's second innings when the tyros Joe Darling (101) and Clem Hill (96) flayed the English bowling and helped the score to a total 408.

That was the end of England's dominance for the whole summer, and even the colonial teams matched them, with NSW winning by a staggering 239 runs.

In the second Test, the first six Australian batsmen got among the runs against a flagging English attack, and Trumble and Noble headed a bowling attack that looked far more penetrating than the older English bowlers. The result was a win by an innings and 55 runs. The third Test story was similar, with Joe Darling scoring 178 before his home crowd in Adelaide. England used eight bowlers, but had to concede a score of 573 runs. Darling became the first batsman to score more than one century in a Test series. Hill (81), Gregory (52) and Iredale (84) were in assistance.

Clem Hill came of age, at least as a batsman, (he was still 48 days short of 21) as he dominated the fourth Test with a peerless 188. He took to the English pacemen with ferocity, often pulling balls wide of the off stump to the square leg boundary. Again it was an easy win, by eight wickets. Hill had shown his promise at this level with 200 for South Australia against England, but this innings was a masterpiece.

Just as England seemed likely to gain respectibility in the fifth Test, setting Australia 275 to win, Joe Darling broke out again for 160, and Australia won by six wickets.

England's downfall has not been helped by the troubles of captain A. E. Stoddart, who missed the first two Tests through illness and because of his mother's death, and who stood down for the fifth Test through poor form. Archie MacLaren has had to carry the captaincy and (with Ranjitsinhji) the batting. The warhorse paceman Tom Richardson has had rhuematism, and only his 8/94 in Australia's first innings of the fifth Test showed him at his best.

Some comfort in the sun. A. E. Stoddart's team enjoy a country sojourn in a stately home in Victoria.

Darling and Hill at the top

Joe Darling: three centuries.

Clem Hill: leg-side assault.

Sydney, March 3. Clem Hill and Joe Darling. The South Australian pair left England in 1896 with very little to their credit, but with youth on their side. How they have stored their experiences, ripened in the Australian sun and blossomed out on the hard pitches of this Australian summer.

Their dominant batting has been the biggest factor between the two teams. Both are hitters, capable of defence, but in their element when hitting out. In Adelaide, Darling hit a six out of the Oval and two fives, one over the heads of the crowd near the entrance gate.

In Sydney in the fifth Test Darling's 160 came in just 171 minutes, with 30 fours. His hundred came in 91 minutes – the fastest in Test cricket.

Hill has been overshadowed on the scoreboard, but the best innings of the series was his superb 188 in the record seventh-wicket partnership of 165 with Hugh Trumble in the fourth Test.

Harry Trott has led the team superbly, and has been consistent with bat and ball, and there have been great batting contributions from McLeod, Gregory and Iredale.

Ernie Jones has troubled the Englishmen throughout with his pace and is the season's top wicket taker, but he did not dominate the Tests. Rather it was the combination of the younger and more vital bowlers, Monty Noble, Hugh Trumble and Bill Howell that made it superior to England. Howell replaced Tom McKibbin, who seems to have lost form due to the accusations of chucking. Both he and Noble have made fine Test beginnings.

In the end Australia's youthful exuberance prevailed, especially in the field.

Trott fades out

Melbourne, March 30. After his great captaincy during the Test series, Harry Trott is now in physical difficulties, and his cricket career may be threatened.

Trott has revealed that he has been troubled with the sight in his right eye, and could scarcely see through it in the fifth Test.

Despite this, Trott has led the side admirably, although his usually reliable batting has been affected, with a 79 his only substantial score.

He has taken seven wickets over the five Tests. He has the solace of immense public popularity and a winning record as captain. He has captained five Test wins and three losses.

Eyes on Trumper

Sydney, March 30. A champion batsman seems to be emerging in New South Wales. Victor Trumper joined the Paddington Cricket Club in 1896 as a fast bowler, but he is making his name as a batsman. This season he became the first batsman to score 1000 runs in the Sydney club competition, scoring six centuries in eight innings and averaging a phenomenal 204.

He has, naturally, forced his way into the NSW side, but he disappointed on his first outing with 0 and 5 against England. Since then he has made 48, 13, 12, 12, 4, 31, 68 and 7. Not a great haul, but his club performance suggests better things to come.

FIRST TEST 1897–98 AUSTRALIA v ENGLAND
Sydney Cricket Ground, Sydney. December 13, 14, 15, 16 ,17, 1897.
Toss: England. England won by 9 wkts.

ENGLAND

Batsman	1st Inns		2nd Inns	
JR Mason b Jones	6		b McKibbin	32
AC MacLaren (c) c Kelly b McLeod	109		not out	50
TW Hayward c Trott b Trumble	72			
W Storer (+) c & b Trott	43			
NF Druce c Gregory b McLeod	20			
GH Hirst b Jones	62			
KS Ranjitsinhji c Gregory b McKibbin	175	(3)	not out	8
E Wainwright b Jones	10			
JT Hearne c & b McLeod	17			
J Briggs run out	1			
T Richardson not out	24			
EXTRAS (LB 11, W 1)	12		(B 5, LB 1)	6
TOTAL	551		1 for 96	

FOW 1st Inns: 26 162 224 256 258 382 422 471 477 551
FOW 2nd Inns: 80

Bowling: *First Innings:* McKibbin 34-5-113-1, Jones 50-8-130-3, McLeod 28-12-80-3, Trumble 40-7-138-1, Trott 23-2-78-1. *Second Innings:* Jones 9-1-28-0, Trumble 14-4-40-0, McKibbin 5-1-22-1.

AUSTRALIA

Batsman	1st Inns		2nd Inns	
J Darling c Druce b Richardson	7		c Druce b Briggs	101
JJ Lyons b Richardson	3	(7)	c Hayward b Hearne	25
FA Iredale c Druce b Hearne	25	(2)	b Briggs	18
C Hill b Hearne	19		b Hearne	96
ES Gregory c Mason b Hearne	46		run out	31
GHS Trott (c) b Briggs	10	(8)	b Richardson	27
JJ Kelly (+) b Richardson	1	(9)	not out	46
H Trumble c Storer b Mason	70	(6)	c Druce b Hearne	2
CE McLeod not out	50	(3)	run out	26
TR McKibbin b Hearne	0	(11)	b Hearne	6
E Jones c Richardson b Hearne	0	(10)	lbw Richardson	3
EXTRAS (B 1, LB 1, NB 4)	6		(B 12, LB 1, W 4, NB 10)	27
TOTAL	237			408

FOW 1st Inns: 8 24 56 57 86 87 138 228 237 237
FOW 2nd Inns: 37 135 191 269 271 318 321 382 390 408

Bowling: *First Innings:* Richardson 27-8-71-3, Hirst 28-7-57-0, Hearne 20.1-7-42-5, Briggs 20-7-42-1, Hayward 3-1-11-0, Mason 2-1-8-1. *Second Innings:* Richardson 41-9-121-2, Hearne 38-8-99-4, Briggs 22-3-86-2, Hayward 5-1-16-0, Hirst 13-3-49-0, Mason 2-0-10-0.

Umpires: C Bannerman & J Phillips

SECOND TEST 1897–98 AUSTRALIA v ENGLAND
Melbourne Cricket Ground, Melbourne. January 1, 3, 4, 5, 1898.
Toss: Australia. Australia won by an innings & 55 runs.

AUSTRALIA

J Darling c Hirst b Briggs	36	
CE McLeod b Storer	112	
C Hill c Storer b Hayward	58	
ES Gregory b Briggs	71	
FA Iredale c Ranjitsinhji b Hirst	89	
GHS Trott (c) c Wainwright b Briggs	79	
MA Noble b Richardson	17	
H Trumble c Hirst b Mason	14	
JJ Kelly (+) c Richardson b Hearne	19	
E Jones run out	7	
TR McKibbin not out	2	
EXTRAS (B 14, W 1, NB 1)	16	
TOTAL	520	

FOW 1st Inns: 97 245 310 374 389 474 493 537 552 573

Bowling: *First Innings:* Richardson 48-12-114-1, Hirst 25-1-89-1, Briggs 40-10-96-3, Hearne 36-6-94-1, Mason 11-1-33-1, Hayward 9-4-23-1, Storer 16-4-55-1.

ENGLAND

Batsman	1st Inns		2nd Inns	
AC MacLaren (c) c Trumble b McKibbin	35		c Trott b Trumble	38
JR Mason b McKibbin	3		b Trumble	3
E Wainwright c Jones b Noble	21	(8)	b Noble	11
KS Ranjitsinhji b Trumble	71	(3)	b Noble	27
TW Hayward c Jones b Trott	23	(4)	c Trumble b Noble	33
W Storer (+) c Kelly b Trumble	51	(5)	c Trumble b Noble	1
GH Hirst b Jones	0	(6)	lbw Trumble	3
NF Druce lbw Trumble	44	(7)	c McLeod b Noble	15
JT Hearne b Jones	1	(10)	c Jones b Noble	0
J Briggs not out	46	(9)	c Trott b Trumble	12
T Richardson b Trumble	3		not out	2
EXTRAS (B 10, LB 3, NB 4)	17		(B 3, LB 1, W 1)	5
TOTAL	315			150

FOW 1st Inns: 10 60 74 133 203 208 223 224 311 315
FOW 2nd Inns: 10 65 71 75 80 115 123 141 148 150

Bowling: *First Innings:* McKibbin 28-7-66-2, Trumble 26.5-5-54-4, Jones 22-5-54-2, Trott 17-3-49-1, Noble 12-3-31-1, McLeod 14-2-44-0. *Second Innings:* Trumble 30.4-12-53-4, McLeod 7-2-13-0, McKibbin 4-0-13-0, Trott 7-0-17-0, Noble 17-1-49-6.

Umpires: C Bannerman & J Phillips

THIRD TEST 1897–98 AUSTRALIA v ENGLAND
Adelaide Oval, Adelaide. January 14, 15, 17, 18, 19, 1898.
Toss: Australia. Australia won by an innings & 13 runs.

AUSTRALIA

CE McLeod b Briggs	.31
J Darling c Storer b Richardson	.178
C Hill c Storer b Richardson	.81
ES Gregory c Storer b Hirst	.52
FA Iredale b Richardson	.84
GHS Trott (c) b Hearne	.3
MA Noble b Richardson	.39
H Trumble not out	.37
JJ Kelly (+) b Stoddart	.22
E Jones run out	.8
WP Howell b Hearne	.16
EXTRAS (B 16, LB 5, NB 1)	.22
TOTAL	.573

FOW 1st Inns: 97 245 310 374 389 474 493 537 552 573

Bowling: *First Innings*: Richardson 56-11-164-4, Briggs 63-26-128-1, Hearne 44.1-15-94-2, Hirst 24.1-6-62-1, Hayward 9-1-36-0, Mason 11-2-41-0, Storer 3-0-16-0, Stoddart 4-1-10-1.

ENGLAND

AC MacLaren b Howell	.14		c Kelly b Noble	.124
JR Mason b Jones	.11		c Jones b Noble	.0
KS Ranjitsinhji c Noble b Trumble	.6		c Trumble b McLeod	.77
W Storer (+) b Howell	.4	(5)	c Hill b McLeod	.6
TW Hayward b Jones	.70	(4)	c & b McLeod	.1
NF Druce c Darling b Noble	.24		b Noble	.27
GH Hirst c Trumble b Noble	.85		lbw McLeod	.6
AE Stoddart (c) c Jones b Howell	.15		c Jones b McLeod	.24
J Briggs c Kelly b Noble	.14		not out	.0
JT Hearne b Howell	.0		c & b McLeod	.4
T Richardson not out	.25		c Jones b Noble	.0
EXTRAS (B 2, LB 6, W 2)	.10		(B 2, LB 6, W 3, NB 2)	.13
TOTAL	.278			.282

FOW 1st Inns: 24 30 34 42 106 172 206 223 224 278
FOW 2nd Inns: 10 152 154 160 212 235 262 278 282 282

Bowling: *First Innings*: Howell 54-23-70-4, Jones 27-3-67-2, Trumble 17-3-39-1, Noble 24.5-5-78-3, Trott 4-0-14-0. *Second Innings*: Howell 40-18-60-0, Noble 33-7-84-5, Trumble 16-5-37-0, McLeod 48-24-65-5, Trott 6-0-18-0, Jones 1-0-5-0.

Umpires: C Bannerman & J Phillips

FIFTH TEST 1897–98 AUSTRALIA v ENGLAND
Sydney Cricket Ground, Sydney. February 26, 28, March 1, 2, 1898.
Toss: England. Australia won by 6 wkts.

ENGLAND

AC MacLaren (c) b Trott	.65	c Darling b Jones	.0
E Wainwright c Hill b Trumble	.49	b Noble	.6
KS Ranjitsinhji c Gregory b Trott	.2	lbw Jones	.12
TW Hayward b Jones	.47	c Worrall b Trumble	.43
W Storer (+) b Jones	.44	c Gregory b Trumble	.31
NF Druce lbw Noble	.64	c Howell b Trumble	.18
GH Hirst b Jones	.44	c Trott b Jones	.7
JR Mason c Howell b Jones	.7	b Trumble	.11
J Briggs b Jones	.0	b Howell	.29
JT Hearne not out	.2	not out	.3
T Richardson b Jones	.1	b Howell	.6
EXTRAS (B 2, LB 5, W 2, NB 1)	.10	(LB 12)	.12
TOTAL	.335		.178

FOW 1st Inns: 111 117 119 197 230 308 318 324 334 335
FOW 2nd Inns: 0 16 30 90 104 121 137 148 172 178

Bowling: *First Innings*: Noble 26-6-57-1, Howell 17-6-40-0, Trumble 26-4-67-1, Jones 26.2-3-82-6, Trott 23-6-56-2, McLeod 11-4-23-0. *Second Innings*: Jones 26-3-61-3, Noble 15-4-34-1, Howell 6.1-0-22-2, Trott 7-1-12-0, Trumble 24-7-37-4.

AUSTRALIA

CE McLeod b Richardson	.64	b Hearne	.4
J Darling c Mason b Briggs	.14	c Wainwright b Richardson	.160
C Hill b Richardson	.8	b Richardson	.2
J Worrall c Ranjitsinhji b Richardson	.26	c Hirst b Hayward	.62
ES Gregory c Storer b Richardson	.21	not out	.22
MA Noble c Storer b Richardson	.31	not out	.15
GHS Trott (c) c Ranjitsinhji b Hearne	.18		
H Trumble b Richardson	.12		
JJ Kelly (+) not out	.27		
WP Howell c MacLaren b Richardson	.10		
E Jones c Storer b Richardson	.1		
EXTRAS (B 5, W 1, NB 1)	.7	(B 6, W 1, NB 4)	.11
TOTAL	.239		.4 for 276

FOW 1st Inns: 36 45 99 132 137 188 188 221 232 239
FOW 2nd Inns: 23 40 233 252

Bowling: *First Innings*: Richardson 36.1-7-94-8, Briggs 17-4-39-1, Hearne 21-9-40-1, Storer 5-1-13-0, Mason 13-7-20-0, Hayward 4-0-12-0, Hirst 4-1-14-0. *Second Innings*: Richardson 21.4-1-110-2, Hearne 15-5-52-1, Hirst 7-0-33-0, Briggs 5-1-25-0, Mason 11-1-27-0, Hayward 3-0-18-1.

Umpires: C Bannerman & J Phillips

FOURTH TEST 1897–98 AUSTRALIA v ENGLAND
Melbourne Cricket Ground, Melbourne. January 29, 31, February 1, 2, 1898.
Toss: Australia. Australia won by 8 wkts.

AUSTRALIA

CE McLeod b Hearne	.1	not out	.64
J Darling c Hearne b Richardson	.12	c Druce b Hayward	.29
C Hill c Stoddart b Hearne	.188	lbw Hayward	.0
ES Gregory b Richardson	.0	not out	.21
FA Iredale c Storer b Hearne	.0		
MA Noble c & b Hearne	.4		
GHS Trott (c) c Storer b Hearne	.7		
H Trumble c Mason b Storer	.46		
JJ Kelly (+) c Storer b Briggs	.32		
E Jones c Hayward b Hearne	.20		
WP Howell not out	.9		
EXTRAS (B 3, W 1)	.4	(NB 1)	.1
TOTAL	.323		.2 for 115

FOW 1st Inns: 1 25 26 32 58 223 283 303 323
FOW 2nd Inns: 50 50

Bowling: *First Innings*: Richardson 26-2-102-2, Hearne 35.4-13-98-6, Hayward 10-4-24-0, Briggs 17-4-38-1, Stoddart 6-1-22-0, Storer 4-0-24-1, Wainwright 3-1-11-0. *Second Innings*: Hearne 7-3-19-0, Briggs 6-1-31-0, Hayward 10-4-24-2, Wainwright 9-2-21-0, Mason 4-1-10-0, Ranjitsinhji 3.4-1-9-0.

ENGLAND

AC MacLaren b Howell	.8	(3)	c Iredale b Trumble	.45
E Wainwright c Howell b Trott	.6		c McLeod b Jones	.2
KS Ranjitsinhji c Iredale b Trumble	.24	(4)	b Noble	.55
TW Hayward c Gregory b Noble	.22	(5)	c & b Trumble	.25
NF Druce lbw Jones	.24	(9)	c Howell b Trott	.16
W Storer (+) c & b Trumble	.2	(7)	c Darling b McLeod	.26
JR Mason b Jones	.30	(8)	b Howell	.26
AE Stoddart (c) c Darling b Jones	.17	(6)	b Jones	.25
J Briggs not out	.21	(1)	c Darling b Howell	.23
JT Hearne c Trott b Jones	.0		not out	.4
T Richardson b Trott	.20		c Trumble b McLeod	.0
EXTRAS	.0		(B 1, LB 11, W 1, NB 1)	.14
TOTAL	.174			.263

FOW 1st Inns: 14 16 60 60 67 103 121 148 148 174
FOW 2nd Inns: 7 63 94 147 157 192 211 259 259 263

Bowling: *First Innings*: Howell 16-7-34-1, Trott 11.1-1-33-2, Noble 7-1-21-1, Trumble 15-4-30-2, Jones 12-2-56-4. *Second Innings*: Howell 30-12-58-2, Jones 25-7-70-2, Trott 12-2-39-1, Trumble 23-6-40-2, Noble 16-6-31-1, McLeod 8.2-4-11-2.

Umpires: C Bannerman & J Phillips

Australian Averages

1897–98 AUSTRALIA v ENGLAND

AUSTRALIA	M	Inn	NO	Runs	H.S	Avrge	Ct	St	Overs	Mds	Runs	Wkt	Avrge
Darling, J	5	8	-	537	178	67.13	5	-	-	-	-	-	-
Gregory, ES	5	8	2	264	71	44.00	5	-	-	-	-	-	-
Hill, C	5	8	-	452	188	56.50	2	-	-	-	-	-	-
Howell, WP	3	3	1	35	16	17.50	4	-	163.1	66	284	9	31.56
Iredale, FA	4	5	-	216	89	43.20	2	-	-	-	-	-	-
Jones, E	5	6	-	39	20	6.50	7	-	198.2	32	553	22	25.14
Kelly, JJ	5	6	2	147	46*	36.75	4	-	-	-	-	-	-
Lyons, JJ	1	2	-	28	25	14.00	-	-	-	-	-	-	-
McKibbin, TR	2	3	1	8	6	4.00	-	-	71.0	13	214	4	53.50
McLeod, CE	5	8	2	352	112	58.67	4	-	116.2	48	236	10	23.60
Noble, MA	4	5	1	106	39	26.50	2	-	150.5	33	385	19	20.26
Trott, GHS	5	6	-	144	79	24.00	6	-	110.1	15	316	7	45.14
Trumble, H	5	6	1	181	70	36.20	4	-	232.3	57	535	19	28.16
Worrall, J	1	2	-	88	62	44.00	1	-	-	-	-	-	-

English Averages

1897–98 AUSTRALIA v ENGLAND

ENGLAND	M	Inn	NO	Runs	H.S	Avrge	Ct	St	Overs	Mds	Runs	Wkt	Avrge
Briggs, J	5	9	3	146	46*	24.33	-	-	190.0	56	485	9	53.89
Druce, NF	5	9	-	252	64	28.00	5	-	-	-	-	-	-
Hayward, TW	5	9	-	336	72	37.33	2	-	53.0	15	164	4	41.00
Hearne, JT	5	9	3	31	17	5.17	2	-	217.0	66	538	20	26.90
Hirst, GH	4	7	-	207	85	29.57	3	-	101.1	18	304	2	152.00
MacLaren, AC	5	10	-	488	124	54.22	1	-	-	-	-	-	-
Mason, JR	5	10	-	129	32	12.90	3	-	54.0	13	149	2	74.50
Ranjitsinhji, KS	5	10	1	457	175	50.78	3	-	3.4	1	9	-	-
Richardson, T	5	9	3	83	25*	13.83	2	-	255.5	50	776	22	35.27
Stoddart, AE	2	4	-	81	25	20.25	1	-	10.0	2	32	1	32.00
Storer, W	5	9	-	208	51	23.11	11	-	28.0	5	108	2	54.00
Wainwright, E	4	7	-	105	49	15.00	2	-	12.0	3	32	-	-

Victor Trumper rising, George Giffen still there

The winning Victorian Sheffield Shield team, captained by Jack Worrall.

Melbourne, April 22. The Shield season has seen even further growth of Australia's cricketing powers. A new player has emerged in Victor Trumper who may yet surpass even the best of our powerful young batsman.

Trumper started against Tasmania when he hit 292 of 839 and, according to *Referee*, 'made every sort of stroke, both off and on, before and behind the wicket, with the grace and power of a master hand.'

Trumper's season then progressed somewhat patchily, with some fine batting, yet few good scores in the Shield, but another double-century against the New Zealanders. For Paddington he made 562 in only three innings. He has topped the first class averages

at 62.35 and is certainly drawing the crowds.

The Shield, however, went to Victoria, due mainly to the pairing of Hugh Trumble and Charles McLeod to open the bowling. They took 55 of the team's 72 wickets and were the tightest of all the Shield bowlers.

New South Wales dropped out early when they lost both of their tour matches in December. South Australia, with Clem Hill, Joe Darling, Jack Lyons and George Giffen heading the batting and Giffen and Ernie Jones the bowling, looked strong, but the rest of the team were probably not Shield class. Giffen remains remarkably durable, figuring high in both the batting and bowling averages.

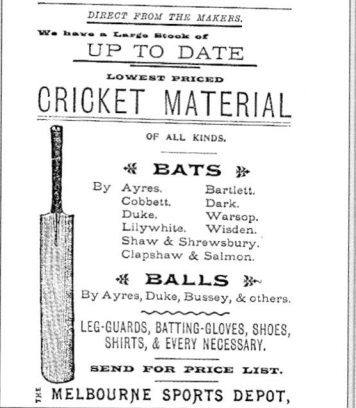
Challenge for old cricket colonies

Perth, April 6. The young Colonies in Australian cricket are starting to make their presence felt, with Queensland, Tasmania and Western Australia all playing first class (but not yet Shield) matches.

New Zealand also sent its first official team over, and it was soundly beaten by both NSW and Victoria.

South Australia has just played the inaugural first class game in Western Australia. WA seemed overawed on the first day, succumbing for 100, but it scored 293 in the second innings and SA had to make 235 to win. The journey from Adelaide to Perth took six days by sea because of rough weather.

Victoria suffered a shock 365-run loss to Tasmania in Hobart, with the island stalwarts Charles Eady (92 and 31 and 12 wickets) and Ken Burn (119 in the second innings) being great contributors. The islanders, however, fared badly on their first visit to NSW.

South Australia's visit to Queensland brought a half holiday on the first day's play at the new Brisbane venue, the Woollangabba Ground. The locals were outclassed, making 100 and 198, to SA's 582.

Long train trips for travelling Shield cricketers

Melbourne, March 15. Colonial cricketers have the prospect of some refreshing visits to other cities, but some long train and boat journeys as well.

For many years now Sydney, Melbourne and Adelaide have been linked by train, but visits to Tasmania, Queensland or Western Australia need a steamer trip. The long voyage of the SS *Paroo* recently left the SA cricketers groggy after battling through a storm in the Bight.

A typical trip is that of NSW on its southern tour. Her players usually leave Sydney on the second Friday in December, and travel by train to Melbourne, a trip of about 18 hours. After a couple of days rest, they entrain to Adelaide for a further 18 hours, arriving on Tuesday. This allows a couple of days rest before the match.

The game over, they leave on Tuesday for Melbourne, where their match, each season, generally starts on Boxing Day.

Australians get a racing start

Manchester, May 26. After the slightly disconcerting loss to Essex two weeks ago, the Australian party has been restored to sparkling form with bat and ball, defeating Lancashire by an innings and 84 runs.

Young Victor Trumper, batsman and assistant to manager Ben Wardill, at last showed some of his wares in a splendidly composed 82 and Hugh Trumble whacked a nice 51 at the end and then took 2/18 and 5/20.

Bill Howell took 2/28 and 3/16 – but this was but a pale reflection of the sensations of his game last week against Surrey. In this match he took all 10 wickets in Surrey's first innings, 10/28 and another five in the second innings 5/29.

Howell's feat was the first by an Australian in England. George Giffen achieved it for the Australians v the Rest in 1883–84 in Sydney.

The win over Lancashire was gained in two days. On the third day Lord Beresford hosted the team at the local races, and did the right thing by advising them to back a horse named Portobello. It also did the right thing by its supporters and came home at long odds. Ernie Jones was especially pleased.

Bill Howell: all 10 wickets.

Trumper, Hill set up win

The young Australian cricketers at last have the lion by the tail.

Lord's, June 17. After outplaying England in the first Test match, the first played at Trent Bridge, Australia came to Lord's in high expectation and fulfilled it, going one up in this first five Test series in England.

The first Test was also W. G. Grace's last. At the age of 50 he was a liability in the field and uncomfortable against the pace of Ernie Jones. W. G. did feature in the best opening stand of the Tests so far for England, a modest 75. Ernie Jones took 5/88 and 2/31 in the draw, and it was he who broke through England's top order in both innings of the second Test. England was 3/20 and 3/24. Jones took a splendid 7/88 in the

first innings and shared the wickets with Frank Laver and Monty Noble in the second, taking 10 for the match.

Of course, it was the tyros Clem Hill and Victor Trumper who took the eye and stole the show in Australia's innings of 421 at Lord's.

Both scored a wonderful 135, Trumper not out, in knocks that have surely written the young men into Australia's cricket future.

Hill, 22, had to battle when Australia was 2/28 and played for four hours with 17 fours. Trumper was able to play in the only way he knows how, with an elegant freedom, and made his runs in just 210 minutes, with 20 fours. Australia won by 10 wickets.

Umpire Barlow's misplaced loyalty

Trent Bridge, June 3. Umpire Dick Barlow, a useful cricketer who played 17 Tests for England, managed to let his heart get in the way of his umpire's head in the first Test.

Australian captain Joe Darling protested to Lord Harris about Barlow's action in recalling England batsman Ranjitsinhji, who had been run out by Frank Laver when Ranji was on 30.

'Ranji' had started to walk towards the pavilion but Barlow had an aberration and called out 'You're not out!'.

Ranji went on to save the Test and play one of his best hands, an innings of 93 not out.

Lord Harris has promised not to use Barlow again in Test matches, saying he had 'misplaced loyalties to his old team'.

Dick Barlow: England's man.

Australia keeps the ashes

Victor Trumper's 300 is hailed

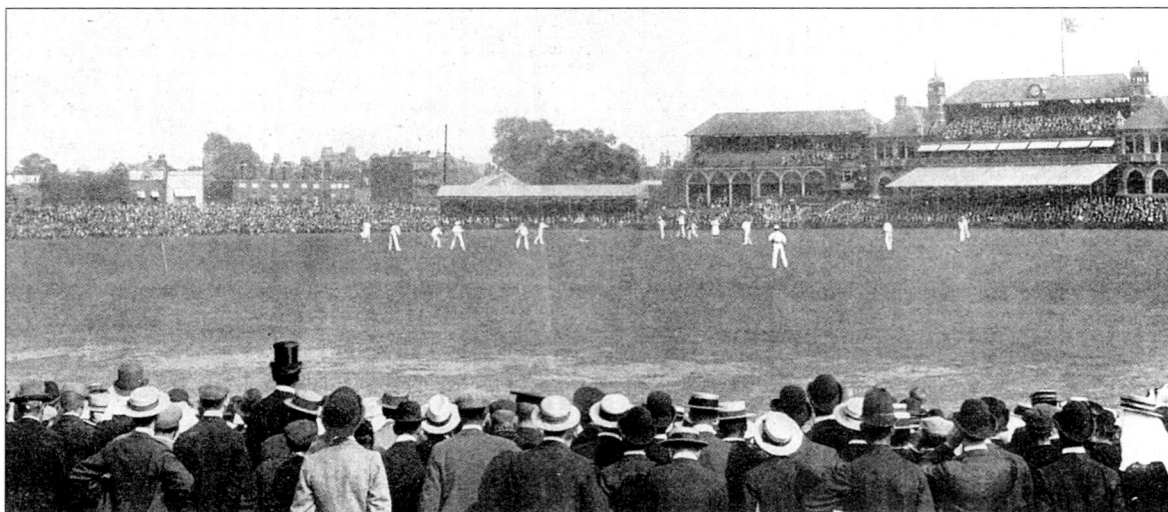
The final Test at the Oval, with a big crowd in attendance to cheer for England as it tries to level the series.

The Oval, Aug. 16. Australia has retained the Ashes, with a fighting draw in the fifth Test, the third close draw in the three matches since Australia's win at Lord's.

England captain Archie MacLaren won the toss and batted on another perfect pitch. Ernie Jones made no impression on openers F. S. Jackson and Tom Hayward who both made centuries. England were 4/435 after the first day.

Australia replied with 352, Syd Gregory 117, and, following on, were never really in trouble losing 5/254 before time ran out.

Jack Worrall was again impressive as an opener, making 55 and 75 with a knee that has been injured for the whole tour.

The compulsory follow-on rule worked to Australia's advantage in the fourth Test at Old Trafford, where it made 196 in reply to England's 372, and, following-on in hot weather on an evenly paced pitch, made 346.

Monty Noble made 89 in over eight hours batting, and was the team's linchpin. The English bowlers just could not winkle him out.

The drawn third Test at Headingley also featured some poor Australian batting, though the wet weather made it more excusable. The game was full of incident. England's John Briggs had an epileptic fit after the first day and was sent to Cheadle Asylum.

Jack Hearne of England performed the first hat-trick by an Englishman in a Test in England, dismissing Clem Hill, Syd Gregory and Monty Noble for ducks.

Jack Worrall, opening the batting in place of Frank Iredale, made 76 in the first innings to help Australia to a modest 172.

The second innings saw Australia in trouble at 6/97 before Hugh Trumble and Frank Laver helped lift the total to 224. Rain then washed out the match.

It is perhaps fortunate for Australia that these Tests were played over three days, because the batting has proved somewhat fragile, and the bowling, Ernie Jones apart, has often semed uninspired.

But illness and injury have played a large part in Australia's batting fortunes in June – the compensation being the 'luck' that made Victor Trumper 14th man.

He has been a revelation, but his equal in the three Tests he played has been the other youngster Clem Hill. Hill made 301 runs in three Tests, Trumper 290 in five. But it was the way Trumper made them that brought joy to every cricket lover's heart.

Brighton, July 29. Of all the stars in the galaxy of Australian batting on this tour, Victor Trumper's is now in the ascendant.

His 300 not out in the draw against Sussex was one of the finest innings ever played in England, and the highest score by an Australian in England, eclipsing former Australian captain Billy Murdoch's 286 not out, coincidentally on the same ground in 1882.

Along with Monty Noble, Trumper has played wonderfully well, especially in the tour matches and has made 11 centuries so far.

Wisden writes that 'very few Australian batsmen coming to England for the first time have approached the form shown by Noble and Trumper'.

Wisden liked Noble's patience, but said that Trumper's free and attractive cricket gave him the more brilliant future.

His elegant 300 was scored in only 380 minutes, and, as *Wisden* remarked, was 'from first to last being of the most perfect character' that it was clear that something phenomenal had come to life on Australian cricket.

He came to the crease with Australia 1/62 chasing 414, of which C. B. Fry contributed 181, and Ranjitsinhji just 5. Joe Darling declared at 4/624.

An observer said that to Trumper on song there was no such thing as a 'good length' ball. They were all 'Trumper-length'.

Trumper's innings of 300 more than the 135 in the second Test confirmed his genius in the eyes of his team-mates.

Great players of the series can be collected on cigarette cards: players like Sam Woods, Pelham Warner, Wilfred Rhodes, Victor Trumper and Ernie Jones.

Australian cricket is a winner as the century closes

London, Sep. 11. As Joe Darling's triumphant Australian team left England's shores in 1899, the *Times* magnanimously remarked how appropriate it was that an Australian team should hold the Ashes as the Australian colonies moved towards federation.

Through beset by a variety of financial, temperamental and skillful vicissitudes since 1877, there had been one Australian cricket team long before the dream of one Australia had ever been thought possible, the *Times* said.

In its own way the gathering together of Australian cricketers in one representative team had proved an ideal for the joining together of the colonies.

Joe Darling's team proved a better model than some had – not only in the aggression and skill of its young batsmen, but in the camaraderie of the dressing room and the evident 'mateship' of the team. Australians didn't distinguish between amateurs and professionals, as the English continued to do, which meant that when on tour Australians 'played together' in all senses of the term. Clem Hill speaks of not only attending music halls in 1899, but when waiting for an incoming batsman at Lord's of six Australians singing a music hall song on the field. It's hard to imagine an English team doing that.

Former umpire Jim Phillips said Australians 'play more in unison, they exchange views in the dressing room, and their captain is thereby materially assisted in many of his plans.'

Australian cricketers grow up with better grounds and facilities, better weather, and perhaps more appreciation. To play for Australia means more than something an English amateur 'just does', or a professional gets paid for.

Part of the attitude difference between Australia and England is 'that the passion for cricket burns like a flame in Australian blood and … the passion is intensified by an unfilial yearning on the part of young Australia to triumphantly thrash the mother country,' or so said the *Review of Reviews* in 1899.

This new national Australian spirit was made manifest in the adulation that Victor Trumper received from everyone, from Sydney boys playing endless games of street cricket (most of whom seem to have been given a bat by Trumper) to poets such as 'Creve Roe' other-

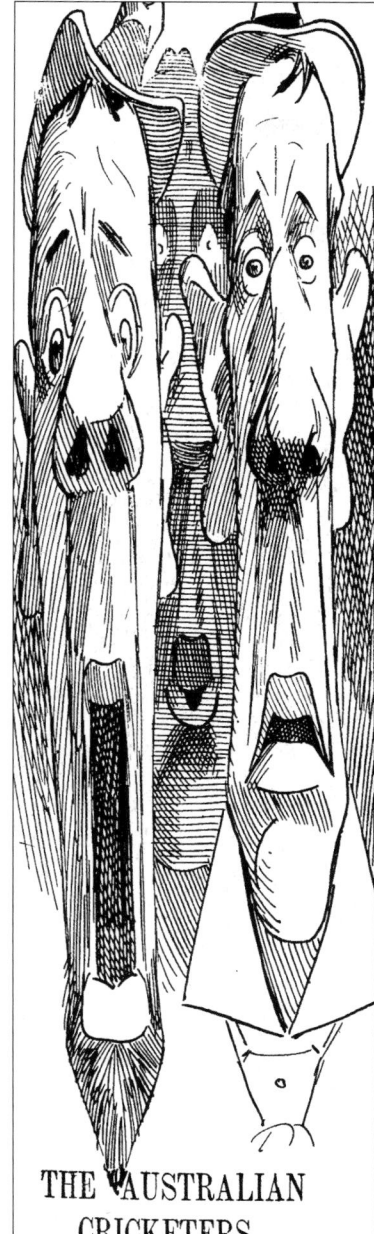

THE AUSTRALIAN CRICKETERS.

The passion for cricket. The Bulletin *sees some long faces in front of a newspaper scoreboard outside the office during the third Test.*

wise known as Victor Daley:

'Ho Statesmen, Patriots, Bards make way!
Your fame has sunk to zero.
For Victor Trumper is today
Our one Australian hero …'

In an 1899 competition the *Bookfellow* called for a quatrain embodying Australia. A. V. G. replied:

'Australia, what are thy distinctive features?
Congested cities, reeking Chinese slums;
The Melbourne Cup; some strange marsupial creatures,
Good cricketers, and – dust, and flies and gums.'

Although Australia had won slightly fewer of the 56 Tests played, there is confidence that the new century might belong to Australia – at least in cricket.

FIRST TEST 1899 ENGLAND v AUSTRALIA
Trent Bridge, Nottingham. June 1, 2, 3, 1899.
Toss: Australia. Match Drawn.

AUSTRALIA

J Darling (c) b Hearne	47		b Rhodes	14
FA Iredale c Hayward b Hearne	6 (4)		run out	20
MA Noble b Rhodes	41 (2)		lbw Rhodes	45
ES Gregory b Hirst	48			
C Hill run out	52 (3)		c Grace b Jackson	80
VT Trumper b Hearne	0 (5)		b Jackson	11
JJ Kelly (+) c Hirst b Hearne	26 (9)		not out	11
F Laver b Rhodes	3 (7)		b Jackson	3
WP Howell c Hayward b Rhodes	0 (10)		not out	4
H Trumble not out	16 (8)		c Ranjitsinhji b Rhodes	38
E Jones c Fry b Rhodes	4 (6)		c Ranjitsinhji b Hearne	3
EXTRAS (B 8, LB 1)	9		(LB 1)	1
TOTAL	252		8 dec	230

FOW 1st Inns: 14 85 109 166 167 229 229 229 248 252
FOW 2nd Inns: 18 111 151 170 173 177 180 226

Bowling: *First Innings*: Rhodes 35.2-13-58-4, Hearne 59-28-71-4, Grace 20-8-31-0, Hirst 24-9-42-1, Jackson 11-3-27-0, Hayward 3-0-14-0. *Second Innings*: Rhodes 20-3-60-3, Hearne 29-10-70-1, Grace 2-0-6-0, Hirst 11-4-20-0, Jackson 26-8-57-3, Hayward 6-2-16-0.

ENGLAND

WG Grace (c) c Kelly b Noble	28		b Howell	1
CB Fry b Jones	50		c Jones b Trumble	9
FS Jackson c Darling b Noble	8		b Howell	0
W Gunn b Jones	14		b Jones	3
KS Ranjitsinhji b Jones	42		not out	93
TW Hayward run out	0		b Trumble	28
JT Tyldesley c Laver b Howell	22		c Kelly b Trumble	10
W Storer (+) b Jones	4		lbw Jones	3
GH Hirst b Howell	6			
W Rhodes c Kelly b Jones	6			
JT Hearne not out	4			
EXTRAS (LB 3, NB 6)	9		(B 5, W 1, NB 2)	8
TOTAL	193		7 for	155

FOW 1st Inns: 75 91 93 116 117 172 176 178 185 193
FOW 2nd Inns: 1 1 10 19 82 140 155

Bowling: *First Innings*: Jones 33-6-88-5, Howell 28.4-12-43-2, Trumble 13-7-17-0, Noble 16-4-36-2. *Second Innings*: Jones 22-9-31-2, Howell 37-18-54-2, Trumble 29-16-39-3, Noble 11-5-23-0.

Umpires: RG Barlow & VA Titchmarsh

SECOND TEST 1899 ENGLAND v AUSTRALIA
Lord's Cricket Ground, London. June 15, 16, 17, 1899.
Toss: England. Australia won by 10 wkts.

ENGLAND

AC MacLaren (c) b Jones	4 (6)		not out	88
CB Fry c Trumble b Jones	13		b Jones	4
KS Ranjitsinhji c & b Jones	8		c Noble b Howell	0
CL Townsend st Kelly b Howell	5		b Jones	8
FS Jackson b Jones	73		c & b Trumble	37
TW Hayward b Noble	1 (1)		c Trumble b Laver	77
JT Tyldesley c Darling b Jones	14		c Gregory b Laver	4
GL Jessop c Trumper b Trumble	51		c Trumble b Laver	4
AFA Lilley (+) not out	19		b Jones	12
W Mead b Jones	7 (11)		lbw Noble	0
W Rhodes b Jones	2 (10)		c & b Noble	2
EXTRAS (B 2, LB 6, W 1)	9		(B 2, LB 2)	4
TOTAL	206			240

FOW 1st Inns: 4 14 20 44 45 66 161 184 194 206
FOW 2nd Inns: 5 6 23 94 160 166 170 212 240 240

Bowling: *First Innings*: Jones 36.1-11-88-7, Howell 14-4-43-1, Noble 15-7-39-1, Trumble 15-9-27-1. *Second Innings*: Jones 36-15-76-3, Howell 31-12-67-1, Noble 19.4-8-37-2, Trumble 15-6-20-1, Laver 16-4-36-3.

AUSTRALIA

J Worrall c Hayward b Rhodes	18		not out	11
J Darling (c) c Ranjitsinhji b Rhodes	9		not out	17
C Hill c Fry b Townsend	135			
ES Gregory c Lilley b Jessop	15			
MA Noble c Lilley b Rhodes	54			
VT Trumper not out	135			
JJ Kelly (+) c Lilley b Mead	9			
H Trumble c Lilley b Jessop	24			
F Laver b Townsend	0			
E Jones c Mead b Townsend	17			
WP Howell b Jessop	0			
EXTRAS (LB 4, NB 1)	5			0
TOTAL	421		0 for	28

FOW 1st Inns: 27 28 59 189 271 306 386 387 421 421
FOW 2nd Inns:

Bowling: *First Innings*: Jessop 37.1-10-105-3, Mead 53-24-91-1, Rhodes 39-10-108-3, Jackson 18-6-31-0, Townsend 15-1-50-3, Ranjitsinhji 2-0-6-0, Hayward 6-0-25-0. *Second Innings*: Jessop 6-0-19-0, Rhodes 5-1-9-0.

Umpires: T Mycroft & WAJ West

THIRD TEST 1899 ENGLAND v AUSTRALIA
Headingley, Leeds. June 29, 30, July 1 (no play), 1899.
Toss: Australia. Match Drawn.

AUSTRALIA

J Worrall run out	76	c (S)JT Tyldesley b Young	16
JJ Kelly (+) c Fry b Briggs	0	(7) c Lilley b Hayward	33
MA Noble run out	0	(5) c Ranjitsinhji b Hearne	0
ES Gregory c Lilley b Hearne	0	c MacLaren b Hearne	0
C Hill c Lilley b Young	34	(3) b Hearne	0
J Darling (c) c Young b Briggs	9	(2) c Fry b Young	16
VT Trumper b Young	12	(6) c Ranjitsinhji b Jackson	32
H Trumble not out	20	run out	56
F Laver st Lilley b Briggs	7	c Lilley b Hearne	45
E Jones b Young	5	c Brown b Hayward	2
WP Howell c Ranjitsinhji b Young	7	not out	2
EXTRAS (B 2)	2	(B 17, LB 3, W 1, NB 1)	22
TOTAL	172		224

FOW 1st Inns: 8 17 24 95 114 131 132 151 164 172
FOW 2nd Inns: 34 34 34 34 39 97 140 213 215 224

Bowling: *First Innings*: Hearne 23-5-69-1, Briggs 30-11-53-3, Young 19.1-11-30-4, Jackson 5-1-18-0. *Second Innings*: Hearne 31.3-12-50-4, Young 26-5-72-2, Jackson 11-6-13-1, Brown 7-0-22-0, Hayward 10-1-45-2.

ENGLAND

JT Brown c Trumble b Noble	27	not out	14
AC MacLaren (c) c & b Trumble	9		
KS Ranjitsinhji c Worrall b Noble	11		
WG Quaife b Jones	20	(2) not out	1
FS Jackson b Trumble	9		
CB Fry b Noble	38		
TW Hayward b Trumble	40		
AFA Lilley (+) c Hill b Trumble	55		
JT Hearne b Trumble	3		
HI Young c Kelly b Trumble	0		
J Briggs			
EXTRAS (B 3, LB 5)	8	(LB 4)	4
TOTAL	9 for 220		0 for 19

FOW 1st Inns: 27 38 53 69 119 119 212 220 220
FOW 2nd Inns:

Bowling *First Innings*: Trumble 39.3-16-60-5, Noble 42-17-82-3, Howell 13-3-29-0, Jones 21-9-34-1, Laver 3-1-7-0. *Second Innings*: Jones 4-2-7-0, Noble 3-1-8-0.

Umpires: W Hearn & M Sherwin

FOURTH TEST 1899 ENGLAND v AUSTRALIA
Old Trafford, Manchester. July 17, 18, 19, 1899.
Toss: England. Match Drawn.

ENGLAND

WG Quaife c Darling b Noble	8	c Iredale b Jones	15
CB Fry b Jones	9	c Iredale b Trumble	4
KS Ranjitsinhji c Worrall b Jones	21	not out	49
AC MacLaren (c) b Noble	8	c Iredale b Trumble	6
FS Jackson c Trumble b Jones	44	not out	14
TW Hayward c Jones b Howell	130		
W Brockwell c Worrall b Noble	20		
AFA Lilley (+) lbw Laver	58		
HI Young b Howell	43		
JT Hearne c Iredale b Trumble	1		
WM Bradley not out	23		
EXTRAS (B 3, LB 3, W 1)	7	(B 4, NB 2)	6
TOTAL	372		3 for 94

FOW 1st Inns: 14 18 47 47 107 154 267 324 337 372
FOW 2nd Inns: 12 39 54

Bowling: *First Innings*: Jones 42-9-136-3, Noble 38-19-85-3, Trumble 29-10-72-1, Howell 19.1-7-45-2, Laver 13-2-27-1. *Second Innings*: Trumble 13-3-33-2, Jones 8-0-33-1, Howell 6-2-22-0.

AUSTRALIA

F Laver c Lilley b Bradley	0	(9) not out	14
JJ Kelly (+) b Young	9	(8) c Lilley b Ranjitsinhji	26
WP Howell b Bradley	0		
J Worrall b Bradley	14	(1) c Brockwell b Young	53
MA Noble not out	60	(6) c & b Hearne	89
ES Gregory lbw Young	5	(5) c Ranjitsinhji b Hearne	1
VT Trumper b Young	14	(4) b Hearne	63
J Darling (c) b Young	4	(6) c (S)W Rhodes b Young	39
H Trumble c MacLaren b Bradley	44	(3) c Ranjitsinhji b Bradley	7
FA Iredale c Lilley b Bradley	31	(7) not out	36
E Jones b Jackson	0		
EXTRAS (B 14, W 1)	15	(B 14, LB 2, W 1, NB 1)	18
TOTAL	196		7 dec 346

FOW 1st Inns: 1 6 14 26 35 53 57 139 195 196
FOW 2nd Inns: 93 117 205 213 255 278 319

Bowling: *First Innings*: Young 29-10-79-4, Bradley 33-13-67-5, Brockwell 6-2-18-0, Hearne 10-6-7-0, Jackson 3.3-1-9-1, Ranjitsinhji 1-0-1-0. *Second Innings*: Young 37-12-81-2, Bradley 46-16-82-1, Brockwell 15-3-36-0, Hearne 47-26-54-3, Jackson 18-8-36-0, Ranjitsinhji 12-5-23-1, Hayward 3-1-10-0, Quaife 3-1-6-0.

Umpires: AB Hide & J Lillywhite jr

FIFTH TEST 1899 ENGLAND v AUSTRALIA
Kennington Oval, London. August 14, 15, 16, 1899.
Toss: England. Match Drawn.

ENGLAND

FS Jackson b Jones	118
TW Hayward c Iredale b McLeod	137
KS Ranjitsinhji c Howell b Jones	54
CB Fry c Worrall b Jones	60
AC MacLaren (c) c Trumper b Trumble	49
CL Townsend b Jones	38
WM Bradley run out	0
WH Lockwood b Trumble	24
AO Jones b Noble	31
AFA Lilley (+) c Iredale b Noble	37
W Rhodes not out	8
EXTRAS (B 9, LB 6, W 4, NB 1)	20
TOTAL	576

FOW 1st Inns: 185 316 318 428 436 436 479 511 551 576

Bowling: *First Innings*: Jones 53-12-164-4, Noble 35.4-12-96-2, Trumble 39-11-107-2, McLeod 48-15-131-1, Howell 15-3-43-0, Worrall 3-0-15-0.

AUSTRALIA

J Worrall c Hayward b Lockwood	55	c Lilley b Hayward	75
H Trumble c & b Jones	24	(7) not out	3
VT Trumper c Lilley b Jones	6	(4) c & b Rhodes	7
MA Noble b Lockwood	9	(3) not out	69
J Darling (c) c Fry b Lockwood	71	(6) run out	6
ES Gregory c Jones b Lockwood	117	(5) b Rhodes	2
FA Iredale b Lockwood	9		
JJ Kelly (+) lbw Jones	4		
CE McLeod not out	31	(2) b Rhodes	77
E Jones b Lockwood	0		
WP Howell b Lockwood	4		
EXTRAS (B 5, LB 10, W 1, NB 6)	22	(B 7, W 4, NB 4)	15
TOTAL	352		5 for 254

FOW 1st Inns: 38 44 85 120 220 242 257 340 340 352
FOW 2nd Inns: 116 208 224 228 243

Bowling: *First Innings*: Bradley 29-12-52-0, Rhodes 25-2-79-0, Lockwood 40.3-17-71-7, Jones 30-12-73-3, Townsend 5-0-16-0, Jackson 14-7-39-0. *Second Innings*: Bradley 17-8-32-0, Rhodes 22-8-27-3, Lockwood 15-7-33-0, Jones 12-2-43-0, Townsend 8-4-9-0, Jackson 13-2-54-0, Hayward 11-3-38-1, Fry 2-1-3-0.

Umpires: W Richards & AA White

Australian Averages

1899 ENGLAND v AUSTRALIA

AUSTRALIA	M	Inn	NO	Runs	H.S	Avrge	Ct	St	Overs	Mds	Runs	Wkt	Avrge
Darling, J	5	10	1	232	71	25.78	3	-	-	-	-	-	-
Gregory, ES	5	8	-	188	117	23.50	1	-	-	-	-	-	-
Hill, C	3	5	-	301	135	60.20	1	-	-	-	-	-	-
Howell, WP	5	7	2	17	7	3.40	1	-	164.0	61	346	8	43.25
Iredale, FA	3	5	1	102	36*	25.50	6	-	-	-	-	-	-
Jones, E	5	7	-	31	9	4.43	3	-	255.1	73	657	26	25.27
Kelly, JJ	5	8	1	118	33	16.86	4	1	-	-	-	-	-
Laver, F	4	7	1	72	45	12.00	1	-	32.0	7	70	4	17.50
McLeod, CE	1	2	1	108	77	108.00	-	-	48.0	15	131	1	131.00
Noble, MA	5	9	2	367	89	52.43	2	-	180.3	73	406	13	31.23
Trumble, H	5	9	3	232	56	38.67	7	-	192.3	78	375	15	25.00
Trumper, VT	5	9	-	280	135*	35.00	2	-	-	-	-	-	-
Worrall, J	4	8	1	318	76	45.43	4	-	3.0	-	15	-	-

English Averages

1899 ENGLAND v AUSTRALIA

ENGLAND	M	Inn	NO	Runs	H.S	Avrge	Ct	St	Overs	Mds	Runs	Wkt	Avrge
Bradley, WM	2	2	1	23	23*	23.00	-	-	125.0	49	233	6	38.83
Briggs, J	1	-	-	-	-	-	-	-	30.0	11	53	3	17.67
Brockwell, W	1	1	-	20	20	20.00	1	-	21.0	5	54	-	-
Brown, JT	1	2	1	41	27	41.00	1	-	7.0	-	22	-	-
Fry, CB	5	8	-	187	60	23.38	5	-	2.0	1	3	-	-
Grace, WG	1	2	-	29	28	14.50	1	-	22.0	8	37	-	-
Gunn, W	1	2	-	17	14	8.50	-	-	-	-	-	-	-
Hayward, TW	5	7	1	413	137	68.83	4	-	39.0	7	148	3	49.33
Hearne, JT	3	3	1	8	4*	4.00	1	-	199.3	87	321	13	24.69
Hirst, GH	1	1	-	6	6	6.00	1	-	35.0	13	62	1	62.00
Jackson, FS	5	8	-	303	118	43.29	1	-	119.3	42	284	5	56.80
Jessop, GL	1	2	-	55	51	27.50	-	-	43.1	10	124	3	41.33
Jones, AO	1	1	-	31	31	31.00	2	-	42.0	14	116	3	38.67
Lilley, AFA	4	5	1	181	58	45.25	13	1	-	-	-	-	-
Lockwood, WH	1	1	-	24	24	24.00	-	-	55.3	24	104	7	14.86
MacLaren, AC	4	6	1	164	88*	32.80	2	-	-	-	-	-	-
Mead, W	1	2	-	7	7	3.50	1	-	53.0	24	91	1	91.00
Quaife, WG	2	4	1	44	20	14.67	-	-	3.0	1	6	-	-
Ranjitsinhji, KS	5	8	2	278	93*	46.33	8	-	15.0	5	30	1	30.00
Rhodes, W	3	4	1	18	8*	6.00	1	-	146.2	37	341	13	26.23
Storer, W	1	2	-	7	4	3.50	-	-	-	-	-	-	-
Townsend, CL	2	3	-	51	38	17.00	-	-	28.0	5	75	3	25.00
Tyldesley, JT	2	4	-	50	22	12.50	-	-	-	-	-	-	-
Young, HI	2	2	-	43	43	21.50	1	-	111.1	38	262	12	21.83

Trumper the great

The ill-fated Gallipoli campaign was still raging on 28 June 1915. On that day the cricket world was stunned and saddened to learn of the death of Victor Trumper, the much-loved free spirit of Australian cricket, whose daring batting had borne all the hallmarks of a master swordsman: swift and unpredictable.

Trumper was only 37 when he succumbed to Bright's disease in a private hospital in Darlinghurst, Sydney.

The Sydney newspapers carried hundreds of tributes to Trumper, alongside those of the Anzacs who had lost their lives. Acknowledging Trumper's stature, the London *Times* issued a poster bearing three words, 'Great Cricketer Dies'.

Trumper's peers, friend and foe alike, spoke glowingly of his astonishing talent during his glory years from 1899 to 1911. One of the most generous compliments came from England captain Archie MacLaren, who told (Sir) Neville Cardus: 'You couldn't set a field for him. He was the most fascinating batsman I have ever seen. He had grace, ease, style and power.'

Ranjitsinhji said: 'Every stroke he made so fascinated me that I couldn't take my eyes off him.'

MacLaren provided a graphic illustration of Trumper's capacity to thrash an attack. The scene was the fourth Test at Old Trafford between Australia and England in June, 1902, on Trumper's second visit to England. Having won the toss, MacLaren sent Australia in, anticipating easy pickings for his bowlers on a rain-affected pitch. MacLaren's plan was to keep Trumper quiet for two hours. The field was set to stop the fours but 'in the second over,' said MacLaren, 'Trumper drove Jackson over the sight-board into the practice ground, and I couldn't ruddy well set one of my long fields out there, could I?' A rampant Trumper scored 103 in 108 minutes before lunch, at which early stage the score was 1/173.

Trumper's whirlwind batting had the dour Mancunian crowd in raptures. It was the first time a player had had the audacity to score a century before lunch in a Test.

Trumper, aged 24, was the top run-scorer on that tour, amassing 2,570 runs at an average of 48.49, a remarkable achievement considering the wretched weather. He scored 11 centuries, with a highest score of 128. Unlike Bradman, 30

years later, he seemed content with a century rather than plundering 200. He was not a greedy man. More than once he surrendered his wicket to some needy bowler.

One of Trumper's maxims was 'spoil a bowler's length and you've got him.' He achieved this with light, nimble footwork: the Fred Astaire of batting.

As early as 1902, Test skipper Darling was aware that Trumper had inherited a weak constitution, which eventually led to his death. 'Unfortunately,' Darling wrote in his memoirs, 'owing to the fact that he did not enjoy the best of health Trumper had many bad days, but when fit and well there was only one cricketer in it as champion of the world, and that was Trumper.'

Scholar, writer and England Test cricketer, C. B. Fry, said Trumper 'had no single style but every style.'

Victor Thomas Trumper was born in the working-class suburb of Paddington on 2 November 1877. He played cricket in the back lanes and backyards of Victorian Sydney. The makeshift pitches were rough and Trumper and his mates soon learnt how to handle 'grubbers' and avoid balls that reared up suddenly. Young Victor spent hours practising alone, playing all manner of shadow shots without a ball, his feet never still.

His career blossomed in 1897, aged 20. Playing for Paddington in grade cricket, he reeled off the following scores: 82, 13, 125, 85, 120 n.o.,191 n.o.,133 and 162, for an average of 204.2.

Some critics considered him too immature for Test cricket but he put them firmly in their place by coming in at number six and scoring 135 not out in the second Test at Lord's in 1899. Trumper's impeccable innings was the first of his six Test hundreds against England. Said one critic: 'He played with astonishing grace and freedom for a young man in only in his second Test'. A month later Trumper flayed the Sussex attack to the tune of 300 not out, then the highest score by an Australian in England.

Trumper scored two Test centuries against Pelham Warner's touring England team in 1903–04, 185 in Sydney and 113 in Adelaide, after which he made two more tours of England in 1905 and 1909.

Victor Trumper's last Test series was against England on home soil in 1911–12 and it produced his last 'ton', 113 in Sydney.

In total, Trumper scored 17,150

Smooth as silk, eyes of a hawk, feet of a dancer: Victor Trumper on the drive.

runs in first class cricket at an average of 45.01, with 43 centuries. In Tests, he made 3,163 runs at 39.04 with eight centuries, six against England and two against South Africa.

In 1903, Trumper opened a sports shop in Sydney. Wrote Neville Cardus: 'As a man he was as generous as Trumper the batsman, not knowing the value of money, just as he seemed not to know the value of runs or averages. One day a man and his son entered Victor's shop. The man wanted to buy a bat for the boy's birthday.

Victor tried a few small sizes then recommended one. He asked the boy when he would be playing his first game. Next Saturday, came the reply: it was now the Monday before.

'So Trumper pretended he would

like to keep the bat a day or two and season it. He used it on the Wednesday in a State match and made 50 or so with it. When the boy called for his bat on the Friday, Victor gave it to him. It's in good condition, I've tested it myself, he said. Bring it back if you don't like it and I'll give you another. The boy, of course, soon found out Victor had used the bat … he was the proudest boy in Australia.'

Cardus also wrote that as a small boy he used to say a prayer: 'Please God, let Victor Trumper score a century today for Australia against England, out of a total of 137 all out.' (He never prayed for Don Bradman – perhaps he didn't have to.)

As Herbie Collins, Australian captain in the mid 1920s, said: 'There'll never be another Trumper.'

The old art of Australian captaincy

Joe Darling, 1899–1903.   *Monty Noble, 1903–09.*   *Clem Hill, 1910–12.*   *Syd Gregory, 1912.*   *Warwick Armstrong, 1914–21.*

Australia's early cricket captains needed to be men of exceptional quality if the team was to succeed not just on the field, but off it as well. The best were men of judgment balanced with a sense of humour, discipline and camaraderie. The worst were indecisive, weak or tactically inept.

The first Australian captain, black-bearded Dave Gregory, was a few years older than his teammates, and commanded respect. Known as Handsome Dave he lead Australia in three Tests, winning two and losing one, as well as the profitable Australian tour of 1878 in which no Tests were played – but each man made £750.

It must also be said that Gregory's intransigence in the 'riot' match between NSW and Lord Harris XI in 1879 almost brought Test cricket to an end after it had just begun.

Billy Murdoch was next, captaining Australia in 14 Tests between 1880 and 1884, and then recalled for the 1890 tour.

Murdoch's stature as a batsman, his amiable disposition, and friendship with W. G. Grace quickly brought relations between Australia and England back on friendly terms. Great English batsman C. B. Fry said that 'every dressing room he entered was relaxed and full of fun … he is simply, genuinely and unaffectedly amusing'.

No wonder Australia won the first Ashes Test in 1882 when all could have been lost. And no wonder he was given a standing ovation at Lords when he made a 'comeback' as captain in 1890.

Australia lost these two Tests, but in his first stint Murdoch won five,

lost five and drew four.

In the 1884–85 series Australia changed its captain with every Test – Murdoch (he fell into disfavour over match payments), Tom Horan, Hugh Massie, Jack Blackham and Tom Horan again, losing the series 3–2.

The MCC organised the next tour to England in 1886, choosing Dr Henry Scott as captain. He was not a commander of men, and this quarrelsome injury-riddled tour was lost 3–0.

Percy McDonnell was an elegant batsman and an excellent practitioner of wet-wicket batting, heading the batting when he was captain for the wet, fractious, depleted tour of 1888. He won only one Test, on that tour, a Ferris/Turner special, in six as captain.

In this period of England ascendancy, Murdoch was recalled in 1890, before the veteran wicketkeeper Jack Blackham was handed the job

Blackham was a great worrier. As captain he was notorious for pacing up and down in the dressing room in worry, being known as the 'Caged Lion'. George Giffen wrote that he 'was far from an ideal captain, on account of his tendency to worry and magnify temporary misfortunes.' In one series he lost a stone in weight between first and third Tests.

Nevertheless he regained the Ashes in 1891–92, losing them in 1893. In all he captained Australia in eight Tests for three wins, three losses and two draws.

George Giffen, the phenomenal all-rounder, was elected captain after Blackham retired through

injury after losing the first Test of the 1894–95 series. Under Giffen Australia won two of four remaining Tests, observers ruminating that he might have done better had he not bowled himself so enthusiastically.

The players of the 1896 tour elected Harry Trott as captain – some compensation for the family for the shock omission of brother 'Alberto' Trott.

Harry Trott was a man *Wisden* said was ' blessed with a humour nothing could ruffle … master of both himself and his team'. He showed himself to be a master of tactics on a successful tour

Trott lost that series 2–1, but made up for it with a 4–1 thrashing of England in Australia in 1897–98, thanks in large part to Clem Hill. Trott then suffered health problems, including the loss of sight in one eye during his last Test. He spent some time in Kew Asylum before returning to play a few games for Victoria between 1901–02 and 1907–08.

Straight talking, widely respected and an outstanding batsman, Joe Darling was Australia's captain for 21 Tests from 1899 in England to Australia's first Test tour to anywhere else – South Africa in 1902–03.

Hugh Trumble took over for two Tests in 1901–02 when Darling was unavailable, winning both.

Darling could be a disciplinarian and frowned on excessive drinking, but was admired by his players for the way he backed them up.

Of his 21 Tests as captain, under Darling Australia won seven, lost four and drew ten.

Monty Noble took over for the

1903–04 series, which England won 3–2, Darling returned for the 1905 tour. Noble finally took over in 1907–08 and 1909, winning both series.

He had the reputation for being a stickler for form and cricket etiquette, and found it hard to suffer fools at all, let alone gladly. He was a successful manager of good teams – winning 8 and losing five, with two draws.

In Clem Hill's period as captain his Australian team beat South Africa 4–1 in 1910–11, and lost by the same margin to England in 1911–12.

A fight with a fellow selector after the first Test in December 1911 at the NSWCA offices in Sydney began a wearisome war between players and various administrative bodies including the Australian Cricket Board. In the short term the effect was Australia under Hill losing the series to a better English team. In the longer term soured relations saw six players including Hill refuse to go to England for the 1912 triangular tournament and Hill's retirement.

Veteran Syd Gregory, battling bankruptcy and aged 42, took what was regarded as the worst Australian team ever to a wet England.

Gregory was too soft-hearted to control the team and though it beat South Africa twice, Australia lost to England and drew the other three. England won the series but Australia under Gregory and an unwanted team manager lost the plot.

And so ended the Golden Age of Australian cricket.

Noble masters twin arts

The play between Queensland and NSW at Brisbane Cricket Ground.

Sydney, Jan. 31. NSW all-rounder Monty Noble beat Victoria with both bat and ball in the final Sheffield Shield match for the season.

Noble's 155 in the second innings put NSW into a strong position after Victoria led by 38 runs on the first innings. His 6/91, which included the first six Victorians to fall, was instrumental in preventing them getting near the 374 required.

Noble finished on top of the bowling averages for the season with 37 wickets at 20.64 and was second behind team-mate Victor Trumper (721 at 72.1) with 694 runs at 69.4.

Both Victoria and NSW had lost one match going into the last game, but NSW had shown more form in its sequence of thumping innings victories including hitting the massive 807 against South Australia – where Noble belted an even 200. And it does have Trumper, and Syd Gregory.

In non-Sheffield Shield games NSW played Queensland and beat them by an innings and 315 runs, with Victor Trumper making a rapid fire 208.

NSW also played Tasmania for the first time in Hobart. This match was closer than expected, the Tasmanians making 420 in their first innings. George Gatehouse made the first century of the 20th century, 105, in his last first class game. NSW lost six wickets chasing 168 in the second innings – a good game by the Vandiemonians.

NSW played and won more matches than any other colony in the last season before Federation.

Joe Darling lost to Tasmanian wilds

Adelaide, July 23. Joe Darling's telegram to the *South Australian Register* has confirmed the rumour that he is leaving South Australia.

It read simply: 'Have purchased property; intend residing in Tasmania.'

The *Register* noted 'Cricket in Australia is far from the stage where a first class man can afford to devote his lifetime to it'. There is plenty requiring Darling's attention at the property, called Stonehenge, including a plethora of rabbits.

Darling may be lost to SA, but his future in international cricket is still in the balance.

Feeble ACC is laid to rest

Melbourne, Jan. 2. The Australasian Cricket Council has finally been dissolved, an event which has been 'on the cards' since the NSWCA withdrew its interest in May 1899.

Evidently the struggle for control of Australian cricket, and the finances flowing from overseas touring, between the NSWCA and the Melbourne Cricket Club is far from over.

The sorry state of the ACC's affairs is made evident by the revelation of a bank balance at the end of just £28.7s. 9d.

Joe Darling, SA delegate to the ACC, noted at the end that 'playing members should have a voice in the control of affairs'. They were in touch with what was going on, and should be represented on a future governing body.

SA in sensational form reversal

Sydney, Jan. 12. SA ended a run of five losses in Sheffield Shield cricket by defeating NSW – thanks to Fred Hack's 158 not out.

The win was a measure of revenge for the massive loss in Adelaide earlier in the season, where NSW made a record total of 807. In that match Victor Trumper contributed a stylish 165, Syd Gregory a thumping 176 and Monty Noble a splendid 200 – his third Shield century in a row, as NSW went on a rampage of big scores.

This time Ernie Jones (9/137 for the match) and George Giffen (5/59 in the first innings) kept NSW down to reasonable scores, while Hack survived four chances.

A dire warning about the length of some matches in Australia.

The vast crowd at the Melbourne Cricket Ground for the Second Test, 1911–12.

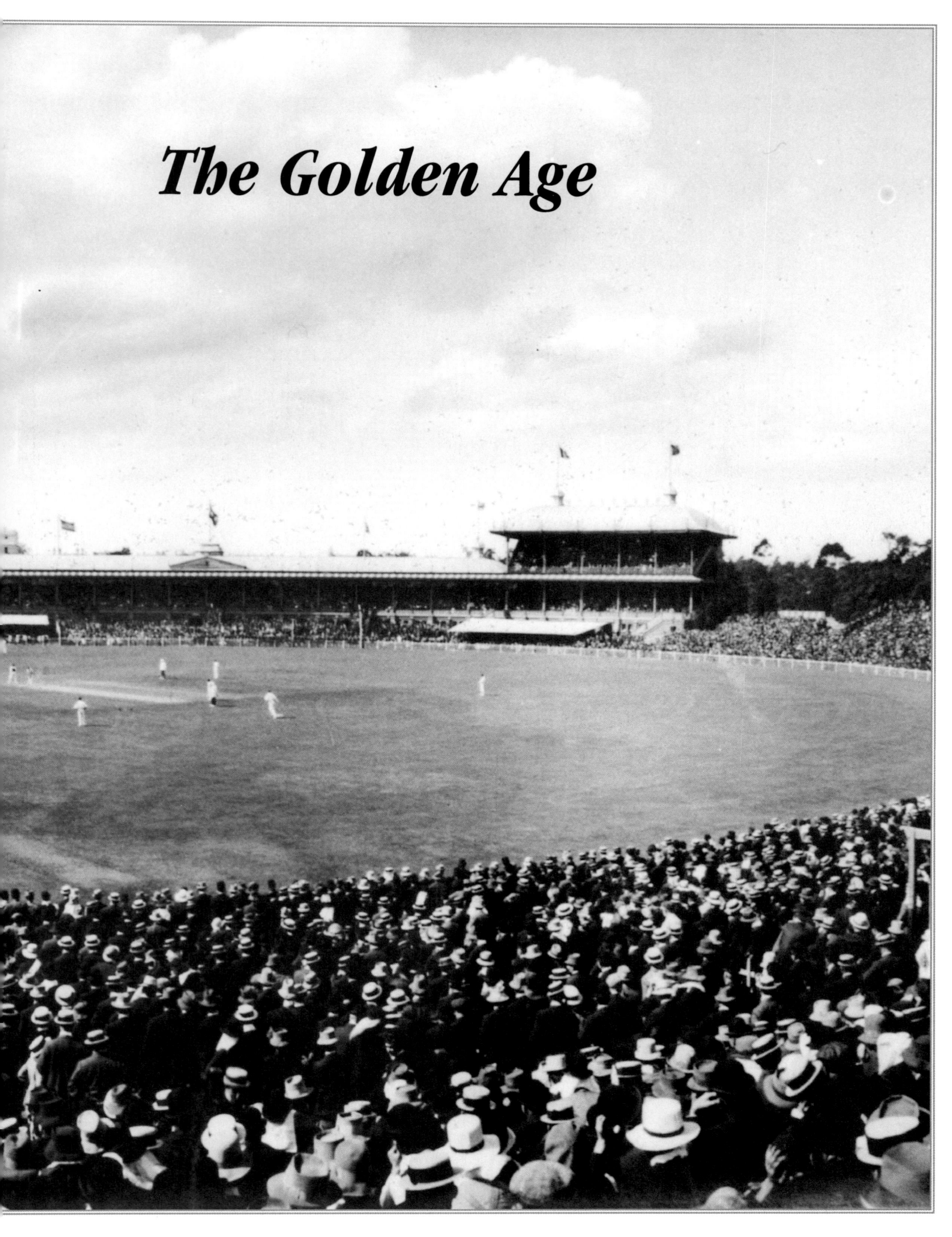

The Golden Age

Clem Hill's 365 in batsman's year

Clem Hill stands proudly before the scoreboard, with his wonderful total of 365.

Sydney, Feb. 5. The fact that a superbly stroked 230 by Victor Trumper can be regarded as brilliant, but not the most brilliant innings on this brief first class season, must mean that his coeval Clem Hill must have done something grand.

Hill did, striking a wonderful 365 not out in South Australia's 576 as it inflicted an innings defeat on NSW in Adelaide in December.

South Australia's win was reversed in January, when NSW scored a record in first class cricket with a total of 918. There were five centuries, Frank Iredale 118, Monty Noble 153, Syd Gregory 168, Reggie Duff 119 and Les Poidevin 140 not out. Victor Trumper, capable of anything on his day, was overshadowed with only 70.

George Giffen took pity on himself as a bowler – in this innings he only bowled 23 overs, 0/119. Fred Jarvis took the most punishment, 49 overs for 2/225.

Giffen is now in the veteran class and a poor season, in which for the first time in years he has not been among the leaders in either the batting or bowling averages, has left the South Australian team surprisingly thin, relying too much on Clem Hill.

For Victoria, young Warwick Armstrong, a tall, slim and confident batsman who goes after the bowling, scored consistently and hit his first century, 118, in the win against South Australia in November.

Vics win Shield in last-day drama

Sydney, Feb. 6. After a match which was full of theatrical moments, Victoria clinched the 1900–1901 Sheffield Shield with a one-wicket win over NSW.

Aside from the no-balling of fast bowler Jack Marsh by controversial umpire Bob Crockett, there was the majesty of a Victor Trumper 230 in less than five hours, an innings without a flaw. It gave Victoria a substantial chase in their second innings.

NSW might have won, had Arthur McBeath not fumbled a ball which would have run out Victoria's last man Saunders, with 9 runs still to get.

Jack Worrall's 90 at the start of Victoria's innings and Hugh Trumble's 63 at the end proved just enough.

Marsh's splint is the end for umpire

Sydney, Feb. 6. Ferociously fast NSW Aboriginal bowler Jack Marsh was no-balled 17 times by umpire Bob Crockett in the second NSW Victoria Shield match this season.

Crockett no-balled Marsh twice in the earlier game, later saying it was for a 'questionable delivery'. No other umpire has a problem with Marsh's whippy action – except umpire William Curran.

When Marsh played in a trial match in front of the NSW selectors earlier in the season, he clean bowled Victor Trumper. Umpire Curran said he would 'call' Marsh in the next innings, so Marsh turned up with his arm in a splint and bearing a doctor's certificate indicating that he could not bend his arm. Curran walked off the ground at lunch, saying he had been humiliated. Victoria won both matches.

Jack Marsh: point proved.

Federal spirit is not forthcoming

Melbourne, Jan. 12. Writing in the *Australasian*, as 'Felix', former Australian player Tom Horan writes: 'Cricket has done much, very much for Federation, and the crowning glory would have been a Test match on the Sydney ground, to celebrate the radiant birth of Australia as a nation.'

A Test match against England 'amid surroundings so coruscatingly brilliant that merely to read of them reminds one of the best and most enchanting picture of oriental splendour' would have been truly fitting.

Felix even missed the speeches: 'Then at the finish of the match, to listen to the rapt oration, flowing free of [NSW Premier] Mr Reid and [Australian PM] Mr Barton' would have been a grand finale.'

Australia fights to Tests lead

The excitement generated by the forthcoming Test can be seen by the crowd at Redfern Station to glimpse and greet the visitors.

Early setbacks for 'weak' tour team

Sydney, Nov. 27. Archie Mac-Laren's team arrived in Australia in a weakened condition, with several of the best English players left at home, and it seems after three matches against the States that it will be in trouble in the Test series.

The tour was originally in the hands of the Marylebone Cricket Club, in liaison with the Melbourne Cricket Club, but the English body withdrew when bowlers Wilfred Rhodes and George Hirst declared themselves unavailable, as did Prince Kumar Ranjitsinhji. Some counties would not release prospective players.

MacLaren then took over to choose and lead the side. His big surprise was the selection of Syd Barnes, a tall, brooding Lancashire Leagues player who has played only a little first class cricket. MacLaren picked him from a net practise at Old Trafford.

Barnes has already shown with 12 wickets against Victoria that his guileful swing bowling is likely to reap rewards.

The English, however, started with a 233-run loss to South Australia (once again the wily George Giffen destroyed them with 13/93) and a loss to NSW.

Adelaide, Jan. 23. Australia now seems on top of England after a four-wicket win in the third Test. England has been badly hurt by the loss of Barnes, who twisted his knee on the second day and seems likely to be out for the rest of the series. His 19 wickets in the first two Tests indicate his value to England.

England was, surprisingly, all over Australia in the first Test, in Sydney, scoring 464 and then bowling Australia out twice. The new attack of Barnes and leg-break bowler Len Braund mystified the Australians.

The tide turned in the second Test in Melbourne, where a wet wicket made batting difficult. Australia was shot out for 112 by left-arm spinner Colin Blythe and Barnes, but the drying pitch proved even more treacherous for the English, who made 67. This was Trumble territory and the lanky spinner had the first three wickets, before Monty Noble had an unplayable spell and took 7/17.

Chasing Australia's 353 (Hill 91, Duff 104), England was 5/157 when rain swept in again. They added 20 more runs, with Hugh Trumble grabbing a hat-trick.

If the weather beat England then, the Australians could take the honours in Adelaide. Clem Hill is the ill-starred hero having made 98 and 97 in his innings, while Hugh Trumble 6/74 in England's second innings, set Australia up for a succesful run chase of 315.

Reg Duff: century in Melbourne.

Outside the Sydney Morning Herald *office, waiting for Adelaide scores.*

QUICK SINGLES

Still feared. George Giffen is now 42, but aided by a 'gluepot' wicket he took 7/62 on November 12, in the England v South Australia match.

Captain's call. In the match against NSW in November England captain Archie MacLaren insisted that the agreement with tour organiser MCC allowed him to appoint one umpire – which the NSWCA allowed, 'under protest'. The MCC has appointed an umpire to tour with the team. MacLaren made 145 in the English win by 53 runs.

Big crowds. Melbourne is slightly ahead of Sydney in attracting cricket crowds. Despite rainy conditions there were 72,000 at the Melbourne Test as against 67,110 in Sydney. But Sydney had the best day attendance, with 34,167 turning out for the Saturday's play.

Nice gesture. When Clem Hill was out for 98 in the third Test in Adelaide, the catcher Johnny Tyldesley urged him to go back, as he had caught the ball on the bike track. Hill reminded him that the fence was the agreed boundary. Hill made 97 in the second innings.

Dusty day. Adelaide Tests seem to be noted for their dust storms. This one, on January 21, swept in from the north, blocking out vision and curtailing play on the fourth day of the match. Players were at times prostrate on the ground before they were forced to leave for the shelter of the dressing room.

Follow-on fiasco. Play was delayed in the NSW v SA Shield match on December 3, while the captains argued over the follow-on rule. SA claimed the ACC rule that the side over 200 runs behind must bat again. NSW claimed the new MCC that a side leading by 150 runs had the option. SA won the argument, NSW the match.

Sewn up. When NSW won the return match against Victoria at Sydney on January 29 it had the Shield sewn up. They were both hard-fought affairs with NSW winning by 42 and 49 runs.

Top total. England made the highest score by a touring team when it rattled up 769 against NSW, MacLaren 167, Hayward 174 and Tyldesely 142. Victor Trumper bowled 40 overs, 1/111. This rather overshadowed NSW's fine innings with Syd Gregory's 147 and 75 on a fourth day 'sticky'. England won by an innings and 128 runs.

Innings declared. For the first time in Australian first class cricket, NSW captain Harold Evers declared an innings closed against Queensland, on April 1, leaving them 233 to win. Match drawn.

A cruise to victory, 4–1

Hugh Trumble: took over as captain.

Clem Hill: stumbling block for England.

Melbourne, March 4. It has been left to Hugh Trumble to guide Australia to a resounding Test series win. After the third Test Joe Darling decided to go back to his farm in Tasmania and leave the winning of the series to others.

His confidence was well placed as Australia won by seven wickets in Sydney and by 32 runs in Melbourne to take the series 4–1 and keep the Ashes.

But the games have been dramatic, and have been followed avidly by the public, both at the grounds and at newspaper offices.

In Sydney England's batting stalwarts MacLaren (92) and Tyldesley (79) helped them to 317, and the fat seemed in the fire when Gilbert 'The Croucher' Jessop snared Australia's first four wickets cheaply, but resistance from Noble (56),

Duff (39), Armstrong (55) Hopkins (43) and Howell, who made 35 off 15 balls, took Australia to 299. Then on a good pitch England surrendered for 99, with Noble (5/54) and Saunders (5/43) bowling unchanged and completely in command.

England held the upper hand briefly in the fifth Test when they bowled Australia out for 144 on a damp pitch. Then MacLaren and Jessop opened like a whirlwind to post 50 runs in 20 minutes and the game looked like getting away from Australia. Trumble took 5/62 in keeping the tourists to 189.

Australia batted steadily, with Hill making 87 of 255, to achieve a lead of 210. Rain then affected England's hopes. Noble (6/98) and Trumble (3/64) ran through the tail for a 32-run win.

Eady gets 566

Hobart, March 9. Charles Eady, long the premier batsman in Tasmania, has just completed a mammoth innings – scoring 566 for his club team, Break-O'Day, against Wellington. He took four afternoons to compile the score in 477 minutes, hitting 13 fives and 68 fours, and has created a club cricket record.

The powerfully built solicitor toured England in 1896 but was hampered by illness. His continued good form took him into the Australian side for the fifth Test a month ago. He took 3/30 in England's first innings, but he scored only 5 and 3.

1902 team chosen

Melbourne, March 20. The Melbourne Cricket Club secretary, Major Ben Wardill, has announced the 1902 team to tour England, and there are no surprises.

The team is Joe Darling (captain), Clem Hill, Monty Noble, Reg Duff, Victor Trumper, Warwick Armstrong, Albert Hopkins, Syd Gregory, Hugh Trumble, Jack Kelly, Ernie Jones, Hanson Carter, Bill Howell and Jack Saunders. It was chosen by Trumble, Noble and Hill.

The only debutant is Hanson Carter, deputy wicketkeeper, who has a unique style in crouching behind the stumps.

FIRST TEST 1901–02 AUSTRALIA v ENGLAND
Sydney Cricket Ground, Sydney, December 13, 14, 16, 1901.
Toss: England. England won by an innings & 124 runs.

ENGLAND

AC MacLaren (c) lbw McLeod	116
TW Hayward c Hill b Trumble	69
JT Tyldesley c McLeod b Laver	1
WG Quaife b Howell	21
GL Jessop b McLeod	24
AO Jones c Kelly b Noble	9
AFA Lilley (+) c Laver b McLeod	84
LC Braund c Jones b McLeod	58
JR Gunn c & b Jones	21
SF Barnes not out	26
C Blythe c Trumble b Laver	20
EXTRAS (B 6, LB 7, W 1, NB 1)	15
TOTAL	464

FOW 1st Inns: 154 163 193 220 236 272 396 405 425 464

Bowling: *First Innings:* Jones 36-8-98-1, Noble 33-17-91-1, Howell 21-8-52-1, McLeod 44-17-84-4, Trumble 34-12-85-1, Laver 17-6-39-2, Trumper 1-1-0-0.

AUSTRALIA

ES Gregory c Braund b Blythe	48 (5)	c MacLaren b Braund	43
VT Trumper c & b Barnes	2	c Lilley b Blythe	34
C Hill b Barnes	46	b Braund	0
MA Noble st Lilley b Braund	2	c Lilley b Blythe	14
WP Howell c Braund b Blythe	9 (10)	not out	31
CE McLeod b Barnes	0	b Blythe	0
JJ Kelly (+) b Blythe	0	c Barnes b Blythe	12
J Darling (c) c Quaife b Barnes	39 (1)	c Jessop b Braund	3
F Laver c Quaife b Braund	6	st Lilley b Braund	0
H Trumble not out	5 (8)	c Lilley b Barnes	26
E Jones c Jessop b Barnes	5	c Jones b Braund	2
EXTRAS (B 1, LB 3, NB 2)	6	(B 5, LB 2)	7
TOTAL	168		172

FOW 1st Inns:384485 120 220 242 257 340 340 352
FOW 2nd Inns: 116 208 224 228 243 254 0 0 0 0

Bowling: *First Innings:* Barnes 35.1-9-65-5, Braund 15-4-40-2, Gunn 5-0-27-0, Blythe 16-8-26-3, Jessop 1-0-4-0. *Second Innings:* Barnes 16-2-74-1, Braund 28.4-8-61-5, Blythe 13-5-30-4.

Umpires: R Callaway & RM Crockett

SECOND TEST 1901–02 AUSTRALIA v ENGLAND
Melbourne Cricket Ground, Melbourne. January 1, 2, 3, 4, 1902.
Toss: England. Australia won by 229 runs.

AUSTRALIA

VT Trumper c Tyldesley b Barnes	0 (8)	c Lilley b Barnes	16
J Darling (c) c Lilley b Blythe	19	c Tyldesley b Barnes	23
C Hill b Barnes	15 (7)	c Jones b Barnes	99
H Trumble c Braund b Blythe	16 (1)	c Braund b Barnes	16
MA Noble c Lilley b Blythe	0 (9)	lbw Blythe	16
ES Gregory st Lilley b Blythe	0	c Jones b Barnes	17
RA Duff c Braund b Barnes	32 (10)	b Braund	104
JJ Kelly (+) c Quaife b Barnes	5 (4)	run out	3
WW Armstrong not out	4 (11)	not out	45
WP Howell b Barnes	1 (3)	c Hayward b Barnes	0
E Jones c MacLaren b Barnes	14 (5)	c MacLaren b Barnes	5
EXTRAS (B 6)	6	(B 7, LB 1, NB 1)	9
TOTAL	112		353

FOW 1st Inns: 03234343881859094 112
FOW 2nd Inns:324242424898 128 167 233 353

Bowling: *First Innings:* Barnes 16.1-5-42-6, Blythe 16-2-64-4. *Second Innings:* Barnes 64-17-121-7, Blythe 31-7-85-1, Braund 53.2-17-114-1, Jessop 1-0-9-0, Gunn 6-1-13-0, Jones 1-0-2-0.

ENGLAND

AC MacLaren (c) c Jones b Trumble	13	c Trumble b Noble	1
TW Hayward c Darling b Trumble	0	st Kelly b Trumble	12
JT Tyldesley c Gregory b Trumble	2	c Trumble b Noble	66
WG Quaife b Noble	0	b Noble	25
GL Jessop st Kelly b Noble	27	c Gregory b Noble	32
JR Gunn st Kelly b Noble	0 (9)	c Jones b Trumble	2
AFA Lilley (+) c Trumper b Noble	6 (6)	c Darling b Noble	0
AO Jones c Kelly b Noble	0	c Darling b Trumble	6
LC Braund not out	2 (7)	c Darling b Noble	25
SF Barnes c & b Noble	1	c & b Trumble	0
C Blythe c Trumper b Noble	4	not out	0
EXTRAS (B 6)	6	(B 1, LB 1, NB 4)	6
TOTAL	61		175

FOW 1st Inns: 5161624365151565761
FOW 2nd Inns: 22980 123 123 156 173 175 175 175

Bowling: *First Innings:* Trumble 8-1-38-3, Noble 7.4-2-17-7. *Second Innings:* Jones 12-2-33-0, Noble 26-7-55-6, Trumble 22.5-10-49-4, Howell 15-6-23-0, Armstrong 2-1-3-0, Trumper 2-1-1-0.

Umpires: R Callaway & RM Crockett

THIRD TEST 1901–02 AUSTRALIA v ENGLAND
Adelaide Oval, Adelaide. January 17, 18, 20, 21, 22, 23, 1902.
Toss: England. Australia won by 4 wkts.

ENGLAND

AC MacLaren (c) run out	67	b Trumble	44
TW Hayward run out	90	b Trumble	47
JT Tyldesley c & b Trumble	0	run out	25
GL Jessop c Trumper b Trumble	1 (5)	b Trumble	16
AFA Lilley (+) lbw Trumble	10 (7)	b McLeod	21
WG Quaife c Kelly b Howell	68 (4)	lbw Trumble	44
LC Braund not out	103 (6)	b Howell	17
AO Jones run out	5	c & b Trumble	11
JR Gunn b Noble	24	lbw Trumble	5
SF Barnes c Hill b Noble	5		
C Blythe c Hill b Noble	2 (10)	not out	10
EXTRAS (B 9, W 1, NB 3)	13	(B 7)	7
TOTAL	388		9 for 247

FOW 1st Inns: 149 160 164 171 186 294 302 371 384 388
FOW 2nd Inns: 80 113 126 144 165 204 218 224 247

Bowling: *First Innings*: Trumble 65-23-124-3, Noble 26-10-58-3, Howell 36-10-82-1, Armstrong 18-5-45-0, Trumper 6-3-17-0, McLeod 19-5-49-0. *Second Innings*: Noble 21-7-72-0, Howell 27-9-54-1, Trumble 44-18-74-6, Armstrong 5-0-9-0, McLeod 14-3-31-1.

AUSTRALIA

J Darling (c) c MacLaren b Blythe	1 (5)	c Hayward b Jessop	69
VT Trumper run out	65	b Gunn	25
C Hill c Tyldesley b Braund	98	b Jessop	97
RA Duff lbw Braund	43 (1)	hit wicket b Gunn	4
ES Gregory c Blythe b Braund	55 (4)	c Braund b Gunn	23
WW Armstrong c & b Gunn	9 (8)	not out	9
H Trumble b Gunn	13 (6)	not out	62
WP Howell c Braund b Gunn	3		
MA Noble b Gunn	14 (7)	run out	13
JJ Kelly (+) not out	5		
CE McLeod b Gunn	7		
EXTRAS (B 2, LB 6)	8	(B 9, LB 3, NB 1)	13
TOTAL	321		6 for 315

FOW 1st Inns: 1 138 197 229 260 288 289 302 309 321
FOW 2nd Inns: 5 50 98 194 255 287

Bowling: *First Innings*: Braund 46-9-143-3, Blythe 11-3-54-1, Barnes 7-0-21-0, Gunn 42-14-76-5, Jessop 7-0-19-0. *Second Innings*: Gunn 38-14-88-3, Braund 25-5-79-0, Blythe 41-16-66-0, Hayward 7-0-28-0, Jessop 23-9-41-2.

Umpires: P Argall & RM Crockett

FOURTH TEST 1901–02 AUSTRALIA v ENGLAND
Sydney Cricket Ground, Sydney. February 14, 15, 17, 18, 1902.
Toss: England. Australia won by 7 wkts.

ENGLAND

AC MacLaren (c) c Duff b Saunders	92	c Kelly b Noble	5
TW Hayward b Saunders	41	b Noble	12
JT Tyldesley c Kelly b Noble	79	c Trumble b Saunders	10
WG Quaife c Kelly b Saunders	4	lbw Noble	15
GL Jessop c Noble b Saunders	0	b Saunders	15
LC Braund lbw Trumble	17	b Saunders	0
CP McGahey b Trumble	18	c Kelly b Saunders	13
AFA Lilley (+) c Kelly b Noble	40	c Trumble b Noble	0
AO Jones c Kelly b Trumble	15	c Kelly b Noble	6
JR Gunn not out	0	not out	13
C Blythe b Noble	4	c Kelly b Saunders	8
EXTRAS (B 5, NB 2)	7	(LB 2)	2
TOTAL	317		99

FOW 1st Inns: 73 179 188 188 225 245 267 312 312 317
FOW 2nd Inns: 5 24 36 57 57 57 60 78 88 99

Bowling: *First Innings*: Noble 33.2-12-78-3, Saunders 43-11-119-4, Howell 22-10-40-0, Trumble 38-18-65-3, Armstrong 2-1-8-0. *Second Innings*: Saunders 24.1-8-43-5, Noble 24-7-54-5.

AUSTRALIA

H Trumble (c) c MacLaren b Jessop	6	lbw Blythe	25
VT Trumper c Braund b Jessop	7	c Lilley b Gunn	30
C Hill c Jones b Jessop	21	not out	12
ES Gregory c Braund b Jessop	5 (5)		
MA Noble lbw Braund	56		
RA Duff c Lilley b Blythe	39 (1)	not out	51
WW Armstrong b Braund	55		
AJY Hopkins c Lilley b Braund	43		
JJ Kelly (+) not out	24		
WP Howell c MacLaren b Gunn	35 (4)	c (S)HG Harnett b Gunn	0
JV Saunders b Braund	0		
EXTRAS (B 7, NB 1)	8	(LB 1, NB 2)	3
TOTAL	299		3 for 121

FOW 1st Inns: 7 18 30 48 119 160 205 252 288 299
FOW 2nd Inns: 50 105 105

Bowling: *First Innings*: Braund 60-25-118-4, Jessop 26-5-68-4, Gunn 16-5-48-1, Blythe 37-17-57-1. *Second Innings*: Jessop 7-0-23-0, Braund 15-2-55-0, Blythe 6-0-23-1, Gunn 8.3-1-17-2.

Umpires: C Bannerman & R Callaway

FIFTH TEST 1901–02 AUSTRALIA v ENGLAND
Melbourne Cricket Ground, Melbourne. February 28, March 1, 3, 4, 1902.
Toss: Australia. Australia won by 32 runs.

AUSTRALIA

VT Trumper b Blythe	27	c McGahey b Braund	18
RA Duff b Braund	10	c & b Braund	28
C Hill c Jones b Gunn	28	c Lilley b Hayward	87
ES Gregory c Jones b Gunn	25	b Gunn	41
MA Noble lbw Hayward	7	c MacLaren b Gunn	16
H Trumble (c) c Quaife b Hayward	3 (7)	b Blythe	22
WW Armstrong not out	17 (6)	lbw Braund	20
AJY Hopkins c Lilley b Hayward	4	c MacLaren b Blythe	0
JJ Kelly (+) c Gunn b Hayward	0	not out	11
CJ Eady b Gunn	5	c Gunn b Braund	3
JPF Travers c Braund b Gunn	9	c & b Braund	1
EXTRAS (B 7, W 1, NB 1)	9	(B 3, LB 1, NB 4)	8
TOTAL	144		255

FOW 1st Inns: 16 54 81 98 104 108 112 112 124 144
FOW 2nd Inns: 30 52 131 149 208 224 249 249 255 255

Bowling: *First Innings*: Jessop 1-0-13-0, Braund 10-2-33-1, Blythe 9-2-29-1, Hayward 16-9-22-4, Gunn 17-6-38-4. *Second Innings*: Hayward 22-4-63-1, Braund 26.1-4-95-5, Gunn 28-11-53-2, Blythe 13-3-36-2.

ENGLAND

AC MacLaren (c) c & b Trumble	25	run out	49
GL Jessop c Hopkins b Trumble	35 (4)	c Trumper b Trumble	16
WG Quaife c Trumble b Noble	3	lbw Noble	4
JT Tyldesley c Kelly b Eady	13 (5)	c Eady b Trumble	36
TW Hayward c Trumper b Travers	19 (2)	c Travers b Trumble	15
LC Braund c Hopkins b Trumble	32	c Hill b Noble	2
AFA Lilley (+) c Eady b Trumble	41	c Duff b Noble	9
CP McGahey b Trumble	0	c Hill b Noble	7
AO Jones c Kelly b Eady	10	c & b Noble	28
JR Gunn lbw Eady	8	c Hill b Noble	4
C Blythe not out	0	not out	5
EXTRAS (B 1, LB 2)	3	(LB 2, NB 1)	3
TOTAL	189		178

FOW 1st Inns: 50 62 64 91 96 164 168 173 186 189
FOW 2nd Inns: 40 64 87 87 93 104 120 157 161 178

Bowling: *First Innings*: Noble 26-4-80-1, Trumble 25-4-62-5, Travers 8-2-14-1, Eady 8.3-2-30-3. *Second Innings*: Noble 33-4-98-6, Trumble 30.3-7-64-3, Eady 2-0-13-0.

Umpires: C Bannerman & RM Crockett

Australian Averages

1901–02 AUSTRALIA v ENGLAND

AUSTRALIA	M	Inn	NO	Runs	H.S	Avrge	Ct	St	Overs	Mds	Runs	Wkt	Avrge
Armstrong, WW	4	7	4	159	55	53.00	-	-	27.0	7	65	-	-
Darling, J	3	6	-	154	69	25.67	4	-	-	-	-	-	-
Duff, RA	4	8	1	311	104	44.43	2	-	-	-	-	-	-
Eady, CJ	1	2	-	8	5	4.00	2	-	10.3	2	43	3	14.33
Gregory, ES	5	10	1	269	55	29.89	2	-	-	-	-	-	-
Hill, C	5	10	-	521	99	52.10	6	-	-	-	-	-	-
Hopkins, AJY	2	3	-	47	43	15.67	2	-	121.0	43	251	3	83.67
Howell, WP	4	7	1	79	35	13.17	1	-	48.0	10	131	1	131.00
Jones, E	2	4	-	26	14	6.50	4	-	-	-	-	-	-
Kelly, JJ	5	8	3	60	24*	12.00	13	3	-	-	-	-	-
Laver, F	1	2	-	6	6	3.00	1	-	17.0	6	39	2	19.50
McLeod, CE	2	3	-	7	7	2.33	1	-	77.0	25	164	5	32.80
Noble, MA	5	9	-	138	56	15.33	3	-	230.0	68	608	32	19.00
Saunders, JV	1	1	-	0	0	0.00	-	-	67.1	19	162	9	18.00
Travers, JPF	1	2	-	10	9	5.00	1	-	8.0	2	14	1	14.00
Trumble, H	5	9	2	169	62*	24.14	10	-	267.2	93	561	28	20.04
Trumper, VT	5	10	-	219	65	21.90	5	-	9.0	5	18	-	-

English Averages

1901–02 AUSTRALIA v ENGLAND

ENGLAND	M	Inn	NO	Runs	H.S	Avrge	Ct	St	Overs	Mds	Runs	Wkt	Avrge
Barnes, SF	3	4	1	32	26*	10.67	2	-	138.2	33	323	19	17.00
Blythe, C	5	9	4	53	20	10.60	1	-	193.0	63	470	18	26.11
Braund, LC	5	9	2	256	103*	36.57	12	-	279.1	76	738	21	35.14
Gunn, JR	5	9	2	77	24	11.00	3	-	160.3	52	360	17	21.18
Hayward, TW	5	9	-	305	90	33.89	2	-	45.0	13	113	5	22.60
Jessop, GL	5	9	-	166	35	18.44	2	-	66.0	14	177	6	29.50
Jones, AO	5	9	-	90	28	10.00	6	-	1.0	-	2	-	-
Lilley, AFA	5	9	-	211	84	23.44	11	3	-	-	-	-	-
MacLaren, AC	5	9	-	412	116	45.78	8	-	-	-	-	-	-
McGahey, CP	2	4	-	38	18	9.50	1	-	-	-	-	-	-
Quaife, WG	5	9	-	184	68	20.44	4	-	-	-	-	-	-
Tyldesley, JT	5	9	-	232	79	25.78	3	-	-	-	-	-	-

Trumble's thumb is an early casualty

Birmingham, May 27. There is an air of gloom over the Australian camp as the players prepare for the Test series against England.

The dark feelings are scarcely relieved by the rain and dark skies that hang over Birmingham, and have been a part of the picture ever since the tourists arrived.

Test players on their first tour to England, Warwick Armstrong, Reg Duff, Bert Hopkins and Jack Saunders, must wish for the sunshine and hard flat pitches they left behind. How did cricket get invented in this damp foggy place?

The English say that this has been the wettest spring they can remember, but they tend to say that about every season when the Australian cricketers are around.

This time there are casualties – five of the touring party have been ill with a particularly virulent influenza, and this has created a greater burden for the team. Some sick men have had to leave their beds to make up the numbers.

In addition, it is now known that Hugh Trumble will not be taking part in the first Test, and has an uncertain tour future. He stopped a fierce Clem Hill drive in the nets before the first match, and his fractured thumb is still unhealed.

Seven matches have now been played for four wins and three draws. The batting form of Victor Trumper and Monty Noble carries some hope for the Test battles ahead, but the bowling looks weak, with the only genuine fast bowler Ernie Jones failing to get among the wickets on the soft pitches.

Joe Darling and Hugh Trumble lead the troops onto English soil.

Disaster, then recovery

Scenes captured at Edgbaston as Australia stumbles to a first Test draw.

Sheffield, July 5. Australia have fought for a creditable third-Test victory at Bramall Lane in Sheffield and are leading the series after what could easily have been a disastrous beginning in the first two Tests, which were both drawn.

The win in the third Test was largely created by the outstanding second innings batting of Clem Hill (119) and Victor Trumper (62). Their work helped Australia to a lead of 338, and Monty Noble led the Australian bowling, adding six second innings wickets to his haul of 5/51 in the first innings. While Hill's century came from his usual confident hitting, it was Trumper who caught the eye. He breezed to 62 in just 50 minutes, finding spaces in the field that would seem beyond other batsmen.

Australia won by 143 runs and can look ahead with confidence.

The match did little for the health of the influenza-ridden Australian team, as it was played in a pea soup fog, acrid from the smoke stacks of this industrial city. The lights in the pavilion were on by day, but did nothing to help the on-field vision.

But there was more self-made gloom than this at Edgbaston, Birmingham, in the first Test, when the tourists were humiliated on a treacherous drying pitch, being shot out for 36 after England had made 376 (Tyldesley 138). Only rain saved Australia. Wilfred Rhodes took 7/17 as the great

names of Australia fell – Duff 2, Hill 1, Gregory 0, Darling 3, Noble 3, Armstrong 0 etc. Only Trumper (18) reached double figures.

Then followed the humiliation against Yorkshire, where the County side achieved a five-wicket win at Leeds after England bowlers Hirst and Jackson had removed the Australians for 23.

The second Test was abandoned on the third day, after only 38 overs of play, as rain had interrupted the first two days.

The English practice of playing three-day Tests, instead of the timeless Tests in Australia, had therefore brought a stalemate in two Tests.

England would almost certainly have won one of them.

An amazing catching feat in the first Test, as Len Braund darts from the off to catch Australia's Clem Hill.

Two magnificent Tests lift the series

Australia by three runs in day of drama

At Old Trafford Trumper and Duff put on 135 in 78 minutes before lunch.

Gilbert Jessop saves day for England

England hero Gilbert Jessop, one of the biggest hitters the game has seen.

Manchester, July 26. The air at Old Trafford has been electric all day as the England and Australian teams have struggled to take the fourth Test match and the Ashes. The pendulum swung from day to day and achieved the closest margin yet in Anglo-Australian Tests – Australia by three runs.

England seemed to have the match in hand on the rain-affected, turning pitch as they had only 124 to get on the last day. By lunch they had grafted to 5/100 and the game seemed won.

But then the England batsmen, faced with the impeccable flight and length of Hugh Trumble and the sharp off-breaks of Jack Saunders, seemed to lose their nerve. Trumble took 6/53 and Saunders 4/52 in a magnificent match-winning display of their subtle arts.

The England collapse brought the satisfaction that had been buzzing in the stands to a stunned silence.

Pity poor Fred Tate, who came out as the last man, with only eight runs needed. His entrance was delayed by 40 minutes as a shower of rain had driven the players from the field at 9/116.

Tate, however, sent a wave of joy through the crowd as he sent the first ball for four – a stroke as precious on this pitch as a brisk 50 in dry conditions. But he essayed a similar stroke at the next ball, and was bowled through the gate. The Australians ran in to celebrate, while Wilfred Rhodes and Tate walked off in solemn silence.

The Australians whooped and ran from the field 'like dervishes' in a sight of delight unseen on an England cricket field before.

The heroics of this day have overshadowed the whole drama of a magnificent match. It began with an astounding innings from Victor Trumper, who had 103 before lunch in an amazing first-morning score of 1/173. Although he was out for 104 Trumper had great allies in Duff (54), Hill (65) and Darling (51). The captain's hand included the first two hits for six – out of the ground – in Tests in England.

The Australian score was matched by 262 from England, in which Stanley Jackson played a lone hand with 128.

But rain affected the second innings, and Australia's fall for 86 brought England's fateful run chase.

The Oval, Aug. 13. All England is saluting a new hero – Gilbert Laird Jessop – after he rescued his team from the jaws of defeat and spurred it to a slender win over the Australians in the fifth Test.

This Test must always be remembered as Jessop's match. His strength wrenched it from a miserable close to the series for England, to a triumph that will burn until the next Ashes series is contested.

Australia had the upper hand and was heading for the stable when Jessop came in. With 273 runs to get on a difficult pitch, England was 5/48.

Jessop is known as 'The Croucher' for the way he gets his compact and powerful body down over the bat, but he is also known as one of the biggest hitters the game has seen.

Big hitters are risk takers, and Jessop decided to go all out. Soon the ball was crashing into the fence as he scored 50 in an astounding 43 minutes, this against the tide of the rampant Hugh Trumble and Jack Saunders. He did more. He shot to 104 in 75 minutes – the fastest century in Test cricket so far.

When he left, trapped at short leg off Warwick Armstrong, the score was 7/187, and 76 runs were still wanted. It was left then for Lockwood, Lilley and Wilfred Rhodes to try and stay with George Hirst, who was playing with a calm confidence that seemed to suggest he could stay there.

Rhodes trudged to the wicket with 15 to get, and the whole game on his shoulders again. This time he grafted, and stayed and hit the winning run, to great scenes of excitement.

In all the excitement, the achievement of Hugh Trumble should be noted. With his 64 in the first innings and match bowling figures of 12/173 he became the first Australian to score 50 and take 10 wickets in a Test. And, on any ordinary day, he should have won the match for Australia.

But as the London *Times* said: 'As long as cricket lasts Mr Jessop's great performance will be remembered.' As will the two close results, this by a solitary wicket – and Australia's 2–1 series win. Back home many regard this Australian team, playing England's best at their peak, as Australia's best-ever team.

Trumper's bumper season

'Tell yer wot! You be England, and I'll be Victor Trumper.'

London, Sep. 20. Victor Trumper has left great memories in England of batting far above anything seen so far in the Test arena.

The wonder of his efforts can be set against the quality of the batsmen around him. Australia has had Clem Hill, Reg Duff, Warwick Armstrong, Monty Noble and Joe Darling – all brilliant on their day.

England has had Archie MacLaren, John Tyldesley, Stanley Jackson and the power hitter Gilbert Jessop. None have even bordered on the majesty of Victor Trumper. Only Ranjitsinjhi, with his subtle and fluent strokes, comes into the same category, and he has been missing from this round of Tests.

Clem Hill topped the Australian batting averages in the Tests, with 36.86, behind Jackson's 44.43 for England, but ahead of Trumper's ordinary looking 30.88.

However, Trumper's pre-lunch century on a wet pitch in the fourth Test was a mark of his greatness.

In the 36 matches he played, he scored 2570 runs at 48.49. Trumper has not wanted to be a run-scoring machine. He made 11 centuries, but he tended to give his wicket away after the 100 was up, and let his fellows have a go. Equally, when he failed, he left the field with a rueful smile and no apparent anger.

His team-mates were in no doubt about his mastery. Clem Hill said that, if he was troubled by a bowler, Trumper would take strike, hit the bowler out of the attack, and then let Hill take over again.

Trumper's skill lay in the ease of his stroke play. He was always on the attack, getting perfectly to the pitch of the ball and scoring either with powerful orthodox shots, or a few more of his own making. And he seemed always to get the ball past the fieldsman.

The dominant bowler in Tests, once he got over his broken thumb, was Hugh Trumble. He played in only three Tests but took 26 wickets, four more than England's best Wilfred Rhodes, who played in all Tests. Australia's next best was Jack Saunders, with 18 wickets in four Tests.

Trumble took 140 wickets on the tour, in which he missed the early matches. He would have been handy on those early season damp pitches.

Warwick Armstrong emerged as an all-rounder with a great future, surpassing the other all-rounder Monty Noble with his tour figures of 1087 runs and 81 wickets.

FIRST TEST 1902 ENGLAND v AUSTRALIA
Edgbaston, Birmingham. May 29, 30, 31, 1902.
Toss: England. Match Drawn.

ENGLAND
AC MacLaren (c) run out 9
CB Fry c Kelly b Jones 0
KS Ranjitsinhji b Armstrong 13
FS Jackson b Jones 53
JT Tyldesley lbw Howell 138
AFA Lilley (+) c Jones b Noble 2
GH Hirst c Armstrong b Trumper 48
GL Jessop c Hopkins b Trumper 6
LC Braund b Jones 14
WH Lockwood not out 52
W Rhodes not out 38
EXTRAS (LB 3) 3
TOTAL ....9 dec 376

FOW 1st Inns: 5 13 35 112 121 212 230 264 295

Bowling: *First Innings:* Jones 28-9-76-3, Noble 44-15-112-1, Trumper 13-5-35-2, Armstrong 25-6-64-1, Howell 26-8-58-1, Hopkins 6-2-28-0.

AUSTRALIA
VT Trumper b Hirst	18	c Braund b Rhodes	14
RA Duff c Jessop b Rhodes	2	c Fry b Braund	15
C Hill c Braund b Hirst	1	not out	10
ES Gregory lbw Hirst	0	not out	1
J Darling (c) c Jessop b Rhodes	3		
MA Noble st Lilley b Rhodes	3		
WW Armstrong c Lilley b Rhodes	0		
AJY Hopkins c Lilley b Rhodes	5		
JJ Kelly (+) not out	1		
E Jones c Jackson b Rhodes	0		
WP Howell c Fry b Rhodes	0		
EXTRAS (B 3)	3	(LB 4, W 1, NB 1)	6
TOTAL	36	2 for 46	

FOW 1st Inns: 9 10 14 17 25 25 31 35 35 36
FOW 2nd Inns: 16 41

Bowling: *First Innings:* Hirst 11-4-15-3, Rhodes 11-3-17-7, Braund 1-0-1-0. *Second Innings:* Hirst 9-6-10-0, Rhodes 10-5-9-1, Braund 5-0-14-1, Jackson 4-2-7-0.

Umpires: W Hearn & J Phillips

SECOND TEST 1902 ENGLAND v AUSTRALIA
Lord's Cricket Ground, London. June 12, 13 (no play),14 (no play), 1902.
Toss: England. Match Drawn.

ENGLAND
AC MacLaren (c) not out 47
CB Fry c Hill b Hopkins 0
KS Ranjitsinhji b Hopkins 0
FS Jackson not out 55
JT Tyldesley
AFA Lilley (+)
GH Hirst
GL Jessop
LC Braund
WH Lockwood
W Rhodes
   EXTRAS 0
TOTAL ....2 for 102

FOW 1st Inns: 0 0

Bowling: *First Innings:* Jones 11-4-31-0, Hopkins 9-3-18-2, Saunders 3-0-15-0, Trumper 8-1-33-0, Armstrong 5-0-5-0, Noble 2-2-0-0.

AUSTRALIA
VT Trumper
RA Duff
AJY Hopkins
C Hill
ES Gregory
J Darling (c)
MA Noble
WW Armstrong
JJ Kelly (+)
E Jones
JV Saunders

Umpires: CE Richardson & VA Titchmarsh

THIRD TEST 1902 ENGLAND v AUSTRALIA
Bramall Lane, Sheffield. July 3, 4, 5, 1902.
Toss: Australia. Australia won by 143 runs.

AUSTRALIA

VT Trumper b Braund	1	c Lilley b Jackson	62
RA Duff c Lilley b Barnes	25	c Hirst b Rhodes	1
C Hill c Rhodes b Barnes	18	c MacLaren b Jackson	119
J Darling (c) c Braund b Barnes	0	c Braund b Barnes	0
ES Gregory c Abel b Barnes	11	run out	29
MA Noble c Braund b Rhodes	47	b Jackson	8
AJY Hopkins c Braund b Barnes	27	not out	40
WW Armstrong c & b Braund	25	b Rhodes	26
JJ Kelly (+) b Barnes	0	c Hirst b Rhodes	0
H Trumble c & b Jackson	32	b Rhodes	0
JV Saunders not out	0	b Rhodes	1
EXTRAS (B 3, LB 5)	8	(LB 3)	3
TOTAL	194		289

FOW 1st Inns: 3 39 39 52 73 127 137 137 194 194
FOW 2nd Inns: 20 80 80 187 214 225 277 287 287 289

Bowling: *First Innings*: Hirst 15-1-59-0, Braund 13-4-34-2, Barnes 20-9-49-6, Jackson 5.1-1-11-1, Rhodes 13-3-33-1. *Second Innings*: Hirst 10-1-40-0, Braund 12-0-58-0, Barnes 12-4-50-1, Jackson 17-2-60-3, Rhodes 17.1-3-63-5, Jessop 4-0-15-0.

ENGLAND

AC MacLaren (c) b Noble	31 (4)	c Trumper b Noble	63
R Abel b Noble	38	c Hill b Noble	8
JT Tyldesley c Armstrong b Noble	22	b Trumble	14
FS Jackson c Gregory b Saunders	3 (6)	b Noble	14
CB Fry st Kelly b Saunders	1	lbw Trumble	4
AFA Lilley (+) b Noble	8 (7)	b Noble	9
LC Braund st Kelly b Saunders	0 (8)	c Armstrong b Noble	9
GH Hirst c Trumble b Saunders	8 (9)	b Noble	0
GL Jessop c Saunders b Noble	12 (1)	lbw Trumble	55
W Rhodes not out	7	not out	7
SF Barnes c Darling b Saunders	7	b Trumble	5
EXTRAS (B 4, LB 3, NB 1)	8	(B 4, LB 1, W 1, NB 1)	7
TOTAL	145		195

FOW 1st Inns: 61 86 101 101 102 106 110 130 131 145
FOW 2nd Inns: 14 75 84 98 162 165 174 174 186 195

Bowling: *First Innings*: Trumble 18-10-21-0, Saunders 15.3-4-50-5, Trumper 4-1-8-0, Noble 19-6-51-5, Armstrong 5-2-7-0. *Second Innings*: Trumble 21.5-3-49-4, Saunders 12-0-68-0, Trumper 6-0-19-0, Noble 21-4-52-6.

Umpires: J Phillips & W Richards

FIFTH TEST 1902 ENGLAND v AUSTRALIA
Kennington Oval, London. August 11, 12, 13, 1902.
Toss: Australia. England won by 1 wkt.

AUSTRALIA

VT Trumper b Hirst	42	run out	2
RA Duff c Lilley b Hirst	23	b Lockwood	6
C Hill b Hirst	11	c MacLaren b Hirst	34
J Darling (c) c Lilley b Hirst	3	c MacLaren b Lockwood	15
MA Noble c & b Jackson	52	b Braund	13
ES Gregory b Hirst	23	b Braund	9
WW Armstrong b Jackson	17	b Lockwood	21
AJY Hopkins c MacLaren b Lockwood	40	c Lilley b Lockwood	3
H Trumble not out	64 (10)	not out	7
JJ Kelly (+) c Rhodes b Braund	39 (11)	lbw Lockwood	0
JV Saunders lbw Braund	0 (9)	c Tyldesley b Rhodes	2
EXTRAS (B 5, LB 3, NB 2)	10	(B 7, LB 2)	9
TOTAL	324		121

FOW 1st Inns: 47 63 69 82 126 174 175 256 324 324
FOW 2nd Inns: 6 9 31 71 75 91 99 114 115 121

Bowling: *First Innings*: Lockwood 24-2-85-1, Rhodes 28-9-46-0, Hirst 29-5-77-5, Braund 16.5-5-29-2, Jackson 20-4-66-2, Jessop 6-2-11-0. *Second Innings*: Lockwood 20-6-45-5, Rhodes 22-7-38-1, Hirst 5-1-7-1, Braund 9-1-15-2, Jackson 4-3-7-0.

ENGLAND

AC MacLaren (c) c Armstrong b Trumble	10	b Saunders	2
LCH Palairet b Trumble	20	b Saunders	6
JT Tyldesley b Trumble	33	b Saunders	0
TW Hayward b Trumble	0	c Kelly b Saunders	7
FS Jackson c Armstrong b Saunders	2	c & b Trumble	49
LC Braund c Hill b Trumble	22	c Kelly b Trumble	2
GL Jessop b Trumble	13	c Noble b Armstrong	104
GH Hirst c & b Trumble	43	not out	58
WH Lockwood c Noble b Saunders	25	lbw Trumble	2
AFA Lilley (+) c Trumper b Trumble	0	c Darling b Trumble	16
W Rhodes not out	0	not out	6
EXTRAS (B 13, LB 2)	15	(B 4, LB 6)	11
TOTAL	183		9 for 263

FOW 1st Inns: 31 36 62 67 67 83 137 179 183 183
FOW 2nd Inns: 5 5 10 31 48 157 187 214 248

Bowling: *First Innings*: Trumble 31-13-65-8, Saunders 23-7-79-2, Noble 7-3-24-0. *Second Innings*: Trumble 33.5-4-108-4, Saunders 24-3-105-4, Noble 5-0-11-0, Armstrong 4-0-28-1.

Umpires: CE Richardson & AA White

FOURTH TEST 1902 ENGLAND v AUSTRALIA
Old Trafford, Manchester. July 24, 25, 26, 1902.
Toss: Australia. Australia won by 3 runs.

AUSTRALIA

VT Trumper c Lilley b Rhodes	104	c Braund b Lockwood	4
RA Duff c Lilley b Lockwood	54	b Lockwood	3
C Hill c Rhodes b Lockwood	65	b Lockwood	0
MA Noble c & b Rhodes	2 (6)	c Lilley b Lockwood	4
ES Gregory b Lilley b Rhodes	3	lbw Tate	24
J Darling (c) c MacLaren b Rhodes	51 (4)	c Palairet b Rhodes	37
AJY Hopkins c Palairet b Lockwood	0	c Tate b Lockwood	2
WW Armstrong b Lockwood	5	b Rhodes	3
JJ Kelly (+) not out	4	not out	2
H Trumble c Tate b Lockwood	0	lbw Tate	4
JV Saunders b Lockwood	3	c Tyldesley b Rhodes	0
EXTRAS (B 5, LB 2, W 1)	8	(B 1, LB 1, NB 1)	3
TOTAL	299		86

FOW 1st Inns: 135 175 179 183 256 256 288 292 292 299
FOW 2nd Inns: 7 9 10 64 74 76 77 79 85 86

Bowling: *First Innings*: Rhodes 25-3-104-4, Jackson 11-0-58-0, Tate 11-1-44-0, Braund 9-0-37-0, Lockwood 20.1-5-48-6. Second Innings: Rhodes 14.4-5-26-3, Tate 5-3-7-2, Braund 11-3-22-0, Lockwood 17-5-28-5.

ENGLAND

LCH Palairet c Noble b Saunders	6	b Saunders	17
R Abel c Armstrong b Saunders	6 (5)	b Trumble	21
JT Tyldesley c Hopkins b Saunders	22	c Armstrong b Saunders	16
AC MacLaren (c) b Trumble	1 (2)	c Duff b Trumble	35
KS Ranjitsinhji lbw Trumble	2 (4)	lbw Trumble	4
FS Jackson c Duff b Trumble	128	c Gregory b Saunders	7
LC Braund b Noble	65	st Kelly b Trumble	3
AFA Lilley b Noble	7	c Hill b Trumble	4
WH Lockwood run out	7	b Trumble	0
W Rhodes c & b Trumble	5	not out	4
FW Tate not out	5	b Saunders	4
EXTRAS (B 6, LB 2)	8	(B 5)	5
TOTAL	262		120

FOW 1st Inns: 12 13 14 30 44 185 203 214 235 262
FOW 2nd Inns: 44 68 72 92 97 107 109 109 116 120

Bowling: First Innings: Trumble 43-16-75-4, Saunders 34-5-104-3, Noble 24-8-47-2, Trumper 6-4-6-0, Armstrong 5-2-19-0, Hopkins 2-0-3-0. *Second Innings*: Trumble 25-9-53-6, Saunders 19.4-4-52-4, Noble 5-3-10-0.

Umpires: J Moss & T Mycroft

Australian Averages

1902 ENGLAND v AUSTRALIA

AUSTRALIA	M	Inn	NO	Runs	H.S	Avrge	Ct	St	Overs	Mds	Runs	Wkt	Avrge
Armstrong, WW	5	7	-	97	26	13.86	7	-	44.0	10	123	2	61.50
Darling, J	5	7	-	109	51	15.57	2	-	-	-	-	-	-
Duff, RA	5	8	-	129	54	16.13	2	-	-	-	-	-	-
Gregory, ES	5	8	1	100	29	14.29	2	-	-	-	-	-	-
Hill, C	5	8	1	258	119	36.86	4	-	-	-	-	-	-
Hopkins, AJY	5	7	1	117	40*	19.50	2	-	17.0	5	49	2	24.50
Howell, WP	1	1	-	0	0	0.00	-	-	26.0	8	58	1	58.00
Jones, E	2	1	-	0	0	0.00	1	-	39.0	13	107	3	35.67
Kelly, JJ	5	7	3	46	39	11.50	3	3	-	-	-	-	-
Noble, MA	5	7	-	129	52	18.43	3	-	127.0	41	307	14	21.93
Saunders, JV	4	6	1	6	3	1.20	1	-	131.1	23	473	18	26.28
Trumble, H	3	6	2	107	64*	26.75	4	-	172.4	55	371	26	14.27
Trumper, VT	5	8	-	247	104	30.88	2	-	37.0	11	101	2	50.50*f*

English Averages

1902 ENGLAND v AUSTRALIA

ENGLAND	M	Inn	NO	Runs	H.S	Avrge	Ct	St	Overs	Mds	Runs	Wkt	Avrge
Abel, R	2	4	-	73	38	18.25	1	-	-	-	-	-	-
Barnes, SF	1	2	-	12	7	6.00	-	-	32.0	13	99	7	14.14
Braund, LC	5	7	-	115	65	16.43	8	-	76.5	13	210	7	30.00
Fry, CB	3	4	-	5	4	1.25	2	-	-	-	-	-	-
Hayward, TW	1	2	-	7	7	3.50	-	-	-	-	-	-	-
Hirst, GH	4	5	1	157	58*	39.25	2	-	79.0	18	208	9	23.11
Jackson, FS	5	8	1	311	128	44.43	3	-	61.1	12	209	6	34.83
Jessop, GL	4	5	-	190	104	38.00	2	-	10.0	2	26	-	-
Lilley, AFA	5	7	-	46	16	6.57	11	1	-	-	-	-	-
Lockwood, WH	4	5	1	86	52*	21.50	-	-	81.1	18	206	17	12.12
MacLaren, AC	5	8	-	198	63	28.29	5	-	-	-	-	-	-
Palairet, LCH	2	4	-	49	20	12.25	2	-	-	-	-	-	-
Ranjitsinhji, KS	3	4	-	19	13	4.75	-	-	-	-	-	-	-
Rhodes, W	5	7	6	67	38*	67.00	4	-	140.5	38	336	22	15.27
Tate, FW	1	2	1	9	5*	9.00	2	-	16.0	4	51	2	25.50
Tyldesley, JT	5	7	-	245	138	35.00	2	-	-	-	-	-	-

South Africa shows its fighting spirit

Johannesburg, Oct. 14. South Africa has surprised the Australians by matching them blow for blow in the first Test encounter between the two countries.

With only eightTests in its entire cricket history (against Australia's 65) it was expected that the South Africans would easily succumb to the more experienced Australians.

But they are, like the Australians, an athletic sporting breed, nurtured by the sun and the hard work of families in the pioneering years.

They made 454 in the first innings, and had Australia following on after its score of 296. Only a savagely brilliant 154 by Clem Hill (which included 100 before lunch on the third day) saved the Australian position.

Perhaps the sea voyage, the excitement of the Cape Town landing, the immediate train journey into the interior and the matting wicket may have told against the Australians. But there was no doubting the South African spirit.

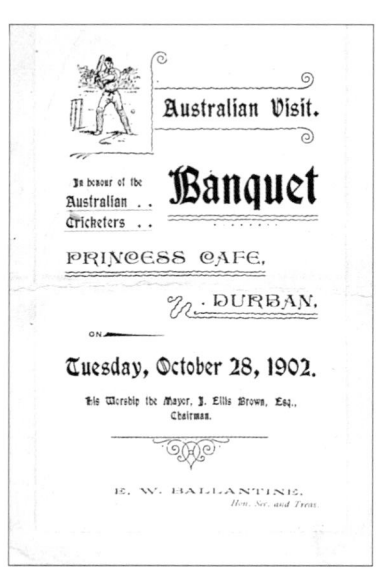

Part of South Africa's welcome.

Jimmy Sinclair's big hitting

Century maker. The powerfully built Jimmy Sinclair displays his big hitting style.

Cape Town, Nov. 11. Australia have won the three-Test series against South Africa, 2–0, but the enthusiastic crowds have had plenty to enjoy in the sterling efforts of the local players.

Their hero is the big-hitting batsman Jimmy Sinclair, who has topped off his efforts with 101 in 80 minutes in the second Test in Johannesburg – the fastest Test century yet played. He got his first 50 in 35 minutes, with six towering sixes. It did not seem to matter that it was a doomed effort, as South Africa lost the Test when it capitulated for 85 in the first innings.

Sinclair has now scored three centuries in the five Tests he has played. He made his maiden century in 1899 against England, and in this series has had scores of 44, 19, 101, 18, 0 and 104. But he has not had the support that would give South Africa a line-up to match the great opening stands of Victor Trumper and Reg Duff, or the consistent scoring of Clem Hill, and Warwick Armstrong.

Armstrong kept Australia in the second Test after a bad start, which saw South Africa leading by 65 on the first innings. Armstrong then scored 159 not out in his second knock, to give Australia some runs to play with. The knockout blow was delivered by spinners Jack Saunders and Bill Howell in the second innings, in which the home side made 85. Howell took 4/18 and 5/81, while Saunders had 4/37 and 2/73.

Spinner Bill Howell likes the matting

Cape Town, Nov. 11. It has been like Old Home Week for Bill Howell In South Africa. The burly off-spinner learned his cricket on the matting wickets of the Penrith district, and he has discovered that he can still get outstanding results with the ball that spins and skids through.

He missed the first Test, but in the five matches he has played he has taken a phenomenal 48 wickets at an average of 9.60.

His best haul was against a 15 of Western Province, when he seemed to be playing skittles as he took 17/54. Howell is remarkable for the number he bowls out. Of his Test wickets he bowled 11 out of 14 victims. In the third Test, which Australia won by 10 wickets, Howell took 4/18 and 5/51.

Howell's rush of form has been in great contrast to his efforts in England, where the softer pitches seemed to nullify his work on the ball, and he was selected only for the first Test.

He will, however, be remembered there for his 1899 game against Surrey, when he took all 10 Surrey wickets for 28.

Banquets, bonuses

Sydney, Dec. 15. The Australian team has been well received on return from its lengthy and mightily successful trips to England and South Africa. There have been dinners, receptions and speeches in number. More importantly there has been money, a tour bonus of £800 for each player for the English tour, plus £250 for South Africa. This is four years pay for the working man.

Victor Trumper has been further singled out, receiving a purse of 100 guineas by a subscription of the people of Sydney.

FIRST TEST 1902–03 SOUTH AFRICA v AUSTRALIA
Old Wanderers, Johannesburg. October 11, 13, 14, 1902.
Toss: South Africa. Match Drawn.

SOUTH AFRICA

Batsman	1st	2nd
WA Shalders c & b Jones	19	c Kelly b Jones ... 0
LJ Tancred c Duff b Trumper	97	b Armstrong ... 24
CB Llewellyn b Trumper	90 (6)	not out ... 4
JH Sinclair c & b Hopkins	44	b Armstrong ... 19
CMH Hathorn c Gregory b Jones	45 (3)	c Armstrong b Noble ... 31
CJE Smith b Hopkins	13 (5)	not out ... 16
HM Taberer (c) b Hopkins	2	
AW Nourse c Hopkins b Noble	72	
EA Halliwell (+) c Darling b Jones	57	
PG Thornton not out	1	
GA Rowe c Jones b Noble	4	
EXTRAS (B 5, LB 4, NB 1)	10	(B 4, LB 3) ... 7
TOTAL	454	4 for 101

FOW 1st Inns: 31 204 223 296 304 306 325 449 449 454
FOW 2nd Inns: 5 44 74 90

Bowling: *First Innings*: Jones 21-5-78-3, Armstrong 13-3-88-0, Trumble 23-1-103-0, Trumper 12-0-62-2, Hopkins 12-1-59-3, Noble 14-2-54-2. *Second Innings*: Jones 7-3-22-1, Armstrong 7-2-24-2, Trumble 11-3-24-0, Hopkins 2-0-17-0, Noble 5-1-7-1.

AUSTRALIA

Batsman	1st	2nd
VT Trumper c Rowe b Llewellyn	63	b Taberer ... 37
WW Armstrong b Sinclair	11 (4)	c Halliwell b Thornton ... 59
C Hill c Nourse b Sinclair	76	c & b Sinclair ... 142
RA Duff not out	82 (2)	c Halliwell b Rowe ... 15
MA Noble b Sinclair	1 (6)	not out ... 53
J Darling (c) st Halliwell b Sinclair	0 (5)	b Llewellyn ... 14
ES Gregory lbw Llewellyn	0	b Llewellyn ... 4
AJY Hopkins c Tancred b Llewellyn	1	lbw Llewellyn ... 30
H Trumble c Thornton b Llewellyn	13	not out ... 0
JJ Kelly (+) c Halliwell b Llewellyn	25	
E Jones c Sinclair b Llewellyn	0	
EXTRAS (B 22, LB 2)	24	(B 13, LB 5) ... 18
TOTAL	296	7 dec 372

FOW 1st Inns: 60 106 195 196 196 199 217 242 296 296
FOW 2nd Inns: 42 67 231 277 281 297 354

Bowling: *First Innings*: Rowe 5-1-28-0, Taberer 4-1-23-0, Llewellyn 22-3-92-6, Sinclair 20-1-129-4. *Second Innings*: Rowe 11-1-55-1, Taberer 6-1-25-1, Llewellyn 26-3-124-3, Sinclair 23-2-115-1, Nourse 8-2-15-0, Thornton 4-0-20-1.

Umpires: F Hearne & A Soames

THIRD TEST 1902–03 SOUTH AFRICA v AUSTRALIA
Newlands, Cape Town. November 8, 10, 11, 1902.
Toss: Australia. Australia won by 10 wkts.

AUSTRALIA

Batsman	1st	2nd
RA Duff c Tancred b Kotze	34	not out ... 20
VT Trumper b Llewellyn	70	not out ... 38
C Hill not out	91	
WW Armstrong b Llewellyn	3	
MA Noble c Smith b Sinclair	9	
AJY Hopkins b Llewellyn	16	
ES Gregory c Smith b Llewellyn	11	
J Darling (c) b Llewellyn	1	
JJ Kelly (+) b Kotze	1	
WP Howell b Llewellyn	2	
JV Saunders run out	4	
EXTRAS (B 6, LB 4)	10	(NB 1) ... 1
TOTAL	252	0 for 59

FOW 1st Inns: 100 121 129 142 179 223 226 227 230 252
FOW 2nd Inns:

Bowling: *First Innings*: Llewellyn 30.5-4-97-6, Kotze 17-1-49-2, Sinclair 12-0-55-1, Middleton 8-1-28-0, Nourse 3-0-13-0. *Second Innings*: Llewellyn 4-1-19-0, Kotze 2.5-1-16-0, Sinclair 2-0-22-0, Middleton 1-0-1-0.

SOUTH AFRICA

Batsman	1st	2nd
LJ Tancred b Howell	0	c & b Howell ... 2
WA Shalders c Darling b Saunders	11	c Darling b Hopkins ... 40
CJE Smith b Saunders	16	c & b Trumper ... 45
JH Sinclair b Howell	0	st Kelly b Saunders ... 104
PS Twentyman-Jones b Howell	0	b Hopkins ... 0
CB Llewellyn b Howell	0	st Kelly b Howell ... 8
CMH Hathorn run out	19	st Kelly b Saunders ... 18
AW Nourse b Saunders	15	b Howell ... 5
EA Halliwell (c+) run out	13	b Howell ... 1
JJ Kotze b Saunders	2	b Howell ... 0
J Middleton not out	0	not out ... 0
EXTRAS (B 4, LB 3)	7	(LB 1, NB 1) ... 2
TOTAL	85	225

FOW 1st Inns: 12 12 12 12 14 36 60 79 83 85
FOW 2nd Inns: 2 81 115 115 134 216 221 225 225 225

Bowling: *First Innings*: Howell 17-6-18-4, Saunders 12.2-2-37-4, Noble 4-0-23-0. *Second Innings*: Howell 26-6-81-5, Saunders 17.1-3-73-2, Noble 6-3-6-0, Trumper 6-1-26-1, Hopkins 8-0-37-2.

Umpires: WH Creese & F Hearne

SECOND TEST 1902–03 SOUTH AFRICA v AUSTRALIA
Old Wanderers, Johannesburg. October 18, 20, 21, 1902.
Toss: Australia. Australia won by 159 runs.

AUSTRALIA

Batsman	1st	2nd
VT Trumper b Kotze	18 (3)	c Shalders b Sinclair ... 13
RA Duff b Middleton	43 (4)	b Sinclair ... 44
C Hill st Halliwell b Kotze	6 (8)	c Kotze b Llewellyn ... 12
WW Armstrong run out	49 (1)	not out ... 159
MA Noble c Kotze b Llewellyn	5	lbw Llewellyn ... 24
J Darling (c) c Anderson b Llewellyn	6	b Llewellyn ... 4
ES Gregory b Kotze	1 (2)	c Llewellyn b Kotze ... 13
AJY Hopkins c Nourse b Llewellyn	20 (9)	c Llewellyn b Nourse ... 8
JJ Kelly (+) c Halliwell b Llewellyn	16 (10)	c Hathorn b Llewellyn ... 9
WP Howell c Nourse b Llewellyn	0 (11)	b Llewellyn ... 9
JV Saunders not out	0 (7)	b Sinclair ... 1
EXTRAS (B 10, W 1)	11	(B 8, LB 5) ... 13
TOTAL	175	309

FOW 1st Inns: 29 35 125 125 138 138 140 172 172 175
FOW 2nd Inns: 40 87 143 180 188 201 238 263 290 309

Bowling: *First Innings*: Kotze 20-2-64-3, Middleton 13-3-27-1, Llewellyn 18.1-3-43-5, Sinclair 4-0-30-0. *Second Innings*: Kotze 17-2-71-1, Middleton 4-0-15-0, Llewellyn 31.4-9-73-5, Sinclair 26-0-118-3, Nourse 3-0-19-1.

SOUTH AFRICA

Batsman	1st	2nd
LJ Tancred lbw Noble	19	c Kelly b Howell ... 29
WA Shalders b Howell	42 (3)	b Saunders ... 3
CMH Hathorn c Armstrong b Noble	12 (2)	b Saunders ... 1
JH Sinclair b Howell	101	b Howell ... 18
CJE Smith c Kelly b Trumper	12 (6)	b Howell ... 4
CB Llewellyn c & b Trumper	10 (5)	b Saunders ... 0
AW Nourse c & b Trumper	5 (8)	not out ... 18
EA Halliwell (+) c Kelly b Noble	4 (9)	b Saunders ... 0
JH Anderson (c) c Howell b Saunders	32 (7)	c Darling b Saunders ... 11
JJ Kotze b Saunders	0 (11)	st Kelly b Saunders ... 0
J Middleton not out	0 (10)	b Saunders ... 0
EXTRAS (B 3)	3	(LB 1) ... 1
TOTAL	240	85

FOW 1st Inns: 58 66 91 136 154 170 179 231 240 240
FOW 2nd Inns: 4 20 46 51 51 66 66 77 77 85

Bowling: *First Innings*: Trumper 12-1-60-3, Saunders 9-1-32-2, Howell 13-1-52-2, Noble 15-2-75-3, Armstrong 2-0-16-0, Hopkins 2-1-2-0. *Second Innings*: Trumper 3-0-27-0, Saunders 11-2-34-7, Howell 8-3-23-3.

Umpires: F Hearne & FE Smith

Australian Averages

1902–03 SOUTH AFRICA v AUSTRALIA

AUSTRALIA	M	Inn	NO	Runs	H.S	Avrge	Ct	St	Overs	Mds	Runs	Wkt	Avrge
Armstrong, WW	3	5	1	281	159*	70.25	2	-	22.0	5	128	2	64.00
Darling, J	3	5	-	25	14	5.00	4	-	-	-	-	-	-
Duff, RA	3	6	2	238	82*	59.50	1	-	-	-	-	-	-
Gregory, ES	3	5	-	29	13	5.80	1	-	-	-	-	-	-
Hill, C	3	5	1	327	142	81.75	-	-	-	-	-	-	-
Hopkins, AJY	3	5	-	75	30	15.00	2	-	24.0	2	115	5	23.00
Howell, WP	2	3	-	11	9	3.67	2	-	64.0	16	174	14	12.43
Jones, E	1	1	-	0	0	0.00	2	-	28.0	8	100	4	25.00
Kelly, JJ	3	4	-	51	25	12.75	4	4	-	-	-	-	-
Noble, MA	3	5	1	92	53*	23.00	-	-	44.0	8	165	6	27.50
Saunders, JV	2	3	1	5	4	2.50	-	-	49.3	8	176	15	11.73
Trumble, H	1	2	1	13	13	13.00	-	-	34.0	4	127	-	-
Trumper, VT	3	6	1	239	70	47.80	3	-	33.0	2	175	6	29.17

South African Averages

1902–03 SOUTH AFRICA v AUSTRALIA

SOUTH AFRICA	M	Inn	NO	Runs	H.S	Avrge	Ct	St	Overs	Mds	Runs	Wkt	Avrge
Anderson, JH	1	2	-	43	32	21.50	1	-	-	-	-	-	-
Halliwell, EA	3	5	-	75	57	15.00	4	2	-	-	-	-	-
Hathorn, CMH	3	6	-	126	45	21.00	-	-	-	-	-	-	-
Kotze, JJ	2	4	-	2	2	0.50	2	-	56.5	6	200	6	33.33
Llewellyn, CB	3	6	1	113	90	22.60	2	-	132.4	23	448	25	17.92
Middleton, J	2	4	3	1	1*	1.00	-	-	26.0	4	71	1	71.00
Nourse, AW	3	5	1	115	72	28.75	3	-	14.0	2	47	1	47.00
Rowe, GA	1	1	-	4	4	4.00	1	-	16.0	2	83	1	83.00
Shalders, WA	3	6	-	115	42	19.17	1	-	-	-	-	-	-
Sinclair, JH	3	6	-	286	104	47.67	2	-	87.0	3	469	9	52.11
Smith, CJE	3	6	1	106	45	21.20	2	-	-	-	-	-	-
Taberer, HM	1	2	-	2	2	2.00	-	-	10.0	2	48	1	48.00
Tancred, LJ	3	6	-	171	97	28.50	2	-	-	-	-	-	-
Thornton, PG	1	1	1	1	1*	-	-	-	4.0	-	20	1	20.00
Twentyman-Jones, PS	1	2	-	0	0	0.00	-	-	-	-	-	-	-

Trumper, Duff season's best

Trumper's big hit at Redfern Oval, which broke the shoe factory window.

Sydney, March 24. Trumper and Duff. Trumper and Duff! You hear their names on the trams and trains in Sydney, Melbourne and Adelaide. Their names are all over the papers. You would think that no one else played cricket but Trumper and Duff.

And in truth they have absolutely dominated the Shield season. In the match against Victoria at the end of January they rampaged to an opening stand of 267, and helped the side to a five-wicket win.

Only two weeks before they hit an absolute pinnacle, putting on 298 runs in 133 minutes, with Duff going to 178 and Trumper 132.

Needless to say, NSW has won the Shield again, with four wins, while South Australia has trailed the field. Duff, who finished the season with 194 against Lord Hawke's XI, visiting after a tour of New Zealand, has an aggregate from nine innings of 786 runs, at an average of 87.33. Trumper scored 446 runs for 49.55, but even Reg Duff acknowledges that Trumper is the master. He reinforced this by scoring 335 for Paddington against Redfern at the Redfern oval, making his runs in only 180 minutes. Members of the nearby bowling club stopped play to protect themselves and to watch his thrilling batting, while windows were smashed in the surrounding houses. One hit travelled 150 yards to break a factory window.

The season has also been notable for the appearance of Warwick Armstrong as second on the run aggregate and batting averages, and sixth on the bowling lists, with 23 wickets. The leading wicket-taker is another Victorian Jack Saunders with 32 at 20.81.

Giffen, at 43, gets a Golden Double

Adelaide, Feb. 28. It's that man again. George Giffen, noted for amazing all-round feats for South Australia, has come up with another golden double at the age of 43. He has had the outstanding figures of 15 wickets (7/75 and 8/110) and 178 (81 and 97) runs against Victoria. This is the ninth time he has got the 100 runs and 10 wickets double and it is his sixth haul of 15 or more wickets. He is not yet thinking of retirement.

Despite all this the more even Victoria side, with a brilliant bowler in Jack Saunders (5/88 and 8/106) won the match by 38 runs, although Giffen and Joe Travers almost stole it with a last-wicket stand of 101.

Outspoken Worrall falls on his sword

Melbourne, Dec. 20. Wherever Jack Worrall goes can trouble be far behind. The Victorian selector, and former player and captain, has withdrawn from the team for the first match because Warwick Armstrong, Hugh Trumble and Jack Saunders refused to play with him.

The trouble arose out of an article for the London *Sportsman*, which has now filtered back to Australia, in which he accused Saunders and Monty Noble of being chuckers. Worrall has been asked to explain by the VCA, and has subsequently apologised to the players. He says he regrets the article, but he is noted for causing controversy.

'Plum' Warner is leader of a small visit from England

Adelaide, March 31. A team sponsored by Lord Hawke and under the captaincy of P. F. 'Plum' Warner has finished its engagements in Australia in a quite remarkable fashion.

Despite a first innings score of 553, and a 9/85 by George Thompson in South Australia's first innings, it contrived to lose the match by 97 runs. Harry Hay, a replacement bowler for SA took 9/67 with a hat-trick in the tourists' second innings, and then SA dashed to a winning score of 454. The match was played at Unley Oval, as the Adelaide Oval was occupied with a bicycle race. The tourists lost to Victoria and had a rain-interrupted draw with NSW.

The Unley Oval at Adelaide attracts a fashionable crowd from both town and country, to watch the match against Lord Hawke's visiting team from England.

England has a smashing start

AUSTRALIA V. ENGLAND
3RD. TEST MATCH PLAYED AT ADELAIDE. JAN.1904
WON BY AUSTRALIA BY 216 RUNS
Warner and Foster Batting

The scene at the Adelaide Oval for the third Test, with a crowd of 18,000 in attendance on the second day.

Adelaide, Jan. 20. This has been a wonderful Test series. Great weather, great crowds and great cricket. The only speck on the blue horizon is that England is only one Test up after dominating the first two games.

England came with a strong team, which seemed settled under the benign captaincy of Pelham 'Plum' Warner. He has a strong armoury in the bowling of Wilfred Rhodes, George Hirst, Ted Arnold, Len Braund and the mysterious Bernard Bosanquet, and experienced batsmen.

They showed their wares in the first two Tests. In the high scoring Sydney match Reg Foster got a debut 287, and, even with Victor Trumper's chanceless second innings 185, England won by five wickets, and left with memories of a hostile crowd after Clem Hill's run out. Hill's protest did not help matters, and as missiles began to land on the ground it seemed that Warner was going to lead his team from the field of play.

In Melbourne, the England top order got away to a slow and steady start to set up a winning score of 315. That was the difference, as the rest of the match was marred by rain and a sticky wicket and the wickets tumbled at a rate of about 10 runs per batsman. It should be said that Trumper's 74 in Australia's first innings 122 was of the highest calibre.

In the third Test in Adelaide the victorious Australians completely outbatted England, with Duff (79), Trumper (113), Hill (88) and Noble (59) setting up the first innings total of 388, and Trumper (59), Noble (65) and Syd Gregory (112) leading in the second innings 351. England could only graft 245 and 278, although they had the benefit of a flat wicket.

Reg Foster: debut double century.

Vics out for 15

Melbourne, Feb. 9. Victoria has been humiliated in its match against the MCC, managing only 15 runs in its second innings. It is the lowest score yet in first class cricket in Australia.

The Victorians, respectable in the first innings, were caught on a rain-soaked and drying wicket. They lost 4/0 in the first two overs, with Wilfred Rhodes missing a hat-trick when Harry Trott (who top-scored with 9) was dropped.

The innings lasted 45 minutes, and England went on to win by eight wickets.

A cartoon depiction of the angry crowd in the hill area throwing missiles onto the Sydney Cricket Ground, after Clem Hill was pronounced to be run out for 51 in the Australian second innings.

Bosie beats the bats

"CAPSTAN" CIGARETTES.

Destroyer: B. J. T. Bosanquet.

The MCG wicket: Norman Lindsay's view.

Sydney, March 3. Australia was never in the hunt in the fourth Test, and England has regained the Ashes after eight years. The weather was a factor throughout, with the pitch difficult at times, but in the end the Australian batting was too brittle.

Monty Noble's medium-paced off-spinners always looked threatening, and the crowd of over 34,000 on the second day was abuzz with Australia's prospects as England was out for 249. They also hooted England's slow play and rain interruptions.

Australia's capitulation for 131 came as a shock, particularly as the last four wickets fell for 34 runs. Reg Duff (47) and Clem Hill (33) seemed to have got Australia away to a reasonable start, although Trumper was beautifully bowled for 7 by the leg-spinner Len Braund,

who has had an outstanding series.

There was no one to tear through the England second innings, and the openers Hayward (53) and Warner (31) saw them on the path to victory.

Eventually, Australia faced a deficit of 378, but failed even to start a run-chase, as Bosanquet took advantage of the wearing wicket. Bowling either side of the lunch break on the sixth day he had 5/12 at one stage and finished with 6/32. On his way to the pavilion 'keeper Jim Kelly muttered: 'There's a man out there bowling leg-breaks that turn in from the off.'

Only Monty Noble (53) offered any real resistance on Australia's behalf. As captain he has led by example throughout the series, and is figuring highly in both the batting and the bowling averages.

Hat-trick Hugh

Melbourne, March 8. Hugh Trumble has announced his retirement from first class cricket, and he ended his great career in the best possible way – with a hat-trick. As Australia cruised to an anticlimactic 218-run victory in the fifth Test, Trumble whipped through Albert Knight, Bernard Bosanquet and Arthur Lilley to win the plaudits of the small last-day crowd and his team-mates. He had taken 7/28 from 6.5 overs, showing all his tricks of flight, turn and varying pace.

Trumble's first hat-trick, also at the MCG, came in the second Test in 1901–02, when he again took the last three wickets of the match.

Cotter impresses

Melbourne, March 9. Australia has lacked an express pace bowler since Ernie Jones, but it seems that young NSW bowler Albert 'Tibby' Cotter is to take up the mantle. He took 6/40 in England's first innings in the fifth Test, and finished the match with 8/65.

He is powerfully built with thick arms and wrists and bowls with a powerful 'spear-throwing' action that brings his whole body behind the ball. He has, at times, been troubled with his run-up and length, but at 21 he is still learning his craft. There is no doubt that he means to menace the batsman, and likes to try the short ball that rises uncomfortably into the body.

FIRST TEST 1903–04 AUSTRALIA v ENGLAND
Sydney Cricket Ground, Sydney. December 11, 12, 14, 15, 16, 17, 1903.
Toss: Australia. England won by 5 wkts.

AUSTRALIA

RA Duff c Lilley b Arnold	3	(3)	c Relf b Rhodes	84
VT Trumper c Foster b Arnold	1	(5)	not out	185
C Hill c Lilley b Hirst	5	(4)	run out	51
MA Noble (c) c Foster b Arnold	133	(6)	st Lilley b Bosanquet	22
WW Armstrong b Bosanquet	48	(7)	c Bosanquet b Rhodes	27
AJY Hopkins b Hirst	39	(8)	c Arnold b Rhodes	20
WP Howell c Relf b Arnold	5	(10)	c Lilley b Arnold	4
ES Gregory b Bosanquet	23	(1)	c Lilley b Rhodes	43
F Laver lbw Rhodes	4		c Relf b Rhodes	6
JJ Kelly (+) c Braund b Rhodes	10	(2)	b Arnold	13
JV Saunders not out	11		run out	2
EXTRAS (NB 3)	3		(B 10, LB 15, W 2, NB 1)	28
TOTAL	285			485

FOW 1st Inns: 2 9 12 118 200 207 259 263 271 285
FOW 2nd Inns: 36 108 191 254 334 393 441 468 473 485

Bowling: *First Innings:* Hirst 24-8-47-2, Arnold 32-7-76-4, Braund 26-9-39-0, Bosanquet 13-0-52-2, Rhodes 17.2-3-41-2, Relf 6-1-27-0. *Second Innings:* Hirst 29-1-79-0, Arnold 28-2-93-2, Rhodes 40.2-10-94-5, Bosanquet 23-1-100-1, Braund 12-2-56-0, Relf 13-5-35-0.

ENGLAND*f*

TW Hayward b Howell	15		st Kelly b Saunders	91
PF Warner (c) c Kelly b Laver	0		b Howell	8
JT Tyldesley b Noble	53		c Noble b Saunders	9
EG Arnold c Laver b Armstrong	27			
RE Foster c Noble b Saunders	287	(4)	st Kelly b Armstrong	19
LC Braund b Howell	102	(5)	c Noble b Howell	0
GH Hirst b Howell	0	(6)	not out	60
BJT Bosanquet c Howell b Noble	2	(7)	not out	1
AFA Lilley (+) c Hill b Noble	4			
AE Relf c Armstrong b Saunders	31			
W Rhodes not out	40			
EXTRAS (B 6, LB 7, W 1, NB 2)	16		(B 3, LB 1, W 2)	6
TOTAL	577		5 for 194	

FOW 1st Inns: 0 49 73 117 309 311 318 332 447 577
FOW 2nd Inns: 21 39 81 82 181

Bowling: *First Innings:* Saunders 36.2-8-125-2, Laver 37-12-119-1, Howell 31-7-111-3, Noble 34-8-99-3, Armstrong 23-3-47-1, Hopkins 11-1-40-0, Trumper 7-2-12-0, Gregory 2-0-8-0. *Second Innings:* Noble 12-2-37-0, Howell 31-18-35-2, Saunders 18.5-3-51-2, Laver 16-4-37-0, Armstrong 18-6-28-1.

Umpires: RM Crockett & AC Jones

SECOND TEST 1903–04 AUSTRALIA v ENGLAND
Melbourne Cricket Ground, Melbourne. January 1 ,2, 4, 5, 1904.
Toss: England. England won by 185 runs.

ENGLAND

PF Warner (c) c Duff b Trumble	68		c Trumper b Saunders	3
TW Hayward c Gregory b Hopkins	58		c Trumper b Trumble	0
JT Tyldesley c Trumble b Howell	97		c Trumble b Howell	62
RE Foster retired hurt	49			
LC Braund c Howell b Trumble	20	(4)	b Saunders	3
AE Knight b Howell	2	(7)	lbw Trumble	0
GH Hirst c Noble b Howell	7	(5)	c Gregory b Howell	4
W Rhodes lbw Trumble	2	(6)	lbw Trumble	9
AFA Lilley (+) c Howell b Trumble	4	(8)	st Kelly b Trumble	0
AE Relf not out	3	(9)	not out	10
A Fielder b Howell	1	(10)	c Hill b Trumble	4
EXTRAS (LB 3, W 1)	4		(B 7, LB 1)	8
TOTAL	9 for 315		9 for 103	

FOW 1st Inns: 122 132 277 279 297 306 306 314 315
FOW 2nd Inns: 5 7 27 40 74 74 74 90 103

Bowling: *First Innings:* Trumble 50-10-107-4, Noble 6-3-4-0, Saunders 16-3-60-0, Howell 34.5-14-43-4, Armstrong 25-6-43-0, Hopkins 20-2-50-1, Trumper 1-0-4-0. *Second Innings:* Trumble 10.5-2-34-5, Saunders 8-0-33-2, Howell 8-3-25-2, Hopkins 2-1-3-0.

AUSTRALIA

VT Trumper c Tyldesley b Rhodes	74		c Relf b Rhodes	35
RA Duff st Lilley b Rhodes	10		c Braund b Rhodes	8
C Hill c Rhodes b Hirst	5		c Relf b Rhodes	20
MA Noble (c) c(S)H Strudwick b Rhodes	0		not out	31
ES Gregory c Hirst b Rhodes	1		c Rhodes b Hirst	0
AJY Hopkins c(S)H Strudwick b Relf	18		c & b Rhodes	7
H Trumble c(S)H Strudwick b Rhodes	0		c Braund b Rhodes	0
WW Armstrong c Braund b Rhodes	1		c Hayward b Rhodes	0
JJ Kelly (+) run out	8		c Lilley b Rhodes	7
WP Howell c Fielder b Rhodes	0		c Hirst b Rhodes	3
JV Saunders not out	2		c Fielder b Hirst	0
EXTRAS (LB 1)	1			0
TOTAL	122			111

FOW 1st Inns: 14 23 23 33 67 73 97 105 116 122
FOW 2nd Inns: 14 59 73 77 86 90 90 102 105 111

Bowling: *First Innings:* Rhodes 15.2-3-56-7, Hirst 8-1-33-1, Relf 2-0-12-1, Braund 5-0-20-0. *Second Innings:* Rhodes 15-0-68-8, Hirst 13.4-4-38-2, Relf 1-0-5-0.

Umpires: P Argall & RM Crockett

THIRD TEST 1903–04 AUSTRALIA v ENGLAND
Adelaide Oval, Adelaide. January 15, 16, 18, 19, 20, 1904.
Toss: Australia. Australia won by 216 runs.

AUSTRALIA
VT Trumper b Hirst	113	lbw Rhodes	59
RA Duff b Hirst	79	c Braund b Hirst	14
C Hill c Lilley b Arnold	88	b Fielder	16
MA Noble (c) st Lilley b Arnold	59	c Bosanquet b Braund	65
ES Gregory c Tyldesley b Arnold	8	c Rhodes b Braund	112
AJY Hopkins b Bosanquet	0 (7)	run out	7
WW Armstrong lbw Rhodes	10 (6)	c Hirst b Bosanquet	39
H Trumble b Bosanquet	4	c & b Bosanquet	9
CE McLeod run out	8	b Bosanquet	2
JJ Kelly (+) lbw Bosanquet	1	st Lilley b Bosanquet	13
WP Howell not out	3	not out	1
EXTRAS (B 7, LB 5, W 3)	15	(B 8, LB 2, W 3, NB 1)	14
TOTAL	388		351

FOW 1st Inns: 129 272 296 308 310 343 360 384 384 388
FOW 2nd Inns: 48 81 101 263 289 320 324 326 350 351

Bowling: *First Innings*: Fielder 7-0-33-0, Arnold 27-4-93-3, Rhodes 14-3-45-1, Bosanquet 30.1-4-95-3, Braund 13-1-49-0, Hirst 15-1-58-2. *Second Innings*: Hirst 13-1-36-1, Arnold 19-3-74-0, Bosanquet 15.5-0-73-4, Rhodes 21-4-46-1, Fielder 25-11-51-1, Braund 21-6-57-2.

ENGLAND
PF Warner (c) c McLeod b Trumble	48	c & b Trumble	79
TW Hayward b Howell	20	lbw Hopkins	67
JT Tyldesley c Kelly b Hopkins	0 (4)	c Noble b Hopkins	10
RE Foster c Howell b Noble	21 (5)	b McLeod	16
LC Braund c Duff b Hopkins	13 (6)	b Howell	25
GH Hirst c Trumper b Trumble	58 (7)	b Trumble	44
BJT Bosanquet c Duff b Hopkins	10 (9)	c Trumper b Hopkins	10
W Rhodes c Armstrong b McLeod	9 (10)	run out	8
EG Arnold not out	23 (3)	b Hopkins	1
AFA Lilley (+) run out	28 (8)	c & b Howell	0
A Fielder b Trumble	6	not out	14
EXTRAS (B 4, LB 1, W 4)	9	(LB 2, W 2)	4
TOTAL	245		278

FOW 1st Inns: 47 48 88 99 116 146 173 199 234 245
FOW 2nd Inns: 148 150 160 160 195 231 231 256 256 278

Bowling: *First Innings*: McLeod 24-6-56-1, Trumble 28-9-49-3, Howell 13-4-28-1, Hopkins 24-5-68-3, Armstrong 10-3-25-0, Noble 3-0-10-1. *Second Innings*: Howell 20-5-52-2, McLeod 25-4-46-1, Trumble 33-8-73-2, Hopkins 28.1-9-81-4, Armstrong 7-2-15-0, Trumper 4-0-7-0.

Umpires: P Argall & RM Crockett

FIFTH TEST 1903–04 AUSTRALIA v ENGLAND
Melbourne Cricket Ground, Melbourne. March 5, 7, 8, 1904.
Toss: Australia. Australia won by 218 runs.

AUSTRALIA
RA Duff b Braund	9 (7)	c Warner b Rhodes	31
VT Trumper c & b Braund	88 (5)	b Hirst	0
C Hill c Braund b Rhodes	16 (6)	c Warner b Hirst	16
MA Noble (c) c Foster b Arnold	29 (8)	st Lilley b Rhodes	19
PA McAlister st Lilley b Braund	36 (1)	c Foster b Arnold	9
DRA Gehrs c & b Braund	3 (10)	c & b Hirst	5
AJY Hopkins c Knight b Braund	32 (9)	not out	25
CE McLeod c Braund b Braund	8 (2)	c Bosanquet b Braund	0
H Trumble c Foster b Braund	6 (11)	c Arnold b Hirst	0
JJ Kelly (+) not out	6 (3)	c & b Arnold	24
A Cotter b Braund	6 (4)	b Hirst	0
EXTRAS (B 4, LB 4)	8	(B 1, LB 3)	4
TOTAL	247		133

FOW 1st Inns: 13 67 142 144 159 218 221 231 235 247
FOW 2nd Inns: 9 9 13 13 43 49 92 115 133 133

Bowling: *First Innings*: Hirst 19-6-44-0, Braund 29.1-6-81-8, Rhodes 12-1-41-1, Arnold 18-4-46-1, Bosanquet 4-0-27-0. *Second Innings*: Rhodes 15-2-52-2, Arnold 8-3-23-2, Braund 4-1-6-1, Hirst 16.5-4-48-5.

ENGLAND
TW Hayward b Noble	0		
W Rhodes c Gehrs b Cotter	3 (8)	not out	16
EG Arnold c Kelly b Noble	0 (10)	c Duff b Trumble	19
PF Warner (c) c McAlister b Cotter	1 (5)	c & b Trumble	11
JT Tyldesley c Gehrs b Noble	10 (3)	c Hopkins b Cotter	15
RE Foster b Cotter	18 (2)	c Trumper b Trumble	30
GH Hirst c McAlister b Trumble	0 (6)	c McAlister b Trumble	1
LC Braund c Hopkins b Noble	5 (1)	c McAlister b Cotter	0
AE Knight b Cotter	0 (4)	c Kelly b Trumble	0
BJT Bosanquet c Noble b Cotter	16 (7)	c Gehrs b Trumble	4
AFA Lilley (+) not out	6 (9)	lbw Trumble	0
EXTRAS (B 1, NB 1)	2	(B 1, LB 4)	5
TOTAL	61		9 for 101

FOW 1st Inns: 0 0 4 5 23 26 36 36 48 61
FOW 2nd Inns: 0 24 38 47 54 61 61 61 101

Bowling: *First Innings*: Noble 15-8-19-4, Cotter 15.2-2-40-6, McLeod 1-1-0-0. *Second Innings*: Cotter 5-0-25-2, Noble 6-2-19-0, Trumble 6.5-0-28-7, McLeod 5-0-24-0.

Umpires: P Argall & RM Crockett

FOURTH TEST 1903–04 AUSTRALIA v ENGLAND
Sydney Cricket Ground, Sydney. February 26, 27, 29 (no play), March 1, 2, 3, 1904.
Toss: England. England won by 157 runs.

ENGLAND
PF Warner (c) b Noble	0 (9)	not out	31
TW Hayward c McAlister b Trumble	18	lbw Trumble	52
JT Tyldesley c Gregory b Noble	16 (4)	b Cotter	5
RE Foster c McAlister b Noble	19 (1)	c Noble b Hopkins	27
AE Knight not out	70	c McAlister b Cotter	9
LC Braund c Trumble b Noble	39	c McLeod b Hopkins	19
GH Hirst b Noble	25	c Kelly b McLeod	18
BJT Bosanquet b Hopkins	12	c Hill b McLeod	7
EG Arnold lbw Noble	0 (3)	c Kelly b Noble	0
AFA Lilley (+) c Hopkins b Trumble	24	b McLeod	6
W Rhodes st Kelly b Noble	10	c McAlister b Cotter	29
EXTRAS (B 6, LB 7, W 2, NB 1)	16	(B 1, LB 6)	7
TOTAL	249		210

FOW 1st Inns: 4 34 42 66 155 185 207 208 237 249
FOW 2nd Inns: 49 50 57 73 106 120 138 141 155 210

Bowling: *First Innings*: Cotter 14-1-44-0, Noble 41.1-10-100-7, Trumble 43-20-58-2, Hopkins 8-3-22-1, McLeod 8-5-9-0. *Second Innings*: Trumble 28-10-49-1, Noble 19-8-40-1, McLeod 20-5-42-3, Hopkins 14-5-31-2, Cotter 18.3-3-41-3.

AUSTRALIA
VT Trumper b Braund	7 (4)	lbw Arnold	12
RA Duff b Arnold	47	b Arnold	19
C Hill c Braund b Arnold	33	st Lilley b Bosanquet	26
PA McAlister c Arnold b Rhodes	2 (1)	b Hirst	1
AJY Hopkins b Braund	9 (7)	st Lilley b Bosanquet	0
CE McLeod b Rhodes	18 (8)	c Lilley b Bosanquet	6
JJ Kelly (+) c Foster b Arnold	5 (10)	c Foster b Bosanquet	10
MA Noble (c) not out	6 (5)	not out	53
ES Gregory c Foster b Rhodes	2 (6)	lbw Bosanquet	0
H Trumble c Lilley b Rhodes	0 (9)	st Lilley b Bosanquet	0
A Cotter c Tyldesley b Arnold	0	b Hirst	34
EXTRAS (B 1, W 1)	2	(B 10)	10
TOTAL	131		171

FOW 1st Inns: 28 61 72 97 101 116 124 126 130 131
FOW 2nd Inns: 7 35 59 76 76 76 86 90 114 171

Bowling: *First Innings*: Hirst 13-1-36-0, Braund 11-2-27-2, Rhodes 11-3-33-4, Arnold 14.3-5-28-4, Bosanquet 2-1-5-0. *Second Innings*: Hirst 18.5-2-32-2, Braund 16-3-24-0, Arnold 12-3-42-2, Rhodes 11-7-12-0, Bosanquet 15-1-51-6.

Umpires: P Argall & RM Crockett

Australian Averages

1903–04 AUSTRALIA v ENGLAND
AUSTRALIA	M	Inn	NO	Runs	H.S	Avrge	Ct	St	Overs	Mds	Runs	Wkt	Avrge
Armstrong, WW	3	6	-	125	48	20.83	2	-	83.0	20	158	2	79.00
Cotter, A	2	4	-	40	34	10.00	-	-	52.5	6	150	11	13.64
Duff, RA	5	10	-	304	84	30.40	4	-	-	-	-	-	-
Gehrs, DRA	1	2	-	8	5	4.00	3	-	-	-	-	-	-
Gregory, ES	4	8	-	189	112	23.63	3	-	2.0	-	8	-	-
Hill, C	5	10	-	276	88	27.60	3	-	-	-	-	-	-
Hopkins, AJY	5	10	1	157	39	17.44	3	-	107.1	26	295	11	26.82
Howell, WP	3	6	2	16	5	4.00	1	-	137.5	51	294	14	21.00
Kelly, JJ	5	10	1	97	24	10.78	6	4	-	-	-	-	-
Laver, F	1	2	-	10	6	5.00	1	-	53.0	16	156	1	156.00
McAlister, PA	2	4	-	48	36	12.00	7	-	-	-	-	-	-
McLeod, CE	3	6	-	42	18	7.00	-	-	83.0	21	177	5	35.40
Noble, MA	5	10	3	417	133	59.57	7	-	136.1	41	328	16	20.50
Saunders, JV	2	4	2	15	11*	7.50	-	-	79.1	14	269	6	44.83
Trumble, H	4	8	-	21	9	2.63	5	-	199.4	59	398	24	16.58
Trumper, VT	5	10	1	574	185*	63.78	6	-	12.0	2	23	-	-

English Averages

1903–04 AUSTRALIA v ENGLAND
ENGLAND	M	Inn	NO	Runs	H.S	Avrge	Ct	St	Overs	Mds	Runs	Wkt	Avrge
Arnold, EG	4	7	1	70	27	11.67	4	-	158.3	31	475	18	26.39
Bosanquet, BJT	4	8	1	62	16	8.86	4	-	103.0	7	403	16	25.19
Braund, LC	5	10	-	226	102	22.60	9	-	137.1	30	359	13	27.62
Fielder, A	2	4	1	25	14*	8.33	2	-	32.0	11	84	1	84.00
Foster, RE	5	9	1	486	287	60.75	8	-	-	-	-	-	-
Hayward, TW	5	9	-	321	91	35.67	1	-	-	-	-	-	-
Hirst, GH	5	10	1	217	60*	24.11	4	-	170.2	29	451	15	30.07
Knight, AE	3	6	1	81	70*	16.20	1	-	-	-	-	-	-
Lilley, AFA	5	9	1	72	28	9.00	8	9	-	-	-	-	-
Relf, AE	2	3	2	44	31	44.00	5	-	22.0	6	79	1	79.00
Rhodes, W	5	9	2	126	40*	18.00	5	-	172.0	36	488	31	15.74
Tyldesley, JT	5	10	-	277	97	27.70	3	-	-	-	-	-	-
Warner, PF	5	10	1	249	79	27.67	2	-	-	-	-	-	-

A new Board of Control

Melbourne, May 6. A body has been established called the Australian Board of Control for International Cricket.

Its secretary is William Percy McElhone, the strongman of NSW cricket. He is legal adviser to the NSW Cricket Association.

The new body has come into being through McElhone's co-operation with the Victorian Cricket Association. Queensland and South Australian delegates attended the conference at Wesley College, at which the Board was voted into being, but Queensland has not yet been invited onto the Board and SA is keeping its options open until the Board defines what it means by 'financial control'.

Essentially international cricket affairs are now deemed to be conducted by NSW and Victoria for their State bodies. The move may put an end to the Melbourne Cricket Club's influence as the premier cricket body in organising overseas tours.

It will be a crucial matter that the Marylebone Cricket Club,

NSW strongman Billy McElhone.

England's premier body, recognises the new Australian entity.

The Australian team now in England is under the captaincy of Joe Darling, no friend of McElhone and the people he describes as 'freeloaders who appear at New South Wales matches.' He may sway the English administrators.

Batsmen have the best of season

Sydney, April 25. Batsmen have again had the best of the domestic Shield season, and some new names have emerged in Vernon Ransford of Victoria, Edgar Waddy of NSW and Algy Gehrs of South Australia. Gehrs has been chosen for the 1905 tour of England on the strength of his 170 against Victoria and his audacious stroke play.

Waddy is considered unlucky. He had a better overall performance than Gehrs, with an average of 50.87, while the young and elegant

Ransford was better again with 61.00.

The highest run-scorer for the season was Warwick Armstrong with a total of 460 and an average of 57.50.

Victoria started with dash, scoring 437 (Armstrong 164) against South Australia and 573 (Armstrong 200, the highest individual score of the season, and Ransford 152) against Queensland, but its performances fell away against the very strong NSW team.

All-powerful NSW keeps Shield grip

Sydney, Feb. 1. NSW has lost only one Shield match of its last 16, and none this season, so they are entitled to the firm grip they hold on the Sheffield Shield at the end of this season's matches. Their key has been consistency, while their opponents have had good individuals in poorer teams.

They have largely been without the services of their premier batsman Victor Trumper, who was only available for the domestic games.

But there has been the usual batting depth in the presence of captain Monty Noble, Reg Duff, Syd Gregory, Albert Hopkins (all Test players) and a strong attack through Noble, Hopkins, Bill Howell, Frank Johnson and the new boy, Albert 'Tibby' Cotter, a genuine speedster.

The young Johnson topped the averages with 27 wickets, but the fearsome Cotter has been preferred for the England tour.

Victoria and South Australia won only one game each, against each other. Neither state could get close to NSW.

A long journey

Melbourne, Dec. 19. On the long train journey back from Victoria to Brisbane, the visiting Queensland cricketers will have some cause for satisfaction.

They lost their first match in Victoria, but Gilbert Morton from Maryborough made 135 in a creditable first-innings total of 280. It was his debut first class match. Victoria then swamped the Queenslanders with 573, but the bowlers stuck to their guns and got the last six wickets for 141.

Cricket at the grass-roots level, as seen by noted artist Frank Reynolds.

A wholesome image for cocoa.

Australia seems all at sea

Manchester, July 26. Bamboozled by Bosie, and thrashed by Jackson. The Australian team has now been forced to bend to the superiority of England and return home without a Test win and without the Ashes.

A team which looked so good on paper – Darling, Noble, Trumper, Hill, Darling, Armstrong and all – proved to be no match for the solid England batting and the superior bowling.

The Australian batting line-up is a proven one, but it seemed at sea in the Tests. The bowling just did not have the penetration with Cotter, the only bowler of genuine pace, pitching short and out of form. So much was left to the defensive medium pace of Armstrong, McLeod and Noble.

The die was cast in the first Test at Trent Bridge. Australia seemed set on its usual course when Laver got 7/64 as England fell for 196. But the Australian batting was merely good enough to get a slender first innings lead, and England's former captain Archie MacLaren (140 not out) led the charge to 5/426 declared against a seemingly impotent attack.

The Australians then reckoned without the extraordinary spinners of Bernard Bosanquet, who had them completely tied up.

'Bosie' showed perfect control of his 'googly' ball, which he delivers

with his usual leg-break action, but puts a reverse spin on it by rolling his wrist right over, giving it an extra 'tweak' so that it breaks to the off.

The groping batsmen failed to pick it time after time and he finished with 8/107 to take England to victory of 213 runs.

Rain saved the Australians in the second and third Tests, but scores of over 600 against Hampshire and Somerset and 556 against Sussex put them in good heart for the fourth Test in Manchester.

They were not kept in suspense as to their fate, as England amassed 446 in its first innings, with skipper, the Hon. F. S. Jackson scoring 113 on top of his 144 not out at Leeds. He has at his disposal two other born leaders in MacLaren and C.B. Fry. Australia surrendered meekly, with only captain Joe Darling (73) and Reg Duff (60) getting worthwhile scores as 20 wickets fell for 366.

The fifth Test was a draw – with Reg Duff's 146 the only bright Australian light.

Impressions of the third Test at Leeds by English press artist Frank Gillott.

The Lord's ground is packed to the fences for the Test match.

Old men of cricket. Australian captain Joe Darling, 34, and Dr W. G. Grace, captain of the Gentlemen of England, at the age of 57.

Darling, a great Captain

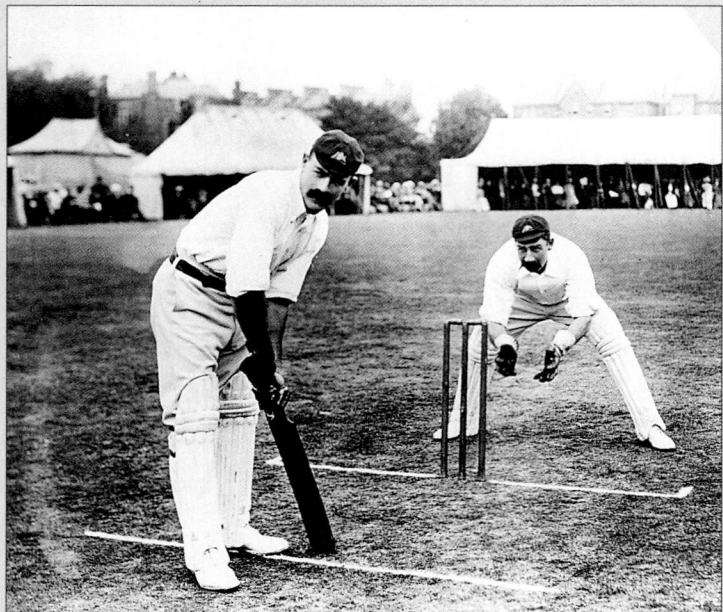

Joe Darling, a strong batsman and a resolute and respected Captain.

Three times the leader of an Australian team to England during the early years of Test cricket, Joe Darling had the respect of his English rivals. He was a model of integrity and fair play, and could mix it in the high social circles that surrounded English cricket and with players in the pavilion.

He was a forceful left hander and a reliable run scorer, but he could defend steadily when he played the opening role. He led Australia in Test series against England and won three of them – two away in 1899 and 1902 and one at home in 1901–02. In 1905, however, England won all five tosses and the two deciding matches, and on returning home Darling retired from Test cricket.

Darling was the son of John Darling, a farmer and member of the South Australian Legislative Council. While Darling Snr introduced the Bill in Parliament that created the parklands housing the Adelaide Oval, he was opposed to his son 'wasting his time' on sport.

Joe, however, became devoted to the game at Prince Alfred College. On the day before his 15th birthday he scored 252 for his school against St Peter's College. The innings got him into a combined Victoria/SA team that played Australia in 1886.

His father sent him to Roseworthy Agricultural College and then to one of the family properties. He returned to Adelaide and cricket two years later, when he opened a sports store in Rundle Street.

He blossomed in the Australian summer of 1897–98, scoring 7 and 101 in Sydney, 36 in Melbourne, 178 in Adelaide, 12 and 29 at Melbourne and 14 and 160 in Sydney as Australia took the series 4–1. He made his 160 in 165 minutes, with 30 fours, as Australia won by six wickets.

His father was his greatest supporter, and gave him £100 when he made a century against Stoddart's team. In Adelaide in 1897–98 he gave him £79 – one for the century and £78 for the runs over 100. 'He bats better when the silver is up,' he said.

At the end of his Test career he had played in 34 Tests over a decade and had the useful average of 28.56 with three Test centuries.

Apart from Test cricket Joe Darling revelled in the District game when he averaged 144 for East Torrens in 1899–1900, and scored 235 not out for Adelaide against Port Adelaide in 1897.

He sold his Adelaide shop in 1908 and left to farm in Tasmania on a midlands property 'Stonehenge'. Darling worked on the eradication of rabbits from Tasmania and was the first Tasmanian farmer to sow sub clover.

He held a seat in the Tasmanian Parliament from 1921 until his death in 1946. His conduct in Parliament was as straight and forthright as his batting.

Darling died on 2 January 1946, and left a family of 10 sons and five daughters.

FIRST TEST 1905 ENGLAND v AUSTRALIA
Trent Bridge, Nottingham. May 29, 30, 31, 1905.
Toss: England. England won by 213 runs.

ENGLAND

TW Hayward b Cotter	5		c Darling b Armstrong	47
AO Jones b Laver	4	(4)	b Duff	30
JT Tyldesley c Duff b Laver	56		c & b Duff	61
AC MacLaren c Kelly b Laver	2	(2)	c	
Duff b Laver	140			
FS Jackson (c) b Cotter	0		not out	82
BJT Bosanquet b Laver	27		b Cotter	6
JR Gunn b Cotter	8			
GL Jessop b Laver	0			
AFA Lilley (+) c & b Laver	37			
W Rhodes c Noble b Laver	29	(7)	not out	39
EG Arnold not out	2			
EXTRAS (B 21, LB 5)	26		(B 11, LB 9, W 1)	21
TOTAL	196			5 dec 426

FOW 1st Inns: 6 24 40 49 98 119 119 139 187 196
FOW 2nd Inns: 145 222 276 301 313

Bowling: *First Innings*: Cotter 23-2-64-3, Laver 31.3-14-64-7, McLeod 8-2-19-0, Armstrong 6-3-4-0, Noble 3-0-19-0. *Second Innings*: Cotter 17-1-59-1, Laver 34-7-121-1, McLeod 28-9-84-0, Armstrong 52-24-67-1, Noble 7-1-31-0, Duff 15-2-43-2.

AUSTRALIA

RA Duff c Hayward b Gunn	1		c & b Bosanquet	25
VT Trumper retired hurt	13			
C Hill b Jackson	54	(5)	c & b Bosanquet	8
MA Noble c Lilley b Jackson	50	(3)	st Lilley b Bosanquet	7
WW Armstrong st Lilley b Rhodes	27	(4)	c Jackson b Bosanquet	6
J Darling (c) c Bosanquet b Jackson	0	(2)	b Bosanquet	40
A Cotter c & b Jessop	45		b Rhodes	18
ES Gregory c Jones b Jackson	2	(6)	c Arnold b Bosanquet	51
CE McLeod b Arnold	4		lbw Bosanquet	13
F Laver c Jones b Jackson	5	(8)	st Lilley b Bosanquet	5
JJ Kelly (+) not out	1	(10)	not out	6
EXTRAS (B 16, LB 2, W 1)	19		(B 4, LB 3, W 2)	9
TOTAL	9 for 221			9 for 188

FOW 1st Inns: 1 129 130 130 200 204 209 216 221
FOW 2nd Inns: 62 75 82 93 100 139 144 175 188

Bowling: *First Innings*: Arnold 11-2-39-1, Gunn 6-2-27-1, Jessop 7-2-18-1, Bosanquet 7-0-29-0, Rhodes 18-6-37-1, Jackson 14.5-2-52-5. *Second Innings*: Rhodes 30-8-58-1, Bosanquet 32.4-2-107-8, Arnold 4-2-7-0, Jackson 5-3-6-0, Jessop 1-0-1-0.

Umpires: J Carlin & J Phillips

SECOND TEST 1905 ENGLAND v AUSTRALIA
Lord's Cricket Ground, London. June 15, 16, 17 (no play), 1905.
Toss: England. Match Drawn.

ENGLAND

AC MacLaren b Hopkins	56		b Armstrong	79
TW Hayward b Duff	16		c Laver b McLeod	8
JT Tyldesley c Laver b Armstrong	43		b Noble	12
CB Fry c Kelly b Hopkins	73		not out	36
FS Jackson (c) c Armstrong b Laver	29		b Armstrong	0
AO Jones b Laver	1		c Trumper b Armstrong	5
BJT Bosanquet c & b Armstrong	6		not out	4
W Rhodes b Hopkins	15			
AFA Lilley (+) lbw McLeod	0			
S Haigh b Laver	14			
EG Arnold not out	7			
EXTRAS (B 20, LB 2)	22		(B 2, LB 4, NB 1)	7
TOTAL	282			5 for 151

FOW 1st Inns: 59 97 149 208 210 227 257 258 258 282
FOW 2nd Inns: 18 63 136 136 146

Bowling: *First Innings*: McLeod 20-7-40-1, Laver 34-8-64-3, Armstrong 30-11-41-2, Noble 34-13-61-0, Duff 7-4-14-1, Hopkins 15-4-40-3. *Second Innings*: McLeod 15-5-33-1, Laver 10-4-39-0, Armstrong 10-2-30-3, Noble 13-2-31-1, Hopkins 2-0-11-0.

AUSTRALIA

VT Trumper b Jackson	31
RA Duff c Lilley b Rhodes	27
C Hill c Bosanquet b Jackson	7
MA Noble c Fry b Jackson	7
WW Armstrong lbw Jackson	33
J Darling (c) c Haigh b Arnold	41
ES Gregory c Jones b Rhodes	5
AJY Hopkins b Haigh	16
CE McLeod b Haigh	0
F Laver not out	4
JJ Kelly (+) lbw Rhodes	2
EXTRAS (B 3, LB 5)	8
TOTAL	181

FOW 1st Inns: 57 73 73 95 131 138 171 175 175 181

Bowling: *First Innings*: Haigh 12-3-40-2, Rhodes 16.1-1-70-3, Jackson 15-0-50-4, Arnold 7-3-13-1.

Umpires: J Phillips & W Richards

THIRD TEST 1905 ENGLAND v AUSTRALIA
Headingley, Leeds. July 3, 4, 5, 1905.
Toss: England. Match Drawn.

ENGLAND

TW Hayward b McLeod	26	c Hopkins b Armstrong	60
CB Fry c Noble b McLeod	32	c Kelly b Armstrong	30
JT Tyldesley b Laver	0	st Kelly b Armstrong	100
D Denton c Duff b McLeod	0	c Hill b Armstrong	12
FS Jackson (c) not out	144	c Duff b Armstrong	17
GH Hirst c Trumper b Laver	35	not out	40
BJT Bosanquet b Duff	20	not out	22
AFA Lilley (+) b Noble	11		
S Haigh c Noble b Armstrong	11		
A Warren run out	7		
C Blythe b Armstrong	0		
EXTRAS (B 10, LB 1, W 2, NB 2)	15	(B 1, LB 6, W 6, NB 1)	14
TOTAL	301	5 dec	295

FOW 1st Inns: 51 54 57 64 133 201 232 282 301 301
FOW 2nd Inns: 80 126 170 202 258

Bowling: *First Innings*: Armstrong 26.3-6-44-2, Noble 23-6-59-1, Laver 29-10-61-2, McLeod 37-13-88-3, Hopkins 9-4-21-0, Duff 4-1-13-1. *Second Innings*: Armstrong 51-14-122-5, Noble 20-3-68-0, Laver 10-4-29-0, McLeod 23-6-62-0.

AUSTRALIA

VT Trumper b Warren	8	c Hirst b Warren	0
RA Duff c Lilley b Blythe	48	b Hirst	17
C Hill c & b Hirst	7	c Warren b Haigh	33
MA Noble c Hayward b Warren	2	st Lilley b Bosanquet	62
WW Armstrong c Hayward b Warren	66	lbw Blythe	32
J Darling (c) c Bosanquet b Warren	5	b Blythe	2
AJY Hopkins c Lilley b Jackson	36	b Blythe	17
ES Gregory run out	4	not out	32
CE McLeod b Haigh	8	not out	10
JJ Kelly (+) not out	1		
F Laver b Warren	3		
EXTRAS (B 4, LB 1, W 2)	7	(B 11, W 6, NB 2)	19
TOTAL	195	7 for	224

FOW 1st Inns: 26 33 36 96 105 161 166 191 191 195
FOW 2nd Inns: 0 36 64 117 121 152 199

Bowling:First Innings: Hirst 7-1-37-1, Warren 19.2-5-57-5, Blythe 8-0-36-1, Jackson 4-0-10-1, Haigh 11-5-19-1, Bosanquet 4-0-29-0. *Second Innings:* Hirst 10-2-26-1, Warren 20-4-56-1, Blythe 24-11-41-3, Jackson 8-2-10-0, Haigh 14-4-36-1, Bosanquet 15-1-36-1.

Umpires: J Phillips & VA Titchmarsh

FIFTH TEST 1905 ENGLAND v AUSTRALIA
Kennington Oval, London. August 14, 15, 16, 1905.
Toss: England. Match Drawn.

ENGLAND

AC MacLaren c Laver b Cotter	6 (3)	c Kelly b Armstrong	6
TW Hayward hit wicket b Hopkins	59	lbw Armstrong	2
JT Tyldesley b Cotter	16 (4)	not out	112
CB Fry b Cotter	144 (5)	c Armstrong b Noble	16
FS Jackson (c) c Armstrong b Laver	76 (6)	b Cotter	31
RH Spooner b Cotter	0 (7)	c (S)DRA Gehrs b Noble	79
GH Hirst c Noble b Laver	5		
EG Arnold c Trumper b Cotter	40 (1)	b Cotter	0
W Rhodes b Cotter	36		
AFA Lilley (+) b Cotter	17		
W Brearley not out	11		
EXTRAS (B 11, LB 1, W 1, NB 7)	20	(B 4, LB 5, W 1, NB 5)	15
TOTAL	430	6 dec	261

FOW 1st Inns: 12 32 132 283 291 306 322 394 418 430
FOW 2nd Inns: 0 8 13 48 103 261

Bowling: *First Innings*: Cotter 40-4-148-7, Noble 18-6-51-0, Armstrong 27-7-76-0, McLeod 13-2-47-0, Laver 17-3-41-2, Hopkins 11-2-32-1, Duff 4-1-15-0. *Second Innings*: Cotter 21-2-73-2, Noble 14.3-3-56-2, Armstrong 30-13-61-2, McLeod 11-2-27-0, Laver 3-0-18-0, Hopkins 1-0-11-0.

AUSTRALIA

VT Trumper b Brearley	4	c Spooner b Brearley	28
RA Duff c & b Hirst	146	b Arnold	34
C Hill c Rhodes b Brearley	18	b Arnold	34
MA Noble c MacLaren b Jackson	25	b Hirst	3
WW Armstrong c(S)AO Jones b Hirst	18	not out	32
J Darling (c) b Hirst	57	not out	12
AJY Hopkins b Brearley	1 (2)	run out	10
CE McLeod b Brearley	0		
JJ Kelly (+) run out	42		
A Cotter c Fry b Brearley	6		
F Laver not out	15		
EXTRAS (B 17, LB 9, W 1, NB 4)	31	(B 4, LB 1)	5
TOTAL	363	4 for	124

FOW 1st Inns: 5 44 159 214 237 247 265 293 304 363
FOW 2nd Inns: 27 49 58 92

Bowling: *First Innings*: Hirst 23-6-86-3, Brearley 31.1-8-110-5, Arnold 9-0-50-0, Rhodes 21-2-59-0, Jackson 9-1-27-1. *Second Innings*: Hirst 9-2-32-1, Brearley 11-2-41-1, Arnold 9-2-17-1, Rhodes 8-0-29-0.
Umpires: J Phillips & JE West

FOURTH TEST 1905 ENGLAND v AUSTRALIA
Old Trafford, Manchester. July 24, 25, 26, 1905.
Toss: England. England won by an innings & 80 runs.

ENGLAND

AC MacLaren c Hill b McLeod	14
TW Hayward c Gehrs b McLeod	82
JT Tyldesley b Laver	24
CB Fry b Armstrong	17
FS Jackson (c) c Cotter b McLeod	113
RH Spooner c & b McLeod	52
GH Hirst c Laver b McLeod	25
EG Arnold run out	25
W Rhodes not out	27
AFA Lilley (+) lbw Noble	28
W Brearley c Darling b Noble	0
EXTRAS (B 17, LB 20, W 1, NB 1)	39
TOTAL	446

FOW 1st Inns: 24 77 136 176 301 347 382 387 446 446

Bowling: *First Innings*: Cotter 26-4-83-0, McLeod 47-8-125-5, Armstrong 48-14-93-1, Laver 21-5-73-1, Noble 15.5-3-33-2.

AUSTRALIA

MA Noble b Brearley	7 (4)	c Rhodes b Brearley	10
VT Trumper c Rhodes b Brearley	11	lbw Rhodes	30
C Hill c Fry b Arnold	0	c (S)AO Jones b Arnold	27
WW Armstrong b Rhodes	29 (5)	b Brearley	9
RA Duff c MacLaren b Brearley	11 (1)	c Spooner b Brearley	60
J Darling (c) c Tyldesley b Jackson	73	c Rhodes b Brearley	0
DRA Gehrs b Arnold	0 (8)	c & b Rhodes	11
CE McLeod b Brearley	6 (9)	c Arnold b Rhodes	6
A Cotter c Fry b Jackson	11 (10)	run out	6
F Laver b Rhodes	24 (11)	not out	6
JJ Kelly (+) not out	16 (7)	c Rhodes b Arnold	5
EXTRAS (B 9)	9	(B 4, NB 1)	5
TOTAL	197		169

FOW 1st Inns: 20 21 27 41 88 93 146 146 166 197
FOW 2nd Inns: 55 121 122 133 133 146 146 158 158 169

Bowling: *First Innings*: Hirst 2-0-12-0, Brearley 17-3-72-4, Arnold 14-2-53-2, Rhodes 5.5-1-25-2, Jackson 7-0-26-2. *Second Innings*: Hirst 7-2-19-0, Brearley 14-3-54-4, Arnold 15-5-35-2, Rhodes 11.3-3-36-3, Jackson 5-0-20-0.

Umpires: J Carlin & JE West

Australian Averages

1905 ENGLAND v AUSTRALIA

AUSTRALIA	M	Inn	NO	Runs	H.S	Avrge	Ct	St	Overs	Mds	Runs	Wkt	Avrge
Armstrong, WW	5	9	1	252	66	31.50	4	-	280.3	94	538	16	33.63
Cotter, A	3	5	-	80	45	16.00	1	-	127.0	13	427	13	32.85
Darling, J	5	9	1	230	73	28.75	2	-	-	-	-	-	-
Duff, RA	5	8	-	335	146	41.88	5	-	30.0	8	85	4	21.25
Gehrs, DRA	1	2	-	11	11	5.50	1	-	-	-	-	-	-
Gregory, ES	3	5	1	94	51	23.50		-	-	-	-	-	-
Hill, C	5	9	-	188	54	20.89	2	-	-	-	-	-	-
Hopkins, AJY	3	5	-	80	36	16.00	1	-	38.0	10	115	4	28.75
Kelly, JJ	5	7	4	73	42	24.33	4	1	-	-	-	-	-
Laver, F	5	7	3	62	24	15.50	5	-	189.3	55	510	16	31.88
McLeod, CE	5	8	1	47	13	6.71	1	-	202.0	54	525	10	52.50
Noble, MA	5	9	-	173	62	19.22	4	-	148.2	37	409	6	68.17
Trumper, VT	5	8	1	125	31	17.86	3	-	-	-	-	-	-

English Averages

1905 ENGLAND v AUSTRALIA

ENGLAND	M	Inn	NO	Runs	H.S	Avrge	Ct	St	Overs	Mds	Runs	Wkt	Avrge
Arnold, EG	4	5	2	74	40	24.67	2	-	69.0	16	214	7	30.57
Blythe, C	1	1	-	0	0	0.00	-	-	32.0	11	77	4	19.25
Bosanquet, BJT	3	6	2	85	27	21.25	5	-	58.4	3	201	9	22.33
Brearley, W	2	2	1	11	11*	11.00	-	-	73.1	16	277	14	19.79
Denton, D	1	2	-	12	12	6.00	-	-	-	-	-	-	-
Fry, CB	4	7	1	348	144	58.00	4	-	-	-	-	-	-
Gunn, JR	1	1	-	8	8	8.00	-	-	6.0	2	27	1	27.00
Haigh, S	2	2	-	25	14	12.50	1	-	37.0	12	95	4	23.75
Hayward, TW	5	9	-	305	82	33.89	3	-	-	-	-	-	-
Hirst, GH	3	4	1	105	40*	35.00	3	-	58.0	13	212	6	35.33
Jackson, FS	5	9	2	492	144*	70.29	1	-	67.5	8	201	13	15.46
Jessop, GL	1	1	-	0	0	0.00	1	-	8.0	2	19	1	19.00
Jones, AO	2	4	-	40	30	10.00	3	-	-	-	-	-	-
Lilley, AFA	5	5	-	93	37	18.60	4	4	-	-	-	-	-
MacLaren, AC	4	7	-	303	140	43.29	2	-	-	-	-	-	-
Rhodes, W	4	5	2	146	39*	48.67	6	-	110.3	21	314	10	31.40
Spooner, RH	2	3	-	131	79	43.67	1	-	-	-	-	-	-
Tyldesley, JT	5	9	1	424	112*	53.00	1	-	-	-	-	-	-
Warren, A	1	1	-	7	7	7.00	1	-	39.2	9	113	6	18.83

NSW rebels back in fold

Trumper's XI poses with a XV from Maryborough, Queensland, on 21 May 1906, during his 'unauthorised' tour.

NSW has bumper crop of run-getters

Sydney, Jan. 30. NSW batsman Sunny Jim Mackay ended the season with a modest 50 in his state's thumping 145-run win over Victoria, giving NSW its fifth Sheffield Shield in succession.

Modest, that is for Sunny Jim. Mackay has scored 902 runs in just six first class matches and nine innings this summer, for an average of 112.75. His highest score was 203 against Queensland.

The aggregate is the best in first class competition since Victor Trumper's 990 in 1903–04 – but the great man played 21 innings.

Mackay, 24, is untrained but has a quick eye and twinkling feet. He is regarded by many judges, such as Clem Hill, as the best bat to emerge in Australia since Trumper himself. He was unlucky not to be given the same opportunity as Trumper in England on the 1905 tour.

Monty Noble also had a wonderful season, knocking up 631 crisply cut and driven runs at 90.14, including 123 in the win over Victoria.

The illustrious Victor Trumper also hit a hundred in this match, one of only two in which he was able to participate.

With NSW having four of the top eight batsmen, and three of the top five bowlers no wonder it was undefeated.

Batsman 'Sunny Jim' Mackay.

Sydney, Aug. 10. The NSW Cricket Association has lifted its ban on the 10 players suspended after they had agreed to play against England in a team sponsored by the Melbourne Cricket Club earlier this year.

The players, Victor Trumper, Tibby Cotter, Monty Noble, Sunny Jim Mackay, Austin Diamond, Reggie Duff, Rev. Mick Waddy, George Garnsey, Hanson Carter, Bert Hopkins – would have formed quite a useful basis for an Australian team, to say the least.

The MCC arrangement had remained secret for several months but when it leaked out, it caused consternation in the Victorian Cricket Association whose irascible secretary Ernie Bean accused the MCC of treachery, and of wanting to take over the game.

The NSWCA's equally determined secretary Billy McElhone, representing the rabidly anti-MCC forces, was incensed.

The players were brought before the NSWCA one by one and asked to repudiate their written agreement – under threat of suspension.

All refused except the Rev Waddy. Sunny Jim Mackay, after his sensational Shield season, felt so aggrieved that he has since gone to play in South Africa.

Trumper himself took off on his 'unauthorised' tour of Queensland, helped not by the NSWCA or Queensland authorities but by the entrepreneur J. C. Williamson.

This team, playing in places such as Charters Towers, Townsville and Mount Morgan was greeted by the cricket-starved people of the bush like heroes.

South Australian players Joe Darling and Clem Hill said they would not play in NSW unless the players were reinstated.

Billy McElhone declared in May that 'the Association and not the players run the sport'. Monty Noble replied that players who had been denied representation on the new Australian cricket board could not be disloyal to it or the NSWCA.

In Melbourne, the MCC resigned from the VCA in April.

The reinstatement and other compromises hopefully point towards a better organisation of Australian cricket.

SA part of new cricket board

Melbourne, April 20. South Australia joined the Australian Board of Control for International Cricket at a meeting at Young and Jackson's Hotel on the basis that it would host a regular Test match in Adelaide.

The meeting also agreed to the terms of an England tour in 1907–08, underwriting it to the tune of £10,000.

This agreement has finally put paid to ambitions the Melbourne Cricket Club might have had to run international cricket – but the role of the players has not been finally clarified.

Tasmania will join later in the year, and WA has been granted observer status.

The Board was mooted on 9 January 1905 by the dominant – and regarded by some as devious – administrative personalities in Australian cricket, Ernie Bean from the VCA and Billy McElhone from the NSWCA, and met on 4 May 1905 in Melbourne.

SA declined to join with Victoria, NSW and Queensland at that time over the matter of financial control, and players, formerly in control of overseas touring, were not invited.

NSW is dominant cricketing state

Perth, March 28. Despite New South Wales' dominance of the Sheffield Shield matches during this season, it was defeated by non-Shield State WA in its first visit to Western Australia, by just five runs.

NSW won the first game by two wickets.

This loss by less than a full-strength team can be regarded as beneficial to Australian cricket and does not take the gloss off NSW's sixth Shield win in succession.

The only close match was against Victoria at the MCG in December when a wonderful 168 not out by Warwick Armstrong nearly gave NSW a big enough target for Victorian leg-spinner Tom Warne to bowl Victoria to a win.

It was not to be.

In the other five Shield games NSW, led by Test player Albert Hopkins, won by an innings. Austin Diamond's 210 not out was the highest score of the season. Up-and-coming all-rounder Charlie Macartney shone with both bat and ball. Macartney took 30 wickets and made 405 runs.

M'Dougall tops the score

Thomas E. Spencer has published his famous verse 'How M'Dougall Topped the Score' in book form.

'Nine wickets down for seventeen, with fifty more to win!'
Our captain heaved a heavy sigh – and sent M'Dougall in.
'Ten pounds to one you'll lose it!' cried a barracker from town;
But M'Dougall said I'll tak' it mon!' and planked the money down.
He held the bat the wrong side out, and Johnson with a grin,
Stepped lightly to the bowling crease, and sent a 'wobbler' in;
M'Dougall spooned it softly back, and Johnson waited there,
But M'Dougall crying 'Fetch it' started running like a hare.
Molongo shouted 'Victory! He's out as sure as eggs'.
When Pincher started through the crowd, and ran through Johnson's legs.
He seized the ball like lightning; then ran behind a log,
And M'Dougall kept on running, while Molongo chased the dog.
They chased him up, they chased him down, they chased him round, and then
He darted through a slip-rail as the scorer shouted 'Ten!'
M'Dougall puffed; Molongo swore; excitement was intense;
As the scorer marked down 'Twenty', Pincher cleared a barbed-wire fence.
'Let us head him!' shrieked Molongo, 'Brain the mongrel with a bat!'
'Run it out! Good old M'Dougall!' yelled the men of Piper's Flat.
And M'Dougall kept on jogging, and then Pincher doubled back,
And the scorer counted 'Forty' as they raced across the track.
When the scorer shouted 'Fifty!' then they knew the chase could cease;
And M'Dougall gasped out 'Drop it!' as he dropped within his crease.
Then Pincher dropped the ball, and, as instinctively he knew
Discretion was the wiser plan, he disappeared from view …
And the critics say they never saw a cricket match like that
When M'Dougall broke the record in the game at Piper's Flat.
And the folk are jubilating as they never were before;
For we played Molongo cricket, and M'Dougall topped the score!

1907–08

ENGLAND IN AUSTRALIA

QUICK SINGLES

Grounds wrangle. The NSWCA will be forced to pay the SCG Trustees 18 per cent of Test gate takings. A threat to use the University ground was stymied when the University Senate said the applause would disturb the professors.

Armstrong out. Warwick Armstrong has stood out of the match against NSW ending January 7, over Victoria's failure to pay him a higher rate of pay as a senior player.

Played out. The London *Tribune* of January 17 suggests Test matches in Australia should be cut to four days, to discourage stonewalling. But Australian matches are played to a finish, in contrast to the situation in England where they are limited to just three days. That does encourage stonewalling.

No news. The English public is in the dark over the progress of the Adelaide Test. Cables relaying the Test news have been 'delayed' in Canada.

Silver cane. England all-rounder John Crawford has been presented with a silver-mounted cane, made from palmwood and inscribed by the Queensland Cricket Association, for his 21st birthday on December 1.

Close to cricket. Australian all-rounder Warwick Armstrong's working day is as pavilion clerk at the Melbourne Cricket Ground, where he is in charge of a staff of 24 men, and also arranges practice for members.

Caught out. England players Joe Hardstaff, Arthur Fielder and Wilfred Rhodes have each been fined £1 in the Melbourne Magistrates Court for being unlawfully at the Old White Heart hotel on Sunday, December 29.

Flying bail. The Brisbane *Courier Mail* of January 7 reports that a ball from James Higgins of the Milton Cricket Club sent a bail flying 51 yards off the wicket. The distance was measured by four players.

Back at work. Roger Hartigan, the hero of the third Test in Adelaide, is unavailable for the fourth Test, because he is unable to get an extension of leave from his job with a woolbroking firm.

Gunn – a handy man standing by

Sydney, Dec. 19. George Gunn came out to Australia for his health. His aim was to act as scorer for the English team, use the Australian sun to dry out his consumptive lungs and check on the sales of Gunn and Moore bats for his uncle William.

But his health is good, while the England captain Arthur Jones has pneumonia and is in hospital in Brisbane.

Called to duty in the first Test, rather than the young member of the touring party, Jack Hobbs, Gunn nearly swung it England's way with innings of 119 and 74

However, the other England bats did not back him up and Australian scraped in by two wickets.

The match revolved around Tibby Cotter, who took 6/101 in England's first innings and was involved in the 56-run ninth-wicket stand with Gerry Hazlitt that carried Australia to victory.

WA welcomes its illustrious visitors

Perth, Oct. 29. After years of rejected invitations and lobbying, the Western Australians finally have the English team playing on their soil.

Their arrival has been greeted with celebration and banqueting, and the building of a new press box and scoreboard at the WACA ground. Former Test fast bowler Ernie Jones, playing for WA, says the board is the equal of Sydney and Melbourne.

The cricket has been watched with great interest by about 9000 spectators over the three days, but the game has been one-sided. England opener Frederick Fane made 133 of England's 402, and WA managed 152 and 116.

It was slow play for Kangaroo.

Test is nearly a tie

The English team in Melbourne for the second nail-biting Test match.

Melbourne, Jan. 7. After six days of cautious batting on a slowish MCG pitch, the second Test bubbled up into a nail-biting finish today. Victory to Australia seemed a formality when Warwick Armstrong had English wicketkeeper Joe Humphries lbw for 16, ending his ninth-wicket stand of 34 with fast bowler Sydney Barnes.

With 39 to win, in came Arthur Fielder, a known rabbit with the bat, to join Barnes.

With Barnes knocking the ball around and Fielder clinging on for dear life the last pair slowly got the score to 281, level with the Australians.

Then came the climactic moment, as the batsmen lurched forward for a suicidal winning run. Gerry Hazlitt had the ball in hand only 10 yards from the stumps with the batsmen stranded, but his wild throw missed wicketkeeper Hanson Carter and the Englishmen scampered to victory.

Hazlitt, who as a batsman partnered Tibby Cotter to an Australian victory in the first Test, is usually an excellent fieldsman.

Despite the slow play, the match has always been absorbing, and has been followed by a crowd totalling 91,386 over six days.

Australia made a good start with Trumper and the new all-rounder Charles Macartney putting on 84, Captain Monty Noble top-scored with 61, but the Australians could only total 266, and Jack Hobbs (83) and Ken Hutchings (126) carried England to a 116-run lead. But Australia had a much stronger second innings, with Trumper (63), Macartney (54), Noble (64), McAlister (77) and Carter (53) contributing to a total of 397.

England had 282 to get, and in a battle of attrition their chances seemed to have gone until the wonderful recovery led by Barnes. The imperturbable Staffordshire bowler also had 5/72 in Australia's second innings, so England can ultimately thank him for this narrowest of wins.

England's saviours Barnes and Fielder, the last pair in the second Test.

Victoria breaks the Shield deadlock

Sydney, Jan. 31. In a classic seven-day battle, Victoria has inflicted the first Shield defeat on New South Wales in Sydney, and in doing so has wrested back the Sheffield Shield after six seasons.

The match was a stern, high scoring battle for five days, but rain prevented play on day six and softened the wicket, described by the *Sydney Morning Herald* for the first few days as being in 'splendid run getting order'.

The rain made it ripe for exploitation by veteran Jack Saunders. He obliged with 6/61 and Victoria were 211-run winners. The first three innings yielded three centuries and two double centuries. Warwick Armstrong made 110 in Victoria's 402, then Monty Noble (176) and Syd Gregory (201) carried NSW to 461.

Not to be outdone, the Victorians compiled 511 with Frank Tarrant, back from England, scoring 206 and Vern Ransford 126. Even then there was a another century to come, as despite NSW's meagre 241 in the last, Monty Noble made a great 123.

'In the Ladies Stand' – a report

Melbourne, Feb. 10. The *Argus* reporter has this to say about women at the cricket during the fourth Test at the MCG:

'Women and cricket are rivals, as are women and tobacco. One notes the resentment of a girl whose lover forgets her in the excitement of the game. She does not know an umpire from a leg glance, a 'googly' from a wicketkeeper, but she does know that she has her best hat on, and George's allegiance is momentarily dead. That is one type. But then there is another who does not know, but pretends to, with painful results. 'Oh! Trumper's got four extras,' she exclaims as the figures move upon the board whose mysteries are not for her sex...

'The girl who sets herself up as one continuous interrogation mark has some charm at first, but becomes wearisome to her escort then. After each over she wants every player pointed out, and then forgets them before the next over.

During the interval a photographer took the field and pointed his camera at the 'ladies' stand.' In a twinkling of an eye 2000 hands went up to their owners hair.'

It's Trumper at last

Clem Hill: 160 in the heat.

Sydney, Feb. 27. The sun seems to have resumed its correct place in the heavens and all seems right with the world today: Victor Trumper has at last thrashed the English bowling.

He has been a long time coming this season, and his failings have only been tolerated because Australia has had an armchair ride through the last three Tests to take the series 4–1.

It took the last innings of the series for Trumper to join in and show his incomparable batting skills. His last five hands have produced scores of 4, 0, 0, 0 and 10. The fates were kind to him again

Armstrong: valuable century.

Jack O'Connor: 8/150 on debut.

yesterday – he had scored only one when he was dropped by Rhodes off a ball from Barnes that kicked and caught the shoulder of the bat.

But four hours later he had 166, produced in a masterful manner against a worthy bowling attack. He was particularly strong on the on side, scoring 117 of his runs with drives, sweeps, pulls and hooks.

Australia scored 422, but even then England had a chance to take the Test as Barnes (6/70) had run through Australia for 137 in its first innings. England needed a moderate 279 to win. But it was never in the race after its first six batsmen were back in the pavilion for 87.

England was in a similar position in the heat-struck third Test in Adelaide, leading on the first innings but then brought down by a big Australian second innings.

This time it was Roger Hartigan, (116 on debut) and Clem Hill (160) who took Australia to 506. They batted in 107-degree and 111-degree heat on the fourth and fifth days in compiling an eighth wicket stand of 243. Hill had gone in ninth because of influenza and was 'sick on the field' several times.

In the fourth Test the Ashes came back to Australia. England was caught on a sticky in the first innings, and then put to rest by a painstaking 133 by Warwick Armstrong. Young Jack Hobbs has been outstanding among the England batsmen. George Gunn knocked up another century, 122 not out for England in the first innings of the fifth Test.

Board tightens its grip on the game

Sydney, May 30. The Australian Board of Control, under the iron fist of Billy McElhone, now seems to be firmly in charge of international cricket, despite rumblings from the players over its methods and decisions.

Having staged the Test series the Board has now distributed the small profits to the only two States that staged the Test matches – Victoria and NSW.

Joe Darling, now living in Tasmania, says it is scandalous that a State which has produced three Test players should not get some reward, particularly as it was admitted to the Board last year.

The Board has also blocked Queensland's push for inclusion in the Sheffield Shield, on a 7–5 vote, presumably due to opposition from SA and Victorian delegates concerned about long travel.

Fiji tour goes on despite the Board

Sydney, May 30. The Fijian tour of Australia was not meant to go ahead, but it is as well that it did because the players, with their sulus and bare feet, have attracted good crowds to their 26 matches.

The Board of Control had originally disapproved the tour on the grounds that it would contravene the White Australia policy. Later the Board approved the tour, but none of the matches were of first class standing. The Fijians were lucky to play against George Giffen who had been persuaded to come out of retirement for one game in Adelaide. Giffen wished he hadn't because he took some punishment from the wristy Fijian batsmen.

Captains Arthur Jones and Monty Noble say farewell to the series.

Noble – all-round captain

Johnnie Moyes wrote in 1959 that Monty Noble was the most accomplished all-round cricketer that Australia had produced.

Moyes knew of George Giffen and had seen Jack Gregory and Keith Miller at close hand.

But he had no hesitation about Noble, a man who played 42 Tests for Australia and had accumulated 1997 runs and 121 wickets on his retirement in 1909.

At that stage Noble had been a NSW regular for 12 years and a Test player for 11 years.

He was 37 with a lot of cricket ahead of him if he chose to play on, but he was driven from the Test arena by the bad feeling and backbiting that stemmed from the Board of Control, which was to further disrupt the game.

Noble was man of character who believed in fair play and set an impeccable example for his players.

He went out of Tests on a high note, having won his two series as captain, but played on for NSW until 1919.

Montague Alfred Noble learned his cricket in the fertile cricketing suburb of Paddington, where his father managed a hotel.

Adopting a grip learned from US baseballers, he held the ball between thumb and forefinger, and was able to impart subtle variations of swing and off-spin. On a worn or wet pitch he was a terrifying proposition.

His batting was orthodox and solid. He was capable of hitting out, but equally of holding his wicket in tense situations and in poor conditions. His best Test effort was in 1901–02, when he took 13/77 at the MCG.

On his first tour of England in 1899 he saved Australia in the third Test, scoring 60 not out in the first innings and then, in the follow-on, making 89 in just on 320 minutes.

By contrast he smashed up 284 in a partnership of 428 with Warwick Armstrong in 1902. He scored over 200 seven times.

But his captaincy stamped him as one of the greatest of the Australians.

He studied the game and his opponents intensely and had iron discipline on the field.

He had supreme confidence in himself as a batsman and expected to stay in and make runs. He expected his players to do the same.

Monty Noble: greatest all-rounder.

This martinet on the field never lost his air of command of the play, but he was a genial and friendly man and invoked harmony, good humour and sportsmanship in his players.

He believed firmly that he should not berate any of his players in front of their fellows as this would create a lack of confidence in the team.

He believed instead that a player should be left alone, to let the lesson sink in, and follow that later with a quiet sympathetic talk.

He supported the team against the machinations of the cricket board, but took no pleasure in his situation.

Noble took a job with a bank as a youngster, but left when he was refused time off to play cricket. He put himself through dentistry and practiced for many years.

One of his patients was Bill Ferguson, who gained his 40-year job as scorer and baggage handler while sitting in Noble's dentist chair.

Ferguson sent his sister for treatment, and at 40, Noble found a wife, with whom he had four children and a happy marriage.

Later in life he became a writer and broadcaster, and wrote three books, *Gilligan's Men*, *The Game's the Thing* and *Those Ashes*.

His reputation was such that he has a grandstand named for him at the Sydney Cricket Ground – the first-ever cricketer to be so honoured.

FIRST TEST 1907–08 AUSTRALIA v ENGLAND
Sydney Cricket Ground, Sydney. December 13, 14, 16, 17, 18 (no play), 19, 1907.
Toss: England. Australia won by 2 wkts.

ENGLAND

FL Fane (c) c Trumper b Cotter	2	c Noble b Saunders	33
RA Young (+) c Carter b Cotter	13 (7)	b Noble	3
G Gunn c Hazlitt b Cotter	119	c Noble b Cotter	74
KL Hutchings c & b Armstrong	42	c Armstrong b Saunders	17
LC Braund b Cotter	30 (6)	not out	32
J Hardstaff sr b Armstrong	12 (5)	b Noble	63
W Rhodes run out	1 (2)	c McAlister b Macartney	29
JN Crawford b Armstrong	31	c Hazlitt b Cotter	5
SF Barnes b Cotter	1	b saunders	11
C Blythe b Cotter	5	c Noble b Saunders	15
A Fielder not out	1	lbw Armstrong	6
EXTRAS (B 7, LB 6, W 1, NB 2)	16	(B 2, LB 3, W 1, NB 7)	12
TOTAL	273		300

FOW 1st Inns: 11 18 91 208 221 223 246 253 271 273
FOW 2nd Inns: 56 82 105 218 223 227 241 262 293 300

Bowling: *First Innings*: Cotter 21.5-0-101-6, Hazlitt 9-2-32-0, Saunders 11-0-42-0, Armstrong 26-10-63-3, Macartney 3-0-5-0, Noble 6-1-14-0. *Second Innings*: Cotter 26-1-101-2, Saunders 23-6-68-4, Armstrong 27-14-33-1, Macartney 14-2-39-1, Hazlitt 4-2-24-0, Noble 15-5-23-2.

AUSTRALIA

VT Trumper b Fielder	43	b Barnes	3
PA McAlister c Hutchings b Barnes	3 (7)	b Crawford	41
C Hill c Gunn b Fielder	87	b Fielder	1
MA Noble (c) c Braund b Fielder	37	b Barnes	27
WW Armstrong c Braund b Fielder	7	b Crawford	44
VS Ransford c Braund b Rhodes	24	c & b Blythe	13
CG Macartney c Young b Fielder	35 (2)	c Crawford b Fielder	9
H Carter (+) b Braund	25	c Young b Fielder	61
GR Hazlitt not out	18 (10)	not out	34
A Cotter b Braund	2 (9)	not out	33
JV Saunders c Braund b Fielder	9		
EXTRAS (B 4, LB 2, W 2, NB 2)	10	(B 6, LB 3)	9
TOTAL	300		8 for 275

FOW 1st Inns: 4 72 164 171 184 222 253 279 281 300
FOW 2nd Inns: 7 12 27 75 95 124 185 219

Bowling: *First Innings*: Fielder 30.2-4-82-6, Barnes 22-3-74-1, Blythe 12-1-33-0, Braund 17-2-74-2, Crawford 5-1-14-0, Rhodes 5-2-13-1. *Second Innings*: Fielder 27.3-4-88-3, Barnes 30-7-63-2, Blythe 19-5-55-1, Crawford 8-2-33-2, Rhodes 7-3-13-0, Braund 7-2-14-0.

Umpires: RM Crockett & W Hannah

SECOND TEST 1907–08 AUSTRALIA v ENGLAND
Melbourne Cricket Ground, Melbourne. January 1, 2, 3, 4, 6, 7, 1908.
Toss: Australia. England won by 1 wkt.

AUSTRALIA

VT Trumper c Humphries b Crawford	49	lbw Crawford	63
CG Macartney b Crawford	37 (6)	c Humphries b Barnes	54
C Hill b Fielder	16	b Fielder	3
MA Noble (c) c Braund b Rhodes	61 (2)	b Crawford	64
WW Armstrong c Hutchings b Crawford	31	b Barnes	77
PA McAlister run out	10 (4)	run out	15
VS Ransford run out	27	c Hutchings b Barnes	18
A Cotter b Crawford	17 (9)	lbw Crawford	27
H Carter (+) not out	15 (8)	c Fane b Barnes	53
GR Hazlitt b Crawford	1	b Barnes	3
JV Saunders b Fielder	0	not out	0
EXTRAS (LB 1, W 1)	2	(B 12, LB 8)	20
TOTAL	266		397

FOW 1st Inns: 84 93 111 168 197 214 240 261 265 266
FOW 2nd Inns: 126 131 135 162 268 303 312 361 392 397

Bowling: *First Innings*: Fielder 27.5-4-77-2, Barnes 17-7-30-0, Rhodes 11-0-37-1, Braund 16-5-41-0, Crawford 29-1-79-5. *Second Innings*: Fielder 27-6-74-1, Crawford 33-6-125-3, Barnes 27.4-4-72-5, Braund 18-2-68-0, Rhodes 16-6-38-0.

ENGLAND

FL Fane (c) b Armstrong	13	b Armstrong	50
JB Hobbs b Cotter	83	b Noble	28
G Gunn lbw Cotter	15	lbw Noble	0
KL Hutchings b Cotter	126	c Cotter b Macartney	39
LC Braund b Cotter	49	b Armstrong	30
J Hardstaff sr b Saunders	12	c Ransford b Cotter	19
W Rhodes b Saunders	32	run out	15
JN Crawford c Ransford b Saunders	16	c Armstrong b Saunders	10
SF Barnes c Hill b Armstrong	14	not out	38
J Humphries (+) b Cotter	6	lbw Armstrong	16
A Fielder not out	6	not out	18
EXTRAS (B 3, LB 3, W 1, NB 3)	10	(B 9, LB 7, W 1, NB 2)	19
TOTAL	382		9 for 282

FOW 1st Inns: 27 61 160 268 287 325 353 360 369 382
FOW 2nd Inns: 54 54 121 131 162 196 198 209 243

Bowling: *First Innings*: Cotter 33-4-142-5, Saunders 34-7-100-3, Noble 9-3-26-0, Armstrong 34.2-15-36-2, Hazlitt 13-1-34-0, Macartney 12-2-34-0. *Second Innings*: Cotter 28-3-82-1, Saunders 30-9-58-1, Armstrong 30.4-10-53-3, Noble 22-7-41-2, Hazlitt 2-1-8-0, Macartney 9-3-21-1.

Umpires: P Argall & RM Crockett

THIRD TEST 1907–08 AUSTRALIA v ENGLAND
Adelaide Oval, Adelaide. January 10, 11, 13, 14, 15, 16, 1908.
Toss: Australia. Australia won by 245 runs.

AUSTRALIA

VT Trumper b Fielder	4	b Barnes	0
MA Noble (c) c Hutchings b Barnes	15	c Gunn b Fielder	65
CG Macartney lbw Braund	75	b Barnes	9
PA McAlister c Hutchings b Crawford	28	c Hutchings b Crawford	17
WW Armstrong c Humphries b Fielder	17	c Hutchings b Braund	34
VS Ransford b Barnes	44 (7)	c Rhodes b Braund	25
C Hill c Humphries b Barnes	5 (9)	c Gunn b Crawford	160
RJ Hartigan b Fielder	48	c (S)RA Young b Barnes	116
H Carter (+) lbw Hutchings	24 (10)	not out	31
JDA O'Connor not out	10 (6)	b Crawford	20
JV Saunders b Fielder	1	run out	0
EXTRAS (B 3, LB 5, W 3, NB 3)	14	(B 20, LB 7, W 2)	29
TOTAL	285		506

FOW 1st Inns: 11 35 114 140 160 191 215 273 275 285
FOW 2nd Inns: 7 35 71 127 135 179 180 423 501 506

Bowling: *First Innings*: Fielder 27.5-5-80-4, Barnes 27-8-60-3, Rhodes 15-5-35-0, Crawford 14-0-65-1, Braund 9-1-26-1, Hutchings 2-1-5-1. *Second Innings*: Fielder 23-3-81-1, Barnes 42-9-83-3, Crawford 45.5-4-113-3, Braund 23-3-85-2, Rhodes 27-9-81-0, Hutchings 7-0-34-0.

ENGLAND

JB Hobbs c Carter b Saunders	26	not out	23
FL Fane (c) run out	48	b Saunders	0
G Gunn b O'Connor	65	c Trumper b O'Connor	11
KL Hutchings c & b Macartney	23	b O'Connor	0
LC Braund b Macartney	0	c Hartigan b O'Connor	47
J Hardstaff sr b O'Connor	61	c Macartney b Saunders	72
W Rhodes c Carter b O'Connor	38	c Armstrong b O'Connor	9
JN Crawford b Armstrong	62	c & b Saunders	7
SF Barnes c & b Armstrong	12	c McAlister b Saunders	8
J Humphries (+) run out	7	b O'Connor	1
A Fielder not out	0	c Ransford b Saunders	1
EXTRAS (B 12, LB 2, W 2, NB 5)	21	(B 3, NB 1)	4
TOTAL	363		183

FOW 1st Inns: 58 98 138 138 194 277 282 320 363 363
FOW 2nd Inns: 8 9 15 128 138 146 162 177 182 183

Bowling: *First Innings*: O'Connor 40-8-110-3, Saunders 36-6-83-1, Noble 18-4-38-0, Armstrong 18-4-55-2, Macartney 18-3-49-2, Hartigan 2-0-7-0. *Second Innings*: O'Connor 21-6-40-5, Saunders 21.4-4-65-5, Armstrong 10-1-43-0, Macartney 4-1-17-0, Noble 7-1-14-0.

Umpires: RM Crockett & J Laing

FIFTH TEST 1907–08 AUSTRALIA v ENGLAND
Sydney Cricket Ground, Sydney. February 21, 22, 24, 25, 26, 27, 1908.
Toss: England. Australia won by 49 runs.

AUSTRALIA

MA Noble (c) b Barnes	35	lbw Rhodes	34
CG Macartney c Crawford b Barnes	1 (5)	c Jones b Crawford	12
JDA O'Connor c Young b Crawford	9 (2)	b Barnes	6
ES Gregory c & b Barnes	44	b Crawford	56
C Hill c Hutchings b Barnes	12 (6)	c Young b Crawford	44
WW Armstrong c & b Crawford	3 (7)	c Gunn b Crawford	32
VT Trumper c Braund b Barnes	10 (3)	c Gunn b Rhodes	166
VS Ransford c Gunn b Barnes	11	not out	21
RJ Hartigan c & b Crawford	1	b Crawford	5
H Carter (+) not out	1	c Hobbs b Rhodes	22
JV Saunders c Young b Barnes	0	c Young b Rhodes	0
EXTRAS (B 9, LB 1)	10	(B 21, LB 3)	24
TOTAL	137		422

FOW 1st Inns: 10 46 46 64 73 94 124 129 137 137
FOW 2nd Inns: 25 52 166 192 300 342 373 387 422 422

Bowling: *First Innings*: Rhodes 10-5-15-0, Barnes 22.4-6-60-7, Crawford 18-4-52-3. *Second Innings*: Barnes 27-6-78-1, Crawford 36-10-141-5, Rhodes 37.4-7-102-4, Braund 20-3-64-0, Hobbs 7-3-13-0.

ENGLAND

JB Hobbs b Saunders	72	c Gregory b Saunders	13
FL Fane b Noble	0	b Noble	46
G Gunn not out	122	b Macartney	0
KL Hutchings run out	13	b Macartney	2
J Hardstaff sr c O'Connor b Saunders	17	b Saunders	8
JN Crawford c Hill b Saunders	6 (10)	not out	24
LC Braund st Carter b Macartney	31 (6)	c Noble b Saunders	0
W Rhodes c Noble b Armstrong	10 (7)	b Noble	69
RA Young (+) st Carter b Macartney	0 (8)	c O'Connor b Saunders	11
AO Jones (c) b Macartney	0 (9)	b Armstrong	34
SF Barnes run out	1	b Saunders	11
EXTRAS (B 6, LB 3)	9	(B 5, LB 6)	11
TOTAL	281		229

FOW 1st Inns: 1 135 168 189 197 245 264 271 271 281
FOW 2nd Inns: 21 26 30 51 57 87 123 176 198 229

Bowling: *First Innings*: Noble 28-9-62-1, Saunders 35-5-114-3, O'Connor 6-0-23-0, Macartney 15.1-3-44-3, Armstrong 12-2-29-1. *Second Innings*: Noble 24-6-56-2, Saunders 35.1-5-82-5, Macartney 15-4-24-2, Armstrong 18-7-27-1, O'Connor 13-3-29-0.

Umpires: W Hannah & AC Jones

FOURTH TEST 1907–08 AUSTRALIA v ENGLAND
Melbourne Cricket Ground, Melbourne. February 7, 8, 10, 11, 1908.
Toss: Australia. Australia won by 308 runs.

AUSTRALIA

MA Noble (c) b Crawford	48	b Crawford	10
VT Trumper c Crawford b Fielder	0	b Crawford	0
C Hill b Barnes	7	run out	25
PA McAlister c Jones b Fielder	37	c Humphries b Fielder	4
ES Gregory c Fielder b Crawford	10	lbw Fielder	29
WW Armstrong c Crawford	32	not out	133
VS Ransford c Braund b Fielder	51	c Humphries b Rhodes	54
CG Macartney c Hardstaff b Fielder	12	c Gunn b Crawford	29
H Carter (+) c & b Crawford	2	c Braund b Fielder	66
JDA O'Connor c Fielder b Crawford	1	c Humphries b Barnes	18
JV Saunders not out	1	c Jones b Fielder	2
EXTRAS (B 1, LB 10, NB 1)	12	(B 7, LB 2, NB 6)	15
TOTAL	214		385

FOW 1st Inns: 1 14 89 103 105 196 196 198 212 214
FOW 2nd Inns: 4 21 28 65 77 162 217 329 374 385

Bowling: *First Innings*: Fielder 22-3-54-4, Barnes 23-11-37-1, Braund 12-3-42-0, Crawford 23.5-3-48-5, Rhodes 5-0-21-0. *Second Innings*: Barnes 35-13-69-1, Crawford 25-5-72-3, Fielder 31-2-91-4, Rhodes 24-5-66-1, Braund 7-0-48-0, Hutchings 2-0-24-0.

ENGLAND

JB Hobbs b Noble	57	c & b Saunders	0
G Gunn c & b Saunders	13	b Saunders	43
J Hardstaff sr c Carter b O'Connor	8	c Carter b Saunders	39
KL Hutchings b Saunders	8	b Noble	3
LC Braund run out	0	b Macartney	10
W Rhodes c McAlister b Saunders	0	c Carter b O'Connor	2
JN Crawford b Saunders	1	c Carter b O'Connor	0
AO Jones (c) b Noble	3	c Saunders b O'Connor	31
SF Barnes c O'Connor b Noble	3	not out	22
J Humphries (+) not out	3	c Carter b Saunders	11
A Fielder st Carter b Saunders	1	b Armstrong	20
EXTRAS (B 1, LB 2, NB 1)	4	(LB 4, NB 1)	5
TOTAL	105		186

FOW 1st Inns: 58 69 88 90 90 92 96 100 103 105
FOW 2nd Inns: 0 61 64 79 85 85 128 132 146 186

Bowling: *First Innings*: O'Connor 6-1-40-1, Armstrong 1-0-4-0, Macartney 6-1-18-0, Saunders 15.2-8-28-5, Noble 6-0-11-3. *Second Innings*: Saunders 26-2-76-4, O'Connor 21-3-58-3, Noble 12-6-14-1, Armstrong 3.1-0-18-1, Macartney 6-1-15-1.

Umpires: P Argall & RM Crockett

Australian Averages

1907–08 AUSTRALIA v ENGLAND

AUSTRALIA	M	Inn	NO	Runs	H.S	Avrge	Ct	St	Overs	Mds	Runs	Wkt	Avrge
Armstrong, WW	5	10	1	410	133*	45.56	5	-	180.1	63	361	14	25.79
Carter, H	5	10	3	300	66	42.86	8	3	-	-	-	-	-
Cotter, A	2	4	1	79	33*	26.33	1	-	108.5	8	426	14	30.43
Gregory, ES	2	4	-	139	56	34.75	1	-	-	-	-	-	-
Hartigan, RJ	2	4	-	170	116	42.50	1	-	2.0	-	7	-	-
Hazlitt, GR	2	4	2	56	34*	28.00	2	-	28.0	6	98	-	-
Hill, C	5	10	-	360	160	36.00	5	-	-	-	-	-	-
Macartney, CG	5	10	-	273	75	27.30	2	-	102.1	20	266	10	26.60
McAlister, PA	4	8	-	155	41	19.38	3	-	-	-	-	-	-
Noble, MA	5	10	-	396	65	39.60	5	-	147.0	42	299	11	27.18
O'Connor, JDA	3	6	1	65	20	13.00	3	-	107.0	21	300	12	25.00
Ransford, VS	5	10	1	288	54	32.00	3	-	-	-	-	-	-
Saunders, JV	5	9	2	13	9	1.86	4	-	267.1	52	716	31	23.10
Trumper, VT	5	10	-	338	166	33.80	2	-	-	-	-	-	-

English Averages

1907–08 AUSTRALIA v ENGLAND

ENGLAND	M	Inn	NO	Runs	H.S	Avrge	Ct	St	Overs	Mds	Runs	Wkt	Avrge
Barnes, SF	5	10	2	121	38*	15.13	1	-	273.2	74	626	24	26.08
Blythe, C	1	2	-	20	15	10.00	1	-	31.0	6	88	1	88.00
Braund, LC	5	10	1	233	49	25.89	8	-	129.0	21	462	5	92.40
Crawford, JN	5	10	1	162	62	18.00	6	-	237.4	36	742	30	24.73
Fane, FL	4	8	-	192	50	24.00	1	-	-	-	-	-	-
Fielder, A	4	8	4	53	20	13.25	2	-	216.3	31	627	25	25.08
Gunn, G	5	10	-	462	122*	51.33	7	-	-	-	-	-	-
Hardstaff sr, J	5	10	-	311	72	31.10	1	-	-	-	-	-	-
Hobbs, JB	4	8	1	302	83	43.14	1	-	7.0	3	13	-	-
Humphries, J	3	6	-	44	16	8.80	7	-	-	-	-	-	-
Hutchings, KL	5	10	-	273	126	27.30	8	-	11.0	1	63	1	63.00
Jones, AO	2	4	-	68	34	17.00	3	-	-	-	-	-	-
Rhodes, W	5	10	-	205	69	20.50	1	-	157.4	42	421	7	60.14
Young, RA	2	4	-	27	13	6.75	6	-	-	-	-	-	-

1908–09

AUSTRALIAN DOMESTIC

NSW run spree wins Shield

Sydney, Jan. 29. NSW won the Sheffield Shield by defeating Victoria in a record-breaking match at the SCG.

Victoria had won the previous encounter at the MCG (as well as last season's Sheffield Shield) by an innings and 47 runs. NSW's star batting lineup 'unaccountably' collapsed in its second innings to a not especially potent Victorian attack of Gerry Hazlitt, Frank Laver, Warwick Armstrong and Jack Saunders.

The wicket was a trifle damp.

In the return match, the first of the seven centuries scored in the six-day run glut was knocked up by Warren Bardsley. After Bert Hopkins went with the score on 42, Bardsley and Monty Noble put on 304 – an Australian second wicket partnership record. Bardsley finished with 192, Noble 213, and then Sid Gregory knocked up a fast 179 in just over 200 minutes.

Even the tail got into the act, with Syd Emery and Charlie Kelleway having an 86-run partnership – NSW finishing with 815.

Victoria made quite a good fist of batting – with Vernon Ransford becoming the first Victorian to score a century in each innings with 182 and 110, and Peter McAlister making 108 in the first innings and Warwick Armstrong 171 in the second. Victoria made 468 and 487.

Bert Hopkins: NSW all-rounder.

Monty Noble batted steadily for 69 not out in the NSW second innings, and they won by six wickets on the sixth day.

This wasn't the only large NSW total this season. Against SA in December, Noble hit up 213 and Bert Hopkins 218 (dropped on nought) in a total of 713.

Victoria finished last on the Shield table but would have finished equal on top with two wins with both NSW and SA had it won the match.

If only.

Huge school scores as bats hit out

Jimmy Prout made the world school-boy record score of 459, for Wesley College in Melbourne.

Sydney, March 19. Australia's younger batsman have shown some mighty form in school games in recent weeks.

The finals of the Sydney public schools' competition resulted in a win for Sydney Grammar with a record score of 916 against Shore's not inconsiderable 301 and miserable 96. Grammar won by an innings and 519.

For Shore, Claude Tozer, nephew of Australian all-rounder Dr Percie Charlton, knocked up 140. (Charlton also starred as a junior – taking seven wickets in a match against the 1887–88 touring England team.)

Tozer's effort was overshadowed by Eric Barbour of Grammar, who made 356 as an opener. Frank Farrer hit 229 in 210 minutes.

Grammar's big score eclipsed the 710 made the previous week in Melbourne by Wesley College in its win over Geelong College.

For Wesley Jimmy Prout made 459, a 'world record' for schoolboy cricket.

Darling hits out at administrators

Adelaide, Sep. 28. At the 'valedictory dinner' given to him by the SACA upon his retirement, former Australian captain and champion of players' rights, Joe Darling made a characteristically straight-talking, hard-hitting speech.

In it he remarked: 'During my cricket experience here in South Australia, this Association has shown more consideration for their players than any other Association in Australia.

'It has been a pleasure to play for the SACA and be treated with respect as players should be. We often asked for reasonable things and they were granted. If other Associations had treated the players so well we would not be seeing the problems that are now existing in NSW.'

The *Bulletin* replied on behalf of the slighted NSWCA which it said was hard up 'because it has treated the crowd Darling represents with lavish generosity' that is, the players. The players 'who have mostly been in revolt against it of late years, ought to get down on their marrowbones and worship it'.

The NSWCA, said the *Bulletin*, had done a great deal to foster the game in and around Sydney – with the result that 'Sydney turns out easily the biggest crowd of high class cricketers' in the land.

Or so says the *Bulletin*.

Noble leads Test turnaround

Noble leads Australia out at Lord's in the second Test, having won the toss and sent England in to bat.

Rebellion on tour team is quelled

AUSTRALIAN CRICKET TEAM, 1909
FIXTURES

DATE.	MATCH versus	PLAYED AT
May 6, 7, 8	Notts	Nottingham
" 10, 11, 12	Northants	Northampton
" 13, 14, 15*	Essex	Leyton
" 17, 18, 19	Surrey	Oval
" 20, 21, 22	M.C.C.	Lords
" 24, 25, 26	Oxford University	Oxford
" 27, 28, 29	**ENGLAND (First Test Match)**	Birmingham
June 31, 1, 2	Leicestershire	Leicester
" 3, 4, 5	Cambridge University	Cambridge
" 7, 8, 9	Hampshire	Southampton
" 10, 11, 12	Somerset	Bath
" 14, 15, 16	**ENGLAND (Second Test Match)**	Lords
" 17, 18, 19	Match to be arranged	Bradford
" 21, 22, 23	Yorkshire	Manchester
" 24, 25, 26	Lancashire and Yorkshire	Edinburgh
" 28, 29, 30	Scotland	Leeds
July 1, 2, 3	**ENGLAND (Third Test Match)**	
" 5, 6, 7	Warwickshire	Birmingham
" 8, 9, 10	Worcestershire	Worcester
" 12, 13, 14	Gloucestershire	Bristol
" 15, 16, 17	Surrey	Oval
" 19, 20, 21	Yorkshire	Sheffield
" 22, 23, 24	Derbyshire	Derby
" 26, 27, 28	**ENGLAND (Fourth Test Match)**	Manchester
" 29, 30, 31	Yorkshire and Lancashire	Hull
Aug. 2, 3, 4	South Wales	Cardiff
" 5, 6, 7	Lancashire	Liverpool
" 9, 10, 11	**ENGLAND (Fifth Test Match)**	Oval
" 12, 13, 14	West of England	Exeter
" 16, 17, 18	Gloucestershire	Cheltenham
" 19, 20, 21	Kent	Canterbury
" 23, 24, 25	Middlesex	Lords
" 26, 27, 28	Sussex	Brighton
" 30, 31, 1	M.C.C.	Lords
Sept. 2, 3, 4	Essex	Leyton
" 6, 7, 8	England XI.	Uttoxeter
" 9, 10, 11	England XI.	Scarborough
" 13, 14, 15	South of England	Hastings

R. F. STEEL, DEL., "THE BLOCK," MELBOURNE.

The 1909 Australian fixtures.

London, April 1. The appointment by the Board of Control of Peter McAlister as vice-captain to Monty Noble for the 1909 tour, despite his poor Test record, in addition to the position of treasurer with the job of supervising the players' chosen manager, Frank Laver, has been cause for unhappiness in the 1909 Australian team.

The players and captain Monty Noble felt that they were being spied upon by the Board.

Noble called for a player vote on the captaincy on arrival in London to confirm his position.

The players responded by electing him and not allowing McAlister to function as vice-captain.

As this was the first tour under the Board's control, many aspects of the tour were different and not altogether satisfactory from the players' point of view.

Play is undertaken six days a week, players are roomed together on an arbitrary basis, and the Board had refused cash advances for players' kit before the start of the tour.

Worst of all was having McAlister delegated to oversee the finances – he was regarded as a 'Board man', not a 'player's man'.

Nevertheless Noble, one of the finest captains Australia has had, has been able to bind a team of 16, including eight on their first tour of England, into a formidable if underrated team.

Leeds, July 3. Australia, and in particular its captain Monty Noble, have retained a hand on the Ashes urn after a second victory in the Test series.

The win by 126 runs at Headingley follows the nine-wicket win at Lord's last month.

What the *Times* took to calling Australia's 'feeble' batting after the initial capitulation to Hirst and Blythe on a wet wicket at Edgbaston showed what it was made of at Lord's where Vernon Ransford made 143 not out.

The *Times* might consider what adjective to use for an England batting line-up which when sent in by Noble at Lord's only managed 269, and scored even fewer in the second innings when confronted by Warwick Armstrong's seemingly mysterious deliveries. He took 6/35 and England only managed 121.

Australia's batting may not have been as powerful as it has been – Victor Trumper has not yet been as glorious as he can be – but it has been far more effective than England's.

And then there is Monty Noble, in charge of a more settled team.

Noble's astute captaincy may be measured by the manner in which he studies opposing batsmen's techniques and favoured strokes and tailors the bowler for them in the conditions.

His manipulation of bowlers, Frank Laver, Bill Whitty, Bert Hopkins and, in particular Charlie Macartney, has lifted them to another level.

Noble said to him in the first England innings of the second Test: 'You go on and get them out and I'll bowl at the other end to keep the runs down.'

Macartney took 7/58 and Noble 0/22 from 13 overs. England was all out for 119.

He and wicketkeeper Hanson Carter have a great understanding about field placements.

When Macartney was seen chatting to a girl on the third-man boundary, Noble shifted him into the slips. As a result of such discipline, the Australian fielding has been on a higher level than has England's.

QUICK SINGLES

The 'Kachaball' machine. A new cricket fielding machine is now in use in England. Hailed as a valuable adjunct to all cricket grounds, it assists in the aim of attaining smart and reliable fielding.

Trumper AWOL. Victor Trumper was out at stumps one day during the match against Hampshire, and next morning went for a stroll on the Southampton docks, and spent the morning aboard the White Star liner *Adriatic*. Unfortunately Australia was all out, caught on a sticky and several Hampshire wickets had fallen before Vic's return. Next day the whole team toured the ship.

Lob bowler. Australia just managed to beat Worcestershire in its opening match, despite a six-wicket haul by G. H. Simpson-Hayward. He is one of the last English county bowlers who employs the lob ball as his main delivery.

Hopkins to the rescue. Facing the ignominy of defeat by Archie MacLaren's understrength Lancashire, Bert Hopkins took 6/15 in the Lancastrians second innings to give Australia a win by 47 runs.

Trumper's ton. Victor Trumper showed a welcome return to his old style and form with a brilliant 113 against Derbyshire in July. Australia won by ten wickets.

Imperial conference. Peter McAlister joined Dr Leslie Poidevin, the former NSW player, at a meeting with England and South African representatives at Lord's in July as the official Australian delegation to what then became known as the Imperial Cricket Conference.

Crawford recruited. Victor Trumper helped SA recruit champion Surrey all rounder Jack Crawford to play for the state and become resident master at St Peter's College at a salary of £160.

Poidevin's pointers. Dr Leslie Poidevin says: 'The English boys are over-coached

… too much attention to style … After all, you play the game to make runs not strokes … The English fielding in the fifth Test was not up to the standard of the Irish tourists in Toronto!'

Ceylon capers. An Australian party led by Monty Noble arrived in Colombo in late October, and played an entertaining draw.

Noble creed: Australian captain Monty Noble has impressed critics with his leadership. He has retained great control of his players, used his bowlers shrewdly and has worked out his tactics carefully. He says: Reputation is wat other people believe you to be; character is what you know yourself to be.

Ceylon complaint. Peter McAlister, leading a second Australian contingent home, lost a match in Ceylon. The Australian party was the subject of a letter of complaint from the Ceylon cricket authorities, apparently over their behaviour.

A happy ending to series

The victorious 1909 Australian team on a motoring tour of Scotland.

The Oval, Aug. 11. Australia has retained the Ashes with a draw in the fifth Test, taking the series 2–1.

The fourth Test at Old Trafford was notable for the unprecedented bowling of Frank Laver, who took the best bag by a visiting player in a Test in England 18.2 overs, seven maidens, 8/31.

Laver bowled his medium pacers with extreme accuracy and 'puzzling flight.' The match petered out to a draw, but Australia had already retained the Ashes.

Monty Noble won his fifth toss in a row (equalling F. S. Jackson's feat in 1905). The wicket was good.

Although Australia made 325 thanks to left hander Warren Bardsley's 136, England scored 352. Australia made light of this deficit thanks to another 130 from Bardsley, and quick runs from Sid Gregory and Noble.

A declaration at 5/339 had England on the back foot.

Warren Bardsley became the first batsman to score a century in each innings of a Test match.

England's eccentric selection and captaincy procedures should not outweigh Monty Noble's moulding of an effective and efficient Australian team.

Frank Laver gets a 'please explain'

Sydney, Nov. 30. Frank Laver, manager of the 1909 Australians, has been asked to show his books of account to the Board of Control.

The Board was interested in discovering how much money the players 'really' made above and beyond what was 'declared'.

Laver replied that Peter McAlister was the treasurer of the tour, and that any books he, Laver, had kept were purely personal mementos. He was happy to answer any Board questions.

For his part McAlister said he had not kept any books because Laver had refused him information.

It is unlikely that the situation of a player elected manager and a Board appointed treasurer will arise again.

The tour grossed £13,228, of which the Board retained £1003. After expenses £7359 was divided between 16 players, about £450 each.

Former East Melbourne team-mates and now bitter adversaries: Frank Laver and Peter McAlister.

FIRST TEST 1909 ENGLAND v AUSTRALIA
Edgbaston, Birmingham. May 27, 28, 29, 1909.
Toss: Australia. England won by 10 wkts.

AUSTRALIA

A Cotter c Hirst b Blythe	2 (9)	c Tyldesley b Hirst 15
W Bardsley c MacLaren b Hirst	2 (6)	c Thompson b Blythe 6
WW Armstrong b Hirst	24 (7)	c Jessop b Blythe 0
VT Trumper c Hirst b Blythe	10 (5)	c Rhodes b Hirst 1
MA Noble (c) c Jessop b Blythe	15 (1)	c Jones b Hirst 11
ES Gregory c Rhodes b Blythe	0 (3)	c Thompson b Blythe 43
VS Ransford b Hirst	1 (4)	b Blythe 43
CG Macartney c MacLaren b Blythe	10 (2)	lbw Blythe 1
H Carter (+) lbw Hirst	0 (8)	c Hobbs b Hirst 1
JDA O'Connor lbw Blythe	8	c Lilley b Hirst 13
WJ Whitty not out	0	not out 9
EXTRAS (LB 1, NB 1)	2	(B 7, LB 1) 8
TOTAL	74	151

FOW 1st Inns: 5 7 30 46 47 52 58 59 71 74
FOW 2nd Inns: 4 16 97 99 103 103 106 123 125 151

Bowling: *First Innings*: Hirst 23-8-28-4, Blythe 23-6-44-6. *Second Innings*: Hirst 23.5-4-58-5, Blythe 24-3-58-5, Thompson 4-0-19-0, Rhodes 1-0-8-0.

ENGLAND

AC MacLaren (c) b Macartney	5	
JB Hobbs lbw Macartney	0 (1)	not out 62
JT Tyldesley b O'Connor	24	
CB Fry b Macartney	0 (2)	not out 35
AO Jones c Carter b Armstrong	28	
GH Hirst lbw Armstrong	15	
GL Jessop b Armstrong	22	
W Rhodes not out	15	
AFA Lilley (+) c Ransford b Armstrong	0	
GJ Thompson run out	6	
C Blythe c Macartney b Armstrong	1	
EXTRAS (B 4, LB 1)	5	(B 5, LB 3) 8
TOTAL	121	0 for 105

FOW 1st Inns: 0 13 13 61 61 90 103 107 116 121
FOW 2nd Inns:

Bowling: *First Innings*: Whitty 17-5-43-0, Macartney 17-6-21-3, Noble 1-0-2-0, O'Connor 5-2-23-1, Armstrong 15.3-7-27-5. *Second Innings*: Whitty 5-1-18-0, Macartney 11-2-35-0, O'Connor 3.2-1-17-0, Armstrong 13-5-27-0.

Umpires: J Carlin & F Parris

SECOND TEST 1909 ENGLAND v AUSTRALIA
Lord's Cricket Ground, London. June 14, 15, 16, 1909.
Toss: Australia. Australia won by 9 wkts.

ENGLAND

TW Hayward st Carter b Laver	16	run out 6
JB Hobbs c Carter b Laver	19	c & b Armstrong 9
JT Tyldesley lbw Laver	46	st Carter b Armstrong 3
G Gunn lbw Cotter	1	b Armstrong 0
JH King c Macartney b Cotter	60	b Armstrong 4
AC MacLaren (c) c Armstrong b Noble	7 (8)	b Noble 24
GH Hirst b Cotter	31	b Armstrong 1
AO Jones b Cotter	8 (6)	lbw Laver 26
AE Relf c Armstrong b Noble	17 (10)	b Armstrong 3
AFA Lilley (+) c Bardsley b Noble	47 (9)	not out 25
S Haigh not out	1	run out 5
EXTRAS (B 8, LB 3, W 3, NB 2)	16	(B 2, LB 3, NB 10) 15
TOTAL	269	121

FOW 1st Inns: 23 41 44 123 149 175 199 205 258 269
FOW 2nd Inns: 16 22 22 23 34 41 82 90 101 121

Bowling: *First Innings*: Laver 32-9-75-3, Macartney 8-3-10-0, Cotter 23-1-80-4, Noble 24.2-9-42-3, Armstrong 20-6-46-0. *Second Innings*: Laver 13-4-24-1, Cotter 18-3-35-0, Noble 5-1-12-1, Armstrong 24.5-11-35-6.

AUSTRALIA

PA McAlister lbw King	22	not out 19
F Laver b Hirst	14	
W Bardsley b Relf	46 (2)	c Lilley b Relf 0
WW Armstrong c Lilley b Relf	12	
VS Ransford not out	143	
VT Trumper c MacLaren b Relf	28	
MA Noble (c) c Lilley b Relf	32	
ES Gregory c Lilley b Relf	14 (3)	not out 18
A Cotter run out	0	
CG Macartney b Hirst	5	
H Carter (+) b Hirst	7	
EXTRAS (B 16, LB 8, W 1, NB 2)	27	(B 4) 4
TOTAL	350	1 for 41

FOW 1st Inns: 18 84 90 119 198 269 317 317 342 350
FOW 2nd Inns: 4

Bowling: *First Innings*: Hirst 26.5-2-83-3, King 27-5-99-1, Relf 45-14-85-5, Haigh 19-5-41-0, Jones 2-0-15-0. *Second Innings*: Hirst 8-1-28-0, Relf 7.4-4-9-1.

Umpires: CE Dench & J Moss

THIRD TEST 1909 ENGLAND v AUSTRALIA
Headingley, Leeds. July 1, 2, 3, 1909.
Toss: Australia. Australia won by 126 runs.

AUSTRALIA

PA McAlister lbw Hirst	3	c Sharp b Barnes	5
ES Gregory b Barnes	46	b Hirst	0
VS Ransford run out	45	lbw Barnes	24
MA Noble (c) b Hirst	3 (5)	c Rhodes b Barnes	31
W Bardsley hit wicket b Rhodes	30 (7)	c Lilley b Barnes	2
WW Armstrong c Lilley b Brearley	21 (4)	b Rhodes	45
VT Trumper not out	27 (6)	b Barnes	2
CG Macartney c Fry b Rhodes	4	b Brearley	18
A Cotter b Rhodes	2	c MacLaren b Rhodes	19
H Carter (+) lbw Rhodes	1	c Lilley b Barnes	30
F Laver c Lilley b Brearley	0	not out	13
EXTRAS (LB 4, W 1, NB 1)	6	(B 15, LB 2, NB 1)	18
TOTAL	188		207

FOW 1st Inns: 6 86 100 104 140 154 167 169 171 188
FOW 2nd Inns: 0 14 52 118 122 126 127 150 183 207

Bowling: *First Innings:* Hirst 26-6-65-2, Barnes 25-12-37-1, Brearley 14.1-1-42-2, Rhodes 8-2-38-4. *Second Innings:* Hirst 17-3-39-1, Barnes 35-16-63-6, Brearley 24.1-6-36-1, Rhodes 19-3-44-2, Sharp 1-0-7-0.

ENGLAND

CB Fry lbw Cotter	1	b Cotter	7
JB Hobbs b Macartney	12	b Cotter	30
JT Tyldesley c Armstrong b Macartney	55	c & b Macartney	7
J Sharp st Carter b Macartney	61	b Cotter	11
AC MacLaren (c) b Macartney	17	c Cotter b Macartney	1
W Rhodes c Carter b Laver	12	c Armstrong b Macartney	16
GH Hirst b Macartney	4 (8)	b Cotter	0
AFA Lilley (+) not out	4 (7)	lbw Cotter	2
SF Barnes b Macartney	1	b Macartney	1
W Brearley b Macartney	6	not out	4
GL Jessop			
EXTRAS (B 1, LB 4, NB 4)	9	(B 1, LB 1, W 1, NB 5)	8
TOTAL	9 for 182		9 for 87

FOW 1st Inns: 8 31 137 146 157 169 171 174 182
FOW 2nd Inns: 17 26 60 61 61 82 82 82 87

Bowling: *First Innings:* Cotter 17-1-45-1, Macartney 25.3-6-58-7, Armstrong 16-5-33-0, Laver 13-4-15-1, Noble 13-5-22-0. *Second Innings:* Cotter 16-2-38-5, Macartney 16.5-5-27-4, Armstrong 3-1-8-0, Laver 2-0-6-0.

Umpires: W Richards & WAJ West

FIFTH TEST 1909 ENGLAND v AUSTRALIA
Kennington Oval, London. August 9, 10, 11, 1909.
Toss: Australia. Match Drawn.

AUSTRALIA

ES Gregory b Carr	1	run out	74
W Bardsley b Sharp	136	lbw Barnes	130
MA Noble (c) lbw Carr	2	c MacLaren b Barnes	55
WW Armstrong lbw Carr	15	c Woolley b Carr	10
VS Ransford b Carr	3	not out	36
VT Trumper c Rhodes b Barnes	73	st Lilley b Carr	20
CG Macartney c Rhodes b Sharp	50	not out	4
AJY Hopkins c Rhodes b Sharp	21		
A Cotter b Carr	7		
H Carter (+) lbw Carr	4		
F Laver not out	8		
EXTRAS (B 1, LB 3, NB 1)	5	(B 4, LB 3, W 1, NB 2)	10
TOTAL	325		5 dec 339

FOW 1st Inns: 9 27 55 58 176 259 289 300 304 325
FOW 2nd Inns: 180 267 268 294 335

Bowling: *First Innings:* Carr 34-2-146-5, Barnes 19-3-57-2, Sharp 16.3-3-67-3, Woolley 4-1-6-0, Hayes 4-0-10-0, Rhodes 12-3-34-0. *Second Innings:* Carr 35-1-136-2, Barnes 27-7-61-2, Sharp 12-0-34-0, Woolley 6-0-31-0, Hayes 2-0-14-0, Rhodes 14-1-35-0, Hutchings 4-0-18-0.

ENGLAND

RH Spooner b Cotter	13	c & b Macartney	3
AC MacLaren (c) lbw Cotter	15	st Carter b Armstrong	54
W Rhodes c Carter b Cotter	66 (2)	not out	35
CB Fry run out	62	not out	0
J Sharp c Gregory b Hopkins	105		
FE Woolley b Cotter	8		
EG Hayes lbw Armstrong	4 (3)	c (S)RJ Hartigan b Armstrong	9
KL Hutchings c Macartney b Cotter	59		
AFA Lilley (+) not out	2		
SF Barnes c Carter b Hopkins	0		
DW Carr b Cotter	0		
EXTRAS (B 8, LB 4, NB 6)	18	(LB 2, NB 1)	3
TOTAL	352		3 for 104

FOW 1st Inns: 15 36 140 187 201 206 348 348 351 352
FOW 2nd Inns: 14 27 88

Bowling: *First Innings:* Cotter 27.4-1-95-6, Armstrong 31-7-93-1, Laver 8-1-13-0, Macartney 16-2-49-0, Hopkins 15-2-51-2, Noble 8-1-29-0, Gregory 1-0-4-0. *Second Innings:* Cotter 8-1-21-0, Armstrong 7-4-8-2, Macartney 8-2-11-1, Hopkins 8-0-40-0, Gregory 2-0-21-0.

Umpires: J Moss & W Richards

FOURTH TEST 1909 ENGLAND v AUSTRALIA
Old Trafford, Manchester. July 26, 27, 28, 1909.
Toss: Australia. Match Drawn.

AUSTRALIA

ES Gregory b Blythe	21	b Hirst	5
W Bardsley b Barnes	9	c MacLaren b Blythe	35
VS Ransford lbw Barnes	4 (7)	not out	54
MA Noble (c) b Blythe	17	b Blythe	13
VT Trumper c Hutchings b Barnes	2 (6)	c Tyldesley b Rhodes	48
WW Armstrong not out	32 (5)	lbw Rhodes	30
AJY Hopkins b Blythe	3 (8)	c Barnes b Rhodes	9
CG Macartney b Barnes	5 (3)	b Rhodes	51
A Cotter c Tyldesley b Blythe	17	c MacLaren b Rhodes	4
H Carter (+) lbw Barnes	13	lbw Barnes	12
F Laver b Blythe	11		
EXTRAS (B 6, LB 7)	13	(B 9, LB 8, NB 1)	18
TOTAL	147		9 dec 279

FOW 1st Inns: 13 21 45 48 58 66 86 110 128 147
FOW 2nd Inns: 16 77 106 126 148 237 256 262 279

Bowling: *First Innings:* Hirst 7-0-15-0, Barnes 27-9-56-5, Blythe 20.3-5-63-5. *Second Innings:* Hirst 12-3-32-1, Barnes 22.3-5-66-1, Blythe 24-5-77-2, Sharp 1-0-3-0, Rhodes 25-0-83-5.

ENGLAND

PF Warner b Macartney	9	b Hopkins	25
RH Spooner c & b Cotter	25	b Laver	58
JT Tyldesley c Armstrong b Laver	15	b Hopkins	11
J Sharp c Armstrong b Laver	3	not out	8
W Rhodes c Carter b Laver	5	not out	0
KL Hutchings b Laver	9		
AC MacLaren (c) lbw Laver	16		
AFA Lilley (+) not out	26		
GH Hirst c Hopkins b Laver	1		
SF Barnes b Laver	0		
C Blythe b Laver	1		
EXTRAS (B 2, LB 3, NB 4)	9	(B 2, LB 4)	6
TOTAL	119		3 for 108

FOW 1st Inns: 24 39 44 50 63 72 99 103 103 119
FOW 2nd Inns: 78 90 102

Bowling: *First Innings:* Noble 8-2-11-0, Macartney 18-6-31-0, Laver 18.2-7-31-8, Cotter 8-1-37-1. *Second Innings:* Macartney 7-2-16-0, Laver 21-12-25-1, Cotter 5-0-14-0, Armstrong 10-6-16-0, Hopkins 12-4-31-2.

Umpires: W Richards & WAJ West

Australian Averages

1909 ENGLAND v AUSTRALIA

AUSTRALIA	M	Inn	NO	Runs	H.S	Avrge	Ct	St	Overs	Mds	Runs	Wkt	Avrge
Armstrong, WW	5	9	1	189	45	23.63	7	-	140.2	52	293	14	20.93
Bardsley, W	5	10	-	396	136	39.60	1	-	-	-	-	-	-
Carter, H	5	8	-	68	30	8.50	6	4	-	-	-	-	-
Cotter, A	5	8	-	66	19	8.25	2	-	122.4	10	365	17	21.47
Gregory, ES	5	10	1	222	74	24.67	1	-	3.0	-	25	-	-
Hopkins, AJY	2	3	-	33	21	11.00	-	-	35.0	6	122	4	30.50
Laver, F	4	5	2	46	14	15.33	-	-	107.2	37	189	14	13.50
Macartney, CG	5	9	1	148	51	18.50	5	-	127.2	34	258	16	16.13
McAlister, PA	2	4	1	49	22	16.33	-	-	-	-	-	-	-
Noble, MA	5	9	-	179	55	19.89	4	-	59.2	18	118	4	29.50
O'Connor, JDA	1	2	-	21	13	10.50	-	-	8.2	3	40	1	40.00
Ransford, VS	5	9	3	353	143*	58.83	1	-	-	-	-	-	-
Trumper, VT	5	9	1	211	73	26.38	-	-	-	-	-	-	-
Whitty, WJ	1	2	2	9	9*	-	-	-	22.0	6	61	-	-

English Averages

1909 ENGLAND v AUSTRALIA

ENGLAND	M	Inn	NO	Runs	H.S	Avrge	Ct	St	Overs	Mds	Runs	Wkt	Avrge
Barnes, SF	3	4	-	2	1	0.50	1	-	155.3	52	340	17	20.00
Blythe, C	2	2	-	2	1	1.00	-	-	91.3	19	242	18	13.44
Brearley, W	1	2	1	10	6	10.00	-	-	38.2	7	78	3	26.00
Carr, DW	1	1	-	0	0	0.00	-	-	69.0	3	282	7	40.29
Fry, CB	3	6	2	140	62	35.00	1	-	-	-	-	-	-
Gunn, G	1	2	-	1	1	0.50	-	-	-	-	-	-	-
Haigh, S	1	2	1	6	5	6.00	-	-	19.0	5	41	-	-
Hayes, EG	1	2	-	13	9	6.50	-	-	6.0	-	24	-	-
Hayward, TW	1	2	-	22	16	11.00	-	-	-	-	-	-	-
Hirst, GH	4	6	-	52	31	8.67	2	-	143.4	27	348	16	21.75
Hobbs, JB	3	6	1	132	62*	26.40	1	-	-	-	-	-	-
Hutchings, KL	2	2	-	68	59	34.00	1	-	4.0	-	18	-	-
Jessop, GL	2	1	-	22	22	22.00	2	-	-	-	-	-	-
Jones, AO	2	3	-	62	28	20.67	1	-	2.0	-	15	-	-
King, JH	1	2	-	64	60	32.00	-	-	27.0	5	99	1	99.00
Lilley, AFA	5	7	4	106	47	35.33	9	1	-	-	-	-	-
MacLaren, AC	5	7	-	85	24	12.14	7	-	-	-	-	-	-
Relf, AE	1	2	-	20	17	10.00	-	-	52.4	18	94	6	15.67
Rhodes, W	5	7	2	168	66	33.60	6	-	79.0	9	242	11	22.00
Sharp, J	3	6	-	188	105	47.00	3	-	30.3	3	111	3	37.00
Spooner, RH	2	4	-	99	58	24.75	-	-	-	-	-	-	-
Thompson, GJ	1	1	-	6	6	6.00	2	-	4.0	-	19	-	-
Tyldesley, JT	4	7	-	161	55	23.00	-	-	-	-	-	-	-
Warner, PF	1	2	-	34	25	17.00	-	-	-	-	-	-	-
Woolley, FE	1	1	-	8	8	8.00	1	-	10.0	1	37	-	-

On Tour With Frank Laver

Frank Laver was a man of many talents, which were in evidence on the 1909 Australian tour of England. He was the elected player-manager of the team, he took 8/31 in the fourth Test. He had made 341 for East Melbourne in 1902–03 and 143 for Australia against Somerset on his first tour in 1899. He was also a talented photographer and journalist writing for the *Sporting and Dramatic News* (London) and publishing *An Australian Cricketer on Tour*, an account of the 1899 and 1905 trips. These are his photographs from albums presented by his family to the MCC Museum.

The SS Orontes *with the Australian team on board is given a rousing farewell in Melbourne.*
Jack O'Connor rides in a dog cart during a visit to Brighton, around the time of the match against Sussex in August 1909 (right).

The Australians stopped at Naples on the way to England. They are pictured examining the excavated ruins of the ancient city of Pompeii.

Cricket wasn't the only sport for spectators. The Henley Royal Regatta in July was just as popular as the Lord's Test match.

Cricket is never far away, as Syd Gregory bowls one up in a London Park.

The Pavilion at Lord's, probably after Australia had won the match, the winning runs, astonishingly, struck by Peter McAlister.

The 'Australian Visitors' Stand' at Old Trafford during the fourth Test – scene of Laver's great bowling feat of 8/31.

The Australians on a boat trip in Scotland, where they 'holidayed' after the second Test. In a match in Glasgow a Scotsman put a ball through Vernon Ransford's defence and said: 'That was a bonny wee ba.'

1909–10

AUSTRALIAN DOMESTIC

Ill-will drives Noble out of game

Sydney, Jan. 13. Monty Noble, the Australian captain, has written to the Board of Control:

'The exigencies of my business demand that close personal attention be given it. It is with the greatest regret, therefore, that I am compelled to retire from first class cricket and sever connections with a game in which I have been so keenly interested.'

Behind this facade lay Noble's deep unhappiness with the way he and the players had been treated by the Board, especially in the connection between Peter McAlister and the Board and the 1909 tour.

Noble, as captain of Australia was understandably aggrieved at being second-guessed and reported on by McAlister to the Board.

At 37 Noble has 'done it all' anyway. He is regarded as the greatest all-rounder Australia has so far produced.

He has scored 1997 runs including a Test century – 133 at the SCG in 1903–04. His 121 Test wickets included 7/17 and 6/60 at the MCG in 1901–02.

Noble led Australia to victory over England both at home in 1907–08 (4–1) and on tour in 1909 (2–1). In all, as skipper, he won 8 Tests out of 15.

Noble played 42 Test matches between 1897 and 1909 taking 6/49 against England on his debut, at the MCG.

In the Sheffield Shield, Noble has played 51 matches, made 4896 runs and taken 158 wickets.

The dream: 'Hope of the side'

SA revives to win Shield

SA import Jack Crawford.

Patient Charlie Kelleway.

Sydney, Jan. 11. Solly Hill, the fifth of the Hill brothers to play for South Australia, has made 62 in a partnership with English import Jack Crawford (73 not out) to win the final Sheffield Shield game against NSW by seven wickets.

The win gave SA its second Sheffield Shield win and the first for 15 years, going a long way to justifying Crawford's acquisition

This is Solly Hill's first season in Shield cricket.

Brother Clem had to go home to Adelaide after last week's game against Victoria where his 185 and 43 (and Solly's 58) were not enough to prevent an exciting win by Victoria, their first and only win for the season.

NSW lacked Victor Trumper who was ill, and were bundled out for 92, Bill Whitty taking 5/43. South Australia replied with a modest 207, Edgar Mayne making 61.

NSW's second innings of 289 included 108 from Charlie Kelleway.

Former Surrey champion Jack Crawford has proved his worth to SA by taking 7/92 in this innings, followed by his 73 not out.

South Australia beat Victoria by an innings and 209 runs in the first encounter, Clem Hill 176, and NSW by an innings and 4 runs, Clem Hill 205 in December.

Crawford earned his keep in this, his first match, with 6/59 in the NSW second innings.

Armstrong leads tour of NZ

Wellington, March 1. Warwick Armstrong's Australian representative team has met with unexpected resistance in its short tour of New Zealand.

After winning two matches Australia was outplayed by Canterbury in Christchurch.

The first unofficial 'Test 'was also played in Christchurch, but Armstrong sent in the New Zealanders on a damp pitch, batted when it was playing well, and then bowled after it had rained in the NZ second innings.

Australia won by nine wickets.

The second unofficial 'Test' was won by Australia by 162 runs, mostly as a result of excellent bowling from Bill Whitty 6/28 in the second innings and the Tasmanian newcomer Ashley Facy's 7/71 in the first innings.

The reality: 'Out first ball.'

South Africa fight back to win first Test

South Africans bring new interest

Adelaide, Nov. 1. The South African team has arrived, the first team not from England to play a Test match series in Australia.

Though relatively unknown, the South Africans promise a new kind of cricket excitement to Australians, as their bowling attack is composed almost entirely of 'googlers' or exponents of the new art of the 'bosie'.

They are leg-break over-the-wrist bowlers with the ability to bowl the one that comes back the other way.

A. E. (Ernie) Vogler has a variety of deliveries and took 10 wickets in an innings in a South African first class match

R. O. (Reggie) Schwarz only bowls the googly, a slow flighted delivery that zips and bounces off the pitch.

Aubrey Faulkner bowls his leg-breaks and bosies at close to a medium pace, has a deceptive yorker and is also a hard hitting batsman

Last of the quartet is Charles 'Buck' Llewellyn, distinguished by being a left-arm bowler who played very well for South Africa against Australia in 1902–03.

How well can the bowlers do on turf wickets having been brought up on 'the mat'?

The incomparable Victor Trumper square drives for his hundredth run at the Melbourne Cricket Ground during the second Test.

Adelaide, Jan. 13. In a run-feast on a benign Adelaide pitch, South Africa held their nerve to score their first Test win against Australia, dismissing the locals for 339 in the second innings to win by 38 runs.

The 1646 runs scored is now the highest aggregate in Test cricket.

After the second Test, which the South Africans lost from a winning position, this win is very heartening as it flows from the attacking bats of the team, not the mysteries of their bowling.

The form of Aubrey Faulkner has been nothing short of a sensation – his scores so far of 62, 43, 204, 8, 56 and 115 show him to be a batsman of world class. Indeed the 204

at Melbourne stands comparison with the innings of the nonpareil Victor Trumper.

Trumper's 159 in Melbourne and 214 in Adelaide were diamonds – flawless and brilliant.

Cricket recorded: 'Probably Trumper has never played a better innings than his 214 not out, which is almost the equivalent of saying probably no better innings has ever been played.'

Clem Hill hit up 191 and Warren Bardsley 132 on the first day in the first Test in Sydney which must have seemed extremely ominous for the South Africans. Australia was 6/494 at stumps. Then, when Tibby Cotter took 6/96 and Bill Whitty 4/33, things must have

looked even more dark.

Whitty's swing was responsible for the destruction of the 'Afrikanders' in the second Test in Melbourne.

Australia had made 348, South Africa replied with 506 thanks to Faulkner's 204, and when Australia was all out for 327 (despite Trumper) the South Africans needed only 170 to win.

Whitty (with help from Cotter 4/47) bowled them out for 80.

His 6/17 from 16 overs was the most sensational spell in recent Australian cricket, except for Monty Noble's 7/17 in 1901–02.

Australia leads the series 2–1. The last two Tests in Melbourne and Sydney now hold more interest.

Aubrey Faulkner, South Africa.

Bowlers were out-googlied

Sydney, March 7. Australia has unleashed its own googly exponent Dr Herbert (Ranji) Hordern in the fourth Test to good effect (8/105 for the match) and while he spun his web once again in the fifth Test, it was not quite as mysterious as it was in the fourth. In the final Test match he took 6/190.

But this is better than the South African trio (Ernie Vogler has not played since the first Test). While they have all been successful in other matches, in the Tests their length and line have been found wanting.

Reggie Schwarz's 6/46 in the fifth Test is the only outstanding analysis.

The lack of a fast bowler of Bill Whitty's calibre has proved a major problem for the South Africans. Whitty's series tally of 37 wickets at 17.08 sets a high standard for all other bowlers.

While Victor Trumper takes the biscuit for the Tests with 661 runs at 94.43, his best ever, Aubrey Faulkner has done very well with the bat for South Africa making 732 runs at 73.2

The tale of the two final Tests is told by those figures, added to which Clem Hill and Warwick Armstrong made centuries in the fourth Test and Vernon Ransford 95. Charlie Macartney chimed in with 137 in the fifth Test at Sydney.

Australia's scores of 328, 578, 364 and 3/198 indicate how much the South African bowling lacked penetration.

But as they are generally 'Saturday afternoon cricketers' at home, not playing as frequently at so high a standard as the Australian

Warren Bardsley, 94 in fifth Test.

players, they have performed more than creditably.

Australia, however, clinched the series, winning by 530 runs in Melbourne and by seven wickets in Sydney.

The visitors played 22 first class matches, winning 12 and losing seven including four Tests.

213,603 people watched the Tests – a very large total – but the receipts of £8891 do not cover the £10,000 guaranteed to the tourists. The State associations will have to make up the difference.

Billy Murdoch dies during Test

MCG, Feb. 18. Felix of the *Australasian* was present at the MCG on the second day of the fourth Test against South Africa when former Australian captain and the best batsman of his era, W. L. (Billy) Murdoch collapsed and died, aged 57.

At luncheon in the MCC committee room he put his hand to his forehead and was asked by his neighbour Major Morkham 'What's the matter?'

Murdoch replied 'Neuralgia, I think. I have a pain here.'

These were the last words uttered by the grand old champion. He sank back unconscious. The end came at Dr Moore's Private Hospital at about five o'clock.

A turkey dinner to celebrate Gordon's win in 1910–11 Sydney First Grade Premiership.

FIRST TEST 1910–11 AUSTRALIA v SOUTH AFRICA
Sydney Cricket Ground, Sydney. December 9, 10, 12 (no play), 13, 14, 1910.
Toss: Australia. Australia won by an innings & 114 runs.

AUSTRALIA

VT Trumper run out	27
W Bardsley b Pearse	132
C Hill (c) b Pearse	191
DRA Gehrs b Pearse	67
WW Armstrong b Schwarz	48
VS Ransford b Schwarz	11
CG Macartney b Schwarz	1
C Kelleway not out	14
H Carter (+) st Sherwell b Schwarz	5
A Cotter st Sherwell b Schwarz	0
WJ Whitty c Snooke b Sinclair	15
EXTRAS (B 12, LB 4, NB 1)	17
TOTAL	528

FOW 1st Inns: 52 276 420 427 445 453 499 511 511 528
Bowling: *First Innings*: Llewellyn 14-0-54-0, Sinclair 19.4-0-80-1, Schwarz 25-6-102-5, Vogler 15-0-87-0, Faulkner 12-0-71-0, Nourse 12-0-61-0, Pearse 12-0-56-3.

SOUTH AFRICA

LA Stricker b Cotter	2	(7)	lbw Whitty	4
JW Zulch b Cotter	4	(4)	run out	1
COC Pearse c Trumper b Cotter	16	(10)	run out	31
AW Nourse c Kelleway b Cotter	5	(6)	not out	64
GA Faulkner c Kelleway b Whitty	62		c Bardsley b Whitty	43
CB Llewellyn b Cotter	0	(8)	c Macartney b Whitty	19
SJ Snooke b Whitty	3	(3)	b Cotter	4
JH Sinclair b Cotter	1	(2)	b Cotter	6
RO Schwarz c Trumper b Whitty	61		c Carter b Whitty	0
PW Sherwell (c+) not out	8	(1)	c Whitty b Kelleway	60
AEE Vogler b Whitty	0		b Kelleway	0
EXTRAS (LB 7, NB 5)	12		(LB 1, NB 7)	8
TOTAL	174			240

FOW 1st Inns: 5 10 29 38 38 44 49 149 174 174
FOW 2nd Inns: 24 28 44 98 124 144 183 185 237 240

Bowling: *First Innings*: Cotter 20-2-69-6, Whitty 24-11-33-4, Armstrong 8-3-16-0, Kelleway 9-1-33-0, Macartney 7-4-11-0. *Second Innings*: Whitty 21-4-75-4, Macartney 5-1-12-0, Cotter 17-2-73-2, Armstrong 9-1-35-0, Kelleway 15.1-4-37-2.

Umpires: RM Crockett & WG Curran

SECOND TEST 1910–11 AUSTRALIA v SOUTH AFRICA
Melbourne Cricket Ground, Melbourne. December 31, 1910, January 2, 3, 4, 1911.
Toss: Australia. Australia won by 89 runs.

AUSTRALIA

VT Trumper b Pegler	34		b Faulkner	159
W Bardsley c Snooke b Sinclair	85		st Sherwell b Schwarz	14
C Hill (c) b Llewellyn	39		b Schwarz	0
DRA Gehrs b Llewellyn	4		st Sherwell b Schwarz	22
CG Macartney run out	7		c Snooke b Llewellyn	5
VS Ransford run out	58		c Sinclair b Schwarz	23
WW Armstrong c Sherwell b Faulkner	75	(8)	b Llewellyn	29
C Kelleway c Faulkner b Stricker	18	(7)	b Pegler	48
H Carter (+) not out	15		c Sherwell b Llewellyn	0
A Cotter c Stricker b Schwarz	3		c (S)JMM Commaille b Llewellyn	15
WJ Whitty c Nourse b Faulkner	6		not out	5
EXTRAS (LB 3, NB 1)	4		(LB 6, NB 1)	7
TOTAL	348			327

FOW 1st Inns: 59 160 164 164 183 262 309 337 340 348
FOW 2nd Inns: 35 35 89 94 176 237 279 279 305 327

Bowling: *First Innings*: Nourse 8-3-24-0, Snooke 5-1-19-0, Pegler 10-0-43-1, Schwarz 13-0-66-1, Llewellyn 10-0-69-2, Sinclair 13-1-53-1, Stricker 10-0-36-1, Faulkner 10.4-0-34-2. *Second Innings*: Nourse 5-1-18-0, Snooke 8-1-24-0, Schwarz 22-2-76-4, Llewellyn 16-0-81-4, Pegler 6.3-1-24-1, Sinclair 8-0-32-0, Faulkner 12-1-55-1, Stricker 2-1-10-0.

SOUTH AFRICA

PW Sherwell (c+) c Carter b Cotter	24		b Whitty	16
JW Zulch b Cotter	42	(8)	not out	6
GA Faulkner c Armstrong b Whitty	204		c Kelleway b Whitty	8
AW Nourse b Kelleway	33		lbw Cotter	2
LA Stricker b Armstrong	26	(2)	lbw Cotter	0
CB Llewellyn b Armstrong	5		b Cotter	17
SJ Snooke b Whitty	77		c Armstrong b Whitty	9
JH Sinclair not out	58	(5)	lbw Whitty	3
RO Schwarz b Whitty	0		c Kelleway b Cotter	0
COC Pearse b Armstrong	6		c Kelleway b Whitty	0
SJ Pegler lbw Armstrong	8		lbw Whitty	0
EXTRAS (B 2, LB 10, W 2, NB 9)	23		(B 6, LB 3, NB 3)	12
TOTAL	506			80

FOW 1st Inns: 34 141 251 298 312 402 469 469 482 506
FOW 2nd Inns: 1 28 31 34 46 66 69 77 80 80

Bowling: *First Innings*: Cotter 43-5-158-2, Whitty 29-6-81-3, Kelleway 17-3-67-1, Armstrong 48-9-134-4, Macartney 16-5-43-0. *Second Innings*: Cotter 15-3-47-4, Whitty 16-7-17-6, Armstrong 1-0-4-0.

Umpires: RM Crockett & W Hannah

THIRD TEST 1910–11 AUSTRALIA v SOUTH AFRICA
Adelaide Oval, Adelaide. January 7, 9, 10, 11, 12, 13, 1911.
Toss: South Africa. South Africa won by 38 runs.

SOUTH AFRICA

PW Sherwell (c+) lbw Armstrong	11		lbw Whitty	1
JW Zulch c Macartney b Whitty	105		c Carter b Whitty	14
GA Faulkner c Hill b Armstrong	56		c Armstrong b Whitty	115
AW Nourse b Cotter	10		c Armstrong b Kelleway	39
CMH Hathorn b Whitty	9 (10)		b Whitty	2
CB Llewellyn run out	43		b Whitty	80
SJ Snooke c Kelleway b Cotter	103 (8)		run out	25
JH Sinclair c Armstrong b Kelleway	20 (9)		c Hill b Whitty	29
LA Stricker c Kelleway b Armstrong	48 (5)		b Macartney	6
RO Schwarz b Armstrong	15 (11)		not out	11
SJ Pegler not out	24 (7)		c Cotter b Kelleway	26
EXTRAS (B 6, LB 10, W 4, NB 18)	38		(B 4, LB 2, W 1, NB 5)	12
TOTAL	482			360

FOW 1st Inns: 31 166 189 191 205 303 338 400 429 482
FOW 2nd Inns: 10 29 106 119 228 273 317 319 327 360

Bowling: *First Innings*: Cotter 38-4-100-2, Whitty 34-7-114-2, Armstrong 42.4-9-103-4, Kelleway 24-6-72-1, Macartney 27-9-51-0, Gehrs 1-0-4-0. *Second Innings*: Whitty 39.2-5-104-6, Cotter 23-3-64-0, Armstrong 33-9-90-0, Kelleway 23-4-64-2, Macartney 12-3-26-1.

AUSTRALIA

CG Macartney b Llewellyn	2 (9)		lbw Schwarz	0
C Kelleway c Sherwell b Llewellyn	47 (4)		c Sherwell b Sinclair	65
VS Ransford b Llewellyn	50 (5)		c Llewellyn b Schwarz	0
W Bardsley lbw Nourse	54 (2)		c & b Faulkner	58
VT Trumper not out	214 (1)		b Llewellyn	28
DRA Gehrs c Schwarz b Faulkner	20 (8)		c Sherwell b Schwarz	22
C Hill (c) c Snooke b Schwarz	16 (3)		c Schwarz b Sinclair	55
WW Armstrong b Sinclair	30 (7)		b Schwarz	48
H Carter (+) lbw Schwarz	17 (6)		c Llewellyn b Faulkner	11
A Cotter c Snooke b Llewellyn	8		not out	36
WJ Whitty c Sherwell b Sinclair	1		c Schwarz b Pegler	11
EXTRAS (B 4, LB 2)	6		(LB 5)	5
TOTAL	465			339

FOW 1st Inns: 7 94 111 229 276 319 384 430 458 465
FOW 2nd Inns: 63 122 170 171 187 263 285 285 292 339

Bowling: *First Innings*: Llewellyn 31-4-107-4, Pegler 20-2-92-0, Schwarz 19-2-68-2, Faulkner 11-0-59-1, Stricker 1-0-4-0, Sinclair 25.5-3-86-2, Nourse 12-2-43-1. *Second Innings*: Snooke 5-0-21-0, Nourse 5-0-31-0, Llewellyn 12-0-48-1, Pegler 10.4-0-58-1, Schwarz 15-3-48-4, Faulkner 15-3-56-2, Sinclair 21-2-72-2.

Umpires: RM Crockett & GA Watson

FOURTH TEST 1910–11 AUSTRALIA v SOUTH AFRICA
Melbourne Cricket Ground, Melbourne. February 17, 18, 20, 21, 1911.
Toss: South Africa. Australia won by 530 runs.

AUSTRALIA

VT Trumper b Faulkner	7 (6)		c Sherwell b Vogler	87
W Bardsley c Schwarz b Pegler	82 (3)		run out	15
C Hill (c) b Llewellyn	11 (5)		st Sherwell b Pegler	100
WW Armstrong run out	48		c Sherwell b Vogler	132
DRA Gehrs st Sherwell b Vogler	9 (2)		c Snooke b Faulkner	58
C Kelleway run out	59 (1)		run out	18
VS Ransford lbw Schwarz	75		b Faulkner	95
A Cotter b Pegler	10		c (S)COC Pearse b Vogler	0
HV Hordern c Vogler b Pegler	7		c (S)COC Pearse b Schwarz	24
H Carter (+) run out	5		c Snooke b Faulkner	2
WJ Whitty not out	0		not out	39
EXTRAS (B 7, LB 7, W 1)	15		(B 4, LB 3, NB 1)	8
TOTAL	328			578

FOW 1st Inns: 9 24 126 146 182 289 310 317 328 328
FOW 2nd Inns: 48 88 106 260 403 418 420 491 496 578

Bowling: *First Innings*: Llewellyn 15-1-65-1, Faulkner 18-2-82-1, Schwarz 15-2-34-1, Vogler 8-2-30-1, Sinclair 14-2-40-0, Pegler 17.4-3-40-3, Stricker 5-1-18-0, Nourse 2-0-4-0. *Second Innings*: Sinclair 13-1-71-0, Schwarz 38-4-168-1, Pegler 17-1-88-1, Faulkner 28.2-5-101-3, Zulch 3-0-26-0, Nourse 7-0-31-0, Snooke 2-0-12-0, Stricker 3-0-14-0, Vogler 15-3-59-3.

SOUTH AFRICA

JW Zulch run out	2		c Trumper b Cotter	15
LA Stricker b Hordern	4		c Carter b Cotter	0
GA Faulkner c Gehrs b Hordern	20		b Whitty	80
AW Nourse not out	92		c & b Hordern	28
SJ Snooke b Whitty	1		b Hordern	7
JH Sinclair b Hordern	0		lbw Hordern	19
RO Schwarz b Whitty	18		c Carter b Whitty	1
PW Sherwell (c+) c(S)TJ Matthews b Whitty	41		c Kelleway b Hordern	0
CB Llewellyn b Whitty	7			
SJ Pegler c Hill b Cotter	15 (9)		c Gehrs b Hordern	8
AEE Vogler b Cotter	0 (10)		not out	2
EXTRAS (B 4, LB 1)	5		(B 7, LB 1, W 2, NB 1)	11
TOTAL	205			9 for 171

FOW 1st Inns: 7 23 36 37 38 65 156 171 205 205
FOW 2nd Inns: 2 25 88 108 151 158 161 165 171

Bowling: *First Innings*: Cotter 6.5-0-16-2, Whitty 22-5-78-4, Hordern 15-1-39-3, Armstrong 8-2-25-0, Kelleway 11-1-42-0. *Second Innings*: Cotter 6-1-22-2, Whitty 9-2-32-2, Kelleway 8-0-25-0, Hordern 14.2-2-66-5, Armstrong 3-0-15-0.

Umpires: RM Crockett & W Hannah

FIFTH TEST 1910–11 AUSTRALIA v SOUTH AFRICA
Sydney Cricket Ground, Sydney. March 3, 4, 6, 7, 1911.
Toss: South Africa. Australia won by 7 wkts.

AUSTRALIA

C Kelleway c Snooke b Llewellyn	2 (5)		not out	24
CG Macartney lbw Schwarz	137		c Nourse b Schwarz	56
HV Hordern lbw Sinclair	50			
W Bardsley c & b Sinclair	94 (1)		b Nourse	39
WJ Whitty c Nourse b Llewellyn	13			
VT Trumper b Schwarz	31 (3)		not out	74
C Hill (c) st Sherwell b Schwarz	13			
WW Armstrong c Pearse b Schwarz	0			
VS Ransford st Sherwell b Schwarz	6 (4)		b Nourse	0
A Cotter st Sherwell b Schwarz	8			
H Carter (+) not out	1			
EXTRAS (B 7, LB 2)	9		(B 1, LB 3, W 1)	5
TOTAL	364			3 for 198

FOW 1st Inns: 2 126 271 296 317 346 346 351 361 364
FOW 2nd Inns: 74 134 134

Bowling: *First Innings*: Llewellyn 25-0-92-2, Faulkner 12-2-38-0, Sinclair 27-6-83-2, Pegler 6-1-31-0, Schwarz 11.4-0-47-6, Nourse 5-1-26-0, Pearse 9-0-36-0, Zulch 1-0-2-0. *Second Innings*: Pearse 3-0-14-0, Llewellyn 8-1-43-0, Schwarz 9-0-42-1, Sinclair 6-1-22-0, Pegler 4-0-22-0, Faulkner 5-0-18-0, Nourse 8.1-0-32-2.

SOUTH AFRICA

COC Pearse b Whitty	0 (11)		lbw Hordern	2
JW Zulch st Carter b Hordern	15		b Ransford	150
GA Faulkner c Armstrong	52 (4)		b Cotter	92
AW Nourse b Armstrong	3 (5)		c Cotter b Whitty	28
LA Stricker c Macartney b Hordern	19 (6)		b Cotter	42
JH Sinclair c Ransford b Hordern	1 (8)		c & b Whitty	12
SJ Snooke b Hordern	18		c Carter b Whitty	12
CB Llewellyn c Carter b Kelleway	24 (9)		b Whitty	3
RO Schwarz run out	13 (10)		not out	6
PW Sherwell (c+) c Bardsley b Whitty	5 (1)		b Armstrong	14
SJ Pegler not out	0 (3)		c Cotter b Hordern	26
EXTRAS (B 1, LB 9)	10		(B 3, LB 4, W 2, NB 5)	14
TOTAL	160			401

FOW 1st Inns: 4 47 70 81 87 115 128 144 160 160
FOW 2nd Inns: 19 64 207 278 357 368 385 392 398 401

Bowling: *First Innings*: Cotter 8-2-24-0, Whitty 11.1-3-32-2, Hordern 21-3-73-4, Kelleway 4-1-4-1, Armstrong 6-1-17-2. *Second Innings*: Cotter 18-1-60-2, Armstrong 26-4-68-1, Hordern 30.1-1-117-2, Whitty 27-5-66-4, Kelleway 7-1-46-0, Macartney 10-0-21-0, Ransford 4-2-9-1.

Umpires: RM Crockett & AC Jones

Australian Averages

1910–11 AUSTRALIA v SOUTH AFRICA AUSTRALIA	M	Inn	NO	Runs	H.S	Avrge	Ct	St	Overs	Mds	Runs	Wkt	Avrge
Armstrong, WW	5	8	-	410	132	51.25	5	-	184.4	38	507	11	46.09
Bardsley, W	5	9	-	573	132	63.67	2	-	-	-	-	-	-
Carter, H	5	8	2	56	17	9.33	7	1	-	-	-	-	-
Cotter, A	5	8	1	80	36*	11.43	3	-	194.5	23	633	22	28.77
Gehrs, DRA	4	7	-	202	67	28.86	2	-	1.0	-	4	-	-
Hill, C	5	8	-	425	191	53.13	3	-	-	-	-	-	-
Hordern, HV	2	3	-	81	50	27.00	1	-	80.3	7	295	14	21.07
Kelleway, C	5	9	2	295	65	42.14	8	-	118.1	21	390	7	55.71
Macartney, CG	4	7	-	208	137	29.71	3	-	77.0	22	164	1	164.00
Ransford, VS	5	9	-	318	95	35.33	1	-	4.0	2	9	1	9.00
Trumper, VT	5	9	2	661	214*	94.43	3	-	-	-	-	-	-
Whitty, WJ	5	8	3	90	39*	18.00	2	-	232.3	55	632	37	17.08

South African Averages

1910–11 AUSTRALIA v SOUTH AFRICA SOUTH AFRICA	M	Inn	NO	Runs	H.S	Avrge	Ct	St	Overs	Mds	Runs	Wkt	Avrge
Faulkner, GA	5	10	-	732	204	73.20	2	-	124.0	13	514	10	51.40
Hathorn, CMH	1	2	-	11	9	5.50	-	-	-	-	-	-	-
Llewellyn, CB	5	9	-	198	80	22.00	2	-	131.0	6	559	14	39.93
Nourse, AW	5	10	2	304	92*	38.00	3	-	64.1	7	270	3	90.00
Pearse, COC	3	6	-	55	31	9.17	1	-	24.0	-	106	3	35.33
Pegler, SJ	4	8	2	107	26	17.83	1	-	91.5	8	398	7	56.86
Schwarz, RO	5	10	2	132	61	16.50	4	-	167.4	19	651	25	26.04
Sherwell, PW	5	10	1	180	60	20.00	8	9	-	-	-	-	-
Sinclair, JH	5	10	1	149	58*	16.56	1	-	147.3	16	539	8	67.38
Snooke, SJ	5	10	-	259	103	25.90	8	-	20.0	2	76	-	-
Stricker, LA	5	10	-	151	48	15.10	1	-	21.0	2	82	1	82.00
Vogler, AEE	2	4	1	2	2*	0.67	1	-	38.0	5	176	4	44.00

Ranji Hordern a new googly wizard

Sydney, Dec. 21. Dr Herbert Hordern is known as 'Ranji' to his team-mates because of his dark complexion.

But the mysterious spin he applies to the ball and the mesmeric effect he has on batsman would suggest he has been schooled in the land of snake charmers. He is the first genuine googly bowler in Australia, and bowls at nearly medium pace.

The England batsmen had been told that they might spot a raised little finger as he turned his leg break into a googly.

It seems they were concentrating too hard on the finger, and not enough on the ball, as he finished with 12/175 to give Australia a win in the first Test by 146 runs.

Another winning factor was Victor Trumper's 113, which set up a first-innings lead of 129.

This is Hordern's third Test and his cricket has been limited because of his dental practice.

He studied in America and went to England twice, with teams from Pennsylvania University and Philadelphia. It was there that he worked on the googly, which he put to good effect against South Africa last summer, taking 14 wickets in two Tests.

England shows its brilliance

The crowd of 31,453 at the Melbourne Cricket Ground on Saturday watch England take control in the second Test.

Sydney, March 1. Australian cricket seems to be at a low ebb following the 4–1 Test drubbing at the hands of England.

Perhaps Australia had a chance in the second Test. Hordern had taken a quick 4/27 to restrict a rampant England to a modest first innings of 265, but with Australia kept to 184 and 299 the visitors needed just 219 to win in the second innings.

Jack Hobbs, who proved to be the master batsman of the series, took Hordern on and tamed him as he made a superlative 126 not out. Hobbs is not a big man, but he strokes the ball calmly and comfortably, splitting the field with his precision.

After that the series was all downhill. The Australian batsmen could

not mount a concerted resistance to England's brilliant opening bowlers Sid Barnes (34 series wickets) and Frank Foster (32). The only one anywhere near their best form and figures for Australia was Hordern, with 32 wickets.

Barnes at 38 remained a master of swing and cut, and showed plenty ill-temper too. When the crowd heckled him for placing his field slowly, he flung down the ball in disgust and had to be persuaded by his captain to continue.

Hobbs' average of 82.15 more than doubled the best Australian (Armstrong at 32.40) and Wilfred Rhodes and George Gunn were also well ahead.

The pattern began in the second Test when Barnes bowled Bardsley with the first ball of the match and

had 5/6 from seven overs of his opening spell.

The third Test was highlighted by Hobbs' 187, carrying him to an unbroken sequence of over 300 runs. Despite Clem Hill's second innings 98 and Warren Bardsley's 63, England romped in by seven wickets.

With Australian morale affected by matters on and off the field, the fourth and fifth Tests were lost. In the fourth, Hobbs (178) and Rhodes (179) made a first-wicket stand of 323 in a total of 589, and in the fifth Frank Woolley made 133 and had a seventh-wicket stand with Joe Vine of 143 in 147 minutes. From 6/162, England made 324 – a decisive total. Woolley compounded Australia's woes in taking eight field catches.

'Ranji' Hordern: master of spin.

Boardroom brawl

Sydney, Feb. 3. Australian cricket captain Clem Hill last night struck his fellow selector Peter McAlister and then fought with him for 20 minutes in the NSWCA office. The two were eventually dragged apart by selector Frank Iredale and Board secretary Sydney Smith, with McAlister bleeding profusely.

McAlister was appointed to the first Board of Control selection panel in 1909 to choose the 1909 team to England, and created some controversy when, aged 40, he became vice-captain and treasurer of that team ahead of other younger players.

Clem Hill was appointed captain of Australia for the 1910–11 series against South Africa.

The fight brings to a head the ill feeling that exists between the Board and the players, particularly the fierce enmity that has arisen between Hill and McAlister.

Two weeks ago six leading players wrote to the Board saying that its decison to send a Board selected manager on the 1912 tour of England was unconstitutional. The players asked for the procedure of the 1909 tour, in which 14 players would be selected and would then select their own player manager. They warned that: 'failing compliance with our request, we have to inform you with much regret that none of us will be available for selection or to play if selected ... yours truly, C. Hill, W. W. Armstrong, V. T. Trumper, V.S. Ransford, A. Cotter, H. Carter.'

With these stakes on the table it is not surprising that there was tension surrounding any contact with Hill and the Board. But the flash point came over the selection of the team for the fourth Test against England and was inflamed by a telegram sent to Hill in reply to his recommendation of the inclusion of Charles Macartney in the team.

McAlister wrote: 'My team forwarded yesterday. Still oppose Macartney's inclusion ... if Iredale agrees with you favour yourself standing down not Minnett.'

When they met in Sydney, McAlister continued to be hostile to Hill, who warned him not to keep insulting him. Hill said later: 'I told him that if he kept on insulting me I would pull his nose. He said that I was the worst captain he had ever seen, and, as he had aggravated me beyond endurance, I gave him a gentle slap on the face.

'He said I had hit him when his hands were down. I said my hands were down now, as I put my hands behind my back. He rushed at me like a bull, and then I admit I fought him. Messrs Iredale and Smith held him back, and as I went out he called out that I was a coward, but as the others prevented him from leaving the room, the matter ended.

'I told Mr Smith that I could no longer continue as a selector any longer with McAlister. He asked me to put my resignation in writing, and I did so.'

Hill also said: 'There are some things a man can't stand. If they go too far I will retire from the game altogether. I do not want to do it because, as I've said before, I want to go to England with the team, but they leave no other course open to me.'

Iredale and McAlister are now picking the fourth Test team.

The jolly scene at the central Victorian city of Ballarat, as the MCC party enjoys a country sojourn after the rigours of Test-match cricket.

Six defectors defy Board

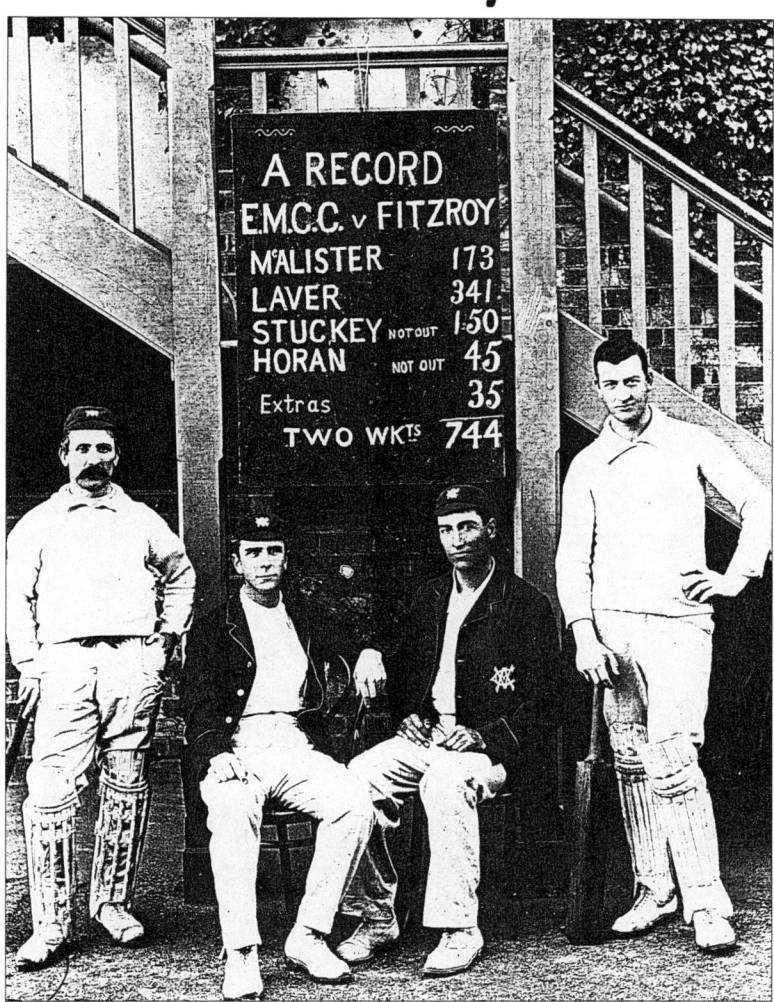

Happier days. Fred Laver and Peter McAlister ... arch enemies now over Cricket Board matters, but once associated with this massive partnership for the East Melbourne club. Laver is a declared players' man.

Sydney, March 15. The Australian team for England is now on the water – leaving behind its best players, despite strenuous efforts from sporting, Government and business figures to have them included.

The Australian Cricket Board has won the day, appointing its own manager to conduct the tour. Board strongman William McElhone says the Melbourne Cricket Club has stirred up the trouble.

Clem Hill, the former captain, has said in a letter to the *Sydney Morning Herald*: 'If it is considered desirable that the control of Australian cricket should be placed in the hands of one man, by all means do it openly, but do not pretend to invest the Board with control, when you know an individual controls the Board'.

Another ex-captain Monty Noble had described the body as 'a democratic body being ruled and governed by a despot.' But in a published letter recently he acknowledged the need for Board control, but was 'strongly against the present personnel.'

The English captain Pelham Warner, anxious for the success of the forthcoming triangular tour, tried vainly to overcome the impasse, pleading with the defecting players and taking the matter up with the Prime Minister, Andrew Fisher, State Governors and the Governor General. For a time he persuaded the Board to delay the announcement .

But there has been no change in the situation. Syd Gregory will lead the team, and 10 of the 15 players now on the water have not been to England before.

It is widely regarded as the weakest Australian team to tour England – an oft-heard remark which, happily, is often proved wrong.

The team is: Syd Gregory (capt.), W. Bardsley, W. Carkeek, S. H. Emery, G. R. Hazlitt, C. B. Jennings, C. Kelleway, J. W. McLaren, C. G. Macartney, T. J. Matthews, R. E. Mayne, R. B. Minnett, D. B. M. Smith, H. W. Webster and W.J. Whitty.

Clem Hill – a great career goes sour

Clem Hill was predestined to be a cricketer. His father made the first century on the Adelaide Oval and there were seven brothers among the cricketing Hills.

He rose to the cricketing heights with all his genetic imprinting overstamped with an iron will, a keen eye and natural ability to hit the ball truly and hard.

His captain Joe Darling showed his promise with a record for St Peter's College of 252. Hill, at 16, surpassed it with 360. He was in the Colonial team at the age of 17, and in 1895–96, he topped the South Australian batting averages at 56.37.

The next step was England, as his 206 not out against NSW was just in time for his late inclusion. Tom Garrett, a selector, recognised the worth of the confident left-hander. So he was off to England at 19 and on the path to a career that saw him score 3412 runs in 49 Tests at 39.21 and 17,216 first class runs at 43.47. He was Australia's biggest-scoring batsman in the years before Ponsford and Bradman, with seven centuries and 19 scores of over 50.

Hill was solidly and powerfully built, a handsome figure with a direct gaze and a straightforward style about him. As he rose to be captain of South Australia and Australia he was revered by his team-mates.

Said Johnnie Moyes: 'As long as he was there we thought everything would turn out all right.'

But there was nothing fancy in his style. He had an awkward, crouched style with his hands low on the bat, as if he was going to club the ball like a slogger. But he saw the ball early, was light on his feet, moved quickly and cleanly to position and hit with ease.

Hill revelled in fast bowling and made his biggest scores in Australia. He was an undoubted success in England as well. His forte was his square and late cutting, and he could carve up a fast bowling attack with this audacious off side play. But he was adept on the leg side and drove with immense power. And he was a fighter, never one to surrender his wicket.

Perhaps his most courageous feat was in the 1907–08 series against England where in the third Test he batted at number nine because of heat stroke, but proceeded to make 160 in five hours in a match-winning partnership with Roger Hartigan.

Clem Hill: 'a proper man'.

He captained Australia 10 times, but he was unfortunate to be around at the time that the Board of Control for International Cricket was seeking to control overseas tours under its own terms.

Hill, like many of his team-mates had little time for the men of the Board and he was not one to hide his feelings.

His career came to an abrupt end as he was a leader in the defection of six players from the 1912 tour because they could not select their own manager.

The poor form of his 1911–12 team was an added component that led to the cricket brawl that made headlines and saw him resign as a selector and bow out of Test cricket.

But horse racing was a great replacement. Growing up in Adelaide, a city of racecourses, Hill had always had a love of horses and a great knowledge of racing.

He became a stipendiary steward and then handicapper for the South Australian Jockey Club. Hill took his family to Melbourne in 1937 when he took the post of handicapper for the Victorian Amateur Turf Club.

When he was suffering ill-health he moved to Geelong, as handicapper for the Geelong Amateur Turf Club.

He died aged 68 as a result of injuries sustained getting off a tram.

FIRST TEST 1911–12 AUSTRALIA v ENGLAND
Sydney Cricket Ground, Sydney. December 15, 16, 18, 19, 20, 21, 1911.
Toss: Australia. Australia won by 146 runs.

AUSTRALIA

W Bardsley c Strudwick b Douglas	30		b Foster	12
C Kelleway c & b Woolley	20		b Douglas	70
C Hill (c) run out	46		b Foster	65
WW Armstrong st Strudwick b Hearne	60		b Foster	28
VT Trumper c Hobbs b Woolley	113		c & b Douglas	14
VS Ransford c Hearne b Barnes	26		c Rhodes b Barnes	34
RB Minnett c Foster b Barnes	90	(8)	b Douglas	17
HV Hordern not out	17	(7)	b Foster	18
A Cotter c & b Barnes	6		lbw Douglas	2
H Carter (+) b Foster	13		c Gunn b Foster	15
WJ Whitty b Foster	0		not out	9
EXTRAS (B 9, LB 15, NB 2)	26		(B 16, LB 7, NB 1)	24
TOTAL	447			308

FOW 1st Inns: 44 77 121 198 278 387 420 426 447 447
FOW 2nd Inns: 29 150 169 191 218 246 268 274 283 308

Bowling: First Innings: Foster 29-6-105-2, Douglas 24-5-62-1, Barnes 35-5-107-3, Hearne 10-1-44-1, Woolley 21-2-77-2, Rhodes 8-0-26-0. *Second Innings:* Foster 31.3-5-92-5, Douglas 21-3-50-4, Barnes 30-8-72-1, Woolley 6-1-15-0, Hearne 13-2-51-0, Rhodes 3-1-4-0.

ENGLAND

JB Hobbs c Hill b Whitty	63		c Carter b Cotter	22
SP Kinneir b Kelleway	22		c Trumper b Hordern	30
G Gunn b Cotter	4		c Whitty b Hordern	62
W Rhodes c Hill b Hordern	41	(5)	c Trumper b Hordern	0
CP Mead c & b Hordern	0	(4)	run out	25
JW Hearne c Trumper b Kelleway	76	(7)	b Hordern	43
FR Foster b Hordern	56	(6)	c Ransford b Hordern	21
FE Woolley b Hordern	39		c Armstrong b Cotter	7
JWHT Douglas (c) c Trumper b Hordern	0		b Hordern	32
SF Barnes b Kelleway	9		b Hordern	14
H Strudwick (+) not out	0		not out	12
EXTRAS (B 3, LB 3, W 1, NB 1)	8		(B 14, LB 8, NB 1)	23
TOTAL	318			291

FOW 1st Inns: 45 53 115 129 142 231 293 293 310 318
FOW 2nd Inns: 29 69 141 141 148 167 177 263 276 291

Bowling: First Innings: Cotter 19-0-88-1, Whitty 28-13-60-1, Kelleway 16.5-3-46-3, Hordern 27-4-85-5, Armstrong 9-3-28-0, Minnett 2-1-3-0. *Second Innings:* Whitty 20-8-41-0, Cotter 27-3-71-2, Hordern 42.2-11-90-7, Kelleway 19-6-27-0, Armstrong 15-3-39-0.

Umpires: RM Crockett & WG Curran

SECOND TEST 1911–12 AUSTRALIA v ENGLAND
Melbourne Cricket Ground, Melbourne. December 30, 1911, January 1, 2, 3, 1912.
Toss: Australia. England won by 8 wkts.

AUSTRALIA

C Kelleway lbw Barnes	2		c Gunn b Foster	13
W Bardsley b Barnes	0		run out	16
C Hill (c) b Barnes	4		c Gunn b Barnes	0
WW Armstrong c Smith b Barnes	4		b Foster	90
VT Trumper b Foster	13		b Barnes	2
VS Ransford c Smith b Hitch	43		c Smith b Foster	32
RB Minnett c Hobbs b Barnes	2	(8)	b Foster	34
HV Hordern not out	49	(7)	c Mead b Foster	31
A Cotter run out	14		c Hobbs b Foster	41
H Carter (+) c Smith b Douglas	29		b Barnes	16
WJ Whitty b Woolley	14		not out	0
EXTRAS (B 5, LB 4, NB 1)	10		(B 14, LB 7, W 1, NB 2)	24
TOTAL	184			299

FOW 1st Inns: 0 5 8 11 33 38 80 97 140 184
FOW 2nd Inns: 28 34 34 38 135 168 232 235 298 299

Bowling: First Innings: Foster 16-2-52-1, Barnes 23-9-44-5, Hitch 7-0-37-1, Douglas 15-4-33-1, Hearne 1-0-8-0, Woolley 0.1-0-0-1. *Second Innings:* Foster 38-9-91-6, Barnes 32.1-7-96-3, Douglas 10-0-38-0, Hearne 1-0-5-0, Woolley 3-0-21-0, Hitch 5-0-21-0, Rhodes 2-1-3-0.

ENGLAND

W Rhodes c Trumper b Cotter	61		c Carter b Cotter	28
JB Hobbs c Carter b Cotter	6		not out	126
JW Hearne c Carter b Cotter	114	(4)	not out	12
G Gunn lbw Armstrong	10	(3)	c Carter b Whitty	43
CP Mead c Armstrong b Whitty	11			
FR Foster c Hill b Cotter	9			
JWHT Douglas (c) b Hordern	9			
FE Woolley c Ransford b Hordern	23			
EJ Smith (+) b Hordern	5			
SF Barnes lbw Hordern	1			
JW Hitch not out	0			
EXTRAS (B 2, LB 10, NB 4)	16		(B 5, LB 5)	10
TOTAL	265			2 for 219

FOW 1st Inns: 10 137 174 213 224 227 258 260 262 265
FOW 2nd Inns: 57 169

Bowling: First Innings: Cotter 22-2-73-4, Whitty 19-2-47-1, Hordern 23.1-1-66-4, Kelleway 15-7-27-0, Armstrong 15-6-20-1, Minnett 5-0-16-0. *Second Innings:* Cotter 14-5-45-1, Whitty 18-3-37-1, Hordern 17-0-66-0, Armstrong 8-1-22-0, Kelleway 7-0-15-0, Minnett 2-0-13-0, Ransford 1.1-0-11-0.

Umpires: RM Crockett & DA Elder

THIRD TEST 1911–12 AUSTRALIA v ENGLAND
Adelaide Oval, Adelaide. January 12, 13, 15, 16, 17, 1912.
Toss: Australia. England won by 7 wkts.

AUSTRALIA

W Bardsley c Smith b Barnes	.5		b Foster	.63
C Kelleway b Foster	.1		b Douglas	.37
HV Hordern c Rhodes b Foster	.25 (7)		c & b Barnes	.5
VS Ransford not out	.8 (8)		b Hitch	.38
WW Armstrong b Foster	.33		b Douglas	.25
VT Trumper b Hitch	.26 (11)		not out	.1
C Hill (c) st Smith b Foster	.0 (4)		c Hitch b Barnes	.98
RB Minnett b Foster	.0 (6)		c Hobbs b Barnes	.38
TJ Matthews c Mead b Barnes	.5		b Barnes	.53
A Cotter b Barnes	.11		b Barnes	.15
H Carter (+) c Gunn b Douglas	.8 (3)		c Smith b Woolley	.72
EXTRAS (B 3, LB 6, NB 2)	.11		(B 26, LB 3, NB 2)	.31
TOTAL	.133			.476

FOW 1st Inns: 6 6 65 84 88 88 97 113 123 133
FOW 2nd Inns: 86 122 279 303 342 360 363 447 475 476

Bowling: *First Innings*: Foster 26-9-36-5, Barnes 23-4-71-3, Douglas 7-2-7-1, Hearne 2-0-6-0, Hitch 2-1-2-1. *Second Innings*: Foster 49-15-103-1, Barnes 46.4-7-105-5, Douglas 29-10-71-2, Hearne 10-0-61-0, Hitch 11-0-69-1, Woolley 7-1-30-1, Rhodes 1-0-6-0.

ENGLAND

JB Hobbs c Hordern b Minnett	.187		lbw Hordern	.3
W Rhodes lbw Cotter	.59		not out	.57
G Gunn c Hill b Cotter	.29		c Cotter b Kelleway	.45
JW Hearne c Hill b Kelleway	.12		c Kelleway b Matthews	.2
CP Mead c & b Hordern	.46		not out	.2
FR Foster b Armstrong	.71			
JWHT Douglas (c) b Minnett	.35			
FE Woolley b Cotter	.20			
EJ Smith (+) c(S)J Vine b Cotter	.22			
SF Barnes not out	.2			
JW Hitch c(S)CG Macartney b Hordern	.0			
EXTRAS (B 7, LB 1, NB 3)	.18		(B 1, LB 1, NB 1)	.3
TOTAL	.501			.3 for 112

FOW 1st Inns: 147 206 260 323 350 435 455 492 501 501
FOW 2nd Inns: 5 102 105

Bowling: *First Innings*: Cotter 43-11-125-4, Hordern 47.1-5-143-2, Kelleway 23-3-46-1, Matthews 33-8-72-0, Minnett 17-3-54-2, Armstrong 14-0-43-1. *Second Innings*: Cotter 5-0-21-0, Hordern 11-3-32-1, Armstrong 6-1-12-0, Minnett 4-1-12-0, Matthews 9.2-3-24-1, Kelleway 7-3-8-1.

Umpires: RM Crockett & GA Watson

FOURTH TEST 1911–12 AUSTRALIA v ENGLAND
Melbourne Cricket Ground, Melbourne. February 9, 10, 12, 13, 1912.
Toss: England. England won by an innings & 225 runs.

AUSTRALIA

C Kelleway c Hearne b Woolley	.29		c Smith b Barnes	.5
HV Hordern b Barnes	.19 (11)		c Foster b Douglas	.5
W Bardsley b Foster	.0		b Foster	.3
VT Trumper b Foster	.17		b Barnes	.28
C Hill (c) c Hearne b Barnes	.22		b Douglas	.11
WW Armstrong b Barnes	.7		b Douglas	.11
RB Minnett c Rhodes b Foster	.56		b Douglas	.7
VS Ransford c Rhodes b Foster	.4		not out	.29
TJ Matthews c Gunn b Barnes	.3 (10)		b Foster	.10
A Cotter b Barnes	.15 (9)		c Mead b Foster	.8
H Carter (+) not out	.6 (2)		c Hearne b Douglas	.38
EXTRAS (B 1, LB 5, NB 7)	.13		(B 9, LB 2, NB 7)	.18
TOTAL	.191			.173

FOW 1st Inns: 53 53 69 74 83 124 152 165 170 191
FOW 2nd Inns: 12 20 76 86 101 112 117 127 156 173

Bowling: *First Innings*: Foster 22-2-77-4, Barnes 29.1-4-74-5, Woolley 11-3-22-1, Rhodes 2-1-1-0, Hearne 1-0-4-0. *Second Innings*: Foster 19-3-38-3, Barnes 20-6-47-2, Douglas 17.5-6-46-5, Hearne 3-0-17-0, Woolley 2-0-7-0.

ENGLAND

JB Hobbs c Carter b Hordern	.178
W Rhodes c Carter b Minnett	.179
G Gunn c Hill b Armstrong	.75
JW Hearne c Armstrong b Minnett	.0
FR Foster c Hordern b Armstrong	.50
JWHT Douglas (c) c Bardsley b Armstrong	.0
FE Woolley c Kelleway b Minnett	.56
CP Mead b Hordern	.21
J Vine not out	.4
EJ Smith (+) c Matthews b Kelleway	.7
SF Barnes c Hill b Hordern	.2
EXTRAS (B 2, LB 4, W 4, NB 9)	.19
TOTAL	.589

FOW 1st Inns: 323 425 425 486 486 513 565 579 589 589

Bowling: *First Innings*: Cotter 37-5-125-0, Kelleway 26-2-80-1, Armstrong 36-12-93-3, Matthews 22-1-68-0, Hordern 47.5-5-137-3, Minnett 20-5-59-2, Ransford 2-1-8-0.

Umpires: RM Crockett & WA Young

FIFTH TEST 1911–12 AUSTRALIA v ENGLAND
Sydney Cricket Ground, Sydney. February 23, 24, 26 (no play), 27, 28, 29 (no play), March 1, 1912.
Toss: England. England won by 70 runs.

ENGLAND

JB Hobbs c Ransford b Hordern	.32		c Hazlitt b Hordern	.45
W Rhodes b Macartney	.8		lbw Armstrong	.30
G Gunn st Carter b Hordern	.52		b Hordern	.61
JW Hearne c Macartney b Armstrong	.4		b Hordern	.18
FR Foster st Carter b Hazlitt	.15		b McLaren	.4
JWHT Douglas (c) c Ransford b Hordern	.18		b Armstrong	.8
FE Woolley not out	.133		c Armstrong b Hazlitt	.11
J Vine b Hordern	.36		not out	.6
EJ Smith (+) b Hordern	.0		b Hordern	.13
SF Barnes c Hordern b Hazlitt	.5		b Hordern	.4
JW Hitch c Hill b Hazlitt	.4		c Ransford b Armstrong	.4
EXTRAS (B 10, LB 4, W 1, NB 2)	.17		(B 8, NB 2)	.10
TOTAL	.324			.214

FOW 1st Inns: 15 69 83 114 125 162 305 305 312 324
FOW 2nd Inns: 76 76 105 110 146 178 186 201 209 214

Bowling: *First Innings*: McLaren 16-2-47-0, Macartney 12-3-26-1, Hordern 37-8-95-5, Hazlitt 31-6-75-3, Armstrong 25-8-42-1, Minnett 8-1-22-0. *Second Innings*: Macartney 7-0-28-0, Hazlitt 12-2-52-1, Armstrong 17.3-7-35-3, Hordern 25-5-66-5, McLaren 8-1-23-1, Minnett 1-1-0-0.

AUSTRALIA

VT Trumper c Woolley b Barnes	.5		c Woolley b Barnes	.50
ES Gregory c Gunn b Douglas	.32		c Smith b Barnes	.40
C Hill (c) c Smith b Hitch	.20		b Foster	.8
WW Armstrong b Woolley b Barnes	.33		b Barnes	.33
RB Minnett c Douglas b Hitch	.0		c Woolley b Barnes	.61
VS Ransford c Hitch b Foster	.29		b Woolley	.9
H Carter (+) c(S)CP Mead b Barnes	.11 (8)		c Woolley b Foster	.23
CG Macartney c & b Woolley	.26 (7)		c Woolley b Foster	.27
HV Hordern b Woolley	.0		run out	.4
GR Hazlitt run out	.1		c Rhodes b Foster	.4
JW McLaren not out	.0		not out	.0
EXTRAS (B 14, LB 2, W 2, NB 1)	.19		(B 22, LB 8, W 1, NB 2)	.33
TOTAL	.176			.292

FOW 1st Inns: 17 59 81 82 133 133 171 175 176 176
FOW 2nd Inns: 88 101 117 209 220 231 278 287 287 292

Bowling: *First Innings*: Foster 16-0-55-1, Barnes 19-2-56-3, Hitch 9-0-31-2, Douglas 7-0-14-1, Woolley 2-1-1-2. *Second Innings*: Foster 30.1-7-43-4, Barnes 39-12-106-4, Douglas 9-0-34-0, Hitch 6-1-23-0, Woolley 16-5-36-1, Rhodes 2-0-17-0.

Umpires: RM Crockett & AC Jones

Australian Averages

1911–12 AUSTRALIA v ENGLAND

AUSTRALIA	M	Inn	NO	Runs	H.S	Avrge	Ct	St	Overs	Mds	Runs	Wkt	Avrge
Armstrong, WW	5	10	-	324	90	32.40	4	-	145.3	41	334	9	37.11
Bardsley, W	4	8	-	129	63	16.13	1	-	-	-	-	-	-
Carter, H	5	10	1	231	72	25.67	7	2	-	-	-	-	-
Cotter, A	4	8	-	112	41	14.00	1	-	167.0	26	548	12	45.67
Gregory, ES	1	2	-	72	40	36.00	-	-	-	-	-	-	-
Hazlitt, GR	1	2	-	5	4	2.50	1	-	43.0	8	127	4	31.75
Hill, C	5	10	-	274	98	27.40	8	-	-	-	-	-	-
Hordern, HV	5	10	2	173	49*	21.63	5	-	277.3	42	780	32	24.38
Kelleway, C	4	8	-	177	70	22.13	2	-	113.5	24	249	6	41.50
Macartney, CG	1	2	-	53	27	26.50	1	-	19.0	3	54	1	54.00
Matthews, TJ	2	4	-	71	53	17.75	1	-	64.2	12	164	1	164.00
McLaren, JW	1	2	2	0	0*	-	-	-	24.0	3	70	1	70.00
Minnett, RB	5	10	-	305	90	30.50	1	-	59.0	12	179	5	35.80
Ransford, VS	5	10	2	252	43	31.50	5	-	3.1	1	19	-	-
Trumper, VT	5	10	1	269	113	29.89	5	-	-	-	-	-	-
Whitty, WJ	2	4	2	23	14	11.50	1	-	85.0	26	185	3	61.67

English Averages

1911–12 AUSTRALIA v ENGLAND

ENGLAND	M	Inn	NO	Runs	H.S	Avrge	Ct	St	Overs	Mds	Runs	Wkt	Avrge
Barnes, SF	5	7	1	35	14	5.83	2	-	297.0	64	778	34	22.88
Douglas, JWHT	5	7	-	102	35	14.57	2	-	139.5	30	355	15	23.67
Foster, FR	5	7	-	226	71	32.29	2	-	276.4	58	692	32	21.63
Gunn, G	5	9	-	381	75	42.33	6	-	-	-	-	-	-
Hearne, JW	5	9	-	281	114	35.13	4	-	41.0	3	196	1	196.00
Hitch, JW	3	4	1	8	4	2.67	2	-	40.0	2	183	5	36.60
Hobbs, JB	5	9	1	662	187	82.75	4	-	-	-	-	-	-
Kinneir, SP	1	2	-	52	30	26.00	-	-	-	-	-	-	-
Mead, CP	4	6	1	105	46	21.00	3	-	-	-	-	-	-
Rhodes, W	5	9	1	463	179	57.88	5	-	18.0	3	57	-	-
Smith, EJ	4	5	-	47	22	9.40	9	1	-	-	-	-	-
Strudwick, H	1	2	2	12	12*	-	1	1	-	-	-	-	-
Vine, J	2	3	2	46	36	46.00	-	-	-	-	-	-	-
Woolley, FE	5	7	1	289	133*	48.17	7	-	68.1	13	209	8	26.13

The triangular series ends in a debacle

Heralding the "Tests," or testing our Heraldry.   Design for a Coat of Arms.

The first Triangular Test series ends with the smile on the face of the victorious British lion.

The Oval, Aug. 22. Variously described as 'unrepresentative', 'the worst Australian team ever', and 'the McElhone XI' so named after the powerful Board of Control individual who faced down the demands of the Big Six, Australia was soundly defeated by England in the last of the six Tests in this unhappy series.

While Australia managed to defeat South Africa twice, the weather spoiled the third Test against them and the first two Tests against England – with Australia in the worse position in two of these games. No bowler other than Bill Whitty (aside from Jimmy Matthews' double hat-trick in the first Test) made any impression. Whitty took 25 wickets in the Tests.

And only two batsmen, Warren Bardsley and Charlie Kelleway, made consistent runs. Bardsley hit 392 at 65.33 and Kelleway, described by *Wisden* as 'a weariness to the flesh', 360 at 60.

The first Test was against South Africa at Old Trafford and was over in just two days – spoiling the box-office attraction of the South Africans, and resulting in low attendances throughout. Kelleway and Bardsley hit centuries, and Jimmy Matthews 49 not out, before taking his unique double hat-trick.

The Lord's Test against England was drawn, but not before Charlie Macartney was out on 99.

Australia then defeated South Africa by ten wickets, also at Lord's, in three days, with centuries from Kelleway and Bardsley.

The second match with England at Old Trafford was ruined by rain, Australia facing only 13 overs in its first innings.

Australia's second innings of 65 in the final Test was a capitulation.

England won the series with four victories from six matches, while Australia won two Tests and lost one.

South Africa won none.

Gerry Hazlitt: 7/25 at the Oval.

Bill Whitty: 5/55 at Old Trafford.

Warren Bardsley: two centuries.

A double hat-trick to Jimmy Matthews

'Hat-trick' Jimmy Matthews.

Old Trafford, May 28. T. J. 'Jimmy' Matthews, playing in his first Test, has performed a unique bowling feat – a double hat-trick, one in each innings of the same match on the same day.

Bowling slow-medium leg breaks 'of the W. W. Armstrong type', says *Cricket*, 'real leg-breaks mixed with some that don't break at all … his best ball is one which pitches on the leg stump and is apt to take the off bail. The straight'uns are good for lbw, and a slower-flighted ball is handy for caught and bowled.'

All were demonstrated in the first Test against South Africa. Matthews took the last three wickets of the first innings, and did it again, at 5/70. South African wicketkeeper Tom Ward was the hat-trick bunny on each occasion.

Captain 'hurt' by team's behaviour

London, Oct. 27. Syd 'Little Tich' Gregory, who was recalled at the age of 42 to lead the depleted Australian team on his eighth tour of England, has played a record 58th Test match.

Gregory as captain was astute on the field, but lacked the authority to control the players off it.

One of his team-mates said: 'Syd Gregory, who is one of the finest fellows that ever played the game, has done his best, both by example and by personal persuasion, to keep the men in check, but they got beyond all control, and have completely defied his authority.

Syd, however is too good a fellow to 'squeal'. He says nothing, but he feels a lot, and I believe that he is deeply hurt about the matter.'

Gregory made his Test debut in England in 1890.

Australian captain Syd Gregory.

Jack Hobbs and Wilfred Rhodes: they are as prolific batting in England as they were down under.

Australia is disgraced

The 1912 Australian Board of Control – determined to do just that.

London, Oct. 30. Cricket Board-imposed tour manager George Crouch received a telegram from William McElhone while still in England suggesting that the tour be called off, because of reports received in Sydney about some players' behaviour.

Crouch has done nothing about this telegram, as he has been unable to do anything much about controlling the players who have been widely reported as carrying on in an appalling and drunken manner on the way home.

On a trip to Ireland, stewards on the ferry refused to serve brawling Australians more liquor. Drunken cricketers are said to have collapsed on the deck, and only revived with difficulty.

On the boat from America, passengers on the SS *Marama* told the Sydney *Sun* 'that the conduct of the [two] cricketers in question was such that it should not be allowed to pass without investigation.'

Warren Bardsley and Charlie Macartney were not part of this group as they did not tour America with the others.

'It is alleged,' said the *Sun* 'that the cricketers referred to became continually intoxicated during the homeward voyage, and on several occasions made public exhibitions of themselves, not by any means calculated to do credit to the good name of Australian cricket.

'The night before the steamer left Auckland a gang of roysterers kept the whole ship awake … [and] other incidents during the trip from Vancouver served to make every true Australian on board feel ashamed.

The three culprits

Melbourne, Dec. 12. Following submission of 1912 tour manager George Crouch's report to the Board of Control, detailing much of the misbehaviour on tour, the Board summoned three players to explain incidents on the tour.

They were hat-trick hero Jimmy Matthews, wicketkeeper 'Barlow' Carkeek, and batsman Dave Smith, who played two Tests for a total of 30 runs. Smith declined to appear, claiming ill health.

While the deliberations were kept secret, the Board Secretary Syd Smith announced that in future the Board reserved the right to assess whether a player was worthy of representing Australia for reasons other than cricket.

Loss to 'Philly'

Bermuda, Oct. 15. Amazingly, Australia has lost its first match against the Philadelphians. Philadelphia made 185 in its first innings, although Jimmy Matthews took yet another hat-trick .

Only Bill Whitty and 'Barlow' Carkeek topped 20 in the Australians' reply of 122, J. Barton King taking 5/40. Then Whitty and Emery bundled the locals out for 74, leaving Australia to make 138 for a win.

Australia needed 12 in the last over, from J. Barton King. A single, then Whitty hit a four, King bowled one that went for four byes – three to get – and then King beat Whitty all ends up.

Philadelphia won by two runs.

FIRST TEST 1912 ENGLAND v AUSTRALIA
Lord's Cricket Ground, London. June 24, 25, 26, 1912.
Toss: England. Match Drawn.

ENGLAND
JB Hobbs b Emery 107
W Rhodes c Carkeek b Kelleway 59
RH Spooner c Bardsley b Kelleway 1
CB Fry (c) run out 42
PF Warner b Emery 4
FE Woolley c Kelleway b Hazlitt 20
FR Foster c Macartney b Whitty 20
JW Hearne not out 21
EJ Smith (+) not out 14
SF Barnes
H Dean
    EXTRAS (B 16, LB 4, NB 2) 22
TOTAL ....7 dec 310

FOW 1st Inns: 112 123 197 211 246 255 285

Bowling: *First Innings*: Whitty 12-2-69-1, Hazlitt 25-6-68-1, Matthews 13-4-26-0, Kelleway 21-5-66-2, Emery 12-1-46-2, Macartney 7-1-13-0.

AUSTRALIA
CB Jennings c Smith b Foster 21
C Kelleway b Rhodes 61
CG Macartney c Smith b Foster 99
W Bardsley lbw Rhodes 21
ES Gregory (c) c Foster b Dean 10
DBM Smith not out 24
TJ Matthews b Dean 0
GR Hazlitt b Rhodes 19
SH Emery
WJ Whitty
W Carkeek (+)
    EXTRAS (B 17, LB 5, W 1, NB 4) 27
TOTAL ....7 for 282

FOW 1st Inns: 27 173 226 233 243 243 282

Bowling: *First Innings*: Foster 36-18-42-2, Barnes 31-10-74-0, Dean 29-10-49-2, Hearne 12-1-31-0, Rhodes 19.2-5-59-3.

Umpires: J Moss & AE Street

THIRD TEST 1912 ENGLAND v AUSTRALIA
Kennington Oval, London. August 19,20,21,22, 1912.
Toss: England. England won by 244 runs.

ENGLAND
JB Hobbs c Carkeek b Macartney ...66 / c Matthews b Whitty 32
W Rhodes b Minnett ....49 / b Whitty 4
RH Spooner c Hazlitt b Macartney ..1 / c Jennings b Whitty 0
CB Fry (c) c Kelleway b Whitty ....5 / c Jennings b Hazlitt 79
FE Woolley lbw Minnett ....62 / b Hazlitt 4
JW Hearne c Jennings b Whitty .....1 / c Matthews b Hazlitt 14
JWHT Douglas lbw Whitty ....18 / lbw Hazlitt 24
FR Foster b Minnett ....19 / not out 3
EJ Smith (+) b Whitty ....4 / b Hazlitt 0
SF Barnes c Jennings b Minnett ....7 / c Whitty b Hazlitt 0
H Dean not out ....0 / b Hazlitt 0
    EXTRAS (B 2, LB 10, NB 1) ....13 / (B 14, NB 1) 15
TOTAL ....245 / 175

FOW 1st Inns: 107 109 127 131 144 180 216 233 239 245
FOW 2nd Inns: 7 7 51 56 91 170 171 171 175 175

Bowling: *First Innings*: Whitty 38-12-69-4, Matthews 14-5-43-0, Hazlitt 26-10-48-0, Macartney 19-6-22-2, Minnett 10.1-3-34-4, Kelleway 7-2-16-0. *Second Innings*: Whitty 33-13-71-3, Matthews 10-3-21-0, Hazlitt 21.4-8-25-7, Macartney 22-5-43-0.

AUSTRALIA
ES Gregory (c) c Rhodes b Barnes ...1 (5) / c Douglas b Dean 1
C Kelleway lbw Woolley ....43 / c Douglas b Dean 0
CG Macartney b Barnes ....4 / b Dean 30
W Bardsley b Barnes ....30 / run out 14
CB Jennings c & b Woolley ....0 (1) / c Fry b Woolley 14
RB Minnett c Rhodes b Woolley ......0 / lbw Woolley 4
DBM Smith c Smith b Woolley ....6 / c Douglas b Dean 0
TJ Matthews c Fry b Barnes ....2 / c & b Woolley 1
WJ Whitty c Foster b Barnes ....0 / b Woolley 3
GR Hazlitt not out ....2 / c Dean b Woolley 5
W Carkeek (+) c Barnes b Woolley ...5 / not out 0
    EXTRAS (B 12, LB 6) ....18 / (B 1, LB 5, W 1) 7
TOTAL ....111 / 65

FOW 1st Inns: 9 19 90 90 92 96 104 104 104 111
FOW 2nd Inns: 0 46 46 47 51 51 51 54 65 65

Bowling: *First Innings*: Barnes 27-15-30-5, Dean 16-7-29-0, Foster 2-0-5-0, Woolley 9.4-3-29-5. *Second Innings*: Barnes 4-1-18-0, Dean 9-2-19-4, Woolley 7.4-1-20-5, Rhodes 2-1-1-0.

Umpires: J Moss & AE Street

SECOND TEST 1912 ENGLAND v AUSTRALIA
Old Trafford, Manchester. July 29, 30, 31 (no play), 1912.
Toss: England. Match Drawn.

ENGLAND
JB Hobbs b Whitty 19
W Rhodes b Whitty 92
RH Spooner b Whitty 1
CB Fry (c) c(S)JW McLaren b Matthews 19
JW Hearne b Hazlitt 9
FE Woolley c Kelleway b Whitty 13
FR Foster c & b Matthews 13
EJ Smith (+) c Emery b Hazlitt 4
S Haigh c Kelleway b Hazlitt 9
SF Barnes not out 1
JW Hitch b Hazlitt 4
    EXTRAS (B 9, LB 9, NB 1) 19
TOTAL 203

FOW 1st Inns: 37 39 83 140 155 181 185 189 199 203

Bowling: *First Innings*: Hazlitt 40.5-12-77-4, Whitty 27-15-43-4, Kelleway 6-1-19-0, Matthews 12-4-23-2, Emery 7-1-22-0.

AUSTRALIA
CB Jennings not out 9
C Kelleway not out 3
ES Gregory (c)
W Bardsley
CG Macartney
RE Mayne
TJ Matthews
SH Emery
WJ Whitty
GR Hazlitt
W Carkeek (+)
    EXTRAS (B 2) 2
TOTAL ....0 for 14

FOW 1st Inns:

Bowling: *First Innings*: Foster 1-0-3-0, Haigh 6-4-3-0, Woolley 6-3-6-0.

Umpires: G Webb & WAJ West

Australian Averages
1912 ENGLAND v AUSTRALIA

AUSTRALIA	M	Inn	NO	Runs	H.S	Avrge	Ct	St	Overs	Mds	Runs	Wkt	Avrge
Bardsley, W	3	3	-	51	31	17.00	1	-	-	-	-	-	-
Carkeek, W	3	2	1	5	5	5.00	2	-	-	-	-	-	-
Emery, SH	2	-	-	-	-	-	1	-	19.0	2	68	2	34.00
Gregory, ES	3	3	-	12	10	4.00	-	-	-	-	-	-	-
Hazlitt, GR	3	3	1	26	19	13.00	1	-	113.3	36	218	12	18.17
Jennings, CB	3	4	-	44	21	14.67	4	-	-	-	-	-	-
Kelleway, C	3	4	1	107	61	35.67	4	-	34.0	8	101	2	50.50
Macartney, CG	3	3	-	133	99	44.33	1	-	48.0	12	78	2	39.00
Matthews, TJ	3	3	-	3	2	1.00	3	-	49.0	16	113	2	56.50
Mayne, RE	1	-	-	-	-	-	1	-	-	-	-	-	-
Minnett, RB	1	2	-	4	4	2.00	-	-	10.1	3	34	4	8.50
Smith, DBM	2	3	1	30	24*	15.00	-	-	-	-	-	-	-
Whitty, WJ	3	2	-	3	3	1.50	1	-	110.0	42	252	12	21.00

English Averages
1912 ENGLAND v AUSTRALIA

ENGLAND	M	Inn	NO	Runs	H.S	Avrge	Ct	St	Overs	Mds	Runs	Wkt	Avrge
Barnes, SF	3	3	1	8	7	4.00	1	-	62.0	26	122	5	24.40
Dean, H	2	2	1	0	0*	0.00	1	-	54.0	19	97	6	16.17
Douglas, JWHT	1	2	-	42	24	21.00	3	-	-	-	-	-	-
Foster, FR	3	4	1	55	20	18.33	2	-	39.0	18	50	2	25.00
Fry, CB	3	4	-	145	79	36.25	2	-	-	-	-	-	-
Haigh, S	1	1	-	9	9	9.00	-	-	6.0	4	3	-	-
Hearne, JW	3	4	1	45	21*	15.00	-	-	12.0	1	31	-	-
Hitch, JW	1	1	-	4	4	4.00	-	-	-	-	-	-	-
Hobbs, JB	3	4	-	224	107	56.00	-	-	-	-	-	-	-
Rhodes, W	3	4	-	204	92	51.00	2	-	21.2	6	60	3	20.00
Smith, EJ	3	4	1	22	14*	7.33	3	-	-	-	-	-	-
Spooner, RH	3	4	-	3	1	0.75	-	-	-	-	-	-	-
Warner, PF	1	1	-	4	4	4.00	-	-	-	-	-	-	-
Woolley, FE	3	4	-	99	62	24.75	2	-	23.2	7	55	10	5.50

FIRST TEST 1912 AUSTRALIA v SOUTH AFRICA
Old Trafford, Manchester. May 27, 28, 1912.
Toss: Australalia. Australia won by an innings & 88 runs.

AUSTRALIA
CB Jennings c Schwarz b Pegler 32
C Kelleway c Ward b Pegler 114
CG Macartney b Pegler 21
W Bardsley c & b White 121
ES Gregory (c) st Ward b Pegler 37
RB Minnett c & b Schwarz 12
TJ Matthews not out 49
SH Emery b Schwarz 1
GR Hazlitt lbw Schwarz 0
W Carkeek (+) b Pegler 4
WJ Whitty st Ward b Pegler 33
    EXTRAS (B 14, LB 9, W 1) 24
TOTAL 448

FOW 1st Inns: 62 92 294 314 328 375 376 376 385 448

Bowling: *First Innings*: Faulkner 16-2-55-0, Nourse 14-1-62-0, Pegler 45.3-9-105-6, Schwarz 32-0-142-3, Hartigan 9-0-31-0, White 6-1-29-1.

SOUTH AFRICA
GPD Hartigan c Carkeek b Emery ....25 | b Kelleway 4
HW Taylor c Carkeek b Whitty ....0 (5) | b Matthews 21
AW Nourse b Whitty ....17 | c Bardsley b Whitty 18
SJ Snooke b Whitty ....7 | b Whitty 9
GA Faulkner not out ....122 (2) | b Kelleway 0
GC White lbw Whitty ....22 | c Carkeek b Kelleway 9
F Mitchell (c) b Whitty ....11 | b Kelleway 0
RO Schwarz b Hazlitt ....19 | c & b Matthews 0
R Beaumont b Matthews ....31 (10) | b Kelleway 17
SJ Pegler lbw Matthews ....0 (11) | not out 8
TA Ward (+) lbw Matthews ....0 (9) | c & b Matthews 0
  EXTRAS (B 2, LB 5, W 1, NB 3) ....11 | (B 5, LB 1, NB 3) 9
TOTAL ....265 | 95

FOW 1st Inns: 4 30 42 54 143 167 200 265 265 265
FOW 2nd Inns: 1 22 22 43 70 70 70 70 78 95

Bowling: *First Innings*: Hazlitt 16-4-46-1, Whitty 34-12-55-5, Emery 37-10-94-1, Kelleway 11-3-27-0, Matthews 12-3-16-3, Minnett 6-2-16-0. *Second Innings*: Kelleway 14.2-4-33-5, Whitty 6-3-15-2, Matthews 8-1-38-3.

Umpires: G Webb & AA White

THIRD TEST 1912 AUSTRALIA v SOUTH AFRICA
Trent Bridge, Nottingham. August 5, 6, 7 (no play), 1912.
Toss: South Africa. Match Drawn.

SOUTH AFRICA
LJ Tancred (c) c Kelleway b Matthews 30
HW Taylor b Whitty 2
AW Nourse b Whitty 64
GA Faulkner c Kelleway b Emery 15
CB Llewellyn b Emery 12
LA Stricker lbw Macartney 37
SJ Snooke b Kelleway 20
GC White not out 59
R Beaumont b Hazlitt 2
SJ Pegler b Hazlitt 26
TA Ward (+) c Emery b Matthews 24
    EXTRAS (B 30, LB 7, NB 1) 38
TOTAL 329

FOW 1st Inns: 2 79 116 140 154 196 225 232 282 329

Bowling: *First Innings*: Whitty 30-10-64-2, Minnett 8-3-12-0, Hazlitt 28-10-48-2, Matthews 20.5-7-27-2, Emery 21-1-87-2, Kelleway 8-2-18-1, Macartney 13-2-35-1.

AUSTRALIA
CB Jennings run out 9
C Kelleway c Faulkner b Pegler 37
CG Macartney c Faulkner b Llewellyn 34
W Bardsley run out 56
ES Gregory (c) b Pegler 18
RB Minnett c Nourse b Faulkner 31
TJ Matthews b Pegler 21
SH Emery b Faulkner 5
GR Hazlitt not out 2
WJ Whitty b Pegler 0
W Carkeek (+) st Ward b Faulkner 1
    EXTRAS (B 2, LB 3) 5
TOTAL 219

FOW 1st Inns: 19 61 101 127 171 199 212 216 216 219

Bowling: *First Innings*: Pegler 36-6-80-4, Faulkner 20.1-2-43-3, Taylor 12-5-19-0, Llewellyn 22-3-60-1, Nourse 4-1-12-0.
Umpires: G Webb & WAJ Wes

SECOND TEST 1912 AUSTRALIA v SOUTH AFRICA
Lord's Cricket Ground, London. July 15, 16, 17, 1912.
Toss: South Africa. Australia won by 10 wkts.

SOUTH AFRICA
GA Faulkner b Whitty ....5 (6) | c & b Matthews 6
LJ Tancred lbw Matthews ....31 | c Bardsley b Hazlitt 19
GC White c Carkeek b Minnett ....0 | b Matthews 18
CB Llewellyn c Jennings b Minnett ....8 | b Macartney 59
AW Nourse b Hazlitt ....11 | lbw Kelleway 10
HW Taylor c Kelleway b Hazlitt ......93 (7) | not out 10
LA Stricker lbw Kelleway ....48 (1) | b Hazlitt 13
F Mitchell (c) b Whitty ....12 | b Matthews 3
RO Schwarz b Whitty ....0 | c Macartney b Matthews 1
SJ Pegler c Bardsley b Whitty ....25 | c Kelleway b Macartney 14
TA Ward (+) not out ....1 | b Macartney 7
  EXTRAS (B 12, LB 14, W 1, NB 2) ....29 | (B 9, LB 4) 13
TOTAL ....263 | 173

FOW 1st Inns: 24 25 35 56 74 171 203 213 250 263
FOW 2nd Inns: 28 54 62 102 134 136 142 146 163 173

Bowling: *First Innings*: Minnett 15-6-49-2, Whitty 31-9-68-4, Hazlitt 19-9-47-2, Matthews 13-5-32-1, Kelleway 11-3-38-1. *Second Innings*: Whitty 9-0-41-0, Hazlitt 13-1-39-2, Matthews 13-2-29-4, Kelleway 8-1-22-1, Macartney 14.1-5-29-3.

AUSTRALIA
CB Jennings b Nourse ....0 | not out 22
C Kelleway lbw Faulkner ....102 |
CG Macartney b Nourse ....9 |
W Bardsley lbw Llewellyn ....164 |
ES Gregory (c) b Llewellyn ....5 |
RE Mayne st Ward b Pegler ....23 (2) | not out 25
RB Minnett b Pegler ....39 |
TJ Matthews c Faulkner b Pegler ....9 |
GR Hazlitt b Nourse ....0 |
W Carkeek (+) not out ....6 |
WJ Whitty lbw Pegler ....3 |
  EXTRAS (B 24, LB 3, W 2, NB 1) ....30 | (B 1) 1
TOTAL ....390 | ....0 for 48

FOW 1st Inns: 0 14 256 277 316 353 375 379 381 390
FOW 2nd Inns:

Bowling: *First Innings*: Nourse 36-12-60-3, Pegler 29.5-7-79-4, Schwarz 11-1-44-0, Faulkner 28-3-86-1, Llewellyn 19-2-71-2, Taylor 2-0-12-0, Stricker 3-1-8-0. *Second Innings*: Nourse 6.1-2-22-0, Pegler 4-1-15-0, Faulkner 2-0-10-0.

Umpires: J Moss & AE Street

Australian Averages

1912 AUSTRALIA v SOUTH AFRICA

AUSTRALIA	M	Inn	NO	Runs	H.S	Avrge	Ct	St	Overs	Mds	Runs	Wkt	Avrge
Bardsley, W	3	3	-	341	164	113.67	3	-	-	-	-	-	-
Carkeek W	3	3	1	11	6*	5.50	4	-	-	-	-	-	-
Emery, SH	2	2	-	6	5	3.00	1	-	58.0	11	181	3	60.33
Gregory, ES	3	3	-	60	37	20.00	-	-	-	-	-	-	-
Hazlitt, GR	3	3	1	2	2*	1.00	-	-	76.0	24	180	7	25.71
Jennings, CB	3	4	1	63	32	21.00	1	-	-	-	-	-	-
Kelleway, C	3	3	-	253	114	84.33	4	-	52.2	13	138	8	17.25
Macartney, CG	3	3	-	64	34	21.33	-	-	27.1	7	64	4	16.00
Matthews, TJ	3	3	1	79	49*	39.50	3	-	66.5	18	142	13	10.92
Mayne, RE	1	2	1	48	25*	48.00	-	-	-	-	-	-	-
Minnett, RB	3	3	-	82	39	27.33	-	-	29.0	11	77	2	38.50
Whitty, WJ	3	3	-	36	33	12.00	-	-	110.0	34	243	13	18.69

South African Averages

1912 AUSTRALIA v SOUTH AFRICA

SOUTH AFRICA	M	Inn	NO	Runs	H.S	Avrge	Ct	St	Overs	Mds	Runs	Wkt	Avrge
Beaumont, R	2	3	-	50	31	16.67	-	-	-	-	-	-	-
Faulkner, GA	3	5	1	148	122*	37.00	3	-	66.1	7	194	4	48.50
Hartigan, GPD	1	2	-	29	25	14.50	-	-	9.0	-	31	-	-
Llewellyn, CB	2	3	-	79	59	26.33	-	-	41.0	5	131	3	43.67
Mitchell, F	2	4	-	26	12	6.50	-	-	-	-	-	-	-
Nourse, AW	3	5	-	120	64	24.00	1	-	60.1	16	156	3	52.00
Pegler, SJ	3	5	1	73	26	18.25	-	-	115.2	23	279	14	19.93
Schwarz, RO	2	4	-	20	19	5.00	2	-	43.0	1	186	3	62.00
Snooke, SJ	2	3	-	36	20	12.00	-	-	-	-	-	-	-
Stricker, LA	2	3	-	98	48	32.67	-	-	3.0	1	8	-	-
Tancred, LJ	2	3	-	80	31	26.67	-	-	-	-	-	-	-
Taylor, HW	3	5	1	126	93	31.50	-	-	14.0	5	31	-	-
Ward, TA	3	5	1	32	24	8.00	1	4	-	-	-	-	-
White, GC	3	5	1	108	59*	27.00	1	-	6.0	-	29	1	29.00

Shield to South Australia

Adelaide, March 4. South Australia wrapped up their third Sheffield Shield win by defeating Victoria by 166 runs.

Prominent in the win, as he has been all season, was Surrey all-rounder and import Jack Crawford.

In his best performance of the season, Crawford made 163 in just 171 minutes in the SA first innings of 368, and followed it up with a devastating spell of medium-pace bowling, taking 8/66 in Victoria's first innings of 209.

Edgar Mayne followed up Crawford's work with a steadying 106 of 222 in the second innings, Victoria then being dismissed for 215 on a wet wicket, Warwick Armstrong not out on 17.

Jack Ryder did not play in this match but he has had an outstanding debut season making 521 runs and taking 35 wickets – the second highest of the season. Leading wicket taker was Hugh Massie's son Jack with 59 at 18.66.

This was South Australia's second win in Shield matches over Victoria – its only loss was to NSW in Sydney in January, where a Victor Trumper special, 201 not out, was the difference. SA scored 412 in the

Jack Crawford: matchwinner.

fourth innings to fall 84 runs short. A. G. 'Johnnie' Moyes made 95.

Victoria played three matches at the same time at the end of January – a Shield match against NSW at the SCG, a game against Tasmania at the MCG, and a Colts match against NSW at the East Melbourne ground featuring several players who played in the 'firsts' this season. The Victorians lost the two major games.

'Big Ship' makes waves in Victoria

Melbourne, Nov. 1. The 1912 affair continued to simmer beneath the 1912–13 season, with a 'pamphlet war' and efforts made to undermine the stay-at-home players, the Big Six.

Warwick Armstrong was 'white-anted' by Board of Control and VCA delegate Ernie Bean as Victorian captain. Fast bowler Jim Kyle, asked to find someone else, refused because Armstrong had always treated him well. 'If this goes on in big cricket I don't care if I ever play for Victoria again.'

Hordern retires

Sydney Sep. 30. Widely regarded as Australia's best 'googly' bowler, Dr H. V. 'Ranji' Hordern has decided to protect the hands and fingers he needs as a dentist, and retire from first class cricket.

In just seven Test matches Hordern took 46 wickets at 23.36, 32 of them against England in the five Tests of 1911–12, with a best of 7/90. Hordern could bat, putting on 124 with Charlie Macartney in 1910–11. He also toured with the Philadelphia and Pennsylvania University teams while in America.

Victor Trumper is captain of a New South Wales team, which played in Tasmania in his benefit year.

Macartney loves the SCG

Charlie Macartney's championship season. He's in devastating form.

Sydney, Feb. 9. The small but powerfully built right-hander Charlie Macartney must wish he could play every match at the Sydney Cricket Ground. He's been in devastating form there.

He has played five matches at the SCG this season and has scored 195 against Queensland, 117 and 54 against South Australia, 142 against New Zealand, 201 against Victoria, and 110 against Tasmania.

In his other two matches he managed 53 against Victoria at the MCG and 15 and 5 not out against SA in Adelaide.

The 'Governor General' is always on the lookout for runs, and this season made 892 of them at 111.5.

Like a good wine, he seems to be getting better with age.

He recently has accepted a five year contract in South Australia.

New Zealand 'Trumpered'

Auckland, March 31. Victor Trumper has been a major part of the Australian team's triumphant march through New Zealand this month.

Trumper scored 1246 runs in 15 innings, including a record eighth-wicket partnership of 433 with Arthur Sims, the New Zealand tour organiser who was playing with the Australians.

In this innings against Canterbury, Trumper made 293, which included 44 fours and three sixes, in about three hours.

If the Kiwis thought they'd copped a pasting on their tour of Australia earlier in the season, they could have had little idea of what would happen with a team that included legends such as Trumper, Warwick Armstrong, Monty Noble, Herbie Collins, Vernon Ransford, Arthur Mailey and Frank Laver.

In the match against a New Zealand representative side at Eden Park, Trumper made an imperious 81 before going out lbw trying his trick shot.

Australia made 6/610 and defeated NZ, 269 and 228, by an innings and 113 runs.

WA set to join Board of Control

Melbourne, Nov. 14. The Board of Control passed a motion at its Annual General Meeting to invite WA to send a representative to the Board.

Other motions passed set out that the Board would in future net all profits arising from Test matches for distribution to affiliated cricket associations.

Also that the Board had final approval of Selection Committee recommendations for Australian teams and could direct the committee to chose another player if the Board did not approve one 'for the reasons other than cricket ability only'.

And that managers and treasurer of touring teams to England would be appointed by the Board, thus putting an end to player control of touring funds.

Australian team for South Africa

Jack Ryder, picked for South Africa.

Melbourne, June 20. Australian selectors Clem Hill, Ernie Bean and Les Poidevin have chosen the team to tour South Africa in 1914–15. Warwick Armstrong is captain.

The original team chosen was Tom Andrews (NSW), Eric Barbour (NSW), Warren Bardsley (NSW), Fred Baring (Vic.), William Carkeek (Vic.), Gerry Hazlitt (Vic.), Charles Kelleway (NSW), Charlie Macartney (NSW), Edgar Mayne (SA), 'Johnnie' Moyes (SA), Jack Ryder (Vic.) and Bill Whitty (SA)

Hazlitt and Barbour dropped out, and were replaced by Roy Park (Vic.) and Bert Folkard (NSW).

'Old Mac' does a spot of curating at the East Melbourne Cricket Ground.

Victor Trumper dies aged 37

Sydney, July 1. Victor Trumper, 37, the greatest batsman of the age, who died of a chronic and insidious kidney disease in St Vincent's Hospital on June 28, a week after admission, in the presence of his wife Annie, has been buried at Waverley Cemetery.

In these dark wartime days, the loss of such a sunny batsman and happy and generous character felt even worse.

His funeral at Waverley was attended by every cricketer who could get there, and a vast crowd of cricket followers, paying their last respects to a man who gave so much enjoyment to so many for Paddington, NSW and Australia.

Trumper's batsmanship has been described as being all style and grace, and as not comprising a single style but being all style. Looking for Trumper by adding up statistics is like looking for Mozart by adding up the notes, an admirer said.

The pall bearers included Monty Noble, Syd Gregory, Tibby Cotter, Charles 'Terror' Turner, Charlie Macartney and Warren Bardsley.

Trumper leaves a wife Annie, nine-year-old daughter Nancy, 18-month-old son Victor Jr, and an estate valued at £5.

The style of the immortal Victor Trumper, the greatest batsman of the age.

Victoria makes a Shield comeback

Adelaide, Feb. 22. After finishing on the bottom of the Shield table for the past three seasons, Victoria won this wartime Sheffield Shield competition, beating SA by 10 wickets.

The left-arm bowling of big Bert 'Dainty' Ironmonger, with his 36 first class wickets at 17.52, was decisive.

On the batting side with Warwick Armstrong's steadying influence, Roy Park averaged 51 in four matches, and Jack Ryder hit 445 runs at 74.16 in five games.

The only match lost was against NSW at the MCG, which lasted only two days after heavy rain on Christmas day.

Victoria beat SA by 247 runs, Ironmonger taking 13 wickets, then won a close game against NSW, by 16 runs, Ryder top-scoring in both innings.

A feature of the final match against SA was Ryder's highest score for the season, a hard-hitting 151.

Park (62) and Ryder passed SA's first-innings score of 143 for the first wicket.

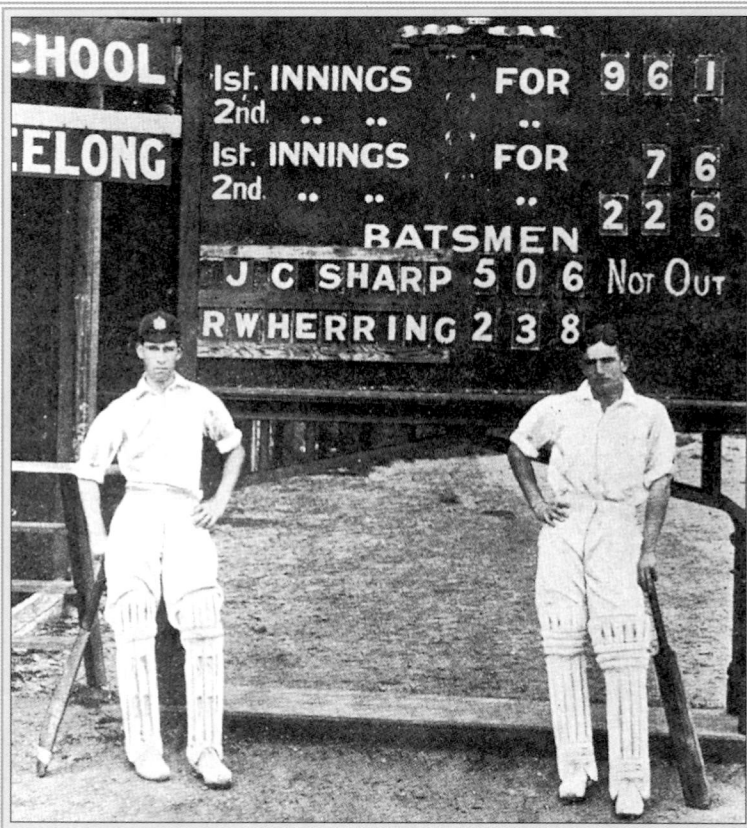

Melbourne Grammar boy J. C Sharp (left) knocked up 506 not out against Geelong College in 1914–15. His partner R. W. Herring made 238 of the total 961. Melbourne Grammar won by an innings and 647 runs.

QUICK SINGLES

To the sportsmen of Victoria. A meeting of 2500, sponsored by MCC, VFL and the Government at the Melbourne Town Hall on 24 February 1915, passed a motion 'that it is the duty of the sportsmen of Victoria to respond at once to the Empire's call by enlisting where possible'. 44 did so on the night.

Massie wounded. Giant NSW fast bowler 'Jack' Massie has been badly wounded at Gallipoli.

Patriotic matches. The first Patriotic Match between Victoria and the Next XV, was played at the MCG on Boxing Day 1915, raising £830.

Cricketer's Tribute. As part of the appeal for Sick and Wounded Soldiers' Funds, an auction of cricket memorabilia was held at Scott's Hotel on 21 January 1916. Jack Blackham donated the ball from the 1882 Ashes test. Racing identity John Wren offered £50 on condition that a £1 subscribers list was opened, and the ball be donated to a national museum. It raised £617. A 1903–04 Trumper bat fetched £57 15s. Billy Murdoch's 1890 autograph bat raised £73 10s. A total of £3255 was raised.

'Felix' dies. Tom Horan, who played 15 Tests for Australia, and became Australia's leading cricket writer, wrote his last story for the *Australasian* on March 25 and died of dropsy on 16 April 1916, aged 62.

'Tibby' Cotter killed. Tibby Cotter, the Australian fast bowler who played 21 Tests and took 89 wickets, was killed in the charge of the Light Horse at Beersheba, Palestine on 31 October 1917. Before the charge he had foraged some fish for dinner. His mate 'Blue' said his last words were 'Blue, you can have the fish supper on your own.'

AIF in England. A team formed from Australian servicemen, captained by Herbie Collins, and still in England, played 28 first class matches in the summer of 1919. Jack Gregory is the star fast bowler.

Interstate cricket resumes. Three matches were played between Victoria, NSW and SA, from December 1918.

Major Onslow batting in difficult conditions (shell-fire) at Shell Green, Gallipoli, on 17 December 1915.

Sportsmen, including cricketers, were called to enlist in the Sportsmen's Thousand organised by racing identity John Wren in 1916.

Tibby Cotter's grave at Beersheba.

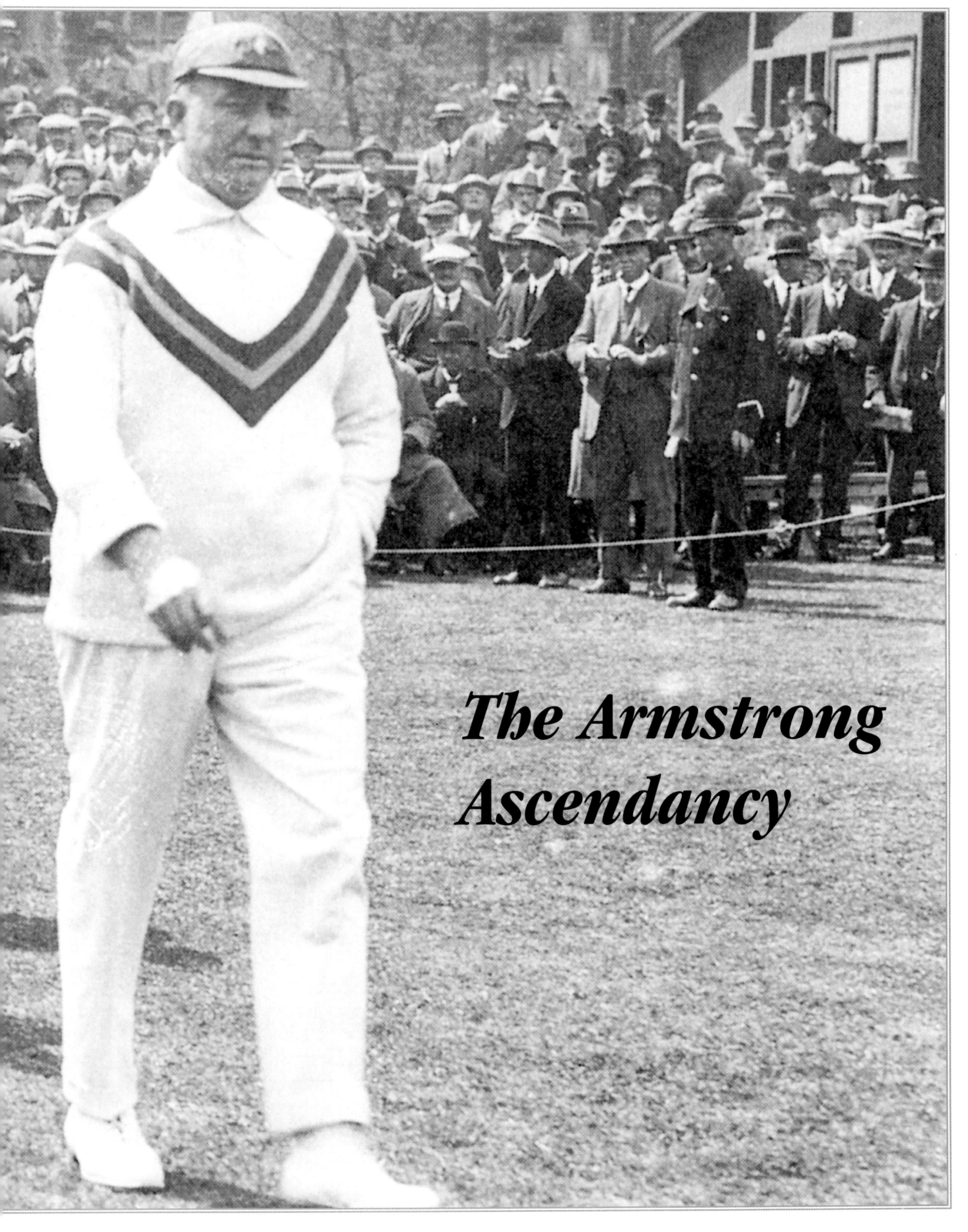

The Armstrong Ascendancy

First AIF team brings on cricket revival

C.S.Winning   C.T.Docker   J.M.Gregory   E.A.Bull   J.T.Murray   E.J.Long   A.W.Lampard
W.S.Stirling   C.E.Pellew   H.L.Collins   Howard Lacy   C.B.Willis   W.L.Trenerry
W.A.Oldfield *Capt.*   J.M.Taylor

The AIF team in England lost only four of 34 matches in 1919, and won 12 of 28 first class games, reviving the game with their spirit and sportsmanship. They were greeted by large crowds wherever they played.

Adelaide, Jan. 2. The victorious Australian Imperial Forces team has nearly arrived home for Christmas, at last, after an all-conquering time in England and South Africa, having agreed to play the three senior States before being demobbed.

However, the team found that the South Australians have already decamped to play Victoria in Melbourne and will have to go there to play.

The AIF tour began with AIF Order No. 1539 on 31 January 1919, which set up an AIF Sports Control Board and cricket team from among the tens of thousands of men still in France and Britain.

Some games had been played in London in 1918 between England and the Dominions. Australian soldier cricketers who played included Charlie Kelleway, Roy Park, Johnnie Moyes and Charlie Macartney.

Trials for the AIF team were held in February, and the first team was then captained for a few matches by Captain Kelleway, but he was 'sacked' by Field Marshall Birdwood, and replaced by the supposedly better-behaved Lance Corporal Herbie Collins.

The AIF team of officers and men played 28 first class and four other matches between May and September, winning 15, drawing

13, and losing just four. One of these was a defeat by a near Test strength Gentlemen of England side at Lord's.

They were greeted by large crowds wherever they played.

The team reluctantly agreed to a request from South Africa to play there on the way home.

Two unofficial Tests against a South African team were played at the Old Wanderers ground at Johannesburg.

Both resulted in easy victories – by eight wickets, and an innings and 129 runs.

Herbie Collins made 235 and took 5/52, and Jack Gregory 5/72 in the first match.

The AIF team among friends outside a guest house. They easily won both unofficial four day 'Tests' in South Africa.

Jack Gregory – the big crowd-puller

Sydney, Feb. 3. Jack Gregory produced one of the great all-round performances in Australian cricket in the last of the three AIF matches against the State teams.

The match against Queensland was substituted for the game against SA – who had already departed Adelaide before the AIF arrived at Christmas time.

Against NSW Gregory blasted 122 in 170 minutes in the first innings, took 5/65 from 15.3 overs, then knocked up 102 in 101 minutes and took another 3/65 as the soldiers' team won by 203 runs.

Gregory also demonstrated his prowess in the slips with three athletic catches.

The successful attacking cricket of the AIF team is proving very attractive to the cricket starved barrackers all over the country.

This crowd-pleaser at the SCG followed Gregory's first class debut in Australia, when he destroyed Victoria with 7/22 on a damp MCG pitch.

The AIF team had the best of a draw with Queensland in a game called off at tea on the last day because of the weather.

The other notable performance in the AIF team was from captain Herbie Collins who scored 135 against Queensland and 129 against NSW.

All-rounder Jack Gregory in action.

Shield – NSW scrapes in

Victoria's Dr Roy Park.

Tom Andrews: 247 not out.

Adelaide, March 3. At the end of the first post-war Sheffield Shield season, both NSW and Victoria finished with an equal number of wins, three each.

NSW won with a better 'quotient'. The 'quotient' is the formula which determines who wins when teams are on equal points.

It is derived by dividing the overall team batting average by the overall team bowling average.

NSW scored 2432 runs for 54 wickets lost, and conceded 2129 while taking 78 wickets – a quotient of 1.650.

Victoria scored 2583 runs for 62 wickets, conceding 2551 runs and taking 70 wickets.

Crucial matches were the NSW-Victoria games at their home grounds. Victoria beat NSW at the MCG, but 'only' by 116 runs – Edgar Mayne making 131, Roy Park 92 and Jack Ryder taking 5/56.

NSW started with a promising opening partnership of 216 from Warren Bardsley, 106, and Charlie Kelleway, 104, but fell short.

In the return match at the SCG, NSW won by a much better margin, an innings and 88 runs, thanks to 247 not out from Tom Andrews. Hunter 'Stork' Hendry cleaned up the Vics with 7/34.

South Australia did not prove competitive, losing to NSW by an innings and 330 runs in Adelaide, and six wickets in Sydney.

Against Victoria they went down by 10 wickets in Melbourne.

In Adelaide they lost by just six wickets.

Shield returns with 8-ball overs

Melbourne, Oct. 17. The Board of Control's Interstate Conference – a committee of the state cricket associations delegates dealing with domestic concerns – set up on 6 December 1918 – will not proceed with VCA secretary Ernie Bean's suggestion that the Sheffield Shield be abandoned.

Bean wanted interstate matches played for 'the joy of competing' on a 'pride only basis'. While the VCA at first agreed to support Bean's idea, its delegates voted against it at this meeting.

The conference also agreed that in future Australian cricket would employ eight ball overs, and that play would take place from 11 a.m. to 6 p.m.

A chance to dine with the AIF team.

QUICK SINGLES

Brother v brother. In the NSW v AIF game at the SCG, two sets of brothers played, named Trenerry and Docker. W.L. Trenerry and C.T. Docker played for the AIF and E. Trenerry and K.B. Docker for NSW.

Curator retires. Charley Checkett has retired as curator of the Adelaide Oval after 36 years, his reason 'rheumatism having developed through moisture from the ground'. He was presented with a testimonial of £186 5s 6d. The new curator will have to deal with white ants eating the perimeter fence.

Diggers practice. Warming up for the AIF v Victoria game at the Brunswick Street Oval against Fitzroy, the AIF made 550 in a day. Cyril Docker made 100 in 22 minutes. Nip Pellew hit 10 sixes, four in one over.

Ground returns. Victoria played Queensland at the Exhibition Ground, the first first class match there for 23 years, and won by 153 runs.

Play suspended. Before the Victoria v AIF game two buglers sounded the Last Post. The *Argus* said: 'It was a wonderful sight – the vast bareheaded crowd standing motionless while the solemn tribute to those gone West was paid.'

Locker-room tea leaf. C. E. R. Maddock (Queensland) was absent on the final day of his side's match against the AIF. Maddock was in court charged with stealing 12s 9-1/2d and other items from the players' change rooms.

Park tops aggregate. Victoria's Dr Roy Park made 648 runs from five first class matches at 72 with a highest score 228, edging out Tom Andrews of NSW with 609 runs at 87 from six matches boosted by his 247 not out.

Stork's bag. Hunter 'Stork' Hendry took 29 wickets at 18.13 to win the bowling aggregate ahead of Warwick Armstrong's 25 at 24.6.

Laver dies. Controversial and underrated, Frank Laver died on 24 September 1919, aged just 49. Laver managed Australian teams and was also a keen diarist and amateur photographer. Dave Gregory also died, on 4 August 1919, aged 74. He was Australia's captain for the first-ever Test in 1877 in Melbourne.

All-round greatness. Playing for the AIF, all-rounder Jack Gregory took 20 wickets in his three matches against the states at 14.89, and made 375 runs at 75. In all AIF matches in his first year of first class play, he took 198 wickets – 131 in 25 matches in England, 47 in eight mat... in South Africa, and his 20 in A... He also scored 1727 runs wi... centuries.

Typhus delays Test

The Australians are getting ready for the first Test series since the War.

Adelaide, Nov. 9. The first England side to tour Australia since the prewar season of 1911–12, had its return to the crease delayed by a bout of typhus.

A passenger on the ship bringing the England team out contracted typhus, which meant that everyone, including the England squad, was quarantined for a week.

A previous invitation to tour in the season 1919–20 was declined by the Marylebone Cricket Club because of its 'unseemly haste' after the War – which cut a melancholy swathe through generations of young English cricketers.

J. W. H. T. Douglas is the England captain. Douglas won an Olympic gold medal in boxing at the 1908 London Games, defeating the Australian legend Snowy Baker in the middleweight division.

Douglas is one of only seven players who have toured Australia before – but the others include the eminent batsmen Jack Hobbs and Patsy Hendren and the all-rounder Wilfred Rhodes.

Among the newcomers, Cecil Parkin's clever off-breaks look promising – though supporters say the England batting looks more suited to Australian conditions than their bowling.

The England team travelled to Adelaide for their first match by train, a journey of four days. The match saw an easy English win. 'Jack' Russell (156) and 'Nutty' Hearne (182) hitting big hundreds and Parkin taking 8/55.

MCG groundsman Bert Luttrell, J. W. H. T. Douglas and Warwick Armstrong.

Public up in arms – no Armstrong

Melbourne, Feb. 15. Rumblings in the public over the dropping of Victorian and Australian captain Warwick Armstrong from the Victorian team surfaced again at a public meeting at the Melbourne Town Hall – even while the Big Ship was sailing through 123 not out for Australia in the fourth Test.

This extraordinary fracas began when Armstrong travelled with the Victorian team to Sydney, but withdrew on medical advice because of a leg injury.

He was promptly dropped by the selectors, who included a couple of his old enemies from 1912, Ernie Bean and Peter McAlister, for the next game against the MCC.

At the public meeting, outrage was expressed by Senator Guthrie who said he had once caught McAlister out and now he was going to boot him out. Martin Hannah MLA said that the selectors had resurrected an old vendetta, using their tyrannical power to crush a great player. 'Kaiserism was not dead,' he said.

Victoria lost that game to NSW, and then lost the game against the MCC. While these matches were taking place, wild meetings were held.

During the MCC match a public meeting in Richmond Park outside the MCG drew more than 8000 people. The *Herald* said many of these came from inside the ground – 'the ranks of the members were depleted as suddenly and as drastically as if a machine gun had been sprayed upon them.'

Victoria has no further matches this season, and Armstrong will content himself with captaining Australia.

The mysterious death of Dr Tozer

Sydney, Dec. 22. NSW batsman Dr Claude Tozer had some unwelcome news for a patient of his after the fourth day's play in the first Test.

Dr Tozer called upon Mrs Dorothy Mort and told her that he was ending their romance because he wished to marry another. Mrs Mort shot him dead, and then wounded herself.

Dr Tozer, born in 1890, was a promising batsman who played four games for NSW before the war, and two in 1919–20.

He made a hundred against Queensland and was tipped to captain NSW.

Australia thrashes a weakened England

Sydney, March 1. Australia completed a 5–0 whitewash of England with the nine-wicket win in the fifth Test at the SCG. This is the first time a victory by one side in all Tests has been achieved in a five-match series, and is a measure of the difference between the two sides.

Australia put seven Test debutants under the captaincy of Warwick Armstrong for the first Test, but somehow they seemed vastly experienced and too good for England.

Jack Gregory, Herbie Collins, Arthur Mailey, Nip Pellew, Jack Ryder, Bert Oldfield and Johnny Taylor joined Charlie Macartney, Warren Bardsley and Charlie Kelleway and the captain at the MCG, and won by 377 runs.

Armstrong hit a chanceless 158 on debut as captain, Collins a century on debut, both in the second innings. Gregory and Mailey took six wickets each for the match. An aggregate crowd of 111,202 people attended the five days.

The second Test was perhaps most notable for a duck, rather than Gregory's 'double' – an even hundred runs and 7/69, or either of the other centuries by Jack Ryder or Jack Hobbs. The latter was itself a masterpiece of batsmanship on a very difficult wicket.

The duck was achieved by local Victorian hero, Dr Roy Park, called into the side from acting as 12th man after Charlie Macartney came down with gastritis.

Park was given a thunderous standing ovation, perhaps the biggest heard at the MCG, and was promptly bowled first ball. The crowd then cheered him off, and was still cheering when next batsman Johnny Taylor was taking block.

Crowds of 105,525 attended three days and one session.

Ominously for England, another fast bowler joined Jack Gregory for the first time in the third Test – the former Tasmanian Ted McDonald.

But the match was won by batsmen, and Mailey, who has proved an enigma, bowling mysteries to most English batsmen. Mailey took 5/160 and 5/142 in large England scores of 447 and 370, with another century to Hobbs.

Australia just outscored England – batting first with 354, Collins 162, and then 582 with centuries to Kelleway, Armstrong, and Pellew.

The fourth Test at the MCG was more of the same – the same Mailey, with 4/115 and an extraor-

dinary 9/121, the same old Armstrong (123) with his third century in a sparkling partnership with Jack Gregory (77) of 145 for the sixth wicket in the second innings, same result – Australia by eight wickets.

Armstrong was suffering from malaria at the time, and took no further part in the game.

Charlie Macartney back from illness knocked up his highest Test score, 170, in the fifth Test, Mailey took another five-wicket haul in the England second innings and Australia won by nine wickets, watched by 63,421 barrackers.

Or perhaps not so happy – accusations flew about after the match when it was revealed that two English players had sent reports to England of unfair 'barracking' of Hobbs, who had batted with an incapacitating thigh injury.

But the *Australasian* had it right when in an editorial comment it said 'opinions held by hysterical amateur special correspondents to the contrary, the Australian cricket "barracker" is not a very dreadful person. He is often a nuisance, and frequently vulgar. Occasionally witty, he has usually a keen sense of fair play, and except when

smarting under a sense of injustice, is not vicious. ... the great body of those present treated Hobbs with consideration and sympathy.'

Journalist Donald McDonald agreed. 'I never heard a remark which could, by any stretch of the imagination, be interpreted as a jeer against a crippled man' – except when news emerged that Fender and Wilson were the player correspondents concerned. They were barracked without ~

Jack Gregory's 15 ca~ series was a record Mailey's 36 wickets of 26.28 was one s'

The considerable bulk of Warwick Armstrong is behind the ball as he drives four of his 1069 runs for the season.

It's 'Gulliver' in flannels

Armstrong's III, with Bill and Tom Tootell v Boys of Mentone XVIII.

Mentone, Feb. 3. While the whole Victorian cricket world was in a state of consternation over Warwick Armstrong being 'dropped' for the game against the touring England side, the great man slipped quietly out of town to fulfill another cricketing engagement – a promise to play the Boys of Mentone, a Melbourne suburb.

A regiment of boys and 500 spectators gathered at the Mentone Reserve to witness the great match. Armstrong had Bill Tootell aged 8, and Tom Tootell aged 6 on his side.

There were 18 Boys ranging in age from 6 to 15 and in height from 3 ft 6 in to 6 feet.

Armstrong changed in the shed, and the boys watched in silent awe as he drew from his capacious flannels his famous American dollar with which he has won three tosses in a row in the first three Tests. Billy Godby was asked to call, and like J. W. H. T. Douglas, called wrong. Armstrong sent the Boys in to bat.

He bowled 36 overs of googlies, took 16/144 as the Boys were dis-[...]ed for 145.

Batting, Armstrong's III lost both openers for three, but as the 'last man gets his tucker' rule applied, Armstrong batted on, making 13 from precise pushes and glides.

But with the score on 17, Billy Godby aged 11, put one straight through the Australian captain, who was clean bowled for 13. The little bowler stood proud but abashed, and his team-mates wanted to box his ears for ending the game so soon.

Armstrong said: 'It's a long time since any man bowled me for so small a score. That ball you bowled me with is the ball that was used in the Test game played at Nottingham, England, in 1909. Keep it boy, to remind you of the day you got me cheap.'

Charlie Smith, skipper of the Boys, handed Armstrong a pipe to remember the day by. Armstrong said, a trifle huskily: 'Thank you boys, I'll never forget you nor the happy time we have had together today.'

No wonder Armstrong is revered by cricket followers, young and old, throughout the land.

FIRST TEST 1920–21 AUSTRALIA v ENGLAND
Sydney Cricket Ground, Sydney. December 17, 18, 20, 21, 22, 1920.
Toss: Australia. Australia won by 377 runs.

AUSTRALIA

CG Macartney b Waddington	19	(3) b Douglas	69
HL Collins run out	70	c Waddington b Douglas	104
W Bardsley c Strudwick b Hearne	22	(1) b Hearne	57
C Kelleway run out	33	(6) c Russell b Woolley	78
WW Armstrong (c) st Strudwick b Woolley	12	(7) b Parkin	158
JM Gregory c Strudwick b Woolley	8	(9) run out	0
JM Taylor lbw Hearne	34	(4) c Woolley b Parkin	51
CE Pellew c Hendren b Hearne	36	(5) lbw Woolley	16
J Ryder run out	5	(8) run out	6
WAS Oldfield (+) c Hobbs b Parkin	7	c Strudwick b Parkin	16
AA Mailey not out	10	not out	0
EXTRAS (B 4, LB 6, NB 1)	11	(B 17, LB 7, NB 2)	26
TOTAL	267		581

FOW 1st Inns: 40 80 140 162 173 176 244 249 250 267
FOW 2nd Inns: 123 234 241 282 332 519 536 540 578 581

Bowling: *First Innings*: Hitch 10-0-37-0, Waddington 18-3-35-1, Parkin 26.5-5-58-1, Hearne 34-8-77-3, Woolley 23-7-35-2, Douglas 3-0-14-0. *Second Innings*: Hitch 8-0-40-0, Waddington 23-4-53-0, Parkin 35.3-5-102-3, Hearne 42-7-124-1, Douglas 26-3-79-2, Woolley 36-10-90-2, Rhodes 22-2-67-0.

ENGLAND

CAG Russell b Kelleway	0	c Oldfield b Gregory	5
JB Hobbs b Gregory	49	lbw Armstrong	59
JW Hearne c Gregory b Mailey	14	b Gregory	57
EH Hendren c Gregory b Ryder	28	b Kelleway	56
FE Woolley c Mailey b Ryder	52	st Oldfield b Mailey	16
JWHT Douglas (c) st Oldfield b Mailey	21	c Armstrong b Mailey	7
W Rhodes c Gregory b Mailey	3	c Ryder b Mailey	45
JW Hitch c Kelleway b Gregory	3	c Taylor b Gregory	19
A Waddington run out	7	b Kelleway	3
CH Parkin not out	4	b Kelleway	4
H Strudwick (+) lbw Gregory	2	not out	1
EXTRAS (B 3, LB 4)	7	(B 6, LB 3)	9
TOTAL	190		281

FOW 1st Inns: 0 50 70 144 145 158 165 180 188 190
FOW 2nd Inns: 5 105 149 170 178 231 264 271 279 281

Bowling: *First Innings*: Kelleway 6-2-10-1, Gregory 23.1-3-56-3, Mailey 23-4-95-3, Ryder 6-1-20-2, Armstrong 1-0-2-0. *Second Innings*: Kelleway 15.5-3-45-3, Gregory 33-6-70-3, Macartney 3-0-7-0, Mailey 24-2-105-3, Ryder 17-6-24-0, Armstrong 10-0-21-1.

Umpires: RM Crockett & AC Jones

SECOND TEST 1920–21 AUSTRALIA v ENGLAND
Melbourne Cricket Ground, Melbourne. December 31, 1920, January 1, 3, 4, 1921.
Toss: Australia. Australia won by an innings & 91 runs.

AUSTRALIA

HL Collins c Hearne b Howell	64
W Bardsley c Strudwick b Woolley	51
RL Park b Howell	0
JM Taylor c Woolley b Parkin	68
WW Armstrong (c) lbw Douglas	39
C Kelleway c Strudwick b Howell	9
CE Pellew b Parkin	116
J Ryder c Woolley b Douglas	13
JM Gregory c Russell b Woolley	100
WAS Oldfield (+) c & b Rhodes	24
AA Mailey not out	8
EXTRAS (B 1, LB 3, W 1, NB 2)	7
TOTAL	499

FOW 1st Inns: 116 116 118 194 220 251 282 455 469 499

Bowling: *First Innings*: Howell 37-5-142-3, Douglas 24-1-83-2, Parkin 27-0-116-2, Hearne 14-0-38-0, Woolley 27-8-87-2, Rhodes 8.3-1-26-1.

ENGLAND

JB Hobbs c Ryder b Gregory	122	b Kelleway	20
W Rhodes b Gregory	7	c Collins b Armstrong	28
JWH Makepeace lbw Armstrong	4	c Gregory b Armstrong	4
EH Hendren c Taylor b Gregory	67	c & b Collins	1
CAG Russell c Collins b Gregory	0	c Armstrong b Collins	5
FE Woolley b Gregory	5	b Ryder	50
JWHT Douglas (c) lbw Gregory	15	b Gregory	9
CH Parkin c Mailey b Gregory	4	c Taylor b Armstrong	9
H Strudwick (+) not out	21	c Oldfield b Armstrong	24
H Howell st Oldfield b Armstrong	5	not out	0
JW Hearne			
EXTRAS (NB 1)	1	(B 3, LB 3, NB 1)	7
TOTAL	9 for 251		9 for 157

FOW 1st Inns: 20 32 174 185 201 208 213 232 251
FOW 2nd Inns: 36 53 54 58 70 104 141 151 157

Bowling: *First Innings*: Kelleway 19-1-54-0, Gregory 20-1-69-7, Armstrong 24.3-8-50-2, Ryder 14-2-31-0, Park 1-0-9-0, Collins 9-0-37-0. *Second Innings*: Kelleway 12-1-25-1, Gregory 12-0-32-1, Armstrong 15.2-5-26-4, Collins 17-5-47-2, Ryder 10-2-17-1, Pellew 1-0-3-0.

Umpires: RM Crockett & DA Elder

THIRD TEST 1920–21 AUSTRALIA v ENGLAND
Adelaide Oval, Adelaide. January 14, 15, 17, 18, 19, 20, 1921.
Toss: Australia. Australia won by 119 runs.

AUSTRALIA

HL Collins c Rhodes b Parkin	162		c Hendren b Parkin	24
W Bardsley st Strudwick b Douglas	14		b Howell	16
C Kelleway c Fender b Parkin	4		b Howell	147
JM Taylor run out	5 (6)		c Strudwick b Fender	38
WW Armstrong (c) c Strudwick b Douglas	11		b Howell	121
CE Pellew run out	35 (7)		c Strudwick b Parkin	104
JM Gregory c Strudwick b Fender	10 (8)		not out	78
J Ryder c Douglas b Parkin	44 (4)		c Woolley b Howell	3
WAS Oldfield (+) lbw Parkin	50		b Rhodes	10
EA McDonald b Parkin	2		b Rhodes	4
AA Mailey not out	3		b Rhodes	13
EXTRAS (B 6, LB 8)	14		(B 5, LB 10, W 4, NB 5)	24
TOTAL	354			582

FOW 1st Inns: 32 45 55 96 176 209 285 347 349 354
FOW 2nd Inns: 34 63 71 265 328 434 477 511 570 582

Bowling: *First Innings*: Howell 26-1-89-0, Douglas 24-6-69-2, Parkin 20-2-60-5, Woolley 21-6-47-0, Fender 12-0-52-1, Rhodes 5-1-23-0. *Second Innings*: Howell 34-6-115-4, Douglas 19-2-61-0, Woolley 38-4-91-0, Parkin 40-8-109-2, Fender 22-0-105-1, Rhodes 25.5-8-61-3, Hobbs 7-2-16-0.

ENGLAND

JB Hobbs c & b Mailey	18		b Gregory	123
W Rhodes run out	16		lbw McDonald	4
JWH Makepeace c Gregory b Armstrong	60		c & b McDonald	30
EH Hendren b Gregory	36		b Mailey	51
FE Woolley c Kelleway b Gregory	79		b Gregory	0
CAG Russell not out	135		b Mailey	59
JWHT Douglas (c) lbw Mailey	60		c Armstrong b Gregory	32
PGH Fender b McDonald	2		c Ryder b Mailey	42
CH Parkin st Oldfield b Mailey	12 (10)		st Oldfield b Mailey	17
H Strudwick (+) c Pellew b Mailey	9 (9)		c Armstrong b Mailey	1
H Howell c Gregory b Mailey	2		not out	4
EXTRAS (B 8, LB 5, NB 5)	18		(LB 3, NB 4)	7
TOTAL	447			370

FOW 1st Inns: 25 49 111 161 250 374 391 416 437 447
FOW 2nd Inns: 20 125 183 185 243 292 308 321 341 370

Bowling: *First Innings*: McDonald 24-1-78-1, Gregory 36-5-108-2, Kelleway 11-4-25-0, Mailey 32.1-3-160-5, Armstrong 23-10-29-1, Ryder 6-0-29-0. *Second Innings*: McDonald 24-0-95-2, Kelleway 8-2-16-0, Mailey 29.2-3-142-5, Armstrong 16-1-41-0, Ryder 9-2-19-0, Gregory 20-2-50-3.

Umpires: RM Crockett & DA Elder

FIFTH TEST 1920–21 AUSTRALIA v ENGLAND
Sydney Cricket Ground, Sydney. February 25, 26, 28, March 1, 1921.
Toss: England. Australia won by 9 wkts.

ENGLAND

JB Hobbs lbw Gregory	40 (5)		c Taylor b Mailey	34
W Rhodes c Carter b Kelleway	26		run out	25
JWH Makepeace c Gregory b Mailey	3		c Gregory b Kelleway	7
EH Hendren c Carter b Gregory	5 (6)		st Carter b Mailey	13
FE Woolley b McDonald	53 (1)		c & b Kelleway	1
CAG Russell c Gregory b Mailey	19 (8)		c Gregory b Armstrong	35
JWHT Douglas (c) not out	32		c & b Mailey	68
PGH Fender c Gregory b Kelleway	2 (9)		c Kelleway b McDonald	40
ER Wilson c Carter b Kelleway	5 (4)		st Carter b Mailey	5
CH Parkin c Taylor b Kelleway	9		c Gregory b Mailey	36
H Strudwick (+) b Gregory	2		not out	5
EXTRAS (B 3, LB 2, W 1, NB 2)	8		(B 3, LB 5, NB 3)	11
TOTAL	204			280

FOW 1st Inns: 54 70 74 76 125 161 164 172 201 204
FOW 2nd Inns: 1 14 29 75 82 91 160 224 251 280

Bowling: *First Innings*: Gregory 16.1-4-42-3, McDonald 11-2-38-1, Kelleway 20-6-27-4, Mailey 23-1-89-2. *Second Innings*: McDonald 25-3-58-1, Kelleway 14-3-29-2, Mailey 36.2-5-119-5, Gregory 16-3-37-0, Ryder 2-2-0-0, Armstrong 8-2-26-1.

AUSTRALIA

HL Collins c Fender b Parkin	5		c Strudwick b Wilson	37
W Bardsley c Fender b Douglas	7		not out	50
CG Macartney c Hobbs b Fender	170		not out	2
JM Taylor c Hendren b Douglas	32			
JM Gregory c Strudwick b Fender	93			
WW Armstrong (c) c Woolley b Fender	0			
J Ryder b Fender	2			
C Kelleway c Strudwick b Wilson	32			
H Carter (+) c Woolley b Fender	17			
AA Mailey b Wilson	5			
EA McDonald not out	3			
EXTRAS (B 18, LB 6, NB 2)	26		(B 3, NB 1)	4
TOTAL	392			1 for 93

FOW 1st Inns: 16 22 89 287 287 313 356 384 384 392
FOW 2nd Inns: 91

Bowling: *First Innings*: Douglas 16-0-84-2, Parkin 19-1-83-1, Woolley 15-1-58-0, Wilson 14.3-4-28-2, Fender 20-1-90-5, Rhodes 7-0-23-0. *Second Innings*: Parkin 9-1-32-0, Woolley 11-3-27-0, Fender 1-0-2-0, Rhodes 7.2-1-20-0, Wilson 6-1-8-1.

Umpires: RM Crockett & DA Elder

FOURTH TEST 1920–21 AUSTRALIA v ENGLAND
Melbourne Cricket Ground, Melbourne. February 11, 12, 14, 15, 16, 1921.
Toss: England. Australia won by 8 wkts.

ENGLAND

JB Hobbs c Carter b McDonald	27		lbw Mailey	13
W Rhodes c Carter b Gregory	11		c Gregory b Mailey	73
JWH Makepeace c Collins b Mailey	117		lbw Mailey	54
EH Hendren c Carter b Mailey	30		b Kelleway	32
FE Woolley lbw Kelleway	29		st Carter b Mailey	0
JWHT Douglas (c) c & b Mailey	50		st Carter b Mailey	60
A Waddington b Mailey	0 (8)		st Carter b Mailey	6
PGH Fender c Gregory b Kelleway	3 (7)		c Collins b Mailey	59
A Dolphin (+) b Kelleway	1		c Gregory b Mailey	0
CH Parkin run out	10		c Bardsley b Mailey	4
H Howell not out	0		not out	0
EXTRAS (B 1, LB 5)	6		(B 5, LB 5, W 1, NB 3)	14
TOTAL	284			315

FOW 1st Inns: 18 61 104 164 270 273 274 275 284
FOW 2nd Inns: 32 145 152 152 201 305 307 307 315 315

Bowling: *First Innings*: McDonald 19-2-46-1, Gregory 18-1-61-1, Mailey 29.2-1-115-4, Ryder 10-5-10-0, Armstrong 5-1-9-0, Kelleway 18-2-37-3. *Second Innings*: Gregory 14-4-31-0, Kelleway 23-8-47-1, Mailey 47-8-121-9, McDonald 23-2-77-0, Ryder 10-3-25-0.

AUSTRALIA

HL Collins c Rhodes b Woolley	59		c Rhodes b Parkin	32
W Bardsley b Fender	56		run out	38
J Ryder lbw Woolley	7		not out	52
JM Taylor hit wicket b Fender	2			
JM Gregory c Dolphin b Parkin	77 (4)		not out	76
CE Pellew b Fender	12			
WW Armstrong (c) not out	123			
C Kelleway b Fender	27			
H Carter (+) b Fender	13			
AA Mailey run out	13			
EA McDonald b Woolley	0			
EXTRAS (B 1, LB 6, W 1, NB 5)	13		(B 5, LB 5, W 2, NB 1)	13
TOTAL	389			2 for 211

FOW 1st Inns: 117 123 128 133 153 298 335 335 376 389
FOW 2nd Inns: 71 81

Bowling: *First Innings*: Howell 17-2-86-0, Douglas 4-0-17-0, Waddington 5-0-31-0, Parkin 22-5-64-1, Fender 32-3-122-5, Woolley 32.1-14-56-3. *Second Innings*: Howell 10-1-36-0, Douglas 5-1-13-0, Woolley 14-4-39-0, Parkin 12-2-46-1, Fender 13.2-2-39-0, Rhodes 10-2-25-0.

Umpires: RM Crockett & DA Elder

Australian Averages

1920–21 AUSTRALIA v ENGLAND

AUSTRALIA	M	Inn	NO	Runs	H.S	Avrge	Ct	St	Overs	Mds	Runs	Wkt	Avrge
Armstrong, WW	5	7	1	464	158	77.33	4	-	102.5	27	204	9	22.67
Bardsley, W	5	9	1	311	57	38.88	1	-	-	-	-	-	-
Carter, H	2	2	-	17	17	8.50	6	5	-	-	-	-	-
Collins, HL	5	9	-	557	162	61.89	5	-	26.0	5	84	2	42.00
Gregory, JM	5	8	2	442	100	73.67	15	-	208.2	29	556	23	24.17
Kelleway, C	5	7	-	330	147	47.14	4	-	146.5	32	315	15	21.00
Macartney, CG	2	4	-	260	170	86.67	-	-	3.0	-	7	-	-
Mailey, AA	5	7	4	52	13	17.33	5	-	244.1	27	946	36	26.28
McDonald, EA	3	4	1	9	4	3.00	1	-	126.0	10	392	6	65.33
Oldfield, WAS	3	5	-	107	50	21.40	2	5	-	-	-	-	-
Park, RL	1	1	-	0	0	0.00	-	-	1.0	-	9	-	-
Pellew, CE	4	6	-	319	116	53.17	1	-	1.0	-	3	-	-
Ryder, J	5	8	1	132	52*	18.86	3	-	84.0	23	175	3	58.33
Taylor, JM	5	7	-	230	68	32.86	5	-	-	-	-	-	-

English Averages

1920–21 AUSTRALIA v ENGLAND

ENGLAND	M	Inn	NO	Runs	H.S	Avrge	Ct	St	Overs	Mds	Runs	Wkt	Avrge
Dolphin, A	1	2	-	1	1	0.50	1	-	-	-	-	-	-
Douglas, JWHT	5	10	1	354	68	39.33	-	-	121.0	13	420	8	52.50
Fender, PGH	3	6	-	148	59	24.67	3	-	100.2	6	410	12	34.17
Hearne, JW	2	2	-	71	57	35.50	1	-	90.0	15	239	4	59.75
Hendren, EH	5	10	-	319	67	31.90	3	-	-	-	-	-	-
Hitch, JW	1	2	-	22	19	11.00	-	-	18.0	-	77	-	-
Hobbs, JB	5	10	-	505	123	50.50	2	-	7.0	2	16	-	-
Howell, H	3	6	4	11	5	5.50	-	-	124.0	15	468	7	66.86
Makepeace, JWH	4	8	-	279	117	34.88	-	-	-	-	-	-	-
Parkin, CH	5	10	1	109	36	12.11	-	-	211.2	29	670	16	41.88
Rhodes, W	5	10	-	238	73	23.80	4	-	85.4	15	245	4	-
Russell, CAG	4	8	1	258	135*	36.86	2	-	-	-	-	-	-
Strudwick, H	4	8	3	65	24	13.00	12	2	-	-	-	-	-
Waddington, A	2	4	-	16	7	4.00	1	-	46.0	7	119	-	-
Wilson, ER	1	2	-	10	5	5.00	-	-	20.3	5	3	-	-

1921

AUSTRALIA IN ENGLAND

QUICK SINGLES

Fixture fiddled. On the voyage to England aboard the *Osterley*, Armstrong told his players that the fixture had been arranged by 'a mob of novices'. The team was expected to traipse all over England, usually playing a county the day before a Test match was to begin. Manager Sydney Smith has rearranged three games before the first three Tests.

Flying visit. While the rest of the team travelled from France to England by boat train, Hanson Carter and Syd Smith became the first Australians to fly in, from Paris to Cricklewood aerodrome in March.

Hobbs displays Aussie bat. Appendicitis-ridden batting great Jack Hobbs displayed a rough-hewn outsize weapon, a bat with the bark on the back and wattle leaves painted on the front, in his Fleet Street shop window. It is a souvenir from the Adelaide Sports Club. He won't be needing it this summer.

The master Macartney. Against Nottingham in June, Charlie Macartney hit 345 in just under four hours, with 47 fours and four sixes. Notts captain Arthur Carr bowled one over to switch bowlers – Macartney hit each ball for four.

Trumper memorial:. Victor Trumper at last had a simple marble memorial in the 'bob' section of the SCG laid without ceremony in July by friends and admirers.

Player turnover. England used 30 players in five Tests, Australia employed just 13.

Runs and wickets. Four players took 100 wickets on tour – McDonald 138, Mailey 134, Gregory 116 and Armstrong 100. Six players made over a thousand runs – Macartney 2317, Bardsley 2005, Armstrong 1213, Andrews 1212, Gregory 1135, Taylor 1019. Armstrong and Gregory achieved the 'double'.

Tour worth a bonus. The 1921 Australian tour reaped a large profit of £35,644 8s 4d. The Board of Control has decided to grant a £200 bonus to each of the fifteen players, plus £100 to Bill Ferguson, baggage man and scorer.

Arthur Mailey – 10/66 and all that

Arthur Mailey: the googly great.

Gloucester, Aug. 19. When Arthur Mailey bowled Gloucestershire out in the second innings, taking all ten wickets for 66, it was entirely appropriate that he should do so.

Johnnie Moyes wrote that his bowling 'was a mixture of spin, flight and humour.'

Last season when England captain J. W. H. T. Douglas took field glasses to try and divine Mailey's mysteries from behind his arm, he didn't reckon on having his footwork befuddled by Mailey's sense of humour.

'Sometimes I am attacked by waves of accuracy; and I don't trust them,' Mailey said of himself.

'As regards humour, I fancy he had many a chuckle when a ball spun prodigiously, landed half way down the pitch, or went towards the batsman on the full and then did something entirely unexpected,' wrote Moyes.

Mailey 'always declared that a ball which is spinning like a top must be treated with care, regardless of the length.'

Aside from 10/66 Mailey took the great 9/121 against England at the MCG in 1920–21.

In the match against Gloucestershire, Mailey took 3/21 in the first innings. In the second innings Armstrong declared he 'was going to get among these cheap wickets' but was belted all round the Cheltenham College ground to the increasing laughter of his fielders. It was only then that he sheepishly handed the ball to Mailey.

Rampaging Australians 2–0

Lord's, June 14. The calls in the London *Times* for an England victory in the second Test at Lord's as 'a matter of national importance' have fallen on deaf ears.

England has been lashed to another defeat, by eight wickets, following the dispiriting loss in the first Test by 10 wickets.

This time it was the last stroke of the day that seems to sum up the England performance.

Big fast bowler Fred Durston let a delivery slip out of his hand, and it dribbled half way up the pitch. Warren Bardsley batting for Australia in the second innings waved fielders away and smote the ball to the boundary, and marched off with his smiling partner 'Nip' Pellew.

Once again Australia proved too talented, too athletic and too well-captained by the colossus of Australian cricket, Warwick Armstrong for England.

They did it without batting all that well – Bardsley excepted.

England's exception was elegant Frank Woolley whose pair of nineties – 95 and 93, were both ended by Arthur Mailey.

But it was the fast bowling duo of Jack Gregory and Ted McDonald which laid out the plans the Australians had for England.

Jack Gregory's third over in the first Test 'destroyed the morale of English cricket for the best part of a season' wrote one commentator.

Gregory took three wickets. When he bowled what was solemnly declared by the *Cricketer* 'to be a ball which would have bowled the best batsman in the world at any time of an innings', the victim 'Patsy' Hendren said it was a statement he 'would have

John Bull in need of comfort.

gladly endorsed with his initials and the date if in the heat and horror of the moment he could have recalled either to his memory'.

In this England innings of 112, which lasted just 37 overs, Gregory and McDonald built their image as destroyers of batsmen.

Ernest Tyldesley in the second innings mistimed a hook from a short fast one from Gregory and was struck on the jaw. He was not knocked out but he was bowled out – the ball had rebounded onto the stumps.

England batted better in the third Test, but all these matches reinforced the idea that three-day Test matches, with or without rain, require extra special bowling efforts in order to gain a result.

The 1921 Australian Test team, mostly under the coveted baggy green cap.

Yet another series win: 3–0

The Oval, Aug. 16. Warwick Armstrong has, as captain, experienced just his second draw in Test cricket – following eight consecutive victories.

This unaccustomed sensation followed the more familiar one of a win in the third Test at Headingley, which wrapped up the series and the Ashes.

This game was memorable for a Charlie Macartney century, and a bludgeoning 77 from the skipper. Hobbs did not bat for England. He was absent with appendicitis.

The Hon. Lionel Tennyson was also hurt, and batted one handed in an extraordinary innings for 63 from 106 balls that gave England hearts a flutter of hope.

The fourth Test lost one of three scheduled days to rain, which left a draw as the only possible result.

At 341 for 4 Tennyson, the England captain, wanted to declare and have twenty minutes at the Australians. He had neglected or did not know Law 55 as amended in 1914 which stated that in a two-day match (which this had become) an innings could not be closed later than 100 minutes before the scheduled close of play. Armstrong, as reminded by 'keeper Hanson Carter, knew that to be the case and smoked his pipe for 20 minutes while the mess was sorted out. Play resumed – and Armstrong who had bowled the last over before the interruption, bowled again directly after it. In preventing the breaking of one law, Armstrong broke another.

The final day's play was enlivened by a pitch drying after overnight rain, and Australia struggled to 175, the day saved by 40 from Herbie Collins in over four hours. It was said he moved not a muscle on his leathery face, and only others as were necessary.

In the fifth Test Phil Mead made 182 for England, the highest score in the series so far.

Australia batted to within 14 runs of England and with three hours play remaining in the match, Armstrong bowled everyone except the 'keeper while England rattled on 2/244. In this fag end of the match, he patrolled the outfield and idly picked up a piece of blowing newspaper for a few seconds. Armstrong said he read it 'to see who we were playing.'

It was England, it was a draw, Armstrong had won the series with surely the most capable team of Australians to land in England.

RIP, an English cartoonist, magnifies the Australian team's personalities.

Frank Woolley plays-on to Arthur Mailey, to be out for 37 in the third Test.

MacLaren shows it can be done

Eastbourne, Aug. 25. Archie MacLaren the 49-year-old pre-war England captain had written to the *Manchester Guardian* cricket correspondent Neville Cardus saying 'I think I know how to beat Armstrong's lot'.

He had his opportunity at the Eastbourne gala, with a collection of Cambridge chums, new prospects and South African Aubrey Faulkner, who had played so well against Australia before the war.

Armstrong and his merry men, who hadn't lost a game for six months and 34 matches, travelled overnight to play.

All seemed well when they bundled MacLaren's men out for 43, but they then struggled against Faulkner's googlies and young swing bowler Michael Falcon. All out 174.

Then, by some strange turn of the cricketing fates, Aubrey Faulkner was supported by sufficient young blades to hit up a wonderful 153 of the team's 326. Australia needed 196 – but could not get them, thanks to Charles Gibson's 6/64.

Australia lost by 28 runs, Armstrong himself googlied out lbw by a beaut straight one from Faulkner.

Their win, acknowledged generously by Armstrong, meant nothing to the triumphant Australians.

But it sent a warm, late summer's glow through English cricket – that there was hope, after all.

Cricket conference plays with rules

London, Aug. 15. At the meeting of the Imperial Cricket Conference, Australian delegates manager Sydney Smith and captain Warwick Armstrong put a number of proposals.

They included the appointing of umpires on the morning of the match to 'remove them from temptation' in regard to betting on cricket, and moving from six to eight ball overs.

The eight-ball over was introduced in Australia in 1918–19. The six-ball over had been the norm from 1889–90.

At the ICC meeting, Australia also called for an extra 10 minutes rolling before play of any pitch affected by rain.

These proposals will be pl___ before a special general the MCC and are unlikely to succeed.

Big Warwick – The Colossus of Cricket

Warwick Windridge Armstrong was born in Kyneton, Victoria on 22 May 1879. His father, a solicitor, was in partnership with the South Melbourne cricketer Albert Major, who played for Victoria against Lord Harris' England XI in 1879.

The Armstrongs moved to Melbourne in 1898 and Warwick turned out for South Melbourne – in cricket and then in football.

He made 665 runs at 95 that season and took 12 wickets at 15.16 for South, and was picked in two games for Victoria – the try-out games against Tasmania (4/78) and New Zealand (nothing special).

In football, he played for South Melbourne in the 1899 Grand Final which the 'blood stained angels' lost to Fitzroy – by a point. This was one of the slim, tall utility player's 13 games in 1899 and 1900, in which he kicked 18 goals.

In the 1899–1900 cricket season Armstrong made his first big score, 270 for South Melbourne against Melbourne, who recruited him as a playing member of the MCC staff, a job which he held until 1921, supervising up to 25 staff and acting as a 'ground' bowler for members.

In 1903–04 he made 812 runs at an average of 135.33 and took 7/6 against South Melbourne. He also made a record district cricket score of 438 against University. His aggregate of 840 in 1905–06 and 1452 in 1915–16 created records he held for nearly 40 years.

Armstrong did not consolidate his place in the Victorian team until he hit 118, the first of his 23 centuries for Victoria, against SA in November 1900.

He made his debut for Australia in the second Test in January 1902, making 45 not out in a 10th-wicket partnership of 120 with Reggie Duff. He played the four last Tests for modest returns.

But he was picked for the great 1902 side which toured England, where he made over a thousand runs and took 81 wickets – the runs included a partnership of 428 against Sussex. He was named a *Wisden* Cricketer of the Year.

He returned with Joe Darling's 1905 team growing in girth and stature, and was the W. G. Grace of Australia – and rightly so.

Armstrong topped both batting and bowling averages, scoring 2002 runs at 48.82 which included a gargantuan innings of 303 not out against Somerset, and 130 wickets at 17.6 with his straight but craftily

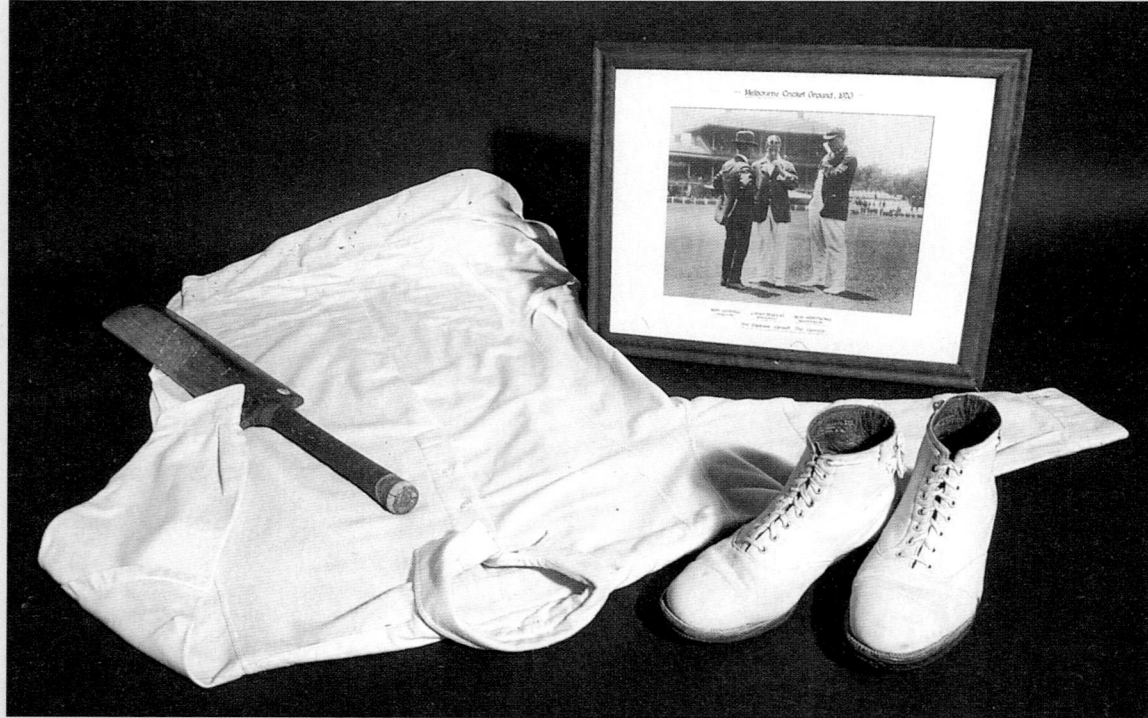

The Big Ship's big shirt, big boots, big bat … now at the MCC Museum.

flighted leggies.

In the 1905–06 Australian season Armstrong made 165 for Victoria against SA, and in the next season 168 against NSW. In 1907–08 he made 1033 runs at 73.78. He was the big man of Australian cricket by now, as Johnnie Moyes later wrote, he was 'a cricketer who mattered'.

He carried this form into the 1909 tour taking more wickets than anyone, 126 at 16.23 and coming second to Warren Bardsley in the batting with 1480 runs at 43.42.

This was to be Armstrong's last tour before the triumph of 1921. In between was the 1912 rumpus, where Armstrong was one of the 'Big Six' who stood out of the tour on the principle that the Board of Control had broken its word about a player-appointed manager – and player control of tour finances.

Armstrong first captained Victoria in 1910–11, lost it in 1911–12, had it back in 1914–15.

He was also captain of Australia in the 1920–21 series which resumed postwar international cricket. It notched up the first-ever 5–0 victory in Tests and he was appointed, but by only one vote, captain of the 1921 touring team.

Armstrong was sacked as captain of Victoria in the middle of the 1920–21 season, as part of the continuing war by Ernie Bean and sections of the VCA against him, a hangover from 1912. This event,

bizarre by even Australian cricket standards, caused an enormous uproar in the cricket public, and made a national hero of Armstrong.

He played in the fourth Test in Melbourne, despite a recurrence of malaria. Coming in at 5/153, he delighted the crowd with a grand 123 not out. Armstrong, it was said, noticed the teetotal Bean gloating as he walked out to bat.

The punchline, according to some, was that when Armstrong came back in Bean was drunk!

As his stature grew, so did his bulk. He was now 'The Big Ship'.

As for his size, Ray Robinson observed: 'No ball that Armstrong drove, and no deck-chair he sat on was ever the same again.'

On the trip to England in 1921, Armstrong tried to keep his weight within 20 stone by stoking the ship for two hours a day. He failed, clocking into the tour at 22 stone.

Like a battleship, Armstrong went into cricket politics with all guns blazing. At the Imperial Cricket Conference in 1921, he suggested that Test umpires not be appointed until the day of the match.

Asked why by Lord Harris, Armstrong said: 'The umpires are paid little for their services and, as there is a lot of betting on Tests, it would be wise to remove them from temptation.'

Next day, Lord Harris said he could find no evidence of betting

on cricket. 'People don't do it.'

Armstrong, puffing on his pipe, looked his Lordship squarely in the eyes and said: 'You don't think so, my Lord? If you'd like £500 on the next Test I can arrange it for you.'

Towards the end of the fifth Test in 1921, with no result possible and Australia having retained the Ashes 3–0, Armstrong placed himself in the outfield, where he picked up a windblown piece of newspaper and began reading it. Asked why, he grinned and said: 'To see who we were playing.'

This tour was a triumph – losing only two of 38 matches. Armstrong himself did the 'double' of 1405 runs and 106 wickets, and went down in history as the only player to bowl two consecutive overs in a Test after a kerfuffle over the rules of declarations.

Cantankerous, a man of strong opinions, a disciplinarian, a wonderful hitter – his team-mates loved and respected him.

Jack Gregory said Armstrong was 'the BIG man in cricket' and that his 'happiest moments in cricket were with that great leader and cricketer, the greatest of my time.'

Armstrong continued to play first class cricket until the end of the 1922 season in Australia, and for Melbourne until 1927.

He moved to Sydney in 1934, and died on 13 July 1947, leaving an estate of more than £100,000.

Australia's twin destroyers

THERE WERE TWO REASONS FOR ENGLAND'S COLLAPSE!
ONE WAS McDONALD!
THE OTHER WAS GREGORY!!

Jack Gregory destroyed England's cricket hopes with three wickets in one over in the first innings of the first Test. He was formidable with Ted McDonald.

Jack Morrison Gregory, born on 14 August 1895, in North Sydney, was a member of the famous Australian cricketing family. Four Gregorys, representing two generations, played Test cricket for Australia over a period of 50 years. Four more played for NSW.

Jack Gregory, a nephew of Dave Gregory, Australia's first captain, was the last and greatest of the dynasty.

When Jack died in 1973, Bill O'Reilly wrote: 'Gregory assumed a cricket stature of such magnetic appeal that one can truthfully say that Don Bradman has been the only Australian to reach the same plane.'

Educated at Shore, Jack was a hurdler of promise at school and played cricket for North Sydney in a lower grade. When World War One broke out, he joined the AIF, rising to the rank of Lieutenant in the artillery and serving in France.

At war's end, the strapping Gregory (he was 6ft 4 in tall) joined the AIF cricket team in England led by Lance Corporal Herbie Collins.

As a boy he was encouraged to bat left-handed, swiping the ball into the next-door orchard, conveniently placed at mid-wicket. Big hits meant fruit for the Gregory sideboard.

With his long, bounding run, giant delivery side and high action, Gregory had the capacity to make the ball lift awkwardly. Apart from his lusty batting, he had another weapon in his armoury – acrobatic slips fielding.

Gregory joined forces with the lithe, rhythmical Tasmanian-born Ted McDonald in 1920–21 to form one of the most formidable fast bowling attacks in cricket history.

He destroyed England's cricket hopes with three wickets in one over in the first innings of the first Test in 1921.

Gregory took 22 wickets in 1924–25 when Australia won the Ashes for the third time straight since the war.

Unfortunately, McDonald had left Australia to play in the Lancashire league, thus splitting a great hunting partnership.

Gregory played in all five Tests in England in 1926 but was ineffective because of his knee injury, which had reduced him to a stock bowler, and he took only three Test wickets.

Gregory's career came to an abrupt end in 1928–29. He broke down in the first Test against England in Brisbane – which was Don Bradman's first appearance for Australia.

Bradman clearly recalled Gregory limping into the dressing room, tears in his eyes and saying 'Boys, I'm through. I've played my last game.'.

Gregory's brief career yielded impressive statistics – 1146 Test runs at 36.96 with two centuries and 85 wickets at 31.15.

In all first class matches, he totalled 5661 runs at 36.52 (13 centuries) and captured 504 wickets at 20.99. He snared 37 catches.

In 1928 he married Phyllis Ethel von Alwyn (the 1927 Miss Australia). He died in 1973, ending a great cricketing dynasty.

FIRST TEST 1921 ENGLAND v AUSTRALIA
Trent Bridge, Nottingham. May 28, 30, 1921.
Toss: England. Australia won by 10 wkts.

ENGLAND

Batsman	1st Innings	Runs	2nd Innings	Runs
DJ Knight	c Carter b Gregory	8	run out	38
P Holmes	b McDonald	30	c Taylor b McDonald	8
GE Tyldesley	b Gregory	0	b Gregory	7
EH Hendren	b Gregory	0	b McDonald	7
JWHT Douglas (c)	c Gregory b Armstrong	11	c Hendry b McDonald	13
FE Woolley	c Hendry b McDonald	20	c Carter b Hendry	34
VWC Jupp	c Armstrong b McDonald	8	c Pellew b Gregory	15
W Rhodes	c Carter b Gregory	19	c Carter b McDonald	10
H Strudwick (+)	c Collins b Gregory	0	b Hendry	0
H Howell	not out	0	not out	4
TL Richmond	c & b Gregory	4	b McDonald	2
EXTRAS	(B 6, LB 6)	12	(B 4, LB 3, NB 2)	9
TOTAL		112		147

FOW 1st Inns: 18 18 18 43 77 78 101 107 108 112
FOW 2nd Inns: 23 41 60 63 76 110 138 138 140 147

Bowling: *First Innings*: Gregory 19-5-58-6, McDonald 15-5-42-3, Armstrong 3-3-0-1. *Second Innings*: Gregory 22-8-45-2, McDonald 22.4-10-32-5, Macartney 5-2-10-0, Armstrong 27-10-33-0, Hendry 9-1-18-2.

AUSTRALIA

Batsman	1st Innings	Runs	2nd Innings	Runs
W Bardsley	lbw Woolley	66	not out	8
HL Collins	lbw Richmond	17		
CG Macartney	lbw Douglas	20 (2)	not out	22
JM Taylor	c Jupp b Douglas	4		
WW Armstrong (c)	b Jupp	11		
JM Gregory	lbw Richmond	14		
CE Pellew	c & b Rhodes	25		
H Carter (+)	b Woolley	33		
TJE Andrews	c & b Rhodes	6		
HSTL Hendry	not out	12		
EA McDonald	c Knight b Woolley	10		
EXTRAS	(B 8, LB 5, NB 1)	14		0
TOTAL		232		0 for 30

FOW 1st Inns: 49 86 98 126 138 152 183 202 212 232
FOW 2nd Inns:

Bowling: *First Innings*: Howell 9-3-22-0, Douglas 13-2-34-2, Richmond 16-3-69-2, Woolley 22-8-46-3, Jupp 5-0-14-1, Rhodes 13-3-33-2. *Second Innings*: Jupp 3.1-0-13-0, Richmond 3-0-17-0.

Umpires: HR Butt & J Moss

SECOND TEST 1921 ENGLAND v AUSTRALIA
Lord's Cricket Ground, London. June 11, 13, 14, 1921.
Toss: England. Australia won by 8 wkts.

ENGLAND

Batsman	1st Innings	Runs	2nd Innings	Runs
DJ Knight	c Gregory b Armstrong	7	c Carter b Gregory	1
AE Dipper	b McDonald	11	b McDonald	40
FE Woolley	st Carter b Mailey	95	c Hendry b Mailey	93
EH Hendren	b McDonald	0	c Gregory b Mailey	10
JWHT Douglas (c)	b McDonald	34	b Gregory	14
AJ Evans	b McDonald	4	lbw McDonald	14
LH Tennyson	st Carter b Mailey	5	not out	74
NE Haig	c Carter b Gregory	3	b McDonald	0
CH Parkin	b Mailey	0	c Pellew b McDonald	11
H Strudwick (+)	c McDonald b Mailey	8	b Gregory	12
FJ Durston	not out	6	b Gregory	2
EXTRAS	(B 1, LB 11, W 1, NB 1)	14	(B 4, LB 3, NB 5)	12
TOTAL		187		283

FOW 1st Inns: 20 24 25 108 120 145 156 157 170 187
FOW 2nd Inns: 3 97 124 165 165 198 202 235 263 283

Bowling: *First Innings*: Gregory 16-1-51-1, McDonald 20-2-58-4, Armstrong 18-12-9-1, Mailey 14.2-1-55-4. *Second Innings*: Gregory 26.2-4-76-4, McDonald 23-3-89-4, Armstrong 12-6-19-0, Mailey 25-4-72-2, Hendry 4-0-15-0.

AUSTRALIA

Batsman	1st Innings	Runs	2nd Innings	Runs
W Bardsley	c Woolley b Douglas	88	not out	63
TJE Andrews	c Strudwick b Durston	9	lbw Parkin	49
CG Macartney	c Strudwick b Durston	31	b Durston	8
CE Pellew	b Haig	43	not out	5
JM Taylor	lbw Douglas	36		
WW Armstrong (c)	b Durston	0		
JM Gregory	c & b Parkin	52		
HSTL Hendry	b Haig	5		
H Carter (+)	b Durston	46		
AA Mailey	c & b Parkin	5		
EA McDonald	not out	17		
EXTRAS	(B 2, LB 5, NB 3)	10	(B 3, LB 2, NB 1)	6
TOTAL		342		2 for 131

FOW 1st Inns: 19 73 145 191 192 230 263 277 289 342
FOW 2nd Inns: 103 114

Bowling: *First Innings*: Durston 24.1-2-102-4, Douglas 9-1-53-2, Parkin 20-5-72-2, Haig 20-4-61-2, Woolley 11-2-44-0. *Second Innings*: Durston 9.3-0-34-1, Douglas 6-0-23-0, Parkin 9-0-31-1, Haig 3-0-27-0, Woolley 3-0-10-0.

Umpires: J Moss & W Phillips

THIRD TEST 1921 ENGLAND v AUSTRALIA
Headingley, Leeds. July 2, 4, 5, 1921.
Toss: Australia. Australia won by 219 runs.

AUSTRALIA

W Bardsley c Woolley b Douglas	6	b Jupp	25
TJE Andrews c Woolley b Douglas	19	b Jupp	92
CG Macartney lbw Parkin	115	c & b Woolley	30
CE Pellew c Hearne b Woolley	52 (5)	c Ducat b White	16
JM Taylor c Douglas b Jupp	50 (6)	c Tennyson b White	4
JM Gregory b Parkin	1 (8)	c Jupp b White	3
WW Armstrong (c) c Brown b Douglas	77	not out	28
HSTL Hendry b Parkin	0 (9)	not out	11
H Carter (+) b Jupp	34 (4)	lbw Parkin	47
EA McDonald not out	21		
AA Mailey c & b Parkin	6		
EXTRAS (B 16, LB 7, NB 3)	26	(B 10, LB 4, NB 3)	17
TOTAL	407	7 dec	273

FOW 1st Inns: 22 45 146 255 256 271 271 333 388 407
FOW 2nd Inns: 71 139 193 223 227 227 230

Bowling: *First Innings*: Douglas 20-3-80-3, White 25-4-70-0, Parkin 20.1-0-106-4, Hearne 5-0-21-0, Jupp 18-2-70-2, Woolley 5-0-34-1. *Second Innings*: Douglas 11-0-38-0, White 11-3-37-3, Jupp 13-2-45-2, Parkin 20-0-91-1, Woolley 18-4-45-1.

ENGLAND

FE Woolley b Gregory	0 (4)	b Mailey	37
HTW Hardinge lbw Armstrong	25	c Gregory b McDonald	5
JW Hearne b McDonald	7	c Taylor b McDonald	27
A Ducat c Gregory b McDonald	3 (6)	st Carter b Mailey	2
JWHT Douglas b Armstrong	75	b Gregory	8
VWC Jupp c Carter b Gregory	14 (7)	c Carter b Armstrong	28
G Brown (+) c Armstrong b Mailey	57 (1)	lbw Gregory	46
JC White b McDonald	1 (9)	not out	6
LH Tennyson (c) c Gregory b McDonald	63 (8)	b Armstrong	36
CH Parkin not out	5	b Mailey	4
JB Hobbs			
EXTRAS (LB 3, NB 6)	9	(B 3)	3
TOTAL	9 for 259		9 for 202

FOW 1st Inns: 0 13 30 47 67 164 165 253 259
FOW 2nd Inns: 15 57 98 124 126 128 190 197 202

Bowling: *First Innings*: Gregory 21-6-47-2, McDonald 26.1-0-105-4, Armstrong 19-4-44-2, Mailey 17-4-38-1, Hendry 10-4-16-0. *Second Innings*: Gregory 14-1-55-2, McDonald 15-2-67-2, Armstrong 3-0-6-2, Mailey 20.2-3-71-3.
Umpires: HR Butt & A Millward

FOURTH TEST 1921 ENGLAND v AUSTRALIA
Old Trafford, Manchester. July 23 (no play), 25, 26, 1921.
Toss: England. Match Drawn.

ENGLAND

CAG Russell b Gregory	101		
G Brown (+) c Gregory b Armstrong	31		
FE Woolley c Pellew b Armstrong	41		
CP Mead c Andrews b Hendry	47		
GE Tyldesley not out	78		
PGH Fender not out	44		
C Hallows	(1)	not out	16
CH Parkin	(2)	c Collins b Andrews	23
CWL Parker	(3)	not out	3
LH Tennyson (c)			
JWHT Douglas			
EXTRAS (B 12, LB 5, NB 3)	20	(LB 2)	2
TOTAL	4 dec 362		1 for 44

FOW 1st Inns: 65 145 217 260
FOW 2nd Inns: 36

Bowling: *First Innings*: Gregory 23-5-79-1, McDonald 31-1-112-0, Macartney 8-2-20-0, Hendry 25-5-74-1, Armstrong 33-13-57-2. *Second Innings*: Hendry 4-1-12-0, Andrews 5-0-23-1, Pellew 3-0-6-0, Taylor 1-0-1-0.

AUSTRALIA

W Bardsley b Parkin	3
HL Collins lbw Parkin	40
CG Macartney b Parker	13
TJE Andrews c Tennyson b Fender	6
JM Taylor b Fender	4
CE Pellew c Tyldesley b Parker	17
WW Armstrong (c) b Douglas	17
JM Gregory b Parkin	29
H Carter (+) b Parkin	0
HSTL Hendry c Russell b Parkin	4
EA McDonald not out	8
EXTRAS (B 22, LB 5, NB 7)	34
TOTAL	175

FOW 1st Inns: 9 33 44 48 78 125 161 161 166 175

Bowling: *First Innings*: Parkin 29.4-12-38-5, Woolley 39-22-38-0, Parker 28-16-32-2, Fender 15-6-30-2, Douglas 5-2-3-1.

Umpires: J Moss & AE Street

FIFTH TEST 1921 ENGLAND v AUSTRALIA
Kennington Oval, London. August 13, 15, 16, 1921.
Toss: England. Match Drawn.

ENGLAND

CAG Russell c Oldfield b McDonald	13	not out	102
G Brown (+) b Mailey	32	c Mailey b Taylor	84
GE Tyldesley c Macartney b Gregory	39		
FE Woolley run out	23		
CP Mead not out	182		
A Sandham b McDonald	21		
LH Tennyson (c) b McDonald	51		
PGH Fender c Armstrong b McDonald	0 (3)	c Armstrong b Mailey	6
JW Hitch b McDonald	18 (4)	not out	51
JWHT Douglas not out	21		
CH Parkin			
EXTRAS (LB 3)	3	(B 1)	1
TOTAL	8 dec 403		2 for 244

FOW 1st Inns: 27 54 84 121 191 312 312 339
FOW 2nd Inns: 158 173

Bowling: *First Innings*: Gregory 38-5-128-1, McDonald 47-9-143-5, Mailey 30-4-85-1, Armstrong 12-2-44-0. *Second Innings*: Gregory 3-0-13-0, McDonald 6-0-20-0, Mailey 18-2-77-1, Pellew 9-3-25-0, Andrews 8-0-44-0, Taylor 7-1-25-1, Collins 7-0-39-0.

AUSTRALIA

HL Collins hit wicket b Hitch	14
W Bardsley b Hitch	22
CG Macartney b Douglas	61
TJE Andrews lbw Parkin	94
JM Taylor c Woolley b Douglas	75
CE Pellew c Woolley b Parkin	1
WW Armstrong (c) c Brown b Douglas	19
JM Gregory st Brown b Parkin	27
WAS Oldfield (+) not out	28
EA McDonald st Brown b Woolley	36
AA Mailey b Woolley	0
EXTRAS (B 6, LB 3, W 2, NB 1)	12
TOTAL	389

FOW 1st Inns: 33 54 162 233 239 288 311 338 389 389

Bowling: *First Innings*: Hitch 19-3-65-2, Douglas 30-2-117-3, Fender 19-3-82-0, Parkin 23-4-82-3, Woolley 11-2-31-2.
Umpires: J Moss & W Phillips

Australian Averages

1921 ENGLAND v AUSTRALIA

AUSTRALIA	M	Inn	NO	Runs	H.S	Avrge	Ct	St	Overs	Mds	Runs	Wkt	Avrge
Andrews, TJE	5	7	-	275	94	39.29	1	-	13.0	-	67	1	67.00
Armstrong, WW	5	6	1	152	77	30.40	4	-	127.0	50	212	8	26.50
Bardsley, W	5	8	2	281	88	46.83	-	-	-	-	-	-	-
Carter, H	4	5	-	160	47	32.00	8	3	-	-	-	-	-
Collins, HL	3	3	-	71	40	23.67	2	-	7.0	-	39	-	-
Gregory, JM	5	6	-	126	52	21.00	8	-	182.2	35	552	19	29.05
Hendry, HSTL	4	5	2	32	12*	10.67	3	-	52.0	11	135	3	45.00
Macartney, CG	5	8	1	300	115	42.86	1	-	13.0	4	30	-	-
Mailey, AA	3	3	-	11	6	3.67	1	-	124.4	18	398	12	33.17
McDonald, EA	5	5	3	92	36	46.00	1	-	205.5	32	668	27	24.74
Oldfield, WAS	1	1	1	28	28*	-	1	-	-	-	-	-	-
Pellew, CE	5	7	1	159	52	26.50	3	-	12.0	3	31	-	-
Taylor, JM	5	6	-	173	75	28.83	2	-	8.0	1	26	1	26.00

English Averages

1921 ENGLAND v AUSTRALIA

ENGLAND	M	Inn	NO	Runs	H.S	Avrge	Ct	St	Overs	Mds	Runs	Wkt	Avrge
Brown, G	3	5	-	250	84	50.00	2	2	-	-	-	-	-
Dipper, AE	1	2	-	51	40	25.50	-	-	-	-	-	-	-
Douglas, JWHT	5	7	1	176	75	29.33	1	-	94.0	10	348	11	31.64
Ducat, A	1	2	-	5	3	2.50	1	-	-	-	-	-	-
Durston, FJ	1	2	1	8	6*	8.00	-	-	33.4	2	136	5	27.20
Evans, AJ	1	2	-	18	14	9.00	-	-	-	-	-	-	-
Fender, PGH	2	3	1	50	44*	25.00	-	-	34.0	9	112	2	56.00
Haig, NE	1	2	-	3	3	1.50	-	-	23.0	4	88	2	44.00
Hallows, C	1	1	1	16	16*	-	-	-	-	-	-	-	-
Hardinge, HTW	1	2	-	30	25	15.00	-	-	-	-	-	-	-
Hearne, JW	1	2	-	34	27	17.00	1	-	5.0	-	21	-	-
Hendren, EH	2	4	-	17	10	4.25	-	-	-	-	-	-	-
Hitch, JW	1	2	1	69	51*	69.00	-	-	19.0	3	65	2	32.50
Hobbs, JB	1	-	-	-	-	-	-	-	-	-	-	-	-
Holmes, P	1	2	-	38	30	19.00	-	-	-	-	-	-	-
Howell, H	1	2	2	4	4*	-	-	-	9.0	3	22	-	-
Jupp, VWC	2	4	-	65	28	16.25	2	-	39.1	4	142	5	28.40
Knight, DJ	2	4	-	54	38	13.50	1	-	-	-	-	-	-
Mead, CP	2	2	1	229	182*	229.00	-	-	-	-	-	-	-
Parker, CWL	1	1	1	3	3*	-	-	-	28.0	16	32	2	16.00
Parkin, CH	4	5	1	43	23	10.75	3	-	121.5	21	420	16	26.25
Rhodes, W	1	2	-	29	19	14.50	2	-	13.0	3	33	2	16.50
Richmond, TL	1	2	-	6	4	3.00	-	-	19.0	3	86	2	43.00
Russell, CAG	2	3	1	216	102*	108.00	1	-	-	-	-	-	-
Sandham, A	1	1	-	21	21	21.00	-	-	-	-	-	-	-
Strudwick, H	2	4	-	20	12	5.00	2	-	-	-	-	-	-
Tennyson, LH	4	5	1	229	74*	57.25	2	-	-	-	-	-	-
Tyldesley, GE	3	4	1	124	78*	41.33	1	-	-	-	-	-	-
White, JC	1	2	1	7	6*	7.00	-	-	36.0	7	107	3	35.67
Woolley, FE	5	8	-	343	95	42.88	6	-	109.0	38	248	7	35.43

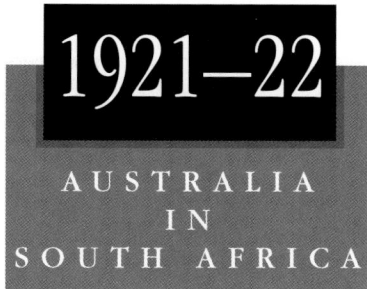

1921–22

AUSTRALIA IN SOUTH AFRICA

Herbie Collins is in charge again

Herbie Collins: a double century.

Cape Town, Nov. 29. Herbie Collins took over the Australian captaincy for the short six-match, three-Test tour of South Africa on the way home from England.

Warwick Armstrong's recurrent malaria and his battered legs meant that he was unable to play another month. Collins has had experience in South Africa, having led the triumphant AIF Australians to victory in 1919.

Collins repeated his 1919 form with another double century, this time in the second Test, and was widely regarded as the best of the Australian batsmen.

Even his occasional left-arm spinners were highly rated. Collins is an astute and popular captain who looks as old as the hills, and when needed, is about as immovable.

But in the mood he can score as freely as any player. In the six matches he made the most runs of anyone, 548 at 60.88.

Australia beat the three provincial teams quite easily: Transvaal by nine wickets, Natal by 194 runs (Collins 135) and Western Province by eight wickets.

The Australian baggy green cap fits Collins and he will wear it well into the future.

Gregory hits fastest 100 in Test cricket

Cape Town, Nov. 29. Australia won the third and final Test in a most unlikely manner, giving a 1–0 result with two draws in the three Test series.

Batting a second time, Australia opened with the unique pair of 'keeper Hanson Carter and that wily batter Arthur Mailey.

Mailey took strike, patted the first ball away confidently, took the single, and Australia won the game by 10 wickets.

Before this jovial bit of batting, Jack Ryder finally added a century, 142, to his fine scores of 78, 58 and 56 made in his prior three Test innings. Some would say that it was about time that he was given a chance on this tour – not having played in a Test in England.

But in terms of batting in this Test series, the innings of Jack Gregory in the second Test at Johannesburg earlier in the month takes the cake.

This was the innings of a whirlwind – 100 of 119 scored in just 70 minutes from 67 balls, the fastest hundred in all of Test cricket.

What Herbie Collins, the man who made 40 in four hours in England made of it was not apparent. But what is. Collins simply went on to make 203 himself. Australia 450.

The Australian batting contrasted with what South Africa had to do to save the match following on 207 behind. Dave Nourse made a well compiled 111. And Charlie Frank batted for 518 minutes over three days making 152 in an innings that made Collins look like a dasher – and Gregory out of this world.

This is how a South African newspaper cartoonist views Jack Gregory.

In the first Test at Durban, the Australians were well on top, due to Charlie Macartney's second innings 117, and Jack Gregory's 6/77 in the South African first innings.

Stumps had been agreed to be at 5 p.m. on the final day – when South Africa were on the ropes at 7/184, still 207 behind.

Perhaps Collins might have declared earlier than at 7/324.

These matches were played on matting, a surface most Australians would not have seen since boyhood.

FIRST TEST 1921–22 SOUTH AFRICA v AUSTRALIA
Lord's, Durban. November 5, 7, 8, 9, 1921.
Toss: Australia. Match Drawn.

AUSTRALIA

HL Collins (c) b Carter	31		c Chapman b Nupen	47
JM Gregory b Blanckenberg	51	(4)	b Blanckenberg	6
CG Macartney c Nourse b Nupen	59		c Ward b Marx	116
W Bardsley b Blanckenberg	5	(2)	lbw Carter	23
TJE Andrews b Blanckenberg	3	(6)	not out	35
J Ryder not out	78	(5)	b Blanckenberg	58
JM Taylor b Carter	18		b Carter	11
HSTL Hendry c Nourse b Chapman	23		b Carter	13
H Carter (+) c Nourse b Blanckenberg	9		not out	1
EA McDonald b Carter	2			
AA Mailey b Blanckenberg	2			
EXTRAS (B 16, LB 2)	18		(B 12, LB 1, NB 1)	14
TOTAL	299		7 dec	324

FOW 1st Inns: 85 95 116 128 175 214 276 291 296 299
FOW 2nd Inns: 1 43 82 112 131 179 182

Bowling: *First Innings*: Marx 3-0-6-0, Nourse 11-1-36-0, Nupen 15-2-42-1, Chapman 11-0-51-1, Blanckenberg 24.4-6-78-5, Carter 20-1-68-3. *Second Innings*: Marx 6-0-20-1, Nourse 8-1-32-0, Nupen 16-3-59-1, Chapman 6-1-33-0, Blanckenberg 30-3-100-2, Carter 21-3-66-3.

SOUTH AFRICA

HW Taylor (c) c Hendry b Gregory	1	(4)	c & b McDonald	29
JW Zulch c Gregory b Macartney	80	(5)	c Taylor b McDonald	17
CN Frank c Gregory b McDonald	1	(1)	c Gregory b Mailey	38
AW Nourse c Hendry b Gregory	32	(6)	not out	31
WVS Ling b Gregory	33	(7)	c Gregory b McDonald	28
WFE Marx c Macartney b Gregory	0	(3)	c Carter b Mailey	28
HW Chapman c Gregory b Hendry	4	(8)	b Gregory	2
EP Nupen c & b Hendry	6	(9)	not out	0
TA Ward (+) not out	22	(2)	b Gregory	0
JM Blanckenberg c Ryder b Gregory	28			
CP Carter c Mailey b Gregory	14			
EXTRAS (B 4, LB 3, NB 4)	11		(LB 8, NB 3)	11
TOTAL	232		7 for	184

FOW 1st Inns: 2 9 62 136 136 154 154 163 214 232
FOW 2nd Inns: 1 43 82 112 131 179 182

Bowling: *First Innings*: Gregory 25.1-4-77-6, McDonald 20-5-55-1, Mailey 17-2-55-0, Macartney 11-6-13-1, Hendry 7-0-21-2. *Second Innings*: Gregory 19-7-28-2, McDonald 34-17-64-3, Mailey 31-10-54-2, Ryder 8-3-17-0, Hendry 4-0-20-0.

Umpires: FW Grey & AG Laver

THIRD TEST 1921–22 SOUTH AFRICA v AUSTRALIA
Newlands, Cape Town. November 26, 28, 29, 1921.
Toss: South Africa. Australia won by 10 wkts.

SOUTH AFRICA

CN Frank b Ryder	21		b Macartney	23
JW Zulch c Ryder b Macartney	50	(3)	c & b Macartney	40
PAM Hands c Gregory b Ryder	0	(6)	c Andrews b Macartney	19
HW Taylor (c) c Andrews b McDonald	26		run out	17
AW Nourse c Mayne b Mailey	11		st Carter b Mailey	31
WVS Ling b McDonald	0	(7)	b Macartney	35
WFE Marx st Carter b Mailey	11	(8)	run out	16
JM Blanckenberg st Carter b Mailey	25	(9)	c Carter b Mailey	20
TA Ward (+) b McDonald	2	(2)	b McDonald	4
CP Carter not out	19		not out	1
N Reid c Mayne b Mailey	11		b Macartney	6
EXTRAS (LB 2, NB 2)	4		(B 1, LB 2, NB 1)	4
TOTAL	180			216

FOW 1st Inns: 50 54 82 106 107 110 143 146 151 180
FOW 2nd Inns: 10 58 84 92 122 162 182 203 209 216

Bowling: *First Innings*: Gregory 15-9-11-0, McDonald 19-3-53-3, Macartney 24-10-47-1, Ryder 16-7-25-2, Mailey 14-1-40-4. *Second Innings*: Gregory 9-1-29-0, McDonald 13-2-35-1, Macartney 24.3-10-44-5, Ryder 7-0-15-0, Mailey 26-0-89-2, Collins 1-1-0-0.

AUSTRALIA

HL Collins (c) b Blanckenberg	54			
W Bardsley lbw Blanckenberg	30			
CG Macartney c Nourse b Blanckenberg	44			
J Ryder c Taylor b Carter	142			
JM Gregory c Hands b Blanckenberg	29			
RE Mayne lbw Reid	15			
TJE Andrews c Hands b Carter	10			
CE Pellew c Nourse b Reid	6			
H Carter (+) not out	31	(2)	not out	0
EA McDonald c Ward b Carter	4			
AA Mailey c Taylor b Nourse	14	(1)	not out	1
EXTRAS (B 9, LB 5, NB 3)	17			0
TOTAL	396		0 for	1

FOW 1st Inns: 71 108 153 201 242 281 320 358 361 396
FOW 2nd Inns:

Bowling: *First Innings*: Marx 7-1-29-0, Nourse 30-5-89-1, Blanckenberg 31-5-82-4, Carter 26-5-104-3, Reid 21-3-63-2, Taylor 5-2-12-0. *Second Innings*: Hands 0.1-0-1-0.

Umpires: HV Adams & AG Laver

SECOND TEST 1921–22 SOUTH AFRICA v AUSTRALIA
Old Wanderers, Johannesburg. November 12, 14, 15, 16, 1921.
Toss: Australia. Match Drawn.

AUSTRALIA

HL Collins (c) c Lindsay b Carter	203		not out	5
W Bardsley c Ward b Marx	8		not out	2
J Ryder b Blanckenberg	56			
JM Gregory st Ward b Carter	119			
TJE Andrews st Ward b Carter	3			
JM Taylor c Nupen b Marx	11			
RE Mayne b Carter	1			
HSTL Hendry b Carter	15			
WAS Oldfield (+) b Marx	2			
EA McDonald not out	9			
AA Mailey st Ward b Carter	4			
EXTRAS (B 3, LB 15, NB 1)	19			0
TOTAL	450		0 for	7

FOW 1st Inns: 15 128 337 347 382 383 407 422 446 450
FOW 2nd Inns:

Bowling: *First Innings*: Marx 21-0-85-3, Nupen 16-0-86-0, Carter 29.5-4-91-6, Blanckenberg 21-2-105-1, Nourse 7-1-44-0, Ling 3-0-20-0. *Second Innings*: Marx 1-0-4-0, Nupen 0.4-0-3-0.

SOUTH AFRICA

JW Zulch hit wicket b McDonald	4		b Gregory	2
CN Frank run out	1		c Collins b Mailey	152
NV Lindsay hit wicket b Gregory	6		b Gregory	29
HW Taylor (c) c Mailey b Gregory	47		c Hendry b Gregory	80
AW Nourse c(S)CE Pellew b McDonald	64		c Gregory b Ryder	111
WVS Ling c Hendry b Gregory	0		st Oldfield b Ryder	19
WFE Marx c Macartney b Gregory	36	(8)	c Bardsley b Mailey	34
TA Ward (+) c Taylor b Collins	7	(9)	not out	9
JM Blanckenberg b Gregory	45	(7)	c Andrews b Mailey	4
EP Nupen b Mailey	22		not out	13
CP Carter not out	0			
EXTRAS (B 4, LB 4, NB 3)	11		(B 10, LB 5, NB 4)	19
TOTAL	243		8 dec	472

FOW 1st Inns: 6 6 16 95 109 135 164 189 243 243
FOW 2nd Inns: 6 44 149 355 387 393 446 450

Bowling: *First Innings*: Gregory 19.3-1-71-4, McDonald 19-7-43-2, Mailey 22-4-72-2, Hendry 12-2-37-0, Collins 6-2-9-1. *Second Innings*: Gregory 28-7-68-3, McDonald 44-14-121-0, Mailey 43-8-113-3, Hendry 23-6-58-0, Collins 15-12-7-0, Taylor 11-4-19-0, Mayne 1-0-1-0, Ryder 30-9-66-2.

Umpires: SL Harris & AG Laver

Australian Averages

1921–22 SOUTH AFRICA v AUSTRALIA

AUSTRALIA	M	Inn	NO	Runs	H.S	Avrge	Ct	St	Overs	Mds	Runs	Wkt	Avrge
Andrews, TJE	3	4	1	51	35*	17.00	3	-	-	-	-	-	-
Bardsley, W	3	5	1	68	30	17.00	1	-	-	-	-	-	-
Carter, H	2	4	3	41	31*	41.00	2	3	-	-	-	-	-
Collins, HL	3	5	1	340	203	85.00	2	-	22.0	15	16	1	16.00
Gregory, JM	3	4	-	205	119	51.25	7	-	115.4	29	284	15	18.93
Hendry, HSTL	2	3	-	51	23	17.00	5	-	46.0	8	136	2	68.00
Macartney, CG	2	3	-	219	116	73.00	2	-	59.3	26	104	7	14.86
Mailey, AA	3	4	1	21	14	7.00	2	-	153.0	25	423	13	32.54
Mayne, RE	2	2	-	16	15	8.00	2	-	1.0	-	1	-	-
McDonald, EA	3	3	1	15	9*	7.50	1	-	149.0	48	371	10	37.10
Oldfield, WAS	1	1	-	2	2	2.00	-	1	-	-	-	-	-
Pellew, CE	1	1	-	6	6	6.00	-	-	-	-	-	-	-
Ryder, J	3	4	1	334	142	111.33	2	-	61.0	19	113	4	28.25
Taylor, JM	2	3	-	40	18	13.33	2	-	11.0	4	19	-	-

South African Averages

1921–22 SOUTH AFRICA v AUSTRALIA

SOUTH AFRICA	M	Inn	NO	Runs	H.S	Avrge	Ct	St	Overs	Mds	Runs	Wkt	Avrge
Blanckenberg, JM	3	5	-	122	45	24.40	-	-	106.4	16	365	12	30.42
Carter, CP	3	4	3	34	19*	34.00	-	-	96.5	13	329	15	21.93
Chapman, HW	1	2	-	6	4	3.00	1	-	17.0	1	84	1	84.00
Frank, CN	3	6	-	236	152	39.33	-	-	-	-	-	-	-
Hands, PAM	1	2	-	19	19	9.50	2	-	0.1	-	1	-	-
Lindsay, NV	1	2	-	35	29	17.50	1	-	-	-	-	-	-
Ling, WVS	3	6	-	115	35	19.17	-	-	3.0	-	20	-	-
Marx, WFE	3	6	-	125	36	20.83	-	-	38.0	1	144	4	36.00
Nourse, AW	3	6	1	280	111	56.00	5	-	56.0	8	201	1	201.00
Nupen, EP	2	4	-	41	22	20.50	-	-	47.4	5	190	2	95.00
Reid, N	1	2	-	17	11	8.50	-	-	21.0	3	63	2	31.50
Taylor, HW	3	6	-	200	80	33.33	2	-	5.0	2	12	-	-
Ward, TA	3	6	2	44	22*	11.00	2	3	-	-	-	-	-
Zulch, JW	3	6	-	193	80	32.17	-	-	-	-	-	-	-

Shield wrapped up for Vics

Adelaide, Feb. 28. Victoria wrapped up its first Sheffield Shield win since the War with a massive win over South Australia – which hasn't won a game in four seasons.

Victoria played this match without in-form batsmen Jack Ryder and Roy Park, nor fast bowler Ted McDonald.

And Bill Woodfull, who injured his hand fielding, did not bat until number eight – by which time the revelation of the season, ex-NSW player Frank O'Keeffe, had knocked up 180 runs, including a 144-run opening stand with Edgar Mayne (85).

Les Cody made 107 and Vernon Ransford 129 in Victoria's 625, enough to beat SA by the huge margin of an innings and 232.

The Victorian season flourished around the splendid batting of Park (122 and 53 v NSW), Ryder (242 v SA) and O'Keeffe, who made 87, 79 and the 180 in his two matches.

Ted McDonald took 25 wickets in his three Shield games.

NSW played its first two matches without its Australian stars, had its return match against Queensland over the New Year at the SCG washed out, and was unable to avenge a 165-run defeat in early December at the 'Gabba.

Jack Ryder: tall streak of talent.

Arthur Mailey is as well liked for his impish cartoons as he is for whimsical leg breaks. He is just back from England where he took 146 wickets at 19.78.

Suburban fields alive with cricket

Melbourne, March 1. Cricket in all states is in a ferment of reorganisation.

The VCA held a conference to coordinate country cricket under its aegis, as grade associations were being formed throughout the state.

The VCA noted, accurately enough, that there are 'one thousand teams under our auspices playing each Saturday.'

The NSWCA introduced the system of 16 first grade clubs this season, purchased property in George Street for £22,165 and began the City v Country match.

The SACA celebrated its Jubilee, and in WA district cricket was reorganised around six first grade clubs in Perth.

Johnnie Moyes – 218 in 83 mins

Sydney, March 25. A. G. 'Johnnie' Moyes scored 218 for his NSW district club Gordon against Central Cumberland – in an incredible 83 minutes.

NSWCA secretary Frank Iredale said 'There is nothing in the records to compare with this rapid rate of scoring.'

He scored 50 in 20 minutes, 100 in 40 minutes, 150 in 62 minutes and 200 in 72 minutes.

Moyes was first out, the score being 1/263.

Moyes hit seven sixes and 36 fours. He last played first class cricket – for Victoria – in 1920, and is still only 29 years old.

A journalist by trade, Moyes is destined for higher honours.

Battling WA now taking a stand

Perth, March 31. The WACA has installed 2000 new seats at the WACA ground, and work has begun on a new grandstand.

3000 feet of drains have been laid under the playing surface.

A new press box has also been built, providing better conditions for reporters.

Best of all, the State government has granted finance to the WACA to purchase the land from which it takes the soil to prepare its hard and fast wickets.

These major improvements are designed to favour Western Australia's early entry to the Sheffield Shield.

Ponsford scores 429 in Victoria's 1059

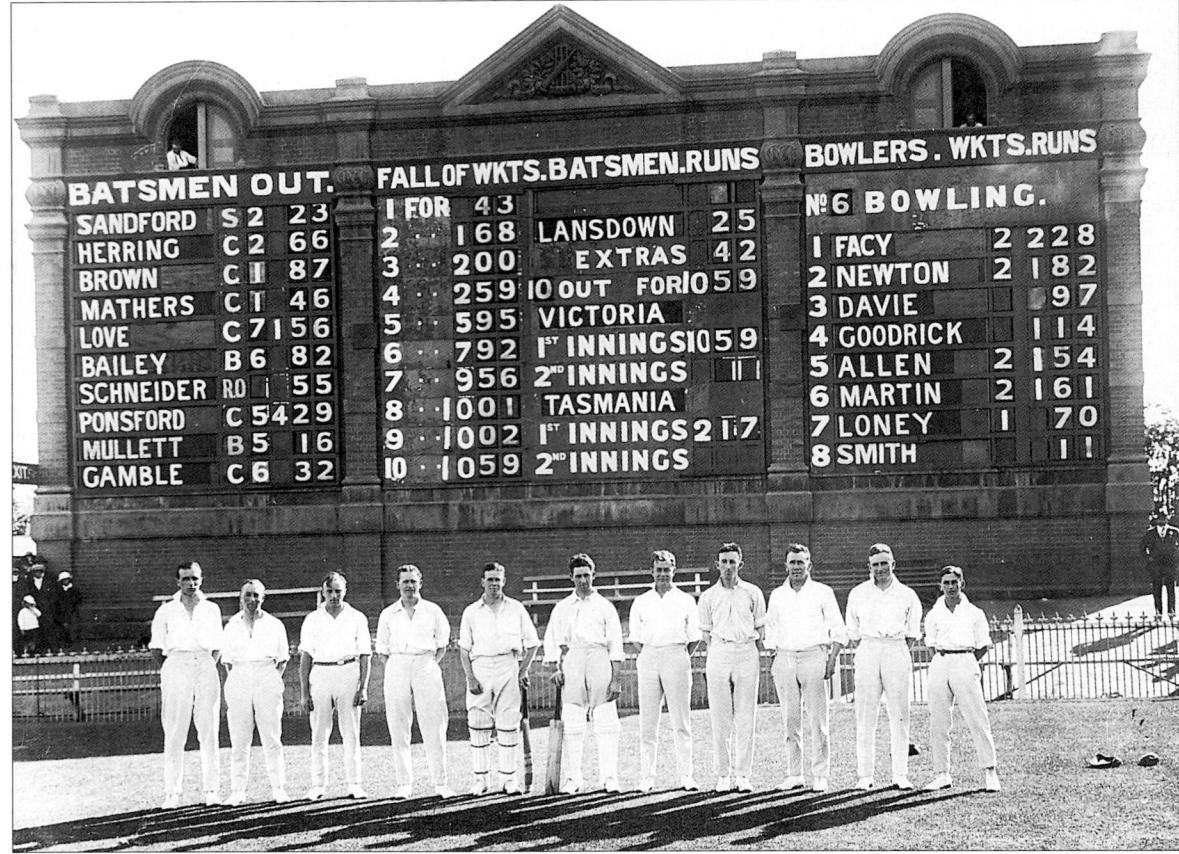

Bill Ponsford and his Victorian team-mates stand before the scoreboard showing the record score.

MCG, Feb. 6. Bill Ponsford was appointed captain of the Victorian 'hopefuls' in just his third first class game, against Tasmania. He responded with the highest innings in first class cricket in history, a little matter of 429 runs.

Along the way, in the words of the Melbourne *Herald*, he 'passed records like a fast car shooting past milestones.' Warwick Armstrong's 250 for Victoria was topped, Charlie Gregory's Australian record of 383, and then Archie MacLaren's world record of 424 went for six.

Ponsford, who took just 477 minutes for this gargantuan effort and hit 42 fours, didn't quite make it to the schoolboy record of 506 scored by J. C. Sharp in 1914–15. Also present in the Victorian team was R. W. Herring, who made a modest 238 in that partnership.

Ponsford gave two hard chances, at 60 and 115. They were the only imperfections in an innings of unique stature. Ponsford hit the run that made Victoria the first team to score over 1000 runs in an innings. He was out at 8/1001 and

Victoria went on to make 1059, their highest team score, eclipsing NSW's 918 against SA in January 1901.

Every Victorian batsman reached double figures, and 'Hammy' Love also plundered the meagre Tasmanian attack for 156 runs. 506 runs were made by Victoria on the second day.

Victoria won by an innings and 666 runs, Tasmania's scores being 217 and 176. Perhaps young Bill might now get a chance in the Shield team.

NSW win Shield

Adelaide, Feb. 20. Victoria easily beat South Australia in the final Sheffield Shield game, Bill Ponsford making 108 in his first game for the Victorian 'firsts' and Bill Woodfull 123 and 94.

Both Victoria and NSW finished with three wins and one loss to each other each, but NSW won the Shield with a better 'quotient'. This was the result of better overall batting by NSW.

Allan Kippax, Herbie Collins, Tom Andrews and 'Stork' Hendry were the main NSW run-getters. Vic Richardson (SA) had the biggest aggregate of Australian batsmen with 758 runs at an average of 75.8.

Queensland press

Brisbane, Dec. 5. Rain washed out the third day's play in the Queensland v NSW encounter.

The match ended in a draw, Otto Nothling for NSW failing to score on his debut.

And despite NSW's support at the Board of Control, the same gloomy outlook faces Queensland's latest request to join the Sheffield Shield competition.

The other states, particularly South Australia, will not yet allow Queensland in, despite standards and playing conditions in Brisbane being at least as good as they are in Adelaide.

SA has not won a game since before WWI.

MacLaren's team

Adelaide, March 17. Archie MacLaren's team of England hopefuls has passed through Australia again, this time on its way back to England.

On the way to New Zealand it had three heavy losses against SA, Victoria and NSW; on the way back it played three draws.

From the spectators' point of view, the highlight has been the sweet hitting of Percy Chapman, who is regarded as Test material, while in the game which finished today, they were impressed by the power of Arthur Richardson, who made 280.

Last week four Victorians made centuries in an innings.

NSW on tour in NZ

Bert Oldfield, on tour in New Zealand.

Wellington, March 30. NSW, led by Charlie Macartney, has completed a 'clean sweep' of New Zealand cricket in the short tour just completed, winning eight and drawing four matches.

The NSW side included Bert Oldfield, Arthur Mailey, Warren Bardsley, Tom Andrews, 'Stork' Hendry and Alan Kippax.

NSW defeated the combined NZ sides twice, by eight wickets, and by an innings and 126.

The sorriest sight in cricket – a victim of injustice.

Huge crowds follow Shield

SCG, Jan. 30. A total of 53,611 people watched, a trifle glumly, as Victoria's batsmen steered their State to an eight-wicket win over NSW and victory in the Sheffield Shield.

The biggest daily crowd, on Australia Day, was 25,408, larger than any single day at the corresponding match just after Christmas at the MCG. At that match 89,386 turned up to watch Victoria win a close encounter by just 43 runs.

The Sydney match started a day late because of a wet wicket, with Clarrie Grimmett omitted from the Victorian team. It was marked by a pair of 110s from Bill Ponsford, making three centuries for him in three innings.

Victorian captain Edgar Mayne, having a wonderful season, carried his bat for 154 runs in Victoria's first innings.

Only Tommy Andrews with 96 of 217 in the first innings saved NSW from a much heavier defeat. They batted better for 321 in their second dig, Herbie Collins 81, but on a flat pitch no one made enough impression to trouble Victoria.

It was much closer in the first match where Victoria's first innings of 285, with Mayne 106, was nearly matched by NSW 268 and Collins' 108. In the second innings Victoria made 412 with Bill Woodfull 117 and contributions right down the order. Once again NSW fell just a few runs short making 386, Charlie Kelleway 98, and lost by 43 runs on the sixth day.

These games between the top two states decided the Shield, as SA failed to win a match.

Bill Ponsford shows the Big Bertha bat.

For SA, this is the sixth season in succession in which they have not won – a remarkably dismal performance despite flashes of brilliance from Arthur and unrelated namesake Victor Richardson.

Both scored centuries in SA's best Shield performance – a loss by only 98 runs to Victoria at the MCG.

It was largely thanks also to some excellent bowling by veteran paceman Bill Whitty, who took 5/49 in Victoria's first innings.

For NSW Alan Kippax hit 32 fours in his 248 in the game against SA at the SCG in January. It was the highest score in a high-scoring season.

Victoria to lose a promising spinner

Adelaide, May 30. Clarrie Grimmett has agreed to terms with SACA and will play for South Australia. The leg-spinner was born in New Zealand, migrated to Sydney in 1914, and has played for Victoria infrequently between 1919 and this season.

After a puzzling attitude from the Victorian selectors, Grimmett has played just five games for Victoria, but impressed SA with 8/86 against them in February's Shield game.

The SACA formed a 'get Grimmett' sub-committee, and approached one Harold Fisher, a cricket supporter who promised £100 a year for an imported player.

After an offer of £7 per week, Grimmett agreed to a three-year contract at £10 per week, plus removal costs.

Victorian may rue the day, but in SA Grimmett will have the chance to show his whole back of tricks. Australian cricket will benefit.

Grimmett had one game for Victoria this season, taking 9/98 against SA.

Clarrie Grimmett is headed for SA.

QUICK SINGLES

Queensland capers. Queensland embarked on extensive southern tour this season, after playing a draw with NSW in Brisbane at the end of November, which included a first-ever game against SA in Adelaide after Christmas. SA won a rare victory for them, by ten wickets.

Great partnership. Edgar Mayne and Bill Ponsford created a record partnership for any wicket with an opening stand of 456 for Victoria against Queensland. Mayne made 209 and Ponsford 248 in Victoria's 2/538 at the MCG in December. Queensland, still waiting for admittance to the shield competition, showed they had a way to go, scoring 162 and 135.

New Colts. South Australia and Victorian Colts drew at the MCG in February – with prospect Hans Ebeling from the MCC taking 7/43.

Tasmania tossed. Stan Wootton made a hundred on debut (105) for a depleted Victorian 'second' XI against Tasmania in the annual match in Hobart in February. The Vics won by five wickets.

Delegate Richardson. SA Captain Vic Richardson lead a successful player delegation to the SACA in April over payment of 'loss of time' money. Players will in future be paid for lost wages rather than a flat maximum of £1 per day.

Ponsford's top perch. Bill Ponsford played in five first class matches in 1923–24, making 777 runs at the respectable average of 111. Team-mate Edgar Mayne had the second-highest aggregate in Shield games, 576 at 82.28.

Hartkopf best bowler. Victorian leg-break bowler Bert Hartkopf emerged as the best bowler this season. His 26 wickets at 24.57 indicates the dominance of the bat.

WA bereft. Western Australia was unable to arrange any first class cricket this season. Last season Western Australia drew a match against the touring England team, but were twice defeated by an innings at the WACA by NSW.

Grandstand grandstanding. Naming of the new and extended grandstands at the Adelaide Oval is causing heartburn. In August the stands were named after SACA stalwarts John Cresswell, B. V. Scrymgour, E. T. Smith and Mostyn Evan. In September after an agitated AGM Scrymgour and Smith were removed. No players have been adjudged worthy of the honour at this stage.

Ted McDonald qualifies. Former Australian fast bowler Ted McDonald finally qualified to play for Lancashire in the 1924 season after playing Lancashire League cricket since 1922. He took 205 wickets at 18.67.

Rescue acts retain the Ashes

Maurice Tate bowls to Bill Ponsford, who made 128 in the second Test. He was bowled by Tate in both innings.

QUICK SINGLES

Eight-ball over. In keeping with the Australian decision of the 1918–19 season, the 1924–25 Test series will be played with eight-ball overs, for the first time.

Unique double. In the Australian XI v MCC match in Brisbane in December, Queensland all-rounder Ron Oxenham achieved a unique pair of dismissals. In the first innings he was stumped Bert Strudwick bowled 'Tich' Freeman. All eleven Englishmen bowled in the second innings, with Freeman keeping. Oxenham was then stumped Freeman – bowled Strudwick. It was Strudwick's first and probably last first class wicket.

Board in control. At the Board of Control meeting on New Year's Eve, it declined an England request to downgrade Tasmanian fixtures from first class status, after Ponsford beat Maclaren's record score. And not to agree to Lord Harris' MCC demand to give up the eight-ball over.

Colonial reunion. At the fourth Test a reunion was held attended by many Australian greats – including Warwick Armstrong, Clem Hill, Fred Spofforth, Jack Blackham, Hugh Trumble and Jack Worrall. Blackham, Spofforth and Trumble inspected the wicket at the tea interval on Saturday to the great cheers of the crowd.

Covered wickets. Former England captain Archie MacLaren, when interviewed in South Africa in February about the 1924–25 tour, said: 'Wickets were not covered [in my day] as today, which favours bigger scoring. Those now in charge of Australian cricket have put gates first and cricket nowhere by covering the whole of the wicket after each day's play to prevent rain touching the wicket.'

Final performance. In the VCA District Final in march, Don Blackie 11/82, and Bert 'Dainty' Ironmonger 9/57 took every wicket between them for St Kilda against Richmond.

Grimmett entree. At tea during the match between Fitzroy and Clarrie Grimmett's old club Prahran at the Brunswick Street Oval in March, the modest bowler was presented with a pair of inscribed silver entree dishes.

Adelaide, Jan. 23. England, which commenced the tour of Australia with such high hopes, must now reconcile itself to the reality of being 3–0 down, and to not having beaten Australia since 1912.

There have been glimmers of opportunity, but with no bowler able to back up the magnificent Maurice Tate, and even with Jack Hobbs, Herbert Sutcliffe and Patsy Hendren, the Australians had too many good players.

In this game it was Jack Ryder who came to the rescue at 6/119 in the first innings, after making a magnificent 201 not out, in over six and a half hours, with partnerships of 134, 108 and 73 for the 8th, 9th and 10th wickets.

This last-wicket stand was with the alleged rabbit Arthur Mailey, who made a stylish 27.

Mailey had come to the rescue before, in a record last-wicket partnership of 127 in the first Test. Mailey was 46 not out then, helping Johnny Taylor to 108, and Australia to a match-winning second innings of 452.

Even in the close-run second Test at the MCG, Australia was 3/47 and 3/27 and yet became the first team to score 600 in a Test innings, winning the game by 81 runs on the seventh day.

Rescuers were Bill Ponsford (128), the first batsman to score centuries in his first two Tests, and Vic Richardson, who made 138 in his second match for Australia.

In the second Test, Herbert Sutcliffe and Jack Hobbs also joined the record books. They became the first batsmen to bat undefeated through a whole uninterrupted day's play, in a partnership of 283.

Gregory catches Jack Hobbs out.

Is England just a three-man team?

Sydney, March 4. Australia might have won the series but England's three best players clearly had the best individual performances on either side.

Maurice Tate took an extraordinary 38 wickets at 23.18, including five hauls of five wickets and one of 10.

Herbert Sutcliffe scored 734 runs in five Tests with four hundreds, at 81.56, and Jack Hobbs 573 runs at 63.67 with three centuries.

No Australians were close – Arthur Mailey took 24 wickets at 41.63 and Johnny Taylor made 541 runs at 54.10, but it just shows that in cricket, eleven good performances will beat three slightly better ones.

Bill Ponsford: looks impassable

England fights, but Grimmett new weapon

An astounding catch: Hobbs, caught Oldfield bowled Gregory 0, in the fifth Test played at the SCG. Oldfield had moved yards to the leg side.

Sydney, March 4. Australia wrapped up the series with an innocuous-looking but lethal secret weapon in the form of Clarrie Grimmett, whose 11 wickets (5/45 and 6/37) is the most outstanding debut performance by an Australian bowler.

Grimmett's crafty, deceptive hand grenades, especially the topspinner and the wrong'un, were too much for England. He bowled just two in the match for two wickets.

Grimmett's co-debutant Alan Kippax batted well with Bill Ponsford in Australia's first innings, making 42 in a partnership of 105 that steered Australia from the brink at 5/103.

Back in Melbourne it had been a different story.

England made 548 on a good batting strip over two days with Herbert Sutcliffe stroking a chanceless 148, his fourth century of the series, the first time a batsman had scored four centuries in one series.

Bert Oldfield became the first wicketkeeper to take five wickets in an innings, another first.

Then it rained on and off on the third day, making batting more difficult and the English bowlers thrived. Australia could only manage 269 and 250.

Maurice Tate exploited the conditions in the second innings, taking 5/75 for England and giving his country its first win over Australia since 1912.

Clarrie Grimmett sends down a leather hand grenade in the fifth Test.

Tests are on radio

Melbourne, Jan. 1. The Melbourne *Sun News Pictorial* reports that for the first time listeners to the wireless 'will obtain a first-hand description of every incident in the second Test match which begins at the MCG today.

'The 3AR broadcasting station has secured the services of the Victorian captain Edgar Mayne, and will describe the progress of the game.

'A special landline has been run from the studio in Elizabeth Street to the MCG, where a special observer from 3AR will transmit over the telephone a complete description of the match.'

Av. 146.6, dropped

Sydney, Jan. 30. Selectors are tough in NSW. Harry Rock made 127 and 27 not out, and 235 and 51 for NSW, for an average 146.6 this season, but with the return of the Test players to their home state, he was unceremoniously dumped.

Rock, a right-handed medical student, has made the most of his opportunities.

Unfortunately not just the selectors stand in his way. He has also missed some matches because of examinations.

The experience of Alan Kippax points to the career choices which bright young batsmen who are also bright young men must make.

It's Kippax at last

Sydney, Feb. 26. If the selection of Clarrie Grimmett in the fifth Test side was a slight though welcome surprise, the selection of the silken stylist Alan Kippax was a surprise that was long, long overdue.

Thus far this season, Kippax has been in dazzling form for NSW, scoring 115 against an Australian XI in October, 127 against SA, 82 not out against the MCC, 122 against SA in the return match, and 212 against Victoria in January.

Even his 46 run out, in the SCG run-feast against the MCC a few days ago, was an innings of class and maturity. He made 853 runs in 1924–25 at 77.54.

Tour makes profit

Melbourne, March 30. The England tour has generated huge attendances and huge profits for the Board of Control, the MCC and for the government.

A total of over 1,043,070 watched the tourist's first class and Test matches, the first time more than a million people have attended cricket in Australia.

Total receipts were £95,171, with government amusement tax of £8479, and the Marylebone Cricket Club share being £35,120.

The Board of Control's Syd Smith noted, 'The interest displayed in the game during the past season was phenomenal.'

Vics win Shield yet again

Alan Kippax completes an on-drive as he compiles 122 for NSW against SA.

Melbourne, Feb. 3. In a season that has had the 'distraction' of an England touring team playing 17 first class matches, the battle for the Sheffield Shield took something of a back seat.

Games were fitted in where the touring and Test program permitted. The two Victoria versus NSW games were scheduled between the third Test in Adelaide, which ended on January 23, and the Victoria v MCC game at the MCG which begins on February 6, and is directly followed by the fourth Test on February 13.

The result of all this is that Victoria won the Shield by defeating NSW in the first game, at the

SCG, January 24–29, which was played without Test players, and lost the return encounter at the MCG today, played with them. But that didn't matter.

South Australia recorded its first win in the Sheffield Shield since 1913–14, defeating NSW by 161 runs in Adelaide, Clarrie Grimmett bamboozling the NSW bats in the second innings with 6/103. Victoria won both games against SA.

Victoria's win over NSW in the SCG encounter was despite the two big, and long, innings by Harry Rock (235) and Alan Kippax (212 not out) in a total of 614. Victoria replied with 502 (Arthur Liddicut 132, Carl Willis 100) but then NSW was bundled out for 152. Kippax fell for 40 to leg-spinner Albert Hartkopf (3/45) and Rock for 51 to aged, but ageless off-spinner Don Blackie (2/29), making his first class debut at the age of 42 years and 294 days.

Bill Woodfull (120 not out) and 'Stork' Hendry knocked off most of the required runs.

The second game, at the MCG was a relatively low-scoring affair, with entirely new elevens from the first game, with the Test players back in. Arthur Mailey and Charlie Kelleway got Victoria out for 155 in the second innings.

It was reported that Victoria wanted Warwick Armstrong to lead the team in this game, but he 'was not within reach'.

What it feels like to be lbw first ball.

Herbie Collins ... poker-faced captain

In Ray Robinson's immortal phrase, Herbie Collins possessed 'by card-table habit' a face which 'revealed no more than the sphinx's inscrutable smile tells camels.'

He was an impregnable right-hand bat who scored, it seemed, with imperceptible nudges and tickles. But against South Africa in 1921 he displayed a diverting array of strokes and made over 200 in a day.

Collins took over the Australian team from Warwick Armstrong for the South African stopover tour in 1921–22, and retained the job for the 1924–25 series against England – which Australia won 4–1. But he had already captained an equally formidable Australian team – the 1919 AIF side, which swept all before it in England, Collins as joyful as the rest – which included Jack Gregory.

Collins' Test career began at the age of nearly 32. He played 19 Tests, made 1352 runs at the very good batsman's average of 45.06, and made four hundreds.

Herbie Collins was born in Paddington on 21 January 1889, and first played cricket under Monty Noble for that team.

He made the NSW team in 1909, and by 1912–13 was among Australia's leading run-getters, with 598 runs, including 282 against Tasmania. Next season he was third in the aggregates, behind Charlie Macartney and Warwick Armstrong.

He enlisted in the AIF in 1915, and served in Palestine and France, and was invited to join the AIF team in 1919, taking over as captain while still a lance corporal.

He was Armstrong's vice-captain in 1921, where he made his Test debut, becoming the fifth Australian to make a century on debut.

When he wasn't playing cricket or attending the opera at Covent Garden, Collins was busy gambling or winning the toss.

It happened so many times that in 1924–25 rival captain Arthur Gilligan got down on his knees and inspected the coin to see if it was a two-up special, a double header.

Said Arthur Mailey, 'Collins' hunting grounds were the race-track, the dog-track, Monte Carlo, a baccarat joint at King's Cross, a two-up school in the Flanders trenches and anywhere a quiet game of poker was being played.'

There are endless stories about

Herbie Collins on the bag.

his gambling proficiency – and high standards.

In 1924–25, just as the Australian team was leaving its hotel for the Adelaide Oval on the last morning of the third Test (England needed 27 to win with two wickets in hand), 'a fabulous-looking race-course man, smoking a cigar called to see Collins.' They had a chat and Collins went over to Mailey.

'This fellow says it's worth a 100 quid if we lose the match. Let's throw him downstairs,' Collins said.

One look at the fellow's displacement put them off that tack. 'I'd better ring the hall porter, then,' said Collins, always cool in a crisis. The big fellow must have heard the conversation. He made himself scarce and Australia won the Test by 11 runs to go 3–up in the series.

Collins captained Australia on the losing tour of England in 1926 and retired, injured, after it.

He became a bookmaker and later a stipendiary steward.

Collins declared that in the depression years, he had tried to find work without success, and had trouble finding enough money to care for himself and his invalid mother. He received assistance from the NSW Cricketer's Fund.

Collins enlisted in the second AIF in 1940, and transferred to the reserve at the end of 1941.

Herbie Collins died of cancer on 28 May 1959.

'Leave our flies alone!'

Yabba is a great seller of bunnies as well as barracker of them.

'Barracking' is as old as organised team sport in Australia: evidence may be found in accounts of football matches in Melbourne from the 1860s onwards.

Barracking is vocal support of a team, not mere abuse of the umpire in football, or an opponent in cricket. Barracking is funny and apt; abuse is an excuse for swearing in a public place.

In cricket the first evidence of barracking in Australia is not barracking at all, but abuse of visiting teams such as during the Sydney Riot of 1879, and abusive behaviour in Melbourne in the 1880s. However, over-the-fence commentary at a sparsely attended cricket match must have been going on in Australia and England long before any journalist noticed.

But with the renewed popularity of cricket and the bigger crowds which included the democratic gamut of Australians, barracking and abuse reached new heights, or depths in the 1890s.

A. E. Stoddart, the English captain of 1897–98 spoke about the 'evil of barracking' some of it directed at Ranjitsinhji at the end of the tour. He was supported by Australian captain Harry Trott, who thought that a few more barrackers ought to be jailed as an example.

Other cases followed. In 1911–12 potentially dangerous situations were defused by the good humour of England captain J. W. H. T. Douglas. And in 1920–21 two English players complained to an English paper about alleged barracking of injured Jack Hobbs. Commentators put the problem English players had with barracking to a lack of a sense of humour, and an inability of the Gentlemen (and aristocrats) to take a bit of Australian democratic ribbing.

Most spectators were not barrackers. But some are, and the most legendary barracker of them all was Yabba, Stephen Harold Gascoine, rabbito of Balmain.

Yabba was born in 1878, and probably was part of the cricket crowds of the 1890s. He said he fought and was wounded in the Boer War.

His fame as well as penetrating voice were recognised in the 1920s and 1930s when he took up station on the fence in front of the Hill at the SCG for every day of just about every Test and Shield match.

Yabba was inimitable in his time because of the range and appropriateness of his comments. He knew the game well, and could pick his moment. Once when the Nawab of Pataudi was finding it difficult to score, he told the umpire, who was a gas meter reader, 'Put a penny in him George, he's stopped registering.'

He advised Bodyline captain Douglas Jardine, waving a fly away, 'Hey Jardine, leave our flies alone!'

When an umpire raised his hand, for a long time to a somnolent attendant to move the sightboard, he called: 'It's no use umpire, you'll have to wait till playtime like the rest of us.'

Some famous barracking expressions are of ancient lineage. 'Get a bag' dates back to the 1890s and ''Av a go, yer mug!' to the 1880s. 'Bowl 'im a pianer and see if he can play that!' predates Yabba.

By the end Yabba was a legend. Jack Hobbs walked over to him on his last appearance at the SCG to shake his hand. Yabba died in 1942.

FIRST TEST 1924–25 AUSTRALIA v ENGLAND
Sydney Cricket Ground, Sydney. December 19, 20, 22, 23, 24, 26, 27, 1924.
Toss: Australia. Australia won by 193 runs.

AUSTRALIA

HL Collins (c) c Hendren b Tate	114 (4)	c Chapman b Tate	60
W Bardsley c Woolley b Freeman	21	b Tate	22
WH Ponsford b Gilligan	110 (5)	c Woolley b Freeman	27
AJ Richardson b Hearne	22 (1)	c & b Freeman	98
JM Taylor c Strudwick b Tate	43 (8)	b Tate	108
VY Richardson b Freeman	42	c Hendren b Tate	18
C Kelleway c Woolley b Tate	17 (3)	b Gilligan	23
HSTL Hendry c Strudwick b Tate	3 (7)	c Strudwick b Tate	22
JM Gregory c Strudwick b Tate	0	c Woolley b Freeman	2
WAS Oldfield (+) not out	39	c Strudwick b Gilligan	18
AA Mailey b Tate	21	not out	46
EXTRAS (B 10, LB 8)	18	(B 2, LB 5, W 1)	8
TOTAL	450		452

FOW 1st Inns: 46 236 275 286 364 374 387 387 388 450
FOW 2nd Inns: 40 115 168 210 241 260 281 286 325 452

Bowling: *First Innings:* Tate 55.1-11-130-6, Gilligan 23-0-92-1, Freeman 49-11-124-2, Hearne 12.1-3-28-1, Woolley 9-0-35-0, Hobbs 2-0-13-0, Chapman 2-0-10-0. *Second Innings:* Gilligan 27-6-114-2, Tate 33.7-8-98-5, Freeman 37-4-134-3, Hearne 25-2-88-0, Chapman 3-1-10-0.

ENGLAND

JB Hobbs c Kelleway b Gregory	115	c Hendry b Mailey	57
H Sutcliffe c VY Richardson b Mailey	59	c Gregory b Mailey	115
JW Hearne c(S)TJE Andrews b Mailey	7	b Gregory	0
FE Woolley b Gregory	0 (6)	c Mailey b Gregory	123
EH Hendren not out	74	c Gregory b Hendry	9
A Sandham b Mailey	7 (7)	c Oldfield b Mailey	2
APF Chapman run out	13 (4)	c Oldfield b Hendry	44
MW Tate c(S)TJE Andrews b Mailey	7	c Ponsford b Kelleway	0
AER Gilligan (c) b Gregory	1	b Kelleway	1
AP Freeman b Gregory	0	not out	50
H Strudwick (+) lbw Gregory	6	c Oldfield b Hendry	2
EXTRAS (B 1, LB 5, NB 3)	9	(B 4, LB 3, NB 1)	8
TOTAL	298		411

FOW 1st Inns: 157 171 172 202 235 254 272 274 274 298
FOW 2nd Inns: 110 127 195 212 262 269 270 276 404 411

Bowling: *First Innings:* Gregory 28.7-2-111-5, Kelleway 14-3-44-0, Mailey 31-2-129-4, Hendry 5-1-5-0, AJ Richardson 1-1-0-0. *Second Innings:* Gregory 28-2-115-2, Kelleway 21-5-60-2, Mailey 32-0-179-3, AJ Richardson 5-0-13-0, Hendry 10.7-2-36-3.

Umpires: AC Jones & AP Williams

SECOND TEST 1924–25 AUSTRALIA v ENGLAND
Melbourne Cricket Ground, Melbourne. January 1, 2, 3, 5, 6, 7, 8, 1925.
Toss: Australia. Australia won by 81 runs.

AUSTRALIA

HL Collins (c) c Strudwick b Tate	9	b Hearne	30
W Bardsley c Strudwick b Gilligan	19	lbw Tate	2
AJ Richardson run out	14	b Tate	9
WH Ponsford b Tate	128	b Tate	4
JM Taylor run out	72	b Tate	90
VY Richardson run out	138	c Strudwick b Hearne	8
C Kelleway c Strudwick b Gilligan	32	c & b Hearne	17
AEV Hartkopf c Chapman b Gilligan	80	lbw Tate	0
JM Gregory c Gilligan b Tate	44	not out	36
WAS Oldfield (+) not out	39	lbw Hearne	39
AA Mailey lbw Douglas	1	b Tate	3
EXTRAS (B 18, LB 5, NB 1)	24	(B 11, LB 1)	12
TOTAL	600		250

FOW 1st Inns: 22 47 47 208 301 424 439 499 599 600
FOW 2nd Inns: 3 13 27 106 126 166 168 168 239 250

Bowling: *First Innings:* Tate 45-10-142-3, Douglas 19.5-0-95-1, Tyldesley 35-3-130-0, Gilligan 26-1-114-3, Hearne 13-1-69-0, Woolley 11-3-26-0. *Second Innings:* Tate 33.3-8-99-6, Gilligan 11-2-40-0, Tyldesley 2-0-6-0, Hearne 29-5-84-4, Douglas 4-0-9-0.

ENGLAND

JB Hobbs b Mailey	154	lbw Mailey	22
H Sutcliffe b Kelleway	176	c Gregory b Mailey	127
FE Woolley b Gregory	0 (5)	lbw AJ Richardson	50
JW Hearne b Mailey	9	lbw Gregory	23
EH Hendren c Oldfield b Kelleway	32 (6)	b Gregory	18
APF Chapman c Oldfield b Gregory	28 (9)	not out	4
JWHT Douglas c Collins b AJ Richardson	8 (8)	b Mailey	14
RK Tyldesley c Collins b Gregory	5 (7)	c Ponsford b Mailey	0
MW Tate b AJ Richardson	34 (11)	b Gregory	0
AER Gilligan (c) not out	17	c & b Mailey	0
H Strudwick (+) b Hartkopf	4 (3)	lbw Gregory	22
EXTRAS (B 4, LB 4, NB 4)	12	(B 6, LB 2, NB 2)	10
TOTAL	479		290

FOW 1st Inns: 283 284 305 373 404 412 418 453 458 479
FOW 2nd Inns: 36 75 121 211 254 255 280 289 289 290

Bowling: *First Innings:* Gregory 34-4-124-3, Kelleway 30-10-62-2, Mailey 34-5-141-2, Hartkopf 26-1-120-1, AJ Richardson 14-6-20-2. *Second Innings:* Gregory 27.3-6-87-4, Kelleway 18-4-42-0, AJ Richardson 22-7-35-1, Mailey 24-2-92-5, Hartkopf 4-1-14-0, Collins 11-3-10-0.

Umpires: RM Crockett & C Garing

THIRD TEST 1924–25 AUSTRALIA v ENGLAND
Adelaide Oval, Adelaide. January 16, 17, 19, 20, 21, 22, 23, 1925.
Toss: Australia. Australia won by 11 runs.

AUSTRALIA
HL Collins (c) b Tate	3		b Freeman	26	
AJ Richardson b Kilner	69		c Kilner b Woolley	14	
JM Gregory b Freeman	6	(9)	c Hendren b Woolley	2	
JM Taylor lbw Tate	0		b Freeman	34	
WH Ponsford c Strudwick b Gilligan	31		c Hendren b Kilner	43	
VY Richardson c Whysall b Kilner	4	(7)	c Tate b Woolley	0	
J Ryder not out	201	(3)	c & b Woolley	88	
TJE Andrews b Kilner	72	(6)	c Whysall b Kilner	1	
C Kelleway c Strudwick b Woolley	16	(8)	not out	22	
WAS Oldfield (+) lbw Kilner	47		b Kilner	4	
AA Mailey st Strudwick b Hendren	27		c Sutcliffe b Kilner	5	
EXTRAS (LB 9, NB 4)	13		(B 4, LB 4, NB 3)	11	
TOTAL	489			250	

FOW 1st Inns: 10 19 22 114 118 119 253 308 416 489
FOW 2nd Inns: 36 63 126 215 216 217 217 220 242 250

Bowling: *First Innings*: Tate 18-1-43-2, Gilligan 7.7-1-17-1, Freeman 18-0-107-1, Woolley 43-5-135-1, Kilner 56-7-127-4, Hobbs 3-0-11-0, Hendren 5.1-0-27-1, Whysall 2-0-9-0. *Second Innings*: Tate 10-4-17-0, Kilner 22.1-7-51-4, Freeman 17-1-94-2, Woolley 19-1-77-4.

ENGLAND
WW Whysall b Gregory	9	(5)	c & b Gregory	75	
MW Tate c Andrews b Mailey	27	(8)	b Mailey	21	
H Strudwick (+) c Gregory b Kelleway	1	(11)	not out	2	
APF Chapman c Gregory b Kelleway	26	(6)	c Ryder b Kelleway	58	
JB Hobbs c Gregory b Mailey	119	(1)	b Collins b AJ Richardson	27	
H Sutcliffe c Oldfield b Ryder	33	(2)	c Ponsford b Mailey	59	
FE Woolley c Andrews b Mailey	16	(3)	b Kelleway	21	
EH Hendren c Taylor b Gregory	92	(4)	lbw Kelleway	4	
R Kilner lbw AJ Richardson	6	(7)	c VY Richardson b AJ Richardson	24	
AER Gilligan (c) c Collins b AJ Richardson	9	(9)	c VY Richardson b Gregory	31	
AP Freeman not out	6	(10)	c Oldfield b Mailey	24	
EXTRAS (B 8, LB 10, NB 3)	21		(B 5, LB 5, W 1, NB 6)	17	
TOTAL	365			363	

FOW 1st Inns: 15 18 67 69 159 180 297 316 326 365
FOW 2nd Inns: 63 92 96 155 244 254 279 312 357 363

Bowling: *First Innings*: Gregory 26.2-0-111-3, Kelleway 15-6-24-1, Mailey 44-5-133-3, Richardson 21-7-42-2, Ryder 6-2-15-1, Collins 5-1-19-0. *Second Innings*: Gregory 23-6-71-2, Collins 9-4-19-0, Kelleway 22-4-57-3, Ryder 2-0-11-0, Richardson 25-5-62-2, Mailey 30.2-4-126-3.

Umpires: RM Crockett & DA Elder

FIFTH TEST 1924–25 AUSTRALIA v ENGLAND
Sydney Cricket Ground, Sydney. February 27, 28, March 2, 3, 4, 1925.
Toss: Australia. Australia won by 307 runs.

AUSTRALIA
HL Collins (c) c Strudwick b Gilligan	1	(7)	lbw Tate	28	
J Ryder b Kilner	29		b Gilligan	7	
JM Gregory run out	29	(1)	lbw Hearne	22	
TJE Andrews c Whysall b Kilner	26	(3)	c Woolley b Hearne	80	
JM Taylor c Whysall b Tate	15	(4)	st Strudwick b Tate	25	
WH Ponsford c Woolley b Kilner	80	(5)	run out	5	
AF Kippax b Kilner	42	(6)	c Whysall b Woolley	8	
C Kelleway lbw Tate	9		c Whysall b Tate	73	
WAS Oldfield (+) c Strudwick b Tate	29		not out	65	
AA Mailey b Tate	14		b Tate	0	
CV Grimmett not out	12		b Tate	0	
EXTRAS (B 2, LB 5, NB 2)	9		(B 6, LB 4, W 1, NB 1)	12	
TOTAL	295			325	

FOW 1st Inns: 3 55 64 99 103 208 239 239 264 295
FOW 2nd Inns: 7 43 110 130 152 156 209 325 325 325

Bowling: *First Innings*: Tate 39.5-6-92-4, Gilligan 13-1-46-1, Kilner 38-4-97-4, Hearne 7-0-33-0, Woolley 5-0-18-0. *Second Innings*: Tate 39.3-6-115-5, Gilligan 15-2-46-1, Kilner 34-13-54-0, Hearne 22-0-84-2, Woolley 8-1-14-1.

ENGLAND
JB Hobbs c Oldfield b Gregory	0		st Oldfield b Grimmett	13	
H Sutcliffe c Mailey b Kelleway	22		b Gregory	0	
A Sandham run out	4		lbw Grimmett	15	
FE Woolley b Grimmett	47		c Andrews b Kelleway	28	
EH Hendren c Ponsford b Gregory	10		c Oldfield b Grimmett	10	
JW Hearne lbw Grimmett	16		lbw Grimmett	24	
WW Whysall lbw Grimmett	8		st Oldfield b Grimmett	18	
R Kilner st Oldfield b Grimmett	24		c Ponsford b Collins	1	
MW Tate b Ryder	25		c Mailey b Kelleway	33	
AER Gilligan (c) st Oldfield b Grimmett	5		not out	0	
H Strudwick (+) not out	1		c Mailey b Grimmett	0	
EXTRAS (LB 5, NB 1)	5		(B 1, LB 3)	4	
TOTAL	167			146	

FOW 1st Inns: 0 15 28 58 96 109 122 157 163 167
FOW 2nd Inns: 3 31 32 60 84 99 100 146 146 146

Bowling: *First Innings*: Gregory 9-1-42-2, Kelleway 15-1-38-1, Mailey 5-0-13-0, Ryder 7-0-24-1, Grimmett 11.7-2-45-5. *Second Innings*: Gregory 10-0-53-1, Kelleway 7-1-16-2, Grimmett 19.4-3-37-6, Collins 8-2-36-1.

Umpires: RM Crockett & DA Elder

FOURTH TEST 1924–25 AUSTRALIA v ENGLAND
Melbourne Cricket Ground, Melbourne. February 13, 14, 16, 17, 18, 1925.
Toss: England. England won by an innings & 29 runs.

ENGLAND
JB Hobbs st Oldfield b Ryder	66
H Sutcliffe lbw Mailey	143
JW Hearne c Bardsley b Richardson	44
FE Woolley st Oldfield b Mailey	40
EH Hendren b Ryder	65
APF Chapman st Oldfield b Mailey	12
WW Whysall st Oldfield b Kelleway	76
R Kilner lbw Kelleway	74
AER Gilligan (c) c Oldfield b Kelleway	0
MW Tate c Taylor b Mailey	8
H Strudwick (+) not out	7
EXTRAS (B 6, LB 2, W 3, NB 2)	13
TOTAL	548

FOW 1st Inns: 126 232 284 307 346 394 527 527 529 548

Bowling: *First Innings*: Gregory 22-1-102-0, Kelleway 29-5-70-3, Mailey 43.6-2-186-4, Ryder 25-3-83-2, Richardson 26-8-76-1, Collins 6-1-18-0.

AUSTRALIA
HL Collins (c) c Kilner b Tate	22		c Whysall b Kilner	1	
AJ Richardson b Hearne	19	(9)	lbw Hearne	3	
J Ryder b Tate	0	(5)	lbw Woolley	38	
W Bardsley run out	24	(2)	b Tate	0	
WH Ponsford c Strudwick b Hearne	21	(8)	b Tate	19	
JM Taylor c Hendren b Woolley	86	(4)	c Woolley b Gilligan	68	
TJE Andrews c Hearne b Kilner	35	(6)	c Strudwick b Tate	3	
C Kelleway lbw Kilner	1	(7)	c Strudwick b Tate	42	
JM Gregory c Woolley b Hearne	38	(3)	c Sutcliffe b Kilner	45	
WAS Oldfield (+) c Chapman b Kilner	3		b Tate	8	
AA Mailey not out	4		not out	8	
EXTRAS (B 13, LB 2, NB 1)	16		(B 15)	15	
TOTAL	269			250	

FOW 1st Inns: 38 38 64 74 109 170 172 244 257 269
FOW 2nd Inns: 5 5 64 133 190 195 225 234 238 250

Bowling: *First Innings*: Tate 16-2-70-2, Gilligan 6-1-24-0, Hearne 19.3-1-77-3, Kilner 13-1-29-3, Woolley 9-1-53-1. *Second Innings*: Tate 25.5-6-75-5, Kilner 16-3-41-2, Hearne 20-0-76-1, Woolley 6-0-17-1, Gilligan 7-0-26-1.

Umpires: RM Crockett & DA Elder

Australian Averages

1924–25 AUSTRALIA v ENGLAND
AUSTRALIA	M	Inn	NO	Runs	H.S	Avrge	Ct	St	Overs	Mds	Runs	Wkt	Avrge
Andrews, TJE	3	6	-	217	80	36.17	3	-	-	-	-	-	-
Bardsley, W	3	6	-	88	24	14.67	1	-	-	-	-	-	-
Collins, HL	5	10	-	294	114	29.40	4	-	39.0	11	102	1	102.00
Gregory, JM	5	10	1	224	45	24.89	6	-	208.4	22	816	22	37.09
Grimmett, CV	1	2	1	12	12*	12.00	-	-	31.3	5	82	11	7.45
Hartkopf, AEV	1	2	-	80	80	40.00	-	-	30.0	2	134	1	134.00
Hendry, HSTL	1	2	-	25	22	12.50	1	-	15.7	3	41	3	13.67
Kelleway, C	5	10	1	252	73	28.00	1	-	171.0	39	413	14	29.50
Kippax, AF	1	2	-	50	42	25.00	-	-	-	-	-	-	-
Mailey, AA	5	10	3	129	46*	18.43	5	-	244.0	20	999	24	41.63
Oldfield, WAS	5	10	3	291	65*	41.57	10	8	-	-	-	-	-
Ponsford, WH	5	10	-	468	128	46.80	5	-	-	-	-	-	-
Richardson, AJ	4	8	-	248	98	31.00	-	-	114.0	34	248	8	31.00
Richardson, VY	3	6	-	210	138	35.00	3	-	-	-	-	-	-
Ryder, J	3	6	1	363	201*	72.60	1	-	40.0	5	133	4	33.25
Taylor, JM	5	10	-	541	108	54.10	2	-	-	-	-	-	-

English Averages

1924–25 AUSTRALIA v ENGLAND
ENGLAND	M	Inn	NO	Runs	H.S	Avrge	Ct	St	Overs	Mds	Runs	Wkt	Avrge
Chapman, APF	4	7	1	185	58	30.83	3	-	5.0	1	20	-	-
Douglas, JWHT	1	2	-	22	14	11.00	-	-	23.5	3	104	1	104.00
Freeman, AP	2	4	2	80	50*	40.00	-	-	121.0	16	459	8	57.38
Gilligan, AER	5	9	2	64	31	9.14	1	-	135.7	14	519	10	51.90
Hearne, JW	4	7	-	123	44	17.57	2	-	147.4	12	539	11	49.00
Hendren, EH	5	9	-	314	92	39.25	5	-	5.1	-	27	1	27.00
Hobbs, JB	5	9	-	573	154	63.67	-	-	5.0	-	24	-	-
Kilner, R	3	5	-	129	74	25.80	2	-	179.1	35	399	17	23.47
Sandham, A	2	4	-	28	15	7.00	-	-	-	-	-	-	-
Strudwick, H	5	9	3	45	22	7.50	16	2	-	-	-	-	-
Sutcliffe, H	5	9	-	734	176	81.56	2	-	-	-	-	-	-
Tate, MW	5	9	-	155	34	17.22	1	-	316.0	62	881	38	23.18
Tyldesley, RK	1	2	-	5	5	2.50	-	-	37.0	3	136	-	-
Whysall, WW	3	5	-	186	76	37.20	7	-	2.0	-	9	-	-
Woolley, FE	5	9	-	325	123	36.11	9	-	110.0	11	375	8	46.88

NSW wraps up the Shield

Alan Kippax makes one of his 585 runs in the 1924–25. season.

Sydney, Jan. 27. NSW has wrapped up the Sheffield Shield in the most emphatic manner possible, defeating Victoria in the last match by an innings and 96 runs.

This is NSW's 17th Shield in the 30 years of competition

The one NSW innings totalled 708, Herbie Collins making 143 and Alan Kippax 271 not out. Bill Woodfull (126) and Bill Ponsford (138) were the only obstacles to an overwhelming win, and season.

NSW scored three wins by an innings, and the other match, against South Australia, was won by the modest amount of 541 runs.

This match has some record breaking aspects to it. NSW made 642 and 593, SA 475 and 219, the highest aggregate of runs, 1929, in any first class match in Australia.

Clarrie Grimmett toiled away for SA bowling 106 overs in total (394 balls – a record) for the depressing match figures of 10/394, also a record.

These matches, while showing Grimmett to be Australia's best bowler, also showed how bare is the bowling cupboard.

It was South Australian veteran Bill Whitty's last match, and Jack Gregory struggled in the game against Victoria.

No fast bowlers are prominent in Australian cricket at the present time.

Slow bowlers, including Grimmett, Arthur Mailey, and even Arthur Richardson's off-breaks have taken the most wickets – while NSW amassed scores of 554, 705, 642, 593 and 708.

WA team goes east

Adelaide, Nov. 23. Western Australia lost its fourth first class match on its first tour to the eastern states to South Australia, by nine wickets.

The SA team was almost a second eleven, as it had rested all but three of the team which had just defeated Victoria.

In the other matches WA lost to NSW by an innings and 234 runs, with Charlie Macartney, Harry Rock and Alan Kippax knocking up centuries for NSW.

Victoria defeated WA by an innings and 282 in the only first class match to be played at the Brunswick Street Oval, Bill Ponsford scoring 158.

In the first match of the tour in early November, WA lost to a full-strength SA side by an innings and 281 runs. There is clearly yet some distance for WA standards to travel.

Kippax out, after brilliant season

Sydney, Jan. 27. The only apparent reason that Alan Kippax, 28, who scored 271 not against Victoria, has been excluded from the 1926 team to tour Australia is that he had one of his very few failures in the Australian XI v The Rest selection trial in December.

But Arthur Richardson, the 37-year-old who has taken Kippax's place, also failed in what was a farcical trial.

Monty Noble has described Kippax's non-selection as 'a crime against the cricketing youth of Australia'.

The decision not to take such an artistic and graceful batsman to England where his deft footwork and elegant cutting would have been seen to advantage is widely regarded as a 'muddle-headed' selection.

It would appear that interstate jealousies, old friendships, and selection 'deals' count for more with the present Australian selectors – Herbie Collins, Clem Hill, and Jack Ryder – than picking the best team on its merits.

Kippax this season has scored 585 runs in eight innings, including his 271 not out, for an average of 83.57.

Arthur Richardson had 18 innings for 904 including a less worthwhile 227 against Western Australia, for an average of 50.22.

Victor Richardson might also count himself unlucky – but he made 56 in the trial match.

The figures would appear to speak for themselves.

Cricket is played the length and breadth of the land in 1925, even in Walhalla in Victoria, where a flat place was created by removing the top of a mountain.

Macartney whirlwind innings gets win

One of the quick-footed Charlie Macartney's drives, in his memorable 151 in the first Test at Trent Bridge, Nottingham.

Leeds, July 13. Too much thinking nearly brought about a result in the third Test, yet another farcical three day match. That there was no result was not caused by the rain, which was the case for the first Test at Trent Bridge when only 17.2 overs were bowled in the entire game. Nor was it the result of three days of hot sun which highlighted Australia's lack of a penetrating fast bowler (Jack Gregory is injured and is a shadow of his former greatness) in the second Test at Lord's, which allowed England to declare at 3/475.

This time it was a muddle in the middle as the English selectors who dropped Harold Larwood from the squad inspected the pitch – which was not the one prepared for the match but a damp, marked adjacent strip. Then England captain A. W. Carr, in consultation with local experts, put Australia in. All seemed well for England when Warren Bardsley fell to Maurice Tate for a duck, but that brought Charlie Macartney to the crease, without batting gloves. Dropped by Carr off his second ball, he proceeded to play an innings the like of which had not been seen, wrote the *Times*, since Trumper got a hundred before lunch at Manchester in 1904. Macartney made 112 before lunch.

He went on to 151, Bill Woodfull got 141 and the much-maligned Arthur Richardson a maiden test hundred, total 494.

Arthur Mailey's cartoon 'Grandmother's funeral' – all roads lead to Lord's.

Grimmett, Mailey carry the bowling

London, Aug. 25. On a tour where the front-line faster bowlers were injured or ill, the wicket-taking burden fell on slow bowlers Clarrie Grimmett and Arthur Mailey.

The spin duo not only has had to take Test wickets, but has had to do the bowling work in the other tour games as well.

Jack Gregory's injured knee resulted in him taking just 36 wickets, and the other fast medium hope, Sam Everett managed just 27 wickets.

Grimmett took 116 at 17.2, and Mailey 141 at 18.7. Even off-spinner Arthur Richardson took 63 wickets, and Charlie Macartney's left-arm 'slowies' obtained 56 valuable wickets.

This lack of pace bowling in Australia was made worse by the loss of Ted McDonald to Lancashire League cricket.

Oh, for a Harold Larwood.

Rain, injuries and strikes on a depressing tour

London, Sep. 1. The only god smiling on the Australian tour has been Jupiter Pluvius, because rain, and not sunshine has followed the team around.

English society itself is under a cloud after the General Strike and its aftermath, and could do with a sunny cricketing revival.

The Australian situation has been different, marked by indifferent form, injury and illness.

Jack Gregory's knee and attendant muscle strains have rendered the great man of 1921 a very sad shadow. He went without a wicket in the first four Tests. Herbie Collins the 'unflappable and almost unbowlable' missed the third and fourth Tests as he was in hospital with neuritis.

Collins, Bardsley take the field.

Illness struck all members of the squad at one time or another.

All this rubbed off on the team's attitude, which was not as aggressive as it had been in the past.

The Australians won only two and drew 11 of the 13 matches leading to the first Test, preferring to use them as warm-ups. Armstrong's 1921 sides would never have done that. In all, the Australians won only 12 matches in the six-month tour – and most importantly did not win a Test.

Bail (E.H.M. Baillie) summing up the tour in the *Sporting Globe* said, 'Some of those now in England will not be Test men in two year's time, and if all that we hear about the probable retirement of others is true we will have to find almost a new team. One thing that stands out above everything else is the need for discovering new bowlers, if such a thing is possible. Where are they to be found?'

Hobbs, Sutcliffe, Rhodes get the urn

Arthur Mailey bowls a chagrined Jack Hobbs with a slow full toss on the leg stump. The Australians are nonplussed.

London, Aug. 18. Australia had not beaten England at the Oval since the Ashes Test of 1882 – and did not do so on this occasion, losing the Ashes in a defeat of some magnitude – 289 runs, despite leading on the first innings.

After four farcical three-day Test draws, the fifth was to be played out to a result, as they are in Australia.

Weather should not be as much of a factor. The Oval ground staff cover the bowler's approaches, though not the pitch, at the conclusion of each day's play.

Once again the Australian bowling was exposed, especially in the little matter of getting either Jack Hobbs or Herbert Sutcliffe out.

A first-innings opening partnership of 53 was as good as could be hoped, but in the second innings it was 172. Hobbs got an even hundred and Sutcliffe went on to 161. Despite rumblings in the

English camp about dissension ('Committee In Blunderland', 'England Quarrels worth 100 runs to Australia' were two newspaper comments) after Percy Chapman replaced Arthur Carr as captain, Frank Woolley was also dropped and 48-year-old Wilfred Rhodes selected, it was England who outbluffed the sphinx, Herbie Collins.

The appointment of Chapman, the epitome of English amateurism, prompted Arthur Mailey to waggishly appear on the first morning in his dinner jacket. This was naturally against the strict team rules. Stern and generally officious manager Syd Smith bided his time and kept his rebuke till after the day's play – in which Mailey took six wickets.

There was to be no rebuke. 'Five wickets wouldn't have done it,' said Mailey.

After England's moderate 280 and Australia's little-better 302, day

three dawned with Hobbs and Sutcliffe at the wicket, after overnight rain. Collins thought the damp wicket would be too dangerous for the injured Gregory, and opened the bowling with Arthur Richardson.

He was played with exaggerated caution, by the wily Englishmen, prompting Collins to bowl him for 41 overs.

By comparison the potential matchwinner Gregory could only bowl 18. England made 436.

This left Australia 415 to win, with all the time in the world.

But rain, Larwood (3/14 including Macartney and Woodfull), Maurice Tate only 1/12 – but it was that danger-man Jack Gregory) and especially Wilfred Rhodes (4/44 including Bardsley, Collins and Ponsford) who made the difference in the conditions.

Australia was all out for 125, losing the Test by 289 runs.

Bill Ponsford is snapped up by Harold Larwood off the bowling of Wilfred Rhodes for 12.

The Governor General

Charles Macartney was born with cricket in his blood. He graced the game during one of Australia's richest eras, from 1907 until 1926.

Charles George Macartney was born in West Maitland on 27 June 1886, and moved to Sydney in 1898. Aged just five, his grandfather, George Moore, who had played against W. G. Grace, used to bowl at him with green apples from his orchard.

Thus began one of cricket's more fruitful, entertaining careers. Macartney wanted to play for Australia and, though something of a stonewaller early on, he soon abandoned that approach and developed into a dashing batsman in the Trumper mould, adventurous and a crowd-pleaser.

Macartney preferred to get off the mark with a thumping straight drive, preferably at the bowler's head ('It rattles 'em') to establish his authority. Macartney put his audacious approach down to the days when he and his brother practiced on the Chatswood Oval. The family's dog, Towser, was a fine fielder, so the teenage Macs could hit the ball as hard and often as they chose.

Macartney was 19 when he was selected to play for NSW cricket against Queensland and he did sufficiently well, making 56 and taking 3/80.

Macartney played his first series against England in Australia in 1907–08. In the beginning he was more of a bowler than a batsmen, showing excellent control with his left-arm slows. The occasional quicker ball was also part of his armoury.

It was during this season that Macartney was dubbed the 'Governor-General', because of his lordly manner when he came out to bat. Asked why he replied: 'I suppose it was because I was cocky.'

Macartney was hardly in vice-regal form in his first series in 1907–08.

He did well enough in the second Test, opening with Trumper. They put on 84 in the first innings and 126 in the second, Macartney scoring 37 and 54. Macartney followed with 75 in the third Test, after which the runs dried up as he dropped down the order.

He made his first tour to England in 1909 distinguishing himself in the Leeds Test with match-winning figures of 7/58 and 4/27.

Macartney – a noble bearing.

Macartney was still out of sorts at the start of the 1910–11 series against the touring South Africans. He managed only 15 runs in five innings in the first three Tests, and was dropped from the fourth. He then belted 119 and 126 for NSW against the tourists, and registered his first Test century, and 137, in the fifth Test at the SCG.

Curiously, Macartney played in only one Test, the fifth, against the visiting Englishmen in 1911–12 but he went to England in 1912 for the Triangular series with South Africa. He scored 99 against England at Lord's.

When World War One broke out he enlisted and served in France. After the war, illness kept Macartney out of the second, third and fourth Tests against the English tourists in 1920–21. He scored his first century against England, 170, in the fifth Test.

Macartney was in rare form in England in 1921, at one stage scoring four centuries in a row, including 345 in a day against Nottingham at Trent Bridge.

After he had reached 200, Macartney signalled the pavilion with a wave of his bat. 'What do you want Charles?' asked Notts skipper A. W. Carr, 'a drink?' 'No,' replied Macartney. 'I want a heavier bat. I'm going to have a dip.' One of the Notts bowlers nearly fainted.

Illness kept him idle in 1924–25 but he regained his fitness for the 1926 tour of England and, at the age of 40, proceeded to play one of his grandest innings, again in at Leeds. This time Macartney made a glorious 151.

Macartney was in sparkling form on his last tour. He scored three consecutive Test centuries, 133 not out, his 151, then 109 in the fourth Test.

He died in 1958.

FIRST TEST 1926 ENGLAND v AUSTRALIA
Trent Bridge, Nottingham. June 12, 14 (no play), 15 (no play), 1926.
Toss: England. Match Drawn.

ENGLAND

JB Hobbs not out	19
H Sutcliffe not out	13
FE Woolley	
JW Hearne	
EH Hendren	
APF Chapman	
R Kilner	
AW Carr (c)	
MW Tate	
CF Root	
H Strudwick (+)	
EXTRAS	0
TOTAL	0 for 32

FOW 1st Inns:

Bowling: *First Innings*: Gregory 8-1-18-0, Macartney 8.2-2-14-0, Richardson 1-1-0-0.

AUSTRALIA
HL Collins (c)
W Bardsley
CG Macartney
JM Taylor
TJE Andrews
WM Woodfull
J Ryder
JM Gregory
AJ Richardson
WAS Oldfield (+)
AA Mailey

Umpires: RD Burrows & F Chester

SECOND TEST 1926 ENGLAND v AUSTRALIA
Lord's Cricket Ground, London. June 26, 28, 29, 1926.
Toss: Australia. Match Drawn.

AUSTRALIA

HL Collins (c) b Root	1		c Sutcliffe b Larwood	24
W Bardsley not out	193			
CG Macartney c Sutcliffe b Larwood	39		not out	133
WM Woodfull c Strudwick b Root	13	(6)	c Root b Woolley	0
TJE Andrews c & b Kilner	10	(4)	b Root	9
JM Gregory b Larwood	7	(2)	c Sutcliffe b Root	0
JM Taylor c Carr b Tate	9			
AJ Richardson b Kilner	35			
J Ryder c Strudwick b Tate	28	(7)	not out	0
WAS Oldfield (+) c Sutcliffe b Kilner	19	(5)	c Sutcliffe b Tate	11
AA Mailey lbw Kilner	1			
EXTRAS (B 12, LB 16)	28		(B 5, LB 12)	17
TOTAL	383			5 for 194

FOW 1st Inns: 11 84 127 158 187 208 282 338 379 383
FOW 2nd Inns: 2 125 163 187 194

Bowling: *First Innings*: Tate 50-12-111-2, Root 36-11-70-2, Kilner 34.5-11-70-4, Larwood 32-2-99-2, Woolley 2-0-5-0. *Second Innings*: Tate 25-11-38-1, Root 19-9-40-2, Kilner 22-2-49-0, Larwood 15-3-37-1, Woolley 7-1-13-1.

ENGLAND

JB Hobbs c Richardson b Macartney	119
H Sutcliffe b Richardson	82
FE Woolley lbw Ryder	87
EH Hendren not out	127
APF Chapman not out	50
AW Carr (c)	
R Kilner	
MW Tate	
H Larwood	
CF Root	
H Strudwick (+)	
EXTRAS (B 4, LB 4, W 1, NB 1)	10
TOTAL	3 dec 475

FOW 1st Inns: 182 219 359

Bowling: *First Innings*: Gregory 30-3-125-0, Macartney 33-8-90-0, Mailey 30-6-96-0, Richardson 48-18-73-1, Ryder 25-3-70-1, Collins 2-0-11-0.

Umpires: LC Braund & AE Street

THIRD TEST 1926 ENGLAND v AUSTRALIA
Headingley, Leeds. July 10, 12, 13, 1926.
Toss: England. Match Drawn.

AUSTRALIA

W Bardsley (c) c Sutcliffe b Tate	0
WM Woodfull b Tate	141
CG Macartney c Hendren b Macaulay	151
TJE Andrews lbw Kilner	4
AJ Richardson run out	100
JM Taylor c Strudwick b Geary	4
JM Gregory c Geary b Kilner	26
J Ryder b Tate	42
WAS Oldfield (+) lbw Tate	14
CV Grimmett c Sutcliffe b Geary	1
AA Mailey not out	1
EXTRAS (B 2, LB 4, NB 4)	10
TOTAL	494

FOW 1st Inns: 0 235 249 378 385 423 452 485 492 494

Bowling: *First Innings*: Tate 51-13-99-4, Macaulay 32-8-123-1, Kilner 37-6-106-2, Geary 41-5-130-2, Woolley 4-0-26-0.

ENGLAND

JB Hobbs c Andrews b Mailey	49	b Grimmett	88
H Sutcliffe c & b Grimmett	26	b Richardson	94
FE Woolley run out	27	c Macartney b Grimmett	20
EH Hendren c Andrews b Mailey	0	not out	4
AW Carr (c) lbw Macartney	13		
APF Chapman b Macartney	15	(5) not out	42
R Kilner c Ryder b Grimmett	36		
MW Tate st Oldfield b Grimmett	5		
G Geary not out	35		
GG Macaulay c & b Grimmett	76		
H Strudwick (+) c Gregory b Grimmett	1		
EXTRAS (B 4, LB 6, NB 1)	11	(B 5, LB 1)	6
TOTAL	294		3 for 254

FOW 1st Inns: 59 104 108 110 131 140 175 182 290 294
FOW 2nd Inns: 156 208 210

Bowling: *First Innings*: Gregory 17-5-37-0, Macartney 31-13-51-2, Grimmett 39-11-88-5, Richardson 20-5-44-0, Mailey 21-4-63-2. *Second Innings*: Gregory 6-2-12-0, Grimmett 29-10-59-2, Macartney 4-1-13-0, Richardson 16-7-22-1, Mailey 18-2-80-0, Ryder 9-2-26-0, Andrews 4-0-36-0.

Umpires: HR Butt & W Reeves

FOURTH TEST 1926 ENGLAND v AUSTRALIA
Old Trafford, Manchester. July 24, 26, 27, 1926.
Toss: Australia. Match Drawn.

AUSTRALIA

WM Woodfull c Hendren b Root	117
W Bardsley (c) c Tyldesley b Stevens	15
CG Macartney b Root	109
TJE Andrews c(S)APF Chapman b Stevens	8
WH Ponsford c & b Kilner	23
AJ Richardson c Woolley b Stevens	0
J Ryder c Strudwick b Root	3
JM Gregory c Kilner b Root	34
WAS Oldfield (+) not out	12
CV Grimmett c Stevens b Tate	6
AA Mailey b Tate	1
EXTRAS (B 2, LB 1, W 1, NB 3)	7
TOTAL	335

FOW 1st Inns: 29 221 252 256 257 266 300 317 329 335

Bowling: *First Innings*: Tate 36.2-7-88-2, Root 52-27-84-4, Kilner 28-12-51-1, Stevens 32-3-86-3, Woolley 2-0-19-0.

ENGLAND

JB Hobbs c Ryder b Grimmett	74
H Sutcliffe c Oldfield b Mailey	20
GE Tyldesley c Oldfield b Macartney	81
FE Woolley c Ryder b Mailey	58
EH Hendren not out	32
GTS Stevens c Bardsley b Mailey	24
R Kilner not out	9
AW Carr (c)	
MW Tate	
CF Root	
H Strudwick (+)	
EXTRAS (B 4, LB 3)	7
TOTAL	5 for 305

FOW 1st Inns: 58 135 225 243 272

Bowling: *First Innings*: Gregory 11-4-17-0, Grimmett 38-9-85-1, Mailey 27-4-87-3, Ryder 15-3-46-0, Richardson 17-3-43-0, Macartney 8-5-7-1, Andrews 9-5-13-0.

Umpires: H Chidgey & HI Young

FIFTH TEST 1926 ENGLAND v AUSTRALIA
Kennington Oval, London. August 14, 16, 17, 18, 1926.
Toss: England. England won by 289 runs.

ENGLAND

JB Hobbs b Mailey	37	b Gregory	100
H Sutcliffe b Mailey	76	b Mailey	161
FE Woolley b Mailey	18	lbw Richardson	27
EH Hendren b Gregory	8	c Oldfield b Grimmett	15
APF Chapman (c) st Oldfield b Mailey	49	b Richardson	19
GTS Stevens c Andrews b Mailey	17	c Mailey b Grimmett	22
W Rhodes c Oldfield b Mailey	28	lbw Grimmett	14
G Geary run out	9	c Oldfield b Gregory	1
MW Tate b Grimmett	23	not out	33
H Larwood c Andrews b Grimmett	0	b Mailey	5
H Strudwick (+) not out	4	c Andrews b Mailey	2
EXTRAS (B 6, LB 5)	11	(B 19, LB 18)	37
TOTAL	280		436

FOW 1st Inns: 53 91 108 189 213 214 231 266 266 280
FOW 2nd Inns: 172 220 277 316 373 375 382 425 430 436

Bowling: *First Innings*: Gregory 15-4-31-1, Grimmett 33-12-74-2, Mailey 33.5-3-138-6, Macartney 7-4-16-0, Richardson 7-2-10-0. *Second Innings*: Gregory 18-1-58-2, Grimmett 55-17-108-3, Mailey 42.5-6-128-3, Macartney 26-16-24-0, Richardson 41-21-81-2.

AUSTRALIA

WM Woodfull b Rhodes	35	c Geary b Larwood	0
W Bardsley c Strudwick b Larwood	2	(4) c Woolley b Rhodes	21
CG Macartney b Stevens	25	c Geary b Larwood	16
WH Ponsford run out	2	(2) c Larwood b Rhodes	12
TJE Andrews b Larwood	3	(6) c Tate b Larwood	15
HL Collins (c) c Stevens b Larwood	61	(5) c Woolley b Rhodes	4
AJ Richardson c Geary b Rhodes	16	(8) b Rhodes	4
JM Gregory c Stevens b Tate	73	(7) c Sutcliffe b Tate	9
WAS Oldfield (+) not out	33	b Stevens	23
CV Grimmett b Tate	35	not out	8
AA Mailey c Strudwick b Tate	2	b Geary	6
EXTRAS (B 5, LB 12)	17	(LB 7)	7
TOTAL	302		125

FOW 1st Inns: 9 44 51 59 90 122 229 231 298 302
FOW 2nd Inns: 1 31 31 35 63 83 83 87 114 125

Bowling: *First Innings*: Tate 37.1-17-40-3, Larwood 34-11-82-3, Geary 27-8-43-0, Stevens 29-3-85-1, Rhodes 25-15-35-2. *Second Innings*: Tate 9-4-12-1, Larwood 14-3-34-3, Geary 6.3-2-15-1, Stevens 3-1-13-1, Rhodes 20-9-44-4.

Umpires: F Chester & HI Young

Australian Averages

1926 ENGLAND v AUSTRALIA

AUSTRALIA	M	Inn	NO	Runs	H.S	Avrge	Ct	St	Overs	Mds	Runs	Wkt	Avrge
Andrews, TJE	5	6	-	49	15	8.17	5	-	13.0	5	49	-	-
Bardsley, W	5	5	1	231	193*	57.75	1	-	-	-	-	-	-
Collins, HL	3	4	-	90	61	22.50	-	-	2.0	-	11	-	-
Gregory, JM	5	6	-	149	73	24.83	1	-	105.0	20	298	3	99.33
Grimmett, CV	3	4	1	50	35	16.67	2	-	194.0	59	414	13	31.85
Macartney, CG	5	6	1	473	151	94.60	1	-	117.2	49	215	4	53.75
Mailey, AA	5	5	1	9	6	2.25	1	-	172.4	25	592	14	42.29
Oldfield, WAS	5	6	2	112	33*	28.00	5	2	-	-	-	-	-
Ponsford, WH	2	3	-	37	23	12.33	-	-	-	-	-	-	-
Richardson, AJ	5	5	-	155	100	31.00	1	-	150.0	57	273	4	68.25
Ryder, J	4	4	1	73	42	24.33	3	-	49.0	8	142	1	142.00
Taylor, JM	3	2	-	13	9	6.50	-	-	-	-	-	-	-
Woodfull, WM	5	6	-	306	141	51.00	-	-	-	-	-	-	-

English Averages

1926 ENGLAND v AUSTRALIA

ENGLAND	M	Inn	NO	Runs	H.S	Avrge	Ct	St	Overs	Mds	Runs	Wkt	Avrge
Carr, AW	4	1	-	13	13	13.00	1	-	-	-	-	-	-
Chapman, APF	4	5	2	175	50*	58.33	-	-	-	-	-	-	-
Geary, G	2	3	1	45	35*	22.50	4	-	74.3	15	188	3	62.67
Hearne, JW	1	-	-	-	-	-	-	-	-	-	-	-	-
Hendren, EH	5	6	3	186	127*	62.00	2	-	-	-	-	-	-
Hobbs, JB	5	7	1	486	119	81.00	-	-	-	-	-	-	-
Kilner, R	4	4	1	45	36	45.00	3	-	121.5	31	276	7	39.43
Larwood, H	2	2	-	5	5	2.50	1	-	95.0	19	252	9	28.00
Macaulay, GG	1	1	-	76	76	76.00	-	-	32.0	8	123	1	123.00
Rhodes, W	1	2	-	42	28	21.00	-	-	45.0	24	79	6	13.17
Root, CF	3	-	-	-	-	-	1	-	107.0	47	194	8	24.25
Stevens, GTS	2	3	-	63	24	21.00	3	-	64.0	7	184	5	36.80
Strudwick, H	5	3	1	7	4*	3.50	8	-	-	-	-	-	-
Sutcliffe, H	5	7	1	472	161	78.67	8	-	-	-	-	-	-
Tate, MW	5	3	1	61	33*	30.50	1	-	208.3	64	388	13	29.85
Tyldesley, GE	1	1	-	81	81	81.00	-	-	-	-	-	-	-
Woolley, FE	5	6	-	237	87	39.50	3	-	15.0	1	63	1	63.00

QUICK SINGLES

Ashes repercussions. Loss of the Ashes has had harsh repercussions. Herbie Collins was dropped as captain of his club Waverley and of NSW. The Gordon club in Sydney dropped team manager Syd Smith as delegate to the NSWCA, and therefore Board of Control positions – because Kelleway had not been selected for the tour. Clem Hill was removed as a selector.

New Shield formula. Because of the odd number of matches this season with Queensland playing SA once only, the Sheffield Shield will be awarded on a 'percentage' basis of wins from matches played.

Blackie's back. Don Blackie playing for St Kilda against Fitzroy in December took all ten wickets. He had 3/63 and captured the last seven for one run.

Australia v The Rest. The 1926 Australian XI played The Rest in February, the team including Alan Kippax, Archie Jackson, Leo O'Connor and Vic Richardson as a benefit for Charlie Macartney in February, and raised £2598. The Australian XI won by seven wickets.

NSW revenge. NSW regained its pride by dismissing a second-string Victorian team for 35 and 181, after totting up 469, with Alan Kippax 217 not out at the SCG in January.

Queensland's second win. Its second win for the season was scored when Queensland defeated Victoria at the Exhibition Ground in Brisbane by 234 runs.

Ponsford predominant. Bill Ponsford's first class season amounted to 1229 runs from ten innings in six matches – an average of 122.9.

SA's Shield. Despite Ponsford, it was South Australia which won the Shield for 1926–27 on percentage, winning three and losing two matches. Vic Richardson made 727 runs and leg spinners Clarrie Grimmett (with 30 wickets) and Norm Williams (35) were the stars.

Malayans win. A team lead by Bill Woodfull was defeated by Malaya in June in Kuala Lumpur. 'Australia' won the return match in Singapore.

That man again: Ponsford 352, Vic 1107

Melbourne, Dec. 29. Bill Ponsford's run-scoring machine has been in good order this season, with scores of 214 and 84 v SA, and 151 v Queensland, but he saved something special for Christmas.

Dismissing NSW for 221 on Christmas Eve, Victoria had two days rest, and then scored 1/573 on the second day, with Ponsford a dominant 334 not out and 'Stork' Hendry 86 not out. Bill Woodfull had already gone for 133, at 1/375.

Next day Ponsford went to 352 in 363 minutes, Hendry made his hundred, bringing Jack Ryder to the crease. Ryder proceeded to display what Woodfull said was 'the most terrific hitting I think anybody has witnessed in cricket', 295 in 245 minutes, six sixes and 33 fours. When Ryder was on 275, NSW leg-spinner Tommy Andrews said to captain Alan Kippax 'I know his weak spot!' The next five balls were 4, 6, 4, 6, out.

Andrews figures of 2/148 were only exceeded by Arthur Mailey's 4/362, his worst from 64 overs.

Victoria's total of 1107 is a first class record. The Vics won by an innings and 656 runs.

Big news at the MCG – a world-record score with Victoria winning by 656 runs.

Queensland is off to a great start in Shield competition

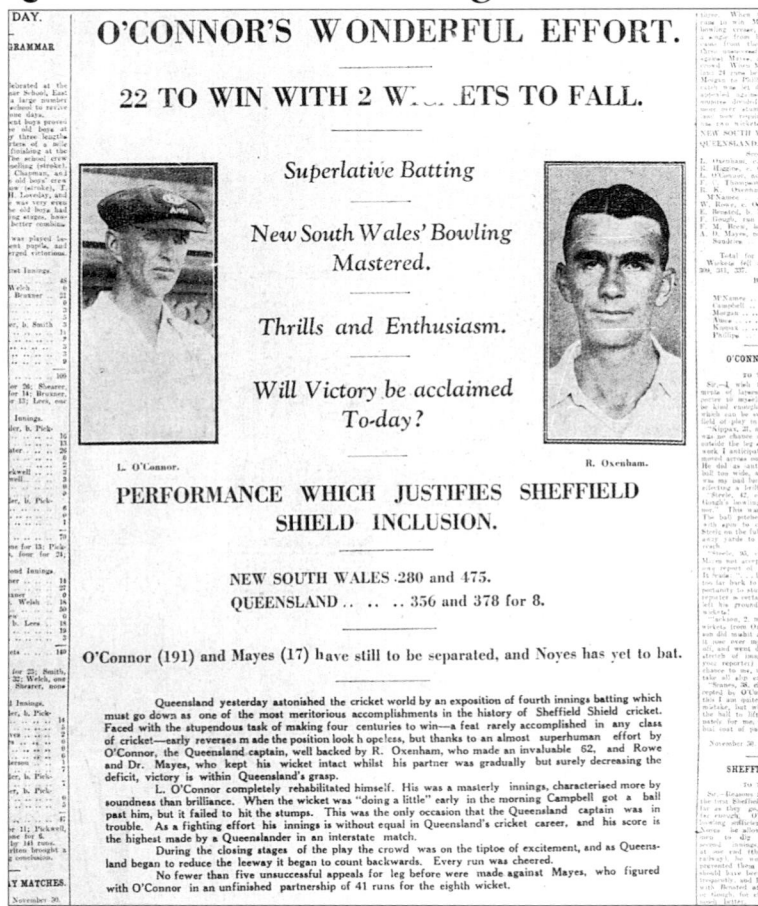

Big news in Brisbane – the Brisbane Courier looks forward to a successful days play in the northern State's first Shield match.

Sydney, Dec. 11. Following a heroic performance in their first Shield match against NSW at the Exhibition Ground in Brisbane, Queensland defeated NSW in Sydney, to record their first win in the Sheffield Shield.

NSW is without its 1926 Test players, who are still on their way back from England, but they do have one player who perhaps should have gone – Alan Kippax, who hit three centuries, 127 and 131 in Brisbane, and 182 in Sydney; and one young star of the future, 17-year-old Archie Jackson, who made 86 in his first match in Brisbane and a sparkling even hundred runs in Sydney.

But the honours in the two matches must go to the Queenslanders. In the first game chasing 400 runs in the fourth innings they fell just eight runs short, when Leo O'Connor, captain, 'keeper and hero, was run out on 196.

Cecil Thompson goes down in the record books as Queensland's first Shield century maker with a first-innings 134.

O'Connor hit a hundred in each innings of the Sydney match, 103 and 143 not out.

Queensland won by five wickets, showing that they will not be Shield 'easybeats'.

And again! World record 437

Melbourne, Feb. 7. Victoria has walked away with the Sheffield Shield through the efforts of one man – the amazing Bill Ponsford. He has broken his own record, with 437 runs against Queensland in December, and has scored a phenomenal 1217 for the season at an average of 152.12.

His dominance was so great early in the season that he achieved the target of 1000 runs in four innings, between December 16 and January 3. He scored 133 against South Australia, 437 against Queensland, 202 and 38 against NSW and then 336 against South Australia.

The monumental innings against Queensland, surpassing his 429 made against Tasmania in February 1923, was achieved in 621 minutes.

It all ended after tea on the second day when he was out caught and bowled by Gordon Amos, to the stunned silence of the second day crowd of 10,977, who had come to watch this phenomenon at work.

'Stork' Hendry contributed 129 of a 314-run partnership with 'Ponny'.

The Queensland players clapped him from the field, all smiles and temporarily unconcerned by the task of chasing nearly 800 runs.

In the end Victoria won by an innings and 197 runs, the second of four outright wins that set up the Shield victory.

NSW building up with young bats

Sydney, Jan. 10. New South Wales has unearthed two super young batsmen who should carry their Shield fortunes for years to come. Archie Jackson at 18 is already in his second Shield season. He had the brilliant double of 131 and 122 against South Australia, displaying power and artistry amazing in one so young.

Donald Bradman, at the age of 19, seems made of the same brilliant stamp. He made 118 on his first class debut in Adelaide, getting his first Shield game because Jackson had a boil on his knee. He finished the season against Victoria with a blazing 134 not out.

Both batsman have been overshadowed this season by the NSW captain Alan Kippax, who has three Shield centuries to his credit, including 315 not out against Queensland. Kippax made 926 runs at 84.18 for the season – compared to Bill Ponsford's 1217 at 152.12 for the Shield winners.

Ponsford the impassable. Bill Ponsford's solid physique, fine technique and broad bat have again brought heartbreak for bowlers this season.

Young NSW batsman Don Bradman shows his concentration as he executes a late cut. He scored 118 against South Australia in his first Shield game.

The Bradman era

England too seasoned: 4–1

The site of the first Queensland Test, the Brisbane Exhibition Ground, is in a natural amphitheatre.

Melbourne, March 16. English and Australian cricket have seemed hopelessly out of balance in the one–sided Test series, which England has won 4–1.

Australia seemed well capable of matching England in batting, with the big scoring and proven men in Woodfull, Ponsford and Kippax supported by all-rounder and captain Jack Ryder and the exciting Don Bradman and Archie Jackson.

But the bowling has been substandard all season. Both Jack Gregory and Charles Kellaway were expected to carry the fast bowling work, but Gregory damaged his knee cartilage and Kelleway suffered food poisoning in the first Test. After that many combinations were tried, but nothing to rip the heart out of the top of an innings. In the end it became an old men's game with Bert Ironmonger and Don Blackie, both 46, doing duty in the spinning area, alongside the crafty Clarrie Grimmett.

But England has a seasoned side in all departments – magnificent batsmen in 46-year-old Hobbs and his opening partner Bert Sutcliffe, a rising star in Walter Hammond and sound middle-order men in both Douglas Jardine and 'Patsy' Hendren.

But in bowling they have been all over Australia, with brilliant fast men in Maurice Tate and the muscular miner Harold Larwood, and the best figures of all from left-arm spinner Jack 'Farmer' White – 8/126 in Australia's second innings in the fourth Test.

Throughout the series Australia used 14 bowlers to England's seven. Despite some fine efforts from Australians the die seemed cast in the first Test, which England won by a mammoth 675 runs after Australia scored a miserable 66. Australia did improve in each Test until a very close 12-run loss in the fourth Test and a face-saving win in the fifth Test, where Tim Wall's eight wickets and Bradman's 123 restored the balance somwhat. But it took eight days – and is the longest first class match on record in Australia.

New Australian cap Don Bradman is lbw to Maurice Tate for 18 in the first innings of the first Test.

Exciting young batsmen

Archie Jackson: a wonderful stylist and building a healthy average.

Melbourne, March 16. The very dismal Test results have not dampened the excitement over the batting of two of Australia's finest prospects.

Leaping over Ponsford, Woodfull and Kippax for batting style and daring are youngsters Don Bradman and Archie Jackson.

Bradman has been outstanding, despite his poor result in the first Test and relegation to 12th man for the second. He has scored two Test centuries since then and has had an amazing first class season, amassing a record 1690 runs at 93.8.

At one stage he had consecutive innings of 131, 133 not out, 87, 132 not out, 1 and 71 not out for NSW. He also scored 340 not out against Victoria.

Jackson has not been as prolific, but has a healthy average of 49.60. He captured the public imagination with his 164 on debut in the fourth Test in Adelaide. At 19 years and 152 days he became the youngest player to score a century in England–Australia Tests.

The nation was tuned to the radio, as the young men batted together for Australia for the first time, making a partnership of 82.

Jackson is all Golden Age grace, while Bradman is a very efficient modern run-making machine. Australia needs both.

Don Blackie called up at the age of 46

Adelaide, Feb. 8. When other men may be thinking about taking up bowls, St Kilda and Victorian teammates Bert Ironmonger and Don Blackie, both 46, have been at the pinnacle of cricket in the last few weeks, playing together in the second Test for Australia.

The old Victorian spinners have had their share of success, with Blackie snaring 4/148 and Ironmonger 2/142 in England's massive innings of 636. Blackie took a wonderful 6/98 in England's first innings in the third Test.

Don Blackie: a late call.

Marathon Test to Australia

Melbourne, March 16. The feast of cricket this summer has been topped off by the longest Test yet played. It took eight days (33 hours and 17 minutes of cricket) to get a result in the fifth Test.

It was gratifying to the crowds, which totalled 213,794 over the match, that Australia finally scored a victory – by five wickets. It was equally gratifying that Australia might have found a new fast bowler when this commodity has been in fearfully short supply.

Tim Wall laboured for 3/126 in England's first innings, but showed distinct promise with 5/66 in the second. Two other bowlers, Percy Hornibrook of Queensland and Alan Fairfax of NSW were also tried, as the selectors have to find the solution before the next encounter with England.

The match was full of contrasts. Jack Hobbs, at 46, played a fabulous innings of 164, his 15th Test century and his 12th against Australia. In his second-innings 65 he became the first player to score 5000 runs in Tests. Maurice Leyland made 137 in England's first innings of 519.

As Hobbs so stylishly staved off the darkness of a career's end, Bradman, at 20, was the bright, rising sun as he scored 123 and 57 not out, just two more of the string of amazing scores that have made him the most talked-about cricketer of the season. And England also had someone to grasp the mantle in Walter Hammond, who made 905 runs in Tests, at an average of 113.12. He is classical in his strokeplay, but powerful and at times daringly brilliant.

As a change from the bowling of Larwood and Tate that has kept England winning this season,

Tim Wall: bowling hope.

George Geary took a hand for England with 5/105 as Australia moved to 491.

But by now we were in the fifth day of the match, and players and audience alike must have been contemplating other pressing engagements. England obliged by succumbing for a modest 257 and Australia was left with 285 to get, having opened with nightwatchmen Oldfield and Hornibrook on the evening of the sixth day. Bradman and Ryder were in occupation at the end just after lunch on the eighth day.

The jury, of more eactly, the selectors, will still have open minds on Hornibrook and Fairfax, but Walls is England-bound. He is an athletic young man who is likely to blast batsmen out with his pace.

Hornibrook is a tall left-arm spinner who can vary his pace to suit the conditions.

Former Test players get together for a yarn at the MCG during the fifth Test. Present are Vernon Ransford, Clem Hill, Monty Noble, Hugh Trumble, Jack Gregory, Joe Darling, John Worrall, Warwick Armstrong and Peter McAlister.

NSW youth policy pays off

Archie Jackson shows his artistry with a powerful on-drive.

Adelaide, March 6. New South Wales has struck a fine balance of youth, experience and all round talent to take out the Sheffield Shield this year.

It had a clear-cut win over Victoria, with Queensland showing improvement to be third ahead of South Australia.

The deeds of Archie Jackson and Don Bradman were a major factor for NSW, but their Alan Kippax, the captain, also had a superb season, with a highest score of 260 when he made an amazing 10th-wicket stand of 307 with Hal Hooker in Melbourne.

Hooker has led the bowling, and has been assisted by another new boy Alan Fairfax, an all-rounder who made his way from his Shield debut this season to a place in the fifth Test.

The tall, slim Fairfax is a fine stroke player, but he owes his Test place to his lively medium-pace bowling.

NSW also seems to have some promising players coming along in Jack Fingleton, a solid batsman, and Stan McCabe, a brilliant stroke player, who both made their debuts during the season.

The busiest bowler of the season has been the off-spinner Clarrie Grimmett, who bowled some marathon Test spells as well as doing duty for South Australia when he was available.

Victoria began with two outright wins, but often had their big guns in Ponsford, Woodfull, Ryder and Hendry unavailable through Test duty or injury. The bowling of both Blackie and Ironmonger could not compensate for their loss.

However primitive the field and skimpy the equipment, the bat and ball game has an endless fascination for players world-wide.

Jack Ryder – a long reign

Always keen on practice, Jack Ryder is at work in the nets during the Test series.

Jack Ryder – 'The King of Collingwood' – undoubtably got the most out of his cricket. While not the greatest batsman of his time, he played some vital and memorable innings.

He was not always secure in his Test place, but he toured England twice and South Africa, and he captained his country.

He was not a great bowler, but with his awkward medium-paced lifters, took wickets for Australia and Victoria. Despite playing only 20 Tests he had great longevity, playing for Victoria in 1912–13 and captaining Frank Tarrant's touring team to India in 1935.

Ryder was tall and lean with whipcord strength. He loved to play attacking cricket and was a particularly strong driver of the ball.

He had a taciturn nature, but was always a popular and fair player, and was particularly loved in his native area of the working-class suburb of Collingwood in Melbourne. Although he was seen as having some batting deficiencies compared to many of his brilliant contemporaries, he made up for that with his fighting qualities and had the highly creditable Test average of 51.62.

Even though his side was being slaughtered by A. P. F. Chapman's touring team in 1928–29, and particularly by the batting onslaught of Walter Hammond, he topped the Australian averages with 492 Test runs at 54.66.

Before World War One he had established himself as an all-rounder of great promise, and was rewarded with Test places against the 1920–21 touring side

from England, and a trip with Warwick's Armstrong's 1921 side. In that powerful team he did not get a Test, although he finished fourth in the batting averages.

He hit a century in South Africa and batted four times for 334 runs.

Yet he failed in England in 1926, and the team he captained in 1928–29 was the only one in which he managed to hold his place for the series.

But the only real cloud in Jack Ryder's long summer of cricket came in 1930, when he was an Australian selector.

With his pads on waiting to bat for Victoria in the last match of the Shield season, Ryder scanned the final selection list drawn up by his fellows Charles Dolling and Dick Jones.

He was out of the tour, too old at 41 and with Bill Woodfull preferred as captain.

Ryder went out under gloomy skies and made 100 not out, having been advised by 'Stork' Hendry:

'You make a hundred and show these bastards sitting in the stand what a mistake they've made'.

A tremendous rumpus broke out. Ryder said nothing in public, and never spoke to Dick Jones again.

But Ryder's influence on Australian cricket was far from over. He became a selector again from 1946 to 1970, sharing the task with the likes of Sir Donald Bradman, and continuing until he was over 80.

He led the parade of Australian Test players before the Centenary Test, and died soon afterwards, aged 87.

The art of batsmanship

Don Bradman's square cut: ferocity and grace in equal measure.

The elements of batting have been set down by the best: by people like Hobbs, Hammond and Bradman himself. Footwork, the grip, the array of strokes, forward play and back play, attack and defence – the technicalities are endless.

More subtle than these, more mysterious than the practice are the gifts of physique, eyesight, judgment, timing and temperament that make a great batsman.

A. G. 'Johnnie' Moyes, the noted ABC commentator and writer, played with and watched the great players from early in the century until the 1950s. He makes these comments:

Victor Trumper: 'Undoubtably the most wonderful batsman in the world, and there are many who claim we have yet to see his equal. Never mind how bad the pitch after rain and sun, he was always likely to get 50 runs, his skill in pulling amounting to genius. But there was another factor as well, for Trumper would never reach for the ball.'

Charles Macartney: 'The cheekiest batsman I have ever seen. He possessed all the known strokes, but wrapped in that smallish frame was an ambition to be different, and a resolve that no bowler could subdue him.'

Clem Hill: 'His late and square cutting, his powerful off-side strokes, and his facility in getting the ball away on the on side were features of his batting which raised him to the highest level. He walked to the wicket like one who was master of his fate.'

Bill Ponsford: 'Accumulated runs like a miser hoards wealth.

Almost infallible against spin. He sidled down the pitch like a crab, was always in the right place, seemed to know just what spin had been imparted.'

Bill Woodfull: 'Almost unbowlable. His back swing was a mere gesture to convention, like a man opening the door an inch or two, then closing it hurriedly so that nothing could enter.'

Alan Kippax: 'A cultured and skilful player not always treated well by selection committees. He was by nature a charmer, could cut, drive and hook with delightful certainty, and there was a beauty about his batting ...'

Archie Jackson: 'His batting was all beauty. Runs flowed from his bat with a perfection of timing, and every time he swung his bat he held one enthralled, this lovable youth who was the nearest in style to Trumper ...'

Don Bradman: 'His figures are so fantastic and overpowering that they can never be ignored.

'His stance at the wicket was easy and comfortable, and he was able to watch the approaching bowler clearly with both eyes.

'His footwork was fast and clever ...

'Bradman played all strokes well, but the hook and the square cut were the two which gave me the greatest thrill ... a combination of grace and ferocity.'

Stan McCabe: 'There have been few batsmen in Australian cricket who could spreadeagle a field as could McCabe.

'He could play all the strokes, hit tremendously hard with a minimum of effort, and had the priceless gift of placing.'

FIRST TEST 1928–29 AUSTRALIA v ENGLAND
Exhibition Ground, Brisbane. November 30, December 1, 3, 4, 5, 1928.
Toss: England. England won by 675 runs.

ENGLAND

Batsman	1st	2nd
JB Hobbs run out	49	lbw Grimmett ... 11
H Sutcliffe c Ponsford b Gregory	38	c (S)RK Oxenham b Ironmonger ... 32
CP Mead lbw Grimmett	8	lbw Grimmett ... 73
WR Hammond c Woodfull b Gregory	44	c (S)FC Thompson b Ironmonger ... 28
DR Jardine c Woodfull b Ironmonger	35	not out ... 65
EH Hendren c Ponsford b Ironmonger	169	c Ponsford b Grimmett ... 45
APF Chapman (c) c Kelleway b Gregory	50	c Oldfield b Grimmett ... 27
MW Tate c Ryder b Grimmett	26	c Bradman b Grimmett ... 20
H Larwood lbw Hendry	70	c Ponsford b Grimmett ... 37
JC White lbw Grimmett	14	
G Duckworth (+) not out	5	
EXTRAS (LB 13, NB 3)	13	(LB 3, NB 1) ... 4
TOTAL	521	8 dec 342

FOW 1st Inns: 85 95 108 161 217 291 319 443 495 521
FOW 2nd Inns: 25 69 117 165 228 263 285 342

Bowling: *First Innings*: Gregory 41-3-142-3, Kelleway 34-9-77-0, Grimmett 40-2-167-3, Ironmonger 44.3-18-79-2, Ryder 6-2-23-0, Hendry 10-1-20-1. *Second Innings*: Hendry 27-6-79-0, Grimmett 44.1-9-131-6, Ironmonger 50-20-85-2, Ryder 14-3-43-0.

AUSTRALIA

Batsman	1st	2nd
WM Woodfull c Chapman b Larwood	0	not out ... 30
WH Ponsford b Larwood	2	c Duckworth b Larwood ... 6
AF Kippax c & b Tate	16	c & b Larwood ... 15
HSTL Hendry lbw Larwood	30	c Larwood b White ... 6
C Kelleway b Larwood	8	
J Ryder (c) c Jardine b Larwood	33 (5)	c Larwood b Tate ... 1
DG Bradman lbw Tate	18 (6)	c Chapman b White ... 1
WAS Oldfield (+) lbw Tate	2 (7)	c Larwood b Tate ... 5
CV Grimmett not out	7 (8)	c Chapman b White ... 1
H Ironmonger b Larwood	4 (9)	c Chapman b White ... 0
JM Gregory		
EXTRAS (B 1, LB 1)	2	(NB 1) ... 1
TOTAL	9 for 122	8 for 66

FOW 1st Inns: 0 7 24 40 71 101 105 116 122
FOW 2nd Inns: 6 33 46 47 49 62 66 66

Bowling: *First Innings*: Larwood 14.4-4-32-6, Tate 21-6-50-3, Hammond 15-5-38-0. *Second Innings*: Larwood 7-0-30-2, Tate 11-3-26-2, Hammond 1-0-2-0, White 6.3-2-7-4.

Umpires: DA Elder & GA Hele

SECOND TEST 1928–29 AUSTRALIA v ENGLAND
Sydney Cricket Ground, Sydney. December 14, 15, 17, 18, 19, 29, 1928.
Toss: Australia. England won by 8 wkts.

AUSTRALIA

Batsman	1st	2nd
WM Woodfull lbw Geary	68	run out ... 111
VY Richardson b Larwood	27	c Hendren b Tate ... 0
AF Kippax b Geary	9 (4)	lbw Tate ... 10
WH Ponsford retired hurt	5	
HSTL Hendry b Geary	37 (3)	lbw Tate ... 112
J Ryder (c) lbw Geary	25 (5)	c Chapman b Larwood ... 79
OE Nothling b Larwood	8 (6)	run out ... 44
WAS Oldfield (+) not out	41 (7)	lbw Tate ... 0
CV Grimmett run out	9 (8)	c Chapman b Geary ... 18
DD Blackie b Geary	8 (9)	not out ... 11
H Ironmonger c Duckworth b Larwood	1 (10)	b Geary ... 0
EXTRAS (B 4, LB 9, W 2)	15	(B 5, LB 6, W 1) ... 12
TOTAL	9 for 253	9 for 397

FOW 1st Inns: 51 65 152 153 171 192 222 251 253
FOW 2nd Inns: 0 215 234 246 347 348 370 397 397

Bowling: *First Innings*: Larwood 26.2-4-77-3, Tate 21-9-29-0, White 38-10-79-0, Geary 18-5-35-5, Hammond 5-0-18-0. *Second Innings*: Larwood 35-5-105-1, Tate 46-14-99-4, Geary 31.4-11-55-2, White 30-5-83-0, Hammond 9-0-43-0.

ENGLAND

Batsman	1st	2nd
JB Hobbs c Oldfield b Grimmett	40	
H Sutcliffe c Hendry b Ironmonger	11	
WR Hammond b Ironmonger	251	
DR Jardine run out	28	
EH Hendren c Richardson b Blackie	74	
APF Chapman (c) c Ryder b Blackie	20	
H Larwood c Ryder b Grimmett	43	
G Geary lbw Blackie	66 (1)	b Hendry ... 8
MW Tate lbw Blackie	25 (2)	c (S)DG Bradman b Hendry ... 4
G Duckworth (+) not out	39 (3)	not out ... 2
JC White st Oldfield b Hendry	29 (4)	not out ... 2
EXTRAS (B 2, LB 3, W 4, NB 1)	10	0
TOTAL	636	2 for 16

FOW 1st Inns: 37 65 148 293 341 432 496 523 592 636
FOW 2nd Inns: 8 13

Bowling: *First Innings*: Nothling 42-15-60-0, Grimmett 64-14-191-2, Ironmonger 68-21-142-2, Blackie 59-10-148-4, Hendry 23.1-4-52-1, Ryder 11-3-22-0, Kippax 5-3-11-0. *Second Innings*: Nothling 4-0-12-0, Hendry 3-2-4-2.

Umpires: DA Elder & GA Hele

THIRD TEST 1928–29 AUSTRALIA v ENGLAND
Melbourne Cricket Ground, Melbourne. December 29, 31, 1928 January 1, 2, 3, 4, 5, 1929.
Toss: Australia. England won by 3 wkts.

AUSTRALIA
WM Woodfull c Jardine b Tate	7	c Duckworth b Tate	107
VY Richardson c Duckworth b Larwood	3	b Larwood	5
HSTL Hendry c Jardine b Larwood	23	st Duckworth b White	12
AF Kippax c Jardine b Larwood	100	b Tate	41
J Ryder (c) c Hendren b Tate	112	b Geary	5
DG Bradman b Hammond	79	c Duckworth b Geary	112
WAS Oldfield (+) b Geary	3	b White	7
EL A'Beckett c Duckworth b White	41	b White	6
RK Oxenham b Geary	15	b White	39
CV Grimmett c Duckworth b Geary	5	not out	4
DD Blackie not out	2	b White	0
EXTRAS (B 4, LB 3)	7	(B 6, LB 7)	13
TOTAL	397		351

FOW 1st Inns: 5 15 57 218 282 287 373 383 394 397
FOW 2nd Inns: 7 60 138 143 201 226 252 345 351 351

Bowling: *First Innings*: Larwood 37-3-127-3, Tate 46-17-87-2, Geary 31.5-4-83-3, Hammond 8-4-19-1, White 57-30-64-1, Jardine 1-0-10-0. *Second Innings*: Larwood 16-3-37-1, Tate 47-15-70-2, White 56.5-20-107-5, Geary 30-4-94-2, Hammond 16-6-30-0.

ENGLAND
JB Hobbs c Oldfield b A'Beckett	20	lbw Blackie	49
H Sutcliffe b Blackie	58	lbw Grimmett	135
WR Hammond c A'Beckett b Blackie	200 (4)	run out	32
APF Chapman (c) b Blackie	24 (6)	c Woodfull b Ryder	5
EH Hendren c A'Beckett b Hendry	19	b Oxenham	45
DR Jardine c & b Blackie	62 (3)	b Grimmett	33
H Larwood c & b Blackie	0		
G Geary lbw Grimmett	1	not out	4
MW Tate c Kippax b Grimmett	21 (7)	run out	0
G Duckworth (+) b Blackie	3 (9)	not out	0
JC White not out	8		
EXTRAS (B 1)	1	(B 15, LB 14)	29
TOTAL	417		7 for 332

FOW 1st Inns: 28 161 201 238 364 364 381 385 391 417
FOW 2nd Inns: 105 199 257 318 326 328 328

Bowling: *First Innings*: A'Beckett 37-7-92-1, Hendry 20-8-35-1, Grimmett 55-14-114-2, Oxenham 35-11-67-0, Blackie 44-13-94-6, Ryder 4-0-14-0. *Second Innings*: A'Beckett 22.5-39-0, Hendry 23-5-33-0, Blackie 39-11-75-1, Oxenham 28-10-44-1, Grimmett 42-12-96-2, Ryder 5.5-1-16-1.

Umpires: DA Elder & GA Hele

FIFTH TEST 1928–29 AUSTRALIA v ENGLAND
Melbourne Cricket Ground, Melbourne. March 8, 9, 11, 12, 13, 14, 15, 16, 1929.
Toss: England. Australia won by 5 wkts.

ENGLAND
JB Hobbs lbw Ryder	142	c Fairfax b Grimmett	65
DR Jardine c Oldfield b Wall	19	c Oldfield b Wall	0
WR Hammond c Fairfax b Wall	38 (4)	c Ryder b Fairfax	16
GE Tyldesley c Hornibrook b Ryder	31 (5)	c Oldfield b Wall	21
G Duckworth (+) c Fairfax b Hornibrook	12 (11)	lbw Oxenham	9
EH Hendren c Hornibrook b Fairfax	95	b Grimmett	1
M Leyland c Fairfax b Oxenham	137	not out	53
H Larwood b Wall	4 (3)	b Wall	11
G Geary b Hornibrook	4	b Wall	3
MW Tate c(S)EL A'Beckett b Hornibrook	15 (8)	c Fairfax b Hornibrook	54
JC White (c) not out	9 (10)	c Oxenham b Wall	4
EXTRAS (B 4, LB 6, W 1, NB 2)	13	(B 19, LB 1)	20
TOTAL	519		257

FOW 1st Inns: 64 146 235 240 261 401 409 428 470 519
FOW 2nd Inns: 1 19 75 119 123 131 212 217 231 257

Bowling: *First Innings*: Wall 49-8-123-3, Hornibrook 48-8-142-3, Oxenham 45.1-15-86-1, Grimmett 25-11-40-0, Fairfax 27-4-84-1, Ryder 18-5-29-2, Kippax 3-1-2-0. *Second Innings*: Wall 26-5-66-5, Hornibrook 19-5-51-1, Fairfax 7-0-20-1, Grimmett 24-7-66-2, Oxenham 10.3-1-34-1.

AUSTRALIA
WM Woodfull c Geary b Larwood	102 (3)	b Hammond	35
A Jackson run out	30 (4)	b Geary	46
AF Kippax c Duckworth b White	38 (5)	run out	28
J Ryder (c) c Tate b Hammond	30 (6)	not out	57
DG Bradman c Tate b Geary	123 (7)	not out	37
AG Fairfax lbw Geary	65		
RK Oxenham c Duckworth b Geary	7		
WAS Oldfield (+) c & b Geary	6 (1)	b Hammond	48
CV Grimmett not out	38		
TW Wall c Duckworth b Geary	9		
PM Hornibrook lbw White	26 (2)	b Hammond	18
EXTRAS (B 6, LB 9, W 2)	17	(B 12, LB 6)	18
TOTAL	491		5 for 287

FOW 1st Inns: 54 143 203 203 386 399 409 420 432 491
FOW 2nd Inns: 51 80 129 158 204

Bowling: *First Innings*: Larwood 34-7-83-1, Tate 62-26-108-0, Geary 81-36-105-5, White 75.3-22-136-2, Hammond 16-3-31-1, Leyland 3-0-11-0. *Second Innings*: Larwood 32.1-5-81-0, Tate 38-13-76-0, White 18-8-28-0, Geary 20.5-5-31-1, Hammond 26-8-53-3.

Umpires: GA Hele & AC Jones

FOURTH TEST 1928–29 AUSTRALIA v ENGLAND
Adelaide Oval, Adelaide. February 1, 2, 4, 5, 6, 7, 8, 1929.
Toss: England. England won by 12 runs.

ENGLAND
JB Hobbs c Ryder b Hendry	74	c Oldfield b Hendry	1
H Sutcliffe st Oldfield b Grimmett	64	c Oldfield b A'Beckett	17
WR Hammond not out	119	c & b Ryder	177
DR Jardine lbw Grimmett	1	c Woodfull b Oxenham	98
EH Hendren b Blackie	13	c Bradman b Blackie	11
APF Chapman (c) c A'Beckett b Ryder	39	c Woodfull b Blackie	0
G Duckworth (+) c Ryder b Grimmett	5 (11)	lbw Oxenham	1
H Larwood b Hendry	3 (7)	lbw Oxenham	5
G Geary run out	3 (8)	c & b Grimmett	6
MW Tate b Grimmett	2 (9)	lbw Oxenham	47
JC White c Ryder b Grimmett	0 (10)	not out	4
EXTRAS (B 3, LB 7, W 1)	11	(B 6, LB 10)	16
TOTAL	334		383

FOW 1st Inns: 143 143 149 179 246 263 270 308 312 334
FOW 2nd Inns: 1 21 283 296 297 302 327 337 381 383

Bowling: *First Innings*: A'Beckett 31-8-44-0, Hendry 31-14-49-2, Grimmett 52.1-12-102-5, Oxenham 35-14-51-0, Blackie 29-6-57-1, Ryder 5-1-20-1. *Second Innings*: A'Beckett 27-9-41-1, Hendry 28-11-56-1, Oxenham 47.4-21-67-4, Blackie 39-11-70-2, Grimmett 52-15-117-1, Ryder 5-1-13-1, Kippax 2-0-3-0.

AUSTRALIA
WM Woodfull c Duckworth b Tate	1	c Geary b White	30
A Jackson lbw White	164	c Duckworth b Geary	36
HSTL Hendry c Duckworth b Larwood	2	c Tate b White	5
AF Kippax b White	3	c Hendren b White	51
J Ryder (c) lbw White	63	c & b White	87
DG Bradman c Larwood b Tate	40	run out	58
EL A'Beckett hit wicket b White	36	c Hammond b White	21
RK Oxenham c Chapman b White	15	c Chapman b White	12
WAS Oldfield (+) b Tate	32	not out	15
CV Grimmett b Tate	4	c Tate b White	9
DD Blackie not out	3	c Larwood b White	0
EXTRAS (LB 5, W 1)	6	(B 9, LB 3)	12
TOTAL	369		336

FOW 1st Inns: 1 6 19 145 227 287 323 336 365 369
FOW 2nd Inns: 65 71 74 211 224 258 308 320 336 336

Bowling: *First Innings*: Larwood 37-6-92-1, Tate 42-10-77-4, White 60-16-130-5, Geary 12-3-32-0, Hammond 9-1-32-0. *Second Innings*: Larwood 20-4-60-0, Tate 37-9-75-0, White 64.5-21-126-8, Hammond 14-3-21-0, Geary 16-2-42-1.

Umpires: DA Elder & GA Hele

Australian Averages

1928–29 AUSTRALIA v ENGLAND

AUSTRALIA	M	Inn	NO	Runs	H.S	Avrge	Ct	St	Overs	Mds	Runs	Wkt	Avrge
A'Beckett, EL	2	4	-	104	41	26.00	3	-	117.0	29	216	2	108.00
Blackie, DD	3	6	3	24	11*	8.00	2	-	210.0	51	444	14	31.71
Bradman, DG	4	8	1	468	123	66.86	2	-	-	-	-	-	-
Fairfax, AG	1	1	-	65	65	65.00	5	-	34.0	4	104	2	52.00
Gregory, JM	1	-	-	-	-	-	-	-	41.0	3	142	3	47.33
Grimmett, CV	5	9	3	95	38*	15.83	1	-	398.2	96	***	23	44.52
Hendry, HSTL	4	8	-	227	112	28.38	1	-	165.1	51	328	8	41.00
Hornibrook, PM	1	2	-	44	26	22.00	2	-	67.0	13	193	4	48.25
Ironmonger, H	2	4	-	5	4	1.25	-	-	162.3	59	306	6	51.00
Jackson, A	2	4	-	276	164	69.00	-	-	-	-	-	-	-
Kelleway, C	1	1	-	8	8	8.00	1	-	34.0	9	77	-	-
Kippax, AF	5	10	-	311	100	31.10	1	-	10.0	4	16	-	-
Nothling, OE	1	2	-	52	44	26.00	-	-	46.0	15	72	-	-
Oldfield, WAS	5	10	2	159	48	19.88	8	2	-	-	-	-	-
Oxenham, RK	3	5	-	88	39	17.60	1	-	201.2	72	349	7	49.86
Ponsford, WH	2	3	-	13	6	6.50	4	-	-	-	-	-	-
Richardson, VY	2	4	-	35	27	8.75	1	-	-	-	-	-	-
Ryder, J	5	10	-	492	112	54.67	8	-	68.5	16	180	5	36.00
Wall, TW	1	1	-	9	9	9.00	-	-	75.0	13	189	8	23.63
Woodfull, WM	5	10	1	491	111	54.56	5	-	-	-	-	-	-

English Averages

1928–29 AUSTRALIA v ENGLAND

ENGLAND	M	Inn	NO	Runs	H.S	Avrge	Ct	St	Overs	Mds	Runs	Wkt	Avrge
Chapman, APF	4	7	-	165	50	23.57	8	-	-	-	-	-	-
Duckworth, G	5	9	4	76	39*	15.20	13	1	-	-	-	-	-
Geary, G	4	8	1	95	66	13.57	3	-	240.3	70	477	19	25.11
Hammond, WR	5	9	1	905	251	113.13	1	-	119.0	30	287	5	57.40
Hendren, EH	5	9	-	472	169	52.44	3	-	-	-	-	-	-
Hobbs, JB	5	9	-	451	142	50.11	-	-	-	-	-	-	-
Jardine, DR	5	9	1	341	98	42.63	4	-	1.0	-	10	-	-
Larwood, H	5	8	-	173	70	21.63	6	-	259.1	41	724	18	40.22
Leyland, M	1	2	-	190	137	190.00	-	-	3.0	-	11	-	-
Mead, CP	1	2	-	81	73	40.50	-	-	-	-	-	-	-
Sutcliffe, H	4	7	-	355	135	50.71	-	-	-	-	-	-	-
Tate, MW	5	10	-	214	54	21.40	5	-	371.0	122	697	17	41.00
Tyldesley, GE	1	2	-	52	31	26.00	-	-	-	-	-	-	-
White, JC	5	8	4	70	29	17.50	1	-	406.4	134	760	25	30.40

Vics win Shield despite NSW bats

Adelaide, Feb. 17. NSW has the glamour, but Victoria has the Shield. Despite fireworks from the NSW batting line-up this season, Victoria has shown that a champion team will beat a team of champions.

What NSW lacked in its bowling line-up Victoria had in abundance, with Bert Ironmonger and Don Blackie, both aged 47, carrying the bowling with their wily spin, and the support of medium pacer Ted a'Beckett.

Batsmen Jack Ryder and Bill Ponsford batted solidly, and they were backed up across the team by a'Beckett, Hunter Hendry, John Scaife and Reginald Ellis.

Don Bradman, Alan Kippax, Stan McCabe and Arthur Allsop shone like stars for NSW.

Each team had one win in their head-on encounters.

Bitter Ryder not for English tour

Perth, March 24. Jack Ryder, dignified and taciturn, is not one to speak out on his own behalf. But plenty of people are doing it for him. The press has generally condemned his omission from the touring side to England, the Australian team which he so recently captained with application, if not with success.

The people of Collingwood, his home base, have turned out in protest.

But Ryder, at 41, has been dropped by the selection committee on which he had a vote. Bill Woodfull, much younger and with captaincy experience, has been preferred. Woodfull sportingly relinquished the captaincy of Victoria in favour of Ryder, and none of the animosity against the selectors is aimed at him. People just feel sorry for Ryder. Also for Ron Oxenham, the Queensland all-rounder who might have gone instead of Victoria's Ted a'Beckett. Queensland has two representatives, fast bowler Alan Hurwood and spinner Percy Hornibrook.

Don Bradman, 452 not out

Don Bradman hits out on his way to 452 not out. He might have made 500.

Sydney, Jan. 7. Alan Kippax declared and stopped the slaughter as Don Bradman might have made 500 or even 600 against Queensland. He was certainly well settled in when Alan Kippax declared the NSW innings at 8/761. Bradman was 452 not out, and the Queenslanders had the sporting grace to chair him from the field, smiling broadly and definitely looking fit enough to carry on.

But they were so undone by the onslaught that they capitulated in their final innings for 84, leaving NSW the winners by 685.

Bradman's innings was fast, certain and a technical masterpiece.

The only half-chances came on 264 and on 345, when the 'keeper and first slip got tangled up over a snick.

Bradman reached 100 in just 104 minutes, 200 in 185 minutes, 300 in 288 minutes and 400 in 377 minutes, and passed Ponsford's previous record as he went on to his score in 415 minutes. He had partnerships of 272 with Kippax (115), 156 with McCabe (60) and 180 with Allsopp (66).

Bradman has been remarkable again, with three other centuries and many scores close to the 100. His runs aggregate threatens to almost double those of his rivals.

Shield bowling honours to Clarrie Grimmett

Perth, March 24. South Australian leg-spinner Clarrie Grimmett has easily topped the season's bowling, taking 36 more wickets than his nearest rival, Arthur Hurwood of Queensland.

His haul of 82 wickets included two efforts of seven wickets in an innings, with his best being 7/136 in the decisive match against New South Wales.

Grimmett has had six seasons with South Australia after he failed over seven seasons to get a regular berth in the Victorian team. He has topped the bowling four times for his adopted State.

He is now 40 but shows no sign of retirement or losing his powers, and is the main bowling weapon for the forthcoming Test tour of England.

Clarrie Grimmett: streets ahead.

QUICK SINGLES

A close go. Queensland runs NSW close in the first Shield match, going down by 23 runs. Ron Oxenham has a fine match for Queensland, scoring 49 and 117 and taking 5/72 in NSW first innings with his medium-pace bowling.

Spun out. Veteran Victorian spin bowlers Don Blackie and Bert Ironmonger take 16 wickets between them for 211 as Victoria beats the MCC (en route to NZ) by seven wickets. Blackie has 6/82 and 7/25.

Batted out. The MCC goes on to NSW and suffers an onslaught from Jackson (149), Bradman (157), Kippax (108) Allsop (117) and McCabe (90) in a total of 629. MCC replies with 469 (Frank Woolley 219) and the match fizzles out to a draw. 1607 runs were scored at 73.04 per wicket.

Queensland first. Arthur Gilligan's MCC team, beset by injuries, tries to cancel its match with Queensland, and then submits to a Queensland victory by five wickets, 248 and 5/183 to MCC 171 and 259. The winning runs were achieved with three minutes to spare.

Selection bids. Ryder's XI plays Woodfull's XI in December as a selection tryout for the England tour. Batsman dominate with Jackson 182, Ponsford 131, Kippax 170 and Bradman 124 and 225. Clarrie Grimmett takes 7/173.

SA surprise. The great performances of Brian Hone (126), David Pritchard (148) and Clarrie Grimmett (7/136) give SA victory over NSW in the first Shield encounter this season, in December.

Jackson ill. NSW batsman Archie Jackson becomes ill during the NSW v SA match with tuberculosis, spending several days in Adelaide hospital after

the match, which ended on December 24.

Time runs out. NSW, with 402 and 2/145, has a moral win over Victoria (229 and 343) in the New Year's match, but runs out of time with 36 runs needed.

Young one. Leonard John Junor, aged 15 years and 265 days, is selected for Victoria to play Western Australia and makes 41 and 6.

Average 113.28. Don Bradman ends the season with 1586 runs in 16 innings, at an average of 113.28. He scored five centuries, taking his total to 14 in only three seasons.

No O'Reilly. Ryder and Oxenham were not the only surprise omissions from the team to tour England. NSW is upset at the absence of leg-spinning school teacher Bill O'Reilly, unable to press his claims after having been posted by the Education Department to remote Kandos.

Bradman casts his shadow

London, May 30. Don Bradman has silenced his English critics as he has blazed through the early County matches and achieved the rare feat of 1000 runs before the end of May, starting with a 236 against Worcestershire and other scores of 185 and 252 not out.

Bradman says he got the most satisfaction from his 252 not out against Surrey, captained by former England Test player Percy Fender, his sternest critic from the previous Australian summer. Fender had written that Bradman was 'brilliant but unsound' and that he would be found out on the softer English pitches. He had to watch helplessly, however, as Bradman took special pleasure in proving him wrong. He absolutely flogged the bowling, scoring his second 100 in a mere 80 minutes.

Woodfull and Ponsford have also been among the runs in a series of games. The other concern for England is crafty Clarrie Grimmett, who took 10/37 against Yorkshire.

A sense of foreboding – England's captain Percy Chapman is suitably concerned at the effect Don Bradman may have. Bradman silenced his critics.

Copley's catch helps England to shock win

Let the Tests begin. Stan McCabe and Don Bradman step out with the Australian team at Notts. But confidence alone does not win Tests.

Nottingham, June 17. Australia is on the back foot to England after losing the first Test by 93 runs. The home team can thank their staunch opening batsmen, the veteran Jack Hobbs and Herbert Sutcliffe. But the unlikely hero was ground staff substitute, the 24-year-old Sydney Copley, who turned the match on the last day with a brilliant catch. England gained a first-innings lead of 164 as it ran through the Australian side on the treacherous wicket after rain on the second day. England then made 302 to set up a 429 target for Australia.

Bradman and McCabe were together at 3/229 in the early afternoon and it seemed that they might overwhelm the bowling as they had made 77 in 70 minutes.

But McCabe mis-hit a drive and Copley, a second-XI player substituting for Sutcliffe, took a running and diving catch low down at mid-on from Tate's bowling.

Bradman pushed on to 131, but misjudged a googly from leg-spinner Walter Robins, leaving it alone and watching it take the off stump. The run chase petered out, an hour early and 93 runs short. It will take more than just Bradman.

Grimmett took 5/107 and 5/94.

For England's Percy Chapman it was the ninth successive win in Test matches under his captaincy.

It's Woodfull and Bradman!

London, July 1. This has been a match of brave captains, brilliant young batsmen and fine spin bowling. In the end the scoring power of Bradman and the spin of Clarrie Grimmett made the difference and took Australia to a seven-wicket win in the second Test at Lord's.

But it may have been Bill Woodfull's inspiring captain's knock of 155 that set the stage for the onslaught of Bradman, Kippax and Co. and a record Test score of 6/729.

He had a big task ahead when he went to the wicket with Bill Ponsford, as England had made 425. K. S. Duleepsinhji had made 173 on debut, emulating his uncle K. S. Ranjitsinhji, who made 175 in his first Test against Australia in 1897. Watching in the stand as 'Duleep' holed out to Bradman off Grimmett, 'Ranji' muttered 'the boy was always careless.'

Ponsford (81) was out 162 runs later, on the first ball he faced after shaking hands with the King. He may have been a mite distracted.

Then it was Woodfull and Bradman pressing on to 1/393 before Woodfull went. Bradman then dominated the tiring England attack as he made his 254, reaching 50 on 46 minutes, 100 in 106 minutes and 200 in 234 minutes.

It was England's captain Percy Chapman who took a brilliant catch to dismiss Bradman, and then propped up England's rearguard in making 121 in the second innings.

Like Ponsford, he may have been distracted on dismissal – for he had swallowed a bluebottle.

Bill Woodfull on-drives on his way to his second-Test score of 155.

Cricket stops Australia

All Australia is staying close to the radio to hear the Test news.

Sydney, Aug. 20. Australian cricket lovers have been living a night-and-day existence as they follow the fortunes of the Test matches in England. The Australian Broadcasting Commission team is providing a commentary on the play from regular cables it receives from England.

Bed is only for bachelors, as husbands have been despatched to the living room to listen to the radio reports.

In the dawn crowds can be found outside newspaper offices, where the scores are posted on a noticeboard. There were thousands of people waiting outside the *Sydney Morning Herald* office on June 17, when the news came through that Australia had won the second Test.

In these hard times of the Depression it is the cricket that has provided some cheer against the background of poverty and unemployment. The country has been told by English expert Sir Otto Niemeyer that it must tighten its belt if it is to get out of trouble.

Asked what he thought of the national mood of the Australian people, he said there was not enough pessimism. 'It might have been better if they had not won the last Test match,' he said.

Cricket lovers know that one foreign debt has been redeemed by the Australian Test players.

Bowler needed

London, May 30. Apparently satisfied with the glut of runs scored by the batsmen, the Australian Board of Control has turned down a request to send another bowler to join the touring party in England.

The Board was responding to a cable from the manager William Kelly and selectors, saying: 'It is imperative in Australia's interest that another bowler of the type of Ironmonger or Chilvers should be chosen for the England tour.'

Bert Ironmonger of Victoria is a left-arm spinner with Test experience and Hugh Chilvers is an orthodox leg-spinner who had success with NSW last season. They are seen as ideal partners for Clarrie Grimmett, who has baffled many of the England players with his leg spin.

The social round

London, May 26. The Australian cricketers are enjoying a constant social life, mixed in with matches, practice and sport.

Today Don Bradman went to the Imperial Advertising Co.

Bradman was given a camera, film, safety razor, pocket knife and wrist watch.

He and Stan McCabe went to the theatre in the afternoon and then walked around London, taking in the sights.

The team went to a dinner hosted by the Surrey County Cricket Club. Guest speakers included Sir Pelham Warner, Lord Chelms-ford and H. D. Leveson-Gower. Many players also spoke by radio phone to their relatives in Australia, where the team's exploits are creating much happiness.

As well as partaking in the busy life of a cricket tour, Don Bradman is writing his enlightening life story for the London Star.

Old England

London, June 17. England does not lack for experience as she goes through this Test series. The average age of the team is a staggering 35 years.

The old men of the team are Jack Hobbs, 47, Frank Woolley, 43, and 'Patsy' Hendren, 41. Herbert Sutcliffe is 36, Maurice Tate, 35, and spinner Dick Tyldesley, 33. One of the babies of the side is the captain, Percy Chapman, at 30.

The Australians are no spring chickens either, with an average age of 30.

The old men in this team are Clarrie Grimmett, 39, Victor Richardson, 36, and Bert Oldfield 35, and there are four others over 30. The young ones are McCabe, aged a mere 20, Bradman, 22, and Alan Fairfax, 24.

Bradman's 300 runs in a day

Leeds, July 15. Don Bradman has placed himself among the immortals of cricket. He has, in one innings, joined Victor Trumper and Charles Macartney in making 100 before lunch; surpassed Reg Foster's record Test score of 287, reached 1000 Test runs in seven matches, 2000 runs for the season and scored 300 runs in one day's play.

Bradman's amazing innings has been watched with rapt attention and heartfelt applause by the crowd at Headingley for the third Test. When he passed Foster's score the *Daily Express* recorded 'the enthusiasm was so terrific that play had to be stopped until the noise diminished'.

Bradman seemed to take it all in his stride, standing with his cap removed and his bat raised, smiling and at his ease. He said he was gratified that he had scored quickly and entertained the crowd.

He made his 105 before lunch, coming in after Ponsford had got out for one, 115 in the two-hour second session before tea and and was 309 not out at stumps. He had a quiet night, playing gramophone records alone in his hotel room, and the next day set off at the same brisk pace.

But at 334, on a faster-playing wicket, he snicked an outswinger from Maurice Tate and was out. Bradman had batted 383 minutes and hit 46 fours. Australia's total at the end of its first innings was 566.

Had Bradman read the papers in the morning his usual quiet demeanour might have been disturbed. The *Times*, for instance, said: 'To mention the strokes from which he scored most of his runs is to go through the whole range of strokes known to modern batsmen. It was, in fact, an innings so glorious that it might well be classed as incomparable …'

The astounding innings brought a wave of euphoria in Australia, and a concrete expression of it arrived by telegram in Bradman's hands while he was fielding. It announced a gift from an admirer in Australia, in recognition of the wonderful innings.

Bradman's effort would surely have brought victory in a timeless Test, but rain intervened on the third day, and the game petered out, enlivened only by Walter Hammond's 113, in which he passed 1000 runs against Australia in his 14th innings. For Australia, Grimmett's 5/135 was off a marathon 56.2 overs.

Master of all he surveys: a tribute to Bradman's innings of 334.

Bradman is feted by the crowd as he returns to the pavilion after his great innings.

Australians storm home with batting spree at the Oval

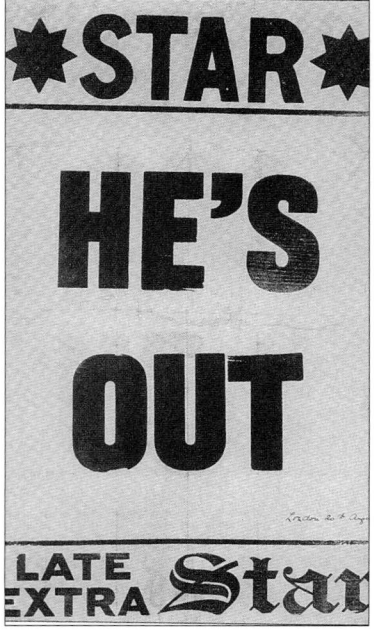

Unbelievable news from the Star.

The Oval, Aug. 22. The Ashes have been emphatically won with another invincible batting display by the Australians. Needless to say, Don Bradman has been at the forefront, this time with 232.

In this timeless fifth Test batting has been more about concentration than quick runs. Herbert Sutcliffe took all day to make 131 on the first day, his 161 the foundation for England's seemingly competitive total of 405.

It became apparent, however, that this would not be enough. Bill Ponsford (110) and Bill Woodfull (54), who have given Australia some fine starts in the series, were at it again, surrendering the first wicket for 163.

Then Bradman took over, batting with calm assurance rather than racing the clock. He was joined by Alan Kippax (28), Archie Jackson (73), Stan McCabe (54) and Alan Fairfax (53) in a run-feast that realised 695.

England leg-spinner Ian Peebles had the only consolation, taking 6/204, in a marathon spell of 71 overs. Peebles may have got Bradman cheaply on the damp pitch at Old Trafford in the fourth Test, but the great man had worked him out this time. Peebles' figures were indicative of a spinner's wicket.

The last word came from Queensland's Percy Hornibrook, a tall left-arm spinner who ripped through England, taking 7/92 as Australia won by an innings and 39 runs.

Don's wave of adulation

Sydney, Nov. 30. Don Bradman has been caught up in a burst of fan worship reserved only for film stars or royalty. His every public utterance is chronicled, his movements are charted and his life is programmed from dawn to dusk.

His promotable quality as the cricketer of the age has been a boon for his boss, the sports store proprietor Mick Simmonds, and he has not been slow in making the most of having Bradman at his behest.

He gained permission to separate Bradman from the rest of the team when the *Oronsay* docked in Adelaide, and bring him to Melbourne and Sydney by air. Crowds flocked at the airports, but they have flocked further to Mick Simmonds stores, grabbing up boots, gloves, bats, pads and cricket clothing which have Donald Bradman's endorsement. Schoolboy cricketers are being 'Bradmanised' from top to toe, and hoping that their play will do credit to the great man's name.

Bradman himself has been available to newspaper and radio, and has appeared in shopping centres, halls, cinemas and at 'welcome home' gatherings, staged around Australia now that the team is home. An accomplished pianist, he has written a song, 'Every Day's a Rainbow Day For Me'. He will be the subject of a film on his exploits. But he has retained the same even and modest demeanour that has characterised his career.

Crowds have been bigger than usual at the cricket, especially any match where Bradman is playing.

If you still haven't seen him bat, this is your chance.

The Jack Ryder testimonial match had a Saturday crowd of 44,434 at the Melbourne Cricket Ground. Bradman made 73 in the first innings and 29 in the second, a modest contribution for him. But in his second innings he passed the total of 4000 first class runs from the calendar year.

Vic Richardson, however, on radio, said: 'We could have played any team without Bradman, but we could not have played the blind school without Clarrie Grimmett.'

A run-feast for Ginger Meggs as his dog Mike snaffles the ball.

FIRST TEST 1930 ENGLAND v AUSTRALIA
Trent Bridge, Nottingham. June 13, 14, 16, 17, 1930.
Toss: England. England won by 93 runs.

ENGLAND

JB Hobbs c Richardson b McCabe	78	st Oldfield b Grimmett	74
H Sutcliffe c Hornibrook b Fairfax	29	retired hurt	58
WR Hammond lbw Grimmett	8	lbw Grimmett	4
FE Woolley st Oldfield b Grimmett	0	b Wall	5
EH Hendren b Grimmett	5	c Richardson b Wall	72
APF Chapman (c) c Ponsford b Hornibrook	52	b Wall	29
H Larwood b Grimmett	18 (9)	b Grimmett	7
RWV Robins not out	50	b McCabe	4
MW Tate b Grimmett	13 (7)	c Kippax b Grimmett	24
RK Tyldesley c Fairfax b Wall	1	b Grimmett	5
G Duckworth (+) lbw Fairfax	4	not out	14
EXTRAS (B 4, LB 7, NB 1)	12	(B 5, LB 1)	6
TOTAL	270		9 for 302

FOW 1st Inns: 53 63 63 71 153 188 218 241 242 270
FOW 2nd Inns: 125 137 147 211 250 260 283 283 302

Bowling: *First Innings*: Wall 17-4-47-1, Fairfax 21.4-5-51-2, Grimmett 32-6-107-5, Hornibrook 12-3-30-1, McCabe 7-3-23-1. *Second Innings*: Grimmett 30-4-94-5, Wall 26-4-67-3, Fairfax 15-4-58-0, Hornibrook 11-4-35-0, McCabe 14-3-42-1.

AUSTRALIA

WM Woodfull (c) c Chapman b Tate	2	c Chapman b Larwood	4
WH Ponsford b Tate	3	b Tate	39
AG Fairfax c Hobbs b Robins	14 (7)	c Robins b Tate	14
DG Bradman b Tate	8 (3)	b Robins	131
AF Kippax not out	64 (4)	c Hammond b Robins	23
SJ McCabe c Hammond b Robins	4 (5)	c (S)SH Copley b Tate	49
VY Richardson b Tyldesley	37 (6)	lbw Tyldesley	29
WAS Oldfield (+) c Duckworth b Robins	4	c Hammond b Tyldesley	11
CV Grimmett st Duckworth b Robins	0	c Hammond b Tyldesley	0
PM Hornibrook lbw Larwood	0	c Duckworth b Robins	5
TW Wall b Tyldesley	0	not out	8
EXTRAS (B 4, LB 4)	8	(B 17, LB 5)	22
TOTAL	144		335

FOW 1st Inns: 4 6 16 57 61 105 134 140 141 144
FOW 2nd Inns: 12 93 152 229 267 296 316 322 324 335

Bowling: *First Innings*: Larwood 15-8-12-1, Tate 19-8-20-3, Tyldesley 21-8-53-2, Robins 17-4-51-4. *Second Innings*: Larwood 5-1-9-1, Tate 50-20-69-3, Robins 17.2-1-81-3, Tyldesley 35-10-77-3, Hammond 29-5-74-0, Woolley 3-1-3-0.

Umpires: J Hardstaff sr & WR Parry

SECOND TEST 1930 ENGLAND v AUSTRALIA
Lord's Cricket Ground, London. June 27, 28, 30, July 1, 1930.
Toss: England. Australia won by 7 wkts.

ENGLAND

JB Hobbs c Oldfield b Fairfax	1	b Grimmett	19
FE Woolley c Wall b Fairfax	41	hit wicket b Grimmett	28
WR Hammond b Grimmett	38	c Fairfax b Grimmett	32
KS Duleepsinhji c Bradman b Grimmett	173	c Oldfield b Hornibrook	48
EH Hendren c McCabe b Fairfax	48	c Richardson b Grimmett	9
APF Chapman (c) c Oldfield b Wall	11	c Oldfield b Fairfax	121
GOB Allen b Fairfax	3	lbw Grimmett	57
MW Tate c McCabe b Wall	54	c Ponsford b Grimmett	10
RWV Robins c Oldfield b Hornibrook	5	not out	11
JC White not out	23	run out	10
G Duckworth (+) c Oldfield b Wall	18	lbw Fairfax	0
EXTRAS (B 2, LB 7, NB 1)	10	(B 16, LB 13, W 1)	30
TOTAL	425		375

FOW 1st Inns: 13 53 105 209 236 239 337 363 387 425
FOW 2nd Inns: 45 58 129 141 147 272 329 354 372 375

Bowling: *First Innings*: Wall 29.4-2-118-3, Fairfax 31-6-101-4, Grimmett 33-4-105-2, Hornibrook 26-6-62-1, McCabe 9-1-29-0. *Second Innings*: Wall 25-2-80-0, Fairfax 12.4-2-37-2, Grimmett 53-13-167-6, Hornibrook 22-6-49-1, Bradman 1-0-1-0, McCabe 3-1-11-0.

AUSTRALIA

WM Woodfull (c) st Duckworth b Robins	155	not out	26
WH Ponsford c Hammond b White	81	b Robins	14
DG Bradman c Chapman b White	254	c Chapman b Tate	1
AF Kippax b White	83	c Duckworth b Robins	3
SJ McCabe c Woolley b Hammond	44	not out	25
VY Richardson c Hobbs b Tate	30		
WAS Oldfield (+) not out	43		
AG Fairfax not out	20		
CV Grimmett			
PM Hornibrook			
TW Wall			
EXTRAS (B 6, LB 8, W 5)	19	(B 1, LB 2)	3
TOTAL	6 dec 729		3 for 72

FOW 1st Inns: 162 393 585 588 643 672
FOW 2nd Inns: 16 17 22

Bowling: *First Innings*: Allen 34-7-115-0, Tate 64-16-148-1, White 51-7-158-3, Robins 42-1-172-1, Hammond 35-8-82-1, Woolley 6-0-35-0. *Second Innings*: Tate 13-6-21-1, Hammond 4.2-1-6-0, Robins 9-1-34-2, White 2-0-8-0.

Umpires: F Chester & TW Oates

THIRD TEST 1930 ENGLAND v AUSTRALIA
Headingley, Leeds. July 11, 12, 14, 15, 1930.
Toss: Australia. Match Drawn.

AUSTRALIA
WM Woodfull (c) b Hammond	.50	
A Jackson c Larwood b Tate	.1	
DG Bradman c Duckworth b Tate	.334	
AF Kippax c Chapman b Tate	.77	
SJ McCabe b Larwood	.30	
VY Richardson c Larwood b Tate	.1	
EL A'Beckett c Chapman b Geary	.29	
WAS Oldfield (+) c Hobbs b Tate	.2	
CV Grimmett c Duckworth b Tyldesley	.24	
TW Wall b Tyldesley	.3	
PM Hornibrook not out	.1	
EXTRAS (B 5, LB 8, W 1)	.14	
TOTAL	.566	

FOW 1st Inns: 2 194 423 486 491 508 519 544 565 566

Bowling: *First Innings:* Larwood 33-3-139-1, Tate 39-9-124-5, Geary 35-10-95-1, Tyldesley 33-5-104-2, Hammond 17-3-46-1, Leyland 11-0-44-0.

ENGLAND
JB Hobbs c A'Beckett b Grimmett	.29	run out	.13
H Sutcliffe c Hornibrook b Grimmett	.32	not out	.28
WR Hammond c Oldfield b McCabe	.113	c Oldfield b Grimmett	.35
KS Duleepsinhji b Hornibrook	.35	c Grimmett b Hornibrook	.10
M Leyland c Kippax b Wall	.44	not out	.1
G Geary run out	.0		
G Duckworth (+) c Oldfield b A'Beckett	.33		
APF Chapman (c) b Grimmett	.45		
MW Tate c Jackson b Grimmett	.22		
H Larwood not out	.10		
RK Tyldesley c Hornibrook b Grimmett	.6		
EXTRAS (B 9, LB 10, NB 3)	.22	(LB 8)	.8
TOTAL	.391		.3 for 95

FOW 1st Inns: 53 64 123 206 206 289 319 370 375 391
FOW 2nd Inns: 24 72 94

Bowling: *First Innings:* Wall 40-12-70-1, A'Beckett 28-8-47-1, Grimmett 56.2-16-135-5, Hornibrook 41-7-94-1, McCabe 10-4-23-1. *Second Innings:* Wall 10-3-20-0, A'Beckett 11-4-19-0, Grimmett 17-3-33-1, Hornibrook 11.5-5-14-1, McCabe 2-1-1-0.

Umpires: W Bestwick & TW Oates

FOURTH TEST 1930 ENGLAND v AUSTRALIA
Old Trafford, Manchester. July 25, 26, 28, 29 (no play), 1930.
Toss: Australia. Match Drawn.

AUSTRALIA
WM Woodfull (c) c Duckworth b Tate	.54
WH Ponsford b Hammond	.83
DG Bradman c Duleepsinhji b Peebles	.14
AF Kippax c Chapman b Nichols	.51
SJ McCabe lbw Peebles	.4
VY Richardson b Hammond	.1
AG Fairfax lbw Goddard	.49
WAS Oldfield (+) b Nichols	.2
CV Grimmett c Sutcliffe b Peebles	.50
PM Hornibrook c Duleepsinhji b Goddard	.3
TW Wall not out	.1
EXTRAS (B 23, LB 3, NB 7)	.33
TOTAL	.345

FOW 1st Inns: 106 138 184 189 190 239 243 330 338 345

Bowling: *First Innings:* Nichols 21-5-33-2, Tate 30-11-39-1, Goddard 32.1-14-49-2, Peebles 55-9-150-3, Leyland 8-2-17-0, Hammond 21-6-24-2.

ENGLAND
JB Hobbs c Oldfield b Wall	.31
H Sutcliffe c Bradman b Wall	.74
WR Hammond b Wall	.3
KS Duleepsinhji c Hornibrook b McCabe	.54
M Leyland b McCabe	.35
APF Chapman (c) c Grimmett b Hornibrook	.1
MW Tate c Ponsford b McCabe	.15
MS Nichols not out	.7
IAR Peebles c Richardson b McCabe	.6
G Duckworth (+) not out	.0
TWJ Goddard	
EXTRAS (B 13, LB 12)	.25
TOTAL	.8 for 251

FOW 1st Inns: 108 115 119 192 199 222 237 247

Bowling: *First Innings:* Wall 33-9-70-3, Fairfax 13-5-15-0, Grimmett 19-2-59-0, Hornibrook 26-9-41-1, McCabe 17-3-41-4.

Umpires: F Chester & J Hardstaff sr

FIFTH TEST 1930 ENGLAND v AUSTRALIA
Kennington Oval, London. August 16, 18, 19, 20, 21 (no play), 22, 1930.
Toss: England. Australia won by an innings & 39 runs.

ENGLAND
JB Hobbs c Kippax b Wall	.47	b Fairfax	.9
H Sutcliffe c Oldfield b Fairfax	.161	c Fairfax b Hornibrook	.54
WW Whysall lbw Wall	.13	c Hornibrook b Grimmett	.10
KS Duleepsinhji c Fairfax b Grimmett	.50	c Kippax b Hornibrook	.46
WR Hammond b McCabe	.13	c Fairfax b Hornibrook	.60
M Leyland b Grimmett	.3	b Hornibrook	.20
RES Wyatt (c) c Oldfield b Fairfax	.64	b Hornibrook	.7
MW Tate st Oldfield b Grimmett	.10	run out	.0
H Larwood lbw Grimmett	.19	c McCabe b Hornibrook	.9
G Duckworth (+) b Fairfax	.3	b Hornibrook	.15
IAR Peebles not out	.3	not out	.0
EXTRAS (LB 17, NB 2)	.19	(B 16, LB 3, NB 2)	.21
TOTAL	.405		.251

FOW 1st Inns: 68 97 162 190 197 367 379 379 391 405
FOW 2nd Inns: 17 37 118 135 189 207 208 220 248 251

Bowling: *First Innings:* Wall 37-6-96-2, Fairfax 31-9-52-3, Grimmett 66.2-18-135-4, McCabe 22-4-49-1, Hornibrook 15-1-54-0. *Second Innings:* Wall 12-2-25-0, Fairfax 10-3-21-1, Grimmett 43-12-90-1, Hornibrook 31.2-9-92-7, McCabe 3-1-2-0.

AUSTRALIA
WM Woodfull (c) c Duckworth b Peebles	.54
WH Ponsford b Peebles	.110
DG Bradman c Duckworth b Larwood	.232
AF Kippax c Wyatt b Peebles	.28
A Jackson c Sutcliffe b Wyatt	.73
SJ McCabe c Duckworth b Hammond	.54
AG Fairfax not out	.53
WAS Oldfield (+) c Larwood b Peebles	.34
CV Grimmett lbw Peebles	.6
TW Wall lbw Peebles	.0
PM Hornibrook c Duckworth b Tate	.7
EXTRAS (B 22, LB 18, NB 4)	.44
TOTAL	.695

FOW 1st Inns: 159 190 263 506 570 594 670 684 684 695

Bowling: *First Innings:* Larwood 48-6-132-1, Tate 65.1-12-153-1, Peebles 71-8-204-6, Wyatt 14-1-58-1, Hammond 42-12-70-1, Leyland 16-7-34-0.

Umpires: J Hardstaff sr & WR Parry

Australian Averages

1930 ENGLAND v AUSTRALIA
AUSTRALIA	M	Inn	NO	Runs	H.S	Avrge	Ct	St	Overs	Mds	Runs	Wkt	Avrge
A'Beckett, EL	1	1	-	29	29	29.00	1	-	39.0	12	66	1	66.00
Bradman, DG	5	7	-	974	334	139.14	2	-	1.0	-	1	-	-
Fairfax, AG	4	5	2	150	53*	50.00	5	-	134.2	34	335	12	27.92
Grimmett, CV	5	5	-	80	50	16.00	2	-	349.4	78	925	29	31.90
Hornibrook, PM	5	5	1	16	7	4.00	5	-	196.1	50	471	13	36.23
Jackson, A	2	2	-	74	73	37.00	1	-					
Kippax, AF	5	7	1	329	83	54.83	4	-					
McCabe, SJ	5	7	1	210	54	35.00	3	-	87.0	21	221	8	27.63
Oldfield, WAS	5	6	-	96	43*	19.20	12	3	-	-	-	-	-
Ponsford, WH	4	6	-	330	110	55.00	3	-					
Richardson, VY	4	5	-	98	37	19.60	4	-					
Wall, TW	5	5	2	12	8*	4.00	1	-	229.4	44	593	13	45.62
Woodfull, WM	5	7	1	345	155	57.50	-	-					

English Averages

1930 ENGLAND v AUSTRALIA
ENGLAND	M	Inn	NO	Runs	H.S	Avrge	Ct	St	Overs	Mds	Runs	Wkt	Avrge
Allen, GOB	1	2	-	60	57	30.00	-	-	34.0	7	115	-	-
Chapman, APF	4	6	-	259	121	43.17	7	-	-	-	-	-	-
Duckworth, G	5	8	2	87	33	14.50	10	2	-	-	-	-	-
Duleepsinhji, KS	4	7	-	416	173	59.43	2	-	-	-	-	-	-
Geary, G	1	1	-	0	0	0.00	-	-	35.0	10	95	1	95.00
Goddard, TWJ	1	-	-	-	-	-	-	-	32.1	14	49	2	24.50
Hammond, WR	5	9	-	306	113	34.00	5	-	148.2	35	302	5	60.40
Hendren, EH	2	4	-	134	72	33.50	-	-	-	-	-	-	-
Hobbs, JB	5	9	-	301	78	33.44	3	-					
Larwood, H	3	5	1	63	19	15.75	3	-	101.0	18	292	4	73.00
Leyland, M	3	5	1	103	44	25.75	-	-	35.0	9	95	-	-
Nichols, MS	1	1	-	7	7*	-	-	-	21.0	5	33	2	16.50
Peebles, IAR	2	3	2	9	6	9.00	-	-	126.0	17	354	9	39.33
Robins, RWV	1	2	-	70	50*	35.00	1	-	85.2	7	338	10	33.80
Sutcliffe, H	4	7	-	436	161	87.20	2	-	-	-	-	-	-
Tate, MW	5	8	-	148	54	18.50	-	-	280.1	82	574	15	38.27
Tyldesley, RK	2	3	-	12	6	4.00	-	-	89.0	23	234	7	33.43
White, JC	1	2	-	33	23*	33.00	-	-	53.0	7	166	3	55.33
Whysall, WW	1	2	-	23	13	11.50	-	-	-	-	-	-	-
Woolley, FE	2	4	-	74	41	18.50	1	-	9.0	1	38	-	-
Wyatt, RES	1	2	-	71	64	35.50	1	-	14.0	1	58	1	58.00

Clarrie Grimmett – masterly and miserly

Clarrie Grimmett, a New Zealander by birth, walked like Groucho Marx, invented the flipper and, according to Sir Neville Cardus, 'bowled like a miser'.

A little thin on top, Grimmett bowled for Australia in his baggy, green cap as though he had been born wearing it.

A small, wiry man with a round-arm action, he was a late starter, making his Test debut at the age of 33. But he was well rehearsed.

Once selected, he wasted no time dominating centre stage with his wiles, becoming the first Australian to take more than 200 wickets in Test cricket, 13 of them in his last Test in Durban in 1935–36.

Born near Dunedin on Christmas Day, 1891, Clarence Victor Grimmett, began his working life as a signwriter and seemed destined for a lifetime in that occupation. But he was a nomad. After a brief spell in New Zealand's Plunkett Shield, he bobbed up in Sydney but was restricted to grade cricket.

His next move was to Victoria, where he took 228 wickets in four seasons with Prahran in district cricket, but couldn't get a game for Victoria, thanks to selector Ernest Bean, who 'had it in for Kiwis'.

In 1923–24 he moved to South Australia after impressing the South Australians with 8/86 for Victoria against SA.

Once established in his new home, he wasted no time exposing the folly of Bean and the NSW selectors by taking 142 wickets against Victoria and 188 against NSW. Grimmett dismissed 183 Queenslanders, becoming the first bowler to take 500 wickets against the three states.

Grimmett had a variety of nicknames – 'The Fox' because of his relentless pursuit of victims, the 'Scarlet Pimpernel' because of the aura of mystery that surrounded him, and 'Grum', adopted by his great friend and partner-in-spin, Bill O'Reilly, after a journalist misspelled his name as 'Grummett'.

Grimmett, who guarded his well-practised secrets jealously, wrote a book on how to take wickets but only revealed how he took them. 'It was as valuable as reading about "the wind on the art of blowing",' noted one critic.

'Grum' had two great bowling partners, as diverse a pair as two masters of the art of spin could be. The first was Arthur Mailey, who 'bowled like a millionaire', in the words of Cardus – erratic and for-

Clarrie Grimmett:the first Australian to take 200 wickets in Tests.

ever experimenting, but also lethal. They were the mainstays of Australia's bowling for a spell.

The second was O'Reilly himself, as wily as Grimmett and as hellbent on seeing Englishmen heading for the pavilion.

O'Reilly watched 'Grum' like a hawk, learning every trick of technique and temperament he had to offer. 'While he was at the other end, I knew full well that no batsman would be allowed the slightest respite,' O'Reilly said. They were in complete harmony and earned the figures to prove it. In the 15 Tests in which they played together, they took an astonishing 162 wickets, Grimmett 83 and O'Reilly 79, an average of almost 11 a match.

Grimmett first played for Australia in the fifth Test against Arthur Gilligan's Englishmen at the MCG in 1924–25. He was an immediate success, taking 5/45 and 6/37. Australia, under Herbie Collins,

won the match by 307 runs and retained the Ashes 4–1.

The 1926 tour of England was not a happy one on the field for Australia, which lost the Ashes 1–0. Despite unresponsive wickets and three-day Tests, Grimmett managed 116 wickets on tour (13 in Tests). Mailey did slightly better with 141 wickets overall and 14 in the Tests.

With the retirement of Mailey, Grimmett took over bowling into the wind when Percy Chapman's team toured Australia in 1928–29. England retained the Ashes 4–1 but Grimmett did his bit with 23 wickets.

With Bradman in full flight and Grimmett at the height of his powers, Australia won back the Ashes 2–1 in England in 1930. Grimmett, often at his best overseas, took a total of 10/201 in the first Test at Trent Bridge and 29 wickets in the series. He met Bosanquet (who asked 'Am I

responsible for you?') and they talked for hours. Grimmett's tour haul was 144 wickets at 16.85, including 10/37 in one innings against Yorkshire.

In the two home series that followed, against the West Indies and South Africa, he captured 33 wickets in each, but he was out of sorts in the bodyline tour of 1932–33, taking only five wickets in three Tests, after which he was dropped. O'Reilly, never one to hide his feelings, said the decision to drop Grimmett was 'hopelessly wrong'.

Back in England in 1934, Grimmett claimed 23 Test wickets and O'Reilly 28. They were described as the greatest spin combination cricket had seen, so who would have thought that Grimmett's record haul of 44 Test wickets at 14.59 apiece in South Africa in 1935–36 would signal his swansong?

For some unaccountable reason, he was dropped from the 1936–37 home series against England. So he retired from Test cricket with a record 216 wickets at an average of 24.21 in 37 matches. He continued to play for South Australia until he was 50 and ended his first-class career with 1402 wickets at 22.18 in 239 matches. He captured 668 wickets for SA.

O'Reilly was furious with the treatment meted out to Grimmett, who took no fewer than 59 wickets in his last seven Tests. 'Even today,' O'Reilly wrote in 1985, 'his omission from the 1936–37 and 1938 series makes me boil with rage. How could the selectors have been so stupid? No better bowler ever breathed.'

It was O'Reilly who introduced the teetotal Grimmett to the joys of a quiet beer or two after a day's play. 'In later years he expressed to me his regret at the pleasure he had missed early in his career, and it is a source of no little pride that I was able to help him overcome his earlier shortcomings,' O'Reilly said.

Clarrie Grimmett died on 2 May 1980, having passed on his secrets to the younger generation. He showed Bruce Dooland (SA) how to bowl the flipper which skids through low, and Cecil Pepper (NSW) and Richie Benaud (Australian captain) also adopted it. More recently, of course, Shane Warne has used it to great effect.

As Ray Robinson said: 'The little signwriter from New Zealand finally wrote his name in large print in cricket history.'

Bradman

The boy Bradman

When George and Emily Bradman left their farm at Yeo Yeo to settle in Bowral, a comfortable town 80 miles south-west of Sydney, the youngest of their five children, Donald George, was not yet three years old. He had been born on 27 August 1908, at Cootamundra.

Young Don was ball-mad, but his playmates lived some distance from the Bradmans, so he began playing games on his own – tennis, football and cricket. His sister Lillian taught him the piano.

In their backyard, the Bradmans had a 800-gallon water tank set on a round brick stand. Underfoot was concrete. As Bradman recalled in his book *Farewell To Cricket*: 'Armed with a cricket stump as a bat, I would throw a golf ball at this brick stand and try to hit the ball on the rebound. The ball came back at great speed and to hit it was no easy task.'

Though done for amusement, Bradman came to understand how this primitive ritual 'must have developed the coordination of brain, eye and muscle which was to serve me so well in important matches later on.'

He organised 'Test' matches, featuring the stars of the day, Jack Gregory, Herbie Collins etc., and often 'incurred his mother's displeasure' for finishing a match when he was wanted at meal time. Another drill, in which he threw a golf ball to hit a rounded fence rail, sharpened his fielding. The ball flew back at different angles, providing sharp catching practice.

Don Bradman was 11 when he played in his first match, on a dirt pitch at Glebe Park, Bowral. The circumstances were daunting. The bowler was on a hat-trick, but the little fellow was equal to the challenge and made 55 not out.

In his debut for Bowral High School, played on matting, the little right-hander, displaying fleet-footed precision and an extraordinary degree of coolness for one so young, startled onlookers with a dazzling 115 out of a total of 156. It was his first century. He was 12 years old. But cricket was not his only pursuit. He played tennis and football for the school and won four events at the sports carnival in his age group – the 100, 220, 440 and 880 yards.

Bradman's first bat was a gift from Bowral team-member Sid Cupitt. It was cracked and Don's father had to saw three inches off the bottom.

Another boyhood landmark, one that fired Don's enthusiasm, was a two-day trip to Sydney with his father to watch the fifth Test between Australia and England in 1921. He saw Macartney make 170 at the SCG. The memory of a flashing Macartney drive never diminished, and Bradman told his father: 'I shall never be satisfied until I play on this ground.'

His first big score was in the wings. In 1925–26, aged 17, he became a regular member of the Bowral team. On the first Saturday of the match against Wingello, Bradman was 234 not out at stumps, the last 50 including four 6s and six 4s. His innings had occupied less than three hours. Blessed with a little luck early on – a somnolent slips fielder getting on in years twice dropped him off a promising leg-spin bowler called O'Reilly – he was bowled first ball the following Saturday by O'Reilly.

Bradman's mother promised him a new bat if he made 100 in the final against Moss Vale. He made sure of it by scoring 300. The match lasted five Saturdays, prompting the *Sydney Sun* to report 'At last, it's over'. His mother was amused when he thought he was entitled to three bats.

Bradman's season, which yielded 1318 runs at an average of 101.3, had not gone unnoticed in high places. On 6 October 1926, he received a letter from the NSW cricket association inviting him to attend practice at the SCG the following Monday at 4 p.m.

Not long after, using the bat his mother had given him, Bradman made his debut in first grade Sydney cricket, scoring 110 for St George. Then it was back to Bowral for the final of the Pickard Cup against old foe Moss Vale.

Bradman was in deadly form, flogging the bowling to the tune of 320 not out. A Sydney paper said: 'This is a great performance. Bradman is scarcely a stylist ... but with his eye and temperament he should develop into a champion.'

Bradman the batsman

Early in the summer of 1927–28, Don Bradman, only just 19, was called upon at the last moment to join the NSW party on its southern trip to Adelaide and Melbourne for Sheffield Shield matches.

The team travelled by train, an arduous trip via Broken Hill. Bradman had difficulty sleeping and, being a new colt, was on the receiving end of practical jokes.

Unfazed, he cheerfully resolved to respond with his bat. Once more his luck was in. Archie Jackson had to withdraw from the match against South Australia because of a boil on his knee, and Bradman was chosen to replace him.

The SA players were keen to see how 'the Bowral wonder', as Bradman had been dubbed, would cope with the wily spin of Clarrie Grimmett. They were impressed when Bradman, batting at no. 7, hit Grimmett for two fours in his first over. At stumps on day one, he was 65 not out in 105 minutes. He completed his century the next day, his 118 making him the 20th Australian to score a century on debut. Said one paper under the headline 'Bradman's brilliant debut': 'If some of the so-called champions used their feet to slow bowlers as this youngster does, cricket would have a much larger following.'

Back in Sydney, and playing his first Shield game at the SCG, against Queensland, he was out for a duck, bowled first ball. It taught him a salutary lesson. Before the ball was delivered, he had decided to push it gently to mid-on for a single, as the well-set Alan Kippax had just done so easily. Bradman decided there and then never to make up his mind which shot to play before the ball was bowled.

He had one other concern – his unusual grip. By turning his left hand, his wrist was behind the handle, meaning the bat sloped at 45 degrees to the ground. While handicapping his play somewhat between mid-off and point, it enabled him to keep the ball down when playing the cut and, in particular, the pull, which was to yield him hundreds, even thousands of runs. He weighed the pros and cons and decided to stick with his grip.

Bradman was primarily a back-foot player, his lack of inches (5 ft 6 3/4) restricting his reach on the drive. And because his grip reduced the chances of lofting the ball, he hit few 6s for such a prolific scorer.

As a good-looking young man just out of his teens with an engaging smile that masked an

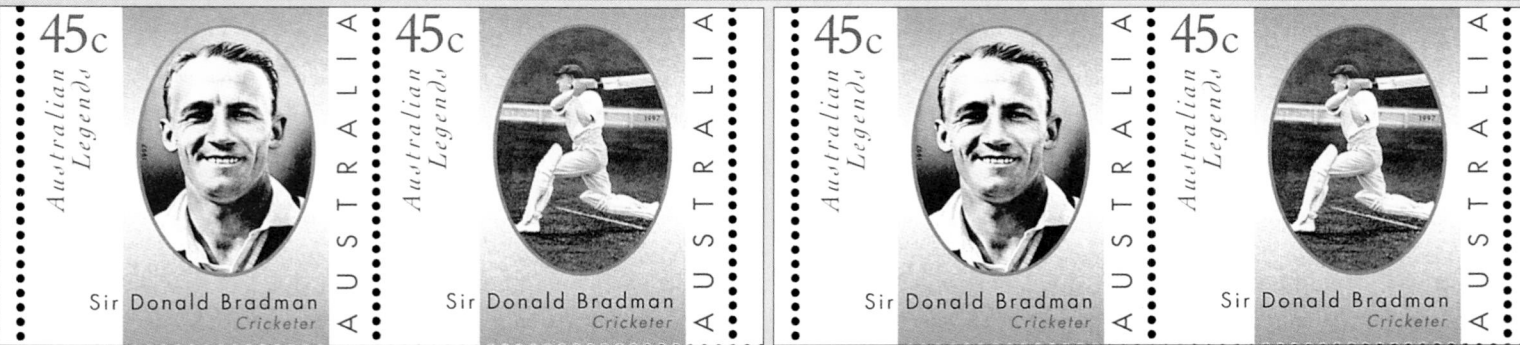

unquenchable desire to succeed, Bradman made his Test debut in the first match of the Ashes series against Percy Chapman's England side at the Exhibition ground, Brisbane, in December 1928. He scored 18 in the first innings – deceived by Maurice Tate's slower ball – and one in the second knock on a sticky wicket, conditions he was not used to. The one bright feature was his lively fielding.

Dropped to 12th man for the second Test, Bradman returned for the third in Melbourne and made 79 and 112, his first Test century. He was aged 20 and 129 days, making him the youngest Test 'centurion' up to that time.

It had come at a time of crisis for Australia and acted as a launching pad for a career that would attain rare heights. With growing confidence, he blazed a trail of unprecedented run-making the following season, 1929–30, culminating in a world record 452 not out in a phenomenal 415 minutes for NSW against Queensland.

One newspaper wrote: 'Today, he can, with safety, pack his bag and label it: D. Bradman, Australian XI, England.' Needless to say, he was a member of Bill Woodfull's team that left Fremantle on the Orient liner *Orford* in early March 1930.

Captain Bradman
Don Bradman was captain of Australia in five Test series, four against England and one against India. He did not lose a rubber but, in his own words, 'lost a great deal of sleep.' He did not claim to have 'any special ability as a captain', saying he learnt from his experiences through hard work and application. There were no short cuts. He was mindful that he had no mortgage on making the right decision at the right time.

Because of Hitler's ambitions, Bradman's term at the helm was divided into two periods. He was 28 when he became captain in 1936–37 and, after leading the Australians in England in 1938, had

intended to retire after one more series.

But World War II swept everyone's plans to one side. Test cricket would not see the light of day again until 1946. At the end of hostilities in 1945, Bradman, aged 37, was in poor health with chronic fibrositis, the result of the relentless pressure he had imposed on himself in 12 years of first class cricket. Also, the firm he worked for had gone bankrupt.

Despite these setbacks, Bradman was only too aware that cricket needed a good start after the war and he made it known he was 'anxious to assist if possible'. His wife's encouragement, and his doctor's diagnosis that everything would be alright if he did not overexert himself, settled the issue. Bradman resumed the captaincy, leading Australia at home against Wally Hammond's Englishmen in 1946–47 and India in 1947–48.

As skipper, Bradman had one distinct advantage over his rivals – his own batting – but he was conscious from the outset that his capacity to succeed in such a demanding role was limited. As vice-captain to Bill Woodfull in England in 1934, he had led the side infrequently and, in his early days at Bowral, older players had charge of the local side.

Bradman's decision in 1933–34 to accept a six-year contract with an Adelaide stockbroking firm was fortuitous, though Bradman and his wife of three years, Jesse Menzies, did not settle in Adelaide until April 1935, because of his near-fatal illness (acute appendicitis) in London after the 1934 tour.

On medical advice, Bradman spent most of 1935 recuperating and was not considered for the Australian tour of South Africa in 1935–36. The victorious Australians were led by the debonair South Australian captain, Vic Richardson.

With Richardson away, Bradman was invited to lead SA in the Sheffield Shield. He also took over the reins of grade side Kensington. He was an immediate success with

both teams. The young players at Kensington were thrilled to have such a star in their presence. They found him determined but friendly. He spent arduous hours coaching.

His first match as captain of SA was against his old team, NSW. He scored 117 and later 233 against Queensland and 357 against Victoria. SA won the shield and former SA and Test player Clem Hill described him as a 'great captain'.

Before the start of the 1936–37 season against the England tourists, led by the popular Australian-born Gubby Allen, Bradman was appointed captain and a selector. Bradman had a horror start as captain. He lost the toss at the 'Gabba, watched his main strike bowler Ernie McCormick break down and was out for a duck in the second innings on a sticky wicket. England romped home by 322 runs and won the second Test in Sydney by an innings, rain once again coming to its aid. Bradman made his second successive duck and the critics were not impressed with the scoreboard – England 2, Australia 0 and in grave danger of losing the Ashes. One newspaper reported that Bradman, the spotlight now focused on him all the time and his anxiety level full to overflowing, was not getting the loyal support of all his players. McCabe issued a statement saying the players were behind him.

Things turned around for Australia and Bradman in the third Test in Melbourne. With rain a factor for the third time and England batting on a sticky wicket, the shrewd Bradman told his bowlers not to get England out. When Allen declared (too late, as it turned out) towards the end of play on Saturday, the wicket was still unfriendly. Bradman gambled and opened the second innings with tail-enders Bill O'Reilly and a stunned 'Chuck' Fleetwood-Smith. O'Reilly was out first ball, but Fleetwood-Smith survived, joking that he 'had the game by the throat'.

By Monday the wicket had lost its fire and, with Bradman back to his

fluent best with 270, Australia won. Bradman's improvisation had paid off. This time Allen's captaincy was under fire. He might have clinched the series 3–0 if he had declared England's second innings sooner and exposed Australia to the damp wicket. Australia won the next two Tests, the captain contributing 212 and 169, to retain the Ashes 3–2 and Bradman had come through his first baptism of fire with his reputation enhanced.

After the war, fears of illness worried Bradman, but they soon faded. 'Instead', he wrote in *Farewell to Cricket*: 'I became fired with a zeal I had not previously experienced.' When the 17-man team assembled to sail to England on the *Strathaird* in March 1948, Bradman told them he had their welfare at heart. He was the figurehead and it was essential for them to pull together as a unit – free of bickering and strife. Happiness, he told them, comes from within. And they were happy.

Bradman celebrated his 40th birthday during the match against the Gentlemen of England at Lord's. It was his last appearance at the mecca of cricket and he obliged with a grand 150, after which he threw his wicket away. Presentations, a giant cake and the crowd singing 'happy birthday' made it a memorable occasion for 'The Don'. Australia, as usual, won and after two festival matches Bradman's 'Invincibles' left England with an unparelleled record – 23 wins (15 by an innings) in 31 matches – a 72 per cent winning record. This bettered the 58 per cent achieved by Armstrong's all-conquering team in 1921.

The only aspect of the game over which Bradman had no control was the toss. He won only 10 out of 24 in his career, but he never lost the match after winning the toss.

As captain of his country, Bradman made 3147 Test runs at an average of 103.1, with 13 centuries (eight of them in consecutive matches – three in 1936–38, three in 1938 and two in 1946–47).

West Indies spirited, but go down 4–0

'Protocol' causes a few early problems

Adelaide, Dec. 12. The West Indies is an unknown place to most Australians. It is British, they play cricket and now they are in Australia. Some are white, while others are black.

These facts have caused some difficulties for the administrators of Australian cricket. The secretary of the Board of Control, Bill Jeanes, found that he had to get the approval of the Department of Home Affairs before the 11 black men in the side could enter the country.

Taking a line through the 'Gentlemen and Players' conventions of old, the administrators put the seven whites and 11 blacks of the party into separate hotels in Sydney. The tourists complained and from then on this polite and friendly team has moved as one.

Further problems have arisen with the knowledge that the West Indians, white and black alike, are mostly very religious and Roman Catholic. They don't play golf on Sundays, going to church instead and on other days as well. The captain G. C. 'Jack' Grant is a lay missionary.

The star player, based on performances against England last season, is George Headley, who made three centuries and a double century in the four-Test series.

Harman Griffith: pace bowler.

The friendly West Indies team: happy tourists but without much success.

Melbourne, Feb. 14. The West Indian cricketers have not had much luck on their first Australian tour, but they have certainly been crowd-pleasers, displaying in enterprise and good spirits what they lack in skill and experience.

They suffered three big losses at the hands of the States before they got to the first Test. George Headley – the 'Black Bradman' – has been making runs and Learie Constantine taking wickets, but the rest seemed all at sea on the hard Australian turf wickets. The West Indian natural wicket is matting.

Spin seemed to have the batsmen baffled, and they succumbed to the wiles of Hugh Chilvers, Bert Ironmonger and Clarrie Grimmett. Ironmonger took 13/118 to leave them stranded in Victoria, even though Headley made 131.

The first Test went the same way, with Clarrie Grimmett dominating proceedings with 7/87 and 4/96.

The second Test in Sydney was an unlucky one for the tourists as they were caught on a sticky wicket after Australia has made 369, mostly on a perfect strip. The visitors made 107 and 90.

The men from the Caribbean had a morale-boosting win against Queensland before the third Test. They weathered the fearsome pace of Eddie Gilbert to make 309 and 265, with Learie Constantine making 75 and 97. Constantine showed his worth with seven wickets (4/33 and 3/23) as the bowlers combined to dislodge Queensland for 167 and 188.

The third Test in Brisbane, however, let Australia in for a run-feast. Don Bradman had been quiet in the series so far, but he blazed forth with 223, the highest score by an Australian in a home Test, surpassing Victor Trumper's 214 not out against South Africa in 1910–11. Australia made 558, and the West Indies succumbed meekly for 193 and 148, even though Headley showed he was getting the hang of the wickets and the bowling with 102 not out of 193.

The fourth Test at the MCG was all Bert Ironmonger's, on his home ground. He took 7/23 and 4/56, enabling Australia to win by an innings and 96 runs. Ironmonger got Headley cheaply in both innings while another Bradman century, 152 in even time, put the match out of West Indian reach.

Even though Australia leads the series 4–0, the cavalier West Indians will always be welcome here.

George Headley: batting honours.

West Indies win: Bradman 0

Don Bradman looks back at stumps shattered by Herman Griffith's ball.

Sydney, Feb. 4. The West Indies have brought off a remarkable win against Australia in the fifth Test. Credit must be distributed throughout the team, but captain Jackie Grant deserves most, as he twice declared to give his bowlers a chance to exploit the drying pitch after rain.

The West Indies bats were 2/299 after the first day. Freddie Martin (123) came together with George Headley (102) for a 152-run partnership, which was carried on by Grant (62).

Overnight rain delayed the start on day two and then the Indies lost 4/19. Grant immediately shut up shop on 6/350.

Enter George Francis, a fast bowler with success behind him at home and in England, and with an uncomplicated way of bowling – at the stumps and very fast. He and Martin had the ball kicking awkwardly from a patch at the south-

ern end and broke into the top order, having Australia reeling at 5/89. On better conditions on the next day, Bradman (43) and Alan Fairfax (54) helped Australia make a respectable total of 224, and the West Indies battled to get 5/124 at stumps.

Rain prevent any play on day four. The Australians had 251 to win and were facing a pitch which 'bumped and kicked at both ends', according to the *Sydney Morning Herald* correspondent.

Then came the sensation. Bradman came in with the score on 49 and left without any change. Herman Griffith bowled him around his legs with a vicious swinging, kicking ball. It was Bradman's first duck on the Test arena.

After that only Keith Rigg (44) and Alan Fairfax (66) offered resistance and Australia fell 31 runs short of the target.

Victoria keeps the Shield

Adelaide, Feb. 24. Victoria has retained the Sheffield Shield by drawing with South Australia. A loss would have handed the Shield to NSW. SA at least kept the match alive, leading on the first innings and setting Victoria 221 to win. Victoria was 4/131 at stumps.

Bert Ironmonger, aged nearly 49, had match figures of 12/195. Without him and Bill Woodfull, who made 177 to carry the Victorian first innings, the cause might have been lost.

This season has been the first in which all Shield matches have been restricted to four days, and more than the usual number of draws have resulted. Now the main race is for first-innings points, and the avoidance of an outright loss.

The Queensland team has improved greatly and has finished third on the table.

The Victorian cause was possibly helped by the two points it and Queensland each obtained for their abandoned match.

SA suffered greatly from some early defeats. It again has the best bowler in the competition in the ageless Clarrie Grimmett, whose 74 first class wickets was approached only by Bert Ironmonger's 68. Bradman and Bill Ponsford were the premier batsmen.

Players revolt leads to suspension

Brisbane, Jan 4. A players' revolt against the Queensland Cricket Association led to the suspension of all but three players, Eddie Gilbert, Cecil Thomson and Gordon Bourne, on the eve of the final Sheffield Shield match against Victoria.

This is the upshot of a simmering row between the captain Frank Gough and QCA officials, and also between the players and Gough. The man at the heart of it is an innocent Aborigine named Eddie Gilbert, a fearsome fast bowler but a newcomer to city life and cricket politics.

Gough was sent on Queensland's southern tour this year with the title of 'selector', but with instructions that the team was to include Gilbert. Gough had been against the selection of Gilbert for the

southern tour, and he had threatened to withdraw from the team – but seemed to yield to the QCA's wishes.

When the team got to Sydney, however, he left Gilbert out of the side.

A team meeting then overruled Gough.

But the team, with Bourne and Alex Hurwood omitted, was still not the QCA's liking, and they were all required to front the Board on their return, 'and express regret at their actions' although some did not attend. In fact, only Ron Oxenham did.

The Queensland line-up for the final match was peculiar, with many suspended and 10 other players declining invitations.

Fortunately, perhaps, rain prevented play against Victoria.

Without doubt, the most coveted symbol of achievement in Australian cricket – the green Test cap. This one is the property of wicketkeeper Bert Oldfield.

To England, but not for cricket. South Australia's gifted batsman Brian Hone has won a Rhodes Scholarship and will go to Oxford.

A familiar face in a different guise. Warwick Armstrong attends a meeting at Randwick racecourse.

FIRST TEST 1930–31 AUSTRALIA v WEST INDIES
Adelaide Oval, Adelaide. December 12, 13, 15, 16, 1930.
Toss: West Indies. Australia won by 10 wkts.

WEST INDIES

CA Roach st Oldfield b Hurwood	56	b Hurwood	9
LS Birkett c & b Grimmett	27	st Oldfield b Grimmett	64
GA Headley c Wall b Grimmett	0	st Oldfield b Grimmett	11
FR Martin b Grimmett	39	run out	3
LN Constantine c Wall b Grimmett	1	b Grimmett	14
GC Grant (c) not out	53	not out	71
EL Bartlett lbw Grimmett	84	c Grimmett b Hurwood	11
I Barrow (+) c Bradman b Grimmett	12	lbw Bradman	27
GN Francis lbw Hurwood	5	b Hurwood	3
OC Scott c Fairfax b Grimmett	3	c Kippax b Hurwood	8
HC Griffith b Hurwood	1	st Oldfield b Grimmett	10
EXTRAS (B 6, LB 8, NB 1)	15	(B 16, LB 2)	18
TOTAL	296		249

FOW 1st Inns: 58 58 118 123 131 245 269 290 295 296
FOW 2nd Inns: 15 47 52 74 115 138 203 208 220 249

Bowling: *First Innings*: Wall 16-0-64-0, Fairfax 11-1-36-0, Grimmett 48-19-87-7, Hurwood 36.1-14-55-3, McCabe 12-3-32-0, Bradman 4-0-7-0. *Second Innings*: Wall 10-1-20-0, Hurwood 34-11-86-4, Grimmett 38-7-96-4, McCabe 8-2-15-0, Bradman 5-1-8-1, Fairfax 3-2-6-0.

AUSTRALIA

WH Ponsford c Birkett b Francis	24	not out	92
A Jackson c Barrow b Francis	31	not out	70
DG Bradman c Grant b Griffith	4		
AF Kippax c Barrow b Griffith	146		
SJ McCabe c & b Constantine	90		
WM Woodfull (c) run out	6		
AG Fairfax not out	41		
WAS Oldfield (+) c Francis b Scott	15		
CV Grimmett c Barrow b Scott	0		
A Hurwood c Martin b Scott	0		
TW Wall lbw Scott	0		
EXTRAS (B 2, LB 10, NB 7)	19	(B 8, W 1, NB 1)	10
TOTAL	376		0 for 172

FOW 1st Inns: 56 59 64 246 269 341 374 374 374 376
FOW 2nd Inns:

Bowling: *First Innings*: Francis 18-7-43-2, Constantine 22-0-89-1, Griffith 28-4-69-2, Martin 29-3-73-0, Scott 20.5-2-83-4. *Second Innings*: Francis 10-1-30-0, Griffith 10-1-20-0, Martin 11-0-28-0, Constantine 9.3-3-27-0, Scott 13-0-55-0, Birkett 2-0-2-0.

Umpires: GA Hele & AG Jenkins

SECOND TEST 1930–31 AUSTRALIA v WEST INDIES
Sydney Cricket Ground, Sydney. January 1, 2 (no play), 3, 5, 1931.
Toss: Australia. Australia won by an innings & 172 runs.

AUSTRALIA

WH Ponsford b Scott	183
A Jackson c Francis b Griffith	8
DG Bradman c Barrow b Francis	25
AF Kippax c Bartlett b Griffith	10
SJ McCabe lbw Scott	31
WM Woodfull (c) c Barrow b Constantine	58
AG Fairfax c Constantine b Francis	15
WAS Oldfield (+) run out	0
CV Grimmett b Scott	12
A Hurwood c Martin b Scott	5
H Ironmonger not out	3
EXTRAS (B 6, LB 5, W 5, NB 3)	19
TOTAL	369

FOW 1st Inns: 12 52 69 140 323 341 344 361 364 369

Bowling: *First Innings*: Francis 27-3-70-2, Constantine 18-2-56-1, Griffith 28-4-57-2, Martin 18-1-60-0, Scott 15.4-0-66-4, Birkett 10-1-41-0.

WEST INDIES

CA Roach run out	7	c Kippax b McCabe	25
LS Birkett c Hurwood b Fairfax	3	c McCabe b Hurwood	8
GA Headley b Fairfax	14	c Jackson b Hurwood	2
FR Martin lbw Grimmett	10	c McCabe b Hurwood	0
GC Grant (c) c Hurwood b Ironmonger	6	not out	15
LN Constantine c Bradman b Grimmett	12	b Hurwood	8
I Barrow (+) c Jackson b Fairfax	17	c McCabe b Ironmonger	10
GN Francis b Grimmett	8	c Oldfield b Ironmonger	0
OC Scott not out	15	c Woodfull b Ironmonger	17
HC Griffith c Kippax b Grimmett	8	lbw Grimmett	0
EL Bartlett			
EXTRAS (B 6, NB 1)	7	(B 1, LB 2, W 1, NB 1)	5
TOTAL	9 for 107		9 for 90

FOW 1st Inns: 3 26 36 36 57 63 80 88 107
FOW 2nd Inns: 26 32 32 42 53 67 67 90 90

Bowling: *First Innings*: Fairfax 13-4-19-3, Hurwood 5-1-7-0, Grimmett 19.1-3-54-4, Ironmonger 13-3-20-1. *Second Innings*: Fairfax 5-1-21-0, Hurwood 11-2-22-4, McCabe 7-0-20-1, Ironmonger 4-1-13-3, Grimmett 3.3-1-9-1.

Umpires: EG Borwick & WG French

THIRD TEST 1930–31 AUSTRALIA v WEST INDIES
Exhibition Ground, Brisbane. January 16, 17, 19, 20, 1931.
Toss: Australia. Australia won by an innings & 217 runs.

AUSTRALIA

WH Ponsford c Birkett b Francis	109
A Jackson lbw Francis	0
DG Bradman c Grant b Constantine	223
AF Kippax b Birkett	84
SJ McCabe c Constantine b Griffith	8
WM Woodfull (c) c Barrow b Griffith	17
AG Fairfax c Sealy b Scott	9
RK Oxenham lbw Griffith	48
WAS Oldfield (+) not out	38
CV Grimmett c Constantine b Francis	4
H Ironmonger c Roach b Griffith	2
EXTRAS (B 2, LB 7, NB 7)	16
TOTAL	558

FOW 1st Inns: 1 230 423 431 441 462 468 543 551 558

Bowling: *First Innings*: Francis 26-4-76-3, Constantine 26-2-74-1, Griffith 33-4-133-4, Scott 24-1-125-1, Martin 27-3-85-0, Sealy 3-0-32-0, Birkett 7-0-16-1, Grant 1-0-1-0.

WEST INDIES

CA Roach lbw Oxenham	4	b McCabe	1
FR Martin lbw Grimmett	21	lbw Oxenham	11
GA Headley not out	102	c Oldfield b Ironmonger	28
JED Sealy c McCabe b Ironmonger	3 (9)	not out	16
GC Grant (c) c McCabe b Grimmett	8 (6)	run out	10
LN Constantine c Fairfax b Ironmonger	9 (4)	b Oxenham	7
LS Birkett lbw Oxenham	8 (5)	b Grimmett	13
I Barrow (+) st Oldfield b Grimmett	19 (7)	st Oldfield b Grimmett	17
OC Scott b Oxenham	0 (8)	lbw Grimmett	15
GN Francis b Oxenham	8	c Oldfield b Grimmett	7
HC Griffith lbw Grimmett	8	c Bradman b Grimmett	12
EXTRAS (B 1, LB 2)	3	(B 5, LB 4, NB 2)	11
TOTAL	193		148

FOW 1st Inns: 5 36 41 60 94 116 159 162 182 193
FOW 2nd Inns: 13 29 47 58 72 82 94 112 128 148

Bowling: *First Innings*: Fairfax 7-2-13-0, Oxenham 30-15-39-4, Ironmonger 26-15-43-2, Grimmett 41.3-9-95-4. *Second Innings*: Fairfax 6-2-6-0, McCabe 7-1-16-1, Oxenham 18-5-37-2, Ironmonger 15-8-29-1, Grimmett 14.3-3-49-5.

Umpires: JP Orr & AE Wyeth

FOURTH TEST 1930–31 AUSTRALIA v WEST INDIES
Melbourne Cricket Ground, Melbourne. February 13, 14, 1931.
Toss: West Indies. Australia won by an innings & 122 runs.

WEST INDIES

CA Roach c Kippax b Grimmett	20	lbw Fairfax	7
FR Martin lbw Ironmonger	17 (6)	c Oldfield b Fairfax	10
GA Headley c Jackson b Ironmonger	33	c Fairfax b Ironmonger	11
LS Birkett c McCabe b Ironmonger	0	c Jackson b Ironmonger	13
EL Bartlett st Oldfield b Ironmonger	9 (7)	b Fairfax	6
GC Grant (c) c Oldfield b Ironmonger	0 (5)	c McCabe b Ironmonger	3
LN Constantine c Jackson b Grimmett	7 (2)	c Kippax b Fairfax	10
I Barrow (+) c Fairfax b Ironmonger	0	c Oxenham b Ironmonger	13
OC Scott run out	11	not out	20
GN Francis not out	0 (11)	c Jackson b Grimmett	0
HC Griffith c Fairfax b Ironmonger	0 (10)	b Grimmett	4
EXTRAS (NB 2)	2	(B 3, LB 6, NB 1)	10
TOTAL	99		107

FOW 1st Inns: 32 51 53 81 81 88 88 88 99 99
FOW 2nd Inns: 8 32 36 49 60 60 67 92 97 107

Bowling: *First Innings*: Fairfax 5-0-14-0, Oxenham 6-1-14-0, Ironmonger 20-7-23-7, Grimmett 19-7-46-2. *Second Innings*: Fairfax 14-2-31-4, Ironmonger 17-4-56-4, Grimmett 4.4-0-10-2.

AUSTRALIA

WM Woodfull (c) run out	83
WH Ponsford st Barrow b Constantine	24
DG Bradman c Roach b Martin	152
A Jackson c Birkett b Constantine	15
SJ McCabe run out	2
AG Fairfax c Birkett b Martin	16
AF Kippax b Martin	24
RK Oxenham c Constantine b Griffith	0
WAS Oldfield (+) not out	1
H Ironmonger	
CV Grimmett	
EXTRAS (B 7, LB 3, NB 1)	11
TOTAL	8 dec 328

FOW 1st Inns: 50 206 265 275 286 325 326 328

Bowling: *First Innings*: Francis 13-0-51-0, Griffith 8-1-33-1, Scott 11-0-47-0, Constantine 25-4-83-2, Martin 30.2-3-91-3, Birkett 2-0-12-0.

Umpires: AN Barlow & J Richards

FIFTH TEST 1930–31 AUSTRALIA v WEST INDIES
Sydney Cricket Ground, Sydney. February 27, 28, March 2, 3 (no play), 4, 1931.
Toss: West Indies. West Indies won by 30 runs.

WEST INDIES

FR Martin not out	123	c McCabe b Grimmett ... 20
CA Roach lbw Grimmett	31	c Oldfield b Ironmonger ... 34
GA Headley lbw McCabe	105	b Oxenham ... 30
GC Grant (c) c McCabe b Ironmonger	62	not out ... 27
JED Sealy c Kippax b Grimmett	4	run out ... 7
LN Constantine c McCabe b Ironmonger	0	c Bradman b Ironmonger ... 4
EL Bartlett b Grimmett	0	not out ... 0
I Barrow (+) not out	7	
OC Scott		
GN Francis		
HC Griffith		
EXTRAS (B 6, LB 5, W 1, NB 6)	18	(B 1, LB 1) ... 2
TOTAL	6 dec 350	5 dec 124

FOW 1st Inns: 70 222 332 337 338 341
FOW 2nd Inns: 46 66 103 113 124

Bowling: *First Innings*: Fairfax 21-2-60-0, Oxenham 24-10-51-0, Ironmonger 42-16-95-2, Grimmett 33-7-100-3, McCabe 15-5-26-1. *Second Innings*: McCabe 7-2-17-0, Oxenham 10-4-14-1, Grimmett 18-4-47-1, Ironmonger 16-7-44-2.

AUSTRALIA

WM Woodfull (c) c Constantine b Martin	22	c Constantine b Griffith ... 18
WH Ponsford c Bartlett b Francis	7	c Constantine b Martin ... 28
DG Bradman c Francis b Martin	43	b Griffith ... 0
AF Kippax c Sealy b Constantine	3 (5)	c Roach b Constantine ... 10
KE Rigg c Barrow b Francis	14 (6)	c Barrow b Constantine ... 16
SJ McCabe c Headley b Francis	21 (7)	c Grant b Martin ... 44
AG Fairfax st Barrow b Scott	54 (8)	not out ... 60
RK Oxenham c Barrow b Francis	0 (9)	lbw Scott ... 14
WAS Oldfield (+) run out	36 (4)	lbw Griffith ... 0
CV Grimmett not out	15	c Constantine b Griffith ... 12
H Ironmonger b Griffith	1	run out ... 4
EXTRAS (B 1, LB 7)	8	(B 3, LB 7, W 2, NB 2) ... 14
TOTAL	224	220

FOW 1st Inns: 7 66 69 89 89 130 134 196 215 224
FOW 2nd Inns: 49 49 53 53 65 76 155 180 214 220

Bowling: *First Innings*: Francis 19-6-48-4, Griffith 13.2-3-31-1, Martin 27-3-67-2, Constantine 10-2-28-1, Scott 10-1-42-1. *Second Innings*: Francis 16-2-32-0, Constantine 17-2-50-2, Martin 18-4-44-2, Griffith 13.3-3-50-4, Scott 11-0-30-1.

Umpires: HJ Armstrong & WG French

Australian Averages

1930–31 AUSTRALIA v WEST INDIES

AUSTRALIA	M	Inn	NO	Runs	H.S	Avrge	Ct	St	Overs	Mds	Runs	Wkt	Avrge
Bradman, DG	5	6	-	447	223	74.50	4	-	9.0	1	15	1	15.00
Fairfax, AG	5	6	2	195	60*	48.75	5	-	85.0	16	206	7	29.43
Grimmett, CV	5	5	1	43	15*	10.75	2	-	239.2	61	593	33	17.97
Hurwood, A	2	2	-	5	5	2.50	2	-	86.1	28	170	11	15.45
Ironmonger, H	4	4	1	10	4	3.33	-	-	153.0	61	323	22	14.68
Jackson, A	4	5	1	124	70*	31.00	6	-	-	-	-	-	-
Kippax, AF	5	6	-	277	146	46.17	6	-	-	-	-	-	-
McCabe, SJ	5	6	-	196	90	32.67	10	-	56.0	13	126	3	42.00
Oldfield, WAS	5	6	2	90	38*	22.50	6	7	-	-	-	-	-
Oxenham, RK	3	4	-	62	48	15.50	1	-	88.0	35	155	7	22.14
Ponsford, WH	5	7	1	467	183	77.83	-	-	-	-	-	-	-
Rigg, KE	1	2	-	30	16	15.00	-	-	-	-	-	-	-
Wall, TW	1	1	-	0	0	0.00	2	-	26.0	1	84	-	-
Woodfull, WM	5	6	-	204	83	34.00	1	-	-	-	-	-	-

West Indian Averages

1930–31 AUSTRALIA v WEST INDIES

WEST INDIES	M	Inn	NO	Runs	H.S	Avrge	Ct	St	Overs	Mds	Runs	Wkt	Avrge
Barrow, I	5	9	1	122	27	15.25	9	2	-	-	-	-	-
Bartlett, EL	4	6	1	110	84	22.00	2	-	-	-	-	-	-
Birkett, LS	4	8	-	136	64	17.00	4	-	21.0	1	71	1	71.00
Constantine, LN	5	10	-	72	14	7.20	9	-	127.3	15	407	8	50.88
Francis, GN	5	8	1	31	8	4.43	3	-	129.0	23	350	11	31.82
Grant, GC	5	10	4	255	71*	42.50	3	-	1.0	-	1	-	-
Griffith, HC	5	8	-	43	12	5.38	-	-	133.5	20	393	14	28.07
Headley, GA	5	10	1	336	105	37.33	1	-	-	-	-	-	-
Martin, FR	5	10	1	254	123*	28.22	2	-	160.2	17	448	7	64.00
Roach, CA	5	10	-	194	56	19.40	3	-	-	-	-	-	-
Scott, OC	5	8	2	89	20*	14.83	-	-	105.3	4	448	11	40.73
Sealy, JED	2	4	1	30	16*	10.00	2	-	3.0	-	32	-	-

Was Gilbert the fastest?

Eddie Gilbert: Short, wiry, with long arms and a lightning action.

A hero in Queensland, Eddie Gilbert was the most feared fast bowler in Australia for several seasons, from his debut year in 1930–31 to 1934–35.

His life after that was not very good. Signs of mental instability brought about his admission to a psychiatric hospital in 1949. He died there in 1978. Sir Donald Bradman was among past cricketers present at his funeral.

How distant that sombre service was from 1931 when Bradman, at the peak of his supreme batting powers, faced the tearaway bowler.

Eddie Gilbert did not look all that fearsome, 5 feet 8 inches tall and weighing around nine stone. If you looked again, it was a wiry, well-muscled frame, with oddly long arms, a lot of the length on the hand side of the wrist joint.

On this morning he had just shot Wendell Bill out, caught behind, with his first ball.

In came Eddie on a short and whippy run, over came the arm and ... Bradman dodged a rising ball, which took his cap off his head.

In again ... Bradman down to avoid another head-high bumper.

In again ... Bradman's bat was knocked from his hands.

In he came again and ... the ball sailed over the wicketkeeper, bounced once and into the sightscreen.

In again ... this time Bradman got his bat to it, trying to hook, and edged an off-side catch to keeper Len Waterman. Bradman said that Gilbert was the fastest bowler he had faced. In reply to commiserations he said, 'Luckiest duck I ever made.'

Eddie Gilbert developed his bowling playing as a youngster with the Barambah Aboriginal team. In October 1930 he took 6/82 for Queensland Colts against NSW. He was brought to Brisbane, living 'under protection' and returning to Barambah between games. Those who knew him say that off the field he was shy, quiet and courteous.

On the field he was a dynamo, but was not always very fit and could easily go off the boil and become erratic. That season Gilbert had his best first class haul, 7/91 against the West Indies.

But Gilbert's reputation as a possible chucker was in the open. In his ninth match, in 1931–32, he was called by Melbourne umpire Andrew Barlow eight times. A film was made of his action, but even in slow motion, it was such a blur that it was impossible to detect a throw. Many felt that he produced a whip like action, similar to the launching of the Aboriginal woomera spear from its sling.

The controversy affected Gilbert's cricket and, in his conscious efforts to avoid being called, he often lost his venom.

It was suggested that he be called to Test duty in 1932–33 to counter the English bodyline onslaught.

Gilbert missed the next season, but in 1934–35 he played in only two matches and was back to his best, taking 14 wickets.

He bowled again the next year, but by 1936–37 his first class services were over.

In his 22 first class matches he had taken 89 wickets at an average of 31.

Rampant Australians outclass South Africa

Melbourne, Feb. 15. Don Bradman has, naturally enough, figured largely in the minds of the South African tourists – from the morning of the first Test in Brisbane last November when he was dropped twice before he was 25, and went on to make 226 – until the first morning of this fifth Test when Bradman did not appear at all.

Bradman twisted his ankle when his sprigs caught the coir matting in the dressing room on the way out. He did not field in the first South African innings, and did not bat in the Australian first innings either.

The tourists were 4–0 down before this fifth Test, rain interrupting the drawn game they played the week before against Victoria. Bradman's non-appearance must have lured them into thinking things were looking up.

Instead, South Melbourne champion footballer Laurie Nash took 4/18 in his first Test, and Bert 'Dainty' Ironmonger turned in the extraordinary figures in modern cricket of 7.2 overs, five maidens, six runs, five wickets.

South Africa made 36 in an hour and a half.

Australia, batting Bradmanless before lunch on the first day, also found conditions difficult because they managed only 153 runs, Jack Fingleton in his debut making a valuable 40, and Alan Kippax 42.

The second day saw no play at all because of rain, and South Africa, resuming at 1/5 on the third day, made just 45.

Ironmonger once again proved unplayable and returned the figures of 15.3 overs, seven maidens, 18 runs, 6 wickets – a total of 11/24 for the match.

Shots like this saw Stan McCabe make 783 runs at 97 in 1931–32.

Bradman did one thing – he took a catch off Ironmonger.

South Africa was generally outplayed in all the Test matches.

But they had their chances.

They dropped catches off Bradman and they led on the first innings in the third Test at the MCG, but generally speaking their batting was no match for the wiles of Clarrie Grimmett with 14 wickets in the fourth Test, Bert Ironmonger, or Bill O'Reilly 3/19 in the fifth Test.

Only Ken Viljoen hit a century – 111 in the third Test.

South Africa has won just three first class matches – two against South Australia and one against Tasmania – so far on the tour.

Bradman's record

Adelaide, Feb. 2. Don Bradman hit the highest Test score in Australia with 299 not out in the fourth Test, improving on R. E. Foster's 287 for England in 1903–04.

Bradman's partner, Queensland fast bowler 'Pud' Thurlow was run out going for the 300th run. Bradman made 806 runs in four Tests at an average of 201.5.

Bradman scored 226 in the first Test, 112 and 1 in the second, and 167 in the third, before his 299.

Bradman also averaged 170 against the South Africans.

Clarrie Grimmett's 7/116 and 7/83 was also the best bowling performance by an Australian in a Test played in Australia.

Commercialism by players was frowned upon by the Board of Control, but that didn't prevent the flow of commerce.

An average Shield game for Stan ...

Sydney, March 22. NSW batsman Stan McCabe preserved his Shield average of 438 in the game against SA – by not batting.

McCabe strained his hip fielding on the first day and took no further part in the game.

His Sheffield Shield scores have been: against Victoria, 106 and 103 not out, and against Queensland 229 not out. Bert Ironmonger was the only successful bowler.

In all, McCabe played 10 first class matches this season for 783 runs at 87. By contrast Don Bradman made 1403 runs at 116.91 – but his Shield average was a more human 42.6.

Gilbert livens up Shield

Don Bradman gets out the the way of a very quick Eddie Gilbert thunderbolt.

Sydney, March 22. NSW has now won the Shield – despite losing their last match to SA – but nothing in the intervening season matched the very first over.

The Sheffield Shield season got off to the liveliest start possible with the first over faced by NSW, from Queensland Aboriginal fast bowler Eddie Gilbert in November.

Gilbert's arm action is so fast it seems a blur of motion, and at his quickest, is the quickest around.

That day Gilbert dismissed Wendell Bill first ball, and Don Bradman with his sixth ball, the intervening four being most uncomfortable for the champion. Gilbert can only be used in short spells, and NSW, thanks to Stan McCabe with 229, went on to win the match. Gilbert bagged 4/74.

Gilbert's short spell was even shorter in Queensland's second match, against Victoria at the MCG. He was called for throwing by umpire Barlow from square leg eight times in his two overs after tea on the first day, and five times in his only over the next morning. Gilbert also bowled a wide – giving him a 14-ball over and the wicket of Jack Ryder. Queensland won this game, their first win over Victoria.

NSW and SA battled for the Shield, both winning four of their six games.

Victoria and Bert Ironmonger missed Don Blackie who was out for most of the season through injury – Ironmonger found his Shield wickets more costly than those he took in Tests.

In 1932, Arthur Mailey took a Board-sanctioned but unofficial team to North America on a tour of 52 matches in 100 days. Players included a honeymooning Don Bradman, and Vic Richardson as captain. They had a great time at places like Niagara, Moose Jaw and Hollywood.

FIRST TEST 1931–32 AUSTRALIA v SOUTH AFRICA
Brisbane Cricket Ground, Brisbane. November 27, 28, 30 (no play), December 1 (no play), 2, 3, 1931.
Toss: Australia. Australia won by an innings & 163 runs.

AUSTRALIA

WM Woodfull (c) lbw Vincent	.76
WH Ponsford c Mitchell b Bell	.19
DG Bradman lbw Vincent	.226
AF Kippax c Cameron b Vincent	.1
SJ McCabe c Vincent b Morkel	.27
HC Nitschke c Cameron b Bell	.6
RK Oxenham b Bell	.1
WAS Oldfield (+) not out	.56
CV Grimmett b Bell	.14
TW Wall lbw Quinn	.14
H Ironmonger b Quinn	.2
EXTRAS (B 5, LB 1, W 1, NB 1)	.8
TOTAL	.450

FOW 1st Inns: 32 195 211 292 316 320 380 407 446 450

Bowling: *First Innings*: Bell 42-5-120-4, Morkel 13-1-57-1, Quinn 38.3-6-113-2, Vincent 34-0-100-3, McMillan 10-0-52-0.

SOUTH AFRICA

JAJ Christy b Wall	.24	c McCabe b Ironmonger	.15
SH Curnow b Ironmonger	.11	b Grimmett	.8
B Mitchell run out	.58	b Wall	.0
HB Cameron (c+) st Oldfield b Grimmett	.4	b Ironmonger	.21
HW Taylor b Wall	.41	c Oxenham b Ironmonger	.47
EL Dalton c & b Ironmonger	.11	b Wall	.6
Q McMillan c Oxenham b Ironmonger	.0 (8)	c Nitschke b Wall	.0
DPB Morkel c McCabe b Ironmonger	.3 (7)	b Wall	.5
CL Vincent c Nitschke b Grimmett	.10	c (S)KE Rigg b Wall	.1
NA Quinn c(S)KE Rigg b Ironmonger	.1	c McCabe b Ironmonger	.0
AJ Bell not out	.1	not out	.0
EXTRAS (B 2, LB 4)	.6	(B 6, LB 5, NB 3)	.14
TOTAL	.170		.117

FOW 1st Inns: 25 44 49 129 140 140 152 157 169 170
FOW 2nd Inns: 16 29 34 78 97 111 111 117 117 117

Bowling: *First Innings*: Wall 28-14-39-2, McCabe 11-4-16-0, Grimmett 41.1-21-49-2, Ironmonger 47-29-42-5, Oxenham 11-5-18-0. *Second Innings*: Wall 15.1-7-14-5, Ironmonger 30-16-44-4, Grimmett 15-3-45-1.

Umpires: EG Borwick & GA Hele

SECOND TEST 1931–32 AUSTRALIA v SOUTH AFRICA
Sydney Cricket Ground, Sydney. December 18, 19, 21, 1921.
Toss: South Africa. Australia won by an innings & 155 runs.

SOUTH AFRICA

JAJ Christy c Nitschke b Grimmett	.14	c Woodfull b Ironmonger	.41
B Mitchell b McCabe	.1	c Oldfield b Wall	.24
DPB Morkel st Oldfield b Grimmett	.20	lbw Grimmett	.17
HB Cameron (c+) b Wall	.11	b Wall	.0
HW Taylor c Lee b Grimmett	.7	c Grimmett b Ironmonger	.6
KG Viljoen b Ironmonger	.37	b Grimmett	.0
EL Dalton b Grimmett	.21	c Bradman b Ironmonger	.14
CL Vincent not out	.31	c Ponsford b Grimmett	.35
LS Brown b McCabe	.2	c Wall b Lee	.8
NA Quinn lbw McCabe	.5	st Oldfield b Grimmett	.1
AJ Bell b McCabe	.0	not out	.1
EXTRAS (LB 3, W 1)	.4	(B 5, LB 8, NB 1)	.14
TOTAL	.153		.161

FOW 1st Inns: 6 31 36 54 62 91 136 143 153 153
FOW 2nd Inns: 70 89 89 100 100 100 122 144 160 161

Bowling: *First Innings*: Wall 18-4-46-1, McCabe 12-5-13-4, Grimmett 24-12-28-4, Ironmonger 12-1-38-1, Lee 7-1-24-0. *Second Innings*: Wall 18-5-31-2, McCabe 3-0-25-0, Grimmett 20.3-7-44-4, Ironmonger 19-10-22-3, Lee 13-4-25-1.

AUSTRALIA

WM Woodfull (c) c Mitchell b Vincent	.58
WH Ponsford b Quinn	.5
KE Rigg b Bell	.127
DG Bradman c Viljoen b Morkel	.112
SJ McCabe c Christy b Vincent	.79
HC Nitschke b Bell	.47
PK Lee c Cameron b Brown	.0
WAS Oldfield (+) c Cameron b Bell	.8
CV Grimmett not out	.9
TW Wall c Morkel b Bell	.6
H Ironmonger c Cameron b Bell	.0
EXTRAS (B 5, LB 12, W 1)	.18
TOTAL	.469

FOW 1st Inns: 6 143 254 347 432 433 444 457 469 469

Bowling: *First Innings*: Bell 46.5-6-140-5, Quinn 42-10-95-1, Brown 29-3-100-1, Vincent 24-5-75-2, Morkel 12-2-33-1, Mitchell 1-0-8-0.

Umpires: EG Borwick & GA Hele

THIRD TEST 1931–32 AUSTRALIA v SOUTH AFRICA
Melbourne Cricket Ground, Melbourne. December 31, 1931 January 1, 2, 4, 5, 6, 1932.
Toss: Australia. Australia won by 169 runs.

AUSTRALIA
WM Woodfull (c) c Cameron b Bell	.7	c Mitchell b McMillan	.161
WH Ponsford b Bell	.7	c Mitchell b Bell	.34
DG Bradman c Cameron b Quinn	.2	lbw Vincent	.167
AF Kippax c Bell b Quinn	.52	c Curnow b McMillan	.67
SJ McCabe c Morkel b Bell	.22	c Mitchell b McMillan	.71
KE Rigg c Mitchell b Bell	.68	c Mitchell b Vincent	.1
EL A'Beckett c Mitchell b Quinn	.6	b Vincent	.4
WAS Oldfield (+) c Vincent b Quinn	.0	lbw McMillan	.0
CV Grimmett c Morkel b Bell	.9	not out	.16
TW Wall not out	.6	b Vincent	.12
H Ironmonger run out	.12	b Quinn	.0
EXTRAS (B 1, LB 4, W 1, NB 1)	.7	(B 17, LB 3, NB 1)	.21
TOTAL	.198		.554

FOW 1st Inns: 11 16 25 74 135 143 143 173 179 198
FOW 2nd Inns: 54 328 408 519 521 521 524 530 550 554

Bowling: *First Innings*: Bell 26.1-9-69-5, Quinn 31-3-42-4, Morkel 3-0-12-0, Vincent 12-1-32-0, McMillan 2-0-22-0, Christy 3-0-14-0. *Second Innings*: Bell 36-6-101-1, Quinn 36.4-6-113-1, Vincent 55-16-154-4, McMillan 33-3-150-4, Morkel 4-0-15-0.

SOUTH AFRICA
SH Curnow b Grimmett	.47	b Grimmett	.9
B Mitchell c McCabe b Wall	.17	c & b Grimmett	.46
JAJ Christy c McCabe b Ironmonger	.16	c Oldfield b Ironmonger	.63
HW Taylor lbw Grimmett	.11	b Grimmett	.38
DPB Morkel lbw Ironmonger	.33	b Ironmonger	.4
HB Cameron (c+) st Oldfield b Ironmonger	.39	lbw Ironmonger	.13
KG Viljoen c Wall b McCabe	.111	b Ironmonger	.2
CL Vincent c Oldfield b Wall	.16	c Ponsford b Grimmett	.34
Q McMillan c Oldfield b Wall	.29	c Wall b Grimmett	.1
NA Quinn b McCabe	.11	not out	.0
AJ Bell not out	.10	b Grimmett	.0
EXTRAS (B 3, LB 13, NB 2)	.18	(B 8, LB 6, NB 1)	.15
TOTAL	.358		.225

FOW 1st Inns: 39 79 89 108 163 183 225 329 336 358
FOW 2nd Inns: 18 120 133 138 178 186 188 208 225 225

Bowling: *First Innings*: Wall 37-5-98-3, A'Beckett 18-5-29-0, Grimmett 63-23-100-2, Ironmonger 49-26-72-3, McCabe 21.3-4-41-2. *Second Innings*: Wall 13-3-35-0, A'Beckett 3-1-6-0, Grimmett 46-14-92-6, Ironmonger 42-18-54-4, McCabe 10-1-21-0, Bradman 1-0-2-0.

Umpires: EG Borwick & GA Hele

FOURTH TEST 1931–32 AUSTRALIA v SOUTH AFRICA
Adelaide Oval, Adelaide. January 29, 30, February 1, 2, 1932.
Toss: South Africa. Australia won by 10 wkts.

SOUTH AFRICA
SH Curnow c Ponsford b Grimmett	.20	b McCabe	.3
B Mitchell c & b McCabe	.75	c O'Reilly b Grimmett	.95
JAJ Christy c O'Reilly	.7	b Grimmett	.51
HW Taylor c Rigg b Grimmett	.78	b O'Reilly	.84
HB Cameron (c+) lbw Grimmett	.52	b O'Reilly	.4
DPB Morkel c & b Grimmett	.0 (8)	b Grimmett	.15
KG Viljoen c & b Grimmett	.0	b Grimmett	.1
CL Vincent not out	.48 (6)	b Grimmett	.5
Q McMillan c & b Grimmett	.19	c Hunt b Grimmett	.3
NA Quinn c Ponsford b Grimmett	.1	b Grimmett	.1
AJ Bell lbw O'Reilly	.2	not out	.0
EXTRAS (LB 2, NB 4)	.6	(B 4, LB 3, NB 5)	.12
TOTAL	.308		.274

FOW 1st Inns: 27 45 165 202 204 204 243 286 300 308
FOW 2nd Inns: 22 103 224 232 240 246 262 268 274 274

Bowling: *First Innings*: Thurlow 27-6-53-0, McCabe 17-6-34-1, O'Reilly 39.4-10-74-2, Grimmett 47-11-116-7, Hunt 10-1-25-0. *Second Innings*: Thurlow 12-1-33-0, McCabe 14-1-51-1, O'Reilly 42-13-81-2, Grimmett 49.2-17-83-7, Hunt 6-1-14-0.

AUSTRALIA
WM Woodfull (c) c Morkel b Bell	.82	not out	.37
WH Ponsford b Quinn	.5	not out	.27
DG Bradman not out	.299		
AF Kippax run out	.0		
SJ McCabe c Vincent b Bell	.2		
KE Rigg c Taylor b Bell	.35		
WAS Oldfield (+) lbw Vincent	.23		
CV Grimmett b Bell	.21		
WA Hunt c Vincent b Quinn	.0		
WJ O'Reilly b Bell	.23		
HM Thurlow run out	.0		
EXTRAS (B 18, LB 3, W 1, NB 1)	.23	(B 4, LB 5)	.9
TOTAL	.513		.0 for 73

FOW 1st Inns: 9 185 191 194 308 357 418 421 499 513
FOW 2nd Inns:

Bowling: *First Innings*: Bell 40-2-142-5, Quinn 37-5-114-2, Vincent 34-5-110-1, McMillan 9-0-53-0, Morkel 18-1-71-0. *Second Innings*: Quinn 3-0-5-0, Morkel 2-0-5-0, McMillan 7.2-0-23-0, Vincent 7-0-31-0.

Umpires: EG Borwick & GA Hele

FIFTH TEST 1931–32 AUSTRALIA v SOUTH AFRICA
Melbourne Cricket Ground, Melbourne. February 12, 13(no play), 15, 1932.
Toss: South Africa. Australia won by an innings & 72 runs.

SOUTH AFRICA
B Mitchell c Rigg b McCabe	.2 (4)	c Oldfield b Ironmonger	.4
SH Curnow c Oldfield b Nash	.3	c Fingleton b Ironmonger	.16
JAJ Christy c Grimmett b Nash	.4 (1)	b Nash	.0
HW Taylor c Kippax b Nash	.0 (7)	c Bradman b Ironmonger	.2
KG Viljoen c(S)LS Darling b Ironmonger	.1 (8)	c Oldfield b O'Reilly	.0
HB Cameron (c+) c McCabe b Nash	.11 (5)	c McCabe b O'Reilly	.0
DPB Morkel c Nash b Ironmonger	.1 (6)	c Rigg b Ironmonger	.0
CL Vincent c Nash b Ironmonger	.1 (9)	not out	.8
Q McMillan st Oldfield b Ironmonger	.0 (10)	c Oldfield b O'Reilly	.0
NA Quinn not out	.5 (11)	c Fingleton b Ironmonger	.5
AJ Bell st Oldfield b Ironmonger	.0 (3)	c McCabe b O'Reilly	.6
EXTRAS (B 2, LB 3, NB 3)	.8	(B 3, LB 1)	.4
TOTAL	.36		.45

FOW 1st Inns: 7 16 16 17 19 25 31 31 33 36
FOW 2nd Inns: 0 12 25 30 30 30 32 32 33 45

Bowling: *First Innings*: Nash 12-6-18-4, McCabe 4-1-4-1, Ironmonger 7.2-5-6-5. *Second Innings*: Nash 7-4-4-1, Ironmonger 15.3-7-18-6, O'Reilly 9-5-19-3.

AUSTRALIA
WM Woodfull (c) b Bell	.0
JHW Fingleton c Vincent b Bell	.40
KE Rigg c Vincent b Quinn	.22
AF Kippax c Curnow b McMillan	.42
SJ McCabe c Cameron b Bell	.0
LJ Nash b Quinn	.13
WAS Oldfield (+) c Curnow b McMillan	.11
CV Grimmett c Cameron b Quinn	.9
WJ O'Reilly c Curnow b McMillan	.13
H Ironmonger not out	.0
DG Bradman	
EXTRAS (LB 3)	.3
TOTAL	.9 for 153

FOW 1st Inns: 0 51 75 75 112 125 131 148 153

Bowling: *First Innings*: Bell 16-0-52-3, Quinn 19.3-4-29-3, Vincent 11-2-40-0, McMillan 8-0-29-3.

Umpires: EG Borwick & GA Hele

Australian Averages

1931–32 AUSTRALIA v SOUTH AFRICA
AUSTRALIA	M	Inn	NO	Runs	H.S	Avrge	Ct	St	Overs	Mds	Runs	Wkt	Avrge
A'Beckett, EL	1	2	-	10	6	5.00	-	-	21.0	6	35	-	-
Bradman, DG	5	5	1	806	299*	201.50	2	-	1.0	-	2	-	-
Fingleton, JHW	1	1	-	40	40	40.00	1	-	-	-	-	-	-
Grimmett, CV	5	6	2	78	21	19.50	5	-	306.0	108	557	33	16.88
Hunt, WA	1	1	-	0	0	0.00	1	-	16.0	2	39	-	-
Ironmonger, H	4	5	1	14	12	3.50	7	-	221.5	112	296	31	9.55
Kippax, AF	4	5	-	162	67	32.40	1	-	-	-	-	-	-
Lee, PK	1	1	-	0	0	0.00	1	-	20.0	5	49	1	49.00
McCabe, SJ	5	6	-	201	79	33.50	9	-	92.3	22	205	9	22.78
Nash, LJ	1	1	-	13	13	13.00	3	-	19.0	10	22	5	4.40
Nitschke, HC	2	2	-	53	47	26.50	3	-	-	-	-	-	-
O'Reilly, WJ	2	2	-	36	23	18.00	1	-	90.4	28	174	7	24.86
Oldfield, WAS	5	6	1	98	56*	19.60	8	6	-	-	-	-	-
Oxenham, RK	1	1	-	1	1	1.00	2	-	11.0	5	18	-	-
Ponsford, WH	4	6	-	97	34	19.40	1	-	-	-	-	-	-
Rigg, KE	4	5	-	253	127	50.60	3	-	-	-	-	-	-
Thurlow, HM	1	1	-	0	0	0.00	-	-	39.0	7	86	-	-
Wall, TW	3	4	1	38	14	12.67	3	-	129.1	38	263	13	20.23
Woodfull, WM	5	7	1	421	161	70.17	1	-	-	-	-	-	-

South African Averages

1931–32 AUSTRALIA v SOUTH AFRICA
SOUTH AFRICA	M	Inn	NO	Runs	H.S	Avrge	Ct	St	Overs	Mds	Runs	Wkt	Avrge
Bell, AJ	5	10	5	20	10*	4.00	1	-	207.0	28	624	23	27.13
Brown, LS	1	2	-	10	8	5.00	-	-	29.0	3	100	1	100.00
Cameron, HB	5	10	-	155	52	15.50	9	-	-	-	-	-	-
Christy, JAJ	5	10	-	235	63	23.50	1	-	3.0	-	14	-	-
Curnow, SH	4	8	-	117	47	14.63	4	-	-	-	-	-	-
Dalton, EL	2	4	-	52	21	13.00	-	-	-	-	-	-	-
McMillan, Q	4	8	-	52	29	6.50	-	-	69.2	3	329	7	47.00
Mitchell, B	5	10	-	322	95	32.20	8	-	1.0	-	8	-	-
Morkel, DPB	5	10	-	98	33	9.80	4	-	52.0	4	193	2	96.50
Quinn, NA	5	10	-	30	11	3.75	-	-	207.4	44	511	13	39.31
Taylor, HW	5	10	-	314	84	31.40	1	-	-	-	-	-	-
Viljoen, KG	4	8	-	152	111	19.00	1	-	-	-	-	-	-
Vincent, CL	5	10	3	189	48*	27.00	6	-	177.0	29	542	10	54.20

McCabe: gallant and gifted

It was clear from a very tender age that Stan McCabe would play for Australia, such was the ease of his shot making. He was something of a late bloomer at Test level, however, and the public had to exercise a fair degree of patience before he unveiled his true might. But when his hour arrived he produced three of the greatest innings ever played in Test cricket.

Wrote Jim Swanton: 'McCabe averaged 48 with the bat over 62 Test innings, and it is safe to say he would have made many, many more runs had they been needed. Going in at no. 4 after Woodfull, Ponsford and Bradman, I suppose he must have sat with his pads on longer than anyone before or since. Was there ever a more powerful quartet?'

Stanley Joseph McCabe was born in the NSW bush town of Grenfell, on 16 July 1910.

Stan's first 'big' game was for NSW Colts in Brisbane in 1928. Stan opened the innings and made 32.

His first Shield game for NSW followed and he played well, scoring 60 and 34.

His form for NSW in 1928–29 earned him a place in Bill Woodfull's team that toured England in 1930. He was only 19, Bradman 22.

In 1931–32, McCabe, still only 21, began to show the form expected of him. He had a brilliant run of scores in Shield matches, averaging a remarkable 438 for New South Wales.

In the first Test of the 'Bodyline' tour, McCabe played the first of his trilogy of memorable innings.

Before a crowd of 40,000 in Sydney, Australia got away to a shaky start in its first innings, losing its first three wickets for 82.

Enter McCabe.

In the next 242 minutes, stretching over two days, McCabe scored 187 not out, putting the much-heralded England express bowlers Larwood and Bill Voce to the sword in cavalier fashion.

Wisden described his maiden Test hundred as 'a remarkable exhibition of courage and craftsmanship'.

McCabe suffered appendicitis in the 1933–34 season and played in only three matches.

He recovered in time for selection in the 1934 team to tour England.

Australia regained the Ashes in

The craftsman Stan McCabe.

England in 1934 and McCabe scored eight centuries, more than any of his team-mates, including 137 in the third Test at Old Trafford.

His 240 against Surrey at the Oval was his highest score, and remained so until the end of his first class career in 1942.

McCabe, by now captain of NSW, was in sparkling form on the 1935–36 tour of South Africa, with 149 in the first Test in Durban, then 189 not out in the second Test in Johannesburg.

During his unbeaten 189, the second of his great trilogy, he scored 50 in 41 minutes.

He headed the batting averages with 420 runs at 84.

McCabe added to his list of centuries with 112 in the first Test against England at the MCG in 1936–37, but the best was yet to come.

His most famous innings was in the first Test against England at Trent Bridge in 1938, when he scored 232 in even time.

His captain, Don Bradman, was enthralled with McCabe's play, saying to him: 'If I could play an innings like that I'd be a proud man, Stan.'

McCabe's innings contained hardly a false shot and for sheer beauty ranked with the best ever played.

None of McCabe's 'great three-some' was a matchwinner, but that does not diminish their quality – and glory.

McCabe died in 1968 at the age of 58.

Ageless spin merchant

When Bert Ironmonger was a boy at Pine Mountain near Ipswich in Queensland he cut off the top of his left index finger with a chaff cutter. No hospital close by so his sister shoved it into a bag of flour, and sealed the wound.

With this truncated finger, big, and clumsy-looking, 'Dainty' Ironmonger literally fired out batsmen with his darting and accurate left-arm spinners.

Born in 1882, he matured slowly and some say majestically in first class cricket. He played for Queensland against Victoria in 1910, toured south in December 1913, where he was invited by Warwick Armstrong to become a ground bowler at the Melbourne Cricket Club.

Ironmonger made his debut for Victoria against Tasmania in February 1914, and his Sheffield Shield debut in 1914–15.

He had to wait until the 1928–29 season and the age of 46 years and 237 days to play his first Test for Australia.

Ironmonger went on to play 14 Tests against England, South Africa and West Indies and unusually, took more wickets, 74, than he scored runs, 42.

By the time he first played Test cricket Ironmonger had given up ground bowling, and first taken the licence of the Royal Derby Hotel in Fitzroy in Melbourne.

Robert Coleman wrote: 'There followed a romance straight from 1930s Hollywood.' Living across the road from the pub was an Irishman who worked as a gripman on the cable trams. Regularly on Friday nights he would dally at the Royal Derby and, as often as not, stay a little too long. He was a widower and at closing time Bert would say, 'Now come on, Tom, I'll take you home to your daughter.' On 14 May 1921, he married the daughter, Elizabeth (Bess) Tierney.

Of Bess and Bert was the story first told, of her ringing the MCG and being told that Bert had just gone in to bat, and saying 'That's all right, I'll hang on.'

(It was also said that when the MCG horse saw Bert go in to bat it backed itself into the shafts of the heavy roller.)

They moved to Sydney, owning a Balmain pub later in 1921, and Ironmonger played two seasons of grade cricket for Balmain.

They returned to Melbourne in 1923, broke, and opened an unin-

Accurate Bert 'Dainty' Ironmonger.

sured tobacconists and barber shop in St Kilda, which was robbed. He lost everything and gave up the business life. He then worked for the St Kilda Council.

Ironmonger's bowling partnership with the right-arm spinner Don Blackie for St Kilda was the stuff of legend. Blackie, who also was born in 1882, played just three Tests, in 1928–29, taking 14 wickets. The second Test was the only occasion where Blackie and Ironmonger (and Grimmett) played together for Australia – and England made 636. But Blackie and Ironmonger were the reason why their club St Kilda won five District competitions between 1923–24 and 1931–32.

Ironmonger's most devastating Test performance was against South Africa in the fifth Test of 1931–32, when on a suitable MCG pitch he took 5/6 and 6/18, which prompted a newspaper to remark that talk of 'patriarchal age, of moths, silverfish and creaking joints' had gone on long enough. 'This Methuselah business has been carried far enough.' With that performance Ironmonger stepped into the 'gallery of immortals'.

In all, Ironmonger played eight seasons with Melbourne, two with Balmain and 11 with St Kilda, taking 890 wickets at 13. In 96 first class matches he took 464 wickets at 21.5, and in Tests 74 at 17.97.

The St Kilda Cricket club named a grandstand the 'Blackie–Ironmonger' Stand in honour of the old, (perhaps oldest) firm.

Don Blackie died in 1955 aged 73, and Ironmonger in 1971 at 88.

England has plan to combat Bradman

Perth, Oct. 20. The 22nd England team has arrived in Australia for a tour of 17 first class matches, under the captaincy of Australophobe, the introverted Douglas Jardine. It is believed he has a plan to combat Don Bradman. Bradman had, of course, put the English bowlers to the sword in 1930, and no Englishman, especially Jardine, thinks they have much hope on Australian wickets if Bradman is not stopped.

The question is how to do it. Jardine had seen Bradman's contemptuous 252 not out against Surrey in 1930 – contemptuous because the Surrey side was captained by Percy Fender who had disparaged Bradman's ability in 1928–29. The dismissive style of Bradman in this game had some impact on Jardine, already ill-disposed to Australia and Australians. 'Plum' Warner wrote of Jardine whom he had nominated as captain, 'He is a queer fellow. When he sees a cricket ground with an Australian on it he goes mad.'

Jardine's anti-Bradman idea is firstly based on 'leg-theory', that is, balls pitched on the leg stump with a field weighted on the leg side are difficult to score from – especially fuller-pitched deliveries. Second, there was a feeling in England that Bradman somehow 'drew away' from Larwood short-pitched deliveries while he was merrily making 232 in the fifth Test in 1930.

Larwood said: 'Don didn't like the balls rising on his body. He kept drawing away.'

These two ideas were the sketch of the plan that Jardine will use

Haughty captain Douglas Jardine.

with his battery of four fast bowlers — Larwood, Bill Voce, Bill Bowes and 'Gubby' Allen. How much the captain has told the bowlers and other members of the team on the boat or beforehand is not known.

Percy Fender probably suggested he try it against Bradman, as Fender's own 'off-theory' had been an abject failure. Bowling on or outside the off stump to Bradman was asking him to whack the ball

over the midwicket boundary. Perhaps bowling on the other side of the wicket would at least slow him down.

Jardine had seen leg theory at work. The Notts captain Arthur Carr, a fellow 'Australophobe', had asked his fast bowlers Larwood and Voce to bowl 'leg theory' occasionally since 1931.

Leg theory is aimed at restricting a batsman's shotmaking.

Bill Bowes had used it against Jack Hobbs, and also bounced the ball at Hobbs' head in August 1932.

This caused Plum Warner to write 'That is not bowling. Indeed it is not cricket.'

Warner also wrote, in the 1930 edition of the *Badminton*, 'It is always possible … to prevent your opponents winning, by instructing your bowlers to bowl a good length outside the leg stump, with six or seven men on the on-side, but for ourselves, and we believe the vast majority of cricketers, we regard such tactics as unsportsmanlike, and quite contrary to the spirit and traditions of the game, and we would scorn such a manoeuvre, and would rather suffer a hundred defeats than put it into practice'.

It remains to be seen whether this idea of Jardine's will work against Bradman, or whether the batsman will find a way of scoring against it.

A lot will depend on the effective combination of sheer speed (Larwood is apparently some yards faster than he was on his last tour), the number of short-pitched balls bowled at or outside leg stump and where the field is placed.

Cricketer and noted cartoonist Arthur Mailey retained the Christmas spirit in drawing the England greeting card.

Jack Fingleton (left) and Don Bradman (right) stride out to face the music.

Not quite the cricketers' traditional version of 'leg theory', but may restrict runs in other ways.

The 'scone theory' is unveiled in Sydney

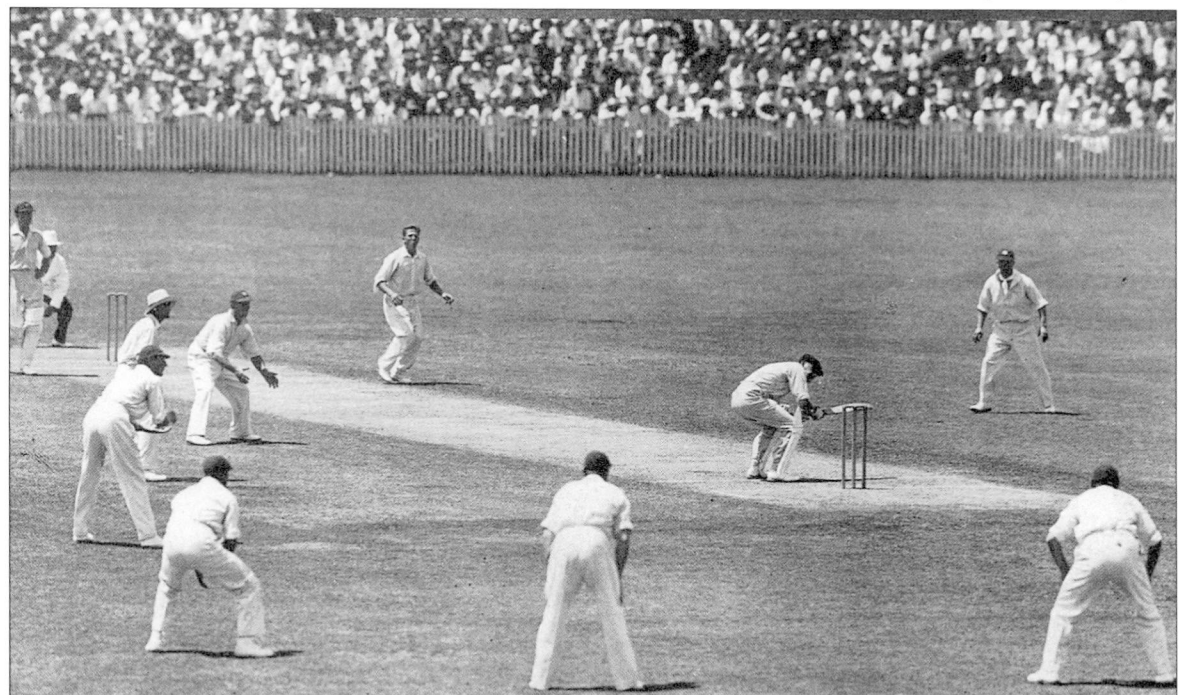

England fast bowler Harold Larwood bowls at Bill Woodfull at the 'Gabba in the fourth Test to a standard Bodyline field. Two not in the picture are back for the hook shot. England took the Ashes with its six-wicket win.

Half of England's pace battery Bill Voce (left) and Harold Larwood (right). Bill Bowes and 'Gubby' Allen completed the quartet, their mission to stop Bradman.

Sydney, Nov. 29. After a couple of uneventful matches – a draw against WA, and an easy win over an Australian XI through the agency of spinner Hedley Verity – England has unveiled its weapon against Don Bradman, Stan McCabe, Jack Fingleton and the other Australian batsmen.

In two matches at the MCG, one against Victoria, a second against the Australian XI, and against NSW at the SCG, England has used the fast leg theory seemingly directed at the batsman's body and head or 'scone'.

This type of bowling, according to NSW victim Bill O'Reilly, has become known to the players as 'scone theory'. 'When they started having a ping at us 'we'd say "Hullo, the scone's on."'

Jack Fingleton, who carried his bat for 119 not out in NSW's first innings, was blue with bruises, and said he took no pleasure in his century.

He was disillusioned by the English tactics, and commented frankly: 'I was conscious of a hurt, and it was not from the physical pummeling I had taken from Voce. It was the consciousness of a crashed ideal.

'Playing against England in actuality had proved vastly different from what boyish dreams and adventure had imagined it to be.'

England defeated NSW by an innings and 44 runs, Herbert Sutcliffe making 182, and Voce taking 5/69 and 5/85.

Ominous draw

Melbourne, Nov. 22. A huge crowd, totalling 109,501 over four days – the largest non-Test attendance in Australia – saw an Australian XI including Don Bradman and Bill Woodfull, on top in a draw against England's four fast bowlers, who were bowling fast and short leg theory.

Woodfull was hit over the heart, but continued to bat.

The MCC made 282 in its first innings, and in reply the Australian XI struggled to 218, with Bradman out lbw to Larwood for 36.

Rain on the third and fourth days changed the game and Lisle Nagel of Victoria bowled the MCC out for 60, taking 8/32. The match was abandoned because of the rain on the fourth day. The Australian XI was at 2/19, needing a further 106 to win. Larwood, ominously, captured 2/5 from 3.7 overs.

No press work

Melbourne, Nov. 30. The impasse over the conflict between Don Bradman's contract to comment on radio and write for Frank Packer's *Sun* newspaper group, and the Board of Control's rule that players should not write for newspapers unless they were solely employed as journalists has been resolved.

Bradman had sought permission to write, and has done so, threatening not to make himself available for Test cricket.

Now Bradman has been released from his newspaper contract by the *Sun* group.

He will still be heard on the wireless.

The talented and young Sid Barnes (aged 16) has showed promise batting for Petersham this season.

McCabe the magnificent defies England

Sydney, Dec. 17. With Don Bradman indisposed and not playing in the first Test, Australia needed someone young and brave to stand up to England's leg theory. Australia was 4/87, Bill Woodfull, Bill Ponsford, Jack Fingleton and Alan Kippax were out. Kippax exclaimed back in the dressing room of Harold Larwood, 'He's too bloody fast for me.'

For his part, the 22-year-old McCabe said to his Dad: 'If I happen to get hit out there, keep Mum from jumping the fence,' and proceeded to play one of the greatest innings in Test Cricket, against a ferocious mixture of short balls on the line of the body, and sheer speed on a fast pitch.

McCabe smacked Larwood's first short ball to the square leg fence, and adopted the same method with all the other bowlers as well.

For the sufficiently skilled player, for the brave and the lucky, this was the answer to England's intimidating bowling.

McCabe had the lot, and made an undefeated 187.

Stan McCabe wields his magic willow at the MCG, pulling Verity for four. He made a glorious 187 not out.

Bradman and O'Reilly even up the Test series

Melbourne, Jan. 3. After a fortnight's beach holiday recuperating from the strains of national idolatry and expectation, Don Bradman walked slowly onto the MCG to the sustained roar of the greatest sporting crowd in the world. This sound lasted for minutes. First ball, Bradman faced Bill Bowes and, expecting a fast Bodyline bouncer, got into position to hook. It was short but it was slow and Bradman bottom edged it into his stumps. Out for a duck in an awful hush.

The pressure on Bradman in the second innings cannot be imagined, but he played one of his great innings, 103 not out, helped by the unlikely Bert Ironmonger to achieve that feat. Though the pitch was slower, Larwood was at his fastest. Arthur Mailey said that Bradman's innings 'stood out from those of his team-mates like a diamond set in a piece of glass.'

In the meantime, Bill O'Reilly had exploited the special qualities of the pitch and the hot weather with a pair of spells; 34.3 overs 5/65 in England's first innings of 169, and 24 overs 5/66 in the even more miserable second innings of 139.

Bert Ironmonger (4/26) also played his part, taking special satisfaction in getting England captain Douglas Jardine for a duck.

Bill O'Reilly bowls England opener Herbert Sutcliffe for 33 in the second innings as he takes 5/66, and 10 wickets for the match. O'Reilly made the most of the special qualities of the pitch and the hot weather.

Adelaide drama – game at crisis point

Woodfull reels in pain as he takes a blow to the chest.

Adelaide, Jan. 19. The 'bodyline' tactics of England captain Douglas Jardine in the third Test have brought relations between Australia and England to crisis point.

The incident began with Larwood's last ball of his second over to Australian captain Bill Woodfull.

This delivery jumped up from short of a length outside the off stump and fizzed back in at Woodfull, who had expected it to fly harmlessly by. It struck him above the heart, he staggered and dropped his bat.

The Adelaide Oval, from the members stand to the outer ground, erupted in scenes of unprecedented outrage. Jardine and Larwood were hooted and counted out.

What followed was unmitigated stupidity if it was not deliberate provocation.

Woodfull recovered and continued his innings. Larwood had had an orthodox field for his first two overs, but either he or Jardine (both have denied responsibility) changed to a bodyline field for Woodfull in the third over.

This reinforced the notion in the crowd that 'bodyline' was really and truly a method directed at the body of a batsman, even one injured like Woodfull.

All hell broke loose. If one barracker had jumped the fence to 'do something' about the incident, he would have been followed by many more of the 50,962 present.

Bert Oldfield staggers after deflecting a short ball from Larwood to his head. He has a fractured skull, but sportingly claims it was a mistake.

That evening, England Manager 'Plum' Warner came to offer sympathy, but instead received a succinct and devastating message from Woodfull.

'I don't want to see you, Mr Warner,' said Woodfull. 'There are two teams out there on the oval. One is playing cricket, the other is not. This game is too good to be spoilt. It is time some people got out of it.'

That was Saturday. Sunday was a rest day. On Monday, the Australian innings resumed, and wicket-keeper Bert Oldfield deflected a short one from Larwood into his head, fracturing his skull. He sportingly claimed that it was his own mistake.

In response to Woodfull's complaint, the Board of Control, acting on a majority of 8/5, telegrammed the MCC in London at 3.12 p.m. on January 18, saying that bodyline bowling was detrimental to the interests of the game, and that 'in our opinion it is unsportsmanlike'.

Bodyline had moved to the political arena.

Panorama of the Adelaide Oval during the third Test. If one spectator had jumped the fence it's likely more than 50,000 would have followed.

England on its winning way to regain the Ashes

Sydney, Feb. 28. After taking the Ashes by winning the fourth Test at the 'Gabba by six wickets, England reinforced its superiority in this series when Walter Hammond hoisted off-spinner Phillip Lee over long off for six, for an eight-wicket victory in the fifth Test at the SCG.

Australia made its highest score against bodyline bowling in the first innings, but managed only 182 in the second innings despite Larwood breaking a big toe. He finished that over to Woodfull, of all people, rolling his arm over standing at the bowlers end. Woodfull patted the balls back to him. Jardine made Larwood stay on the ground until Bradman was dismissed by Verity and then Bradman and Larwood walked off together.

It had been a torrid series for Bradman. His average was only half what it normally is in Test cricket – 56.6.

R. E. Wilmot wrote that Bradman 'felt himself that he must take the gifts the gods offered while he had the chance, and as he expressed it, 'I thought I had better hit Verity before Larwood hit me.'

He whacked a bouncer from Larwood back over his head in Sydney with a tennis smash shot that bounced once into the sight screen.

Tim Wall takes all 10 NSW wickets

Sydney, Feb. 6. SA fast bowler Thomas 'Tim' Wall, in a remarkable spell of 5.4 overs after lunch on the first day of the NSW v SA match, advanced his figures from 1/31 to 10/36.

This 10-wicket haul is the first in Sheffield Shield cricket and the first in Australia since George Giffen, also a South Australian, did it for an Australian XI against a Combined XI in February 1884.

Giffen's analysis was 26 overs, 10/66 – coincidentally the same as Arthur Mailey's feat in England in 1921.

Wall's haul included Don Bradman, Stan McCabe, Bill Brown and Jack Fingleton.

NSW made just 113, but got back into the match by dismissing SA for 114.

Bradman finished off the game in the second innings – with the ball. He had Wall stumped.

NSW won the match – and the Sheffield Shield.

Bodyline results in war of 'cable cricket'

The kangaroo's farewell.

Melbourne, Feb. 8. The bodyline business has resulted in an unprecedented series of cables between the Australian Board of Control and the Marylebone Cricket Club, with the assertion that bodyline is unsportsmanlike being received with indignation in England. This reaction may, to some extent be put down to a lack of appreciation of exactly how dangerous bodyline has been, how thoroughgoing has been Douglas Jardine's use of it, and a misunderstanding of how importantly it has been regarded by all Australians.

The first cable, sent by the Board of Control on 18 January stated 'Bodyline bowling assumed such proportions as to menace the best interest of the game, making protection of body by batsmen the main consideration and causing intensely bitter feelings amongst players as well as injury. In our opinion it is unsportsmanlike and unless stopped at once is likely to upset friendly relations existing between Australia and England.'

The MCC replied, 'We deplore your cable. We deprecate your opinion that there has been unsportsmanlike play. We have fullest confidence in captain, team and managers and are convinced that they would do nothing to infringe either the laws of cricket, or the spirit of the game.

'We have no evidence that our confidence has been misplaced. Much as we regret accidents to Woodfull and Oldfield, we understand that in neither case was the bowler to blame.

'If the Australian Board of Control wishes to propose a new law or rule, it shall receive our careful consideration in due course.

'We hope the situation is not now as serious as your cable would seem to indicate but if it is such as to jeopardise the good relations between English and Australian cricketers, and you consider it desirable to cancel remainder of program, we would consent, but with great reluctance.'

The Australian Board of Control sent another cable on January 30:

'We appreciate your difficulty in dealing with this matter without having seen the actual play.

'We unanimously agree that "body-line" bowling, as adopted in some games on the present tour, is opposed to the spirit of cricket, and unnecessarily dangerous to players.

'We are deeply concerned that the ideals of the game shall be preserved, and we have therefore appointed a committee to report on the means necessary to eliminate such bowling from Australian cricket, beginning with 1933–34 season …

'We do not consider it necessary to cancel the remainder of the program …'

The MCC noted that 'with pleasure' in a reply, but 'May we accept this as a clear indication that the good sportsmanship of our team is not in question?

'We are sure you will appreciate how impossible it would be to play any Test match in the spirit we all desire unless both sides were satisfied there was no reflection upon their sportsmanship.'

There was a happy ending – the remaining Tests went ahead with good feeling.

The coffin of Archie Jackson, who died of tuberculosis on February 16 at the tragically early age of 24, is carried by his Australian team-mates Vic Richardson, Bill Woodfull, Alan Kippax, Bert Oldfield. Out of picture are Bill Ponsford and Don Bradman. Graceful and elegant, Jackson could have been a batsman to rival the very best, but died a legend.

How peace was restored

RIP Bodyline? Some bowlers will be sad to see it go, but it served its purpose.

Melbourne, March 1. The semi-public exchanges between the Australian Board of Control and the Marylebone Cricket Club obscured a murky process whereby pressure at the highest level was brought on both the Board and the MCC, especially the Board, to compromise, for the sake not only of cricket, but also the economic and diplomatic relationship between the two countries.

On February 1, England manager 'Plum' Warner cabled the British representative in Australia Ernest Crutchley the following: 'Have under consideration cancellation of remaining matches of tour including Test owing to failure of Board to withdraw stigma of word unsportsmanlike in their first cable. Beg you use your influence to get word withdrawn. Matter very urgent.'

In addition, Douglas Jardine has indicated that he would not play in the fourth Test unless the stigma was removed.

Crutchley telephoned the Australian Prime Minister Joseph Lyons the same day. The PM called in Board chairman Dr Alan Robertson, again on the same day, and Robertson cabled Board Secretary Bill Jeanes. 'Prime Minister interviewed me today. Stated that British representative had seen him and asked him to get us to withdraw word objected to. If not likelihood of England pulling right out. If we do withdraw has no doubt attack [bowling] would be modified. Government afraid successful conversions endangered.'

'Conversions' referred to the rolling-over of British banks' loans to Australian governments – which

had once been threatened by NSW Premier Jack Lang, who threatened to repudiate the loans and was sacked by Governor Sir Phillip Game in May 1932. The implication was that bodyline might threaten the confidence of British banks in Australia, and the loans might not be rolled-over. True or not, it was a powerful persuader for the Board.

Other activity was also taking place. The Governor of South Australia, Sir Alexander Hore-Ruthven, was in England, but the acting Governor Sir George Murray invited Warner and local cricket officials to a meeting in Adelaide.

Warner reportedly said that he 'emphatically condemned' bodyline, but that 'on the field Jardine was in complete control.' Murray then cabled Hore-Ruthven in London, who in turn visited the British Minister responsible for Dominion Affairs, James Thomas, on January 31. Thomas met the MCC on February 1.

Exactly what transpired at this meeting is not known, but a week later the Board cabled the 'withdrawal' of the unsportsmanlike comment on February 8.

'We do not regard the sportsmanship of your team as being in question,' cabled the Board, however '... a particular class of bowling is not in the best interests of cricket,' and they hoped the 'remaining Tests would be played with the traditional good feeling.'

And the tour and Test matches proceeded.

And so did bodyline – Jardine still used it in the fifth Test when the series and Ashes had already been decided.

THIRD TEST 1932–33 AUSTRALIA v ENGLAND
Adelaide Oval, Adelaide. January 13, 14, 16, 17, 18, 19, 1933.
Toss: England. England won by 338 runs.

ENGLAND

H Sutcliffe c Wall b O'Reilly	9	c (S)LPJ O'Brien b Wall	7
DR Jardine (c) b Wall	3	lbw Ironmonger	56
WR Hammond c Oldfield b Wall	2 (5)	b Bradman	85
LEG Ames (+) b Ironmonger	3 (7)	b O'Reilly	69
M Leyland b O'Reilly	83 (6)	c Wall b Ironmonger	42
RES Wyatt c Richardson b Grimmett	78 (3)	c Wall b O'Reilly	49
E Paynter c Fingleton b Wall	77 (10)	not out	1
GOB Allen lbw Grimmett	15 (4)	lbw Grimmett	15
H Verity c Richardson b Wall	45 (8)	b O'Reilly	40
W Voce b Wall	8 (11)	b O'Reilly	8
H Larwood not out	3 (9)	c Bradman b Ironmonger	8
EXTRAS (B 1, LB 7, NB 7)	15	(B 17, LB 11, NB 4)	32
TOTAL	341		412

FOW 1st Inns: 4 16 16 30 186 196 228 324 336 341
FOW 2nd Inns: 7 91 123 154 245 296 394 395 403 412

Bowling: *First Innings*: Wall 34.1-10-72-5, O'Reilly 50-19-82-2, Ironmonger 20-6-50-1, Grimmett 28-6-94-2, McCabe 14-3-28-0. *Second Innings*: Wall 29-6-75-1, O'Reilly 50.3-21-79-4, Ironmonger 57-21-87-3, Grimmett 35-9-74-1, McCabe 16-0-42-0, Bradman 4-0-23-1.

AUSTRALIA

JHW Fingleton c Ames b Allen	0	b Larwood	0
WM Woodfull (c) b Allen	22	not out	73
DG Bradman c Allen b Larwood	8 (4)	c & b Verity	66
SJ McCabe c Jardine b Larwood	8 (5)	c Leyland b Allen	7
WH Ponsford b Voce	85 (3)	c Jardine b Larwood	3
VY Richardson b Allen	28	c Allen b Larwood	21
WAS Oldfield (+) retired hurt	41		
CV Grimmett c Voce b Allen	10 (7)	b Allen	6
TW Wall b Hammond	6 (8)	b Allen	0
WJ O'Reilly b Larwood	0 (9)	b Allen	5
H Ironmonger not out	0 (10)	b Allen	0
EXTRAS (B 2, LB 11, NB 1)	14	(B 4, LB 2, W 1, NB 5)	12
TOTAL	9 for 222		9 for 193

FOW 1st Inns: 1 18 34 51 131 194 212 222 222
FOW 2nd Inns: 3 12 100 116 171 183 183 192 193

Bowling: *First Innings*: Larwood 25-6-55-3, Allen 23-4-71-4, Hammond 17.4-4-30-1, Voce 14-5-21-1, Verity 16-7-31-0. *Second Innings*: Larwood 19-3-71-4, Allen 17.2-5-50-4, Voce 4-1-7-0, Hammond 9-3-27-0, Verity 20-12-26-1.

Umpires: EG Borwick & GA Hele

FIFTH TEST 1932–33 AUSTRALIA v ENGLAND
Sydney Cricket Ground, Sydney. February 23, 24, 25, 27, 28, 1933.
Toss: Australia. England won by 8 wkts.

AUSTRALIA

VY Richardson c Jardine b Larwood	0	c Allen b Larwood	0
WM Woodfull (c) b Larwood	14	b Allen	67
DG Bradman b Larwood	48	b Verity	71
LPJ O'Brien c Larwood b Voce	61	c Verity b Voce	5
SJ McCabe c Hammond b Verity	73	c Jardine b Voce	4
LS Darling b Verity	85	c Wyatt b Verity	7
WAS Oldfield (+) run out	52	c Wyatt b Verity	5
PK Lee c Jardine b Verity	42	b Allen	15
WJ O'Reilly b Allen	19	b Verity	1
HH Alexander not out	17	lbw Verity	0
H Ironmonger b Larwood	1	not out	0
EXTRAS (B 13, LB 9, W 1)	23	(B 4, NB 3)	7
TOTAL	435		182

FOW 1st Inns: 0 59 64 163 244 328 385 414 430 435
FOW 2nd Inns: 0 115 135 139 148 161 177 178 178 182

Bowling: *First Innings*: Larwood 32.2-10-98-4, Voce 24-4-80-1, Allen 25-1-128-1, Hammond 8-0-32-0, Verity 17-3-62-3, Wyatt 2-0-12-0. *Second Innings*: Larwood 11-0-44-1, Allen 11.4-2-54-2, Hammond 3-0-10-0, Voce 10-0-34-2, Verity 19-9-33-5.

ENGLAND

DR Jardine (c) c Oldfield b O'Reilly	18	c Richardson b Ironmonger	24
H Sutcliffe c Richardson b O'Reilly	56	not out	75
WR Hammond lbw Lee	101 (4)	not out	75
H Larwood c Ironmonger b Lee	98		
M Leyland run out	42 (3)	b Ironmonger	0
RES Wyatt c Ironmonger b O'Reilly	51 (2)	not out	61
LEG Ames (+) run out	4		
E Paynter b Lee	9		
GOB Allen c Bradman b Lee	48		
H Verity c Oldfield b Alexander	4		
W Voce not out	7		
EXTRAS (B 7, LB 7, NB 2)	16	(B 6, LB 1, NB 1)	8
TOTAL	454		2 for 168

FOW 1st Inns: 31 153 245 310 330 349 374 418 434 454
FOW 2nd Inns: 43 43

Bowling: *First Innings*: Alexander 35-1-129-1, McCabe 12-1-27-0, O'Reilly 45-7-100-3, Ironmonger 31-13-64-0, Lee 40.2-11-111-4, Darling 7-5-3-0, Bradman 1-0-4-0. *Second Innings*: Alexander 11-2-25-0, O'Reilly 15-5-32-0, Ironmonger 26-12-34-2, Lee 12.2-3-52-0, McCabe 5-2-10-0, Darling 2-0-7-0.

Umpires: EG Borwick & GA Hele

FOURTH TEST 1932–33 AUSTRALIA v ENGLAND
Brisbane Cricket Ground, Brisbane. February 10, 11, 13, 14, 15, 16, 1933.
Toss: Australia. England won by 6 wkts.

AUSTRALIA

VY Richardson st Ames b Hammond	83	c Jardine b Verity	32
WM Woodfull (c) b Mitchell	67	c Hammond b Mitchell	19
DG Bradman b Larwood	76	c Mitchell b Larwood	24
SJ McCabe c Jardine b Allen	20 (5)	b Verity	22
WH Ponsford b Larwood	19 (4)	c Larwood b Allen	0
LS Darling c Ames b Allen	17	run out	39
EH Bromley c Verity b Larwood	26	c Hammond b Allen	7
HSB Love (+) lbw Mitchell	5	lbw Larwood	3
TW Wall not out	6	c Jardine b Allen	2
WJ O'Reilly c Hammond b Larwood	6	b Larwood	4
H Ironmonger st Ames b Hammond	8	not out	0
EXTRAS (B 5, LB 1, NB 1)	7	(B 13, LB 9, NB 1)	23
TOTAL	340		175

FOW 1st Inns: 133 200 233 264 267 292 315 317 329 340
FOW 2nd Inns: 46 79 81 91 136 163 169 169 171 175

Bowling: *First Innings*: Larwood 31-7-101-4, Allen 24-4-83-2, Hammond 23-5-61-2, Mitchell 16-5-49-2, Verity 27-12-39-0. *Second Innings*: Larwood 17.3-3-49-3, Allen 17-3-44-3, Hammond 10-4-18-0, Verity 19-6-30-2, Mitchell 5-0-11-1.

ENGLAND

DR Jardine (c) c Love b O'Reilly	46	lbw Ironmonger	24
H Sutcliffe lbw O'Reilly	86	c Darling b Wall	2
WR Hammond b McCabe	20 (4)	c Bromley b Ironmonger	14
RES Wyatt c Love b Ironmonger	12		
M Leyland c Bradman b O'Reilly	12 (3)	c McCabe b O'Reilly	86
LEG Ames (+) c Darling b Ironmonger	17 (5)	not out	14
GOB Allen c Love b Wall	13		
E Paynter c Richardson b Ironmonger	83 (6)	not out	14
H Larwood b McCabe	23		
H Verity not out	23		
TB Mitchell lbw O'Reilly	0		
EXTRAS (B 6, LB 12, NB 3)	21	(B 2, LB 4, NB 2)	8
TOTAL	356		4 for 162

FOW 1st Inns: 114 157 165 188 198 216 225 264 356 356
FOW 2nd Inns: 5 78 118 138

Bowling: *First Innings*: Wall 33-6-66-1, O'Reilly 67.4-27-120-4, Ironmonger 43-19-69-3, McCabe 23-7-40-2, Bromley 10-4-19-0, Bradman 7-1-17-0, Darling 2-0-4-0. *Second Innings*: Wall 7-1-17-1, O'Reilly 30-11-65-1, Ironmonger 35-13-47-2, McCabe 7.4-2-25-0.

Umpires: EG Borwick & GA Hele

Australian Averages

AUSTRALIA	M	Inn	NO	Runs	H.S	Avrge	Ct	St	Overs	Mds	Runs	Wkt	Avrge
Alexander, HH	1	2	1	17	17*	17.00	-	-	46.0	3	154	1	154.00
Bradman, DG	4	8	1	396	103*	56.57	3	-	12.0	1	44	1	44.00
Bromley, EH	1	2	-	33	26	16.50	1	-	10.0	4	19	-	-
Darling, LS	2	4	-	148	85	37.00	2	-	11.0	5	14	-	-
Fingleton, JHW	3	6	-	150	83	25.00	3	-	-	-	-	-	-
Grimmett, CV	3	6	-	42	19	7.00	1	-	147.0	41	326	5	65.20
Ironmonger, H	4	8	3	13	8	2.60	2	-	245.1	96	405	15	27.00
Kippax, AF	1	2	-	27	19	13.50	-	-	2.0	1	3	-	-
Lee, PK	1	2	-	57	42	28.50	-	-	52.4	14	163	4	40.75
Love, HSB	1	2	-	8	5	4.00	3	-	-	-	-	-	-
McCabe, SJ	5	10	1	385	187*	42.78	4	-	92.5	17	215	3	71.67
Nagel, LE	1	2	1	21	21*	21.00	-	-	43.4	9	110	2	55.00
O'Brien, LPJ	2	4	-	87	61	21.75	2	-	-	-	-	-	-
O'Reilly, WJ	5	10	-	61	19	6.10	1	-	383.4	144	724	27	26.81
Oldfield, WAS	4	7	2	136	52	27.20	6	1	-	-	-	-	-
Ponsford, WH	3	6	-	141	85	23.50	-	-	-	-	-	-	-
Richardson, VY	5	10	-	279	83	27.90	7	-	-	-	-	-	-
Wall, TW	4	8	1	42	20	6.00	4	-	170.1	33	409	16	25.56
Woodfull, WM	5	10	1	305	73*	33.89	-	-	-	-	-	-	-

English Averages

ENGLAND	M	Inn	NO	Runs	H.S	Avrge	Ct	St	Overs	Mds	Runs	Wkt	Avrge
Allen, GOB	5	7	-	163	48	23.29	7	-	171.0	29	593	21	28.24
Ames, LEG	5	8	1	113	69	16.14	8	2	-	-	-	-	-
Bowes, WE	1	2	2	4	4*	-	-	-	23.0	2	70	1	70.00
Hammond, WR	5	9	1	440	112	55.00	6	-	120.5	27	291	9	32.33
Jardine, DR	5	9	-	199	56	22.11	9	-	-	-	-	-	-
Larwood, H	5	7	1	145	98	24.17	2	-	220.2	42	644	33	19.52
Leyland, M	5	9	-	306	86	34.00	2	-	-	-	-	-	-
Mitchell, TB	1	1	-	0	0	0.00	1	-	21.0	5	60	3	20.00
Nawab of Pataudi sr	2	3	-	122	102	40.67	-	-	-	-	-	-	-
Paynter, E	3	5	2	184	83	61.33	-	-	-	-	-	-	-
Sutcliffe, H	5	9	1	440	194	55.00	1	-	-	-	-	-	-
Verity, H	4	5	1	114	45	28.50	3	-	135.0	54	271	11	24.64
Voce, W	4	6	2	29	8	7.25	3	-	133.3	24	407	15	27.13
Wyatt, RES	5	9	2	327	78	46.71	2	-	2.0	-	12	-	-

1934 England tour will proceed

London, Dec. 14. While the Interstate Conference agreed to ban bodyline bowling, the MCC in London has not. However the MCC and the Board of Control in negotions over playing conditions for the 1934 tour eventually and grudgingly came up with forms of words that were agreeable.

The tour will proceed.

MCC to Board, 12 June 1933:

The MCC 'considers that the term 'body-line' bowling is misleading and improper …

'The term 'bodyline' would appear to imply a direct attack by the bowler on the batsman. The Committee consider that such an implication applied to the English bowling in Australia is improper and incorrect. Such action … would be an offence against the spirit of the game and would immediately be condemned.'

Board of Control to MCC, Sep. 22:

'We note that you consider a form of bowling which amounted to a direct attack by the bowler on the batsman would be against the spirit of the game …

'We feel that while the type of bowling to which exception has been taken in Australia, strictly was not in conflict with the Laws of Cricket, yet its continued practice would not be in the best interests of the game. May we assume that you concur in this point of view and that the teams may thus take the field in 1934 with that knowledge?'

MCC to Board, Oct. 9:

'We … agree and have always agreed that a form of bowling which is obviously a direct attack by the bowler on the batsman would be an offence against the spirit of the game. Your team can certainly take the field with the knowledge and the full assurance that cricket will be played here in the same spirit as in the past …'

Board to MCC, Nov. 16:

'We … assume that your cable is intended to give the assurance asked for in our cablegram of September 22. It is on this understanding that we are sending a team in 1934.'

Big bats star in Shield

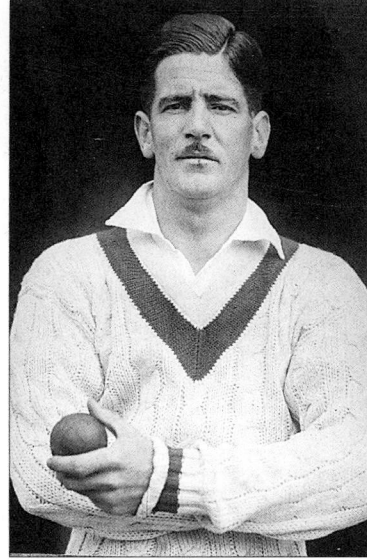
'Chuck' Fleetwood-Smith (Victoria).

Bill Brown (NSW) – a double century.

Sydney, Jan. 30. Victoria won the Sheffield Shield by batting out the last day, following on after NSW made a quick 672 and dismissed Victoria for 407.

Victoria lost on the first innings, but NSW needed outright points to win the Shield.

Don Bradman, in his last match for NSW, continued his merry way this season with a century in 87 minutes, the last 118 of his 128 in just 58 minutes.

His other scores include 200 and 253 in the NSW games against Queensland, and 187 against Victoria in the first match.

In this game Jack Fingleton made 145 after retiring hurt with cramp on 78 when the score was 0/148. That brought Bradman to join Bill Brown, with the result that the first wicket stand was 340, but involved two partnerships. Brown made 205, and Fingleton returned to finish with 145.

Len Darling for Victoria failed in the first innings but made 93 in the second to stave off outright defeat.

Darling has been Victoria's most consistent batsman with Bill Woodfull, this season making 828 runs at 48. Woodfull made 818 at 62.92.

Bradman topped everything with 1192 runs (from just 11 innings) at 132.44. Brown made 878 at 67.53, Alan Kippax 863 at 71.91.

Outstanding young batsman from Tasmania Clayvel 'Jack' Badcock who made his debut at 15 in 1930, made centuries in four consecutive matches, including a wonderful 274 against Victoria.

Badcock also made over 800 runs, 803 at 89.22 from 10 innings.

Bradman moves to South Australia and new career

Adelaide, March 14. Don Bradman, who is 25 years old, officially starts his new cricket life and new career in South Australia, in the stockbroking firm of H. W. Hodgetts & Co.

His salary of £700 per year (and £500 when out of Australia, where he is at present) compares most favourably with the 10/- he received playing Sheffield Shield cricket in Sydney for NSW.

Bradman has had trouble enough fulfilling his contractual commitments with the Sydney *Sun*, radio 2UE as well as meeting the Board of Control's guidelines for players.

These contracts finished on February 1, and his new situation will lead to a more secure and settled life for Australia's batting phenomenon.

South Australia hope to obtain a leader as well as the country's best batsman – they have won only one Shield since World War One.

Negotiations commenced in December 1933, after Bradman had indicated that he was receptive to the idea, and that SA were in a position to subsidise the employment of a player of Bradman's quality.

Harry Hodgetts is a SACA committeeman, and Board of Control delegate, as well as stockbroker, but he must wait until Bradman returns from the 1934 tour of England before he begins to repay his 'investment'.

Rumours are rife that other players might be lured to jobs – and cricket – in South Australia.

Old bowlers' benefit. A match between Vic Richardson's XI and Bill Woodfull's XI at the MCG in November for the benefit of old Victorian and Australian bowlers Don Blackie and Bert Ironmmonger saw a total of 44,545 spectators and £908 raised for each player.

And as for the Rest. Another benefit match was played at the SCG in aid of Herbie Collins, Charlie Kelleway and Tom Andrews. It raised £500 for each champion and saw a thrilling win to the Rest over NSW when Laurie Nash hit 4, 2, dot, 6, dot, and ran a leg bye from the sixth ball for the winning run.

First ball. John Davey, the South Australian fast medium bowler became the first player from his state to take a wicket with his first ball in first class

cricket – and it was a big one– that of the Test and Victorian opener, Bill Ponsford.

Really O'Reilly. Bill O'Reilly took the best figures in matches between NSW and Victoria with a spellbinding 35 overs, 9/50 in December. Alan McGilvray, on debut, spoiled O'Reilly's party by bowling Lisle Nagel. The match was drawn.

Not bad, Badcock. 'Jack' Badcock scored his maiden first class century for Tasmania aged 19, and Arthur Allsopp became the first player to score a century on debut for two states. Allsopp made one for NSW in 1928–29, and 123 for Victoria in the win against Tasmania over Christmas.

First women's Test. England defeated Australia by nine wickets in the first women's Test match at the 'Gabba in December.

Bradman out at last. Don Bradman is out for the first time since Clarrie Grimmett got him – 517 runs ago. Since that 90 v SA, Bradman made 187 not out and 77 not out against Victoria, and in January made 253 against Queensland. On 139 he passed 1000 runs in a season for a record sixth time.

NZ tour off. With the 1934 team to England on the water, the NZ Cricket Council has declined an offer of a visit from a team to have been captained by Vic Richardson, as it lacked drawcards. The tour was to have taken place in March–April.

Ironmonger's last match. Bert 'Dainty' Ironmonger retired after the NSW v Victoria game in January, playing his 85th and last first class match at the age of 51 years and 298 days. He had taken 464 first class wickets at an average of 21.50.

Spin is the king with series in balance

Joy at last for Bill O'Reilly as substitute fielder Charles Barnett catches Leyland (153) in the third Test at Old Trafford.

Manchester, July 10. It has been a time of cricketing convention so far in this Test series. There has been fine batting, but none of the searing double and triple centuries that have dominated and shaped past games. Indeed, even Don Bradman has been subdued (he has not yet made a 50) and the Australian batting has been carried by the likes of Stan McCabe, Bill Brown and Arthur Chipperfield. England has had fine efforts from Maurice Leyland, Les Ames and Patsy Hendren.

The dominant factor so far has been the bowling, and the efforts on both sides have left the teams at one game all and the series poised for a desperate finish.

In the first Test it was the Australians who carried the day.

England was set with 379 to win after spinner Clarrie Grimmett and Bill O'Reilly had taken nine first-innings wickets.

The final innings saw O'Reilly switch ends to allow Grimmett to attack a fancied dust spot. O'Reilly hit similar pay dirt from the other end. He made the ball 'bite like a whiting' as he took 7/54.

In the second Test Hedley Verity displayed the art of left-arm ortho-dox spin as Australia was caught on a sticky after England had made 440. Australia had got to 2/192, with Bill Brown on 103, when overnight rain changed the face of things on the third day. Verity took 14 wickets for 80 runs, six in the last hour, to claim a crushing victory for England. Australia had reeled to 284 in the first innings

and 118 in the second. Verity bowled with perfect length and direction, and from his height he made the ball bounce chest-high off the damaged pitch.

The third Test was more of a batsman's affair as the sun blazed down on Old Trafford Manchester. Australia looked likely early, as O'Reilly took three wickets, Cyril Walters, Bob Wyatt and Walter Hammond, in four balls. Hendren desperately staved off the hat-trick and then went on to 132 and a partnership with Maurice Leyland (153) that took the score to 5/340. England made 627.

Australia, thanks to McCabe (137), Brown (72) and Bill Woodfull (73), scored 441 to put a win out of reach for England, and keep the series square.

Many hands on deck at the ABC as Charles Moses (sitting left) tells the radio public what's happening in the Test match.

Bradman seals the Ashes

Bradman takes a first-ball four from Bill Bowes at Headingley during the fourth Test, and Australia's fortune is restored.

London, Aug. 22. Don Bradman has emerged from a comparatively quiet period with the bat to reveal all his old splendour and wrest the Test series and the Ashes from England at the Oval.

Even Bradman's team-mates were worried as the usual flow of runs dried up. Bradman had scored only 137 in five innings in the first three Tests.

He has more than made up for his run of outs. In the drawn fourth Test at Leeds he had his usual treat for the Yorkshire crowd, scoring 304 to match his 334 in 1930.

It was 47 minutes slower than the 1930 whirlwind, and there was no 300 in a day, but it was no less authoritative for that.

Bradman had to weather some hostile bowling at the start, as Australia was in a tight position 3/39. Bill Bowes had just got Bert Oldfield and Bill Woodfull out for ducks.

There was a hush over the ground, as Bradman faced the first ball, and a great roar as he moved right behind it and drove it off his toes wide of mid-on for four. The Australian dressing room was all smiles.

With Bill Ponsford (181) Bradman moved the score to 427 and Australia was safe, with a first-innings score of 584 in reply to England's 200. Rain on the last day was all that saved England.

Ponsford and Bradman did it again in the fifth Test with a second-wicket partnership of 451, a record for any wicket in Test cricket. Bradman's 244 took 316 minutes,

Australia was in a tight position the time of the partnership, while opener Ponsford was at the wicket for 460 minutes and was out when the score had reached 574.

Ponsford was out in the same fashion as in the fourth Test, hit wicket, when those who knew his play thought he was certain to stay, in what may possibly be his last match, and top Bradman's Test-record 334.

Australia closed at 701 and, with time to spare in this timeless Ashes-deciding Test, added 327 in the second innings, but only needed four days for the job. England could only manage 321 and 145 and was beaten by 562 runs.

Clarrie Grimmett capped off a great season in tandem with his fellow leggie Bill O'Reilly, taking 5/64 in England's short-lived last innings.

Bodyline echo

Nottingham, Aug. 13. With a packed crowd cheering him along, Nottingham's unforgiving and unreconstructed bodyline bowler Bill Voce bowled embarrassing 'scone balls' to a leg-theory field against the touring Australians.

Bill Woodfull, still in his pads after having batted throughout the onslaught, went straight to the Notts secretary and told him the Australians would not play if Voce took the field in the second innings. Voce developed a 'leg strain' and did not take the field, while the Australians were hooted and jeered.

The Australians meet the King at Balmoral Castle, Scotland.

Don Bradman is gravely ill: anxious nation awaits news

London, Sep. 20. Australia's batting hero Don Bradman is gravely ill in hospital, suffering with post-operative complications after the removal of an appendix several days ago.

The news of Bradman's illness has swept all other matters into second place on the front pages of newspapers in both Australia and England.

The King has asked for regular bulletins on his progress, and many would-be donors have phoned the Park Lane nursing home, offering blood.

Bradman, was diagnosed with a gangrenous appendix after he became ill and suffered acute pain at the team hotel. After consulting a local doctor, he was operated on by a distinguished Australian-born surgeon, Sir Douglas Shields.

The Sydney Morning Herald *reports.*

Arrangements have been made for Bradman's wife Jessie to go immediately to London by ship.

The aviator Sir Charles Kingsford Smith offered to fly her to London if need be, but encouraging news several days after the operation has convinced her to go by ship. She did fly to Perth to catch the *Maloja* just before it sailed, with the trip put at her disposal by the P & O shipping company.

Bradman, however, is not out of danger, although a drop in temperature is indicating improvement. He is extremely weak and feverish, and has been in a sleepy state for several days.

Bradman has been the second appendicitis sufferer among the Australians, as all-rounder Ern Bromley was forced to withdraw from the team earlier in the tour.

Bradman's next season in Australia looks in doubt.

Woodfull was 'the great unbowlable'

Bill Woodfull was loved by his players. He was the skipper, and they trusted him to see them through the toughest situation.

Bill O'Reilly wrote of that testing time of bodyline: 'As I made my diffident way from the dressing room door, my captain, Woodfull, God bless him, said, "Listen carefully, Tiger, I want you, above all, not to get hit." What a relief! Could any shivering batsman ever have been presented with a more reassuring exit than that? I have always been quick to offer him my undying gratitude for those few kind words in my biggest moment of crisis.'

The bodyline series was Woodfull's time of crisis and he came through it well, with example, courage, dignity and moral fury over the treatment meted out to his men. He had to lead them through it without flinching. In the Adelaide Test Woodfull carried his bat through the second innings, making 73 not out in 'four hours of grinding patience and weariness and unsubmissive courage ... avoiding the bumpers when he could and letting them hit him when he couldn't,' according to Ronald Mason in *Ashes in the Mouth*, the story of the Bodyline tour.

Woodfull's words, albeit supposed to be private, to England manager 'Plum' Warner – 'There are two teams out there, but only one of them is playing cricket' – are probably the best known of all cricket quotations.

They were a turning point for the better in Anglo–Australian cricket relations as they began the clearing of the air when the very game was endangered.

Woodfull led his team on the next tour of England, with such diplomacy and assurance that it seemed that bodyline never happened. But he quickly moved to protect his men when it surfaced again in a 1934 game against Nottingham, threatening to leave the field of play if Bill Voce came out in the second innings.

His captaincy was so important that it might be forgotten that he was one of Australia's most consistent and effective opening batman, who made more runs (2300 in 35 Tests) than his more celebrated partner Bill Ponsford (2122 in 29 Tests).

They dominated the scene in Victoria, with Woodfull as captain from 1927 until he and Ponsford both retired with a benefit match

Woodfull: the unbowlable batsman.

at the MCG in November 1934. Typically, he yielded the State captaincy to Jack Ryder in 1928–29 series, when Ryder was chosen as captain of the Australian team.

William Maldon Woodfull came from the small town of Maldon in central Victoria. He was a heavy-set man who as a youth suffered from muscular problems which prevented war service. He came to cricket late, playing in local teams, but his application and high scoring soon had him playing in Melbourne and in the Victorian team in 1921–22 at the age of 24.

He made his entrance in Test cricket in 1926, when he was said to be the last man chosen for the England tour. He was the highest runmaker on that tour, with 1809 at an average of 53.5, and he let his presence be felt early with 141 in his third Test innings.

He was not a pretty batsman, with his short backlift and pushing shots, but he was so difficult to dislodge that he became known as 'the great unbowlable'.

For Victoria he made the 13, 392 runs at an average of 65.00. Of his era only Ponsford made more, 13,819 at 65.18.

He had to be talked into taking the Australian captaincy when Jack Ryder was displaced in 1930.

Woodfull retired after the 1934 series, having won back the Ashes. He became headmaster of Melbourne High School.

After having refused a knighthood for services to cricket (he apparently said he wouldn't accept it for mere cricket), he was was awarded the OBE for services to education. He died in 1965, aged 67.

FIRST TEST 1934 ENGLAND v AUSTRALIA
Nottingham. June 8, 9, 11, 12, 1934.
Toss: Australia. Australia won by 238 runs.

AUSTRALIA

WM Woodfull (c) c Verity b Farnes	26	b Farnes	2
WH Ponsford c Ames b Farnes	53	b Hammond	5
WA Brown lbw Geary	22	c Ames b Verity	73
DG Bradman c Hammond b Geary	29	c Ames b Farnes	25
SJ McCabe c Leyland b Farnes	65	c Hammond b Farnes	88
LS Darling b Verity	4	c Hammond b Farnes	14
AG Chipperfield c Ames b Farnes	99	c Hammond b Farnes	4
WAS Oldfield (+) c Hammond b Mitchell	20	not out	10
CV Grimmett b Geary	39 (10)	not out	3
WJ O'Reilly b Farnes	7 (9)	c Verity b Geary	18
TW Wall not out	0		
EXTRAS (B 4, LB 5, NB 1)	10	(B 22, LB 9)	31
TOTAL	374	8 dec	273

FOW 1st Inns: 77 88 125 146 153 234 281 355 374 374
FOW 2nd Inns: 2 32 69 181 219 231 244 267

Bowling: *First Innings*: Farnes 40.2-10-102-5, Geary 43-8-101-3, Hammond 13-4-29-0, Verity 34-9-65-1, Mitchell 21-4-62-1, Leyland 1-0-5-0. *Second Innings*: Farnes 25-3-77-5, Geary 23-5-46-1, Hammond 12-5-25-1, Verity 17-8-48-1, Mitchell 13-2-46-0.

ENGLAND

CF Walters (c) lbw Grimmett	17	b O'Reilly	46
H Sutcliffe c Chipperfield b Grimmett	62	c Chipperfield b O'Reilly	24
WR Hammond c McCabe b O'Reilly	25	st Oldfield b Grimmett	16
Nawab of Pataudi sr c McCabe b Wall	12	c Ponsford b Grimmett	10
M Leyland c & b Grimmett	6 (6)	c Oldfield b O'Reilly	18
EH Hendren b O'Reilly	79 (5)	c Chipperfield b O'Reilly	3
LEG Ames (+) c Wall b O'Reilly	7	b O'Reilly	12
G Geary st Oldfield b Grimmett	53	c Chipperfield b Grimmett	0
H Verity b O'Reilly	0	not out	0
K Farnes b Grimmett	1	c Oldfield b O'Reilly	0
TB Mitchell not out	1	lbw O'Reilly	4
EXTRAS (B 5)	5	(B 4, LB 3, NB 1)	8
TOTAL	268		141

FOW 1st Inns: 45 102 106 114 145 165 266 266 266 268
FOW 2nd Inns: 51 83 91 103 110 134 135 137 137 141

Bowling: *First Innings*: Wall 33-7-82-1, McCabe 7-2-7-0, Grimmett 58.3-24-81-5, O'Reilly 37-16-75-4, Chipperfield 3-0-18-0. *Second Innings*: Wall 13-2-27-0, McCabe 2-0-7-0, Grimmett 47-28-39-3, O'Reilly 41.4-24-54-7, Chipperfield 4-1-6-0.

Umpires: F Chester & A Dolphin

SECOND TEST 1934 ENGLAND v AUSTRALIA
Lord's Cricket Ground, London. June 22, 23, 25, 1934.
Toss: England. England won by an innings & 38 runs.

ENGLAND

CF Walters c Bromley b O'Reilly	82
H Sutcliffe lbw Chipperfield	20
WR Hammond c & b Chipperfield	2
EH Hendren c McCabe b Wall	13
RES Wyatt (c) c Oldfield b Chipperfield	33
M Leyland b Wall	109
LEG Ames (+) c Oldfield b McCabe	120
G Geary c Chipperfield b Wall	9
H Verity st Oldfield b Grimmett	29
K Farnes b Wall	1
WE Bowes not out	10
EXTRAS (LB 12)	12
TOTAL	440

FOW 1st Inns: 70 78 99 130 182 311 359 409 410 440

Bowling: *First Innings*: Wall 49-7-108-4, McCabe 18-3-38-1, Grimmett 53.3-13-102-1, O'Reilly 38-15-70-1, Chipperfield 34-10-91-3, Darling 6-2-19-0.

AUSTRALIA

WM Woodfull (c) b Bowes	22	c Hammond b Verity	43
WA Brown c Ames b Bowes	105	c Walters b Bowes	2
DG Bradman c & b Verity	36 (4)	c Ames b Verity	13
SJ McCabe c Hammond b Verity	34 (3)	c Hendren b Verity	19
LS Darling c Sutcliffe b Verity	0	b Hammond	10
AG Chipperfield not out	37	c Geary b Verity	14
EH Bromley c Geary b Verity	4	c & b Verity	1
WAS Oldfield (+) c Sutcliffe b Verity	23	lbw Verity	0
CV Grimmett b Bowes	9	c Hammond b Verity	0
WJ O'Reilly b Verity	4	not out	8
TW Wall lbw Verity	0	c Hendren b Verity	1
EXTRAS (B 1, LB 9)	10	(B 6, NB 1)	7
TOTAL	284		118

FOW 1st Inns: 68 141 203 204 205 218 258 273 284 284
FOW 2nd Inns: 10 43 57 94 94 95 95 95 112 118

Bowling: *First Innings*: Farnes 12-3-43-0, Bowes 31-5-98-3, Geary 22-4-56-0, Verity 36-15-61-7, Hammond 4-1-6-0, Leyland 4-1-10-0. *Second Innings*: Farnes 4-2-6-0, Bowes 14-4-24-1, Verity 22.3-8-43-8, Hammond 13-0-38-1.

Umpires: F Chester & J Hardstaff sr

THIRD TEST 1934 ENGLAND v AUSTRALIA
Old Trafford, Manchester. July 6, 7, 9, 10, 1934.
Toss: England. Match Drawn.

ENGLAND

CF Walters c Darling b O'Reilly	52	not out	50
H Sutcliffe c Chipperfield b O'Reilly	63	not out	69
RES Wyatt (c) b O'Reilly	0		
WR Hammond b O'Reilly	4		
EH Hendren c & b O'Reilly	132		
M Leyland c(S)BA Barnett b O'Reilly	153		
LEG Ames (+) c Ponsford b Grimmett	72		
JL Hopwood b O'Reilly	2		
GOB Allen b McCabe	61		
H Verity not out	60		
EW Clark not out	2		
EXTRAS (B 6, LB 18, W 2)	26	(B 2, LB 1, W 1)	4
TOTAL	9 dec 627		0 dec 123

FOW 1st Inns: 68 68 72 149 340 482 492 510 605
FOW 2nd Inns:

Bowling: *First Innings*: Wall 36-3-131-0, McCabe 32-3-98-1, Grimmett 57-20-122-1, O'Reilly 59-9-189-7, Chipperfield 7-0-29-0, Darling 10-0-32-0. *Second Innings*: Wall 9-0-31-0, McCabe 13-4-35-0, O'Reilly 13-4-25-0, Grimmett 17-5-28-0.

AUSTRALIA

WA Brown c Walters b Clark	72	c Hammond b Allen	0
WH Ponsford c Hendren b Hammond	12	not out	30
SJ McCabe c Verity b Hammond	137	not out	33
WM Woodfull (c) run out	73		
LS Darling b Verity	37		
DG Bradman c Ames b Hammond	30		
WAS Oldfield (+) c Wyatt b Verity	13		
AG Chipperfield c Walters b Verity	26		
CV Grimmett b Verity	0		
WJ O'Reilly not out	30		
TW Wall run out	18		
EXTRAS (B 20, LB 13, W 4, NB 6)	43	(B 1, LB 2)	3
TOTAL	491		1 for 66

FOW 1st Inns: 34 230 242 320 378 409 411 419 454 491
FOW 2nd Inns: 1

Bowling: *First Innings*: Clark 40-9-100-1, Allen 31-3-113-0, Hammond 28.3-6-111-3, Verity 53-24-78-4, Hopwood 38-20-46-0. *Second Innings*: Allen 6-0-23-1, Clark 4-1-16-0, Hopwood 9-5-16-0, Hammond 2-1-2-0, Verity 5-4-2-0, Hendren 1-0-4-0.

Umpires: J Hardstaff sr & FI Walden

FIFTH TEST 1934 ENGLAND v AUSTRALIA
Kennington Oval, London. August 18, 20, 21, 22, 1934.
Toss: Australia. Australia won by 562 runs.

AUSTRALIA

WA Brown b Clark	10	c Allen b Clark	1
WH Ponsford hit wicket b Allen	266	c Hammond b Clark	22
DG Bradman c Ames b Bowes	244	b Bowes	77
SJ McCabe b Allen	10	c Walters b Clark	70
WM Woodfull (c) b Bowes	49	b Bowes	13
AF Kippax lbw Bowes	28	c Walters b Clark	8
AG Chipperfield b Bowes	3	c Woolley b Clark	16
WAS Oldfield (+) not out	42	c Hammond b Bowes	0
CV Grimmett c Ames b Allen	7	c Hammond b Bowes	14
HI Ebeling b Allen	2	c Allen b Bowes	41
WJ O'Reilly b Clark	7	not out	15
EXTRAS (B 4, LB 14, W 2, NB 13)	33	(B 37, LB 8, W 1, NB 4)	50
TOTAL	701		327

FOW 1st Inns: 21 472 488 574 626 631 638 676 682 701
FOW 2nd Inns: 13 42 192 213 224 236 236 256 272 327

Bowling: *First Innings*: Bowes 38-2-164-4, Allen 34-5-170-4, Clark 37.2-4-110-2, Hammond 12-0-53-0, Verity 43-7-123-0, Wyatt 4-0-28-0, Leyland 3-0-20-0. *Second Innings*: Allen 16-2-63-0, Clark 20-1-98-5, Hammond 7-1-18-0, Verity 14-3-43-0, Bowes 11.3-3-55-5.

ENGLAND

CF Walters c Kippax b O'Reilly	64	b McCabe	1
H Sutcliffe c Oldfield b Grimmett	38	c McCabe b Grimmett	28
FE Woolley c McCabe b O'Reilly	4	c Ponsford b McCabe	0
WR Hammond c Oldfield b Ebeling	15	c & b O'Reilly	43
RES Wyatt (c) b Grimmett	17 (6)	c Ponsford b Grimmett	22
M Leyland b Grimmett	110 (5)	c Brown b Grimmett	17
LEG Ames (+) retired hurt	33		
GOB Allen b Ebeling	19 (7)	st Oldfield b Grimmett	26
H Verity b Ebeling	11 (8)	c McCabe b Grimmett	1
EW Clark not out	2	not out	2
WE Bowes	(9)	c Bradman b O'Reilly	2
EXTRAS (B 4, LB 3, NB 1)	8	(LB 1, NB 2)	3
TOTAL	8 for 321		9 for 145

FOW 1st Inns: 104 108 111 136 142 263 311 321
FOW 2nd Inns: 1 3 67 89 109 122 138 141 145

Bowling: *First Innings*: Ebeling 21-4-74-3, McCabe 6-1-21-0, Grimmett 49.3-13-103-3, O'Reilly 37-10-93-2, Chipperfield 4-0-22-0. *Second Innings*: Ebeling 10-5-15-0, McCabe 5-3-5-2, Grimmett 26.3-10-64-5, O'Reilly 22-9-58-2.

Umpires: F Chester & FI Walden

FOURTH TEST 1934 ENGLAND v AUSTRALIA
Headingley, Leeds. July 20, 21, 23, 24, 1934.
Toss: England. Match Drawn.

ENGLAND

CF Walters c & b Chipperfield	44	b O'Reilly	45
WW Keeton c Oldfield b O'Reilly	25	b Grimmett	12
WR Hammond b Wall	37	run out	20
EH Hendren b Chipperfield	29	lbw O'Reilly	42
RES Wyatt (c) st Oldfield b Grimmett	19	b Grimmett	44
M Leyland b O'Reilly	16	not out	49
LEG Ames (+) c Oldfield b Grimmett	9	c Brown b Grimmett	8
JL Hopwood lbw O'Reilly	8	not out	2
H Verity not out	4		
TB Mitchell st Oldfield b Grimmett	9		
WE Bowes c Ponsford b Grimmett	0		
EXTRAS (LB 2)	2	(B 1, LB 6)	7
TOTAL	200		6 for 229

FOW 1st Inns: 43 85 135 135 168 170 189 189 200 200
FOW 2nd Inns: 28 70 87 152 190 213

Bowling: *First Innings*: Wall 18-1-57-1, McCabe 4-2-3-0, Grimmett 30.4-11-57-4, O'Reilly 35-16-46-3, Chipperfield 18-6-35-2. *Second Innings*: Wall 14-5-36-0, McCabe 5-4-5-0, Grimmett 56.5-24-72-3, O'Reilly 51-25-88-2, Chipperfield 9-2-21-0.

AUSTRALIA

WA Brown b Bowes	15
WH Ponsford hit wicket b Verity	181
WAS Oldfield (+) c Ames b Bowes	0
WM Woodfull (c) b Bowes	0
DG Bradman b Bowes	304
SJ McCabe b Bowes	27
LS Darling b Bowes	12
AG Chipperfield c Wyatt b Verity	1
CV Grimmett run out	15
WJ O'Reilly not out	11
TW Wall lbw Verity	1
EXTRAS (B 8, LB 9)	17
TOTAL	584

FOW 1st Inns: 37 39 39 427 517 550 551 557 574 584

Bowling: *First Innings*: Bowes 50-13-142-6, Hammond 29-5-82-0, Mitchell 23-1-117-0, Verity 46.5-15-113-3, Hopwood 30-7-93-0, Leyland 5-0-20-0.

Umpires: A Dolphin & J Hardstaff sr

Australian Averages

1934 ENGLAND v AUSTRALIA

AUSTRALIA	M	Inn	NO	Runs	H.S	Avrge	Ct	St	Overs	Mds	Runs	Wkt	Avrge
Bradman, DG	5	8	-	758	304	94.75	1	-	-	-	-	-	-
Bromley, EH	1	2	-	5	4	2.50	1	-	-	-	-	-	-
Brown, WA	5	9	-	300	105	33.33	2	-	-	-	-	-	-
Chipperfield, AG	5	8	1	200	99	28.57	8	-	79.0	19	222	5	44.40
Darling, LS	4	6	-	77	37	12.83	1	-	16.0	2	51	-	-
Ebeling, HI	1	2	-	43	41	21.50	-	-	31.0	9	89	3	29.67
Grimmett, CV	5	8	1	87	39	12.43	1	-	396.3	148	668	25	26.72
Kippax, AF	1	2	-	36	28	18.00	1	-	-	-	-	-	-
McCabe, SJ	5	9	1	483	137	60.38	6	-	92.0	22	219	4	54.75
O'Reilly, WJ	5	8	4	100	30*	25.00	2	-	333.4	128	698	28	24.93
Oldfield, WAS	5	8	2	108	42*	18.00	8	6	-	-	-	-	-
Ponsford, WH	4	7	-	569	266	94.83	5	-	-	-	-	-	-
Wall, TW	4	5	1	20	18	5.00	1	-	172.0	25	472	6	78.67
Woodfull, WM	5	8	-	228	73	28.50	-	-	-	-	-	-	-

English Averages

1934 ENGLAND v AUSTRALIA

ENGLAND	M	Inn	NO	Runs	H.S	Avrge	Ct	St	Overs	Mds	Runs	Wkt	Avrge
Allen, GOB	2	3	-	106	61	35.33	2	-	87.0	10	369	5	73.80
Ames, LEG	5	7	1	261	120	43.50	10	-	-	-	-	-	-
Bowes, WE	3	3	1	12	10*	6.00	-	-	144.3	27	483	19	25.42
Clark, EW	2	3	3	6	2*	-	-	-	101.2	15	324	8	40.50
Farnes, K	2	3	-	2	1	0.67	-	-	81.2	18	228	10	22.80
Geary, G	2	3	-	62	53	20.67	2	-	88.0	17	203	4	50.75
Hammond, WR	5	8	-	162	43	20.25	12	-	120.3	23	364	5	72.80
Hendren, EH	4	6	-	298	132	49.67	3	-	1.0	-	4	-	-
Hopwood, JL	2	3	1	12	8	6.00	-	-	77.0	32	155	-	-
Keeton, WW	1	2	-	37	25	18.50	-	-	-	-	-	-	-
Leyland, M	5	8	1	478	153	68.29	1	-	13.0	1	55	-	-
Mitchell, TB	2	3	1	14	9	7.00	-	-	57.0	7	225	1	225.00
Nawab of Pataudi sr	1	2	-	12	12	11.00	-	-	-	-	-	-	-
Sutcliffe, H	4	7	1	304	69*	50.67	2	-	-	-	-	-	-
Verity, H	5	7	3	103	60*	25.75	5	-	271.2	93	576	24	24.00
Walters, CF	5	9	1	401	82	50.13	5	-	-	-	-	-	-
Woolley, FE	1	2	-	4	4	2.00	1	-	-	-	-	-	-
Wyatt, RES	4	6	-	135	44	22.50	2	-	4.0	-	28	-	-

Bradmania

Across three decades Don Bradman was more than a famous cricketer. To the public eye he was the spirit of Australia. His deeds, his humble background, his modesty and good manners captured the hearts of Australians and helped to carry the country through the Depression of the early 30s. A fever of Bradmania grew around him, and every appearance, on or off the cricket field, drew throngs of people. He remained set in his goals and unshaken in his character, but his obligation to the people took him into strange circumstances – into songwriting, film and theatre appearances, writing, press and radio interviews and advertising. His name was a guarantee of success.

The young Bradman in the 1920s, slight and good-looking, his smile masking an iron will, discipline and immense physical endurance.

Toby jugs of many varieties carried the features of the super batsman.

Commercial potteries found a saleable image in Bradman for the mantlepiece.

Bradman, a good pianist, wrote a work that seemed appropriate to his life and outlook – 'Every Day is a Rainbow Day for Me'.

Chilling news. Bradman's scores made headlines.

Bradman's power is evident in this off-drive.

A press coup. Words on the Tests sold papers.

The Bradman bat; light and beautifully balanced.

At ease in the crowd. Bradman and rival England captain Walter Hammond take the field.

1934–35

AUSTRALIAN DOMESTIC

Vics still Shield leaders

Batsmen Jack Fingleton and Bill Brown: the outstanding openers of this season.

Adelaide, Feb. 19. SA defeated Victoria in the last Sheffield Shield match of the season by 107 runs, but Victoria had already secured the trophy with five outright wins from the previous five games. This was an outstanding result for Victoria given the retirements of great servants such as Bill Woodfull, Bill Ponsford and Bert Ironmonger.

Victoria defeated NSW twice despite NSW having the top opening pair of Jack Fingleton and Bill Brown. Their stands of 249, 124, 64, 130, 145 and 177 have been very consistent.

Fingleton and Brown were the outstanding batsmen in a season bereft of Bradman. The figures of ordinary mortals were revealed –

Fingleton 880 runs at 58.66 and Brown 683 at 45.53. Victoria's Len Darling was third in the aggregates – with 634 runs at 70.44 from two fewer matches.

Against Victoria in the second match in January, Brown and Fingleton only managed stands of eight and nine, and Victoria won by 213 runs. This result was mainly due to the extraordinary performance of 'Chuck' Fleetwood-Smith who took 15 wickets, quite inexpensively, the first Victorian to achieve the feat in a Shield game. His figures were 7/113 and 8/113.

Fleetwood-Smith took eight wickets in a match against SA, and became the first bowler to take 60 wickets in a Shield season.

The remnants of bodyline: Harold Larwood's worn-out boots.

Big send-off for Ponsford, Woodfull

Melbourne, Nov. 20. Bill Woodfull and Bill Ponsford showed that they will be missed from Australian first class cricket when they shared a bright century stand for Woodfull's XI in a their benefit match and final first class game. Woodfull made 111 and Ponsford 83 in a stand of 132 before 22,637 of their supporters and well-wishers at the MCG.

A total attendance of 43,878 raised £1042 for each player.

Woodfull's XI defeated Richardson's XI by seven wickets, with Bill Brown knocking up a 102 in the second innings, despite a nice double by 'Jack' Badcock of 64 and 87 and 107 from Vic Richardson for his team.

New stand at MCG

Melbourne, Dec. 1. The Melbourne Cricket Club has agreed to spend £100,000 on a new Southern Stand at the MCG, increasing ground capacity to 100,000.

Much criticism has been made of the ground when it contains big crowds and one Member of Parliament has suggested that if there was another Larwood in the 1936–37 England team there would also be a riot. Ladies, who are increasingly in attendance at the cricket, find it uncomfortable.

The new stand will be 1250 feet in length and house 35,000 spectators in better comfort than before, and contain dressing rooms for cricketers and footballers, and refreshments booths.

Badcock a hit in SA

Adelaide, Dec. 27. Ex-Tasmanian prodigy 'Jack' Badcock made a quiet debut for SA with innings of 5 and 17 against NSW in November, but has repaid some of the faith SACA has shown in him with a fine 137 in SA's record score of 644 against Queensland. Vic Richardson (185), Carl Nitchske (116) and Roy Lonergan (137) also hit hundreds in this innings.

Clarrie Grimmett took 16/289 in the match, the best Shield return since George Giffen's 16/168 in 1894–95.

Badcock and his lawyer, the Tasmanian delegate to the Board of Control Harold Bushby, struck a deal with SA's delegate Harry Hodgetts last season at the same time as Don Bradman signed on.

Badcock's batting will help to compensate for Bradman's absence from the team while he recovers from illness.

Vic Richardson leads by example

Kimberley, Feb. 1. Undoubtedly one of the reasons why the Australian tour of South Africa was so successful was because it was so happy – 'the happiest I was ever on,' said Bill O'Reilly. And the reason was the captain, veteran Victor York Richardson.

Although a trifle past his prime as a batsman at 41, as a leader he has proved the most successful captain since Warwick Armstrong, and less prickly with local officialdom on tour than was the 'Big Ship'.

Only once was there a problem. Playing against Griqualand West in the Kimberley on an extremely hot afternoon in February, the bowlers wanted a beer with drinks. An official in the dressing room refused to 'allow beer on the field of play'. 12th man Arthur Chipperfield came and spoke to Richardson who was on the field. Richardson went inside, and a few minutes later the bowlers got their beers.

No wonder the players like him.

Vic Richardson played 14 of the 16 matches and made 443 runs at 34 – but he played only 14 innings. The dominant Australian team rarely had to bat twice, and sometimes didn't need anyone much after Fingleton, Brown, McCabe and Chipperfield.

The Richardson-led team was undefeated on tour, winning 13 of 16 matches, ten by an innings.

Vic Richardson: happy Captain

South Africa in a spin

The Australians were undefeated in South Africa.in a series on turf wickets.

Durban, March 3. Australia took just two days to wrap up its first full Test series played in South Africa, winning by an innings and six runs.

The winner of this Test series, the first to be played in South Africa entirely on turf wickets, was to become the champion of the British Empire, as the South African part-timers had just beaten England at home and away.

Due to untimely deaths, retirements and cricket exhaustion, South Africa was never able to field its best team.

Australia won the series 4–0, with a draw in the second Test at Old Wanderers in Johannesburg, when Dudley Nourse hit his magnificent 231 in the second innings, leaving Australia 399 to win.

Stan McCabe played an attacking innings the like of which has rarely been seen in attempting this big total. He had made 189 not out, in 165 minutes when the South African captain Herbie Wade appealed against the light – a storm was brewing, it was dark and his fieldsmen couldn't see McCabe's flashing strokes. They were in danger. The appeal at 2.40 p.m. was upheld, in good humour, and a few minutes later the rain came down. The match was abandoned as a draw at 4.55.

Australia would have won had the weather not intervened.

Aside from the batting of McCabe, Jack Fingleton and Bill Brown also scored over 400 runs and provided the foundation for Australian dominance.

Don's back

Adelaide, March 3. Don Bradman began his recuperation by playing his first match for SA against an English MCC XI on its way to a Test tour of New Zealand with a quiet 15 and 50. The MCC won two matches, including one against an Australian XI, drew two and lost one. Bradman improved, making 117 against NSW, 233 against Queensland, then 357 against Victoria. In the second match against Victoria SA won the Shield and the match by an innings and 190 runs, thanks, not to Bradman., but to 'Jack' Badcock's 325. Bradman topped the lot against Tasmania with 369 – beating Clem Hill's old SA record of 365.

The MCC sent Christmas cards home from Australia on their way to New Zealand.

QUICK SINGLES

Olympic cricket. On their way to Perth to play WA, and then tour South Africa, the Australian XI train stopped at Kalgoorlie where the Mayor at a civic reception, said 'And now I want to wish you and your team, Mr Chipperfield, all the best of successes at the Olympic Games.'

Grave visit. Before playing Natal in Durban, the Australians took time to visit the grave of Australian fast bowler and Light Horseman Jack Ferris on November 17, the anniversary of his death from enteric fever there during the Boer War.

Sporting gesture. In the Transvaal game, Australia needed one run to win when rain fell so heavily players could not see the ball. Bowler Eiulf Nupen sportingly bowled four wides to give Australia the win.

Fast bowler's lament. Australian quick bowler, Ernie McCormick, after playing at Cape Town in December asked where he could get a wreath. Asked what he wanted it for, he replied 'I want to lay it on the Newlands pitch – it's the deadest thing I've ever struck.'

Underarm tactics. Against Transvaal in December, Bill O'Reilly was advised by a member of the big crowd at Johannesburg to bowl underarm to Bruce Mitchell who had taken 147 minutes to make 38. Instead 'Tiger' bowled him a perfect leg-spinner which pitched outside leg and hit off.

Grimmett's record. When Clarrie Grimmett caught and bowled Dudley Nourse in the second innings of the third Test at Newlands, Cape Town, he became Test cricket's leading wicket-taker. He passed Syd Barnes' 189, a record that had stood since 1914.

Flying visit. In February before the fourth Test some Australian players broke the Board of Control contract by flying at dawn in a Junkers aeroplane from Johannesburg to the Kruger National Park 200 miles away to spend the day looking at lions, before returning safely that night.

New ball game. As a benefit for the family of 'Jock' Cameron, who tragically died before the series began, the Australians agreed to play baseball against Transvaal in March. They won 12/5. Stan McCabe made three 'safe hits' and commented 'How can you miss, they're all full tosses.'

That man Clarrie again. Grimmett takes 44 wickets at 14.59 against South Africa, the second-highest Test haul since England's Sydney Barnes took 49 (at 10.93) also against South Africa in 1913–14.

FIRST TEST 1935–36 SOUTH AFRICA v AUSTRALIA
Kingsmead, Durban. December 14, 16, 17, 18, 1935.
Toss: South Africa. Australia won by 9 wkts.

SOUTH AFRICA

B Mitchell b Fleetwood-Smith	19	run out	19
IJ Siedle lbw O'Reilly	31	b Grimmett	59
EAB Rowan c & b Grimmett	66	b Grimmett	49
KG Viljoen b Fleetwood-Smith	4	b Fleetwood-Smith	1
AD Nourse b McCormick	30	c Fingleton b O'Reilly	91
HF Wade (c) b O'Reilly	31	lbw O'Reilly	11
EL Dalton st Oldfield b Fleetwood-Smith	4	c Darling b Grimmett	5
ABC Langton b Grimmett	0	not out	12
F Nicholson (+) not out	16	b O'Reilly	0
RJ Crisp b Fleetwood-Smith	35	b O'Reilly	16
JB Robertson b O'Reilly	9	c Richardson b O'Reilly	9
EXTRAS (B 1, LB 2)	3	(B 8, LB 1, NB 1)	10
TOTAL	248		282

FOW 1st Inns: 45 59 71 108 168 185 186 187 234 248
FOW 2nd Inns: 65 86 89 207 233 242 242 242 263 282

Bowling: *First Innings*: McCabe 10-1-28-0, McCormick 15-4-50-1, Grimmett 28-10-48-2, O'Reilly 33.2-17-55-3, Fleetwood-Smith 28-6-64-4. *Second Innings*: McCormick 6-0-26-0, McCabe 2-0-5-0, Grimmett 52-20-83-3, O'Reilly 17-5-49-5, Fleetwood-Smith 37-7-101-1, Chipperfield 1-0-8-0.

AUSTRALIA

WA Brown c Langton b Robertson	66	c Crisp b Dalton	55
JHW Fingleton c Nicholson b Crisp	2	not out	36
SJ McCabe c Rowan b Langton	149	not out	7
LS Darling c Viljoen b Crisp	60		
VY Richardson (c) b Langton	2		
AG Chipperfield b Crisp	109		
WAS Oldfield (+) lbw Langton	0		
WJ O'Reilly c Rowan b Robertson	11		
CV Grimmett c Nicholson b Robertson	15		
EL McCormick not out	2		
LO Fleetwood-Smith b Langton	1		
EXTRAS (B 5, LB 2, W 1, NB 4)	12	(B 3, LB 1)	4
TOTAL	429		1 for 102

FOW 1st Inns: 12 173 269 277 299 299 329 412 428 429
FOW 2nd Inns: 93

Bowling: *First Innings*: Crisp 36-7-87-3, Langton 48.2-10-113-4, Robertson 55-11-143-3, Dalton 6-0-25-0, Mitchell 17-2-49-0. *Second Innings*: Crisp 6-1-10-0, Langton 9-0-29-0, Robertson 13-4-24-0, Mitchell 7-0-23-0, Dalton 1.3-0-12-1.

Umpires: JC Collings & WJ Routledge

THIRD TEST 1935–36 SOUTH AFRICA v AUSTRALIA
Newlands, Cape Town. January 1 (no play), 2, 3, 4, 1936.
Toss: Australia. Australia won by an innings & 78 runs.

AUSTRALIA

WA Brown c & b Robertson	121
JHW Fingleton c Wade b Balaskas	112
SJ McCabe c & b Balaskas	0
LS Darling lbw Balaskas	12
VY Richardson (c) lbw Crisp	14
AG Chipperfield b Langton	30
WAS Oldfield (+) b Robertson	8
CV Grimmett not out	30
WJ O'Reilly b Balaskas	17
EL McCormick not out	0
LO Fleetwood-Smith	
EXTRAS (B 14, LB 4)	18
TOTAL	8 dec 362

FOW 1st Inns: 233 235 251 259 299 313 313 361

Bowling: *First Innings*: Crisp 14-2-30-1, Langton 30-2-94-1, Robertson 29-8-75-2, Balaskas 38-1-126-4, Mitchell 4-0-19-0.

SOUTH AFRICA

IJ Siedle lbw Grimmett	1	b Grimmett	59
HF Wade (c) c & b McCabe	0	lbw Fleetwood-Smith	31
EAB Rowan b Grimmett	12	c Richardson b O'Reilly	19
B Mitchell c Fingleton b O'Reilly	14 (5)	b Grimmett	0
KG Viljoen st Oldfield b Fleetwood-Smith	14 (6)	c O'Reilly b Grimmett	23
AD Nourse not out	44 (4)	c & b Grimmett	25
F Nicholson (+) b Fleetwood-Smith	0	c & b O'Reilly	4
ABC Langton b Grimmett	3	b O'Reilly	4
RJ Crisp b Grimmett	0	c Richardson b O'Reilly	0
XC Balaskas b Grimmett	0 (11)	b Grimmett	2
JB Robertson run out	1 (10)	not out	12
EXTRAS (LB 13)	13	(B 1, LB 2)	3
TOTAL	102		182

FOW 1st Inns: 0 12 21 29 86 88 95 95 95 102
FOW 2nd Inns: 87 97 137 137 139 146 156 156 174 182

Bowling: *First Innings*: McCormick 2-1-3-0, McCabe 2-1-9-1, O'Reilly 11-4-24-1, Grimmett 17-4-32-5, Fleetwood-Smith 6.2-0-21-2. *Second Innings*: McCormick 2-0-8-0, Grimmett 36.4-17-56-5, Fleetwood-Smith 24-4-80-1, O'Reilly 25-15-35-4.

Umpires: RGA Ashman & JC Collings

SECOND TEST 1935–36 SOUTH AFRICA v AUSTRALIA
Old Wanderers, Johannesburg. December 24, 26, 27, 28, 1935.
Toss: South Africa. Match Drawn.

SOUTH AFRICA

B Mitchell c Oldfield b McCormick	8 (4)	c Oldfield b McCabe	45
IJ Siedle c Chipperfield b McCormick	22	b Grimmett	34
EAB Rowan lbw Grimmett	38	lbw Grimmett	13
AD Nourse b McCormick	0 (5)	c McCormick b McCabe	231
AW Briscoe b O'Reilly	15 (6)	b McCormick	16
HF Wade (c) b O'Reilly	0 (1)	lbw Grimmett	30
ABC Langton c Fingleton b O'Reilly	7 (8)	b McCormick	16
F Nicholson (+) st Oldfield b Grimmett	27 (7)	lbw Fleetwood-Smith	29
RJ Crisp b Grimmett	8	b O'Reilly	35
JB Robertson b O'Reilly	17	b McCormick	3
EG Bock not out	9	not out	2
EXTRAS (LB 6)	6	(B 13, LB 19, NB 5)	37
TOTAL	157		491

FOW 1st Inns: 11 46 50 68 70 78 112 126 139 157
FOW 2nd Inns: 50 89 90 219 291 397 440 454 466 491

Bowling: *First Innings*: McCormick 16-5-36-3, O'Reilly 20.2-9-54-4, Grimmett 15-5-29-3, McCabe 6-2-11-0, Fleetwood-Smith 6-2-21-0. *Second Innings*: McCormick 26-3-129-3, O'Reilly 35.3-15-91-1, Grimmett 58-28-111-3, McCabe 9-1-30-2, Fleetwood-Smith 21-5-93-1.

AUSTRALIA

JHW Fingleton c & b Langton	62	b Mitchell	40
WA Brown c Crisp b Robertson	51	c Nicholson b Crisp	6
SJ McCabe c Robertson b Langton	34	not out	189
LS Darling run out	42	not out	37
VY Richardson (c) b Langton	2		
AG Chipperfield c Rowan b Langton	0		
WAS Oldfield (+) c Briscoe b Mitchell	40		
CV Grimmett b Mitchell	7		
WJ O'Reilly b Mitchell	0		
EL McCormick b Mitchell	4		
LO Fleetwood-Smith not out	5		
EXTRAS (LB 3)	3	(LB 2)	2
TOTAL	250		2 for 274

FOW 1st Inns: 105 127 168 170 174 209 241 241 242 250
FOW 2nd Inns: 17 194

Bowling: *First Innings*: Crisp 15-1-49-0, Langton 32-6-85-4, Mitchell 7.3-0-26-4, Bock 14-2-49-0, Robertson 13-0-38-1. *Second Innings*: Crisp 17-3-62-1, Langton 22-6-54-0, Mitchell 15-1-73-1, Robertson 13-3-41-0, Bock 9-0-42-0.

Umpires: RGA Ashman & JC Collings

FOURTH TEST 1935–36 SOUTH AFRICA v AUSTRALIA
Old Wanderers, Johannesburg. February 15, 17, 1936.
Toss: South Africa. Australia won by an innings & 184 runs.

SOUTH AFRICA

IJ Siedle lbw Grimmett	44	b McCormick	0
HF Wade (c) b McCormick	39	b McCormick	2
AD Nourse c Oldfield b McCormick	3 (5)	b McCormick	3
KG Viljoen b O'Reilly	33 (3)	st Oldfield b Grimmett	7
RL Harvey b O'Reilly	5 (6)	c Darling b Grimmett	17
B Mitchell st Oldfield b Grimmett	16 (4)	not out	48
ABC Langton lbw O'Reilly	7 (8)	lbw Grimmett	9
F Nicholson (+) b Grimmett	0 (7)	b Grimmett	0
EP Nupen b O'Reilly	1	b Grimmett	6
XC Balaskas lbw O'Reilly	0	c O'Brien b Grimmett	3
EQ Davies not out	0	c Oldfield b Grimmett	3
EXTRAS (LB 5, W 4)	9	(LB 3)	3
TOTAL	157		98

FOW 1st Inns: 81 91 96 128 137 153 154 155 157 157
FOW 2nd Inns: 0 5 21 24 49 50 76 82 82 98

Bowling: *First Innings*: McCormick 11-0-37-2, McCabe 5-2-21-0, Grimmett 26.4-6-70-3, O'Reilly 21-11-20-5. *Second Innings*: McCormick 12-2-28-3, McCabe 2-1-1-0, Grimmett 19.5-9-40-7, O'Reilly 10-3-26-0.

AUSTRALIA

JHW Fingleton c Langton b Davies	108
WA Brown lbw Langton	34
SJ McCabe b Davies	40
LPJ O'Brien b Balaskas	59
WAS Oldfield (+) c Balaskas b Nupen	44
LS Darling c Wade b Balaskas	16
AG Chipperfield lbw Balaskas	39
VY Richardson (c) b Davies	21
CV Grimmett lbw Balaskas	4
WJ O'Reilly not out	56
EL McCormick c Mitchell b Davies	13
EXTRAS (B 1, LB 4)	5
TOTAL	439

FOW 1st Inns: 99 179 184 260 282 333 352 368 370 439

Bowling: *First Innings*: Davies 24.4-4-75-4, Langton 30-5-88-1, Balaskas 44-4-165-4, Nupen 14-1-53-1, Mitchell 14-1-53-0.

Umpires: RGA Ashman & JC Collings

FIFTH TEST 1935–36 SOUTH AFRICA v AUSTRALIA
Kingsmead, Durban. February 28, 29, March 2, 3, 1936.
Toss: South Africa. Australia won by an innings & 6 runs.

SOUTH AFRICA

IJ Siedle c Fingleton b Grimmett 36	c Brown b Grimmett 46
HF Wade (c) c Richardson b Grimmett 26	b O'Reilly 25
B Mitchell c & b Grimmett 10	not out 72
AD Nourse lbw Grimmett 50	b O'Reilly 41
KG Viljoen c Chipperfield b McCormick 56	lbw Grimmett 25
RL Harvey c Oldfield b McCormick 28	c Richardson b Grimmett 1
ABC Langton st Oldfield b Grimmett 1	b Grimmett 3
XC Balaskas st Oldfield b Grimmett 2	c Richardson b Grimmett 0
RJ Crisp b Grimmett 0 (11)	c Richardson b O'Reilly 0
EA Van der Merwe (+) not out 7 (9)	c Richardson b Grimmett 0
EQ Davies b McCormick 0 (10)	c Richardson b O'Reilly 2
EXTRAS (B 1, LB 5) 6	(B 5, LB 7) 12
TOTAL 222	227

FOW 1st Inns: 44 57 124 125 178 183 199 199 220 222
FOW 2nd Inns: 63 73 146 196 206 212 220 220 227 227

Bowling: *First Innings*: McCormick 20.1-8-37-3, McCabe 7-0-20-0, Grimmett 45-18-100-7, O'Reilly 37-15-59-0. *Second Innings*: McCormick 15-1-64-0, McCabe 2-0-11-0, Grimmett 48-23-73-6, O'Reilly 40.1-18-47-4, Chipperfield 8-1-20-0.

AUSTRALIA

JHW Fingleton b Crisp 118
WA Brown c Langton b Mitchell 84
SJ McCabe c & b Mitchell 1
LPJ O'Brien c Van der Merwe b Balaskas 48
LS Darling lbw Mitchell 62
AG Chipperfield c Balaskas b Mitchell 18
VY Richardson (c) b Crisp 45
WAS Oldfield (+) c Crisp b Langton 29
CV Grimmett c Siedle b Mitchell 14
WJ O'Reilly c Siedle b Langton 13
EL McCormick not out 0
EXTRAS (B 19, LB 3, NB 1) 23
TOTAL 455

FOW 1st Inns: 162 164 240 316 333 361 423 433 451 455

Bowling: *First Innings*: Davies 18-0-54-0, Crisp 19-2-65-2, Langton 33-9-69-2, Balaskas 51-4-157-1, Mitchell 25.5-2-87-5.

Umpires: JC Collings & WJ Routledge

Australian Averages

1935–36 SOUTH AFRICA v AUSTRALIA

AUSTRALIA	M	Inn	NO	Runs	H.S	Avrge	Ct	St	Overs	Mds	Runs	Wkt	Avrge
Brown, WA	5	7	-	417	121	59.57	1	-	-	-	-	-	-
Chipperfield, AG	5	5	-	196	109	39.20	2	-	9.0	1	28	-	-
Darling, LS	5	6	1	229	62	45.80	2	-	-	-	-	-	-
Fingleton, JHW	5	7	1	478	118	79.67	4	-	-	-	-	-	-
Fleetwood-Smith, LO	3	2	1	6	5*	6.00	-	-	122.2	24	380	9	42.22
Grimmett, CV	5	5	1	70	30*	17.50	3	-	346.1	140	642	44	14.59
McCabe, SJ	5	7	2	420	189*	84.00	1	-	45.0	8	136	3	45.33
McCormick, EL	5	5	3	19	13	9.50	1	-	125.1	24	418	15	27.87
O'Brien, LPJ	2	2	-	107	59	53.50	1	-	-	-	-	-	-
O'Reilly, WJ	5	5	1	97	56*	24.25	2	-	250.2	112	460	27	17.04
Oldfield, WAS	5	5	-	121	44	24.20	5	7	-	-	-	-	-
Richardson, VY	5	5	-	84	45	16.80	9	-	-	-	-	-	-

South African Averages

1935–36 SOUTH AFRICA v AUSTRALIA

SOUTH AFRICA	M	Inn	NO	Runs	H.S	Avrge	Ct	St	Overs	Mds	Runs	Wkt	Avrge
Balaskas, XC	3	6	-	4	2	0.67	3	-	133.0	9	448	9	49.78
Bock, EG	1	2	2	11	9*	-	-	-	23.0	2	91	-	-
Briscoe, AW	1	2	-	31	16	15.50	1	-	-	-	-	-	-
Crisp, RJ	4	8	-	94	35	11.75	3	-	107.0	16	303	7	43.29
Dalton, EL	1	2	-	9	5	4.50	-	-	7.3	-	37	1	37.00
Davies, EQ	2	4	1	5	3	1.67	-	-	42.4	4	129	4	32.25
Harvey, RL	2	4	-	51	28	12.75	-	-	-	-	-	-	-
Langton, ABC	5	10	1	62	16	6.89	4	-	204.2	38	532	12	44.33
Mitchell, B	5	10	2	251	72*	31.38	2	-	90.2	6	330	10	33.00
Nicholson, F	4	8	1	76	29	10.86	3	-	-	-	-	-	-
Nourse, AD	5	10	1	518	231	57.56	-	-	-	-	-	-	-
Nupen, EP	1	2	-	7	6	3.50	-	-	14.0	1	53	1	53.00
Robertson, JB	3	6	1	51	17	10.20	2	-	123.0	26	321	6	53.50
Rowan, EAB	3	6	-	197	66	32.83	3	-	-	-	-	-	-
Siedle, IJ	5	10	-	332	59	33.20	2	-	-	-	-	-	-
Van der Merwe, EA	1	2	1	7	7*	7.00	1	-	-	-	-	-	-
Viljoen, KG	4	8	-	163	56	20.38	1	-	-	-	-	-	-
Wade, HF	5	10	-	195	39	19.50	2	-	-	-	-	-	-

The Maharajah requests …

His Highness the Maharajah of Patiala's Team of Australian Cricketers.

Patiala, April 18. The first tour of India by an Australian team, organised by Frank Tarrant at the request of the Maharajah of Patiala, concluded with an Indian win over the Australians at Madras.

The tour began with an inquiry to the Board of Control by Tarrant on behalf of the Maharajah in January, asking the Board to nominate a team which would not interfere with the Test side in South Africa, and which would be entirely at the expense of the Maharajah.

The Board initially rejected the request as 'presumptuous', but five months later, after tremendous public pressure, relented by permitting Tarrant to select a team of players who had retired and were not required for the Sheffield Shield. Not every retired player who wanted to tour was allowed, but eventually Jack Ryder, Charlie Macartney, 'Stork' Hendry, Bert Ironmonger, Wendell Bill and Lisle Nagel went with a number of slightly younger grade cricketers.

The team left Australia on October 8, for a tour of 23 matches including 17 first class games, losing just three.

They were to be styled the 'Maharajah of Patiala's team of Australian Cricketers' and under no circumstances were they to play anything that resembled a Test match against an 'All India' team.

The 'Australians', as the became known, were a great success on and off the field. They became popular with the locals, making it known that they will not take advantage of any club facilities offered by a social institution

The Maharajah: cricket patron.

which does not accord to Indians the same status as themselves.'

The first non-'Test' between 'All-India' and the 'Australians' was played on matting in Bombay over four days from December 5.

Australia won by nine wickets, Jack Ryder 104, and the second 'Test' in Calcutta by eight wickets. In the third match, at Lahore, Wazir Ali batted and captained All-India to a 68-run win which the *Hindu* reported 'caused the atmosphere to vibrate with triumphant joy.'

It did likewise in the fourth, at Madras, where the Australians failed to score the 141 runs required for victory, a spinner called Nissar taking 6/36. The non-series finished two–all.

Jack Ryder predicted that India would one day become a powerful force in world cricket.

Bradman now the Aussie skipper

Sydney, Nov. 24. Don Bradman, having captained SA to a Sheffield Shield victory last season, been appointed an Australian selector, and captained the Australian XI against the MCC, is a 'cert' to be appointed Australian captain in the first Test in Brisbane. Bradman the batsman is the drawcard, and may be counted an even bigger one as captain.

Vic Richardson, to the disappointment of his many admirers and supporters, will go from Australian captain beating South Africa 4–0, to 'just' a player for SA: chocolates to boiled lollies.

Douglas Jardine, Bradman's nemesis, has been replaced by 'Gubby' Allen, the bodyline bowler who would not bowl it. Jardine, writing in the London *Evening Standard* asked, in hope, whether 'the cares of captaincy might put some curb on Bradman's prolific bat. It is at least reasonable to assume that his new role cannot increase his scoring ability.'

In the match against the MCC Bradman scored a modest 63. It was 'Jack' Badcock who caught the eye with a stylish 182. Fingleton and Brown took up where they left off in South Africa.

Wicket plays tricks: Australia out for 58

Brisbane, Dec. 9. Don Bradman's first taste of Test captaincy has been a sour one, after Australia was caught on a classic 'sticky' on the last day, being dismissed for 58.

No day was entirely satisfactory from the Australian point of view. Bill Brown had to be made 12th man as he had an injured thumb, and Ernie McCormick came down with lumbago after just eight overs and 3/26 on the first day.

Maurice Leyland made that day worse with 126.

Day three was better when Jack Fingleton scored exactly 100.

Day four saw Australia having to bat in very bad light. Fingleton appealed against it, but was turned down and then was out first ball. Five more appeals were made, and after 1.4 overs, the 'light' was granted, Australia 1/3.

And that night it rained. England took 8/55 in 10.5 overs to win. McCormick did not bat.

No Imperial game

Melbourne, Dec. 31. The suggestion of former Australian captain Monty Noble that there should be a special Test match played on the 150th anniversary of the founding of NSW (and Australia), has been rejected by the Board of Control.

Noble's suggestion was for an 'Imperial' team comprising players from England, West Indies, New Zealand and South Africa to play matches in 1938.

Despite government pressure since April, delegates from States other than NSW saw no merit in the matter.

Jack Badcock: 8 and 0 on debut.

Arthur Chipperfield: sole survivor on 26.

Fingleton's fourth

Brisbane, Dec. 7. Jack Fingleton's century – an even 100 runs – in the first Test against England was his fourth hundred in four innings in as many Tests. He is the first batsman to achieve this feat.

The Brisbane hundred out of a total of 234 was a fighting knock, the three in South Africa part of match-winning opening partnerships with Bill Brown. In the third Test Fingleton's 112 was in a stand of 233, in the fourth Test he made 108, and the opening partnership was 99, and in fifth Test, 118 and the first wicket fell at 162.

Queensland gaffes

Brisbane, Dec. 1. England drew with Queensland in the warm-up to the first test at the 'Gabba, but there was a slight chill in the pavilion. The distinguished former England player and captain C. B. Fry (so regal in appearance that he was seriously offered the job as King of Albania) was refused admittance because he was writing for an English newspaper.

Journalists sat elsewhere, majestic of appearance or not. Fry would have thought highly of Charles Barnett's aggressive personal best innings of 259 for MCC.

The MCC Christmas card expressed the feelings of good sportsmanship and good cricket in this reconciliation tour.

QUICK SINGLES

Bradman v Richardson. Vic Richardson's South African XI was pitted against an XI drawn from the 'rest' and captained by Don Bradman as a benefit for Warren Bardsley and Jack Gregory at the SCG in October. Bradman's XI won by six wickets, mainly due to Bradman's 212 against Grimmett, and the success of new leg-spinner Frank Ward who took 7/127 and 5/100 against Richardson's side. The match raised £1411 and was suggestive for the selectors.

'Keeping's off. Two unusual incidents in the NSW v Queensland Shield match at the 'Gabba in October. Queensland 'keeper Don Tallon was out on 96 but NSW 'keeper Bert Oldfield said that a boundary given as byes had actually been 'touched' by Tallon. Scores were adjusted so Tallon got his century, and Oldfield a clean sheet. Secondly, Tallon while keeping was obscured by a batsman, and unable to take a return which went to the boundary. The batsmen did not claim the runs, but later NSW captain Alan McGilvray did claim the four. NSW won a close game by just one wicket.

Dressing room dressing down. Messages were received in the Australian change room by five players after the conclusion of the third Test. O'Reilly, McCabe, Darling, O'Brien and Fleetwood-Smith were summoned to a hear a lecture about fitness, drinking, and supporting the captain from Board of Control chairman Dr Allan Robertson. O'Reilly asked whether anyone was being charged and when no one was, O'Reilly said 'In that case this is all tiggy touchwood and we may as well leave.'

No bread rise. The Melbourne *Sun News Pictorial* reported during the third Test:

'There will be no rise in bread prices while the Test cricket is on. A meeting of the Master Bakers' Council that was to take place yesterday to consider an increase has been postponed until Thursday afternoon, as the Council were unanimous that watching Bradman yesterday was more entertaining than risking the wrath of housewives by raising prices.'

News direct to England. English wireless listeners were able to get the bad news direct from the ground for the first time when Alan Kippax spoke by radio-telephone direct to the BBC for ten minutes at the end of each day's play in the fourth Test in Adelaide.

Victoria's Shield. Victoria with 24 points recaptures the Sheffield Shield easily from SA (17).

Big crowds. More than 95,000 spectators watch the five Test matches.

Is Bradman jinxed? Another Test disaster

Bradman late-cuts with his usual sureness as he makes one of his 17 runs in the second innings of the second Test.

Sydney, Dec. 22. Australian captain Don Bradman must wonder what he had done to displease the weather gods, because Australia was caught once again on a 'sticky' wicket after England piled on 426 in two days, Walter Hammond looking as unshakable as a mountain in making 231 not out.

In the England innings the wicket played very well. It rained on the third day, the rest day, on the uncovered pitch, and rained again on the next morning, which is when 'Gubby' Allen declared. This was the first occasion where a first

innings had been declared closed in a Test in Australia.

Australia was shot out for 80, which would have been less had not Bill O'Reilly been given a chance to slog the England leg-spinner Jim Sims for two sixes, top-scoring with 37 not out.

England captain 'Gubby' Allen's decision to enforce the follow-on looked a little bit shaky at the end of the third day, with Australia at 1/145 and Bradman 57 not out and Fingleton 67 not out, but in the event they were out quickly next day, and only Stan McCabe with a

typical hard-hitting 93 offered much resistance.

Bradman at 26 passed Clem Hill's record of runs against England, with 2661. 'Jack' Badcock got out of his sickbed in the second innings to come in at number 11.

Australia at 324 was only good enough to lose by an innings and 22 runs.

Two successive losses caused some talk about players alleged drinking habits and the staging of late-night parties during Test matches. Wiser heads looked to injuries, selection and the weather.

British brigade

Melbourne, Jan. 2. The Board of Control entertained Lord Somers, visiting President of the Marylebone Cricket Club, the two teams, and visiting journalists at a Gala Dinner at the Windsor Hotel.

Lord Somers is in Australia 'on a friendly visit'.

The journalists, many of whom are distinguished former cricketers, include Neville Cardus, C. B. Fry, Bruce Harris, Gilbert Mant, Jack Hobbs, Ross Slater and William Pollock – a far cry from the small, undistinguished and unfortunate contingent which was in Australia for Bodyline.

None would have been too pleased to report that England was all out for 76 on this day.

Victorian Shield

Adelaide, March 15. Victoria clinched the Sheffield Shield in the last match of the season, by defeating South Australia in Adelaide, with Don Bradman playing. Despite a good wicket, bowlers dominated. 'Chuck' Fleetwood Smith took 6/66 in SA's first innings of 182. Bradman made 31.

Victoria only did marginally better, making 213, with opener Ian Lee carrying his bat for 103 not out, and Waite 4/35. But Ernie McCormick gave an extraordinary performance of 9/40, dismissing the home side for 79, Bradman 8.

Victoria went through the season undefeated, and won the Shield with three outright wins, plus three first innings wins.

Record crowds to see the Tests

The Captains toss.

Melbourne, March 3. Test cricket has never been more popular in Australia, and nowhere in the world is it more popular than it is here. A total of 957,550 spectators paid £87,318 over the five Test matches.

Figures for each Test are:

Attendance at the first Test Brisbane, 72,818, receipts £10,336.

Second Test, Sydney, 126,947, £12,038

Third Test, Melbourne, 350,534, £29,169.

Fourth Test, Adelaide, 171,135, £17,504.

Fifth Test, Melbourne, 236,116, £18,271.

Some 1.3 million people saw the English team play in all games with receipts of more than £110,000. While so-called 'Bradmania' had something to do with it, big attendances also reflected the end of the Depression, and recovery from the trauma cricket experienced over Bodyline.

The menu from the gala dinner for Lord Somers at the Windsor Hotel.

Alan McGilvray was captain of NSW in the 1936–37 season.

Australia bolts in, 3–2

Adelaide Oval during the third Test – no rain in sight and happy spectators.

Melbourne, March 3. A measure of the great success of the Test series has been that 12,000 people went to the MCG on the morning of the last day, with England 8/165, were admitted free, and watched 'Chuck' Fleetwood-Smith bowl the two balls required for victory. They went home happy.

Australia had recovered from two down, to win the next three.

The weather played a big part in helping England win the first two, but then assisted Australia in the third and fifth Tests at Melbourne.

Big Morrie Sievers had the best of the conditions in the third Test when he took 5/21 on a 'sticky' in England's first innings of 9/76 declared. Sievers was instructed not to curtail the English innings by taking any more wickets.

That was in front of 65,235 spectators, who admired the cunning of

captain Don Bradman in then sending in Bill O'Reilly, Frank Ward and Fleetwood-Smith as nightwatchmen while the wicket dried.

Next day a mammoth 87,798 saw Jack Fingleton make 136, and the great man himself 248 of his 270 runs in a partnership of 346.

There was no rain in Adelaide, where Australia levelled the series, just another Bradman double century, some sparkle from Stan McCabe (88 and 55), and the debut of elegant Ross Gregory with 23 and 50. Fleetwood-Smith took 10 wickets.

And so to the series decider, a beautiful 100 from 'Jack' Badcock, a mere 169 from Bradman, and another 'special' from Stan McCabe. Then the rain came and spiced up the pitch especially for O'Reilly.

It wasn't all Test cricket – the Melbourne Cricket Club were District Premiers in 1936–37. The team included Ebeling, Rigg, Campbell, Fleetwood-Smith, Ponsford, Ley, Beames, Kinnear, Gardiner (hidden), Collie and Nagel. No

---

FIRST TEST 1936–37 AUSTRALIA v ENGLAND
Brisbane Cricket Ground, Brisbane. December 4, 5, 7, 8, 9, 1936.
Toss: England. England won by 322 runs.

ENGLAND

TS Worthington c Oldfield b McCormick	0	st Oldfield b McCabe 8
CJ Barnett c Oldfield b O'Reilly	69	c Badcock b Ward 26
AE Fagg c Oldfield b McCormick	4	st Oldfield b Ward 27
WR Hammond c Robinson b McCormick	0	hit wicket b Ward 25
M Leyland b Ward	126	c Bradman b Ward 33
LEG Ames (+) c Chipperfield b Ward	24	b Sievers 9
J Hardstaff jr c McCabe b O'Reilly	43 (8)	st Oldfield b Ward 20
RWV Robins c(S)WA Brown b O'Reilly	38 (9)	c Chipperfield b Ward 0
GOB Allen (c) c McCabe b O'Reilly	35 (7)	c Fingleton b Sievers 68
H Verity c Sievers b O'Reilly	7	lbw Sievers 19
W Voce not out	4	not out 2
EXTRAS (B 1, LB 3, NB 4)	8	(B 14, LB 4, NB 1) 19
TOTAL	358	256

FOW 1st Inns: 0 20 20 119 162 252 311 311 343 358
FOW 2nd Inns: 17 50 82 105 122 144 205 205 247 256

Bowling: *First Innings*: McCormick 8-1-26-3, Sievers 16-5-42-0, O'Reilly 40.6-13-102-5, Ward 36-3-138-2, Chipperfield 11-3-32-0, McCabe 2-0-10-0. *Second Innings*: Sievers 19.6-9-29-3, McCabe 6-1-14-1, Ward 46-16-102-6, O'Reilly 35-15-59-0, Chipperfield 10-2-33-0.

AUSTRALIA

JHW Fingleton b Verity	100	b Voce 0
CL Badcock b Allen	8	c Fagg b Allen 0
DG Bradman (c) c Worthington b Voce	38 (5)	c Fagg b Allen 0
SJ McCabe c Barnett b Voce	51 (6)	c Leyland b Allen 7
RH Robinson c Hammond b Voce	2 (7)	c Hammond b Voce 3
AG Chipperfield c Ames b Voce	7 (8)	not out 26
MW Sievers b Allen	8 (3)	c Voce b Allen 5
WAS Oldfield (+) c Ames b Voce	6 (4)	b Voce 10
WJ O'Reilly c Leyland b Voce	3	b Allen 0
FA Ward c Hardstaff b Allen	0	b Voce 1
EL McCormick not out	1	
EXTRAS (B 4, LB 1, NB 5)	10	(NB 6) 6
TOTAL	234	9 for 58

FOW 1st Inns: 13 89 166 176 202 220 229 231 231 234
FOW 2nd Inns: 0 3 7 7 16 20 35 41 58

Bowling: *First Innings*: Allen 16-2-71-3, Voce 20.6-5-41-6, Hammond 4-0-12-0, Verity 28-11-52-1, Robins 17-0-48-0. *Second Innings*: Voce 6.3-0-16-4, Allen 6-0-36-5.

Umpires: EG Borwick & JD Scott

SECOND TEST 1936–37 AUSTRALIA v ENGLAND
Sydney Cricket Ground, Sydney. December 18, 19, 21, 22, 1936.
Toss: England. England won by an innings & 22 runs.

ENGLAND

AE Fagg c Sievers b McCormick	11
CJ Barnett b Ward	57
WR Hammond not out	231
M Leyland lbw McCabe	42
LEG Ames (+) c(S)RH Robinson b Ward	29
GOB Allen (c) lbw O'Reilly	9
J Hardstaff jr b McCormick	26
H Verity not out	0
JM Sims	
RWV Robins	
W Voce	
EXTRAS (B 8, LB 2, W 1, NB 4)	21
TOTAL	6 dec 426

FOW 1st Inns: 27 118 247 351 368 424

Bowling: *First Innings*: McCormick 20-1-79-2, Sievers 16.2-4-30-0, Ward 42-8-132-2, O'Reilly 41-17-86-1, Chipperfield 13-2-47-0, McCabe 9-1-31-1.

AUSTRALIA

JHW Fingleton c Verity b Voce	12	b Sims 73
LPJ O'Brien c Sims b Voce	0	c Allen b Hammond 17
DG Bradman (c) c Allen b Voce	0	b Verity 82
SJ McCabe c Sims b Voce	0	lbw Voce 93
AG Chipperfield c Sims b Allen	13	b Voce 21
MW Sievers c Voce b Verity	4 (7)	run out 24
WAS Oldfield (+) b Verity	1 (8)	c Ames b Voce 1
WJ O'Reilly not out	37 (9)	b Hammond 3
EL McCormick b Allen	10 (10)	lbw Hammond 0
FA Ward b Allen	0 (11)	not out 1
CL Badcock	(6)	lbw Allen 2
EXTRAS (B 1, LB 1, NB 1)	3	(LB 3, NB 4) 7
TOTAL	9 for 80	324

FOW 1st Inns: 1 1 1 16 28 30 31 80 80
FOW 2nd Inns: 38 162 186 220 226 318 319 323 323 324

Bowling: *First Innings*: Voce 8-1-10-4, Allen 5.7-1-19-3, Verity 3-0-17-2, Hammond 4-0-6-0, Sims 2-0-20-0, Robins 1-0-5-0. *Second Innings*: Voce 19-4-66-3, Allen 19-4-61-1, Hammond 15.7-3-29-3, Sims 17-0-80-1, Verity 19-7-55-1, Robins 7-0-26-0.

Umpires: EG Borwick & JD Scott

THIRD TEST 1936–37 AUSTRALIA v ENGLAND
Melbourne Cricket Ground, Melbourne. January 1, 2, 4, 5, 6, 7, 1937.
Toss: Australia. Australia won by 365 runs.

AUSTRALIA
JHW Fingleton c Sims b Robins	.38	(6)	c Ames b Sims	.136
WA Brown c Ames b Voce	.1	(5)	c Barnett b Voce	.20
DG Bradman (c) c Robins b Verity	.13	(7)	c Allen b Verity	.270
KE Rigg c Verity b Allen	.16		lbw Sims	.47
SJ McCabe c Worthington b Voce	.63	(8)	lbw Allen	.22
LS Darling c Allen b Verity	.20	(9)	b Allen	.0
MW Sievers st Ames b Robins	.1	(10)	not out	.25
WAS Oldfield (+) not out	.27	(11)	lbw Verity	.7
WJ O'Reilly c Sims b Hammond	.4	(1)	c & b Voce	.0
FA Ward st Ames b Hammond	.7	(3)	c Hardstaff b Verity	.18
LO Fleetwood-Smith		(2)	c Verity b Voce	.0
EXTRAS (B 2, LB 6, NB 2)	.10		(B 6, LB 2, W 1, NB 10)	.19
TOTAL	.9 dec 200			.564

FOW 1st Inns: 7 33 69 79 122 130 183 190 200
FOW 2nd Inns: 0 3 38 74 97 443 511 511 549 564

Bowling: *First Innings*: Voce 18-3-49-2, Allen 12-2-35-1, Sims 9-1-35-0, Verity 14-4-24-2, Robins 7-0-31-2, Hammond 5.3-0-16-2. *Second Innings*: Voce 29-2-120-3, Hammond 22-3-89-0, Allen 23-2-84-2, Verity 37.7-9-79-3, Robins 11-2-46-0, Sims 23-1-109-2, Worthington 4-0-18-0.

ENGLAND
TS Worthington c Bradman b McCabe	.0		c Sievers b Ward	.16
CJ Barnett c Darling b Sievers	.11		lbw O'Reilly	.23
WR Hammond c Darling b Sievers	.32		b Sievers	.51
M Leyland c Darling b O'Reilly	.17		not out	.111
JM Sims c Brown b Sievers	.3	(10)	lbw Fleetwood-Smith	.0
LEG Ames (+) b Sievers	.3	(5)	b Fleetwood-Smith	.19
RWV Robins b Sievers	.3	(8)	b O'Reilly	.61
J Hardstaff jr b O'Reilly	.3	(6)	c Ward b Fleetwood-Smith	.17
GOB Allen (c) not out	.0	(7)	c Sievers b Fleetwood-Smith	.11
H Verity c Brown b O'Reilly	.0	(9)	c McCabe b O'Reilly	.11
W Voce not out	.0		c Bradman b Fleetwood-Smith	.0
EXTRAS (B 5, LB 1, NB 1)	.7		(LB 3)	.3
TOTAL	.9 dec 76			.323

FOW 1st Inns: 0 14 56 68 71 71 76 76 76
FOW 2nd Inns: 29 65 117 155 179 195 306 322 323 323

Bowling: *First Innings*: McCabe 2-1-7-1, Sievers 11.2-5-21-5, O'Reilly 12-5-28-3, Fleetwood-Smith 3-1-13-0. *Second Innings*: Ward 12-1-60-1, McCabe 8-0-32-0, O'Reilly 21-6-65-3, Fleetwood-Smith 25.6-2-124-5, Sievers 12-2-39-1.

Umpires: EG Borwick & JD Scott

FIFTH TEST 1936-37–AUSTRALIA v ENGLAND
Melbourne Cricket Ground, Melbourne. February 26, 27, March 1, 2, 3, 1937.
Toss: Australia. Australia won by an innings & 200 runs.

AUSTRALIA
JHW Fingleton c Voce b Farnes	.17
KE Rigg c Ames b Farnes	.28
DG Bradman (c) b Farnes	.169
SJ McCabe c Farnes b Verity	.112
CL Badcock c Worthington b Voce	.118
RG Gregory c Verity b Farnes	.80
WAS Oldfield (+) c Ames b Voce	.21
LJ Nash c Ames b Farnes	.17
WJ O'Reilly b Voce	.1
EL McCormick not out	.17
LO Fleetwood-Smith b Voce	.13
EXTRAS (B 1, LB 5, W 1, NB 4)	.11
TOTAL	.604

FOW 1st Inns: 42 54 303 346 507 544 563 571 576 604

Bowling: *First Innings*: Allen 17-0-99-0, Farnes 28.5-5-96-6, Voce 29-3-123-3, Hammond 16-1-62-0, Verity 41-5-127-1, Worthington 6-0-60-0, Leyland 3-0-26-0.

ENGLAND
CJ Barnett c Oldfield b Nash	.18		lbw O'Reilly	.41
TS Worthington hit wicket b Fleetwood-Smith	.44		c Bradman b McCormick	.6
J Hardstaff jr c McCormick b O'Reilly	.83		b Nash	.1
WR Hammond c Nash b O'Reilly	.14		c Bradman b O'Reilly	.56
M Leyland b O'Reilly	.7		c McCormick b Fleetwood-Smith	.28
RES Wyatt c Bradman b O'Reilly	.38		run out	.9
LEG Ames (+) b Nash	.19		c McCabe b McCormick	.11
GOB Allen (c) c Oldfield b Nash	.0		c Nash b O'Reilly	.7
H Verity c Rigg b Nash	.17		not out	.2
W Voce st Oldfield b O'Reilly	.3		c Badcock b Fleetwood-Smith	.1
K Farnes not out	.0		c Nash b Fleetwood-Smith	.0
EXTRAS (LB 12, NB 1)	.13		(LB 3)	.3
TOTAL	.239			.165

FOW 1st Inns: 33 96 130 140 202 236 236 236 239 239
FOW 2nd Inns: 9 10 70 121 142 142 153 162 165 165

Bowling: *First Innings*: McCormick 13-1-54-0, Nash 17.5-1-70-4, O'Reilly 23-7-51-5, Fleetwood-Smith 18-3-51-1. *Second Innings*: McCormick 9-0-33-2, Nash 7-1-34-1, O'Reilly 19-6-58-3, McCabe 1-0-1-0, Fleetwood-Smith 13.2-3-36-3.

Umpires: EG Borwick & JD Scott

FOURTH TEST 1936-37 AUSTRALIA v ENGLAND
Adelaide Oval, Adelaide. January 29, 30, February 1, 2, 3, 4, 1937.
Toss: Australia. Australia won by 148 runs.

AUSTRALIA
JHW Fingleton run out	.10		lbw Hammond	.12
WA Brown c Allen b Farnes	.42		c Ames b Voce	.32
KE Rigg c Ames b Farnes	.20	(5)	c Hammond b Farnes	.7
DG Bradman (c) b Allen	.26	(3)	c & b Hammond	.212
SJ McCabe c Allen b Robins	.88	(4)	c Wyatt b Robins	.55
RG Gregory lbw Hammond	.23		run out	.50
AG Chipperfield not out	.57		c Ames b Hammond	.31
WAS Oldfield (+) run out	.5		c Ames b Hammond	.1
WJ O'Reilly c Leyland b Allen	.7		c Hammond b Farnes	.1
EL McCormick c Ames b Hammond	.4		b Hammond	.1
LO Fleetwood-Smith b Farnes	.1		not out	.4
EXTRAS (LB 2, NB 3)	.5		(B 10, LB 15, W 1, NB 1)	.27
TOTAL	.288			.433

FOW 1st Inns: 26 72 73 136 206 226 249 271 283 288
FOW 2nd Inns: 21 88 197 237 372 422 426 427 429 433

Bowling: *First Innings*: Voce 12-0-49-0, Allen 16-0-60-2, Farnes 20.6-1-71-3, Hammond 6-0-30-2, Verity 16-4-47-0, Robins 7-1-26-1. *Second Innings*: Farnes 24-2-89-2, Hammond 15.2-1-57-5, Allen 14-1-61-0, Voce 20-2-86-1, Verity 37-17-54-0, Robins 6-0-38-1, Barnett 5-1-15-0, Leyland 2-0-6-0.

ENGLAND
H Verity c Bradman b O'Reilly	.19		b Fleetwood-Smith	.17
CJ Barnett lbw Fleetwood-Smith	.129		c Chipperfield b Fleetwood-Smith	.21
WR Hammond c McCormick b O'Reilly	.20	(4)	b Fleetwood-Smith	.39
M Leyland c Chipperfield b Fleetwood-Smith	.45	(5)	c Chipperfield b Fleetwood-Smith	.32
RES Wyatt c Fingleton b O'Reilly	.3	(6)	c Oldfield b McCabe	.50
LEG Ames (+) b McCormick	.52	(7)	lbw Fleetwood-Smith	.0
J Hardstaff jr c & b McCormick	.20	(3)	b O'Reilly	.43
GOB Allen (c) lbw Fleetwood-Smith	.11		c Gregory b McCormick	.9
RWV Robins c Oldfield b O'Reilly	.10		b McCormick	.4
W Voce c Rigg b Fleetwood-Smith	.8		b Fleetwood-Smith	.1
K Farnes not out	.0		not out	.7
EXTRAS (B 6, LB 2, W 1, NB 4)	.13		(B 12, LB 2, NB 6)	.20
TOTAL	.330			.243

FOW 1st Inns: 53 108 190 195 259 299 304 318 322 330
FOW 2nd Inns: 45 50 120 149 190 190 225 231 235 243

Bowling: *First Innings*: McCormick 21-2-81-2, McCabe 9-2-18-0, Fleetwood-Smith 41.4-10-129-4, O'Reilly 30-12-51-4, Chipperfield 9-1-24-0, Gregory 3-0-14-0. *Second Innings*: McCormick 13-1-43-2, McCabe 5-0-15-1, Fleetwood-Smith 30-1-110-6, O'Reilly 26-8-55-1.

Umpires: EG Borwick & JD Scott

Australian Averages

1936–37 AUSTRALIA v ENGLAND

AUSTRALIA	M	Inn	NO	Runs	H.S	Avrge	Ct	St	Overs	Mds	Runs	Wkt	Avrge
Badcock, CL	3	4	-	128	118	32.00	2	-	-	-	-	-	-
Bradman, DG	5	9	-	810	270	90.00	7	-	-	-	-	-	-
Brown, WA	2	4	-	95	42	23.75	2	-	-	-	-	-	-
Chipperfield, AG	3	6	2	155	57*	38.75	5	-	43.0	8	136	-	-
Darling, LS	1	2	-	20	20	10.00	3	-	-	-	-	-	-
Fingleton, JHW	5	9	-	398	136	44.22	2	-	-	-	-	-	-
Fleetwood-Smith, LO	3	4	1	18	13	6.00	-	-	131.4	20	463	19	24.37
Gregory, RG	2	3	-	153	80	51.00	1	-	3.0	-	14	-	-
McCabe, SJ	5	9	-	491	112	54.56	4	-	42.0	5	128	4	32.00
McCormick, EL	4	6	2	33	17*	8.25	4	-	84.0	6	316	11	28.73
Nash, LJ	1	1	-	17	17	17.00	3	-	24.5	2	104	5	20.80
O'Brien, LPJ	1	2	-	17	17	8.50	-	-	-	-	-	-	-
O'Reilly, WJ	5	9	1	56	37*	7.00	1	-	247.6	89	555	25	22.20
Oldfield, WAS	5	9	1	79	27*	9.88	7	4	-	-	-	-	-
Rigg, KE	3	5	-	118	47	23.60	2	-	-	-	-	-	-
Robinson, RH	1	2	-	5	3	2.50	1	-	-	-	-	-	-
Sievers, MW	3	6	1	67	25*	13.40	4	-	75.2	25	161	9	17.89
Ward, FA	3	6	1	27	18	5.40	1	-	136.0	20	432	11	39.27

English Averages

1936–37 AUSTRALIA v ENGLAND

ENGLAND	M	Inn	NO	Runs	H.S	Avrge	Ct	St	Overs	Mds	Runs	Wkt	Avrge
Allen, GOB	5	9	1	150	68	18.75	6	-	128.7	12	526	17	30.94
Ames, LEG	5	9	-	166	52	18.44	13	2	-	-	-	-	-
Barnett, CJ	5	9	-	395	129	43.89	2	-	5.0	1	15	-	-
Fagg, AE	2	3	-	42	27	14.00	2	-	-	-	-	-	-
Farnes, K	2	4	3	7	7*	7.00	1	-	73.3	8	256	11	23.27
Hammond, WR	5	9	1	468	231*	58.50	5	-	88.4	8	301	12	25.08
Hardstaff jr, J	5	9	-	256	83	28.44	2	-	-	-	-	-	-
Leyland, M	5	9	1	441	126	55.13	3	-	5.0	-	32	-	-
Robins, RWV	4	6	-	113	61	18.83	1	-	56.0	3	220	4	55.00
Sims, JM	2	2	-	3	3	1.50	4	-	51.0	2	244	3	81.33
Verity, H	5	9	2	75	19	10.71	4	-	195.7	57	455	10	45.50
Voce, W	5	8	3	19	8	3.80	4	-	162.1	20	560	26	21.54
Worthington, TS	3	6	-	74	44	12.33	3	-	10.0	-	78	-	-
Wyatt, RES	2	4	-	100	50	25.00	1	-	-	-	-	-	-

O'Reilly is King of Spin this season

A typical Bill O'Reilly curly one.

Perth, March 21. It wasn't just the large number of wickets that Bill O'Reilly took in the 1937–38 season that made him the leading bowler in Australia – it was the miserly way he took them.

His 64 wickets cost only 784 runs, at an average of just 12.25. By contrast 'Chuck' Fleetwood-Smith also took 64 wickets but at a cost of 1436 runs, at 22.43.

As well as the extraordinary 9/41 and 5/57 against South Australia, O'Reilly's figures include 5/57 and 4/61 against a New Zealand XI, 5/34 against Tasmania and 5/12 against WA for the Australian XI.

Clarrie Grimmett took 41 wickets at 21.56, and his SA spinning rival Frank Ward 51 at 21.56.

O'Reilly was consulted before the NSW v SA Shield game in Sydney by Don Bradman about which he would prefer in England in 1938.

O'Reilly is a well known admirer of Grimmett.

States beat NZ

Sydney, Nov. 22. Returning from the 1–0 loss in the three-Test series against England in 1937, the New Zealand side stopped off in Australia for another three matches.

They played against NSW, Victoria and SA, in order to recoup some of the costs of the England tour.

NZ lost to SA by 10 wickets before 6562 people who paid £310; then to Victoria by five wickets, crowd 7845, takings £263; and to NSW by eight wickets, crowd 11,778, gate £448. The three local associations gave NZ the whole gate; not the 75 per cent previously agreed.

NZ had no answer to the spin of Frank Ward, Clarrie Grimmett and Bill O'Reilly.

NSW wraps up Shield

The NSW Sheffield Shield team in Brisbane in November. Back row: J. G. Lush, L. C. Hynes, W. J. O'Reilly, E. S. White, A. G. Cheetham, J. H. Fingleton. Front row: V. Jackson, A. G. Chipperfield, S. J. McCabe (capt.), P. C. Harrison (manager), S. G. Barnes, W. A. Oldfield, R. G. Beattie.

Sydney, Jan. 19. NSW won the Sheffield Shield for the first time since 1932–33 by defeating main rivals SA for the second time.

Bill O'Reilly had a quiet match by his standards, and did not manage to dismiss either of SA's main scoring weapons, Don Bradman or 'Jack' Badcock.

The NSW bowlers shared the wickets around in the SA first innings, Les O'Brien getting Badcock for 6, and Bradman for 44 in a meagre 187. Stan McCabe's 82, Arthur Chipperfield's 63 and some handy down-the-order runs from O'Reilly got NSW to 295.

Bradman, who despite a cut thumb, took over behind the stumps after Charles Walker broke his thumb, had the satisfaction of eventually stumping O'Reilly from the bowling of Frank Ward.

SA's second innings was better, both Badcock and Bradman getting centuries in a total of 334, but

NSW managed the required 227, winning the game by four wickets – and the Shield.

The first match, played in Adelaide in December, was much better for O'Reilly.

O'Reilly posted his best figures, and the best by a NSW bowler, in taking 9/41 from 33.6 overs, and in the words of the *Adelaide Advertiser*, 'Bradman was pinned to the crease by O'Reilly.' It was a magnificent tribute to the bowler.

Bradman did manage a modest 91 and 62, despite O'Reilly's prowess.

In the second innings, O'Reilly followed up by cleaning up the tail as well as Bradman, taking 5/57.

Three outright wins – the other was over Queenland – and points for a first-innings advantage gave NSW a clear lead on the Shield table, 21 points to 14. Victoria managed one win and Queensland none.

New faces for '38

Melbourne, Feb. 7. The Australian team chosen to tour England reflects the state of Australian cricket – a plethora of leg-spinners, a paucity of genuinely fast bowlers, a prodigy of batsmen.

Clarrie Grimmett was controversially not selected, but Frank Ward, Bill O'Reilly, 'Chuck' Fleetwood-Smith and left-armer Ted White were.

Ben Barnett, was preferred to Bert Oldfield is the wicketkeeper. The captain is Don Bradman, to bat with some of the following: Stan McCabe, Bill Brown, Jack Fingleton, 'Jack' Badcock, Arthur Chipperfield, Sid Barnes and Lindsay Hassett.

Ernie McCormick and Merv Waite are the quick bowlers selected.

1938

AUSTRALIA IN ENGLAND

QUICK SINGLES

New faces. Newcomers to the Australian team for England are Sid Barnes (NSW), Lindsay Hassett (Vic.), Merv Waite (SA), Ted White (NSW) and Charles Walker (SA). Considered unlucky are batsman Ross Gregory (Vic.) and fast bowler 'Ginty' Lush (NSW).

Barnes out. Sid Barnes, who slipped on a wet deck en route to England, has been found on arrival to have a broken wrist. He will miss the early Tests.

Dream run. Australia has a run of big scores – 541 at Worcester, 679 at Oxford, 708 versus Cambridge, 502 against MCC, 406 at Northampton and 528 against Surrey.

New for England: The first Test sees the inclusion of new England caps, batsmen Bill Edrich, Len Hutton and Denis Compton, and leg-spinner Douglas Wright.

Record protected: Australia's vigorous fielding frustrates English opener Charles Barnett as he tries for 100 before lunch in the first Test. He got to 99.

Slow play. Intent on saving the first Test, Jack Fingleton and Bill Brown are booed for slowness. Fingleton sits down until the noise subsides.

McAlister dies. Former Test player and Board of Control member Peter McAlister, famous for his fist fight with Clem Hill in 1912, dies at the age of 69.

No play. The third Test at Old Trafford in rainy Manchester scheduled for July 8 to 12 is a complete washout. Not a ball was bowled.

Six on trot. Bradman's 103 in the fourth Test extends to six his record for centuries in successive Tests.

Stranger on field. Having recovered from a hand injury, Charles Walker takes the field against Somerset on July 27, with team-mates jokingly asking who he is.

Only two losses. The Australians won 20 of their 36 matches and had two defeats, at the hands of England in a Test match, and to Leveson-Gowers' XI in a light-hearted game at Scarborough.

McCabe's 232 prevents disaster

Stan McCabe reaches 100 with a lofted single. The onslaught is about to begin. McCabe's batting skill has saved Australia.

Nottingham, June 14. What a cricketer is Stan McCabe! His fighting spirit and batting skill have brought Australia from the brink of disaster in the first Test to an honourable draw.

After England had scored 658, with three centuries and a double century, and Australia was 3/134, it seemed just a question of shutting the gate.

This was the first Test match in which four batsman made centuries in the same innings, and one of them was a double century, 216 not out to Eddie Paynter. The doughty left-hander was the perfect foil for the spin of Bill O'Reilly and 'Chuck' Fleetwood-Smith, and

he was around to help Denis Compton make 100 in his first Test against Australia.

Another new boy to Ashes Tests was Len Hutton, who made 100 and had an opening partnership of 219 with Charles Barnett (126).

Into Australia's trouble walked McCabe, sturdy, imperturbable, a man with a mission. He took the bowling on and soon had England on the defensive as he reeled off four after four, putting himself in a scoring position even to balls of immaculate line and length.

His glorious 232 was made in under four hours, and as wickets tumbled around him the tempo of his innings increased.

He made his second 100 in 80 minutes, the last 50 of it in 24 minutes.

Bradman was so impressed he called to his team-mates: 'Come and watch this. You'll never see anything like this again.'

Finally he was left with tail-ender Fleetwood-Smith and it was time for some real action. Farming the strike and hitting out he scored 72 of the last 77 runs, finally getting out to a Compton catch off Verity. Australia was 411.

The second-innings batsmen did not let McCabe's great work go to waste, with Bill Brown scoring 133 and Bradman 144 in 6/427. Seven batsmen made centuries in the Test.

Bradman's 1000 in seven innings

Southhampton, May 27. Don Bradman has surpassed himself, in scoring 1000 runs in only seven innings. He started out with his usual double century (258) at Worcester, and joined W. G. Grace and Jack Hobbs when, for the sixth time, he made centuries (or more) in successive innings.

He then scored 137 against Cambridge and 278 against the MCC, dominating the bowling right to the eve of the first Test. His average is 170.15 at this stage.

Another outstanding early performance was from the spinner 'Chuck' Fleetwood-Smith, who took 8/98 and 3/38 in the first match against Worcestershire.

This team brings you cricket through the night from 3DB. Somewhere in there are Ray Robinson, Norm Spencer, Harry Marks, Eric Welch, Keith Rigg and Jack Ryder, and the famous Ricketty Kate, who 'goes off' when a wicket falls.

Australia wins agonising fourth Test

Denis Compton's gone, caught by Ben Barnett off O'Reilly for 15 in his second innings at Headingley, Leeds.

Leeds, July 25. Australia had to hold out on a wet pitch in an agonising last day as they crept to a target of 107. Hold out they did, under threatening skies, and the Ashes were won.

The record shows that Australia won by five wickets, but does not reveal the pacing in the dressing room and the anxious concentration on every ball as England fought for the breakthrough.

The man of the day was Lindsay Hassett, correct and watchful as he made 33 and took Australia within 14 runs of victory. He was instructed not to appeal against the light as he peered into the growing gloom.

It all seemed in vain as the rain came again with Australia nine runs from the target. But play resumed and Ben Barnett and 'Jack' Badcock knocked off the deficit.

The architects of the win, and the champions of the tour, were, once again, Don Bradman and Bill O'Reilly. In a low-scoring match Bradman crafted 102 first-innings runs on the difficult wicket, to extend to six his sequence of centuries in consecutive matches.

It was also his third century in successive Test innings at Leeds, his happy hunting ground in England. Despite their support for England, he is almost a god to the cricket-loving Yorkshire crowds. At the end, even with the sombre realisation that the Ashes were lost, a crowd of 25,000 gathered outside the pavilion shouting 'We want Bradman.' He received a great ovation when he appeared.

O'Reilly twice rent the English innings asunder, taking 5/66 and 5/56. He was well supported by Fleetwood-Smith, who took seven wickets and increased his reputation for bowling the occasional unreadable ball.

The Australians held a private dinner at the hotel to celebrate the victory.

Wayward Ernie

Leeds, July 25. Ernie McCormick, the cheerful joker of the Australian team, has had a shocking tour. He cannot get his run-up right and had had so many no-balls against him that sometimes he counts for an extra batsman on the other side.

He has a reputation as the fastest bowler Australia has produced, but Bradman has had to use him sparingly, although he did have a good second Test, taking seven wickets.

All was revealed in the very first match against Worcestershire, when he was no-balled 17 times in two overs. Things went from bad to worse, as he changed his approach run several times, watched slow motion films and put markers down along his route to the wicket.

Any time is Cricket Time
WITH A MANTEL MODEL
"HIS MASTER'S VOICE"
BAKELITE RECEIVER

"HIS MASTER'S VOICE"
TRUE · TO · LIFE
RADIOS AND RADIOGRAMS

Cricket and pipe in bed – good show!

Big workload

London, Aug. 24. It is as well that Bill O'Reilly loves to bowl. With McCormick a liability and Merv Waite not breaking through, the Australian attack has revolved around the master spinners O'Reilly and 'Chuck' Fleetwood-Smith.

O'Reilly bowled 56 overs in one innings in the first Test, 37 and 29 in the second, got a break when the third Test was abandoned, bowled 34 and 21 in the fourth and a mammoth 85 in the fifth, with England grinding out the huge score of 903 on a pitch made for batting.

With his long run-up and the fast pace of his spinners it has been a gruelling task. No one can dispute that O'Reilly has earned his nickname 'Tiger'.

'No wives' edict bristles players

Jessie Bradman: made England trip.

Nottingham, June 20. A 'players revolt' in the Australian team has led to the Board of Control reversing its edict on players' wives joining them at the end of the cricket tour.

The Board had ruled that the tour ended when the players arrived back in Australia, rather than when the last match finished in England.

It was particularly disturbing for Don Bradman, as he had arranged for his wife Jessie to come, expecting the same courtesy that had been extended to the wife of Bill Woodfull in 1934.

He told the press he was 'very disappointed' with the decision, and it is known that he was seething over it, and that the team supported him to a man.

The players themselves, seeing Bradman's distress, held a meeting without him, and cabled the Board of Control asking that the decision be reversed.

The response has Bradman all smiles, and has opened the way for all players to be reunited with their wives if they wish.

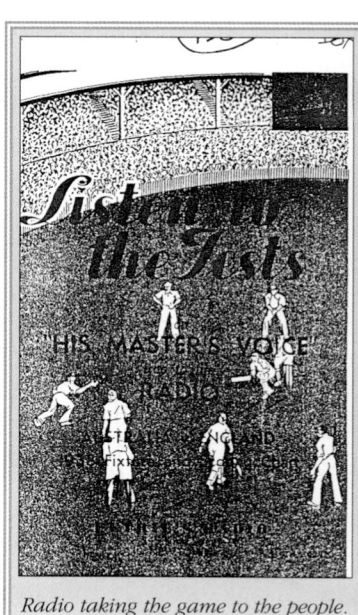

Radio taking the game to the people.

Hutton, 364, leads the way as Test records fall

A pull from Len Hutton has the field ducking for safety.

Record run-maker Len Hutton and Charles Fleetwood-Smith tussle light-heartedly for a souvenir stump at the end of the fifth Test at the Oval.

London, Aug. 24. It has been long, it has been dour, but it has been done. Len Hutton has made 364 runs to surpass Don Bradman's Test record of 334, and also bring a Test win to England.

It took the 22-year-old from Yorkshire 13 hours and 20 minutes (as against Bradman's six hours and 23 minutes), and it contained only one blemish. When he was on 40 he jumped out to Fleetwood-Smith, missed and turned round to see Ben Barnett fumble the easiest of stumping chances. He had hit 35 fours, but scored most of his runs with deflections and cuts. He passed 334 with a late cut for four, and Bradman was the first to shake his hand in congratulation.

England made a record score of 903, and another record went with the 382-run partnership between Hutton and Maurice Leyland.

At the end of his 85 overs Australian Bill O'Reilly's spinning finger was bleeding, and 'Chuck' Fleetwood-Smith had 1/298 after bowling 87 overs. 'Where's the groundsman's hut. I'd like to shoot him now,' said O'Reilly, who had toiled on a featherbed pitch rolled to perfection for batting.

Despite this, Australia capitulated for 201 and 123. Perhaps, with the Ashes in place and no hope of a win, they were temporarily sick and tired of cricket.

Don Bradman was a casualty of the affair, stumbling in an O'Reilly footmark while bowling leg-breaks, and suffering a flake fracture of an ankle.

Australian Averages

1938 ENGLAND v AUSTRALIA

AUSTRALIA	M	Inn	NO	Runs	H.S	Avrge	Ct	St	Overs	Mds	Runs	Wkt	Avrge
Badcock, CL	4	8	1	32	9	4.57	1	-	-	-	-	-	-
Barnes, SG	1	2	-	74	41	37.00	1	-	38.0	3	84	1	84.00
Barnett, BA	4	8	1	195	57	27.86	3	2	-	-	-	-	-
Bradman, DG	4	6	2	434	144*	108.50	-	-	2.2	1	6	-	-
Brown, WA	4	8	1	512	206*	73.14	3	-	-	-	-	-	-
Chipperfield, AG	1	1	-	1	1	1.00	-	-	8.4	-	51	-	-
Fingleton, JHW	4	6	-	123	40	20.50	2	-	-	-	-	-	-
Fleetwood-Smith, L	4	5	3	30	16*	15.00	-	-	217.5	34	727	14	51.93
Hassett, AL	4	8	-	199	56	24.88	1	-	13.0	2	52	-	-
McCabe, SJ	4	8	-	362	232	45.25	4	-	103.0	19	293	2	146.50
McCormick, EL	3	3	-	2	2	0.67	3	-	114.0	20	345	10	34.50
O'Reilly, WJ	4	5	1	60	42	15.00	-	-	263.0	78	610	22	27.73
Waite, MG	2	3	1	11	8	3.67	1	-	92.0	23	190	1	190.00
Ward, FA	1	2	1	9	7*	9.00	-	-	30.0	2	142	-	-

Bradman, Hardstaff offer a hand.

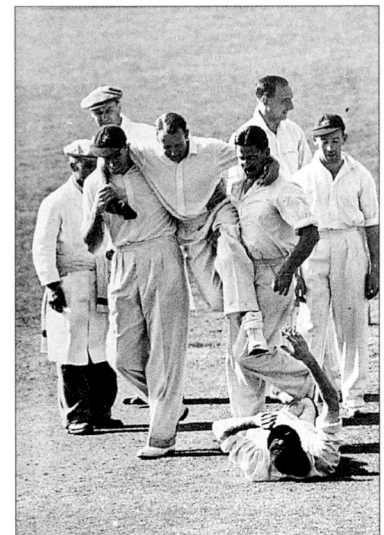

Bradman is carried off, hurt.

English Averages

1938 ENGLAND v AUSTRALIA

ENGLAND	M	Inn	NO	Runs	H.S	Avrge	Ct	St	Overs	Mds	Runs	Wkt	Avrge
Ames, LEG	2	3	-	135	83	45.00	2	-	-	-	-	-	-
Barnett, CJ	3	5	-	215	126	43.00	3	-	1.0	-	10	-	-
Bowes, WE	2	2	-	3	3	1.50	-	-	75.4	12	188	10	18.80
Compton, DCS	4	6	1	214	102	42.80	4	-	-	-	-	-	-
Edrich, WJ	4	6	-	67	28	11.17	4	-	35.2	6	139	4	34.75
Farnes, K	4	3	1	14	7	7.00	-	-	179.4	32	581	17	34.18
Hammond, WR	4	6	-	403	240	67.17	8	-	33.0	13	67	-	-
Hardstaff jr, J	2	3	1	184	169*	92.00	1	-	-	-	-	-	-
Hutton, L	3	4	-	473	364	118.25	1	-	-	-	-	-	-
Leyland, M	1	1	-	187	187	187.00	1	-	8.1	-	30	1	30.00
Paynter, E	4	6	2	407	216*	101.75	3	-	-	-	-	-	-
Price, WFF	1	2	-	6	6	3.00	2	-	-	-	-	-	-
Sinfield, RA	1	1	-	6	6	6.00	-	-	63.0	16	123	2	61.50
Verity, H	4	6	2	52	25*	13.00	2	-	154.1	53	354	14	25.29
Wellard, AW	1	2	-	42	38	21.00	-	-	32.0	3	126	3	42.00
Wood, A	1	1	-	53	53	53.00	3	-	-	-	-	-	-
Wright, DVP	3	5	2	39	22	13.00	2	-	120.0	20	426	12	35.50

FIRST TEST 1938 ENGLAND v AUSTRALIA
Trent Bridge, Nottingham. June 10, 11, 13, 14, 1938.
Toss: England. Match Drawn.

ENGLAND

CJ Barnett b McCormick	126
L Hutton lbw Fleetwood-Smith	100
WJ Edrich b O'Reilly	5
WR Hammond (c) b O'Reilly	26
E Paynter not out	216
DCS Compton c Badcock b Fleetwood-Smith	102
LEG Ames (+) b Fleetwood-Smith	46
H Verity b Fleetwood-Smith	3
RA Sinfield lbw O'Reilly	6
DVP Wright not out	1
K Farnes	
EXTRAS (B 1, LB 22, NB 4)	27
TOTAL	8 dec 658

FOW 1st Inns: 219 240 244 281 487 577 597 626

Bowling: *First Innings*: McCormick 32-4-108-1, O'Reilly 56-11-164-3, McCabe 21-5-64-0, Fleetwood-Smith 49-9-153-4, Ward 30-2-142-0.

AUSTRALIA

JHW Fingleton b Wright	9		c Hammond b Edrich	40
WA Brown c Ames b Farnes	48		c Paynter b Verity	133
DG Bradman (c) c Ames b Sinfield	51		not out	144
SJ McCabe c Compton b Verity	232		c Hammond b Verity	39
FA Ward b Farnes	2	(8)	not out	7
AL Hassett c Hammond b Wright	1	(5)	c Compton b Verity	2
CL Badcock b Wright	9	(6)	b Wright	5
BA Barnett (+) c Wright b Farnes	22	(7)	lbw Sinfield	31
WJ O'Reilly c Paynter b Farnes	9			
EL McCormick b Wright	2			
LO Fleetwood-Smith not out	5			
EXTRAS (B 10, LB 10, W 1)	21		(B 5, LB 16, NB 5)	26
TOTAL	411			6 for 427

FOW 1st Inns: 34 111 134 144 151 194 263 319 334 411
FOW 2nd Inns: 89 259 331 337 369 417

Bowling: *First Innings*: Farnes 37-11-106-4, Hammond 19-7-44-0, Sinfield 28-8-51-1, Wright 39-6-153-4, Verity 7.3-0-36-1. *Second Innings*: Farnes 24-2-78-0, Hammond 12-6-15-0, Sinfield 35-8-72-1, Wright 37-8-85-1, Verity 62-27-102-3, Edrich 13-2-39-1, Barnett 1-0-10-0.

Umpires: F Chester & E Robinson

Third Test scheduled for July 8 at Old Trafford was washed out.

SECOND TEST 1938 ENGLAND v AUSTRALIA
Lord's Cricket Ground, London. June 24, 25, 27, 28, 1938.
Toss: England. Match Drawn.

ENGLAND

CJ Barnett c Brown b McCormick	18		c McCabe b McCormick	12
L Hutton c Brown b McCormick	4		c McCormick b O'Reilly	5
WJ Edrich b McCormick	0	(4)	c McCabe b McCormick	10
WR Hammond (c) b McCormick	240	(6)	c (S)MG Waite b McCabe	2
E Paynter lbw O'Reilly	99		run out	43
DCS Compton lbw O'Reilly	6	(7)	not out	76
LEG Ames (+) c McCormick b Fleetwood-Smith	83	(8)	c McCabe b O'Reilly	6
H Verity b O'Reilly	5	(3)	b McCormick	11
AW Wellard c McCormick b O'Reilly	4		b McCabe	38
DVP Wright b Fleetwood-Smith	6		not out	10
K Farnes not out	5			
EXTRAS (B 1, LB 12, W 1, NB 10)	24		(B 12, LB 12, W 1, NB 4)	29
TOTAL	494			8 for 242

FOW 1st Inns: 12 20 31 253 271 457 472 476 483 494
FOW 2nd Inns: 25 28 43 64 76 128 142 216

Bowling: *First Innings*: McCormick 27-1-101-4, McCabe 31-4-86-0, Fleetwood-Smith 33.5-2-139-2, O'Reilly 37-6-93-4, Chipperfield 8.4-0-51-0. *Second Innings*: McCormick 24-5-72-3, O'Reilly 29-10-53-2, McCabe 12-1-58-2, Fleetwood-Smith 7-1-30-0.

AUSTRALIA

JHW Fingleton c Hammond b Wright	31	c Hammond b Wellard	4
WA Brown not out	206	b Verity	10
DG Bradman (c) b Verity	18	not out	102
SJ McCabe c Verity b Farnes	38	c Hutton b Verity	21
AL Hassett lbw Wellard	56	b Wright	42
CL Badcock b Wellard	0	c Wright b Edrich	0
BA Barnett (+) c Compton b Verity	8	c Paynter b Edrich	14
AG Chipperfield lbw Verity	1		
WJ O'Reilly b Farnes	42		
EL McCormick c Barnett b Farnes	0		
LO Fleetwood-Smith c Barnett b Verity	7		
EXTRAS (B 1, LB 8, NB 6)	15	(B 5, LB 3, W 2, NB 1)	11
TOTAL	422		6 for 204

FOW 1st Inns: 69 101 152 276 276 307 308 393 393 422
FOW 2nd Inns: 8 71 111 175 180 204

Bowling: *First Innings*: Farnes 43-6-135-3, Wellard 23-2-96-2, Wright 16-2-68-1, Verity 35.4-9-103-4, Edrich 4-2-5-0. *Second Innings*: Farnes 13-3-51-0, Wellard 9-1-30-1, Verity 13-5-29-2, Wright 8-0-56-1, Edrich 5.2-0-27-2.

Umpires: EJ Smith & FI Walden

FOURTH TEST 1938 ENGLAND v AUSTRALIA
Headingley, Leeds. July 22, 23, 25, 1938.
Toss: England. Australia won by 5 wkts.

ENGLAND

WJ Edrich b O'Reilly	12	st Barnett b Fleetwood-Smith	28
CJ Barnett c Barnett b McCormick	30	c Barnett b McCormick	29
J Hardstaff jr run out	4	b O'Reilly	11
WR Hammond (c) b O'Reilly	76	c Brown b O'Reilly	0
E Paynter st Barnett b Fleetwood-Smith	28	not out	21
DCS Compton b O'Reilly	14	c Barnett b O'Reilly	15
WFF Price (+) c McCabe b O'Reilly	0	lbw Fleetwood-Smith	6
H Verity not out	25	b Fleetwood-Smith	0
DVP Wright c Fingleton b Fleetwood-Smith	22	c Waite b Fleetwood-Smith	0
K Farnes c Fingleton b Fleetwood-Smith	2	b O'Reilly	7
WE Bowes b O'Reilly	3	lbw O'Reilly	0
EXTRAS (LB 4, NB 3)	7	(LB 4, W 1, NB 1)	6
TOTAL	223		123

FOW 1st Inns: 29 34 88 142 171 171 172 213 215 223
FOW 2nd Inns: 60 73 73 73 96 116 116 116 123 123

Bowling: *First Innings*: McCormick 20-6-46-1, Waite 18-7-31-0, O'Reilly 34.1-17-66-5, Fleetwood-Smith 25-7-73-3, McCabe 1-1-0-0. *Second Innings*: McCormick 11-4-18-1, Waite 2-0-9-0, O'Reilly 21.5-8-56-5, Fleetwood-Smith 16-4-34-4.

AUSTRALIA

JHW Fingleton b Verity	30		lbw Verity	9
WA Brown b Wright	22		lbw Farnes	9
BA Barnett (+) c Price b Farnes	57	(7)	not out	15
DG Bradman (c) b Bowes	103	(3)	c Verity b Wright	16
SJ McCabe b Farnes	1	(4)	c Barnett b Wright	15
CL Badcock b Bowes	4		not out	5
AL Hassett c Hammond b Wright	13	(5)	c Edrich b Wright	33
MG Waite c Price b Farnes	3			
WJ O'Reilly c Hammond b Farnes	2			
EL McCormick b Bowes	0			
LO Fleetwood-Smith not out	2			
EXTRAS (B 2, LB 3)	5		(B 4, LB 1)	5
TOTAL	242			5 for 107

FOW 1st Inns: 28 87 128 136 145 195 232 240 240 242
FOW 2nd Inns: 17 32 50 61 91

Bowling: *First Innings*: Farnes 26-3-77-4, Bowes 35.4-6-79-3, Wright 15-4-38-2, Verity 19-6-30-1, Edrich 3-0-13-0. *Second Innings*: Farnes 11.3-4-17-1, Bowes 11-0-35-0, Verity 5-2-24-1, Wright 5-0-26-3.

Umpires: F Chester & EJ Smith

FIFTH TEST 1938 ENGLAND v AUSTRALIA
Kennington Oval, London. August 20, 22, 23, 24, 1938.
Toss: England. England won by an innings & 579 runs.

ENGLAND

L Hutton c Hassett b O'Reilly	364
WJ Edrich lbw O'Reilly	12
M Leyland run out	187
WR Hammond (c) lbw Fleetwood-Smith	59
E Paynter lbw O'Reilly	0
DCS Compton b Waite	1
J Hardstaff jr not out	169
A Wood (+) c & b Barnes	53
H Verity not out	8
K Farnes	
WE Bowes	
EXTRAS (B 22, LB 19, W 1, NB 8)	50
TOTAL	7 dec 903

FOW 1st Inns: 29 411 546 547 555 770 876

Bowling: *First Innings*: Waite 72-16-150-1, McCabe 38-8-85-0, O'Reilly 85-26-178-3, Fleetwood-Smith 87-11-298-1, Barnes 38-3-84-1, Hassett 13-2-52-0, Bradman 2.2-1-6-0.

AUSTRALIA

WA Brown c Hammond b Leyland	69	c Edrich b Farnes	15
CL Badcock c Hardstaff b Bowes	0	b Bowes	9
SJ McCabe c Edrich b Farnes	14	c Wood b Farnes	2
AL Hassett c Compton b Edrich	42	lbw Bowes	10
SG Barnes b Bowes	41	lbw Verity	33
BA Barnett (+) c Wood b Bowes	2	b Farnes	46
MG Waite b Bowes	8	c Edrich b Verity	0
WJ O'Reilly c Wood b Bowes	0	not out	7
LO Fleetwood-Smith not out	16	c Leyland b Farnes	0
DG Bradman (c)			
JHW Fingleton			
EXTRAS (B 4, LB 2, NB 3)	9	(B 1)	1
TOTAL	8 for 201		8 for 123

FOW 1st Inns: 0 19 70 145 147 160 160 201
FOW 2nd Inns: 15 18 35 41 115 115 117 123

Bowling: *First Innings*: Farnes 13-2-54-1, Bowes 19-3-49-5, Edrich 10-2-55-1, Verity 5-1-15-0, Leyland 3.1-0-11-1, Hammond 2-0-8-0. *Second Innings*: Farnes 12.1-1-63-4, Bowes 10-3-25-2, Verity 7-3-15-2, Leyland 5-0-19-0.

Umpires: F Chester & FI Walden

'Tiger' O'Reilly defies description ...

'Bill O'Reilly was a fighter,' wrote English essayist and Somerset trundler, Raymond Robertson-Glasgow. 'He looked as if, under necessary circumstances, he might have founded or sacked a city. It was a face and form as you might have seen in a picture of explorers or pioneers. At cricket he would have bowled till his boots burst and after. If only one cricket ball was left in the world, and that came to pieces in his hand, he would whiz down a leg-break with the largest fragment. He had the inspired joy of battle ...'

Sir Donald Bradman, who first faced O'Reilly in a country game in 1925, rated him the finest bowler he had ever faced. On bush concrete pitches, on which the tall, gangling O'Reilly learnt his craft, he was 'almost unplayable', according to 'The Don', although he made 234 not out against him at their first meeting, thanks to two early dropped catches. When play resumed the next weekend O'Reilly bowled him first ball.

O'Reilly's action almost defied description. Robertson-Glasgow put it best, saying: 'During his run-up, a sort of gulumph, the right arm worked like a piston; at delivery the head was held low.' Then there was the incredible accuracy.

O'Reilly, born at White Cliffs in far western NSW in 1905, played for Australia from 1931–32 until the outbreak of World War II, and in one Test in New Zealand in 1945–46, in which he took 5/14 and 3/19. His entry into the Test arena was delayed by his job as a school teacher and might not have eventuated at all had the NSW captain, Reg Bettington, himself a spinner, not withdrawn from a Shield match against Queensland. O'Reilly took his place and within a few weeks was playing for Australia against the touring South Africans.

He was at his best against the old foe, England, taking 102 wickets in 19 matches at an average of 25.36. Three times he took 10 wickets in a match. In all Tests he captured 144 wickets at 22.59 apiece and in all first class games 774 wickets at 16. As a left-handed batsman he did not take it too seriously and he was safe in the field for a big man.

After making his Test debut against South Africa in 1932, O'Reilly played in all five 'bodyline' Tests in 1932–33, taking 27 wickets for 26.8. With 5/63 and 5/66, he was largely responsible for Australia's

only win in the series, at the MCG.

When his playing days were over he retired to the press box. His forthright opinions in the *Sydney Morning Herald* and the *Age* attracted a wide audience and he was at his trenchant best during the Packer upheaval. One day cricket – he dubbed it the pyjama game – was anathema to him. O'Reilly believed a bowler's job was to get wickets, not to stop batsmen from scoring.

O'Reilly followed in his father's footsteps as a teacher. The family moved to Marengo when Bill was only three. Marengo, O'Reilly said in his autobiography, *'Tiger'*, played no vital part in his cricket education. It was when his father moved to Wingello, 30 kilometres north of Goulburn in 1917 that O'Reilly, then aged 12, developed a passion for the game. Wingello was a cricket town. 'Everyone was a cricket crank,' said O'Reilly.

A critical point in his career occurred in the early 1920s when his older brother Jack moved to Sydney. One afternoon while practising at the North Sydney nets Jack watched the world famous spinner Arthur Mailey intently and learnt enough to write to Bill, explaining how to bowl a 'bosie'.

Within a couple of days teenager Bill had taught himself the simple mechanics of changing the spin from anticlockwise to clockwise without any discernible changed movement of the hand. He did it with a tennis ball and 'the bosie became my most prized possession. I practised it day in, day out.'

In 1921, Bill became a boarder at St Patrick's College, Goulburn, and in no time he was a member of the school's football, cricket, tennis and athletics teams. O'Reilly won a two-year scholarship to the Sydney Teachers College. In his spare time he played for the David Jones second XI and was lucky enough to play against journalist Johnnie Moyes, who wrote about him glowingly. Selection in the state practice squad followed and he played his first Shield game for NSW against Queensland in Brisbane in 1927.

O'Reilly played a lot of cricket with and against Bradman.

'On the cricket field we had the greatest respect for each other,' O'Reilly said in his book. 'But off the field we had not much in common. You could say we did not like each other, but it would be closer to the truth to say we chose to have

Bill O'Reilly: inspired by the battle.

little to do with each other.

I don't think that this arose from the ego-laden encounters of our younger days. It was more the product of the chemistry arising from our different backgrounds.

'Don was a teetotaller, ambitious, conservative and meticulous. I was outspoken and gregarious, an equally ambitious young man of Irish descent.'

O'Reilly's first Test was against South Africa at the Adelaide Oval in January 1932. Playing in the same match was fellow spinner, Clarrie Grimmett, 14 years his senior. O'Reilly watched as Grimmett ripped through the Springboks, taking 14 wickets. O'Reilly took a modest 4. It was the start of a long partnership and friendship. Said O'Reilly: 'Clarrie and I bowled in perfect harmony. With him at the other end, I knew full well that no batsmen would be allowed the slightest respite.'

O'Reilly produced his greatest spell of bowling in the first Test at Nottingham in 1934. He took 11/129, defeating England almost single-handedly, giving Australia a flying start in its bid to regain the Ashes. Grimmett had to settle for 6 wickets.

An inspired spell by O'Reilly followed at Manchester. With England 0/68, O'Reilly dismissed Walters (52), Wyatt (0) and Hammond (4)

in four balls. O'Reilly ended with 7/189 of 59 overs as England amassed 9/627 declared. Australia easily won the fifth Test as the Oval to take the series 2–1, O'Reilly and Grimmett collecting 12 wickets between them.

In the series, O'Reilly took 28 wickets at 24.9 apiece.

With Grimmett dropped, O'Reilly had 'Chuck' Fleetwood-Smith as a spinning partner in England in 1938. O'Reilly soon realised the English had taken precautions to prevent the Australian spinners from dominating the series and was not looking forward to it. Nevertheless Australia was 1–up coming to the fifth Test at the Oval. 'You could smell the cow dung a mile away,' said O'Reilly. 'There was no way we were going to win. The pitch was dosed to the eyeballs.'

This was the Test in which Len Hutton scored 364 in 13 plus hours. O'Reilly sent down 85 overs for 3/187 and Fleetwood-Smith 87 overs for 1/298 in England's 7/903 declared. England won by an innings.

Even though he took 23 wickets in four Tests (the third was washed out) O'Reilly had to bowl 263 overs. It was a long and tiring tour and, as it turned out, his last to England as a player.

He wrote later: 'I did not look forward to the 1938 tour of England with the eager anticipation of younger days. You can take it from me that cricket quickly ceases to be fun once you have settled into the round eternal of six days cricket per week through a four-and-a-half months tour. As you rise from your couch each morning you eventually find yourself saying, 'Oh god! Not another day's cricket.'

On his retirement, O'Reilly blamed the English for the dearth of leg-spinners in the post-war years. They couldn't handle them so changed the rules to allow a new ball after 55 eight-ball overs, then after 85 six-ball overs. The battle, he said must be won if cricket was ever going to recover the majesty it had lost as a result of the banishment.

In 1985 he wrote: 'Cricket has suffered a great deal because of the discrimination against leg-spin in favour of fast bowling, and I will go on saying it until I die.'

O'Reilly died on 6 October 1992, but he lived long enough to see the emergence of Shane Warne, who has spread the gospel.

Don Tallon equals record for 'keeper dismissals

Don Tallon: record-breaking keeper.

Brisbane, Feb. 8. Don Tallon, the Queensland wicketkeeper, made seven dismissal in Victoria's first innings – the first time this feat has been achieved in Australia.

Queensland won the match on the back of 215 by Bill Brown, the first time the Bananalanders have beaten Victoria in 13 matches since 1932.

Tallon, whom most observers felt should have gone to England in 1938, is making the Australian selectors look a bit sick. He made 12 dismissals – six in each innings –in the game against NSW in December. This equalled a record set in England in 1868.

He can also bat – he scored 115 against SA at the 'Gabba in January.

MCC centenary

Melbourne, Dec. 14. The Melbourne Cricket Club, founded in 1838, celebrated its centenary, and that of the first cricket match played in Melbourne, with a period costume game after Saturday's play in a celebratory match between Bradman's 1938 Australians and Keith Rigg's XI at the MCG.

Afterwards, with the Members' Stand lit with fairy lights, invited guests and players watched a replica of Captain Smyth's Redcoats of the 80th Regiment, which played in the original game, march to the wicket for the 'toss', and a re-enactment game.

A period ball was held on Tuesday night, with ladies admitted to the Lounge and dining room for the first time.

Bradman hits six in a row

Adelaide, Feb. 25. Recovered from the broken foot he suffered in the fifth Test in England, Don Bradman emphasised and re-emphasised his brilliance as he compiled a record of centuries unsurpassed in the annals of the game. Six centuries in six innings in six matches.

Little-known bowler Frank Thorn disappointed the crowd of 17,777 – a Shield record at the Adelaide oval – on the second day when he had Bradman caught for 5, denying the Don a new record of seven in a row.

Despite this, SA won the Shield, as Victoria needed first-innings points to take it for themselves.

Bradman's run began with a scintillating partnership with Stan McCabe in the game to celebrate the Melbourne Cricket Club's Centenary, played at the MCG in December. Bradman's XI was the 1938 Australians against Keith Rigg's XI. Bradman scored 118 for his team, McCabe 105.

Next century was for SA against NSW, 143 in 270 minutes, which included 91 singles. 'Jack' Badcock hit 271 not out – showing he too had recovered from his single figure trauma in the 1938 Test series.

Appropriately, over Christmas when SA played Queensland in Adelaide, a bowler named Christ (Charles Christ, that is) took Bradman's wicket – but only after he had scored 225 (Badcock 100) in SA's win by an innings and 20 runs.

The fourth century was for SA against Victoria at the MCG in late December, where chasing Victoria's 499 (Lindsay Hassett 211), Bradman made a century in 91 minutes. This was also Bradman's

Don Bradman – hits six in a row.

22nd first class century in the calendar year 1938. He has an aggregate of 3838 runs at an average of 112.88 for 1938.

His fifth century was against Queensland where he scored a chanceless 186 – this time Bradman was finally caught Christ, bowled Les Tallon.

The record-equalling 'ton' was against NSW in Sydney where he made 135 not out.

Englishman C. B. Fry had scored six consecutive centuries in 1901. The Australian record was four by Bradman himself in 1931–32 and Charlie Macartney in England in 1921.

As Bradman has made centuries in his last two innings in Australia before the 1938 tour, he has scored eight consecutive centuries in Australia. Records may be made to be broken, but this is one that is hardly likely ever to be.

Cricket is flourishing all over the country – not least in north Queensland, where the Townsville Bulletin Cricket Club had a successful season.

Cricket still on despite the war

Sydney, March 11. Taking Prime Minister Robert Menzies' advice for the Australian people 'to carry on in a normal way', the Sheffield Shield season of 1939–40 has proceeded as usual, except for a number of players 'joining up'.

A match between Sheffield Shield winners NSW and 'the Rest' was played at the SCG in March for the benefit of patriotic funds. A total of 30,505 people attended the three days, raising £1886, with servicemen and women in uniform allowed in for half price.

NSW won the competitive match by two wickets after trailing on the first innings. Lindsay Hassett hit a quick 136 for the Rest, while the eternal Clarrie Grimmett took 5/65 to dismiss NSW 70 runs behind. Hassett made another 75, also quickly and with Bill Brown's 97 saw the Rest to a 323-run lead.

But Mort Cohen, Stan McCabe and Sid Barnes saw NSW home by two wickets.

Don Bradman only made a modest contribution – 25 and 2. He is expected to enlist, probably in the RAAF, in coming months.

Bradman, Grimmett dominate scene

Sydney, Jan. 30. NSW won the Sheffield Shield for 1939–40, the last to be contested 'for the duration', but it was SA's champions Don Bradman and Clarrie Grimmett who stole the show.

NSW won the Shield by defeating Victoria by 177 runs in this match, and just as significantly defeating SA by 237 runs earlier in January.

Despite two superb 122's from Victoria's Lindsay Hassett, the leggies of Bill O'Reilly and Cecil Pepper were too much for the other Victorian batsmen. Second-innings centuries from Stan McCabe (114) and Sid Barnes (135 not out) enabled NSW to declare at 5/492. Victoria's 326 was 177 short of the victory target.

In the SA game Don Bradman was restricted to 39 and 40, and 'Jack' Badcock to 40 and 20, and while Grimmett took 6/118 and 5/111, the South Australians could not score sufficient runs to trouble NSW.

During the rest of the season, however, Bradman was head and shoulders above the rest.

He scored 1475 runs at 122.91, including 251 not out, and 90 not out in SA's win over NSW, 138

Ben Barnett: Victorian stalwart.

against Queensland, 267 against Victoria, and 209 not out against Western Australia.

Grimmett, apparently ageless and indestructible, took 73 wickets at 22.65 in the season, ahead of O'Reilly's 55 – though 'Tiger's' average was his usual miserly 15.12.

In the end NSW finished one outright win ahead of SA.

An empty street, a kerosine tin, bat and ball, and the kids can play all day, dreaming of Tests and glories to come.

Sgt Observer Ross Gregory was killed in action on 10 June 1942 near Ghafargon, Assam in India. Other bright cricketing lives sadly lost in WWII included Ken Ridings, 17 May 1943; Glen Baker, 15 December 1943; and Charlie Walker, 18 December 1942.

Members of the Australian 9th Division take time out for street cricket during the siege of Tobruk in 1941.

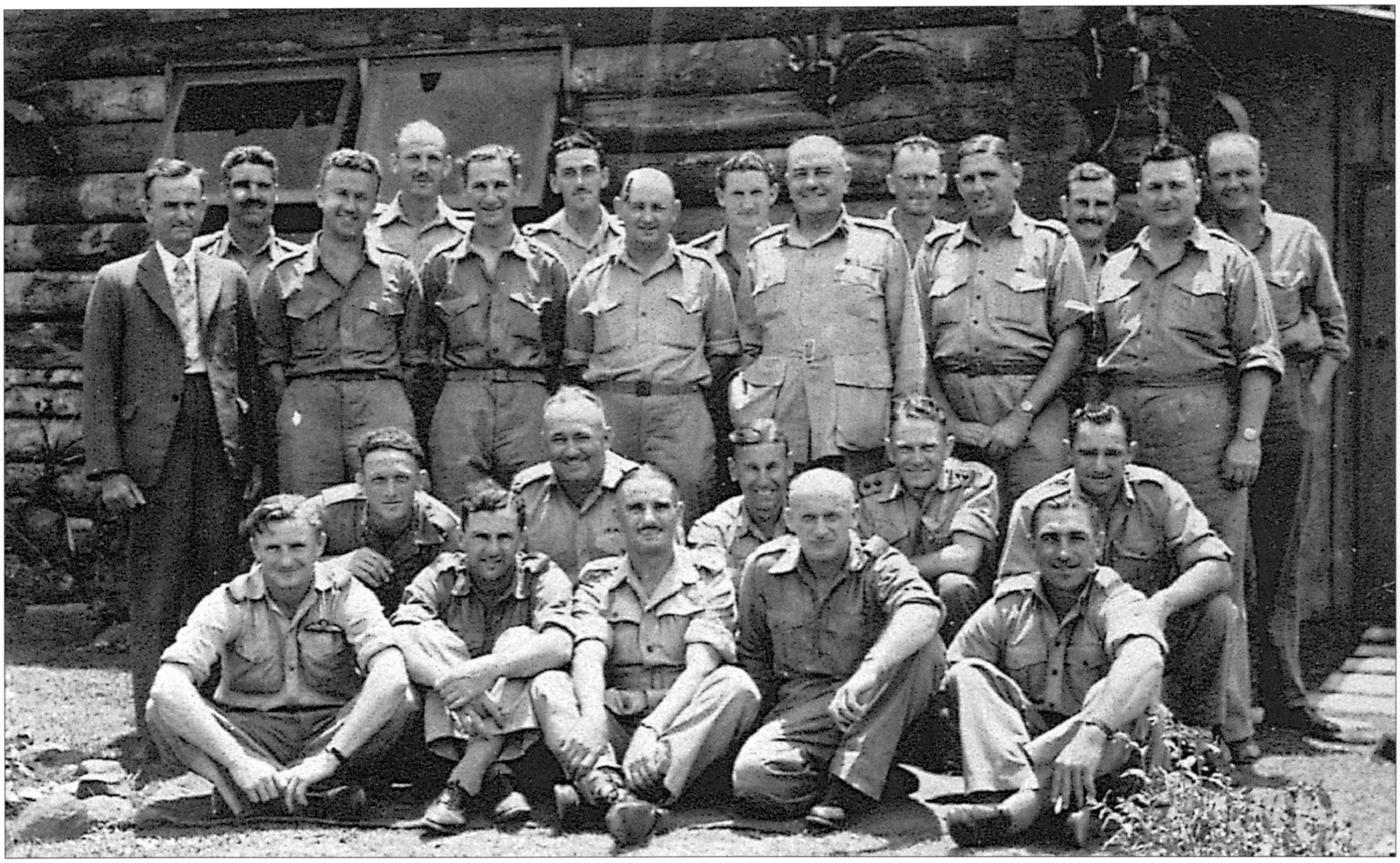

And they could play entertaining cricket too: members of the Army Entertainment Group late in WWII included first class cricketers Ron Saggers, Stan McCabe, Bill Alley, Lincoln Hynes, Bill O'Reilly, Bert Wright, Jack Chegwyn, Sid Barnes, Don Tallon, Colin McCool, Clarrie Grimmett and Vic Jackson.

Cricket revived by Victory 'Test' series

The sensational all-rounder from Victoria Keith Miller hits another four in the Victory Test at Lord's.

Manchester, Aug. 22. Over 367,000 people enjoyed the spirit – and the cricket – of the five 'Victory' Tests played by the Australian Services team against England between May and August. The happy result of the series was 'all square' with two close wins each and one draw.

As Australian captain Lindsay Hassett said at the conclusion of the fifth Test, 'This is cricket as it should be. These games have shown that international cricket can be played as between real friends – so let's have no more talk of "war" in cricket.'

All results were close. Australia went into the match against the cream of English cricket with only Hassett having played in a Test.

They were half expecting to make fools of themseves. Yet with 70 minutes to go, they needed just 107 runs to win. Hassett opened with R. S. 'Dick' Whitington, who was out for a duck. Cecil Pepper came in and a couple of run-outs later, including Keith Miller (105 in the first innings), six runs were required with six wickets in hand and six balls to play. Pepper and Charles Price needed only four deliveries to clinch victory by six wickets, and joy for all and sundry.

England won a closely contested second Test at Bramall Lane, Sheffield, by 41 runs after making only 147 in the first innings.

At Lord's, Australia won the third Test by four wickets, the difference between the two sides being

Miller's hostile spell in the second England innings, where he took a couple of wickets and hit John Dewes in the arm, causing the crowd to call out 'Get off, Larwood!'

The fourth Test, also at Lord's, was drawn, Keith Miller notching another hundred.

The fifth Test was a low-scoring affair at Old Trafford, with Australia 173, England 243 and then Australia 6/69 – before Bob Cristofani thumped 110 not out, from 141 scored. He received a standing ovation. A lead of 210 gave Australia a tiny chance to win, but England scored the runs, losing four wickets. Cristofani played just three Tests but made 164 runs, and took 14 wickets. Miller played five Tests for 443 runs and 10 wickets.

Spirit of goodwill for Indian tour

Madras, Dec. 10. The Services team arrived in Bombay on October 22 for a six-week tour.

Captain Lindsay Hassett said on arrival: 'We have come to India to play cricket, not win trophies.'

The team played three matches against a representative Indian side.

There were two high scoring draws at Bombay in November – Keith Carmody 113 and Jack Pettiford 124, Cecil Pepper 95; and in Calcutta – Dick Whitington 155 and Jack Pettiford 101.

The third match in Madras in December was lost to India by six wickets, despite Lindsay Hassett's 143 and Cecil Pepper taking 4/118 from 41 overs.

The Australian Services XI blazer badge incorporated the insignia of the three services: Army, Air Force and Navy. The only naval player, Melbourne's Dr Ted Cordner, played in the Probables v Possibles game in May 1945.

Keith Miller, the matchwinner

A tall man with broad shoulders, Miller bowled with fire or a sense of fun, delivering a hair-raising bumper or, when least expected, an off-spinner or leg break. Len Hutton said he would rather face the fearsome speed of Ray Lindwall because he knew what to expect from Lindwall.

When batting, Miller backed his eye and timing 'with characteristic panache' against the best of bowlers.

In 55 Tests from 1946 until 1956, he scored 2958 runs at an average of 36.97 with seven centuries and took 170 wickets at 22.97. His highest Test score, 147, was made against the West Indies, one of three centuries he achieved in the Caribbean in 1955. In all first class games, Miller made 14,183 runs at 48.9 with 41 hundreds, and captured 497 wickets at 22.30. He took 136 catches, 38 of them in Tests.

Against England, he played in 29 Tests, scoring 1511 runs (average 33.57) and taking 87 wickets at 22.40. With Ray Lindwall after World War II, the pair revived many memories of Gregory and McDonald after World War I.

Unfortunately for Australia, Miller and Lindwall were not always able to work together because of injuries, but they claimed 197 English wickets and were at their destructive best against England at the Oval in 1948, taking 13/97. With Lindwall hurt in the first Test at Trent Bridge in 1948, Miller with his high action established himself as a great bowler in his own right, capturing 3/38 and 4/125, dismissing Hutton and Compton in both innings.

Keith Ross Miller, born on November 28, 1919, in the Melbourne suburb of Sunshine, was named after two famous Australian aviators, Sir Ross and Sir Keith Smith.

As a boy, Miller often spent Saturday afternoons at St Kilda Cricket Ground watching Bill Ponsford bat. 'Ponny' always seemed to be batting. Miller was small for his age and wanted to be a jockey.

But by the time he was 18 he was well over 6 feet tall and had developed into an all-round athlete. He played 50 games of Australian Rules football for St Kilda and also represented Victoria. In cricket, he was little more than 18 when he made his first class debut for Victoria in February, 1938, and

scored 181 against Tasmania at the MCG. By 1939–40, he was a regular member of the Victorian Shield team and made 108 in his fourth match, against South Australia. After that innings, the wily Clarrie Grimmett, a South Australian, advised him to take up bowling. 'It's more satisfying than batting'. Clem Hill also made an observation: 'This boy will play for Australia'.

When John Arlott, Sergeant of Police, poet and occasional BBC broadcaster, encountered RAAF Sergeant Pilot Miller in the Australian's favorite watering hole, the Seven Bells, in Brighton in 1943, Miller 'was busy living life in case he ran out of it'.

In the course of several convivial evenings, Arlott later recalled, cricket was hardly mentioned. A year later Miller crash landed his Mosquito aircraft, causing the back injury that plagued his bowling career.

Flying Officer Miller lifted the spirits of all those around him in 1945 with his dazzling batting in the five Victory Tests between Australia (led by Warrant Officer Lindsay Hassett) and England (Wally Hammond).

He did not let his growing army of fans down, topping the Victory Test averages with 443 runs at 63.28. He scored 105 in the first Test, 118 in the fourth, and for good measure captured 3/44 and 3/42 in Australia's four wicket win in the third encounter. Veteran judges said he bowled faster than anyone since Larwood.

After his successes in the Victory Tests he was back in August to play for the Dominions against England at Lord's. In the second innings, he hit a glorious 185 in only 165 minutes with seven sixes and 13 fours. His sixes were aimed at the Pavilion and one broke into the famous Long Room. 'Plum' Warner said: 'In an experience of first class cricket over nearly 60 years, I have never seen such hitting.' Raymond Robertson-Glasgow said: 'He is a story-book batsman; were he not fine fact, he would be first-rate fiction.'

On his return to Australia, Miller played in all five Tests against Wally Hammond's 1946–47 touring side, taking the bowling honours with 7/60 and 2/17, as well as making 79 in Australia's innings win in the first Test in Brisbane.

His first Test century, 141 not out, was posted in Adelaide and he

Keith Miller doing what he did best with the ball – putting everything into it.

finished second to Bradman in the averages with 384 runs at 76.8 and second to Lindwall in bowling with 16 wickets (20.87).

Miller did nothing of note against the touring Indians, who were soundly defeated in 1947–48, but against the old enemy, England, in 1948 his enthusiasm returned. He was used sparingly and ended with 13 Test wickets at 23.15 apiece.

An example of his distaste for one-sided contests came at Essex when Australia scored 721 in a day. He let himself be bowled first ball.

'By now,' wrote Arlott in 1948, 'Miller was an immense spectator attraction throughout England. He could infuriate a crowd in a matter of seconds by tossing his long hair forward over his face and sweeping it back with an elaborate gesture, or by bowling a bouncer: or he could charm them by a wave, a brilliant catch, an expansive stroke. Disapproving elders sent him hairpins by post but the young, especially the girls, worshipped him. At the heart of the admiration for him lay admiration for his immense cricketing gifts. He did not display them consistently but in Test after Test he produced a great innings or a magnificent bowling spell ...'

In all matches in 1948, he made 1088 runs at 47.3, with a highest score of 202 not out. His 56 wickets cost 17.58 each.

Miller's omission from the 1949–50 team to tour South Africa caused a rumpus. It was said that Bradman, by now a selector, was annoyed with Miller for bowling

bouncers at him in a testimonial match. As it turned out, Miller went when Bill Johnston was injured and 'Nugget', as Miller was known, reacted as only he could by ripping through South Africa in the first Test in Johannesburg, taking 5/40 in the home side's first innings of 137. Then, in the last Test, he took 4/42, reducing the locals to 158.

Miller's highpoint in 1950–51 against the touring Englishmen was in the third Test. He broke the back of the England batting with 4/34 then dashed off an unbeaten 145 not out. He topped the batting averages with 350 at 43.75 and his 17 wickets cost 17.7 apiece.

Five more Test centuries came Miller's way before he quit the Test scene – 129 against the West Indies in Sydney in 1951–52, 109 at Lord's in 1953, the year Australia lost the Ashes, and three against the West Indies in the Caribbean in 1955 – 147, 137 and 109.

Miller's last tour of England in 1956 was highlighted by Jim Laker's 19 wickets in the dust at Old Trafford and his own 10/152 at his old hunting ground, Lord's. Laker claimed Miller's wicket six times, though the Australian fought hard to score 41 and 26 in the third Test. In 1948 at Lord's, Miller had hit Laker for five sixes; now it was the Englishman's turn. Miller's 21 Test wickets in 1956 put him second only to Laker (46).

One of the greatest disappointments of Miller's career was his failure to win the captaincy of his country. Because of his spirit and attacking nature, he was tipped to succeed Hassett in 1954–55 – the season 'Typhoon' Tyson tore the heart out of Australia's batting – but he was overlooked in favor of Ian Johnson despite the fact he had led NSW to victory over England and NSW to two Sheffield Shield wins. A third consecutive Shield win came in 1956. The highest office Miller attained was vice-captain twice to Johnson – on the first visit to the West Indies in 1955 and in England in 1956.

Miller was awarded an MBE in 1956 and elected in the first eleven of the Australian Cricket Hall of Fame in 1996.

Of the tributes that have flowed Miller's way, none is more appropriate than Arlott's: 'If I had my choice of a player to win a match off the last ball, whether it required a catch, a six or a wicket, I would pick one player – Keith Ross Miller.

First New Zealand Test lasts two days

Wellington, March 30. After some 20 tours across the Tasman in 75 years, Australia and New Zealand finally played a Test match – in part to make up for the promised match cancelled in 1940.

Some controversy greeted the Australian team and who was to captain it. Don Bradman was unavailable, Lindsay Hassett was not favoured, and Bill Brown got the job.

The tourists overwhelmed all opposition in four games before the Test match, with Sid Barnes, Keith Miller, Hassett, and Brown thumping centuries and fast bowler Ray Lindwall being impressive.

New Zealand was hampered by the absence of some leading players, who were still coming back from the war. Captain Walter Hadlee, however, was in good form, having belted 198 for Otago against the Australian attack.

Hadlee won the toss and decided to bat on the damp pitch. Bill O'Reilly (5/14), Ernie Toshack (4/12) and Lindwall with his first Test wicket dismissed NZ for 42 before lunch.

Australia declared at 8/199 next

The Australian team in Wellington, New Zealand, in 1946.

morning. The Australian attack of Lindwall, Toshack, O'Reilly, Miller and Colin McCool had NZ out for 54 in 32.2 overs. The two balls were bowled by McCool, who ended the innings with his first wicket – and second ball – in Test cricket.

It was a disappointing result. Australia put on a batting display in the afternoon for the crowd of 16,000.

Bill O'Reilly decided that his 40-year-old knees had had enough Test cricket, and tossed his boots out of the dressing room window after the match to mark his retirement.

In 27 Tests 'Tiger' took a total of 144 wickets at 22.59.

No Shield but Service team tours

Hobart, Feb. 1. The Australian Services team, suffering what captain Lindsay Hassett calls 'cricket exhaustion', finally concluded their war service, and six-State tour of Australia with a draw in Tasmania.

In all they played 64 games in nine months in England, India, Ceylon and Australia for 27 wins and 12 losses – two of them to Victoria and NSW, the other matches against the States were drawn.

The Services team came up against a few players relishing the chance to get back into big cricket after the war – fresh bowlers such as Ray Lindwall, Ian Johnson, Ernie Toshack, Colin McCool and Bruce Dooland.

Batsmen too, such as Sid Barnes, Bill Alley, Ken Meuleman and Bill Brown were anxious to get back at it. Even Don Bradman, recovering from illness and injury knocked up a recuperative hundred for SA against the Services.

Victoria had wanted to resume the Sheffield Shield competition for 1945–46 season, but will have to wait until next year. Games were played between NSW, Victoria, SA and Queensland before the NZ tour.

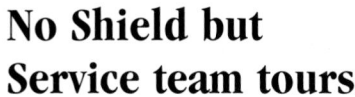

ONLY TEST 1945–46 NEW ZEALAND v AUSTRALIA
Basin Reserve, Wellington. March 29, 30, 1946.
Toss: New Zealand. Australia won by an innings & 103 runs.

NEW ZEALAND

WA Hadlee (c) c Miller b Toshack	6	b Miller	3
WM Anderson b Lindwall	4	b Lindwall	1
VJ Scott c Barnes b O'Reilly	14	c Tallon b Miller	4
WM Wallace c Barnes b Toshack	10	run out	14
EWT Tindill (+) b Toshack	1	lbw Toshack	13
CG Rowe b O'Reilly	0	b O'Reilly	0
LA Butterfield lbw O'Reilly	0	lbw O'Reilly	0
DAN McRae c Hassett b O'Reilly	0 (9)	c Meuleman b McCool	8
C Burke lbw Toshack	1 (8)	b Toshack	3
J Cowie st Tallon b O'Reilly	2	c Toshack b O'Reilly	0
DC Cleverley not out	1	not out	1
EXTRAS (B 3)	3	(B 5, NB 2)	7
TOTAL	42		54

FOW 1st Inns: 7 15 37 37 37 37 37 39 40 42
FOW 2nd Inns: 3 5 12 36 37 37 39 41 42 54

Bowling: *First Innings*: Lindwall 8-1-13-1, Toshack 19-13-12-4, O'Reilly 12-5-14-5. *Second Innings*: Lindwall 9-3-16-1, Toshack 10-5-6-2, O'Reilly 7-1-19-3, Miller 6-2-6-2, McCool 0.2-0-0-1.

AUSTRALIA

WA Brown (c) c Rowe b Burke	67
KD Meuleman b Cowie	0
SG Barnes b Cowie	54
KR Miller c Hadlee b Burke	30
AL Hassett c Tindill b Cowie	19
CL McCool c Hadlee b Cowie	7
IW Johnson not out	7
D Tallon (+) c Scott b Cowie	5
RR Lindwall c Anderson b Cowie	0
WJ O'Reilly	
ERH Toshack	
EXTRAS (B 5, LB 3, NB 2)	10
TOTAL	8 for 199

FOW 1st Inns: 9 118 142 174 186 186 196 199

Bowling: *First Innings*: McRae 14-3-44-0, Cowie 21-8-40-6, Cleverley 15-1-51-0, Butterfield 13-6-24-0, Burke 11-2-30-2.

Umpires: HW Gourlay & MF Pengelly

The Life of O'Reilly

The unique O'Reilly bowling action, with the stoop at the point of delivery. He was advised to change it, but his career figures give the answer to his critics. He took 144 wickets in 27 Tests at an average of 22.59.

Bill O'Reilly was a meticulous man, a school teacher, a company secretary and a highly individual, humorous and even cantakerous writer on the game. He kept his records and photos, and presented them to the New South Wales Cricket Association. He was also one of Australia's greatest bowlers, despite a relatively short career

Married to Molly Herbert at St Francis Xavier's Church, in Paddington, Sydney, on 6 May 1933. The best man (standing next to Molly) is NSW and Test opening batman, Jack Fingleton.

Signing the register; the beginning of a half-century partnership.

of 27 Tests. His nickname was 'Tiger' and he bowled his fast leg-spinners with sustained ferocity, rising to fever pitch when his temper was up. Off the field he was a great team man, fun-loving and with a rich sense of humour. He had a full and happy cricketing and private life, and left a pile of pictures for his admirers to enjoy.

A happy man about the house.

Bill O'Reilly, next to the teacher, with his team at St Patrick's College, Goulburn.

A Test hero mobbed by schoolboys as he leaves the cricket field in Hobart.

With Don Bradman at the opening of the Don Bradman Oval at Bowral.

The scribe in the straw hat.

A tribute to one of cricket's finest. At the opening of the Bill O'Reilly Stand at the Sydney Cricket Ground in 1985.

Bump ball and storms batter England

Brisbane, Dec. 4. After tune-up games against the States in a leisurely anticlockwise tour of Australia to Brisbane, England were quietly confident their more experienced team would account well for itself in the first Test, provided it had an ounce of luck.

Three things happened in Brisbane which demonstrated that luck was the one thing England did not have.

First Bradman won the first toss of the series, second he was given not out at 28 to a 'catch' off Bill Voce and went on to make 187, and third, England had just commenced its second innings when one of two tremendous thunderstorms unloaded on the 'Gabba, turning the uncovered pitch into a lake and then a diabolical 'sticky'.

Losing the toss meant England had to bat when the pitch drained after the downpour – it was so heavy that the stumps were seen floating around on the 'lake'.

When play eventually resumed, England was bundled out for 172 (Toshack 6/82) and Australia won by an innings and 332 runs.

As for the Bradman 'catch' – some close to the wicket thought that Jack Ikin had 'made it'.

But Bradman waited for the umpire's decision. The umpire agreed with his view that it was a bump ball.

Bradman's 187 was perhaps not the most fluent innings he ever played, but it gradually served to roll back the years to the Bradman of old.

Black tie required

Melbourne, Jan. 4. Dinner jackets were required dress at the formal dinner given by the Board of Control during the third Test at the Windsor Hotel. Just as well the England party had been reminded to pack their formal gear by the Board.

While negotiations on tour conditions were taking place the MCC asked the Australian Board whether 'it was thought desirable that players should take dress clothes' because 'such clothes are, at the present time, very expensive here in Britain, and purchase of them would involve the surrender of a number of clothing coupons'.

The Board replied that players might feel 'uncomfortable if they were not able to "dress".'

Australia is a land of milk and honey compared to the war-ravaged England they left behind, not least in the occasions to 'dress'.

NOV 10-16
VOLUME 8, No. 43 NOV. 9, 1946

The ABC weekly

A.B.C. CRICKET COVERAGE —See P. 5

NEW A.B.C. SESSION FOR WOMEN
(SEE PAGE 3)

JOURN... ...RALIAN BROADCASTING COMMISSION
...re ...for transmi... by post as a newspaper.

Ready for the Tests: ABC radio commentator and former Australian captain Vic Richardson looks thoughtfully at England fast bowler Bill Voce.

Queensland 'keeper Don Tallon took his Test chance with both hands.

Film, radio deal

Melbourne, Dec. 31. Film and radio rights of the season's cricket have been negotiated. Twentieth Century Fox paid £40 to each state association for the film rights to all games, while Movietone and British Empire Films paid £25 each for the Test matches.

Radio rights were negotiated with the Federation of Commercial Broadcasting Association. The NSWCA will be paid £1200, VCA, SACA and QCA £800 and WACA and TCA £150.

Listeners in England could tune in to the 'short wave' to hear E. W. Swanton at 8 a.m. local time, 10 p.m. London time. On December 5 he said that no play would be possible because the 'Gabba was under water. They woke next morning to find 15 wickets had fallen and England had lost the first Test.

Barnes, Bradman make 234 – each

Sydney, Dec. 19. The absence of Ray Lindwall in the second Test (due to chickenpox) posed England's batsmen a new problem – could they use their feet to spinners Ian Johnson (6/42) and Colin McCool (3/73)? Answer: no.

But, chasing England's modest 255, Australia was 3/96 and then 4/159 when Don Bradman, batting down the list with a leg injury joined not-out opener Sid Barnes.

Six and a half hours later Bradman was out for 234, and four balls later Barnes was also out on 234, on purpose it's said, as he wished to be remembered for making the same score as the Master.

Their partnership of 405 is a new record for the fifth wicket. E. W. Swanton wrote 'though Bradman had to play almost entirely off the back foot, he always seemed to have two or three strokes to Barnes' one.' Barnes' repertoire of powerful hooks and cuts served him well for over ten hours batting, and an Australian win by an innings.

Bradman on Board

Don Bradman, a portrait by Ivor Hele.

Melbourne, Jan. 4. Don Bradman, now a SACA delegate to the Board of Control, spoke on a number of matters at the Board meeting which commenced on December 30, the day before the third Test.

Bradman has had to fit in attendance at the meeting with playing in the Test, and has succeeded admirably at both.

He has put the players' point of view on a number of issues, ranging from the type of ball to be used to players' hotel rooms.

In the new post-war era it is seen as a refreshing change to have a current Australian captain able to speak on behalf of the players' welfare, particularly one with such experience of cricket and of dealing with the Board, as Bradman had before the war.

Hard lesson for old England

Lindsay Hassett makes a graceful leg-side shot in the third Test. Edrich, Evans and Hammond can only watch it go.

Sydney, March 5. After the two high scoring draws in Melbourne and Adelaide, England came to Sydney still seeking a consolation win in the series. Remarkably, the draw in the third Test was the first in Australia since 1882.

But luck turned against the older English team – they are several years older on average than the Australians – as it had in the first Test. This time bad luck was in the form of illness to Len Hutton, who retired ill on 122 in the first innings of 280 and could not bat in the second. Even so this innings and the bowling of bouncy leg spinner Doug Wright who nabbed 7/105 in Australia's first innings, took England to 253 and a lead of 27. Had Hutton been able to bat in the second innings no doubt England would have made more than 186.

The second piece of bad luck was Bill Edrich uncharacteristically dropping Don Bradman in the second innings when he had scored just 2. Bradman went on to steer Australia to a five wicket win with 63.

Arthur Morris, after failing in the first two Tests and scoring 21 in the first innings of the third Test, found form with a vengeance, hitting 155, 122 and 124 not out, in his next three innings and 57 in the fifth Test.

His pair of hundreds in the Adelaide Test accompanied 147 and 103 not out from Denis Compton, the first time two players have achieved this double in a Test.

The Melbourne match was remarkable for other less-heralded batsmen. Colin McCool's match-saving 104 not out in the first innings preceded a seventh-wicket partnership of 154 between Don Tallon (92) and Ray Lindwall (100).

Australia won the series 3–0 in front of huge and enthusiastic crowds, especially at the MCG. The tour made a profit of £39,722 and was played in a friendly and attractive way – despite some murmurings about Keith Miller's use of the bumper.

Memberships rise

Perth, March 31. The first real post-war season and the appeal of an England tour has sent membership and receipts of state cricket associations soaring.

In Perth membership of the WACA increased by 1186 and the ground had 100 additional seats installed.

In Adelaide membership rose to 3837 and the SACA had to create a waiting list for the first time.

In Melbourne the MCC profit on cricket matches was £17,992 while membership rose to 7085. The VCA profit was £9502.

In NSW it was the same story - the trustees of the SCG had a newly created waiting list of 5000, and the NSWCA recorded assets of £79,800. The QCA spent a large sum on the 'Gabba and was in profit by £1433.

Vics win Shield

Melbourne, March 30. Victoria dominated the 1946–47 Sheffield Shield season, winning five of six matches outright, while the other was a rained-off draw.

With or without Test players called up, Victoria scored 548, 543, 8/560, 466, 356 and 3/450

It had the dominant batsmen in Lindsay Hassett and Keith Miller, who scored at a phenomenal rate.

Hassett made 128, 126, 114, 200 and 190 during the season, Miller 141 not out, 188, 153, and 206 not out. Sam Loxton also scored a double century – 232 not out, Doug Ring 145 and Merv Harvey 136.

George Tribe was the outstanding Victorian bowler – he took 6/49 against England, 7/85 and 6/68 against SA, and 7/100 and 5/71 against NSW.

State of the game

Sydney, March 31. The NSWCA commissioned a report on the state of cricket in NSW from selectors, headed by 'Chappie' Dwyer.

While acknowledging the success of the season just past, the report saw long term problems for cricket as it competed with rival outdoor pastimes such as golf, tennis and surfing. There was competition from gambling and racing.

There was 'the increased competition for jobs among young people – who were concentrating less on cricket – and a reluctance of employers to give cricketers time off to play or practise'.

A loss of interest at schools was another long term problem, as was the loss of open space around Sydney. Other Associations took note.

'Professional' cricketers' pay

Melbourne, Jan. 18. The *Sporting Globe's* Hec de Lacy asked in an article whether players are paid enough considering that cricket has become close to a full-time summer job. He said the public want to see the best players, but employers might become reluctant to release them for so much time.

Victorian Sheffield Shield players each receive 30 shillings a day expenses, plus loss of time on an employer's certificate up to £1 a day. Board and residence and travel are paid by the VCA.

Test players are paid £40 a match and 30 shillings a day for board and residence. Touring England, players receive £600 and 30 shillings a day out-of-pocket expenses. All board and travel is found.

The question is, are these payments sufficient to keep the best players in the game for long enough, and to set them up for life after cricket?

George Tribe at backyard practice.

Bradman speaks his mind to pressman

Sydney, March 10. Australian captain Don Bradman spoke freely to English cricket writer E.W. 'Jim' Swanton after the fifth Test, before Swanton joined the English team on the flying boat at Rose Bay in Sydney Harbour to go to NZ.

Bradman told Swanton that he thought that Australia would be strong, but had 'turned out better than he'd hoped with batting to meet all demands, well-varied bowling, and almost everyone capable of making a hundred.' He said they had a natural aggressive spirit.

He praised the 'sheer artistry, the classical style and power' of an innings by Miller.

He said the quick resumption of Test cricket after the war had justified itself – psychologically, technically and financially.

Of the Englishmen, he liked leg-spinner Doug Wright and thought that Alec Bedser was better than Maurice Tate in 1928–29, and that England needed a genuine fast bowler.

Bradman still wanted the change in the lbw law that he had advocated in the 1939 *Wisden* – that a batsman could be out even if his pads extended outside the line of the off stump.

He said that the most vital consideration in cricket was the mental attitude of the player 'who can if he chooses spoil any game by his interpretation of its character.'

On pitches – he said that too often they were too good, they should be 'true' but reasonably nat-ural. He did not offer an opinion whether Australian wickets ought to be covered. He said he preferred to bat on English pitches though most Australian batsmen did not.

He could not yet say whether he would or would not go to England in 1948. He would love to, but then had to look after himself and at the present time rated it 'unlikely'. Which is bad news for Australians.

Bradman took a swipe at a few jealous critics who had seen nothing satisfactory in anything he had ever done, and whose 'intent was so obvious that it was laughable.'

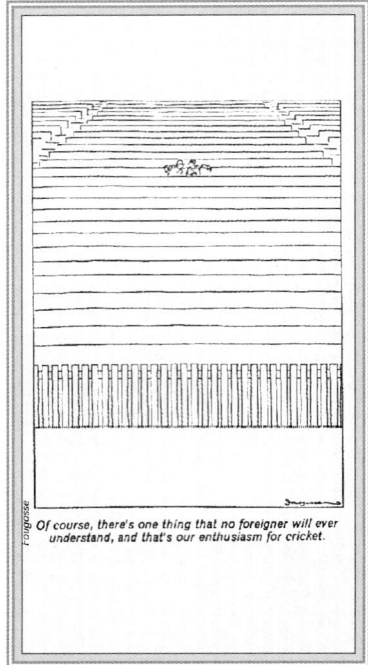
Of course, there's one thing that no foreigner will ever understand, and that's our enthusiasm for cricket.

FIRST TEST 1946–47 AUSTRALIA v ENGLAND
Brisbane Cricket Ground, Brisbane. November 29, 30, December 2, 3, 4, 1946.
Toss: Australia. Australia won by an innings & 332 runs.

AUSTRALIA

SG Barnes c Bedser b Wright	31
AR Morris c Hammond b Bedser	2
DG Bradman (c) b Edrich	187
AL Hassett c Yardley b Bedser	128
KR Miller lbw Wright	79
CL McCool lbw Wright	95
IW Johnson lbw Wright	47
D Tallon (+) lbw Edrich	14
RR Lindwall c Voce b Wright	31
GE Tribe c Gibb b Edrich	1
ERH Toshack not out	1
EXTRAS (B 5, LB 11, W 2, NB 11)	29
TOTAL	645

FOW 1st Inns: 9 46 322 428 465 596 599 629 643 645

Bowling: *First Innings*: Voce 28-9-92-0, Bedser 41-5-159-2, Wright 43.6-4-167-5, Edrich 25-2-107-3, Yardley 13-1-47-0, Ikin 2-0-24-0, Compton 6-0-20-0.

ENGLAND

L Hutton b Miller	7	c Barnes b Miller	0
C Washbrook c Barnes b Miller	6	c Barnes b Miller	13
WJ Edrich c McCool b Miller	16	lbw Toshack	7
DCS Compton lbw Miller	17	c Barnes b Toshack	15
WR Hammond (c) lbw Toshack	32	b Toshack	23
JT Ikin c Tallon b Miller	0	b Tribe	32
NWD Yardley c Tallon b Toshack	29	c Hassett b Toshack	0
PA Gibb (+) b Miller	13	lbw Toshack	11
W Voce not out	1	c Hassett b Tribe	18
AV Bedser lbw Miller	0	c & b Toshack	18
DVP Wright c Tallon b Toshack	4	not out	10
EXTRAS (B 8, LB 3, W 2, NB 3)	16	(B 15, LB 7, W 1, NB 2)	25
TOTAL	141		172

FOW 1st Inns: 10 25 49 56 56 121 134 136 136 141
FOW 2nd Inns: 0 13 33 62 65 65 112 114 143 172

Bowling: *First Innings*: Lindwall 12-4-23-0, Miller 22-4-60-7, Toshack 16.5-11-17-3, Tribe 9-2-19-0, McCool 1-0-5-0, Barnes 1-0-1-0. *Second Innings*: Miller 11-3-17-2, Toshack 20.7-2-82-6, Tribe 12-2-48-2.

Umpires: EG Borwick & JD Scott

SECOND TEST 1946–47 AUSTRALIA v ENGLAND
Sydney Cricket Ground, Sydney. December 13, 14, 16, 17, 18, 19, 1946.
Toss: England. Australia won by an innings & 33 runs.

ENGLAND

L Hutton c Tallon b Johnson	39	hit wicket b Miller	37
C Washbrook b Freer	1	c McCool b Johnson	41
WJ Edrich lbw McCool	71	b McCool	119
DCS Compton c Tallon b McCool	5	c Bradman b Freer	54
WR Hammond (c) c Tallon b McCool	1	c Toshack b McCool	37
JT Ikin c Hassett b Johnson	60	b Freer	17
NWD Yardley c Tallon b Johnson	25	b McCool	35
TPB Smith lbw Johnson	4	c Hassett b Johnson	2
TG Evans (+) b Johnson	5	st Tallon b McCool	9
AV Bedser b Johnson	14	not out	3
DVP Wright not out	15	c Tallon b McCool	0
EXTRAS (B 4, LB 11)	15	(B 8, LB 6, W 1, NB 2)	17
TOTAL	255		371

FOW 1st Inns: 10 88 97 99 148 187 197 205 234 255
FOW 2nd Inns: 49 118 220 280 309 327 346 366 369 371

Bowling: *First Innings*: Miller 9-2-24-0, Freer 7-1-25-1, Toshack 7-2-6-0, Tribe 20-3-70-0, Johnson 30.1-12-42-6, McCool 23-2-73-3. *Second Innings*: Miller 11-3-37-1, Freer 13-2-49-2, Toshack 6-1-16-0, Tribe 12-0-40-0, Johnson 29-7-92-2, McCool 32.4-4-109-5, Barnes 3-0-11-0.

AUSTRALIA

SG Barnes c Ikin b Bedser	234
AR Morris b Edrich	5
IW Johnson c Washbrook b Edrich	7
AL Hassett c Compton b Edrich	34
KR Miller c Evans b Smith	40
DG Bradman (c) lbw Yardley	234
CL McCool c Hammond b Smith	12
D Tallon (+) c & b Wright	30
FW Freer not out	28
GE Tribe not out	25
ERH Toshack	
EXTRAS (LB 7, W 1, NB 2)	10
TOTAL	8 dec 659

FOW 1st Inns: 24 37 96 159 564 564 595 617

Bowling: *First Innings*: Bedser 46-7-153-1, Edrich 26-3-79-3, Wright 46-8-169-1, Smith 37-1-172-2, Ikin 3-0-15-0, Compton 6-0-38-0, Yardley 9-0-23-1.

Umpires: EG Borwick & JD Scott

THIRD TEST 1946–47 AUSTRALIA v ENGLAND
Melbourne Cricket Ground, Melbourne. January 1, 2, 3, 4, 6, 7, 1947.
Toss: Australia. Match Drawn.

AUSTRALIA

SG Barnes lbw Bedser	.45	c Evans b Yardley	.32
AR Morris lbw Bedser	.21	b Bedser	.155
DG Bradman (c) b Yardley	.79	c & b Yardley	.49
AL Hassett c Hammond b Wright	.12	b Wright	.9
KR Miller c Evans b Wright	.33	c Hammond b Yardley	.34
IW Johnson lbw Yardley	.0 (7)	run out	.0
CL McCool not out	.104 (6)	c Evans b Bedser	.43
D Tallon (+) c Evans b Edrich	.35	c & b Wright	.92
RR Lindwall b Bedser	.9	c Washbrook b Bedser	.100
B Dooland c Hammond b Edrich	.19	c Compton b Wright	.1
ERH Toshack c Hutton b Edrich	.6	not out	.2
EXTRAS (NB 2)	.2	(B 14, LB 2, NB 3)	.19
TOTAL	.365		.536

FOW 1st Inns: 32 108 143 188 188 192 255 272 355 365
FOW 2nd Inns: 68 159 177 242 333 335 341 495 511 536

Bowling: *First Innings*: Voce 10-2-40-0, Bedser 31-4-99-3, Wright 26-2-124-2, Yardley 20-4-50-2, Edrich 10.3-2-50-3. *Second Innings*: Voce 6-1-29-0, Bedser 34.3-4-176-3, Wright 32-3-131-3, Yardley 20-0-67-3, Edrich 18-1-86-0, Hutton 3-0-28-0.

ENGLAND

L Hutton c McCool b Lindwall	.2	c Bradman b Toshack	.40
C Washbrook c Tallon b Dooland	.62	b Dooland	.112
WJ Edrich lbw Lindwall	.89	lbw McCool	.13
DCS Compton lbw Toshack	.11	run out	.14
WR Hammond (c) c & b Dooland	.9	b Lindwall	.26
JT Ikin c Miller b Dooland	.48	c Hassett b Miller	.5
NWD Yardley b McCool	.61	not out	.53
TG Evans (+) b McCool	.17 (9)	not out	.0
W Voce lbw Dooland	.0		
AV Bedser not out	.27 (8)	lbw Miller	.25
DVP Wright b Johnson	.10		
EXTRAS (B 8, LB 12, NB 2)	.15	(B 15, LB 6, W 1)	.22
TOTAL	.351		.7 for 310

FOW 1st Inns: 8 155 167 176 179 292 298 298 324 351
FOW 2nd Inns: 138 163 186 197 221 249 294

Bowling: *First Innings*: Lindwall 20-1-64-2, Miller 10-0-34-0, Toshack 26-5-88-1, McCool 19-3-53-2, Dooland 27-5-69-4, Johnson 6.5-1-28-1. *Second Innings*: Lindwall 16-2-59-1, Miller 11-0-41-2, Toshack 16-5-39-1, McCool 24-9-41-1, Dooland 21-1-84-1, Johnson 12-4-24-0.

Umpires: EG Borwick & JD Scott

FOURTH TEST 1946–47 AUSTRALIA v ENGLAND
Adelaide Oval, Adelaide. January 31, February 1, 3, 4, 5, 6, 1947.
Toss: England. Match Drawn.

ENGLAND

L Hutton lbw McCool	.94	b Johnson	.76
C Washbrook c Tallon b Dooland	.65	c Tallon b Lindwall	.39
WJ Edrich c & b Dooland	.17	c Bradman b Toshack	.46
WR Hammond (c) b Toshack	.18	c Lindwall b Toshack	.22
DCS Compton c & b Lindwall	.147	not out	.103
J Hardstaff jr b Miller	.67	b Toshack	.9
JT Ikin c Toshack b Dooland	.21	lbw Toshack	.1
NWD Yardley not out	.18	c Tallon b Lindwall	.18
AV Bedser b Lindwall	.2	c Tallon b Miller	.3
TG Evans (+) b Lindwall	.0	not out	.10
DVP Wright b Lindwall	.0		
EXTRAS (B 4, LB 5, W 2)	.11	(B 5, LB 3, W 2, NB 3)	.13
TOTAL	.460		.8 dec 340

FOW 1st Inns: 137 173 196 202 320 381 455 460 460 460
FOW 2nd Inns: 100 137 178 188 207 215 250 255

Bowling: *First Innings*: Lindwall 23-5-52-4, Miller 16-0-45-1, Toshack 30-13-59-1, McCool 29-1-91-1, Johnson 22-3-69-0, Dooland 33-1-133-3. *Second Innings*: Lindwall 17.1-4-60-2, Miller 11-0-34-1, Toshack 36-6-76-4, McCool 19-3-41-0, Johnson 25-8-51-1, Dooland 17-2-65-0.

AUSTRALIA

MR Harvey b Bedser	.12	b Yardley	.31
AR Morris c Evans b Bedser	.122	not out	.124
DG Bradman (c) b Bedser	.0	not out	.56
AL Hassett c Hammond b Wright	.78		
KR Miller not out	.141		
IW Johnson lbw Wright	.52		
CL McCool c Bedser b Yardley	.2		
D Tallon (+) b Wright	.3		
RR Lindwall c Evans b Yardley	.20		
B Dooland c Bedser b Yardley	.29		
ERH Toshack run out	.0		
EXTRAS (B 16, LB 6, W 2, NB 4)	.28	(LB 2, NB 2)	.4
TOTAL	.487		.1 for 215

FOW 1st Inns: 18 18 207 222 372 389 396 423 486 487
FOW 2nd Inns: 116

Bowling: *First Innings*: Bedser 30-6-97-3, Edrich 20-3-88-0, Wright 32.4-1-152-3, Yardley 31-7-101-3, Ikin 2-0-9-0, Compton 3-0-12-0. *Second Innings*: Bedser 15-1-68-0, Edrich 7-2-25-0, Wright 9-0-49-0, Yardley 13-0-69-1.

Umpires: EG Borwick & JD Scott

FIFTH TEST 1946–47 AUSTRALIA v ENGLAND
Sydney Cricket Ground, Sydney. February 28, March 1 (no play), 3, 4, 5, 1947.
Toss: England. Australia won by 5 wkts.

ENGLAND

L Hutton retired hurt	.122		
C Washbrook b Lindwall	.0	b McCool	.24
WJ Edrich c Tallon b Lindwall	.60	st Tallon b McCool	.24
LB Fishlock b McCool	.14 (1)	lbw Lindwall	.0
DCS Compton hit wicket b Lindwall	.17 (4)	c Miller b Toshack	.76
NWD Yardley (c) c Miller b Lindwall	.2	b McCool	.11
JT Ikin b Lindwall	.0 (5)	st Tallon b McCool	.0
TG Evans (+) b Lindwall	.29 (7)	b Miller	.20
TPB Smith b Lindwall	.2 (8)	c Tallon b Lindwall	.24
AV Bedser not out	.10 (9)	st Tallon b McCool	.4
DVP Wright c Tallon b Miller	.7 (10)	not out	.1
EXTRAS (B 7, LB 8, W 1, NB 1)	.17	(B 1, LB 1)	.2
TOTAL	.9 dec 280		.9 dec 186

FOW 1st Inns: 1 151 188 215 225 225 244 269 280
FOW 2nd Inns: 0 42 65 65 85 120 157 184 186

Bowling: *First Innings*: Lindwall 22-3-63-7, Miller 15.3-2-31-1, Tribe 28-2-95-0, Toshack 16-4-40-0, McCool 13-0-34-1. *Second Innings*: Lindwall 12-1-46-2, Miller 6-1-11-1, Tribe 14-0-58-0, Toshack 4-1-14-1, McCool 21.4-5-44-5, Barnes 3-0-11-0.

AUSTRALIA

SG Barnes c Evans b Bedser	.71	c Evans b Bedser	.30
AR Morris lbw Bedser	.57	run out	.17
DG Bradman (c) b Wright	.12	c Compton b Bedser	.63
AL Hassett c Ikin b Wright	.24	c Ikin b Wright	.47
KR Miller c Ikin b Wright	.23	not out	.34
RA Hamence not out	.30	c Edrich b Wright	.1
CL McCool c Yardley b Wright	.3	not out	.13
D Tallon (+) c Compton b Wright	.0		
RR Lindwall c Smith b Wright	.0		
GE Tribe c Fishlock b Wright	.9		
ERH Toshack run out	.5		
EXTRAS (B 7, LB 6, NB 6)	.19	(B 4, LB 1, NB 4)	.9
TOTAL	.253		.5 for 214

FOW 1st Inns: 126 146 146 187 218 230 230 233 245 253
FOW 2nd Inns: 45 51 149 173 180

Bowling: *First Innings*: Bedser 27-7-49-2, Edrich 7-0-34-0, Smith 8-0-38-0, Wright 29-4-105-7, Yardley 5-2-8-0. *Second Innings*: Bedser 22-4-75-2, Edrich 2-0-14-0, Smith 2-0-8-0, Wright 22-1-93-2, Yardley 3-1-7-0, Compton 1.2-0-8-0.

Umpires: EG Borwick & JD Scott

Australian Averages

1946–47 AUSTRALIA v ENGLAND

AUSTRALIA	M	Inn	NO	Runs	H.S	Avrge	Ct	St	Overs	Mds	Runs	Wkt	Avrge
Barnes, SG	4	6	-	443	234	73.83	4	-	7.0	-	23	-	-
Bradman, DG	5	8	1	680	234	97.14	3	-	-	-	-	-	-
Dooland, B	2	3	-	49	29	16.33	2	-	98.0	9	351	8	43.88
Freer, FW	1	1	1	28	28*	-	-	-	20.0	3	74	3	24.67
Hamence, RA	1	2	1	31	30*	31.00	-	-	-	-	-	-	-
Harvey, MR	1	2	-	43	31	21.50	-	-	-	-	-	-	-
Hassett, AL	5	7	-	332	128	47.43	5	-	-	-	-	-	-
Johnson, IW	4	5	-	106	52	21.20	-	-	124.6	35	306	10	30.60
Lindwall, RR	4	5	-	160	100	32.00	-	-	122.1	20	367	18	20.39
McCool, CL	5	7	2	272	104*	54.40	3	-	182.0	27	491	18	27.28
Miller, KR	5	7	2	384	141*	76.80	3	-	122.3	15	334	16	20.88
Morris, AR	5	8	1	503	155	71.86	-	-	-	-	-	-	-
Tallon, D	5	6	-	174	92	29.00	16	4	-	-	-	-	-
Toshack, ERH	5	5	2	14	6	4.67	3	-	178.4	50	437	17	25.71
Tribe, GE	3	3	1	35	25*	17.50	-	-	95.0	9	330	2	165.00

English Averages

1946–47 AUSTRALIA v ENGLAND

ENGLAND	M	Inn	NO	Runs	H.S	Avrge	Ct	St	Overs	Mds	Runs	Wkt	Avrge
Bedser, AV	5	10	3	106	27*	15.14	3	-	246.3	38	876	16	54.75
Compton, DCS	5	10	1	459	147	51.00	4	-	16.2	-	78	-	-
Edrich, WJ	5	10	-	462	119	46.20	1	-	115.3	13	483	9	53.67
Evans, TG	4	8	2	90	29	15.00	9	-	-	-	-	-	-
Fishlock, LB	1	2	-	14	14	7.00	1	-	-	-	-	-	-
Gibb, PA	1	2	-	24	13	12.00	1	-	-	-	-	-	-
Hammond, WR	4	8	-	168	37	21.00	6	-	-	-	-	-	-
Hardstaff jr, J	1	2	-	76	67	38.00	-	-	-	-	-	-	-
Hutton, L	5	9	1	417	122*	52.13	1	-	3.0	-	28	-	-
Ikin, JT	5	10	-	184	60	18.40	4	-	7.0	-	48	-	-
Smith, TPB	2	4	-	32	24	8.00	1	-	47.0	1	218	2	109.00
Voce, W	2	4	-	19	9	9.50	1	-	44.0	12	161	-	-
Washbrook, C	5	10	-	363	112	36.30	2	-	-	-	-	-	-
Wright, DVP	5	8	3	47	15*	9.40	2	-	240.2	23	990	23	43.04
Yardley, NWD	5	10	2	252	61	31.50	3	-	114.0	15	372	10	37.20

India brings new cricket style out to Australian fields

Perth, Oct. 6. It's been a long time coming, but at last an Indian cricket team has arrived in Australia to play Test cricket.

While India first toured England in 1932, and has made two subsequent tours, Australian cricket lovers have been deprived of their elegant batsmen and guileful spinners until now.

An unofficial Australian team sponsored by the Maharajah of Patiala visited in 1935–36, and the Services team played three unofficial 'Tests' in 1945 (losing one) but that is the extent of Australia's cricket contact.

The party of 17 players is captained by Lala Amarnath, but unfortunately the brilliant bats Vijay Merchant and Rusi Modi were unable to come. Merchant had made 155 not out, and Modi 203 against the 1945 Services side. However Amarnath is a batsman of the highest quality – he also hit a hundred in 1945, and in 'Vinoo' Mankad India has a genuine all-rounder who did the double in England in 1946 – 1000 runs and 100 wickets. Vijay Hazare is also a batsman of quality – twice in the 1939–40 season in India he made over 300.

India will play five Tests and 14 matches altogether.

Indian all-rounder Mulvantri Himatial Mankad is known as 'Vinoo' to his cricket friends.

Bradman and Toshack set winning note

Sid Barnes traps Indian captain Lala Amarnath lbw at the MCG in the first official Test between Australia and India.

Brisbane, Dec. 4. Australia completed an overwhelming victory over India in the first official Test between the two countries on the sixth day – the fifth day was abandoned because of rain, and on three of the other days only two hours play was possible.

Given Ernie Toshack's bowling and Don Bradman's batting this was all that was required – but the weather nearly caused a riot on the second day.

Several hundred spectators had travelled long distances to Brisbane from the canefields of North Queensland and did not take kindly to being given tickets for Monday's play, when they would have to go back north on the Sunday. They had spend upwards of £5 to see cricket – and they wanted cricket or their money back.

On day two, play started at 4.52 p.m., and while Indian captain Amarnath was cheered, Australia's captain Don Bradman was hooted when he and Keith Miller resumed their innings. Cries of 'Knock 'em over' and 'Come on, Mankad' were heard. Evidently the crowd blamed Bradman and not Amarnath for the delay in play.

Bradman was not knocked over – at least not until he made 185, and even then he hit his own wicket. With a whirlwind 58 from Miller, Australia made 8/358 before Bradman declared.

Ray Lindwall made a mess of India in his first over, a maiden, taking two wickets, and at 53 India had lost 5 wickets.

Enter Ernie Toshack with his left-arm medium-to-slow varieties of cutters, stoppers and fizzers.

He bowled just 19 deliveries, taking one wicket in his first over, three in his second at a cost of two runs, and a fifth with the third ball of his third over – 5/2.

India's second innings extended from the third day to the sixth, but only totalled 98 runs. Toshack was once again the destroyer, taking 6/29 from 17 overs.

Barnes locked out – again. Out-of-favour opening batsman Sid Barnes' troubles with turnstile attendants continued in Brisbane when he was refused entry to Australia's final practice session, despite being identified by players and pressmen.

Fair weather bats. Indian great Duleepsinjhi said in December that 'Australians and Indians have a lot to learn about how to play on a sticky wicket. They are fair-weather batsmen.'

Too many 'keepers. Stan Sismey, one of the best 'keepers in the country, can't get a game for NSW while Ron Saggers is in the team, And Saggers can't play for Australia while Don Tallon has the job.

Alley for Lancashire. NSW all rounder Bill Alley played his last Sydney grade game in December before going to Lancashire League club Coine.

Cheaper cricket. Chairman of the SCG Trust Dick Jones says that 3/3d and 5/11d is too much to pay for Test cricket. He wants pass outs for another day if two hours cricket aren't seen, family tickets and other innovations. 'I want to bring about a better understanding between the people who pay for the sport and the people who stage it', he said in December.

Lindwall's bunny. Indian opener Vinoo Mankad has had a wretched start to the series, being dismissed by Ray Lindwall for 0, 7, 5, and 5 in the first two Tests.

Indian 'coach'. Indian captain Lala Amarnath said in January that: 'Frequently after a game Bradman has come to tell our players over a cup of tea of faults they had made in batting, fielding or bowling, and how they can correct them'.

Ten bob a run. Don Bradman has been offered 10 shillings a run in the fifth Test by Jim Burton of the Kedron Park Hotel. 'This will certainly be Don's last big game in Australia,' he said, hoping to pay out on 'a couple of hundred'.

Toshack not wanted. Ernie Toshack, resting his injured ankle from his Australian duties in February, turned up to play for his club side Petersham 12 minutes before play was due to start. He was told in no uncertain terms he was not included in the side – because he had not acknowledged his selection earlier in the week. A team does need discipline.

Indian tour becomes a rout

The Indian team: Standing (l. to r.) are W. Ferguson (scorer), C.R. Rangachary, G. Kishenchand, J.K. Irani, K.M. Rangnekar, Rai Singh, P.K. Sen, M.S. Ranvirsinjhi, D.G. Phadkar, H.R. Adhikary, T.A. Langridge (masseur). Seated: C.T. Sarwate, Gul Mahomed, S.W. Sohoni, V.S. Hazare, L. Amarnath, P. Gupta (manager), V. Mankad, C.S. Nayudu, Amir Elahi.

Melbourne, Feb. 10. 'Vinoo' Mankad spoiled Bill Brown's Test match – again – by running him out on 99, this time not at the bowler's end, but with a smart return to the 'keeper.

Mankad then went on to a painstaking 111, which with Vijay Hazare's 72 not out overnight on the third day, looked like helping India stave off the follow-on.

That was about the best moment for India in the fifth Test, as they went down by the large margin of an innings and 177 runs.

For Australia the highlight was the magnificent 153 made in refreshing style by 19 year old Neil Harvey. He is the youngest Australian Test centurion and probably the only one who has brought up his hundred with an all run five.

It's a 'Mankad'

Sydney, Dec. 17. 'Vinoo' Mankad ran out Australian opener Bill Brown – at the bowler's end in the second Test, without warning.

This caused a stir at the ground, at the time, but observers such as the *Sporting Globe's* Hec de Lacy say Brown deserved what he got.

He had been warned by Mankad for overzealous backing-up in the India v Australian XI game, but persisted and was run out.

To do it again in the Test match was bound to add injury to insult. Sportsmanship does not come into it, says de Lacy, Brown was two yards out of his crease, trying to make a short single even shorter.

Arthur Morris in the first Test was warned by Mankad, desisted, and was not run out.

Since the rained-out draw in the second Test in Sydney, where only 10 hours play was possible, Australia has demonstrated a crushing superiority over the Indians.

India has proved to be among the most popular teams ever to visit Australia, having been accosted by people apparently sick of Australia winning all the time, wishing them luck and hoping they can pull off a win.

No such luck at Melbourne where only cramp could get out Bradman, and Keith Miller entertained with three sixes in his cameo innings of 29.

In Adelaide, Australia scored 674, its highest total in Australia, with a Bradman double century and a Lindsay Hassett 198, and while

John Bradman (fourth from right, leaning on radio) and his mates wait around the radio for Dad's hundredth hundred.

Hazare achieved the distinction of a century in each innings for India, they were still defeated by an innings and 16 runs.

Mankad and Hazare with two hundreds apiece, and all-rounder Phadkar with one have shown something with the bat, but captain Lala Amarnath has been a failure.

Ray Lindwall and Keith Miller have made India's top order batting look shaky indeed.

The bowling (and too frequently, the fielding) has been a problem, being unable to seriously limit the Australian scoring, especially by Don Bradman.

Australia had to bat twice only once in the Tests, and Bradman made 185, 13, 132 and 127 not out, 201 and 57 retired hurt. Not bad for an 'old' man.

100 hundreds

Sydney, Nov. 17. The Indian cricketers have got their wish, expressed before the tour, that Don Bradman would score his hundredth hundred against them.

The 'cricketing colossus' made the record, the first Australian to do so, in his 295th innings, a feat approached by no other batsman.

Captaining an Australian XI he played carefully until the last over before tea on the second day when, on 99, Indian captain Lala Amarnath threw the ball to Gogumal Kishenchand for his first over of the tour. Bradman pushed the second ball to the leg side for a single, and a hundred hundreds. He finished with 172 and 26, not enough to win the match. India won by 47 runs.

Press query on covering wickets

Melbourne, Dec. 10. Indian captain Lala Amarnath, who declined the offer of covered wickets in Tests in Australia, must have regretted it after the unsatisfactory, even unsavoury events in Brisbane. But covering wickets may not be the answer.

Critics ask the proponents of covered wickets the question: 'Cover with what? There isn't a wicket covering in Australia that isn't a menace in itself,' writes Hec De Lacy in the *Sporting Globe*.

'Cricket is played on a ground as well as a wicket'. Old pitches take the run-off from the centre pitch tarpaulin, turning them into dangerous quagmires.

'Before the Australian Board can talk intelligently to visiting teams on the need to cover Test wickets, it must devise a uniform and satisfactory means of covering a wicket.

'Rain inflicts a loss of gate money, and this rather than the actual quality of cricket conditions has become the burden of Australian officials.

'If it were possible to protect a wicket against rain so well that it was almost perfect, where would the quality of conditions be?

'Bowlers and fieldsmen would be slithering around on a sloppy ground, while batsmen enjoyed the paradise of a perfect turf.

'There are two sides to covering wickets – the bowler's and the batsman's.'

WA wins Shield in its first season

Brisbane, Feb. 10. Western Australia has won the Sheffield Shield, on percentage, at its first attempt by defeating Queensland outright at the 'Gabba by 183 runs.

Tom O'Dwyer took 5/52 for WA and Doug Watt made 129 in WA's 445.

WA played fewer games than the other states. The Shield win is decided on percentages.

WA's first game was equally dramatic. It defeated SA by an innings and 124 runs, after skipper Keith Carmody made 198.

NSW defeated WA in Sydney after Keith Miller – having transferred from Victoria made 170 in 180 minutes.

Earlier in the season Ken Meuleman struck 206 for Victoria against Tasmania, recalling the form that made him 12th man for Australia twice last season.

Sid Barnes, the cricket enigma

Sid Barnes ranks among the best batsmen to have played for Australia. His quality can be gauged by Don Bradman's reaction to a near loss to Yorkshire in 1948 – 'Either Sid or I had better play in every match.'

And yet Barnes only played in 13 Tests, his career interrupted by war. And he left some bitter memories, with his biting comments in his Sydney newspaper column, and in his book *Eyes on the Ashes*, a sour report on the 1953 Tour of England.

He left Test cricket voluntarily, declaring himself unavailable for the 1949–50 tour because he could not afford to accept the £450 tour allowance and lose money in business.

Barnes was a 'hustler', always on the lookout for a deal. Also a prankster and crowd-pleaser, he could be volatile and moody off the field.

His cricketing skill, however was never challenged. He was a powerful and flamboyant opening batsman, an outstanding short leg fieldsman, and could also do duty as a wicketkeeper and a fizzing leg-break bowler. In his short post-war career he was inclined towards caution, eliminating some of his best shots.

Before the war he showed himself to be a powerful batsman with all the strokes – driving, pulling, hooking and cutting with ease and strength. He was chunky and broad shouldered, and very quick. His renowned attribute was his ability to read the ball right onto the bat.

He was in no way a classical bat, facing up in a crouch with his bottom hand jammed low on the bat. He took the bat back towards slip, before bringing it through in a loop to meet the ball, and he made an odd flourish after a defensive stroke – 'like taking a soup spoon out of a bowl', according to writer Ray Robinson.

Barnes was brought up in poor circumstances in the Sydney suburb of Stanmore. Cricket was his way up the ladder, and he was playing as a wicketkeeper/batsman with Petersham in his late teens. He was in the NSW team at 20. In that 1937–1938 summer he was at his unfettered best, becoming only the fourth batsman in a 'Shield-only' summer to score 1000 first class runs in a season. In one district game for Petersham

Sid Barnes is carried from the field at Old Trafford after being struck in the ribs by the ball while fielding at silly mid-on, during the 1948 series.

he hit 40 runs in an over from the NSW fast bowler John 'Ginty' Lush.

After only eight Shield games he was picked for England. A ship board accident left him with a broken wrist.

The tour had a lasting effect on him, however, as he became more gentlemanly in his manner. He spoke more carefully and became the best dressed man in the Australian team.

His marriage to the daughter of a theological professor added to his image as a man-about-town.

But he never became an establishment man, and was always capable of the outrageous, and clowning for the crowd.

He would start to walk towards the pavilion when he hit a bump ball, and hook imaginary balls into the air when a bowler was testing his run up.

While he was a boisterous part of the Test team, he always seemed to have another agenda, with private meetings and deals.

Barnes' determination to stay in at all costs gave rise to a monumental Test innings in 1946–47, when he crawled to 234. He was out on exactly the same score as Bradman, and the pair also claimed the world record fifth-wicket partnership of 405. Barnes later claimed that he wanted his score to equal Bradman's, so that it would be remembered.

His 17 years of cricket gave him only 13 Tests, and in that sphere he had an average of 63.05 – up among the greats. A longer career, and a more attacking approach, might have yielded even better figures.

FIRST TEST 1947–48 AUSTRALIA v INDIA
Brisbane Cricket Ground, Brisbane. November 28, 29, December 1, 2, 3 (no play), 4, 1947.
Toss: Australia. Australia won by an innings & 226 runs.

AUSTRALIA
WA Brown c Irani b Amarnath 11
AR Morris hit wicket b Sarwate 47
DG Bradman (c) hit wicket b Amarnath 185
AL Hassett c Gul b Mankad 48
KR Miller c Mankad b Amarnath 58
CL McCool c Sohoni b Amarnath 10
RR Lindwall st Irani b Mankad 7
D Tallon (+) not out 3
IW Johnson c Rangnekar b Mankad 6
ERH Toshack not out 0
WA Johnston
EXTRAS (B 5, LB 1, NB 1) 7
TOTAL ....8 dec 382

FOW 1st Inns: 38 97 198 318 344 373 373 380

Bowling: *First Innings*: Sohoni 23-4-81-0, Amarnath 39-10-84-4, Mankad 34-3-113-3, Sarwate 5-1-16-1, Hazare 11-1-63-0, Nayudu 3-0-18-0.

INDIA

MH Mankad c Tallon b Lindwall	.0	b Lindwall	.7
CT Sarwate c Johnston b Miller	12	b Johnston	26
Gul Mahomed b Lindwall	.0	b Toshack	13
HR Adhikari c McCool b Johnston	.8	lbw Toshack	13
G Kishenchand c Tallon b Johnston	.1	c Bradman b Toshack	.0
VS Hazare c Brown b Toshack	10	c Morris b Toshack	18
L Amarnath (c) c Bradman b Toshack	22	b Toshack	.5
KM Rangnekar c Miller b Toshack	.1	c Hassett b Toshack	.0
SW Sohoni c Miller b Toshack	.2	c Brown b Miller	.4
CS Nayudu not out	.0	c Hassett b Lindwall	.6
JK Irani (+) c Hassett b Toshack	.0	not out	.2
EXTRAS (B 1, LB 1)	.2	(B 3, NB 1)	.4
TOTAL	58		98

FOW 1st Inns: 0 0 19 23 23 53 56 58 58 58
FOW 2nd Inns: 14 27 41 41 72 80 80 89 94 98

Bowling: *First Innings*: Lindwall 5-2-11-2, Johnston 8-4-17-2, Miller 6-1-26-1, Toshack 2.3-1-2-5. *Second Innings*: Lindwall 10.7-2-19-2, Johnston 9-6-11-1, Miller 10-2-30-1, Toshack 17-6-29-6, Johnson 3-1-5-0.

Umpires: AN Barlow & EG Borwick

SECOND TEST 1947–48 AUSTRALIA v INDIA
Sydney Cricket Ground, Sydney. December 12, 13, 15(no play), 16(no play), 17, 18(no play), 1947. Toss: India. Match Drawn.

INDIA

MH Mankad b Lindwall	.5	b Lindwall	.5
CT Sarwate b Johnston	.0 (3)	c Johnson b Johnston	.3
Gul Mahomed c Brown b Miller	29 (4)	c Bradman b Johnson	.5
VS Hazare b Miller	16 (5)	not out	13
L Amarnath (c) b Johnson	25 (7)	c Morris b Johnson	14
G Kishenchand b Johnson	44 (8)	c McCool b Johnston	.0
HR Adhikari lbw Johnston	.0 (9)	not out	.0
DG Phadkar c Miller b McCool	51 (6)	c Tallon b Miller	.2
CS Nayudu c & b McCool	.6		
Amir Elahi c Miller b McCool	.4 (2)	c Miller b Johnston	13
JK Irani (+) not out	.1		
EXTRAS (B 5, LB 2)	.7	(B 3, LB 3)	.6
TOTAL	188		7 for 61

FOW 1st Inns: 2 16 52 57 94 95 165 174 182 188
FOW 2nd Inns: 17 19 26 29 34 53 55

Bowling: *First Innings*: Lindwall 12-3-30-1, Johnston 17-4-33-2, Miller 9-3-25-2, McCool 18-2-71-3, Johnson 14-3-22-2. *Second Innings*: Lindwall 5-1-13-1, Johnston 13-5-15-3, Miller 6-2-5-1, Johnson 13-7-22-2.

AUSTRALIA
WA Brown run out 18
AR Morris lbw Amarnath 10
DG Bradman (c) b Hazare 13
AL Hassett c Adhikari b Hazare 6
KR Miller lbw Phadkar 17
RA Hamence c Adhikari b Mankad 25
IW Johnson lbw Phadkar 1
CL McCool b Phadkar 9
RR Lindwall b Hazare 0
D Tallon (+) c Irani b Hazare 6
WA Johnston not out 0
EXTRAS (B 1, LB 1) 2
TOTAL 107

FOW 1st Inns: 25 30 43 48 86 92 92 97 105 107

Bowling: *First Innings*: Phadkar 10-2-14-3, Amarnath 14-4-31-1, Mankad 9-0-31-1, Hazare 13.2-3-29-4.

Umpires: AN Barlow & EG Borwick

THIRD TEST 1947–48 AUSTRALIA v INDIA
Melbourne Cricket Ground, Melbourne. January 1, 2, 3, 5, 1948.
Toss: Australia. Australia won by 233 runs.

AUSTRALIA

SG Barnes b Mankad 12 (4)	c Sen b Amarnath 15
AR Morris b Amarnath 45 (5)	not out 100
DG Bradman (c) lbw Phadkar 132 (6)	not out 127
AL Hassett lbw Mankad 80	
KR Miller lbw Mankad 29	
RA Hamence st Sen b Amarnath 25	
RR Lindwall b Amarnath 26	
D Tallon (+) c Mankad b Amarnath ...2	
B Dooland not out 21 (2)	lbw Phadkar 6
IW Johnson lbw Mankad 16 (1)	c Hazare b Amarnath 0
WA Johnston run out 5 (3)	lbw Amarnath 3
EXTRAS (B 1) 1	(B 3, NB 1) 4
TOTAL 394	.......................4 dec 255

FOW 1st Inns: 29 99 268 289 302 339 341 352 387 394
FOW 2nd Inns: 1 11 13 32

Bowling: *First Innings*: Phadkar 15-1-80-1, Amarnath 21-3-78-4, Hazare 16.1-0-62-0, Mankad 37-4-135-4, Sarwate 3-0-16-0, Nayudu 2-0-22-0. *Second Innings*: Phadkar 10-1-28-1, Amarnath 20-3-52-3, Hazare 11-1-55-0, Mankad 18-4-74-0, Sarwate 5-0-41-0, Gul 1-0-1-0.

INDIA

MH Mankad c Tallon b Johnston 116	b Johnston 13
CT Sarwate c Tallon b Johnston 36	b Johnston 1
Gul Mahomed c & b Dooland 12	c Morris b Johnson 28
VS Hazare c Tallon b Barnes 17	c Barnes b Miller 10
L Amarnath (c) lbw Barnes 0	b Lindwall 8
DG Phadkar not out 55	c Barnes b Johnston 13
HR Adhikari st Tallon b Johnson 26	c Lindwall b Johnson 1
K Rai Singh c Barnes b Johnson 2	c Tallon b Johnston 24
KM Rangnekar c & b Johnson 6	c Hamence b Johnson 18
P Sen (+) b Johnson 4	c Hassett b Johnson 2
CS Nayudu not out 4	not out 0
EXTRAS (B 9, LB 3, NB 1) 13	(B 6, LB 1) 7
TOTAL ....9 dec 291	125

FOW 1st Inns: 124 145 188 188 198 260 264 280 284
FOW 2nd Inns: 10 27 44 60 60 69 100 107 125 125

Bowling: *First Innings*: Lindwall 12-0-47-0, Miller 13-2-46-0, Johnston 12-0-33-2, Johnson 14-1-59-4, Dooland 12-0-68-1, Barnes 6-1-25-2. *Second Innings*: Lindwall 3-0-10-1, Miller 7-0-29-1, Johnston 10-1-44-4, Johnson 5.7-0-35-4.

Umpires: AN Barlow & H Elphinston

FOURTH TEST 1947–48 AUSTRALIA v INDIA
Adelaide Oval, Adelaide. January 23, 24, 26, 27, 28, 1948.
Toss: Australia. Australia won by an innings & 16 runs.

AUSTRALIA

SG Barnes lbw Mankad 112
AR Morris b Phadkar 7
DG Bradman (c) b Hazare 201
AL Hassett not out 198
KR Miller b Rangachari 67
RN Harvey lbw Rangachari 13
CL McCool b Phadkar 27
IW Johnson b Rangachari 22
RR Lindwall b Rangachari 2
D Tallon (+) lbw Mankad 1
ERH Toshack lbw Hazare 8
EXTRAS (B 8, LB 6, NB 2) 16
TOTAL 674

FOW 1st Inns: 20 256 361 503 523 576 634 640 641 674

Bowling: *First Innings*: Phadkar 15-0-74-2, Amarnath 9-0-42-0, Rangachari 41-5-141-4, Mankad 43-8-170-2, Sarwate 22-1-121-0, Hazare 21.3-1-110-2.

INDIA

MH Mankad b McCool 49	c Tallon b Lindwall 0
CT Sarwate b Miller 1	b Toshack 11
P Sen (+) b Miller 0 (10)	not out 0
L Amarnath (c) c Bradman b Johnson ..46 (3)	b Lindwall 0
VS Hazare lbw Johnson 116 (4)	b Lindwall 145
Gul Mahomed st Tallon b Johnson 4 (5)	b Barnes 34
DG Phadkar lbw Toshack 123 (6)	lbw Lindwall 14
G Kishenchand b Lindwall 10 (7)	b Lindwall 0
HR Adhikari run out 2 (8)	lbw Miller 51
KM Rangnekar st Tallon b Johnson 8 (9)	b Lindwall 0
CR Rangachari not out 0	c McCool b Lindwall 0
EXTRAS (B 11, LB 8, NB 3) 22	(B 18, LB 3, NB 1) 22
TOTAL 381	277

FOW 1st Inns: 6 6 69 124 133 321 353 359 375 381
FOW 2nd Inns: 0 0 33 99 139 139 271 273 273 277

Bowling: *First Innings*: Lindwall 21-6-61-1, Miller 9-1-39-2, McCool 28-2-102-1, Johnson 23.1-5-64-4, Toshack 18-2-66-1, Barnes 9-0-23-0, Bradman 1-0-4-0. *Second Innings*: Lindwall 16.5-4-38-7, Miller 9-3-13-1, McCool 4-0-26-0, Johnson 20-4-54-0, Toshack 25-8-73-1, Barnes 18-4-51-1.

Umpires: EG Borwick & RR Wright

FIFTH TEST 1947–48 AUSTRALIA v INDIA
Melbourne Cricket Ground, Melbourne. February 6, 7, 9, 10, 1948.
Toss: Australia. Australia won by an innings & 177 runs.

AUSTRALIA

SG Barnes run out 33
WA Brown run out 99
DG Bradman (c) retired hurt 57
KR Miller c Sen b Phadkar 14
RN Harvey c Sen b Mankad 153
SJE Loxton c Sen b Amarnath 80
RR Lindwall c Phadkar b Mankad 35
D Tallon (+) c Sen b Sarwate 37
LJ Johnson not out 25
DT Ring c Kishenchand b Hazare 11
WA Johnston not out 23
EXTRAS (B 4, LB 4) 8
TOTAL ....8 dec 575

FOW 1st Inns: 48 182 219 378 457 497 527 544

Bowling: *First Innings*: Phadkar 9-0-58-1, Amarnath 23-1-79-1, Rangachari 17-1-97-0, Hazare 14-1-63-1, Mankad 33-2-107-2, Sarwate 18-1-82-1, Nayudu 13-0-77-0, Adhikari 1-0-4-0.

INDIA

MH Mankad c Tallon b Loxton 111	c Tallon b Lindwall 0
CT Sarwate b Lindwall 0	lbw Johnston 10
HR Adhikari c Tallon b Loxton 38	c Bradman b Loxton 17
VS Hazare lbw Lindwall 74	c & b Johnston 10
L Amarnath (c) c Barnes b Ring 12 (6)	c Johnson b Ring 8
DG Phadkar not out 56 (5)	lbw Johnston 0
Gul Mahomed c Lindwall b Johnson ...1	c Barnes b Ring 4
G Kishenchand b Ring 14	c Barnes b Johnson 0
CS Nayudu c Bradman b Ring 2	c Brown b Ring 0
P Sen (+) b Johnson 13	b Johnson 10
CR Rangachari b Johnson 0	not out 0
EXTRAS (B 6, LB 2, NB 2) 10	(B 6, LB 1, NB 1) 8
TOTAL 331	67

FOW 1st Inns: 3 127 206 231 257 260 284 286 331 331
FOW 2nd Inns: 0 22 28 35 51 51 56 56 66 67

Bowling: *First Innings*: Lindwall 25-5-66-2, Johnson 30-8-66-3, Loxton 19-1-61-2, Johnston 8-4-14-0, Ring 36-8-103-3, Miller 3-0-10-0, Barnes 2-1-1-0. *Second Innings*: Lindwall 3-0-9-1, Johnson 5.2-2-8-3, Loxton 4-1-10-1, Johnston 7-0-15-2, Ring 5-1-17-3.

Umpires: AN Barlow & GC Cooper

Australian Averages

1947–48 AUSTRALIA v INDIA

AUSTRALIA	M	Inn	NO	Runs	H.S	Avrge	Ct	St	Overs	Mds	Runs	Wkt	Avrge
Barnes, SG	3	4	-	172	112	43.00	6	-	35.0	6	100	3	33.33
Bradman, DG	5	6	2	715	201	178.75	6	-	1.0	-	4	-	-
Brown, WA	3	3	-	128	99	42.67	4	-	-	-	-	-	-
Dooland, B	1	2	1	27	21*	27.00	1	-	12.0	-	68	1	68.00
Hamence, RA	2	2	-	50	25	25.00	1	-	-	-	-	-	-
Harvey, RN	2	2	-	166	153	83.00	-	-	-	-	-	-	-
Hassett, AL	4	4	1	332	198*	110.67	4	-	-	-	-	-	-
Johnson, IW	4	5	-	45	22	9.00	2	-	93.0	21	261	16	16.31
Johnson, LJ	1	1	1	25	25*	-	2	-	35.2	10	74	6	12.33
Johnston, WA	4	4	2	31	23*	15.50	1	-	84.0	24	182	16	11.38
Lindwall, RR	5	5	-	70	35	14.00	2	-	113.4	23	304	18	16.89
Loxton, SJE	1	1	-	80	80	80.00	-	-	23.0	2	71	3	23.67
McCool, CL	3	3	-	46	27	15.33	4	-	50.0	4	199	4	49.75
Miller, KR	5	5	-	185	67	37.00	5	-	72.0	14	223	9	24.78
Morris, AR	4	5	1	209	100*	52.25	3	-	-	-	-	-	-
Ring, DT	1	1	-	11	11	11.00	-	-	41.0	9	120	6	20.00
Tallon, D	5	5	-	49	37	12.25	11	3	-	-	-	-	-
Toshack, ERH	2	2	1	8	8	8.00	-	-	62.3	17	170	13	13.08

Indian Averages

1947–48 AUSTRALIA v INDIA

INDIA	M	Inn	NO	Runs	H.S	Avrge	Ct	St	Overs	Mds	Runs	Wkt	Avrge
Adhikari, HR	5	10	1	156	51	17.33	2	-	1.0	-	4	-	-
Amarnath, L	5	10	-	140	46	14.00	-	-	126.0	21	366	13	28.15
Amir Elahi	1	2	-	17	13	8.50	-	-	-	-	-	-	-
Gul Mahomed	5	10	-	130	34	13.00	1	-	1.0	-	1	-	-
Hazare, VS	5	10	1	429	145	47.67	1	-	86.6	7	382	7	54.57
Irani, JK	2	3	2	3	2*	3.00	2	1	-	-	-	-	-
Kishenchand, G	4	8	-	69	44	8.63	1	-	-	-	-	-	-
Mankad, MH	5	10	-	306	116	30.60	2	-	174.0	21	630	12	52.50
Nayudu, CS	4	7	3	18	4	4.50	-	-	18.0	-	117	-	-
Phadkar, DG	4	8	2	314	123	52.33	1	-	59.0	4	254	8	31.75
Rai Singh, K	1	2	-	26	24	13.00	-	-	-	-	-	-	-
Rangachari, CR	2	4	2	0	0*	0.00	-	-	58.0	6	238	4	59.50
Rangnekar, KM	3	6	-	33	18	5.50	-	-	-	-	-	-	-
Sarwate, CT	5	10	-	100	36	10.00	-	-	53.0	3	276	2	138.00
Sen, P	3	6	1	29	13	5.80	5	1	-	-	-	-	-
Sohoni, SW	1	2	-	6	4	3.00	1	-	23.0	4	81	-	-

A formidable team to face the old foe

Don Bradman and his team are greeted by a barrage of photographers on arrival at Tilbury Dock, London.

Tilbury, April 16. The Australian team has been beseiged by press photographers even before it has left the ship. Excitement is running high in England at the first Australian Test Tour since the end of World War ll.

Four of the 17 Australians – Bradman, Barnes, Hassett and Brown – have toured before, while Miller played in the 'Victory Tests' at the end of the war. So, despite the 1946–47 tour to Australia, the visiting side is more unknown to the English public than for most tours, and the press is more active than usual in profiling the players.

They may discover that this is the best team to leave Australia.

The opening spots are between Arthur Morris, Sid Barnes and Bill Brown. Although Morris has never been to England, his play in Australia suggests he might be the best of this trio.

Bradman is 40, and the best known as well as simply the best batsman of the series. The unknown batting quantities are Ron Hamence from South Australia Neil Harvey of Victoria, a 19-year-old with quick footwork and a flashing bat.

The all-rounders are the pugnacious Sam Loxton of Victoria and the mercurial Miller, who sometimes looks likely to win a match by his deeds alone. Wicketkeepers Don Tallon and Ron Saggers have good batting records.

The spearhead bowler Ray Lindwall is of great interest to the English press, but the players on the 1946 tour will remember his rhythmical run up and the pace that yielded him 18 wickets in four Tests. Miller's shock bowling makes him a feared partner.

They will give way to the tall, dark country men, Bill Johnston from Victoria, with his swinging left-arm deliveries and Ern Toshack of NSW – known as 'The Black Prince' – a left-arm spinner who can deliver cut, spin or an alarming drifting ball. The looped off-spin of Victoria's Ian Johnson and the leg spin of Doug Ring (Victoria) and Colin McCool (NSW) add to the variety.

Tests on wireless

London, April 10. The British Broadcasting Corporation will provide a live description of the Test matches to home listeners and also in an across-the-world cable hook-up which will carry the descriptions to Australia.

Because of 'atmospherics' which might affect the airwaves, and the distance of the link to the Antipodes, the radio commentary there may be marred by static and rises and falls in the volume.

The BBC has paid the English governing body, the Marylebone Cricket Club, £250 for the right to broadcast the Tests and transmit to Australia. The broadcast in Australia will start at 10 p.m., Eastern Standard Time.

Don Bradman's dream coat – his 1948 blazer.

Cricket, not war

London, April 16. Don Bradman, in a speech to the British Institute of Journalists, has appealed to the press to regard the Test matches as a sporting contest, rather than a minor war.

He said there was no place in the game for unfortunate incidents, which were blown up by the press. 'Most of these incidents do not originally occur in the minds of the players themselves.' The players on both sides were friendly, he said.

Bradman also refuted the suggestion that the Australians avoided risks.

He pointed out that only three players had made a Test century before lunch, and they were all Australians.

Australians have a heavy social life

London, April 22. The Australian cricket team has had an extraordinary 12 days, overwhelmed by hospitality. The manager Keith Johnson has had to roster players 'on duty' for sessions of autograph signing. Don Bradman has been inundated with fan mail.

The team has only had time to practice for an hour or two each day since its arrival.

On April 11, the day after the ship docked, the team was entertained at an Australia House reception. On April 12 it was a 'lay day', with golf at Burnham Beeches.

On April 13 the team practised and then lunched at the Royal Empire Society. That night they were guests at the musical *Annie Get Your Gun*.

April 14 was highlighted by a three-hour lunch given by the British Sportsman's Club. On April 15 a lunch was hosted by the London District of the Institute of Journalists, where Bradman made a speech in which it was said he quipped and jested 'with the same easy grace that he wields his bat.'

April 16 included dinner at the Cricket Writers' Club at the Public Schools' Club, and on April 18 the entire Australian team was seated alongside the Royal box for the FA Cup at Wembley.

On the following Monday Don Bradman and Keith Johnson went on to St Paul's Cathedral for the Royal Silver Jubilee service, and then the team were guests of the Lord Mayor of London for dinner at the Mansion House.

The players are now in Worcester and happy to go to bed early. The real business of cricket is about to begin.

A distraction. So this is the way to keep England batting?

Sparkling form and barrage of sixes

A beautiful souvenir. The Worcester Vase depicts one of cricket's most atmospheric grounds.

Nottingham, June 4. The English County teams have mostly succumbed easily to the Australian cricket team in the pre-Test matches. At Worcester Don Bradman refrained from scoring the double century that he notched up on his previous three visits, contenting himself with 107, while Arthur Morris made 138. Keith Miller dominated the second match against Leicester, with a sparkling 202.

Against the Yorkshire team Bradman rested himself and Sid Barnes. On the damp pitch 35 wickets fell for a total of 325 runs. In its second innings Australia needed 60 to win. It lost 6/31, and only big hitting by Tallon and Harvey saved the day.

Bradman was unimpressed: 'That's it then', he said. 'Either Sid or I will have to play in every match'.

On to Surrey and a huge win, by an innings and 296 runs, with Barnes making 176, Bradman 146 and Hassett 110. Alec Bedser toiled for 4/104, but left Bradman in no doubt that he would be a danger.

The heavy program had Australia playing another eight matches before tomorrow's first Test. They won six and drew two, and absolutely thrashed Essex, scoring a world record 721 in a day, with four centuries.

Aussies go two up

Lord's, June 29. Australia has taken a firm grip on the Test series with resounding wins over England at Trent Bridge, Nottingham, and at Lord's.

The first Test was virtually over on the first day when the English batsmen succumbed for 165. The first blow was when Len Hutton was clean bowled by Miller for three. Miller struck a similar blow soon afterwards in dismissing Denis Compton. Miller finished with 3/38, but Bill Johnston with 5/36 was the main destroyer.

At 8/74 England was facing humiliation, but Jim Laker (63) and Alec Bedser (22) held on. Factors in England's poor showing were a greasy wicket and overcast skies.

The Australian innings was slow, lasting until well into the third day, but realised 509, with Bradman 138 and Hassett 137.

England showed its batting mettle in its second innings, with 74 to Hutton and a gritty 187 from Compton, full of near misses. The crowd had earlier demonstrated against a Miller bumper which had hit Hutton, and it howled again when a Miller bumper caused Compton to tread on his wicket.

In the end England was 441, leaving Australia only 98 to get, and Barnes and Hassett scurried to that total, fearing rain was on the way.

Bradman was out for 0 in the second innings, the second time he was caught down the leg-side off Bedser. The crowd, and the press, made much of the supposed flaw in the super-batsman's make-up.

In the second Test England started well, having Barnes back in the pavilion for 0, and Bradman for 38, again caught by Len Hutton off

Just brilliant. Keith Miller catches 'Young Joe' Hardstaff at Trent Bridge.

Bedser, but the tail wagged to the extent that the score, from 6/225, mounted to 350. Arthur Morris (105) showed growing skills on the green-top wicket.

England followed with 215, with only Compton and skipper Norman Yardley showing form.

Australia hammered the nails in with 7/460 declared in the next innings, Barnes making amends for his first innings with 141.

Ray Lindwall was the destroyer in the England first innings with 5/70, and combined with Ern Toshack to wreck the second innings for 186. Washbrook was dismissed by an amazing catch by Tallon. A full toss from Toshack just grazed his flashing bat and went into Tallon's glove at ground level.

The 1948 Australians sing Happy Birthday to Don Bradman at Lord's, Aug. 27.

Australia's last innings miracle at Leeds

A bumper Yorkshire crowd. 10,000 wait outside the ground at Headingley, while 40,000 were inside for the extraordinary match.

Young Neil Harvey in characteristic form – no cap and a maiden century.

Leeds, July 27. Australia has scored an astonishing 404 in less than a day in the final innings to win the fourth Test.

Australia had to rewrite the record books to win, becoming the first team to score more than 400 runs in the final innings to secure victory.

The English team came to Headingley with the series still alive, and a moral win in the drawn third Test. Hutton was back, and the batting looked stronger.

And so it proved, as Hutton (81) and Washbrook (143) made a tremendous start, seeing off the opening barrage by Miller and Lindwall and then getting amongst the spinners to carry the score to 169.

After Lindwall spreadeagled Hutton's stumps Washbrook and Edrich carried on.

At lunch England on the second day was 2/360. With Bradman reduced to trying Arthur Morris' leg spin, Edrich and Bedser were finding the range for sixes. Then Bedser, perhaps conscious of a looming century, played a quiet caught and bowled to Ian Johnson and England was 3/423.

From then on it was all downhill for England – all out for 496.

Australia lost Morris for 6. Bradman came in to a hero's welcome, with an avenue of spectators two-thirds of the way to the pitch. He briskly took his score to 31, with Hassett on 13 and Australia 1/63 at stumps.

The third day will surely be remembered as a classic of Test cricket. Pollard got Hassett with a ball that popped and took the edge. When Bradman faced Pollard he seemed to be waiting to deal with a similar rising ball, but it shot under his bat and bowled him. There was tumult in the crowd.

Neil Harvey came out in his first Test innings at 3/63, and with the pitch looking dangerous. Keith Miller was on 3 at the other end, but obviously ignited by the challenge.

Soon Miller and Harvey were driving and cutting, getting 50 in 43 minutes. When Laker came on and troubled Harvey, Miller gained the strike and hit him for six and two imperious off-drives for four. Harvey began to deal with Laker in like fashion.

The thrilling partnership came to an end when Miller, trying to hit Yardley out of the ground, got an edge and Godfrey Evans snared the ball in his fingertips. Harvey carried on to score his maiden Test century and go to 112.

England's failure to break a late partnership between Loxton (93) and Lindwall (77) ruined their Test, as Australia's innings ended on 458, on the third over of the fourth day.

England set about posting a formidable total for Australia to chase, and Hutton (57), Washbrook (65), Edrich (54) and Crompton (66) fulfilled their roles as senior batsmen.

It was 8/362 at stumps, but Yardley batted for a few overs on the fifth morning to give himself the choice of rollers. He hoped that the heavy roller would break the pitch up and help Laker. And so Australia was left with 404 runs to win in 344 minutes.

It seemed that Hassett and Morris were not moving fast enough, scoring 32 in 45 minutes.

Bradman set about building the score. The score was 1/121 at lunch.

Then came the onslaught as Hutton and Compton could not keep up a semblance of Test standard. Morris hit seven fours in two overs, and quickly went to a century. Bradman followed, after surviving two chances put down off Compton. The fielding was woeful with four chances dropped.

At tea Australia had a further 112 runs to make. Morris was caught off the bowling of Yardley for 182, but The Don was there at the end, triumphant on 173, and congratulating Neil Harvey on hitting the winning runs.

The Don and the King. Don Bradman conversing with King George VI – he has been criticised for having his hands in his pockets.

Farewell – out second ball

Don Bradman looks ruefully back at his stumps for the last time in a Test.

The Oval, Aug. 18. Don Bradman today walked to the wicket for the last time in Test matches. The applause from the capacity crowd rose to a crescendo as the English captain Norman Yardley called for three cheers for Bradman, and then shook him by the hand.

Bradman seemed quite moved by the reception, and took some time to compose himself before he settled over his bat to face the leg-spinner Eric Hollies. He had four runs to make, to have an average of 100 in all his Test cricket.

Hollies' first ball had him going back on his stumps and playing defensively. He said later that he hardly saw the ball, so stirred were his emotions.

The next was a wrong'un on a perfect length – Bradman went forward and was bowled off an inside edge. A mighty roar went up.

Bradman looked back at his stumps, and seemed unable to believe what he saw there. Then he turned and walked slowly away. The roar subsided into a sympathetic hush, and then prolonged applause as his slight, athletic figure went through the gate.

Bradman's Test career had ended with an average of 99.94.

The rest of the match was all anticlimax, as England had made 52 in its first innings, its lowest score at Lord's since 1888, and was already staring at defeat, with Australia 2/153 at stumps.

The England side succumbed to Ray Lindwall, who took 6/20.

Only Len Hutton (30) reached double figures, and he was out at the end to one of the finest catches taken, with Tallon diving to leg to scoop up a fine glance of Lindwall.

The next day was a muted affair, despite the fact that Arthur Morris played an outstanding innings of 196 run out, while the rest of the Australians fell around him and the score reached only 389. His best shots were through the covers, where he comes through the ball with fine timing.

Hollies finished with 5/131 of 56 overs, and had many Englishmen wondering why his leg spin hadn't been employed throughout the Test series.

England put up a second innings fight in the top order, with Hutton (64), Edrich (28) and Compton (39), but then fell apart again to be all out for 188. Bill Johnston (4/40) and Lindwall again (3/50) were the destroyers.

Catch of the century. Don Tallon catches Len Hutton off a delighted Ray Lindwall.

FIRST TEST 1948 ENGLAND v AUSTRALIA
Trent Bridge, Nottingham. June 10, 11, 12, 14, 15, 1948.
Toss: England. Australia won by 8 wkts.

ENGLAND

L Hutton b Miller	3	b Miller	74
C Washbrook c Brown b Lindwall	6	c Tallon b Miller	1
WJ Edrich b Johnston	18	c Tallon b Johnson	13
DCS Compton b Miller	19	hit wicket b Miller	184
J Hardstaff jr c Miller b Johnston	0	c Hassett b Toshack	43
CJ Barnett b Johnston	8	c Miller b Johnston	6
NWD Yardley (c) lbw Toshack	3	c & b Johnston	22
TG Evans (+) c Morris b Johnston	12	c Tallon b Johnston	50
JC Laker c Tallon b Miller	63	b Miller	4
AV Bedser c Brown b Johnston	22	not out	3
JA Young not out	1	b Johnston	9
EXTRAS (B 5, LB 5)	10	(B 12, LB 17, NB 3)	32
TOTAL	165		441

FOW 1st Inns: 9 15 46 46 48 60 74 74 163 165
FOW 2nd Inns: 5 39 150 243 264 321 405 413 423 441

Bowling: *First Innings*: Lindwall 13-5-30-1, Miller 19-8-38-3, Johnston 25-11-36-5, Toshack 14-8-28-1, Johnson 5-1-19-0, Morris 3-1-4-0. *Second Innings*: Miller 44-10-125-4, Johnston 59-12-147-4, Toshack 33-14-60-1, Johnson 42-15-66-1, Barnes 5-2-11-0.

AUSTRALIA

SG Barnes c Evans b Laker	62	not out	64
AR Morris b Laker	31	b Bedser	9
DG Bradman (c) c Hutton b Bedser	138	c Hutton b Bedser	0
KR Miller c Edrich b Laker	0		
WA Brown lbw Yardley	17		
AL Hassett b Bedser	137 (4)	not out	21
IW Johnson b Laker	21		
D Tallon (+) c & b Young	10		
RR Lindwall c Evans b Yardley	42		
WA Johnston not out	17		
ERH Toshack lbw Bedser	19		
EXTRAS (B 9, LB 4, W 1, NB 1)	15	(LB 2, W 1, NB 1)	4
TOTAL	509		2 for 98

FOW 1st Inns: 73 121 121 185 305 338 365 472 476 509
FOW 2nd Inns: 38 48

Bowling: *First Innings*: Edrich 18-1-72-0, Bedser 44.2-12-113-3, Barnett 17-5-36-0, Young 60-28-79-1, Laker 55-14-138-4, Compton 5-0-24-0, Yardley 17-6-32-2. *Second Innings*: Edrich 4-0-20-0, Bedser 14.3-4-46-2, Young 10-3-28-0.

Umpires: F Chester & E Cooke

SECOND TEST 1948 ENGLAND v AUSTRALIA
Lord's Cricket Ground, London. June 24, 25, 26, 28, 29, 1948.
Toss: Australia. Australia won by 409 runs.

AUSTRALIA

SG Barnes c Hutton b Coxon	0	c Washbrook b Yardley	141
AR Morris c Hutton b Coxon	105	b Wright	62
DG Bradman (c) c Hutton b Bedser	38	c Edrich b Bedser	89
AL Hassett b Yardley	47	b Yardley	0
KR Miller lbw Bedser	4	c Bedser b Laker	74
WA Brown lbw Yardley	24	c Evans b Coxon	32
IW Johnson c Evans b Edrich	4 (8)	not out	9
D Tallon (+) c Yardley b Bedser	53		
RR Lindwall b Bedser	15 (7)	st Evans b Laker	25
WA Johnston st Evans b Wright	29		
ERH Toshack not out	20		
EXTRAS (B 3, LB 7, NB 1)	11	(B 22, LB 5, NB 1)	28
TOTAL	350		7 dec 460

FOW 1st Inns: 3 87 166 173 216 225 246 275 320 350
FOW 2nd Inns: 122 296 296 329 416 445 460

Bowling: *First Innings*: Bedser 43-14-100-4, Coxon 35-10-90-2, Edrich 8-0-43-1, Wright 21.3-8-54-1, Laker 7-3-17-0, Yardley 15-4-35-2. *Second Innings*: Bedser 34-6-112-1, Coxon 28-3-82-1, Edrich 2-0-11-0, Wright 19-4-69-1, Laker 31.2-6-111-2, Yardley 13-4-36-2, Compton 3-0-11-0.

ENGLAND

L Hutton b Johnson	20	c Johnson b Lindwall	13
C Washbrook c Tallon b Lindwall	8	c Tallon b Toshack	37
WJ Edrich b Lindwall	5	c Johnson b Toshack	2
DCS Compton c Miller b Johnston	53	c Miller b Johnston	29
HE Dollery b Lindwall	0	b Lindwall	37
NWD Yardley (c) b Lindwall	44	b Toshack	11
A Coxon c & b Johnson	19	lbw Toshack	0
TG Evans (+) c Miller b Johnston	9	not out	24
JC Laker c Tallon b Johnson	28	b Lindwall	0
AV Bedser b Lindwall	9	c Hassett b Johnston	9
DVP Wright not out	13	c Lindwall b Toshack	4
EXTRAS (LB 3, NB 4)	7	(B 16, LB 4)	20
TOTAL	215		186

FOW 1st Inns: 17 32 46 46 133 134 145 186 197 215
FOW 2nd Inns: 42 52 65 106 133 133 141 141 158 186

Bowling: *First Innings*: Lindwall 27.4-7-70-5, Johnston 22-4-43-2, Johnson 35-13-72-3, Toshack 18-11-23-0. *Second Innings*: Lindwall 23-9-61-3, Johnston 33-15-62-2, Johnson 2-1-3-0, Toshack 20.1-6-40-5.

Umpires: DE Davies & CN Woolley

THIRD TEST 1948 ENGLAND v AUSTRALIA
Old Trafford, Manchester. July 8, 9, 10, 12 (no play), 13, 1948.
Toss: England. Match Drawn.

ENGLAND

C Washbrook b Johnston	11	not out	85
GM Emmett c Barnes b Lindwall	10	c Tallon b Lindwall	0
WJ Edrich c Tallon b Lindwall	32	run out	53
DCS Compton not out	145	c Miller b Toshack	0
JF Crapp lbw Lindwall	37	not out	19
HE Dollery b Johnston	1		
NWD Yardley (c) c Johnson b Toshack	22		
TG Evans (+) c Johnston b Lindwall	34		
AV Bedser run out	37		
R Pollard b Toshack	3		
JA Young c Bradman b Johnston	4		
EXTRAS (B 7, LB 17, NB 3)	27	(B 9, LB 7, W 1)	17
TOTAL	363	3 dec 174	

FOW 1st Inns: 22 28 96 97 119 141 216 337 352 363
FOW 2nd Inns: 1 125 129

Bowling: *First Innings*: Lindwall 40-8-99-4, Johnston 45.5-13-67-3, Loxton 7-0-18-0, Toshack 41-20-75-2, Johnson 38-16-77-0. *Second Innings*: Lindwall 14-4-37-1, Johnston 14-3-34-0, Loxton 8-2-29-0, Toshack 12-5-26-1, Johnson 7-3-16-0, Miller 14-7-15-0.

AUSTRALIA

AR Morris c Compton b Bedser	51	not out	54
IW Johnson c Evans b Bedser	1	c Crapp b Young	6
DG Bradman (c) lbw Pollard	7	not out	30
AL Hassett c Washbrook b Young	38		
KR Miller lbw Pollard	31		
SG Barnes retired hurt	1		
SJE Loxton b Pollard	36		
D Tallon (+) c Evans b Edrich	18		
RR Lindwall c Washbrook b Bedser	23		
WA Johnston c Crapp b Bedser	3		
ERH Toshack not out	0		
EXTRAS (B 5, LB 4, NB 3)	12	(NB 2)	2
TOTAL	9 dec 221	1 for 92	

FOW 1st Inns: 3 13 82 135 139 172 208 219 221
FOW 2nd Inns: 10

Bowling: *First Innings*: Bedser 36-12-81-4, Pollard 32-9-53-3, Edrich 7-3-27-1, Yardley 4-0-12-0, Young 14-5-36-1. *Second Innings*: Bedser 19-12-27-0, Pollard 10-8-6-0, Edrich 2-0-8-0, Young 21-12-31-1, Compton 9-3-18-0.

Umpires: F Chester & D Davies

FOURTH TEST 1948 ENGLAND v AUSTRALIA
Headingley, Leeds. July 22, 23, 24, 26, 27, 1948.
Toss: England. Australia won by 7 wkts.

ENGLAND

L Hutton b Lindwall	81	c Bradman b Johnson	57
C Washbrook c Lindwall b Johnston	143	c Harvey b Johnston	65
WJ Edrich c Morris b Johnson	111	lbw Johnston	54
AV Bedser c & b Johnson	79 (9)	c Hassett b Miller	17
DCS Compton c Saggers b Lindwall	23 (4)	c Miller b Johnston	66
JF Crapp b Toshack	5 (5)	b Lindwall	18
NWD Yardley (c) b Miller	25 (6)	c Harvey b Johnston	7
K Cranston b Loxton	10 (7)	c Saggers b Johnston	0
TG Evans (+) c Hassett b Loxton	3 (8)	not out	47
JC Laker c Saggers b Loxton	4	not out	15
R Pollard not out	0		
EXTRAS (B 2, LB 8, W 1, NB 1)	12	(B 4, LB 12, NB 3)	19
TOTAL	496	8 dec 365	

FOW 1st Inns: 168 268 423 426 447 473 486 490 496 496
FOW 2nd Inns: 129 129 232 260 277 278 293 330

Bowling: *First Innings*: Lindwall 38-10-79-2, Miller 17.1-2-43-1, Johnston 38-12-86-1, Toshack 35-6-112-1, Loxton 26-4-55-3, Johnson 33-9-89-2, Morris 5-0-20-0. *Second Innings*: Lindwall 26-6-84-2, Miller 21.5-5-53-1, Johnston 29-5-95-4, Loxton 10-2-29-0, Johnson 21-2-85-1.

AUSTRALIA

AR Morris c Cranston b Bedser	6	c Pollard b Yardley	182
AL Hassett c Crapp b Pollard	13	c & b Compton	17
DG Bradman (c) b Pollard	33	not out	173
KR Miller c Edrich b Yardley	58	lbw Cranston	12
RN Harvey b Laker	112	not out	4
SJE Loxton b Yardley	93		
IW Johnson c Cranston b Laker	10		
RR Lindwall c Crapp b Bedser	77		
RA Saggers (+) st Evans b Laker	5		
WA Johnston c Edrich b Bedser	13		
ERH Toshack not out	12		
EXTRAS (B 9, LB 14, NB 3)	26	(B 6, LB 9, NB 1)	16
TOTAL	458	3 for 404	

FOW 1st Inns: 13 65 68 189 294 329 344 355 403 458
FOW 2nd Inns: 57 358 396

Bowling: *First Innings*: Bedser 31.2-4-92-3, Pollard 38-6-104-2, Cranston 14-1-51-0, Edrich 3-0-19-0, Laker 30-8-113-3, Yardley 17-6-38-2, Compton 3-0-15-0. *Second Innings*: Bedser 21-2-56-0, Pollard 22-6-55-0, Cranston 7.1-0-28-1, Laker 32-11-93-0, Yardley 13-1-44-1, Compton 15-3-82-1, Hutton 4-1-30-0.

Umpires: HG Baldwin & F Chester

FIFTH TEST 1948 ENGLAND v AUSTRALIA
Kennington Oval, London. August 14, 16, 17, 18, 1948.
Toss: England. Australia won by an innings & 149 runs.

ENGLAND

L Hutton c Tallon b Lindwall	30	c Tallon b Miller	64
JG Dewes b Miller	1	b Lindwall	10
WJ Edrich c Hassett b Johnston	3	b Lindwall	28
DCS Compton c Morris b Lindwall	4	c Lindwall b Johnston	39
JF Crapp c Tallon b Miller	0	b Miller	9
NWD Yardley (c) b Lindwall	7	c Miller b Johnston	9
AJ Watkins lbw Johnston	0	c Hassett b Ring	2
TG Evans (+) b Lindwall	1	b Lindwall	8
AV Bedser b Lindwall	0	b Johnston	0
JA Young b Lindwall	0	not out	3
WE Hollies not out	0	c Morris b Johnston	0
EXTRAS (B 6)	6	(B 9, LB 4, NB 3)	16
TOTAL	52	188	

FOW 1st Inns: 2 10 17 23 35 42 45 45 47 52
FOW 2nd Inns: 20 64 125 153 164 167 178 181 188 188

Bowling: *First Innings*: Lindwall 16.1-5-20-6, Miller 8-5-5-2, Johnston 16-4-20-2, Loxton 2-1-1-0. *Second Innings*: Lindwall 25-3-50-3, Miller 15-6-22-2, Johnston 27.3-12-40-4, Loxton 10-2-16-0, Ring 28-13-44-1.

AUSTRALIA

SG Barnes c Evans b Hollies	61
AR Morris run out	196
DG Bradman (c) b Hollies	0
AL Hassett lbw Young	37
KR Miller st Evans b Hollies	5
RN Harvey c Young b Hollies	17
SJE Loxton c Evans b Edrich	15
RR Lindwall c Edrich b Young	9
D Tallon (+) c Crapp b Hollies	31
DT Ring c Crapp b Bedser	9
WA Johnston not out	0
EXTRAS (B 4, LB 2, NB 3)	9
TOTAL	389

FOW 1st Inns: 20 64 125 153 164 167 178 181 188 188

Bowling: *First Innings*: Bedser 31.2-9-61-1, Watkins 4-1-19-0, Young 51-16-118-2, Hollies 56-14-131-5, Compton 2-0-6-0, Edrich 9-1-38-1, Yardley 5-1-7-0.

Umpires: HG Baldwin & D Davies

Australian Averages

1948 ENGLAND v AUSTRALIA

AUSTRALIA	M	Inn	NO	Runs	H.S	Avrge	Ct	St	Overs	Mds	Runs	Wkt	Avrge
Barnes, SG	4	6	2	329	141	82.25	1	-	5.0	2	11	-	-
Bradman, DG	5	9	2	508	173*	72.57	2	-	-	-	-	-	-
Brown, WA	2	3	-	73	32	24.33	2	-	-	-	-	-	-
Harvey, RN	2	3	1	133	112	66.50	2	-	-	-	-	-	-
Hassett, AL	5	8	1	310	137	44.29	6	-	-	-	-	-	-
Johnson, IW	4	6	1	51	21	10.20	5	-	183.0	60	427	7	61.00
Johnston, WA	5	5	2	62	29	20.67	-	-	309.2	91	630	27	23.33
Lindwall, RR	5	6	-	191	77	31.83	3	-	222.5	57	530	27	19.63
Loxton, SJE	3	3	-	144	93	48.00	-	-	63.0	11	148	3	49.33
Miller, KR	5	7	-	184	74	26.29	8	-	138.1	43	301	13	23.15
Morris, AR	5	9	1	696	196	87.00	4	-	8.0	1	24	-	-
Ring, DT	1	1	-	9	9	9.00	-	-	28.0	13	44	1	44.00
Saggers, RA	1	1	-	5	5	5.00	3	-	-	-	-	-	-
Tallon, D	4	4	-	112	53	28.00	12	-	-	-	-	-	-
Toshack, ERH	4	4	3	51	20*	51.00	-	-	173.1	70	364	11	33.09

English Averages

1948 ENGLAND v AUSTRALIA

ENGLAND	M	Inn	NO	Runs	H.S	Avrge	Ct	St	Overs	Mds	Runs	Wkt	Avrge
Barnett, CJ	1	2	-	14	8	7.00	-	-	17.0	5	36	-	-
Bedser, AV	5	9	1	176	79	22.00	1	-	274.3	75	688	18	38.22
Compton, DCS	5	10	1	562	184	62.44	2	-	37.0	6	156	1	156.00
Coxon, A	1	2	-	19	19	9.50	-	-	63.0	13	172	3	57.33
Cranston, K	1	2	-	10	10	5.00	2	-	21.1	1	79	1	79.00
Crapp, JF	3	6	1	88	37	17.60	6	-	-	-	-	-	-
Dewes, JG	1	2	-	11	10	5.50	-	-	-	-	-	-	-
Dollery, HE	2	3	-	38	37	12.67	-	-	-	-	-	-	-
Edrich, WJ	5	10	-	319	111	31.90	5	-	53.0	5	238	3	79.33
Emmett, GM	1	2	-	10	10	5.00	-	-	-	-	-	-	-
Evans, TG	5	9	2	188	50	26.86	8	4	-	-	-	-	-
Hardstaff jr, J	1	2	-	43	43	21.50	-	-	-	-	-	-	-
Hollies, WE	1	2	1	0	0*	0.00	-	-	56.0	14	131	5	26.20
Hutton, L	4	8	-	342	81	42.75	5	-	4.0	1	30	-	-
Laker, JC	3	6	1	114	63	22.80	1	-	155.2	42	472	9	52.44
Pollard, R	2	2	1	3	3	3.00	1	-	102.0	29	218	5	43.60
Washbrook, C	4	8	-	356	143	50.86	3	-	-	-	-	-	-
Watkins, AJ	1	2	-	2	2	1.00	-	-	4.0	1	19	-	-
Wright, DVP	1	2	-	17	13*	17.00	-	-	40.3	12	123	2	61.50
Yardley, NWD	5	9	-	150	44	16.67	1	-	84.0	22	204	9	22.67
Young, JA	3	5	2	17	9	5.67	2	-	156.0	64	292	5	58.40

Season of testimonials for stalwarts of old

Sir Donald Bradman receives the plaudits of the crowd as he walks on the Sydney Cricket Ground for his last first class match there, in the Oldfield–Kippax testimonial. He made 53 runs.

Adelaide, March 8. The cricket lovers of Australia have turned out this season to farewell some of the great cricketers of recent years, but the focus has been on Sir Donald Bradman. He played in his own testimonial, and in the Oldfield–Kippax match.

His last appearance, however, was at the ground where he played his opening first class innings, at the Adelaide Oval. Appearing in the Arthur Richardson testimonial he made a rather scratchy 30, not unexpected for a 41-year-old who has had no batting practice. But there were those in the crowd who remembered his debut on the same ground in 1927, when he made 118 runs in his first innings.

Bradman's career had just failed to overlap with that of Arthur Richardson, and it is unusual that a benefit match should be held for a cricketer who retired so long ago. But the word is around that, due to some bad investment advice, Richardson is in difficult circumstances. The match raised over £2130.

The most publicised match was The Don's own testimonial, played at the Melbourne Cricket Ground in December. It was a light-hearted affair, with runs galore and a tied result, with each side having a two-innings total of 836 runs.

But that did not stop the entertainment or the adulation for Bradman from an official attendance of 94,035 people. The SACA Bradman testimonial fund will receive some £5185 from the match.

He was the subject of a bit of a fiddle by one of the most reliable of Australian fieldsmen, Colin McCool. Bradman was on 97 when he skyed the ball to midwicket, where McCool ran around under it like a demented squirrel, muffed the catch and 'accidentally' kicked the ball into the deep. Bradman got to his century and went on to 123.

The Oldfield–Kippax testimonial was at the Sydney Cricket Ground. Both men had played with him in his first match in Adelaide and in his first Test. He made 53 before a packed stadium, as £6030 was raised.

NSW too strong

Sydney, March 30. New South Wales continues to have the strongest Shield side, despite the loss of Sid Barnes this season. Its only loss has been to Victoria, where Lindsay Hassett, Neil Harvey and Ian Johnson have been the backbone of the team. But NSW has Ray Lindwall and Arthur Miller, Arthur Morris and promising newcomers in bowler Alan Walker and batsman Jack Moroney.

Ian Johnson topped the bowling this season, with 43 wickets, while Lindsay Hassett has the highest score of the season with 205 against Queensland.

Knighthood at end of playing days

Melbourne, March 15. Sir Donald Bradman was knighted today by the Governor-General, Sir William McKell, at a ceremony at Government House.

Sir Donald was knighted in the New Year honours for services to cricket. He came over from Adelaide with Lady Bradman for the ceremony.

After the investiture he chatted with the other recipients of honours and with the Governor, who is an ardent cricket follower and has his own stories of watching the great Victor Trumper in club cricket in Sydney.

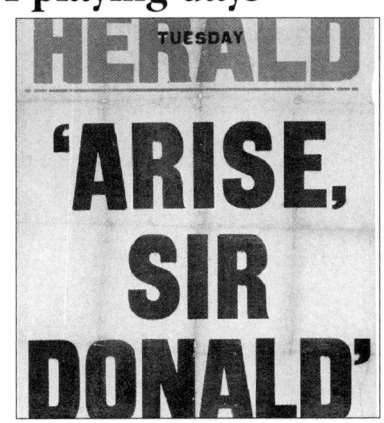

The Herald *poster on the day of Sir Donald's investiture.*

The Friendly Fifties

Dashing Keith Miller carries the fight to the old foe, England.

1949–50

AUSTRALIA IN SOUTH AFRICA

QUICK SINGLES

Battle revives Shield. Victoria took 5/14 on the second last day of the Shield game against NSW after trailing on the first innings, late in December, in front of 10,466 – a crowd which would have been much larger had a radio broadcast been permitted. Crowds would have flocked with NSW in trouble, had they known.

New-ball tactic criticised. Lindsay Hassett's tactic of taking the new ball immediately it was available, when the spinners had done the damage in the first Test at Johannesburg was criticised by the *Age's* Percy Beames. He thought this tactic was 'wavering'.

Team for N.Z. tipped. The *Sun* in January predicted that the Board of Control team of 'certainties' for N.Z. were Bill Brown, Ken Meuleman, Roy Howard, Jim de Courcy, Wally Driver, Doug Ring, Jack Iverson, Len Johnson and Stan Sismey and Alan Davidson.

WA to be retained in Shield. The Interstate Conference has agreed to WA staying in the Sheffield Shield for another season. WA are currently 'on probation'.

Storybook finish. NSW 19-year-old batsman Jim Burke batted with a broken finger and with fast bowler Tom Brooks in a last-wicket partnership of 17 runs to defeat Queensland at the SCG in January.

Two times Test. Melbourne will get the second Test match over the Christmas period, not over the New Year as has become usual in recent years, and the fifth Test (to be played to a finish if it will decide the series) when England visits later in 1950.

Test broadcast times. The third Test in South Africa will be broadcast on 3AR from 9.15 to 9.25 p.m. – a lunch summary, then from 11.18 to 11.50 p.m. ball-to-ball, and tea summary; stumps summary at 6.10 a.m. 3AW and 3XY will broadcast scores at intervals throughout the night.

NSW wins Shield. Ron James led NSW to a Shield win without their Test players. The only loss was to Victoria in Melbourne, despite 162 not out from Jim Burke.

Miller dropped, but still tours

Lindsay Hassett – happy captain.

Durban, Dec. 15. The cricketing contest between Australia and South Africa has resumed for the first time in 13 years, since the happy tour of South Africa by Vic Richardson's team in 1935–36.

Lindsay Hassett captains a side which has arrived with some selection surprises. It was picked by Australian selectors Don Bradman, 'Chappie' Dwyer and Jack Ryder and did not include Keith Miller.

However a car accident involving Bill Johnston very early in the tour resulted in an SOS being sent to Miller. He has flown out to join the team, rectifying the mystery of his non-selection.

Hassett is reported to have only gained the captaincy by a single vote of the Board of Control, a surprising result, given cricketing logic, Bradman's apparent assumption of who his successor would be and Hassett's arduous commitment with the 1945 Services' team. Miller was also considered by outsiders to be a contender.

Hassett possesses the friendliness and sense of fun that made Vic Richardson's tour such a success.

With Sid Barnes, and Bill Brown unavailable, Ernie Toshack and Miller were not selected some new faces are in the team.

The new players include rugby union international and fast bowler Alan Walker, punishing opening bat Jack Moroney, opener and excellent fielder Ken Archer from Queensland and versatile medium pacer and off-spinner Geff Noblet.

Since arriving in South Africa in October, the Australian team has scored six wins and three draws in first class matches in the leisurely build-up to the first Test in Johannesburg.

It's Johnson and Johnston

Johannesburg, Dec. 28. It might have been different, if South Africa's 19-year-old Cuan McCarthy had been a lucky sort of bowler, rather than an unlucky one. He did get Arthur Morris for a duck – and while Jack Moroney was run out also for a duck, McCarthy had Keith Miller and Lindsay Hassett dropped when they hadn't scored, and a bit later Sam Loxton was 'morally' bowled at least six times.

But none of this happened, instead Hassett became Bradman with the bat as well as with the captaincy and made 112 – one of his greatest innings for Australia. By the final two overs of that day – which was Christmas Eve, Hassett was so tired he could barely lift his bat, and went to bed at 8 p.m. – without a Christmas drink!

McCarthy had 2/90 – whereas in South Africa's first innings Miller took 5/40, and 'Big Bill' Johnston, having overcome the effects of his

Arthur Morris pads up.

car smash, took 2/21 and 6/44 on a tricky last-day pitch.

Ian Johnson backed his 66 with bowling figures of 3/37 and 3/54.

Neil Harvey the South African hero

The 1949–50 Australian team was warmly welcomed in South Africa.

Cape Town, Jan. 4. Some observers noted that during the brilliant innings of 178 by Neil Harvey that the black South Africans in the 'outer' have cheered his every run. Harvey is their hero, not the white South African bowlers.

But this was an innings where Harvey was everyone's hero, including the other crowd sitting at the white table-clothed tables under the elms, drinking tea and eating sandwiches.

Australia was off to a much better start in this Test, giving Harvey, batting number five, a solid platform of 4/276.

Arthur Morris 42, Jack Moroney 87, Keith Miller 58 and Lindsay Hassett 57 provided solid support to Australia's cause, and to Harvey. The result was easily foreseen when Australia were 4/312 on the first day, which was New Year's Eve.

Colin McCool contributed 49 on the second day, and then took 5/41 with his leg breaks in the South African first innings. Only Dudley Nourse and Eric Rowan provided much resistance.

In the second innings the South African upper order, following on, was 'Johnstoned' before the tail was absolutely 'Lindwalled' – 5/32.

Dramatic fight in classic third Test

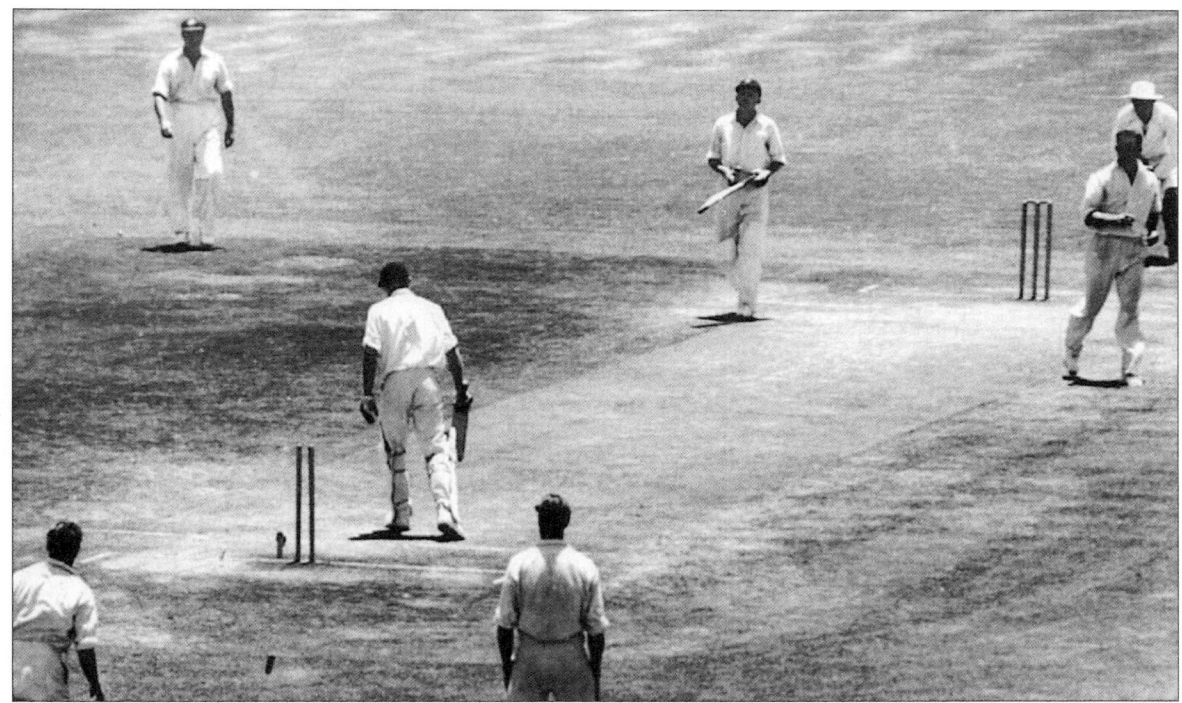

Ray Lindwall broke a stump as he bowled out South Africa's 'Tufty' Mann at Ellis Park in the fourth Test.

Durban, Jan. 24. A team that made just 75 in its first innings, 236 behind its opponent, would be considered most unlikely to win a Test match. But Lindsay Hassett's wise and cunning captaincy snared a tremendous win in just those circumstances, in the third Test at Kingsmead.

Eric Rowan made a patient but very slow 143 in South Africa's first innings, putting on 167 for the third wicket with Dudley Nourse (66). South Africa made 2/240 on the first day. After heavy overnight rain the pitch was treacherous, and had the home side scored more quickly, it could have declared and had Australia out twice on the second day.

As it happened, Hassett instructed his bowlers to 'get Nourse early', and then let the South Africans bat as long as they wanted to. They meandered to 311 all out, and Hugh Tayfield (7/23) bundled Australia out for 75.

South Africa decided not to enforce the follow-on, and were shot out by Johnston and Johnson on the gradually improving pitch for 99 – Australia needed 336.

Neil Harvey, as might have been predicted, got nearly half of them himself, 151 not out on a pitch hardly any better than the one on which South Africa made 99.

Thank heavens for Harvey, as Australia had lost 4/95 (Morris 44, Moroney 10, Miller 10, Hassett 11) when the young left-hander came in. Harvey, showing great patience batted for 330 minutes to give Australia a five-wicket win. McCool was 39 not out.

Neil Harvey hits four Test 100s

Port Elizabeth, March 6. Neil Harvey scored his fourth century in as many Tests with a sparkling 116 in the fifth Test.

Observers such as team-mate Keith Miller could not imagine that there is a greater or more brilliant batsman in the world at the present time than 21-year-old Harvey.

'Rarely in Test history had brilliance, grace and consistency been so effectively welded in one batsman,' said Miller.

Harvey's perfectly executed hooks, dazzling cover drives, square drives and delicately played late cuts and leg glances have charmed all spectators on this tour in his 178, 151, 100, and 116 in the four past Tests. He has averaged 132 in Tests on this tour.

Percy Beames wrote in the *Age*, that the fourth Test century 'was truly a magnificent performance by one so young, on whom Bradman's mantle has fallen.

'Harvey has risen to such a great height that he lacks respect for any bowling. The only hope an opposing side has for his dismissal is to allow his brilliance to run riot – a costly hope.'

In the fifth Test there were also the little matters of 157 from Arthur Morris and 167 from the captain Lindsay Hassett in Australia's 7/549.

Geff Noblet, replacing Ray Lindwall, took 3/21 on debut as the bowlers disposed of South Africa for 158 and 132, to complete a 4–0 demolition.

Jack Moroney's tedious two ton crawl

Johannesburg, Feb. 14. Lindsay Hassett's captaincy has been slightly criticised by elements of the South African press for failing to declare the second Australian innings on the last day and settling for a draw, rather than giving South Africa a target, however improbable.

In the dressing room on that last morning of the fourth Test with Australia due to bat, Hassett asked: 'Any volunteers to bat?' The only volunteers were Bill Johnston, who hadn't batted in the first innings, and 12th man Ken Archer.

Hassett said: 'Right, then, normal order' – which gave Jack Moroney the opportunity to score his second century of the game, but batting 'like a purposeless porpoise'. Keith Miller noted that 'Moroney showed no signs of animation and no indication that he had any goal in mind except to stay at the wicket and annoy everybody, including his partners. We include his partners, because one or two of them (including Miller himself) made abnormal attempts to give Jack the strike from time to time to help him to reach his second century, but he refused to avail himself of the opportunities offered.'

The crowd believed that a declaration at tea would have been the sporting thing to do, for to have to endure Moroney in a match that no longer had any competitive interest was too much to be borne.

Moroney's second century somewhat overshadowed his first in the match where he (118) and Arthur Morris (111) put on an opening stand of 214.

However, a sublime innings of exactly 100 by Neil Harvey (who threw away his hand to give Miller a chance to clobber a couple of sixes) was worth the price of entry to two Test matches.

An old foe is welcome. Harold Larwood (left), Bodyline terror, is greeted by Jack Fingleton, who encouraged his emigration to Australia with his family.

Neil Harvey, the left-handed genius

There are plenty of admirers of the style of young Neil Harvey.

When surveying his team for the 1948 tour, Don Bradman said that the 19-year-old left-hander Neil Harvey possessed 'the brilliance and daring of youth, and the likelihood of rapid improvement.'

On that very tour he saw his words come true. Harvey did not make the powerful Test XI until the fourth Test, and only because Sid Barnes was hurt.

He came out when Australia was in a tough position in the first innings, 3/68 (Bradman, Hassett, Morris gone) chasing 496.

Harvey sparred and missed at his first few balls and was called for a talk with his partner Keith Miller, who was batting with aggression. The Miller confidence rubbed off and Harvey began to display his natural gifts – driving with superb timing, cutting, hooking and pulling.

By the time Miller (58) left, Australia was 4/189, and Harvey then combined with Sam Loxton (93) before he was out for 112 and the score was 5/294.

Two days later he was four not out, shaking the hand of Don Bradman (173) as they achieved their final-day score of 404 and the Test was won.

From that time, until his retirement in 1962, Harvey was an automatic selection for Australia, invariably at first drop behind such stalwarts as Arthur Morris, Lindsay Hassett, Colin McDonald, Jim Burke, Bob Simpson and Bill Lawry.

He combined a solidity of technique and temperament with the ability to completely destroy the bowling once he was set.

Small in stature, he drove with authority and hooked with great power. His timing was built on brilliant footwork, and he was happy to get down the wicket to the spin bowlers.

Through all this Harvey was always modest, cheerful and unruffled. He neat physique was matched with a ready smile.

He was one of the surest cover fieldsmen of all time, pouncing on seemingly unstoppable balls and sending them back to the 'keeper with a precise right-handed throw.

In his 79 Tests Harvey had a very fine average of 48.42, the tenth-best of all Australian cricketers. To add to his value it was reckoned that his fielding saved at least 50 runs in the average opposing innings.

On top of that he was a popular easygoing man, the ideal vice-captain who set a standard of behaviour that kept touring parties cheerful but well settled.

Neil Harvey was bound to play cricket, as he came from a dedicated cricket family.

His father had played grade cricket in Newcastle before settling in Fitzroy, Melbourne, and raising six sons and a daughter in industrial, inner-city Fitzroy.

All the Harvey boys played cricket, graduating from the tennis ball and kerosene tin in Argyle Street, to club cricket with the District team of Fitzroy. All the brothers played with the Fitzroy Firsts; four of them, Mick, Mervyn, Ray and Neil played for Victoria; and two of them, Mervyn and Neil, played Test cricket.

FIRST TEST 1949–50 SOUTH AFRICA v AUSTRALIA
Ellis Park, Johannesburg. December 24, 26, 27, 28, 1949.
Toss: Australia. Australia won by an innings & 85 runs.

AUSTRALIA

AR Morris c Tayfield b McCarthy	0
J Moroney run out	0
KR Miller b Mann	21
AL Hassett (c) b Watkins	112
RN Harvey b Watkins	34
SJE Loxton st Wade b Tayfield	101
CL McCool b Tayfield	31
IW Johnson c Cheetham b Mann	66
RA Saggers (+) lbw McCarthy	14
RR Lindwall c Nel b Tayfield	21
WA Johnston not out	1
EXTRAS (B 5, LB 5, W 2)	12
TOTAL	413

FOW 1st Inns: 0 2 71 163 200 283 320 372 408 413

Bowling: *First Innings*: McCarthy 25-2-90-2, Watkins 19-3-56-2, Smith 13-0-70-0, Tayfield 28-3-93-3, Mann 28.4-4-92-2.

SOUTH AFRICA

EAB Rowan b Miller	60	lbw McCool	32
OE Wynne lbw Johnston	3	c Saggers b Johnston	33
JD Nel b Johnson	4	c Saggers b Johnston	14
AD Nourse (c) c Hassett b Johnson	0	c Saggers b Johnson	36
WW Wade (+) b Miller	2	b Johnston	11
JE Cheetham lbw Johnston	10	c Hassett b Johnston	35
JC Watkins c Hassett b Miller	36	c Miller b Johnson	0
HJ Tayfield lbw Miller	6	c Miller b Johnson	0
NBF Mann b Miller	0	lbw Johnston	13
VI Smith not out	1	c McCool b Johnston	1
CN McCarthy b Johnson	0	not out	1
EXTRAS (LB 14, NB 1)	15	(B 9, LB 3, W 1, NB 2)	15
TOTAL	137		191

FOW 1st Inns: 14 32 40 47 82 112 122 122 133 137
FOW 2nd Inns: 50 83 113 133 141 142 142 184 186 191

Bowling: *First Innings*: Lindwall 10-1-22-0, Johnston 12-4-21-2, Miller 15-3-40-5, Johnson 18.2-6-37-3, Loxton 1-0-2-0. *Second Innings*: Lindwall 8-1-25-0, Johnston 20.1-5-44-6, Miller 11-1-27-0, Johnson 14-0-54-3, Loxton 3-0-11-0, McCool 9-3-15-1.

Umpires: RGA Ashman & D Collins

SECOND TEST 1949–50 SOUTH AFRICA v AUSTRALIA
Newlands, Cape Town. December 31, January 2, 3, 4, 1950.
Toss: Australia. Australia won by 8 wkts.

AUSTRALIA

AR Morris c Watkins b Tayfield	42	c & b Mann	24
J Moroney c Cheetham b Mann	87	lbw Mann	19
KR Miller b Watkins	58 (4)	not out	16
AL Hassett (c) c & b Mann	57		
RN Harvey c Wade b Mann	178 (3)	not out	23
SJE Loxton b Tayfield	35		
CL McCool not out	49		
IW Johnson c Watkins b Mann	0		
RR Lindwall not out	8		
RA Saggers (+)			
WA Johnston			
EXTRAS (B 8, LB 4)	12	(B 5)	5
TOTAL	7 dec 526		2 for 87

FOW 1st Inns: 68 172 215 276 416 502 502
FOW 2nd Inns: 37 44

Bowling: *First Innings*: McCarthy 24-2-98-0, Watkins 12-2-59-1, Mann 28-3-105-4, Tayfield 37-4-141-2, Smith 25-0-111-0. *Second Innings*: McCarthy 4-1-18-0, Watkins 2-0-10-0, Mann 8-1-23-2, Tayfield 6-1-31-0.

SOUTH AFRICA

EAB Rowan lbw McCool	67	c Harvey b Johnston	3
OE Wynne c Johnson b Miller	13	c Saggers b Johnston	10
JD Nel lbw Johnson	38	c McCool b Johnson	19
AD Nourse (c) c Johnston b Miller	65	lbw McCool	114
WW Wade (+) c Saggers b Loxton	4	b Johnston	11
JE Cheetham c McCool b Miller	3	c Saggers b Lindwall	27
JC Watkins st Saggers b McCool	35	c Saggers b Lindwall	9
HJ Tayfield st Saggers b McCool	15	b Lindwall	75
NBF Mann b McCool	16	b Lindwall	46
VI Smith not out	11	lbw Lindwall	4
CN McCarthy st Saggers b McCool	0	not out	0
EXTRAS (B 2, LB 8, W 1)	11	(B 3, LB 10, NB 2)	15
TOTAL	278		333

FOW 1st Inns: 33 92 154 169 194 203 241 250 278 278
FOW 2nd Inns: 5 16 61 80 141 159 225 327 332 333

Bowling: *First Innings*: Lindwall 12-2-33-0, Johnston 17-3-53-0, Johnson 12-1-61-0, Miller 17-3-54-3, Loxton 6-0-25-1, McCool 11.4-1-41-5. *Second Innings*: Lindwall 15.4-2-32-5, Johnston 24-2-70-3, Johnson 24-5-91-1, Miller 11-0-43-0, McCool 21-3-71-1, Loxton 4-1-6-0, Harvey 3-1-5-0.

Umpires: RGA Ashman & D Collins

THIRD TEST 1949–50 SOUTH AFRICA v AUSTRALIA
Kingsmead, Durban. January 20, 21, 23, 24, 1950.
Toss: South Africa. Australia won by 5 wkts.

SOUTH AFRICA

EAB Rowan c Johnston b Miller	143	c Saggers b Lindwall	4
OE Wynne b Johnston	18	b Johnson	29
JD Nel c & b Johnson	14	lbw Johnston	20
AD Nourse (c) c Saggers b Johnston	66	c McCool b Johnson	27
WW Wade (+) b Lindwall	24	b Johnson	0
NBF Mann b Johnston	9 (9)	lbw Johnson	0
JE Cheetham c Hassett b Johnston	4 (6)	c Hassett b Johnson	1
JC Watkins b Lindwall	5 (7)	st Saggers b Johnson	2
HJ Tayfield run out	15 (8)	b Johnson	3
VI Smith b Lindwall	1	b Johnson	4
CN McCarthy not out	0	not out	2
EXTRAS (B 3, LB 7, NB 2)	12	(B 5, LB 1, NB 1)	7
TOTAL	311		99

FOW 1st Inns: 32 75 242 264 283 289 293 304 308 311
FOW 2nd Inns: 9 51 85 85 88 90 93 93 93 99

Bowling: *First Innings*: Lindwall 19-3-47-3, Miller 24-5-73-1, McCool 13-3-35-0, Johnston 31.2-5-75-4, Loxton 6-1-31-0, Johnson 16-5-38-1. *Second Innings*: Lindwall 4-1-7-1, Miller 7-0-12-0, Johnston 18.2-6-39-4, Johnson 17-2-34-5.

AUSTRALIA

AR Morris c Smith b Tayfield	25	hit wicket b Tayfield	44
J Moroney b Tayfield	10	lbw Tayfield	10
IW Johnson lbw Tayfield	2		
KR Miller b Tayfield	2 (3)	lbw Mann	10
AL Hassett (c) lbw Tayfield	2 (4)	lbw Mann	11
RA Saggers (+) c Cheetham b Mann	2		
CL McCool lbw Mann	1	not out	39
RR Lindwall b Mann	7		
RN Harvey c & b Tayfield	2 (5)	not out	151
SJE Loxton c Cheetham b Tayfield	16 (6)	b Mann	54
WA Johnston not out	2		
EXTRAS (B 3, LB 1)	4	(B 7, LB 9, NB 1)	17
TOTAL	75		5 for 336

FOW 1st Inns: 31 35 37 39 42 45 46 53 63 75
FOW 2nd Inns: 14 33 59 95 230

Bowling: *First Innings*: McCarthy 6-2-8-0, Watkins 4-1-9-0, Mann 10-1-31-3, Tayfield 8.4-1-23-7. *Second Innings*: McCarthy 12-3-32-0, Watkins 6-2-10-0, Mann 51.6-13-101-3, Tayfield 49-5-144-2, Smith 5-0-32-0.

Umpires: JV Hart-Davis & BV Malan

FOURTH TEST 1949–50 SOUTH AFRICA v AUSTRALIA
Ellis Park, Johannesburg. February 10, 11, 13, 14, 1950.
Toss: Australia. Match Drawn.

AUSTRALIA

AR Morris c Fullerton b McCarthy	111	c Mann b McCarthy	19
J Moroney c Fullerton b Melle	118	not out	101
KR Miller c Fullerton b Melle	84 (4)	not out	33
RR Lindwall b Melle	5		
AL Hassett (c) b McCarthy	53		
RN Harvey not out	56 (3)	b Melle	100
SJE Loxton b Melle	6		
CL McCool st Fullerton b Tayfield	8		
IW Johnson c(S)JB Roothman b Melle	3		
RA Saggers (+) not out	5		
WA Johnston			
EXTRAS (B 8, LB 7, NB 1)	16	(B 5, LB 1)	6
TOTAL	8 for 465		2 for 259

FOW 1st Inns: 214 265 273 382 392 418 437 440
FOW 2nd Inns: 28 198

Bowling: *First Innings*: McCarthy 31-4-113-2, Melle 33-3-113-5, Tayfield 31-4-103-1, Mann 25-2-85-0, Begbie 7-0-35-0. *Second Innings*: McCarthy 13-1-56-1, Melle 12-0-58-1, Tayfield 14-2-88-0, Mann 8-1-32-0, Begbie 3-0-19-0, Rowan 1-1-0-0, Nourse 1-1-0-0.

SOUTH AFRICA

EAB Rowan b Lindwall	55
JD Nel run out	25
RG Draper c Saggers b Johnston	15
AD Nourse (c) c Saggers b Lindwall	5
DW Begbie c McCool b Miller	24
PL Winslow c & b Miller	19
GM Fullerton (+) c Hassett b McCool	88
HJ Tayfield c Johnson b Miller	40
NBF Mann b Lindwall	52
MG Melle lbw McCool	14
CN McCarthy not out	2
EXTRAS (B 7, LB 5, NB 1)	13
TOTAL	352

FOW 1st Inns: 84 86 96 115 145 148 213 307 345 352

Bowling: *First Innings*: Lindwall 26-3-82-3, Johnston 29-5-68-1, Miller 28-3-75-3, Loxton 10-2-22-0, Johnson 18-4-52-0, McCool 7-0-29-2, Hassett 1-0-5-0, Harvey 3-0-6-0.

Umpires: D Collins & DT Drew

FIFTH TEST 1949–50 SOUTH AFRICA v AUSTRALIA
St George's Park, Port Elizabeth. March 3, 4, 6, 1950.
Toss: Australia. Australia won by an innings & 259 runs.

AUSTRALIA

AR Morris c Winslow b Melle	157
J Moroney c Nourse b Melle	7
KR Miller c Nourse b Tayfield	22
RN Harvey b Begbie	116
AL Hassett (c) c McCarthy b Mann	167
SJE Loxton c Rowan b Mann	43
CL McCool c Fullerton b Tayfield	6
IW Johnson not out	26
RA Saggers (+) not out	4
WA Johnston	
G Noblet	
EXTRAS (B 1)	1
TOTAL	7 dec 549

FOW 1st Inns: 16 49 236 350 449 485 545

Bowling: *First Innings*: McCarthy 29-3-121-0, Melle 23-2-132-2, Tayfield 25-1-103-2, Mann 36-4-154-2, Begbie 4-0-38-1.

SOUTH AFRICA

EAB Rowan b Johnson	40	c McCool b Miller	0
JD Nel b Miller	0	lbw Johnston	5
RG Draper c Johnston b Miller	7	b Johnson	3
AD Nourse (c) c McCool b Miller	37	b Johnson	55
DW Begbie c Saggers b Noblet	1	b Johnston	5
PL Winslow lbw Noblet	0 (7)	st Saggers b Johnson	11
GM Fullerton (+) st Saggers b McCool	18 (6)	c Saggers b Loxton	24
HJ Tayfield st Saggers b McCool	6	st Saggers b McCool	7
MG Melle b Miller	0 (10)	c Harvey b McCool	6
NBF Mann b Noblet	41 (9)	lbw Johnson	6
CN McCarthy not out	2	not out	4
EXTRAS (B 5, NB 1)	6	(B 3, LB 3)	6
TOTAL	158		132

FOW 1st Inns: 3 19 71 84 84 95 104 113 117 158
FOW 2nd Inns: 0 3 12 24 63 88 113 115 126 132

Bowling: *First Innings*: Miller 14-3-42-4, Johnston 3-0-12-0, Noblet 17.1-7-21-3, Johnson 11-1-48-1, McCool 5-1-29-2. *Second Innings*: Miller 8-0-24-1, Johnston 6-1-10-3, Noblet 9-2-16-0, Johnson 7-1-21-3, McCool 14.2-2-48-2, Loxton 4-2-7-1.

Umpires: D Collins & BV Malan

Australian Averages

1949–50 SOUTH AFRICA v AUSTRALIA

AUSTRALIA	M	Inn	NO	Runs	H.S	Avrge	Ct	St	Overs	Mds	Runs	Wkt	Avrge
Harvey, RN	5	8	3	660	178	132.00	2	-	6.0	1	11	-	-
Hassett, AL	5	6	-	402	167	67.00	6	-	1.0	-	5	-	-
Johnson, IW	5	5	1	97	66	24.25	3	-	137.2	25	436	18	24.22
Johnston, WA	5	2	2	3	2*	-	3	-	160.5	31	392	23	17.04
Lindwall, RR	4	4	1	41	21	13.67	-	-	94.4	13	248	12	20.67
Loxton, SJE	5	6	-	255	101	42.50	-	-	34.0	6	104	2	52.00
McCool, CL	5	6	2	134	49*	33.50	7	-	80.6	13	268	13	20.62
Miller, KR	5	8	2	246	84	41.00	3	-	135.0	18	390	17	22.94
Moroney, J	5	8	1	352	118	50.29	-	-	-	-	-	-	-
Morris, AR	5	8	-	422	157	52.75	-	-	-	-	-	-	-
Noblet, G	1	-	-	-	-	-	-	-	26.1	9	37	3	12.33
Saggers, RA	5	4	2	25	14	12.50	13	8	-	-	-	-	-

South African Averages

1949–50 SOUTH AFRICA v AUSTRALIA

SOUTH AFRICA	M	Inn	NO	Runs	H.S	Avrge	Ct	St	Overs	Mds	Runs	Wkt	Avrge
Begbie, DW	2	3	-	30	24	10.00	-	-	14.0	-	92	1	92.00
Cheetham, JE	3	6	-	80	35	13.33	4	-	-	-	-	-	-
Draper, RG	2	3	-	25	15	8.33	-	-	-	-	-	-	-
Fullerton, GM	2	3	-	130	88	43.33	4	1	-	-	-	-	-
Mann, NBF	5	9	-	183	52	20.33	3	-	195.2	29	623	16	38.94
McCarthy, CN	5	9	7	10	4*	5.00	-	-	144.0	18	536	5	107.20
Melle, MG	2	3	-	21	14	7.00	-	-	68.0	5	303	8	37.88
Nel, JD	5	9	-	139	38	15.44	1	-	-	-	-	-	-
Nourse, AD	5	9	-	405	114	45.00	2	-	1.0	1	0	-	-
Rowan, EAB	5	9	-	404	143	44.89	1	-	1.0	1	0	-	-
Smith, VI	3	6	2	22	11*	5.50	1	-	43.0	1	213	-	-
Tayfield, HJ	5	9	-	167	75	18.56	2	-	198.4	21	726	17	42.71
Wade, WW	3	6	-	52	24	8.67	1	1	-	-	-	-	-
Watkins, JC	3	6	-	87	36	14.50	2	-	43.0	8	144	3	48.00
Winslow, PL	2	3	-	30	19	10.00	1	-	-	-	-	-	-
Wynne, OE	3	6	-	106	33	17.67	-	-	-	-	-	-	-

1950–51

ENGLAND IN AUSTRALIA

Brisbane 'sticky' a stopper for England

Brisbane, Dec. 5. The question of whether Australia, the pitch, the weather, or even Len Hutton won this amazing first Test match is a matter for the cricket scholars – suffice to say that on the scoreboard it was Australia, by just 70 runs.

But between Australia's modest first innings of 228, which occupied the whole of the first day, and the fall of the last English wicket, that of England leg-spinner Doug Wright, lay many strange stories.

First of all it rained heavily on the scheduled day two, and 35,000 angry patrons were locked out of the ground, and then it rained some more on the Sunday rest day – the result being a classic Brisbane 'sticky dog', also described by one player as a 'pig of a wicket'.

That meant England's Cyril Washbrook was top score in England's 7/68 declared with 19.

Australia's turn. Neil Harvey top-scored here with 12, in 7/32 declared. Lindsay Hassett said to England captain Freddie Brown: 'It's your move, old chap.' Hassett's inspired declaration meant England were batting again. By the end of the day they were 6/30 with 163 still to get on the last day, Hutton not out.

In a great defensive innings Hutton was 62 not out at the end, and England had added 92, but Hutton ran out of partners, and England was 70 short.

Australia won the game, but England has shown that it will be a more than worthy opponent this summer.

The dirt on pitches

Melbourne, Dec. 30. Low scoring in Australian cricket since World War II, especially in the light of the sub-200 innings totals at the MCG in the second Test, has led observers such as E. H. M. Baillie in the *Sporting Globe* to question whether it is the fault of the wickets.

Baillie says that while there has been some deterioration in the past 20 years, it has not been as bad as some make out. Good wickets of today were not much different from good wickets in the past, he wrote.

But they are not as fast as they once were. Perhaps it is the fault of the soils used. The Bulli soil in Sydney, the hill soil in Adelaide and the black Merri Creek soil for the MCG are all sourced from slightly different locations these days.

Tense battle in Christmas Test

Melbourne, Dec. 27. Alec Bedser and Trevor Bailey showed an unanticipated effectiveness on the seemingly benign MCG pitch, taking four wickets each and limiting Australia to a very modest 194, with only captain Lindsay Hassett getting past 50.

Similarly, in England's first innings only captain Freddie Brown with 62 got over 50 as England crept past Australia's modest score. Jack Iverson took four wickets with his mysterious deliveries. There were then two days off for Christmas, but the rest did little for Australia's batting.

Australia once again fell cheaply in the second innings – after Bedser picked up Ken Archer for 46, and Neil Harvey was run out for 32, the crucial dismissal was that of Hassett by Freddie Brown. Brown took 4/26, and Australia was all out 181. England then lost two wickets.

The young England players were taking inspiration from big hearted 40 year old Freddie Brown, who with bat and ball has shown the way to take on the Australians.

England needed only 151 runs on the last day, eight wickets in hand. Len Hutton took nearly three hours for 40, and the other batsman played cautiously as Bill Johnston picked them off. In a day of increasing tension, Johnston had Doug Wright leg before and England fell 28 runs short.

Neither side reached 200 in seaming conditions before Christmas, and slow and low conditions after two days of fierce sun after it.

Miller a match for injured England

Sydney, Jan. 9. Hec de Lacy, writing in the *Sporting Globe*: 'I've just watched the world's greatest bowler dismiss the world's greatest batsmen in what may easily have been the world's greatest "shock" over.'

Ten minutes before tea, 'the score book recorded it. Hutton lbw bowled Miller. Compton b. Miller. Parkhouse two near misses the scorebook will not record. After tea, Simpson was caught Loxton b. Miller. Four overs, two maidens, 5 runs – and three wickets.'

Even without the ball in hand, Miller was in the game, snapping up a lightning-reflex catch to dismiss Cyril Washbrook.

England was all out for 290, which would have been less but for another lion-hearted innings from captain Freddie Brown.

Trevor Bailey had a broken thumb, and Doug Wright had an injured leg – and neither could bowl.

Miller wasn't done.

He came in when Australia was 3/122 and proceeded to make 145 essential rather than swashbuckling runs, including a partnership of 150 with Ian Johnson (77).

In England's second innings Miller and Lindwall were only needed for 10 overs before Hassett brought on the mystery spin of Jack Iverson, who proceeded to bowl 19.4 overs of unplayables, taking 6/27.

Australia won the match by an innings and 13 runs, and has taken the series 3–0.

An aerial view of the WACA ground in Perth, where England drew in its initial first class game in Australia, against Western Australia, in October.

278

Big innings from Morris and Hutton

Adelaide, Feb. 8. Former England fast bowler Bill Bowes wrote after the second day's play: 'How one's courage and hopes rise and fall in a Test match. Half an hour after lunch I felt England was in for a blistering, then in a few overs I felt we could beat you. We had you, the last five wickets adding only 61 and your total 371 instead of the expected 500. If the wicket holds we have got more than a fighting chance.'

Arthur Morris overcame an indifferent series, and the hoodoo of Alec Bedser (who has dismissed him in four out of five innings this season) with a remorseless 206 in 462 minutes which included 23 fours.

Bowes would not have been unhappy with what happened to England, after restraining Australia, and after watching Len Hutton conquer the Svengali of spin, Jack Iverson.

Morris's innings was overshadowed in brilliance by one of the best played by Len Hutton, who carried his bat for 156 in 370 minutes out of a meagre total of 272.

Australia was in the box seat after a sparkling 68 from Neil Harvey, a solid 99 from Keith Miller and an entertaining 101 not out by Jim Burke in his first Test.

England lost wickets steadily in its second innings and batted without captain Freddie Brown who had rammed a tram pole in his car in North terrace after a Government House reception. Bill Johnston took 4/73, making 20 for the series so far.

England break a 13-year drought

Melbourne, Feb. 28. England has scored its first win over Australia since 1938. This time Len Hutton contributed a relatively paltry 79 and 60 not out, compared to the 364 he notched back then, but perhaps there was equal satisfaction in the England camp. This win, after all, has come after four successive, if somewhat unlucky, defeats.

The hero with the bat for England was the enigmatic Reg Simpson, who made 156 not out, of 320 in England's first innings. He had made only one score of over 50 in the rest of the series.

Australia made 217 in its first innings and 197 in its second, low totals mainly due to the persistently accurate bowling of Alec Bedser who took 5/46 and 5/95.

England lost £5000 in profit from the abandoned second day's play, and is now unlikely to make as much as the £17,500 it took home in 1946–47.

Hutton made 533 runs in the series at 88.83 and was head and shoulders above all other batsmen for consistency and sheer class.

Apart from Hutton, and Bedser, the main hero for England in the series and this game was captain 'bulldog' Freddie Brown.

Journalists thought Brown was the gutsiest and probably the best England captain ever to come to Australia. Former skipper Arthur Gilligan said 'I've got to hand it to Brown. He's a marvel. Just imagine: he's as lame as a duck one minute, goes to bowl, and gets Harvey, Miller and Morris for no score!'

A rare event in the 1950–51 series: Len Hutton has a swing and a miss.

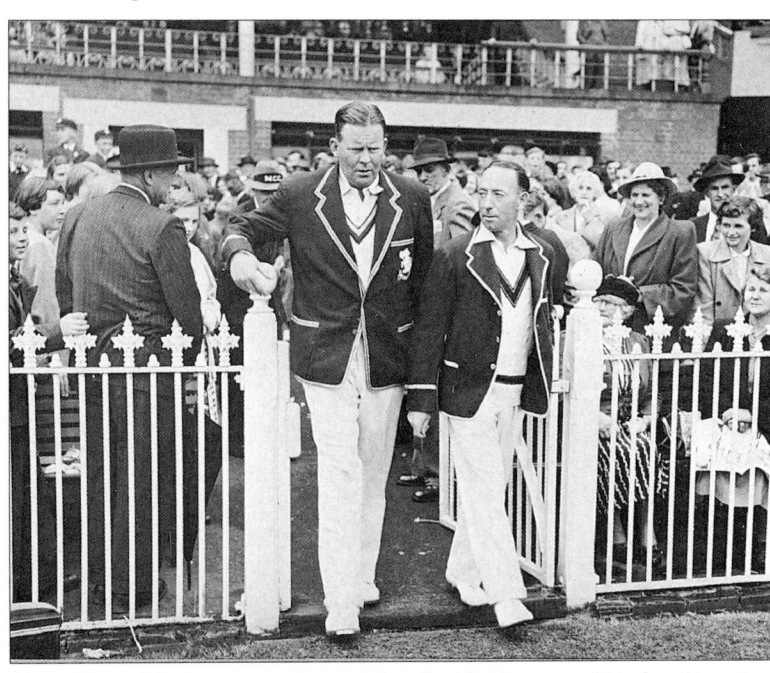

Two of Test cricket's most popular captains, Freddie Brown and Lindsay Hassett, go out to toss a coin on the first morning of the Melbourne Test.

A win at last. England captain Freddie Brown earns the gratitude of John Bull, who has been starved of success.

Jack Iverson's big season

Melbourne, Feb. 28. A month ago Jack Iverson said that the fifth Test would be his last, and that at the age of 36 he would retire. But everything about 'Big Jake's' career has been remarkable so it would not surprise if he popped up again.

A big, shambly man of 6ft 3in. and 15 stone, Iverson burst onto the cricket scene like a meteor, and seems to have disappeared as fast. In his one season of Test cricket, Australia won 4–1 and Iverson took 21 wickets at 15.24.

This season has been just his fourth. In his first season, 1947–48, he played for the sub-district team Brighton and they won the premiership. In 1948–49 he shifted to Melbourne, was leading wicket-taker, and they won the premiership. In 1949–50, the same thing occurred for Victoria.

His extraordinary career only commenced after World War II. Iverson was born in 1915, and went to Geelong College, where he once bowled Lindsay Hassett. He served in the Middle East in the same regiment as Hassett, and later in New Guinea developed his unique flicking style of spinning, with a table tennis ball. He has big hands, long fingers and could squeeze out a cricket ball using the same method, flicking it both ways between his second and third fingers.

Inspired by blind cricketers he saw in 1946, Iverson joined Brighton thirds late that year. He played his first game at 31. By the

Jack Iverson – Svengali of spin.

end of 1946–47 he was in the firsts. Victoria called him up in 1949–50 and he took 6/47 against WA, then 7/77 against SA. At the end of this season he went to NZ with an Australian 'seconds' team, and bamboozled the Kiwis, taking 75 wickets at 7.73.

Women cricketers are out in force, bringing new hazards for the umpire.

FIRST TEST 1950–51 AUSTRALIA v ENGLAND
Brisbane Cricket Ground, Brisbane. December 1, 2 (no play), 4, 5, 1950.
Toss: Australia. Australia won by 70 runs.

AUSTRALIA

Batsman	1st		2nd	
J Moroney c Hutton b Bailey	0		lbw Bailey	0
AR Morris lbw Bedser	25		c Bailey b Bedser	0
RN Harvey c Evans b Bedser	74	(6)	c Simpson b Bedser	12
KR Miller c McIntyre b Wright	15	(7)	c Simpson b Bailey	8
AL Hassett (c) b Bedser	8		lbw Bailey	3
SJE Loxton c Evans b Brown	24	(4)	c Bailey b Bedser	0
RR Lindwall c Bedser b Bailey	41	(8)	not out	0
D Tallon (+) c Simpson b Brown	5			
IW Johnson c Simpson b Bailey	23	(3)	lbw Bailey	8
WA Johnston c Hutton b Bedser	1			
JB Iverson not out	1			
EXTRAS (B 5, LB 3, NB 3)	11		(NB 1)	1
TOTAL	228		7 dec	32

FOW 1st Inns: 0 69 116 118 129 156 172 219 226 228
FOW 2nd Inns: 0 0 0 12 19 31 32

Bowling: *First Innings*: Bailey 12-4-28-3, Bedser 16.5-4-45-4, Wright 16-0-81-1, Brown 11-0-63-2. *Second Innings*: Bailey 7-2-22-4, Bedser 6.5-2-9-3.

ENGLAND

Batsman	1st		2nd	
RT Simpson b Johnston	12		b Lindwall	0
C Washbrook c Hassett b Johnston	19		c Loxton b Lindwall	6
TG Evans (+) c Iverson b Johnston	16	(6)	c Loxton b Johnston	5
DCS Compton c Lindwall b Johnston	3	(9)	c Loxton b Johnston	0
JG Dewes c Loxton b Miller	1	(3)	b Miller	9
L Hutton not out	8	(8)	not out	62
AJW McIntyre b Johnston	1		run out	7
FR Brown (c) c Tallon b Miller	4	(10)	c Loxton b Iverson	17
TE Bailey not out	1	(4)	c Johnston b Iverson	7
AV Bedser		(5)	c Harvey b Iverson	0
DVP Wright			c Lindwall b Iverson	2
EXTRAS (LB 2, NB 1)	3		(B 6, NB 1)	7
TOTAL	7 dec 68			122

FOW 1st Inns: 28 49 52 52 56 57 67
FOW 2nd Inns: 0 16 22 23 23 30 46 46 77 122

Bowling: *First Innings*: Lindwall 1-0-1-0, Johnston 11-2-35-5, Miller 1-1-29-2. *Second Innings*: Lindwall 7-3-21-2, Johnston 11-2-30-2, Miller 7-3-21-1, Iverson 13-3-43-4.

Umpires: AN Barlow & H Elphinston

SECOND TEST 1950–51 AUSTRALIA v ENGLAND
Melbourne Cricket Ground, Melbourne. December 22, 23, 26, 27, 1950.
Toss: Australia. Australia won by 28 runs.

AUSTRALIA

Batsman	1st		2nd	
KA Archer c Bedser b Bailey	26		c Bailey b Bedser	46
AR Morris c Hutton b Bedser	2		lbw Wright	18
RN Harvey c Evans b Bedser	42		run out	31
KR Miller lbw Brown	18		b Bailey	14
AL Hassett (c) b Bailey	52		c Bailey b Brown	19
SJE Loxton c Evans b Close	32		c Evans b Brown	2
RR Lindwall lbw Bailey	8		c Evans b Brown	7
D Tallon (+) not out	7		lbw Brown	0
IW Johnson c Parkhouse b Bedser	0		c Close b Bedser	23
WA Johnston c Hutton b Bedser	0		b Bailey	6
JB Iverson b Bailey	1		not out	0
EXTRAS (B 4, LB 2)	6		(B 10, LB 5)	15
TOTAL	194			181

FOW 1st Inns: 6 67 89 93 177 177 192 193 193 194
FOW 2nd Inns: 43 99 100 126 131 151 151 156 181 181

Bowling: *First Innings*: Bailey 17.1-5-40-4, Bedser 19-3-37-4, Wright 8-0-63-0, Brown 9-0-28-1, Close 6-1-20-1. *Second Innings*: Bedser 16.3-2-43-2, Bailey 15-3-47-2, Wright 9-0-42-1, Brown 12-2-26-4, Close 1-0-8-0.

ENGLAND

Batsman	1st		2nd	
RT Simpson c Johnson b Miller	4		b Lindwall	23
C Washbrook lbw Lindwall	21		b Iverson	8
JG Dewes c Miller b Johnston	8	(5)	c Harvey b Iverson	5
L Hutton c Tallon b Iverson	12		c Lindwall b Johnston	40
WGA Parkhouse c Hassett b Miller	9	(6)	lbw Johnston	28
DB Close c Loxton b Iverson	0	(7)	lbw Johnston	1
FR Brown (c) c Johnson b Iverson	62	(8)	b Lindwall	8
TE Bailey b Lindwall	12	(3)	b Johnson	0
TG Evans (+) c Johnson b Iverson	49		b Lindwall	2
AV Bedser not out	4		not out	14
DVP Wright lbw Johnston	2		lbw Johnston	2
EXTRAS (B 8, LB 6)	14		(B 17, LB 2)	19
TOTAL	197			150

FOW 1st Inns: 11 33 37 54 54 61 126 153 194 197
FOW 2nd Inns: 21 22 52 82 92 95 122 124 134 150

Bowling: *First Innings*: Lindwall 13-2-46-2, Miller 13-0-39-2, Johnston 9-1-28-2, Iverson 18-3-37-4, Johnson 5-1-19-0, Loxton 4-1-14-0. *Second Innings*: Lindwall 12-1-29-3, Miller 5-2-16-0, Johnson 13-3-24-1, Iverson 20-4-36-2, Johnston 13.7-1-26-4.

Umpires: GC Cooper & RR Wright

THIRD TEST 1950–51 AUSTRALIA v ENGLAND
Sydney Cricket Ground, Sydney. January 5, 6, 8, 9, 1951.
Toss: England. Australia won by an innings & 13 runs.

ENGLAND
L Hutton lbw Miller	62	c Tallon b Iverson	9
C Washbrook c Miller b Johnson	18	b Iverson	34
RT Simpson c Loxton b Miller	49	c Tallon b Iverson	0
DCS Compton b Miller	0	c Johnson b Johnston	23
WGA Parkhouse c Morris b Johnson	25	run out	15
FR Brown (c) b Lindwall	79	b Iverson	18
TE Bailey c Tallon b Johnson	15 (8)	not out	0
TG Evans (+) not out	23 (7)	b Johnson	14
AV Bedser b Lindwall	3	b Iverson	4
JJ Warr b Miller	4	b Iverson	0
DVP Wright run out	0		
EXTRAS (LB 10, NB 2)	12	(B 1, LB 5)	6
TOTAL	290		9 for 123

FOW 1st Inns: 34 128 128 137 187 258 267 281 286 290
FOW 2nd Inns: 32 40 45 74 91 119 119 123 123

Bowling: *First Innings*: Lindwall 16-0-60-2, Miller 15.7-4-37-4, Johnston 21-5-50-0, Iverson 10-1-25-0, Johnson 31-8-94-3, Loxton 5-0-12-0. *Second Innings*: Lindwall 4-1-12-0, Miller 6-2-15-0, Johnston 13-6-31-1, Iverson 19.4-8-27-6, Johnson 10-2-32-1.

AUSTRALIA
KA Archer c Evans b Bedser	48
AR Morris b Bedser	0
AL Hassett (c) c Bedser b Brown	70
RN Harvey b Bedser	39
KR Miller not out	145
SJE Loxton c Bedser b Brown	17
D Tallon (+) lbw Bedser	18
IW Johnson b Brown	77
RR Lindwall lbw Brown	1
WA Johnston run out	0
JB Iverson run out	1
EXTRAS (B 3, LB 7)	10
TOTAL	426

FOW 1st Inns: 1 122 122 190 223 252 402 406 418 426

Bowling: *First Innings*: Bedser 43-4-107-4, Warr 36-4-142-0, Brown 44-4-153-4, Compton 6-1-14-0.

Umpires: AN Barlow & H Elphinston

FOURTH TEST 1950–51 AUSTRALIA v ENGLAND
Adelaide Oval, Adelaide. February 2, 3, 5, 6, 7, 8, 1951.
Toss: Australia. Australia won by 274 runs.

AUSTRALIA
KA Archer c Compton b Bedser	0	c Bedser b Tattersall	32
AR Morris b Tattersall	206	run out	16
AL Hassett (c) c Evans b Wright	43	lbw Wright	31
RN Harvey b Bedser	43	b Brown	68
KR Miller c Brown b Wright	44	b Wright	99
JW Burke b Tattersall	12	not out	101
IW Johnson c Evans b Bedser	16	c Evans b Warr	3
RR Lindwall lbw Wright	1	run out	31
D Tallon (+) b Tattersall	1	c Hutton b Compton	5
WA Johnston c Hutton b Wright	0	not out	9
JB Iverson not out	0		
EXTRAS (B 2, LB 1, W 1, NB 1)	5	(B 7, LB 1)	8
TOTAL	371		8 dec 403

FOW 1st Inns: 0 95 205 281 310 357 363 366 367 371
FOW 2nd Inns: 26 79 95 194 281 297 367 378

Bowling: *First Innings*: Bedser 26-4-74-3, Warr 16-2-63-0, Wright 25-1-99-4, Tattersall 25.5-5-95-3, Brown 3-0-24-0, Compton 1-0-11-0. *Second Innings*: Bedser 25-6-62-0, Warr 21-0-76-1, Wright 21-2-109-2, Tattersall 27-2-116-1, Brown 3-1-14-1, Compton 4.6-1-18-1.

ENGLAND
L Hutton not out	156	c (S)SJE Loxton b Johnston	45
C Washbrook c Iverson b Lindwall	2	lbw Johnston	31
RT Simpson b Johnston	29	c Burke b Johnston	61
DCS Compton c Tallon b Lindwall	5	c (S)SJE Loxton b Johnston	0
DS Sheppard b Iverson	9	lbw Miller	41
FR Brown (c) b Miller	16		
TG Evans (+) c Burke b Johnston	13 (6)	c Johnson b Miller	21
AV Bedser lbw Iverson	7 (7)	c Morris b Miller	0
R Tattersall c Harvey b Iverson	0 (8)	c Morris b Johnson	6
JJ Warr b Johnston	0 (9)	b Johnson	0
DVP Wright lbw Lindwall	14 (10)	not out	0
EXTRAS (B 15, LB 5, NB 1)	21	(B 15, LB 3, W 2, NB 3)	23
TOTAL	272		9 dec 228

FOW 1st Inns: 7 80 96 132 161 195 206 214 219 272
FOW 2nd Inns: 74 90 90 181 221 221 228 228 228

Bowling: *First Innings*: Lindwall 13.3-0-51-3, Miller 13-2-36-1, Johnston 25-4-58-3, Iverson 26-4-68-3, Johnson 15-2-38-0. *Second Innings*: Lindwall 10-2-35-0, Miller 13-4-27-3, Johnston 27-4-73-4, Johnson 25.6-6-63-2, Burke 3-1-7-0.

Umpires: AN Barlow & AF Cocks

FIFTH TEST 1950–51 AUSTRALIA v ENGLAND
Melbourne Cricket Ground, Melbourne. February 23, 24 (no play), 26, 27, 28, 1951.
Toss: Australia. England won by 8 wkts.

AUSTRALIA
JW Burke c Tattersall b Bedser	11	c Hutton b Bedser	1
AR Morris lbw Brown	50	lbw Bedser	4
AL Hassett (c) c Hutton b Brown	92	b Wright	48
RN Harvey c Evans b Brown	1	lbw Wright	52
KR Miller c & b Brown	7	c & b Brown	0
GB Hole b Bedser	18	b Bailey	63
IW Johnson lbw Bedser	1	c Brown b Wright	0
RR Lindwall c Compton b Bedser	21	b Bedser	14
D Tallon (+) c Hutton b Bedser	1	not out	2
WA Johnston not out	12	b Bedser	1
JB Iverson c Washbrook b Brown	0	c Compton b Bedser	0
EXTRAS (B 2, LB 1)	3	(B 2, LB 8, W 1, NB 1)	12
TOTAL	217		197

FOW 1st Inns: 23 111 115 123 156 166 184 187 216 217
FOW 2nd Inns: 5 6 87 89 142 142 192 196 197 197

Bowling: *First Innings*: Bedser 22-5-46-5, Bailey 9-1-29-0, Brown 18-4-49-5, Wright 9-1-50-0, Tattersall 11-3-40-0. *Second Innings*: Bedser 20.3-4-59-5, Bailey 15-3-32-1, Wright 15-2-56-3, Tattersall 5-2-6-0.

ENGLAND
L Hutton b Hole	79	not out	60
C Washbrook c Tallon b Miller	27	c Lindwall b Johnston	7
RT Simpson not out	156	run out	15
DCS Compton c Miller b Lindwall	11	not out	11
DS Sheppard c Tallon b Miller	1		
FR Brown (c) b Lindwall	6		
TG Evans (+) b Miller	1		
AV Bedser b Lindwall	11		
TE Bailey c Johnson b Iverson	5		
DVP Wright lbw Iverson	3		
R Tattersall b Miller	10		
EXTRAS (B 9, LB 1)	10	(LB 2)	2
TOTAL	320		2 for 95

FOW 1st Inns: 40 171 204 205 212 213 228 236 246 320
FOW 2nd Inns: 32 62

Bowling: *First Innings*: Lindwall 21-1-77-3, Miller 21.7-5-76-4, Johnston 12-1-55-0, Iverson 20-4-52-2, Johnson 11-1-40-0, Hole 5-0-10-1. *Second Innings*: Lindwall 2-0-12-0, Miller 2-0-5-0, Iverson 12-2-32-0, Johnston 11-3-36-1, Johnson 1-0-1-0, Hole 1-0-3-0, Hassett 0.6-0-4-0.

Umpires: AN Barlow & H Elphinston

Australian Averages

1950–51 AUSTRALIA v ENGLAND
AUSTRALIA	M	Inn	NO	Runs	H.S	Avrge	Ct	St	Overs	Mds	Runs	Wkt	Avrge
Archer, KA	3	5	-	152	48	30.40	2	-	-	-	-	-	-
Burke, JW	2	4	1	125	101*	41.67	2	-	3.0	1	7	-	-
Harvey, RN	5	9	-	362	74	40.22	3	-	-	-	-	-	-
Hassett, AL	5	9	-	366	92	40.67	2	-	0.6	-	4	-	-
Hole, GB	1	2	-	81	63	40.50	-	-	6.0	-	13	1	13.00
Iverson, JB	5	7	3	3	1*	0.75	2	-	138.4	29	320	21	15.24
Johnson, IW	5	9	-	151	77	16.78	6	-	111.6	23	311	7	44.43
Johnston, WA	5	8	2	29	12*	4.83	1	-	153.7	29	422	22	19.18
Lindwall, RR	5	9	1	124	41	15.50	4	-	99.3	10	344	15	22.93
Loxton, SJE	3	5	-	75	32	15.00	7	-	9.0	1	26	-	-
Miller, KR	5	9	1	350	145*	43.75	3	-	97.6	23	301	17	17.71
Moroney, J	1	2	-	0	0	0.00	-	-	-	-	-	-	-
Morris, AR	5	9	-	321	206	35.67	3	-	-	-	-	-	-
Tallon, D	5	8	2	39	18	6.50	8	-	-	-	-	-	-

English Averages

1950–51 AUSTRALIA v ENGLAND
ENGLAND	M	Inn	NO	Runs	H.S	Avrge	Ct	St	Overs	Mds	Runs	Wkt	Avrge
Bailey, TE	4	7	2	40	15	8.00	4	-	75.1	18	198	14	14.14
Bedser, AV	5	8	2	43	14*	7.17	5	-	195.0	34	482	30	16.07
Brown, FR	5	8	-	210	79	26.25	4	-	109.0	12	389	18	21.61
Close, DB	1	2	-	1	1	0.50	1	-	7.0	1	28	1	28.00
Compton, DCS	4	8	1	53	23	7.57	3	-	11.6	2	43	1	43.00
Dewes, JG	2	4	-	23	9	5.75	-	-	-	-	-	-	-
Evans, TG	5	9	1	144	49	18.00	11	-	-	-	-	-	-
Hutton, L	5	10	4	533	156*	88.83	9	-	-	-	-	-	-
McIntyre, AJW	1	2	-	8	7	4.00	1	-	-	-	-	-	-
Parkhouse, WGA	2	4	-	77	28	19.25	1	-	-	-	-	-	-
Sheppard, DS	2	3	-	51	41	17.00	-	-	-	-	-	-	-
Simpson, RT	5	10	1	349	156*	38.78	4	-	-	-	-	-	-
Tattersall, R	2	3	-	16	10	5.33	1	-	68.5	12	257	4	64.25
Warr, JJ	2	4	-	4	4	1.00	-	-	73.0	6	281	1	281.00
Washbrook, C	5	10	-	173	34	17.30	1	-	-	-	-	-	-
Wright, DVP	5	7	1	23	14	3.83	-	-	103.0	6	500	11	45.45

West Indies in thrilling Test win: series alive

Three 'W's lead West Indies

Alf Valentine spins a web.

Sydney, Oct. 20. The West Indies team has arrived in Australia for the first time since 1930–31 with something of a reputation. They demolished England in 1950, 3–1.

Opener Alan Rae had two centuries, but it was the 'Three W's', Clyde Walcott, Everton Weekes and Frank Worrell who caught the eye of discerning spectators with devastating batting.

Walcott hit 168, Weekes 129, and Worrell 261 and 138, which added greatly to their reputations. Weekes made four centuries in succession against India in 1948–49.

Walcott, a burly right hander, attracted attention in 1945–46 when he made 314 not out in a 574-run stand with Worrell (255 not out) for Barbados v Trinidad. At 19, Worrell (308 not out) put on 502 with present tour captain John Goddard.

And then there are the bowlers, Alf Valentine and Sonny Ramadhin.

Valentine is the taller of the two, a 21-year-old left-arm leg-spinner, who can bowl an immaculate length seemingly for hours on end. In England at Trent Bridge he bowled 92 overs for 3/141.

Ramadhin is a small right-arm finger spinner who turns them from the leg and the off seemingly with the same action.

Everton Weekes catches Ken Archer at the Sydney Cricket Ground from the bowling of Gerry Gomez.

Adelaide, Dec. 25. The West Indies had a wonderful Christmas present, defeating Australia by six wickets in the third Test. This was a match of sensations, beginning with the non-selection of Sid Barnes, the proposal of the selectors to name Phil Ridings after Lindsay Hassett pulled a muscle at training, and the Board not allowing it. As a result of that, Hassett had to act as 12th man – leaving Australia with only five batsmen.

Arthur Morris made his debut as captain and won the toss, deciding to bat on a pitch that had a 'sporty' damp patch at one end. Clyde Walcott was also injured, and the West Indies selectors also decided to go in without a recognised fast bowler.

As it happened Frank Worrell's medium-paced 'straights' were devastating. He took 6/38 at one end and John Goddard 3/26 at the other. Australia achieved its lowest post-war total – just 82.

But the West Indies found the conditions just as trying – and they were all out for 105, Bill Johnston 6/62. Before the day was over Australia had lost 2/21 and 22 wickets had fallen on the first day for 209.

Doug Ring, who had come in as nightwatchman, hit out next day for 67, and Australia eventually set the West Indies a target of 233, which was achieved for the loss of four wickets, after a couple of palpitations with the dismissals of Worrell (28) and Weekes (29).

Australia had lost just its second post-war Test.

But Australia won the first two against the West Indies, who had a limited preparation before the Tests began, including one first class game, against Queensland at the 'Gabba.

The first two Tests were disappointing from a West Indian viewpoint, but they were competetive and Sonny Ramadhin's 5/90 off 40 overs in Brisbane was described by Keith Miller and R. S. Whitington as 'the greatest individual bowling performance seen in Test cricket since the days of Bill O'Reilly.'

But the West Indies batting has yet to really 'come off' against the pace and hostility of Lindwall and Miller.

QUICK SINGLES

Lindwall's big over. Ray Lindwall had a look at three balls of an Alf Valentine over then hit 2, 6, 4, 4, 4 for a total of 22 from his 61 in the first Test.

Iverson's ankle. Jack Iverson bowled 29 overs, 2/124 for Victoria against Queensland with no pain in his troublesome ankle. However, he said he was 'inclined to drop the ball short and then the batsmen cracked me.'

Johnson tops 400. Victorian Ian Johnson has taken his 400th first class wicket in the second innings against NSW in December. Recent Australian Test bowlers have taken more first class wickets than any other bowlers in Australia. They are Ray Lindwall 353, Doug Ring 334, Bill Johnston 325 and Keith Miller 260.

Fifty centuries. Lindsay Hassett brought up his 50th first class century with his fourth Test 102. Sir Donald Bradman scored 117 first class centuries.

Fergie honoured. Bill Ferguson, the veteran scorer here with the West Indies team, was honoured with life membership of the West Coburg Bowling Club in January.

Richardson's return. Arthur Richardson, who played Test cricket for Australia in the 1920s, made a comeback at age 63, playing for Broken Hill against Norwood in January. He took 2/23.

Too much Test cricket. Test cricket has been weakened through too much of it being played. Hec de Lacy says 'to make it all possible, the backbone of Australian cricket – the Sheffield Shield games and club games – have been sacrificed. Shield cricket is in a particularly parlous state. To bring South Africa here next summer is to court disaster. Their cricket is an embarrassment.'

Sporting capital. Melbourne stands out as the sporting capital of Australia. Receipts and attendances for the four-day fourth Test were double the five days of the Sydney second Test – 168,904 and £20,165 to 88,379 and £11,997.

NSW's Shield. NSW made certain of the Sheffield Shield with an outright defeat of WA in January by 250 runs. Ray Lindwall took his 100th wicket in Shield cricket when he bowled Keith Carmody and WA's Charlie Puckett took six to become the first West Australian player to take 100. He has 103 wickets.

Day in, day out. Arthur Morris, with a brilliant 253 for NSW, was on the field for the entire match against Queensland in Brisbane in mid-October.

Barnes chosen but Board of Control vetoes selection

Sid Barnes – out of favour.

Melbourne, Dec. 20. Apparently using a rule first promulgated in the wake of the 1912 fiasco, the Board of Control has overridden the selectors, Sir Donald Bradman, 'Chappie' Dwyer and Jack Ryder, and not allowed Sid Barnes to play in the third Test.

Barnes, who last played for Australia in 1948 and has a Test average of 63, has made a 'comeback' with a brilliant 107 for NSW against Victoria on December 8.

A few Australian newspapers, such as the *Sporting Globe* on December 19, defended the Board's decision saying that 'only the Board knows the full background of a man nominated for international honours. They need not brand a man by giving reasons, but if they have the slightest doubt about his credentials then they must reject him'.

English newspapers have not been so coy about names and reasons. Alan Hoby in the *Sunday Express* alleges that the Board of Control has consigned Barnes to the 'doghouse' for 'daring to be different'.

'Barnes is too ebullient, too brutally outspoken and, ironically enough, far too puckish and cheeky for the graveyard solemnities of international cricket,' he wrote.

'Is it that pompous officialdom cannot forget the time when Barnes the Jester produced a toy bat in the Bradman testimonial …

'Or that other occasion when Barnes the Cameraman snapped Bradman making a duck?

'Or the occasion when Barnes the Comedian picked up a stray dog and offered it, with a huge grin, to the umpire, who was not amused?… Irritating? Possibly. Teasing? Maybe. Malicious? No. Entertaining? Yes'.

Johnston and Ring stop the nation

Melbourne, Jan. 4. In one of the most memorable and exciting finishes to a Test match at the MCG, or anywhere else, tail-enders Doug Ring and Bill Johnston poked, edged, snicked, tapped, patted and slogged the 38 runs required for a one-wicket series-clinching victory to Australia.

Dick Whitington told the story of the bored American watching his first game of cricket and hardly understanding a thing. Thirty minutes before the finish he got up and left. Puzzled, Whitington tracked him down after the match. He was in the bar of the Grey Smith Stand, alone. The barman said Whitington should look after him, for he was stressed and could not stand the strain.

All the guile and wiles of Sonny Ramadhin and Alf Valentine just couldn't separate the unlikely pair of Ring and Johnston. 30,000 fans watched nervously as the partnership began at 5 p.m. after the fighting five-hour century of captain Lindsay Hassett.

Few believed Johnston would stay the distance with his Richmond club-mate Ring, but stay he did, not out seven in the 35 minutes it took Ring to score the other 31 runs. He held the bat like a twig in his big hands, but seemed to have little idea about weilding it.

With three runs needed, Ring said to Johnston, who was on strike, 'hit the next ball on the off hard. It will go through the covers somewhere and we'll be all right.' 'Oh no,' replied Johnston (echoing

Happy tail-enders Bill Johnston and Doug Ring after their match-winning stand.

words from the first Ashes Test) 'we'll get them in singles.'

It fell to Johnston to turn the eighth ball of Frank Worrell's ninth over to leg and win the match. Until then the West Indies looked set to win the game and square the series with one Test to play in Sydney. Frank Worrell had made a

century in the West Indies' first innings of 272, and they had bowled Australia out for a paltry 216. The tourists' second innings 203 was disappointing but seemed likely to be just enough before Johnston, anxious, Test average 10, walked to the crease, to play out his teasing fate.

Australians accused of borderline 'Bodyline'

Sydney, Jan. 30. The bowling of Keith Miller and Ray Lindwall in the fifth Test raised the hitherto banished spectre of bodyline. But this time the bodies were in West Indian boots.

Lindwall bowled a dozen bumpers, described as 'vicious', at Everton Weekes, in an attempt to unsettle him. Two short-leg fieldsmen were there to collect the 'crumbs' and Neil Harvey was at long leg for the hook shot.

This was hardly a bodyline field, but it might have been considered intimidatory. Lindwall was not spoken to, but Keith Miller was in Brisbane in the first Test where he was bowling medium pace by comparison.

The question was whether Lindwall was using, as the rule book says, 'systematic and persistent short pitched balls in line with the batsman's body'.

Ray Lindwall: accused, with Keith Miller, of borderline 'Bodyline'.

New boys blooded

Melbourne, Dec. 26. Colin McDonald is keeping his fingers crossed about being chosen for the fifth Test team, after a string of good opening performances for Victoria. Newspapermen are howling for his selection after the poor opening stands of Australia this year.

McDonald made his debut in 1947–48, but has been somewhat erratic until this season where 43 and 207 not out, on top of scores of 105, 25, 53 and 45 have been more consistent – as well as brilliant.

The other young player putting his name forward is the batting leg spinner Richie Benaud, from NSW. In the game against SA earlier in the month he made his first Shield century 117, and bowled well. 'Adelaidian' said in the *Sporting Globe* on December 5: 'Benaud, with his all-round ability, should go a long way in the game.'

Spin bowling back in style

Neil Harvey survives a confident West Indies appeal for lbw, off Ramadhin.

Melbourne, Dec. 5. West Indian spin wizard Sonny Ramadhin has offered some advice to spin bowlers.

'You would like to be a spin bowler, young man? Then let me tell you something. Forget the idea – get it right out of your head – unless you have two things.

'First is love of cricket and the intention of playing the game for fun, to be able to laugh at yourself and put more into the game in the way of friendship than you expect to get out of it.

'Secondly, you must always be working at the fingers of your bowling hand to strengthen them until they are tough as wire rope and as supple as plastic.

'I am forever working on my fingers to toughen them up as I walk down the street. I am always stretching the web between the index and middle fingers. My grip must be like a vice.'

Sid Barnes wins his libel case

Sydney, Aug. 22. The Sid Barnes libel case has been settled in the former Australian batsman's favour.

He sought no damages but was awarded costs in the case against Jacob L. Raith, whose letter to the Sydney *Daily Mirror* was found to be libellous of him. Raith was ordered to pay costs.

Barnes brought the case against Raith in order to bring into the open the Board of Control's reasons for excluding him from Test cricket.

Barnes had issued a public statement earlier this year to elicit a Board response but none was forthcoming.

Raith came to the rescue with his letter, stating: 'The Board would not have excluded Mr. Barnes from the Australian XI capriciously, but only for a matter of sufficiently serious nature. In declining to publish reasons, the Board may have acted kindly towards him.'

Under cross examination by Raith's counsel, Smyth QC, Board members, secretary Bill Jeanes,

chairman Aubrey Oxlade, selector Edmund Dwyer and 1948 tour manager Keith Johnson failed to provide any serious reason for excluding Barnes, save that he was supposed to have jumped a turnstile, had given a sarcastic commentary on his 'home movie' of the 1948 tour and had done the dreadful thing of taking his cap off and bowing to the crowd, to the great embarrassment of the Board.

Smyth was not impressed with such reasons, and exclaimed: 'Did you ever hear such tommyrot?'

As a result, Raith, who had defended his action on the basis of 'Truth and Public Benefit', withdrew.

Smyth admitted that 'seldom in the history of libel actions had such a plea failed so completely and utterly. The Board has presented an awful image of the chaos and bigotry under which Australian cricket was administered …

'My client foolishly, as it turns out, believed that this Board was an impartial body of cricket administrators.'

FIRST TEST 1951–52 AUSTRALIA v WEST INDIES
Brisbane Cricket Ground, Brisbane. November 9, 10, 12, 13, 1951.
Toss: West Indies. Australia won by 3 wkts.

WEST INDIES

AF Rae b Lindwall	0		lbw Johnson	25
JB Stollmeyer c Langley b Johnston	8		st Langley b Johnson	10
FMM Worrell b Johnston	37		st Langley b Ring	20
EC Weekes c Langley b Ring	35		c Hole b Johnston	70
RJ Christiani c Ring b Lindwall	22	(6)	b Ring	6
CL Walcott (+) lbw Lindwall	0	(8)	st Langley b Ring	4
RE Marshall b Johnson	28	(9)	c Hassett b Miller	30
GE Gomez c Langley b Lindwall	22	(7)	c Harvey b Ring	55
JDC Goddard (c) b Miller	45	(5)	c & b Ring	0
S Ramadhin not out	16		not out	2
AL Valentine st Langley b Ring	2		c Morris b Ring	13
EXTRAS (LB 1)	1		(B 8, LB 2)	10
TOTAL	216			245

FOW 1st Inns: 0 18 63 92 95 112 150 170 207 216
FOW 2nd Inns: 23 50 88 88 96 153 184 229 230 245

Bowling: *First Innings*: Lindwall 20-4-62-4, Miller 14-3-40-1, Johnston 17-2-49-2, Ring 14-2-52-2, Johnson 5-1-12-1. *Second Innings*: Lindwall 10-0-36-0, Miller 8-2-19-1, Johnston 16-4-41-1, Hole 1-0-3-0, Johnson 18-1-56-2, Ring 16-2-80-6.

AUSTRALIA

KA Archer c Goddard b Valentine	20	b Gomez	4
AR Morris c Rae b Valentine	33	c Gomez b Ramadhin	48
AL Hassett (c) b Ramadhin	6	lbw Ramadhin	35
RN Harvey lbw Valentine	18	b Ramadhin	42
KR Miller c & b Valentine	46	b Valentine	4
GB Hole lbw Valentine	20	not out	45
RR Lindwall b Gomez	61	b Ramadhin	29
IW Johnson not out	16	b Ramadhin	8
DT Ring c Walcott b Gomez	0	not out	6
GRA Langley (+) lbw Worrell	0		
WA Johnston run out	2		
EXTRAS (B 4)	4	(B 3, LB 11, NB 1)	15
TOTAL	226		7 for 236

FOW 1st Inns: 30 53 80 85 129 188 215 215 216 226
FOW 2nd Inns: 8 69 126 143 149 203 225

Bowling: *First Innings*: Worrell 8-0-38-1, Gomez 7.5-2-10-2, Valentine 25-4-99-5, Ramadhin 24-5-75-1. *Second Innings*: Worrell 2-1-2-0, Gomez 3-0-12-1, Valentine 40.7-6-117-1, Ramadhin 40-9-90-5.

Umpires: AN Barlow & H Elphinston

SECOND TEST 1951–52 AUSTRALIA v WEST INDIES
Sydney Cricket Ground, Sydney. November 30, December 1, 3, 4, 5, 1951.
Toss: Australia. Australia won by 7 wkts.

WEST INDIES

AF Rae c Johnson b Johnston	17	c Ring b Miller	9
JB Stollmeyer c Johnson b Lindwall	36	b Johnson	35
FMM Worrell b Johnson	64	c Langley b Lindwall	20
EC Weekes b Lindwall	5	b Johnson	56
CL Walcott (+) c Langley b Ring	60	st Langley b Johnson	10
RJ Christiani b Hole	76	c Hassett b Miller	30
GE Gomez lbw Johnston	54	c Miller b Lindwall	41
JDC Goddard (c) c Johnson b Johnston	33	not out	57
PE Jones lbw Lindwall	1	c Miller b Johnston	7
S Ramadhin b Lindwall	0	b Johnston	3
AL Valentine not out	0	b Miller	1
EXTRAS (B 12, LB 3, NB 1)	16	(B 9, LB 12)	21
TOTAL	362		290

FOW 1st Inns: 33 84 99 139 218 286 359 360 360 362
FOW 2nd Inns: 19 52 102 130 141 210 230 246 268 290

Bowling: *First Innings*: Lindwall 26-2-66-4, Johnston 25.4-2-80-3, Johnson 14-3-48-1, Miller 21-3-72-0, Ring 17-1-71-1, Hole 4-1-9-1. *Second Innings*: Lindwall 17-3-59-2, Johnston 24-5-61-2, Johnson 23-2-78-3, Miller 13.2-2-50-3, Ring 7-0-21-0.

AUSTRALIA

KA Archer c Weekes b Gomez	11	lbw Worrell	47
AR Morris c Walcott b Jones	11	st Walcott b Ramadhin	30
AL Hassett (c) c Christiani b Jones	132	not out	46
RN Harvey c Gomez b Goddard	39	lbw Worrell	1
KR Miller b Valentine	129	not out	6
GB Hole b Valentine	1		
RR Lindwall run out	48		
IW Johnson c Walcott b Jones	5		
DT Ring c Ramadhin b Valentine	65		
GRA Langley (+) not out	15		
WA Johnston b Valentine	28		
EXTRAS (B 12, LB 18, NB 3)	33	(B 6, LB 1)	7
TOTAL	517		3 for 137

FOW 1st Inns: 19 27 106 341 345 348 372 457 485 517
FOW 2nd Inns: 49 123 125

Bowling: *First Innings*: Jones 27-5-68-3, Gomez 18-2-47-1, Worrell 11-0-60-0, Valentine 30.5-3-111-4, Ramadhin 41-7-143-0, Goddard 24-6-55-1. *Second Innings*: Jones 5-1-16-0, Gomez 5-1-9-0, Worrell 2-0-7-2, Ramadhin 12.3-1-53-1, Valentine 10-0-45-0.

Umpires: AN Barlow & H Elphinston

THIRD TEST 1951–52 AUSTRALIA v WEST INDIES
Adelaide Oval, Adelaide. December 22, 24, 25, 1951.
Toss: Australia. West Indies won by 6 wkts.

AUSTRALIA
JW Burke c Stollmeyer b Worrell	3 (9)	b Valentine	15
AR Morris (c) b Worrell	1 (5)	b Valentine	45
RN Harvey c Guillen b Gomez	10 (6)	c Guillen b Ramadhin	9
KR Miller c Ramadhin b Worrell	4 (7)	lbw Gomez	35
GB Hole c Worrell b Goddard	23 (8)	c Weekes b Gomez	25
RR Lindwall b Worrell	2 (10)	not out	8
IW Johnson c Stollmeyer b Worrell	11 (1)	c Marshall b Valentine	16
DT Ring c Christiani b Goddard	5 (4)	run out	67
GRA Langley (+) b Worrell	5 (2)	b Valentine	23
G Noblet b Goddard	8 (3)	c Weekes b Valentine	0
WA Johnston not out	7	lbw Valentine	0
EXTRAS (LB 3)	3	(B 8, LB 4)	12
TOTAL	82		255

FOW 1st Inns: 4 5 15 39 41 43 58 62 72 82
FOW 2nd Inns: 16 20 81 148 162 172 227 240 255 255

Bowling: *First Innings*: Gomez 5-3-5-1, Worrell 12.7-3-38-6, Goddard 8-1-36-3. *Second Innings*: Gomez 7-2-17-2, Worrell 9-2-29-0, Goddard 1-0-7-0, Valentine 27.5-6-102-6, Ramadhin 25-4-76-1, Marshall 5-1-12-0.

WEST INDIES
RE Marshall c Burke b Johnston	14	c Langley b Ring	29
JB Stollmeyer b Johnston	17	c Miller b Ring	47
JDC Goddard (c) c Langley b Lindwall	0		
FMM Worrell b Miller	6 (3)	c Noblet b Johnston	28
EC Weekes b Johnston	26 (4)	c & b Ring	29
GE Gomez c Langley b Johnston	4 (5)	not out	46
RJ Christiani b Johnston	4 (6)	not out	42
SC Guillen (+) b Noblet	9		
DE Atkinson c Burke b Johnston	15		
S Ramadhin not out	5		
AL Valentine b Noblet	0		
EXTRAS (LB 5)	5	(B 6, LB 5, W 1)	12
TOTAL	105		4 for 233

FOW 1st Inns: 25 26 34 44 51 55 85 87 101 105
FOW 2nd Inns: 72 85 141 141

Bowling: *First Innings*: Lindwall 4-0-18-1, Johnston 12-0-62-6, Miller 5-1-13-1, Noblet 3.5-0-7-2. *Second Innings*: Lindwall 13-1-40-0, Johnston 19-4-50-1, Miller 5-0-12-0, Noblet 13-1-30-0, Ring 16.5-3-62-3, Johnson 7-1-27-0.

Umpires: MJ McInnes & RR Wright

FIFTH TEST 1951–52 AUSTRALIA v WEST INDIES
Sydney Cricket Ground, Sydney. January 25, 26, 28, 29, 1952.
Toss: Australia. Australia won by 202 runs.

AUSTRALIA
CC McDonald c Worrell b Gomez	32	b Ramadhin	62
GR Thoms b Gomez	16	hit wicket b Worrell	28
AL Hassett (c) c Guillen b Gomez	2	c Worrell b Valentine	64
RN Harvey b Gomez	18	c Guillen b Worrell	8
KR Miller c Rae b Worrell	20	c Weekes b Valentine	69
GB Hole c Guillen b Worrell	1	b Worrell	62
R Benaud c Stollmeyer b Gomez	3	c (S)KR Rickards b Worrell	19
RR Lindwall c Worrell b Gomez	0	c Walcott b Gomez	21
DT Ring c Atkinson b Gomez	4	b Gomez	12
GRA Langley (+) c Weekes b Worrell	6	b Gomez	8
WA Johnston not out	13	not out	6
EXTRAS (LB 1)	1	(B 10, LB 8)	18
TOTAL	116		377

FOW 1st Inns: 39 49 54 77 78 91 91 97 99 116
FOW 2nd Inns: 55 138 152 216 287 326 347 353 370 377

Bowling: *First Innings*: Worrell 12.2-1-42-3, Gomez 18-3-55-7, Atkinson 6-2-18-0. *Second Innings*: Worrell 23-2-95-4, Gomez 18.2-3-58-3, Atkinson 8-0-25-0, Ramadhin 34-8-102-1, Valentine 30-6-79-2.

WEST INDIES
AF Rae c Langley b Johnston	11	c Harvey b Ring	25
JB Stollmeyer (c) lbw Johnston	10	lbw Lindwall	104
CL Walcott b Lindwall	1	c Langley b Miller	12
EC Weekes c Langley b Lindwall	0	c Langley b Lindwall	21
RJ Christiani c & b Miller	7 (6)	c Johnston b Lindwall	4
FMM Worrell b Miller	6 (5)	run out	18
GE Gomez b Miller	11	b Miller	2
DE Atkinson b Miller	6	hit wicket b Lindwall	2
SC Guillen (+) not out	13	b Lindwall	6
S Ramadhin b Johnston	0	not out	3
AL Valentine c Langley b Miller	6	b Benaud	0
EXTRAS (B 3, LB 3, W 1)	7	(B 4, LB 11, W 1)	16
TOTAL	78		213

FOW 1st Inns: 17 18 18 34 34 51 56 59 60 78
FOW 2nd Inns: 48 83 147 191 192 194 200 205 212 213

Bowling: *First Innings*: Lindwall 8-1-20-2, Johnston 14-3-25-3, Miller 7.6-1-26-5. *Second Innings*: Lindwall 21-4-52-5, Johnston 10-2-30-0, Miller 19-2-57-2, Ring 13-1-44-1, Benaud 4.3-0-14-1.

Umpires: H Elphinston & MJ McInnes

FOURTH TEST 1951–52 AUSTRALIA v WEST INDIES
Melbourne Cricket Ground, Melbourne. December 31, 1951, January 1, 2, 3, 1952.
Toss: West Indies. Australia won by 1 wkt.

WEST INDIES
KR Rickards b Miller	15 (4)	lbw Johnston	22
JB Stollmeyer c Langley b Miller	7 (8)	lbw Miller	54
FMM Worrell b Lindwall	108 (8)	b Johnston	30
EC Weekes c Johnson b Johnston	1 (5)	lbw Johnson	2
GE Gomez c Langley b Miller	37 (7)	b Johnston	52
RJ Christiani run out	37	b Miller	33
JDC Goddard (c) b Miller	21 (3)	lbw Lindwall	0
SC Guillen (+) not out	22 (1)	c Johnston b Lindwall	0
J Trim run out	0	run out	0
S Ramadhin c Langley b Johnston	1	run out	0
AL Valentine c Lindwall b Miller	14	not out	1
EXTRAS (B 2, LB 6, W 1)	9	(B 4, LB 5)	9
TOTAL	272		203

FOW 1st Inns: 16 29 30 102 194 221 237 242 248 272
FOW 2nd Inns: 0 0 53 60 97 128 190 194 194 203

Bowling: *First Innings*: Lindwall 18-2-72-1, Miller 19.3-1-60-5, Johnston 20-1-59-2, Ring 9-0-43-0, Johnson 7-0-23-0, Hole 2-0-6-0. *Second Innings*: Lindwall 17-2-59-2, Miller 16-1-49-2, Johnston 14.3-2-51-3, Ring 7-1-17-0, Johnson 5-0-18-1.

AUSTRALIA
J Moroney lbw Ramadhin	26	lbw Ramadhin	5
AR Morris b Trim	6	lbw Valentine	12
AL Hassett (c) run out	15	lbw Valentine	102
RN Harvey c & b Ramadhin	83	b Valentine	33
KR Miller b Trim	47	hit wicket b Valentine	2
GB Hole b Valentine	2	c Gomez b Worrell	13
RR Lindwall lbw Trim	13	c Guillen b Ramadhin	29
IW Johnson c Guillen b Trim	1	c Guillen b Ramadhin	6
DT Ring b Trim	6	not out	32
GRA Langley (+) not out	0	lbw Valentine	1
WA Johnston b Gomez	1	not out	7
EXTRAS (B 12, LB 4)	16	(B 14, LB 4)	18
TOTAL	216		9 for 260

FOW 1st Inns: 17 48 49 173 176 208 209 210 215 216
FOW 2nd Inns: 27 93 106 109 147 192 218 218 222

Bowling: *First Innings*: Trim 12-2-34-5, Gomez 13.3-7-25-1, Valentine 23-8-50-1, Ramadhin 17-4-63-2, Goddard 8-0-28-0. *Second Innings*: Trim 10-3-25-0, Gomez 9-1-18-0, Valentine 30-9-88-5, Ramadhin 39-15-93-3, Worrell 9-1-18-1.

Umpires: MJ McInnes & RR Wright

Australian Averages

1951–52 AUSTRALIA v WEST INDIES
AUSTRALIA	M	Inn	NO	Runs	H.S	Avrge	Ct	St	Overs	Mds	Runs	Wkt	Avrge
Archer, KA	2	4	-	82	47	20.50	2	-	-	-	-	-	-
Benaud, R	1	2	-	22	19	11.00	-	-	4.3	-	14	1	14.00
Burke, JW	1	2	-	18	15	9.00	2	-	-	-	-	-	-
Harvey, RN	5	10	-	261	83	26.10	2	-	-	-	-	-	-
Hassett, AL	4	8	1	402	132	57.43	2	-	-	-	-	-	-
Hole, GB	5	9	-	192	62	24.00	1	-	7.0	1	18	1	18.00
Johnson, IW	4	7	1	63	16*	10.50	4	-	79.0	8	262	8	32.75
Johnston, WA	5	8	4	64	28	16.00	2	-	171.7	25	508	23	22.09
Langley, GRA	5	8	2	58	23	9.67	16	5	-	-	-	-	-
Lindwall, RR	5	9	1	211	61	26.38	1	-	154.0	19	484	21	23.05
McDonald, CC	1	2	-	94	62	47.00	-	-	-	-	-	-	-
Miller, KR	5	10	1	362	129	40.22	5	-	128.3	16	398	20	19.90
Moroney, J	1	2	-	31	26	15.50	-	-	-	-	-	-	-
Morris, AR	4	8	-	186	48	23.25	1	-	-	-	-	-	-
Noblet, G	1	2	-	8	8	4.00	1	-	16.5	1	37	2	18.50
Ring, DT	5	9	2	197	67	28.14	4	-	99.5	10	390	13	30.00
Thoms, GR	1	2	-	44	28	22.00	-	-	-	-	-	-	-

West Indian Averages

1951–52 AUSTRALIA v WEST INDIES
WEST INDIES	M	Inn	NO	Runs	H.S	Avrge	Ct	St	Overs	Mds	Runs	Wkt	Avrge
Atkinson, DE	2	3	-	23	15	7.67	1	-	14.0	2	43	-	-
Christiani, RJ	5	10	1	261	76	29.00	2	-	-	-	-	-	-
Goddard, JDC	4	7	1	156	57*	26.00	-	-	41.0	7	126	4	31.50
Gomez, GE	5	10	1	324	55	36.00	3	-	104.2	24	256	18	14.22
Guillen, SC	3	5	2	50	22*	16.67	8	-	-	-	-	-	-
Jones, PE	1	2	-	8	7	4.00	-	-	32.0	6	84	3	28.00
Marshall, RE	2	4	-	101	30	25.25	1	-	5.0	1	12	-	-
Rae, AF	3	6	-	87	25	14.50	2	-	-	-	-	-	-
Ramadhin, S	5	9	4	30	16*	6.00	3	-	232.3	53	695	14	49.64
Rickards, KR	1	2	-	37	22	18.50	-	-	-	-	-	-	-
Stollmeyer, JB	5	10	-	328	104	32.80	3	-	-	-	-	-	-
Trim, J	1	2	-	0	0	0.00	-	-	22.0	5	59	5	11.80
Valentine, AL	5	9	2	37	14	5.29	1	-	217.1	42	691	24	28.79
Walcott, CL	1	2	-	13	12	6.50	-	-	-	-	-	-	-
Weekes, EC	5	10	-	245	70	24.50	5	-	-	-	-	-	-
Worrell, FMM	5	10	-	337	108	33.70	4	-	89.1	10	329	17	19.35

QUICK SINGLES

Poor kangaroo. After a visit to Perth's Kings Park and its wonderful wildflowers, South African captain 'Happy Jack' Cheetham said at a Mayoral reception, 'Yesterday I was introduced to the kangaroo paw. When we come back to Perth to catch the boat home after our Australian journey I think it may be a case of the poor kangaroo'.

Interchange. When Richie Benaud was injured in the third Test, the *Sporting Globe* suggested that he be allowed to be replaced by a player allowed to bat *and* bowl. It called the present 12th man rule a 'farce'.

Another tyro. 16-year-old Bob Simpson replaced Sid Barnes, who withdrew in favour of youth in the NSW team to play Victoria in January. He made 69.

'Bomber' Coombes. Ex-11th Squadron RAAF Ron Coombes, playing for Elwood RSL, bombed Malvern, making 54 in two overs in a one day game. In one over he made 38, scoring 6, 4, 6, 6, 4, 2, 6, 4.

No barracking. Umpire Mackinnon warned the crowd about their barracking of the incredibly stodgy NSW batting at the SCG in the game against SA in February. Jim Burke and Jim de Courcy were singled out.

Harvey is the greatest. South Africans must be sick of the sight of Harvey. In 1949–50 he made 660 runs in the Test series at a modest average of 132. In this series he has scored a record 834 runs with four centuries, including his best yet, 205, for an average of 92.67.

SA wins Shield. Unbeaten SA wins its seventh Sheffield Shield. Captain Phil Ridings played in SA's last win in 1938-39.

Australian team named. No surprises in the 17-man team to tour England in 1953 except that Arthur Morris is vice-captain to Lindsay Hassett rather than Keith Miller. Other members are Ron Archer, Richie Benaud, Ian Craig, Alan Davidson, Jim de Courcy, Neil Harvey, Jack Hill, Graeme Hole, Bill Johnston, Gil Langley, Ray Lindwall, Colin McDonald, Doug Ring, and Don Tallon.

South Africa on terms with big Test win

Melbourne, Dec. 30. 'Amazingly sustained and brilliant catching and great off-spin bowling by 24-year-old Hugh Tayfield' were the main factors in South Africa's astonishing win over Australia in the second Test, wrote Percy Beames in the *Age*.

This is South Africa's first victory over Australia in over 42 years.

One example of the South African fielding was from Tayfield himself. Arthur Morris belted one through captain Jack Cheetham at silly point, who managed to knock it up behind Tayfield who was bowling, and had to double back, dive and take the catch inches above the ground.

A second great catch was by Russell Endean, who caught a head-high 'skimmer' from Keith Miller that everyone thought was going for six. That is the sort of fielding we have seen from these highly tuned cricket athletes.

Bill O'Reilly said after Tayfield's 6/84 and 7/81 that he 'must surely lay claim to top ranking in the world's rating of off-spinners.

Only Tayfield looked like breaking the partnership near the end of the Australian second innings. Doug Ring (45), whose memories of last season's tail-end heroics must have flashed before his eyes, and aggressive Richie Benaud (53), playing in his second Test, looked for a while as if they might pull Australia out of the hole Tayfield was digging.

While the win will do wonders for South African cricket, who were hardly rated before they came to Australia, it sends a strong message to Australia that it is time for a changing of the guard. More young Benauds are required.

O'Reilly noticed in Australia's first-Test win that there were a number of players whose 'galloping days are over', after the equally brilliant field effort by the South Africans in the first Test.

Hugh Tayfield: South African spinner.

An extraordinary catch by Hugh Tayfield off his own bowling, after Arthur Morris drove the ball at captain Jack Cheetham. The ball bounced off Cheetham's hands (top), and Tayfield turned and ran to snare the catch at ground level.

'Baby' batsman is given Test duty

Sydney, Feb. 1. Great things have been predicted of young NSW batsman Ian Craig, just selected for his first Test match, since he was first picked for NSW aged 16 last season.

Writers were given to flights of fancy, for example R. S. Whitington wrote 'the promise of Craig must have been as beautiful and promising as the sight of the stars over Bethlehem to the wise men. Here at last was a young man who could change the horizon of the cricket world and cause cricket lovers to flock to watch him as they flocked, like so many children from Hamelin town, after Bradman.'

His promise was realised when he made 213 not out, the youngest batsman ever to achieve the feat, for NSW against South Africa on January 2. This demonstrated that he had overcome a tendency to 'nibble' outside the off stump, and had the stamina to go with his classical stroke play.

Whitington again: 'He was impervious to applause or criticism from the crowd, or at least he never allowed it to affect his concentration. His favourite stroke was the late cut, and Bradman, perhaps, played it little better. His leg glancing was stamped with all the precision of a minting machine, his cover drives surged over the field like surf over the flat beach of Bondi. His hooks were so safe a fisherman might have called them "gaffs".'

This is a great weight for a boy batsman to carry into a Test match.

No Cup at cricket

Adelaide, Nov. 4. Forced to follow on in the game against South Australia, South African captain Jack Cheetham caused some chagrin among the punting section of the cricket crowd by refusing to allow the broadcast of the Melbourne Cup over the Adelaide Oval loudspeakers.

Cheetham said it would disturb the concentration of his batsmen, and 'they don't broadcast the cricket at the Melbourne Cup, do they?' This had been done at the Queensland v West Indies match last season. While the crowd was very sparse at Adelaide, the failure to broadcast the Cup cannot be blamed. Some of those present had their portable wirelesses.

The race was won by the New Zealand stayer Dalray, ridden by Bill Williamson. Dalray, the top weight, started favourite at 5/1.

A sacrifice by Morris

Wells' view in the Age, *Melbourne: the kangaroo is now a laughing 'stock'.*

Melbourne, Feb. 12. On day one of the drawn fifth Test, Arthur Morris sacrificed his wicket for the ineffable Neil Harvey when Morris was on 99, and Harvey repaid him with a superb 205. Harvey had stroked the ball into the covers and called for a single, which was not on. Morris, who initially had not moved, saw what was happening, called Harvey through – he was already half-way down the pitch, and jogged down to be run out by yards. It was the greatest self sacrifice seen on an Australian cricket field, and denied Morris, who has been in scratchy form, his 11th Test century.

On the second day, Harvey carried on to his 205, and made most of it with 17-year-old Ian Craig.

During Craig and Harvey's partnership of 148, how much confidence must Craig have gained in his splendid 53 watching the still young master blast his way to his highest Test score. Craig showed his quality when he also made 47 in the second innings.

The question remains that with such terrific batting, how Australia could have lost the match, and only draw the series?

The answer lay in the selection decision to rest Ray Lindwall and Keith Miller for the tour of England, replacing them with Geff Noblet and Ron Archer. Noblet was ineffectual in both South African innings, and Archer only bowled five overs in the second, leaving Bill Johnston to do the bulk of the work.

South Africa's catching was also a feature in Australia's second innings 205, and Hugh Tayfield added another six wickets to total 30 for the series.

Australia was 2–1 after winning the third Test in Sydney, Lindwall taking 11 wickets and Miller five, and having the best of a draw in Adelaide where Colin McDonald (154), Lindsay Hassett (163), and the inevitable Harvey 84 (and 116) set up a match where young Richie Benaud was given a good long bowl for the first time – 44 overs for 4/118 in the first innings and 14 overs for 1/28 in an effort to force a win in the second.

He was less used and not as successfully in the fifth Test loss, bowling 15 overs in each innings, but on this occasion every bowler had trouble winkling the South Africans out.

But the win has been good for cricket, adding another first class Test nation to the roster.

Cheetham's troops do the training

Sydney, Jan. 13. As well as some glorious batting, and some wily bowling from the South Africans, the aspect of cricket which has impressed Australians has been their fielding. On arrival in Perth, captain Jack Cheetham asked: 'How many batsmen have scored a century in Test cricket without giving a chance? The answer given by manager Ken Viljoen was 'Precious few'.

Cheetham, unsure how the batting and bowling would stand up, decided to adopt a third mode of attack – fielding.

He instituted an army-like discipline at the WACA, where the South Africans practised during October, putting as much emphasis on fielding as on batting and bowling in the nets.

Cheetham was in command of the nets, Viljoen in charge of the fielding – which meant he must be given some of the credit for its success. Viljoen played 27 Tests for South Africa before and after the war, and was regarded as a brilliant out-fielder.

They even went so far as taking packed lunches to the ground six days a week, so as to have more time for training.

This dedication was unheard of in touring sides. One journalist noted with alarm that: 'All the normal pleasures and relaxations enjoyed by the average touring cricket team were eliminated, including golf.'

The laugh's on Sid Barnes. The joke of appearing dressed in 'civvies' carrying cigars, iced towels and a radio when 12th man in the NSW v SA game at the Adelaide Oval in November 1952 was the last straw for cricket officialdom. He was not considered for Australia again.

Ian Craig: 'This kid's good!'

'When 17-year-old Ian Craig moved smartly down-wicket and drove South African Percy Mansell to the extra cover fence eyes of the old timers widened. When he repeated the dose a few balls later they exclaimed: "This kid's good!" Ian had won his battle at the MCG in the fifth Test. Here was a lad with the cover drive of a Victor Trumper and with ice in his veins, the level head of an old timer.

'He made only 53 but he made them like a champion. He showed no signs of a swelled head, no flashness.

'Craig sold himself to his public for what he is – a level headed young fellow with dynamite in his willow and purpose in his life.

'He was with Neil Harvey, whose sustained brilliance would have cheapened the great. But Craig did not suffer by comparison. His hand fitted into Harvey's glove.'

So reported the *Sporting Globe's* Hec de Lacy on 11 February 1953 when Ian Craig made his Test debut, the youngest Australian ever, at 17 years and 239 days. So much promise. Craig had forced his way into the side by making 213 not out against South Africa in January 1953, following a series of good scores for NSW, including 91 on debut in the 1951–52 season.

His 213 made the frail lad, at 16 years and 249 days, the youngest player to score a double century in the world – younger than Bradman.

It was ironic, or perhaps fateful, that Craig was batting with Harvey on his Test debut. Harvey had been Australia's youngest century maker at 19 years and 121 days in 1948, and he went on to play 79 Tests and make 21 hundreds in 6149 runs at an average 48.41.

Craig played just 11 matches, five of them as captain, and made 358 runs at 19.88.

His first Test innings proved to be his highest score.

Harvey started batting with Bradman and he was never expected to be the 'next' Bradman but Craig carried such hopes. He was light-framed and neat – Ray Robinson wrote of 'the grace of his movements which made him the Bambi of the fielding side'. He had a slightly unorthodox grip, and favoured on-side shots.

He was one of the unluckiest cricketers with illness, study and

Ian Craig: career cut short.

career decisions interfering with the progress of his cricket.

In 1953 he was not picked to play in any Tests, and his form in tour matches was modest.

In the domestic season in 1953–54 Craig had a poor season and he missed 1954–55 with National Service and pharmacy studies, but was chosen to tour England in 1956 (he was not yet 21) and suffered food poisoning, missing the first three Tests. It was his luck to play in the fourth 'Laker's' Test at Manchester, when Australia was caught on a sticky and Laker took 19 wickets. Craig with 38 in the second innings was the only batsman to look like staying with Colin McDonald.

On the way home from this tour he made 0 and 18 in Australia's nine-wicket loss to Pakistan, and 40 in the first Test and 36 and 6 in the third Test against India. (Harvey made 140 in the second test in which Craig did not play. After this he became NSW's youngest captain (22 years) and then Australian captain for a tour of New Zealand in 1957.

Having completed his pharmacy studies, Craig was made captain of the Australian Test side to tour South Africa in 1957–58. His scores were 14 and 17, 0, 52 and 0, 3, and 17. Australia won the series 3–0, and was on the way back to international respectability after the shambles of the early 1950s. Much of it was due to Craig's captaincy.

He retired for business reasons when he was just combining experience with his undoubted talent. He was not yet 27.

FIRST TEST 1952–53 AUSTRALIA v SOUTH AFRICA
Brisbane Cricket Ground, Brisbane. December 5, 6, 8, 9, 10, 1952.
Toss: Australia. Australia won by 96 runs.

AUSTRALIA

CC McDonald c & b Watkins	27	st Waite b Tayfield	17
AR Morris lbw Watkins	29	c Melle b Tayfield	58
RN Harvey c(S)GAS Innes b Melle	109 (4)	run out	52
AL Hassett (c) c Waite b Watkins	55 (3)	c McGlew b Melle	17
KR Miller b Watkins	3	lbw Tayfield	3
GB Hole c Tayfield b Melle	8	lbw Melle	42
RR Lindwall lbw Melle	5	not out	38
GRA Langley (+) c Tayfield b Melle	17	b Watkins	27
DT Ring c Mansell b Melle	13	b Melle	4
IW Johnson lbw Melle	7	lbw Watkins	13
WA Johnston not out	1	c McGlew b Tayfield	0
EXTRAS (B 1, LB 3, NB 2)	6	(B 2, LB 4)	6
TOTAL	280		277

FOW 1st Inns: 55 56 211 216 231 237 252 272 273 280
FOW 2nd Inns: 48 75 115 123 160 198 246 251 276 277

Bowling: *First Innings:* Melle 20.5-0-71-6, Watkins 24-8-41-4, Murray 14-1-63-0, Tayfield 15-3-59-0, Mansell 8-0-40-0. *Second Innings:* Melle 26-2-95-3, Watkins 26-13-47-2, Murray 13-7-13-0, Tayfield 33.3-5-116-4.

SOUTH AFRICA

DJ McGlew c Johnson b Miller	9	lbw Lindwall	69
JHB Waite (+) lbw Ring	39	st Langley b Johnson	14
WR Endean c Langley b Ring	14	lbw Lindwall	12
KJ Funston b Ring	33	c Langley b Johnston	65
RA McLean c Miller b Johnson	13	b Lindwall	38
JE Cheetham (c) c Langley b Lindwall	26	b Johnston	18
JC Watkins c Miller b Ring	25	hit wicket b Johnson	1
PNF Mansell c Lindwall b Ring	31	b Lindwall	4
ARA Murray lbw Johnston	18	not out	11
HJ Tayfield lbw Ring	3	c Langley b Johnson	1
MG Melle not out	7	b Lindwall	4
EXTRAS (B 3)	3	(B 2, NB 1)	3
TOTAL	221		240

FOW 1st Inns: 13 39 88 103 113 153 177 195 211 221
FOW 2nd Inns: 20 57 153 170 209 210 215 226 227 240

Bowling: *First Innings:* Lindwall 12-0-48-1, Miller 10-0-46-1, Johnston 7.6-2-21-1, Ring 21-2-72-6, Johnson 12-3-31-1. *Second Innings:* Lindwall 30-8-60-5, Johnston 26-5-62-2, Ring 17-3-58-0, Johnson 30-7-52-3, Hole 3-0-5-0, Harvey 1-1-0-0.

Umpires: H Elphinston & RR Wright

SECOND TEST 1952–53 AUSTRALIA v SOUTH AFRICA
Melbourne Cricket Ground, Melbourne. December 24, 26, 27, 29, 30, 1952.
Toss: South Africa. South Africa won by 82 runs.

SOUTH AFRICA

DJ McGlew b Lindwall	46	st Langley b Ring	13
JHB Waite (+) c Lindwall b Miller	0	c Hole b Miller	62
WR Endean c Benaud b Lindwall	2	not out	162
KJ Funston c Ring b Miller	9	run out	26
RA McLean c Lindwall b Ring	27	lbw Miller	42
JE Cheetham (c) c Johnston b Miller	15	lbw Johnston	6
JC Watkins c Langley b Benaud	19	b Johnston	3
PNF Mansell b Lindwall	24	b Miller	18
ARA Murray c Johnston b Benaud	51	st Langley b Ring	23
HJ Tayfield c Langley b Miller	23	lbw Lindwall	22
MG Melle not out	4	b Lindwall	0
EXTRAS (B 4, LB 3)	7	(B 1, LB 5, W 4, NB 1)	11
TOTAL	227		388

FOW 1st Inns: 2 9 27 63 93 112 126 156 207 227
FOW 2nd Inns: 23 134 196 261 284 290 317 353 388 388

Bowling: *First Innings:* Lindwall 14-2-29-3, Miller 21-3-62-4, Johnston 12-2-37-0, Ring 18-1-72-1, Benaud 6.6-1-20-2. *Second Innings:* Lindwall 31.5-4-87-2, Miller 22-5-51-3, Johnston 31-9-77-2, Ring 31-5-115-2, Benaud 6-0-23-0, Hole 7-0-24-0.

AUSTRALIA

CC McDonald c(S)ERH Fuller b Mansell	82	c Mansell b Murray	23
AR Morris c & b Tayfield	43	c Watkins b Melle	1
RN Harvey c Cheetham b Tayfield	11 (4)	c Watkins b Tayfield	60
AL Hassett (c) c Melle b Mansell	18 (3)	lbw Tayfield	21
KR Miller c Endean b Tayfield	52	b Tayfield	31
GB Hole c Waite b Mansell	13 (7)	b Tayfield	25
R Benaud b Tayfield	5 (8)	c Melle b Tayfield	45
RR Lindwall run out	1 (9)	b Melle	19
DT Ring c McGlew b Tayfield	14 (10)	c Melle b Tayfield	53
GRA Langley (+) not out	2 (6)	b Tayfield	4
WA Johnston lbw Tayfield		not out	0
EXTRAS (NB 2)	2	(B 1, LB 6, NB 1)	8
TOTAL	243		290

FOW 1st Inns: 84 98 155 158 188 211 219 239 243 243
FOW 2nd Inns: 3 34 76 131 139 148 181 216 277 290

Bowling: *First Innings:* Melle 14-0-73-0, Watkins 6-1-15-0, Murray 3-1-11-0, Tayfield 29.4-9-84-6, Mansell 19-3-58-3. *Second Innings:* Melle 11-2-39-2, Watkins 10-2-34-0, Murray 23-7-59-1, Tayfield 37.1-13-81-7, Mansell 14-2-69-0.

Umpires: H Elphinston & MJ McInnes

THIRD TEST 1952–53 AUSTRALIA v SOUTH AFRICA
Sydney Cricket Ground, Sydney. January 9, 10, 12, 13, 1953.
Toss: South Africa. Australia won by an innings & 38 runs.

SOUTH AFRICA

DJ McGlew run out	24	c Langley b Lindwall	9
JHB Waite (+) c Morris b Johnston	32	c Hole b Lindwall	0
WR Endean b Lindwall	18	lbw Miller	71
KJ Funston b Ring	56	c Hole b Miller	16
RA McLean b Lindwall	0 (6)	c Benaud b Lindwall	65
JE Cheetham (c) c Johnston b Miller	5 (5)	c Morris b Lindwall	5
ARA Murray c(S)JH De Courcy b Miller	4	c Hole b Benaud	17
JC Watkins c(S)JH De Courcy b Miller	17	c Miller b Johnston	48
PNF Mansell b Lindwall	8	c Hole b Benaud	0
HJ Tayfield not out	3		
MG Melle c Langley b Lindwall	1 (10)	not out	0
EXTRAS (B 1, LB 3, W 1)	5	(LB 1)	1
TOTAL	173		9 dec 232

FOW 1st Inns: 54 65 83 83 115 142 144 156 172 173
FOW 2nd Inns: 9 10 60 68 167 167 232 232 232

Bowling: *First Innings*: Lindwall 14.2-1-40-4, Miller 17-1-48-3, Johnston 18-5-46-1, Ring 12-4-23-1, Hole 2-0-11-0. *Second Innings*: Lindwall 20-3-72-4, Miller 18-6-33-2, Johnston 14.6-0-51-1, Ring 12-1-54-0, Benaud 5-1-21-2.

AUSTRALIA

CC McDonald c Endean b Tayfield	67
AR Morris b Watkins	18
AL Hassett (c) c Funston b Murray	2
RN Harvey c Watkins b Murray	190
KR Miller lbw Tayfield	55
GB Hole run out	5
R Benaud lbw Melle	0
DT Ring b Tayfield	58
RR Lindwall b Murray	1
GRA Langley (+) c Mansell b Murray	20
WA Johnston not out	7
EXTRAS (B 3, LB 12, W 1, NB 4)	20
TOTAL	443

FOW 1st Inns: 40 49 162 330 344 350 374 379 425 443

Bowling: *First Innings*: Melle 23-3-98-1, Watkins 12-5-16-1, Murray 51.2-11-169-4, Tayfield 38-9-94-3, Mansell 7-0-46-0.

Umpires: H Elphinston & MJ McInnes

FOURTH TEST 1952–53 AUSTRALIA v SOUTH AFRICA
Adelaide Oval, Adelaide. January 24, 26, 27, 28, 29, 1953.
Toss: Australia. Match Drawn.

AUSTRALIA

CC McDonald st Waite b Tayfield	154	b Mansell	15
AR Morris c Endean b Fuller	1	c Endean b Melle	77
AL Hassett (c) c McGlew b Mansell	163		
RN Harvey c Tayfield b Fuller	84 (3)	c Endean b Watkins	116
KR Miller c Waite b Tayfield	9		
GB Hole c & b Mansell	59 (4)	not out	6
R Benaud b Melle	6 (5)	not out	18
DT Ring c McLean b Tayfield	28		
RR Lindwall lbw Tayfield	2		
GRA Langley (+) not out	5		
WA Johnston run out	11		
EXTRAS (B 1, LB 7)	8	(B 1)	1
TOTAL	530		3 dec 233

FOW 1st Inns: 2 277 356 387 439 448 494 505 517 530
FOW 2nd Inns: 42 199 209

Bowling: *First Innings*: Melle 26-1-105-1, Fuller 25-2-119-2, Tayfield 44-6-142-4, Mansell 32-1-113-2, McGlew 2-0-9-0, Watkins 6-1-34-0. *Second Innings*: Melle 10-1-50-1, Fuller 3-0-12-0, Tayfield 14-1-65-0, Mansell 7-0-40-1, McGlew 1-0-7-0, Watkins 12-1-58-1.

SOUTH AFRICA

DJ McGlew c Hole b Johnston	26	c Langley b Johnston	54
WR Endean c Langley b Benaud	56 (4)	b Harvey	17
RA McLean c Hassett b Ring	11	c Hole b Benaud	17
JHB Waite (+) c Hole b Benaud	44 (2)	b Hole	20
KJ Funston c & b Benaud	92	lbw Johnston	17
JC Watkins b Benaud	76	b Morris	21
JE Cheetham (c) b Johnston	6	not out	13
PNF Mansell c Hole b Johnston	33	not out	2
HJ Tayfield b Johnston	16		
ERH Fuller c & b Johnston	0		
MG Melle not out	9		
EXTRAS (B 12, LB 4, NB 2)	18	(B 16)	16
TOTAL	387		6 for 177

FOW 1st Inns: 62 79 100 208 270 296 350 374 378 387
FOW 2nd Inns: 81 95 109 127 158 166

Bowling: *First Innings*: Lindwall 13-0-47-0, Johnston 49.3-17-110-5, Miller 2.1-1-1-0, Ring 30-8-88-1, Benaud 44-9-118-4, Hole 3-1-5-0. *Second Innings*: Johnston 24-4-67-2, Ring 11-3-25-0, Benaud 14-5-28-1, Hole 9-4-17-1, Harvey 7-2-9-1, Morris 5-0-11-1, Hassett 1-0-1-0, McDonald 1-0-3-0.

Umpires: MJ McInnes & RR Wright

FIFTH TEST 1952–53 AUSTRALIA v SOUTH AFRICA
Melbourne Cricket Ground, Melbourne. February 6, 7, 9, 10, 11, 12, 1953.
Toss: Australia. South Africa won by 6 wkts.

AUSTRALIA

CC McDonald c McLean b Mansell	41	c Watkins b Fuller	11
AR Morris run out	99	lbw Tayfield	44
RN Harvey c Cheetham b Fuller	205	b Fuller	7
AL Hassett (c) run out	40	c Endean b Mansell	30
ID Craig c Keith b Fuller	53	c Endean b Tayfield	47
RG Archer c Waite b Fuller	18	c Watkins b Tayfield	0
R Benaud c & b Tayfield	20	c Watkins b Fuller	30
DT Ring b Tayfield	14	c Endean b Mansell	0
GRA Langley (+) b Murray	2	not out	26
WA Johnston c Endean b Tayfield	12	c Cheetham b Fuller	5
G Noblet not out	13	b Fuller	1
EXTRAS (LB 3)	3	(B 7, LB 1)	8
TOTAL	520		209

FOW 1st Inns: 122 166 269 417 450 459 490 493 495 520
FOW 2nd Inns: 36 44 70 128 129 152 152 187 193 209

Bowling: *First Innings*: Fuller 19-4-74-3, Watkins 23-3-72-0, Tayfield 35.4-4-129-3, Murray 25-3-84-1, Mansell 22-0-114-1, Keith 9-0-44-0. *Second Innings*: Fuller 30.2-4-66-5, Watkins 14-4-33-0, Tayfield 32-8-73-3, Mansell 8-3-29-2.

SOUTH AFRICA

WR Endean c Langley b Johnston	16	b Johnston	70
JHB Waite (+) run out	64	c Archer b Noblet	18
JC Watkins b Archer	92	b Ring	50
KJ Funston lbw Johnston	16	b Benaud	35
HJ Keith b Johnston	10	not out	40
RA McLean lbw Noblet	81	not out	76
JE Cheetham (c) c McDonald b Johnston	66		
PNF Mansell lbw Johnston	52		
ARA Murray c & b Johnston	17		
HJ Tayfield c Benaud b Ring	17		
ERH Fuller not out	0		
EXTRAS (B 1, LB 3)	4	(B 2, LB 6)	8
TOTAL	435		4 for 297

FOW 1st Inns: 31 129 189 189 239 290 401 402 435 435
FOW 2nd Inns: 42 124 174 191

Bowling: *First Innings*: Noblet 30-6-65-1, Archer 33-4-97-1, Johnston 46-8-152-6, Ring 19.1-1-62-1, Benaud 15-3-55-0. *Second Innings*: Noblet 24-9-44-1, Archer 5-0-23-0, Johnston 38-7-114-1, Ring 13-2-55-1, Benaud 15-4-41-1, Hassett 0.5-0-12-0.

Umpires: MJ McInnes & RR Wright

Australian Averages

1952–53 AUSTRALIA v SOUTH AFRICA

AUSTRALIA	M	Inn	NO	Runs	H.S	Avrge	Ct	St	Overs	Mds	Runs	Wkt	Avrge
Archer, RG	1	2	-	18	18	9.00	1	-	38.0	4	120	1	120.00
Benaud, R	4	7	1	124	45	20.67	4	-	105.6	23	306	10	30.60
Craig, ID	1	2	-	100	53	50.00	-	-	-	-	-	-	-
Harvey, RN	5	9	-	834	205	92.67	1	-	8.0	3	9	1	9.00
Hassett, AL	5	8	-	346	163	43.25	1	-	1.5	-	13	-	-
Hole, GB	4	7	1	158	59	26.33	9	-	24.0	5	62	1	62.00
Johnson, IW	1	2	-	20	13	10.00	1	-	42.0	10	83	4	20.75
Johnston, WA	5	8	3	36	12	7.20	5	-	266.7	59	737	21	35.10
Langley, GRA	5	8	3	103	27	20.60	11	3	-	-	-	-	-
Lindwall, RR	4	6	1	66	38*	13.20	3	-	134.7	18	383	19	20.16
McDonald, CC	5	9	-	437	154	48.56	1	-	1.0	-	3	-	-
Miller, KR	4	6	-	153	55	25.50	3	-	90.1	16	241	13	18.54
Morris, AR	5	9	-	370	99	41.11	2	-	5.0	-	11	1	11.00
Noblet, G	1	2	1	14	13*	14.00	-	-	54.0	15	109	2	54.50
Ring, DT	5	8	-	184	58	23.00	1	-	184.1	30	624	13	48.00

South African Averages

1952–53 AUSTRALIA v SOUTH AFRICA

SOUTH AFRICA	M	Inn	NO	Runs	H.S	Avrge	Ct	St	Overs	Mds	Runs	Wkt	Avrge
Cheetham, JE	5	9	1	160	66	20.00	3	-	-	-	-	-	-
Endean, WR	5	10	1	438	162*	48.67	9	-	-	-	-	-	-
Fuller, ERH	2	2	1	0	0*	0.00	-	-	77.2	10	271	10	27.10
Funston, KJ	5	10	-	365	92	36.50	1	-	-	-	-	-	-
Keith, HJ	1	2	-	50	40*	50.00	1	-	9.0	-	44	-	-
Mansell, PNF	5	9	1	172	52	21.50	4	-	117.0	9	509	9	56.56
McGlew, DJ	4	8	-	250	69	31.25	4	-	3.0	-	16	-	-
McLean, RA	5	10	-	370	81	41.11	2	-	-	-	-	-	-
Melle, MG	4	7	4	25	9*	8.33	-	-	130.5	9	531	14	37.93
Murray, ARA	4	7	1	141	51	23.50	-	-	129.2	30	399	6	66.50
Tayfield, HJ	5	7	1	85	23	14.17	5	-	278.4	58	843	30	28.10
Waite, JHB	5	10	-	293	64	29.30	4	2	-	-	-	-	-
Watkins, JC	5	10	-	352	92	35.20	7	-	133.0	38	350	8	43.75

England thwarted in first Test

Nottingham, June 16. Rain forced the abandonment of the fourth day's play in the first Test, and prevented England batting until 4.30 on the final afternoon when they needed 187 runs with nine wickets in hand to win the match.

Alec Bedser and Ray Lindwall provided some thrilling cricket on the days when play was possible.

After Bedser disposed of Graeme Hole with the second ball of the match, Lindsay Hassett and Arthur Morris put on 124, Hassett going on to 115 in over six hours in the gloom. Bedser took 7/55 in the first innings then 7/44 in the second, when Australia collapsed for 123.

Ray Lindwall kept Australia in the match with 5/57 in England's 144, taking three of them when the score was 17, and having 5/5 at one stage. Alan Davidson in his debut Test, took 2/22.

TV stops England, radio Australia

Melbourne, June 20. While English cricket fanatics could stay out of the rain by watching the cricket on new-fangled television, Australian radio listeners-in were subjected to the 'earthquake' of cricket, the BBC relay from Trent Bridge.

A wireless critic wrote in the Melbourne *Age:* 'This week normal values went haywire. Music and drama – what were they in face of the excitement brewed by an old game that defies all precedent by getting younger? How could we sit calmly listening to sounds generated by strings and brass when the fate of a nation was being determined by another magical sound, the crack of bat on ball?

'Sleep? How could a listener leave his set while the great game was being played out and the result was anybody's guess?

'And who could fail to dwell on every word uttered at the lunch and tea adjournments by that army of experts and old-timers who recalled the great matches of the past and the great men who took part in them?' And during the rain.

Barnacle Bailey holds out Australia

England captain Len Hutton survives a confident appeal for lbw off Lindwall in the rain-affected Trent Bridge Test.

Lord's, June 30. Before the Test match began, confident Australians were asking how good could England be when the selectors recalled well-liked ex-captain Freddie Brown to the team as an all-rounder at the age of 42. At the end of it, they were wondering where 33-year-old left hander Willie Watson had sprung from as Watson made a century (109) on debut against Australia, and with Trevor Bailey (71) defied everything from Miller's thunderbolts to Benaud's teasers for five and a half hours on the last day.

It was alleged by Sid Barnes, in England writing for the *Daily Mirror*, that the Australians on this day took the game a bit too easily because they had begun celebrations a day (or a night) early.

This Test looked as if it would be Australia's from the moment Ray Lindwall hit a fast 50 on the fourth day, giving Australia a lead of 342. England was 3/20 at the end of the day, Lindwall having removed first innings century maker Len Hutton for 5 and Don Kenyon (2).

However at times England seemed as if she could also force a victory, particularly when Hutton and Denis Compton put on a hundred in the first innings, after Hutton had done the same with Tom Graveney. Being 2/279 chasing Australia's 346 (complete with another Hassett hundred) was a strong position. But soon after Bill Johnston disposed of Hutton, Lindwall took 3/8 and England were all out for 372, a lead of just 26.

Australia's position became even more promising when Keith Miller struck a well-judged 109.

But no Australian bowler could make an impact on that last-day pitch, the match ending in a stubborn draw – with Freddie Brown coming in to whack a satisfying 28 runs in what may well be his last Test innings.

Pipe openers. On the way to England the 1953 Australians played three matches in Australia – against Tasmania, a Combined XI and WA. Neil Harvey made 148 in the innings defeat of Tasmania. (Ian Craig 59), Richie Benaud (167) and Alan Davidson (90) thrashed the Combined XI bowlers – and the youngsters Benaud (100 not out) and Craig showed what they could do in the draw in WA.

Radio cover. 3AW will commence its Test broadcast at 8.45 p.m. with complete coverage of the day's play at Lord's, with commentary from Ian Johnson and George Hele. A variety show will be broadcast in the luncheon break compered by Norman Banks.

Charges upset tourists. Australian cricketers are upset at suggestions in the Sydney press that the Board of Control might ask manager George Davies for 'a special report on players' conduct'. Mr. Davies said on June 28 that he had no such request and 'sees no occasion to make one'. The players ridicule reports of misbehaviour. One senior player said: 'This is the quietest mob I have ever travelled with.'

Record attendance. 86,000 people paid £29,261 at the first Test at Trent Bridge – record figures for England.

Lancastrian boycott. A Manchester clergyman returned his paid-for seats at Old Trafford for the third Test in protest against the dropping of Lancastrian Cyril Washbrook – an 'outrage' and an example of 'partisan Test selection'.

Put in. Lindsay Hassett was the first Australian captain to send the opposition in to bat in England since the fourth Test in 1909.

Double closure. Tom Dollery, the Warwickshire captain, established a record, of sorts, when he closed each innings in the match against the Australians at Birmingham in August. This had never happened before in 75 years.

The double. Ray Lindwall became the fourth player to achieve the double of 1000 runs and 100 test wickets when he scored 52 in the fifth Test.

Five in a row. Lindsay Hassett called correctly for five Tests in a row, but lost the series. Len Hutton therefore became the first Test captain to lose five tosses but win the series.

World record. England's opening bowler Alec Bedser passed Clarrie Grimmett's record of 216 Test wickets, which has stood since 1936, with his 6/95 in Australia's first innings in the fourth Test at Leeds.

England's Ashes after 20 years

The cheerful English multitude swarm over the Oval after they celebrate the return of the Ashes.

Wet Old Trafford saves Australia

Manchester, July 14. Old Trafford lived up to its gloomy meteorological tradition with yet another drawn Test match. Rain interfered with play for the ninth successive time, a sequence which has seen one Test match abandoned in 1938, and play on nine individual days abandoned as well.

In this match, less than 14 hours play was possible, which was enough time for Neil Harvey to record his second century (122) against England – making a total of 11 hundreds. His partner Graeme Hole contributed 66.

A draw looked inevitable when England avoided the follow-on with a wagging tail. With just a bit more time, England may have pulled off an improbable win. Australia was 8/35 when time ran out, Johnny Wardle taking 4/7, Jim Laker 2/11.

It's that man again

Leeds, July 28. After Ray Lindwall bowled Len Hutton and Dennis Compton for ducks, while taking 5/54 in getting England out for 167, Australia made 266, and had England 6/167 – before Bailey. Trevor Bailey, thorn in Australia's side at Lord's, batted for 262 minutes making 38 runs and using up enough time to prevent an Australian run chase – 177 runs in 115 minutes. He wasn't the only 'brick-wall batter'. Bill Edrich also took 225 minutes over his 50. Bailey later bowled half a dozen overs of 'leg theory' to stop the forlorn chase. At the close Australia, having had a go, was 4/147.

Benaud's flurry

Scarborough, Aug. 30. Despite the loss of the Ashes in the fifth Test, Australia had a prolific and successful tour. In fact, it only lost one match in the 35 played. At Scarborough Richie Benaud hit 11 sixes in his 135 when Australia made 320 in 220 minutes, defeating Tom Pearce's XI.

On the tour Neil Harvey made 2040 runs at 65.8, Keith Miller 1433 at 51.77, Arthur Morris 1302 at 38.29 and Lindsay Hassett 1236 at 44.14.

Of the bowlers, Ray Lindwall took 85 wickets at 16.43, Bill Johnston 75 at 21.06, Doug Ring 68 at 19.98 and Benaud 57 at 22.28.

The real batting star on paper was Bill Johnston, whose 102 runs on tour for only once out, giving a Bradmanesque average of 102, was contrived by Hassett and the rest of the team.

The Oval, Aug. 19. Moments after Denis Compton hit a four from the unlikely bowling of Arthur Morris, England was filled with delirium, and Australia is filled with early morning gloom.

England had won the Ashes for the first time since the Bodyline series of 1932–33, and the first time at home since 1926.

Newspapers increased their circulation and the last hours of the match were beamed direct over radio and television – the BBC had cancelled all normal programs to give the game extended coverage.

In city offices and West End clubs, tickertapes recorded every run. London streets were blocked as crowds gathered beneath blackboard scores in shop windows.

It was a long-awaited national triumph that made cricket supreme in England again. While the result was a substantial eight wickets, it was a close-run thing right up until Australia batted a second time.

England, in an all-round batting performance, led Australia by 31 runs, with 306 to Australia's 275 on the third day. Overnight and intermittent rain during the morning had softened the pitch, and a hot sun turned it into an ideal surface for Tony Lock and Jim Laker to cast their spells upon, which they did to great effect. Lock 5/45 and Laker 4/75 – Australia all out a second time for 162. By the end of the day, England was 1/38.

Despite the weather, this close-fought series has been seen by nearly 550,000 people, and thousands poured into the Oval on the

Tony Lock is clapped in at the Oval after his match-winning five-wicket bag.

last morning to be part of the great Coronation-year triumph.

The ground was crowded before play, but a constant stream filled it to joyful capacity by mid-morning as the England batsmen Peter May and Bill Edrich resumed their quest for the 94 runs required.

Bill Johnston seemed most likely to be able to exploit the wicket in the morning session, but his return was 18 overs, 11 maidens, 24 runs, 0 wickets. He had a number of edges, and one dropped chance, but the wicket became more benign by the minute.

Lindwall bowled with all his guile for 75 minutes but could find nothing in the pitch: 11 overs, four maidens, 30 runs, 0 wickets.

Hassett brought Keith Miller on to bowl off-spinners, and after driving for four, Peter May clipped one off his toes straight to Alan Davidson at short fine leg. That made the score 2/88 and still 44 to get.

All England was on tenterhooks as Compton walked to the wicket. Lindwall came back into the attack – he'd got Compton twice in the fourth Test – but still the score slowly mounted, reaching 2/101 at lunch.

After lunch, with nine needed, Hassett brought himself on to bowl. He went for four. Then Arthur Morris bowled five balls ... before pandemonium broke loose.

Australia had played entertaining cricket on tour, and the team made many friends, but lost the Test that mattered.

Board blamed for loss

Melbourne, Aug. 22. 'Having watched, ball by ball, the rise and fall of Australia's post-war cricket, I'd like to believe that the Ashes were on loan to England for return to Australia in 1954–55.

'I'm not so sure. There's an ineptitude, a lack of vision in cricket's high places. There's disunity where there should be drive, and political issues to be ironed out before we can hope to get down to tin tacks on our promotion,' writes Hec de Lacy in a feature article in the *Sporting Globe*, after Australia lost the Ashes. De Lacy put into words what many despairing cricket followers have been thinking.

'The lack of public relations in cricket as far as the Board of Control is concerned is lamentable. The approach to public questions is far too often autocratic and rude.

'There's an alienation of public sympathy and energy which does nothing to offset the loss of cricket's popularity among young men.

'Promising school cricketers today are turning to tennis while the grand old men of the game still rebuff public relations and goodwill with a grumble or a grunt. One would think that all things in cricket began and ended in the septuagenarian era.

'Progress is retarded by cliques – and it was a clique that upset the best Australian selection committee we had for years in Sir Donald Bradman and Messrs Jack Ryder and E. A. Dwyer.

'NSW still smarts about the defeat of Mr Dwyer as an Australian selector last season. Sir Donald had retired through family illness. Selection plans were thrown into the pot. Only Mr Ryder remained…

'Harmony can only be restored by resignations in certain administrative quarters,' said de Lacy.

King Willow's Coronation

SOME OF THE "CROWN JEWELS" – "SPARKLERS?"

ENGLANDS CRICKET CROWN 1953

WELLS

FIRST TEST 1953 ENGLAND v AUSTRALIA
Trent Bridge, Nottingham. June 11, 12, 13, 15 (no play), 16, 1953.
Toss: Australia. Match Drawn.

AUSTRALIA

GB Hole b Bedser	0	b Bedser	5
AR Morris lbw Bedser	67	b Tattersall	60
AL Hassett (c) b Bedser	115	c Hutton b Bedser	5
RN Harvey c Compton b Bedser	0	c Graveney b Bedser	2
KR Miller c Bailey b Wardle	55	c Kenyon b Bedser	5
R Benaud c Evans b Bailey	3	b Bedser	0
AK Davidson b Bedser	4	c Graveney b Tattersall	6
D Tallon (+) b Bedser	0	c Simpson b Tattersall	15
RR Lindwall c Evans b Bailey	0	c Tattersall b Bedser	12
JC Hill b Bedser	0	c Tattersall b Bedser	4
WA Johnston not out	0	not out	4
EXTRAS (B 2, LB 2, NB 1)	5	(LB 5)	5
TOTAL	249		123

FOW 1st Inns: 2 124 128 237 244 244 246 247 248 249
FOW 2nd Inns: 28 44 50 64 68 81 92 106 115 123

Bowling: *First Innings*: Bedser 38.3-16-55-7, Bailey 44-14-75-2, Wardle 35-16-55-1, Tattersall 23-5-59-0. *Second Innings*: Bedser 17.2-7-44-7, Bailey 5-1-28-0, Wardle 12-3-24-0, Tattersall 5-0-22-3.

ENGLAND

L Hutton (c) c Benaud b Davidson	43	not out	60
D Kenyon c Hill b Lindwall	8	c Hassett b Hill	16
RT Simpson lbw Lindwall	0	not out	28
DCS Compton c Morris b Lindwall	0		
TW Graveney c Benaud b Hill	22		
PBH May c Tallon b Hill	9		
TE Bailey lbw Hill	13		
TG Evans (+) c Tallon b Davidson	8		
JH Wardle not out	29		
AV Bedser lbw Lindwall	2		
R Tattersall b Lindwall	0		
EXTRAS (B 5, LB 3)	8	(B 8, LB 4, W 2, NB 2)	16
TOTAL	144		1 for 120

FOW 1st Inns: 17 17 17 76 82 92 107 121 136 144
FOW 2nd Inns: 26

Bowling: *First Innings*: Lindwall 20.4-2-57-5, Johnston 18-7-22-0, Hill 19-8-35-3, Davidson 15-7-22-2. *Second Innings*: Lindwall 16-4-37-0, Johnston 18-9-14-0, Hill 12-3-26-1, Benaud 5-0-15-0, Davidson 5-1-7-0, Morris 2-0-5-0.

Umpires: D Davis & H Elliott

SECOND TEST 1953 ENGLAND v AUSTRALIA
Lord's Cricket Ground, London. June 25, 26, 27, 29, 30, 1953.
Toss: Australia. Match Drawn.

AUSTRALIA

AL Hassett (c) c Bailey b Bedser	104	c Evans b Statham	3
AR Morris st Evans b Bedser	30	c Statham b Compton	89
RN Harvey lbw Bedser	59 (4)	b Bedser	21
KR Miller b Wardle	25 (3)	b Wardle	109
GB Hole c Compton b Wardle	13	lbw Brown	47
R Benaud lbw Wardle	0	c Graveney b Bedser	5
AK Davidson c Statham b Bedser	76	c & b Brown	15
DT Ring lbw Wardle	18	lbw Brown	7
RR Lindwall b Statham	9	b Bedser	50
GRA Langley (+) c Watson b Bedser	1	b Brown	9
WA Johnston not out	3	not out	0
EXTRAS (B 4, LB 4)	8	(B 8, LB 5)	13
TOTAL	346		368

FOW 1st Inns: 65 190 225 229 240 280 291 330 331 346
FOW 2nd Inns: 3 168 227 235 248 296 305 308 362 368

Bowling: *First Innings*: Bedser 42.4-8-105-5, Statham 28-7-48-1, Brown 25-7-53-0, Bailey 16-2-55-0, Wardle 29-8-77-4. *Second Innings*: Bedser 31.5-8-77-3, Statham 15-3-40-1, Wardle 46-18-111-1, Brown 27-4-82-4, Bailey 10-4-24-0, Compton 3-0-21-1.

ENGLAND

L Hutton (c) c Hole b Johnston	145	c Hole b Lindwall	5
D Kenyon c Davidson b Lindwall	3	c Hassett b Lindwall	2
TW Graveney b Lindwall	78	c Langley b Johnston	2
DCS Compton c Hole b Benaud	57	lbw Johnston	33
W Watson st Langley b Johnston	4	c Hole b Ring	109
TE Bailey c & b Miller	2	c Benaud b Ring	71
FR Brown c Langley b Lindwall	22	c Hole b Benaud	28
TG Evans (+) b Lindwall	0	not out	11
JH Wardle b Davidson	23	not out	0
AV Bedser b Lindwall	1		
JB Statham not out	17		
EXTRAS (B 11, LB 1, W 1, NB 7)	20	(B 7, LB 6, W 2, NB 6)	21
TOTAL	372		7 for 282

FOW 1st Inns: 9 177 279 291 301 328 328 332 341 372
FOW 2nd Inns: 6 10 12 73 236 246 282

Bowling: *First Innings*: Lindwall 23-4-66-5, Miller 25-6-57-1, Johnston 35-11-91-2, Ring 14-2-43-0, Benaud 19-4-70-1, Davidson 10.5-2-25-1. *Second Innings*: Lindwall 19-3-26-2, Johnston 29-10-70-2, Ring 29-5-84-2, Miller 17-8-17-0, Benaud 17-6-51-1, Davidson 14-5-13-0, Hole 1-1-0-0.

Umpires: HG Baldwin & FS Lee

THIRD TEST 1953 ENGLAND v AUSTRALIA
Old Trafford, Manchester. July 9, 10, 11, 13 (no play), 14, 1953.
Toss: Australia. Match Drawn.

AUSTRALIA

AL Hassett (c) b Bailey	26	c Bailey b Bedser	8
AR Morris b Bedser	1	c Hutton b Laker	0
KR Miller b Bedser	17	st Evans b Laker	6
RN Harvey c Evans b Bedser	122 (7)	b Wardle	0
GB Hole c Evans b Bedser	66 (4)	c Evans b Bedser	2
JH De Courcy lbw Wardle	41 (5)	st Evans b Wardle	8
AK Davidson st Evans b Laker	15 (6)	not out	4
RG Archer c Compton b Bedser	5	lbw Wardle	0
RR Lindwall c Edrich b Wardle	1	b Wardle	4
JC Hill not out	8	not out	0
GRA Langley (+) c Edrich b Wardle	8		
EXTRAS (B 6, LB 1, NB 1)	8	(LB 3)	3
TOTAL	318	8 for 35	

FOW 1st Inns: 15 48 48 221 256 285 290 291 302 318
FOW 2nd Inns: 8 12 18 18 31 31 31 35

Bowling: *First Innings*: Bedser 45-10-115-5, Bailey 26-4-83-1, Wardle 28.3-10-70-3, Laker 17-3-42-1. *Second Innings*: Laker 9-5-11-2, Bedser 4-1-14-2, Wardle 5-2-7-4.

ENGLAND

L Hutton (c) lbw Lindwall	66
WJ Edrich c Hole b Hill	6
TW Graveney c De Courcy b Miller	5
DCS Compton c Langley b Archer	45
JH Wardle b Lindwall	5
W Watson b Davidson	16
RT Simpson c Langley b Davidson	31
TE Bailey c Hole b Hill	27
TG Evans (+) not out	44
JC Laker lbw Hill	5
AV Bedser b Morris	10
EXTRAS (B 8, LB 8)	16
TOTAL	276

FOW 1st Inns: 19 32 126 126 149 149 209 231 243 276

Bowling: *First Innings*: Lindwall 20-8-30-2, Archer 15-8-12-1, Hill 35-7-97-3, Miller 24-11-38-1, Davidson 20-4-60-2, Harvey 3-2-2-0, Hole 2-0-16-0, Morris 1-0-5-1.

Umpires: D Davis & H Elliott

FIFTH TEST 1953 ENGLAND v AUSTRALIA
Kennington Oval, London. August 15, 17, 18, 19, 1953.
Toss: Australia. England won by 8 wkts.

AUSTRALIA

AL Hassett (c) c Evans b Bedser	53	lbw Laker	10
AR Morris lbw Bedser	16	lbw Lock	26
KR Miller lbw Bailey	1 (5)	c Trueman b Laker	0
RN Harvey c Hutton b Trueman	36	b Lock	1
GB Hole c Evans b Trueman	37 (3)	lbw Laker	17
JH De Courcy c Evans b Trueman	5	run out	4
RG Archer c & b Bedser	10	c Edrich b Lock	49
AK Davidson c Edrich b Laker	22	b Lock	21
RR Lindwall c Edrich b Laker	62	c Compton b Laker	12
GRA Langley (+) c Edrich b Lock	18	c Trueman b Lock	2
WA Johnston not out	9	not out	6
EXTRAS (B 4, NB 2)	6	(B 11, LB 3)	14
TOTAL	275		162

FOW 1st Inns: 38 41 107 107 118 160 160 207 245 275
FOW 2nd Inns: 23 59 60 61 61 85 135 140 144 162

Bowling: *First Innings*: Bedser 29-3-88-3, Trueman 24.3-3-86-4, Bailey 14-3-42-1, Lock 9-2-19-1, Laker 5-0-34-1. *Second Innings*: Bedser 11-2-24-0, Trueman 2-1-4-0, Laker 16.5-2-75-4, Lock 21-9-45-5.

ENGLAND

L Hutton (c) b Johnston	82	run out	17
WJ Edrich lbw Lindwall	21	not out	55
PBH May c Archer b Johnston	39	c Davidson b Miller	37
DCS Compton c Langley b Lindwall	16	not out	22
TW Graveney c Miller b Lindwall	4		
TE Bailey b Archer	64		
TG Evans (+) run out	28		
JC Laker c Langley b Miller	1		
GAR Lock c Davidson b Lindwall	4		
FS Trueman b Johnston	10		
AV Bedser not out	22		
EXTRAS (B 9, LB 5, W 1)	15	(LB 1)	1
TOTAL	306		2 for 132

FOW 1st Inns: 37 137 154 167 170 210 225 237 262 306
FOW 2nd Inns: 24 88

Bowling: *First Innings*: Lindwall 32-7-70-4, Miller 34-12-65-1, Johnston 45-16-94-3, Davidson 10-1-26-0, Archer 10.3-2-25-1, Hole 11-6-11-0. *Second Innings*: Lindwall 21-5-46-0, Miller 11-3-24-1, Johnston 29-14-52-0, Archer 1-1-0-0, Hassett 1-0-4-0, Morris 0.5-0-5-0.

Umpires: D Davies & FS Lee

FOURTH TEST 1953 ENGLAND v AUSTRALIA
Headingley, Leeds. July 23, 24, 25, 27, 28, 1953.
Toss: Australia. Match Drawn.

ENGLAND

L Hutton (c) b Lindwall	0	c Langley b Archer	25
WJ Edrich lbw Miller	10	c De Courcy b Lindwall	64
TW Graveney c Benaud b Miller	55	b Lindwall	3
DCS Compton c Davidson b Lindwall	0	lbw Lindwall	61
W Watson b Lindwall	24	c Davidson b Miller	15
RT Simpson c Langley b Lindwall	15	c De Courcy b Miller	0
TE Bailey run out	7	c Hole b Davidson	38
TG Evans (+) lbw Miller	25	c Lindwall b Miller	1
JC Laker c Lindwall b Archer	10	c Benaud b Davidson	48
GAR Lock b Davidson	9	c Morris b Miller	8
AV Bedser not out	0	not out	3
EXTRAS (B 8, LB 4)	12	(B 1, LB 8)	9
TOTAL	167		275

FOW 1st Inns: 0 33 36 98 108 110 133 149 167 167
FOW 2nd Inns: 57 62 139 167 171 182 239 244 258 275

Bowling: *First Innings*: Lindwall 35-10-54-5, Miller 28-13-39-2, Davidson 20.4-7-23-1, Archer 18-4-27-1, Benaud 8-1-12-0. *Second Innings*: Lindwall 54-19-104-3, Miller 47-19-63-4, Archer 25-12-31-1, Davidson 29.3-15-36-2, Hole 3-1-6-0, Benaud 19-8-26-0.

AUSTRALIA

AL Hassett (c) c Lock b Bedser	37	b Lock	4
AR Morris c Lock b Bedser	10	st Evans b Laker	38
RN Harvey lbw Bailey	71 (4)	lbw Bedser	34
KR Miller c Edrich b Bailey	5		
GB Hole c Lock b Bedser	53 (3)	c Graveney b Bailey	33
JH De Courcy lbw Lock	10	not out	13
R Benaud b Bailey	7		
AK Davidson c Evans b Bedser	2 (5)	not out	17
RG Archer not out	31		
RR Lindwall b Bedser	9		
GRA Langley (+) c Hutton b Bedser	17		
EXTRAS (B 4, LB 8, W 2)	14	(B 3, LB 4, W 1)	8
TOTAL	266		4 for 147

FOW 1st Inns: 27 70 84 168 183 203 203 208 218 266
FOW 2nd Inns: 27 54 111 117

Bowling: *First Innings*: Bedser 28.5-2-95-6, Bailey 22-4-71-3, Lock 23-9-53-1, Laker 9-1-33-0. *Second Innings*: Bedser 17-1-65-1, Lock 8-1-48-1, Laker 2-0-17-1, Bailey 6-1-9-1.

Umpires: F Chester & FS Lee

Australian Averages

1953 ENGLAND v AUSTRALIA

AUSTRALIA	M	Inn	NO	Runs	H.S	Avrge	Ct	St	Overs	Mds	Runs	Wkt	Avrge
Archer, RG	3	5	1	95	49	23.75	1	-	69.3	27	95	4	23.75
Benaud, R	3	5	-	15	7	3.00	5	-	68.0	19	174	2	87.00
Davidson, AK	5	10	2	182	76	22.75	5	-	125.0	42	212	8	26.50
De Courcy, JH	3	6	1	81	41	16.20	3	-	-	-	-	-	-
Harvey, RN	5	10	-	346	122	34.60	-	-	3.0	2	2	-	-
Hassett, AL	5	10	-	365	115	36.50	2	-	1.0	-	4	-	-
Hill, JC	2	4	2	12	8*	6.00	1	-	66.0	18	158	7	22.57
Hole, GB	5	10	-	273	66	27.30	8	-	17.0	8	33	-	-
Johnston, WA	3	6	6	22	9*	-	-	-	174.0	67	343	7	49.00
Langley, GRA	4	6	-	55	18	9.17	8	1	-	-	-	-	-
Lindwall, RR	5	9	-	159	62	17.67	2	-	240.4	62	490	26	18.85
Miller, KR	5	9	-	223	109	24.78	3	-	186.0	72	303	10	30.30
Morris, AR	5	10	-	337	89	33.70	2	-	3.5	-	15	1	15.00
Ring, DT	1	2	-	25	18	12.50	-	-	43.0	7	127	2	63.50
Tallon, D	1	2	-	15	15	7.50	2	-	-	-	-	-	-

English Averages

1953 ENGLAND v AUSTRALIA

ENGLAND	M	Inn	NO	Runs	H.S	Avrge	Ct	St	Overs	Mds	Runs	Wkt	Avrge
Bailey, TE	5	7	-	222	71	31.71	3	-	143.0	33	387	8	48.38
Bedser, AV	5	6	3	38	22*	12.67	1	-	265.1	58	682	39	17.49
Brown, FR	1	2	-	50	28	25.00	1	-	52.0	11	135	4	33.75
Compton, DCS	5	8	1	234	61	33.43	4	-	3.0	-	21	1	21.00
Edrich, WJ	3	5	1	156	64	39.00	6	-	-	-	-	-	-
Evans, TG	5	7	2	117	44*	23.40	11	5	-	-	-	-	-
Graveney, TW	5	7	-	169	78	24.14	4	-	-	-	-	-	-
Hutton, L	5	9	1	443	145	55.38	4	-	-	-	-	-	-
Kenyon, D	2	4	-	29	16	7.25	1	-	-	-	-	-	-
Laker, JC	3	4	-	64	48	16.00	1	-	58.5	11	212	9	23.56
Lock, GAR	2	3	-	21	9	7.00	3	-	61.0	21	165	8	20.63
May, PBH	2	3	-	85	39	28.33	1	-	-	-	-	-	-
Simpson, RT	3	5	1	74	31	18.50	1	-	-	-	-	-	-
Statham, JB	1	1	-	17	17*	-	2	-	43.0	10	88	2	44.00
Tattersall, R	1	1	-	2	2	2.00	2	-	28.0	5	81	3	27.00
Trueman, FS	1	1	-	10	10	10.00	2	-	26.3	4	90	4	22.50
Wardle, JH	3	4	2	57	29*	28.50	-	-	155.3	57	344	13	26.46
Watson, W	3	5	-	168	109	33.60	-	-	-	-	-	-	-

Morris, steady as a rock

Arthur Morris, the champion left-hand opening batsman, began his career bowling left-arm wrist spinners for St George in Sydney grade cricket and batting down the order.

It was Bill O'Reilly who noticed the potential of young Arthur Robert Morris as a batsman in those early days at St George. He suggested that the curly haired youngster with the strong wrists and powerful forearms should open the batting.

Morris was 16 when he made his first century, against Sydney University, and he was only 18 when he earned a special place in *Wisden* by becoming the first player to score a century in each innings on debut in first class cricket. His attractive 148 and 111 for NSW against Queensland at the SCG in December 1940 made him world famous. In the first innings he shared an opening stand of 261 with Test partner-to-be, Sid Barnes. World War II put Morris' career on hold for the best part of six years. He joined the Army and served in New Guinea.

Born on 19 January 1922, Morris was 24 when he returned to Sheffield Shield cricket in 1946–47. He was soon in good form, producing a variety of majestic shots on either side of the wicket. He was a fierce hooker, as Victoria's Keith Miller discovered at the SCG one afternoon. The devil-may-care Miller, intent on testing the mettle of Morris, bowled an over of bouncers to him. Morris hooked four in a row to the boundary, and took 24 off the over.

A lovely innings of 115 for an Australian XI against the touring MCC side earned Morris a place in the Test team in 1946–47 and, after a quiet start at the top level, he scored 122 and 124 not out in the fourth encounter against England in Adelaide.

Morris scored an unbeaten Test 100 against the visiting Indians in 1947–48 and was one of three openers, with Barnes and Bill Brown, chosen for the 1948 tour of England under Don Bradman.

Morris secured his Test berth with a hard-hitting 184, which contained 26 fours, against Sussex a week before the first Test at Nottingham.

He had to call on all his courage and skill in the second Test at Lord's. With Barnes (0) steady and Bradman (38) out, Morris posted

Arthur Morris: the dependable one.

his maiden Test hundred in England with 105 in 200 minutes.

In the fourth Test at Leeds he shared a memorable partnership of 303 with Bradman as Australia swept to a seven-wicket win, scoring a record last-innings score of 3/404 to do so. Morris made 182 and Bradman 173 not out.

Morris was Australia's most consistent player in the Tests, scoring 696 runs at an average of 87.00. Bradman averaged 72.57. Morris scored 1922 runs in all matches at 71.18 with seven centuries, three of them in Tests. His highest score was 290 against Gloucestershire.

Morris occupies another special spot in *Wisden*, having the distinction of scoring a hundred on debut in four countries – England, South Africa, the West Indies and at home.

Morris captained Australia twice, standing in once for Lindsay Hassett in 1951–52 and in 1954–55 when skipper Ian Johnson and vice-captain Keith Miller were injured. Both matches were lost. He led NSW 26 times.

His premature retirement in 1955 aged 33 was the result of the death of his wife Valerie, who was only 35.

He made a brief comeback to big cricket for a Commonwealth side against India in Calcutta in 1963.

His shot making was so spectacular that Norm O'Neill implored his team-mates to come out of the rooms and watch.

Lindwall's perfect action

Good judges are unanimous that Ray Lindwall had no peer as an all-round fast bowler. Others may have been quicker. Others had a higher action, but Lindwall combined several qualities that placed him in a class of his own.

He once bowled Len Hutton, one of England's finest openers, with his slower ball – the fourth of the match. Don Bradman said Lindwall's outstanding attribute was his control of direction.

Lindwall attacked the stumps or deceived opponents with late outswing where top 'keeper Don Tallon came into his own. Of the 86 wickets he took on the 1948 tour of England 43 were clean bowled, 11 lbw and 14 caught behind.

Lindwall was a true all-rounder, but because he played in such strong sides after the war there was little need for his aggressive batting. However, on one occasion at the MCG against England in 1946–47 when Australia was in a bit of a spot, Lindwall (100) and Tallon (92) put on 154 exhilarating runs in 87 minutes.

Ray Lindwall at full stretch.

Lindwall's run-up of 18 metres was characterised by power, grace and balance. A lethal bouncer was part of his armoury.

Raymond Russell Lindwall, who was born on October 3, 1921, was a fine sportsman. He once ran 100 yards in 10.6 seconds and at 15 scored 219 and 110 in a day, playing for a junior side in the morning and the seniors in the afternoon.

He made his debut for NSW in November 1941 in a war-proceeds match against Queensland. After war service in the Pacific Islands, he showed he was over a bout of malaria by taking 9/80 against South Australia and scoring 134 not out. at the SCG against Queensland, which remained his highest score.

From 1946 on, he was a regular in Test sides. His new-ball partner in more than 35 tests was the cavalier 'Nugget' Miller. They roomed together on tour and there have been few more lethal duos. If an opening batsman wasn't on the receiving end of a searing Lindwall yorker or outswinger he had to combat a Miller leg-break or vicious off-cutter.

Lindwall made his Test debut against England at the 'Gabba in 1946–47.

In England in 1948, after satisfying umpires that a longer run-up

had cured his back-foot drag, Lindwall was at his peak. Nursed by Bradman, he did not hit top pace until a fortnight before the first Test.

He pulled a leg muscle in the first Test at Trent Bridge but took 8/131 (5/70 and 3/61) in the second Test at Lord's, 5/136 at Old Trafford and 4/163 at Leeds. He saved his best performance for the fifth Test at the Oval, routing England for 52 with 6/20. He rounded off a decisive season with 3/50 in the second innings for a series aggregate of 27 wickets at 19.62.

Lindwall toured England again in 1953 and 1956 but was not 'The Invincible' force of '48. But there were bright Test cameos, such as his 5/32 in South Africa In 1949–50 and a stylish century, 118, against the West Indies in Bridgetown in 1954–55.

Lindwall left NSW for Queensland in 1954–55 and played there until 1959–60, the last five years as captain. By then he was a clever medium-pace bowler, deploying the outswinger cleverly. He captained Australia in one Test against India in 1956–57 for a draw. He played his final Tests against Pakistan and India on the tour of the sub-continent in 1959–60.

Lindwall played in 61 Tests, taking 228 wickets at 23.03 with a best of 7/38 and 12 hauls of five wickets.

Lindwall was an Australian selector from 1979–1983, was made a life member of the MCC in 1960 and received the MBE in 1965. He was a keen golfer and in his latter years ran a florist shop with his wife. He died on 23 June 1996, aged 72.

Lindsay Hassett – captain, diplomat, prankster, batsman

Taking over as Australian captain from Don Bradman was probably the most difficult job in cricket at the time, not only because the team the new captain inherited would be without the great batsman, but also because Australia would have great expectations.

A big man would be required to fill this big role. But, by one vote, the Board of Control chose a small man – but whose slight 5 ft 6 1/2 inches was packed with a huge heart, immense cricket talent and a droll sense of humour that would have made him a packet on the stage if he had not chosen cricket as a career.

Lindsay Hassett has an enviable record as a Test batsman, making over 3000 runs at 46.56 in a career abbreviated (like many others) by World War II. He made his first of 10 Test centuries when he was 32. He had a great record as captain winning 14, and losing only four (six draws), making some of the most audacious declarations in Test history grounded in his profound understanding of the essence of a cricket match. Some, if not most of the great cricket stories are told about him, or by him.

Keith Miller said that Hassett made more friends in and around cricket than anyone he knew.

Arthur Lindsay Hassett was born in Geelong on August 28, 1913, and became a star sportsman at Geelong College. In 1930–31 while still at school he made 147 for Victorian Country against the touring West Indies side.

He played his first game for Victoria against South Australia in February 1933, hitting Clarrie Grimmett for four from his first ball and going out lbw to the next.

His Victorian career was slow to get started – the first substantial scores were 82 and 71 not out against NSW in December 1936. His initial first class century was 127 not out for Victoria against New Zealand in November 1937. In 1937–38 he made 693 runs at 53.3, to earn a berth on the 1938 tour of England under Bradman.

Hassett was an immediate success in the tour games, making 43, 146, 148 and 220 not out in his first four matches, and averaging 53.16 for the tour – though he did less well in the Tests.

In the 1938–39 Shield season he batted brilliantly for 967 runs at 74.38. In the 1939–40 season, before joining up, Hassett made 122 in each innings, repeatedly

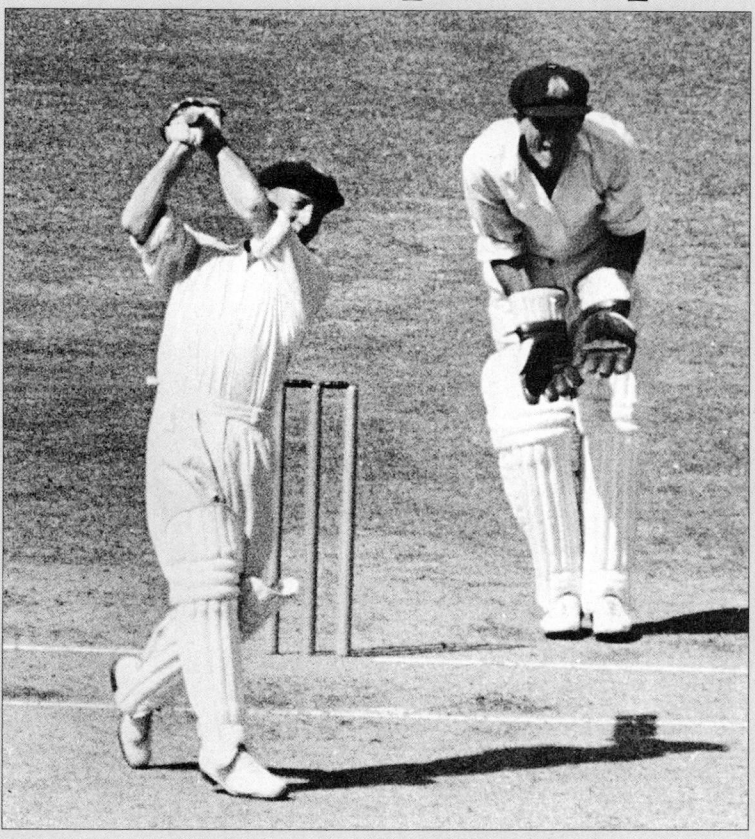

Lindsay Hassett was a fluent strokemaker with timing making up for strength.

hoisting Bill O'Reilly over his head to the SCG boundary.

Hassett was gunner in the 2/2 Anti-Aircraft Regiment in Egypt in 1941, and captained an AIF side to three memorable victories against teams from other forces, and made a couple of handy centuries.

In 1945 Hassett found himself attached to the AIF Reception Centre in England, among many other cricketers. When an AIF side was formed to help restore the game and give entertainment to the war-weary English people, in the manner of the famed 1919 AIF team, Hassett was the logical choice as captain.

This AIF side proceeded to play the five 'Victory Tests' in England, a series in India and then a tour of the Australian states over nine months playing 64 games for 27 wins. During this arduous tour, Hassett established that he was the supreme diplomat of Australian cricket, making a few more centuries and charming everyone he made contact with – and all for his army pay of 12 shillings a day.

Unaccountably and ungratefully Hassett was not appointed captain of the Australian Test side which went to New Zealand in March 1946, a tour for which Bradman was unavailable.

He was back with the 1948 side averaging 44 in the Tests. In 1949, Hassett only gained the captaincy for the South African tour by one vote. He celebrated by making 112 in his first Test as captain. In the third Test he conspired to keep South Africa batting on the 'sticky' that had seen Australia dismissed for 75 (236 behind), until the pitch improved, and won the match.

In Brisbane in 1950 against England he declared Australia's second innings at 7/32 (Freddie Brown had declared just before at 7/68) and bowled England out for 122 to win the match.

Hassett was one of the most popular Australian skippers, and certainly a whimsical fellow whose company was much sought after. Late one evening in 1948, a spacious, chauffeured sedan was making its way steadfastly back to London, having picked up its four passengers at a private black-tie function in Surrey.

It was barely midnight, too early to be calling it a day. 'Excuse me, driver,' said the small, dapper man in the front seat. Why don't we call in at the next mansion?' 'Yes, sir,' replied the driver.

The sedan duly turned off the highway and made its way along the drive of a large, two-storey home, parking outside the huge front door. A light was on. The small man got out of the car and rang the front doorbell. Dogs barked, servants stirred. Upstairs a window creaked open and a distinguished-looking figure looked down. 'Good god, what do you think you're doing?' he said churlishly.

'Just thought we'd pop in,' replied the small man. The awakened Lord of the Manor looked down more closely and asked, 'I say, aren't you Lindsay Hassett?'

'Yes, sir,' replied the vice-captain of the 1948 team. 'Don't move, I'll be right down.'

With that the butler materialised, lit the fire, and produced the port and cigars. The Lord of the Manor appeared resplendent in silk dressing gown.

It was 2 a.m. before Hassett, Keith Miller, Ian Johnson and Bill Johnston were allowed to take their leave. Needless to say the L of the M dined out to the point of boredom about the night Lindsay Hassett and Co. called in for one for the road.

During his address at one function, former Prime Minister Sir Robert Menzies noticed Hassett along the table.

'Lindsay Hassett is one of the outstanding interjectors I have known. He should have entered politics,' said Sir Robert.

'When I was PM I used to organise cricket matches between overseas teams and my own side, which Lindsay captained ... After play I used to invite both teams to a dinner at the Hotel Canberra ....'

Menzies paused. 'And mighty frugal do's they were too,' said Hassett, with his impish smile.

Hassett, one of Australia's most accomplished batsmen from an early age, scored 3073 in 43 Tests at 46.56 with 10 centuries. His highest score was 198 not out against India.

He retired from cricket after losing the Ashes in 1953, continuing in his sports store in Melbourne, where generations of small boys used to buy bats from a bloke they could look, with awe, in the eye.

He soon joined the ABC to become as dry and discerning in his comments as he was in his cricket, retiring to universal dismay in 1981, disappointed with what cricket had become.

He became a keen fisherman, and died at his haven at Bateman's Bay on 16 June 1993.

NSW just wins in exciting Shield season

The NSW team in Adelaide, November 1953: (from left, top row, standing) R. Briggs, I. Craig, RR Lindwall, R. Simpson, R. Benaud, J. Burke, G, Trueman, J. Clark, (Sitting) R. Roxby, KR Miller (captain), FW Bennett (manager), AR Morris (vice captain), J De Courey.

Adelaide, March 2. Victoria had to defeat South Australia outright in the last Sheffield Shield game of the season in order to win the trophy – but only managed first-innings points, despite a marathon bowling effort by Ian Johnson.

SA took a long time making 315 (Neil Dansie 101, Johnson 6/85), and Victoria just as long in making 401, with Colin McDonald a chanceless career-best 229. By the time SA declared at 9/305 (Johnson 6/99), Victoria needed 220 in three hours, and lost 6/148 without threatening to win. Victoria and NSW each won four games, but NSW had two first innings wins, winning the Shield by two points.

NSW had in their turn defeated SA by five wickets, in February on the strength of Richie Benaud's (9/103) and Bob Simpson's (6/121) leg spin bowling, and an opening stand of 161 between Bill Watson (82 on debut) and Ron Briggs (136).

During the Shield season Benaud made 811 runs at 62.3 and took 35 wickets at 30.5.

Against each other Victoria and NSW shared a win. NSW defeated Victoria by nine wickets at the MCG after Christmas with the season's largest crowd – 19,593 on Boxing Day, and 21,169 on the next day of play, the 28th.

Victoria reversed the result at the SCG in January, winning by five wickets.

Hassett testimonial

Melbourne, Jan. 19. In the absence of international cricket, the match between Lindsay Hassett's XI and Arthur Morris' XI at the MCG was the representative 'match of the season'. 46,859 supporters of Lindsay Hassett raised £5503 and the players raised 1801 runs with 20 sixes and 189 fours as Ian Craig hit 106, Graeme Hole 97 for Morris' winning team, and Hassett made 126 for his side. Star hitter was Keith Miller who made a century in each innings for the first time, 100 and 101. Match scores: Morris' XI 562 and 399 defeated Hassett's XI 415 and 425. A shade is drawn over the bowling figures in this enjoyable carnival game.

And now they are airborne. The Victorian team leaves for Brisbane.

South provides another captain

Captain Ian Johnson in action.

Melbourne, Oct. 30. Perhaps the fact that Ian Johnson once played for the South Melbourne Cricket Club was the least important factor in his being appointed captain of Australia, but it at least showed that he came from a distinguished lineage.

Five captains before him had played for South: Jack Blackham, Harry Trott, Warwick Armstrong, Bill Woodfull and Lindsay Hassett.

Blackham had three wins, three losses, and two draws; Trott five wins and three losses; Armstrong eight wins and no losses; Woodfull 14 wins and seven losses, four draws; Hassett 14 wins, four losses and six draws.

And Johnson's rival in NSW eyes was Keith Miller – but of course he also had played his club cricket with South Melbourne.

Johnson had not been chosen for the 1953 tour of England, but after a 'rev-up' by Hassett played remarkably well for Victoria in 1953–54, taking 45 first class wickets and topping the averages.

When he was appointed Australian captain Johnson was in charge of a first class side for just the 13th time. Previously Hassett had stood down as captain to give Johnson more experience.

Johnson's elevation to the captaincy makes him doubly rare, first as an Australian off-spin bowler, and also as a bowler who is a captain.

Harvey, Morris stand takes first Test

Brisbane, Dec. 1. For men bereft of practice and form, Arthur Morris and Neil Harvey did well in their first outing against the vaunted pace attack of England, but not without some painful moments.

'Johnnie' Moyes overheard a bit of barracking on the scratchy first day of the first Test, with Morris being painfully slow. 'One dear old soul called out, "Don't take any notice of them, Arthur. You stay there even if you don't make another run before Monday." And a tough old cattleman replied, "Good gracious, Mum! Don't make it Monday. Let him get another one tomorrow, as we wouldn't be here after the weekend."'

Arthur did, 153 of them altogether, outshining the usually sublime Neil Harvey. No barracking of Neil, but after Morris departed (419 minutes) Harvey brought up his first hundred against England in Australia, and then arriving at some point of energy, 'was now in tremendous form, and cover-hit and drove with atomic power.'

England's fielding was below standard, with uncountable dropped catches (more than 12) and the poor decision to go into the match without a spinner on a dry pitch. Australia bowled out their side of professionals and young tyros twice, including Len Hutton himself for 4 and 13.

A story did the rounds that the 'Gabba groundsman led Hutton 'up the garden path' in regard to the state of the pitch, and in winning the toss Hutton sent Australia in. Hutton scotched this rumour – which only makes the decision to send Australia in an even more baffling piece of misjudgment.

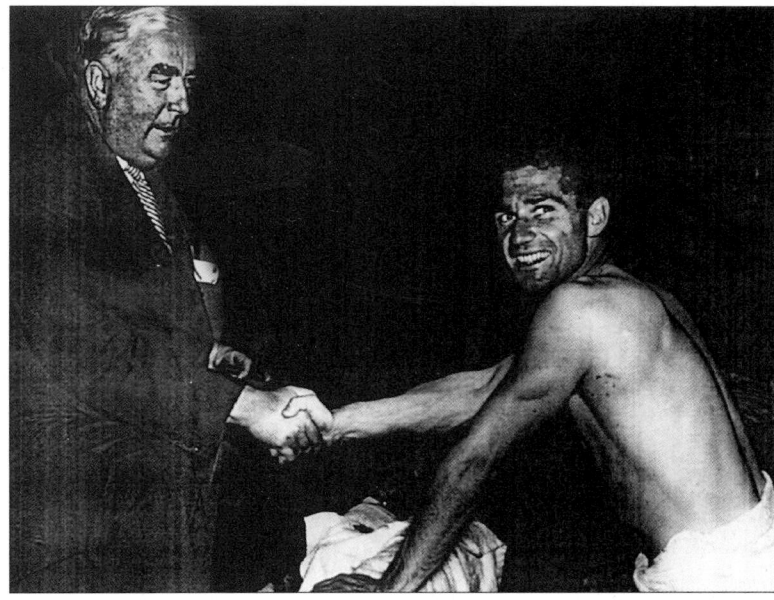

Cricket-loving Australian Prime Minister Robert Menzies congratulates Neil Harvey.

Anguish for Edrich as he swings and misses a long hop from Bill Johnston.

Press 'army' puts strain on resources

Perth, Oct. 7. Cricket journalist E. W. Swanton noted on his arrival for the England tour that they had needed the largest Orient liner, the *Orsova*, to bring the players and the press corps to Australia.

The English press contingent was nearly twice the size of a cricket team – 23 – and when added to the locals, some 40 of them at tour matches, and 80 or more for Tests, was larger than some crowds.

The BBC has had special telephone lines installed at Test venues so that John Arlott can report directly to his listeners on the English defence of the Ashes.

Pitch watered

Melbourne, Jan. 3. The pitch at the MCG has been illegally watered on the rest day of the third Test. Only the goodwill of the captains enabled the Test to continue, as they agreed to ignore the action taken by curator Jack House. With temperatures hovering around 105 degrees with a 50 m.p.h. wind, House decided that the widening cracks in the pitch might prevent the Test from continuing anyway, and ordered the watering.

The action might have gone unnoticed, but House told Percy Beames of the *Age*.

MCC officials interrogated all and sundry and denied any watering had taken place. The newspaper stuck by its report. Johnnie Moyes wrote: 'The improvement in the turf favoured England without a doubt' and 'I offer no opinion on the matter, except to say that the pitch recovered in a most amazing fashion. As to the reason … no comment.'

The old cricketers are still around. Bodyline hero Stan McCabe, in his Sydney sports store.

'Typhoon' Tyson England's Test trump

Melbourne, Jan. 5. Before the second Test in Sydney, Frank Tyson made a crucial change in his run-up. Instead of the unsuccessful 35-yard marathon he cut it down to an 18–20 yard rhythmical sprint he said he had used in League cricket when he started out.

The results were promising in the game against Victoria, and even more so in the Sydney Test, after which 'Johnnie' Moyes wrote 'with his shortened run Tyson gained more precise control without losing much in speed. And he showed far greater intelligence than in Brisbane, where he was too short of a length. This time he attacked, gave the batsmen little respite, and in general forced them to play.

'As he hit the stumps five times, he was clearly master of the batsmen – not perhaps one of the immortals, so far, but a proper lad who had developed so tremendously in a few weeks.'

Tyson took 10 wickets in the match, Australia lost eight batsman for 113 runs on a day when they only needed 151 to win.

The batsman in Australia's fragile line-up whom Tyson could not get was Neil Harvey, who stood, with 92 not out, in the second innings 'a symbol of the soundness and fighting spirit which had once featured Australian batsmanship.'

The third Test was worse. Australia needed 240 runs in the second innings to win. At close of play on the third day Australia was 2/75 with Harvey and Richie Benaud at the crease.

But in 80 minutes of agony, the following morning, Australia lost 8/36 on 'a day of mourning and humiliation, not because Australia was beaten, but because of the feebleness of the display – out for 111. Tyson had six wickets for 16 during those 80 minutes, and seven for 27 runs for the innings – magnificent figures. He had speed, life, control and the will to succeed.'

He had Harvey caught down the leg side by 'keeper Godfrey Evans.

'One never likes to depreciate the work of a bowler, but without doubt poor batting helped. Some were out off strokes which should never have been played, especially by batsmen who had developed 'pitch complex'. How the wheel had turned! Not so long ago it was the Australian fast bowlers who had made the English batsmen finger their shirt-buttons anxiously. Now England possessed the men of violence, and Australian batsmen had no answer.

The terrifying power of a Typhoon – Frank Tyson bowls to Arthur Morris.

Is this the reason? Frank Tyson has bowled superbly since he was KO'd in Sydney.

Fast bowlers but slow over rates

Sydney, Dec. 31. England captain Len Hutton is the first modern 'professional' to captain England, and equipped with a medium to fast pace bowling battery, his apprehension about making a mistake has led to a dreary over rate.

Partly due to the plodding way bowlers such as Brian Statham and Frank Tyson turned and walked back to their marks, starting from their distant fielding positions, and partly due to the punctilious way Hutton sets his fields (sometimes requiring three conferences with the bowler in an over), the over rate has decreased the attractiveness of the cricket. In the first Test, on the Monday afternoon, Australia bowled 51 overs in 213 minutes, England on the Friday managed 56 overs in 300 minutes.

As a tactic to break the concentration and rhythm of the Australian batsmen, especially against Neil Harvey it has proved less than successful and has caused a good deal of agitation in the crowd who feel cheated of anything up to 10 overs a day of entertainment.

Hot crowd but cold pies at MCG

Melbourne, Jan. 8. Calls have been made for the State Government to take over the MCG and set up a stadium that will really belong to the people, not merely serve as a club for the privileged few.

That was the message from the *Sporting Globe* after the MCG system buckled under the strain of 300,270 patrons over the five days of the sensational third Test.

The *Globe* cited 'The watering of the pitch, the disgusting and unhealthy "conveniences" for both women and men and the fact that hot pies and cold beer were even more scarce than runs for Australian batsmen against Frank Tyson.'

There is growing public regret that the Olympic Games are not being held at a rebuilt Carlton ground.

There's a growing autocracy at the MCC that scorns public opinion and needs – even in the holy of holies, the members' reserve, there was pungent criticism of the facilities and public services available.

A lot of things will have to improved for the Olympic Games. Ex-boxer Merv Williams said the hardest fight he had had in his life was to get a feed at the MCG during the cricket.

It's all England – again

Top-scoring England batsman Peter May plays a copybook straight drive.

Sydney, March 3. Australia surrendered, once again, in the fourth Test in Adelaide, but not Keith Miller.

Perhaps with a desire to make up with the ball what he along with his team-mates had failed to achieve with the bat, he took a wicket in each of his first three overs as England chased the 94 runs it required to win, and retain the Ashes.

Miller removed Bill Edrich in his first over, Len Hutton in his second, and Colin Cowdrey in his third and later brilliantly caught Peter May in the covers off the bowling of Bill Johnston.

But these happenings merely brought to life a Test that had been dead since Australia began its slide to be dismissed for an England-pleasing score of 111 – Nelson.

Some critics have blamed the pitch for the difficulties in batting, but both teams made over 300 in the first innings, and Australia collapsed in the second. Australia's plight was put down to technically inferior batsmanship.

In Sydney in the fifth Test it was perhaps fortunate that the first three days of the Test were lost to rain because surely any additional time would have meant another England win.

As it was, Australia only managed 221 in reply to England's modest 7/371 and was forced to follow-on.

In 22 overs on the second innings it contrived to lose 6/118 with some lusty hitting from Miller, Richie Benaud and Peter Burge (Burge's first touch of a cricket ball in Test cricket was holding a catch off Ray Lindwall's bowling, dismissing Len Hutton).

The only positive thing to come out of the fifth Test was Ray Lindwall taking his hundredth wicket against England.

Purists objected to the seeming fact that Trevor Bailey managed to get bowled off his pads – but maybe he thought he could hit the ball – he had made 72.

Aussie cricket spirit is a myth

Melbourne, March 5. John Arlott, writing in the *Sporting Globe,* has had some hard things to say about Australian cricket.

'I came on this first trip to Australia with respect – at times almost with awe for Australian cricket, and an immense personal liking for a number of players I knew. I go back to England with that liking undimmed but with much of the respect gone.

'I was brought up to believe in the immense powers of resistance and of fight-back instinctive in the Australian cricketer.

'They have been the sides never beaten until the last ball is bowled, producing tail-enders as batsmen of tough defence and shrewd attack. On this tour I have seen them routed by fast bowling.

'That perhaps is not in isolation alarming. There is no true fast bowling in Australia's domestic cricket at the moment, and it is hard on Test players to have to take their practice and reconstruct their timing against speed in Test matches only. But in the fifth Test the Australian batting looked second rate against two very ordinary spin bowlers.

'Australia's batting has folded with the deflated feebleness of a punctured balloon. The fact is they have not fought. Secondly they have batted incorrectly. Show me the Australian batsman who has played straight in this series.

'If the England side were a great one, the matter would be different: it is not.

'Behind it all is the decline of cricket as a sport in Australia. Fewer and fewer young men are playing cricket – fewer and fewer young men or old are watching it.

'Good cricket demands constant practice. There is little room at the top; small chance in the crowded competition and small fixture list of the Australian State sides.'

The captains and the coin.

FIRST TEST 1954–55 AUSTRALIA v ENGLAND
Brisbane Cricket Ground, Brisbane. November 26, 27, 29, 30, December 1, 1954.
Toss: England. Australia won by an innings & 154 runs.

AUSTRALIA

LE Favell c Cowdrey b Statham	23
AR Morris c Cowdrey b Bailey	153
KR Miller b Bailey	49
RN Harvey c Bailey b Bedser	162
GB Hole run out	57
R Benaud c May b Tyson	34
RG Archer c Bedser b Statham	0
RR Lindwall not out	64
GRA Langley (+) b Bailey	16
IW Johnson (c) not out	24
WA Johnston	
EXTRAS (B 11, LB 7, NB 1)	19
TOTAL	8 dec 601

FOW 1st Inns: 51 123 325 456 463 464 545 572

Bowling: *First Innings*: Bedser 37-4-131-1, Statham 34-2-123-2, Tyson 29-1-160-1, Bailey 26-1-140-3, Edrich 3-0-28-0.

ENGLAND

L Hutton (c) c Langley b Lindwall	4	lbw Miller	13
RT Simpson b Miller	2	run out	9
WJ Edrich c Langley b Archer	15	b Johnston	88
PBH May b Lindwall	1	lbw Lindwall	44
MC Cowdrey c Hole b Johnston	40	b Benaud	10
TE Bailey b Johnston	88	c Langley b Lindwall	23
FH Tyson b Johnston	7	not out	37
AV Bedser b Johnson	5	c Archer b Johnson	5
KV Andrew (+) b Lindwall	6	b Johnson	5
JB Statham b Johnson	11 (11)	c Harvey b Benaud	14
DCS Compton not out	2 (10)	c Langley b Benaud	0
EXTRAS (B 3, LB 6)	9	(B 7, LB 2)	9
TOTAL	190		257

FOW 1st Inns: 4 10 11 25 107 132 141 156 181 190
FOW 2nd Inns: 22 23 147 163 181 220 231 242 243 257

Bowling: *First Innings*: Lindwall 14-4-27-3, Miller 11-5-19-1, Archer 4-1-14-1, Johnson 19-5-46-3, Benaud 12-5-28-0, Johnston 16.1-5-47-2. *Second Innings*: Lindwall 17-3-50-2, Miller 12-2-30-1, Archer 15-4-28-0, Johnson 17-5-38-2, Benaud 8.1-1-43-3, Johnston 21-8-59-1.

Umpires: C Hoy & MJ McInnes

THIRD TEST 1954–55 AUSTRALIA v ENGLAND
Melbourne Cricket Ground, Melbourne. December 31, 1954, January 1, 3, 4, 5, 1955.
Toss: England. England won by 128 runs.

ENGLAND

L Hutton (c) c Hole b Miller	12	lbw Archer	42
WJ Edrich c Lindwall b Miller	4	b Johnston	13
PBH May c Benaud b Lindwall	0	b Johnston	91
MC Cowdrey b Johnson	102	b Benaud	7
DCS Compton c Harvey b Miller	4	c Maddocks b Archer	23
TE Bailey c Maddocks b Johnston	30	not out	24
TG Evans (+) lbw Archer	20	c Maddocks b Miller	22
JH Wardle b Archer	0	b Johnson	38
FH Tyson b Archer	6	c Harvey b Johnston	6
JB Statham b Archer	3	c Favell b Johnston	0
R Appleyard not out	1	b Johnston	6
EXTRAS (B 9)	9	(B 2, LB 4, W 1)	7
TOTAL	191		279

FOW 1st Inns: 14 21 29 41 115 169 181 181 190 191
FOW 2nd Inns: 40 96 128 173 185 211 257 273 273 279

Bowling: *First Innings*: Lindwall 13-0-59-1, Miller 11-8-14-3, Archer 13.6-4-33-4, Benaud 7-0-30-0, Johnston 12-6-26-1, Johnson 11-3-20-1. *Second Innings*: Lindwall 18-3-52-0, Miller 18-6-35-1, Archer 24-7-50-2, Benaud 8-2-25-1, Johnston 24.5-2-85-5, Johnson 8-2-25-1.

AUSTRALIA

LE Favell lbw Statham	25	b Appleyard	30
AR Morris lbw Tyson	3	c Cowdrey b Tyson	4
KR Miller c Evans b Statham	7 (5)	c Edrich b Tyson	6
RN Harvey b Appleyard	31	c Evans b Tyson	11
GB Hole b Tyson	11 (6)	c Evans b Statham	5
R Benaud c(S)JV Wilson b Appleyard	15 (3)	b Tyson	22
RG Archer b Wardle	23	b Statham	15
LV Maddocks (+) c Evans b Statham	47	b Tyson	0
RR Lindwall b Statham	13	lbw Tyson	0
IW Johnson (c) not out	33	not out	4
WA Johnston b Statham	11	c Evans b Tyson	0
EXTRAS (B 7, LB 3, NB 2)	12	(B 1, LB 13)	14
TOTAL	231		111

FOW 1st Inns: 15 38 43 65 92 115 134 151 205 231
FOW 2nd Inns: 23 57 77 86 87 97 98 98 110 111

Bowling: *First Innings*: Tyson 21-2-68-2, Statham 16.3-0-60-5, Bailey 9-1-33-0, Appleyard 11-3-38-2, Wardle 6-0-20-1. *Second Innings*: Tyson 12.3-1-27-7, Statham 11-1-38-2, Bailey 3-0-14-0, Appleyard 4-1-17-1, Wardle 1-0-1-0.

Umpires: C Hoy & MJ McInnes

SECOND TEST 1954–55 AUSTRALIA v ENGLAND
Sydney Cricket Ground, Sydney. December 17, 18, 20, 21, 22, 1954.
Toss: Australia. England won by 38 runs.

ENGLAND

L Hutton (c) c Davidson b Johnston	30	c Benaud b Johnston	28
TE Bailey b Lindwall	0	c Langley b Archer	6
PBH May c Johnston b Archer	5	b Lindwall	104
TW Graveney c Favell b Johnston	21	c Langley b Johnston	0
MC Cowdrey c Langley b Davidson	23	c Archer b Benaud	54
WJ Edrich c Benaud b Archer	10	b Archer	29
FH Tyson b Lindwall	0	b Lindwall	9
TG Evans (+) c Langley b Archer	3	c Lindwall b Archer	4
JH Wardle c Burke b Johnston	35	lbw Lindwall	8
R Appleyard c Hole b Davidson	8	not out	19
JB Statham not out	14	c Langley b Johnston	25
EXTRAS (LB 5)	5	(LB 6, NB 4)	10
TOTAL	154		296

FOW 1st Inns: 14 19 58 63 84 85 88 99 111 154
FOW 2nd Inns: 18 55 55 171 222 232 239 249 250 296

Bowling: *First Innings*: Lindwall 17-3-47-2, Archer 12-7-12-3, Davidson 12-3-34-2, Johnston 13.3-1-56-3. *Second Innings*: Lindwall 31-10-69-3, Archer 22-9-53-3, Davidson 13-2-52-0, Johnston 19.3-2-70-3, Benaud 19-3-42-1.

AUSTRALIA

LE Favell c Graveney b Bailey	26	c Edrich b Tyson	16
AR Morris (c) c Hutton b Bailey	12	lbw Statham	10
JW Burke c Graveney b Bailey	44	b Tyson	14
RN Harvey c Cowdrey b Tyson	12	not out	92
GB Hole b Tyson	12	b Tyson	0
R Benaud lbw Statham	20	c Tyson b Appleyard	12
RG Archer c Hutton b Tyson	49	b Tyson	6
AK Davidson b Statham	20	c Evans b Statham	5
RR Lindwall c Evans b Tyson	19	b Tyson	8
GRA Langley (+) b Bailey	5	b Statham	0
WA Johnston not out	0	c Evans b Tyson	11
EXTRAS (B 5, LB 2, NB 2)	9	(LB 7, NB 3)	10
TOTAL	228		184

FOW 1st Inns: 18 65 100 104 122 141 193 213 224 228
FOW 2nd Inns: 27 34 77 77 102 122 127 136 145 184

Bowling: *First Innings*: Statham 18-1-83-2, Bailey 17.4-3-59-4, Tyson 13-2-45-4, Appleyard 7-1-32-0. *Second Innings*: Statham 19-6-45-3, Bailey 6-0-21-0, Tyson 18.4-1-85-6, Appleyard 6-1-12-1, Wardle 4-2-11-0.

Umpires: MJ McInnes & RR Wright

FOURTH TEST 1954–55 AUSTRALIA v ENGLAND
Adelaide Oval, Adelaide. January 28, 29, 31, February 1, 2, 1955.
Toss: Australia. England won by 5 wkts.

AUSTRALIA

CC McDonald c May b Appleyard	48	b Statham	29
AR Morris c Evans b Tyson	25	c & b Appleyard	16
JW Burke c May b Tyson	18	b Appleyard	5
RN Harvey c Edrich b Bailey	25	b Appleyard	7
KR Miller c Bailey b Appleyard	44	b Statham	14
R Benaud c May b Appleyard	15 (7)	lbw Tyson	1
LV Maddocks (+) run out	69 (6)	lbw Statham	2
RG Archer c May b Tyson	21	c Evans b Tyson	3
AK Davidson c Evans b Bailey	5	lbw Wardle	23
IW Johnson (c) c Statham b Bailey	41 (11)	not out	3
WA Johnston not out	0 (10)	c Appleyard b Tyson	3
EXTRAS (B 3, LB 7, W 2)	12	(B 4, LB 1)	5
TOTAL	323		111

FOW 1st Inns: 59 86 115 129 175 182 212 229 321 323
FOW 2nd Inns: 24 40 54 69 76 77 79 83 101 111

Bowling: *First Innings*: Tyson 26.1-4-85-3, Statham 19-4-70-0, Bailey 12-3-39-3, Appleyard 23-7-58-3, Wardle 19-5-59-0. *Second Innings*: Tyson 15-2-47-3, Statham 12-1-38-3, Appleyard 12-7-13-3, Wardle 4.2-1-8-1.

ENGLAND

L Hutton (c) c Davidson b Johnston	80	c Davidson b Miller	5
WJ Edrich b Johnson	21	b Miller	0
PBH May c Archer b Benaud	1	c Miller b Johnston	26
MC Cowdrey c Maddocks b Davidson	79	c Archer b Miller	4
DCS Compton lbw Miller	44	not out	34
TE Bailey c Davidson b Johnston	38	lbw Johnston	15
TG Evans (+) c Maddocks b Benaud	37	not out	6
JH Wardle c & b Johnson	23		
FH Tyson c Burke b Benaud	1		
R Appleyard not out	10		
JB Statham c Maddocks b Benaud	0		
EXTRAS (B 1, LB 2, NB 4)	7	(B 3, LB 4)	7
TOTAL	341		5 for 97

FOW 1st Inns: 60 63 162 232 232 283 321 323 336 341
FOW 2nd Inns: 3 10 18 49 90

Bowling: *First Innings*: Miller 11-4-34-1, Archer 3-0-12-0, Johnson 36-17-46-2, Davidson 25-8-55-1, Johnston 27-11-60-2, Benaud 36.6-6-120-4, Burke 2-0-7-0. *Second Innings*: Miller 10.4-2-40-3, Archer 4-0-13-0, Davidson 2-0-7-0, Johnston 8-2-20-2, Benaud 6-2-10-0.

Umpires: MJ McInnes & RR Wright

FIFTH TEST 1954–55 AUSTRALIA v ENGLAND
Sydney Cricket Ground, Sydney. February 25 (no play), 26 (no play), 28 (no play), March 1, 2, 3, 1955.
Toss: Australia. Match Drawn.

ENGLAND
L Hutton (c) c Burge b Lindwall	6
TW Graveney c & b Johnson	111
PBH May c Davidson b Benaud	79
MC Cowdrey c Maddocks b Johnson	0
DCS Compton c & b Johnson	84
TE Bailey b Lindwall	72
TG Evans (+) c McDonald b Lindwall	10
JH Wardle not out	5
FH Tyson	
R Appleyard	
JB Statham	
EXTRAS (B 1, LB 3)	4
TOTAL	7 for 371

FOW 1st Inns: 6 188 188 196 330 359 371

Bowling: First Innings: Lindwall 20.6-5-77-3, Miller 15-1-71-0, Davidson 19-3-72-0, Johnson 20-5-68-3, Benaud 20-4-79-1.

AUSTRALIA
WJ Watson b Wardle	18	c Graveney b Statham	3
CC McDonald c May b Appleyard	72	c Evans b Graveney	37
LE Favell b Tyson	1	c Graveney b Wardle	9
RN Harvey c & b Tyson	13	c & b Wardle	1
KR Miller run out	19	b Wardle	28
PJP Burge c Appleyard b Wardle	17	not out	18
R Benaud b Wardle	7	b Hutton	22
LV Maddocks (+) c Appleyard b Wardle	32		
AK Davidson c Evans b Wardle	18		
IW Johnson (c) run out	11		
RR Lindwall not out	2		
EXTRAS (B 10, LB 1)	11		0
TOTAL	221		6 for 118

FOW 1st Inns: 52 53 85 129 138 147 157 202 217 221
FOW 2nd Inns: 14 27 29 67 87 118

Bowling: First Innings: Tyson 11-1-46-2, Statham 9-1-31-0, Appleyard 16-2-54-1, Wardle 24.4-6-79-5. Second Innings: Tyson 5-2-20-0, Statham 5-0-11-1, Wardle 12-1-51-3, Graveney 6-0-34-1, Hutton 0.6-0-2-1.

Umpires: MJ McInnes & RR Wright

Australian Averages

1954–55 AUSTRALIA v ENGLAND

AUSTRALIA	M	Inn	NO	Runs	H.S	Avrge	Ct	St	Overs	Mds	Runs	Wkt	Avrge
Archer, RG	4	7	-	117	49	16.71	4	-	97.6	32	215	13	16.54
Benaud, R	5	9	-	148	34	16.44	3	-	116.7	23	377	10	37.70
Burge, PJP	1	2	1	35	18*	35.00	1	-	-	-	-	-	-
Burke, JW	2	4	-	81	44	20.25	2	-	2.0	-	7	-	-
Davidson, AK	3	5	-	71	23	14.20	5	-	71.0	16	220	3	73.33
Favell, LE	4	7	-	130	30	18.57	2	-	-	-	-	-	-
Harvey, RN	5	9	1	354	162	44.25	3	-	-	-	-	-	-
Hole, GB	3	5	-	85	57	17.00	3	-	-	-	-	-	-
Johnson, IW	4	6	4	116	41	58.00	3	-	111.0	37	243	12	20.25
Johnston, WA	4	6	2	25	11	6.25	1	-	141.4	37	423	19	22.26
Langley, GRA	2	3	-	21	16	7.00	9	-	-	-	-	-	-
Lindwall, RR	4	6	2	106	64*	26.50	2	-	130.6	28	381	14	27.21
Maddocks, LV	3	5	-	150	69	30.00	7	-	-	-	-	-	-
McDonald, CC	2	4	-	186	72	46.50	1	-	-	-	-	-	-
Miller, KR	4	7	-	167	49	23.86	1	-	88.4	28	243	10	24.30
Morris, AR	4	7	-	223	153	31.86	-	-	-	-	-	-	-
Watson, WJ	1	2	-	21	18	10.50	-	-	-	-	-	-	-

English Averages

1954–55 AUSTRALIA v ENGLAND

ENGLAND	M	Inn	NO	Runs	H.S	Avrge	Ct	St	Overs	Mds	Runs	Wkt	Avrge
Andrew, KV	1	2	-	11	6	5.50	-	-	-	-	-	-	-
Appleyard, R	4	5	3	44	19*	22.00	4	-	79.0	22	224	11	20.36
Bailey, TE	5	9	1	296	88	37.00	2	-	73.4	8	306	10	30.60
Bedser, AV	1	2	-	10	5	5.00	1	-	37.0	4	131	1	131.00
Compton, DCS	4	7	2	191	84	38.20	-	-	-	-	-	-	-
Cowdrey, MC	5	9	-	319	102	35.44	4	-	-	-	-	-	-
Edrich, WJ	4	8	-	180	88	22.50	3	-	3.0	-	28	-	-
Evans, TG	4	7	1	102	37	17.00	13	-	-	-	-	-	-
Graveney, TW	2	3	-	132	111	44.00	4	-	6.0	-	34	1	34.00
Hutton, L	5	9	-	220	80	24.44	2	-	0.6	-	2	1	2.00
May, PBH	5	9	-	351	104	39.00	6	-	-	-	-	-	-
Simpson, RT	1	2	-	11	9	5.50	-	-	-	-	-	-	-
Statham, JB	5	7	1	67	25	11.17	1	-	143.3	16	499	18	27.72
Tyson, FH	5	7	1	66	37*	11.00	2	-	151.0	16	583	28	20.82
Wardle, JH	4	6	1	109	38	21.80	1	-	70.6	15	229	10	22.90

Bill Johnston – great bowler, no batsman

Paradoxically, Bill Johnston, Australia's best left-arm pace bowler, is now as much remembered for his batting as for his bowling. The story of his winning partnership with Richmond team-mate Doug Ring in the fourth Test against the West Indies on 3 January 1952 ranks high in the annals of Australia's last-ditch, or last-wicket, stands. Ring made 32 not out and Johnston 7 not out, including the winning run.

Typical of Johnston's sunny and seemingly carefree attitude to the game of cricket was his remark after the match. Asked whether he was nervous or afraid, Big Bill said: 'Certainly not. Everybody expected me to make a duck and besides, I knew we didn't have a chance.'

Captain Lindsay Hassett thought so – he went off to have a shower and watched the unlikely victory naked, when his towel slipped.

Johnston's mum was told that the last pair didn't have a hope in hell of winning. And from the silent Punt Road end of the MCG, in the old Southern Stand most near to the Richmond ground, came the old football cry 'Eat 'em alive, Tigers.' Which is what they did, baffling the West Indies with their happy-go-lucky batting. The picture of them coming off the ground carrying souvenir stumps and wearing the grins of happy men is a treasure of Australian cricket.

Bill Johnston was born near Beeac in Victoria's Western District in 1922, and came to Melbourne in 1939, and started playing for Richmond thirds. By the end of the season he was in the firsts, playing with Ernie McCormick.

After the war he rejoined Richmond with Doug Ring for the 1945–46 season, and played for Victoria in that non-Shield season as well.

Johnston was 6 ft 2 1/2 inches tall, and lanky – hence 'Big' Bill, and began bowling slow left-arm leg-breaks with changes of pace.

It was in this season that both Jack Ryder and Don Bradman urged him to use his occasional 'quick' ball eight times an over, and he became a fast-medium bowler of quite lethal dimensions.

Coming in from a short seven-pace run-up Johnston bowled sharp rearing deliveries on an impeccable length with an occasional slower spinning delivery from the same run-up and action.

Big Bill Johnston's style.

His Test debut was against India in 1947–48 where he took 16 wickets in five Tests. He was effective with new and old balls, and by the 1948 tour of England he formed a fearsome trio with Keith Miller and Ray Lindwall. On this tour he was the only bowler who took over one hundred wickets (102) with his deceptive pace and late swing. In South Africa he topped the bowling averages with 56 wickets at 13.75.

Back in England in 1953 he took 75 wickets to Lindwall's 85, and averaged 102 with the bat. This Bradmanesque average was contrived by captain Lindsay Hassett and team-mates, as be batted 17 times, 16 not outs for a total of 102. This included a top score of 27 not out against the Gentlemen, at Lord's. Big Bill's batting which Jack Pollard described as 'usually last man in, with a gangling lope that radiated fun' averaged 12.68 in first class matches and 11.37 in tests which is not the batting of a complete rabbit.

In Test cricket his powers declined somewhat after a knee injury in 1953 in England, but against that country in 1954–55 he was close to his best with 19 wickets in the series at 22.26. His last Test and first class season was against the West Indies in 1954–55.

Bill Johnston is one of the most universally loved and respected Australian cricketers. He was described by Keith Miller as 'the most popular character in cricket … He is a great bloke in every way.'

Big scoring as Australia takes the lead

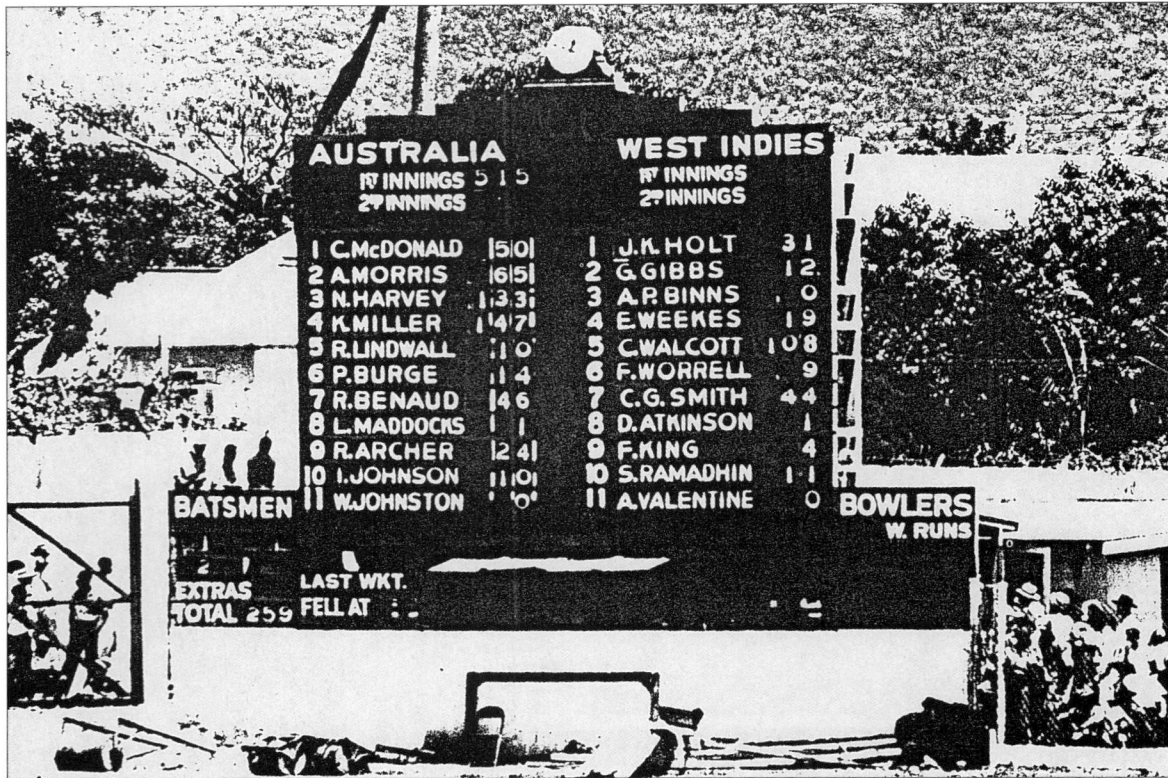

The scoreboard tells an encouraging story midway through the first Test at Sabina Park, Jamaica.

Kingston, March 31. Centuries to Neil Harvey and Keith Miller set Australia on the path to a runaway win in the first Test in the West Indies.

At the opening all the colour of a Caribbean cricketing day included a radio car circling outside the ground protesting the appointment of the white Denis Atkinson instead of the black Frank Worrell as captain. The voice was that of the United African National Council.

This did not deter the Australians as they set about thrashing the West Indies attack.

Colin McDonald (50) took a number of bumpers from Frank King with his usual stoicism as he and Arthur Morris (65) set up a first wicket partnership of 102. Then Harvey and Miller showed no mercy, particularly to the idols of the West Indies, the spinners Sonny Ramadhin and Alf Valentine. The bumper onslaught was taken up by King again with the new ball, giving rise to a fear of reprisals, stated in the *Daily Gleaner* – 'If Australia want to retaliate and start a bumper war we are heavily outnumbered.'

Miller's punishing 147 and Harvey's 133 took a fearful toll. As the West Indies attack wore out, its three main bowlers each with a century against their names, Australia moved to 9/515 declared.

There was no bumper retaliation, but the West Indies batsman were largely outclassed in two innings of 259 and 275, distinguished by 109 from Clyde Walcott in the first innings and a second-innings 104 from Test debutant Collie Smith.

Diplomatic skills put Aussies on side in West Indies

Kingston, March 31. Having danced into the night at the welcoming cocktail pary, Australian captain Ian Johnson has become the Calypso Captain. And having swept a young Jamaican boy into his arms as he left the field at the end of the first Test, he is also seen as a great man by the family-loving Jamaicans.

Having talked affably to reporters and on the radio, Keith Miller is an idol of unparalleled stature.

The Australians, well briefed on behaviour but naturally friendly, have wiped off West Indian resentment over the patronising and lordly English who toured here last season and left a bitter taste behind them.

The first Australian tour of the West Indies is off to a great start.

The Governor of Jamaica, Sir Hugh Foot, meets the Australian team before the first

Johnson bowls up a big series lead

Australian opener Colin McDonald is caught well short of the crease by Frank Worrell's fast return.

Georgetown, April 29. The Test series is in Australia's keeping, as a dramatic bowling spell by Ian Johnson shredded the West Indies second innings and opened the path to an eight wicket win in the third Test.

With a lead of 75 in the first innings, Australia was not the dominant batting force which compiled another mammoth score in the second Test.

The pitch was playing well and the West Indies went into the second innings knowing that they had the batting skill to take on the

Australian bowling, particularly the fearsome fast men, Lindwall and Miller.

But the slump came from a less likely source, particularly as Johnson's first wicket came from a rank full toss which West Indies captain Jeff Stollmeyer inexplicably played back into the hands of the bowler.

The West Indies were reeling at 3/25, but got to 150 before Johnson began to tie them up. The fresh breeze created ideal conditions for his floating off spinners and the batsmen could not read his length.

Of his 7/44 he had three out stumped, as the batsmen danced forward gleefully to the high, floating ball only to be left stranded.

Australian wicketkeeper Gil Langley had a wonderful time, and his five wickets in an innings equalled the world record of his illustrious predecessor Bert Oldfield, set in 1924–25 against England, when Clarrie Grimmett gave him four stumpings.

Another bowling highlight came in the first innings, when Richie Benaud picked up three tail-end wickets in four balls.

Bowlers dropped

Kingston, June 10. Since 1950, when they were the architects of a thrilling series win over England, Sonny Ramadhin and Alf Valentine, have been the wizards of West Indies cricket.

Now the spin twins are in disgrace, after some monumental Australian innings. Valentine was out of the third Test, and they have both been excluded from the fifth Test. The thought is that Valentine's spinning finger is worn, and that Ramadhin can now be read by the Australians. The Australians, says Keith Miller, don't think Ramadhin has been 'exploded', but they are not arguing over the West Indies selection process.

Johnson and Miller come to grips

Bridgetown, May 20. The fourth Test here has seen some explosions of scoring on the field, and one highly volatile situation in the dressing room.

The game started out placidly enough, indeed the ease with which the batsmen scored deadened any sense of drama.

Australia made 668, with six batsmen scoring over 50 and centuries from Keith Miller (137) and Ray Lindwall (118).

Then Australia began to mow down the West Indians, and they were 6/146 when Miller had Everton Weekes and Collie Smith in one over.

Miller is renowned for his bowl-

ing when he has a head of steam up, but inexplicably Ian Johnson took him out of the attack.

The next wicket fell at 494, after Denis Atkinson and Clairemonte Depieza had stayed together throughout a whole day's play.

Their stand of 347 was a world record for the seventh wicket.

The heat between the players arose from Ray Lindwall's refusal of an Ian Johnson request to bowl, and Miller's support of Lindwall.

In the dressing room Miller told Johnson he couldn't 'captain a team of schoolboys' and Johnson invited him 'outside.'

Wiser heads prevailed, and the match was drawn.

Walcott, Weekes & Co. create batting excitement

Kingston, June 17. The West Indies crowds have been loud in their disappointment at Australia's dominance in the series, but their batsmen have given them a lot to sing about. There have been some thrilling performances, particularly from Clyde Walcott.

In the first Test he made 108 of 259 in the first innings, in the second Test a century in each innings and in the fifth another century in each innings. He has finished the series with the highest aggregate score of 827, and an average of 82.70.

But it has been the quality that lingers beyond the scores. He could score anywhere, but his off driving and cutting was superb.

Everton Weekes has not been as dominant as usual, but he had one fine century in the second Test. And the West Indian cup ran over when Denis Atkinson (219) and Clairemont Depieza (122) batted all day in the fourth Test.

Five centuries in Australia's 8/758

Kingston, June 11. Seven centuries in one Test match. The fifth Test resulted in an unprecedented run feast, and a series win to Australia, 3–0.

The West Indies' lack of bowling penetration became acute in this match.

After the home side scored a creditable 357 (Walcott 155) they were powerless against the rampaging Australian batsman. McDonald (127), Harvey (204), Miller (109), Archer (128) and Benaud (121) picked them off at will in a score of 8/758 declared. Such was their authority that Benaud got his century in 78 minutes, the third fastest in Test history.

Another ignominious record was that all the bowlers got a 'century', apart from Garfield Sobers, who took 1/99.

The West Indies have used up to nine bowlers in some Tests as they have tried to contain the Australians. This time, without Valentine and Ramadhin, they used six, but were even less effective.

The final innings of this timeless match was a formality, but Walcott showed that the talent was not all on one side as he scored his second century of the match 110, and young Sobers made 64 not out.

Ian Johnson – a late developer

Ian Johnson was, according to Sir Donald Bradman the best Australian off-spinner he had played against. He had a high jumping and looping action and gave the ball a real twist. Bradman said he had a particularly deceptive delivery in which he spun the ball from the palm of his hand. 'I never knew another off-spinner who did it,' said Sir Don.

Johnson learned this delivery from his father, William James Johnson (1884–1941), a slow-bowling wine and spirit merchant who played for North Melbourne and had one game for Victoria against Tasmania in 1924, and became an Australian selector.

On debut for South Melbourne seconds in 1933, a 15-year-old Ian Johnson so impressed the prescient *Sun News Pictorial* columnist 'Sundowner', that he predicted that Bill might one day have the pleasure of picking his son for Australia. Bill Johnson died in 1941 but he did choose him as a member for the Victorian team. Ian made his Victorian debut, also against Tasmania, in 1935.

Ian William Johnson was born in North Melbourne on 8 December 1917, but the family later moved to Middle Park, tying him to the South Melbourne Cricket Club where his team-mates included Lindsay Hassett and Keith Miller.

Johnson joined the RAAF in 1941, when he was a regular in the Victorian team, and flew Beaufighters with 22 Squadron. He married the daughter of Dr Roy Park, fellow Victorian selector with his father, in 1942.

He was chosen for the Ashes series against England in 1946–47. He did not bowl in the first Test (he made 47) but in the second Test was instrumental in winning the match, taking 6/42 in England's first innings.

On the 1948 tour Bradman often relied on Johnson to take wickets in a side that included Miller, Lindwall and Bill Johnston. Johnson was the third highest wicket-taker on the tour with 85 and 18.38. In four Tests, however, he took only seven wickets at 61, dismissing Hutton twice.

Johnson had a good series against South Africa in 1949–50 taking 18 Test wickets at 24 runs. But by the time it came to pick the team to tour England under Lindsay Hassett in 1953, Johnson gave the appearance of being jaded and covered that tour as a journalist.

Ian Johnson – a diplomatic and popular captain and administrator.

When Lindsay Hassett retired both as Victorian and Australian captain after he returned in 1953, Johnson was appointed captain of Victoria.

Hassett had a 'man-to-man' with his former school and team-mate, and told him that if he put his mind to it he could soon become the captain of Australia. As a result Johnson went into training, and at 36 made one of the more meritorious comebacks in Australian cricket history, being appointed Australian captain for the first Test in 1954–55. It was his 29th Test and he was 36 years old.

First up, he had the misfortune to captain Australia against Typhoon Tyson in 1954–55, and again in 1956 on the 'Laker'-made dust bowl pitches.

Despite some indifferent form with the ball, Johnson excelled as a captain, making tremendously popular tours of the West Indies, India and Pakistan .

In 17 Tests as captain, Johnson's sides won seven and lost five, with five draws. In 45 Tests he did 'the double' of 1000 runs and 109 wickets. Johnson played 77 games for Victoria.

After he retired in 1956 he worked as a TV commentator for GTV 9 on the Olympic games, the Davis Cup and the 1957 VFL season. He became Secretary of the Melbourne Cricket Club in May 1957, where he served with distinction and with a kindly disposition toward staff and members for 25 years, in changing sporting times.

FIRST TEST 1954–55 WEST INDIES v AUSTRALIA
Sabina Park, Kingston. March 26, 28, 29, 30, 31, 1955.
Toss: Australia. Australia won by 9 wkts.

AUSTRALIA
CC McDonald st Binns b Valentine .50 (3) / not out .7
AR Morris lbw Valentine .65 / c Gibbs b Weekes .1
RN Harvey b Walcott .133
KR Miller lbw Walcott .147
RR Lindwall lbw Ramadhin .10
PJP Burge c & b Atkinson .14
LV Maddocks (+) b Valentine .1 (1) / not out .12
R Benaud b Walcott .46
RG Archer c Walcott b Holt .24
IW Johnson (c) not out .18
WA Johnston not out .0
EXTRAS (B 3, LB 3, W 1) .7 / .0
TOTAL .9 dec 515 / 1 for 20

FOW 1st Inns: 102 137 361 391 417 430 435 475 506
FOW 2nd Inns: 6

Bowling: *First Innings*: King 28-7-122-0, Worrell 7-2-13-0, Atkinson 23-9-46-1, Ramadhin 46-12-112-1, Valentine 54-20-113-3, Smith 11-0-27-0, Walcott 26-9-50-3, Gibbs 3-1-5-0, Holt 3-0-20-1. *Second Innings*: Weekes 2.2-0-8-1, King 2-0-10-0, Gibbs 1-0-2-0.

WEST INDIES
JK Holt c Benaud b Lindwall .31 / c Maddocks b Benaud .60
GL Gibbs lbw Archer .12 / b Johnston .0
AP Binns (+) c Burge b Archer .0 (7) / lbw Miller .0
EC Weekes run out .19 / c & b Benaud .1
CL Walcott c Benaud b Miller .108 / c Archer b Lindwall .39
FMM Worrell b Johnston .9 (8) / b Archer .9
OG Smith lbw Lindwall .44 (3) / c Harvey b Miller .104
DE Atkinson (c) c Harvey b Miller .1 (6) / c Benaud b Miller .30
FM King c Maddocks b Lindwall .4 / b Lindwall .21
S Ramadhin not out .12 / c Lindwall b Archer .3
AL Valentine b Lindwall .0 / not out .2
EXTRAS (B 14, LB 2, NB 3) .19 / (B 5, NB 1) .6
TOTAL .259 / .275

FOW 1st Inns: 27 27 56 75 101 239 240 243 253 259
FOW 2nd Inns: 20 122 132 209 213 213 239 253 270 275

Bowling: *First Innings*: Lindwall 24-6-61-4, Archer 19-8-39-2, Johnston 23-4-75-1, Benaud 19-7-29-0, Miller 16-5-36-2. *Second Innings*: Lindwall 16.1-3-63-2, Archer 12-3-44-2, Johnston 16-3-54-1, Benaud 23-7-44-2, Miller 28-9-62-3, Harvey 1-0-2-0.

Umpires: P Burke & TA Ewart

SECOND TEST 1954–55 WEST INDIES v AUSTRALIA
Queen's Park Oval, Port-of-Spain. April 11, 12, 13, 14, 15, 16, 1955.
Toss: West Indies. Match Drawn.

WEST INDIES
JK Holt c Johnston b Lindwall .25 / lbw Archer .21
JB Stollmeyer (c) b Lindwall .14 / b Johnson .42
CL Walcott st Langley b Benaud .126 / c Watson b Archer .110
EC Weekes c Johnson b Benaud .139 / not out .87
OG Smith b Benaud .0 / c Langley b Archer .0
GS Sobers c Langley b Lindwall .47 / not out .8
CA McWatt (+) c Benaud b Miller .4
FM King b Lindwall .2
S Ramadhin b Lindwall .0
LS Butler c Johnson b Lindwall .16
AL Valentine not out .4
EXTRAS (B 1, LB 3, NB 1) .5 / (LB 3, NB 2) .5
TOTAL .382 / .4 for 273

FOW 1st Inns: 39 40 282 282 323 355 360 360 361 382
FOW 2nd Inns: 40 103 230 236

Bowling: *First Innings*: Lindwall 24.5-3-95-6, Miller 28-8-96-1, Archer 9-0-42-0, Johnston 7-2-29-0, Johnson 19-5-72-0, Benaud 17-3-43-3. *Second Innings*: Lindwall 17-0-70-0, Miller 11-0-52-0, Archer 8-1-37-3, Johnston 7-0-31-0, Johnson 7-2-26-1, Benaud 12-2-52-0.

AUSTRALIA
CC McDonald c Walcott b Valentine .110
AR Morris c King b Butler .111
RN Harvey lbw King .133
WJ Watson lbw Ramadhin .27
R Benaud c Walcott b Ramadhin .5
KR Miller run out .3
RG Archer c McWatt b Valentine .84
IW Johnson (c) c McWatt b Butler .66
RR Lindwall not out .37
GRA Langley (+) c King b Walcott .9
WA Johnston not out .1
EXTRAS (B 5, LB 6, W 1, NB 2) .14
TOTAL .9 dec 600

FOW 1st Inns: 191 259 328 336 345 439 529 570 594

Bowling: *First Innings*: Butler 40-7-151-2, King 37-7-98-1, Holt 1-1-0-0, Ramadhin 32-8-90-2, Valentine 49-12-133-2, Walcott 19-5-45-1, Sobers 3-1-10-0, Smith 15-1-48-0, Stollmeyer 5-0-11-0.

Umpires: HBC Jordan & EN Lee Kow

THIRD TEST 1954–55 WEST INDIES v AUSTRALIA
Bourda, Georgetown. April 26, 27, 28, 29, 1955.
Toss: West Indies. Australia won by 8 wkts.

WEST INDIES

JK Holt c & b Miller	.12	c Langley b Miller	.6
JB Stollmeyer (c) c Archer b Miller	.16	c & b Johnson	.17
CL Walcott c & b Archer	.8	hit wicket b Lindwall	.73
EC Weekes c Archer b Benaud	.81	c Langley b Johnson	.0
FMM Worrell c Johnson b Archer	.9	hit wicket b Benaud	.56
GS Sobers c Watson b Johnson	.12 (8)	b Johnson	.11
DE Atkinson b Lindwall	.13	st Langley b Johnson	.16
CC Depeiza (+) not out	.16 (6)	st Langley b Johnson	.13
NE Marshall b Benaud	.0	c (S)LE Favell b Johnson	.8
S Ramadhin c Archer b Benaud	.0	st Langley b Johnson	.2
FM King c Langley b Benaud	.13	not out	.0
EXTRAS (B 1, LB 1)	.2	(B 1, LB 2, NB 2)	.5
TOTAL	.182		.207

FOW 1st Inns: 23 30 42 52 83 124 156 156 160 182
FOW 2nd Inns: 25 25 25 150 162 175 186 204 204 207

Bowling: *First Innings:* Lindwall 12-0-44-1, Miller 9-1-33-2, Archer 10-0-46-2, Johnson 9-1-42-1, Benaud 3.5-1-15-4. *Second Innings:* Lindwall 18-1-54-1, Miller 9-3-18-1, Archer 12-3-43-0, Johnson 22.2-10-44-7, Benaud 14-3-43-1.

AUSTRALIA

CC McDonald b Atkinson	.61	b Atkinson	.31
AR Morris c Sobers b Atkinson	.44	c Walcott b Marshall	.38
RN Harvey c Holt b Ramadhin	.38	not out	.41
WJ Watson c & b Ramadhin	.6	not out	.22
KR Miller c Depeiza b Sobers	.33		
R Benaud c(S)OG Smith b Marshall	.68		
RG Archer st Depeiza b Sobers	.2		
IW Johnson (c) c Stollmeyer b Sobers	.0		
RR Lindwall b Atkinson	.2		
GRA Langley (+) not out	.1		
WA Johnston			
EXTRAS (LB 2)	.2	(NB 1)	.1
TOTAL	.9 dec 257		.2 for 133

FOW 1st Inns: 71 135 147 161 215 231 231 238 257
FOW 2nd Inns: 70 70

Bowling: *First Innings:* King 12-1-37-0, Worrell 9-2-17-0, Ramadhin 26-9-55-2, Atkinson 37-13-85-3, Marshall 33.3-16-40-1, Stollmeyer 1-0-1-0, Sobers 16-10-20-3. *Second Innings:* King 3-0-10-0, Worrell 7-2-20-0, Ramadhin 9-1-29-0, Atkinson 15.5-5-32-1, Marshall 13-6-22-1, Sobers 11-4-19-0.

Umpires: ES Gillette & EN Lee Kow

FIFTH TEST 1954–55 WEST INDIES v AUSTRALIA
Sabina Park, Kingston. June 11, 13, 14, 15, 16, 17, 1955.
Toss: West Indies. Australia won by an innings & 82 runs.

WEST INDIES

JK Holt c Langley b Miller	.4	c Langley b Benaud	.21
HA Furlonge c Benaud b Lindwall	.4	c (S)AK Davidson b Miller	.28
CL Walcott c Langley b Miller	.155 (4)	c Langley b Lindwall	.110
EC Weekes b Benaud	.56 (9)	not out	.36
FMM Worrell c Langley b Lindwall	.61 (7)	b Johnson	.12
OG Smith c Langley b Miller	.29	c & b Benaud	.16
GS Sobers not out	.35 (5)	c Favell b Lindwall	.64
DE Atkinson (c) run out	.8	c Langley b Archer	.4
CC Depeiza (+) c Langley b Miller	.0 (3)	b Miller	.7
FM King b Miller	.0	c Archer b Johnson	.6
DT Dewdney b Miller	.2	lbw Benaud	.0
EXTRAS (LB 2, W 1)	.3	(B 8, LB 6, W 1)	.15
TOTAL	.357		.319

FOW 1st Inns: 5 13 95 204 268 327 341 347 347 357
FOW 2nd Inns: 47 60 65 244 244 268 273 283 289 319

Bowling: *First Innings:* Lindwall 12-2-64-2, Miller 25.2-3-107-6, Archer 11-1-39-0, Benaud 24-5-75-1, Johnson 22-7-69-0. *Second Innings:* Lindwall 19-6-51-2, Miller 19-3-58-2, Archer 27-6-73-1, Benaud 29.5-10-76-3, Johnson 23-10-46-2.

AUSTRALIA

CC McDonald b Worrell	.127
LE Favell c Weekes b King	.0
AR Morris lbw Dewdney	.7
RN Harvey c Atkinson b Smith	.204
KR Miller c Worrell b Atkinson	.109
RG Archer c Depeiza b Sobers	.128
RR Lindwall c Depeiza b King	.10
R Benaud c Worrell b Smith	.121
IW Johnson (c) not out	.27
GRA Langley (+)	
WA Johnston	
EXTRAS (B 8, LB 7, W 9, NB 1)	.25
TOTAL	.8 dec 758

FOW 1st Inns: 0 7 302 373 593 597 621 758

Bowling: *First Innings:* Dewdney 24-4-115-1, King 31-1-126-2, Atkinson 55-20-132-1, Smith 52.4-17-145-2, Worrell 45-10-116-1, Sobers 38-12-99-1.

Umpires: P Burke & TA Ewart

FOURTH TEST 1954–55 WEST INDIES v AUSTRALIA
Kensington Oval, Bridgetown. May 14, 16, 17, 18, 19, 20, 1955.
Toss: Australia. Match Drawn.

AUSTRALIA

CC McDonald run out	.46	b Smith	.17
LE Favell c Weekes b Atkinson	.72	run out	.53
RN Harvey c Smith b Worrell	.74	c Valentine b Smith	.27
WJ Watson c Depeiza b Dewdney	.30	b Atkinson	.0
KR Miller c Depeiza b Dewdney	.137	lbw Atkinson	.10
R Benaud c Walcott b Dewdney	.1	b Sobers	.5
RG Archer b Worrell	.98	lbw Atkinson	.28
RR Lindwall c Valentine b Atkinson	.118 (9)	lbw Atkinson	.10
IW Johnson (c) b Dewdney	.23 (8)	c Holt b Smith	.57
GRA Langley (+) b Sobers	.53	not out	.28
JC Hill not out	.8	c Weekes b Atkinson	.1
EXTRAS (B 1, LB 2, W 4, NB 1)	.8	(B 9, LB 4)	.13
TOTAL	.668		.249

FOW 1st Inns: 108 126 226 226 233 439 483 562 623 668
FOW 2nd Inns: 71 72 73 87 107 119 151 177 241 249

Bowling: *First Innings:* Worrell 40-7-120-2, Dewdney 33-5-125-4, Walcott 26-10-57-0, Valentine 31-9-87-0, Ramadhin 24-3-84-0, Atkinson 48-14-108-2, Smith 22-8-49-0, Sobers 11.5-6-30-1. *Second Innings:* Worrell 7-0-25-0, Dewdney 10-4-23-0, Valentine 6-1-16-0, Ramadhin 2-0-10-0, Atkinson 36.2-16-56-5, Smith 34-12-71-3, Sobers 14-3-35-1.

WEST INDIES

JK Holt b Lindwall	.22	lbw Hill	.49
GS Sobers c Hill b Johnson	.43	lbw Archer	.11
CL Walcott c Langley b Benaud	.15	b Benaud	.83
EC Weekes c Langley b Miller	.44	run out	.6
FMM Worrell run out	.16	c Archer b Miller	.34
OG Smith c Langley b Miller	.2	b Lindwall	.11
DE Atkinson (c) c Archer b Johnson	.219	not out	.20
CC Depeiza (+) b Benaud	.122	not out	.11
S Ramadhin c & b Benaud	.10		
DT Dewdney b Johnson	.0		
AL Valentine not out	.2		
EXTRAS (B 5, LB 4, W 2, NB 4)	.15	(B 6, LB 2, W 1)	.9
TOTAL	.510		.6 for 234

FOW 1st Inns: 52 69 105 142 143 147 494 504 504 510
FOW 2nd Inns: 38 67 81 154 193 207

Bowling: *First Innings:* Lindwall 25-3-96-1, Miller 22-2-113-2, Archer 15-4-44-0, Johnson 35-13-77-3, Hill 24-9-71-0, Benaud 31.1-6-73-3, Harvey 4-0-16-0, Watson 1-0-5-0. *Second Innings:* Lindwall 8-1-39-1, Miller 21-3-66-1, Archer 7-1-11-1, Johnson 14-4-30-0, Hill 11-2-44-1, Benaud 11-3-35-1.

Umpires: HBC Jordan & EN Lee Kow

Australian Averages

1954–55 WEST INDIES v AUSTRALIA

AUSTRALIA	M	Inn	NO	Runs	H.S	Avrge	Ct	St	Overs	Mds	Runs	Wkt	Avrge
Archer, RG	5	6	-	364	128	60.67	8	-	130.0	27	418	11	38.00
Benaud, R	5	6	-	246	121	41.00	8	-	184.5	47	485	18	26.94
Burge, PJP	1	1	-	14	14	14.00	1	-	-	-	-	-	-
Favell, LE	2	3	-	125	72	41.67	1	-	-	-	-	-	-
Harvey, RN	5	7	1	650	204	108.33	2	-	5.0	-	18	-	-
Hill, JC	1	2	1	9	8*	9.00	1	-	35.0	11	115	1	115.00
Johnson, IW	5	6	2	191	66	47.75	4	-	151.2	52	406	14	29.00
Johnston, WA	4	2	2	1	1*	-	1	-	53.0	9	189	2	94.50
Langley, GRA	4	4	2	91	53	45.50	16	4	-	-	-	-	-
Lindwall, RR	5	6	1	187	118	37.40	1	-	176.0	25	637	20	31.85
Maddocks, LV	1	2	1	13	12*	13.00	2	-	-	-	-	-	-
McDonald, CC	5	8	1	449	127	64.14	-	-	-	-	-	-	-
Miller, KR	5	6	-	439	147	73.17	1	-	188.2	37	641	20	32.05
Morris, AR	4	6	-	266	111	44.33	-	-	-	-	-	-	-
Watson, WJ	3	5	1	85	30	21.25	2	-	1.0	-	5	-	-

West Indian Averages

1954–55 WEST INDIES v AUSTRALIA

WEST INDIES	M	Inn	NO	Runs	H.S	Avrge	Ct	St	Overs	Mds	Runs	Wkt	Avrge
Atkinson, DE	4	8	1	311	219	44.43	2	-	215.1	77	459	13	35.31
Binns, AP	1	2	-	0	0	0.00	-	1	-	-	-	-	-
Butler, LS	1	1	-	16	16	16.00	-	-	40.0	7	151	2	75.50
Depeiza, CC	3	6	2	169	122	42.25	5	1	-	-	-	-	-
Dewdney, DT	2	3	-	2	2	0.67	-	-	67.0	13	263	5	52.60
Furlonge, HA	1	2	-	32	28	16.00	-	-	-	-	-	-	-
Gibbs, GL	1	2	-	12	12	6.00	1	-	4.0	1	7	-	-
Holt, JK	5	10	-	251	60	25.10	2	-	4.0	1	20	1	20.00
King, FM	4	7	1	46	21	7.67	-	-	113.0	16	403	3	134.33
Marshall, NE	1	2	-	8	8	4.00	-	-	46.3	22	62	2	31.00
McWatt, CA	1	1	-	4	4	4.00	2	-	-	-	-	-	-
Ramadhin, S	4	6	1	27	12*	5.40	-	-	139.0	33	380	5	76.00
Smith, OG	4	8	-	206	104	25.75	1	-	134.4	38	340	5	68.00
Sobers, GS	5	8	2	231	64	38.50	1	-	93.5	36	213	6	35.50
Stollmeyer, JB	2	4	-	89	42	22.25	1	-	6.0	-	12	-	-
Valentine, AL	3	4	3	8	4*	8.00	2	-	140.0	42	349	5	69.80
Walcott, CL	5	10	-	827	155	82.70	5	-	71.0	24	152	4	38.00
Weekes, EC	5	10	-	469	139	58.63	3	-	2.2	-	8	1	8.00
Worrell, FMM	4	8	2	206	61	25.75	2	-	115.0	23	311	3	103.67

First subcontinent Tests approved

Brothers in arms. Ray, Mervyn and Neil Harvey are at the forefront for Victoria.

Sydney, Sep. 15. The influence of Sir Donald Bradman on the Australian Board of Control has been felt in the speedy adoption of a plan for the Australian team to play Test matches in India and Pakistan after its 1956 tour of England.

The matter of the tour and the first Test appearances of an Australian team on the subcontinent gained a head of steam at the Imperial Cricket Conference held at Lord's in July. The glaring absence of any Australian team in India or Pakistan, apart from the unofficial 1935 tour under Jack Ryder, gave rise to informal discussion. The Indian and Pakistan Boards soon sent letters of requests for the Tests. Sir Donald broke through the usual concern over the 'difficulties' of such tours with a complete outline of dates and places, luggage control, travel and financial implications. He was backed up by Board Secretary Jack Ledward, who had visited the Marylebone Cricket Club during the year and attended the ICC. Their thoroughness won the day.

Testimonial is a Test trial match

Sydney, Jan. 15. The celebration of the careers of Johnny Taylor and Arthur Mailey in a testimonial match has had an underlying seriousness, as the Test selectors have used it as a trial match for contenders for the tour of England.

While there might be some concern over the bowling, there were batting riches on display, with centuries from Jim Burke (192), Ken Mackay (143), Richie Benaud (101) and John Rutherford (113). Rutherford is likely to be the first tourist from WA. Neil Harvey, a tour certainty, made 96.

Mailey and Taylor came out in a lunch break in their coats and ties, and Mailey clean bowled Taylor with his only ball. 'I should have always bowled with my coat on', said the great spinner.

Shield win to NSW

Sydney, March 15. Keith Miller's all powerful NSW team has won the Sheffield Shield for the third season in a row. Victoria has been the only State to put pressure on the New South Welshmen, but Miller, Richie Benaud, Pat Crawford and Alan Davidson have had outstanding seasons for NSW, and so have Victoria's stalwarts Ian Johnson, Colin McDonald and Neil Harvey.

The remarkable match of the season belonged to Miller. Against South Australia in November he recorded his best-ever figures in Shield cricket, taking an astonishing 7/12.

Scorer Bill given £200 for trouble

Sydney, Sep. 15. Bill Ferguson has been voted a gift of £200 from the Board of Control in recognition of 50 years as scorer/baggage-man for Australian teams.

'Fergie' has had a lot of travel, mostly by sea, estimated at about 600,000 miles. He has scored more than 200 Test matches, not only for Australia, but for England, South Africa and the West Indies as well.

He has, apart from his official duties as scorer and baggage handler for his teams, devoted himself to the convenience of the champions of the game – never with undue deference and always with a smile. He has shaken hands with each of the last five monarchs of England.

He got the job in a peculiar way, in the dentist's chair of Monty Noble in 1905. The young insurance clerk knew that a scorer's job was going, and he asked Noble to put in a word for him. He received £2 a week for his trouble, but he had found his vocation. (He later sent along his sister as a patient, inadvertently becoming the agent of a long and happy marriage.)

His days on tour are long and responsible – laundry, herding the team to pack and be on time, organising transport and baggage, dealing with letters and piles of books for autograph hunters – and, of course, scoring. Apart from his scorebooks he has invented the 'wheel', which shows where batsmen have taken their runs.

'Fergie' has never had much money. A baseball match between South African and Australian cricketers in 1950 raised £1000, and the West Indies arranged another match in Sydney which brought in £600.

But, as he says, it has been a labour of love.

The umpire who confessed he wasn't looking.

Miller and Benaud put Australia ahead

Lord's, June 26. Keith Miller has now reached the warhorse stage of his cricketing life, but the whiff of battle against 'the old enemy' has stirred him to produce his best Test bowling performance.

With the Australian attack for the second Test at Lord's reduced by an early injury to frontline bowler Pat Crawford, Miller was left to carry the attack with medium pacer Ron Archer. They had already lost the preferred spearhead in Alan Davidson, who fell while running in to bowl in the drawn first Test. Crawford, seen by many as the logical successor to Ray Lindwall, had delivered only 29 balls when he limped off the field with a pulled thigh muscle.

A challenge has always brought out the best in Miller, who has been criticised for periods of disinterest on the field.

But first Australia was held together by the opening partnership of 137 by Colin McDonald and Jim Burke, the highest opening stand since 1930. Their effort became vital as the rest succumbed for a total of 285.

But then Miller got his momentum going, and, using his short run, he crashed through five

Neil Harvey's leg glance off Trueman goes no further than into the right hand of Trevor Bailey. He had made 10, after a duck in the first innings.

England bats for 72 runs, as they limped to 171.

Despite Fred Trueman's 5/90 in Australia's second innings, Australia got to 257 and a comfortable lead, with Richie Benaud holding the bottom order together with a spirited 97. Benaud was beginning to show the benefit of his tour experiences, bowling well in support of Miller and taking a brilliant

one-handed catch to dismiss Cowdrey in the first innings.

The last innings completed the rout, with Miller taking 5/80 and Ron Archer 4/71, as England could score only 186. Captain Peter May was the only England batsman to perform creditably throughout the Test, with 63 and 53.

Australian 'keeper Gil Langley claimed a Test-record nine victims.

Surrey breaks a 44-year drought

London, May 18. In an ominous portent Surrey has beaten Australia, the first County to do so in 44 years.

The Australian batsmen were bamboozled by the spin of Jim Laker and Tony Lock.

Laker took 10 wickets for 88 in Australia's first innings 220. It was the first time an English bowler had taken 10 wickets against Australia since another Surrey player, Edward Barrett, did so in 1878. The ultimate destroyer was Lock, who took 7/49 in Australia's miserable second innings of 107 runs.

Surrey had only to make 20 runs to clinch the historic victory.

The pitch was a little conducive to spin, but was not a horror stretch. Ian Johnson bowled on it without great effect. The difference may be that his spinners loop and bounce, while the Englishmen dig them in from a lower trajectory.

The loss follows some promising play by the Australians. Richie Benaud made 160 against Worcester, and then Keith Miller had a monumental innings of 281 at Leicester, while Colin McDonald made 195. Neil Harvey made 225 against an MCC team.

A classic off-drive from the batting star of the second Test, Richie Benaud.

Washbrook back to bolster England

Ron Archer: several quick wickets.

Leeds, July 17. At the age of 41, England selector Cyril Washbrook had the temerity to put his name forward for England's third Test team, and was roundly criticised by the English press for doing so. When he joined Peter May at the crease England was 3/17 and Ron Archer had all three wickets. When May left, having made 101, England was 4/204. Washbrook went on to 98 and England to a first innings total of 325.

The deteriorating pitch had the Australians helpless against the spin of Jim Laker and Tony Lock, who garnered nine wickets between them in each innings as Australia made 143 and 140. Only McDonald, Miller and Harvey got past 30.

Spinners wanted but not invited

Manchester, July 31. It is too late to think of the talented Australian spinners languishing in the British counties when they might have helped their Test team.

It has been long apparent that this has been a spinners' series, but Ian Johnson's looping off-breaks and Richie Benaud leg-breaks have not been as effective as the flatter spinners of the English pair, Jim Laker and Tony Lock.

But there are two others in the wings, Bruce Dooland of South Australia and Victoria's George Tribe, who might have made the difference. Leg-spinner Dooland has had 8/20 for Notts against Worcestershire this season and Tribe's darting left-arm spinners are in the same mould as those of Tony Lock.

Australia spun out by Laker

Manchester, July 31. You could call the pitch at Old Trafford a shocker, and many did. You could rail against groundsmen preparing a pitch specifically to suit the home side, and many did. They were mostly in the Australian dressing room and the press contingent.

You could also call the fourth Test a triumph for English cricket, and Jim Laker the bowler of the century. Many did, and they were all in the England dressing room or in the English media army.

This was undoubtedly Laker's match, and the finest bowling analysis in first class cricket history. His 19/90 was the most wickets taken, and included the only instance of a bowler taking 10 wickets in a Test innings. It was also the only instance of two first class 10 wicket hauls in a season, as Laker had 10/88 in the Australia v Surrey match.

His 39 wickets for the Test series so far has already equalled Alec Bedser's record of 39 for England v Australia Tests, with a game to play.

The pitch was looking suspicious enough on day one, but England made a fine start with the first three batsmen contributing 297 between them, but it began to break up as they got to the total of 459. The groundsman sweeping the pitch at lunchtime on the first day raised clouds of dust, and by the time the Australians were in it was a cracked and flaking dustbowl.

This was a paradise for Laker, who is a good spinner at the best of times and lethal on anything damp, drying or breaking up.

McDonald and Burke, who are turning into a good combination, gave resistance to the tune of 48 runs, but then it was a procession, with four ducks, to 84 all out. Laker had 9/37 and, amazingly, his equally adept spinning partner Tony Lock had only one wicket.

But the best was yet to come for England. Burke and McDonald tried to hold out again, but McDonald retired with a jarred knee at 28, and the floodgates were open.

As Laker took wicket after wicket with his subtly flighted off-spinners, McDonald returned and fought gamely for 89 runs as everything fell around him. Although he has never been a stylist, he is a master of concentration and the stubborn, dead bat. His innings lasted 337 minutes, and was one of the finest seen in Tests in the defence of a lost cause.

England's triumph hurt in Australia, as Sam Wells' cartoon in the Age *demonstrates.*

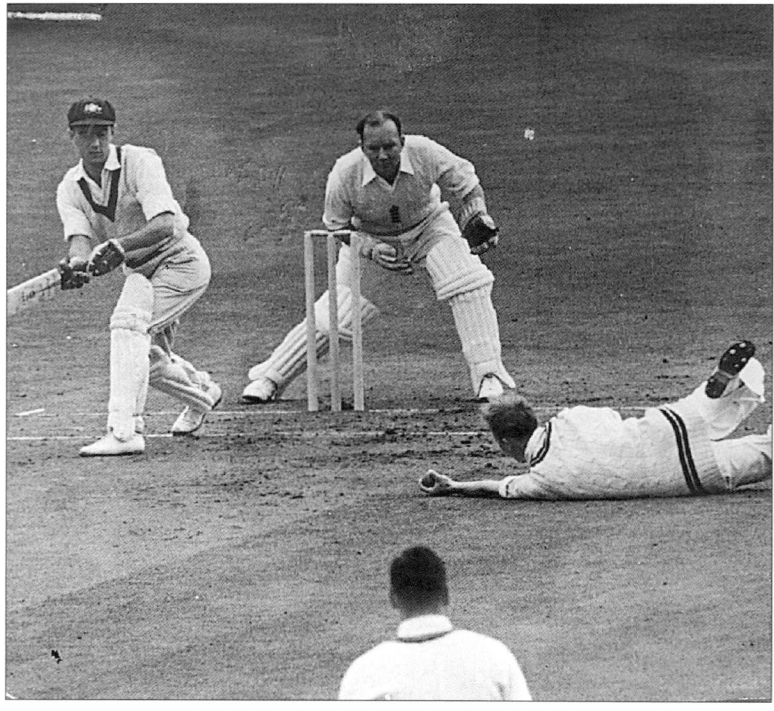

Not a good tour. Ian Craig is caught Lock, bowled Laker in the fifth Test.

One-Test Wonders

Victorian batsman Roy Park.

Hans Ebeling: had endeavour.

Colin Guest: brief understudy.

Les Joslin: boy wonder.

How does it feel? You are selected for Australia and go through days of back slapping excitement as the Test approaches. Your name is in the papers and your selection is analysed in the newspapers, and in bar rooms and living rooms around the country. The future beckons.

You walk to the wicket, a shaky legged mixture of fear and determination, and take block. The bowler starts his run, your concentration narrows and crash, you are bowled, first ball.

You walk back, head bowed. Commiserations are offered, but you grow ever more lonely as your team runs up 499.

There is no second innings, and no more Tests for you. Two other players score their maiden centuries. If only you had met that first ball with the bat, you might have got one too.

This happened to Roy Park in the 1920–21 season in front of his home-town crowd – the sort of crowd that cheered his 58 Victorian Football League games with University and Melbourne, and watched him make 586 runs in the previous cricket season at an average of 83.71. He was everything exemplary in a sportsman, courageous and talented and with brains to boot, having combined a medical degree with sport.

If only, too, he had not been up with a patient half the night and had a good night's sleep. The 'if onlys' pile up for the One-Test Wonders.

They all have two things in common – they had one chance, and that they were good enough to play for Australia. But cricket, particularly for a batsman, is the cruellest of games.

The bowler has his own form of purgatory. Colin Guest, for example, was one of those striving to fill the glaring holes in the Australian line-up after the Lindwall and Miller era was well over. He looked right – tall, broad shouldered and with a beautiful, free-flowing action that had the ball zipping off the pitch, a natural outswinger, but with an in-dipper in the armoury.

Guest had taken 7/95 and 3/39 against Western Australia, 5/36, again against WA and 6/100 against Queensland. He was ripe, and became third paceman to Alan Davidson and Graham McKenzie in the third Test at the SCG in 1962.

He had the same number of overs as McKenzie in the first innings and a better analysis – 0/51 against 'Garth's' 0/52. In the next innings he got just two overs as 'Davo' and Garth ripped into England. Just a couple of wickets might have made the difference.

There are 40 men in the narrow band of One-Test Wonders, just as there are a group of '12th men – no Tests', 'toured but no Tests', 'two Tests and out'. What the one-Test men would have given for that second Test – it only needs a good game with good fortune, to get that third, fourth and fifth chance.

But, in days of less intensity, some of the early men just came and went due more to circumstances than cricket.

Frank Allen was known as 'the bowler of the century'. He declined to play in the first of all Tests to go to an agricultural show, but appeared for his one Test in 1879, where he took 4/80.

Dashing Arthur Coningham had the credentials, and had played one Test in Melbourne, but he was so volatile off and on the field and subject to long disappearances, that he was ignored.

There was only one Test in England in 1880 and Tom Groube played in it, making 11 and 0. Back in Australia his legal practice took precedence over cricket and he played in only two first class games, but he racked up phenomenal scores for East Melbourne.

Lucky were those of the One-Test list who achieved the ultimate schoolboy dream of being chosen for the tour. At least there were, for them, always chances to force their way into the touring side, and being a part of the tour group carried its own honour.

Men like Les Joslin, Ian Callen and Jack Wilson may only have got one Test, but they got a lot of memories on the way.

Les Joslin burst onto the Shield scene in 1967–68 and seemed assured of success with his brilliant and aggressive left hand batting. He made it to the fifth Test against India, scoring 7 and 2, and into the tour party to England in 1968.

Ian Callen started in Sheffield Shield cricket with 25 wickets for Victoria, and took six wickets in his first test against India in 1977–78. On the tour of the Caribbean which followed he took only 11 wickets, and did not get a Test. A back injury ended his first class career.

Genial Jack Wilson from South Australia was a surprise selection for England in 1956, when it was thought his left-arm googlies might worry the Englishmen. They didn't, although he had match figures of 12/61 against Gloucester. He languished in many a dressing room, and got his only Test on the way

home, against India at Bombay. He took 1/64.

The meteors, like Roy Park, had their one Test at home and were immediately consigned to cricket history.

Merv Harvey got his Test chance a year before his illustrious brother Neil, 10 years younger. He opened the batting in the fourth Test against England in 1946–47, scoring 12 and 31, but figuring in a partnership of 113 with Arthur Morris. Surely enough for another chance? Sorry.

Ken Eastwood, of Footscray and Victoria, was another with plenty of experience, when he broke into Test cricket. At the age of 35 he was picked for the seventh, and deciding, Test against England in 1970–71. He had been scoring prolifically at State level, and was suddenly seen as a better bet than Bill Lawry. Making 5 and 0 he did nothing but hasten Lawry's retirement. And England won.

Perhaps the most important of the One-Test Wonders is Hans Ebeling, a Victorian bowler who toured England in 1934, and playing in the fifth Test, taking three wickets in the first innings (Walter Hammond, Gubby Allan and Hedley Verity) and making 41 in the second innings, before playing second fiddle to the spinners Grimmett and O'Reilly. Ebeling captained Victoria and had a 57-year association with the Melbourne Cricket Club, culminating in the Presidency.

The Centenary Test was Ebeling's brainchild, and he worked tirelessly for the success of one of the greatest games of cricket and the great reunion of past players of England and Australia.

Too old, say the critics

London, July 27. There is no doubt among the Australian writers watching the Test series that Australia was not good enough.

The general feeling is that there are too many veterans in the Australian side, and that it's time for a changing of the guard.

Percy Millard, for the Melbourne *Herald* says Ian Johnson, Keith Miller, Ray Lindwall and Gil Langley have served Australia well, but should not be considered for the South African tour in 1957–58.

Instead, a young team should be built around Richie Benaud as captain, with the only tourists remaining being Colin McDonald, Jim Burke, Neil Harvey, Ian Craig, Ron Archer, Alan Davidson, Len Maddocks, and possibly Peter Burge.

He says that John Rutherford, Ken Mackay, Pat Crawford and Jack Wilson are not up to Test standard.

He cites the youth policy of the South African team of 1952–53, which brought together enthusiasm, fitness and teamwork.

Harvey and Lindwall were cited as the great disappointments of the 1956 tour.

Harvey, with a Test batting average of 61, managed to average only 22 in this series to see his average drop to 56. He has played well in England before, and it seems he must re-examine his technique.

Lindwall struggled with injury and managed only seven wickets in the four Tests he played. He is clearly in the twilight of an illustrious career.

The successes were openers McDonald and Burke, who made many starts, but saw their work frit-

Australian captain Ian Johnson and veteran all-rounder Keith Miller at Buckingham Palace to receive the MBE.

tered away, and Keith Miller, who battled injury to be the most successful bowler and a useful batsman.

Bill O'Reilly, for the *Sydney Morning Herald*, said that batting had been far below that standard Englishmen have come to expect from visiting Australian sides.

O'Reilly said no Australian made a Test century, with the highest score being Richie Benaud's 97 in the second Test.

Conceding that Ian Johnson and Richie Benaud were not effective as bowlers, O'Reilly insists that Australia must go all out for spin bowling before the next tour to England.

He said it was pitiable to watch Johnson try to get Alan Davidson and Ron Archer to adapt their bowling to the spinning wickets.

Phone bonanza

Leeds, July 17. The Test tour has proved a bonanza for the British Post Office, which received 380,000 calls for scores of the Leeds Test. Multiply this by five Tests, and there's a bit of revenue to be had from this score service.

The British office worker, imprisoned and too timorous to bring a portable radio to work, can look industrious under the eyes of the management as he sneaks a phone call for the cricket scores.

In Australia it can all be done for the cost of a radio licence, and listeners have the option of the crackly version from the ABC, via short wave, or the various commercial variety shows, which fill the long night with scores, song, commentary and inanity.

Segregation policy

London, April 1. The manager of the Australian team, Bill Dowling, has taken the strict 'no wives on tour' policy of the Australian Board of Control to the letter. He has caused some heartache in his efforts to keep Pat Crawford away from his wife on the way to England.

Mrs Crawford, ill and pregnant, was inadvertently booked to England on the same ship as the team and had travelled from Melbourne to Perth.

When Dowling found that she was on board the ship he told Crawford that his tour contract could be cancelled.

Mrs Crawford disembarked to stay in a hotel for a week and await the next ship.

FIRST TEST 1956 ENGLAND v AUSTRALIA
Trent Bridge, Nottingham. June 7, 8 (no play), 9, 11, 12, 1956.
Toss: England. Match Drawn.

ENGLAND

PE Richardson c Langley b Miller	81	c Langley b Archer	73
MC Cowdrey c Miller b Davidson	25	c Langley b Miller	81
TW Graveney c Archer b Johnson	8 (4)	not out	10
PBH May (c) c Langley b Miller	73		
W Watson lbw Archer	0 (3)	c Langley b Miller	8
TE Bailey c Miller b Archer	14		
TG Evans (+) c Langley b Miller	0 (5)	not out	8
JC Laker not out	9		
GAR Lock lbw Miller	4		
R Appleyard not out	1		
AE Moss			
EXTRAS (B 5, LB 1)	6	(B 4, LB 1, W 2, NB 1)	8
TOTAL	8 dec 217		3 dec 188

FOW 1st Inns: 53 72 180 181 201 203 213 214
FOW 2nd Inns: 151 163 178

Bowling: *First Innings*: Lindwall 15-4-43-0, Miller 33-5-69-4, Davidson 9.4-1-22-1, Archer 31-10-51-2, Johnson 14-7-26-1, Burke 1-1-0-0. *Second Innings*: Miller 19-2-58-2, Archer 9-0-46-1, Johnson 12-2-29-0, Burke 3-1-6-0, Benaud 18-4-41-0.

AUSTRALIA

CC McDonald lbw Lock	1	c Lock b Laker	6
JW Burke c Lock b Laker	11	not out	58
RN Harvey lbw Lock	64	b Lock	3
PJP Burge c(S)JM Parks b Lock	7 (5)	not out	35
KR Miller lbw Laker	0 (4)	lbw Laker	4
RG Archer c Lock b Appleyard	33		
R Benaud b Appleyard	17		
IW Johnson (c) c Bailey b Laker	12		
RR Lindwall c Bailey b Laker	0		
GRA Langley (+) not out	0		
AK Davidson			
EXTRAS (LB 3)	3	(B 10, LB 3, NB 1)	14
TOTAL	9 dec 148		3 for 120

FOW 1st Inns: 10 12 33 36 90 110 148 148 148
FOW 2nd Inns: 13 18 41

Bowling: *First Innings*: Moss 4-3-1-0, Bailey 3-1-8-0, Laker 29.1-11-58-4, Lock 36-16-61-3, Appleyard 11-4-17-2. *Second Innings*: Bailey 9-3-16-0, Laker 30-19-29-2, Lock 22-11-23-1, Appleyard 19-6-32-0, Graveney 6-3-6-0.

Umpires: TJ Bartley & JS Buller

SECOND TEST 1956 ENGLAND v AUSTRALIA
Lord's Cricket Ground, London. June 21, 22, 23, 25, 26, 1956.
Toss: Australia. Australia won by 185 runs.

AUSTRALIA

CC McDonald c Trueman b Bailey	78	c Cowdrey b Bailey	26
JW Burke st Evans b Laker	65	c Graveney b Trueman	16
RN Harvey c Evans b Bailey	0	c Bailey b Trueman	10
PJP Burge b Statham	21	b Trueman	14
KR Miller b Trueman	28 (7)	c Evans b Trueman	30
KD Mackay c Bailey b Laker	38 (5)	c Evans b Statham	31
RG Archer b Wardle	28 (6)	c Evans b Bailey	1
R Benaud b Statham	5	c Evans b Trueman	97
IW Johnson (c) c Evans b Trueman	6	lbw Bailey	17
GRA Langley (+) c Bailey b Laker	14	not out	7
WPA Crawford not out	0	lbw Bailey	0
EXTRAS (LB 2)	2	(B 2, LB 2, NB 4)	8
TOTAL	285		257

FOW 1st Inns: 137 137 151 185 196 249 255 265 285 285
FOW 2nd Inns: 36 47 69 70 79 112 229 243 257 257

Bowling: *First Innings*: Statham 35-9-70-2, Trueman 28-6-54-2, Bailey 34-12-72-2, Laker 29.1-10-47-3, Wardle 20-7-40-1. *Second Innings*: Statham 26-5-59-1, Trueman 28-2-90-5, Bailey 24.5-8-64-4, Laker 7-3-17-0, Wardle 7-2-19-0.

ENGLAND

PE Richardson c Langley b Miller	9	c Langley b Archer	21
MC Cowdrey c Benaud b Mackay	23	lbw Benaud	27
TW Graveney b Miller	5	c Langley b Miller	18
PBH May (c) b Benaud	63 (5)	c Langley b Miller	53
W Watson c Benaud b Miller	6 (4)	b Miller	18
TE Bailey b Miller	32	c Harvey b Archer	18
TG Evans (+) st Langley b Benaud	0	c Langley b Miller	20
JC Laker b Archer	12	c Langley b Archer	4
JH Wardle c Langley b Archer	0	b Miller	0
FS Trueman c Langley b Miller	7	b Archer	2
JB Statham not out	0	not out	0
EXTRAS (LB 14)	14	(LB 5)	5
TOTAL	171		186

FOW 1st Inns: 22 32 60 87 128 128 161 161 170 171
FOW 2nd Inns: 35 59 89 91 142 175 180 184 184 186

Bowling: *First Innings*: Miller 34.1-9-72-5, Crawford 4.5-2-4-0, Archer 23-9-47-2, Mackay 11-3-15-1, Benaud 9-2-19-2. *Second Innings*: Miller 36-12-80-5, Archer 31.2-8-71-4, Benaud 28-14-27-1, Johnson 4-2-3-0.

Umpires: D Davies & FS Lee

THIRD TEST 1956 ENGLAND v AUSTRALIA
Headingley, Leeds. July 12, 13, 14 (no play), 16, 17, 1956.
Toss: England. England won by an innings & 42 runs.

ENGLAND
PE Richardson c Maddocks b Archer 5
MC Cowdrey c Maddocks b Archer 0
ASM Oakman b Archer 4
PBH May (c) c Lindwall b Johnson 101
C Washbrook lbw Benaud 98
GAR Lock c Miller b Benaud 21
DJ Insole c Mackay b Benaud 5
TE Bailey not out 33
TG Evans (+) b Lindwall 40
JC Laker b Lindwall 5
FS Trueman c & b Lindwall 0
     EXTRAS (B 4, LB 9) 13
TOTAL 325

FOW 1st Inns: 2 8 17 204 226 243 248 301 321 325

Bowling: *First Innings*: Lindwall 33.4-11-67-3, Archer 50-24-68-3, Mackay 13-3-29-0, Benaud 42-9-89-3, Johnson 29-8-59-1.

AUSTRALIA
CC McDonald c Evans b Trueman 2   b Trueman 6
JW Burke lbw Lock 41   b Laker 16
RN Harvey c Trueman b Lock 11   c & b Lock 69
PJP Burge lbw Laker ....2 (5)   lbw Laker 5
KD Mackay c Bailey b Laker .....2 (8)   b Laker 2
KR Miller b Laker ....41 (4)   c Trueman b Laker 26
RG Archer b Laker ....4 (9)   c Washbrook b Lock 1
R Benaud c Oakman b Laker ......30 (6)   b Lock 1
LV Maddocks (+) c Trueman b Lock ..0 (10) lbw Lock 0
IW Johnson (c) c Richardson b Lock .0 (7)   c Oakman b Laker 3
RR Lindwall not out 0   not out 0
     EXTRAS (B 4, LB 6) 10   (B 7, LB 4) 11
TOTAL 143 140

FOW 1st Inns: 2 40 59 59 63 69 142 143 143 143
FOW 2nd Inns: 10 45 108 120 128 136 138 140 140 140

Bowling: *First Innings*: Trueman 8-2-19-1, Bailey 7-2-15-0, Laker 29-10-58-5, Lock 27.1-11-41-4.
Second Innings: Trueman 11-3-21-1, Bailey 7-2-13-0, Laker 41.3-21-55-6, Lock 40-23-40-3.

Umpires: JS Buller & D Davies

FOURTH TEST 1956 ENGLAND v AUSTRALIA
Old Trafford, Manchester. July 26, 27, 28, 30, 31, 1956.
Toss: England. England won by an innings & 170 runs.

ENGLAND
PE Richardson c Maddocks b Benaud 104
MC Cowdrey c Maddocks b Lindwall 80
DS Sheppard b Archer 113
PBH May (c) c Archer b Benaud 43
TE Bailey b Johnson 20
C Washbrook lbw Johnson 6
ASM Oakman c Archer b Johnson 10
TG Evans (+) st Maddocks b Johnson 47
JC Laker run out 3
GAR Lock not out 25
JB Statham c Maddocks b Lindwall 0
     EXTRAS (B 2, LB 5, W 1) 8
TOTAL 459

FOW 1st Inns: 174 195 288 321 327 339 401 417 458 459

Bowling: *First Innings*: Lindwall 21.3-6-63-2, Miller 21-6-41-0, Archer 22-6-73-1, Johnson 47-10-151-4, Benaud 47-17-123-2.

AUSTRALIA
CC McDonald c Lock b Laker 32   c Oakman b Laker 89
JW Burke c Cowdrey b Lock 22   c Lock b Laker 33
RN Harvey b Laker 0   c Cowdrey b Laker 0
ID Craig lbw Laker 8   lbw Laker 38
KR Miller c Oakman b Laker ....6 (6)   b Laker 0
KD Mackay c Oakman b Laker .....0 (5)   c Oakman b Laker 0
RG Archer st Evans b Laker 0   c Oakman b Laker 0
R Benaud c Statham b Laker 0   b Laker 18
RR Lindwall not out 6   c Lock b Laker 8
LV Maddocks (+) b Laker ....4 (11)   lbw Laker 2
IW Johnson (c) b Laker ....0 (10)   not out 1
     EXTRAS 0   (B 12, LB 4) 16
TOTAL 84 205

FOW 1st Inns: 48 48 62 62 62 73 73 78 84 84
FOW 2nd Inns: 28 55 114 124 130 130 181 198 203 205

Bowling: *First Innings*: Statham 6-3-6-0, Bailey 4-3-4-0, Laker 16.4-4-37-9, Lock 14-3-37-0. *Second Innings*: Statham 16-10-15-0, Bailey 20-8-31-0, Laker 51.2-23-53-10, Lock 55-30-69-0, Oakman 8-3-21-0.

Umpires: D Davies & FS Lee

FIFTH TEST 1956 ENGLAND v AUSTRALIA
Kennington Oval, London. August 23, 24, 25, 27 (no play), 28, 1956.
Toss: England. Match Drawn.

ENGLAND
PE Richardson c Langley b Miller 37   c Langley b Lindwall 34
MC Cowdrey c Langley b Lindwall 0   c Benaud b Davidson 8
DS Sheppard c Archer b Miller 24   c Archer b Miller 62
PBH May (c) not out 83   not out 37
DCS Compton c Davidson b Archer 94   not out 35
GAR Lock c Langley b Archer 0
C Washbrook lbw Archer 0
TG Evans (+) lbw Miller 0
JC Laker c Archer b Miller 4
FH Tyson c Davidson b Archer 3
JB Statham b Archer 0
     EXTRAS (W 2) 2   (B 3, LB 3) 6
TOTAL 247   ....3 dec 182

FOW 1st Inns: 1 53 66 222 222 222 223 231 243 247
FOW 2nd Inns: 17 100 108

Bowling: *First Innings*: Lindwall 18-5-36-1, Miller 40-7-91-4, Davidson 5-1-16-0, Archer 28.2-7-53-5, Johnson 9-2-28-0, Benaud 9-2-21-0. *Second Innings*: Lindwall 12-3-29-1, Miller 22-3-56-1, Davidson 5-0-18-1, Archer 13-3-42-0, Johnson 4-1-7-0, Benaud 1-0-10-0, Burke 4-2-14-0.

AUSTRALIA
CC McDonald c Lock b Tyson 3   lbw Statham 0
JW Burke b Laker 8   lbw Laker 1
RN Harvey c May b Lock 39   c May b Lock 1
ID Craig c Statham b Lock 2   c Lock b Laker 7
IW Johnson (c) b Laker ....12 (6)   c Lock b Laker 10
AK Davidson c May b Laker 8
KR Miller c Washbrook b Statham ...61 (5)   not out 7
RG Archer c Tyson b Laker 0
R Benaud b Statham ....32 (7)   not out 0
RR Lindwall not out 22
GRA Langley (+) lbw Statham 0
     EXTRAS (B 6) 6   (B 1) 1
TOTAL 202   ....5 for 27

FOW 1st Inns: 3 17 20 35 47 90 111 154 202 202
FOW 2nd Inns: 0 1 5 10 27

Bowling: *First Innings*: Statham 21-8-33-3, Tyson 14-5-34-1, Laker 32-12-80-4, Lock 25-10-49-2. *Second Innings*: Statham 2-1-1-1, Laker 18-14-8-3, Lock 18.1-11-17-1.

Umpires: TJ Bartley & D Davies

Australian Averages

1956 ENGLAND v AUSTRALIA

AUSTRALIA	M	Inn	NO	Runs	H.S	Avrge	Ct	St	Overs	Mds	Runs	Wkt	Avrge
Archer, RG	5	8	-	82	33	10.25	6	-	207.4	67	451	18	25.06
Benaud, R	5	9	1	200	97	25.00	3	-	154.0	48	330	8	41.25
Burge, PJP	3	6	1	84	35*	16.80	-	-	-	-	-	-	-
Burke, JW	5	10	1	271	65	30.11	-	-	8.0	4	20	-	-
Craig, ID	2	4	-	55	38	13.75	-	-	-	-	-	-	-
Crawford, WPA	1	2	1	0	0*	0.00	-	-	4.5	2	4	-	-
Davidson, AK	2	1	-	8	8	8.00	2	-	19.4	2	56	2	28.00
Harvey, RN	5	10	-	197	69	19.70	1	-	-	-	-	-	-
Johnson, IW	5	9	1	61	17	7.63	-	-	119.0	32	303	6	50.50
Langley, GRA	3	4	2	21	14	10.50	18	1	-	-	-	-	-
Lindwall, RR	4	6	4	36	22*	18.00	2	-	100.1	29	238	7	34.00
Mackay, KD	3	6	-	73	38	12.17	1	-	24.0	6	44	1	44.00
Maddocks, LV	2	4	-	6	6	1.50	5	1	-	-	-	-	-
McDonald, CC	5	10	-	243	89	24.30	-	-	-	-	-	-	-
Miller, KR	5	10	1	203	61	22.56	3	-	205.1	44	467	21	22.24

English Averages

1956 ENGLAND v AUSTRALIA

ENGLAND	M	Inn	NO	Runs	H.S	Avrge	Ct	St	Overs	Mds	Runs	Wkt	Avrge
Appleyard, R	1	1	1	1	1*	-	-	-	30.0	10	49	2	24.50
Bailey, TE	4	5	1	117	33*	29.25	6	-	108.5	39	223	6	37.17
Compton, DCS	1	2	1	129	94	129.00	-	-	-	-	-	-	-
Cowdrey, MC	5	8	-	244	81	30.50	3	-	-	-	-	-	-
Evans, TG	5	7	1	115	47	19.17	7	2	-	-	-	-	-
Graveney, TW	2	4	1	41	18	13.67	1	-	6.0	3	6	-	-
Insole, DJ	1	1	-	5	5	5.00	-	-	-	-	-	-	-
Laker, JC	5	6	1	37	12	7.40	-	-	283.5	127	442	46	9.61
Lock, GAR	4	4	1	46	25*	15.33	10	-	237.2	115	337	15	22.47
May, PBH	5	7	2	453	101	90.60	3	-	-	-	-	-	-
Moss, AE	1	-	-	-	-	-	-	-	4.0	3	1	-	-
Oakman, ASM	2	2	-	14	10	7.00	7	-	8.0	3	21	-	-
Richardson, PE	5	8	-	364	104	45.50	1	-	-	-	-	-	-
Sheppard, DS	2	3	-	199	113	66.33	-	-	-	-	-	-	-
Statham, JB	3	4	2	0	0*	0.00	-	-	106.0	36	184	7	26.29
Trueman, FS	2	3	-	9	7	3.00	4	-	75.0	13	184	9	20.44
Tyson, FH	1	1	-	3	3	3.00	1	-	14.0	5	34	1	34.00
Wardle, JH	1	2	-	0	0	0.00	-	-	27.0	9	59	1	59.00
Washbrook, C	3	3	-	104	98	34.67	2	-	-	-	-	-	-
Watson, W	2	4	-	32	18	8.00	-	-	-	-	-	-	-

Fazal humbles Australians

Karachi, Oct. 17. Australia has been brought low by Pakistan in an extraordinary Test match, in which the essential boredom of the play has been overridden by the high national fervour surrounding Pakistan's success.

The national hero is Fazal Mahmood, the fast-medium bowler who bedazzled the Australians with his persistence, his swing, his leg and off-cutters.

He took six wickets in Australia's dismal first innings and seven in the second. His haul of 13/114 is a record for Pakistan. Mahmood's support came from Khan Mohammad, who took the other seven wickets with his swinging deliveries.

The Australians, unaccustomed to matting and in the hot house environment of Karachi for the first time, made heavy weather of the whole business.

They managed only 80 runs in what has been recorded as the slowest day of Test cricket. Pakistan was 2/15 at stumps, but the next day Waqar Hassan (67) and Wazir Mohammad (69) set up their victory with a 104 run partnership that helped carry the score to 199.

Mahmood: the danger man.

Still in with a chance the Australian batsmen could do nothing to break the control of Fazal and Khan. They limped along to score 187, with only the young all-rounders Richie Benaud (67) and Alan Davidson (37) boosting the score to some respectability.

Pakistan, to nationwide delight, had ticked off the 69 runs required for the loss of one wicket.

ONLY TEST 1956–57 PAKISTAN v AUSTRALIA
National Stadium, Karachi. October 11, 12, 13, 15, 17, 1956.
Toss: Australia. Pakistan won by 9 wkts.

AUSTRALIA

CC McDonald c Imtiaz b Fazal	17	b Fazal	3
JW Burke c Mathias b Fazal	4	c Mathias b Fazal	10
RN Harvey lbw Fazal	2	b Fazal	4
ID Craig c Imtiaz b Fazal	0	lbw Fazal	18
KR Miller c Wazir b Fazal	21	b Khan	11
RG Archer c Imtiaz b Khan	10	c Fazal b Khan	27
R Benaud c Waqar b Fazal	4	b Fazal	56
AK Davidson c Kardar b Khan	3	c Imtiaz b Khan	37
RR Lindwall c Mathias b Khan	2	lbw Fazal	0
IW Johnson (c) not out	13	b Fazal	0
GRA Langley (+) c Waqar b Khan	1	not out	13
EXTRAS (LB 2, NB 1)	3	(LB 2, NB 6)	8
TOTAL	80		187

FOW 1st Inns: 19 23 24 43 48 52 56 65 76 80
FOW 2nd Inns: 6 10 23 46 47 111 141 141 143 187

Bowling: *First Innings:* Fazal 27-11-34-6, Khan 26.1-9-43-4. *Second Innings:* Fazal 48-17-80-7, Khan 40.5-13-69-3, Zulfiqar 9-1-18-0, Kardar 12-5-12-0.

PAKISTAN

Hanif Mohammad c Langley b Miller	0	c Harvey b Davidson	5
Alimuddin c Lindwall b Archer	10	not out	34
Gul Mahomed b Davidson	12	not out	27
Imtiaz Ahmed (+) c McDonald b Benaud	15		
Waqar Hassan c Langley b Miller	6		
Wazir Mohammad c & b Johnson	67		
AH Kardar (c) lbw Johnson	69		
W Mathias b Johnson	0		
Fazal Mahmood not out	10		
Zulfiqar Ahmed c Langley b Lindwall	0		
Khan Mohammad b Johnson	3		
EXTRAS (B 5, LB 2)	7	(LB 1, NB 2)	3
TOTAL	199		1 for 69

FOW 1st Inns: 3 15 24 35 70 174 174 189 190 199
FOW 2nd Inns: 7

Bowling: *First Innings:* Lindwall 27-8-42-1, Miller 17-5-40-2, Archer 4-0-18-1, Davidson 6-4-6-1, Benaud 17-5-36-1, Johnson 20.3-3-50-4. *Second Innings:* Lindwall 16-8-22-0, Miller 12-4-18-0, Archer 3.5-3-1-0, Davidson 9-5-9-1, Johnson 7.5-2-16-0.

Umpires: Daud Khan & Idris Beg

Benaud, Lindwall get seven each

Madras, Oct. 23. A return to a turf wicket seems to have restored Australia to cricket normality and it has little difficulty in wrapping up the first Test against India with more than a day to spare.

Playing at Corporation Stadium before a noisy, capacity crowd, the Australians seemed at ease on turf, after having been humbled on matting at Karachi.

The match featured a reversal of the usual bowling fortunes.

Spinner Richie Benaud dominated on the first day with 7/72, getting turn and bounce off the bare and dry wicket, while speedster Ray Lindwall took a last-day haul usually reserved for spinners.

Lindwall left the ground with a stomach complaint, not unusual for visitors, after nine overs in the first innings. Benaud and fast bowler Pat Crawford, who ripped out the middle order with 3/32, had India all out for 161.

India had its spinners, too, in 'Vinoo' Mankad and 'Baloo' Gupte, who had Australia 8/200. But Ian Johnson (73) and Pat Crawford (36) put on 87 for the ninth wicket to boost the score to 319.

Lindwall was back to his old form with 7/43 as Australia won by an innings and 5 runs.

Spinner Richie Benaud: back on turf.

Burke, 160, and Harvey in charge

Jim Burke: slow but steady.

Bombay, Oct. 31. After his dismal experiences in England, Neil Harvey seemed to relish the heat of India and the faster wicket at Brabourne Stadium to give an exhibition of his brilliant batting in the second Test.

He was second fiddle to Jim Burke on the scoreboard, but took only 73 overs to make his 140, while Burke laboured to his score of 161 off 154 overs.

With new cap John Rutherford, the first Test player from Western Australia, making 30 as an opener and Peter Burge and Ray Lindwall making a solid contribution, Australia got to 523 and a 274 run lead on the first innings.

The Indian first innings of 251 was remarkable in that four players contributed 228 of them, with Gulabrai Ramchand making 109. Seven players made fewer than 10 runs apiece, even though the Australian bowling looked thin with Crawford off the field and Miller and Ian Johnson out of action.

Lindwall was doing duty as Australia's captain for the first time in his long career, in the absense of Johnson. He did not seem to relish the task of manipulating the attack. In the end he used eight bowlers.

India saved the day in its second innings, as Pankaj Roy and 'Polly' Umrigar led a battle that lasted over four sessions and yielded only five wickets.

Umrigar batted for six hours to make 78 and he had support right down the line as India held out to be 5/250 at stumps. Again Lindwall had to use eight men in his pop-gun attack.

Johnson gets his 1000 runs at end

Calcutta, Nov. 6. Ian Johnson has made it clear that this is his last Test for Australia, and he occupied the batting crease for just long enough in his last innings to make a rounded ending to his career. His 28 runs took his Test runs to 1000 and gave him the coveted double of 100 (actually 109) wickets and 1000 runs in his 47 Tests. This was just one more highlight of a good match for Australia.

It did not look promising at the start on this spinners' wicket, as Indian off-break bowler Ghulam Ahmed took the first big haul of 7/49 and Australia was all out 177.

But again Richie Benaud was around to exploit the conditions, and he had 6/36 as India fell for 136. He was well supported by the revitalised Ray Lindwall. The match continued to be all spin, as 35 of the 49 wickets fell to the turning ball. Australian pacemen had only five overs in the whole match, so keen was Johnson to get spin on to worry the senior batsmen.

Ahmed and 'Vinoo' Mankad went to work on Australia's second innings and again Australia was out cheaply, with a lead of only 222. In two innings only Peter Burge and Neil Harvey had exceeded 50.

But Benaud was lying in wait with his leg spin, and this time he had an ally in the form of part time bowler Jim Burke who picked 4/37 to back up Benaud's 5/53.

Benaud's match tally of 11/53 brings his wicket tally in three Tests to 23.

Peter Burge: respectable score.

FIRST TEST 1956–57 INDIA v AUSTRALIA
MA Chidambaram Stadium (Chepauk), Madras. October 19, 20, 22, 23, 1956.
Toss: India. Australia won by an innings & 5 runs.

INDIA

MH Mankad c McDonald b Benaud	27	c Langley b Lindwall 11
Pankaj Roy c Harvey b Benaud	13	c Harvey b Lindwall 9
PR Umrigar (c) c Craig b Benaud	31	c Langley b Lindwall 25
VL Manjrekar lbw Benaud	41 (5)	b Crawford 16
GS Ramchand b Crawford	0 (6)	lbw Johnson 28
HR Adhikari c Burke b Crawford	5 (7)	lbw Lindwall 0
AG Kripal Singh c Harvey b Crawford	13 (8)	not out 20
NS Tamhane (+) not out	9 (4)	c Crawford b Benaud 5
JM Patel c Johnson b Benaud	3	b Lindwall 0
Ghulam Ahmed c Harvey b Benaud	11	c Burge b Lindwall 13
SP Gupte c McDonald b Benaud	4	b Lindwall 8
EXTRAS (LB 4)	4	(B 10, LB 5, NB 3) 18
TOTAL	161	153

FOW 1st Inns: 41 44 97 98 106 134 134 137 151 161
FOW 2nd Inns: 18 22 39 63 99 100 113 119 143 153

Bowling: *First Innings*: Lindwall 9-1-15-0, Crawford 26-8-32-3, Benaud 29.3-10-72-7, Mackay 20-9-25-0, Johnson 15-10-13-0. *Second Innings*: Lindwall 22.5-9-43-7, Crawford 12-6-18-1, Benaud 20-5-59-1, Johnson 9-5-15-1.

AUSTRALIA

CC McDonald st Tamhane b Mankad	29
JW Burke c Tamhane b Gupte	10
RN Harvey b Mankad	37
ID Craig c Ramchand b Mankad	40
PJP Burge lbw Patel	35
KD Mackay c Tamhane b Ghulam	29
R Benaud b Ghulam	6
RR Lindwall c Adhikari b Gupte	8
IW Johnson (c) c Roy b Gupte	73
WPA Crawford st Tamhane b Mankad	34
GRA Langley (+) not out	10
EXTRAS (B 5, LB 3)	8
TOTAL	319

FOW 1st Inns: 12 58 97 152 186 186 198 200 287 319

Bowling: *First Innings*: Ramchand 5-1-12-0, Umrigar 4-0-17-0, Gupte 28.3-6-89-3, Ghulam 38-17-67-2, Mankad 45-15-90-4, Patel 14-3-36-1.

Umpires: DD Desai & MG Vijayasarathi

SECOND TEST 1956–57 INDIA v AUSTRALIA
Brabourne Stadium, Bombay. October 26, 27, 29, 30, 31, 1956.
Toss: India. Match Drawn.

INDIA

MH Mankad c Burge b Lindwall	0	c Burke b Benaud 16
Pankaj Roy c Burge b Crawford	31	c Maddocks b Benaud 79
PR Umrigar (c) b Crawford	8	c & b Lindwall 78
VL Manjrekar c Harvey b Benaud	55	b Rutherford 30
JM Ghorpade b Crawford	0	
GS Ramchand c(S)CC McDonald b Mackay	109	c Maddocks b Wilson 16
DG Phadkar c Maddocks b Benaud	1	not out 3
HR Adhikari c Davidson b Mackay	33 (5)	not out 22
NS Tamhane (+) c Harvey b Davidson	5	
JM Patel c Maddocks b Mackay	6	
SP Gupte not out	0	
EXTRAS (LB 1, NB 2)	3	(B 1, LB 1, NB 4) 6
TOTAL	251	5 for 250

FOW 1st Inns: 0 18 74 74 130 140 235 240 251 251
FOW 2nd Inns: 31 121 191 217 242

Bowling: *First Innings*: Lindwall 22-7-60-1, Crawford 12-3-28-3, Davidson 9-1-24-1, Benaud 25-6-54-2, Mackay 14.2-5-27-3, Wilson 15-6-39-0, Burke 2-0-12-0, Rutherford 1-0-4-0. *Second Innings*: Lindwall 23-9-40-1, Crawford 13-4-24-0, Davidson 14-9-18-0, Benaud 42-15-98-2, Mackay 17-6-22-0, Wilson 21-11-25-1, Burke 2-0-6-0, Rutherford 5-2-11-1.

AUSTRALIA

JW Burke c Umrigar b Mankad	161
JW Rutherford c Tamhane b Gupte	30
RN Harvey c(S)RG Nadkarni b Patel	140
PJP Burge c Patel b Gupte	83
KD Mackay c Roy b Patel	26
AK Davidson lbw Ramchand	16
R Benaud c(S)RG Nadkarni b Gupte	2
RR Lindwall (c) not out	48
LV Maddocks (+) not out	8
JW Wilson	
WPA Crawford	
EXTRAS (B 2, LB 4, NB 3)	9
TOTAL	7 dec 523

FOW 1st Inns: 57 261 398 432 459 462 470

Bowling: *First Innings*: Phadkar 39-9-92-0, Ramchand 18-2-78-1, Patel 39-10-111-2, Gupte 38-13-115-3, Mankad 46-9-118-1.

Umpires: AR Joshi & BJ Mohoni

THIRD TEST 1956–57 INDIA v AUSTRALIA
Eden Gardens, Calcutta. November 2, 3, 5, 6, 1956.
Toss: India. Australia won by 94 runs.

AUSTRALIA

CC McDonald b Ghulam	3	lbw Ramchand	0
JW Burke c Manjrekar b Ghulam	10	c Contractor b Ghulam	2
RN Harvey c Tamhane b Ghulam	7	c Umrigar b Mankad	69
ID Craig c Tamhane b Gupte	36	b Ghulam	6
PJP Burge c Ramchand b Ghulam	58	c Ramchand b Ghulam	22
KD Mackay lbw Mankad	5	hit wicket b Mankad	27
R Benaud b Ghulam	24	b Gupte	21
RR Lindwall b Ghulam	8	c Tamhane b Mankad	28
IW Johnson (c) c Ghulam b Mankad	1	st Tamhane b Mankad	5
WPA Crawford c Contractor b Ghulam	18	not out	1
GRA Langley (+) not out	1		
EXTRAS (B 6)	6	(B 6, LB 2)	8
TOTAL	177	9 dec	189

FOW 1st Inns: 6 22 25 93 106 141 152 157 163 177
FOW 2nd Inns: 0 9 27 59 122 149 159 188 189

Bowling: *First Innings*: Ramchand 2-1-1-0, Umrigar 16-3-30-0, Ghulam 20.3-6-49-7, Gupte 23-11-35-1, Mankad 25-4-56-2. *Second Innings*: Ramchand 2-1-6-1, Umrigar 20-9-21-0, Ghulam 29-5-81-3, Gupte 7-1-24-1, Mankad 9.4-1-49-4.

INDIA

Pankaj Roy b Lindwall	13	lbw Burke	24
NJ Contractor lbw Benaud	22	b Johnson	20
PR Umrigar (c) c Burge b Johnson	5	c Burke b Benaud	28
VL Manjrekar b Harvey b Benaud	33	c Harvey b Benaud	22
MH Mankad lbw Benaud	4	c Harvey b Benaud	24
GS Ramchand st Langley b Benaud	2	b Burke	3
AG Kripal Singh c Mackay b Benaud	14	b Benaud	0
P Bhandari lbw Lindwall	17	c Harvey b Burke	2
NS Tamhane (+) b Benaud	5	b Benaud	0
Ghulam Ahmed c Mackay b Lindwall	10	b Burke	0
SP Gupte not out	1	not out	0
EXTRAS (B 7, LB 1, NB 2)	10	(B 5, LB 5, NB 3)	13
TOTAL	136		136

FOW 1st Inns: 15 20 76 80 82 98 99 115 135 136
FOW 2nd Inns: 44 50 94 99 102 121 134 136 136 136

Bowling: *First Innings*: Lindwall 25.2-12-32-3, Crawford 3-3-0-0, Johnson 12-2-27-1, Benaud 29-10-52-6, Harvey 1-1-0-0, Burke 8-3-15-0. *Second Innings*: Lindwall 12-7-9-0, Crawford 2-1-1-0, Johnson 14-5-23-1, Benaud 24.2-6-53-5, Burke 17-4-37-4.

Umpires: G Ayling & BJ Mohoni

Australian Averages

1956–57 INDIA v AUSTRALIA

AUSTRALIA	M	Inn	NO	Runs	H.S	Avrge	Ct	St	Overs	Mds	Runs	Wkt	Avrge
Benaud, R	3	4	-	53	24	13.25	-	-	169.5	52	388	23	16.87
Burge, PJP	3	4	-	198	83	49.50	4	-	-	-	-	-	-
Burke, JW	3	4	-	183	161	45.75	3	-	29.0	7	70	4	17.50
Craig, ID	2	3	-	82	40	27.33	1	-	-	-	-	-	-
Crawford, WPA	3	3	1	53	34	26.50	1	-	68.0	25	103	7	14.71
Davidson, AK	1	1	-	16	16	16.00	1	-	23.0	10	42	1	42.00
Harvey, RN	3	4	-	253	140	63.25	10	-	1.0	1	0	-	-
Johnson, IW	2	3	-	79	73	26.33	1	-	50.0	22	78	3	26.00
Langley, GRA	2	2	2	11	10*	-	2	1	-	-	-	-	-
Lindwall, RR	3	4	1	92	48*	30.67	1	-	114.1	45	199	12	16.58
Mackay, KD	3	4	-	87	29	21.75	2	-	51.2	20	74	3	24.67
Maddocks, LV	1	1	1	8	8*	-	4	-	-	-	-	-	-
McDonald, CC	2	3	-	32	29	10.67	2	-	-	-	-	-	-
Rutherford, JW	1	1	-	30	30	30.00	-	-	6.0	2	15	1	15.00
Wilson, JW	1	-	-	-	-	-	-	-	36.0	17	64	1	64.00

Indian Averages

1956–57 INDIA v AUSTRALIA

INDIA	M	Inn	NO	Runs	H.S	Avrge	Ct	St	Overs	Mds	Runs	Wkt	Avrge
Adhikari, HR	2	4	1	60	33	20.00	1	-	-	-	-	-	-
Bhandari, P	1	2	-	19	17	9.50	-	-	-	-	-	-	-
Contractor, NJ	1	2	-	42	22	21.00	2	-	-	-	-	-	-
Ghorpade, JM	1	1	-	0	0	0.00	-	-	-	-	-	-	-
Ghulam Ahmed	2	4	-	34	13	8.50	1	-	87.3	28	197	12	16.42
Gupte, SP	3	5	3	13	8	6.50	-	-	96.3	31	263	8	32.88
Kripal Singh, AG	2	4	1	47	20*	15.67	-	-	-	-	-	-	-
Manjrekar, VL	3	6	-	197	55	32.83	1	-	-	-	-	-	-
Mankad, MH	3	6	-	82	27	13.67	-	-	125.4	29	313	11	28.45
Patel, JM	2	3	-	9	6	3.00	1	-	53.0	13	147	3	49.00
Phadkar, DG	1	2	1	4	3*	4.00	-	-	39.0	9	92	-	-
Ramchand, GS	3	6	-	158	109	26.33	3	-	27.0	5	97	2	48.50
Roy, Pankaj	3	6	-	169	79	28.17	2	-	-	-	-	-	-
Tamhane, NS	3	5	1	24	9*	6.00	6	3	-	-	-	-	-
Umrigar, PR	3	6	-	175	78	29.17	2	-	40.0	12	68	-	-

The fine art of leg spin

Leg spin has its own language, – bosie, googly, wrong'un, flipper, and toppie, zooter, fizzer are among the little wonders that can be conjured by a right-arm spinner, releasing the ball over the wrist. It is also a long and strong Australian tradition in bowling. Leggies have been as effective as quicks.

The spin is imparted both by the twisting motion of the wrist and action on the ball by the fingers on release – a sort of flicking motion. Shane Warne is said to 'rip' the ball with his powerful shoulder turn, wrists and fingers, so imparting fearful spin.

Leg spin bowling is now back in vogue, following the drought of some 30 years in which the pacemen dominated the scene.

Great leg-spinner Bill O'Reilly railed against this in his newspaper coverage of Test cricket. O'Reilly wanted to see the magic of spin, the battle of the minds and the absorbing spectacle of the probing bat and spinning ball.

Consider the armoury of the leg spin bowler – he has the variety of spin he can impart, from stock leg spinner to the opposite-spinning googly. He has the width of the crease, from over the wicket to around the wicket. He has pace, he has flight, he has length and he has bounce. He bowls to either left or right-handed batsmen, in varying conditions of the pitch, the light, the wind, the temperature. He orders his field placement. There is room here for thought and innovation.

One great development was the introduction of the 'bosie', or the googly, by English bowler Bernard Bosanquet in 1900. The uncertainty over which way the ball would spin took the leg spinners art to a new pitch. 'Ranji' Hordern, a Sydney dentist, cultivated the same googly skills with great effect, but like Bosanquet he played only seven Tests. It seemed that both men had other fields to conquer.

Arthur Mailey and Clarrie Grimmett wanted to stay longer in the game, particularly Grimmett, who resented being dropped from Tests at the age of 45.

Mailey and Grimmett, whose careers overlapped, were a great contrast in styles, and were known as 'the millionaire and the miser'.

Mailey gave the ball air, and liked to tease the batsman, offering him runs while he found the fatal flaw.

Richie Benaud: master at work.

Grimmett, with his low-slung round-arm style, didn't give up any runs voluntarily, and nagged at the batsman as he worked through the spinners' box of tricks. He was all leg-spinner, working at his craft, ever alert for a batting weakness or the hint of an advantage from the pitch. Mailey conceded 33.4 runs for each Test wicket, compared to Grimmett's 24.21.

O'Reilly, who worked in tandem with Grimmett for five years from 1931, was a charmer off the field, but a fiercely aggressive bowler, with a jerky, arm-swinging run-up and a stoop on delivery.

Grimmett, who tried everything, brought the flipper to the art – a ball that seems to come from the back of the hand, but is released underneath. It looks like a long hop until its pace and bounce have gone through the batsman's defences.

Grimmett taught it to Bruce Dooland, who passed the technique on to Richie Benaud. It became Benaud's creature as he worked on it, waiting over a year before he tried it in a match.

Benaud was a master at exploiting weaknesses, and placing his field to extract the maximum toll. He had a flowing run to the wicket and a powerful shoulder action, and he could spin the ball prodigously, usually with looping flight. He was accurate and mean with runs, but prepared to experiment.

The flipper has passed down to Shane Warne.

The House of Harvey

There was not much room in the home of Horace and Elsie Harvey at 198 Argyle Street, Fitzroy, with six cricket-loving boys and daughter Rita filling the house.

But there was the lane next door for endless cricket matches on the cobblestones and between two high brick walls. That laneway yielded two Test cricketers, the illustrious Neil and his older brother Merv.

Ray and Mick Harvey joined the other two in Sheffield Shield cricket.

198 Argyle Street, Fitzroy, Victoria.

Neil Harvey, aged 12: captain and 'keeper in the State School team.

The young dasher at Fitzroy.

Time for tuition from a Test batsman for the kids in the lane.

Horace, Elsie and Neil's fiancée Iris listen to the first Test in England in 1953.

Craig's mettle and Kline's hat-trick

The 1957–58 Australians under the captaincy of Ian Craig. It is the fifth team to tour South Africa undefeated.

Durban, Jan. 29. A fighting innings by captain Ian Craig rescued Australia in the first innings of the third Test, after he had won the toss and decided to bat on a pitch described as 'fiery'. His decision was criticised by some of of the Australian press. Craig batted for 212 minutes in making 52 of Australia's paltry 163.

Bowlers Neil Adcock and Trevor Goddard dominated batsmen who had scored 449 against them in the second Test. In South Africa's slow innings of 384, 'Jackie' McGlew scored his second century in three tests, a marathon innings of 105 in 575 minutes which had the side-effect of playing South Africa out of the match. His partnership of 231 with John Waite (134) was a record against Australia in this drawn game. Richie Benaud took five wickets. Jim Burke and Neil Harvey batted solidly, but Ian Craig scored (another) duck in Australia's second innings.

Events in this match did not match the spectacular conclusion to the second Test at Newlands in Cape Town.

That Test was set up by a methodical opening stand of 190 by Colin McDonald (99) and Jim Burke. Burke went on with 'Slasher' Mackay (63) to make 189.

Scoring was so slow that Ian Craig sent hard-hitting Richie Benaud in to speed things up, which he did for 33.

The Australian spinners Benaud and Lindsay Kline disposed of South Africa for 209, after Alan Davidson removed the sticky McGlew and Ian Meckiff had to leave the field with an injured shoulder after 5.4 overs.

Following on 240 behind, South Africa collapsed to be all out for 99. Benaud bowled magnificently for 5/49, and Lindsay Kline had every bowler's dream come true, when he finished the innings and the Test match with a hat-trick.

Up-country games

Salisbury, Nov. 30. Australia's tour of southern Africa has extended to two games in Rhodesia. The first was in the capital, Salisbury where Ian Craig made the first century of the tour (113) followed by Richie Benaud with 117 not out and Alan Davidson 100 not out. Australia won by an innings.

Craig made another hundred and Jim Burke 106 in the second game, at Bulawayo in the south.

Before this game, the Australians had played for the first time at Kitwe in Northern Rhodesia, where Benaud baffled the opposition with 9/16 from ten overs.

Several more matches will be played before the first Test.

NSW wins Shield

Sydney, Jan. 29. NSW wrapped up the Sheffield Shield with a 10-wicket win over Victoria at the SCG. This season the Shield has been decided by a new system to encourage results and 'positive' cricket – more points for outright results. Only two fieldsmen may be stationed behind square leg. Along with an extraordinary season from Norm O'Neill, captain Sid Carroll had a great year, making 700 runs art 50, and bowlers Johnnie Martin and Peter Philpott took 25 wickets and 23 wickets each.

NSW defeated WA outright, drew with Queensland twice, won and lost to SA and defeated Victoria twice for four outright wins.

O'Neill's great season

Sydney, Jan. 29. Norm O'Neill turned the disappointment of not being chosen for South Africa into a season of great opportunity. His 233 against Victoria simply emphasised that he is a class above any batsman in Australia. 'It was an innings that, with its pulverising power and its rich variety of stroke play, was worthy of Bradman himself,' said the Sydney *Sun-Herald*.

O'Neill hit 38 fours in his 244-minute innings, which was given a standing ovation by the good first-day crowd of 8310.

O'Neill has notched up 1005 runs at 83.75, becoming only the third Australian after Bradman and Bill Ponsford to top a thousand runs.

Benaud star of Test wins

Port Elizabeth, March 4. Richie Benaud capped off a marvellous tour with bat and ball by taking his fourth five-wicket haul in the fifth Test at St George's Park, wrapping up the Test series for Australia.

His 5/82 included his 100th Test wicket, and with another economical five-wicket performance from Alan Davidson, South Africa was dismissed for 144 in the second innings leaving Australia just 68 to win. At 2/53 Ian Craig sent Benaud in to bat with Wally Grout to score the winning runs.

Australia has won the series 3–0 and can thank the all-round ability of Benaud, with bat, ball and in the field for most of its success.

The delivery with which he bowled South African captain Clive van Ryneveld was a beauty. It pitched on the leg stump and took the off and was a spectacular 100th Test wicket. Equally satisfying was the 'flipper' that trapped Trevor Goddard, and the straight flighted 'toppie' that bowled Jackie McGlew, trying to use his feet. Benaud has joined the select band of Test players who have done the double of a thousand runs and a hundred Test wickets.

His attacking batting on this tour has been splendid, most notably his fast 100 batting at number four in the fourth Test, and his 122 in the first Test draw.

In the second South African innings of the fourth Test, Benaud broke through the stubborn opening partnership of Jackie McGlew and Russell Endean, having Endean caught by Bob Simpson, and then repeating the dose with number three Trevor Goddard, for a duck. The same pairing removed McGlew, but only after he had made 70.

In the end, Benaud captured 5/84, dismissing South Africa for 198 in the follow-on. Australia required

Richie Benaud hard hitting style.

just one run to win by 10 wickets. Victory. With nine wickets and a century, it was Benaud's match.

Overall Benaud made 817 runs on the tour, including four first class centuries, at an average of 51 – and was the outstanding batsman. His 106 wickets at 19.4 in first class matches saw him pipping Alan Davidson as the best bowler.

In Tests he took 30 wickets at 21.9. Davidson took 25 at 17.

This was the fifth time Australia had toured South Africa without losing a match.

Percy Beames in the *Age* writes that if 'Ian Craig's young, rebuilt team had failed, the Australian selectors would have been in a pretty pickle to choose the next Test side' to play England next summer. As it stands, selectors must 'reinforce spots never exposed by South Africa' – in particular, support for Davidson in the fast bowling department.

Ian Meckiff: played four Tests.

Lindsay Kline: poor wicket haul.

FIRST TEST 1957–58 SOUTH AFRICA v AUSTRALIA
New Wanderers Stadium, Johannesburg. December 23, 24, 26, 27, 28, 1957.
Toss: South Africa. Match Drawn.

SOUTH AFRICA

DJ McGlew (c) c Simpson b Meckiff	108	c Simpson b Meckiff ...6
TL Goddard b Meckiff	90	c Grout b Davidson ...5
JD Nel b Meckiff	4	c Grout b Davidson ...7
JHB Waite (+) c Burge b Benaud	115	c Grout b Burke ...59
WR Endean lbw Meckiff	50 (6)	c Meckiff b Davidson ...77
RA McLean b Meckiff	50 (5)	c Grout b Davidson ...0
KJ Funston lbw Mackay	12	b Meckiff ...27
HJ Tayfield b Davidson	18	c Grout b Meckiff ...3
PS Heine b Mackay	7	c Grout b Davidson ...2
VI Smith not out	2	not out ...1
NAT Adcock		c Simpson b Davidson ...0
EXTRAS (B 8, LB 4, W 1, NB 1)	14	(B 5, LB 7, W 1, NB 1) ...14
TOTAL	9 dec 470	...201

FOW 1st Inns: 176 182 237 341 412 436 461 465 470
FOW 2nd Inns: 6 19 19 19 148 193 196 199 199 201

Bowling: *First Innings*: Davidson 32-4-115-1, Meckiff 31-3-125-5, Mackay 20.6-3-54-2, Benaud 27-7-115-1, Kline 20-6-47-0. *Second Innings*: Davidson 17.4-4-34-6, Meckiff 26-3-52-3, Mackay 11-1-29-0, Benaud 2-0-15-0, Kline 8-2-18-0, Burke 14-3-39-1.

AUSTRALIA

CC McDonald c Tayfield b Smith	75	st Waite b Smith ...25
JW Burke c Waite b Heine	16	retired hurt ...10
KD Mackay c Waite b Heine	3	not out ...65
ID Craig (c) b Heine	14	b Tayfield ...17
PJP Burge c Waite b Heine	0	b Tayfield ...14
RB Simpson lbw Tayfield	60	not out ...23
R Benaud c Heine b Adcock	122	
AK Davidson c(S)ERH Fuller b Heine	24	
ATW Grout (+) c Endean b Tayfield	21	
I Meckiff c Smith b Heine	11	
LF Kline not out	6	
EXTRAS (B 4, LB 11, NB 1)	16	(B 6, LB 2) ...8
TOTAL	368	3 for 162

FOW 1st Inns: 34 40 56 62 151 177 244 313 355 368
FOW 2nd Inns: 44 85 118

Bowling: *First Innings*: Heine 14.2-3-58-6, Adcock 23-3-106-1, Goddard 16-5-57-0, Tayfield 29-9-101-2, Smith 9-2-30-1. *Second Innings*: Heine 8-2-17-0, Adcock 3-0-11-0, Goddard 12-6-24-0, Tayfield 33-12-70-2, Smith 16-8-25-1, McGlew 1-0-7-0.

Umpires: A Birkett & JH McMenamin

SECOND TEST 1957–58 SOUTH AFRICA v AUSTRALIA
Newlands, Cape Town. December 31, 1957 January 1, 2, 3, 1958.
Toss: Australia. Australia won by an innings & 141 runs.

AUSTRALIA

CC McDonald c Waite b Fuller	99
JW Burke b Tayfield	189
RN Harvey c Goddard b Adcock	15
ID Craig (c) b Goddard	0
KD Mackay lbw Tayfield	63
R Benaud c McGlew b Tayfield	33
AK Davidson c & b Tayfield	21
RB Simpson c Funston b Tayfield	3
ATW Grout (+) run out	0
I Meckiff not out	11
LF Kline lbw Fuller	5
EXTRAS (B 1, LB 6, NB 3)	10
TOTAL	449

FOW 1st Inns: 190 215 220 350 399 408 412 412 434 449

Bowling: *First Innings*: Adcock 27-5-80-1, Goddard 29-9-57-1, Fuller 34.2-3-125-2, Tayfield 51-18-120-5, Westcott 4-0-22-0, Van Ryneveld 7-0-35-0.

SOUTH AFRICA

DJ McGlew c Mackay b Davidson	30	c McDonald b Davidson ...0
TL Goddard lbw Benaud	29	not out ...56
RJ Westcott c Simpson b Davidson	0	c Davidson b Benaud ...18
JHB Waite (+) c Simpson b Kline	7	c Benaud b Davidson ...8
RA McLean c Harvey b Kline	38	c Burke b Benaud ...2
WR Endean c Davidson b Burke	21	b Benaud ...5
KJ Funston c & b Benaud	2	b Benaud ...8
CB Van Ryneveld (c) b Benaud	43	c Burke b Benaud ...1
ERH Fuller c Harvey b Benaud	5	c Benaud b Kline ...0
HJ Tayfield c Benaud b Kline	21	lbw Kline ...0
NAT Adcock not out	0	c Simpson b Kline ...0
EXTRAS (B 6, LB 5, W 1, NB 1)	13	(LB 1) ...1
TOTAL	209	...99

FOW 1st Inns: 61 61 70 103 118 121 146 164 209 209
FOW 2nd Inns: 0 56 69 74 80 88 98 99 99 99

Bowling: *First Innings*: Meckiff 5.4-1-18-0, Davidson 18-5-31-2, Benaud 35-6-95-4, Kline 19.1-5-29-3, Burke 9-2-23-1. *Second Innings*: Davidson 15-6-18-2, Benaud 21-6-49-5, Kline 10.4-2-18-3, Burke 6-4-7-0, Mackay 5-3-6-0.

Umpires: D Collins & V Costello

THIRD TEST 1957–58 SOUTH AFRICA v AUSTRALIA
Kingsmead, Durban. January 24, 25, 27, 28, 29, 1958.
Toss: Australia. Match Drawn.

AUSTRALIA

CC McDonald c Goddard b Adcock	28	lbw Tayfield	33
JW Burke c Waite b Adcock	2	b Goddard	83
RN Harvey c Waite b Adcock	6	b Adcock	68
ID Craig (c) b Goddard	52	c Goddard b Tayfield	0
RB Simpson b Goddard	17 (8)	c Tayfield b Van Ryneveld	4
KD Mackay hit wicket b Adcock	32 (5)	not out	52
R Benaud lbw Adcock	5 (6)	b Van Ryneveld	20
AK Davidson c Waite b Heine	12 (7)	c McGlew b Tayfield	4
ATW Grout (+) b Heine	2	not out	3
LF Kline c Goddard b Adcock	0		
RA Gaunt not out	0		
EXTRAS (NB 7)	7	(B 19, LB 5, NB 1)	25
TOTAL	163	7 for 292	

FOW 1st Inns: 13 19 54 87 131 142 161 163 163 163
FOW 2nd Inns: 92 170 179 221 261 274 289

Bowling: *First Innings*: Heine 17.4-4-30-2, Adcock 18-2-43-6, Goddard 23-12-25-2, Tayfield 21-7-41-0, Van Ryneveld 3-0-17-0. *Second Innings*: Heine 14-1-40-0, Adcock 15-1-34-1, Goddard 42-18-62-1, Tayfield 59-24-94-3, Van Ryneveld 17-1-37-2.

SOUTH AFRICA

DJ McGlew c Grout b Gaunt	105
RJ Westcott b Gaunt	0
WR Endean c Simpson b Benaud	15
JHB Waite (+) b Davidson	134
TL Goddard lbw Davidson	45
KJ Funston c Grout b Mackay	27
CB Van Ryneveld (c) not out	32
RA McLean c Grout b Benaud	11
HJ Tayfield st Grout b Benaud	0
PS Heine c Burke b Benaud	7
NAT Adcock c Grout b Benaud	0
EXTRAS (B 2, LB 5, NB 1)	8
TOTAL	384

FOW 1st Inns: 6 28 259 259 313 356 371 371 383 384

Bowling: *First Innings*: Davidson 34-8-62-2, Gaunt 27-2-87-2, Mackay 35-5-77-1, Benaud 50.7-13-114-5, Kline 17-6-36-0.

Umpires: V Costello & W Marais

FIFTH TEST 1957–58 SOUTH AFRICA v AUSTRALIA
St George's Park, Port Elizabeth. February 28, March 1, 3, 4, 1958.
Toss: South Africa. Australia won by 8 wkts.

SOUTH AFRICA

DJ McGlew c Simpson b Davidson	14 (7)	b Benaud	20
TL Goddard c Harvey b Meckiff	17	lbw Benaud	33
WR Endean c McDonald b Davidson	2 (1)	c Simpson b Davidson	23
JHB Waite (+) c Harvey b Davidson	17 (3)	b Davidson	0
KJ Funston c Grout b Davidson	20 (4)	c Simpson b Davidson	4
CB Van Ryneveld (c) c Burke b Kline	26	b Benaud	5
CGV Burger lbw Kline	3 (8)	not out	37
PR Carlstein c & b Kline	32 (9)	lbw Benaud	1
HJ Tayfield c Burke b Kline	66 (5)	c Grout b Davidson	2
PS Heine lbw Benaud	3	lbw Benaud	15
NAT Adcock not out	3	b Davidson	0
EXTRAS (B 4, LB 5, NB 2)	11	(B 2, LB 2)	4
TOTAL	214	144	

FOW 1st Inns: 28 30 36 57 86 96 105 191 198 214
FOW 2nd Inns: 55 55 63 63 70 70 97 99 131 144

Bowling: *First Innings*: Davidson 20-6-44-4, Meckiff 18-4-76-1, Benaud 12-2-34-1, Mackay 11-3-16-0, Kline 13.6-3-33-4. *Second Innings*: Davidson 26.1-8-38-5, Meckiff 16-8-20-0, Benaud 33-14-82-5.

AUSTRALIA

CC McDonald c Waite b Adcock	58	c Tayfield b Adcock	4
JW Burke c Endean b Adcock	8		
RN Harvey lbw Heine	15	c & b Tayfield	22
ID Craig (c) c Endean b Tayfield	17		
R Benaud c & b Goddard	43 (4)	not out	6
RB Simpson c Carlstein b Tayfield	23		
KD Mackay not out	77		
AK Davidson lbw Heine	4		
ATW Grout (+) c Endean b Goddard	25 (2)	not out	35
I Meckiff c Waite b Heine	8		
LF Kline c Goddard b Tayfield	0		
EXTRAS (B 2, LB 4, NB 7)	13	(B 1)	1
TOTAL	291	2 for 68	

FOW 1st Inns: 13 37 124 145 194 199 239 265 278 291
FOW 2nd Inns: 4 53

Bowling: *First Innings*: Heine 30-3-68-3, Adcock 24-1-81-2, Goddard 23-9-48-2, Tayfield 30.3-12-81-3. *Second Innings*: Heine 3-0-12-0, Adcock 4-0-18-1, Goddard 1-0-8-0, Tayfield 4-1-25-1, Van Ryneveld 0.4-0-4-0.

Umpires: V Costello & W Marais

FOURTH TEST 1957–58 SOUTH AFRICA v AUSTRALIA
New Wanderers Stadium, Johannesburg. February 7, 8, 10, 11, 12, 1958.
Toss: Australia. Australia won by 10 wkts.

AUSTRALIA

CC McDonald lbw Tayfield	26	not out	1
JW Burke c Waite b Heine	81	not out	0
RN Harvey c Waite b Goddard	5		
R Benaud c Endean b Heine	100		
ID Craig (c) b Heine	3		
ATW Grout (+) lbw Adcock	7		
KD Mackay not out	83		
RB Simpson c Waite b Adcock	6		
AK Davidson c Burger b Heine	62		
I Meckiff c Endean b Heine	26		
LF Kline c Waite b Heine	1		
EXTRAS (LB 1)	1		0
TOTAL	401	0 for 1	

FOW 1st Inns: 43 52 210 213 222 222 234 315 393 401
FOW 2nd Inns:

Bowling: *First Innings*: Heine 37.5-6-96-6, Adcock 17-3-37-2, Goddard 43-10-136-1, Tayfield 49-17-107-1, Van Ryneveld 3-0-24-0. *Second Innings*: McLean 0.4-0-1-0.

SOUTH AFRICA

DJ McGlew c Grout b Meckiff	1	c Simpson b Benaud	70
WR Endean lbw Davidson	22	c Simpson b Benaud	38
HJ Tayfield lbw Benaud	27 (9)	st Grout b Kline	0
TL Goddard c & b Meckiff	9 (3)	c Simpson b Benaud	0
KJ Funston c Craig b Kline	70 (4)	not out	64
RA McLean c Grout b Davidson	9 (5)	c Grout b Davidson	0
CGV Burger st Grout b Kline	21	c McDonald b Kline	1
JHB Waite (+) lbw Benaud	12 (6)	c Grout b Benaud	10
PS Heine c & b Benaud	24 (10)	c Meckiff b Benaud	1
NAT Adcock b Benaud	0 (11)	run out	3
CB Van Ryneveld (c) not out	0 (8)	lbw Kline	0
EXTRAS (B 3, W 2, NB 3)	8	(LB 8, W 2, NB 1)	11
TOTAL	203	198	

FOW 1st Inns: 17 27 46 104 115 166 166 186 194 203
FOW 2nd Inns: 78 78 147 148 161 180 180 182 183 198

Bowling: *First Innings*: Meckiff 21-3-38-2, Davidson 19-2-39-2, Mackay 11-5-11-0, Benaud 20.2-0-70-4, Kline 9-1-37-2. *Second Innings*: Meckiff 13-2-24-0, Davidson 20-4-44-1, Benaud 41-8-84-5, Kline 16-6-27-3, Burke 15-10-8-0.

Umpires: A Birkett & JH McMenamin

Australian Averages

1957–58 SOUTH AFRICA v AUSTRALIA

AUSTRALIA	M	Inn	NO	Runs	H.S	Avrge	Ct	St	Overs	Mds	Runs	Wkt	Avrge
Benaud, R	5	8	1	329	122	54.83	5	-	242.1	56	658	30	21.93
Burge, PJP	1	2	-	14	14	7.00	1	-	-	-	-	-	-
Burke, JW	5	8	2	389	189	64.83	5	-	44.0	19	77	2	38.50
Craig, ID	5	7	-	103	52	14.71	1	-	-	-	-	-	-
Davidson, AK	5	6	-	127	62	21.17	2	-	201.5	47	425	25	17.00
Gaunt, RA	1	1	1	0	0*	-	-	-	27.0	2	87	2	43.50
Grout, ATW	5	7	2	93	35*	18.60	16	3	-	-	-	-	-
Harvey, RN	4	6	-	131	68	21.83	4	-	-	-	-	-	-
Kline, LF	5	5	1	12	6*	3.00	1	-	113.3	31	245	15	16.33
Mackay, KD	5	7	4	375	83*	125.00	1	-	93.6	20	193	3	64.33
McDonald, CC	5	9	1	349	99	43.63	3	-	-	-	-	-	-
Meckiff, I	4	4	1	56	26	18.67	3	-	130.4	24	353	11	32.09
Simpson, RB	5	7	1	136	60	22.67	13	-	-	-	-	-	-

South African Averages

1957–58 SOUTH AFRICA v AUSTRALIA

SOUTH AFRICA	M	Inn	NO	Runs	H.S	Avrge	Ct	St	Overs	Mds	Runs	Wkt	Avrge
Adcock, NAT	5	8	2	6	3*	1.00	-	-	131.0	15	410	14	29.29
Burger, CGV	2	4	1	62	37*	20.67	1	-	-	-	-	-	-
Carlstein, PR	1	2	-	33	32	16.50	1	-	-	-	-	-	-
Endean, WR	5	9	-	253	77	28.11	6	-	-	-	-	-	-
Fuller, ERH	1	2	-	5	5	2.50	-	-	34.2	3	125	2	62.50
Funston, KJ	5	9	1	234	70	29.25	1	-	-	-	-	-	-
Goddard, TL	5	9	1	284	90	35.50	6	-	189.0	69	417	7	59.57
Heine, PS	4	7	-	59	24	8.43	1	-	124.3	19	321	17	18.88
McGlew, DJ	5	9	-	354	108	39.33	2	-	1.0	-	7	-	-
McLean, RA	4	7	-	110	50	15.71	4	-	0.4	-	1	-	-
Nel, JD	1	2	-	11	7	5.50	-	-	-	-	-	-	-
Smith, VI	1	2	2	3	2*	-	-	-	25.0	10	55	2	27.50
Tayfield, HJ	5	9	-	137	66	15.22	5	-	276.3	100	639	17	37.59
Van Ryneveld, CB	4	7	2	107	43	21.40	-	-	30.4	1	117	2	58.50
Waite, JHB	5	9	-	362	134	40.22	13	1	-	-	-	-	-
Westcott, RJ	2	3	-	18	18	6.00	-	-	4.0	-	22	-	-

Richie Benaud: the complete cricketer

Richie Benaud's cricketing career as a captain and a player was distinguished by a sense of purpose. He never drifted on the field, but worked and planned for success. Every ball he bowled had planning behind it, and was destined to take a wicket if the execution, the conditions and the batsman's failings coincided.

As he walked back to bowl, for a more urgent and vigorous run-up than is usual in a spinner, you could see in the concentrated expression that there was a lot of thinking going on.

He batted and fielded the same way, as a hard-hitting all-rounder and a gully fielding specialist of the highest standard, but his thinking and his manner as a captain permeated the whole Australian team and took it to a winning pitch over four successive Test series.

Both the intensity of his cricket, his strong and reserved personality and his public relations skills combined to put Australia in the forefront of the renaissance of cricket that occurred through the late 50s and into the 60s.

He remains, as the major cricket commentator for the Nine Network and the BBC, a central part of the international game today.

Benaud, and his younger brother John, were destined for the game. Their father Lou, a school teacher, played Sydney district cricket for many years with Penrith, and is one of a select few cricketers to have taken 20 wickets in one match (against St Mary's in 1922–23). He was a slow leg-break bowler and he naturally passed on the mysteries of the craft. John went on to State and Test cricket as a batsman.

The Benaud boys went to Parramatta High School and both were academic as well as sporting, winning cadetships in journalism. Richie impressed with his leg-breaks and his powerful batting as a youthful district cricketer, and he was selected for New South Wales at the age of 18 in the summer of 1948–49. He played his first Test for Australia against the West Indies in 1951–52.

Australia was well on top of the West Indians and Benaud's inclusion for the fifth Test in Sydney was a nod towards the future by the selectors. Young Richie made 1 and 19 (bowled by the man who was to be his most gallant adversary, Frank Worrell), and got his only

Richie Benaud at the Sydney Cricket Ground for his last Test innings, against South Africa in 1963–64.

wicket by bowling one of cricket's great 'rabbits', Alf Valentine.

He played four Tests in the subsequent South African tour of Australia, but his 10 wickets and his batting were not an inspirational beginning. He continued to perform modestly on his first tour of England in 1953. Through three more series without notable success the selectors stuck by him.

But there was steady improvement, and a century in the fifth Test against the West Indies in Jamaica in 1954–55 (in a score of 8/758 dec.) was an indication of a return on investment, as was 7/72 against India in Madras in 1956–57.

The slow maturing bore rich fruit in South Africa in 1957–58, when Benaud took 30 Test wickets and made 327 in seven innings (once not out) for an average of 54.5. In

all matches on that tour he took 106 wickets, a record in a South African first class summer, and made 817 runs.

He was a senior member of the team. He was suddenly elevated to the captaincy for the England tour of Australia in 1958–59, when Ian Craig, who had led in South Africa and New Zealand, contracted hepatitis. He guided Australia to four resounding wins and a draw. Benaud took 31 wickets and Australia regained the Ashes.

His bowling was now at its peak, the reward of long sessions of practice. He had a high and fluent action, gaining plenty of bounce, and he worked on subtle variations of flight and spin. He supplemented his leg-break and wrong'un with a new weapon, the 'flipper'. In the summer of 1959–60, with

tours from India and Pakistan for four Tests each, Benaud showed his mastery by taking 47 wickets

The outstanding teams that faced each other on the 1960–61 tour by the West Indies, and the charismatic leadership of Benaud and Worrell, brought a glory to cricket that was reminiscent of the Bradman years.

There was a natural empathy between the captains and the strong competitive approach between the brilliant players on both sides never broke down into sledging or unsporting behaviour.

Like Worrell, Benaud was a natural leader, able to be close to his team, but to maintain discipline through the force of his personality. His intensity and his enthusiasm for the game rubbed off on his players, and they worked for the team rather than for themselves.

He was able to extract some heroic performances from his star bowler Alan Davidson, urging him to keep going through fatigue and injury. Apart from their bowling Davidson and Benaud became a batting force in the bottom half of the order, with their aggression and batting skills often taking their toll of flagging attacks.

Both were genuine all-rounders, but the demands and the successes of bowling had some effect on their batting consistency.

Benaud flew the Australian flag triumphantly through England in the winter of 1961, and had his finest hour as a bowler when England looked set to win the fourth Test and go 2–1 up in the series.

England needed little more than 100 to win with nine wickets in hand. Benaud took the ball and bowled around the wicket into the rough, dismissing Ted Dexter, Brian Close, Peter May and Raman Subba Row in five overs. He finished with 6/70 and Australia won by 45 runs and had the Ashes safe.

He had played in 63 Tests, and became the only player to that time to have taken more than 200 wickets and scored 2000 runs. He led Australia in 27 Tests, and lost only four. His record of 248 Test wickets was not beaten until Dennis Lillee overtook him in 1980–81.

But it was his heroic style that will be remembered by those who saw him, his suavity and leadership character that instilled pride in Australians. He is now a sage and respected commentator in world cricket.

The slowest half-century in history

Richie Benaud is captain, Harvey is disappointed

Melbourne, Nov. 30. Richie Benaud has been appointed captain of Australia for the first Test in Brisbane.

Benaud replaces Ian Craig who has been forced to take the rest of the season off after two ducks in two games showed the after-effects of a bout of hepatitis.

The duck habit passed from Craig to his vice-captain in South Africa, Neil Harvey, who upon being appointed captain of the Australian XI team against the touring England side, scored one in the 345-run loss.

No one with cricket nous could blame Harvey for this – Ray Robinson said that England fast bowlers gouged holes in the pitch 'as big as a meat dish'.

Benaud has recently captained NSW in Craig's absence, while Harvey was captain of Victoria in 1956–57.

In the tied Shield game between NSW and Victoria that season, he outsmarted Benaud when NSW only needed 16 to win.

Harvey, twice overlooked as captain in favour of Craig, and now Benaud, told his new captain: 'I'll be playing for you.'

Now TV at Tests

Melbourne, Jan. 10. The ABC paid £5000 for the rights to show two hours of each day's play at the first Test match in Brisbane – the first TV broadcast of Test cricket in Australia. Now two commercial stations, ATN-7 in Sydney and GTV-9 in Melbourne, are cooperating to transmit the third Test from Sydney to Melbourne, paying £1333 for the privilege.

Last night, when Graham Kennedy said 'Come in Sydney' and they did, almost instantaneously on his show 'In Melbourne Tonight', it was the first time television had bridged the gap between the two cities in a 'live' telecast. The signal is transmitted via five special mobile units on mountain tops stationed on the 600-mile route between the two cities.

At last! Peter May is caught by Wally Grout off Ian Meckiff.

Second-Test revenge: Davidson gets Lock.

Brisbane, Dec. 10. There must be something in the pitch or in the Brisbane air, because incredibly slow scoring is the order of the day whoever plays.

Sir Donald Bradman, casting his eye over the formidable names on paper, of the England bowling line-up – Jim Laker, Frank Tyson, Fred Trueman, Brian Statham, Tony Lock and Trevor Bailey said 'I hope we can give you a good game.' Sir Donald can never have imagined batting as slowly as this against any bowling.

The game against Queensland last week was a nightmare preview of the Test. England made 151, Raman Subba Row scoring 51 in 143 minutes, and Trevor 'Barnacle' Bailey made 33 in 189 minutes. This was bettered, if that is the word, by Ken 'Slasher' Mackay with 18 in 133 minutes and Peter Burge 11 in 107 minutes.

Norm O'Neill made his long-awaited Test debut for Australia.

It was Australia's bowlers Alan Davidson, Ian Meckiff and captain Richie Benaud who bowled England out for 134. This innings took the whole day, less two overs in 12 minutes, in which the Australians made 0/8. Bailey made 27 in two hours.

England captain Peter May appeared to have lost a tactical battle by winning the toss and batting, and in not (a) getting on or getting out and (b) declaring the innings closed to give his bowlers ten overs at Australia under the same dubious conditions.

As it was, Australia's seemingly brittle line-up was bundled out for 186, only Colin McDonald and O'Neill making more than 30. Only 148 runs were made for the day.

On the third and fourth days, only 228 runs were made in total.

The main culprit was Bailey, who made the slowest half-century in first class history – taking three minutes short of six hours to do it. He went on, if 'went' is the right word, to 68 in 458 minutes.

In a low-scoring match, Australia was left with the interesting target of 147 to win in a day's play. Jim Burke almost matched the slowness of Bailey – his 28 not out occupied the entire innings time of 250 minutes.

Play was so slow that Colin McDonald played a ball onto his stumps which did not dislodge a bail. Luckily Norm O'Neill showed the sluggards what to do, hitting 71 not out in 113 minutes.

English press in chucking whinge

Melbourne, Feb. 18. When the England team first came across the bowling of Ian Meckiff, in the Victoria v England match on November 7, where he took a modest 4/69, 'the batsmen were strongly inclined to think that he threw. However, it was said he didn't throw particularly well, and no official comment or complaint was made,' wrote E. W. 'Jim' Swanton, the London *Daily Telegraph* cricket correspondent.

By the time Meckiff took a match-winning 6/38 on January 5, attitudes had changed.

Swanton wrote in his preview of the match that 'the most remarkable aspect of Australian cricket on the tour had been the increase in doubtful actions,' and he named the three 'offenders' – Meckiff, Jim Burke and Keith Slater.

Swanton sought to explain or even to excuse the England batsmen's ineptitude, writing 'it is characteristic of the chuckers that the flight of the ball is harder to pick up.'

Of Meckiff's Melbourne performance, Swanton wrote 'I never saw anything so blatant as Meckiff's action as, with the swell of the crowd in his ears, he came up full pelt from the bottom end towards the pavilion.'

When Gordon Rorke, a very fast bowler with a huge drag played in the fourth Test Brian Chapman of the London *Daily Express* wrote he was 'a honey of a chucker'.

Things might have been viewed differently by the jackals of Fleet Street had England played more brightly, and if Typhoon Tyson had not bowled like a zephyr.

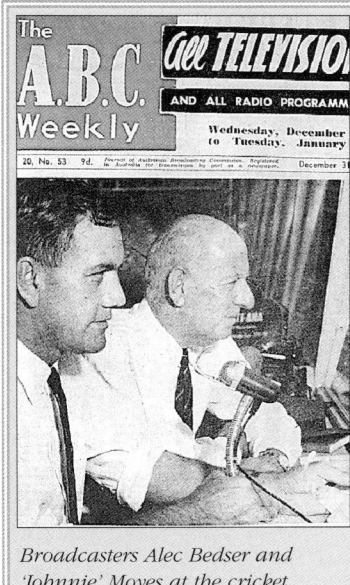

Broadcasters Alec Bedser and 'Johnnie' Moyes at the cricket.

Australia on top in all departments

The wide-angle view at the MCG during the second Test – a total of 244,948 attended over the five days.

Melbourne, Feb. 18. England's woes continued to the very end of the tour, when Peter Loader and Brian Statham were injured in a car crash just before the fifth Test, and could not be considered. It is doubtful whether they would have made much difference as the damage to England had been done by the ultra defensive batting tactics, ineffective bowling, poor fielding and plain old bad luck.

Australia, rejuvenated under Richie Benaud's aggressive leadership, had young and young-at-heart batsmen, such as Norm O'Neill, Neil Harvey and Colin McDonald, and tearaway fast bowlers such as Ian Meckiff and Gordon Rorke to unsettle the England bats. The 'chucking' and 'dragging' controversies overshadowed the fact that most wickets in the series were taken by Benaud and Alan Davidson, and that the old warhorse Ray Lindwall could be recalled for the last two Tests and take seven wickets.

Fast bowlers were in sensational form in the second Test. Davidson took three wickets in his second

Lindwall's return

Melbourne, Feb. 18. Ray Lindwall capped his return to Test cricket with his 216th wicket, taking him past Clarrie Grimmett as Australia's leading wicket-taker.

The record was achieved with the fourth delivery of his first over in the second innings – bowling Trevor Bailey for the second frame in his pair of spectacles in this match – a great relief of the MCG crowd, who like Bailey more the less they see of him at the crease. Lindwall also had his wicket in the first innings, and in the second innings of his comeback match, the fourth Test in Adelaide.

Lindwall has taken seven wickets in his two comeback Tests, the first he has played since the third Test in India in 1956–57.

over to have England rocking at 3/7. Statham took 7/57 in 28 hostile overs, confining Australia to a lead of only 41 runs (Neil Harvey a chanceless 167).

But then England collapsed in 30.2 lethal overs from Meckiff and Davidson.

Benaud was England's nemesis in the third Test at Sydney, taking nine wickets in the drawn match. On the batting side Australia put in a good all-round performance, and England was saved by a five-hour 92 from Peter May, and a six-hour 100 not out from Colin Cowdrey. This was the slowest Test century achieved in an Ashes contest.

The 'chucking' controversy was given a stir with the selection of Keith Slater, whose faster ball was thought by some to occasionally

have been thrown.

Australia won back the Ashes with a third victory in the fourth Test, built around an opening stand of 171 between Colin McDonald (eventually out for 170) and Jim Burke (66).

McDonald was involved in an umpiring controversy with umpire Mel McInnes who first gave him out run out, then recalled him saying he wasn't in the correct position to adjudicate.

McDonald had a further brush with fate, when a bail was discovered dislodged after he had played a ball from Fred Trueman when he was just 12.

The bail must have been knocked off while running. The ruling was that it had come off after the shot had been played.

Alan Davidson and Ian Meckiff deserve the praise for their bowling efforts in Melbourne, when they took 18 wickets between them.

The matter of 'chucking'

Adelaide, Feb. 1. During the Adelaide Test, the Australian Board of Control met and rejected all complaints about umpire Mel McInnes, noting that in their opinion 'the objections raised were neither tangible nor reasonable.'

In the opinion of 'Johnnie' Moyes McInnes was 'one of the three outstanding umpires in Australian cricket history... There are many who think that a vendetta was declared against him purely because he was a strong man who insisted that the game be played under the laws as he knew them.'

McInnes was dropped from the fifth Test 'for Mel's own peace of mind,' as an official told Moyes.

Complaints had not only to do with some bad decisions, which McInnes freely admitted, but also with the question of 'chucking'. England captain Peter May, manager Freddie Brown and assistant manager Desmond Eager attended to discuss grievances.

Brown told the Board 'I would like to make it perfectly clear ... I am definitely not raising any objection regarding the action of any Australian bowler ... However I must make a point to you. I have visited 15 schools on this tour and at practically every one there were around four or five boys ... who had suspicious actions.'

Sir Donald Bradman said, 'Mr. Brown, there are two points. First, whether the umpires are

Gordon Rorke, the dragger.

interpreting the law correctly; and secondly, whether the law should be altered. In my opinion it must be one or the other.'

Brown said: 'You are quite right. My own view is that the law is difficult to interpret, and I believe that change in the law would be of considerable benefit and would make it easier for the umpires to interpret...'

For his part, umpire McInnes suggests that the words 'or jerked' be deleted from Law 26, which says 'the ball must be bowled, not thrown or jerked.'

Richie Benaud hands Peter May his cap. May would rather it be the Ashes.

FIRST TEST 1958–59 AUSTRALIA v ENGLAND
Brisbane Cricket Ground, Brisbane. December 5, 6, 8, 9, 10. 1958.
Toss: England. Australia won by 8 wkts.

ENGLAND
PE Richardson c Mackay b Davidson	11	c & b Benaud	8
CA Milton b Meckiff	5	c Grout b Davidson	17
TW Graveney c Grout b Davidson	19 (4)	run out	36
PBH May (c) c Grout b Meckiff	26 (5)	lbw Benaud	4
MC Cowdrey c Kline b Meckiff	13 (6)	c Kline b Meckiff	28
TE Bailey st Grout b Benaud	27 (3)	b Mackay	68
TG Evans (+) c Burge b Davidson	4	lbw Davidson	4
GAR Lock c Davidson b Benaud	5	b Meckiff	1
JC Laker c Burke b Benaud	13	b Benaud	15
JB Statham c Grout b Mackay	2	c McDonald b Benaud	3
PJ Loader not out	6	not out	0
EXTRAS (LB 1, W 1, NB 1)	3	(B 10, LB 4)	14
TOTAL	134		198

FOW 1st Inns: 16 16 62 75 79 83 92 112 116 134
FOW 2nd Inns: 28 34 96 102 153 161 169 190 198 198

Bowling: *First Innings*: Davidson 16-4-36-3, Meckiff 17-5-33-3, Mackay 8-1-16-1, Benaud 18.4-9-46-3. *Second Innings*: Davidson 28-12-30-2, Meckiff 19-7-30-2, Mackay 9-6-7-1, Benaud 39.2-10-66-4, Kline 14-4-34-0, Burke 10-5-17-0.

AUSTRALIA
CC McDonald c Graveney b Bailey	42	c Statham b Laker	15
JW Burke c Evans b Loader	20	not out	28
RN Harvey lbw Loader	14	c Milton b Lock	23
NC O'Neill c Graveney b Bailey	34	not out	71
PJP Burge c Cowdrey b Bailey	2		
KD Mackay c Evans b Laker	16		
R Benaud (c) lbw Loader	16		
AK Davidson lbw Laker	25		
ATW Grout (+) b Statham	2		
I Meckiff b Loader	5		
LF Kline not out	4		
EXTRAS (B 4, LB 1, NB 1)	6	(B 2, LB 3, NB 5)	10
TOTAL	186		2 for 147

FOW 1st Inns: 55 65 88 94 122 136 162 165 178 186
FOW 2nd Inns: 20 58

Bowling: *First Innings*: Statham 20-2-57-1, Loader 19-4-56-4, Bailey 13-2-35-3, Laker 10.1-3-15-2, Lock 10-4-17-0. *Second Innings*: Statham 6-1-13-0, Loader 9-1-27-0, Bailey 5-1-21-0, Laker 17-3-39-1, Lock 14.7-5-37-1.

Umpires: C Hoy & MJ McInnes

SECOND TEST 1958–59 AUSTRALIA v ENGLAND
Melbourne Cricket Ground, Melbourne. December 31, 1958, January 1, 2, 3, 5, 1958.
Toss: England. Australia won by 8 wkts.

ENGLAND
PE Richardson c Grout b Davidson	3	c Harvey b Meckiff	2
TE Bailey c Benaud b Meckiff	48	c Burke b Meckiff	14
W Watson b Davidson	0	b Davidson	7
TW Graveney lbw Davidson	0	c Davidson b Meckiff	3
PBH May (c) b Meckiff	113	c Davidson b Meckiff	17
MC Cowdrey c Grout b Davidson	44	c Grout b Meckiff	12
TG Evans (+) c Davidson b Meckiff	4	run out	11
GAR Lock st Grout b Benaud	5	c & b Davidson	6
JC Laker not out	22	c Harvey b Davidson	3
JB Statham b Davidson	13	not out	8
PJ Loader b Davidson	1	b Meckiff	0
EXTRAS (B 1, LB 2, W 3)	6	(B 1, LB 1, NB 2)	4
TOTAL	259		87

FOW 1st Inns: 7 7 7 92 210 218 218 233 253 259
FOW 2nd Inns: 3 14 21 27 44 57 71 75 80 87

Bowling: *First Innings*: Davidson 25.5-7-64-6, Meckiff 24-4-69-3, Mackay 9-2-16-0, Benaud 29-7-61-1, Kline 11-2-43-0. *Second Innings*: Davidson 15-2-41-3, Meckiff 15.2-3-38-6, Benaud 1-0-4-0.

AUSTRALIA
CC McDonald c Graveney b Statham	47	lbw Statham	5
JW Burke b Statham	3	not out	18
RN Harvey b Loader	167 (4)	not out	7
NC O'Neill c Evans b Statham	37		
KD Mackay c Evans b Statham	18		
RB Simpson lbw Loader	0		
R Benaud (c) lbw Statham	0		
AK Davidson b Statham	24		
ATW Grout (+) c May b Loader	8 (3)	st Evans b Laker	12
I Meckiff b Statham	0		
LF Kline not out	1		
EXTRAS (LB 3)	3		0
TOTAL	308		2 for 42

FOW 1st Inns: 11 137 255 257 261 262 295 300 300 308
FOW 2nd Inns: 6 26

Bowling: *First Innings*: Statham 28-6-57-7, Loader 27.2-4-97-3, Bailey 16-0-50-0, Laker 12-1-47-0, Lock 17-2-54-0. *Second Innings*: Statham 5-1-11-1, Loader 5-1-13-0, Laker 4-1-7-1, Lock 3.1-1-11-0.

Umpires: MJ McInnes & RR Wright

THIRD TEST 1958–59 AUSTRALIA v ENGLAND
Sydney Cricket Ground, Sydney. January 9, 10, 12, 13, 14, 15, 1959.
Toss: England. Match Drawn.

ENGLAND

TE Bailey lbw Meckiff	8	c (S)RB Simpson b Benaud	25
CA Milton c Meckiff b Davidson	8	c Davidson b Benaud	8
TW Graveney c Harvey b Benaud	33	lbw Davidson	22
PBH May (c) c Mackay b Slater	42	b Burke	92
MC Cowdrey c Harvey b Benaud	34	not out	100
ER Dexter lbw Slater	1	c Grout b Benaud	11
R Swetman (+) c Mackay b Benaud	41	lbw Burke	5
GAR Lock lbw Mackay	21 (9)	not out	11
FS Trueman c Burke b Benaud	18 (8)	st Grout b Benaud	0
JC Laker c Harvey b Benaud	2		
JB Statham not out	0		
EXTRAS (B 4, LB 5, W 2)	11	(B 11, LB 1, W 1)	13
TOTAL	219	7 dec	287

FOW 1st Inns: 19 23 91 97 98 155 194 200 202 219
FOW 2nd Inns: 30 37 64 246 262 269 270

Bowling: *First Innings*: Davidson 12-3-21-1, Meckiff 15-2-45-1, Benaud 33.4-10-83-5, Slater 14-4-40-2, Mackay 8-3-19-1. *Second Innings*: Davidson 33-11-65-1, Meckiff 3-1-7-0, Benaud 33-7-94-4, Slater 18-5-61-0, Mackay 11-2-21-0, Burke 11-3-26-2.

AUSTRALIA

CC McDonald c Graveney b Lock	40	b Laker	16
JW Burke c Lock b Laker	12	b Laker	7
RN Harvey b Laker	7	not out	18
NC O'Neill c Swetman b Laker	77	not out	7
LE Favell c Cowdrey b Lock	54		
KD Mackay b Trueman	57		
R Benaud (c) b Laker	6		
AK Davidson lbw Lock	71		
ATW Grout (+) c Statham b Laker	14		
KN Slater not out	1		
I Meckiff b Lock	2		
EXTRAS (B 5, LB 10, NB 1)	16	(B 6)	6
TOTAL	357	2 for	54

FOW 1st Inns: 26 52 87 197 199 208 323 353 355 357
FOW 2nd Inns: 22 33

Bowling: *First Innings*: Statham 16-2-48-0, Trueman 18-3-37-1, Lock 43.2-9-130-4, Laker 46-9-107-5, Bailey 5-0-19-0. *Second Innings*: Statham 2-0-6-0, Trueman 4-1-9-0, Lock 11-4-23-0, Laker 8-3-10-2.

Umpires: C Hoy & MJ McInnes

FIFTH TEST 1958–59 AUSTRALIA v ENGLAND
Melbourne Cricket Ground, Melbourne. February 13, 14, 16, 17, 18, 1959.
Toss: Australia. Australia won by 9 wkts.

ENGLAND

PE Richardson c & b Benaud	68	lbw Benaud	23
TE Bailey c Davidson b Lindwall	0	b Lindwall	0
PBH May (c) c Benaud b Meckiff	11	c Harvey b Lindwall	4
MC Cowdrey c Lindwall b Davidson	22	run out	46
TW Graveney c McDonald b Benaud	19	c Harvey b Davidson	54
ER Dexter c Lindwall b Meckiff	6	c Grout b Davidson	6
R Swetman (+) c Grout b Davidson	1	lbw Lindwall	9
JB Mortimore not out	44	b Rorke	11
FS Trueman c & b Benaud	21	b Rorke	36
FH Tyson c Grout b Benaud	9	c Grout b Rorke	6
JC Laker c Harvey b Davidson	2	not out	5
EXTRAS (LB 4, W 4)	8	(B 9, LB 3, W 2)	14
TOTAL	205		214

FOW 1st Inns: 0 13 61 109 112 124 128 191 203 205
FOW 2nd Inns: 0 12 78 105 131 142 158 172 182 214

Bowling: *First Innings*: Davidson 12.5-2-38-3, Lindwall 14-2-36-1, Meckiff 15-2-57-2, Rorke 6-1-23-0, Benaud 17-5-43-4. *Second Innings*: Davidson 21-1-95-2, Lindwall 11-2-37-3, Meckiff 4-0-13-0, Rorke 12.4-2-41-3, Benaud 6-1-14-1.

AUSTRALIA

CC McDonald c Cowdrey b Laker	133	not out	51
JW Burke c Trueman b Tyson	16	lbw Tyson	13
RN Harvey c Swetman b Trueman	13	not out	1
NC O'Neill c Cowdrey b Trueman	0		
KD Mackay c Graveney b Laker	23		
AK Davidson b Mortimore	17		
R Benaud (c) c Swetman b Laker	64		
ATW Grout (+) c Trueman b Laker	74		
RR Lindwall c Cowdrey b Trueman	0		
I Meckiff c & b Trueman	2		
GF Rorke not out	0		
EXTRAS (B 5, LB 4)	9	(LB 4)	4
TOTAL	351	1 for	69

FOW 1st Inns: 41 83 83 154 207 209 324 327 329 351
FOW 2nd Inns: 66

Bowling: *First Innings*: Trueman 25-0-92-4, Tyson 20-1-73-1, Bailey 14-2-43-0, Laker 30.5-4-93-4, Mortimore 11-1-41-1. *Second Innings*: Trueman 6.7-0-45-0, Tyson 6-0-20-1.

Umpires: L Townsend & RR Wright

FOURTH TEST 1958–59 AUSTRALIA v ENGLAND
Adelaide Oval, Adelaide. January 30, 31, February 2, 3, 4, 5, 1959.
Toss: England. Australia won by 10 wkts.

AUSTRALIA

CC McDonald b Trueman	170		
JW Burke c Cowdrey b Bailey	66	not out	16
RN Harvey run out	41		
NC O'Neill b Statham	56		
LE Favell b Statham	4 (1)	not out	15
KD Mackay c Evans b Statham	4		
R Benaud (c) b Trueman	46		
AK Davidson c Bailey b Tyson	43		
ATW Grout (+) lbw Trueman	9		
RR Lindwall b Trueman	19		
GF Rorke not out	2		
EXTRAS (B 2, LB 8, W 4, NB 2)	16	(B 4, LB 1)	5
TOTAL	476	0 for	36

FOW 1st Inns: 171 276 286 294 369 388 407 445 473 476
FOW 2nd Inns:

Bowling: *First Innings*: Statham 23-0-83-3, Trueman 30.1-6-90-4, Tyson 28-1-100-1, Bailey 22-2-91-1, Lock 25-0-96-0. *Second Innings*: Statham 4-0-11-0, Trueman 3-1-3-0, Lock 2-0-8-0, Cowdrey 1.3-0-9-0.

ENGLAND

PE Richardson lbw Lindwall	4	lbw Benaud	43
TE Bailey c Davidson	4 (6)	c Grout b Lindwall	6
PBH May (c) b Benaud	37	lbw Rorke	59
MC Cowdrey b Rorke	84	b Lindwall	8
TW Graveney c Benaud b Rorke	41	not out	53
W Watson b Rorke	25 (2)	c Favell b Benaud	40
FS Trueman c Grout b Benaud	0	c Grout b Davidson	0
GAR Lock c Grout b Benaud	5	b Rorke	9
FH Tyson c & b Benaud	0	c Grout b Benaud	33
TG Evans (+) c Burke b Benaud	4 (11)	c Benaud b Davidson	0
JB Statham not out	36 (10)	c O'Neill b Benaud	2
EXTRAS (LB 2, NB 1)	3	(B 5, LB 5, W 3, NB 4)	17
TOTAL	240		270

FOW 1st Inns: 7 11 74 170 173 180 184 184 188 240
FOW 2nd Inns: 89 110 125 177 198 199 222 268 270 270

Bowling: *First Innings*: Davidson 12-0-49-1, Lindwall 15-0-66-1, Rorke 18.1-7-23-3, Benaud 27-6-91-5, O'Neill 2-1-8-0. *Second Innings*: Davidson 8.3-3-17-2, Lindwall 26-6-70-2, Rorke 34-7-78-2, Benaud 29-10-82-4, Burke 4-2-6-0.

Umpires: MJ McInnes & RR Wright

Australian Averages

1958–59 AUSTRALIA v ENGLAND

AUSTRALIA	M	Inn	NO	Runs	H.S	Avrge	Ct	St	Overs	Mds	Runs	Wkt	Avrge
Benaud, R	5	5	-	132	64	26.40	8	-	233.2	65	584	31	18.84
Burge, PJP	1	1	-	2	2	2.00	1	-	-	-	-	-	-
Burke, JW	5	10	3	199	66	28.43	4	-	25.0	10	49	2	24.50
Davidson, AK	5	5	-	180	71	36.00	7	-	183.5	45	456	24	19.00
Favell, LE	2	3	1	73	54	36.50	1	-	-	-	-	-	-
Grout, ATW	5	6	-	119	74	19.83	17	3	-	-	-	-	-
Harvey, RN	5	9	3	291	167	48.50	8	-	-	-	-	-	-
Kline, LF	2	2	2	5	4*	-	2	-	25.0	6	77	-	-
Lindwall, RR	2	2	-	19	19	9.50	2	-	66.0	10	209	7	29.86
Mackay, KD	5	5	-	118	57	23.60	3	-	45.0	14	79	3	26.33
McDonald, CC	5	9	1	519	170	64.88	2	-	-	-	-	-	-
Meckiff, I	4	4	-	9	5	2.25	1	-	112.2	24	292	17	17.18
O'Neill, NC	5	7	2	282	77	56.40	1	-	2.0	1	8	-	-
Rorke, GF	2	2	2	2	2*	-	-	-	70.5	17	165	8	20.63
Simpson, RB	1	1	-	0	0	0.00	-	-	-	-	-	-	-
Slater, KN	1	1	1	1	1*	-	-	-	32.0	9	101	2	50.50

English Averages

1958–59 AUSTRALIA v ENGLAND

ENGLAND	M	Inn	NO	Runs	H.S	Avrge	Ct	St	Overs	Mds	Runs	Wkt	Avrge
Bailey, TE	5	10	-	200	68	20.00	1	-	75.0	7	259	4	64.75
Cowdrey, MC	5	10	1	391	100*	43.44	6	-	1.3	-	9	-	-
Dexter, ER	2	4	-	18	11	4.50	-	-	-	-	-	-	-
Evans, TG	3	6	-	27	11	4.50	5	1	-	-	-	-	-
Graveney, TW	5	10	1	280	54	31.11	5	-	-	-	-	-	-
Laker, JC	4	7	2	62	22*	12.40	-	-	127.6	24	318	15	21.20
Loader, PJ	2	4	2	7	6*	3.50	-	-	60.2	10	193	7	27.57
Lock, GAR	4	8	1	60	21	8.57	1	-	126.2	25	376	5	75.20
May, PBH	5	10	-	405	113	40.50	1	-	-	-	-	-	-
Milton, CA	2	4	-	38	17	9.50	-	-	-	-	-	-	-
Mortimore, JB	1	2	1	55	44*	55.00	-	-	11.0	1	41	1	41.00
Richardson, PE	4	8	-	162	68	20.25	-	-	-	-	-	-	-
Statham, JB	4	7	3	64	36*	16.00	2	-	104.0	12	286	12	23.83
Swetman, R	2	4	-	56	41	14.00	3	-	-	-	-	-	-
Trueman, FS	3	6	-	75	36	12.50	3	-	87.0	11	276	9	30.67
Tyson, FH	2	4	-	48	33	12.00	-	-	54.0	2	193	3	64.33
Watson, W	2	4	-	72	40	18.00	-	-	-	-	-	-	-

Australia is on top in tedious cricket

Karachi, Dec. 9. Cricket has a different flavour in Pakistan than the Australians have been used to, but they have come through some trying experiences with two Test wins and a draw.

The first Test in Dacca, East Pakistan, was remarkable for the monsoonal rain which destroyed the pitch and created a soggy and deep green outfield, instead of the usual yellow grass.

A matting wicket was dragged over the sodden strip, causing captain Richie Benaud concern that it might not be pulled tight enough to give the batsmen a chance on an even surface. Benaud had Lindsay Kline monitor the laying of the strip by the ground staff.

The nemesis of Australia's first Pakistan game in 1956–57, Fazal Mahmood, was lying in wait for the Australians, and only a stout hand of 96 by Neil Harvey allowed them to get to 225 and lead by 25 runs.

But then, with the fast bowlers making no headway, Australia found an ace up its sleeve in the shape of Ken Mackay. The accurate medium pacer reverted to flat and snaking off-spin, bringing the *Pakistan Observer* to comment: 'Mackay had so hypnotised the batsman that it was almost sacrilegious to handle him roughly.' Mackay took 6/42 in Pakistan's 134, and Australia had only 112 to get.

The second Test in Lahore was characterised by terribly slow play. Pakistan took nearly all day to make 146 in yet another poor start.

Pakistan's star batsman Hanif Mahommad made runs in each Test.

The shining light for Australia was Norman O'Neill, who made 134, using powerful on side shots, and the match seemed won as Australia led by 245 runs.

Pakistan batsman Saeed Ahmed however was determined to cling to the crease and on the fourth day only 150 runs were scored in 385 minutes. Ahmed made 166 and he was aided by slowcoach Shuja-ud-Din, who made 45 in 318 minutes.

In the end Australia had only two hours to make 122, and got there with 12 minutes to spare.

The third Test was even slower, trying the patience of even the cricket-mad Karachi crowd.

There was never the hope of a result.

US President sees the slowest day of cricket ever played

Colin McDonald, doughty opening batsman, has played some courageous innings.

Karachi, Dec. 8. What luck for US President Dwight D. Eisenhower! A day at the cricket as a welcome relief from affairs of state and discussions with the severe President of Pakistan, Field Marshal Mohammad Ayub Khan.

'Ike' was the first of his exalted number to watch a Test match, although he may have some memories of the game played among the English as he plotted the invasion of Normandy in 1945.

If it seemed a cheery diversion then it must have stunned the President today. He happened on the second slowest day's play in Test history, as 104 runs were scored for the loss of five Pakistan wickets. At one stage Pakistan scored 27 runs in 130 minutes.

Conversation must have been stilted in the Presidential box, with words such as 'incomprehensible', 'dull' and 'ridiculous' being studiously avoided.

FIRST TEST 1959-60 PAKISTAN v AUSTRALIA
National Stadium, Dacca. November 13, 14, 15, 17, 18, 1959.
Toss: Australia. Australia won by 8 wkts.

PAKISTAN

Hanif Mohammad b Mackay	66	b Benaud	19
Ijaz Butt c Grout b Davidson	0	b Mackay	20
Saeed Ahmed c Harvey b Davidson	37	b Mackay	15
W Mathias c & b Benaud	4	lbw Mackay	1
D Sharpe run out	56	lbw Mackay	35
Wazir Mohammad c Meckiff b Benaud	0	lbw Benaud	5
Imtiaz Ahmed (+) b Davidson	13	b Mackay	4
Israr Ali st Grout b Benaud	7 (9)	b Benaud	0
Shujauddin not out	2 (8)	not out	16
Fazal Mahmood (c) b Benaud	1	c & b Mackay	4
Nasim-ul-Ghani b Benaud	5	c McDonald b Benaud	0
EXTRAS (B 5, LB 1, NB 3)	9	(B 7, LB 5, NB 2)	14
TOTAL	200		134

FOW 1st Inns: 3 75 82 145 146 170 184 191 193 200
FOW 2nd Inns: 32 57 62 68 81 94 117 128 133 134

Bowling: *First Innings*: Davidson 23.5-7-42-4, Meckiff 10-2-33-0, Lindwall 15-1-31-0, Benaud 38-10-69-4, Mackay 19-12-16-1. *Second Innings*: Davidson 11-3-23-0, Meckiff 3-1-8-0, Lindwall 2-0-5-0, Benaud 39.3-26-42-4, Mackay 45-27-42-6.

AUSTRALIA

CC McDonald lbw Fazal	19	not out	44
LE Favell b Israr	0	c & b Israr	4
RN Harvey b Fazal	96	b Fazal	30
NC O'Neill b Nasim-ul-Ghani	2	not out	26
PJP Burge c Imtiaz b Nasim-ul-Ghani	0		
R Benaud (c) lbw Nasim-ul-Ghani	16		
KD Mackay b Fazal	7		
AK Davidson lbw Israr	4		
ATW Grout (+) not out	66		
RR Lindwall lbw Fazal	4		
I Meckiff b Fazal	2		
EXTRAS (LB 9)	9	(B 3, LB 3, NB 2)	8
TOTAL	225	2 for	112

FOW 1st Inns: 0 51 53 53 112 134 143 151 189 225
FOW 2nd Inns: 12 65

Bowling: *First Innings*: Fazal 35.5-11-71-5, Israr 23-5-85-2, Nasim-ul-Ghani 17-4-51-3, Shujauddin 3-0-9-0. *Second Innings*: Fazal 20.1-4-52-1, Israr 9-0-20-1, Nasim-ul-Ghani 10-2-16-0, Shujauddin 8-4-12-0, Saeed 1-0-4-0.

Umpires: Khwaja Saeed Ahmed & AA Qureshi

THIRD TEST 1959-60 PAKISTAN v AUSTRALIA
National Stadium, Karachi. December 4,5,6,8,9, 1959.
Toss: Pakistan. Match Drawn.

PAKISTAN

Hanif Mohammad lbw Lindwall	51 (4)	not out	101
Imtiaz Ahmed (+) b Davidson	18	c Harvey b Davidson	9
Saeed Ahmed c Harvey b Lindwall	91	c Harvey b Davidson	8
Shujauddin c O'Neill b Benaud	5 (6)	c Favell b Mackay	4
D Sharpe c Burge b Benaud	4	c Mackay b Lindwall	26
Ijaz Butt c Grout b Benaud	58 (1)	not out	8
W Mathias c Favell b Mackay	43	c Davidson b Benaud	13
Intikhab Alam run out	0	c Burge b Mackay	6
Fazal Mahmood (c) c Harvey b Benaud	7	c Benaud b Davidson	11
Mohammad Munaf not out	4	not out	4
Munir Malik st Grout b Benaud	0		
EXTRAS (LB 3, NB 3)	6	(LB 2, NB 2)	4
TOTAL	287	8 dec	194

FOW 1st Inns: 36 124 143 149 181 265 267 276 287 287
FOW 2nd Inns: 11 25 25 78 91 124 159 179

Bowling: *First Innings*: Davidson 26-5-59-1, Lindwall 25-6-72-2, Benaud 49.5-17-93-5, Mackay 27-8-53-1, O'Neill 4-1-4-0. *Second Innings*: Davidson 34-8-70-3, Lindwall 17-10-14-1, Benaud 26-13-48-1, Mackay 32.4-11-58-2.

AUSTRALIA

CC McDonald b Intikhab	19	lbw Munir	30
GB Stevens c Mathias b Fazal	13	c Imtiaz b Intikhab	28
ATW Grout (+) c & b Intikhab	20		
KD Mackay c Ijaz b Fazal	40		
RN Harvey c Imtiaz b Fazal	54 (3)	not out	13
NC O'Neill b Munir	6 (4)	not out	7
LE Favell c Sharpe b Fazal	10		
PJP Burge c Sharpe b Mohammad	12		
R Benaud (c) c Imtiaz b Munir	18		
AK Davidson not out	39		
RR Lindwall c Imtiaz b Fazal	23		
EXTRAS (LB 1, NB 2)	3	(LB 3, NB 2)	5
TOTAL	257	2 for	83

FOW 1st Inns: 29 33 82 106 122 145 174 184 207 257
FOW 2nd Inns: 54 76

Bowling: *First Innings*: Fazal 30.2-12-74-5, Mohammad 8-0-42-1, Intikhab 19-4-49-2, Munir 22-5-76-2, Shujauddin 3-0-13-0. *Second Innings*: Fazal 10.5-16-0, Mohammad 3-0-10-0, Intikhab 6-1-13-1, Munir 9-1-24-1, Shujauddin 2-1-9-0, Saeed 3-0-6-0.

Umpires: Khwaja Saeed Ahmed & Munawar Hussain

SECOND TEST 1959-60 PAKISTAN v AUSTRALIA
Lahore Stadium, Lahore. November 21,22,23,25,26, 1959.
Toss: Pakistan. Australia won by 7 wkts.

PAKISTAN

Hanif Mohammad c Grout b Meckiff	49 (5)	b Kline	18
Imtiaz Ahmed (c+) b Davidson	18	c O'Neill b Kline	54
Saeed Ahmed c Grout b Meckiff	17	st Grout b Kline	166
Alimuddin b Meckiff	8 (1)	b Kline	7
D Sharpe c Grout b Kline	12 (6)	st Grout b Kline	1
Waqar Hassan c Grout b Davidson	12 (7)	b Kline	4
Shujauddin b Benaud	17 (4)	lbw O'Neill	45
Israr Ali lbw Benaud	0 (10)	not out	0
Nasim-ul-Ghani c Stevens b Davidson	6 (8)	b Benaud	15
Mohammad Munaf c Grout b Davidson	5 (9)	c Davidson b Kline	19
Haseeb Ahsan not out	0	c Grout b Benaud	4
EXTRAS (B 1, LB 1)	2	(B 31, LB 2)	33
TOTAL	146		366

FOW 1st Inns: 39 56 92 109 115 120 121 126 142 146
FOW 2nd Inns: 45 87 256 312 319 324 325 362 362 366

Bowling: *First Innings*: Davidson 19-2-48-4, Meckiff 19-7-45-3, Benaud 16-6-36-2, Kline 12-6-15-1. *Second Innings*: Davidson 35-9-56-0, Meckiff 22-4-44-0, Benaud 54.4-22-92-2, Kline 44-21-75-7, O'Neill 13.5-3-37-1, Mackay 6-1-21-0, Harvey 5-2-8-0.

AUSTRALIA

CC McDonald c Imtiaz b Haseeb	42		
GB Stevens c Imtiaz b Mohammad	9	c Alimuddin b Mohammad	8
RN Harvey lbw Mohammad	43	b Mohammad	37
NC O'Neill st Imtiaz b Shujauddin	134	not out	43
LE Favell b Israr	32 (1)	b Israr	4
ATW Grout (+) lbw Nasim-ul-Ghani	12		
R Benaud (c) b Haseeb	29 (5)	not out	21
AK Davidson c Imtiaz b Israr	47		
KD Mackay c Imtiaz b Haseeb	26		
LF Kline not out	0		
I Meckiff			
EXTRAS (B 5, LB 5, NB 7)	17	(B 6, LB 4)	10
TOTAL	9 dec 391	3 for	123

FOW 1st Inns: 27 83 114 213 247 310 311 391 391
FOW 2nd Inns: 13 15 77

Bowling: *First Innings*: Mohammad 31-8-100-2, Israr 13-5-29-2, Nasim-ul-Ghani 21-3-72-1, Shujauddin 20-2-58-1, Haseeb 33.3-8-115-3. *Second Innings*: Mohammad 10-2-38-2, Israr 5-1-20-1, Nasim-ul-Ghani 3.3-0-18-0, Shujauddin 3-0-16-0, Haseeb 4-0-21-0.

Umpires: Khwaja Saeed Ahmed & AA Qureshi

Australian Averages

1959-60 PAKISTAN v AUSTRALIA

AUSTRALIA	M	Inn	NO	Runs	H.S	Avrge	Ct	St	Overs	Mds	Runs	Wkt	Avrge
Benaud, R	3	4	1	84	29	28.00	2	-	224.0	94	380	18	21.11
Burge, PJP	2	2	-	12	12	6.00	2	-					
Davidson, AK	3	3	1	90	47	45.00	2	-	148.5	34	298	12	24.83
Favell, LE	3	5	-	50	32	10.00	2	-					
Grout, ATW	3	3	1	98	66*	49.00	8	4					
Harvey, RN	3	6	-	273	96	54.60	5	-	5.0	2	8	-	-
Kline, LF	1	1	1	0	0*	-	-	-	56.0	27	90	8	11.25
Lindwall, RR	2	2	-	27	23	13.50	-	-	59.0	17	122	3	40.67
Mackay, KD	3	3	-	73	40	24.33	2	-	129.4	59	190	10	19.00
McDonald, CC	3	5	1	154	44*	38.50	1	-					
Meckiff, I	2	1	-	2	2	2.00	1	-	54.0	14	130	3	43.33
O'Neill, NC	3	6	3	218	134	72.67	-	-	17.0	6	41	1	41.00
Stevens, GB	2	4	-	58	28	14.50	1	-	-	-	-	-	-

Pakistani Averages

1959-60 PAKISTAN v AUSTRALIA

PAKISTAN	M	Inn	NO	Runs	H.S	Avrge	Ct	St	Overs	Mds	Runs	Wkt	Avrge
Alimuddin	1	2	-	15	8	7.50	1	-					
Fazal Mahmood	2	4	-	23	11	5.75	-	-	96.2	32	213	11	19.36
Hanif Mohammad	3	6	1	304	101*	60.80	-	-	-	-	-	-	-
Haseeb Ahsan	1	2	1	4	4	4.00	-	-	37.3	8	136	3	45.33
Ijaz Butt	2	4	-	86	58	21.50	1	-					
Imtiaz Ahmed	3	6	-	116	54	19.33	9	1					
Intikhab Alam	1	2	-	6	6	3.00	-	-	25.0	5	62	3	20.67
Israr Ali	2	4	1	8	7	2.67	1	-	50.0	11	154	6	25.67
Mathias, W	2	4	-	61	43	15.25	1	-					
Mohammad Munaf	2	4	2	32	19	16.00	-	-	52.0	10	190	5	38.00
Munir Malik	1	1	-	0	0	0.00	-	-	31.0	6	100	3	33.33
Nasim-ul-Ghani	2	4	-	26	15	6.50	1	-	51.3	9	157	4	39.25
Saeed Ahmed	3	6	-	334	166	55.67	-	-	4.0	-	10	-	-
Sharpe, D	3	6	-	134	56	22.33	2	-					
Shujauddin	3	6	2	89	45	22.25	-	-	39.0	7	117	1	117.00
Waqar Hassan	1	2	-	16	12	8.00	-	-					
Wazir Mohammad	1	2	-	5	5	2.50	-	-					

1959-60

AUSTRALIA IN INDIA

Gordon Rorke is downed by illness

Bombay, Jan. 6. Fast bowler Gordon Rorke has been sent back to Australia, suffering from extreme stomach illness, which has been diagnosed as hepatitis. The big man has lost eight kilos in weight since the tour began.

He, along with the other members of the team, have been suffering with stomach upsets as the tour has progressed through Pakistan and India. Rorke became too ill to continue in the second Test at Kanpur, and was taken to hospital. He did not play in any of the Pakistan Tests, but took two wickets in the first Test against India, without ever achieving the fierce pace and bounce that made him one of the most promising bowlers to emerge in recent years.

Two other players, Lindsay Kline and Gavin Stevens, are on the sick list, and unlikely to remain active on the tour.

The third Test in Bombay, played to a lifeless draw, was more notable off the field, with players on both sides suffering from stomach cramps and gastric illness.

Gordon Rorke: ill on the field.

Hero Patel

Jasubhai Patel: hero for India.

Kanpur, Dec. 24. The Australian Board of Control may have contributed to India's first victory over Australia in 13 Tests. With the Green Park pitch soft from protracted rain, the Indian Board offered Australia a matting pitch to make the contest 'more fair and even'. Australia declined.

Australian bowlers made good use of the pitch, but the Indian hero was Jasubhai Patel, who took 9/69 in the first innings with his off-spinners. With Australia needing 225 to win, Patel took 5/55 in the miserable total of 105. Australia started out at 2/58 and expected to cruise to victory, but Patel and 'Polly' Umrigar, who took 4/27, never allowed them a start. In the morning session eight wickets fell for 46.

Australia is in command

Madras, Jan. 17. After a drawn third Test in Bombay, Australia virtually sealed the series against India with an innings win in Madras.

Although depleted by the intense heat and gastric illness, the tourists fought strongly for their victory.

Richie Benaud won the toss for the first time and Australia had the luxury of batting first on a batsman's wicket. They were rewarded with 342, as Les Favell took the opening role to record his maiden century, and Ken Mackay held together the tail with a watchful 89. As seems the case on the subcontinent, Favell took all day to make his 100, and Mackay's innings lasted 210 minutes.

The best bowler was a paceman, Ramakant 'Tiny' Desai, who took 4/93, while Rameshchandra Nadkarni had 3/75.

Alan Davidson and Benaud, however, proved the superior bowling force and India was forced to follow-on after making 149. Benaud continued his good form with 5/43 and Davidson made the first break, having Pankaj Roy for 1, in his 3/36. Benaud, Meckiff and Mackay completed the humiliation as India could manage only 139 in the second innings.

The fifth Test in Calcutta seemed like another cakewalk when India made 194 and Australia replied with 331. Norm O'Neill confirmed his status with his second series century, making 113.

Indian resistance left Australia with 203 to get, in 150 minutes, but they fell behind in the chase, and were content with the draw and the series win.

Nadkarni: a useful series.

Davidson: led strong attack.

QUICK SINGLES

Big farewell. About 10,000 Pakistanis turn up at Karachi airport to farewell the Australian cricketers as they leave on December 10.

India down. The Indian team has just returned from England, where it was beaten in all five Tests.

Classic catch. Second Test scene. Nari Contractor swung to leg off Alan Davidson and Neil Harvey, at fine leg, ducked. The ball somehow stuck in the hollow of Harvey's bent knee, and he claimed the catch.

Caribbean run-fest. Playing against England in Barbados, Garfield Sobers (226) and Frank Worrell (197 not out) share a record fourth-wicket stand of 399 for the West Indies – the second highest for that wicket in Tests. The record (411)

was set by England's Peter May and Colin Cowdrey v West Indies in 1957.

Simpson's match. Bob Simpson (formerly of NSW) was on the field for the entire match as WA thrashed NSW by an innings and 105 runs. He made 236 not out in WA's 4/487, declared and then took 5/45 when NSW followed on. In WA's only innings, he shared a record unbeaten fifth-wicket stand of 301 with Ken Meuleman (153 not out).

Again. A week later, in the match ending December 22, Bob Simpson makes 230 not out as WA beat Queensland by an innings and seven runs.

Three in four. Victoria has a rare victory over the dominant NSW, by 214 runs, after John Power takes three wickets in four balls.

Grout's record. Wally Grout figures in eight dismissals for Queensland against

WA on February 12, a world first class record for a wicketkeeper.

NSW Shield. NSW steadies towards the end of the season to just hold the Sheffield Shield for a record seventh season. It beats Victoria, by two points, with WA third. Bob Simpson (WA) dominates the batting with 902 runs at an average of 300.66, while Johnny Martin (NSW) is the best bowler with 45 wickets.

Final tally. Ray Lindwall, in his last Test, takes 3/110 in the fifth Test in India to move his Australian-record wicket haul to 228, eight behind Alec Bedser's world record.

The Seconds. An Australian 'Second XI' toured New Zealand. The team was Ian Craig (captain), Len Maddocks, Brian Booth, Barry Fisher, Ron Gaunt, John Lill, Johnny Martin, Ian Quick, John Shaw, Bob Simpson, Keith Slater, and Grahame Thomas.

FIRST TEST 1959–60 INDIA v AUSTRALIA
Feroze Shah Kotla Ground, Delhi. December 12, 13, 14, 16, 1959.
Toss: India. Australia won by an innings & 127 runs.

INDIA

Pankaj Roy c Grout b Davidson	0	c Benaud b Kline	99
NJ Contractor b Davidson	41	c Favell b Benaud	34
PR Umrigar c Grout b Davidson	0 (5)	c Favell b Kline	32
AA Baig b Rorke	9 (3)	run out	5
CG Borde c Grout b Meckiff	14 (4)	c Davidson b Benaud	0
GS Ramchand (c) c Grout b Kline	20	c Davidson b Kline	6
RG Nadkarni b Rorke	1	lbw Benaud	7
PG Joshi (+) b Benaud	15	c Davidson b Kline	8
Surendranath not out	24	c Davidson b Benaud	0
VM Muddiah lbw Benaud	0	not out	0
RB Desai c O'Neill b Benaud	0	c Meckiff b Benaud	0
EXTRAS (B 6, LB 2, NB 3)	11	(B 8, LB 5, NB 2)	15
TOTAL	135		206

FOW 1st Inns: 4 8 32 66 69 70 100 131 135 135
FOW 2nd Inns: 121 132 132 172 187 192 202 206 206 206

Bowling: *First Innings*: Davidson 14-9-22-3, Meckiff 17-4-52-1, Rorke 14-5-30-2, Kline 9-3-15-1, Benaud 3.4-3-0-3, O'Neill 1-0-4-0, Mackay 1-0-1-0. *Second Innings*: Davidson 14-5-16-0, Meckiff 14-3-33-0, Rorke 7-3-5-0, Kline 24-12-42-4, Benaud 46-18-76-5, O'Neill 5-0-19-0, Harvey 1-1-0-0.

AUSTRALIA

CC McDonald b Surendranath	20
LE Favell b Surendranath	39
RN Harvey lbw Nadkarni	114
NC O'Neill run out	39
KD Mackay c Joshi b Umrigar	78
AK Davidson c Baig b Desai	25
R Benaud (c) c Borde b Umrigar	20
ATW Grout (+) b Umrigar	42
LF Kline c & b Ramchand	14
I Meckiff not out	45
GF Rorke c(S)BK Kunderan b Umrigar	7
EXTRAS (B 11, LB 13, NB 1)	25
TOTAL	468

FOW 1st Inns: 53 64 143 275 318 353 398 402 443 468

Bowling: *First Innings*: Desai 34.3-3-123-1, Ramchand 7-1-27-1, Surendranath 38-8-101-2, Borde 15-3-49-0, Muddiah 13-4-32-0, Nadkarni 20-6-62-1, Umrigar 15.3-1-49-4.

Umpires: SK Ganguli & Mahomed Yunus

SECOND TEST 1959–60 INDIA v AUSTRALIA
Green Park (Modi Stadium), Kanpur. December 19, 20, 21, 23, 24, 1959.
Toss: India. India won by 119 runs.

INDIA

Pankaj Roy c Harvey b Benaud	17	c Benaud b Davidson	8
NJ Contractor c Jarman b Benaud	24	c Harvey b Davidson	74
PR Umrigar c Davidson b Kline	6	c Rorke b Davidson	14
AA Baig b Davidson	19	c Harvey b Benaud	36
CG Borde c Kline b Davidson	20	c O'Neill b Meckiff	44
GS Ramchand (c) c Mackay b Benaud	24	b Harvey	5
RB Kenny b Davidson	0	c Jarman b Davidson	51
RG Nadkarni c Harvey b Davidson	25	lbw Davidson	46
NS Tamhane (+) b Benaud	1	c Harvey b Davidson	0
JM Patel c Kline b Davidson	4 (11)	b Davidson	0
Surendranath not out	8 (10)	not out	4
EXTRAS (LB 2, NB 2)	4	(B 7, LB 2)	9
TOTAL	152		291

FOW 1st Inns: 38 47 51 77 112 112 126 128 141 152
FOW 2nd Inns: 32 72 121 147 153 214 286 286 291 291

Bowling: *First Innings*: Davidson 20.1-7-31-5, Meckiff 8-2-15-0, Benaud 25-8-63-4, Rorke 2-1-3-0, Kline 15-7-36-1. *Second Innings*: Davidson 57.3-23-93-7, Meckiff 18-4-37-1, Benaud 38-15-81-1, Kline 7-3-14-0, Mackay 10-5-14-0, Harvey 12-3-31-1, O'Neill 2-0-12-0.

AUSTRALIA

CC McDonald b Patel	53	st Tamhane b Patel	34
GB Stevens c & b Patel	25	c Kenny b Patel	7
RN Harvey b Patel	51	c Nadkarni b Umrigar	25
NC O'Neill b Borde	16	c Nadkarni b Umrigar	5
KD Mackay lbw Patel	0	lbw Umrigar	0
AK Davidson b Patel	41	b Patel	8
R Benaud (c) b Patel	7	c Ramchand b Patel	0
BN Jarman (+) lbw Patel	1	b Umrigar	0
LF Kline b Patel	9	b Patel	0
I Meckiff not out	1	not out	14
GF Rorke c Baig b Patel	0		
EXTRAS (B 9, LB 2, NB 4)	15	(B 5, LB 7)	12
TOTAL	219		9 dec 105

FOW 1st Inns: 71 128 149 159 159 174 186 216 219 219
FOW 2nd Inns: 12 49 59 61 78 78 79 84 105

Bowling: *First Innings*: Surendranath 4-0-13-0, Ramchand 6-3-14-0, Patel 35.5-16-69-9, Umrigar 15-1-40-0, Borde 15-1-61-1, Nadkarni 2-0-7-0. *Second Innings*: Surendranath 4-2-4-0, Ramchand 3-0-7-0, Patel 25.4-7-55-5, Umrigar 25-11-27-4.

Umpires: SK Ganguli & AR Joshi

THIRD TEST 1959–60 INDIA v AUSTRALIA
Brabourne Stadium, Bombay. January 1, 2, 3, 5, 6, 1960.
Toss: India. Match Drawn.

INDIA

Pankaj Roy b Davidson	6	b Meckiff	57
NJ Contractor c Benaud b Meckiff	108	b Lindwall	43
PR Umrigar c Harvey b Davidson	0		
AA Baig c Grout b Davidson	50 (5)	c Mackay b Lindwall	58
CG Borde b Meckiff	26 (4)	b Meckiff	1
GS Ramchand (c) lbw Meckiff	0		
RB Kenny b Meckiff	20 (6)	not out	55
BK Kunderan (+) lbw Lindwall	19 (3)	hit wicket b Meckiff	2
RG Nadkarni	18 (7)	not out	1
SA Durani c Stevens b Benaud	18		
GM Guard c Benaud b Davidson	7		
EXTRAS (B 9, LB 4, NB 4)	17	(LB 9)	9
TOTAL	289		5 dec 226

FOW 1st Inns: 21 21 154 199 199 203 229 246 272 289
FOW 2nd Inns: 95 99 111 112 221

Bowling: *First Innings*: Davidson 34.5-9-62-4, Lindwall 23-7-56-1, Mackay 6-3-11-0, Meckiff 38-12-79-4, Benaud 41-24-64-1. *Second Innings*: Davidson 14-4-25-0, Lindwall 23-7-56-2, Mackay 6-4-6-0, Meckiff 28-8-67-3, Benaud 24-10-36-0, O'Neill 3-1-16-0, Harvey 3-1-11-0.

AUSTRALIA

CC McDonald b Nadkarni	36		
GB Stevens b Nadkarni	22		
RN Harvey b Nadkarni	102		
NC O'Neill c(S)MM Sood b Borde	163		
LE Favell b Nadkarni	1		
ATW Grout (+) b Nadkarni	31 (1)	not out	22
R Benaud (c) lbw Nadkarni	14 (3)	not out	12
AK Davidson not out	9		
KD Mackay b Borde	1		
RR Lindwall not out	1		
I Meckiff	(2)	b Roy	0
EXTRAS (B 4, LB 3)	7		0
TOTAL	8 dec 387		1 for 34

FOW 1st Inns: 60 63 270 282 358 376 379 380
FOW 2nd Inns: 4

Bowling: *First Innings*: Guard 33-7-93-0, Ramchand 35-13-85-0, Umrigar 8-2-19-0, Nadkarni 51-11-105-6, Borde 13-1-78-2. *Second Innings*: Guard 1-0-1-0, Roy 2-0-6-1, Contractor 2-1-5-0, Baig 2-0-13-0, Durani 1-0-9-0.

Umpires: HE Chowdhury & ND Nagarwalla

FOURTH TEST 1959–60 INDIA v AUSTRALIA
MA Chidambaram Stadium (Chepauk), Madras. January 13, 14, 15, 17, 1960.
Toss: Australia. Australia won by an innings & 55 runs.

AUSTRALIA

CC McDonald b Patel	16
LE Favell st Kunderan b Nadkarni	101
RN Harvey b Desai	11
NC O'Neill b Desai	40
PJP Burge b Desai	35
KD Mackay st Kunderan b Patel	89
AK Davidson lbw Nadkarni	6
ATW Grout (+) c Milkha Singh b Nadkarni	2
R Benaud (c) b Borde	25
I Meckiff c Roy b Desai	8
LF Kline not out	0
EXTRAS (B 3, LB 5, NB 1)	9
TOTAL	342

FOW 1st Inns: 58 77 147 197 216 239 249 308 329 342

Bowling: *First Innings*: Desai 41-10-93-4, Ramchand 15-6-26-0, Nadkarni 44-15-75-3, Patel 37-12-84-2, Borde 16-1-55-1.

INDIA

Pankaj Roy c Grout b Davidson	1	c O'Neill b Meckiff	3
BK Kunderan (+) b Benaud	71 (4)	b Benaud	33
RB Kenny b Mackay	33	c Grout b Meckiff	1
NJ Contractor c Kline b Benaud	7 (2)	c Meckiff b Kline	41
CG Borde c Grout b Kline	3	c Davidson b Benaud	1
GS Ramchand (c) c Harvey b Benaud	13 (8)	st Grout b Benaud	22
AG Milkha Singh b Davidson	16 (6)	b Harvey	9
RG Nadkarni c Kline b Benaud	3 (7)	run out	18
MM Sood st Grout b Davidson	0	b Davidson	3
RB Desai c McDonald b Benaud	0	not out	0
JM Patel not out	0	c Kline b Davidson	0
EXTRAS (B 1, NB 1)	2	(B 4, LB 2, NB 1)	7
TOTAL	149		138

FOW 1st Inns: 20 95 111 114 130 130 145 148 149 149
FOW 2nd Inns: 7 11 54 62 78 100 127 138 138 138

Bowling: *First Innings*: Davidson 19-6-36-3, Meckiff 7-4-21-0, Benaud 32.1-14-43-5, Kline 15-8-21-1, Harvey 1-0-9-0, Mackay 3-0-17-1. *Second Innings*: Davidson 19-7-33-2, Meckiff 22-10-33-2, Benaud 35-19-43-3, Kline 12-5-13-1, Harvey 13-7-8-1, Mackay 4-3-1-0.

Umpires: ND Sane & MG Vijayasarathi

FIFTH TEST 1959–60 INDIA v AUSTRALIA
Eden Gardens, Calcutta. January 23, 24, 25, 27, 28, 1960.
Toss: India. Match Drawn.

INDIA

BK Kunderan (+) b Mackay	12		b Davidson	0
NJ Contractor b Benaud	36		c Davidson b Benaud	30
Pankaj Roy c Grout b Davidson	33		lbw Benaud	39
RG Nadkarni c Burge b Lindwall	2	(6)	c Grout b Lindwall	29
RB Kenny c Grout b Lindwall	7	(8)	c Grout b Mackay	62
CD Gopinath b Benaud	39	(5)	c Grout b Benaud	0
CG Borde b Benaud	6		b Meckiff	50
GS Ramchand (c) b Davidson	12	(9)	b Benaud	9
ML Jaisimha not out	20	(4)	b Mackay	74
RB Desai c Grout b Davidson	17		not out	17
JM Patel run out	0		c Benaud b Davidson	12
EXTRAS (B 5, LB 1, W 1, NB 3)	10		(B 11, LB 4, NB 2)	17
TOTAL	194			339

FOW 1st Inns: 30 59 71 83 112 131 142 158 194 194
FOW 2nd Inns: 0 67 78 78 123 206 289 294 316 339

Bowling: *First Innings*: Davidson 16-2-37-3, Meckiff 17-5-28-0, Mackay 11-5-16-1, Lindwall 16-6-44-2, Benaud 29.3-12-59-3. *Second Innings*: Davidson 36.2-13-76-2, Meckiff 21-2-41-1, Mackay 21-7-36-2, Lindwall 20-3-66-1, Benaud 48-23-103-4.

AUSTRALIA

LE Favell b Desai	26		not out	62
ATW Grout (+) b Patel	50			
RN Harvey c Jaisimha b Patel	17		c & b Contractor	36
NC O'Neill c Kunderan b Desai	113			
PJP Burge b Desai	60			
CC McDonald lbw Borde	27	(2)	run out	6
KD Mackay b Patel	18			
RR Lindwall c Kunderan b Desai	10			
AK Davidson b Borde	4			
R Benaud (c) c & b Borde	3	(4)	not out	10
I Meckiff not out	0			
EXTRAS (LB 3)	3		(B 1, LB 5, NB 1)	7
TOTAL	331			2 for 121

FOW 1st Inns: 76 76 116 266 273 299 323 325 328 331
FOW 2nd Inns: 20 104

Bowling: *First Innings*: Desai 36-4-111-4, Ramchand 10-1-37-0, Patel 26-2-104-3, Nadkarni 22-10-36-0, Borde 13.1-4-23-3, Jaisimha 4-0-17-0. *Second Innings*: Desai 11-4-18-0, Ramchand 3-2-4-0, Patel 7-1-15-0, Nadkarni 7-4-10-0, Borde 13-1-45-0, Jaisimha 6-2-13-0, Contractor 5-1-9-1.

Umpires: SK Ganguli & ND Sane

Australian Averages

1959–60 INDIA v AUSTRALIA

AUSTRALIA	M	Inn	NO	Runs	H.S	Avrge	Ct	St	Overs	Mds	Runs	Wkt	Avrge
Benaud, R	5	8	2	91	25	15.17	5	-	322.2	146	568	29	19.59
Burge, PJP	2	2	-	95	60	47.50	1	-	-	-	-	-	-
Davidson, AK	5	6	1	93	41	18.60	7	-	244.5	85	431	29	14.86
Favell, LE	4	5	1	229	101	57.25	2	-	-	-	-	-	-
Grout, ATW	4	5	1	147	50	36.75	14	2	-	-	-	-	-
Harvey, RN	5	7	-	356	114	50.86	7	-	30.0	12	59	2	29.50
Jarman, BN	1	2	-	1	1	0.50	2	-	-	-	-	-	-
Kline, LF	3	4	1	23	14	7.67	5	-	82.0	38	141	8	17.63
Lindwall, RR	2	2	1	11	10	11.00	-	-	82.0	23	222	6	37.00
Mackay, KD	5	6	-	186	89	31.00	2	-	62.0	27	102	4	25.50
McDonald, CC	5	7	-	192	53	27.43	1	-	-	-	-	-	-
Meckiff, I	5	6	4	68	45*	34.00	2	-	190.0	54	406	12	33.83
O'Neill, NC	5	6	-	376	163	62.67	3	-	11.0	1	51	-	-
Rorke, GF	2	2	-	7	7	3.50	1	-	23.0	9	38	2	19.00
Stevens, GB	2	3	-	54	25	18.00	1	-	-	-	-	-	-

Indian Averages

1959–60 INDIA v AUSTRALIA

INDIA	M	Inn	NO	Runs	H.S	Avrge	Ct	St	Overs	Mds	Runs	Wkt	Avrge
Baig, AA	3	6	-	177	58	29.50	2	-	2.0	-	13	-	-
Borde, CG	5	10	-	165	50	16.50	2	-	85.1	11	311	7	44.43
Contractor, NJ	5	10	-	438	108	43.80	1	-	7.0	2	14	1	14.00
Desai, RB	3	6	2	34	17*	8.50	-	-	122.3	21	345	9	38.33
Durani, SA	1	1	-	18	18	18.00	-	-	1.0	-	9	-	-
Gopinath, CD	1	2	-	39	39	19.50	-	-	-	-	-	-	-
Guard, GM	1	1	-	7	7	7.00	-	-	34.0	7	94	-	-
Jaisimha, ML	1	2	1	94	74	94.00	1	-	10.0	2	30	-	-
Joshi, PG	1	2	-	23	15	11.50	1	-	-	-	-	-	-
Kenny, RB	4	8	1	229	62	32.71	1	-	-	-	-	-	-
Kunderan, BK	3	6	-	137	71	22.83	2	2	-	-	-	-	-
Milkha Singh, AG	1	2	-	25	16	12.50	1	-	-	-	-	-	-
Muddiah, VM	1	2	1	0	0*	0.00	-	-	13.0	4	32	-	-
Nadkarni, RG	5	10	2	150	46	18.75	2	-	146.0	46	295	10	29.50
Patel, JM	3	6	1	16	12	3.20	1	-	131.3	38	327	19	17.21
Ramchand, GS	5	9	-	111	24	12.33	2	-	79.0	26	200	1	200.00
Roy, Pankaj	5	10	-	263	99	26.30	1	-	2.0	-	6	1	6.00
Sood, MM	1	2	-	3	3	1.50	-	-	-	-	-	-	-
Surendranath	2	4	3	36	24*	36.00	-	-	46.0	10	118	2	59.00
Tamhane, NS	1	2	-	1	1	0.50	-	1	-	-	-	-	-
Umrigar, PR	3	5	-	52	32	10.40	-	-	63.3	15	135	8	16.88

Davo – master of pace

Alan Davidson: carried a big physical burden, but never gave in.

A memorable sight in Test cricket of the 50s and early 60s is of Alan Davidson limping back to his bowling crease, there to be met by his skipper Richie Benaud for earnest consultation. Davo would square his shoulders and run in for just one more over, and one more, and one more.

Despite his workload and genuine physical distress, that same beautiful late-swinging delivery would be produced, that ball that hit the pitch and cut alarmingly, either way and off a length. When the pitch was right, Davidson seemed to be bowling hand grenades. They weren't overly fast, but they did things that scared the hell out of batsmen and had them groping, jamming, fending and blocking to keep the ball off the edge and out of the stumps.

Davidson did carry a severe load, as the change bowler who was elevated to the spearhead position with the retirement of Ray Lindwall and Keith Miller. He had a number of partners – Gordon Rorke, the luckless Ian Meckiff, Ron Gaunt, Frank Misson, Des Hoare, until Graham 'Garth' McKenzie came along to take some of the pressure.

Some of his deeds will stay in the mind's eye of all who saw them – his stupendous bowling in the Tied Test of 1961, when he took 5/135 in the first innings and 6/87 in the second. He became the first player to take 10 wickets and score 100 runs in a match,

and in the series he took 33 wickets in four Tests at 18.54, and also scored 212 runs in seven knocks (30.3).

This was an advance on some very productive work in previous Test series. Against South Africa in 1957–58 he took 23 wickets. Against England in Australia in 1958–59 he took 24, in 1961 in England he took 23 wickets and in Australia in 1962–63 he took 24.

In 44 Tests he took 186 wickets, and all the time he was likely to score runs as a hard-hitting tailender.

His best batting effort was in England when he made 77 not out as he and Garth McKenzie added 98 for the last wicket at Manchester to set up the Ashes victory.

Davidson came from Gosford, north of Sydney, and was keen on cricket as a small boy, making his own pitch and practising his leg-breaks. But he was needed to fill a pace bowling spot in a local team, and success put leg breaks out of his mind. He went to Sydney in the summer of 1948–49 at the age of 20 and got into the NSW side.

He was not overly successful early, and it was not until he went with an Australian Second XI to New Zealand that his ability to crash through a batting line-up was realised. In a match against Wairarapa he took 10/29 off 81 deliveries, and made 157 not out. He was soon back in the NSW side, then on his way to England for the 1953 tour.

The wicketkeepers

Ask the unanswerable question. Who was the best wicketkeeper for Australia? The one name in the Australian Cricket Hall of Fame is of Jack Blackham, who kept in the first-ever Test in 1877, and was behind the stumps for Australia in 35 Tests and more often for Victoria in a career lasting from 1874 to 1894.

He used an erect, rather than crouching, style and operated with meagre equipment to bowling which, at its fastest, was no faster than today's medium pace. Could he have been better than the three other contenders for top billing – Bert Oldfield, Don Tallon and Rodney Marsh? We have to rely on contemporary reports to have a look at the work of Blackham.

George Giffen toured with Blackham and played with and against him. He was obviously in awe of Blackham's brilliance. He says: 'He was peerless as a wicketkeeper. One could not help admiring him as he stood behind the stumps at a critical period of the game. With eyes as keen as a hawk, and regardless of knocks, he would take the fastest bowling with marvellous dexterity, and woe betide the batsman who even so much as lifted the heel of his back foot as he played forward and missed the ball. I have seen him do some marvellous things. For instance, when the 1884 Australian XI defeated the Gentlemen of England by 46 runs, he stumped the last three batsmen.'

Certainly Blackham's ratio of stumpings, and those of Oldfield and Tallon, are amazing compared with later wicketkeepers. Of 60 Test dismissals he had 24 stumped, and of 451 first class dismissals, 179 were stumped.

By comparison, Rod Marsh had 810 first class dismissals, with 61 stumped, and only 12 stumpings in 355 Test dismissals. The game has changed, with really quick bowling forcing the wicketkeeper back and being conducive to catches in the cordon rather than stumpings.

Those who followed Blackham in the early years never attracted quite the same praise. And there were not many between him and Oldfield, who started in 1919. Wicketkeepers tend to stamp the 'reserved' sign on the job and to hold it against all comers. There have been only 28 'keepers for Australia in Test history.

James Joseph 'Stumper' Kelly had

Don Tallon – only 17 Tests, but considered by some to be the best.

the job after Blackham and kept it for 36 Tests, in a career which went from 1896 to 1906. He was the first to keep to an innings of 500 runs without a bye, and the first to make eight dismissals in a Test (in Sydney in 1901–2), a record which was not surpassed until 1956.

Kelly's successor was Hanson Carter, from NSW, who had the job from 1907 to 1921, with a break in 1912 when he joined the 'rebels' who refused to tour.

Carter introduced the crouch as the bowler came to the crease. He stood a yard further back than Blackham or Kelly, which made him less effective as a stumper, but enabled him to pick up snicks and deflections. Like all 'keepers at Test level, he snared amazing catches with his skill and anticipation.

Oldfield took over from Carter, and he seems to be the bridge between the old timers and the 'keepers of today. He brought polish and stylish technique to the job, moving to the ball with grace, making positions on his feet where

other 'keepers, before and after, dived and lunged.

Oldfield was so dedicated to his craft that he would not go the pictures in case they affected his eyesight, and insisted that staff in his Sydney sports store throw objects to him instead of passing them.

The great England batsman Jack Hobbs described him as 'the best 'keeper of his time' and 'an artist in everything he did behind the wicket.' Oldfield was so complete and so economical that it seems he was only noticed on the rare occasions when something went wrong.

He was not one to appeal if he believed a batsman was not out, and if he stood silently when the slips cordon was in uproar, the umpire had an extra gauge for his judgement. He knew his business and took pride in it.

If Oldfield was the master craftsman, Don Tallon was said by some to be the supreme artist of them all.

He served a long apprenticeship to Oldfield and only had 17 Tests, but he left an indelible mark. He

was lean and suntanned with a lined and taciturn face, and he learned from Oldfield the art of economy and unobtrusive performance.

When he moved it was with lightning speed and he figured in some amazing catches and stumpings.

His catch at the Oval of Len Hutton off Lindwall, wide down the leg side, is among the very greatest. Don Bradman, who had seen a lot of Oldfield, described Tallon after that 1948 tour, as the best Australian 'keeper he had seen. His departure from the game, in 1953, was hastened by the onset of a slight deafness, which prevented him from hearing snicks.

The honor roll is short but illustrious. Tubby Gil Langley gave his all in 26 Tests, and had a record in 1956 when he dismissed nine batsmen in the Lord's Test.

Len Maddocks had a brief and neat stint in there when Langley was injured. Genial Wally Grout was a reliable performer through the Benaud years with 52 Tests, and has the record for six victims in a Test innings. He ignored a heart warning to go with the team to the West Indies, and he died young, at the age of 41.

Barry Jarman and Brian Taber had brief reigns before the job went to Western Australian Rod Marsh.

Judges were appalled that this bulky, apparently slow moving figure should have been preferred to the agile Taber. And his early fumbles won him the nickname 'Old Iron Gloves' from opponents. But he was fearless and effective keeping to the most lethal combination in Australian fast bowling, Lillee and Thomson.

He became the epitome of reliability, high spirits and team leadership for 14 years under the Chappell brothers. The change in the game, in which he played 96 Tests for a world record 355 dismissals is indicated by the fact that he had only 12 stumpings. His most common feature in the scorebooks was 'caught Marsh, bowled Lillee' – 95 times. His aggression was tempered with an innate sportsmanship.

Ian Healy, the incumbent from 1988–89 onwards, got the job after only six matches and had a less than convincing start. But he has improved into a top-class 'keeper adept at working with the spin of Shane Warne and others.

Young Ian Chappell takes an astounding catch to dismiss Indian captain Pataudi.

Benaud and beyond

Tied Test – cricket is alive

Brisbane, Dec. 14. On the evening of the third day of this extraordinary Test match Australian captain Richie Benaud and vice-captain Neil Harvey agreed over a quiet ale that it would probably be a draw. Two days to go and if the West Indies batted as they had in the first innings Australia would never get them out, and the West Indies surely couldn't get Australia out. A draw seemed the likeliest result.

Garfield 'Gary' Sobers had plundered a sensational 132 on the first day, inventing shots as the bowlers devised ways to bowl at him – one a back-foot drive for six off an Ian Meckiff slower ball. Sobers said the shot was 'made from being tricked by one ball and deciding not to be tricked by the next one like it.'

Out for 453, the West Indies were confronted by Norm O'Neill, who parried with a slower but seemingly match-winning century of his own – 181, after Bob Simpson (92) and Colin McDonald (57) had survived a fiery onslaught from Wes Hall. Australia finished with 505.

On the evening of the next day Benaud was buoyant. The West Indies were 9/259, Hall and Alf Valentine at the crease. Knock them over and a bit over 200 to get – should be easy.

However, the game had another twist in its tale, as the West Indian bowlers, notably Wes Hall, had Australia 2/7, then 4/49 and 6/92.

At the tea interval Sir Donald Bradman asked Benaud: 'What are you going for Richie – a win or a draw?' 'We're going for a win, of course,' he replied. 'I'm very

Norm O'Neill scores four of his 181 runs in Australia's first innings of 505.

pleased to hear it,' said Sir Don.

And go for it Benaud and Davidson did through the last session, adding 50 before drinks, with the crowd of 4000 or so gripped with frenzy, and 84 afterwards. With two overs to go, Australia was 6/226 and needed seven to win. Then Davidson was run out for a heroic 80 by an incredible Joe Solomon throw.

With one over left Australia (7/227) needed six to win. The drama mounting with each delivery. Benaud (52) and Grout (2) fell in the first six balls, as five runs were added – Australia 9/232, scores tied. Meckiff and Kline batting. Enter Solomon again. He throws down the stumps as Meckiff sprints for the winning run. Out. All out for 232. A tie!

How the game was all tied up in fateful last over

Brisbane, Dec. 14. Wally Grout had the strike the first ball of Wes Hall's last over. Hall took the ball and paced back to his mark, in the distance near the sight screen. He ran in on his athletic run-up, and exploded at the crease, a flurry of arms and legs, and hurled the ball down the pitch.

The first ball took Grout fair in the stomach, and he dropped his bat. Benaud, at the other end, was running for the single as Grout stumbled through.

Ball two was a bumper, and Benaud thought that it was a chance for four of the runs needed, and almost certain victory. He hooked, or tried to, and the ball took his glove as Gerry Alexander jubilantly took the catch.

'All yours Wal,' said Benaud. 'Thanks very much', muttered Grout. Five to win, six balls left.

Ian Meckiff played the third ball, and missed the fourth but they ran a bye as it whistled through to 'keeper Alexander.

Ball five was rising on a good length which Grout attempted to hook, but only managed to top edge it towards Rohan Kanhai at backward square leg – but Wes Hall, fired-up and desperate to win charged at the ball, took it from Kanhai's grasp, and dropped it.

Ball six, three runs needed. Meckiff swiped outside-in towards the mid-wicket boundary, scampering two runs, turning for the third as Conrad Hunte picked up the ball and threw in a single

action eighty yards from the stumps. A perfect throw to Alexander. Grout, out.

Ball seven, one wicket left, scores are tied. West Indies' skipper Frank Worrell, fielding at mid-on, talks to Hall. The weather was not mentioned – the not inconsiderable matter of a no-ball was.

Lindsay Kline was facing. Hall bowled, and Kline met the ball with the full face of the bat and turned it to forward square leg. They ran.

But Joe Solomon pounced as the batsmen crossed, Meckiff racing to the danger end, as Solomon threw and hit the stumps again, from side on. Umpire Hoy raised his finger – it was a tie – the first in 502 Test matches played around the world.

Great professionalism and good luck gave Ron Lovitt one of the best cricket pictures ever taken, as Joe Solomon throws down the wicket.

Neil Harvey out in the second innings and the West Indians celebrate.

Last frame gets a great picture

Brisbane, Dec. 14. Melbourne *Age* photographer Ron Lovitt had his camera, known as a Long Tom, with a specially adapted auto Graflex fitted with a 101 cm focal length lens on a makeshift 'grandstand' at the 'Gabba. The sheet film was contained in two magazines, each containing 12 negatives. They had to be unloaded and reloaded in a dark room during lunch or long breaks in play. At 5.55 p.m. Wes Hall starts the last eight-ball over. The first six balls yield five runs, two wickets. All photographers including Lovitt are out of film halfway through the over. No time to reload. Lovitt searches in his camera bag and finds an old double-dark slide containing two negatives, he hopes. He slips the slide into the camera and 'captures' Grout's dismissal. One negative left. Two balls left. Seventh ball. Kline nudges the ball to square leg and the batsmen take off for the winning run. Lovitt waits. Solomon pounces on the ball and throws. Lovitt clicks as the ball hits the stumps from side on. Meckiff is run out by a whisker. It's all there, West Indies players dancing, Kline looking back and, on the edge of the negative, Joe Solomon, arm outstretched, throwing the ball.

West Indies captain Frank Worrell.

Joe Solomon's unhappy hat trick

Melbourne, Jan. 3. Australia won the second Test with time to spare after a curiously subdued and even defensive performance from the West Indies batsmen.

No game could live up to the heroics of the first Tied Test, but a number of incidents enlivened proceedings for the 150,265 Melbourne cricket lovers who attended.

Main item was the incident of Joe Solomon's cap. Solomon opened the batting with Conrad Hunte in the second innings after Richie Benaud enforced the follow-on. Solomon bats inside the batting crease, and in jerking his head out of the way of a delivery which had bounced and spun, his cap fell off and dislodged a bail.

Wally Grout spontaneously appealed, Benaud joined in, and Solomon was given out, hit wicket.

The crowd, knowledgeable in cricket ethics as well as the ambiguity of the ancient law, hooted and booed the decision, and kept it up whenever Benaud bowled.

Keith Butler in the *Adelaide Advertiser* wrote: 'There are some things which are done and some which are not, and the crowd, with the underdog, obviously thought that this was one thing that was not done.'

Despite the law specifically saying a batsman is out if his cap breaks the wicket, the crowd, and some senior cricketers place this rule in the same 'not cricket' category as 'Mankading' a batsman without warning.

The other incident, just to show that the bails have minds of their own, was later in the same innings

Joe Solomon's fateful cap.

where a Benaud delivery struck the wicket when Gerry Alexander was on 25 – without knocking off a bail.

Left-arm wrist spinner Johnny Martin took three wickets in four balls – those of Kanhai, Sobers and Worrell, in the second innings.

Sobers, spinners win for Windies

Sydney, Jan. 18. Gary Sobers said of himself in the second Test that 'Gary Sobers caught a couple of catches but didn't set the show alight. You get matches like this. No excuses. They happen'. In the third Test Frank Worrell 'won the toss and we had a fair start. I am not proud of my showing at Melbourne and am determined to settle in to this game. I think I was around 160 not out at close of play [actually 152].'

The *Sydney Morning Herald* said it was 'one of the greatest exhibitions of controlled hitting seen on the SCG'. 'Johnnie' Moyes wrote that 'Sobers ran to his most superlative form with strokes of power and beauty flowing from his bat. Those who had not previously seen him in action revelled in his lovely batsmanship, and were particularly impressed by the uncanny manner in which he found the gaps… magnificent batting from a master technician.

'The next day in the Pavilion, Frank reminded me how I had got out a few times hooking the ball. He says: "Gary, try to cut out the hook shots." So I go in, not knowing he has second sight. About the third ball Alan Davidson sends down is a short bouncer. Between thinking about hooking and having an automatic reflex of wanting to hook, I played the shot a bit too late. The ball hit the top of my bat, flew high in the air, and I was out - caught and bowled for 168. Second innings I scored one. That's how it goes! But it was a tremendous game, well fought out and we won by about 200 runs' [actually 222].

There was also the little matter of

Wily off-spinner Lance Gibbs.

Lance Gibbs taking 3/46 and 6/66 and Alf Valentine 4/67 and 4/86.

For the record, the West Indies scored 339 and 326 (Alexander 108 and Worrell a lovely 82) and Australia a miserable 202. Australia lost its last six wickets in the second innings for 44.

The Australian team, second Test 1960–61. Rear: R. Simpson, F. Misson, I. Meckiff, I. Favell, J. Martin. Front: A. Davidson, N. O'Neill, R. Benaud and C. McDonald, W. Grout. Inset: N. Harvey.

West Indies team 1960–61. Back row: P. Lashley, C. Watson, C. W. Smith, T. W. Dewdney, W. Hall, J. Hendriks, L. Gibbs, E. Alves (masseur). Middle row: G. E. Gomez (mgr), K. T. Ramadhin, F. C. M. Alexander, F. M. Worrell, G. Sobers, A. L. Valentine, M. Marshall (asst. mgr). Front row: C. C. Hunte, R. B. Kanhai, J. Solomon, S. Nurse.

Rabbit Lindsay Kline keeps his end up

Adelaide, Feb. 1. The fourth Test was played in tremendous heat. The West Indian first innings featured a savage knock of 117 from Rohan Kanhai and a glorious 115 by Gary Sobers (Benaud's 200th Test wicket) out of 432 in the second innings. Australia, chasing an improbable 460, was 9/207 with 110 minutes remaining – it seemed that the West Indies would win and lead the series.

Enter Lindsay Kline to join 'Slasher' Mackay. Norm O'Neill and Johnny Martin had bowled to Kline in the nets as the wickets tumbled. O'Neill said: 'We had him out in every possible way ... I couldn't imagine the worst batsman in the world being in so much trouble against me.'

A female onlooker in the nets declared to Kline that he didn't stand a chance.

Kline marched straight from the nets to the middle. His team-mates went for showers, and started packing their bags. O'Neill said: 'A few optimists sat and watched the game. I also sat and watched, but I was not optimistic. I just wanted to see which way Lindsay would get out.'

Time marched on, and Worrell used every bowler, and crowded Kline with fieldsmen around the bat. Kline stayed and stayed.

Wes Hall bowled the last over to Mackay. Five balls caused no trouble – the next two from round the wicket were blocked. With the last, Hall missed his run, then bowled a no-ball unheard by spectators, who invaded the field.

After it was cleared Hall bowled what really was the last ball, which Mackay allowed to hit his chest. It was finally all over – one of the most exciting and tense draws in cricket history.

With the field crowding the pitch, Lindsay Kline plays a dead bat and survives one more ball ...

Slasher Mackay saves the day with his last-over heroics.

Grout not out in fifth Test decider

Melbourne, Feb. 15. This remarkable series climaxed in another tense finish as Australia struggled to a two-wicket win, after yet another controversial umpiring decision.

At tea on the fifth day the game was up for grabs. Peter Burge hit out after the interval, and then Sobers finally caught Davidson for 12 – 6/236. Burge on 53 played one on from Valentine – 7/248, bringing Wally Grout to the wicket.

Six runs later, Valentine bowled to Grout, who cut the ball and the batsmen set off. 'Keeper Gerry Alexander pointed to a bail lying on the ground. Umpire Col Egar who was standing at the bowler's end conferred with umpire Colin Hoy. Hoy made it clear that Grout had not hit the wicket with his bat, and nor had Alexander dislodged the bail. How did it fall? The alternative was that the ball had done the work, yet Egar, unsighted, gave Grout the benefit of the doubt. This upset the West Indies, for if Grout had been out – 8/254, anything might have happened. Grout gave his opinion by committing 'suicide' and Johnny Martin and Ken Mackay hung on, shakily, for the two runs required.

Australian cricket fans love the spirit of the Windies

Melbourne, Feb. 15. The Board of control has donated a perpetual trophy for competition between Australia and the West Indies, to be called the Frank Worrell trophy. 'I doubt if there could be a finer name for such a trophy,' said Richie Benaud. 'Worrell captured the imagination of the Australian public in this series, for allied to his great cricketing ability he is also a charming personality, and a gentleman in every way. To say it was a pleasure and privilege to be associated with him in a Test series is to understate the position.'

But it takes two to tango, and Richie Benaud's attacking captaincy and brighter cricket philosophy will be forever joined with Worrell's after this magnificent series. Australia won it, after the narrow two-wicket win in the fifth Test, but was not necessarily the better team.

'Johnnie' Moyes said the impact the West Indies made on Australian cricket 'was amazing: they turned the world upside down; they arrived almost unhonoured and unsung; they took away with them the esteem, affection, and admiration of all sections of the community. They proved what so many of us had declared – that people will go to see cricket played as a game and an entertainment'

Never more so than in the fifth Test, where an astounding 90,800 attended on the second day, and 274,424 for the match.

16 February 1961: A ticker-tape parade in Bourke Street, Melbourne, after the fifth Test. Frank Worrell and Gerry Alexander pass the GPO as well-wishers cheer them on their way. It was 'a send-off so magnificent and so sincere, we shall treasure it to the end of our days,' said Gary Sobers.

FIRST TEST 1960–61 AUSTRALIA v WEST INDIES
Brisbane Cricket Ground, Brisbane. December 9 ,10, 12, 13, 14, 1960.
Toss: West Indies. Match Tied.

WEST INDIES

CC Hunte c Benaud b Davidson	24	c Simpson b Mackay	39
CW Smith c Grout b Davidson	7	c O'Neill b Davidson	6
RB Kanhai c Grout b Davidson	15	c Grout b Davidson	54
GS Sobers c Kline b Meckiff	132	b Davidson	14
FMM Worrell (c) c Grout b Davidson	65	c Grout b Davidson	65
JS Solomon hit wicket b Simpson	65	lbw Simpson	47
PD Lashley c Grout b Kline	19	b Davidson	0
FCM Alexander (+) c Davidson b Kline	60	b Benaud	5
S Ramadhin c Harvey b Davidson	12	c Harvey b Simpson	6
WW Hall st Grout b Kline	50	b Davidson	18
AL Valentine not out	0	not out	7
EXTRAS (LB 3, W 1)	4	(B 14, LB 7, W 2)	23
TOTAL	453		284

FOW 1st Inns: 23 42 65 239 243 283 347 366 452 453
FOW 2nd Inns: 13 88 114 127 210 210 241 250 253 284

Bowling: *First Innings*: Davidson 30-2-135-5, Meckiff 18-0-129-1, Mackay 3-0-15-0, Benaud 24-3-93-0, Simpson 8-0-25-1, Kline 17.6-6-52-3. *Second Innings*: Davidson 24.6-4-87-6, Meckiff 4-1-19-0, Benaud 31-6-69-1, Mackay 21-7-52-1, Kline 4-0-14-0, Simpson 7-2-18-2, O'Neill 1-0-2-0.

AUSTRALIA

CC McDonald c Hunte b Sobers	57	b Worrell	16
RB Simpson b Ramadhin	92	c (S)LR Gibbs b Hall	0
RN Harvey b Valentine	15	c Sobers b Hall	5
NC O'Neill c Valentine b Hall	181	c Alexander b Hall	26
LE Favell run out	45	c Solomon b Hall	7
KD Mackay b Sobers	35	b Ramadhin	28
AK Davidson c Alexander b Hall	44	run out	80
R Benaud (c) lbw Hall	10	c Alexander b Hall	52
ATW Grout (+) lbw Hall	4	run out	2
I Meckiff run out	4	run out	2
LF Kline not out	3	not out	0
EXTRAS (B 2, LB 8, W 1, NB 4)	15	(B 2, LB 9, NB 3)	14
TOTAL	505		232

FOW 1st Inns: 84 138 194 278 381 469 484 489 496 505
FOW 2nd Inns: 1 7 49 49 57 92 226 228 232 232

Bowling: *First Innings*: Hall 29.3-1-140-4, Worrell 30-0-93-0, Sobers 32-0-115-2, Valentine 24-6-82-1, Ramadhin 15-1-60-1. *Second Innings*: Hall 17.7-3-63-5, Worrell 16-3-41-1, Sobers 8-0-30-0, Valentine 10-4-27-0, Ramadhin 17-3-57-1.

Umpires: CJ Egar & C Hoy

SECOND TEST 1960–61 AUSTRALIA v WEST INDIES
Melbourne Cricket Ground, Melbourne. December 30, 31, 1960, January 2, 3, 1961.
Toss: Australia. Australia won by 7 wkts.

AUSTRALIA

CC McDonald c Watson b Hall	15	c Sobers b Hall	13
RB Simpson c Alexander b Hall	49	not out	27
RN Harvey c Sobers b Worrell	12	c Alexander b Hall	0
NC O'Neill c Sobers b Worrell	40	lbw Watson	0
LE Favell c Nurse b Sobers	51	not out	24
KD Mackay b Ramadhin	74		
AK Davidson b Hall	35		
R Benaud (c) b Hall	2		
ATW Grout (+) b Watson	5		
JW Martin b Valentine	55		
FM Misson not out	0		
EXTRAS (LB 7, W 1, NB 2)	10	(B 4, LB 1, NB 1)	6
TOTAL	348		3 for 70

FOW 1st Inns: 35 60 105 155 189 242 244 251 348 348
FOW 2nd Inns: 27 27 30

Bowling: *First Innings*: Hall 12-2-51-4, Watson 12-1-73-1, Sobers 17-1-88-1, Worrell 9-0-50-2, Valentine 11.1-1-55-1, Ramadhin 5-0-21-1. *Second Innings*: Hall 9.4-0-32-2, Watson 9-1-32-1.

WEST INDIES

CC Hunte c Simpson b Misson	1	c Grout b O'Neill	110
JS Solomon c Grout b Davidson	0	hit wicket b Benaud	4
SM Nurse c Grout b Davidson	70	run out	3
RB Kanhai c Harvey b Davidson	84	c Misson b Martin	25
GS Sobers c Simpson b Benaud	9	c Simpson b Martin	0
FMM Worrell (c) b Misson	0	c Simpson b Martin	0
FCM Alexander (+) c Favell b Davidson	5	c Grout b Davidson	72
S Ramadhin b Davidson	0	st Grout b Benaud	3
WW Hall b Davidson	5	b Davidson	4
CD Watson c McDonald b Benaud	4	run out	5
AL Valentine not out	1	not out	0
EXTRAS (NB 2)	2	(B 2, LB 2, W 1, NB 2)	7
TOTAL	181		233

FOW 1st Inns: 1 1 124 139 142 160 160 166 177 181
FOW 2nd Inns: 40 51 97 99 99 186 193 206 222 233

Bowling: *First Innings*: Davidson 22-4-53-6, Misson 11-0-36-2, Benaud 27.2-10-58-2, Martin 8-1-32-0, Simpson 1-1-0-0. *Second Innings*: Davidson 15.4-2-51-2, Misson 12-3-36-0, Benaud 20-3-49-2, Martin 20-3-56-3, Simpson 8-0-24-0, O'Neill 5-1-10-1.

Umpires: CJ Egar & C Hoy

THIRD TEST 1960–61 AUSTRALIA v WEST INDIES
Sydney Cricket Ground, Sydney. January 13, 14, 16, 17, 18, 1961.
Toss: West Indies. West Indies won by 222 runs.

WEST INDIES
CC Hunte c Simpson b Meckiff	34	c O'Neill b Davidson	1	
CW Smith c & b Benaud	16	c Simpson b Benaud	55	
RB Kanhai c Grout b Davidson	21	c Martin b Davidson	3	
GS Sobers c & b Davidson	168	c Grout b Davidson	1	
FMM Worrell (c) c Davidson b Benaud	22	lbw Benaud	82	
SM Nurse c Simpson b Benaud	43	c & b Mackay	11	
JS Solomon c Simpson b Benaud	14	c Harvey b Benaud	1	
FCM Alexander (+) c Harvey b Benaud	0	lbw Mackay	108	
LR Gibbs c Grout b Davidson	0	st Grout b Benaud	18	
WW Hall c Grout b Davidson	10	b Mackay	24	
AL Valentine not out	0	not out	10	
EXTRAS (B 6, LB 4, W 1)	11	(B 4, LB 7, W 1)	12	
TOTAL	339		326	

FOW 1st Inns: 48 68 89 152 280 329 329 329 329 339
FOW 2nd Inns: 10 20 22 123 144 159 166 240 309 326

Bowling: *First Innings*: Davidson 21.6-4-80-5, Meckiff 13-1-74-1, Mackay 14-1-40-0, Benaud 23-3-86-4, Martin 8-1-37-0, Simpson 2-0-11-0. *Second Innings*: Davidson 8-1-33-3, Meckiff 5-2-12-0, Mackay 31.4-5-75-3, Benaud 44-14-113-4, Martin 10-0-65-0, Simpson 4-0-16-0.

AUSTRALIA
CC McDonald b Valentine	34	c Alexander b Valentine	27	
RB Simpson c Kanhai b Hall	10	b Sobers	12	
RN Harvey c Sobers b Hall	9	c Sobers b Gibbs	85	
NC O'Neill c Sobers b Sobers	71	c Sobers b Gibbs	70	
LE Favell c Worrell b Valentine	16	b Gibbs	2	
KD Mackay c Solomon b Gibbs	39	c Nurse b Gibbs	0	
AK Davidson c Worrell b Valentine	16 (10)	b Valentine	1	
R Benaud (c) c & b Valentine	3 (7)	c & b Valentine	24	
JW Martin c Solomon b Gibbs	0 (8)	b Valentine	5	
ATW Grout (+) c Hunte b Gibbs	0 (9)	b Gibbs	0	
I Meckiff not out	0	not out	6	
EXTRAS (B 1, LB 2, NB 1)	4	(B 3, LB 6)	9	
TOTAL	202		241	

FOW 1st Inns: 17 40 65 105 155 194 200 200 202 202
FOW 2nd Inns: 27 83 191 197 197 202 209 220 234 241

Bowling: *First Innings*: Hall 13-0-53-2, Worrell 9-4-18-0, Gibbs 23-6-46-3, Valentine 24.2-6-67-4, Sobers 5-2-14-1. *Second Innings*: Hall 8-0-35-0, Worrell 4-0-7-0, Gibbs 26-5-66-5, Sobers 9-1-38-1, Valentine 25.2-7-86-4.

Umpires: CJ Egar & C Hoy

FOURTH TEST 1960–61 AUSTRALIA v WEST INDIES
Adelaide Oval, Adelaide. January 27, 28, 30, 31, February 1, 1961.
Toss: West Indies. Match Drawn.

WEST INDIES
CC Hunte lbw Hoare	6	run out	79	
CW Smith c & b Benaud	28	c Hoare b Mackay	46	
RB Kanhai c Simpson b Benaud	117	lbw Benaud	115	
GS Sobers b Benaud	1	run out	20	
FMM Worrell (c) c Misson b Hoare	71	c Burge b Mackay	53	
SM Nurse c & b Misson	49	c Simpson b Benaud	5	
JS Solomon c & b Benaud	22 (8)	not out	16	
FCM Alexander (+) not out	63 (7)	not out	87	
LR Gibbs b Misson	18			
WW Hall c Hoare b Benaud	5			
AL Valentine lbw Misson	0			
EXTRAS (B 3, LB 3, W 5, NB 2)	13	(B 2, LB 6, W 2, NB 1)	11	
TOTAL	393		6 dec 432	

FOW 1st Inns: 12 83 91 198 271 288 316 375 392 393
FOW 2nd Inns: 66 229 263 270 275 388

Bowling: *First Innings*: Hoare 16-0-68-2, Misson 17.5-2-79-3, Mackay 2-0-11-0, Benaud 27-5-96-5, Kline 21-3-109-0, Simpson 5-0-17-0. *Second Innings*: Hoare 13-0-88-0, Misson 28-3-106-0, Mackay 12-0-72-2, Benaud 27-3-107-2, Kline 12-2-48-0.

AUSTRALIA
CC McDonald c Hunte b Gibbs	71	run out	2	
LE Favell c Alexander b Worrell	1	c Alexander b Hall	4	
NC O'Neill c Alexander b Sobers	11	c & b Sobers	65	
RB Simpson c Alexander b Hall	85	c Alexander b Hall	3	
PJP Burge c Sobers	45	c Alexander b Valentine	49	
R Benaud (c) c Solomon b Gibbs	77	c & b Sobers	17	
KD Mackay lbw Gibbs	29	not out	62	
ATW Grout (+) c Sobers b Gibbs	2	lbw Worrell	42	
FM Misson b Gibbs	0	c Solomon b Worrell	1	
DE Hoare c Sobers	35	b Worrell	0	
LF Kline not out	0	not out	15	
EXTRAS (B 2, LB 3, NB 7)	12	(B 9, LB 1, NB 3)	13	
TOTAL	366		9 for 273	

FOW 1st Inns: 9 45 119 213 221 281 281 281 366 366
FOW 2nd Inns: 6 7 31 113 129 144 203 207 207

Bowling: *First Innings*: Hall 22-3-85-1, Worrell 7-0-34-1, Sobers 24-3-64-3, Gibbs 35.6-4-97-5, Valentine 21-4-74-0. *Second Innings*: Hall 13-4-61-2, Worrell 17-9-27-3, Sobers 39-11-87-2, Gibbs 28-13-44-0, Valentine 20-7-40-1, Solomon 3-2-1-0.

Umpires: CJ Egar & C Hoy

FIFTH TEST 1960–61 AUSTRALIA v WEST INDIES
Melbourne Cricket Ground, Melbourne. February 10, 11, 13, 14, 15, 1961.
Toss: Australia. Australia won by 2 wkts.

WEST INDIES
CW Smith c O'Neill b Misson	11	lbw Davidson	37	
CC Hunte c Simpson b Davidson	31	c Grout b Davidson	52	
RB Kanhai c Harvey b Davidson	38	c Misson b Benaud	31	
GS Sobers c Grout b Simpson	64 (5)	c Grout b Simpson	21	
FMM Worrell (c) c Grout b Martin	10 (7)	c Grout b Davidson	7	
PD Lashley c Misson b Benaud	41 (8)	lbw Martin	18	
FCM Alexander (+) c McDonald b Misson	11 (6)	c Mackay b Davidson	73	
JS Solomon run out	45 (4)	run out	36	
LR Gibbs c Burge b Misson	11	c O'Neill b Simpson	8	
WW Hall b Misson	21	c Grout b Simpson	21	
AL Valentine not out	0	not out	3	
EXTRAS (B 4, LB 4, W 1)	9	(B 5, LB 8, W 1)	14	
TOTAL	292		321	

FOW 1st Inns: 18 75 81 107 200 204 221 235 290 292
FOW 2nd Inns: 54 103 135 173 201 218 262 295 304 321

Bowling: *First Innings*: Davidson 27-4-89-1, Misson 14-3-58-4, Mackay 1-0-1-0, Benaud 21.7-5-55-2, Martin 8-0-29-1, Simpson 18-3-51-1. *Second Innings*: Davidson 24.7-4-84-5, Misson 10-1-58-0, Mackay 10-2-21-0, Benaud 23-4-53-1, Martin 10-1-36-1, Simpson 18-4-55-2.

AUSTRALIA
RB Simpson c Gibbs b Sobers	75	b Gibbs	92	
CC McDonald lbw Sobers	91	c Smith b Gibbs	11	
NC O'Neill b Gibbs	10 (4)	c Alexander b Worrell	48	
PJP Burge c Sobers b Gibbs	68 (5)	b Valentine	53	
KD Mackay c Alexander b Hall	19 (8)	not out	3	
RN Harvey c Alexander b Sobers	5	c Smith b Worrell	12	
AK Davidson c Alexander b Sobers	24	c Sobers b Worrell	12	
R Benaud (c) b Gibbs	3 (3)	b Valentine	6	
JW Martin c Kanhai b Sobers	15 (10)	not out	1	
FM Misson not out	12			
ATW Grout (+) c Hunte b Gibbs	14 (9)	c Smith b Valentine	5	
EXTRAS (B 4, LB 8, NB 8)	20	(B 3, LB 9, NB 3)	15	
TOTAL	356		8 for 258	

FOW 1st Inns: 146 181 181 244 260 309 309 319 335 356
FOW 2nd Inns: 50 75 154 176 200 236 248 256

Bowling: *First Innings*: Hall 15-1-56-1, Worrell 11-2-44-0, Sobers 44-7-120-5, Gibbs 38.4-18-74-4, Valentine 13-3-42-0. *Second Innings*: Hall 5-0-40-0, Worrell 31-16-43-3, Sobers 13-2-32-0, Gibbs 41-19-68-2, Valentine 21.7-4-60-3.

Umpires: CJ Egar & C Hoy

Australian Averages
1960–61 AUSTRALIA v WEST INDIES

AUSTRALIA	M	Inn	NO	Runs	H.S	Avrge	Ct	St	Overs	Mds	Runs	Wkt	Avrge
Benaud, R	5	9	-	194	77	21.56	3	-	268.1	56	779	23	33.87
Burge, PJP	2	4	-	215	68	53.75	2	-	-	-	-	-	-
Davidson, AK	4	7	-	212	80	30.29	3	-	173.7	25	612	33	18.55
Favell, LE	4	8	1	150	51	21.43	1	-	-	-	-	-	-
Grout, ATW	5	9	-	72	42	8.00	20	3	-	-	-	-	-
Harvey, RN	4	8	-	143	85	17.88	6	-	-	-	-	-	-
Hoare, DE	1	2	-	35	35	17.50	2	-	29.0	-	156	2	78.00
Kline, LF	2	4	4	18	15*	-	1	-	54.6	11	223	3	74.33
Mackay, KD	5	9	2	289	74	41.29	2	-	94.4	15	287	6	47.83
Martin, JW	3	5	1	76	55	19.00	1	-	64.0	6	255	5	51.00
McDonald, CC	5	10	-	337	91	33.70	2	-	-	-	-	-	-
Meckiff, I	2	4	2	12	6*	6.00	-	-	40.0	4	234	2	117.00
Misson, FM	3	4	2	13	12*	6.50	5	-	92.5	12	373	9	41.44
O'Neill, NC	5	10	-	522	181	52.20	4	-	6.0	1	12	1	12.00
Simpson, RB	5	10	-	445	92	49.44	13	-	71.0	10	217	6	36.17

West Indian Averages
1960–61 AUSTRALIA v WEST INDIES

WEST INDIES	M	Inn	NO	Runs	H.S	Avrge	Ct	St	Overs	Mds	Runs	Wkt	Avrge
Alexander, FCM	5	10	2	484	108	60.50	16	-	-	-	-	-	-
Gibbs, LR	3	5	-	55	18	11.00	1	-	192.2	65	395	19	20.79
Hall, WW	5	9	-	158	50	17.56	-	-	144.6	14	616	21	29.33
Hunte, CC	5	10	-	377	110	37.70	4	-	-	-	-	-	-
Kanhai, RB	5	10	-	503	117	50.30	2	-	-	-	-	-	-
Lashley, PD	2	4	-	78	41	19.50	-	-	-	-	-	-	-
Nurse, SM	3	6	-	181	70	30.17	2	-	-	-	-	-	-
Ramadhin, S	2	4	-	21	12	5.25	-	-	37.0	4	138	3	46.00
Smith, CW	4	8	-	206	55	25.75	3	-	-	-	-	-	-
Sobers, GS	5	10	-	430	168	43.00	12	-	191.0	27	588	15	39.20
Solomon, JS	5	10	1	250	65	27.78	5	-	3.0	2	1	-	-
Valentine, AL	5	9	8	21	10*	21.00	1	-	170.4	42	533	14	38.07
Watson, CD	1	2	-	9	9	4.50	1	-	21.0	2	105	2	52.50
Worrell, FMM	5	10	-	375	82	37.50	2	-	134.0	34	357	10	35.70

Gag on Benaud mystifies press

London, June 8. Richie Benaud is an accomplished speaker, so it is surprising that the Australian team management will not allow him to speak to the press after the first day's play at Edgbaston.

If ever a cricketer knows a newspaper's needs, it must surely be Benaud, who has served 'time' as a police roundsman with the *Sydney Sun*. He knows that journalists need headlines.

There are rumours of a rift now that responsibility for public comment in the Australian camp has been taken over by team manager, Sid Webb.

Benaud's eloquent post-match commentaries and interpretations were much appreciated by the English press.

And while Webb, a Queen's Counsel, should be able to handle curly questions, newsmen say they would have preferred the cricketer to the QC.

Bill Lawry a find

Bill Lawry hooks at Lord's.

London, June 24. In a rare tribute during the second Test at Lord's today, the huge crowd of 30,000 people rose to acknowledge a magnificent effort by young Australian batsman Bill Lawry, a left-hander on his first tour.

Playing in only his second Test, Lawry's 130 runs scored in just over six hours have given Australia a lead of 80 runs with two wickets in hand.

He also takes his personal tally over the past two months to 1000 runs, which is a remarkable performance by the gangly newcomer, who shows great heart and patience at the crease.

Harvey wins 'Battle of Ridge'

Neil Harvey, captaining the side for the first time, meets the Queen.

London, June 27. In his first experience of Test captaincy, Neil Harvey has led Australia to a five-wicket victory in the second Test at Lord's.

Harvey, a veteran of 70 Test matches since 1947, finally gained his chance after Richie Benaud was declared unfit to play due to a shoulder injury which he sustained early in the tour.

England won the toss for the eighth time in a row, and decided to bat on what it thought would be a spinner's pitch.

The wicket seemed different, with less grass than usual and bare patches, but nobody imagined it would be so full of life on the first day.

Much to everyone's surprise, Australia's left-arm fast bowler Alan Davidson not only found his pace, but noticed a small ridge in the pitch at the Nursery end. He unleashed his missiles at this spot, taking 5/42 as the Queen and the Duke of Edinburgh watched England's first innings fall for a mere 206.

Coming in to bat at 5.30 p.m., Australia's Colin McDonald was bowled by Brian Statham for 4. Bob Simpson then went for a duck, leaving the inexperienced Bill Lawry to carry the side.

And carry it he did, notching up his maiden Test century before tea on the second day and making 130 before being caught by John Murray off Ted Dexter.

To cap off the innings, Graham McKenzie celebrated his 20th birthday with a fine Test debut 34, bringing Australia's total to 340.

McKenzie also took 5/37 in England's second innings.

Apart from Barrington's 66 and Pullar's 42, poor batting in England's second innings resulted in just 202 runs, leaving only 71 runs for Australia to make on the fourth day. The tourists lost five wickets in achieving the target.

The ridge pitch is now being investigated by a team of English architects, who are armed with theodolites and spirit levels, and will attempt to prevent such a massacre occurring again.

A fine on-drive bt Ted Dexter

Fred Trueman has a purple patch

Leeds, July 8. From a sound position of 2/183 at tea on the first day of the third Test at Headingley, Australia was all out for 237 by stumps that night.

In an extraordinary collapse, Australia lost 7/21 in just 50 minutes, on a pitch described by the *Times* as 'an unkempt garden path a few days after being sprayed with weedkiller.'

At first the visitors' tally was built up gradually by the invariably successful opening pair of Colin McDonald (54) and Bill Lawry (28). By tea, Neil Harvey had reached 66 and Norman O'Neill was on 27.

When fiery Fred Trueman took the new ball the blitz began. O'Neill was his first victim, caught by Colin Cowdrey in the gully for 27. Then came Harvey (73), caught by Tony Lock. Peter Burge fell for 5, caught by Cowdrey off a ball from Les Jackson.

Trueman's next over with the new ball saw Bob Simpson lbw for 2 and Richie Benaud bowled first ball. Then he had Wally Grout caught behind for three. In six devastating overs Trueman had taken 5 wickets for 16 runs.

And that wasn't all. In Australia's dismal second innings of 120, one explosive 25-minute spell of just 24 balls from Trueman saw him capture the wickets of O'Neill, Harvey, Simpson, Benaud and Mackay – without conceding a single run.

Nobody spoke of weedkiller now. The purple on the pitch was Freddie Trueman, with match figures of 11/88 in England's eight-wicket win.

And Australian batsmen are terrified he'll be back, full of fire and speed to poison their path again.

Fred Trueman: Roy Ulyett's view.

Ashes won in gripping match

Richie Benaud produces a superb ball to bowl England captain Peter May for a duck.

Manchester, Aug. 1. Australia retained the Ashes today in a thrilling climax to the fourth Test at Old Trafford.

Once again, Bill Lawry gave Australia a fine start, picking up 64 runs on the first day, which ended with Australia at 4/124.

A model of concentration in a batsman, young Lawry held his ground while more experienced comrades fell around him. The loss of his wicket for 74, lbw off the fast bowling of Brian Statham, signalled Australia's first innings collapse.

From 5/174 at 12.30 p.m. on the second day, Australia was all out for 190 at one o'clock. Statham took 5/53.

A 111-run partnership between Geoffrey Pullar and Peter May gave England the upper hand by the end of day two. But there were warning signs in the air.

From the city end Australian captain Richie Benaud was flying his leg-breaks into the breeze. He seemed to have recovered from that troublesome shoulder injury which kept him out of the second Test and almost bowled May for 37. Benaud was looking dangerous again.

Before lunch on the third day Bob Simpson dived to catch May on 95, after he was tempted by an outswinger from Alan Davidson.

Once again, Lawry took up the mantle in Australia's second innings, making his century by mid-afternoon.

On the final day, Ted Dexter hit fifteen fours as England chased victory. When he reached his century with two hours of play remaining, England had nine wickets in hand and needed only 132 runs to win.

But Benaud refused to accept the inevitable, and his solo effort was of the calibre of of Fred Trueman's match-winning bowling in the third Test. In a magnificent leg-break attack he turned the match on its head, taking 6/70 in 30 overs, eleven of them maidens. By 5.40 p.m. England was all out, beaten by 54 runs and a captain who never said die.

Plunder by Australia in the fifth Test

The Oval, Aug. 22. Safe in the knowledge that Australia has retained the Ashes, batsmen have finally reaped the spoils in the fifth Test at the Oval.

In reply to England's tentative first innings total of 256, Australia's confident 494 runs was highlighted by outstanding displays from Norman O'Neill (117) and Peter Burge (181).

O'Neill came to the crease on the second day with Australia at 2/15. Partnered first by Bob Simpson, then Burge, O'Neill loosened up with some magnificent cover drives, then stretched out all over the ground.

His running between wickets, always flat out for the first run in

the hope of a second, was likened to Bradman by the *Times*.

O'Neill had tea at 99, nervously perhaps, but showed little fear as he passed the century soon after the break and went on to 117.

The aggressive, gum-chewing Burge then settled in, sweeping and cutting to claim his maiden Test century by noon the following day. And the flavour remained, as he moved up to a brilliant 181, the highest individual score of the series.

England's batsmen also found their feet. Subba Row's second innings 137 was well supported by Ken Barrington's 83, but rain eventually forced England to play for a draw.

Grout's record

The Oval, Aug. 23. Shortly after 5 p.m. yesterday, Australian wicketkeeper Wally Grout came of age when he caught John Murray, to claim his 21st victim for the England–Australia series.

Grout's 21 is a new record for wicketkeepers in an Ashes series.

The previous record of 20 was set by in Australia by fellow Queenslander Don Tallon in 1946–7.

Grout has proved a worthy successor to Tallon. His speed, consistency, agility and uncanny capacity to read the play are the hallmarks of wicketkeeping greatness.

He is also a handy lower-middle-order batsman.

Garth – bowling superhero

They called him 'Garth.' He was big, broad, and burly. A ladykiller. A real-life superhero like his comic strip namesake.

Graham McKenzie was a natural. At high school in Perth he excelled at cricket, running, hockey, swimming and Australian Rules football.

He captained Western Australia's schoolboy hockey sides in 1956, and again in 1957, when WA beat every State in Australia and McKenzie was named best and fairest.

Playing cricket for Claremont-Cottlesloe in the summer of 1959–60, he scored over 500 runs and took 49 wickets for an average of 11.89. During that season he also made his first century at the WACA, taking just 105 minutes to reach the ton.

Early in the 1960–61 West Indies tour, young McKenzie was first picked for WA. Showing scant respect for the likes of Frank Worrell and Garfield Sobers, he took 4/41 in eleven overs.

Worrell was stunned. Facing his first delivery from McKenzie, he had no idea that the big 19-year-old could put such explosive pace on the ball from a casual nine or ten-stride run-up. He said later that the Australian selectors ought to consider McKenzie for inclusion in the 1961 Ashes tour.

There wasn't much need for prompting. McKenzie starred for WA in Shield games that summer, and in his first week of teaching at John Forrest High School the news came that 'Garth' was in.

Naturally, the newspapers had a field day. The new 'baby' of the Australian side bounced in at 97 kgs, with 33 cm biceps, 66 cm thighs, and a 109 cm chest. Soon, everybody knew of his arrival.

And if they didn't know then, they knew after the first Test at Lord's, where he took 5/37.

No first, faltering steps for this boy. He ran before he crawled.

In fact, he never did crawl, come to think of it. When McKenzie dismissed England batsman Colin Cowdrey in the Lord's Test, Cowdrey was on 127 and had hit three successive balls for four. McKenzie once again made his steady, deliberate approach, then stung Cowdrey with what the *Times* described as a 'particularly fast ball … short, into the bargain, and it seemed to come back at Cowdrey as he tried to get his bat out of the way.'

Aggressive outswingers with a

McKenzie: all round sportsman.

deceptive change of pace became McKenzie's hallmarks.

Early problems with accuracy and control were mastered by the 1964 Ashes tour, when he took 29 wickets. That kind of skill had to be used by Australian captains, but not too much.

Overbowling in the India and Pakistan tours in 1964–65 led to exhaustion. Even Garth was human.

But he broke all the records. He had taken 100 Test wickets by the age of 23, 150 by 26 and 200 by 27, in each case being the youngest Australian to do so.

And he broke all the batsmen, too, sometimes physically. He sent England's Geoff Boycott to hospital with a fractured forearm, and West Indian 'Jackie' Hendriks almost died during brain surgery in May 1965 after being hit on the head. Fortunately, Hendriks made a full recovery after the accident.

McKenzie's brilliant Test career was hit for six by the selectors' decision to drop him after the second Test against India in January 1968, where he had taken 10 wickets. His biographer, Ed Jaggard, describes this as 'one of the most staggering decisions in post-war Australian cricket.'

McKenzie signed with Leicestershire in 1969, and later joined Kerry Packer's troupe. He also played for the International Wanderers in South Africa.

In 60 tests between 1961 and 1971, McKenzie took 246 wickets at an average of 29.78. His best was 8/71 against the West Indies in 1968–69.

Australia probably lost Garth McKenzie too soon, but his deeds inspired a generation of cricketers – perhaps, even, another young Western Australian called Dennis Lillee.

FIRST TEST 1961 ENGLAND v AUSTRALIA
Edgbaston, Birmingham. June 8, 9, 10, 12, 13, 1961.
Toss: England. Match Drawn.

ENGLAND

G Pullar b Davidson	17	c Grout b Misson 28
R Subba Row c Simpson b Mackay	59	b Misson 112
ER Dexter c Davidson b Mackay	10	st Grout b Simpson 180
MC Cowdrey (c) b Misson	13	b Mackay 14
KF Barrington c Misson b Mackay	21	not out 48
MJK Smith c Lawry b Mackay	0	not out 1
R Illingworth c Grout b Benaud	15	
JT Murray (+) c Davidson b Benaud	16	
DA Allen run out	11	
FS Trueman c Burge b Benaud	20	
JB Statham not out	7	
Extras (B 3, LB 3)	6	(LB 18) 18
TOTAL	195	............4 for 401

FOW 1st Inns: 36 53 88 121 121 122 153 156 181 195
FOW 2nd Inns: 93 202 239 400

Bowling: *First Innings*: Davidson 26-6-70-1, Misson 15-6-47-1, Mackay 29-10-57-4, Benaud 14.3-8-15-3. *Second Innings*: Davidson 31-10-60-0, Misson 28-6-82-2, Simpson 34-12-87-1, Mackay 41-13-87-1, Benaud 20-4-67-0.

AUSTRALIA

WM Lawry c Murray b Illingworth	57
CC McDonald c Illingworth b Statham	22
RN Harvey lbw Allen	114
NC O'Neill b Statham	82
PJP Burge lbw Allen	25
RB Simpson c & b Trueman	76
AK Davidson c & b Illingworth	22
KD Mackay c Barrington b Statham	64
R Benaud (c) not out	36
ATW Grout (+) c Dexter b Trueman	5
FM Misson	
Extras (B 8, LB 4, NB 1)	13
TOTAL	9 dec 516

FOW 1st Inns: 47 106 252 299 322 381 469 501 516

Bowling: *First Innings*: Trueman 36.5-1-136-2, Statham 43-6-147-3, Illingworth 44-12-110-2, Allen 24-4-88-2, Dexter 5-1-22-0.

Umpires: JS Buller & FS Lee

SECOND TEST 1961 ENGLAND v AUSTRALIA
Lord's Cricket Ground, London. June 22, 23, 24, 26, 1961.
Toss: England. Australia won by 5 wkts.

ENGLAND

G Pullar b Davidson	11	c Grout b Misson 42
R Subba Row lbw Mackay	48	c Grout b Davidson 8
ER Dexter c McKenzie b Misson	27	b McKenzie 17
MC Cowdrey (c) c Grout b McKenzie	16	c Mackay b Misson 7
PBH May c Grout b Davidson	17	c Grout b McKenzie 22
KF Barrington c Mackay b Davidson	4	lbw Davidson 66
R Illingworth b Misson	13	c Harvey b Simpson 0
JT Murray (+) lbw Mackay	18	c Grout b McKenzie 25
GAR Lock c Grout b Davidson	5	b McKenzie 1
FS Trueman b Davidson	25	c Grout b McKenzie 0
JB Statham not out	11	not out 2
Extras (LB 9, W 2)	11	(B 1, LB 10, W 1) 12
TOTAL	206	202

FOW 1st Inns: 26 87 87 111 115 127 156 164 167 206
FOW 2nd Inns: 33 63 67 80 127 144 191 199 199 202

Bowling: *First Innings*: Davidson 24.3-6-42-5, McKenzie 26-7-81-1, Misson 16-4-48-2, Mackay 12-3-24-2. *Second Innings*: Davidson 24-8-50-2, McKenzie 29-13-37-5, Misson 17-2-66-2, Mackay 8-6-5-0, Simpson 19-10-32-1.

AUSTRALIA

WM Lawry c Murray b Dexter	130	c Murray b Statham 1
CC McDonald b Statham	4	c Illingworth b Trueman 14
RB Simpson c Illingworth b Trueman	0 (6)	c Illingworth b Statham 15
RN Harvey (c) c Barrington b Trueman	27 (3)	c Murray b Trueman 4
NC O'Neill b Dexter	1 (4)	b Statham 0
PJP Burge c Murray b Statham	46 (5)	not out 37
AK Davidson lbw Trueman	6	not out 0
KD Mackay c Barrington b Illingworth	54	
ATW Grout (+) lbw Dexter	0	
GD McKenzie b Trueman	34	
FM Misson not out	25	
Extras (B 1, LB 12)	13	0
TOTAL	340	5 for 71

FOW 1st Inns: 5 6 81 88 183 194 238 238 291 340
FOW 2nd Inns: 15 15 19 19 58

Bowling: *First Innings*: Statham 44-10-89-2, Trueman 34-3-118-4, Dexter 24-7-56-3, Lock 26-13-48-0, Illingworth 11.3-5-16-1. *Second Innings*: Statham 10.5-3-31-3, Trueman 10-0-40-2.

Umpires: CS Elliott & WE Phillipson

THIRD TEST 1961 ENGLAND v AUSTRALIA
Headingley, Leeds. July 6, 7, 8, 1961.
Toss: Australia. England won by 8 wkts.

AUSTRALIA

CC McDonald st Murray b Lock	54	b Jackson	1
WM Lawry lbw Lock	28	c Murray b Allen	28
RN Harvey c Lock b Trueman	73	c Dexter b Trueman	53
NC O'Neill c Cowdrey b Trueman	27	c Cowdrey b Trueman	19
PJP Burge c Cowdrey b Jackson	5	lbw Allen	0
KD Mackay lbw Jackson	6 (9)	c Murray b Trueman	0
RB Simpson lbw Trueman	2 (6)	b Trueman	3
AK Davidson not out	22 (7)	c Cowdrey b Trueman	7
R Benaud (c) b Trueman	0 (8)	b Trueman	1
ATW Grout (+) c Murray b Trueman	3	c & b Jackson	7
GD McKenzie b Allen	8	not out	0
Extras (B 7, LB 2)	9	(LB 2)	2
TOTAL	237		120

FOW 1st Inns: 65 113 187 192 196 203 203 204 208 237
FOW 2nd Inns: 4 49 99 102 102 105 109 109 120 120

Bowling: *First Innings*: Trueman 22-5-58-5, Jackson 31-11-57-2, Allen 28-12-45-1, Lock 29-5-68-2. *Second Innings*: Trueman 15.5-5-30-6, Jackson 13-5-26-2, Allen 14-6-30-2, Lock 10-1-32-0.

ENGLAND

G Pullar b Benaud	53	not out	26
R Subba Row lbw Davidson	35	b Davidson	6
MC Cowdrey c Grout b McKenzie	93	c Grout b Benaud	22
PBH May (c) c & b Davidson	26	not out	8
ER Dexter b Davidson	28		
KF Barrington c Simpson b Davidson	6		
JT Murray (+) b McKenzie	6		
FS Trueman c Burge b Davidson	4		
GAR Lock lbw McKenzie	30		
DA Allen not out	5		
HL Jackson run out	8		
Extras (LB 5)	5		0
TOTAL	299		2 for 62

FOW 1st Inns: 59 145 190 223 239 248 252 286 291 299
FOW 2nd Inns: 14 45

Bowling: *First Innings*: Davidson 47-23-63-5, McKenzie 27-4-64-3, Mackay 22-4-34-0, Benaud 39-15-86-1, Simpson 14-5-47-0. *Second Innings*: Davidson 11-6-17-1, McKenzie 5-0-15-0, Mackay 1-0-8-0, Benaud 6-1-22-1.

Umpires: JS Buller & JG Langridge

FOURTH TEST 1961 ENGLAND v AUSTRALIA
Old Trafford, Manchester. July 27, 28, 29, 31, August 1, 1961.
Toss: Australia. Australia won by 54 runs.

AUSTRALIA

WM Lawry lbw Statham	74	c Trueman b Allen	102
RB Simpson c Murray b Statham	4	c Murray b Flavell	51
RN Harvey c Subba Row b Statham	19	c Murray b Dexter	35
NC O'Neill hit wicket b Trueman	11	c Murray b Statham	67
PJP Burge b Flavell	15	c Murray b Dexter	23
BC Booth c Close b Statham	46	lbw Dexter	9
KD Mackay c Murray b Statham	11	c Close b Allen	18
AK Davidson c Barrington b Dexter	0	not out	77
R Benaud (c) b Dexter	2	lbw Allen	1
ATW Grout (+) c Murray b Dexter	2	c Statham b Allen	0
GD McKenzie not out	1	b Flavell	32
Extras (B 4, LB 1)	5	(B 6, LB 9, W 2)	17
TOTAL	190		432

FOW 1st Inns: 8 51 89 106 150 174 185 185 189 190
FOW 2nd Inns: 113 175 210 274 290 296 332 334 334 432

Bowling: *First Innings*: Trueman 14-1-55-1, Statham 21-3-53-5, Flavell 22-8-61-1, Dexter 6.4-2-16-3. *Second Innings*: Statham 44-9-106-1, Trueman 32-6-92-0, Flavell 29.4-4-65-2, Allen 38-25-58-4, Dexter 20-4-61-3, Close 8-1-33-0.

ENGLAND

G Pullar b Davidson	63	c O'Neill b Davidson	26
R Subba Row c Simpson b Davidson	2	b Benaud	49
ER Dexter c Davidson b McKenzie	16	c Grout b Benaud	76
PBH May (c) c Simpson b Davidson	95	b Benaud	0
DB Close lbw McKenzie	33	c O'Neill b Benaud	8
KF Barrington c O'Neill b Simpson	78	lbw Mackay	5
JT Murray (+) c Grout b Mackay	24	c Simpson b Benaud	4
DA Allen c Booth b Simpson	42	c Simpson b Benaud	10
FS Trueman c Harvey b Simpson	3	c Benaud b Simpson	8
JB Statham c Mackay b Simpson	8	b Davidson	8
JA Flavell not out	0	not out	0
Extras (B 2, LB 4, W 1)	7	(B 5, W 2)	7
TOTAL	367		201

FOW 1st Inns: 3 43 154 212 212 272 358 362 367 367
FOW 2nd Inns: 40 150 150 158 163 171 171 189 193 201

Bowling: *First Innings*: Davidson 39-11-70-3, McKenzie 38-11-106-2, Mackay 40-9-81-1, Benaud 35-15-80-0, Simpson 11.4-4-23-4. *Second Innings*: Davidson 14.4-1-50-2, McKenzie 4-1-20-0, Benaud 32-11-70-6, Simpson 8-4-21-1, Mackay 13-7-33-1.

Umpires: JG Langridge & WE Phillipson

FIFTH TEST 1961 ENGLAND v AUSTRALIA
Kennington Oval, London. August 17, 18, 19, 21, 22, 1961.
Toss: England. Match Drawn.

ENGLAND

G Pullar b Davidson	8	c Grout b Mackay	13
R Subba Row lbw Gaunt	12	c & b Benaud	137
MC Cowdrey c Grout b Davidson	0 (5)	c Benaud b Mackay	3
PBH May (c) c Lawry b Benaud	71	c O'Neill b Mackay	33
ER Dexter c Grout b Gaunt	24 (3)	c Gaunt b Mackay	0
KF Barrington c Grout b Gaunt	53	c O'Neill b Benaud	83
JT Murray (+) c O'Neill b Mackay	27	c Grout b Benaud	40
GAR Lock c Grout b Mackay	3	c Benaud b Mackay	0
DA Allen not out	22	not out	42
JB Statham b Davidson	18	not out	9
JA Flavell c Simpson b Davidson	14		
Extras (B 1, LB 2, W 1)	4	(B 6, LB 3, W 1)	10
TOTAL	256		8 for 370

FOW 1st Inns: 18 20 20 67 147 193 199 202 238 256
FOW 2nd Inns: 33 33 83 90 262 283 283 355

Bowling: *First Innings*: Davidson 34.1-8-83-4, Gaunt 24-3-53-3, Benaud 17-4-35-1, Mackay 39-14-75-2, Simpson 4-2-6-0. *Second Innings*: Davidson 29-7-67-0, Gaunt 22-7-33-0, Mackay 68-21-121-5, Benaud 51-18-113-3, Simpson 2-0-13-0, O'Neill 4-1-13-0, Harvey 1-1-0-0.

AUSTRALIA

WM Lawry c Murray b Statham	0
RB Simpson b Allen	40
RN Harvey lbw Flavell	13
NC O'Neill c(S)MJ Stewart b Allen	117
PJP Burge b Allen	181
BC Booth c Subba Row b Lock	71
KD Mackay c Murray b Flavell	5
AK Davidson lbw Statham	17
R Benaud (c) b Allen	6
ATW Grout (+) not out	30
RA Gaunt b Statham	3
Extras (B 10, LB 1)	11
TOTAL	494

FOW 1st Inns: 0 15 88 211 396 401 441 455 472 494

Bowling: *First Innings*: Statham 38.5-10-75-3, Flavell 31-5-105-2, Dexter 24-2-68-0, Allen 30-6-133-4, Lock 42-14-102-1.

Umpires: CS Elliott & FS Lee

Australian Averages

1961 ENGLAND v AUSTRALIA

AUSTRALIA	M	Inn	NO	Runs	H.S	Avrge	Ct	St	Overs	Mds	Runs	Wkt	Avrge
Benaud, R	4	6	1	45	36*	9.00	4	-	214.3	76	488	15	32.53
Booth, BC	2	3	-	126	71	42.00	1	-	-	-	-	-	-
Burge, PJP	5	8	1	332	181	47.43	2	-	-	-	-	-	-
Davidson, AK	5	8	3	151	77*	30.20	4	-	280.2	86	572	23	24.87
Gaunt, RA	1	1	-	3	3	3.00	-	-	46.0	10	86	3	28.67
Grout, ATW	5	7	1	47	30*	7.83	20	1	-	-	-	-	-
Harvey, RN	5	8	-	338	114	42.25	2	-	1.0	1	0	-	-
Lawry, WM	5	8	-	420	130	52.50	2	-	-	-	-	-	-
Mackay, KD	5	7	-	158	64	22.57	3	-	273.0	87	525	16	32.81
McDonald, CC	3	5	-	95	54	19.00	-	-	-	-	-	-	-
McKenzie, GD	3	5	2	75	34	25.00	1	-	129.0	36	323	11	29.36
Misson, FM	2	1	1	25	25*	-	1	-	76.0	18	243	7	34.71
O'Neill, NC	5	8	-	324	117	40.50	6	-	4.0	1	13	-	-
Simpson, RB	5	8	-	191	76	23.88	7	-	92.4	37	229	7	32.71

English Averages

1961 ENGLAND v AUSTRALIA

ENGLAND	M	Inn	NO	Runs	H.S	Avrge	Ct	St	Overs	Mds	Runs	Wkt	Avrge
Allen, DA	4	6	3	132	42*	44.00	-	-	134.0	53	354	13	27.23
Barrington, KF	5	9	1	364	83	45.50	4	-	-	-	-	-	-
Close, DB	1	2	-	41	33	20.50	2	-	8.0	1	33	-	-
Cowdrey, MC	4	8	-	168	93	21.00	4	-	-	-	-	-	-
Dexter, ER	5	9	-	378	180	42.00	2	-	79.4	16	223	9	24.78
Flavell, JA	2	3	-	14	14	14.00	-	-	82.4	17	231	5	46.20
Illingworth, R	2	3	-	28	15	9.33	5	-	55.3	17	126	3	42.00
Jackson, HL	1	1	-	8	8	8.00	1	-	44.0	16	83	4	20.75
Lock, GAR	3	5	-	39	30	7.80	1	-	107.0	33	250	3	83.33
May, PBH	4	8	1	272	95	38.86	-	-	-	-	-	-	-
Murray, JT	5	8	-	160	40	20.00	17	1	-	-	-	-	-
Pullar, G	5	10	-	287	63	31.89	-	-	-	-	-	-	-
Smith, MJK	1	2	-	1	1*	1.00	-	-	-	-	-	-	-
Statham, JB	4	7	4	59	18	19.67	1	-	201.4	41	501	17	29.47
Subba Row, R	5	10	-	468	137	46.80	2	-	-	-	-	-	-
Trueman, FS	4	6	-	60	25	10.00	2	-	164.4	21	529	20	26.45

Imports lead bumper Shield season

Caribbean fast bowler Wes Hall, in Queensland to play Sheffield Shield, talks to the future of Australian cricket.

Perth, March 6. A splash of Caribbean colour has encouraged huge interest in Sheffield Shield cricket this season.

Attendances have nearly doubled in Adelaide, where West Indies champion Gary Sobers, playing for South Australia, scored 251 runs against NSW in February.

He also took 6/72 in the bowling that match, making his all-round performance one of the most remarkable exhibitions in Shield history.

Sobers not only topped the batting for South Australia with 769 runs this season, he also headed the bowling, taking 35 wickets at an average of 21.97.

Fellow West Indian Wes Hall was even better, taking 43 wickets for Queensland.

'Man, this wicket should give me plenty of lift,' Hall exclaimed when he first set eyes on the 'Gabba pitch in November.

And how right he was. In one of the best fast spells ever seen at the ground, he took 6/29 from 12 overs against SA on January 13.

In similar burst against Victoria a fortnight later, he took 7/76 and went past Len Johnson's 1949–50 Queensland Shield bowling record of 39 wickets.

Adding to the feats of Sobers and Hall was another West Indian, Rohan Kanhai, who made 533 runs

for Western Australia.

Tiny Kanhai came to WA with a big reputation as the most spectacular batsman in the world.

Against South Australia at Adelaide in early November, Kanhai showed his greatness with a majestic 135 in a record third-wicket partnership of 223 runs with Barrie Shepherd (92).

But he could not always make up for local deficiencies. Coming to the crease with WA at 3/15 against NSW on November 28, he added a determined 81, but did not have enough support.

Thanks to the imports, Sheffield Shield has enjoyed its best trading year since Bradman.

No to centenary

Melbourne, Dec. 1. There is now no hope of a commemorative Test match being staged next month to mark the centenary of the first game played by an English team in Australia, which was held in Melbourne in January 1862.

The idea of a centenary Test originated with the New South Wales Cricket Association Secretary, Alan Barnes.

He officially proposed some months ago that one of the Tests scheduled in the forthcoming England tour of Australia might be designated the 'Centenary Test'.

It seems, however, that Australian cricket authorities do not want the extra pressures of a celebration of the past to distract its players from the present.

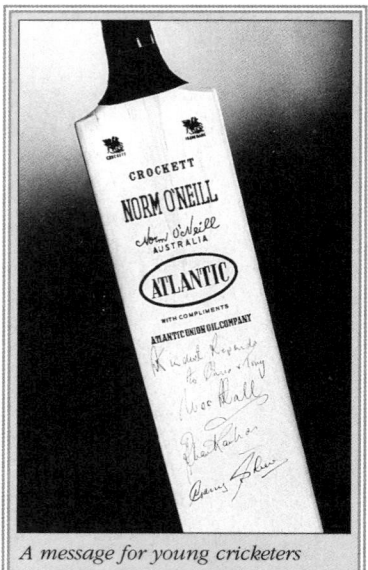

A message for young cricketers from Wes Hall and friends.

NSW Test team

Perth, March 5. The last game of the Sheffield Shield season ended today with a seven-wicket win to Victoria over Western Australia. The result determined which team finished at the bottom.

Final points were: New South Wales, 64; Queensland, 36; South Australia, 30; Victoria, 24; and Western Australia, 22.

The champion NSW team, which was led by Richie Benaud, had no fewer than nine experienced Test representatives in its line-up, including Neil Harvey, Alan Davidson and Norman O'Neill.

South Australia has been the only side to beat NSW this season, thanks largely to an outstanding 251 runs from West Indies import Garfield Sobers.

1962–63

ENGLAND IN AUSTRALIA

A mixed start for team of gentlemen

Brisbane, Nov. 29. A large question mark looms over the England side on the eve of the first Test against Australia.

England began the tour last month with a resounding ten-wicket victory over Western Australia, and followed up with a massive 7/633 against an Australian eleven in Melbourne.

Then came a puzzling loss by an innings and 80 runs to New South Wales, which has had all the experts guessing.

The England team is captained by the Sussex captain, Edward Ralph Dexter, known as 'Lord' Ted. He is a dashing right-handed batsman of aristocratic demeanour, born in Milan, Italy.

He is an adventurous type whose pastimes include motorbike riding and flying private aeroplanes. And he dabbles in horses and hounds, of course.

He is also a talented amateur golfer, and on dull days fielding in the outfield doesn't mind practising his golf swing, much to the amusement of the crowd.

Supporting Dexter will be champion batsman Michael Colin Cowdrey, who incidentally bears the initials MCC, prophetically bestowed on him by his cricket-loving father at Bangalore three decades ago.

With the Duke of Norfolk managing the team, England is no doubt hoping that the old Empire will continue to hold its head high in the colonies.

Sir Donald Bradman, captain of the Prime Minister's XI, gets a word of encouragement from Mr Menzies.

England's shock victory

Ted Dexter is caught and bowled by Richie Benaud for 70 at the 'Gabba.

Melbourne, Jan. 3. Champagne is flowing tonight in the England camp after the tourists won the second Test by seven wickets, with a little over an hour to spare.

The victory is England's first Test win in Australia since 1954–55.

Ever the diplomat, England captain Lord Ted Dexter told the cheering crowds his side was lucky to win.

'Rubbish,' yelled the gallery, as calls went out for 'the parson', Reverend David Sheppard, who made amends for a first-innings duck with 113 glorious runs that proved decisive in England's win.

Australian captain Richie Benaud described the match as one of the best he had ever seen.

Coming into the final day needing 234 runs to win, Dexter was quietly confident his men could do the job. The pitch was still playing well, and England's batting form seemed adequate. Dexter himself had made 93 runs in the first innings, and Colin Cowdrey 113.

The match turned on the fourth day when opener Bill Lawry was bowled by Dexter for 57.

Lawry had proved almost impenetrable at the crease. His 57 runs in the second innings were useful, but unbelievably dreary. He was at the crease for 304 minutes, and the 275 minutes it took him to reach his 50 is the slowest Australian half-century on record.

The crawl was in marked contrast to the first Test in Brisbane, where 14 fifties were scored by batsmen, equalling a long-standing record which was set during the fourth Test at Leeds in July 1948.

Australia was victorious on that occasion, and might have taken the honours this time at the 'Gabba, but for a resolute 99 by Dexter, which held off a desperate, last-day grab for victory by Benaud's men.

Dexter may have erred tactically in not bringing Fred Trueman on earlier at the MCG. When he was brought into the England bowling attack, he took 5/62 and kept Australia's score down to 248.

After a draw in Brisbane and a loss today, Australia looks to its batsmen for improvement. Peter Burge, Bob Simpson, Norman O'Neill and Neil Harvey have all played dismally.

Simpson, Davidson bring Australia back

Sydney, Jan. 16. The Ashes series now stands at one–all following Australia's commanding eight-wicket victory in the third Test yesterday.

Australia easily found the 65 runs it needed to win after England's second innings collapsed for 104.

From the outset, this Test was full of drama. Seven English wickets fell on the first day for just 256 runs.

At one stage, England was 3/201 and looked set to make a big score.

But then Colin Cowdrey, on 85 runs, succumbed to one of Bob Simpson's leg-breaks. Simpson had already claimed the wicket of England opener Geoff Pullar (53).

Cowdrey was enjoying easy pickings, and heading untroubled for his century when Simpson sent a low one down.

Carelessly, Cowdrey tried to back cut the ball, only to find himself caught behind by Barry Jarman.

After that unexpected success, Richie Benaud decided to give Simpson another over.

This time it was Peter Parfitt. He didn't seem to do anything to stop Simpson's first ball, which simply spun across the bat to Bill Lawry at short leg slip. Out for a duck.

At that stage Benaud took the new ball and gave it to speedsters Alan Davidson and Graham McKenzie.

Just 23 balls later Davidson bowled Ken Barrington lbw, following up next delivery with a late inswinger that took the wicket of

Batting one-armed, with an injured right shoulder: England's John Murray managed 3 not out in the third Test.

John Murray for a duck.

When England's innings ended at 279 next day, Simpson's figures were 5/57.

A moderate first-innings batting performance by Australia (319) left the door open for England, whose brilliant off-spinner, Fred Titmus, destroyed the Australian innings right through the order, to get the outstanding haul of 7/79 from 37 overs with 14 maidens. At one

stage he took 4/5.

England's deplorable second-innings effort of 104 runs gave the game to Australia.

Davidson bowled England apart in its second innings. He had dismissed Geoff Pullar (0) and David Sheppard (12) when Ted Dexter came to the crease.

Three times in Davidson's second over to Dexter, the usually reliable English captain hit out and missed.

Each delivery went dangerously close to the stumps.

In Davidson's next over, a less-confident Dexter edged a fast, low ball into the slips, where a diving catch by Simpson finished the job.

England collapsed after the fall of Dexter's wicket for 11, and Davidson ended England's second innings with figures of 5/25.

England was all out for 104, leaving Australia just 67 to win.

'Ron's on The Hill today — he likes to get a bit of practice in at the nets.'

There was a new diversion for the patrons of the outer during this Test series. The beer can was on sale and it proved a remarkably adaptable vessel. You could drink its contents and then use it as a two-can viewing platform, as an ever-available missile or other things besides. As the Benier cartoon saw it, the crowds soon got up to speed on the can and its uses.

'Cricket dull? It's jolly good fun.'

Molnar, too, could see varieties of diversions on a pleasant afternoon on the Hill at the Sydney Cricket Ground, with cricket sometimes taking second place.

Series dies with dull draws

Sydney, Feb. 21. What was billed as the 'big Test' turned out to be the 'big flop' yesterday, when Australia successfully played for a draw in the fifth Test to retain the Ashes.

After an earlier dismal draw in the fourth Test at Adelaide, and also in the first Test in Brisbane, crowds were keen to see some life in Test cricket this summer. They didn't mind showing their disappointment when it failed to arrive.

Australian batsmen were greeted with jeers, boos, and general abuse.

Unfortunately, the brunt of their attack was 'boring' Bill Lawry, who made a staunch defence yesterday.

Scoring 45 runs in four long hours was not the Sydney crowd's idea of entertainment.

They could have gone to Circular Quay if they wanted to watch a barnacle all day.

Many felt Lawry's stand was relieved only by the rattling of beer cans and the din of slow handclapping that filtered down from the hill and rang around the ground like a chant – a kind of meditative mantra that only seemed to deepen the batsman's trance.

The people wanted action, and yesterday Test cricket failed to deliver.

After all, they had been promised a win by both captains, and when England's Ted Dexter declared at 8/268, Australia could have made a dash, needing 241 runs in 240 minutes.

But because the odds were not overwhelmingly in Australia's favour, Australian captain Richie Benaud wisely decided not to take the bait.

After Neil Harvey, Bob Simpson,

Captains Richie Benaud and Ted Dexter get together.

Brian Booth and Norman O'Neill were dismissed for 70 runs, Benaud felt Australia had little choice but to play for the draw.

Lawry and Peter Burge dug in deep. Very deep. Burge had scored a century in the first innings, but there were no sweep shots yesterday. He didn't go out of his depth, and stayed between the flags, safe as a Bondi bather.

Lawry was barely alive, a brick wall at the crease. The 36 minutes he took to move from 40 to 41 runs was almost excruciating. People were dying on their seats.

'Give him out, give him out!' the crowd cried every time a ball hit his bulky pads.

Their pleas were futile. Not even a bomb would have blown Bill Lawry off the wicket yesterday.

At the end of this tedious day, Australia was only 89 runs short of a victory. But the Ashes were safe for another series.

Davo, Harvey reach the end

Sydney, Feb. 22. Neil Harvey and Alan Davidson, two of Australia's greatest cricketers, bowed out of the game yesterday.

Unfortunately, injuries have dogged Davidson throughout his cricket career, and he tore a hamstring during the fourth Test in Adelaide, but was pronounced fit for the final Test at Sydney.

He ended a marvellous career on a high note, taking a wicket on his last delivery when he had Alan Smith caught on 1 by Bob Simpson at first slip.

Davidson retires after 44 Tests with figures of 186 wickets and 1328 runs, making him one of Australia's greatest all-rounders.

Among many memorable performances, he took 24 wickets against England in 1958–59, and 33 wickets against the West Indies in 1960–61.

In the Tied Test at Brisbane in December 1960, Davidson became the first player to score 100 runs and take 10 wickets in a Test.

His good friend, Neil Harvey, also played in that historic game.

Harvey succumbed quietly yesterday, losing his wicket at 28 to a beautiful spinner from David Allen. He was still in good form, and had taken six catches in the Test.

In 79 Tests since 1947, Harvey made 6149 runs and 21 centuries. No other Australian has played in as many Tests, and only Sir Donald Bradman made more centuries.

Australians will miss the familiar sound of Harvey's shots hitting the boundary fences, and the familiar tousled black hair of the characteristically capless champion.

And old hands will never forget the fifth Test in Melbourne in February 1953, when Harvey made

Sam Wells on Neil Harvey's career.

a career-best tally of 205 against South Africa.

Some say the daring way he attacked down the pitch was reminiscent of the great Victor Trumper. And, like Trumper, he made some prodigious scores, including 254 for Fitzroy against St Kilda in 1951–52.

Harvey would have made an excellent Australian captain, but fate decreed otherwise.

All good things must come to an end, and Australian cricket will be much the poorer for the loss of Neil Harvey and Alan Davidson.

Sponsors on field

Melbourne, Jan. 2. Is nothing sacred? Cricket's hallowed pitch has been invaded by advertising.

The Australian Board of Control has negotiated sponsorship deals with Shell petroleum and the British Tobacco Company, and their presence will be felt and seen around the grounds.

Cricket is an expensive sport to run, and the Board has moved with the times by obtaining a slice of the corporate pounds and pence now becoming available in the sporting arena.

Another sign of the Board's more 'professional' attitude has been its readiness to allow televising of interstate matches and of each day's final session in host cities.

Brighter cricket call

Melbourne, May 10. The chairman of the Australian Board of Control, Sir Donald Bradman, has written to State cricket associations calling for a 'more aggressive, positive approach' in matches.

Sir Donald is concerned at the trend of dull draws which characterised the Ashes series this season, making the game slow and uninteresting.

ABC television viewers turned from cricket to the more exciting Davis Cup tennis, and Sydney crowds abused players in the fifth Test at Sydney. It is believed Sir Donald has recommended numerous changes at the club cricket level which will hopefully ensure a brighter future for the game.

Alan Davidson, the 'claw,' performing a miracle at Old Trafford in 1961.

NSW denied 10th Shield

Melbourne, Feb. 26. In a dramatic final day's play at the MCG yesterday, Victoria beat Queensland outright to take the Sheffield Shield for the first time in 12 years.

The win, by an innings and 28 runs, gives Victoria an unassailable lead on the Shield table, ending almost a decade of NSW domination.

But it nearly didn't come off. In its first innings, Victoria compiled a massive 4/633 (dec.), but looked like failing to stitch up a victory.

Queensland made 384 in its first innings and Victoria went into the final day needing 13 wickets.

Queensland was 7/95 in its second innings at 3.30 p.m., when tailenders Wally Grout, Barry Fisher and Wes Hall made a solid, last-ditch stand, adding 126 runs.

With just 14 minutes remaining, Hall appealed against the light, which was by no means good. The umpires knocked him back.

So Bill Lawry took the new ball and gave it to fast bowler Ian Meckiff. Two balls later it was all over. When Meckiff dismissed Hall lbw for 36, ending with figures of 3/26, it heralded a changing of the guard in Sheffield Shield cricket.

Cartoonist Sam Wells' view.

Several factors are behind Victoria's success this season. Batsmen Bob Cowper and Jack Potter have both had a wonderful summer, and Cowper leads the Shield averages.

Not far behind is 21-year-old opener, Ian Redpath, whose first-innings 261 against Queensland is the highest Shield score by a Victorian on the MCG for 35 years.

Victoria has also reaped the benefits of Lawry's able captaincy, and of a splendid fast-bowling trio in Ian Meckiff, Colin Guest and Alan Connolly.

The famous Sydney 'Hill', as seen by Russell Drysdale.

FIRST TEST 1962–63 AUSTRALIA v ENGLAND
Brisbane Cricket Ground, Brisbane. November 30, December 1, 3, 4, 5, 1962.
Toss: Australia. Match Drawn.

AUSTRALIA

WM Lawry c Smith b Trueman	5	c Sheppard b Titmus	98
RB Simpson c Trueman b Dexter	50	c Smith b Dexter	71
NC O'Neill c Statham b Trueman	19	lbw Statham	56
RN Harvey b Statham	39	c Statham b Dexter	57
PJP Burge c Dexter b Trueman	6	not out	47
BC Booth c Dexter b Titmus	112	not out	19
AK Davidson c Trueman b Barrington	23		
KD Mackay not out	86		
R Benaud (c) c Smith b Knight	51		
GD McKenzie c & b Knight	4		
BN Jarman (+) c Barrington b Knight	2		
EXTRAS (B 5, LB 1, NB 1)	7	(B 4, LB 10)	14
TOTAL	404	4 dec 362	

FOW 1st Inns: 5 46 92 101 140 194 297 388 392 404
FOW 2nd Inns: 136 216 241 325

Bowling: *First Innings*: Statham 16-1-75-1, Trueman 18-0-76-3, Knight 17.5-2-65-3, Titmus 33-8-91-1, Dexter 10-0-46-1, Barrington 12-3-44-1. *Second Innings*: Trueman 15-0-59-0, Statham 16-1-67-1, Knight 14-1-63-0, Titmus 26-3-81-1, Dexter 16-0-78-2.

ENGLAND

G Pullar c & b Benaud	33	c & b Davidson	56
DS Sheppard b McKenzie b Benaud	31	c Benaud b Davidson	53
ER Dexter (c) b Benaud	70	b McKenzie	99
MC Cowdrey c Lawry b Simpson	21	c & b Benaud	9
KF Barrington c Burge b Benaud	78	c McKenzie b Davidson	23
AC Smith (+) c Jarman b McKenzie	21		
PH Parfitt c Davidson b Benaud	80 (6)	c Jarman b McKenzie	4
FJ Titmus c Simpson b Benaud	21 (7)	not out	3
BR Knight c Davidson b McKenzie	0 (8)	not out	4
FS Trueman c Jarman b McKenzie	19		
JB Statham not out	8		
EXTRAS (B 4, LB 2, W 1)	7	(B 15, LB 10, NB 2)	27
TOTAL	389	6 for 278	

FOW 1st Inns: 62 65 145 169 220 297 361 362 362 389
FOW 2nd Inns: 114 135 191 257 257 261

Bowling: *First Innings*: Davidson 21-4-77-0, McKenzie 25.3-2-78-3, Mackay 28-7-55-0, Benaud 42-12-115-6, Simpson 18-6-52-1, O'Neill 1-0-5-0. *Second Innings*: Davidson 20-6-43-3, McKenzie 20-4-61-2, Benaud 27-7-71-1, Mackay 7-0-28-0, Simpson 7-0-48-0, O'Neill 2-2-0-0.

Umpires: CJ Egar & EF Wykes

SECOND TEST 1962–63 AUSTRALIA v ENGLAND
Melbourne Cricket Ground, Melbourne. December 29, 31, January 1, 2, 3 1963.
Toss: Australia. England won by 7 wkts.

AUSTRALIA

WM Lawry b Trueman	52	b Dexter	57
RB Simpson c Smith b Coldwell	38	b Trueman	14
NC O'Neill c Graveney b Statham	19	c Cowdrey b Trueman	0
RN Harvey b Coldwell	0	run out	10
PJP Burge lbw Titmus	23	b Statham	14
BC Booth c Barrington b Titmus	27	c Trueman b Statham	103
AK Davidson c Smith b Trueman	40	c Smith b Titmus	17
KD Mackay lbw Titmus	49	lbw Trueman	9
R Benaud (c) c Barrington b Titmus	36	c Cowdrey b Trueman	4
GD McKenzie b Trueman	16	b Trueman	0
BN Jarman (+) not out	10	not out	11
EXTRAS (B 2, LB 4)	6	(B 4, LB 5)	9
TOTAL	316	248	

FOW 1st Inns: 62 111 112 112 155 164 237 289 294 316
FOW 2nd Inns: 30 30 46 69 161 193 212 228 228 248

Bowling: *First Innings*: Trueman 23-1-83-3, Statham 22-2-83-1, Coldwell 17-2-58-2, Barrington 6-0-23-0, Dexter 6-1-10-0, Titmus 15-2-43-4, Graveney 3-1-10-0. *Second Innings*: Trueman 20-1-62-5, Statham 23-1-52-2, Coldwell 25-2-60-0, Titmus 14-4-25-1, Dexter 9-2-18-1, Barrington 5-0-22-0.

ENGLAND

DS Sheppard lbw Davidson	0	run out	113
G Pullar b Davidson	11	c Jarman b McKenzie	5
ER Dexter (c) c Simpson b Benaud	93	run out	52
MC Cowdrey c Burge b McKenzie	113	not out	58
KF Barrington lbw McKenzie	35	not out	0
TW Graveney run out	41		
FJ Titmus c Jarman b Davidson	15		
AC Smith (+) not out	6		
FS Trueman c O'Neill b Davidson	6		
JB Statham b Davidson	1		
LJ Coldwell c Benaud b Davidson	1		
EXTRAS (B 4, LB 4, NB 1)	9	(B 5, LB 3, NB 1)	9
TOTAL	331	3 for 237	

FOW 1st Inns: 0 19 194 254 255 292 315 324 327 331
FOW 2nd Inns: 5 129 233

Bowling: *First Innings*: Davidson 23.1-4-75-6, McKenzie 29-3-95-2, Mackay 6-2-17-0, Benaud 18-3-82-1, Simpson 7-1-34-0, O'Neill 5-1-19-0. *Second Innings*: Davidson 19-2-53-0, McKenzie 20-3-58-1, Benaud 14-1-69-0, Mackay 9-0-34-0, Simpson 2-0-10-0, Booth 0.2-0-4-0.

Umpires: CJ Egar & WJ Smyth

THIRD TEST 1962–63 AUSTRALIA v ENGLAND
Sydney Cricket Ground, Sydney. January 11, 12, 14, 15, 1963.
Toss: England. Australia won by 8 wkts.

ENGLAND
G Pullar c Benaud b Simpson	53	b Davidson	0
DS Sheppard c McKenzie b Davidson	3	c Simpson b Davidson	12
ER Dexter (c) c Lawry b Benaud	32	c Simpson b Davidson	11
MC Cowdrey c Jarman b Simpson	85	c Simpson b Benaud	8
KF Barrington lbw Davidson	35	b McKenzie	21
PH Parfitt c Lawry b Simpson	0	c O'Neill b McKenzie	28
FJ Titmus b Davidson	32	c Booth b O'Neill	6
JT Murray (+) lbw Davidson	0	not out	3
FS Trueman b Simpson	32	c Jarman b McKenzie	9
JB Statham c Benaud b Simpson	0	b Davidson	2
LJ Coldwell not out	2	c Sheppard b Davidson	0
Extras (LB 3, W 2)	5	(B 2, LB 2)	4
TOTAL	279		104

FOW 1st Inns: 4 65 132 201 203 221 221 272 272 279
FOW 2nd Inns: 0 20 25 37 53 71 90 100 104 104

Bowling: *First Innings*: Davidson 24.5-7-54-4, McKenzie 15-3-52-0, Guest 16-0-51-0, Benaud 16-2-60-1, Simpson 15-3-57-5. *Second Innings*: Davidson 10.6-2-25-5, McKenzie 14-3-26-3, Guest 2-0-8-0, Benaud 19-10-29-1, O'Neill 7-5-7-1, Simpson 4-2-5-0.

AUSTRALIA
WM Lawry c Murray b Coldwell	8	b Trueman	8
RB Simpson b Titmus	91	not out	34
RN Harvey c Barrington b Titmus	64	lbw Trueman	15
BC Booth c Trueman b Titmus	16	not out	5
NC O'Neill b Titmus	3		
BK Shepherd not out	71		
BN Jarman (+) run out	0		
AK Davidson c Trueman b Titmus	15		
R Benaud (c) c & b Titmus	15		
GD McKenzie lbw Titmus	4		
CEJ Guest b Statham	11		
Extras (B 10, LB 11)	21	(B 5)	5
TOTAL	319		2 for 67

FOW 1st Inns: 14 174 177 187 212 216 242 274 280 319
FOW 2nd Inns: 28 54

Bowling: *First Innings*: Trueman 20-2-68-0, Statham 21.2-2-67-1, Coldwell 15-1-41-1, Titmus 37-14-79-7, Barrington 8-0-43-0. *Second Innings*: Statham 3-0-15-0, Trueman 6-1-20-2, Dexter 3.2-0-27-0.

Umpires: LP Rowan & WJ Smyth

FIFTH TEST 1962–63 AUSTRALIA v ENGLAND
Sydney Cricket Ground, Sydney. February 15, 16, 18, 19, 20, 1963.
Toss: England. Match Drawn.

ENGLAND
DS Sheppard c & b Hawke	19	c Harvey b Benaud	68
MC Cowdrey c Harvey b Davidson	2 (5)	c Benaud b Davidson	53
KF Barrington c Harvey b Benaud	101	c Grout b McKenzie	94
ER Dexter (c) c Simpson b O'Neill	47	st Grout b Benaud	6
TW Graveney c Harvey b McKenzie	14 (6)	c & b Davidson	3
R Illingworth c Grout b Davidson	27 (2)	c Hawke b Benaud	18
FJ Titmus c Grout b Hawke	34	not out	12
FS Trueman c Harvey b Benaud	30	c Harvey b McKenzie	8
AC Smith (+) b Simpson	6	c Simpson b Davidson	1
DA Allen c Benaud b Davidson	14		
JB Statham not out	17		
Extras (B 4, LB 6)	10	(B 1, LB 4)	5
TOTAL	321		8 dec 268

FOW 1st Inns: 5 39 129 177 189 224 276 286 293 321
FOW 2nd Inns: 40 137 145 239 247 249 257 268

Bowling: *First Innings*: Davidson 25.6-4-43-3, McKenzie 27-4-57-1, Hawke 20-1-51-2, Benaud 34-9-71-2, Simpson 18-4-51-1, O'Neill 10-0-38-1. *Second Innings*: Davidson 28-1-80-3, McKenzie 8-0-39-2, Hawke 9-0-38-0, Benaud 30-8-71-3, Simpson 4-0-22-0, Harvey 3-0-13-0.

AUSTRALIA
WM Lawry c Smith b Trueman	11	not out	45
RB Simpson c Trueman b Titmus	32	b Trueman	0
BC Booth b Titmus	11 (5)	b Allen	0
NC O'Neill c Graveney b Allen	73	c Smith b Allen	17
PJP Burge lbw Titmus	103 (6)	b Allen	52
RN Harvey c(S)PH Parfitt b Statham	22 (3)	b Allen	28
AK Davidson c Allen b Dexter	15		
R Benaud (c) c Graveney b Allen	57		
GD McKenzie c & b Titmus	0		
NJN Hawke c Graveney b Titmus	14		
ATW Grout (+) not out	0		
Extras (B 6, LB 5)	11	(B 4, LB 6)	10
TOTAL	349		4 for 152

FOW 1st Inns: 28 50 71 180 231 271 299 303 347 349
FOW 2nd Inns: 0 39 70 70

Bowling: *First Innings*: Trueman 11-0-33-1, Statham 18-1-76-1, Dexter 7-1-24-1, Titmus 47.2-9-103-5, Allen 43-15-87-2, Illingworth 5-1-15-0. *Second Innings*: Trueman 3-0-6-1, Statham 4-1-8-0, Dexter 4-1-11-0, Allen 19-11-26-3, Titmus 20-7-37-0, Barrington 8-3-22-0, Graveney 4-0-24-0, Illingworth 10-5-8-0.

Umpires: CJ Egar & LP Rowan

FOURTH TEST 1962–63 AUSTRALIA v ENGLAND
Adelaide Oval, Adelaide. January 25, 26, 28, 29, 30, 1963.
Toss: Australia. Match Drawn.

AUSTRALIA
WM Lawry b Illingworth	10	c Graveney b Trueman	16
RB Simpson c Smith b Statham	0	c Smith b Dexter	71
RN Harvey c Statham b Dexter	154	c Barrington b Statham	6
BC Booth c Cowdrey b Titmus	34	c Smith b Dexter	77
NC O'Neill c Cowdrey b Dexter	100	c Cowdrey b Trueman	23
AK Davidson b Statham	46 (10)	b Statham	2
BK Shepherd c Trueman b Statham	10 (6)	c Titmus b Dexter	13
KD Mackay c Smith b Trueman	1 (7)	c Graveney b Trueman	3
R Benaud (c) b Dexter	16 (8)	c Barrington b Trueman	48
GD McKenzie c Sheppard b Titmus	15 (9)	c Smith b Statham	13
ATW Grout (+) not out	1	not out	16
Extras (LB 5, W 1)	6	(B 1, LB 4)	5
TOTAL	393		293

FOW 1st Inns: 2 16 101 295 302 331 336 366 383 393
FOW 2nd Inns: 27 37 170 175 199 205 228 254 258 293

Bowling: *First Innings*: Trueman 19-1-54-1, Statham 21-5-66-3, Illingworth 20-3-85-1, Dexter 23-1-94-3, Titmus 20.1-2-88-2. *Second Innings*: Trueman 23.3-3-60-4, Statham 21-2-71-3, Dexter 17-0-65-3, Titmus 24-5-69-0, Illingworth 5-1-23-0.

ENGLAND
G Pullar b McKenzie	9	c Simpson b McKenzie	3
DS Sheppard st Grout b Benaud	30	c Grout b Mackay	1
KF Barrington b Simpson	63	not out	132
MC Cowdrey c Grout b McKenzie	13	run out	32
ER Dexter (c) c Grout b McKenzie	61	c Simpson b Benaud	10
TW Graveney c Booth b McKenzie	22	not out	36
FJ Titmus not out	59		
R Illingworth c Grout b McKenzie	12		
AC Smith (+) c Lawry b Mackay	13		
FS Trueman c Benaud b Mackay	38		
JB Statham b Mackay	1		
Extras (B 5, LB 5)	10	(B 4, W 5)	9
TOTAL	331		4 for 223

FOW 1st Inns: 17 84 117 119 165 226 246 275 327 331
FOW 2nd Inns: 2 4 98 122

Bowling: *First Innings*: Davidson 3.4-0-30-0, McKenzie 33-3-89-5, Mackay 27.6-8-80-3, Benaud 18-3-82-1, Simpson 8-1-40-1. *Second Innings*: McKenzie 14-0-64-1, Mackay 8-2-13-1, Benaud 15-3-38-1, O'Neill 8-0-49-0, Simpson 10-1-50-0, Lawry 1-1-0-0, Harvey 1-1-0-0.

Umpires: CJ Egar & A Mackley

Australian Averages

1962–63 AUSTRALIA v ENGLAND

AUSTRALIA	M	Inn	NO	Runs	H.S	Avrge	Ct	St	Overs	Mds	Runs	Wkt	Avrge
Benaud, R	5	7	-	227	57	32.43	9	-	233.0	58	688	17	40.47
Booth, BC	5	10	2	404	112	50.50	2	-	0.2	-	4	-	-
Burge, PJP	3	6	2	245	103	61.25	2	-	-	-	-	-	-
Davidson, AK	5	7	-	158	46	22.57	4	-	175.6	30	480	24	20.00
Grout, ATW	2	3	3	17	16*	-	7	2	-	-	-	-	-
Guest, CEJ	1	1	-	11	11	11.00	-	-	18.0	-	59	-	-
Harvey, RN	5	10	-	395	154	39.50	6	-	4.0	1	13	-	-
Hawke, NJN	1	1	-	14	14	14.00	-	-	29.0	1	89	2	44.50
Jarman, BN	3	4	2	23	11*	11.50	7	-	-	-	-	-	-
Lawry, WM	5	10	1	310	98	34.44	4	-	1.0	1	0	-	-
Mackay, KD	3	5	1	148	86*	37.00	-	-	85.6	19	227	4	56.75
McKenzie, GD	5	7	-	52	16	7.43	3	-	205.3	25	619	20	30.95
O'Neill, NC	5	9	-	310	100	34.44	2	-	33.0	8	118	2	59.00
Shepherd, BK	2	3	1	94	71*	47.00	-	-	-	-	-	-	-
Simpson, RB	5	10	1	401	91	44.56	9	-	93.0	18	369	8	46.13

English Averages

1962–63 AUSTRALIA v ENGLAND

ENGLAND	M	Inn	NO	Runs	H.S	Avrge	Ct	St	Overs	Mds	Runs	Wkt	Avrge
Allen, DA	1	1	-	14	14	14.00	1	-	62.0	26	113	5	22.60
Barrington, KF	5	10	2	582	132*	72.75	6	-	39.0	6	154	1	154.00
Coldwell, LJ	2	3	1	3	2*	1.50	-	-	57.0	5	159	3	53.00
Cowdrey, MC	5	10	1	394	113	43.78	5	-	-	-	-	-	-
Dexter, ER	5	10	-	481	99	48.10	2	-	95.2	6	373	11	33.91
Graveney, TW	3	5	1	116	41	29.00	6	-	7.0	1	34	-	-
Illingworth, R	2	3	-	57	27	19.00	-	-	40.0	10	131	1	131.00
Knight, BR	1	2	1	4	4*	4.00	1	-	31.5	3	128	3	42.67
Murray, JT	1	2	1	3	3*	3.00	1	-	-	-	-	-	-
Parfitt, PH	2	4	-	112	80	28.00	-	-	-	-	-	-	-
Pullar, G	3	6	-	170	56	21.25	-	-	-	-	-	-	-
Sheppard, DS	5	10	-	330	113	33.00	3	-	-	-	-	-	-
Smith, AC	4	5	1	47	21	11.75	13	-	-	-	-	-	-
Statham, JB	5	6	2	29	17*	7.25	3	-	165.2	16	580	13	44.62
Titmus, FJ	5	8	3	182	59*	36.40	3	-	236.3	54	616	21	29.33
Trueman, FS	5	7	-	142	38	20.29	7	-	158.3	9	521	20	26.05

Ian Meckiff is chucked out

Brisbane, Dec. 11. Australian fast bowler Ian Meckiff was no-balled by square leg umpire Col Egar four times in the second over of South Africa's innings.

Australia had batted first and made 435 in a day and a half, Brian Booth 169, Norm O'Neill 82. Graham McKenzie bowled the first over without incident.

Meckiff did not bowl again in the innings, and captain Richie Benaud said after the sensational day's play that Meckiff would not bowl again in the Test.

The crowd angrily supported Meckiff throughout the rest of that day, and stopped play for two minutes after tea with a chant, 'We want Meckiff... We want Meckiff.' The bowler himself was consigned miserably to the outfield, there to contemplate the tatters of his career.

At stumps, spectators surged onto the ground and chaired Meckiff from the field, and then formed a passage for umpire Egar to leave, booing him bitterly.

Percy Beames reported in the *Age* that Egar's decision 'dumbfounded and stunned' every Australian player' and that even the 'imperturbable Benaud was left aghast and shocked by the boldness of umpire Egar's action'.

Meckiff had been recalled to the Test side by selectors Sir Donald Bradman, Jack Ryder and Dudley Seddon for the first time since the third Test against the West Indies in January 1961 – to the surprise of many, as despite his speed he had achieved only modest returns.

Lindsay Hassett, also writing in the *Age*, firmly stated: 'It is common knowledge that at the start of this summer all umpires were instructed to call any bowler whose action even hinted at illegality, regardless of what happened in previous seasons'.

Umpire Egar had watched Meckiff bowl some 119 overs in Test and Shield matches before this game, and the Board of Control directive would seem to justify his decision.

It would also scotch the conspiracy theorists who maintained that Meckiff was chosen as a scapegoat to show that Australia was determined to clean up its act with regard to 'chucking'.

Hassett said, 'My own view is that Meckiff's action can be doubted only rarely, and generally when he is tired and loses balance at the moment of delivery. But I have no doubt that Egar's action was hon-

Ian Meckiff's bowling action reveals his characteristic 'bent arm' delivery.

estly, even if wrongly, conceived. I would defy anyone to detect any difference in the deliveries.'

Meckiff had been 'called' twice last season, and his action was controversial during England's 1958–59 tour.

Opinions differed on Benaud's actions in not giving Meckiff a chance to bowl at the other end, Hassett saying that Benaud 'took the easy way out'.

Percy Beames, on the other hand, thought Benaud did the right thing because he believed that umpire Lou Rowan at the other end would also have 'called' Meckiff. He believed, too, that the embarrassment had gone on long enough.

For his part, Meckiff said during the Test that he would see the game out, but would retire from all forms of cricket at the end of it.

And, by the way, the first Test was a draw – though some would say that someone lost badly.

Norm O'Neill was injured in the first Test and missed Australia's win at the MCG in the second Test.

Benaud makes way for Bob Simpson

Bradman advises the new captain.

Melbourne, Jan. 6. A depleted Australian line-up – without the services of injured stars Brian Booth, Norm O'Neill and Richie Benaud – gave new captain Bob Simpson a successful initiation, by winning the second Test.

Simpson boldly sent South Africa in after winning the toss, and, despite Eddie Barlow's second successive century, bowled them out for a modest 274.

Bill Lawry and debutant Ian Redpath put on 219 for the first wicket, Lawry going on to 157 and Redpath unluckily out for 97. Simpson himself made a duck, but 55 not out in the second innings saw Australia home by a surprisingly wide margin of eight wickets.

Benaud had indicated before the Test that he was not going to be available for the 1964 tour of England, and has now offered to withdraw from the captaincy for the rest of the South African visit, in order that Simpson might establish himself in the role.

Benaud said that he would be available to assist Australian cricket with his experience in any other capacity, including playing in the South African Tests when fit.

Benaud remarked that 'the wonderful performance of Simpson and his team in this present Test has made it clear to me that we have the nucleus of a very fine team.'

Simpson was worried before the game about whether he could handle the side effectively while fielding in the slips. However, afterwards he said he had no problem, and would continue to play in his specialist position.

Classic batting for South African win

South Africa 1963–64. Back: McLennan (baggage master), Barlow, Halse, Seymour, R.G. Pollock, P.M Pollock, Bland, Lindsay, D. B Pithey, Partridge. Front: A. J Pithey, Waite, Goddard (capt.), Vilkjoen (mgr), Van Der Merwe, Farrer, Carlstein.

Adelaide, Jan. 29. Graham Pollock, the 19-year-old South African batsman, added a monumental 175 to the sublime 122 he made in the drawn third Test in Sydney. The first innings Lindsay Hassett said was of 'unusual brilliance ... in recent years; the only innings I have seen to match Pollock's in power and grace was Garfield Sobers's century ... in the first Test in Brisbane in 1960–61, and that was a truly great exhibition.

Pollock's knock was accompanied by Eddie Barrow who made a snick-filled 201 in a partnership of 341 that broke just about every record South Africans could think of. In four tests Barlow has now scored 576 runs in six innings with one not out, for an average of 115.

Barlow's part in South Africa's win was not over, however. He was called upon to bowl at 5.30 p.m. on the fourth day and proceeded to take 3/5 from fifteen balls, helping plunge Australia from a possible rescue position at 5/301 to certain defeat at 9/310.

Barry Shepherd and Richie Benaud were in occupation, and had put on 91 with little perturbation when Shepherd top-edged a hook shot off Barlow and South African 'keeper Denis Lindsay raced 40 yards towards fine leg, got his gloves under the ball and crashed to the ground – but held the catch. Two balls later Benaud dragged one from Barlow from outside off stump onto his wicket.

Cricket writers criticised the Australian team for its 'surrender', contrasting it with the defiant West Indies attitude in 1960–61.

Grout passes Bert Oldfield's record of Test dismissals

Adelaide, Jan. 27. When Wally Grout caught South Africa's Tony Pithey from the bowling of Neil Hawke, it was his 131st dismissal in Test cricket, passing Bert Oldfield's Australian record of 130.

Grout achieved this in his 33rd Test – it took Oldfield 54, which tells a little of Grout's concentration and efficiency behind the stumps. But both are 'keepers of the highest standard, and can only take the chances that come their way. Grout went one better in this match, catching Colin Bland as well.

He has quickly eaten up wicket-keeping records, and set the new standard at six dismissals in his first Test v South Africa in 1957–58. In 1960–61 he set a new record for England v Australia Tests with 21 dismissals in the series. He took 23 in the 1960–61 West Indies series.

Wally Grout snaps one up in front of Bob Simpson at the MCG.

Time alone saves Australia

Richie Benaud leaves the field after his final Test, at the Sydney Cricket Ground.

Sydney, Feb. 12. The fifth Test fizzled out to a tame draw when South African openers Trevor Goddard and Eddie Barlow made 76 of the 171 runs required to win in the 85 minutes left.

Had the South African bowlers managed to separate Tom Veivers and Neil Hawke sooner, the result might have been different. Australia was 9/225 and looking down the barrel – the off-spinner Michael Seymour was a torment – and there would have been plenty of time to get the 125 runs necessary for South Africa to win the match and the series.

But Veivers and Hawke, who came together at 2.49 p.m., survived until the balance between time and runs tipped Australia's way, 20 minutes after tea. By then Australia had made 270 runs.

However it was a 'moral' win in this match, and in the series overall. Had the South Africans caught better they would certainly have won. Goddard was the outstanding all-rounder, Peter Pollock and Joe Partridge the best opening bowlers, and Barlow, Graeme Pollock and Colin Bland tremendous batsmen. Australia's batting was patchy and with Alan Davidson missing, the Australian pace attack lacked a genuine wicket-taker.

Sobers and SA win Sheffield Shield

Adelaide, Feb. 24. South Australia, or more accurately, Gary Sobers with some help from Rex Sellers' 46 wickets, defeated Victoria inside three days and won the Sheffield Shield for the first time since the 1952–53 season.

Sobers made 124 and took 6/71 to round out a season in which he topped both batting and bowling averages with 973 runs at 74.8 and 47 wickets at 28.2. Sobers' highest score was 195 against WA in Perth in January.

Ian Chappell also made good runs, and was unlucky not to be picked to tour England.

South Australia won four matches outright and another on the first innings. In addition to the match against Victoria, SA defeated WA by an innings and 102 runs in Adelaide in November, and by nine wickets in Perth in January; defeated NSW by two wickets in Sydney in January, and lost to Queensland in Adelaide in December. A draw with first-innings points was achieved against Queensland, and a loss to Victoria.

Victoria was second with three outright wins and three draws with first-innings points.

FIRST TEST 1963–64 AUSTRALIA v SOUTH AFRICA
Brisbane Cricket Ground, Brisbane. December 6, 7, 9 (no play), 10, 11, 1963.
Toss: Australia. Match Drawn.

AUSTRALIA

WM Lawry c RG Pollock b Barlow	43	not out	87
RB Simpson c Waite b PM Pollock	12	c (S)KC Bland b Partridge	34
NC O'Neill c Barlow b PM Pollock	82	not out	19
PJP Burge run out	13		
BC Booth c Barlow b PM Pollock	169		
R Benaud (c) lbw Goddard	43		
GD McKenzie c PM Pollock b Goddard	39		
TR Veivers c Goddard b PM Pollock	14		
ATW Grout (+) c Seymour b PM Pollock	6		
I Meckiff b PM Pollock	7		
AN Connolly not out	1		
Extras (B 1, LB 5)	6	(LB 4)	4
TOTAL	435		1 dec 144

FOW 1st Inns: 39 73 88 208 310 394 415 427 434 435
FOW 2nd Inns: 83

Bowling: *First Innings*: PM Pollock 22.6-0-95-6, Partridge 25-3-87-0, Goddard 24-6-52-2, Barlow 9-0-71-1, Seymour 11-0-39-0, Pithey 23-6-85-0. *Second Innings*: PM Pollock 6-0-26-0, Partridge 17-1-50-1, Goddard 7-0-34-0, Pithey 5-0-30-0.

SOUTH AFRICA

TL Goddard (c) c Meckiff b Benaud	52	not out	8
EJ Barlow b Benaud	114	c Simpson b McKenzie	0
PR Carlstein c & b Benaud	0	not out	1
RG Pollock b McKenzie	25		
DT Lindsay lbw Benaud	17		
JHB Waite (+) lbw Connolly	66		
PL Van der Merwe b O'Neill	17		
DB Pithey c Meckiff b Veivers	18		
PM Pollock lbw Benaud	8		
MA Seymour b Simpson	10		
JT Partridge not out	3		
Extras (B 3, LB 5, NB 8)	16	(B 4)	4
TOTAL	346		1 for 13

FOW 1st Inns: 74 78 120 157 239 272 321 325 335 346
FOW 2nd Inns: 1

Bowling: *First Innings*: McKenzie 23-1-88-1, Meckiff 1-0-8-0, Connolly 19-4-46-1, Veivers 34-15-48-1, Benaud 33-10-68-5, Simpson 18.5-5-52-1, O'Neill 7-0-20-1. *Second Innings*: McKenzie 3.3-1-3-1, Connolly 1-0-2-0, Benaud 2-1-4-0.

Umpires: CJ Egar & LP Rowan

SECOND TEST 1963–64 AUSTRALIA v SOUTH AFRICA
Melbourne Cricket Ground, Melbourne. January 1, 2, 3, 4, 6, 1964.
Toss: Australia. Australia won by 8 wkts.

SOUTH AFRICA

TL Goddard (c) b Grout b McKenzie	17	lbw Hawke	8
EJ Barlow c Connolly b McKenzie	109	run out	54
AJ Pithey lbw Connolly	21	c Grout b Connolly	76
RG Pollock c Simpson b McKenzie	16	c Martin b Connolly	2
JHB Waite (+) c Grout b Hawke	14	b McKenzie	77
PL Van der Merwe st Grout b Martin	14	c Grout b Martin	31
KC Bland run out	50	c & b Martin	22
DB Pithey c Grout b McKenzie	0	c Martin b Hawke	4
PM Pollock c Simpson b Martin	14 (10)	b Hawke	0
MA Seymour not out	7 (11)	not out	11
JT Partridge run out	9 (9)	b McKenzie	12
Extras (LB 3)	3	(B 2, LB 3, W 2, NB 2)	9
TOTAL	274		306

FOW 1st Inns: 26 74 100 129 179 201 201 256 256 274
FOW 2nd Inns: 35 83 85 213 233 273 282 282 282 306

Bowling: *First Innings*: McKenzie 19-1-82-4, Hawke 20-2-77-1, Connolly 18-2-62-1, Martin 16-3-44-2, Veivers 5-1-6-0. *Second Innings*: McKenzie 25-1-81-2, Connolly 18-2-49-2, Hawke 19-1-53-3, Martin 27-4-83-2, Simpson 12-2-31-0.

AUSTRALIA

WM Lawry c(S)PR Carlstein b Partridge	157	b Partridge	20
IR Redpath b Partridge	97	c Van der Merwe b Barlow	25
RB Simpson (c) b PM Pollock	0	not out	55
PJP Burge c Bland b PM Pollock	23	not out	26
BK Shepherd c DB Pithey b Barlow	96		
ATW Grout (+) c Waite b PM Pollock	3		
TR Veivers c Waite b Partridge	19		
GD McKenzie c Partridge b Seymour	2		
NJN Hawke b Barlow	24		
JW Martin c DB Pithey b Partridge	17		
AN Connolly not out	0		
Extras (B 1, LB 2, NB 6)	9	(B 5, LB 2, W 1, NB 2)	10
TOTAL	447		2 for 136

FOW 1st Inns: 219 222 270 291 301 340 357 413 439 447
FOW 2nd Inns: 33 75

Bowling: *First Innings*: Pollock 20.5-1-98-3, Partridge 34-4-108-4, Bland 11-2-35-0, Goddard 21-2-70-0, Pithey 5-1-20-0, Seymour 19-2-56-1, Barlow 7.6-0-51-2. *Second Innings*: Partridge 17-1-49-1, Barlow 11-0-49-1, Goddard 1-1-0-0, Pithey 6-0-18-0, Bland 2-0-6-0, Van der Merwe 0.1-0-4-0.

Umpires: CJ Egar & LP Rowan

THIRD TEST 1963–64 AUSTRALIA v SOUTH AFRICA
Sydney Cricket Ground, Sydney. January 10, 11, 13, 14, 15, 1964.
Toss: Australia. Match Drawn.

AUSTRALIA

RB Simpson (c) c Goddard b PM Pollock	58	lbw Halse	31
WM Lawry b Partridge	23	c RG Pollock b Goddard	89
NC O'Neill c Goddard b Halse	3	c Barlow b Partridge	88
PJP Burge b Partridge	36	c Waite b PM Pollock	13
BC Booth b Partridge	75	b Partridge	16
BK Shepherd c Waite b PM Pollock	0	c Waite b Partridge	11
R Benaud c Bland b PM Pollock	43	c DB Pithey b PM Pollock	90
GD McKenzie c Goddard b Partridge	3	c Van der Merwe b Partridge	76
NJN Hawke c Goddard b PM Pollock	2	not out	6
ATW Grout (+) c Partridge b PM Pollock	1	c Bland b Partridge	8
AN Connolly not out	3		
Extras (B 5, LB 6, W 1, NB 1)	13	(B 8, LB 8, W 1, NB 5)	22
TOTAL	260		9 dec 450

FOW 1st Inns: 59 66 108 128 129 229 238 248 256 260
FOW 2nd Inns: 58 198 235 235 259 264 424 436 450

Bowling: *First Innings*: PM Pollock 18-2-83-5, Partridge 19.6-2-88-4, Goddard 10-1-24-0, Halse 11-1-36-1, Bland 2-0-7-0, Barlow 2-0-9-0. *Second Innings*: PM Pollock 24-0-129-2, Partridge 32.5-4-123-5, Halse 15-2-58-1, Bland 1-0-7-0, Barlow 1-0-5-0, DB Pithey 16-1-86-0, Goddard 11-3-20-1.

SOUTH AFRICA

TL Goddard (c) c Connolly b Benaud	80	lbw Simpson	84
EJ Barlow c Grout b Connolly	6	c Simpson b Hawke	35
AJ Pithey c Grout b Hawke	9 (6)	not out	53
RG Pollock c McKenzie b Connolly	122	c Grout b Hawke	42
JHB Waite (+) b McKenzie	8		
PL Van der Merwe b McKenzie	0 (7)	not out	13
KC Bland c McKenzie b Benaud	51 (5)	c Benaud b O'Neill	85
DB Pithey c Lawry b Benaud	10 (3)	b McKenzie	7
PM Pollock c Grout b Hawke	1		
JT Partridge b McKenzie	7		
CG Halse not out	1		
Extras (B 3, LB 4)	7	(B 2, LB 5)	7
TOTAL	302		5 for 326

FOW 1st Inns: 10 58 137 162 162 244 277 278 300 302
FOW 2nd Inns: 57 67 141 201 291

Bowling: *First Innings*: McKenzie 19-2-70-3, Connolly 19-2-66-2, Hawke 18-1-56-2, Simpson 9-2-32-0, O'Neill 3-0-16-0, Benaud 24.1-4-55-3. *Second Innings*: McKenzie 14-2-61-1, Connolly 13-0-41-0, Benaud 30-8-61-0, Hawke 19-5-43-2, O'Neill 16-1-59-1, Simpson 23-8-48-1, Booth 1-0-3-0, Shepherd 1-0-3-0.

Umpires: CJ Egar & LP Rowan

FIFTH TEST 1963–64 AUSTRALIA v SOUTH AFRICA
Sydney Cricket Ground, Sydney. February 7, 8, 10, 11, 12, 1964.
Toss: South Africa. Match Drawn.

AUSTRALIA

WM Lawry b Halse	13	c Waite b PM Pollock	12
RB Simpson (c) c Lindsay b Partridge	28	lbw Partridge	31
NC O'Neill b PM Pollock	21 (7)	b PM Pollock	6
PJP Burge b Partridge	56	c Partridge b Seymour	39
BC Booth not out	102 (3)	c (S)PR Carlstein b Seymour	87
BK Shepherd lbw Partridge	1	c Bland b Goddard	12
R Benaud b Goddard	11 (5)	c (S)PR Carlstein b Seymour	3
TR Veivers b Partridge	43	c Barlow b Goddard	39
GD McKenzie b Partridge	0	c Bland b PM Pollock	0
NJN Hawke c Lindsay b Partridge	0 (11)	not out	16
ATW Grout (+) c Waite b Partridge	29 (10)	c Barlow b Partridge	14
Extras (LB 2, NB 5)	7	(B 5, LB 4, NB 2)	11
TOTAL	311		270

FOW 1st Inns: 42 44 103 142 144 179 263 263 265 311
FOW 2nd Inns: 29 49 132 152 181 189 207 209 225 270

Bowling: *First Innings*: PM Pollock 22-5-75-1, Partridge 31.1-6-91-7, Halse 14-3-40-1, Goddard 16-1-67-1, Barlow 9-1-31-0. *Second Innings*: PM Pollock 11-1-35-3, Partridge 32-5-85-2, Halse 7-0-22-0, Barlow 1-0-8-0, Seymour 38-9-80-3, Goddard 24.7-10-29-2.

SOUTH AFRICA

TL Goddard (c) c Grout b Veivers	93	not out	44
EJ Barlow c Benaud b O'Neill	5	not out	32
AJ Pithey c Grout b McKenzie	49		
RG Pollock c & b Veivers	17		
KC Bland c Booth b Benaud	126		
JHB Waite (+) c Simpson b McKenzie	19		
DT Lindsay c(S)AN Connolly b Benaud	65		
PM Pollock c Lawry b Benaud	6		
MA Seymour c Benaud b McKenzie	0		
JT Partridge lbw Benaud	6		
CG Halse not out	10		
Extras (B 4, LB 4, W 1, NB 6)	15		0
TOTAL	411		0 for 76

FOW 1st Inns: 18 142 157 182 223 341 365 368 389 411
FOW 2nd Inns:

Bowling: *First Innings*: McKenzie 37-4-110-3, Hawke 22-4-69-0, O'Neill 2-0-2-1, Benaud 49-10-118-4, Veivers 35-5-97-2. *Second Innings*: McKenzie 4-0-16-0, Benaud 8-2-25-0, Veivers 8-0-19-0, Hawke 4-0-16-0.

Umpires: CJ Egar & LP Rowan

FOURTH TEST 1963–64 AUSTRALIA v SOUTH AFRICA
Adelaide Oval, Adelaide. January 24, 25, 27, 28, 29, 1964.
Toss: Australia. South Africa won by 10 wkts.

AUSTRALIA

RB Simpson (c) b Goddard	78	c Lindsay b Halse	34
WM Lawry c Partridge b PM Pollock	14	c Goddard b PM Pollock	38
NC O'Neill c Goddard b PM Pollock	0	c Partridge b Halse	66
PJP Burge c Halse b PM Pollock	91	run out	20
BC Booth c Lindsay b Goddard	58	lbw PM Pollock	24
BK Shepherd lbw Goddard	70	c Lindsay b Barlow	78
R Benaud b Partridge	7	b Barlow	34
GD McKenzie c Lindsay b Goddard	12	c & b Barlow	4
ATW Grout (+) c PM Pollock b Goddard	0	c Pithey b Halse	23
NJN Hawke not out	0	c Carlstein b Seymour	0
RA Gaunt run out	1	not out	2
Extras (B 1, LB 8, NB 5)	14	(LB 4, W 1, NB 3)	8
TOTAL	345		331

FOW 1st Inns: 35 37 141 225 279 290 333 333 344 345
FOW 2nd Inns: 72 81 125 178 210 301 301 302 310 331

Bowling: *First Innings*: PM Pollock 21-1-96-3, Partridge 22-4-76-1, Halse 13-1-54-0, Goddard 24.6-4-60-5, Seymour 12-2-38-0, Bland 1-0-7-0. *Second Innings*: PM Pollock 14-1-73-2, Partridge 17-3-76-0, Goddard 21-3-64-0, Halse 13.3-0-50-3, Seymour 19-1-54-1, Barlow 5-2-6-3.

SOUTH AFRICA

TL Goddard (c) b Hawke	34	not out	34
EJ Barlow lbw Hawke	201	not out	47
AJ Pithey c Grout b Hawke	0		
RG Pollock b Hawke	175		
KC Bland c Grout b Gaunt	33		
PR Carlstein c Benaud b Gaunt	37		
DT Lindsay (+) b Simpson	41		
PM Pollock c Benaud b Hawke	21		
MA Seymour c Simpson b Hawke	3		
JT Partridge b McKenzie	6		
CG Halse not out	19		
Extras (B 7, LB 8, W 3, NB 7)	25	(W 1)	1
TOTAL	595		0 for 82

FOW 1st Inns: 70 70 411 437 500 501 559 568 575 595
FOW 2nd Inns:

Bowling: *First Innings*: Gaunt 24-2-115-2, McKenzie 30.1-2-156-1, Hawke 39-5-139-6, Benaud 20-1-101-0, Simpson 10-1-59-1. *Second Innings*: Gaunt 4-0-22-0, McKenzie 4-0-22-0, Hawke 6-0-20-0, Benaud 3-1-17-0.

Umpires: CJ Egar & LP Rowan

Australian Averages

1963–64 AUSTRALIA v SOUTH AFRICA

AUSTRALIA	M	Inn	NO	Runs	H.S	Avrge	Ct	St	Overs	Mds	Runs	Wkt	Avrge
Benaud, R	4	7	-	231	90	33.00	6	-	169.1	37	449	12	37.42
Booth, BC	4	7	1	531	169	88.50	1	-	1.0	-	3	-	-
Burge, PJP	5	9	1	317	91	39.63	-	-					
Connolly, AN	3	3	3	4	3*	-	2	-	88.0	10	266	6	44.33
Gaunt, RA	1	2	1	3	2*	3.00	-	-	28.0	2	137	2	68.50
Grout, ATW	5	8	-	84	29	10.50	13	1	-	-	-	-	-
Hawke, NJN	4	7	3	48	24	12.00	-	-	147.0	18	473	14	33.79
Lawry, WM	5	10	1	496	157	55.11	2	-	-	-	-	-	-
Martin, JW	1	1	-	17	17	17.00	3	-	43.0	7	127	4	31.75
McKenzie, GD	5	8	-	136	76	17.00	2	-	178.4	14	689	16	43.06
Meckiff, I	1	1	-	7	7	7.00	2	-	1.0	-	8	-	-
O'Neill, NC	4	8	1	285	88	40.71	2	-	28.0	1	97	3	32.33
Redpath, IR	1	2	-	122	97	61.00	-	-	-	-	-	-	-
Shepherd, BK	4	7	-	268	96	38.29	1	-	1.0	-	3	-	-
Simpson, RB	5	10	1	361	78	40.11	6	-	72.5	18	222	3	74.00
Veivers, TR	3	4	-	115	43	28.75	1	-	82.0	21	170	3	56.67

South African Averages

1963–64 AUSTRALIA v SOUTH AFRICA

SOUTH AFRICA	M	Inn	NO	Runs	H.S	Avrge	Ct	St	Overs	Mds	Runs	Wkt	Avrge
Barlow, EJ	5	10	2	603	201	75.38	6	-	45.6	3	230	7	32.86
Bland, KC	4	6	-	367	126	61.17	5	-	17.0	2	62	-	-
Carlstein, PR	2	3	-	38	37	19.00	1	-	-	-	-	-	-
Goddard, TL	5	10	3	454	93	64.86	7	-	160.5	31	420	11	38.18
Halse, CG	3	3	3	30	19*	-	1	-	73.3	7	260	6	43.33
Lindsay, DT	3	3	-	123	65	41.00	6	-	-	-	-	-	-
Partridge, JT	5	6	1	43	12	8.60	5	-	247.4	33	833	25	33.32
Pithey, AJ	4	6	1	208	76	41.60	1	-	-	-	-	-	-
Pithey, DB	3	5	-	39	18	7.80	3	-	55.0	8	239	-	-
Pollock, PM	5	5	-	50	21	8.33	2	-	159.3	11	710	25	28.40
Pollock, RG	5	7	-	399	175	57.00	2	-	-	-	-	-	-
Seymour, MA	4	5	2	31	11*	10.33	1	-	99.0	14	267	5	53.40
Van der Merwe, PL	3	5	1	75	31	18.75	2	-	0.1	-	4	-	-
Waite, JHB	4	5	-	184	77	36.80	8	-	-	-	-	-	-

Grey cricket under grey English skies

Simpson's men an unknown quantity

London, April 19. Asked on arrival at the airport what margin he would like to win by, Australian captain Bob Simpson said 'One up in the last Test' would do him.

As this is alleged to be the 'second worst' Australian team to tour England – the 1912 side is the universal pick of the worst – a series win would be welcome.

Simpson had four fast-medium bowlers, which included the lion-hearted Graham McKenzie, Neil Hawke and Alan Connolly – none of whom had impressed against South Africa, and Grahame Corling, who has only played a handful of first class matches.

But McKenzie is deceptively fast and never stops giving his all, the others are of the type that generally do well on softer English wickets where swing and cut are as important as sheer speed.

In the batting Simpson thought that with himself, Norm O'Neill, Brian Booth, Bill Lawry and Peter Burge there was a good core of players and that in Ian Redpath (97 on Test debut), Bob Cowper and Jack Potter were young batsmen of great promise. This team wasn't '1948' but it was much better than '1912'.

Wally Grout earned the crowd's approval for declining to take the bails off when Fred Titmus fell after colliding with Neil

Lord's, June 23. Wet, wet, wet. That's the word on cricket in England so far. The Australians obtained little practice on the field, though a good deal in receptions, cocktail parties, luncheons and formal dinners before the first first class match at Worcester on April 29. This game was a draw, as were six of the nine others played before the first Test. The Australians won three including the match against MCC at Lord's – virtually a Test trial for Australia and England. Grahame Corling and Graham McKenzie bowled with unprecedented ferocity (in this match) with the second new ball and the MCC collapsed from 1/124 to all out 229. Then Ian Redpath (56), Norm O'Neill (151) and Bob Simpson tore the MCC attack to shreds, making 6/358 and eventually winning by an innings and 119 runs. Perhaps the team isn't as bad as its critics thought.

The first Test was at Nottingham and was the first seen there in eight years. The third day was lost to rain, after England had opened with Geoff Boycott in his first Test and oddly, Fred Titmus. Highlight of this dull draw was Wally Grout deciding not to run out Titmus after Neil Hawke had knocked him over on his follow through as they attempted a single.

The second Test at Lord's lost two whole days, and more, to rain. Highlight of a low-scoring draw was a six from Graham McKenzie that went over the Mound Stand and into a street beyond, where it knocked off the spectacles of a passer-by.

No Chappell. Percy Beames wrote in the *Age* on February 14 that the selectors had done a creditable job in picking the touring 17, but might have selected 20-year-old Ian Chappell rather than 31-year-old Peter Burge.

Questioning pitches. The tour agreement on covering pitches says that pitches may be covered until the first ball is bowled, on each night of the match, and if necessary all of Sunday. In addition, if rain falls during play, 'the umpires shall order the pitch to be completely covered from the time they decide that sufficient rain has fallen on the pitch to ensure that no further play is possible on that day.' This compromise with the Australian position is disliked by Australians, reports the *Times* on June 8.

CND slogans. Campaign for Nuclear Disarmament campaigners climbed into the Worcester ground on the night of April 28 before the Australian game, daubing the ground and surrounds with slogans and symbols.

Redpath a 'chucker'. Ian Redpath, the young batsman, was called for 'throwing' when he bowled one over at the end of the game against Glamorgan at Cardiff on May 19.

A long bowl. In the fourth Test Tom Veivers bowled 95.1 overs in the England innings taking 3/155 – three short of Sonny Ramadhin's record number of overs. A scheme to break the record near the end of the match failed when Veivers 'accidentally' bowled John Price.

Did you catch it? When Ted Dexter was on 108 in the fourth Test, he popped a catch to point where Peter Burge dived forward and appeared to catch it. Walking off Dexter said, 'Oh, I say Peter, did you catch it?' Burge replied, 'Well Ted, I really don't know.' Umpire Syd Buller then said, 'Well if he doesn't know if he caught it we had better play on.' Dexter made 174.

Test profit. 354,436 people saw the five Tests enabling the tour to make a £30,000 profit for the Australian Board of Control.

Holland defeats Australia. In an extraordinary one day match at The Hague on August 29, Australia 197 all out were defeated by Holland 7/201. Jack Potter received a fractured skull and flew back to Australia.

Simmo tops averages. Bob Simpson scored 1714 runs on tour at an average of 57.13. Brian Booth made 1551 at 55.39 and Bill Lawry 1601 at 42.13. Simmo also took 32 wickets at 32.40. Graham McKenzie took 88 wickets at 22.68, Neil Hawke 83 at 19.86 and Tom Veivers 52 wickets at 36.17.

Norm O'Neill hits a characteristic four. But he is not having a good series, with only moderate scores in the first two Tests. He missed the third Test through injury.

Dexter's blue hands Test to Peter Burge

Leeds, July 6. An injury to Norm O'Neill saw Bob Simpson open in the third Test with Bill Lawry, with Ian Redpath at three, and Bob Cowper in for his first Test. Peter Burge was at four. His 59 in the second innings of the second Test was promising.

England struggled to 268, and Australia replied with 3/129 with some aggressive batting from Lawry (78). Soon it was 7/178, all Australian batsmen struggling against spin, especially that of Fred Titmus. Neil Hawke joined Burge, on 33. They took the score to 187, when England captain Ted Dexter made a fateful decision and took the new ball. Fred Trueman and Jack Flavell then served up what one observer said was 'a dish that they [the batsmen] found most delectable, of balls demanding to be hit'. And they were.

Burge gave a magnificent display of hooking, cutting and cover driving to put Australia in the ascendancy. Hawke was out off the last ball of the day, but he had made his highest Test score of 37, and Australia was on 283.

Next day it was more of the same with Wally Grout driving as if he were on a highway. He and Burge added 89 for the ninth wicket when Grout went for 37. Burge was last out after plundering 160. The last three wickets put on 211.

Peter Burge slashes Fred Titmus to the boundary in his match-winning 160.

Trueman first to 300 Test wickets

The Oval, Aug. 18. Tom Veivers nearly broke Sonny Ramadhin's record for the number of overs bowled in an innings with his 95.1 in the fourth Test, but it was other bowlers who were record makers in the fifth Test. Veivers bowled 'only' 47 overs in England's second innings.

Geoff Boycott made his first Test century for England in this innings (113) as the match petered out to another wet and soggy draw.

For the other bowlers there were compensations.

Graham McKenzie equalled Clarrie Grimmett's old record of 29 wickets in a series against England, in England. One of them was Ted Dexter, playing what has been announced as his last Test innings.

For Australia, Neil Hawke came of age as a bowler, taking 6/47 in England's first innings.

But the bowling highlight was England's with Freddie Trueman, recalled for this test, taking 4/87, and becoming the first bowler to pass 300 wickets. He now has 301.

Trueman had 0/80 when Dexter brought him back on the third day, bowling from his short run. With his second over of the new spell, things changed.

Victim 298 was Ian Redpath, and next ball 'Garth' McKenzie. Neil Hawke saved the hat-trick and went on to score 14, but after lunch was Trueman's 300th.

Deadly Bob Simpson grinds on to 311 – and a dull draw

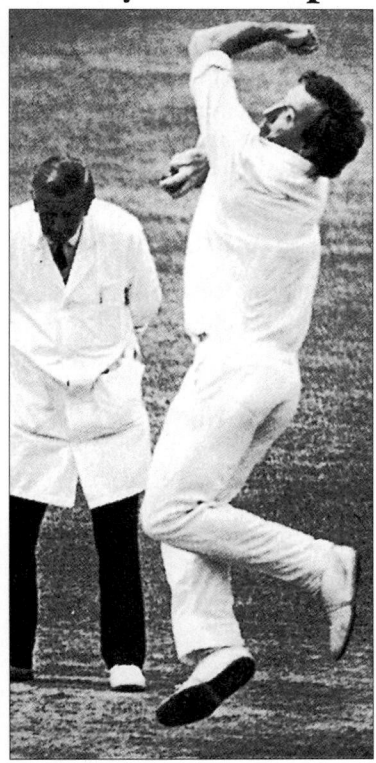

Graham McKenzie's 29 wickets equals the Clarrie Grimmett record.

Manchester, July 28. One down with two to play in the series England needed a win to have a chance of winning the Ashes. A draw would not do – which is perhaps the background to the vitriol that descended upon the Australians, especially captain Bob Simpson, after a drawn-out draw proved to be the result.

'They're playing for a draw,' said the papers, 'They're killing cricket', after Australia made 8/656 in 778 minutes. The Australians maintained that they were going flat out for a win, having lived down the 'worst team to visit England' image, they hoped for a decisive win in the series. Simpson's strategy was to get as many runs as he could in the first innings and try and bowl England out twice.

England dropped Fred Trueman after his disappointing bowling in the third Test – but it was hard to see how that was an attacking move. One of his replacements, John Price, did get Bob Simpson – but Simpson had already made 311 and Price took 3/183.

This was Simpson's first century in Test cricket. Simpson had scored over 40 centuries in first class cricket and said: 'Nobody can describe the feeling of relief that flowed through me when the magical three-digit number went up on the scoreboard. I don't know of any player who was on the international scene as long as I without scoring a century. I was feeling a bit silly about it by this stage.'

It took two days and 40 minutes, and was classed as 'belonging to the weirder regions of record compiling, like pole squatting, or a-coast to-coast race on stilts' by one Fleet Street wit.

Had that been the case with Simpson he might have gone on to chase Bradman's record, but did not, he said, because it wasn't in the team's interests, and 'I did not think I was a good enough player to have broken Bradman's record.'

England replied to Australia's 8/656 with 611, including slower innings than Simpson's by both Ted Dexter (174) and Ken Barrington (256).

Congratulations all round – Trueman takes his 301st Test wicket.

Simpson's long innings

Robert Baddeley Simpson was born in Marrickville, Sydney on 3 February 1936. As a teenager in Sydney, Simpson was a natural sportsman and a dasher with the bat. The son of Scottish migrants – his father played first division soccer in Scotland – Simpson quickly earned a reputation for making quick 40s and 50s then surrendering his wicket with a rash shot.

He first played for NSW aged 16, coming on as 12th man at the SCG. He asked captain Keith Miller where he should field. Miller, no stickler for putting the 12th man in a non-catching position, directed Simpson to the slips where he stayed for the rest of his career.

After four seasons for NSW, Simpson moved to WA in 1956. He toured New Zealand under Ian Craig in 1957, then went to South Africa in 1957–58, making 671 runs at 47.92 but failing in the Tests with only 136 runs in six completed innings. He made a duck in his only Test appearance against England in 1958–59, but took it out on opposing Sheffield Shield bowlers. Advised by Neil Harvey to open the batting for WA, he scored in turn 98 v Victoria, 236 not out v NSW, 230 not out v Queensland, 79 v SA and 98 and 161 not out v NSW – 902 runs at the remarkable average of 300.66.

Picked to tour England in 1961, Simpson, also a useful right-arm leg-break bowler, made 1947 runs with six hundreds but a Test century eluded him until 1964 when, as captain, he batted for more than two days at Old Trafford for 311.

The stocky Simpson was a grand square cutter and a good driver. He seldom played the hook stroke, except against Wesley Hall in Melbourne in 1961 when, in a show of strength, he took 18 off an over. After his retirement in 1967–68, he continued to play grade cricket in Sydney until his recall to the captaincy in 1977 in the wake of the World Series Cricket 'revolution'.

Simpson took over from Benaud during the 1963–64 South African tour of Australia. He was captain 25 times until mid-way through the 4–0 win over India in 1967–68 when he handed the reins to Lawry.

Simpson was a man of strong convictions. If he took a risk, as

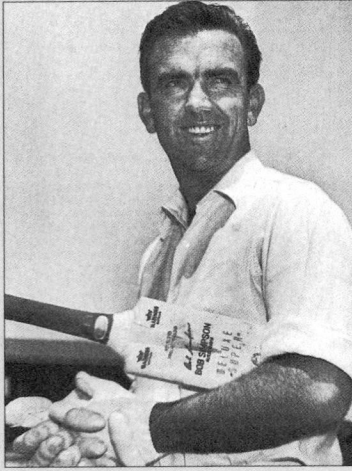

Bob Simpson: long innings.

he did with Peter Burge in England in 1964, and it came off, up went the shutters. Facing defeat at Leeds, Simpson prevailed upon Burge to attack. Burge made 160 and Australia won, the only result in the series. In the next Test, Simpson deprived England of any hope of equalising by scoring 311 in 12 hours, 42 minutes, the longest innings ever played against England.

In the West Indies in 1965, Simpson became even more negative in the face of Charlie Griffith's hostile bowling. He was bitter after being subjected to a bumper barrage, saying he was 'chucked out'.

The WSC upheaval resulted in Simpson, aged 41, being recalled to the captaincy in 1977–78 against India. Leading a young team, his purposeful leadership helped Australia win 3–2. At ease against the Indian spinners, Simpson scored two centuries, 176 and 100.

Back in the West Indies in 1977–78, it took a lot of courage for a man of his age to face the Windies pace attack. He made only 189 runs and lost the series 3–1, but won back a lot of friends. In all, Simpson led Australia 39 times for 12 wins and 12 losses. In 1986 Simpson became coach of the Australian Test team for 10 years. His firm approach was not enjoyed by all, but he helped weld Australia into a strong team.

In 62 Tests (39 of them as captain) Simpson made 4869 runs at an average of 46.81. He hit 10 centuries with a highest score of 311. Simpson also captured 71 wickets in Tests (average 42.26) with his leg-spinners and took 110 catches, mostly fielding in slips.

FIRST TEST 1964 ENGLAND v AUSTRALIA
Trent Bridge, Nottingham. June 4, 5, 6 (no play), 8, 9, 1964.
Toss: England. Match Drawn.

ENGLAND

Batsman		1st		2nd	
G Boycott c Simpson b Corling	48		lbw McKenzie	17	
FJ Titmus c Redpath b Hawke	16		c O'Neill b McKenzie	68	
ER Dexter (c) c Grout b Hawke	9	(1)	b McKenzie	33	
MC Cowdrey b Hawke	32	(3)	lbw Corling	33	
KF Barrington c Lawry b Veivers	22	(4)	c & b Veivers	1	
PJ Sharpe not out	35		c Hawke b Veivers	19	
JM Parks (+) c Booth b Veivers	15	(5)	c Grout b McKenzie	4	
FS Trueman c Simpson b Veivers	0	(7)	lbw McKenzie	3	
DA Allen c Grout b McKenzie	21	(8)	not out	0	
LJ Coldwell not out	0		c Booth b Corling	7	
JA Flavell	(9)		(B 2, LB 2, W 1, NB 3)	8	
Extras (B 5, LB 11, NB 2)	18				
TOTAL	8 dec 216			9 dec 193	

FOW 1st Inns: 38 70 90 135 141 164 165 212
FOW 2nd Inns: 90 95 147 175 179 180 186 187 193

Bowling: *First Innings*: McKenzie 28-7-53-1, Corling 23-7-38-1, Hawke 35-15-68-3, Veivers 16-2-39-3. *Second Innings*: McKenzie 24-5-53-5, Hawke 19-5-53-0, Corling 15.5-4-54-2, Veivers 8-0-25-2.

AUSTRALIA

Batsman	1st		2nd
WM Lawry c Barrington b Coldwell	11		run out	3
IR Redpath b Trueman	6		c Parks b Flavell	2
NC O'Neill b Allen	26		retired hurt	24
PJP Burge lbw Trueman	31		not out	4
BC Booth run out	0		not out	6
RB Simpson (c) c Barrington b Titmus	50		
TR Veivers c Trueman b Flavell	8		
GD McKenzie c Parks b Coldwell	4		
NJN Hawke not out	10		
ATW Grout (+) c Parks b Coldwell	13		
GE Corling b Trueman	3		
Extras (LB 1, NB 5)	6		(NB 1)	1
TOTAL	168		2 for 40

FOW 1st Inns: 8 37 57 61 91 118 137 141 165 168
FOW 2nd Inns: 3 25

Bowling: *First Innings*: Trueman 20.3-3-58-3, Coldwell 22-3-48-3, Allen 16-8-22-1, Titmus 4-1-6-1. *Second Innings*: Trueman 5-0-28-0, Flavell 4.2-0-11-1.

Umpires: JS Buller & CS Elliott

SECOND TEST 1964 ENGLAND v AUSTRALIA
Lord's Cricket Ground, London. June 18 (no play), 19 (no play), 20, 22, 23, 1964.
Toss: England. Match Drawn.

AUSTRALIA

Batsman	1st		2nd
WM Lawry b Trueman	4		c Dexter b Gifford	20
IR Redpath c Parfitt b Coldwell	30		lbw Titmus	36
NC O'Neill c Titmus b Dexter	26		c Parfitt b Trueman	22
PJP Burge lbw Dexter	1		c Parfitt b Titmus	59
BC Booth lbw Trueman	14		not out	2
RB Simpson (c) c Parfitt b Trueman	0		not out	15
TR Veivers b Gifford	54		
GD McKenzie b Trueman	10		
ATW Grout (+) c Dexter b Gifford	14		
NJN Hawke not out	5		
GE Corling b Trueman	0		
Extras (B 8, LB 5, NB 5)	18		(B 8, LB 4, NB 2)	14
TOTAL	176		4 for 168

FOW 1st Inns: 8 46 58 84 84 88 132 163 167 176
FOW 2nd Inns: 35 76 143 148

Bowling: *First Innings*: Trueman 25-8-48-5, Coldwell 23-7-51-1, Gifford 12-6-14-2, Dexter 7-1-16-2, Titmus 17-6-29-0. *Second Innings*: Trueman 18-6-52-1, Coldwell 19-4-59-0, Dexter 3-0-5-0, Gifford 17-9-17-1, Titmus 17-7-21-2.

ENGLAND

Batsman	1st
ER Dexter (c) b McKenzie	2
JH Edrich c Redpath b McKenzie	120
MC Cowdrey c Burge b Hawke	10
KF Barrington lbw McKenzie	5
PH Parfitt lbw Corling	20
PJ Sharpe lbw Hawke	35
JM Parks (+) c Simpson b Hawke	12
FJ Titmus b Corling	15
FS Trueman b Corling	8
N Gifford c Hawke b Corling	5
LJ Coldwell not out	6
Extras (LB 7, NB 1)	8
TOTAL	246

FOW 1st Inns: 2 33 42 83 138 170 227 229 235 246

Bowling: *First Innings*: McKenzie 26-8-69-3, Corling 27.3-9-60-4, Hawke 16-4-41-3, Veivers 9-4-17-0, Simpson 21-8-51-0.

Umpires: JS Buller & JF Crapp

THIRD TEST 1964 ENGLAND v AUSTRALIA
Headingley, Leeds. July 2, 3, 4, 6, 1964.
Toss: England. Australia won by 7 wkts.

ENGLAND

G Boycott c Simpson b Corling	38	c Simpson b Corling	4
JH Edrich c Veivers b McKenzie	3	c Grout b McKenzie	32
ER Dexter (c) c Grout b McKenzie	66 (5)	c Redpath b Veivers	17
KF Barrington b McKenzie	29	lbw Veivers	85
PH Parfitt b Hawke	32 (3)	c Redpath b Hawke	6
K Taylor c Grout b Hawke	9 (8)	b Veivers	15
JM Parks (+) c Redpath b Hawke	68 (6)	c Booth b McKenzie	23
FJ Titmus b Burge b McKenzie	3 (9)	c Cowper b Corling	14
FS Trueman c Cowper b Hawke	4 (10)	not out	12
N Gifford not out	1 (7)	b McKenzie	1
JA Flavell c Redpath b Hawke	5	c Simpson b Corling	5
Extras (LB 9, NB 1)	10	(B 6, LB 6, W 1, NB 2)	15
TOTAL	268		229

FOW 1st Inns: 17 74 129 138 163 215 232 260 263 268
FOW 2nd Inns: 13 88 145 156 169 184 192 199 212 229

Bowling: *First Innings*: McKenzie 26-7-74-4, Hawke 31.3-11-75-5, Corling 24-7-50-1, Veivers 17-3-35-0, Simpson 5-0-24-0. *Second Innings*: McKenzie 28-8-53-3, Corling 17.5-6-52-3, Hawke 13-1-28-1, Veivers 30-12-70-3, Simpson 1-0-11-0.

AUSTRALIA

WM Lawry run out	78	c Gifford b Trueman	1
RB Simpson (c) b Gifford	24	c Barrington b Titmus	30
IR Redpath b Gifford	20	not out	58
PJP Burge c(S)A Rees b Trueman	160	b Titmus	8
BC Booth st Parks b Titmus	4	not out	12
RM Cowper b Trueman	2		
TR Veivers c Parks b Titmus	8		
GD McKenzie b Titmus	0		
NJN Hawke c Parfitt b Trueman	37		
ATW Grout (+) lbw Titmus	37		
GE Corling not out	2		
Extras (B 1, LB 8, W 2, NB 6)	17	(B 1, LB 1)	2
TOTAL	389		3 for 111

FOW 1st Inns: 50 124 129 154 157 178 178 283 372 389
FOW 2nd Inns: 3 45 64

Bowling: *First Innings*: Trueman 24.3-2-98-3, Flavell 29-5-97-0, Gifford 34-15-62-2, Dexter 19-5-40-0, Titmus 50-24-69-4, Taylor 2-0-6-0. *Second Innings*: Trueman 7-0-28-1, Titmus 27-19-25-2, Gifford 20-5-47-0, Dexter 3-0-9-0.

Umpires: CS Elliott & WFF Price

FIFTH TEST 1964 ENGLAND v AUSTRALIA
Kennington Oval, London. August 13, 14, 15, 17, 18 (no play), 1964.
Toss: England. Match Drawn.

ENGLAND

G Boycott b Hawke	30	c Redpath b Simpson	113
RW Barber b Hawke	24	lbw McKenzie	29
ER Dexter (c) c Booth b Hawke	23	c Simpson b McKenzie	25
MC Cowdrey c Grout b McKenzie	20 (5)	not out	93
KF Barrington c Simpson b Hawke	47 (6)	not out	54
PH Parfitt b McKenzie	3		
JM Parks (+) c Simpson b Corling	10		
FJ Titmus c Grout b Hawke	8 (4)	b McKenzie	56
FS Trueman c Redpath b Hawke	14		
TW Cartwright c Grout b McKenzie	0		
JSE Price not out	0		
Extras (LB 3)	3	(B 6, LB 4, NB 1)	11
TOTAL	182		4 for 381

FOW 1st Inns: 44 61 82 111 117 141 160 173 174 182
FOW 2nd Inns: 80 120 200 255

Bowling: *First Innings*: McKenzie 26-6-87-3, Corling 14-2-32-1, Hawke 25.4-8-47-6, Veivers 6-1-13-0. *Second Innings*: McKenzie 38-5-112-3, Corling 25-4-65-0, Hawke 39-8-89-0, Veivers 47-15-90-0, Simpson 14-7-14-1.

AUSTRALIA

RB Simpson (c) c Dexter b Cartwright	24
WM Lawry c Trueman b Dexter	94
NC O'Neill c Parfitt b Cartwright	11
PJP Burge lbw Titmus	25
BC Booth c Trueman b Price	74
IR Redpath b Trueman	45
ATW Grout (+) b Cartwright	20
TR Veivers not out	67
GD McKenzie c Cowdrey b Trueman	0
NJN Hawke c Cowdrey b Trueman	14
GE Corling c Parfitt b Trueman	0
Extras (B 4, LB 1)	5
TOTAL	379

FOW 1st Inns: 45 57 96 202 245 279 343 343 367 379

Bowling: *First Innings*: Trueman 33.3-6-87-4, Price 21-2-67-1, Cartwright 62-23-110-3, Titmus 42-20-51-1, Barber 6-1-23-0, Dexter 13-1-36-1.

Umpires: JF Crapp & CS Elliott

FOURTH TEST 1964 ENGLAND v AUSTRALIA
Old Trafford, Manchester. July 23, 24, 25, 27, 28, 1964.
Toss: Australia. Match Drawn.

AUSTRALIA

WM Lawry run out	106	not out	0
RB Simpson (c) c Parks b Price	311	not out	4
IR Redpath lbw Cartwright	19		
NC O'Neill b Price	47		
PJP Burge c Price b Cartwright	34		
BC Booth c & b Price	98		
TR Veivers c Edrich b Rumsey	22		
ATW Grout (+) c Dexter b Rumsey	0		
GD McKenzie not out	0		
GE Corling			
NJN Hawke			
Extras (B 1, LB 9, NB 9)	19		0
TOTAL	8 dec 656		0 for 4

FOW 1st Inns: 201 233 318 382 601 646 652 656
FOW 2nd Inns:

Bowling: *First Innings*: Rumsey 35.5-4-99-2, Price 45-4-183-3, Cartwright 77-32-118-2, Titmus 44-14-100-0, Dexter 4-0-12-0, Mortimore 49-13-122-0, Boycott 1-0-3-0. *Second Innings*: Barrington 1-0-4-0, Titmus 1-1-0-0.

ENGLAND

G Boycott b McKenzie	58
JH Edrich c Redpath b McKenzie	6
ER Dexter (c) b Veivers	174
KF Barrington lbw McKenzie	256
PH Parfitt c Grout b McKenzie	12
JM Parks (+) c Hawke b Veivers	60
FJ Titmus c Simpson b McKenzie	9
JB Mortimore c Burge b McKenzie	12
TW Cartwright b McKenzie	4
JSE Price b Veivers	1
FE Rumsey not out	3
Extras (B 5, LB 11)	16
TOTAL	611

FOW 1st Inns: 15 126 372 417 560 589 594 602 607 611

Bowling: *First Innings*: McKenzie 60-15-153-7, Corling 46-11-96-0, Hawke 63-28-95-0, Simpson 19-4-59-0, Veivers 95.1-36-155-3, O'Neill 10-0-37-0.

Umpires: JS Buller & WFF Price

Australian Averages

1964 ENGLAND v AUSTRALIA

AUSTRALIA	M	Inn	NO	Runs	H.S	Avrge	Ct	St	Overs	Mds	Runs	Wkt	Avrge
Booth, BC	5	8	3	210	98	42.00	4	-	-	-	-	-	-
Burge, PJP	5	8	1	322	160	46.00	3	-	-	-	-	-	-
Corling, GE	5	4	1	5	3	1.67	-	-	193.1	50	447	12	37.25
Cowper, RM	1	1	-	2	2	2.00	2	-	-	-	-	-	-
Grout, ATW	5	5	-	84	37	16.80	10	-	-	-	-	-	-
Hawke, NJN	5	4	2	66	37	33.00	3	-	242.1	80	496	18	27.56
Lawry, WM	5	9	1	317	106	39.63	1	-	-	-	-	-	-
McKenzie, GD	5	5	1	14	10	3.50	-	-	256.0	61	654	29	22.55
O'Neill, NC	4	6	1	156	47	31.20	1	-	10.0	-	37	-	-
Redpath, IR	5	8	1	216	58*	30.86	9	-	-	-	-	-	-
Simpson, RB	5	8	2	458	311	76.33	10	-	60.0	19	159	1	159.00
Veivers, TR	5	5	1	159	67*	39.75	2	-	228.1	73	444	11	40.36

English Averages

1964 ENGLAND v AUSTRALIA

ENGLAND	M	Inn	NO	Runs	H.S	Avrge	Ct	St	Overs	Mds	Runs	Wkt	Avrge
Allen, DA	1	2	-	24	21	12.00	-	-	16.0	8	22	1	22.00
Barber, RW	1	2	-	53	29	26.50	-	-	6.0	1	23	-	-
Barrington, KF	5	8	1	531	256	75.86	3	-	1.0	-	4	-	-
Boycott, G	4	6	-	291	113	48.50	-	-	1.0	-	3	-	-
Cartwright, TW	2	2	-	4	4	2.00	-	-	139.0	55	228	5	45.60
Coldwell, LJ	2	3	3	6	6*	-	-	-	64.0	14	158	4	39.50
Cowdrey, MC	3	5	1	188	93*	47.00	2	-	-	-	-	-	-
Dexter, ER	5	8	-	384	174	48.00	4	-	49.0	7	118	3	39.33
Edrich, JH	3	4	-	161	120	40.25	1	-	-	-	-	-	-
Flavell, JA	2	3	-	17	7	5.67	-	-	49.2	8	136	2	68.00
Gifford, N	2	3	1	7	5	3.50	-	-	83.0	35	140	5	28.00
Mortimore, JB	1	1	-	12	12	12.00	-	-	49.0	13	122	-	-
Parfitt, PH	4	5	-	73	32	14.60	7	-	-	-	-	-	-
Parks, JM	5	7	-	207	68	29.57	5	1	-	-	-	-	-
Price, JSE	2	2	1	1	1	1.00	-	-	66.0	6	250	4	62.50
Rumsey, FE	1	1	1	3	3*	-	-	-	35.5	4	99	2	49.50
Sharpe, PJ	2	3	1	71	35*	35.50	-	-	-	-	-	-	-
Taylor, K	1	2	-	24	15	12.00	-	-	2.0	-	6	-	-
Titmus, FJ	5	8	-	138	56	17.25	1	-	202.0	92	301	10	30.10
Trueman, FS	4	6	1	42	14	8.40	3	-	133.3	25	399	17	23.47

Classic battle in the heat of Bombay

Calcutta, Oct. 22. Graham 'Garth' McKenzie was the outstanding bowler of the three-Test series against India.

He had bowled more overs in Tests than anyone in England, and was only outbowled by the indefatigable spinner Tom Veivers in the oppressive heat, illness and inconsistent umpiring of this Indian tour.

McKenzie bowled 108.3 overs to Veivers' 163.4, but even in this spinner's paradise took 13 wickets to Veivers' 11.

McKenzie said that he was pleased to get so many wickets in the drawn series, one win each and one draw, on slow pitches. McKenzie tried always to keep the ball up putting pressure on the Indian batsmen. The umpiring affected McKenzie less than the other bowlers because, he said, 'Luckily I managed to bowl a few of my wickets'.

In the first Test in Madras McKenzie was the reason Australia won, taking 6/58 and 4/33, which with the solid batting of Bob Simpson, Bill Lawry – and Tom Veivers' 74 batting at number eight.

The Indian slow bowler 'Bapu' Nadkarni – famous as the man who bowled 131 balls in a row without a run being scored from them, against England at Madras in 1963–64 – bowled well, taking eleven wickets for the match.

Indian captain the Nawab of Pataudi emulated his father in his first Test by making a century on debut against Australia – 128. His father made 102 for England in a Sydney Test in 1932.

The second Test at Bombay was a closely contested match which

Just like Dad: The Nawab of Pataudi made a century in his first Test against Australia.

Norm O'Neill in Bombay hospital

Bombay, Oct. 16. Norm O'Neill will remain in hospital while the Australian team travels to Calcutta for the third Test.

O'Neill is suffering from a very serious viral infection of the stomach and has been advised by an English specialist that he must have more rest in hospital.

Getting food and clean water was a constant problem for the Australians. Tom Veivers and Bill Lawry were ill with dysentery in the first Test and struggled to bat. Most of the rest of the team had stomach trouble at one time or another.

O'Neill's illness is by far the most serious, and he will miss the Test in

Australia lost by two wickets. McKenzie said: 'We lost the match … playing against extremely high odds. It almost amounted to eleven men playing against 13. The umpires were very bad'.

Norm O'Neill was in the side but did not play because of a bad viral stomach illness, which meant Australia batted one short. Veivers bowled 91.4 overs in the match. With the umpiring and against the odds, Australia lost a close fought game by two wickets.

This match belonged to the enigmatic and handsome medium-paced wrist-spinner Bhagwat Subrahmanya Chandrasekhar ('Chandra'), who took hauls of 4/50 and 4/73.

Two days of the third Test match in Calcutta were lost to the monsoon rain, with Australia 1/143, and the game and series were drawn.

Simpson and Lawry opened with stands of 97 and 115, giving Australia good starts, but in the first innings Australia managed just 77 more, spun out by Salim Aziz Durani.

It was both a relief and a disappointment for the match to end this way, because Australia were heading to a favourable position but with the sickness and heat of the tour, Australian players were happy to have a couple more days rest before flying to Pakistan.

'Chandra': the Indian medium-pace wrist-spinner was spot on in the second Test.

FIRST TEST 1964–65 INDIA v AUSTRALIA
MA Chidambaram Stadium (Chepauk), Madras. October 2, 3, 4, 6, 7, 1964.
Toss: Australia. Australia won by 139 runs.

AUSTRALIA

WM Lawry b Nadkarni	62	c (S)RF Surti b Nadkarni	41
RB Simpson (c) st Indrajitsinhji b Durani	30	run out	77
NC O'Neill b Durani	40	b Nadkarni	0
PJP Burge b Nadkarni	20	lbw Nadkarni	60
BC Booth lbw Nadkarni	8	c Indrajitsinhji b Durani	29
JW Martin c Indrajitsinhji b Kripal Singh	20 (8)	c Nadkarni b Ranjane	39
IR Redpath c Hanumant b Nadkarni	10 (6)	c Indrajitsinhji b Nadkarni	0
TR Veivers b Kripal Singh	0 (7)	c Nawab b Nadkarni	74
GD McKenzie not out	8	c Sardesai b Ranjane	27
ATW Grout (+) c Jaisimha b Nadkarni	0	c Hanumant b Nadkarni	12
NJN Hawke b Kripal Singh	0	not out	1
Extras (LB 6, NB 7)	13	(B 15, LB 11, NB 11)	37
TOTAL	211		397

FOW 1st Inns: 66 127 139 161 174 203 203 203 209 211
FOW 2nd Inns: 91 91 175 228 232 237 301 374 392 397

Bowling: *First Innings*: Ranjane 7-0-30-0, Jaisimha 4-1-13-0, Durani 21-5-68-2, Kripal Singh 18-5-43-3, Borde 4-2-13-0, Nadkarni 18-6-31-5. *Second Innings*: Ranjane 12-1-53-2, Jaisimha 9-2-13-0, Nadkarni 54.4-21-91-6, Durani 40-9-102-1, Kripal Singh 38-13-91-0, Borde 5-2-10-0.

INDIA

ML Jaisimha lbw McKenzie	29	b McKenzie	0
KS Indrajitsinhji (+) c Grout b Hawke	4	b Hawke	0
DN Sardesai b McKenzie	0	c Redpath b Martin	14
VL Manjrekar c Grout b Martin	33	c Simpson b O'Neill	40
Hanumant Singh c Grout b Martin	0 (6)	c O'Neill b Veivers	94
Nawab of Pataudi jr (c) not out	128 (7)	b McKenzie	1
CG Borde c Simpson b McKenzie	49 (8)	b McKenzie	0
SA Durani c Grout b McKenzie	5 (10)	c O'Neill b Veivers	10
RG Nadkarni lbw Hawke	3	c Simpson b Hawke	20
AG Kripal Singh b McKenzie	0 (5)	b McKenzie	1
VB Ranjane c Redpath b McKenzie	2	not out	0
Extras (B 13, LB 9, NB 1)	23	(B 11, LB 2)	13
TOTAL	276		193

FOW 1st Inns: 12 13 55 56 76 218 232 249 256 276
FOW 2nd Inns: 0 0 23 24 117 130 130 168 191 193

Bowling: *First Innings*: McKenzie 32.3-8-58-6, Hawke 33-13-55-2, Redpath 2-1-1-0, Simpson 12-3-23-0, Martin 26-11-63-2, Booth 10-4-14-0, Veivers 10-2-20-0, O'Neill 7-3-19-0. *Second Innings*: McKenzie 20-9-33-4, Hawke 17-7-26-2, Martin 16-4-43-1, Veivers 10-4-18-2, Simpson 5-3-9-0, Booth 3-0-10-0, O'Neill 9-3-41-1.

Umpires: MV Nagendra & S Roy

SECOND TEST 1964–65 INDIA v AUSTRALIA
Brabourne Stadium, Bombay. October 10, 11, 12, 14, 15, 1964.
Toss: Australia. India won by 2 wkts.

AUSTRALIA

WM Lawry c Indrajitsinhji b Durani	16	lbw Chandrasekhar	68
RB Simpson (c) b Chandrasekhar	27	c Hanumant b Surti	20
BC Booth b Chandrasekhar	1 (5)	st Indrajitsinhji b Nadkarni	74
PJP Burge c Chandrasekhar b Borde	80	b Chandrasekhar	0
RM Cowper lbw Nadkarni	20 (3)	c Indrajitsinhji b Nadkarni	81
TR Veivers c Borde b Chandrasekhar	67	lbw Chandrasekhar	0
BN Jarman (+) c Durani b Surti	78	b Chandrasekhar	0
JW Martin c Nadkarni b Chandrasekhar	0	c Surti b Nadkarni	16
GD McKenzie b Nadkarni	17	c Surti b Nadkarni	4
AN Connolly not out	0	not out	0
NC O'Neill			
Extras (B 7, LB 4, NB 3)	14	(B 4, NB 7)	11
TOTAL	9 dec 320		9 dec 274

FOW 1st Inns: 35 36 53 142 146 297 303 304 320
FOW 2nd Inns: 59 121 121 246 247 247 257 265 274

Bowling: *First Innings*: Surti 18-1-70-1, Jaisimha 8-1-20-0, Durani 20-5-78-1, Chandrasekhar 26-10-50-4, Nadkarni 24.5-6-65-2, Borde 7-0-23-1. *Second Innings*: Surti 21-5-77-1, Jaisimha 11-4-18-0, Chandrasekhar 30-11-73-4, Durani 15-3-48-0, Nadkarni 20.4-10-33-4, Borde 2-0-14-0.

INDIA

DN Sardesai c Simpson b Connolly	3	lbw McKenzie	56
ML Jaisimha b Veivers	66	c Jarman b Connolly	0
SA Durani c Jarman b Simpson	12	c Cowper b Simpson	31
VL Manjrekar c Cowper b Veivers	59 (8)	c Simpson b Connolly	39
Hanumant Singh b Veivers	14 (6)	b McKenzie	11
Nawab of Pataudi jr (c) c McKenzie b Veivers	86 (7)	c Burge b Connolly	53
CG Borde c Simpson b Martin	4 (9)	not out	30
RF Surti c Jarman b Connolly	21 (5)	c Booth b Veivers	10
RG Nadkarni c Jarman b Martin	34 (4)	c Simpson b Veivers	0
KS Indrajitsinhji (+) c(S)IR Redpath b Connolly	23	not out	3
BS Chandrasekhar not out	0		
Extras (B 4, LB 8, NB 6)	18	(B 15, LB 8)	23
TOTAL	341		8 for 256

FOW 1st Inns: 7 30 142 149 181 188 255 293 331 341
FOW 2nd Inns: 4 70 71 99 113 122 215 224

Bowling: *First Innings*: McKenzie 22-2-49-0, Connolly 22.3-5-66-3, Martin 34-11-72-2, Simpson 13-1-40-1, Veivers 48-20-68-4, Cowper 13-3-28-0. *Second Innings*: McKenzie 21-6-43-2, Connolly 18-8-24-3, Simpson 24-12-34-1, Veivers 43.4-12-82-2, Martin 14-2-35-0, Cowper 4-0-14-0, Booth 4-3-1-0.

Umpires: HE Chowdhury & SK Raghunatha Rao

THIRD TEST 1964–65 INDIA v AUSTRALIA
Eden Gardens, Calcutta. October 17, 18, 20, 21 (no play), 22 (no play), 1964.
Toss: India. Match Drawn.

AUSTRALIA

WM Lawry b Durani	50	not out	47
RB Simpson (c) lbw Surti	67	c Hanumant b Surti	71
RM Cowper c Nadkarni b Durani	4	not out	14
PJP Burge c Hanumant b Durani	4		
BC Booth b Durani	0		
IR Redpath not out	32		
TR Veivers c Nawab b Durani	2		
BN Jarman (+) b Durani	1		
GD McKenzie st Indrajitsinhji b Surti	0		
RHD Sellers b Surti	0		
AN Connolly c Hanumant b Chandrasekhar	0		
Extras (B 1, LB 8, NB 5)	14	(B 6, NB 5)	11
TOTAL	174		1 for 143

FOW 1st Inns: 97 104 109 109 145 165 167 167 169 174
FOW 2nd Inns: 115

Bowling: *First Innings*: Surti 21-7-38-3, Jaisimha 5-3-2-0, Durani 28-11-73-6, Chandrasekhar 28.5-15-39-1, Nadkarni 2-0-8-0. *Second Innings*: Surti 10-2-37-1, Jaisimha 2-1-4-0, Durani 18-3-59-0, Chandrasekhar 8-3-27-0, Nadkarni 8-6-5-0.

INDIA

DN Sardesai c Veivers b Booth	42
ML Jaisimha c Booth b Simpson	57
SA Durani c Simpson b Veivers	12
VL Manjrekar lbw Veivers	9
Hanumant Singh c Burge b Veivers	5
Nawab of Pataudi jr (c) b Simpson	2
RG Nadkarni b McKenzie	24
CG Borde not out	68
RF Surti c Sellers b Simpson	9
KS Indrajitsinhji (+) st Jarman b Booth	2
BS Chandrasekhar b Simpson	1
Extras (B 4)	4
TOTAL	235

FOW 1st Inns: 60 97 119 127 129 133 166 187 196 235

Bowling: *First Innings*: McKenzie 13-1-31-1, Connolly 8-4-10-0, Veivers 52-18-81-3, Sellers 5-1-17-0, Booth 18-10-33-2, Cowper 6-0-14-0, Simpson 28-12-45-4.

Umpires: SP Pan & B Satyaji Rao

Australian Averages

1964–65 INDIA v AUSTRALIA AUSTRALIA	M	Inn	NO	Runs	H.S	Avrge	Ct	St	Overs	Mds	Runs	Wkt	Avrge
Booth, BC	3	5	-	112	74	22.40	2	-	35.0	17	58	2	29.00
Burge, PJP	3	5	-	164	80	32.80	2	-	-				
Connolly, AN	2	3	2	0	0*	0.00	-	-	48.3	17	100	6	16.67
Cowper, RM	2	4	1	119	81	39.67	2	-	23.0	3	56	-	-
Grout, ATW	1	2	-	12	12	6.00	4	-	-				
Hawke, NJN	1	2	1	1	1*	1.00	-	-	50.0	20	81	4	20.25
Jarman, BN	2	3	-	79	78	26.33	4	1	-				
Lawry, WM	3	6	1	284	68	56.80	-	-	-				
Martin, JW	2	4	-	75	39	18.75	-	-	90.0	28	213	5	42.60
McKenzie, GD	3	5	1	56	27	14.00	1	-	108.3	26	214	13	16.46
O'Neill, NC	2	2	-	40	40	20.00	2	-	16.0	6	60	1	60.00
Redpath, IR	2	3	1	42	32*	21.00	2	-	2.0	1	1	-	-
Sellers, RHD	1	1	-	0	0	0.00	1	-	5.0	1	17	-	-
Simpson, RB	3	6	-	292	77	48.67	8	-	82.0	31	151	6	25.17
Veivers, TR	3	5	-	143	74	28.60	1	-	163.4	56	269	11	24.4

Indian Averages

1964–65 INDIA v AUSTRALIA INDIA	M	Inn	NO	Runs	H.S	Avrge	Ct	St	Overs	Mds	Runs	Wkt	Avrge
Borde, CG	3	5	2	151	68*	50.33	1	-	18.0	4	60	1	60.00
Chandrasekhar, BS2	2	2	1	2	1*	2.00	1	-	92.5	39	189	9	21.00
Durani, SA	3	5	-	70	31	14.00	1	-	142.0	36	428	10	42.80
Hanumant Singh	3	5	-	124	94	24.80	6	-	-				
Indrajitsinhji, KS	3	5	1	32	23	8.00	5	3	-				
Jaisimha, ML	3	5	-	152	66	30.40	1	-	39.0	12	70	-	-
Kripal Singh, AG	1	2	-	1	1	0.50	-	-	56.0	18	134	3	44.67
Manjrekar, VL	3	5	-	180	59	36.00	-	-	-				
Nadkarni, RG	3	5	-	81	34	16.20	3	-	128.1	49	233	17	13.71
Nawab of Pataudi jr	3	5	1	270	128*	67.50	2	-	-				
Ranjane, VB	1	2	1	2	2	2.00	-	-	19.0	1	83	2	41.50
Sardesai, DN	3	5	-	115	56	23.00	-	-	-				
Surti, RF	2	3	-	40	21	13.33	2	-	70.0	15	222	6	37.00

PAKISTAN IN AUSTRALIA

Six debutants, two 100s in Karachi

Majid Khan makes debut.

Karachi, Oct. 29. Pakistan fielded six new players, including Khalid Ibadulla, Asif Iqbal and Majid Khan in just the fifth Test between the two countries.

After a 249-run opening stand between Ibadulla (166) and Abdul Kadir (95) it was clear that there were plenty of runs in the pitch.

However, a great spell from Graham McKenzie on the second morning saw Pakistan slump from 3/284 to 7/302. Stout batting from the tail (Intikhab Alam 53 and Asif Iqbal 41) saw Pakistan to a record total of 414.

Australian captain Bob Simpson scored his second Test century, a chanceless 153 in 408 minutes.

The rest of the Australian batting was mediocre, only Peter Burge passing 50. Just before tea on the third day Australia lost 4/5 to be 9/320, and was all out for 352, 62 behind. But instead of forcing the pace on the fourth day to leave time to bowl Australia out, Pakistan crawled to 8/279 and declared.

That left Australia with 342 to win in 290 minutes. Bob Simpson used the time to make another century, 115, the first Australian to achieve this feat in Pakistan.

Dour Melbourne struggle

Melbourne, Dec. 8. Pakistan agreed to the suggestion of the VCA in October that the scheduled tour game against Victoria become a Test match. Pakistan are to play a Test series in New Zealand, and have played three-day matches against Queensland, NSW and SA, all draws.

Australia picked SA batsman Ian Chappell and googly bowler David Sincock for their first Tests.

Pakistan has seemed more determined not to lose than to risk a win on this tour, and batted sedately on the first day against the pace of Graham McKenzie. Hanif Mohammad, world first class record holder with 499, scored a solid century. But McKenzie really took the palm with his third wicket of the day, that of Nasim-ul-Ghani, McKenzie's hundredth wicket in Test cricket. Hanif was David Sincock's first Test wicket after an erratic 16 overs which cost 64 runs. He finished with 3/67, which might have saved his bacon for the forthcoming West Indies tour.

Australia replied with 448, thanks mainly to Bob Cowper (83) and Tom Veivers (88). Ian Chappell scored just 11 good-looking runs in his first Test appearance, but Barry Shepherd and Brian Booth contributed half-centuries.

Hanif top-scored again in the second Pakistani innings of 326, which left Australia to make 166 runs in 127 minutes, a difficult but not impossible task. Pakistan had kept up a passive resistance as Australia, through big Barry Shepherd, advanced to 2/88 in 71 minutes.

Then bowler Ariuf Butt slipped

Bob Cowper – in fine touch.

and fell as he came in to bowl, and Hanif appealed against the light and rain, which had been falling for half an hour or so. Umpires Colin Egar and Bill Smyth agreed, and that was the end of the game. Shepherd threw his bat to the ground in disgust. He, at least, thought Australia could get the remaining 78 runs in the hour or so left to play.

The umpires evidently thought that the 30 minutes of play that was granted was sufficient – it was a more lenient approach than is normal in Test matches.

Only 33,067 people watched this dour struggle of a Test match. More excitement will certainly be needed to bring the crowds back.

Big year, Simpson and McKenzie

Melbourne, Dec. 31. Bob Simpson and Graham McKenzie had record-breaking years in calendar 1964.

Simpson played 14 Tests in four countries, and made 1381 runs – beating Denis Compton's 1159 runs in nine Tests in three countries in 1947. His highest score was the 311 in England.

McKenzie, too, played 14 Tests and took 71 wickets, also a record.

McKenzie equalled Clarrie Grimmett's haul of 29 by an Australian in England sending down a near record, for a fast bowler, of 256 overs in the series.

He remained fit and seemingly fresh all year, taking 50 of his 71 wickets between June and October.

Bob Simpson – triple century.

QUICK SINGLES

Not yet. Tasmania has had its application to join the Sheffield Shield turned down again – but Victoria and NSW agreed to resume playing matches with Tasmania between their own Shield commitments.

Now on Sundays. Queensland Cricket Association announced in August that they wanted to play cricket on Sundays, which was agreed by the Board. The matches between Queensland and WA will be the first.

Now no running on the pitch. The Australian Board of Control adopted an experimental rule concerning persistent running on the pitch by bowlers in October. After being warned by the umpires, offenders will be liable to be taken off and not allowed to bowl again in that innings.

Shepherd outscores Victoria. The WA captain Barry Shepherd made 215 not out in the draw against Victoria, who made 208 in their first innings.

Once a 'keeper. Pakistan captain Hanif Mohammad took the gloves in the Melbourne Test after a 12-year absence, and took two catches. Regular 'keeper Abdul Kadir was injured. Hanif started his career as a gloveman, but his remarkable batting feats eventually forced him to give up the gloves.

Walters in great stand. Young 19-year-old NSW batsman Doug Walters (253) and 22-year-old Lyn Marks put on 378 in 307 minutes for NSW in Adelaide in February. Walters also took 7/63.

Windies team announced. In February the Board announced the team for the tour to the West Indies. Peter Burge and Tom Veivers asked not to be considered. Bob Simpson was named captain, Brian

Booth vice-captain, and Peter Allan, Bob Cowper, Wally Grout, Neil Hawke, Bill Lawry, Barry Jarman, Graham McKenzie, Laurie Mayne, Norm O'Neill, Peter Philpott, Barrie Shepherd, David Sincock, Grahame Thomas and Sam Trimble.

Helmets on. The Australian Cricket Society presented each member of the Australian touring team with a protective helmet against the potentially lethal bowling of Wes Hall and Charlie Griffith. The helmets will not be used, says manager Bob Parish.

Sincock at last. After five years of being hailed as 'the next big thing' in spin bowling, left-arm googly bowler David Sincock made an interesting Test debut against Pakistan at the MCG. He took 3/67 in the first innings, and a worrying 1/102 in the second. It is said he could spin the ball on an ice rink, but his direction can be wayward.

NSW wins Sheffield Shield

Perth, Feb. 15. NSW secured the Sheffield Shield with a five-wicket win over Western Australia at the WACA, in the last game of the season, finishing two points clear of Victoria and South Australia.

NSW made 302 (Des Hoare taking 8/98 for WA) and 5/156 to WA's 184 and 273 (Doug Walters 5/92 for NSW.)

From its eight matches NSW won three outright, two on the first innings and lost three on the first innings. Victoria and SA had two outright wins each, but Victoria had only one outright loss.

Perhaps the best match of the season was that between NSW and SA, which had indicated its batting power in the game against Queensland.

On New Year's Day, Queensland was bowled out for 148. NSW replied with 360, after which Peter Burge made 242 not out for Queensland with 26 fours. He declared at 6/517, leaving NSW to make 306 in 195 minutes.

Norm O'Neill belted 96 runs in 99 minutes. But after Ross Duncan grabbed four wickets in 14 balls, NSW just managed to hold on for the draw at 9/258.

NSW followed up a week later in the game against SA at the SCG. SA made 391 in its first innings, Ian Chappell 123 and Neil Hawke 77 not out. NSW was seven runs short on the first innings, despite 148 from Graeme Thomas and 121 from Bob Simpson. SA then made 268, Alan Shiell 110, setting NSW to get 276 in 220 minutes.

With Simpson 142 not out and O'Neill 133 not out they got there in just 43 overs.

Bill Lawry made 246 against SA over the new year, in Victoria's 111-run win.

In the Christmas Victoria v NSW match at the MCG, it was virtually a one-innings chase for first-innings points when Lawry made 140 and Bob Cowper 192 in a 225-run second-wicket partnership. Victoria scored 5/549.

NSW made a valiant pursuit of the Victorian total, with Simpson contributing 121. At tea on the last day NSW was 6/515, but lost Thomas for 162, and then folded to be all out for 536.

Bill Lawry was best overall with the bat, making 788 runs at 98.50, and Alan Connolly best with the ball – 29 wickets at 27.72.

ONLY TEST 1964–65 AUSTRALIA v PAKISTAN
Melbourne Cricket Ground, Melbourne. December 4, 5, 7, 8, 1964.
Toss: Australia. Match Drawn.

PAKISTAN

Abdul Kadir (+) c Chappell b McKenzie ...0 (7)	c Jarman b Hawke	...35
Mohammad Ilyas run out ...6	lbw McKenzie	...3
Saeed Ahmed c Chappell b Hawke ...80	c Chappell b McKenzie	...24
Javed Burki c Simpson b McKenzie ...29	b Hawke	...47
Hanif Mohammad (c) c McKenzie b Sincock ...104	st Jarman b Veivers	...93
Nasim-ul-Ghani b McKenzie ...27	b Sincock	...10
Asif Iqbal c McKenzie b Hawke ...1 (8)	c Jarman b Hawke	...15
Intikhab Alam b Shepherd b Hawke ...13 (9)	c Simpson b Hawke	...61
Afaq Hussain not out ...8 (10)	not out	...13
Arif Butt c Chappell b Sincock ...7 (1)	c Jarman b McKenzie	...12
Farooq Hamid b Sincock ...0	b McKenzie	...3
Extras (B 4, LB 4, W 3, NB 1) ...12	(B 5, LB 2, W 2, NB 1)	...10
TOTAL ...287		...326

FOW 1st Inns: 0 18 112 127 225 226 255 275 287 287
FOW 2nd Inns: 6 37 46 130 152 198 229 267 323 326

Bowling: *First Innings*: McKenzie 22-5-66-3, Hawke 21-1-69-3, Sincock 17.6-0-67-3, Simpson 9-1-21-0, Chappell 15-2-49-0, Veivers 3-2-3-0. *Second Innings*: McKenzie 24.4-1-74-4, Hawke 21-2-72-4, Sincock 28-5-102-1, Chappell 11-2-31-0, Veivers 12-4-37-1.

AUSTRALIA

RB Simpson (c) b Arif ...47	c Hanif b Arif	...1
WM Lawry c Hanif b Arif ...41	run out	...19
IM Chappell c Hanif b Farooq ...11		
BK Shepherd c(S)Ghulam Ahmed b Asif ...55 (3)	not out	...43
BC Booth c Hanif b Arif ...57		
RM Cowper c Intikhab b Saeed ...83		
TR Veivers c Hanif b Arif ...88 (4)	not out	...16
BN Jarman (+) b Arif ...33		
DJ Sincock b Arif ...7		
GD McKenzie b Arif ...1		
NJN Hawke not out ...1		
Extras (B 6, LB 3, W 1, NB 14) ...24	(B 2, LB 4, W 2, NB 1)	...9
TOTAL ...448		...2 for 88

FOW 1st Inns: 81 105 105 200 233 372 418 434 446 448
FOW 2nd Inns: 12 55

Bowling: *First Innings*: Farooq 19-1-82-1, Asif 19-1-90-2, Arif 21.3-1-89-6, Afaq 9-1-45-0, Intikhab 10-0-51-0, Saeed 10-0-31-1, Nasim-ul-Ghani 4-0-36-0. *Second Innings*: Farooq 4-0-25-0, Asif 2-0-25-0, Arif 5.5-0-29-1.

Umpires: CJ Egar & WJ Smyth

ONLY TEST 1964–65 PAKISTAN v AUSTRALIA
National Stadium, Karachi. October 24, 25, 27, 28, 29, 1964.
Toss: Pakistan. Match Drawn.

PAKISTAN

Khalid Ibadulla c Grout b McKenzie ...166	c Redpath b McKenzie	...3
Abdul Kadir (+) run out ...95	hit wicket b Veivers	...26
Saeed Ahmed c Redpath b Martin ...7 (4)	c (S)RH Sellers b Martin	...35
Javed Burki hit wicket b Veivers ...8 (5)	c Grout b Cowper	...62
Hanif Mohammad (c) c & b McKenzie ...2 (6)	c McKenzie b Booth	...40
Shafqat Rana c Grout b McKenzie ...0 (7)	lbw McKenzie	...24
Nasim-ul-Ghani c Redpath b Hawke ...15 (8)	c Grout b Veivers	...22
Majid Khan lbw Martin ...0		
Intikhab Alam c Grout b McKenzie ...53	not out	...21
Asif Iqbal c Booth b McKenzie ...41 (3)	c & b Simpson	...36
Pervez Sajjad not out ...3		
Extras (B 9, LB 12, NB 3) ...24	(B 1, LB 6, NB 3)	...10
TOTAL ...414		...8 dec 279

FOW 1st Inns: 249 266 284 296 296 301 302 334 383 414
FOW 2nd Inns: 13 65 81 118 202 224 236 236

Bowling: *First Innings*: McKenzie 30-9-69-6, Hawke 20-2-84-1, Martin 36-11-106-2, Veivers 16-5-33-0, Simpson 30-8-69-0, Booth 5-2-15-0, Redpath 1-0-14-0. *Second Innings*: McKenzie 25-5-62-2, Hawke 6-2-20-0, Martin 17-4-42-1, Veivers 30-16-44-2, Simpson 20-5-47-1, Booth 13-4-18-1, Cowper 11-3-36-1.

AUSTRALIA

WM Lawry hit wicket b Majid ...7	c Khalid b Majid	...22
RB Simpson (c) c Pervez b Saeed ...153	c Khalid b Nasim-ul-Ghani	...115
IR Redpath lbw Intikhab ...19	not out	...40
PJP Burge c Majid b Pervez ...54	not out	...28
BC Booth c Asif b Majid ...15		
RM Cowper b Asif ...16		
TR Veivers st Abdul b Saeed ...25		
JW Martin b Asif ...26		
ATW Grout (+) c Asif b Saeed ...0		
GD McKenzie lbw Intikhab ...2		
NJN Hawke not out ...8		
Extras (B 12, LB 8, NB 7) ...27	(LB 14, NB 8)	...22
TOTAL ...352		...2 for 227

FOW 1st Inns: 10 78 194 228 257 315 315 315 320 352
FOW 2nd Inns: 54 173

Bowling: *First Innings*: Majid 30-9-55-2, Asif 23.5-5-68-2, Pervez 22-5-52-1, Intikhab 28-5-83-2, Nasim-ul-Ghani 4-0-17-0, Saeed 19-5-41-3, Khalid 7-3-9-0. *Second Innings*: Majid 16-3-42-1, Asif 12-4-28-0, Pervez 8-2-17-0, Intikhab 16-3-48-0, Nasim-ul-Ghani 12-3-24-1, Saeed 13-6-28-0, Khalid 2-0-14-0, Javed 2-1-3-0, Shafqat 1-0-1-0.

Umpires: Daud Khan & Shujauddin

Australian Averages

1964–65 PAKISTAN v AUSTRALIA

AUSTRALIA	M	Inn	NO	Runs	H.S	Avrge	Ct	St	Overs	Mds	Runs	Wkt	Avrge
Booth, BC	2	2	-	72	57	28.50	1	-	18.0	6	33	1	33.00
Burge, PJP	1	2	1	82	54	82.00	-	-	-	-	-	-	-
Chappell, IM	1	1	-	11	11	11.00	4	-	26.0	4	80	-	-
Cowper, RM	2	2	-	109	83	54.50	-	-	11.0	3	36	1	36.00
Grout, ATW	1	1	-	0	0	0.00	5	-	-	-	-	-	-
Hawke, NJN	2	2	2	9	8*	-	-	-	68.0	7	245	8	30.63
Jarman, BN	1	1	-	33	33	33.00	3	1	-	-	-	-	-
Lawry, WM	2	4	-	89	41	22.25	-	-	-	-	-	-	-
Martin, JW	1	1	-	26	26	26.00	-	-	53.0	15	148	3	49.33
McKenzie, GD	2	2	-	3	2	1.50	4	-	101.4	20	271	15	18.06
Redpath, IR	2	2	1	59	40*	59.00	-	-	1.0	-	14	-	-
Shepherd, BK	1	2	1	98	55	98.00	1	-	-	-	-	-	-
Simpson, RB	2	4	-	316	153	79.00	3	-	59.0	14	137	1	137.00
Sincock, DJ	1	1	-	7	7	7.00	-	-	45.6	5	169	4	42.25
Veivers, TR	2	3	1	129	88	64.53	-	-	61.0	27	117	3	39.00

Pakistani Averages

1964–65 PAKISTAN v AUSTRALIA

PAKISTAN	M	Inn	NO	Runs	H.S	Avrge	Ct	St	Overs	Mds	Runs	Wkt	Avrge
Abdul Kadir	2	4	-	156	95	39.00	-	1	-	-	-	-	-
Afaq Hussain	1	2	2	21	13*	-	-	-	9.0	1	45	-	-
Arif Butt	1	2	-	19	12	9.50	-	-	27.0	1	118	7	16.86
Asif Iqbal	2	4	-	93	41	22.25	2	-	56.5	10	211	4	52.75
Farooq Hamid	1	2	-	3	3	1.50	-	-	23.0	1	107	1	107.00
Hanif Mohammad	2	4	-	239	104	59.75	5	-	-	-	-	-	-
Intikhab Alam	2	4	1	148	61	43.33	1	-	54.0	8	182	91.00	
Javed Burki	2	4	-	146	62	36.20	-	-	2.0	1	3	-	-
Khalid Ibadulla	1	2	-	169	166	84.50	2	-	9.0	3	23	-	-
Majid Khan	1	1	-	0	0	0.00	-	-	46.0	12	97	3	32.33
Mohammad Ilyas	1	2	-	9	6	4.50	-	-	-	-	-	-	-
Nasim-ul-Ghani	2	4	-	74	27	18.50	1	-	20.0	3	77	1	77.00
Pervez Sajjad	1	1	1	3	3*	-	1	-	30.0	7	69	1	69.00
Saeed Ahmed	2	4	-	146	80	36.50	-	-	42.0	11	100	4	25.00
Shafqat Rana	1	2	-	24	24	12.00	-	-	1.0	-	1	-	-

Australia 'bumped' off

Gary Sobers, captaining the West Indies for the first time, displays his batting skills.

Port-of-Spain, April 1. Gary Sobers noted after the crowd swarmed on the Queen's Park Oval on the sixth day of a disappointing draw, that the 'pitch ought to be dug up'. After all, just three innings had been completed, batting had been sedate and the over rate slow, with nearly more bumpers bowled than runs scored.

Only on the second day did the batting measure up to the ability of the batsmen, when Basil Butcher and Gary Sobers put on 160. Butcher was a revelation, outshining even the glorious Sobers in stroke play.

This was matched by the Australian fielding. Richie Benaud reflected that he had 'never seen a better team exhibition than that put up by the Australians … they saved probably 70 runs in the field'.

In fact both Sobers (69) and Butcher (117) were run out by the sharp fielding of Brian Booth.

Booth then made 117 himself, and Bob Cowper 143, as Australia set themselves the task of overhauling the West Indies' first innings of 429, which they achieved. Benaud was of the opinion that with slightly better catching, slightly faster over rates and a slightly faster pitch a result might have been achieved. It was a disappointment that the attacking spirit of 1960–61, even after just two Tests played, seemed absent.

The first Test at Sabina Park Jamaica saw Gary Sobers win his first Test as captain, giving the West Indies their first win over Australia at home.

This was a relatively low-scoring game, a bowler's match where the Australians had a good deal of trouble with the bumper business, especially from the dubious action of Charlie Griffith. Wes Hall was fast enough but with his legitimate action had to bowl so short in order to get the ball up that batsmen had some chance of getting out of the way. Griffith, with the ball appearing suddenly from behind his ear and his 'whippy' style, could get them up from just short of a length. Benaud said that he did think a lot were bowled, though 'I didn't think they got within the confines of unfair play'.

However, Australia could hardly blame the unsettling bowling of Griffith for its loss – the batting wasn't quite up to the bowling of Hall – who took nine wickets in the match to Griffith's four.

Griffith's action is under scrutiny

Kingston, March 10. Richie Benaud, after taking his own photographs of West Indian paceman Charlie Griffith in the first Test, wrote in the Sydney *Sun* and the local paper the Jamaica *Gleaner*, that he 'throws. I am quite convinced of this having watched him in action in the first Test match.

'There were occasions when Griffith bowled at half pace and was obviously making a great effort to conform to the laws with regard to throwing.

'There were others where I caught my breath at the sheer speed of the ball as it hurtled down the pitch from his wide-open bent-armed action…

'No one minds seeing Wes Hall in full cry – this is one of the greatest sights in the game. This is what I would like to see from Griffith in future games – an action like Wes Hall and bowling just as fast and there could be no worries from anyone.'

This article caused consternation in Jamaica, where the view is that because Griffith had not been 'called' by an umpire in a Test match, he is 'not guilty', and that Benaud is attempting psychological warfare because Australia lost.

Charlie Griffith's suspect action.

Worrell trophy to Windies

Bridgetown, May 11. Despite high-scoring batting, timely declarations and Australia having its best match of the tour, the fourth Test at Kensington Oval in Barbados finished in a draw. Therefore, after the West Indies' Lance Gibbs-inspired win in the third Test, the home side has won the series and the Frank Worrell Trophy.

Australian captain Bob Simpson declared the Australian second innings closed after 20 minutes on the final day, leaving the West Indies 253 to win at a bit less than a run a minute. At one stage the West Indies needed just 39 runs in the last 35 minutes, but lost Conrad Hunte and then first-innings double centurion Seymour Nurse for a duck. Joe Solomon and Gary Sobers needed 12 runs from what tuned out to be the last over. Graham McKenzie accidentally, perhaps, bowled a wide, making sure this was the last over, and Solomon could only score two runs.

But the West Indies only needed the draw, while Australia needed a win to stay in the series.

Simpson and Bill Lawry got Australia off to a magnificent start with an opening stand of 382, before Simpson was finally bowled by Wes Hall for 201. He and Lawry had withstood some fierce bowling, which resulted in Griffith being officially warned for intimidatory bowling after five bumpers in six balls to Simpson, and Lawry had had his cheekbone 'grazed' by another one.

Australia was in a position to pull off a surprising win in the third Test in Georgetown – but that was before lanky Lance Gibbs turned the game in the space of 21 balls on the afternoon of the third day. Australia, in particular Neil Hawke

Bill Lawry bowled round his legs by Lance Gibbs.

who followed his 6/72 in the first innings with 4/43 in the second, and Peter Philpott also with four second-innings wickets, routed the might of West Indies batting for 180. This left Australia with an improbable but not impossible 357 to win, and plenty of time to do it.

At tea on the fourth day Australia had lost only Bob Simpson for 23. Then, after tea, came Gibbs. He

bowled Lawry round his legs, had Cowper stumped, O'Neill gave Sobers a catch at leg slip and Brian Booth did the same to 'keeper Jackie Hendricks – 4/5 in 21 balls, and that was just about that for Australia. Laurie Mayne survived one ball, and the match continued for a few minutes on the fifth day – to give Gibbs his sixth wicket, and the West Indies the trophy.

Umpire Gomez is called to duty

Georgetown, April 20. In one of the more farcical events in cricket history, former West Indian all-rounder and current selector Gerry Gomez was called in to umpire the third Test at Bourda, British Guiana.

The bizarre business has its origins in the rivalry between the different component countries of the West Indies, which means that no Test panel of umpires is available for the whole series.

It transpired that Cortez Jordan from Trinidad was rumoured to stand in the Test in British Guiana with local man Cecil Kippins.

When this actually happened the British Guiana umpires' Board at a protest meeting decided that Kippins would not be allowed to stand 'unless a fellow Guianese is permitted to stand with him.'

Richie Benaud said: 'It was one of those situations where Gilbert and Sullivan were at their best.'

It soon became clear that the West Indies board was not going to fly in an umpire from elsewhere. The day before the Test was supposed to begin there was only one umpire. Faced with this, the West Indies Board decided on Gerry Gomez – fair man, excellent cricketer, but also a radio announcer with commitments.

Australian captain Bob Simpson was given an ultimatum the night before the game, to which he agreed. Farce was piled on when at 1.15 p.m. on the first day yet another umpire turned up ready for duty.

Fortunately the Board, with the bemused agreement of Simpson, let Gomez continue for the whole match. It is, however, slightly unusual to have an umpire who is a selector for one side being called upon to adjudicate over the action of a bowler like Charlie Griffith.

Last Test win saves face for Australia

Port-of-Spain, May 17. David Sincock was brought in to play his first Test of the series for the injured Norm O'Neill, and aside from the embarrassing moment when he dropped Rohan Kanhai, bowled sufficient good balls to take four wickets in Australia's win over the newly crowned 'world champions'.

Kanhai provided the batting highlight with a magnificent 121 that went some way to hiding the paltry West Indies total of 224 on another slow pitch.

Australia struggled to a lead of 70. Observers thought this was a good lead, but would not be enough. If

the West Indies could set Australia 200 or so in their second innings on the pitch that was beginning to play tricks, then the West Indies might well go three up.

They didn't expect to see Neil Hawke take the early wickets, Sincock a couple in the middle, and then Graham McKenzie, in his most lethal spell of the tour, bowl Gary Sobers and clean up the tail to finish with 5/33. He took three wickets in four balls to close out the match, leaving a somewhat stunned opener Conrad Hunte at the other end on 60 not out.

Simpson and Lawry got the required 63 with little fuss.

Bob Simpson and Bill Lawry are joined by a third man – and would-be opener.

It all happens for Bill Lawry

Bill Lawry, who grew up in the Melbourne suburb of Northcote, was named after Prime Minister William Morris Hughes. He had none of Hughes' feisty characteristics as a leader, though like Hughes he loved a good scrap. Lawry, the batsman, revealed his exceptional fighting qualities early in his career. He played for Melbourne District club Northcote First XI aged 16, and struggled for a few seasons before becoming established in the Victorian team. He played for the VCA Colts and then the Victorian Second XI in 1954 aged 17. Lawry made 155 for a Victorian Seconds side in November 1955, and played his first Sheffield Shield game against WA. He turned 19 during the match.

But big scores were not forthcoming for Victoria until a defiant 266 against NSW earned him a berth on the boat to England in 1961. From then, the tall hawk-like figure, a plumber and owner of racing pigeons in private life, became Mr Reliable.

He was a great success in England in 1961, scoring two Test centuries – 130 at Lord's and 102 at Old Trafford for an average of 52.5. The London tabloid press, revelling in a spot of class consciousness, greeted his century at cricket's Mecca with headlines such as 'Plumber's ton at Lord's'. With 2019 runs at an average of 61.18 (nine centuries), Lawry was the success story of Richie Benaud's '61 side that retained the Ashes.

Known as 'The Phantom' – someone discovered some Phantom comics in his bag when he was a teenager playing in the Victorian seconds – and dubbed 'The corpse with pads on' by English cricket writer Ian Woolridge, Lawry gave new meaning to the concept of concentration. He made seven centuries against England, four against the West Indies one each against India and South Africa. He carried his bat five times in first class matches.

One of Lawry's finest hours was in the 1965–66 Melbourne district final when he compiled 282 to lead Northcote to victory over Essendon, which had scored 9/514 declared. The left-hander batted for three Saturdays until victory was secure.

The imperturbable Lawry took over the captaincy from Simpson

Bill Lawry – 'The Phantom'.

during India's 1967–68 tour and promptly won the last two Tests for a 4–0 result. He retained the Ashes in England in 1968 (1–all) scoring 135 at the Oval, and had a resounding 3–1 win over Gary Sobers' West Indians at home in 1968–69, this time with three centuries, 105 in Brisbane, 205 at the MCG and 151 in Sydney. The tide turned against him, however, with a heavy 4–0 defeat in South Africa in 1969–70.

The writing was on the wall for Lawry mid-way through the spiteful England tour of Australia in 1970–71. Led by the implacable Ray Illingworth, England had Snow, whose fast bowling was never less than menacing, and a Lawry bat-alike in Geoff Boycott. Lawry had to call on all his concentration with the bat, apart from the captaincy. When Australia folded for 116 in Sydney, Lawry carried his bat for 60, the second time he had done so in a Test.

The selectors decided it was time for a fresh approach. Lawry was axed on the eve of the final Test in 1971. Lawry heard the news on the radio, and was not even picked as a batsman, which caused an outcry.

On his retirement, Lawry managed the Victorian team and became an enthusiastic Channel 9 commentator on the game. Lawry's favourite cry, 'It's all happening,' has become synonymous with any action-packed pursuit, one day cricket or otherwise.

Defiant and single-minded, he was one of the best – he scored more runs and made more centuries than any other opener.

Lawry scored 5234 runs at 47.15 in 67 Tests, including 25 as captain, and took 30 catches.

WEST INDIES

Batsman	1st Innings		2nd Innings	
CC Hunte c Grout b Philpott	41		c Simpson b Mayne	81
SM Nurse c Grout b Hawke	15		run out	17
RB Kanhai c Philpott b McKenzie	17		c & b Philpott	16
BF Butcher b Mayne	39		c Booth b Philpott	71
GS Sobers (c) lbw Simpson	30	(6)	c Simpson b Philpott	27
JS Solomon c Grout b Mayne	0	(7)	c Grout b Mayne	76
JL Hendriks (+) b Philpott	11	(8)	b O'Neill	30
AW White not out	57	(9)	st Grout b Philpott	3
WW Hall b Hawke	9	(10)	b Mayne	16
CC Griffith b Mayne	6	(11)	not out	1
LR Gibbs b Mayne	6	(5)	b Mayne	5
Extras (B 4, LB 3, W 1)	8		(B 20, LB 7, W 1, NB 2)	30
TOTAL	239			373

FOW 1st Inns: 48 70 82 149 149 149 181 211 229 239
FOW 2nd Inns: 50 78 194 211 226 247 311 314 372 373

Bowling: *First Innings*: McKenzie 20-2-70-1, Hawke 14-4-47-2, Mayne 17.2-2-43-4, Philpott 14-2-56-2, Simpson 4-2-15-1. *Second Innings*: McKenzie 33-7-56-0, Hawke 18-5-25-0, Mayne 23.4-5-56-4, Philpott 47-10-109-4, Simpson 15-2-36-0, Cowper 9-1-27-0, O'Neill 7-0-34-1.

AUSTRALIA

Batsman	1st Innings		2nd Innings	
WM Lawry lbw Hall	19		b Griffith	17
RB Simpson (c) c Kanhai b Hall	11		c Hendriks b Hall	16
RM Cowper c Nurse b Hall	26	(4)	lbw Hall	2
NC O'Neill c Butcher b White	40	(5)	c Nurse b Gibbs	22
BC Booth b Griffith	2	(6)	b Griffith	56
G Thomas b Griffith	23	(7)	b Hall	15
PI Philpott c White b Hall	22	(8)	c Kanhai b Sobers	9
NJN Hawke not out	45	(3)	b Solomon	33
ATW Grout (+) c Nurse b Hall	5		lbw Hall	2
GD McKenzie b White	0		c Hall b White	20
LC Mayne b Sobers	9		not out	11
Extras (B 2, LB 8, NB 5)	15		(NB 13)	13
TOTAL	217			216

FOW 1st Inns: 32 39 42 80 96 136 176 192 193 217
FOW 2nd Inns: 39 40 43 75 144 167 180 184 192 216

Bowling: *First Innings*: Hall 24-0-60-5, Griffith 20-2-59-2, Sobers 20.4-7-30-1, White 15-4-34-2, Gibbs 16-8-19-0. *Second Innings*: Hall 19-5-45-4, Griffith 14-3-36-2, Gibbs 9-1-21-1, Sobers 17-2-64-1, Solomon 5-0-23-1, White 14.5-8-14-1.

Umpires: O Davies & D Sang Hue

WEST INDIES

Batsman	1st Innings	2nd Innings	
CC Hunte c Simpson b McKenzie	89	b Philpott	53
BA Davis c Simpson b McKenzie	54	c Simpson b O'Neill	58
RB Kanhai c Grout b Cowper	27	c McKenzie b Philpott	53
BF Butcher run out	117	c Thomas b Mayne	47
GS Sobers (c) run out	69	lbw Simpson	24
JS Solomon not out	31	c Booth b Simpson	48
JL Hendriks (+) c Philpott b O'Neill	2	c Grout b Hawke	22
AW White c Grout b Philpott	7	lbw Hawke	4
WW Hall c Booth b O'Neill	4	c Mayne b Simpson	37
CC Griffith b O'Neill	12	not out	18
LR Gibbs st Grout b O'Neill	1	c Booth b Simpson	1
Extras (B 4, LB 9, W 2, NB 1)	16	(B 11, LB 8, NB 2)	21
TOTAL	429		386

FOW 1st Inns: 116 164 205 365 372 380 393 404 425 429
FOW 2nd Inns: 91 166 166 236 266 323 327 328 382 386

Bowling: *First Innings*: McKenzie 36-9-94-2, Hawke 23-4-50-0, Mayne 17-0-65-0, Philpott 36-10-82-1, Booth 2-0-5-0, Simpson 8-1-28-0, Cowper 12-1-48-1, O'Neill 17.4-3-41-4. *Second Innings*: McKenzie 21-5-62-0, Mayne 11-2-37-1, Hawke 21-4-42-2, Philpott 28-4-57-2, O'Neill 24-6-65-1, Simpson 36.5-5-83-4, Booth 5-1-14-0, Cowper 1-0-5-0.

AUSTRALIA

Batsman	1st Innings
WM Lawry c Davis b Griffith	1
RB Simpson (c) b Griffith	30
RM Cowper run out	143
NC O'Neill c Sobers b Hall	36
BC Booth c Hendriks b Griffith	117
G Thomas c Hendriks b Hall	61
PI Philpott c Sobers b Gibbs	19
NJN Hawke c Hall b Sobers	39
ATW Grout (+) c Hendriks b Sobers	35
GD McKenzie c Butcher b Sobers	13
LC Mayne not out	1
Extras (B 8, LB 3, NB 10)	21
TOTAL	516

FOW 1st Inns: 15 60 288 306 372 415 431 489 511 516

Bowling: *First Innings*: Hall 35-6-104-2, Griffith 33-5-81-3, Sobers 27.5-5-75-3, Gibbs 66-22-129-1, White 52-15-104-0, Hunte 2-1-2-0.

Umpires: CZ Bain & R Gosein

THIRD TEST 1964–65 WEST INDIES v AUSTRALIA
Bourda, Georgetown. April 14, 15, 17, 19, 20, 1965.
Toss: West Indies. West Indies won by 212 runs.

WEST INDIES
CC Hunte c McKenzie b Philpott	31	c Grout b Hawke	38	
BA Davis b Hawke	28	b McKenzie	17	
RB Kanhai b Hawke	89	b McKenzie	0	
BF Butcher run out	49	b Hawke	18	
SM Nurse c & b Hawke	42	st Grout b Philpott	6	
GS Sobers (c) c Grout b Hawke	45	c Simpson b Philpott	42	
JS Solomon c Grout b Hawke	0	c Simpson b Philpott	17	
JL Hendriks (+) not out	31	c Grout b Hawke	2	
WW Hall c Mayne b Hawke	7	not out	20	
CC Griffith lbw O'Neill	19	c Thomas b Philpott	13	
LR Gibbs b O'Neill	2	b Hawke	1	
Extras (B 7, LB 1, W 1, NB 3)	12	(LB 3, W 1, NB 2)	6	
TOTAL	355		180	

FOW 1st Inns: 56 68 203 210 290 290 297 309 353 355
FOW 2nd Inns: 31 31 62 69 125 129 146 146 176 180

Bowling: *First Innings*: McKenzie 23-2-92-0, Hawke 32-8-72-6, Mayne 12-1-54-0, Philpott 26-5-75-1, O'Neill 6.2-1-26-2, Simpson 7-1-23-0, Cowper 1-0-1-0. *Second Innings*: McKenzie 21-7-53-2, Hawke 20.4-7-43-4, Simpson 17-9-19-0, Mayne 2-1-6-0, Philpott 16-3-49-4, O'Neill 1-0-4-0.

AUSTRALIA
RB Simpson (c) b Sobers	7	b Griffith	23	
WM Lawry run out	20	b Gibbs	22	
RM Cowper c Hendriks b Gibbs	41	st Hendriks b Gibbs	30	
NC O'Neill b Griffith	27	c Sobers b Gibbs	16	
PI Philpott c Butcher b Sobers	5 (8)	c Sobers b Gibbs	6	
BC Booth c Sobers b Gibbs	37 (5)	c Hendriks b Gibbs	0	
G Thomas b Hall	8 (6)	st Hendriks b Solomon	5	
NJN Hawke c Sobers b Hall	0 (7)	c Hendriks b Sobers	14	
ATW Grout (+) run out	19	b Sobers	8	
GD McKenzie not out	3	b Gibbs	6	
LC Mayne b Gibbs	5	not out	0	
Extras (LB 1, NB 6)	7	(B 4, LB 4, NB 6)	14	
TOTAL	179		144	

FOW 1st Inns: 11 68 71 85 116 127 130 170 171 179
FOW 2nd Inns: 31 88 91 104 109 115 130 130 144 144

Bowling: *First Innings*: Hall 13-2-43-2, Sobers 12-2-38-2, Griffith 14-2-40-1, Gibbs 25.5-9-51-3. *Second Innings*: Hall 2-1-1-0, Griffith 6-1-30-1, Sobers 19-7-39-2, Gibbs 22.2-9-29-6, Solomon 9-2-31-1.

Umpires: GE Gomez & HBC Jordan

FIFTH TEST 1964–65 WEST INDIES v AUSTRALIA
Queen's Park Oval, Port-of-Spain. May 14, 15, 17, 1965.
Toss: West Indies. Australia won by 10 wkts.

WEST INDIES
CC Hunte c Grout b Hawke	1	not out	60	
BA Davis c McKenzie b Hawke	4	lbw Hawke	8	
RB Kanhai c Hawke b Cowper	121	b Hawke	9	
BF Butcher lbw Hawke	2	c Cowper b Sincock	26	
SM Nurse c McKenzie	9	lbw Hawke	1	
GS Sobers (c) b Sincock	18	b McKenzie	8	
WV Rodriguez c & b Sincock	9	st Grout b Sincock	1	
DW Allan (+) run out	11	c Cowper b McKenzie	7	
WW Hall b Philpott	29	b McKenzie	8	
CC Griffith c Sincock b Philpott	11	b McKenzie	0	
LR Gibbs not out	0	b McKenzie	0	
Extras (B 4, LB 2, W 2, NB 1)	9	(B 2, W 1)	3	
TOTAL	224		131	

FOW 1st Inns: 2 18 26 64 100 114 162 202 217 224
FOW 2nd Inns: 12 22 63 66 87 92 103 131 131 131

Bowling: *First Innings*: McKenzie 14-0-43-1, Hawke 13-3-42-3, Sincock 15-1-79-2, Philpott 7.3-0-25-2, Cowper 6-0-26-1. *Second Innings*: McKenzie 17-7-33-5, Hawke 13-2-31-3, Sincock 18-0-64-2.

AUSTRALIA
WM Lawry c Allan b Griffith	3	not out	18	
RB Simpson (c) b Griffith	72	not out	34	
RM Cowper lbw Sobers	69			
BC Booth lbw Griffith	0			
G Thomas c Allan b Griffith	38			
BK Shepherd c(S)CA Davis b Gibbs	38			
NJN Hawke b Griffith	3			
PI Philpott b Gibbs	10			
ATW Grout (+) c Griffith b Gibbs	14			
DJ Sincock not out	17			
GD McKenzie b Griffith	8			
Extras (B 12, LB 3, W 1, NB 6)	22	(B 4, W 1, NB 6)	11	
TOTAL	294		0 for 63	

FOW 1st Inns: 5 143 143 167 222 230 248 261 270 294
FOW 2nd Inns:

Bowling: *First Innings*: Hall 14-2-46-0, Griffith 20-6-46-6, Gibbs 44-17-71-3, Rodriguez 13-2-44-0, Sobers 37-13-65-1. *Second Innings*: Griffith 6-0-19-0, Hall 4-0-7-0, Gibbs 4-2-7-0, Sobers 2-0-7-0, Rodriguez 1-0-8-0, Kanhai 1-0-4-0.

Umpires: HBC Jordan & CP Kippins

FOURTH TEST 1964–65 WEST INDIES v AUSTRALIA
Kensington Oval, Bridgetown. May 5, 6, 7, 8, 10, 11, 1965.
Toss: Australia. Match Drawn.

AUSTRALIA
WM Lawry c Sobers b Solomon	210	retired hurt	58	
RB Simpson (c) b Hall	201	c Nurse b Sobers	5	
RM Cowper b Sobers	102	c & b Hall	4	
NC O'Neill c Kanhai b Gibbs	51	not out	74	
BC Booth b Gibbs	5	c Sobers b Gibbs	17	
G Thomas not out	27	b Gibbs	1	
BK Shepherd lbw Hall	4			
NJN Hawke not out	8			
GD McKenzie				
ATW Grout (+)				
PI Philpott				
Extras (B 10, LB 12, W 2, NB 18)	42	(B 11, LB 3, W 1, NB 1)	16	
TOTAL	6 dec 650		4 dec 175	

FOW 1st Inns: 382 522 583 604 615 631
FOW 2nd Inns: 7 13 160 175

Bowling: *First Innings*: Hall 27-3-117-2, Griffith 35-3-131-0, Sobers 37-7-143-1, Gibbs 73-17-168-2, Solomon 14-1-42-1, Hunte 3-1-7-0. *Second Innings*: Hall 8-0-31-1, Sobers 20-11-29-1, Gibbs 18.2-3-61-2, Griffith 7-0-38-0.

WEST INDIES
CC Hunte c Simpson b McKenzie	75	c Grout b McKenzie	81	
BA Davis b McKenzie	8	c (S)DJ Sincock b Philpott	68	
RB Kanhai c Hawke b McKenzie	129	lbw McKenzie	1	
BF Butcher c Simpson b O'Neill	9	c Booth b Philpott	27	
SM Nurse c Simpson b Hawke	201 (6)	lbw Hawke	0	
GS Sobers (c) c Grout b McKenzie	55 (5)	not out	34	
JS Solomon c McKenzie b Hawke	1	not out	6	
JL Hendriks (+) retired hurt	4			
WW Hall c Simpson b Hawke	9			
CC Griffith run out	54			
LR Gibbs not out	3			
Extras (B 13, LB 12, W 1, NB 5)	31	(B 19, LB 3, W 2, NB 1)	25	
TOTAL	9 dec 573		5 for 242	

FOW 1st Inns: 13 99 299 445 448 453 474 539 573
FOW 2nd Inns: 145 146 183 216 217

Bowling: *First Innings*: McKenzie 47-11-114-4, Hawke 49-11-135-3, Philpott 45-17-102-0, O'Neill 26-13-60-1, Simpson 15-3-44-0, Cowper 21-6-64-0, Booth 6-2-17-0, Shepherd 3-1-6-0. *Second Innings*: McKenzie 24-6-60-2, Hawke 15-4-37-1, Philpott 24-7-74-2, Cowper 8-4-19-0, Booth 5-1-12-0, Simpson 9-4-15-0.

Umpires: HBC Jordan & CP Kippins

Australian Averages

1964–65 WEST INDIES v AUSTRALIA

AUSTRALIA	M	Inn	NO	Runs	H.S	Avrge	Ct	St	Overs	Mds	Runs	Wkt	Avrge
Booth, BC	5	8	-	234	117	29.25	5	-	18.0	4	48	-	-
Cowper, RM	5	8	-	417	143	52.13	2	-	58.0	12	190	2	95.00
Grout, ATW	5	6	-	83	35	13.83	14	4	-	-	-	-	-
Hawke, NJN	5	7	2	142	45*	28.40	3	-	218.4	52	524	24	21.83
Lawry, WM	5	9	2	368	210	52.57	-	-	-	-	-	-	-
Mayne, LC	3	5	3	26	11*	13.00	2	-	83.0	11	261	9	29.00
McKenzie, GD	5	6	1	50	20	10.00	4	-	256.0	56	677	17	39.82
O'Neill, NC	4	7	1	266	74*	44.33	-	-	82.0	23	230	9	25.56
Philpott, PI	5	6	-	71	22	11.83	3	-	243.3	58	629	18	34.94
Shepherd, BK	2	2	-	42	38	21.00	-	-	3.0	1	6	-	-
Simpson, RB	5	9	1	399	201	49.88	11	-	111.5	27	263	5	52.60
Sincock, DJ	1	1	-	17	17*	-	2	-	33.0	1	143	4	35.75
Thomas, G	5	8	1	178	61	25.43	2	-	-	-	-	-	-

West Indian Averages

1964–65 WEST INDIES v AUSTRALIA

WEST INDIES	M	Inn	NO	Runs	H.S	Avrge	Ct	St	Overs	Mds	Runs	Wkt	Avrge
Allan, DW	1	2	-	18	11	9.00	2	-	-	-	-	-	-
Butcher, BF	5	10	-	405	117	40.50	3	-	-	-	-	-	-
Davis, BA	4	8	-	245	68	30.63	1	-	-	-	-	-	-
Gibbs, LR	5	9	2	19	6	2.71	-	-	278.3	88	556	18	30.89
Griffith, CC	5	9	2	134	54	19.14	1	-	155.0	22	480	15	32.00
Hall, WW	5	9	1	133	37	16.63	3	-	146.0	19	454	16	28.38
Hendriks, JL	4	7	2	102	31*	20.40	7	2	-	-	-	-	-
Hunte, CC	5	10	1	550	89	61.11	-	-	5.0	2	9	-	-
Kanhai, RB	5	10	-	462	129	46.20	3	-	1.0	-	4	-	-
Nurse, SM	4	8	-	291	201	36.38	4	-	-	-	-	-	-
Rodriguez, WV	1	2	-	10	9	5.00	-	-	14.0	2	52	-	-
Sobers, GS	5	10	1	352	69	39.11	8	-	192.3	54	490	12	40.83
Solomon, JS	4	8	2	179	76	29.83	4	-	28.0	3	96	3	32.00
White, AW	2	4	1	71	57*	23.67	1	-	81.5	27	152	3	50.67

Doug Walters a huge new talent

Melbourne, Jan. 5. Two Tests between Australia and England have now been played, both drawn. In the first, it was rain; in the second, slow batting.

But deep in all that dullness has emerged a most exciting prospect for Australian cricket. Nineteen-year-old Doug Walters, a sports goods salesman nicknamed 'Bikki', made 155 in his Test debut at the 'Gabba last month, and followed up with 115 in Melbourne. The only other Australian to score a century in his first two Tests against England was the great Bill Ponsford, way back in 1924–25.

The young batsman from Dungog, NSW is a real threat to England. Walters has told the press that he thinks milking cows on his parents' dairy farm has strengthened his wrists. But he does come from a cricketing family.

Even his mother Colleen played the game, and after milking 115 cows twice a day, the whole family would settle down to a good old game on a makeshift pitch made of ant bed soil.

Australia's newest Test star isn't mentioning all those times he was clean bowled by Mum, but maybe England captain Mike Smith would like a word with her.

In the first Test Walters was on 94 when a small dog ran onto the 'Gabba and held up play for three minutes. It was not a problem for the country boy.

Debutant Doug Walters shows his style as he hooks to the boundary.

Congratulations for England's Colin Cowdrey, who made 104 in the second Test.

Allan takes all 10 against Victoria

Perth, Jan. 26. Queensland fast bowler Peter Allan, who took 10/61 against Victoria at the MCG two weeks ago, is unlikely to play in the fourth Test in Adelaide.

Playing in the WA v Queensland Sheffield Shield game in Perth today, Allan left the field with what was later revealed to be an injured leg.

There has been a cloud over Allan's form ever since his first-innings triumph in Melbourne.

He was taken out of the Queensland attack later in that match after appearing to have difficulty with his run-up from the members' end.

Allan seemed to slip when approaching the crease, so he changed to bowling around the wicket.

Whether that episode is related to Allan's withdrawal today is unclear, but he will be examined by a Perth specialist tomorrow morning.

Simpson, Lawry save series

A flying catch from Ian Chappell ends the first innings of England opener Geoff Boycott.

Cowper marches to monumental 307

Triple-centurion Bob Cowper.

Adelaide, Feb. 2. A record 244-run opening partnership by Bob Simpson and Bill Lawry in the fourth Test has kept alive Australia's hopes of retaining the Ashes.

Australia arrived in Adelaide looking vulnerable after England won the third Test in Sydney to go one game ahead in the series. Sydney was England's first win by an innings in Australia since 1936–37, and was highlighted by a magnificent performance from its top-order batting trio of Geoff Boycott (84), Bob Barber (185), and John Edrich (103).

Unfortunately, Australia was without Bob Simpson in Sydney, who had been forced to withdraw suffering from chicken pox.

Australia also lost the toss in Sydney and had to follow on after making just 221 in its first innings, in reply to England's 488.

Australia could make little headway batting in the final stages on a scarred, uneven pitch that favoured England slow bowlers Fred Titmus and David Allen.

Titmus's bowling figures showed England's growing advantage. He took 0/40 in Australia's first innings, then 5/40 in the second.

Boycott and Edrich's opening partnership of 234 runs in Sydney looked unlikely to be matched for a long time, but now Lawry and Simpson have bettered that remarkable tally on the smooth, well-grassed Adelaide surface.

England batted first in Adelaide and was all out for 241.

Australian fast bowler Graham McKenzie captured most of the wickets (6/48).

Simpson batted in wonderful form, hitting a six and eighteen fours in 545 minutes. He was finally caught by Titmus (b. Jeff Jones) on 225. He and Lawry employed some aggressive run-getting moves to counter England's 'go slow' tactics. They ran 95 singles together.

Simpson, still recovering from chicken pox and also a more recent stomach upset, was hardly fit enough to be making many quick singles. His effort speaks volumes for his leadership.

Melbourne, Feb. 18. Test cricket records fell in the fifth Test yesterday, as Australian batsman Bob Cowper amassed 307 runs.

Along the way Cowper passed Sir Donald Bradman's 299 not out, which was the highest Test score made by any player in Australia.

Cowper had no idea he had broken Bradman's record, until Sir Donald came into the rooms at tea and congratulated him. His marvellous score comes after being recently dropped by the selectors.

It was a steady, stout innings. Cowper was at the crease for 727 minutes, one of the longest stints in cricket history, before he was finally bowled by Barry Knight.

A draw was inevitable after rain affected the second-last day of play, leaving the series at one–all.

How cartoonist Paul Rigby sees some irony on the impact of big-hitting English opener, Bob Barber, on Australia.

Stepping out for his last Test: Wally Grout, Australian wicketkeeper.

Stacky hit hard and often

Keith Stackpole's batting was based on the ethos that the harder you hit the ball, the more likely you were to score runs and the less likely you were to be caught.

For an Australian opening batsman in the 1960s it was a philosophy that was unheard of. There had been West Indian openers who were bent on all-out aggression, and the Englishman Bob Barber had successfully applied the tactic in the 1965–66 tour.

A heavily built and powerful man, he claimed that he was 'as blind as a bat' in one eye and had hammer toes and high arches on both feet.

Born in the tough Melbourne inner-suburb of Collingwood, his father was a footballer and cricketer for the Magpies. The elder Stackpole was a good enough first class batsman to score more than 1000 runs for Victoria including two centuries. From the moment his son held a cricket bat, Keith senior told him to hit the ball hard.

Collingwood prematurely elevated the chubby 16-year-old to the Firsts so he could play alongside his father in the veteran's last game. Nervous at the new level, he was unable to dispatch generous full tosses offered by Ian Johnson, and went out for a duck in the next over.

It is an oft-forgotten fact that, due to the absence of Bill Lawry on Test duties, Stackpole opened for Victoria in his Sheffield Shield debut and top-scored with 83.

He settled in to a batting place lower down the order and filled another void as Victoria's spinner – a role he admitted was 'a not-too-onerous task as our side depended mostly on fast and medium-pace bowlers.'

The then Prime Minister Sir Robert Menzies offered to sponsor tuition of Victoria's most promising spinner by the great Clarrie Grimmett. The story made national headlines, but the week at the master's side only convinced Stackpole of his inadequacies as a spinner.

As a middle-order batsman for Victoria he scored consistently enough to win a Test place late in the series against England in 1965–66. He earned a trip to South Africa the following summer and in the second Test at Cape Town he hammered 134, including a century between lunch and tea.

Keith Stackpole: a fast starter.

But apart from this gem Stackpole's visits to the crease were unproductive. Back in Australia his form continued to be indifferent and he was dumped for the home series against India and the English tour.

With his career at the crossroads he worked hard to reduce his weight over winter. A century for Victoria against the West Indies earned a Test recall, but in the first two Tests the runs still didn't come.

Redpath's sparse returns as an opener prompted Stackpole's rise up the list – a decision suddenly announced by Lawry as the Australian fieldsmen walked off the ground. Stackpole was so nervous that he could hardly buckle up his pads, but composed himself to make a quick-fire 68.

His fast starts gave a new dimension to Australia's batting. He followed the dictum of his mentor at Collingwood, Jack Ryder, who had taught Stackpole that if you had a bat in your hand you were meant to show the bowler who was boss.

From 1969 to 1973 he hit six centuries for Australia. His home crowd loved him and it was one of his greatest delights when he scored a Test century on the MCG in 1973–74 against New Zealand.

In his autobiography he said that he would spend half of a 15-minute net session concentrating on defence.

'People don't realise that for seven and a half minutes of most sessions I practised being a stonewaller.'

'Which was long enough.'

FIRST TEST 1965–66 AUSTRALIA v ENGLAND
Brisbane Cricket Ground, Brisbane. December 10, 11 (no play), 13, 14, 15, 1965.
Toss: Australia. Match Drawn.

AUSTRALIA

WM Lawry c Parks b Higgs	166
IR Redpath b Brown	17
RM Cowper c Barrington b Brown	22
PJP Burge b Brown	0
BC Booth (c) c & b Titmus	16
KD Walters c Parks b Higgs	155
TR Veivers not out	56
NJN Hawke not out	6
PI Philpott	
PJ Allan	
ATW Grout (+)	
Extras (LB 2, NB 3)	5
TOTAL	6 dec 443

FOW 1st Inns: 51 90 90 125 312 431

Bowling: *First Innings*: Brown 21-4-71-3, Higgs 30-6-102-2, Titmus 38-9-99-1, Allen 39-12-108-0, Barber 5-0-42-0, Boycott 4-0-16-0.

ENGLAND

RW Barber c Walters b Hawke	5	c Veivers b Walters	34
G Boycott b Philpott	45	not out	63
JH Edrich c Lawry b Philpott	32	c Veivers b Philpott	37
KF Barrington b Hawke	53	c Booth b Cowper	38
MJK Smith (c) b Allan	16	not out	10
JM Parks (+) c Redpath b Philpott	52		
FJ Titmus st Grout b Philpott	60		
DA Allen c Cowper b Walters	3		
DJ Brown b Philpott	3		
K Higgs lbw Allan	4		
WE Russell not out	0		
Extras (B 4, NB 3)	7	(B 2, LB 2)	4
TOTAL	280		3 for 186

FOW 1st Inns: 5 75 86 115 191 221 232 253 272 280
FOW 2nd Inns: 46 114 168

Bowling: *First Innings*: Allan 21-6-58-2, Hawke 16-7-44-2, Walters 10-1-25-1, Philpott 28.1-3-90-5, Cowper 7-4-7-0, Veivers 11-1-49-0. *Second Innings*: Allan 3-0-25-0, Hawke 10-2-16-0, Walters 5-1-22-1, Philpott 14-1-62-1, Veivers 12-0-37-0, Cowper 6-0-20-1.

Umpires: CJ Egar & LP Rowan

SECOND TEST 1965–66 AUSTRALIA v ENGLAND
Melbourne Cricket Ground, Melbourne. December 30, 31, 1965 January 1, 3, 4, 1966.
Toss: Australia. Match Drawn.

AUSTRALIA

RB Simpson (c) c Edrich b Allen	59		c Barrington b Knight	67
WM Lawry c Cowdrey b Allen	88		c Smith b Barber	78
PJP Burge b Jones	5	(4)	c Edrich b Boycott	120
RM Cowper c Titmus b Jones	99	(3)	lbw Jones	5
BC Booth lbw Jones	23		b Allen	10
KD Walters c Parks b Knight	22		c & b Barrington	115
TR Veivers run out	19		st Parks b Boycott	3
PI Philpott b Knight	10		b Knight	2
ATW Grout (+) c Barber b Knight	11		c Allen b Barrington	16
GD McKenzie not out	12		run out	2
AN Connolly c Parks b Knight	0		not out	0
Extras (B 2, LB 7, NB 1)	10		(B 1, LB 3, W 1, NB 3)	8
TOTAL	358			426

FOW 1st Inns: 93 109 203 262 297 318 330 342 352 358
FOW 2nd Inns: 120 141 163 176 374 382 385 417 426 426

Bowling: *First Innings*: Jones 24-4-92-3, Knight 26.5-2-84-4, Titmus 31-7-93-0, Allen 20-4-55-2, Barber 6-1-24-0. *Second Innings*: Jones 20-1-92-1, Knight 21-4-61-2, Titmus 22-6-43-0, Allen 18-3-48-1, Barber 17-0-87-1, Barrington 7.4-0-47-2, Boycott 9-0-32-1, Smith 2-0-8-0.

ENGLAND

G Boycott c McKenzie b Walters	51	not out	5
RW Barber c Grout b McKenzie	48	not out	0
JH Edrich c & b Veivers	109		
KF Barrington c Burge b Veivers	63		
MC Cowdrey c Connolly b Cowper	104		
MJK Smith (c) c Grout b McKenzie	41		
JM Parks (+) c Cowper b McKenzie	71		
BR Knight c Simpson b McKenzie	1		
FJ Titmus not out	56		
DA Allen c Grout b Connolly	2		
IJ Jones b McKenzie	1		
Extras (B 4, LB 5, W 2)	11		0
TOTAL	558		0 for 5

FOW 1st Inns: 98 110 228 333 409 443 447 540 551 558
FOW 2nd Inns:

Bowling: *First Innings*: McKenzie 35.5-3-134-5, Connolly 37-5-125-1, Philpott 30-2-133-0, Walters 10-2-32-1, Simpson 16-4-61-0, Veivers 12-3-46-2, Cowper 3-0-16-1. *Second Innings*: Connolly 1-0-3-0, McKenzie 1-0-2-0.

Umpires: CJ Egar & WJ Smyth

THIRD TEST 1965–66 AUSTRALIA v ENGLAND
Sydney Cricket Ground, Sydney. January 7, 8, 10, 11, 1966.
Toss: England. England won by an innings & 93 runs.

ENGLAND
G Boycott c & b Philpott	.84	
RW Barber b Hawke	.185	
JH Edrich c & b Philpott	.103	
KF Barrington c McKenzie b Hawke	.1	
MC Cowdrey c Grout b Hawke	.6	
MJK Smith (c) c Grout b Hawke	.6	
DJ Brown c Grout b Hawke	.1	
JM Parks (+) c Grout b Hawke	.13	
FJ Titmus c Grout b Walters	.14	
DA Allen not out	.50	
IJ Jones b Hawke	.16	
Extras (B 3, LB 8, W 2, NB 2)	.15	
TOTAL	.488	

FOW 1st Inns: 234 303 309 309 317 328 358 395 433 488

Bowling: *First Innings*: McKenzie 25-2-113-0, Hawke 33.7-6-105-7, Walters 10-1-38-1, Philpott 28-3-86-2, Sincock 20-1-98-0, Cowper 6-1-33-0.

AUSTRALIA
WM Lawry c Parks b Jones	.0	c Cowdrey b Brown	.33
G Thomas c Titmus b Brown	.51	c Cowdrey b Titmus	.25
RM Cowper st Parks b Allen	.60	c Boycott b Titmus	.0
PJP Burge c Parks b Brown	.6	run out	.1
BC Booth (c) c Cowdrey b Jones	.8	b Allen	.27
DJ Sincock c Parks b Brown	.29 (7)	b Smith b Allen	.27
KD Walters st Parks b Allen	.23 (6)	not out	.35
NJN Hawke c Barber b Brown	.0 (9)	c Smith b Titmus	.2
ATW Grout (+) b Brown	.0 (10)	c Smith b Allen	.3
GD McKenzie c Cowdrey b Barber	.24 (11)	c Barber b Titmus	.12
PI Philpott not out	.5 (8)	lbw Allen	.5
Extras (B 7, LB 8)	.15	(B 3, LB 1)	.4
TOTAL	.221		.174

FOW 1st Inns: 0 81 91 105 155 174 174 174 203 221
FOW 2nd Inns: 46 50 51 86 86 119 131 135 140 174

Bowling: *First Innings*: Jones 20-6-51-2, Brown 17-1-63-5, Boycott 3-1-8-0, Titmus 23-8-40-0, Barber 2.1-1-2-1, Allen 19-5-42-3. *Second Innings*: Jones 7-0-35-0, Brown 11-2-32-1, Titmus 17.3-4-40-4, Allen 20-8-47-4, Barber 5-0-16-0.

Umpires: CJ Egar & LP Rowan

FIFTH TEST 1965–66 AUSTRALIA v ENGLAND
Melbourne Cricket Ground, Melbourne. February 11, 12, 14, 15 (no play), 16, 1966.
Toss: England. Match Drawn.

ENGLAND
G Boycott c Stackpole b McKenzie	.17	lbw McKenzie	.1
RW Barber run out	.17	b McKenzie	.20
JH Edrich c McKenzie b Walters	.85	b McKenzie	.3
KF Barrington c Grout b Walters	.115	not out	.32
MC Cowdrey c Grout b Walters	.79	not out	.11
MJK Smith (c) c Grout b Walters	.0		
JM Parks (+) run out	.89		
FJ Titmus not out	.42		
BR Knight c Grout b Hawke	.13		
DJ Brown c & b Chappell	.12		
IJ Jones not out	.4		
Extras (B 9, LB 2, NB 1)	.12	(LB 2)	.2
TOTAL	.9 dec 485		.3 for 69

FOW 1st Inns: 36 41 219 254 254 392 419 449 474
FOW 2nd Inns: 6 21 34

Bowling: *First Innings*: McKenzie 26-5-100-1, Hawke 35-5-109-1, Walters 19-3-53-4, Simpson 5-1-20-0, Stackpole 10-2-43-0, Veivers 15-3-78-0, Chappell 17-4-70-1. *Second Innings*: McKenzie 6-2-17-3, Hawke 4-1-22-0, Walters 2-0-16-0, Stackpole 3-0-10-0, Chappell 2-0-2-0.

AUSTRALIA
WM Lawry c Edrich b Jones	.108
RB Simpson (c) b Brown	.4
G Thomas c Titmus b Jones	.19
RM Cowper b Knight	.307
KD Walters c & b Barber	.60
IM Chappell c Parks b Jones	.19
KR Stackpole b Knight	.9
TR Veivers b Titmus	.4
NJN Hawke not out	.0
GD McKenzie	
ATW Grout (+)	
Extras (B 6, LB 5, NB 2)	.13
TOTAL	.8 dec 543

FOW 1st Inns: 15 36 248 420 481 532 543 543

Bowling: *First Innings*: Brown 31-3-134-1, Jones 29-1-145-3, Knight 36.2-4-105-2, Titmus 42-12-86-1, Barber 16-0-60-1.

Umpires: CJ Egar & LP Rowan

FOURTH TEST 1965–66 AUSTRALIA v ENGLAND
Adelaide Oval, Adelaide. January 28, 29, 31, February 1, 1966.
Toss: England. Australia won by an innings & 9 runs.

ENGLAND
G Boycott c Chappell b Hawke	.22	lbw McKenzie	.12
RW Barber c Grout b McKenzie	.0	c Grout b Hawke	.19
JH Edrich c Simpson b McKenzie	.5	c Simpson b Hawke	.1
KF Barrington lbw Walters	.60	c Chappell b Hawke	.102
MC Cowdrey run out	.38	c Grout b Stackpole	.35
MJK Smith (c) b Veivers	.29	c McKenzie b Stackpole	.5
JM Parks (+) c Stackpole b McKenzie	.49	run out	.16
FJ Titmus lbw McKenzie	.33	c Grout b Hawke	.53
DA Allen c Simpson b McKenzie	.2	not out	.0
DJ Brown c Thomas b McKenzie	.1	c & b Hawke	.0
IJ Jones not out	.0	c Lawry b Veivers	.8
Extras (LB 2)	.2	(LB 2, NB 8)	.10
TOTAL	.241		.266

FOW 1st Inns: 7 25 33 105 150 178 210 212 222 241
FOW 2nd Inns: 23 31 32 114 123 163 244 253 257 266

Bowling: *First Innings*: McKenzie 21.7-4-48-6, Hawke 23-2-69-1, Walters 14-0-50-1, Stackpole 5-0-30-0, Chappell 4-1-18-0, Veivers 13-3-24-1. *Second Innings*: McKenzie 18-4-53-1, Hawke 21-6-54-5, Walters 9-0-47-0, Chappell 22-4-53-0, Stackpole 14-3-33-2, Veivers 3.7-0-16-1.

AUSTRALIA
RB Simpson (c) c Titmus b Jones	.225
WM Lawry b Titmus	.119
G Thomas b Jones	.52
TR Veivers c Parks b Jones	.1
PJP Burge c Parks b Jones	.27
KD Walters c Parks b Brown	.0
IM Chappell c Edrich b Jones	.17
KR Stackpole c Parks b Jones	.43
NJN Hawke not out	.20
ATW Grout (+) b Brown	.4
GD McKenzie lbw Titmus	.1
Extras (B 4, LB 3)	.7
TOTAL	.516

FOW 1st Inns: 244 331 333 379 383 415 480 501 506 516

Bowling: *First Innings*: Jones 29-3-118-6, Brown 28-4-109-1, Boycott 7-3-33-0, Titmus 37-6-116-3, Allen 21-1-103-0, Barber 4-0-30-0.

Umpires: CJ Egar & LP Rowan

Australian Averages

1965–66 AUSTRALIA v ENGLAND

AUSTRALIA	M	Inn	NO	Runs	H.S	Avrge	Ct	St	Overs	Mds	Runs	Wkt	Avrge
Allan, PJ	1	-	-	-	-	-	-	-	24.0	6	83	2	41.50
Booth, BC	3	5	-	84	27	16.80	1	-	-	-	-	-	-
Burge, PJP	4	6	-	159	120	26.50	1	-	-	-	-	-	-
Chappell, IM	2	2	-	36	19	18.00	3	-	45.0	9	143	1	143.00
Connolly, AN	1	2	1	0	0*	0.00	1	-	38.0	5	128	1	128.00
Cowper, RM	4	6	-	493	307	82.17	2	-	22.0	5	76	2	38.00
Grout, ATW	5	5	-	34	16	6.80	15	1	-	-	-	-	-
Hawke, NJN	4	5	3	28	20*	14.00	1	-	142.7	29	419	16	26.19
Lawry, WM	5	7	-	592	166	84.57	2	-	-	-	-	-	-
McKenzie, GD	4	5	1	51	24	12.75	4	-	133.4	20	467	16	29.19
Philpott, PI	3	4	1	22	10	7.33	2	-	100.1	9	371	8	46.38
Redpath, IR	1	1	-	17	17	17.00	1	-	-	-	-	-	-
Simpson, RB	3	4	-	355	225	88.75	4	-	21.0	5	81	-	-
Sincock, DJ	1	2	-	56	29	28.00	-	-	20.0	1	98	-	-
Stackpole, KR	2	2	-	52	43	26.00	4	-	32.0	5	116	2	58.00
Thomas, G	3	4	-	147	52	36.75	1	-	-	-	-	-	-
Veivers, TR	4	5	1	83	56*	20.75	3	-	66.7	10	250	4	62.50
Walters, KD	5	7	-	410	155	68.33	1	-	79.0	8	283	9	31.44

English Averages

1965–66 AUSTRALIA v ENGLAND

ENGLAND	M	Inn	NO	Runs	H.S	Avrge	Ct	St	Overs	Mds	Runs	Wkt	Avrge
Allen, DA	4	5	2	62	50*	20.67	1	-	137.0	33	403	9	44.78
Barber, RW	5	9	1	328	185	41.00	4	-	55.1	2	261	3	87.00
Barrington, KF	5	8	1	464	115	66.29	3	-	7.4	-	47	2	23.50
Boycott, G	5	9	2	300	84	42.86	1	-	23.0	4	89	2	44.50
Brown, DJ	4	5	-	17	12	3.40	1	-	108.0	14	409	11	37.18
Cowdrey, MC	4	6	1	267	104	53.40	5	-	-	-	-	-	-
Edrich, JH	5	8	-	375	109	46.88	4	-	-	-	-	-	-
Higgs, K	1	1	-	4	4	4.00	-	-	30.0	6	102	2	51.00
Jones, IJ	4	5	2	29	16	9.67	-	-	129.0	15	533	15	35.53
Knight, BR	2	2	-	14	13	7.00	-	-	83.7	10	250	8	31.25
Parks, JM	5	6	-	290	89	48.33	12	3	-	-	-	-	-
Russell, WE	1	1	1	0	0*	-	-	-	-	-	-	-	-
Smith, MJK	5	7	1	107	41	17.83	4	-	2.0	-	8	-	-
Titmus, FJ	5	6	2	258	60	64.50	5	-	210.3	52	517	9	57.44

Lindsay's match, Sth Africans show strength

First-Test century for South African wicketkeeper, Denis Lindsay.

Walters a 'Nasho'

Johannesburg, Dec. 22. Australia begins the first Test against South Africa tomorrow without Peter Burge and Doug Walters. Both have declared themselves unavailable.

Walters was told last summer to expect an Army call for a medical check 'very soon'.

It came soon enough. Walters was fit, of course, and as a result he was signed up for two years of compulsory national service.

Some would say he would have been much fitter to play cricket for his country, but that's the law. Walters has taken it well.

Loss to Transvaal

Johannesburg, Dec. 18. Australia's hopes of defeating South Africa are looking grim following mixed results in lead up games.

The most ominous result, a 76-run defeat by Transvaal,was the first time since 1902 that Australia has been beaten on South African soil. Transvaal captain Ali Bacher was in scintillating form, scoring 235 runs in the second innings.

Strong wins over Western Province and Eastern Province followed that upset, but then Australia lost by 190 runs against a South African eleven.

Johannesburg, Dec. 29. South Africa has won the first Test against Australia after an outstanding performance by Denis Lindsay averted almost certain defeat.

The match began badly for South Africa, who slumped to 5/41 after only 90 minutes of play.

Lindsay, the South African wicketkeeper, came in at number seven and saved the day with a resolute 69 runs, the best South African score of the innings, which ended at 199.

Australia made 325 in reply, but Lindsay was once again in great form, this time behind the stumps, where he took six catches.

There was now no doubt that Lindsay had his 'eye in'. He was hot, and Australia's hopes of victo-ry collapsed in the second innings when Lindsay hit five sixes and 25 fours in a magnificent 182 runs, the highest score ever made on the Wanderers' ground. It was also his maiden Test century.

Lindsay was aided by Graeme Pollock, who hit out for a cool 90 runs before being bowled by Bob Cowper.

South Africa's second innings tally of 620 runs is its highest score in Test cricket.

Any chances Australia had of saving the match on the final day ended when South Africa claimed Australia's first four wickets in the opening 25 minutes.

The biggest blow was losing captain Bob Simpson, run out off the second ball of the day (48).

South Africa's 35-year-old veteran bowler, Trevor Goddard, did most of the damage, taking 6/53 from 32.5 overs. He dismissed Bob Cowper (1), Keith Stackpole (9), Tom Veivers (55), Brian Taber (7), Garth McKenzie (34), and Neil Hawke (13).

Unfortunately, Hawke was injured earlier in the Test, when he broke down during a bowling spell with a suspected groin injury.

McKenzie's 5/46 in Australia's first innings gives Australian bowlers some hope for the second Test, provided Lindsay is not still on the boil, of course.

Interest in South Africa has never been higher, the first Test breaking all records with an aggregate attendance of 110,676.

QUICK SINGLES

Christmas cheer. Australian team manager Bill Jacobs says allegations that 'a wild champagne Christmas party' was responsible for Australia's loss in the first Test are a 'pack of lies'. The Australian cricketers' private function at the Wanderer's Club was 'Christmas dinner, the type which would be taking place all over the world,' Jacobs explained. 'We thoroughly enjoyed ourselves,' he added.

First at home. South Africa's win in the first Test was its first home victory against Australia in 22 attempts over the 64 years since series began.

Sub-standard. The Australian team in Durban for the third Test had to change in the Kingsmead dressing rooms then drive five miles to a school ground for a centre-wicket workout. The Kingsmead practice wickets were 'too dangerous'.

Black and white. A storm is brewing in South Africa over the possibility of England playing Basil D'Oliveira, a South-African-born naturalised Briton, in its forthcoming tour of South Africa. Mr P. M. Le Roux, Minister of the Interior, says the MCC must cancel the tour if the coloured D'Oliveira is selected: 'Our policy is clear. We will not allow mixed teams to compete against our white teams.'

Pollock warns Lawry. The bouncer from South African fast bowler Peter Pollock that sent Bill Lawry to hospital in the third Test came after Lawry had protested twice about Pollock following through down the pitch. On both occasions Pollock was warned by the umpires.

Support for rumours. Stories of rowdy, unbecoming behaviour by the Australian tourists continued with the allegation that an Australian Test player walked into a club gathering wearing only an athletic support. The team has closed ranks on the matter and tight-lipped 'No comments' are the order of the day.

Lindsay's record hauls. In the fourth Test, South Africa's Denis Lindsay made his third century of the series and passed 585 runs, smashing the previous highest Test series aggregate by a wicketkeeper, set in 1963–64 by India's Budhi Kunderan (526). Lindsay finished the series with 606 runs and 24 catches.

Pollock's ton. Ian Redpath's fifth Test dismissal by Peter Pollock gave the South African speedster his 100th Test wicket. Pollock made his Test debut at Kingsmead against New Zealand in 1961–62, achieving match figures of 9/99.

Shield debuts. Victoria has won their fourth Sheffield Shield since the War, a highlight being a magnificent 202 runs against South Australia by Paul Sheahan on debut. Greg Chappell made 53 on debut for South Australia.

New Board head

Melbourne, Sep. 8. Victorian Bob Parish was yesterday elected chairman of the Australian Board of Control

He is likely to move quickly to update cricket administration, which has not been known for its readiness to accept change.

Parish comes to the post with wide experience, both as a cricketer and as an administrator.

From 1935–36 he played in 14 seasons for Prahran, capturing 195 wickets. Best known as a medium-paced bowler, he also made a fine century against NTCA in 1938.

Parish became Prahran delegate to the VCA in 1950, and was elected club president at Prahran in 1954.

He has been Victorian delegate to the ACB since 1957, and managed the Australian team that toured the West Indies in 1965.

Aussie grip slipping

On top: Bob Simpson drives past Trevor Goddard in the second Test.

Durban, Jan. 26. Australian blood continued to drip heavily on the pitch at Kingsmead Ground yesterday, when the tourists lost the third Test by 8 wickets.

The pattern was set in the first innings as Australian batsman Bill Lawry tried to hook one of Peter Pollock's bouncers, but missed.

The ball hit Lawry on the top of his head, splitting his scalp. Bleeding profusely, he was taken to hospital, later returning to the crease with ten stitches and a head covered in bandages.

Lawry is nothing if not tough, and stayed on for another 146 minutes, making 44 runs to be top-scorer in a dismal Australian innings of 147. Australia then fought hard when forced to follow on, trailing by 153 runs.

That total was exactly the score made by Bob Simpson in the second Test at Cape Town, which Australia won by six wickets despite a sizzling 209 runs from Graeme Pollock.

Simpson couldn't repeat his Cape Town triumph, but stood firm for a determined 94 runs before being dismissed lbw to Pat Trimborn.

Equally grim, Ian Redpath batted for 369 minutes to score a valiant 80, but after his wicket fell Australia collapsed to be all out for 334. South African 'keeper Denis Lindsay is still in magnificent form, making 137 runs and claiming six catches.

History was not on the side of Australia when Simpson elected to field – the first time a captain had done so at Durban since 1930–31.

Simpson v Umpire Kidson

Port Elizabeth, Feb. 23. Australian players are angry at newspaper criticism that the team has disintegrated under Bob Simpson's leadership, which has been characterised by several personal confrontations with the South Africans, and one umpire in particular.

As Australia goes into the fifth Test 2–1 down in the series, Simpson declares: 'We are a very happy team, no matter what the outcome.'

He argues that South Africa is much stronger than had been anticipated, and he denies that there is division in the Australian camp.

Former Test opening batsman, Dick Whitington, has been an outspoken critic of Simpson's style.

Writing in the Melbourne *Sun* a few weeks ago, Whitington attacked Simpson's sportsmanship after Simpson stood his ground and glared when given out by Umpire Hayward Kidson in the first innings of the third Test at Durban.

It was the third time he had been given out by Kidson in the series, and afterwards the Australians objected to Kidson's appointment for the two remaining Tests.

In a fiery tour for the Australian captain, he has criticised South African crowds for being 'unsporting', and had an altercation with a photographer in Johannesburg who was trying to snap 'Garth' McKenzie after the first Test.

Perhaps Simpson has been feeling the pressure on this tour, but allegations of the team being split into factions over his leadership seem far from true. Still, winning more matches could only help.

Tables turned: Bob Simpson (18) is caught by Trevor Goddard.

One day match

Johannesburg, March 30. Australia returns home from South Africa having lost the series 3–1.

Australia's defeat by seven wickets in the fifth Test was followed by yet another disappointment, a loss by three wickets to South Africa in a 60-overs match at Johannesburg.

After batting first, Australia reached 8/323 with Bill Lawry contributing 91, but once again it was South Africa's Graeme Pollock (132) who proved Australia's undoing. South Africa's final score was 7/327.

The crowd of over 11,000 surpassed expectations and suggests there may be a future for limited-over cricket, which was trialled in England in 1963.

One of the livelier moments on the South African tour, when two teams went out to field.

McKenzie the lone force

Port Elizabeth, March 1. Former Australian Test captain Richie Benaud has declared that the Australian team to tour South Africa made 'history.'

They're the 'worst ever', Benaud says, because they are the only Australian touring team to lose three Tests in a five-match series.

Benaud feels that Graham McKenzie's bowling performances are among the few highlights for Australia, the others being Bob Simpson's consistent batting and Brian Taber's fine catching.

McKenzie's efforts included 5/46 in the first Test, 5/65 in the second, and 5/65 in the fifth.

Simpson admits that Australia did not deserve to win the series. 'We let too many opportunities go,' he said. But it was also a very good South African side, with outstanding batting from Denis Lindsay and Graeme Pollock, and fierce fast bowling by Peter Pollock.

South African captain Peter van der Merwe said South Africa had been trying for a long time to win a series against Australia and now that the moment has finally arrived, 'we are very proud and also a little humble.' After the fifth Test Simpson handed his cap to

Graham 'Garth' McKenzie winds up.

Peter van der Merwe.

'Cricket needs to be loved,' Simpson said, and maybe the South Africans loved it more. Their officials and players have vigorously promoted the game in recent years, especially among schoolboys.

Simpson's safari, which arrived in South Africa with great expectations, failed in the end to capture the prize.

New blood rises in New Zealand

Wellington, Feb. 28. Australia's 'second eleven', which has played ten matches in New Zealand under the captaincy of Les Favell, returns home with two wins, two losses and six draws.

New Zealand won the series of four unofficial 'Tests,' with a 159-run win in New Plymouth. The three other matches were draws.

'We were out-batted, out-bowled and out-fielded,' said Favell.

But mainly, Australia was out-bowled. New Zealand bowlers Victor Pollard and Bryan Yuile took 38 wickets between them.

For Australia, the triumph of the tour has been the performance of a number of new players who grabbed the chance to represent their country, and have now staked their claim.

The confident, elegant style of batsman Paul Sheahan, who made 135 in one innings, suggests he has a brilliant future.

Young Victorian slow bowler Bob Bitmead took 6/11 in the opening match against Otago in Dunedin, but had to return to Australia due to his father's death.

Bitmead showed great promise, as did the NSW right-arm spinner John Gleeson, who proved he

Barry Jarman: 'keeper in New Zealand.

could deliver an amazing variety of spin.

The New Zealand batsmen found Gleeson's best deliveries almost impossible to pick.

Geoff Davies was a champion schoolboy cricketer in NSW, and his effort in New Zealand proved he has the ability to succeed at the highest level. He is a capable all-rounder, with a keen eye and firm hand in slips.

FIRST TEST 1966–67 SOUTH AFRICA v AUSTRALIA
New Wanderers Stadium, Johannesburg. December 23, 24, 26, 27, 28, 1966.
Toss: South Africa. South Africa won by 233 runs.

SOUTH AFRICA

Batsman	1st	2nd
TL Goddard c Taber b Hawke	5	c Simpson b Hawke 13
EJ Barlow c Taber b McKenzie	13	c Taber b Renneberg 50
A Bacher c Cowper b McKenzie	5	run out 63
RG Pollock c McKenzie b Renneberg	5	b Cowper 90
KC Bland lbw McKenzie	0	c Simpson b Chappell 32
HR Lance hit wicket b McKenzie	44	c Simpson b McKenzie 70
DT Lindsay (+) c Taber b Renneberg	69	c Chappell b Stackpole 182
PL Van der Merwe (c) c Taber b Simpson	19	c Chappell b Simpson 76
R Dumbrill c Chappell b Simpson	19	c Taber b Chappell 29
PM Pollock c Taber b McKenzie	6	st Taber b Simpson 2
AH McKinnon not out	0	not out 0
Extras (B 11, W 3)	14	(B 7, LB 5, W 1) 13
TOTAL	199	620

FOW 1st Inns: 14 31 31 35 41 151 156 190 199 199
FOW 2nd Inns: 29 87 178 228 268 349 570 614 620 620

Bowling: *First Innings*: McKenzie 21.5-6-46-5, Hawke 8-1-25-1, Renneberg 16-3-54-2, Chappell 2-0-16-0, Veivers 9-1-13-0, Cowper 6-0-21-0, Simpson 4-1-10-2. *Second Innings*: McKenzie 39-4-118-1, Renneberg 32-8-96-1, Hawke 14.2-1-46-1, Veivers 18-3-59-0, Simpson 16.1-3-66-2, Chappell 21-3-91-2, Cowper 16-2-56-1, Stackpole 21-6-75-1.

AUSTRALIA

Batsman	1st	2nd
RB Simpson (c) c Goddard b PM Pollock	65	run out 48
WM Lawry c Lindsay b Goddard	98	b McKinnon 27
IR Redpath c Lindsay b Barlow	41	c Van der Merwe b Barlow 21
RM Cowper c Lindsay b Barlow	0	c Lindsay b Goddard 1
KR Stackpole c Lindsay b Barlow	0	b Goddard 9
IM Chappell c Lindsay b Goddard	37	c Lindsay b Dumbrill 34
TR Veivers b Lance	18	b Goddard 55
HB Taber (+) c Lindsay b McKinnon	13	b Goddard 7
GD McKenzie run out	16	c (S)MJ Procter b Goddard 34
NJN Hawke not out	18	c (S)MJ Procter b Goddard 13
DA Renneberg c Goddard b McKinnon	9	not out 2
Extras (LB 5, W 2, NB 3)	10	(LB 6, W 2, NB 2) 10
TOTAL	325	261

FOW 1st Inns: 118 204 207 207 218 267 267 294 299 325
FOW 2nd Inns: 62 97 98 110 112 183 210 212 248 261

Bowling: *First Innings*: Pollock 25-6-74-1, Dumbrill 18-3-55-0, Goddard 26-11-39-2, Lance 17-6-35-1, McKinnon 27.2-9-73-2, Barlow 17-3-39-3. *Second Innings*: Pollock 18-3-33-0, Dumbrill 16-6-43-1, Barlow 15-1-47-1, Goddard 32.5-14-53-6, McKinnon 30-14-64-1, Pollock 3-1-5-0, Lance 3-0-6-0.

Umpires: LM Baxter & HC Kidson

SECOND TEST 1966–67 SOUTH AFRICA v AUSTRALIA
Newlands, Cape Town. December 31, 1966 January 2, 3, 4, 5, 1967.
Toss: Australia. Australia won by 6 wkts.

AUSTRALIA

Batsman	1st	2nd
RB Simpson (c) c Lance b Barlow	153	c Goddard b PM Pollock 18
WM Lawry lbw PM Pollock	10	c PM Pollock b Goddard 39
IR Redpath lbw McKinnon	54	not out 69
RM Cowper c Van der Merwe b Lance	36	c Lindsay b Goddard 4
IM Chappell c Lindsay b Goddard	49	b McKinnon 7
TR Veivers lbw PM Pollock	30	not out 35
KR Stackpole c Lindsay b Barlow	134	
GD Watson c Lance b Barlow	50	
GD McKenzie c & b Barlow	11	
HB Taber (+) not out	2	
DA Renneberg b Barlow	2	
Extras (B 2, LB 7, W 2)	11	(LB 5, NB 3) 8
TOTAL	542	4 dec 180

FOW 1st Inns: 21 138 216 310 316 368 496 537 438 542
FOW 2nd Inns: 49 81 98 119

Bowling: *First Innings*: PM Pollock 22-4-84-2, Dumbrill 11-2-36-0, Goddard 42-15-79-1, Barlow 33.3-9-85-5, Pithey 22-5-59-0, McKinnon 38-16-93-1, Lance 20-1-95-1. *Second Innings*: PM Pollock 12-2-42-1, Barlow 2-1-1-0, Goddard 29.1-10-67-2, McKinnon 22-5-62-1.

SOUTH AFRICA

Batsman	1st	2nd
TL Goddard c Stackpole b McKenzie	7	lbw Simpson 37
EJ Barlow c Redpath b McKenzie	19	run out 17
A Bacher b McKenzie	0	c Simpson b McKenzie 4
RG Pollock c Taber b Simpson	209	b Simpson 4
HR Lance c Simpson b Chappell	2	run out 53
DT Lindsay (+) c & b Renneberg	5	c Simpson b Cowper 81
PL Van der Merwe (c) c Cowper b Simpson	50	lbw Chappell 18
DB Pithey c Taber b McKenzie	4	c Redpath b Renneberg 55
R Dumbrill c Chappell b McKenzie	6 (10)	b McKenzie 1
PM Pollock c Stackpole b Veivers	41 (9)	not out 75
AH McKinnon not out	6	b McKenzie 8
Extras (LB 4)	4	(B 5, LB 9) 14
TOTAL	353	367

FOW 1st Inns: 12 12 41 66 85 197 242 258 343 353
FOW 2nd Inns: 45 60 60 64 183 211 245 331 345 367

Bowling: *First Innings*: McKenzie 33-10-65-5, Renneberg 18-6-51-1, Watson 11-2-27-0, Chappell 13-4-51-1, Simpson 24-9-59-2, Veivers 8.1-2-32-1, Cowper 6-0-28-0, Stackpole 14-2-36-0. *Second Innings*: McKenzie 39.3-11-67-3, Renneberg 24-2-63-1, Simpson 39-12-99-2, Chappell 39-17-71-1, Veivers 7-2-21-0, Cowper 10-2-21-1, Stackpole 8-4-11-0.

Umpires: G Goldman & HC Kidson

THIRD TEST 1966–67 SOUTH AFRICA v AUSTRALIA
Kingsmead, Durban. January 20, 21, 23, 24, 25, 1967.
Toss: Australia. South Africa won by 8 wkts.

SOUTH AFRICA
EJ Barlow c & b McKenzie	0	c Redpath b McKenzie	22
TL Goddard b Cowper	19	c Taber b Cowper	33
A Bacher c Taber b McKenzie	47	not out	60
RG Pollock c Redpath b Cowper	2	not out	67
HR Lance c Taber b Cowper	13		
DT Lindsay (+) c Chappell b Hawke	137		
MJ Procter b Renneberg	1		
PL Van der Merwe (c) run out	42		
DB Pithey b Hawke	15		
PM Pollock not out	12		
PHJ Trimborn run out	..0		
Extras (B 3, LB 2, NB 5)	10	(LB 2, NB 1)	3
TOTAL	300		2 for 185

FOW 1st Inns: 0 53 57 83 90 94 197 286 287 300
FOW 2nd Inns: 52 58

Bowling: *First Innings*: McKenzie 31-7-93-2, Hawke 18-1-69-2, Renneberg 21-4-58-1, Cowper 37-14-57-3, Redpath 4-0-13-0. *Second Innings*: McKenzie 20-7-36-1, Renneberg 11-1-27-0, Hawke 14-6-22-0, Cowper 17-9-29-1, Simpson 4-0-21-0, Chappell 7-0-39-0, Stackpole 2-0-8-0.

AUSTRALIA
RB Simpson (c) c Lindsay b Procter	6	lbw Trimborn	94
WM Lawry c Lindsay b Barlow	44	c Lindsay b Lance	34
IR Redpath c Barlow b Goddard	7	c Barlow b PM Pollock	80
RM Cowper c Goddard b Trimborn	19	c Lindsay b Lance	40
KR Stackpole c Lindsay b Barlow	24 (7)	c RG Pollock b PM Pollock	35
TR Veivers b Goddard	6	c Lindsay b Procter	0
IM Chappell run out	..5 (5)	c RG Pollock b Procter	25
GD McKenzie lbw Procter	17	b Procter	8
HB Taber (+) c Bacher b Barlow	4 (10)	c Trimborn b Procter	0
NJN Hawke not out	9 (9)	b Goddard	5
DA Renneberg b Procter	0	not out	0
Extras (B 1, NB 5)	6	(B 4, LB 4, NB 5)	13
TOTAL	147		334

FOW 1st Inns: 14 37 45 74 88 96 132 137 137 147
FOW 2nd Inns: 94 159 224 266 266 317 320 334 334 334

Bowling: *First Innings*: Pollock 13-4-35-0, Procter 14-4-27-3, Trimborn 14-3-35-1, Goddard 17-6-26-2, Barlow 11-4-18-3. *Second Innings*: Pollock 19-5-58-2, Procter 29.1-7-71-4, Barlow 14-5-28-0, Trimborn 28-9-47-1, Pithey 28-12-55-0, Goddard 27-15-23-1, Lance 15-4-39-2.

Umpires: JG Draper & HC Kidson

FIFTH TEST 1966–67 SOUTH AFRICA v AUSTRALIA
St George's Park, Port Elizabeth. February 24, 25, 27, 28, 1967.
Toss: South Africa. South Africa won by 7 wkts.

AUSTRALIA
RB Simpson (c) c Lindsay b PM Pollock	12	lbw Goddard	35
WM Lawry run out	0	c Bacher b Barlow	25
IM Chappell c Bacher b Procter	11	lbw Goddard	15
IR Redpath c Du Preez b PM Pollock	26	lbw PM Pollock	28
RM Cowper c Lindsay b Trimborn	60	b Barlow	54
KR Stackpole c RG Pollock b Goddard	24	c Lindsay b Trimborn	19
JW Martin lbw Goddard	0	c Lindsay b Goddard	20
GD Watson c Barlow b Goddard	0	b PM Pollock	9
GD McKenzie c Trimborn b Du Preez	14	c RG Pollock b Trimborn	29
HB Taber (+) c Bacher b Procter	20	c Goddard b Trimborn	30
DA Renneberg not out	0	not out	0
Extras (W 1, NB 5)	6	(LB 2, W 1, NB 11)	14
TOTAL	173		278

FOW 1st Inns: 4 17 27 89 137 137 137 137 173 173
FOW 2nd Inns: 50 74 79 144 166 207 207 229 268 278

Bowling: *First Innings*: PM Pollock 17-2-57-2, Procter 15.1-3-36-2, Trimborn 18-4-37-1, Goddard 10-3-13-3, Barlow 4-2-9-0, Lance 8-4-15-0, Du Preez 2-2-0-1. *Second Innings*: PM Pollock 15-0-42-2, Procter 16-3-59-0, Goddard 36-12-63-3, Barlow 15-3-52-2, Du Preez 8-4-29-0, Trimborn 10.1-4-12-3, Lance 5-2-7-0.

SOUTH AFRICA
TL Goddard c Taber b McKenzie	74	c Taber b McKenzie	59
EJ Barlow lbw McKenzie	46	c Chappell b McKenzie	15
A Bacher c Taber b McKenzie	3	c Martin b Chappell	40
RG Pollock b Cowper	105	not out	33
HR Lance c Renneberg b Simpson	21	not out	28
DT Lindsay (+) c Redpath b McKenzie	1		
MJ Procter hit wicket b McKenzie	0		
PL Van der Merwe (c) lbw Watson	8		
PM Pollock c Lawry b Cowper	13		
JH Du Preez lbw Cowper	0		
PHJ Trimborn not out	0		
Extras (B 1, LB 3, W 1)	5	(LB 1, W 2, NB 1)	4
TOTAL	276		3 for 179

FOW 1st Inns: 112 124 125 175 201 201 226 271 271 276
FOW 2nd Inns: 28 109 118

Bowling: *First Innings*: McKenzie 35-13-65-5, Renneberg 19-6-44-0, Watson 18-3-58-1, Cowper 19.3-9-27-3, Martin 17-1-64-0, Simpson 8-2-13-1. *Second Innings*: McKenzie 17-5-38-2, Renneberg 12-1-38-0, Watson 3-0-10-0, Cowper 12-4-26-0, Martin 5-0-25-0, Simpson 5-0-10-0, Chappell 7.1-2-28-1.

Umpires: JG Draper & HC Kidson

FOURTH TEST 1966–67 SOUTH AFRICA v AUSTRALIA
New Wanderers Stadium, Johannesburg. February 3, 4, 6, 7 (no play), 8, 1967.
Toss: Australia. Match Drawn.

AUSTRALIA
WM Lawry c Bacher b Trimborn	17	b Procter	2
RB Simpson (c) c Du Preez b Goddard	24	c Bacher b Procter	28
IR Redpath c Lindsay b Barlow	14 (4)	c Trimborn b PM Pollock	46
RM Cowper c Trimborn b Procter	25 (5)	b Du Preez	16
IM Chappell lbw Goddard	0 (6)	not out	13
KR Stackpole b Goddard	4 (7)	c Goddard b Du Preez	5
TR Veivers c Lindsay b Procter	19 (8)	c Lindsay b Goddard	21
GD Watson c Lance b Procter	17 (9)	b Goddard	0
GD McKenzie c RG Pollock b Procter	11 (10)	not out	0
HB Taber (+) c Trimborn b PM Pollock	4 (3)	lbw Goddard	14
DA Renneberg not out	0		
Extras (LB 6, W 1, NB 1)	8	(LB 2, NB 1)	3
TOTAL	143		8 for 148

FOW 1st Inns: 33 59 59 59 69 103 108 139 139 143
FOW 2nd Inns: 11 41 58 94 116 125 148 148

Bowling: *First Innings*: PM Pollock 12.1-3-21-1, Procter 18-7-32-4, Goddard 19-6-36-3, Trimborn 10-3-21-1, Barlow 11-6-25-1. *Second Innings*: PM Pollock 14-6-24-1, Procter 17-6-38-2, Barlow 7-3-20-0, Goddard 16.3-9-23-3, Trimborn 7-3-14-0, Du Preez 14-6-22-2, Lance 3-1-4-0.

SOUTH AFRICA
TL Goddard c Stackpole b Renneberg	47
EJ Barlow c Taber b Renneberg	4
A Bacher c Taber b Watson	22
RG Pollock c Taber b Cowper	22
HR Lance lbw Watson	30
DT Lindsay (+) c Simpson b Renneberg	131
MJ Procter lbw Simpson	16
PL Van der Merwe (c) c Taber b Renneberg	12
JH Du Preez c Simpson b Renneberg	0
PM Pollock not out	34
PHJ Trimborn not out	11
Extras (LB 3)	3
TOTAL	9 dec 332

FOW 1st Inns: 8 39 86 120 177 210 266 272 299

Bowling: *First Innings*: McKenzie 39-7-96-0, Renneberg 25-3-97-5, Watson 20-4-67-2, Cowper 15-7-36-1, Simpson 6-0-33-1.

Umpires: JG Draper & HC Kidson

Australian Averages

1966–67 SOUTH AFRICA v AUSTRALIA
AUSTRALIA	M	Inn	NO	Runs	H.S	Avrge	Ct	St	Overs	Mds	Runs	Wkt	Avrge
Chappell, IM	5	10	1	196	49	21.78	6	-	89.1	26	296	5	59.20
Cowper, RM	5	10	-	255	60	25.50	2	-	138.3	47	301	10	30.10
Hawke, NJN	2	4	2	45	18*	22.50	-	-	54.2	9	162	4	40.50
Lawry, WM	5	10	-	296	98	29.60	1	-	-	-	-	-	-
Martin, JW	1	2	-	20	20	10.00	1	-	22.0	1	89	-	-
McKenzie, GD	5	9	1	140	34	17.50	2	-	275.2	70	624	24	26.00
Redpath, IR	5	10	1	386	80	42.89	5	-	4.0	-	13	-	-
Renneberg, DA	5	8	5	13	9	4.33	2	-	178.0	34	528	11	48.00
Simpson, RB	5	10	-	483	153	48.30	8	-	106.1	27	311	10	31.10
Stackpole, KR	5	9	-	254	134	28.22	3	-	45.0	12	130	1	130.00
Taber, HB	5	9	1	94	30	11.75	19	1	-	-	-	-	-
Veivers, TR	4	8	1	184	55	26.29	-	-	42.1	8	125	1	125.00
Watson, GD	3	5	-	76	50	15.20	-	-	52.0	9	162	3	54.00

South African Averages

1966–67 SOUTH AFRICA v AUSTRALIA
SOUTH AFRICA	M	Inn	NO	Runs	H.S	Avrge	Ct	St	Overs	Mds	Runs	Wkt	Avrge
Bacher, A	5	9	1	244	63	30.50	6	-	-	-	-	-	-
Barlow, EJ	5	9	-	186	50	20.67	4	-	129.3	37	324	15	21.60
Bland, KC	1	2	-	32	32	16.00	-	-	-	-	-	-	-
Du Preez, JH	2	2	-	0	0	0.00	2	-	24.0	12	51	3	17.00
Dumbrill, R	2	4	-	55	29	13.75	-	-	45.0	11	134	1	134.00
Goddard, TL	5	9	-	294	74	32.67	6	-	255.3	101	422	26	16.23
Lance, HR	5	8	1	261	70	37.29	3	-	71.0	18	201	4	50.25
Lindsay, DT	5	7	-	606	182	86.57	24	-	-	-	-	-	-
McKinnon, AH	2	4	3	14	8	14.00	-	-	117.2	44	292	5	58.40
Pithey, DB	2	3	-	74	55	24.67	-	-	50.0	17	114	-	-
Pollock, PM	5	7	3	183	75*	45.75	1	-	167.1	35	470	12	39.17
Pollock, RG	5	9	2	537	209	76.71	5	-	3.0	1	5	-	-
Procter, MJ	3	3	-	17	16	5.67	-	-	109.2	30	263	15	17.53
Trimborn, PHJ	3	3	2	13	11*	13.00	5	-	87.1	26	166	7	23.71
Van der Merwe, PL	5	7	-	225	76	32.14	2	-	-	-	-	-	-

Indians are cheerful, but outclassed

Sydney, Jan. 31. India has been completely outclassed in the Test series against Australia that ended today in Sydney.

The tourists lost all four Tests by substantial margins, and the home side's dominance was so great that selectors were able to experiment with the team in the last two Tests.

India struggled in the state games leading up to the first Test and suffered a crucial blow when its captain, the Nawab of Pataudi, pulled a hamstring in the opening match against Western Australia.

The Indian batting was always vulnerable and suffered from inconsistency at the top of the order. Ajit Wadekar, Chandrakant Borde, Syed Abid Ali and 'keeper Farokh Engineer all showed ability at times, but in every Test India suffered slumps at critical stages.

The Nawab of Pataudi was clearly the best batsman in the party and the 26-year-old's courage won the hearts of Australian crowds who were aware that he had overcome the loss of vision in one eye due to a car accident.

He was rushed back into the team for the second Test when he was clearly not 100 per cent fit, and took on the Australian attack with an aggressive 75 and 85.

In both innings his score could have been greater if his leg injury had not restricted his running between wickets. In six Test innings he was never dismissed for less than 48.

The only other Indian batsman to take up the cudgels against Australia was Jaisimha, who was flown out as a reinforcement and immediately scored an aggressive century at Brisbane.

Nadkarni can't stop a drive from retiring Australian skipper, Bobby Simpson.

Lawrie Mayne was an unlikely hero of Western Australia's Sheffield Shield win, leaving Bill Lawry confused and cartoonist Langoulant delighted. Mayne had been out of the WA side for over a year. He regained his place when Jim Hubble injured his ankle when his foot was tangled in the nets. Mayne responded with 20 wickets in the last three games.

Simpson quits, Lawry in

Farokh Engineer in a brilliant attempt to catch Jarman off Prasanna.

Brisbane, Jan. 20. The Brisbane crowd was quick to chastise new Australian captain Bill Lawry for his extended use of fellow Victorians Alan Connolly and Bob Cowper at the bowling crease.

One wag yelled: 'Hey Lawry! Give Gleeson a bowl – his grandmother lives in Geelong.'

Lawry has taken over as Australian Test captain following the retirement of his opening partner Bob Simpson.

Lawry has captained Victoria for six years and under his leadership the state has won two Sheffield Shields. He is a hard, unrelenting character who is renowned for never conceding an inch to opponents.

Simpson, who turns 32 next month, informed selectors of his decision after leading Australia to victory in the second Test and scoring his second century of the series.

He leaves the game at a time when he is scoring runs as well as ever and is rated Australia's best batsman. In the next 18 months Australia will tour England and play the West Indies at home and Simpson says that the new captain needs time to settle in to the role.

Although he has told selectors that he would be available as a player for the rest of the series, Simpson was surprised to be omitted for the third Test, although selectors have said that he will return for a farewell in the fourth, and last, Test in Sydney.

Team for tour visits Queensland

Brisbane, Jan. 15. Australian selectors have created a strange precedent in standing down ace fast bowler Graham McKenzie from the side for the third and fourth Tests against India.

McKenzie brought India to its knees in the second Test when he took the first five wickets and had the tourists 5/26. He finished with 10 wickets for the game.

With one eye on the forthcoming tour to England, the selectors have opted to use the last two Tests against the hapless Indians as a trial for fast bowling places.

New boy Eric Freeman will play in Brisbane and fellow South Australian Neil Hawke will take the new ball in Sydney.

Several Australian players are believed to be concerned at the unprecedented decision to 'rest' McKenzie and former skipper Bob Simpson, two of the country's best players, in order to audition youngsters for the English tour.

It has always been the Australian policy to pick the best available players and an additional concern is the fact that McKenzie is a full-time professional cricketer and loses match payments.

At 26 he has 174 Test wickets and is well on the way to breaking Richie Benaud's Test record of 248, but is being denied the chance to boost his tally.

The action is seen as a slight to the Indians and as an insult to the lion-hearted McKenzie who has carried the country's bowling workload since the retirement of Alan Davidson.

Indian mysteries of spin

Sydney, Jan. 31. The Indian team may have struggled on this tour, but the magical qualities of the team's spinners have entranced the Australian public.

India's opening bowlers have generally looked innocuous and usually have been given token use of the new ball before handing over to the spin brigade.

Leading the way has been the bouncy little off-spinner Erapally Prasanna who consistently spun the ball more than any player on either side. His clever use of flight has deceived the Australian batsmen through the air, and his record of 25 wickets in four Tests entitles him to a ranking among the best spin bowlers to come to this country since World War II.

Prasanna came to Australia as the second-ranked spinner behind Bhagwat Chandrasekhar, but the talented leg-spinner did not show anything of his best form before injuring his foot early in the second Test.

The absence of Chandrasekhar placed responsibility on veteran Bapu Nadkarni and the young Sikh, Bishen Bedi. Bedi's colourful

Erapally Prasanna spins one down.

turbans and obvious joy in his craft made him a popular figure.

He is an off-spinner whose easy, loose-limbed style indicated that he could comfortably bowl for long spells, and he looks to have a big future.

Backing up the front-line spinners is Rusi Surti, who will play for Queensland next season.

Australian Averages

1967–68 AUSTRALIA v INDIA AUSTRALIA	M	Inn	NO	Runs	H.S	Avrge	Ct	St	Overs	Mds	Runs	Wkt	Avrge
Chappell, IM	4	7	-	212	151	30.29	7	-	44.0	6	175	1	175.00
Connolly, AN	3	5	1	26	14	6.50	5	-	73.3	16	250	8	31.25
Cowper, RM	4	7	-	485	165	69.29	4	-	103.4	32	239	13	18.38
Freeman, EW	2	4	-	45	18	11.25	-	-	51.1	5	197	7	28.14
Gleeson, JW	4	7	2	66	18*	13.20	3	-	108.0	33	257	9	28.56
Hawke, NJN	1	2	-	5	4	2.50	-	-	24.0	4	73	-	-
Jarman, BN	4	7	-	136	65	19.43	11	1	-	-	-	-	-
Joslin, LR	1	2	-	9	7	4.50	-	-	-	-	-	-	-
Lawry, WM	4	7	-	369	100	52.71	3	-	-	-	-	-	-
McKenzie, GD	2	3	-	33	28	11.00	-	-	72.4	7	312	13	24.00
Redpath, IR	3	5	-	180	79	36.00	7	-	-	-	-	-	-
Renneberg, DA	3	5	2	9	8*	3.00	-	-	66.2	8	302	12	25.17
Sheahan, AP	4	7	-	318	81	45.43	3	-	-	-	-	-	-
Simpson, RB	3	5	-	294	109	58.80	7	-	76.0	20	213	13	16.38
Walters, KD	2	4	2	254	94*	127.00	1	-	24.0	3	86	2	43.00

Indian Averages

1967–68 AUSTRALIA v INDIA INDIA	M	Inn	NO	Runs	H.S	Avrge	Ct	St	Overs	Mds	Runs	Wkt	Avrge
Abid Ali, S	4	8	-	299	81	37.38	4	-	73.0	5	302	8	37.75
Bedi, BS	2	4	1	12	8	4.00	2	-	79.0	17	223	4	55.75
Borde, CG	4	8	-	166	69	20.75	4	-	-	-	-	-	-
Chandrasekhar, BS2	4	2	1	1	1*	0.50	-	-	47.1	4	174	1	174.00
Desai, RB	1	2	1	27	14	27.00	4	-	12.0	-	63	-	-
Engineer, FM	4	8	-	215	89	26.88	8	3	-	-	-	-	-
Jaisimha, ML	2	4	-	188	101	47.00	-	-	4.0	-	17	1	17.00
Kulkarni, UN	3	6	3	12	7	4.00	-	-	46.2	2	200	5	40.00
Nadkarni, RG	3	6	-	43	17	7.17	-	-	71.4	18	211	3	70.33
Nawab of Pataudi jr3	6	-	339	85	56.50	1	-	-	-	-	-	-	
Prasanna, EAS	4	8	1	108	26	15.43	1	-	197.5	34	686	25	27.44
Sardesai, DN	2	4	-	18	11	4.50	-	-	-	-	-	-	-
Subramanya, V	2	4	-	97	75	24.25	-	-	6.0	-	37	-	-
Surti, RF	4	8	-	367	70	45.88	4	-	117.4	18	528	15	35.20
Wadekar, AL	4	8	-	212	99	26.50	5	-	-	-	-	-	-

FIRST TEST 1967–68 AUSTRALIA v INDIA
Adelaide Oval, Adelaide. December 23, 25, 26, 27, 28, 1967.
Toss: Australia. Australia won by 146 runs.

AUSTRALIA

RB Simpson (c) c & b Abid Ali	55	b Surti	103
WM Lawry c Engineer b Abid Ali	42	c Engineer b Kulkarni	0
AP Sheahan lbw Prasanna	81	lbw Prasanna	35
RM Cowper c Engineer b Abid Ali	92	b Abid Ali	108
IR Redpath c Borde b Prasanna	0 (7)	lbw Surti	34
IM Chappell c Borde b Prasanna	2 (5)	b Surti	13
BN Jarman (+) b Abid Ali	34 (6)	c & b Surti	17
GD McKenzie c Borde b Abid Ali	5	run out	28
JW Gleeson lbw Abid Ali	1	not out	18
AN Connolly not out	7	c (S)RB Desai b Surti	0
DA Renneberg b Chandrasekhar	1	run out	0
Extras (B 20, LB 10, NB 30)	15	(B 5, LB 6, NB 2)	13
TOTAL	335		369

FOW 1st Inns: 99 109 227 227 235 311 319 324 330 335
FOW 2nd Inns: 0 61 233 263 263 295 322 364 365 369

Bowling: *First Innings*: Kulkarni 5-0-25-0, Surti 7-0-30-0, Abid Ali 17-2-55-6, Nadkarni 17-2-68-0, Chandrasekhar 27.1-3-72-1, Prasanna 17-2-60-3, Subramanya 2-0-10-0.
Second Innings: Kulkarni 4-1-12-1, Surti 20.1-6-74-5, Abid Ali 16-2-61-1, Nadkarni 9.4-3-24-0, Chandrasekhar 13-1-67-0, Prasanna 25.2-5-109-1, Subramanya 1-0-9-0.

INDIA

FM Engineer (+) c Jarman b McKenzie	89	run out	19
DN Sardesai c Redpath b Renneberg	1	c Jarman b Renneberg	11
AL Wadekar st Jarman b Connolly	28	c Jarman b Renneberg	0
CG Borde (c) lbw Gleeson	69	b Renneberg	12
RF Surti b Simpson	70	c Redpath b Gleeson	53
RG Nadkarni lbw Gleeson	3 (8)	b McKenzie	15
S Abid Ali c & b Connolly	33 (6)	lbw Renneberg	33
V Subramanya b Connolly	7 (7)	run out	75
EAS Prasanna c Lawry b McKenzie	1	not out	18
UN Kulkarni lbw Connolly	0 (11)	c Chappell b Renneberg	2
BS Chandrasekhar not out	1 (10)	c Simpson b Gleeson	0
Extras (NB 5)	5	(B 3, LB 8, NB 2)	13
TOTAL	307		251

FOW 1st Inns: 19 80 129 250 259 272 287 288 291 307
FOW 2nd Inns: 24 24 46 49 104 159 209 232 236 251

Bowling: *First Innings*: McKenzie 15-1-70-2, Renneberg 6-0-45-1, Connolly 12.4-1-54-4, Gleeson 13-4-36-2, Chappell 10-1-41-0, Simpson 12-2-42-1, Cowper 3-0-14-0. *Second Innings*: McKenzie 17-2-91-1, Renneberg 14.2-2-39-5, Connolly 3-0-21-0, Gleeson 16-4-38-2, Chappell 5-0-24-0, Simpson 5-0-25-0.

Umpires: CJ Egar & LP Rowan

SECOND TEST 1967–68 AUSTRALIA v INDIA
Melbourne Cricket Ground, Melbourne. December 30, 1967, January 1, 2, 3, 1968.
Toss: India. Australia won by an innings & 4 runs.

INDIA

DN Sardesai b McKenzie	1	b McKenzie	5
FM Engineer (+) c Connolly b McKenzie	9	c Chappell b Renneberg	42
S Abid Ali c Jarman b McKenzie	4 (8)	lbw Cowper	21
AL Wadekar c Connolly b McKenzie	6 (3)	c Sheahan b Simpson	99
RF Surti lbw Simpson	30 (4)	c Jarman b McKenzie	43
CG Borde c Redpath b McKenzie	0	c Redpath b Renneberg	6
Nawab of Pataudi jr (c) c Jarman b Renneberg	75	c Redpath b Simpson	85
V Subramanya b McKenzie	5 (9)	lbw McKenzie	10
EAS Prasanna c Chappell b Renneberg	14 (5)	c Chappell b Simpson	21
RB Desai not out	13	c Simpson b Connolly	14
BS Chandrasekhar c Jarman b McKenzie	0	not out	0
Extras (B 8, LB 2, NB 6)	16	(B 1, LB 4, NB 1)	6
TOTAL	173		352

FOW 1st Inns: 2 10 18 25 25 47 72 146 162 173
FOW 2nd Inns: 11 66 182 194 217 227 276 292 346 352

Bowling: *First Innings*: McKenzie 21.4-2-66-7, Renneberg 15-4-37-2, Connolly 13-3-33-0, Gleeson 5-0-9-0, Chappell 1-0-7-0, Simpson 2-0-5-1. *Second Innings*: McKenzie 19-2-85-3, Renneberg 14-1-98-2, Connolly 11.7-2-48-1, Gleeson 14-5-37-0, Chappell 4-0-14-0, Simpson 14-3-44-3, Cowper 8-2-20-1.

AUSTRALIA

RB Simpson (c) b Surti	109
WM Lawry st Engineer b Prasanna	100
AP Sheahan c Engineer b Surti	24
RM Cowper b Prasanna	12
IM Chappell c Wadekar b Surti	151
IR Redpath run out	26
BN Jarman (+) b Prasanna	65
GD McKenzie c(S)BS Bedi b Prasanna	0
JW Gleeson c Borde b Prasanna	13
AN Connolly c(S)BS Bedi b Prasanna	5
DA Renneberg not out	8
Extras (B 3, LB 10, NB 3)	16
TOTAL	529

FOW 1st Inns: 191 233 246 274 329 463 463 500 508 529

Bowling: *First Innings*: Desai 12-0-63-0, Surti 29.3-4-150-3, Abid Ali 20-0-106-0, Chandrasekhar 7-0-35-0, Prasanna 34-6-141-6, Subramanya 3-0-18-0.

Umpires: CJ Egar & LP Rowan

THIRD TEST 1967–68 AUSTRALIA v INDIA
Brisbane Cricket Ground, Brisbane. January 19, 20, 22, 23, 24, 1968.
Toss: India. Australia won by 39 runs.

AUSTRALIA

WM Lawry (c) c Bedi b Nadkarni	64	c Engineer b Surti	45
IR Redpath c Wadekar b Prasanna	41	lbw Prasanna	79
RM Cowper b Nadkarni	51	b Surti	25
AP Sheahan st Engineer b Surti	58	c Surti b Bedi	26
IM Chappell b Surti	17	b Prasanna	27
KD Walters c Wadekar b Kulkarni	93	not out	62
BN Jarman (+) lbw Prasanna	2	c & b Prasanna	9
EW Freeman b Surti	18	c Surti b Prasanna	8
JW Gleeson run out	15	c Abid Ali b Surti	1
AN Connolly c Nawab b Kulkarni	14	b Prasanna	0
DA Renneberg not out	0	c Surti b Prasanna	0
Extras (B 1, LB 1, NB 4)	6	(B 1, LB 10, NB 1)	12
TOTAL	379		294

FOW 1st Inns: 76 148 160 215 239 250 277 323 378 379
FOW 2nd Inns: 116 136 162 196 240 266 284 293 294 294

Bowling: *First Innings*: Kulkarni 8.2-1-37-2, Surti 26-2-102-3, Prasanna 38-6-114-2, Bedi 23-4-71-0, Abid Ali 2-0-9-0, Nadkarni 14-5-34-2, Jaisimha 1-0-6-0. *Second Innings*: Kulkarni 4-0-22-0, Surti 16-4-59-3, Prasanna 33.4-9-104-6, Bedi 14-4-44-1, Abid Ali 1-0-6-0, Nadkarni 15-5-47-0.

INDIA

FM Engineer (+) c Gleeson b Freeman	2	c Jarman b Renneberg	0
S Abid Ali c Redpath b Freeman	2	c Jarman b Connolly	47
AL Wadekar c Jarman b Renneberg	1	c Connolly b Cowper	11
RF Surti c Cowper b Chappell	52	b Cowper	64
Nawab of Pataudi jr (c) lbw Freeman	74	b Walters	48
ML Jaisimha c Lawry b Cowper	74	c Gleeson b Cowper	101
CG Borde c & b Connolly	12	c Redpath b Cowper	63
RG Nadkarni b Cowper	17	lbw Gleeson	2
EAS Prasanna c Walters b Cowper	24	b Gleeson	4
BS Bedi not out	2	c Lawry b Gleeson	0
UN Kulkarni c Cowper b Connolly	7	not out	1
Extras (B 6, LB 4, NB 2)	12	(B 4, LB 6, NB 4)	14
TOTAL	279		355

FOW 1st Inns: 2 5 9 137 139 165 209 268 270 279
FOW 2nd Inns: 17 48 61 154 191 310 313 323 333 355

Bowling: *First Innings*: Renneberg 10-1-40-1, Freeman 21-1-56-3, Walters 6-0-22-0, Connolly 15-4-43-2, Gleeson 15-7-20-0, Cowper 15-5-31-3, Chappell 18-4-55-1. *Second Innings*: Renneberg 7-0-43-1, Freeman 8-2-29-0, Walters 11-2-33-1, Connolly 18-6-51-1, Gleeson 21-6-50-3, Cowper 39.6-8-104-4, Chappell 5-1-31-0.

Umpires: CJ Egar & LP Rowan

FOURTH TEST 1967–68 AUSTRALIA v INDIA
Sydney Cricket Ground, Sydney. January 26, 27, 29, 30, 31, 1968.
Toss: India. Australia won by 144 runs.

AUSTRALIA

WM Lawry (c) c Engineer b Prasanna	66	c (S)V Subramanya b Nadkarni	52
RM Cowper b Abid Ali	32	st Engineer b Prasanna	165
AP Sheahan c & b Bedi	72 (4)	c Wadekar b Jaisimha	22
KD Walters not out	94 (5)	run out	5
LR Joslin c Wadekar b Prasanna	7 (6)	c Abid Ali b Bedi	2
RB Simpson b Bedi	7 (3)	run out	20
IM Chappell run out	0	lbw Prasanna	2
BN Jarman (+) c Engineer b Surti	4	run out	5
EW Freeman lbw Kulkarni	11	c (S)RC Saxena b Prasanna	8
NJN Hawke c Engineer b Kulkarni	1	c Abid Ali b Prasanna	4
JW Gleeson lbw Prasanna	14	not out	4
Extras (B 2, LB 4, NB 3)	9	(B 1, LB 1, NB 1)	3
TOTAL	317		292

FOW 1st Inns: 61 136 219 228 239 242 256 275 277 317
FOW 2nd Inns: 111 166 222 240 243 260 271 278 286 292

Bowling: *First Innings*: Kulkarni 17-0-73-2, Surti 11-1-64-1, Abid Ali 15-1-58-1, Jaisimha 2-0-9-0, Bedi 21-4-42-2, Prasanna 20.6-5-62-3. *Second Innings*: Kulkarni 8-0-31-0, Surti 8-1-49-0, Abid Ali 2-0-7-0, Jaisimha 1-0-2-1, Bedi 21-5-66-1, Prasanna 29.3-4-96-4, Nadkarni 16-3-38-1.

INDIA

FM Engineer (+) c Chappell b Walters	17	c Simpson b Gleeson	37
S Abid Ali hit wicket b Gleeson	78	c Simpson b Cowper	81
AL Wadekar c & b Cowper	49	lbw Cowper	18
RF Surti b Simpson	29	c Chappell b Simpson	26
Nawab of Pataudi jr (c) c Simpson b Freeman	51	c Chappell b Simpson	6
ML Jaisimha c Jarman b Simpson	0	c Gleeson b Cowper	13
RG Nadkarni c Sheahan b Simpson	0 (8)	c Sheahan b Simpson	6
EAS Prasanna c Cowper b Freeman	26 (9)	b Simpson	0
CG Borde lbw Freeman	0 (7)	c Simpson b Cowper	4
BS Bedi c Simpson b Freeman	8	b Simpson	2
UN Kulkarni not out	1	not out	1
Extras (B 4, LB 2, NB 3)	9	(LB 3)	3
TOTAL	268		197

FOW 1st Inns: 56 111 178 178 184 184 236 236 367 268
FOW 2nd Inns: 83 120 145 164 175 180 193 193 195 197

Bowling: *First Innings*: Hawke 18-2-51-0, Freeman 18.1-2-86-4, Walters 4-0-20-1, Gleeson 12-3-40-1, Cowper 12-5-21-1, Simpson 20-10-38-3, Chappell 1-0-3-0. *Second Innings*: Hawke 6-2-22-0, Freeman 4-0-26-0, Walters 3-1-11-0, Gleeson 12-4-27-1, Cowper 25.6-12-49-4, Simpson 23-5-59-5.

Umpires: CJ Egar & LP Rowan

A morale-boosting win

Barry Jarman takes a great catch to dismiss John Edrich.

Manchester, June 11. Australia has confounded the critics by comfortably winning the first Test at Manchester.

This team has the youngest average age of any Australian touring team and has been tagged the weakest of all time. Ten of the 17-man squad have never toured England before.

Plenty of responsibility fell on the shoulders of young batsmen Ian Chappell, Paul Sheahan and Doug Walters, who were all new to English conditions. Walters has played just a handful of first class games in the past two seasons.

On the first day of the series it was Chappell, Sheahan and Walters who helped their skipper Bill Lawry build a score of 4/319 by stumps that laid the foundation for victory.

England openers Edrich and Boycott began well with an opening stand of 86, but the home side collapsed in the face of McKenzie's pace and the off-spin of surprise packet Bob Cowper (4/48), who is only a part-time tweaker for his state side.

Walters always looked wary of the pitch, but in scoring his second eighty of the match helped set England a target of 413 – a fourth-innings total never achieved by an England side to win a Test against Australia.

Despite a cavalier, but belated knock of 87 not out by D'Oliveira, the home side went down by 159 runs.

Bill Lawry hooks in characteristic style in his first English Test.

200th game but Australia's shame

Lord's, June 25. The 200th Test between Australia and England was meant to be a celebration of cricket's oldest rivalry, but for Australia it was the scene of a shameful batting performance.

First the Billy Bunter-like figure of Colin Milburn smashed 83, including two sixes and 12 fours, to humble the visiting attack.

Worse was to follow when England bowlers David Brown and Barry Knight exploited the dull, heavy conditions on a greenish pitch to shoot Australia out for 78.

There have been reports that some of the Aussies fleetingly attended the wedding breakfast of a journalist on the rest day before the collapse, which may have affected them.

Cowdrey – 100 Tests

Boycott is lbw to Gleeson.

Edgbaston, July 16. The unassuming English skipper Colin Cowdrey has achieved an unprecedented landmark in playing his 100th Test.

The *Times* says he is almost 'too nice a chap' to be a dominating cricketer. 'It is almost as if he were afraid he would hurt the bowler's feelings if he did him real violence.'

In *Boys' Own* style, Cowdrey scored a century in his 100th Test; strangely enough it was his first against the Aussies in England.

He tore a thigh muscle in the middle of the innings, and his opposing skipper was also in the wars. Bill Lawry had his finger broken in John Snow's first over.

As commentator Jack Fingleton said, the rain is the only certainty in England, and again it caused the game to fizzle to a draw with only 90 minutes play on the last day.

A nailbiter goes to England

Stand-in skipper gets the Ashes

Leeds, July 30. Barry Jarman made sure the photographers' cameras were clicking when he tossed with England's Tom Graveney.

After all it isn't every day you see two vice-captains leading their respective countries.

Skippers Colin Cowdrey (thigh) and Bill Lawry (broken finger) were ruled out and their deputies were doubtful up until the last minute as Jarman was recovering from a broken finger and Graveney from a gashed hand.

It seemed Graham McKenzie would lead Australia and England would be captained by Ted Dexter, whose only recent involvement in cricket until a fortnight ago was as a commentator.

Lord Ted's preparation was a bit of jogging and a hit with Sussex that produced a double century.

Even the imperious Dexter couldn't spark an English win and once again the match was drawn as England never seriously threatened to reach the 327 target.

Rain brings on gloomy cricket

London, Aug. 31. All the worst jokes about English weather have come to haunt the touring Australians.

It has been a miserable summer and the Australian team has lost 100 hours of play overall. As captain Bill Lawry points out in *Australian Cricket* magazine, the previous team in 1964 made 14,000 runs on tour. This side was at the crease only long enough to score 7000.

'If you go to England as a top player you expect to bat 50 times. Ian Redpath, who played every game, batted 33 times. This was the difference.'

With 10 players new to English conditions it was essential that the batsmen spent plenty of time at the crease. Instead, the first game was washed out altogether and by the time the first day of the fourth match was washed out, the Aussies had lost 49 hours out of a possible 60 hours of play.

Of the three drawn Tests, two were ruined by the weather.

Lack of cricket also meant a big drop in revenue and Australian manager Bob Parish asked his board for permission to overturn rules and play on Sundays. For the first time Australia played on Sunday in three different county games.

England jump for joy as Graham McKenzie is given out.

Another one gone! John Gleeson bowled by Derek Underwood.

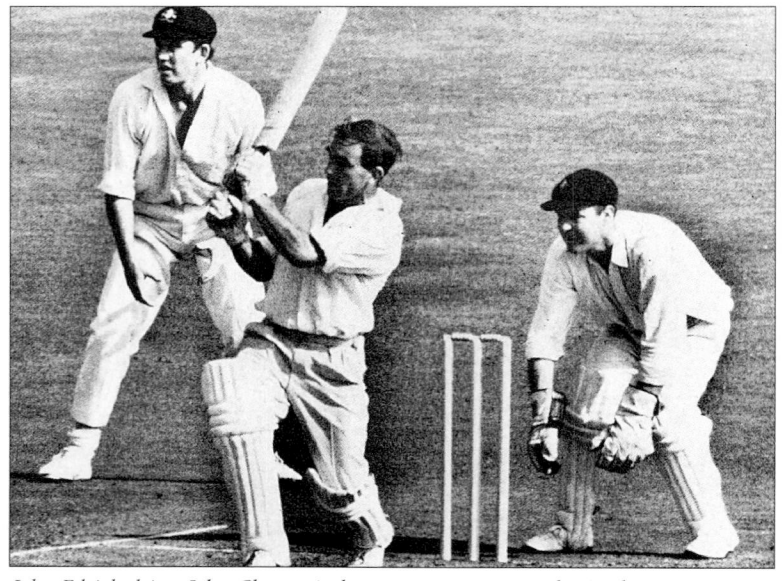
John Edrich drives John Gleeson in his century innings at the Oval.

The Oval, Aug. 27. England has squared the series with a dramatic win in the fifth Test at the Oval.

The Australian opener John Inverarity was the final wicket to fall when he was trapped lbw for 56 by Derek Underwood, with just six minutes to spare.

Throughout this English summer the Australians have cursed the weather, but they were quite content to see the rain arrive on the last day.

When they went to lunch the rain was pelting down and a third of the ground was covered in a sheet of water.

As one player remarked 'on any other ground at any time, and in any other match it would probably have taken at least a day and a half before day would have been possible.'

Instead the Australians were confronted by the sight of a hundred spectators armed with blankets and brooms, and spiking the flooded areas, to make the ground playable. Within an hour and a half it was declared fit for play.

Australia resumed on 5/85 at 4.45 p.m. and needed to survive just 75 minutes. It took 40 minutes to capture the sixth wicket, Barry Jarman, and with each batsman ringed by all nine fielders England pressed harder for victory.

Left-arm Derek Underwood was virtually unplayable on the drying pitch and the ball almost stopped on pitching. Switched to the pavilion end he removed the last four batsmen for just six runs in 27 deliveries.

The gallant Inverarity had batted for four hours for his 56 runs. To their credit the Australians never tried stalling tactics in the tense final session. England's 226-run victory ends the series at one-all, which was probably a fair reflection of the contest.

This Australian team was thought too raw to succeed in England and although their batting has been patchy, their youth has given them the edge in a critically important area – fielding.

Jack Fingleton wrote: 'The English are slow and unsure. The flannels of the two teams tell the story. The English leave the field spotless at the knees whereas the Australians have green stains because they fling themselves at the ball.'

The athleticism of brilliant cover fieldsman Paul Sheahan has been recognised by an award of £100 for best fielder in the series.

A 'corpse with pads on'

London, Aug. 27. He is the man who gets under the skin of the English cricketing press more than any other.

One writer has dubbed Bill Lawry 'the corpse with pads on' in describing his dour style.

In the fifth Test he ground out 135 in seven and a half hours – Australia's only hundred of the series – and prompted calls from former great Keith Miller to abandon the Ashes concept.

His wicket was the most sought after prize and when the burly Colin Milburn snapped him up in the second innings, John Woodcock of the *Times* wrote: 'If the English side could have thrown Milburn aloft they would have.'

Woodcock did recognise Lawry's powers of concentration: 'Lawry is a great battler and a wonderfully sound judge of length. All too often he has been the rock on which England have foundered.'

Strangely enough in the first Test Lawry changed the course of the game by belting a couple of sixes from Pocock, which forced the Englishman out of the attack at a critical stage.

Bill Lawry in uniform.

Ian Chappell looks the goods

London, Aug. 27. In a disappointing tour for batsmen, South Australian Ian Chappell has made his mark as the side's most successful run-getter.

The grandson of former Test skipper Vic Richardson topped the first class averages, and was only just behind Bill Lawry in the Test averages.

His willingness to battle through demanding situations has impressed good judges such as Jack Fingleton who wrote: 'Chappell is a rare fighter even if he sometimes twists his feet into some agitated knots.'

This has been his first complete Ashes series (he played two Tests in 1965–66) and it has been a revelation to him. When Australia played for a draw in the fourth Test to secure the Ashes he hurled his cap in the rooms and said 'If that's Test cricket you can stick it up your jumper,' and Lawry told him firmly: 'We've done what we came over here to do, and that was to win the Ashes.'

Chappell's batting on this tour has secured his place in the side at a time when many were starting to question whether he had the capacity to continue at this level.

Of the other Australian batsmen, Walters and Sheahan began impressively in the first Test, but

Ian Chappell: fierce cutter.

were gradually overcome by the conditions as the series progressed. Bob Cowper impressed on his first tour of England in 1964, but this time had a tour that could only be described as 'fair'.

One of the most notable victims of the damp conditions was young Les Joslin who could manage only 344 runs at an average of 21.5 – a confidence-shattering experience.

FIRST TEST 1968 ENGLAND v AUSTRALIA
Old Trafford, Manchester. June 6, 7, 8, 10, 11, 1968.
Toss: Australia. Australia won by 159 runs.

AUSTRALIA

WM Lawry (c) c Boycott b Barber	81	c Pocock b D'Oliveira	16
IR Redpath lbw Snow	8	lbw Snow	8
RM Cowper b Snow	0	c & b Pocock	37
KD Walters lbw Barber	81	lbw Pocock	86
AP Sheahan c D'Oliveira b Snow	88	c Graveney b Pocock	8
IM Chappell run out	73	c Knott b Pocock	9
BN Jarman (+) c & b Higgs	12	b Pocock	41
NJN Hawke c Knott b Snow	5	c Edrich b Pocock	0
GD McKenzie c Cowdrey b D'Oliveira	0	c Snow b Barber	0
JW Gleeson c Knott b Higgs	0	run out	2
AN Connolly not out	0	not out	2
Extras (LB 7, NB 2)	9	(B 2, LB 9)	11
TOTAL	357		220

FOW 1st Inns: 29 29 173 174 326 341 351 353 357 357
FOW 2nd Inns: 24 24 106 122 140 211 211 214 214 220

Bowling: *First Innings*: Snow 34-5-97-4, Higgs 35.3-11-80-2, D'Oliveira 25-11-38-1, Pocock 25-5-77-0, Barber 11-0-56-2. *Second Innings*: Snow 17-2-51-1, Higgs 23-8-41-0, D'Oliveira 5-3-7-1, Pocock 33-10-79-6, Barber 10-1-31-1.

ENGLAND

JH Edrich run out	49	c Jarman b Cowper	38
G Boycott c Jarman b Cowper	35	c Redpath b McKenzie	11
MC Cowdrey (c) c Lawry b McKenzie	4	c Jarman b McKenzie	11
TW Graveney c McKenzie b Cowper	2	c Jarman b Gleeson	33
DL Amiss c Cowper b McKenzie	0	b Cowper	0
RW Barber c Sheahan b McKenzie	20	c Cowper b Hawke	46
BL D'Oliveira b Connolly	9	not out	87
APE Knott (+) c McKenzie b Cowper	5	lbw Connolly	4
JA Snow not out	18	c Lawry b Connolly	2
K Higgs lbw Cowper	2	c Jarman b Gleeson	0
PI Pocock c Redpath b Gleeson	6	lbw Gleeson	10
Extras (B 9, LB 3, W 3)	15	(B 5, LB 6)	11
TOTAL	165		253

FOW 1st Inns: 86 87 89 90 97 120 137 137 144 165
FOW 2nd Inns: 13 25 91 91 105 185 214 218 219 253

Bowling: *First Innings*: McKenzie 28-11-33-3, Hawke 15-7-18-0, Connolly 28-15-26-1, Gleeson 6.3-2-21-1, Cowper 26-11-48-4, Chappell 1-0-4-0. *Second Innings*: McKenzie 18-3-52-2, Hawke 8-4-15-1, Connolly 13-4-35-2, Gleeson 30-14-44-3, Cowper 39-12-82-2, Chappell 2-0-14-0.

Umpires: JS Buller & CS Elliott

SECOND TEST 1968 ENGLAND v AUSTRALIA
Lord's Cricket Ground, London. June 20, 21, 22, 24, 25, 1968.
Toss: England. Match Drawn.

ENGLAND

JH Edrich c Cowper b McKenzie	7
G Boycott c Sheahan b McKenzie	49
C Milburn c Walters b Gleeson	83
MC Cowdrey (c) c Cowper b McKenzie	45
KF Barrington c Jarman b Connolly	75
TW Graveney c Jarman b Connolly	14
BR Knight not out	27
APE Knott (+) run out	33
JA Snow not out	0
DJ Brown	
DL Underwood	
Extras (B 7, LB 5, W 1, NB 5)	18
TOTAL	7 dec 351

FOW 1st Inns: 10 142 147 244 271 330 351

Bowling: *First Innings*: McKenzie 45-18-111-3, Hawke 35-7-82-0, Connolly 26.3-8-55-2, Walters 3-2-2-0, Cowper 8-2-40-0, Gleeson 27-11-43-1.

AUSTRALIA

WM Lawry (c) c Knott b Brown	0	c Brown b Snow	28
IR Redpath c Cowdrey b Brown	4	b Underwood	53
RM Cowper b Graveney b Snow	8	c Underwood b Barrington	32
KD Walters c Knight b Brown	26	b Underwood	0
AP Sheahan c Knott b Knight	6	not out	0
IM Chappell lbw Knight	7	not out	12
NJN Hawke c Cowdrey b Knight	2		
GD McKenzie b Brown	5		
JW Gleeson c Cowdrey b Brown	14		
BN Jarman (+) retired hurt	0		
AN Connolly not out	0		
Extras (LB 2, NB 4)	6	(NB 2)	2
TOTAL	9 dec 78		4 for 127

FOW 1st Inns: 1 12 23 46 52 58 63 78 78
FOW 2nd Inns: 66 93 97 115

Bowling: *First Innings*: Snow 9-5-14-1, Brown 14-5-42-5, Knight 10.4-5-16-3. *Second Innings*: Snow 12-5-30-1, Brown 19-9-40-0, Knight 16-9-35-0, Underwood 18-15-8-2, Barrington 2-0-12-1.

Umpires: JS Buller & AE Fagg

THIRD TEST 1968 ENGLAND v AUSTRALIA
Edgbaston, Birmingham. July 11 (no play), 12, 13, 15, 16, 1968.
Toss: England. Match Drawn.

ENGLAND

JH Edrich c Taber b Freeman	88	c Cowper b Freeman	64
G Boycott lbw Gleeson	36	c Taber b Connolly	31
MC Cowdrey (c) b Freeman	104		
KF Barrington lbw Freeman	0		
TW Graveney b Connolly	96 (3)	not out	39
BR Knight c Chappell b Connolly	6 (4)	b Connolly	1
APE Knott (+) b McKenzie	4 (5)	not out	4
R Illingworth lbw Gleeson	27		
DJ Brown b Connolly	0		
JA Snow c Connolly b Freeman	19		
DL Underwood not out	14		
Extras (B 4, LB 6, W 1, NB 4)	15	(LB 2, NB 1)	3
TOTAL	409	3 dec	142

FOW 1st Inns: 80 188 189 282 293 323 374 374 376 409
FOW 2nd Inns: 57 131 134

Bowling: *First Innings*: McKenzie 47-14-115-1, Freeman 30.5-8-78-4, Connolly 35-8-84-3, Gleeson 46-19-84-2, Cowper 7-1-25-0, Walters 7-3-8-0. *Second Innings*: McKenzie 18-1-57-0, Freeman 9-2-23-1, Connolly 15-3-59-2.

AUSTRALIA

WM Lawry (c) retired hurt	6		
IR Redpath b Brown	0	lbw Snow	22
RM Cowper b Snow	57 (1)	not out	25
IM Chappell b Knight	71 (3)	not out	18
KD Walters c & b Underwood	46		
AP Sheahan b Underwood	4		
HB Taber (+) c Barrington b Illingworth	16		
EW Freeman b Illingworth	6		
GD McKenzie not out	0		
JW Gleeson c Illingworth b Underwood	3		
AN Connolly b Illingworth	0		
Extras (B 1, LB 10, NB 2)	13	(LB 1, NB 2)	3
TOTAL	9 dec 222		1 for 68

FOW 1st Inns: 10 121 165 176 213 213 219 222 222
FOW 2nd Inns: 44

Bowling: *First Innings*: Snow 17-3-46-1, Brown 13-2-44-1, Knight 14-2-34-1, Underwood 25-9-48-3, Illingworth 22-10-37-3. *Second Innings*: Snow 9-1-32-1, Brown 6-1-15-0, Underwood 8-4-14-0, Illingworth 5.2-2-4-0.

Umpires: CS Elliott & H Yarnold

FIFTH TEST 1968 ENGLAND v AUSTRALIA
Kennington Oval, London. August 22, 23, 24, 26, 27, 1968.
Toss: England. England won by 226 runs.

ENGLAND

JH Edrich b Chappell	164	c Lawry b Mallett	17
C Milburn b Connolly	8	c Lawry b Connolly	18
ER Dexter b Gleeson	21	b Connolly	28
MC Cowdrey (c) lbw Mallett	16	b Mallett	35
TW Graveney c Redpath b McKenzie	63	run out	12
BL D'Oliveira c Inverarity b Mallett	158	c Gleeson b Connolly	9
APE Knott (+) c Jarman b Mallett	28	run out	34
R Illingworth lbw Connolly	8	b Gleeson	10
JA Snow run out	4	c Sheahan b Gleeson	13
DL Underwood not out	9	not out	1
DJ Brown c Sheahan b Gleeson	2	b Connolly	1
Extras (B 1, LB 11, W 1)	13	(LB 3)	3
TOTAL	494		181

FOW 1st Inns: 28 84 113 238 359 421 458 468 489 494
FOW 2nd Inns: 23 53 67 90 114 126 149 179 179 181

Bowling: *First Innings*: McKenzie 40-8-87-1, Connolly 57-12-127-2, Walters 6-2-17-0, Gleeson 41.2-8-109-2, Mallett 36-11-87-3, Chappell 21-5-54-1. *Second Innings*: McKenzie 4-0-14-0, Connolly 22.4-2-65-4, Mallett 25-4-77-2, Gleeson 7-2-22-2.

AUSTRALIA

WM Lawry (c) c Knott b Snow	135	c Milburn b Brown	4
RJ Inverarity c Milburn b Snow	1	lbw Underwood	56
IR Redpath c Cowdrey b Snow	67	lbw Underwood	8
IM Chappell c Knott b Brown	10	lbw Underwood	2
KD Walters c Knott b Brown	5	c Knott b Underwood	1
AP Sheahan b Illingworth	14	c Snow b Illingworth	24
BN Jarman (+) st Knott b Illingworth	0	b D'Oliveira	21
GD McKenzie b Brown	12 (9)	c Brown b Underwood	0
AA Mallett not out	43 (8)	c Brown b Underwood	0
JW Gleeson c Dexter b Underwood	19	b Underwood	5
AN Connolly b Underwood	3	not out	0
Extras (B 4, LB 7, NB 4)	15	(LB 4)	4
TOTAL	324		125

FOW 1st Inns: 7 136 151 161 185 188 237 269 302 324
FOW 2nd Inns: 4 13 19 29 65 110 110 110 120 125

Bowling: *First Innings*: Snow 35-12-67-3, Brown 22-5-63-3, Illingworth 48-15-87-2, Underwood 54.3-21-89-2, D'Oliveira 4-2-3-0. *Second Innings*: Snow 11-5-22-0, Brown 8-3-19-1, Underwood 31.3-19-50-7, Illingworth 28-18-29-1, D'Oliveira 5-4-1-1.

Umpires: CS Elliott & AE Fagg

FOURTH TEST 1968 ENGLAND v AUSTRALIA
Headingley, Leeds. July 25, 26, 27, 29, 30, 1968.
Toss: Australia. Match Drawn.

AUSTRALIA

RJ Inverarity b Snow	8	lbw Illingworth	34
RM Cowper b Snow	27	st Knott b Illingworth	5
IR Redpath b Illingworth	92	c Edrich b Snow	48
KD Walters c Barrington b Underwood	42	c Graveney b Snow	56
IM Chappell b Brown	65	c Barrington b Underwood	81
AP Sheahan c Knott b Snow	38	st Knott b Illingworth	31
BN Jarman (c+) c Dexter b Brown	10	st Knott b Illingworth	4
EW Freeman b Underwood	21	b Illingworth	10
GD McKenzie lbw Underwood	1	c Snow b Illingworth	10
JW Gleeson not out	2	c Knott b Underwood	7
AN Connolly c Graveney b Underwood	0	not out	0
Extras (LB 5, NB 1)	5	(B 13, LB 8, NB 5)	26
TOTAL	315		312

FOW 1st Inns: 10 104 152 188 248 267 307 309 315 315
FOW 2nd Inns: 28 81 119 198 273 281 283 296 311 312

Bowling: *First Innings*: Snow 35-3-98-3, Brown 35-4-99-2, Illingworth 29-15-47-1, Underwood 27.4-13-41-4, Dexter 7-0-25-0. *Second Innings*: Snow 24-3-51-2, Brown 27-5-79-0, Illingworth 51-22-87-6, Underwood 45.1-22-52-2, Dexter 1-0-3-0, Barrington 6-1-14-0.

ENGLAND

JH Edrich c Jarman b McKenzie	62	c Jarman b Connolly	65
RM Prideaux c Freeman b Gleeson	6 4	b McKenzie	2
ER Dexter b McKenzie	10	b Connolly	38
TW Graveney (c) c Cowper b Connolly	37	c & b Cowper	41
KF Barrington b Connolly	49	not out	46
KWR Fletcher c Jarman b Connolly	0	not out	23
APE Knott (+) lbw Freeman	4		
R Illingworth c Gleeson b Connolly	6		
JA Snow b Connolly	0		
DJ Brown b Cowper	14		
DL Underwood not out	45		
Extras (B 1, LB 7, NB 3)	11	(LB 7, NB 8)	15
TOTAL	302		4 for 230

FOW 1st Inns: 123 136 141 209 215 235 237 241 241 302
FOW 2nd Inns: 4 81 134 168

Bowling: *First Innings*: McKenzie 39-20-61-2, Freeman 22-6-60-1, Gleeson 25-5-68-1, Connolly 39-13-72-5, Chappell 4-1-6-0, Cowper 18-10-24-1. *Second Innings*: McKenzie 25-2-65-1, Freeman 6-1-25-0, Gleeson 11-4-26-0, Connolly 31-10-68-2, Cowper 5-0-22-1, Chappell 5-3-6-0, Inverarity 1-0-3-0.

Umpires: JS Buller & AE Fagg

Australian Averages

1968 ENGLAND v AUSTRALIA

AUSTRALIA	M	Inn	NO	Runs	H.S	Avrge	Ct	St	Overs	Mds	Runs	Wkt	Avrge
Chappell, IM	5	10	2	348	81	43.50	1	-	33.0	9	84	1	84.00
Connolly, AN	5	8	5	5	3	1.67	1	-	267.1	75	591	23	25.70
Cowper, RM	4	8	1	191	57	27.29	7	-	103.0	36	241	8	30.13
Freeman, EW	2	3	-	37	21	12.33	1	-	67.5	17	186	6	31.00
Gleeson, JW	5	8	1	52	19	7.43	2	-	193.5	65	417	12	34.75
Hawke, NJN	2	3	-	7	5	2.33	-	-	58.0	18	115	1	115.00
Inverarity, RJ	2	4	-	99	56	24.75	1	-	1.0	-	3	-	-
Jarman, BN	4	7	1	88	41	14.67	11	-	-	-	-	-	-
Lawry, WM	4	7	1	270	135	45.00	4	-	-	-	-	-	-
Mallett, AA	1	2	1	43	43*	43.00	-	-	61.0	15	164	5	32.80
McKenzie, GD	5	8	1	32	12	4.57	2	-	264.0	77	595	13	45.77
Redpath, IR	5	10	-	310	92	31.00	3	-	-	-	-	-	-
Sheahan, AP	5	9	1	213	88	26.63	4	-	-	-	-	-	-
Taber, HB	1	1	-	16	16	16.00	2	-	-	-	-	-	-
Walters, KD	5	9	-	343	86	38.11	1	-	16.0	7	27	-	-

English Averages

1968 ENGLAND v AUSTRALIA

ENGLAND	M	Inn	NO	Runs	H.S	Avrge	Ct	St	Overs	Mds	Runs	Wkt	Avrge
Amiss, DL	1	2	-	0	0	0.00	-	-	-	-	-	-	-
Barber, RW	1	2	-	66	46	33.00	-	-	21.0	1	87	3	29.00
Barrington, KF	3	4	1	170	75	56.67	3	-	8.0	1	26	1	26.00
Boycott, G	3	5	-	162	49	32.40	1	-	-	-	-	-	-
Brown, DJ	4	4	-	17	14	4.25	3	-	144.0	34	401	12	33.42
Cowdrey, MC	4	6	-	215	104	35.83	5	-	-	-	-	-	-
D'Oliveira, BL	2	4	1	263	158	87.67	1	-	39.0	20	49	3	16.33
Dexter, ER	2	4	-	97	38	24.25	1	-	8.0	-	28	-	-
Edrich, JH	5	9	-	554	164	61.56	2	-	-	-	-	-	-
Fletcher, KWR	1	2	1	23	23*	23.00	1	-	-	-	-	-	-
Graveney, TW	5	9	-	337	96	42.13	4	-	-	-	-	-	-
Higgs, K	1	2	-	2	2	1.00	1	-	58.3	19	121	2	60.50
Illingworth, R	3	4	-	51	27	12.75	1	-	183.2	82	291	13	22.38
Knight, BR	2	3	-	34	27*	17.00	1	-	40.4	16	85	4	21.25
Knott, APE	5	8	-	116	34	16.57	11	4	-	-	-	-	-
Milburn, C	2	3	-	109	83	36.33	2	-	-	-	-	-	-
Pocock, PI	1	2	-	16	10	8.00	2	-	58.0	15	156	6	26.00
Prideaux, RM	1	2	-	66	64	33.00	-	-	-	-	-	-	-
Snow, JA	5	7	2	56	19	11.20	3	-	203.0	44	508	17	29.88
Underwood, DL	4	4	4	69	45*	-	2	-	209.5	103	302	20	15.10

Droll Doug Walters stands tall

Doug Walters had a lot in common with Stan McCabe, a hero of the 1930s. Both were born in the NSW 'bush'. Both were gifted stroke players, matchwinners when the occasion called for bold batting, and both played for Australia at the age of 19.

The modest, droll Walters, one of Australia's most popular cricketers, was not the first young player to be labelled 'a second Bradman'.

He certainly began with a flourish, scoring more than 1000 runs in his first 11 Tests, including centuries in his first two Tests, against England, in 1965–66.

But he could not sustain that pace. There was a carefree gaiety about his batting, rather than a ruthless desire for runs. Of his 15 Test centuries, only two progressed beyond 200 – 242 against the West Indies in Sydney in 1969 and 250 (his highest Test score) against New Zealand in Christchurch in 1976–77.

Walters eschewed practice. He smoked and played cards in the dressing room while waiting to bat. One day his team-mates were staggered when he announced he was going to loosen up. He got to his feet, picked up a dart and threw it at the board and said: 'That'll do.'

In his era he had few peers as an attacking player, off the front foot or the back. Three times he made a century in a session and his spanking drives, cuts and hooks and innovative shots of his own making yielded him 5375 Test runs at an average of 48.26.

When he retired in 1981, only three Australians had made more Test runs – Greg Chappell, Bradman and Neil Harvey.

Walters was not a success in England, despite making 81 and 86 in his first Test there in 1968. In five Tests on that first visit he made 343 runs at 38.11. He joked that he scored his first century on Denham golf course. In four tours he averaged less than 26 in Tests and did not make a Test century. His highest Test score was a dashing 88 at Old Trafford in 1977.

As a bowler, Walters earned a reputation for breaking troublesome partnerships with his lively medium-pace deliveries. He claimed many notable scalps. In 1965–66, in the fifth Test against England, he dismissed John Edrich, Cowdrey, Barrington and skipper Mike Smith for 53 runs. In the field Walters was brisk and had a safe pair of hands.

The son of a dairy farmer, Kevin Douglas Walters was born at Dungog (north-west of Newcastle) on 21 December 1945. His father Ted played B-grade cricket. His mother Maud kept wickets for the local women's team. His older brother Warren helped him fashion a pitch on the farm with the tractor.

Walters first came to prominence with 140 not out for NSW Colts against Queensland, hitting one six right out of the SCG Ground No. 2 into the Kippax Lake 60 metres from the ground. In Adelaide in 1964–65 he shared with Lyn Marks the second highest partnership in Sheffield Shield history – 378 v South Australia. His contribution was 253 and, for good measure, he took 7/63.

He won Test selection the next season after scoring 129 for NSW against the touring Englishmen at the SCG on 27 November 1965. NSW was 2/4 when he came in and reeled off a superb century in 193 minutes.

A little over a fortnight later, he scored 155 against England in his Test debut in Brisbane. He reached his century in 242 minutes and his innings lasted 322 minutes and included 11 fours and a 6.

With Bill Lawry (166), Walters put on 187 for the fifth wicket. Not satisfied with 155 on debut, Walters cracked 115 in the next Test at the MCG, ending the series with 410 runs at at 68.33.

Two years National Service training prevented Walters touring South Africa in 1966–67 and he resumed his Test career in 1968 with 93 and 62 not out against India in Brisbane.

Some critics said Walters was not the same player after doing his National Service. He scoffed at that, saying his form against the West Indies in 1968–69 was the best of his career. The figures proved it. In four Tests he made 699 runs, including 242 and 103 in Sydney – the first player to score a double century and a century in the same Test. In the first innings he shared a record fourth-wicket stand of 336 with Bill Lawry.

He scored three centuries in a row for NSW in 1972–73: 159, 133 and 176 (plus 5/61) and he took that form to the West Indies in 1973, scoring 497 runs in five Tests at 71.00, including a century between lunch and tea at Port-of-Spain.

Doug Walters – the people's choice, who believed in attack.

His hundred between tea and stumps against England in Perth in 1975 has become part of cricket folklore. He needed a 6 off the last ball, bowled by Bob Willis, to post his century and, to the delight of the crowd, promptly hooked it over the fence. He was given a standing ovation as he left the ground but no such greeting awaited him in the dressing rooms.

Not a soul was in sight as he entered. He didn't know whether to laugh or cry. Presently, captain Ian Chappell appeared and admonished him for playing such an outrageous shot off the last ball. Then Chappelli put his arms around him and the rest of the team materialised.

Though a great favorite with the crowds – for his flair and epitomisation of the typical 'ocker' – the poker-faced Walters didn't seek adulation. But such was his appeal at the SCG, his home ground, that he had his own wee slice of the Hill – a tarpaulin poster proclaiming 'The Doug Walters Stand'. In time, a permanent stand was built in his honor.

Though he didn't know it at the time, Walters was to leave the cricket scene prematurely after the summer of 1980–81. That was the season he returned to establishment cricket after an indifferent stint with Packer cricket. In six Tests against New Zealand and India in 1980–81 he made 397 runs at 56.70, including a sparkling 107 against the Kiwis. The selectors must have thought long and hard about taking him to England in 1981. They decided not to, based on his past performances. Walters took the rejection in good grace and announced his retirement.

Australia wrests back Test supremacy

Sponsorship enters the cricket arena

Melbourne, Dec. 1. The latest trends in English cricket are sure to have an effect in Australia.

As manager of the Australian team that toured the UK, Bob Parish noted the increasing involvement of sponsors and promoters in the game.

The Board sought a sponsor for the series against the West Indies and tobacco company W. D. and H. O. Wills offered to put up $20,000 on the condition they could erect signs on the perimeter fence at each end of the ground. But the ground authorities at Melbourne and Sydney refused permission and the offer was withdrawn.

A freak catch

Melbourne, Dec. 30. It was a knockout catch in more ways than one in the West Indian second innings of the Melbourne Test.

Seymour Nurse racked up 74 runs before spinner Johnny Gleeson fed up a long hop which the West Indian eagerly hoped to despatch to square leg. But the ball cannoned off the head of short-leg fieldsman Eric Freeman as he ducked for cover, and dollied into the waiting hands of Keith Stackpole, standing at square leg.

It signalled the end for the West Indies, who added just 37 more runs.

Melbourne, Dec. 30. Australia squared the Test series at one-all in a comprehensive second-Test victory at Melbourne.

It was an emphatic rebound after the West Indies' solid win in the opening Test at Brisbane. That has been the only high spot in the tourists' itinerary so far as they have struggled to find form and overcome the march of old age.

Veteran fast bowlers Wes Hall and Charlie Griffith are both on the wrong side of 30 and are clearly no longer the force they once were. Hall missed a month of cricket after tearing back ligaments while fielding and has still not played a Test while Griffiths broke down after just 12 overs in the first Test.

Captain Gary Sobers, laboring under a shoulder problem himself, was so short of bowling resources that he threw the ball to young batsman Clive Lloyd and the part-time off-spinner ended a 217-run partnership by snaring century-makers Ian Chappell and Bill Lawry.

Lloyd then showed why he had come to Australia with such a glittering reputation as a batsman and cruised effortlessly to a score of 129 that included 18 fours and a six. Set 366 to win in ten and a half hours Australia could not counter Sobers and Lance Gibbs on the spinning pitch.

Australia hit back immediately in the second Test and bowling on a pitch that had sweated under the covers. Graham McKenzie took 8/71 – the best bowling figures in a West Indies v Australia clash – then Lawry and Chappell set up victory with another mammoth stand of 298.

What a wicket! Graham McKenzie's 200th Test wicket was that of the great Gary Sobers in the second Test, bowled by a superb delivery.

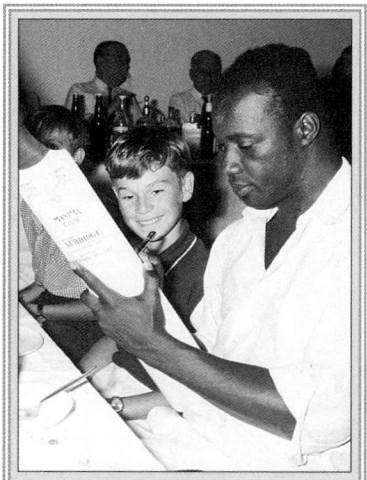

Wes Hall, the giant West Indies paceman, signs a Lindsay Hassett bat for a small admirer.

Keep out. Sydney crowds let Test 'keeper Barry Jarman know their feelings about who should keep for the Test team when he struggled behind the stumps. They wanted their man, Brian Taber, and Jarman commented that he had a sore back after the game 'where 28,000 people have been jumping on it.' Taber won his place when Jarman was dumped for the fifth Test.

Standing aside. Doug Walters asked to be relieved of the NSW captaincy midway through the season saying he needed to devote more time to his own cricket, business and domestic activities. Brian Taber replaced him and in his first match in charge he equalled the world wicketkeeping record with 12 dismissals (10 caught, 2 stumped). It was even more amazing as only 17 South Australian wickets fell in the match.

Up the list. The decision to use Keith Stackpole as a Test opener has revitalised the Victorian's career. He relished the change from batting down the order. 'You get lazy waiting so long,' he said. But he admits that he was too nervous to buckle up his pads when Bill Lawry suddenly told him he was about to open in the third Test.

At the double. Sixteen of the world's best players took part in a double wicket competition around Australia just prior to the start of the season. The highly publicised event, in which players compete in teams of two, was organised by former Test skipper Bob Simpson and proved popular with crowds.

A sad passing. The cricket world was saddened by the premature death of former keeper Wally Grout at the age of 41. He retired from cricket in 1966, but it was revealed that he had suffered a heart attack in 1964 just months before taking part in the trip to the West Indies.

Back again. West Indian batsman Rohan Kanhai accepted an offer to coach in Tasmania in 1969–70. After the last West Indian tour he spent a year with WA. Approaches were made to Gary Sobers to lure him back to South Australia where he performed so brilliantly for three Sheffield Shield seasons, but he knocked back the offer because of his heavy cricketing workload.

Instant hit. Young Rodney Marsh became the fourth Western Australian to score a century on his first class debut when he hit 104 against the West indies after making a duck in the first innings. Although a 'keeper for his district club, Marsh was picked as a batsman with Gordon Becker behind the stumps – but he has promise with the gloves at the higher level.

Sheahan and Connolly hold on in close one

Adelaide, Jan. 29. Adelaide has once again provided the stage for a thrilling draw between Australia and West Indies.

The drama did not stretch out for as long as the Ken Mackay–Lindsay Kline stand of 1960–61, but the tension was certainly real for the last 26 balls as Paul Sheahan and no. 11 batsman Alan Connolly held out the West Indies attack.

Sheahan needed to hold on, as his own bad calling had combined with the brilliant fielding of the West Indies to run out Doug Walters, Eric Freeman and Barry Jarman at a crucial stage on the last day.

This was a free-scoring match in which the scoring rate never fell below 52 runs an hour. Although conditions were perfect for batting, the West Indies batted carelessly yet again and it was only a classic, even time century by Sobers that kept their first innings respectable.

All of Australia's top order batsmen contributed to a commanding first-innings lead and the prospect of a huge defeat stared the visitors in the face.

Suddenly the West Indies batting clicked and showed the application that had been sorely lacking. The Australian bowlers were pummelled and for the first time in the series spinner John Gleeson was belted out of the attack and left with the sorry figures of 1/176.

Late on the fourth day Australia looked to have stemmed the tide, but then Jackie Hendriks and David Holford added a fine ninth-wicket stand of 122 which stretched out the Australian target to 360 runs.

Graham McKenzie swings one away in his 59 in the first innings.

Sobers's decision to bat on into the fifth day cost him 15 minutes of time that later proved crucial. Lawry, Stackpole, Chappell and Walters gave Australia a great start and with an hour remaining the team needed 62 runs from 120 balls with seven wickets standing. But the late collapse of the lower order left Sheahan and Connolly purely clinging to their wickets.

The West Indies has been unable to staunch the flow of runs from the Aussie bats, particularly Ian Chappell, who has had an amazing sequence against the tourists. Even when Chappell 'failed' with a 33 in the third Test in Sydney, the team made over 500 and won the game by 10 wickets.

Charlie Griffith 'does a Mankad' on hapless Ian Redpath

Adelaide, Jan. 29. Australian batsman Ian Redpath was run out in sensational fashion during his team's run chase on the last day of the fourth Test.

West Indies bowler Charlie Griffith ran in to bowl, held onto the ball and ran out the non-striker as he drifted out of the crease.

Redpath admits that he went 'walkabout', but Griffith did not give the traditional warning.

At tea West Indies captain Gary Sobers apologised to the Australian captain Bill Lawry for Griffith's action.

The action evokes memories of Indian bowler Vinoo Mankad, who twice ran out Australia's Bill Brown in the Test series 20 years ago. This type of dismissal has entered the Australian cricketing vernacular as 'a Mankad'.

Charlie Griffith 'Mankads' Ian Redpath on the final day.

Talented Windies are lacking lustre

Sydney, Feb. 20. The 1968–69 West Indians have found it hard to emulate their predecessors.

No team in the modern era has had such an impact as the 1960–61 West Indians. Just six members of that side made this trip, but the men from the Caribbean have not been able to recapture the public's imagination.

The magnificent batting of Gary Sobers has maintained the stellar heights of the past, but Rohan Kanhai was well short of his best and the others were inconsistent, apart from Basil Butcher. Joey Carew was a surprise packet.

In the field too many catches have been dropped and the bowling lacked a sharp edge.

Crowds are down

Sydney, Feb. 1. Veteran fast bowler Wes Hall has admitted in *Australian Cricket* magazine that he is disappointed with the crowds that the West Indies have attracted this season.

'Having played in the 1960–61 series where you had 98,000 people in Melbourne, I would say that I am a bit disappointed.

'But youngsters nowadays have got other interests. There's always the beach, and people have got more money.'

Total attendance for the series was 428,940, paying $277,668 which was well below the targets of 755,000 and $488,000 which the Australian Cricket Board had budgeted for, based on the returns of the 1960–61 tour.

Chappell torments West Indies

Sydney, Feb. 20. Ian Chappell has haunted the West Indies this summer In all first class matches he has averaged 82 and has totalled 1476 runs. More than 1000 of those runs have been peeled off the West Indian attack.

His amazing run against them began with 188 not out for a Combined XI in the second match of the tour. On the following weekend he pillaged the visitors again in scoring 123 for SA.

There was no let-up in the Test series, with 117 and 50 at Brisbane followed by 180 in another outing for SA against the Caribbean bowlers.

His 165 in the Melbourne Test was his fifth century against the tourists inside eight weeks.

Walters gets 242 then 103

Four of Doug Walters' wonderful match total of 345.

Sydney, Feb. 19. Doug Walters has created a Test record by scoring a double century and a century in the one game.

His 242 and 103 were scored before an adoring home crowd in Sydney, setting up a 382 run victory that gave Australia a 3–1 win in the series. As the series could still be squared by the West Indies, this Test was to be played over six days.

Walters began this summer needing to affirm his Test place after a disappointing tour of England. A thigh injury kept him out of the first Test, then he picked up the threads immediately, scoring centuries in the third and fourth Tests before building up to the crescendo in Sydney.

In six Test innings his lowest score was 50, and he built a Bradman-esque average of 116.50.

Australia slumped to 3/51 in the first innings, but a 336-run stand by Walters and Bill Lawry crushed West Indian spirits.

Walters gave his captain a 90-minute start and quickly passed him. Frank Tyson has described his innings as 'the supreme example of an eye player in superlative form.'

Milburn gets crowds, but SA wins

Brisbane, March 1. Roly-poly Englishman Colin Milburn produced an electrifying performance against Queensland in Brisbane, when he scored a searing 243.

The 18-stone Western Australian opener began steadily, scoring 61 out of 92 by lunch, then savaged the bowlers to an extent rarely seen. Between lunch and tea he scored 181 runs off 134 balls, and was dismissed immediately after tea. His 243 included 38 fours and four sixes, a couple of which landed in the street.

In the dressing room, burly Queenslander Peter Burge congratulated Milburn 'on behalf of all fat men'. Queensland fieldsman Geoff Gray dropped Milburn three times and in one attempt was forced into the pickets chest first by the power of the stroke.

The match against South Australia provided a graphic illustration of his batting ferocity. When WA needed 146 to win in even time, Milburn and partner Derek Chadwick reached the target with 16 minutes to spare – Milburn belting one six and ten fours in his 82 not out.

Milburn scored a record 940 runs this season, but it wasn't enough to win the Shield for WA. They came second to South Australia.

Australian cricket judges are amazed that Milburn has not held down a regular place in the English team.

THIRD TEST 1968–69 AUSTRALIA v WEST INDIES
Sydney Cricket Ground, Sydney. January 3, 4, 7, 8, 1968.
Toss: West Indies. Australia won by 10 wkts.

WEST INDIES

RC Fredericks c Chappell b McKenzie	26	c Redpath b Connolly	43
MC Carew c Jarman b McKenzie	30	c Jarman b Freeman	10
RB Kanhai b McKenzie	17	c Chappell b McKenzie	69
BF Butcher b Stackpole	28	c & b Gleeson	101
SM Nurse c Redpath b Connolly	3	c Stackpole b McKenzie	17
GS Sobers (c) b Freeman	49	c Chappell b Gleeson	36
CH Lloyd c Jarman b Freeman	50	c Stackpole b Freeman	13
JL Hendriks (+) c Stackpole b Freeman	4 (9)	c Connolly b Gleeson	22
RM Edwards b Connolly	10 (8)	b Freeman	0
WW Hall c Gleeson b McKenzie	33	st Jarman b Gleeson	5
LR Gibbs not out	1	not out	1
Extras (B 2, LB 10, NB 1)	13	(LB 3, NB 4)	7
TOTAL	264		324

FOW 1st Inns: 49 72 79 85 143 181 216 217 236 264
FOW 2nd Inns: 20 123 127 168 243 263 264 318 323 324

Bowling: *First Innings*: McKenzie 22.1-3-85-4, Connolly 16-1-54-2, Freeman 13-2-57-3, Walters 2-1-3-0, Gleeson 18-7-45-0, Stackpole 4-2-7-1. *Second Innings*: McKenzie 24-2-80-2, Connolly 23-7-54-1, Freeman 15-3-59-3, Gleeson 26-5-91-4, Stackpole 5-0-33-0.

AUSTRALIA

WM Lawry (c) c Carew b Edwards	29		
KR Stackpole c Gibbs b Hall	58	not out	21
IM Chappell c Kanhai b Gibbs	33		
IR Redpath st Hendriks b Carew	80		
KD Walters b Gibbs	118		
AP Sheahan c Lloyd b Hall	47 (1)	not out	21
BN Jarman (+) c Fredericks b Hall	0		
EW Freeman b Edwards	76		
GD McKenzie run out	10		
JW Gleeson not out	42		
AN Connolly run out	37		
Extras (B 5, LB 11, W 1)	17		0
TOTAL	547		0 for 42

FOW 1st Inns: 68 95 153 235 345 349 387 418 474 547
FOW 2nd Inns:

Bowling: *First Innings*: Hall 26-2-113-3, Edwards 25-1-139-2, Sobers 21-4-109-0, Gibbs 37.6-6-124-2, Carew 12-1-45-1. *Second Innings*: Hall 2-0-8-0, Edwards 1-0-7-0, Carew 2-0-9-0, Lloyd 2-0-8-0, Kanhai 1-0-10-0.

Umpires: CJ Egar & LP Rowan

FIFTH TEST 1968–69 AUSTRALIA v WEST INDIES
Sydney Cricket Ground, Sydney. February 14, 15, 16, 18, 19, 20, 1969.
Toss: West Indies. Australia won by 382 runs.

AUSTRALIA

WM Lawry (c) b Griffith	151	c Fredericks b Griffith	17
KR Stackpole b Hall	20	c Carew b Hall	6
IM Chappell lbw Sobers	1	c Hendriks b Hall	10
IR Redpath c Nurse b Sobers	0	c Sobers b Gibbs	132
KD Walters b Gibbs	242	c Fredericks b Gibbs	103
AP Sheahan c Fredericks b Griffith	27	c Hendriks b Sobers	34
EW Freeman c Hendriks b Griffith	56	c Carew b Sobers	15
GD McKenzie b Gibbs	19	c Carew b Sobers	40
HB Taber (+) lbw Hall	48	not out	15
JW Gleeson c Hendriks b Hall	45	not out	5
AN Connolly not out	1		
Extras (LB 2, W 1, NB 6)	9	(B 4, LB 6, W 1, NB 6)	17
TOTAL	619		8 dec 394

FOW 1st Inns: 43 51 51 387 435 453 483 543 614 619
FOW 2nd Inns: 21 36 40 250 301 329 329 388

Bowling: *First Innings*: Hall 35.7-3-157-3, Griffith 37-1-175-3, Sobers 28-4-94-2, Gibbs 40-8-133-2, Carew 10-2-44-0, Lloyd 2-1-7-0. *Second Innings*: Hall 12-0-47-0, Griffith 14-0-41-1, Gibbs 33-2-133-2, Sobers 26-3-117-3, Carew 5-0-26-0, Lloyd 2-0-13-0.

WEST INDIES

RC Fredericks c Taber b Connolly	39	c Taber b McKenzie	0
MC Carew c Taber b Freeman	64	b Connolly	3
RB Kanhai c Taber b Connolly	44	c Connolly b McKenzie	18
GS Sobers (c) c Taber b Connolly	13 (5)	c Redpath b Gibbs	113
BF Butcher c Sheahan b McKenzie	10 (4)	c Gleeson b Stackpole	31
CH Lloyd b McKenzie	53	c Freeman b Stackpole	11
SM Nurse c Stackpole b Connolly	9	b Gleeson	137
JL Hendriks (+) c Taber b McKenzie	1	c Stackpole b McKenzie	16
CC Griffith c Freeman b Gleeson	27	b Gleeson	15
WW Hall b Gleeson	1	c Sheahan b Chappell	0
LR Gibbs not out	4	not out	0
Extras (B 2, LB 4, NB 8)	14	(B 1, LB 5, NB 2)	8
TOTAL	279		352

FOW 1st Inns: 100 154 159 179 179 190 193 257 259 279
FOW 2nd Inns: 0 10 30 76 102 220 284 351 352 352

Bowling: *First Innings*: McKenzie 22.6-2-90-3, Connolly 17-2-61-4, Freeman 12-2-48-1, Gleeson 19-8-53-2, Chappell 6-1-13-0. *Second Innings*: McKenzie 16-1-93-3, Connolly 18-4-72-1, Stackpole 7-0-57-2, Gleeson 15.2-1-84-3, Freeman 2-0-16-0, Chappell 6-0-22-1.

Umpires: CJ Egar & LP Rowan

FOURTH TEST 1968–69 AUSTRALIA v WEST INDIES
Adelaide Oval, Adelaide. January 24, 25, 27, 28, 29, 1968.
Toss: West Indies. Match Drawn.

WEST INDIES

RC Fredericks lbw Connolly	17	c Chappell b Connolly	23
MC Carew c Chappell b Gleeson	36	c Chappell b Connolly	90
RB Kanhai lbw Connolly	11	b Connolly	80
BF Butcher c Chappell b Gleeson	52	c Sheahan b McKenzie	118
SM Nurse c & b McKenzie	5 (6)	lbw Gleeson	40
GS Sobers (c) b Freeman	110 (7)	c Walters b Connolly	52
CH Lloyd c Lawry b Gleeson	10 (8)	c Redpath b Connolly	42
DAJ Holford c McKenzie b Freeman	6 (9)	c Stackpole b McKenzie	80
CC Griffith b Freeman	7 (5)	run out	24
JL Hendriks (+) not out	10	not out	37
LR Gibbs c Connolly b Freeman	4	b McKenzie	1
Extras (B 5, LB 2, NB 1)	8	(B 5, LB 12, NB 12)	29
TOTAL	276		616

FOW 1st Inns: 21 39 89 107 199 215 228 261 264 276
FOW 2nd Inns: 35 167 240 304 376 404 476 492 614 616

Bowling: *First Innings*: McKenzie 14-1-51-1, Connolly 13-3-61-2, Freeman 10.3-0-52-4, Gleeson 25-5-91-3, Stackpole 3-1-13-0. *Second Innings*: McKenzie 22.2-4-90-3, Connolly 34-7-122-5, Freeman 18-3-96-0, Gleeson 35-2-176-1, Stackpole 12-3-44-0, Chappell 14-0-50-0, Walters 1-0-6-0, Redpath 1-0-3-0.

AUSTRALIA

WM Lawry (c) c Butcher b Sobers	62	c (S)CA Davis b Sobers	89
KR Stackpole c Hendriks b Holford	62	c Hendriks b Gibbs	50
IM Chappell c Sobers b Gibbs	76	lbw Griffith	96
IR Redpath lbw Carew	45	run out	9
KD Walters c & b Griffith	110	run out	50
AP Sheahan b Gibbs	51	not out	11
EW Freeman lbw Griffith	33	run out	1
BN Jarman (+) c Hendriks b Gibbs	4	run out	4
GD McKenzie c Nurse b Holford	59	c (S)GS Camacho b Gibbs	4
JW Gleeson b Gibbs	17	lbw Griffith	0
AN Connolly not out	1	not out	6
Extras (B 3, LB 6, NB 5)	14	(B 8, LB 10, NB 1)	19
TOTAL	533		9 for 339

FOW 1st Inns: 89 170 248 254 347 424 429 465 529 533
FOW 2nd Inns: 86 185 215 304 315 318 322 333 333

Bowling: *First Innings*: Sobers 28-4-106-1, Griffith 22-4-94-2, Holford 18.5-0-118-2, Gibbs 43-8-145-4, Carew 9-3-30-1, Lloyd 6-0-26-0. *Second Innings*: Griffith 19-2-73-2, Sobers 22-1-107-1, Gibbs 26-7-79-2, Holford 15-1-53-0, Carew 2-0-8-0.

Umpires: CJ Egar & LP Rowan

Australian Averages

1968–69 AUSTRALIA v WEST INDIES

AUSTRALIA	M	Inn	NO	Runs	H.S	Avrge	Ct	St	Overs	Mds	Runs	Wkt	Avrge
Chappell, IM	5	8	-	548	165	68.50	10	-	45.0	2	152	3	50.67
Connolly, AN	5	7	4	48	37	16.00	3	-	192.0	39	628	20	31.40
Freeman, EW	4	6	-	183	76	30.50	3	-	88.3	11	391	13	30.08
Gleeson, JW	5	8	3	120	45	24.00	5	-	250.6	57	844	26	32.46
Inverarity, RJ	1	2	-	14	9	7.00	2	-	-	-	-	-	-
Jarman, BN	4	6	-	40	17	6.67	12	1	-	-	-	-	-
Lawry, WM	5	8	-	667	205	83.38	1	-	-	-	-	-	-
Mallett, AA	1	2	-	25	19	12.50	1	-	18.0	2	86	1	86.00
McKenzie, GD	5	8	1	175	59	25.00	2	-	206.1	27	758	30	25.27
Redpath, IR	5	8	-	291	132	36.38	9	-	1.0	-	3	-	-
Sheahan, AP	5	9	2	257	51	36.71	5	-	-	-	-	-	-
Stackpole, KR	5	9	-	265	62	33.13	7	-	61.0	19	251	4	62.75
Taber, HB	1	2	1	63	48	63.00	6	-	-	-	-	-	-
Walters, KD	4	6	-	699	242	116.50	1	-	3.0	-	9	-	-

West Indian Averages

1968–69 AUSTRALIA v WEST INDIES

WEST INDIES	M	Inn	NO	Runs	H.S	Avrge	Ct	St	Overs	Mds	Runs	Wkt	Avrge
Butcher, BF	5	10	-	405	118	40.50	2	-	-	-	-	-	-
Camacho, GS	2	4	-	57	40	14.25	1	-	-	-	-	-	-
Carew, MC	5	10	-	427	90	47.44	6	-	59.0	9	238	3	79.33
Davis, CA	1	2	-	28	18	14.00	-	-	24.0	-	94	1	94.00
Edwards, RM	2	4	1	40	21	13.33	-	-	52.0	2	274	3	91.33
Fredericks, RC	4	8	-	271	76	33.88	4	-	-	-	-	-	-
Gibbs, LR	5	10	5	28	17	5.60	2	-	292.2	52	923	24	38.46
Griffith, CC	3	6	-	82	27	13.67	1	-	104.0	8	430	8	53.75
Hall, WW	2	4	-	39	33	9.75	-	-	75.7	5	325	8	40.63
Hendriks, JL	5	10	3	118	37*	16.86	9	2	-	-	-	-	-
Holford, DAJ	2	4	-	96	80	24.00	3	-	72.5	8	290	4	72.50
Kanhai, RB	5	10	-	371	94	37.10	2	-	1.0	-	10	-	-
Lloyd, CH	4	8	-	315	129	39.38	2	-	22.0	2	78	2	39.00
Nurse, SM	5	10	-	348	137	34.80	3	-	-	-	-	-	-
Sobers, GS	5	10	-	497	113	49.70	6	-	206.1	37	733	18	40.72

First Test blood to Australia

Rusi Surti is out lbw to Alan Connolly in the first Test at Bombay.

Bombay, Nov. 9. Bill Lawry's Australian team has overcome its first big hurdle on the Indian tour by notching a win in the first Test at Bombay.

A tour of India must be the toughest assignment that can face a Test cricketer, and this trip is placing a great deal of pressure on the Australians.

Originally it was intended that the Australians would complete the second half of this tour in Pakistan, but its cricketing authority could not pay the normal guarantee to the Australian Board.

The South Africans quickly volunteered to invite Australia for a four-Test series and thus the Australians were committed to playing nine Tests in 13 weeks across two different continents.

Events surrounding the first Test gave a hint of possible turmoil. There was public outcry when India's selectors dropped spinner Venkataraghavan and before the Test, medium-pacer Guha agreed to step down to let Venkataraghavan play.

The spinner was in the midst of the chaos that erupted on the fourth day. With India sliding to defeat on 7/114 umpire Shambu Pan gave Venkataraghavan out, caught behind by Taber off Connolly. Radio commentators said that Lawry should be a sportsman and recall the batsman. That enraged many of the crowd armed with transistor radios.

Rocks, bottles and fruit were showered onto the ground and the next batsman, Prasanna, took 10 minutes to emerge from the dressing room. When he did, he was accompanied by the Chief of Police.

Behind the stands the crowd set fire to cars, tennis nets and other equipment and smoke billowed across the ground in such a thick screen that the scorer ran onto the field complaining he could not see the game. With his side on top, Lawry was determined to stay on the field and at the end of the day India was 9/125.

Officials restricted the number of people allowed into the ground on the following day, and in an eerie silence Australia took the last wicket and then knocked off the required runs.

Riots, death make tense cricket on sub-continent

Calcutta, Dec. 20. Incident follows incident on this tour and reports coming out of the subcontinent are being exaggerated because no English or Australian reporters are there, and only the Indian view is being expressed.

In Australia, Richie Benaud has raised questions over the veracity of Indian reporting.

Still, there is no doubt that there is an unpleasant aspect to this trip.

It began with the Bombay riot over Venkataraghavan's dismissal, and even the more reasonable elements on the Indian side consider that Lawry was too dogmatic in continuing the game amidst thick smoke and with the backdrop of a rioting crowd.

At the height of the riot Ian Chappell suggested to Lawry that it may be a good idea to leave the field, but the skipper only said: 'Hell, we need a wicket badly.'

Other smaller incidents have not helped – such as Lawry hurling down his cap in disgust when umpires refused to let him squeeze in an extra over before a lunch break.

The Australian skipper seems to be constantly on the look out for umpiring mistakes, and this probably stems from his experience in the brief tour of 1964.

The volatility of Indian crowds is well known, but it has shown an even darker side this trip. On the Australians' very first night in India 3000 demonstrators mounted an anti-Vietnam protest against Doug Walters because he had been a National Serviceman.

There was tragedy on the night before the Calcutta Test when six people died in a riot among people queuing for tickets.

At various times the Australians' bus has been pelted with stones and players have been forced to lie on the floor for protection. There is a strong belief that the disturbances are politically motivated because they only seem to occur in certain parts of the country, but the mysteries of Indian politics are beyond the understanding of outsiders.

Meanwhile, the Indian press is keen to pounce on Lawry for any perceived transgression. When he pulled away from facing a delivery at Bangalore because a woman in a brightly colored sari walked in front of the sight-screen he was even accused of insulting Indian womenhood!

Riot threatens Calcutta test

Bill Lawry and Keith Stackpole hold the fort at Calcutta.

Calcutta, Dec. 16. Six people were killed when tension surrounding the fourth Test at Calcutta bubbled over into tragedy.

With the series level at one–all and the Australians holding a 111-run lead, there was unprecedented demand for tickets and 30,000 people lined up overnight seeking the 8000 tickets that were available. When latecomers tried to grab tickets in the morning, there was a wild melee that left six people dead and 100 injured.

Those who did get into the game were dismayed to see their team bundled out for 161. The Calcutta crowd vented its anger at the home captain and shouts of 'Shame Pataudi' filled the air.

As Australia only needed 42 for victory some of the rowdier elements in the second tier of the grandstand began to leave and showered those below with bottles and other rubbish. They streamed onto the ground and stopped play.

During this shambles Lawry clashed with a photographer. After telling him to get off the ground, Lawry ran at the photographer, prodding him with his bat and the man fell on his camera.

The secretary of the Indian Press photographers Association has instructed his members to wear black armbands at the Australians' next match as a form of protest.

Ashley Mallett's turn in land of spin

Madras, Dec. 28. Ashley Mallett has relished his role as Australia's principal spinner in the fifth Test.

He had the home team in trouble right from the start of its first innings with four of the first five wickets as the Indians slumped to 5/56.

Mallett's off-spin claimed 10 wickets for the match and brings his tally to 28 for the series. He asserted himself at the right time for Australia as Johnnie Gleeson struggled and was dropped after three Tests.

India was faced with a modest target of 249 to win the final Test, but Mallett sparked a collapse. He has made the most of his chances on this tour and is now a much better bowler than he was at the start. In the past he has been under-used by Lawry, but has bowled 298 overs in this series.

Ashley Mallett and Paul Sheahan shake after Australia's win in the fifth Test at Madras.

FIRST TEST 1969–70 INDIA v AUSTRALIA
Brabourne Stadium, Bombay. November 4, 5, 7, 8, 9, 1969.
Toss: India. Australia won by 8 wkts.

INDIA

DN Sardesai b McKenzie	20	c Taber b Gleeson	3
FM Engineer (+) c Redpath b McKenzie	19	c McKenzie b Mallett	28
AV Mankad b McKenzie	74	b Gleeson	8
CG Borde c Chappell b McKenzie	2	c Redpath b Gleeson	18
Nawab of Pataudi jr (c) c Lawry b Gleeson	95	c Stackpole b Gleeson	0
AL Wadekar lbw Connolly	9	c McKenzie b Stackpole	46
RF Surti st Taber b Gleeson	4	lbw Connolly	13
S Abid Ali c Stackpole b McKenzie	3	lbw Connolly	2
S Venkataraghavan c Taber b Connolly	2	c Taber b Connolly	9
EAS Prasanna not out	12	b Mallett	3
BS Bedi c McKenzie b Gleeson	7	not out	1
Extras (B 15, LB 4, NB 5)	24	(B 4, NB 2)	6
TOTAL	271		137

FOW 1st Inns: 39 40 42 188 239 245 246 249 252 271
FOW 2nd Inns: 19 37 55 56 59 87 89 114 125 137

Bowling: *First Innings*: McKenzie 29-7-69-5, Connolly 31-11-55-2, Gleeson 35.4-18-52-3, Walters 6-0-13-0, Mallett 30-19-43-0, Stackpole 3-1-8-0, Chappell 1-0-7-0. *Second Innings*: McKenzie 16-4-33-0, Connolly 20-10-20-3, Gleeson 32-17-56-4, Mallett 21-9-22-2, Stackpole 1.2-1-0-1.

AUSTRALIA

WM Lawry (c) b Prasanna	25	b Surti	2
KR Stackpole c Surti b Prasanna	103	lbw Surti	11
IM Chappell b Prasanna	31	not out	31
KD Walters c Venkataraghavan b Bedi	48	not out	22
IR Redpath c Wadekar b Venkataraghavan	77		
AP Sheahan lbw Venkataraghavan	14		
GD McKenzie c Borde b Prasanna	16		
HB Taber (+) c Surti b Bedi	5		
AA Mallett not out	10		
JW Gleeson c Borde b Prasanna	0		
AN Connolly c(S)ED Solkar b Bedi	8		
Extras (B 4, NB 4)	8	(B 1)	1
TOTAL	345		2 for 67

FOW 1st Inns: 81 164 167 285 297 322 322 337 337 345
FOW 2nd Inns: 8 13

Bowling: *First Innings*: Abid Ali 18-3-52-0, Surti 9-2-23-0, Venkataraghavan 31-11-67-2, Bedi 62.4-33-74-3, Prasanna 49-19-121-5. *Second Innings*: Abid Ali 3-0-14-0, Surti 4-1-9-2, Bedi 9-5-11-0, Prasanna 9-3-20-0, Mankad 0.5-0-10-0, Venkataraghavan 1-0-2-0.

Umpires: I Gopalakrishnan & SP Pan

SECOND TEST 1969–70 INDIA v AUSTRALIA
Green Park (Modi Stadium), Kanpur. November 15, 16, 18, 19, 20, 1969.
Toss: India. Match Drawn.

INDIA

FM Engineer (+) c & b Stackpole	77	c Gleeson b Connolly	21
AV Mankad c & b Mallett	64	b McKenzie	68
AL Wadekar c Mallett b Connolly	27	c Chappell b Connolly	12
GR Viswanath c Redpath b Connolly	0	lbw Mallett	137
Nawab of Pataudi jr (c) c Redpath b McKenzie	38	lbw McKenzie	0
A Gandotra c Taber b Connolly	13	c Chappell b Gleeson	8
ED Solkar b Connolly	44	c Taber b McKenzie	35
S Venkataraghavan run out	17	not out	20
S Guha lbw Mallett	6	not out	1
EAS Prasanna c McKenzie b Mallett	22		
BS Bedi not out	1		
Extras (LB 5, NB 6)	11	(LB 1, NB 9)	10
TOTAL	320		7 dec 312

FOW 1st Inns: 111 167 171 171 197 239 285 287 315 320
FOW 2nd Inns: 43 94 125 125 147 257 306

Bowling: *First Innings*: McKenzie 25-7-70-1, Connolly 36-13-91-4, Gleeson 29-5-79-0, Mallett 51.5-30-58-3, Stackpole 2-1-4-1, Walters 2-1-7-0. *Second Innings*: McKenzie 34-13-63-3, Connolly 36-7-69-2, Gleeson 35-11-74-1, Mallett 36-18-62-1, Stackpole 7-1-21-0, Walters 3-1-7-0, Lawry 1-0-6-0.

AUSTRALIA

KR Stackpole run out	40	not out	37
WM Lawry (c) c Solkar b Venkataraghavan	14	not out	56
IM Chappell lbw Prasanna	16		
KD Walters b Bedi	53		
IR Redpath c Guha b Solkar	70		
AP Sheahan c Engineer b Guha	114		
AA Mallett b Venkataraghavan	4		
GD McKenzie lbw Prasanna	0		
HB Taber (+) c Viswanath b Venkataraghavan	1		
JW Gleeson b Guha	13		
AN Connolly not out	7		
Extras (B 4, LB 7, NB 5)	16	(NB 2)	2
TOTAL	348		0 for 95

FOW 1st Inns: 48 56 93 140 271 287 290 297 331 348
FOW 2nd Inns:

Bowling: *First Innings*: Guha 21.2-6-55-2, Solkar 19-7-44-1, Bedi 49-21-82-1, Prasanna 39-18-71-2, Venkataraghavan 37-16-76-3, Viswanath 1-0-4-0. *Second Innings*: Guha 5-1-7-0, Solkar 12-3-37-0, Nawab 1-0-4-0, Venkataraghavan 4-1-11-0, Prasanna 15-6-17-0, Bedi 3-1-8-0, Viswanath 1-0-4-0, Mankad 1-1-0-0, Gandotra 1-0-5-0, Wadekar 1-1-0-0.

Umpires: AM Mamsa & B Satyaji Rao

THIRD TEST 1969–70 INDIA v AUSTRALIA
Feroze Shah Kotla Ground, Delhi. November 28, 29, 30, December 2, 1969.
Toss: Australia. India won by 7 wkts.

AUSTRALIA
KR Stackpole st Engineer b Bedi	.61	b Prasanna	.9
WM Lawry (c) b Guha	.6	not out	.49
IM Chappell b Bedi	.138	c Solkar b Bedi	.0
KD Walters c Solkar b Prasanna	.4	b Bedi	.0
IR Redpath c Bedi b Prasanna	.6	b Bedi	.4
AP Sheahan b Bedi	.4	c Venkataraghavan b Prasanna	.15
HB Taber (+) st Engineer b Bedi	.46	c & b Prasanna	.7
AA Mallett b Venkataraghavan	.2 (9)	c Venkataraghavan b Prasanna	.0
GD McKenzie lbw Prasanna	.20 (8)	lbw Bedi	.7
JW Gleeson c Solkar b Prasanna	.1	c Viswanath b Bedi	.1
AN Connolly not out	.4	c & b Prasanna	.11
Extras (B 2, LB 1, NB 1)	.4	(B 4)	.4
TOTAL	.296		.107

FOW 1st Inns: 33 100 105 117 133 251 260 283 291 296
FOW 2nd Inns: 15 16 16 24 61 81 88 89 92 107

Bowling: *First Innings*: Guha 14-0-47-1, Solkar 11-1-43-0, Bedi 42-15-71-4, Prasanna 38.4-9-111-4, Venkataraghavan 14-4-20-1. *Second Innings*: Guha 2-0-7-0, Solkar 1-1-0-0, Bedi 23-11-37-5, Prasanna 24.2-10-42-5, Venkataraghavan 8-2-17-0.

INDIA
FM Engineer (+) b Connolly	.38	c McKenzie b Mallett	.6
AV Mankad c Walters b Mallett	.97	b Mallett	.7
AL Wadekar c & b Stackpole	.22 (4)	not out	.91
GR Viswanath b Gleeson	.29 (5)	not out	.44
S Venkataraghavan c Walters b Mallett	.0		
Nawab of Pataudi jr (c) c Chappell b Mallett	.8		
A Roy c Taber b Mallett	.0		
ED Solkar not out	.13		
S Guha b Mallett	.0		
EAS Prasanna lbw Gleeson	.1		
BS Bedi b Mallett	.6 (3)	b Connolly	.20
Extras (B 3, LB 1, NB 5)	.9	(B 9, LB 2, NB 2)	.13
TOTAL	.223		3 for 181

FOW 1st Inns: 85 124 176 177 197 202 207 207 208 223
FOW 2nd Inns: 13 18 61

Bowling: *First Innings*: McKenzie 12-4-22-0, Connolly 20-4-43-1, Gleeson 34-14-62-2, Mallett 32.3-10-64-6, Stackpole 10-4-23-1. *Second Innings*: McKenzie 13.4-5-19-0, Connolly 16-5-35-1, Gleeson 12-5-24-0, Mallett 29-10-60-2, Stackpole 8-4-13-0, Chappell 2-0-17-0.

Umpires: I Gopalakrishnan & S Roy

FIFTH TEST 1969–70 INDIA v AUSTRALIA
Nehru (Corporation) Stadium, Madras. December 24, 25, 27, 28, 1969.
Toss: Australia. Australia won by 77 runs.

AUSTRALIA
KR Stackpole c Solkar b Venkataraghavan	.37	b Amarnath	.4
WM Lawry (c) c Bedi b Prasanna	.33	b Prasanna	.2
IM Chappell b Prasanna	.4	b Amarnath	.5
KD Walters c Venkataraghavan b Bedi	.102	c Solkar b Prasanna	.1
AP Sheahan c Solkar b Prasanna	.1 (6)	st Engineer b Prasanna	.8
IR Redpath c Engineer b Prasanna	.33 (5)	lbw Prasanna	.63
HB Taber (+) lbw Venkataraghavan	.10	c Solkar b Prasanna	.0
GD McKenzie lbw Venkataraghavan	.0	lbw Venkataraghavan	.24
LC Mayne c Chauhan b Venkataraghavan	.10	c Viswanath b Prasanna	.13
AA Mallett not out	.2	not out	.11
AN Connolly c & b Solkar	.11	c Engineer b Venkataraghavan	.8
Extras (B 11, LB 2)	.13	(B 8, LB 5, NB 1)	.14
TOTAL	.258		.153

FOW 1st Inns: 60 69 78 82 184 219 225 243 245 258
FOW 2nd Inns: 4 12 15 16 24 24 57 107 140 153

Bowling: *First Innings*: Amarnath 7-0-21-0, Solkar 8.2-5-8-1, Bedi 26-10-45-1, Prasanna 40-13-100-4, Venkataraghavan 34-13-71-4. *Second Innings*: Amarnath 24-11-31-2, Solkar 4-2-2-0, Venkataraghavan 12.5-2-26-2, Prasanna 31-14-74-6, Bedi 9-5-6-0.

INDIA
CPS Chauhan c Chappell b Mallett	.19	c Redpath b McKenzie	.1
AV Mankad c Taber b Mayne	.0	c Redpath b McKenzie	.10
AL Wadekar c Chappell b Mallett	.12	c Stackpole b Mayne	.55
GR Viswanath b Mallett	.6	c Redpath b Mallett	.59
FM Engineer (+) c Connolly b Mallett	.32	c & b McKenzie	.3
Nawab of Pataudi jr (c) c Sheahan b McKenzie	.59	c Chappell b Mallett	.4
ED Solkar c Taber b Mallett	.11	c & b Mallett	.12
M Amarnath not out	.16	c Taber b Mayne	.0
S Venkataraghavan run out	.2	b Mallett	.13
EAS Prasanna c Chappell b McKenzie	.0	c McKenzie b Mallett	.5
BS Bedi	..not out		.0
Extras (LB 5, W 1)	.6	(LB 4, W 5)	.9
TOTAL	9 dec 163		.171

FOW 1st Inns: 0 30 33 40 96 128 158 163 163
FOW 2nd Inns: 3 12 114 119 135 142 144 159 169 171

Bowling: *First Innings*: McKenzie 16.4-8-19-2, Mayne 7-2-21-1, Connolly 14-5-26-0, Mallett 25-7-91-5. *Second Innings*: McKenzie 24-9-45-3, Mayne 18-8-32-2, Mallett 29.2-12-53-5, Connolly 9-4-18-0, Stackpole 5-2-14-0.

Umpires: I Gopalakrishnan & B Satyaji Rao

FOURTH TEST 1969–70 INDIA v AUSTRALIA
Eden Gardens, Calcutta. December 12, 13, 14, 16, 1969.
Toss: Australia. Australia won by 10 wkts.

INDIA
FM Engineer (+) c Stackpole b McKenzie	.0	c Redpath b Freeman	.10
AV Mankad c Stackpole b McKenzie	.9	c Taber b McKenzie	.20
AL Wadekar c Freeman b McKenzie	.0	lbw Freeman	.62
GR Viswanath c Taber b Mallett	.54	b Freeman	.5
Nawab of Pataudi jr (c) c Chappell b Mallett	.15 (6)	c Connolly b Mallett	.1
A Roy c Taber b McKenzie	.18 (7)	c Sheahan b Connolly	.19
ED Solkar c Taber b McKenzie	.42 (5)	lbw Connolly	.21
S Venkataraghavan c Stackpole b Mallett	.24	b Connolly	.0
EAS Prasanna run out	.26	c Stackpole b Freeman	.0
S Guha b McKenzie	.4 (11)	not out	.1
BS Bedi not out	.9 (10)	c Chappell b Connolly	.7
Extras (B 5, LB 1, W 1, NB 4)	.11	(B 6, LB 4, NB 5)	.15
TOTAL	.212		.161

FOW 1st Inns: 0 0 22 64 103 103 154 178 184 212
FOW 2nd Inns: 29 31 40 90 93 141 141 142 159 161

Bowling: *First Innings*: McKenzie 33.4-12-67-6, Freeman 17-6-43-0, Connolly 17-5-27-0, Mallett 27-9-55-3, Stackpole 2-0-9-0. *Second Innings*: McKenzie 18-4-34-1, Freeman 26-7-54-4, Connolly 16.1-3-31-4, Mallett 17-5-27-1.

AUSTRALIA
WM Lawry (c) c Solkar b Bedi	.35	not out	.17
KR Stackpole run out	.41	not out	.25
IM Chappell c Wadekar b Bedi	.99		
KD Walters st Engineer b Bedi	.56		
IR Redpath c Wadekar b Bedi	.0		
AP Sheahan run out	.32		
EW Freeman c Prasanna b Bedi	.29		
HB Taber (+) b Bedi	.2		
GD McKenzie c Nawab b Bedi	.0		
AA Mallett not out	.2		
AN Connolly c Guha b Solkar	.31		
Extras (B 4, LB 2, NB 2)	.8		.0
TOTAL	.335		0 for 42

FOW 1st Inns: 65 84 185 185 257 279 302 302 302 335
FOW 2nd Inns:

Bowling: *First Innings*: Guha 19-5-55-0, Solkar 9.1-1-28-1, Prasanna 49-15-116-0, Venkataraghavan 16-6-30-0, Bedi 50-19-98-7. *Second Innings*: Guha 3-1-25-0, Wadekar 2-0-17-0.

Umpires: SP Pan & J Reuben

Australian Averages

1969–70 INDIA v AUSTRALIA
AUSTRALIA	M	Inn	NO	Runs	H.S	Avrge	Ct	St	Overs	Mds	Runs	Wkt	Avrge
Chappell, IM	5	8	1	324	138	46.29	10	-	3.0	-	24	-	-
Connolly, AN	5	7	2	80	31	16.00	2	-	215.1	67	415	17	24.41
Freeman, EW	1	1	-	29	29	29.00	1	-	43.0	13	97	4	24.25
Gleeson, JW	3	4	-	15	13	3.75	1	-	177.4	70	347	10	34.70
Lawry, WM	5	10	3	239	56*	34.14	1	-	1.0	-	6	-	-
Mallett, AA	5	7	4	31	11*	10.33	3	-	298.4	129	535	28	19.11
Mayne, LC	1	2	-	23	13	11.50	-	-	25.0	10	53	3	17.67
McKenzie, GD	5	7	-	69	24	9.86	1	-	222.0	73	441	21	21.00
Redpath, IR	5	7	-	253	77	36.14	8	-	-	-	-	-	-
Sheahan, AP	5	7	-	188	114	26.86	2	-	-	-	-	-	-
Stackpole, KR	5	10	2	368	103	46.00	9	-	38.2	14	92	3	30.67
Taber, HB	5	7	-	71	46	10.14	13	1	-	-	-	-	-
Walters, KD	5	8	1	286	102	40.86	2	-	11.0	2	27	-	-

Indian Averages

1969–70 INDIA v AUSTRALIA
INDIA	M	Inn	NO	Runs	H.S	Avrge	Ct	St	Overs	Mds	Runs	Wkt	Avrge
Abid Ali, S	1	2	-	5	3	2.50	-	-	21.0	3	66	-	-
Amarnath, M	1	2	1	16	16*	16.00	-	-	31.0	11	52	2	26.00
Bedi, BS	5	8	4	51	20	12.75	2	-	273.4	120	432	21	20.57
Borde, CG	1	2	-	20	18	10.00	2	-	-	-	-	-	-
Chauhan, CPS	1	2	-	20	19	10.00	1	-	-	-	-	-	-
Engineer, FM	5	10	-	234	77	23.40	3	4	-	-	-	-	-
Gandotra, A	1	2	-	21	13	10.50	-	-	1.0	-	5	-	-
Guha, S	3	5	2	12	6	4.00	2	-	64.2	13	196	3	65.33
Mankad, AV	5	10	-	357	97	35.70	-	-	1.5	1	10	-	-
Nawab of Pataudi jr	5	9	-	220	95	24.44	1	-	1.0	-	4	-	-
Prasanna, EAS	5	8	1	69	26	9.86	3	-	295.0	107	672	26	25.85
Roy, A	2	3	-	37	19	12.33	-	-	-	-	-	-	-
Sardesai, DN	1	2	-	23	20	11.50	-	-	-	-	-	-	-
Solkar, ED	4	7	1	178	44	29.67	10	-	64.3	20	162	3	54.00
Surti, RF	1	2	-	17	13	8.50	2	-	13.0	3	32	2	16.00
Venkataraghavan, S	5	9	1	87	24	10.88	4	-	157.5	55	320	12	26.67
Viswanath, GR	4	8	-	334	137	47.71	3	-	2.0	-	8	-	-
Wadekar, AL	5	10	1	336	91*	37.33	3	-	3.0	1	17	-	-

Skittled by South Africa, 4–0

Johhny Gleeson bowls to South African all-rounder 'Tiger' Lance at the Kingsmead ground in Durban.

Port Elizabeth, March 10. A drained and distracted Australian team has been mauled by the fit and success-hungry South Africans.

The South Africans won all four tests on their home soil and clearly established themselves as the top Test country in the world.

The Springboks' batting had depth and awesome quality, while the brilliant all-rounder Mike Procter headed an aggressive attack that proved too much for the Australians.

Australia's batsmen had only a matter of days to adjust from the slow, spinning wickets of India to the greenish, seaming tracks of South Africa and they were blasted aside in the Tests.

It was a sign of things to come when veteran Peter Pollock snared the wickets of Lawry and Chappell in the space of just four deliveries in the first Test. Australia was shot out for 164 and only Doug Walters (73) showed anything like his true ability.

The pattern of dramatic batting collapses continued throughout the series.

The South Africans could afford what seemed a luxury in Australian eyes, by leaving out 'keeper Denis Lindsay who had been the Aussies' nemesis three years earlier.

Despite indifferent first class form he returned for the last two Tests and added even more to the depth of the batting.

Graeme Pollock was dismissed for 1 and 4 in the last Test, but by then the damage had been done as he had already scored more than 500 runs in the first three games. Barry Richards was not far behind him in aggregate and effectiveness after his 140 in the second Test, with veteran Eddie Barlow and new boy Lee Irvine making significant contributions.

Dropped catches

Port Elizabeth, March 10. Outplayed in all departments, the Aussies have been especially humiliated in the area of fielding.

When yet another catch was put down late in the fourth Test off Johnny Gleeson it was estimated that 13 chances had been missed off the wily spinner's bowling.

Gleeson has been Australia's best bowler in this series and South Africans rate him the only Aussie that would earn a place in their side. The most costly miss off Gleeson's bowling was when Pollock was put down at 104 in the Second Test. He went on to make 274. By contrast, the South Africa's fielding has been sharp .

Near thing

Cape Town, Feb. 16. Australia's rapidly evaporating confidence took another body blow when they scraped out of the match against lowly provincial side Border.

Border is rated 10th of the 11 Currie Cup sides and its strong showing was largely due the innings of former Test batsman Bill 'Buster' Farrer who made a dazzling 154 out of 299 in the first innings. Sadly for the 33-year-old Farrer the nearest Test selector was hundreds of miles away. Australia had a trademark batting collapse on the last day, but in the finish, tail-enders Connolly and Mallett saw them through to the target in the midst of pouring rain.

Chappell's nightmare

Durban, Feb. 9. Australian skipper Bill Lawry placed a huge yoke on the neck of his vice-captain Ian Chappell when he told the press upon the team's arrival in South Africa that he thought Ian Chappell was the best batsman in the world on all types of wickets.

For his part, Chappell says he is not taking it too seriously. But with yet another first-innings duck in the second Test, the local press is throwing the statement back in Lawry's face.

Meanwhile, in Barry Richards and Graeme Pollock, South Africa possesses probably the two best batsmen in the world and they dismembered the visiting attack.

Lawry aloof and isolated

The captains toss: South African skipper Ali Bacher looks happier than his glum Australian counterpart Bill Lawry.

Port Elizabeth, March 10. At the end of a sorely testing and personally troubled tour, Bill Lawry stands as a lone and pilloried figure.

Nobody doubts his courage and fighting qualities as a batsman, but the Australian captaincy demands a large dose of diplomacy and even Lawry's closest admirers within the team admit that he is deficient in that area.

In South Africa he was visibly riled by inconsistent umpires and at one stage gave a hand gesture to the hooting crowd.

A beaten team always struggles to maintain good morale and Lawry's uncompromising attitude has grated on some members of the side. Lawry has never liked hanging around for a drink with the opposition, and after the final day of the fourth Test some Australians were critical that he had left the ground at stumps.

The captain's troubles began on the arduous tour of India, and he is known to be critical of the security arrangements on the sub-continent.

'B Team' boasts Greg Chappell, Lillee

Wellington, April 1. In the wake of the Test team's slaughter in South Africa there was plenty of scope for the next batch of players to show their wares in the Australian B team tour of New Zealand at the close of the Sheffield Shield season.

Two players have emerged from the tour with strong credentials for places in the main team.

Young West Australian quickie Dennis Lillee was not daunted by the softer, slower wickets of New Zealand, and although he played in only one of the three unofficial 'Tests', he topped the first class bowling averages.

Greg Chappell was by far the best and most consistent batsman in the touring party and looked more than ready to take the next step. In addition to his copybook batting style, Chappell has the will and determination to stay at the crease for long batting stints.

The team was led by the cheerful veteran Sam Trimble who must be one of the unluckiest players never to get a Test for Australia. In the third representative match Trimble took eight hours to make a fighting 213, as all others fell around him and the side was bowled out for 353.

Steady Vics win shield

Melbourne, Feb. 16. Victoria has been a model of consistency in fighting its way to take the Sheffield Shield of 1969–70.

The Vics entered the campaign without six players involved in the India/South African tour: Bill Lawry, Paul Sheahan, Ian Redpath, Alan Connolly, Keith Stackpole and Ray Jordon, but the return of Cowper after a year in WA on business was a surprise boost.

Cowper in top form would have been more than handy in the Test line-up if available, but he has not scored as freely in Australia as would have been expected with the best bowlers overseas. Still, his captaincy was always sound.

Ken Eastwood relished the chance to play a regular part instead of the emergency role that has been his lot in recent times. He scored two centuries and consistently propelled Victoria to a flying start.

The tall Alan Thomson used his stiff-armed windmill action to tremendous effect and he took more wickets than any other bowler in Australia. Graeme Watson and Bob Cowper made good contributions to the batting output early in the campaign.

WA captain Tony Lock took his side to second spot on the Shield table.

Australian Averages													
1969–70 SOUTH AFRICA v AUSTRALIA													
AUSTRALIA	M	Inn	NO	Runs	H.S	Avrge	Ct	St	Overs	Mds	Runs	Wkt	Avrge
Chappell, IM	4	8	-	92	34	11.50	5	-	-	-	-	-	-
Connolly, AN	4	8	2	83	36	13.83	1	-	214.2	57	522	20	26.10
Freeman, EW	2	4	-	51	18	12.75	-	-	67.0	12	257	4	64.25
Gleeson, JW	4	8	1	63	24	9.00	2	-	255.0	68	740	19	38.95
Lawry, WM	4	8	-	193	83	24.13	6	-	-	-	-	-	-
Mallett, AA	1	2	-	24	19	12.00	-	-	87.1	26	205	6	34.17
Mayne, LC	2	4	-	27	13	6.75	1	-	100.3	16	314	7	44.86
McKenzie, GD	3	6	-	31	19	5.17	1	-	110.5	21	333	1	333.00
Redpath, IR	4	8	2	283	74*	47.17	1	-	1.0	1	0	-	-
Sheahan, AP	4	8	-	247	67	30.88	-	-	-	-	-	-	-
Stackpole, KR	4	8	-	187	71	23.38	4	-	21.0	2	75	2	37.50
Taber, HB	4	8	3	109	30*	21.80	16	2	-	-	-	-	-
Walters, KD	4	8	-	258	74	32.25	3	-	43.0	6	145	5	29.00

South African Averages													
1969–70 SOUTH AFRICA v AUSTRALIA													
SOUTH AFRICA	M	Inn	NO	Runs	H.S	Avrge	Ct	St	Overs	Mds	Runs	Wkt	Avrge
Bacher, A	4	7	-	217	73	31.00	2	-	-	-	-	-	-
Barlow, EJ	4	7	-	360	127	51.43	8	-	94.0	27	257	11	23.36
Chevalier, GA	1	2	1	0	0*	0.00	-	-	42.1	11	100	5	20.00
Gamsy, D	2	3	1	39	30*	19.50	5	-	-	-	-	-	-
Goddard, TL	3	5	-	58	17	11.60	2	-	126.3	58	203	9	22.56
Irvine, BL	4	7	-	353	102	50.43	2	-	-	-	-	-	-
Lance, HR	3	5	-	139	61	27.80	2	-	30.0	10	77	1	77.00
Lindsay, DT	2	4	-	109	60	27.25	10	-	-	-	-	-	-
Pollock, PM	4	7	3	74	36*	18.50	2	-	115.0	39	258	15	17.20
Pollock, RG	4	7	-	517	274	73.86	4	-	3.0	1	8	-	-
Procter, MJ	4	7	1	209	48	34.83	4	-	143.0	50	353	26	13.58
Richards, BA	4	7	-	508	140	72.57	3	-	12.0	3	26	1	26.00
Seymour, MA	1	2	-	0	0	0.00	-	-	30.0	8	68	2	34.00
Traicos, AJ	3	4	2	8	5*	4.00	4	-	78.2	24	207	4	51.75
Trimborn, PHJ	1	1	-	0	0	0.00	2	-	37.2	5	91	4	22.75

FIRST TEST 1969–70 SOUTH AFRICA v AUSTRALIA
Newlands, Cape Town. January 22, 23, 24, 26, 27, 1970.
Toss: South Africa. South Africa won by 170 runs.

SOUTH AFRICA
BA Richards b Connolly	29	c Taber b Connolly	32
TL Goddard c Taber b Walters	16	c Lawry b Mallett	17
A Bacher (c) lbw Connolly	57	lbw Gleeson	16
RG Pollock c Chappell b Walters	49	c Walters b Connolly	50
EJ Barlow c Chappell b Gleeson	127	c Taber b Gleeson	16
BL Irvine c Gleeson b Mallett	42	c Walters b Connolly	19
MJ Procter b Mallett	22	c Taber b Connolly	48
D Gamsy (+) not out	30	c Taber b Gleeson	2
PM Pollock lbw Mallett	1	b Gleeson	25
MA Seymour c Lawry b Mallett	0	c Lawry b Connolly	0
GA Chevalier c Chappell b Mallett	0	not out	0
Extras (B 2, LB 5, NB 2)	9	(B 1, LB 4, NB 2)	7
TOTAL	382		232

FOW 1st Inns: 21 96 111 187 281 323 363 364 374 382
FOW 2nd Inns: 75 130 131 136 161 188 198 228 239 280

Bowling: *First Innings*: McKenzie 30-8-74-0, Connolly 29-12-62-2, Walters 8-1-19-2, Gleeson 45-17-92-1, Mallett 55.1-16-126-5. *Second Innings*: McKenzie 8-0-29-0, Connolly 26-10-47-5, Mallett 32-10-79-1, Gleeson 30-11-70-4.

AUSTRALIA
KR Stackpole c Barlow b Procter	19	c Barlow b Goddard	29
WM Lawry (c) b PM Pollock	2	lbw Procter	83
IM Chappell c Chevalier b PM Pollock	0	b Chevalier	13
KD Walters c Irvine b PM Pollock	73	c Irvine b Procter	4
IR Redpath c Barlow b Procter	0	not out	47
AP Sheahan c Barlow b Chevalier	8	b Seymour	16
HB Taber (+) lbw Seymour	11	lbw Procter	15
GD McKenzie c RG Pollock b PM Pollock	5 (9)	c RG Pollock b Chevalier	19
AA Mallett c Goddard b Chevalier	19 (8)	c PM Pollock b Procter	5
JW Gleeson b Goddard	17	b Richards	10
AN Connolly not out	0	b Chevalier	25
Extras (B 1, NB 9)	10	(B 7, LB 2, NB 5)	14
TOTAL	164		280

FOW 1st Inns: 5 5 38 39 58 92 123 134 164 164
FOW 2nd Inns: 75 130 131 136 161 188 198 228 239 280

Bowling: *First Innings*: Procter 12-4-30-2, PM Pollock 12-4-20-4, Goddard 19.4-9-29-1, Chevalier 11-2-32-2, Seymour 11-2-28-1, Barlow 1-0-15-0. *Second Innings*: Procter 17-4-47-4, PM Pollock 18-12-19-0, Goddard 32-12-66-1, Chevalier 31.1-9-68-3, Seymour 19-6-40-1, Barlow 6-2-14-0, Richards 6-1-12-1.

Umpires: G Goldman & WW Wade

SECOND TEST 1969–70 SOUTH AFRICA v AUSTRALIA
Kingsmead, Durban. February 5, 6, 7, 9, 1970.
Toss: South Africa. South Africa won by an innings & 129 runs.

SOUTH AFRICA
BA Richards b Freeman	140
TL Goddard c Lawry b Gleeson	17
A Bacher (c) b Connolly	9
RG Pollock c & b Stackpole	274
EJ Barlow lbw Freeman	1
BL Irvine b Gleeson	13
HR Lance st Taber b Gleeson	61
MJ Procter c Connolly b Stackpole	32
D Gamsy (+) lbw Connolly	7
PM Pollock not out	36
AJ Traicos not out	5
Extras (B 1, LB 3, NB 23)	27
TOTAL	9 dec 622

FOW 1st Inns: 88 126 229 231 281 481 558 575 580

Bowling: *First Innings*: McKenzie 25.5-3-92-0, Connolly 33-7-104-2, Freeman 28-4-120-2, Gleeson 51-9-160-3, Walters 9-0-44-0, Stackpole 21-2-75-2.

AUSTRALIA
KR Stackpole c Gamsy b Goddard	27	lbw Traicos	71
WM Lawry (c) lbw Barlow	15	c Gamsy b Goddard	14
IM Chappell c Gamsy b Barlow	0	c Gamsy b PM Pollock	14
KD Walters c Traicos b Barlow	4	c RG Pollock b Traicos	74
IR Redpath c Richards b Procter	4	not out	74
AP Sheahan c Traicos b Goddard	62	c Barlow b Procter	4
EW Freeman c Traicos b PM Pollock	5	b Barlow	18
HB Taber (+) c & b PM Pollock	6	c Lance b Barlow	0
GD McKenzie c Traicos b Procter	1	lbw Barlow	4
JW Gleeson not out	4	c Gamsy b Procter	24
AN Connolly c Bacher b Traicos	14	lbw Procter	0
Extras (LB 5, NB 10)	15	(B 9, LB 8, NB 22)	39
TOTAL	157		336

FOW 1st Inns: 44 44 44 48 56 79 100 114 139 157
FOW 2nd Inns: 65 83 151 208 222 264 264 268 336 336

Bowling: *First Innings*: Procter 11-2-39-2, PM Pollock 10-3-31-2, Goddard 7-4-10-2, Barlow 10-3-24-3, Traicos 8.2-3-27-1, Lance 2-0-11-0. *Second Innings*: PM Pollock 21.3-4-45-1, Procter 18.5-5-62-3, Barlow 31-10-63-3, Traicos 30-8-70-2, Goddard 17-7-30-1, Richards 3-1-8-0, Lance 7-4-11-0, RG Pollock 3-1-8-0.

Umpires: CMP Coetzee & JG Draper

THIRD TEST 1969–70 SOUTH AFRICA v AUSTRALIA
New Wanderers Stadium, Johannesburg. February 19, 20, 21, 23, 24, 1970.
Toss: South Africa. South Africa won by 307 runs.

SOUTH AFRICA
BA Richards c Taber b Connolly	65	c Taber b Mayne	35
TL Goddard c Walters b Connolly	6 (9)	c Taber b Connolly	2
A Bacher (c) lbw Mayne	30	b Connolly	15
RG Pollock c Taber b Freeman	52	b Freeman	87
EJ Barlow st Taber b Gleeson	6 (2)	c Lawry b Gleeson	110
BL Irvine c Stackpole b Gleeson	79 (5)	c Lawry b Gleeson	73
HR Lance run out	8	lbw Gleeson	30
DT Lindsay (+) c Stackpole b Gleeson	0 (6)	b Gleeson	6
MJ Procter c Chappell b Walters	22 (8)	not out	36
PM Pollock c Taber b Walters	0	c Taber b Gleeson	1
AJ Traicos not out	1	lbw Mayne	0
Extras (LB 7, W 1, NB 2)	10	(LB 8, NB 5)	13
TOTAL	279		408

FOW 1st Inns: 56 85 141 162 170 194 194 238 246 279
FOW 2nd Inns: 76 102 241 269 275 349 372 375 380 408

Bowling: *First Innings*: Mayne 26.5-8-83-1, Connolly 30-10-49-2, Freeman 20-4-60-1, Gleeson 21.4-2-61-3, Walters 5-1-16-2. *Second Innings*: Connolly 32-6-83-2, Mayne 18.3-1-77-2, Gleeson 45-15-125-5, Freeman 19-4-77-1, Walters 7-1-33-0.

AUSTRALIA
KR Stackpole c Lindsay b Procter	5	c Lindsay b Procter	1
WM Lawry (c) c Lindsay b PM Pollock	1	c RG Pollock b Barlow	17
IR Redpath lbw Procter	0	b Goddard	66
IM Chappell c Lance b Goddard	34	b Barlow	0
KD Walters c Procter b PM Pollock	64	b Procter	15
AP Sheahan b PM Pollock	44	b Procter	0
EW Freeman c Goddard b PM Pollock	10	run out	18
LC Mayne run out	0	c Procter b Traicos	2
HB Taber (+) not out	26	not out	18
JW Gleeson b Procter	0	b Goddard	0
AN Connolly c Richards b PM Pollock	3	c Richards b Goddard	36
Extras (LB 4, W 1, NB 10)	15	(W 2, NB 3)	5
TOTAL	202		178

FOW 1st Inns: 7 7 12 109 112 139 140 194 195 202
FOW 2nd Inns: 11 43 43 73 73 122 124 126 126 178

Bowling: *First Innings*: Procter 21-5-48-3, PM Pollock 23.2-10-39-5, Barlow 12-5-31-0, Goddard 26-10-41-1, Lance 3-1-5-0, Traicos 6-3-23-0. *Second Innings*: Procter 14-8-24-3, PM Pollock 15-4-56-0, Barlow 7-3-17-2, Goddard 24.5-16-27-3, Traicos 17-4-49-1.

Umpires: CMP Coetzee & AJ Warner

FOURTH TEST 1969–70 SOUTH AFRICA v AUSTRALIA
St George's Park, Port Elizabeth. March 5, 6, 7, 9, 10, 1970.
Toss: South Africa. South Africa won by 323 runs.

SOUTH AFRICA
BA Richards c Taber b Connolly	81	c Chappell b Mayne	126
EJ Barlow c McKenzie b Connolly	73	c Stackpole b Walters	27
A Bacher (c) run out	17	hit wicket b McKenzie	73
RG Pollock c Taber b Gleeson	1	b Mayne	4
BL Irvine c Redpath b Gleeson	25	c Gleeson b Mayne	102
DT Lindsay (+) c Taber b Connolly	43	b Connolly	60
HR Lance b Mayne	21	run out	19
MJ Procter c Taber b Connolly	26	c Mayne b Gleeson	23
PM Pollock not out	4	not out	7
PHJ Trimborn b Connolly	0		
AJ Traicos c Taber b Connolly	2		
Extras (B 4, LB 3, NB 11)	18	(LB 9, NB 20)	29
TOTAL	311		8 dec 470

FOW 1st Inns: 157 158 159 183 208 259 294 305 305 311
FOW 2nd Inns: 73 199 213 279 367 440 440 470

Bowling: *First Innings*: McKenzie 27-7-66-0, Mayne 27.4-4-71-1, Connolly 28.2-9-47-6, Walters 9-1-19-0, Gleeson 32-9-90-2. *Second Innings*: Mayne 29-6-83-3, Connolly 36-3-130-1, McKenzie 20-3-72-1, Gleeson 30.2-5-142-1, Walters 5-2-14-1, Redpath 1-1-0-0.

AUSTRALIA
KR Stackpole c Barlow b Procter	15	b Procter	20
WM Lawry (c) c Lindsay b Lance	18	c Lindsay b Barlow	43
IR Redpath c Trimborn b Procter	55	c Barlow b Procter	37
IM Chappell c Procter b Trimborn	17	c Trimborn b Barlow	14
KD Walters c Lindsay b Trimborn	1	b Procter	23
AP Sheahan c Procter b PM Pollock	67	c Lindsay b Procter	46
HB Taber (+) lbw Barlow	3	not out	30
LC Mayne b Procter	13	c Lindsay b Procter	12
GD McKenzie c Barlow b PM Pollock	0	c Lindsay b Procter	2
JW Gleeson b Lindsay b PM Pollock	8	b Procter	0
AN Connolly not out	2	c Bacher b Trimborn	3
Extras (LB 3, W 1, NB 9)	13	(LB 2, NB 14)	16
TOTAL	212		246

FOW 1st Inns: 27 46 80 82 152 177 191 195 208 212
FOW 2nd Inns: 22 98 116 130 189 207 234 243 243 246

Bowling: *First Innings*: PM Pollock 14-2-46-3, Procter 25.1-11-30-3, Barlow 9-1-27-1, Lance 8-1-32-1, Trimborn 17-1-47-2, Traicos 3-1-17-0. *Second Innings*: PM Pollock 1.1-0-2-0, Procter 24-11-73-6, Trimborn 20.2-4-44-2, Barlow 18-3-66-2, Traicos 14.5-21-0, Lance 10-4-18-0, Richards 3-1-6-0.

Umpires: CMP Coetzee & AJ Warner

Lucky Stacky stars in first Test draw

Left: Keith Stackpole is adjudged not out and, right, Doug Walters belts another boundary.

Brisbane, Dec. 2. England finished on top in the drawn first Test, which finished here today.

It did not take long for controversy to erupt in this series and provide grist for the mill of the English tabloid press. After just 30 runs were on the board in the first session, Australia's Keith Stackpole lunged for a quick single and had his wicket thrown down by Geoffrey Boycott.

Umpire Lou Rowan gave him not out, but TV replays indicated that Stackpole was just short of his crease. A still shot published the next day showed Stackpole's bat across the line but not grounded. By stumps he was 175 not out and the English press was busily trotting out its usual line about incompetent Australian umpiring.

Stackpole reached 207 the following day and Doug Walters made an unusually restrained 112. The most disturbing part of the Australian innings was the loss of the last seven wickets for 15 runs in the space of 45 minutes – a collapse typical of those in South Africa the previous season.

In response, England's dour professionalism ground out a score that put it slightly ahead on the first innings. All batsmen had good starts, but none went on to a hundred. Australia plodded to 2/56 at stumps on the fourth day and the only remote chance of a result was the possibility of an English victory.

The dogged Lawry was still there and he was in his element, batting in siege-like conditions and taking five and a half hours to score 84. His approach seemed to rub off on every other batsman.

By the time England returned to the batting crease there was only an hour left with a target of 172. Had the English bowlers managed to get through their overs more quickly there may have been more time to force the issue.

Australian selectors introduced three new faces in this game. Leg-spinner Terry Jenner toiled hard and unorthodox speedster Alan 'Froggie' Thomson found the going tough at Test level after having taken 120 wickets from his 22 first class matches. Burly 'keeper Rodney Marsh will add much-needed depth to the batting.

Some Test cricket greats gather at the 'Gabba for the first Test. From left: Bill O'Reilly, Sid Barnes, Bob Simpson, Richie Benaud, Ray Lindewall, Lindsay Hassett, Jack Fingelton and Frank Tyson.

WACA and Greg Chappell shine in sun

The WACA ground was full to overflowing with a colourful crowd for the first Test match staged in Western Australia.

Perth, Dec. 16. Australia has a new Test batting star after Greg Chappell's confident and chanceless century on debut at Perth.

The young South Australian's performance was the highlight of the first Test match ever to be played in Western Australia. Perth's daily attendances showed an increase on those in Brisbane for the previous Test. The WACA has taken out substantial loans to build two new grandstands and renovate the ground in other ways.

The WACA pitch was perfect for batting … perhaps too good, as it lacked the extra pace usually associated with Perth pitches. Lindsay Hassett remarked that 'you can scarcely get a decent Test attack from the two sides.'

The only time that a result seemed likely was on the third day when John Snow lived up to his aggressive reputation and had Australia reeling at 5/107. Redpath and Greg Chappell rescued the innings, and although Redpath was sometimes disconcerted by pace his young partner remained unperturbed.

Boycott and Snow star in big English win

Sydney, Jan. 14. The hardbitten professionalism of John Snow and Geoff Boycott has proved too much for Australia in the fourth Test and England's 299-run victory has given it a 1–0 lead in the series.

Australia was never in serious contention apart from a brief period on the first day when spinners Ashley Mallett and John Gleeson were able to keep the Englishmen to a reasonable total.

The English fast bowlers removed Lawry and makeshift opener Ian Chappell with only 38 runs on the board, and from that moment the home team was on the back foot. Evoking memories of his match-winning performance at the Oval in 1968, Derek Underwood mesmerised the Australian batsmen.

In England's second innings Geoff Boycott sacrificed his partner John Edrich in a run-out, but made up for it by scoring 142 not out as a follow-up to his 77 in the first innings. Set 416 runs to win, Australia was in immediate trouble when a vicious Snow lifter removed Chappell on the first ball that he faced. Bowling with perfect rhythm and finding a couple of danger spots on the pitch, Snow simply mowed down the Australians, except for Bill Lawry, who remained 60 not out.

The fast bowler's fraternity: John Snow gets one to rise from as good length to Graham McKenzie in the fourth Test. It hit 'Garth' in the face, and he retired hurt with blood pouring from the wounds. He did not take any further part in the game.

One day game drags the crowds

Melbourne, Jan. 5. The first ever one day international clash in Australia was gleefully welcomed by cricket starved Victorians.

The match was only arranged after the third Test was washed out and the 40-over-a-side game was played on the day that had been scheduled as the last of the Test match.

Before now, limited-overs matches have only been played at grade or district level in Australia. Last season a domestic one day competition between states was held, as a result of the success of English matches, which have been running since 1963.

The Melbourne Test is usually the major money-spinner for Australian cricket and the Test wipeout was a major blow. A healthy attendance of 46,006 paid $33,984 to watch the one day clash and saw England score 190 in 39.4 eight-ball overs. John Edrich top scored with 82 and Mallett took 4/34. Australia achieved the target in 34.6 overs and Ian Chappell made 60 and Doug Walters 41 in its score of 5/191.

The international concept has so impressed cricketing authorities that there are suggestions that a World Cup could take place.

Chappell century brings an invasion

Melbourne, Jan. 26. The unruly behaviour of the Melbourne crowd has been condemned after 2000 fans stampeded onto the MCG to congratulate Ian Chappell on his century in the sixth Test.

Chappell was badly shaken by the incident and his cap was souvenired along with Colin Cowdrey's white hat and a stump. Chappell told the *Age*: 'I was petrified I would fall and be trampled under all those feet. If it hadn't been for a couple of strong spectators who tried to protect me, I'm sure I would have fallen.'

Melbourne Cricket Club secretary Ian Johnson called it a disgraceful performance and said: 'The adults were either sheer exhibitionists or drunken louts.'

In the final half hour of the day the crowd made a continuous racket with empty beer cans in protest against the slow batting of Englishmen Boycott and Edrich, and at one stage the umpires conferred before allowing the game to continue.

Lawry's decision to declare when Rodney Marsh was on 92 was also widely criticised as it prevented him from becoming the first Australian 'keeper to score a Test century.

D'Oliveira and Luckhurst both scored centuries for England and Luckhurst's effort was particularly heroic as he batted for most of the innings with his left hand in plaster and three fingers of the glove bound together.

Despite the various incidents, one writer has described the drawn game as the 'Ho-Hum Test'.

Geoff Boycott loses his cap but not his head facing Dennis Lillee in Perth.
He made 70 and 50 – dismissed by Johnny Gleeson on both occasions.

Bill Lawry sacked as captain

Brothers Ian and Greg Chappell played together for the first time in a Test match in Perth, and look to be fixtures in the Australian team.

Adelaide, Feb. 3. The Australian selectors have sent shockwaves through the game with their decision to dump Bill Lawry as Australian captain.

A regular Australian captain has never been dropped in mid-series.

Lawry has not only been dropped as captain, but has been omitted from the side altogether.

While the merits of dropping Lawry can be debated, the fact that he heard of the announcement over the radio is seen as shabby handling of a man who has been a loyal servant of the Australian game.

Lawry's form has not been good in recent times, but he is still the man whose wicket England values most. With Australia still hoping to square the series in the final Test in Sydney, it seems odd that the team will go into the game with a new opener, 35-year-old Ken Eastwood, to replace Lawry.

Indeed an Australian team without Lawry will not seem the same. Since starting 10 years ago he has missed only one Test, when injured, and has been a cornerstone of the batting line-up. The decision to drop him entirely may have been motivated by a desire to give his successor Ian Chappell a smoother entry to the job.

Speculation over Lawry's sacking has focused on a number of issues. The Australians have not won any of their last eight Tests, and Lawry's defensive approach as captain and as a batsman is seen is one major reason.

A siege mentality has permeated all parts of his game, and his scoring rate has ground down to an agonising 13 runs an hour

Yet just two Tests ago he carried his bat through an innings and his average this series is a healthy 40.

The seeds of his dismissal may have been sown during the Indian and South African tour, when he clashed with umpires, opponents and the press. Although some of his transgressions were blown out of proportion it is worrying for the Australian Cricket Board, which was unimpressed by a blunt report that Lawry submitted at the end of the tour. His decision to go public with a series of newspaper articles also antagonised the higher echelons of the game.

Australia escaped with a draw in the sixth Test at Adelaide thanks to the stubborn last day stand between Stackpole and Ian Chappell, and the side is now definitely in a rebuilding phase.

Newcomer Dennis Lillee took an impressive 5/84 in his debut and could take over the mantle as head of the attack.

Illingworth leads England off over Snow incident

Sydney, Feb. 17. England skipper Ray Illingworth marched his team off the Sydney Cricket Ground after wild scenes on the second day of the seventh Test.

Trouble was brewing early in the afternoon when the Saturday crowd on the Hill erupted into a brawl 15 minutes before tea and police were pelted with cans. The real trouble began when Australian tail-ender Terry Jenner ducked into a bouncer from John Snow and had to leave the field with blood pouring from a gash on his head.

Umpire Rowan warned Snow for intimidatory bowling and after an animated discussion between Snow, Rowan and Illingworth the paceman snatched his cap and stomped away towards his fielding position under the Paddington Hill. In a provocative action, Snow walked right to the fence and swapped comments with jeering spectators.

One drunken barracker grabbed Snow by the shirt as cans flew in his direction. Illingworth sprawled on the ground near the wicket, then signalled to the rest of the team to follow him off the ground, without a word to either the umpires or the batsmen, Greg Chappell and Dennis Lillee, who stood their ground in the middle of the field.

Within minutes Illingworth's team re-emerged after having been told by the umpires that the game could be awarded to Australia if they did not return.

The Snow incident should not be allowed to detract from a pressure-filled game that has been the highlight of a lacklustre series. On the opening day a rookie Australian attack of Dennis Lillee, Tony Dell, Terry Jenner and Kerry O'Keefe, with only three Tests experience between them, bundled out England for 184, its lowest score of the series.

By the fourth afternoon Australia had been set a total of 223 to win and Snow, the villain of the match in Australian eyes, again figured in the drama. He bowled Eastwood for a duck but in the fifth over crashed into the fence while trying to take a catch in the outfield and was put out of the game with a broken hand.

That England was able to win without Snow and the injured Geoff Boycott was a performance that warranted a 2–0 record in the series.

Seventh Test: Tail-ender Terry Jenner is felled by a fast one from John Snow.

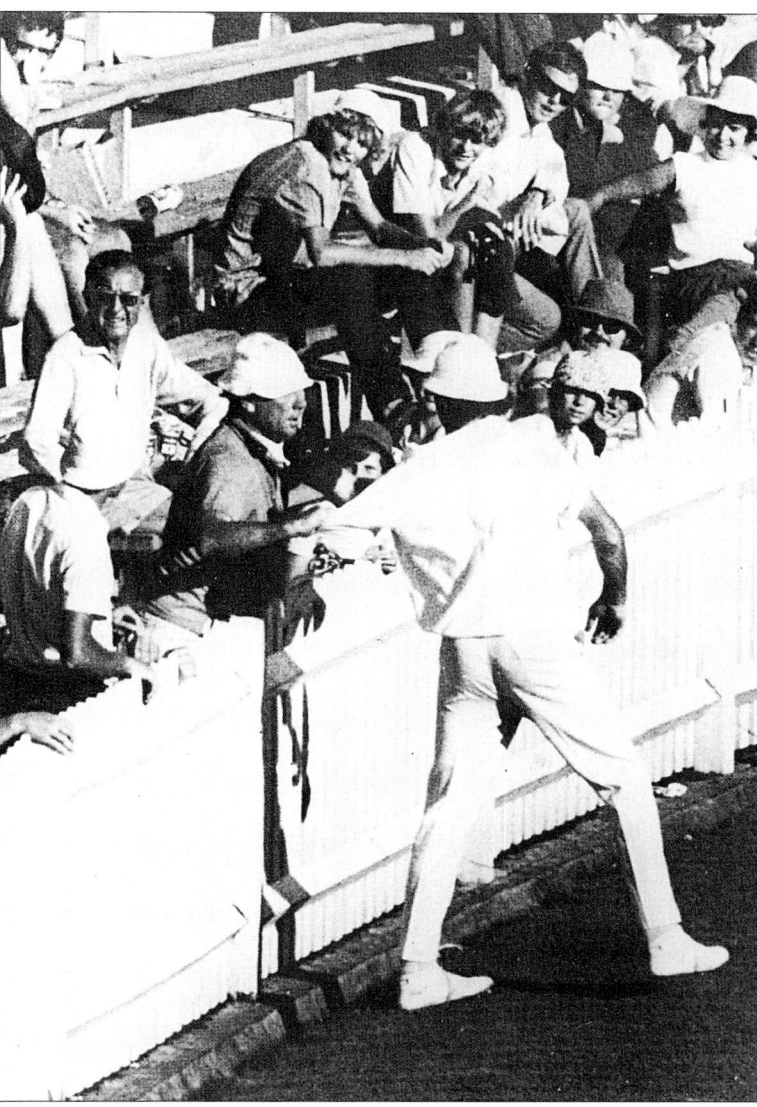

Snow strays too close for comfort to the boundary fence and has his shirt tugged by an aggrieved barracker in the public stand.

Umpire Lou Rowan has a discussion over intimidatory bowling with John Snow.

Cans were thrown onto the ground and Snow, provocatively placed by Illingworth at fine leg, shouts in defiance at the howling crowd.

All out: Illingworth leads his team from the field and returns when the cans have been cleared, under threat of forfeiting the match.

Boycott, Stackpole the best

Sydney, Feb. 17. Two batsmen whose styles are as different as chalk and cheese have topped the batting averages for their respective countries.

Geoff Boycott and Keith Stackpole both had splendid series.

Boycott has loomed as immovable for the Australian bowlers. His love of occupying the crease is already assuming legendary proportions. He averaged 93.85 in the Test series and scored a whopping 1535 runs in all first class matches.

His dogged approach will never win the crowd's affection, and has been known to anger teammates at times, but this self-absorbed man could not care less. So great is his self-belief that he is said to have invited the Australian paceman Alan Thomson to give him batting practice in the nets.

He had to sit out the last Test after his arm was broken by a ball from Graham McKenzie in a one day game.

Aussie Keith Stackpole is Boycott's antithesis. He attacks from the moment he takes block and openly admits that he has no interest in playing long innings, unless he is scoring at a fast pace.

Ian Redpath was Australia's second-best batsman, averaging 49.70.

His average of 52 is well below Boycott's but he has had to contend with a much stronger attack. Like most Australian batsmen his reputation was severely battered by the South African tour, but at the end of this series he stands as one of the foundations of the Australian batting line-up for the future.

FIRST TEST 1970–71 AUSTRALIA v ENGLAND
Brisbane Cricket Ground, Brisbane. November 27, 28, 29, December 1, 2, 1970.
Toss: Australia. Match Drawn.

AUSTRALIA

Batsman	1st	2nd
WM Lawry (c) c Knott b Snow	4	c Snow b Fletcher 84
KR Stackpole c Knott b Snow	207	c Knott b Shuttleworth 8
IM Chappell run out	59	st Knott b Illingworth 10
KD Walters b Underwood	112	c Luckhurst b Snow 7
IR Redpath c Illingworth b Underwood	22	c & b Underwood 28
AP Sheahan c Knott b Underwood	0	c Shuttleworth b Snow 36
RW Marsh (+) b Snow	9	b Shuttleworth 14
TJ Jenner c Cowdrey b Snow	0	c Boycott b Shuttleworth 2
GD McKenzie not out	3	b Shuttleworth 1
JW Gleeson c Cowdrey b Snow	0	b Shuttleworth 6
AL Thomson b Snow	0	not out 4
Extras (B 7, LB 4, NB 6)	17	(B 4, LB 3, NB 7) 14
TOTAL	433	214

FOW 1st Inns: 12 163 372 418 418 421 422 433 433 433
FOW 2nd Inns: 30 47 64 137 152 193 199 201 208 214

Bowling: *First Innings*: Snow 32.3-6-114-6, Shuttleworth 27-6-81-0, D'Oliveira 16-2-63-0, Illingworth 11-1-47-0, Underwood 28-6-101-3, Cowdrey 1-0-10-0. *Second Innings*: Snow 20-3-48-2, Shuttleworth 17.5-2-47-5, D'Oliveira 7-5-7-0, Underwood 20-10-23-1, Illingworth 18-11-19-1, Fletcher 9-1-48-1, Cowdrey 2-0-8-0.

ENGLAND

Batsman	1st	2nd
G Boycott c Marsh b Gleeson	37	c & b Jenner 16
BW Luckhurst run out	74	not out 20
APE Knott (+) c Lawry b Walters	73	
JH Edrich c Chappell b Jenner	79	
MC Cowdrey c Chappell b Gleeson	28	
KWR Fletcher c Marsh b McKenzie	34	
BL D'Oliveira c Sheahan b McKenzie	57	
R Illingworth (c) c Marsh b Thomson	8	
JA Snow c Marsh b Walters	34	
DL Underwood not out	2	
K Shuttleworth c Lawry b Walters	7	
Extras (B 2, LB 7, NB 22)	31	(LB 3) 3
TOTAL	464	1 for 39

FOW 1st Inns: 92 136 245 284 336 346 371 449 456 464
FOW 2nd Inns: 39

Bowling: *First Innings*: McKenzie 28-5-90-2, Thomson 43-8-136-1, Gleeson 42-15-97-2, Jenner 24-5-86-1, Stackpole 4-0-12-0, Walters 5.5-0-12-3. *Second Innings*: Thomson 4-0-20-0, McKenzie 3-0-6-0, Jenner 4.6-2-9-1, Stackpole 4-3-1-0.

Umpires: TF Brooks & LP Rowan

Australian Averages

1970–71 AUSTRALIA v ENGLAND

AUSTRALIA	M	Inn	NO	Runs	H.S	Avrge	Ct	St	Overs	Mds	Runs	Wkt	Avrge
Chappell, GS	6	8	1	243	108	34.71	3	-	93.0	15	255	5	51.00
Chappell, IM	7	12	-	452	111	37.67	7	-	3.0	-	10	1	10.00
Connolly, AN	2	2	-	14	14	7.00	2	-	27.0	3	81	1	81.00
Dell, AR	1	2	2	6	3*	-	-	-	42.7	11	97	5	19.40
Duncan, JRF	1	1	-	3	3	3.00	-	-	14.0	4	30	-	-
Eastwood, KH	1	2	-	5	5	2.50	-	-	5.0	-	21	1	21.00
Gleeson, JW	6	7	-	42	16	6.00	4	-	221.0	57	605	14	43.21
Jenner, TJ	2	4	-	36	30	9.00	2	-	65.6	15	176	6	29.33
Lawry, WM	6	10	2	324	84	40.50	3	-	-	-	-	-	-
Lillee, DK	2	3	-	16	10	5.33	2	-	62.3	5	199	8	24.88
Mallett, AA	3	3	-	38	28	12.67	-	-	56.7	8	188	6	31.33
Marsh, RW	7	9	1	215	92*	26.88	11	3	-	-	-	-	-
McKenzie, GD	4	5	3	28	11*	14.00	1	-	110.4	14	351	7	50.14
O'Keeffe, KJ	2	3	-	42	27	14.00	-	-	100.0	30	260	6	43.33
Redpath, IR	7	12	2	497	171	49.70	5	-	-	-	-	-	-
Sheahan, AP	2	3	-	38	36	12.67	1	-	-	-	-	-	-
Stackpole, KR	7	12	-	627	207	52.25	9	-	92.5	20	261	2	130.50
Thomson, AL	4	5	4	22	12*	22.00	-	-	189.7	33	654	12	54.50
Walters, KD	7	12	2	373	112	37.30	3	-	61.5	8	181	7	25.86

English Averages

1970–71 AUSTRALIA v ENGLAND

ENGLAND	M	Inn	NO	Runs	H.S	Avrge	Ct	St	Overs	Mds	Runs	Wkt	Avrge
Boycott, G	6	10	3	657	142*	93.86	4	-	1.0	-	7	-	-
Cowdrey, MC	4	4	-	82	40	20.50	3	-	6.0	-	36	-	-
D'Oliveira, BL	7	10	-	369	117	36.90	4	-	114.0	28	290	6	48.33
Edrich, JH	7	11	2	648	130	72.00	5	-	-	-	-	-	-
Fletcher, KWR	5	9	-	225	80	25.00	3	-	20.0	1	101	1	101.00
Hampshire, JH	2	4	-	92	55	23.00	2	-	-	-	-	-	-
Illingworth, R	7	10	1	333	53	37.00	4	-	132.0	43	349	10	34.90
Knott, APE	7	9	2	222	73	31.71	21	3	-	-	-	-	-
Lever, P	6	6	-	83	36	13.83	5	-	143.5	25	439	13	33.77
Luckhurst, BW	6	9	1	455	131	56.88	5	-	-	-	-	-	-
Shuttleworth, K	3	2	-	9	7	4.50	1	-	75.5	13	242	7	34.57
Snow, JA	7	7	1	141	38	23.50	2	-	225.5	47	708	31	22.84
Underwood, DL	6	6	3	16	8*	5.33	4	-	194.6	50	520	16	32.50
Willis, RGD	4	5	3	37	15*	18.50	3	-	88.0	16	329	12	27.42

SECOND TEST 1970–71 AUSTRALIA v ENGLAND
W.A.C.A. Ground, Perth. December 11, 12, 13, 15, 16, 1970.
Toss: Australia. Match Drawn.

ENGLAND

Batsman	1st	2nd
G Boycott c McKenzie b Gleeson	70	st Marsh b Gleeson 50
BW Luckhurst b McKenzie	131	c Stackpole b Walters 19
JH Edrich run out	47	not out 115
APE Knott (+) c Stackpole b Thomson	24 (8)	not out 30
KWR Fletcher b Walters	22 (4)	lbw Gleeson 0
MC Cowdrey c & b GS Chappell	40 (5)	c Marsh b Thomson 1
BL D'Oliveira c Stackpole b Thomson	8 (6)	b Gleeson 31
R Illingworth (c) b McKenzie	34 (7)	c Marsh b Stackpole 29
JA Snow not out	4	
K Shuttleworth b McKenzie	2	
P Lever b McKenzie	2	
Extras (LB 8, W 1, NB 4)	13	(B 2, LB 3, NB 7) 12
TOTAL	397	6 for 287

FOW 1st Inns: 171 243 281 291 310 327 389 389 393 397
FOW 2nd Inns: 60 98 98 101 152 209

Bowling: *First Innings*: McKenzie 31.4-4-66-4, Thomson 24-4-118-2, GS Chappell 24-4-54-1, Gleeson 32-10-78-1, Walters 11-1-35-1, Stackpole 11-2-33-0. *Second Innings*: McKenzie 18-2-50-0, Thomson 25-3-71-1, Gleeson 32-11-68-3, Stackpole 15-3-43-1, Walters 7-1-26-1, GS Chappell 4-1-17-0.

AUSTRALIA

Batsman	1st	2nd
WM Lawry (c) c Illingworth b Snow	0	not out 38
KR Stackpole c Lever b Snow	5	c (S)JH Hampshire b Snow 0
IM Chappell c Knott b Snow	50	c (S)JH Hampshire b Snow 17
KD Walters c Knott b Lever	7	b Lever 8
IR Redpath c & b Illingworth	171	not out 26
AP Sheahan run out	2	
GS Chappell c Luckhurst b Shuttleworth	108	
RW Marsh (+) c D'Oliveira b Shuttleworth	44	
GD McKenzie c Lever b D'Oliveira	7	
JW Gleeson c Knott b Snow	15	
AL Thomson not out	12	
Extras (B 5, LB 4, NB 10)	19	(B 4, LB 4, NB 3) 11
TOTAL	440	3 for 100

FOW 1st Inns: 5 8 17 105 107 326 393 408 426 440
FOW 2nd Inns: 0 20 40

Bowling: *First Innings*: Snow 33.5-3-143-4, Shuttleworth 28-4-105-2, Lever 21-3-78-1, D'Oliveira 17-1-41-1, Illingworth 13-2-43-1, Boycott 1-0-7-0, Fletcher 1-0-4-0. *Second Innings*: Snow 9-4-17-2, Shuttleworth 3-1-9-0, Lever 5-2-10-1, D'Oliveira 4-2-5-0, Illingworth 4-2-12-0, Fletcher 4-0-18-0, Cowdrey 3-0-18-0.

Umpires: TF Brooks & LP Rowan

THIRD TEST 1970–71 AUSTRALIA v ENGLAND
Melbourne Cricket Ground, Melbourne. December 31 (no play), 1970, January 1 (no play), 2 (no play), 1971.
Toss: England. Match Abandoned.

FOURTH TEST 1970–71 AUSTRALIA v ENGLAND
Sydney Cricket Ground, Sydney. January 9, 10, 11, 13, 14, 1971.
Toss: England. England won by 299 runs.

ENGLAND

G Boycott c Gleeson b Connolly	77	not out	142
BW Luckhurst lbw Gleeson	38	c IM Chappell b McKenzie	5
JH Edrich c Gleeson b GS Chappell	55	run out	12
KWR Fletcher c Walters b Mallett	23	c Stackpole b Mallett	8
BL D'Oliveira c Connolly b Mallett	0	c IM Chappell b GS Chappell	56
R Illingworth (c) b Gleeson	25	st Marsh b Mallett	53
APE Knott (+) st Marsh b Mallett	6	not out	21
JA Snow c Lawry b Gleeson	37		
P Lever c Connolly b Mallett	36		
DL Underwood c GS Chappell b Gleeson	0		
RGD Willis not out	15		
Extras (B 5, LB 2, W 1, NB 12)	20	(B 9, LB 4, NB 9)	22
TOTAL	332	5 for 319	

FOW 1st Inns: 116 130 201 205 208 219 262 291 291 332
FOW 2nd Inns: 7 35 48 181 276

Bowling: *First Innings*: McKenzie 15-3-74-0, Connolly 13-2-43-1, Gleeson 29-7-83-4, GS Chappell 11-4-30-1, Mallett 16.7-5-40-4, Walters 3-1-11-0, Stackpole 7-2-31-0. *Second Innings*: McKenzie 15-0-65-1, Connolly 14-1-38-0, GS Chappell 15-5-24-1, Gleeson 23-4-54-0, Mallett 19-1-85-2, Stackpole 6-1-17-0, Walters 2-0-14-0.

AUSTRALIA

WM Lawry (c) c Edrich b Lever	9	not out	60
IM Chappell c Underwood b Snow	12	c D'Oliveira b Snow	0
IR Redpath c Fletcher b D'Oliveira	64	c Edrich b Snow	6
KD Walters c Luckhurst b Illingworth	55	c Knott b Lever	3
GS Chappell c & b Underwood	15	b Snow	2
KR Stackpole c Boycott b Underwood	33	c Lever b Snow	30
RW Marsh (+) c D'Oliveira b Underwood	8	c Willis b Snow	0
AA Mallett b Underwood	4	c Knott b Willis	6
GD McKenzie not out	11	retired hurt	6
JW Gleeson c Fletcher b D'Oliveira	0	b Snow	0
AN Connolly b Lever	14	c Knott b Snow	0
Extras (NB 11)	11	(B 2, NB 1)	3
TOTAL	236	9 for 116	

FOW 1st Inns: 14 38 137 160 189 199 208 208 219 236
FOW 2nd Inns: 1 11 14 21 66 66 86 116 116

Bowling: *First Innings*: Snow 14-6-23-1, Willis 9-2-26-0, Lever 8.6-1-31-2, Underwood 22-7-66-4, Illingworth 14-3-59-1, D'Oliveira 9-2-20-2. *Second Innings*: Snow 17.5-5-40-7, Lever 11-1-24-1, Underwood 8-2-17-0, D'Oliveira 7-3-16-0, Illingworth 9-5-9-0, Willis 3-2-1-1, Fletcher 1-0-6-0.

Umpires: TF Brooks & LP Rowan

SIXTH TEST 1970–71 AUSTRALIA v ENGLAND
Adelaide Oval, Adelaide. January 29, 30, February 1, 2, 3, 1971.
Toss: England. Match Drawn.

ENGLAND

G Boycott run out	58	not out	119
JH Edrich c Stackpole b Lillee	130	b Thomson	40
KWR Fletcher b Thomson	80	b Gleeson	5
APE Knott (+) c Redpath b Lillee	7		
BL D'Oliveira c Marsh b GS Chappell	47 (4)	c Walters b Thomson	5
JH Hampshire c Lillee b GS Chappell	55 (5)	lbw Thomson	3
R Illingworth (c) b Lillee	24 (6)	not out	48
JA Snow b Lillee	38		
P Lever b Thomson	5		
DL Underwood not out	1		
RGD Willis c Walters b Lillee	4		
Extras (B 1, LB 5, W 4, NB 11)	21	(LB 4, W 1, NB 8)	13
TOTAL	470	4 dec 233	

FOW 1st Inns: 107 276 289 289 385 402 458 465 465 470
FOW 2nd Inns: 103 128 143 151

Bowling: *First Innings*: Thomson 29.7-6-94-2, Lillee 28.3-0-84-5, Walters 9-2-29-0, GS Chappell 18-1-54-2, Gleeson 19-1-78-0, Mallett 20-1-63-0, Stackpole 12-2-47-0. *Second Innings*: Lillee 7-0-40-0, Thomson 19-2-79-3, Walters 3-0-5-0, GS Chappell 5-0-27-0, Gleeson 16-1-69-1, Mallett 1-1-0-0.

AUSTRALIA

KR Stackpole b Underwood	87	b Snow	136
WM Lawry (c) c Knott b Snow	10	c Knott b Willis	21
IM Chappell c Knott b Snow	2	c Willis b Underwood	104
IR Redpath c Lever b Illingworth	9	not out	21
KD Walters c Knott b Lever	8	not out	36
GS Chappell c Edrich b Lever	0		
RW Marsh (+) c Knott b Willis	28		
AA Mallett c Illingworth b Snow	28		
JW Gleeson c Boycott b Willis	16		
DK Lillee c Boycott b Lever	10		
AL Thomson not out	6		
Extras (LB 2, NB 3)	5	(B 2, LB 3, NB 5)	10
TOTAL	235	3 for 328	

FOW 1st Inns: 61 117 131 141 145 163 180 219 221 235
FOW 2nd Inns: 65 267 271

Bowling: *First Innings*: Snow 21-4-73-2, Lever 17.1-2-49-4, Underwood 21-6-45-1, Willis 12-3-49-2, Illingworth 5-2-14-1. *Second Innings*: Snow 17-3-60-1, Lever 17-4-49-0, Willis 13-1-48-1, Illingworth 14-7-32-0, Underwood 35-7-85-1, D'Oliveira 15-4-28-0, Fletcher 4-0-16-0.

Umpires: TF Brooks & MG O'Connell

FIFTH TEST 1970–71 AUSTRALIA v ENGLAND
Melbourne Cricket Ground, Melbourne. January 21, 22, 23, 25, 26, 1971.
Toss: Australia. Match Drawn.

AUSTRALIA

KR Stackpole c Lever b D'Oliveira	30	c Knott b Willis	18
WM Lawry (c) c Snow b Willis	56	c (S)KJ Shuttleworth b Snow	42
IM Chappell c Luckhurst b Snow	111	b Underwood	30
IR Redpath b Snow	72	c Knott b Snow	5
KD Walters b Underwood	55	not out	39
GS Chappell c Edrich b Willis	3	not out	20
RW Marsh (+) not out	92		
KJ O'Keeffe c Luckhurst b Illingworth	27		
JW Gleeson c Cowdrey b Willis	5		
JRF Duncan c Edrich b Illingworth	3		
AL Thomson not out	0		
Extras (B 10, LB 17, NB 12)	39	(B 8, LB 3, NB 4)	15
TOTAL	9 dec 493	4 dec 169	

FOW 1st Inns: 64 266 269 310 314 374 471 477 480
FOW 2nd Inns: 51 84 91 132

Bowling: *First Innings*: Snow 29.6-9-94-2, Lever 25-6-79-0, D'Oliveira 22-6-71-1, Willis 20-5-73-3, Underwood 19-4-78-1, Illingworth 13-0-59-2. *Second Innings*: Snow 12-4-21-2, Lever 12-1-53-0, Willis 10-1-42-1, Underwood 12-0-38-1.

ENGLAND

G Boycott c Redpath b Thomson	12	not out	76
BW Luckhurst b Walters	109	not out	74
JH Edrich c Marsh b Thomson	9 (2)		
MC Cowdrey c & b Gleeson	13		
BL D'Oliveira c Marsh b Thomson	117		
R Illingworth (c) c Redpath b Gleeson	41		
APE Knott (+) lbw Stackpole	19		
JA Snow b IM Chappell	1		
P Lever run out	19		
DL Underwood c & b Gleeson	5		
RGD Willis not out	5		
Extras (B 17, LB 14, NB 11)	42	(B 1, LB 8, NB 2)	11
TOTAL	392	0 for 161	

FOW 1st Inns: 40 64 88 228 306 340 354 362 379 392
FOW 2nd Inns:

Bowling: *First Innings*: Thomson 34.5-110-3, Duncan 14-4-30-0, GS Chappell 8-0-21-0, O'Keeffe 31-11-71-0, Gleeson 25-7-60-3, Stackpole 17.5-4-41-1, Walters 5-2-7-1, Chappell 3-0-10-1. *Second Innings*: Thomson 11-5-26-0, Walters 7-1-14-0, Gleeson 3-1-18-0, O'Keeffe 19-3-45-0, Stackpole 13-2-28-0, GS Chappell 5-0-19-0.

Umpires: MG O'Connell & LP Rowan

SEVENTH TEST 1970–71 AUSTRALIA v ENGLAND
Sydney Cricket Ground, Sydney. February 12, 13, 14, 16, 17, 1971.
Toss: Australia. England won by 62 runs.

ENGLAND

JH Edrich c GS Chappell b Dell	30	c IM Chappell b O'Keeffe	57
BW Luckhurst c Redpath b Walters	0	c Lillee b O'Keeffe	59
KWR Fletcher c Stackpole b O'Keeffe	33	c Stackpole b Eastwood	20
JH Hampshire c Marsh b Lillee	10	c IM Chappell b O'Keeffe	24
BL D'Oliveira b Dell	1	c IM Chappell b Lillee	47
R Illingworth (c) b Jenner	42	lbw Lillee	29
APE Knott (+) c Stackpole b O'Keeffe	27	b Dell	15
JA Snow b Jenner	7	c Stackpole b Dell	20
P Lever c Jenner b O'Keeffe	4	c Redpath b Jenner	17
DL Underwood not out	8	c Marsh b Dell	0
RGD Willis b Jenner	11	not out	2
Extras (B 4, LB 4, W 1, NB 2)	11	(B 3, LB 3, NB 6)	12
TOTAL	184	302	

FOW 1st Inns: 5 60 68 69 98 145 156 165 165 184
FOW 2nd Inns: 94 130 158 165 234 251 276 298 299 302

Bowling: *First Innings*: Lillee 13-5-32-1, Dell 16-8-32-2, Walters 4-0-10-1, GS Chappell 3-0-9-0, Jenner 16-3-42-3, O'Keeffe 24-8-48-3. *Second Innings*: Lillee 14-0-43-2, Dell 26.7-3-65-5, Walters 5-0-18-0, O'Keeffe 26-8-96-3, Jenner 21-5-39-1, Eastwood 5-0-21-1, Stackpole 3-1-8-0.

AUSTRALIA

KH Eastwood c Knott b Lever	5	b Snow	0
KR Stackpole b Snow	6	b Illingworth	67
RW Marsh (+) c Willis b Lever	4 (7)	b Underwood	16
IM Chappell (c) b Willis	25 (3)	c Knott b Lever	6
IR Redpath c & b Willis	59 (4)	c Hampshire b Illingworth	14
KD Walters st Knott b Underwood	42 (5)	c D'Oliveira b Willis	1
GS Chappell b Willis	65 (6)	st Knott b Illingworth	30
KJ O'Keeffe c Knott b Illingworth	3	c (S)KJ Shuttleworth b D'Oliveira	12
TJ Jenner b Lever	30	c Fletcher b Underwood	4
DK Lillee c Knott b Willis	6	c Hampshire b D'Oliveira	0
AR Dell not out	3	not out	3
Extras (LB 5, W 1, NB 10)	16	(B 2, NB 5)	7
TOTAL	264	160	

FOW 1st Inns: 11 13 32 66 147 162 178 235 239 264
FOW 2nd Inns: 0 22 71 82 96 131 142 154 154 160

Bowling: *First Innings*: Snow 18-2-68-1, Lever 14.6-3-43-3, D'Oliveira 12-2-24-0, Willis 12-1-58-3, Underwood 16-3-39-2, Illingworth 11-3-16-1. *Second Innings*: Snow 2-1-7-1, Lever 12-2-23-1, D'Oliveira 5-1-15-2, Willis 9-1-32-1, Underwood 13.6-5-28-2, Illingworth 20-7-39-3, Fletcher 1-0-9-0.

Umpires: TF Brooks & LP Rowan

Chappell's Charges

1971-72

REST OF THE WORLD IN AUSTRALIA

South African tour is called off

Sydney, Sep. 8. The Australian Board of Control for International Cricket has issued a statement cancelling the proposed South African tour of Australia this summer.

Violent protests during the recent South African rugby tour of Australia have highlighted the strong feeling that exists in the community against South Africa's apartheid policies.

In making its decision, the Board has been mindful of the views of politicians, police, religious leaders, union officials and ground administrators.

All the evidence suggests that, had the tour gone ahead, massive demonstrations would have interrupted the matches.

There is little doubt that politics and sport should be separated, but the Board believes it is prudent to accept the realities of the situation.

The Board commends the South African Cricket Association's strong stand against its government's racial policies, and hopes the South African Government will soon relax its laws.

In the meantime, the Australian cricket authorities are urgently discussing alternatives for the coming season.

Graeme Watson is accidentally hit in the head by Tony Greig and suffers severe injuries.

Lillee, Massie, new finds

Melbourne, Feb. 5. Australian cricket officials are delighted with results of the 'World XI' tour which was organised to replace the cancelled South African tour this summer. Attendance figures of around 400,000 could scarcely have been bettered had the Springboks made the trip.

In the unofficial series, the World XI won two matches, Australia one, and there were two draws.

The highlights for Australia are the performances of bowlers Bob Massie (7/76 at Sydney) and Dennis Lillee (8/29 at Perth).

Lillee's spell comprised 7.1 overs. At one stage he captured six wickets for no runs off 15 balls.

With Lillee's pace and Massie's swing, Australia now has a bowling attack to take on the world's best. Australia's batsmen also put in some fine performances against the World XI. Ian Chappell scored four centuries, and his brother Greg made 197 at Sydney.

Obviously one of the attractions for the public has been the chance to see champions from six countries in the World XI, which includes: Garfield Sobers and Clive Lloyd (West Indies); Intikhab Alam and Zaheer Abbas (Pakistan); Graeme and Peter Pollock (South Africa); Sunil Gavaskar and Bishen Bedi (India); Tony Greig (England); and Bob Cunis (NZ).

The World XI was plagued by injuries, 35 to be precise, according to team manager Bill Jacobs.

But that didn't prevent some unforgettable performances. Sobers' 254 runs in 376 minutes at the MCG was hailed by Sir

A big six from Ian Chappell, as bowler Bishen Bedi looks on in the Australia v World XI in Brisbane in December.

Donald Bradman as 'probably the best ever seen in Australia'.

'The people who saw Sobers enjoyed one of the historic events of cricket,' Sir Donald said. 'They were privileged to have such an experience.'

Sobers hit two sixes and 33 fours in six hours and sixteen minutes.

Peter Pollock, who with Sobers added 186 for the eighth wicket, said afterwards: 'It was my greatest cricket experience. There can be no greater cricketer.'

As the World XI won the Melbourne international by 97 runs, Australian batsman Graeme Watson fought for his life in hospital after being hit in the face by a full toss from Tony Greig. He needed 40 pints of blood.

WA shield winner

Melbourne, March 6. Western Australia has won the Sheffield Shield by one point from South Australia.

WA appeared set for victory after a five-wicket win over South Australia in Perth on March 1 gave it a six-point lead in the competition. Victoria's defeat of SA today, in which Bob Rowan took 7/36, has sealed the Shield for Western Australia.

Seventy-one of WA's 128 dismissals were taken by its devastating bowling trio of Bob Masssie (25 at 24.28), Dennis Lillee (24 at 18.75), and Graham McKenzie (22 at 22.31).

Batsman Ross 'Roscoe' Edwards made 586 runs for WA at 58.60, while John Inverarity made 641 at 53.41.

Western Australian players look set to dominate selection for the Ashes tour later this year.

'Walk!' Victoria's Alan Thomson tells WA's Rod Marsh to move on.

QUICK SINGLES

New Shield system. Sheffield Shield cricket is being played under a new bonus points system this season. Points are awarded for outright wins, and bonus points can be earned in the first 65 overs of the first innings of each side, on the basis of one to the batting side for every 25 runs scored after 150 and one to the fielding side for every two wickets taken. There are now no points for draws or first-innings leads.

World beater. Sensational fast bowler Dennis 'the menace' Lillee single-handedly destroyed the World XI in the second international in Perth, taking 8/29. 'I'm a little tired,' he said afterwards.

Pair of sevens. Bob Massie took 7/76 for Australia against the World XI in the fourth international in Sydney. His effort was echoed by seven catches dropped.

AUSTRALIA v WORLD XI scores

First International at Brisbane Nov 26 – Dec 1. Australia 4/389 dec. (K Stackpole 132, I Chappell 145) and 3/220 dec. (I Chappell 106) v World XI 4/285 dec. I(H Ackerman 112, R Kanhai 101) and 4/108 (Z Abbas 32; D Lillee 2/38). Match drawn.

Second International at Perth, Dec 10–12. Australia 349 (K Stackpole 55, I Chappell 56, K D Walters 125; A Greig 4/94) d World XI 59 (Lillee 8/29) and 279 (R Kanhai 118, Z Abbas 51; D Lillee 4/63, G McKenzie 4/66).
Australia won by an innings and 11 runs.

Third International at Melbourne, Jan 1–6. World XI 184 (S Gavaskar 38, A Greig 66, Intikhab 38; Lillee 5/48) and 514 (Z Abbas 86, G Sobers 254, P Pollock 54; D Lillee 3/133, T Jenner 4/87) d Australia 285 (G Chappell 115; G Sobers 3/67, A Greig 4/41) and 317 (I Chappell 41,

J Benaud 42, K D Walters 127; Intinkhab 3/83, Bedi 4/81).
World XI won by 96 runs.

Fourth International at Sydney, Jan 8–12. Australia 312 (K Stackpole 104, J Benaud 54, R Marsh 77; Bedi 4/85, Intikhab 3/75) and 546 (I Chappell 119, G Chappell 197, K O'Keefe 54; Intiokhab 4/132) v World XI 277 (R Pollock 37, F Engineer 36, Intikhab 73; R Massie 7/76) and 5/173 (H Ackerman 87, S Gavaskar 68; K O'Keefe 3/34).
Match drawn.

Fifth International at Adelaide, Jan 28 – Feb 1. Australia 311 (J Benaud 99, G Chappell 85, R Marsh 54; A Greig 6/30, Intikhab 3/95) and 201 (I Chappell 111 not out; Bedi 3/54, Intikhab 4/78) lost to World XI 367 (Z Abbas 73, R Pollock 136; A Mallett 4/116) and 1/146 (H Ackerman 79, S Gavaskar 50).
World XI won by nine wickets.

Adventurous Australians strike a snag

Caught Marsh, bowled Lillee. A fate which befell England's Alan Knott three times in the 1972 series.

Manchester, June 14. A record ninth-wicket stand by Australia's Rod Marsh and John Gleeson at Old Trafford yesterday was not enough to prevent England winning the first Test by 89 runs. It was England's first win over Australia in the opening Test of a home series since 1930.

Gleeson and Marsh came together at 147 for 8. Their ninth-wicket partnership of 104 runs in 80 minutes is the best made by Australians in a Test in England.

For a few moments it almost seemed possible that Australia might snatch victory, but all hopes were dashed when Marsh was caught for 91 by Alan Knott, off the bowling of Tony Greig.

Marsh again almost became the first Australian 'keeper to make a Test century.

Apart from Keith Stackpole, he was the only Australian batsman who looked comfortable on the seaming Old Trafford pitch. He also took five catches in England's second innings.

England's batting was generally lacklustre. Tony Greig was best in both innings (57 and 62).

Australia's fast bowler Dennis Lillee captured 6/66 in England's second innings, three of these off four balls in his final over.

The first-Test loss has been a blow to Australia, which was boosted by three wins and seven draws in its ten lead-up matches.

Bob Massie's 6/31 against Worcestershire gave Australia great heart, but injury prevented him making his Test debut.

Lillee is fighting fit. Since April he has been a familiar figure running the streets at dawn near Covent Garden Markets.

Perhaps the most disappointing aspect of Australia's play was its fielding. Three catches went down in slips on the first day – Geoffrey Boycott on five, John Edrich on 44 and Tony Greig before scoring.

Long hair, flares, the odd card game and a purple suit

London, June 26. Lord's has seen more than its share of purple over the years. Dukes, Duchesses, Kings and Queens, Knights of the Realm.

But the blue bloods saw red when that brash Australian captain, Ian Chappell, 'graced' the balcony at Lord's in a purple jump suit.

Dear me! Gentle folk in the members enclosure were horrified.

Still, it was a change from that ghastly mauve safari suit he usually sports.

Chappell's colonials are a motley lot. They wear flared trousers, hair over the ears, and sideburns. Why, even their moustaches droop.

But at least the public don't have to see their dressing room antics. The infernal pranks and carry-on, the beer and cigarettes and cribbage games. And all that yelling and laughter.

It wouldn't have happened in the good old days.

Australian cricketers keep their cards close to their chests.

Massie's massacre at Lord's

Bob Massie: magician at Lord's.

England's immovable Geoff Boycott looks pained, bowled by Bob Massie for 11.

Lord's, June 14. They're calling it 'Massie's Match.' Never before has a bowler taken 16 wickets in his first Test.

Only four other bowlers have taken eight wickets in an innings, and Australia's Bob Massie has just done it twice in the second Test at Lord's, which Australia has won by eight wickets. His figures of 8/84 and 8/53 are extraordinary.

The young Western Australian bank clerk is a fast-medium bowler with an uncanny ability to swing the ball. He has obviously benefited from playing with Kilmarnock in Scotland last summer.

Massie perfectly understood the pitch and conditions.

He bowled like some kind of machine. His easy, gliding action was smooth and controlled, hypnotic and bewitching.

And as the England batsmen fell to his spell, he changed the pace, swinging the ball both ways with sharp, steady, and subtle swerves. Then they were gone.

Time after time Massie's magic was questioned by batsmen. What was his sleight of hand?

They checked the ball. Perhaps it was damaged?

They checked the ball again. Perhaps he was rubbing it with oil?

And they checked the ball again.

No, he didn't have a string attached.

And he didn't steer it by radio either. But it certainly looked that way.

He tricked them all. Well, all but one, that is. The only England batsmen not to have his wicket taken by Massie in the second Test was Brian Luckhurst. He was dismissed by Dennis Lillee in both innings, for 1 and 4.

The people rose to their feet as Massie walked back to the rooms. And then a hush descended on Lord's.

'Who was that man?' they whispered.

Runs galore but Test a fizzer

Nottingham, July 19. The third Test at Trent Bridge has ended in a disappointing draw despite some marvellous cricket and high individual scoring on both sides.

Unusually, England sent Australia in to bat first. Opener Keith Stackpole showed how much he relished the chance by making 114 runs on the first day.

Australia was all out for 315 in the first innings, but England made only 189 in reply.

In Australia's second innings Ross Edwards showed he was more than a pipe-smoking accountant by building up 170 runs not out in just under six hours.

England opener Brian Luckhurst was caught on 96 by Greg Chappell off his brother Ian's bowling, but the pitch was too dead for Australia to have any chance of victory.

Ross Edwards at Trent Bridge.

No to Lillee

Melbourne, Sep. 25. The Australian Cricket Board will not let Western Australian fast bowler Dennis Lillee play next season with English county side Derbyshire.

Lillee was approached by the Derbyshire County Cricket Club during the Ashes tour.

Like many other leading Australian cricketers, Lillee is interested in playing during the English summer of 1973.

Australian players who are making their mark in English county cricket include Lillee's fellow Western Australian Graham McKenzie, and Terry Jenner, Ian Redpath, Marshall Rosen and John Maclean.

Lillee is reported to be stunned that his formal request to the Board has been rejected.

How Australian cartoonist Rigby saw Bob Massie's bowling feat of 16 wickets in the test at Lord's.

Pitched out at Headingley

Peter Parfitt makes a spectacular lunge to catch Doug Walters at Headingley.

Leeds, July 29. England retained the Ashes today, after winning the fourth Test at Headingley by nine wickets. It is the first time since 1961 that a Test has been all over in only three days of play.

Australian captain Ian Chappell won the toss, but possibly miscalculated by batting first. The pitch had been drenched by rain before the match. It was devoid of grass, yet the field was green and lush.

Questions were asked about the pitch preparation, which certainly favoured the England spin bowlers, Ray Illingworth and Derek Underwood, who were able to dictate terms from the outset.

Underwood came on at 1.00 pm on the first day, when Australia was 56 for one. By the time he finished, the score was 146 for eight. Underwood took 4/37 in 31 overs.

Keith Stackpole's first-innings tally of 52 runs was the best Australian batsmen could muster.

Illingworth brought himself into the bowling before lunch on the first day, a remarkable time for a spinner, but not on this pitch.

Australia was all out in their first innings for 146.

The pitch seemed to get slower hour by hour. It was no track for the Australian speedsters, Dennis Lillee and Bob Massie.

Only Ashley Mallett's 5/43 kept

The elegant style of Paul Sheahan.

Australia's hopes alive. The quiet off-spinner, 'Rowdy' to his mates, certainly made some noise early in England's first innings. England was 112 for six at lunch on day two, but in the afternoon put on 79 runs for the loss of one wicket.

Australia failed by 10 runs to better its miserable first innings score.

England might have won by an innings, had not Australia's Paul Sheahan stayed firm at the crease to notch up 41 not out in Australia's second innings. Of the others, only Keith Stackpole passed 20.

Lillee, Marsh on high note

London, Aug. 17. The highlight of Australia's five-wicket victory in the fifth Test at the Oval has been the devastating combination of Australian bowler Dennis Lillee and wicketkeeper Rod Marsh.

Lillee's figures of 5/58 and 5/23 take him to 31 wickets, a new record for Australia in England. Marsh added four catches to take his series tally to 23 dismissals, another new record.

In England's first innings Lillee proved that lightning does strike twice. He captured three wickets in four balls, a feat achieved by only a handful of players, yet it was the second time this series for Lillee. He is shaping as one of the great fast bowlers.

On the second and third days the Chappell brothers, Ian and Greg, set up the Australian victory with 118 and 113 runs respectively. The Chappells made a magnificent third-wicket stand of 201.

It is the first time brothers have made centuries in the same Test.

England was deprived of three of its leading bowlers due to injury, however.

John Snow suffered a bruised arm from a Lillee bouncer. Basil D'Oliveira strained his back, and

Dennis Lillee: batsmen beware.

Ray Illingworth twisted his ankle in a foothole late on the fifth day.

The match was only the second six-day Test in England, the other being the fifth Test between Australia and England in 1930, when a full day was lost due to rain. Australia won that too.

A diving Greg Chappell catches the important wicket of Basil D'Oliveira.

Sussex breaks 84-year drought

Manchester, June 7. In the lead-up to the first Test at Old Trafford, England's hopes were boosted by an extrordinary win over Australia by the Sussex county side.

Sussex had not beaten Australia since 1888. Australian captain Ian Chappell is a gambler, however, and when he closed Australia's innings at 2 for 262, the county didn't need to think twice about the rare carrot

Chappell had dangled before it.

Requiring 261 in 180 minutes, Sussex gave it everything.

With nothing to lose, Sussex's leading batsman, the South African-born Tony Greig, hit three sixes in one over. At one stage he made 36 runs from just 18 balls.

The 6ft 7in. Greig looked good for his Test debut in the first Test at Old Trafford tomorrow.

McGilvray the voice of cricket

London, Aug. 10. Thanks to satellite communication, the fifth Test between England and Australia will be telecast live in Australia.

Until now, the only solace for cricket fans on cold winter evenings in Australia has been the smooth voice of ABC radio commentator Alan McGilvray, who began as a broadcaster back in 1935.

Sir Robert Menzies once told

McGilvray: 'you always tell us the state of play, who hit the ball, where it went, what runs resulted, and what the state of the game is.'

High praise indeed.

Back in 1938 McGilvray had to 'manufacture' radio commentaries in the studio from telegrams sent from England. It was so informative and exciting that people thought he must have been there.

Massie's figures near the top

London, Aug. 20. Bob Massie, the 25-year-old bank clerk from Perth, Western Australia, has earned a place in cricket history with his remarkable bowling feats during the Australian tour of England.

Most of the English press had never heard of Massie until that unforgettable second Test at Lord's when he captured 16 wickets for 137 runs on debut.

Things must be good in Australia. This man was working the Western Australian scoreboard last December when Australia played the World XI in Perth. Now they give him a game and he virtually bowls out the English Test team twice.

Ironically, he has been in England for three seasons, playing for Kilmarnock during the Australian winter. He has even married a local girl.

Not many remember his first match in the Western Union competition, when he took all 10 wickets. Not many noticed when he took 6/31 at Worcester in April. Now everybody knows his name.

Massie's 8/84 and 8/53 at Lord's take him into the record books.

No Australian bowler has ever made such a fine debut. No Australian has ever taken so many wickets in a Test, and in over 700 Test matches played, only two other bowlers have bettered his figures.

The English off-spinner Jim Laker claimed 19/90 against Australia at Old Trafford in 1956.

Bob Massie seasons in England.

Laker's effort broke the old record of 17 wickets that England's Sydney Barnes set in December 1912 against South Africa at Johannesburg.

Barnes, like Massie, was a right-arm medium-fast bowler with an exceptional ability to swing the ball. Many consider him to be the best bowler in the history of the game.

Barnes played local league cricket and the odd first class match until he was aged well into his sixties.

One-eyed English cricket fans are hoping Bob Massie doesn't leave it that long before deciding to rest on his laurels.

Sponsorship, one dayers catching on

Melbourne, Sep. 15. As members of the Australian Test team begin to arrive home from England, cricket administrators are delighted to hear that the recent series established a new record for receipts.

Takings for the five-Test competition were £246,000, a £4000 increase on the 1968 tour.

But gate figures are only part of the success story. This series has seen the arrival of marketing men in a big way.

The MCC has reaped nearly £600,000 from sponsorship deals with various firms who have recognised the commercial potential of linking their name with cricket.

The windfall has benefited the county sides, who will each receive payouts of £25,000.

Nearly £100,000 was paid by English television and radio stations for broadcasting rights.

Gillette and Benson and Hedges committed over £200,000, and the Prudential Insurance Group provided £30,000 for three 55-over matches to replace a sixth Test.

England won the best-of-three Prudential Trophy series two–nil. Special awards for 'Man of the Match' and 'Man of the Series' look like catching on, as does the limited-over game itself, if attendance figures of 55,000 are any guide.

Purists scoff at limited over cricket, but there is no doubt that the public like the attacking play that the format encourages. They also like to see a result, which limited-over cricket guarantees.

Australian officials have now seen the potential to bring new money into the game, and hopefully it won't be too long before our cricketers will reap the benefits.

Not all Australian players will continue to accept financial hardship merely for the baggy green cap.

FIRST TEST 1972 ENGLAND v AUSTRALIA
Old Trafford, Manchester. June 8, 9, 10, 12, 13, 1972.
Toss: England. England won by 89 runs.

ENGLAND

G Boycott c Stackpole b Gleeson	8	lbw Gleeson	47
JH Edrich run out	49	c Marsh b Watson	26
BW Luckhurst b Colley	14	c Marsh b Colley	0
MJK Smith lbw Lillee	10	c Marsh b Lillee	34
BL D'Oliveira b GS Chappell	23	c Watson b Lillee	37
AW Greig lbw Colley	57	b GS Chappell	62
APE Knott (+) c Marsh b Lillee	18	c Marsh b Lillee	1
R Illingworth (c) not out	26	c IM Chappell b Lillee	14
JA Snow b Colley	3	lbw Lillee	0
N Gifford run out	15	c Marsh b Lillee	0
GG Arnold c Francis b Gleeson	1	not out	0
Extras (B 10, LB 9, W 2, NB 4)	25	(B 4, LB 8, NB 1)	13
TOTAL	249		234

FOW 1st Inns: 50 86 99 118 127 190 200 209 243 249
FOW 2nd Inns: 60 65 81 140 182 192 234 234 234 234

Bowling: *First Innings*: Lillee 29-14-40-2, Colley 33-3-83-3, GS Chappell 16-6-28-1, Walters 5-1-7-0, Watson 4-2-8-0, Gleeson 24.4-10-45-2, Inverarity 9-3-13-0. *Second Innings*: Lillee 30-8-66-6, Colley 23-3-68-1, GS Chappell 21.2-6-42-1, Watson 5-0-29-1, Gleeson 7-3-16-1.

AUSTRALIA

KR Stackpole lbw Arnold	53	b Greig	67
BC Francis lbw D'Oliveira	27	lbw Snow	6
IM Chappell (c) c Smith b Greig	0	c Knott b Snow	7
GS Chappell c Greig b Snow	24	c D'Oliveira b Arnold	23
GD Watson c Knott b Arnold	2	c & b Snow	0
KD Walters c Illingworth b Snow	17	b Greig	20
RJ Inverarity c Knott b Arnold	4	c Luckhurst b D'Oliveira	3
RW Marsh (+) c Edrich b Arnold	8	c Knott b Greig	91
DJ Colley b Snow	1	c Greig b Snow	4
JW Gleeson b Snow	0	b Greig	30
DK Lillee not out	1	not out	0
Extras (B 1, LB 4)	5	(W 1)	1
TOTAL	142		252

FOW 1st Inns: 68 69 91 99 119 124 134 137 137 142
FOW 2nd Inns: 9 31 77 78 115 120 136 147 251 252

Bowling: *First Innings*: Snow 20-7-41-4, Arnold 25-4-62-4, Greig 7-1-21-1, D'Oliveira 6-1-13-1. *Second Innings*: Snow 27-2-87-4, Arnold 20-2-59-1, Greig 19.2-7-53-4, D'Oliveira 16-4-23-1, Gifford 3-0-29-0.

Umpires: CS Elliott & TW Spencer

SECOND TEST 1972 ENGLAND v AUSTRALIA
Lord's Cricket Ground, London. June 22, 23, 24, 26, 1972.
Toss: England. Australia won by 8 wkts.

ENGLAND

G Boycott b Massie	11	b Lillee	6
JH Edrich lbw Lillee	10	c Marsh b Massie	6
BW Luckhurst b Lillee	1	c Marsh b Lillee	4
MJK Smith b Massie	34	c Edwards b Massie	30
BL D'Oliveira lbw Massie	32	c GS Chappell b Massie	3
AW Greig c Marsh b Massie	54	c IM Chappell b Massie	3
APE Knott (+) c Colley b Massie	43	c GS Chappell b Massie	12
R Illingworth (c) lbw Massie	30	c Stackpole b Massie	12
JA Snow b Massie	37	c Marsh b Massie	0
N Gifford c Marsh b Massie	3	not out	16
JSE Price not out	4	c GS Chappell b Massie	19
Extras (LB 6, W 1, NB 6)	13	(W 1, NB 4)	5
TOTAL	272		116

FOW 1st Inns: 22 23 28 84 97 193 200 260 265 272
FOW 2nd Inns: 12 16 18 25 31 52 74 74 81 116

Bowling: *First Innings*: Lillee 28-3-90-2, Massie 32.5-7-84-8, Colley 16-2-42-0, GS Chappell 6-1-18-0, Gleeson 9-1-25-0. *Second Innings*: Lillee 21-6-50-2, Massie 27.2-9-53-8, Colley 7-1-8-0.

AUSTRALIA

KR Stackpole c Gifford b Price	5	not out	57
BC Francis b Snow	0	c Knott b Price	9
IM Chappell (c) c Smith b Snow	56	c Luckhurst b D'Oliveira	6
GS Chappell b D'Oliveira	131	not out	7
KD Walters c Illingworth b Snow	1		
R Edwards c Smith b Illingworth	28		
JW Gleeson c Knott b Greig	1		
RW Marsh (+) c Greig b Snow	50		
DJ Colley c Greig b Price	25		
RAL Massie c Knott b Snow	0		
DK Lillee not out	2		
Extras (LB 7, NB 2)	9	(LB 2)	2
TOTAL	308		2 for 81

FOW 1st Inns: 0 0 0 0 0 0 0 0 0 0
FOW 2nd Inns: 20 51

Bowling: *First Innings*: Snow 32-13-57-5, Price 26.1-5-87-2, Greig 29-6-74-1, D'Oliveira 17-5-48-1, Gifford 11-4-20-0, Illingworth 7-2-13-1. *Second Innings*: Snow 8-2-15-0, Price 7-0-28-1, Greig 3-0-17-0, D'Oliveira 8-3-14-1, Luckhurst 0.5-0-5-0.

Umpires: DJ Constant & AE Fagg

THIRD TEST 1972 ENGLAND v AUSTRALIA
Trent Bridge, Nottingham. July 13, 14, 15, 17, 18, 1972.
Toss: England. Match Drawn.

AUSTRALIA

KR Stackpole c Parfitt b Greig	114	c Luckhurst b Snow	12
BC Francis c Smith b Lever	10		
IM Chappell (c) c Knott b Snow	34	lbw Illingworth	50
GS Chappell c Parfitt b Snow	26	b Snow	72
KD Walters c Parfitt b Snow	2	c Gifford b Snow	7
R Edwards c Knott b Snow	13 (2)	not out	170
RW Marsh (+) c D'Oliveira b Gifford	41 (6)	not out	7
DJ Colley c Greig b D'Oliveira	54		
RAL Massie c Parfitt b Snow	0		
JW Gleeson not out	6		
DK Lillee c Knott b Greig	0		
Extras (B 4, LB 6, NB 5)	15	(LB 4, W 1, NB 1)	6
TOTAL	315	4 dec	324

FOW 1st Inns: 16 98 157 165 189 227 289 298 315 315
FOW 2nd Inns: 15 139 285 295

Bowling: *First Innings*: Snow 31-8-92-5, Lever 26-8-61-1, Greig 38.4-9-88-2, D'Oliveira 18-5-41-1, Gifford 5-1-18-1. *Second Innings*: Snow 24-1-94-3, Lever 19-3-76-0, Greig 12-1-46-0, D'Oliveira 7-0-12-0, Gifford 15-1-49-0, Illingworth 15-4-41-1.

ENGLAND

BW Luckhurst lbw Lillee	23	c GS Chappell b IM Chappell	96
JH Edrich c Marsh b Colley	37	b Massie	15
PH Parfitt b Massie	0	b Lillee	46
MJK Smith b Lillee	17	lbw Lillee	15
BL D'Oliveira lbw Lillee	29	not out	50
N Gifford c Marsh b Massie	16		
AW Greig c Marsh b Massie	7 (6)	not out	36
APE Knott (+) c Marsh b Massie	13		
R Illingworth (c) not out	24		
JA Snow c Marsh b Lillee	6		
P Lever c Walters b Colley	9		
Extras (B 5, LB 2, W 1, NB 13)	21	(B 17, LB 9, W 4, NB 2)	32
TOTAL	189	4 for	290

FOW 1st Inns: 55 60 74 111 133 145 145 155 166 189
FOW 2nd Inns: 50 167 200 201

Bowling: *First Innings*: Lillee 29-15-35-4, Massie 30-10-43-4, Colley 23.3-5-68-2, Gleeson 6-1-22-0. *Second Innings*: Lillee 25-10-40-2, Massie 36-13-49-1, Colley 19-6-43-0, IM Chappell 12-5-26-1, Gleeson 30-13-49-0, GS Chappell 9-4-16-0, Stackpole 17-7-35-0.

Umpires: AEG Rhodes & TW Spencer

FIFTH TEST 1972 ENGLAND v AUSTRALIA
Kennington Oval, London. August 10, 11, 12, 14, 15, 16, 1972.
Toss: England. Australia won by 5 wkts.

ENGLAND

B Wood c Marsh b Watson	26	lbw Massie	90
JH Edrich lbw Lillee	8	b Lillee	18
PH Parfitt b Lillee	51	b Lillee	18
JH Hampshire c Inverarity b Mallett	42	c IM Chappell b Watson	20
BL D'Oliveira c GS Chappell b Mallett	4	c IM Chappell b Massie	43
AW Greig c Stackpole b Mallett	16	c Marsh b Lillee	29
R Illingworth (c) c GS Chappell b Lillee	0	lbw Lillee	31
APE Knott (+) c Marsh b Lillee	92	b Lillee	63
JA Snow c Marsh b Lillee	3	c Stackpole b Mallett	14
GG Arnold b Inverarity	22	lbw Mallett	4
DL Underwood not out	3	not out	0
Extras (LB 8, W 1, NB 8)	17	(B 11, LB 8, NB 7)	26
TOTAL	284		356

FOW 1st Inns: 25 50 133 142 145 145 159 181 262 284
FOW 2nd Inns: 56 81 114 194 205 270 271 333 356 356

Bowling: *First Innings*: Lillee 24.2-7-58-5, Massie 27-5-69-0, Watson 12-4-23-1, Mallett 23-4-80-3, GS Chappell 2-0-18-0, Inverarity 4-0-19-1. *Second Innings*: Lillee 32.2-8-123-5, Massie 32-10-77-2, Watson 19-8-32-1, Mallett 23-7-66-2, Inverarity 15-4-32-0.

AUSTRALIA

GD Watson c Knott b Arnold	13	lbw Arnold	6
KR Stackpole b Snow	18	c Knott b Greig	79
IM Chappell (c) c Snow b Arnold	118	c (S)RGD Willis b Underwood	37
GS Chappell c Greig b Illingworth	113	lbw Underwood	16
R Edwards b Underwood	79	lbw Greig	1
AP Sheahan c Hampshire b Underwood	5	not out	44
RW Marsh (+) b Underwood	0	not out	43
RJ Inverarity c Greig b Underwood	28		
AA Mallett run out	5		
RAL Massie b Arnold	4		
DK Lillee not out	0		
Extras (LB 8, W 1, NB 7)	16	(LB 6, NB 10)	16
TOTAL	399	5 for	242

FOW 1st Inns: 24 34 235 296 310 310 383 387 399 399
FOW 2nd Inns: 16 132 136 137 171

Bowling: *First Innings*: Arnold 35-11-87-3, Snow 34.5-5-111-1, Greig 18-9-25-0, D'Oliveira 9-4-17-0, Underwood 38-16-90-4, Illingworth 17-4-53-1. *Second Innings*: Arnold 15-5-26-1, Snow 6-1-21-0, Greig 25.3-10-49-2, Underwood 35-11-94-2, Illingworth 8.5-2-26-0, Parfitt 2-0-10-0.

Umpires: AE Fagg & AEG Rhodes

FOURTH TEST 1972 ENGLAND v AUSTRALIA
Headingley, Leeds. July 27, 28, 29, 1972.
Toss: Australia. England won by 9 wkts.

AUSTRALIA

KR Stackpole c Knott b Underwood	52	lbw Underwood	28
R Edwards c Knott b Snow	0	c Knott b Arnold	0
IM Chappell (c) c & b Illingworth	26	c Knott b Arnold	0
GS Chappell lbw Underwood	12	c D'Oliveira b Underwood	13
AP Sheahan c Illingworth b Underwood	0	not out	41
KD Walters b Illingworth	4	c Parfitt b Underwood	3
RW Marsh (+) c Illingworth b Underwood	1	c Knott b Underwood	1
RJ Inverarity not out	26	c Illingworth b Underwood	0
AA Mallett lbw Snow	20	b Illingworth	9
RAL Massie b Arnold	0 (11)	b Illingworth	18
DK Lillee c Greig b Arnold	0 (10)	b Underwood	7
Extras (LB 2, NB 3)	5	(LB 12, NB 4)	16
TOTAL	146		136

FOW 1st Inns: 10 79 93 93 97 98 98 145 146 146
FOW 2nd Inns: 5 7 31 51 63 69 69 93 111 136

Bowling: *First Innings*: Arnold 9.5-2-28-2, Snow 13-5-11-2, Greig 10-1-25-0, Illingworth 21-11-32-2, Underwood 31-16-37-4, D'Oliveira 2-1-8-0. *Second Innings*: Arnold 6-1-17-2, Snow 10-2-26-0, Underwood 21-6-45-6, Illingworth 19.1-5-32-2.

ENGLAND

BW Luckhurst c GS Chappell b Mallett	18	not out	12
JH Edrich c IM Chappell b Mallett	45	lbw Lillee	4
PH Parfitt c Marsh b Lillee	2	not out	0
KWR Fletcher lbw Mallett	5		
BL D'Oliveira b Mallett	12		
AW Greig c GS Chappell b Inverarity	24		
APE Knott (+) st Marsh b Mallett	0		
R Illingworth (c) lbw Lillee	57		
JA Snow st Marsh b Inverarity	48		
DL Underwood c IM Chappell b Inverarity	5		
GG Arnold not out	0		
Extras (B 19, LB 15, W 4, NB 8)	46	(LB 3, NB 2)	5
TOTAL	263	1 for	21

FOW 1st Inns: 43 52 66 76 108 108 128 232 246 263
FOW 2nd Inns: 7

Bowling: *First Innings*: Lillee 26.1-10-39-2, Massie 14-4-34-0, Mallett 52-20-114-5, Inverarity 33-19-26-3, IM Chappell 3-2-1-0, GS Chappell 2-0-3-0. *Second Innings*: Lillee 5-2-7-1, Mallett 5-1-9-0.

Umpires: DJ Constant & CS Elliott

Australian Averages

1972 ENGLAND v AUSTRALIA

AUSTRALIA	M	Inn	NO	Runs	H.S	Avrge	Ct	St	Overs	Mds	Runs	Wkt	Avrge
Chappell, GS	5	10	1	437	131	48.56	8	-	56.2	17	125	2	62.50
Chappell, IM	5	10	-	334	118	33.40	6	-	15.0	7	27	1	27.00
Colley, DJ	3	4	-	84	54	21.00	1	-	121.3	20	312	6	52.00
Edwards, R	4	7	1	291	170*	48.50	1	-					
Francis, BC	3	5	-	52	27	10.40	1	-					
Gleeson, JW	3	4	1	37	30	12.33	-	-	76.4	28	157	3	52.33
Inverarity, RJ	3	5	1	61	28	15.25	1	-	61.0	26	90	4	22.50
Lillee, DK	5	7	4	10	7	3.33	-	-	249.5	83	548	31	17.68
Mallett, AA	2	3	-	34	20	11.33	-	-	103.0	32	269	10	26.90
Marsh, RW	5	9	2	242	91	34.57	21	2					
Massie, RAL	4	5	-	22	18	4.40	-	-	199.1	58	409	23	17.78
Sheahan, AP	2	4	2	90	44*	45.00	-	-					
Stackpole, KR	5	10	1	485	114	53.89	4	-	17.0	7	35	-	-
Walters, KD	4	7	-	54	20	7.71	1	-	5.0	1	7	-	-
Watson, GD	2	4	-	21	13	5.25	1	-	40.0	14	92	3	30.67

English Averages

1972 ENGLAND v AUSTRALIA

ENGLAND	M	Inn	NO	Runs	H.S	Avrge	Ct	St	Overs	Mds	Runs	Wkt	Avrge
Arnold, GG	3	5	2	28	22	9.33	-	-	110.5	25	279	13	21.46
Boycott, G	2	4	-	72	47	18.00	-	-					
D'Oliveira, BL	5	9	1	233	50*	29.13	3	-	83.0	23	176	5	35.20
Edrich, JH	5	10	-	218	49	21.80	1	-					
Fletcher, KWR	1	1	-	5	5	5.00	-	-					
Gifford, N	3	5	1	50	16*	12.50	2	-	34.0	6	116	1	116.00
Greig, AW	5	9	-	288	62	36.00	8	-	162.3	44	398	10	39.80
Hampshire, JH	1	2	-	62	42	31.00	1	-					
Illingworth, R	5	8	2	194	57	32.33	6	-	88.0	28	197	7	28.14
Knott, APE	5	8	-	229	92	28.63	17	-					
Lever, P	1	1	-	9	9	9.00	-	-	45.0	11	137	1	137.00
Luckhurst, BW	4	8	1	168	96	24.00	3	-	0.5	-	5	-	-
Parfitt, PH	3	6	1	117	51	23.40	5	-	2.0	-	10	-	-
Price, JSE	1	2	-	23	19	23.00	-	-	33.1	5	115	3	38.33
Smith, MJK	3	6	-	140	34	23.33	4	-					
Snow, JA	5	8	-	111	48	13.88	2	-	205.5	46	555	24	23.13
Underwood, DL	2	3	2	8	5	8.00	-	-	125.0	49	266	16	16.63
Wood, B	1	2	-	116	90	58.00	-	-					

'Tangles' Walker to the rescue

New boy Thommo makes awful debut

The new boy: bowler Jeff Thomson.

Melbourne, Jan. 4. Young NSW fast bowler Jeff Thomson failed to live up to selectors' expectations in his debut in the second Test against Pakistan at the MCG.

He has not been selected for the third Test in Sydney.

The well-built Thomson did not intimidate anyone at this first appearance, his figures of 0/100 suggesting that he was either injured or perhaps his debut was premature.

Doyen of Australian cricket writers, Ray Robinson, at the second Test in Melbourne.

Sydney, Jan. 12. If ever Pakistan had a chance of winning their first Test in Australia it was yesterday.

All that was needed was a score of 159 runs in the second innings.

The Pakistanis, who don't celebrate with champagne for religious reasons, had already rung the milkman. Everything was set.

Then along came Max. Max Walker, that is, a huge, awkward-looking six feet four, pigeon-chested, wrong-footed, right-arm medium-fast bowling giant, who usually answers to the name 'Tanglefoot'. Or just 'Tangles' for short.

And did he tangle with the Pakistani batsmen.

In his last 30 balls Walker took five wickets while conceding only three runs, ending with figures of 6/15 and steering home an Australian victory by 52 runs.

Walker is a Tasmanian who made his Test debut at the MCG after Christmas, where his figures were 2/112 and 3/39.

Until recently, he has been an Australian Rules footballer in Melbourne, where he has played 85 games with the Melbourne Football Club.

He is known as a useful defender and ruckman, but his brilliant bowling performance yesterday suggests he may have an even brighter future in cricket.

Thanks to Walker, Australia has finished the three-Test series against Pakistan three wins to nil.

But it almost didn't come off.

The Pakistani side led by Intikhab Alam is certainly the best ever to have set foot in this country.

All arms and legs: Max Walker.

Seven specialist batsmen were in the line-up: Zaheer Abbas, Sadiq Muhammad, Saeed Ahmed, Asif Iqbal, Mustaq Muhammad, Talat Ali Malik and Majid Khan.

Australia, on the other hand, lost its key opening batsman Keith Stackpole with a back injury, which stopped him playing in the first and second Tests.

His replacement, Ian Redpath, was caught on 2 by Wasim off the bowling of Masood in the first Test. So Australian captain Ian Chappell took on the job himself, making 196 runs before being unluckily caught by Iqbal just one hit short of his double century.

Rod Marsh became the first Australian wicketkeeper to make a Test century, scoring 118 in Australia's big total of 585. In Pakistan's second innings Marsh took six catches, while Ashley Mallett captured 8/59 with his tricky off-spin deliveries.

Australia's fast bowler, Dennis Lillee, took 4/49 in the Pakistan first innings, aided by Bob Massie (4/70). One of Lillee's deliveries broke Talat Ali's thumb, which meant he had to bat one-handed in the second innings and miss the remainder of the series.

Unfortunately, the series involved three Test matches in three weeks, and Pakistan had no real opportunity to draw new blood.

Australia didn't appreciate the punishing schedule either, and Chappell complained.

In the second Test at the MCG Chappell declared at 5/441 in the first innings, but then Pakistan made 8/574 dec. in reply, with Sadiq (137) and Majid (158) making a second-wicket partnership of 195 runs. Paul Sheahan and John Benaud both made centuries in Australia's second innings, but at stumps on day four Pakistan needed only 2 wickets and 283 runs to win.

Pakistan's first victory over Australia since Karachi in 1964 seemed possible. But Pakistan's batsmen panicked, forgetting their basics in a comedy of errors.

'We mulled it,' said Intikhab Alam. That was the story of the series.

QUICK SINGLES

Fighting Words. Pakistan captain Intikhab Alam denies that his batsmen have a Lillee complex. 'We will treat Dennis Lillee the same way Sir Donald Bradman treated Larwood,' he says.

Work before play. Both Ashley Mallett and Paul Sheahan have declared themselves unavailable for the West Indies tour in February, citing employment reasons. Mallett begins as a journalist with an Adelaide suburban newspaper next month, and Sheahan has been appointed senior mathematics master at Geelong Grammar. 'After all, I'm a school teacher playing cricket,' Sheahan says, 'not the other way round.'

New record set. Pakistan's first innings 8/574 dec. in the second Test in Melbourne breaks their old record against Australia, 414 at Karachi in 1964.

An angry 100. John Benaud was told he would not be selected for the third Test just before he went out to bat in the second innings of the second Test. He smashed 97 before lunch on his way to 142, in a partnership of 233 with Paul Sheahan (127).

Panikstan. No, it's not a misprint. That was the headline in the Melbourne *Sun* newspaper after Pakistan's experienced batsmen, Mustaq and Asif, looked like a couple of backyard cricketers playing tip-pity runs when Asif ran Mustaq out in the second Test.

In the head and legs. Australian wicket-keeper Rod Marsh says confidence is the key to his brilliant batting and catching form against Pakistan. He has also given up drinking beer during the winter and watched his diet. Now the man known as 'Bacchus' weighs only 13 stone 5 lbs, and says most of the weight is in his legs. 'I'm only a 12-stoner from the waist up,' he argues.

Needling not cricket. Mr T. C. J. Caldwell, the chairman of the Australian Cricket Board, says needling and bad language are on the rise on the cricket field. Umpires will be instructed to take disciplinary action against offenders.

Board hears Chappell. Australian captain Ian Chappell has been given the chance to address the Board of Control on various issues, including players' wishes for shorter overseas tours, better match payments, more rest days, better food on tour, penalties for slow over rates in Sheffield Shield games, and creation of a player liaison delegate to facilitate routine Board and player communications.

Rabbits alive-oh. Bowlers Bob Massie and Jim Watkins, a first-gamer, kept Australia in the third Test with a partnership of 83 for the ninth wicket.

FIRST TEST 1972–73 AUSTRALIA v PAKISTAN
Adelaide Oval, Adelaide. December 22, 23, 24, 26, 27, 1972.
Toss: Pakistan. Australia won by an innings & 114 runs.

PAKISTAN

Batsman	Dismissal 1	R		Dismissal 2	R
Sadiq Mohammad	c GS Chappell b Massie	11		c & b Mallett	81
Talat Ali	retired hurt	7	(11)	c Edwards b Mallett	0
Zaheer Abbas	c Marsh b Lillee	7		c Marsh b O'Keeffe	0
Majid Khan	c Sheahan b Massie	11		c IM Chappell b Mallett	11
Mushtaq Mohammad	c GS Chappell b Lillee	3		lbw Mallett	32
Saeed Ahmed	c Marsh b Massie	36	(2)	lbw Mallett	39
Asif Iqbal	c Marsh b Massie	16	(6)	c GS Chappell b Mallett	0
Intikhab Alam (c)	c Edwards b Lillee	64	(7)	c GS Chappell b Lillee	30
Wasim Bari (+)	c Redpath b Mallett	72	(8)	c O'Keeffe b Mallett	9
Salim Altaf	not out	17	(9)	not out	9
Asif Masood	c Marsh b Lillee	0	(10)	c Marsh b Mallett	1
Extras	(B 4, LB 3, W 4, NB 2)	13		(B 3, LB 4, W 1, NB 3)	11
TOTAL	9 dec	257			214

FOW 1st Inns: 30 30 33 74 95 104 208 255 257
FOW 2nd Inns: 88 89 111 162 162 182 182 211 214 214

Bowling: *First Innings*: Lillee 20.3-7-49-4, Massie 24-3-70-4, GS Chappell 11-2-29-0, Mallett 12-3-52-1, O'Keeffe 8-1-44-0. *Second Innings*: Lillee 15-3-53-1, Massie 9-3-26-0, GS Chappell 4-0-21-0, Mallett 23.6-6-59-8, O'Keeffe 14-1-44-1.

AUSTRALIA

Batsman	Dismissal	R
AP Sheahan	b Asif	44
IR Redpath	c Wasim b Asif	2
IM Chappell (c)	c Asif b Majid	196
GS Chappell	lbw Salim	28
R Edwards	lbw Asif	89
J Benaud	lbw Salim	24
RW Marsh (+)	b Mushtaq	118
KJ O'Keeffe	b Mushtaq	40
AA Mallett	c(S)Sarfraz Nawaz b Majid	0
DK Lillee	c Saeed b Mushtaq	14
RAL Massie	not out	12
Extras	(B 2, LB 12, NB 4)	18
TOTAL		585

FOW 1st Inns: 3 103 158 330 390 413 533 534 566 585
Bowling: *First Innings*: Asif 19-1-110-3, Salim 25-1-83-2, Asif 14-0-76-0, Intikhab 18-2-115-0, Saeed 3-0-28-0, Majid 20-1-88-2, Mushtaq 11.2-0-67-3.

Umpires: MG O'Connell & N Townsend

THIRD TEST 1972–73 AUSTRALIA v PAKISTAN
Sydney Cricket Ground, Sydney. January 6, 7, 8, 10, 11, 1973.
Toss: Pakistan. Australia won by 52 runs.

AUSTRALIA

Batsman	Dismissal 1	R		Dismissal 2	R
KR Stackpole	c Wasim b Sarfraz	28		c Intikhab b Salim	9
IR Redpath	run out	79		c Nasim-ul-Ghani b Sarfraz	18
IM Chappell (c)	lbw Sarfraz	43		c Wasim b Sarfraz	27
GS Chappell	b Majid	30	(6)	lbw Sarfraz	6
R Edwards	c Wasim b Salim	69	(4)	lbw Salim	3
KD Walters	b Asif	19	(5)	lbw Salim	6
RW Marsh (+)	c Wasim b Salim	15		c Zaheer b Salim	0
MHN Walker	c Majid b Sarfraz	5		c Mushtaq b Sarfraz	16
JR Watkins	b Asif	3		c Zaheer b Intikhab	36
DK Lillee	b Sarfraz	2	(11)	not out	0
RAL Massie	b Salim	2	(10)	c Sadiq b Mushtaq	42
Extras	(B 18, LB 8, W 4, NB 9)	39		(B 10, LB 3, NB 8)	21
TOTAL		334			184

FOW 1st Inns: 56 138 196 220 271 315 324 327 329 334
FOW 2nd Inns: 29 31 34 44 70 73 94 101 184 184

Bowling: *First Innings*: Asif 18-1-80-1, Salim 21.5-3-71-3, Sarfraz 19-3-53-4, Majid 18-1-66-1, Asif 2-0-11-1, Intikhab 2-0-13-0. *Second Innings*: Asif 3-0-15-0, Salim 20-5-60-4, Sarfraz 21-7-56-4, Intikhab 4-2-9-1, Asif 2-0-10-0, Mushtaq 3.1-0-13-1.

PAKISTAN

Batsman	Dismissal 1	R	Dismissal 2	R
Sadiq Mohammad	c GS Chappell b Lillee	30	c Edwards b Massie	6
Nasim-ul-Ghani	c Redpath b GS Chappell	64	b Lillee	5
Zaheer Abbas	c Marsh b Massie	14	c Redpath b Lillee	47
Majid Khan	b Massie	0	lbw Walker	12
Mushtaq Mohammad	c Walker b GS Chappell	121	c Marsh b Lillee	15
Asif Iqbal	c Marsh b GS Chappell	65	c Marsh b Walker	5
Intikhab Alam (c)	c Marsh b Massie	9	c Watkins b Walker	8
Wasim Bari (+)	b GS Chappell	1	c Edwards b Walker	0
Salim Altaf	c Marsh b Walker	12	c Massie b Walker	0
Sarfraz Nawaz	b GS Chappell	12	c Redpath b Walker	1
Asif Masood	not out	1	not out	3
Extras	(B 12, LB 10, W 6, NB 3)	31	(LB 2, W 1, NB 1)	4
TOTAL		360		106

FOW 1st Inns: 56 79 83 131 270 279 280 336 349 360
FOW 2nd Inns: 7 11 52 83 88 93 95 95 103 106

Bowling: *First Innings*: Lillee 10-2-34-1, Massie 28-6-123-3, Walker 16-2-65-1, GS Chappell 18.6-5-61-5, Walters 9-3-25-0, Watkins 6-1-21-0, IM Chappell 1-1-0-0. *Second Innings*: Lillee 23-5-68-3, Massie 7-4-19-1, Walker 16-8-15-6.

Umpires: TF Brooks & JR Collins

SECOND TEST 1972–73 AUSTRALIA v PAKISTAN
Melbourne Cricket Ground, Melbourne. December 29, 30, 1972, January 1, 2, 3, 1973.
Toss: Australia. Australia won by 92 runs.

AUSTRALIA

Batsman	Dismissal 1	R		Dismissal 2	R
IR Redpath	c Saeed b Intikhab	135		c Wasim b Salim	6
AP Sheahan	run out	23		c Sarfraz b Asif	127
IM Chappell (c)	c Wasim b Sarfraz	66	(4)	st Wasim b Majid	9
GS Chappell	not out	116	(5)	run out	62
J Benaud	c Sarfraz b Intikhab	13	(3)	c Wasim b Salim	142
RW Marsh (+)	c Wasim b Sarfraz	74		c Asif b Asif	3
KJ O'Keeffe				b Sarfraz	24
AA Mallett				c Wasim b Sarfraz	8
MHN Walker				run out	11
JR Thomson				not out	19
DK Lillee				c Mushtaq b Intikhab	2
Extras	(B 1, LB 6, NB 7)	14		(LB 3, NB 9)	12
TOTAL	5 dec	441			425

FOW 1st Inns: 60 183 273 295 441
FOW 2nd Inns: 18 251 288 298 305 375 391 392 418 425

Bowling: *First Innings*: Asif 17-0-97-0, Salim 9-0-49-0, Sarfraz 22.5-4-100-2, Intikhab 16-0-101-2, Majid 21-2-80-0. *Second Innings*: Asif 12-0-100-2, Salim 14-0-50-2, Sarfraz 22-2-99-2, Intikhab 15.6-3-70-1, Majid 17-1-61-1, Mushtaq 7-0-33-0.

PAKISTAN

Batsman	Dismissal 1	R	Dismissal 2	R
Sadiq Mohammad	lbw Lillee	137	c Marsh b Walker	5
Saeed Ahmed	c GS Chappell b Walker	50	c Mallett b Lillee	6
Zaheer Abbas	run out	51	run out	25
Majid Khan	c Marsh b Walker	158	c Marsh b Lillee	47
Mushtaq Mohammad	c Marsh b O'Keeffe	60	run out	13
Asif Iqbal	c Lillee b Mallett	7	c Redpath b Walker	37
Intikhab Alam (c)	c Sheahan b Mallett	8	c IM Chappell b Mallett	48
Wasim Bari (+)	b Mallett	7	b Walker	0
Salim Altaf	not out	13	b O'Keeffe	10
Sarfraz Nawaz	not out	0	run out	8
Asif Masood				1
Extras	(B 12, LB 7, W 1, NB 3)	23		0
TOTAL	8 dec	574		200

FOW 1st Inns: 128 323 395 416 429 519 541 572
FOW 2nd Inns: 11 15 80 83 128 138 138 161 181 200

Bowling: *First Innings*: Lillee 16.6-1-90-1, Thomson 17-1-100-0, Walker 24-1-112-2, Mallett 38-4-124-3, O'Keeffe 23-1-94-1, Chappell 5-0-21-0, Redpath 1-0-10-0. *Second Innings*: Lillee 11-1-59-2, Thomson 2-0-10-0, Walker 14-3-59-3, Mallett 17.5-3-56-1, O'Keeffe 9-4-10-1, Chappell 3-0-16-0, Chappell 1-0-10-0.

Umpires: JR Collins & PR Enright

Australian Averages

1972–73 AUSTRALIA v PAKISTAN

AUSTRALIA	M	Inn	NO	Runs	H.S	Avrge	Ct	St	Overs	Mds	Runs	Wkt	Avrge
Benaud, J	2	3	-	179	142	59.67	-	-	-	-	-	-	-
Chappell, GS	3	5	1	242	116*	60.50	6	-	34.6	7	121	5	24.20
Chappell, IM	3	5	-	341	196	68.20	2	-	9.0	1	37	-	-
Edwards, R	2	3	-	161	89	53.67	4	-	-	-	-	-	-
Lillee, DK	3	4	1	18	14	6.00	1	-	96.1	19	353	12	29.42
Mallett, AA	2	2	-	8	8	4.00	2	-	91.3	16	291	13	22.38
Marsh, RW	3	5	-	210	118	42.00	16	-	-	-	-	-	-
Massie, RAL	2	3	1	56	42	28.00	1	-	68.0	16	238	8	29.75
O'Keeffe, KJ	2	2	-	64	40	32.00	1	-	54.0	7	192	3	64.00
Redpath, IR	3	5	-	240	135	48.00	5	-	1.0	-	10	-	-
Sheahan, AP	2	3	-	194	127	64.67	2	-	-	-	-	-	-
Stackpole, KR	1	2	-	37	28	18.50	-	-	-	-	-	-	-
Thomson, JR	1	1	-	19	19*	-	-	-	19.0	1	110	-	-
Walker, MHN	2	3	-	32	16	10.67	1	-	70.0	14	231	12	19.25
Walters, KD	1	2	-	25	19	12.50	-	-	9.0	3	25	-	-
Watkins, JR	1	2	1	39	36	39.00	1	-	6.0	1	21	-	-

Pakistani Averages

1972–73 AUSTRALIA v PAKISTAN

PAKISTAN	M	Inn	NO	Runs	H.S	Avrge	Ct	St	Overs	Mds	Runs	Wkt	Avrge
Asif Iqbal	3	6	-	130	65	21.67	2	-	18.0	-	97	1	97.00
Asif Masood	3	5	3	6	3*	3.00	-	-	69.0	2	403	5	80.60
Intikhab Alam	3	6	-	227	68	37.83	1	-	55.6	7	308	4	77.00
Majid Khan	3	6	-	239	158	39.83	1	-	76.0	5	295	4	73.75
Mushtaq Mohammad	3	6	-	244	121	40.67	2	-	21.3	-	113	4	28.25
Nasim-ul-Ghani	1	2	-	69	64	34.50	1	-	-	-	-	-	-
Sadiq Mohammad	3	6	-	270	137	45.00	1	-	-	-	-	-	-
Saeed Ahmed	2	4	-	131	50	32.75	2	-	3.0	-	28	-	-
Salim Altaf	3	6	3	61	17*	20.33	-	-	89.5	9	313	11	28.45
Sarfraz Nawaz	2	4	-	21	12	7.00	-	-	84.5	16	308	12	25.67
Talat Ali	1	2	1	7	7*	7.00	-	-	-	-	-	-	-
Wasim Bari	3	6	-	80	72	13.33	10	1	-	-	-	-	-
Zaheer Abbas	3	6	-	144	51	24.00	2	-	-	-	-	-	-

Fighting series win to Australia

Lillee injured

Port-of-Spain, March 23. Australia's fast bowling hope, Dennis Lillee, failed a fitness test today and will not play in the third Test.

'Naturally, we are disappointed,' said the Australian captain, Ian Chappell.

Lillee sent down eight balls at quarter pace to Keith Stackpole. He grimaced in pain after each delivery.

X-rays show he has damaged the vertebrae in his lower back.

An orthopaedic surgeon at the Queen Elizabeth Hospital in Bridgetown says Lillee will need rest and special back exercises. It seems likely he will be sent home.

Georgetown, April 12. Australia leads the world in cricket, following a resounding 10-wicket win over the West Indies in the fourth Test at Bourda Oval. The victory gives Australia an unbeatable 2–nil lead in the series.

Australian captain Ian Chappell felt the game was in the balance after three days of play, when Australia had been dismissed for 341, in reply to the West Indies first innings of 366.

Clive Lloyd hit a magnificent 178 for the West Indies, but Chappell was also in brilliant form (109).

He could sniff victory, and thanks to bowlers Jeff Hammond (4/38) and Max Walker (4/45) the West Indies were dismissed for only 109 in their second innings, their lowest total at home, and Australia finished the job in the opening hour of the final day.

The first two Tests, at Kingston and Bridgetown, were played on dead pitches and ended in draws. The West Indies had drawn in 10 successive Tests leading up to the the third Test at Port-of-Spain, but this time the result was different.

Australia triumphed by 44 runs, without its key fast bowler Dennis Lillee. Australia had a lead of just 52 runs after the first innings, which was highlighted by a splendid 112 from Doug Walters.

Alvin Kallicharan shaped up as the most dangerous of the West Indies batsmen, hitting eight fours to reach his half-century in 140 minutes. Then he tried to cut a short ball from Terry Jenner, and a diving catch from Greg Chappell at short leg ended Kallicharan's innings at 53.

Ian Chappell had originally thought there was no life in this pitch, but was proved mistaken by Australia's spinners, Jenner and Kerry O'Keefe.

'I am confident we can get the first result of the series,' Chappell said after the third day.

And he backed that prediction with an aggressive 97 runs in Australia's second innings, all the more courageous because he played with a sprained ankle.

Kallicharan loomed again as the danger in the second innings, and at lunch on the final day the West Indies were only 66 runs short of victory with six wickets in hand.

It looked all over. But not to Ian Chappell. The Australian captain chose lunch to address his troops. Unofficial reports suggest he spoke to them in a way that any trooper would, in colourful terms, let us say, strong enough to ensure they understood the message.

Strong enough for more than one to gag on his sandwiches. But nobody choked after lunch.

Kallicharan was dismissed on 91 and Australia took the last five wickets for 21 runs.

Kensington Oval, Bridgetown, Barbados, the colourful palm-fringed scene of the drawn second Test between Australia and the West Indies.

Sobers refuses

Bridgetown, March 9. Former West Indies captain Garry Sobers has refused to provide selectors with a doctor's certificate confirming his fitness for the second Test against Australia.

West Indies chairman of selectors Jeff Stollmeyer has issued a statement saying selectors were not convinced Sobers was ready for a Test comeback.

Sobers, who is now 36, underwent a knee operation last July, and has also recently suffered an eye infection. He says he is surprised that he was omitted, but was not consulted by the selectors. They suggest Sobers should have consulted them.

The Prime Minister of Trinidad has criticised the selectors for letting protocol stand in the way of the world's greatest all-rounder.

QUICK SINGLES

Sheahan stars. Victorian opening batsman Paul Sheahan belted South Australia's Ashley Mallett over the MCG sight-screen when he scored 196 not out in the Sheffield Shield in December.

WA Shield win. In the final Sheffield Shield match of the season Western Australia thrashed South Australia by an innings and 47 runs, to win the Shield for the fourth time (with 95 points) from South Australia (79), NSW (72), Victoria (64), and Queensland (60).

A new Commandment. In the first Test at Sabina Park, in Kingston, Jamaica, the Australian opener Keith Stackpole had so little trouble with the bowling of Uton Dowe (1/96) that some West Indies fans arrived the next day with a large banner, proclaiming: 'Dowe shalt not bowl.'

100 on debut. West Indies batsman Maurice Foster joined the select band of players who have made a century on debut. He made 125 in a 210-run partnership with Rohan Kanhai.

Marathon Maxie. Max Walker bowled superbly on a flat pitch to contain the West Indies in the second Test. His lengthy spell of 51.4 overs yeilded 5/97.

Willett will not play. On the eve of the first Test, West Indies team manager Clyde Walcott has announced that slow left-arm spinner Elquemado Willett would not be considered for the match. Willett took seven wickets against Australia in a lead-up match at Montego Bay, including Ian Chappell's for 8.

Balls milestone. West Indies off-spinner Lance Gibbs became the first bowler to deliver 20,000 balls in Test cricket, during the fifth Test in Trinidad.

Cricket's big five. The cricketing 'bible' *Wisden* has named four Australians among its top five cricketers of the year. They are: Greg Chappell; Dennis Lillee; Bob Massie; and Keith Stackpole. The fifth is English fast bowler John Snow.

Lille on Lillee. Injured Australian bowler Dennis Lillee was treated at the Queen Elizabeth Hospital in Bridgetown, Barbados, by a local orthopaedic surgeon, Dr Shirin Lille, who said that Lillee's vertebrae problem was serious: 'It will take some time to knit properly, hence the importance of the rest and exercises.'

Moot point. E. W. Swanton, writing in London's *Daily Telegraph*, said after the fourth Test that no side stood out as world champions. 'Though India has claims not easily refuted,' he said, 'on neutral soil … I would back this Australian side, augmented by Mallett and Sheahan, against them.'

Chappelli: the skipper who loved a scrap

Ian Chappell was one of Australia's most successful cricket captains. He loved the heat of battle whether locking horns with the authorities or hooking a John Snow bouncer to the boundary.

The stockily built Chappell played a leading role in Australia's revival as a cricket power in the 1970s. He played in 71 Tests in a row from 1965 to 1975, after which he became deeply involved in the organisation of the breakaway World Series Cricket.

Chappell's batting was rugged and aggressive. A right-hander, he was a powerful driver on either side of the wicket. He played the cut shot boldly, glanced deftly and defended well. He was a compulsive hooker, which often led to his downfall. His grandmother told him to give it up.

From the moment he appeared from the pavilion, bat in hand, Chappell looked as though he meant business. Often capless and with his collar turned up, he would look skywards to adjust his eyes to the light and walk busily to the crease. Once there, he would begin a ritual of fidgeting, forever adjusting his equipment, a restless storehouse of energy.

He was a useful leg-spin bowler, but bowled less as his career progressed. He played baseball for Australia in 1964 and 1966, and in between had a season in Lancashire League cricket.

After a disappointing start to his Test career, Chappell eventually established himself at number three in the batting order, where only the most reliable survive.

He scored his first Test hundred (151) in his 10th Test, against India at the MCG in 1967–68, and greater consistency followed in England in 1968 with four half-centuries – 73, 71, 65 and 81 – in five Tests, batting at four, five or six. He topped the tour averages, making 1261 runs at 48.5 with a top score of 202 not out against Warwickshire.

He made 5345 Test runs at an average of 42.42 with 14 hundreds and a highest score of 196. At first slip he was quick and safe, taking 105 catches.

As a bluntly spoken captain in 30 Tests from 1971 until 1975, Chappell was worshipped by his players. He came along at a time when conservatism had given way to the pop culture of the 70s, with its trademarks of irreverence, long hair, jeans and sloppy dressing. In 1972, his appearance on the Lord's balcony in a purple jumpsuit had the MCC members muttering into their medallions.

Chappell, who had been vice-captain to Bill Lawry, led Australia for the first time in the heated seventh Test at the MCG in 1971.

Chappell celebrated his captaincy with four centuries in the highly successful series against the Rest of the World XI in 1971–72, the year Dennis Lillee established himself as a great fast bowler.

With Lillee as his main strike bowler, Chappell squared the 1972 series in England 2–all.

Australia followed the 1972 series with good wins over Pakistan and the West Indies, after which Chappell scaled his Everest by regaining the Ashes 4–1 on home soil in 1974–75.

He quit the captaincy at the end of 1975 after retaining the Ashes 1–0 in England. In 1976 he was named one of *Wisden*'s Cricketers of the Year.

Chappelli went out in a blaze of glory at the Oval in 1975. After announcing he was tossing in the captaincy, he made 192 in his last Test in 442 minutes, coming in at 1/7 and sharing a second-wicket stand of 277 with Rick McCosker (127). Chappelli scored 419 runs in the four Tests at 69.8.

He played under his brother Greg in Australia's 5–1 humiliation of the West Indies in 1975–76, scoring 156 in Perth.

He completed a highly rewarding season by leading SA to victory in the 1975–76 Sheffield Shield.

After that, Packer cricket occupied his time. To this day he is a commentator on Packer's Channel 9. He made a brief comeback to Test ranks in 1979–80, playing in three Tests during joint Australian tours by the Windies and England. He bowed out with 75 and 26 not out against England at the MCG.

Born in Adelaide on 26 September 1943, Ian Michael Chappell was the oldest of three sons of grade cricketer Martin and Jeanne Chappell.

Jeanne Chappell was a daughter of debonair Australian Test captain and great all-round sportsman, Victor Richardson.

Ian may not have endeared himself to traditionalists, but his record speaks volumes for his talent. He scored 19,680 runs in first class cricket at 48.35 with 59 centuries and a top score of 205 not out. He scored 7665 for South Australia at an average of 53.23 with 22 hun-

Chappelli: unorthodox, fiery, aggressive and successful – a players' captain.

dreds. He took 176 first class wickets at 37.57 (best 5/29) and 312 catches.

Chappelli first played in the one-off Test against Pakistan at the MCG in 1964–65, making 11 and catching Abdul Kadir off McKenzie the first time he touched a ball at international level. It was 13 months before he got another Test chance, against England at the Adelaide Oval. He made only 17 batting at number seven. He failed in South Africa in 1966–67, scoring only 196 runs in nine completed Test innings and his average after nine Tests was a dismal 19.80.

He was vice-captain in Lawry's team that crashed 4–0 in South Africa. Lauded by Lawry as the best batsman in the world, Chappell responded abysmally with 92 runs in eight innings.

After that there were no more batting hiccups, and plenty of solid centuries.

In New Zealand in 1973–74 he and Greg became the first brothers to score a century in each innings of a Test. Chappelli made 145 and 121 and Greg 247 not out and 133. They shared a stand of 264 in the first innings.

During his two years with WSC he did not temper his behaviour. In 1979 he pleaded guilty to 'unlawful assault on an official' during a riot-ridden tour of the West Indies. The WSC players backed him.

More trouble was in store for him on his return to establishment cricket. In his last first class season in 1979–80 he was suspended for abusing an umpire in Hobart, and again for the same offence in Adelaide. In a SA v NSW match, fast bowler Len Pascoe took offence at references Chappell made to his ancestry.

No one suggested Chappelli invented sledging, but he gave it a new dimension. On retirement from playing, he was suspended briefly by Channel 9 for swearing on air.

As for the 'tweeds' incident at the Adelaide Oval in 1975, when he was accused of pointing his backside at the committee enclosure, Chappelli pleaded innocence. He said a thigh-pad attachment was sticking into his leg and he thought he could fix it by undoing his pants and leaving them loose. 'In doing so, my tweeds slipped down further.'

The spirit of Australia

Doug Walters, 112 in the third Test.

Rod Marsh, 97 in the first Test.

Port-of-Spain, April 27. Lady Velda Worrell yesterday presented the Sir Frank Worrell trophy to Australian captain Ian Chappell.

Who would have imagined that the five-Test West Indies v Australia series would end this way? Immediately following the first Test both captains agreed it was perfectly feasible the series could end without a single result.

The teams seemed well-matched in terms of ability and all of the pitches looked dead for bowlers.

'Getting results in this series is going to be very hard work,' Ian Chappell said.

Yet Australia achieved a seemingly impossible 44-run win in the third Test and a commanding 10-wicket victory in the fourth.

So what made the difference?

Chappell himself has been a key. He never stopped attacking, often against the odds.

Two days before the third Test, Chappell twisted his right ankle while playing tennis. But the pain didn't stop him making 97 runs in Australia's second innings. Some said he shouldn't have played, and certainly he must have wondered that himself when unable to bend and dive while fielding in slips.

Chappell's century in the fourth Test built the Australian innings, and his pep talk at lunch on the final day inspired the players to seize a memorable victory out of almost certain defeat.

After the fourth Test the Australian team manager, Bill Jacobs, paid tribute to Chappell's leadership: 'They have come through to win the series without Dennis Lillee and Bob Massie, with the new Test players, Max Walker and Jeff Hammond, bowling magnificently in their place.' Jacobs might also have added Terry Jenner and Kerry O'Keefe.

Leadership, guts, determination, and never say die. That was the difference.

Dennis Lillee's back puts him out

Port-of-Spain, April 26. A disappointing draw in the rain-affected fifth Test means Australia has finished its 12-match West Indies tour without a single loss.

Except, that is, for the loss of fast bowler Dennis Lillee, who is now in medical care.

Lillee broke down in the first Test at Kingston, where he finished wicketless (0/132) after 32 overs of bowling.

At first it was thought Lillee's back was jarred, and he was given physiotherapy at his hotel. Specialist radiologist Dr Rudy Webster believed the problem was muscular, and prescribed rest.

But back injuries are notoriously difficult to diagnose. Lillee failed fitness tests before the second Test at Bridgetown, and again at Port-of-Spain before the third Test.

It seemed likely that some kind of vertebrae damage was causing Lillee to writhe in pain after each delivery, and he played no further part in the tour.

Medical experts have expressed a range of opinions on the cause of Lillee's problem.

Unfortunately, the one common feature is that all the specialists seem to agree he should not be playing cricket, which is a terrible blow for Australia and the young bowler who took 8/29 against the World XI last year.

FIRST TEST 1972–73 WEST INDIES v AUSTRALIA
Sabina Park, Kingston. February 16, 17, 18, 20, 21, 1973.
Toss: Australia. Match Drawn.

AUSTRALIA

KR Stackpole b Foster	44	c Rowe b Holder	142
IR Redpath b Gibbs	46	c Kanhai b Gibbs	60
IM Chappell (c) c Dowe b Inshan	19	not out	38
GS Chappell c Kallicharran b Gibbs	42	not out	14
R Edwards c & b Gibbs	63		
KD Walters c Kanhai b Gibbs	72		
RW Marsh (+) hit wicket b Dowe	97		
KJ O'Keeffe not out	19		
DK Lillee			
JR Hammond			
MHN Walker			
Extras (B 6, LB 12, W 1, NB 7)	26	(LB 2, NB 4)	6
TOTAL	7 dec 428		2 dec 260

FOW 1st Inns: 66 106 128 179 271 365 428
FOW 2nd Inns: 161 230

Bowling: *First Innings*: Holder 26-5-55-0, Dowe 21-3-96-1, Foster 44-18-84-1, Gibbs 41-14-85-4, Inshan 25-5-82-1. *Second Innings*: Dowe 21-4-72-0, Holder 19-5-34-1, Inshan 4-0-28-0, Foster 22-7-71-0, Gibbs 15-4-40-1, Fredericks 1-0-9-0.

WEST INDIES

RC Fredericks c O'Keeffe b Walker	31	c Marsh b GS Chappell	21
GA Greenidge b Walker	0		
LG Rowe c Stackpole b Walker	76	c GS Chappell b Hammond	4
AI Kallicharran c Marsh b Hammond	50	not out	7
RB Kanhai (c) c Marsh b Hammond	84		
MLC Foster b Walker	125 (5)	not out	18
TM Findlay (+) c Marsh b Walker	12 (2)	c Marsh b GS Chappell	13
Inshan Ali c Marsh b Walker	10		
VA Holder lbw Hammond	12		
LR Gibbs c O'Keeffe b Hammond	5		
UG Dowe not out	5		
Extras (LB 9, NB 9)	18	(B 1, W 1, NB 2)	4
TOTAL	428		3 for 67

FOW 1st Inns: 6 49 165 165 375 385 400 417 423 428
FOW 2nd Inns: 35 36 42

Bowling: *First Innings*: Lillee 26-4-112-0, Walker 39-10-114-6, Hammond 28.5-5-79-4, O'Keeffe 18-1-71-0, IM Chappell 11-3-30-0, GS Chappell 2-0-4-0. *Second Innings*: Lillee 6-1-20-0, Walker 6-3-8-0, Hammond 10-4-17-1, GS Chappell 10-4-18-2, Walters 1-1-0-0.

Umpires: R Gosein & D Sang Hue

SECOND TEST 1972–73 WEST INDIES v AUSTRALIA
Kensington Oval, Bridgetown. March 9, 10, 11, 13, 14, 1973.
Toss: Australia. Match Drawn.

AUSTRALIA

KR Stackpole c Kanhai b Holder	1	b Foster	53
IR Redpath c Kanhai b Boyce	6	c Greenidge b Gibbs	20
IM Chappell (c) run out	72	not out	106
GS Chappell c Murray b Holder	106		
R Edwards c Murray b Boyce	15		
KD Walters c Kanhai b Gibbs	1 (4)	not out	102
RW Marsh (+) c Rowe b Willett	78		
KJ O'Keeffe b Willett	21		
JR Hammond lbw Boyce	0		
TJ Jenner not out	10		
MHN Walker b Gibbs	0		
Extras (NB 14)	14	(B 1, LB 6, NB 12)	19
TOTAL	324		2 dec 300

FOW 1st Inns: 2 19 148 189 194 218 264 283 320 324
FOW 2nd Inns: 79 108

Bowling: *First Innings*: Holder 21-5-49-2, Boyce 22-5-68-3, Foster 15-4-35-0, Willett 37-11-79-2, Gibbs 36-9-79-2. *Second Innings*: Holder 21-5-52-0, Boyce 18-4-54-0, Willett 28-15-45-0, Foster 13-4-29-1, Gibbs 25-10-55-1, Fredericks 1-0-3-0, Greenidge 7-0-24-0, Kanhai 6.1-1-19-0.

WEST INDIES

RC Fredericks lbw Hammond	98	not out	22
GA Greenidge lbw Walker	9	not out	10
LG Rowe c Stackpole b Walker	16		
AI Kallicharran b Walker	14		
RB Kanhai (c) lbw IM Chappell	105		
MLC Foster b Jenner	12		
DL Murray (+) c Redpath b Jenner	90		
KD Boyce lbw Walker	10		
ET Willett c Stackpole b Jenner	0		
VA Holder b Walker	1		
LR Gibbs not out	0		
Extras (B 13, LB 5, W 4, NB 14)	36	(LB 2, W 1, NB 1)	4
TOTAL	391		0 for 36

FOW 1st Inns: 19 77 118 162 179 344 385 386 391 391
FOW 2nd Inns:

Bowling: *First Innings*: Hammond 31-9-114-1, Walker 51.4-20-97-5, GS Chappell 22-11-37-0, Jenner 28-9-65-3, O'Keeffe 10-3-18-0, Walters 2-0-7-0, IM Chappell 8-3-17-1. *Second Innings*: Hammond 4-1-10-0, Walker 4-3-1-0, O'Keeffe 6-2-15-0, Stackpole 5-3-6-0.

Umpires: HBC Jordan & D Sang Hue

THIRD TEST 1972–73 WEST INDIES v AUSTRALIA
Queen's Park Oval, Port-of-Spain. March 23, 24, 25, 27, 28, 1973.
Toss: Australia. Australia won by 44 runs.

AUSTRALIA

KR Stackpole c Foster b Boyce	0	c Fredericks b Boyce	18
IR Redpath run out	66	c Kanhai b Willett	44
GS Chappell c Kallicharran b Gibbs	56 (4)	c & b Gibbs	1
KD Walters c Fredericks b Inshan	112 (5)	c Gibbs b Willett	32
R Edwards lbw Boyce	12 (6)	b Gibbs	14
IM Chappell (c) c & b Inshan	8 (3)	c & b Willett	97
RW Marsh (+) b Inshan	14	b Inshan	8
KJ O'Keeffe run out	37	c Kallicharran b Gibbs	7
TJ Jenner lbw Gibbs	2	b Gibbs	6
MHN Walker b Gibbs	0 (11)	not out	23
JR Hammond not out	2 (10)	c Kanhai b Gibbs	19
Extras (B 10, LB 7, NB 6)	23	(B 5, LB 7)	12
TOTAL	332		281

FOW 1st Inns: 1 108 181 240 257 262 312 321 321 332
FOW 2nd Inns: 31 96 99 156 185 208 231 231 248 281

Bowling: *First Innings*: Boyce 18-4-54-2, Lloyd 7-3-13-0, Gibbs 38-11-79-3, Willett 19-3-62-0, Inshan 41.1-11-89-3, Foster 6-2-12-0. *Second Innings*: Boyce 10-1-41-1, Lloyd 3-1-11-0, Gibbs 45-14-102-5, Inshan 21-2-82-1, Willett 28-15-33-3.

WEST INDIES

RC Fredericks c IM Chappell b Jenner	16	c Redpath b Stackpole	76
MLC Foster lbw Jenner	25 (6)	c GS Chappell b O'Keeffe	34
AI Kallicharran c GS Chappell b Jenner	53	c Marsh b Walker	91
CH Lloyd c & b GS Chappell	20 (5)	c Stackpole b O'Keeffe	15
RB Kanhai (c) c Redpath b O'Keeffe	56 (4)	b GS Chappell	14
DL Murray (+) lbw Hammond	40 (2)	c Redpath b Walker	7
KD Boyce c Marsh b O'Keeffe	12	c IM Chappell b O'Keeffe	11
Inshan Ali c Marsh b Walker	15	b Walker	2
ET Willett not out	4	b O'Keeffe	3
LR Gibbs c O'Keeffe b Jenner	6	not out	0
LG Rowe			
Extras (B 17, LB 11, W 1, NB 4)	33	(B 19, LB 13, NB 7)	39
TOTAL	9 dec 280		9 dec 289

FOW 1st Inns: 33 44 100 149 206 230 265 267 280
FOW 2nd Inns: 39 141 177 219 268 274 281 288 289

Bowling: *First Innings*: Walker 30-8-55-1, Hammond 7-3-7-1, Jenner 38.3-7-98-4, O'Keeffe 28-10-62-2, GS Chappell 14-8-16-1, Stackpole 2-0-8-0, Chappell 2-1-1-0. *Second Innings*: Walker 25-6-43-3, Hammond 6-3-12-0, Jenner 15-2-46-0, O'Keeffe 24.1-5-57-4, GS Chappell 32-10-65-1, Stackpole 11-4-27-1.

Umpires: R Gosein & D Sang Hue

FIFTH TEST 1972–73 WEST INDIES v AUSTRALIA
Queen's Park Oval, Port-of-Spain. April 21, 22, 23, 25, 26, 1973.
Toss: Australia. Match Drawn.

AUSTRALIA

IR Redpath c Fredericks b Gibbs	36	c Boyce b Foster	24
R Edwards c Fredericks b Jumadeen	74	c Kallicharran b Inshan	14
IM Chappell (c) c Kallicharran b Inshan	56	c Kallicharran b Gibbs	37
GS Chappell c Fredericks b Gibbs	41	c Fredericks b Gibbs	31
KD Walters c Fredericks b Gibbs	70	c Murray b Gibbs	27
J Benaud c & b Inshan	8	c Davis b Inshan	36
RW Marsh (+) c Inshan b Jumadeen	56	not out	21
KJ O'Keeffe b Inshan	37	c Lloyd b Gibbs	0
TJ Jenner not out	27	not out	11
JR Hammond not out	6		
MHN Walker			
Extras (B 5, LB 1, NB 2)	8	(B 13, LB 2, W 1, NB 1)	17
TOTAL	8 dec 419		7 dec 218

FOW 1st Inns: 50 159 169 280 281 293 379 395
FOW 2nd Inns: 37 49 101 114 157 195 197

Bowling: *First Innings*: Boyce 10-3-21-0, Lloyd 12-6-19-0, Davis 5-0-22-0, Gibbs 52-15-114-3, Jumadeen 40-8-89-2, Inshan 44-4-124-3, Foster 8-3-15-0, Fredericks 2-0-7-0. *Second Innings*: Lloyd 3-0-16-0, Davis 5-0-16-0, Foster 3-1-3-1, Inshan 19-2-68-2, Gibbs 32-12-66-4, Jumadeen 18-5-32-0.

WEST INDIES

RC Fredericks c Edwards b Jenner	73	c Marsh b Hammond	8
MLC Foster c Marsh b Walker	29	c IM Chappell b Walker	19
CA Davis c Marsh b Walker	25	b Benaud	24
AI Kallicharran c Hammond b Jenner	32	c O'Keeffe b Benaud	26
RB Kanhai (c) b Jenner	3 (6)	not out	16
CH Lloyd c Redpath b Walker	59 (7)	not out	22
DL Murray (+) c Marsh b Walker	34 (5)	c IM Chappell b Jenner	7
KD Boyce b Jenner	31		
Inshan Ali c GS Chappell b Walker	0		
RR Jumadeen not out	11		
LR Gibbs c Hammond b Jenner	6		
Extras (B 6, LB 4, W 1, NB 5)	16	(B 10, NB 3)	13
TOTAL	319		5 for 135

FOW 1st Inns: 48 88 151 171 180 270 271 271 303 319
FOW 2nd Inns: 25 30 81 86 96

Bowling: *First Innings*: Hammond 21-4-76-0, Walker 37-10-75-5, GS Chappell 7-2-21-0, Walters 3-2-5-0, Jenner 32.2-9-90-5, O'Keeffe 11-1-36-0. *Second Innings*: Walker 17-8-24-1, Hammond 15-8-25-1, Jenner 17-7-33-1, GS Chappell 6-2-11-0, O'Keeffe 10-5-17-0, Benaud 4-1-12-2.

Umpires: R Gosein & D Sang Hue

FOURTH TEST 1972–73 WEST INDIES v AUSTRALIA
Bourda, Georgetown. April 6, 7, 8, 10, 11, 1973.
Toss: West Indies. Australia won by 10 wkts.

WEST INDIES

RC Fredericks c IM Chappell b Walters	30	c Marsh b Hammond	6
GA Greenidge b Walters	22	b Hammond	24
AI Kallicharran run out	13	c Walker b Hammond	8
CH Lloyd b Hammond	178	c Marsh b Hammond	3
RB Kanhai (c) c O'Keeffe b Hammond	57	lbw Walker	23
CA Davis lbw Walker	5	c Marsh b Walker	16
DL Murray (+) c IM Chappell b Hammond	1	c Marsh b Walker	3
KD Boyce c Edwards b Walters	23	c GS Chappell b Walters	10
ET Willett lbw Walters	12	not out	3
VA Holder not out	9	b Walters	3
LR Gibbs b Walters	1	b Walker	7
Extras (B 5, LB 6, W 2, NB 2)	15	(LB 3)	3
TOTAL	366		109

FOW 1st Inns: 55 56 90 277 307 310 337 347 356 366
FOW 2nd Inns: 12 30 39 42 77 82 91 95 100 109

Bowling: *First Innings*: Hammond 33-6-110-3, Walker 38-11-77-1, GS Chappell 16-4-56-0, Walters 18.2-1-66-5, O'Keeffe 8-1-27-0, Jenner 7-0-15-0, IM Chappell 1-1-0-0. *Second Innings*: Hammond 16-4-38-4, Walker 23.3-4-45-4, Walters 13-3-23-2.

AUSTRALIA

KR Stackpole lbw Boyce	1	not out	76
IR Redpath c Fredericks b Holder	22	not out	57
IM Chappell (c) b Gibbs	109		
GS Chappell b Willett	51		
KD Walters c Murray b Gibbs	81		
R Edwards c Murray b Boyce	13		
RW Marsh (+) lbw Willett	23		
KJ O'Keeffe b Gibbs	5		
TJ Jenner c Kallicharran b Boyce	10		
JR Hammond run out	1		
MHN Walker not out	2		
Extras (B 9, LB 7, W 4, NB 3)	23	(LB 2)	2
TOTAL	341		0 for 135

FOW 1st Inns: 5 36 157 229 262 306 316 334 336 341
FOW 2nd Inns:

Bowling: *First Innings*: Holder 35-6-64-1, Boyce 24.4-6-69-3, Davis 6-0-15-0, Willett 27-3-88-2, Gibbs 36-15-67-3, Lloyd 7-1-15-0. *Second Innings*: Holder 7-2-21-0, Boyce 8-1-33-0, Gibbs 5-4-9-0, Willett 6-2-20-0, Kanhai 5-1-15-0, Greenidge 4-0-15-0, Lloyd 5-1-15-0, Davis 3-2-5-0.

Umpires: CP Kippins & D Sang Hue

Australian Averages

1972–73 WEST INDIES v AUSTRALIA

AUSTRALIA	M	Inn	NO	Runs	H.S	Avrge	Ct	St	Overs	Mds	Runs	Wkt	Avrge
Benaud, J	1	2	-	44	36	22.00	-	-	4.0	1	12	2	6.00
Chappell, GS	5	8	1	342	106	48.86	6	-	109.0	41	228	4	57.00
Chappell, IM	5	9	-	542	109	77.43	6	-	22.0	8	48	1	48.00
Edwards, R	5	7	-	205	74	29.29	2	-	-	-	-	-	-
Hammond, JR	5	5	2	28	19	9.33	2	-	171.5	47	488	15	32.53
Jenner, TJ	4	6	3	66	27*	22.00	-	-	137.5	34	347	13	26.69
Lillee, DK	1	-	-	-	-	0-	-	-	32.0	5	132	-	-
Marsh, RW	5	7	1	297	97	49.50	17	-	-	-	-	-	-
O'Keeffe, KJ	5	7	-	126	37	21.00	4	-	115.1	28	303	6	50.50
Redpath, IR	5	10	1	381	66	42.33	5	-	-	-	-	-	-
Stackpole, KR	4	8	1	335	142	47.86	4	-	18.0	7	41	1	41.00
Walker, MHN	5	4	2	25	23*	12.50	4	-	271.1	83	539	26	20.73
Walters, KD	5	8	1	497	112	71.00	-	-	37.2	7	101	7	14.43

West Indian Averages

1972–73 WEST INDIES v AUSTRALIA

WEST INDIES	M	Inn	NO	Runs	H.S	Avrge	Ct	St	Overs	Mds	Runs	Wkt	Avrge
Boyce, KD	4	6	-	97	31	16.17	1	-	110.4	24	340	9	37.78
Davis, CA	2	4	-	70	25	17.50	1	-	19.0	2	58	-	-
Dowe, UG	1	1	1	5	5*	-	-	1	42.0	7	168	1	168.00
Findlay, TM	1	2	-	25	13	12.50	-	-	-	-	-	-	-
Foster, MLC	4	7	1	262	125	43.67	1	-	111.0	39	249	3	83.00
Fredericks, RC	5	10	1	381	98	42.33	9	-	4.0	-	19	-	-
Gibbs, LR	5	7	2	25	7	5.00	3	-	325.0	108	696	26	26.77
Greenidge, GA	2	3	1	65	24	16.25	1	-	11.0	-	39	-	-
Holder, VA	3	4	1	25	12	8.33	-	-	129.0	28	275	4	68.75
Inshan Ali	3	4	-	27	15	6.75	3	-	154.1	24	473	10	47.30
Jumadeen, RR	1	1	1	11	11*	-	-	-	58.0	13	121	2	60.50
Kallicharran, AI	5	9	-	294	91	36.75	7	-	-	-	-	-	-
Kanhai, RB	5	8	1	358	105	51.14	7	-	11.1	2	34	-	-
Lloyd, CH	3	6	-	297	178	59.40	1	-	37.0	12	89	-	-
Murray, DL	4	7	-	182	90	26.00	5	-	-	-	-	-	-
Rowe, LG	3	3	-	96	76	32.00	2	-	-	-	-	-	-
Willett, ET	3	5	2	19	12	6.33	-	-	145.0	49	327	7	46.71

Greg Chappell is lured to Queensland

Brisbane, Oct. 19. Queensland has pulled off the cricketing coup of the year by tempting Greg Chappell to abandon his native South Australia for a place in the sun.

The South Australian Cricket Association was unable to counter the attractive Queensland deal, which appealed to Chappell in cricket, business and personal terms.

Chappell was named by cricketing 'bible' *Wisden* as one of the five Cricketers of the Year in April.

He leads the Queensland State side against New South Wales today.

Wisden said Chappell typified the new young breed of Australian cricketers and had confirmed his place as Australia's number one batsman in England last year, when he made 131 in the second Test at Lord's and shared a 200-run partnership with his brother Ian at the Oval.

Australian Cricket Board – new name

Sydney, Sep. 8. The Australian Board of Control for International Cricket has adopted a new name and new rules following recommendations from the Board's Constitution Review Committee.

The Board, which was established in 1905, has overall responsibility for control of cricket in Australia and organises overseas tours, law changes and umpiring. It will now be officially known by the simpler title: Australian Cricket Board.

In other changes, the Board has abolished its Interstate Conference and has given the Western Australian Cricket Association a second delegate. It is the first time since the Second World War that State representation has been altered.

All television, radio and sponsorship negotiations affecting cricket will be the responsibility of the Australian Cricket Board.

New Zealand confounds critics, but robbed

Sydney, Jan. 11. New Zealand has been prevented from almost certain victory in the second Test when rain washed out play on two days of the match.

Rain clouds looked ominous as Ian Chappell sent the Kiwis in to bat on a green pitch.

The New Zealand opener, John Parker, soon made Chappell regret his decision. Parker brought up his 50 in 105 minutes, and just before tea he reached his century with a fine lofted drive over midwicket. He was out, caught by Rod Marsh off Max Walker for 108 soon after play resumed.

New Zealand was all out for 312 just before lunch on the second day, after the opening hour was lost due to rain.

That afternoon, the Kiwis revelled in the damp, heavy conditions, especially in slips, where Australian opener Keith Stackpole gave an easy catch to John Morrison and was out for 8, off the bowling of Richard Hadlee.

A few balls later, Paul Sheahan was caught on 7, after snicking one of Bryan Andrews' outswingers. Greg Chappell lasted only six balls before catching an edge off an Andrews delivery.

It is hard to believe this is the same side that Australia thrashed a week ago, after which the former Australian wicketkeeper Ray Jordan wrote in the Melbourne *Truth*: 'the opposition is so feeble it provides no experience for our up-and-coming players.'

Things got better for Australia, but not much. Ian Chappell (45), Doug Walters (41) and Ian Davis (29) were the only batsmen who

NZ's John Parker is caught for a duck by Rod Marsh off Geoff Dymock.

lived up to the name. Australia was all out for 162 and at stumps at the end of day two, New Zealand was 0/10 in its second innings.

But then the rains came, completely washing out the third day's play.

'We will go flat out for a win,' announced New Zealand captain Bevan Congden.

In a formidable second innings, Morrison posted a confident 117 runs, aided by Brian Hastings (83). Congden declared at 9/305 after tea on the fourth day.

At stumps, Australia was 2/30 and on the ropes, and there would have been a knockout in the final round, but the fight didn't go on. The heavens opened, and steady, soaking rain drenched the SCG for all of the final day.

Turner, Hadlee lead New Zealand win

Christchurch, March 14. For the first time in fourteen Tests, Australia has been beaten. New Zealand's five-wicket win in the second Test is the first time it has triumphed over Australia.

There will be no panic, says captain Ian Chappell, but the historic victory signals that New Zealand is rising as a power in world cricket.

Australia was most disappointing in its first innings. With the exception of Ian Redpath (71), and Rod Marsh (38), all wickets fell cheaply. Richard Collinge (3/70) caught and bowled Redpath, and also bowled Keith Stackpole (4) and Ashley Mallett (1). Richard Hadlee (3/59) accounted for Ian Chappell (20), Greg Chappell (25), Ian Davis (5) and Doug Walters (6).

New Zealand's victory was set up by opening batsman Glenn Turner, who made a splendid 101 runs in a first-innings total of 255, in reply to Australia's 223.

The game was still in the balance, but Australia made a poor start to its second innings. Stackpole was caught early for 9 by Ken Wadsworth off a fiery delivery from Collinge. Ian Chappell (1) was bowled by Collinge in the next over. Greg Chappell snicked a Richard Hadlee delivery and was caught on 6 at first slip by Coney.

Christchurch was not a Test for the Chappell boys, and perhaps that partially explains Australia's defeat.

This Test belonged to New

NZ fast bowler Richard Hadlee.

Zealand's brothers, Richard and Dayle Hadlee, who together claimed eight of Australia's second-innings wickets, taking 4/71 and 4/75 respectively. They took 12 wickets for the match.

Richard Hadlee's dismissal of Australia's mainstay, Ian Redpath, caused a sensation. Redpath was on 58 when he square cut Hadlee to backward point, where the ball was caught by Hedley Howard. Redpath refused to move, but then

umpire John Hastie raised his finger. Dismayed, Redpath walked.

Apparently, Redpath thought he heard a 'no ball' call. But it seems the noise was Hadlee, who grunted as he unleashed his delivery.

Tensions increased between the two sides as the match progressed.

Any hopes of an Australian win were thwarted again by Turner, who backed up his first-innings century with 110 in the second, to give New Zealand victory.

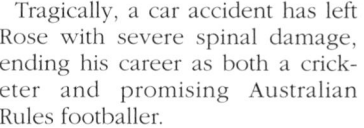
Glenn Turner: 101 and 110.

1455 runs in Test

Wellington, March 7. Cricket statisticians are big winners in the drawn first Test at Basin Reserve.

Runs, runs and more runs sum up the game. A New Zealand Test record of one thousand, four hundred and fifty-five, to be precise. That's the aggregate of Australia's first innings (511), second innings (460), and New Zealand's only innings (484).

Australia's Chappell brothers made 646 and five of the seven centuries scored. Ian Chappell contributed 266 runs (145 and 121), while Greg Chappell's 380 (247 and 133) is a new record for the most runs scored in any Test match by an individual. Just three other batsmen have made double and single centuries in a Test, and the only other time brothers each scored centuries in both innings of a first class match was England's Reg and Frank Foster back in 1899.

New Zealand's century makers were Bevan Congdon and (132) and Bryan Hastings (101).

Sign of the times: fence advertising.

Australians turn ugly in NZ

Christchurch, March 13. New Zealand captain Bevan Congdon has demanded an apology from Australian captain Ian Chappell.

With just 12 minutes to go before stumps on the fourth day of the second Test, New Zealand's Brian Hastings lofted Ashley Mallett to the fence for what should have been four runs. Unfortunately, umpire Bob Monteith signalled a six.

After a vigorous protest from Ian Chappell, the decision was reversed to a four. New Zealand batsman Glenn Turner then appeared to make a comment to Chappell, who responded with a shout and a one-digit gesticulation.

New Zealand representatives later claimed that the verbal part of Chappell's response went: 'Keep your —— out of it, you little ——'.

Cricket authorities will find little excuse for such antics.

Victoria wins an even Shield year

Sydney, Feb. 12. Victoria has won the Sheffield Shield in one of the closest seasons for years.

The Victorian win, from Queensland (98) and NSW (90) is a fitting end to the glorious career of Victorian captain Keith Stackpole, who has announced his retirement.

Stackpole had more bad days than good in his final summer at the crease, but apart from the Shield win his personal highlight was probably the magnificent 145 runs he scored against Western Australia in early December.

Another highlight for Victoria was the arrival of young Robert Rose, who signalled his potential as a Test representative in October when he made 118 not out and 88 against the strong Queensland side, which included Greg Chappell and the brilliant Pakistani import, Majid Khan.

Tragically, a car accident has left Rose with severe spinal damage, ending his career as both a cricketer and promising Australian Rules footballer.

Greg Chappell has topped the batting averages with 1013 runs at 92.09, followed by Victoria's Paul Sheahan (671 at 61.00) and SA's Ian Chappell (869 at 57.93).

In the third match of the series, Victorian left-arm spinner Ray Bright took 6/61 against South Australia, and together with pace bowlers Max Walker and Alan Hurst, added up to a formidable Victorian bowling combination.

Victoria's 105-point winning total is the highest since the bonus points system was introduced.

Explosive action: Alan Hurst (Vic.).

FIRST TEST 1973–74 AUSTRALIA v NEW ZEALAND
Melbourne Cricket Ground, Melbourne. December 29, 30, 1973, January 1, 2, 1974.
Toss: Australia. Australia won by an innings & 25 runs.

AUSTRALIA
KR Stackpole c Parker b Shrimpton 122
AP Sheahan c Wadsworth b DR Hadlee 28
IM Chappell (c) c RJ Hadlee b Shrimpton 54
GS Chappell c Wadsworth b Congdon 60
KD Walters c Wadsworth b DR Hadlee 79
IC Davis c Wadsworth b DR Hadlee 15
RW Marsh (+) c Parker b DR Hadlee 6
KJ O'Keeffe not out 40
GJ Gilmour b Congdon 52
AA Mallett
AR Dell
Extras (LB 4, W 1, NB 1) 6
TOTAL ....8 dec 462

FOW 1st Inns: 75 203 212 304 345 363 381 462

Bowling: *First Innings*: RJ Hadlee 25-4-104-0, Andrews 19-2-100-0, DR Hadlee 20-2-102-4, O'Sullivan 22-3-80-0, Shrimpton 7-0-39-2, Congdon 8.5-1-31-2.

NEW ZEALAND
GM Turner c Gilmour b Dell 6
JM Parker c IM Chappell b O'Keeffe ....27 (1)   c IM Chappell b Walters 23
MJF Shrimpton c Marsh b Gilmour 16   b Walters 22
BF Hastings b O'Keeffe 1   c Marsh b Mallett 22
BE Congdon (c) st Marsh b Mallett 31   c Marsh b Mallett 14
JFM Morrison c Marsh b Gilmour ....44 (2)   c Marsh b Walters 16
KJ Wadsworth (+) c GS Chappell b Gilmour ....80 (6)   c Stackpole b Mallett 30
RJ Hadlee c Marsh b Gilmour ....9 (7)   c IM Chappell b O'Keeffe 6
DR Hadlee run out ....2 (8)   c & b O'Keeffe 37
DR O'Sullivan c Davis b Mallett ....6 (9)   c & b Mallett 8
B Andrews not out ....0 (10)   not out 5
Extras (B 8, LB 5, NB 2) 15   (B 8, LB 9) 17
TOTAL 237   ....9 dec 200

FOW 1st Inns: 19 47 51 56 100 189 215 230 237 237
FOW 2nd Inns: 37 54 83 109 113 134 150 188 200

Bowling: *First Innings*: Dell 22-7-54-1, Gilmour 22-4-75-4, GS Chappell 4-2-4-0, Mallett 16.7-2-46-2, IM Chappell 1-0-3-0, O'Keeffe 14-4-40-2. *Second Innings*: Dell 5-0-9-0, Gilmour 3-0-16-0, GS Chappell 7-3-18-0, Mallett 24-4-63-4, O'Keeffe 29.6-12-51-2, Walters 13-4-26-3.

Umpires: TF Brooks & JR Collins

THIRD TEST 1973–74 AUSTRALIA v NEW ZEALAND
Adelaide Oval, Adelaide. January 26, 27, 28, 30 (no play), 31 1974.
Toss: Australia. Australia won by an innings & 57 runs.

AUSTRALIA
KR Stackpole c Parker b DR Hadlee 15
AJ Woodcock c Coney b Cairns 27
IM Chappell (c) c RJ Hadlee b Cairns 22
GS Chappell b Congdon 42
KD Walters b O'Sullivan 94
IC Davis c Congdon b O'Sullivan 15
RW Marsh (+) st Wadsworth b O'Sullivan 132
KJ O'Keeffe lbw RJ Hadlee 85
AA Mallett c Wadsworth b O'Sullivan 11
AG Hurst c Hastings b O'Sullivan 16
G Dymock not out 0
Extras (B 3, LB 6, NB 9) 18
TOTAL 477

FOW 1st Inns: 21 67 73 173 221 232 400 452 472 477

Bowling: *First Innings*: RJ Hadlee 28-3-102-1, DR Hadlee 21-2-76-1, Cairns 21-4-73-2, O'Sullivan 35.5-4-148-5, Congdon 15-1-60-1.

NEW ZEALAND
JM Parker c Marsh b Dymock 0   c IM Chappell b Dymock 22
GM Turner lbw Hurst 20   c O'Keeffe b Dymock 34
JFM Morrison c IM Chappell b O'Keeffe 40   c IM Chappell b Dymock 4
BF Hastings c Woodcock b O'Keeffe 23   c Stackpole b Dymock 7
BE Congdon (c) run out 13   not out 71
JV Coney c Marsh b Dymock 0   b Dymock 17
KJ Wadsworth (+) lbw IM Chappell 48   c Marsh b O'Keeffe 16
DR Hadlee c GS Chappell b Mallett 29   c GS Chappell b Mallett 0
RJ Hadlee c IM Chappell b Mallett 20   c Marsh b O'Keeffe 15
DR O'Sullivan b O'Keeffe 2   c IM Chappell b Dymock 4
BL Cairns not out 4   c IM Chappell b Mallett 0
Extras (B 4, LB 4, NB 3) 11   (B 2, LB 8, NB 2) 12
TOTAL 218 202

FOW 1st Inns: 1 35 84 89 107 110 176 209 214 218
FOW 2nd Inns: 56 65 65 73 105 130 143 170 197 202

Bowling: *First Innings*: Hurst 19-3-56-1, Dymock 19-5-44-2, Walters 1-0-2-0, Mallett 23-6-46-2, O'Keeffe 24.3-9-55-3, IM Chappell 1-0-4-1. *Second Innings*: Hurst 10-2-17-0, Dymock 27-7-58-5, Walters 3-0-17-0, Mallett 21.5-9-47-2, O'Keeffe 28-12-51-3.

Umpires: JR Collins & PR Enright

SECOND TEST 1973–74 AUSTRALIA v NEW ZEALAND
Sydney Cricket Ground, Sydney. January 5, 6, 7 (no play), 9, 10 (no play), 1974.
Toss: Australia. Match Drawn.

NEW ZEALAND
JM Parker c Marsh b Walker 108   c Marsh b GS Chappell 11
JFM Morrison c GS Chappell b Walters 28   c Davis b IM Chappell 117
MJF Shrimpton b Walters 0   c & b Walters 28
BE Congdon (c) c Marsh b Walters 4   b Gilmour 17
BF Hastings c Marsh b Walker 16   b GS Chappell 83
JV Coney c Stackpole b O'Keeffe ....45 (7)   c Davis b GS Chappell 11
KJ Wadsworth (+) c Marsh b Walters ....54 (6)   c GS Chappell b Gilmour 2
DR Hadlee c & b GS Chappell ....14 (9)   not out 18
RJ Hadlee c IM Chappell b GS Chappell ....17 (8)   run out 1
DR O'Sullivan not out 3   lbw Gilmour 1
B Andrews c Marsh b Gilmour 17
Extras (LB 2, NB 4) 6   (B 4, LB 11, W 1) 16
TOTAL 312   ....9 dec 305

FOW 1st Inns: 78 78 90 113 193 221 268 292 293 312
FOW 2nd Inns: 23 94 120 244 255 276 282 292 305

Bowling: *First Innings*: Gilmour 18.6-3-70-1, Walker 22-2-71-2, GS Chappell 19-2-76-2, Walters 11-0-39-4, Mallett 8-2-30-0, O'Keeffe 8-2-20-1. *Second Innings*: Gilmour 21.2-1-70-3, GS Chappell 16-3-54-3, Walters 11-0-54-1, Mallett 14-1-65-0, O'Keeffe 10-0-40-0, IM Chappell 3-0-6-1.

AUSTRALIA
AP Sheahan c Coney b Andrews 7   not out 14
KR Stackpole c Morrison b RJ Hadlee 8   lbw RJ Hadlee 2
IM Chappell (c) c Hastings b DR Hadlee 45   lbw RJ Hadlee 6
GS Chappell c Coney b Andrews 0   not out 8
KD Walters c Coney b DR Hadlee 41
IC Davis c Andrews b RJ Hadlee 29
RW Marsh (+) c Wadsworth b DR Hadlee 10
KJ O'Keeffe c Wadsworth b RJ Hadlee 9
GJ Gilmour c Wadsworth b Congdon 3
AA Mallett lbw RJ Hadlee 0
MHN Walker not out 2
Extras (LB 5, NB 3) 8 0
TOTAL 162   ....2 for 30

FOW 1st Inns: 20 20 21 98 115 133 150 157 160 162
FOW 2nd Inns: 10 22

Bowling: *First Innings*: RJ Hadlee 9.4-2-33-4, Andrews 9-1-40-2, DR Hadlee 13-3-52-3, Congdon 13-2-29-1. *Second Innings*: RJ Hadlee 4.3-0-16-2, Andrews 4-0-14-0.

Umpires: PR Enright & MG O'Connell

Australian Averages

1973–74 AUSTRALIA v NEW ZEALAND

AUSTRALIA	M	Inn	NO	Runs	H.S	Avrge	Ct	St	Overs	Mds	Runs	Wkt	Avrge
Chappell, GS	3	4	1	110	60	36.67	6	-	46.0	10	152	5	30.40
Chappell, IM	3	4	-	127	54	31.75	10	-	5.0	-	13	2	6.50
Davis, IC	3	3	-	59	29	19.67	3	-	-	-	-	-	-
Dell, AR	1	-	-	-	-	-	-	-	27.0	7	63	1	63.00
Dymock, G	1	1	1	0	0*	-	-	-	46.0	12	102	7	14.57
Gilmour, GJ	2	2	-	55	52	27.50	1	-	65.0	8	231	8	28.88
Hurst, AG	1	1	-	16	16	16.00	-	-	29.0	5	73	1	73.00
Mallett, AA	3	2	-	11	11	5.50	-	-	107.4	22	297	10	29.70
Marsh, RW	3	3	-	148	132	49.33	16	1	-	-	-	-	-
O'Keeffe, KJ	3	3	1	134	85	67.00	2	-	114.1	39	257	11	23.36
Sheahan, AP	2	3	1	49	28	24.50	-	-	-	-	-	-	-
Stackpole, KR	3	4	-	147	122	36.75	3	-	-	-	-	-	-
Walker, MHN	1	1	1	2	2*	-	-	-	22.0	2	71	2	35.50
Walters, KD	3	3	-	214	94	71.33	1	-	39.0	4	138	8	17.25
Woodcock, AJ	1	1	-	27	27	27.00	1	-	-	-	-	-	-

New Zealand Averages

1973–74 AUSTRALIA v NEW ZEALAND

NEW ZEALAND	M	Inn	NO	Runs	H.S	Avrge	Ct	St	Overs	Mds	Runs	Wkt	Avrge
Andrews, B	2	3	2	22	17	22.00	1	-	32.0	3	154	2	77.00
Cairns, BL	1	2	1	4	4*	4.00	-	-	21.0	4	73	2	36.50
Coney, JV	2	4	-	81	45	20.25	4	-	-	-	-	-	-
Congdon, BE	3	6	1	150	71*	30.00	1	-	36.5	4	120	4	30.00
Hadlee, DR	3	6	1	100	37	20.00	-	-	54.0	7	230	8	28.75
Hadlee, RJ	3	6	-	68	20	11.33	2	-	66.7	9	255	7	36.43
Hastings, BF	3	6	-	152	83	25.33	2	-	-	-	-	-	-
Morrison, JFM	3	6	-	249	117	41.50	1	-	-	-	-	-	-
O'Sullivan, DR	3	6	1	24	8	4.80	-	-	57.5	7	228	5	45.60
Parker, JM	3	6	-	191	108	31.83	3	-	-	-	-	-	-
Shrimpton, MJF	2	4	-	66	28	16.50	-	-	7.0	-	39	2	19.50
Turner, GM	2	3	-	60	34	20.00	-	-	-	-	-	-	-
Wadsworth, KJ	3	6	-	230	80	38.33	8	1	-	-	-	-	-

FIRST TEST 1973–74 NEW ZEALAND v AUSTRALIA
Basin Reserve, Wellington. March 1, 2, 3, 5, 6, 1974.
Toss: Australia. Match Drawn.

AUSTRALIA

KR Stackpole b Webb	10	b Collinge	27
IR Redpath c Coney b Hadlee	19	c Howarth b Congdon	93
IM Chappell (c) c Wadsworth b Webb	145	c Hadlee b Howarth	121
GS Chappell not out	247	c Wadsworth b Collinge	133
IC Davis c Wadsworth b Hadlee	16	c Wadsworth b Howarth	8
KD Walters c Howarth b Collinge	32	c Morrison b Hadlee	8
RW Marsh (+) lbw Congdon	22	c Collinge b Congdon	17
KJ O'Keeffe c Howarth b Congdon	2		
MHN Walker not out	22		
AA Mallett not out	4		
G Dymock			
Extras (B 1, LB 4, NB 15)	20	(B 4, LB 4, W 1, NB 16)	25
TOTAL	6 dec 511		8 for 460

FOW 1st Inns: 13 55 319 359 431 511
FOW 2nd Inns: 67 208 294 318 359 414 433 433

Bowling: *First Innings:* Webb 21-1-114-2, Collinge 24-3-103-1, Hadlee 27-7-107-2, Howarth 21-0-113-0, Congdon 12.5-0-54-1. *Second Innings:* Webb 19-0-93-0, Collinge 19-3-60-2, Hadlee 21-2-106-1, Howarth 25-3-97-2, Congdon 13-1-60-3, Coney 2-0-13-0, Hastings 2-0-6-0.

NEW ZEALAND

GM Turner c Redpath b O'Keeffe	79
JM Parker lbw Walker	10
JFM Morrison b Walker	66
BE Congdon (c) c Davis b Mallett	132
BF Hastings c IM Chappell b Dymock	101
JV Coney c GS Chappell b Walker	13
KJ Wadsworth (+) b Dymock	5
DR Hadlee c Davis b O'Keeffe	9
RO Collinge run out	2
HJ Howarth not out	29
MG Webb c O'Keeffe b Dymock	12
Extras (B 10, LB 5, NB 11)	26
TOTAL	484

FOW 1st Inns: 28 136 169 398 409 423 423 430 437 484

Bowling: *First Innings:* Walker 41-11-107-3, Dymock 35-7-77-3, Walters 8-1-39-0, Mallett 41-8-117-1, O'Keeffe 33-9-83-2, GS Chappell 7-0-27-0, IM Chappell 4-0-8-0.

Umpires: DEA Copps & FR Goodall

SECOND TEST 1973–74 NEW ZEALAND v AUSTRALIA
Lancaster Park, Christchurch. March 8, 9, 10, 12, 13, 1974.
Toss: New Zealand. New Zealand won by 5 wkts.

AUSTRALIA

KR Stackpole b Collinge	4	c Wadsworth b Collinge	9
IR Redpath c & b Collinge	71	c Howarth b RJ Hadlee	58
IM Chappell (c) b RJ Hadlee	20	b Collinge	1
GS Chappell c Howarth b Congdon	25	c Coney b RJ Hadlee	6
IC Davis lbw RJ Hadlee	5	c Congdon b RJ Hadlee	50
KD Walters b RJ Hadlee	6	lbw DR Hadlee	65
RW Marsh (+) b Congdon	38	c & b DR Hadlee	4
KJ O'Keeffe c Wadsworth b Congdon	3	not out	23
MHN Walker not out	18	c Howarth b DR Hadlee	4
AA Mallett b Collinge	1 (11)	c Wadsworth b RJ Hadlee	11
G Dymock c Congdon b DR Hadlee	13 (10)	c Wadsworth b DR Hadlee	0
Extras (B 1, LB 6, NB 12)	19	(B 16, LB 4, NB 8)	28
TOTAL	223		259

FOW 1st Inns: 8 45 101 120 128 181 190 194 196 223
FOW 2nd Inns: 12 26 33 139 142 160 232 238 239 259

Bowling: *First Innings:* RJ Hadlee 14-2-59-3, Collinge 21-4-70-3, DR Hadlee 12.2-2-42-1, Congdon 11-2-33-3. *Second Innings:* RJ Hadlee 18.4-3-71-4, Collinge 9-0-37-2, DR Hadlee 20-2-75-4, Congdon 9-3-26-0, Howarth 11-2-22-0.

NEW ZEALAND

GM Turner c Stackpole b GS Chappell	101	not out	110
JM Parker lbw Dymock	18	c Marsh b Walker	26
JFM Morrison c Marsh b GS Chappell	12	lbw Walker	0
BE Congdon (c) c IM Chappell b Walker	8	run out	2
BF Hastings c Marsh b Walker	19	b Mallett	46
JV Coney c Marsh b Dymock	15	c Marsh b GS Chappell	14
KJ Wadsworth (+) c Marsh b Mallett	24	not out	9
DR Hadlee c Marsh b Dymock	11		
RJ Hadlee lbw Walker	23		
HJ Howarth c IM Chappell b Walker	0		
RO Collinge not out	1		
Extras (B 4, LB 8, NB 11)	23	(B 4, LB 14, NB 5)	23
TOTAL	255		5 for 230

FOW 1st Inns: 59 90 104 136 171 213 220 241 242 255
FOW 2nd Inns: 51 55 62 177 206

Bowling: *First Innings:* Walker 19.6-5-60-4, Dymock 24-6-59-3, Walters 7-1-34-0, GS Chappell 20-2-76-2, Mallett 3-1-3-1. *Second Innings:* Walker 28-10-50-2, Dymock 25-5-84-0, GS Chappell 17.6-5-38-1, Mallett 13-4-35-1.

Umpires: JBR Hastie & RL Monteith

THIRD TEST 1973–74 NEW ZEALAND v AUSTRALIA
Eden Park, Auckland. March 22, 23, 24, 1974.
Toss: New Zealand. Australia won by 297 runs.

AUSTRALIA

KR Stackpole c Parker b RJ Hadlee	0	c Congdon b Collinge	0
IR Redpath c Wadsworth b Collinge	13	not out	159
IM Chappell (c) c Turner b Collinge	37	lbw Collinge	35
GS Chappell c Howarth b Collinge	0	c Wadsworth b Howarth	38
IC Davis c Hastings b Collinge	0	c Parker b Howarth	5
KD Walters not out	104	c Parker b Congdon	5
RW Marsh (+) c Hastings b Collinge	45	c RJ Hadlee b Howarth	47
KJ O'Keeffe c Morrison b Congdon	0	c Burgess b Collinge	32
GJ Gilmour c Morrison b Congdon	1	b RJ Hadlee	4
MHN Walker c Burgess b Congdon	7	b RJ Hadlee	0
AA Mallett c Turner b Congdon	7	c Parker b Collinge	6
Extras (B 4, LB 1, NB 2)	7	(B 4, LB 4, W 1, NB 6)	15
TOTAL	221		346

FOW 1st Inns: 0 32 37 37 64 150 154 162 191 221
FOW 2nd Inns: 2 69 118 132 143 230 315 330 330 346

Bowling: *First Innings:* RJ Hadlee 9-1-45-1, Collinge 18-4-82-5, DR Hadlee 9-0-41-0, Congdon 10.2-0-46-4. *Second Innings:* RJ Hadlee 9-1-50-2, Collinge 16.4-0-84-4, DR Hadlee 7-0-48-0, Congdon 19-1-66-1, Howarth 28-5-83-3.

NEW ZEALAND

GM Turner c GS Chappell b Mallett	41	c IM Chappell b Walker	72
JM Parker lbw Gilmour	11	c Marsh b Gilmour	34
JFM Morrison c Marsh b Walker	9	c Marsh b Gilmour	0
BE Congdon (c) lbw Gilmour	4	c Marsh b Walker	4
BF Hastings b Gilmour	0	lbw Walker	1
MG Burgess c Marsh b Gilmour	7	c Stackpole b Walker	6
KJ Wadsworth (+) c Marsh b Gilmour	0	c GS Chappell b Mallett	21
HJ Howarth c Gilmour b Mallett	0 (10)	not out	3
DR Hadlee b Mallett	4 (8)	c Walters b Mallett	4
RJ Hadlee c IM Chappell b Mallett	13 (9)	b O'Keeffe	1
RO Collinge not out	8	c IM Chappell b O'Keeffe	4
Extras (B 4, LB 1, NB 10)	15	(B 3, LB 2, NB 3)	8
TOTAL	112		158

FOW 1st Inns: 16 28 34 40 62 62 63 72 102 112
FOW 2nd Inns: 107 107 112 115 116 127 145 147 147 158

Bowling: *First Innings:* Walker 10-4-11-1, Gilmour 15-3-64-5, Mallett 5.2-0-22-4. *Second Innings:* Walker 19-8-39-4, Gilmour 16-0-52-2, Mallett 13-6-51-2, O'Keeffe 5-1-8-2.

Umpires: DEA Copps & WRC Gardiner

Australian Averages

1973–74 NEW ZEALAND v AUSTRALIA

AUSTRALIA	M	Inn	NO	Runs	H.S	Avrge	Ct	St	Overs	Mds	Runs	Wkt	Avrge
Chappell, GS	3	6	1	449	247*	89.80	3	-	44.6	7	141	3	47.00
Chappell, IM	3	6	-	359	145	59.83	6	-	4.0	-	8	-	-
Davis, IC	3	6	-	84	50	14.00	2	-	-	-	-	-	-
Dymock, G	2	2	-	13	13	6.50	-	-	84.0	18	220	6	36.67
Gilmour, GJ	1	2	-	5	4	7.50	1	-	31.0	3	116	7	16.57
Mallett, AA	3	5	1	29	11	7.25	-	-	75.2	19	228	9	25.33
Marsh, RW	3	6	-	173	47	28.83	13	-	-	-	-	-	-
O'Keeffe, KJ	3	5	1	60	32	15.00	1	-	38.0	10	91	4	22.75
Redpath, IR	3	6	1	413	159*	82.60	1	-	-	-	-	-	-
Stackpole, KR	3	6	-	50	27	8.33	2	-	-	-	-	-	-
Walker, MHN	3	5	2	51	22*	17.00	-	-	117.6	38	267	14	19.07
Walters, KD	3	6	1	220	104*	44.00	-	-	15.0	2	73	-	-

New Zealand Averages

1973–74 NEW ZEALAND v AUSTRALIA

NEW ZEALAND	M	Inn	NO	Runs	H.S	Avrge	Ct	St	Overs	Mds	Runs	Wkt	Avrge
Burgess, MG	1	2	-	13	7	6.50	2	-	-	-	-	-	-
Collinge, RO	3	4	2	15	8*	7.50	2	-	107.4	14	436	17	25.65
Coney, JV	2	3	-	42	15	14.00	2	-	2.0	-	13	-	-
Congdon, BE	3	5	-	150	132	30.00	3	-	74.7	7	285	12	23.75
Hadlee, DR	3	4	-	28	11	7.00	2	-	96.2	13	419	8	52.38
Hadlee, RJ	2	3	-	37	23	12.33	1	-	50.4	7	225	10	22.50
Hastings, BF	3	5	-	167	101	33.40	2	-	2.0	-	6	-	-
Howarth, HJ	3	4	2	32	29*	16.00	1	-	85.0	10	315	5	63.00
Morrison, JFM	3	5	-	87	66	17.40	3	-	-	-	-	-	-
Parker, JM	3	5	-	99	34	19.80	4	-	-	-	-	-	-
Turner, GM	3	5	1	403	110*	100.75	2	-	-	-	-	-	-
Wadsworth, KJ	3	5	-	59	24	14.75	10	-	-	-	-	-	-
Webb, MG	1	1	-	12	12	12.00	-	-	40.0	1	207	2	103.50

Pace attack shatters England

'Ashes to Ashes, dust to dust, if Lillee don't get ya, Thomson must!'

Rigby's cartoon graphically expressed the opinion of Australian cricket followers over the deeds of the dynamic duo.

Perth, Dec. 17. In just over two weeks of cricket England discovered, to its consternation, that Dennis Lillee has returned from injury better and faster than ever – and that worse (for them), he has a twin in 'terror' in Jeff Thomson.

At least one observer, Richie Benaud, noted that in the beginning it was England who thought she had the faster and more lethal bowlers in Bob Willis, Mike Hendrick and Peter Lever and began the 'bumper war' on the suspect first day pitch in Brisbane.

The preparation of the pitch had, extraordinarily, been taken over by Brisbane Mayor Clem Jones, and was dubious at one end.

England captain Mike Denness said 'Not many of the England team didn't get a touch of Thomson on the gloves or on the body.' As the speedster admitted himself, he didn't know where the balls were headed either.

In the second Test England flew in the 41-year-old Colin Cowdrey, following injuries to Dennis Amiss (broken finger) and John Edrich (back) and immediately put him in the side. England also called up 42-year-old Fred Titmus.

At drinks in the afternoon session of the first day it seemed as if Ian Chappell's decision to put England in might have misfired, when Cowdrey and David Lloyd had reached 1/99. But they were 4/133 at tea, and all out for 208 before stumps.

Not that it was all the work of Lillee and Thomson – some blinding catching off the bowling of Doug Walters and Ian Chappell was required to break the stubborn partnership of Alan Knott and Fred Titmus. As for Cowdrey, he batted over two hours for 22 before Thommo knocked his leg stump over.

Day two was something of a contrast as Australia built to a strong position with four wickets down just before tea. Doug Walters joined Ross Edwards, and after the interval provided a vintage Walters innings of audacious pull shots and thumping drives, culminating in a glorious pull off Bob Willis' last ball of the day for six, and a century in a session. He was out to Willis from the second ball he faced next morning.

Ross Edwards went on to score a patient hundred, and Australia's total of 481 was easily good enough to win within three and half days of play.

Doug Walters hits Bob Willis for six in the second Test – bringing up a century in a session for the third time.

The 1974–75 Australians, ready for the Tests with England. From left R. Marsh, W. Edwards, G. Dymock, R. McCosker, A. Mallett, M. Walker, G. Chappell, D. Lillee, I. Redpath, T. Jenner, I. Chappell, D. Walters.

Australia gets Ashes back

'Keeper caught: Rod Marsh catches England counterpart Alan Knott in the third Test at the MCG.

Sydney, Jan. 9. The third Test in Melbourne had wound its way through three innings of not very inspiring batting, peppered with some good wickets to Lillee, Thomson and Willis. At the beginning of the last day Australia needed 246 to win with a whole day's play to get them. But good bowling from Tony Greig and Bob Willis had Australia in early trouble, and just after tea Australia was 6/171 when Doug Walters fell.

All possible results for the game were open when the last fifteen overs of the game started. Rod Marsh and Max Walker took the score along to 207 before Marsh was out and seven overs had been bowled. Walker and Lillee gathered runs quietly, perhaps too slowly. The second-last over was a

maiden bowled by Underwood, leaving an improbable 14 runs required off the last. Greig bowled the last over, Walker took three runs, Lillee was caught and the match was an unadventurous draw.

Australia would have to wait until the fourth Test to take the series and the Ashes. Again it was close-run thing, with Australia waiting until the tenth over of the last fifteen before taking the final wicket, and winning by 171 runs. England's near-hero was acting-captain John Edrich, who took a sickening blow from Lillee on the first ball he received, and went to hospital. He returned and batted for two and half hours for 33, but ran out of partners, starting with Tony Greig who batted as if the game were already lost.

Centuries to Ian Redpath and Greg Chappell had, however put the match out of England's reach on the fourth day. Rick McCosker did not bat in the second innings, having received a fearful blow to the forehead from John Edrich in the first innings, fielding close in on the leg side.

Greg Chappell in particular was in imperious mood – in the eyes of one observer 'letting loose a masterful, savage yet beautiful period of batting'.

It was a more refined innings than that of Doug Walters in Perth, and with the solid rock of Redpath at the other end, enabled Ian Chappell to declare 400 in front – Greg Chappell 144, Redpath 105.

Australia won back the Ashes, which it had lost in 1972.

One day game

Melbourne, Jan. 1. In almost a replica of the first one day international match in Australia, played four years ago on 1 January 1971, one team scored 190 and the other 191. This time however the boot was on the other foot, and Australia lost by three wickets.

This game the second official one day international played in Australia, was watched by a good crowd of 18,827 who paid $18,156 to watch Australia make their 190 in 34.5 overs. England made 7/191 in 37.1 overs, Wally Edwards bowling a-no ball with his first ball to give England the win.

Ian (42) and Greg (44) Chappell did best for Australia with the bat, and Alan Hurst best with the ball, with 2/27 from his eight overs.

England flowers with Lillee and Thommo off scene

Melbourne, Feb. 13. When Jeff Thomson injured his shoulder in a social tennis match on the rest day of the fifth Test in Adelaide, all that happened was that Dennis Lillee and Max Walker redoubled their efforts in the second innings to bowl Australia to a comfortable 163-run victory.

The game began in conditions favouring England: a damp and tricky pitch for Derek Underwood and Fred Titmus to bowl on. They had Australia 5/84.

But the lower order, Terry Jenner (74) Max Walker(41) Lillee 26) and Ashley Mallett (23) chipped in to get Australia to a decent 304, with Underwood taking 7/113.

That score gave Lillee and Thomson something to work with, and wickets fell steadily.

Australia's second innings 5/272 put the home side the mandatory 400 in front. And Lillee and Walker did the rest.

But when it came to the sixth Test, Thomson was not available because of his shoulder injury, and Lillee broke down on second day having bowled just six overs.

In addition Australia had been caught on a pitch with a wet patch at one end caused by a groundsman's error when lifting the covers before play. Peter Lever found the spot and took 6/38.

Denness (188) and Keith Fletcher (146) then took complete control on then flat pitch. Australia batted 9 and a half hours in the second innings, Greg Chappell 102, but lost after lunch on the fifth day by an innings and four runs.

Colin Cowdrey ruefully watches Greg Chappell take a great catch.

A pair of impeccably attired umpires walked out into the MCG when the third Test was interrupted for bad light – but they were bogus blokes with beards who, unlike the real umpires, wanted play to recommence.

Lillee 'n' Thommo – fast and fearful pair

Dennis Lillee, whose boyhood hero was the great West Indies fast bowler Wesley Hall, was a tall, strapping man with a classical style – long, menacing run-up, a high bounding action and a copybook follow through. Appeals were accompanied by steely glares. His black moustache added to the aura of venom. He had everything – inswingers, outswingers and, above all, fierce determination.

Jeff Thomson, or 'Thommo' was broad of shoulder and adopted a quick-footed approach to the wicket, tucking his right hand behind his back just before delivery. Then, with a slinging action, he hurled deceptively fast deliveries at unsuspecting batsmen. His missiles lifted alarmingly, even on placid pitches. Intimidation was his stock in trade. In grade cricket in Sydney he once put a batsman into intensive care. He had scant respect for authority and was a favourite with the crowds.

Dennis Keith Lillee was born at Subiaco, Perth on 18 July 1949. Thirteen months later Jeffrey Robert Thomson was born at Greenacre, Sydney on 16 August 1950.

Lillee played his first game for WA in 1969–70. It was on a dead-flat pitch at the 'Gabba and his first victim was noted Queensland opener Sam Trimble, caught close in. Lillee took 15 wickets on WA's four-match tour of the eastern states.

Lillee's Test debut followed late next season, in 1970–71, with 5/84 in England's first innings in the sixth Test in Adelaide. Lillee's WA teammate and buddy, Rod Marsh, also came into Test cricket in 1970–71. In 1983–84, when they retired, 95 Test batsmen had been given their marching orders – c. Marsh, b. Lillee – easily a Test record.

Lillee produced one of his greatest performances in 1971–72 when he tore through a strong Rest of the World XI with 8/29 in Perth, at one stage taking 6/0. The team was led by Sobers, who described Lillee as the fastest bowler he had faced, and included Gavaskar, Lloyd and Pollock.

Lillee was close to his peak in England in 1972, taking 31 wickets at 17.83. Thanks to him, Australia squared the series 2–all.

The next year, 1973, Lillee's career was in jeopardy with severe back problems diagnosed as stress fractures of the lower lumber vertebrae. He was out of cricket for over

a year but worked diligently at restoring his strength, and by 1974–75 was back to his fiery best against England, taking 25 wickets.

Thommo made his Test debut against Pakistan in 1972 after only six matches for NSW, and had the unflattering figures of 0/100. It was later discovered he had a broken bone in his foot. He moved to Queensland in 1974–75, the season he first partnered Lillee.

After taking 29 wickets at 30.66 against the West Indies in 1975–76, Thomson collided heavily with team-mate Alan Turner trying to catch Pakistan's Zaheer Abbas in the first Test in Adelaide in late December, 1976. He was never quite the same again, saying the accident cost him his 'zing'.

With different opening partners in the absence of Lillee, he still managed to take 26 wickets in England in 1977 and a total of 41 against India and the West Indies in 1977–78 and 1978.

After stints with WSC and Middlesex, Thomson was called up for the last four Tests of the 1982–83 Ashes series at home. Lillee and Terry Alderman were injured and Thommo immediately obliged with 5/73 and, overall, 22 wickets at 18.68 in Australia's 2–1 win.

With the bat, few will forget his great last-wicket stand with Allan Border that took Australia to within three runs of victory in the Melbourne Test.

Thomson spent the rest of his career until 1985–86 playing for Queensland and he became the first Queenslander to take 300 Shield wickets.

Sharing the new ball, Lillee and Thomson played together in 25 Tests from 1974 to 1983, capturing 214 wickets at an average of 25.89. Lillee's contribution was 116 wickets at 24.80, Thomson's 98 at 27.19. Their strike rate together was a phenomenal 8.56 wickets per Test. Such was their dominance, Australia won 14 of these 25 Tests with only three losses.

In three consecutive series, from 1974 until 1976, two against England and the other against the West Indies, they spearheaded Australia to nine Test wins out of 14 with only one loss, taking a total of 153 wickets at 23.82.

After one inauspicious Test together against Pakistan in 1972–73, they foreshadowed Australia's return to pre-eminence with an explosive 13/203 in the

Dennis Lillee: 355 Test wickets.

first Test against old foe England at the 'Gabba in 1974–75. Thomson ended the series with 33 wickets at 17.90 and Lillee 25 at 23.14. They took 10 or more wickets in the first five Tests.

Thomson injured his shoulder playing tennis during the fifth Test and missed the last encounter. With Lillee also injured, England won by an innings.

Both were fit again for the 1975 tour of England, however, and took 37 wickets in four Tests, Australia retaining the Ashes 1–0. The following season in Australia, 1975–76, they blitzed the West Indians 5–1. Even though Lillee missed the Sydney Test, they dismissed 56 Windies batsmen at an average of 27.54, their best yield being 13/239 at the MCG.

The severe shoulder injury to Thomson suffered while fielding, followed by Lillee's decision to join WSC in 1977, broke up the partnership for the best part of three years.

They were eventually reunited in 1979–80 for two Tests. Then in 1981–82 they took 58 wickets against Pakistan, the West Indies and New Zealand in nine Tests. The three-Test series with NZ was their swansong and yielded a modest 13 wickets.

After WSC Lillee returned to the Australian side for six Tests at home against England and the West Indies in 1979–80. He captured 35 wickets, including one bag of 11/138. His effort in taking 39 wickets at 22.30 in the six Tests in England in 1981 spoke volumes for his tenacity and pluck, for he was unwell for most of the tour. Thomson was overlooked for that

Jeff Thomson: 200 Test wickets.

tour and played for Middlesex. Lillee, though a tail-end batsman, was no rabbit and scored 73 not out against England at Lord's in 1975.

Lillee's volatility sometimes got the better of him, as it did against Pakistan at the WACA in November 1981. On the fourth day of the first Test, Lillee clashed with Javed Miandad, kicking the Pakistani captain after a mid-pitch confrontation in which Lillee veered into Miandad, who was completing a run. After much politicking, Lillee apologised.

In the twilight of his career, Lillee bowled at a more economical pace but no less effectively, combining clever use of cutters and swing. His last 29 Tests yielded 146 wickets (5.03 per match).

In all first class matches, Lillee took 882 wickets at an average of 23.46. In 70 Tests he captured a world record 355 wickets at 23.92, including 23 hauls of five-wickets and seven of 10 wickets. His best haul was 7/83 in the Boxing Day Test at the MCG in 1981. He also took 79 wickets in 'Supertests' against top oppositon.

Few Test bowlers have averaged five wickets or better a Test. Lillee's average was 5.07. His world record has since been passed by five players, of whom only Sir Richard Hadlee (431 wickets) has an equivalent strike rate – 5.01 wickets a Test. Lillee scored 905 runs in Tests at an average of 13.71.

Since his retirement, Lillee has been involved in coaching, passing on his art to players all over the world. He was inducted into Cricket's Hall of Fame in 1996.

Skipper's views on season

Melbourne, Feb. 14. After the loss in the sixth Test, Australian captain Ian Chappell said 'They'll probably knock back our bonus, now we lost. It's a hard life.' After a comprehensive 4–1 win in the series, somehow that's doubtful.

Chappell may well be right when he also said that he thought that six Tests was too many, in particular with regard to the bowlers. 'We're getting to the stage where the strain of too much Test cricket will start to tell on the bowlers … I think a fast bowler is only good for a certain number of test matches in his career. Having these long series one after the other lessens their bowling life.'

Mike Denness on the other hand was less reflective about the state of the game, and more concerned with the tour just past and the 1975 Australian tour to England,

He said England's bowlers had done a good job, but the batsmen, himself included, had not 'got anywhere near enough runs.

'But I'd like to think we can win back the Ashes … it will be a very tough job … but it can be done.' MCC manager Alec Bedser blamed

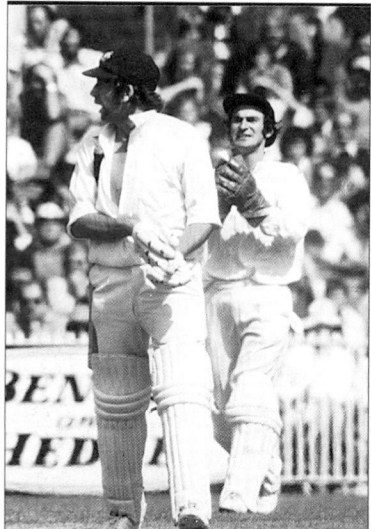

Ian Chappell leaves the field.

England's woes on injury. 'You lost a couple of players in the last Test and looked what happened,' he said with a grin.

Chappell said that 'We should do all right in England. Attack wise, we're pretty right.'

And as for Thommo? 'He'll do all right in England. Don't make any mistake about that.'

FIRST TEST 1974–75 AUSTRALIA v ENGLAND
Brisbane Cricket Ground, Brisbane. November 29, 30, December 1, 3, 4, 1974.
Toss: Australia. Australia won by 166 runs.

AUSTRALIA

IR Redpath b Willis	5	b Willis	25
WJ Edwards c Amiss b Hendrick	4	c Knott b Willis	5
IM Chappell (c) c Greig b Willis	90	c Fletcher b Underwood	11
GS Chappell c Fletcher b Underwood	58	b Underwood	71
R Edwards c Knott b Underwood	32	c Knott b Willis	53
KD Walters c Lever b Willis	3	not out	62
RW Marsh (+) c Denness b Hendrick	14	not out	46
TJ Jenner c Lever b Willis	12		
DK Lillee c Knott b Greig	15		
MHN Walker not out	41		
JR Thomson run out	23		
Extras (LB 4, NB 8)	12	(B 1, LB 7, W 1, NB 6)	15
TOTAL	309		5 dec 288

FOW 1st Inns: 7 10 110 197 202 205 228 229 257 309
FOW 2nd Inns: 15 39 59 173 190

Bowling: *First Innings*: Willis 21.5-3-56-4, Lever 16-1-53-0, Hendrick 19-3-64-2, Greig 16-2-70-1, Underwood 20-6-54-2. *Second Innings*: Willis 15-3-45-3, Lever 18-4-58-0, Hendrick 13-2-47-0, Underwood 26-6-63-2, Greig 13-2-60-0.

ENGLAND

DL Amiss c Jenner b Thomson	7	c Walters b Thomson	25
BW Luckhurst c Marsh b Thomson	1	c IM Chappell b Lillee	3
JH Edrich c IM Chappell b Thomson	48	b Thomson	6
MH Denness (c) lbw Walker	6	c Walters b Thomson	27
KWR Fletcher b Lillee	17	c GS Chappell b Jenner	19
AW Greig c Marsh b Lillee	110	b Thomson	2
APE Knott (+) c Jenner b Walker	12	b Thomson	19
P Lever c IM Chappell b Walker	4	c Redpath b Lillee	14
DL Underwood c Redpath b Walters	25	c Walker b Jenner	30
RGD Willis not out	13	not out	3
M Hendrick c Redpath b Walker	4	b Thomson	0
Extras (B 5, LB 2, W 3, NB 8)	18	(B 8, LB 3, W 2, NB 5)	18
TOTAL	265		166

FOW 1st Inns: 9 10 33 57 130 162 168 226 248 265
FOW 2nd Inns: 18 40 44 92 94 94 115 162 163 166

Bowling: *First Innings*: Lillee 23-6-73-2, Thomson 21-5-59-3, Walker 24.5-2-73-4, Walters 6-1-18-1, Jenner 6-1-24-0. *Second Innings*: Lillee 12-2-25-2, Thomson 17.5-3-46-6, Walker 9-4-32-0, Jenner 16-5-45-2, Walters 2-2-0-0.

Umpires: RC Bailhache & TF Brooks

Australian Averages

1974–75 AUSTRALIA v ENGLAND

AUSTRALIA	M	Inn	NO	Runs	H.S.	Avrge	Ct	St	Overs	Mds	Runs	Wkt	Avrge
Chappell, GS	6	11	-	608	144	55.27	14	-	-	-	-	-	-
Chappell, IM	6	12	1	387	90	35.18	11	-	22.0	3	83	1	83.00
Dymock, G	1	2	-	0	0	0.00	-	-	39.0	6	130	1	130.00
Edwards, R	5	9	1	261	115	32.63	-	-	-	-	-	-	-
Edwards, WJ	3	6	-	68	30	11.33	-	-	-	-	-	-	-
Jenner, TJ	2	3	1	100	74	50.00	3	-	42.0	10	136	3	45.33
Lillee, DK	6	8	2	88	26	14.67	2	-	182.6	36	596	25	23.84
Mallett, AA	5	7	2	61	31	12.20	9	-	140.6	47	339	17	19.94
Marsh, RW	6	11	2	313	55	34.78	18	1	-	-	-	-	-
McCosker, RB	3	5	-	202	80	40.40	1	-	-	-	-	-	-
Redpath, IR	6	12	1	472	105	42.91	11	-	-	-	-	-	-
Thomson, JR	5	5	2	65	24*	21.67	3	-	175.1	34	592	33	17.94
Walker, MHN	6	8	3	221	41*	44.20	5	-	218.7	46	684	23	29.74
Walters, KD	6	11	2	383	103	42.56	5	-	56.3	14	175	5	35.00

SECOND TEST 1974–75 AUSTRALIA v ENGLAND
W.A.C.A. Ground, Perth. December 13, 14, 15, 17, 1974.
Toss: Australia. Australia won by 9 wkts.

ENGLAND

D Lloyd c GS Chappell b Thomson	49	c GS Chappell b Walker	35
BW Luckhurst c Mallett b Walker	27 (7)	c Mallett b Lillee	23
MC Cowdrey b Thomson	22 (2)	lbw Thomson	41
AW Greig c Mallett b Walker	23	c GS Chappell b Thomson	32
KWR Fletcher c Redpath b Lillee	4	c Marsh b Thomson	0
MH Denness (c) c GS Chappell b Lillee	2 (3)	c Redpath b Thomson	20
APE Knott (+) c Redpath b Walters	51 (6)	c GS Chappell b Lillee	18
FJ Titmus c Redpath b Walters	10	c GS Chappell b Mallett	61
CM Old c GS Chappell b IM Chappell	7	c Thomson b Mallett	43
GG Arnold run out	1	c Mallett b Thomson	4
RGD Willis not out	4	not out	0
Extras (W 3, NB 5)	8	(LB 4, W 1, NB 11)	16
TOTAL	208		293

FOW 1st Inns: 44 99 119 128 132 132 194 201 202 208
FOW 2nd Inns: 62 106 124 124 154 156 219 285 293 293

Bowling: *First Innings*: Lillee 16-4-48-2, Thomson 15-6-45-2, Walker 20-5-49-2, Mallett 10-3-35-0, Walters 2.3-0-13-2, IM Chappell 2-0-10-1. *Second Innings*: Lillee 22-5-59-2, Thomson 25-4-93-5, Walker 24-7-76-1, Walters 9-4-17-0, Mallett 11.1-4-32-2.

AUSTRALIA

IR Redpath st Knott b Titmus	41	not out	12
WJ Edwards c Lloyd b Greig	30	lbw Arnold	0
IM Chappell (c) c Knott b Arnold	25	not out	11
GS Chappell c Greig b Willis	62		
R Edwards b Arnold	115		
KD Walters c Fletcher b Willis	103		
RW Marsh (+) c Lloyd b Titmus	41		
MHN Walker c Knott b Old	19		
DK Lillee b Old	11		
AA Mallett c Knott b Old	0		
JR Thomson not out	11		
Extras (B 7, LB 14, NB 2)	23		0
TOTAL	481		1 for 23

FOW 1st Inns: 64 101 113 192 362 416 449 462 462 481
FOW 2nd Inns: 4

Bowling: *First Innings*: Willis 22-0-91-2, Arnold 27-1-129-2, Old 22.6-3-85-3, Greig 9-0-69-1, Titmus 28-3-84-2. *Second Innings*: Willis 2-0-8-0, Arnold 1.7-0-15-1.

Umpires: RC Bailhache & TF Brooks

English Averages

1974–75 AUSTRALIA v ENGLAND

ENGLAND	M	Inn	NO	Runs	H.S.	Avrge	Ct	St	Overs	Mds	Runs	Wkt	Avrge
Amiss, DL	5	9	-	175	90	19.44	3	-	-	-	-	-	-
Arnold, GG	4	7	1	22	14	3.67	-	-	141.1	23	528	14	37.71
Cowdrey, MC	5	9	-	165	41	18.33	3	-	-	-	-	-	-
Denness, MH	5	9	-	318	188	35.33	6	-	-	-	-	-	-
Edrich, JH	4	7	1	260	70	43.33	2	-	-	-	-	-	-
Fletcher, KWR	5	9	-	324	146	36.00	3	-	-	-	-	-	-
Greig, AW	6	11	-	446	110	40.55	12	-	167.5	19	681	17	40.06
Hendrick, M	2	4	2	12	8*	6.00	-	-	34.6	6	119	2	59.50
Knott, APE	6	11	1	364	106*	36.40	22	1	-	-	-	-	-
Lever, P	2	3	1	24	14	12.00	2	-	61.0	8	214	9	23.78
Lloyd, D	4	8	-	196	49	24.50	6	-	-	-	-	-	-
Luckhurst, BW	2	4	-	54	27	13.50	-	-	-	-	-	-	-
Old, CM	2	3	-	50	43	16.67	-	-	51.6	4	210	6	35.00
Titmus, FJ	4	8	-	138	61	17.25	-	-	122.3	30	360	7	51.43
Underwood, DL	5	9	-	111	30	12.33	-	-	185.0	42	595	17	35.00
Willis, RGD	5	10	5	76	15	15.20	1	-	140.4	15	522	17	30.71

THIRD TEST 1974–75 AUSTRALIA v ENGLAND
Melbourne Cricket Ground, Melbourne. December 26, 27, 28, 30, 31, 1974.
Toss: Australia. Match Drawn.

ENGLAND

Batsman	1st		2nd
DL Amiss c Walters b Lillee	4	c IM Chappell b Mallett	90
D Lloyd c Mallett b Thomson	14	c & b Mallett	44
MC Cowdrey lbw Thomson	35	c GS Chappell b Lillee	8
JH Edrich c Marsh b Mallett	49	c Marsh b Thomson	4
MH Denness (c) c Marsh b Mallett	8	c IM Chappell b Thomson	2
AW Greig run out	28	c GS Chappell b Lillee	60
APE Knott (+) b Thomson	52	c Marsh b Thomson	4
FJ Titmus c Mallett b Lillee	10	b Mallett	0
DL Underwood c Marsh b Walker	9	c IM Chappell b Mallett	4
RGD Willis c Walters b Thomson	13	b Thomson	15
M Hendrick not out	8	not out	0
Extras (LB 2, W 1, NB 9)	12	(B 2, LB 9, W 2)	13
TOTAL	242		244

FOW 1st Inns: 4 34 110 110 141 157 176 213 232 242
FOW 2nd Inns: 115 134 152 156 158 165 178 182 238 244

Bowling: *First Innings*: Lillee 20-2-70-2, Thomson 22.4-4-72-4, Walker 24-10-36-1, Walters 7-2-15-0, Mallett 15-3-37-2. *Second Innings*: Lillee 17-3-55-2, Thomson 17-1-71-4, Walker 11-0-45-0, Mallett 24-6-60-4.

AUSTRALIA

Batsman	1st		2nd
IR Redpath c Knott b Greig	55	run out	39
WJ Edwards c Denness b Willis	29	lbw Greig	0
GS Chappell c Greig b Willis	2 (4)	lbw Titmus	61
R Edwards c Cowdrey b Titmus	1 (5)	c Lloyd b Titmus	10
KD Walters c Lloyd b Greig	36 (6)	c Denness b Greig	32
IM Chappell (c) lbw Willis	36 (3)	lbw Willis	0
RW Marsh (+) c Knott b Titmus	44	c Knott b Greig	40
MHN Walker c Knott b Willis	30	not out	23
DK Lillee not out	2	c Denness b Greig	14
AA Mallett run out	0	not out	0
JR Thomson b Willis	2		
Extras (B 2, LB 2)	4	(B 6, LB 9, NB 4)	19
TOTAL	241		8 for 238

FOW 1st Inns: 65 67 68 121 126 173 237 237 238 241
FOW 2nd Inns: 4 5 106 120 121 171 208 235

Bowling: *First Innings*: Willis 21.7-4-61-5, Hendrick 2.6-1-8-0, Underwood 22-6-62-0, Greig 24-2-63-2, Titmus 22-11-43-2. *Second Innings*: Willis 14-2-56-1, Greig 18-2-56-4, Titmus 29-10-64-2, Underwood 19-7-43-0.

Umpires: RC Bailhache & TF Brooks

FIFTH TEST 1974–75 AUSTRALIA v ENGLAND
Adelaide Oval, Adelaide. January 25 (no play),26, 27, 29, 30, 1975.
Toss: England. Australia won by 163 runs.

AUSTRALIA

Batsman	1st		2nd
IR Redpath c Greig b Underwood	21	b Underwood	52
RB McCosker c Cowdrey b Underwood	35	c Knott b Arnold	11
IM Chappell (c) c Knott b Underwood	0	c Knott b Underwood	41
GS Chappell lbw Underwood	5	c Greig b Underwood	18
KD Walters c Willis b Underwood	55	not out	71
RW Marsh (+) c Greig b Underwood	6	c Greig b Underwood	55
TJ Jenner b Underwood	74	not out	14
MHN Walker run out	41		
DK Lillee b Willis	26		
AA Mallett not out	23		
JR Thomson b Arnold	5		
Extras (B 4, LB 4, NB 5)	13	(LB 4, NB 6)	10
TOTAL	304		5 dec 272

FOW 1st Inns: 52 52 58 77 84 164 241 259 295 304
FOW 2nd Inns: 16 92 128 133 245

Bowling: *First Innings*: Willis 10-0-46-1, Arnold 12.2-3-42-1, Underwood 29-3-113-7, Greig 10-0-63-0, Titmus 7-1-27-0. *Second Innings*: Willis 5-0-27-0, Arnold 20-1-71-1, Underwood 26-5-102-4, Titmus 13-1-53-0, Greig 2-0-9-0.

ENGLAND

Batsman	1st		2nd
DL Amiss c IM Chappell b Lillee	0	c Marsh b Lillee	0
D Lloyd c Marsh b Lillee	4	c Walters b Walker	5
MC Cowdrey c Walker b Thomson	26	c Mallett b Lillee	3
MH Denness (c) c Marsh b Thomson	51	c Jenner b Lillee	14
KWR Fletcher c IM Chappell b Thomson	40	lbw Lillee	63
AW Greig c Marsh b Lillee	19	lbw Walker	20
APE Knott (+) c Lillee b Mallett	5	not out	106
FJ Titmus c GS Chappell b Mallett	11	lbw Jenner	20
DL Underwood c Lillee b Mallett	0	c IM Chappell b Mallett	0
GG Arnold b Lillee	0	b Mallett	0
RGD Willis not out	11	b Walker	3
Extras (LB 2, NB 3)	5	(B 3, LB 3, NB 1)	7
TOTAL	172		241

FOW 1st Inns: 2 19 66 90 130 147 155 156 161 172
FOW 2nd Inns: 0 8 10 33 76 144 212 213 217 241

Bowling: *First Innings*: Lillee 12.5-2-49-4, Thomson 15-1-58-3, Walker 5-1-18-0, Jenner 5-0-28-0, Mallett 9-4-14-3. *Second Innings*: Lillee 14-3-69-4, Walker 20-3-89-3, Mallett 25-10-36-2, Jenner 15-4-39-1, IM Chappell 1-0-1-0.

Umpires: RC Bailhache & TF Brooks

FOURTH TEST 1974–75 AUSTRALIA v ENGLAND
Sydney Cricket Ground, Sydney. January 4, 5, 6, 8, 9, 1975.
Toss: Australia. Australia won by 171 runs.

AUSTRALIA

Batsman	1st		2nd
IR Redpath hit wicket b Titmus	33	c (S)CM Old b Underwood	105
RB McCosker c Knott b Greig	80		
IM Chappell (c) c Knott b Arnold	53 (2)	c Lloyd b Willis	5
GS Chappell c Greig b Arnold	84 (3)	c Lloyd b Arnold	144
R Edwards b Greig	15 (6)	not out	17
KD Walters lbw Arnold	1 (4)	b Underwood	5
RW Marsh (+) b Greig	30 (5)	not out	7
MHN Walker c Greig b Arnold	30		
DK Lillee b Arnold	8		
AA Mallett lbw Greig	31		
JR Thomson not out	24		
Extras (LB 4, W 1, NB 11)	16	(LB 2, W 1, NB 3)	6
TOTAL	405		4 dec 289

FOW 1st Inns: 96 142 199 251 255 305 310 332 368 405
FOW 2nd Inns: 15 235 242 280

Bowling: *First Innings*: Willis 18-2-80-0, Arnold 29-7-86-5, Greig 22.7-2-104-4, Underwood 13-3-54-0, Titmus 16-2-65-1. *Second Innings*: Willis 11-1-52-1, Arnold 22-3-78-1, Greig 12-1-64-0, Underwood 12-1-65-2, Titmus 7.3-2-24-0.

ENGLAND

Batsman	1st		2nd
DL Amiss c Mallett b Walker	12	c Marsh b Lillee	37
D Lloyd c Thomson b Lillee	19	c GS Chappell b Lillee	26
MC Cowdrey c McCosker b Thomson	22	c IM Chappell b Walker	1
JH Edrich (c) c Marsh b Walters	50	not out	33
KWR Fletcher c Redpath b Walker	24	c Redpath b Thomson	11
AW Greig c GS Chappell b Thomson	9	st Marsh b Mallett	54
APE Knott (+) b Thomson	82	c Redpath b Mallett	10
FJ Titmus c Marsh b Walters	22	c Thomson b Mallett	4
DL Underwood c Walker b Lillee	27	c & b Walker	5
RGD Willis b Thomson	2	b Lillee	12
GG Arnold not out	3	c GS Chappell b Mallett	14
Extras (B 15, LB 7, W 1)	23	(B 13, LB 3, NB 5)	21
TOTAL	295		228

FOW 1st Inns: 36 46 69 108 123 180 240 273 285 295
FOW 2nd Inns: 68 70 74 103 136 156 158 175 201 228

Bowling: *First Innings*: Lillee 19.1-2-66-2, Thomson 19-3-74-4, Walker 23-2-77-2, Mallett 1-0-8-0, Walters 7-2-26-2, IM Chappell 4-0-21-0. *Second Innings*: Lillee 21-5-65-2, Thomson 23-7-74-2, Walker 16-5-46-2, Mallett 16.5-9-21-4, IM Chappell 3-2-1-0.

Umpires: RC Bailhache & TF Brooks

SIXTH TEST 1974–75 AUSTRALIA v ENGLAND
Melbourne Cricket Ground, Melbourne. February 8, 9, 10, 12, 13, 1975.
Toss: Australia. England won by an innings & 4 runs.

AUSTRALIA

Batsman	1st		2nd
IR Redpath c Greig b Lever	1	c Amiss b Greig	83
RB McCosker c Greig b Lever	0	c Cowdrey b Arnold	76
IM Chappell (c) c Knott b Old	65	c Knott b Greig	50
GS Chappell c Denness b Lever	1	b Lever	102
R Edwards c Amiss b Lever	0	c Knott b Arnold	18
KD Walters c Edrich b Old	12	b Arnold	3
RW Marsh (+) b Old	29	c Denness b Lever	1
MHN Walker not out	20	c & b Greig	17
DK Lillee c Knott b Lever	12 (11)	not out	0
AA Mallett b Lever	7 (9)	c Edrich b Greig	0
G Dymock c Knott b Greig	0 (10)	c Knott b Lever	0
Extras (B 2, LB 1, NB 2)	5	(B 9, LB 5, W 4, NB 5)	23
TOTAL	152		373

FOW 1st Inns: 0 5 19 23 50 104 115 141 149 152
FOW 2nd Inns: 111 215 248 289 297 306 367 373 373 373

Bowling: *First Innings*: Arnold 6-2-24-0, Lever 11-2-38-6, Old 11-0-50-3, Greig 8.7-1-35-1. *Second Innings*: Arnold 23-6-83-3, Lever 16-1-65-3, Old 18-1-75-0, Underwood 18-5-39-0, Greig 31.7-7-88-4.

ENGLAND

Batsman	1st
DL Amiss lbw Lillee	0
MC Cowdrey c Marsh b Walker	7
JH Edrich c IM Chappell b Walker	70
MH Denness (c) c & b Walker	188
KWR Fletcher c Redpath b Walker	146
AW Greig c(S)TJ Jenner b Walker	89
APE Knott (+) c Marsh b Walker	5
CM Old b Dymock	0
DL Underwood b Walker	11
GG Arnold c Marsh b Walker	0
P Lever not out	6
Extras (B 4, LB 2, NB 1)	7
TOTAL	529

FOW 1st Inns: 4 18 167 359 507 507 508 514 514 529

Bowling: *First Innings*: Lillee 6-2-17-1, Walker 42.2-7-143-8, Dymock 39-6-130-1, Walters 23-3-86-0, Mallett 29-8-96-0, IM Chappell 12-1-50-0.

Umpires: RC Bailhache & TF Brooks

Windies win first World Cup

Gary Gilmour gets Australia into final

Leeds, June 18. How things have changed at Headingley! The dust-bowl on which Derek Underwood (10/82) wrecked Australia in the fourth Test in 1972, was a green, seamer's delight today for the Australia v England semi-final of the first World Cup.

And who better to exploit it than burly left-arm seamer Gary Gilmour, who, in the words of Greg Chappell, 'bent the ball like a safety pin, in the air and off the pitch.'

Gilmour took a match-winning 6/14, reducing England to a miserable 94 all out in 36 of the scheduled 60 overs.

Gilmour, whose immense natural talent too often goes missing, then turned his hand to extricating Australia with the bat as it set about scoring the 94 runs needed for victory and a place in the final against the West Indies at Lord's.

When Australia slumped to 6/39, it seemed England may yet prevail.

Enter that man again – genial 'Gus' Gilmour, a southpaw with the bat as well as with the ball. His confidence riding higher than a wave during a southerly blow at Bondi, he took to Snow as though he were a Sunday park bowler. With Doug Walters playing a supporting role, Gilmour (28 not out) saw Australia to victory.

To skipper Ian Chapell, this victory was almost as good as winning the final itself. He knew the final against the West Indies would be a thriller.

World Cup scores

Preliminary rounds: Australia 7/278 (Turner 101, Walters 59) d Pakistan 205 by 73 runs at Leeds

Australia 5/328 d Sri Lanka 4/276 by 52 runs at the Oval.

Australia 192 lost to West Indies 3/195 by seven wickets at the Oval.

Semi-final, at Leeds: Australia 6/94 (Gilmour 28 not out) d England 93 (Gilmour 6/14) by four wickets.

Final: Australia 274 (I. Chappell 62, Turner 40; Boyce 4/50) lost to West Indies 8/291 (Lloyd 102, Kanhai 55; Gilmour 5/48) by 17 runs.

Lord's, June 21. Critics of limited-over cricket were applauding tonight, won over by an enthralling final of the first World Cup, in which the West Indies defeated Australia by 17 runs before a colourful, cheerful crowd of 26,000 at the headquarters of cricket.

Wrote John Woodcock in the *Times*: 'The curtain calls lasted until 9 p.m. By the time the last of the speeches had been made and the last of the lights put out, it was past midnight. The final had been a piece of theatre; of drama, tragedy, carnival and farce …'

Hero of the occasion was the West Indies captain, the tall bespectacled Clive Lloyd, who wields his bat like a bludgeon.

His 102 with 12 cracking fours and two 6s will long be remembered by those lucky enough to be at Lord's. It came after the Windies, sent in by Ian Chappell, had slumped to 3/50.

With Rohan Kanhai (55) in a supporting role, Lloyd saw the Windies to a respectable 8/291 off 60 overs. For Australia, Gary Gilmour took 5/48.

If the Australian fielding had been sharper, Lloyd would have departed at 26, when Ross Edwards just failed to hold a low catch at midwicket.

Giving chase, the Australians, 1/80 off 20 overs, might have won had they refrained from running each other out.

Viv Richards' deadly aim and some fatal hesitation by the Australians led to Ian Chappell (62), Alan Turner (40) and Greg Chappell being run out after the score had been 3/162.

Even at 9/233, with seven overs to go, all was not lost for Australia. The pitch was playing easily and Lillee and Thomson, not your usual run of rabbits, were enjoying themselves amid what Woodcock described as the crowd's 'rocking, rolling, shouting and clanging.'

For 40 minutes, the two fast bowlers swung, missed, defended, clouted and ran, adding 41 until Thomson, the striker, was run out, diving for his ground after being sent back by Lillee.

It was some time before Thomson emerged from the throng of chanting West Indian supporters, minus bat, gloves and sweater, but with his pride intact. A gallant loser, like all the Australians.

But the trophy was off to the Caribbean, in the safe hands of the Man of the Match, Clive Lloyd.

West Indies' inspiring captain Clive Loyd cracks a ball down the ground for 4, during his magnificent 102 in the World Cup final at Lord's.

World Cup gets Royal approval. The Queen, Prince Charles and the Duke of Edinburgh at an informal get-together with players from all the teams, before the preliminary matches got underway.

Mike Denness puts England on sticky

The 1975 Australians in London present a motley picture – long hair, broad lapels and flared trousers are in vogue.

Birmingham, July 14. The axe is about to fall on England captain Mike Denness. Appointed for the first Test only, he gambled by inviting Australia to bat, then suffered the indignity of having his team beaten by an innings and 85 runs with a day and a half left.

Next please. Odds-on favorite for his job is South African-born beanstalk Tony Greig, a good all-rounder who speaks with a South African accent.

Greig was marginally more successful than Denness in the Edgbaston debacle, scoring 8 and 7 and taking 1/43 with his medium-pace deliveries. Denness troubled the scorer to the tune of 3 and 8 in England's miserable 101 and 173, made on a rain-affected pitch that favoured the Australian pace trio of Dennis Lillee, Jeff Thomson and Max Walker. Their counterparts, Geoff Arnold and John Snow, a former scourge of Australia and recalled after a two-year break, had less favourable conditions.

Australia began by posting a first-innings score of 359 after looking vulnerable at 5/186. Rod Marsh (61) and Ross Edwards (56) steadied the ship after Rick McCosker (59) and Ian Chappell (52) had launched it successfully. Thommo, with a Test best of 49, gave the stern a breezy finale.

Then it rained and England, batting on a green-tinged wicket, was soon in trouble, Lillee claiming the hapless Dennis Amiss for 4. Amiss has fallen to Lillee for 0, 0, 0, 4 in their past four meetings. It was a procession all the way, England edging into three figures – 101. Lillee, economical and fast, took 5/15 off 15 overs and Walker 5/48.

Following on, England was destroyed by Thomson (5/35). Keith Fletcher's 51 was the only half century for poor old England.

Tony Greig is the new England captain

London, July 16. As expected, Tony Greig, the 29-year-old Sussex captain, will lead England in the second Test at Lord's. He phoned deposed captain Mike Denness to tell him of the news.

After the Edgbaston thrashing, England must come up with suitable support for Greig, regarded by the Australians as a tough opponent and fine player.

Greig was born in South Africa and lived there until 1966 when he moved to Sussex. His father was Scottish and his mother South African. Some say he should not lead England but he regards himself as English.

He has scored five Test centuries in 39 Tests and last year took 24 Test wickets in the Windies. Standing 6ft 7in., he lifts his bat while taking strike. He will help to pick the team for Lord's.

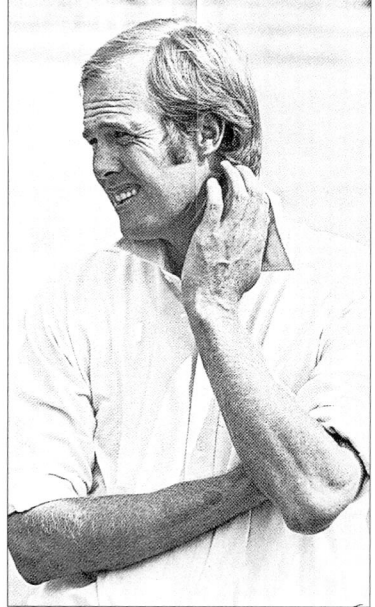

Tony Greig, new skipper.

Lillee the batsman

Lord's, Aug. 5. Dennis Lillee usually confronts a crisis with a bag of wickets. In the second Test, he scored a timely 73 not out off 103 balls as Australia struggled to match England's first innings of 315, which was propped up by new captain Tony Greig's 96 after Lillee had 'roared' with 4/33.

Australia managed 268, Ross Edwards contributing 99. Lillee's 73 was his highest first class score and he added 69 with Ashley Mallett for the last wicket. England then laboured to 7/436 declared, John Edrich scoring 175.

Greig set Australia a target of 484 to win in 500 minutes! With a draw inevitable, Australia ended with a rain-delayed 3/329. On day four, a Navy cook, Michael Angelow, became the first streaker in an England Test. He hurdled the stumps at 3.20 p.m.

Cricket pitched out at Leeds

Huge runs in longest game

Ian Chappell and Tony Greig examine the horror strip after vandals had done their dirty work.

Leeds, Aug. 19. Vandals have sabotaged the third Test, angering cricket lovers of both sides just as the series was coming to life.

With a full day to play and the game delicately poised, saboteurs broke into the ground overnight. They lifted the covers and dug holes in the pitch, filling the holes with oil and spraying it on the pitch, which was unplayable.

Officials and captains Ian Chappell and Tony Greig, after conferring with the head groundsman, took the only course possible – abandoning the game.

Australia, 1–up in the four-Test series, will retain the Ashes. There is widespread indignation that vandals, campaigning for the release of a convicted criminal, should use cricket as a vehicle for their grievances. Unfortunately, a policeman on night duty at the ground did not detect the vandals.

The day should have started with Australia needing 225 runs to win with seven wickets in hand – Rick McCosker on 95 and Doug Walters on 25. It seems the match was doomed anyway, for it rained from noon until 4 p.m.

For the record, England made 298 (Gary Gilmour 6/85), after which left-arm orthodox spinner Phil Edmonds, making his debut, took 5/28 and sent Australia packing for 135. England, batting again, made 291, giving Australia a stiff target of 444. At stumps on day four, the last day as it turned out, Australia was in good shape at 3/220. Or was it? We'll never know.

Good shot, no runs for Greg Chappell.

London, Sep. 3. When England followed on in the fourth Test at the Oval, few thought the match would go the full distance of six days. Are there two Englands? Why should a team that scores only 191 in its first innings, then amass 538?

After winning the toss, Ian Chappell chose to bat on a placid pitch. At 1/7, however, he found himself at the crease. With Rick McCosker, deprived of a century at Leeds, Chappell put on 277 for the second wicket in 344 minutes. McCosker went for 127 and Chappell for 192, his highest Test score against England. Brother Greg Chappell made nought in a total of 9/532 declared.

Jeff Thomson (4/50), Max Walker (4/63) and Dennis Lillee (2/44) went about their work vigorously and had England's batsmen coming and going like tube trains at nearby Kennington station – out for 191.

Then came the turnabout, led by Bob Woolmer, who ground his way to a century in 349 minutes, and was out for 149. Support roles were played by opener John Edrich 96, Graham Roope (77), and David Steele, who added 66 to his impressive Leeds double of 73 and 92. Grand total 538, Lillee toiling long and hard for 4/91 and Doug Walters helping out nicely with 4/34 off 10.5 overs. With 85 minutes in which to make 198, Australia was not to be tempted and ended with 2/40, retaining the Ashes 1–0 in a series that had more drama than the result indicates.

MOVES TO RESTRICT AUST. FAST BOWLERS ON ENGLISH TOUR!

ISN'T IT RAINING YET?

'Also ensure that those colonial scoundrels bowl underarm and make the ball bounce twice before arriving at the gentleman batsman!'

The money game – Players v Board

If Dennis Lillee is disenchanted with his salary, he doesn't show it at the MCG as he thunders in to bowl from the outer end.

He admits that the chant of 'Lill-ee, Lill-ee' from the rowdy folk in Bay 13 spurs him on. But there must be more to it than that. Playing for one's country has fired generations of Davis Cup players, Olympians and cricketers for peanuts.

Lillee would probably do it for nothing, but believes that money is better than poverty, if only from the point of view of self-respect. He has told a journalist that he believes players should be contracted to the Australian Cricket Board and be paid $25,000 to $30,000 a year.

A far cry from the $180 a match he received on his Test debut against England in Adelaide in 1971. His 5/84 cost the Board $36 per wicket.

The Board disagrees with Lillee on contracts. Secretary Alan Barnes says: 'The players are not professional. They are invited to play and if they don't like the conditions there are 500,000 other cricketers in Australia who would love to take their place.'

Lillee could argue that his professionalism enabled him to overcome a severe back injury suffered in 1972–73.

Meanwhile, Australian Test captain Ian Chappell is going in to bat for his players with the vigor of a Warwick Armstrong, who took on the Marylebone Cricket Club in 1921 and achieved two off-field victories – a rest day before each Test and drinks to be served in the dressing room at Lord's.

Chappell, who believes players are paid 'fish and chips money', has already tasted success as an advocate.

As Test captain, he attended the Board meeting in Melbourne the day before the sixth Australia v England Test at the MCG in 1974–75 and was told that on top of the $200 match fee for that series, each player would receive a $200 bonus per match and a sponsor's bonus of $157 – a grand total of $557 for each game.

In contrast to Barnes, the cricketers argue that professionalism is at hand, hastened by the aeroplane, which has resulted in an abundance of fixtures. From November 1970 until February 1975 – 51 months – Australia played in 31 Tests, five more than Bill O'Reilly managed in 78

Ian Chappell: vigorous advocate.

months from 1932–38 when players travelled by ship.

As a result of the huge success of the first World Cup, in which the West Indies beat Australia at Lord's, there is growing speculation of limited-over cricket ad infinitum. Not to mention sponsors and more money.

The Australians were less than sanguine about a quick resolution to their money problems. after the 1975 tour of England, despite retaining the Ashes.

On hearing the Board had made a profit of $78,000, they pointed out that their take, $2734 apiece, $182 a week for the 105-day tour, would leave them out of pocket.

Team manager Fred Bennett told them their bid for a match fee of $500 for the 1975–76 Test series at home against the West Indies would be put to the new Australian Cricket Board. The Board fixed the fee at $400.

In *Cricketer Annual*, editor Eric Beecher says that cricket requires a mediating force between the players and the administrators to resolve the cool climate. 'The gap, which has probably always existed, has been widened by players' requests for more money.'

There is a feeling that if the Board doesn't act soon over money, cricket will throw up a Jack Kramer, who caused an upheaval in tennis in the 1950s with his pro troupe. It lead to Open tennis, but only after much disruption and agony.

While agreeing with the sentiment, Ian Chappell did not say: 'Money is the most important thing in the world.' He didn't have to – these words were penned by George Bernard Shaw.

Arise, Sir Garfield

Arise Sir Garfield St Aubrun Sobers, dubbed cricket's latest knight.

Australian Averages

1975 ENGLAND v AUSTRALIA

AUSTRALIA	M	Inn	NO	Runs	H.S	Avrge	Ct	St	Overs	Mds	Runs	Wkt	Avrge
Chappell, GS	4	7	2	106	73*	21.20	9	-	12.0	2	53	-	-
Chappell, IM	4	6	-	429	192	71.50	2	-	29.0	8	82	1	82.00
Edwards, R	4	6	1	253	99	50.60	-	-	2.0	-	20	-	-
Gilmour, GJ	1	1	-	6	6	6.00	-	-	51.2	15	157	9	17.44
Lillee, DK	4	4	2	115	73*	57.50	-	-	207.0	72	460	21	21.90
Mallett, AA	4	4	3	23	14	23.00	5	-	161.0	57	386	9	42.89
Marsh, RW	4	5	-	133	61	26.60	14	1	-	-	-	-	-
McCosker, RB	4	7	2	414	127	82.80	1	-	-	-	-	-	-
Thomson, JR	4	4	-	82	49	20.50	3	-	175.1	56	457	16	28.56
Turner, A	3	5	-	77	37	15.40	2	-	-	-	-	-	-
Walker, MHN	4	4	-	25	13	6.25	1	-	204.1	59	486	14	34.71
Walters, KD	4	5	1	125	65	31.25	7	-	12.5	3	40	5	8.00

English Averages

1975 ENGLAND v AUSTRALIA

ENGLAND	M	Inn	NO	Runs	H.S	Avrge	Ct	St	Overs	Mds	Runs	Wkt	Avrge
Amiss, DL	2	4	-	19	10	4.75	1	-	-	-	-	-	-
Arnold, GG	1	2	2	6	6*	-	-	1	33.0	3	91	3	30.33
Denness, MH	1	2	-	11	8	5.50	1	-	-	-	-	-	-
Edmonds, PH	2	4	1	32	13*	10.67	-	-	81.1	20	224	6	37.33
Edrich, JH	4	8	-	428	175	53.50	1	-	-	-	-	-	-
Fletcher, KWR	2	4	-	79	51	19.75	2	-	-	-	-	-	-
Gooch, GA	2	4	-	37	31	9.25	2	-	-	-	-	-	-
Greig, AW	4	8	-	284	96	35.50	4	-	97.0	23	322	8	40.25
Hampshire, JH	1	2	-	14	14	7.00	1	-	-	-	-	-	-
Knott, APE	4	8	1	261	69	37.29	4	-	-	-	-	-	-
Lever, P	1	1	-	4	4	4.00	-	-	35.0	5	138	2	69.00
Old, CM	3	6	1	60	25*	12.00	4	-	91.0	22	283	7	40.43
Roope, GRJ	1	2	-	77	77	38.50	1	-	-	-	-	-	-
Snow, JA	4	7	-	84	34	12.00	-	-	135.5	31	355	11	32.27
Steele, DS	3	6	-	365	92	60.83	4	-	11.4	5	21	2	10.50
Underwood, DL	4	7	3	16	10	4.00	1	-	131.0	51	266	6	44.33
Wood, B	3	6	-	146	52	24.33	-	-	6.0	2	16	-	-
Woolmer, RA	2	4	-	218	149	54.50	1	-	34.0	9	72	2	36.00

FIRST TEST 1975 ENGLAND v AUSTRALIA
Edgbaston, Birmingham. July 10, 11, 12, 14, 1975.
Toss: England. Australia won by an innings & 85 runs.

AUSTRALIA

RB McCosker b Arnold	.59	
A Turner c Denness b Snow	.37	
IM Chappell (c) c Fletcher b Snow	.52	
GS Chappell lbw Old	.0	
R Edwards c Gooch b Old	.56	
KD Walters c Old b Greig	.14	
RW Marsh (+) c Fletcher b Arnold	.61	
MHN Walker c Knott b Snow	.7	
JR Thomson c Arnold b Underwood	.49	
DK Lillee c Knott b Arnold	.3	
AA Mallett not out	.3	
Extras (B 1, LB 8, NB 9)	.18	
TOTAL	.359	

FOW 1st Inns: 80 126 135 161 186 265 286 332 343 359

Bowling: *First Innings*: Arnold 33-3-91-3, Snow 33-6-86-3, Old 33-7-111-2, Greig 15-2-43-1, Underwood 7-3-10-1.

ENGLAND

JH Edrich lbw Lillee	.34	c Marsh b Walker	.5
DL Amiss b Lillee	.4	c (S)GJ Gilmour b Thomson	.5
KWR Fletcher c Mallett b Walker	.6	c Walters b Lillee	.51
MH Denness (c) c GS Chappell b Walker	.3	b Thomson	.8
GA Gooch c Marsh b Walker	.0	c Marsh b Thomson	.0
AW Greig c Marsh b Walker	.8	c Marsh b Walker	.7
APE Knott (+) b Lillee	.14	c McCosker b Thomson	.38
DL Underwood b Lillee	.10 (10)	b Mallett	.3
CM Old c GS Chappell b Walker	.13 (8)	c Walters b Lillee	.7
JA Snow lbw Lillee	.0 (9)	c Marsh b Thomson	.34
GG Arnold not out	.0	not out	.6
Extras (LB 3, W 5, NB 1)	.9	(LB 5, W 2, NB 2)	.9
TOTAL	.101		.173

FOW 1st Inns: 9 24 46 46 54 75 78 87 97 101
FOW 2nd Inns: 7 18 20 52 90 100 122 141 167 173

Bowling: *First Innings*: Lillee 15-8-15-5, Thomson 10-3-21-0, Walker 17.3-5-48-5, Mallett 3-1-8-0. *Second Innings*: Lillee 20-8-45-2, Walker 24-9-47-2, Thomson 18-8-38-5, Mallett 13.2-6-34-1.

Umpires: HD Bird & AE Fagg

SECOND TEST 1975 ENGLAND v AUSTRALIA
Lord's Cricket Ground, London. July 31, August 1, 2, 4, 5, 1975.
Toss: England. Match Drawn.

ENGLAND

B Wood lbw Lillee	.6	c Marsh b Thomson	.52
JH Edrich lbw Lillee	.9	c Thomson b Mallett	.175
DS Steele b Thomson	.50	c & b Walters	.45
DL Amiss lbw Lillee	.0	c GS Chappell b Lillee	.10
GA Gooch c Marsh b Lillee	.6	b Mallett	.31
AW Greig (c) c IM Chappell b Walker	.96	c Walters b IM Chappell	.41
APE Knott (+) lbw Thomson	.69	not out	.22
RA Woolmer c Turner b Mallett	.33	b Mallett	.31
JA Snow c Walker b Mallett	.11		
DL Underwood not out	.0		
P Lever lbw Walker	.4		
Extras (B 3, LB 1, W 4, NB 23)	.31	(LB 18, W 2, NB 9)	.29
TOTAL	.315		.7 dec 436

FOW 1st Inns: 10 29 31 49 145 222 288 309 310 315
FOW 2nd Inns: 111 215 249 315 380 387 436

Bowling: *First Innings*: Lillee 20-4-84-4, Thomson 24-7-92-2, Walker 21.4-7-52-2, Mallett 22-4-56-2. *Second Innings*: Lillee 33-10-80-1, Thomson 29-8-73-1, Walker 37-8-95-0, Mallett 36.4-10-127-3, IM Chappell 10-2-26-1, Walters 2-0-6-1.

AUSTRALIA

RB McCosker c & b Lever	.29	lbw Steele	.79
A Turner lbw Snow	.9	c Gooch b Greig	.21
IM Chappell (c) c Knott b Snow	.2	lbw Greig	.86
GS Chappell lbw Snow	.4	not out	.73
R Edwards lbw Woolmer	.99	not out	.52
KD Walters c Greig b Lever	.2		
RW Marsh (+) c Amiss b Greig	.3		
MHN Walker b Snow	.5		
JR Thomson b Underwood	.17		
DK Lillee not out	.73		
AA Mallett lbw Steele	.14		
Extras (LB 5, NB 6)	.11	(B 4, NB 14)	.18
TOTAL	.268		.3 for 329

FOW 1st Inns: 21 29 37 54 56 64 81 133 199 268
FOW 2nd Inns: 50 169 222

Bowling: *First Innings*: Snow 21-4-66-4, Lever 15-0-83-2, Woolmer 13-5-31-1, Greig 15-5-47-1, Underwood 13-5-29-1, Steele 0.4-0-1-1. *Second Innings*: Snow 19-3-82-0, Lever 20-5-55-0, Greig 26-6-82-2, Underwood 31-14-64-0, Woolmer 3-1-3-0, Steele 9-4-19-1, Wood 1-0-6-0.

Umpires: WE Alley & TW Spencer

THIRD TEST 1975 ENGLAND v AUSTRALIA
Headingley, Leeds. August 14, 15, 16, 18, 19 (no play), 1975.
Toss: England. Match Drawn.

ENGLAND

B Wood lbw Gilmour	.9	lbw Walker	.25
JH Edrich c Mallett b Thomson	.62	b Mallett	.35
DS Steele c Walters b Thomson	.73	c GS Chappell b Gilmour	.92
JH Hampshire lbw Gilmour	.14 (7)	c GS Chappell b Thomson	.0
KWR Fletcher c Mallett b Lillee	.8 (4)	c GS Chappell b Lillee	.14
AW Greig (c) run out	.51 (5)	c & b Mallett	.49
APE Knott (+) lbw Gilmour	.14 (8)	c Thomson b Lillee	.31
PH Edmonds not out	.13 (9)	c (S)A Turner b Gilmour	.8
CM Old b Gilmour	.5 (6)	st Marsh b Mallett	.10
JA Snow c Walters b Walker	.0	c Marsh b Gilmour	.9
DL Underwood c GS Chappell b Gilmour	.0	not out	.0
Extras (B 4, LB 15, W 11, NB 9)	.39	(B 5, LB 2, W 2, NB 9)	.18
TOTAL	.288		.291

FOW 1st Inns: 25 137 159 189 213 268 269 284 284 288
FOW 2nd Inns: 55 70 103 197 209 210 272 276 285 291

Bowling: *First Innings*: Lillee 28-12-53-1, Thomson 22-8-53-2, Gilmour 31.2-10-85-6, Walker 18-4-54-0, IM Chappell 2-0-4-0. *Second Innings*: Lillee 20-5-48-2, Gilmour 20-5-72-3, Thomson 20-6-67-1, Walker 15-4-36-1, Mallett 19-4-50-3.

AUSTRALIA

RB McCosker c Hampshire b Old	.0	not out	.95
RW Marsh (+) b Snow	.25	b Underwood	.12
IM Chappell (c) b Edmonds	.35	lbw Old	.62
GS Chappell c Underwood b Edmonds	.13	c Steele b Edmonds	.12
R Edwards lbw Edmonds	.0		
KD Walters b Edmonds	.19 (5)	not out	.25
GJ Gilmour c Greig b Underwood	.6		
MHN Walker c Old b Edmonds	.0		
JR Thomson c Steele b Snow	.16		
DK Lillee b Snow	.11		
AA Mallett not out	.1		
Extras (LB 5, W 1, NB 3)	.9	(B 4, LB 8, NB 2)	.14
TOTAL	.135		.3 for 220

FOW 1st Inns: 8 53 78 78 81 96 104 107 128 135
FOW 2nd Inns: 55 161 174

Bowling: *First Innings*: Snow 18.5-7-22-3, Old 11-3-30-1, Greig 3-0-14-0, Wood 5-2-10-0, Underwood 19-12-22-1, Edmonds 20-7-28-5. *Second Innings*: Old 17-5-61-1, Snow 15-6-21-0, Underwood 15-4-40-1, Edmonds 17-4-64-1, Greig 9-3-20-0.

Umpires: DJ Constant & AE Fagg

FOURTH TEST 1975 ENGLAND v AUSTRALIA
Kennington Oval, London. August 28, 29, 30, September 1, 2, 3, 1975.
Toss: Australia. Match Drawn.

AUSTRALIA

RB McCosker c Roope b Old	.127	not out	.25
A Turner c Steele b Old	.2	c Woolmer b Greig	.8
IM Chappell (c) c Greig b Woolmer	.192		
GS Chappell c Knott b Old	.4	not out	.4
R Edwards c Edrich b Snow	.44 (3)	c Old b Underwood	.2
KD Walters b Underwood	.65		
RW Marsh (+) c & b Greig	.32		
MHN Walker c Steele b Greig	.13		
JR Thomson c Old b Greig	.0		
DK Lillee not out	.28		
AA Mallett not out	.5		
Extras (LB 5, W 2, NB 17)	.24	(LB 1)	.1
TOTAL	.9 dec 532		.2 for 40

FOW 1st Inns: 7 284 286 356 396 441 477 477 501
FOW 2nd Inns: 22 33

Bowling: *First Innings*: Old 28-7-74-3, Steele 2-1-1-0, Woolmer 18-3-38-1, Edmonds 38-7-118-0, Underwood 44-13-96-1, Greig 24-5-107-3, Snow 27-4-74-1. *Second Innings*: Old 2-0-7-0, Snow 2-1-4-0, Edmonds 6.1-2-14-0, Underwood 2-0-5-1, Greig 5-2-9-1.

ENGLAND

B Wood b Walker	.32	lbw Thomson	.22
JH Edrich lbw Walker	.12	b Lillee	.96
DS Steele b Lillee	.39	c Marsh b Lillee	.66
GRJ Roope c Turner b Walker	.0	b Lillee	.77
RA Woolmer c Mallett b Thomson	.5	lbw Walters	.149
AW Greig (c) c Marsh b Lillee	.17	c Marsh b Lillee	.15
APE Knott (+) lbw Walker	.9	c Marsh b Walters	.64
PH Edmonds c Marsh b Thomson	.4 (9)	run out	.7
CM Old not out	.25 (8)	c IM Chappell b Walters	.0
JA Snow c GS Chappell b Thomson	.30	c & b Walters	.0
DL Underwood c GS Chappell b Thomson	.0	not out	.3
Extras (LB 3, W 3, NB 12)	.18	(B 2, LB 15, W 5, NB 17)	.39
TOTAL	.191		.538

FOW 1st Inns: 45 78 83 96 103 125 131 147 190 191
FOW 2nd Inns: 77 202 209 331 371 522 522 533 533 538

Bowling: *First Innings*: Lillee 19-7-44-2, Thomson 22.1-7-50-4, Walker 25-7-63-4, Mallett 3-1-16-0. *Second Innings*: Lillee 52-18-91-4, Thomson 30-9-63-1, Walker 46-15-91-0, Mallett 64-31-95-0, IM Chappell 17-6-52-0, GS Chappell 12-2-53-0, Walters 10.5-3-34-4, Edwards 2-0-20-0.

Umpires: HD Bird & TW Spencer

Chappell's captaincy handover an easy family matter

Brisbane, Dec. 1. When Ian Chappell announced on September 3, the last day of the final test at the Oval against England, that he would be retiring as Australian captain but would be available as a player, few imagined the handover to brother Greg would be smooth as it has been.

The form of both players has been outstanding. Greg Chappell has copped some backhanded criticism because he is supposed to be lucky that the side is ticking like clockwork.

But as he said 'This was Ian's great contribution of course. The side was running itself. I don't think it would have mattered if Billy the Goose had taken over really. You'd really have to try to bugger it up to ruin Ian's good work quickly.'

Dennis Lillee downs old mate

Perth, Nov. 18. Dennis Lillee has demonstrated that the Australian fast bowler's fraternity only applies when they are in the same team.

On day three of the Sheffield Shield game against Victoria he bowled a short lifter at Australian team-mate Max Walker and struck him below the left eye, fracturing his cheekbone, and causing him to be taken off on a stretcher.

Victoria collapsed in its second innings to be all out for 122, Lillee taking 5/58 plus Walker.

Aside from anything else this meant the lion-hearted Walker was unable to bowl in WA's second innings. The Sandgropers made the 162 required for victory against an attack of Alan Hurst and Trevor Laughlin – with the third bowler used being Ian Redpath. They lost six wickets in doing so and Rod Marsh was dropped on one, before going on to record 76.

Marsh also equalled the world record for first class dismissals in a match by a 'keeper, taking eleven catches for the game – six off them off Lillee.

First Tests ignites crowds

Greg Chappell, Dennis Lillee and Fred Bennett celebrate after the first Test.

Perth, Dec. 16. Some hot batting under the hot sun enabled the West Indies to square the series at a win apiece on the fast and true pitch at the WACA. Roy Fredericks gave one of the great displays of power hitting when he blazed a hundred of his 169 in 116 minutes off just 71 balls after lunch on the second day.

Clive Lloyd followed with an equally powerful 149 in 219 minutes as the West Indies posted a 260-run lead. That it wasn't a greater lead may be laid at the door of Ian Chappell, whose 156 was the major part of Australia's first innings of 329.

Andy Roberts with 14 overs of sustained pace, hostility and accuracy destroyed Australia's second innings, with 7/54. West Indies won by an innings and 87 runs, and the first Test at Brisbane seemed some time ago.

Or so it must have seemed to Greg Chappell, who in his first Test as captain scored a century in each innings, a first in Test cricket, as the West Indies policy is attack at all costs – which meant attack at a great deal of cost.

At lunch on the first day the West Indies had scored 125 – but had lost six wickets as well, but were all out 214. Two centuries from Alvin Kallicharran and Lawrence Rowe saw the West Indies to 370 in the second innings but that was never going to be enough. Ian Chappell's patient 74 and Greg's imperious 109 saw Australia home by eight wickets. The big crowd went home happy.

Thommo's $633,000 Queensland deal

Brisbane, Jan. 20. Jeff Thomson has signed a $633,000 deal to play cricket and work in Queensland for radio station 4IP for ten years in the most lucrative contract offered to a cricketer anywhere in the world.

Thommo says the new contract won't go to his head.

'Am I the same Thommo now as I was a couple of years ago … Too right I'm the same bloke, but with one major exception – I reckon I'm far more responsible now than then. I sure had nothing to beat …

'Few people believe me when I say I hadn't seen a Sheffield Shield or Test match until I played in them. I honestly cannot remember ever wanting to wear the NSW blue or the green and gold cap of Australia…'

Hello hello, what's all this then?

Australia romps in as Windies self-destruct

Ian Chappell catches Lawrence Rowe from the bowling of Jeff Thomson in the third Test at the MCG.

Melbourne, Feb. 5. One newspaper story which appeared after just three days of the sixth Test was headed: 'Woeful Windies – It was just a massacre at the MCG. The West Indies cricketers are becoming an embarrassment.'

That was after Gary Gilmour destroyed the West Indies chase for Australia's modest 351 (Ian Redpath 101) with 5/34 from ten overs. Dennis Lillee chimed in for the other five for 63. West Indies all out 160.

Viv Richards made 50 of them and then 98 of the second innings 326 (with Clive Lloyd a defiant 91 not out), after Greg Chappell set them a mammoth 492 at lunch on the fourth day. Rick McCosker was 109 not out, and Ian Redpath made another 70 in his final Test.

Australia had won the series 5–1, a humiliation for a team which had come with such high hopes and possessed such great talent.

Highlight of the other Tests were the huge crowds at the third Test in Melbourne where the first day's attendance came close to breaking the world-record crowd for one day of Test cricket, with 85,596.

And debutante Gary Cosier, a 'reject' from Victorian cricket, dropped Roy Fredericks on the first morning with his first touch of a ball in Test cricket, but made up for it by completing a hundred on the morning of day three.

Jeff Thomson took nine wickets for the match in the fourth Test and Greg Chappell made 182 magnificent runs in a seven-wicket win. In the fifth Test in Adelaide, Redpath and Alan Turner made centuries, Graham Yallop made 47 and 43 in his second Test and Australia won by 190 runs.

Paulsen gets 8/71

Perth, Dec. 9. In an amazing match of runs and ruins, WA legspinner Bob Paulsen bowled his side to a 115-run win with a startling 8/71 in the second innings.

WA was 188 behind on the first innings after making 291 (Ian Brayshaw a quick 100), to which the West Indies replied with a pounding 479 – Roy Fredericks 108, Alvin Kallicharran 175 and Viv Richards 105. A strong WA second innings anchored by Kim Hughes 102 saw the deficit become a 333 lead – which was gettable, except for Paulsen.

It appeared that the West Indian batsmen could not 'read' his array of leggies and wrong'uns, with predictable (in hindsight) results.

'Redders' quits while on top

Melbourne, Feb. 5. Ian Redpath, man of the match in the sixth Test after he made 101 and 70, announced his retirement. He is 34 and is the Australian vice-captain, and will leave a big hole in the Australian top order. In this series he has made 575 runs at 52.27, the second-highest aggregate behind Greg Chappell's 702 (at 117).

Richie Benaud wrote in the Melbourne *Herald* 'I am sorry to see 'Redders' has given big cricket away. Cricketers do not come any better, more versatile or as better team men.'

Redpath had the reputation for being a bit slow and stodgy, but that was because he saw his role as a top-order batsman. He was really a free flowing stylist in disguise – one who once hit 32 off one over against Orange Free State in 1969–70 in South Africa.

SA win Shield

Brisbane March 5. A wash-out of the last two days of the Shield match between Queensland and South Australia did not stop last year's wooden spooners, South Australia, from taking the trophy.

Under Ian Chappell, SA dragged itself up by its bootstraps. Early in the season Chappell told his mixture of old stagers such as Terry Jenner and Ashley Mallett, and young tyros such as Gary Cosier, Wayne Prior, David Hookes and RickDarling that 'if everyone, especially the young players, really wanted to, we could win the Shield.' This they did with five wins.

The team spirit and will to win sometimes overflowed, but the cricket was of a very high standard.

One million season

Melbourne, Feb. 10. Big crowds for all six Test matches saw a total 'box office' of $1,110,685 – the first million-dollar series.

The first Test attendance in Brisbane was 64,383; second Test in Perth 65,974; third Test in Melbourne 222,755; fourth Test in Sydney 160,499; fifth Test in Adelaide 103,819; and the sixth Test in Melbourne 119,619.

This makes a total of 737,049 people who watched Test cricket in Australia in 1975–76.

The slump in Melbourne attendance may be put down to the fact that the series was already decided.

Despite this, the West Indies Board has asked for an extra $100,000 for the tour.

Lance Gibbs with the trophy for breaking the world record number of wickets in Tests – Gary Gilmour in the sixth Test was his 309th.

Ian Redpath loses his cap hooking Andy Roberts in his fifth-Test 103 at Adelaide.

Four great Australian captains line up during the making of a coaching film. From left: Ian Chappell, Bill Lawry, Bob Simpson and Richie Benaud.

FIRST TEST 1975–76 AUSTRALIA v WEST INDIES
Brisbane Cricket Ground, Brisbane. November 28, 29, 30, December 2, 1975.
Toss: West Indies. Australia won by 8 wkts.

WEST INDIES
RC Fredericks c Marsh b Gilmour	46	c Marsh b Gilmour	7
CG Greenidge lbw Lillee	0	c McCosker b Gilmour	0
LG Rowe run out	28	(4) c IM Chappell b Jenner	107
AI Kallicharran c Turner b Lillee	4	(5) b Mallett	101
IVA Richards c Gilmour b Lillee	0	(7) run out	12
CH Lloyd (c) c Marsh b Gilmour	7	c Redpath b Jenner	0
DL Murray (+) c Mallett b Gilmour	66	(8) c & b Mallett	55
MA Holding c GS Chappell b Gilmour	34	(3) c Turner b Lillee	19
Inshan Ali c Redpath b Thomson	12	b Lillee	24
AME Roberts c IM Chappell b Mallett	3	lbw Lillee	3
LR Gibbs not out	11	not out	4
Extras (B 1, NB 2)	3	(B 4, LB 15, W 5, NB 14)	38
TOTAL	214		370

FOW 1st Inns: 3 63 70 70 81 99 171 199 199 214
FOW 2nd Inns: 6 12 50 248 248 269 275 346 348 370

Bowling: *First Innings*: Lillee 11-0-84-3, Thomson 10-0-69-1, Gilmour 12-1-42-4, Jenner 4-1-15-0, Mallett 0.5-0-1-1. *Second Innings*: Lillee 16-3-72-3, Gilmour 11-4-26-2, Thomson 18-3-89-0, Mallett 21.4-6-70-2, Jenner 20-2-75-2.

AUSTRALIA
IR Redpath run out	39	b Gibbs	26
A Turner b Roberts	81	not out	74
IM Chappell lbw Gibbs	41	not out	109
GS Chappell (c) c Greenidge b Roberts	123		
RB McCosker c Kallicharran b Inshan	1	(1) c Murray b Roberts	2
RW Marsh (+) c Murray b Gibbs	48		
GJ Gilmour c Lloyd b Gibbs	13		
TJ Jenner not out	6		
DK Lillee b Roberts	1		
JR Thomson lbw Gibbs	4		
AA Mallett c Fredericks b Gibbs	0		
Extras (LB 5, NB 4)	9	(B 5, LB 2, NB 1)	8
TOTAL	366		2 for 219

FOW 1st Inns: 99 142 178 195 317 350 354 361 366 366
FOW 2nd Inns: 7 60

Bowling: *First Innings*: Roberts 25-2-85-3, Holding 20-4-81-0, Gibbs 38-7-102-5, Inshan 17-1-67-1, Lloyd 6-1-22-0. *Second Innings*: Roberts 14-2-47-1, Holding 10-0-46-0, Gibbs 20-8-48-1, Inshan 10-0-57-0, Fredericks 2-0-12-0, Kallicharran 0.2-0-1-0.

Umpires: RC Bailhache & TF Brooks

Australian Averages

1975–76 AUSTRALIA v WEST INDIES
AUSTRALIA	M	Inn	NO	Runs	H.S	Avrge	Ct	St	Overs	Mds	Runs	Wkt	Avrge
Chappell, GS	6	11	5	702	182*	117.00	7	-	21.2	-	69	3	23.00
Chappell, IM	6	12	2	449	156	44.90	7	-	12.6	4	54	2	27.00
Cosier, GJ	3	3	-	174	109	58.00	-	-	12.0	1	51	-	-
Gilmour, GJ	5	7	-	185	95	26.43	4	-	97.6	17	406	20	20.30
Jenner, TJ	1	1	1	6	6*	-	-	-	24.0	3	90	2	45.00
Lillee, DK	5	6	3	77	25	25.67	1	-	129.3	7	712	27	26.37
Mallett, AA	6	8	2	66	18*	11.00	8	-	119.1	19	506	11	46.00
Marsh, RW	6	8	-	236	56	29.50	26	-	-	-	-	-	-
McCosker, RB	4	8	2	172	109*	28.67	3	-	-	-	-	-	-
Redpath, IR	6	11	-	575	103	52.27	8	-	-	-	-	-	-
Thomson, JR	6	7	-	63	44	9.00	3	-	150.5	15	831	29	28.66
Turner, A	6	12	-	439	136	36.58	4	-	-	-	-	-	-
Walker, MHN	3	4	-	13	8	3.25	2	-	79.3	14	320	11	29.09
Yallop, GN	3	5	1	179	57	44.75	1	-	-	-	-	-	-

West Indian Averages

1975–76 AUSTRALIA v WEST INDIES
WEST INDIES	M	Inn	NO	Runs	H.S	Avrge	Ct	St	Overs	Mds	Runs	Wkt	Avrge
Baichan, L	1	2	-	23	20	11.50	-	-	-	-	-	-	-
Boyce, KD	4	7	2	240	95*	48.00	1	-	82.2	6	361	9	40.11
Fredericks, RC	6	11	-	417	169	37.91	4	-	13.0	1	62	1	62.00
Gibbs, LR	6	11	6	43	13	8.60	4	-	232.5	48	652	16	40.75
Greenidge, CG	2	4	-	11	8	2.75	1	-	1.0	1	0	-	-
Holder, VA	3	6	1	82	24	16.40	1	-	109.0	7	513	13	39.46
Holding, MA	5	9	-	95	34	10.56	3	-	140.5	15	614	10	61.40
Inshan Ali	1	2	-	36	24	18.00	-	-	27.0	1	124	1	124.00
Julien, BD	3	5	1	124	46*	31.00	2	-	68.4	8	303	11	27.55
Kallicharran, AI	6	11	-	421	101	38.27	3	-	3.1	1	21	1	21.00
Lloyd, CH	6	11	1	469	149	46.90	5	-	17.0	4	56	-	-
Murray, DL	6	11	-	342	66	31.09	17	-	-	-	-	-	-
Richards, IVA	6	11	-	426	101	38.73	6	-	8.1	-	44	-	-
Roberts, AME	5	9	-	40	17	4.44	-	-	141.6	15	580	22	26.36
Rowe, LG	6	11	-	270	107	24.55	2	-	1.0	-	6	-	-

SECOND TEST 1975–76 AUSTRALIA v WEST INDIES
W.A.C.A. Ground, Perth. December 12, 13, 14, 16, 1975.
Toss: Australia. West Indies won by an innings & 87 runs.

AUSTRALIA
RB McCosker lbw Roberts	0	c Rowe b Roberts	13
A Turner c Gibbs b Roberts	23	c Murray b Roberts	0
IM Chappell b Holding	156	c (S)CG Greenidge b Roberts	20
GS Chappell (c) c Murray b Julien	13	c Rowe b Roberts	43
IR Redpath c Murray b Julien	33	lbw Roberts	0
RW Marsh (+) c Julien b Boyce	23	c Murray b Roberts	39
GJ Gilmour c Julien b Gibbs	45	c Fredericks b Roberts	3
MHN Walker c Richards b Holding	1	c (S)CG Greenidge b Julien	3
DK Lillee not out	12	c Lloyd b Julien	4
JR Thomson b Holding	0	b Julien	9
AA Mallett b Holding	0	not out	18
Extras (B 12, LB 5, NB 6)	23	(B 13, LB 2, NB 2)	17
TOTAL	329		169

FOW 1st Inns: 0 37 70 149 189 277 285 329 329 329
FOW 2nd Inns: 0 25 45 45 124 128 132 142 146 169

Bowling: *First Innings*: Roberts 13-1-65-2, Boyce 12-2-53-1, Holding 18.7-1-88-4, Julien 12-0-51-2, Gibbs 14-4-49-1. *Second Innings*: Roberts 14-3-54-7, Holding 10.6-1-53-0, Julien 10.1-1-32-3, Boyce 2-0-8-0, Fredericks 1-0-2-0, Gibbs 3-1-3-0.

WEST INDIES
RC Fredericks c GS Chappell b Lillee	169
BD Julien c Mallett b Gilmour	25
LG Rowe c Marsh b Thomson	19
AI Kallicharran c IM Chappell b Walker	57
IVA Richards c Gilmour b Thomson	12
CH Lloyd (c) b Gilmour	149
DL Murray (+) c Marsh b Lillee	63
MA Holding c Marsh b Thomson	0
KD Boyce not out	49
AME Roberts b Walker	0
LR Gibbs run out	13
Extras (B 2, LB 16, NB 11)	29
TOTAL	585

FOW 1st Inns: 91 134 258 297 461 461 522 548 548 585

Bowling: *First Innings*: Lillee 20-0-123-2, Thomson 17-0-128-3, Gilmour 14-0-103-2, Walker 17-1-99-2, Mallett 26-4-103-0, IM Chappell 1.4-1-0-0.

Umpires: RR Ledwidge & MG O'Connell

THIRD TEST 1975–76 AUSTRALIA v WEST INDIES
Melbourne Cricket Ground, Melbourne. December 26, 27, 28, 30, 1975.
Toss: Australia. Australia won by 8 wkts.

WEST INDIES

RC Fredericks c McCosker b Thomson	59	b GS Chappell	26
CG Greenidge c Marsh b Thomson	3	c Marsh b Walker	8
LG Rowe c IM Chappell b Thomson	0	c Marsh b Lillee	8
AI Kallicharran c Marsh b Thomson	20	c Marsh b Lillee	32
IVA Richards b Lillee	41	c Marsh b Thomson	36
CH Lloyd (c) c GS Chappell b Thomson	2	c Lillee b Mallett	102
DL Murray (+) c Walker b Lillee	24	c Marsh b Lillee	22
BD Julien c Mallett b Lillee	18	b Walker	27
VA Holder b Walker	24	run out	15
AME Roberts c Marsh b Lillee	6	c Mallett b IM Chappell	5
LR Gibbs not out	0	not out	5
Extras (LB 4, W 1, NB 22)	27	(B 8, LB 4, NB 14)	26
TOTAL	224		312

FOW 1st Inns: 22 22 91 103 108 167 172 199 218 224
FOW 2nd Inns: 14 48 48 99 151 229 278 288 297 312

Bowling: *First Innings*: Lillee 14-2-56-4, Thomson 11-1-62-5, Walker 13-1-46-1, Cosier 4-0-15-0, Mallett 5-1-18-0. *Second Innings*: Lillee 15-1-70-3, Walker 19-1-74-2, GS Chappell 7-1-23-1, IM Chappell 5.2-3-7-1, Thomson 9-0-51-1, Mallett 14-0-61-1.

AUSTRALIA

IR Redpath b Roberts	102 (3)	c (S)KD Boyce b Julien	9
A Turner b Roberts	21	b Roberts	7
RB McCosker c Murray b Julien	4 (1)	not out	22
IM Chappell c Kallicharran b Gibbs	35	not out	13
GS Chappell (c) c Murray b Julien	52		
GJ Cosier c Kallicharran b Roberts	109		
RW Marsh (+) c & b Gibbs	56		
MHN Walker c Murray b Roberts	1		
DK Lillee c Richards b Holder	25		
JR Thomson lbw Julien	44		
AA Mallett not out	3		
Extras (B 5, LB 6, NB 22)	33	(LB 1, NB 3)	4
TOTAL	485		2 for 55

FOW 1st Inns: 49 61 151 188 302 390 392 415 471 485
FOW 2nd Inns: 23 36

Bowling: *First Innings*: Roberts 32-2-126-4, Holder 27-2-123-1, Julien 28.3-5-120-3, Gibbs 30-9-81-2, Richards 1-0-2-0. *Second Innings*: Roberts 3-0-19-1, Julien 3-0-13-1, Greenidge 1-1-0-0, Rowe 1-0-6-0, Kallicharran 0.7-0-13-0.

Umpires: RC Bailhache & JR Collins

FIFTH TEST 1975–76 AUSTRALIA v WEST INDIES
Adelaide Oval, Adelaide. January 23, 24, 26, 27, 28, 1976.
Toss: Australia. Australia won by 190 runs.

AUSTRALIA

IR Redpath b Gibbs	103	c Lloyd b Gibbs	65
A Turner b Boyce	26	c Richards b Gibbs	136
GN Yallop c Richards b Holder	47	lbw Holder	43
IM Chappell lbw Holder	42	run out	23
GS Chappell (c) c Richards b Holder	4	not out	48
GJ Cosier c Murray b Holder	37		
RW Marsh (+) b Roberts	24 (6)	c Murray b Holder	1
GJ Gilmour c Holding b Gibbs	95 (7)	c Fredericks b Holder	0
AA Mallett c Fredericks b Holding	5 (8)	c Murray b Gibbs	11
JR Thomson c Murray b Holder	6		
DK Lillee not out	16		
Extras (B 1, LB 9, W 1, NB 2)	13	(LB 7, NB 11)	18
TOTAL	418		7 dec 345

FOW 1st Inns: 43 171 190 199 259 272 327 355 362 418
FOW 2nd Inns: 148 253 261 302 318 318 345

Bowling: *First Innings*: Roberts 12-1-54-1, Holding 22-3-126-1, Boyce 7-0-40-1, Holder 21-1-108-5, Gibbs 26-4-77-2. *Second Innings*: Roberts 4-0-24-0, Holding 14-0-55-0, Boyce 5-0-22-0, Holder 23-2-115-3, Gibbs 32.5-5-106-3, Fredericks 1-0-5-0.

WEST INDIES

RC Fredericks lbw Gilmour	0	lbw Lillee	10
IVA Richards c Yallop b Thomson	30	b Lillee	101
LG Rowe run out	7	c GS Chappell b Thomson	15
AI Kallicharran lbw Thomson	76	c Redpath b Mallett	67
CH Lloyd (c) lbw Lillee	6	b Mallett	5
DL Murray (+) c Mallett b Lillee	18	c Marsh b Thomson	6
KD Boyce not out	95	c (S)MHN Walker b Mallett	69
MA Holding c Mallett b Thomson	8	c IM Chappell b Gilmour	10
VA Holder lbw Thomson	0	c Marsh b Gilmour	7
AME Roberts c Redpath b IM Chappell	17	c & b Gilmour	0
LR Gibbs b Gilmour	3	not out	0
Extras (LB 1, NB 13)	14	(B 1, LB 2, W 1, NB 5)	9
TOTAL	274		299

FOW 1st Inns: 0 21 50 78 110 149 171 171 239 274
FOW 2nd Inns: 23 55 182 189 212 216 265 285 299 299

Bowling: *First Innings*: Gilmour 8.2-1-37-2, Thomson 11-0-68-4, Lillee 10-0-68-2, Cosier 5-0-23-0, Mallett 5-0-37-0, IM Chappell 2-0-23-1, GS Chappell 1-0-4-0. *Second Innings*: Lillee 14-0-64-2, Thomson 12-2-66-2, Gilmour 10.4-1-44-3, GS Chappell 5-0-21-0, Mallett 20-3-91-3, IM Chappell 1-0-4-0.

Umpires: TF Brooks & MG O'Connell

FOURTH TEST 1975–76 AUSTRALIA v WEST INDIES
Sydney Cricket Ground, Sydney. January 3, 4, 5, 7, 1976.
Toss: Australia. Australia won by 7 wkts.

WEST INDIES

RC Fredericks c IM Chappell b Thomson	48	c Turner b Gilmour	24
BD Julien not out	46 (9)	lbw Walker	8
AI Kallicharran c Redpath b Thomson	9 (2)	c Walker b Thomson	7
LG Rowe b Walker	67	c Marsh b Thomson	7
IVA Richards c IM Chappell b GS Chappell	44 (3)	c Thomson b Gilmour	2
CH Lloyd (c) c Turner b Walker	51	c Marsh b Thomson	19
DL Murray (+) c Thomson b Walker	32	b Thomson	50
KD Boyce c & b Mallett	16	c Redpath b Thomson	0
MA Holding hit wicket b Thomson	2 (5)	b Thomson	9
AME Roberts c Marsh b Walker	4	b Walker	2
LR Gibbs c Marsh b GS Chappell	5	not out	0
Extras (B 5, LB 14, W 9, NB 3)	31		0
TOTAL	355		128

FOW 1st Inns: 44 87 160 213 233 259 321 321 346 355
FOW 2nd Inns: 23 32 33 47 52 95 95 120 126 128

Bowling: *First Innings*: Thomson 25-5-117-3, Gilmour 13-2-54-0, Walker 21-8-70-4, Cosier 3-1-13-0, Mallett 13-4-50-1, IM Chappell 1-0-10-0, GS Chappell 4.2-0-10-2. *Second Innings*: Thomson 15-4-50-6, Gilmour 12-4-40-2, Walker 9.3-3-31-2, GS Chappell 2-0-5-0, Mallett 1-0-2-0.

AUSTRALIA

IR Redpath c Murray b Holding	25	b Boyce	28
A Turner c Lloyd b Boyce	53	c Murray b Holding	15
GN Yallop c Murray b Julien	16	not out	16
IM Chappell c Murray b Holding	4	c (S)CG Greenidge b Kallicharran	9
GS Chappell (c) not out	182		6
GJ Cosier b Holding	28		
RW Marsh (+) c Gibbs b Julien	38		
GJ Gilmour run out	20		
MHN Walker c Lloyd b Roberts	8		
JR Thomson c Richards b Roberts	0		
AA Mallett lbw Roberts	13		
Extras (B 3, LB 8, W 2, NB 5)	18	(LB 4, W 4)	8
TOTAL	405		3 for 82

FOW 1st Inns: 70 93 103 103 202 319 348 377 377 405
FOW 2nd Inns: 45 51 67

Bowling: *First Innings*: Roberts 20.6-3-94-3, Holding 21-2-79-3, Boyce 16-1-75-1, Gibbs 18-3-52-0, Julien 15-2-87-2. *Second Innings*: Roberts 4-1-12-0, Holding 7-0-33-1, Boyce 4-0-14-1, Kallicharran 2-1-7-1, Gibbs 1-0-4-0, Richards 0.1-0-4-0.

Umpires: TF Brooks & RR Ledwidge

SIXTH TEST 1975–76 AUSTRALIA v WEST INDIES
Melbourne Cricket Ground, Melbourne. January 31, February 1, 2, 4, 5, 1976.
Toss: Australia. Australia won by 165 runs.

AUSTRALIA

IR Redpath c Holding b Gibbs	101	c (S)CG Greenidge b Holder	70
A Turner c Gibbs b Holder	30	lbw Boyce	21
RB McCosker b Boyce	21	not out	109
IM Chappell b Gibbs	1	c Holder b Boyce	31
GS Chappell (c) c Boyce b Fredericks	68	not out	54
GN Yallop c Holding b Boyce	57		
RW Marsh (+) b Holding	7		
GJ Gilmour lbw Gibbs	9		
AA Mallett lbw Boyce	16		
JR Thomson lbw Holder	0		
DK Lillee not out	19		
Extras (B 4, LB 11, NB 7)	22	(B 5, LB 9, NB 1)	15
TOTAL	351		3 dec 300

FOW 1st Inns: 44 92 96 220 250 261 277 317 323 351
FOW 2nd Inns: 53 132 190

Bowling: *First Innings*: Boyce 17.2-1-75-3, Holding 16-4-51-1, Holder 20-2-86-3, Lloyd 7-2-20-0, Fredericks 6-0-29-1, Gibbs 24-4-68-2. *Second Innings*: Boyce 19-2-74-2, Holding 1-0-2-0, Holder 18-0-81-1, Lloyd 4-1-14-0, Fredericks 3-1-14-0, Gibbs 26-3-62-0, Richards 7-0-38-0.

WEST INDIES

RC Fredericks c Thomson b Gilmour	22	b Thomson	6
IVA Richards c Marsh b Lillee	50	c GS Chappell b Lillee	98
L Baichan c GS Chappell b Gilmour	3	b Thomson	20
AI Kallicharran b Gilmour	4	c McCosker b Lillee	44
CH Lloyd (c) c Redpath b Lillee	37	not out	91
LG Rowe c Marsh b Gilmour	6	c Redpath b Mallett	6
DL Murray (+) c Marsh b Lillee	5	c Marsh b Lillee	5
KD Boyce lbw Gilmour	0	c GS Chappell b Mallett	11
MA Holding b Lillee	9	c Gilmour b Mallett	4
VA Holder not out	14	b Thomson	22
LR Gibbs c Marsh b Lillee	2	c Marsh b Thomson	0
Extras (LB 5, W 1, NB 6)	12	(B 6, LB 10, NB 3)	19
TOTAL	160		326

FOW 1st Inns: 44 49 53 99 110 113 118 140 151 160
FOW 2nd Inns: 6 53 170 175 186 199 226 238 326 326

Bowling: *First Innings*: Thomson 9-0-51-0, Lillee 11.3-0-63-5, Gilmour 10-3-34-5. *Second Innings*: Thomson 12.5-0-80-4, Lillee 18-1-112-3, Gilmour 7-1-26-0, GS Chappell 2-0-6-0, IM Chappell 2-0-10-0, Mallett 13-1-73-3.

Umpires: TF Brooks & MG O'Connell

Board says no to exclusive TV rights

Melbourne, Jan. 15. The Australian Cricket Board has been advised by the UK Test and County Cricket Board that Kerry Packer's GTV 9 television network has made a substantial offer to broadcast the forthcoming England v Australia Test series.

According to the ACB, a joint arrangement with the ABC would be preferable in view of the ABC's support for Australian cricket over the years, and the fact that the ABC could guarantee national coverage in Australia.

Reports that the ACB has 'denied' television rights to GTV 9 are incorrect. GTV 9 approached the ACB in March 1976 with a view to obtaining cricket television rights, but no mention was made then of an 'exclusive' arrangement.

The ACB negotiated its standard three-year agreement with the ABC in May 1976, and when commercial broadcasting rights were subseqently opened for negotiation, GTV 9 formally sought exclusive status. The Board could not accept this in view of its established policy and the fact that the ABC had already negotiated a non-exclusive arrangement.

Benson & Hedges to sponsor cricket

Melbourne, Jan. 30. The Australian Cricket Board has finalised a sponsorship arrangement with the Benson and Hedges Company.

The $350,000 contract, signed with the support of the players, begins with the Australian tour of New Zealand and ends in 1978–79.

In a 'better deal', each member of the 35-day tour of New Zealand will receive $2430, and for the 134-day tour of England, each of the 17 players will take home $10,890.

In the current series against Pakistan, players receive a base fee of $400 per five-day Test, plus $75 expenses and a bonus of $250 for each Test.

As well as to match fees, the Board will allocate sponsorship funds to the players as prize money.

Crunch for Thommo

Jeff Thomson sees his chance for a caught and bowled to dismiss Zaheer Abbas and veers to midwicket where he crashes into Alan Turner, who also had his eyes on the ball. The result is a trip to hospital.

Melbourne, Jan. 6. For the Pakistanis, there's no escape. With Jeff Thomson in hospital after a sickening collision with team-mate Alan Turner in the drawn first Test in Adelaide, Dennis Lillee had to go it alone in the second Test.

And the fiery Perth express, urged on by the big MCG crowd, rose to Olympian heights with 6/82 and 4/53. Australia won by a mammoth 348 runs after Gary Cosier with a cavalier 168 and Greg Chappell (121) had spearheaded it to a first-innings total of 8/517 declared.

Chasing such a big score, Pakistan made a grand start to be 2/270, then lost 8/63 (five of them to Lillee) to be 333 all out. After closing its second innings at 8/315, Australia demolished the tourists for 151.

Meanwhile, Thomson has had a pin inserted in his right shoulder and will miss the Centenary Test. He and Turner crashed into each other in Adelaide trying to catch Zaheer Abbas at short midwicket. Neither saw the other coming. The ball fell to ground.

Thomson, bowling as fast as ever, had 2/34 off 8.5 overs when the accident happened.

Speed men up for Pakistan Test win

Sydney, Jan. 18. Pakistani speed merchants, Imran Khan and Sarfraz Nawaz, no doubt peeved by Dennis Lillee's jibes that they weren't good enough to dismiss Australia for reasonably low scores twice in the same match, are dining out tonight on their success.

They not only dismissed Australia for 211 and 180, but sat back and watched their batsmen, led by century-maker Asif Iqbal (120), hit Pakistan to an eight-wicket win in the third Test, thus levelling the series at 1–all. It was Pakistan's first win on Australian soil.

The handsome Imran, a Rhodes Scholar, and the fiery Sarfraz humbled the pride of Australia's batting, Imran taking 6/102 and 6/63 and Sarfraz 3/42 and 3/77.

Imran's 12-wicket haul is a Pakistani record in Australia.

Imran Khan, who took 12/165.

QUICK SINGLES

Home side hooted. Australian batsmen Gary Cosier and Rod Marsh were booed off the ground in Adelaide after playing it safe in the drawn first Test against Pakistan. Needing 56 to win in the compulsory last 15 overs, they concentrated on keeping their wickets intact and protecting the tail-enders. Australia, 6/261, finished only 24 runs short of victory.

Beefy in form. Big boy Gary Cosier's 168 in the second Test took only 228 minutes with 20 fours. He put on 171 with Greg Chappell (121) for the fifth wicket. A year ago Cosier scored 109 v the Windies at the MCG.

The King is dead. Former Test captain Jack Ryder died on April 3 and, as a mark of respect, many shopkeepers in his beloved Collingwood closed their doors the day of the funeral. Ryder, who was 87, played in 20 Tests and scored 295 in

Victoria's record Sheffield Shield score of 1107 in 1926–27.

Bay 13 barrackers. The cry of 'Lill-ee, Lill-ee' from Bay 13 at the MCG is Dennis Lillee's secret weapon. 'You've no idea how the crowd lifted me. I'd say it added a couple of yards to my pace,' he said after taking 10 wickets in Australia's second-Test win.

Uneducated Aussies. Colonel Shuja, Pakistan's manager, says half the Australian team is illiterate and that Dennis Lillee should keep his trap shut. He accused Greg Chappell and Lillee of waging psychological war against Pakistan in their newspaper columns. 'My boys have been to the best Universities, half your lads are illiterate,' he said.

Two honoured. Former Test captain Ian Johnson and Test opening batsman/journalist Jack Fingleton have been awarded the OBE in the New Year honors. They

have contributed much to cricket; Johnson as secretary of the Melbourne Cricket Club, and Fingleton as an author.

Table dance. A jubilant Pakistani skipper Mushtaq Mohammad tried his hand at table-top dancing when his team celebrated its third Test win. Veteran of 41 Tests, he said it was 'the best win of my career.'

Thommo's dozen. Before his Test injury, Queenslander Jeff Thomson ran through New South Wales in a Shield game, taking 12/112.

WA's Shield. Western Australia wins the Sheffield Shield for the sixth time with 138 points. Victoria was second with 91, followed by Queensland (83), NSW (82) and SA (62).

Newcomer. Allan Border plays five matches for NSW in his first season and makes 128 runs at an average of 18.28 with a highest score of 68.

FIRST TEST 1976–77 AUSTRALIA v PAKISTAN
Adelaide Oval, Adelaide. December 24, 26, 27, 28, 29, 1976.
Toss: Pakistan. Match Drawn.

PAKISTAN
Majid Khan c McCosker b Thomson	15	lbw Lillee	47
Mudassar Nazar b Marsh b Gilmour	13	c Marsh b O'Keeffe	22
Zaheer Abbas c Walters b O'Keeffe	85	c Davis b Lillee	101
Mushtaq Mohammad (c) c McCosker b Thomson	18	c Marsh b Lillee	37
Javed Miandad b O'Keeffe	15	b Gilmour	54
Asif Iqbal c Marsh b O'Keeffe	0	not out	152
Imran Khan b Chappell	48	b O'Keeffe	5
Salim Altaf c Davis b Chappell	16	c Turner b Lillee	21
Wasim Bari (+) run out	21	lbw Lillee	0
Sarfraz Nawaz c Marsh b Lillee	29	c Lillee b O'Keeffe	0
Iqbal Qasim not out	1	run out	4
Extras (LB 6, NB 5)	11	(B 14, LB 1, NB 8)	23
TOTAL	272		466

FOW 1st Inns: 19 56 98 140 152 157 220 221 271 272
FOW 2nd Inns: 58 92 182 236 293 298 368 378 379 466

Bowling: *First Innings*: Lillee 19-1-104-1, Thomson 8.5-2-34-2, Gilmour 14.2-1-55-1, Walters 3-0-12-0, O'Keeffe 19.5-42-3, Chappell 7-2-14-2. *Second Innings*: Lillee 47.7-10-163-5, Chappell 11-3-31-0, O'Keeffe 53-12-166-3, Cosier 5-1-11-0, Walters 2-1-5-0, Gilmour 14-1-67-1.

AUSTRALIA
IC Davis c Mushtaq b Javed	105	b Sarfraz	0
A Turner c Zaheer b Imran	33	c Sarfraz b Javed	48
RB McCosker b Mushtaq	65	c Wasim b Iqbal	42
GS Chappell (c) c Zaheer b Javed	52	c Mushtaq b Iqbal	70
KD Walters c Javed b Sarfraz	107	c Wasim b Iqbal	51
GJ Cosier c Asif b Javed	33 (7)	not out	25
RW Marsh (+) b Mushtaq	36 (8)	not out	13
GJ Gilmour c Iqbal b Mushtaq	3 (6)	b Iqbal	5
KJ O'Keeffe not out	3		
DK Lillee c Majid b Mushtaq	0		
JR Thomson			
Extras (LB 4, NB 13)	17	(B 1, LB 3, NB 3)	7
TOTAL	9 dec 454		6 for 261

FOW 1st Inns: 63 188 244 278 366 445 451 451 454
FOW 2nd Inns: 0 92 100 201 219 228

Bowling: *First Innings*: Sarfraz 24-3-75-1, Salim 15-0-71-0, Imran 22-2-92-1, Iqbal 14-0-56-0, Javed 25-3-85-3, Mushtaq 19.4-2-58-4. *Second Innings*: Sarfraz 8-1-24-1, Imran 5-0-25-0, Mushtaq 9-1-50-0, Javed 21-6-71-1, Iqbal 30-6-84-4.

Umpires: RC Bailhache & MG O'Connell

SECOND TEST 1976–77 AUSTRALIA v PAKISTAN
Melbourne Cricket Ground, Melbourne. January 1, 2, 3, 5, 6, 1977.
Toss: Australia. Australia won by 348 runs.

AUSTRALIA
IC Davis c Imran b Asif	56	c Asif b Iqbal	88
A Turner b Asif	82	lbw Imran	5
RB McCosker lbw Asif	0	st Wasim b Iqbal	105
GS Chappell (c) c Wasim b Iqbal	121	c Majid b Imran	67
KD Walters st Wasim b Iqbal	42	b Imran	0
GJ Cosier c Asif b Majid	168	b Imran	8
RW Marsh (+) lbw Iqbal	2	st Wasim b Iqbal	13
GJ Gilmour st Wasim b Iqbal	0	not out	7
KJ O'Keeffe not out	28		
MHN Walker			
DK Lillee	(9)	b Imran	6
Extras (B 3, LB 7, W 1, NB 7)	18	(B 2, LB 11, NB 3)	16
TOTAL	8 dec 517		8 dec 315

FOW 1st Inns: 134 134 151 227 398 400 400 517
FOW 2nd Inns: 6 182 223 226 244 301 301 315

Bowling: *First Innings*: Imran 22-0-115-0, Salim 17-2-117-0, Asif 13-1-79-0, Asif 16-3-52-3, Javed 2-0-15-0, Iqbal 21-5-111-4, Majid 1.6-0-10-1. *Second Innings*: Salim 6-1-28-0, Imran 25.5-2-122-5, Iqbal 25-2-119-3, Majid 2-0-12-0, Mushtaq 3-0-18-0.

PAKISTAN
Majid Khan c Marsh b Lillee	76	b Lillee	35
Sadiq Mohammad c McCosker b O'Keeffe	105	c Walters b Gilmour	0
Zaheer Abbas b Gilmour	90	lbw Walker	58
Mushtaq Mohammad (c) lbw Lillee	9	c Chappell b Lillee	4
Javed Miandad lbw Lillee	0	c Turner b O'Keeffe	10
Asif Iqbal c(S)KJ Hughes b Gilmour	35	lbw Lillee	6
Imran Khan c Marsh b Lillee	5	c & b O'Keeffe	28
Salim Altaf c Chappell b Lillee	0	b O'Keeffe	0
Wasim Bari (+) lbw Lillee	0	c Walker b O'Keeffe	2
Iqbal Qasim run out	1	c Marsh b Lillee	1
Asif Masood not out	0	not out	0
Extras (LB 2, NB 5)	7	(B 1, LB 6)	7
TOTAL	333		151

FOW 1st Inns: 113 241 270 285 292 303 303 303 332 333
FOW 2nd Inns: 4 86 99 104 120 124 128 136 145 151

Bowling: *First Innings*: Lillee 23-4-82-6, Gilmour 16.1-2-78-2, Walker 22-1-93-0, O'Keeffe 21-4-63-1, Cosier 2-0-10-0. *Second Innings*: Lillee 14-1-53-4, Gilmour 3-0-19-1, Walker 9-2-34-1, O'Keeffe 18.1-5-38-4.

Umpires: TF Brooks & MG O'Connell

THIRD TEST 1976–77 AUSTRALIA v PAKISTAN
Sydney Cricket Ground, Sydney. January 14, 15, 16, 18, 1977.
Toss: Australia. Pakistan won by 8 wkts.

AUSTRALIA
IC Davis b Sarfraz	20	c Haroon b Imran	25
A Turner c Wasim b Sarfraz	0	c Majid b Imran	11
RB McCosker c Mushtaq b Sarfraz	8	c Wasim b Imran	8
GS Chappell (c) c Zaheer b Imran	28	c Wasim b Sarfraz	5
KD Walters c Mushtaq b Imran	2	c Wasim b Imran	38
GJ Cosier c Wasim b Imran	50	c Wasim b Sarfraz	4
RW Marsh (+) c & b Imran	14	run out	41
GJ Gilmour c Javed b Sarfraz	32	c Zaheer b Imran	0
KJ O'Keeffe c Asif b Imran	1	c Haroon b Imran	7
DK Lillee lbw Javed	14	c Zaheer b Imran	27
MHN Walker not out	34	not out	3
Extras (B 5, NB 3)	8	(B 7, NB 4)	11
TOTAL	211		180

FOW 1st Inns: 3 26 28 38 100 125 138 146 159 211
FOW 2nd Inns: 32 41 51 61 75 99 99 115 177 180

Bowling: *First Innings*: Sarfraz 16-4-42-3, Imran 26-6-102-6, Asif 15-5-53-0, Mushtaq 2-1-2-0, Iqbal 4-3-2-0, Javed 1.2-0-2-1. *Second Innings*: Imran 19.7-3-63-6, Sarfraz 15-3-77-3, Javed 5-0-27-0, Iqbal 2-1-2-0.

PAKISTAN
Majid Khan c Marsh b Walker	48	not out	26
Sadiq Mohammad c Cosier b Walker	25	c Marsh b Lillee	0
Zaheer Abbas c Turner b Lillee	5	c Walters b Lillee	4
Mushtaq Mohammad (c) c Turner b Lillee	9	not out	0
Haroon Rashid c Marsh b Gilmour	57		
Asif Iqbal b Gilmour	120		
Javed Miandad c Walters b Walker	64		
Imran Khan c Turner b Gilmour	0		
Sarfraz Nawaz c Turner b Walker	13		
Wasim Bari (+) c Walters b Lillee	5		
Iqbal Qasim not out	0		
Extras (B 6, LB 6, NB 2)	14	(B 1, NB 1)	2
TOTAL	360		2 for 32

FOW 1st Inns: 42 51 77 111 205 320 322 339 360 360
FOW 2nd Inns: 1 22

Bowling: *First Innings*: Lillee 22.3-0-114-3, Gilmour 16-1-81-3, Walker 29-4-112-4, O'Keeffe 11-2-32-0, Walters 4-1-7-0. *Second Innings*: Lillee 4-0-24-2, Walker 3.2-1-6-0.

Umpires: TF Brooks & RR Ledwidge

Australian Averages

1976–77 AUSTRALIA v PAKISTAN

AUSTRALIA	M	Inn	NO	Runs	H.S	Avrge	Ct	St	Overs	Mds	Runs	Wkt	Avrge
Chappell, GS	3	6	-	343	121	57.17	2	-	18.0	5	45	2	22.50
Cosier, GJ	3	6	1	288	168	57.60	1	-	7.0	1	21	-	-
Davis, IC	3	6	-	294	105	49.00	2	-	-	-	-	-	-
Gilmour, GJ	3	6	1	47	32	9.40	-	-	63.3	5	300	8	37.50
Lillee, DK	3	4	-	47	27	11.75	1	-	130.2	16	540	21	25.71
Marsh, RW	3	6	1	119	41	23.80	11	-	-	-	-	-	-
McCosker, RB	3	6	-	228	105	38.00	3	-	-	-	-	-	-
O'Keeffe, KJ	3	4	2	39	28*	19.50	1	-	122.1	28	341	11	31.00
Thomson, JR	1	-	-	-	-	-	-	-	8.5	2	34	2	17.00
Turner, A	3	6	-	179	82	29.83	6	-	-	-	-	-	-
Walker, MHN	2	2	2	37	34*	-	1	-	63.2	8	245	5	49.00
Walters, KD	3	6	-	240	107	40.00	5	-	9.0	2	24	-	-

Pakistani Averages

1976–77 AUSTRALIA v PAKISTAN

PAKISTAN	M	Inn	NO	Runs	H.S	Avrge	Ct	St	Overs	Mds	Runs	Wkt	Avrge
Asif Iqbal	3	5	1	313	152*	78.25	3	-	31.0	8	105	3	35.00
Asif Masood	1	2	2	0	0*	-	1	-	13.0	1	79	-	-
Haroon Rashid	1	1	-	57	57	57.00	2	-	-	-	-	-	-
Imran Khan	3	5	-	86	48	17.20	2	-	120.4	13	519	18	28.83
Iqbal Qasim	3	5	2	7	4	2.33	1	-	96.0	17	374	11	34.00
Javed Miandad	3	5	-	148	64	29.60	2	-	54.2	9	200	5	40.00
Majid Khan	3	6	1	247	76	49.40	3	-	3.6	-	22	1	22.00
Mudassar Nazar	1	2	-	35	22	17.50	-	-	-	-	-	-	-
Mushtaq Mohammad	3	6	1	77	37	15.40	3	-	33.4	4	128	4	32.00
Sadiq Mohammad	2	4	-	130	105	32.50	-	-	-	-	-	-	-
Salim Altaf	2	4	-	37	21	9.25	-	-	38.0	3	216	-	-
Sarfraz Nawaz	2	3	-	42	29	14.00	1	-	63.0	11	218	8	27.25
Wasim Bari	3	5	-	28	21	5.60	10	4	-	-	-	-	-
Zaheer Abbas	3	6	-	343	101	57.17	5	-	-	-	-	-	-

Walters fires, Lillee rampant

Just in case there's a snick! Not quite. Skipper Greg Chappell employed a nine-man slips cordon for Dennis Lillee towards the end of the Auckland Test so that he could get a picture for the cover of his book.

Auckland, March 1. Doug Walters and Dennis Lillee have been at their best in the two-Test series against New Zealand.

In the drawn first Test in Christchurch, in which the bat prevailed, Walters treated the crowd to a vintage knock of 250, his highest Test score and 11th Test century. He surpassed his previous highest Test score of 242 against the West Indies in Sydney in 1968–69.

With Gus Gilmour, whose pugnacious 101 included 20 fours and a 6, he put on 217 for the seventh wicket as Australia piled on 552 in its first innings.

New Zealand took up the challenge, Hedley Howarth (61) taking the long handle to Lillee in the Kiwis' first innings of 357 and Bevan Congdon contributing 107 not out in the second innings.

If the wicket was on the slow side, the opposite applied at Eden Park, Auckland. One look at the grassy pitch was all that Greg Chappell required. On winning the toss, he had no hesitation in inviting the Kiwis to bat.

A rampant Lillee soon quelled their excitement, mowing down the home side for 229 (Geoff Howarth 59) and 175 with a career-best of 11/123 (5/51 and 6/72) less than two months after humbling Pakistan at the MCG with 10/135. Only Richard Hadlee, who scored 44 in the first innings, offered spirited resistance in the second knock, hitting a breezy 81 after the Kiwis had slumped to 5/31.

The Australian batting was resolute. No Walters magic this time, in fact only 16. Rick McCosker (84), the in-form Gilmour (64) and Greg Chappell (58) anchored the tourists to a match-winning total of 377. After Lillee's superb second-innings spell, in which he crashed through the top order, an Australian victory (by 10 wickets) was a formality. Though they lost the two-Test series 1–0 and their captain Glenn Turner made only 78 in four hands, the Kiwis agreed it had been one hell of a month.

Strange visitors to the rooms

Auckland, March 1. Dennis Lillee, according to reports, is about to have an affair with television – on the Channel 9 show 'A Current Affair'.

His managers, John Cornell and Austin Robertson, who bobbed up in the dressing rooms during the Auckland Test, are arranging a contract for Lillee.

Cornell, better known as Paul Hogan's offsider 'Strop' on TV, is also an entrepreneur.

In 1976, according to the *Age*'s Peter McFarline, he came up with the idea of a series of televised games, which 'could lead to a major confrontation between the players and the Australian Cricket Board.'

Packer secures TV Test rights

Sydney, Feb. 16. Kerry Packer has upped the ante and won the rights to televise the forthcoming Tests in England, starting in June.

Initially, Packer offered the Test and County Cricket Board $118,000 for exclusive rights.

The Australian Cricket Board preferred a joint ABC/Packer arrangement, in view of the ABC's proven commitment to cricket and its capacity to provide national coverage.

The TCCB was prepared to offer exclusive live rights to the ABC for $120,000, but the ABC felt this was too much.

Packer then doubled his offer to $236,000, which the TCCB accepted.

$2340 pay for month's work

Melbourne, March 4. The successful Australians have returned from their NZ tour, having made a profit of $35,000 for their hosts.

As for themselves, the Australian players were paid $2430 each for a month's work. Rewarded at this rate per month (which they aren't), the players would earn $30,000 a year – not a lot for top-class entertainers.

Still, even allowing for inflation, it is appreciably more than Ian Chappell earned in 1975–76. He described the $4800 he received for five months' work – Sheffield Shield matches and six Tests against the West Indies (449 runs at 44.9) as 'fish and chips money'.

Australian women win Test series in England

The Australian women's cricket team (pictured at Edgbaston) of 1976 was the first to play at Lord's. The first Test at Old Trafford was a draw; as was the second at Edgbaston. The third Test, at the Oval, was the first to be played over four days. England made just 134 in the first innings. Australia followed with 379 – the highest score in Anglo–Australian women's Test cricket. England then batted for nearly two days to save the game. On August 4 England and Australia played a one day match at Lord's.

FIRST TEST 1976–77 NEW ZEALAND v AUSTRALIA
Lancaster Park, Christchurch. February 18, 19, 20, 22, 23, 1977.
Toss: New Zealand. Match Drawn.

AUSTRALIA

A Turner b Chatfield	3	lbw DR Hadlee 20
IC Davis c GP Howarth b RJ Hadlee	34	c Lees b RJ Hadlee 22
RB McCosker c Parker b DR Hadlee	37	not out 77
GS Chappell (c) c Turner b RJ Hadlee	44	c Parker b HJ Howarth 0
GJ Cosier b RJ Hadlee	23	run out 2
KD Walters c HJ Howarth b DR Hadlee	250	not out 20
RW Marsh (+) c Parker b HJ Howarth	2	
GJ Gilmour b Chatfield	101	
KJ O'Keeffe run out	8	
DK Lillee c RJ Hadlee b Chatfield	19	
MHN Walker not out	10	
Extras (B 7, LB 10, NB 4)	21	(LB 10, NB 3) 13
TOTAL	552	..............................4 dec 154

FOW 1st Inns: 9 76 78 112 205 208 425 454 504 552
FOW 2nd Inns: 37 67 68 82

Bowling: *First Innings*: RJ Hadlee 29-1-155-3, Chatfield 31-4-125-3, DR Hadlee 24.5-1-130-2, HJ Howarth 19-2-94-1, Congdon 7-0-27-0. *Second Innings*: RJ Hadlee 13-4-41-1, Chatfield 11-1-34-0, DR Hadlee 8-0-28-1, HJ Howarth 10-0-37-1, Congdon 1-0-1-0.

NEW ZEALAND

GM Turner (c) c Turner b O'Keeffe	15	c & b O'Keeffe 36
GP Howarth c Marsh b O'Keeffe	42	c Marsh b Gilmour 28
BE Congdon c Gilmour b Walker	23	not out 107
JM Parker c Marsh b O'Keeffe	34	c McCosker b Walker 21
MG Burgess c Marsh b Walker	66	c McCosker b Walker 39
GN Edwards c Gilmour b O'Keeffe	34	c Marsh b Walker 15
WK Lees (+) c Marsh b Lillee	14	c Marsh b Lillee 3
RJ Hadlee c Marsh b O'Keeffe	3 (9)	c Cosier b Walker 15
HJ Howarth b Walker	61 (8)	b Lillee 0
DR Hadlee not out	37	not out 8
EJ Chatfield b Lillee	5	
Extras (LB 9, W 2, NB 12)	23	(LB 12, W 1, NB 8) 21
TOTAL	357	...............................8 for 293

FOW 1st Inns: 60 65 91 189 193 220 223 265 338 357
FOW 2nd Inns: 70 70 128 218 238 245 245 260

Bowling: *First Innings*: Lillee 31.2-6-119-2, Walker 26-7-66-3, Gilmour 10-0-48-0, O'Keeffe 28-5-101-5. *Second Innings*: Lillee 18-1-70-2, Walker 25-4-65-4, Gilmour 10-0-48-1, O'Keeffe 20-4-56-1, Chappell 11-0-33-0.

Umpires: DEA Copps & FR Goodall

SECOND TEST 1976–77 NEW ZEALAND v AUSTRALIA
Eden Park, Auckland. February 25, 26, 27, March 1, 1977.
Toss: Australia. Australia won by 10 wkts.

NEW ZEALAND

GM Turner (c) c Marsh b Walker	4	c Walters b Lillee 23
GP Howarth c McCosker b Lillee	59	c Turner b Lillee 2
BE Congdon c Marsh b Lillee	25	c McCosker b Lillee 1
JM Parker c Cosier b Lillee	20	c Turner b Walker 5
MG Burgess c Marsh b Walters	1	b Walker 38
GN Edwards (+) c Lillee b Gilmour	51	c Marsh b Lillee 0
RJ Hadlee c McCosker b Lillee	44	b Chappell 81
BL Cairns b Chappell	2	c Lillee b Walker 7
HJ Howarth b Walker	5	lbw Lillee 6
PJ Petherick c Marsh b Lillee	4	b Lillee 1
EJ Chatfield not out	0	not out 4
Extras (LB 7, NB 7)	14	(B 4, LB 2, NB 1) 7
TOTAL	229	175

FOW 1st Inns: 6 63 112 113 121 177 202 211 228 229
FOW 2nd Inns: 10 12 23 31 31 136 162 163 169 175

Bowling: *First Innings*: Lillee 17.3-4-51-5, Walker 24-6-60-2, Gilmour 7-0-56-1, Chappell 13-4-28-1, Walters 4-1-20-1, O'Keeffe 1-1-0-0. *Second Innings*: Lillee 15.7-2-72-6, Walker 17-4-70-3, Gilmour 1-0-11-0, Chappell 9-4-15-1.

AUSTRALIA

IC Davis b Chatfield	13	not out 6
A Turner c Edwards b Cairns	30	not out 20
RB McCosker c Edwards b Cairns	84	
GS Chappell (c) run out	58	
GJ Cosier c & b Cairns	21	
KD Walters c Hadlee b Chatfield	16	
RW Marsh (+) lbw Hadlee	4	
GJ Gilmour b Chatfield	64	
KJ O'Keeffe c Congdon b Hadlee	32	
DK Lillee not out	23	
MHN Walker c Turner b Chatfield	9	
Extras (B 9, LB 9, NB 5)	23	(LB 1, NB 1) 2
TOTAL	377	...............................0 for 28

FOW 1st Inns: 31 56 171 202 217 221 245 338 364 377
FOW 2nd Inns:

Bowling: *First Innings*: Hadlee 28-2-147-2, Chatfield 27.1-3-100-4, Cairns 28-9-69-3, Congdon 5-1-8-0, HJ Howarth 5-1-16-0, Petherick 4-2-14-0. *Second Innings*: Hadlee 2-0-11-0, Chatfield 1.5-0-15-0.

Umpires: DEA Copps & WRC Gardiner

Australian Averages

1976–77 NEW ZEALAND v AUSTRALIA

AUSTRALIA	M	Inn	NO	Runs	H.S	Avrge	Ct	St	Overs	Mds	Runs	Wkt	Avrge
Chappell, GS	2	3	-	102	58	34.00	-	-	33.0	8	76	2	38.00
Cosier, GJ	2	3	-	46	23	15.33	2	-	-	-	-	-	-
Davis, IC	2	4	1	75	34	25.00	-	-	-	-	-	-	-
Gilmour, GJ	2	2	-	165	101	82.50	2	-	28.0	-	163	2	81.50
Lillee, DK	2	2	1	42	23*	42.00	2	-	82.4	13	312	15	20.80
Marsh, RW	2	2	-	6	4	3.00	13	-	-	-	-	-	-
McCosker, RB	2	3	1	198	84	99.00	5	-	-	-	-	-	-
O'Keeffe, KJ	2	2	-	40	32	20.00	1	-	49.0	10	157	6	26.17
Turner, A	2	4	1	73	30	24.33	3	-	-	-	-	-	-
Walker, MHN	2	2	1	19	10*	19.00	-	-	92.0	21	261	12	21.75
Walters, KD	2	3	1	286	250	143.00	1	-	4.0	1	20	1	20.00

New Zealand Averages

1976–77 NEW ZEALAND v AUSTRALIA

NEW ZEALAND	M	Inn	NO	Runs	H.S	Avrge	Ct	St	Overs	Mds	Runs	Wkt	Avrge
Burgess, MG	2	4	-	144	66	36.00	-	-	-	-	-	-	-
Cairns, BL	1	2	-	9	7	4.50	1	-	28.0	9	69	3	23.00
Chatfield, EJ	2	3	2	9	5	9.00	-	-	70.6	8	274	7	39.14
Congdon, BE	2	4	1	156	107*	52.00	1	-	13.0	1	36	-	-
Edwards, GN	2	4	-	100	51	25.00	2	-	-	-	-	-	-
Hadlee, DR	1	2	2	45	37*	-	-	-	32.5	1	158	3	52.67
Hadlee, RJ	2	4	-	143	81	35.75	2	-	72.0	7	354	6	59.00
Howarth, GP	2	4	-	131	59	32.75	1	-	-	-	-	-	-
Howarth, HJ	2	4	-	72	61	18.00	1	-	34.0	3	147	2	73.50
Lees, WK	1	2	-	17	14	8.50	1	-	-	-	-	-	-
Parker, JM	2	4	-	80	34	20.00	3	-	-	-	-	-	-
Petherick, PJ	1	2	-	5	4	2.50	-	-	4.0	2	14	-	-
Turner, GM	2	4	-	78	36	19.50	2	-	-	-	-	-	-

Test by television

Centenary Test: a celebration

Ebeling's brainchild

Melbourne, March 17. The Centenary Test was the brainchild of former Melbourne Cricket Club President, Hans Ebeling, who played in one Test for Australia in 1934. Although the notion of a match had been floating around cricket circles since 1963, it was Ebeling who saw the project to fruition, taking the MCC proposal to the VCA, and then to the Australian Cricket Board via Ray Steele in 1973. Here the idea was taken up with enthusiasm by Bob Parish, who negotiated with the English authorities.

Hans Ebeling – a great idea.

Poster for the big game.

Melbourne, March 17. What memories to take from the Centenary Test!

We will remember the fierce bowling of both sides in the first innings, with Dennis Lillee at his best; the sickening blow to Rick McCosker's jaw, and his brave return; David Hookes in his first Test, taking five successive fours; Derek Randall's perpetual motion while making 174 to put victory within England's grasp; Rod Marsh's sporting recall of Randall.

We will remember the men in the stands – more that 200 former Test cricketers from England and Australia – many of them old and frail. 'The cumulative effect of all these men under the same roof, lunching, dining, watching the play, reminiscing, recalling old triumphs – and failures – across 40 or 50 years, produced an atmosphere of almost unbelievable nostalgia,' wrote John Arlott.

And we will remember the Melbourne Cricket Ground, packed with cricket lovers, bathed in autumn sunshine, the perfect place for cricket and the place where Test cricket began.

The pace with which the wickets fell on the first two days had the organisers concerned, however, and there were contingency plans for an exhibition match in place for the fifth day, when the Queen was to pay a visit.

The Australian top order bats collapsed, as much through rash batting as through the sustained pace bowling and sharp fielding of England. Rick McCosker, Ian Davis, Gary Cosier, Gary Gilmour and Doug Walters could only muster 27 between them. McCosker was hurt when a ball from Willis reared and broke his jaw, on its way onto the stumps.

It was left to Greg Chappell, who made a valiant 40, new boy David Hookes (17) and Rod Marsh (28) to push some runs into the scoresheet. Australia finished with 138.

But Australia roared back into the game with Dennis Lillee and Max Walker bowling at their peak. The crowd roared the familiar chant 'Lillee, Lillee' with each ball of his 13.3 overs, and he rewarded them by breaking the top order and then cleaning up the tail to finish with 6/26. Walker took 4/24, and Rod Marsh took four catches to surpass Wally Grout's record for an

Australian wicketkeeper of 187 dismissals. England was out for 95.

The second innings were a complete contrast, with batsmen getting their heads over the ball and working for runs. Even so, Australia seemed in a precarious position after the second day on 3/104, with Cosier, Chappell and makeshift opener Kerry O'Keefe back in the pavilion.

Davis and Walters, however, seemed on top of the bowling on the third day and stayed for 45 minutes until Davis went for 68. Hookes and Walters were there at lunch, but Walters surrendered soon afterwards, for a subdued but important 66. He was replaced by Rod Marsh, who began to hit the ball robustly and cleanly.

Then came the over that brought the match alive, and reportedly brought tears to the eyes of a lot of former Test players in the Member's stand. Tony Greig went around the wicket to Hookes. The bronzed and blond South Australian played the first two balls defensively, then hit five consecutive fours. He lofted the third ball high over mid-off, swung the fourth fine down the leg side,

The angelic-looking David Hookes sends a Tony Greig delivery to the devil.

Derek Randall: nearly won it.

# of cricket

cover-drove the fifth, sent the sixth through mid-wicket to bring up his 50, and again bisected the covers off the seventh ball. The last ball was played to cover, but fielded.

The drama ended as Hookes fell next ball to Underwood for 56.

Rod Marsh continued his best batting form to carry the score to 8/353. Then came another moment of drama as Rick McCosker, his jaw wired and his head swathed in bandages, came out, with Kerry O'Keefe as runner. At stumps, Marsh stood at 95 and on the threshhold of the first century by an Australian wicketkeeper against England. The next day, after Marsh had his century, McCosker's wicket fell at 25 and Australia declared at 9/419, 463 runs ahead.

England fought back. After Bob Woolmer went, Mike Brearley was joined by the scarecrow figure of Derek Randall, coming off an average in India of 12.28. England was 2/191 at stumps, with 272 to win.

By lunch on the fifth day England had jumped to favoritism. It was 2/267 and the Australian bowling was looking thin, with Lillee under a heavy workload and Gary Gilmour injured.

The balance altered soon after lunch when Greg Chappell bowled Amiss with a ball that kept low and Keith Fletcher fell to Lillee for 1. Greig joined Randall and the pendulum began to swing again.

Then another great moment when Marsh seemed to hold a diving chance. Umpire Tom Brooks signalled Randall out, but Marsh ran forward and signalled he had not taken the ball cleanly. It was instinctive sportsmanship.

Randall added 13 more, and seemed to be leading the charge to victory, but was caught by a diving Cosier off O'Keefe for 174.

Evading one Lillee bouncer he ducked and completed a backward double somersault. Another glancing blow from a bouncer caused him to raise his cap and bow to the bowler.

Greig and Knott, two fighting cricketers, were at the crease at tea, with England on 5/354 and needing just 109 to win. But when Greig went England was in trouble. Knott could not keep the tail-enders with him, and was finally out, with England 45 runs short – exactly the same margin as in the first Test in 1877.

ONLY TEST 1976–77 AUSTRALIA v ENGLAND
Melbourne Cricket Ground, Melbourne. March 12, 13, 14, 16, 17, 1977.
Toss: England. Australia won by 45 runs.

AUSTRALIA

	1st		2nd
IC Davis lbw Lever	5	c Knott b Greig	68
RB McCosker b Willis	4 (10)	c Greig b Old	25
GJ Cosier c Fletcher b Lever	10 (4)	c Knott b Lever	4
GS Chappell (c) b Underwood	40 (3)	b Old	2
DW Hookes c Greig b Old	17 (6)	c Fletcher b Underwood	56
KD Walters c Greig b Willis	4 (5)	c Knott b Greig	66
RW Marsh (+) c Knott b Old	28	not out	110
GJ Gilmour c Greig b Old	4	b Lever	16
KJ O'Keeffe c Brearley b Underwood	0 (2)	c Willis b Old	14
DK Lillee not out	10 (9)	c Amiss b Old	25
MHN Walker b Underwood	2	not out	8
Extras (B 4, LB 2, NB 8)	14	(LB 10, NB 15)	25
TOTAL	138		9 dec 419

FOW 1st Inns: 11 13 23 45 51 102 114 117 136 138
FOW 2nd Inns: 33 40 53 132 187 244 277 353 407

Bowling: *First Innings*: Lever 12-1-36-2, Willis 8-0-33-2, Old 12-4-39-3, Underwood 11.6-2-16-3.
Second Innings: Lever 21-1-95-2, Willis 22-0-91-0, Old 27.6-2-104-4, Greig 14-3-66-2, Underwood 12-2-38-1.

ENGLAND

	1st		2nd
RA Woolmer c Chappell b Lillee	9	lbw Walker	12
JM Brearley c Hookes b Lillee	12	lbw Lillee	43
DL Underwood c Chappell b Walker	7 (10)	b Lillee	7
DW Randall c Marsh b Lillee	4 (3)	c Cosier b O'Keeffe	174
DL Amiss c O'Keeffe b Walker	4 (4)	b Chappell	64
KWR Fletcher c Marsh b Walker	4 (5)	c Marsh b Lillee	1
AW Greig c Marsh b Walker	18 (6)	c Cosier b O'Keeffe	41
APE Knott (+) lbw Lillee	15 (7)	lbw Lillee	42
CM Old c Marsh b Lillee	3 (8)	c Chappell b Lillee	2
JK Lever c Marsh b Lillee	11 (9)	lbw O'Keeffe	4
RGD Willis not out	1	not out	5
Extras (B 2, LB 2, W 1, NB 2)	7	(B 8, LB 4, W 3, NB 7)	22
TOTAL	95		417

FOW 1st Inns: 19 30 34 40 40 61 65 78 86 95
FOW 2nd Inns: 28 113 279 290 346 369 380 385 410 417

Bowling: *First Innings*: Lillee 13.3-2-26-6, Walker 15-3-54-4, O'Keeffe 1-0-4-0, Gilmour 5-3-4-0.
Second Innings: Lillee 34.4-7-139-5, Walker 22-4-83-1, Gilmour 4-0-29-0, O'Keeffe 33-6-108-3, Chappell 16-7-29-1, Walters 3-2-7-0.

Umpires: TF Brooks & MG O'Connell

Great days at the MCG. Who could have predicted that the one-hundredth Test would have the same result as the first – Australia by 45 runs.

A great catch by Mike Brearley sees Kerry O'Keeffe depart for a duck.

Rod Marsh thanks goodness that he had a lucky escape with fellow 'keeeper Alan Knott.

Derek Randall demonstrates how to pull the ball on the ground in his great second-innings knock.

Rick McCosker comes out to face the music again in the Australian second innings.

Geoff Cook's whimsical poster was a great souvenir of the Centenary Test.

200 of the greatest Test players from Australia and England came to the Melbourne Cricket Ground for the great match and the celebration.

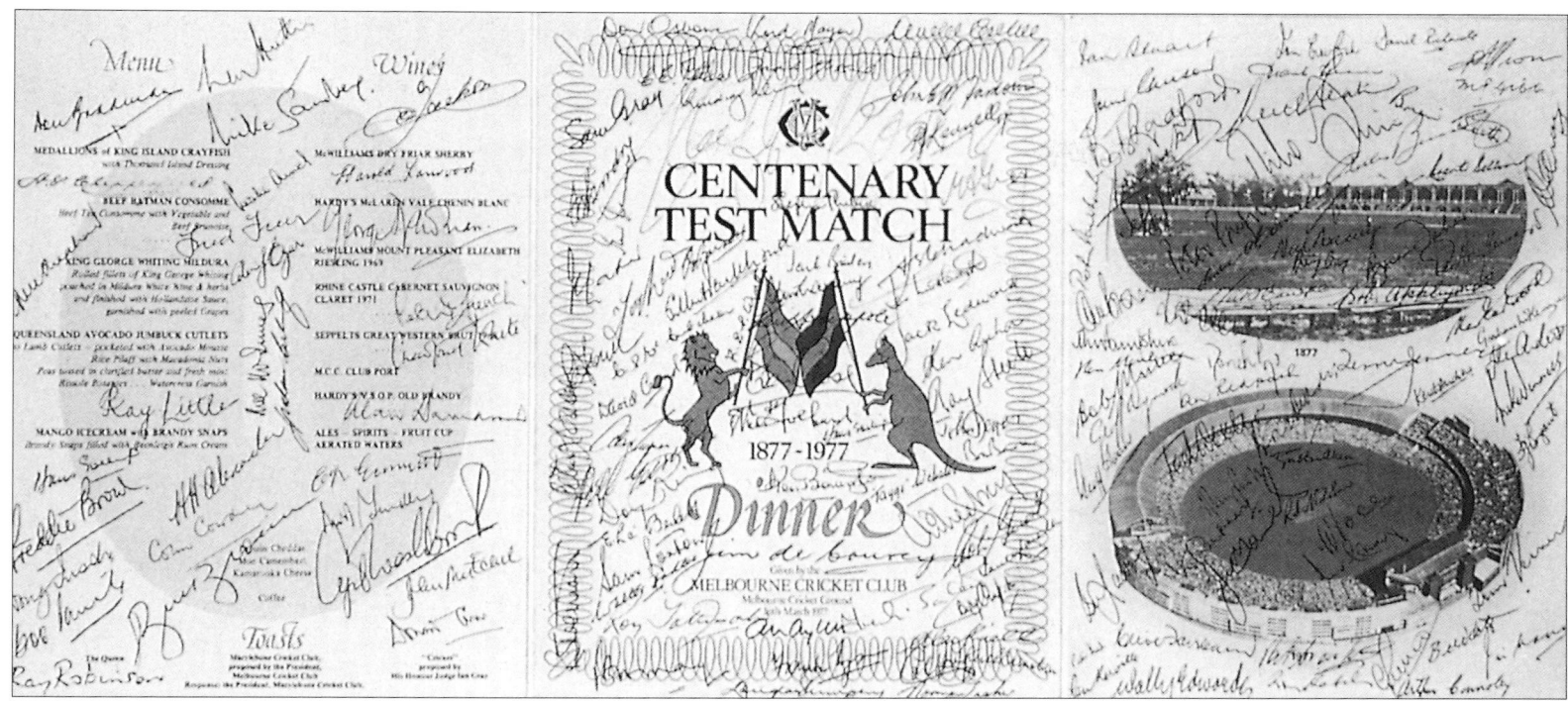

The Centenary dinner, hosted by the Melbourne Cricket Club, provided an opportunity for cricket autograph hunting on a grand scale.

Australia Post released a stamp series which underlined the importance of the Centenary Test, and the game of cricket, to the Australian story.

A critical moment. Derek Randall is out for 174, caught by Gary Cosier off Kerry O'Keeffe.

Packer's cat gets out of the bag

A new-look Test team for England

Melbourne, March 20. The Australian squad of 17 players for the Jubilee tour of England contains some shocks, and the overall impression is that it lacks experience. Ten of the players have never been to England, and the team is enormously weakened by the absence of Dennis Lillee.

Batsmen Kim Hughes and Craig Serjeant, wicketkeeper Richie Robinson and bowlers Mick Malone and Ray Bright have had no Test match experience, and six of the front-line batsmen have only played 22 Tests between them.

There is surprise at the omission of all-rounder Gary Gilmour, who has shown himself capable of running through a side with his bowling. His poor Centenary Test probably counted against him, but his replacement, Geoff Dymock, at 31, has not succeeded at Test level and has no great batting record.

The team is: Greg Chappell (capt.), Rod Marsh (v.c.), Ray Bright, Gary Cosier, Ian Davis, Geoff Dymock, David Hookes, Kim Hughes, Mick Malone, Rick McCosker, Kerry O'Keeffe, Len Pascoe, Richie Robinson, Craig Serjeant, Jeff Thomson, Max Walker and Doug Walters.

The ugly Australians. A decidedly scruffy Australian team lines up behind captain Greg Chappell and manager Len Maddocks.

London, May 9. The news is out. Kerry Packer has signed up 35 of the world's top cricketers and plans to play a series of 'Supertests' and one day games in Australia next summer.

All but four of the Australian team touring England at the moment have signed up with the Packer organisation. Those on the 'outer' are Geoff Dymock, Gary Cosier, Kim Hughes and Craig Sergeant.

The news has stunned the ICC and other cricket bodies, including the Australian Cricket Board.

The manager of the Australian touring party, Len Maddocks, has been in telephone consultation with the ACB. He has subsequently told the press that the current tour was 'on' and no player would be recalled.

The news came out today after a party at the home of the English captain Tony Greig. Greig today issued a statement admitting he had signed with Mr Packer. He had apparently been alerted by fast bowler John Snow that Australian journalists Peter McFarline and Alan Shiell were about to break the story.

Similarly, it is known that the *Daily Mail* cricket writer Ian Wooldridge had pieced together the story, and was ready to go to press, despite denials from his good friend Richie Benaud.

Benaud, it transpires, is under contract to Mr Packer to manage the Supertest series in Australia.

The 35 players are being paid between $16,500 and $35,000 per year on contracts extending for three years.

They include 18 Australians, 13 of whom are touring England. The extra five are Ian Chappell, Ian Redpath and Ross Edwards (all retired from representative cricket), Dennis Lillee (unavailable to tour), and all-rounder Gary Gilmour.

Other contracted players are:

England: Tony Greig, Derek Underwood, Alan Knott, John Snow.

South Africa: Barry Richards, Mike Procter, Graeme Pollock, Eddie Barlow, Denys Hobson.

Pakistan: Mushtaq Mohammad, Asif Iqbal, Majid Khan, Imran Khan.

West Indies: Andy Roberts, Clive Lloyd, Vivien Richards, Michael Holding.

Roy Ullyett

LILLEE NOT TO TOUR ENGLAND

A disappointed English batsman.

QUICK SINGLES

Still standing. The Australian team lands in London on April 22. Rod Marsh and Doug Walters are the worse for wear, having beaten the Qantas 'Sydney to London drinking record'.

A wet start. Torrential rain on May 2 wipes out the opening first class match of the tour, against Surrey.

Slow going. Icy wind and rain allow only five hours of play in three days to May 5, with Australia making 7/240 against Glamorgan (Serjeant 50, Hughes 80).

Yet again. Game against Sussex washed out on May 12. Australia 1/111 (Serjeant 55).

And again. Not a ball bowled in match against Hampshire, ending on May 16. England's wettest spring for 100 years.

Idle hands. Australians claim a record on May 16. Of 88 hours of scheduled play in their first five games, they have been on the field for only 22 hours.

Saved by stand. Australia struggles to a draw against Glamorgan on May 19, after being 6/39. Kerry O'Keeffe (26 not out) and Ray Bright (21 not out) hold on until stumps.

Sour apples. Australia loses Somerset match, ending May 24, despite centuries to Hookes and Chappell. Young Somerset all-rounder Ian Botham impresses, and West Indians Joel Garner and Viv Richards boost Somerset team.

One day loss. England wins the Prudential Trophy one day series ending June 6, two matches to one.

Begorrah. A hook from Craig Serjeant crashes through the bar room window at Leinster Country Ground, Dublin, on June 8, showering drinkers and cricketers with shards of broken glass.

Packer meet. International Cricket Conference meets in emergency session on June 14 and decides it wants to confer with Kerry Packer on his plans.

Not this Bird. Famous English umpire Dicky Bird announces on July 15 that he has declined an offer to officiate in the Packer Supertests.

Rock-bottom. An Australian side is beaten for the first time ever by the Minor Counties in a two-day match at Sunderland on August 7.

Captain quits. Greg Chappell resigns from the Australian captaincy on August 30, as he is to be involved with planned Packer cricket circus.

Packer gets runs. Kerry Packer bats eighth for the Australian Press team against the English Press and makes 2 not out.

How the deal was done

The full story of cricket's best-kept secret can now be told. It had its genesis in Kerry Packers' dealing with the Australian Cricket Board, which effectively shut out his bid for television rights to Australian cricket.

In late 1976 former journalists and sports managers, John Cornell ('Strop' of the Paul Hogan TV show) and Austin Robertson, put to Packer the idea of a series of TV matches with 'personality' players, mostly out of first class cricket. Packer took it a further step, suggesting they sign up the best in the world.

With his backing and money, they set out to get the players, with Dennis Lillee as their chief advisor and assistant. Lillee was the first to sign, for a contract worth $105,000. That same day he took 5/44 against South Australia.

Intakhab Alam, who was touring with the Pakistan team, was next and the revolution was underway. The next rich signing ground was New Zealand, where Australia was playing a short Test series. Cornell and Robertson gained the agreement of most members of the Australian team, masquerading as representatives of the program 'A Current Affair' to mask their frequent appearances around the dressing rooms.

The two go-betweens have had a hectic time in the last few months. After the Centenary Test they moved among the players, handing some of them envelopes of 'theatre tickets', which turned out to be cheques.

They went to the West Indies in April, meeting up with an extra persuader, Tony Greig, and taking just four days to sign up the players. After that, a trip to the English camp, where again the signatures came easily, and back to Australia to round up Hookes, Chappell, Bright, Robinson, Thomson and Marsh.

The press reaction, in England and around the world, has been immediate, and reflected shock and horror at the split at the top of cricket. Ian Woolridge described the rebel players as the 'Dogs of Cricket'.

Jubilee Test an honourable draw

Greg Chappell falls in evading a Bob Willis bouncer at Old Trafford.

Lord's, June 21. After a see-sawing battle, in which England had the upper hand on the last day, Australia has held on to force a draw in the Jubilee Test match at Lords. Australia needed 226 to win in 105 minutes, plus 20 overs, but at 5/71 was in dire peril of losing.

Resolute defence by Rod Marsh (6 not out) and Kerry O'Keeffe (8 not out) was required to see Australia out of danger.

The match tilted Australia's way after the first innings, which left them 80 runs ahead, despite the fine bowling of England's Bob Willis, who took 7/87. Chappell (66), Serjeant (81) and Doug Walters (53) had added some spine to an innings which took Australia to 5/256 before they were bundled out for 296.

England's second innings, however, showed more resolution, and at one stage was 5/286. Bob Woolmer had followed his first innings 76 with 120, and Tony Greig spanked 91 runs. Then a game that seemed headed for a draw came to life, as England lost four wickets for 0, surrendering its last six wickets for 19 runs.

Jeff Thomson proved his worth when he was needed, with 4/86 and match figures of 8/127. He was well supported by the tearaway Len Pascoe and the steady, probing bowling of Max Walker.

But the chase for victory went awry due to rash shots, with only David Hookes (50) shining.

Tony Greig dropped as England captain

London, May 14. The UK Cricket Council has dropped Tony Greig from the captaincy of England because of his involvement with Packer cricket, saying: 'His action has inevitably impaired the trust which existed between the cricket authorities and the captain of the England side.

The council has yet to rule on the eligibility of the four English rebels – Greig, Alan Knott, John Snow and Derek Underwood, for the Tests against Australia.

Greig, captain for 14 Tests and regarded as a leader in the revival of English cricket, is unrepentant, despite attacks from the British press, some alluding to his upbringing in South Africa.

Former captain Colin Cowdrey wrote: 'Alas, a sickening temptation has been put in his way, and in the moment of euphoria after his trimphant march through India and the excitement of the Centenary Test, he succumbed.'

England's Tony Greig: in disgrace.

Stand-off between Board and Packer

London, June 22. A meeting between the International Cricket Confence and promoter Kerry Packer has foundered on Mr Packer's demand for exclusive television right to Australian cricket after the 1978–79 season. The ICC told Mr Packer that it had no jurisdiction over Australian domestic arrangements. It refused to include them for discussion in any Packer-proposed 'working committee'.

Earlier Mr Packer seemed agreeable to the points put to him by the committee, namely that the program and grounds for the Packer games be acceptable to the 'home' authority and that the Packer season be over six weeks and 'under the control of the home authority', with players available for Test and first class matches.

Mr Packer said that he saw 'no insurmountable problems' but then dropped his TV-rights bombshell.

Faded hotels dampen the spirit

Leeds, Aug. 11. The Australian players, for once in reasonable quarters at the Post House Hotel, Leeds, have responded with a keener mood and brighter spirits as they prepare for the fourth Test.

The quality of the Aussie digs has been such that captain Greg Chappell publicly complained. 'Most of the hotels are so bad, they are depressing. They have had a bad effect, expecially on the younger team members.

'Perhaps because the Australian Cricket Board gave the players a pay rise recently, they cut costs in other areas.'

Earlier in the tour it was the Dudley Hotel at Hove, known to the players as the 'Deadly Dudley', which epitomised the hotels – all gloom, old furniture, peeling paint and bad plumbing.

Chappell also singled out hotels at Scarborough, Chesterfield and Northampton for special comment. The rooms did not have baths; paint was peeling from the walls and ceilings; it was appalling.'

The Scarborough Hotel was of such a poor standard that it captured the attention of the authorities only the day after the team's departure. The state of the kitchen was such that the hotel has been charged.

Chappell pointed out that teams touring Australia always had first-class accomodation. 'And if they don't like it, they can change,' he said, referring to a change in hotels make by the Pakistan team in Melbourne last summer.

England captain Mike Brearley brings a new idea to the game with a home-designed helmet.

Boycott and Co. grind life out

Geoff Boycott happily owns up to scoring a hundred hundreds in front of his unquestioning Yorkshire fans.

London, Aug. 30. It has been a dismal summer for Australian cricketers in England, and a dismal winter for those who stayed up late in Australia to watch England completely dominate the series.

While Geoff Boycott is loved in Yorkshire and at least admired in England for his ability to compile big scores, his grafting style of play has been an irritant to partisan Australians, as he has ground the bowlers in to the turf.

His 100th first class century was the cause of national celebration in England, and unrelieved gloom in Australia, especially as it accompanied a decline in the Australian team's performance and morale.

Bob Woolmer (137), Derek Randall (79) and Tony Greig (76) did the job in the nine-wicket win in the second Test, when England compiled 437 and 1/82 in reply to Australia's 297 and 218. Only Greg Chappell's 112 in the second innings (more than half the total score) gave some comfort to the Australians.

Then Boycott was brought onto the stage and with successive scores of 107, 80 not out and 191 put paid to any remaining hopes in the third and fourth Tests, which England won by seven wickets, and then an innings and 85 runs.

Boycott's early partners crashed around him in the first innings of the third Test, and at one stage England was 5/82, but he found a stalwart companion in wicketkeeper Alan Knott who made his highest Test score of 135. Knott went on to be Boycott's best partner in the fourth Test, compiling 57 as the pair added 123 runs for the sixth wicket.

Australia's bowling has lacked variety and penetration, with Jeff Thomson below his fiery best, Max Walker merely workmanlike, Len Pascoe pitching too short and the spinners failing to cause real trouble. Thomson's 100th Test wicket in the drawn fifth Test was the only cause for muted celebration.

The continued and inexplicable omission of the young and enthusiastic Mick Malone from the Test team, finally rectified in the more promising fifth Test, has made the Australian bowling look stale and predictable.

The Australians have obviously been unsettled by the furore that has surrounded their almost complete defection to the impending Packer Circus, and their morale has been low, despite many team meetings and attempts to create a sense of purpose.

A sample of Australia's failings came in the third Test at Nottingham, when Ian Botham ripped the heart out of the innings with five wickets in 34 balls, as Australia slumped from 0/74 to 8/155, with the batsman slashing imprudently outside the off stump. The batsman wanted to hit their way out of trouble, rather than displaying the will to fight for the hard runs.

The Australians finally came into some form in the fifth Test, when Mick Malone was brought into the side and snared five wickets to have England all out for 214 after an opening stand of 88. The Australian tail wagged for once (Hookes 85, Marsh 57, Walker 78 not out and Malone 46) to give the tourists 385 and a 171-run lead. But rain had shortened the match to the point that there was no hope of a result.

Of the batsman only Greg Chappell can stand tall. Doug Walters was again unable to get going in England. He has failed to make 1000 runs on any of his four tours, and this time he made only 235 in five Tests, and has a Test average of 26.5.

Walters, on the hard, fast pitches of Australia, is a crisp strokemaker, but the soft pitches and humid airs of England he seems to grope for the ball.

The new hope of the side, the dashing David Hookes, seems to have a similar problem, and the bold strokemaker of the Centenary Test made only 283 in nine Test innings, with an 85 in the fifth Test his only worthwhile innings.

Rick McCosker had a great third Test, with 51 and 107, but he, Ian Davis and Craig Serjeant could not run into consistent form.

In a most dismal tour, the team won only five of the 22 matches it played.

Australian cricket has been becalmed in England in advance of the cricket storms that lie ahead.

# of Australia

A disappointing last Test innings in England for Doug Walters.

The end for Greg Chappell, caught and bowled Derek Underwood for 39.

ICC ban on Packer Players

The game divided – between the old tradition and a brave new world?

London, July 26. A meeting of the International Cricket Conference has today announced that players who compete for the Packer organisation in any of the so-called Supertest cricket matches will be ineligible to play in any Test competition thereafter. The decision is binding for all governing bodies of the cricket countries, and the ban can only be lifted by the ICC.

The meeting's communique tersely stated: 'It is hereby resolved that any match arranged, or to be arranged by J. P. Sport Pty Ltd, Mr Kerry Packer, Mr Richie Benaud or associated companies or persons, to take place in Australia or elsewhere between 1 October 1977 and 31 March 1979 is disapproved.'

The communique leaves open the question as to whether the rebel players will be eligible to play at club, State, Province or County level.

The news has been greeted by the players and press alike without surprise, but with the realisation that the world's finest cricketers will not again appear for the countries at recognised Test level.

Meanwhile, plans for the World Series Packer tour in Australia have advanced to the point that two pitches are being prepared in hot-house conditions outside the Waverley Park football ground in Melbourne.

They are being grown using the same Merri Creek soil as is employed for the MCG pitches, by Melbourne curator Jack Maley. The pitches are in tubs, so that they can be transported to the centre of the ground and placed in a trench, or sent to other venues.

Averages show team of dismal performers

London, Aug. 30. The only credit the Australians could take from the 1977 Ashes series was some sort of form in the first and fifth Tests. For the rest they were completely outplayed. The abysmal batting averages for the tour point up the Australian weakness. The great batsman Greg Chappell, who has at times been compared to Bradman, had an under-average series, with an average of 41.22. David Hookes was the only other tourist to average better than 30 – 31.44.

The remainder of the Australian batsman can be ranked as failures. Craig Sergeant, Doug Walters, Ian David, Rick McCosker and 'keeper Rod Marsh might have been expected to do something with the bat. They never came to terms with their task, although McCosker joined Chappell as the only other player to score a Test century.

Gary Cosier was a virtual passenger, never displaying enough form or application to warrant a Test place.

England's superiority in batting was so evident. Geoff Boycott played in only three games, but towered over over all others with 442 from five innings and an average of 147.33.

Australia's best bowler was Jeff Thomson with 27 wickets, while Walker bowled without luck for 14 wickets. Mick Malone played in the last Test and showed what might have been with 6/77.

Willis, with 27 wickets, led a more potent bowling line-up.

And, for once, England was sharp in the field, where Australia was only sloppy and dispirited.

Is there anyone out there?

Australian v West Indies in 1952. Broadcasting for the ABC are 'Johnny' Moyes, Ernest Eytles, Alan McGilvray, Vic Richardson and Bernard Kerr.

Cricket might have been invented for the wireless, and vice versa. They were made for each other, as entertainment, as news and as a kind of art form which overcame the dreaded 'tyranny of distance' for Australians starved of cricket on winter's nights down under.

From the very beginning of radio in Australia proprietors of commercial stations, and later the ABC, saw the potential of cricket.

The first cricket broadcasts from a ground were heard on 2BL Sydney in December 1924, when progress scores of Herbie Collins' and Bill Ponsford's hundreds were broadcast at 15-minute intervals. The first 'ball-by-ball' broadcasts was by Edgar Mayne from the MCG on 1 January 1925 at the second Test, Bill Ponsford and Vic Richardson making hundreds.

By 1930 when Bill Woodfull captained Don Bradman on his extraordinary tour of England, the demand for up-to-the-minute details was insatiable. It was not possible to broadcast direct from England. David Worrall of 3DB in Melbourne and Oswald Anderson 2UW in Sydney decided to cover the cricket by reading telegrams of play from the first Test at Trent Bridge. After a few hours on the first night, Worrall began to wonder whether anyone was listening. He said 'Is anyone out there listening? Should we close down now or carry on until stumps?' The switchboard lit up, and telegrams poured in.

Soon Worrall developed a variety-show format to accompany the scores – a precursor of the many comedy sports shows on radio and TV in the 1980s and 1990s.

Comedy and music was used to fill the gaps between cables. By 1934 3DB used particular songs

for different cricketing occasions. A doll named Rickety Kate was on the studio wall and the fall of a wicket her eyes would light up as a signal for the studio audience to sing songs to mourn or celebrate.

By 1938 there was competition in the form of serious cricket broadcasting from the ABC, but 3DB kept up its own variety of ball-by-ball description until 1956, by then under the management of Ron Casey, using experts such as Vic Richardson and Lindsay Hassett.

The ABC began its famous 'synthetic' broadcasts of the cricket in 1934. Rather than offer a variety show, Charles Moses and the team, including Alan McGilvray, recreated the sounds and feel of a Test match in the studio with pencils tapping wood, and sound effects simulating applause.

In 1948 short-wave broadcasting from England to Australia was possible for the first time, and the advertisement-free sound of cricket wafted across the atmosphere for the first time.

Something in the order of 70 per cent of Australian radios were tuned in at some time to the 1947–48 series – and 90 per cent of households had radios. It was a big national audience – the most important shared event in the life of the post-war Australian community.

The ABC broadcast every series Australia was involved in, at home, and away, from 1932–33 when it first offered a national ball-by-ball description, through the 1950s.

The intimacy, portability, accuracy and sheer entertainment value means ABC radio has made cultural heroes of commentators such as McGilvray, and in recent years, of Tim Lane.

FIRST TEST 1977 ENGLAND v AUSTRALIA
Lord's Cricket Ground, London. June 16, 17, 18, 20, 21, 1977.
Toss: England. Match Drawn.

ENGLAND

DL Amiss b Thomson	4	b Thomson	0
JM Brearley (c) c Robinson b Thomson	9	c Robinson b O'Keeffe	49
RA Woolmer run out	79	c Chappell b Pascoe	120
DW Randall c Chappell b Walker	53 (7)	c McCosker b Thomson	0
AW Greig b Pascoe	5 (4)	c O'Keeffe b Pascoe	91
GD Barlow c McCosker b Walker	1 (5)	lbw Pascoe	5
APE Knott (+) c Walters b Thomson	8 (6)	c Walters b Walker	8
CM Old c Marsh b Walker	9	c Walters b Walker	0
JK Lever b Pascoe	8	c Marsh b Thomson	3
DL Underwood not out	11	not out	12
RGD Willis b Thomson	17	c Marsh b Thomson	0
Extras (B 1, LB 3, W 1, NB 7)	12	(B 5, LB 9, W 1, NB 2)	17
TOTAL	216		305

FOW 1st Inns: 12 13 111 121 134 155 171 183 189 216
FOW 2nd Inns: 0 132 224 263 286 286 286 286 305 305

Bowling: *First Innings*: Thomson 20.5-5-41-4, Pascoe 23-7-53-2, Walker 30-6-66-3, O'Keeffe 10-3-32-0, Chappell 3-0-12-0. *Second Innings*: Thomson 24.4-3-86-4, Pascoe 26-2-96-3, Walker 35-13-56-2, Chappell 12-2-24-0, O'Keeffe 15-7-26-1.

AUSTRALIA

RD Robinson b Lever	11	c Woolmer b Old	4
RB McCosker b Old	23	b Willis	1
GS Chappell (c) c Old b Willis	66	c Lever b Old	24
CS Serjeant c Knott b Willis	81 (6)	c Amiss b Underwood	3
KD Walters c Brearley b Willis	53	c (S)AGE Ealham b Underwood	10
DW Hookes c Brearley b Old	11 (4)	c & b Willis	50
RW Marsh (+) lbw Willis	1	not out	6
KJ O'Keeffe c(S)AGE Ealham b Willis	12	not out	8
MHN Walker c Knott b Willis	4		
JR Thomson b Willis	6		
LS Pascoe not out	3		
Extras (LB 7, W 1, NB 17)	25	(NB 8)	8
TOTAL	296		6 for 114

FOW 1st Inns: 25 51 135 238 256 264 265 284 290 296
FOW 2nd Inns: 5 5 48 64 71 102

Bowling: *First Innings*: Willis 30.1-7-78-7, Lever 19-5-61-1, Underwood 25-6-42-0, Old 35-10-70-2, Woolmer 5-1-20-0. *Second Innings*: Willis 10-1-40-2, Old 14-0-46-2, Underwood 10-3-16-2, Lever 5-2-4-0.

Umpires: HD Bird & WL Budd

SECOND TEST 1977 ENGLAND v AUSTRALIA
Old Trafford, Manchester. July 7, 8, 9, 11, 12, 1977.
Toss: Australia. England won by 9 wkts.

AUSTRALIA

RB McCosker c Old b Willis	2	c Underwood b Willis	0
IC Davis c Knott b Old	34	c Lever b Willis	12
GS Chappell (c) c Knott b Greig	44	b Underwood	112
CS Serjeant lbw Lever	14	c Woolmer b Underwood	8
KD Walters c Greig b Miller	88	lbw Greig	10
DW Hookes c Knott b Lever	5	c Brearley b Miller	28
RW Marsh (+) c Amiss b Miller	36	c Randall b Underwood	1
RJ Bright c Greig b Lever	12	c & b Underwood	0
KJ O'Keeffe c Knott b Willis	12	not out	24
MHN Walker b Underwood	9	c Greig b Underwood	6
JR Thomson not out	14	c Randall b Underwood	1
Extras (LB 15, NB 12)	27	(LB 1, W 1, NB 14)	16
TOTAL	297		218

FOW 1st Inns: 4 80 96 125 140 238 246 272 272 297
FOW 2nd Inns: 0 30 74 92 146 147 147 202 212 218

Bowling: *First Innings*: Willis 21-8-45-2, Lever 25-8-60-3, Old 20-3-57-1, Underwood 20.2-7-53-1, Greig 13-4-37-1, Miller 10-3-18-2. *Second Innings*: Willis 16-2-56-2, Lever 4-1-11-0, Underwood 32.5-13-66-6, Old 8-1-26-0, Greig 12-6-19-1, Miller 9-2-24-1.

ENGLAND

DL Amiss c Chappell b Walker	11	not out	28
JM Brearley (c) c Chappell b Thomson	6	c Walters b O'Keeffe	44
RA Woolmer c Davis b O'Keeffe	137	not out	0
DW Randall lbw Bright	79		
AW Greig c & b Walker	76		
APE Knott (+) c O'Keeffe b Thomson	39		
G Miller c Marsh b Thomson	6		
CM Old c Marsh b Walker	37		
JK Lever b Bright	10		
DL Underwood b Bright	10		
RGD Willis not out	1		
Extras (B 9, LB 9, NB 7)	25	(LB 3, NB 7)	10
TOTAL	437		1 for 82

FOW 1st Inns: 19 23 165 325 348 366 377 404 435 437
FOW 2nd Inns: 75

Bowling: *First Innings*: Thomson 38-11-73-3, Walker 54-15-131-3, Bright 35.1-12-69-3, O'Keeffe 36-11-114-1, Chappell 6-1-25-0. *Second Innings*: Thomson 8-2-24-0, Walker 7-0-17-0, O'Keeffe 9.1-4-25-1, Bright 5-2-6-0.

Umpires: WE Alley & TW Spencer

THIRD TEST 1977 ENGLAND v AUSTRALIA
Trent Bridge, Nottingham. July 28, 29, 30, August 1, 2, 1977.
Toss: Australia. England won by 7 wkts.

AUSTRALIA

RB McCosker c Brearley b Hendrick	51	c Brearley b Willis	107
IC Davis c Botham b Underwood	33	c Greig b Willis	9
GS Chappell (c) b Botham	19	b Hendrick	27
DW Hookes c Hendrick b Willis	17	lbw Hendrick	42
KD Walters c Hendrick b Botham	11	c Randall b Greig	28
RD Robinson c Brearley b Greig	11	lbw Underwood	34
RW Marsh (+) lbw Botham	0	c Greig b Willis	0
KJ O'Keeffe not out	48	not out	21
MHN Walker c Hendrick b Botham	0	b Willis	17
JR Thomson c Knott b Botham	21	b Willis	0
LS Pascoe c Greig b Hendrick	20	c Hendrick b Underwood	0
Extras (B 4, LB 2, NB 6)	12	(B 1, LB 5, W 1, NB 17)	24
TOTAL	243		309

FOW 1st Inns: 79 101 131 133 153 153 153 155 196 243
FOW 2nd Inns: 18 60 154 204 240 240 270 307 308 309

Bowling: *First Innings*: Willis 15-0-58-1, Hendrick 21.2-6-46-2, Botham 20-5-74-5, Greig 15-4-35-1, Underwood 11-5-18-1. *Second Innings*: Willis 26-6-88-5, Hendrick 32-14-56-2, Botham 25-5-60-0, Greig 9-2-24-1, Underwood 27-15-49-2, Miller 5-2-5-0, Woolmer 3-0-3-0.

ENGLAND

JM Brearley (c) c Hookes b Pascoe	15	b Walker	81
G Boycott c McCosker b Thomson	107	not out	80
RA Woolmer lbw Pascoe	0		
DW Randall run out	13 (5)	not out	19
AW Greig b Thomson	11 (4)	b Walker	0
G Miller c Robinson b Pascoe	13		
APE Knott (+) c Davis b Thomson	135 (3)	c O'Keeffe b Walker	2
IT Botham b Walker	25		
DL Underwood b Pascoe	7		
M Hendrick b Walker	1		
RGD Willis not out	2		
Extras (B 9, LB 7, W 3, NB 16)	35	(B 2, LB 2, W 1, NB 2)	7
TOTAL	364		3 for 189

FOW 1st Inns: 34 34 52 64 82 297 326 357 357 364
FOW 2nd Inns: 154 156 158

Bowling: *First Innings*: Thomson 31-6-103-3, Pascoe 32-10-80-4, Walters 3-0-5-0, Chappell 8-0-19-0, O'Keeffe 11-4-43-0, Walker 39.2-12-79-2. *Second Innings*: Thomson 16-6-34-0, Pascoe 22-6-43-0, O'Keeffe 19.2-2-65-0, Walker 24-8-40-3.

Umpires: HD Bird & DJ Constant

FOURTH TEST 1977 ENGLAND v AUSTRALIA
Headingley, Leeds. August 11, 12, 13, 15, 1977.
Toss: England. England won by an innings & 85 runs.

ENGLAND

JM Brearley (c) c Marsh b Thomson	0
G Boycott c Chappell b Pascoe	191
RA Woolmer c Chappell b Thomson	37
DW Randall lbw Pascoe	20
AW Greig b Thomson	43
GRJ Roope c Walters b Thomson	34
APE Knott (+) lbw Bright	57
IT Botham b Bright	0
DL Underwood c Bright b Pascoe	6
M Hendrick c Robinson b Pascoe	4
RGD Willis not out	5
Extras (B 5, LB 9, W 3, NB 22)	39
TOTAL	436

FOW 1st Inns: 0 82 105 201 275 398 398 412 422 436

Bowling: *First Innings*: Thomson 34-7-113-4, Walker 48-21-97-0, Pascoe 34.4-10-91-4, Walters 3-1-5-0, Bright 26-9-66-2, Chappell 10-2-25-0.

AUSTRALIA

RB McCosker run out	27	c Knott b Greig	12
IC Davis lbw Hendrick	0	c Knott b Greig	19
GS Chappell (c) c Brearley b Hendrick	4	c Greig b Willis	36
DW Hookes lbw Botham	24	lbw Hendrick	21
KD Walters c Knott b Botham	4	lbw Woolmer	15
RD Robinson c Greig b Hendrick	20	b Hendrick	20
RW Marsh (+) c Knott b Botham	2	c Randall b Hendrick	63
RJ Bright not out	9	c Greig b Hendrick	5
MHN Walker c Knott b Botham	7	b Willis	30
JR Thomson b Botham	0	b Willis	0
LS Pascoe b Hendrick	0	not out	0
Extras (LB 3, W 1, NB 2)	6	(B 1, LB 4, W 4, NB 18)	27
TOTAL	103		248

FOW 1st Inns: 8 26 52 57 66 77 87 100 100 103
FOW 2nd Inns: 31 35 63 97 130 167 179 244 245 248

Bowling: *First Innings*: Willis 5-0-35-0, Hendrick 15.3-2-41-4, Botham 11-3-21-5. *Second Innings*: Willis 14-7-32-3, Hendrick 22.5-6-54-4, Greig 20-7-64-2, Botham 17-3-47-0, Woolmer 8-4-8-1, Underwood 8-3-16-0.

Umpires: WE Alley & WL Budd

FIFTH TEST 1977 ENGLAND v AUSTRALIA
Kennington Oval, London. August 25 (no play),26, 27, 29, 30, 1977.
Toss: Australia. Match Drawn.

ENGLAND

JM Brearley (c) c Marsh b Malone	39	c Serjeant b Thomson	4
G Boycott c McCosker b Walker	39	not out	25
RA Woolmer lbw Thomson	15	c Marsh b Malone	6
DW Randall c Marsh b Malone	3	not out	20
AW Greig c Bright b Malone	0		
GRJ Roope b Thomson	38		
APE Knott (+) c McCosker b Malone	6		
JK Lever lbw Malone	3		
DL Underwood b Thomson	20		
M Hendrick b Thomson	15		
RGD Willis not out	24		
Extras (LB 6, W 1, NB 5)	12	(W 2)	2
TOTAL	214		2 for 57

FOW 1st Inns: 86 88 104 104 106 122 130 169 174 214
FOW 2nd Inns: 5 16

Bowling: *First Innings*: Thomson 23.2-3-87-4, Malone 47-20-63-5, Walker 28-11-51-1, Bright 3-2-1-0. *Second Innings*: Thomson 5-1-22-1, Malone 10-4-14-1, Walker 8-2-14-0, Bright 3-2-5-0.

AUSTRALIA

CS Serjeant lbw Willis	0
RB McCosker lbw Willis	32
GS Chappell (c) c & b Underwood	39
KJ Hughes c Willis b Hendrick	1
DW Hookes c Knott b Greig	85
KD Walters b Willis	4
RW Marsh (+) lbw Hendrick	57
RJ Bright lbw Willis	16
MHN Walker not out	78
MF Malone b Lever	46
JR Thomson b Willis	17
Extras (B 1, LB 6, NB 3)	10
TOTAL	385

FOW 1st Inns: 0 54 67 84 104 184 236 252 352 385

Bowling: *First Innings*: Willis 29.3-5-102-5, Hendrick 37-5-93-2, Lever 22-6-61-1, Underwood 35-9-102-1, Greig 8-2-17-1.

Umpires: DJ Constant & TW Spencer

Australian Averages

1977 ENGLAND v AUSTRALIA

AUSTRALIA	M	Inn	NO	Runs	H.S	Avrge	Ct	St	Overs	Mds	Runs	Wkt	Avrge
Bright, RJ	3	5	1	42	16	10.50	2	-	72.1	27	147	5	29.40
Chappell, GS	5	9	-	371	112	41.22	6	-	39.0	5	105	-	-
Davis, IC	3	6	-	107	34	17.83	2	-	-	-	-	-	-
Hookes, DW	5	9	-	283	85	31.44	1	-	-	-	-	-	-
Hughes, KJ	1	1	-	1	1	1.00	-	-	-	-	-	-	-
Malone, MF	1	1	-	46	46	46.00	-	-	57.0	24	77	6	12.83
Marsh, RW	5	9	1	166	63	20.75	9	-	-	-	-	-	-
McCosker, RB	5	9	-	255	107	28.33	5	-	-	-	-	-	-
O'Keeffe, KJ	3	6	4	125	48*	62.50	3	-	100.3	31	305	3	101.67
Pascoe, LS	3	5	2	23	20	7.67	-	-	137.4	35	363	13	27.92
Robinson, RD	3	6	-	100	34	16.67	4	-	-	-	-	-	-
Serjeant, CS	3	5	-	106	81	21.20	1	-	-	-	-	-	-
Thomson, JR	5	8	1	59	21	8.43	-	-	200.5	44	583	23	25.35
Walker, MHN	5	8	1	151	78*	21.57	1	-	273.2	88	551	14	39.36
Walters, KD	5	9	-	223	88	24.78	5	-	6.0	1	10	-	-

English Averages

1977 ENGLAND v AUSTRALIA

ENGLAND	M	Inn	NO	Runs	H.S	Avrge	Ct	St	Overs	Mds	Runs	Wkt	Avrge
Amiss, DL	2	4	1	43	28*	14.33	2	-	-	-	-	-	-
Barlow, GD	1	2	-	6	5	3.00	-	-	-	-	-	-	-
Botham, IT	2	2	-	25	25	12.50	1	-	73.0	16	202	10	20.20
Boycott, G	3	5	2	442	191	147.33	-	-	-	-	-	-	-
Brearley, JM	5	9	-	247	81	27.44	7	-	-	-	-	-	-
Greig, AW	5	7	-	226	91	32.29	9	-	77.0	25	196	7	28.00
Hendrick, M	3	3	-	20	15	6.67	5	-	128.4	33	290	14	20.71
Knott, APE	5	7	-	255	135	36.43	12	-	-	-	-	-	-
Lever, JK	3	4	-	24	10	6.00	2	-	75.0	22	197	5	39.40
Miller, G	2	2	-	19	13	9.50	-	-	24.0	7	47	3	15.67
Old, CM	2	3	-	46	37	15.33	2	-	77.0	14	199	5	39.80
Randall, DW	5	8	2	207	79	34.50	4	-	-	-	-	-	-
Roope, GRJ	2	2	-	72	38	36.00	-	-	-	-	-	-	-
Underwood, DL	5	6	2	66	20	16.50	3	-	169.1	61	362	13	27.85
Willis, RGD	5	6	4	49	24*	24.50	2	-	166.4	36	534	27	19.78
Woolmer, RA	5	8	1	394	137	56.29	2	-	16.0	5	31	1	31.00

It's Simpson and Co.

Cartoonist Bill Mitchell takes this view of Bob Simpson's Test cricket recall.

Sydney, Oct. 17. Following Greg Chappell's defection to World Series Cricket, former Australian captain Bob Simpson has agreed to return to Test cricket and captain Australia against India this summer.

Ironically, the last time Simpson played in a Test series was against India in 1967–68, where he scored centuries in Melbourne and Sydney, held six catches, and took 3/39 and 5/59.

Since then, Simpson has continued to play grade cricket in Sydney for the Western Suburbs. But he is now aged 41, and naturally has a few reservations about the comeback.

'Right now I think I am more nervous than when I started batting against Wes Hall and Charlie Griffith,' he said.

Simpson says he has received comeback offers almost annually since 1968, and was 'very sceptical' when the Australian Cricket Board made their approach over lunch at Sydney's Angus Steak House in September.

He agreed that after all the upheaval of the past 12 months there was a need for someone experienced to lead Australia, and was flattered that the Board considered he was that person.

Aggressive fast bowler Jeff Thomson will be Simpson's deputy in a young and inexperienced team that includes Test debutants Graham Yallop, Craig Sergeant, Peter Toohey, David Ogilvie, Wayne Clark, Paul Hibbert and a new wicketkeeper, Steve Rixon.

As a result, many new players will be blooded in Sheffield Shield cricket this season.

The old skipper leads his boys to a 2–0 advantage

Perth, Dec. 22. Two Tests down, and it's two close wins to Australia over India. At the WACA ground yesterday, the margin was two wickets, while in the first Test in Brisbane a fortnight ago, Australia won by just 16 runs.

The veteran Australian skipper, Bob Simpson, made a shaky start to his Test comeback, scoring only seven runs in his first innings at Brisbane, but followed up with 89 in the next. His 176 at Perth leaves no doubt. The old stager hasn't lost his touch.

Simpson's 89 in Brisbane clinched the first Test, where India's Bishen Bedi took 5/55 in Australia's first-innings total of 166. Peter Toohey made a fine Test debut, batting consistently for 82 and 57.

India had to chase 341 runs in the last two days, and almost got there.

The pitch in Perth was better suited to Australian fast bowler Jeff Thomson (4/101 & 2/65), although Bedi still managed to take five wickets in each innings.

Perth was a high-scoring affair. Centuries were made by India's Sunil Gavaskar (127) and Mohinder Armanath (100), and also by Australians Bob Simpson (176) and Tony Mann, who came in as a nightwatchman and made 105.

At 41, Simpson is the oldest Australian to score a century in a home Test. 'Although my reflexes may be slightly slower,' Simpson says, 'experience counts.'

It counts sufficiently for Australia to be two–nil up, in fact.

The subcontinent's prayers will soon be answered for India's turbaned spin magician, Bishen Bedi, seen warming up.

Sponsorship swells ACB funds

Melbourne, Dec. 15. Televised coverage of cricket has doubled, perhaps trebled, the commercial value of the sport, and companies are clamouring to promote their business via cricket.

Poor player payments have been a sore point for years, but thanks to a prod from World Series Cricket, the Australian Cricket Board has now negotiated lucrative sponsorship deals which have funded significant player payment increases.

Foremost among these deals, Benson and Hedges has provided an $800,000 major sponsorship package. New South Wales has been sponsored by Tooheys Brewery and Victoria by Federated Insurance.

Hookesy rejects $50,000 from SACA

Adelaide, Oct. 19. Batsman David Hookes has rejected an offer promising $50,000 per year if he leaves World Series Cricket and continues playing cricket with South Australia.

The president of the South Australian Cricket Association, Philip Ridings, is disappointed by Hookes' decision to knock back such a rewarding and permanent contract.

Last season Hookes made five centuries in his six appearances for South Australia in the Sheffield Shield, won by WA.

Spinners salute. India's Bishen Bedi (left) and Bhagwat Chandra, at the third Test in Melbourne.

Chandra leads the charge

Veteran Australian captain Bob Simpson is out lbw (4) to Chandra.

Sydney, Jan. 13. India has come back with a vengeance in the past two Tests, trouncing Australia by 222 runs at Melbourne in the third Test last week, and by an innings and 2 runs yesterday at the SCG.

India's outstanding spin attack has done all the damage to Australia.

The Indian captain, Bishen Bedi, ended with figures of 2/71 and 4/58 in Melbourne, and 3/49 and 2/62 in the fourth Test in Sydney. His partner, Bhagwat Subrahmanya Chandrasekhar (Chandra for short), was even better, taking 6/52 twice at Melbourne, and 4/30 and 2/85 in Sydney. Erapally Prasanna took 1/14 and 4/51 in Sydney.

More than anything else, Chandra's extraordinary bowling at Melbourne was responsible for India's first-ever Test win in Australia. His batting, however, left room for improvement (0 and 0).

Chandra's team-mate, Sunil Gavaskar, also made a duck in his first innings, but soon made amends with 118 in the second innings, his third century of the tour.

Gavaskar made 49 in the fourth Test, where Australia was let down by an abysmal first-innings total of 131. The pitch was damp due to torrential rain which drenched the SCG before the match, and Australia died a slow and painful death in a Scotch mist – not the kind of conditions to be expected in Sydney.

When Bedi complained about a damp spot on the Randwick end of the pitch, the heavy roller wasn't good enough. So the curator took out his handkerchief to finish the job with a series of gentle pats.

Such tenderness! But it did little to pacify the Indian captain.

If Australia had a hero in the fourth Test, it was Peter Toohey, who tore his ankle ligaments while fielding. Toohey was almost lame, but batted courageously with a runner to notch up 85 runs in Australia's second innings.

The series now stands at two Tests–all, and changes may have to be made if Australia is to win the deciding Test in Adelaide.

Australia scrapes home in thriller

Adelaide, Feb. 4. The 'grand old man' of Australian cricket couldn't have asked for a better 42nd birthday present than a win over India in the fifth Test.

It's true that Simpson did make a rather substantial contribution to his own present, making a century in Australia's first innings and 50 in the second. But everybody else chipped in too.

Australia amassed 505 runs in its first innings. Graham Yallop top-scored with 121 runs, and other fine batting performances were made by Rick Darling (65), Peter Toohey (60), and even the tail-enders, Bruce Yardley (22), Jeff Thomson (24) and Ian Callen (22 not out).

India made only 269 in reply, but the Indian bowlers were revitalised by their rest day on New Year's Eve, which they spent at Hill-Smith's Barossa Valley vineyard. The Australians might have had greater difficulty in the same circumstances.

Refreshed and fortified by the break, India came out on the fourth day and tipped Australia out for 256. Karsan Ghavri ended the day with figures of 4/45.

At lunch on the sixth day India needed 58 to win with two wickets in hand, but Australia dismissed the Indian spinners, Bedi (16) and Chandra (2) to snatch victory by 47 runs. A leg-spinner from the birthday boy snuffed the last candle in the Test and the series.

Indian wicketkeeper Syed Kirmani stumped Australia's Graeme Wood (39) in the fifth Test at Adelaide.

War of words over WSC

Some cheers for WSC cricket. Ian Chappell is on hand to pour the drinks.

Melbourne, Feb. 13. The first season of World Series Cricket has ended with more than 350,000 people attending the 73 WSC games played this summer.

Now Kerry Packer has had the audacity to offer 14 of his WSC players to the Australian Cricket Board, in case they need them for the forthcoming West Indies tour.

Back in October, VCA President Ray Steele accused Packer of exploiting the game for his own private benefit, and not wanting to 'put anything back into it.'

Then Greg Chappell was not selected by Queensland for the Gillette Cup.

'I have directed all my energy towards the betterment of Queensland cricket,' Chappell said, 'only to be treated shabbily in what

I believe to be retaliation for having signed with World Series Cricket.'

In November the Federal Court ruled that WSC could not use the word 'Test' to describe its matches, or call its Australian team the 'Australian' side. By a ruling in the NSW Equity Court, WSC was prevented from using the Sydney Cricket Ground.

But WSC had a win in the High Court in London with a decision that WSC players could not be prevented from playing county cricket in England.

On a more personal level, the Australian captain Bob Simpson has said 'slobs' were included in some recent Australian sides. WSC's Ian Chappell has taken offence at this and has accused Simpson of 'mud-slinging'.

Tasmania in Shield

Devonport, March 7. A draw with New South Wales yesterday leaves Tasmania with three losses and two draws in its debut Sheffield Shield season.

The strong improvement by the islanders during the summer was demonstrated by their amazing 84-run victory over India at Christmas. Tasmanian fast bowler Dennis Baker took 5/45 in that game, and experts are predicting that under the coaching of Jack Simmons Tasmania will soon have a Test cricketer or two among its ranks.

The Shield this year has been won convincingly by Western Australia (seven wins and two draws). The only team WA didn't beat was Queensland.

David Ogilvie went a long way towards replacing Greg Chappell by making six centuries for Queensland.

A new world. Cricket's old order and the WSC apocalypse.

FIRST TEST 1977–78 AUSTRALIA v INDIA
Brisbane Cricket Ground, Brisbane. December 2, 3, 4, 6, 1977.
Toss: Australia. Australia won by 16 runs.

AUSTRALIA

PA Hibbert c Kirmani b Amarnath	13	lbw Madan Lal	2
GJ Cosier c Madan Lal b Amarnath	19	c Prasanna b Madan Lal	0
AD Ogilvie c Viswanath b Bedi	5	b Chandrasekhar	46
CS Serjeant c Gavaskar b Bedi	0	b Amarnath	0
RB Simpson (c) c Gavaskar b Bedi	7	c Viswanath b Amarnath	89
PM Toohey st Kirmani b Bedi	82	c Bedi b Chandrasekhar	57
AL Mann lbw Madan Lal	19	c Amarnath b Madan Lal	29
SJ Rixon (+) c Amarnath b Bedi	9	c Kirmani b Madan Lal	6
WM Clark c Gavaskar b Chandrasekhar	4	b Madan Lal	12
JR Thomson b Chandrasekhar	3	not out	41
AG Hurst not out	0	run out	26
EXTRAS (B 3, LB 1, W 1)	5	(B 6, LB 11, NB 2)	19
TOTAL	166		327

FOW 1st Inns: 24 33 33 43 49 90 107 112 132 166
FOW 2nd Inns: 0 6 7 100 184 233 237 246 277 327

Bowling: *First Innings*: Madan Lal 10-3-27-1, Amarnath 13-4-43-2, Bedi 13.7-3-55-5, Prasanna 4-2-2-0, Chandrasekhar 6-1-34-2. *Second Innings*: Madan Lal 19-2-72-5, Amarnath 8-1-24-2, Bedi 18.5-2-71-0, Prasanna 20-4-59-0, Chandrasekhar 26-6-82-2.

INDIA

SM Gavaskar c Cosier b Clark	3	c Rixon b Clark	113
DB Vengsarkar hit wicket b Thomson	48	b Clark	1
M Amarnath lbw Clark	0	c Rixon b Thomson	47
GR Viswanath c Hurst b Mann	45	c Ogilvie b Thomson	35
BP Patel c Serjeant b Clark	13	lbw Thomson	3
AV Mankad c Rixon b Thomson	0	b Hurst	21
S Madan Lal b Clark	4 (8)	c Rixon b Clark	2
SMH Kirmani (+) c Ogilvie b Thomson	11 (7)	c Serjeant b Hurst	55
EAS Prasanna c Thomson b Mann	23	c Hibbert b Clark	8
BS Bedi (c) not out	2	not out	26
BS Chandrasekhar lbw Mann	0	c Rixon b Thomson	0
EXTRAS (NB 4)	4	(LB 6, NB 7)	13
TOTAL	153		324

FOW 1st Inns: 11 15 90 108 110 112 119 149 151 153
FOW 2nd Inns: 7 88 147 151 196 243 251 275 318 324

Bowling: *First Innings*: Thomson 16-1-54-3, Clark 18-5-46-4, Hurst 7-0-31-0, Cosier 3-1-6-0, Mann 6-0-12-3. *Second Innings*: Thomson 19.7-1-76-4, Clark 26-1-101-4, Hurst 15-3-50-2, Simpson 4-0-22-0, Mann 15-3-52-0, Cosier 5-1-10-0.

Umpires: TF Brooks & MG O'Connell

SECOND TEST 1977–78 AUSTRALIA v INDIA
W.A.C.A. Ground, Perth. December 16, 17, 18, 20, 21, 1977.
Toss: India. Australia won by 2 wkts.

INDIA

SM Gavaskar c Rixon b Clark	4	b Clark	127
CPS Chauhan c Gannon b Simpson	88	c Ogilvie b Thomson	32
M Amarnath c Gannon b Thomson	90	c Rixon b Simpson	100
GR Viswanath b Thomson	38	c Rixon b Clark	1
DB Vengsarkar c Rixon b Clark	49	c Hughes b Gannon	9
BP Patel c Rixon b Thomson	3	b Gannon	27
SMH Kirmani (+) c Rixon b Thomson	38	lbw Gannon	2
S Venkataraghavan c Simpson b Gannon	37	c Hughes b Gannon	14
S Madan Lal b Gannon	43	b Thomson	3
BS Bedi (c) b Gannon	3	not out	0
BS Chandrasekhar not out	0	not out	0
EXTRAS (B 1, NB 8)	9	(B 1, LB 4, NB 10)	15
TOTAL	402		9 dec 330

FOW 1st Inns: 14 163 224 229 235 311 319 383 391 402
FOW 2nd Inns: 47 240 244 283 287 289 327 328 330

Bowling: *First Innings*: Thomson 24-1-101-4, Clark 17-0-95-2, Gannon 16.6-1-84-3, Mann 11-0-63-0, Simpson 11-0-50-1. *Second Innings*: Thomson 21.5-3-65-2, Gannon 18-2-77-4, Clark 18-1-83-2, Mann 8-0-49-0, Simpson 8-2-41-1.

AUSTRALIA

J Dyson c Patel b Bedi	53	c Vengsarkar b Bedi	4
CS Serjeant c Kirmani b Madan Lal	13	c Kirmani b Madan Lal	12
AD Ogilvie b Bedi	27 (4)	b Bedi	47
PM Toohey st Kirmani b Bedi	0 (5)	c Amarnath b Bedi	83
RB Simpson (c) c Vengsarkar b Venkataraghavan	176 (6)	run out	39
SJ Rixon (+) c Kirmani b Amarnath	50 (8)	lbw Bedi	23
KJ Hughes c Patel b Bedi	28	lbw Madan Lal	0
AL Mann c Vengsarkar b Bedi	7 (3)	c Kirmani b Bedi	105
WM Clark c Patel b Chandrasekhar	15	not out	5
JR Thomson c Amarnath b Venkataraghavan	0	not out	6
JB Gannon not out	0		
EXTRAS (LB 25)	25	(B 8, LB 10)	18
TOTAL	394		8 for 342

FOW 1st Inns: 19 61 65 149 250 321 341 388 388 394
FOW 2nd Inns: 13 33 172 195 295 296 330 330

Bowling: *First Innings*: Madan Lal 15-1-54-1, Amarnath 16-2-57-1, Chandrasekhar 33.6-6-114-1, Bedi 31-6-89-5, Venkataraghavan 23-4-55-2. *Second Innings*: Madan Lal 11-0-44-2, Amarnath 3-0-22-0, Bedi 30.2-6-105-5, Chandrasekhar 15-0-67-0, Venkataraghavan 28-9-86-0.

Umpires: RC Bailhache & RA French

THIRD TEST 1977–78 AUSTRALIA v INDIA
Melbourne Cricket Ground, Melbourne. December 30, 31, 1977, January 2, 3, 4, 1978.
Toss: India. India won by 222 runs.

INDIA
SM Gavaskar c Rixon b Thomson	0	c Serjeant b Gannon	118
CPS Chauhan c Mann b Clark	0	run out	20
M Amarnath c Simpson b Clark	72	b Cosier	41
GR Viswanath c Rixon b Thomson	59	lbw Clark	54
DB Vengsarkar c Simpson b Thomson	37	c Cosier b Clark	6
AV Mankad c Clark b Gannon	44	c Clark	38
SMH Kirmani (+) lbw Simpson	29	c Thomson b Mann	29
KD Ghavri c Rixon b Gannon	6	c Simpson b Clark	6
EAS Prasanna c Clark	0	c Rixon b Gannon	11
BS Bedi (c) not out	2	not out	12
BS Chandrasekhar b Clark	0	lbw Cosier	0
EXTRAS (LB 3, NB 4)	7	(LB 1, NB 7)	8
TOTAL	256		343

FOW 1st Inns: 0 0 105 174 180 234 254 254 256 256
FOW 2nd Inns: 40 89 187 198 265 286 294 315 343 343

Bowling: *First Innings*: Thomson 16-2-78-3, Clark 19.2-2-73-4, Gannon 14-2-47-2, Cosier 12-3-25-0, Simpson 3-1-11-1, Mann 5-1-15-0. *Second Innings*: Clark 29-3-96-4, Gannon 22-4-88-2, Cosier 12.7-2-58-2, Thomson 18-4-47-0, Mann 4-0-24-1, Simpson 3-0-22-0.

AUSTRALIA
J Dyson b Ghavri	0	lbw Bedi	12
GJ Cosier c Chauhan b Chandrasekhar	67	b Chandrasekhar	34
AD Ogilvie lbw Ghavri	6	c Chauhan b Bedi	0
CS Serjeant b Chandrasekhar	85	b Chandrasekhar	17
RB Simpson (c) b Chandrasekhar	2	lbw Chandrasekhar	4
PM Toohey c Viswanath b Bedi	14	c Chauhan b Chandrasekhar	14
AL Mann c Gavaskar b Bedi	11	c Gavaskar b Chandrasekhar	18
SJ Rixon (+) lbw Chandrasekhar	11	c & b Chandrasekhar	12
WM Clark lbw Chandrasekhar	3	c Ghavri b Bedi	33
JR Thomson c Ghavri b Chandrasekhar	0	c & b Bedi	7
JB Gannon not out	0	not out	3
EXTRAS (B 6, LB 7, NB 1)	14	(B 6, LB 4)	10
TOTAL	213		164

FOW 1st Inns: 0 18 122 124 166 178 202 211 211 213
FOW 2nd Inns: 42 42 52 60 77 98 115 122 151 164

Bowling: *First Innings*: Ghavri 9-0-37-2, Gavaskar 2-0-7-0, Bedi 15-2-71-2, Chandrasekhar 14.1-2-52-6, Prasanna 10-1-32-0. *Second Innings*: Ghavri 4-0-29-0, Amarnath 3-0-10-0, Prasanna 8-4-5-0, Bedi 16.1-5-58-4, Chandrasekhar 20-3-52-6.

Umpires: RA French & MG O'Connell

FOURTH TEST 1977–78 AUSTRALIA v INDIA
Sydney Cricket Ground, Sydney. January 7, 8, 9, 11, 12, 1978.
Toss: Australia. India won by an innings & 2 runs.

AUSTRALIA
J Dyson lbw Chandrasekhar	26		c & b Chandrasekhar	6
GJ Cosier b Amarnath	17		b Bedi	68
PM Toohey run out	4	(6)	c (S)Madan Lal b Ghavri	85
CS Serjeant c Ghavri b Bedi	4		b Prasanna	1
RB Simpson (c) c Kirmani b Chandrasekhar	38		lbw Prasanna	33
KJ Hughes b Bedi	17	(3)	c Vengsarkar b Bedi	19
AL Mann b Bedi	0		c & b Prasanna	0
SJ Rixon (+) lbw Chandrasekhar	17		c Viswanath b Chandrasekhar	11
WM Clark c Gavaskar b Chandrasekhar	0		b Prasanna	10
JR Thomson not out	1		b Ghavri	16
JB Gannon c Amarnath b Prasanna	0		not out	0
EXTRAS (LB 5, NB 2)	7		(B 5, LB 6, NB 3)	14
TOTAL	131			263

FOW 1st Inns: 29 34 46 61 84 84 125 125 130 131
FOW 2nd Inns: 26 87 88 106 171 171 194 221 257 263

Bowling: *First Innings*: Ghavri 7-1-25-0, Amarnath 7-4-6-1, Bedi 13-3-49-3, Chandrasekhar 15-3-30-4, Prasanna 7.4-2-14-1. *Second Innings*: Ghavri 12.7-3-42-2, Amarnath 5-3-9-0, Chandrasekhar 24-3-85-2, Bedi 28-8-62-2, Prasanna 29-11-51-4.

INDIA
SM Gavaskar c Rixon b Thomson	49
CPS Chauhan c Mann b Clark	42
M Amarnath c Gannon b Clark	9
GR Viswanath b Thomson	79
DB Vengsarkar c Rixon b Cosier	48
AV Mankad b Thomson	16
SMH Kirmani (+) b Cosier	42
KD Ghavri c Serjeant b Thomson	64
EAS Prasanna not out	25
BS Bedi (c) not out	1
BS Chandrasekhar	
EXTRAS (LB 9, NB 12)	21
TOTAL	8 dec 396

FOW 1st Inns: 29 34 46 61 84 84 125 125

Bowling: *First Innings*: Thomson 27-8-83-4, Clark 21-3-66-2, Gannon 20-4-65-0, Mann 20-0-101-0, Simpson 4-0-34-0, Cosier 9-1-26-2.

Umpires: RC Bailhache & TF Brooks

FIFTH TEST 1977–78 AUSTRALIA v INDIA
Adelaide Oval, Adelaide. January 28, 29, 30, February 1, 2, 3, 1978.
Toss: Australia. Australia won by 47 runs.

AUSTRALIA
GM Wood st Kirmani b Chandrasekhar	39		c Vengsarkar b Bedi	8
WM Darling c Vengsarkar b Chandrasekhar	65		b Bedi	56
GN Yallop c Gavaskar b Amarnath	121		b Bedi	24
PM Toohey c Gavaskar b Chandrasekhar	60		c Kirmani b Prasanna	10
RB Simpson (c) c Viswanath b Ghavri	100		lbw Ghavri	51
GJ Cosier b Ghavri	1		st Kirmani b Bedi	34
SJ Rixon (+) b Bedi	32		run out	13
B Yardley c & b Ghavri	22		c Vengsarkar b Ghavri	26
JR Thomson c Ghavri b Chandrasekhar	24	(11)	c Amarnath b Ghavri	3
WM Clark b Chandrasekhar	0	(9)	lbw Ghavri	1
IW Callen not out	22	(10)	not out	4
EXTRAS (B 4, LB 14, NB 1)	19		(B 5, LB 15, W 3, NB 3)	26
TOTAL	505			256

FOW 1st Inns: 89 110 230 334 337 406 450 457 458 505
FOW 2nd Inns: 17 84 95 107 172 210 214 240 248 256

Bowling: *First Innings*: Ghavri 22-2-93-3, Amarnath 12-0-45-1, Bedi 34-1-127-1, Prasanna 10-1-48-0, Chandrasekhar 29.4-0-136-5, Gaekwad 5-0-37-0. *Second Innings*: Ghavri 10.5-2-45-4, Amarnath 4-0-12-0, Prasanna 34-7-68-1, Bedi 20-3-53-4, Chandrasekhar 14-0-52-0.

INDIA
SM Gavaskar c Toohey b Thomson	7	c Rixon b Callen	29
CPS Chauhan c Cosier b Clark	15	c Wood b Yardley	32
M Amarnath c Cosier b Thomson	0	c Callen b Yardley	86
GR Viswanath c Rixon b Callen	89	c Simpson b Clark	73
DB Vengsarkar c Rixon b Callen	44	c Toohey b Yardley	78
AD Gaekwad c Rixon b Callen	27	c & b Yardley	12
SMH Kirmani (+) run out	48	b Clark	51
KD Ghavri c Simpson b Clark	3	c (S)KJ Hughes b Callen	23
EAS Prasanna not out	15	not out	10
BS Bedi (c) c(S)KJ Hughes b Clark	6	c Cosier b Callen	16
BS Chandrasekhar c & b Clark	2	c Rixon b Simpson	2
EXTRAS (B 4, LB 1, NB 8)	13	(B 6, LB 11, NB 16)	33
TOTAL	269		445

FOW 1st Inns: 89 110 230 334 337 406 450 457 458 505
FOW 2nd Inns: 40 79 210 256 323 348 415 417 442 445

Bowling: *First Innings*: Thomson 3.3-1-12-2, Clark 20.7-6-62-4, Callen 22-0-83-3, Cosier 4-3-4-0, Yardley 23-6-62-0, Simpson 9-0-33-0. *Second Innings*: Callen 33-5-108-3, Clark 29-6-79-2, Yardley 43-6-134-4, Simpson 23.4-6-70-1, Cosier 13-6-21-0.

Umpires: RA French & MG O'Connell

Australian Averages

1977–78 AUSTRALIA v INDIA

AUSTRALIA	M	Inn	NO	Runs	H.S	Avrge	Ct	St	Overs	Mds	Runs	Wkt	Avrge
Callen, IW	1	2	2	26	22*	-	1	-	55.0	5	191	6	31.83
Clark, WM	5	10	1	83	33	9.22	2	-	198.1	27	701	28	25.04
Cosier, GJ	4	8	-	240	68	30.00	5	-	58.7	17	150	4	37.50
Darling, WM	1	2	-	121	65	60.50	-	-	-	-	-	-	-
Dyson, J	3	6	-	101	53	16.83	-	-	-	-	-	-	-
Gannon, JB	3	5	4	3	3*	3.00	3	-	90.6	13	361	11	32.82
Hibbert, PA	1	2	-	15	13	7.50	1	-	-	-	-	-	-
Hughes, KJ	2	4	-	64	28	16.00	2	-	-	-	-	-	-
Hurst, AG	1	2	1	26	26	26.00	1	-	22.0	3	81	2	40.50
Mann, AL	4	8	-	189	105	23.63	2	-	69.0	4	316	4	79.00
Ogilvie, AD	3	6	-	131	47	21.83	3	-	-	-	-	-	-
Rixon, SJ	5	10	-	184	50	18.40	22	-	-	-	-	-	-
Serjeant, CS	4	8	-	132	85	16.50	4	-	-	-	-	-	-
Simpson, RB	5	10	-	539	176	53.90	6	-	65.4	9	283	4	70.75
Thomson, JR	5	10	3	101	41*	14.43	2	-	145.7	21	516	22	23.45
Toohey, PM	5	10	-	409	85	40.90	2	-	-	-	-	-	-
Wood, GM	1	2	-	47	39	23.50	1	-	-	-	-	-	-
Yallop, GN	1	2	-	145	121	72.50	-	-	-	-	-	-	-
Yardley, B	1	2	-	48	26	24.00	1	-	66.0	12	196	4	49.00

Indian Averages

1977–78 AUSTRALIA v INDIA

INDIA	M	Inn	NO	Runs	H.S	Avrge	Ct	St	Overs	Mds	Runs	Wkt	Avrge
Amarnath, M	5	9	-	445	100	49.44	6	-	71.0	14	228	7	32.57
Bedi, BS	5	9	6	68	26*	22.67	2	-	219.7	39	740	31	23.87
Chandrasekhar, BS	5	8	2	4	2	0.67	2	-	197.3	24	704	28	25.14
Chauhan, CPS	4	7	-	229	88	32.71	3	-	-	-	-	-	-
Gaekwad, AD	1	2	-	39	27	19.50	-	-	5.0	-	37	-	-
Gavaskar, SM	5	9	-	450	127	50.00	8	-	2.0	-	7	-	-
Ghavri, KD	3	5	-	102	64	20.40	5	-	65.4	8	271	11	24.64
Kirmani, SMH	5	9	-	305	55	33.89	8	4	-	-	-	-	-
Madan Lal, S	2	4	-	52	43	13.00	2	-	55.0	6	197	9	21.89
Mankad, AV	3	5	-	119	44	23.80	1	-	-	-	-	-	-
Patel, BP	2	4	-	46	27	11.50	3	-	-	-	-	-	-
Prasanna, EAS	4	7	3	92	25*	23.00	2	-	122.4	32	279	6	46.50
Vengsarkar, DB	5	9	-	320	78	35.56	7	-	-	-	-	-	-
Venkataraghavan, S	1	2	-	51	37	25.50	-	-	51.0	13	141	2	70.50
Viswanath, GR	5	9	-	473	89	52.56	5	-	-	-	-	-	-

QUICK SINGLES

Simmo's sixtieth. On March 13 Australian captain Bob Simpson scored the sixtieth century of his first class career in a match between Australia and Barbados at Bridgetown. The game was drawn, but Australia amassed 511 runs in its first innings. Craig Sergeant also made a century.

Six-step starter. In Jeff Thomson's first over against the West Indies at Antigua on February 22, he was no-balled for overstepping six times.

Blood match. On the first day of the Guyana v Australia match on March 25, Guyana fast bowler Colin Croft delivered a vicious bouncer which broke the jaw of Australian batsman Graham Yallop. Another Croft bouncer hit Bruce Yardley on the back of the head. Yardley, who was carried to the dressing room dazed and bleeding, required three stitches.

A googly dozen. Victorian spin merchant Jim Higgs claimed 12 wickets in Australia's first West Indies tour match against the Leeward Islands in February. Australia won the game by 183 runs, after Higgs' googlies left the local batsmen looking completely confused. Spin is not a notable commodity in the West Indies these days.

Sang saw and said. When Australia played Jamaica at Kingston in April, umpire Sang Hue twice called no-ball for throwing to Australia's Bruce Yardley. Captain Bob Simpson removed Yardley from the bowling, but later said: 'I am extremely disappointed that umpire Sang Hue has taken this action, especially when he has seen Yardley bowl in two matches before.'

Not noticed. The riot in the fifth Test at Kingston overshadowed some brilliant batting performances from Australia's Peter Toohey (122 and 97) and Graeme Wood (90), and also from West Indians Alvin Kallicharan (126) and Larry Gomes (121).

TV man repairs. During the WSC walkout in the West Indies, the WSC chief and Australian media magnate Kerry Packer flew to Barbados, where he appeared on television discussing the poor payments West Indies players received.

Young Australians blitzed in West Indies

Bridgetown, March 20. The relatively inexperienced Australian team has been crushed in the first two West Indies Tests.

Australian captain Bob Simpson has asked critics to be patient. Australia narrowly won the recent series against India, but on the Carribean campaign 'we are in against a very experienced side,' Simpson warns.

The West Indian captain, Clive Lloyd, has commented that he thinks the WSC Australians would have been superior opponents.

Australia lost the first Test at Port-of-Spain by an innings and 106 runs. In a shattering defeat, Australia was all out on the first day for 90 runs. Only two batsmen, Peter Toohey (20) and Gary Cosier (46), reached double figures.

At the end of the Australian first innings, scoreboard totals told a terrible tale. In batting order: 2, 3, 2, 20, 0, 46, 1, 2, 0, 0, 0.

The three West Indies fast bowlers who did the damage were Andy Roberts (2/62), Colin Croft (4/15) and Joel Garner (3/35). It was a vicious and powerful pace attack unlike anything most of these Australians had ever met.

Toohey was hit in the face by one of Roberts' rising deliveries and needed three stitches above his right eye. Despite doctor's advice Toohey returned to face Joel Garner in the afternoon, but the 6ft 8in. 'big bird' took only five balls to strike Toohey's middle stump and send him back to the pavilion.

It was all over in two and a half days. The West Indies made 405

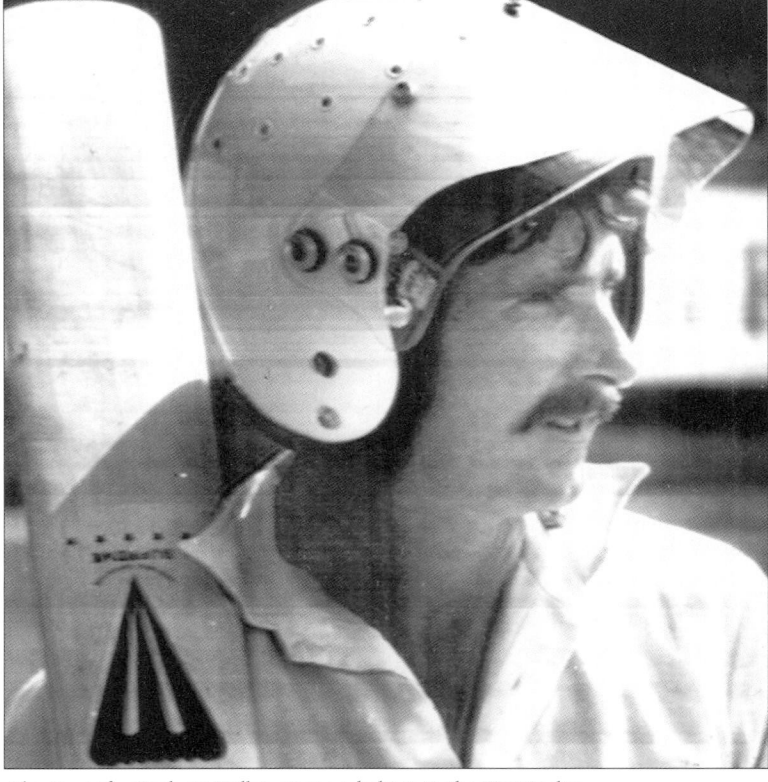

Playing safe: Graham Yallop wears a helmet in the West Indies.

runs, including 127 from Alvin Kallicharan, and Australia could manage only 209 in its second innings, despite a respectable 81 by Graham Yallop.

When Yallop came back at Bridgetown in the second Test he gave notice that he wasn't going to be intimidated. Yallop wore a helmet, the first time a player has done so in Test cricket.

Unfortunately, the story was not much different for Australia, which lost by nine wickets. The one gleam of hope was bowler Jeff Thomson, who took 6/77 in 13 overs which showed the West Indies that fast, aggressive bowling was not a Carribean monopoly.

The West Indies do seem to have a specialty in the short-pitched department, though. In just one over, Joel Garner sent down five bumpers. Umpires might look to their counting skills, or some official complaints could be made.

Australian women win World Cup

Hyderabad, Jan. 14. Australia's women cricketers have defeated England to win the final of the second World Cup, staged in India this month.

The victory makes amends for Australia's loss to England in the inaugural cup in 1973. Seven countries participated in 1973, but this time four countries competed and six matches were played. Australia and England each defeated India and New Zealand to reach the final.

The play-off saw England bat first to reach 8/96, but they were no match for the Australian women, who lost two wickets in passing the England total in 31.3 overs. Australia's Margaret Jennings scored 57 not out. Janette Tredrea was 37 not out, and her sister Sharon took 4/25.

At the grave of former West Indian captain, Sir Frank Worrell (1924–67), Bob Simpson and Australian team members join Sir Frank's widow in tribute.

Player walkout weakens Windies

Georgetown, March 30. The West Indies have selected a new side to play Australia in the third Test at Georgetown, Guyana following the withdrawal of the West Indies' WSC players over the past few days.

In a sensational fortnight, on March 21 the leading West Indies players Richard Austin, Colin Croft and Desmond Haynes signed with WSC.

Then, on March 27, West Indies captain Clive Lloyd resigned as a protest against the selectors dropping Haynes and Deryck Murray, who has led players in a quest for better pay and conditions.

In the wake of Lloyd's resignation, the last WSC players in the West Indies team withdrew their services, in support of Lloyd.

Colin Croft, Joel Garner, Gordon Greenidge, Viv Richards and Andy Roberts advised the West Indies Cricket Board by a telegram which said they were each 'unavailable'.

Alvin Kallicharan has been named captain of the new West Indies side.

The ledger looks a little more balanced now that both sides are minus their WSC players, and Australia appears to have its best chance of winning in the third Test at Georgetown.

The problem is that even without WSC players, the West Indies team still has some classy batsmen in Kallicharan and Larry Gomes. Kallicharan has been playing Test cricket since the early 1970s.

But in Bob Simpson Australia boasts a captain who began playing first class cricket before some of the West Indies players were born.

West Indies' Clive Lloyd at the crease.

Young Aussies summon up a thrilling win

Cartoonist Norm Mitchell's view of the third Test win by Bob Simpson's young Australian team.

Georgetown, April 4. Australia may have lacked experience and confidence in this West Indies tour, but courage has had its reward in a fighting three-wicket win over the West Indies in the third Test today.

The Australian captain, Bob Simpson, says he has never known a more desperate Test match.

'It was so utterly vital I just couldn't watch,' Simpson said. 'We had to win today or the tour wasn't worthwhile anymore.'

And it was not just the tour at stake. Players were on the line.

'Some of them on the thresholds of their careers were facing the possibility that they wouldn't play Test cricket anymore,' Simpson said. 'I've never known a situation quite like this. It meant everything to win here.'

After electing to bat first, the West Indies collapsed in their first innings to be all out for 205. Two Australian bowlers, the fast Jeff Thomson (4/57) and fast-medium

Wayne Clark (4/64), kept the pressure on all day. Thomson's furious dismissal of West Indies skipper Alvin Kallicharan (0) was a marvellous morale booster for the Australians.

Australia began batting badly, and at one stage was 5/90, but strong performances by Simpson (67), Steve Rixon (54), and Graeme Wood (50) helped Australia to a first-innings lead of 81 runs.

On the third day, the West Indies batted their way back into the match. Maiden Test centuries by Basil Williams (100) and Larry Gomes (101) lifted the West Indies second-innings total to an almost unbeatable 439.

But Australia refused to accept defeat. From 3/22 on the fourth day, Graeme Wood and Craig Sergeant both went on to make centuries, adding 251 runs to snatch an unbelievable victory that has restored some of the lost pride of Australian cricket.

Riots and boycotts mar Test match

Kingston, May 4. The fifth Test between Australia and the West Indies has been declared a draw following riots which interrupted play and prevented an almost certain Australian victory.

Australia's batsmen hit out in brilliant form here, and on the fifth day Australia had one hour to capture just one wicket after West Indies tail-ender Vanburn Holder was caught by Steve Rixon.

But the crowd rioted when Holder disputed the umpire's decision. At first, bottles were tossed over the fence. Then anything else

at hand. Someone tried to burn the grandstand down. Another dug a hole in the pitch.

One hundred police charged onto the ground to protect the players and umpires, who huddled mid-field for 25 minutes.

Play was abandoned, and an attempt to resume the following day was stymied when umpire Ralph Gosein refused to participate. There is speculation that the WSC players' boycott had angered local crowds. All that was needed was a spark to take matters beyond the control of police.

The spinner's art: Jim Higgs.

Aussie women at the wicket

Betty Wilson, a natural athlete, learnt to throw a ball at primary school in the Melbourne suburb of Collingwood in the 1920s and used to watch the Collingwood women's team play at Clifton Hill.

In the days of the depression, women's cricket began to attract a strong following. As a small face in a crowd of up to 3000, she sometimes returned the ball from the boundary. Not exactly over the stumps, but mighty well.

Everyone was impressed. By the time she was 10, Betty, the daughter of a bootmaker, was playing for Collingwood.

Wilson, an attacking bat and off-spin bowler, developed into the greatest woman cricketer Australia has produced. In 1954–55 when Frank 'Typhoon' Tyson was wrecking Australia at the MCG, someone cried out 'Send Betty Wilson in.'

The war restricted Wilson's Test career to 11 matches. She peaked against England in 1957–58 with a world first (male or female) by taking 10 wickets and making a century in the same match.

She routed England for 35 at St Kilda, taking 7/7 (including a hat-trick), made an even 100, then took 4/49 as the tourists held on for a draw.

Even if women's cricket struggled in the rough and tumble of the colonial days, it slowly won acceptance.

By the 1930s it was no longer deemed unladylike to take the new ball and be a 'Demon bowler', as Sydney's Molly Flaherty was known. She was a member of the team that toured England in 1937 and her pace and lift astounded spectators there. Against Kent, she took 7/32.

Feminists like Vida Goldstein championed the game's cause in Australia and the phenomenal success of Don Bradman helped spread its popularity.

More and more clubs were formed as the 1930s progressed, but World War Two stifled the game and it was not until the 1970s that interest was renewed thanks to government grants and sponsorship. As a result, more and more young women were attracted to the game in the 1980s and 1990s.

Appropriate dress sparked much debate as long ago as the 1930s. The AWCC, founded in 1931, opted for culottes, a divided skirt, rather than trousers.

If the 1934–45 tour by England

Betty Wilson and Una Paisley go out to bat in Adelaide in 1934–35.

was something of a novelty, that image soon disappeared. Players of the standing of Peggy Antonio, Betty Wilson, Una Paisley, and Sharon Tredrea etc. earned the respect of the critics from Yabba (the famous barracker at the Sydney Cricket Ground) to Test bowler Bill O'Reilly.

'This is cricket, this is – leave the girls alone,' was Yabba's firm response to a fellow barracker who made reference to 'powder puffs' during a women's match at the SCG in the late 1930s.

In 1949, Bill O'Reilly was so impressed with the standard of play, he wrote: 'From this time onward I shall steadfastly refrain from saying that "so and so batted or bowled like a woman".'

And Zoe Goss' dismissal of Brian Lara (caught and stumped by Steve Rixon!) in a televised celebrity match at the SCG in 1994 certainly was no laughing matter.

In that one fun match, Goss, who made 29 with some fine shots, took two wickets (Dujon as well as Lara) and fielded well, gave women's cricket a credibility it previously had not enjoyed among the cricket community at large.

Viewers saw for themselves Goss' all-round talent and enthusiasm for the game. She was coached in Perth by Dennis Lillee, and her achievements demonstrate that women's cricket deserves to be taken seriously across the board – though that battle has yet to be won.

FIRST TEST 1977–78 WEST INDIES v AUSTRALIA
Queen's Park Oval, Port-of-Spain. March 3, 4, 5, 1978.
Toss: West Indies. West Indies won by an innings & 106 runs.

AUSTRALIA

GM Wood c Haynes b Croft	2		lbw Roberts	32
CS Serjeant c Murray b Croft	3		lbw Garner	40
GN Yallop c Richards b Croft	2		b Roberts	81
PM Toohey b Garner	20			
RB Simpson (c) lbw Garner	0		b Parry	14
GJ Cosier c Greenidge b Croft	46	(4)	lbw Garner	19
SJ Rixon (+) run out	1	(6)	lbw Roberts	0
B Yardley c Murray b Roberts	2	(7)	not out	7
JR Thomson c Austin b Roberts	0	(8)	b Parry	4
WM Clark b Garner	0	(9)	b Roberts	0
JD Higgs not out	0	(10)	b Roberts	2
EXTRAS (B 4, LB 6, NB 4)	14		(B 6, LB 1, W 1, NB 2)	10
TOTAL	90			9 dec 209

FOW 1st Inns: 7 10 16 23 45 75 75 84 90 90
FOW 2nd Inns: 59 90 149 194 194 194 200 201 209

Bowling: *First Innings*: Roberts 12-4-26-2, Croft 9.1-5-15-4, Garner 15-7-35-3. *Second Innings*: Roberts 16.3-3-56-5, Croft 13-1-55-0, Garner 17-5-39-2, Parry 17-1-49-2.

WEST INDIES

CG Greenidge b Yardley	43
DL Haynes c Rixon b Higgs	61
IVA Richards lbw Thomson	39
AI Kallicharran b Yardley	127
CH Lloyd (c) b Thomson	86
RA Austin c(S)TJ Laughlin b Thomson	2
DL Murray (+) c Rixon b Higgs	21
DR Parry b Yardley	0
AME Roberts st Rixon b Higgs	7
J Garner c Cosier b Higgs	0
CEH Croft not out	4
EXTRAS (LB 9, NB 6)	15
TOTAL	405

FOW 1st Inns: 87 143 143 313 324 385 385 391 391 405

Bowling: *First Innings*: Thomson 21-6-84-3, Clark 16-3-41-0, Higgs 24.5-3-91-4, Simpson 16-2-65-0, Yardley 19-1-64-3, Cosier 13-2-45-0.

Umpires: R Gosein & D Sang Hue

SECOND TEST 1977–78 WEST INDIES v AUSTRALIA
Kensington Oval, Bridgetown. March 17, 18, 19, 1978.
Toss: West Indies. West Indies won by 9 wkts.

AUSTRALIA

WM Darling c Richards b Croft	4		c Murray b Croft	8
GM Wood lbw Croft	69		run out	56
GN Yallop c Austin b Croft	47		c Lloyd b Garner	14
CS Serjeant c Murray b Parry	4		c Murray b Roberts	2
RB Simpson (c) c Murray b Croft	9	(7)	c Murray b Roberts	17
GJ Cosier c Murray b Roberts	1	(5)	c Croft b Roberts	8
SJ Rixon (+) lbw Garner	16	(6)	c Lloyd b Roberts	0
B Yardley b Garner	74		b Garner	43
JR Thomson b Garner	12		c Richards b Garner	11
WM Clark b Garner	0		lbw Garner	0
JD Higgs not out	4		not out	0
EXTRAS (B 3, LB 4, NB 3)	10		(B 1, LB 8, NB 10)	19
TOTAL	250			178

FOW 1st Inns: 13 105 116 134 135 149 161 216 216 250
FOW 2nd Inns: 21 62 69 80 95 99 154 167 173 178

Bowling: *First Innings*: Roberts 18-2-79-1, Croft 18-3-47-4, Garner 16.1-2-65-4, Parry 12-4-44-1, Austin 1-0-5-0. *Second Innings*: Roberts 18-5-50-4, Croft 15-4-53-1, Garner 15-3-56-4.

WEST INDIES

CG Greenidge c Cosier b Thomson	8		not out	80
DL Haynes c Rixon b Higgs	66		c Yardley b Higgs	55
IVA Richards c Clark b Thomson	23			
AI Kallicharran c Yardley b Thomson	8			
CH Lloyd (c) c Serjeant b Clark	42			
RA Austin c Serjeant b Clark	20			
DL Murray (+) c Darling b Thomson	60			
DR Parry c Serjeant b Simpson	27	(3)	not out	3
AME Roberts lbw Thomson	4			
J Garner not out	5			
CEH Croft lbw Thomson	3			
EXTRAS (LB 3, NB 19)	22		(LB 2, W 1)	3
TOTAL	288			1 for 141

FOW 1st Inns: 16 56 71 154 172 198 263 269 282 288
FOW 2nd Inns: 131

Bowling: *First Innings*: Thomson 13-1-77-6, Clark 24-3-77-2, Cosier 9-4-24-0, Higgs 16-4-46-1, Simpson 7-1-30-1, Yardley 2-0-12-0. *Second Innings*: Thomson 6-1-22-0, Clark 7-0-27-0, Higgs 13-4-34-1, Yardley 10.5-2-55-0.

Umpires: R Gosein & SE Parris

THIRD TEST 1977–78 WEST INDIES v AUSTRALIA
Bourda, Georgetown. March 31, April 1, 2, 4, 5, 1978.
Toss: West Indies. Australia won by 3 wkts.

WEST INDIES
AE Greenidge lbw Thomson	56	b Clark		11
AB Williams lbw Clark	10	c Serjeant b Clark		100
HA Gomes b Clark	4 (5)	c Simpson b Yardley		101
AI Kallicharran (c) b Thomson	0 (6)	b Yardley		22
IT Shillingford c Clark b Laughlin	3 (7)	c & b Thomson		16
DA Murray (+) c Ogilvie b Clark	21 (3)	lbw Simpson		16
S Shivnarine c Rixon b Thomson	53 (8)	b Cosier		63
N Phillip c Yardley b Simpson	15 (9)	st Rixon b Yardley		4
VA Holder c Laughlin b Clark	1 (10)	lbw Clark		31
DR Parry not out	21 (4)	lbw Clark		51
ST Clarke b Thomson	6	not out		5
EXTRAS (LB 2, NB 13)	15	(B 4, LB 5, NB 10)		19
TOTAL	205			439

FOW 1st Inns: 31 36 48 77 84 130 165 166 193 205
FOW 2nd Inns: 36 95 172 199 249 285 355 369 431 439

Bowling: *First Innings*: Thomson 16.2-1-57-4, Clark 24-6-64-4, Laughlin 10-4-34-1, Cosier 2-1-1-0, Simpson 8-1-34-1. *Second Innings*: Thomson 20-2-83-1, Clark 34.4-4-124-4, Yardley 30-6-96-3, Simpson 19-4-70-1, Cosier 6-1-14-1, Laughlin 7-1-33-0.

AUSTRALIA
WM Darling c Greenidge b Phillip	15	c Williams b Clarke		0
GM Wood lbw Holder	50	run out		126
AD Ogilvie c & b Phillip	4	lbw Clarke		0
GJ Cosier lbw Clarke	9 (6)	b Phillip		0
CS Serjeant b Clarke	0	c (S)SFAF Bacchus b Phillip		124
RB Simpson (c) run out	67 (4)	c Murray b Clarke		4
TJ Laughlin c Greenidge b Parry	21 (8)	c & b Parry		24
SJ Rixon (+) c Holder b Phillip	54 (7)	not out		39
B Yardley b Clarke	33	not out		15
JR Thomson c & b Phillip	3			
WM Clark not out	2			
EXTRAS (LB 12, W 1, NB 15)	28	(B 8, LB 4, W 2, NB 16)		30
TOTAL	286		7 for	362

FOW 1st Inns: 28 36 77 85 90 142 237 256 268 286
FOW 2nd Inns: 11 13 22 273 279 290 338

Bowling: *First Innings*: Phillip 18-0-76-4, Holder 17-1-40-1, Clarke 22-3-57-3, Gomes 3-0-8-0, Parry 15-2-39-1, Shivnarine 8-0-38-0. *Second Innings*: Clarke 27-5-83-3, Phillip 19-2-65-2, Holder 20-3-55-0, Parry 17-1-61-1, Shivnarine 18-2-68-0.

Umpires: R Gosein & CF Vyfhuis

FIFTH TEST 1977–78 WEST INDIES v AUSTRALIA
Sabina Park, Kingston. April 28, 29, 30, May 2, 3 1978.
Toss: Australia. Match Drawn.

AUSTRALIA
GM Wood c Parry b Phillip	16	c Bacchus b Jumadeen		90
AD Ogilvie c Shivnarine b Holder	0	st Murray b Parry		43
PM Toohey c Williams b Holder	122	st Murray b Jumadeen		97
GN Yallop c(S)HG Gordon b Shivnarine	57	not out		23
CS Serjeant b Holder	26	not out		32
RB Simpson (c) c Murray b Foster	46			
TJ Laughlin c(S)HG Gordon b Jumadeen	35			
SJ Rixon (+) not out	13			
B Yardley b Jumadeen	7			
JR Thomson c Murray b Jumadeen	4			
JD Higgs c Foster b Jumadeen	0			
EXTRAS (LB 5, W 1, NB 11)	17	(B 5, LB 8, NB 7)		20
TOTAL	343		3 dec	305

FOW 1st Inns: 0 38 171 217 266 308 324 335 343 343
FOW 2nd Inns: 65 245 246

Bowling: *First Innings*: Phillip 32-5-90-1, Holder 31-8-63-3, Parry 5-0-15-0, Jumadeen 38.4-6-72-4, Foster 32-10-68-1, Shivnarine 9-2-13-1. *Second Innings*: Phillip 17-1-64-0, Holder 18-2-41-0, Jumadeen 23-2-90-2, Parry 18-3-60-1, Foster 7-1-22-0, Shivnarine 3-1-8-0.

WEST INDIES
AB Williams c Serjeant b Laughlin	17	c Wood b Yardley		19
SFAF Bacchus c Yardley b Thomson	5	c Simpson b Thomson		21
DA Murray (+) c Wood b Laughlin	12 (6)	b Yardley		10
HA Gomes b Thomson	115 (3)	c Rixon b Higgs		1
AI Kallicharran (c) c Ogilvie b Laughlin	6	lbw Higgs		126
MLC Foster c Rixon b Laughlin	8 (4)	run out		5
S Shivnarine st Rixon b Higgs	53	c Yallop b Yardley		27
DR Parry lbw Higgs	4	c Serjeant b Yardley		0
N Phillip c Rixon b Simpson	26	not out		26
VA Holder lbw Laughlin	24	c Rixon b Higgs		6
RR Jumadeen not out	4	not out		0
EXTRAS (LB 1, NB 5)	6	(B 14, LB 1, NB 2)		17
TOTAL	280		9 for	258

FOW 1st Inns: 13 28 41 47 63 159 173 219 276 280
FOW 2nd Inns: 42 43 43 59 88 179 181 242 258

Bowling: *First Innings*: Thomson 22-4-61-2, Laughlin 25.4-4-101-5, Yardley 14-4-27-0, Simpson 10-0-38-1, Higgs 19-3-47-2. *Second Innings*: Thomson 15-1-53-1, Laughlin 10-1-34-0, Higgs 28.4-10-67-3, Yardley 29-17-35-4, Simpson 11-4-44-0, Yallop 3-1-8-0.

Umpires: R Gosein & W Malcolm

FOURTH TEST 1977–78 WEST INDIES v AUSTRALIA
Queen's Park Oval, Port-of-Spain. April 15, 16, 17, 18, 1978.
Toss: Australia. West Indies won by 198 runs.

WEST INDIES
AE Greenidge c Wood b Clark	6	c Thomson b Yardley		69
AB Williams c Yallop b Higgs	87	c Yallop b Simpson		24
DA Murray (+) c Wood b Yardley	4	lbw Clark		4
HA Gomes c Simpson b Clark	30	c Simpson b Higgs		14
AI Kallicharran (c) c Yallop b Clark	92	c & b Clark		27
SFAF Bacchus b Higgs	9	c Wood b Yardley		7
S Shivnarine c Simpson b Thomson	10	c Serjeant b Simpson		11
DR Parry st Rixon b Higgs	22	c Serjeant b Yardley		65
N Phillip c Rixon b Thomson	3	c Wood b Yardley		46
VA Holder b Thomson	7	b Simpson		0
RR Jumadeen not out	0	not out		2
EXTRAS (B 7, LB 1, W 2, NB 12)	22	(B 1, LB 13, NB 7)		21
TOTAL	292			290

FOW 1st Inns: 7 16 111 166 185 242 258 262 291 292
FOW 2nd Inns: 36 51 79 134 151 151 204 273 280 290

Bowling: *First Innings*: Thomson 23-8-64-3, Clark 24-6-65-3, Yardley 18-5-48-1, Higgs 16.5-2-53-3, Simpson 15-4-40-0. *Second Innings*: Thomson 15-1-76-0, Clark 21-4-62-2, Simpson 14-2-45-3, Higgs 21-7-46-1, Yardley 30.2-15-40-4.

AUSTRALIA
GM Wood c Murray b Phillip	16	lbw Holder		17
WM Darling c Jumadeen b Holder	10	b Phillip		6
PM Toohey c Williams b Parry	40	c Bacchus b Jumadeen		17
GN Yallop c Murray b Jumadeen	75	c Kallicharran b Parry		18
CS Serjeant st Murray b Jumadeen	49	c Bacchus b Jumadeen		4
RB Simpson (c) lbw Holder	36	lbw Jumadeen		6
SJ Rixon (+) c Murray b Holder	21	not out		13
B Yardley c Williams b Holder	22	b Parry		3
JR Thomson b Holder	0	b Parry		1
WM Clark b Holder	4	b Parry		0
JD Higgs not out	0	b Parry		4
EXTRAS (B 4, LB 2, NB 11)	17	(LB 2, NB 3)		5
TOTAL	290			94

FOW 1st Inns: 23 43 92 193 204 254 275 275 289 290
FOW 2nd Inns: 9 42 44 60 72 76 80 86 88 94

Bowling: *First Innings*: Phillip 17-0-73-1, Holder 13-4-28-6, Jumadeen 24-4-83-2, Parry 30-5-77-1, Shivnarine 6-1-12-0. *Second Innings*: Phillip 7-0-24-1, Holder 11-3-16-1, Jumadeen 15-3-34-3, Parry 10.4-4-15-5.

Umpires: R Gosein & CF Vyfhuis

Australian Averages

1977–78 WEST INDIES v AUSTRALIA
AUSTRALIA	M	Inn	NO	Runs	H.S	Avrge	Ct	St	Overs	Mds	Runs	Wkt	Avrge
Clark, WM	4	7	1	6	4	1.00	3	-	150.4	26	460	15	30.67
Cosier, GJ	3	6	-	83	46	13.83	2	-	30.0	8	84	1	84.00
Darling, WM	3	6	-	43	15	7.17	1	-	-	-	-	-	-
Higgs, JD	4	7	4	10	4*	3.33	-	-	139.2	33	384	15	25.60
Laughlin, TJ	2	3	-	80	35	26.67	1	-	52.4	10	202	6	33.67
Ogilvie, AD	2	4	-	47	43	11.75	2	-	-	-	-	-	-
Rixon, SJ	5	9	3	157	54	26.17	9	4	-	-	-	-	-
Serjeant, CS	5	10	1	284	124	31.56	8	-	-	-	-	-	-
Simpson, RB	5	9	-	199	67	22.11	5	-	100.0	18	366	7	52.29
Thomson, JR	5	8	-	35	12	4.38	2	-	151.2	25	577	20	28.85
Toohey, PM	3	5	-	296	122	59.20	-	-	-	-	-	-	-
Wood, GM	5	10	-	474	126	47.40	6	-	-	-	-	-	-
Yallop, GN	4	8	1	317	81	45.29	4	-	3.0	1	8	-	-
Yardley, B	5	9	2	206	74	29.43	4	-	153.1	50	377	15	25.13

West Indian Averages

1977–78 WEST INDIES v AUSTRALIA
WEST INDIES	M	Inn	NO	Runs	H.S	Avrge	Ct	St	Overs	Mds	Runs	Wkt	Avrge
Austin, RA	2	2	-	22	20	11.00	2	-	1.0	-	5	-	-
Bacchus, SFAF	2	4	-	42	21	10.50	3	-	-	-	-	-	-
Clarke, ST	1	2	1	11	6	11.00	-	-	49.0	8	140	6	23.33
Croft, CEH	2	2	1	7	4*	7.00	1	-	55.1	13	170	9	18.89
Foster, MLC	1	2	-	13	8	6.50	1	-	39.0	11	90	1	90.00
Garner, J	2	2	1	5	5*	5.00	-	-	63.1	17	195	13	15.00
Gomes, HA	3	6	-	265	115	44.17	-	-	3.0	-	8	-	-
Greenidge, AE	2	4	-	142	69	35.50	2	-	-	-	-	-	-
Greenidge, CG	2	3	1	131	80*	65.50	1	-	-	-	-	-	-
Haynes, DL	2	3	-	182	66	60.67	1	-	-	-	-	-	-
Holder, VA	3	6	-	69	31	11.50	-	-	110.0	21	248	11	22.55
Jumadeen, RR	2	4	4	6	4*	-	1	-	100.4	15	279	11	25.36
Kallicharran, AI	5	8	-	408	127	51.00	1	-	-	-	-	-	-
Lloyd, CH	2	2	-	128	86	64.00	2	-	-	-	-	-	-
Murray, DA	3	6	-	67	21	11.17	6	3	-	-	-	-	-
Murray, DL	2	2	-	81	60	40.50	8	-	-	-	-	-	-
Parry, DR	5	9	2	193	65	27.57	2	-	124.4	20	360	12	30.00
Phillip, N	3	6	1	120	46	24.00	2	-	110.0	8	392	9	43.56
Richards, IVA	2	2	-	62	39	31.00	3	-	-	-	-	-	-
Roberts, AME	2	2	-	11	7	5.50	-	-	64.3	14	211	12	17.58
Shillingford, IT	1	2	-	19	16	9.50	-	-	-	-	-	-	-
Shivnarine, S	3	6	-	217	63	36.17	1	-	44.0	6	139	1	139.00
Williams, AB	3	6	-	257	100	42.83	4	-	-	-	-	-	-

World Series comes in from the cold

Sydney, Nov. 28. The tide of cricketing popularity has been turned with tonight's amazing attendance at the Sydney Cricket ground.

Last year WSC played its games at Sydney Showground, VFL Park in Melbourne, Football Park in Adelaide and Gloucester Park in Perth.

It needed a genuine cricket ground and the first opportunity came when the NSW Labor government stripped the NSWCA of its total control of the SCG. WSC offered $200,000 to use the ground for 17 days in the 1978–79 season. Kerry Packer was even prepared to budget $1 million on flood-lighting, but the Sydney Cricket Trust insisted on paying itself.

Then there were other incursions when WSC secured the 'Gabba and the Adelaide Oval.

But Sydney was the biggest coup. Certainly the novelty of the controversial new floodlights explained a part of the attraction, but the Establishment cricketing powers could not ignore 50,000 people.

By the tea break 30,000 people had passed throught the turnstiles and the crowd was sure to swell further with the Australians due to bat second. As the crowd hit 44,000 Packer gave approval to open the gates and let in the huge queues of people outside the ground.

They saw Australia comfortably wipe off the target of just 129 thanks largely to Ian Davis, who hit a neat 42 and set the platform for his team to win by five wickets.

Earlier in the afternoon Greg Chappell had snared 5/13 and Dennis Lillee grabbed 4/12 to bundle out the West Indies for 128.

Night cricket, complete with a white ball, has been just one of a series of WSC innovations this season. Coloured clothing has been another radical move with the Australians wearing pastel yellow, the World XI pastel blue, and the West Indies coral red.

A cornerstone of the intense marketing campaign has been the 'C'mon Aussie, C'mon' jingle that has been used in all promotion of the Supertests and one day matches. It is known that Kerry Packer believes that patriotism can be a powerful force and the jingle is rapidly becoming an anthem for crowds at WSC matches, even though it is played *ad nauseum* whenever an Australian does something of note.

Lessons have been learned from the first season, and departing batsmen do not have to suffer the painful theme music and ever-

Gone again. Tony Greig was one of the driving forces in getting World Series Cricket off the ground, but he has had a tough year at the batting crease. Here he is bowled by Dennis Lillee, but there are few to witness his demise.

present interviewers that they had to endure last year.

The down-side to the patriotic fervour whipped up for the Australians is that crowds are much smaller for the West Indies–World XI games in which Australia is not involved.

In general the Australian press still tends to give more attention to traditional cricket. English pressmen in Australia for the Ashes tour are even harder to win over.

John Woodcock lamented in the *Times* that the Australians who had been discredited initially had been rebuilt into idols. But others like Alan Lee called the landmark Sydney night game a 'wild and wonderful experience'.

Tony Greig checks the texture of the controversial 'hot-house' wickets before they are transported to VFL Park and put in place.

West Indies bumper war

West Indian Viv Richards, who struggled for form this summer.

The fearsome West Indian fast bowler, 'whispering death' Michael Holding.

Antigua, April 10. Whatever the traditionalists may say about World Series Cricket nobody can deny its intensity.

The WSC tour of the West Indies concluded today, marking the close of a bumper war that had its origins in Australia earlier in the summer.

The four-pronged West Indian speed attack of Andy Roberts, Michael Holding, Colin Croft and Wayne Daniel is as ferocious a quartet as has ever been seen on a cricket field. The nature of the WSC game has developed into a series of salvos fired by the respective fast-bowling batteries and has left all batsmen shell-shocked.

Some, such as Pakistani Majid Khan, have been left with more tangible reminders of battle. Majid was hit by a Roberts bouncer at VFL Park and left with a fractured cheekbone.

The Supertest Grand Final in Australia was a bitter contest, with both Australia and the World XI stocked to the brim with bowlers willing to drop the ball short at every opportunity. Big South African Garth Le Roux is always aggressive in approach and Imran Khan, Clive Rice and Mike Procter had similar intentions.

Dennis Lillee and Len Pascoe gave as good as they got for Australia, and in the West Indies were joined by Jeff Thomson, free to play after his court-imposed restriction.

Makeshift Australian opener Trevor Chappell was the first casualty in Jamaica, struck on the jaw by a fierce bouncer from Roberts.

On the opposing side, Lawrence Rowe suffered a fractured cheekbone courtesy of a Lillee delivery, as the resounding crack of his earguard was heard around his home ground.

Just when the Australians were mounting a rearguard action in the second Supertest they were thwarted by an unexpected threat at Bridgetown when the Barbados crowd pelted the ground with bottles causing the game to be abandoned.

The old tenet about fast bowlers not bowling bumpers at their opposite numbers has gone by the wayside these days.

Dennis Lillee quickly recognised the need for head protection by donning a helmet in Australia and in the Supertest at Trinidad he was confident enough to hook a Holding bouncer into the grandstand for six.

Earlier in the summer Tony Greig wrote that the competition in WSC was so intense that teams could no longer afford to let opposition tailenders hang around. 'Consequently the pace bowlers are dishing out an unprecedented amount of bouncers to the rabbits'.

Batsmen at all levels in WSC competition knew only too well that once they hit a slump it was incredibly difficult to dig themselves out of the hole because of the incessant pace bowling.

While the aggressive pace bowling is popular with TV watchers, it threatens to undermine the overall quality of batting if it continues unchecked by umpires. Keen judges believe it would be wise for WSC to restrict the number of bouncers per over.

West Indies Supertest shorts

How do you tame them? When Australia bundled out the home side for 188 in the first Supertest it seemed that they would crack the West Indies. A second-innings 197 run slaughter by Clive Lloyd put paid to those thoughts, and Andy Roberts rubbed salt in the wounds by making 89. His previous best score at international level had been 33.

Bottles stop game. Barbados had generally been free of crowd disturbances, but that changed in the second Supertest. Chasing victory on the fifth day, Roy Fredericks and Viv Richards were motoring along until Fredericks was controversially given out lbw. Even before he left the field the bottles started hailing down. It took 50 minutes for the ground to be cleared as the crowd called for Fredericks' return. But when Richards and Lloyd came down the steps the bottles were hurled again and the game was abandoned.

Stumpy's stand. Nuggetty opener Bruce 'Stumpy' Laird blunted the mighty West Indian attack at Trinidad with a knock of 122. He had only reached double figures three times in his previous nine innings. His courageous effort set up the Australian victory that squared the series.

Spun out. Kerry O'Keeffe's mission on the Caribbean tour was supposedly to be used as second spinner on the traditionally turning pitch at Trinidad. But he never made it that far, on account of being struck by a car while jogging along the street. A fractured tibia resulted in him flying home to Australia.

Off again, on again. After a week of rain, Guyana's cricket fans were bouyed by suggestions that the fourth Supertest would start on time and would be something special. A ground announcer stated that the match would get under way, but by mid-afternoon the ground was still not ready and the crowd rioted, causing $20,000 damage. The game was abandoned, but a midnight conference between officials and players enabled the match to go ahead.

Cop that. On the day after the crowd explosion, Ian Chappell landed in hot water when he spotted the announcer whose statement had ignited the Guyana riot. Chappell punched him in the stomach and was charged by the local police chief, who saw the incident.

Just made it. The only interest in the dying stages of the drawn fifth Supertest centred on whether Rodney Marsh would reach his century. He did so, with just one over in the match remaining.

Master bowler. They will never be accepted as part of the official record, but Dennis Lillee's 79 wickets in 15 Supertests were hard-earned against the toughest competition possible. The mighty fast bowler was a hero for WSC crowds and showed the champion's ability to pull out something extra just when his team needed it most. In a bouncer war he had an extra ingredient – guile.

Greg Chappell Australia's best

Antigua, April 10. The fifth Supertest ended in a draw today, but it was not without its highlights. Yet again Greg Chappell was at the heart of the Australian batting performance.

In the pressure-cooker atmosphere of the West Indies he has stood head and shoulders above all other batsmen – no mean feat, as some of the world's finest batsmen have been on show.

Chappell has shot 631 runs off the West Indian pace battery, almost 300 clear of the next highest scorer in either side.

Even more surprising is the fact that Chappell was a doubtful starter for this tour as he was suffering from palsy. He could have easily pulled out of the trip, but was determined to prove that he could make runs against the West Indies pace quartet after a disappointing summer in Australia where he averaged just 26 in the Supertests against the West Indians and the World XI.

One factor in the turnaround may have been the fact that a red ball was used in the West Indies instead of the white employed in Australia. Chappell says that he saw the red ball much quicker and easier, even though others attest that they see the white ball quicker.

In preparation for this tour Chappell spent many hours with Richie Benaud reviewing videos of his batting, and his decision to go back to the basics has reaped three centuries.

The West Indians got him cheaply in the first clash, but since then he has had only one failure at the crease with a 90 and 85 to go with the hundreds.

For Dennis Lillee the West Indies has been the location of two career turning points.

Australia against the odds

Australia's fast bowling hero Rod Hogg sends down another thunderbolt.

Brisbane, Dec. 6. Australia's worst nightmares about being slaughtered by England came to life in the opening 85 minutes of the first Test.

The side, depleted by World Series Cricket defections, was powerless to stop a ruthlessly professional England.

In humid, overcast conditions that were ideal for swing bowling the Australians slumped to 6/26 as English pacemen Bob Willis, Ian Botham and Chris Old made the top-order batsmen look out of their depth.

None of the first six Australians could reach double figures and it was left to wicketkeeper John McLean and fast bowler Rodney Hogg to take up the fight with their bats. Hogg then capped off a personally satisfying day by blasting out English openers Boycott and Gooch and sounding a warning that the visitors would not have things all their own way.

The young Australians clawed back some respectability through aggressive fast bowling by Hogg and Alan Hurst, then centuries by Graham Yallop and Kim Hughes

But the torrid first 85 minutes

meant that Australia was always behind the eightball, and by mid afternoon on the fifth day England was celebrating its opening win.

English skipper Mike Brearley said Australia should not be too disappointed at the way they were defeated, but with the cricket public sizing up which camp it will follow, the loss was a blow for authorities.

In the second Test at Perth, Hogg had two batsmen back in the pavillion with just three runs on the board, but Boycott showed typical stubbornness to steer England out of trouble along with the more entertaining David Gower, who made a fine century.

In a season where the traditional game is trying to be more attractive, Boycott's 448 minutes at the crease did not produce a single boundary in his score of 77.

Australia's batting crumbled in both innings with only Peter Toohey, Graeme Wood and Gary Cosier showing resistance. Toohey's 81 not out was reminiscent of his fellow New South Welshman Doug Walters.

The home team is badly in need of a win to restore some credibility in response to WSC.

10/66 and all that for Rodney Hogg

Melbourne, Jan. 3. There have been few moments as exhilarating for an Australian cricket crowd as the opening overs bowled by Rodney Hogg in England's first innings of the third Test.

Coming after a late-order Australian batting collapse, Hogg had only a couple of overs at the Englishmen before lunch and he wrought havoc by bowling Boycott then capturing Brearley lbw.

The MCG crowd was in raptures at the departure of the dreaded Yorkshireman and the prim skipper in the space of just a few deliveries.

After the crushing defeats in the opening two Tests, Hogg's furious spell was a much-wanted show of defiance that could not have been any more poignant had it been scripted. His sustained pace did not stop there and his match figures of 10/66 off 34 overs brought England to its knees on a pitch that was described diplomatically by the English captain as 'curious'.

While all the credit has gone to Hogg, the efforts of Graeme Wood should not be overlooked. The young West Australian scored an even 100 – his first Test century – in a match where no other batsman even reached the half-century mark.

Hogg was well supported in the attack by the workhorse Geoff Dymock and to a lesser extent by Alan Hurst.

Each of the Australian batsmen made starts in their innings including young debutant Allan Border, who made 29 in his first innings and was sadly run out for a duck in the second innings.

Graeme Wood after his fighting century at Melbourne.

England's Ashes, but Hogg a marvel

Australia's great find of the series – Rodney Hogg tearing in to bowl.

Sydney, Feb.14. A nine-wicket loss in the sixth Test has ended a miserable series for Australia.

Rodney Hogg is one Australian who has taken the fight to the Englishmen from the first ball he delivered.

Hogg has proven his credentials as a Test cricketer while most of those around him have looked well out of their depth. His 41 wickets in the series broke the previous series record by an Australian held by Arthur Mailey with 36 wickets in the 1920–21 series.

Hogg's pinpoint accuracy and sustained pace has constantly put England under the hammer. He is an interesting character, with a wilful streak and a readiness to buck authority. His apparent dislike of 'The Poms' has been a winner with crowds.

Born not far from the MCG, Hogg was playing district cricket by the age of 16 and was in the state squad at 18. But by the age of 24 he had not played state cricket and headed to South Australia.

He provided the much-needed hero that traditional authorities were praying for, and when a hoax telegram pretended to make an appointment for World Series Cricket he said sharply: 'They'd be wasting my time and theirs. I have a two year contract with the Board and have no desire to be a hack bowler up the bush for Packer.'

Just four years ago he watched Lillee and Thomson from the outer. Now the MCG Bay 13 mob shout 'Hoggyyyy, Hoggyyy' with as much fervour as they once uttered Lillee's name.

Darling survives blow to the heart

Adelaide, Jan. 27. Australian opener Rick Darling owes his life to England spinner, John Emburey.

Darling was struck under the heart by a ball from Bob Willis that lifted viciously, and collapsed on the pitch.

Emburey was first on the scene and could not find any sign of respiration or pulse. He struck Darling on the chest and the opener started breathing again. Umpire Max O'Connell then applied mouth to mouth resuscitation. The team physiotherapist found that Darling had swallowed his chewing gum and was only moments from death.

Darling was taken from the field on a stretcher, but will be OK to resume his innings tomorrow.

Controversial umpire Tom Brooks announced his retirement at Perth.

Melbourne fans leave no doubt of their opinion of England's opener.

Young Kangaroos showed fighting spirit in Tests

Yallop with Prime Minister Fraser.

Sydney, Feb. 10. The young Australian side has battled insurmountable odds this series, yet has kept going in the best traditions of the Anzac spirit.

Captain Graham Yallop showed that sort of tenacity in scoring his 121 on the opening day of the sixth Test. No other Australian progressed beyond 15 in the total of 178. Thrust into the captaincy role at the start of this series after just eight Tests, Yallop is an introverted man who has found the going tough.

However, he led by example with his batting, which yielded two centuries, and with his demeanour on and off the field.

There is a glimmer of hope for the future in the continued development of Kim Hughes, and Allan Border is a gritty little customer who had some good moments in his debut series. These two, along with Peter Toohey, may provide the backbone of future batting.

In the bowling ranks all the attention has focused on Hogg's record-breaking efforts, but Alan Hurst's 25 wickets have provided sturdy back-up. Right-arm googly spinner Jim Higgs also did well, with 19 wickets.

Probably no action displayed the Aussie spirit better than the response of Rick Darling less than 24 hours after he had almost died on the pitch in Adelaide. On his return to the crease he promptly belted Ian Botham for six.

You see some funny things happen on a cricket ground.

FIRST TEST 1978–79 AUSTRALIA v ENGLAND
Brisbane Cricket Ground, Brisbane. December 1, 2, 3, 5, 6, 1978.
Toss: Australia. England won by 7 wkts.

AUSTRALIA

GM Wood c Taylor b Old	7 (2)	lbw Old	19
GJ Cosier run out	1 (1)	b Willis	0
PM Toohey b Willis	1	lbw Botham	1
GN Yallop (c) c Gooch b Willis	7	c & b Willis	102
KJ Hughes c Taylor b Botham	4	c Edmonds b Willis	129
TJ Laughlin c(S)JK Lever b Willis	2	lbw Old	5
JA Maclean (+) not out	33	lbw Miller	15
B Yardley c Taylor b Willis	17	c Brearley b Miller	16
RM Hogg c Taylor b Botham	36	b Botham	16
AG Hurst c Taylor b Botham	0	b Botham	0
JD Higgs b Old	1	not out	1
EXTRAS (B 1, NB 6)	7	(B 9, LB 5, NB 22)	36
TOTAL	116		339

FOW 1st Inns: 2 5 14 22 24 26 53 113 113 116
FOW 2nd Inns: 0 2 49 219 228 261 310 339 339 339

Bowling: *First Innings*: Willis 14-2-44-4, Old 9.7-1-24-2, Botham 12-1-40-3, Gooch 1-0-1-0, Edmonds 1-1-0-0. *Second Innings*: Willis 27.6-3-69-3, Botham 26-5-95-3, Old 17-1-60-2, Miller 34-12-52-2, Edmonds 12-1-27-0.

ENGLAND

G Boycott c Hughes b Hogg	13	run out	16
GA Gooch c Laughlin b Hogg	2	c Yardley b Hogg	2
DW Randall c Laughlin b Hurst	75	not out	74
RW Taylor (+) lbw Hurst	20		
JM Brearley (c) c Maclean b Hogg	6 (4)	c Maclean b Yardley	13
DI Gower c Maclean b Hurst	44 (5)	not out	48
IT Botham c Maclean b Hogg	49		
G Miller lbw Hogg	27		
PH Edmonds c Maclean b Hogg	1		
CM Old not out	29		
RGD Willis c Maclean b Hurst	8		
EXTRAS (B 7, LB 4, NB 1)	12	(B 12, LB 3, NB 2)	17
TOTAL	286		3 for 170

FOW 1st Inns: 2 38 111 120 120 215 219 226 266 286
FOW 2nd Inns: 16 37 74

Bowling: *First Innings*: Hurst 27.4-6-93-4, Hogg 28-8-74-6, Laughlin 22-6-54-0, Yardley 7-1-34-0, Cosier 5-1-10-0, Higgs 6-2-9-0. *Second Innings*: Hogg 12.5-2-35-1, Hurst 10-4-17-0, Yardley 13-1-41-1, Laughlin 3-0-6-0, Higgs 12-1-43-0, Cosier 3-0-11-0.

Umpires: RA French & MG O'Connell

Australian Averages
1978–79 AUSTRALIA v ENGLAND

AUSTRALIA	M	Inn	NO	Runs	H.S	Avrge	Ct	St	Overs	Mds	Runs	Wkt	Avrge
Border, AR	3	6	2	146	60*	36.50	3	-	31.0	13	50	1	50.00
Carlson, PH	2	4	-	23	21	5.75	2	-	46.0	10	99	2	49.50
Cosier, GJ	2	4	-	52	47	13.00	2	-	12.0	3	35	-	-
Darling, WM	4	8	-	221	91	27.63	4	-	-	-	-	-	-
Dymock, G	3	6	1	28	11	5.60	-	-	114.1	19	269	7	38.43
Higgs, JD	5	10	4	46	16	7.67	-	-	196.6	47	468	19	24.63
Hilditch, AMJ	1	2	-	4	3	2.00	2	-	-	-	-	-	-
Hogg, RM	6	12	-	95	36	7.92	-	-	217.4	60	527	41	12.85
Hughes, KJ	6	12	-	345	129	28.75	4	-	-	-	-	-	-
Hurst, AG	6	12	2	44	17*	4.40	2	-	204.2	44	577	25	23.08
Laughlin, TJ	1	2	-	7	5	3.50	2	-	25.0	6	60	-	-
Maclean, JA	4	8	1	79	33*	11.29	18	-	-	-	-	-	-
Toohey, PM	5	10	1	149	81*	16.56	5	-	-	-	-	-	-
Wood, GM	6	12	-	344	100	28.67	6	-	-	-	-	-	-
Wright, KJ	2	4	-	37	29	9.25	7	1	-	-	-	-	-
Yallop, GN	6	12	-	391	121	32.58	3	-	-	-	-	-	-
Yardley, B	4	8	1	148	61*	21.14	4	-	113.2	12	389	7	55.57

English Averages
1978–79 AUSTRALIA v ENGLAND

ENGLAND	M	Inn	NO	Runs	H.S	Avrge	Ct	St	Overs	Mds	Runs	Wkt	Avrge
Botham, IT	6	10	-	291	74	29.10	11	-	158.4	25	567	23	24.65
Boycott, G	6	12	-	263	77	21.92	2	-	1.0	-	6	-	-
Brearley, JM	6	12	1	184	53	16.73	5	-	-	-	-	-	-
Edmonds, PH	1	1	-	1	1	1.00	1	-	13.0	2	27	-	-
Emburey, JE	4	7	1	67	42	11.17	6	-	144.4	49	306	16	19.13
Gooch, GA	6	11	-	246	74	22.36	9	-	6.0	1	15	-	-
Gower, DI	6	11	1	420	102	42.00	4	-	-	-	-	-	-
Hendrick, M	5	9	4	34	10	6.80	3	-	145.0	30	299	19	15.74
Lever, JK	1	2	-	24	14	12.00	-	-	15.1	2	48	5	9.60
Miller, G	6	10	-	234	64	23.40	1	-	177.1	54	346	23	15.04
Old, CM	1	1	1	29	29*	-	-	-	26.7	2	84	4	21.00
Randall, DW	6	12	2	385	150	38.50	4	-	-	-	-	-	-
Taylor, RW	6	10	2	208	97	26.00	18	2	-	-	-	-	-
Willis, RGD	6	10	2	88	24	11.00	3	-	140.3	23	461	20	23.05

SECOND TEST 1978–79 AUSTRALIA v ENGLAND
W.A.C.A. Ground, Perth. December 15, 16, 17, 19, 20, 1978.
Toss: Australia. England won by 166 runs.

ENGLAND

G Boycott lbw Hurst	77	lbw Hogg	23
GA Gooch c Maclean b Hogg	1	lbw Hogg	43
DW Randall c Wood b Hogg	0	c Cosier b Yardley	45
JM Brearley (c) c Maclean b Dymock	17	c Maclean b Hogg	0
DI Gower b Hogg	102	c Maclean b Hogg	12
IT Botham lbw Hurst	11	c Wood b Yardley	30
G Miller b Hogg	40	c Toohey b Yardley	25
RW Taylor (+) c Hurst b Yardley	12 (9)	c Maclean b Hogg	2
JK Lever c Cosier b Hurst	14 (8)	c Maclean b Hurst	10
RGD Willis c Yallop b Hogg	2	not out	3
M Hendrick not out	7	b Dymock	1
EXTRAS (B 6, LB 9, W 3, NB 8)	26	(LB 6, NB 8)	14
TOTAL	309		208

FOW 1st Inns: 3 3 41 199 219 224 253 295 300 309
FOW 2nd Inns: 58 93 93 135 151 176 201 201 206 208

Bowling: *First Innings*: Hogg 30.5-9-65-5, Dymock 34-4-72-1, Hurst 26-7-70-3, Yardley 23-1-62-1, Cosier 4-2-14-0. *Second Innings*: Hogg 17-2-57-5, Dymock 16.3-2-53-1, Hurst 17-5-43-1, Yardley 16-1-41-3.

AUSTRALIA

GM Wood lbw Lever	5 (2)	c Taylor b Lever	64
WM Darling run out	25 (1)	c Boycott b Lever	5
KJ Hughes b Willis	16	c Gooch b Willis	12
GN Yallop (c) b Willis	3	c Taylor b Hendrick	3
PM Toohey not out	81	c Taylor b Hendrick	0
GJ Cosier c Gooch b Willis	4	lbw Miller	47
JA Maclean (+) c Gooch b Miller	0	c Brearley b Miller	1
B Yardley c Taylor b Hendrick	12	c Botham b Lever	7
RM Hogg c Taylor b Willis	18	b Miller	0
G Dymock b Hendrick	11	not out	6
AG Hurst c Taylor b Willis	5	b Lever	5
EXTRAS (LB 7, W 1, NB 2)	10	(LB 3, W 4, NB 4)	11
TOTAL	190		161

FOW 1st Inns: 8 34 38 60 78 79 100 128 185 190
FOW 2nd Inns: 8 36 58 58 141 143 143 147 151 161

Bowling: *First Innings*: Lever 7-0-20-1, Botham 11-2-46-0, Willis 18.5-5-44-5, Hendrick 14-1-39-2, Miller 16-6-31-1. *Second Innings*: Willis 12-1-36-1, Lever 8.1-2-28-4, Botham 11-1-54-0, Hendrick 8-3-11-2, Miller 7-4-21-3.

Umpires: RC Bailhache & TF Brooks

THIRD TEST 1978–79 AUSTRALIA v ENGLAND
Melbourne Cricket Ground, Melbourne. December 29, 30, 1978, January 1, 2, 3 1979.
Toss: Australia. Australia won by 103 runs.

AUSTRALIA

GM Wood c Emburey b Miller	100 (2)	b Botham	34
WM Darling run out	33 (1)	c Randall b Miller	21
KJ Hughes c Taylor b Botham	0	c Gower b Botham	48
GN Yallop (c) c Hendrick b Botham	41	c Taylor b Miller	16
PM Toohey c Randall b Miller	32	c Botham b Embury	20
AR Border c Brearley b Hendrick	29	run out	0
JA Maclean (+) b Botham	8	c Hendrick b Embury	10
RM Hogg c Randall b Miller	0	b Botham	1
G Dymock b Hendrick	0	c Brearley b Hendrick	6
AG Hurst b Hendrick	0 (11)	not out	0
JD Higgs not out	1 (10)	st Taylor b Embury	0
EXTRAS (LB 8, W 6)	14	(B 4, LB 6, NB 1)	11
TOTAL	258		167

FOW 1st Inns: 65 65 126 189 247 250 250 251 252 258
FOW 2nd Inns: 55 81 101 136 136 152 157 167 167 167

Bowling: *First Innings*: Willis 13-2-47-0, Botham 20.1-4-68-3, Hendrick 23-3-50-3, Embury 14-1-44-0, Miller 19-6-35-3. *Second Innings*: Willis 7-0-21-0, Botham 15-4-41-0, Hendrick 14-4-25-1, Miller 14-5-39-2, Embury 21.2-12-30-3.

ENGLAND

G Boycott b Hogg	1	lbw Hurst	38
JM Brearley (c) lbw Hogg	1	c Maclean b Dymock	0
DW Randall lbw Hurst	13	lbw Hogg	2
GA Gooch c Border b Dymock	25	lbw Hogg	40
DI Gower lbw Dymock	29	lbw Dymock	49
IT Botham c Darling b Higgs	22	c Maclean b Higgs	10
G Miller b Hogg	7	c Hughes b Higgs	1
RW Taylor (+) b Hogg	1	c Maclean b Hogg	5
JE Embury b Hogg	0	not out	7
RGD Willis c Darling b Dymock	19	c Yallop b Hogg	3
M Hendrick not out	6	b Hogg	0
EXTRAS (B 6, LB 4, NB 9)	19	(B 10, LB 7, W 1, NB 6)	24
TOTAL	143		179

FOW 1st Inns: 2 3 40 52 81 100 101 101 120 143
FOW 2nd Inns: 1 6 71 122 163 163 167 171 179 179

Bowling: *First Innings*: Hogg 17-7-30-5, Hurst 12-2-24-1, Dymock 15.6-4-38-3, Higgs 19-9-32-1. *Second Innings*: Hogg 17-5-36-5, Hurst 11-1-39-1, Dymock 18-4-37-2, Higgs 16-2-29-2, Border 5-0-14-0.

Umpires: RA French & MG O'Connell

FIFTH TEST 1978–79 AUSTRALIA v ENGLAND
Adelaide Oval, Adelaide. January 27, 28, 29, 31, February 1, 1979.
Toss: Australia. England won by 205 runs.

ENGLAND

G Boycott c Wright b Hurst	6	c Hughes b Hurst	49
JM Brearley (c) c Wright b Hogg	2	lbw Carlson	9
DW Randall c Carlson b Hurst	4	c Yardley b Hurst	15
GA Gooch c Hurst b Hogg	1	b Carlson	18
DI Gower b Hurst	9	lbw Higgs	21
IT Botham c Wright b Higgs	74	c Yardley b Hurst	7
G Miller lbw Hogg	31	c Wright b Hurst	64
RW Taylor (+) run out	4	c Wright b Hogg	97
JE Embury b Higgs	4	b Hogg	42
RGD Willis c Darling b Hogg	24	c Wright b Hogg	12
M Hendrick not out	0	not out	3
EXTRAS (B 1, LB 4, W 3, NB 2)	10	(B 1, LB 16, W 2, NB 4)	23
TOTAL	169		360

FOW 1st Inns: 10 12 16 18 27 80 113 136 147 169
FOW 2nd Inns: 31 57 97 106 130 132 267 336 347 360

Bowling: *First Innings*: Hogg 10.4-1-26-4, Hurst 14-1-65-3, Carlson 9-1-34-0, Yardley 4-0-25-0, Higgs 3-1-9-2. *Second Innings*: Hogg 27.6-7-59-3, Hurst 37-9-97-4, Carlson 27-8-41-2, Yardley 20-6-60-0, Higgs 28-4-75-1, Border 3-2-5-0.

AUSTRALIA

WM Darling c Willis b Botham	15 (2)	b Botham	18
GM Wood c Randall b Embury	35 (1)	run out	9
KJ Hughes c Embury b Hendrick	4	c Gower b Hendrick	46
GN Yallop (c) b Hendrick	0	b Hendrick	36
AR Border c Taylor b Botham	11	b Willis	1
PH Carlson c Taylor b Botham	0	c Gower b Hendrick	21
B Yardley b Botham	28	c Brearley b Willis	0
KJ Wright (+) lbw Embury	29	c Embury b Miller	0
RM Hogg b Willis	0	b Miller	2
JD Higgs run out	16	not out	3
AG Hurst not out	17	b Willis	13
EXTRAS (B 1, LB 3, NB 5)	9	(LB 1, NB 10)	11
TOTAL	164		160

FOW 1st Inns: 5 10 22 24 72 94 114 116 133 164
FOW 2nd Inns: 31 36 115 120 121 121 124 130 147 160

Bowling: *First Innings*: Willis 11-1-55-1, Hendrick 19-1-45-2, Botham 11.4-0-42-4, Embury 12-7-13-2. *Second Innings*: Willis 12-3-41-3, Hendrick 14-6-19-3, Botham 14-4-37-1, Miller 18-3-36-2, Embury 9-5-16-0.

Umpires: RC Bailhache & MG O'Connell

FOURTH TEST 1978–79 AUSTRALIA v ENGLAND
Sydney Cricket Ground, Sydney. January 6, 7, 8, 10, 11, 1979.
Toss: England. England won by 93 runs.

ENGLAND

G Boycott c Border b Hurst	8	lbw Hogg	0
JM Brearley (c) b Hogg	17	b Border	53
DW Randall c Wood b Hurst	0	lbw Hogg	150
GA Gooch c Toohey b Higgs	18	c Wood b Higgs	22
DI Gower c Maclean b Hurst	7	c Maclean b Hogg	34
IT Botham c Yallop b Hogg	59	c Wood b Higgs	6
G Miller c Maclean b Hurst	4	lbw Hogg	17
RW Taylor (+) c Border b Higgs	10	not out	21
JE Embury c Wood b Higgs	0	c Darling b Higgs	14
RGD Willis not out	7	c Toohey b Higgs	0
M Hendrick b Hurst	10	c Toohey b Higgs	7
EXTRAS (B 1, LB 1, W 2, NB 8)	12	(B 5, LB 3, NB 14)	22
TOTAL	152		346

FOW 1st Inns: 18 18 35 51 66 70 94 98 141 152
FOW 2nd Inns: 0 111 169 237 267 292 307 334 334 346

Bowling: *First Innings*: Hogg 11-3-36-2, Dymock 13-1-34-0, Hurst 10.6-2-28-5, Higgs 18-4-42-3. *Second Innings*: Hogg 28-10-67-4, Dymock 17-4-35-0, Hurst 19-3-43-0, Higgs 59.6-15-148-5, Border 23-11-31-1.

AUSTRALIA

GM Wood b Willis	0 (2)	run out	27
WM Darling c Botham b Miller	91 (1)	c Gooch b Hendrick	13
KJ Hughes c Embury b Willis	48	c Embury b Miller	15
GN Yallop (c) c Botham b Hendrick	44	c & b Hendrick	1
PM Toohey c Gooch b Botham	1	b Miller	5
AR Border not out	60	not out	45
JA Maclean (+) lbw Embury	12	c Botham b Miller	0
RM Hogg run out	6 (9)	c Botham b Embury	0
G Dymock b Botham	5 (8)	b Embury	0
JD Higgs c Botham b Hendrick	11	lbw Embury	0
AG Hurst run out	0	b Embury	0
EXTRAS (B 2, LB 3, NB 11)	16	(LB 1, NB 1)	2
TOTAL	294		111

FOW 1st Inns: 1 126 178 179 210 235 245 276 290 294
FOW 2nd Inns: 38 44 45 59 74 76 85 85 105 111

Bowling: *First Innings*: Willis 9-2-33-2, Botham 28-3-87-2, Hendrick 24-4-50-2, Miller 13-2-37-1, Embury 29-10-57-1, Gooch 5-1-14-0. *Second Innings*: Willis 2-0-8-0, Hendrick 10-3-17-2, Embury 17.2-7-46-4, Miller 20-7-38-3.

Umpires: RC Bailhache & RA French

SIXTH TEST 1978–79 AUSTRALIA v ENGLAND
Sydney Cricket Ground, Sydney. February 10, 11, 12, 14, 1979.
Toss: Australia. England won by 9 wkts.

AUSTRALIA

GM Wood c Botham b Hendrick	15	c Willis b Miller	29
AMJ Hilditch run out	3	c Taylor b Hendrick	1
KJ Hughes c Botham b Willis	16	c Gooch b Embury	7
GN Yallop (c) c Gower b Botham	121	c Taylor b Miller	17
PM Toohey c Taylor b Botham	8	c Gooch b Embury	0
PH Carlson c Gooch b Botham	2	c Botham b Embury	0
B Yardley b Embury	7	not out	61
KJ Wright (+) st Taylor b Embury	3	c Boycott b Miller	5
RM Hogg c Embury b Miller	9	b Miller	7
JD Higgs not out	9	c Botham b Embury	2
AG Hurst b Botham	0	c & b Miller	4
EXTRAS (LB 3, NB 2)	5	(B 3, LB 6, NB 1)	10
TOTAL	198		143

FOW 1st Inns: 18 19 67 101 109 116 124 159 198 198
FOW 2nd Inns: 8 28 48 48 82 114 130 136 143

Bowling: *First Innings*: Willis 11-4-48-1, Hendrick 12-2-21-1, Botham 9.7-1-57-4, Embury 18-3-48-2, Miller 9-3-13-1, Boycott 1-0-6-0. *Second Innings*: Willis 3-0-15-0, Hendrick 7-3-22-1, Embury 24-4-52-4, Miller 27.1-6-44-5.

ENGLAND

G Boycott c Hildtch b Hurst	19	c Hughes b Higgs	13
JM Brearley (c) c Toohey b Higgs	46	not out	20
DW Randall lbw Hogg	7	not out	0
GA Gooch st Wright b Higgs	74		
DI Gower c Wright b Higgs	65		
IT Botham c Carlson b Yardley	23		
G Miller lbw Hurst	18		
RW Taylor (+) not out	36		
JE Embury c Hildtch b Hurst	0		
RGD Willis b Higgs	10		
M Hendrick c & b Yardley	0		
EXTRAS (B 3, LB 5, NB 2)	10	(NB 2)	2
TOTAL	308		1 for 35

FOW 1st Inns: 37 46 115 182 233 247 270 280 306 308
FOW 2nd Inns: 31

Bowling: *First Innings*: Hogg 18-6-42-1, Hurst 20-4-58-3, Yardley 25-2-105-2, Carlson 10-1-24-0, Higgs 30-8-69-4. *Second Innings*: Yardley 5.2-0-21-0, Higgs 5-1-12-1.

Umpires: AR Crafter & DG Weser

Sarfraz supreme as Australia folds

Melbourne, March 15. Sarfraz Nawaz has produced one of the greatest bowling spells in Test history to pluck an amazing win out of the fire for Pakistan.

In just 33 deliveries he took 7/1 after Australia had been on the verge of winning an entertaining game. At 4.30 p.m. the home side had seven wickets in hand and needed just 77 runs to win.

Allan Border and Kim Hughes had looked in total command until Border was bowled at 3/305 and Sarfraz wrought havoc to finish with personal figures of 9/86. The other wicket was that of Graham Yallop, who was run out.

It would have been an heroic win to Australia, who went into this Test with five players who totalled just seven Tests between them. Compare that with the Pakistani team that included WSC stars Sarfraz, Asif Iqbal, Majid Khan, Javed Miandad, Imran Khan, Haroon Rashid and Mushtaq Mohammad.

The Pakistanis were on the back foot from the first day when Rod Hogg, fresh after a three-week rest, cut through the top order.

Imran Khan was just as effective for Pakistan and when they batted again the visitors rediscovered their batting form, led by a century from Majid Khan.

Set a mammoth 382 to win, the Australians went confidently about their task, starting well thanks to openers Andrew Hilditch and debutant Dav Whatmore.

Then came the spell from Sarfraz. Bowling slow medium cutters off a reduced run, he snared five batsmen for ducks. It was, as Mushtaq described it, 'a miracle'.

Pakistan's captain Mushtaq Mohammad hits out at Melbourne.

QUICK SINGLES

Short but not sweet. The brief Pakistani tour of Australia spanned just 25 days, after they had toured New Zealand. The seven WSC members of the side all wore their WSC shirts when warming up for a game against NSW and were ordered by their manager to cover the rebel insignia.

Just not cricket. Rodney Hogg was involved in a heated incident on the second day of the second Test when he played a defensive shot several yards onto the off side then walked a couple of paces to prod the pitch. Miandad picked up the ball and broke the stumps and umpire Harvey gave Hogg out. As he walked off in disgust Hogg was recalled by Pakistan captain Mushtaq, but Harvey overruled Mushtaq and Hogg headed to the pavilion.

Border unbroken. Young batsman Allan Border scored his first century in first class cricket in a bizarre NSW innings against WA. Fellow NSW bats were left battered by balls that kicked up at them. Steve Rixon broke his hand, David Johnston fractured a knuckle and Bob Vidler broke a forearm. NSW had to declare at 7/408 because all three had their arms in casts or slings.

Day of shame. Pakistan tail-ender Sikander Bakht was stunned when Alan Hurst performed a 'Mankad' on him as he backed up on the last day. Australian 12th man Trevor Laughlin had alerted Hurst to the Pakistani's habit of cribbing three or four yards down the pitch and when Hurst ran in to bowl he gently tapped the stumps and Sikander was on his way. Hurst then told him: 'You've cheated. So you're out.'

Badly handled. Andrew Hilditch went into the record books as only the second Test batsman ever to be dismissed 'handled ball', at Perth. Fellow batsman Rick Darling had driven to mid-off and bowler Sarfraz fumbled the return which rolled five yards away. Hilditch picked it up and threw it back, but Sarfraz did not even catch it and immediately appealed. Test selector Neil Harvey accused Sarfraz of cheating and called it the worst incident he had ever seen.

Kim Hughes makes right decision

Perth, March 29. The truncated Pakistani visit may have only encompassed two Tests, but it has provided more than its share of controversy.

Australia's seven-wicket victory today squared the series at one-all, but came on a day when two incidents left a bitter taste in the mouths of true cricket lovers. Australia's Alan Hurst ran out Sikander Bakht in 'Mankad' style, then Sarfraz appealed successfully against Andrew Hilditch for a 'handled the ball' decision.

Australia went into the match without injured captain Graham Yallop, and Kim Hughes thus became the first Western Australian to lead an Australian Test side.

After the second day, Hughes was also incapacitated after treading on a ball at practice and severely twisting his ankle. This left 22-year-old Andrew Hilditch in charge in just his third Test.

On the first day Hughes took the courageous decision to send Pakistan in and it proved a match-winning move. Alan Hurst was the man who assumed the mantle this time and Hogg took a back seat.

Hurst's tally of nine wickets for the game was instrumental in the Australian success.

Flamboyant Rick Darling made the most of his recall with two scores over 70 and brilliant fielding efforts that ran out Mushtaq and Asif.

After their dramatic collapse in Melbourne nothing would be a surprise. This time, though, Border and 31-year-old rookie Jeff Moss saw them through to victory.

West Indian Rohan Kanhai continued his love affair with Australia by playing District cricket for North Melbourne.

The Cricket War Over

Melbourne, May 30. Cricket's most divisive conflict is over at last.

At noon today, the Chairman of the Australian Cricket Board, Bob Parish, issued a statement that signalled a truce to end the two-year rift that has ravaged the game.

The agreement between the ACB and PBL Sports, Kerry Packer's organisation, grants PBL rights to promote cricket for the next 10 years, and has secured telecasting rights for Channel 9 for the next three years. The WSC logo will be worn by Australian players in one day international matches.

Selection will again be the responsibility of the ACB and no player will be penalised for having been part of Packer's troupe for the past two years.

Cricket will never be the same again, with day/night matches and coloured clothing for one day matches among the WSC innovations that will now become part of the game.

India has been asked to defer its tour scheduled for next season to pave the way for the West Indies to come to Australia along with England.

The deal gives the ACB $1.5 million per year, but is not indexed to inflation.

There were hints that a settlement was in the wind three months ago and Packer's presence at the Australia v Pakistan Test in Melbourne was a public indication that the two parties would come together. With WSC's increased acceptance by the public in the 1979–80 season it was obvious that established cricket could no longer withstand a divided market.

There are those in England who believe that the war should have been continued, but the deep financial reserves of the Packer organisation would have meant that the ACB could have faced disaster.

The biggest beneficiaries of the agreement are the players, whose salaries will never return to the unrealistic payments of pre-1977.

FIRST TEST 1978–79 AUSTRALIA v PAKISTAN
Melbourne Cricket Ground, Melbourne. March 10, 11, 12, 14, 15, 1979.
Toss: Australia. Pakistan won by 71 runs.

PAKISTAN

Batsman	1st Innings		2nd Innings	
Majid Khan	c Wright b Hogg	1	b Border	108
Mohsin Khan	c Hilditch b Hogg	14	c & b Hogg	14
Zaheer Abbas	b Hogg	11	b Hogg	59
Javed Miandad	b Hogg	19	c Wright b Border	16
Asif Iqbal	c Wright b Clark	9	lbw Hogg	44
Mushtaq Mohammad (c)	c Wright b Hurst	36	c (S)JD Higgs b Sleep	28
Wasim Raja	b Hurst	13	c Wright b Hurst	28
Imran Khan	c Wright b Hurst	33	c Clark b Hurst	28
Sarfraz Nawaz	c Wright b Sleep	35	lbw Hurst	1
Wasim Bari (+)	run out	0	not out	8
Sikander Bakht	not out	5		
EXTRAS	(B 2, LB 7, W 1, NB 10)	20	(B 4, LB 6, NB 9)	19
TOTAL		196	9 dec	353

FOW 1st Inns: 2 22 28 40 83 99 122 173 177 196
FOW 2nd Inns: 30 165 204 209 261 299 330 332 353

Bowling: *First Innings*: Hogg 17-4-49-4, Hurst 20-4-55-3, Clark 17-4-56-1, Sleep 7.7-2-16-1. *Second Innings*: Hogg 19-2-75-3, Clark 21-6-47-0, Hurst 19.5-1-115-3, Sleep 8-0-62-1, Border 14-5-35-2.

AUSTRALIA

Batsman	1st Innings		2nd Innings	
GM Wood	not out	5 (6)	c Wasim b Sarfraz	0
AMJ Hilditch	c Javed b Imran	3	b Sarfraz	62
AR Border	b Imran	20	b Sarfraz	105
GN Yallop (c)	b Imran	25	run out	8
KJ Hughes	run out	19	c Mohsin b Sarfraz	84
DF Whatmore	lbw Sarfraz	43 (1)	b Sarfraz	15
PR Sleep	c Wasim b Imran	10	b Sarfraz	0
KJ Wright (+)	c Imran b Wasim	9	not out	1
WM Clark	c Mushtaq b Wasim	9	b Sarfraz	0
RM Hogg	run out	9	lbw Sarfraz	0
AG Hurst	c & b Sarfraz	0	c Wasim b Sarfraz	0
EXTRAS	(B 1, LB 5, W 2, NB 8)	16	(B 13, LB 13, NB 9)	35
TOTAL		168		310

FOW 1st Inns: 11 53 63 97 109 140 152 167 167 168
FOW 2nd Inns: 49 109 128 305 305 306 308 309 310 310

Bowling: *First Innings*: Imran 18-8-26-4, Sarfraz 21.6-6-39-2, Sikander 10-1-29-0, Mushtaq 7-0-35-0, Wasim 5-0-23-2. *Second Innings*: Imran 27-9-73-0, Sarfraz 35.4-7-86-9, Sikander 7-0-29-0, Mushtaq 11-0-42-0, Majid 9-1-34-0, Wasim 3-0-11-0.

Umpires: RC Bailhache & CE Harvey

Australian Averages

1978–79 AUSTRALIA v PAKISTAN

AUSTRALIA	M	Inn	NO	Runs	H.S	Avrge	Ct	St	Overs	Mds	Runs	Wkt	Avrge
Border, AR	2	4	1	276	105	92.00	1	-	18.0	5	44	2	22.00
Clark, WM	1	2	-	9	9	4.50	1	-	38.0	10	103	1	103.00
Darling, WM	1	2	-	154	79	77.00	-	-	-	-	-	-	-
Dymock, G	1	1	1	5	5*	-	-	-	44.6	9	137	4	34.25
Hilditch, AMJ	2	4	-	135	62	33.75	4	-	-	-	-	-	-
Hogg, RM	2	3	-	12	9	4.00	-	-	75.0	13	257	10	25.70
Hughes, KJ	2	3	-	112	84	37.33	-	-	-	-	-	-	-
Hurst, AG	2	3	-	16	16	5.33	-	-	87.4	11	325	15	21.67
Moss, JK	1	2	1	60	38*	60.00	-	-	-	-	-	-	-
Sleep, PR	1	2	-	10	10	5.00	-	-	15.7	2	78	2	39.00
Whatmore, DF	2	3	-	73	43	24.33	1	-	-	-	-	-	-
Wood, GM	1	2	1	5	5*	5.00	-	-	-	-	-	-	-
Wright, KJ	2	3	1	26	16	13.00	14	-	-	-	-	-	-
Yallop, GN	1	2	-	33	25	16.50	-	-	-	-	-	-	-
Yardley, B	1	2	-	20	19	10.00	2	-	28.0	5	94	1	94.00

Pakistani Averages

1978–79 AUSTRALIA v PAKISTAN

PAKISTAN	M	Inn	NO	Runs	H.S	Avrge	Ct	St	Overs	Mds	Runs	Wkt	Avrge
Asif Iqbal	2	4	1	222	134*	74.00	1	-	-	-	-	-	-
Haroon Rashid	1	2	-	51	47	25.50	-	-	-	-	-	-	-
Imran Khan	2	4	-	90	33	22.50	1	-	94.0	23	285	7	40.71
Javed Miandad	2	4	1	183	129*	61.00	1	-	4.0	-	20	1	20.00
Majid Khan	2	4	-	109	108	27.25	1	-	9.0	1	34	-	-
Mohsin Khan	1	2	-	28	14	14.00	1	-	-	-	-	-	-
Mudassar Nazar	1	2	-	30	25	15.00	-	-	26.1	4	83	3	27.67
Mushtaq Mohammad	2	4	-	88	36	22.00	1	-	18.0	-	77	-	-
Sarfraz Nawaz	2	4	-	66	35	16.50	1	-	111.3	21	322	13	24.77
Sikander Bakht	2	3	1	5	5*	2.50	-	-	27.5	2	91	1	91.00
Wasim Bari	2	4	1	8	8*	2.67	6	-	-	-	-	-	-
Wasim Raja	1	2	-	41	28	20.50	-	-	8.0	-	34	2	17.00
Zaheer Abbas	2	4	-	117	59	29.25	1	-	-	-	-	-	-

SECOND TEST 1978–79 AUSTRALIA v PAKISTAN
W.A.C.A. Ground, Perth. March 24, 25, 26, 28, 29, 1979.
Toss: Australia. Australia won by 7 wkts.

PAKISTAN

Batsman	1st Innings		2nd Innings	
Majid Khan	c Hilditch b Hogg	0	c (S)TJ Laughlin b Hogg	0
Mudassar Nazar	c Wright b Hurst	5	c Hilditch b Hurst	25
Zaheer Abbas	c Wright b Hurst	29	c Wright b Hogg	18
Javed Miandad	not out	129	c Wright b Hurst	19
Haroon Rashid	c Border b Hurst	4	c Yardley b Dymock	47
Asif Iqbal	run out	35	not out	134
Mushtaq Mohammad (c)	run out	23	lbw Yardley	1
Imran Khan	c Wright b Dymock	14	c Wright b Hurst	15
Sarfraz Nawaz	c Wright b Hurst	27	c Yardley b Hurst	3
Wasim Bari (+)	c Hilditch b Dymock	0	c Whatmore b Hurst	0
Sikander Bakht	b Dymock	0	run out	0
EXTRAS	(LB 3, W 3, NB 5)	11	(B 3, LB 8, NB 12)	23
TOTAL		277		285

FOW 1st Inns: 0 27 41 49 90 176 224 276 277 277
FOW 2nd Inns: 0 35 68 86 152 153 245 263 263 285

Bowling: *First Innings*: Hogg 19-2-88-1, Hurst 23-4-61-4, Dymock 21.6-4-65-3, Yardley 14-2-52-0. *Second Innings*: Hogg 20-5-45-2, Hurst 24.7-2-94-5, Dymock 23-5-72-1, Yardley 14-3-42-1, Border 4-0-9-0.

AUSTRALIA

Batsman	1st Innings		2nd Innings	
WM Darling	lbw Mudassar	75	run out	79
AMJ Hilditch	c Zaheer b Imran	41	handled ball	29
AR Border	c Majid b Javed	85	not out	66
KJ Hughes (c)	lbw Sikander	9		
JK Moss	c Wasim b Mudassar	22	not out	38
DF Whatmore	c Asif b Imran	15		
KJ Wright (+)	c Wasim b Mudassar	16		
B Yardley	b Sarfraz	19 (4)	run out	1
G Dymock	not out	5		
RM Hogg	b Imran	3		
AG Hurst	c Wasim b Sarfraz	16		
EXTRAS	(B 3, LB 4, W 1, NB 13)	21	(LB 13, NB 10)	23
TOTAL		327	3 for	236

FOW 1st Inns: 96 143 161 219 246 273 297 301 304 327
FOW 2nd Inns: 87 153 155

Bowling: *First Innings*: Imran 32-5-105-3, Sarfraz 35.1-7-112-2, Sikander 10.5-1-33-1, Mudassar 16-2-48-3, Javed 2-0-8-1. *Second Innings*: Imran 17-1-81-0, Sarfraz 19-1-85-0, Mudassar 10.1-2-35-0, Javed 2-0-12-0.

Umpires: AR Crafter & MG O'Connell

West Indies' sweet success in World Cup

Jubilant West Indies supporters go into calypso mode as they celebrate their team's second World Cup triumph.

Lord's, June 23. The all-powerful West Indian team has stamped its mark as the world's top cricketing country with an easy win in today's Prudential World Cup final. It is the second time that the West Indians have taken the crown, after winning the initial title four years ago.

Things started badly for the West Indians in the final when England's fast bowlers Botham, Hendrick and Old used the conditions to move the ball considerably and had the defending champions 4/99.

Then Viv Richards (138) and Collis King (86) took advantage of England's decision to play an extra batsman and share the fifth bowler duties between batsmen Wayne Larkins, Geoff Boycott and Graham Gooch.

King, in particular, was very severe on the part-timers, hitting three sixes and 10 fours.

The 139 run partnership between King and Richards turned the game, and English skipper Brearley admitted to feeling 'helpless' when they were in full flight. In the end the West Indies achieved the sizeable innings of 9/286 and England needed to get away to a flying start.

That sort of start was not forthcoming from openers Geoff Boycott and Mike Brearley. It took Boycott 17 overs to reach double figures before finishing with 64. When Brearley was dismissed England needed a massive 158 from the remaining 22 overs – a virtually impossible task.

Derek Randall and Graham Gooch tried to push the scoring rate along before being dismissed and opening the way for giant fast bowlers Joel Garner and Colin Croft to rip through the home team. Garner's final figures of 5/38 included a spell during which he took 5/4 in 11 balls and was twice on a hat-trick.

A sell-out crowd of 25,000 watched the final. The West Indies and Pakistan had no hesitation in using their players with WSC connections during the competition, but the Australian team was chosen from non-WSC men.

News of the WSC–ACB settlement came through just a couple of days after the Australians arrived in London and many players will be keenly aware that they will not have a future at international level now that all players are once again available.

By the time the final was played Australia's players were at home watching it on their TV screens, and were grateful they did not have to meet the West Indies. It has been said that the 'contest' would have been like the Battle of Little Big Horn.

The Aussies threw away their match against England by four ungainly run-outs. Apart from openers Rick Darling (25) and Andrew Hilditch (47) only Allan Border (34) offered resistance.

Rodney Hogg's fierce opening bowling assault sent Geoff Boycott and Derek Randall back to the pavilion with only five runs on the board, but the Englishmen reached the target with 13 overs to spare.

Australia went into the match against Pakistan without strike bowler Rodney Hogg who had bronchial trouble, and the team was never in the race. The bowling situation was worsened further by the erratic spell from Alan Hurst who foolishly tried to 'bounce' the Pakistanis and was hammered to all parts of the ground. In 12 overs he took 1/65 and bowled five wides, four no-balls and several long hops.

Australia's sole win for the tournament came against lowly Canada.

Gavaskar, Dev lead Indian whitewash

Quick change. Before the first Test clash in Madras, both Australia and India had little time to adapt to the local conditions. Coming out of their winter, the Australians had only two warm-up games. The Indians began the first Test just a week after walking off the Oval in their previous Test against England.

Now for the bad news. Spin bowler Venkataraghavan found out on the plane trip back from England that he had lost the captaincy when the flight captain made the announcement over the PA system. Sunil Gavaskar was appointed as captain for the series against Australia.

In your face. Expert close-in fielder Yajurvindra Singh had a miserable first Test. It started when he missed Allan Border on 0 at backward square leg off Kapil Dev. Border went on to make 162. In the second innings Yajurvindra was smashed in the face by a full-blooded sweep from Hilditch.

Grumpy Hogg. Rodney Hogg's bowling rhythm was thrown out of gear on this tour and problems erupted in the second Test after he was no-balled 14 times for over-stepping and he kicked down the stumps in frustration. Captain Kim Hughes made an immediate apology to the umpires and convinced Hogg to do the same at the end of the day's play.

Pained finish. The Australian team limped to the finish of the tour. Bruce Yardley pulled out of the last Test through an injury suffered at practice, and of the eleven that went onto the field Yallop, Higgs and Darling all had stomach ailments. Yallop only played because India permitted the Australians to start the game with a substitute, and Higgs could not last for the whole of the first day.

Ghouse that. Umpire Mohammad Ghouse's rejection of Rodney Hogg's lbw appeal against Kapil Dev in the sixth Test sparked an angry response. Hogg looked disheartened after the incident and at the end of the day Hughes told the press that the decision was 'the most dishonest piece of umpiring I have ever seen'. Ghouse umpired in both the third and the sixth Tests.

Young Australian batsman Kim Hughes had a good tour, showing class against the spinners and topping the averages.

Bombay, Nov. 7. India sealed its first series win over Australia with a comfortable victory in the sixth Test here today.

While the 2–0 win is a historic feat for Indian cricket, the Australians were not completely disgraced in what is their last campaign before the return of the World Series Cricket players. However the series did show the gulf between the depleted Australian team and other full-strength international outfits.

India's success was based on its batting depth, spearheaded by Gundappa Viswanath and Sunil Gavaskar. Young fast bowler Kapil Dev headed an attack that adapted to the conditions better than all of the Australian bowlers apart from Geoff Dymock.

The Queensland veteran has been a brave and willing workhorse in conditions that offered little to fast bowlers. It was left to him to shoulder the burden after Alan Hurst returned home in mid-tour with a back injury, and with Rodney Hogg's form falling away on the demoralising pitches.

From Australia's viewpoint the batting of Kim Hughes, Allan Border and to a lesser extent Graham Yallop was a cause for optimism. Hughes' technique against the spinners has been sound and always positive, while Border's continued development as a Test batsman shows that he is a cut above the others who have come and gone through this side in the past two years of turbulence.

The scheduling of the tour, starting in September, meant that cricket was at the mercy of the monsoon season and the first two Tests were badly affected by the weather.

Australian leg-spinner Jim Higgs took 7/143 in a marathon spell in the first Test, but the Indians mastered his bowling after that.

Australia's poor fielding and undisciplined batting led to the loss in the third Test. They could not handle the pitch's uneven bounce and the task of occupying the crease for five hours was beyond them, apart from resolute efforts by Hilditch and Whatmore.

It was Whatmore and all-rounder Peter Sleep who saw Australia through to the safety of a draw in the fourth Test.

Australia's insipid performance in the final Test was out of character with the resolve they had shown earlier in the series. The players looked like a group that was pre-occupied with the thought of going home.

Geoff Dymock gets all 11 out

Kanpur, Oct. 7. Hard-working Queenslander Geoff Dymock has completed the unusual feat of dismissing every opposition batsman at least once in the third Test match, which Australia lost by 153 runs.

The probing medium pacer took 5/99 and 7/67 and by a statistical oddity the only batsman he snared twice was tailender Srinivas Venkataraghavan.

It is perhaps misleading to describe Dymock as a late bloomer as he has been a valuable journeyman on the Shield scene for a decade. Although he made his Test debut in 1973–74, Dymock has had to queue up behind Lillee, Thomson, Walker, Gilmour and others in the line for a Test place.

Now 34 years old, the left-armer has developed an inswinger comparatively late in his career and this has added a new dimension to his bowling.

When Alan Hurst's crippling back problems meant that he had to be flown home after the second Test, young New South Wales fast bowler Geoff Lawson was sent as a replacement. But Dymock's ability

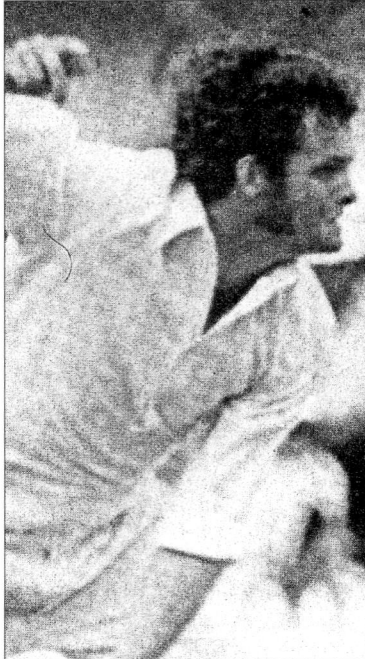

Determined medium pacer Geoff Dymock has been a great workhorse for Australia.

to lift his game a cog has meant that Lawson has only been needed for one first class game.

FIRST TEST 1979–80 INDIA v AUSTRALIA
Nehru (Corporation) Stadium, Madras. Sepeptember 11, 12, 14, 15, 16, 1979.
Toss: Australia. Match Drawn.

AUSTRALIA

AMJ Hilditch c Venkataraghavan b Kapil	4	lbw Doshi	55
GM Wood lbw Doshi	33	c Chauhan b Kapil	2
AR Border run out	162	b Venkataraghavan	50
KJ Hughes (c) c Venkataraghavan b Doshi	100	lbw Venkataraghavan	36
GN Yallop c Yajurvindra b Doshi	18	run out	2
DF Whatmore c Venkataraghavan b Doshi	20	c Chauhan b Doshi	8
KJ Wright (+) b Venkataraghavan	20	b Venkataraghavan	5
G Dymock lbw Kapil	16	not out	28
RM Hogg c Kapil b Doshi	3	not out	8
AG Hurst c Kirmani b Doshi	0		
JD Higgs not out	1		
EXTRAS (B 1, LB 7, W 1, NB 4)	13	(B 11, LB 4, NB 3)	18
TOTAL	390		7 for 212

FOW 1st Inns: 8 75 297 318 339 352 369 375 376 390
FOW 2nd Inns: 2 103 123 127 146 156 175

Bowling: *First Innings*: Kapil 25.4-3-95-2, Ghavri 20-4-49-0, Yajurvindra 9-1-29-0, Venkataraghavan 46-16-101-1, Doshi 43-10-103-6. *Second Innings*: Kapil 9-3-30-1, Ghavri 17.4-8-23-0, Doshi 42-15-64-2, Venkataraghavan 45-10-77-3.

INDIA

SM Gavaskar (c) c Wood b Hogg	50
CPS Chauhan c Wright b Higgs	26
SMH Kirmani (+) c Border b Hogg	57
GR Viswanath c Hughes b Higgs	17
DB Vengsarkar c Whatmore b Higgs	65
Yashpal Sharma lbw Higgs	52
Yajurvindra Singh c Wright b Yallop	15
Kapil Dev c Hurst b Higgs	83
KD Ghavri not out	23
S Venkataraghavan lbw Higgs	4
DR Doshi c Hogg b Higgs	3
EXTRAS (B 2, LB 5, NB 23)	30
TOTAL	425

FOW 1st Inns: 80 89 122 221 240 281 371 394 417 425

Bowling: *First Innings*: Hogg 22-1-85-2, Hurst 23-8-51-0, Dymock 24-6-65-0, Higgs 41.3-12-143-7, Border 14-4-30-0, Yallop 6-1-21-1.

Umpires: MV Gothoskar & Swaroop Kishen

1979–80 INDIA v AUSTRALIA

AUSTRALIA	M	Inn	NO	Runs	H.S	Avrge	Ct	St	Overs	Mds	Runs	Wkt	Avrge
Border, AR	6	12	-	521	162	43.42	4	-	52.0	16	110	3	36.67
Darling, WM	5	9	1	158	59	19.75	-	-	-	-	-	-	-
Dymock, G	5	9	2	103	31*	14.71	-	-	212.4	46	580	24	24.17
Higgs, JD	6	9	3	36	11	6.00	1	-	227.3	62	702	14	50.14
Hilditch, AMJ	6	12	-	313	85	26.08	3	-	-	-	-	-	-
Hogg, RM	6	10	2	54	19	6.75	2	-	194.2	39	591	11	53.73
Hughes, KJ	6	12	2	594	100	59.40	5	-	-	-	-	-	-
Hurst, AG	2	2	-	0	0	0.00	1	-	52.0	11	144	-	-
Sleep, PR	2	4	-	85	64	21.25	-	-	41.0	8	145	-	-
Whatmore, DF	5	10	-	220	77	22.00	12	-	5.0	2	11	-	-
Wood, GM	2	4	-	83	33	20.75	1	-	-	-	-	-	-
Wright, KJ	6	11	4	156	55*	22.29	10	3	-	-	-	-	-
Yallop, GN	6	12	1	423	167	38.45	-	-	16.0	2	62	1	62.00
Yardley, B	3	5	1	154	61*	38.50	1	-	159.0	49	381	10	38.10

1979–80 INDIA v AUSTRALIA

INDIA	M	Inn	NO	Runs	H.S	Avrge	Ct	St	Overs	Mds	Runs	Wkt	Avrge
Amarnath, M	1	1	-	2	2	2.00	2	-	7.0	2	12	-	-
Chauhan, CPS	6	8	-	380	84	47.50	6	-	9.0	1	22	1	22.00
Doshi, DR	6	4	1	3	3	1.00	-	-	306.2	87	630	27	23.33
Gavaskar, SM	6	8	-	425	123	53.13	4	-	4.0	1	10	-	-
Ghavri, KD	6	6	-	148	86	37.00	4	-	201.4	48	556	11	50.55
Kapil Dev	6	7	1	212	83	35.33	3	-	223.1	53	625	28	22.32
Kirmani, SMH	6	7	2	285	101*	57.00	11	3	-	-	-	-	-
Narasimha Rao, MV2	3	2	-	35	20*	17.50	3	-	39.0	4	120	2	60.00
Vengsarkar, DB	6	8	-	372	112	46.50	4	-	-	-	-	-	-
Venkataraghavan, S3	4	3	1	9	4*	4.50	3	-	146.0	44	308	6	51.33
Viswanath, GR	6	8	-	518	161*	74.00	4	-	3.3	-	11	1	11.00
Yadav, NS	5	4	1	18	18	6.00	1	-	234.3	63	577	24	24.04
Yajurvindra Singh	1	1	-	15	15	15.00	1	-	9.0	1	29	-	-
Yashpal Sharma	6	8	2	304	100*	50.67	2	-	-	-	-	-	-

SECOND TEST 1979–80 INDIA v AUSTRALIA
M Chinnaswamy Stadium, Bangalore. September 19, 20, 22, 23, 24, 1979.
Toss: Australia. Match Drawn.

AUSTRALIA

AMJ Hilditch c(S)Arun Lal b Yadav	62	lbw Yadav	3
WM Darling b Kapil	7		
AR Border c Yadav b Doshi	44	b Yadav	19
KJ Hughes (c) c Ghavri b Kapil	86	not out	13
GN Yallop c Viswanath b Yadav	12	not out	6
B Yardley c & b Ghavri	47		
GM Wood c Kirmani b Ghavri	18 (2)	c Viswanath b Yadav	30
KJ Wright (+) not out	16		
RM Hogg lbw Venkataraghavan	19		
JD Higgs lbw Yadav	1		
AG Hurst b Yadav	0		
EXTRAS (B 5, LB 6, NB 10)	21	(LB 5, NB 1)	6
TOTAL	333		3 for 77

FOW 1st Inns: 21 99 137 159 258 294 294 332 333 333
FOW 2nd Inns: 13 53 62

Bowling: *First Innings*: Ghavri 19-5-68-2, Kapil 25-4-89-2, Venkataraghavan 20-6-43-1, Yadav 22.5-6-49-4, Doshi 28-6-63-1. *Second Innings*: Ghavri 3-1-9-0, Kapil 3-2-1-0, Venkataraghavan 8-2-18-0, Yadav 15.4-4-32-3, Doshi 8-4-11-0.

INDIA

SM Gavaskar (c) c Hilditch b Yardley	10
CPS Chauhan c Hilditch b Yardley	31
DB Vengsarkar lbw Yardley	112
SMH Kirmani (+) st Wright b Higgs	30
GR Viswanath not out	161
Yashpal Sharma c Border b Yardley	37
Kapil Dev not out	38
KD Ghavri	
NS Yadav	
S Venkataraghavan	
DR Doshi	
EXTRAS (B 12, LB 8, W 1, NB 17)	38
TOTAL	5 dec 457

FOW 1st Inns: 22 61 120 279 372

Bowling: *First Innings*: Hogg 32-6-118-0, Hurst 29-3-93-0, Yardley 44-16-107-4, Higgs 37-9-95-1, Yallop 2-0-6-0.

Umpires: PR Punjabi & KB Ramaswamy

THIRD TEST 1979–80 INDIA v AUSTRALIA
Green Park (Modi Stadium), Kanpur. October 2, 3, 4, 6, 7, 1979.
Toss: India. India won by 153 runs.

INDIA

Batsman	1st Inns	Dismissal	2nd Inns
SM Gavaskar (c) lbw Dymock	76	c Whatmore b Yardley	12
CPS Chauhan c & b Hogg	58	c Yardley b Dymock	84
DB Vengsarkar lbw Hogg	52	c Whatmore b Dymock	20
GR Viswanath c(S)PR Sleep b Dymock	44	c Whatmore b Yardley	52
Yashpal Sharma b Hogg	0	c Wright b Dymock	0
Kapil Dev c Hughes b Border	5	b Dymock	10
SMH Kirmani (+) c Whatmore b Hogg	4	b Dymock	45
KD Ghavri c Whatmore b Dymock	5	c (S)PR Sleep b Hogg	25
NS Yadav lbw Dymock	0	c Whatmore b Dymock	18
S Venkataraghavan c Border b Dymock	1	not out	4
DR Doshi not out	0	b Dymock	0
EXTRAS (B 5, LB 6, NB 15)	26	(B 11, LB 9, NB 21)	41
TOTAL	271		311

FOW 1st Inns: 114 201 206 214 231 239 246 246 256 271
FOW 2nd Inns: 24 48 161 163 177 256 261 302 311 311

Bowling: *First Innings*: Dymock 35-7-99-5, Hogg 26-3-66-4, Yardley 20-6-54-0, Higgs 7-4-23-0, Border 3-2-3-1. *Second Innings*: Dymock 28.4-5-67-7, Hogg 19-4-49-1, Yardley 40-15-82-2, Border 2-1-4-0, Higgs 22-7-68-0.

AUSTRALIA

Batsman	1st Inns	Dismissal	2nd Inns
AMJ Hilditch c Chauhan b Ghavri	1	b Doshi	23
B Yardley c Yashpal b Ghavri	29 (8)	lbw Kapil	5
AR Border c Viswanath b Venkataraghavan	24 (6)	b Yadav	8
KJ Hughes (c) b Yadav	50	lbw Kapil	1
GN Yallop hit wicket b Kapil	89 (3)	c Kirmani b Ghavri	15
KJ Wright (+) lbw Kapil	6 (7)	b Yadav	11
DF Whatmore c Gavaskar b Doshi	14 (5)	b Yadav	33
WM Darling c Kirmani b Ghavri	59 (2)	lbw Kapil	4
G Dymock run out	11	st Kirmani b Yadav	6
RM Hogg b Yadav	10	lbw Kapil	6
JD Higgs not out	3	not out	8
EXTRAS (LB 2, NB 6)	8	(B 1, LB 2, NB 2)	5
TOTAL	304		125

FOW 1st Inns: 1 51 75 168 175 192 246 263 294 304
FOW 2nd Inns: 13 32 37 49 74 93 104 106 113 125

Bowling: *First Innings*: Kapil 27-5-78-2, Ghavri 23.3-5-65-3, Venkataraghavan 18-6-56-1, Doshi 16-5-32-1, Yadav 25-3-65-2. *Second Innings*: Kapil 16.2-5-30-4, Ghavri 11-0-28-1, Venkataraghavan 9-4-13-0, Doshi 12-5-14-1, Yadav 12-0-35-0.

Umpires: SN Hanumantha Rao & Mohammad Ghouse

FOURTH TEST 1979–80 INDIA v AUSTRALIA
Feroze Shah Kotla Ground, Delhi. October 13, 14, 16, 17, 18, 1979.
Toss: India. Match Drawn.

INDIA

Batsman	1st Inns
SM Gavaskar (c) lbw Higgs	115
CPS Chauhan c Whatmore b Dymock	19
DB Vengsarkar st Wright b Higgs	26
GR Viswanath st Wright b Higgs	131
Yashpal Sharma not out	100
Kapil Dev c Whatmore b Dymock	29
MV Narasimha Rao c Wright b Dymock	5
SMH Kirmani (+) b Dymock	35
KD Ghavri not out	8
NS Yadav	
DR Doshi	
EXTRAS (B 6, LB 12, NB 24)	42
TOTAL	7 for 510

FOW 1st Inns: 38 108 267 338 395 415 467

Bowling: *First Innings*: Dymock 42.2-8-135-4, Hogg 33-8-91-0, Yallop 5-0-21-0, Border 4-2-5-0, Higgs 47-11-150-3, Sleep 13-1-66-0.

AUSTRALIA

Batsman	1st Inns	Dismissal	2nd Inns
AMJ Hilditch c Kirmani b Yadav	29	c Kirmani b Ghavri	85
WM Darling c Kirmani b Kapil	19	c Kirmani b Kapil	7
AR Border c Narasimha Rao b Kapil	24	c Narasimha Rao b Ghavri	46
KJ Hughes (c) c Kirmani b Kapil	18	c & b Ghavri	40
DF Whatmore lbw Yadav	77 (6)	lbw Kapil	54
PR Sleep c Chauhan b Narasimha Rao	17 (7)	c (S)Arun Lal b Chauhan	64
GN Yallop c Chauhan b Narasimha Rao	21 (5)	b Doshi	25
KJ Wright (+) not out	55	b Yadav	15
G Dymock c Kirmani b Kapil	0	not out	31
RM Hogg b Yadav	0	run out	0
JD Higgs lbw Doshi	11	c Vengsarkar b Viswanath	7
EXTRAS (B 4, LB 4, NB 19)	27	(B 13, LB 9, W 1, NB 16)	39
TOTAL	298		413

FOW 1st Inns: 32 72 93 116 160 225 228 242 246 298
FOW 2nd Inns: 20 147 156 205 241 318 344 395 395 413

Bowling: *First Innings*: Ghavri 22-8-58-0, Kapil 32-7-82-5, Doshi 13.3-5-29-1, Yadav 27-10-56-2, Narasimha Rao 12-1-46-2. *Second Innings*: Kapil 20-7-48-2, Ghavri 30-8-74-3, Narasimha Rao 19-3-50-0, Doshi 34-11-69-1, Yadav 36-10-101-1, Gavaskar 4-1-10-0, Chauhan 5-1-11-1, Viswanath 3.3-0-11-1.

Umpires: PR Punjabi & KB Ramaswamy

FIFTH TEST 1979–80 INDIA v AUSTRALIA
Eden Gardens, Calcutta. October 26, 27, 28, 30, 31, 1979.
Toss: Australia. Match Drawn.

AUSTRALIA

Batsman	1st Inns	Dismissal	2nd Inns
AMJ Hilditch c Kirmani b Kapil	0	b Ghavri	29
GN Yallop c Gavaskar b Yadav	167	lbw Kapil	4
AR Border lbw Kapil	54	st Kirmani b Doshi	6
KJ Hughes (c) lbw Kapil	92	not out	64
DF Whatmore b Kapil	4	c Vengsarkar b Doshi	4
WM Darling st Kirmani b Doshi	39	c Gavaskar b Yadav	7
B Yardley not out	61	c Narasimha Rao b Yadav	12
KJ Wright (+) lbw Doshi	0	not out	12
G Dymock lbw Doshi	3		
RM Hogg c Yashpal b Doshi	0		
JD Higgs lbw Kapil	1		
EXTRAS (B 7, LB 7, NB 7)	21	(B 9, LB 4)	13
TOTAL	442		6 dec 151

FOW 1st Inns: 0 97 303 311 347 396 396 418 426 442
FOW 2nd Inns: 21 39 53 62 81 115

Bowling: *First Innings*: Kapil 32-9-74-5, Ghavri 24-3-85-0, Yadav 42-8-135-1, Narasimha Rao 8-0-24-0, Doshi 43-10-92-4, Chauhan 4-0-11-0. *Second Innings*: Kapil 11-3-33-1, Ghavri 13.3-5-39-1, Doshi 22-6-50-2, Yadav 11-6-16-2.

INDIA

Batsman	1st Inns	Dismissal	2nd Inns
SM Gavaskar (c) lbw Hogg	14	c Hilditch b Dymock	25
CPS Chauhan c Border b Higgs	39	c Wright b Dymock	50
DB Vengsarkar c Hughes b Yardley	89	c Wright b Dymock	2
GR Viswanath c Wright b Yardley	96	lbw Dymock	7
Yashpal Sharma c Wright b Hogg	22	not out	85
MV Narasimha Rao run out	10	not out	20
Kapil Dev c Hughes b Dymock	30		
SMH Kirmani (+) not out	13		
KD Ghavri c Wright b Yardley	1		
NS Yadav c Wright b Yardley	0		
DR Doshi b Dymock	0		
EXTRAS (B 12, LB 9, W 4, NB 8)	33	(B 4, LB 7)	11
TOTAL	347		4 for 200

FOW 1st Inns: 15 132 256 290 290 305 341 342 346 347
FOW 2nd Inns: 52 54 70 123

Bowling: *First Innings*: Dymock 26.4-8-56-2, Hogg 26-2-103-2, Yardley 42-11-91-4, Higgs 28-12-56-1, Border 2-0-8-0, Yallop 1-1-0-0. *Second Innings*: Hogg 8.2-1-26-0, Dymock 25-7-63-4, Yardley 13-1-47-0, Higgs 16-3-51-0, Yallop 1-0-2-0.

Umpires: SN Hanumantha Rao & Swaroop Kishen

SIXTH TEST 1979–80 INDIA v AUSTRALIA
Wankhede Stadium, Bombay. November 3, 4, 6, 7, 1979.
Toss: India. India won by an innings & 100 runs.

INDIA

Batsman	1st Inns
SM Gavaskar (c) c Hughes b Border	123
CPS Chauhan b Dymock	73
DB Vengsarkar c Whatmore b Border	6
GR Viswanath c & b Higgs	10
SMH Kirmani (+) not out	101
Yashpal Sharma c Whatmore b Hogg	8
M Amarnath hit wicket b Hogg	2
Kapil Dev c Whatmore b Higgs	17
KD Ghavri c(S)GD Porter b Dymock	86
NS Yadav not out	0
DR Doshi	
EXTRAS (B 3, LB 12, NB 17)	32
TOTAL	8 dec 458

FOW 1st Inns: 192 222 231 240 272 281 327 454

Bowling: *First Innings*: Dymock 31-5-95-2, Hogg 28-14-53-2, Higgs 29-4-116-2, Border 27-7-60-2, Sleep 28-7-79-0, Whatmore 5-2-11-0, Yallop 1-0-12-0.

AUSTRALIA

Batsman	1st Inns	Dismissal	2nd Inns
AMJ Hilditch run out	13	b Kapil	9
GN Yallop c Gavaskar b Yadav	60	c Amarnath b Ghavri	4
AR Border c Vengsarkar b Yadav	23	b Doshi	61
KJ Hughes (c) c Vengsarkar b Doshi	14	c Ghavri b Kapil	80
DF Whatmore lbw Doshi	6	lbw Kapil	0
WM Darling c(S)RMH Binny b Yadav	16	retired hurt	0
PR Sleep b Yadav		c Kapil b Doshi	3
KJ Wright (+) not out	11	lbw Doshi	5
G Dymock c Chauhan b Doshi	1	c Viswanath b Yadav	7
RM Hogg c Amarnath b Doshi	5	not out	3
JD Higgs b Doshi	0	b Kapil	4
EXTRAS (B 1, LB 2, NB 7)	10	(LB 12, NB 10)	22
TOTAL	160		9 dec 198

FOW 1st Inns: 28 77 110 118 124 125 144 145 158 160
FOW 2nd Inns: 11 17 149 154 159 176 183 187 198

Bowling: *First Innings*: Kapil 8-0-26-0, Ghavri 8-1-30-0, Doshi 19.5-4-43-5, Amarnath 5-1-11-0, Yadav 21-7-40-4. *Second Innings*: Kapil 14.1-5-39-4, Ghavri 10-0-28-1, Amarnath 2-1-1-0, Yadav 22-9-48-1, Doshi 25-6-60-3.

Umpires: JD Ghosh & Mohammad Ghouse

Lillee's alumbat is a bother

Perth, Dec. 15. The Australian Cricket Board has severely reprimanded fast bowler Dennis Lillee for his behaviour in the first Test between Australia and England, when Lillee was the star of a sensational sideshow involving an aluminium bat.

'Your behaviour was reprehensible,' the Board told Lillee today. 'As a senior player it is your responsibility to set an example and not to denigrate the game.'

The incident occurred on the second morning of the Test, after Lillee walked to the pitch carrying one of the 'Combat' aluminium cricket bats that he is promoting.

He faced four balls from England's Ian Botham and scored three runs with the bat before England captain Mike Brearley went to speak with umpires Max O'Connell and Don Weser.

Brearley alleged the metal bat was damaging the ball.

Australia's 12th man, Rodney Hogg, acting under instructions from captain Greg Chappell, then emerged from the boundary carrying two traditional willow bats.

Lillee rejected both and returned to the boundary with Hogg.

Moments later Lillee was back, once again with the aluminium bat. Play remained at a standstill while

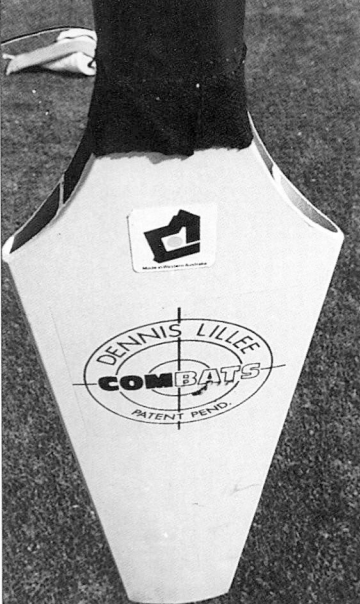

Dennis Lillee's aluminium cricket bat.

Lillee and the umpires conversed, after which he threw the aluminium bat away, apparently in anger, but then he graciously accepted a willow bat from Chappell with what seemed to be a smile.

The incident wasted 15 minutes of play, and while Lillee may have lost his bat, he hasn't lost his smile. Everybody knows about those aluminium bats now.

PBL saturates the cricket calendar

Sydney, Nov. 30. How much cricket is enough? Maybe there can never be too much, if the people who have moved into cricket this year continue to have their way.

Under an agreement signed in May, the rift between World Series Cricket and the Australian Cricket Board was ended when the ACB gave exclusive cricket promotion rights for 10 years to PBL Sports, a company associated with Kerry Packer's Channel Nine television network.

PBL have certainly ensured that cricket fans will not be starved of top grade cricket in season 1979–80.

A six-Test series against India has just been completed. England and the West Indies are each about to play three Tests on Australian soil. And the Sheffield Shield and twenty limited-overs games must somehow be squeezed in before Australia tours Pakistan in February–March.

As part of the PBL deal, the Board has agreed to consider introducing 30-yard circles, coloured clothing and day/night fixtures in limited-overs matches. Selection and playing conditions will remain under the Board's control. But who will control the marketing men?

The art of cricket is splendidly portrayed in Alan Fearnley's painting of the Melbourne Cricket Ground, looking north.

Bruce Laird in blazing opening

Bruce Laird (92 & 75) at Brisbane.

Brisbane, Dec. 5. For a small man, new Australian opening batsman Bruce Laird is big on runs.

In the first Test between Australia and the West Indies, Laird made 92 and 75, which is the highest number of runs without a century from any batsman in his Test debut.

Most of Laird's aggregate was built up by clever singles, and he looked set to make a century in both innings but for the West Indies' giant bowler, Joel Garner.

In the first innings Laird edged Garner just as the light was fading. The ball was caught behind by Deryck Murray. In the second, Laird was caught on 75 by Malcolm Marshall, off a Garner delivery.

Goliath stopped David here, but the little man will be back.

Viv Richards a whirlwind

Melbourne, Jan. 2. Viv Richards is the star of a resounding West Indies victory over Australia in the second Test at the MCG.

The free-flowing West Indian batsman was at his magnificent best in Melbourne, scoring 96 runs in just 110 balls on the second day of the Test. At one stage he hit 45 runs from 36 balls.

Richards is a thrilling player who refuses to be intimidated by bowlers. After being struck in the mouth by one of Rodney Hogg's bouncers, he was unperturbed and answered in the best possible way, by hitting the next ball for one of the most glorious sixes seen at the MCG in a long time.

The West Indies made 397 in their first innings and won the Test by 10 wickets. It is the first time that the West Indies have defeated Australia in Melbourne.

Australia collapsed on the first day to be all out for 156 in its first innings and could manage only 259 in the second.

The West Indies fast bowlers did all the damage. Colin Croft and Michael Holding each claimed six wickets for the match.

Croft came close to a hat-trick in the first innings, while Holding surprised everyone with the pace he achieved from what seemed to be just a long, loping run. He packs a punch in his final leap.

The pair were ably assisted by Andy Roberts, who took 3/64 in the second innings, and Joel Garner (3/33 and 2/56).

In contrast, Australian fast man Rodney Hogg proved expensive. Hogg's figures were 0/59 off six

Viv Richards: backyard brilliance.

overs. Back problems may have been to blame, however.

Dennis Lillee was in better form (3/96), and Australia's best bowler was Geoff Dymock, who held firm for 34 overs to end with match figures of 4/106. In his old age, Dymock has perfected a formidable inswinger.

Crowds failed to be impressed. The attendance of 89,045 is the worst Christmas Test aggregate in Melbourne for many years.

ACB and ABC at legal odds

Sydney, Dec. 21. The Australian Broadcasting Commission has launched legal action in the Federal Court against PBL Marketing and World Series Cricket, alleging breaches of the Trade Practices Act.

It is believed that the dispute concerns the television rights to broadcast cricket, which have now been acquired by Kerry Packer's PBL for his Channel Nine network.

As part of the deal reached between the Australian Cricket Board and PBL in May, the Board agreed to let PBL arrange a contract for televising the cricket program over the next three years, at least.

By taking legal action, the ABC hopes to gain the right to telecast cricket in country areas, which will not be serviced by Packer's stations.

Windies administer sound thrashing

Adelaide, Jan. 30. Today in the third Test the West Indies have given Australia one of the most severe thrashings in the history of Test cricket. It has been a terrible punishment. Just brutal.

And it all began on Australia Day, when those West Indian bully boys, Clive Lloyd and Viv Richards, got together. Talk about humiliation. Lloyd made 121 runs and Richards was almost invincible, hitting 13 fours and 76 runs.

It really hurt when Richards slashed Len Pascoe to the boundary three times in a row. Then the West Indies fast bowlers took their turn and Australia's Chappell brothers became the whipping boys.

Andy Roberts dismissed Ian Chappell for 2 runs, and followed up next ball with Greg, out first ball for a duck. Take that! And that! Oh, the rest was just pain, and more pain.

Australia's best bowling hope, Dennis Lillee, took five wickets in the West Indies first innings, but batting late on the second day he was hit on the finger by one of Michael Holding's fiery fast ones. And did it sting.

With a black and blue finger, Lillee was useless bowling in the second innings (0/75), where the West Indies made 448 runs and Alvin Kallicharran (106) belted the Australia's bowlers red and raw.

Australia had no hope of making 574 runs in its second innings.

Beaten by 408 runs, the Australians can hardly walk back to the rooms. And they can't sit down either.

Who said cricket wasn't fun anymore? High jinks from Peter Laker (left) and Bob Simpson, who kicks over his stumps in the annual 'Press Test'.

After a stunning shot from Clive Lloyd this seagull was taken off the field by pall-bearer Dennis Lillee.

Border gets 100, and two on 99

Perth, Dec. 20. As sure as there's something magical about 100 runs, there's something diabolical about 99.

Three batsmen reached 99 in the first Test between Australia and England. Only one went past.

That was Australia's Allan Border, who top-scored in the match with 115 in Australia's second innings.

Border, a gritty left-handed batsman from Sydney, was unimpressive in the recent Test against the West Indies, where he made 1 and 7. Now, against England, he has more than made amends. His 115 was a dogged performance that sealed the win for Australia.

Much of the groundwork was laid in Australia's first innings by Kim Hughes, who held firm against a devastating fast bowling attack from England's Ian Botham (6/78).

Botham almost wrecked Australia's chances, but Hughes was resolute. It was unfortunate that Hughes ended an otherwise cool innings at 99. Some typically tight bowling from Derek Underwood seemed to be more than Hughes could stand on the edge of his milestone. He lashed out at one ball, and that was it – caught at backward square by the England captain, Mike Brearley.

England opener Geoffrey Boycott knew how Hughes felt. But at least he knew it wasn't his fault.

Boycott was left at 99 not out when his side was bowled out for 215 runs in their second innings.

Australia won the Test by 138 runs. There was a minor fiasco on the second day when Australia's Dennis Lillee attempted to use an aluminium bat. The word is that he may be hearing from the ACB in the next mail. And it might not be a Christmas card.

Allan Border: century sealed win.

Storms over the SCG

England captain Mike Brearley was forced to bat on a nightmare pitch.

Sydney, Jan. 8. The second Test between Australia and England has been something of a disaster all round, but most of all for England, whose six-wicket loss gives Australia an unbeatable two–nil lead in the series.

There is dismay in the Australian camp because English authorities refused to put the Ashes up for grabs in this three-Test series.

'We won them,' Australian captain Greg Chappell says defiantly.

But not officially. The Ashes will stay in England.

From start to finish, the Sydney Test has been a stormy affair in more ways than one.

Dark clouds were gathering on New Year's Eve, and on New Year's Day the heavens opened.

Unfortunately, the SCG ground staff had left the wickets uncovered and the ground was utterly soaked.

Staff had also watered the pitch before the downpour. The result was it was still drying out on the opening day of the Test.

There seemed little hope of a start, but at 3 p.m. the call was made. Brearley lost the toss and Chappell sent England in to bat.

Australian bowlers Dennis Lillee and Geoff Dymock had a field day.

Lillee took 4/40 and Dymock, 4/42. With a little help from Bruce Pascoe (1/14) and Greg Chappell (1/19), England was all out for 123. And that sums up the way it went. One, two, three. They just fell over at the crease.

The pitch was green in patches and Australia's fast bowlers enjoyed a dangerous advantage at the outset.

David Gower made a valiant stand in England's second innings, and was unlucky to be stranded on 98 when Bob Willis was caught by Greg Chappell at first slip.

Greg Chappell was Man of the Match with 98 not out in Australia's second innings. But despite Australia's win, he is still annoyed that the Test went ahead before the pitch was ready.

Fortune fell on the flip of a coin.

Lillee gets his 200th Test wicket

Melbourne, Feb. 7. Dennis Lillee may like to bat with aluminium, but when he bowls it's gold.

Sponsors have given Lillee a set of gold goblets after his 11-wicket haul for Australia in the third Test against England at the MCG. Lillee's match figures were 11/138. He was Man of the Match and also claimed his 200th wicket in Test cricket when he bowled John Lever in England's first innings.

Lillee had to leave the field on the opening day because of sinus trouble, but he certainly came good as the match progressed.

England jumped to a powerful start, thanks to opening batsmen Graham Gooch (99) and Geoff Boycott (25). England was 1/170 by mid afternoon on the first day and the wicket looked a batsman's beauty.

But Gooch fell victim to '99 madness', when he dashed for a crazy single and ran himself out.

It was just the break that Australia needed. A sustained bowling attack from Lillee (6/60), Len Pascoe (2/71) and Geoff Dymock (1/54) saw England collapse to be all out for 306 in the first innings.

Australia scored 477 in reply, with Greg Chappell (114) setting up a first-innings lead of 71 runs.

Lillee took 5/78 in England's second innings (273), which left an easy 103 run chase for Australia.

Apart from Gooch (51), Ian Botham was the only other England batsman able to fight off Lillee.

Botham scored his fifth Test century to end at 119 not out, which earned him a London sponsor's bonus of 100 bottles of champagne. It was a pity England had nothing else to celebrate, because Dennis Lillee had a beautiful set of goblets.

Ian Botham: brilliant batting.

FIRST TEST 1979–80 AUSTRALIA v WEST INDIES
Brisbane Cricket Ground, Brisbane. December 1, 2, 3, 4, 5, 1979.
Toss: West Indies. Match Drawn.

AUSTRALIA
BM Laird c Murray b Garner	92 (2)	c (S)MD Marshall b Garner 75
RB McCosker c Kallicharran b Croft	14 (1)	b Holding 33
AR Border c Murray b Garner	1	c Richards b Garner 7
GS Chappell (c) c King b Roberts	74	b Croft 124
KJ Hughes b Croft	3	not out 130
DW Hookes c Holding b Croft	43	b Roberts 37
RW Marsh (+) c Murray b Garner	3	c Kallicharran b King 19
RJ Bright b Holding	13	not out 2
DK Lillee lbw Garner	0	
RM Hogg b Roberts	8	
JR Thomson not out	0	
EXTRAS (B 1, LB 4, NB 12)	17	(B 2, LB 11, W 2, NB 6) 21
TOTAL	268	6 dec 448

FOW 1st Inns: 19 26 156 174 228 242 246 252 268 268
FOW 2nd Inns: 40 55 179 297 371 442

Bowling: *First Innings*: Roberts 18.1-5-50-2, Holding 16-3-53-1, Croft 25-6-80-3, Garner 22-5-55-4, King 5-1-13-0. *Second Innings*: Roberts 27-5-70-1, Holding 30-4-91-1, Croft 28-3-106-1, Garner 41-13-75-2, King 22-6-50-1, Kallicharran 18-0-32-0.

WEST INDIES
CG Greenidge c Marsh b Lillee	34	c McCosker b Thomson 0
DL Haynes c Marsh b Thomson	42	lbw Hogg 4
IVA Richards c Marsh b Lillee	140	
AI Kallicharran c Marsh b Thomson	38	not out 10
LG Rowe b Chappell	50 (3)	b Hogg 3
CL King c Marsh b Lillee	0 (5)	not out 8
DL Murray (c+) c McCosker b Thomson	21	
AME Roberts run out	7	
J Garner lbw Lillee	60	
MA Holding b Bright	11	
CEH Croft not out	2	
EXTRAS (B 5, LB 3, NB 28)	36	(B 5, W 1, NB 9) 15
TOTAL	441	3 for 40

FOW 1st Inns: 68 93 198 317 317 341 365 366 385 441
FOW 2nd Inns: 2 15 16

Bowling: *First Innings*: Lillee 29.1-8-104-4, Hogg 25-6-55-0, Thomson 24-4-90-3, Chappell 12-2-25-1, Bright 32-9-97-1, Border 5-1-19-0, Hookes 5-2-15-0. *Second Innings*: Hogg 5-2-11-2, Thomson 3-2-3-1, Bright 4-3-8-0, Lillee 2-0-3-0.

Umpires: RC Bailhache & AR Crafter

SECOND TEST 1979–80 AUSTRALIA v WEST INDIES
Melbourne Cricket Ground, Melbourne. December 29, 30, 31, 1979, January 1, 1980.
Toss: Australia. West Indies won by 10 wkts.

AUSTRALIA
JM Wiener lbw Garner	40	c Murray b Croft 24
BM Laird c Lloyd b Holding	16	c Garner b Holding 69
AR Border c Richards b Garner	17	lbw Holding 15
GS Chappell (c) c Murray b Garner	19	c Murray b Roberts 22
KJ Hughes c Rowe b Holding	4	lbw Roberts 70
PM Toohey c Roberts b Holding	10	c Murray b Croft 7
RW Marsh (+) c Kallicharran b Holding	0	b Croft 7
DK Lillee c Lloyd b Croft	12	c & b Roberts 0
G Dymock c Kallicharran b Croft	7	c Lloyd b Garner 17
RM Hogg c Greenidge b Croft	14	c Holding b Garner 11
JD Higgs not out	0	not out 0
EXTRAS (B 9, LB 4, W 2, NB 2)	17	(B 2, LB 10, NB 5) 17
TOTAL	156	259

FOW 1st Inns: 38 69 97 108 112 118 123 133 143 156
FOW 2nd Inns: 43 88 121 187 205 228 228 233 258 259

Bowling: *First Innings*: Roberts 14-1-39-0, Holding 14-3-40-4, Croft 13.3-4-27-3, Garner 15-7-33-3. *Second Innings*: Roberts 21-1-64-3, Holding 23-7-61-2, Croft 22-2-61-3, Garner 20.4-2-56-2.

WEST INDIES
CG Greenidge c Higgs b Dymock	48	not out 9
DL Haynes c Hughes b Lillee	29	not out 9
IVA Richards c Toohey b Dymock	96	
AI Kallicharran c Laird b Higgs	39	
LG Rowe b Lillee	26	
CH Lloyd (c) c Marsh b Dymock	40	
DL Murray (+) b Dymock	24	
AME Roberts lbw Lillee	54	
J Garner c Dymock b Higgs	29	
MA Holding not out	0	
CEH Croft lbw Higgs	0	
EXTRAS (LB 4, NB 7)	11	(LB 4) 4
TOTAL	397	0 for 22

FOW 1st Inns: 46 156 215 226 250 305 320 390 396 397
FOW 2nd Inns:

Bowling: *First Innings*: Lillee 36-7-96-3, Hogg 6-0-59-0, Dymock 31-2-106-4, Higgs 34.4-4-122-3, Chappell 5-2-3-0. *Second Innings*: Lillee 3-0-9-0, Dymock 3-0-5-0, Hughes 1-1-0-0, Toohey 0.2-0-4-0.

Umpires: AR Crafter & CE Harvey

THIRD TEST 1979–80 AUSTRALIA v WEST INDIES
Adelaide Oval, Adelaide. January 26, 27, 28, 29, 30, 1980.
Toss: Australia. West Indies won by 408 runs.

WEST INDIES
CG Greenidge lbw Lillee	6	st Marsh b Mallett 76
DL Haynes c Lillee b Mallett	28	c Marsh b Pascoe 27
IVA Richards c Marsh b Lillee	76	b Border 74
AI Kallicharran c IM Chappell b Mallett	9	b Mallett 106
LG Rowe c Lillee b Dymock	40	c Marsh b Dymock 43
CH Lloyd (c) lbw Lillee	121 (7)	c Marsh b Dymock 40
DL Murray (+) c Marsh b Dymock	4 (8)	c GS Chappell b Dymock 28
AME Roberts b Lillee	9 (9)	c Laird b Dymock 8
J Garner c Hughes b Lillee	16 (10)	not out 1
MA Holding b Pascoe	9 (11)	lbw Dymock 1
CEH Croft not out	1 (6)	c Border b Pascoe 12
EXTRAS (B 2, NB 7)	9	(B 1, LB 10, NB 21) 32
TOTAL	328	448

FOW 1st Inns: 11 115 115 126 239 252 300 303 326 328
FOW 2nd Inns: 12 21 71 83 98 130 131 135 159 165

Bowling: *First Innings*: Lillee 24-3-78-5, Dymock 25-7-74-2, Pascoe 15.3-1-90-1, Mallett 27-5-77-2. *Second Innings*: Lillee 26-6-75-0, Pascoe 25-3-93-2, Dymock 33.5-7-104-5, Mallett 38-7-134-2, Border 4-2-10-1.

AUSTRALIA
JM Wiener c Haynes b Holding	3	c Murray b Roberts 8
BM Laird c Garner b Croft	52	lbw Garner 36
IM Chappell c Greenidge b Roberts	2	c Murray b Holding 4
GS Chappell (c) c Garner b Roberts	0	lbw Croft 31
KJ Hughes c Lloyd b Croft	34	lbw Garner 11
AR Border b Roberts	54	c Greenidge b Roberts 24
RW Marsh (+) c Murray b Croft	5	not out 23
DK Lillee c Haynes b Holding	16	c Kallicharran b Croft 0
G Dymock c Rowe b Croft	10	c Richards b Holding 2
AA Mallett c Rowe b Garner	0	b Holding 12
LS Pascoe not out	5	b Holding 5
EXTRAS (B 1, LB 14, NB 7)	22	(LB 2, W 2, NB 5) 9
TOTAL	203	165

FOW 1st Inns: 23 26 26 83 110 127 165 188 189 203
FOW 2nd Inns: 12 21 71 83 98 130 131 135 159 165

Bowling: *First Innings*: Roberts 16.5-3-43-3, Holding 15-5-31-2, Garner 18-4-43-1, Richards 2-0-7-0, Croft 22-4-57-4. *Second Innings*: Roberts 15-5-30-2, Holding 13-2-40-4, Garner 11-3-39-2, Croft 11-1-47-2.

Umpires: MW Johnson & MG O'Connell

Australian Averages

1979–80 AUSTRALIA v WEST INDIES
AUSTRALIA	M	Inn	NO	Runs	H.S	Avrge	Ct	St	Overs	Mds	Runs	Wkt	Avrge
Border, AR	3	6	-	118	54	19.67	1	-	9	3	29	1	29.00
Bright, RJ	1	2	1	15	13	15.00	-	-	36	12	105	1	105.00
Chappell, GS	3	6	-	270	124	45.00	1	-	17	4	28	1	28.00
Chappell, IM	1	2	-	6	4	3.00	1	-	-	-	-	-	-
Dymock, G	2	4	-	36	17	9.00	-	-	92.5	16	289	11	26.27
Higgs, JD	1	2	2	0	0*	-	1	-	34.4	4	122	3	40.67
Hogg, RM	2	3	-	33	14	11.00	-	-	36	8	125	2	62.50
Hookes, DW	1	2	-	80	43	40.00	-	-	5	2	15	0	-
Hughes, KJ	3	6	1	252	130*	50.40	2	-	1	1	0	0	-
Laird, BM	3	6	-	340	92	56.67	2	-	-	-	-	-	-
Lillee, DK	3	5	-	28	16	5.60	2	-	120.1	24	365	12	30.42
Mallett, AA	1	2	-	12	12	6.00	-	-	65	12	211	4	52.75
Marsh, RW	3	6	1	57	23*	11.40	11	1	-	-	-	-	-
McCosker, RB	1	2	-	47	33	23.50	2	-	-	-	-	-	-
Pascoe, LS	1	2	1	10	5*	10.00	-	-	40.3	4	183	3	61.00
Thomson, JR	1	1	1	0	0*	-	-	-	27	6	93	4	23.25
Toohey, PM	1	2	-	17	10	8.50	1	-	0.2	0	4	0	-
Wiener, JM	2	4	-	75	40	18.75	-	-	-	-	-	-	-

West Indian Averages

1979–80 AUSTRALIA v WEST INDIES
WEST INDIES	M	Inn	NO	Runs	H.S	Avrge	Ct	St	Overs	Mds	Runs	Wkt	Avrge
Croft, CEH	3	4	2	15	12	7.50	-	-	121.3	20	378	16	23.63
Garner, J	3	4	1	106	60	35.33	3	-	127.4	34	301	14	21.50
Greenidge, CG	3	6	1	173	76	34.60	3	-	-	-	-	-	-
Haynes, DL	3	6	1	139	42	27.80	2	-	-	-	-	-	-
Holding, MA	3	4	1	22	11	7.33	2	-	111.0	24	319	14	22.79
Kallicharran, AI	3	5	1	202	106	50.50	5	-	18.0	-	32	-	-
King, CL	1	2	1	8	8*	8.00	1	-	27.0	7	63	1	63.00
Lloyd, CH	2	3	-	201	121	67.00	4	-	-	-	-	-	-
Murray, DL	3	6	-	77	28	19.25	10	-	-	-	-	-	-
Richards, IVA	3	4	-	386	140	96.50	3	-	2.0	-	7	-	-
Roberts, AME	3	4	-	78	54	19.50	-	-	112.0	20	296	11	26.91
Rowe, LG	3	5	-	162	50	32.40	3	-	-	-	-	-	-

FIRST TEST 1979-80 AUSTRALIA v ENGLAND
W.A.C.A. Ground, Perth. December 14, 15, 16, 18, 19, 1979.
Toss: England. Australia won by 138 runs.

AUSTRALIA

JM Wiener run out	11	c Randall b Underwood	58
BM Laird lbw Botham	0	c Taylor b Underwood	33
AR Border lbw Botham	4	c Taylor b Willis	115
GS Chappell (c) c Boycott b Botham	19	st Taylor b Underwood	43
KJ Hughes c Brearley b Underwood	99	c Miller b Botham	4
PM Toohey c Underwood b Dilley	19	c Taylor b Botham	3
RW Marsh (+) c Taylor b Dilley	42	c Gower b Botham	4
RJ Bright c Taylor b Botham	17	lbw Botham	12
DK Lillee c Taylor b Botham	18	c Willey b Dilley	19
G Dymock b Botham	5	not out	20
JR Thomson not out	1	b Botham	8
EXTRAS (B 4, LB 3, NB 2)	9	(B 4, LB 5, W 2, NB 7)	18
TOTAL	244		337

FOW 1st Inns: 2 17 20 88 127 186 219 219 243 244
FOW 2nd Inns: 91 100 168 183 191 204 225 303 323 337

Bowling: *First Innings*: Dilley 18-1-47-2, Botham 35-9-78-6, Willis 23-7-47-0, Underwood 13-4-33-1, Miller 11-2-30-0. *Second Innings*: Botham 45.5-14-98-5, Dilley 18-3-50-1, Willis 26-7-52-1, Miller 10-0-36-0, Underwood 41-14-82-3, Willey 1-0-1-0.

ENGLAND

DW Randall c Hughes b Lillee	0	lbw Dymock	1
G Boycott lbw Lillee	0	not out	99
P Willey c Chappell b Dymock	9	lbw Dymock	12
DI Gower c Marsh b Lillee	17	c Thomson b Dymock	23
G Miller c Hughes b Thomson	25	c Chappell b Thomson	8
JM Brearley (c) c Marsh b Lillee	64 (7)	c Marsh b Bright	11
IT Botham c Toohey b Thomson	15 (6)	c Marsh b Lillee	18
RW Taylor (+) b Chappell	14	b Lillee	15
GR Dilley not out	38	c Marsh b Dymock	16
DL Underwood lbw Dymock	13	c Wiener b Dymock	0
RGD Willis b Dymock	11	c Chappell b Dymock	0
EXTRAS (LB 7, NB 15)	22	(LB 3, W 1, NB 8)	12
TOTAL	228		215

FOW 1st Inns: 1 12 14 41 74 90 123 185 203 228
FOW 2nd Inns: 8 26 64 75 115 141 182 211 211 215

Bowling: *First Innings*: Lillee 28-11-73-4, Dymock 29.1-14-52-3, Chappell 11-6-5-1, Thomson 21-3-70-2, Bright 2-0-6-0. *Second Innings*: Lillee 23-5-74-2, Dymock 17.2-4-34-6, Chappell 6-4-6-0, Thomson 11-3-30-1, Bright 23-11-30-1, Wiener 8-3-22-0, Border 2-0-7-0.

Umpires: MG O'Connell & DG Weser

SECOND TEST 1979-80 AUSTRALIA v ENGLAND
Sydney Cricket Ground, Sydney. January 4, 5, 6, 8, 1980.
Toss: Australia. Australia won by 6 wkts.

ENGLAND

GA Gooch b Lillee	18	c GS Chappell b Dymock	4
G Boycott b Dymock	8	c McCosker b Pascoe	18
DW Randall c GS Chappell b Lillee	0 (6)	c Marsh b GS Chappell	25
P Willey c Wiener b Dymock	8 (3)	b Pascoe	3
JM Brearley (c) c Pascoe b Dymock	7 (4)	c Marsh b Pascoe	0
DI Gower b GS Chappell	3 (7)	not out	98
IT Botham c GS Chappell b Pascoe	27 (8)	c Wiener b GS Chappell	0
RW Taylor (+) c Marsh b Lillee	10 (9)	b Lillee	8
GR Dilley not out	22 (10)	b Dymock	4
RGD Willis c Wiener b Dymock	3 (11)	c GS Chappell b Lillee	1
DL Underwood c Border b Lillee	12 (5)	c Border b Dymock	43
EXTRAS (NB 5)	5	(B 1, LB 10, W 1, NB 2)	14
TOTAL	123		237

FOW 1st Inns: 10 13 31 38 41 74 75 90 98 123
FOW 2nd Inns: 6 21 29 77 105 156 174 211 218 237

Bowling: *First Innings*: Lillee 13.3-4-40-4, Dymock 17-6-42-4, Pascoe 9-4-14-1, GS Chappell 4-1-19-1, Higgs 1-0-3-0. *Second Innings*: Lillee 24.3-6-63-2, Dymock 28-8-48-3, Pascoe 23-3-76-3, GS Chappell 21-10-36-2.

AUSTRALIA

RB McCosker c Gower b Willis	1	c Taylor b Underwood	41
JM Wiener run out	22	b Underwood	13
IM Chappell c Brearley b Gooch	42	c Botham b Underwood	9
GS Chappell (c) c Taylor b Underwood	3	not out	98
KJ Hughes c Taylor b Botham	18	c Dilley b Willis	47
AR Border c Gooch b Botham	15	not out	2
RW Marsh (+) c Underwood b Gooch	7		
DK Lillee c Brearley b Botham	5		
G Dymock c Taylor b Botham	4		
LS Pascoe not out	10		
JD Higgs b Underwood	2		
EXTRAS (B 2, LB 12, W 2)	16	(LB 8, W 1)	9
TOTAL	145		4 for 219

FOW 1st Inns: 18 52 71 92 100 114 121 129 132 145
FOW 2nd Inns: 31 51 98 203

Bowling: *First Innings*: Botham 17-7-29-4, Willis 11-3-30-1, Underwood 13.2-3-39-2, Dilley 5-1-13-0, Willey 1-0-2-0, Gooch 11-4-16-2. *Second Innings*: Willis 12-2-26-1, Botham 23.3-12-43-0, Underwood 26-6-71-3, Dilley 12-0-33-0, Willey 4-0-17-0, Gooch 8-2-20-0.

Umpires: RC Bailhache & WJ Copeland

THIRD TEST 1979-80 AUSTRALIA v ENGLAND
Melbourne Cricket Ground, Melbourne. February 1, 2, 3, 5, 6, 1980.
Toss: England. Australia won by 8 wkts.

ENGLAND

GA Gooch run out	99	b Mallett	51
G Boycott c Mallett b Dymock	44	b Lillee	7
W Larkins c GS Chappell b Pascoe	25	lbw Pascoe	3
DI Gower lbw Lillee	0	b Lillee	11
P Willey lbw Pascoe	1	c Marsh b Lillee	2
IT Botham c Marsh b Lillee	8 (7)	not out	119
JM Brearley (c) not out	60 (6)	c Border b Pascoe	10
RW Taylor (+) b Lillee	23	c Border b Lillee	32
DL Underwood c IM Chappell b Lillee	3	b Pascoe	0
JK Lever b Lillee	22	c Marsh b Lillee	12
RGD Willis c GS Chappell b Lillee	4	c GS Chappell b Pascoe	2
EXTRAS (B 1, LB 2, NB 14)	17	(B 2, LB 12, NB 10)	24
TOTAL	306		273

FOW 1st Inns: 116 170 175 177 177 192 238 242 296 306
FOW 2nd Inns: 25 46 64 67 88 92 178 179 268 273

Bowling: *First Innings*: Lillee 33.1-9-60-6, Dymock 28-6-54-1, Mallett 35-9-104-0, Pascoe 32-7-71-2. *Second Innings*: Lillee 33-6-78-5, Dymock 11-2-30-0, Pascoe 29.5-3-80-4, Mallett 14-1-45-1, Border 4-0-16-0.

AUSTRALIA

RB McCosker c Botham b Underwood	33	lbw Botham	2
BM Laird c Gower b Underwood	74	c Boycott b Underwood	25
IM Chappell c & b Underwood	75	not out	26
KJ Hughes c Underwood b Botham	15		
AR Border c & b Lever	63		
GS Chappell (c) c Larkins b Lever	114 (4)	not out	40
RW Marsh (+) c Botham b Lever	17		
DK Lillee c Willey b Lever	8		
G Dymock b Botham	19		
AA Mallett lbw Botham	25		
LS Pascoe not out	1		
EXTRAS (B 13, LB 12, W 1, NB 7)	33	(LB 8, NB 2)	10
TOTAL	477		2 for 103

FOW 1st Inns: 52 179 196 219 345 411 421 432 465 477
FOW 2nd Inns: 20 42

Bowling: *First Innings*: Lever 53-15-111-4, Botham 39.5-15-105-3, Willis 21-4-61-0, Underwood 53-19-131-3, Willey 13-2-36-0. *Second Innings*: Willis 5-3-8-0, Botham 12-5-18-1, Underwood 14-2-49-1, Lever 7.4-3-18-0.

Umpires: RC Bailhache & PM Cronin

Australian Averages

1979-80 AUSTRALIA v ENGLAND

AUSTRALIA	M	Inn	NO	Runs	H.S	Avrge	Ct	St	Overs	Mds	Runs	Wkt	Avrge
Border, AR	3	5	1	199	115	49.75	4	-	6	-	23	-	-
Bright, RJ	1	2	-	29	17	14.50	-	-	25	11	36	1	36.00
Chappell, GS	3	6	2	317	114	79.25	10	-	42	21	66	4	16.50
Chappell, IM	2	4	1	152	75	50.67	1	-	-	-	-	-	-
Dymock, G	3	4	1	48	20*	16.00	-	-	130.3	34	260	17	15.29
Higgs, JD	1	1	-	2	2	2.00	-	-	1	-	3	-	-
Hughes, KJ	3	5	-	183	99	36.60	2	-	-	-	-	-	-
Laird, BM	2	4	-	132	74	33.00	-	-	-	-	-	-	-
Lillee, DK	3	4	-	50	19	12.50	-	-	155.1	35	388	23	16.87
Mallett, AA	1	1	-	25	25	25.00	-	-	49	10	149	1	149.00
Marsh, RW	3	4	-	70	42	17.50	11	-	-	-	-	-	-
McCosker, RB	2	4	-	77	41	19.25	1	-	-	-	-	-	-
Pascoe, LS	2	2	2	11	10*	-	-	1	93.5	17	241	10	24.10
Thomson, JR	1	2	1	9	8	9.00	-	-	32	6	100	3	33.33
Toohey, PM	1	2	-	22	19	11.00	1	-	-	-	-	-	-
Wiener, JM	2	4	-	104	58	26.00	4	-	8	3	22	-	-

English Averages

1979-80 AUSTRALIA v ENGLAND

ENGLAND	M	Inn	NO	Runs	H.S	Avrge	Ct	St	Overs	Mds	Runs	Wkt	Avrge
Botham, IT	3	6	1	187	119*	37.40	3	-	173.1	62	371	19	19.53
Boycott, G	3	6	1	176	99*	35.20	2	-	-	-	-	-	-
Brearley, JM	3	6	1	171	64	34.20	3	-	-	-	-	-	-
Dilley, GR	2	4	2	80	38*	40.00	1	-	53.0	5	143	3	47.67
Gooch, GA	2	4	-	172	99	43.00	1	-	19.0	6	36	2	18.00
Gower, DI	3	6	1	152	98*	30.40	3	-	-	-	-	-	-
Larkins, W	1	2	-	28	25	14.00	-	-	-	-	-	-	-
Lever, JK	1	2	-	34	22	17.00	1	-	60.4	18	129	4	32.25
Miller, G	1	2	-	33	25	16.50	1	-	21.0	2	66	-	-
Randall, DW	2	4	-	26	25	6.50	1	-	-	-	-	-	-
Taylor, RW	3	6	-	102	32	17.00	10	1	-	-	-	-	-
Underwood, DL	3	6	-	71	43	11.83	4	-	160.2	48	405	13	31.15
Willey, P	3	6	-	35	12	5.83	2	-	19.0	2	56	-	-
Willis, RGD	3	6	-	21	11	3.50	-	-	98.0	26	224	3	74.67

QUICK SINGLES

Brighter prospects. The left-arm orthodox slow bowler, Ray Bright, who has carried the drinks on several overseas tours, was extraordinarily successful in Pakistan. Bright's match aggregate of 10/111 in the first Test at Karachi is his best performance.

No trouble. Prior to the Pakistan tour, Australian captain Greg Chappell feared that political and military unrest could affect the Tests. Special procedures were planned with the Australian Department of Foreign Affairs, and the Pakistan Prime Minister gave a personal guarantee there would be no trouble. The series was uninterrupted.

Border's boundaries. Against the Punjab Governor's XI at Multan in March, Allan Border hit 27 fours in his magnificent 178-run tally.

History not repeated. In 1976 at the National Stadium in Karachi, Pakistani batsman Majid Khan scored a century before lunch against New Zealand. He did not repeat that feat against Australia at the same ground in 1980, but he did manage 89 runs in Pakistan's first innings.

Fast man fizzles. The prolific Australian wicket-taker, Dennis Lillee, did not have a happy tour of Pakistan. In the three-Test series Lillee captured only three wickets for 303 runs from 102 overs.

A pair of sevens. Australian wicket-keeper Rod Marsh dismissed nine Pakistani batsmen on the 1980 tour, seven by catches and two by stumpings. Allan Border also took seven catches.

Brilliant bowling. In a drawn match between the BCCP President's XI and Australia in February, Australian spinner Ray Bright returned match figures of 11/122.

Ten ton tour. In just five first class matches played between Australia and Pakistan on the 1980 tour, ten superb centuries were scored, including a double century from Pakistan's Taslim Arif (210) in the second Test. Three centuries were made by Australia's Allan Border (178 v Punjab, and 150 not out and 153 v Pakistan at Lahore).

Australian Cricket Team, Pakistan 1980. Top: M. Mason (physiotherapist.), D. W. Hookes, G. Beard, G. N. Yallop, D. K. Lillee, M. F. Malone, G. F. Lawson, J. M. Wiener, G. Dymock, H. Torode (physician). Seated: R. J. Bright, R. W. Marsh, K. J. Hughes, F. W. Bennett (manager), G. S. Chappell (captain), A. R. Border, B. M. Laird.

First Test pitch made for spinners

Karachi, March 3. Pakistan won the first Test against Australia by seven wickets yesterday at the National Stadium.

If ever there was a spinner's pitch, it was this one. The Australian fast men, Dennis Lillee and Geoff Dymock, couldn't manage a wicket in the match. But the Pakistani spinner, Iqbal Qasim, claimed 11 scalps, and Australia's Ray Bright had 10 around his neck by the end of the game. Almost everyone in the Pakistani side had a spin in Australia's first innings, but the main attackers were Qasim (4/69) and Tauseef Ahmed (4/64).

Kim Hughes batted well for 85 of Australia's plodding 225-run total, but the team could muster only 140 runs in its second innings, where Qasim took 7/49 and Ahmed cleaned up the rest (3/62). Quasim bowled 34 maidens in the match.

Majid Khan (89) and Taslim Arif (58) both batted well for Pakistan but succumbed to turning balls from Bright, who took 7/87 and 3/24.

Allan Border's 58 not out in the second innings was the other 'bright' spot for Australia.

Second Test is a batsman's paradise

Faisalabad, March 11. To everything there is a season, a wise man once said, and in the space of a week batsmen have found their way from the hell of Karachi in the first Test to some kind of heaven.

The second Test between Pakistan and Australia was drawn, but the match has been a memorable one.

Rain prevented play on the first day, then just 12 wickets were lost over the remaining four days. Each side batted for only one innings, and 999 runs were amassed, 617 by Australia and 382 by Pakistan.

For Australia, Greg Chappell batted for over seven hours and scored 235 runs. Graham Yallop was at the wicket for eight and a half hours to make his 172, and Kim Hughes (88) and Rod Marsh (71) were amongst the runs for Australia.

The Pakistanis who piled on the runs were Taslim Arif (210 not out) and Javed Miandad (106 not out).

Every Australian team member had a bowl in the Pakistan innings.

The only other time a whole side bowled in a Test innings was in a similar match between England and Australia at the Oval in 1884.

Border scores 150 in both innings

Lahore, March 24. Australia's Allan Border yesterday completed an extraordinary double in the third Test at Gaddafi Stadium. Border scored 150 not out in Australia's first innings and 153 in the second.

Greg Chappell, who was playing in his sixtieth Test, made half centuries in both innings and scored his 5000th run in Test cricket.

Julien Wiener batted well for Australia in the first innings, when he made 93, but was caught by Mudassar Nazar at 4 in the second.

At stumps on the third day Pakistan was 5/224 and 183 runs behind.

Majid Khan's 110 runs not out kept Pakistan in the match. Majid and Imran Khan added 111 runs for the eighth wicket, which is a new Australia v Pakistan record.

When Australia replied to Pakistan's first innings 420, ten Pakistanis bowled, but the Australian batsmen dug in deep and the Test ended in a draw.

The match belongs to Allan Border. For his pair of 150's he batted for 10 hours and hit seven sixes and 32 fours.

FIRST TEST 1979–80 PAKISTAN v AUSTRALIA
National Stadium, Karachi. February 27, 28, 29, March 2, 1980.
Toss: Australia. Pakistan won by 7 wkts.

AUSTRALIA

BM Laird lbw Imran	.6	c Javed b Iqbal	.23
GN Yallop c Taslim b Tauseef	.12	c Majid b Iqbal	.16
KJ Hughes c Majid b Tauseef	.85	st Taslim b Tauseef	.8
GS Chappell (c) st Taslim b Iqbal	.20	c Taslim b Tauseef	.13
DW Hookes c Majid b Iqbal	.0	lbw Iqbal	.0
AR Border lbw Iqbal	.30	not out	.58
RW Marsh (+) c Haroon b Tauseef	.13	c Mudassar b Iqbal	.1
GR Beard b Imran	.9	b Iqbal	.4
RJ Bright c Majid b Iqbal	.15	c Majid b Iqbal	.0
DK Lillee not out	.12	lbw Iqbal	.5
G Dymock c Wasim b Tauseef	.3	b Tauseef	.0
EXTRAS (B 8, LB 9, NB 3)	.20	(B 4, LB 5, W 1, NB 2)	.12
TOTAL	.225		.140

FOW 1st Inns: 8 39 93 93 161 177 181 199 216 225
FOW 2nd Inns: 38 51 55 59 89 90 106 108 139 140

Bowling: *First Innings*: Imran 16-4-28-2, Sarfraz 13-4-20-0, Mudassar 2-0-6-0, Iqbal 30-12-69-4, Tauseef 30.2-9-64-4, Majid 2-0-13-0, Wasim 2-0-5-0. *Second Innings*: Sarfraz 7-2-7-0, Mudassar 2-0-4-0, Iqbal 42-22-49-7, Tauseef 34-11-62-3, Majid 1-1-0-0, Wasim 4-1-6-0.

PAKISTAN

Taslim Arif (+) c Marsh b Bright	.58	b Bright	.8
Haroon Rashid b Bright	.6	b Bright	.10
Zaheer Abbas c Lillee b Bright	.8	not out	.18
Javed Miandad (c) c Border b Chappell	.40	b Bright	.21
Wasim Raja c(S)GF Lawson b Chappell	.0	not out	.12
Majid Khan c Border b Bright	.89		
Mudassar Nazar c Border b Bright	.29		
Imran Khan c Border b Chappell	.9		
Sarfraz Nawaz c Chappell b Bright	.17		
Iqbal Qasim not out	.14		
Tauseef Ahmed b Bright	.0		
EXTRAS (LB 12, NB 10)	.22	(LB 3, NB 4)	.7
TOTAL	.292		.3 for 76

FOW 1st Inns: 34 44 120 121 134 210 238 266 292 292
FOW 2nd Inns: 17 26 60

Bowling: *First Innings*: Lillee 28-4-76-0, Dymock 5-2-5-0, Bright 46.5-17-87-7, Beard 17-8-39-0, Chappell 20-3-49-3, Yallop 2-0-14-0. *Second Innings*: Lillee 11-2-22-0, Dymock 2-0-9-0, Bright 11-5-24-3, Beard 1.1-0-14-0.

Umpires: Mahboob Shah & Shakoor Rana

THIRD TEST 1979–80 PAKISTAN v AUSTRALIA
Gaddafi Stadium, Lahore. March 18, 19, 21, 22, 23, 1980.
Toss: Australia. Match Drawn.

AUSTRALIA

JM Wiener b Iqbal	.93	c Mudassar b Imran	.4
BM Laird b Tauseef	.17	c Taslim b Tauseef	.63
KJ Hughes b Iqbal	.1	c Iqbal b Imran	.0
GS Chappell (c) lbw Imran	.56	b Iqbal	.57
GN Yallop lbw Iqbal	.3	c & b Wasim	.34
AR Border not out	.150	st Javed b Azhar	.153
RW Marsh (+) b Iqbal	.8	run out	.13
GR Beard lbw Imran	.39	c (S)Sultan Rana b Taslim	.49
RJ Bright not out	.26	not out	.10
DK Lillee		not out	.1
G Dymock			
EXTRAS (B 4, LB 6, NB 4)	.14	(LB 4, NB 3)	.7
TOTAL	.7 for 407		.8 for 391

FOW 1st Inns: 50 53 136 153 204 218 298
FOW 2nd Inns: 4 7 115 149 192 223 357 390

Bowling: *First Innings*: Imran 28-7-86-2, Sarfraz 28-6-67-0, Mudassar 6-1-16-0, Iqbal 39-10-90-4, Tauseef 21-3-81-1, Wasim 14-3-45-0, Azhar 2-1-1-0, Javed 2-0-5-0, Majid 2-0-2-0. *Second Innings*: Imran 12-3-30-2, Sarfraz 14-5-42-0, Iqbal 34-8-111-1, Tauseef 26-3-72-1, Majid 9-3-24-0, Javed 4-0-14-0, Wasim 9-1-42-1, Taslim 5-0-28-1, Azhar 1-0-1-1, Mudassar 2-0-20-0.

PAKISTAN

Mudassar Nazar c Yallop b Lillee	.59
Taslim Arif (+) c Marsh b Bright	.31
Iqbal Qasim c Marsh b Lillee	.5
Azmat Rana c Chappell b Beard	.49
Javed Miandad (c) c Marsh b Bright	.14
Wasim Raja c Border b Lillee	.55
Majid Khan not out	.110
Azhar Khan b Bright	.14
Imran Khan c Chappell b Bright	.56
Sarfraz Nawaz st Marsh b Bright	.5
Tauseef Ahmed	
EXTRAS (LB 4, W 1, NB 17)	.22
TOTAL	.9 for 420

FOW 1st Inns: 37 53 133 161 177 270 299 310 420

Bowling: *First Innings*: Lillee 42-9-114-3, Dymock 24-6-66-0, Bright 56-14-172-5, Beard 10-5-26-1, Chappell 8-3-20-0.

Umpires: Amanullah Khan & Khizer Hayat

SECOND TEST 1979–80 PAKISTAN v AUSTRALIA
Iqbal Stadium, Faisalabad. March 6 (no play), 7, 8, 10, 11 1980.
Toss: Australia. Match Drawn.

AUSTRALIA

JM Wiener b Ehteshamuddin	.5
BM Laird c Taslim b Sarfraz	.0
KJ Hughes c Ehteshamuddin b Tauseef	.88
GS Chappell (c) lbw Sarfraz	.235
GN Yallop b Wasim	.172
AR Border run out	.4
RW Marsh (+) lbw Tauseef	.71
GR Beard c Sarfraz b Tauseef	.13
RJ Bright b Wasim	.5
DK Lillee lbw Wasim	.0
G Dymock not out	.0
EXTRAS (B 11, LB 10, NB 3)	.24
TOTAL	.617

FOW 1st Inns: 1 21 200 417 434 561 585 592 612 617

Bowling: *First Innings*: Sarfraz 49-13-119-2, Ehteshamuddin 18-2-59-1, Iqbal 56-11-156-0, Tauseef 33-3-77-3, Wasim 30-6-100-3, Majid 22-2-66-0, Javed 3-0-16-0.

PAKISTAN

Taslim Arif (+) not out	.210
Haroon Rashid lbw Dymock	.21
Zaheer Abbas run out	.19
Javed Miandad (c) not out	.106
Wasim Raja	
Majid Khan	
Mudassar Nazar	
Sarfraz Nawaz	
Iqbal Qasim	
Ehteshamuddin	
Tauseef Ahmed	
EXTRAS (B 7, LB 4, NB 15)	.26
TOTAL	.2 for 382

FOW 1st Inns: 87 159

Bowling: *First Innings*: Lillee 21-4-91-0, Dymock 20-5-49-1, Bright 33-9-71-0, Border 3-2-3-0, Beard 15-4-30-0, Hughes 8-1-19-0, Laird 2-1-3-0, Chappell 6-3-5-0, Wiener 5-1-19-0, Marsh 10-1-51-0, Yallop 3-0-15-0.

Umpires: Javed Akhtar & Khalid Aziz

Australian Averages

1979–80 PAKISTAN v AUSTRALIA

AUSTRALIA	M	Inn	NO	Runs	H.S	Avrge	Ct	St	Overs	Mds	Runs	Wkt	Avrge
Beard, GR	3	5	-	114	49	22.80	-	-	43.1	17	109	1	109.00
Border, AR	3	5	2	395	153	131.67	5	-	3.0	2	3	-	-
Bright, RJ	3	5	2	56	26*	18.67	-	-	146.5	45	354	15	23.60
Chappell, GS	3	5	-	381	235	76.20	3	-	34.0	9	74	3	24.67
Dymock, G	3	3	1	3	3	1.50	-	-	51.0	13	129	1	129.00
Hookes, DW	1	2	-	0	0	0.00	-	-	-	-	-	-	-
Hughes, KJ	3	5	-	182	88	36.40	-	-	8.0	1	19	-	-
Laird, BM	3	5	-	109	63	21.80	-	-	2.0	1	3	-	-
Lillee, DK	3	4	2	18	12*	9.00	1	-	102.0	19	303	3	101.00
Marsh, RW	3	5	-	106	71	21.20	4	1	10.0	1	51	-	-
Wiener, JM	2	3	-	102	93	34.00	-	-	5.0	1	19	-	-
Yallop, GN	3	5	-	237	172	47.40	1	-	5.0	-	29	-	-

Pakistani Averages

1979–80 PAKISTAN v AUSTRALIA

PAKISTAN	M	Inn	NO	Runs	H.S	Avrge	Ct	St	Overs	Mds	Runs	Wkt	Avrge
Azhar Khan	1	1	-	14	14	14.00	-	-	3.0	1	2	1	2.00
Azmat Rana	1	1	-	49	49	49.00	-	-	-	-	-	-	-
Ehteshamuddin	1	-	-	-	-	-	1	-	18.0	2	59	1	59.00
Haroon Rashid	2	3	-	37	21	12.33	1	-	-	-	-	-	-
Imran Khan	2	2	-	65	56	32.50	-	-	56.0	14	144	6	24.00
Iqbal Qasim	3	2	1	19	14*	19.00	1	-	201.0	63	475	16	29.69
Javed Miandad	3	4	1	181	106*	60.33	1	1	9.0	-	35	-	-
Majid Khan	3	2	1	199	110*	199.00	5	-	36.0	6	105	-	-
Mudassar Nazar	3	2	-	88	59	44.00	2	-	12.0	1	46	-	-
Sarfraz Nawaz	3	2	-	22	17	11.00	1	-	111.0	30	255	2	127.50
Taslim Arif	3	4	1	307	210*	102.33	4	2	5.0	-	28	1	28.00
Tauseef Ahmed	3	1	-	0	0	0.00	-	-	144.2	29	356	12	29.67
Wasim Raja	3	3	1	67	55	33.50	2	-	59.0	11	198	4	49.50
Zaheer Abbas	2	3	1	45	19	22.50	-	-	-	-	-	-	-

Centenary Test a damp squib

Lord's, Sep. 2. Much water has flowed beneath cricket's bridge since the glories of Melbourne's Centenary Test in 1977. But after the reconciliation between official cricket and the commercial variety was achieved, and Australia and England were able to celebrate the centenary of Test cricket played in England with teams fully representative of each country's talent, it was hoped festivities would extend onto the playing field.

In this game the water, having flowed under the bridge, proceeded to precipitate onto the ground at Lord's, causing the loss of ten hours of play in the first three days.

It also caused apoplexy in some MCC members, who jostled umpires David Constant and Harold 'Dickie' Bird when, on the third day they made five pitch inspections and decided play could not commence because of a couple of damp spots on the old pitch area. On returning from the fifth inspection it appeared that the umpires were manhandled.

Play did not commence on this day until 3.45 p.m., and the umpires emerged from the Long Room under police escort. Apologies were profuse from the MCC to umpires and captains, though nothing was directed at the full house of spectators who sat in the sunshine all day waiting.

As to the game, it was marked by two glorious innings from Man of the Match Kim Hughes, two declarations from Greg Chappell, the second leaving England to get 370 to win in just over 360 minutes.

Unlike the England of the Melbourne Centenary Test, this team made no attempt, and Geoff Boycott crawled to 128 not out, passing Len Hutton and Don Bradman's Test aggregates along the way. Derek Randall he is not.

This was in contrast to the delights of Kim Hughes, who in his second-innings 84 danced down the wicket to Chris Old and smote a ball onto the MCC pavilion roof. His first-innings century contained an array of entertaining strokes that made the waiting of the spectators worthwhile. Dennis Lillee and Len Pascoe displayed fast bowling fireworks in front of 200 ex-Test players.

ONLY TEST 1980 ENGLAND v AUSTRALIA
Lord's Cricket Ground, London. August 28, 29, 30, September 1, 2, 1980.
Toss: Australia. Match Drawn.

AUSTRALIA

GM Wood st Bairstow b Emburey	112	lbw Old	8
BM Laird c Bairstow b Old	24	c Bairstow b Old	6
GS Chappell (c) c Gatting b Old	47	b Old	59
KJ Hughes c Athey b Old	117	lbw Botham	84
GN Yallop lbw Hendrick	2		
AR Border not out	56 (5)	not out	21
RW Marsh (+) not out	16		
LS Pascoe			
AA Mallett			
DK Lillee			
RJ Bright			
EXTRAS (B 1, LB 8, NB 2)	11	(B 1, LB 8, NB 2)	11
TOTAL	5 dec 385		4 dec 189

FOW 1st Inns: 64 150 260 267 320
FOW 2nd Inns: 15 28 139 189

Bowling: *First Innings*: Old 35-9-91-3, Hendrick 30-6-67-1, Botham 22-2-89-0, Emburey 38-9-104-1, Gooch 8-3-16-0, Willey 1-0-7-0. *Second Innings*: Old 20-6-47-3, Hendrick 15-4-53-0, Emburey 9-2-35-0, Botham 9.2-1-43-1.

ENGLAND

GA Gooch c Bright b Lillee	8	lbw Lillee	16
G Boycott c Marsh b Lillee	62	not out	128
CWJ Athey b Lillee	9	c Laird b Pascoe	1
DI Gower b Lillee	45	b Mallett	35
MW Gatting lbw Pascoe	12	not out	51
IT Botham (c) c Wood b Pascoe	0		
P Willey lbw Pascoe	5		
DL Bairstow (+) lbw Pascoe	6		
JE Emburey lbw Pascoe	3		
CM Old not out	24		
M Hendrick c Border b Mallett	5		
EXTRAS (B 6, LB 8, NB 12)	26	(B 3, LB 2, NB 8)	13
TOTAL	205		3 for 244

FOW 1st Inns: 10 41 137 151 158 163 164 173 200 205
FOW 2nd Inns: 19 43 124

Bowling: *First Innings*: Lillee 15-4-43-4, Pascoe 18-5-59-5, Chappell 2-0-2-0, Bright 21-6-50-0, Mallett 7.2-3-25-1. *Second Innings*: Lillee 19-5-53-1, Pascoe 17-1-73-1, Bright 25-9-44-0, Mallett 21-2-61-1.

Umpires: HD Bird & DJ Constant

Over 200 Test players, past and present, assembled in front of the Pavilion – and the covers – before the commencement of play in the Centenary Test at Lord's.

Lillee the key to Kiwi wickets

New Zealand opener Bruce Edgar: snapped up by Australia's Kim Hughes off Dennis Lillee for 51 in Brisbane.

Melbourne, Dec. 30. Dennis Lillee is no longer Australia's fastest bowler – that honor lies with Rod Hogg – but the great Western Australian has humbled New Zealand with a menacing blend of swing, direction and lift.

Australia won the three-Test series 2–0, though NZ came close to salvaging a win in the drawn third Test on a lifeless MCG pitch, which Australian skipper Greg Chappell desribed as 'a disgrace'. But NZ express bowler Richard Hadlee managed to extract some

bounce from it, capturing 3/89 and 6/57. NZ, needing 193 to win in its second innings, ended with 6/128.

Lillee began the series in Brisbane quietly, his 2/36 playing second fiddle to Jim Higgs' 4/59 and Len Pascoe's 3/41 in the Kiwis' first innings of 225. Australia replied with 305 (opener Graeme Wood a fine 111), after which Lillee seized the baton, so to speak, and with 16 balls fired out Wright (1), McEwan (0) and Howarth (4). NZ, 3/14, never recovered, succumbing for 142. Lillee finished with 6/53.

Australia's 10-wicket win shattered the Kiwis, who folded again in Perth in the second Test, scoring 196 and 121. This time Lillee, on his fast, home turf, took 5/63 and 2/14 in Australia's eight-wicket win. Lillee's seven wickets took his Test haul to 229, one more than the legendary Ray Lindwall (228) and only 19 fewer than Richie Benaud's Australian record of 248.

Another local hero, Rod Marsh, hit a timely 91 in Australia's first innings of 265 in Perth and took six catches to be Man of the Match.

Higgs incident upsets NZ captain

Melbourne, Dec. 27. New Zealand is angry with umpire Robin Bailhache for giving Jim Higgs a 'life' in the third Test.

Bailhache ruled Higgs not out after the Australian number 11 had gloved a Lance Cairns lifter to 'keeper Warren Lees. NZ was leaving the field, unaware Bailhache had signalled a no-ball for 'intimidatory bowling'.

NZ skipper Geoff Howarth argued with Bailhache. Higgs had been batting for 28 minutes when Cairns sounded him out with a short one. Higgs (6 not out) stayed for another 68 minutes as Doug Walters raced from 77 to 107. So Australia made 321, not 279 had Higgs been out.

NZ feels it has been robbed.

Kiwi skippper Geoff Howarth: upset.

New ACB chairman

Melbourne, Sep. 30. Former South Austrlian captain and chairman of the Australian selectors, Phil Ridings, is the new chairman of the Australian Cricket Board. He takes over from Bob Parish, who held the post from 1975 to 1980.

Regarded as a tough, disciplined skipper, Ridings has a fine administrative record. He follows in the footsteps of Charles Eady and Sir Donald Bradman as successful cricketers who made the transition to board chairman.

As a national selector, Ridings voted against his own inclusion in the 1953 team to tour England. Co-selector Bill Brown wanted him to tour. Ridings scored 5653 runs for SA at 36.23 with nine centuries.

FIRST TEST 1980–81 AUSTRALIA v NEW ZEALAND
Brisbane Cricket Ground, Brisbane. November 28, 29, 30, 1980.
Toss: Australia. Australia won by 10 wkts.

NEW ZEALAND

JG Wright c Marsh b Pascoe	29	c Walters b Lillee	1
BA Edgar c Marsh b Lawson	20	c Hughes b Lillee	51
PE McEwan c Border b Lillee	6	c Hughes b Lillee	0
GP Howarth (c) c & b Higgs	65	c Wood b Lillee	4
JM Parker b Pascoe	52	c Dyson b Lawson	4
MG Burgess c Chappell b Pascoe	0	c Wood b Lillee	2
IDS Smith (+) c Hughes b Lillee	7	c Hughes b Pascoe	7
RJ Hadlee b Marsh b Higgs	10 (9)	not out	51
BL Cairns c Border b Higgs	0 (10)	c Border b Lillee	0
JG Bracewell not out	6 (8)	c Border b Lawson	0
BP Bracewell b Higgs	0	b Pascoe	8
EXTRAS (LB 18, W 5, NB 7)	30	(B 4, LB 4, W 1, NB 5)	14
TOTAL	225		142

FOW 1st Inns: 64 71 76 193 193 209 209 210 221 225
FOW 2nd Inns: 6 9 14 30 34 58 61 114 114 142

Bowling: *First Innings*: Lillee 18-7-36-2, Pascoe 19-4-41-3, Lawson 12-2-39-1, Chappell 4-1-18-0, Higgs 16.1-3-59-4, Walters 1-0-2-0. *Second Innings*: Lillee 15-1-53-6, Pascoe 13.1-2-30-2, Lawson 8-0-26-2, Higgs 5-1-19-0.

AUSTRALIA

GM Wood c Parker b JG Bracewell	111	not out	32
J Dyson lbw Cairns	30	not out	24
GS Chappell (c) c McEwan b Cairns	35		
KJ Hughes c Wright b Hadlee	9		
AR Border run out	36		
KD Walters b Cairns	17		
RW Marsh (+) b Hadlee	8		
DK Lillee c Parker b Cairns	24		
GF Lawson c(S)SL Boock b Hadlee	16		
LS Pascoe b Cairns	5		
JD Higgs not out	1		
EXTRAS (B 1, LB 7, NB 5)	13	(B 2, LB 2, NB 3)	7
TOTAL	305		0 for 63

FOW 1st Inns: 80 145 160 225 235 250 258 299 299 305
FOW 2nd Inns:

Bowling: *First Innings*: Hadlee 37-8-83-3, BP Bracewell 22-8-71-0, Cairns 38.5-11-87-5, JG Bracewell 18-5-51-1. *Second Innings*: Hadlee 6-0-28-0, BP Bracewell 3-3-0-0, Cairns 7.3-3-16-0, JG Bracewell 5-0-12-0.

Umpires: RC Bailhache & MW Johnson

THIRD TEST 1980–81 AUSTRALIA v NEW ZEALAND
Melbourne Cricket Ground, Melbourne. December 26, 27, 28, 29, 30, 1980.
Toss: New Zealand. Match Drawn.

AUSTRALIA

GM Wood c Lees b Hadlee	0	c Lees b Hadlee	21
J Dyson b Troup	13	lbw Cairns	16
GS Chappell (c) c Coney b Hadlee	42	b Hadlee	78
KJ Hughes c Parker b Hadlee	51	b Hadlee	30
AR Border c Cairns b Coney	45	c Lees b Hadlee	9
KD Walters b Coney	107	run out	2
RW Marsh (+) c Parker b Coney	1	lbw Cairns	0
DK Lillee b Cairns	27	c Coney b Bracewell	8
RM Hogg run out	0	b Hadlee	12
LS Pascoe b Cairns	0	not out	0
JD Higgs not out	6	b Hadlee	0
EXTRAS (B 7, LB 13, W 3, NB 6)	29	(B 6, LB 4, NB 2)	12
TOTAL	321		188

FOW 1st Inns: 0 32 75 159 190 192 261 261 261 321
FOW 2nd Inns: 25 64 111 128 131 131 149 185 188 188

Bowling: *First Innings*: Hadlee 39-8-89-3, Troup 26-5-54-1, Cairns 35-6-83-2, Bracewell 9-0-38-0, Coney 12.3-6-28-3. *Second Innings*: Hadlee 27.2-7-57-6, Troup 11-1-31-0, Cairns 33-13-65-2, Bracewell 15-5-22-1, Coney 1-0-1-0.

NEW ZEALAND

JG Wright c Chappell b Higgs	4	c Wood b Hogg	44
BA Edgar lbw Higgs	21	run out	25
GP Howarth b Hogg	65	lbw Chappell	20
JM Parker c Marsh b Pascoe	56	lbw Chappell	1
MG Burgess (c) lbw Pascoe	49 (6)	not out	10
JV Coney not out	55 (5)	lbw Hogg	3
JG Bracewell c Chappell b Pascoe	0		
WK Lees (+) lbw Hogg	4 (7)	b Lillee	7
RJ Hadlee c Border b Hogg	9 (8)	not out	5
BL Cairns lbw Higgs	18		
GB Troup c Hughes b Hogg	1		
EXTRAS (B 13, LB 12, NB 10)	35	(B 2, LB 8, W 1, NB 2)	13
TOTAL	317		6 for 128

FOW 1st Inns: 27 32 157 163 247 247 264 280 316 317
FOW 2nd Inns: 50 95 97 101 101 121

Bowling: *First Innings*: Lillee 21-4-49-0, Hogg 26.2-9-60-4, Higgs 29-6-87-3, Pascoe 26-6-75-3, Border 4-1-6-0, Chappell 2-0-5-0. *Second Innings*: Lillee 13-3-30-1, Hogg 8-1-14-2, Higgs 12-4-24-0, Pascoe 11-1-35-0, Chappell 7-4-7-2, Border 2-1-5-0, Hughes 1-1-0-0.

Umpires: RC Bailhache & AR Crafter

SECOND TEST 1980–81 AUSTRALIA v NEW ZEALAND
W.A.C.A. Ground, Perth. December 12, 13, 14, 1980.
Toss: Australia. Australia won by 8 wkts.

NEW ZEALAND

JG Wright b Pascoe	10	c Marsh b Hogg	3
BA Edgar c Border b Lillee	0	c Hughes b Pascoe	0
JM Parker c Chappell b Hogg	3 (4)	c Hughes b Hogg	18
PE McEwan c Marsh b Lillee	8 (5)	c Marsh b Lillee	16
JV Coney b Hogg	71 (6)	c Marsh b Higgs	0
MG Burgess (c) c Hughes b Lillee	43 (7)	lbw Higgs	18
WK Lees (+) c Marsh b Pascoe	5 (8)	not out	25
RJ Hadlee c Hughes b Pascoe	23 (9)	c Chappell b Higgs	0
JG Bracewell lbw Lillee	6 (3)	run out	16
BL Cairns c Pascoe b Lillee	13	c Border b Higgs	6
GB Troup not out	0	c Marsh b Lillee	0
EXTRAS (LB 3, W 2, NB 9)	14	(LB 12, W 2, NB 5)	19
TOTAL	196		121

FOW 1st Inns: 6 13 24 28 116 133 171 177 196 196
FOW 2nd Inns: 0 27 38 63 64 73 115 115 121 121

Bowling: *First Innings*: Lillee 23.5-5-63-5, Hogg 16-5-29-2, Pascoe 20-3-61-3, Chappell 7-3-5-0, Higgs 5-1-13-0, Walters 2-0-11-0. *Second Innings*: Lillee 15.1-7-14-2, Pascoe 10-1-30-1, Hogg 10-2-25-2, Chappell 3-1-7-0, Walters 2-1-1-0, Higgs 8-2-25-4.

AUSTRALIA

GM Wood c Bracewell b Hadlee	0	c Lees b Hadlee	0
J Dyson c Bracewell b Cairns	28	not out	25
GS Chappell (c) c Cairns b Troup	12	c Lees b Hadlee	13
KJ Hughes c Lees b Hadlee	3	not out	16
AR Border b Cairns	10		
KD Walters c Coney b Hadlee	55		
RW Marsh (+) c Coney b Hadlee	91		
DK Lillee c & b Hadlee	8		
RM Hogg b Cairns	3		
LS Pascoe not out	30		
JD Higgs c Coney b Cairns	7		
EXTRAS (B 3, LB 4, W 1, NB 10)	18	(LB 1)	1
TOTAL	265		2 for 55

FOW 1st Inns: 0 22 25 50 68 156 176 187 244 265
FOW 2nd Inns: 3 31

Bowling: *First Innings*: Hadlee 27-8-87-5, Troup 22-5-57-1, Cairns 28.1-7-88-4, Bracewell 4-1-15-0. *Second Innings*: Hadlee 11.1-4-20-2, Troup 1-0-1-0, Cairns 5-2-17-0, Bracewell 5-0-16-0.

Umpires: AR Crafter & DG Weser

Australian Averages

1980–81 AUSTRALIA v NEW ZEALAND

AUSTRALIA	M	Inn	NO	Runs	H.S	Avrge	Ct	St	Overs	Mds	Runs	Wkt	Avrge
Border, AR	3	4	-	100	45	25.00	7	-	6.0	2	11	-	-
Chappell, GS	3	5	-	180	78	36.00	5	-	23.0	9	42	2	21.00
Dyson, J	3	6	2	136	30	34.00	1	-	-	-	-	-	-
Higgs, JD	3	4	2	14	7	7.00	1	-	75.1	17	227	11	20.64
Hogg, RM	2	3	-	15	12	5.00	-	-	60.2	17	128	10	12.80
Hughes, KJ	3	5	-	109	51	27.25	9	-	1.0	1	0	-	-
Lawson, GF	1	1	-	16	16	16.00	-	-	20.0	2	65	3	21.67
Lillee, DK	3	4	-	67	27	16.75	-	-	106.0	27	245	16	15.31
Marsh, RW	3	4	-	100	91	25.00	10	-	-	-	-	-	-
Pascoe, LS	3	4	2	35	30*	17.50	1	-	99.1	17	272	12	22.67
Walters, KD	3	4	-	181	107	45.25	1	-	5.0	1	14	-	-
Wood, GM	3	6	1	164	111	32.80	3	-	-	-	-	-	-

New Zealand Averages

1980–81 AUSTRALIA v NEW ZEALAND

NEW ZEALAND	M	Inn	NO	Runs	H.S	Avrge	Ct	St	Overs	Mds	Runs	Wkt	Avrge
Bracewell, BP	1	2	-	8	8	4.00	-	-	25.0	11	71	-	-
Bracewell, JG	3	5	1	28	16	7.00	2	-	56.0	11	154	2	77.00
Burgess, MG	3	6	1	122	49	24.40	-	-	-	-	-	-	-
Cairns, BL	3	5	-	37	18	7.40	2	-	147.3	42	356	13	27.38
Coney, JV	2	4	1	129	71	43.00	5	-	13.3	6	29	3	9.67
Edgar, BA	3	6	-	117	51	19.50	-	-	-	-	-	-	-
Hadlee, RJ	3	6	2	98	51*	24.50	1	-	147.3	35	364	19	19.16
Howarth, GP	2	4	-	154	65	38.50	-	-	-	-	-	-	-
Lees, WK	2	4	1	41	25*	13.67	6	-	-	-	-	-	-
McEwan, PE	2	4	-	30	16	7.50	1	-	-	-	-	-	-
Parker, JM	3	6	-	134	56	22.33	4	-	-	-	-	-	-
Smith, IDS	1	2	-	14	7	7.00	-	-	-	-	-	-	-
Troup, GB	2	3	1	1	1	0.50	-	-	60.0	11	143	2	71.50
Wright, JG	3	6	-	91	44	15.17	1	-	-	-	-	-	-

Chappell's underarm ball rocks cricket

Melbourne, Feb. 1. 'Trevor Chappell takes a well-judged catch running back – he's got the ball and he's going to bowl the last over. The man coming in is the well-loved Richard Hadlee. I doubt we can ask for a better finish – New Zealand 6/221, six balls to go, 15 runs required for victory – 52,000 people and I doubt that any have left the ground.'

With these words, Channel 9 commentator, former Test captain Ian Chappell, set the scene at the MCG for one of cricket's blackest moments – the underarm ball bowled by his younger brother Trevor, a medium-pace trundler.

The hot day that began brightly for Australian captain Greg Chappell, who top-scored with 90 in Australia's 4/235, was to become an inferno of controversy in this, the third final of the best-of-five WSC Cup (India missed out).

With the final tied at 1–all, the Australian total off 50 overs seemed enough until NZ openers John Wright and Bruce Edgar put on 85. Wright's fall for 42 heralded a collapse and only the gutsy Edgar kept NZ alive. Coming to the last over, Greg Chappell, at deep mid-on, looked angry. The fielding had been poor. His mood worsened when Hadlee clouted the first ball of Trevor Chappell's last over for 4. Next ball, Hadlee was lbw – 7/225. New batsman, 'keeper Ian Smith, scored two twos then had his middle stump knocked back. NZ 8/229 with one ball to go.

Enter Brian McKechnie, a beefy rugby All-Black – just the man to hit a 6 and tie the game, a scenario not lost on Greg Chappell, who walked up to his brother and asked him: 'How are you at bowling your underarms?' 'Oh, I don't know,' said Trevor, buoyed by two quick wickets after being belted for 49 runs. 'Well, you're about to find out.' As required, Greg Chappell told umpire Don Weser of his intentions. Weser informed McKechnie, who dropped his bat in disbelief. Rod Marsh said to T. Chappell: 'No, mate don't do it.'

With that, T. Chappell bowled the ball as though at a bowling alley. McKechnie blocked it, then flung his bat in the air in disgust. Edgar, 102 not out in a losing 8/229, made a rude, two-finger gesture to T. Chappell. Most of the crowd of 52,990 booed. NZ skipper Geoff Howarth burst on to the ground in his socks to have a piece of the umpires. For Australia, up 2–1, it was a Pyrrhic victory.

Under instructions, Trevor Chappell delivers the infamous underarm ball to Kiwi batsman Brian McKechnie.

Condemnation loud and clear: 'cowardice'

Melbourne, Feb. 1. Sam Loxton, a member of Don Bradman's 1948 team, and currently a national selector, was close to tears. As Greg Chappell, the villain in the underarm saga that has rocked cricket, prepared to take a shower, Loxton put a hand on his shoulder and said: 'You might have won the game but you've lost a lot of friends.'

As Loxton left, team wit Doug Walters attempted to ease the tension: 'Just goes to show you. I never thought a cricket match was over until the last over was bowled.'

Condemnation has followed Greg Chappell's decision to instruct his brother Trevor to bowl the last ball of the third WSC final underarm.

The media on both sides of the Tasman immediately condemned Australia's lack of sportsmanship. The Prime Ministers of both countries have weighed in.

The trenchant Kiwi premier, Robert Muldoon, said: 'It is the most disgusting incident I can recall in the history of cricket, a game I thought was played by gentlemen. Look, if the bloody Australians want it, they'll get it fair between the eyes.' It was 'an act of cowardice' and it was appropriate that the Australians wore yellow.

Australia's Malcolm Fraser, a more staid leader, said the underarm was a serious mistake and 'contrary to the traditions of the game'.

Former Australian captain Richie Benaud said on television: 'It was the most gutless thing I have ever seen on a cricket field.'

Said the *Age* in Melbourne: 'Australian cricket today is in disgrace and the country's reputation as a sporting nation has been severely damaged.'

The sober London *Times* said: 'There could not be a lonelier man in the cricket world than Greg Chappell.'

At a press conference after the game, a weary Chappell defended his action, saying: 'If it is written in the rules of the game it is fair play.' But he feared the worst.

Back at the hotel, Chappell spoke by phone to his wife Judy in Brisbane. She backed him but his son Stephen, almost six, thought he had done the wrong thing. He is reported to have told his father: 'I don't think you should have done it. I feel sorry for you.'

Chappell decided to quit Melbourne that night and flew to Sydney with Lillee, Walters and Len Pascoe to prepare for the fourth final in Sydney.

In Adelaide, Sir Donald Bradman is examining the rules.

Short Tests costing advertising money

Melbourne, Feb. 11. PBL Marketing has lost six lucrative days of revenue from television advertising because of Australia's Test dominance this summer.

At peak times, this is worth $8000 for a 30-second time slot.

Of the six Tests played against New Zealand and India, Australia won three of them inside three days. Five days were allotted for each. The first two Tests against NZ were resolved in three days, Australia winning by 10 wickets in Brisbane and by eight wickets in Perth. A similar fate awaited India in the first Test in Sydney. It was walloped by an innings and four runs. Also, crowds were down, averaging 47,555 for each Test.

New scoreboard

Melbourne, March 27. Of all the cricket scoreboards in the world, the MCG has the most distinctive. Perched at the western end of the ground, it records in detail the events below for all to see all the time.

But it is about to be replaced next season by a computer-controlled Mitsubishi 'Diamond Vision' scoreboard rather like a huge colour TV that can show pictures and replays at the push of a button.

It will measure 10.85 metres by 7.235 metres, and contain 38,500 pixels – individual cathode ray tubes with a life expectancy of 10,000 hours each.

Shield starvation

Perth, March 10. Another Sheffield Shield season has ended, with success going to Western Australia and crowds depressingly small.

Only four times have aggregate attendances over four days exceeded 10,000 – three times in Perth and once in Brisbane.

The average daily attendance in 1980–81 was 1944 spectators.

A far cry from the immediate post-war years. Old timers recall that in those days up to 30,000 used to attend the MCG on Boxing Day alone for the traditional NSW v Victoria match.

This season Western Australia was able to field up to eight Test players as well as South African Ken McEwan.

One record was established, in Brisbane on January 9, when Queensland and Tasmania participated in the 1000th Shield game. Queensland won by nine wickets, Martin Kent scoring 171.

India fights on after slump for draw

Indian opening batsman Chetandra Chauhan is caught Marsh, bowled Lillee for 97 in Adelaide.

Adelaide, Jan. 27. After being put to the sword in the first Test in Sydney, first by Greg Chappell's imperious 204 then by Dennis Lillee's match-winning haul of 7/165, India has shown remarkable pluck to salvage a draw in the second Test.

After a first innings run-fest, India was facing its second straight loss when it slumped to 8/128 in its second innings on the Adelaide Oval.

The victory target of 331 was out of the question as Yav Yadav joined fellow tail-ender Karsan Ghavri with 31 minutes to go.

An Australian win seemed a formality but the gritty Indians managed to survive, though it might have been a different story had Greg Chappell called on Lillee and Pascoe. Instead, Chappell relied on his own leg-breaks and the spin of Bruce Yardley and Allan Border to try to finish off the tourists.

The spinners bowled 18 of the last 20 overs – Lillee had only two – and Yadav and Ghavri, raised on a diet of slow bowling, were still there at the end having added just seven runs. Of India's 8/135, Yadav made precisely nought not out off 28 balls and Ghavri seven not out from 36 balls.

Greg Chappell's captaincy was criticised but not by the Indians, who now go to Melbourne 1–down but with pride restored.

Early on in Adelaide, Australia looked set for a repeat of its innings win in Sydney, Kim Hughes thrilling the small crowd with a dazzling 213 in 383 minutes with 21 fours. His innings was highlighted by audacious footwork as he punished spinners Dilip Doshi and Yav Yadav with cracking drives. Australia made 528 but India replied handsomely with 419, courtesy of an exhilarating 174 by willowy Bombay batsman Sandeep Patil, who hit 22 fours and his first 50 in 70 minutes. Australia then declared at 7/221, setting India 331 to win.

Chappell contrite

Sydney, Feb. 2. Greg Chappell regrets the underarm incident at the MCG yesterday.

On the eve of the fourth WSC Cup final against NZ, a statement attributed to him was read to a press conference. Chappell was not present. He was at a friend's place with Dennis Lillee.

Chappell's statement said: 'I have always played cricket within the rules of the game. I took a decision yesterday which, whilst within the laws of cricket, in the cool light of day I recognise as not being within the spirit of the game. The decision was made whilst I was under pressure and in the heat of the moment. I regret the decision. It is something I would not do again.'

With 500 Test runs behind him, Doug Walters is still dealing the cards as he relaxes in the dressing room.

Kapil's 5/28 spearheads Indian victory

Kapil Dev, smiling hero of India's 59-run win at the MCG, is congratulated by team-mates.

Melbourne, Feb. 11. India has staged an astonishing comeback to square the three-Test series with Australia 1–all. It seemed inconceivable that Australia could lose the third Test at the MCG after scoring 419 in its first innings, Allan Border making a fine 124.

Needing only 143 in its second innings to win and take the series 2–0, Australia capitulated for 83 in 203 minutes to lose by 59 runs.

Last-day hero for India was Kapil Dev with 5/28 off 16.4 overs. He achieved his match-winning analysis in spite of a thigh injury.

Kapil, only just 22, is no stranger to the spotlight. The tall, handsome all-rounder is the youngest player to achieve the Test double of 1000 runs and 100 wickets.

Kapil did not strike until Australia had lost 4/40 to the spin of Doshi and the medium pace of left-hander Ghavri. Then, in quick succession, Kapil claimed the wickets of Border (9), Marsh (3), Yardley (7), Lillee (4) and Higgs (0).

Australian captain Greg Chappell, who made a duck in Australia's lamentable second innings, said the home side's 'degree of determination was a cause for some concern.' Doug Walters top-scored with 18 not out.

Kapil was not Man of the Match. That honor went to his team-mate Gundappa Viswanath, who cracked a lovely, free-flowing 114 in 274 minutes in India's first innings of 237. A little fellow, 'Vishy' has strong wrists and scintillating timing. But for him India would have been lucky to reach three figures.

The tourists were more consistent in their second knock, scoring 324. 'Vishy' chipped in with a nice 30.

Angry Gavaskar near to forfeit

Melbourne, Feb. 11. It's just as well the Indian manager, Wing-Commander Shahid Durrani, pulled rank on the fourth day of the third Test at the MCG. Otherwise, India might have been deprived of a meritorious 59-run win.

India, which trailed by 182 on the first innings, was going along merrily at 0/165 in its second innings when captain Sunil Gavaskar was adjudged lbw to Lillee for 70. 'Sunny' by name but not by disposition in this instance, Gavaskar argued with umpire Rex Whitehead, saying he had edged the ball into his pads. Eventually he trudged off towards the pavilion, stopping half-way and motioning fellow opener Chetan Chauhan to accompany him.

The attempted 'walk-off' was averted by Durrani, who waved Chauhan back to the wicket as new batsman Dilip Vengsarkar made his way onto the ground, passing an irate Gavaskar, who has had a lean Test series with only 118 runs in six hands. Gavaskar has scored 23 Test centuries – five against Australia, three here in 1977–78.

He said after India's win he regretted his action, adding that 'something snapped'. The incident upset Chauhan, soon out for 85.

Lillee breaks through the 250-wicket mark and sets new Australian record

Melbourne, Feb. 11. It is a measure of Dennis Lillee's greatness that the dead pitch at the MCG has in no way thwarted his charge to a place of pre-eminence in Australian Test history.

Yesterday's tearaway fast bowler is now operating within his physical limitations, relying on impeccable control. This has not reduced his strike rate, especially at the MCG, where he has taken more than six wickets in each of 11 Tests there.

The giant ground seems to bring out the giant in him. It certainly did in the third Test against India. His 4/65 in the tourists' first innings took his Test haul to 247 and, when he had skipper Sunil Gavaskar lbw in the second innings, he had equalled Richie Benaud's Australian record of 248. Twenty minutes later he left Benaud's mark astern when he had India's other opener Chetan Chauhan caught. He raised his hands in triumph to Benaud in the Channel 9 commentary box.

Two more wickets for a match haul of 8/169 took Lillee through the 250 barrier to 251. Though he is 31, there are plenty more to come.

Applause as Australia's greatest wicket-taker, Dennis Lillee, leaves the field.

FIRST TEST 1980–81 AUSTRALIA v INDIA
Sydney Cricket Ground, Sydney. January 2, 3, 4, 1981.
Toss: India. Australia won by an innings & 4 runs.

INDIA

SM Gavaskar (c) c Marsh b Lillee	0	c Marsh b Hogg	10
CPS Chauhan c Border b Pascoe	20	c Walters b Pascoe	36
DB Vengsarkar c Marsh b Lillee	22	c Marsh b Pascoe	34
GR Viswanath b Hogg	26	st Marsh b Higgs	24
Yashpal Sharma c Marsh b Pascoe	6	c Walters b Lillee	4
SM Patil retired hurt	65 (8)	c Wood b Lillee	4
Kapil Dev c Marsh b Pascoe	22 (6)	c (S)SF Graf b Higgs	19
SMH Kirmani (+) c Walters b Lillee	27 (7)	not out	43
RMH Binny c Marsh b Pascoe	3	lbw Lillee	0
KD Ghavri c Wood b Lillee	7	c Hogg b Higgs	21
DR Doshi not out	0	c Lillee b Higgs	0
EXTRAS (LB 1, NB 2)	3	(B 2, LB 3, W 1)	6
TOTAL	9 dec 201		201

FOW 1st Inns: 0 36 62 70 78 145 183 186 201
FOW 2nd Inns: 21 74 92 110 120 126 144 144 201 201

Bowling: *First Innings*: Lillee 20.2-3-86-4, Hogg 14-1-51-4, Pascoe 19-6-61-4. *Second Innings*: Lillee 18-2-79-3, Hogg 9-1-24-1, Pascoe 11-2-35-2, Higgs 18-8-45-4, Walters 6-3-12-0.

AUSTRALIA

GM Wood c Kirmani b Kapil	9
J Dyson c Gavaskar b Kapil	0
GS Chappell (c) c Kapil b Ghavri	204
KJ Hughes c Kirmani b Kapil	24
AR Border c Kirmani b Kapil	31
KD Walters c Viswanath b Ghavri	67
RW Marsh (+) c Binny b Ghavri	12
DK Lillee c Doshi b Ghavri	5
RM Hogg not out	26
LS Pascoe c Doshi b Ghavri	7
JD Higgs b Kapil	2
EXTRAS (B 4, LB 3, W 3, NB 9)	19
TOTAL	406

FOW 1st Inns: 3 14 95 169 341 355 363 366 376 406

Bowling: *First Innings*: Kapil 36.1-7-97-5, Ghavri 30-7-107-5, Binny 15-1-70-0, Doshi 27-0-103-0, Chauhan 1-0-10-0.

Umpires: MW Johnson & RV Whitehead

THIRD TEST 1980–81 AUSTRALIA v INDIA
Melbourne Cricket Ground, Melbourne. February 7, 8, 9, 10, 11, 1981.
Toss: Australia. India won by 59 runs.

INDIA

SM Gavaskar (c) c Hughes b Pascoe	10	lbw Lillee	70
CPS Chauhan c Yardley b Pascoe	0	c Yardley b Lillee	85
DB Vengsarkar c Border b Lillee	12	c Marsh b Pascoe	41
GR Viswanath c Chappell b Yardley	114	b Lillee	30
SM Patil c Hughes b Lillee	23	c Chappell b Yardley	36
Yashpal Sharma c Marsh b Lillee	4	b Pascoe	9
Kapil Dev c Hughes b Pascoe	5 (8)	b Yardley	0
SMH Kirmani (+) c Marsh b Lillee	25 (7)	not out	9
KD Ghavri run out	0	run out	11
NS Yadav not out	20		
DR Doshi c Walters b Yardley	0 (10)	b Lillee	7
EXTRAS (B 1, LB 8, W 6, NB 9)	24	(B 11, LB 8, NB 7)	26
TOTAL	237		9 dec 324

FOW 1st Inns: 0 22 43 91 99 115 164 190 230 237
FOW 2nd Inns: 165 176 243 245 260 296 296 308 324

Bowling: *First Innings*: Lillee 25-6-65-4, Pascoe 22-11-29-3, Chappell 5-2-9-0, Yardley 13-3-45-2, Higgs 19-2-65-0. *Second Innings*: Lillee 32.1-5-104-4, Pascoe 29-4-80-2, Higgs 15-3-41-0, Yardley 31-11-65-2, Border 2-0-8-0.

AUSTRALIA

J Dyson c Kirmani b Kapil	16	c Kirmani b Ghavri	3
GM Wood c Doshi b Ghavri	10	st Kirmani b Doshi	10
GS Chappell (c) c & b Ghavri	76	b Ghavri	0
KJ Hughes c Chauhan b Yadav	24	b Doshi	16
AR Border b Yadav	124 (6)	c Kirmani b Kapil	9
KD Walters st Kirmani b Doshi	78 (7)	not out	18
RW Marsh (+) c(S)Kirti Azad b Doshi	45 (8)	b Kapil	3
B Yardley lbw Doshi	0 (5)	b Kapil	7
DK Lillee c & b Patil	19	b Kapil	4
LS Pascoe lbw Patil	3	run out	6
JD Higgs not out	1	lbw Kapil	0
EXTRAS (B 12, LB 6, NB 5)	23	(LB 5, NB 2)	7
TOTAL	419		83

FOW 1st Inns: 30 32 81 189 320 356 356 413 413 419
FOW 2nd Inns: 11 11 18 40 50 55 61 69 79 83

Bowling: *First Innings*: Kapil 19-7-41-1, Doshi 52-14-109-3, Ghavri 39-4-110-2, Yadav 32-6-100-2, Chauhan 2-0-8-0, Patil 12.3-4-28-2. *Second Innings*: Ghavri 8-4-10-2, Patil 2-0-5-0, Doshi 22-9-33-2, Kapil 16.4-4-28-5.

Umpires: MW Johnson & RV Whitehead

SECOND TEST 1980–81 AUSTRALIA v INDIA
Adelaide Oval, Adelaide. January 23, 24, 25, 26, 27, 1981.
Toss: India. Match Drawn.

AUSTRALIA

J Dyson c Gavaskar b Kapil	30	lbw Ghavri	28
GM Wood c Doshi b Yadav	125	c Patil b Doshi	3
GS Chappell (c) c Chauhan b Doshi	36	st Kirmani b Doshi	52
KJ Hughes c Yashpal b Yadav	213	b Kapil	53
AR Border c Gavaskar b Kapil	57	b Doshi	7
KD Walters c Viswanath b Yadav	20	not out	33
RW Marsh (+) run out	0	c Kirmani b Yadav	23
B Yardley c Viswanath b Doshi	12	c Vengsarkar b Yadav	2
DK Lillee c Kapil b Doshi	2	not out	10
RM Hogg c & b Yadav	11		
LS Pascoe not out	1		
EXTRAS (LB 13, W 1, NB 7)	21	(B 2, LB 5, NB 3)	10
TOTAL	528		7 dec 221

FOW 1st Inns: 84 152 234 363 393 399 435 461 505 528
FOW 2nd Inns: 5 74 118 138 165 204 208

Bowling: *First Innings*: Kapil 32-5-112-2, Ghavri 27-4-106-0, Doshi 48-6-146-3, Yadav 42.4-6-143-4. *Second Innings*: Kapil 17-3-55-1, Doshi 33-11-49-3, Yadav 29-6-70-2, Ghavri 11-2-37-1.

INDIA

SM Gavaskar (c) b Pascoe	23	c Chappell b Pascoe	5
CPS Chauhan c Marsh b Lillee	97	c Marsh b Pascoe	11
NS Yadav c Chappell b Yardley	16 (10)	not out	0
GR Viswanath lbw Hogg	3	b Pascoe	16
DB Vengsarkar lbw Lillee	2 (3)	c Chappell b Border	37
SM Patil lbw Hogg	174 (5)	lbw Lillee	9
Yashpal Sharma c Marsh b Lillee	47 (6)	lbw Yardley	13
Kapil Dev c Border b Lillee	2 (7)	c Marsh b Lillee	7
SMH Kirmani (+) b Pascoe	6 (8)	c Marsh b Chappell	14
KD Ghavri c Wood b Yardley	3 (9)	not out	7
DR Doshi not out	6		
EXTRAS (B 11, LB 10, W 2, NB 17)	40	(B 7, LB 1, NB 8)	16
TOTAL	419		8 for 135

FOW 1st Inns: 77 112 115 130 238 385 393 399 409 419
FOW 2nd Inns: 13 16 44 57 90 103 126 128

Bowling: *First Innings*: Lillee 34-10-80-4, Hogg 28-6-100-2, Pascoe 17-2-62-2, Yardley 44.4-16-90-2, Chappell 6-2-14-0, Walters 3-0-21-0, Border 4-1-11-0, Hughes 1-0-1-0. *Second Innings*: Lillee 19-7-38-2, Pascoe 11-2-32-3, Border 9-5-9-1, Chappell 9-6-4-1, Yardley 24-13-25-1, Hogg 3-0-11-0.

Umpires: AR Crafter & RV Whitehead

Australian Averages

1980–81 AUSTRALIA v INDIA

AUSTRALIA	M	Inn	NO	Runs	H.S	Avrge	Ct	St	Overs	Mds	Runs	Wkt	Avrge
Border, AR	3	5	-	228	124	45.60	3	-	15.0	6	28	1	28.00
Chappell, GS	3	5	-	368	204	73.60	5	-	20.0	10	27	1	27.00
Dyson, J	3	5	-	77	30	15.40	-	-					
Higgs, JD	2	3	1	3	2	1.50	-	-	52.0	13	151	4	37.75
Hogg, RM	2	2	-	37	26*	37.00	1	-	54.0	8	186	4	46.50
Hughes, KJ	3	5	-	330	213	66.00	3	-	1.0	-	1	-	
Lillee, DK	3	5	1	40	19	10.00	1	-	148.3	33	452	21	21.52
Marsh, RW	3	5	-	83	45	16.60	15	1					
Pascoe, LS	3	4	1	17	7	5.67	-	-	109.0	27	299	16	18.69
Walters, KD	3	5	2	216	78	72.00	4	-	9.0	3	33	-	
Wood, GM	3	5	-	157	125	31.40	3	-					
Yardley, B	2	4	-	21	12	5.25	2	-	112.4	43	225	7	32.14

Indian Averages

1980–81 AUSTRALIA v INDIA

INDIA	M	Inn	NO	Runs	H.S	Avrge	Ct	St	Overs	Mds	Runs	Wkt	Avrge
Binny, RMH	1	2	-	3	3	1.50	1	-	15.0	1	70	-	
Chauhan, CPS	3	6	-	249	97	41.50	2	-	3.0	-	18	-	
Doshi, DR	3	5	2	13	7	4.33	4	-	182.0	40	440	11	40.00
Gavaskar, SM	3	6	-	118	70	19.67	3	-					
Ghavri, KD	3	6	2	49	21	12.25	1	-	115.0	21	370	10	37.00
Kapil Dev	3	6	-	55	22	9.17	2	-	120.5	26	333	14	23.79
Kirmani, SMH	3	6	1	124	43*	24.80	7	3					
Patil, SM	3	6	1	311	174	62.20	2	-	14.3	4	33	2	16.50
Vengsarkar, DB	3	6	-	148	41	24.67	1	-					
Viswanath, GR	3	6	-	213	114	35.50	3	-					
Yadav, NS	2	3	2	36	20*	36.00	1	-	103.4	18	313	8	39.13
Yashpal Sharma	3	6	-	83	47	13.83	1	-					

Ex-skipper Botham revives England

Australia looks set for Ashes glory

Nottingham, June 21. Dennis Lillee, only a month away from his 32nd birthday, is like a vintage car – purring along as powerfully as ever. Ably assisted by swing bowler Terry Alderman, 25, on his first tour of England, Lillee has given Australia a wonderful start in its bid to regain the Ashes.

Kim Hughes' tourists have won the first Test, a low-scoring affair on a sporting pitch, by four wickets.

Though Australia was headed on the first innings, 185 to 179, Lillee and Alderman soon rectified that state of affairs, dismissing openers Graham Gooch (6) and the rock-like Geoff Boycott (4) in the first 16 minutes of England's second innings. Despite a breezy 33 by skipper Ian Botham, the slide continued until Lillee (5/46) and Alderman (5/62) had routed the home side on their own for 125.

Alderman (9/130) took most wickets in the match but it was Lillee, sporting a yellow headband, whose 8/80 earned him the $700 as Man of the Match. But not before Australia, requiring 132 runs to win, achieved the target a trifle shakily for the loss of six wickets, John Dyson (38) and Trevor Chappell (20 not out) being the steadiest of the batsman. The match yielded only two half centuries – Allan Border (63) and Mike Gatting (52).

Kim Hughes: victorious.

The axe of Damocles fell, but Botham went on to bigger and better things.

Leeds, July 21. Ian Botham is a national hero again, back to his ebullient self, two weeks after being pilloried as a failed captain. And sharing favoritism with him in the hallelujah stakes is fast bowler Bob Willis.

Between them, they have restored England's pride with a gripping 18-run victory in the third Test, its first win in 13 Tests. Not since England did so in 1894–95 has a team won a Test after following on.

How Australia contrived to lose this match defies logic. Certainly, after England had followed on 227 behind and was 7/135 in its second innings, there was every justifica-

The faces say it all – English jubilation at another Botham wicket.

tion for Fleet Street headlines such as 'England sinking fast' ... 'Australia set for kill'. But it was England which was to do the slaying, courtesy of Botham, a veritable St George with the bat.

Coming to the wicket at 5/105 with England facing an innings defeat, he played one of the greatest hands in Test history – 149 not out in 219 minutes off 148 balls with 27 boundaries and a six. Having abdicated the captaincy after the drawn Lord's Test, Botham was a free spirit again, clouting the Australian bowlers to all parts of the Leeds turf and hitting a century between tea and

stumps on day four. It was as though a brutal Bradman had materialised.

When Botham had run out of partners, England had surged to 356 all out in 396 minutes, leaving Australia only 130 for victory.

England's new skipper Mike Brearley didn't have to call on his Cambridge education to know that lanky Bob Willis was his man as he tossed him the new ball.

Willis would oblige with 8/43 and, helped by bad batting, fired Australia out for 111 after it was 1/56. To rub it in, Australian skipper Kim Hughes made 0 - caught Botham, bowled Willis.

Up with Grace. Mike Brearley, recalled to the captaincy at Leeds, established an England record with his ninth win over Australia, one more than W. G. Grace. Said Brearley after the Leeds win: 'Ian Botham and Bob Willis were magnificent. One gave us a chance and the other took us to the limit.'

Rare double. With 6/95 in Australia's first innings and 149 not out at Leeds, Ian Botham became the second player, after Australia's Jack Gregory (7/69 and 100 in 1920–21), to score a century and take five wickets in an innings of an Ashes Test.

England 500/1: According to Bob Willis, Ian Botham, whose 12-match reign as Test captain had produced not one win, refused to admit England was beaten at Leeds even though the bookmakers were offering 500/1 after day three. 'At a barbecue on the Sunday, Ian pledged he

would have a go at the Aussie bowlers on Monday,' said Willis.

'Keeping records. Rod Marsh and Bob Taylor set records for wicketkeepers at Leeds. Marsh overtook Alan Knott's record of 263 Test dismissals and Taylor passed fellow Englishman John Murray's tally of 1270 first class catches.

No day of rest. The first Test at Trent Bridge is notable as the first Test match in England to include play on a Sunday, and also as the first five-day Test in England that does not contain a rest-day.

Chappell trio unique. At Trent Bridge Trevor Chappell followed in the footsteps of brothers Ian and Greg as an Australian Test cricketer. The Chappells are the first trio of brothers to represent Australia.

Low-scoring Test. No batsman scored a fifty in the fourth Test at Edgbaston, the first time this has occurred in a Test since England played the West Indies in 1935.

Dennis dries up. The second Test saw Dennis Lillee bowl 48.4 overs before claiming his first wicket. After a wicketless first innings (in which Geoff Lawson's 43.1 overs produced 7/81), Lillee took three in the second for unflattering match figures of 3/184.

Doubles on debut. Mike Whitney, making his Test debut at Old Trafford, took a pair in both innings and made a pair in his own.

Headingley haul. England's Bob Willis set a record for Headingley Tests with his 8/43 in the third Test.

Dirk did well. In making his Test debut at the Oval, Australia's Dirk Wellham scored 24 and 103. The last time an Australian scored a century on Test debut in England was when Henry Graham did so in the only Australian innings of the 1893 Lord's Test. Wellham also scored a century in his first class debut for NSW against Victoria in 1980–81.

Australia drifts to Ashes defeat: 2–1 down

Birmingham, Aug. 2. That man Ian Botham, 'Guy the Gorilla' to his team-mates, has produced another strong-arm performance, giving England a 29-run win in the fourth Test and a 2–1 lead with two to go.

Meek batting has been Australia's downfall and unless there is a remarkable turnabout in this area the Ashes will stay put.

At Leeds last month, Botham destroyed Australia with the bat, setting up an unlikely England win. Here, he did it alone, with the ball, a vivid reminder of his great all-round talent. Seldom has he bowled with such devastating effect, his 14 overs producing 5/11 and reducing Australia's second innings to tatters. Under the heading 'Somerset Superman' the *Daily Express* said Botham had pulled off the greatest cricket upset 'for nearly a fortnight'.

As was the case at Leeds, Australia led on the first innings, but only by 68. When spinner Ray Bright (5/68) helped reduce England to 219 in its second innings, Australia needed 151 to win.

At 4/105, all seemed well, Border having made 40. Botham, reluctant to bowl, was persuaded to do so and promptly took 5/1 off 28 balls as Australia nosedived to be all out for 121 – the last six wickets falling for 16 runs in 47 minutes.

Australian skipper Kim Hughes, whose first dig of 46 was the second highest in the match, said: 'We fell apart under pressure. I'll have to think how I'm going to lift the team.' Just how remains to be seen.

A bright moment for Australia, as Yallop and Lillee combine for a wicket.

Australian press are not impressed

London, Aug. 17. The British press is rejoicing in Australia's plight. Ian Botham's trilogy of match-winning Test performances – 149 not out, 5/11 and 118 – has given the headline writers here a month of unmitigated glee.

If the Australians were not 'awful and appalling', they were 'miserable and pathetic'.

After the Leeds debacle when Australia, odds-on, was pipped on the post by a 500/1 shot, the *Daily Express* said 'the humiliated tourists didn't know what to think'.

In a despatch to the Melbourne *Herald*, former Australian Test captain Richie Benaud said it was an insult to Botham to say that he only played well because he had stood down as captain.

'I certainly didn't see anything wildly exciting from the new skipper (Mike Brearley) that Botham would not have produced had he still been in charge.'

Benaud said Australia erred at Leeds by not having Alderman bowl around the wicket to Dilley earlier in England's second innings, when Australia had the match 'won'. When Alderman did, thus changing the angle, he bowled Dilley – but not before the Englishman had made 56 and, with Botham (149), put on a crucial 117 for the eighth wicket. As a result, England recovered from 7/135 to 356 all out, and had a target to bowl to – and won.

'There was a touch of panic, or at best a lack of thinking (by captain Kim Hughes) in the Australian side,' Benaud said.

Rod Marsh and Dennis Lillee: in the money at long odds

Leeds, July 20. Who can resist odds of 500/1? Not Australian Test players Rod Marsh and Dennis Lillee, it seems.

With England teetering towards an innings defeat at tea on the fourth day of the third Test, Ladbroke's flashed the odds about a home-side victory on the scoreboard – England 500/1.

'I reckon the Poms have a real chance of getting up,' Lillee said sarcastically, and gave bus driver Peter Tribe £10.

Just as Tribe was heading for the Ladbroke's tent, Marsh, finding the odds irresistible, indicated he'd have a £5 bet on the Poms.

The rest, as they say, is history. Lillee and Marsh won £7500 and broke the bank.

They were accused of 'playing dead'. Said Allan Border: 'That's scurrilous. In a word, bullshit.'

Just a couple of punters: Rod Marsh and Dennis Lillee.

Fifth Test a record breaker

Manchester, Aug. 18. In a record-breaking finale, England retained the Ashes with a 103-run victory over Australia in the fifth Test.

Allan Border (123), batting with a broken finger, took 377 minutes to record the slowest Test century by an Australian.

Among other milestones, Chris Tavare (78) made the slowest fifty in English first class cricket, Geoff Boycott passed Colin Cowdrey's aggregate of 7624 runs, Alan Knott became the first to make 100 Test dismissals against Australia, Ian Botham smashed six sixes in his 118 off 86 balls, Dennis Lillee dismissed Bob Willis to take his 150th Ashes series wicket and Terry Alderman broke Lillee's record of 31 wickets in an Ashes series in England.

Alderman, Border best on tour

The 1981 Australian touring team, led by Kim Hughes.

London, Aug. 20. Australia's 3–1 defeat by England had its brighter moments, notably the batting of Allan Border, who provided much-needed solidarity, and the bowling of Test rookie Terry Alderman, dubbed 'the king of swing'.

The left-handed Border, 26, came to England with six Test centuries to his credit and added two more – 123 not out and 106 not out in the last two of the six-Test series.

He was the only Test regular to average more than 50, and did so handsomely with 533 runs at 59.22,

while all around him failed. No other regular bettered 29.00.

Alderman, 25, the likeable Perth purveyor of medium-pace, took 42 wickets at 21.16 – the biggest haul by an Australian in a Test series against England. Dennis Lillee, the old war-horse, supported him superbly with 39 wickets.

In the land of the seamer Alderman had immediate impact, taking 4/68 and 5/62 in Australia's first-Test win. Lillee remarked: 'I was surprised at his stamina. I wish I was as young and bowling as well.'

FIRST TEST 1981 ENGLAND v AUSTRALIA
Trent Bridge, Nottingha<None>m. June 18, 19, 20, 21, 1981.
Toss: Australia. Australia won by 4 wkts.

ENGLAND

GA Gooch c Wood b Lillee 10	c Yallop b Lillee 6
G Boycott c Border b Alderman 27	c Marsh b Alderman 4
RA Woolmer c Wood b Lillee 0	c Marsh b Alderman 0
DI Gower c Yallop b Lillee 26	c (S)MF Kent b Lillee 28
MW Gatting lbw Hogg 52	lbw Alderman 15
P Willey c Border b Alderman 10	lbw Lillee 13
IT Botham (c) b Alderman 1	c Border b Lillee 33
PR Downton (+) c Yallop b Alderman 8	lbw Alderman 3
GR Dilley b Hogg 34	c Marsh b Alderman 13
RGD Willis c Marsh b Hogg 0	c Chappell b Lillee 1
M Hendrick not out 6	not out 0
EXTRAS (LB 6, W 1, NB 4) 11	(LB 8, NB 1) 9
TOTAL 185	125

FOW 1st Inns: 13 13 57 67 92 96 116 159 159 185
FOW 2nd Inns: 12 12 13 39 61 94 109 113 125 125

Bowling: *First Innings*: Lillee 13-3-34-3, Alderman 24-7-68-4, Hogg 11.4-1-47-3, Lawson 8-3-25-0. *Second Innings*: Lillee 16.4-2-46-5, Alderman 19-3-62-5, Hogg 3-1-8-0.

AUSTRALIA

GM Wood lbw Dilley 0	c Woolmer b Willis 8
J Dyson c Woolmer b Willis 5	c Downton b Dilley 38
GN Yallop b Hendrick 13	c Gatting b Botham 6
KJ Hughes (c) lbw Willis 7	lbw Dilley 22
TM Chappell b Hendrick 17	not out 20
AR Border c & b Botham 63	b Dilley 20
RW Marsh (+) c Boycott b Willis 19	lbw Dilley 0
GF Lawson c Gower b Botham 14	not out 5
DK Lillee c Downton b Dilley 12	
RM Hogg c Boycott b Dilley 0	
TM Alderman not out 12	
EXTRAS (B 4, LB 8, W 1, NB 4) 17	(B 1, LB 6, NB 6) 13
TOTAL 179	.....6 for 132

FOW 1st Inns: 0 21 21 33 64 89 110 147 153 179
FOW 2nd Inns: 20 40 77 80 122 122

Bowling: *First Innings*: Dilley 20-7-38-3, Willis 30-14-47-3, Hendrick 20-7-43-2, Botham 16.5-6-34-2. *Second Innings*: Dilley 11.1-4-24-4, Willis 13-2-28-1, Hendrick 20-7-33-0, Botham 10-1-34-1.

Umpires: WE Alley & DJ Constant

Australian Averages

1981 ENGLAND v AUSTRALIA

AUSTRALIA	M	Inn	NO	Runs	H.S	Avrge	Ct	St	Overs	Mds	Runs	Wkt	Avrge
Alderman, TM	6	9	5	22	12*	5.50	8	-	325.0	76	893	42	21.26
Border, AR	6	12	3	533	123*	59.22	12	-	-	-	-	-	-
Bright, RJ	5	9	-	127	33	14.11	4	-	191.4	82	390	12	32.50
Chappell, TM	3	6	1	79	27	15.80	2	-	-	-	-	-	-
Dyson, J	5	10	-	206	102	20.60	2	-	-	-	-	-	-
Hogg, RM	2	3	1	0	0*	0.00	1	-	40.4	8	123	4	30.75
Hughes, KJ	6	12	-	300	89	25.00	3	-	-	-	-	-	-
Kent, MF	3	6	-	171	54	28.50	6	-	-	-	-	-	-
Lawson, GF	3	5	1	38	14	9.50	-	-	106.1	30	285	12	23.75
Lillee, DK	6	10	3	153	40*	21.86	1	-	311.4	81	870	39	22.31
Marsh, RW	6	11	-	216	52	19.64	23	-	-	-	-	-	-
Wellham, DM	1	2	-	127	103	63.50	-	-	-	-	-	-	-
Whitney, MR	2	4	-	4	4	1.00	-	-	78.0	16	246	5	49.20
Wood, GM	6	12	1	310	66	28.18	4	-	-	-	-	-	-
Yallop, GN	6	12	-	316	114	26.33	7	-	8.0	2	17	-	-

English Averages

1981 ENGLAND v AUSTRALIA

ENGLAND	M	Inn	NO	Runs	H.S	Avrge	Ct	St	Overs	Mds	Runs	Wkt	Avrge
Allott, PJW	1	2	1	66	52*	66.00	-	-	23.0	4	88	4	22.00
Botham, IT	6	12	1	399	149*	36.27	12	-	272.3	81	700	34	20.59
Boycott, G	6	12	-	392	137	32.67	2	-	3.0	2	2	-	-
Brearley, JM	4	8	-	141	51	17.63	4	-	-	-	-	-	-
Dilley, GR	3	6	2	150	56	37.50	1	-	98.0	24	275	14	19.64
Downton, PR	1	2	-	11	8	5.50	2	-	-	-	-	-	-
Emburey, JE	4	7	2	134	57	26.80	1	-	193.5	58	399	12	33.25
Gatting, MW	6	12	-	370	59	30.83	8	-	3.0	1	13	-	-
Gooch, GA	5	10	-	139	44	13.90	1	-	10.0	4	28	-	-
Gower, DI	5	10	-	250	89	25.00	3	-	-	-	-	-	-
Hendrick, M	2	3	3	6	6*	-	-	-	100.2	28	221	6	36.83
Knott, APE	2	4	1	178	70*	59.33	6	-	-	-	-	-	-
Larkins, W	1	2	-	58	34	29.00	-	-	-	-	-	-	-
Old, CM	2	4	1	63	29	21.00	-	-	84.0	27	175	5	35.00
Parker, PWG	1	2	-	13	13	6.50	-	-	-	-	-	-	-
Tavare, CJ	2	4	-	179	78	44.75	1	-	-	-	-	-	-
Taylor, RW	3	6	-	23	9	3.83	13	-	-	-	-	-	-
Willey, P	4	8	-	179	82	22.38	1	-	16.0	3	35	1	35.00
Willis, RGD	6	10	2	43	13	5.38	2	-	252.4	56	666	29	22.97
Woolmer, RA	2	4	-	30	21	7.50	-	-	-	-	-	-	-

SECOND TEST 1981 ENGLAND v AUSTRALIA
Lord's Cricket Ground, London. July 2, 3, 4, 6, 7, 1981.
Toss: Australia. Match Drawn.

ENGLAND

GA Gooch c Yallop b Lawson 44	lbw Lawson 20
G Boycott c Alderman b Lawson 17	c Marsh b Lillee 60
RA Woolmer c Marsh b Lawson 21	lbw Alderman 9
DI Gower c Marsh b Lawson 27	c Alderman b Lillee 89
MW Gatting lbw Bright 59	c Wood b Bright 16
P Willey c Border b Alderman 82 (7)	c Chappell b Bright 12
JE Emburey run out 31	
IT Botham (c) lbw Lawson 0 (6)	b Bright 0
RW Taylor (+) c Hughes b Lawson 0	b Lillee 9
GR Dilley not out 7 (8)	not out 27
RGD Willis c Wood b Lawson 5	
EXTRAS (B 2, LB 3, W 3, NB 10) 18	(B 2, LB 8, NB 13) 23
TOTAL 311	.....8 dec 265

FOW 1st Inns: 60 65 134 187 284 293 293 293 298 311
FOW 2nd Inns: 31 55 178 217 217 217 242 265

Bowling: *First Innings*: Lillee 35.4-7-102-0, Alderman 30.2-7-79-1, Lawson 43.1-14-81-7, Bright 15-7-31-1. *Second Innings*: Lillee 26.4-8-82-3, Alderman 17-2-42-1, Lawson 19-6-51-1, Bright 36-18-67-3.

AUSTRALIA

GM Wood c Taylor b Willis 44	not out 62
J Dyson c Gower b Botham 7	lbw Dilley 1
GN Yallop b Dilley 1	c Botham b Willis 3
KJ Hughes (c) c Willis b Emburey 42	lbw Dilley 4
TM Chappell c Taylor b Dilley 2	c Taylor b Botham 5
AR Border c Gatting b Botham 64	not out 12
RW Marsh (+) lbw Dilley 47	
RJ Bright lbw Emburey 33	
GF Lawson lbw Willis 5	
DK Lillee not out 40	
TM Alderman c Taylor b Willis 5	
EXTRAS (B 6, LB 11, W 6, NB 32) 55	(W 1, NB 2) 3
TOTAL 345	.....4 for 90

FOW 1st Inns: 62 62 69 81 167 244 257 268 314 345
FOW 2nd Inns: 2 11 17 62

Bowling: *First Innings*: Willis 27.4-9-50-3, Dilley 30-8-106-3, Botham 26-8-71-2, Gooch 10-4-28-0, Emburey 25-12-35-2. *Second Innings*: Willis 12-3-35-1, Dilley 7.5-1-18-2, Emburey 21-10-24-0, Botham 8-3-10-1.

Umpires: DO Oslear & KE Palmer

THIRD TEST 1981 ENGLAND v AUSTRALIA
Headingley, Leeds. July 16, 17, 18, 20, 21, 1981.
Toss: Australia. England won by 18 runs.

AUSTRALIA

J Dyson b Dilley	102	c Taylor b Willis	34
GM Wood lbw Botham	34	c Taylor b Botham	10
TM Chappell c Taylor b Willey	27	c Taylor b Willis	8
KJ Hughes (c) c & b Botham	89	c Botham b Willis	0
RJ Bright b Dilley	7 (8)	b Willis	19
GN Yallop c Taylor b Botham	58 (5)	c Gatting b Willis	0
AR Border lbw Botham	8 (6)	b Old	0
RW Marsh (+) b Botham	28 (7)	c Dilley b Willis	4
GF Lawson c Taylor b Botham	13	c Taylor b Willis	1
DK Lillee not out	3	c Gatting b Willis	17
TM Alderman not out	0	not out	0
EXTRAS (B 4, LB 13, W 3, NB 12)	32	(LB 3, W 1, NB 14)	18
TOTAL	9 dec 401		111

FOW 1st Inns: 55 149 196 220 332 354 357 396 401
FOW 2nd Inns: 13 56 58 58 65 68 74 75 110 111

Bowling: *First Innings*: Willis 30-8-72-0, Old 43-14-91-0, Dilley 27-4-78-2, Botham 39.2-11-95-6, Willey 13-2-31-1, Boycott 3-2-2-0. *Second Innings*: Botham 7-3-14-1, Dilley 2-0-11-0, Willis 15.1-3-43-8, Old 9-1-21-1, Willey 3-1-4-0.

ENGLAND

GA Gooch lbw Alderman	2	c Alderman b Lillee	0
G Boycott b Lawson	12	lbw Alderman	46
JM Brearley (c) c Marsh b Alderman	10	c Alderman b Lillee	14
DI Gower c Marsh b Lawson	24	c Border b Alderman	9
MW Gatting lbw Lillee	15	lbw Alderman	1
P Willey b Lawson	8	c Dyson b Lillee	33
IT Botham c Marsh b Lillee	50	not out	149
RW Taylor (+) c Marsh b Lillee	5	c Bright b Alderman	1
GR Dilley c & b Lillee	13	b Alderman	56
CM Old c Border b Alderman	0	b Lawson	29
RGD Willis not out	1	c Border b Alderman	2
EXTRAS (B 6, LB 11, W 6, NB 11)	34	(B 5, LB 3, W 3, NB 5)	16
TOTAL	174		356

FOW 1st Inns: 12 40 42 84 87 112 148 166 167 174
FOW 2nd Inns: 0 18 37 41 105 133 135 252 319 356

Bowling: *First Innings*: Lillee 18.5-7-49-4, Alderman 19-4-59-3, Lawson 13-3-32-3. *Second Innings*: Lillee 25-6-94-3, Alderman 35.3-6-135-6, Lawson 23-4-96-1, Bright 4-0-15-0.

Umpires: DGL Evans & BJ Meyer

FOURTH TEST 1981 ENGLAND v AUSTRALIA
Edgbaston, Birmingham. July 30, 31, August 1, 2, 1981.
Toss: England. England won by 29 runs.

ENGLAND

G Boycott c Marsh b Alderman	13	c Marsh b Bright	29
JM Brearley (c) c Border b Lillee	48	lbw Lillee	13
DI Gower c Hogg b Alderman	0	c Border b Bright	23
GA Gooch c Marsh b Bright	21	b Bright	21
MW Gatting c Alderman b Lillee	21	b Bright	39
P Willey b Bright	16	b Bright	5
IT Botham c Marsh b Alderman	26	c Marsh b Lillee	3
JE Emburey b Hogg	3 (9)	not out	37
RW Taylor (+) b Alderman	0 (10)	lbw Alderman	8
CM Old not out	11 (8)	c Marsh b Alderman	23
RGD Willis c Marsh b Alderman	13	c Marsh b Alderman	2
EXTRAS (B 1, LB 5, W 1, NB 10)	17	(LB 6, W 1, NB 9)	16
TOTAL	189		219

FOW 1st Inns: 29 29 60 101 126 145 161 161 165 189
FOW 2nd Inns: 18 52 89 98 110 115 154 167 217 219

Bowling: *First Innings*: Lillee 18-4-61-2, Alderman 23.1-8-42-5, Hogg 16-3-49-1, Bright 12-4-20-2. *Second Innings*: Lillee 26-9-51-2, Alderman 22-5-65-3, Hogg 10-3-19-0, Bright 34-17-68-5.

AUSTRALIA

GM Wood run out	38	lbw Old	2
J Dyson b Old	1	lbw Willis	13
AR Border c Taylor b Old	2	c Gatting b Emburey	40
RJ Bright lbw Alderman	27 (8)	lbw Botham	5
KJ Hughes (c) lbw Old	47 (4)	c Emburey b Willis	5
GN Yallop b Emburey	30 (5)	c Botham b Emburey	30
MF Kent c Willis b Emburey	46 (6)	b Botham	10
RW Marsh (+) b Emburey	2 (7)	b Botham	4
DK Lillee b Emburey	18	c Taylor b Botham	3
RM Hogg run out	0	not out	0
TM Alderman not out	3	b Botham	0
EXTRAS (B 4, LB 19, NB 21)	44	(B 1, LB 2, NB 11)	14
TOTAL	258		121

FOW 1st Inns: 5 14 62 115 166 203 220 253 253 258
FOW 2nd Inns: 2 19 29 87 105 114 114 120 121 121

Bowling: *First Innings*: Willis 19-3-63-0, Old 21-8-44-3, Emburey 26.5-12-43-4, Botham 20-1-64-1. *Second Innings*: Willis 20-6-37-2, Old 11-4-19-1, Emburey 22-10-40-2, Botham 14-9-11-5.

Umpires: HD Bird & DO Oslear

FIFTH TEST 1981 ENGLAND v AUSTRALIA
Old Trafford, Manchester. August 13, 14, 15, 16, 17, 1981.
Toss: England. England won by 103 runs.

ENGLAND

GA Gooch lbw Lillee	10	b Alderman	5
G Boycott c Marsh b Alderman	10	lbw Alderman	37
CJ Tavare c Alderman b Whitney	69	c Kent b Alderman	78
DI Gower c Yallop b Whitney	23	c Bright b Lillee	1
JM Brearley (c) lbw Alderman	2 (6)	c Marsh b Alderman	3
MW Gatting c Border b Lillee	32 (5)	lbw Alderman	11
IT Botham c Bright b Lillee	0	c Marsh b Whitney	118
APE Knott c Border b Alderman	13	c Dyson b Lillee	59
JE Emburey c Border b Alderman	1	c Kent b Whitney	57
PJW Allott not out	52	c Hughes b Bright	14
RGD Willis c Hughes b Lillee	11	not out	5
EXTRAS (LB 6, W 2)	8	(B 1, LB 12, NB 3)	16
TOTAL	231		404

FOW 1st Inns: 19 25 57 62 109 109 131 137 175 231
FOW 2nd Inns: 7 79 80 98 104 253 282 356 396 404

Bowling: *First Innings*: Lillee 24.1-8-55-4, Alderman 29-5-88-4, Whitney 17-3-50-2, Bright 16-6-30-0. *Second Innings*: Lillee 46-13-137-2, Alderman 52-19-109-5, Bright 26.4-12-68-1, Whitney 27-6-74-2.

AUSTRALIA

GM Wood lbw Allott	19	c Knott b Allott	6
J Dyson c Botham b Willis	0	run out	5
KJ Hughes (c) lbw Willis	4	lbw Botham	43
GN Yallop c Botham b Willis	0	b Emburey	114
MF Kent c Knott b Emburey	52 (6)	c Brearley b Emburey	2
AR Border c Gower b Botham	11 (5)	not out	123
RW Marsh (+) c Botham b Willis	1	c Knott b Willis	47
RJ Bright c Knott b Botham	22	c Knott b Willis	5
DK Lillee c Gooch b Botham	13	c Botham b Allott	28
MR Whitney b Allott	0 (11)	c Gatting b Willis	0
TM Alderman not out	2 (10)	lbw Botham	0
EXTRAS (NB 6)	6	(LB 9, W 2, NB 18)	29
TOTAL	130		402

FOW 1st Inns: 20 24 24 24 58 59 104 125 126 130
FOW 2nd Inns: 7 24 119 198 206 296 322 373 378 402

Bowling: *First Innings*: Willis 14-0-63-4, Allott 6-1-17-2, Botham 6.2-1-28-3, Emburey 4-0-16-1. *Second Innings*: Willis 30.5-2-96-3, Allott 17-3-71-2, Botham 36-16-86-2, Emburey 49-9-107-2, Gatting 3-1-13-0.

Umpires: DJ Constant & KE Palmer

SIXTH TEST 1981 ENGLAND v AUSTRALIA
Kennington Oval, London. August 27, 28, 29, 31, September 1, 1981.
Toss: England. Match Drawn.

AUSTRALIA

GM Wood c Brearley b Botham	66	c Knott b Hendrick	21
MF Kent c Gatting b Botham	54	c Brearley b Botham	7
KJ Hughes (c) hit wicket b Botham	31	lbw Hendrick	6
GN Yallop c Botham b Willis	26	b Hendrick	35
AR Border not out	106	c Tavare b Emburey	84
DM Wellham b Willis	24	lbw Botham	103
RW Marsh (+) c Botham b Willis	12	c Gatting b Botham	52
RJ Bright c Brearley b Botham	3	b Botham	11
DK Lillee b Willis	11	not out	8
TM Alderman b Botham	0		
MR Whitney b Botham	4 (10)	c Botham b Hendrick	0
EXTRAS (B 4, LB 6, W 1, NB 4)	15	(B 1, LB 8, W 1, NB 7)	17
TOTAL	352		9 dec 344

FOW 1st Inns: 120 125 169 199 260 280 303 319 320 352
FOW 2nd Inns: 26 36 41 104 205 291 332 343 344

Bowling: *First Innings*: Willis 31-6-91-4, Hendrick 31-8-63-0, Botham 47-13-125-6, Emburey 23-2-58-0. *Second Innings*: Willis 10-0-41-0, Botham 42-9-128-4, Hendrick 29.2-6-82-4, Emburey 23-3-76-1.

ENGLAND

G Boycott c Yallop b Lillee	137	lbw Lillee	0
W Larkins c Alderman b Lillee	34	c Alderman b Lillee	24
CJ Tavare c Marsh b Lillee	24	c Kent b Whitney	8
MW Gatting b Lillee	53	c Kent b Lillee	56
JM Brearley (c) c Bright b Alderman	0 (6)	c Marsh b Lillee	51
PWG Parker c Kent b Alderman	0 (5)	c Kent b Alderman	13
IT Botham c Yallop b Whitney	3	lbw Alderman	16
APE Knott (+) b Lillee	36	not out	70
JE Emburey lbw Lillee	0	not out	5
RGD Willis b Alderman	3		
M Hendrick not out	0		
EXTRAS (LB 9, W 3, NB 12)	24	(B 2, LB 5, W 2, NB 9)	18
TOTAL	314		7 for 261

FOW 1st Inns: 61 131 246 248 248 256 293 293 302 314
FOW 2nd Inns: 0 18 88 101 127 144 237

Bowling: *First Innings*: Lillee 31.4-4-89-7, Alderman 35-4-84-3, Whitney 23-3-76-0, Bright 21-6-41-0. *Second Innings*: Lillee 30-10-70-4, Alderman 19-6-60-2, Whitney 11-4-46-1, Bright 27-12-50-0, Yallop 8-2-17-0.

Umpires: HD Bird & BJ Meyer

Spirited battle with Pakistan, Wood hero

Melbourne, Dec. 15. Pakistan had a consolation victory in the third and final Test at the MCG, on a pitch which Australian captain Greg Chappell declared not to be up to Test standard – while the match was still in progress.

Not surprisingly, Australia capitulated for 125 in the second innings, with Chappell recording yet another duck.

First-innings hero Graeme Wood followed his first-innings century with just one run in the second innings.

Bruce Yardley was the definite star with the ball, taking a career-best 7/187 from a marathon 66 overs in Pakistan's big total of 8/500.

Few people witnessed these events. In one of the most poorly attended Melbourne Tests in recent memory, just 33,743 people watched a match which went into a fifth day.

Dennis Lillee, who passed 300 Test wickets in the second Test, finished the series on 305. Lance Gibbs' record is in sight – but in the third Test he failed to take a wicket. This is just the third time in his career that this has happened.

Greg Chappell put the events and the poor personal form of the first Test behind him and scored a magnificent double century at the 'Gabba, his fourth in Tests, in Australia's commanding second-Test total of 9/512.

Chappell could celebrate his 200 with a can of beer as a fan of the local hero jumped the fence and outsprinted two policemen to deliver his gift.

It did not have the desired effect, because Chappell was out for 201 shortly afterwards.

This was after an excellent opening stand of 109 from Bruce Laird (44) and Graeme Wood (72).

Australia's 221-run lead would have been even more substantial except for the brave effort of Zaheer Abbas, batting with a painful rib injury for 80, and the lion-hearted effort of Imran Khan with the ball, bowling 40 overs for 4/92.

By contrast Sarfraz Nawaz took two tail-end wickets for 121, from 35 overs.

Imran was named Man of the Series, heading the bowling for Pakistan with 16 wickets at 19.5.

Dennis Lillee, who was once again the outstanding bowler for Australia, ended with match figures of 9/132.

Feisty left-hander Graeme Wood strikes a boundary in his defiant century in the third Test at the MCG.

Tempers rise as something goes wrong with Perth match

Umpire Tony Crafter steps between Dennis Lillee and Javed Miandad to prevent escalation of the ugly first Test incident which saw Lillee suspended for two limited-overs matches – an inadequate punishment, in the view of many people.

Perth, Nov. 16. Dennis Lillee has not been suspended from any Test matches following his confrontation with Pakistani captain Javed Miandad in the first Test. Lillee told a journalist that if he was, he would retire from Test cricket, and that he was unfairly painted as the aggressor when he was really responding to a whack from Miandad.

Lillee says that Miandad had hit him, or poked him with his bat in the ribs as he was ambling a single from Lillee's bowling. Lillee was walking back to his mark.

Lillee maintains he 'tapped on the pad' with his boot 'as if to say 'what do you think you are doing? You can't get away with that!' It wasn't a vicious kick. But when Miandad responded by waving his bat, Lillee shaped up, and a picture was taken and flashed around the world.

Lillee says he was wrong to retaliate but was also annoyed that the instigator of the incident got off with an unblemished reputation. Lillee was suspended for two one day matches.

Australia won the first Test after a Lillee-inspired Pakistan collapse, where he took 5/18 in nine overs. Miandad made a defiant 79.

FIRST TEST 1981–82 AUSTRALIA v PAKISTAN
W.A.C.A. Ground, Perth. November 13, 14, 15, 16, 17, 1981.
Toss: Pakistan. Australia won by 286 runs.

AUSTRALIA
BM Laird c Wasim b Imran	.27	c Wasim b Imran 85
GM Wood lbw Sikander	.33	b Iqbal 49
GS Chappell (c) lbw Imran	.22	b Imran 6
KJ Hughes b Sarfraz	.14	c Majid b Imran 106
GN Yallop c & b Iqbal	.20	c Imran b Sikander 38
AR Border c Wasim b Sarfraz	.3	c Mudassar b Sikander 37
RW Marsh (+) c Iqbal b Sikander	.16	c Mansoor b Wasim 47
B Yardley c Wasim b Imran	.9	st Wasim b Iqbal 22
DK Lillee c Wasim b Wasim	.16	not out 4
JR Thomson b Imran	.2	not out 5
TM Alderman not out	.0	
EXTRAS (LB 5, W 1, NB 12)	.18	(B 1, LB 9, W 1, NB 14) 25
TOTAL	.180	....8 dec 424

FOW 1st Inns: 45 81 89 113 119 136 154 165 180 180
FOW 2nd Inns: 92 105 192 262 327 360 412 416

Bowling: *First Innings*: Imran 31.4-8-66-4, Sarfraz 27-10-43-2, Sikander 21-4-47-2, Iqbal 3-1-6-1, Wasim 1-1-0-1. *Second Innings*: Imran 39-12-90-3, Sikander 23-3-79-2, Sarfraz 27-5-88-0, Wasim 20-3-58-1, Iqbal 26-4-81-2, Javed 1-0-2-0, Mudassar 2-1-1-0.

PAKISTAN
Mudassar Nazar c Marsh b Lillee	.0	lbw Alderman 5
Rizwan-uz-Zaman lbw Alderman	.0	c Marsh b Alderman 8
Mansoor Akhtar c Marsh b Alderman	.6	c Hughes b Thomson 36
Javed Miandad (c) c Hughes b Alderman	.6	b Yardley 79
Majid Khan c Marsh b Lillee	.3	c Marsh b Yardley 0
Wasim Raja c Thomson b Lillee	.4	c Hughes b Yardley 48
Imran Khan c Yardley b Lillee	.4	c Alderman b Yardley 31
Sarfraz Nawaz c Marsh b Alderman	.26	c & b Yardley 9
Wasim Bari (+) c Marsh b Lillee	.1	c Border b Yardley 20
Iqbal Qasim c Alderman b Thomson	.5	c Alderman b Lillee 4
Sikander Bakht not out	.3	not out 0
EXTRAS (NB 4)	.4	(LB 1, NB 15) 16
TOTAL	.62	256

FOW 1st Inns: 1 1 14 17 21 25 25 26 57 62
FOW 2nd Inns: 8 27 96 99 174 198 229 236 254 256

Bowling: *First Innings*: Lillee 9-3-18-5, Alderman 10.2-2-36-4, Thomson 2-1-4-1. *Second Innings*: Lillee 20-3-78-1, Alderman 16-4-43-2, Thomson 12-4-35-1, Yardley 25.5-5-84-6.

Umpires: AR Crafter & MW Johnson

SECOND TEST 1981–82 AUSTRALIA v PAKISTAN
Brisbane Cricket Ground, Brisbane. November 27, 28, 29, 30, December 1, 1981.
Toss: Australia. Australia won by 10 wkts.

PAKISTAN
Mudassar Nazar c Marsh b Lillee	.36	c Laird b Lillee 33
Mohsin Khan c Border b Chappell	.11	c Marsh b Lillee 43
Majid Khan c Chappell b Lillee	.29	c Chappell b Yardley 15
Javed Miandad (c) b Lillee	.20	lbw Alderman 38
Zaheer Abbas b Lillee	.80	lbw Yardley 0
Wasim Raja c Laird b Lillee	.43	b Lillee 36
Imran Khan c Marsh b Alderman	.0	c Wellham b Yardley 3
Ijaz Faqih b Yardley	.34	c Chappell b Thomson 21
Sarfraz Nawaz c Border b Alderman	.4	c Alderman b Yardley 13
Wasim Bari (+) c Marsh b Thomson	.7	not out 4
Sikander Bakht not out	.1	b Thomson 2
EXTRAS (B 12, LB 1, W 1, NB 12)	.26	(B 2, LB 3, W 1, NB 9) 15
TOTAL	.291	223

FOW 1st Inns: 40 60 105 111 236 237 245 263 285 291
FOW 2nd Inns: 72 90 115 115 177 178 189 216 219 223

Bowling: *First Innings*: Lillee 20-3-81-5, Alderman 25-6-74-2, Thomson 15-2-52-1, Chappell 3-1-6-1, Yardley 15-1-51-1, Border 1-0-1-0. *Second Innings*: Lillee 19-4-51-4, Alderman 15-3-37-0, Thomson 15-3-43-2, Yardley 24-4-77-4.

AUSTRALIA
BM Laird c Zaheer b Ijaz	.44	not out 3
GM Wood c Mudassar b Wasim	.72	not out 0
GS Chappell (c) c Zaheer b Sikander	.201	
AR Border b Imran	.36	
KJ Hughes b Imran	.28	
DM Wellham b Imran	.36	
RW Marsh (+) c Zaheer b Imran	.27	
B Yardley b Sarfraz	.2	
DK Lillee b Sarfraz	.5	
JR Thomson not out	.22	
TM Alderman not out	.5	
EXTRAS (B 1, LB 5, W 2, NB 17)	.25	0
TOTAL	.9 dec 512	....0 for 3

FOW 1st Inns: 109 149 219 298 429 448 469 470 492
FOW 2nd Inns:

Bowling: *First Innings*: Imran 40-6-92-4, Sarfraz 35-4-121-2, Sikander 24-2-81-1, Ijaz 22-1-76-1, Wasim 17-0-68-1, Mudassar 2-0-10-0, Javed 3-0-18-0, Majid 9-1-21-0. *Second Innings*: Imran 1.2-1-2-0, Sikander 1-0-1-0.

Umpires: AR Crafter & MW Johnson

THIRD TEST 1981–82 AUSTRALIA v PAKISTAN
Melbourne Cricket Ground, Melbourne. December 11, 12, 13, 14, 15, 1981.
Toss: Pakistan. Pakistan won by an innings & 82 runs.

PAKISTAN
Mudassar Nazar c Lillee b Yardley	.95
Mohsin Khan c Thomson b Yardley	.17
Majid Khan c Wood b Yardley	.74
Javed Miandad (c) lbw Yardley	.62
Zaheer Abbas c & b Yardley	.90
Wasim Raja c Laird b Yardley	.50
Imran Khan not out	.70
Sarfraz Nawaz c Yardley b Chappell	.0
Wasim Bari (+) b Yardley	.8
Iqbal Qasim not out	.16
Sikander Bakht	
EXTRAS (B 1, LB 5, NB 12)	.18
TOTAL	.8 dec 500

FOW 1st Inns: 40 181 201 329 363 443 444 456

Bowling: *First Innings*: Lillee 36.3-9-104-0, Alderman 27-8-62-0, Thomson 25-2-85-0, Yardley 66-16-187-7, Border 4-1-16-0, Chappell 9-2-17-1, Hughes 3-1-2-0, Laird 1-0-9-0.

AUSTRALIA
BM Laird lbw Iqbal	.35	c Sarfraz b Iqbal 52
GM Wood c Mohsin b Sarfraz	.100	c Wasim b Sarfraz 1
GS Chappell (c) c Wasim b Wasim	.22	c Javed b Sarfraz 0
AR Border run out	.7	run out 1
KJ Hughes c & b Iqbal	.34	c Majid b Iqbal 11
DM Wellham c Mudassar b Sarfraz	.26	b Sarfraz 13
RW Marsh (+) c Mudassar b Imran	.31	c Mohsin b Iqbal 21
B Yardley b Yardley	.20	b Imran 0
DK Lillee lbw Imran	.1	c Wasim b Iqbal 4
JR Thomson not out	.3	b Imran 17
TM Alderman lbw Imran	.1	not out 4
EXTRAS (B 4, LB 6, NB 3)	.13	(B 1) 1
TOTAL	.293	125

FOW 1st Inns: 75 118 127 173 232 235 286 288 289 293
FOW 2nd Inns: 1 9 13 29 77 78 78 92 121 125

Bowling: *First Innings*: Imran 24.1-7-41-3, Sarfraz 14-3-43-2, Wasim 37-7-73-1, Iqbal 55-17-104-3, Sikander 2-0-9-0, Majid 2-0-10-0. *Second Innings*: Imran 14.1-5-21-2, Sarfraz 15-10-11-3, Iqbal 24-11-44-4, Wasim 13-2-34-0, Majid 4-1-5-0, Javed 2-0-9-0.

Umpires: RC Bailhache & RA French

Australian Averages

1981–82 AUSTRALIA v PAKISTAN

AUSTRALIA	M	Inn	NO	Runs	H.S	Avrge	Ct	St	Overs	Mds	Runs	Wkt	Avrge
Alderman, TM	3	4	3	10	5*	10.00	4	-	93.2	23	252	8	31.50
Border, AR	3	5	-	84	37	16.80	3	-	5.0	1	17	-	-
Chappell, GS	3	5	-	251	201	50.20	3	-	12.0	3	23	2	11.50
Hughes, KJ	3	5	-	193	106	38.60	3	-	3.0	1	2	-	-
Laird, BM	3	6	-	246	85	49.20	1	-	1.0	-	9	-	-
Lillee, DK	3	5	1	39	16	9.75	1	-	104.3	22	332	15	22.13
Marsh, RW	3	5	-	142	47	28.40	11	-	-	-	-	-	-
Thomson, JR	3	5	3	49	22*	24.50	2	-	69.0	12	219	5	43.80
Wellham, DM	2	3	-	75	36	25.00	1	-	-	-	-	-	-
Wood, GM	3	6	1	255	100	51.00	-	-	-	-	-	-	-
Yallop, GN	1	2	-	58	38	29.00	-	-	-	-	-	-	-
Yardley, B	3	5	-	53	22	10.60	4	-	130.5	26	399	18	22.17

Pakistani Averages

1981–82 AUSTRALIA v PAKISTAN

PAKISTAN	M	Inn	NO	Runs	H.S	Avrge	Ct	St	Overs	Mds	Runs	Wkt	Avrge
Ijaz Faqih	1	2	-	55	34	27.50	-	-	22.0	1	76	1	76.00
Imran Khan	3	5	1	108	70*	27.00	1	-	150.2	39	312	16	19.50
Iqbal Qasim	2	3	1	25	16*	12.50	3	-	108.0	33	235	10	23.50
Javed Miandad	3	5	-	205	79	41.00	1	-	6.0	-	29	-	-
Majid Khan	3	5	-	121	74	24.20	2	-	15.0	2	36	-	-
Mansoor Akhtar	1	2	-	42	36	21.00	1	-	-	-	-	-	-
Mohsin Khan	2	3	-	71	43	23.67	2	-	-	-	-	-	-
Mudassar Nazar	3	5	-	169	95	33.80	4	-	4.0	1	11	-	-
Rizwan-uz-Zaman	1	2	-	8	8	4.00	-	-	-	-	-	-	-
Sarfraz Nawaz	3	5	-	52	26	10.40	1	-	118.0	32	306	9	34.00
Sikander Bakht	3	4	3	6	3*	6.00	-	-	71.0	9	217	5	43.40
Wasim Bari	3	5	-	40	20	10.00	8	1	-	-	-	-	-
Wasim Raja	3	5	-	181	50	36.20	-	-	88.0	13	233	4	58.25
Zaheer Abbas	2	3	-	170	90	56.67	3	-	-	-	-	-	-

A million-fan season soon

Melbourne, March 1. The astonishing drawing-power of the one day games, the West Indies and 'controversial' Australian personalities such as Dennis Lillee in his testimonial year saved the 1981–82 season from financial and attendance mediocrity.

Following the disappointing three-Test series against Pakistan where attendances totalled 29,879 at the WACA, 33,768 at the 'Gabba, and a dreadful 25,342 at the MCG (total 88,989), something needed to happen to save the summer. And it did – the West Indies arrived with Viv Richards, Clive Lloyd, Gordon Greenidge, Joel Garner, Michael Holding and Malcolm Marshall – and set the one day series alight, a blaze which continued into the three-Test series in which the Windies retained the Frank Worrall Trophy.

435,000 fans attended the 15 one day qualifying matches and the four finals, paying over $2 million.

And 356,000 saw the three Tests against the West Indies, in stark contrast to the attendance at the Pakistan games. 133,964 in four days at the MCG, 115,161 at the SCG and 107,768 at Adelaide.

The players from all three countries shared to an extent in this success. Top Australian players appear to have grossed around $50,000 from the season, when match

Viv Richards plays one of his typically imperious hook shots to the fence.

provident fund, sponsorship and promotional payments are totalled.

Australia gained $101,500 from their Benson & Hedges prize-money over the season. The West Indies received $90,000 and Pakistan $47,000.

The lion's share of prizemoney in World Series Cup matches went to the West Indies ($63,500). Australia earned $38,500 and Pakistan ended up with $23,000.

Records in gripping Test

Melbourne, Dec. 30. Dennis Lillee's career best performance of 7/83 saw him surge past Lance Gibbs' world record for the number of Test dismissals in the low scoring, topsy-turvy first Test.

The MCG wicket played a major part in the difficulties both sides had with the bat.

It was low and slow from the start, and got lower and slower as the game wore on, producing grubbers and shooters in the West Indies second innings. Had Australia batted last the result might well have been different.

Kim Hughes' somewhat chancy but sparkling and adventurous 100 not out in Australia's first innings came after a sensational Boxing Day collapse.

Bruce Laird, Graeme Wood, Greg Chappell and Allan Border were all out for 26. Chappell's duck was his fourth in succession and he was one of Michael Holding's five victims in the first innings.

Another six in Australia's second innings gave Holding his best figures in Australia. The innings was also memorable for David Murray, whose nine catches behind the stumps was a record for a West Indian against Australia.

If the Boxing Day crowd was stunned by Australia's collapse they were overjoyed by an even worse one by the West Indies –

A jubilant Rod Marsh and Dennis Lillee – Australia's deadly duo.

who slumped to 4/10 in the 35 minutes play before stumps, Lillee taking three including bowling Viv Richards with the final delivery of the day.

The crowd, ecstatic at the heroic performance, stayed for over half an hour chanting Lill-eee! Lill-eee! Next day, Jeff Dujon was Lillee's record-equalling 309th wicket, and Larry Gomes the record-breaking victim.

Cheers as the crowd in the MCG's Southern Stand rises to welcome a departing West Indian batsman to the dressing room during the Boxing Day Test.

Dyson marathon brings draw

Sydney, Jan. 6. Bad light and John Dyson prevented the West Indies from squaring the series in Sydney. Australia was outplayed from the beginning when Clive Lloyd won the toss and batted, and contributed 40 to his team's solid first-innings total of 384.

The star of the West Indies first innings, however, was Gordon Greenidge, who plundered 66 off 116 balls, despite hobbling with a knee injury. He couldn't move easily, so he smashed the ball instead. Larry Gomes by contrast batted steadily for nearly six hours in compiling 126.

Australia's 267 featured an excellent 63 from Graeme Wood, a welcome 53 from out-of-form Allan Border and a thumping 45 from Bruce Yardley.

It was Yardley's terrific 7/98 that restricted the West Indies' second innings to 255, giving Australia a very remote chance of victory.

John Dyson, recalled at Dirk Wellham's expense, took two of the most spectacular chances seen at the SCG – an outstretched one-hander one to get rid of Sylvester Clarke on the midwicket boundary was especially memorable.

Dyson, sent in to open in place of injured Graeme Wood, and dropped before he had scored, batted all day to save Australia and score 127 not out.

Rod Marsh congratulates Bruce 'Roo' Yardley on his seventh wicket.

With Bruce Laird, Dyson put on 104 in three hours, saw Greg Chappell score another duck and batted an hour each with Border, Kim Hughes and Wood, who came in at no. 6.

Failing light prevented the last seven overs being bowled, but by then Australia was 4/200, and had been steered into the calm waters of a draw.

Pitch problems

Melbourne, Jan. 1. Bill Lawry in the Melbourne *Sunday Observer* called the MCG pitch a 'calypso conspiracy of doctored wickets', apparently subscribing to the theory that the low and slow MCG pitch had been prepared to take the sting out of the West Indies fast bowlers.

This idea seems questionable when Australia is able to fight fire with fire using Dennis Lillee and Terry Alderman – as they did in the first Test.

The MCG pitch deserves criticism and has received it from all three Test captains to have played on it this year, but the reason is the tired soil and the increased use in the football season.

The pitch lacked grass, plays low and inhibits shot-making as well as fast bowling. Its fiercest critic, Greg Chappell, has been having a bad time of it. Chappell scored 22 and 0 against Pakistan and 0 and 6 against the West Indies. At first glance, however, those results would seem to have given the bowlers an advantage.

Finals for Shield

Adelaide, March 1. At a meeting of members of the Cricket Committee of the Australian Cricket Board and the State captains it was recommended that there be a Sheffield Shield final next season between the two teams topping the table, on the ground of the top side.

This season's Shield was won by South Australia after a nine-wicket win over Victoria, before the best crowd of the season, 15,010.

SA grabbed the $56,000 prize-money by winning four of the last five Shield games outright.

Rick Darling (726) and Jeff Crowe (657) made most of the runs for SA, supported by captain David Hookes, 'keeper Kevin Wright and opener Wayne Phillips.

NSW also did well towards the end of the season, defeating Victoria by eight wickets. They might have lost the Shield by allowing Tasmania to take first-innings points when Stuart Saunders hit 84 batting at number nine. NSW won outright, but gained 12, not the maximum 16 points – losing the Shield by two.

Windies too hot in Adelaide

Adelaide, Feb. 3. Clive Lloyd won the toss and sent Australia in on a lively Adelaide wicket that observers thought was about as fast as Perth. On this track the West Indian fast men Andy Roberts and Michael Holding worked up fearsome pace, and had Australia in desperate trouble at 4/17. Greg Chappell, after an understandably nervous start, made 61 and Allan Border 78 in an innings full of purpose and concentration. Australia struggled to 238.

When Dennis Lillee broke down with a groin strain after just 4.5 overs Australia was up against it. The West Indies made 389 as Lillee watched from the dressing room with Greg Chappell and Kim Hughes, both also injured. Despite gutsy efforts from Jeff Thomson and Bruce Yardley, the lack of bowling firepower told on the Australians, who couldn't dismiss Larry Gomes, 124 not out.

In Australia's second innings, 2/35 became 2/201 as Bruce Laird and Kim Hughes, batting with a broken foot, added 162 before Laird was out. Allan Border then made a studied 126 before a stunning collapse on the fifth morning, when Australia lost 6/34 – with Joel Garner taking 4/5 from nine overs with seven maidens.

The West Indies were left with a one-day task of scoring 236 runs

Joel 'Big Bird' Garner celebrates one his five wickets in Melbourne.

and did it with professional timing – winning at 6.16 p.m. with 17 balls remaining and five wickets in hand.

Clive Lloyd, in possibly his last Test in Australia, was the hero, and was rightly chaired shoulder-high from the ground. The win squared the series, meaning that the West Indies retain the Frank Worrell Trophy.

A flock of ducks

Adelaide Feb. 3. Greg Chappell has scored 'ducks' in five successive international matches.

In the third Test against Pakistan he made 22 and 0, then made ducks in one day games against Pakistan on December 17 in Sydney and against the West Indies in Perth on December 20. He scored 0 and 6 in the first West Indies Test at the MCG, and in the second Test in Adelaide on January 2–6 he made 12 and 0.

He did make 201 in Brisbane in November.

Sir Donald Bradman, Test average 99.94, photographed for the first time with Viv Richards – the player with the second-highest Test average, currently 62.01.

Greg Chappell's prospects in NZ.

FIRST TEST 1981–82 AUSTRALIA v WEST INDIES
Melbourne Cricket Ground, Melbourne. December 26, 27, 28, 29, 30, 1981.
Toss: Australia. Australia won by 58 runs.

AUSTRALIA

BM Laird c Murray b Holding	4	lbw Croft	64
GM Wood c Murray b Roberts	3	c Murray b Garner	46
GS Chappell (c) c Murray b Holding	0	c Murray b Garner	6
AR Border c Murray b Holding	4	b Holding	66
KJ Hughes not out	100	b Holding	8
DM Wellham c(S)AL Logie b Croft	17	lbw Holding	2
RW Marsh (+) c Richards b Garner	21	c Murray b Holding	2
B Yardley b Garner	21	b Garner	13
DK Lillee c Gomes b Holding	1	c Murray b Holding	0
GF Lawson b Holding	2	not out	0
TM Alderman c Murray b Croft	10	b Holding	1
EXTRAS (B 1, LB 6, NB 8)	15	(B 5, LB 4, W 1, NB 4)	14
TOTAL	198		222

FOW 1st Inns: 4 4 8 26 59 115 149 153 155 198
FOW 2nd Inns: 82 106 139 184 190 199 215 218 220 222

Bowling: *First Innings*: Holding 17-3-45-5, Roberts 15-6-40-1, Garner 20-6-59-2, Croft 16.1-3-39-2. *Second Innings*: Holding 21.3-5-62-6, Roberts 18-4-31-0, Croft 20-2-61-1, Garner 18-5-37-3, Richards 5-0-17-0.

WEST INDIES

DL Haynes c Border b Lillee	1	c Lillee b Yardley	28
SFAF Bacchus c Wood b Alderman	1	lbw Alderman	0
CEH Croft lbw Lillee	0 (11)	not out	0
IVA Richards c Marsh b Lillee	2 (3)	b Alderman	0
CH Lloyd (c) c Alderman b Yardley	29 (4)	c Border b Lawson	19
HA Gomes c Chappell b Lillee	55 (5)	b Yardley	24
PJL Dujon b Hughes b Lillee	41 (6)	c Marsh b Yardley	43
DA Murray (+) not out	32 (7)	c Marsh b Yardley	10
AME Roberts c Marsh b Lillee	18 (8)	lbw Lillee	10
MA Holding c & b Alderman	2 (9)	lbw Lillee	7
J Garner c Laird b Lillee	7 (10)	lbw Lillee	0
EXTRAS (B 1, LB 3, NB 9)	13	(B 1, LB 10, NB 9)	20
TOTAL	201		161

FOW 1st Inns: 3 5 6 10 62 134 147 174 183 201
FOW 2nd Inns: 4 4 38 80 88 116 150 154 154 161

Bowling: *First Innings*: Lillee 26.3-3-83-7, Alderman 18-3-54-2, Lawson 9-2-28-0, Chappell 2-2-0-0, Yardley 7-2-23-1. *Second Innings*: Lillee 27.1-8-44-3, Alderman 9-3-23-2, Lawson 17-3-36-1, Yardley 21-7-38-4.

Umpires: RC Bailhache & AR Crafter

THIRD TEST 1981–82 AUSTRALIA v WEST INDIES
Adelaide Oval, Adelaide. January 30, 31, February 1, 2, 3, 1982.
Toss: West Indies. West Indies won by 5 wkts.

AUSTRALIA

BM Laird c Dujon b Roberts	2	c Dujon b Croft	78
GM Wood c Garner b Roberts	5	c & b Holding	6
J Dyson c Dujon b Holding	1	c Lloyd b Garner	10
KJ Hughes c Greenidge b Holding	5 (5)	c Bacchus b Garner	84
GS Chappell (c) c Garner b Holding	61 (7)	lbw Holding	7
AR Border c Dujon b Roberts	78 (4)	c Dujon b Roberts	126
RW Marsh (+) c Dujon b Holding	39 (6)	c Haynes b Holding	38
B Yardley b Croft	8	b Garner	6
DK Lillee b Roberts	2	c Dujon b Garner	1
JR Thomson not out	18	c Bacchus b Garner	0
LS Pascoe b Holding	10	not out	0
EXTRAS (B 1, LB 2, W 1, NB 5)	9	(B 7, LB 10, NB 13)	30
TOTAL	238		386

FOW 1st Inns: 3 8 8 17 122 193 206 209 210 238
FOW 2nd Inns: 10 35 201 267 362 373 383 383 383 386

Bowling: *First Innings*: Holding 25-5-72-5, Roberts 19-7-43-4, Croft 23-4-60-1, Garner 17-4-44-0, Gomes 7-3-10-0. *Second Innings*: Holding 29-9-70-3, Roberts 24-7-64-1, Garner 35-15-56-5, Croft 32-4-90-1, Gomes 14-1-38-0, Richards 18-3-38-0.

WEST INDIES

CG Greenidge c Border b Thomson	8	c Marsh b Thomson	52
DL Haynes c Marsh b Thomson	26	c Marsh b Thomson	4
IVA Richards c Laird b Yardley	42	b Pascoe	50
HA Gomes not out	124	b Pascoe	21
SFAF Bacchus c Laird b Pascoe	0 (6)	c Lillee b Pascoe	27
CH Lloyd (c) c Marsh b Thomson	53 (5)	not out	77
CEH Croft b Thomson	0		
PJL Dujon (+) c Thomson b Yardley	51 (7)	not out	0
AME Roberts c(S)DW Hookes b Yardley	42		
MA Holding b Yardley	3		
J Garner c Wood b Yardley	12		
EXTRAS (B 4, LB 7, W 3, NB 14)	28	(LB 2, W 1, NB 5)	8
TOTAL	389		5 for 239

FOW 1st Inns: 12 72 85 92 194 194 283 365 369 389
FOW 2nd Inns: 7 107 114 176 235

Bowling: *First Innings*: Lillee 4.5-3-4-0, Thomson 29-1-112-4, Yardley 40.5-10-132-5, Pascoe 30-3-94-1, Border 5-0-19-0. *Second Innings*: Thomson 19.1-4-62-2, Pascoe 22-3-84-3, Yardley 16-0-68-0, Lillee 4-0-17-0.

Umpires: RC Bailhache & MW Johnson

SECOND TEST 1981–82 AUSTRALIA v WEST INDIES
Sydney Cricket Ground, Sydney. January 2, 3, 4, 5, 6, 1982.
Toss: West Indies. Match Drawn.

WEST INDIES

CG Greenidge c Laird b Lillee	66	c Yardley b Lillee	8
DL Haynes lbw Thomson	15	lbw Lillee	51
IVA Richards c Marsh b Lillee	44	c Border b Alderman	22
HA Gomes c Chappell b Yardley	126	c Border b Yardley	43
CH Lloyd (c) c Marsh b Thomson	40	c Hughes b Yardley	57
PJL Dujon c & b Thomson	44	c & b Yardley	48
DA Murray (+) b Yardley	13	c Laird b Yardley	1
MA Holding lbw Lillee	9	c Dyson b Yardley	5
ST Clarke b Yardley	14	c Dyson b Yardley	5
J Garner c Marsh b Lillee	1 (11)	b Yardley	0
CEH Croft not out	0 (10)	not out	4
EXTRAS (LB 3, NB 9)	12	(LB 1, W 5, NB 5)	11
TOTAL	384		255

FOW 1st Inns: 37 128 133 229 325 346 363 379 380 384
FOW 2nd Inns: 29 52 112 179 208 225 231 246 255 255

Bowling: *First Innings*: Lillee 39-6-119-4, Alderman 30-9-73-0, Thomson 20-1-93-3, Yardley 26.2-3-87-3, Border 1-1-0-0. *Second Innings*: Lillee 20-6-50-2, Alderman 12-2-46-1, Yardley 31.4-6-98-7, Thomson 15-3-50-0.

AUSTRALIA

BM Laird c Dujon b Garner	14	c Murray b Croft	38
GM Wood c Murray b Holding	63 (6)	not out	7
J Dyson lbw Holding	28 (2)	not out	127
GS Chappell (c) c Dujon b Holding	12 (3)	c Murray b Croft	0
TM Alderman b Clarke	0		
KJ Hughes b Garner	16 (4)	lbw Gomes	13
AR Border not out	53 (5)	b Gomes	9
RW Marsh (+) c Holding b Gomes	17		
B Yardley b Holding	45		
DK Lillee c Garner b Holding	4		
JR Thomson run out	8		
EXTRAS (B 1, LB 2, W 2, NB 2)	7	(B 2, LB 1, NB 3)	6
TOTAL	267		4 for 200

FOW 1st Inns: 38 108 111 112 128 141 172 242 246 267
FOW 2nd Inns: 104 104 149 169

Bowling: *First Innings*: Holding 29-9-64-5, Clarke 16-4-51-1, Garner 20-4-52-2, Croft 20-7-53-0, Richards 13-7-21-0, Gomes 9-1-19-1. *Second Innings*: Holding 19-6-31-0, Clarke 16-9-25-0, Croft 27-5-58-2, Garner 12-3-27-0, Richards 13-3-33-0, Gomes 15-7-20-2.

Umpires: RA French & MW Johnson

Australian Averages

1981–82 AUSTRALIA v WEST INDIES

AUSTRALIA	M	Inn	NO	Runs	H.S	Avrge	Ct	St	Overs	Mds	Runs	Wkt	Avrge
Alderman, TM	2	3	-	11	10	3.67	2	-	69.0	17	196	5	39.20
Border, AR	3	6	1	336	126	67.20	5	-	6.0	1	19	-	-
Chappell, GS	3	6	-	86	61	14.33	2	-	2.0	2	0	-	-
Dyson, J	2	4	1	166	127*	55.33	2	-	-	-	-	-	-
Hughes, KJ	3	6	1	226	100*	45.20	2	-	-	-	-	-	-
Laird, BM	3	6	-	200	78	33.33	5	-	-	-	-	-	-
Lawson, GF	1	2	1	2	2	2.00	-	-	26.0	5	64	1	64.00
Lillee, DK	3	5	-	8	4	1.60	2	-	121.3	26	317	16	19.81
Marsh, RW	3	5	-	117	39	23.40	10	-	-	-	-	-	-
Pascoe, LS	1	2	1	10	10	10.00	-	-	52.0	6	178	4	44.50
Thomson, JR	2	3	1	26	18*	13.00	2	-	83.1	9	317	9	35.22
Wellham, DM	1	2	-	19	17	9.50	-	-	-	-	-	-	-
Wood, GM	3	6	1	130	63	26.00	2	-	-	-	-	-	-
Yardley, B	3	5	-	93	45	18.60	2	-	142.5	28	446	20	22.30

West Indian Averages

1981–82 AUSTRALIA v WEST INDIES

WEST INDIES	M	Inn	NO	Runs	H.S	Avrge	Ct	St	Overs	Mds	Runs	Wkt	Avrge
Bacchus, SFAF	2	4	-	28	27	7.00	2	-	-	-	-	-	-
Clarke, ST	1	2	-	19	14	9.50	-	-	32.0	13	76	1	76.00
Croft, CEH	3	5	3	4	4*	2.00	-	-	138.1	25	361	7	51.57
Dujon, PJL	3	6	1	227	51	45.40	9	-	-	-	-	-	-
Garner, J	3	5	-	20	12	4.00	3	-	122.0	37	275	12	22.92
Gomes, HA	3	6	1	393	126	78.60	1	-	45.0	12	87	3	29.00
Greenidge, CG	2	4	-	134	66	33.50	1	-	-	-	-	-	-
Haynes, DL	3	6	-	125	51	20.83	1	-	-	-	-	-	-
Holding, MA	3	5	-	26	9	5.20	2	-	140.3	37	344	24	14.33
Lloyd, CH	3	6	1	275	77*	55.00	1	-	-	-	-	-	-
Murray, DA	2	4	1	56	32*	18.67	12	-	-	-	-	-	-
Richards, IVA	3	6	-	160	50	26.67	1	-	49.0	13	109	-	-
Roberts, AME	2	3	-	70	42	23.33	-	-	76.0	24	178	6	29.67

Greg Chappell, all style and elegance

Greg Chappell was 22 years old when he launched his majestic Test career with a century.

Chappell – tall, slender and graceful – had made 11 first class centuries, nine for South Australia and two for Somerset, when he was selected for the second Test against England in December 1970. It was played at Perth, hosting its first Test.

Australia was a perilous 5/107 in its first innings – his older brother Ian having contributed 50 – when the upright figure of Greg Chappell in his brand new baggy green cap, made his way to the crease.

When he left after making 108 in 272 minutes – a watchful knock that blossomed as he gained confidence – Australia was 6/326. He had shared a 219-run stand with Ian Redpath (171) and the crowd gave him a standing ovation. The next day the *Age* carried a picture of Chappell executing an off-drive with all the elegance reserved for the most gifted. Over the next decade, shots of such grandeur became a familiar sight. The second 50 of Chappell's innings in Perth took only 58 minutes. He clouted paceman Peter Lever for 4, 2, 2, 4, 2, 2 in one over.

Early in his career Chappell, a right-hander, was mainly an onside player. Unrelenting practice and a modification of his grip suggested by Sir Donald Bradman, resulted in more fluent off-side shots and in the 1970s he was probably the finest batsman in the world. He scored most of his runs in the arc from cover to midwicket. Unlike his older brother Ian, he rarely used the hook shot.

Greg Chappell's arrival as a force coincided with a hectic and turbulent period in cricket history. In 17 years of establishment cricket from 1965 until 1984, he played in 321 first class matches (87 of them Tests) and more than 100 limited over games. So heavy was the schedule, he did not see his son Stephen until he was three months old. As well, his health at times was less than robust because of tonsillitis.

Chappell had succeeded his brother Ian as captain of Australia when the Packer revolution erupted in 1977. The demanding post-WSC program is said to have clouded his judgment in the infamous underarm incident against New Zealand in the World Series Cup limited-over decider at the MCG in 1981.

Greg Chappell, master batsman.

Chappell's act stunned those who saw him as basically a traditionalist. He issued a statement saying he had made the decision under pressure in the heat of the moment and regretted it. 'It is something I would not do again,' he said.

That unpleasant episode marred an otherwise exemplary reign as Test captain. Forthright but fair, he led Australia 48 times for 21 wins and 13 losses.

Chappell, born on 17 August 1948 and christened Gregory Stephen, showed a respect for the traditions of cricket from the age of four when his grandfather, Vic Richardson, himself a Test captain, played backyard cricket with him.

When Greg, formally attired in pads, cap, gloves etc. was bowled by his grandfather, he would retire to the shed, change, dress again and reappear as a fresh player – the next man in. This ritual delighted Vic Richardson.

Chappell was shy (and small) when he was enrolled at Adelaide's Prince Alfred College, the training ground for champions Joe Darling, Clem Hill and brother Ian. The school coach, Chester Bennett, who had played for SA and WA, instilled into Greg the need to strive for perfection.

Chappell made his debut for South Australia in 1966–67, scoring 53 and 62 not out against Victoria. The same season he posted his first Sheffield Shield century, 104 against Queensland in Brisbane, which was to become his new home in 1973 when he accepted an offer to play for Queensland.

After his initial Test season, he flourished against the popular World XI, whose visit in 1971–72 was hastily arranged to take the place of the aborted South African tour. He made 425 runs at 106.25 and took that form with him to England in 1972 under the captaincy of Ian Chappell. Greg's patient innings of 131 in the second Test at Lord's, made after Australia had crashed to 2/7, paved the way for Australia's eight-wicket win and was described by Trevor Bailey as 'quite the most magnificent innings of the season'.

Before finishing the tour with 1260 runs at an average of 70, another grand knock was in store in the fifth Test at the Oval when Greg scored 113. He and Ian Chappell (118) put on 231 for the third wicket and, with Lillee (5/85 and 5/123) strutting his stuff, Australia squared the series at 2–all. That win heralded the revival of Australian cricket, resulting in 21 wins and only four losses in nine series up to the 1977 tour of England.

On the 1972–73 tour of the West Indies, Chappell made 1100 first class runs at 69.37, including 106 in the second Test at Bridgetown. With Lillee's breakdown after the first Test, he bowled extensively. He took only two wickets but his 97 overs were economical.

The Chappells created history in Wellington in March 1974, Greg scoring 247 not out and 133 and Ian 145 and 121 against NZ – the first time brothers had scored two centuries in the same match. In the first innings they put on 264 for the third wicket.

Australia regained the Ashes decisively in 1974–75, Lillee and Thomson crashing through the England batting and Greg Chappell contributing 606 runs at 55.2 in the 4–1 triumph. Greg scored 144 in Sydney and 102 in Melbourne.

Chappell's next milestone was his 123 and 109 not out in his first Test as captain, against the West Indies in 1975–76. That achievement came in the first Test in Brisbane and was followed by an imposing 182 not out in the fourth Test in Sydney.

The 1977 tour of England was a trying one for Chappell. Deprived of his brother's sure batting and Lillee's presence after the first Test, his team lost the Ashes 3–0. In May on that tour, news of Kerry Packer's plans to sign 50 or so of the world's best players for his cricket troupe was leaked to the press. Chappell signed for a healthy sum.

After cricket peace was restored, Chappell was reinstated as captain when England under Brearley played three tests in Australia in 1979–80. Chappell had his 'revenge', winning 3–0, but the Ashes were not at stake. Chappell was in sparkling form, scoring 317 runs at 79.25. A month later he made his highest Test score to date, 235 in 435 minutes, on the 1980 tour of Pakistan, but he pulled out of the 1981 tour of England saying he needed a rest. His decision followed the underarm incident against NZ.

In November 1981 he thrashed the Pakistan attack in Brisbane, scoring 201 after which came his 'duck period' when he scored seven noughts (five in successive matches) in 15 innings – Tests and limited-over games.

When Chappell made 176 against New Zealand in Christchurch in March 1982, the sighs of relief could be heard across the Tasman.

Chappell eventually regained the Ashes in 1982–83, defeating Bob Willis' tourists 2–1. He cracked 117 in Perth, his happy hunting ground, and 115 in Adelaide. The 1983–84 Test series against Pakistan was to be his last. His 150 not out in the second Test in Brisbane took him to within 83 runs of Bradman's Test aggregate of 6996 runs. He announced after the fourth Test his intention to retire at season's end. With one Test to go, the fifth at the SCG, Chappell was still 68 runs short of Bradman's total, having scored only 6, 4 and 5 in the third and fourth encounters.

In a storybook ending he went out the way he came in, with a century in Australia's 10-wicket win. His careful 182 in Sydney exorcised the failures of the immediate past and saw him top 7000 runs, the first Australian to do so.

On retirement Chappell was a member of the ACB for four years and involved himself in business and TV commentary.

Honours and tempers even in New Zealand

Christchurch, March 23. Greg Chappell, the New Zealand *bête noire* after the 'underarm incident', was named 'Sportsman of the Series' after some brilliant batting and equally brilliant diplomacy over six weeks, three Tests, three one day internationals, much rain, injuries and assorted other misadventures.

Chappell made 108 in the first one dayer at Auckland, but more importantly for the tour, New Zealand won the game – in front of the largest crowd assembled at a cricket match in New Zealand – over 42,000.

The first Test in Wellington was affected by rain, with less than eleven hours play in the whole match. New Zealand opener Bruce Edgar batted for 336 minutes over five days – surely the slowest 55 in Test history, in terms of days.

New Zealand won the second Test, dismissing Australia for 210 on a placid pitch, then rubbing it in with a Bruce Edgar 161 in a total of 387. Australia's first innings went from bad (4/120) to mad when Chappell and Border were run out off successive balls – all out 210. Worse followed in Australia's second innings where 4/202 became all out 280. Chappell went out from the first ball of the final day to Richard Hadlee, who took 5/63.

Australia squared the series in the third Test at Christchurch, where Chappell made a wonderful 176.

Rod Marsh makes a vehement appeal for lbw against Richard Hadlee – not out.

Stirrers have their say at the official picture ceremony in Auckland – and the Kiwis won the game, too.

FIRST TEST 1981–82 NEW ZEALAND v AUSTRALIA
Basin Reserve, Wellington. February 26 (no play), 27, 28, March 1 (no play), 2, 1982.
Toss: Australia. Match Drawn.

NEW ZEALAND
BA Edgar lbw Alderman	55
JG Wright c Chappell b Yardley	38
JFM Morrison b Thomson	15
GP Howarth (c) not out	58
JV Coney lbw Yardley	1
MD Crowe run out	9
RJ Hadlee b Thomson	21
IDS Smith (+) c Chappell b Yardley	11
BL Cairns not out	19
MC Snedden	
EJ Chatfield	
EXTRAS (B 5, LB 19, W 4, NB 11)	39
TOTAL	7 dec 266

FOW 1st Inns: 86 120 149 162 186 212 246

Bowling: *First Innings*: Thomson 26-13-35-2, Alderman 44-20-93-1, Lillee 15-5-32-0, Chappell 8-2-18-0, Yardley 23-10-49-3.

AUSTRALIA
GM Wood b Cairns	41
BM Laird not out	27
J Dyson not out	12
GS Chappell (c)	
KJ Hughes	
AR Border	
RW Marsh (+)	
B Yardley	
DK Lillee	
JR Thomson	
TM Alderman	
EXTRAS (LB 2, NB 3)	5
TOTAL	1 for 85

FOW 1st Inns: 65

Bowling: *First Innings*: Hadlee 7-2-15-0, Snedden 8-1-24-0, Cairns 11-4-20-1, Chatfield 8-5-7-0, Crowe 4-1-14-0.

Umpires: FR Goodall & SJ Woodward

THIRD TEST 1981–82 NEW ZEALAND v AUSTRALIA
Lancaster Park, Christchurch. March 19, 20, 21, 22, 1982.
Toss: New Zealand. Australia won by 8 wkts.

AUSTRALIA
BM Laird c Smith b Troup	12	c Edgar b Snedden	31
GM Wood c Hadlee b Snedden	64	c Coney b Hadlee	15
J Dyson c Crowe b Hadlee	1	not out	14
GS Chappell (c) c Smith b Coney	176	not out	3
KJ Hughes b Hadlee	12		
AR Border b Snedden	6		
RW Marsh (+) c Cairns b Hadlee	23		
B Yardley c Cairns b Hadlee	8		
JR Thomson b Hadlee	25		
DK Lillee c & b Hadlee	7		
TM Alderman not out	0		
EXTRAS (B 2, LB 8, NB 8)	18	(B 2, LB 2, NB 2)	6
TOTAL	353		2 for 69

FOW 1st Inns: 50 57 82 128 145 237 256 340 352 353
FOW 2nd Inns: 24 60

Bowling: *First Innings*: Hadlee 28.5-5-100-6, Troup 11-1-53-1, Snedden 18-2-89-2, Cairns 21-3-74-0, Coney 8-2-15-1, Morrison 3-0-4-0. *Second Innings*: Hadlee 8-2-10-1, Cairns 9-1-28-0, Coney 1-0-2-0, Snedden 4-0-15-1, Morrison 2-1-6-0, Wright 1-0-2-0, Crowe 0.3-0-0-0.

NEW ZEALAND
BA Edgar c Dyson b Alderman	22	c Marsh b Alderman	11
JG Wright c Marsh b Lillee	13	b Alderman	141
JFM Morrison lbw Thomson	8	lbw Chappell	4
GP Howarth (c) c Alderman b Thomson	9	c Wood b Border	41
JV Coney b Lillee	0	b Border	0
MD Crowe c Marsh b Lillee	0	b Yardley	9
RJ Hadlee c Marsh b Thomson	40	c Alderman b Yardley	0
IDS Smith (+) b Thomson	0	c Wood b Yardley	0
BL Cairns run out	3	lbw Yardley	16
MC Snedden b Alderman	32	b Border	20
GB Troup not out	0	not out	8
EXTRAS (B 8, LB 2, W 1, NB 11)	22	(B 4, LB 7, W 2, NB 9)	22
TOTAL	149		272

FOW 1st Inns: 33 57 57 57 67 82 82 87 149 149
FOW 2nd Inns: 21 36 129 133 162 166 166 215 249 272

Bowling: *First Innings*: Thomson 21-5-51-4, Alderman 19.2-3-62-2, Lillee 12-6-13-3. *Second Innings*: Chappell 18-5-30-1, Alderman 23-5-66-2, Thomson 19-5-54-0, Yardley 27-7-80-4, Border 10.3-4-20-3.

Umpires: FR Goodall & DA Kinsella

SECOND TEST 1981–82 NEW ZEALAND v AUSTRALIA
Eden Park, Auckland. March 12, 13, 14, 15, 16, 1982.
Toss: New Zealand. New Zealand won by 5 wkts.

AUSTRALIA
BM Laird c Smith b Troup	38	lbw Hadlee	39
GM Wood c Smith b Cairns	9	c Snedden b Cairns	100
J Dyson b Snedden	33	b Cairns	33
KJ Hughes c Smith b Troup	0	b Cairns	17
GS Chappell (c) run out	32	c Edgar b Hadlee	24
AR Border run out	0	c Howarth b Morrison	38
RW Marsh (+) b Troup	33	c Crowe b Hadlee	3
B Yardley b Hadlee	25	c Coney b Hadlee	0
JR Thomson lbw Hadlee	13	lbw Hadlee	4
DK Lillee c Crowe b Troup	9	c Smith b Morrison	5
TM Alderman not out	0	not out	0
EXTRAS (LB 2, NB 16)	18	(B 4, LB 5, NB 8)	17
TOTAL	210		280

FOW 1st Inns: 19 75 76 120 120 131 173 187 203 210
FOW 2nd Inns: 4 17 44 97 103 0 0 0 0 0

Bowling: *First Innings*: Hadlee 20-7-38-2, Troup 18.3-3-82-4, Cairns 17-7-38-1, Snedden 12-5-26-1, Howarth 1-0-8-0. *Second Innings*: Hadlee 28-9-63-5, Troup 15-4-31-0, Cairns 44-10-85-3, Snedden 8-2-22-0, Coney 4-1-6-0, Morrison 35-16-52-2, Howarth 4-2-4-0.

NEW ZEALAND
BA Edgar c & b Yardley	161	c Lillee b Yardley	29
JG Wright c Yardley b Lillee	4	c Laird b Alderman	4
JFM Morrison b Lillee	11	c Marsh b Lillee	8
GP Howarth (c) run out	56	c Chappell b Yardley	19
JV Coney b Yardley	73 (6)	not out	5
MD Crowe c Wood b Lillee	2		
RJ Hadlee c Chappell b Yardley	25	not out	6
IDS Smith (+) lbw Yardley	5		
BL Cairns c Lillee b Alderman	14 (5)	b Border	34
MC Snedden not out	18		
GB Troup c Border b Alderman	4		
EXTRAS (B 4, LB 7, W 1, NB 2)	14	(LB 4)	4
TOTAL	387		5 for 109

FOW 1st Inns: 15 35 122 276 291 326 345 352 366 387
FOW 2nd Inns: 4 17 44 97 103

Bowling: *First Innings*: Thomson 23-8-52-0, Alderman 24.3-5-59-2, Lillee 39-7-106-3, Yardley 56-22-142-4, Border 3-0-11-0, Chappell 5-2-3-0. *Second Innings*: Lillee 13-5-32-1, Alderman 7-0-31-0, Yardley 7.4-2-40-2, Border 2-1-3-1.

Umpires: BA Bricknell & SJ Woodward

Australian Averages

1981–82 NEW ZEALAND v AUSTRALIA

AUSTRALIA	M	Inn	NO	Runs	H.S	Avrge	Ct	St	Overs	Mds	Runs	Wkt	Avrge
Alderman, TM	3	3	3	1	1*	-	2	-	117.5	33	311	8	38.88
Border, AR	3	3	-	44	38	14.67	1	-	15.3	5	34	4	8.50
Chappell, GS	3	4	1	235	176	78.33	4	-	31.0	9	51	1	51.00
Dyson, J	3	5	2	93	33	31.00	1	-	-	-	-	-	-
Hughes, KJ	3	3	-	29	17	9.67	-	-	-	-	-	-	-
Laird, BM	3	5	1	147	39	36.75	1	-	-	-	-	-	-
Lillee, DK	3	3	-	21	9	7.00	2	-	79.0	23	183	7	26.14
Marsh, RW	3	3	-	59	33	19.67	5	-	-	-	-	-	-
Thomson, JR	3	3	-	42	25	14.00	-	-	89.0	31	192	6	32.00
Wood, GM	3	5	-	229	100	45.80	3	-	-	-	-	-	-
Yardley, B	3	3	-	33	25	11.00	2	-	113.4	41	311	13	23.92

New Zealand Averages

1981–82 NEW ZEALAND v AUSTRALIA

NEW ZEALAND	M	Inn	NO	Runs	H.S	Avrge	Ct	St	Overs	Mds	Runs	Wkt	Avrge
Cairns, BL	3	5	1	86	34	21.50	2	-	102.0	25	245	5	49.00
Chatfield, EJ	1	-	-	-	-	-	-	-	8.0	5	7	-	-
Coney, JV	3	5	1	79	73	19.75	2	-	13.0	3	23	1	23.00
Crowe, MD	3	4	-	20	9	5.00	3	-	4.3	1	14	-	-
Edgar, BA	3	5	-	278	161	55.60	2	-	-	-	-	-	-
Hadlee, RJ	3	5	-	92	40	23.00	2	-	91.5	25	226	14	16.14
Howarth, GP	3	5	1	183	58*	45.75	1	-	5.0	2	12	-	-
Morrison, JFM	3	5	-	46	15	9.20	-	-	40.0	17	62	2	31.00
Smith, IDS	3	4	-	16	11	4.00	6	-	-	-	-	-	-
Snedden, MC	3	3	1	70	32	35.00	1	-	50.0	10	176	4	44.00
Troup, GB	2	3	2	12	8*	12.00	-	-	44.3	8	166	5	33.20
Wright, JG	3	5	-	200	141	40.00	-	-	1.0	-	2	-	-

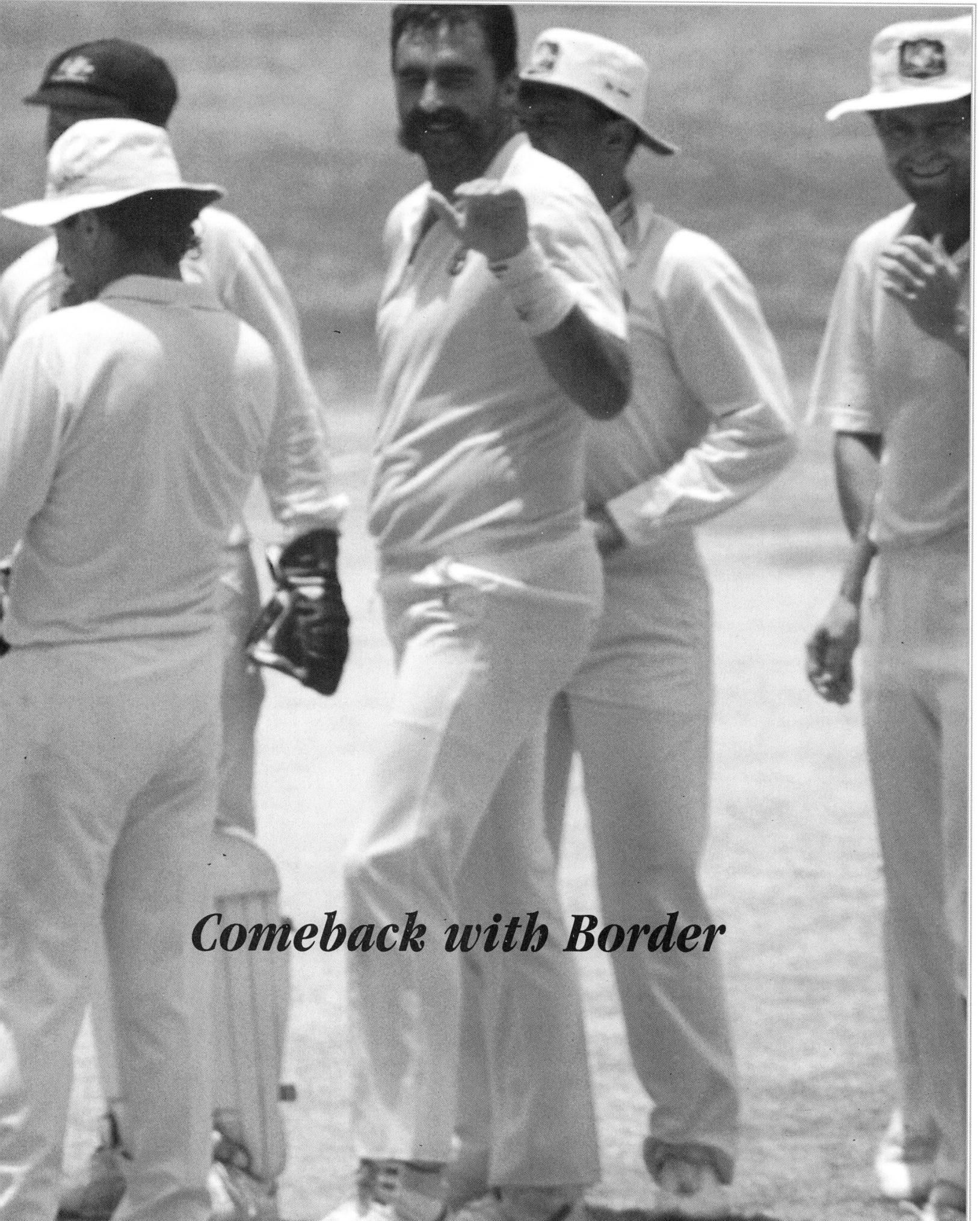

Comeback with Border

Qadir spins through timid Australia: 3–0

Hard work for part-time skipper

Lahore, Oct. 20. After Greg Chappell stepped aside for the six-week tour of Pakistan, Kim Hughes was given what seemed to be a wonderful opportunity to captain Australia. But now he knows he drew the short straw.

Key players were missing from the start. There was no Chappell, and the fast bowlers, Len Pascoe and Dennis Lillee, also withdrew.

Then there was illness. Rod Marsh was late arriving due to his son's sickness, and Bruce Yardley caught the flu early in the tour.

And there were ugly crowds. If they didn't like the play, they threw stones, potatoes, and anything else. Hughes had to lead his players off the field in three matches.

And umpire problems. In one incident in the first Test Hughes had to intervene when Australian fast bowler Geoff Lawson twice tried to grab his hat from umpire Mahboob Shah's pocket at the end of an over, but Shah refused to give it back.

And player problems. In another dispute between Jeff Thomson and umpire Rana, Thomson simply walked away from Hughes in what seemed to be a huff.

Oh yes, a captain's lot is not a happy one. Just ask Kim Hughes.

Lahore, Oct. 19. Abdul Qadir, Pakistan's spin magician, ended the Test series between Australia and Pakistan today with an aggregate 22 wickets. The series has been a disaster for Australia, which has lost all three Tests and failed to win a single match on tour.

Quadir's looping leg-spinners and googlies were devastating in the first two Tests, where he claimed match figures of 7/156 and 11/218.

After Qadir's effort at Karachi in the first Test, Australian skipper Kim Hughes said: 'He provided the best piece of attacking spin bowling I have ever seen, and he will be a danger man throughout the series.'

When Qadir took five wickets on the fourth day he ended any hopes Australia had of winning.

Timid batting from Australia's middle order characterised every Test, and Hughes lamented that it always seemed to be a case of 'four-out, all-out'.

The Australians were abysmal in the field. Six catches were dropped in the first Test, two of these by the usually reliable Allan Border.

'I am as frustrated as I am disappointed,' Hughes declared.

The heat was almost unbearable and Australia's players found it difficult to concentrate.

The crowd was also out of control. Hughes was forced to lead his players off the field twice during this Test after missiles were thrown at his players.

In the second Test at Iqbal Stadium, Faisalabad, Qadir dismissed Bruce Laird twice (for 8 and 60), and Allan Border (31), Kim

Kim Hughes - no match for Abdul Quadir in Pakistan.

Hughes twice (11 and 7), Rod Marsh (0), Ray Bright (0), John Dyson (43), Peter Sleep (29), Geoff Lawson (0) and Jeff Thomson (11).

The only Australian batsman to emerge with any credibility was Greg Ritchie, who stood his ground for 295 minutes and was 106 not out at the end of the Australian innings.

Australia's loss at Faisalabad by an innings and three runs was its worst of the series.

Qadir was less successful in the third Test here at Lahore (2/86 & 2/102), but he passed the ball to

fellow spinner Imran Khan (4/45 & 4/35).

Australia made an excellent start thanks to opener Graeme Wood (85), but once again the 'four-out, all-out' principle seemed to be operating. Three middle-order wickets went for 20 runs at one stage. Again it was a disaster in the field, where five catches were dropped.

Pakistan won the third Test by nine wickets. It is only the third time an Australian team has lost every match in a three-Test series.

The outrageous Max 'Tangles' Walker is retiring from first class cricket.

QUICK SINGLES

Hat trickery. Pakistani bowler Tahir Naqqash was twice on a hat-trick in the first Test when he claimed 4 for 2 in eight balls. Australia's Geoff Lawson was twice on a different kind of hat-trick, when at the end of his over near tea on the second day he made two attempts to reclaim his hat from the pocket of umpire Mahboob Shah. Shah refused to give him the hat, telling Lawson to apologise for an outburst earlier in the match.

Feeding frenzy. Australia's Kim Hughes said 'we won't be treated like animals in a zoo' as he walked his team off the field in the first Test. Just before lunch the Australians were pelted with potatoes, onions and stones by the crowd. Later in the day, spectators demolished part of the fence and invaded the field, causing a 25-minute interruption.

Ritchie's wrong return. When 2000 Pakistani spectators went berserk during the first Test, Australia had trouble convincing the umpires of the gravity of the situation, so Greg Ritchie picked up a rock which had been thrown on the field and tossed it in the direction of umpire Hayat. The rock accidentally hit Hayat on the leg, necessitating some fast talking from Hughes.

Pakistan on a roll. Pakistan's convincing victories in the first and second Tests were the first time that Pakistan had recorded successive Test wins over Australia. The record run was then extended in the third Test.

Unusual four. In his unbeaten 106 over 195 minutes a Faisalabad, Australia's Greg Ritchie hit three sixes and nine fours. One of his boundaries was hit off a stationary ball which had slipped from the hand of bowler Abdul Qadir.

Deaf Jeff. In the third Test Australia's Jeff Thomson was no-balled several times in succession, and kicked over the stumps. He was spoken to by umpire Rana, who also asked Australian captain Kim Hughes to intervene. Thomson ignored them both.

No wins for Australia. Of the nine first class matches played on Australia's 1982 Pakistan tour, Pakistan won six matches, including all three Tests. Two matches were drawn, and the third International at Karachi had to be abandoned due to crowd disturbances.

Poor touch. Pakistani opening batsman Mohsin Khan handled the ball during the first Test at Karachi. In a reflex action, Mohsin knocked the ball aside when it rebounded towards his stumps after a poor defensive shot. He is only the third player in Test history to lose his wicket in this unusual way.

FIRST TEST 1982–83 PAKISTAN v AUSTRALIA
National Stadium, Karachi. September 22, 23, 24, 26, 27, 1982.
Toss: Australia. Pakistan won by 9 wkts.

AUSTRALIA

GM Wood c Wasim b Imran	0	c (S)Salim Malik b Abdul	17
BM Laird run out	32	c Mansoor b Imran	3
J Dyson b Iqbal	87	b Abdul	6
KJ Hughes (c) c Wasim b Iqbal	54 (5)	c Wasim b Abdul	14
AR Border not out	55 (4)	c (S)Salim Malik b Abdul	8
GM Ritchie c Haroon b Abdul	4	b Iqbal	17
RW Marsh (+) b Tahir	19	lbw Imran	32
B Yardley c Javed b Tahir	0	lbw Abdul	0
RJ Bright c Haroon b Tahir	2	not out	32
GF Lawson c Wasim b Tahir	0	run out	11
JR Thomson st Wasim b Abdul	14	c Wasim b Iqbal	18
EXTRAS (B 4, LB 10, W 1, NB 2)	17	(B 2, LB 19)	21
TOTAL	284		179

FOW 1st Inns: 0 71 169 202 211 249 249 255 255 284
FOW 2nd Inns: 10 29 32 45 72 72 73 137 160 179

Bowling: *First Innings*: Imran 23-3-38-1, Tahir 16-3-61-4, Mudassar 13-0-33-0, Abdul 21.4-1-80-2, Iqbal 26-10-55-2. *Second Innings*: Imran 12-5-17-2, Tahir 7-3-17-0, Iqbal 21.5-6-48-2, Abdul 26-7-76-5.

PAKISTAN

Mohsin Khan handled ball	58	not out	14
Mansoor Akhtar c Bright b Thomson	32 (3)	not out	26
Haroon Rashid c Laird b Yardley	82		
Javed Miandad b Lawson	32		
Zaheer Abbas c Marsh b Lawson	91		
Mudassar Nazar not out	52 (2)	c Border b Thomson	5
Imran Khan (c) c Yardley b Bright	1		
Tahir Naqqash st Marsh b Bright	15		
Wasim Bari (+) b Bright	0		
Abdul Qadir run out	29		
Iqbal Qasim not out	2		
EXTRAS (B 4, LB 8, W 1, NB 12)	25	(NB 2)	2
TOTAL	9 dec 419		1 for 47

FOW 1st Inns: 43 168 188 277 328 329 351 353 404
FOW 2nd Inns: 5

Bowling: *First Innings*: Thomson 29-5-103-1, Lawson 39-10-93-2, Bright 36-8-96-3, Yardley 23-2-98-1, Border 1-0-4-0. *Second Innings*: Thomson 3-1-16-1, Bright 5-0-14-0, Yardley 3-1-9-0, Hughes 0.1-0-6-0.

Umpires: Khizer Hayat & Mahboob Shah

SECOND TEST 1982–83 PAKISTAN v AUSTRALIA
Iqbal Stadium, Faisalabad. September 30, October 1, 2, 4, 5, 1982.
Toss: Pakistan. Pakistan won by an innings & 3 runs.

PAKISTAN

Mohsin Khan c Marsh b Lawson	76
Mudassar Nazar c Hughes b Border	79
Mansoor Akhtar c Marsh b Lawson	111
Javed Miandad c Laird b Lawson	6
Zaheer Abbas b Sleep	126
Haroon Rashid c Laird b Lawson	51
Imran Khan (c) not out	24
Tahir Naqqash not out	15
Wasim Bari (+)	
Abdul Qadir	
Iqbal Qasim	
EXTRAS (B 4, LB 1, NB 8)	13
TOTAL	6 dec 501

FOW 1st Inns: 123 181 201 356 428 482

Bowling: *First Innings*: Thomson 23-5-79-0, Lawson 33-6-97-4, Sleep 36-3-158-1, Bright 41-15-107-0, Border 11-3-47-1.

AUSTRALIA

BM Laird lbw Abdul	8	c Mudassar b Abdul	60
GM Wood c Wasim b Mudassar	49 (7)	c Wasim b Iqbal	22
J Dyson c Mudassar b Iqbal	23 (2)	c Iqbal b Abdul	43
AR Border c Javed b Imran	9 (3)	c Haroon b Abdul	31
KJ Hughes (c) c Imran b Abdul	11 (4)	lbw Abdul	7
GM Ritchie run out	34 (5)	not out	106
PR Sleep lbw Imran	0 (6)	c Mohsin b Abdul	29
RW Marsh (+) c Wasim b Abdul	0	run out	8
RJ Bright c Haroon b Abdul	0	c (S)Salim Malik b Iqbal	0
GF Lawson c Zaheer b Iqbal	14	lbw Abdul	0
JR Thomson not out	1	st Wasim b Abdul	11
EXTRAS (B 8, LB 6, W 2, NB 3)	19	(LB 7, W 1, NB 5)	13
TOTAL	168		330

FOW 1st Inns: 20 82 96 113 123 123 124 124 167 168
FOW 2nd Inns: 73 125 133 162 218 290 309 309 310 330

Bowling: *First Innings*: Tahir 15-4-21-0, Imran 14-6-16-2, Abdul 42-14-76-4, Iqbal 25-11-28-2, Mudassar 7-2-8-1. *Second Innings*: Tahir 9-1-25-0, Imran 10-5-20-0, Abdul 50.4-12-142-7, Iqbal 46-18-97-2, Mudassar 9-3-26-0, Zaheer 3-0-5-0, Javed 1-0-2-0.

Umpires: Khizer Hayat & Mahboob Shah

THIRD TEST 1982–83 PAKISTAN v AUSTRALIA
Gaddafi Stadium, Lahore. October 14, 15, 16, 18, 19, 1982.
Toss: Pakistan. Pakistan won by 9 wkts.

AUSTRALIA

GM Wood c Javed b Abdul	85	c Mudassar b Jalal-ud-din	30
BM Laird lbw Abdul	28	lbw Tahir	6
J Dyson b Jalal-ud-din	10	lbw Tahir	51
AR Border lbw Imran	9	st Wasim b Abdul	6
KJ Hughes (c) b Tahir	29	st Wasim b Abdul	39
GM Ritchie lbw Imran	26	lbw Imran	18
RW Marsh (+) c(S)Iqbal Qasim b Imran	1	c Mudassar b Jalal-ud-din	12
B Yardley c Haroon b Jalal-ud-din	40	b Imran	21
GF Lawson not out	57	c (S)Iqbal Qasim b Imran	9
JR Thomson lbw Jalal-ud-din	0	not out	5
TM Alderman b Imran	7	c Zaheer b Imran	0
EXTRAS (B 1, LB 13, W 5, NB 5)	24	(B 4, LB 5, NB 8)	17
TOTAL	316		214

FOW 1st Inns: 85 120 140 140 197 202 203 264 264 316
FOW 2nd Inns: 21 55 64 138 157 170 189 203 214 214

Bowling: *First Innings*: Imran 24.2-10-45-4, Tahir 18-4-65-1, Mudassar 6-1-17-0, Jalal-ud-din 19-4-77-3, Abdul 37-7-86-2, Zaheer 2-0-2-0. *Second Innings*: Imran 20-6-35-4, Tahir 16-3-39-2, Abdul 35-7-102-2, Jalal-ud-din 16-8-15-2, Mudassar 2-0-5-0, Zaheer 1-0-1-0.

PAKISTAN

Mohsin Khan b Border	135	lbw Lawson	14
Mudassar Nazar lbw Lawson	23	not out	39
Abdul Qadir c Laird b Yardley	1		
Mansoor Akhtar lbw Lawson	12 (3)	not out	2
Javed Miandad c Hughes b Alderman	138		
Zaheer Abbas c Yardley b Alderman	52		
Haroon Rashid c Ritchie b Thomson	15		
Imran Khan (c) not out	39		
Tahir Naqqash not out	7		
Wasim Bari (+)			
Jalal-ud-din			
EXTRAS (B 3, LB 13, W 2, NB 27)	45	(B 4, LB 5)	9
TOTAL	7 dec 467		1 for 64

FOW 1st Inns: 92 93 119 269 392 402 442
FOW 2nd Inns: 55

Bowling: *First Innings*: Thomson 19-1-73-1, Lawson 35-4-91-2, Alderman 34-4-144-2, Yardley 27-6-102-1, Border 4-1-12-1. *Second Innings*: Thomson 5-0-24-0, Lawson 7-1-21-1, Alderman 3-0-10-0.

Umpires: Javed Akhtar & Shakoor Rana

Australian Averages

1981–82 AUSTRALIA v PAKISTAN

AUSTRALIA	M	Inn	NO	Runs	H.S	Avrge	Ct	St	Overs	Mds	Runs	Wkt	Avrge
Alderman, TM	3	4	3	10	5*	10.00	4	-	93.2	23	252	8	31.50
Border, AR	3	5	-	84	37	16.80	3	-	5.0	1	17	-	-
Chappell, GS	3	5	-	251	201	50.20	3	-	12.0	3	23	2	11.50
Hughes, KJ	3	5	-	193	106	38.60	3	-	3.0	1	2	-	-
Laird, BM	3	6	1	246	85	49.20	3	-	1.0	-	9	-	-
Lillee, DK	3	5	1	39	16	9.75	1	-	104.3	22	332	15	22.13
Marsh, RW	3	5	-	142	47	28.40	11	-	-	-	-	-	-
Thomson, JR	3	5	3	49	22*	24.50	2	-	69.0	12	219	5	43.80
Wellham, DM	2	3	-	75	36	25.00	1	-	-	-	-	-	-
Wood, GM	3	6	1	255	100	51.00	1	-	-	-	-	-	-
Yallop, GN	1	2	-	58	38	29.00	-	-	-	-	-	-	-
Yardley, B	3	5	-	53	22	10.60	4	-	130.5	26	399	18	22.17

Pakistani Averages

1981–82 AUSTRALIA v PAKISTAN

PAKISTAN	M	Inn	NO	Runs	H.S	Avrge	Ct	St	Overs	Mds	Runs	Wkt	Avrge
Ijaz Faqih	1	2	-	55	34	27.50	-	-	22.0	1	76	1	76.00
Imran Khan	3	5	1	108	70*	27.00	1	-	150.2	39	312	16	19.50
Iqbal Qasim	2	3	1	25	16*	12.50	3	-	108.0	33	235	10	23.50
Javed Miandad	3	5	-	205	79	41.00	1	-	6.0	-	29	-	-
Majid Khan	3	5	-	121	74	24.20	2	-	15.0	2	36	-	-
Mansoor Akhtar	1	2	-	42	36	21.00	1	-	-	-	-	-	-
Mohsin Khan	2	3	-	71	43	23.67	2	-	-	-	-	-	-
Mudassar Nazar	3	5	-	169	95	33.80	4	-	4.0	1	11	-	-
Rizwan-uz-Zaman	1	2	-	8	8	4.00	-	-	-	-	-	-	-
Sarfraz Nawaz	3	5	-	52	26	10.40	1	-	118.0	32	306	9	34.00
Sikander Bakht	3	4	3	6	3*	6.00	-	-	71.0	9	217	5	43.40
Wasim Bari	3	5	1	40	20	10.00	8	1	-	-	-	-	-
Wasim Raja	3	5	-	181	50	36.20	-	-	88.0	13	233	4	58.25
Zaheer Abbas	2	3	-	170	90	56.67	-	-	-	-	-	-	-

Australia finds the winning formula

Adelaide, Dec. 15. Australia moves to a two–nil lead in the Ashes series after a solid eight-wicket win over England today in the third Test.

England sent Australia in to bat on a pitch that turned out to be almost perfect for scoring. Greg Chappell came in at number three to make his first Test century at the Adelaide Oval. He ended with 115 runs and was ably partnered by Kim Hughes (88).

Despite a fine second-innings 114 from England's David Gower, the Test was probably decided in the first innings when England lost its last seven wickets for 35 runs in one hour's play. It got better, but not much. In its second innings England lost seven wickets for 68 runs.

The Australian fast bowler, Geoff Lawson, took 9/22 for the match. His fiery, short-pitched deliveries intimidated England's batsmen.

England captain Bob Willis lamented: 'As a country, we have not played this sort of bowling for almost ten years.'

Lawson also thrashed England in the second Test at Brisbane, taking 11 wickets for the match, which Australia won by seven wickets. The highlight of the second Test was a splendid debut Test century for Australia by South-African-born Kepler Wessels (162).

Wessels did not play in the drawn first Test at Perth, where centuries were made by Chappell (117) and England's Derek Randall (115).

Out for a duck! A stunned Ian Botham walks from the crease as his destroyer, Geoff Lawson, inspects the damage with unrestrained glee.

Alderman hurt in shameful attack by pro-England yobbo

Perth, Nov. 14. In a disgraceful episode during the first Test at the WACA ground yesterday, a group of rowdy spectators invaded the playing arena when England passed 400 in its first innings.

Some of the hooligans were waving Union Jacks. One of them headed towards Australia's Terry Alderman and struck him across the back of the head. Infuriated, Alderman chased his assailant for about 20 metres and grappled with the man. The bowler fell heavily, dislocating his shoulder.

After Dennis Lillee and Allan Border rushed to aid their teammate, the culprit was held until police arrived.

Greg Chappell took the Australian side off the field while the police made 26 arrests. Tragically, Alderman had to be carried off on a stretcher.

The offenders will be charged and probably fined, but the victim is likely to pay the higher price.

His shoulder badly damaged, Australia's Terry Alderman is carried off the field after attempting to tackle a lout who invaded the field and attacked him.

Series a delight for statisticians

Brisbane, Dec. 2. The cricket milestones just keep on coming.

The first Test saw Ian Botham's 250th Test wicket; his 3000th run; and Bruce Yardley's 100th wicket. The second saw Kepler Wessel's record Test debut aggregate; Rod Marsh's 300th catch and a new Ashes record of six in an innings; Australia becoming the first side to hold 19 catches in a Test; David Gower's 3000th run; Allan Border's 1000th against England; Derek Randall's 1000th against Australia; a new Australian record of 52 extras; and a new world record of 35 no-balls set by Australia.

Whew! Cricket statisticians are jumping over their notebooks.

Bob's big blunder

Adelaide, Dec. 12. The precedents were there, if only England captain Bob Willis had cared to notice.

The first time England invited Australia to bat first at the Adelaide Oval was when Peter May made the mistake in December 1959. The result: Australia scored 476 in its first innings and won by 10 wickets.

The second time was January 1975, when Mike Denness did the deed. Result: 304 first-innings runs and a 163-run victory to Australia.

And it's looking like a case of third time unlucky for England, because Australia's first innings in Adelaide has just ended at 438.

May's mistake. Denness's disaster. And now Bob's blunder. Oh dear!

There's life in the parks for old Test players. North Melbourne coach Gary Cosier celebrates a wicket.

Border and Thommo fail in heroic stand

So near and yet so far: end of the line for a still-focused Allan Border.

Melbourne, Dec. 30. In one of the closest results in Test cricket history, England beat Australia in the fourth Test by just three runs this morning.

It was a historic match. Australia's Rod Marsh took his 27th catch for the 1982–83 Ashes series, to break J. H. B. Waite's world record set in 1961–62.

Scores were so even that each innings was within a ten-run range.

It was the 250th Test between Australia and England and the 75th Test staged at the MCG, which is a record for any ground in cricket history. It was also the first Test to be played on the relaid MCG wicket, and the first to be played with the MCG's multi-million dollar electronic scoreboard, which features instant video playback.

But most of all, the match was memorable for the last-wicket partnership between Australia's Allan Border and tail-ender Jeff Thomson, who together added 70 runs in 128 minutes. Border took 38 minutes to get off the mark late yesterday, and when he and Thomson came to the crease this morning, Australia needed 37 runs to win. England needed one wicket.

The first nine overs this morning produced: 0, 2, 0, 1, 0, 1, 3, 1, 3.

They declined to play 29 seemingly easy singles and the tension was almost unbearable when, just four runs short of victory, England's Ian Botham came into the attack. Thomson edged Botham's first ball to Chris Tavare at second slip. Tavare fumbled, but Geoff Miller dived to snatch the catch and withhold victory from Australia.

Under 25's on tour

Perth, May 30. The Young Australia team, captained by WA's Mike Veletta, has returned home after an eight-match tour of Zimbabwe.

Among the fourteen promising players who made up the team, several who show potential as Test cricketers are Tony Dodemaide, Craig McDermott and Ian Healy.

McDermott is a fast bowler from Ipswich in Queensland. He is tall and athletic, with a devastating inswinger.

Healy, another Queenslander, looks like a teenaged version of Wally Grout, and if he maintains his consistency should make it to the top as a 'keeper/batsman.

Dodemaide is safe bat and solid bowler from Williamstown in Victoria.

Bruce Yardley congratulates Australian wicketkeeper Rod Marsh (left), who has established a new world record with 28 catches over the five-Test series, including nine dismissals in the second Test and eight in the third.

Ashes regained in fifth Test

Sydney, Jan. 8. Australia won back the Ashes yesterday when the fifth Test was drawn at the SCG.

In a sensational first over, Australian opening batsman John Dyson appeared to be run out, but was not given out by umpire Johnston.

Television footage later showed Dyson was at least 30 centimetres out of his ground. He eventually scored 79 runs.

Kim Hughes made a magnificent century in Australia's second innings and went on to make 137 before finally succumbing to a catch by Ian Botham off the bowling of Eddie Hemmings.

Hemmings took six wickets in the Test and bowled 26 maiden overs.

For Australia, Jeff Thomson captured seven wickets. He has been a magnificent replacement for the injured bowlers, Dennis Lillee and Terry Alderman.

After the Test, Greg Chappell announced that he would be temporarily stepping down as Australia's captain.

English cricket officials would not permit the actual Ashes to travel from their hallowed sanctuary at Lord's, so the Australians have made their own by burning one of the bails in the dressing rooms and placing its ashes in an urn, inscribed: 'The Ashes. English cricket dies again. Fondly accepted by Greg Chappell and Co. at the Sydney Cricket Ground on January 7, 1983.'

'Toey' out of Africa

Melbourne, Jan. 15. The former South African bowler, Hugh 'Toey' Tayfield is in Australia, covering the Test series for Johannesburg's *Star* newspaper.

Tayfield earned his nickname from his habit of stubbing his toe in the ground before bowling. But now it seems 'Toey' is stubbing cheques. There are rumours he is working undercover for a big cricket sponsor and is offering Test players up to $100,000 to play in a five-week tour of South Africa.

Someone else has approached Kim Hughes, and now it's the Australian Cricket Board who are 'toey'.

NSW's Shield win

Perth, March 8. New South Wales won the Sheffield Shield today, defeating Western Australia by 54 runs.

WA looked to have the match won, but lost its last six wickets for just 52 runs. NSW has not won the Shield since 1965–66.

It is the first time that the Shield has been decided by a final in which the top two teams play off.

To secure the Shield, the second team must obtain an outright victory, which is a tall order at the best of times, so there are obviously great advantages to the team that finishes top of the table before the final.

Dennis Lillee: the fresh flower of Australian fast bowling in 1969.

He's still here, but fighting injury after the first Test.

FIRST TEST 1982–83 AUSTRALIA v ENGLAND
W.A.C.A. Ground, Perth. November 12, 13, 14, 16, 17, 1982.
Toss: Australia. Match Drawn.

ENGLAND

G Cook c Dyson b Lillee	1	c Border b Lawson	7
CJ Tavare c Hughes b Yardley	89	c Chappell b Yardley	9
DI Gower c Dyson b Alderman	72	lbw Lillee	28
AJ Lamb c Marsh b Yardley	46	c Marsh b Lawson	56
IT Botham c Marsh b Lawson	12	b Lawson	0
DW Randall c Wood b Yardley	78	b Lawson	115
G Miller c Marsh b Lillee	30 (8)	c Marsh b Yardley	0
DR Pringle b Lillee	0 (9)	not out	47
RW Taylor (+) not out	29 (7)	b Yardley	31
RGD Willis (c) c Lillee b Yardley	26	b Lawson	0
NG Cowans b Yardley	4	lbw Chappell	36
EXTRAS (B 7, LB 9, W 2, NB 6)	24	(B 5, LB 11, W 2, NB 11)	29
TOTAL	411		358

FOW 1st Inns: 14 109 189 204 304 323 342 357 406 411
FOW 2nd Inns: 10 51 77 80 151 228 242 292 292 358

Bowling: *First Innings*: Lillee 38-13-96-3, Alderman 43-15-84-1, Lawson 29-6-89-1, Chappell 3-0-11-0, Yardley 42.4-15-107-5. *Second Innings*: Lillee 33-12-89-1, Lawson 32-5-108-5, Yardley 41-10-101-3, Border 7-2-21-0, Chappell 2.3-1-8-1, Hookes 1-0-2-0.

AUSTRALIA

GM Wood c & b Willis	29	c Taylor b Willis	0
J Dyson lbw Miller	52	c Cowans b Willis	12
AR Border c Taylor b Botham	8	not out	32
GS Chappell (c) c Lamb b Willis	117	not out	22
KJ Hughes c Willis b Miller	62		
DW Hookes lbw Miller	56		
RW Marsh (+) c Cook b Botham	0		
GF Lawson b Miller	50		
B Yardley c Lamb b Willis	17		
DK Lillee not out	2		
TM Alderman			
EXTRAS (B 4, LB 1, W 1, NB 25)	31	(LB 1, NB 6)	7
TOTAL	9 dec 424		2 for 73

FOW 1st Inns: 63 76 123 264 311 311 374 414 424
FOW 2nd Inns: 2 22

Bowling: *First Innings*: Willis 31.5-4-95-3, Botham 40-10-121-2, Cowans 13-2-54-0, Pringle 10-1-37-0, Miller 33-11-70-4, Cook 4-2-16-0. *Second Innings*: Willis 6-1-23-2, Botham 6-1-17-0, Cowans 3-1-15-0, Miller 4-3-8-0, Pringle 2-0-3-0, Lamb 1-1-0-0.

Umpires: AR Crafter & MW Johnson

SECOND TEST 1982–83 AUSTRALIA v ENGLAND
Brisbane Cricket Ground, Brisbane. November 26, 27, 28, 30, December 1, 1982.
Toss: Australia. Australia won by 7 wkts.

ENGLAND

CJ Tavare c Hughes b Lawson	1	c Marsh b Lawson	13
G Fowler c Yardley b Lawson	7	c Marsh b Thomson	83
DI Gower c Wessels b Lawson	18	c Marsh b Thomson	34
AJ Lamb c Marsh b Lawson	72	c Wessels b Thomson	12
IT Botham c Rackemann b Yardley	40 (6)	c Marsh b Thomson	15
DW Randall c Lawson b Rackemann	37 (5)	c Yardley b Thomson	4
G Miller c Marsh b Lawson	0	c Marsh b Lawson	60
RW Taylor (+) c Lawson b Rackemann	1	c Hookes b Lawson	3
EE Hemmings not out	15	b Lawson	18
RGD Willis (c) c Thomson b Yardley	1	not out	10
NG Cowans c Marsh b Lawson	10	c Marsh b Lawson	5
EXTRAS (LB 2, W 1, NB 14)	17	(B 8, LB 8, W 1, NB 35)	52
TOTAL	219		309

FOW 1st Inns: 8 13 63 141 152 152 178 191 195 219
FOW 2nd Inns: 54 144 165 169 194 201 226 285 295 309

Bowling: *First Innings*: Lawson 18.3-4-47-6, Rackemann 21-8-61-2, Thomson 8-0-43-0, Yardley 17-5-51-2. *Second Innings*: Lawson 35.3-11-87-5, Rackemann 12.2-3-35-0, Thomson 31-6-73-5, Yardley 40.4-21-50-0, Chappell 6-2-8-0, Hookes 2-0-4-0.

AUSTRALIA

KC Wessels b Willis	162	b Hemmings	46
J Dyson b Botham	1	retired hurt	4
AR Border c Randall b Willis	0	c Botham b Hemmings	15
GS Chappell (c) run out	53	c Lamb b Cowans	8
KJ Hughes c Taylor b Botham	0	not out	39
DW Hookes c Taylor b Miller	28	not out	66
RW Marsh (+) c Taylor b Botham	11		
B Yardley c Tavare b Willis	53		
GF Lawson c Hemmings b Willis	6		
CG Rackemann b Willis	4		
JR Thomson not out	5		
EXTRAS (B 2, LB 8, NB 8)	18	(B 2, LB 5, NB 5)	12
TOTAL	341		3 for 190

FOW 1st Inns: 4 11 94 99 130 171 271 310 332 341
FOW 2nd Inns: 60 77 83

Bowling: *First Innings*: Willis 29.4-3-66-5, Botham 22-1-105-3, Cowans 6-0-36-0, Hemmings 33.3-6-81-0, Miller 19.3-4-35-1. *Second Innings*: Willis 4-1-24-0, Botham 15.5-1-70-0, Hemmings 29-9-43-2, Cowans 9-1-31-1, Miller 3-0-10-0.

Umpires: RC Bailhache & MW Johnson

THIRD TEST 1982–83 AUSTRALIA v ENGLAND
Adelaide Oval, Adelaide. December 10, 11, 12, 14, 15, 1982.
Toss: England. Australia won by 8 wkts.

AUSTRALIA
KC Wessels c Taylor b Botham	44	c Taylor b Botham	1
J Dyson c Taylor b Botham	44	not out	37
GS Chappell (c) c Gower b Willis	115 (4)	not out	26
KJ Hughes run out	88		
GF Lawson c Botham b Willis	2 (3)	c Randall b Willis	14
AR Border c Taylor b Pringle	26		
DW Hookes c Botham b Hemmings	37		
RW Marsh (+) c Hemmings b Pringle	3		
B Yardley c Gower b Botham	38		
RM Hogg not out	14		
JR Thomson c & b Botham	3		
EXTRAS (LB 6, NB 18)	24	(NB 5)	5
TOTAL	438		2 for 83

FOW 1st Inns: 76 138 264 270 315 355 359 391 430 438
FOW 2nd Inns: 3 37

Bowling: *First Innings*: Willis 25-8-76-2, Botham 36.5-5-112-4, Pringle 33-5-97-2, Miller 14-2-33-0, Hemmings 48-17-96-1. *Second Innings*: Willis 8-1-17-1, Botham 10-2-45-1, Hemmings 4-1-5-0, Pringle 1.5-0-11-0.

ENGLAND
CJ Tavare c Marsh b Hogg	1	c Wessels b Thomson	0
G Fowler c Marsh b Lawson	11	c Marsh b Lawson	37
DI Gower c Marsh b Lawson	60	b Hogg	114
AJ Lamb c Marsh b Lawson	82	c Chappell b Yardley	8
IT Botham c Wessels b Thomson	35	c Dyson b Yardley	58
DW Randall b Lawson	0	c Marsh b Lawson	17
G Miller c Yardley b Hogg	7	lbw Lawson	17
RW Taylor (+) c Chappell b Yardley	2 (9)	not out	3
DR Pringle not out	1 (8)	c Marsh b Thomson	9
EE Hemmings b Thomson	0	c Wessels b Lawson	4
RGD Willis (c) b Thomson	1	c Marsh b Lawson	10
EXTRAS (LB 5, NB 11)	16	(B 7, LB 6, W 3, NB 15)	31
TOTAL	216		304

FOW 1st Inns: 1 21 140 181 181 194 199 213 213 216
FOW 2nd Inns: 11 90 118 247 247 272 277 289 290 304

Bowling: *First Innings*: Lawson 18-4-56-4, Hogg 14-2-41-2, Thomson 14.5-3-51-3, Yardley 21-7-52-1. *Second Innings*: Lawson 24-6-66-5, Thomson 13-3-41-2, Yardley 37-12-90-2, Hogg 19-5-53-1, Border 8-2-14-0, Hookes 3-1-9-0.

Umpires: RA French & MW Johnson

FIFTH TEST 1982–83 AUSTRALIA v ENGLAND
Sydney Cricket Ground, Sydney. January 2, 3, 4, 6, 7, 1983.
Toss: Australia. Match Drawn.

AUSTRALIA
KC Wessels c Willis b Botham	19	lbw Botham	53
J Dyson c Taylor b Hemmings	79	c Gower b Willis	2
GS Chappell (c) lbw Willis	35	c Randall b Hemmings	11
KJ Hughes c Cowans b Botham	29	c Botham b Hemmings	137
DW Hookes c Botham b Hemmings	17	lbw Miller	19
AR Border c Miller b Hemmings	89	c Botham b Cowans	83
RW Marsh (+) c & b Miller	3	c Taylor b Miller	41
B Yardley b Cowans	24	c Botham b Hemmings	0
GF Lawson c & b Botham	6	not out	13
JR Thomson c Lamb b Botham	0	c Gower b Miller	12
RM Hogg not out	0	run out	0
EXTRAS (B 3, LB 8, W 2)	13	(LB 7, NB 4)	11
TOTAL	314		382

FOW 1st Inns: 39 96 150 173 210 219 262 283 291 314
FOW 2nd Inns: 23 38 82 113 262 350 357 358 382 382

Bowling: *First Innings*: Willis 20-6-57-1, Cowans 21-3-67-1, Botham 30-8-75-4, Hemmings 27-10-68-3, Miller 17-7-34-1. *Second Innings*: Willis 10-2-33-1, Cowans 13-1-47-1, Hemmings 47-16-116-3, Miller 49.3-12-133-3, Botham 10-0-35-1, Cook 2-1-7-0.

ENGLAND
G Cook c Chappell b Hogg	8	lbw Lawson	2
CJ Tavare c Lawson	0	lbw Yardley	16
DI Gower c Chappell b Lawson	70 (4)	c Hookes b Yardley	24
AJ Lamb b Lawson	0 (5)	c & b Yardley	29
DW Randall b Thomson	70 (6)	b Thomson	44
IT Botham c Wessels b Thomson	5 (7)	lbw Thomson	32
G Miller lbw Thomson	34 (8)	not out	21
RW Taylor (+) lbw Thomson	0 (9)	not out	28
EE Hemmings c Border b Yardley	29 (3)	c Marsh b Yardley	95
RGD Willis (c) c Border b Thomson	1		
NG Cowans not out	0		
EXTRAS (B 4, LB 4, NB 12)	20	(B 1, LB 10, W 1, NB 11)	23
TOTAL	237		7 for 314

FOW 1st Inns: 8 23 24 146 163 169 170 220 232 237
FOW 2nd Inns: 3 55 104 155 196 260 261

Bowling: *First Innings*: Lawson 20-2-70-3, Hogg 16-2-50-1, Thomson 14.5-2-50-5, Yardley 14-4-47-1. *Second Innings*: Lawson 15-1-50-1, Hogg 13-6-25-0, Yardley 37-6-139-4, Thomson 12-3-30-2, Border 16-3-36-0, Hookes 2-1-5-0, Chappell 1-0-6-0.

Umpires: RA French & MW Johnson

FOURTH TEST 1982–83 AUSTRALIA v ENGLAND
Melbourne Cricket Ground, Melbourne. December 26, 27, 28, 29, 30, 1982.
Toss: Australia. England won by 3 runs.

ENGLAND
G Cook c Chappell b Thomson	10	c Yardley b Thomson	26
G Fowler c Chappell b Hogg	4	b Hogg	65
CJ Tavare c Yardley b Thomson	89	b Hogg	0
DI Gower c Marsh b Hogg	18	c Marsh b Lawson	3
AJ Lamb c Dyson b Yardley	83	c Marsh b Hogg	26
IT Botham c Wessels b Yardley	27	c Chappell b Thomson	46
G Miller c Border b Yardley	10	lbw Lawson	14
DR Pringle c Wessels b Hogg	9	c Marsh b Lawson	42
RW Taylor (+) c Marsh b Yardley	1	lbw Thomson	37
RGD Willis (c) not out	6	not out	8
NG Cowans c Lawson b Hogg	3	b Lawson	10
EXTRAS (B 3, LB 6, W 3, NB 12)	24	(B 2, LB 9, NB 6)	17
TOTAL	284		294

FOW 1st Inns: 11 25 56 217 227 259 262 268 278 284
FOW 2nd Inns: 40 41 45 128 129 160 201 262 280 294

Bowling: *First Innings*: Lawson 17-6-48-0, Hogg 23.3-6-69-4, Yardley 27-9-89-4, Thomson 13-2-49-2, Chappell 1-0-5-0. *Second Innings*: Lawson 21.4-6-66-4, Hogg 22-5-64-3, Thomson 21-3-74-3, Yardley 15-2-67-0, Chappell 1-0-6-0.

AUSTRALIA
KC Wessels b Willis	47	b Cowans	14
J Dyson lbw Cowans	21	c Tavare b Botham	31
GS Chappell (c) c Lamb b Cowans	0	c (S)IJ Gould b Cowans	2
KJ Hughes b Willis	66	c Taylor b Miller	48
AR Border b Botham	2 (6)	not out	62
DW Hookes c Taylor b Pringle	53 (5)	c Willis b Cowans	68
RW Marsh (+) b Willis	53	lbw Cowans	13
B Yardley b Miller	9	b Cowans	0
GF Lawson c Fowler b Miller	0	c Cowans b Pringle	7
RM Hogg not out	8	lbw Cowans	4
JR Thomson b Miller	1	c Miller b Botham	21
EXTRAS (LB 8, NB 19)	27	(B 5, LB 9, W 1, NB 3)	18
TOTAL	287		288

FOW 1st Inns: 55 55 83 89 180 261 276 276 278 287
FOW 2nd Inns: 37 39 71 171 173 190 190 202 218 288

Bowling: *First Innings*: Willis 15-2-38-3, Botham 18-3-69-1, Cowans 16-0-69-2, Pringle 15-2-40-1, Miller 15-5-44-3. *Second Innings*: Willis 17-0-57-0, Cowans 26-6-77-6, Botham 25.1-4-80-2, Pringle 12-4-26-1, Miller 16-6-30-1.

Umpires: AR Crafter & RV Whitehead

Australian Averages

1982–83 AUSTRALIA v ENGLAND
AUSTRALIA	M	Inn	NO	Runs	H.S	Avrge	Ct	St	Overs	Mds	Runs	Wkt	Avrge
Alderman, TM	1	-	-	-	-	-	-	-	43.0	15	84	1	84.00
Border, AR	5	9	2	317	89	45.29	4	-	31.0	7	71	-	-
Chappell, GS	5	10	2	389	117	48.63	8	-	14.3	3	44	1	44.00
Dyson, J	5	10	-	283	79	35.38	4	-	-	-	-	-	-
Hogg, RM	3	5	3	26	14*	13.00	-	-	107.3	26	302	11	27.45
Hookes, DW	5	8	1	344	68	49.14	2	-	8.0	2	20	-	-
Hughes, KJ	5	8	1	469	137	67.00	2	-	-	-	-	-	-
Lawson, GF	5	8	1	98	50	14.00	3	-	230.4	51	687	34	20.21
Lillee, DK	1	1	1	2	2*	-	1	-	71.0	25	185	4	46.25
Marsh, RW	5	7	-	124	53	17.71	28	-	-	-	-	-	-
Rackemann, CG	1	1	-	4	4	4.00	-	-	33.2	11	96	2	48.00
Thomson, JR	4	6	1	42	21	8.40	1	-	127.4	22	411	22	18.68
Wessels, KC	4	8	-	386	162	48.25	8	-	-	-	-	-	-
Wood, GM	1	2	-	29	29	14.50	1	-	-	-	-	-	-
Yardley, B	5	7	-	141	53	20.14	6	-	292.2	91	793	22	36.05

English Averages

1982–83 AUSTRALIA v ENGLAND
ENGLAND	M	Inn	NO	Runs	H.S	Avrge	Ct	St	Overs	Mds	Runs	Wkt	Avrge
Botham, IT	5	10	-	270	58	27.00	9	-	213.5	35	729	18	40.50
Cook, G	3	6	-	54	26	9.00	1	-	6.0	3	23	-	-
Cowans, NG	4	7	1	68	36	11.33	3	-	107.0	14	396	11	36.00
Fowler, G	3	6	-	207	83	34.50	1	-	-	-	-	-	-
Gower, DI	5	10	-	441	114	44.10	4	-	-	-	-	-	-
Hemmings, EE	3	6	1	157	95	31.40	2	-	188.3	59	409	9	45.44
Lamb, AJ	5	10	-	414	83	41.40	5	-	1.0	1	0	-	-
Miller, G	5	10	1	193	60	21.44	3	-	171.0	50	397	13	30.54
Pringle, DR	3	6	2	108	47*	27.00	-	-	73.5	12	214	4	53.50
Randall, DW	4	8	-	365	115	45.63	3	-	-	-	-	-	-
Tavare, CJ	5	10	-	218	89	21.80	2	-	-	-	-	-	-
Taylor, RW	5	10	3	135	37	19.29	13	-	-	-	-	-	-
Willis, RGD	5	9	3	63	26	10.50	4	-	166.3	28	486	18	27.00

Greg Chappell's perfect stance.

Hookesy makes an almighty century

Kandy, April 23. Sri Lanka will long remember the Australian batsman, David Hookes, who made a whirlwind 143 runs not out in Australia's first innings, which was declared closed at 4/514 today.

Hookes faced 152 balls and hit two sixes and 17 fours.

So fast was his scoring rate that he made a century in a session this afternoon, when he took his tally from 43 to 143 after lunch.

Hookes is a very aggressive left-handed batsman who made his first class cricket debut in the 1975–76 season, and came to prominence late in 1977–78 when he hit five centuries in six innings while playing for South Australia in the Sheffield Shield.

He captained South Australia to a win in the Shield last year.

Hookes made a memorable Test debut in the centenary Test in Melbourne, where his brilliant 56 runs innings included hitting five successive fours off England's Tony Greig.

He is an explosive, natural talent of outstanding promise. Last season Hookes made 1424 runs at an average of 64.72.

ONLY TEST 1982–83 SRI LANKA v AUSTRALIA
Asgiriya Stadium, Kandy. April 22, 23, 24, 26, 1983.
Toss: Australia. Australia won by an innings & 38 runs.

AUSTRALIA
KC Wessels c Dias b De Silva	141	
GM Wood c Ratnayake b Ranatunga	4	
GN Yallop lbw De Mel	98	
GS Chappell (c) lbw De Mel	66	
DW Hookes not out	143	
AR Border not out	47	
RD Woolley (+)		
TG Hogan		
B Yardley		
DK Lillee		
RM Hogg		
EXTRAS (LB 11, W 1, NB 3)	15	
TOTAL	4 dec 514	

FOW 1st Inns: 43 213 290 359

Bowling: *First Innings*: De Mel 23-3-113-2, Ratnayake 28-4-108-0, Ranatunga 19-2-72-1, De Silva 44-7-122-1, Guneratne 17-1-84-0.

SRI LANKA
S Wettimuny c Woolley b Lillee	0		b Hogan	96
ERNS Fernando c Woolley b Hogg	0		c Woolley b Lillee	3
RL Dias c Border b Lillee	4		b Hogan	10
LRD Mendis (c) c Hookes b Yardley	74	(5)	c Border b Yardley	6
RS Madugalle c & b Yardley	9	(6)	b Yardley	0
A Ranatunga c Lillee b Yardley	90	(7)	b Hogan	32
DS De Silva c Hogan b Yardley	26	(8)	c Woolley b Hogan	5
ALF De Mel c Hookes b Hogan	29	(9)	c Yallop b Hogan	0
RG De Alwis (+) c Border b Yardley	3	(10)	run out	9
RJ Ratnayake c Woolley b Border	14	(4)	run out	30
RPW Guneratne not out	0		not out	0
EXTRAS (B 4, LB 5, W 1, NB 12)	22		(B 6, LB 7, NB 1)	14
TOTAL	271			205

FOW 1st Inns: 1 5 9 46 142 220 224 247 270 271
FOW 2nd Inns: 17 59 120 151 155 155 162 164 191 205

Bowling: *First Innings*: Lillee 19-3-67-2, Hogg 12-4-31-1, Chappell 1-0-2-0, Yardley 25-7-88-5, Hogan 11-1-50-1, Border 4.5-0-11-1. *Second Innings*: Lillee 11-3-40-1, Hogg 3-2-7-0, Yardley 26-6-78-2, Hogan 25.2-6-66-5.

Umpires: CEB Anthony & HC Felsinger

A Test for Sri Lanka, at last

Graham Yallop scores a stylish 98 runs in the inaugural Test against Sri Lanka.

Kandy, April 27. The inaugural Test between Sri Lanka and Australia has ended in a comfortable win to Australia by an innings and 38 runs.

The match showed the huge gulf that exists between the Sri Lankan newcomers and a Test-hardened side like Australia.

Sri Lanka became a member of the ICC in April 1981 and toured Australia in February 1983, playing matches against NSW, Victoria, Tasmania and the ACT.

An Australia/Sri Lanka tradition already exists. Billy Murdoch's Australian team visited Sri Lanka, when it was known as Ceylon, as far back as 1884, and other Australian teams played there in 1890, 1896, 1912 and 1914.

Don Bradman never played in India, but he did participate in a couple of Sri Lankan matches in 1930 and 1948. Both were memorable: the first because Bradman made only 40 runs against All-Ceylon; the second because he made only 20 and the pitch was later found to be two yards short!

There was nothing wrong with the pitch at Asgiriya Stadium for Sri Lanka's historic first Test against Australia this week.

Australia faced little opposition and declared at 4/514 in its only innings. David Hookes top-scored with 143 runs, closely followed by Kepler Wessels (141) and Graham Yallop (98).

Sri Lanka began rather badly when both opening batsmen, Wettimuny and Fernando, went out for ducks, caught by wicket-keeper Roger Woolley.

Arjuna Ranatunga saved face with a creditable 90 runs, and Wettimuny made some amends with 96 in Sri Lanka's second innings, but overall Sri Lanka were no match for Australia's slow bowlers.

Bruce Yardley destroyed Sri Lanka's first innings (5/88) and Tom Hogan took the honours in the second with 5/66.

Zimbabwe shock stops Australia

World Cup results

GROUP A

9 June **Eng** d **NZ** by 106 runs; 9 June **Pak** d **Sri Lanka** by 50 runs; 11 June **Eng** d **Sri Lanka** by 47 runs; 11–12 June **NZ** d **Pak** by 52 runs; 13 June **Pak** d **Eng** by 8 wkts; 13 June **Sri Lanka** d **NZ** by 5 wkts; 13 June **Eng** d **NZ** by 2 wkts; 16 June **Pak** d **Sri Lanka** by 11 runs;18 June **NZ** d **Sri Lanka** by 3 wkts; 18 June **Pak** d **Eng** by 7 wkts; 20 June **Pak** d **NZ** by 11 runs; 20 June **Sri Lanka** d **Eng** by 9 wkts.

GROUP B

9–10 June **India** d **West Indies** by 34 runs.

9 June at Trent Bridge. **Zimbabwe** d **Australia** by 13 runs; **Zimbabwe** 6/239, Dave Houghton 69, Dennis Lillee 2/47, Graham Yallop 2/28. **Australia** 226, Kepler Wessels 76, DAG Fletcher 4/42.

11 June **India** d Zim by 5 wkts.

11–12 June at Headingley **West Indies** d **Australia** by 101 runs; **West Indies** 9/252 Viv Richards 78, Geoff Lawson 3/29. **Australia** 151 David Hookes 45, Winston Davis 7/51.

13 June at Trent Bridge **Australia** d **India** by 162 runs; **Australia** 320 Trevor Chappell 110, Graham Yallop 66 n.o., Kapil Dev 5/43. **India** 158 Kapil Dev 40, Ken Macleay 6/39.

13 June at Worcester **West Indies** d **Zimbabwe** by 8 wkts.

15 June **West Indies** d **India** by 66 runs.

16 June at Southampton **Australia** d **Zimbabwe** by 22 runs; **Australia** 272, Graeme Wood 73, John Traicos 2/28. **Zimbabwe** 240, Dave Houghton 84, Rod Hogg 3/40.

18 June at Lord's. **West Indies** d **Australia** by 7 wkts; **Australia** 6/273, Kim Hughes 69, **West Indies** 3/276 Viv Richards 95 n.o., Gordon Greenidge 90.

18 June at Tunbridge Wells. **India** d **Zimbabwe** by 31 runs.

20 June at Chelmsford **India** d **Australia** by 118 runs; **India** 247 Yashpal Sharma 40, Rod Hogg 3/40. **Australia** 129, Madan Lal 4/20.

20 June at Edgbaston. **West Indies** d **Zimbabwe** by 10 wkts.

SEMI FINALS

22 June **India** d **Eng** by 6 wkts; **West Indies** d **Pakistan** by 8 wkts.

FINAL

25 June at Lord's **India** d **West Indies** by 43 runs.

London, June 25. How the mighty have fallen. Little Zimbabwe, playing in its first World Cup, defeated Australia by 13 runs on June 9. Australia never recovered, winning only two matches in its Group B, comprising India, Zimbabwe and West Indies.

One win was in the return match against Zimbabwe, the other was over eventual winners India, which featured 110 from Trevor Chappell and 6/39 from Ken Macleay. But the truth is Australia isn't consistently in the top flight of one day nations at the moment.

At lunch in the first match against Zimbabwe, they were 5/94, but Australia dropped five catches to let cricket's newcomers reach 6/239.

Then Australia's middle order collapsed (yet again) to give Zimbabwe its historic victory.

Australia fell to the West Indies by 101 runs at Leeds on June 11. The Australian innings lasted only 30.3 overs as Winston Davis (7/51) murdered the Australian batsmen.

The West Indies lost only three wickets to Australia in a second encounter on June 18 at Lord's.

Australia failed to reach the semi-finals, and it was little consolation that the Australians defeated Zimbabwe by 32 runs in the return bout. In that match Rodney Hogg and Trevor Chappell claimed four wickets for one run.

Graeme Wood is caught by Zimbabwe wicketkeeper Dave Houghton.

The Indian team led by brilliant fast bowler Kapil Dev, seated in the centre of the front row, defeated the West Indies to take the 1983 World Cup at Lord's. Australia defeated India in a preliminary match but did not earn a place in the final.

Tortured Pakistan on the 'Rack' in Perth

Kim Hughes – a model of concentration in charge of Australia.

Perth, Nov. 14. Kim Hughes led a full-strength Australian side on Australian turf for the first time at the WACA. Greg Chappell, Dennis Lillee and Rod Marsh might have had reservations about Hughes' leadership, but they could have had none about the rest of the youthful team.

Wayne Phillips scored a century in his first Test innings, and his 158 fell just seven short of the highest-ever debut century by an Australian, that of Charles Bannerman in the very first Test in 1877.

Graham Yallop's 141 was perhaps less uninhibited than Phillips' free-wheeling approach but it was an innings of great drives and sweeps and control.

After Australia had compiled 9/436 in the brisk time of 505 minutes, it was the turn of the tyro bowlers. Carl Rackemann, in his second Test, took 5/32 in the first innings, including 5/14 in one spell of 34 balls. He took 6/86 after Pakistan was invited to follow on.

The Pakistani first innings was destroyed by Rodney Hogg who took three wickets in ten balls in a spell that was the quickest and most terrifying seen at the WACA since Thommo in his heyday.

The second day of the game was marred by rain, and by a crackpot who dug two small holes in the pitch, about 30 centimetres in front of the popping crease at the southern end. He left a note but its contents were kept secret. Play commenced at 2 p.m. that day.

Pakistan suffers internal problems

Perth, Nov. 11. Pakistan is being led for the first few Tests at least by Zaheer Abbas, not by Imran Khan, who has an injury preventing him from bowling. This appears to one of the more straightforward selection decisions. But all is not what it seems. As a preliminary to the five-Test Australian tour, three Tests were played against India – and this caused ructions as a training-camp location and team were first chosen and then abandoned.

Then Chairman of Selectors Haseeb Ahsan demanded Imran undergo a fitness test, but was overruled by the Board. Board President Air Marshal Nur Khan also vetoed Zaheer's appointment, upon which the entire selection committee resigned. For his part Zaheer arrived late in Australia and will depart early before the one day series – for 'family reasons'.

A delighted Qasim Omar shakes hands with everyone after his maiden Test century in Adelaide. Omar bore multiple bruises, courtesy of Dennis Lillee.

Yallop's touch of greatness

Kim Hughes shared a 203-run partnership with Graham Yallop in the fourth Test.

Melbourne, Dec. 30. In the fourth Test at the MCG, Pakistan has shown its best batting of the tour – 470, including a superb 152 from Mohsin Khan from just 239 balls. Imran Khan played his first Test for nearly a year and made a bright 83.

Australia made a tentative start. Kepler Wessels and Wayne Phillips were gone with 70 on the board, but Graham Yallop showed a touch of greatness with his 268 runs. He partnered Kim Hughes (94), then Allan Border (32) and Greg Matthews (75).

The partnership with Hughes of 203 was a record against Pakistan. By the time he was ninth out, Yallop had made the third-highest innings on the MCG, scored his third double century of the season, surpassed Greg Chappell's highest score against Pakistan and proved himself as the batsman of the summer. He dominated the Pakistani attack and already has 524 runs from five innings.

After Australia made 555 a draw was on the cards, and was inevitable by the time Zaheer (50 in 148 minutes) and Imran (70 in 222 minutes) batted out the last day. Even Rod Marsh had a bowl, and stumps were drawn half an hour early.

Greg Matthews celebrates bowling Zaheer Abbas at the MCG.

Big three leave with records

Sydney, Jan. 6. Australia won the Test and the series against Pakistan, but the big news was the retirements of three of the biggest names in Australian cricket – Greg Chappell, Dennis Lillee and Rod Marsh. The way they played in this match not only demonstrated their true stature in the game, but perhaps that there were a few games still left in them.

Greg Chappell became one of the few players to make a century in his first and last Tests, and also broke Sir Donald Bradman's aggregate of Test runs for Australia and passed the 7000 mark. Chappell modestly and correctly pointed to the fact that he played a few more Tests than the Don to do it. But as his brother remarked, 'Greg is every inch a champion.'

So is Dennis Lillee. The last thing he did in Test cricket was take a wicket, making a world record 355 victims – coincidentally the same number as his partner in crime, Rod Marsh. Lillee took eight wickets in his last match, and Marsh made six catches – two c. Marsh b. Lillee classics. Another spectacular catch, Greg Chappell's snaring of Mudassar Nazar off the bowling of Geoff Lawson, was a record-equalling 120th catch – he finished with 122.

It was a very emotional game with first Chappell, after day two, then Lillee the next day and finally Marsh after the match announcing their retirements.

The game itself was a bit of an anticlimax as the realisation sank in for cricket followers that a great turning point in Australian cricket had been reached. However, the Man of the Series, Geoff Lawson, was going about his business, taking 5/95 and 4/48.

Australia won the match by ten wickets. But it was Greg Chappell, with 182 glorious runs, who was Man of the Match.

Greg Chappell – the master batsman.

Geoff Lawson traps Zaheer Abbas lbw.

South Africa looms as enticing target

Melbourne, Aug. 26. The allure of large contracts, said to be upwards of $100,000 to participate in 'rebel' tours of South Africa, has provoked a response from the Australian Cricket Board.

It has insisted that contracts to 'Key Players' be signed immediately, in order to secure them for the 1983–84 and 1984–85 seasons. As these contracts are worth just $12,000, this has caused some perturbation among the players.

One such tour of South Africa was apparently mooted while the

Australians were in England. It seems there was a meeting between Ali Bacher of the South African Cricket Union, Graham Yallop and Kepler Wessels, but unfortunately for them the story was leaked, which scotched the idea.

The Board also met with the secretaries of the State Associations on July 28 to discuss the matter – as well as the performance of Australia.

The contract matter seems likely to drag on through the season.

Yallop: Unhappy champion

In his controversial book *Lambs to the Slaughter*, Graham Yallop describes the atmosphere in the dressing room after he was selected for his first Test match in 1975–76. His selection was a surprise even to him. He replaced Rick McCosker.

'The dropping of McCosker angered Ian Chappell and his team-mates, and I copped the brunt of their annoyance. I may have been an unassuming guy at the time, but I was rudely awakened to the facts of life at Test level – thanks, or rather no thanks, to Chappell and the rest of the team. I was not exactly welcomed with open arms into the team. In fact I was lucky to discover my locker in the Australian dressing rooms. To top it off, Chappell figured that if I was selected to replace McCosker that's exactly what I would do ...'

Yallop was thrown in at the deep end at no. 3., ahead of the Chappells against Andy Roberts and Michael Holding – and had the satisfaction of being not out 16 in Australia's seven-wicket win in the fourth Test.

Yallop retained his place for the next two Tests, making 16, 16 not out, 47 and 43, and 57 – and showing that he had the determination and the ability to succeed at Test level. His career was long but up and down (or in-and-out), through the turbulent time of World Series Cricket and South Africa's isolation. He suffered injuries, he was dropped – but eventually captained Australia.

Although Yallop somehow came to be regarded as weak and genteel – perhaps because he went to Carey Grammar, where he was coached by Frank Tyson – he was an underestimated, durable cricketer. He played for Richmond in 1970–71, made his debut for Victoria in 1972–73, and was captain for three seasons from 1977, winning two Sheffield Shields.

After his initial three Tests against the West Indies in 1975–76, he was dropped for 1976–77 and the 1977 tour of England. He returned to the Australian side for the fifth Test against India in 1977–78 and scored a stylish 121, which assured him of a place on the tough tour of the West Indies. He made 317 runs at 45 in the Tests and had his jaw broken by Colin Croft after a brilliant 118 against Guyana.

He was appointed, dragooned

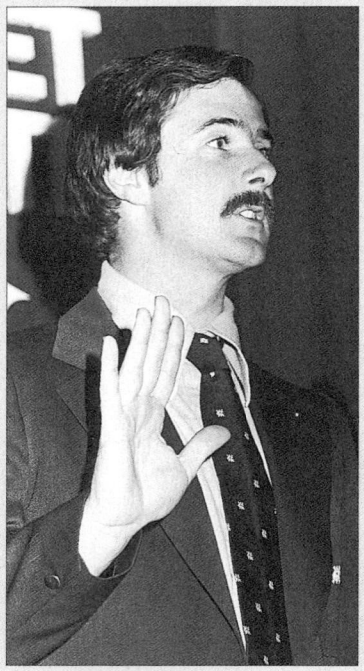

Graham Yallop: brilliant, tragic.

even, into the Australian captaincy in the post-Packer series of 1978–79, succeeding Bob Simpson.

Yallop's inferior team was whipped 5–1, but his batting stood up well. He made two centuries and more runs than any other Australian. He was then summarily dropped – as captain. He toured India successfully under Kim Hughes, but was dropped for the next summer's Test series.

Yallop was captain of Victoria in one further season in 1982–83, when it failed to win a game but Yallop had a great Ponsfordian year, scoring 1254 runs, breaking the 55-year-old record.

When called upon he went to Pakistan under Greg Chappell in 1979–80, contributing a splendid 172 in the second Test. A player less committed to Australian cricket might not have gone.

His career highlights after this include a brilliant 114 at Old Trafford on the 1981 Ashes tour, and a sensational series against Pakistan in Australia in 1983–84, including 268 at the MCG.

After a knee operation he joined the 'rebel' tours of South Africa in 1985–1987. This resulted in a suspension from first class cricket by the ACB. He played District cricket until 1991.

In another era Yallop might have been a great Australian batsman. In his era he was unhappy, perhaps tragic.

FIRST TEST 1983–84 AUSTRALIA v PAKISTAN
W.A.C.A. Ground, Perth. November 11, 12, 13, 14, 1983.
Toss: Pakistan. Australia won by an innings & 9 runs.

AUSTRALIA

KC Wessels c Wasim b Azeem	12
WB Phillips c Tahir b Mohammad	159
GN Yallop b Azeem	141
KJ Hughes (c) b Abdul	16
AR Border c Wasim b Azeem	32
GS Chappell c Azeem b Abdul	17
RW Marsh (+) c Wasim b Azeem	24
GF Lawson c Mohammad b Abdul	9
DK Lillee c Wasim b Azeem	0
RM Hogg not out	7
CG Rackemann	
EXTRAS (LB 9, W 3, NB 7)	19
TOTAL	9 dec 436

FOW 1st Inns: 34 293 321 369 386 404 424 424 436

Bowling: *First Innings*: Tahir 22-6-76-0, Azeem 27.3-5-100-5, Mudassar 15-1-39-0, Mohammad 29-5-91-1, Abdul 32-4-121-3.

PAKISTAN

Mohsin Khan c Marsh b Hogg	8	c Border b Rackemann	24
Mudassar Nazar c Phillips b Lillee	1	c Chappell b Rackemann	27
Qasim Omar c Yallop b Rackemann	48	c Marsh b Rackemann	65
Javed Miandad c Phillips b Hogg	0	lbw Rackemann	46
Zaheer Abbas (c) c Phillips b Hogg	0	c Marsh b Rackemann	30
Wasim Raja c Chappell b Rackemann	14	c Marsh b Lawson	4
Wasim Bari (+) c Chappell b Rackemann	0	c Marsh b Lawson	7
Tahir Naqqash not out	29	c Marsh b Rackemann	26
Abdul Qadir b Rackemann	5	run out	18
Mohammad Nazir c Chappell b Rackemann	16	c Border b Hogg	18
Azeem Hafeez c Border b Lawson	1	not out	0
EXTRAS (LB 3, NB 4)	7	(B 4, LB 7, W 2, NB 20)	33
TOTAL	129		298

FOW 1st Inns: 7 13 15 15 65 68 90 105 124 129
FOW 2nd Inns: 62 63 188 197 206 218 257 267 281 298

Bowling: *First Innings*: Lillee 13-3-26-1, Hogg 12-4-20-3, Rackemann 8-0-32-5, Lawson 7.2-0-48-1.
Second Innings: Lillee 29-6-56-0, Hogg 21.1-2-72-1, Rackemann 26-6-86-6, Lawson 13-1-53-2, Chappell 9-1-20-0.

Umpires: MW Johnson & PJ McConnell

SECOND TEST 1983–84 AUSTRALIA v PAKISTAN
Brisbane Cricket Ground, Brisbane. November 25, 26, 27, 28, 29 (no play), 1983.
Toss: Pakistan. Match Drawn.

PAKISTAN

Mohsin Khan c Chappell b Lawson	2	b Lawson	37
Mudassar Nazar c Marsh b Lawson	24	c Wessels b Rackemann	18
Qasim Omar c Hughes b Lawson	17	not out	11
Javed Miandad c Marsh b Hogg	6	c Phillips b Rackemann	5
Zaheer Abbas (c) c Border b Lawson	56	not out	3
Wasim Raja c Hughes b Rackemann	27		
Wasim Bari (+) c Border b Rackemann	2		
Abdul Qadir b Rackemann	0		
Rashid Khan not out	13		
Mohammad Nazir c Marsh b Hogg	1		
Azeem Hafeez b Lawson	2		
EXTRAS (LB 3, W 1, NB 2)	6	(LB 6, NB 2)	8
TOTAL	156		3 for 82

FOW 1st Inns: 10 39 46 62 124 128 128 146 147 156
FOW 2nd Inns: 57 59 74

Bowling: *First Innings*: Lawson 17.1-1-49-5, Hogg 15-2-43-2, Rackemann 10-3-28-3, Lillee 8-1-33-0.
Second Innings: Hogg 3-0-11-0, Lawson 10-3-24-1, Rackemann 8-1-31-2, Lillee 2-0-10-0.

AUSTRALIA

KC Wessels c Qasim b Azeem	35
WB Phillips b Rashid	46
GN Yallop c Wasim b Rashid	33
KJ Hughes (c) c Mohammad b Azeem	53
AR Border c Wasim b Rashid	118
GS Chappell not out	150
RW Marsh (+) b Azeem	1
GF Lawson b Abdul	49
DK Lillee	
CG Rackemann	
RM Hogg	
EXTRAS (B 2, LB 6, W 1, NB 15)	24
TOTAL	7 dec 509

FOW 1st Inns: 56 120 124 232 403 406 509

Bowling: *First Innings*: Azeem 37-7-152-3, Rashid 43-10-129-3, Mudassar 16-2-47-0, Abdul 32-5-112-1, Mohammad 24-6-50-0, Wasim 3-0-11-0.

Umpires: RA French & MW Johnson

THIRD TEST 1983–84 AUSTRALIA v PAKISTAN
Adelaide Oval, Adelaide. December 9, 10, 11, 12, 13, 1983.
Toss: Australia. Match Drawn.

AUSTRALIA

KC Wessels c Zaheer b Abdul	179	c Wasim b Sarfraz	2
WB Phillips c Wasim b Azeem	12	c Mudassar b Abdul	54
GN Yallop c Qasim b Sarfraz	68	c Javed b Abdul	14
KJ Hughes (c) c Wasim b Azeem	30	c Mudassar b Azeem	106
AR Border not out	117	lbw Azeem	66
GS Chappell c Wasim b Sarfraz	6	run out	4
RW Marsh (+) c Mohsin b Sarfraz	2	retired hurt	33
TG Hogan run out	2	c Qasim b Salim	8
GF Lawson c Wasim b Azeem	4	not out	7
DK Lillee c Sarfraz b Azeem	25	not out	4
RM Hogg c Javed b Azeem	5		
EXTRAS (LB 7, W 4, NB 4)	15	(B 3, LB 4, W 1, NB 4)	12
TOTAL	465		7 for 310

FOW 1st Inns: 21 163 219 353 376 378 383 394 451 465
FOW 2nd Inns: 3 44 121 216 228 293 305

Bowling: *First Innings*: Azeem 38.2-8-167-5, Sarfraz 42-7-105-3, Abdul 20-1-96-1, Mudassar 10-2-45-0, Mohammad 9-0-37-0, Mohsin 3-0-8-0. *Second Innings*: Sarfraz 30-8-69-1, Azeem 19-4-50-2, Abdul 47-9-132-2, Mohammad 27-14-39-0, Javed 3-0-10-0, Mohsin 1-1-0-0, Salim 1-0-3-1, Qasim 1-1-0-0.

PAKISTAN

Mohsin Khan c Phillips b Lawson	149
Mudassar Nazar c Marsh b Lillee	44
Qasim Omar c Marsh b Lillee	113
Javed Miandad lbw Lawson	131
Zaheer Abbas (c) c Yallop b Hogg	46
Salim Malik c Lawson b Hogan	77
Sarfraz Nawaz c Yallop b Lillee	32
Abdul Qadir b Lillee	10
Wasim Bari (+) c Marsh b Lillee	0
Mohammad Nazir not out	5
Azeem Hafeez c Wessels b Lillee	5
EXTRAS (B 1, LB 4, NB 7)	12
TOTAL	624

FOW 1st Inns: 73 306 314 371 557 590 604 612 613 624

Bowling: *First Innings*: Lawson 37-7-127-2, Hogg 34-3-123-1, Lillee 50.2-8-171-6, Hogan 37-8-107-1, Chappell 32-6-82-0, Border 1-0-9-0.

Umpires: AR Crafter & RA French

FOURTH TEST 1983–84 AUSTRALIA v PAKISTAN
Melbourne Cricket Ground, Melbourne. December 26, 27, 28, 29, 30, 1983.
Toss: Pakistan. Match Drawn.

PAKISTAN

Mohsin Khan lbw Lillee	152	c Hughes b Lillee	3
Mudassar Nazar c Marsh b Lawson	7	lbw Matthews	35
Qasim Omar b Maguire	23	b Lawson	9
Javed Miandad c Marsh b Maguire	27	lbw Lillee	11
Zaheer Abbas (6)	44	b Matthews	50
Salim Malik c Maguire b Lawson (8)	35	b Lillee	14
Imran Khan (c) c Marsh b Lillee	83	not out	72
Sarfraz Nawaz c Hughes b Maguire (9)	22	not out	11
Abdul Qadir c Lawson b Matthews (5)	45	b Lawson	12
Wasim Bari (+) not out	6		
Azeem Hafeez c Maguire b Matthews	7		
EXTRAS (LB 11, NB 8)	19	(B 10, LB 9, W 2)	21
TOTAL	470		7 for 238

FOW 1st Inns: 13 64 112 244 294 321 349 457 459 470
FOW 2nd Inns: 3 18 37 73 81 160 213

Bowling: *First Innings*: Lawson 38-8-125-2, Lillee 38-11-113-2, Maguire 29-7-111-3, Matthews 28.4-7-95-2, Chappell 7-3-15-0. *Second Innings*: Lawson 21-3-47-2, Lillee 29-7-71-3, Maguire 12-3-26-0, Matthews 21-8-48-2, Border 5-3-9-0, Chappell 8-3-13-0, Marsh 2-0-3-0, Wessels 2-1-2-0.

AUSTRALIA

KC Wessels c Wasim b Azeem	11
WB Phillips lbw Azeem	35
GN Yallop c Wasim b Sarfraz	268
KJ Hughes (c) lbw Azeem	94
AR Border lbw Abdul	32
GS Chappell c Salim b Abdul	5
RW Marsh (+) c Mudassar b Abdul	0
GRJ Matthews lbw Sarfraz	75
GF Lawson c Mudassar b Abdul	0
JN Maguire c Wasim b Abdul	4
DK Lillee not out	2
EXTRAS (B 15, LB 9, W 2, NB 3)	29
TOTAL	555

FOW 1st Inns: 21 70 273 342 354 354 539 540 553 555

Bowling: *First Innings*: Sarfraz 51-12-106-2, Azeem 35-8-115-3, Abdul 54.3-12-166-5, Mudassar 20-0-76-0, Javed 5-0-16-0, Zaheer 22-5-42-0, Salim 2-1-10-0.

Umpires: AR Crafter & PJ McConnell

FIFTH TEST 1983–84 AUSTRALIA v PAKISTAN
Sydney Cricket Ground, Sydney. January 2, 3, 4, 5, 6, 1984.
Toss: Australia. Australia won by 10 wkts.

PAKISTAN

Mohsin Khan c Border b Lillee	14	c Chappell b Lawson	1
Mudassar Nazar c Chappell b Lawson	84	b Lawson	21
Qasim Omar c Border b Lillee	15	c Marsh b Lawson	26
Abdul Qadir c Hughes b Lawson (9)	4	c Marsh b Lillee	5
Javed Miandad c Lillee b Matthews (4)	16	c Marsh b Lawson	60
Zaheer Abbas c Yallop b Lawson (5)	61	c Marsh b Hogg	33
Imran Khan (c) c Yallop b Lawson (6)	5	c Marsh b Hogg	10
Salim Malik c Lillee b Lawson (7)	54	c Chappell b Lillee	7
Sarfraz Nawaz lbw Lillee (8)	5	c Phillips b Lillee	20
Wasim Bari (+) not out	7	c Phillips b Lillee	20
Azeem Hafeez c Marsh b Lillee	4	not out	2
EXTRAS (B 2, LB 7)	9	(LB 4, NB 1)	5
TOTAL	278		210

FOW 1st Inns: 18 57 67 131 150 158 254 267 267 278
FOW 2nd Inns: 5 47 56 104 132 163 163 173 195 210

Bowling: *First Innings*: Lillee 31.2-10-65-4, Hogg 18-1-61-0, Chappell 8-0-25-0, Lawson 25-5-59-5, Matthews 18-4-59-1. *Second Innings*: Lillee 29.5-5-88-4, Lawson 20-7-48-4, Matthews 7-4-17-0, Hogg 14-2-53-2.

AUSTRALIA

KC Wessels c Wasim b Azeem	3	not out	14
WB Phillips c Salim b Sarfraz	37	not out	19
GN Yallop c Wasim b Mudassar	30		
GS Chappell lbw Mudassar	182		
KJ Hughes (c) lbw Sarfraz	76		
AR Border c Wasim b Mudassar	64		
GRJ Matthews not out	22		
RW Marsh (+) not out	15		
GF Lawson			
RM Hogg			
DK Lillee			
EXTRAS (LB 15, W 1, NB 9)	25	(NB 2)	2
TOTAL	6 dec 454		0 for 35

FOW 1st Inns: 11 66 83 254 407 436
FOW 2nd Inns:

Bowling: *First Innings*: Sarfraz 53-13-132-2, Azeem 36-7-121-1, Mudassar 31-9-81-3, Abdul 34-9-105-0. *Second Innings*: Sarfraz 3-1-7-0, Azeem 2.4-0-28-0.

Umpires: RA French & MW Johnson

Australian Averages

1983–84 AUSTRALIA v PAKISTAN

AUSTRALIA	M	Inn	NO	Runs	H.S	Avrge	Ct	St	Overs	Mds	Runs	Wkt	Avrge
Border, AR	5	6	1	429	118	85.80	7	-	6.0	3	18	-	-
Chappell, GS	5	6	1	364	182	72.80	8	-	64.0	13	155	-	-
Hogan, TG	1	2	-	10	8	5.00	-	-	37.0	8	107	1	107.00
Hogg, RM	4	2	1	12	7*	12.00	-	-	117.1	14	383	9	42.56
Hughes, KJ	5	6	-	375	106	62.50	5	-	-	-	-	-	-
Lawson, GF	5	5	1	69	49	17.25	2	-	188.3	40	580	24	24.17
Lillee, DK	5	4	2	31	25	15.50	2	-	230.3	51	633	20	31.65
Maguire, JN	1	1	-	4	4	4.00	2	-	41.0	10	137	3	45.67
Marsh, RW	5	6	2	75	33*	18.75	21	-	2.0	-	3	-	-
Matthews, GRJ	2	2	1	97	75	97.00	-	-	74.4	23	219	5	43.80
Phillips, WB	5	7	1	362	159	60.33	7	-	-	-	-	-	-
Rackemann, CG	2								52.0	10	177	16	11.06
Wessels, KC	5	7	1	256	179	42.67	2	-	2.0	1	2	-	-
Yallop, GN	5	6	-	554	268	92.33	5	-	-	-	-	-	-

Pakistani Averages

1983–84 AUSTRALIA v PAKISTAN

PAKISTAN	M	Inn	NO	Runs	H.S	Avrge	Ct	St	Overs	Mds	Runs	Wkt	Avrge
Abdul Qadir	5	8	-	99	45	12.38	-	-	219.3	40	732	12	61.00
Azeem Hafeez	5	7	2	21	7	4.20	1	-	195.3	39	733	19	38.58
Imran Khan	2	4	1	170	83	56.67	-	-	-	-	-	-	-
Javed Miandad	5	9	-	302	131	33.56	2	-	8.0	-	26	-	-
Mohammad Nazir	3	4	1	40	18	13.33	2	-	89.0	25	217	1	217.00
Mohsin Khan	5	9	-	390	152	43.33	1	-	4.0	-	8	-	-
Mudassar Nazar	5	9	-	261	84	29.00	4	-	92.0	14	288	3	96.00
Qasim Omar	5	9	-	327	113	40.88	3	-	1.0	-	0	-	-
Rashid Khan	1	1	1	13	13*	-	-	-	43.0	10	129	3	43.00
Salim Malik	3	5	-	187	77	37.40	2	-	3.0	1	13	1	13.00
Sarfraz Nawaz	5	5	1	90	32	22.50	1	-	179.0	41	419	8	52.38
Tahir Naqqash	1	2	1	55	29*	55.00	1	-	22.0	6	76	-	-
Wasim Bari	5	7	2	42	20	8.40	15	-	-	-	-	-	-
Wasim Raja	2	3	-	45	27	15.00	2	-	3.0	-	11	-	-
Zaheer Abbas	5	9	1	323	61	40.38	1	-	22.0	5	42	-	-

Defiant Border carries Australian flag

Port-of-Spain, March 21. Defiant and courageous batting by Allan Border in both innings of the second Test saved Australia from defeat. His 98 and 100 not out were epics of concentration, occupying five hours and 49 minutes in the first innings and four hours 45 minutes in the second.

Border's hundred came with a straight drive to the fence, after which acting West Indian captain Viv Richards shook Border by the hand and acknowledged the game as a draw.

This result seemed most unlikely when the eighth wicket fell. Australia, still 17 behind with three hours to play, had only Rod Hogg and Terry Alderman to come. But they batted with grit – Hogg staying until the score was 238 and an innings defeat was avoided. Alderman batted like a man with a chance to save his life when he entered the field just after tea.

Richards didn't take the new ball for 10 overs, while Alderman survived and Border accumulated. By the time the new ball was taken they were in a groove and were still in it after 280 balls and 105 minutes – when Border made his century. As they left the field the Trinidad crowd gave Border a grand reception. He said he felt like he'd been 'steam ironed'. Some might consider it his finest hour, but he thought of it as his finest ten hours, comparable with the tension he felt when he and Jeff Thomson just failed to beat England in the last-wicket action of December 1982.

The great second-innings ton should not overshadow the first-innings 98, half of which was completed with young Dean Jones in a century stand.

Two draws in the first two Tests is some achievement for this young Australian team. But it may be a different story when all the top Windies fast bowlers are back.

Allan Border: 100 at Queen's Park.

'No-go' Hughes drops his bundle: behaviour 'insulting'

The inexperienced Australian team required reinforcements because of injury in the West Indies in 1984.

Pointe-a-Pierre, March 12. This already bad-tempered tour reached a new low when Australian captain Kim Hughes, protesting against Trinidad and Tobago skipper Nanan's unwillingness to make a game of it by declaring either innings, refused to take runs while batting in the second innings.

He patted back long hops, half volleys and full tosses, and made only 10 runs from 24 overs he faced from mostly part-time bowlers.

At the other end, Wayne Phillips batted the same way and at one stage sat on the ground as the bowler delivered the ball. Phillips also took his pads off in the last over, tucking them under his arm. Hughes refused Nanan's offer to call the game off early – and afterwards said that he had no commitment to Trinidadian cricket or to its supporters.

Hughes was rebuked for this insulting behaviour by the local press, and was admonished by the tour management who fined him $400. The committee comprised manager Colin Egar, Allan Border and Geoff Lawson. Border said: 'It was not brilliant stuff from an international relations viewpoint.'

Clive Lloyd makes flying visit

Melbourne, April 15. Clive Lloyd flew to Melbourne between the fourth and fifth Tests in the West Indies to give evidence in the libel case against the Melbourne *Age*, resulting from an article 'C'mon Dollar C'mon' which was about the one day match played on 19 January 1982.

Australia won the rain-shortened match, and the article alleged that the West Indies threw the match for financial reasons – to ensure an Australia v West Indies final.

Lloyd as West Indian captain brought a libel action against the newspaper. In evidence it was shown that the West Indies played for a guaranteed fee, not based on percentage of gate takings – and could in no way have benefited whoever they played in the final.

Lloyd asserted that by libelling the whole team each player was also libelled, including him. The court found in his favour, awarding damages of $100,000 plus costs against the *Age*. Lloyd returned to the West Indies for the fifth Test.

The *Age* has given notice of appeal, contending that as no individual player was mentioned there could have been no libel of Lloyd. The West Indian captain believes that it would be absurd to think that a team could be held responsible for an action without the individual players in it, especially the captain, being also responsible.

The case is certain to be subject to appeals at the highest possible level.

Big Bird and Border

Kingston, May 2. West Indies giant fast bowler Joel Garner dominated the bowling averages with 31 wickets at the miserly average of 16.87. He bowled 208.5 overs, 53 maidens and took 31/523. His best was 6/60 in the first innings of the second Test.

Partners in crime for the West Indies were Malcolm Marshall, 21 wickets at 22.85 and Michael Holding, 13 at 18.84.

For Australia only Geoff Lawson's 12 wickets stood out – but his cost was 53.16. Rodney Hogg took 9 at 40.55 and Tom Hogan 8 at 60.37.

Allan Border's 521 runs at 74.42 was streets ahead of any other Australian – next best was Wayne Phillips with 258 at 25.8.

For the West Indies, Desmond Haynes made 468 at 93.6, Gordon Greenidge 393 at 78.6 and Richie Richardson 327 from just five innings, at 81.75.

Windies pacemen wrap up the series

Joel Garner: big and fast.

Malcolm Marshall: just fast.

Kingston, May 2. A dispirited and outplayed Australian side was demolished for the third Test in a row by Malcolm Marshall, Joel Garner and Michael Holding.

That this Test was the hundredth home Test for the West Indies and Clive Lloyd's hundredth appearance made it special for them – but for Australia the only special feat was Allan Border scoring another hundred – 41 and 60 not out for the match.

The Test was played after an entertaining game at Castries on St Lucia against the Windward Islands, which Australia, not facing the might of Garner & Co., might have won – but it was followed by two depressing one day internationals where Australia was thumped.

The fifth Test was the most discouraging of all.

Lloyd sent Australia in for the fifth Test in succession, Garner broke Steve Smith's finger, and Gordon Greenidge made a century to add to those by Desmond Haynes (third Test), Richie Richardson (third and fourth) and Viv Richards (fourth).

That's the way it was in the three final Tests – the West Indies batting once and bowling Australia (except for Border) out pretty easily. The exception was the third Test in Bridgetown, where, thanks to an impressive 120 from 'keeper Wayne Phillips (who had replaced the injured Roger Woolley in the second Test) and 68 from Graham Wood, Australia made 429.

The West Indies replied with a stunning 509 (Richardson 131 not out) after retaining his place when Gus Logie caught the flu) and then bowled Australia out for 97. On the final morning Marshall took 3/18 and Holding 3/9, as Australia lost 6/29.

The fourth Test at St John's took place just three days after the depressing collapse at Bridgetown. Rodney Hogg and Wood were injured and could not play, and except for Border's 98 and David Hookes' 51, the batting was unable to cope.

The West Indies made their third score of over 450 in a row, Richardson 154 and Richards 178. Their partnership of 308 was larger than either Australian innings. Richard's innings was the highest scored at the Recreation Ground. Carl Rackemann was an unflagging contributor, at one stage bowling 27 overs in succession, finishing with 5/160. The West Indies won by an innings and 36 runs.

Clive Lloyd holds the Frank Worrell Trophy after the fifth-Test win in Jamaica.

Kim Hughes: brilliant but...

Kim Hughes' place in Australian cricket will be forever stained by the way he left, or abandoned, the captaincy of Australia on 27 November 1985, after the Test in Brisbane against the West Indies.

Australia had been thrashed for the fifth time in five Tests, Hughes had made 34 and 4, and he was not getting the support (perhaps had never had it) of his team-mates.

Hughes played two more Tests. He ended his 70-Test career with an average of 37.41 and nine centuries – career statistics that perhaps demonstrate he was not quite as good as he looked when he was on song with the bat.

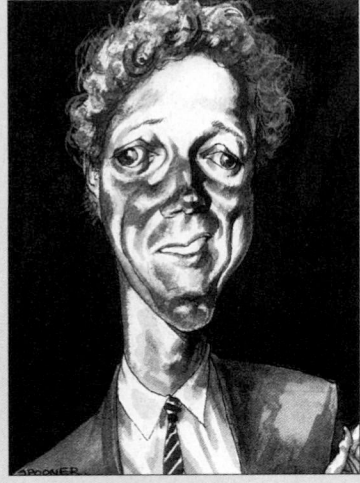

Kim Hughes: teary farewell.

As captain he was given some hard tasks and tours, and won only four of 28 Tests, with 11 draws and 13 losses.

That less-than-satisfactory listing belies not only the promise of Hughes' batting, but also its glorious actuality – as anyone who saw Hughes bat at the 1980 Centenary Test at Lord's would attest. Here it was not a case of a 'good batsman, but ...' No, here was a batsman in a great match, whose audacious driving and cutting illuminated every one of the rain-sodden playing days. One hit onto the pavilion roof lives on in Test cricket memory.

The blonde curly-haired and boyish-looking right-hander was born on Australia Day 1954 in the Western Australian wine-growing region of Margaret River.

He made his Sheffield Shield debut against NSW in 1975–76 with a poised 119 and 60, and seemed the quintessential dashing and elegant young batsman.

He was picked for the 1977 tour of England, and made just one in the drawn fifth Test of that series. He was in and out of the Australian side in the 1977–78 summer, but played in the first test against England at the 'Gabba in 1978–79 where he made 4 and a splendid 129, most of them in partnership with Graham Yallop.

Hughes took over the captaincy from Yallop at the end of the disastrous 1978–79 series, winning one of the two Tests against Pakistan, before taking Australia to a lacklustre performance in the 1979 World Cup, and a tour to India in August 1979. He made 100 in a 222-run partnership with Allan Border in the drawn first Test. Hughes made 92 and 64 not out in the drawn fifth Test.

In 1979–80, the 'reconciliation summer' under Greg Chappell against England, Hughes made 99 in Perth, and against the West Indies in the first Test made 130 not out. He went to Pakistan under Chappell and made two 80s in the Tests.

Hughes' highest score was 213 in the drawn Adelaide Test in January 1981.

Chappell decided not to tour England in 1981, and Hughes became captain again. He made 89 in the Leeds Test where England, through Ian Botham and Bob Willis, won the match after following-on – out-thought and outmotivated by new captain Mike Brearley. This destroyed Australia for the rest of that tour.

Under Chappell again in 1981–82 against Pakistan, Hughes made 106 in Perth, then 100 not out, of 198 on Boxing Day in Melbourne against the West Indies – a Test Australia won.

His reward was to be made captain again for the disastrous and chaotic tour of Pakistan, lost 3–nil.

Hughes hit the winning runs in Brisbane in the second Test in 1982–83 against England, and made 137 in the fifth Test. The Ashes regained – Chappell stepped down as captain. And Kim Hughes's somewhat tragic denouement commenced.

After resigning the captaincy he was soon dropped, and not being chosen for the England tour of 1985, he went to South Africa He made 97 not out in the second unofficial 'Test' at Cape Town. In the winter of 1986 he was in court fighting the WACA decision not to let him play club cricket. He won, and played three seasons in South Africa for Natal.

FIRST TEST 1983–84 WEST INDIES v AUSTRALIA
Bourda, Georgetown. March 2, 3, 4, 6, 7, 1984.
Toss: Australia. Match Drawn.

AUSTRALIA

SB Smith c Dujon b Garner	3	c Dujon b Garner ... 12
KC Wessels c Lloyd b Garner	4	c Lloyd b Daniel ... 20
GM Ritchie c Davis b Harper	78	lbw Garner ... 3
KJ Hughes (c) b Garner	18	c Haynes b Daniel ... 0
AR Border b Garner	5	run out ... 54
DW Hookes c Dujon b Harper	32	b Garner ... 10
WB Phillips (+) c Greenidge b Harper	16	b Daniel ... 76
GF Lawson c Richards b Harper	11	not out ... 35
TG Hogan not out	42	lbw Davis ... 18
TM Alderman lbw Garner	1 (11)	not out ... 3
RM Hogg lbw Garner	52 (10)	b Davis ... 6
EXTRAS (B 2, LB 3, W 1, NB 11)	17	(B 10, LB 15, NB 11) ... 36
TOTAL	279	9 dec 273

FOW 1st Inns: 6 23 55 63 139 166 180 181 182 279
FOW 2nd Inns: 37 41 42 50 60 185 209 249 263

Bowling: *First Innings*: Garner 27.2-10-75-6, Daniel 12-3-60-0, Davis 19-2-45-0, Harper 24-7-56-4, Gomes 15-1-35-0, Richards 5-2-3-0. *Second Innings*: Garner 24-5-67-3, Daniel 27-4-86-3, Davis 14-3-35-2, Harper 15-4-27-0, Gomes 11-2-25-0, Richards 6-2-8-0.

WEST INDIES

CG Greenidge c Wessels b Lawson	16	not out ... 120
DL Haynes lbw Hogg	60	not out ... 103
RB Richardson lbw Lawson	19	
IVA Richards c Phillips b Hogg	8	
HA Gomes c Border b Hogan	10	
CH Lloyd c Phillips b Alderman	36	
PJL Dujon (+) b Hogan	21	
RA Harper b Hogan	10	
J Garner not out	16	
WW Davis c Ritchie b Hogan	11	
WW Daniel lbw Lawson	4	
EXTRAS (LB 3, NB 16)	19	(B 10, LB 13, NB 4) ... 27
TOTAL	230	0 for 250

FOW 1st Inns: 29 72 93 110 154 181 191 203 225 230
FOW 2nd Inns:

Bowling: *First Innings*: Lawson 20.4-4-59-3, Alderman 21-3-64-1, Hogg 12-0-48-2, Hogan 25-9-56-4. *Second Innings*: Hogg 13-0-56-0, Alderman 11-0-43-0, Lawson 18-0-54-0, Hogan 19-2-74-0.

Umpires: DM Archer & DJ Narine

SECOND TEST 1983–84 WEST INDIES v AUSTRALIA
Queen's Park Oval, Port-of-Spain. March 16, 17, 18, 20, 21, 1984.
Toss: West Indies. Match Drawn.

AUSTRALIA

KC Wessels c Gomes b Garner	4	lbw Garner ... 4
WB Phillips (+) c Dujon b Garner	4	run out ... 0
GM Ritchie b Garner	1	b Small ... 26
KJ Hughes (c) c Dujon b Garner	24	lbw Marshall ... 33
AR Border not out	98 (6)	not out ... 100
DW Hookes b Garner	23 (7)	c Richardson b Gomes ... 21
DM Jones c & b Richards	48 (8)	b Richards ... 5
GF Lawson c & b Daniel	14 (9)	b Marshall ... 20
TG Hogan c Greenidge b Daniel	0 (5)	c Logie b Daniel ... 38
RM Hogg c Marshall b Daniel	11	c Garner b Richards ... 9
TM Alderman c Richardson b Garner	1	not out ... 21
EXTRAS (B 6, LB 4, NB 17)	27	(B 6, LB 1, W 1, NB 14) ... 22
TOTAL	255	9 for 299

FOW 1st Inns: 4 7 16 50 85 185 233 233 253 255
FOW 2nd Inns: 1 35 41 114 115 162 196 238 299

Bowling: *First Innings*: Garner 28.1-9-60-6, Marshall 19-4-73-0, Daniel 15-2-40-3, Small 10-3-24-0, Gomes 10-0-33-0, Richards 10-4-15-1. *Second Innings*: Marshall 22-3-73-2, Garner 15-4-35-1, Small 14-2-51-1, Daniel 9-3-11-1, Richards 25-5-65-2, Gomes 27-5-53-1, Logie 0.1-0-4-0.

WEST INDIES

CG Greenidge c Phillips b Hogg	24
DL Haynes run out	53
RB Richardson c Wessels b Alderman	23
IVA Richards (c) c Phillips b Alderman	76
HA Gomes b Lawson	3
AL Logie lbw Hogan	97
PJL Dujon (+) b Hogan	130
MD Marshall lbw Lawson	10
J Garner not out	24
WW Daniel not out	6
MA Small	
EXTRAS (B 7, LB 12, W 2, NB 1)	22
TOTAL	8 dec 468

FOW 1st Inns: 35 93 124 129 229 387 430 462

Bowling: *First Innings*: Lawson 32-3-132-2, Hogg 31-2-103-1, Alderman 35-9-91-2, Hogan 28-3-123-2.

Umpires: DM Archer & CE Cumberbatch

THIRD TEST 1983–84 WEST INDIES v AUSTRALIA
Kensington Oval, Bridgetown. March 30, 31, April 1, 3, 4, 1984.
Toss: West Indies. West Indies won by 10 wkts.

AUSTRALIA
SB Smith c Dujon b Marshall	10	b Marshall	7
GM Wood c Dujon b Holding	68	lbw Garner	20
GM Ritchie c & b Harper	57	c Haynes b Marshall	0
KJ Hughes (c) c Lloyd b Marshall	20	c Lloyd b Holding	25
AR Border c Richardson b Marshall	38 (6)	c Dujon b Holding	8
DW Hookes c Dujon b Garner	30 (7)	b Holding	9
TG Hogan b Garner	40 (5)	c Richardson b Holding	2
WB Phillips (+) c Dujon b Garner	120	b Marshall	1
GF Lawson b Baptiste	10	c Harper b Marshall	2
RM Hogg c Garner b Harper	3	not out	5
TM Alderman not out	2	b Marshall	0
EXTRAS (B 14, LB 8, NB 9)	31	(B 1, LB 6, NB 11)	18
TOTAL	429		97

FOW 1st Inns: 11 114 158 171 223 263 307 330 366 429
FOW 2nd Inns: 13 13 63 65 68 80 85 85 92 97

Bowling: *First Innings*: Garner 33.5-6-110-3, Marshall 26-2-83-2, Holding 30-5-94-2, Baptiste 17-5-34-1, Harper 43-9-86-2. *Second Innings*: Marshall 15.5-1-42-5, Garner 8-4-9-1, Holding 15-4-24-4, Harper 2-1-1-0, Baptiste 3-0-14-0.

WEST INDIES
CG Greenidge run out	64	not out	10
DL Haynes b Hogg	145	not out	11
RB Richardson not out	131		
IVA Richards b Lawson	6		
EAE Baptiste b Lawson	11		
PJL Dujon (+) b Alderman	2		
CH Lloyd (c) b Hogg	76		
MD Marshall b Hogg	10		
RA Harper b Hogg	19		
J Garner c Phillips b Hogg	9		
MA Holding c Smith b Hogg	0		
EXTRAS (LB 25, NB 11)	36		0
TOTAL	509		0 for 21

FOW 1st Inns: 132 277 289 313 316 447 465 493 509 509
FOW 2nd Inns:

Bowling: *First Innings*: Lawson 33.2-4-150-2, Alderman 42.4-6-152-1, Hogg 32.4-4-77-6, Hogan 34-8-97-0, Border 3-1-8-0. *Second Innings*: Lawson 2-1-3-0, Alderman 1.4-0-18-0.

Umpires: DM Archer & LH Barker

FOURTH TEST 1983–84 WEST INDIES v AUSTRALIA
Recreation Ground, St John's. April 7, 8, 9, 11, 1984.
Toss: Australia. West Indies won by an innings & 36 runs.

AUSTRALIA
WB Phillips c Dujon b Garner	5	b Garner	22
GM Ritchie c Holding b Marshall	6	c Dujon b Garner	23
AR Border c Dujon b Baptiste	98	c Greenidge b Baptiste	19
KJ Hughes (c) c Marshall b Harper	24	c Richards b Marshall	29
DM Jones b Harper	1	c Dujon b Garner	11
DW Hookes c Richardson b Baptiste	51	c Greenidge b Holding	29
RD Woolley (+) c Dujon b Baptiste	13	lbw Marshall	8
TG Hogan c Harper b Holding	14	c Baptiste b Garner	6
GF Lawson b Holding	4	not out	17
JN Maguire not out	15	b Marshall	0
CG Rackemann b Holding	12	b Garner	0
EXTRAS (B 5, LB 4, NB 10)	19	(B 19, LB 7, NB 10)	36
TOTAL	262		200

FOW 1st Inns: 14 14 67 78 202 208 217 224 246 262
FOW 2nd Inns: 50 57 97 116 150 167 176 185 185 200

Bowling: *First Innings*: Marshall 18-2-70-1, Garner 18-5-34-1, Holding 19.5-3-42-3, Harper 19-4-58-2, Baptiste 17-2-42-3, Richards 5-0-7-0. *Second Innings*: Marshall 17-5-51-3, Garner 20.5-2-63-5, Holding 14-2-22-1, Baptiste 8-2-14-1, Harper 6-0-24-0.

WEST INDIES
CG Greenidge c Ritchie b Lawson	0
DL Haynes b Lawson	21
RB Richardson c Woolley b Rackemann	154
IVA Richards c Woolley b Rackemann	178
PJL Dujon (+) c Hughes b Rackemann	28
CH Lloyd (c) c Jones b Rackemann	38
MD Marshall c Hookes b Maguire	6
EAE Baptiste b Maguire	6
RA Harper c Ritchie b Maguire	27
J Garner c Hogan b Rackemann	10
MA Holding not out	3
EXTRAS (B 13, LB 13, NB 1)	27
TOTAL	498

FOW 1st Inns: 0 43 351 390 405 426 442 468 491 498

Bowling: *First Innings*: Lawson 29-4-125-2, Rackemann 42.4-8-161-5, Maguire 44-9-121-3, Hogan 30-9-65-0.

Umpires: DM Archer & AE Weekes

FIFTH TEST 1983–84 WEST INDIES v AUSTRALIA
Sabina Park, Kingston. April 28, 29, 30, May 2, 1984.
Toss: West Indies. West Indies won by 10 wkts.

AUSTRALIA
WB Phillips (+) c Dujon b Garner	12	b Garner	2
SB Smith c Greenidge b Marshall	9	not out	60
AR Border c Dujon b Marshall	41	b Holding	8
GM Ritchie c Dujon b Marshall	5	c Greenidge b Marshall	23
KJ Hughes (c) c Harper b Holding	19	c Dujon b Marshall	7
DW Hookes b Harper	36	b Holding	7
GRJ Matthews st Dujon b Harper	7 (2)	b Holding	7
TG Hogan c & b Garner	25 (7)	b Marshall	10
GF Lawson c Harper b Garner	15 (8)	b Marshall	4
RM Hogg not out	1 (9)	b Marshall	14
JN Maguire b Baptiste	9 (10)	b Marshall	0
EXTRAS (B 8, LB 3, W 1, NB 8)	20	(B 17, LB 4, NB 4)	25
TOTAL	199		9 dec 160

FOW 1st Inns: 22 23 34 73 113 124 142 181 190 199
FOW 2nd Inns: 7 15 27 89 109 125 131 159 160

Bowling: *First Innings*: Marshall 18-4-37-3, Garner 17-4-42-3, Holding 12-2-43-1, Baptiste 11-3-40-1, Harper 20-8-26-2. *Second Innings*: Marshall 23-3-51-5, Garner 16.4-6-28-2, Holding 11-4-20-2, Baptiste 6-3-11-0, Harper 9-2-25-0, Richards 2-0-4-0.

WEST INDIES
CG Greenidge c Ritchie b Hogan	127	not out	32
DL Haynes b Hogan	60	not out	15
RB Richardson c Phillips b Lawson	0		
IVA Richards run out	2		
CH Lloyd (c) c Phillips b Lawson	20		
PJL Dujon (+) c Phillips b Lawson	23		
MD Marshall c Hookes b Maguire	19		
EAE Baptiste c Lawson b Maguire	27		
RA Harper c Phillips b Maguire	0		
J Garner c Phillips b Lawson	7		
MA Holding not out	0		
EXTRAS (B 1, LB 11, NB 8)	20	(B 2, LB 3, NB 3)	8
TOTAL	305		0 for 55

FOW 1st Inns: 162 169 174 213 228 260 274 274 297 305
FOW 2nd Inns:

Bowling: *First Innings*: Lawson 30-6-91-3, Hogg 16-2-67-0, Hogan 30-8-68-2, Maguire 16.4-2-57-4, Matthews 2-0-10-0. *Second Innings*: Lawson 5-0-24-0, Hogg 5.2-0-18-0, Maguire 1-0-8-0.

Umpires: DM Archer & LH Barker

Australian Averages

1983–84 WEST INDIES v AUSTRALIA

AUSTRALIA	M	Inn	NO	Runs	H.S	Avrge	Ct	St	Overs	Mds	Runs	Wkt	Avrge
Alderman, TM	3	6	3	44	21*	9.33	-	-	111.2	18	368	4	92.00
Border, AR	5	10	3	521	100*	74.43	-	-	3.0	1	8	-	-
Hogan, TG	5	10	1	195	42*	21.67	1	-	166.0	39	483	8	60.38
Hogg, RM	4	8	2	101	52	16.83	-	-	110.0	8	369	9	41.00
Hookes, DW	5	10	-	248	51	24.80	2	-	-	-	-	-	-
Hughes, KJ	5	10	-	215	33	21.50	1	-	-	-	-	-	-
Jones, DM	2	4	-	65	48	16.25	1	-	-	-	-	-	-
Lawson, GF	5	10	2	132	35*	16.50	1	-	170.0	22	638	12	53.17
Maguire, JN	2	4	1	24	15*	8.00	-	-	61.4	11	186	7	26.57
Matthews, GRJ	1	2	-	14	7	7.00	-	-	2.0	0	10	-	-
Phillips, WB	5	10	-	258	120	25.80	10	-	-	-	-	-	-
Rackemann, CG	1	2	-	12	12	6.00	-	-	42.4	8	161	5	32.20
Ritchie, GM	5	10	-	207	78	20.70	4	-	-	-	-	-	-
Smith, SB	3	5	-	41	12	8.20	1	-	-	-	-	-	-
Wessels, KC	2	4	-	32	20	8.00	2	-	-	-	-	-	-
Wood, GM	1	2	-	88	68	44.00	-	-	-	-	-	-	-
Woolley, RD	1	2	-	21	13	10.50	2	-	-	-	-	-	-

West Indian Averages

1983--84 WEST INDIES v AUSTRALIA

WEST INDIES	M	Inn	NO	Runs	H.S	Avrge	Ct	St	Overs	Mds	Runs	Wk	Avrge
Baptiste, EAE	3	3	-	44	27	14.67	1	-	62.0	15	155	6	25.83
Daniel, WW	2	2	1	10	6*	10.00	1	-	63.0	12	197	7	28.14
Davis, WW	1	1	-	11	11	11.00	1	-	33.0	5	80	2	40.00
Dujon, PJL	5	5	-	204	130	40.80	19	1	-	-	-	-	-
Garner, J	5	5	2	66	24*	22.00	3	-	208.5	55	523	31	16.87
Gomes, HA	2	2	-	13	10	6.50	1	-	63.0	8	146	1	146.00
Greenidge, CG	5	8	3	393	127	78.60	6	-	-	-	-	-	-
Harper, RA	4	4	-	56	27	14.00	5	-	138.0	35	303	10	30.30
Haynes, DL	5	8	3	468	145	93.60	2	-	-	-	-	-	-
Holding, MA	3	3	2	3	3*	3.00	1	-	101.5	20	245	13	18.85
Lloyd, CH	4	4	-	170	76	42.50	4	-	-	-	-	-	-
Logie, AL	1	1	-	97	97	97.00	1	-	0.1	-	4	-	-
Marshall, MD	4	4	-	45	19	11.25	2	-	158.5	24	480	21	22.86
Richards, IVA	5	5	-	270	178	54.00	3	-	53.0	13	102	3	34.00
Richardson, RB	5	5	1	327	154	81.75	5	-	-	-	-	-	-
Small, MA	1	-	-	-	-	-	-	-	24.0	5	75	1	75.00

Rampaging West Indies shatter Australia

PM shattered in memory lane match

Bob Hawke's hook shot.

Canberra, Oct. 15. It was just a social game between the Prime Minister's staff and the Parliamentary press gallery.

Prime Minister Hawke had nudged along to 28 runs and was facing Gary O'Neill of the Melbourne *Herald* when he edged a ball into his eyes.

He fell to the ground, glasses smashed, hands on his face, blood streaming between his fingers.

Fortunately there was no serious damage after fragments were removed at Canberra Hospital.

Hawke returned with a patch over his eye to receive the Bob Hawke Trophy, a bat-wielding garden gnome bearing a striking resemblance to you-know-who.

Adelaide, Dec. 11. Just before tea today, Australia and the West Indies commemorated the centenary of Test cricket at the Adelaide Oval. But for Australia, there was little else to celebrate.

This afternoon Australia lost any hope of taking the series when the West Indies won the third Test by 191 runs. The loss follows Australia's defeat by eight wickets in the second Test at Brisbane, and an innings-and-112-runs massacre at Perth in the first Test.

From the start at Perth, Australia never looked a chance. West Indies batsmen Larry Gomes and Jeffrey Dujon both scored centuries and then Australia was bowled all out for 76 in a first-innings debacle which saw Michael Holding take six wickets and Malcolm Marshall and Joel Garner clean up the rest.

From there, the only way had to be up, but Australia barely got off the ground at Brisbane. This time centuries were made by two other West Indians, captain Clive Lloyd (114) and Richie Richardson (138). Australia's top scorer was Wayne Phillips (44) in the first innings and Kepler Wessels (61) in the second.

The Australians looked better in the third Test this week, especially Geoff Lawson whose analysis of 8/112 was an outstanding performance. But the West Indies maintained their brilliant form. Gomes managed another fine century (120) and Marshall captured five wickets in both innings (5/69 and 5/38).

The West Indies' win today is their 11th consecutive Test victory, a world record.

Clive Lloyd plays his last Test in Australia.

Lloyd bows out. West Indies captain Clive Lloyd retired after the fifth Test in Sydney. Since his Test debut against India in 1966–67, Lloyd played in 110 Tests and made 7515 runs at an average of 46.67, including 19 centuries. He captained the West Indies for 74 Tests.

Dingoes did it. The former Australian opener and captain, Bill Lawry, told an Adelaide Rotary Club luncheon: 'What happened to Kim Hughes in Brisbane was like being dragged down like a dingo in the pack and devoured by your own from within and without.'

Double to NSW. New South Wales, coached by Bob Simpson, won both the Sheffield Shield and the McDonald's Cup in 1984–85. Pakistani 'import' Imran Khan proved a matchwinner in the Shield final when he captured nine wickets for NSW against Queensland.

India World Champs. The seven-country World Championship of Cricket was staged by the VCA in February and March 1985 to mark the 150th anniversary of Victoria. India defeated Pakistan by eight wickets in the final of this unique one-day series. India's Ravi Shastri was Champion of Champions, but did not repeat his recent feat of six sixes in six balls.

TV team. Channel Nine's cricket commentary team used the World Championship of Cricket to pick a hypothetical world's best one-day side. No Australian was selected in the team, which included Sunil Gavaskar, Joel Garner and Imran Khan, and had Richard Hadlee as 12th man.

One-day dominator. West Indian Viv Richards was Player of the Series in the Benson and Hedges World Series competition. His statistics for 11 innings included 651 runs, a highest score of 103 not out, an average of 65.10, and bowling figures of 11/496.

No smiling matter. When the West Indies met Sri Lanka in the World Championship of Cricket, wild deliveries from Sri Lankan speedster Rumesh Ratnayake hit Clive Lloyd on the head, Richie Richardson on the jaw, and Larry Gomes in the mouth. Gomes lost two front teeth.

Hughes dropped. After three ducks in four innings, Kim Hughes was not selected for the fifth Test against the West Indies. Hughes last scored a Test century (106) against Pakistan in Adelaide in 1983–84.

Bob's match. Bob Holland's match figures of 10/144 in the fifth Test were a record against the West Indies in Sydney. Murray Bennett claimed 5/124 in a triumph for the spin combination.

Hughes falls on his sword

Tired of 'constant speculation, criticism and innuendo', Kim Hughes steps down as Australian captain.

Brisbane, Nov. 26. Australian captain Kim Hughes has been subject to intense criticism lately for poor performances on-field by both himself and the team.

After Australia's loss to the West Indies shortly after lunch today, Hughes called a press conference in the dining room at the 'Gabba.

'The Australian cricket captaincy is something I have held very dear to me,' Hughes began, reading from a piece of paper.

'However, playing the game with total enjoyment has always been of greatest importance.'

Eyes half-closed, almost in a trance, he looked up for just a glance, then turned his head back down.

'The constant speculation, criticism and innuendo by former players and sections of the media over the last four or five years have finally taken their toll.'

At that, he seemed to reflect for a moment or two. Everything went quiet.

Hughes was poised, the memories and dreams of a lifetime flashing through his head.

He held the paper, trembling, choking, a tear in his eye.

And pierced his heart with the words: 'It is in the interests of the team, Australian cricket and myself that I have informed the Australian Cricket Board of my decision to stand down as captain.'

There was no going back. He knew it now. And everyone watched in stunned helplessness as he broke down and left the room, unable to proceed. He passed the statement to Bob Merriman, the Australian team manager.

'I look forward to continuing my career,' Merriman read, 'in whatever capacity the selectors and the Board see fit, with the same ability I have displayed as Australian captain.

'Gentlemen, I wish not to discuss this matter any further and I will not be available to answer any further questions.'

The words seemed strangely hollow, for the captain had gone. His corpse was cold.

Most witnesses were like the Australian vice-captain, Allan Border, who says he will never forget the 'gut-wrenching' pain of Hughes' departure.

But there were some who did not weep.

Hughes' resignation immediately followed two heavy defeats at the hands of the West Indies – by an innings and 112 runs in Perth and by eight wickets here in Brisbane.

In neither match did Hughes perform with the bat, scoring 4 and 37 in Perth and 34 and 4 here.

Not since his 76 against Pakistan in Sydney in January 1984 has Hughes posted a half-century in Tests.

One person who knew Hughes was about to resign was vice-captain Allan Border. Hughes had shown a stunned Border his speech during a break in play this morning.

As the tragedy unfolds, Border appears to be the man most likely to step into the captain's shoes. He lacks the bubbling, free-flowing personality of Kim Hughes at the crease, but he is experienced, mentally tough and respected by the players.

He hasn't asked for the job, but there are some who 'have greatness thrust upon them'.

Richards smokes but Hilditch hangs on for the draw

Viv Richards: stylish 208.

Melbourne, Dec. 28. Australia gasped its way to a draw with the West Indies in the fourth Test yesterday, thanks to 339 minutes of defiance by Andrew Hilditch.

The heat was almost unbearable as big Joel Garner dismissed Hilditch's team-mates, Graeme Wood (5), Kepler Wessels (0) and Kim Hughes (0) in the space of five balls for no runs.

But Hilditch (113) hung on to save Australia from its fourth defeat for the series.

A West Indian victory looked almost certain after their huge first innings total (479), which included a double century from Viv Richards (208), who lit up the MCG with three sixes and 22 fours in a dazzling 374-minute display.

The draw suggests the West Indies might yet run out of puff. They have not lost for 27 Tests in a row.

Tom Hughes QC and Clive Lloyd arrive at the NSW Supreme Court during an ongoing libel dispute with the Age. *The matter was settled out of court.*

Spinners bring some joy for Australia in Sydney

Sydney, Jan. 3. A month after taking over the Australian captaincy from Kim Hughes, Allan Border has tasted victory over the West Indies in the fifth Test at the SCG.

The West Indies gambled on the Sydney pitch suiting their armoury of pace bowlers.

They lost. By an innings and 55 runs. It was a terrible miscalculation.

Sydney has traditionally favoured spin, and Australia's selectors wisely let history be their guide. They chose Bob Holland, a 38-year-old leg-spinner from Newcastle, and teamed him up with the left-arm orthodox spinner, Murray Bennett. Both had little Test experience.

The West Indies, on the other hand, were so confident of success with their four pace bowlers that they did not even select off-spinner Roger Harper.

Their mistake was obvious in Australia's first innings, which was highlighted by 173 runs from Kepler Wessels. Australia was at the crease until just before lunch on the third day, when Border declared at 9/471.

The fast bowling of young Craig McDermott claimed the early wickets of West Indians Gordon Greenidge (18) and Richie Richardson (2) before Holland took a turn with the spinning ball.

And what a remarkable turn it

Murray Bennett: five wickets.

was. In 22 overs, Holland bowled seven maidens and took six wickets for a mere 54 runs. Bennett took 2/45 and pitched the West Indies all out for 163 runs.

In the follow-on, West Indies captain Clive Lloyd, playing in his last Test, made a valiant 72 runs, but apart from Viv Richards (58) the West Indies were no match again for Holland (4/90) and Bennett (3/79).

The Test loss ends the West Indies' record unbeaten run of 27 matches. It is the first time in four years that the West Indies have been beaten and the first time they have lost by an innings in 17 years.

And there was light! Night cricket arrives at the MCG on 17 February 1985, the opening night of the Benson and Hedges World Championship of Cricket. A fireworks display hailed Australia's seven-wicket win over England.

FIRST TEST 1984–85 AUSTRALIA v WEST INDIES
W.A.C.A. Ground, Perth. November 9, 10, 11, 12, 1984.
Toss: Australia. West Indies won by an innings & 112 runs.

WEST INDIES

CG Greenidge c Rackemann b Alderman	30
DL Haynes c Yallop b Hogg	56
RB Richardson b Alderman	0
HA Gomes b Hogg	127
IVA Richards c Phillips b Alderman	10
CH Lloyd (c) c Phillips b Alderman	0
PJL Dujon (+) c Phillips b Alderman	139
MD Marshall c Hughes b Hogg	21
MA Holding c Wood b Alderman	1
J Garner c Phillips b Hogg	17
CA Walsh not out	9
EXTRAS (B 1, LB 1, NB 4)	6
TOTAL	416

FOW 1st Inns: 83 83 89 104 104 186 335 337 387 416

Bowling: *First Innings:* Lawson 24-3-79-0, Rackemann 28-3-106-0, Hogg 32-6-101-4, Alderman 39-12-128-6.

AUSTRALIA

KC Wessels c Holding b Garner	13	c Lloyd b Garner	0
J Dyson c Lloyd b Marshall	0	b Marshall	30
GM Wood c Lloyd b Garner	6	c Richardson b Walsh	56
AR Border c Dujon b Holding	15	c Haynes b Marshall	6
KJ Hughes (c) c Marshall b Holding	4	lbw Marshall	37
GN Yallop c Greenidge b Holding	2	c Haynes b Walsh	1
WB Phillips (+) c Marshall b Holding	22	c Dujon b Garner	16
GF Lawson c Dujon b Marshall	1	not out	38
RM Hogg b Holding	0	b Marshall	0
CG Rackemann c Richardson b Holding	0	b Garner	0
TM Alderman not out	0	c Richardson b Holding	23
EXTRAS (B 4, LB 2, NB 7)	13	(LB 7, NB 14)	21
TOTAL	76		228

FOW 1st Inns: 1 18 28 40 46 55 58 63 63 76
FOW 2nd Inns: 4 94 107 107 124 166 168 168 169 228

Bowling: *First Innings:* Marshall 15-5-25-2, Garner 7-0-24-2, Holding 9.2-3-21-6. *Second Innings:* Garner 16-5-52-3, Marshall 21-4-68-4, Holding 11.3-1-53-1, Walsh 20-4-43-2, Gomes 1-0-1-0, Richards 1-0-4-0.

Umpires: AR Crafter & PJ McConnell

SECOND TEST 1984–85 AUSTRALIA v WEST INDIES
Brisbane Cricket Ground, Brisbane. November 23, 24, 25, 26, 1984.
Toss: West Indies. West Indies won by 8 wkts.

AUSTRALIA

J Dyson c Dujon b Holding	13		c Dujon b Marshall	21
KC Wessels b Garner	0		c Gomes b Walsh	61
GM Wood c Marshall b Walsh	20		c Richardson b Holding	3
AR Border c Lloyd b Marshall	17		c (S)RA Harper b Holding	24
KJ Hughes (c) c Marshall b Garner	34		lbw Holding	4
DC Boon c Richardson b Marshall	11		c Holding b Marshall	51
WB Phillips (+) c Dujon b Walsh	44	(8)	c (S)RA Harper b Holding	54
GF Lawson b Garner	14	(9)	c Richards b Marshall	14
TM Alderman c Lloyd b Walsh	0	(7)	c Richardson b Marshall	1
RG Holland c Dujon b Garner	6		b Marshall	0
RM Hogg not out	0		not out	21
EXTRAS (B 4, LB 1, NB 11)	16		(B 4, LB 5, NB 8)	17
TOTAL	175			271

FOW 1st Inns: 1 33 33 81 97 102 122 136 173 175
FOW 2nd Inns: 88 88 99 106 131 212 236 236 271 271

Bowling: *First Innings:* Garner 18.4-5-67-4, Marshall 14.4-5-39-2, Holding 6.2-2-9-1, Walsh 16-5-55-3. *Second Innings:* Marshall 34-7-82-5, Garner 20-4-80-0, Holding 30-7-92-4, Walsh 5-2-7-1, Richards 1-0-1-0.

WEST INDIES

CG Greenidge c Border b Lawson	44			
DL Haynes b Alderman	21	(1)	b Lawson	7
RB Richardson c Phillips b Alderman	138	(2)	c Alderman b Hogg	5
HA Gomes b Holland	13	(3)	not out	9
IVA Richards c Boon b Lawson	6	(4)	not out	3
PJL Dujon (+) c Phillips b Holland	14			
CH Lloyd (c) c Hughes b Alderman	114			
MD Marshall b Lawson	57			
MA Holding b Lawson	1			
J Garner not out	0			
CA Walsh c Phillips b Lawson	0			
EXTRAS (B 2, LB 6, NB 8)	16		(LB 2)	2
TOTAL	424			2 for 26

FOW 1st Inns: 36 99 129 142 184 336 414 423 424 424
FOW 2nd Inns: 6 18

Bowling: *First Innings:* Lawson 30.4-8-116-5, Alderman 29-10-107-3, Hogg 21-3-71-0, Holland 27-5-97-2, Border 5-0-25-0. *Second Innings:* Lawson 5-0-10-1, Hogg 4.1-0-14-1.

Umpires: RA French & MW Johnson

THIRD TEST 1984–85 AUSTRALIA v WEST INDIES
Adelaide Oval, Adelaide. December 7, 8, 9, 10, 11 1984.
Toss: West Indies. West Indies won by 191 runs.

WEST INDIES

CG Greenidge c Hogg b Lawson ...95		lbw Lawson ...4	
DL Haynes c Hughes b Hogg ...0		c Wood b Lawson ...50	
RB Richardson c Border b Lawson ...8	(4)	lbw Hogg ...3	
HA Gomes c Rixon b Lawson ...60	(5)	not out ...120	
IVA Richards c Rixon b Lawson ...0	(6)	c Rixon b Hogg ...42	
CH Lloyd (c) b Lawson ...78	(7)	c Rixon b Lawson ...6	
PJL Dujon (+) lbw Lawson ...77	(8)	c Boon b Holland ...32	
MD Marshall c Rixon b Lawson ...9			
RA Harper c Rixon b Lawson ...9	(3)	c Rixon b Hogg ...26	
J Garner not out ...8			
CA Walsh b Holland ...0			
EXTRAS (B 5, LB 4, NB 3) ...12		(LB 2, NB 7) ...9	
TOTAL ...356		...7 dec 292	

FOW 1st Inns: 4 25 157 157 172 322 331 348 355 356
FOW 2nd Inns: 4 39 45 121 218 225 292

Bowling: *First Innings*: Lawson 40-7-112-8, Hogg 28-7-75-1, Alderman 19-8-38-0, Holland 30.2-5-109-1, Wessels 5-0-13-0. *Second Innings*: Lawson 24-6-69-3, Hogg 21-2-77-3, Holland 18.1-1-54-1, Alderman 12-1-66-0, Border 4-0-24-0.

AUSTRALIA

GM Wood c Greenidge b Harper ...41	(7)	c Dujon b Harper ...19	
J Dyson c Dujon b Walsh ...8		lbw Marshall ...5	
KC Wessels b Marshall ...98	(1)	c Dujon b Harper ...70	
SJ Rixon (+) c Richards b Marshall ...0	(6)	lbw Harper ...16	
KJ Hughes c Dujon b Garner ...0	(2)	b Marshall ...2	
AR Border (c) c Garner b Marshall ...21	(3)	b Marshall ...18	
DC Boon c Dujon b Marshall ...12	(5)	c Harper b Garner ...9	
GF Lawson c Dujon b Garner ...49		c Dujon b Marshall ...2	
RG Holland c Haynes b Walsh ...2		not out ...7	
RM Hogg not out ...7		b Harper ...7	
TM Alderman c Richardson b Marshall ...10		b Marshall ...0	
EXTRAS (B 2, LB 8, NB 26) ...36		(B 7, LB 7, NB 4) ...18	
TOTAL ...284		...173	

FOW 1st Inns: 28 91 91 122 138 145 232 241 265 284
FOW 2nd Inns: 22 70 78 97 123 150 153 153 170 173

Bowling: *First Innings*: Marshall 26-8-69-5, Garner 26-5-61-2, Walsh 24-8-88-2, Harper 21-4-56-1.
Second Innings: Marshall 15.5-4-38-5, Garner 16-2-58-1, Walsh 4-0-20-0, Harper 15-6-43-4.

Umpires: AR Crafter & MW Johnson

FIFTH TEST 1984–85 AUSTRALIA v WEST INDIES
Sydney Cricket Ground, Sydney. December 30, 31, January 1, 2, 1985.
Toss: Australia. Australia won by an innings & 55 runs.

AUSTRALIA

AMJ Hilditch c Dujon b Holding ...2	
GM Wood c Haynes b Gomes ...45	
KC Wessels b Holding ...173	
GM Ritchie run out ...37	
AR Border (c) c Greenidge b Walsh ...69	
DC Boon b Garner ...49	
SJ Rixon (+) c Garner b Holding ...20	
MJ Bennett c Greenidge b Garner ...23	
GF Lawson not out ...5	
CJ McDermott c Greenidge b Walsh ...4	
RG Holland	
EXTRAS (B 7, LB 20, NB 17) ...44	
TOTAL ...9 for 471	

FOW 1st Inns: 12 126 338 342 350 392 450 463 471

Bowling: *First Innings*: Marshall 37-2-111-0, Garner 31-5-101-2, Holding 31-7-74-3, Walsh 38.2-1-118-2, Gomes 12-2-29-1, Richards 7-2-11-0.

WEST INDIES

CG Greenidge c Rixon b McDermott ...18		b Holland ...12	
DL Haynes c Wessels b Holland ...34		lbw McDermott ...3	
RB Richardson b McDermott ...2		c Wood b Bennett ...26	
HA Gomes c Bennett b Holland ...28		c Wood b Lawson ...8	
IVA Richards c Wessels b Holland ...15		b Bennett ...58	
CH Lloyd (c) c Wood b Holland ...33		c Border b McDermott ...72	
PJL Dujon (+) c Hilditch b Bennett ...22		c & b Holland ...8	
MD Marshall st Rixon b Holland ...0		not out ...32	
MA Holding c McDermott b Bennett ...0		c Wessels b Holland ...0	
J Garner c Rixon b Holland ...0		c Rixon b Bennett ...8	
CA Walsh not out ...1		c Bennett b Holland ...4	
EXTRAS (LB 3, NB 7) ...10		(B 2, LB 12, NB 8) ...22	
TOTAL ...163		...253	

FOW 1st Inns: 26 34 72 103 106 160 160 160 160 163
FOW 2nd Inns: 7 31 46 93 153 180 231 231 244 253

Bowling: *First Innings*: Lawson 9-1-27-0, McDermott 9-0-34-2, Bennett 22.5-7-45-2, Holland 22-7-54-6. *Second Innings*: Lawson 6-1-14-1, McDermott 12-0-56-2, Bennett 33-9-79-3, Holland 33-8-90-4.

Umpires: RC Isherwood & MW Johnson

FOURTH TEST 1984-85 AUSTRALIA v WEST INDIES
Melbourne Cricket Ground, Melbourne. December 22, 23, 24, 26, 27 1984.
Toss: Australia. Match Drawn.

WEST INDIES

CG Greenidge c Bennett b Lawson ...10		lbw Lawson ...1	
DL Haynes c Border b Lawson ...13		b McDermott ...63	
RB Richardson b McDermott ...51		b Lawson ...3	
HA Gomes c Matthews b McDermott ...68		c Bennett b McDermott ...18	
IVA Richards c Hughes b Matthews ...208		lbw McDermott ...0	
PJL Dujon (+) b McDermott ...0		not out ...49	
CH Lloyd (c) c Lawson b Matthews ...19		not out ...34	
MD Marshall c Rixon b Hogg ...55			
RA Harper c & b Hogg ...5			
J Garner lbw Lawson ...8			
CA Walsh not out ...18			
EXTRAS (B 1, LB 11, NB 12) ...24		(B 4, LB 9, NB 5) ...18	
TOTAL ...479		...5 dec 186	

FOW 1st Inns: 27 30 153 154 154 223 362 376 426 479
FOW 2nd Inns: 2 12 63 63 100

Bowling: *First Innings*: Lawson 37-9-108-3, Hogg 27-2-96-2, McDermott 27-2-118-3, Bennett 20-0-78-0, Matthews 14.3-2-67-2. *Second Innings*: Lawson 19-4-54-2, Hogg 14-3-40-0, McDermott 21-6-65-3, Bennett 3-0-12-0, Wessels 1-0-2-0.

AUSTRALIA

GM Wood lbw Garner ...12		c Dujon b Garner ...5	
AMJ Hilditch b Harper ...70		b Gomes ...113	
KC Wessels c Dujon b Marshall ...90		b Garner ...0	
KJ Hughes c Dujon b Walsh ...0		lbw Garner ...0	
AR Border (c) c Richards b Walsh ...35		c Dujon b Richards ...41	
GRJ Matthews b Marshall ...5		b Harper ...2	
SJ Rixon (+) c Richardson b Marshall ...0		c Richardson b Harper ...17	
MJ Bennett not out ...22		not out ...3	
GF Lawson c Walsh b Garner ...8		b Walsh ...0	
CJ McDermott b Marshall ...0			
RM Hogg lbw Marshall ...19			
EXTRAS (B 5, LB 7, W 1, NB 22) ...35		(B 6, LB 2, NB 9) ...17	
TOTAL ...296		...8 for 198	

FOW 1st Inns: 38 161 163 220 238 238 240 253 253 296
FOW 2nd Inns: 17 17 17 128 131 162 198 198

Bowling: *First Innings*: Marshall 31.5-6-86-5, Garner 24-6-74-2, Walsh 21-5-57-2, Harper 14-1-58-1, Richards 1-0-9-0. *Second Innings*: Marshall 20-4-36-0, Garner 19-1-49-3, Walsh 18-4-44-1, Harper 22-4-54-2, Richards 6-2-7-1, Gomes 2-2-0-1.

Umpires: PJ McConnell & SG Randell

Australian Averages

1984–85 AUSTRALIA v WEST INDIES

AUSTRALIA	M	Inn	NO	Runs	H.S	Avrge	Ct	St	Overs	Mds	Runs	Wkt	Avrge
Alderman, TM	3	6	1	34	23	6.80	1	-	99.0	31	339	9	37.67
Bennett, MJ	2	3	2	48	23	48.00	4	-	78.5	16	214	5	42.80
Boon, DC	3	5	-	132	51	26.40	2	-	-	-	-	-	-
Border, AR	5	9	-	246	69	27.33	4	-	9.0	-	49	-	-
Dyson, J	3	6	-	77	30	12.83	-	-	-	-	-	-	-
Hilditch, AMJ	2	3	-	185	113	61.67	-	-	-	-	-	-	-
Hogg, RM	4	7	3	54	21*	13.50	2	-	147.1	23	474	11	43.09
Holland, RG	3	4	1	15	7*	5.00	2	-	130.3	26	404	14	28.86
Hughes, KJ	4	8	-	81	37	10.13	4	-	-	-	-	-	-
Lawson, GF	5	9	2	131	49	18.71	6	-	194.4	39	589	23	25.61
Matthews, GRJ	1	2	-	7	5	3.50	1	-	14.3	2	67	2	33.50
McDermott, CJ	2	2	-	4	4	2.00	1	-	69.0	8	273	10	27.30
Phillips, WB	2	4	-	136	54	34.00	7	-	-	-	-	-	-
Rackemann, CG	1	2	-	0	0	0.00	1	-	28.0	3	106	-	-
Ritchie, GM	1	1	-	37	37	37.00	-	-	-	-	-	-	-
Rixon, SJ	3	5	-	53	20	10.60	11	1	-	-	-	-	-
Wessels, KC	5	9	-	505	173	56.11	3	-	6.0	-	15	-	-
Wood, GM	5	9	-	207	56	23.00	5	-	-	-	-	-	-
Yallop, GN	1	2	-	3	2	1.50	1	-	-	-	-	-	-

West Indian Averages

1984–85 AUSTRALIA v WEST INDIES

WEST INDIES	M	Inn	NO	Runs	H.S	Avrge	Ct	St	Overs	Mds	Runs	Wkt	Avrge
Dujon, PJL	5	8	1	341	139	48.71	19	-	-	-	-	-	-
Garner, J	5	6	2	41	17	10.25	2	-	177.4	33	566	19	29.79
Gomes, HA	5	9	2	451	127	64.43	1	-	15.0	4	30	2	15.00
Greenidge, CG	5	8	-	214	95	26.75	5	-	-	-	-	-	-
Harper, RA	2	3	-	40	26	13.33	1	-	72.0	15	211	8	26.38
Haynes, DL	5	9	-	247	63	27.44	4	-	-	-	-	-	-
Holding, MA	3	4	-	2	1	0.50	2	-	88.1	20	249	15	16.60
Lloyd, CH	5	8	1	356	114	50.86	5	-	-	-	-	-	-
Marshall, MD	5	6	-	174	57	34.80	4	-	215.2	45	554	28	19.79
Richards, IVA	5	9	-	342	208	42.75	3	-	16.0	4	32	1	32.00
Richardson, RB	5	9	-	236	138	26.22	9	-	-	-	-	-	-
Walsh, CA	5	6	3	32	18*	10.67	1	-	146.2	29	432	13	33.23

It's one–all as Border leads by example

The second XI

London, May 7. New Australian captain Allan Border bristled with annoyance when Fleet Street reporters suggested that his team represented Australia's 'second eleven'. The implication is that Australia has been crippled by defections to the unofficial South African tour, which was announced a few weeks ago.

Australia's bowling ranks are depleted. Terry Alderman, Carl Rackemann, Rodney Hogg and John Maguire have each signed for South Africa, but Australia still has three outstanding fast bowlers in the form of Geoff Lawson, Craig McDermott and Jeff Thomson.

Rebels in Africa

Canberra, April 16. Prime Minister Bob Hawke has begged Australian cricketers not to participate in the proposed 'rebel' tour of South Africa.

The team, announced three days ago, includes several players selected to play in the forthcoming Ashes tour.

The 'defectors' include Terry Alderman, Wayne Phillips, Rod McCurdy, Murray Bennett, Dirk Wellham, Graeme Wood and Steve Rixon. Kim Hughes and Graham Yallop have also signed following their omission from the Australian team to tour England.

Four centuries

Derby, May 25. The Australian captain, Allan Border, has already made four centuries in lead-up matches on the Ashes tour.

Against Somerset on May 8, Border hit a run a minute to make 106. A few days later he scored 135 in Australia's drawn match against Worcestershire, and followed up on May 25 with 125 against the MCC at Lord's.

Anyone would think his 100 against Derbyshire today would be cause for great celebration. Yet there was his team-mate, Wayne Phillips, looking as though someone had died.

Poor old Phillips had taken the tempting odds that Border would not stretch his three tons to four.

Border gave him a special smile.

Allan Border on the way to making one of eight centuries on the 1985 Australian tour of England. He struck 196 at Lord's and 146 at Old Trafford.

Lord's, July 2. The Ashes series stands at one-all after the second Test at Lord's ended in a four wicket victory to Australia. Today's win was Australia's first triumph in an Ashes Test at Lord's since 1972.

Fast bowler Craig McDermott captured 6/70 in England's first innings of 290, dismissing both England openers lbw.

Allan Border scored 196 in Australia's first innings and never lost concentration, despite five interruptions on the second day.

England's Ian Botham claimed 5/109 in Australia's first innings. It is the 25th time he has done so in a Test.

Botham and Mike Gatting added 131 in England's second innings, but Border turned the match in Australia's favour when he brought on the leg-spinner, Bob Holland, who took 5/68 from 32 overs in his first appearance in a Test in England.

The Australian bowling had no answer in the first Test at Headingley, where England made a massive 533 in its first innings and beat Australia by five wickets. England's Tim Robinson (175) was helped by an extremely fast outfield. Andrew Hilditch (119 and 80) was Australia's best.

The first Test was marred by spectators invading the pitch when England neared victory. England captain David Gower called them a 'pack of mad dogs'.

The trend is alarming. Three weeks ago 250 people were injured and 30 killed when fans rioted at a soccer game between England and Italy in Brussels.

QUICK SINGLES

Packer tempts trio. Australian media magnate Kerry Packer tempted three of Australia's prospective South African 'defectors' to reject the rebel tour. Wayne Phillips, Dirk Wellham and Graeme Wood each accepted lucrative offers from Packer to continue playing for Australia.

New start. The 1985 Ashes series opened at Headingley, Leeds, the first time that Headingley has staged the opening Test in the history of Tests between England and Australia.

Boffin stumped. Such was the popularity of Allan Border's Australians that a match against Oxford and Cambridge Universities at Fenner's, Cambridge, was packed to overflowing. The astonished Dean told Border the attendance was unprecedented.

Beginner's luck. Test rookie Simon O'Donnell had the privilege of hitting the winning runs in the second Test at Lord's.

Terrible tune. During the second Test at Lord's, Allan Border tried not be distracted by the song England's Ian Botham kept singing on the field. Botham sang his own composition, comprising two words: 'Remember 1981.'

Records broken. Ian Botham took five wickets in an innings (for the 25th time) in Australia's first innings at Lord's, breaking Sydney Barnes' 1914 world record. When Botham dismissed Graeme Wood, he achieved his 326th wicket in Test cricket, and passed Bob Willis as England's leading wicket-taker.

Mac's milestone. Craig McDermott took 8/141 in the drawn fourth Test at Old Trafford. At 20 years and 113 days, he is the youngest Australian to take eight wickets in a Test innings.

Boon bombs Essex. The drawn Essex v Australians match in early July was interrupted for 20 minutes on the second day by a bomb scare. The crowd moved onto the field as police and army experts searched the stands and pavilion. Australia's David Boon top-scored with 138.

French cricket. England captain David Gower won the toss in the third Test at Trent Bridge with a 10 Franc coin and elected to bat. England made 456 in its first innings, but the match was drawn.

Lord's record. Allan Border's 196 in the second test at Lord's was the highest score by an Australian Test captain at the famous ground. The previous best was Bill Woodfull's 155 in 1930.

Bridge crossed. In the third Test, Australia's 539-run innings (Wood 172, Ritchie 146) was its highest-ever total at Trent Bridge.

England cruise away to series win

A goodwill tour

The Oval, Sep. 3. Australia may have lost the Ashes, but Allan Border's team has done much to win the hearts and minds of the English cricketing public.

The 'ugly Australian' image has faded under Border's capable leadership. Morale has recovered after the South Africa upheaval and young players like David Boon, Greg Matthews, Craig McDermott, Greg Ritchie and Simon O'Donnell have all been blooded in the best traditions of the game.

Matches have been played in a spirit of fairness and friendly rivalry, and the resounding cheer that Border received from the fans at Lord's yesterday was not just politeness. The public turned out in droves to see Border's Australians. They can come back anytime.

Gower must g… Stay!

London, June 4. Fleet Street has more egg than ink on its front pages today. When Australia wrapped up the Texaco Trophy one day series on June 1, the word went out: 'Gower must go.'

Australia won the first match at Old Trafford by three wickets and the second at Edgbaston by four. England captain David Gower's scores of 3, 1, and 0 were enough to make the press forget how he had recently led England to a rare victory over India on the subcontinent. He had to go.

Now, in the final Texaco Trophy game, Gower has made 102 and inspired his England side to an eight-wicket win.

'Save him,' they cry.

Three days is a long time on Fleet Street.

Allan Border is clean bowled for two by Richard Ellison in the fifth Test.

Commiserations for Allan Border.

The Oval, Sep. 3. Australia has fallen into a heap in the fifth and sixth Tests, England winning both of them by an innings.

England has not achieved successive innings victories over Australia since 1956, and during the last few days at the Oval, Australia was forced to follow on for the first time since 1977.

The England bowler, Richard Ellison, has been the key to his country reclaiming the Ashes 3–1.

Ellison took 6/77 in Australia's first innings at Edgbaston, and 4/27 in the second. His swing bowling under heavy cloud cover on the second day saw him capture the wickets of Kepler Wessels (83), Graeme Wood (19), Bob Holland (0) and Allan Border (45) in the space of 15 balls.

England's 5/595 dec. in its first innings included five centuries. David Gower top-scored with 215.

When Ellison repeated the dose in Australia's second innings, the tourists teetered at 5/36 and were all out for 142, giving Ellison match figures of 10/104.

He captured another seven Australian wickets in the sixth Test, where England's Graham Gooch (196) set up victory with a second-wicket stand of 351 with Gower (157).

Australia certainly deteriorated in these final Tests, but a lucky toss at the Oval allowed England to bat first on what began as an ideal batting wicket.

The pitch would later have suited the Australian leg-spinner Bob Holland. Unfortunately, Holland wasn't picked this time.

Caught off boot

Edgbaston, Aug. 25. The old axiom in cricket that batsmen should be given the benefit of the doubt seemed to be forgotten in the fifth Test.

Australian batsman Wayne Phillips was on 59 when he hit a ball from Phil Edmonds hard and low into the foot of Allan Lamb at silly point. The ball rebounded into the air and was caught by David Gower a few yards away. Gower claimed the catch. Both umpires consulted, then umpire David Shepherd raised the finger.

Australian captain Allan Border argued that nobody could be certain that the ball hit Lamb's boot on the full. He says the dismissal probably cost Australia the Test.

DAILY DRIVEL

ENGLAND OPENERS REACH DOUBLE FIGURES

Big news in England.

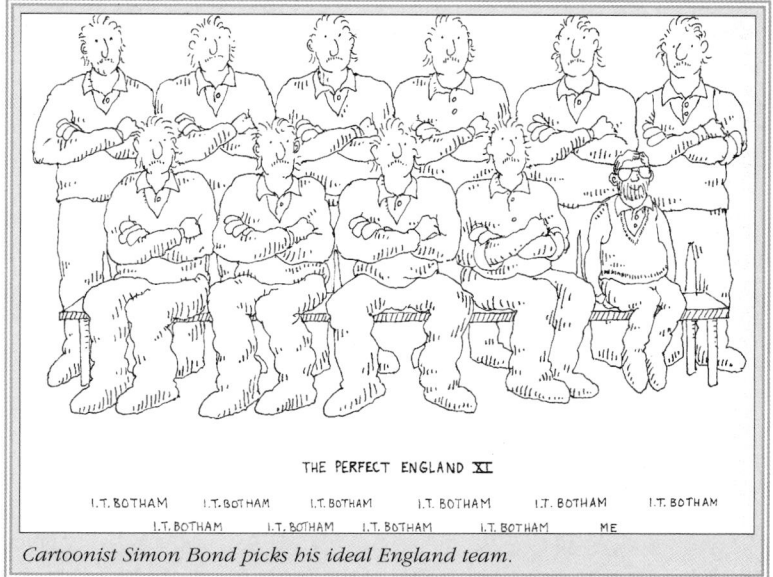

THE PERFECT ENGLAND XI

I.T. BOTHAM I.T. BOTHAM I.T. BOTHAM I.T. BOTHAM I.T. BOTHAM I.T. BOTHAM
I.T. BOTHAM I.T. BOTHAM I.T. BOTHAM I.T. BOTHAM ME

Cartoonist Simon Bond picks his ideal England team.

The report card on Test men

London, Sep. 10. The 1985 Ashes tour is over and Australian cricketers are taking their reports home to an anxious public.

These are the results:

Allan Border: dux of the class with eight centuries, including a match-winning 196 in the Lord's Test and 146 at Old Trafford. An outstanding effort.

David Boon: best in Tests was 61 (Old Trafford), but scored 832 runs on tour, including 206 not out against Northamptonshire.

Bob Holland: his 5/68 sealed Australia's victory at Lord's. He took 29 wickets at an average of 35.06.

Kepler Wessels: 83 at Edgbaston, but failed to reach potential.

Craig McDermott: outstanding bowler (30 Test wickets at 30.03).

Geoff Lawson: 22 wickets, but troubled by bronchial illness.

Greg Ritchie: came of age as a batsman (1097 runs for the tour, 422 of them coming in Tests).

Andrew Hilditch: began confidently (119 and 80 at Headingley) but tapered off.

Wayne Phillips: reliable run-getter and a safe pair of hands, took 21 catches.

A fine hook from Kepler Wessels.

Simon O'Donnell: more consistency needed. Best was 100 not out against the MCC at Lord's.

Graeme Wood: a superb 172 at Trent Bridge.

Jeff Thomson: expensive figures of 3/275 in his two Tests.

Greg Matthews: failed to impress in his only Test. He'll also have to get a decent haircut if he wants to come back next term.

Australian Averages

1985 ENGLAND v AUSTRALIA

AUSTRALIA	M	Inn	NO	Runs	H.S	Avrge	Ct	St	Overs	Mds	Runs	Wkt	Avrge
Bennett, MJ	1	2	-	23	12	11.50	1	-	32.0	8	111	1	111.00
Boon, DC	4	7	-	124	61	17.71	4	-	-	-	-	-	-
Border, AR	6	11	2	597	196	66.33	11	-	11.0	1	37	-	-
Gilbert, DR	1	2	1	1	1	1.00	-	-	21.0	2	96	1	96.00
Hilditch, AMJ	6	11	-	424	119	38.55	3	-	-	-	-	-	-
Holland, RG	4	5	1	15	10	3.75	1	-	172.0	41	465	6	77.50
Lawson, GF	6	9	1	119	53	14.88	2	-	246.0	38	830	22	37.73
Matthews, GRJ	1	2	-	21	17	10.50	2	-	9.0	2	21	-	-
McDermott, CJ	6	9	1	103	35	12.88	2	-	234.2	21	901	30	30.03
O'Donnell, SP	5	8	1	184	48	26.29	3	-	145.4	31	487	6	81.17
Phillips, WB	6	11	1	350	91	35.00	11	-	-	-	-	-	-
Ritchie, GM	6	11	1	422	146	42.20	3	-	1.0	-	10	-	-
Thomson, JR	2	4	4	38	28*	-	1	-	56.0	4	275	3	91.67
Wellham, DM	1	2	-	18	13	9.00	1	-	-	-	-	-	-
Wessels, KC	6	11	-	368	83	33.45	3	-	6.0	2	18	-	-
Wood, GM	5	9	-	260	172	28.89	1	-	-	-	-	-	-

English Averages

1985 ENGLAND v AUSTRALIA

ENGLAND	M	Inn	NO	Runs	H.S	Avrge	Ct	St	Overs	Mds	Runs	Wkt	Avrge
Agnew, JP	1	1	1	2	2*	-	-	-	23.0	2	99	-	-
Allott, PJW	4	5	1	27	12	6.75	-	-	113.0	22	297	5	59.40
Botham, IT	6	8	-	250	85	31.25	8	-	251.4	36	855	31	27.58
Cowans, NG	1	1	1	22	22*	-	-	-	33.0	6	128	2	64.00
Downton, PR	6	7	1	114	54	19.00	19	1	-	-	-	-	-
Edmonds, PH	5	5	-	47	21	9.40	8	-	225.5	59	549	15	36.60
Ellison, RM	2	1	-	3	3	3.00	1	-	75.5	20	185	17	10.88
Emburey, JE	6	6	2	130	33	32.50	3	-	248.4	75	544	19	28.63
Foster, NA	1	2	-	3	3	1.50	-	-	23.0	1	83	1	83.00
Gatting, MW	6	9	3	527	160	87.83	-	-	5.0	-	16	-	-
Gooch, GA	6	9	-	487	196	54.11	4	-	41.2	10	102	2	51.00
Gower, DI	6	9	-	732	215	81.33	6	-	-	-	-	-	-
Lamb, AJ	6	8	1	256	67	36.57	7	-	1.0	-	10	-	-
Robinson, RT	6	9	1	490	175	61.25	5	-	-	-	-	-	-
Sidebottom, A	1	1	-	2	2	2.00	-	-	18.4	3	65	1	65.00
Taylor, LB	2	1	1	1	1*	-	1	-	63.3	11	178	4	44.50
Willey, P	1	2	1	39	36	39.00	-	-	-	-	-	-	-

FIRST TEST 1985 ENGLAND v AUSTRALIA
Headingley, Leeds. June 13, 14, 15, 17, 18, 1985.
Toss: Australia. England won by 5 wkts.

AUSTRALIA

GM Wood lbw Allott	.14 (2)	c Lamb b Botham	.3
AMJ Hilditch c Downton b Gooch	.119 (1)	c Robinson b Emburey	.80
KC Wessels c Botham b Emburey	.36	b Emburey	.64
AR Border (c) c Botham b Cowans	.32	c Downton b Botham	.8
DC Boon lbw Gooch	.14	b Cowans	.22
GM Ritchie b Botham	.46	b Emburey	.1
WB Phillips (+) c Gower b Emburey	.30	c Lamb b Botham	.91
CJ McDermott b Botham	.18 (10)	c Gooch b Emburey	.6
SP O'Donnell b Botham	.0 (8)	c Downton b Botham	.24
GF Lawson c Downton b Allott	.0 (9)	c Downton b Emburey	.15
JR Thomson not out	.4	not out	.2
EXTRAS (LB 13, W 4, NB 1)	.18	(B 4, LB 3, W 1)	.8
TOTAL	.331		.324

FOW 1st Inns: 23 155 201 229 229 284 326 326 327 331
FOW 2nd Inns: 5 144 151 159 160 192 272 307 318 324

Bowling: *First Innings:* Cowans 20-4-78-1, Allott 22-3-74-2, Botham 29.1-8-86-3, Gooch 21-4-57-2, Emburey 6-1-23-2. *Second Innings:* Botham 33-7-107-4, Allott 17-4-57-0, Emburey 43.4-14-82-5, Cowans 13-2-50-1, Gooch 9-3-21-0.

ENGLAND

GA Gooch lbw McDermott	.5	lbw O'Donnell	.28
RT Robinson c Boon b Lawson	.175	b Lawson	.21
DI Gower (c) c Phillips b McDermott	.17	c Border b O'Donnell	.5
MW Gatting c Hilditch b McDermott	.53	c Phillips b Lawson	.12
AJ Lamb b O'Donnell	.38	not out	.31
IT Botham b Thomson	.60	b O'Donnell	.12
P Willey c Hilditch b Lawson	.36	not out	.3
PR Downton (+) c Border b McDermott	.54		
JE Emburey b Lawson	.21		
PJW Allott c Boon b Thomson	.12		
NG Cowans not out	.22		
EXTRAS (B 5, LB 16, W 5, NB 14)	.40	(LB 7, W 1, NB 3)	.11
TOTAL	.533		.5 for 123

FOW 1st Inns: 14 50 186 264 344 417 422 462 484 553
FOW 2nd Inns: 44 59 71 83 110

Bowling: *First Innings:* Lawson 26-4-117-3, McDermott 32-2-134-4, Thomson 34-3-166-2, O'Donnell 27-8-77-1, Border 3-0-16-0, Wessels 3-2-2-0. *Second Innings:* McDermott 4-0-20-0, Lawson 16-4-51-2, O'Donnell 15.4-5-37-3, Thomson 3-0-8-0.

Umpires: BJ Meyer & KE Palmer

SECOND TEST 1985 ENGLAND v AUSTRALIA
Lord's Cricket Ground, London. June 27, 28, 29, July 1, 2, 1985.
Toss: Australia. Australia won by 4 wkts.

ENGLAND

GA Gooch lbw McDermott	.30	c Phillips b McDermott	.17
RT Robinson lbw McDermott	.6	b Holland	.12
DI Gower (c) c Border b McDermott	.86 (5)	c Phillips b McDermott	.22
MW Gatting lbw Lawson	.14 (6)	not out	.75
AJ Lamb c Phillips b Lawson	.47 (7)	c Holland b Lawson	.9
IT Botham c Ritchie b Lawson	.5 (8)	c Border b Holland	.85
PR Downton (+) c Wessels b McDermott	.21 (9)	c Boon b Holland	.0
JE Emburey lbw O'Donnell	.33 (3)	b Lawson	.20
PH Edmonds c Border b McDermott	.21 (10)	c Boon b Holland	.1
NA Foster c Wessels b McDermott	.3 (11)	c Border b Holland	.0
PJW Allott not out	.1 (4)	b Lawson	.0
EXTRAS (B 1, LB 4, W 1, NB 17)	.23	(B 1, LB 12, W 4, NB 3)	.20
TOTAL	.290		.261

FOW 1st Inns: 26 51 99 179 184 211 241 273 283 290
FOW 2nd Inns: 32 34 38 57 77 98 229 229 261 261

Bowling: *First Innings:* Lawson 25-2-91-3, McDermott 29.2-5-70-6, O'Donnell 22-3-82-1, Holland 23-6-42-0. *Second Innings:* McDermott 20-2-84-2, Lawson 23-0-86-3, Holland 32-12-68-5, O'Donnell 5-0-10-0.

AUSTRALIA

GM Wood c Emburey b Allott	.8 (2)	c Lamb b Botham	.6
AMJ Hilditch b Foster	.14 (1)	c Lamb b Botham	.0
KC Wessels lbw Botham	.11	run out	.28
AR Border (c) c Gooch b Botham	.196 (5)	not out	.41
DC Boon c Downton b Botham	.4 (6)	b Edmonds	.1
GM Ritchie lbw Botham	.94 (4)	b Allott	.2
WB Phillips (+) c Edmonds b Botham	.21	c Edmonds b Emburey	.29
SP O'Donnell c Lamb b Edmonds	.48	not out	.9
GF Lawson not out	.5		
CJ McDermott run out	.9		
RG Holland b Edmonds	.0		
EXTRAS (LB 10, W 1, NB 4)	.15	(LB 11)	.11
TOTAL	.425		.6 for 127

FOW 1st Inns: 11 24 80 101 317 347 398 414 425 425
FOW 2nd Inns: 0 9 22 63 65 116

Bowling: *First Innings:* Foster 23-1-83-1, Allott 30-4-70-1, Botham 24-2-109-5, Edmonds 25.4-5-85-2, Gooch 3-1-11-0, Emburey 19-3-57-0. *Second Innings:* Botham 15-0-49-2, Allott 7-4-8-1, Edmonds 16-5-35-1, Emburey 8-4-24-1.

Umpires: HD Bird & DGL Evans

THIRD TEST 1985 ENGLAND v AUSTRALIA
Trent Bridge, Nottingham. July 11, 12, 13, 15, 16, 1985.
Toss: England. Match Drawn.

ENGLAND

GA Gooch c Wessels b Lawson	70	c Ritchie b McDermott ... 48
RT Robinson c Border b Lawson	38	not out ... 77
DI Gower c Phillips b O'Donnell	166	c Phillips b McDermott ... 17
MW Gatting run out	74	not out ... 35
AJ Lamb lbw Lawson	17	
IT Botham c O'Donnell b McDermott	38	
PR Downton (+) c Ritchie b McDermott	0	
A Sidebottom c O'Donnell b Lawson	2	
JE Emburey not out	16	
PH Edmonds b Holland	12	
PJW Allott c Border b Lawson	7	
EXTRAS (LB 12, W 1, NB 3)	16	(B 1, LB 16, NB 2) ... 19
TOTAL	456	... 2 for 196

FOW 1st Inns: 55 171 358 365 416 416 419 419 443 456
FOW 2nd Inns: 79 107

Bowling: *First Innings*: Lawson 39.4-10-103-5, McDermott 35-3-147-2, O'Donnell 29-4-104-1, Holland 26-3-90-1. *Second Innings*: Lawson 13-4-32-0, McDermott 16-2-42-2, Holland 28-9-69-0, O'Donnell 10-2-26-0, Ritchie 1-0-10-0.

AUSTRALIA

GM Wood c Robinson b Botham	172
AMJ Hilditch lbw Allott	47
RG Holland lbw Sidebottom	10
KC Wessels c Downton b Emburey	33
AR Border (c) c Botham b Edmonds	23
DC Boon c & b Emburey	15
GM Ritchie b Edmonds	146
WB Phillips (+) b Emburey	2
SP O'Donnell c Downton b Botham	46
GF Lawson c Gooch b Botham	18
CJ McDermott not out	0
EXTRAS (B 6, LB 7, W 2, NB 12)	27
TOTAL	539

FOW 1st Inns: 87 128 205 234 263 424 437 491 539 539

Bowling: *First Innings*: Botham 34.2-3-107-3, Sidebottom 18.4-3-65-1, Allott 18-4-55-1, Edmonds 66-18-155-2, Emburey 55-15-129-3, Gooch 8.2-2-13-0, Gatting 1-0-2-0.

Umpires: DJ Constant & AGT Whitehead

FIFTH TEST 1985 ENGLAND v AUSTRALIA
Edgbaston, Birmingham. August 15, 16, 17, 19, 20, 1985.
Toss: England. England won by an innings & 118 runs.

AUSTRALIA

GM Wood c Edmonds b Botham	19 (2)	c Robinson b Ellison ... 10
AMJ Hilditch c Downton b Edmonds	39 (1)	c Ellison b Botham ... 10
KC Wessels c Downton b Ellison	83	c Downton b Ellison ... 10
AR Border (c) c Edmonds b Ellison	45 (5)	b Ellison ... 2
GM Ritchie c Botham b Ellison	8 (6)	c Lamb b Emburey ... 20
WB Phillips (+) c Robinson b Ellison	15 (7)	c Gower b Edmonds ... 59
SP O'Donnell c Downton b Taylor	1 (8)	b Botham ... 11
GF Lawson run out	53 (9)	c Gower b Edmonds ... 3
CJ McDermott c Gower b Ellison	35 (10)	c Edmonds b Botham ... 8
JR Thomson not out	28 (11)	not out ... 4
RG Holland c Edmonds b Ellison	0 (4)	lbw Ellison ... 0
EXTRAS (LB 4, W 1, NB 4)	9	(B 1, LB 3, NB 1) ... 5
TOTAL	335	... 142

FOW 1st Inns: 44 92 189 191 207 208 218 276 335 335
FOW 2nd Inns: 10 32 32 35 36 113 117 120 137 142

Bowling: *First Innings*: Botham 27-1-108-1, Taylor 26-5-78-1, Ellison 31.5-9-77-6, Edmonds 20-4-47-1, Emburey 9-2-21-0. *Second Innings*: Botham 14.1-2-52-3, Taylor 13-4-27-0, Ellison 9-3-27-4, Edmonds 15-9-13-2, Emburey 13-5-19-1.

ENGLAND

GA Gooch c Phillips b Thomson	19
RT Robinson b Lawson	148
DI Gower (c) c Border b Lawson	215
MW Gatting not out	100
AJ Lamb c Wood b McDermott	46
IT Botham c Thomson b McDermott	18
PR Downton (+) not out	0
JE Emburey	
RM Ellison	
PH Edmonds	
LB Taylor	
EXTRAS (B 7, LB 20, NB 22)	49
TOTAL	5 dec 595

FOW 1st Inns: 38 369 463 572 592

Bowling: *First Innings*: Lawson 37-1-135-2, McDermott 31-2-155-2, Thomson 19-1-101-1, Holland 25-4-95-0, O'Donnell 16-3-69-0, Border 6-1-13-0.

Umpires: DJ Constant & DR Shepherd

FOURTH TEST 1985 ENGLAND v AUSTRALIA
Old Trafford, Manchester. August 1, 2, 3, 5, 6, 1985.
Toss: England. Match Drawn.

AUSTRALIA

KC Wessels c Botham b Emburey	34 (3)	c & b Emburey ... 50
AMJ Hilditch c Gower b Edmonds	49 (1)	b Emburey ... 40
DC Boon c Lamb b Botham	61 (5)	b Emburey ... 7
AR Border (c) st Downton b Edmonds	8	not out ... 146
GM Ritchie c & b Edmonds	4 (6)	b Emburey ... 31
WB Phillips (+) c Downton b Botham	36 (7)	not out ... 39
GRJ Matthews b Botham	4 (2)	c & b Edmonds ... 17
SP O'Donnell b Edmonds	45	
GF Lawson c Downton b Botham	4	
CJ McDermott lbw Emburey	0	
RG Holland not out	5	
EXTRAS (LB 3, W 1, NB 3)	7	(B 1, LB 6, NB 3) ... 10
TOTAL	257	... 5 for 340

FOW 1st Inns: 71 97 118 122 193 198 211 223 224 257
FOW 2nd Inns: 38 85 126 138 213

Bowling: *First Innings*: Botham 23-4-79-4, Agnew 14-0-65-0, Allott 13-1-29-0, Emburey 24-7-41-2, Edmonds 15.1-4-40-4. *Second Innings*: Botham 15-3-50-0, Allott 6-2-4-0, Edmonds 54-12-122-1, Emburey 51-17-99-4, Agnew 9-2-34-0, Gatting 4-0-14-0, Lamb 1-0-10-0.

ENGLAND

GA Gooch lbw McDermott	74
RT Robinson c Border b McDermott	10
DI Gower (c) c Hilditch b McDermott	47
MW Gatting c Phillips b McDermott	160
AJ Lamb run out	67
IT Botham c O'Donnell b McDermott	20
PR Downton (+) b McDermott	23
JE Emburey not out	31
PH Edmonds b McDermott	1
PJW Allott b McDermott	7
JP Agnew not out	2
EXTRAS (B 7, LB 16, NB 17)	40
TOTAL	9 dec 482

FOW 1st Inns: 21 142 148 304 339 430 448 450 470

Bowling: *First Innings*: Lawson 37-7-114-0, McDermott 36-3-141-8, Holland 38-7-101-0, O'Donnell 21-6-82-0, Matthews 9-2-21-0.

Umpires: HD Bird & DR Shepherd

SIXTH TEST 1985 ENGLAND v AUSTRALIA
Kennington Oval, London. August 29, 30, 31 September 2, 1985.
Toss: England. England won by an innings & 94 runs.

ENGLAND

GA Gooch c & b McDermott	196
RT Robinson b McDermott	3
DI Gower (c) c Bennett b McDermott	157
MW Gatting c Border b Bennett	4
JE Emburey c Wellham b Lawson	9
AJ Lamb c McDermott b Lawson	1
IT Botham c Phillips b Lawson	12
PR Downton (+) b McDermott	16
RM Ellison c Phillips b Gilbert	3
PH Edmonds lbw Lawson	12
LB Taylor not out	1
EXTRAS (B 13, LB 11, NB 26)	50
TOTAL	464

FOW 1st Inns: 20 371 376 403 405 418 425 447 452 464

Bowling: *First Innings*: Lawson 29.2-6-101-4, McDermott 31-2-108-4, Gilbert 21-2-96-1, Bennett 32-8-111-1, Border 2-0-8-0, Wessels 3-0-16-0.

AUSTRALIA

GM Wood lbw Botham	22 (2)	b Botham ... 6
AMJ Hilditch c Gooch b Botham	17 (1)	c Gower b Taylor ... 9
KC Wessels b Emburey	12	c Downton b Botham ... 7
AR Border (c) b Edmonds	38	c Botham b Ellison ... 58
DM Wellham c Downton b Ellison	13	lbw Ellison ... 5
GM Ritchie not out	64	c Downton b Ellison ... 6
WB Phillips (+) b Edmonds	18	c Downton b Botham ... 10
MJ Bennett c Robinson b Ellison	12	c & b Taylor ... 11
GF Lawson c Botham b Taylor	14	c Downton b Ellison ... 7
CJ McDermott run out	25	c Botham b Ellison ... 2
DR Gilbert b Botham	1	not out ... 0
EXTRAS (LB 3, W 2)	5	(B 4, NB 4) ... 8
TOTAL	241	... 129

FOW 1st Inns: 35 52 56 101 109 144 171 192 236 241
FOW 2nd Inns: 13 16 37 51 71 96 114 127 129 129

Bowling: *First Innings*: Botham 20-3-64-3, Taylor 13-1-39-1, Ellison 18-5-35-2, Emburey 19-7-48-1, Edmonds 14-2-52-2. *Second Innings*: Botham 17-3-44-3, Taylor 11.3-1-34-2, Ellison 17-3-46-5, Emburey 1-0-1-0.

Umpires: HD Bird & KE Palmer

The young Allan Border.

Mates: Border (centre) at Brisbane's 'Gabba in 1981.

Allan Border – the soul of modern Australian cricket

London, Sep. 15. Courage, tenacity, spirit, toughness, durability, resourcefulness and intelligence are but a few of the labels now being applied to Australian captain Allan Border.

Who can forget his effort against England in 1981 when he batted with a broken finger for 15 hours in the final two Tests.

The Australian captaincy was thrust upon him last year when Kim Hughes resigned, and Border has held the team together despite some severe beatings.

His defiant 58 in the sixth Test at the Oval was typical of Border. 'AB,' as he is affectionately known, is the captain who always plays a captain's game.

Family man: Allan Border with wife Jane and son Dene.

Coming of age: Border aged 21 at the SCG in 1976.

Another day over and the captain reflects on the state of play. Despite the team cameraderie, the buck stops at the top.

A chat with Sir Donald Bradman.

Celebrating his first Test win as skipper – the fifth Test in Sydney, 1984–85.

The dignity and authority of the captaincy came to sit well with Border.

Border is jubilant as he completes his century in the 1992–93 Boxing Day Test against the West Indies. He batted for nearly six hours.

End of an era. Border leaves the Kingsmead ground, South Africa, in 1994, having made an unbeaten 42 in what would be his last Test innings.

Menacing Hadlee Humbles Australia

Richard Hadlee: performed brilliantly to take 33 wickets in the series.

New Zealand skipper Jeremy Coney is given the low-down by the umpires.

This dismissal of David Hookes triggered Australia's slide to defeat.

Perth, Dec. 4. New Zealand has defeated Australia (2–1) in a Test Series for the first time, thanks to the sustained menace of fast bowler Richard Hadlee.

With 33 wickets in three Tests, Hadlee dominated the Australians. His accuracy had the home team under constant pressure from the opening day of the series, when he took 9/52 and only missed taking all 10 because he caught Geoff Lawson off Vaughan Brown. Hadlee's figures have only been bettered three times in Test cricket.

Hadlee may not bowl at the same speed as the West Indian pace battery, but he is a master at his craft.

Even on a slow third Test pitch in Perth he had the Australians' measure. The home team's bats were guilty of prodding cautiously and not using their feet.

In the first Test, Australia's attack was given a hiding by Martin Crowe (188), and by the next game the opening bowlers were Dave Gilbert and Simon O'Donnell – hardly the most fearsome pair to take the new ball for Australia.

Geoff Lawson missed the second Test with a groin injury and Craig McDermott was dropped, but they weren't missed on the spinners' pitch. Veteran leggie Bob Holland took 10 wickets for the game in Australia's four-wicket win.

Australia achieved their target with just 23 balls to spare thanks to a staunch effort by David Boon who made 81 in 267 minutes.

In the third Test, Australia began badly, with Hadlee pinning down their bats on a relaid WACA wicket that was uncharacteristically slow and low in bounce. The spongy outfield made fours a rarity, but the Australian total of 203 was disap-

pointing. By this stage of the Tests series Australia had been reduced to the tactic of merely keeping Hadlee at bay at all costs and, although it worked in the opening session, he broke through with 3/15 off the next 10 overs.

Thanks to a succession of dropped catches, New Zealand was able to build a solid lead and Australia needed to show the grit that had thus far been absent from their batting. David Boon and Allan Border settled in for a long and dour occupation of the crease.

Not surprisingly it was Hadlee who turned the game when he dismissed the Australian captain. After that the tail crumbled, leaving New Zealand with just 164 to get.

A missed run-out, a botched stumping and dropped catches in the final stages were typical of the Australian fielding in the series.

Captain Grumpy fed up with Australian team's failure

Perth, Dec. 4. The pathetic display by Australia in the final hour of the third Test has even penetrated the armour of the valiant skipper Allan Border.

Tonight he told a press conference: 'You start to wonder whether you are the right man for the job. If there was an obvious choice, who I believed could do a better job, I would be more than happy to stand down.'

Border had hoped his tail-enders would show more resolve, but their collapse hit Border hard and he said: 'I'm finding it increasingly difficult to lift. My own enjoyment of the game is suffering. You start to wonder what you are going to do.'

All-rounder Greg Matthews (right) manages to raise a smile from his skipper Allan Border early in the series. Matthews had just made 130 in Brisbane.

FIRST TEST 1985–86 AUSTRALIA v NEW ZEALAND
Brisbane Cricket Ground, Brisbane. November 8 ,9, 10, 11, 12, 1985.
Toss: New Zealand. New Zealand won by an innings & 41 runs.

AUSTRALIA

KC Wessels lbw Hadlee	70 (2)	c Brown b Chatfield	3
AMJ Hilditch c Chatfield b Hadlee	0 (1)	c Chatfield b Hadlee	12
DC Boon c Coney b Hadlee	31	c Smith b Chatfield	1
AR Border (c) c Edgar b Hadlee	1	not out	152
GM Ritchie c MD Crowe b Hadlee	8	c Coney b Snedden	20
WB Phillips (+) b Hadlee	34	b Hadlee	2
GRJ Matthews b Hadlee	2	c Coney b Hadlee	115
GF Lawson c Hadlee b Brown	8 (9)	c Brown b Chatfield	7
CJ McDermott c Coney b Hadlee	9 (8)	c & b Hadlee	5
DR Gilbert not out	0	c Chatfield b Hadlee	10
RG Holland c Brown b Hadlee	0	b Hadlee	0
EXTRAS (B 9, LB 5, NB 2)	16	(LB 3, NB 3)	6
TOTAL	179		333

FOW 1st Inns: 1 70 72 82 148 150 159 175 179 179
FOW 2nd Inns: 14 16 16 47 67 264 272 291 333 333

Bowling: *First Innings*: Hadlee 23.4-4-52-9, Chatfield 18-6-29-0, Snedden 11-1-45-0, MD Crowe 5-0-14-0, Brown 12.5-1-17-1, Coney 7-5-8-0. *Second Innings*: Hadlee 28.5-9-71-6, Chatfield 32-9-75-3, Snedden 19-3-66-1, MD Crowe 9-2-19-0, Brown 25-5-96-0, Coney 3-1-3-0.

NEW ZEALAND

BA Edgar c Phillips b Gilbert	17
JG Wright lbw Matthews	46
JF Reid c Border b Gilbert	108
MD Crowe b Matthews	188
JV Coney (c) c Phillips b Lawson	22
JJ Crowe c Holland b Matthews	35
VR Brown not out	36
RJ Hadlee c Phillips b McDermott	54
IDS Smith (+) not out	2
MC Snedden	
EJ Chatfield	
EXTRAS (B 2, LB 11, NB 32)	45
TOTAL	7 dec 553

FOW 1st Inns: 36 85 309 363 427 471 549

Bowling: *First Innings*: Lawson 36.5-8-96-1, McDermott 31-3-119-1, Gilbert 39-9-102-2, Matthews 31-5-110-3, Holland 22-3-106-0, Border 0.1-0-0-0, Wessels 1-0-7-0.

Umpires: AR Crafter & RA French

SECOND TEST 1985–86 AUSTRALIA v NEW ZEALAND
Sydney Cricket Ground, Sydney. November 22, 23, 24, 25, 26, 1985.
Toss: Australia. Australia won by 4 wkts.

NEW ZEALAND

JG Wright c O'Donnell b Bright	38	c & b Matthews	43
BA Edgar c Border b Holland	50	c & b Holland	52
JF Reid c Kerr b Holland	7	b Matthews	19
MD Crowe run out	8	b Holland	0
JV Coney (c) c Border b Holland	8	b Holland	7
JJ Crowe b Holland	13	c & b Holland	6
VR Brown lbw Holland	0	b Bright	15
IDS Smith (+) c Hookes b Bright	28	c & b Bright	12
RJ Hadlee lbw Holland	5	lbw Gilbert	26
JG Bracewell not out	83	not out	2
SL Boock lbw Gilbert	37	c Boon b Bright	3
EXTRAS (B 6, LB 8, NB 2)	16	(B 1, LB 4, NB 3)	8
TOTAL	293		193

FOW 1st Inns: 79 92 109 112 128 128 161 166 169 293
FOW 2nd Inns: 100 106 107 119 131 137 162 163 190 193

Bowling: *First Innings*: Gilbert 20.3-6-41-1, O'Donnell 6-2-13-0, Bright 34-12-87-2, Matthews 17-3-32-0, Holland 47-19-106-6. *Second Innings*: Gilbert 9-2-22-1, O'Donnell 5-4-4-0, Holland 41-16-84-3, Matthews 30-11-55-2, Bright 17.5-3-39-3.

AUSTRALIA

WB Phillips (+) b Bracewell	31	c Bracewell b Boock	63
RB Kerr lbw Hadlee	7	c Wright b Bracewell	7
DC Boon lbw Hadlee	0	c Reid b Bracewell	81
AR Border (c) b Bracewell	20	st Smith b Bracewell	11
GM Ritchie c JJ Crowe b Hadlee	89	c MD Crowe b Hadlee	13
DW Hookes run out	0	not out	38
GRJ Matthews c Smith b Hadlee	50	lbw Hadlee	32
SP O'Donnell not out	20	not out	2
RJ Bright lbw Boock	1		
DR Gilbert c Smith b Hadlee	0		
RG Holland st Smith b Boock	0		
EXTRAS (B 5, LB 2, NB 2)	9	(B 3, LB 9, NB 1)	13
TOTAL	227		6 for 260

FOW 1st Inns: 19 22 48 71 71 186 224 225 226 227
FOW 2nd Inns: 27 132 144 163 192 258

Bowling: *First Innings*: Hadlee 24-2-65-5, MD Crowe 5-2-15-0, Bracewell 25-9-51-2, Boock 29.5-14-53-2, Brown 13-3-35-0, Coney 1-0-1-0. *Second Innings*: Hadlee 27.1-10-58-2, MD Crowe 2-1-7-0, Bracewell 30-7-91-3, Boock 22-4-49-1, Brown 7-0-28-0, Coney 9-1-15-0.

Umpires: MW Johnson & BE Martin

THIRD TEST 1985–86 AUSTRALIA v NEW ZEALAND
W.A.C.A. Ground, Perth. November 30, December 1, 2, 3, 4, 1985.
Toss: New Zealand. New Zealand won by 6 wkts.

AUSTRALIA

WB Phillips (+) c Smith b Chatfield	37	c Smith b Chatfield	10
RB Kerr c Smith b Chatfield	17	b Hadlee	0
DC Boon c Bracewell b Hadlee	12	b Hadlee	50
AR Border (c) c Smith b Hadlee	12	b Hadlee	83
GM Ritchie lbw Coney	6	c MD Crowe b Coney	44
DW Hookes c Bracewell b Coney	14	b Bracewell	7
GRJ Matthews b Hadlee	34	lbw Hadlee	14
GF Lawson c JJ Crowe b Hadlee	11	c JJ Crowe b Hadlee	21
CJ McDermott b Chatfield	36	lbw Bracewell	11
DR Gilbert not out	12	b Hadlee	3
RG Holland c MD Crowe b Hadlee	4	not out	0
EXTRAS (LB 6, NB 2)	8	(B 2, LB 5, NB 9)	16
TOTAL	203		259

FOW 1st Inns: 38 63 78 85 85 114 131 159 190 203
FOW 2nd Inns: 3 28 109 195 207 214 234 251 255 259

Bowling: *First Innings*: Hadlee 26.5-6-65-5, Cairns 14-1-50-0, Chatfield 16-6-33-3, Coney 21-11-43-2, Bracewell 6-3-6-0. *Second Innings*: Hadlee 39-11-90-6, Cairns 26-6-59-0, Chatfield 30-9-47-1, Bracewell 28.5-8-47-2, Coney 8-5-9-1.

NEW ZEALAND

JG Wright c Phillips b Lawson	20	b Gilbert	35
BA Edgar c Hookes b McDermott	74	c Border b Matthews	16
JF Reid b Gilbert	7	c Phillips b Gilbert	28
MD Crowe lbw McDermott	71	not out	42
JV Coney (c) c Phillips b Lawson	19	b Gilbert	16
JJ Crowe lbw Holland	17	not out	2
RJ Hadlee c Hookes b Holland	26		
IDS Smith (+) c Matthews b Lawson	12		
JG Bracewell not out	28		
BL Cairns c Ritchie b Holland	0		
EJ Chatfield c Phillips b Lawson	3		
EXTRAS (B 1, LB 7, NB 14)	22	(B 7, LB 7, NB 11)	25
TOTAL	299		4 for 164

FOW 1st Inns: 43 55 184 191 215 253 256 273 276 299
FOW 2nd Inns: 47 77 121 149

Bowling: *First Innings*: Lawson 47-12-79-4, McDermott 33-9-66-2, Gilbert 31-9-75-1, Holland 40-12-63-3, Matthews 5-3-6-0, Hookes 1-0-2-0. *Second Innings*: Lawson 21-7-35-0, Gilbert 23-5-48-3, Matthews 9-3-13-1, McDermott 13-1-27-0, Holland 8-1-27-0.

Umpires: RC Isherwood & PJ McConnell

Australian Averages

1985–86 AUSTRALIA v NEW ZEALAND

AUSTRALIA	M	Inn	NO	Runs	H.S	Avrge	Ct	St	Overs	Mds	Runs	Wkt	Avrge
Boon, DC	3	6	-	175	81	29.17	1	-	-	-	-	-	-
Border, AR	3	6	1	279	152*	55.80	4	-	0.1	-	0	-	-
Bright, RJ	1	1	-	1	1	1.00	1	-	51.5	15	126	5	25.20
Gilbert, DR	3	5	2	25	12*	8.33	-	-	122.3	31	288	8	36.00
Hilditch, AMJ	1	2	-	12	12	6.00	-	-	-	-	-	-	-
Holland, RG	3	5	1	4	4	1.00	3	-	158.0	51	370	13	28.46
Hookes, DW	2	4	1	59	38*	19.67	3	-	1.0	-	2	-	-
Kerr, RB	2	4	-	31	17	7.75	1	-	-	-	-	-	-
Lawson, GF	2	4	-	47	21	11.75	-	-	104.5	27	210	5	42.00
Matthews, GRJ	3	6	-	247	115	41.17	2	-	92.0	25	216	6	36.00
McDermott, CJ	2	4	-	61	36	15.25	-	-	77.0	13	212	3	70.67
O'Donnell, SP	1	2	2	22	20*	-	1	-	11.0	6	17	-	-
Phillips, WB	3	6	-	177	63	29.50	7	-	-	-	-	-	-
Ritchie, GM	3	6	-	180	89	30.00	1	-	-	-	-	-	-
Wessels, KC	1	2	-	73	70	36.50	-	-	1.0	-	7	-	-

New Zealand Averages

1985–86 AUSTRALIA v NEW ZEALAND

NEW ZEALAND	M	Inn	NO	Runs	H.S	Avrge	Ct	St	Overs	Mds	Runs	Wkt	Avrge
Boock, SL	1	2	-	40	37	20.00	-	-	51.5	18	102	3	34.00
Bracewell, JG	2	3	3	113	83*	-	3	-	89.5	27	195	7	27.86
Brown, VR	2	3	1	51	36*	25.50	3	-	57.0	13	176	1	176.00
Cairns, BL	1	1	-	0	0	0.00	-	-	40.0	7	109	-	-
Chatfield, EJ	2	1	-	3	3	3.00	-	-	96.0	30	184	7	26.29
Coney, JV	3	5	-	72	22	14.40	4	-	49.0	23	79	3	26.33
Crowe, JJ	3	5	1	73	35	18.25	3	-	-	-	-	-	-
Crowe, MD	3	5	1	309	188	77.25	4	-	21.0	5	55	-	-
Edgar, BA	3	5	-	209	74	41.80	1	-	-	-	-	-	-
Hadlee, RJ	3	4	-	111	54	27.75	2	-	169.3	42	401	33	12.15
Reid, JF	3	5	-	169	108	33.80	1	-	-	-	-	-	-
Smith, IDS	3	4	1	54	28	18.00	7	2	-	-	-	-	-
Snedden, MC	1	-	-	-	-	-	-	-	30.0	4	111	1	111.00
Wright, JG	3	5	-	182	46	36.40	1	-	-	-	-	-	-

Three draws but India moral victors

New boys liven up cricket scene

Victorian paceman Merv Hughes considers a boundary conceded during his tough initiation into Test cricket.

Melbourne, Feb. 9. New life has been injected into the ailing Australian side by the addition of a fresh batch of rookies.

Five players have appeared in their debut Test this season. Robbie Kerr lasted just two Tests before being dropped, but Merv Hughes, Geoff Marsh, Bruce Reid and Steve Waugh have seized their chance. Queensland's Glenn Trimble and young 'keeper Tim Zoehrer have also had a taste of international cricket in one day matches.

The 203-cm tall Reid has made the best impression so far. He is not a tearaway speedster, but he can whip in an occasional fast bouncer which gains impetus from his great height.

West Australian Geoff Marsh has taken a while to mature, but he is a dogged customer who makes the most of his chances. He has settled in well at the top of the order, batting at No. 3 for his first two Tests before opening in the third game.

Steve Waugh was chosen at the tender age of 20, and although he struggled in his first two Tests, he proved a handy performer in the just-completed one day World Series Cup matches. Another newcomer, Victorian fast bowler Merv Hughes, struggled in his only Test.

Sydney, Jan. 6. The three Test matches between Australia and India have failed to produce a result in the series dubbed the battle for cricket's wooden spoon. India came to Australia after losing a series to Sri Lanka, and Australian cricket was at its lowest ebb after losing to New Zealand.

India had the better of each Test match but was unable to press home the advantage.

Apart from newcomer Bruce Reid, the Australian attack looked innocuous and non-threatening. Indian batting hero Sunil Gavaskar looked invincible in averaging 117.3.

Australia was able to post a decent score of 381 in the first Test in Adelaide thanks to four dropped catches. Bad weather – five hours were lost due to rain – and a batsman's pitch made it clear that the

India's master batsman Sunil Gavaskar shows eagle-like concentration in playing this off-drive.

game would end in a draw a long way from the end, and Gavaskar's six-hour occupation of the crease made it a certainty. Although he retired hurt at 1/97 after a painful blow from McDermott, Gavaskar came back at 5/247 and remained unconquered on 166 at the end of the innings. It was his 31st Test century and strangely enough he had not scored a Test ton for almost two years.

Australia was on the back foot from the start of the second Test and only Greg Matthews' resolute and undefeated century saved the home team from embarrassment.

Frustrated by some dubious umpiring decisions, the Indians were further angered when they thought Border should have been given out on the opening ball of the final day. Border made the most of the reprieve and scored 163. No other Australian progressed past 20.

Bad weather again intervened on the final day, washing out the last session, but India's lack of urgency did not help its cause.

Indian captain Kapil Dev was scathing after the match when he claimed that the umpiring had cost his side victory.

Centuries by each of India's top three batsmen shut out any hope of Australia winning the third Test at the SCG.

Gavaskar, Srikkanth and Amarnath humbled the attack, with Srikkanth hitting Holland out of the attack – a worthy achievement as the spinner had taken 10 wickets in each of his previous two Tests on his home ground.

David Boon is all aggression in playing this hook shot off Kapil Dev. He has emerged as a fine Test batsman.

All style. Geoff Marsh punishes this delivery which strayed down off side.

QUICK SINGLES

Back in trouble. Fast bowler Geoff Lawson entered hospital early in January with severe back pains. The 28-year-old fast bowler was feared to have stress fractures similar to those suffered by Dennis Lillee, and was told to take a year off cricket.

TV or not TV. India's complaints about umpiring decisions were peppered through the summer. Australian captain Allan Border said that electronic replays on scoreboards at Sydney and Melbourne placed too much pressure on the umpires. The suggestion of having a third umpire determining TV replays brought a sharp response from Border, who said that move would make cricket a game for robots.

More Aussies down. Kim Hughes' rebel touring team lost the final Test of its unof-

ficial three-match series after the first two games had been drawn. The 41-year-old South African legend Graeme Pollock showed that he retained his magical skills with a stunning century in the first Test.

Strange programming. Crowds have been down in this series and the Indians have never been a team which has attracted Australian spectators. The programming of three Tests in the space of 25 days was an extremely strange move. The total through the gates for the six Test matches involving Australia against New Zealand and India was a very disappointing 283,109 people.

Tassie record. David Boon's 123 in the first Test made him the first resident Tasmanian to post a Test hundred. In the same innings, Kapil Dev's 8/106 (5/4 from 21 balls) was the best analysis by an Indian in Australia.

Big Bruce. Fast-medium bowler Bruce Reid made his debut for Australia in the first Test, along with Merv Hughes and fellow Western Australian Geoff Marsh. Reid took 4/113. At 6ft 8in., he is the tallest player to have represented Australia.

9000 up. With his 166 not out in the first Test at the Adelaide Oval, Sunil Gavaskar became the first player to score 9000 Test runs. The diminutive Indian batting hero has scored a world record 31 Test hundreds.

Waugh begins. Twenty-year-old Steve Waugh failed badly in his first two Tests, scoring 13 and 5 at the MCG and 8 and 0 at Sydney.

Rare double. In the second Test, Kapil Dev became the third player (after Sir Garfield Sobers and Ian Botham) to achieve the double of 3000 Test runs and 200 wickets.

FIRST TEST 1985–86 AUSTRALIA v INDIA
Adelaide Oval, Adelaide. December 13, 14, 15, 16, 17, 1985.
Toss: Australia. Match Drawn.

AUSTRALIA
WB Phillips (+) c Yadav b Kapil	11			
DC Boon c Vengsarkar b Kapil	123	(1)	not out	11
GR Marsh c Sharma b Binny	5	(2)	not out	2
AR Border (c) b Kapil	49			
GM Ritchie c Kirmani b Kapil	128			
DW Hookes b Yadav	34			
GRJ Matthews lbw Kapil	18			
RJ Bright not out	5			
CJ McDermott lbw Kapil	0			
BA Reid c Gavaskar b Kapil	2			
MG Hughes c Vengsarkar b Kapil	0			
EXTRAS (LB 4, NB 2)	6		(LB 3, NB 1)	4
TOTAL	381			0 for 17

FOW 1st Inns: 19 33 124 241 318 374 375 375 381 381
FOW 2nd Inns:

Bowling: *First Innings*: Kapil 38-6-106-8, Binny 24-7-56-1, Sharma 19-3-70-0, Yadav 27-6-66-1, Shastri 38-11-70-0, Amarnath 3-0-9-0. *Second Innings*: Kapil 3-1-3-0, Sharma 2-0-9-0, Yadav 2-1-2-0, Shastri 1-1-0-0.

INDIA
SM Gavaskar not out	166
K Srikkanth c Ritchie b McDermott	51
C Sharma c Phillips b Reid	54
DB Vengsarkar c Phillips b Hughes	7
M Azharuddin c Phillips b Reid	17
M Amarnath c Marsh b McDermott	37
RJ Shastri b Reid	42
Kapil Dev (c) lbw Bright	38
RMH Binny c Phillips b McDermott	38
SMH Kirmani (+) c Boon b Reid	7
NS Yadav b Hughes b Hookes	41
EXTRAS (B 2, LB 7, W 1, NB 12)	22
TOTAL	520

FOW 1st Inns: 95 131 171 187 247 273 333 409 426 520

Bowling: *First Innings*: McDermott 48-14-131-3, Hughes 38-6-123-1, Reid 53-22-113-4, Bright 44-15-80-1, Matthews 17-2-60-0, Hookes 2-0-4-1.

Umpires: AR Crafter & SG Randell

THIRD TEST 1985–86 AUSTRALIA v INDIA
Sydney Cricket Ground, Sydney. January 2, 3, 4, 5, 6, 1986.
Toss: India. Match Drawn.

INDIA
SM Gavaskar b Holland	172
K Srikkanth b Reid	116
M Amarnath c Bright b Gilbert	138
Kapil Dev (c) b Gilbert	42
DB Vengsarkar not out	37
M Azharuddin not out	59
RJ Shastri	
SMH Kirmani (+)	
C Sharma	
L Sivaramakrishnan	
NS Yadav	
EXTRAS (B 5, LB 9, NB 22)	36
TOTAL	4 dec 600

FOW 1st Inns: 191 415 485 510

Bowling: *First Innings*: Gilbert 37-3-135-2, Reid 34-8-89-1, Bright 41-7-121-0, Holland 21-6-113-1, Matthews 29-2-95-0, Waugh 7-0-33-0.

AUSTRALIA
DC Boon b Kapil	131	(2)	run out	25
GR Marsh c Gavaskar b Shastri	92	(1)	lbw Yadav	28
AR Border (c) c Sharma b Shastri	71	(7)	c Sivaramakrishnan b Yadav	4
GM Ritchie c Kapil b Yadav	14	(3)	not out	17
WB Phillips (+) c Srikkanth b Shastri	14		c Srikkanth b Shastri	22
GRJ Matthews c Amarnath b Yadav	40		c Kapil b Yadav	17
SR Waugh c Sivaramakrishnan b Yadav	8	(4)	lbw Shastri	0
RJ Bright c Kirmani b Shastri	3		not out	0
DR Gilbert c Azharuddin b Yadav	1			
BA Reid st Kirmani b Yadav	4			
RG Holland not out	1			
EXTRAS (LB 14, NB 3)	17		(B 3, LB 2, NB 1)	6
TOTAL	396			6 for 119

FOW 1st Inns: 217 258 276 302 369 387 388 390 395 396
FOW 2nd Inns: 57 57 60 87 111 115

Bowling: *First Innings*: Kapil 25-8-65-1, Shastri 57-21-101-4, Yadav 62.3-21-99-5, Sivaramakrishnan 22-2-79-0, Sharma 13-2-38-0. *Second Innings*: Kapil 7-3-11-0, Yadav 33-22-19-3, Sharma 3-0-11-0, Shastri 25-12-36-2, Sivaramakrishnan 9-0-37-0.

Umpires: PJ McConnell & SG Randell

SECOND TEST 1985–86 AUSTRALIA v INDIA
Melbourne Cricket Ground, Melbourne. December 26, 27, 28, 29, 30, 1985.
Toss: India. Match Drawn.

AUSTRALIA
WB Phillips (+) b Yadav	7	(7)	c Srikkanth b Yadav	13
DC Boon lbw Shastri	14		c & b Kapil	19
GR Marsh c Sivaramakrishnan b Yadav	30	(1)	c Sivaramakrishnan b Shastri	19
AR Border (c) c & b Sivaramakrishnan	11	(3)	st Kirmani b Yadav	163
DW Hookes b Shastri	42	(4)	c Srikkanth b Shastri	0
SR Waugh c Kapil b Sivaramakrishnan	13	(5)	b Shastri	5
GRJ Matthews not out	100	(6)	c Azharuddin b Sivaramakrishnan	16
RJ Bright b Shastri	28		lbw Kapil	20
CJ McDermott c Kapil b Shastri	1		c & b Shastri	2
BA Reid c Srikkanth b Kapil	1		c Sivaramakrishnan b Yadav	13
DR Gilbert c Kirmani b Yadav	4		not out	10
EXTRAS (B 5, LB 6)	11		(B 11, LB 16, NB 1)	28
TOTAL	262			308

FOW 1st Inns: 22 26 41 90 109 127 193 195 216 262
FOW 2nd Inns: 32 54 54 84 126 161 202 205 231 308

Bowling: *First Innings*: Kapil 23-6-38-1, Binny 3-0-11-0, Shastri 37-13-87-4, Yadav 27.5-10-64-3, Sivaramakrishnan 13-2-51-2. *Second Innings*: Kapil 22-7-53-2, Amarnath 3-0-9-0, Shastri 47-13-92-4, Yadav 38.5-15-84-3, Sivaramakrishnan 13-1-43-1.

INDIA
SM Gavaskar b Gilbert	6		b Reid	8
K Srikkanth lbw Gilbert	86		c Bright b Reid	38
M Amarnath c Phillips b Reid	45		not out	3
DB Vengsarkar c & b Matthews	75		not out	1
M Azharuddin b Matthews	37			
RJ Shastri c Phillips b Waugh	49			
Kapil Dev (c) c Hookes b Reid	55			
RMH Binny c Matthews b Reid	0			
SMH Kirmani (+) c Phillips b Waugh	35			
L Sivaramakrishnan c Phillips b Reid	15			
NS Yadav not out	6			
EXTRAS (B 4, LB 15, NB 17)	36		(B 4, LB 1, NB 4)	9
TOTAL	445			2 for 59

FOW 1st Inns: 15 116 172 246 291 370 372 420 425 445
FOW 2nd Inns: 39 57

Bowling: *First Innings*: McDermott 15-5-52-0, Gilbert 22-1-81-2, Reid 38.2-11-100-4, Bright 31-8-76-0, Matthews 31-7-81-2, Waugh 11-5-36-2. *Second Innings*: McDermott 6-1-17-0, Gilbert 4-0-9-0, Reid 8-2-23-2, Bright 7-4-5-0.

Umpires: RA French & RC Isherwood

Australian Averages

1985–86 AUSTRALIA v INDIA

AUSTRALIA	M	Inn	NO	Runs	H.S	Avrge	Ct	St	Overs	Mds	Runs	Wkt	Avrge
Boon, DC	3	6	1	323	131	64.60	1	-	-	-	-	-	-
Border, AR	3	5	-	298	163	59.60	-	-	-	-	-	-	-
Bright, RJ	3	5	2	56	28	18.67	2	-	123.0	34	282	1	282.00
Gilbert, DR	2	3	1	15	10*	7.50	-	-	63.0	4	225	4	56.25
Holland, RG	1	1	1	1	1*	-	-	-	21.0	6	113	1	113.00
Hookes, DW	2	3	-	76	42	25.33	1	-	2.0	-	4	1	4.00
Hughes, MG	1	1	-	0	0	0.00	1	-	38.0	6	123	1	123.00
Marsh, GR	3	6	1	176	92	35.20	1	-	-	-	-	-	-
Matthews, GRJ	3	5	1	191	100*	47.75	2	-	77.0	11	236	2	118.00
McDermott, CJ	2	3	-	3	2	1.00	-	-	69.0	20	200	3	66.67
Phillips, WB	3	5	-	67	22	13.40	8	-	-	-	-	-	-
Reid, BA	3	4	-	20	13	5.00	-	-	133.2	43	325	11	29.55
Ritchie, GM	2	3	1	159	128	79.50	1	-	-	-	-	-	-
Waugh, SR	2	4	-	26	13	6.50	-	-	18.0	5	69	2	34.50

Indian Averages

1985–86 AUSTRALIA v INDIA

INDIA	M	Inn	NO	Runs	H.S	Avrge	Ct	St	Overs	Mds	Runs	Wkt	Avrge
Amarnath, M	3	4	1	223	138	74.33	1	-	6.0	-	18	-	-
Azharuddin, M	3	3	1	113	59*	56.50	2	-	-	-	-	-	-
Binny, RMH	2	2	-	38	38	19.00	-	-	27.0	7	67	1	67.00
Gavaskar, SM	3	4	1	352	172	117.33	2	-	-	-	-	-	-
Kapil Dev	3	3	-	135	55	45.00	5	-	118.0	31	276	12	23.00
Kirmani, SMH	3	2	-	42	35	21.00	3	2	-	-	-	-	-
Sharma, C	2	1	-	54	54	54.00	2	-	37.0	5	128	-	-
Shastri, RJ	3	2	-	91	49	45.50	1	-	205.0	71	386	14	27.57
Sivaramakrishnan, L	2	1	-	15	15	15.00	6	-	57.0	5	210	3	70.00
Srikkanth, K	3	4	-	291	116	72.75	5	-	-	-	-	-	-
Vengsarkar, DB	3	4	2	120	75	60.00	2	-	-	-	-	-	-
Yadav, NS	3	4	1	47	41	47.00	1	-	191.1	75	334	15	22.27

Border follows the greats with twin tons and 6000 runs

Allan Border lashes out with his favorite cut shot.

Christchurch, March 4. Allan Border was disenchanted with his side's efforts earlier this summer, but the smile returned to his face after a splendid personal performance in the drawn second Test.

For the second time in his career Border scored two centuries in a Test and in doing so, passed the 6000 run mark and moved to third on the all-time Australian list behind Greg Chappell and Sir Donald Bradman.

The phlegmatic left-hander is a class above the rest of the team's batsmen. The others would do well to place the same value on their wickets.

Series to New Zealand 1–0

Auckland, March 17. Yet another trademark Australian batting collapse has enabled New Zealand to retain the Trans-Tasman Trophy which it won earlier this summer.

For once the architect of the victory was not Richard Hadlee. Off-spinner John Bracewell, who originally was not even ranked highly enough to make the trip to Australia, took 10 wickets in the match. Since being flown to Australia as a replacement the gritty undertaker has shown his talents to the benefit of the Kiwi side.

On the final day Australia fell apart for just 103 and only David Boon, who carried his bat for 58 not out, could hold his head high.

Geoff Marsh scored his maiden century in the first innings of this match and confirmed his arrival as an opener of substance, batting for a touch over four hours. Australia batted solidly, but slowly on the first day then was skittled on the second morning.

Jeremy Coney's 93 prevented a New Zealand failure as Greg Matthews nagged away with accurate slow bowling and contained the Kiwis. With a first innings lead of 56 Australia should have been well placed to pursue victory, but the second innings disintegration gave New Zealand a soft target.

The first two Tests had ended in draws. Rain interrupted both games, particularly the first Test, when only 80 minutes play was possible on the fourth day and none on the last.

The Marsh–Boon opening stand of 104 was a healthy sign for the Australians, and Matthews made an excellent century.

Australia's batting was patchy

John Bracewell had the match of his life in the third Test, taking 10 wickets and humbling the Aussies.

apart from Border. Relieved of his wicketkeeping duties, Phillips had a fairly quiet series with the bat, and Ritchie's batting fell away after his first Test score of 92.

Young Steve Waugh gave some encouraging signs with his 74 in the second Test, providing great support for his skipper after the Aussies had slumped to 5/74. In addition to his batting Waugh proved a handy medium-pace bowler and he gave his captain an extra option at the bowling crease.

Captain disgusted

Auckland, March 17. Allan Border is reported to be getting grumpier by the day.

The frustrated captain issued an ultimatum to his players after a one day loss in Dunedin – that he would quit as captain unless they started winning.

'They are going to show me whether they really want me to play for Australia and whether they want to play under me,' Border said.

'I'll find out over the next three games and my decision will be made as to my future as a captain and a player after that.

'I don't think it's my captaincy, but if we continue to lose, you've got to start saying, "Right, someone else has to come in."'

Cooking up a partnership: opening pair Geoff Marsh and David Boon show that they get on well on the other side of the fence.

FIRST TEST 1985–86 NEW ZEALAND v AUSTRALIA
Basin Reserve, Wellington. February 21, 22, 23, 24, 25 (no play), 1986.
Toss: New Zealand. Match Drawn.

AUSTRALIA
DC Boon c Smith b Troup 70
GR Marsh c Coney b Chatfield 43
WB Phillips b Gillespie 32
AR Border (c) lbw Hadlee 13
GM Ritchie b Troup 92
GRJ Matthews c Rutherford b Coney 130
SR Waugh c Smith b Coney 11
TJ Zoehrer (+) c(S)JG Bracewell b Coney 18
CJ McDermott b Hadlee 2
BA Reid not out 0
SP Davis c & b Hadlee 0
    EXTRAS (B 2, LB 9, W 4, NB 9) 24
TOTAL 435

FOW 1st Inns: 104 143 166 166 379 414 418 435 435 435

Bowling: *First Innings*: Hadlee 37.1-5-116-3, Chatfield 36-10-96-1, Troup 28-6-86-2, Gillespie 27-2-79-1, Coney 18-7-47-3.

NEW ZEALAND
TJ Franklin c Border b McDermott 0
BA Edgar c Waugh b Matthews 38
JF Reid c Phillips b Reid 32
SR Gillespie c Border b Reid 28
MD Crowe b Matthews 19
KR Rutherford c(S)RJ Bright b Reid 65
JV Coney (c) not out 101
RJ Hadlee not out 72
IDS Smith (+)
GB Troup
EJ Chatfield
    EXTRAS (B 2, LB 6, W 1, NB 15) 24
TOTAL .....6 for 379

FOW 1st Inns: 0 57 94 115 138 247

Bowling: *First Innings*: McDermott 25.3-5-80-1, Davis 25-4-70-0, Reid 31-6-104-3, Matthews 37-10-107-2, Border 4-3-1-0, Waugh 4-1-9-0.

Umpires: FR Goodall & SJ Woodward

SECOND TEST 1985–86 NEW ZEALAND v AUSTRALIA
Lancaster Park, Christchurch. February 28, March 1, 2, 3, 4, 1986.
Toss: New Zealand. Match Drawn.

AUSTRALIA
GR Marsh b Hadlee .....28 (2) lbw Bracewell 15
DC Boon c Coney b Hadlee .....26 (1) c Coney b Troup 6
WB Phillips c Smith b Chatfield .....1 b Hadlee 25
AR Border (c) b Chatfield .....140 not out 114
GM Ritchie lbw Hadlee .....4 c Smith b Bracewell 11
GRJ Matthews c Smith b Hadlee .....6 c (S)JJ Crowe b Hadlee 3
SR Waugh lbw Hadlee .....74 c Smith b Bracewell 1
TJ Zoehrer (+) c Coney b Hadlee .....30 c Rutherford b Bracewell 13
RJ Bright c Smith b Bracewell .....21 not out 21
DR Gilbert b Hadlee 15
BA Reid not out 1
    EXTRAS (B 1, LB 9, NB 8) .....18 (LB 6, W 1, NB 3) 10
TOTAL .....364 .....7 dec 219

FOW 1st Inns: 57 58 58 64 74 251 319 334 358 364
FOW 2nd Inns: 15 32 76 120 129 130 167

Bowling: *First Innings*: Hadlee 44.4-8-116-7, Troup 34-4-104-0, Chatfield 36-13-56-2, Bracewell 27-9-46-1, MD Crowe 2-1-4-0, Coney 9-0-28-0. *Second Innings*: Hadlee 25-4-47-2, Troup 15-0-50-1, Chatfield 17-6-29-0, Bracewell 33-12-77-4, Reid 1-1-0-0, Coney 3-1-10-0.

NEW ZEALAND
JG Wright c Zoehrer b Gilbert .....10 (2) not out 4
BA Edgar lbw Reid .....8 (1) c & b Matthews 9
JF Reid c Zoehrer b Waugh .....2 not out 0
MD Crowe c Waugh b Reid 137
KR Rutherford lbw Gilbert 0
JV Coney (c) c Reid b Waugh 98
RJ Hadlee c Zoehrer b Reid 0
IDS Smith (+) b Waugh 22
JG Bracewell c Marsh b Reid 20
GB Troup lbw Waugh 10
EJ Chatfield not out 2
    EXTRAS (B 6, LB 8, NB 16) .....30 (NB 3) 3
TOTAL .....339 .....1 for 16

FOW 1st Inns: 17 29 29 48 124 191 263 311 331 339
FOW 2nd Inns: 16

Bowling: *First Innings*: Reid 34.3-8-90-4, Gilbert 26-4-106-2, Waugh 23-6-56-4, Bright 18-6-51-0, Matthews 6-1-22-0. *Second Innings*: Gilbert 7-4-9-0, Reid 4-0-7-0, Matthews 3-3-0-1.

Umpires: BL Aldridge & FR Goodall

THIRD TEST 1985–86 NEW ZEALAND v AUSTRALIA
Eden Park, Auckland. March 13, 14, 15, 16, 17, 1986.
Toss: Australia. New Zealand won by 8 wkts.

AUSTRALIA
DC Boon c Coney b Hadlee .....16 (2) not out 58
GR Marsh c Coney b Hadlee .....118 (1) lbw Hadlee 0
WB Phillips c Smith b Bracewell .....62 c Bracewell b Chatfield 15
AR Border (c) c Smith b Chatfield .....17 (5) b Bracewell 6
TJ Zoehrer (+) c Coney b Robertson .....9 (4) lbw Chatfield 1
GM Ritchie c Smith b Chatfield .....56 lbw Chatfield 1
GRJ Matthews c Smith b Bracewell .....5 st Smith b Bracewell 4
SR Waugh c Reid b Bracewell .....1 b Bracewell 0
RJ Bright c Smith b Hadlee .....5 b Bracewell 0
CJ McDermott lbw Bracewell .....9 b Bracewell 6
BA Reid not out .....0 c Hadlee b Bracewell 8
    EXTRAS (B 2, LB 11, NB 3) .....16 (LB 4) 4
TOTAL 314 103

FOW 1st Inns: 25 193 225 225 278 293 294 301 309 314
FOW 2nd Inns: 0 28 35 59 62 62 71 71 71 103

Bowling: *First Innings*: Hadlee 31-12-60-3, Robertson 24-6-91-1, Chatfield 29-10-54-2, Crowe 3-2-4-0, Bracewell 43.3-19-74-4, Coney 5-0-18-0. *Second Innings*: Hadlee 20-7-48-1, Chatfield 18-9-19-3, Bracewell 22-8-32-6.

NEW ZEALAND
JG Wright c Zoehrer b McDermott .....56 c Boon b Matthews 59
BA Edgar lbw Matthews .....24 b Reid 1
KR Rutherford b Matthews .....0 not out 50
MD Crowe lbw Matthews .....0 not out 23
JF Reid c Phillips b Bright 16
JV Coney (c) c Border b McDermott 93
RJ Hadlee b Reid 33
IDS Smith (+) b Waugh 3
JG Bracewell c Boon b Bright 4
GK Robertson st Zoehrer b Matthews 12
EJ Chatfield not out 1
    EXTRAS (B 7, LB 8, NB 1) .....16 (B 18, LB 4, NB 5) 27
TOTAL .....258 .....2 for 160

FOW 1st Inns: 73 73 73 103 107 170 184 203 250 258
FOW 2nd Inns: 6 106

Bowling: *First Innings*: McDermott 17-2-47-2, Reid 19-2-63-1, Matthews 34-15-61-4, Bright 22-4-58-2, Waugh 5-1-14-1. *Second Innings*: McDermott 14-3-29-0, Reid 12.4-2-30-1, Matthews 31-18-46-1, Bright 23-12-29-0, Waugh 4-1-4-0.

Umpires: RL McHarg & SJ Woodward

Australian Averages

1985–86 NEW ZEALAND v AUSTRALIA

AUSTRALIA	M	Inn	NO	Runs	H.S	Avrge	Ct	St	Overs	Mds	Runs	Wkt	Avrge
Boon, DC	3	5	1	176	70	44.00	2	-	-	-	-	-	-
Border, AR	3	5	1	290	140	72.50	3	-	4.0	3	1	-	-
Bright, RJ	2	4	1	47	21*	15.67	-	-	63.0	22	138	2	69.00
Davis, SP	1	1	-	0	0	0.00	-	-	25.0	4	70	-	-
Gilbert, DR	1	1	-	15	15	15.00	-	-	33.0	8	115	2	57.50
Marsh, GR	3	5	-	204	118	40.80	1	-	-	-	-	-	-
Matthews, GRJ	3	5	-	148	130	29.60	1	-	111.0	47	236	8	29.50
McDermott, CJ	2	3	-	17	9	5.67	-	-	56.3	10	156	3	52.00
Phillips, WB	3	5	-	135	62	27.00	2	-	-	-	-	-	-
Reid, BA	3	4	3	9	8	9.00	1	-	101.1	18	294	9	32.67
Ritchie, GM	3	5	-	164	92	32.80	-	-	-	-	-	-	-
Waugh, SR	3	5	-	87	74	17.40	2	-	36.0	9	83	5	16.60
Zoehrer, TJ	3	5	-	71	30	14.20	4	1	-	-	-	-	-

New Zealand Averages

1985–86 NEW ZEALAND v AUSTRALIA

NEW ZEALAND	M	Inn	NO	Runs	H.S	Avrge	Ct	St	Overs	Mds	Runs	Wkt	Avrge
Bracewell, JG	2	2	-	24	20	12.00	1	-	125.3	48	229	15	15.27
Chatfield, EJ	3	2	2	3	2*	-	-	-	136.0	48	254	8	31.75
Coney, JV	3	3	1	292	101*	146.00	7	-	35.0	8	103	3	34.33
Crowe, MD	3	4	1	179	137	59.67	-	-	5.0	3	8	-	-
Edgar, BA	3	5	-	80	38	16.00	-	-	-	-	-	-	-
Franklin, TJ	1	1	-	0	0	0.00	-	-	-	-	-	-	-
Gillespie, SR	1	1	-	28	28	28.00	-	-	27.0	2	79	1	79.00
Hadlee, RJ	3	3	1	105	72*	52.50	2	-	157.5	36	387	16	24.19
Reid, JF	3	5	-	50	32	16.67	1	-	1.0	1	0	-	-
Robertson, GK	1	1	-	12	12	12.00	-	-	24.0	6	91	1	91.00
Rutherford, KR	3	4	-	115	65	38.33	2	-	-	-	-	-	-
Smith, IDS	3	2	-	25	22	12.50	11	1	-	-	-	-	-
Troup, GB	2	2	-	10	10	10.00	-	-	77.0	10	240	3	80.00
Wright, JG	2	4	1	129	59	43.00	-	-	-	-	-	-	-

Tied Test in steamy Madras

Maninder Singh is trapped lbw by Greg Matthews and the Australians rejoice at Test cricket's second tie. The tall Bruce Reid raises his arms in triumph as Geoff Marsh leads the charge to the refreshments.

Madras, Sep. 22. For only the second time in cricket history, a Test match has ended in a tie.

Unlike the 1960–61 tie between Australia and the West Indies, this was not a match played on a knife-edge for five days.

India was totally outplayed for three days, only just avoiding the follow-on and getting a sniff of victory courtesy of a sporting declaration by Allan Border.

Australia got away to a fine start, with David Boon making a century on his first day and Dean Jones and Allan Border following suit. Jones played a heroic innings of 210, enabling Australia to declare early on the third day at 7/574.

Kapil Dev's hundred came off 109 balls and forced Australia to bat again. Border's men made 5/170 off 49 overs in an acrimonious day which was punctuated by verbal abuse between players and confrontations with umpires.

The tension continued on the final day when Border openly argued with umpire Dotiwala. Australians Bright, Matthews and Zoehrer all disputed decisions and early in the match Srikkanth shook his fist under the nose of close-in fieldsman Bright.

Maninder ran 40 yards to remonstrate with Jones after dismissing

him in the second innings.

Chasing 349, India was sitting pretty at tea with 2/193 on the board. Gavaskar and Dev went in quick succession and Australia was back in contention. India was within 17 runs of victory with four wickets in hand when Bright snaffled three wickets.

Maninder Singh, a true no. 11 batsman, came to the crease with four needed from the last over. Shastri managed a two, then a single to level the scores. Maninder had three balls from which to make the winning run, but on the second-last ball of Matthews' 31st over on the trot, was trapped lbw.

Dean Jones endures all for double century in pressure cooker

Madras, Sep. 19. Dean Jones has played one of the most remarkable innings in modern day Test cricket.

His 210 was made in searing heat of 45°C and 60 per cent humidity. Through it all, he kept going despite agonising stomach and leg cramps, repeated vomiting attacks and heat exhaustion.

The marathon knock took 503 minutes from 330 balls. Immediately after he left the field, Jones collapsed and was rushed to hospital and placed on a saline drip. The Australian physiotherapist Errol Alcott was extremely concerned about Jones' well-being in a possible life-threatening situation.

It is no wonder that coach Bob Simpson rates it the most courageous innings he has ever seen.

Jones' temperament and courage were proven by this monumental display. It is the first time an

Australian has made a double century in a Test match in India.

Jones is appearing in only his third Test and has been out of the team for two and a half years. A confident character, he has scored plenty of runs for Victoria in the meantime.

During his saga at the crease, Jones shed seven kilograms. The Victorian suffered hallucinations from about the time he reached 150. After vomiting for the 15th time, Jones was doubled up in agony and told Allan Border he could not go on. The skipper replied that he would get a 'real Australian out here – a Queenslander', as Greg Ritchie was next man in.

By the latter part of the innings Jones could only stand and hammer fours. Running was out of the question. He had batted himself literally to a standstill.

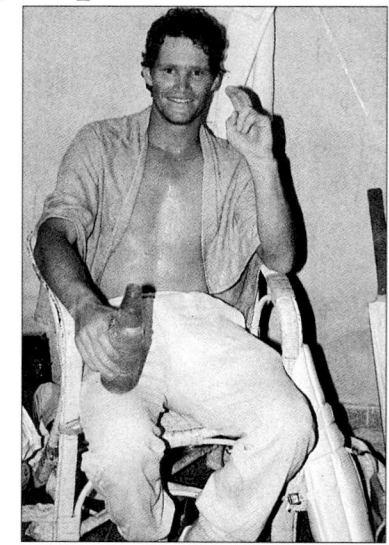

Dean Jones in meltdown mode at tea on the second day of his marathon stay, after he had just completed his double century.

FIRST TEST 1986-87 INDIA v AUSTRALIA
Nehru (Corporation) Stadium, Madras. September 18, 19, 20, 21, 22, 1986.
Toss: Australia. Match Tied.

AUSTRALIA

DC Boon c Kapil b Sharma	122 (2)	lbw Maninder	49	
GR Marsh c Kapil b Yadav	22 (1)	b Shastri	11	
DM Jones b Yadav	210	c Azharuddin b Maninder	24	
RJ Bright c Shastri b Yadav	30			
AR Border (c) c Gavaskar b Shastri	106 (4)	b Maninder	27	
GM Ritchie run out	13 (5)	c Pandit b Shastri	28	
GRJ Matthews c Pandit b Yadav	44 (6)	not out	27	
SR Waugh not out	12 (7)	not out	2	
CJ McDermott				
TJ Zoehrer (+)				
BA Reid				
EXTRAS (B 1, LB 7, W 1, NB 6)	15	(LB 1, NB 1)	2	
TOTAL	7 dec 574		5 dec 170	

FOW 1st Inns: 48 206 282 460 481 544 574
FOW 2nd Inns: 31 81 94 125 165

Bowling: *First Innings*: Kapil 18-5-52-0, Sharma 16-1-70-1, Maninder 39-8-135-0, Yadav 49.5-9-142-4, Shastri 47-8-161-1, Srikkanth 1-0-6-0. *Second Innings*: Sharma 6-0-19-0, Kapil 1-0-5-0, Shastri 14-2-50-2, Maninder 19-2-60-3, Yadav 9-0-35-0.

INDIA

SM Gavaskar c & b Matthews	8	c Jones b Bright	90	
K Srikkanth c Ritchie b Matthews	53	c Waugh b Matthews	39	
M Amarnath run out	1	c Boon b Matthews	51	
M Azharuddin c & b Bright	50	c Ritchie b Bright	42	
RJ Shastri c Zoehrer b Matthews	62 (7)	not out	48	
CS Pandit (+) c Waugh b Matthews	35	b Matthews	39	
Kapil Dev (c) c Border b Matthews	119 (5)	c Bright b Matthews	1	
KS More c Zoehrer b Waugh	4 (9)	lbw Bright	0	
C Sharma c Zoehrer b Reid	30 (8)	c McDermott b Bright	23	
NS Yadav c Border b Bright	19	b Bright	8	
Maninder Singh not out	0	lbw Matthews	0	
EXTRAS (B 1, LB 9, NB 6)	16	(B 1, LB 3, NB 2)	6	
TOTAL	397		347	

FOW 1st Inns: 62 65 65 142 206 220 245 330 387 397
FOW 2nd Inns: 55 158 204 251 253 291 331 334 334 347

Bowling: *First Innings*: McDermott 14-2-59-0, Reid 18-4-93-1, Matthews 28.2-3-103-5, Bright 23-3-88-2, Waugh 11-2-44-1. *Second Innings*: McDermott 5-0-27-0, Reid 10-2-48-0, Matthews 39.5-7-146-5, Bright 25-3-94-5, Border 3-0-12-0, Waugh 4-1-16-0.

Umpires: DN Dotiwalla & V Vikram Raju

SECOND TEST 1986-87 INDIA v AUSTRALIA
Feroze Shah Kotla Ground, Delhi. September 26 (no play), 27 (no play), 28 (no play), 29, 30, 1986.
Toss: Australia. Match Drawn.

AUSTRALIA

GR Marsh c Pandit b Sharma	11
DC Boon c Maninder b Shastri	67
DM Jones st Pandit b Shastri	29
SR Waugh not out	39
TJ Zoehrer (+) not out	52
AR Border (c)	
GRJ Matthews	
RJ Bright	
CJ McDermott	
GM Ritchie	
DR Gilbert	
EXTRAS (LB 2, W 4, NB 3)	9
TOTAL	3 dec 207

FOW 1st Inns: 34 110 118

Bowling: *First Innings*: Kapil 14-5-27-0, Sharma 8-1-34-1, Shastri 21.4-4-44-2, Maninder 19-4-54-0, Yadav 13-1-46-0.

INDIA

SM Gavaskar b Gilbert	4
K Srikkanth run out	26
M Azharuddin c Zoehrer b Waugh	24
DB Vengsarkar not out	22
CS Pandit (+) not out	26
RJ Shastri	
Kapil Dev (c)	
M Amarnath	
C Sharma	
Maninder Singh	
NS Yadav	
EXTRAS (LB 5)	5
TOTAL	3 for 107

FOW 1st Inns: 9 57 59

Bowling: *First Innings*: McDermott 6-1-24-0, Gilbert 11-1-44-1, Waugh 6-0-29-1, Boon 2-1-5-0, Jones 1-1-0-0.

Umpires: VK Ramaswamy & PD Reporter

THIRD TEST 1986-87 INDIA v AUSTRALIA
Wankhede Stadium, Bombay. October 15, 16, 17, 18, 19, 1986.
Toss: Australia. Match Drawn.

AUSTRALIA

GR Marsh c Gavaskar b Kulkarni	101 (2)	b Shastri	20	
DC Boon c Gavaskar b Kulkarni	47 (1)	c More b Shastri	40	
DM Jones c(S)L Sivaramakrishnan b Yadav	35	not out	73	
AR Border (c) st More b Maninder	46	not out	66	
GM Ritchie run out	31			
GRJ Matthews b Yadav	20			
SR Waugh b Yadav	6			
TJ Zoehrer (+) c & b Maninder	21			
RJ Bright lbw Kulkarni	8			
DR Gilbert c(S)L Sivaramakrishnan b Yadav	1			
BA Reid not out	2			
EXTRAS (B 5, LB 12, NB 10)	27	(B 5, LB 5, NB 7)	17	
TOTAL	345		2 for 216	

FOW 1st Inns: 76 151 241 252 295 304 308 340 340 345
FOW 2nd Inns: 64 70

Bowling: *First Innings*: Kulkarni 23-2-85-3, Kapil 6-1-16-0, Shastri 42-16-68-0, Yadav 41.4-8-84-4, Maninder 33-10-72-2, Srikkanth 2-0-3-0. *Second Innings*: Kapil 6-1-24-0, Maninder 20-6-31-0, Shastri 30-8-60-2, Yadav 23-7-52-0, Kulkarni 6-0-29-0, Srikkanth 3-0-10-0.

INDIA

SM Gavaskar c Ritchie b Matthews	103
K Srikkanth c Marsh b Bright	24
KS More (+) c Jones b Matthews	15
M Amarnath c(S)MRJ Veletta b Matthews	35
DB Vengsarkar not out	164
M Azharuddin c(S)MRJ Veletta b Matthews	10
RJ Shastri not out	121
Kapil Dev (c)	
RR Kulkarni	
NS Yadav	
Maninder Singh	
EXTRAS (B 9, LB 15, NB 21)	45
TOTAL	5 dec 517

FOW 1st Inns: 53 119 194 205 219

Bowling: *First Innings*: Reid 32-5-81-0, Gilbert 24-3-75-0, Matthews 52-8-158-4, Bright 38-6-109-1, Border 10-3-29-0, Waugh 14-2-41-0.

Umpires: JD Ghosh & RB Gupta

Australian Averages

1986-87 INDIA v AUSTRALIA

AUSTRALIA	M	Inn	NO	Runs	H.S	Avrge	Ct	St	Overs	Mds	Runs	Wkt	Avrge
Boon, DC	3	5	-	325	122	65.00	1	-	2.0	1	5	-	-
Border, AR	3	4	1	245	106	81.67	2	-	13.0	3	41	-	-
Bright, RJ	3	2	-	38	30	19.00	2	-	86.0	12	291	8	36.38
Gilbert, DR	2	1	-	1	1	1.00	-	-	35.0	4	119	1	119.00
Jones, DM	3	5	1	371	210	92.75	2	-	1.0	1	0	-	-
Marsh, GR	3	5	-	165	101	33.00	1	-	-	-	-	-	-
Matthews, GRJ	3	3	1	91	44	45.50	1	-	120.1	18	407	14	29.07
McDermott, CJ	2	-	-	-	-	-	1	-	25.0	3	110	-	-
Reid, BA	2	1	1	2	2*	-	-	-	60.0	11	222	1	222.00
Ritchie, GM	3	3	-	72	31	24.00	3	-	-	-	-	-	-
Waugh, SR	3	4	3	59	39*	59.00	-	-	35.0	5	130	2	65.00
Zoehrer, TJ	3	2	1	73	52*	73.00	4	-	-	-	-	-	-

Indian Averages

1986-87 INDIA v AUSTRALIA

INDIA	M	Inn	NO	Runs	H.S	Avrge	Ct	St	Overs	Mds	Runs	Wkt	Avrge
Amarnath, M	3	3	-	87	51	29.00	-	-	-	-	-	-	-
Azharuddin, M	3	4	-	126	50	31.50	1	-	-	-	-	-	-
Gavaskar, SM	3	4	-	205	103	51.25	3	-	-	-	-	-	-
Kapil Dev	3	2	-	120	119	60.00	2	-	45.0	12	124	-	-
Kulkarni, RR	1	-	-	-	-	-	-	-	29.0	2	114	3	38.00
Maninder Singh	3	2	1	0	0*	0.00	2	-	130.0	30	352	5	70.40
More, KS	2	3	-	19	15	6.33	1	1	-	-	-	-	-
Pandit, CS	2	3	1	100	39	50.00	3	1	-	-	-	-	-
Sharma, C	2	2	-	53	30	26.50	-	-	30.0	2	123	2	61.50
Shastri, RJ	3	3	2	231	121*	231.00	1	-	154.4	38	383	7	54.71
Srikkanth, K	3	4	-	142	53	35.50	-	-	6.0	-	19	-	-
Vengsarkar, DB	2	2	2	186	164*	-	-	-	-	-	-	-	-
Yadav, NS	3	2	-	27	19	13.50	-	-	136.3	25	359	8	44.88

Botham rampage puts England on front foot

QUICK SINGLES

Unimpressed. Allan Border has never left any doubt about his opinion of one day cricket. He criticised the decision to impose a penalty of 0.1 of a point on Sheffield Shield sides that did not complete 96 overs in a day. 'Let them fiddle with one day cricket, he said. 'From the four-day game we are trying to produce Test cricketers. Now there are going to be times when we get joke cricket played just so teams can get their overs in.'

Costly exercise. The WACA faced a legal bill of $400,000 after losing the case which permitted rebel tourist Kim Hughes to continue to play grade cricket for his club.

Aussie Springbok rebel. Most bizarre situation of the season was Kepler Wessels' inclusion in the Australian rebel side against South Africa, the country of his birth. It came about after negotiations between the South African and Australian boards.

How's that? Michael Haysman had the most remarkable piece of luck imaginable when playing for the rebel Australian XI against the South African President's XI. Stranded out of his crease when his stumps were hit by a direct throw, the bails flew in the air then landed back in the grooves on top of the stumps. Haysman regained his ground and continued the innings.

Drought breaker. The Australian win in the fifth Test ended a 15-Test winless sequence – their longest run without a victory in Test history. The most recent win had been against New Zealand in Sydney in 1985–86.

Unbeatable. South Australians David Hookes and Wayne Phillips made a remarkable unbroken fourth wicket stand of 462 against Tasmania. Hookes' score of 306 not out included 41 fours and two sixes. Phillips finished on 213 not out. The partnership was the biggest for any wicket in Australian cricket, surpassing the 456 by Bill Ponsford and Edgar Mayne for Victoria in 1923–24.

Coaching influence. Bob Simpson's influence since being appointed full-time cricket manager in October is bearing fruit in the Australian team – they look a fitter, tighter unit.

Dean Jones dances out of his crease and is stumped by England 'keeper Jack Richards, as Ian Botham celebrates at first slip.

Brisbane, Nov. 19. Ian Botham has once again proven to be Australia's nemesis in the opening Ashes Test, bludgeoning England to a seven-wicket victory.

Before this game England was seen as a struggling, badly chosen and divided team in contrast to the perception of Australia as a spirited young unit on the upward curve.

Botham has turned the whole equation upside down by lacerating the Australian attack in scoring his first Test century for three years.

It forced Allan Border to retreat in his captaincy and set fields to weather the storm as Botham belted 13 fours and four sixes in his 138 off 174 balls.

Surprisingly, Australia left out Geoff Lawson and banked on novices Bruce Reid, Merv Hughes and Chris Matthews. Hughes copped such a hammering that he has been dumped from the team for the second Test.

Australia was always under the hammer in its first innings and

when Border lost patience and was stumped off Edmonds, the writing was on the wall. Greg Matthews tried hard to see the home team clear of the follow-on, but he ran out of partners. Predictably it was Botham who cracked the Australian tail.

Geoff Marsh confirmed his growing reputation as a 'sticker' by resolutely fighting his way to a century, but had insufficient support.

England needed only 74 to win when it batted a second time.

Allan Lamb is a sombre figure as rain stops play in Melbourne.

Bob Hawke enjoys the Prime Minister's XI match with Colin Cowdrey (right) and leading Victorian and Australian cricket identity, Bob Bennett (left).

The weakest team ever to leave England

London, Nov. 15. It is not the first time that the tag 'weakest team ever to tour' has been affixed to an Ashes team.

In 1986 it has been England's turn to cop the label. Critics said that the fast bowlers Dilley, DeFreitas, Botham, Foster and Small were unlikely to strike fear into the Australians, and that it was hard to see the batsmen making match-winning scores.

One English writer said that there were only three things wrong with the English – 'they can't bat, can't bowl and can't field'.

The British press also had a field day when skipper Mike Gatting slept in and missed the start of the game against Victoria.

Rebels lose 1–0

Port Elizabeth, Feb. 4. Australia's rebel team has been beaten 1–0 in its second tour of South Africa.

The four-match series finished here today. Batsmen John Dyson, Steve Smith and Michael Haysman each had an excellent series, but the Aussie bowlers could not make inroads against the South African batting, apart from the occasional fierce spell from Rodney Hogg.

Peter Kirsten, Ken McEwan and Graeme Pollock took a heavy toll on the Australian attack, with the amazing Pollock stroking a glorious century in the final clash just three weeks short of his 43rd birthday.

One day star Simon O'Donnell about to let fly.

Ashes still in English hands

Geoff Marsh is caught in spectacular fashion by wicketkeeper Jack Richards.

Melbourne, Dec. 28. Australia has failed to regain the Ashes after being humbled in the fourth Test in just three days, and now trails 0–2 with only one Test to go.

It is the first time since 1901–02 that England has won a Test on Australian soil in under three days. The Australians had effectively lost the game by tea on the first day after some poor batting and team selection.

The decision to play all-rounder Greg Matthews left Australia with just five specialist batsmen including David Boon, whose century at Adelaide was the only time he has passed 15 this series.

Allan Border said at the start of this game that Australia would have to play boldly, but his batsmen took this to ridiculous extremes as they slashed wildly and often. Even the normally sober approach of Geoff Marsh went out the window when he played a wayward hook at a Botham ball on the off-stump. In 30 hours at the crease against England this tour he has rarely played the hook-shot, yet decided to do it at a crucial point in the series.

Botham bowled at reduced pace because of a strained intercostal muscle, yet as so often before, he picked up wickets despite looking innocuous at times. He and Gladstone Small simply bowled on the spot and let the Australians self-destruct.

A large Boxing Day crowd saw local boy Dean Jones score 59 with a mix of audacity and luck, but the score of 141 was never going to be enough to win a Test.

England passed that tally for the loss of just one wicket and at 1/163 was looking at a possible score of 500. Instead, it was kept to 349, Chris Broad making his third century in four Tests.

England's dogged professionalism was again evident in its tail-end batting, which added a vital 60 runs for the last two wickets and effectively squelched Australian hopes of making the game a contest.

Australia's only chance of getting back into the game lay with in-form batsmen Border and Marsh digging in for a lengthy stand. They were on track until Border decided to go after Small's bowling. He slashed two fours then was caught at third slip trying to repeat the effort.

Australia's back was effectively broken and the final blow came 40 runs later when Marsh, after 213 minutes of patience tried to take a suicidal single and was run out by several metres. After that the Aussies lost their will, and six wickets dissolved in 80 minutes.

After the thrashing in the opening Test, Australia had shown more gumption in the second and third Tests.

An opening stand of 223 between Bill Athey and Chris Broad ensured that England would never lose the second Test. The game illustrated the deficiencies of both bowling attacks and demonstrated why England and Australia currently find themselves at the bottom of the pile in world cricket.

The bowlers again struggled in the third Test when only 20 wickets fell for the entire game. England went into the game without the injured Botham, but took the negative approach of selecting batsman James Whitaker to replace him.

Against an attack of just four specialist bowlers, David Boon was able to bat his way back to form with a century, after a horror run.

Prisoner of Zenda proves his worth as spinner

Sydney, Jan. 15. Was it the right Taylor? That was the question asked around Australia when Peter Taylor was selected for the Australian team in the fifth Test.

Some mischievous elements in the English press are convinced that the Australian new boy in the fifth Test was meant to be NSW opening bat Mark Taylor, who has steadily built a reputation over the last two Sheffield seasons.

Spin bowler Peter Taylor has only played six first-class matches before this game, and when it was announced that 'Taylor of New South Wales' was in the team, a TV station immediately dispatched its crew to the home of the batsman.

It is reminiscent of the old film about mistaken identity – *The Prisoner of Zenda*, but Australian selector Lawrie Sawle says it is disgraceful to suggest that the wrong player was selected.

If Peter Taylor's selection was a case of mistaken identity between selectors and the board's media liaison people, then it was the best piece of luck all summer for Australia.

The 30-year-old spinner snared eight wickets for the match, scored vital runs (11 and 42), and saved face for Australia, which finally scored a victory, by 55 runs.

The contribution of batsman Dean Jones should not be overlooked as he put his head down to amass 184 not out – the highest Test score in Sydney since Don Bradman and Sid Barnes each scored 234 in 1946–47.

It was Taylor, though, who could do no wrong in this match. He

Mystery man Peter Taylor: made a mighty debut in the fifth Test.

held his nerve as Ian Botham strode to the crease clearly intending to teach the newcomer a lesson. The first two balls went for four, and soon after, Botham heaved a six into the members' stand.

But another attempt at a big hit was caught by Geoff Marsh at forward short leg. England had slumped to 5/119, and a revitalised Australian team was on its way to victory.

Australia grabbed the last wicket in England's second innings with just one over remaining. Leggie Peter Sleep bowled a flipper that took Emburey's middle and leg stumps, to end a memorable match for spinners.

Seven fingers for seven wickets: John Emburey took 7/87 in Australia's second innings in the fifth Test, but Australia still won by 55 runs.

FIRST TEST 1986–87 AUSTRALIA v ENGLAND
Brisbane Cricket Ground, Brisbane. November 14, 15, 16, 18, 19, 1986.
Toss: Australia. England won by 7 wkts.

ENGLAND

BC Broad c Zoehrer b Reid	8	not out	35
CWJ Athey c Zoehrer b CD Matthews	76	c Waugh b Hughes	1
MW Gatting (c) b Hughes	61	c GRJ Matthews b Hughes	12
AJ Lamb lbw Hughes	40	lbw Reid	9
DI Gower c Ritchie b CD Matthews	51	not out	15
IT Botham c Hughes b Waugh	138		
CJ. Richards (+) b CD Matthews	0		
JE Emburey c Waugh b Hughes	8		
PAJ DeFreitas c CD Matthews b Waugh	40		
PH Edmonds not out	9		
GR Dilley c Boon b Waugh	0		
EXTRAS (B 3, LB 19, NB 3)	25	(B 2, NB 3)	5
TOTAL	456		3 for 77

FOW 1st Inns: 15 116 198 198 316 324 351 443 451 456
FOW 2nd Inns: 6 25 40

Bowling: *First Innings*: Reid 31-4-86-1, Hughes 36-7-134-3, CD Matthews 35-10-95-3, Waugh 21-3-76-3, GRJ Matthews 11-2-43-0. *Second Innings*: CD Matthews 4-0-11-0, Hughes 5.3-0-28-2, Reid 6-1-20-1, GRJ Matthews 7-1-16-0.

AUSTRALIA

GR Marsh c Richards b Dilley	56	(2)	b DeFreitas	110
DC Boon c Broad b DeFreitas	10	(1)	lbw Botham	14
TJ Zoehrer (+) lbw Dilley	38	(8)	not out	16
DM Jones lbw DeFreitas	8	(3)	st Richards b Emburey	18
AR Border (c) c DeFreitas b Edmonds	7	(4)	c Lamb b Emburey	23
GM Ritchie c Edmonds b Dilley	41	(5)	lbw DeFreitas	45
GRJ Matthews not out	56	(6)	c & b Dilley	13
SR Waugh c Richards b Dilley	0	(7)	b Emburey	28
CD Matthews c Gatting b Botham	11		lbw Emburey	0
MG Hughes b Botham	0		b DeFreitas	0
BA Reid c Richards b Dilley	3		c Broad b Emburey	2
EXTRAS (B 2, LB 8, W 2, NB 6)	18		(B 5, LB 6, NB 2)	13
TOTAL	248			282

FOW 1st Inns: 27 97 114 126 159 198 204 239 239 248
FOW 2nd Inns: 24 44 92 205 224 262 266 266 275 282

Bowling: *First Innings*: DeFreitas 16-5-32-2, Dilley 25.4-7-68-5, Emburey 34-11-66-0, Edmonds 12-6-12-1, Botham 16-1-58-2, Gatting 1-0-2-0. *Second Innings*: Botham 12-0-34-1, Dilley 19-6-47-1, Emburey 42.5-14-80-5, DeFreitas 17-2-62-3, Edmonds 24-8-46-0, Gatting 2-0-2-0.

Umpires: AR Crafter & MW Johnson

SECOND TEST 1986–87 AUSTRALIA v ENGLAND
W.A.C.A. Ground, Perth. November 28, 29, 30, December 2, 3, 1986.
Toss: England. Match Drawn.

ENGLAND

BC Broad c Zoehrer b Reid	162		lbw Waugh	16
CWJ Athey b Reid	96		c Border b Reid	6
AJ Lamb c Zoehrer b Reid	0	(4)	lbw Reid	2
MW Gatting (c) c Waugh b CD Matthews	14	(3)	b Waugh	70
DI Gower c Waugh b GRJ Matthews	136		c Zoehrer b Waugh	48
IT Botham c Border b Reid	0		c GRJ Matthews b Reid	6
CJ. Richards (+) c Waugh b CD Matthews	133		c Lawson b Waugh	15
PAJ DeFreitas lbw CD Matthews	11		b Waugh	15
JE Emburey not out	5		not out	4
PH Edmonds				
GR Dilley				
EXTRAS (B 4, LB 15, W 3, NB 13)	35		(B 4, LB 9, NB 4)	17
TOTAL	8 dec 592			8 dec 199

FOW 1st Inns: 223 227 275 333 339 546 585 592
FOW 2nd Inns: 8 47 50 123 140 172 190 199

Bowling: *First Innings*: Lawson 41-8-126-0, CD Matthews 29.1-4-112-3, Reid 40-8-115-4, Waugh 24-4-90-0, GRJ Matthews 34-3-124-1, Border 2-0-6-0. *Second Innings*: Reid 21-3-58-3, Lawson 9-1-44-0, Waugh 21.3-4-69-5, CD Matthews 2-0-15-0.

AUSTRALIA

GR Marsh c Broad b Botham	15	(2)	lbw Emburey	49
DC Boon b Dilley	2	(1)	c Botham b Dilley	0
SR Waugh c Botham b Emburey	71			
DM Jones c Athey b Edmonds	27	(3)	run out	69
AR Border (c) c Richards b Dilley	125	(4)	c Lamb b Edmonds	16
GM Ritchie c Botham b Edmonds	33	(5)	not out	24
GRJ Matthews c Botham b Dilley	45	(6)	not out	14
TJ Zoehrer (+) lbw Dilley	29			
GF Lawson b DeFreitas	13			
CD Matthews c Broad b Emburey	10			
BA Reid not out	2			
EXTRAS (B 9, LB 9, NB 11)	29		(B 9, LB 6, NB 10)	25
TOTAL	401			4 for 197

FOW 1st Inns: 4 64 114 128 198 279 334 360 385 401
FOW 2nd Inns: 0 126 142 152

Bowling: *First Innings*: Botham 22-4-72-1, Dilley 24.4-4-79-4, Emburey 43-9-110-2, DeFreitas 24-4-67-1, Edmonds 21-4-55-2. *Second Innings*: Dilley 15-1-53-1, Botham 7.2-4-13-0, DeFreitas 13.4-2-47-0, Emburey 28-11-41-1, Edmonds 27-13-25-1, Gatting 5-3-3-0, Lamb 1-1-0-0.

Umpires: RA French & PJ McConnell

THIRD TEST 1986–87 AUSTRALIA v ENGLAND
Adelaide Oval, Adelaide. December 12, 13, 14, 15, 16, 1986.
Toss: Australia. Match Drawn.

AUSTRALIA

GR Marsh b Edmonds	43 (2)	c & b Edmonds	41
DC Boon c Whitaker b Emburey	103 (1)	lbw DeFreitas	0
DM Jones c Richards b Dilley	93	c Lamb b Dilley	2
AR Border (c) c Richards b Edmonds	70	not out	100
GM Ritchie c Broad b DeFreitas	36	not out	46
GRJ Matthews not out	73		
SR Waugh not out	79		
PR Sleep			
GC Dyer (+)			
MG Hughes			
BA Reid			
EXTRAS (LB 2, NB 15)	17	(B 4, LB 6, NB 2)	12
TOTAL	5 dec 514		3 for 201

FOW 1st Inns: 113 185 311 333 368
FOW 2nd Inns: 1 8 77

Bowling: *First Innings*: Dilley 32-3-111-1, DeFreitas 32-4-128-1, Emburey 46-11-117-1, Edmonds 52-14-134-2, Gatting 9-1-22-0. *Second Innings*: Dilley 21-8-38-1, DeFreitas 16-5-36-1, Emburey 22-6-50-0, Edmonds 29-7-63-1, Gatting 2-1-4-0.

ENGLAND

BC Broad c Marsh b Waugh	116	not out	15
CWJ Athey b Sleep	55	c Dyer b Hughes	12
MW Gatting (c) c Waugh b Sleep	100	b Matthews	0
AJ Lamb c Matthews b Hughes	14	not out	9
DI Gower lbw Reid	38		
JE Emburey c Dyer b Reid	49		
JJ Whitaker c Matthews b Reid	11		
CJ. Richards (+) c Jones b Sleep	29		
PAJ DeFreitas not out	4		
PH Edmonds c Border b Sleep	13		
GR Dilley b Reid	0		
EXTRAS (B 4, LB 14, W 4, NB 4)	26	(B 2, LB 1)	3
TOTAL	455		2 for 39

FOW 1st Inns: 112 273 283 341 341 361 422 439 454 455
FOW 2nd Inns: 21 21

Bowling: *First Innings*: Hughes 30-8-82-1, Reid 28.4-8-64-4, Sleep 47-14-132-4, Matthews 23-1-102-0, Border 1-0-1-0, Waugh 19-4-56-1. *Second Innings*: Hughes 7-2-16-1, Waugh 3-1-10-0, Matthews 8-4-10-1, Sleep 5-5-0-0.

Umpires: AR Crafter & SG Randell

FIFTH TEST 1986–87 AUSTRALIA v ENGLAND
Sydney Cricket Ground, Sydney. January 10, 11, 12, 14, 15, 1987.
Toss: Australia. Australia won by 55 runs.

AUSTRALIA

GR Marsh c Gatting b Small	24 (2)	c Emburey b Dilley	14
GM Ritchie lbw Dilley	6 (1)	c Botham b Edmonds	13
DM Jones not out	184	c Richards b Emburey	30
AR Border (c) c Botham b Edmonds	34	b Edmonds	49
DM Wellham c Richards b Small	17	c Lamb b Emburey	1
SR Waugh c Richards b Small	0	c Athey b Emburey	73
PR Sleep c Richards b Small	9	c Lamb b Emburey	10
TJ Zoehrer (+) c Gatting b Small	12	lbw Emburey	1
PL Taylor c Emburey b Edmonds	11	c Lamb b Emburey	42
MG Hughes c Botham b Edmonds	16	b Emburey	5
BA Reid b Dilley	4	not out	1
EXTRAS (B 13, LB 3, W 2, NB 8)	26	(B 5, LB 7)	12
TOTAL	343		251

FOW 1st Inns: 8 58 149 184 184 200 232 271 338 343
FOW 2nd Inns: 29 31 106 110 115 141 145 243 248 251

Bowling: *First Innings*: Dilley 23.5-5-67-2, Small 33-11-75-5, Botham 23-10-42-0, Emburey 30-4-62-0, Edmonds 34-5-79-3, Gatting 1-0-2-0. *Second Innings*: Dilley 15-4-48-1, Small 8-2-17-0, Edmonds 43-16-79-2, Emburey 46-15-78-7, Botham 3-0-17-0, Gatting 2-2-0-0.

ENGLAND

BC Broad lbw Hughes	6	c & b Sleep	17
CWJ Athey c Zoehrer b Hughes	5	b Sleep	31
MW Gatting (c) lbw Reid	0 (5)	c & b Waugh	96
AJ Lamb c Zoehrer b Taylor	24	c Waugh b Sleep	3
DI Gower c Wellham b Taylor	72 (3)	c Marsh b Border	37
IT Botham c Marsh b Taylor	16	c Wellham b Taylor	0
CJ. Richards (+) c Wellham b Reid	46	b Sleep	38
JE Emburey b Taylor	69	b Sleep	22
PH Edmonds c Marsh b Taylor	3	lbw Sleep	0
GC Small b Taylor	14	c Border b Reid	0
GR Dilley not out	4	not out	2
EXTRAS (B 9, LB 3, W 2, NB 2)	16	(B 8, LB 6, W 1, NB 3)	18
TOTAL	275		264

FOW 1st Inns: 16 17 17 89 119 142 213 219 270 275
FOW 2nd Inns: 24 91 91 102 102 233 257 257 262 264

Bowling: *First Innings*: Hughes 16-3-58-2, Reid 25-7-74-2, Waugh 6-4-6-0, Taylor 26-7-78-6, Sleep 21-6-47-0. *Second Innings*: Hughes 12-3-32-0, Reid 19-8-32-1, Sleep 35-14-72-5, Taylor 29-10-76-2, Border 13-6-25-1, Waugh 6-2-13-1.

Umpires: PJ McConnell & SG Randell

FOURTH TEST 1986–87 AUSTRALIA v ENGLAND
Melbourne Cricket Ground, Melbourne. December 26, 27, 28, 1986.
Toss: England. England won by an innings & 14 runs.

AUSTRALIA

GR Marsh c Richards b Botham	17 (2)	run out	60
DC Boon c Botham b Small	7 (1)	c Gatting b Small	8
DM Jones c Gower b Small	59	c Gatting b DeFreitas	21
AR Border (c) c Richards b Botham	15	c Emburey b Small	34
SR Waugh c Botham b Small	10	b Edmonds	49
GRJ Matthews c Botham b Small	14	b Emburey	0
PR Sleep c Richards b Small	0	run out	6
TJ Zoehrer (+) b Botham	5	c Athey b Edmonds	1
CJ McDermott c Richards b Botham	0	b Emburey	1
MG Hughes c Richards b Botham	2	c Small b Edmonds	8
BA Reid not out	2	not out	0
EXTRAS (B 1, LB 1, W 1, NB 7)	10	(LB 3, W 1, NB 2)	6
TOTAL	141		194

FOW 1st Inns: 16 44 80 108 118 118 129 133 137 141
FOW 2nd Inns: 13 48 113 153 153 175 180 185 189 194

Bowling: *First Innings*: Small 22.4-7-48-5, DeFreitas 11-1-30-0, Emburey 4-0-16-0, Botham 16-4-41-5, Gatting 1-0-4-0. *Second Innings*: DeFreitas 12-1-44-1, Small 15-3-40-2, Botham 7-1-19-0, Edmonds 19.4-5-45-3, Emburey 20-5-43-2.

ENGLAND

BC Broad c Zoehrer b Hughes	112
CWJ Athey lbw Reid	21
MW Gatting (c) c Hughes b Reid	40
AJ Lamb c Zoehrer b Reid	43
DI Gower c Matthews b Sleep	7
IT Botham c Zoehrer b McDermott	29
CJ. Richards (+) c Marsh b Reid	3
PAJ DeFreitas c Matthews b McDermott	7
JE Emburey c & b McDermott	22
PH Edmonds lbw McDermott	19
GC Small not out	21
EXTRAS (B 6, LB 7, W 1, NB 11)	25
TOTAL	349

FOW 1st Inns: 58 163 198 219 251 273 277 289 319 349

Bowling: *First Innings*: McDermott 26.5-4-83-4, Hughes 30-3-94-1, Reid 28-5-78-4, Waugh 8-4-16-0, Sleep 28-4-65-1.

Umpires: AR Crafter & RA French

Australian Averages

1986–87 AUSTRALIA v ENGLAND

AUSTRALIA	M	Inn	NO	Runs	H.S	Avrge	Ct	St	Overs	Mds	Runs	Wkt	Avrge
Boon, DC	4	8	-	144	103	18.00	1		-				-
Border, AR	5	10	1	473	125	52.56	4	-	16.0	6	32	1	32.00
Dyer, GC	1						2	-					-
Hughes, MG	4	6	-	31	16	5.17	2	-	136.3	26	444	10	44.40
Jones, DM	5	10	1	511	184*	56.78	1	-					-
Lawson, GF	1	1	-	13	13	13.00	1	-	50.0	9	170	-	-
Marsh, GR	5	10	-	429	110	42.90	5	-					-
Matthews, CD	2	3	-	21	11	7.00	1	-	70.1	14	233	6	38.83
Matthews, GRJ	4	7	3	215	73*	53.75	6	-	83.0	11	295	2	147.50
McDermott, CJ	1	2	-	1	1	0.50	1	-	26.5	4	83	4	20.75
Reid, BA	5	7	4	14	4	4.67	-	-	198.4	44	527	20	26.35
Ritchie, GM	4	8	2	244	46*	40.67	1	-					-
Sleep, PR	3	4	-	25	10	6.25	1	-	136.0	43	316	10	31.60
Taylor, PL	1	2	-	53	42	26.50	-	-	55.0	17	154	8	19.25
Waugh, SR	5	8	1	310	79*	44.29	8	-	108.3	26	336	10	33.60
Wellham, DM	1	2	-	18	17	9.00	3	-					-
Zoehrer, TJ	4	7	1	102	38	17.00	10	-					-

English Averages

1986–87 AUSTRALIA v ENGLAND

ENGLAND	M	Inn	NO	Runs	H.S	Avrge	Ct	St	Overs	Mds	Runs	Wkt	Avrge
Athey, CWJ	5	9	-	303	96	33.67	3	-					
Botham, IT	4	6	-	189	138	31.50	10	-	106.2	24	296	9	32.89
Broad, BC	5	9	2	487	162	69.57	5	-					
DeFreitas, PAJ	4	5	1	77	40	19.25	1	-	141.4	24	446	9	49.56
Dilley, GR	4	4	2	6	4*	3.00	1	-	176.1	38	511	16	31.94
Edmonds, PH	5	5	1	44	19	11.00	2	-	261.4	78	538	15	35.87
Emburey, JE	5	7	2	179	69	35.80	3	-	315.5	86	663	18	36.83
Gatting, MW	5	9	-	393	100	43.67	5	-	23.0	7	39	-	-
Gower, DI	5	8	-	404	136	57.71	1	-					
Lamb, AJ	5	9	1	144	43	18.00	6	-	1.0	1	0	-	-
Richards, CJ.	5	7	-	264	133	37.71	15	1					
Small, GC	2	3	1	35	21*	17.50	1	-	78.4	23	180	12	15.00
Whitaker, JJ	1	1	-	11	11	11.00	1	-					

Australia, the outsiders, beat the World

World Cup results

GROUP A

Australia 6/270 (50 overs) d India 269 (49.5 overs).

New Zealand 7/242 (50 overs) d Zimbabwe 239 (49.4 overs).

Australia 9/235 (50 overs) d Zimbabwe 139 (42.4 overs).

India 7/252 (50 overs) d New Zealand 8/236 (50 overs).

Zimbabwe 135 (44.2 overs) lost to India 2/136 (27.5 overs).

Australia 4/199 (30 overs) d New Zealand 9/196 (30 overs).

India 6/289 (50 overs) d Australia 233 (49 overs).

Zimbabwe 5/227 (50 overs) lost to New Zealand 6/228 (47.4 overs)

Zimbabwe 7/191 (50 overs) lost to India 3/194 (42 overs).

Australia 8/251 (50 overs) d New Zealand 234 (48.4 overs).

Australia 5/266 (50 overs) d Zimbabwe 6/196 (50 overs).

New Zealand 9/221 (50 overs) lost to India 1/224 (32.1 overs).

GROUP B

Pakistan 6/267 (50 overs) d Sri Lanka 252 (49.2 overs).

West Indies 7/243 (50 overs) lost to England 8/246 (49.3 overs).

Pakistan 7/239 (50 overs) d England 221 (48.4 overs).

West Indies 4/360 (50 overs) d Sri Lanka 4/169 (50 overs).

West Indies 216 (49.3 overs) lost to Pakistan 9/217 (50 overs).

England 4/296 (50 overs) d Sri Lanka 8/158 (45 overs).

England 9/244 (50 overs) lost to Pakistan 3/247 (49 overs).

West Indies 8/236 (50 overs) d Sri Lanka 8/211 (50 overs).

Pakistan 7/297 (50 overs) d Sri Lanka 8/184 (50 overs).

England 5/269 (50 overs) d West Indies 235 (48.1 overs).

Sri Lanka 7/218 (50 overs) lost to England 2/219 (41.2 overs).

West Indies 7/258 (50 overs) d Pakistan 9/230 (50 overs).

SEMI-FINALS

Australia 8/267 (50 overs) (Boon 65, Veletta 48; Imran 3/36) d Pakistan 249 (49 overs). (Miandad 70, Imran 58; McDermott 5/44).

England 6/254 (50 overs) (Gooch 115, Gatting 56; Maninder 3/54) d India 219 (45.3 overs) (Azharuddin 64; Hemmings 4/52, Foster 3/47)

FINAL

Australia 5/253 (50 overs) (Boon 75) d England 8/246 (50 overs) (Athey 58).

The world-beaters: Allan Border's Australians victorious over England in the final at Calcutta.

Calcutta, Nov. 8. Allan Border's young Australian team has won the World Cup – the peak of one day cricket. Urged on by the Indian crowd, Australia beat England by seven runs in the final.

The Indian support at the Eden Gardens stadium was due to Australia having rolled India's arch-rival Pakistan in the semi-final, and also because England put India out of the contest in the other semi.

The Aussies are deserving winners. They have appeared to put more work into their preparation than any of the other teams.

In the final David Boon and Geoff Marsh gave Australia a mighty start. At 1/150 Australia looked on track for a big score, but in the space of three overs England swung the game by having Dean Jones caught for 33, and getting pinch-hitter Craig McDermott after he had swiped 14 runs off eight balls. Boon then went for 75 and the Aussies were 4/168.

Border and Mike Veletta chipped away at the bowling before Border tried one quick single too many and was run out for 31. Veletta's 45 not out came off just 31 balls and Australia finished on 5/253.

England started disastrously, losing Tim Robinson for a duck from the fourth ball. Gooch and Athey laboured, and when skipper Mike Gatting came to the crease at 2/66 there was a need for some urgency in the batting.

He took to Tim May's off-spin, belting a four, reverse sweeping a three and then thumping a six.

Just when he was starting to turn the screws on Australia, Gatting resorted to a reverse sweep against Border and popped an easy catch to 'keeper Greg Dyer. With Gatting gone for 41, England was 3/135.

Allan Lamb's aggression and Athey's determination revived England, which needed 34 runs off the last three overs.

The Australians held their nerve, and McDermott was never going to let them get the 15 runs needed from the last over.

The World Cup finally gave Allan Border something to smile about.

Border is contented after the win over New Zealand at Chandigarh.

Sir Don pulls up stumps at SACA

Sir Donald Bradman is signing off from a long association with the SACA.

On 30 June 1986, Sir Donald Bradman's official contribution to the game at an administrative level ceased.

His knowledge and astute observations have long been a huge influence on Australian cricket, and he drew the curtains on his last official position when he attended his 1713th meeting of the South Australian Cricket Association.

In his first spell as chairman of the national Board, he attended 546 meetings from 1960 to 1963. He was the man frequently called upon to untangle cricket's most demanding problems, and as recently as mid-1985 he was called upon by the Board to solve the problems caused by the South African defections.

In April 1986 the president of the SACA read a letter from Sir Donald which flagged his intention to retire. It stated, 'I would be happy to retire forthwith if the committee so wished, but otherwise I thought it sensible for me to see out the financial year and make my retirement operative from early July'.

He was an SACA member of the Board of Control from 1945 until 1972, acting as Board chairman from 1960 to 1963 and from 1969 to 1972. He was vice-president of the SACA from 1950 to 1965 and then president until 1973. Add in his service as national chairman of selectors, and you have a truly remarkable off-field career.

The Jones boy – folk hero

Dean Jones possessed a style and supreme confidence that was always going to confront and challenge.

Along the way it has brought him an inordinate amount of controversy, but not even his detractors could dispute that he was one of the most exciting batsmen of his era. While the tag of 'best one day batsman in the world' was affixed to him late in his career, it should not be forgotten that he had a fine Test record, scoring 3631 runs at an average of 46.55 and hitting 11 centuries along the way.

Jones was sometimes too impetuous for his own good. Not hesitant to 'needle' an opponent, he sometimes found that the tactic backfired. A graphic instance of this was the time he complained about Curtly Ambrose's wristband. and so riled the giant West Indies paceman that he blasted out of a personal bowling slump and proceeded to destroy Australia at both one day and Test level.

Jones preferred to categorise his approach as being one of nervous energy. 'Some call it arrogance and some reckon Dean Jones is just a bloody big-head,' he wrote, 'but I don't see any point in pretending to be anything I'm not. Anybody who has ever played cricket knows it's very much an individual game once you have a bat in your hand.'

His batting was characterised by nimble footwork and lightning running between wickets.

Jones made his debut at senior District level when just 16 at Carlton, the club where his father Barney was a District legend, having won three premierships.

Jones spent a year in League cricket in Yorkshire when 20 and it added depth to his batting knowledge. On his return to Australia he won a spot in the Victorian side, and although he had a quiet beginning in 1981–82, he had a fine year the following season, scoring 603 runs at an average of 54.81.

A knee injury to Graham Yallop prompted Jones' selection for the Australian team to tour the West Indies in 1984. It was a demanding task for a youngster and he made his Test debut in the second Test when Steve Smith suddenly took ill before the game.

Facing the fearsome Joel Garner and Co. on a wet pitch, Jones made 48 after coming in at 5/85.

This was the time that the rebel South African tours were being

Dean Jones: all hail to the king of one day cricket.

organised and Jones was offered a $200,000 two-year contract by Dr Ali Bacher. His first response was to accept it, but after lengthy arguments with his traditionalist father, he rejected the offer. The fact that he was on a rebel list of prospective players may have affected his chances of Test selection. Left out of Test matches the following summer, he still won inclusion in the national one day side.

Two and a half years passed before he earned another Test chance and in the searing heat at Madras he played an innings of amazing heroism. He knew that the conditions were exceptionally bad when one of the Indians, Srikkanth, remarked how humid it was. Jones realised that if one of the locals thought it was bad then it must have been something out of the ordinary.

Making the situation even worse was the stench from the nearby Buckingham Canal which was little more than an open sewer. Despite all of that, Jones made 210 and prompted Bob Simpson to say: 'I doubt whether there has ever been a more courageous Test innings… I think he has settled something within himself. Deano has a reputation of being a little brittle in his temperament. That's totally wiped now.'

From that moment forward, Jones prospered. A good series against England in 1986–87 produced 511 runs at an average of 56.78, including a dominating 184 not out in Australia's only victory.

He faltered slightly against the probing swing of Richard Hadlee,

but was soon back on track with a fine home series against the West Indies that saw him produce his highest Test score of 216 at Adelaide.

In the 1989 tour of England he scored two centuries and amassed 566 runs at an average of 70.75 to be a key part of the Australian batting rampage.

The run-flow continued, yet after the Sri Lankan tour of 1992–93 he found himself out of the side.

On the surface it looked like a case of other batsmen getting the nod just ahead of him and scoring enough runs to stay in the side. Pro-Jones fans saw more Machiavellian notions lurking in the shadows, and his liking for speaking his mind was said to have counted against him.

He certainly did not endear himself to selectors by making a hasty announcement that he would retire from Test cricket.

The sheer weight of runs for Victoria opened the door to a touring spot to South Africa in 1993–94, but he did not play a Test.

On the shortlist for the 1996 World Cup team, he again missed out and accepted a position in English county cricket. His form did not waver throughout this period and he scored a career-best 324 against South Australia in 1994–95.

Such was the respect for Deano – international batsman and one day king – that even at the age of 35 there was still a cell of public opinion that clamored for Jones to return to the struggling national one day side.

McDermott Whitney survive Tasman Cup Test

Melbourne, Dec. 30. The Trans-Tasman Trophy was first contested in 1985–86, in Allan Border's first series against New Zealand as captain.

Six Tests were played that season, three home and three away. Needless to say, New Zealand won and then retained the trophy 3–1 overall.

Now, in a thrilling final Test, Australia and Allan Border have won the trophy back – and Allan Border has his first series win.

In the end it was thanks to Craig McDermott and Mike Whitney holding out the relentless Richard Hadlee for a total of 29 deliveries that the third Test was saved, securing Australia's 1–0 lead.

Hadlee had equalled Ian Botham's world record 373 Test wickets, taking ten in a match for a record eighth time.

Australia was 16 runs short of a victory that looked probable at 5/209, but unlikely at 9/227. Tony Dodemaide was the outstanding all-rounder for Australia, making a hard-hitting 50 in the first innings and taking 6/58 in NZ's second.

Australia won the series with a nine-wicket win at the 'Gabba – built around Bruce Reid, Merv Hughes and Craig McDermott knocking over New Zealand in the first innings for 186 – and then David Boon scoring a magnificent 143 of Australia's 305. The second-Test draw was notable for Allan Border's 205 after Jeff Crowe declined a 'catch' when he was 53.

Peter Sleep made an important 90 in the third Test, his highest Test score.

Support for States

Sydney, Oct. 1. Both players and state associations are in better financial positions than they have been in previous years with healthy sponsorship agreements having been signed by most states.

NSWCA has signed a $500,000 three year deal with a brewery, as has SA. Tasmania plumped for a $40,000 annual contract with a computer company, and WA signed a long-term arrangement with a local bank worth $2.1m.

WA also promised bonuses to its players – $20,00 for finishing on top of the Shield ladder, and $500 for qualifying for a McDonald's Cup semi final.

The ACB was also in a bonus-paying mood – offering $3000 to the team heading the Shield table, $18,000 for the winning team.

Any team which made a clean sweep in the McDonald's Cup was eligible for an ACB bonus of $17,400.

Craig McDermott's classical fast bowler's action brought him a harvest of Kiwi wickets.

Critical catch

Melbourne, Dec. 26. Australian wicketkeeper Greg Dyer dived down the leg side to catch Andrew Jones in the first innings of the third Test, from the bowling of Craig McDermott. The only trouble with the catch was that when Dyer rolled over the ball clearly (on the TV replays) popped out before being scooped up again.

A somewhat half-hearted appeal to umpire Tony Crafter was initially not acceded to, but square leg umpire Dick French indicated the ball had carried – as it had, and Crafter gave Jones out for 40. Both umpires were unable to see the ball pop out onto the ground.

Many observers felt Dyer must have known what had happened and criticised him for not owning up – recalling Jeff Crowe's action in the second Test in saying he had not caught Allan Border.

Not to mention that of Rod Marsh in the Centenary Test.

One swallow does not make it through the summer

Perth, Nov. 7. A good-length delivery from Tasmanian bowler Peter Faulkner struck a swallow after it pitched, on its way to Graeme Wood. The ball was defended easily by Wood, but the swallow was killed instantly – and was sent for taxidermy. It will be displayed in the planned WACA museum.

Other recorded dead bird balls include the one hit by Greg Chappell, bowling John Inverarity 'in off' at the Adelaide oval in 1969. Inverarity walked but was recalled when the fatal circumstance was noticed. The bird is in the committee room of the Adelaide Oval.

The other case occurred at Lord's in 1936 – a ball from Jahangir Khan knocking a sparrow against the stumps, T. N. Pearce batting, but not dislodging the bails. The bird is on display in the Long Room, mounted on the fatal weapon.

A pen laid down

Sydney, Feb. 2. The great bowler, storyteller and journalist Bill O'Reilly was given a press box presentation at his beloved SCG on the last day of the Bicentennial Test – the day he filed his last regular report for the *Sydney Morning Herald*.

O'Reilly, aged 82, has been writing for the *SMH* for 42 years with wit, passion for cricket and especially on the art of the leg-spinner, providing acute judgement and criticism where it was due.

O'Reilly's feats as a bowler – 144 wickets in 27 Tests – need no amplification here except to say that his prowess on the field gives him a unique authority among present-day cricket writers.

Despite retirement, there is no indication that O'Reilly's output will be affected.

Vintage cricket

Brisbane, April 17. The 1977 Centenary test teams played the last of three one day charity matches – Australia winning the lot – and raising more than $250,000 for charity. David Hookes was out for 94 in this final game trying to hit a six with the scores level.

The games were played in Perth before 19,500, in Adelaide (7363) and in Brisbane (8435). The only player unavailable was Alan Knott who was injured – his place was taken by Bob Taylor.

Bicentennial Test lacks fireworks

England and Australia pose before at a sparsely populated Sydney Cricket Ground before the Bicentennial Test.

Sydney, Feb. 2. The Ashes were not up for grabs in the one-off Test match played between England and Australia at the SCG to mark the bicentenary of European settlement of Australia. Many old Test players were invited, but not all could make it. There were celebration dinners, parades in horse-drawn carriages and the Ashes were displayed for the first time outside Lord's (in a Sydney bank), but the celebratory fizz of the Melbourne Centenary Test was missing here, as it was to some extent in England in the 1980 Centenary there.

The promoters of the game somewhat overenthusiastically claimed the match was a sell-out, telling journalists no tickets were available. However only 103,831 attended – half what was expected.

This was reflected in the cricket where England, not doing terribly well, was determined not to lose, and Australia, on the way back to success, fresh from the triumphs in the one day arena, found it hard to readapt to the long game.

England made just 221 for the loss of two wickets on the dull and even first day, as Chris Broad ground his way to a fourth hundred in seven Tests in Australia in just 14 months. He hardly played an aggressive shot until he was out.

Broad pulled a short one from Steve Waugh onto his stumps on the second day when he was 139. This unaccountably enraged him, and he smashed the stumps with his bat – which obtained him a fine of £500 ($1200) by team management within 30 minutes.

His action was roundly condemned as bringing Test cricket into further danger.

England was all out for 425 after tea – everyone including Mr Extras getting into double figures.

On the third day Australia fell to the persistent though not noticeably dangerous bowling of Graham Dilley, Eddie Hemmings and Neil Foster – with captain Allan Border out for two, hooking at Capel.

The umpires needed to adjudicate in six of the seven dismissals

– only Border's being clear-cut. There were some excellent chances taken by England. Only Dean Jones managed to reach 50. Bad light stopped play at 4.11 p.m. with Australia at 7/164.

All out and following on next day, Australia's batsmen seemed to have awoken from their one day twitches, with David Boon imperturbable in progressing to 184 not out (along the way creating an SCG record for the first wicket against England of 162 with Geoff Marsh 56).

Border, in making, 48 not out reached 7500 runs, pushing Wally Hammond to seventh on the all-time run-makers list.

A considerable amount of time was lost in this match, to Border's chagrin, and Australia saw out an honourable enough draw.

The Test crowd, it was reported, showed as much or more interest in scoreboard updates of a game played between English and Australian 'Living Legends', roaring as the scores of heroes of yesteryear displayed.

Cricket was hot property for sponsors in the 1987–88 season – this welcome cheque was for the NSWCA.

Sri Lankans take a step up

Mike Veletta batted for Australia on the WACA, his home ground.

Perth, Feb. 26. Australia predictably defeated Sri Lanka in the first Test played between the two countries in Australia, and only the second Test played.

The first, played in Kandy in 1982–83 was also won by Australia. In the eyes of some observers the sparse program of games played between the two countries is regrettable, even taking into account the busy cricket schedule of Australia and the requirement that visiting teams be drawcards like the West Indies and England.

A total of only 10,607 patrons watched three days play plus 75 minutes of the fourth day required for the Australian win – by an innings and 108 runs.

But Sri Lanka will surely only improve in the Test arena by play-

ing more Tests, and more three and four-day games against quality opposition. On this tour they played only one – a draw against Victoria.

In further bad news for Sri Lankan cricket it was announced that the Australian tour in April has been cancelled owing to he continuing civil unrest and military action – this tour was to replace the cancelled Test that was not played before the 1987 World Cup.

As to the Test which finished on February 15, it saw Australia make 455 courtesy of Dean Jones's third Test century – after he was dropped by substitute fieldsman Hashan Tillekeratne when on 98. Jones ran the necessary two for his ton.

Border enforced the follow-on for just the second time as captain.

WA take Shield

Perth, March 22. A six over square leg by Wayne Andrews from the bowling of Dirk Tazelaar saw West Australia retain the Sheffield Shield, their 11th in 41 years and ninth in the past 17 seasons.

Queensland's solid first innings of 289, featured 66 from captain Allan Border (after being dropped on nought) but Ian Botham made only nine. Chris Matthews in an outstanding performance took 8/101. His fifth wicket broke Tony Lock's Shield record of 52 wickets in a season. WA's reply was dominated by Graeme Wood's 141 of 344. Terry Alderman took 6/91 in Queensland's disappointing second-innings 216, which set WA 162 to win, which they did for the loss of five wickets.

World Youth Cup

Adelaide, March 13. The inaugural World Youth Cup final in Adelaide has been won by Australia, who defeated Pakistan by five wickets.

The preliminary games, played around country Victoria and South Australia in February and March, were played in the same format as the senior World Cup – that is, one day, fifty overs a side, for players under 20 years of age.

In the final Pakistan made 201, Inzamam-ul-Haq 37, Sarfraz Nawaz 35, Zahoor Elahi 35, Geoff Parker 3/36, Wayne Holdsworth 3/38 in 49.3 overs. Australia made 5/202 in 45.5 overs - Brett Williams (Man of the Match) 108, and Stuart Law 44.

It has been a very successful eight-team tournament.

FIRST TEST 1987–88 AUSTRALIA v NEW ZEALAND
Brisbane Cricket Ground, Brisbane. December 4, 5, 6, 7, 1987.
Toss: Australia. Australia won by 9 wkts.

NEW ZEALAND

KR Rutherford c Veletta b Reid	0	(2)	c Dyer b McDermott	2
JG Wright c Dyer b Hughes	38	(1)	lbw Reid	15
AH Jones b McDermott	4		c Border b Reid	45
MD Crowe c Waugh b Hughes	67		c Jones b Hughes	23
JJ Crowe (c) lbw Waugh	16		lbw Reid	12
DN Patel c Dyer b McDermott	17		c Dyer b Hughes	62
RJ Hadlee c Boon b Hughes	8		c Marsh b McDermott	24
JG Bracewell c Veletta b McDermott	11		c Dyer b McDermott	0
IDS Smith (+) lbw Reid	2		c Veletta b Reid	9
DK Morrison c Waugh b McDermott	0		c Dyer b Waugh	2
EJ Chatfield not out	0		not out	1
EXTRAS (B 1, LB 7, W 4, NB 11)	23		(B 6, LB 1, W 1, NB 9)	17
TOTAL	186			212

FOW 1st Inns: 0 28 80 133 143 153 175 180 181 186
FOW 2nd Inns: 18 20 66 103 104 142 142 152 204 212

Bowling: *First Innings*: Reid 25-10-40-2, McDermott 22.2-6-43-4, Hughes 18-5-40-3, Waugh 22-9-35-1, Sleep 6-1-20-0. *Second Innings*: Reid 25-6-53-4, McDermott 21-2-79-3, Hughes 17-7-57-2, Sleep 14-5-14-0, Waugh 2-1-2-1.

AUSTRALIA

GR Marsh c Bracewell b Hadlee	25	(2)	not out	31
DC Boon run out	143	(1)	lbw Bracewell	24
DM Jones b Hadlee	2		not out	38
AR Border (c) lbw Morrison	9			
MRJ Veletta c Rutherford b Bracewell	4			
SR Waugh c Jones b Morrison	21			
PR Sleep c & b Bracewell	39			
GC Dyer (+) lbw Hadlee	8			
CJ McDermott c Wright b Morrison	22			
MG Hughes c Smith b Morrison	5			
BA Reid not out	8			
EXTRAS (B 3, LB 5, W 2, NB 9)	19		(LB 1, W 1, NB 2)	4
TOTAL	305			1 for 97

FOW 1st Inns: 65 72 110 131 219 219 250 286 291 305
FOW 2nd Inns: 37

Bowling: *First Innings*: Hadlee 31-5-95-3, Morrison 28-7-86-4, Chatfield 34-11-58-0, Bracewell 24.5-3-58-2. *Second Innings*: Hadlee 8-3-14-0, Morrison 8-0-32-0, Bracewell 13-3-32-1, Patel 3.1-0-18-0.

Umpires: AR Crafter & MW Johnson

SECOND TEST 1987–88 AUSTRALIA v NEW ZEALAND
Adelaide Oval, Adelaide. December 11, 12, 13, 14, 15, 1987.
Toss: New Zealand. Match Drawn.

NEW ZEALAND

JJ Crowe (c) c Veletta b Reid	0		c Boon b May	19
JG Wright c Waugh b May	45		b McDermott	8
AH Jones run out	150		c Border b Sleep	64
MD Crowe c(S)MG Hughes b Sleep	137		c Border b Sleep	8
DN Patel c Marsh b McDermott	35		c Boon b May	40
EJ Gray b McDermott	23		c Border b May	14
RJ Hadlee c & b Jones	36	(9)	not out	3
JG Bracewell c Sleep b McDermott	32			
IDS Smith (+) not out	8	(8)	c Dyer b Sleep	5
MC Snedden c Veletta b McDermott	0	(7)	not out	8
DK Morrison				
EXTRAS (B 3, LB 7, W 1, NB 8)	19		(B 2, LB 4, NB 7)	13
TOTAL	9 dec 485			7 for 182

FOW 1st Inns: 0 128 341 346 398 405 473 481 485
FOW 2nd Inns: 16 57 77 139 153 170 179

Bowling: *First Innings*: Reid 7-0-21-1, McDermott 45.5-10-135-4, Waugh 31-11-71-0, May 54-13-134-1, Sleep 34-5-109-1, Jones 3-1-5-1. *Second Innings*: McDermott 10-3-29-1, Waugh 10-4-17-0, Sleep 32-14-61-3, May 30-10-68-3, Jones 3-2-1-0.

AUSTRALIA

DC Boon b Hadlee	6
GR Marsh c Gray b Hadlee	30
DM Jones c Smith b Hadlee	0
AR Border (c) st Smith b Bracewell	205
SR Waugh lbw Snedden	61
PR Sleep c Smith b Morrison	62
MRJ Veletta c(S)KR Rutherford b Bracewell	10
GC Dyer (+) run out	60
CJ McDermott lbw Hadlee	18
TBA May not out	14
BA Reid c Smith b Hadlee	5
EXTRAS (B 2, LB 13, W 1, NB 9)	25
TOTAL	496

FOW 1st Inns: 29 29 85 201 355 380 417 451 489 496

Bowling: *First Innings*: Hadlee 42-16-68-5, Morrison 22-0-89-1, Bracewell 48-8-122-2, Snedden 32-6-89-1, Gray 44-10-102-0, Patel 7-3-11-0.

Umpires: RC Bailhache & SG Randell

THIRD TEST 1987–88 AUSTRALIA v NEW ZEALAND
Melbourne Cricket Ground, Melbourne. December 26, 27, 28, 29, 30, 1987.
Toss: Australia. Match Drawn.

NEW ZEALAND

PA Horne c Dyer b Dodemaide	.7	c Boon b Dodemaide	.27
JG Wright c Dyer b McDermott	.99	b Sleep	.43
AH Jones c Dyer b McDermott	.40	run out	.20
MD Crowe c Veletta b McDermott	.82	c Border b Dodemaide	.79
JJ Crowe (c) lbw McDermott	.6	c Boon b Sleep	.25
DN Patel b McDermott	.0	c Dyer b Dodemaide	.38
JG Bracewell c Dyer b Whitney	.9 (8)	c Veletta b Dodemaide	.1
RJ Hadlee c Dodemaide b Whitney	.11 (7)	lbw Sleep	.29
IDS Smith (+) c Jones b Whitney	.44	c Dyer b Dodemaide	.12
DK Morrison c Border b Whitney	.0	b Dodemaide	.0
EJ Chatfield not out	.6	not out	.1
EXTRAS (B 1, LB 4, NB 8)	.13	(B 2, LB 8, NB 1)	.11
TOTAL	.317		.286

FOW 1st Inns: 32 119 187 221 223 254 254 280 294 317
FOW 2nd Inns: 73 76 158 178 220 272 272 281 285 286

Bowling: *First Innings*: McDermott 35-8-97-5, Whitney 33.3-6-92-4, Dodemaide 20-4-48-1, Waugh 10-1-44-0, Sleep 12-1-31-0. *Second Innings*: McDermott 10-3-43-0, Whitney 20-5-45-0, Dodemaide 28.3-10-58-6, Sleep 26-5-107-3, Jones 8-3-23-0.

AUSTRALIA

DC Boon lbw Hadlee	.10 (2)	c MD Crowe b Morrison	.54
GR Marsh c(S)KR Rutherford b Hadlee	.13 (1)	c Bracewell b Hadlee	.23
DM Jones c Smith b Hadlee	.4	c MD Crowe b Chatfield	.8
AR Border (c) c JJ Crowe b Bracewell	.31	lbw Hadlee	.43
MRJ Veletta lbw Hadlee	.31	c Patel b Bracewell	.39
SR Waugh c Jones b Bracewell	.55	c Patel b Chatfield	.10
PR Sleep lbw Hadlee	.90	lbw Hadlee	.20
GC Dyer (+) run out	.21	c Smith b Hadlee	.4
AIC Dodemaide c Smith b Morrison	.50	lbw Hadlee	.3
CJ McDermott b Morrison	.33	not out	.10
MR Whitney not out	.0	not out	.2
EXTRAS (LB 8, NB 11)	.19	(B 1, LB 9, NB 4)	.14
TOTAL	.357		.9 for 230

FOW 1st Inns: 24 30 31 78 121 170 213 293 354 357
FOW 2nd Inns: 45 59 103 147 176 209 209 216 227

Bowling: *First Innings*: Hadlee 44-11-109-5, Morrison 27.4-5-93-2, Chatfield 30-10-55-0, Bracewell 32-8-69-2, Patel 12-6-23-0. *Second Innings*: Hadlee 31-9-67-5, Morrison 16-2-54-1, Chatfield 21-6-41-2, Bracewell 24-5-58-1.

Umpires: AR Crafter & RA French

ONLY TEST 1987–88 AUSTRALIA v SRI LANKA
W.A.C.A. Ground, Perth. February 12, 13, 14, 15, 1988.
Toss: Australia. Australia won by an innings & 108 runs.

AUSTRALIA

GR Marsh b Labrooy	.53
DC Boon c Ratnayeke	.64
DM Jones lbw Labrooy	.102
AR Border (c) b Ratnayeke	.88
MRJ Veletta c De Alwis b Ratnayeke	.21
SR Waugh c Labrooy b Amalean	.20
GC Dyer (+) c Ramanayake b Amalean	.38
PL Taylor c Amalean b Ratnayeke	.18
AIC Dodemaide not out	.16
CJ McDermott c De Alwis b Amalean	.4
MG Hughes b Amalean	.8
EXTRAS (LB 12, W 5, NB 6)	.23
TOTAL	.455

FOW 1st Inns: 120 133 289 346 346 380 418 434 443 455

Bowling: *First Innings*: Ratnayeke 40-6-98-4, Labrooy 36-5-108-2, Ramanayake 17-2-58-0, Amalean 22.2-1-97-4, Kaluperuma 13-0-62-0, Ranatunga 8-2-18-0, De Silva 1-0-2-0.

SRI LANKA

RS Mahanama c Dyer b Dodemaide	.41	run out	.28
DSBP Kuruppu c Marsh b McDermott	.19	c Dyer b Dodemaide	.3
SMS Kaluperuma lbw McDermott	.0	c & b Hughes	.6
PA De Silva lbw Waugh	.6	lbw Dodemaide	.7
A Ranatunga c & b Waugh	.55	lbw Dodemaide	.45
RS Madugalle (c) c Border b Dodemaide	.6	c Waugh b Hughes	.7
JR Ratnayeke c Marsh b McDermott	.24	c Dyer b Dodemaide	.38
RG De Alwis (+) c Dyer b Waugh	.7	c Waugh b Hughes	.8
CPH Ramanayake c Dyer b Waugh	.9	c Veletta b Hughes	.0
GF Labrooy c Dyer b Dodemaide	.4	b Hughes	.4
KN Amalean not out	.7	not out	.0
EXTRAS (B 1, LB 6, W 2, NB 14)	.23	(LB 6, NB 1)	.7
TOTAL	.194		.153

FOW 1st Inns: 51 51 60 93 104 147 148 181 182 194
FOW 2nd Inns: 36 42 42 66 83 111 130 130 153 153

Bowling: *First Innings*: McDermott 20-3-50-3, Hughes 18-2-61-0, Dodemaide 22.3-6-40-3, Waugh 20-7-33-4, Taylor 2-1-3-0. *Second Innings*: McDermott 4-2-8-0, Hughes 21-7-67-5, Waugh 8-4-14-0, Dodemaide 19.1-7-58-4.

Umpires: RC Bailhache & PJ McConnell

ONLY TEST 1987–88 AUSTRALIA v ENGLAND
Sydney Cricket Ground, Sydney. January 29, 30, 31, February 1, 2, 1988.
Toss: England. Match Drawn.

ENGLAND

BC Broad b Waugh	.139
MD Moxon b Sleep	.40
RT Robinson c Veletta b Dodemaide	.43
MW Gatting (c) c Dyer b Waugh	.13
CWJ Athey c & b Taylor	.37
DJ Capel c Sleep b Taylor	.21
JE Emburey st Dyer b Sleep	.23
BN French (+) st Dyer b Taylor	.47
NA Foster c Border b Taylor	.19
EE Hemmings not out	.8
GR Dilley b Waugh	.13
EXTRAS (B 4, LB 9, W 1, NB 8)	.22
TOTAL	.425

FOW 1st Inns: 93 192 245 262 313 314 346 387 410 425

Bowling: *First Innings*: McDermott 35-8-65-0, Dodemaide 36-10-98-1, Taylor 34-10-84-4, Waugh 22.5-5-51-3, Sleep 45-8-114-2.

AUSTRALIA

DC Boon c French b Foster	.12	not out	.184
GR Marsh c French b Capel	.5	c Athey b Emburey	.56
DM Jones c Emburey b Hemmings	.56	c Moxon b Capel	.24
AR Border (c) c Broad b Capel	.2	not out	.48
MRJ Veletta c Emburey b Hemmings	.22		
SR Waugh c French b Dilley	.27		
PR Sleep c Athey b Foster	.41		
GC Dyer (+) lbw Dilley	.0		
PL Taylor c French b Hemmings	.20		
AIC Dodemaide not out	.12		
CJ McDermott c Foster b Dilley	.1		
EXTRAS (LB 10, W 1, NB 5)	.16	(B 3, LB 7, NB 6)	.16
TOTAL	.214		.2 for 328

FOW 1st Inns: 18 25 34 82 116 147 153 183 209 214
FOW 2nd Inns: 162 218

Bowling: *First Innings*: Dilley 19.1-4-54-3, Foster 19-6-27-2, Emburey 30-10-57-0, Capel 6-3-13-2, Hemmings 22-3-53-3. *Second Innings*: Foster 15-6-27-0, Capel 17-4-38-1, Dilley 13-1-48-0, Hemmings 52-15-107-0, Emburey 38-5-98-1.

Umpires: AR Crafter & PJ McConnell

Australian Averages

1987–88 AUSTRALIA v NEW ZEALAND

AUSTRALIA	M	Inn	NO	Runs	H.S	Avrge	Ct	St	Overs	Mds	Runs	Wkt	Avrge
Boon, DC	3	5	-	237	143	47.40	6	-	-	-	-	-	-
Border, AR	3	4	-	288	205	72.00	6	-	-	-	-	-	-
Dodemaide, AIC	1	2	-	53	50	26.50	1	-	48.3	14	106	7	15.14
Dyer, GC	3	4	-	93	60	23.25	13	-	-	-	-	-	-
Hughes, MG	1	1	-	5	5	5.00	-	-	35.0	12	97	5	19.40
Jones, DM	3	5	1	52	38*	13.00	3	-	14.0	6	29	1	29.00
Marsh, GR	3	5	1	122	31*	30.50	2	-	-	-	-	-	-
May, TBA	1	1	1	14	14*	-	-	-	84.0	23	202	4	50.50
McDermott, CJ	3	4	1	83	33	27.67	-	-	144.1	32	426	17	25.06
Reid, BA	2	2	1	13	8*	13.00	-	-	57.0	16	114	7	16.29
Sleep, PR	3	4	-	211	90	52.75	1	-	124.0	31	342	7	48.86
Veletta, MRJ	3	4	-	84	39	21.00	7	-	-	-	-	-	-
Waugh, SR	3	4	-	147	61	36.75	3	-	75.0	26	169	2	84.50
Whitney, MR	1	2	2	2	2*	-	-	-	53.3	11	137	4	34.25

New Zealand Averages

1987–88 AUSTRALIA v NEW ZEALAND

NEW ZEALAND	M	Inn	NO	Runs	H.S	Avrge	Ct	St	Overs	Mds	Runs	Wkt	Avrge
Bracewell, JG	3	5	-	53	32	10.60	3	-	141.5	27	339	8	42.38
Chatfield, EJ	2	4	4	8	6*	-	-	-	85.0	27	154	2	77.00
Crowe, JJ	3	6	-	78	25	13.00	1	-	-	-	-	-	-
Crowe, MD	3	6	-	396	137	66.00	2	-	-	-	-	-	-
Gray, EJ	1	2	-	37	23	18.50	1	-	44.0	10	102	-	-
Hadlee, RJ	3	6	1	111	36	22.20	-	-	156.0	44	353	18	19.61
Horne, PA	1	2	-	34	27	17.00	-	-	-	-	-	-	-
Jones, AH	3	6	-	323	150	53.83	2	-	-	-	-	-	-
Morrison, DK	3	4	-	2	2	0.50	-	-	101.4	19	354	8	44.25
Patel, DN	3	6	-	192	62	32.00	2	-	22.1	9	52	-	-
Rutherford, KR	1	2	-	2	2	1.00	1	-	-	-	-	-	-
Smith, IDS	3	6	-	80	44	16.00	7	1	-	-	-	-	-
Snedden, MC	1	2	1	8	8*	8.00	-	-	32.0	6	89	1	89.00
Wright, JG	3	6	-	248	99	41.33	1	-	-	-	-	-	-

1988-89

AUSTRALIA IN PAKISTAN

Pakistan's pitch formula gives results

AUSTRALIA CRICKET TEAM PAKISTAN TOUR 1988

The Australian team touring Pakistan in 1988 had to endure 'special' pitches and poor umpiring.

Lahore, Oct. 11. 'I could have written down the scenario before I got here, exactly what was going to happen,' Australian captain Allan Border told the ABC after the third Test.

Australia had lost the first and the other two were drawn with Australia on top.

But even before the first Test the Australian party managed by former umpire Col Egar was upset, and threatening to come home. They were only dissuaded by strong pressure from Australia to see out the tour for the good of cricket.

What Border meant was that the Pakistanis had prepared – or under-prepared – the pitch for the first Test at the National Stadium in Karachi, managed to win the toss, batted for over two days and then dismissed Australia twice on a pitch that took spin like a dog takes a bone.

This kind of analysis leaves out the extraordinary patience and skill of Pakistani captain Javed Miandad (who took over from Imran Khan who refused to play in the series). Miandad batted ten minutes short of ten hours for 211, his fifth double century and survived chances on 126 and 186 – as well as innumerable lbw appeals.

Independent observers agreed that the umpiring by Khizer Hayat in his 21st Test, and Mahboob Shah, officiating for the 18th time, was of a very low and partisan standard.

Pakistan's 469 was its highest score against Australia and also featured Shoaib Mohammad's 94 in a partnership of 196 with Miandad.

In Australia's first innings of just 165, only Peter Taylor was able to read the mysteries of recalled veteran left arm spinner Iqbal Qasim. Taylor was 54 not out, more than double the next highest, that of 'keeper Ian Healy who made 26 in his first Test. Australia was 6/64 and without a prayer.

Iqbal Qasim, who many thought had disappeared from the Pakistani Test scene, bowled 39 overs and took 5/35. Abdul Qadir took 2/54 from 37 overs. Quicker (they weren't fast) bowlers totalled 20 overs – just to take the shine off the ball.

The second innings was a repeat of the first except that the tail failed to wag. 6/80 following on, Peter Taylor being asked to open with Geoff Marsh, a move which failed – Taylor made just two runs.

This time Iqbal Qasim took 4/49 from 25 overs and Abdul Qadir 3/34.

Australia's top score was a miserable 21 from Ian Healy – showing an admirable fighting spirit. He took one catch – Ramiz Raja off the tireless beanstalk Bruce Reid in Pakistan's innings.

After the bitter first-Test defeat, Border had said: 'The next two Tests will be played on bland pitches and will be drawn. It's the same old story in Pakistan.'

And so it came to pass – drawn matches in Faisalabad and at Gadaffi Stadium, Lahore.

Veteran leg spinner Abdul Qadir was better with the ball than the bat – he kept the flame of wrist spin alight – but he scored a first class century in his second match in 1975.

FIRST TEST 1988–89 PAKISTAN v AUSTRALIA
National Stadium, Karachi. September 15, 16, 17, 19, 20, 1988.
Toss: Pakistan. Pakistan won by an innings & 188 runs.

PAKISTAN

Mudassar Nazar b Reid		0
Rameez Raja c Healy b Reid		9
Shoaib Mohammad b Waugh		94
Javed Miandad (c) c Boon b Reid		211
Tauseef Ahmed c Boon b May		35
Salim Malik c Boon b May		45
Ijaz Ahmed c Boon b Reid		12
Aamir Malik not out		17
Salim Yousuf (+) c Wood b May		5
Abdul Qadir c Marsh b May		8
Iqbal Qasim		
EXTRAS (B 16, LB 12, NB 5)		33
TOTAL		9 dec 469

FOW 1st Inns: 0 21 217 284 398 428 444 457 469

Bowling: *First Innings*: Reid 41-10-109-4, Dodemaide 29-13-35-0, Waugh 26-3-94-1, May 40.5-10-97-4, Taylor 16-2-73-0, Border 17-7-33-0.

AUSTRALIA

GR Marsh b Iqbal	8		lbw Tauseef	17
DC Boon c Abdul	14 (3)		b Iqbal	4
DM Jones lbw Iqbal	3 (4)		c Ijaz b Abdul	4
GM Wood c Aamir b Tauseef	23 (5)		lbw Iqbal	15
AR Border (c) c Aamir b Iqbal	4 (6)		b Iqbal	18
SR Waugh lbw Iqbal	0 (7)		st Salim b Iqbal	13
PL Taylor not out	54 (2)		c Ijaz b Aamir	2
IA Healy (+) c Ijaz b Mudassar	26		c Shoaib b Abdul	21
AIC Dodemaide c Ijaz b Salim	8		st Salim b Tauseef	2
TBA May c Salim b Abdul	6		lbw Abdul	0
BA Reid lbw Iqbal	0		not out	8
EXTRAS (B 12, LB 7)	19		(B 6, LB 6)	12
TOTAL	165			116

FOW 1st Inns: 19 23 40 48 54 64 106 139 162 165
FOW 2nd Inns: 4 10 15 46 50 80 93 104 104 116

Bowling: *First Innings*: Mudassar 10-3-15-1, Aamir 2-0-6-0, Iqbal 39-24-35-5, Abdul 37-16-54-2, Tauseef 26-15-28-1, Shoaib 2-1-1-0, Salim 6-4-7-1. *Second Innings*: Mudassar 3-0-5-0, Aamir 2-2-0-1, Iqbal 25-14-49-4, Abdul 13-4-34-3, Tauseef 21.4-13-16-2.

Umpires: Khizer Hayat & Mahboob Shah

SECOND TEST 1988–89 PAKISTAN v AUSTRALIA
Iqbal Stadium, Faisalabad. September 23, 24, 25, 27, 28, 1988.
Toss: Pakistan. Match Drawn.

PAKISTAN

Mudassar Nazar c Marsh b Reid	9		c Border b May	27
Rameez Raja lbw Dodemaide	0		c Boon b Waugh	32
Shoaib Mohammad b Dodemaide	11		st Salim b May	74
Javed Miandad (c) c Boon b May	43		lbw Reid	107
Salim Malik b Dodemaide	0		c Border b Reid	10
Ijaz Ahmed b Reid	122		c Healy b Reid	0
Salim Yousuf (+) c Boon b Dodemaide	62		not out	66
Abdul Qadir b Reid	6 (10)		c Reid b May	13
Tauseef Ahmed not out	35 (8)		c Waugh b Dodemaide	2
Iqbal Qasim c & b Sleep	16 (9)		lbw Reid	28
Salim Jaffar lbw Sleep	0			
EXTRAS (B 2, LB 6, NB 4)	12		(LB 6, NB 13)	19
TOTAL	316			9 dec 378

FOW 1st Inns: 4 20 24 25 144 255 255 267 316 316
FOW 2nd Inns: 64 64 236 264 265 269 274 344 378

Bowling: *First Innings*: Reid 31-8-92-3, Dodemaide 34-6-87-4, Waugh 11-3-36-0, Sleep 5.5-1-24-2, May 19-3-58-1, Border 6-1-11-0. *Second Innings*: Reid 30-6-100-4, Dodemaide 20-4-48-1, Waugh 18-6-44-1, May 34.4-7-126-3, Sleep 13-4-51-0, Border 1-0-3-0.

AUSTRALIA

DC Boon b Mudassar	13 (2)		c Mudassar b Tauseef	15
GR Marsh b Tauseef	51 (1)		b Abdul	9
DM Jones lbw Abdul	16		not out	21
GM Wood lbw Salim	32 (5)		not out	2
AIC Dodemaide c Ijaz b Mudassar	19			
AR Border (c) not out	113			
SR Waugh st Salim b Tauseef	1 (4)		c & b Shoaib	19
PR Sleep b Tauseef	12			
IA Healy (+) c Iqbal b Salim	27			
TBA May c(S)Moin-ul-Atiq b Abdul	14			
BA Reid c Salim b Iqbal	1			
EXTRAS (B 4, LB 15, W 1, NB 2)	22		(B 1)	1
TOTAL	321			3 for 67

FOW 1st Inns: 24 65 122 122 167 170 204 256 318 321
FOW 2nd Inns: 18 30 65

Bowling: *First Innings*: Salim 29-7-69-2, Mudassar 17-4-39-2, Abdul 34-5-84-2, Tauseef 35-10-73-3, Iqbal 14.5-4-37-1. *Second Innings*: Salim 2-0-8-0, Mudassar 2-0-5-0, Abdul 10-1-34-1, Tauseef 11-4-17-1, Shoaib 1-0-2-1.

Umpires: Mahboob Shah & Tariq Ata

THIRD TEST 1988–89 PAKISTAN v AUSTRALIA
Gaddafi Stadium, Lahore. October 7, 8, 9, 10, 11, 1988.
Toss: Australia. Match Drawn.

AUSTRALIA

DC Boon c Shoaib b Salim	43 (2)		c Javed b Salim	28
GR Marsh st Salim b Iqbal	64 (1)		not out	84
DM Jones lbw Tauseef	0		lbw Salim	0
AR Border (c) c Salim b Tauseef	75		c Salim b Tauseef	20
GM Wood lbw Mudassar	15			
PL Taylor st Salim b Abdul	29 (5)		not out	25
SR Waugh c Ijaz b Iqbal	59			
IA Healy (+) lbw Abdul	0			
AIC Dodemaide c Iqbal b Abdul	14			
TBA May not out	13			
BA Reid c Mudassar b Tauseef	8			
EXTRAS (B 4, LB 12, W 4)	20		(LB 4)	4
TOTAL	340			3 dec 161

FOW 1st Inns: 87 88 155 200 231 241 241 294 331 340
FOW 2nd Inns: 71 71 108

Bowling: *First Innings*: Salim 33-9-82-1, Mudassar 15-6-23-1, Abdul 37-10-88-3, Tauseef 50-20-85-3, Iqbal 22-6-42-2, Shoaib 1-0-4-0. *Second Innings*: Salim 14-2-60-2, Mudassar 3-0-8-0, Tauseef 17-2-48-1, Abdul 4-1-26-0, Iqbal 3-0-15-0.

PAKISTAN

Mudassar Nazar c Boon b May	27		c Border b Taylor	49
Rameez Raja c Healy b Reid	64		c Boon b May	21
Shoaib Mohammad run out	13		lbw May	3
Javed Miandad (c) c Healy b Reid	27		c Border b May	24
Salim Malik c & b Dodemaide	26		c Healy b Taylor	13
Ijaz Ahmed b Dodemaide	23		c Taylor b Dodemaide	15
Salim Yousuf (+) c Healy b Reid	1		c Waugh b Taylor	2
Abdul Qadir lbw Dodemaide	18		st Healy b Taylor	6
Iqbal Qasim lbw May	14		not out	10
Tauseef Ahmed c Boon b May	3		not out	1
Salim Jaffar not out	0			
EXTRAS (LB 6, NB 11)	17		(B 6, LB 1, NB 2)	9
TOTAL	233			8 for 153

FOW 1st Inns: 80 104 118 172 172 173 206 228 232 233
FOW 2nd Inns: 36 48 86 107 123 125 131 147

Bowling: *First Innings*: Reid 23-3-53-3, Waugh 18-4-34-0, Dodemaide 26-6-56-3, May 27.2-6-73-3, Taylor 4-2-11-0. *Second Innings*: Dodemaide 12-5-20-1, Waugh 5-1-8-0, May 35-20-39-3, Taylor 28-9-78-4, Border 4-3-1-0.

Umpires: Khizer Hayat & Salim Badar

Australian Averages

1988–89 PAKISTAN v AUSTRALIA

AUSTRALIA	M	Inn	NO	Runs	H.S	Avrge	Ct	St	Overs	Mds	Runs	Wkt	Avrge
Boon, DC	3	6	-	117	43	19.50	10	-	-	-	-	-	-
Border, AR	3	5	1	230	113*	57.50	4	-	28.0	11	48	-	-
Dodemaide, AIC	3	4	-	43	19	10.75	1	-	121.0	34	246	9	27.33
Healy, IA	3	4	-	74	27	18.50	6	2	-	-	-	-	-
Jones, DM	3	6	-	44	21*	8.80	-	-	-	-	-	-	-
Marsh, GR	3	6	1	233	84*	46.60	2	-	-	-	-	-	-
May, TBA	3	4	-	33	14	11.00	-	-	156.5	46	393	14	28.07
Reid, BA	3	4	1	17	8*	5.67	1	-	125.0	27	354	14	25.29
Sleep, PR	1	1	-	12	12	12.00	1	-	18.5	5	75	2	37.50
Taylor, PL	2	4	2	110	54*	55.00	1	-	48.0	13	162	4	40.50
Waugh, SR	3	5	-	92	59	18.40	2	-	78.0	17	216	2	108.00
Wood, GM	3	5	1	87	32	21.75	1	-	-	-	-	-	-

Pakistani Averages

1988–89 PAKISTAN v AUSTRALIA

PAKISTAN	M	Inn	NO	Runs	H.S	Avrge	Ct	St	Overs	Mds	Runs	Wkt	Avrge
Aamir Malik	1	1	1	17	17*	-	1	-	4.0	2	6	1	6.00
Abdul Qadir	3	5	-	51	18	10.20	-	-	135.0	37	320	11	29.09
Ijaz Ahmed	3	5	-	172	122	34.40	6	-	-	-	-	-	-
Iqbal Qasim	3	4	1	68	28	22.67	3	-	103.5	48	178	12	14.83
Javed Miandad	3	5	-	412	211	82.40	1	-	-	-	-	-	-
Mudassar Nazar	3	5	-	112	49	22.40	2	-	50.0	13	95	4	23.75
Rameez Raja	3	5	-	126	64	25.20	-	-	-	-	-	-	-
Salim Jaffar	2	2	1	0	0*	-	-	-	78.0	18	219	5	43.80
Salim Malik	3	5	-	94	45	18.80	-	-	6.0	4	7	1	7.00
Salim Yousuf	3	5	-	136	66*	34.00	4	5	-	-	-	-	-
Shoaib Mohammad	3	5	-	195	94	39.00	3	-	4.0	1	7	1	7.00
Tauseef Ahmed	3	5	2	76	35*	25.33	-	-	160.4	64	267	11	24.27

Windies too good despite big Merv's rage

Perth, Dec. 6. When Merv Hughes vented his anger at the West Indies with a superbly aggressive and lightning fast delivery that thundered into the pads of Gordon Greenidge, Australians everywhere thought something startling was happening, or could happen.

Merv completed an unusual hat-trick. Greenidge out lbw was his third wicket in three consecutive balls over two innings and three overs. He claimed the first wicket (Curtly Ambrose) with the last ball of his 36th over, the second wicket (Patrick Patterson) with the first ball of his 37th over (which ended the West Indian first innings) and Greenidge with the first ball of the second innings.

This was sweet revenge for Australians, after Ambrose broke Geoff Lawson's jaw with a short ball 'in Australia's fighting innings of 8/395.

But as has been generally the case with Australia v West Indies contests, the fightback cannot be sustained for an entire five days.

In the West Indies first innings it was a Viv Richards' 'special' – 146 runs, looking like he would get out at any time. In the second innings it was Desmond Haynes with a crashing and crunching innings of exactly 100 that snuffed Australia out. Hughes took a magnificently aggressive 8/87 to go with his first innings 5/130 – but the Windies made 349.

The hard work of Graham Wood, David Boon and Steve Waugh in the first innings was for nothing as Australia was dismissed for 234 in the second innings, to lose by 169 runs.

The first Test set the scene for the summer – Australia's Allan Border winning the toss and batting, then Patrick Patterson limping from the field after 3.1 overs – but this seeming good fortune was erased by the arrival of Ambrose at the bowling crease, taking three quick wickets including Border, Wood and Geoff Marsh.

The West Indies bounded to a great start with their batting – Haynes and Greenidge putting on a record 135. Richards (68) and Richie Richardson (81) then got the Windies to 394 which proved to be plenty.

Australia were 4/65 and only Steve Waugh's 90 stood in the way of a nine-wicket defeat.

The bowling highlight was a hat-trick to Courtney Walsh, and the wild and wide bowling of Chris Matthews – who sprayed the ball about in his first Test for 0/61.

Geoff Lawson's jaw was broken by a delivery from big Curtly Ambrose.

Merv Hughes growls with pride at his captain after grabbing his hat-trick.

Patterson lifters raise the eyebrows

Melbourne, Dec. 29. Patrick Patterson, recovered from his injury, had the Australians ducking and diving in the third Test at the MCG, taking 5/39 in Australia's second innings disaster – including Allan Border for the equal top score of 20. Patterson's (and Curtly Ambrose's) use of the short ball on the now traditional sub-standard MCG pitch was not lethal but was painfully effective. Australia was never in the hunt after Richie Richardson's flourishing and occasionally majestic 122, and Viv Richard's slamming 63. Steve Waugh took a 'fivefor' but the West Indies made 361.

Schedule slated

Sydney, Jan. 1. Following criticism by Melbourne Cricket Club secretary of the Melbourne Test starting on Christmas Eve rather than on the more popular and traditional Boxing Day, there has been much discussion over the decline of Test cricket crowds.

The Sydney *Sun Herald* published a chart showing a decline in average daily attendances from a high point of 36,631 in 1936–37 v England, to 30,621 in 1960–61 v West Indies, 26,805 in 1974–75 v England, 14,523 in 1984–85 v West Indies to 12,963 so far this season. Although daily averages don't tell the whole story, with the added factor of increased prices, they certainly tell part of it.

The Deano show

Adelaide Feb. 7. Highlight of this match on a flat track was the career-restoring 216 by Dean Jones. He had begun to blossom on the first day, reaching 131 in Australia's 3/283, Allan Border not out 64.

Next morning Border went without adding to his score, and at 7/333, with Tim May coming to the crease, a double century looked beyond hope.

But May added 24 of 50, and then mighty Merv Hughes put on 114 with Jones, seeing him (more like swiping him) to 216 before Jones was run out. Hughes was eventually 72 not out, with Australia in charge of the game.

Richie Richardson played another glorious attacking innings in the Windies first innings and Gordon Greenidge an equally glorious defensive century in the second – the match ended in draw, a result only evident in the last session on the fifth day. A good match.

Bowler Border raises the spirits at SCG

Allan Border's hitherto unsung left arm 'ordinaries' proved to be hand grenades in Sydney. He took 11/96 in the Sydney Test.

Sydney, Jan. 30. Mark Taylor opened the batting for the first time in the fourth Test, joining Peter 'Who' Taylor in the team – and allowing David Boon to bat at three. If the opening stands in this match, 14 and 3, were nothing to write home about, Boon was a spectacular success, making 149 with good support from Allan Border and Dean Jones, as Australia chased the West Indies modest and suspicious 224.

While Peter Taylor dismissed Gordon Greenidge and Trevor Hohns snared Desmond Haynes, it was the part-time left-arm genius of Allan Border who in 26 mysterious and inviting overs snared 7/46. This unlikely event lifted the Australians' depression, which Boon proceeded to turn into a positive expectation of victory.

While Border was slightly less effective with 4/50 in the second innings he did eventually remove the only major scorer, Haynes, for a beautiful 143. His placement on the on side and driving and cutting were a delight. Next highest score was Carl Hooper with 35 – which left Australia with just 82 to win.

Unlikely as it sounds, Border was the first Australian captain to take ten wickets in a match.

There were several disputed bat–pad decisions – Richards given out in the first innings to Border, and Border given not out when on nought, but equally there was a lot of unnecessary appealing.

Merv Hughes's warm-up exercises proved to be an opportunity for mass callisthenics by his legion of fans.

World Series controversy

Viv Richards: 60 not out in the third World Series final.

Sydney, Jan. 18. Pakistan, led by Imran Khan, was the third team in the 1988–89 World Series cup competition, which comprises twelve games and a best-of-three finals sandwiched between the five Test matches. Pakistan beat Australia and the West Indies once, but were playing out of their league to some extent.

Australia, on the other hand, was competitive right from the first match – it lost by two runs, but very nearly won. In the end Australia and the West Indies won five games each and were a total of six runs and 0.02 in run-rate

apart after eight games. Australia won the first final at the MCG in front of 73,575 fans by two runs, batting first, then lost the second at the SCG by a decisive 92 runs – after the spinners were slogged all over the park.

The deciding final was rain affected – Australia making a wonderful 226 from 38 overs – Dean Jones 93 not out. Further rain left the West Indies to score 108 in 18 overs. The slippery ball and the plainly unjust way the target was calculated led to much criticism as the Windies made them in 13.2 overs and won the competition.

Cricket Academy in Adelaide

Adelaide, Feb. 28. The Australian Institute of Sport cricket academy, sponsored by the Commonwealth Bank, began work in Adelaide in May 1988.

Practice for the 20 young players seleceted is at Adelaide's picturesque No. 2 ground. The players stay at St Mark's boarding school nearby.

Coach Jack Potter and assistant Peter Spence have overseen the installation of two all-weather practice nets and the upgrading of the outdoor areas, and have the use of two additional practice lanes at the indoor centre next to the Adelaide Oval administration centre.

Many of the young men were ini-

tially quite homesick, and counselling had to be arranged. Some, while waiting for the promised jobs and having to exist on a government stipend of $10 a week, became even more unhappy.

It proved difficult to find employers willing to allow the academicians time off for two training sessions a day – at 7.30 a.m. and 3.30 p.m.

After a few months the whole arrangement has bedded down well – except that the bowlers have had to work too hard. Every bowler came down with an injury at some stage. Joe Scuderi, Brett Williams, Jamie Cox and Peter Drinnen all made the jump from academy to first class cricket.

FIRST TEST 1988–89 AUSTRALIA v WEST INDIES
Brisbane Cricket Ground, Brisbane. November 18, 19, 20, 21, 1988.
Toss: Australia. West Indies won by 9 wkts.

AUSTRALIA

GR Marsh c Logie b Ambrose	.27	(2)	lbw Ambrose	.2
DC Boon lbw Marshall	.10	(1)	c Dujon b Marshall	.12
MRJ Veletta b Hooper	.37		c Hooper b Walsh	.10
GM Wood c Greenidge b Ambrose	.6	(5)	lbw Walsh	.0
AR Border (c) c Dujon b Ambrose	.4	(6)	c Haynes b Ambrose	.41
SR Waugh lbw Marshall	.4	(4)	c Haynes b Marshall	.90
IA Healy (+) c Logie b Walsh	.27		c Ambrose b Marshall	.28
AIC Dodemaide c Richards b Walsh	.22		c Richards b Marshall	.7
CJ McDermott c Logie b Walsh	.2		not out	.32
CD Matthews c Dujon b Walsh	.1		c (S)KLT Arthurton b Walsh	.32
TBA May not out	.4		c Hooper b Ambrose	.5
EXTRAS (B 1, LB 5, W 1, NB 16)	.23		(B 4, LB 5, NB 21)	.30
TOTAL	.167			.289

FOW 1st Inns: 19 52 64 76 86 126 138 140 150 167
FOW 2nd Inns: 14 16 65 65 157 199 212 212 270 289

Bowling: *First Innings*: Marshall 18-3-39-2, Patterson 3.1-1-5-0, Ambrose 16.5-5-30-3, Walsh 18.3-3-62-4, Hooper 12-2-24-1, Richards 1-0-1-0. *Second Innings*: Marshall 26-2-92-4, Ambrose 26.1-5-78-3, Walsh 19-3-61-3, Richards 11-4-26-0, Hooper 4-0-23-0.

WEST INDIES

CG Greenidge b May	.80	c Healy b Dodemaide	.16
DL Haynes c Healy b Waugh	.40	not out	.30
RB Richardson lbw Dodemaide	.81	not out	.7
CL Hooper c Border b Waugh	.1		
IVA Richards (c) c McDermott b May	.68		
AL Logie c Border b May	.19		
PJL Dujon (+) c May b McDermott	.27		
MD Marshall c Border b McDermott	.11		
CEL Ambrose not out	.19		
CA Walsh lbw McDermott	.0		
BP Patterson lbw Dodemaide	.0		
EXTRAS (B 5, LB 9, W 6, NB 28)	.48	(LB 4, W 3, NB 3)	.10
TOTAL	.394		.1 for 63

FOW 1st Inns: 135 156 162 270 307 359 361 389 393 394
FOW 2nd Inns: 43

Bowling: *First Innings*: McDermott 28-3-99-3, Matthews 21-3-62-0, Dodemaide 16.4-2-60-2, May 29-6-90-3, Waugh 18-2-61-2, Border 1-0-8-0. *Second Innings*: McDermott 4-0-12-0, Matthews 3.5-1-18-0, Dodemaide 5.2-1-15-1, Waugh 6-0-14-0.

Umpires: AR Crafter & PJ McConnell

SECOND TEST 1988–89 AUSTRALIA v WEST INDIES
W.A.C.A. Ground, Perth. December 2, 3, 4, 5, 6, 1988.
Toss: Australia. West Indies won by 169 runs.

WEST INDIES

CG Greenidge b Lawson	.40	lbw Hughes	.0
DL Haynes lbw Hughes	.11	c Healy b Hughes	.100
RB Richardson c Boon b Hughes	.66	c Healy b Hughes	.48
CL Hooper c Boon b Lawson	.26	c Dodemaide b Hughes	.64
IVA Richards (c) c Dodemaide b Lawson	.146	lbw Hughes	.5
AL Logie c Waugh b May	.93	b Hughes	.30
PJL Dujon (+) c Veletta b May	.32	c Dodemaide b Hughes	.9
MD Marshall c Veletta b Hughes	.4	c Healy b Dodemaide	.23
CEL Ambrose c Healy b Hughes	.8	c Wood b Hughes	.15
CA Walsh not out	.0	not out	.17
BP Patterson c Dodemaide b Hughes	.1	not out	.6
EXTRAS (B 1, LB 12, NB 9)	.22	(B 14, LB 9, NB 9)	.32
TOTAL	.449		.9 dec 349

FOW 1st Inns: 16 82 126 180 343 421 426 440 448 449
FOW 2nd Inns: 0 103 216 236 246 259 300 310 341

Bowling: *First Innings*: Lawson 32-7-97-3, Hughes 36.1-7-130-5, Dodemaide 17-1-79-0, Waugh 28-3-90-0, May 10-3-40-2. *Second Innings*: Hughes 37-9-87-8, Dodemaide 24-2-101-1, Waugh 23-1-70-0, May 14-1-68-0.

AUSTRALIA

GR Marsh c Richardson b Walsh	.30	(2)	c Logie b Marshall	.6
DC Boon c Logie b Ambrose	.80	(1)	b Patterson	.4
MRJ Veletta run out	.11		c Dujon b Marshall	.13
GM Wood c Richardson b Ambrose	.111		c Greenidge b Walsh	.42
AR Border (c) c Dujon b Ambrose	.6		b Hooper	.26
SR Waugh c Dujon b Ambrose	.91		c Hooper b Patterson	.26
IA Healy (+) lbw Marshall	.8		c Logie b Ambrose	.52
AIC Dodemaide not out	.7		lbw Ambrose	.11
TBA May c Richards b Ambrose	.2		not out	.8
GF Lawson retired hurt	.0			
MG Hughes		(10)	c Logie b Ambrose	.0
EXTRAS (B 5, LB 9, NB 35)	.49		(B 5, LB 4, NB 37)	.46
TOTAL	.8 dec 395			.9 for 234

FOW 1st Inns: 83 139 152 167 367 374 388 395
FOW 2nd Inns: 14 14 46 93 138 140 190 232 234

Bowling: *First Innings*: Marshall 23-3-84-1, Patterson 16-1-95-0, Walsh 19-3-58-1, Ambrose 23.3-3-72-5, Richards 14-0-43-0, Hooper 5-0-29-0. *Second Innings*: Marshall 12-0-50-2, Patterson 14-2-58-2, Ambrose 17-1-66-3, Walsh 15-1-46-1, Hooper 5-2-5-1.

Umpires: RC Bailhache & TA Prue

THIRD TEST 1988–89 AUSTRALIA v WEST INDIES
Melbourne Cricket Ground, Melbourne. December 24, 26, 27, 28, 29, 1988.
Toss: Australia. West Indies won by 285 runs.

WEST INDIES

CG Greenidge c Healy b Alderman	49	not out	36
DL Haynes c Boon b McDermott	17	lbw Alderman	23
RB Richardson c Taylor b Alderman	26	c & b Waugh	122
CL Hooper c Border b McDermott	38	lbw Alderman	4
IVA Richards (c) c Border b Waugh	12 (6)	lbw Waugh	63
AL Logie lbw Alderman	10 (10)	c Border b Waugh	17
PJL Dujon (+) c Healy b Waugh	26 (5)	c Wood b Alderman	46
MD Marshall c Jones b Waugh	7 (7)	c Alderman b Waugh	19
CEL Ambrose lbw McDermott	44 (8)	c Marsh b McDermott	5
CA Walsh not out	30 (9)	c Marsh b Waugh	6
BP Patterson lbw Alderman	13	not out	3
EXTRAS (B 1, LB 4, NB 3)	8	(LB 1, NB 16)	17
TOTAL	280		9 dec 361

FOW 1st Inns: 68 68 114 137 147 166 185 199 256 280
FOW 2nd Inns: 38 92 191 284 317 324 324 335 356

Bowling: *First Innings*: Hughes 14-3-52-0, Alderman 32.1-9-68-4, McDermott 19-3-62-3, Waugh 21-3-77-3, Taylor 7-3-16-0. *Second Innings*: Hughes 24-8-71-0, Alderman 36-12-78-3, Waugh 24-5-92-5, McDermott 26-3-78-1, Border 1-1-0-0, Taylor 9-1-41-0.

AUSTRALIA

DC Boon run out	23 (2)	lbw Marshall	20
GR Marsh b Patterson	36 (1)	b Patterson	1
DM Jones b Ambrose	28	c (S)RA Harper b Ambrose	18
GM Wood c Haynes b Patterson	12	c Ambrose b Walsh	7
AR Border (c) b Ambrose	0	c Haynes b Patterson	20
SR Waugh c Greenidge b Ambrose	42	c (S)RA Harper b Ambrose	3
IA Healy (+) lbw Patterson	4	c Hooper b Walsh	8
PL Taylor c Greenidge b Ambrose	14	not out	18
CJ McDermott c Marshall b Patterson	28	c (S)KLT Arthurton b Patterson	0
MG Hughes not out	21	c Dujon b Patterson	4
TM Alderman b Walsh	3	c Dujon b Patterson	0
EXTRAS (B 2, LB 14, NB 15)	31	(B 4, LB 5, NB 6)	15
TOTAL	242		114

FOW 1st Inns: 40 103 117 117 150 161 186 190 234 242
FOW 2nd Inns: 7 30 56 58 64 75 104 104 114 114

Bowling: *First Innings*: Marshall 30-8-68-0, Ambrose 27-7-60-4, Walsh 17.3-3-49-1, Patterson 20-2-49-4. *Second Innings*: Marshall 9-3-12-1, Patterson 15.1-3-39-5, Ambrose 13-5-21-2, Walsh 16-7-21-2, Richards 4-1-12-0.

Umpires: AR Crafter & PJ McConnell

FOURTH TEST 1988–89 AUSTRALIA v WEST INDIES
Sydney Cricket Ground, Sydney. January 26, 27, 28, 29, 30, 1989.
Toss: West Indies. Australia won by 7 wkts.

WEST INDIES

CG Greenidge c Waugh b PL Taylor	56	c & b Hughes	4
DL Haynes c Boon b Hohns	75	c MA Taylor b Border	143
RB Richardson c PL Taylor b Border	28	c Hughes b PL Taylor	22
CL Hooper c Marsh b Border	0	c Jones b Hohns	35
IVA Richards (c) c Boon b Border	11	c Jones b Hohns	4
AL Logie b Border	0	c PL Taylor b Hohns	6
PJL Dujon (+) c Hughes b Border	18	run out	9
RA Harper c PL Taylor b Border	17	lbw Border	12
MD Marshall c Marsh b Border	9	c PL Taylor b Border	3
CEL Ambrose c Jones b PL Taylor	1	c Boon b Border	5
CA Walsh not out	4	not out	7
EXTRAS (B 1, W 1, NB 3)	5	(B 1, W 1, NB 4)	6
TOTAL	224		256

FOW 1st Inns: 90 144 156 174 174 174 199 213 220 224
FOW 2nd Inns: 17 56 167 188 198 225 232 244 247 256

Bowling: *First Innings*: Alderman 10-2-17-0, Hughes 10-3-28-0, PL Taylor 25.2-8-65-2, Hohns 24-8-49-1, Border 26-10-46-7, Waugh 4-0-18-0. *Second Innings*: Hughes 18-6-29-1, Alderman 2-0-6-0, Waugh 3-0-10-0, PL Taylor 29-4-91-1, Hohns 34-11-69-3, Border 18.4-3-50-4.

AUSTRALIA

GR Marsh c Dujon b Marshall	2 (2)	b Richards	23
MA Taylor b Ambrose	25 (1)	c Haynes b Ambrose	3
DC Boon c Dujon b Walsh	149	c Harper b Marshall	10
DM Jones b Richards	29	not out	24
AR Border (c) b Marshall	75	not out	16
SR Waugh not out	55		
IA Healy (+) c Logie b Marshall	11		
PL Taylor lbw Marshall	0		
TV Hohns b Marshall	0		
MG Hughes c Dujon b Walsh	12		
TM Alderman run out	9		
EXTRAS (B 6, LB 14, NB 14)	34	(B 3, LB 1, NB 2)	6
TOTAL	401		3 for 82

FOW 1st Inns: 14 43 114 284 335 355 357 357 388 401
FOW 2nd Inns: 3 16 55

Bowling: *First Innings*: Marshall 31-16-29-5, Ambrose 33-5-78-1, Harper 37-9-86-0, Walsh 22.5-5-48-2, Hooper 37-10-72-0, Richards 31-1-68-1. *Second Innings*: Marshall 8-2-17-1, Ambrose 7-1-16-1, Hooper 10.3-2-24-0, Walsh 3-0-9-0, Richards 7-2-12-1.

Umpires: LJ King & TA Prue

FIFTH TEST 1988–89 AUSTRALIA v WEST INDIES
Adelaide Oval, Adelaide. February 3, 4, 5, 6, 7, 1989.
Toss: Australia. Match Drawn.

AUSTRALIA

GR Marsh c Dujon b Ambrose	21 (2)	c Dujon b Ambrose	79
MA Taylor run out	3 (1)	run out	36
DC Boon c Richardson b Ambrose	34	run out	55
DM Jones run out	216	lbw Richards	6
AR Border (c) b Marshall	64 (6)	not out	6
SR Waugh c Dujon b Walsh	12 (5)	run out	8
IA Healy (+) lbw Walsh	0		
TV Hohns c Hooper b Walsh	9		
TBA May c Richardson b Ambrose	24		
MG Hughes not out	72		
MR Whitney c Dujon b Patterson	2		
EXTRAS (LB 18, NB 40)	58	(B 11, LB 13, NB 10)	34
TOTAL	515		4 dec 224

FOW 1st Inns: 7 64 75 289 311 311 333 383 497 515
FOW 2nd Inns: 98 176 187 213

Bowling: *First Innings*: Marshall 23-3-67-1, Patterson 30.5-1-130-1, Ambrose 26-4-93-3, Walsh 33-5-120-3, Hooper 3-0-14-0, Richards 25-1-73-0. *Second Innings*: Marshall 12-2-30-0, Ambrose 15-2-44-1, Walsh 13-2-26-0, Patterson 8-1-29-0, Richards 24-3-64-1, Hooper 3-1-7-0.

WEST INDIES

CG Greenidge b Whitney	12	c Boon b May	104
DL Haynes run out	83	c Healy b Whitney	15
RB Richardson c Jones b Whitney	106	c Border b Whitney	22
CL Hooper c Healy b Whitney	2	b May	0
IVA Richards (c) c Boon b Whitney	69	not out	68
AL Logie c Healy b Hohns	21	not out	2
PJL Dujon (+) b Hohns	28		
MD Marshall c Marsh b Whitney	0		
CEL Ambrose c Boon b Whitney	9		
CA Walsh c Healy b Whitney	4		
BP Patterson not out	9		
EXTRAS (B 6, LB 10, NB 10)	26	(B 3, LB 7, W 1, NB 11)	22
TOTAL	369		4 for 233

FOW 1st Inns: 19 186 190 231 293 315 315 331 346 369
FOW 2nd Inns: 21 87 89 212

Bowling: *First Innings*: Hughes 15-0-86-0, Whitney 30-6-89-7, May 16-6-42-0, Waugh 3-0-17-0, Hohns 47.4-9-106-2, Border 10-2-13-0. *Second Innings*: Hughes 9-5-20-0, Whitney 20-4-60-2, Waugh 9-3-23-0, Hohns 15-3-56-0, May 23-3-60-2, Border 5-3-4-0.

Umpires: RJ Evans & PJ McConnell

Australian Averages

1988–89 AUSTRALIA v WEST INDIES

AUSTRALIA	M	Inn	NO	Runs	H.S	Avrge	Ct	St	Overs	Mds	Runs	Wkt	Avrge
Alderman, TM	2	3	-	12	9	4.00	1	-	80.1	23	169	7	24.14
Boon, DC	5	10	1	397	149	44.11	9	-	-	-	-	-	-
Border, AR	5	10	2	258	75	32.25	7	-	61.4	19	121	11	11.00
Dodemaide, AIC	2	4	1	47	22	15.67	4	-	63.0	6	255	4	63.75
Healy, IA	5	8	-	138	52	17.25	12	-	-	-	-	-	-
Hohns, TV	2	2	-	9	9	4.50	-	-	120.4	31	280	6	46.67
Hughes, MG	4	5	2	109	72*	36.33	4	-	163.1	41	503	14	35.93
Jones, DM	3	6	1	321	216	64.20	5	-	-	-	-	-	-
Lawson, GF	1	1	1	0	0+	-	-	-	32.0	7	97	3	32.33
Marsh, GR	5	10	-	227	79	22.70	5	-	-	-	-	-	-
Matthews, CD	1	2	-	33	32	16.50	-	-	24.5	4	80	-	-
May, TBA	3	5	2	43	24	14.33	1	-	92.0	19	300	7	42.86
McDermott, CJ	2	4	1	62	32*	20.67	1	-	77.0	9	251	7	35.86
Taylor, MA	2	4	-	67	36	16.75	1	-	-	-	-	-	-
Taylor, PL	2	3	1	32	18*	16.00	5	-	70.2	16	213	3	71.00
Veletta, MRJ	2	4	-	71	37	17.75	2	-	-	-	-	-	-
Waugh, SR	5	9	2	331	91	41.38	3	-	139.0	17	472	10	47.20
Whitney, MR	1	1	-	2	2	2.00	-	-	50.0	10	149	9	16.56
Wood, GM	3	6	-	178	111	29.67	2	-	-	-	-	-	-

+ retired hurt

West Indian Averages

1988–89 AUSTRALIA v WEST INDIES

WEST INDIES	M	Inn	NO	Runs	H.S	Avrge	Ct	St	Overs	Mds	Runs	Wkt	Avrge
Ambrose, CEL	5	8	1	106	44	15.14	2	-	204.3	38	558	26	21.46
Dujon, PJL	5	8	-	195	46	24.38	15	-	-	-	-	-	-
Greenidge, CG	5	10	1	397	104	44.11	4	-	-	-	-	-	-
Harper, RA	1	2	-	29	17	14.50	1	-	37.0	9	86	-	-
Haynes, DL	5	10	1	537	143	59.67	5	-	-	-	-	-	-
Hooper, CL	5	9	-	170	64	18.89	5	-	79.3	17	198	2	99.00
Logie, AL	5	9	-	198	93	24.75	4	-	-	-	-	-	-
Marshall, MD	5	8	-	76	23	9.50	1	-	192.0	42	488	17	28.71
Patterson, BP	4	6	2	32	13	10.67	-	-	107.1	11	405	12	33.75
Richards, IVA	5	9	1	446	146	55.75	3	-	117.0	12	299	3	99.67
Richardson, RB	5	10	1	528	122	58.67	4	-	-	-	-	-	-
Walsh, CA	5	8	5	68	30*	22.67	-	-	176.5	32	500	17	29.41

1989

AUSTRALIA IN ENGLAND

Border's boys on a weighty mission

Melbourne, April 27. The Australian Cricket Board has received details of Allan Border's three-year contract, said to be worth $300,000. With that confidence in his future as player and captain he will be able to lead the Australians on the 1989 tour of England from the front.

Border has been involved in the selection of the touring players, and is confident that they will meld into a unified and purposeful outfit.

The squad is strong, and focussed on the job of regaining the Ashes in England, a feat achieved only once before – by Bill Woodfull's 1934 Australians.

The squad is Geoff Marsh, Mark Taylor, Steve Waugh, David Boon, Dean Jones, Trevor Hohns, Geoff Lawson, Merv Hughes, Terry Alderman, Greg Campbell, Ian Healy, Mike Veletta, Tom Moody, Tim May, Carl Rackemann, Tim Zoehrer.

Now that Mark Taylor has established his place, with David Boon at three, Border four, followed by Jones and the more than promising Steve Waugh the team is better balanced and looks to be consistently attacking. It seems to have the bowlers to dispose of England whatever pitches might be in store.

Tasmanian fast-medium bowler Greg Campbell is the only surprise – and he showed some good form in the last summer, taking 36 wickets.

Two Test wins in a row

Celebrating in the traditional manner after the first 'pair' of Test wins since 1948.

Lord's, June 27. Australia has shown it means business with two overwhelming wins, at Headingley and Lord's. The optimism in the English camp has turned to back-biting and gloom, as Terry Alderman mesmerised the batsmen, and Steve Waugh has proved impossible, so far, to remove at all.

But the mood of the series was really set by the captain in the first innings of the first Test. Australia was in some difficulty at 2/57 when Border came out to bat at his favourite number four spot. He was aggressive and even adventurous from the beginning – slapping England quick Phillip DeFreitas over point for six – an accident perhaps, as Border remarked, but an accident with intent.

He went on to make 66, and 60 not out in the second innings, while Mark Taylor made a maiden Test century, followed by Steve Waugh's first as well – a magnificent 177 not out. Merv Hughes started batting with a six from the first ball and rubbed salt into the English wounds with a belting 71 in the total of 601.

Terry Alderman bowled straight from close to the stumps and picked up a 'fivefor', and Hughes bowled with passion and pace at the other end. England made 430, but it never looked enough to save the game, after Border and Australia set 400 plus and 83 overs to survive. 6/88 after lunch on the fifth day from Alderman and Geoff Lawson soon had the writing on the wall: Australia won by 210 runs.

In the second Test at Lord's, if the mixture wasn't quite as before, the match result was. Australia, through Alderman and Hughes, bowled England out for 286, 'keeper Jack Russell adding some frustrating value towards the end with 64 not out – before Australia piled on 528, thanks mainly to the unbowlable Steve Waugh (152) and the ominous return to form of David Boon, (94 – still to score a hundred in England).

England's reply was brave – especially from David Gower who made his 15th Test century. But Hughes finally got him fending one off his body. Alderman made Robin Smith (96) one of his six victims.

Australia made the 119 required for the loss of four wickets. Guess who was not out at the end – Steve Waugh, of course.

They just couldn't get him out: Steve Waugh wasn't dismissed until the third Test.

The battles of the captains

London, Aug. 28. It didn't take long. Despite his courageous batting in the second test, where he made 57 and 106, England captain David Gower is under the hammer.

Terry Brindle wrote in the *Australian*: 'David Gower is unloved by the English public which sees his apparent acceptance of failure as a luxury, unappreciated by professionals who see his as an amateur philosophy on the game and – perhaps most importantly – off side with an English media which creates kings and coffins with equal facility.'

Australia had no such problem with its captain's form, his strategies and tactics, or the support from his team-mates. The ploy of placing a shortish midwicket for Graham Gooch might not have got him out every time, but definitely inhibited his batting. Allan Border's aggressive batting has created the mood, and his bustling, somewhat stern and even authoritarian organisation of his field placements and bowler rotations has shown who is in charge on the field.

On the fourth day of the second Test, after the visit of the Queen, Border told his team: 'Come on, think about it again. If we can pick up a few in this session, we'll be certain of going two–up tomorrow. We can win the Test in this session.'

Border was also glad to be facing David Gower, captain to captain, because he was anxious to exorcise the ghosts of 1985 – and win back the Ashes from the man who took them then.

Gower thought Border was 'mean'. 'He was mean to the opposition, the press and indeed his own players. He sledged pretty fiercely too … it was hyper unfriendly.'

The Australians on the other hand thought Gower's attitude somewhat whimsical – he sent the 12th man to the press box during Australia's marathon opening stand in the fifth Test looking for advice.

Geoff Lawson thought Gower 'seems to have had one plan out on the field and when that hasn't worked he's been stuck… That's the main difference between him and AB … AB has learned to be a good captain; Gower does not appear to too interested in learning'.

At the end Border must have thought back to the selection process in which he was involved, and his comment: 'In this selection, there isn't one bloke that I was concerned about. I knew they'd gel.'

Rain snuffs Australian victory chance

Lovely weather for ducks: the first-day scene at Edgbaston.

Birmingham, July 11. In 1985 Edgbaston was the scene of one of Australia's heaviest defeats in Test cricket, an innings and 118 runs, certainly the most humiliating of that ignominious tour.

It was a venue at which the veterans of that match, Allan Border and Geoff Lawson, had a few ghosts to exorcise.

By contrast David Gower could look back at his 200, and not at the two heavy defeats he has suffered this season.

Thus it was a little surprising when Allan Border, on the Saturday night after much play was lost to rain, declared that Australia had a chance to win, after Dean Jones's blazing 157.

England, at one stage 5/75 (Gower 8 - lbw in the now traditional manner, b. Alderman) looked unlikely to save the follow-on until some stout resistance from Ian Botham, Jack Russell and John Emburey saw them struggle over the line.

Jones's innings was superb. From the moment he arrived at 3/105, three wickets having fallen for 17 runs, he attacked the bowling with relish. One of his hot drives deflected from bowler Paul Jarvis and ran out unlucky David Boon.

A draw was inevitable after the follow-on was saved, Mark Taylor having time to make another half century, but many ghosts had been laid to rest.

Australia eagerly looked forward to Manchester.

Where is that darned ball? asks the Australian slips cordon as it watches a David Gower edge fly out of reach.

Triumph! The Ashes regained

Taylor gets a Boon-hug.

Tim Curtis is caught by David Boon off the bowling of a delighted Terry Alderman at Old Trafford.

Manchester, Aug. 1. The man who became Captain Grumpy in the dark summers after he took over the captaincy became Captain Cheerful upon the high point of his captaincy and cricket career thus far.

Allan Border has regained the Ashes for Australia, in England – from a team that contained the Australians' nemesis in 1981, Ian Botham, and the batsman of 1985, David Gower.

When David Boon whacked Nick Cook to the midwicket boundary and scampered first for souvenir stumps and then off the ground, he too was as happy as Larry.

Congratulations for this joyful turn of events for Australian cricket began to be earned in the days when Border was appointed captain nearly five years ago, and began the Australian team's slow road back to respect and respectability.

Only David Boon remains from the first team Border captained, and it was appropriate that he should be the batsman to offer Border the opportunity to bat at number three in order to score the winning runs. Typically Border turned down the offer and stuck to the game plan.

This time the plan involved a superb whole-team performance with the bat, in which no one made a hundred.

Australia replied to England's modest 260 with 447.

Highlight was perhaps Steve Waugh's 92 – he looked as invincible as ever before he got out – but Mark Taylor also made 85, Border himself making a ferociously determined 80, Dean Jones a sparkling 69 and Geoff Marsh 47. Boon made just 12, but his value to the team is more than with the bat … his smart catch to get rid of Tim Curtis for a duck in the second innings was the start of the rot for England.

In terms of the bowling it was Geoff Lawson's 'turn' in the first innings. He strode in faster and with a longer stride than earlier in the tour and bowled at top pace, taking 6/72. And Trevor Hohns's bemusing leggies disposed of Gower with a flipper, and Botham with deceptive flight. Botham lumbered down the pitch with a rush of first ball blood and was beaten and bowled for a duck. It was not 1981 anymore.

If England had not had a resolute Robin Smith making 143 from 260 in the first innings, and a bulldog

Jack Russell in the second, making 128 from 264, the situation would have been completely catastrophic for England. As it stands, with the Ashes gone, they are in the position of Australia in 1985, sparkless, leaderless, lacking depth and talent.

In England's second innings, batting 187 behind, Terry Alderman started the rot with that catch to Boon, after Graham Gooch took ten from Lawson's first over.

Lawson had his revenge as Gooch snicked one to Alderman and was gone for 13. 2/25. Lawson had Tim Robinson lbw for 12 and it was 3/27. Alderman then had Smith edging to Ian Healy and it was 4/28, Lawson got Gower for 15, 5/38 – Botham was lbw to Alderman (how else?). At 6/59 it looked all over – but Jack Russell and John Emburey (and the weather) frustrated Australia with a 142-run partnership before Alderman bowled his fellow bowler, and Hohns and Hughes wrapped up the tail.

The corks were being loosened by Australians lower down in the batting order as Taylor and Marsh set about making the required 81 runs. Marsh went sweeping at Emburey, but soon it was all over.

Australia won, Border grinned.

Allan Border: in charge.

Allan Border, the man for the hour

'What a brave player this fellow is! So quiet and efficient about everything he does in cricket, so determined to succeed and so professional'.

This appreciation of one of Australia's grandest and pluckiest players did not emanate from a scribe tapping away in the press box. It came from Dennis Lillee, in praise of Allan Border's unbeaten 123, his seventh Test century, in the fifth Test against England at Old Trafford in 1981.

Border batted for 420 minutes that day at Manchester with a broken bone in his hand in a brave attempt to steer Australia to victory after Ian Botham had sent Fleet Street into a frenzy again.

But Allan Robert Border, born in the Sydney suburb of Cremorne on 27 July 1955, had served notice that given the players, he would one day return and finish the job, to restore the Ashes to Australia. That day came at Old Trafford in 1989 when Border's team took an unbeatable 3–0 lead over England. Border was the proudest man in all of England.

Border was elevated to the captaincy in December 1984. By then he had transferred to Queensland and scored 11 Test centuries.

In the next non-stop decade until his retirement from Tests in 1993–94, he led Australia a record 93 times in a row for 32 wins, 22 losses, a tie and 38 draws. Not to mention in 178 one day internationals for 107 wins, 67 defeats, a tie and three no results. When it was all over, family-man Border – he married Jane Hiscox in 1980 – wasted no words: 'It's no picnic being a jet-setting cricketer but it sure beats sitting at home and wondering what the rest of the world's like.'

Border, a stockily built left-hander with strong forearms and supple wrists, was a better batsman than he looked. The proof is in the records – a world record 11,174 Test runs at an average of 50.56, putting him in some pretty fancy company.

Border also had the occasional day out with his under-utilised left-arm orthodox slows (7/46 v West Indies in 1988). His slips fielding and throwing were always of the highest order.

English cricket writer John Woodcock described Border's batting style as 'less technique than modus operandi'. But it was based on the essentials – good footwork, crisp execution, fine judgment in knowing whether to go forward or back and the courage Lillee spoke of.

Border, his feet as nimble as a dancer's, was a superb player of spin, meeting the ball firmly in the middle of the bat while others sought vainly to do so. He also had a gift, a magician's flair for making the willow vanish, so to speak, just when it seemed a gleeful fast bowler was about to find an edge. With a short back-lift he could punch a ball through the covers or wide of point with the best of them or pull a ball viciously to midwicket, over the top if need be. He wasn't graceful but the runs were sweet.

If he often looked troubled as he walked out to bat, a solemn figure in need of a good tailor and sometimes a shave, the scoreboard revealed why. The negligence of others required a period of Bill Lawry stoicism, which makes his Test average of 50-plus all the more remarkable. Once stability had been restored, the artistry of Border, albeit pugnacious, was allowed to flow.

As with so many champion cricketers, Border's career began in the family backyard, with his younger brothers Johnno and Brett.

The future Australian skipper started out as an all-rounder at North Sydney Boys' High School, bowling his slow lefties and batting with zest in the middle order. In 1975 Border got cracking with a century first-up for Mosman. Selection in the NSW Colts' side followed, the first match as a self-confessed 'slack 12th man'.

The advent of World Series Cricket in 1977 helped Border's cause, freeing up places in the NSW Shield side. His first Shield season in 1976–77 produced 'no fairytale performances' and it was not until December 1978 that he scored his maiden first class century, against WA in Perth – a painstaking 135 that occupied a day and 29 minutes. Five days later a score of 114 against Victoria propelled the 23-year-old into the Test team against England, which was leading Australia 2–0.

Warmed by the cheering MCG crowd, a nervous Border made 29 and nought in the third Test, followed by two unbeaten knocks of 60 and 45 in Sydney.

The MCG was the scene of his first Test century, 105 against Pakistan in March 1979 and he

'AB' after his last Test innings, Kingsmead, South Africa, March 1994.

retained his Test spot when the Packer players returned. Under the leadership of Greg Chappell and playing for the first time with Lillee, Thomson and Marsh, the 'rookie' Border made his maiden Test century against England in 1979–80.– 115 in Perth.

In this period one of Border's finest knocks was at the MCG against England in 1982–83, again in a losing cause. After a run of low scores, he joined forces with number 11 Jeff Thomson in a last-wicket stand of 70 that had the nation glued to the telly. Border (62 not out) and Thommo failed by four runs to overhaul England.

Border took over the captaincy during a heated home series against the West Indies in 1984–85. Australia, under Kim Hughes, lost the first two Tests, after which Hughes, in tears, abdicated. Border liked Hughes and thought he was unfairly criticised.

Handicapped by the retirement of Greg Chappell, Lillee and Marsh, Border salvaged a win in the last Test against the Windies. Leadership, he barely had time to observe, was exhilarating and exhausting. Within a few weeks he was leading the Australians in England. The Ashes stayed there but Border showed that for him, at least, captaincy and run-making were compatible. He scored two Test centuries – 196 at Lord's and 146 not out at Old Trafford.

The first two years of his tenure were difficult. Though good company off the field, he was not a natural communicator on it, and was criticised for being too defensive. Things soon changed around and his leadership became more assertive, freer in concept in the 1987 World Cup in India and Pakistan. With Bob Simpson as coach, Australia defeated England in the final but there was trouble ahead in Pakistan in 1988. Border, not the first to do so, blamed partisan umpiring and poorly prepared pitches for Australia's 1–0 defeat. Simpson and manager Col Egar bought into the argument and a magazine writer dubbed a churlish Border 'Captain Grumpy'. The name stuck but Border was made of steely stuff.

Over the next five years he lost his grumpy image and restored Australia's cricket prestige with decisive wins over England in 1990–91 and 1993, two split decisions (1–all) in enthralling engagements with South Africa, two narrow losses to the West Indies, a 2–0 defeat of New Zealand and a 4–0 drubbing of India. His last match as skipper was against South Africa in Durban in March 1994.

When he quit the Test scene, a refreshed Border, free of the urgency and demands of cricket at the top level, had one of his most productive seasons with the bat when Queensland won its first Sheffield Shield in 1994–95. Border made a sparkling 911 runs for the Bananalanders at an average of 65.

When he finally called it a day the next season, aged 40, Border had made 27,131 runs in first class matches at 51.38 with 70 hundreds and a highest score of 205. In Tests, he hit 27 centuries, two fewer than Bradman. Eight of his hundreds were against England, his highest being 200 not out at Leeds in 1993. He averaged a healthy 56.03 against the old foe, again second only to Bradman.

Border captured 39 Test wickets at 39.10 and nabbed 56 catches.

Captain Courageous, as Border will be remembered by most, left Australian cricket in good shape. He was a stickler for the game's finer points and bore no grudges. Australia required at the helm a complete cricketer, an indestructible rock on which the enemy would founder.

Border was the man for the hour.

Celebrations in Australia

Melbourne, Sep. 27. A month of celebrations followed Australia's Ashes win. They included an overwhelming ticker-tape parade in Sydney and an equally enthusiastic parade around the MCG in open cars before the monumental 1989 Grand Final between Geelong and Hawthorn.

The previous Wednesday evening the Prime Minister, Bob Hawke, hosted a dinner at the Southern Cross Hotel to celebrate what was a turning point in Australian cricket history – and the way Australians feel about themselves.

There is nothing like victory over the Old Enemy on their home turf to make an Australian feel that all is well with the world – and the PM was no exception. As a sometime cricketer himself, Hawke knows something of what it takes to be the very best in the world, and as a successful politician something about building a winning team.

He was, like most Australians, prouder on this night, of Allan Border and his men, than he had been of the America's Cup win – which is high praise indeed.

Terry Alderman – wonderful tour

FIRST TEST 1989 ENGLAND v AUSTRALIA
Headingley, Leeds. June 8, 9, 10, 12, 13, 1989.
Toss: England. Australia won by 210 runs.

AUSTRALIA

GR Marsh lbw DeFreitas	.16 (2)	c Russell b Foster	.6
MA Taylor lbw Foster	136 (1)	c Broad b Pringle	.60
DC Boon c Russell b Foster	.9	lbw DeFreitas	.43
AR Border (c) c Foster b DeFreitas	.66	not out	.60
DM Jones c Russell b Newport	.79	not out	.40
SR Waugh not out	177		
IA Healy (+) c & b Newport	.16		
MG Hughes c Russell b Foster	.71		
GF Lawson not out	.10		
GD Campbell			
TM Alderman			
EXTRAS (LB 13, W 1, NB 7)	.21	(B 2, LB 5, W 9, NB 5)	.21
TOTAL	.7 dec 601		.3 dec 230

FOW 1st Inns: 44 57 174 273 411 441 588
FOW 2nd Inns: 14 97 129

Bowling: *First Innings*: DeFreitas 45.3-8-140-2, Foster 46-14-109-3, Newport 39-5-153-2, Pringle 33-5-123-0, Gooch 9-1-31-0, Barnett 6-0-32-0. *Second Innings*: Foster 19-4-65-1, DeFreitas 18-2-76-1, Pringle 12.5-1-60-1, Newport 5-2-22-0.

ENGLAND

GA Gooch lbw Alderman	.13	lbw Hughes	.68
BC Broad b Hughes	.37	lbw Alderman	.7
KJ Barnett lbw Alderman	.80	c Taylor b Alderman	.34
AJ Lamb c Boon b Alderman	125	c Boon b Alderman	.4
DI Gower (c) c Healy b Lawson	.26	c Healy b Lawson	.34
RA Smith lbw Alderman	.66	c Border b Lawson	.0
DR Pringle lbw Campbell	.6	c Border b Alderman	.0
PJ Newport c Boon b Lawson	.36	c Marsh b Alderman	.8
RC Russell (+) c Marsh b Lawson	.15	c Healy b Hughes	.2
PAJ DeFreitas lbw Alderman	.1 (11)	b Hughes	.21
NA Foster not out	.2 (10)	not out	.1
EXTRAS (B 5, LB 7, W 1, NB 10)	.23	(B 4, LB 3, NB 5)	.12
TOTAL	430		191

FOW 1st Inns: 35 81 195 243 323 338 392 421 424 430
FOW 2nd Inns: 17 67 77 134 134 153 153 166 170 191

Bowling: *First Innings*: Alderman 37-7-107-5, Lawson 34.5-6-105-3, Campbell 14-0-82-1, Hughes 28-7-92-1, Waugh 6-2-27-0, Border 2-1-5-0. *Second Innings*: Alderman 20-7-44-5, Lawson 11-2-58-2, Campbell 10-0-42-0, Hughes 9.2-2-36-3, Border 5-3-4-0.

Umpires: JW Holder & DR Shepherd

Australian Averages

1989 ENGLAND v AUSTRALIA

AUSTRALIA	M	Inn	NO	Runs	H.S	Avrge	Ct	St	Overs	Mds	Runs	Wkt	Avrge
Alderman, TM	6	4	3	20	8	20.00	2	-	269.2	68	712	41	17.37
Boon, DC	6	11	3	442	94	55.25	9	-	-	-	-	-	-
Border, AR	6	9	3	442	80	73.67	5	-	24.0	9	44	-	-
Campbell, GD	1	-	-	-	-	-	-	-	24.0	-	124	1	124.00
Healy, IA	6	7	1	103	44	17.17	14	-	-	-	-	-	-
Hohns, TV	5	5	1	127	40	31.75	3	-	134.0	53	300	11	27.27
Hughes, MG	6	5	-	127	71	25.40	-	-	189.2	41	615	19	32.37
Jones, DM	6	9	1	566	157	70.75	4	-	-	-	-	-	-
Lawson, GF	6	5	1	115	74	28.75	-	-	277.1	68	791	29	27.28
Marsh, GR	6	11	-	347	138	31.55	5	-	-	-	-	-	-
Taylor, MA	6	11	1	839	219	83.90	5	-	-	-	-	-	-
Waugh, SR	6	8	4	506	177*	126.50	4	-	57.0	15	208	2	104.00

English Averages

1989 ENGLAND v AUSTRALIA

ENGLAND	M	Inn	NO	Runs	H.S	Avrge	Ct	St	Overs	Mds	Runs	Wkt	Avrge
Atherton, MA	2	4	-	73	47	18.25	1	-	8.0	-	34	-	-
Barnett, KJ	3	5	-	141	80	28.20	-	-	6.0	-	32	-	-
Botham, IT	3	4	-	62	46	15.50	3	-	80.0	15	241	3	80.33
Broad, BC	2	4	-	82	37	20.50	2	-	-	-	-	-	-
Capel, DJ	1	2	-	21	17	10.50	-	-	24.0	2	101	2	50.50
Cook, NGB	3	5	3	45	31	22.50	-	-	103.5	23	282	5	56.40
Curtis, TS	3	5	-	71	41	14.20	1	-	3.0	-	7	-	-
DeFreitas, PAJ	1	2	-	22	21	11.00	-	-	63.3	10	216	3	72.00
Dilley, GR	2	3	1	42	24	21.00	-	-	85.0	12	318	5	63.60
Emburey, JE	3	5	1	131	64	32.75	-	-	152.0	37	342	8	42.75
Foster, NA	3	6	2	68	39	17.00	1	-	167.0	42	421	12	35.08
Fraser, ARC	3	5	-	47	29	9.40	-	-	144.2	30	323	9	35.89
Gatting, MW	1	2	-	22	22	11.00	-	-	-	-	-	-	-
Gooch, GA	5	9	-	183	68	20.33	4	-	31.0	9	72	1	72.00
Gower, DI	6	11	-	383	106	34.82	4	-	-	-	-	-	-
Hemmings, EE	1	2	-	73	38	36.50	-	-	33.0	9	81	-	-
Igglesden, AP	1	1	1	2	2*	-	1	-	37.0	3	146	3	48.67
Jarvis, PW	2	3	-	33	22	11.00	-	-	69.2	8	290	2	145.00
Lamb, AJ	1	2	-	129	125	64.50	-	-	-	-	-	-	-
Malcolm, DE	1	2	-	14	9	7.00	-	-	44.0	2	166	1	166.00
Moxon, MD	1	2	-	18	18	9.00	-	-	-	-	-	-	-
Newport, PJ	1	2	-	44	36	22.00	1	-	44.0	7	175	2	87.50
Pringle, DR	2	3	-	33	27	11.00	-	-	86.2	12	306	5	61.20
Robinson, RT	1	2	-	12	12	6.00	1	-	-	-	-	-	-
Russell, RC	6	11	3	314	128*	39.25	14	4	-	-	-	-	-
Small, GC	1	1	-	59	59	59.00	-	-	60.0	12	198	4	49.50
Smith, RA	5	10	1	553	143	61.44	1	-	-	-	-	-	-
Stephenson, JP	1	2	-	36	25	18.00	-	-	-	-	-	-	-
Tavare, CJ	1	1	-	2	2	2.00	-	-	-	-	-	-	-

SECOND TEST 1989 ENGLAND v AUSTRALIA
Lord's Cricket Ground, London. June 22, 23, 24, 26, 27, 1989.
Toss: England. Australia won by 6 wkts.

ENGLAND

GA Gooch c Healy b Waugh	.60	lbw Alderman	.0
BC Broad lbw Alderman	.18	b Lawson	.20
KJ Barnett c Boon b Hughes	.14	c Jones b Alderman	.3
MW Gatting c Boon b Hughes	.0	lbw Alderman	.22
DI Gower (c) b Lawson	.57	c Border b Hughes	106
RA Smith c Hohns b Lawson	.32	b Alderman	.96
JE Emburey b Alderman	.0 (8)	not out	.36
RC Russell (+) not out	.64 (7)	c Boon b Lawson	.29
NA Foster c Jones b Hughes	.16	lbw Alderman	.4
PW Jarvis c Marsh b Hughes	.6	lbw Alderman	.5
GR Dilley c Border b Alderman	.7	c Boon b Hughes	.24
EXTRAS (LB 9, NB 3)	.12	(B 6, LB 6, NB 2)	.14
TOTAL	286		359

FOW 1st Inns: 31 52 58 131 180 185 191 237 253 286
FOW 2nd Inns: 0 18 28 84 223 274 300 304 314 359

Bowling: *First Innings*: Alderman 20.5-4-60-3, Lawson 27-8-88-2, Hughes 23-6-71-4, Waugh 9-3-49-1, Hohns 7-3-9-0. *Second Innings*: Alderman 38-6-128-6, Lawson 39-10-99-2, Hughes 24-8-44-2, Border 9-3-23-0, Hohns 13-6-33-0, Waugh 7-2-20-0.

AUSTRALIA

GR Marsh c Russell b Dilley	.3 (2)	b Dilley	.1
MA Taylor lbw Foster	.62 (1)	c Gooch b Foster	.27
DC Boon c Russell b Dilley	.94	not out	.58
AR Border (c) c Smith b Emburey	.35	c (S)RJ Sims b Foster	.1
DM Jones lbw Foster	.27	c Russell b Foster	.0
SR Waugh not out	152	not out	.21
IA Healy (+) c Russell b Jarvis	.3		
MG Hughes c Gooch b Foster	.30		
TV Hohns b Emburey	.21		
GF Lawson c Broad b Emburey	.74		
TM Alderman lbw Emburey	.8		
EXTRAS (LB 11, NB 8)	.19	(B 3, LB 4, NB 4)	.11
TOTAL	528		4 for 119

FOW 1st Inns: 6 151 192 221 235 265 331 381 511 528
FOW 2nd Inns: 9 51 61 67

Bowling: *First Innings*: Dilley 34-3-141-2, Foster 45-7-129-3, Jarvis 31-3-150-1, Emburey 42-12-88-4, Gooch 6-2-9-0. *Second Innings*: Dilley 10-2-27-1, Foster 18-3-39-3, Emburey 3-0-8-0, Jarvis 9.2-0-38-0.

Umpires: HD Bird & NT Plews

THIRD TEST 1989 ENGLAND v AUSTRALIA
Edgbaston, Birmingham. July 6, 7, 8, 10, 11, 1989.
Toss: Australia. Match Drawn.

AUSTRALIA

GR Marsh lbw Botham	42 (2)	b Jarvis	42
MA Taylor st Russell b Emburey	43 (1)	c Botham b Gooch	51
DC Boon run out	38	not out	22
AR Border (c) b Emburey	8		
DM Jones c(S)l Foley b Fraser	157		
SR Waugh b Fraser	43		
IA Healy (+) b Fraser	2 (4)	not out	33
MG Hughes c Botham b Dilley	2		
TV Hohns c Gooch b Dilley	40		
GF Lawson b Fraser	12		
TM Alderman not out	0		
EXTRAS (LB 20, NB 17)	37	(B 4, LB 4, NB 2)	10
TOTAL	424		2 for 158

FOW 1st Inns: 88 94 105 201 272 289 299 391 421 424
FOW 2nd Inns: 81 109

Bowling: *First Innings*: Dilley 31-3-123-2, Jarvis 23-4-82-0, Fraser 33-8-63-4, Botham 26-5-75-1, Emburey 29-5-61-2. *Second Innings*: Dilley 10-4-27-0, Fraser 12-0-29-0, Emburey 20-8-37-0, Jarvis 6-1-20-1, Gooch 14-5-30-1, Curtis 3-0-7-0.

ENGLAND

GA Gooch lbw Lawson	8
TS Curtis lbw Hughes	41
DI Gower (c) lbw Alderman	8
CJ Tavare c Taylor b Alderman	2
KJ Barnett c Healy b Waugh	10
IT Botham b Hughes	46
RC Russell c Taylor b Hohns	42
JE Emburey c Boon b Lawson	26
ARC Fraser run out	12
GR Dilley not out	11
PW Jarvis lbw Alderman	22
EXTRAS (B 1, LB 2, NB 11)	14
TOTAL	242

FOW 1st Inns: 17 42 47 75 75 171 171 185 215 242

Bowling: *First Innings*: Alderman 26.3-6-61-3, Lawson 21-4-54-2, Waugh 11-3-38-1, Hughes 22-4-68-2, Hohns 16-8-18-1.

Umpires: HD Bird & JW Holder

FIFTH TEST 1989 ENGLAND v AUSTRALIA
Trent Bridge, Nottingham. August 10, 11, 12, 14, 1989.
Toss: Australia. Australia won by an innings & 180 runs.

AUSTRALIA

GR Marsh c Botham b Cook	138
MA Taylor st Russell b Cook	219
DC Boon st Russell b Cook	73
AR Border (c) not out	65
DM Jones c Gower b Fraser	22
SR Waugh c Gower b Malcolm	0
IA Healy (+) b Fraser	5
TV Hohns not out	19
GF Lawson	
MG Hughes	
TM Alderman	
EXTRAS (B 6, LB 23, W 3, NB 29)	61
TOTAL	6 dec 602

FOW 1st Inns: 329 430 502 543 553 560

Bowling: *First Innings*: Fraser 52.3-18-108-2, Malcolm 44-2-166-1, Botham 30-4-103-0, Hemmings 33-9-81-0, Cook 40-10-91-3, Atherton 7-0-24-0.

ENGLAND

TS Curtis lbw Alderman	2 (2)	lbw Alderman	6
MD Moxon c Waugh b Alderman	0 (5)	lbw Alderman	18
MA Atherton lbw Alderman	0	c & b Hohns	47
RA Smith c Healy b Alderman	101	b Hughes	26
DI Gower (c) c Healy b Lawson	11 (1)	b Lawson	5
RC Russell (+) c Healy b Lawson	20	b Lawson	1
EE Hemmings b Alderman	38	lbw Hughes	35
ARC Fraser b Hohns	29	b Hohns	1
IT Botham c Waugh b Hohns	12		
NGB Cook not out	2 (9)	not out	7
DE Malcolm c Healy b Hughes	9 (10)	b Hughes	5
EXTRAS (LB 18, NB 13)	31	(B 3, LB 6, W 1, NB 6)	16
TOTAL	255		9 for 167

FOW 1st Inns: 1 1 14 37 119 172 214 243 244 255
FOW 2nd Inns: 5 13 67 106 114 120 134 160 167

Bowling: *First Innings*: Alderman 19-2-69-5, Lawson 21-5-57-2, Hohns 18-8-48-2, Hughes 7.5-0-40-1, Waugh 11-4-23-0. *Second Innings*: Alderman 16-6-32-2, Lawson 15-3-51-2, Hughes 12.3-1-46-3, Hohns 12-3-29-2.

Umpires: NT Plews & DR Shepherd

FOURTH TEST 1989 ENGLAND v AUSTRALIA
Old Trafford, Manchester. July 27, 28, 29, 31, August 1, 1989.
Toss: England. Australia won by 9 wkts.

ENGLAND

GA Gooch b Lawson	11	c Alderman b Lawson	13
TS Curtis b Lawson	22	c Boon b Alderman	0
RT Robinson lbw Lawson	0	lbw Lawson	12
RA Smith c Hohns b Hughes	143	c Healy b Alderman	1
DI Gower (c) lbw Hohns	35	c Marsh b Lawson	15
IT Botham b Hohns	0	lbw Alderman	4
RC Russell (+) lbw Lawson	1	not out	128
JE Emburey lbw Hohns	5	b Alderman	64
NA Foster c Border b Lawson	39	b Alderman	6
ARC Fraser lbw Lawson	2	c Marsh b Hohns	3
NGB Cook not out	0	c Healy b Hughes	5
EXTRAS (LB 2)	2	(LB 6, W 2, NB 5)	13
TOTAL	260		264

FOW 1st Inns: 23 23 56 132 140 147 158 232 252 260
FOW 2nd Inns: 10 25 27 28 38 59 201 223 255 264

Bowling: *First Innings*: Alderman 25-13-49-0, Lawson 33-11-72-6, Hughes 17-6-55-1, Hohns 22-7-59-3, Waugh 6-1-23-0. *Second Innings*: Lawson 31-8-81-3, Alderman 27-7-66-5, Hohns 26-15-37-1, Hughes 14.4-2-45-1, Border 8-2-12-0, Waugh 4-0-17-0.

AUSTRALIA

MA Taylor st Russell b Emburey	85 (2)	not out	37
GR Marsh b Russell b Botham	47 (1)	c Robinson b Emburey	31
DC Boon b Fraser	12	not out	10
AR Border (c) c Russell b Foster	80		
DM Jones b Botham	69		
SR Waugh c Curtis b Fraser	92		
IA Healy (+) lbw Foster	0		
TV Hohns c Gower b Cook	17		
MG Hughes b Cook	3		
GF Lawson b Fraser	17		
TM Alderman not out	6		
EXTRAS (B 5, LB 7, W 1, NB 6)	19	(NB 3)	3
TOTAL	447		1 for 81

FOW 1st Inns: 135 143 154 274 362 362 413 423 423 447
FOW 2nd Inns: 62

Bowling: *First Innings*: Foster 34-12-74-2, Fraser 36.5-4-95-3, Emburey 45-9-118-1, Cook 28-6-85-2, Botham 24-6-63-2. *Second Innings*: Foster 5-2-5-0, Fraser 10-0-28-0, Emburey 13-3-30-1, Cook 4.5-0-18-0.

Umpires: JH Hampshire & BJ Meyer

SIXTH TEST 1989 ENGLAND v AUSTRALIA
Kennington Oval, London. August 24, 25, 26, 28, 29, 1989.
Toss: Australia. Match Drawn.

AUSTRALIA

GR Marsh c Igglesden b Small	17 (2)	lbw Igglesden	4
MA Taylor c Russell b Igglesden	71 (1)	c Russell b Small	48
DC Boon c Atherton b Small	46	run out	37
AR Border (c) c Russell b Capel	76	not out	51
DM Jones c Gower b Small	122	b Capel	50
SR Waugh b Igglesden	14	not out	7
IA Healy (+) c Russell b Pringle	44		
TV Hohns c Russell b Pringle	30		
MG Hughes lbw Pringle	21		
GF Lawson b Pringle	2		
TM Alderman not out	6		
EXTRAS (B 1, LB 9, NB 9)	19	(B 2, LB 7, NB 13)	22
TOTAL	468		4 dec 219

FOW 1st Inns: 48 130 149 345 347 386 409 447 453 468
FOW 2nd Inns: 7 100 101 189

Bowling: *First Innings*: Small 40-8-141-3, Igglesden 24-2-91-2, Pringle 24.3-6-70-4, Capel 16-2-66-1, Cook 25-5-78-0, Atherton 1-0-10-0, Gooch 2-1-2-0. *Second Innings*: Small 20-4-57-1, Igglesden 13-1-55-1, Capel 8-0-35-1, Pringle 16-0-53-0, Cook 6-2-10-0.

ENGLAND

GA Gooch lbw Alderman	0	c & b Alderman	10
JP Stephenson c Waugh b Alderman	25	lbw Alderman	11
MA Atherton c Healy b Hughes	12	b Lawson	14
RA Smith b Lawson	11	not out	77
DI Gower (c) c Healy b Alderman	79	c Waugh b Lawson	7
DJ Capel lbw Alderman	4	c Taylor b Hohns	17
RC Russell (+) c Healy b Alderman	12	not out	0
DR Pringle c Taylor b Hohns	27		
GC Small c Jones b Lawson	59		
NGB Cook c Jones b Lawson	31		
AP Igglesden not out	2		
EXTRAS (B 2, LB 7, W 1, NB 13)	23	(LB 1, W 1, NB 5)	7
TOTAL	285		5 for 143

FOW 1st Inns: 1 28 47 80 84 98 169 201 274 285
FOW 2nd Inns: 20 27 51 67 138

Bowling: *First Innings*: Alderman 27-7-66-5, Lawson 29.1-9-85-3, Hughes 23-3-84-1, Hohns 10-1-30-1, Waugh 3-0-11-0. *Second Innings*: Alderman 13-3-30-2, Lawson 15.1-2-41-2, Hughes 8-2-34-0, Hohns 10-2-37-1.

Umpires: HD Bird & KE Palmer

1989–90

NEW ZEALAND/ PAKISTAN/SRI LANKA IN AUSTRALIA

NZ's Mark Greatbatch in slow fight to draw

The elation of Danny Morrison, who dismissed Dean Jones on 99.

QUICK SINGLES

Three nations tour. The 1989–90 summer was the first time in Australian Test cricket history that three nations (New Zealand, Sri Lanka and Pakistan) visited Australia to play Test cricket.

Another Waugh. During the 1989–90 Sheffield Shield season NSW's Mark Waugh top-scored with 967 runs at 80.58. Waugh is the slightly younger twin (by four minutes) of Australian Test star Steve Waugh.

Toe-in triple ton. Batting for Western Australia against South Australia in a Sheffield Shield game at Perth, WA's Geoff Marsh scored 355 not out in ten-and-a-half hours. Remarkably, Marsh was still getting over a broken toe.

TV stumps Board. A WSC match between Australia and Sri Lanka in Perth was delayed for eight minutes while Channel Nine replaced their TV microphone in one of the stumps. A WACA complaint to the ACB met with no comment.

Big brother on hill. Larrikinism at the Sydney Cricket Ground is to be monitored by a new surveillance system, installed before the third Test between Australia and Pakistan. The $1 million system comprises 95 strategically positioned cameras.

Pakis pack up. Against Victoria in January, Pakistani spinner Mustaq Ahmed was banned after three warnings for following through onto the pitch. Pakistan left the field for 30 minutes before it was agreed one of the warnings had been incorrectly given. Victoria won by 59 runs.

Indian failure. Australia competed in the one-day Nehru Cup in India in October, but failed to qualify for the finals after losing to Pakistan (the eventual winners), India and England. Australia beat the West Indies and Sri Lanka in the series.

Bradman Museum. At Bowral, NSW, where Sir Donald Bradman was raised, the Bradman Museum was opened by Sir Donald in October. The museum is near his old 20 Glebe St home and adjoins the ground where the legendary batsman played his early matches.

Perth, Nov. 29. November is the month when New Zealand stayers cross the Tasman to thwart the brightest hopes of Australia.

It's a good thing this one wasn't running at Flemington a few weeks ago. Because marathon man Mark Greatbatch can stay all day. And all of the next day, too.

He came to the pitch at the W.A.C.A. early on the fourth day of the Australia/New Zealand Test. Victory looked almost certain for the Australians, who made a mammoth 9/521 dec. in their only innings and forced New Zealand to follow on after their first innings 231.

But Greatbatch dug in his heels and just kept plodding on. The 462 minutes it took him to reach his century is the slowest first class century ever recorded in Australia.

At stumps yesterday he was undefeated at 146, after batting for 655 minutes and facing 485 balls.

Thanks to Greatbatch's heroic stand, New Zealand has salvaged a respectable draw out of what should have been a disaster.

His innings overshadows two memorable performances by the Australian batsmen, David Boon (200) and Dean Jones (99).

Boon passed the 3000th run mark mark in this Test, his 43rd. It is his first double century in Test cricket.

Boon hit 28 fours and faced 326 balls in 451 minutes, which is eleven minutes less to make his 200 than Greatbatch took for his 100.

Australians have always suspected their Kiwi cousins were slow. Now they know.

New Headquarters

Melbourne, Oct. 11. The Australian Cricket Board has purchased a property in the Melbourne suburb of Jolimont.

The two-storey building, located at 90 Jolimont Street, is just a short walk across the parkland from the Melbourne Cricket Ground.

Jolimont properties rarely come onto the real estate market, and never cheaply. It is believed that the Board paid over $1.5 million for the property, which will be modernised to become the new headquarters for Australian cricket.

The days of cricket being run predominantly by a handful of delegates are long gone. Directors and committee representatives are supported by an ever-growing administration, including the chief executive, general manager, media manager and office staff.

ONLY TEST 1989–90 AUSTRALIA v NEW ZEALAND
W.A.C.A. Ground, Perth. November 24, 25, 26, 27, 28, 1989.
Toss: New Zealand. Match Drawn.

AUSTRALIA
```
MA Taylor c Wright b Morrison .................9
DC Boon c Wright b Snedden .................200
TM Moody c Smith b Snedden .................61
AR Border (c) b Morrison ....................50
DM Jones lbw Morrison ......................99
SR Waugh c Greatbatch b Snedden ...........17
IA Healy (+) c JJ Crowe b Patel ..............28
MG Hughes c Wright b Snedden ..............16
GF Lawson b Morrison .......................1
CG Rackemann not out ......................15
TM Alderman
     EXTRAS (B 1, LB 9, W 2, NB 13) ..........25
TOTAL ..............................9 dec 521
```
FOW 1st Inns: 28 177 316 361 395 449 489 490 521

Bowling: *First Innings*: Morrison 39.1-8-145-4, Cairns 12-2-60-0, Snedden 42-10-108-4, Watson 37-7-118-0, Patel 28-5-80-1.

NEW ZEALAND
```
JG Wright (c) b Rackemann ..........34    c Border b Lawson ...........3
RH Vance b Alderman ................4     c Alderman b Rackemann .....8
MJ Greatbatch c Healy b Hughes .....76    not out ...................146
MD Crowe lbw Alderman ..............62    c Taylor b Moody ..........30
DN Patel c Boon b Hughes ...........0     lbw Alderman ...............7
JJ Crowe c Healy b Rackemann .......7     lbw Hughes ................49
IDS Smith (+) c Lawson b Hughes ....11    c Border b Hughes ..........0
CL Cairns c Healy b Hughes .........1     lbw Hughes ................28
MC Snedden not out ................13     not out ...................33
DK Morrison c Border b Lawson ......3
W Watson lbw Alderman ..............4
     EXTRAS (B 1, LB 6, W 4, NB 5) ..16     (LB 14, NB 4) .............18
TOTAL ............................231                      .....7 for 322
```
FOW 1st Inns: 28 84 173 178 191 204 206 212 226 231
FOW 2nd Inns: 11 11 79 107 189 189 234

Bowling: *First Innings*: Alderman 25.4-7-73-3, Lawson 22-5-54-1, Rackemann 20-4-39-2, Hughes 20-7-51-4, Moody 4-1-6-0, Border 1-0-1-0. *Second Innings*: Alderman 32-14-59-1, Lawson 38-12-88-1, Rackemann 31-21-23-1, Hughes 36-8-92-3, Moody 17-6-23-1, Border 5-2-17-0, Jones 3-2-6-0.

Umpires: RJ Evans & PJ McConnell

De Silva saves Sri Lanka at 'Gabba

Brisbane, Dec. 13. The relatively inexperienced Sri Lankan side has survived the first Test against Australia with a creditable draw.

The Australians came into this Test after a run of nine successive first innings totals over 400, but all that came to an end when Australia managed only 367 this time in.

Australia plunged into problems with a bad batting start from openers David Boon (0) and Mark Taylor (9), but a fine century from Tom Moody (106) aided by Allan Border (56) kept the side afloat.

Sri Lanka's Graeme Labrooy took 5/133 in Australia's innnings.

Australia was stunned by Sri Lanka's first innings (418) in which Aravinda de Silva scored 167 runs.

De Silva may be small, and he has a most unusual chopping style at the crease, but there's no doubt about his ability. He hooks and cuts with plenty of wrist, and his footwork is deceptively fast. He also shows that great batting virtue: patience.

The little Sri Lankan batted for 491 minutes to score his first hundred against Australia, hitting one six and 17 fours. He eventually succumbed, caught by Geoff Lawson when attempting to hook Carl Rackemann.

In Australia's second innings of 375, Mark Taylor scored 164, his third century in ten Tests, and when he hit his 76th run he became the first batsman to score 1000 runs in his Test debut year.

Another milestone in this Test was reached by Australia's Allan Border, who passed Sunil Gavaskar's record of 106 Test appearances in a row.

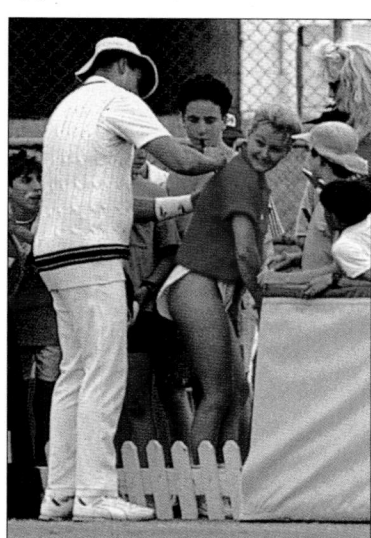

Merv Hughes signs up a few new fans at the 'Gabba.

Bellerive fine venue for first Tasmanian Test

Perfect cricket. Perfect setting. Tasmania's first Test match was a victory for Australia.

Hobart, Dec. 21. The picturesque Bellerive Oval, alongside the Derwent River in the Hobart suburb of Clarence, has now joined the MCG, the 'Gabba, the WACA, the Adelaide Oval, and the SCG. Bellerive Oval became Australia's latest Test cricket venue this week in the second Test between Australia and Sri Lanka.

Fittingly, the first ball was faced by Tasmanian David Boon, who scored 41 in Australia's modest first innings total of 224.

Boon was dismissed by Sri Lankan medium pacer Rumesh Ratnayake, whose 6/66 proved to be the devil's number for Australia.

Tasmania's Greg Campbell (2/41) opened the bowling. Sri Lanka batted well at first and reached 3/146 before Australia's Peter Sleep snared 3/26 in a devastating ten over leg-break spell which included four maidens. Roshan Mahanama (85) and Aravinda de Silva (75) added 128.

Australian fast bowler Merv Hughes (3/68) cleaned up the Sri Lankan tail. When Allan Border caught Ratnayake (0) he passed Greg Chappell's world record of 122 catches in the field.

Sri Lanka was only eight runs behind when Australia began its second innings, but this time Ratnayake didn't find his magic.

Mark Taylor looked in superb touch as he smashed the Sri Lankan attack all over Bellerive. His fine innings ended on 108, and was bettered by Dean Jones (118 not out) and Steve Waugh (134 not our). Jones and Waugh added 260 runs in 234 minutes.

Border (85) declared at 5/513, leaving the Sri Lankans needing 522 in five sessions to win. Aravinda looked the danger again, but after he went for 72 early on the last day, the task proved too great. Hughes took 5/88 in Sri Lanka's second innings (348), giving Australia victory by 173 runs.

Hobart banquet

Hobart, Dec. 17. Tasmania's historic first week of Test cricket has begun with a banquet in Hobart for 500 people.

But the real feast is likely to be enjoyed by many thousands more as cricket fans flock to Bellerive Oval for the second Test between Australia and Sri Lanka.

Cricket was first played at Bellerive Oval early this century on a concrete pitch.

It has been the home ground of the Clarence Cricket Club since the 1950s, when a turf wicket was laid.

The Tasmanian Cricket Association moved its headquarters to Bellerive in 1987 and the ground was then resurfaced. It is now as fine a playing surface as any in Australia.

Catch 123 for Alan Border (R. Ratnayake) is a new world record.

Sri Lanka lost in the bush

Melbourne, Feb. 20. The Sri Lankan touring side has now played 27 matches over the past three months.

The only match won by Sri Lanka was against Pakistan in a one day game at Perth, but there was a narrow loss to Australia by 30 runs on Boxing Day in Melbourne.

Sri Lanka also drew with South Australia, NSW and Tasmania, and the draw with Australia in the first Test at Brisbane was an outstanding performance.

Inexperience may have showed on many occasions, but Sri Lanka proved a competitive, courageous, and far from outclassed rival. Some who saw the tourists in the bush suspect that the day might not be far off when Sri Lanka could humble the giants of cricket.

Conditions have hardly been easy. For most of the past two months the side has been wandering around Australia, competing in the back blocks on cow paddocks, and ranging up and down the highways and airports of Australia.

The Sri Lankans didn't know whether to sing 'On the road again' or 'I've been everywhere, man'.

But they're starting to call Australia home after clocking up over 30,000 kilometres on 22 separate journeys since the second Test.Next time in they'll know their way around a little better.

Sterling stroke: Aravinda de Silva.

FIRST TEST 1989–90 AUSTRALIA v SRI LANKA
Brisbane Cricket Ground, Brisbane. December 8, 9, 10, 11, 12, 1989.
Toss: Sri Lanka. Match Drawn.

AUSTRALIA

DC Boon c Samarasekera b Labrooy	0	(2)
MA Taylor c Wickremasinghe b Ramanayake	9	(1)
TM Moody c Wickremasinghe b Labrooy	106	
AR Border (c) c A Ranatunga b Labrooy	56	
DM Jones lbw Labrooy	15	(4)
SR Waugh c A Ranatunga b Ramanayake	60	(5)
IA Healy (+) lbw Gurusinha	21	(6)
MG Hughes run out	25	
GF Lawson c Wickremasinghe b Labrooy	22	
CG Rackemann not out	5	(7)
TM Alderman c PA De Silva b Gurusinha	18	

2nd Innings:
- lbw Ramanayake 26
- lbw Ramanayake 164
- c A Ranatunga b EAR De Silva 30
- c Ramanayake b PA De Silva 23
- b Gurusinha 57
- not out 26
- not out 23
- b Gurusinha 0

EXTRAS (B 5, LB 8, NB 21) ... 30
(B 5, LB 4, NB 17) ... 26
TOTAL ... 367 .... 6 for 375

FOW 1st Inns: 1 27 185 197 210 247 295 339 339 367
FOW 2nd Inns: 60 124 167 316 324 324

Bowling: *First Innings*: Ratnayeke 8.5-1-17-0, Labrooy 31.1-5-133-5, Ramanayake 26-2-101-2, A Ranatunga 13-1-49-0, EAR De Silva 8-1-21-0, Gurusinha 8.3-1-37-2. *Second Innings*: Labrooy 24-4-69-0, Ramanayake 28-3-81-2, EAR De Silva 39-8-112-1, PA De Silva 15-2-45-1, Gurusinha 10-3-31-2, A Ranatunga 6-0-25-0, Mahanama 1-0-3-0.

SRI LANKA

RS Mahanama lbw Alderman	5
D Ranatunga c Waugh b Lawson	40
AP Gurusinha c Healy b Rackemann	43
EAR De Silva b Alderman	22
PA De Silva c Lawson b Rackemann	167
A Ranatunga (c) lbw Hughes	25
MAR Samarasekera c Moody b Rackemann	18
JR Ratnayeke lbw Hughes	56
AGD Wickremasinghe (+) c Boon b Hughes	2
GF Labrooy lbw Alderman	1
CPH Ramanayake not out	10
EXTRAS (LB 23, W 2, NB 4)	29
TOTAL	418

FOW 1st Inns: 10 80 114 148 201 238 382 386 391 418

Bowling: *First Innings*: Alderman 40-13-81-3, Lawson 33-10-51-1, Rackemann 30.3-6-88-3, Hughes 39-8-123-3, Moody 16-8-15-0, Border 7-0-36-0, Jones 1-0-1-0.

Umpires: AR Crafter & CD Timmins

Australian Averages

1989–90 AUSTRALIA v SRI LANKA

AUSTRALIA	M	Inn	NO	Runs	H.S	Avrge	Ct	St	Overs	Mds	Runs	Wkt	Avrge
Alderman, TM	2	2	-	18	18	9.00	-	-	93.0	27	200	5	40.00
Boon, DC	2	4	-	67	41	16.75	1	-	-	-	-	-	-
Border, AR	2	3	-	165	85	55.00	2	-	12.0	4	38	-	-
Campbell, GD	1	1	-	6	6	6.00	1	-	56.0	17	143	5	28.60
Healy, IA	2	3	1	64	26*	32.00	4	-	-	-	-	-	-
Hughes, MG	2	4	1	105	30	35.00	-	-	92.2	22	279	11	25.36
Jones, DM	2	4	1	159	118*	53.00	1	-	5.0	2	6	-	-
Lawson, GF	1	1	-	22	22	22.00	1	-	33.0	10	51	1	51.00
Moody, TM	2	4	-	147	106	36.75	3	-	18.0	8	24	-	-
Rackemann, CG	1	2	1	5	5*	5.00	-	-	30.3	6	88	3	29.33
Sleep, PR	1	1	1	47	47*	-	-	-	46.0	20	99	5	19.80
Taylor, MA	2	4	-	304	164	76.00	3	-	-	-	-	-	-
Waugh, SR	2	4	1	267	134*	89.00	2	-	6.0	3	6	-	-

SECOND TEST 1989–90 AUSTRALIA v SRI LANKA
Bellerive Oval, Hobart. December 16, 17, 18, 19, 20, 1989.
Toss: Sri Lanka. Australia won by 173 runs.

AUSTRALIA

DC Boon c Mahanama b Ratnayake	41	(2)
MA Taylor c Tillakaratne b Ratnayake	23	(1)
TM Moody c Gurusinha b Ratnayake	6	
AR Border (c) c EAR De Silva b Ratnayeke	24	(5)
DM Jones c Tillakaratne b Ratnayake	3	(6)
SR Waugh c Tillakaratne b Labrooy	16	(7)
PR Sleep not out	47	
IA Healy (+) c Tillakaratne b Gurusinha	17	
MG Hughes b EAR De Silva	27	(4)
GD Campbell c Mahanama b Ratnayake	6	
TM Alderman b Ratnayake	0	

2nd Innings:
- c Ratnayake b Labrooy 0
- c Gurusinha b PA De Silva 108
- c Tillakaratne b Ratnayake 5
- b PA De Silva 85
- not out 118
- not out 134
- c Gurusinha b Ratnayake 30

EXTRAS (LB 7, W 1, NB 6) ... 14
(B 2, LB 5, W 4, NB 22) ... 33
TOTAL ... 224 .... 5 dec 513

FOW 1st Inns: 50 68 83 89 112 123 166 207 224 224
FOW 2nd Inns: 1 10 77 240 253

Bowling: *First Innings*: Ratnayeke 15-2-39-1, Labrooy 19-3-61-1, Ratnayake 19.4-2-66-6, Ramanayake 4-0-21-0, Gurusinha 6-0-20-1, EAR De Silva 9-6-10-1. *Second Innings*: Labrooy 22-3-100-1, Ratnayake 35-5-123-2, Ratnayeke 19-1-86-0, EAR De Silva 21-2-83-0, PA De Silva 18-1-65-2, Ramanayake 10-0-49-0.

SRI LANKA

RS Mahanama c Healy b Sleep	85	
D Ranatunga c Moody b Alderman	2	
AP Gurusinha c Taylor b Alderman	0	
EAR De Silva c Border b Campbell	2	(8)
PA De Silva lbw Campbell	75	(4)
A Ranatunga (c) c Moody b Sleep	21	(5)
HP Tillakaratne (+) c Taylor b Sleep	0	(6)
JR Ratnayeke c Taylor b Hughes	9	(7)
GF Labrooy b Hughes	11	
CPH Ramanayake not out	4	
RJ Ratnayake c Border b Hughes	0	

2nd Innings:
- lbw Campbell 5
- c Healy b Hughes 45
- c (S)AE Tucker b Hughes 20
- b Campbell 50
- c Campbell b Sleep 72
- c Jones b Hughes 38
- c Waugh b Sleep 6
- c Healy b Campbell 75
- b Hughes 5
- not out 2
- lbw Hughes 5

EXTRAS (LB 4, NB 3) ... 7
(B 9, LB 12, NB 4) ... 25
TOTAL ... 216 348

FOW 1st Inns: 11 15 18 146 188 192 193 201 216 216
FOW 2nd Inns: 6 53 94 187 187 208 332 337 337 348

Bowling: *First Innings*: Alderman 23-2-71-2, Campbell 23-9-41-2, Hughes 21.4-6-68-3, Sleep 10-4-26-3, Waugh 6-3-6-0. *Second Innings*: Alderman 30-12-48-0, Campbell 33-8-102-3, Sleep 36-16-73-2, Hughes 31.4-8-88-5, Moody 2-0-9-0, Jones 4-2-5-0, Border 5-4-2-0.

Umpires: LJ King & SG Randell

Sri Lankan Averages

1989–90 AUSTRALIA v SRI LANKA

SRI LANKA	M	Inn	NO	Runs	H.S	Avrge	Ct	St	Overs	Mds	Runs	Wkt	Avrge
De Silva, EAR	2	3	-	74	50	24.67	1	-	77.0	17	226	2	113.00
De Silva, PA	2	3	-	314	167	104.67	1	-	33.0	3	110	3	36.67
Gurusinha, AP	2	3	-	63	43	21.00	3	-	24.3	4	88	5	17.60
Labrooy, GF	2	3	-	17	11	5.67	-	-	96.1	15	363	7	51.86
Mahanama, RS	2	3	-	95	85	31.67	2	-	1.0	-	3	-	-
Ramanayake, CPH	2	3	3	16	10*	-	1	-	68.0	5	252	4	63.00
Ranatunga, A	2	3	-	84	38	28.00	3	-	19.0	1	74	-	-
Ranatunga, D	2	3	-	87	45	29.00	-	-	-	-	-	-	-
Ratnayake, RJ	1	2	-	5	5	2.50	-	-	54.4	7	189	8	23.63
Ratnayeke, JR	2	3	-	140	75	46.67	-	-	42.5	4	142	1	142.00
Samarasekera, MAR	1	1	-	18	18	18.00	1	-	-	-	-	-	-
Tillakaratne, HP	1	2	-	6	6	3.00	5	-	-	-	-	-	-
Wickremasinghe, AGD	1	1	-	2	2	2.00	3	-	-	-	-	-	-

Pakistan loses valiant fight

Not out is the result as Ijaz Ahmed defends against Peter Sleep.

Melbourne, Jan. 17. In a marvellous exhibition of Test cricket, Pakistan lost to Australia in the first Test by 92 runs.

There were only 22 minutes remaining in the match when Australia clinched victory.

It might have finished much earlier, but for an heroic second innings stand from the young Pakistani, Ijaz Ahmed, who held firm against the Australian pace attack for 450 minutes.

Ijaz scored 121 runs, including 11 fours, before losing his wicket to an extraordinary left-handed catch from Geoff Marsh. Ijaz had just hit a beautiful square cut to point, when Marsh dived to take the ball fully stretched.

Pakistani fast bowler Wasim Akram ended with match figures of 11/160. Wasim's dismissal of Terry Alderman (0) was his 100th wicket in Test cricket.

The match was full of tension. Six batsmen were given out leg before wicket and both Wasim and Imran Khan each took two Australian wickets with successive deliveries.

Pakistan deserve great credit for overcoming a deplorable first innings (107) to almost save the match.

Queensland not yet

Sydney, Mar. 28. New South Wales has defeated Queensland in the Sheffield Shield final at the Sydney Cricket Ground.

Queensland seems to have no luck against NSW. In 1984–85, and again in 1985–86, the Queenslanders lost to NSW in thrilling contests.

The last five days show nothing has changed. Mark Taylor scored 127 and 100 for NSW, while Greg Matthews took 5/31 in Queensland's first innings.

One of the problems was that Queensland had selected an all-seam bowling line up, and when Queensland won the toss it had to ask NSW to bat first.

In its first innings NSW scored 360 runs, and Queensland probably lost the match when it could manage only 103 in reply. A horrifying start saw five Queensland batsmen out for ducks, including openers Cantrell and Foley.

Australian cricket legend Sir Donald Bradman in front of the $11m. grandstand named in his honour at the Adelaide Oval.

Jones in Adelaide run glut

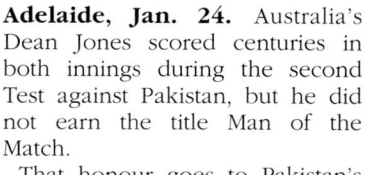

Adelaide, Jan. 24. Australia's Dean Jones scored centuries in both innings during the second Test against Pakistan, but he did not earn the title Man of the Match.

That honour goes to Pakistan's Wasim Akram, who not only captured 5/100 in Australia's first innings, but also scored 52 and 123 in two brilliant innings.

Wasim's second innings stand of 191 with Imran Khan salvaged a draw for Pakistan.

An Australian victory looked likely when Pakistan lost its first five wickets cheaply and crumpled to 4/22 in its second innings. Shoaib Mohammad (0), Ramiz Raja (2), Salim Yousuf (1), Javed Miandad (21) and Ijaz Ahmed (4) all fell to the bowling of Merv Hughes (5/111).

If the second innings belonged to Hughes, the first was seized by Carl Rackemann (4/40).

Rackemann took three wickets in four balls and was superbly aided by the firm hands of wicketkeeper Ian Healy, who held five catches.

As the match progressed, it became clear that Adelaide was yet again a fine pitch for batsmen.

Five centuries and five half-centuries were scored in the Test.

Mark Taylor made 77 in Australia's first innings, but fellow opener Geoff Marsh managed only 13. Marsh broke his thumb catching Ijaz, and courageously padded up.

He was caught by Salim Yousuf

Dean Jones: big scorer at Adelaide.

off the bowling of Wasim.

Dean Jones scored 116 and 121. He showed great style with his full-blooded drives, confidence, and athleticism highlighted by some superb running between the wickets. Jones is the tenth Australian to achieve centuries in both innings of a Test.

In another milestone at Adelaide, Allan Border became the first Australian to captain in 50 Tests.

Border had a quiet match this time, scoring 13 and 8 with the bat, and taking the ball for four tight overs in each innings (1/10 and 0/5).

His dismissal of the potentially dangerous Ijaz (28) was vital.

Seagulls revel as rain washes out three days of Test cricket at the SCG.

FIRST TEST 1989–90 AUSTRALIA v PAKISTAN
Melbourne Cricket Ground, Melbourne. January 12, 13, 14, 15, 16, 1990.
Toss: Pakistan. Australia won by 92 runs.

AUSTRALIA
GR Marsh c Salim b Wasim 30 (2)	c Wasim b Aaqib 24
MA Taylor c Aaqib b Imran 52 (1)	c Aamir b Tauseef 101
DC Boon lbw Wasim 0	run out 21
AR Border (c) c Javed b Wasim 24	not out 62
DM Jones c Salim b Imran 0	lbw Wasim 10
SR Waugh c Salim b Aaqib 20	c Salim b Wasim 3
PR Sleep lbw Wasim 23	b Wasim 0
IA Healy (+) c Shoaib b Aaqib 48	c Ijaz b Wasim 25
MG Hughes c Mansoor b Wasim 8	c Mansoor b Wasim 32
TM Alderman c Aamir b Wasim 1	not out 1
CG Rackemann not out 0	
EXTRAS (LB 9, NB 9) 18	(B 2, LB 10, W 1, NB 20) 33
TOTAL 223	8 dec 312

FOW 1st Inns: 90 90 98 98 131 148 201 223 223 223
FOW 2nd Inns: 73 116 204 216 220 220 260 305

Bowling: *First Innings*: Imran 18-6-53-2, Wasim 30-9-62-6, Aaqib 22.1-7-47-2, Waqar 12-3-27-0, Tauseef 8-1-25-0. *Second Innings*: Wasim 41.4-12-98-5, Aaqib 21-1-55-1, Imran 8-2-21-0, Waqar 22-4-68-0, Tauseef 16-3-58-1.

PAKISTAN
Aamir Malik lbw Alderman 7	c Taylor b Hughes 0
Shoaib Mohammad c Healy b Alderman 6 (3)	c Boon b Hughes 10
Mansoor Akhtar c Taylor b Rackemann 5 (2)	lbw Alderman 14
Javed Miandad c Healy b Alderman 3	lbw Waugh 65
Ijaz Ahmed c Taylor b Hughes 19	c Marsh b Hughes 121
Imran Khan (c) c Alderman b Rackemann 3	lbw Alderman 45
Salim Yousuf (+) c Taylor b Hughes 16	lbw Alderman 38
Wasim Akram c Healy b Hughes 6	c Taylor b Sleep 6
Tauseef Ahmed not out 9	not out 14
Waqar Younis lbw Sleep 18	lbw Alderman 4
Aaqib Javed c Healy b Rackemann 0	lbw Alderman 0
EXTRAS (B 1, LB 4, NB 10) 15	(B 1, LB 7, W 2, NB 9) 19
TOTAL 107	336

FOW 1st Inns: 12 20 20 44 44 65 71 71 106 107
FOW 2nd Inns: 4 23 31 134 218 291 303 328 333 336

Bowling: *First Innings*: Alderman 19-6-30-3, Rackemann 21.5-8-32-3, Hughes 17-7-34-3, Sleep 8-5-6-1. *Second Innings*: Hughes 42-14-79-3, Rackemann 38-13-67-0, Alderman 33.5-6-105-5, Sleep 21-7-64-1, Waugh 3-0-13-1.

Umpires: RJ Evans & PJ McConnell

SECOND TEST 1989–90 AUSTRALIA v PAKISTAN
Adelaide Oval, Adelaide. January 19, 20, 21, 22, 23, 1990.
Toss: Pakistan. Match Drawn.

PAKISTAN
Shoaib Mohammad lbw Hughes 43	c Healy b Hughes 0
Rameez Raja c PL Taylor b Campbell 9	c Waugh b Hughes 2
Salim Yousuf (+) lbw Rackemann 38	c MA Taylor b Hughes 1
Javed Miandad c Healy b Campbell 52 (6)	c PL Taylor b Hughes 21
Ijaz Ahmed c Marsh b Border 28 (4)	c PL Taylor b Hughes 4
Salim Malik c Healy b Hughes 11 (8)	not out 65
Imran Khan (c) c Healy b Rackemann 13 (5)	b PL Taylor 136
Wasim Akram c Border b Campbell 52 (7)	b Campbell 123
Tauseef Ahmed c Healy b Rackemann 0	c Healy b Rackemann 18
Mushtaq Ahmed c Healy b Rackemann 0	b PL Taylor 4
Waqar Younis not out 1	
EXTRAS (B 4, LB 4, W 1, NB 1) 10	(B 4, LB 5, W 1, NB 3) 13
TOTAL 257	9 dec 387

FOW 1st Inns: 27 91 95 166 187 187 241 251 251 257
FOW 2nd Inns: 0 2 7 22 90 281 316 380 387

Bowling: *First Innings*: Hughes 18-5-63-2, Campbell 21.3-2-79-3, PL Taylor 12-0-57-0, Rackemann 21-3-40-4, Border 4-0-10-1. *Second Innings*: Hughes 32-9-111-5, Campbell 29-5-83-1, Rackemann 37-11-85-1, PL Taylor 41.5-13-94-2, Border 4-0-5-0.

AUSTRALIA
GR Marsh c Salim b Wasim 13	
MA Taylor lbw Imran 77 (1)	c (S)Saeed Anwar b Mushtaq 59
DC Boon lbw Wasim 29 (2)	c Rameez b Wasim 5
AR Border (c) b Waqar 13 (3)	c Salim b Waqar 8
DM Jones c Wasim b Imran 116 (4)	not out 121
SR Waugh lbw Wasim 17 (5)	b Tauseef 4
IA Healy (+) c(S)Maqsood Rana b Waqar 12 (6)	c (S)Aamir Malik b Tauseef 27
PL Taylor run out 33 (7)	c Shoaib b Tauseef 1
MG Hughes not out 6 (8)	not out 2
GD Campbell lbw Wasim 0	
CG Rackemann b Wasim 0	
EXTRAS (LB 12, NB 13) 25	(LB 3, NB 3) 6
TOTAL 341	6 for 233

FOW 1st Inns: 82 113 156 188 216 328 328 341 341 341
FOW 2nd Inns: 9 33 106 129 213 229

Bowling: *First Innings*: Wasim 43-10-100-5, Waqar 26-4-66-2, Mushtaq 23-4-69-0, Imran 27-6-61-2, Tauseef 14-1-33-0. *Second Innings*: Wasim 11-3-29-1, Waqar 14-4-42-1, Tauseef 32-6-80-3, Mushtaq 25-5-72-1, Shoaib 1-0-7-0.

Umpires: AR Crafter & LJ King

THIRD TEST 1989–90 AUSTRALIA v PAKISTAN
Sydney Cricket Ground, Sydney. February 3 (no play), 4 (no play), 5, 6 (no play), 7, 8, 1990.
Toss: Australia. Match Drawn.

PAKISTAN
Aamir Malik c Healy b Alderman 7
Rameez Raja c & b Hughes 0
Shoaib Mohammad lbw Alderman 9
Javed Miandad c Jones b Hughes 49
Ijaz Ahmed c MA Taylor b Rackemann 8
Imran Khan (c) not out 82
Wasim Akram c MA Taylor b Alderman 10
Salim Yousuf (+) c Jones b Rackemann 6
Tauseef Ahmed b Alderman 0
Waqar Younis c Veletta b Hughes 16
Nadeem Ghauri b Alderman 0
EXTRAS (B 1, LB 7, NB 4) 12
TOTAL 199

FOW 1st Inns: 2 15 20 51 106 128 154 160 191 199

Bowling: *First Innings*: Alderman 33.5-10-65-5, Hughes 31-16-70-3, Rackemann 22-8-33-2, Taylor 8-1-23-0.

AUSTRALIA
MA Taylor not out 101
MRJ Veletta lbw Waqar 9
TM Moody c Aamir b Tauseef 26
AR Border (c) not out 27
DM Jones
SR Waugh
IA Healy (+)
PL Taylor
MG Hughes
CG Rackemann
TM Alderman
EXTRAS (B 4, LB 5, NB 4) 13
TOTAL .....2 dec 176

FOW 1st Inns: 33 106

Bowling: *First Innings*: Wasim 10-3-29-0, Imran 17-2-32-0, Tauseef 19-3-62-1, Nadeem 8-1-20-0, Waqar 9-4-21-1, Ijaz 2-0-3-0.

Umpires: AR Crafter & PJ McConnell

Australian Averages

1989–90 AUSTRALIA v PAKISTAN
AUSTRALIA	M	Inn	NO	Runs	H.S	Avrge	Ct	St	Overs	Mds	Runs	Wkt	Avrge
Alderman, TM	2	2	1	1	1*	1.00	1	-	86.4	22	200	13	15.38
Boon, DC	2	4	-	55	29	13.75	1	-	-	-	-	-	-
Border, AR	3	5	2	134	62*	44.67	1	-	8.0	-	15	1	15.00
Campbell, GD	1	1	-	0	0	0.00	-	-	50.3	7	162	4	40.50
Healy, IA	3	4	-	112	48	28.00	12		-	-	-	-	-
Hughes, MG	3	4	2	48	32	24.00	1	-	140.0	51	357	16	22.31
Jones, DM	3	4	1	247	121*	82.33	2	-	-	-	-	-	-
Marsh, GR	2	3	-	67	30	22.33	2	-	-	-	-	-	-
Moody, TM	1	1	-	26	26	26.00	-	-	-	-	-	-	-
Rackemann, CG	3	2	1	0	0*	0.00	-	-	139.5	43	257	10	25.70
Sleep, PR	1	2	-	23	23	11.50	-	-	29.0	12	70	2	35.00
Taylor, MA	3	5	1	390	101*	97.50	8	-	-	-	-	-	-
Taylor, PL	2	2	-	34	33	17.00	3	-	61.5	14	174	2	87.00
Veletta, MRJ	1	1	-	9	9	9.00	1	-	-	-	-	-	-
Waugh, SR	3	4	-	44	20	11.00	-	-	3.0	-	13	1	13.00

Pakistani Averages

1989–90 AUSTRALIA v PAKISTAN
PAKISTAN	M	Inn	NO	Runs	H.S	Avrge	Ct	St	Overs	Mds	Runs	Wkt	Avrge
Aamir Malik	2	3	-	14	7	4.67	3	-	-	-	-	-	-
Aaqib Javed	1	2	-	0	0	0.00	-	-	43.1	8	102	3	34.00
Ijaz Ahmed	3	5	-	180	121	36.00	1	-	2.0	-	3	-	-
Imran Khan	3	5	1	279	136	69.75	-	-	70.0	16	167	4	41.75
Javed Miandad	3	5	-	190	65	38.00	1	-	-	-	-	-	-
Mansoor Akhtar	1	2	-	19	14	9.50	2	-	-	-	-	-	-
Mushtaq Ahmed	1	2	-	4	4	2.00	-	-	48.0	9	141	1	141.00
Nadeem Ghauri	1	1	-	0	0	0.00	-	-	8.0	1	20	-	-
Rameez Raja	2	3	-	11	9	3.67	-	-	-	-	-	-	-
Salim Malik	1	2	1	76	65*	76.00	-	-	-	-	-	-	-
Salim Yousuf	3	5	-	99	38	19.80	6	-	-	-	-	-	-
Shoaib Mohammad	3	5	-	68	43	13.60	2	-	1.0	-	7	-	-
Tauseef Ahmed	3	5	2	41	18	13.67	-	-	89.0	14	258	5	51.60
Waqar Younis	3	4	1	39	18	13.00	-	-	83.0	19	224	4	56.00
Wasim Akram	3	5	-	197	123	39.40	2	-	135.4	37	318	17	18.71

NZ ends Australia's run

Wellington, Mar. 20. Australia's undefeated run of 14 Tests in a row came to an end at Basin Reserve yesterday, when New Zealand handed out a nine-wicket beating.

The Australians were unlucky to bat first on a pitch that New Zealand captain John Wright called the slowest he had ever played a Test on.

It was remarkable that any play occurred at all, because the ground was deluged by rain a couple of days before the match began.

Play started at 2p.m. on the first day and Australia was bowled out for 110 runs in just 198 minutes.

Specialist off-spinner Peter Taylor, coming in to bat at number eight, top-scored in Australia's innings with 29. When the going gets slow, the slow get going, it seems.

New Zealand all-rounder Richard Hadlee took 5/39 off 16.2 overs and bowled five maidens. It is the 100th time that Hadlee has taken five or more wickets in an innings.

The New Zealand nightwatchman Martin Snedden broke a world record when he did not

Mark Greatbatch: stonewall style.

score a single run for 94 minutes. He was on six runs for the whole time.

Australia's second innings 269 was only made respectable thanks to Allan Border (78 not out) and the slow man Taylor, yet again, who scored a fine 87.

New Zealand needed just 178 to win, which was achieved largely courtesy of a fine 117 from left-handed opener Wright.

ONLY TEST 1989–90 NEW ZEALAND v AUSTRALIA
Basin Reserve, Wellington. March 15, 16, 17, 18, 19, 1990.
Toss: Australia. New Zealand won by 9 wkts.

AUSTRALIA

MA Taylor lbw Morrison	4	(2)	lbw Hadlee	5
GR Marsh b Morrison	4	(1)	c Rutherford b Bracewell	41
DC Boon lbw Hadlee	0		c Smith b Bracewell	12
AR Border (c) lbw Morrison	1	(5)	not out	78
DM Jones c Wright b Snedden	20	(6)	lbw Morrison	0
SR Waugh b Hadlee	25	(7)	c Greatbatch b Hadlee	25
IA Healy (+) b Snedden	0	(8)	c Rutherford b Bracewell	10
PL Taylor c Wright b Hadlee	29	(4)	c Smith b Morrison	87
GD Campbell lbw Hadlee	4		b Bracewell	0
CG Rackemann not out	6		b Bracewell	1
TM Alderman b Hadlee	4		st Smith b Bracewell	1
EXTRAS (LB 6, NB 7)	13		(LB 6, NB 3)	9
TOTAL	110			269

FOW 1st Inns: 4 9 9 12 38 44 70 87 103 110
FOW 2nd Inns: 27 54 91 194 194 232 261 261 267 269

Bowling: *First Innings*: Hadlee 16.2-5-39-5, Morrison 10-4-22-3, Snedden 15-2-33-2, Rutherford 2-0-8-0, Bracewell 2-1-2-0. *Second Innings*: Hadlee 25-3-70-2, Morrison 24-8-58-2, Snedden 25-5-46-0, Bracewell 34.2-11-85-6, Jones 1-0-4-0.

NEW ZEALAND

TJ Franklin c Marsh b PL Taylor	28		c Healy b Campbell	18
JG Wright (c) c Healy b Alderman	36		not out	117
AH Jones c & b Border	18		not out	33
MC Snedden b Alderman	23			
MJ Greatbatch c Healy b PL Taylor	16			
KR Rutherford c Healy b PL Taylor	12			
JJ Crowe lbw Alderman	9			
RJ Hadlee lbw Campbell	18			
IDS Smith (+) c MA Taylor b Campbell	1			
JG Bracewell not out	19			
DK Morrison c MA Taylor b Alderman	12			
EXTRAS (B 2, LB 5, NB 3)	10		(B 2, LB 10, NB 1)	13
TOTAL	202			1 for 181

FOW 1st Inns: 48 89 89 111 123 150 151 152 171 202
FOW 2nd Inns: 53

Bowling: *First Innings*: Alderman 29-9-46-4, Rackemann 32-17-42-0, PL Taylor 33-19-44-3, Campbell 21-3-51-2, Border 6-3-12-1. *Second Innings*: Alderman 14-8-27-0, Rackemann 15-4-39-0, PL Taylor 11-3-39-0, Campbell 7-2-23-1, Jones 6-3-14-0, Border 10.4-5-27-0.

Umpires: RS Dunne & SJ Woodward

Boon – cricket's folk hero

In every Australian schoolyard. there's a little fat kid. This one made a hundred at Lord's. And just about everywhere else, too.

David Boon was so short and stocky they called him a 'keg on legs.' But what a keg! He played in 107 Tests, made 21 Test centuries and 32 half-centuries, and scored 7422 runs between 1984–85 and 1995–96 at an average of 43.66.

He remains the second highest run-getter in Australian cricket history, behind Allan Border, and took many of his 99 Test catches at short leg, where his lightning reflexes made him one of the best in the world.

In one day cricket, Boon played in 181 matches and scored 5964 runs at an average of 37.04.

He was one mean cricketer. And not just statistically speaking. Boon's handlebar moustache and stony stare terrified even his own team-mates. When Ian Healy first met Boon, it took months for him to realise Boon didn't hate him. Boonie always looked that way.

But underneath was a shy, modest and sincere team man who never shirked his duty. Toughness was his trademark. Against the West Indies in 1991, a vicious bouncer from Patrick Smith hit Boon on the chin. He shook his head, had the physio bandage him, and walked back to the crease. Five stitches at lunch, and the bulldog batted on to another century.

After an Australian win, he would jump on a table or chair to lead the team's victory anthem, 'Under the Southern Cross'.

Boon was born on 29 December 1960 at Launceston, Tasmania, and ABC commentator Neville Oliver remembers him as a 'fiercely determined' five-year-old who used to wander down from Charles Street Primary School to his father Clarrie's newsagency to stock up on chewing gum and other necessities.

'This kid has ice in his veins,' said former Queensland batsman Ken Mackay after Boon debuted for Tasmania in 1978–79.

In November 1985 he made his Test debut against the West Indies at Brisbane, and scored 11 and 56 batting at number 6. Soon he formed a successful opening partnership with Geoff Marsh, who called him 'the gutsiest cricketer with whom I ever played.'

'I'd do the talking,' Marsh said. 'He would just mumble "ummm".'

An Australian legend: 'Boonie'.

Boon was the classic strong, silent type. He was Man of the Match in the 1987 World Cup final against England in Calcutta, scoring 75. His 815 runs at 54.33 in 16 World Cup matches is the record for any Australian.

'Doing a Boonie', became synonymous with any task that called for grit and dependability. Ever the patriot, he stayed at the crease for 492 minutes to make an unbeaten 184 in the Bicentennial Test against England in 1988.

On the 1989 Ashes Tour Boon made 442 runs and reached a peak in 1993 with centuries in three Tests in a row against England.

His highest Test score was 200 against New Zealand in 1989–90.

Australian captain Allan Border described David Boon as his 'rock of Gibraltar,' and if ever one man was an island, it was Boonie. He was named Tasmanian captain in 1985 and whenenver he batted, he carried the pride and hopes of his State on his shoulders.

It was a fitting tribute when the NTCA named the members' stand at Launceston in his honour.

There was sorrow and surprise when he announced his retirement from Test cricket in January 1996.

They say the Tasmanian tiger is extinct. But Boonie will be there when the cheers ring out in the dressing rooms. In the grandstands, loungerooms, backyards and bars, the little battler will be there.

For his is the spirit of green and gold, the call of an Australian son: *Under the Southern Cross I stand A sprig of wattle in my hand A native in my native land Australia, you bloody beauty.*

Rampant Reid routs England

First Test ends in England collapse

Greg Matthews: just makes it.

Brisbane, Nov. 25. Australia has comfortably won the first Test in just three days after it had seemed that the match would be a close contest at stumps on day two.

England had a dramatic collapse reminiscent of the disastrous failures when Australia toured England last year.

Australia ripped through the tourists after David Gower and acting captain Allan Lamb had looked well set.

After a two year absence because of back problems, Bruce Reid showed why he is Australia's best bowler when in good health. The Englishmen had no answer to his accuracy and ability to get the ball to lift from a good length.

On the second day Australian batsmen departed in a similar procession and with seamers Angus Fraser, Gladstone Small and Chris Lewis sharing the wickets, Australia fell 42 runs short of the England first innings of 194.

It has often been said of Terry Alderman that he can only bowl effectively at Perth or in England, but the 34-year-old was devastating here and his 6/47 sent England into a downward spiral.

The sun now appeared for the first time and openers Marsh and Taylor blossomed. With innings scores of 194, 152 and 114 so far in the match, nobody would have predicted the Australians would rattle off the 157 without loss, but they did just that.

Bruce Reid is the spindly mainstay of the Australian fast-bowling fleet.

Melbourne, Dec. 30. Beanpole Australian fast bowler Bruce Reid has given Australia a virtually unassailable 2–0 lead in the Ashes series.

The tall left-armer took 13 wickets in a match which featured the almost mandatory English batting collapse – this time a second-innings disaster of six wickets falling for only three runs. Yet again the Englishmen had Australia on the ropes only to ease the pressure and let the home side bolt away to a comfortable win.

The Australian pair of Geoff Marsh and David Boon repeated their second-innings effort of the Brisbane Test by building a huge partnership and sealing victory.

The Englishmen have been bedevilled by misfortune this tour. No sooner did Captain Graham Gooch return to the side after his hand injury than the team lost his deputy Allan Lamb, who strained a a calf muscle while jogging back to the team motel after making a century in Ballarat.

The MCG pitch was so slow that English 'keeper Jack Russell has said he has never stood closer to the stumps to take the bowling of speedster Devon Malcolm.

The nature of the pitch made England's second innings collapse even more remarkable, after being soundly placed at 1/103.

In what England manager Mickey Stewart describes as '50 minutes of madness' after tea on the fourth day, Reid and Greg Matthews took six wickets in 12 overs while just three runs were scored.

Mark Waugh fires up in Adelaide

Better late than never. Mark Waugh made a classic century on debut.

Adelaide, Jan. 25. 'It was just one of those days when everything hit the middle', is Mark Waugh's description of his magical Test debut in Adelaide today.

Waugh is the 15th Australian batsman to make a century on Test debut, and his grace captivated the Adelaide Oval crowd.

From the time he stroked the third ball he faced for three, Waugh was in charge. That shot came off Phil DeFreitas, who had dismissed Allan Border and Dean Jones in the previous four balls.

By four minutes the younger of the 25-year-old twins, Mark's entry to the Test team had a bitter-sweet side, as he was selected to replace his brother Steve.

He came to the crease with Australia in trouble at 4/104 and fashioned his 138 off just 186 balls.

Greg Matthews kisses his bat on reaching the ton for Australia.

English Press puts boots in again

London, Jan. 30. The Gulf War has dominated newspapers and other media, but English sports writers have still managed to fire plenty of broadsides at their own team.

There was outrage at the report that English players David Gower and John Morris were in a plane that 'buzzed' the Carrara ground during the game between the Englishmen and Queensland. For once the England management agreed with the media and fined the players £1000 each.

Allan Lamb was also attacked for having injured his calf jogging back to the team hotel after a century innings, after he had done the same thing eight months earlier in Barbados.

Parish retires

Melbourne, Sep. 14. After 33 years in cricket administration, Bob Parish has said farewell to his role at the Australian Cricket Board.

A firm and far-sighted leader, Parish was a central figure in the ACB's confrontation with Kerry Packer's World Series Cricket and then was one of the main brokers in the peace settlement. Back in 1957 he was, at the age of 41, the youngest ever member of the Australian Cricket Board. He spent eight years as chairman of the Board of Control/ACB.

During the chaotic days of the 'Cricket War' Parish and his administrative partner Ray Steele did more than anyone else to hold traditional cricket together.

Potter quits college

Adelaide, July 1. Australia's Cricket Academy has suffered a big blow in the resignation of its head coach Jack Potter.

The former Victorian batsman was the first Cricket Academy coach and he has done much in the space of two years to lay the foundations for international success in the next decade.

It is believed that Potter is tired of the constant cricketing politics that are played out in the background to his post.

Potter has one of the most astute cricketing brains in Australia and his individuality has probably rankled with more conservative elements in power.

He has an imaginative eye for talent and one of his charges is young Victorian leg-spinner Shane Warne, whom Potter has taught 'the flipper'.

McDermott back – and how

Craig McDermott grabs the wicket of Alec Stewart in the summer of his triumphant return.

Perth, Feb. 5. Fast bowler Craig McDermott has completed an amazing return to international cricket with a Man of the Match performance in the fifth Test.

Australia won by nine wickets thanks largely to the flying start given to the team by McDermott who took 8/97 on the first day. Thede exceptional figures come on top of a five-wicket haul in the fourth Test a week ago, when McDermott regained his place after a two-year absence.

Knee and back injuries forced him out of the Test side, but continued excellence at Sheffield Shield level enable him to force his way back.

In a display of his iron will, McDermott trained with Australian iron-man champion Trevor Hendy on the long haul back to full fitness.

Although McDermott's first-innings figures in Perth were his best ever performance at Test level, there was a fair sprinkling of half-volleys on leg stump.

At the start of the day he had trouble handling the Fremantle Doctor as the wind was at his back and he fell into the trap of over-pitching.

Captain Border then decided to bowl him into the wind and McDermott responded in grand style.

He took three wickets in his first 18 overs which cost an expensive 80 runs.

But after tea he grabbed five wickets for 17 in 6.4 overs, starting with Allan Lamb, who played a wild cross-bat stroke in the first over of the session.

In the second innings McDermott showed his maturity by learning from his wayward spell and bowling better than his figures of 3/60 indicated.

A key difference between these teams has been Australia's batting strength in the lower order.

England has invariably disintegrated whereas the Australian tail has managed to scratch out handy runs.

In the fourth Test McDermott made his highest Test score of 42 and this match he made 25, and Ian Healy scored 42.

Linking it all has been the middle order pluck of Greg Matthews who has been a model of consistency and a thorn in England's side.

Matthews' batting returns in this series include 128 at Sydney, 65 at Adelaide and 60 here in Perth.

Waugh twins in record romp

Perth, Dec. 21. The Waugh twins have smashed a stack of records in their amazing partnership against a Western Australian side that boasts a Test-strength bowling attack.

Their 464 is a world record partnership for the fifth wicket, an Australian record for any wicket and is the first time that brothers have each scored double-centuries in the same innings of a first class match.

They came together with NSW struggling at 4/137 and Bruce Reid on top with figures of 3/25. By the time Geoff Lawson declared the innings a day later they had been together for 407 minutes. Mark was not out 229 and Steve not out 216.

The Australian batting warrior Steve Waugh.

O'Donnell leads Vics to victory

Melbourne, March 26. Victoria has won its first Sheffield Shield since 1979-80 with a handsome win over New South Wales in the final.

The win is a tribute to their combative skipper Simon O'Donnell who has overcome cancer to return to cricket and re-establish himself as a potent force. Operating in tandem with Tony Dodemaide (5/25) and Paul Reiffel (2/40), O'Donnell (3/34) humbled NSW for 134 in its second innings after Victoria had looked to have blown its chance with a paltry 119 in the first dig. Dodemaide has grabbed 20 wickets in three games since his late-season recall.

Wayne Phillips (91 not out) and Jamie Siddons (124 not out) steered the Vics home with an unbroken third wicket stand of 212.

Australia one day winner in a canter

Melbourne, Jan. 15. Australia wrapped up the Benson and Hedges World Series with ease today after dominating the competition in a manner rarely seen in this type of cricket.

The Aussies won nine of their 10 matches thanks to brilliant fielding and depth in the batting that extended down to no. 9.

Geoff Marsh, David Boon and Mark Taylor ensured consistently good starts. The consistent Marsh scored 46, 45, 37, 51, 82, 61, 29, 7 and 70, but on the second final he was bowled first ball. All-rounder Simon O'Donnell, acknowledged as a one day specialist, played such an important role that he was controversially voted International Cricketer of the Year despite not appearing in a Test all summer.

Cricket with a special country air

Bowral, Dec. 11. Bowral has a special place in Australian cricket lore as the site of Don Bradman's emergence as a batsman.

The Bradman Museum at Bowral honors the world's greatest batsman, and the England side had a delightful stop-over there for a special one day game to raise money for the Bradman Museum and Trust.

The crowd of 5000 warmed to the rustic atmosphere and $40,000 was raised for the Trust.

Former Australian Test batsman Doug Walters came out of retirement to lead the Bradman XI, but because of the fine form of youngsters Darren Lehmann (112 not out) and Michael Bevan (51 not out), he did not get the chance to bat.

Bush bliss at Bowral during the game between the Englishmen and the Bradman XI.

FIRST TEST 1990-91 AUSTRALIA v ENGLAND
Brisbane Cricket Ground, Brisbane. November 23, 24, 25, 1990.
Toss: Australia. Australia won by 10 wkts.

ENGLAND

MA Atherton lbw Reid	.13	b Alderman .15
W Larkins c Healy b Hughes	.12	lbw Reid .0
DI Gower c Healy b Reid	.61	b Hughes .27
AJ Lamb (c) c Hughes b Matthews	.32	lbw Alderman .14
RA Smith b Reid	.7 (6)	c Taylor b Alderman .1
AJ Stewart lbw Reid	.4 (7)	c (S)PE Cantrell b Alderman .6
RC Russell (+) c & b Alderman	.16 (5)	lbw Waugh .15
CC Lewis c Border b Hughes	.20	lbw Alderman .14
GC Small not out	.12	c Alderman b Hughes .15
ARC Fraser c Healy b Alderman	.1	c (S)PE Cantrell b Alderman .0
DE Malcolm c Waugh b Hughes	.5	not out .0
EXTRAS (B 1, LB 7, NB 3)	.11	(LB 3, NB 4) .7
TOTAL	.194	.114

FOW 1st Inns: 23 43 117 123 134 135 167 181 187 194
FOW 2nd Inns: 0 42 46 60 78 84 93 112 114 114

Bowling: *First Innings*: Alderman 18-5-44-2, Reid 18-3-53-4, Hughes 19-5-39-3, Waugh 7-2-20-0, Matthews 16-8-30-1. *Second Innings*: Alderman 22-7-47-6, Reid 14-3-40-1, Hughes 12.1-5-17-2, Matthews 1-1-0-0, Waugh 4-2-7-1.

AUSTRALIA

GR Marsh lbw Fraser	.9 (2)	not out .72
MA Taylor c Lewis b Fraser	.10 (1)	not out .67
DC Boon lbw Small	.18	
AR Border (c) c Atherton b Small	.9	
DM Jones c Small b Lewis	.17	
SR Waugh c Smith b Small	.1	
GRJ Matthews c Small b Malcolm	.35	
IA Healy (+) c Atherton b Lewis	.22	
MG Hughes c Russell b Fraser	.9	
BA Reid b Lewis	.0	
TM Alderman not out	.0	
EXTRAS (B 1, LB 10, NB 11)	.22	(B 3, LB 2, W 3, NB 10) .18
TOTAL	.152	.0 for 157

FOW 1st Inns: 22 35 49 60 64 89 135 150 150 152
FOW 2nd Inns:

Bowling: *First Innings*: Malcolm 17-2-45-1, Fraser 21-6-33-3, Small 16-4-34-3, Lewis 9-0-29-3. *Second Innings*: Fraser 14-2-49-0, Small 15-2-36-0, Malcolm 9-5-22-0, Lewis 6-0-29-0, Atherton 2-0-16-0.

Umpires: AR Crafter & PJ McConnell

SECOND TEST 1990-91 AUSTRALIA v ENGLAND
Melbourne Cricket Ground, Melbourne. December 26, 27, 28, 29, 30, 1990.
Toss: England. Australia won by 8 wkts.

ENGLAND

GA Gooch (c) lbw Alderman	.20	c Alderman b Reid .58
MA Atherton c Boon b Reid	.0	c Healy b Reid .4
W Larkins c Healy b Reid	.64	c Healy b Reid .54
RA Smith c Healy b Hughes	.30	c Taylor b Reid .8
DI Gower c & b Reid	.100	c Border b Matthews .0
AJ Stewart c Healy b Reid	.79	c Marsh b Reid .8
RC Russell (+) c Healy b Hughes	.15	c Jones b Matthews .1
PAJ DeFreitas c Healy b Reid	.3	lbw Reid .0
ARC Fraser c Jones b Alderman	.24	c Taylor b Reid .0
DE Malcolm c Taylor b Reid	.6	lbw Matthews .1
PCR Tufnell not out	.0	not out .0
EXTRAS (LB 2, NB 9)	.11	(B 7, LB 3, NB 6) .16
TOTAL	.352	.150

FOW 1st Inns: 11 30 109 152 274 303 307 324 344 352
FOW 2nd Inns: 17 103 115 122 147 148 148 148 150 150

Bowling: *First Innings*: Alderman 30.4-7-86-2, Reid 39-8-97-6, Hughes 29-7-83-2, Matthews 27-8-65-0, Waugh 6-2-19-0. *Second Innings*: Alderman 10-2-19-0, Reid 22-12-51-7, Hughes 9-4-26-0, Matthews 25-9-40-3, Waugh 7-6-4-0.

AUSTRALIA

GR Marsh c Russell b DeFreitas	.36 (2)	not out .79
MA Taylor c Russell b DeFreitas	.61 (1)	c Atherton b Malcolm .5
DC Boon c Russell b Malcolm	.28 (4)	not out .94
AR Border (c) c Russell b Fraser	.62	
DM Jones c Russell b Fraser	.44	
SR Waugh b Fraser	.19	
GRJ Matthews lbw Fraser	.12	
IA Healy (+) c Russell b Fraser	.5 (3)	c Atherton b Fraser .1
MG Hughes lbw Malcolm	.4	
TM Alderman b Fraser	.0	
BA Reid not out	.3	
EXTRAS (B 4, LB 12, NB 16)	.32	(B 4, LB 12, NB 2) .18
TOTAL	.306	.2 for 197

FOW 1st Inns: 63 133 149 224 264 281 289 298 302 306
FOW 2nd Inns: 9 10

Bowling: *First Innings*: Malcolm 25.5-4-74-2, Fraser 39-10-82-6, Tufnell 21-5-62-0, DeFreitas 25-5-69-2, Atherton 2-1-3-0. *Second Innings*: Malcolm 23-7-52-1, Fraser 20-4-33-1, Tufnell 24-12-36-0, DeFreitas 16-3-46-0, Atherton 3-0-14-0.

Umpires: AR Crafter & PJ McConnell

THIRD TEST 1990-91 AUSTRALIA v ENGLAND
Sydney Cricket Ground, Sydney. January 4, 5, 6, 7, 8, 1991.
Toss: Australia. Match Drawn.

AUSTRALIA

GR Marsh c Larkins b Malcolm	13 (2)	c Stewart b Malcolm	4	
MA Taylor c Russell b Malcolm	11 (1)	lbw Hemmings	19	
DC Boon c Atherton b Gooch	97 (4)	c Gooch b Tufnell	29	
AR Border (c) b Hemmings	78 (5)	c Gooch b Tufnell	20	
DM Jones st Russell b Small	60 (6)	c & b Tufnell	0	
SR Waugh c Stewart b Malcolm	48 (7)	c Russell b Hemmings	14	
GRJ Matthews c Hemmings b Tufnell	128 (8)	b Hemmings	19	
IA Healy (+) c Small b Hemmings	35 (3)	c Smith b Tufnell	69	
CG Rackemann b Hemmings	1	b Malcolm	9	
TM Alderman not out	26	c Gower b Tufnell	1	
BA Reid c Smith b Malcolm	0	not out	5	
EXTRAS (B 5, LB 8, NB 8)	21	(LB 16)	16	
TOTAL	518		205	

FOW 1st Inns: 21 38 185 226 292 347 442 457 512 518
FOW 2nd Inns: 21 29 81 129 129 166 166 189 192 205

Bowling: *First Innings*: Malcolm 45-12-128-4, Small 31-5-103-1, Hemmings 32-7-105-3, Tufnell 30-6-95-1, Gooch 14-3-46-1, Atherton 5-0-28-0. *Second Innings*: Malcolm 6-1-19-2, Small 2-1-6-0, Hemmings 41-9-94-3, Tufnell 37-18-61-5, Atherton 3-1-9-0.

ENGLAND

GA Gooch (c) c Healy b Reid	59	c Border b Matthews	54
MA Atherton c Boon b Matthews	105 (6)	not out	3
W Larkins run out	11	lbw Border	0
RA Smith c Healy b Reid	18 (5)	not out	10
DI Gower c Marsh b Reid	123 (2)	c Taylor b Matthews	36
AJ Stewart lbw Alderman	91 (4)	run out	7
RC Russell (+) not out	30		
GC Small lbw Alderman	10		
EE Hemmings b Alderman	0		
PCR Tufnell not out	5		
DE Malcolm			
EXTRAS (B 1, LB 8, NB 8)	17	(LB 1, NB 2)	3
TOTAL	8 dec 469		4 for 113

FOW 1st Inns: 95 116 156 295 394 426 444 444
FOW 2nd Inns: 84 84 100 100

Bowling: *First Innings*: Alderman 20.1-4-62-3, Reid 35.1-9-79-3, Rackemann 25.5-5-89-0, Matthews 58-16-145-1, Border 19-5-45-0, Waugh 14-3-40-0. *Second Innings*: Alderman 4-0-29-0, Rackemann 3-0-20-0, Matthews 9-2-26-2, Border 9-1-37-1.

Umpires: AR Crafter & PJ McConnell

FIFTH TEST 1990-91 AUSTRALIA v ENGLAND
W.A.C.A. Ground, Perth. February 1, 2, 3, 5, 1991.
Toss: England. Australia won by 9 wkts.

ENGLAND

GA Gooch (c) c Healy b McDermott	13	c Alderman b Hughes	18
MA Atherton c Healy b McDermott	27	c Boon b Hughes	25
AJ Lamb c Border b McDermott	91	lbw McDermott	5
RA Smith c Taylor b McDermott	58	lbw Alderman	43
DI Gower not out	28	c Taylor b Alderman	5
AJ Stewart (+) lbw McDermott	2	c Healy b McDermott	7
PAJ DeFreitas c Marsh b McDermott	5	c Healy b Alderman	5
PJ Newport c Healy b McDermott	0	not out	40
GC Small c Boon b Hughes	0	c Taylor b Hughes	4
PCR Tufnell c Healy b Hughes	0	c Healy b Hughes	8
DE Malcolm c Marsh b McDermott	7	c Jones b McDermott	6
EXTRAS (B 1, LB 6, W 1, NB 5)	13	(B 5, LB 5, NB 6)	16
TOTAL	244		182

FOW 1st Inns: 27 50 191 212 220 226 226 227 227 244
FOW 2nd Inns: 41 49 75 80 114 118 125 134 144 182

Bowling: *First Innings*: Alderman 22-5-66-0, McDermott 24.4-2-97-8, Hughes 17-3-49-2, Waugh 1-0-9-0, Matthews 2-0-16-0. *Second Innings*: McDermott 19.3-2-60-3, Alderman 22-3-75-3, Hughes 20-7-37-4.

AUSTRALIA

GR Marsh c Stewart b Small	1 (2)	not out	63
MA Taylor c Stewart b Malcolm	12 (1)	c Stewart b DeFreitas	19
DC Boon c Stewart b Malcolm	64	not out	30
AR Border (c) lbw DeFreitas	17		
DM Jones b Newport	34		
ME Waugh c Small b Malcolm	26		
GRJ Matthews not out	60		
IA Healy (+) c Lamb b Small	42		
CJ McDermott b Tufnell	25		
MG Hughes c Gooch b Tufnell	0		
TM Alderman lbw DeFreitas	7		
EXTRAS (B 2, LB 8, W 1, NB 8)	19	(LB 5, W 2, NB 1)	8
TOTAL	307		1 for 120

FOW 1st Inns: 1 44 90 113 161 168 230 281 283 307
FOW 2nd Inns: 39

Bowling: *First Innings*: Malcolm 30-4-94-3, Small 23-3-65-2, DeFreitas 16.5-2-57-2, Newport 14-0-56-1, Tufnell 7-1-25-2. *Second Innings*: Malcolm 9-0-40-0, Small 10-5-24-0, DeFreitas 6.2-0-29-1, Newport 6-0-22-0.

Umpires: SG Randell & CD Timmins

FOURTH TEST 1990-91 AUSTRALIA v ENGLAND
Adelaide Oval, Adelaide. January 25, 26, 27, 28, 29, 1991.
Toss: Australia. Match Drawn.

AUSTRALIA

GR Marsh c Gooch b Small	37 (2)	c Gooch b Small	0	
MA Taylor run out	5 (1)	run out	4	
DC Boon c Fraser b Malcolm	49	b Tufnell	121	
AR Border (c) b DeFreitas	12 (7)	not out	83	
DM Jones lbw DeFreitas	0 (4)	lbw DeFreitas	8	
ME Waugh b Malcolm	138 (5)	b Malcolm	23	
GRJ Matthews c Stewart b Gooch	65 (8)	not out	34	
IA Healy (+) c Stewart b DeFreitas	1			
CJ McDermott not out	42			
MG Hughes lbw Small	1 (6)	c Gooch b Fraser	30	
BA Reid c Lamb b DeFreitas	5			
EXTRAS (B 2, LB 23, W 2, NB 4)	31	(B 1, LB 7, W 1, NB 2)	11	
TOTAL	386		6 dec 314	

FOW 1st Inns: 11 62 104 104 124 295 298 358 373 386
FOW 2nd Inns: 1 8 25 64 130 240

Bowling: *First Innings*: Malcolm 38-7-104-2, Fraser 23-6-48-0, Small 34-10-92-2, DeFreitas 26.2-6-56-4, Tufnell 5-0-38-0, Gooch 9-2-23-1. *Second Innings*: Malcolm 21-0-87-1, Small 18-3-64-1, DeFreitas 23-6-61-1, Fraser 26-3-66-1, Tufnell 16-3-28-1.

ENGLAND

GA Gooch (c) c Healy b Reid	87	c Marsh b Reid	117
MA Atherton lbw McDermott	0	c Waugh b Reid	87
AJ Lamb c Healy b McDermott	0	b McDermott	53
RA Smith c & b Hughes	53 (5)	not out	10
DI Gower c Hughes b McDermott	11 (4)	lbw Hughes	16
AJ Stewart (+) c Healy b Reid	11	c Jones b McDermott	9
PAJ DeFreitas c Matthews b McDermott	45	not out	19
GC Small b McDermott	1		
ARC Fraser c Healy b Reid	2		
DE Malcolm c Healy b Reid	2		
PCR Tufnell not out	0		
EXTRAS (B 1, LB 3, NB 13)	17	(B 5, LB 9, W 1, NB 9)	24
TOTAL	229		5 for 335

FOW 1st Inns: 10 11 137 160 176 179 198 215 219 229
FOW 2nd Inns: 203 246 287 287 297

Bowling: *First Innings*: Reid 29-9-53-4, McDermott 26.3-3-97-5, Hughes 22-4-62-1, Waugh 4-1-13-0. *Second Innings*: Reid 23-5-59-2, McDermott 27-5-106-2, Matthews 31-7-100-0, Hughes 14-3-52-1, Waugh 1-0-4-0.

Umpires: LJ King & TA Prue

Australian Averages

1990-91 AUSTRALIA v ENGLAND

AUSTRALIA	M	Inn	NO	Runs	H.S	Avrge	Ct	St	Overs	Mds	Runs	Wkt	Avrge
Alderman, TM	4	5	2	34	26*	11.33	4	-	148.5	33	428	16	26.75
Boon, DC	5	9	2	530	121	75.71	4	-	-	-	-	-	-
Border, AR	5	7	1	281	83*	46.83	4	-	28.0	6	82	1	82.00
Healy, IA	5	7	-	175	69	25.00	24	-	-	-	-	-	-
Hughes, MG	4	5	-	44	30	8.80	3	-	142.1	38	365	15	24.33
Jones, DM	5	7	-	163	60	23.29	4	-	-	-	-	-	-
Marsh, GR	5	10	3	314	79*	44.86	5	-	-	-	-	-	-
Matthews, GRJ	5	7	2	353	128	70.60	1	-	169.0	51	422	7	60.29
McDermott, CJ	2	2	1	67	42*	67.00	-	-	97.4	12	360	18	20.00
Rackemann, CG	1	2	-	10	9	5.00	-	-	28.5	5	109	-	-
Reid, BA	4	5	2	13	5*	4.33	1	-	180.1	49	432	27	16.00
Taylor, MA	5	10	-	213	67*	23.67	8	-	-	-	-	-	-
Waugh, ME	2	3	-	187	138	62.33	1	-	6.0	1	26	-	-
Waugh, SR	3	4	-	82	48	20.50	1	-	38.0	15	90	1	90.00

English Averages

1990-91 AUSTRALIA v ENGLAND

ENGLAND	M	Inn	NO	Runs	H.S	Avrge	Ct	St	Overs	Mds	Runs	Wkt	Avrge
Atherton, MA	5	10	1	279	105	31.00	5	-	15.0	2	70	-	-
DeFreitas, PAJ	3	6	1	77	45	15.40	-	-	113.3	22	318	10	31.80
Fraser, ARC	3	5	-	27	24	5.40	-	-	143.0	31	311	11	28.27
Gooch, GA	4	8	-	426	117	53.25	6	-	23.0	5	69	2	34.50
Gower, DI	5	10	1	407	123	45.22	1	-	-	-	-	-	-
Hemmings, EE	1	1	-	0	0	0.00	1	-	73.0	16	199	6	33.17
Lamb, AJ	3	6	-	195	91	32.50	2	-	-	-	-	-	-
Larkins, W	3	6	-	141	64	23.50	1	-	-	-	-	-	-
Lewis, CC	1	2	-	34	20	17.00	1	-	15.0	-	58	3	19.33
Malcolm, DE	5	7	1	27	7	4.50	-	-	223.5	42	665	16	41.56
Newport, PJ	1	2	1	40	40*	40.00	-	-	20.0	-	78	1	78.00
Russell, RC	3	5	1	77	30*	19.25	9	1	-	-	-	-	-
Small, GC	4	6	1	42	15	8.40	4	-	149.0	33	424	9	47.11
Smith, RA	5	10	2	238	58	29.75	3	-	-	-	-	-	-
Stewart, AJ	5	10	-	224	91	22.40	8	-	-	-	-	-	-
Tufnell, PCR	4	6	4	13	8	6.50	1	-	140.0	45	345	9	38.33

Jones run-out turns the series sour

Geoff Marsh faces a tough task opening the batting against Malcolm Marshall and Curtly Ambrose.

Georgetown, March 27. An incident that combined bad sportsmanship and poor umpiring has left relations between West Indies and Australia at an all-time low.

The rancorous feeling between the two teams has bubbled under the surface in recent years, but the dismissal of Dean Jones in Australia's second innings has brought feelings to a head.

Jones was bowled by a no-ball from Courtney Walsh and headed toward the pavilion oblivious to the call. West Indian fieldsman Carl Hooper charged in and grabbed the ball and uprooted a stump. Seeing what was about to happen, Allan Border at the non-striker's end tried to tell him to get back.

Incredibly, umpire Clyde Cumberbatch gave Jones out. Under laws 38 (2) and 27 (5) Jones should not have been dismissed. Law 38 (2) states that: 'If a no-ball has been called, the striker shall not be given out unless he attempts a run.'

Captains Allan Border and Viv Richards have admitted that they did not know the rule. Australian manager Bob Simpson took a copy of the rules to umpire Cumberbatch at the tea break, but he would not reinstate Jones.

Australia's bad position was worsened – and so were relations.

West Indian methods of pitch preparation are an eye-opener – the pitch is on fire!

Sledging leads to insult by Richards

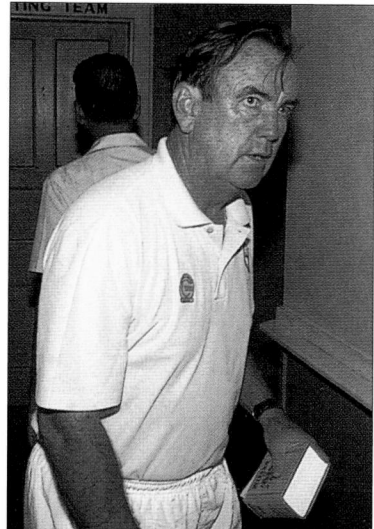

Australian Coach Bob Simpson became embroiled in controversy on this tour.

Bridgetown, April 24. Even the magnificence of a 343-run West Indian victory could not overshadow the acrimony of this series.

At tonight's press conference Viv Richards fired off a scathing attack on Australian coach Bob Simpson, labelling him a 'moaner, a bad loser and a very sour sort of guy.'

Richards was angered by earlier reports that Simpson had focussed on the supposedly brittle West Indian batting.

The Windies captain said: 'I'm not in the business of shouting my mouth off about what we're going to do. I've been hearing what Simpson said the Australians are going to do to us in Australia and before this series. I don't have great respect for Bob Simpson after seeing the way he operates. I'm not the greatest admirer of Bobby Simpson. You treat people as you are treated.'

The sorry litany of disputation continued on the opening day of the fourth Test when Australian 'keeper Ian Healy clashed with West Indian opener Desmond Haynes after Healy led the Australians in a vocal appeal for a catch.

The tension between the two sides is never far from the surface and they do not socialise after the game in the traditional manner of cricket teams down through the ages.

The differences have even spilled to the level of the two countries' respective Boards who have swapped press releases commenting on the behaviour of their opponents. This series had been billed as the championship of the world, but it will be remembered more for its open hostility.

Windies onslaught wins series

Talented West Indian skipper Richie Richardson cuts past the imperturbable David Boon.

Bridgetown, April 24. Australia has been torn apart by a West Indies pace attack bristling with hostility and able to achieve deadly accuracy.

The fifth Test will be a meaningless affair as West Indies thumped Australia by 10 wickets at Guyana and by 343 runs here. The first and third Tests were affected by rain.

Allan Border is in the best position to evaluate the West Indians and he rates the current attack as equal to any he has faced.

'They have bowled better than I thought them capable – especially on the flatter wickets ... They've got an old head in Malcolm Marshall who has been written off – but he still produces the goods all the time. Walsh has improved out of sight with the old ball, Ambrose is one of the best going around, and Patterson has improved 100 per cent. And their strength is not sheer pace, either. It's their persistent line and length which keeps you under pressure,' said Border.

With typical straightforward honesty, Border said 'I thought we had a big chance, but basically we've been blitzed in the Test series. But I'm not totally distraught. I know what we are up against. They are a great side.'

It isn't just the West Indian bowlers who have been on the attack. The batsmen have taken up the fight whenever presented with a challenge. In the second Test Australia took 116 overs to be all out for 348. Then Desmond Haynes and Richie Richardson plundered 297 in 70 overs.

One day win a boost for Australia

Georgetown, March 2. There is some consolation for the bruised and battered Australians, as they have prevailed in the one day series.

Today Australia won its fourth game and could blame their only loss on the weather, which gave the home team a big advantage in the third game.

Opener Geoff Marsh is developing a reputation as the world's pre-eminent player in this form of the game.

In this series he has scored 26, 23, 81, 113 and 106 not out.

The rest of the side has shown great efficiency and maturity in all aspects of the one day format.

Dark clouds over West Indies cricket: Queens Park, Trinidad.

Aussies fight for late win

Allan Border is a favourite wherever he bats.

St John's, May 1. Australia can head home to their winter with a little glow of satisfaction over winning the fifth Test today.

Under less pressure because the series has already been decided, the Australians were virtually unrecognisable from the team that was steamrollered in the previous Test.

Mark Waugh played the best Australian innings of the series with a slashing knock of 139 not out and Dean Jones' 81 ended a long sequence of failures.

Their 187 run partnership set up a handsome first innings score of 403 and fast bowlers Craig McDermott and Merv Hughes then chimed in with valuable support, taking four wickets each and sending the home side on its way for 214.

Only Desmond Haynes, with 84 managed to get going. Later in the game he angrily confronted McDermott and Hughes after being run out on the final day – yet another stain on a series that has been pock-marked by incidents and aggravation that have brought little credit to the competing sides.

A fine second-innings 144 by Mark Taylor set the West Indians a big target and they never seriously looked like achieving it, falling 157 runs short.

Trophy missing

Antigua, May 1. It is perhaps apt that the prized Sir Frank Worrell trophy has gone missing.

When it came to the end of this series nobody could find the trophy named after the much-loved captain who led the West Indian team on their landmark tour of Australia in 1960-61.

That tour was said to have turned around the popularity of the game in Australia – a stark contrast to the nastiness and ill-temper shown here 30 years later.

Someone in the West Indies Board of Control reckons that the trophy went to India for an exhibition and never returned, but no-one is sure.

Better in Bermuda

Somerset Field, May 12. The shell-shocked Australians have had a chance to wind down their Caribbean odyssey in the quieter climes of Bermuda following their bitter clash with West Indies over the past three months.

Australia won all three games concluding with a 93-run victory over Bermuda at Somerset Field.

The 'one day maestro' Geoff Marsh signed off the tour with 107.

In the second match Allan Border scored 100.

It has been a light-hearted end to a demanding tour. In the match against the President's Eleven the Australians used 10 bowlers, including 'keeper Ian Healy.

FIRST TEST 1990–91 WEST INDIES v AUSTRALIA
Sabina Park, Kingston. March 1, 2, 3, 5 (no play), 6, 1991.
Toss: West Indies. Match Drawn.

WEST INDIES

CG Greenidge c & b McDermott	27	c Healy b McDermott 35
DL Haynes b McDermott	8	c Healy b McDermott 84
RB Richardson c Healy b Hughes	15	not out 104
CL Hooper c Marsh b Hughes	0	b McDermott 31
IVA Richards (c) c Hughes b McDermott	11	not out 52
AL Logie not out	77	
PJL Dujon (+) c Marsh b Hughes	59	
MD Marshall lbw McDermott	0	
CEL Ambrose c & b Waugh	33	
CA Walsh lbw McDermott	10	
BP Patterson b Hughes	4	
EXTRAS (LB 6, W 1, NB 13)	20	(B 15, LB 6, W 1, NB 6) 28
TOTAL	264	...................3 for 334

FOW 1st Inns: 33 37 57 68 75 75 144 166 234 264
FOW 2nd Inns: 118 134 216

Bowling: *First Innings*: McDermott 23-3-80-5, Whitney 21-4-58-0, Hughes 21.3-4-67-4, Matthews 11-2-28-0, Waugh 6-1-25-1. *Second Innings*: McDermott 24-10-48-3, Whitney 17-3-55-0, Hughes 22-5-79-0, Matthews 25-2-90-0, Border 10-3-21-0, Waugh 13-6-20-0.

AUSTRALIA

GR Marsh c Dujon b Ambrose	69
MA Taylor c Hooper b Patterson	58
DC Boon not out	109
AR Border (c) c Dujon b Ambrose	31
DM Jones c & b Hooper	0
ME Waugh lbw Marshall	39
GRJ Matthews c Dujon b Patterson	10
IA Healy (+) lbw Walsh	0
CJ McDermott b Patterson	1
MG Hughes c Hooper b Patterson	0
MR Whitney b Patterson	2
EXTRAS (B 4, LB 23, W 4, NB 21)	52
TOTAL	371

FOW 1st Inns: 139 159 227 228 329 357 358 365 365 371

Bowling: *First Innings*: Ambrose 30-3-94-2, Patterson 24-1-83-5, Marshall 22-3-57-1, Walsh 23-4-73-1, Hooper 21-7-37-1.

Umpires: DM Archer & SA Bucknor

SECOND TEST 1990–91 WEST INDIES v AUSTRALIA
Bourda, Georgetown. March 23, 24, 25, 27, 28, 1991.
Toss: Australia. West Indies won by 10 wkts.

AUSTRALIA

MA Taylor lbw Patterson	0	(2)	lbw Ambrose 15
GR Marsh c Hooper b Patterson	94	(1)	b Walsh 22
DC Boon c Dujon b Marshall	7		c Dujon b Marshall 2
AR Border (c) b Marshall	47		c Dujon b Marshall 34
DM Jones b Marshall	34		run out 3
ME Waugh c Dujon b Patterson	71		c Richards b Ambrose 31
GRJ Matthews c Dujon b Ambrose	1		c Dujon b Marshall 16
IA Healy (+) run out	53		run out 47
CJ McDermott lbw Patterson	1		c Dujon b Patterson 4
MG Hughes b Ambrose	0		c Patterson b Walsh 21
MR Whitney not out	1		not out 0
EXTRAS (B 6, LB 8, W 2, NB 23)	39		(B 17, LB 6, W 2, NB 28) 53
TOTAL	348		248

FOW 1st Inns: 3 24 124 188 237 238 339 346 346 348
FOW 2nd Inns: 32 43 67 73 130 161 172 187 241 248

Bowling: *First Innings*: Ambrose 31.4-9-64-2, Patterson 24-1-80-4, Walsh 24-2-81-0, Marshall 23-3-67-3, Hooper 13-3-37-0, Richards 1-0-5-0. *Second Innings*: Ambrose 24-5-45-2, Patterson 14-5-46-1, Walsh 23-4-55-2, Marshall 15-2-31-3, Hooper 18-6-35-0, Richards 4-2-13-0.

WEST INDIES

CG Greenidge lbw McDermott	2	not out 5
DL Haynes c ME Waugh b Border	111	not out 23
RB Richardson lbw McDermott	182	
CL Hooper c ME Waugh b Matthews	62	
IVA Richards (c) b Matthews	50	
AL Logie c Healy b Border	54	
PJL Dujon (+) lbw Border	29	
MD Marshall not out	22	
CEL Ambrose b Border	0	
CA Walsh b Border	1	
BP Patterson lbw Matthews	15	
EXTRAS (B 5, LB 13, NB 23)	41	(LB 2, NB 1) 3
TOTAL	569	.........................0 for 31

FOW 1st Inns: 10 307 353 443 444 529 530 530 532 569
FOW 2nd Inns:

Bowling: *First Innings*: McDermott 36-3-114-2, Whitney 28-4-103-0, Matthews 37.5-6-155-3, Hughes 20-4-93-0, ME Waugh 2-0-18-0, Border 30-11-68-5. *Second Innings*: McDermott 4-1-10-0, Hughes 3.5-0-19-0.

Umpires: CE Cumberbatch & CR Duncan

THIRD TEST 1990–91 WEST INDIES v AUSTRALIA
Queen's Park Oval, Port-of-Spain. April 5, 6, 8, 9, 10, 1991.
Toss: West Indies. Match Drawn.

AUSTRALIA

GR Marsh c Hooper b Ambrose 10 (2)	lbw Marshall 12
MA Taylor c Walsh b Marshall 61 (1)	b Patterson 2
DC Boon c Logie b Patterson 27	b Walsh 29
AR Border (c) run out 43 (5)	not out 27
DM Jones lbw Patterson 21 (4)	not out 39
ME Waugh lbw Marshall 64	
SR Waugh c Dujon b Walsh 26	
IA Healy (+) c Dujon b Marshall 9	
CJ McDermott c Richardson b Patterson 0	
MG Hughes lbw Patterson 0	
BA Reid not out 0	
EXTRAS (B 6, LB 14, NB 13) 33	(B 1, LB 9, NB 4) 14
TOTAL 294	...........3 for 123

FOW 1st Inns: 24 93 116 174 210 268 293 294 294 294
FOW 2nd Inns: 3 49 53

Bowling: *First Innings*: Ambrose 29-7-51-1, Patterson 26-2-50-4, Marshall 18.1-3-55-3, Walsh 30-9-45-1, Hooper 25-5-73-0. *Second Innings*: Ambrose 10-4-11-0, Patterson 7-0-27-1, Marshall 10-3-24-1, Walsh 12-6-11-0, Hooper 13-4-38-0, Richardson 1-0-2-0.

WEST INDIES

CG Greenidge c ME Waugh b Reid 12
DL Haynes b McDermott 1
RB Richardson c MA Taylor b Hughes 30
CL Hooper lbw Hughes 12
AL Logie c ME Waugh b Hughes 1
IVA Richards (c) c SR Waugh b Hughes 2
PJL Dujon (+) lbw McDermott 70
MD Marshall c McDermott b Border 12
CEL Ambrose c Border b ME Waugh 53
CA Walsh not out 12
BP Patterson b McDermott 0
EXTRAS (B 6, LB 7, NB 9) 22
TOTAL 227

FOW 1st Inns: 16 18 46 52 56 86 110 197 225 227

Bowling: *First Innings*: McDermott 14.2-2-36-3, Reid 22-0-79-1, Border 19-5-28-1, Hughes 17-5-48-4, SR Waugh 5-0-10-0, ME Waugh 6-2-9-1, Jones 1-0-4-0.

Umpires: DM Archer & LH Barker

FIFTH TEST 1990–91 WEST INDIES v AUSTRALIA
Recreation Ground, St John's. April 27, 28, 29, May 1, 1991.
Toss: Australia. Australia won by 157 runs.

AUSTRALIA

MA Taylor c Dujon b Hooper 59 (2)	c & b Ambrose 144
GR Marsh c Richardson b Patterson 6 (1)	c Dujon b Ambrose 1
DC Boon c Greenidge b Ambrose 0 (4)	b Walsh 35
AR Border (c) c Dujon b Hooper 59 (5)	b Walsh 5
DM Jones lbw Marshall 81 (6)	b Walsh 8
ME Waugh not out 139 (7)	lbw Walsh 0
IA Healy (+) c Dujon b Marshall 12 (3)	c Logie b Patterson 32
PL Taylor c Dujon b Ambrose 2	b Marshall 4
MG Hughes b Ambrose 1	c Walsh b Ambrose 13
CJ McDermott c Dujon b Walsh 7	c Dujon b Marshall 1
TM Alderman b Walsh 0	not out 0
EXTRAS (B 1, LB 12, W 6, NB 18) 37	(B 11, LB 7, NB 4) 22
TOTAL 403	265

FOW 1st Inns: 10 13 129 156 342 371 381 385 403 403
FOW 2nd Inns: 4 49 142 168 184 184 237 258 265 265

Bowling: *First Innings*: Ambrose 30-6-92-3, Patterson 12-1-44-1, Marshall 22-1-72-2, Walsh 22-1-54-2, Hooper 15-1-82-2, Richards 7-0-46-0. *Second Innings*: Ambrose 16-1-64-3, Walsh 26-2-56-4, Hooper 27-6-61-0, Patterson 1-0-1-1, Marshall 13.1-4-36-2, Richards 8-0-29-0.

WEST INDIES

CG Greenidge lbw McDermott 6	run out 43
DL Haynes lbw McDermott 84	run out 33
RB Richardson b McDermott 3	c Jones b ME Waugh 41
CL Hooper lbw Hughes 12	c ME Waugh b PL Taylor 35
IVA Richards (c) lbw McDermott 0	c Alderman b Border 2
AL Logie c Jones b PL Taylor 24	lbw Alderman 61
PJL Dujon (+) c Jones b Hughes 33	lbw McDermott 4
MD Marshall c Healy b ME Waugh 28	lbw Hughes 51
CEL Ambrose c MA Taylor b Hughes 0	run out 0
CA Walsh not out 11	c Healy b Hughes 0
BP Patterson b Hughes 2	not out 7
EXTRAS (LB 2, NB 11) 13	(B 5, LB 7, W 8) 20
TOTAL 214	297

FOW 1st Inns: 10 22 35 46 114 136 186 195 206 214
FOW 2nd Inns: 76 92 142 145 182 193 271 271 271 297

Bowling: *First Innings*: McDermott 15-4-42-4, Alderman 7-0-42-0, Hughes 17-2-65-4, PL Taylor 11-2-40-1, ME Waugh 5-0-23-1. *Second Innings*: McDermott 17-2-55-1, Alderman 15.4-4-63-1, Hughes 19-5-49-2, PL Taylor 10-0-39-1, Border 15-2-71-1, ME Waugh 5-3-8-1.

Umpires: LH Barker & SA Bucknor

FOURTH TEST 1990–91 WEST INDIES v AUSTRALIA
Kensington Oval, Bridgetown. April 19, 20, 21, 23, 24, 1991.
Toss: Australia. West Indies won by 343 runs.

WEST INDIES

CG Greenidge c Reid b McDermott 10	lbw Hughes 226
DL Haynes c ME Waugh b Hughes 28	c Healy b ME Waugh 40
RB Richardson c Boon b McDermott 1 (4)	lbw ME Waugh 99
CL Hooper c Jones b Hughes 0 (5)	c Healy b ME Waugh 57
IVA Richards (c) c Hughes b McDermott 32 (6)	lbw ME Waugh 25
AL Logie c Taylor b Reid 11 (7)	not out 33
PJL Dujon (+) c Healy b Hughes 10 (8)	c ME Waugh b McDermott 4
MD Marshall c Marsh b Reid 17 (3)	c Healy b McDermott 15
CEL Ambrose not out 19	b Reid 2
CA Walsh c ME Waugh b McDermott 10	c Marsh b Reid 0
BP Patterson c ME Waugh b Hughes 1	not out 4
EXTRAS (LB 3, NB 7) 10	(LB 19, NB 12) 31
TOTAL 149	...........9 dec 536

FOW 1st Inns: 17 21 22 72 89 96 103 125 148 149
FOW 2nd Inns: 129 153 352 454 470 512 522 525 525

Bowling: *First Innings*: McDermott 22-7-49-4, Reid 21-8-50-2, Hughes 16.1-2-44-4, SR Waugh 2-0-3-0. *Second Innings*: McDermott 37.3-8-130-2, Reid 30-4-100-2, Hughes 36-6-125-1, SR Waugh 28-6-77-0, ME Waugh 28-6-80-4, Jones 3-1-5-0.

AUSTRALIA

MA Taylor lbw Ambrose 26 (2)	lbw Marshall 76
GR Marsh c Logie b Ambrose 12 (1)	lbw Ambrose 0
DC Boon c Hooper b Marshall 0	b Ambrose 57
AR Border (c) b Marshall 29	c Dujon b Ambrose 0
DM Jones lbw Marshall 22 (6)	b Hooper 37
ME Waugh not out 20 (7)	b Hooper 3
SR Waugh c Dujon b Patterson 2 (8)	not out 4
IA Healy (+) c Logie b Walsh 2 (9)	b Marshall 0
MG Hughes c Logie b Walsh 3 (5)	c Dujon b Marshall 3
CJ McDermott b Walsh 2	c (S)RIC Holder b Walsh 2
BA Reid b Walsh 0	b Walsh 0
EXTRAS (LB 2, NB 14) 16	(B 3, LB 5, NB 18) 26
TOTAL 134	208

FOW 1st Inns: 24 27 59 95 97 100 106 121 127 134
FOW 2nd Inns: 0 111 111 122 190 200 200 200 208 208

Bowling: *First Innings*: Ambrose 16-5-36-2, Patterson 13-6-22-1, Marshall 16-1-60-3, Walsh 5.1-1-14-4. *Second Innings*: Ambrose 19-7-36-3, Patterson 15-3-56-0, Walsh 14.2-3-37-2, Marshall 17-6-35-3, Hooper 19-4-28-2, Richards 3-0-8-0.

Umpires: DM Archer & LH Barker

Australian Averages

1990–91 WEST INDIES v AUSTRALIA

AUSTRALIA	M	Inn	NO	Runs	H.S	Avrge	Ct	St	Overs	Mds	Runs	Wkt	Avrge
Alderman, TM	1	2	-	0	0*	0.00	1	-	22.4	4	105	1	105.00
Boon, DC	5	9	1	266	109*	33.25	1	-					
Border, AR	5	9	1	275	59	34.38	1	-	74.0	21	188	7	26.86
Healy, IA	5	8	-	155	53	19.38	10	-					
Hughes, MG	5	8	-	41	21	5.13	2	-	172.3	33	589	19	31.00
Jones, DM	5	9	1	245	81	30.63	4	-	4.0	1	9	-	
Marsh, GR	5	9	-	226	94	25.11	4	-					
Matthews, GRJ	2	3	-	27	16	9.00	-	-	73.5	10	273	3	91.00
McDermott, CJ	5	8	-	18	7	2.25	2	-	192.5	40	564	24	23.50
Reid, BA	2	3	1	0	0*	0.00	1	-	73.0	12	229	5	45.80
Taylor, MA	5	9	-	441	144	49.00	3	-					
Taylor, PL	1	2	-	6	4	3.00	-	-	21.0	2	79	2	39.50
Waugh, ME	5	8	2	367	139*	61.17	10	-	65.0	18	183	8	22.88
Waugh, SR	2	3	1	32	26	16.00	1	-	35.0	6	90	-	
Whitney, MR	2	3	2	3	2	3.00	-	-	66.0	11	216	-	

West Indian Averages

1990–91 WEST INDIES v AUSTRALIA

WEST INDIES	M	Inn	NO	Runs	H.S	Avrge	Ct	St	Overs	Mds	Runs	Wkt	Avrge
Ambrose, CEL	5	7	1	115	53	19.17	1	-	205.4	47	493	18	27.39
Dujon, PJL	5	7	-	209	70	29.86	23	-					
Greenidge, CG	5	9	1	366	226	45.75	1	-					
Haynes, DL	5	9	1	412	111	51.50	-	-					
Hooper, CL	5	8	-	199	62	24.88	6	-	151.0	36	391	5	78.20
Logie, AL	5	7	2	261	77*	52.20	4	-					
Marshall, MD	5	7	1	145	51	24.17	-	-	156.2	26	437	21	20.81
Patterson, BP	5	7	2	33	15	6.60	1	-	136.0	19	409	18	22.72
Richards, IVA	5	8	1	174	52*	24.86	2	-	23.0	2	101	-	
Richardson, RB	5	8	1	475	182	67.86	1	-	1.0	-	2	-	
Walsh, CA	5	7	2	44	12*	8.80	2	-	179.3	32	426	17	25.06

India fights in thrilling Tests

Australia gets a good start

Merv Hughes hugs David Boon, and how!

Melbourne, Dec. 29. Left-arm pace bowler Bruce Reid, with match figures of 12/126 in the second Test, has given Australia a 2-0 lead against India. Australia's eight-wicket victory at the MCG followed its 10-wicket drubbing of India in the first Test at the Gabba.

Reid's penetrating bowling, an Australian record in a home series against India, reduced the tourists to 263 and 213 in Melbourne, and solid batting by opener Geoff Marsh (86), Ian Healy (60) and Dean Jones (59) helped set up the win.

India's inadequacy against pace had been revealed in the 'Gabba Test, in which Craig McDermott had match figures of 9/101 and Merv Hughes 7/84. India succumbed for 239 and 156. The Australian top-order batsmen showed early form, Marsh getting 47, Mark Taylor 94 and David Boon 66. In scoring a half century, Boon became the 11th Australian batsman to have scored 4000 Test runs.

In this match, Allan Border, leading Australia for the 63rd time in a row, broke Sunil Gavaskar's record of 125 Test appearances.

Two notable performances for India were Manoj Prabhakar's double of 54 not out and 39 — both top scores — and Kapil Dev's 4/80 in Australia's first innings of 340.

Adelaide, Jan. 29. Outplayed in the first two Tests, India has fought back strongly, though without any semblance of luck.

The fourth Test here was a thriller, Australia scraping home by 38 runs.

The home side, skittled for 145 in its first innings (Kapil Dev 3/33), overcame its problems by keeping India to 225 (McDermott 5/76), then piling on 451 in its second innings. Mark Taylor (100) and David Boon (135) put on 221 for the second wicket, and Border (91 not out) would not surrender. Kapil toiled magnificently, taking 5/130.

Requiring 372 to win, India was in good shape at 6/283 then lost 4/50, all four wickets falling to McDermott with the new ball. He took 5/92, giving him 10/168 for the match, in India's losing total of 333, of which skipper Mohinder Azharuddin made a breezy 106 in only 185 minutes.

India had some appalling misfortune in the previous Test at the SCG, the loss of five hours play on days three and four robbing it of victory.

After bowling Australia out for 313 (Boon 129), India replied with 483 thanks to a stand of 196 — an Indian record for the fifth wicket against Australia — by Ravi Shastri (206) and a lovely unbeaten 148 by Sachin Tendulkar, at 18 the youngest Indian to score a Test hundred in Australia.

Australia then collapsed and was three runs ahead at 8/173 when the match ended in a draw . Shane Warne, on his debut, took 1/150 off in India's only innings.

Geoff Marsh is comprehensively bowled by Subroto Banerjee for eight in the third Test.

Mark Taylor, back leg at full stretch, survives a spirited stumping appeal by Chadrakant Pandit.

QUICK SINGLES

Pace prevails. NSW has won the FAI limited-over cup final in Perth. Batting first, it scored a modest 9/199 (Mark Taylor 50). WA then folded for 130 against the pace of Geoff Lawson, Wayne Holdsworth and the economical Mike Whitney (2/19 from 10 overs).

No-balled. In the 'Gabba Test, India's Manoj Prabhakar was the first bowler to be no-balled under the new ICC regulation prohibiting more than one bouncer at each batsman in the same over. In another first, an ICC referee officiated — former England captain Mike Smith.

Umpire's milestone. Tony Crafter officiated at his 33rd Test, an Australian record, in the fifth Test between Australia and India at the WACA. He made his Test umpiring debut in 1978–79.

Still trying. Queensland, yet to win the Sheffield Shield, had the season's biggest win, defeating Tasmania by an innings and 129 runs.

First 200. Ravi Shastri's 206 in Sydney was the first double century by an Indian in Tests against Australia. The highest Test score by an Indian is Sunil Gavaskar's 236 not out against the West Indies in Madras in 1983–84.

Boom batsman. With his 135 in the fourth Test in Adelaide, David Boon became the first Australian to score five Test hundreds against India. Those with four are Border, Bradman, Harvey and Simpson. Boon made it six with 107 in Perth and finished his outstanding series with 556 runs at 79.43.

Healy milestone. During the fifth Test in Perth, Ian Healy joined Bill Oldfield and Rod Marsh as the only Australian wicketkeepers to complete the double – 100

dismissals and 1000 runs. Craig McDermott with 31 wickets equalled Bishen Bedi's series record.

The stars. In the Tests, Craig McDermott was twice Man of the Match (1st and 4th Tests). Others were Bruce Reid (2nd), Ravi Shastri (3rd) and Mike Whitney (5th).

Waugh dropped. Mark Waugh, whose Shield season has already yielded 762 runs at 69.27, was dropped from the fifth Test against India after disappointing scores of 11, 34, 5, 18, 15 and 0.

WA's Shield. In spite of a third-wicket stand of 204 by the Waugh brothers in the first innings, New South Wales lost the Sheffield Shield final to Western Australia by 44 runs in Perth. Scores: WA 396 (Moody 78; Matthews 3/49) and 344 (Langer 149; Whitney 7/75) d NSW 415 (M. Waugh 163, S. Waugh 113) and 281 (S. Waugh 68; Reid 3/61, Alderman 3/73) by 44 runs.

Whitney cleans up with 7/42

Perth, Feb. 5. Left-arm fast bowler Mike Whitney has become sick of playing third fiddle to McDermott and Hughes.

With only six wickets in two Tests, he conducted the show in the fifth Test, skittling India for 141 in its second innings with 7/27 off 12.1 hostile overs, the best innings analysis by an Australian against India. It followed his 4/68 in India's first innings of 272 and gave him a match haul of 11/95, his best in Tests.

With its 300-run victory, Australia won the series 4-0, thus emulating the successes of the 1947-48 side under Bradman and the 1967-68 team led by Simpson, then Lawry.

The remarkable aspect of India's second innings was that openers Krishnam Srikkanth and Navjot Sidhu put on 82. Then 10 wickets fell for 59. Victoria's Paul Reiffel, making his debut, took 2/34, claiming the valuable wicket of Sachin Tendulkar for five. In the first innings, Tendulkar had charmed the crowd with 114, his second century of the series.

In a match for statisticians, David Boon scored his third 'ton' in three Tests, this time 107 in Australia's first innings of 346, and Kapil Dev became only the second bowler, after Sir Richard Hadlee, to take 400 Test wickets. Dean Jones made 150 not out in Australia's second knock, and local hero Tom Moody 101.

Mike Whitney: destroyer.

Kapil Dev, only the second player to take 400 Test wickets, is clapped off the field in Perth. Mark Taylor was the 400th scalp.

FIRST TEST 1991–92 AUSTRALIA v INDIA
Brisbane Cricket Ground, Brisbane. November 29, 30, December 1, 2, 1991.
Toss: Australia. Australia won by 10 wkts.

INDIA

RJ Shastri c Waugh b McDermott	8	c Healy b McDermott	41
K Srikkanth c Boon b McDermott	13	c Boon b Hughes	0
SV Manjrekar c & b Hughes	17	c Boon b Hughes	5
DB Vengsarkar c Waugh b Hughes	5	lbw Hughes	0
M Azharuddin (c) c Hughes b Whitney	10	c Boon b Hughes	12
SR Tendulkar b Whitney	16	c Healy b McDermott	7
Kapil Dev b McDermott	44	c Waugh b McDermott	25
M Prabhakar not out	54	c Healy b Whitney	39
KS More (+) c Whitney b Hughes	19	lbw McDermott	1
SLV Raju c Healy b McDermott	12	c Healy b Whitney	2
J Srinath c Healy b McDermott	21	not out	12
EXTRAS (B 1, LB 6, NB 13)	20	(LB 4, NB 8)	12
TOTAL	239		156

FOW 1st Inns: 21 24 50 53 67 83 141 186 206 239
FOW 2nd Inns: 0 14 14 32 47 87 136 140 142 156

Bowling: *First Innings*: McDermott 28.1-11-54-5, Whitney 21-2-82-2, Hughes 20-5-34-3, Waugh 1-0-6-0, PL Taylor 18-3-56-0. *Second Innings*: McDermott 25-7-47-4, Hughes 16-4-50-4, Whitney 17.2-3-55-2.

AUSTRALIA

GR Marsh b Srinath	47 (2)	not out	17
MA Taylor c Vengsarkar b Raju	94 (1)	not out	35
DC Boon c More b Prabhakar	66		
AR Border (c) b Kapil	28		
DM Jones b Kapil	0		
ME Waugh c More b Srinath	11		
IA Healy (+) lbw Prabhakar	12		
PL Taylor c Raju b Srinath	31		
MG Hughes b Kapil	11		
CJ McDermott c Azharuddin b Kapil	8		
MR Whitney not out	7		
EXTRAS (LB 15, W 1, NB 9)	25	(LB 4, NB 2)	6
TOTAL	340		0 for 58

FOW 1st Inns: 95 178 244 244 265 278 280 301 316 340
FOW 2nd Inns:

Bowling: *First Innings*: Kapil 34-9-80-4, Prabhakar 37-10-88-2, Srinath 24.4-4-59-3, Raju 31-5-90-1, Tendulkar 1-0-8-0. *Second Innings*: Kapil 9-0-23-0, Prabhakar 2-1-3-0, Srinath 9-5-6-0, Raju 3-1-13-0, Tendulkar 1-0-5-0, Manjrekar 0.5-0-4-0.

Umpires: PJ McConnell & SG Randell

SECOND TEST 1991–92 AUSTRALIA v INDIA
Melbourne Cricket Ground, Melbourne. December 26, 27, 28, 29, 1991.
Toss: India. Australia won by 8 wkts.

INDIA

RJ Shastri c Healy b Reid	23	c Healy b Reid	22
K Srikkanth c Boon b Reid	5	lbw Reid	6
M Prabhakar b Reid	0 (9)	c Healy b Reid	17
SV Manjrekar c Waugh b Reid	25 (3)	c MA Taylor b McDermott	30
DB Vengsarkar c Reid b Hughes	23 (4)	c (S)MR Whitney b McDermott	54
M Azharuddin (c) c Jones b McDermott	22 (5)	c MA Taylor b Reid	2
SR Tendulkar c Waugh b Reid	15	c Border b PL Taylor	40
Kapil Dev c Hughes b McDermott	19	c Healy b Reid	12
KS More (+) not out	67 (10)	lbw Reid	12
SLV Raju c Border b Hughes	31 (6)	c & b McDermott	1
J Srinath c Border b Reid	14	not out	0
EXTRAS (B 1, LB 8, W 6, NB 4)	19	(B 1, LB 6, NB 10)	17
TOTAL	263		213

FOW 1st Inns: 11 11 61 64 109 109 128 151 228 263
FOW 2nd Inns: 13 48 75 78 79 141 155 173 213 213

Bowling: *First Innings*: McDermott 30-6-100-2, Reid 26.2-7-66-6, Hughes 23-6-52-2, Waugh 8-1-16-0, PL Taylor 6-0-20-0. *Second Innings*: McDermott 29-8-63-3, Reid 29-9-60-6, Hughes 19-6-43-0, PL Taylor 11-3-40-1.

AUSTRALIA

GR Marsh c Vengsarkar b Kapil	86 (2)	lbw Prabhakar	10
MA Taylor c Tendulkar b Prabhakar	13 (1)	st More b Raju	60
DC Boon c Srikkanth b Kapil	11	not out	44
AR Border (c) b Kapil	0	not out	5
DM Jones c More b Prabhakar	59		
ME Waugh c More b Shastri	34		
IA Healy (+) lbw Kapil	60		
PL Taylor c More b Prabhakar	11		
MG Hughes c Tendulkar b Kapil	36		
CJ McDermott not out	16		
BA Reid c Kapil b Prabhakar	3		
EXTRAS (LB 9, NB 11)	20	(LB 3, NB 6)	9
TOTAL	349		2 for 128

FOW 1st Inns: 24 55 55 163 211 229 262 326 337 349
FOW 2nd Inns: 16 122

Bowling: *First Innings*: Kapil 35-9-97-5, Prabhakar 34-7-84-4, Srinath 25-3-71-0, Raju 17-3-52-0, Tendulkar 4-1-16-0, Shastri 4-1-20-1. *Second Innings*: Kapil 12-1-30-0, Prabhakar 11-0-38-1, Srinath 8-0-28-0, Raju 6-0-17-1, Shastri 3-1-12-0.

Umpires: LJ King & TA Prue

THIRD TEST 1991–92 AUSTRALIA v INDIA
Sydney Cricket Ground, Sydney. January 2, 3, 4, 5, 6, 1992.
Toss: India. Match Drawn.

AUSTRALIA

GR Marsh b Banerjee	8 (2)	c Pandit b Kapil	4
MA Taylor c Pandit b Banerjee	56 (1)	c Kapil b Shastri	35
DC Boon not out	129	c Azharuddin b Srinath	7
ME Waugh c Prabhakar b Banerjee	5	lbw Prabhakar	18
DM Jones run out	35	c Pandit b Shastri	18
AR Border (c) c Pandit b Kapil	19	not out	53
IA Healy (+) c(S)K Srikkanth b Prabhakar	1	c Prabhakar b Shastri	7
MG Hughes c Pandit b Prabhakar	2	c Prabhakar b Tendulkar	21
CJ McDermott b Prabhakar	1	c Vengsarkar b Shastri	0
SK Warne c Pandit b Kapil	20	not out	1
BA Reid c Tendulkar b Kapil	0		
EXTRAS (B 4, LB 14, W 1, NB 18)	37	(LB 4, W 1, NB 4)	9
TOTAL	313	8 for 173	

FOW 1st Inns: 22 117 127 210 248 251 259 269 313 313
FOW 2nd Inns: 9 31 55 85 106 114 164 171

Bowling: *First Innings*: Kapil 33-9-60-3, Prabhakar 39-12-82-3, Banerjee 18-4-47-3, Srinath 21-5-69-0, Shastri 13-1-37-0. *Second Innings*: Kapil 19-5-41-1, Prabhakar 27-10-53-1, Srinath 12-0-28-1, Shastri 25-8-45-4, Tendulkar 1-0-2-1.

INDIA

RJ Shastri c Jones b Warne	206
NS Sidhu c Waugh b McDermott	0
SV Manjrekar c Waugh b Hughes	34
DB Vengsarkar c Waugh b McDermott	54
M Azharuddin (c) c Boon b McDermott	4
SR Tendulkar not out	148
M Prabhakar c Taylor b Hughes	14
Kapil Dev c Marsh b Hughes	0
CS Pandit (+) run out	9
ST Banerjee c Border b McDermott	3
J Srinath run out	1
EXTRAS (B 1, LB 4, NB 5)	10
TOTAL	483

FOW 1st Inns: 7 86 197 201 397 434 434 458 474 483

Bowling: *First Innings*: McDermott 51-12-147-4, Reid 4-0-10-0, Hughes 41.4-8-104-3, Waugh 14-5-28-0, Warne 45-7-150-1, Border 13-3-39-0.

Umpires: PJ McConnell & SG Randell

FOURTH TEST 1991–92 AUSTRALIA v INDIA
Adelaide Oval, Adelaide. January 25, 26, 27, 28, 29, 1992.
Toss: India. Australia won by 38 runs.

AUSTRALIA

GR Marsh b Prabhakar	8 (2)	b Kapil	5
MA Taylor b Tendulkar	11 (1)	c Raju b Kapil	100
DC Boon b Kapil	19	run out	135
AR Border (c) c Pandit b Tendulkar	0	not out	91
DM Jones c Azharuddin b Raju	41	c Pandit b Kapil	0
ME Waugh lbw Prabhakar	15	c Tendulkar b Kapil	0
IA Healy (+) c Pandit b Kapil	1	c Srikkanth b Kapil	41
MG Hughes c Manjrekar b Kapil	26	lbw Srinath	23
SK Warne st Pandit b Raju	7	c Pandit b Srinath	0
CJ McDermott b Raju	0	b Raju	21
MR Whitney not out	0	c Srinath b Raju	12
EXTRAS (LB 10, NB 7)	17	(LB 15, NB 8)	23
TOTAL	145		451

FOW 1st Inns: 13 36 39 50 77 81 117 141 145 145
FOW 2nd Inns: 10 231 277 277 277 348 383 383 409 451

Bowling: *First Innings*: Kapil 23-11-33-3, Prabhakar 18-3-55-2, Srinath 10-2-26-0, Tendulkar 4-2-10-2, Raju 11.4-7-11-3. *Second Innings*: Kapil 51-12-130-5, Prabhakar 21-5-60-0, Raju 56-15-121-2, Srinath 37-13-76-2, Srikkanth 1-0-5-0, Tendulkar 20-5-44-0.

INDIA

K Srikkanth c Healy b McDermott	17	b McDermott	22
NS Sidhu c Healy b Hughes	27	lbw Hughes	35
SV Manjrekar lbw Hughes	2	run out	45
DB Vengsarkar c Waugh b McDermott	13 (5)	lbw Hughes	4
M Azharuddin (c) lbw McDermott	1 (6)	c Taylor b McDermott	106
SR Tendulkar lbw McDermott	6 (4)	lbw Waugh	17
Kapil Dev c Border b Hughes	56	c Marsh b Hughes	5
M Prabhakar lbw Whitney	33	lbw McDermott	64
CS Pandit (+) c Boon b McDermott	15	c Waugh b McDermott	7
SLV Raju not out	19	not out	8
J Srinath c Healy b Whitney	21	c Warne b McDermott	3
EXTRAS (LB 5, NB 10)	15	(B 3, LB 9, NB 5)	17
TOTAL	225		333

FOW 1st Inns: 30 33 55 64 70 70 135 174 192 225
FOW 2nd Inns: 52 72 97 102 172 182 283 291 327 333

Bowling: *First Innings*: McDermott 31-9-76-5, Whitney 26.2-6-68-2, Hughes 18-5-55-3, Warne 7-1-18-0, Waugh 2-1-3-0. *Second Innings*: McDermott 29.1-8-92-5, Whitney 17-3-59-0, Hughes 23-5-66-3, Waugh 12-2-36-1, Warne 16-1-60-0, Border 3-0-8-0.

Umpires: DB Hair & PJ McConnell

FIFTH TEST 1991–92 AUSTRALIA v INDIA
W.A.C.A. Ground, Perth. February 1, 2, 3, 4, 5, 1992.
Toss: Australia. Australia won by 300 runs.

AUSTRALIA

MA Taylor c Srikkanth b Kapil	2	lbw Kapil	16
WN Phillips c More b Prabhakar	8	c Kapil b Srinath	14
DC Boon c Sidhu b Prabhakar	107	c Kapil b Prabhakar	38
AR Border (c) c Srikkanth b Kapil	59 (8)	not out	20
DM Jones c Srikkanth b Raju	7 (4)	not out	150
TM Moody c Vengsarkar b Prabhakar	50 (5)	c More b Kapil	101
IA Healy (+) c More b Srinath	28 (6)	c More b Raju	7
MG Hughes c Srikkanth b Srinath	24 (7)	c Tendulkar b Srinath	11
PR Reiffel c More b Prabhakar	9		
CJ McDermott c Srikkanth b Prabhakar	31		
MR Whitney not out	1		
EXTRAS (B 1, LB 7, NB 12)	20	(LB 4, NB 6)	10
TOTAL	346	6 dec 367	

FOW 1st Inns: 10 21 138 145 232 259 290 303 339 346
FOW 2nd Inns: 27 31 113 286 298 315

Bowling: *First Innings*: Kapil 40-12-103-2, Prabhakar 32.5-9-101-5, Srinath 25-5-69-2, Tendulkar 5-2-9-0, Raju 23-6-56-1. *Second Innings*: Kapil 28-8-48-2, Prabhakar 32-4-116-1, Srinath 29.3-4-121-2, Raju 24-5-78-1.

INDIA

K Srikkanth c Boon b McDermott	34	c Jones b Whitney	38
NS Sidhu c Healy b Hughes	5	c Jones b Reiffel	35
SV Manjrekar c Jones b Hughes	31	c Healy b Whitney	8
SR Tendulkar c Moody b Whitney	114	c Moody b Reiffel	5
DB Vengsarkar c Taylor b Hughes	1	c Moody b Whitney	4
M Azharuddin (c) c Healy b McDermott	11	lbw Whitney	24
SLV Raju c Taylor b Whitney	1 (10)	c Healy b Whitney	8
Kapil Dev c Hughes b Whitney	4 (7)	lbw Whitney	0
M Prabhakar c Reiffel b Whitney	0 (8)	c Healy b McDermott	3
KS More (+) c Healy b Hughes	43 (9)	c Taylor b Whitney	1
J Srinath not out	5	not out	1
EXTRAS (LB 14, NB 9)	23	(LB 11, NB 3)	14
TOTAL	272		141

FOW 1st Inns: 25 69 100 109 130 135 159 159 240 272
FOW 2nd Inns: 82 90 97 103 111 111 126 129 134 141

Bowling: *First Innings*: McDermott 21-6-47-2, Hughes 26.5-5-82-4, Reiffel 17-5-46-0, Whitney 23-4-68-4, Moody 2-0-15-0. *Second Innings*: McDermott 20-8-44-1, Hughes 12-2-25-0, Reiffel 11-2-34-2, Whitney 12.1-3-27-7.

Umpires: AR Crafter & TA Prue

Australian Averages

1991–92 AUSTRALIA v INDIA

AUSTRALIA	M	Inn	NO	Runs	H.S	Avrge	Ct	St	Overs	Mds	Runs	Wkt	Avrge
Boon, DC	5	9	2	556	135	79.43	8	-	-	-	-	-	-
Border, AR	5	9	4	275	91*	55.00	5	-	16.0	3	47	-	-
Healy, IA	5	8	-	157	60	19.63	19	-	-	-	-	-	-
Hughes, MG	5	8	-	154	36	19.25	4	-	199.3	46	511	22	23.23
Jones, DM	5	8	1	310	150*	44.29	5	-	-	-	-	-	-
Marsh, GR	4	8	1	185	86	26.43	2	-	-	-	-	-	-
McDermott, CJ	5	7	1	77	31	12.83	1	-	264.2	75	670	31	21.61
Moody, TM	1	2	-	151	101	75.50	3	-	2.0	-	15	-	-
Phillips, WN	1	2	-	22	14	11.00	-	-	-	-	-	-	-
Reid, BA	2	2	-	3	3	1.50	1	-	59.2	16	136	12	11.33
Reiffel, PR	1	1	-	9	9	9.00	1	-	28.0	7	80	2	40.00
Taylor, MA	5	10	1	422	100	46.89	7	-	-	-	-	-	-
Taylor, PL	2	2	-	42	31	21.00	-	-	35.0	6	116	1	116.00
Warne, SK	2	4	1	28	20	9.33	1	-	68.0	9	228	1	228.00
Waugh, ME	4	6	-	83	34	13.83	10	-	37.0	9	89	1	89.00
Whitney, MR	3	4	3	20	12	20.00	1	-	116.5	21	359	17	21.12

Indian Averages

1991–92 AUSTRALIA v INDIA

INDIA	M	Inn	NO	Runs	H.S	Avrge	Ct	St	Overs	Mds	Runs	Wkt	Avrge
Azharuddin, M	5	9	-	192	106	21.33	3	-	-	-	-	-	-
Banerjee, ST	1	1	-	3	3	3.00	-	-	18.0	4	47	3	15.67
Kapil Dev	5	9	-	165	56	18.33	4	-	284.0	76	645	25	25.80
Manjrekar, SV	5	9	-	197	45	21.89	1	-	0.5	-	4	-	-
More, KS	3	6	1	143	67*	28.60	10	1	-	-	-	-	-
Pandit, CS	2	3	-	31	15	10.33	10	1	-	-	-	-	-
Prabhakar, M	5	9	1	224	64	28.00	3	-	253.5	61	680	19	35.79
Raju, SLV	4	8	2	82	31	13.67	2	-	171.4	42	438	9	48.67
Shastri, RJ	3	5	-	300	206	60.00	1	-	48.0	11	114	5	22.80
Sidhu, NS	3	5	-	102	35	20.40	1	-	-	-	-	-	-
Srikkanth, K	4	8	-	135	38	16.88	7	-	1.0	-	5	-	-
Srinath, J	5	9	4	78	21	15.60	1	-	201.1	41	553	10	55.30
Tendulkar, SR	5	9	1	368	148*	46.00	5	-	36.0	10	94	3	31.33
Vengsarkar, DB	5	9	-	158	54	17.56	4	-	-	-	-	-	-

Four fast and furious men for Australia

Bruce Reid: talented but injury prone.

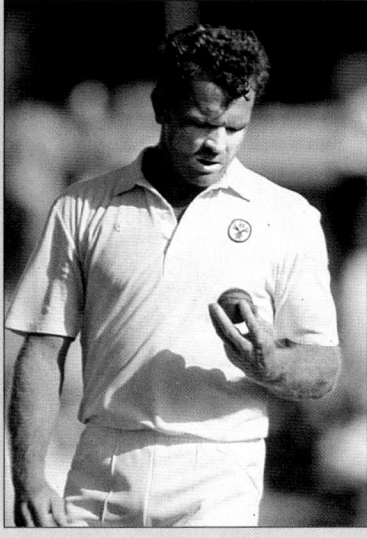

Billy the Kid.

Alderman: swing and seam.

Merv Hughes: toiler and extrovert.

Bruce Reid's Test career spanned the eight seasons from 1985–86 to 1992–93 but injuries restricted him to only 27 Test appearances. A heavy schedule of one day games (84 in all) placed great demands on the willowy frame of this talented left-arm fast-medium bowler.

As it was, he took 113 Test wickets at 24.63 – an average of 4.1 a match – and in all first class games 350 wickets at 26.63.

At 203 cm (6ft 8in.), the gangling Reid had remarkable rhythm for one so tall. His height enabled him to achieve awkward bounce and, like Alan Davidson before him, he was accurate and adept at slanting the ball across right-hand batsmen. He could also get one to nip back off the pitch.

Reid began his first class career with WA in 1984 and, in 1986–87, established himself as a Test bowler with 20 wickets at 26.35 against England. The next season he suffered a back injury against NZ.

In action again in 1990–91, he took 5/49 and 6/94 against SA in Adelaide and played a major role in Australia's 3–0 defeat of England with 27 wickets at 16 apiece. He was in superb form in the second Test in Melbourne, taking 6/97 and a career-best 7/51.

A back strain limited him to two home Tests against India in 1991–92. In Melbourne, he took 6/66 and 6/60, his lift perplexing the tourists.

After taking 5/112 against the West Indies in Brisbane in 1992–93, shoulder problems forced him out. The unassuming Reid retired in 1995–96, having borne his physical burdens with good grace.

Craig McDermott, six feet tall, strong of limb and naturally athletic, was born to bowl fast. A confident young man, he first played for Queensland at 17 and Australia at 19. He made his Test debut at the MCG in December, 1984 in the fourth Test against the West Indies.

His hostile bowling exceeded expectations. He took 3/118 and 3/65, getting Viv Richards lbw for a duck in the second innings.

The redheaded right-hander took 40 wickets in his first eight Tests, including 30 in England in 1985 with 6/70 at Lord's and 8/141 at Old Trafford. By now Australia's number one strike bowler, McDermott suddenly lost all form and was dropped. He was devastated.

For five seasons he was in and out of the side, the bright note being 17 wickets against NZ in 1987–88. But that was merely a rainbow amid the gloom.

He said later that success had come too easily, that immaturity was the problem. He shed unwanted kilos and was recalled for the last two Tests against England in 1990–91. Success was instantaneous – 5/97 in Adelaide and 8/97 and 3/60 in Perth.

In 1991–92 he ripped through the Indians (31 wickets) but illness hit him in 1993 on tour in England. He recovered and in 1994–95 took 32 wickets at 21.09 as Australia retained the Ashes.

Sadly, more injuries forced him to retire in 1995–96. His 291 Test wickets (second only to Lillee's 355), cost 28.63 apiece. In all first class games he had 677 wickets at 28.10. A hard-hitting tailender, he made 940 Test runs at 12.10.

Fast-medium swing bowler Terry Alderman turned into a destructive seamer almost overnight, thanks to a tip from Dennis Lillee in England in 1981. Practising on a lively Edgbaston net wicket, Lillee advised him to bowl faster off a longer run. Alderman, a tall man at 188 cm (6ft 2 in.), found he could hit the seam and the results were remarkable – an Australian record (v England) of 42 wickets in six Tests. Erased were memories of the early days when he was twice dropped by WA after winning his first State cap at 18 in 1974–75.

When Australia regained the Ashes in 1989 in England, Alderman played a key role with 41 wickets, including 10/151 in Australia's 210-run win at Leeds. This achievement was all the more praiseworthy because of a modified action, the result of a nasty incident in 1982 in which he badly injured his shoulder tackling a lout who had invaded the Australia v England Test field in Perth. It took Alderman two seasons to recover.

In his fourth and last series against England, in 1990–91, he took 16 wickets, and he ended his short 41-match Test career with 170 wickets at 27.15. He averaged 4.14 wickets a Test, a higher yield than Lindwall, Miller, Thomson and Benaud.

Alderman played in several of WA's winning Sheffield Shield teams, the last in 1991–92. He retired in 1992–93 with 956 first class wickets, the fourth highest by an Australian, at 23.74.

A sure slips fielder, he took 190 catches (27 in Tests). Alderman, a modest man, was a fine ambassador for the game.

Merv Hughes enjoys good company, especially in *Wisden*. With fellow post-war trundlers – Lindwall, Miller, Benaud and Davidson – he is one of eight Australians who have made 1000 runs and taken 200 wickets in Tests; in Hughes' case 1032 runs at 16.64 (highest score 72 not out) and 212 wickets at 28.38.

When Hughes shuffled in and bowled a 'leggie' at the MCG, he sometimes saw the humor of it all and looked as though he might continue on and join his mates from working-class Footscray in the old Bay 13 where bushy moustaches like his were imitated en masse.

Though his ample girth denied him access to the Ray Lindwall school of flannelled elegance, Hughes was a true toiler. And there was variety. Not only in his callisthenics, bad-guy glares and bouts of dissent, but in the aforementioned leg-break, part of his armoury of outswing and changes of pace.

The popular Hughes first played for Footscray, then for Victoria in 1981–82. He made his Test debut in 1985 against India but was soon axed, his bowling being too wayward. A shorter run-up following a back injury resulted in tighter control and he hit the headlines in Perth late in 1988 with 5/130 and 8/78 against the West Indies – a record haul against them.

On the triumphant 1989 Ashes tour, in support of Alderman and Lawson, he took 18 wickets. He carried the new-ball attack in England in 1993 with 21 wickets, paving the way for Shane Warne to deliver the KO. Hughes retired in 1995 and still enjoys the spotlight with his media appearances.

World Cup comes to the Antipodes

The world's finest. The cream of world cricket line up in Sydney.

WORLD CUP 1992 SCORES

(50 overs unless otherwise noted)

New Zealand 6/248 d Australia 211 (48.1 overs) at Auckland.

England 9/236 d India 227 (49.2 overs) at Perth.

Zimbabwe 4/312 lost to **Sri Lanka** 7/313 (49.2 overs) at New Plymouth.

Pakistan 2/220 lost to **West Indies** 0/221 (46.5 overs) at Melbourne.

Sri Lanka 9/206 lost to **New Zealand** 4/210 (48.2 overs) at Hamilton.

Australia 9/170 (49 overs) lost to **South Africa** 1/171 (46.5 overs) at Sydney.

Pakistan 4/254 (50 overs) d Zimbabwe 7/201 (50 overs) at Hobart.

West Indies 157 (49.2 overs) lost to **England** 4/160 (39.5 overs) at Melbourne.

India 0/1 (0.2 overs) v Sri Lanka at Mackay – no result due to rain.

South Africa 7/190 lost to **New Zealand** 3/191 (34.3 overs) at Auckland.

West Indies 8/264 d Zimbabwe 7/189 at Brisbane.

Australia 9/237 d India 234 (47 overs) at Brisbane.

Pakistan 74 (40.2 overs) No result at Adelaide due to rain.

South Africa 195 lost to **Sri Lanka** 7/198 (49.5 overs) at Wellington.

New Zealand 3/162 (20.5 overs) d Zimbabwe 7/105 (18 overs) at Napier.

India 7/216 (49 overs) d Pakistan 173 (48.1 overs) at Sydney.

South Africa 8/200 d West Indies 136 (38.4 overs) at Christchurch.

Australia 171 (49 overs) lost to **England** 2/173 (40 overs) at Sydney.

India 7/203 (32 overs) d Zimbabwe 1/104 (19.1 overs) at Hamilton.

Sri Lanka 9/189 lost to **Australia** 3/190 (44 overs) at Adelaide.

West Indies 7/203 lost to **New Zealand** 5/206 (48.3 overs) at Auckland.

South Africa 7/211 d Pakistan 8/173 (36 overs) at Brisbane.

England 6/280 d Sri Lanka 174 (44 overs) at Ballarat.

India 197 (49.5 overs) lost to **West Indies** 5/195 (40.2 overs) at Wellington.

Zimbabwe 163 (48.3 overs) lost to **South Africa** 3/164 (45.1 overs) at Canberra.

Pakistan 9/220 d Australia 172 (45.2 overs) at Perth.

India 6/230 lost to **New Zealand** 6/231 (47.1 overs) at Dunedin.

South Africa 4/236 lost to **England** 7/226 (40.5 overs) at Melbourne.

West Indies 8/268 d Sri Lanka 9/177 at Berri.

Australia 6/265 (46 overs) d Zimbabwe 137 (41.4 overs) at Hobart.

England 8/200 lost to **New Zealand** 3/201 (40.5 overs) at Wellington

India 6/180 (30 overs) lost to **South Africa** 4/181 (29.1 overs) at Adelaide

Sri Lanka 6/212 lost to **Pakistan** 6/216 (49.1 overs) at Perth

New Zealand 166 (48.2) lost to **Pakistan** 3/167 (44.4 overs) at Christchurch

Zimbabwe 134 (46.1 overs) d England 125 (49.1 overs) at Albury

Australia 6/216 d West Indies 159 (42.2 overs) at Melbourne

SEMI FINALS: New Zealand 7/262 lost to **Pakistan** 6/264 (49 overs) at Auckland

England 6/252 (45 overs) d South Africa 6/232 (43 overs) at Sydney. Decided on scoring rate.

FINAL: Pakistan 6/249 d England 227 (49.2 overs) at Melbourne

World Cup puts one day game on new level

Melbourne, March 25. Cricket's greatest show has ended at the MCG tonight with Imran Khan's Pakistan proclaimed as World Cup winners.

The game's four-yearly cricketing festival has put the one day form of cricket on a new plane and has generated enormous interest throughout New Zealand and Australia.

In one bizarre sidelight, the *Sydney Morning Herald* newspaper was three and a half hours late on March 19 due to a fight between two of the printing staff - one a New Zealander and one an Australian – over a New Zealand loss which put Australia out of the semis.

Twenty-five games were played in Australia and 14 in New Zealand across a span of 33 days.

Nine countries have battled out the fifth World Cup. It is the first time in these championships that teams have worn coloured clothing and played under lights.

The most contentious issue has been the rules applying to rain-shortened games. The World Cup committee decided that the reduction in the target would be equal to the lowest scoring overs of the team that batted first.

The rule led to a farcical situation in the semi-final between South Africa and England. A mere 12 minutes of heavy rain when South Africa needed 22 from 13 balls, changed their target to 22 from seven balls and then a ludicrous 21 from one ball.

Biggest shock of the tournament was the failure of red-hot favorite Australia to reach the final. Things started badly for Australia when they were well-beaten by New Zealand at Auckland. The Kiwis were the tournament's surprise packet, adopting the unusual tactic of opening the bowling with off-spinner Dipak Patel.

Ironically, Australia played its best game in its last appearance when David Boon scored a century and Mike Whitney took four wickets to put the West Indies out of the tournament.

Australian selectors have been criticised for persisting with Geoff Marsh when he was not scoring quickly enough. They also left Simon O'Donnell out of the squad.

In the end it was down to England and Pakistan before 90,000 people at the MCG and an estimated one billion TV viewers.

Ian Botham is sent on his way for a duck in the final after being caught behind off Wasim Akram.

The fielding of Jonty Rhodes has set new standards in this competition.

Appeal in cricket final.

To the victor the spoils. Pakistan captain Imram Khan with the coveted trophy.

Comeback in Colombo

Colombo, Aug. 22. Australia has won a game in which it was only on top for one session.

But that session was the one that really mattered – the final session.

Veteran spinner Greg Matthews and the young leggie Shane Warne were the bowlers who gave Australia an improbable win by 16 runs, against all the odds.

'It must be the greatest heist since the Great Train Robbery,' said Allan Border after the match. It was Border who took the catch that swung the pendulum Australia's way on the last day.

Aravinda de Silva was batting smoothly with 37 runs from 32 balls, and had taken Sri Lanka within 54 runs of a historic victory, when he suddenly had a rush of blood and skyed a ball from McDermott.

Border sprinted 25 metres, shedding his sunglasses and towelling hat before plucking a fine catch.

Until that moment Sri Lanka had been in charge from the moment Arjuna Ranatunga sent the Australians in to bat on a moist wicket in helpful conditions. The visitors made just 256 then saw their bowlers hammered as three Sri Lankans make centuries.

Most sensational of all was Test debutant Romesh Kaluwitharana whose 132 not out came from just 158 balls.

Trailing on the first innings by 291 runs, Australia's evenness and depth in batting helped to mount a comeback.

The Sri Lankans set out chasing a modest target of 180 and looked like getting there until the de Silva dismissal.

The nagging accuracy of Matthews chipped away at the Sri Lankan batting, but the master stroke from Border was bowling young Warne, who had taken only 1/335 runs from 90 test overs. He calmly took three wickets for no runs within 13 balls, and the match-winning spell was vindication of the selectors' faith in him.

Young Shane Warne repaid the selectors' faith in his leg-spin bowling with a match-winning effort in the first Test.

Four ducks in a row for Waugh

Moratuwa. Sep. 13. The usually brilliant Australian batsman Mark Waugh has scored four ducks in a row. He began the series in good enough fettle, scoring five and 56 in the opening Test, and a century in the next first class game, but he has since fallen into a trough.

A pair in the second Test was the start of the nightmare, then the spiral continued here with a pair of spectacles yet again.

Rated one of the best batsmen in the world, Waugh's flat spot puts him in the company of only five other players who have scored pairs in consecutive Tests. Australians Wayne Clark and Bob Holland were tailenders, as were Englishmen Bobby Peel and Pat Pocock and the South African Bob Crisp.

Waugh's effort is just short of Bob Holland, who was dismissed for zero in his next innings as well, and is the only man to score five consecutive ducks in Tests.

Sri Lanka wins the limited overs

Khettarama, Sep. 5. Sri Lanka has scored a morale-boosting 2–1 win in the three-match limited over series which finished here today.

The enthusiastic Sri Lankans have played wholehearted cricket against an Australian team that has played in uninspired style.

Sri Lanka's attack may not be the most potent in the world, but the batsmen have usually been able to compensate for their deficiencies. The home team's best bat, Aravinda de Silva, was brilliant in the opening one day clash in scoring 105 from 102 balls, and skipper Arjuna Ranatunga joined in the fun by making 45 not out (including a burst of 20 from one Craig McDermott over). In the end Sri Lanka passed the target of 247 with just four balls to spare.

Earlier in the day Australian openers Tom Moody (54) and Mark Taylor (94) had given the Aussies a flying start with a partnership of 109, but the total of 5/247 wasn't enough.

The second one day international was played on a damp, under-prepared pitch at Khettarama stadium. Sri Lanka won the rain-reduced match with de Silva (63 from 61 balls) leading the way again.

Australia finally tasted success in the third game when David Boon (69 not out) guided the tourists to victory in a low-scoring match.

FIRST TEST 1992–93 SRI LANKA v AUSTRALIA
Sinhalese Sports Club, Colombo. August 17, 18, 19, 21, 22 1992.
Toss: Sri Lanka. Australia won by 16 runs.

AUSTRALIA

MA Taylor lbw Wickramasinghe	42 (2)	c Gurusinha b Anurasiri	43
TM Moody lbw Ramanayake	1 (1)	b Ramanayake	13
DC Boon c Ramanayake b Hathurusingha	32	c Ranatunga b Anurasiri	68
DM Jones lbw Hathurusingha	10	run out	57
ME Waugh c Kaluwitharana b Hathurusingha	5	c Kaluwitharana b Wickramasinghe	56
AR Border (c) b Hathurusingha	3	c Gurusinha b Anurasiri	15
GRJ Matthews lbw Ramanayake	6	c Kaluwitharana b Ramanayake	64
IA Healy (+) not out	66	lbw Hathurusingha	12
CJ McDermott c Ranatunga b Ramanayake	22	lbw Ramanayake	40
SK Warne c & b Anurasiri	24	b Anurasiri	35
MR Whitney c & b Wickramasinghe	13	not out	10
EXTRAS (LB 10, W 3, NB 19)	32	(LB 23, W 1, NB 34)	58
TOTAL	256		471

FOW 1st Inns: 8 84 94 96 109 118 124 162 207 256
FOW 2nd Inns: 41 107 195 233 269 319 361 417 431 471

Bowling: *First Innings*: Ramanayake 20-4-51-3, Wickramasinghe 18-4-69-2, Hathurusingha 22-5-66-4, Madurasinghe 10-1-21-0, Gurusinha 2-0-17-0, Anurasiri 12-2-22-1. *Second Innings*: Ramanayake 37-10-113-3, Wickramasinghe 19-0-79-1, Hathurusingha 27-7-79-1, Anurasiri 35-3-127-4, Madurasinghe 14-1-50-0.

SRI LANKA

RS Mahanama c Healy b Waugh	78	c Boon b Matthews	39
UC Hathurusingha c Taylor b Waugh	18	run out	36
AP Gurusinha c Jones b Whitney	137	not out	31
PA De Silva lbw Matthews	6	c Border b McDermott	37
A Ranatunga (c) c Warne b Matthews	127	c Border b McDermott	0
MS Atapattu b Matthews	0	b Matthews	1
RS Kaluwitharana (+) not out	132	b Matthews	4
CPH Ramanayake c Healy b McDermott	0	lbw Matthews	6
GP Wickramasinghe c Matthews b McDermott	21	c Waugh b Warne	2
MAWR Madurasinghe not out	5 (11)	c Matthews b Warne	0
SD Anurasiri	(10)	c Waugh b Warne	1
EXTRAS (B 2, LB 7, W 1, NB 13)	23	(B 2, LB 3, NB 2)	7
TOTAL	8 dec 547		164

FOW 1st Inns: 36 128 137 367 367 463 472 503
FOW 2nd Inns: 76 79 127 132 133 137 147 150 156 164

Bowling: *First Innings*: McDermott 40-9-125-2, Whitney 32-10-84-1, Moody 17-3-44-0, Waugh 17-3-77-2, Warne 22-2-107-0, Matthews 38-11-93-3, Border 4-1-8-0. *Second Innings*: McDermott 14-4-43-2, Whitney 5-2-13-0, Moody 5-0-10-0, Matthews 20-2-76-4, Waugh 2-0-6-0, Warne 5.1-3-11-3.

Umpires: KT Francis & TM Samarasinghe

THIRD TEST 1992–93 SRI LANKA v AUSTRALIA
Tyronne Fernando Stadium, Moratuwa. September 8, 9, 10, 12, 13, 1992.
Toss: Australia. Match Drawn.

AUSTRALIA

TM Moody b Ramanayake	0 (2)	c Tillakaratne b Ramanayake	2
MA Taylor c Ranatunga b Anurasiri	19 (1)	c Mahanama b Liyanage	3
DC Boon c De Silva b Ramanayake	18	lbw Liyanage	0
DM Jones lbw Liyanage	11	b Anurasiri	21
ME Waugh b Ramanayake	0	c Tillakaratne b Liyanage	0
AR Border (c) b Ramanayake	106	lbw Ramanayake	78
GRJ Matthews run out	57	b Ramanayake	96
IA Healy (+) c Jayasuriya b Muralidaran	71	c Jayasuriya b Liyanage	49
CJ McDermott c Tillakaratne b Hathurusingha	10		
SK Warne c Gurusinha b Ramanayake	7		
AIC Dodemaide not out	13 (9)	not out	2
EXTRAS (B 3, LB 9, W 3, NB 10)	25	(LB 4, W 1, NB 15)	20
TOTAL	337		8 for 271

FOW 1st Inns: 0 42 46 57 58 185 252 283 302 337
FOW 2nd Inns: 6 6 6 9 60 132 261 271

Bowling: *First Innings*: Ramanayake 31-3-82-5, Liyanage 17-0-54-1, Hathurusingha 21-8-50-1, Anurasiri 22-2-57-1, Muralidaran 15.1-2-58-1, Jayasuriya 2-0-9-0, Gurusinha 3-0-15-0. *Second Innings*: Ramanayake 22.1-4-75-3, Liyanage 16-3-56-4, Hathurusingha 4-2-3-0, Anurasiri 29-5-49-1, Muralidaran 7-1-26-0, Ranatunga 1-0-9-0, Jayasuriya 7-1-17-0, Mahanama 5-0-27-0.

SRI LANKA

RS Mahanama lbw Matthews	50
UC Hathurusingha c Boon b McDermott	2
AP Gurusinha c Healy b McDermott	0
PA De Silva b Dodemaide	58
HP Tillakaratne (+) c Waugh b Dodemaide	82
A Ranatunga (c) c Jones b McDermott	48
ST Jayasuriya c Boon b McDermott	24
CPH Ramanayake not out	15
DK Liyanage c Moody b Dodemaide	4
SD Anurasiri b Dodemaide	0
M Muralidaran	
EXTRAS (LB 8, W 3, NB 5)	16
TOTAL	9 dec 274

FOW 1st Inns: 4 4 111 116 232 234 262 274 274

Bowling: *First Innings*: McDermott 31-6-89-4, Dodemaide 23.5-9-65-4, Moody 3-0-8-0, Matthews 31-8-64-1, Warne 11-3-40-0.

Umpires: BC Cooray & KT Francis

SECOND TEST 1992–93 SRI LANKA v AUSTRALIA
R.Premadasa (Khettarama) Stadium, Colombo. August 28, 29, 30, September 1, 2, 1992.
Toss: Sri Lanka. Match Drawn.

AUSTRALIA

TM Moody c Kaluwitharana b Liyanage	1 (2)	b Muralidaran	54
MA Taylor c Jayasuriya b Hathurusingha	15 (1)	lbw Hathurusingha	26
DC Boon c Jayasuriya b Liyanage	28	c Mahanama b Anurasiri	15
DM Jones lbw Gurusinha	77	not out	100
ME Waugh c Jayasuriya b Ramanayake	0	lbw Muralidaran	0
AR Border (c) b Liyanage	13	lbw Anurasiri	28
GRJ Matthews c Muralidaran b Ramanayake	55	c Mahanama b Anurasiri	51
IA Healy (+) lbw Gurusinha	0	not out	4
CJ McDermott lbw Muralidaran	9		
AIC Dodemaide not out	16		
MR Whitney lbw Ramanayake	1		
EXTRAS (B 10, LB 14, W 2, NB 6)	32	(B 4, LB 9, NB 5)	18
TOTAL	247		6 dec 296

FOW 1st Inns: 1 34 69 72 109 181 183 200 239 247
FOW 2nd Inns: 61 102 104 104 149 280

Bowling: *First Innings*: Ramanayake 23.3-7-64-3, Liyanage 30-10-66-3, Hathurusingha 9-1-26-1, Gurusinha 9-2-18-2, Anurasiri 8-0-17-0, Muralidaran 17-2-32-1. *Second Innings*: Ramanayake 12-0-49-0, Liyanage 13-1-47-0, Hathurusingha 12-4-12-1, Anurasiri 44-11-66-3, Muralidaran 34-7-109-2.

SRI LANKA

RS Mahanama c Moody b Dodemaide	14	lbw McDermott	69
UC Hathurusingha b Moody	67	c Moody b McDermott	49
AP Gurusinha c Healy b Whitney	29	not out	8
PA De Silva c Healy b McDermott	85		
A Ranatunga (c) c (S)DR Martyn b Dodemaide	18		
ST Jayasuriya c Healy b McDermott	19 (4)	not out	1
RS Kaluwitharana (+) c(S)DR Martyn b Border	1		
CPH Ramanayake c Healy b McDermott	8		
DK Liyanage c Healy b McDermott	4		
SD Anurasiri not out	2		
M Muralidaran not out	0		
EXTRAS (LB 6, NB 5)	11	(LB 6, NB 3)	9
TOTAL	9 dec 258		2 for 136

FOW 1st Inns: 26 67 174 211 240 243 243 255 258
FOW 2nd Inns: 110 129

Bowling: *First Innings*: McDermott 20-4-53-4, Whitney 16-1-49-1, Dodemaide 25-4-74-2, Matthews 10-2-20-0, Waugh 4-0-11-0, Moody 6-1-17-1, Border 11-3-28-1. *Second Innings*: McDermott 19-7-32-2, Whitney 5-2-13-0, Matthews 21-5-59-0, Dodemaide 5-2-11-0, Border 4-0-15-0.

Umpires: I Anandappa & WAU Wickremasinghe

Australian Averages

1992–93 SRI LANKA v AUSTRALIA

AUSTRALIA	M	Inn	NO	Runs	H.S	Avrge	Ct	St	Overs	Mds	Runs	Wkt	Avrge
Boon, DC	3	6	-	161	68	26.83	3	-					
Border, AR	3	6	-	243	106	40.50	2	-	19.0	4	51	1	51.00
Dodemaide, AIC	2	3	3	31	16*	-	-	-	53.5	15	150	6	25.00
Healy, IA	3	6	2	202	71	50.50	7	-					
Jones, DM	3	6	1	276	100*	55.20	2	-					
Matthews, GRJ	3	6	-	329	96	54.83	2	-	120.0	28	312	8	39.00
McDermott, CJ	3	4	-	81	40	20.25	-	-	124.0	30	342	14	24.43
Moody, TM	3	6	-	71	54	11.83	3	-	31.0	4	79	1	79.00
Taylor, MA	3	6	-	148	43	24.67	1	-					
Warne, SK	2	3	-	66	35	22.00	1	-	38.1	8	158	3	52.67
Waugh, ME	3	6	-	61	56	10.17	-	-	23.0	3	94	2	47.00
Whitney, MR	2	3	1	24	13	12.00	-	-	58.0	15	159	2	79.50

Sri Lankan Averages

1992–93 SRI LANKA v AUSTRALIA

SRI LANKA	M	Inn	NO	Runs	H.S	Avrge	Ct	St	Overs	Mds	Runs	Wkt	Avrge
Anurasiri, SD	3	3	1	3	2*	1.50	1	-	150.0	23	338	10	33.80
Atapattu, MS	1	2	-	1	1	0.50	-	-	-	-	-	-	-
De Silva, PA	3	4	-	186	85	46.50	1	-	-	-	-	-	-
Gurusinha, AP	3	5	2	205	137	68.33	3	-	15.0	2	55	2	27.50
Hathurusingha, UC	3	5	-	172	67	34.40	-	-	95.0	27	236	8	29.50
Jayasuriya, ST	2	3	-	22	19	11.00	5	-	9.0	1	26	-	-
Kaluwitharana, RS	2	3	1	137	132*	68.50	4	-					
Liyanage, DK	2	2	-	5	4	2.50	-	-	76.0	14	223	8	27.88
Madurasinghe, MAWR	1	2	1	5	5*	5.00	-	-	24.0	2	71	-	-
Mahanama, RS	3	5	-	250	78	50.00	3	-	5.0	-	27	-	-
Muralidaran, M	2	1	1	0	0*	-	1	-	73.1	12	225	4	56.25
Ramanayake, CPH	3	4	1	29	15*	9.67	1	-	145.4	28	434	17	25.53
Ranatunga, A	2	4	-	193	127	48.25	3	-	1.0	-	9	-	-
Tillakaratne, HP	1	1	-	82	82	82.00	3	-	-	-	-	-	-
Wickramasinghe, GP	1	2	-	23	21	11.50	1	-	37.0	4	148	3	49.33

Australia 1–0, poised to down Windies

Melbourne, Dec. 30. Australia is on the threshold of a long-awaited series win over the West Indies after demolishing the tourists in the second Test here today.

The West Indies were lucky to escape with a draw in the first Test, but in this match they were conclusively beaten, as young Victorian Shane Warne put the spotlight on their well-known deficiencies against leg spin. His final day spell of 7/21 brought the West Indies to their knees.

It was also a triumph for captain Allan Border, who was roundly criticised following the first Test indiscretions which saw him fined for violations of the Code of Conduct.

The skipper also pulled out of a batting slump by hitting his 25th Test century and combining with Mark Waugh to rescue the team after it had teetered at 4/115.

The West Indies needed 359 in the fourth innings and looked well placed on the final morning as Phil Simmons and Richie Richardson were in steady command of the attack.

The turning point came 12 minutes before lunch when Shane Warne's flipper removed Richardson and started an irreversible decline.

'It would have to be close to the best I've ever bowled,' he said tonight.

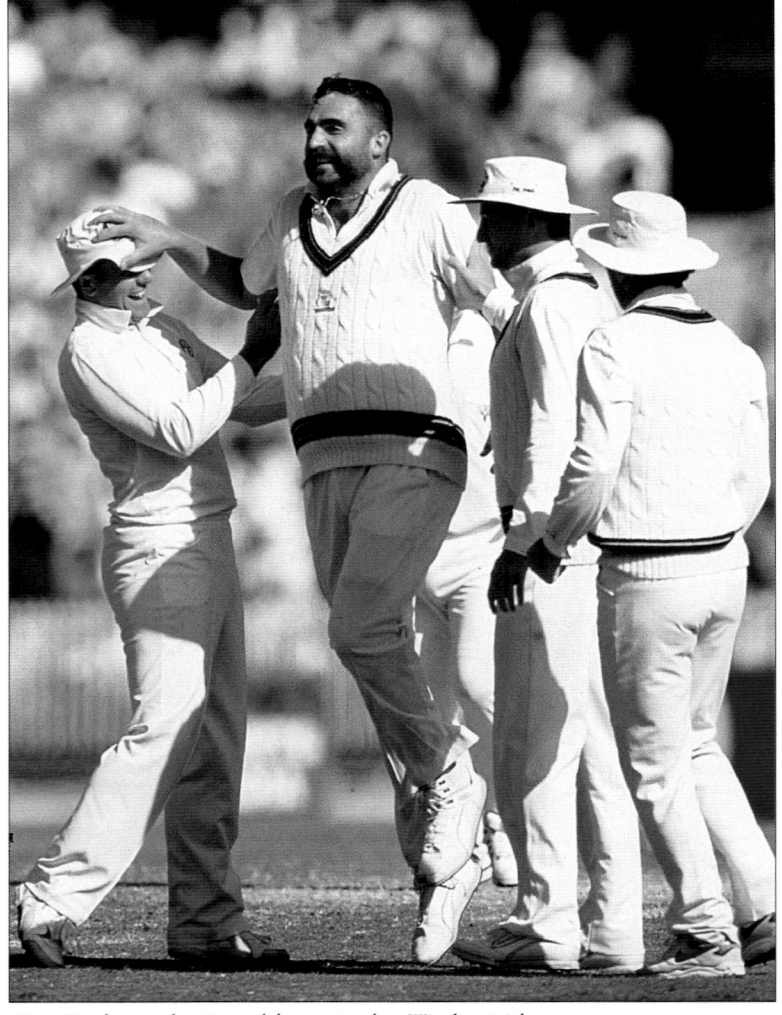

Merv Hughes and mates celebrate another Windies wicket.

Captain's answer is a ton of runs

Melbourne, Dec. 27. Allan Border is at his best when the chips are down, and the Australian skipper has rarely been under as much pressure as he was coming into the second Test match.

Border was reported by umpire Steve Randell for dissent in the first Test match after disputing a disallowed lbw decision against Richie Richardson and pointing to his shin to indicate the ball kept low. Soon after, another clash with Randell added fuel to the fire.

Border showed his disdain by refusing to even attend the disciplinary hearing.

Match referee Raman Subba Row was so furious that he tried to impose a two-match suspension on Border, but was overruled by ICC chairman Sir Colin Cowdrey and Border copped a $2000 fine – the biggest on any player since the code was introduced.

The embattled captain responded by making a gritty century.

Steve Waugh batted at no. 3 and was tested with many short ones.

Shane Warne is new bogey man

Melbourne, Dec. 30. Windies skipper Richie Richardson is trying to play down the destructive efforts of Australia's new leg-spin sensation Shane Warne.

'You have to remember there are a lot of spinners who come in and take a lot of wickets in one match and then you never hear of them again. I don't think our batsmen are afraid of him. We respect him as a Test player, but he's not a worry,' said the West Indian leader.

It is a brave front, but you get the feeling that Warne is more than just a flash in the pan.

The oft-chronicled West Indies dislike for leg spin has reared its head again. Warne's last day spell of 7/21 included the final killer blow of 4/3.

This young man turns the ball prodigiously and to their credit the Australian selectors have stuck by him in the face of media doubts. He has helped his own cause by trimming down in summer training.

Huge scores in drawn third Test

Sydney Jan. 6. A docile Sydney pitch has produced huge scoring in the third Test, which predictably ended in a draw today.

The batting paradise has played the West Indies back into form just when it seemed that the series was sliding away from them.

Australia followed its big first innings of 9/503 declared by bundling out openers Phil Simmons and Desmond Haynes with just 31 on the board.

Standing on the precipice, Richie Richardson and the fast-emerging Brian Lara pulled the side back from the brink with Lara racing to his maiden Test century off just 125 balls in just his fifth Test appearance. He finished with 277.

Their stand of 293 turned the game and the trend of the series. Richardson paid compliments to Lara's knock by saying he could hardly remember his own century: 'It was difficult playing and being a spectator at the same time.'

Three umpires to ease the strain

Melbourne, Sep. 24. The Australian Cricket Board has addressed the problem of umpires coming under too much pressure in first class games by announcing that in the 1992–93 season three umpires will officiate at all State matches, each one controlling two sessions instead of three.

Richie Benaud was critical of the campaign for the use of a 'third' or 'video' umpire in Test matches, on the grounds that it would breed lazy umpiring, was costly and was unfair if not used for all decisions.

In the first one day final Dean Jones objected to the wristband on Curtly Ambrose's bowling arm. Ambrose fired up and took 5/32. Jones made 13.

Australia Day showdown in Adelaide

Australian physiotherapist Errol Alcott and Dr Donald Beard persuade a reluctant David Boon to leave the Adelaide Oval.

Adelaide, Jan. 26. One of the most gripping Test matches of all time ended here today with the West Indies winning by a solitary run – the narrowest victory by any team in Test history.

Only the two tied Tests in Australia and India have been closer than this enthralling match, which had the whole of Australia on the edge of its seat on this Australia Day holiday.

The nation stopped as Australia's batsmen inched towards victory, and TV ratings reached an all-time high.

Australia had the whole of the last day to make 186 for the win that would have ended the West Indies' 13-year domination of world cricket, but in a low-scoring match this was a formidable total.

When Merv Hughes was dismissed just after lunch on the fourth day Australia was 7/74 and seemingly finished. In that period Curtly Ambrose was in rampant mood and mowed down the Australians as four wickets fell in the space of half an hour.

Courageous batting by debutant Justin Langer was the cornerstone of the Australian innings. When he was dismissed for 54 he had batted staunchly for a touch over four hours. It was little consolation to him that only one player had compiled a bigger innings in the match because Australia was 9/144. The 42 runs still required had assumed Everest-like proportions.

Tim May, already an unlikely hero with figures of 5/9 the previous day, now combined with no. 11 Craig McDermott – the man whose batting courage had been questioned by the West Indians.

Ambrose and Bishop were warned for intimidatory bowling as the gallant Aussies soldiered on to the strains of the crowd singing Waltzing Matilda.

With just two needed for victory McDermott swivelled and faintly gloved – according to the umpire but not to millions of TV viewers – a Walsh delivery to 'keeper Murray. Abject misery for the Aussies, unbridled joy for the West Indians.

Sponsorship issue is a smoking gun

Canberra, March 31. The controversial sponsorship of cricket by the Benson and Hedges company will continue to the end of March 1996, but it is in doubt after that.

The Federal Government's tough anti-smoking stance has meant that tobacco and alcohol sponsorship of sporting events is in jeopardy.

The Australian Cricket Board sought assurance that the sponsorship would be allowed to run its term, and was relieved to know that the income will be enabled to flow.

Dressed for success: the winning NSW team poses in period costume for the Sheffield Shield Centenary.

Australia skittled in Perth

Perth, Feb. 1. After its courageous showing in the fourth Test, Australia has been blown away by awesome West Indian fast bowling in Perth.

The game finished just before lunch today – only the third scheduled day of the game.

Australia had no answer to the savage bowling of Curtly Ambrose, who has been a different man since being riled by Dean Jones' complaint about his sweatband in a one day match.

The complaint about the wristband being a distraction may have been legitimate, but Jones' fellow Australian batsmen are all wishing that he had kept his mouth shut.

With the assistance of the famous 'Fremantle Doctor' Ambrose skittled seven Aussies for just one run in the space of 31 balls. Australia went from 2/85 to all out 119. At stumps on the first day the West Indies were 1/135.

Australia worked hard in the field to try and save face, but when it came to their second turn to bat they were again humbled, this time by Ian Bishop.

Australia's nemesis: Curtly Ambrose.

Umpires sue

Perth, Oct. 12. Umpires Terry Prue and Peter McConnell have been awarded $25,000 each by Perth's Supreme Court after sueing the Sydney newspaper the *Sunday Telegraph Mirror*.

In a January 1992 article headed 'Aussie Cheats', the paper accused them of bias and detailed the views of India's Sunil Gavaskar, who said that the pair had made biased decisions in favour of Australia in the series against India.

McConnell told the court he had retired from umpiring 'because of the distress caused by the report'.

More Tests claims

Melbourne, April 1. Melbourne and Sydney are lobbying hard to get more Test matches played in their cities in preference to other states.

Although this makes sense on financial grounds it is sure to ignite the anger of the other states.

Poor Test match attendances in Brisbane and Perth have been a big concern for the ACB. The gulf in attendances is illustrated by the fact that just 31,749 people saw the whole five days of the Brisbane Test, but 49,414 turned up for the first day of the next Test in Melbourne.

NSW players celebrate their defeat of Queensland at the SCG on March 30.

FIRST TEST 1992–93 AUSTRALIA v WEST INDIES
Brisbane Cricket Ground, Brisbane. November 27, 28, 29, 30, December 1, 1992.
Toss: Australia. Match Drawn.

AUSTRALIA

MA Taylor c Williams b Bishop	.7 (2)	c Williams b Walsh	.34
DC Boon c Simmons b Hooper	.48 (1)	c Arthurton b Bishop	.111
SR Waugh c Williams b Ambrose	.10	c Williams b Ambrose	.20
ME Waugh c & b Hooper	.39	c Haynes b Ambrose	.60
DR Martyn c Lara b Ambrose	.36	lbw Ambrose	.15
AR Border (c) run out	.73	c Williams b Walsh	.17
GRJ Matthews c Arthurton b Bishop	.30	lbw Ambrose	.0
IA Healy (+) c Lara b Hooper	.17	c Williams b Bishop	.18
MG Hughes c Bishop b Hooper	.10	c Williams b Ambrose	.1
CJ McDermott c Hooper b Patterson	.3	not out	.16
BA Reid not out	.1	c Richardson b Hooper	.1
EXTRAS (B 3, LB 4, NB 12)	.19	(B 4, LB 2, NB 9)	.15
TOTAL	.293		.308

FOW 1st Inns: 8 21 88 125 180 252 264 285 288 293
FOW 2nd Inns: 64 114 224 250 255 255 280 287 295 308

Bowling: *First Innings*: Ambrose 29.1-12-53-2, Bishop 23-3-51-2, Patterson 19-0-83-1, Walsh 0.5-0-2-0, Hooper 30.1-4-75-4, Simmons 7-2-16-0, Arthurton 3-0-6-0. *Second Innings*: Ambrose 32-8-66-5, Bishop 27-6-58-2, Hooper 28.2-8-63-1, Walsh 24-3-64-2, Patterson 7-0-44-0, Arthurton 1-0-2-0, Simmons 1-0-5-0.

WEST INDIES

DL Haynes c Taylor b Reid	.8	c Healy b McDermott	.1
PV Simmons b Reid	.27	c Healy b Reid	.1
RB Richardson (c) c Matthews b Hughes	.17	c Healy b Hughes	.66
BC Lara st Healy b Matthews	.58	c Taylor b McDermott	.0
KLT Arthurton not out	.157	b McDermott	.0
CL Hooper b SR Waugh	.47	c Boon b Matthews	.32
D Williams (+) c Hughes b Reid	.15	lbw McDermott	.0
IR Bishop b McDermott	.5	not out	.16
CEL Ambrose lbw Reid	.4	c Hughes b Reid	.4
BP Patterson c ME Waugh b Reid	.0		
CA Walsh b Hughes	.17 (10)	not out	.0
EXTRAS (LB 6, NB 10)	.16	(LB 7, NB 6)	.13
TOTAL	.371		.8 for 133

FOW 1st Inns: 25 50 58 170 265 293 307 321 331 371
FOW 2nd Inns: 2 2 3 9 95 96 123 128

Bowling: *First Innings*: McDermott 25-4-93-1, Reid 37-2-112-5, Hughes 18.3-3-58-2, Matthews 27-12-41-1, Border 1-0-7-0, SR Waugh 14-2-46-1, ME Waugh 2-0-8-0. *Second Innings*: McDermott 18-7-35-4, Reid 16-7-39-2, Hughes 13-4-28-1, Matthews 13-4-18-1, SR Waugh 5-2-6-0.

Umpires: TA Prue & SG Randell

SECOND TEST 1992–93 AUSTRALIA v WEST INDIES
Melbourne Cricket Ground, Melbourne. December 26, 27, 28, 29, 30, 1992.
Toss: Australia. Australia won by 139 runs.

AUSTRALIA

DC Boon c Williams b Walsh	.46 (2)	b Simmons	.11
MA Taylor c Lara b Walsh	.13 (1)	b Bishop	.42
SR Waugh c Lara b Ambrose	.38 (4)	c Simmons b Bishop	.1
ME Waugh c Williams b Ambrose	.112 (5)	c Adams b Walsh	.16
DR Martyn c Simmons b Ambrose	.7 (6)	not out	.67
AR Border (c) c Williams b Bishop	.110 (7)	b Bishop	.4
IA Healy (+) c Hooper b Walsh	.24 (8)	c & b Walsh	.8
MG Hughes not out	.9 (9)	c Williams b Ambrose	.15
SK Warne c Adams b Bishop	.1 (3)	c Arthurton b Ambrose	.5
CJ McDermott b Walsh	.17	c Arthurton b Simmons	.4
MR Whitney lbw Bishop	.0	run out	.13
EXTRAS (LB 14, W 1, NB 3)	.18	(B 1, LB 8, NB 1)	.10
TOTAL	.395		.196

FOW 1st Inns: 38 100 104 115 319 362 366 369 394 395
FOW 2nd Inns: 22 40 41 73 90 102 121 154 167 196

Bowling: *First Innings*: Ambrose 35-10-70-3, Bishop 29-2-84-3, Simmons 10-2-23-0, Walsh 39-10-91-4, Hooper 36-3-95-0, Adams 4-0-18-0. *Second Innings*: Ambrose 30-9-57-2, Bishop 20-5-45-3, Walsh 21-7-42-2, Simmons 18-6-34-2, Hooper 2.4-1-9-0.

WEST INDIES

DL Haynes b Hughes	.7	c Healy b Hughes	.5
PV Simmons c Boon b Hughes	.6	c Boon b Warne	.110
RB Richardson (c) c Healy b Hughes	.15	b Warne	.52
BC Lara lbw Whitney	.52	c Boon b Whitney	.4
KLT Arthurton c Healy b McDermott	.71	st Healy b Warne	.13
CL Hooper c & b SR Waugh	.3	c Whitney b Warne	.0
JC Adams c Boon b McDermott	.47	c Taylor b McDermott	.16
D Williams (+) c Healy b McDermott	.0	c ME Waugh b Warne	.0
IR Bishop b McDermott	.9	c Taylor b Warne	.7
CEL Ambrose c McDermott b Warne	.7	not out	.6
CA Walsh not out	.0	c Hughes b Warne	.0
EXTRAS (LB 10, NB 6)	.16	(B 3, LB 2, NB 1)	.6
TOTAL	.233		.219

FOW 1st Inns: 11 28 33 139 144 192 192 206 233 233
FOW 2nd Inns: 9 143 148 165 177 198 206 206 219 219

Bowling: *First Innings*: McDermott 25.1-8-66-4, Hughes 19-5-51-3, Whitney 13-4-27-1, Warne 24-7-65-1, SR Waugh 4-1-14-1. *Second Innings*: McDermott 17-2-66-1, Hughes 18-7-41-1, Whitney 10-2-32-1, Warne 23.2-8-52-7, ME Waugh 3-0-23-0.

Umpires: SG Randell & CD Timmins

THIRD TEST 1992-93 AUSTRALIA v WEST INDIES
Sydney Cricket Ground, Sydney. January 2, 3, 4, 5, 6, 1993.
Toss: Australia. Match Drawn.

AUSTRALIA

DC Boon c Murray b Adams 76	(2)	not out 63	
MA Taylor c Murray b Bishop 20	(1)	not out 46	
SR Waugh c Simmons b Ambrose 100			
ME Waugh run out 57			
DR Martyn b Ambrose 0			
AR Border (c) c Murray b Hooper 74			
GRJ Matthews c Murray b Hooper 79			
IA Healy (+) not out 36			
MG Hughes c Haynes b Bishop 17			
SK Warne c Simmons b Hooper 14			
CJ McDermott			
EXTRAS (B 2, LB 23, NB 5) 30		(B 1, LB 2, NB 5) 8	
TOTAL .....9 dec 503		.....0 for 117	

FOW 1st Inns: 42 160 254 261 270 425 440 469 503
FOW 2nd Inns:

Bowling: *First Innings*: Ambrose 35-8-87-2, Bishop 36-6-87-2, Walsh 30-8-86-0, Hooper 45.4-6-137-3, Adams 15-2-56-1, Simmons 10-2-25-0. *Second Innings*: Ambrose 6-2-10-0, Bishop 4-1-9-0, Simmons 3-2-9-0, Walsh 8-3-13-0, Hooper 10-2-22-0, Adams 8-1-29-0, Arthurton 5-1-14-0, Lara 2-0-4-0, Richardson 1-0-4-0.

WEST INDIES

DL Haynes b Matthews 22	
PV Simmons c Taylor b McDermott 3	
RB Richardson (c) c Warne b Hughes 109	
BC Lara run out 277	
KLT Arthurton c Healy b Matthews 47	
CL Hooper b Warne 21	
JC Adams not out 77	
JR Murray (+) c Healy b Hughes 11	
IR Bishop run out 1	
CEL Ambrose c Martyn b ME Waugh 16	
CA Walsh c Healy b Hughes 0	
EXTRAS (B 4, LB 9, W 1, NB 8) 22	
TOTAL 606	

FOW 1st Inns: 13 31 324 448 481 537 573 577 603 606

Bowling: *First Innings*: McDermott 33-3-119-1, Hughes 16.4-1-76-3, Matthews 59-12-169-2, SR Waugh 11-1-43-0, Warne 41-6-116-1, Border 14-1-41-0, ME Waugh 10-1-29-1.

Umpires: DB Hair & TA Prue

FIFTH TEST 1992-93 AUSTRALIA v WEST INDIES
W.A.C.A. Ground, Perth. January 30, 31, February 1, 1993.
Toss: Australia. West Indies won by an innings & 25 runs.

AUSTRALIA

DC Boon c Richardson b Ambrose 44		b Bishop 52	
JL Langer c Murray b Bishop 10		c (S)AL Logie b Ambrose 1	
SR Waugh c Murray b Bishop 13		c (S)AL Logie b Bishop 0	
ME Waugh c Murray b Ambrose 9		c Richardson b Bishop 21	
DR Martyn c Simmons b Ambrose 13	(6)	c Ambrose b Cummins 31	
AR Border (c) c Murray b Ambrose 0	(7)	b Bishop 0	
IA Healy (+) c Lara b Ambrose 0	(8)	c Murray b Bishop 27	
MG Hughes c Arthurton b Ambrose 0	(9)	c Murray b Walsh 22	
SK Warne run out 13	(5)	c Murray b Ambrose 0	
J Angel c Murray b Ambrose 0		not out 4	
CJ McDermott not out 2		c Lara b Bishop 8	
EXTRAS (LB 8, W 1, NB 6) 15		(B 1, LB 6, NB 5) 12	
TOTAL 119		178	

FOW 1st Inns: 27 58 85 90 90 100 102 104 104 119
FOW 2nd Inns: 13 14 66 67 95 95 130 162 170 178

Bowling: *First Innings*: Ambrose 18-9-25-7, Bishop 11-6-17-2, Walsh 11.2-2-45-0, Cummins 7-0-24-0. *Second Innings*: Ambrose 21-8-54-2, Bishop 16-4-40-6, Walsh 12-2-46-1, Cummins 8-3-31-1.

WEST INDIES

DL Haynes c Healy b Hughes 24	
PV Simmons c SR Waugh b Angel 80	
RB Richardson (c) c Langer b McDermott 47	
BC Lara c Warne b McDermott 16	
KLT Arthurton c SR Waugh b McDermott 77	
JC Adams b Hughes 8	
JR Murray (+) c Healy b ME Waugh 37	
IR Bishop c Healy b ME Waugh 0	
AC Cummins c ME Waugh b Hughes 3	
CEL Ambrose not out 9	
CA Walsh b Hughes 1	
EXTRAS (B 4, LB 10, NB 6) 20	
TOTAL 322	

FOW 1st Inns: 111 136 184 195 205 280 286 301 319 322

Bowling: *First Innings*: McDermott 22-4-85-3, Hughes 25.4-6-71-4, Angel 19-4-72-1, Warne 12-0-51-0, SR Waugh 6-3-8-0, ME Waugh 6-1-21-2.

Umpires: SG Randell & CD Timmins

FOURTH TEST 1992-93 AUSTRALIA v WEST INDIES
Adelaide Oval, Adelaide. January 23, 24, 25, 26, 1993.
Toss: West Indies. West Indies won by 1 run.

WEST INDIES

DL Haynes st Healy b May 45	c Healy b McDermott 11	
PV Simmons c Hughes b SR Waugh 46	b McDermott 10	
RB Richardson (c) lbw Hughes 2	c Healy b Warne 72	
BC Lara c Healy b McDermott 52	c SR Waugh b Hughes 7	
KLT Arthurton c SR Waugh b May 0	c Healy b McDermott 0	
CL Hooper c Healy b Hughes 2	c Hughes b May 25	
JR Murray (+) not out 49	c ME Waugh b May 0	
IR Bishop c ME Waugh b Hughes 13	c ME Waugh b May 6	
CEL Ambrose c Healy b Hughes 0	st Healy b May 1	
KCG Benjamin c ME Waugh b ME Waugh 15	c Warne b May 0	
CA Walsh lbw Hughes 5	not out 0	
EXTRAS (LB 11, NB 12) 23	(LB 2, NB 12) 14	
TOTAL 252	146	

FOW 1st Inns: 84 99 129 130 134 189 206 206 247 252
FOW 2nd Inns: 14 49 63 65 124 137 145 146 146 146

Bowling: *First Innings*: McDermott 16-1-85-1, Hughes 21.3-3-64-5, SR Waugh 13-4-37-1, May 14-1-41-2, Warne 2-0-11-0, ME Waugh 1-0-3-1. *Second Innings*: McDermott 11-0-66-3, Hughes 13-1-43-1, SR Waugh 5-1-8-0, May 6.5-3-9-5, Warne 6-2-18-1.

AUSTRALIA

MA Taylor c Hooper b Bishop 1	(2)	c Murray b Benjamin 7
DC Boon not out 39	(1)	lbw Ambrose 0
JL Langer c Murray b Benjamin 20		c Murray b Bishop 54
ME Waugh c Simmons b Ambrose 0		c Hooper b Walsh 26
SR Waugh c Murray b Ambrose 42		c Arthurton b Ambrose 1
AR Border (c) c Hooper b Ambrose 19		c Haynes b Ambrose 1
IA Healy (+) c Hooper b Ambrose 0		b Walsh 0
MG Hughes c Murray b Hooper 43		lbw Ambrose 0
SK Warne lbw Hooper 0		lbw Bishop 9
TBA May c Murray b Ambrose 6		not out 42
CJ McDermott b Ambrose 14		c Murray b Walsh 18
EXTRAS (B 7, LB 3, NB 19) 29		(B 1, LB 8, NB 13) 22
TOTAL 213		184

FOW 1st Inns: 1 16 46 108 108 112 181 181 197 213
FOW 2nd Inns: 5 16 54 64 72 73 74 102 144 184

Bowling: *First Innings*: Ambrose 28.2-6-74-6, Bishop 18-3-48-1, Benjamin 6-0-22-1, Walsh 10-3-34-0, Hooper 13-4-25-2. *Second Innings*: Ambrose 26-5-46-4, Bishop 17-3-41-2, Benjamin 12-2-32-1, Walsh 19-4-44-3, Hooper 5-1-12-0.

Umpires: DB Hair & LJ King

Australian Averages

1992-93 AUSTRALIA v WEST INDIES

AUSTRALIA	M	Inn	NO	Runs	H.S	Avrge	Ct	St	Overs	Mds	Runs	Wkt	Avrge
Angel, J	1	2	1	4	4*	4.00	-	-	19.0	4	72	1	72.00
Boon, DC	5	10	2	490	111	61.25	5	-	-	-	-	-	-
Border, AR	5	9	-	298	110	33.11	-	-	15.0	1	48	-	-
Healy, IA	5	9	1	130	36*	16.25	19	4	-	-	-	-	-
Hughes, MG	5	9	1	118	43	14.75	5	-	145.2	30	432	20	21.60
Langer, JL	2	4	-	85	54	21.25	1	-	-	-	-	-	-
Martyn, DR	4	7	1	169	67*	28.17	1	-	-	-	-	-	-
Matthews, GRJ	2	3	-	109	79	36.33	1	-	99.0	28	228	4	57.00
May, TBA	1	2	1	48	42*	48.00	-	-	20.5	4	50	7	7.14
McDermott, CJ	5	8	2	82	18	13.67	1	-	167.1	29	615	18	34.17
Reid, BA	1	2	1	2	1*	2.00	-	-	53.0	9	151	7	21.57
Taylor, MA	4	8	1	170	46*	24.29	5	-	-	-	-	-	-
Warne, SK	4	7	-	42	14	6.00	3	-	108.2	23	313	10	31.30
Waugh, ME	5	9	-	340	112	37.78	6	-	22.0	2	84	4	21.00
Waugh, SR	5	9	-	228	100	25.33	5	-	58.0	14	162	3	54.00
Whitney, MR	1	2	-	13	13	6.50	1	-	23.0	6	59	2	29.50

West Indian Averages

1992-93 AUSTRALIA v WEST INDIES

WEST INDIES	M	Inn	NO	Runs	H.S	Avrge	Ct	St	Overs	Mds	Runs	Wkt	Avrge
Adams, JC	3	4	1	148	77*	49.33	2	-	27.0	3	103	1	103.00
Ambrose, CEL	5	8	2	47	16	7.83	1	-	260.3	77	542	33	16.42
Arthurton, KLT	5	8	1	365	157*	52.14	6	-	9.0	1	22	-	-
Benjamin, KCG	1	2	-	15	15	7.50	-	-	18.0	2	54	2	27.00
Bishop, IR	5	8	1	57	16*	8.14	1	-	201.0	39	480	23	20.87
Cummins, AC	1	1	-	3	3	3.00	-	-	15.0	3	55	1	55.00
Haynes, DL	5	8	-	123	45	15.38	3	-	-	-	-	-	-
Hooper, CL	4	7	-	130	47	18.57	7	-	170.5	29	438	10	43.80
Lara, BC	5	8	-	466	277	58.25	6	-	2.0	-	4	-	-
Murray, JR	3	4	1	97	49*	32.33	19	-	-	-	-	-	-
Patterson, BP	1	1	-	0	0	0.00	-	-	26.0	-	127	1	127.00
Richardson, RB	5	8	-	380	109	47.50	3	-	1.0	-	4	-	-
Simmons, PV	5	8	-	283	110	35.38	7	-	49.0	14	112	2	56.00
Walsh, CA	5	8	4	23	17	4.60	1	-	175.1	42	467	12	38.92
Williams, D	2	4	-	15	15	3.75	11	-	-	-	-	-	-

Border passes a mighty milestone

Christchurch, Feb. 28. When Australian captain Allan Border pulled a ball from Rashid Patel for four to reach 50 on day two of the first Test against New Zealand at Lancaster Park, he became the highest run-scorer in Test history.

His score of 88 took his tally to 10,161 – 39 more than Indian opener Sunil Gavaskar, who quit Test cricket in 1986 with 10,122 runs beside his name from 214 innings. Border overtook him in his 240th knock. Sir Donald Bradman was quick to congratulate Border on his achievement.

The record his, Border sat back and watched his team rattle up a first-innings score of 485, which

Another ton: Allan Border's 25th.

surprisingly contained not one century, Border's 88 being top score. Solid in support were Mark Taylor (82), Justin Langer (63) and Steve Waugh (62).

Having put Australia in on a wet pitch, the Kiwis suffered the ignominy of making only 182 and 243, giving Australia victory by an innings and 60 runs, its first win over NZ since 1981–82.

Leg-spinner Shane Warne, in only his eighth Test, earned the Man of the Match award for figures of 3/21 and 4/63, and 22 not out. Merv Hughes also did well, with match figures of 6/106 and 45 runs.

Ken Rutherford's second-innings 102 was a bright spot for NZ.

NZ retains Trophy

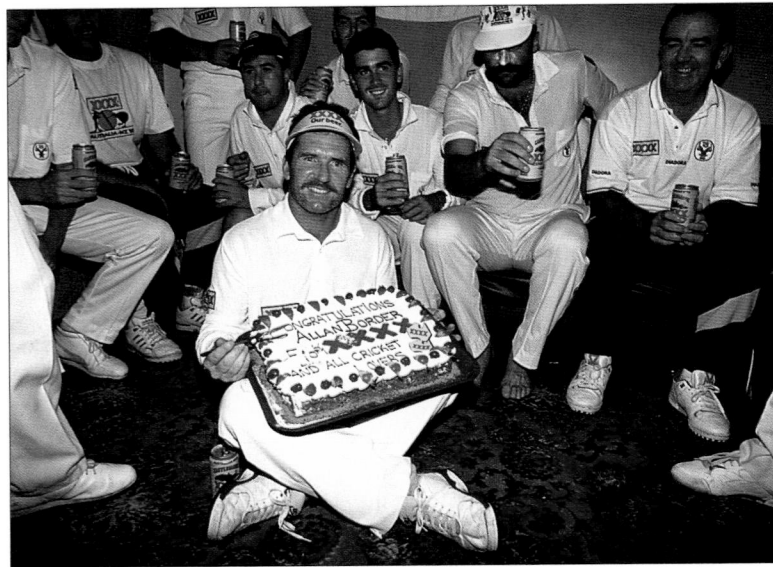

The Australians: good start, poor finish.

Auckland, March 16. With a much-improved showing, New Zealand has retained the Trans-Tasman trophy, defeating Australia by five wickets in the third Test at Eden Park.

The win enabled the home side to level the series at 1–all after the second Test in Wellington had been drawn.

Australia effectively lost the Eden Park match on the first day, nose-diving to 9/139 in conditions that favoured the swing bowling of Danny Morrison. On day two, Australia did not add to its score, Morrison wrapping up the innings and finishing with 6/37 off 18.4 overs. Only Steve Waugh (41) and Merv Hughes (33) scored over 20.

New Zealand also made heavy going of it, after openers John Wright (33) and Mark Greatbatch (32) had put on 60. Persistent bowling by Craig McDermott (2/50), Merv Hughes (3/67) and Shane Warne (4/8 off 15 overs) restricted NZ to 224, a lead of 85. Solid contributions from Ken Rutherford (43) and skipper Martin Crowe (31) saved NZ from total collapse.

With Damien Martyn (74) and Allan Border (71) showing the way, Australia scored 285 in its second innings, giving the Kiwis a victory target of 201.

By stumps on the fourth day they had wiped off 168 of them for the loss of five wickets, Warne having two scalps, including Crowe for 25.

But if Australia thought it might snatch victory it was to be disappointed. Before a crowd of 10,000, which gained free entry, New Zealand knocked off the remaining 33 runs in 29 minutes without any further loss. Rutherford scored a delightful 53 not out in the five-wicket win.

Some people have to take the blame – who better than the selectors

FIRST TEST 1992–93 NEW ZEALAND v AUSTRALIA
Lancaster Park, Christchurch. February 25, 26, 27, 28, 1993.
Toss: New Zealand. Australia won by an innings & 60 runs.

AUSTRALIA

DC Boon c Parore b Owens	.15
MA Taylor c Crowe b Morrison	.82
JL Langer lbw Morrison	.63
ME Waugh c Parore b Patel	.13
SR Waugh lbw Owens	.62
AR Border (c) c Parore b Morrison	.88
IA Healy (+) c Morrison b Owens	.54
MG Hughes c Cairns b Patel	.45
PR Reiffel c Greatbatch b Su'a	.18
SK Warne not out	.22
CJ McDermott c Jones b Cairns	.4
EXTRAS (B 2, LB 6, W 5, NB 6)	.19
TOTAL	.485

FOW 1st Inns: 33 149 170 217 264 363 435 441 480 485

Bowling: *First Innings*: Morrison 36-11-81-3, Su'a 33-5-106-1, Cairns 31.3-9-87-1, Owens 26-9-58-3, Patel 31-3-145-2.

NEW ZEALAND

MJ Greatbatch c Healy b McDermott	.4	c Reiffel b Hughes	.0
JG Wright lbw Warne	.39	b McDermott	.14
AH Jones lbw McDermott	.8	c Border b McDermott	.10
MD Crowe (c) c Taylor b Hughes	.15	lbw Hughes	.14
KR Rutherford b Warne	.57	c Healy b Warne	.102
CL Cairns c Boon b McDermott	.1	c Taylor b Warne	.21
AC Parore (+) c Boon b Reiffel	.6	c Boon b Warne	.5
DN Patel c McDermott b Hughes	.35	b Warne	.8
ML Su'a c Healy b Reiffel	.0	b Hughes	.44
DK Morrison not out	.4	c Healy b Hughes	.19
MB Owens lbw Warne	.0	not out	.0
EXTRAS (B 2, LB 4, W 4, NB 4)	.14	(LB 2, NB 4)	.6
TOTAL	.182		.243

FOW 1st Inns: 4 18 53 124 128 138 150 152 181 182
FOW 2nd Inns: 0 19 24 51 92 110 144 190 242 243

Bowling: *First Innings*: McDermott 21-4-73-3, Hughes 21-10-44-2, Reiffel 18-8-27-2, SR Waugh 4-2-9-0, Warne 22-12-23-3. *Second Innings*: Hughes 24.5-6-62-4, McDermott 19-6-45-2, Reiffel 18-3-59-0, SR Waugh 2-2-0-0, Warne 26-7-63-4, ME Waugh 5-1-12-0.

Umpires: BL Aldridge & CE King

SECOND TEST 1992–93 NEW ZEALAND v AUSTRALIA
Basin Reserve, Wellington. March 4, 5, 6, 7, 8, 1993.
Toss: Australia. Match Drawn.

NEW ZEALAND

MJ Greatbatch c Taylor b Reiffel	.61	b McDermott	.0
JG Wright c Healy b Hughes	.72	(6) not out	.46
AH Jones b Reiffel	.4	(2) lbw Warne	.42
MD Crowe (c) b McDermott	.98	(3) lbw McDermott	.3
KR Rutherford c Healy b Hughes	.32	(4) c Healy b Reiffel	.11
TE Blain (+) b Hughes	.1	(5) c Healy b Warne	.51
CL Cairns c Border b McDermott	.13	lbw McDermott	.14
DN Patel not out	.13	c Healy b ME Waugh	.25
DK Morrison c Warne b McDermott	.2	not out	.0
W Watson c Taylor b Warne	.3		
MB Owens b Warne	.0		
EXTRAS (B 7, LB 11, W 2, NB 10)	.30	(B 8, LB 8, W 1, NB 1)	.18
TOTAL	.329		.7 for 210

FOW 1st Inns: 111 120 191 287 289 307 308 314 329 329
FOW 2nd Inns: 4 9 30 101 131 154 202

Bowling: *First Innings*: McDermott 31-8-66-3, Hughes 35-9-100-3, Reiffel 23-8-55-2, SR Waugh 15-7-28-0, Warne 29-9-59-2, ME Waugh 2-1-3-0. *Second Innings*: McDermott 23-9-54-3, Hughes 11-5-22-0, Warne 40-25-49-2, Reiffel 16-7-27-1, Border 12-5-15-0, ME Waugh 8-3-12-1, Taylor 4-2-15-0, Boon 1-1-0-0.

AUSTRALIA

MA Taylor run out	.50
DC Boon c & b Morrison	.37
JL Langer c Blain b Watson	.24
ME Waugh c & b Owens	.12
SR Waugh c Blain b Morrison	.75
AR Border (c) lbw Morrison	.30
IA Healy (+) c Rutherford b Morrison	.8
MG Hughes c Wright b Morrison	.8
PR Reiffel lbw Morrison	.7
SK Warne c Greatbatch b Morrison	.22
CJ McDermott not out	.7
EXTRAS (LB 14, NB 4)	.18
TOTAL	.298

FOW 1st Inns: 92 105 128 154 229 237 251 258 271 298

Bowling: *First Innings*: Morrison 26.4-5-89-7, Cairns 24-3-77-0, Watson 29-12-60-1, Owens 21-3-54-1, Patel 1-0-4-0.

Umpires: BL Aldridge & RS Dunne

THIRD TEST 1992–93 NEW ZEALAND v AUSTRALIA
Eden Park, Auckland. March 12, 13, 14, 15, 16, 1993.
Toss: Australia. New Zealand won by 5 wkts.

AUSTRALIA

DC Boon lbw Watson	.20 (2)	lbw Su'a	.53
MA Taylor lbw Morrison	.13 (1)	st Blain b Patel	.3
JL Langer c Blain b Morrison	.0	lbw Patel	.0
DR Martyn c Blain b Watson	.1	c Greatbatch b Patel	.74
SR Waugh c Jones b Watson	.41	lbw Patel	.0
AR Border (c) c Blain b Morrison	.0	c Harris b Watson	.71
IA Healy (+) c Jones b Morrison	.0	c Blain b Patel	.24
MG Hughes c Morrison b Patel	.33	not out	.31
PR Reiffel c Blain b Morrison	.9	b Watson	.1
SK Warne not out	.3	c Jones b Morrison	.2
CJ McDermott b Morrison	.6	c Wright b Watson	.10
EXTRAS (LB 7, NB 6)	.13	(B 1, LB 7, NB 8)	.16
TOTAL	.139		.285

FOW 1st Inns: 38 38 39 39 43 48 101 121 133 139
FOW 2nd Inns: 5 8 115 119 160 225 261 271 274 285

Bowling: *First Innings*: Morrison 18.4-5-37-6, Su'a 14-3-27-0, Watson 19-9-47-3, Patel 4-0-21-1. *Second Innings*: Morrison 33-8-81-1, Patel 34-10-93-5, Watson 19-5-43-3, Su'a 18-4-56-1, Harris 2-1-4-0.

NEW ZEALAND

JG Wright c Taylor b McDermott	.33	run out	.33
MJ Greatbatch c Border b Hughes	.32	b Hughes	.29
AH Jones c Healy b Hughes	.20	b Warne	.26
MD Crowe (c) c Taylor b SR Waugh	.31	c Langer b Warne	.25
KR Rutherford st Healy b Warne	.43	not out	.53
CZ Harris c Taylor b Warne	.13	lbw SR Waugh	.0
TE Blain (+) c Healy b McDermott	.15	not out	.24
DN Patel c Healy b Warne	.2		
ML Su'a c SR Waugh b Warne	.3		
DK Morrison not out	.10		
W Watson lbw Hughes	.0		
EXTRAS (B 7, LB 10, NB 5)	.22	(LB 10, NB 1)	.11
TOTAL	.224		.5 for 201

FOW 1st Inns: 60 91 97 144 178 200 205 206 224 224
FOW 2nd Inns: 44 65 109 129 134

Bowling: *First Innings*: McDermott 19-6-50-2, Hughes 24.5-6-67-3, Reiffel 22-6-63-0, Warne 15-12-8-4, SR Waugh 14-6-19-1, Martyn 1-1-0-0. *Second Innings*: McDermott 12-3-38-0, Hughes 15.4-2-54-1, Reiffel 6-1-19-0, Warne 27-8-54-2, Border 6-3-11-0, SR Waugh 6-1-15-1.

Umpires: BL Aldridge & CE King

Australian Averages

1992–93 NEW ZEALAND v AUSTRALIA

AUSTRALIA	M	Inn	NO	Runs	H.S	Avrge	Ct	St	Overs	Mds	Runs	Wkt	Avrge
Boon, DC	3	4	-	125	53	31.25	3		1.0	1	0	-	-
Border, AR	3	4	-	189	88	47.25	3		18.0	8	26	-	-
Healy, IA	3	4	-	86	54	21.50	12	1					
Hughes, MG	3	4	1	117	45	39.00	-		132.2	38	349	13	26.85
Langer, JL	3	4	-	87	63	21.75	1		-				-
Martyn, DR	1	2	-	75	74	37.50			1.0	1	0	-	-
McDermott, CJ	3	4	1	27	10	9.00	1		125.0	36	326	13	25.08
Reiffel, PR	3	4	-	35	18	8.75	1		103.0	33	250	5	50.00
Taylor, MA	3	4	-	148	82	37.00	7		4.0	2	15	-	-
Warne, SK	3	4	2	49	22*	24.50	1		159.0	73	256	17	15.06
Waugh, ME	2	2	-	25	13	12.50	-		15.0	5	27	1	27.00
Waugh, SR	3	4	-	178	75	44.50	1		41.0	18	71	2	35.50

New Zealand Averages

1992–93 NEW ZEALAND v AUSTRALIA

NEW ZEALAND	M	Inn	NO	Runs	H.S	Avrge	Ct	St	Overs	Mds	Runs	Wkt	Avrge
Blain, TE	2	4	1	91	51	30.33	7	1	-	-	-	-	-
Cairns, CL	2	4	-	48	21	12.00	1	-	55.3	12	164	1	164.00
Crowe, MD	3	6	-	186	98	31.00	1	-	-	-	-	-	-
Greatbatch, MJ	3	6	-	126	61	21.00	0	-	-	-	-	-	-
Harris, CZ	1	2	-	13	13	6.50	1	-	2.0	1	4	-	-
Jones, AH	3	6	-	110	42	18.33	4	-	-	-	-	-	-
Morrison, DK	3	5	3	35	19	17.50	3	-	114.2	29	288	17	16.94
Owens, MB	2	3	1	0	0*	0.00	1	-	47.0	12	112	4	28.00
Parore, AC	1	2	-	11	6	5.50	3	-	-	-	-	-	-
Patel, DN	3	5	1	83	35	20.75	-	-	70.0	13	263	8	32.88
Rutherford, KR	3	6	1	298	102	59.60	1	-	-	-	-	-	-
Su'a, ML	2	3	-	47	44	15.67	-	-	65.0	12	189	2	94.50
Watson, W	2	2	-	3	3	1.50	-	-	67.0	26	150	7	21.43
Wright, JG	3	6	1	237	72	47.40	2	-	-	-	-	-	-

Warne's 'ball from hell'

A startled Mike Gatting is bowled by Shane Warne's 'ball from hell'.

Mike Gatting departs, the master of spin a victim of it.

Manchester, June 7. Mike Gatting, regarded as a master of spin bowling, was just the man to face Shane Warne's first ball in Test cricket in England. Or so it seemed, in the first Ashes clash at Old Trafford.

England, replying to Australia's modest 289, of which opener Mark Taylor made a majestic 124, was 1/80 when the blond-haired Warne, with 31 wickets in 11 Tests and precociously talented for one so young (23), took the ball. Gatting was four not out. Warne's first delivery to him was no loosener. Like a wily veteran, he gave it a vigorous tweak out of the back of his hand. It dipped in the air and was a good 18 inches outside the leg stump when it landed and bounced. In Gatting's eyes, its very width made it harmlesss.

To Gatting's astonishment and the delight of Australians everywhere, it fizzed across his portly frame and clipped the off bail. A bewildered Gatting looked back to confirm his worst fears, then departed to read the next day he had been bowled by a 'ball from hell'.

For Australia, it was heaven-sent. When Warne got Robin Smith four runs later, England was on its way to 210 all out. Warne captured 4/51, and really demonstrated to English cricketers, and indeed everyone, that he has 'arrived' in Test cricket.

'Keeper Ian Healy, after a close-up view of 'that ball', celebrated with a maiden Test century, 102 not out in Australia's second innings of 5/432 dec. Then Warne (4/86) and Hughes (4/92) bowled England out for 332 – skipper Graham Gooch scoring a fine 133. Australia, victor by 179 runs and with Warne on the warpath, is a firm favorite to retain the Ashes.

Border leads Australian conquest

Allan Border: victorious again.

Birmingham, Aug. 9. Allan Border, Test cricket's highest run-scorer, achieved another milestone today when Australia defeated England by eight wickets in the fifth Test.

With one Test to go, at the Oval, his side leads 4–0, a post-war record achieved in England only by Bradman (1948) and Border himself, in 1989. For Australia it has been a series of sound leadership, heavy scoring and the Warne factor, not forgetting fast bowlers Merv Hughes (25 wickets to date) and Paul Reiffel in the absence of Craig McDermott, sent home ill.

In the second Test at Lord's, which Australia won by an innings and 62 runs, Mark Taylor (111), Michael Slater (152) and David Boon (162 not out) enabled Border to declare at 4/632 – Australia's second-highest score at

Michael Slater plays a full-blooded cut shot for 4 on his joyful tour of England.

Lord's. Warne (8/159) and Tim May (6/145) spun England out for 205 and 365.

England introduced four new chums in the drawn third Test at Trent Bridge – Ilott, Lathwell, McCague and Thorpe – and stopped Australia's run of seven straight wins. Warne took his 50th Test wicket.

In the fourth Test at Leeds, Border scored his first double century in England (200 not out), and with Steve Waugh (157 not out) put on an unbroken 332, the second-highest fifth-wicket stand in Tests. With Reiffel's match total of 8/152, Australia won by an innings, to secure the Ashes.

And so to Edgbaston where new

skipper Mike Atherton could not stop England's run of losses, this time by eight wickets. Mark Waugh's 137 was his fourth Test century and Warne's 5/82 in England's second innings gave him 29 wickets for the series, equalling Clarrie Grimmett's record for an Australian leg-spinner in England.

Veteran Gooch ends a captain's agony after crushing defeats

Embattled pair: captain Graham Gooch and coach Keith Fletcher at Lord's.

Leeds, July 26. England captain Graham Gooch, a sterling campaigner, has had enough agony. He has stepped down after 34 Tests as skipper in the wake of Australia's overwhelming win by an innings and 148 runs in the fourth Test here. Australia has retained the Ashes, and leads the rubber 3–0.

The much-criticised England selectors, led by Ted Dexter, have chosen opening batsman Mike Atherton to lead the side at Edgbaston. Gooch will play.

On a personal note, Gooch, who celebrated his 40th birthday during the Leeds massacre, has had a good series with two centuries – 133 at Old Trafford and 120 at Trent Bridge. The England bowling has been the weak link, Australia twice having declared in excess of 600.

The new England captain is given a baptism of fire by Merv Hughes.

England's Test win a reviver

The Oval, Aug. 23. England, with a more penetrating attack, has finally broken the drought, winning the sixth Test at the Oval by a whopping 161 runs.

The victory ended an unprecedented run of 18 matches since England's last win over Australia in 1986–87 in Melbourne. As well, it ended a run of nine defeats in 10 matches inflicted by four countries.

New captain Mike Atherton (50 and 42) and his predecessor Graham Gooch (56 and 79) led from the front, and for only the second time in the series England twice topped 300, scoring 380 and 313. Australia made 303 and 229.

Fast-medium seam bowler Angus Fraser (5/87 and 3/44), recalled to the England team, too late in the eyes of some, bowled beautifully and was named Man of the Match. He received splendid support from two other fresh bowlers, fellow 'quicks' Devon Malcolm and Steve Watkin.

The Australian batting for once lacked sparkle, and suffered one or two dubious decisions – Slater and Border the unlucky bunnies as Australia failed to salvage a draw.

Delight at home over success

Triumphant Aussies.

Sydney, Sep. 10. The triumphant Australian cricketers have been given a rousing reception and a ticker-tape parade on their return home after retaining the Ashes 4–1 against the old foe, England.

For long-serving skipper Allan Border it was his third Ashes win, having prevailed 4–0 in 1989 and 3–0 in 1990–91.

FIRST TEST 1993 ENGLAND v AUSTRALIA
Old Trafford, Manchester. June 3, 4, 5, 6, 7, 1993.
Toss: England. Australia won by 179 runs.

AUSTRALIA

MA Taylor c & b Such	124	(2)	lbw Such	9
MJ Slater c Stewart b DeFreitas	58	(1)	c Caddick b Such	27
DC Boon c Lewis b Such	21		c Gatting b DeFreitas	93
ME Waugh c & b Tufnell	6		b Tufnell	64
AR Border (c) st Stewart b Such	17		c & b Caddick	31
SR Waugh b Such	3		not out	78
IA Healy (+) c Such b Tufnell	12		not out	102
BP Julian c Gatting b Such	0			
MG Hughes c DeFreitas b Such	2			
SK Warne not out	15			
CJ McDermott run out	8			
EXTRAS (B 8, LB 8, NB 7)	23		(B 6, LB 14, NB 8)	28
TOTAL	289			5 dec 432

FOW 1st Inns: 128 183 221 225 232 260 264 266 267 289
FOW 2nd Inns: 23 46 155 234 252

Bowling: *First Innings*: Caddick 15-4-38-0, DeFreitas 23-8-46-1, Lewis 13-2-44-0, Such 33.3-9-67-6, Tufnell 28-5-78-2. *Second Innings*: Caddick 20-3-79-1, DeFreitas 24-1-80-1, Such 31-6-78-2, Tufnell 37-4-112-1, Hick 9-1-20-0, Lewis 9-0-43-0.

ENGLAND

GA Gooch (c) c Julian b Warne	65		handled ball	133
MA Atherton c Healy b Hughes	19		c Taylor b Warne	25
MW Gatting b Warne	4		b Hughes	23
RA Smith c Taylor b Warne	4		b Warne	18
GA Hick c Border b Hughes	34		c Healy b Hughes	22
AJ Stewart (+) b Julian	27		c Healy b Warne	11
CC Lewis c Boon b Hughes	9		c Taylor b Warne	43
PAJ DeFreitas lbw Julian	5		lbw Julian	7
AR Caddick c Healy b Warne	7		c Warne b Hughes	25
PM Such not out	14		c Border b Hughes	9
PCR Tufnell c Healy b Hughes	1		not out	0
EXTRAS (B 6, LB 10, NB 5)	21		(LB 11, W 1, NB 4)	16
TOTAL	210			332

FOW 1st Inns: 71 80 84 123 148 168 178 183 203 210
FOW 2nd Inns: 73 133 171 223 230 238 260 299 331 332

Bowling: *First Innings*: McDermott 18-2-50-0, Hughes 20.5-5-59-4, Julian 11-2-30-2, Warne 24-10-51-4, Border 1-0-4-0. *Second Innings*: McDermott 30-9-76-0, Hughes 27.2-4-92-4, Warne 49-26-86-4, Julian 14-1-67-1.

Umpires: HD Bird & KE Palmer

Australian Averages

1993 ENGLAND v AUSTRALIA

AUSTRALIA	M	Inn	NO	Runs	H.S	Avrge	Ct	St	Overs	Mds	Runs	Wkt	Avrge
Boon, DC	6	10	2	555	164*	69.38	5	-	-	-	-	-	-
Border, AR	6	9	1	433	200*	54.13	8	-	27.0	11	35	1	35.00
Healy, IA	6	7	2	296	102*	59.20	21	5	-	-	-	-	-
Hughes, MG	6	5	-	76	38	15.20	2	-	296.2	78	845	31	27.26
Julian, BP	2	3	1	61	56*	30.50	2	-	82.0	16	291	5	58.20
May, TBA	5	4	2	23	15	11.50	2	-	278.0	90	592	21	28.19
McDermott, CJ	2	1	-	8	8	8.00	-	-	48.0	11	126	-	-
Reiffel, PR	3	3	-	62	42	20.67	1	-	140.4	31	396	19	20.84
Slater, MJ	6	10	-	416	152	41.60	2	-	-	-	-	-	-
Taylor, MA	6	10	-	428	124	42.80	11	-	-	-	-	-	-
Warne, SK	6	5	2	113	37	37.67	4	-	439.5	178	877	34	25.79
Waugh, ME	6	10	1	550	137	61.11	9	-	56.0	17	161	1	161.00
Waugh, SR	6	9	4	416	157*	83.20	5	-	32.0	9	82	2	41.00

English Averages

1993 ENGLAND v AUSTRALIA

ENGLAND	M	Inn	NO	Runs	H.S	Avrge	Ct	St	Overs	Mds	Runs	Wkt	Avrge
Atherton, MA	6	12	-	553	99	46.08	1	-	-	-	-	-	-
Bicknell, MP	2	4	-	26	14	6.50	-	-	87.0	17	263	4	65.75
Caddick, AR	4	8	1	101	25	14.43	2	-	153.0	28	488	5	97.60
DeFreitas, PAJ	1	2	-	12	7	6.00	-	-	47.0	9	126	2	63.00
Emburey, JE	1	2	1	92	55*	92.00	-	-	57.0	13	150	3	50.00
Foster, NA	1	2	-	36	20	18.00	-	-	30.0	4	94	-	-
Fraser, ARC	1	2	-	41	28	20.50	1	-	45.5	9	131	8	16.38
Gatting, MW	2	4	-	91	59	22.75	2	-	-	-	-	-	-
Gooch, GA	6	12	-	673	133	56.08	2	-	25.0	6	66	-	-
Hick, GA	3	6	-	256	80	42.67	-	-	25.0	7	52	-	-
Hussain, N	4	8	2	184	71	30.67	2	-	-	-	-	-	-
Ilott, MC	3	5	1	28	15	7.00	-	-	129.0	28	412	8	51.50
Lathwell, MN	2	4	-	78	33	19.50	-	-	-	-	-	-	-
Lewis, CC	2	4	-	52	43	13.00	1	-	58.0	7	238	2	119.00
Malcolm, DE	1	2	2	0	0*	-	-	-	46.0	8	170	6	28.33
Maynard, MP	2	4	-	39	20	9.75	2	-	-	-	-	-	-
McCague, MJ	2	3	-	20	11	6.67	1	-	79.3	13	294	4	73.50
Ramprakash, MR	1	2	-	70	64	35.00	2	-	-	-	-	-	-
Smith, RA	5	10	-	283	86	28.30	2	-	-	-	-	-	-
Stewart, AJ	6	12	-	378	78	31.50	14	2	-	-	-	-	-
Such, PM	5	9	3	56	14*	9.33	1	-	239.5	64	541	16	33.81
Thorpe, GP	3	6	1	230	114*	46.00	5	-	6.0	1	14	-	-
Tufnell, PCR	2	4	2	3	2*	1.50	1	-	104.0	12	319	5	63.80
Watkin, SL	1	2	-	17	13	8.50	1	-	53.0	13	152	6	25.33

SECOND TEST 1993 ENGLAND v AUSTRALIA
Lord's Cricket Ground, London. June 17, 18, 19, 20, 21, 1993.
Toss: Australia. Australia won by an innings & 62 runs.

AUSTRALIA

MA Taylor st Stewart b Tufnell	111
MJ Slater c(S)BF Smith b Lewis	152
DC Boon not out	164
ME Waugh b Tufnell	99
AR Border (c) b Lewis	77
SR Waugh not out	13
IA Healy (+)	
MG Hughes	
SK Warne	
TBA May	
CJ McDermott	
EXTRAS (LB 1, W 1, NB 14)	16
TOTAL	4 dec 632

FOW 1st Inns: 260 277 452 591

Bowling: *First Innings*: Caddick 38-5-120-0, Foster 30-4-94-0, Such 36-6-90-0, Tufnell 39-3-129-2, Lewis 36-5-151-2, Gooch 9-1-26-0, Hick 8-3-21-0.

ENGLAND

GA Gooch (c) c May b Hughes	12		c Healy b Warne	29
MA Atherton b Warne	80		run out	99
MW Gatting b May	5		lbw Warne	59
RA Smith st Healy b May	22		c (S)ML Hayden b May	5
GA Hick c Healy b Hughes	20		c Taylor b May	64
AJ Stewart (+) lbw Hughes	3		lbw May	62
CC Lewis lbw Warne	0		st Healy b May	0
NA Foster c Border b Warne	16		c ME Waugh b Border	20
AR Caddick c Healy b Hughes	21		not out	0
PM Such c Taylor b Warne	7		b Warne	0
PCR Tufnell not out	2		b Warne	0
EXTRAS (LB 8, NB 9)	17		(B 10, LB 13)	23
TOTAL	205			365

FOW 1st Inns: 33 50 84 123 131 132 167 174 189 205
FOW 2nd Inns: 71 175 180 244 304 312 361 361 365 365

Bowling: *First Innings*: Hughes 20-5-52-4, ME Waugh 6-1-16-0, SR Waugh 4-1-5-0, May 31-12-64-2, Warne 35-12-57-4, Border 3-1-3-0. *Second Innings*: Hughes 31-9-75-0, ME Waugh 17-4-55-0, May 51-23-81-4, SR Waugh 2-0-13-0, Warne 48.5-17-102-4, Border 16-9-16-1.

Umpires: BJ Meyer & KE Palmer

THIRD TEST 1993 ENGLAND v AUSTRALIA
Trent Bridge, Nottingham. July 1, 2, 3, 5, 6, 1993.
Toss: England. Match Drawn.

ENGLAND

MN Lathwell c Healy b Hughes	20		lbw Warne	33
MA Atherton c Boon b Warne	11		c Healy b Hughes	9
RA Smith c & b Julian	86		c Healy b Warne	50
AJ Stewart (+) c ME Waugh b Warne	25		lbw Hughes	6
GA Gooch (c) c Border b Hughes	38		c Taylor b Warne	120
GP Thorpe c SR Waugh b Hughes	6	(7)	not out	114
N Hussain c Boon b Warne	71	(8)	not out	47
AR Caddick lbw Hughes	15	(6)	c Boon b Julian	12
MJ McCague c ME Waugh b Hughes	9			
MC Ilott c Taylor b May	6			
PM Such not out	0			
EXTRAS (B 5, LB 23, W 4, NB 2)	34		(B 11, LB 11, NB 9)	31
TOTAL	321		6 dec	422

FOW 1st Inns: 28 63 153 159 174 220 290 304 321 321
FOW 2nd Inns: 11 100 109 117 159 309

Bowling: *First Innings*: Hughes 31-7-92-5, Julian 24-3-84-1, Warne 40-17-74-3, May 14.4-7-31-1, SR Waugh 8-4-12-0, ME Waugh 1-1-0-0. *Second Innings*: Hughes 22-8-41-2, Julian 33-10-110-1, May 38-6-112-0, Warne 50-21-108-3, SR Waugh 1-0-3-0, Border 5-0-11-0, ME Waugh 6-3-15-0.

AUSTRALIA

MJ Slater lbw Caddick	40	(2)	b Such	26
MA Taylor c Stewart b McCague	28	(1)	c Atherton b Such	28
DC Boon b McCague	101		c Stewart b Caddick	18
ME Waugh c McCague b Such	70		b Caddick	1
SR Waugh c Stewart b McCague	13	(6)	not out	47
IA Healy (+) c Thorpe b Ilott	9	(7)	lbw Ilott	5
BP Julian c Stewart b Ilott	5	(8)	not out	56
AR Border (c) c Smith b Such	38	(5)	c Thorpe b Caddick	2
MG Hughes b Ilott	17			
SK Warne not out	35			
TBA May lbw McCague	1			
EXTRAS (B 4, LB 8, W 4)	16		(B 5, LB 5, W 4, NB 5)	19
TOTAL	373		6 for	202

FOW 1st Inns: 55 74 197 239 250 262 284 311 356 373
FOW 2nd Inns: 46 74 75 81 93 115

Bowling: *First Innings*: McCague 32.3-5-121-4, Ilott 34-8-108-3, Such 20-7-51-2, Caddick 22-5-81-1. *Second Innings*: McCague 19-6-58-0, Ilott 18-5-44-1, Such 23-6-58-2, Caddick 16-6-32-3.

Umpires: HD Bird & KE Palmer

FIFTH TEST 1993 ENGLAND v AUSTRALIA
Edgbaston, Birmingham. August 5, 6, 7, 8, 9, 1993.
Toss: England. Australia won by 8 wkts.

ENGLAND

MA Atherton (c) b Reiffel	72	(2)	c Border b Warne	28
GA Gooch c Taylor b Reiffel	8	(1)	b Warne	48
RA Smith b ME Waugh	21		lbw Warne	19
MP Maynard c SR Waugh b May	0		c Healy b May	10
AJ Stewart (+) c & b Warne	45		lbw Warne	5
GP Thorpe c Healy b May	37		st Healy b Warne	60
N Hussain b Reiffel	3		c SR Waugh b May	0
JE Emburey not out	55		c Healy b May	37
MP Bicknell c ME Waugh b Reiffel	14		c SR Waugh b May	0
PM Such b Reiffel	1		not out	7
MC Ilott c Healy b Reiffel	3		b May	15
EXTRAS (B 4, LB 6, NB 7)	17		(B 11, LB 9, NB 2)	22
TOTAL	276			251

FOW 1st Inns: 17 71 76 156 156 160 215 262 264 276
FOW 2nd Inns: 60 104 115 115 124 125 229 229 229 251

Bowling: *First Innings*: Hughes 19-4-53-0, Reiffel 22.5-3-71-6, ME Waugh 15-5-43-1, SR Waugh 5-2-4-0, May 19-9-32-2, Warne 21-7-63-1. *Second Innings*: Hughes 18-7-24-0, Reiffel 11-2-30-0, May 48.2-15-89-5, Warne 49-23-82-5, Border 2-1-1-0, ME Waugh 5-2-5-0.

AUSTRALIA

MA Taylor run out	19	(2)	c Thorpe b Such	4
MJ Slater c Smith b Such	22	(1)	c Thorpe b Emburey	8
DC Boon lbw Emburey	0		not out	38
ME Waugh c Thorpe b Ilott	137		not out	62
AR Border (c) c Hussain b Such	3			
SR Waugh c Stewart b Bicknell	59			
IA Healy (+) c Stewart b Bicknell	80			
MG Hughes b Bicknell	38			
PR Reiffel b Such	20			
SK Warne c Stewart b Emburey	10			
TBA May not out	3			
EXTRAS (B 7, LB 8, NB 2)	17		(B 3, LB 5)	8
TOTAL	408		2 for	120

FOW 1st Inns: 34 39 69 80 233 263 370 379 398 408
FOW 2nd Inns: 12 12

Bowling: *First Innings*: Bicknell 34-9-99-3, Ilott 24-4-85-1, Such 52.5-18-90-3, Emburey 39-9-119-2. *Second Innings*: Bicknell 3-0-9-0, Such 20.3-4-58-1, Emburey 18-4-31-1, Ilott 2-0-14-0.

Umpires: JH Hampshire & DR Shepherd

FOURTH TEST 1993 ENGLAND v AUSTRALIA
Headingley, Leeds. July 22, 23, 24, 25, 26, 1993.
Toss: Australia. Australia won by an innings & 148 runs.

AUSTRALIA

MJ Slater b Ilott	67
MA Taylor lbw Bicknell	27
DC Boon lbw Ilott	107
ME Waugh b Ilott	52
AR Border (c) not out	200
SR Waugh not out	157
IA Healy (+)	
PR Reiffel	
MG Hughes	
SK Warne	
TBA May	
EXTRAS (B 8, LB 22, W 4, NB 9)	43
TOTAL	4 dec 653

FOW 1st Inns: 86 110 216 321

Bowling: *First Innings*: McCague 28-2-115-0, Ilott 51-11-161-3, Caddick 42-5-138-0, Bicknell 50-8-155-1, Gooch 16-5-40-0, Thorpe 6-1-14-0.

ENGLAND

MN Lathwell c Healy b Hughes	0		b May	25
MA Atherton b Reiffel	55		st Healy b May	63
RA Smith c & b May	23		lbw Reiffel	35
AJ Stewart (+) c Slater b Reiffel	5		c ME Waugh b Reiffel	78
GA Gooch (c) lbw Reiffel	59		st Healy b May	26
GP Thorpe c Healy b Reiffel	0		c Taylor b Reiffel	13
N Hussain b Reiffel	15		not out	18
AR Caddick c ME Waugh b Hughes	9		lbw Hughes	12
MP Bicknell c Border b Hughes	12		lbw Hughes	0
MJ McCague c Taylor b Warne	0		b Hughes	11
MC Ilott not out	0		c Border b May	4
EXTRAS (B 2, LB 3, NB 17)	22		(B 5, LB 3, W 1, NB 11)	20
TOTAL	200			305

FOW 1st Inns: 0 43 50 158 158 169 184 195 200 200
FOW 2nd Inns: 60 131 149 202 256 263 279 279 295 305

Bowling: *First Innings*: Hughes 15.5-3-47-3, Reiffel 26-6-65-5, May 15-3-33-1, Warne 23-9-43-1, ME Waugh 3-0-7-0. *Second Innings*: Hughes 30-10-79-3, Reiffel 28-8-87-3, Warne 40-16-63-0, May 27-6-65-4, ME Waugh 2-1-3-0.

Umpires: HD Bird & NT Plews (TV Umpire – B Leadbeater)

SIXTH TEST 1993 ENGLAND v AUSTRALIA
Kennington Oval, London. August 19, 20, 21, 22, 23, 1993.
Toss: England. England won by 161 runs.

ENGLAND

GA Gooch c Border b SR Waugh	56	c Healy b Warne	79
MA Atherton (c) lbw SR Waugh	50	c Warne b Reiffel	42
GA Hick c Warne b May	80	c Boon b May	36
MP Maynard b Warne	20	c Reiffel b Hughes	9
N Hussain c Taylor b Warne	30	c ME Waugh b Hughes	0
AJ Stewart (+) c Healy b Hughes	76	c ME Waugh b Reiffel	35
MR Ramprakash c Healy b Hughes	6	c Slater b Hughes	64
ARC Fraser b Reiffel	28	c Healy b Reiffel	13
SL Watkin c SR Waugh b Reiffel	13	lbw Warne	4
PM Such c ME Waugh b Hughes	4	lbw Warne	10
DE Malcolm not out	0	not out	0
EXTRAS (LB 7, W 1, NB 9)	17	(B 5, LB 12, W 1, NB 3)	21
TOTAL	380		313

FOW 1st Inns: 88 139 177 231 253 272 339 363 374 380
FOW 2nd Inns: 77 157 180 180 186 254 276 283 313 313

Bowling: *First Innings*: Hughes 30-7-121-3, Reiffel 28.5-4-88-2, SR Waugh 12-2-45-2, Warne 20-5-70-2, ME Waugh 1-0-17-0, May 10-3-32-1. *Second Innings*: Hughes 31.2-9-110-3, Reiffel 24-8-55-3, Warne 40-15-78-3, May 24-6-53-1.

AUSTRALIA

MA Taylor c Hussain b Malcolm	70	(2)	b Watkin	8
MJ Slater c Gooch b Malcolm	4	(1)	c Stewart b Watkin	12
DC Boon c Gooch b Malcolm	13		lbw Watkin	0
ME Waugh c Taylor b Fraser	10		c Ramprakash b Malcolm	49
AR Border (c) c Stewart b Fraser	48		c Stewart b Malcolm	17
SR Waugh b Fraser	20		lbw Malcolm	26
IA Healy (+) not out	83		c Maynard b Watkin	5
MG Hughes c Ramprakash b Watkin	7		c Watkin b Fraser	12
PR Reiffel c Maynard b Watkin	0		c & b Fraser	42
SK Warne c Stewart b Fraser	16		lbw Fraser	37
TBA May c Stewart b Fraser	15		not out	4
EXTRAS (B 5, LB 6, W 2, NB 4)	17		(B 2, LB 6, W 2, NB 7)	17
TOTAL	303			229

FOW 1st Inns: 9 30 53 132 164 181 196 196 248 303
FOW 2nd Inns: 23 23 30 92 95 106 142 143 217 229

Bowling: *First Innings*: Malcolm 26-5-86-3, Watkin 28-4-87-2, Fraser 26.4-4-87-5, Such 14-4-32-0. *Second Innings*: Malcolm 20-3-84-3, Watkin 25-9-65-4, Fraser 19.1-5-44-3, Such 9-4-17-0, Hick 8-3-11-0.

Umpires: MJ Kitchen & BJ Meyer (TV Umpire – AA Jones)

Warne, the Sultan of Spin

It takes a great leg-spin bowler to recognise one in the making. When a chubby 22-year-old Victorian leg-spinner with bleached blond hair and an ear-stud made his Test debut against India at the SCG in January 1992, his figures were less than flattering.

In India's score of 483, highlighted by Ravi Shastri's 206 and a masterful 148 not out by wonder-boy Sachin Tendulkar,

Shane Warne's baptism resulted in an unhappy 1/150 off 45 overs.

Still, it was only his seventh first class game and he claimed the wicket of Shastri.

Bill O'Reilly, a leg-spinner without peer and, needless to say, a proponent of guile as opposed to pace, gave Warne the nod of approval, saying: 'His grip, arm and hand action after a short amble to the bowling crease suggest that somewhere in his private locker he does have a wrong'un wisely kept under lock and key for the present.

'He does spin the ball and his leg-break turns enough to keep any batsman on the lookout.'

Indeed he does, as Mike Gatting, England's recognised master of spin bowling discovered in the first Test at Old Trafford in 1993.

With his first ball in a Test in England, Warne bowled Gatting with the so-called 'ball from hell' that pitched 18 inches outside his leg stump and ripped venomously across to nick the off bail.

It was just as well the Australian selectors had had the presence of mind to persevere with Warne, otherwise he might have been deemed a liability and thrown on the well-occupied scrapheap of failed spinners.

Two spells of bowling in 1992 changed his career, the first against Sri Lanka in Colombo and the second against the West Indies at the MCG.

Going into the first Test against Sri Lanka, Warne had taken 1/218 in two Tests. The Sri Lankan batsmen led by centurions Gurusinha, Ranatunga and Kaluwitharana promptly belted him to the tune of 0/107 off 22 overs. With Sri Lanka set to cruise to victory, captain Allan Border pinned his hopes on a downcast Warne, who took teammate Greg Matthews' advice to 'spin it hard'. The aggressive Warne did just that, taking 3/11 off 5.1 overs and bowling Australia to an improbable 16-run win.

That night Warne, who lost 14

Shane Warne in England in 1993, on the tour that made his reputation.

kilograms during the off-season, revealed that after the hammering he had taken in the first innings he thought he might as well 'go back to the beer and junk food' for all the good the hard work was doing him.

All that hard training, however, paid off again on his return home.

Playing against the West Indies for the first time, in Melbourne, his control and direction were better. His first-innings figures of 1/65 off 24 overs were the curtain-raiser. With the West Indies needing 359 to win, Warne got to work on a turning pitch and bamboozled the batsmen, spinning Austrlia to a big win with 7/52 off 23.2 overs.

He was a hero overnight and, though he took only two more wickets in the series, he was 'on the boat' to England, as they say.

After claiming Gatting's wicket with that astonishing first ball, Warne went on to take a total of 34 in England, the fourth-highest haul by an Australian there, and to play

a major role in Australia's 4–1 win in the rubber. He conceded less than two runs an over. Top New Zealand batsman Martin Crowe had warned the Englishmen before the Ashes series that Warne was the best leg-spinner in the world. Now they believed him. Not since the pre-war days of O'Reilly and Clarrie Grimmett had a wrist-spinner had such an impact on a series in England. Graham Gooch was one English batsmen able to distinguish Warne's googly from his leg-break, but Warne still dismissed him five times.

Dubbed the 'Sultan of Spin', Warne's very appearance at the bowling crease sparked excitement among crowds, whether in Tests or in limited-overs games, in which he was also damaging.

Suddenly, on practice ovals all over Australia, boys of all ages sporting baggy baseball gear and caps, were ambling in and 'letting one rip'. Like their fathers before them, they found it more difficult

than they thought, but spin was in. Pace was pedantic.

Shane Keith Warne, born on 13 September 1969, was raised in a bayside suburb in Melbourne.

His cricket skill revealed itself early. He first played for the St Kilda grade side in 1989–90 then had a term with the Australian Cricket Academy in 1990, leaving under a cloud because of an aversion to discipline.

He first played for Victoria in 1991. His first two overs in Shield cricket against WA cost 20 runs and his match figures were 1/120.

His Test debut against India followed only four Shield games in which he took eight wickets.

A schoolmate, Raj Krishnan, put Warne's success down to the fact that: 'He never seemed to feel pressure. Some people do and go back into their shell, but Shane always got more aggressive.'

After his dramatic success in England in 1993, Warne became a mainstay of the Australian team and a household name in the cricketing world. He seemed to lose his 'buzz' for a time, but regained it.

In 1993–94, three Tests at home against NZ and six against South Africa yielded 47 wickets at 19.08.

The Pakistanis thought they had his measure, only to lose 18 wickets for 28.0 in 1994–95.

In the 1994–95 Ashes series, Warne maintained his mastery, capturing 27 England wickets (including a hat-trick) at 20.33

In the West Indies in 1995, when Australia regained the Frank Worrell trophy, he took 15 wickets at 27.06.

He continued to shine in limited-over games, producing a telling example in South Africa in April 1997. He bowled the last over in the fifth game and ensured victory for Australia by restricting the home side to five runs.

As he has shown many times, Warne is a capable batsman, and the only impediment in his temperament is his sometime boorish behaviour, such as his crass send-offs to departing batsmen.

At the end of the 1996–97 season Warne had taken 218 Test wickets at 23.90 with 10 hauls of five wickets. This puts him sixth on the list of Australian bowlers, immediately behind Ray Lindwall (228). Richie Benaud (248) is the only spinner who has taken more Test wickets. In all first class games, Warne has taken 387 wickets at 25.09.

Massacre at Bellerive sets up series win

NZ fights for draw

Mark Taylor: left handed gloves please.

Perth, Nov. 16. New Zealand, battered by injury and ill-luck, gamely fought out the first Test to a draw. Perhaps New Zealand never looked likely to win it, but at 6/198 in its first innings there was always the possibility of Australia losing it.

Ian Healy's steely determination to score his second Test century – in honour, he said, of his grandfather George who died on Friday, put paid to the idea of an Australian collapse, as he made 113 not out in Australia's 398.

New Zealand's innings marked the bowling debut of Glenn McGrath, a tall and quick country boy who took the wicket of Mark Greatbatch.

Andrew Jones played a beautiful Man of the Match innings of 143, mostly off the back foot.

The Australian bowlers lacked penetration and seemed to tire toward the end. The only joy for Australia was McDermott dismissing Ken Rutherford for his 200th Test wicket.

Australia, batting again 21 behind, had a field day with the depleted Kiwi attack. Willie Watson had done a hamstring running a single, and Chris Cairns had a bruised heel and bowled just one over in the second innings.

Australia made hay – Mark Taylor 142 not out, Michael Slater 99 and David Boon 67 not out, which included some controversial umpiring.

Hobart, Nov. 29. New Zealand, chasing Australia's large first innings score of 6/544, lost 13 wickets for 207 runs on the third day of the match in Hobart – eleven of them to spinners Tim May and Shane Warne.

Tim May bowled beautifully in the first innings and took 5/65. Warne snared 3/36.

Following on, New Zealand was all out before lunch on the fourth day, suffering their heaviest defeat in Test cricket in losing by an innings and 222 runs. Shane Warne was at his irrepressible best, taking 6/31 from 19.5 overs. He took the last four wickets for three runs in 14 balls.

Although injury-hit, New Zealand probably had only three Test-class players, captain Ken Rutherford, Andrew Jones and perhaps the unluckiest bowler in world cricket at the moment, Danny Morrison.

Nevertheless, Australia's win was a resounding one, built on the slashing 168 from Michael Slater, the majestic 111 from Mark Waugh – and on David Boon's first century on his home town ground. His glorious 106 cheered up, and was cheered by, all of Hobart. Boon became the fifth Australian to pass 6000 Test runs. Bradman, Harvey, Chappell G., Border, Boon.

New Zealand's morale was not improved by the very late withdrawal of Chris Cairns.

Captain Allan Border wasn't complacent, saying: 'We just cannot give ourselves a big pat on the back. Earlier in the year we fell over in Auckland and that can easily happen in Brisbane.'

Shane Warne took 6/31 in Hobart, and was Man of the Series against New Zealand.

QUICK SINGLES

Centurion censured. New Zealand's first innings centurion Andrew Jones was severely reprimanded by first-Test referee Srinivas Venkataraghavan after he showed dissent at umpire Tony McQuillan (who turned down a bat-pad appeal against Mark Taylor) by hurling the ball into the ground.

All bets off. Bookies had New Zealand at 7/1 to win the first Test in Perth, but of the $100,000 laid with one establishment, $80,000 was for an Australian win. Those punters were nervous at the end of the first day – Australia was 6/229.

Tons all round. Mark Taylor's 143 not out at the WACA completed the set – he is the only player to have made Test centuries at all six Australian Test venues including Bellerive in Hobart. Bradman, G. Chappell, Walters, K. Hughes, Yallop

and Gavaskar have scored centuries at the five mainland venues.

Injured Kiwis fly. Martin Crowe flew home after his gallant second dig ion the first Test for arthroscopic surgery on his knee; replacement batsman David White went home within 10 hours of arrival after injuring his knee. Richard de Groen and Chris Harris flew in to replace injured bowlers Chris Cairns, Dipak Patel and Willie Watson.

Bails off. Winds of up to 78 kph forced umpires Darrell Hair and Bill Sheahan to remove the bails for the final hour of play on the second day of the second Test in Hobart. They had been continually blown off.

Spacious crowds. Only 13,220 watched the Kiwis' demoralisation at Bellerive, less than half the number who watched the first Test played in Hobart against Sri Lanka.

Third Test drubbing. NZ was beaten by less than it was in the second Test, and to that extent improved. It lost by an innings and 96 runs at the 'Gabba, after Australia posted a daunting six declared for 607. Allan Border and Steve Waugh hit hundreds for Australia; the wickets were shared around.

Border at three. In front of an adoring and chanting home town crowd, Allan Border became the third greatest century scorer in Test history with 27 – behind Don Bradman and Sunil Gavaskar.

A third umpire first. Ian Healy became the first player to be given out by a TV umpire when given the two red lights, run out, by Darrell Hair.

Man of the Year. Shane Warne's eight match wickets and 74 not out in the third Test won him the award of Man of the Match and Man of the Series. Warne took 71 wickets in the calendar year.

FIRST TEST 1993-94 AUSTRALIA v NEW ZEALAND
W.A.C.A. Ground, Perth. November 12, 13, 14, 15, 16, 1993.
Toss: New Zealand. Match Drawn.

AUSTRALIA

MA Taylor b Cairns	64 (2)	not out	142
MJ Slater c Patel b Cairns	10 (1)	c Blain b Patel	99
DC Boon c Rutherford b Cairns	0	not out	67
ME Waugh lbw Morrison	36		
AR Border (c) c Rutherford b Morrison	16		
SR Waugh c Blain b Patel	44		
IA Healy (+) not out	113		
PR Reiffel c Jones b Watson	51		
SK Warne c Patel b Cairns	11		
CJ McDermott b Su'a	35		
GD McGrath lbw Su'a	0		
EXTRAS (B 4, LB 7, NB 7)	18	(LB 6, NB 9)	15
TOTAL	398		1 dec 323

FOW 1st Inns: 37 37 100 129 164 198 291 329 398 398
FOW 2nd Inns: 198

Bowling: *First Innings*: Morrison 35-4-113-2, Cairns 28-4-113-4, Watson 24-11-52-1, Su'a 19.5-2-72-2, Patel 8-0-37-1. *Second Innings*: Morrison 25-5-80-0, Patel 39-4-144-1, Cairns 1-0-12-0, Su'a 20-0-71-0, Pocock 2-0-10-0.

NEW ZEALAND

MJ Greatbatch c Healy b McGrath	18	c Healy b McDermott	0
BA Pocock c Boon b McDermott	34	c Healy b McGrath	28
AH Jones c Healy b ME Waugh	143	lbw ME Waugh	45
MD Crowe (c) c Taylor b Reiffel	42	not out	31
KR Rutherford c Healy b McDermott	17	lbw SR Waugh	39
DN Patel c SR Waugh b Reiffel	20	not out	18
CL Cairns b Warne	78		
TE Blain (+) lbw McDermott	36		
ML Su'a not out	14		
DK Morrison lbw McGrath	0		
W Watson retired hurt	0		
EXTRAS (B 1, LB 6, NB 10)	17	(LB 1, NB 4)	5
TOTAL	9 for 419		4 for 166

FOW 1st Inns: 25 100 199 239 275 292 394 413 418
FOW 2nd Inns: 0 66 85 145

Bowling: *First Innings*: McDermott 40-10-127-3, McGrath 39-12-92-2, Reiffel 24-2-75-2, Warne 37.1-6-90-1, ME Waugh 13-5-18-1, SR Waugh 4-0-10-0, Border 2-2-0-0.
Second Innings: McDermott 13-3-40-1, McGrath 16-6-50-1, Reiffel 7-2-25-0, ME Waugh 6-4-17-1, Warne 13-6-23-0, SR Waugh 7-2-10-1.

Umpires: DB Hair & AJ McQuillan (TV Umpire – TA Prue)

SECOND TEST 1993-94 AUSTRALIA v NEW ZEALAND
Bellerive Oval, Hobart. November 26, 27, 28, 29, 1993.
Toss: Australia. Australia won by an innings & 222 runs.

AUSTRALIA

MA Taylor c Jones b Su'a	27
MJ Slater c Morrison b Patel	168
DC Boon c Jones b Doull	106
ME Waugh c Doull b De Groen	111
AR Border (c) c & b Morrison	60
SR Waugh not out	25
IA Healy (+) c Doull b De Groen	1
PR Reiffel not out	23
TBA May	
SK Warne	
CJ McDermott	
EXTRAS (B 7, LB 2, NB 14)	23
TOTAL	6 dec 544

FOW 1st Inns: 65 300 335 485 501 502

Bowling: *First Innings*: Morrison 33-4-125-1, Su'a 24-3-102-1, Doull 21-0-99-1, De Groen 36-9-113-2, Patel 23-3-78-1, Harris 2-0-18-0.

NEW ZEALAND

MJ Greatbatch c May b McDermott	12	c ME Waugh b McDermott	0
BA Pocock lbw ME Waugh	9	st Healy b Warne	15
AH Jones c Healy b May	47	c Border b ME Waugh	18
KR Rutherford (c) c Taylor b May	17	b Warne	55
DN Patel c Taylor b Warne	18	lbw May	16
CZ Harris c ME Waugh b May	4	b May	4
TE Blain (+) c Warne b May	40	c & b Warne	29
ML Su'a c Taylor b Warne	6	b Warne	5
DK Morrison c ME Waugh b May	0	b Warne	0
SB Doull lbw Warne	0	c May b Warne	1
RP De Groen not out	0	not out	3
EXTRAS (B 2, LB 1, NB 9)	12	(B 2, LB 5, NB 8)	15
TOTAL	161		161

FOW 1st Inns: 15 47 84 105 107 117 137 138 139 161
FOW 2nd Inns: 1 29 84 103 111 133 149 149 158 161

Bowling: *First Innings*: McDermott 15-3-29-1, Reiffel 5-1-13-0, SR Waugh 4-1-8-0, ME Waugh 9-4-7-1, May 31.3-10-65-5, Warne 18-5-36-3. *Second Innings*: McDermott 17-8-42-1, Reiffel 12-1-28-0, ME Waugh 4-0-8-1, May 25-13-45-2, Warne 19.5-9-31-6.

Umpires: DB Hair & WP Sheahan (TV Umpire – SG Randell)

THIRD TEST 1993-94 AUSTRALIA v NEW ZEALAND
Brisbane Cricket Ground, Brisbane. December 3, 4, 5, 6, 7 1993.
Toss: New Zealand. Australia won by an innings & 96 runs.

NEW ZEALAND

BA Pocock c Healy b McDermott	0 (2)	c Healy b McDermott	11
BA Young c Healy b ME Waugh	38 (1)	b Warne	53
AH Jones b Warne	56	c Border b Warne	15
KR Rutherford (c) c Boon b McDermott	36	c Warne b McGrath	86
MJ Greatbatch c Healy b McDermott	35	lbw McDermott	2
CL Cairns c & b Warne	5	c Healy b McGrath	16
DN Patel c Boon b May	1 (8)	b Warne	3
TE Blain (+) not out	42 (7)	b McGrath	18
DK Morrison c Healy b Warne	0	not out	20
SB Doull c Healy b McDermott	10	c Taylor b Warne	24
RP De Groen c Border b Warne	3	b May	6
EXTRAS (B 2, LB 3, NB 2)	7	(B 7, LB 12, NB 5)	24
TOTAL	233		278

FOW 1st Inns: 2 96 98 167 170 174 174 178 193 233
FOW 2nd Inns: 34 80 81 84 138 187 218 230 265 278

Bowling: *First Innings*: McDermott 23-11-39-4, McGrath 20-7-45-0, SR Waugh 3-0-13-0, ME Waugh 10-4-14-1, May 21-7-51-1, Warne 28.3-12-66-4. *Second Innings*–McDermott 25-4-63-2, McGrath 21-1-66-3, May 16-3-41-1, Warne 35-11-59-4, ME Waugh 6-1-30-0.

AUSTRALIA

MJ Slater c Blain b Patel	28
MA Taylor c Pocock b Doull	53
DC Boon c Blain b Doull	89
ME Waugh c Greatbatch b Cairns	68
AR Border (c) c Patel b De Groen	105
SR Waugh not out	147
IA Healy (+) run out	15
SK Warne not out	74
TBA May	
CJ McDermott	
GD McGrath	
EXTRAS (B 6, LB 13, NB 9)	28
TOTAL	6 dec 607

FOW 1st Inns: 80 102 227 277 436 465

Bowling: *First Innings*: Morrison 33-3-104-0, Cairns 36-7-128-1, Doull 33-5-105-2, De Groen 46-14-120-1, Patel 33-4-125-1, Jones 2-0-6-0.

Umpires: PD Parker & SG Randell (TV Umpire – DB Hair)

Australian Averages

1993-94 AUSTRALIA v NEW ZEALAND

AUSTRALIA	M	Inn	NO	Runs	H.S	Avrge	Ct	St	Overs	Mds	Runs	Wkt	Avrge
Boon, DC	3	4	1	262	106	87.33	3	-	-	-	-	-	-
Border, AR	3	3	-	181	105	60.33	3	-	2.0	2	0	-	-
Healy, IA	3	3	1	129	113*	64.50	13	1	-	-	-	-	-
May, TBA	2	-	-	-	-	-	2	-	93.3	33	202	9	22.44
McDermott, CJ	3	1	-	35	35	35.00	-	-	133.0	39	340	12	28.33
McGrath, GD	2	1	-	0	0	0.00	-	-	96.0	26	253	6	42.17
Reiffel, PR	2	2	1	74	51	74.00	-	-	48.0	6	141	2	70.50
Slater, MJ	3	4	-	305	168	76.25	-	-	-	-	-	-	-
Taylor, MA	3	4	-	286	142*	95.33	5	-	-	-	-	-	-
Warne, SK	3	2	1	85	74*	85.00	4	-	151.3	49	305	18	16.94
Waugh, ME	3	3	-	215	111	71.67	3	-	48.0	18	94	5	18.80
Waugh, SR	3	3	2	216	147*	216.00	1	-	18.0	3	41	1	41.00

New Zealand Averages

1993-94 AUSTRALIA v NEW ZEALAND

NEW ZEALAND	M	Inn	NO	Runs	H.S	Avrge	Ct	St	Overs	Mds	Runs	Wkt	Avrge
Blain, TE	3	5	1	165	42*	41.25	4	-	-	-	-	-	-
Cairns, CL	2	3	-	99	78	33.00	-	-	65.0	11	253	5	50.60
Crowe, MD	1	2	1	73	42	73.00	-	-	-	-	-	-	-
De Groen, RP	2	4	2	12	6	6.00	-	-	82.0	23	233	3	77.67
Doull, SB	2	4	-	35	24	8.75	2	-	54.0	5	204	3	68.00
Greatbatch, MJ	3	6	-	67	35	11.17	1	-	-	-	-	-	-
Harris, CZ	1	2	-	4	4	2.00	-	-	2.0	-	18	-	-
Jones, AH	3	6	-	324	143	54.00	3	-	2.0	-	6	-	-
Morrison, DK	3	5	1	20	20*	5.00	2	-	126.0	16	422	3	140.67
Patel, DN	3	6	1	76	20	15.20	3	-	103.0	11	384	4	96.00
Pocock, BA	3	6	-	97	34	16.17	1	-	2.0	-	10	-	-
Rutherford, KR	3	6	-	250	86	41.67	2	-	-	-	-	-	-
Su'a, ML	2	3	1	25	14*	12.50	-	-	63.5	5	245	3	81.67
Watson, W	1	1	1	0	0+	-	-	-	24.0	11	52	1	52.00
Young, BA	1	2	-	91	53	45.50	-	-	-	-	-	-	-

Australia falls in the chase

Kepler Wessels back in town

A wet day at the 'G'.

Melbourne, Dec. 30. Torrential rain on Boxing Day prevented the resumption of Test hostilities between Australian and South Africa until 5 p.m. – a few hours added to the 24–year interregnum.

Former Australian opener Kepler Wessels leads a team which promises to be very competitive – fast bowlers Alan Donald and Fanie de Villiers (Brett Schultz is still recovering from a knee injury) are the new Peter Pollock and Mike Proctor, Daryll Cullinan is alleged to be the new Barry Richards, and bowling all-rounder Brian Macmillan, and what might be called a fielding all-rounder Jonty Rhodes are new. W. J. 'Hansie' Cronje is an excellent number three, and touted as the next South African captain.

The rain meant that the first Test failed to do justice to the occasion – 170 from Mark Taylor took four days, and Mark Waugh 84 in an Australian innings that was played for time, not result.

Donald and fast bowler Chris Matthews bowled fast and without luck – Cullinan dropped four chances at slip. The South Africans batted out the draw.

Sydney, Jan. 6. A haul of 12 wickets to Shane Warne in the second Test was small consolation compared to the ten for Man of the Match 'Fanie' de Villiers – especially his six second-innings wickets in Australia's doleful surrender on the last morning.

Chasing just 117 to win, Australia was all out for nelson, 111. Only Craig McDermott overcame the batting yips, and tried to hit out for the runs on the exciting but untrustworthy pitch.

Fittingly, de Villiers, who never gave up, exultantly caught and bowled Glenn McGrath to win the match.

Things began well enough – Shane Warne weaving a deadly spell over South Africa in the first innings, taking 7/56 from 27 overs and at one stage having 7/28 after 15 overs.

Australia's first innings 292 was marked by 92 (another in the 90s to follow his 99 against New Zealand) from Michael Slater and an adventurous 59 from Damien Martyn, fighting for his Test cricketing life, seemed adequate enough – especially when McDermott and Warne dismissed South Africa a second time – for 239.

But the pitch was getting lower and more erratic, and as de Villiers said on the fourth evening, with Australia needing only 60 runs: 'The advantage will be with us if Australia try to get the runs in singles. If we can get a couple of wickets early, this match is not lost'. Which is what happened.

South African hero Fanie de Villiers never gave up hope of victory.

QUICK SINGLES

Double trouble. South African Peter Kirsten was referred to the ICC referee Jackie Hendricks twice in the third Test after questioning Darrell Hair's lbw decisions. He was fined 25 per cent of his match fee for the first offence and a further 50 per cent for the second.

Jones recalled. Dean Jones was recalled to the Australian one day team for the post Christmas set of one dayers, celebrating with a Man of the Match winning 98 against South Africa in Brisbane on January 9.

Border's final game. Extraordinary scenes during the third World Series final at the SCG as the crowd paid tribute to Allan Border in his last match in Australian colours in Australia. Chanting forced him to bowl one last over.

Australia wins World Series. Australia won the best of three World Series finals by winning the two Sydney games after losing at the MCG. Mark Waugh made 107 and 60 and was Player of the Finals.

Not out, no TV. Nightwatchman Fanie de Villiers survived a stumping appeal to the TV umpire in the third Test because the cameras were in the wrong place, and the third umpire could not adjudicate.

NSW Double. NSW added the Mercantile Mutual Cup to its Sheffield Shield win with a big win over WA. Richard Chee Quee made 131 for NSW.

Warne's wonders. In all first class cricket this season, Shane Warne took 63 wickets at 19.92: the highest number and the best average.

Thousands of runs. Six batsmen scored over a thousand first class runs in the season Matt Hayden (1136 at 126.22)

Michael Bevan (1312 at 77.18) Justin Langer (1198 at 70.47) Greg Blewett (1036 at 57.56) Darren Lehmann (1087 at 57.21) and Dene Hills (1068 at 48.55).

Border testimonial. A grand entertaining Testimonial match was played for Allan Border in February at the 'Gabba. In a fitting tribute to AB it attracted 16,000 to the game and TV ratings in the 30s.

Players of the Year. Matt Hayden is the 1993–94 Sheffield Shield Player of the Year, finishing just one point ahead of Michael Bevan.

SuperTest Team surprises. The popular SuperTest team competition was changed this season for the public to choose the best Australian team of all time from a shortlist. Named were: Simpson, Lawry, Bradman, G. Chappell, Border (c), Miller, Marsh, Warne, Lillee, M. Hughes, Thomson.

Steve Waugh leads the way

Adelaide, Feb. 1. Steve Waugh was at his most imperious, the back foot drive operating smoothly, along with the fierce square cut and the impregnable forward defence, making 164 and combining in a 173-run partnership with captain Allan Border.

Fifties from Michael Slater, Mark Taylor and David Boon saw Australia to the strong position of 7/469 declared.

South Africa scored slowly, 198 runs from 97 overs on the third day, with feisty performances from Andrew Hudson and Peter Kirsten, but that man Steve Waugh chipped in with four wickets in the final session to give Australia some hope of enforcing the follow-on.

Shane Warne, with a sore shoulder, took just one wicket – that of the limpet-like Peter Kirsten, but he was out at 270, and Australia had to bat again.

The question after Australia declared at 6/124 was not whether 320 would prove sufficient, but whether South Africa could bat out the final day. They began at 3/18.

One ball before afternoon drinks they were 3/100, but nightwatchman de Villiers skyed McDermott and was out. The floodgates opened. At tea they were 7/116, Shane Warne had taken his hundredth Test wicket, Ian Healy his 200th catch, Peter Kirsten was reported for a second time in the match for dissent, and South Africa suffered some dubious decisions.

Steve Waugh smacks a boundary off the back foot.

NSW wins Shield

Sydney, March 29. NSW retained the Sheffield Shield with a thumping home victory over Tasmania.

Sent in to bat by NSW captain Phil Emery, the young Tasmanians failed to fire. Ricky Ponting was bowled by Brad McNamara for one run, and Michael DiVenuto was scarcely any better with 4.

Ponting had scored 245 for once out in his last game, and big things were, and still are, expected of him.

Tasmanian batsmen were unsure about two or three decision on the first day, captain Rod Tucker saying of umpires Darrell Hair and Terry Prue: 'They do their best and don't intend to make mistakes …'

NSW, especially Michael Bevan (113) and Brad McNamara (128), pounded the Tasmanian attack, making 442.

In the Tasmanian second innings Ponting top-scored with a miserable 28 and DiVenuto made 27, as Tasmania collapsed for 126.

Jonty Rhodes has become one of the world's finest fielders.

Mark Taylor made hay while the sun shone in Melbourne.

Warne is named International Cricketer of the Year

Shane Warne: the wizard.

Sydney, Feb. 1. Shane Warne's exceptional summer followed his exceptional tour of England, and he was named International Cricketer of the Year, winning two cars worth $64,000.

In six Tests this summer he took 15 wickets at 22.40 against South Africa and 18 at 16.94 against New Zealand – achieving the marvellous total of 101 Test wickets in just 23 Tests.

As a limited-overs bowler he proved a revelation, being the leading wicket-taker in the World Series games, 22 at 13.68, coupled with a strike rate of a wicket every 24.55 balls. The only cautionary note has been a shoulder problem, brought on apparently by too much practice of the wrong'un and flipper in the nets at Sydney.

Richie Benaud says Warne 'is the best young leg-spin bowler I have ever seen … and provided his shoulder holds up, will continue to be a force in world cricket.'

FIRST TEST 1993–94 AUSTRALIA v SOUTH AFRICA
Melbourne Cricket Ground, Melbourne. December 26, 27 (no play), 28, 29, 30, 1993.
Toss: Australia. Match Drawn.

AUSTRALIA
MA Taylor b Symcox		170
MJ Slater c Kirsten b Donald		32
SK Warne lbw de Villiers		0
DC Boon b Matthews		25
ME Waugh lbw Matthews		84
AR Border (c) c Richardson b Matthews		2
DR Martyn b Symcox		8
IA Healy (+) not out		7
PR Reiffel		
CJ McDermott		
TBA May		
EXTRAS (B 2, LB 7, NB 5)		14
TOTAL		7 dec 342

FOW 1st Inns: 57 58 127 296 300 327 342

Bowling: *First Innings*: Donald 30-4-108-1, de Villiers 32-6-83-1, Matthews 24-5-68-3, Cronje 13-4-25-0, Symcox 16.5-3-49-2.

SOUTH AFRICA
AC Hudson retired hurt		64
G Kirsten c Taylor b Waugh		16
WJ Cronje c Boon b Warne		71
DJ Cullinan c Border b McDermott		0
JN Rhodes not out		35
KC Wessels (c) not out		63
DJ Richardson (+)		
PL Symcox		
CR Matthews		
PS de Villiers		
AA Donald		
EXTRAS (LB 2, NB 7)		9
TOTAL		3 for 258

FOW 1st Inns: 49 157 157
Bowling: *First Innings*: McDermott 23-5-60-1, Reiffel 21-4-55-0, Waugh 12-3-20-1, May 28-7-58-0, Warne 31-8-63-1.

Umpires: DB Hair & TA Prue (TV Umpire – LJ King)

THIRD TEST 1993–94 AUSTRALIA v SOUTH AFRICA
Adelaide Oval, Adelaide. January 28, 29, 30, 31, February 1, 1994.
Toss: Australia. Australia won by 191 runs.

AUSTRALIA
MA Taylor b G Kirsten	62	(2)	b Snell	38
MJ Slater c Rhodes b Donald	53	(1)	lbw Donald	7
DC Boon c de Villiers b Donald	50		c Hudson b McMillan	38
ME Waugh c Snell b McMillan	2		c Richardson b Donald	12
AR Border (c) c Richardson b McMillan	84		run out	4
SR Waugh c Richardson b Donald	164		c Richardson b Snell	1
IA Healy (+) c Rhodes b McMillan	0		not out	14
PR Reiffel not out	32		not out	2
SK Warne not out	4			
TBA May				
CJ McDermott				
EXTRAS (LB 9, NB 9)	18		(LB 7, NB 1)	8
TOTAL	7 dec 469			6 dec 124

FOW 1st Inns: 83 152 159 183 391 391 464
FOW 2nd Inns: 23 79 91 99 103 109

Bowling: *First Innings*: Donald 38-7-122-3, de Villiers 41-11-105-0, Snell 19-6-44-0, McMillan 30-3-89-3, Cronje 9-3-21-0, G Kirsten 23-8-62-1, PN Kirsten 4-0-17-0.
Second Innings: Donald 11-2-26-2, McMillan 11-0-33-1, Cronje 6-1-20-0, Snell 12-3-38-2.

SOUTH AFRICA
AC Hudson lbw SR Waugh	90		c SR Waugh b McDermott	2
G Kirsten c May b McDermott	43		b Warne	7
WJ Cronje (c) c Healy b Reiffel	0		lbw Warne	3
PN Kirsten c ME Waugh b Warne	79		lbw McMillan	42
JN Rhodes b SR Waugh	5	(6)	lbw May	4
DJ Cullinan b SR Waugh	10	(7)	c Healy b McDermott	5
BM McMillan lbw SR Waugh	2	(8)	lbw Warne	4
DJ Richardson (+) lbw McDermott	6	(9)	c Taylor b May	10
RP Snell c Healy b McDermott	10	(10)	c & b Warne	1
PS de Villiers run out	4	(5)	c Reiffel b McDermott	30
AA Donald not out	1		not out	0
EXTRAS (B 3, LB 10, W 1, NB 9)	23		(B 9, LB 7, W 2, NB 3)	21
TOTAL	273			129

FOW 1st Inns: 100 103 173 179 195 203 222 243 270 273
FOW 2nd Inns: 12 17 18 100 105 113 116 128 128 129

Bowling: *First Innings*: McDermott 27-9-49-3, Reiffel 15-4-36-1, May 25-9-57-0, Warne 44.2-15-85-1, ME Waugh 3-1-7-0, SR Waugh 18-7-26-4. *Second Innings*: McDermott 19-8-33-4, Reiffel 11-4-15-0, Warne 30.5-15-31-4, May 32-20-26-2, SR Waugh 6-3-4-0, Border 4-3-1-0, ME Waugh 3-2-3-0.

Umpires: DB Hair & TA Prue (TV Umpire – SJ Davis)

SECOND TEST 1993–94 AUSTRALIA v SOUTH AFRICA
Sydney Cricket Ground, Sydney. January 2, 3, 4, 5, 6, 1994.
Toss: South Africa. South Africa won by 5 runs.

SOUTH AFRICA
AC Hudson lbw McGrath	0		c Healy b McDermott	1
G Kirsten st Healy b Warne	67		b McDermott	41
WJ Cronje c Waugh b McDermott	41		b McDermott	38
DJ Cullinan b Warne	9	(5)	lbw Warne	2
JN Rhodes lbw Warne	4	(6)	not out	76
KC Wessels (c) c & b Warne	3	(4)	b Warne	18
DJ Richardson (+) c Taylor b Warne	4		lbw McGrath	24
PL Symcox b Warne	7		c Healy b McDermott	4
CR Matthews c Taylor b Warne	0		c Waugh b Warne	4
PS de Villiers c Waugh b McDermott	18		lbw Warne	2
AA Donald not out	0		c Healy b Warne	10
EXTRAS (B 1, LB 4, NB 11)	16		(B 13, LB 1, NB 5)	19
TOTAL	169			239

FOW 1st Inns: 1 91 110 133 134 141 142 142 152 169
FOW 2nd Inns: 2 75 101 107 110 182 188 197 203 239

Bowling: *First Innings*: McDermott 18.1-2-42-2, McGrath 19-5-32-1, Warne 27-8-56-7, May 10-1-34-0. *Second Innings*: McDermott 28-9-62-4, McGrath 14-3-30-1, May 22-4-53-0, Warne 42-17-72-5, Border 3-1-8-0.

AUSTRALIA
MJ Slater b Donald	92	(2)	b de Villiers	1
MA Taylor c Richardson b Donald	7	(1)	c Richardson b de Villiers	27
DC Boon b de Villiers	19		c Kirsten b de Villiers	24
ME Waugh lbw Symcox	7	(5)	lbw Donald	11
AR Border (c) c Richardson b de Villiers	49	(6)	b Donald	7
DR Martyn c Richardson b de Villiers	59	(7)	c Hudson b Donald	6
IA Healy (+) c Richardson b Donald	19	(8)	b de Villiers	1
SK Warne c Rhodes b Symcox	11	(9)	run out	1
CJ McDermott c Cronje b de Villiers	6	(10)	not out	29
TBA May not out	8	(4)	lbw de Villiers	0
GD McGrath b Donald	9		c & b de Villiers	1
EXTRAS (B 1, LB 2, NB 3)	6		(LB 3)	3
TOTAL	292			111

FOW 1st Inns: 10 58 75 179 179 229 250 266 281 292
FOW 2nd Inns: 4 51 51 56 63 72 73 75 110 111

Bowling: *First Innings*: Donald 31.2-8-83-4, de Villiers 36-12-80-4, Matthews 28-11-44-0, Symcox 46-11-82-2. *Second Innings*: Donald 17-5-34-3, de Villiers 23.3-8-43-6, Matthews 6-5-9-0, Symcox 10-3-22-0.

Umpires: SG Randell & WP Sheahan (TV Umpire – IS Thomas)

Australian Averages

1993–94 AUSTRALIA v SOUTH AFRICA
AUSTRALIA	M	Inn	NO	Runs	H.S	Avrge	Ct	St	Overs	Mds	Runs	Wkt	Avrge
Boon, DC	3	5	-	156	50	31.20	1	-	-	-	-	-	-
Border, AR	3	5	-	146	84	29.20	1	-	7.0	4	9	-	-
Healy, IA	3	5	2	41	19	13.67	6	1	-	-	-	-	-
Martyn, DR	2	3	-	73	59	24.33	-	-	-	-	-	-	-
May, TBA	3	2	1	8	8*	8.00	1	-	117.0	41	228	2	114.00
McDermott, CJ	3	2	1	35	29*	35.00	-	-	115.1	33	246	14	17.57
McGrath, GD	1	2	-	10	9	5.00	-	-	33.0	8	62	2	31.00
Reiffel, PR	2	2	2	34	32*	-	1	-	47.0	12	106	1	106.00
Slater, MJ	3	5	-	185	92	37.00	-	-	-	-	-	-	-
Taylor, MA	3	5	-	304	170	60.80	4	-	-	-	-	-	-
Warne, SK	3	4	1	16	11	5.33	2	-	175.1	63	307	18	17.06
Waugh, ME	3	5	-	116	84	23.20	4	-	18.0	6	30	1	30.00
Waugh, SR	1	2	-	165	164	82.50	1	-	24.0	10	30	4	7.50

South African Averages

1993–94 AUSTRALIA v SOUTH AFRICA
SOUTH AFRICA	M	Inn	NO	Runs	H.S	Avrge	Ct	St	Overs	Mds	Runs	Wkt	Avrge
Cronje, WJ	3	5	-	153	71	30.60	1	-	28.0	8	66	-	-
Cullinan, DJ	3	5	-	26	10	5.20	-	-	-	-	-	-	-
De Villiers, PS	3	4	-	54	30	13.50	2	-	132.3	37	311	11	28.27
Donald, AA	3	4	3	11	10	11.00	-	-	127.2	26	373	13	28.69
Hudson, AC	3	5	1	157	90	39.25	2	-	-	-	-	-	-
Kirsten, G	3	5	-	174	67	34.80	2	-	23.0	8	62	1	62.00
Kirsten, PN	1	2	-	121	79	60.50	-	-	4.0	0	17	-	-
Matthews, CR	2	2	-	4	4	2.00	-	-	58.0	21	121	3	40.33
McMillan, BM	1	2	-	6	4	3.00	-	-	41.0	3	122	4	30.50
Rhodes, JN	3	5	2	124	76*	41.33	3	-	-	-	-	-	-
Richardson, DJ	3	4	-	44	24	11.00	10	-	-	-	-	-	-
Snell, RP	1	2	-	11	10	5.50	1	-	31.0	9	82	2	41.00
Symcox, PL	2	2	-	11	7	5.50	-	-	72.5	17	153	4	38.25
Wessels, KC	2	3	1	84	63*	42.00	-	-	-	-	-	-	-

One–all in tough series

Allan Border and Kepler Wessels shared both the Test and the one day series.

Durban, March 29. Typical of the career of Allan Border, cricketer and Australian captain, was that he was 42 not out saving a draw on the last day of his last Test.

With him was Mark Waugh, whose 113 not out could not rescue what was a dull draw, in a series both sides seemed content to leave at one win each.

This Australian three-Test tour was the first in 18 years and was played in the lead up to the elections for the 'new' South Africa, most likely to be led by Nelson Mandela.

President of the 'old' South Africa, F. W. de Klerk, visited the two teams at the exciting first Test at Johannesburg, won by South Africa after a hard-hitting second-innings 122 by Hansie Cronje. Kepler Wessels set Australia 434 to win – a task not made easy by Matt Hayden, a last minute substitute for flu-struck Mark Taylor, batting with a broken thumb. Australia survived until after tea on the fifth day.

Australia levelled the series at Cape Town, thanks to Steve Waugh who made 86 in Australia's 435 then took 5/28 in South Africa's second innings as they crumbled to 164 and a nine-wicket loss.

Warne and Hughes misbehave and cop a blast from ACB

Johannesburg, March 14. Unacceptable behaviour by Shane Warne and Merv Hughes in the first Test has resulted in the Australian Cricket Board adding fines to those already imposed by the ICC referee Donald Carr.

Warne was reported for his unseemly send-off of Andrew Hudson, after bowling him round his legs in the second innings.

Hughes was fined for abusing Gary Kirsten, slamming his bat into an advertising hoarding and poking his bat at a vituperating spectator as he walked from the field after Australia's loss.

This return of the ugly Australian cricketer was greeted with universal disapproval by the cricket public, but not, initially at least, by the Australian tour management.

The initial fines of $250 by the referee were increased by the ACB from distant Melbourne to $4000 each, plus a suspended fine for Hughes of $2000 for the reaction to the spectator.

Not everyone thought the fines were warranted by the offences – expatriate Australian Michael Haysman said on radio: 'I suppose some kids might have seen Hughes mouthing off, but I was very disappointed to see ICC referee Donald Carr jump in and fine the boys. I think it's very sad when someone gets involved outside the playing arena.'

But someone has to, it seems.

Border and Deano make their exits from internationals

Allan Border makes his last Test appearance in the third Test at Durban – another gritty knock.

Bloemfontein, April 8. Dean Jones announced his retirement from international cricket at a press conference after the final one day game against South Africa. Jones was not picked in this match, which was also Allan Border's final appearance for Australia. Australia won the game to square the one day series.

Jones's last game for Australia was at Newlands in Cape Town on April 6 He was given out for eight runs in another dodgey decision of the sort that has plagued his one day innings in South Africa, adding to the feeling that it was time to go.

He told captain Allan Border after this innings of his intention to retire – widely regarded as premature. Jones's pique with selectors extends back to being made 12th man against the West Indies in November 1993.

Dean Jones played 164 one day internationals, averaging 44.62 with a strike rate of 72.49.

FIRST TEST 1993–94 SOUTH AFRICA v AUSTRALIA
The Wanderers, Johannesburg. March 4, 5, 6, 7, 8, 1994.
Toss: South Africa. South Africa won by 197 runs.

SOUTH AFRICA
AC Hudson c Healy b McDermott	17	b Warne		60
G Kirsten b Hughes	47	c Hughes b May		35
WJ Cronje c Border b SR Waugh	21	c SR Waugh b Hughes		122
KC Wessels (c) c Hayden b Hughes	18	c Border b Warne		50
PN Kirsten b May	12	c Boon b May		53
JN Rhodes c ME Waugh b McDermott	69	c Healy b SR Waugh		14
BM McMillan c Boon b May	0 (8)	b Warne		24
DJ Richardson (+) lbw Warne	31 (9)	c Border b Warne		20
CR Matthews c Boon b Hughes	6 (10)	not out		31
PS de Villiers b McDermott	16 (7)	b McDermott		4
AA Donald not out	0	not out		15
EXTRAS (B 1, LB 10, NB 3)	14	(B 13, LB 4, NB 5)		22
TOTAL	251			9 dec 450

FOW 1st Inns: 21 70 103 116 126 126 194 203 249 251
FOW 2nd Inns: 76 123 258 289 324 343 366 403 406

Bowling: *First Innings*: McDermott 15.2-3-63-3, Hughes 20-6-59-3, May 22-5-62-2, SR Waugh 9-2-14-1, Warne 14-4-42-1. *Second Innings*: McDermott 35-3-112-1, Hughes 25-5-86-1, May 39-11-107-2, SR Waugh 10-3-28-1, ME Waugh 6-2-14-0, Warne 44.5-14-86-4.

AUSTRALIA
MJ Slater c Hudson b De Villiers	26 (2)	b De Villiers		41
ML Hayden c Richardson b Donald	15 (1)	b De Villiers		5
DC Boon c De Villiers b Donald	17	b Matthews		83
ME Waugh run out	42	c Richardson b Donald		28
AR Border (c) run out	34	c G Kirsten b McMillan		14
SR Waugh not out	45	c Richardson b Matthews		0
IA Healy (+) b Matthews	11	c & b Donald		30
MG Hughes c G Kirsten b McMillan	7	not out		26
SK Warne lbw Matthews	15	lbw McMillan		1
CJ McDermott lbw Donald	31	b McMillan		10
TBA May lbw De Villiers	2	c G Kirsten b Cronje		11
EXTRAS (B 1, LB 1, NB 1)	3	(LB 5, NB 2)		7
TOTAL	248			256

FOW 1st Inns: 35 56 70 136 142 169 176 201 245 248
FOW 2nd Inns: 18 95 136 164 164 191 219 225 235 256

Bowling: *First Innings*: Donald 19-0-86-3, de Villiers 19.3-1-74-2, McMillan 14-3-46-1, Matthews 15-4-40-2. *Second Innings*: Donald 23-3-71-2, de Villiers 30-11-70-2, McMillan 19-2-61-3, Matthews 20-6-42-2, G Kirsten 4-0-7-0, Cronje 0.3-0-0-1.

Umpires: SB Lambson & DR Shepherd (TV Umpire –CJ Mitchley)

SECOND TEST 1993–94 SOUTH AFRICA v AUSTRALIA
Newlands, Cape Town. March 17, 18, 19, 20, 21, 1994.
Toss: South Africa. Australia won by 9 wkts.

SOUTH AFRICA
AC Hudson run out	102	lbw SR Waugh		49
G Kirsten run out	29	lbw Warne		10
WJ Cronje b McGrath	2	c & b SR Waugh		19
KC Wessels (c) c ME Waugh b McDermott	11	run out		9
PN Kirsten lbw Warne	70	c Taylor b Warne		3
JN Rhodes lbw McGrath	5	c Border b SR Waugh		27
BM McMillan b Warne	74 (8)	lbw SR Waugh		3
DJ Richardson (+) lbw McDermott	34 (9)	c Healy b McGrath		31
CR Matthews not out	7 (10)	not out		0
PS de Villiers c Taylor b Warne	7 (7)	lbw McGrath		0
AA Donald c Healy b McGrath	7	b SR Waugh		0
EXTRAS (LB 6, NB 7)	13	(B 4, LB 6, NB 3)		13
TOTAL	361			164

FOW 1st Inns: 71 78 100 189 198 260 335 339 348 361
FOW 2nd Inns: 33 69 94 97 97 103 164 164 164

Bowling: *First Innings*: McDermott 27-6-80-2, Hughes 20-1-80-0, McGrath 26.1-4-65-3, SR Waugh 9-3-20-0, Warne 47-18-78-3, ME Waugh 10-3-23-0, Border 5-2-9-0. *Second Innings*: McDermott 13-3-39-0, Hughes 5-1-12-0, Warne 30-13-38-3, McGrath 16-6-26-1, SR Waugh 22.3-9-28-5, Border 1-1-0-0, ME Waugh 3-1-11-0.

AUSTRALIA
MJ Slater c PN Kirsten b De Villiers	26 (2)	not out		43
MA Taylor c Richardson b De Villiers	70 (1)	b Donald		14
DC Boon c Richardson b De Villiers	96	not out		32
ME Waugh c PN Kirsten b McMillan	7			
AR Border (c) c Richardson b Matthews	45			
SR Waugh b Matthews	86			
IA Healy (+) c De Villiers b Matthews	61			
MG Hughes lbw Matthews	0			
SK Warne c McMillan b De Villiers	11			
CJ McDermott c PN Kirsten b Matthews	1			
GD McGrath not out	1			
EXTRAS (B 6, LB 17, W 1, NB 7)	31	(B 1, NB 2)		3
TOTAL	435			1 for 92

FOW 1st Inns: 40 145 153 244 310 418 418 430 434 435
FOW 2nd Inns: 30

Bowling: *First Innings*: Donald 35-10-111-0, de Villiers 44.4-11-117-4, Matthews 36-12-80-5, McMillan 29-8-82-1, G Kirsten 4-0-13-0, Cronje 11-4-9-0. *Second Innings*: Matthews 6-1-14-0, de Villiers 6-0-20-0, Donald 5-0-20-1, McMillan 5-0-23-0, Cronje 2-0-4-0, G Kirsten 1.1-0-10-0.

Umpires: KE Liebenberg & DR Shepherd (TV Umpire – SB Lambson)

THIRD TEST 1993–94 SOUTH AFRICA v AUSTRALIA
Kingsmead, Durban. March 25, 26, 27, 28, 29, 1994.
Toss: South Africa. Match Drawn.

AUSTRALIA
MJ Slater c Rhodes b Matthews	20 (2)	lbw Donald		95
MA Taylor lbw Donald	1 (1)	lbw De Villiers		12
DC Boon c G Kirsten b Donald	37	c PN Kirsten b Donald		12
ME Waugh c Richardson b Donald	43 (5)	not out		113
AR Border (c) c Rhodes b McMillan	17 (6)	not out		42
SR Waugh c Wessels b Matthews	64			
IA Healy (+) b Matthews	55			
PR Reiffel lbw De Villiers	13			
SK Warne c Wessels b Matthews	2 (4)	c McMillan b Donald		12
CJ McDermott c Donald b De Villiers	6			
GD McGrath not out	0			
EXTRAS (LB 1, W 1, NB 9)	11	(LB 6, W 1, NB 4)		11
TOTAL	269			4 for 297

FOW 1st Inns: 7 45 81 123 123 215 250 256 269 269
FOW 2nd Inns: 55 81 109 157

Bowling: *First Innings*: Donald 18-1-71-3, de Villiers 24.2-5-55-2, Matthews 29-9-65-4, McMillan 19-5-56-1, Cronje 5-1-8-0, G Kirsten 6-1-13-0. *Second Innings*: Donald 28-8-66-3, de Villiers 24.5-69-1, McMillan 22-6-53-0, Matthews 28-12-56-0, Cronje 18-5-40-0, G Kirsten 3-1-7-0, Rhodes 1-1-0-0.

SOUTH AFRICA
AC Hudson lbw Reiffel	65
G Kirsten c Healy b Reiffel	41
WJ Cronje c SR Waugh b Warne	26
KC Wessels (c) lbw McDermott	1
PN Kirsten b SR Waugh	49
JN Rhodes lbw Warne	78
BM McMillan c Slater b SR Waugh	84
DJ Richardson (+) c Reiffel b Warne	59
CR Matthews lbw Warne	1
PS de Villiers lbw SR Waugh	0
AA Donald not out	0
EXTRAS (B 3, LB 10, NB 5)	18
TOTAL	422

FOW 1st Inns: 100 117 118 155 256 274 417 422 422 422

Bowling: *First Innings*: McDermott 38-11-76-1, Reiffel 30-7-77-2, McGrath 41-11-78-0, Warne 55-20-92-4, SR Waugh 27.2-12-40-3, ME Waugh 11-3-38-0, Border 3-1-8-0.

Umpires: Mahboob Shah & CJ Mitchley (TV Umpire – KE Liebenberg)

Australian Averages

1993–94 SOUTH AFRICA v AUSTRALIA

AUSTRALIA	M	Inn	NO	Runs	H.S	Avrge	Ct	St	Overs	Mds	Runs	Wkt	Avrge
Boon, DC	3	6	1	277	96	55.40	3	-	-	-	-	-	-
Border, AR	3	5	1	152	45	38.00	4	-	9.0	4	17	-	-
Hayden, ML	1	2	-	20	15	10.00	1	-	-	-	-	-	-
Healy, IA	3	4	-	157	61	39.25	5	-	-	-	-	-	-
Hughes, MG	2	3	1	33	26*	16.50	1	-	70.0	13	237	4	59.25
May, TBA	1	2	-	13	11	6.50	-	-	61.0	16	169	4	42.25
McDermott, CJ	3	4	-	48	31	12.00	-	-	128.2	26	370	7	52.86
McGrath, GD	2	2	2	1	1*	-	-	-	83.1	21	169	4	42.25
Reiffel, PR	1	1	-	13	13	13.00	1	-	30.0	7	77	2	38.50
Slater, MJ	3	6	1	251	95	50.20	1	-	-	-	-	-	-
Taylor, MA	2	-	-	97	70	24.25	2	-	-	-	-	-	-
Warne, SK	3	5	-	41	15	8.20	-	-	190.5	69	336	15	22.40
Waugh, ME	3	5	1	233	113*	58.25	2	-	30.0	9	86	-	-
Waugh, SR	3	4	1	195	86	65.00	3	-	77.5	29	130	10	13.00

South African Averages

1993–94 SOUTH AFRICA v AUSTRALIA

SOUTH AFRICA	M	Inn	NO	Runs	H.S	Avrge	Ct	St	Overs	Mds	Runs	Wkt	Avrge
Cronje, WJ	3	5	-	190	122	38.00	-	-	36.3	10	61	1	61.00
De Villiers, PS	3	5	-	27	16	5.40	2	-	148.3	33	405	11	36.82
Donald, AA	3	5	3	22	15*	11.00	2	-	128.0	22	425	12	35.42
Hudson, AC	3	5	-	293	102	58.60	1	-	-	-	-	-	-
Kirsten, G	3	5	-	162	47	32.40	4	-	18.1	2	50	-	-
Kirsten, PN	3	5	-	187	70	37.40	4	-	-	-	-	-	-
Matthews, CR	3	5	3	45	31*	22.50	-	-	134.0	44	297	13	22.85
McMillan, BM	3	5	-	185	84	37.00	2	-	108.0	24	321	6	53.50
Rhodes, JN	3	5	-	193	78	38.60	2	-	1.0	1	0	-	-
Richardson, DJ	3	5	-	175	59	35.00	7	-	-	-	-	-	-
Wessels, KC	3	5	-	89	50	17.80	2	-	-	-	-	-	-

Mark Taylor the new-age skipper

Mark Taylor: popular.

Lahore, Nov. 5. It may be a hard act to follow taking over from Allan Border, but Australia's new captain, Mark Taylor, a good natured fellow, has emerged as a positive skipper and imbued his team with a brighter outlook.

If there is a whiff of victory it must be seized. Defeat in pursuit of higher goals is no disgrace.

After a horror start with a pair in the first Test, Taylor scored 69, 5 not out and 32, and he took on the chin 13 missed chances and the high number of injuries.

Karachi Test slips away

Ian Healy lets one slip past for byes, Shane Warne hangs his head.

Karachi, Oct. 1. Mark Taylor's Australians have almost pulled off the impossible – victory over Pakistan. Not for 35 years, since Richie Benaud's team won by seven wickets in Lahore, has Australia won a Test in Pakistan.

The 1994–95 rubber got away to a thrilling start, Australia scoring a lively 337 with Michael Bevan (82) and Steve Waugh (73) putting on 121 for the fifth wicket. Pakistan replied with a lowly 256. Australia, at 2/171 in its second innings, was in control until pacemen Wasim (5/63) and Waqar (4/69) got busy. Only David Boon (114 not out) survived as Australia crashed to

232 all out.

Still, despite injuries to Glenn McGrath and Tim May, Australia sniffed victory when Pakistan, chasing 315, lost five wickets to Shane Warne and slumped to 9/258 – still 57 behind. Inzamam-ul-Haq and last man in Mushtaq Ahmed crept to within three runs of victory when Warne tempted Inzamam from his crease. The ball spun so sharply it missed the bat and 'keeper Healy, but only a magician could have made the stumping. Four leg-byes (actually byes) resulted, and so Pakistan won by one wicket.

Perhaps next time!

Salim Malik and bribe allegations

Karachi, Oct. 25. A Pakistani judge has cleared Test captain Salim Malik of bribery charges, saying they were 'unfounded'.

Shane Warne reportedly said Malik approached him before the first Test in 1994, offering him and 'Maysie' (Tim May) $225,000 not to bowl well. Pakistan won by a wicket, Warne taking eight wickets. Mark Waugh said Malik spoke to him at a reception before a one day game in Rawalpindi about arranging for four or five Australians to play below their best for $200,000. Warne and May confirmed the offers.

The Pakistani judge criticised the ACB for not sending the three Australians to Pakistan, saying their statements were unsworn and therefore could not be admitted as evidence.

Salim Malik celebrates his 200.

Big scores, draws

Lahore, Nov. 5. After the dramatic finish to the first Test, the remaining two Tests in the Pakistan v Australia rubber became an orgy of run-scoring on pitches seemingly designed to deny a result.

At Rawalpindi, Michael Slater (110) and Steve Waugh (98) launched Australia to a first-innings score of 9/521 dec. and a winning position. But Pakistan captain Salim Malik ended Australia's hopes with a career-best 237 in a marathon innings of 443 minutes, after his team had followed on.

That draw was repeated in Lahore, with Pakistan making 373 (Warne distinquishing himself with 6/136) and Australia 455 (Bevan 91, Mark Waugh 71). Pakistan then batted out the match, scoring 404.

QUICK SINGLES

All-white. The first triangular one day series in Pakistan saw the players decked out in all white and using a red ball. Only 3000 spectators turned out for first game between Australia and South Africa, which proved to be an absorbing confrontation. Australia won by six runs with a score of 6/207 (S. Waugh 56) to South Africa's 8/201 (H. Cronje 98; McDermott 3/32).

Taylor's trials. Mark Taylor became the first Australian captain to score a 'pair' (of ducks) in his first game as captain.

Big stand. Despite 121 not out by Mark Waugh, Australia was thumped by Pakistan in the sixth one day match. The home side scored 1/251 off 39 overs in reply to Australia's 6/250.

Third win. Australia captured its third

one day title this season with a decisive win over Pakistan in the final in Lahore. Scores: Australia 5/269 (Slater 66, Taylor 56) d Pakistan 204 (Basit Ali 63; Fleming 3/32, M. Waugh 2/43) by 65 runs. Australia's other wins were in the WSC series in Australia and in the Centenary Cup in NZ.

Early form. The Australians got away to a good start in their first match against a President's XI. David Boon made 101, Mark Waugh 57, Steve Waugh 53 not out and Michael Bevan 62 not out (second innings). With the ball, Glenn McGrath starred with match figures of 18/81. The game was drawn.

Cautioned. Jo Angel, a last minute replacement for injured Craig McDermott, was cautioned by referee John Reid after the thrilling first Test. With Australia needing one wicket for victory, Angel reacted strongly when

umpire Khizer Hayat rejected an lbw appeal against Inzamam, who, with last-man-in Ahmed, saw Pakistan home to a one-wicket win, keeping intact its unbeaten 30-Test record in Karachi.

Rumblings. The withdrawal of Pakistan's top pacemen, Wasim Akram (back problem) and Waqar Younis (hamstring), before the third Test sparked a controversy, raising the question: were they injured or was it political? For Australia, Phil Emery (NSW) replaced Ian Healy (broken thumb) behind the stumps. Emery had five dismissals in Pakistan's second innings.

Equals record. With 18 Test wickets, Shane Warne equalled Richie Benaud's record haul in Pakistan. Top scorers for Australia were Michael Slater 244 at 48.80 and Michael Bevan 243 at 60.75. Steve Waugh averaged 57.0 and Mark Waugh 55.0.

FIRST TEST 1994–95 PAKISTAN v AUSTRALIA
National Stadium, Karachi. September 28, 29, 30, October 1, 1994.
Toss: Australia. Pakistan won by 1 wkt.

AUSTRALIA

MJ Slater lbw Wasim	.36	(2)	lbw Mushtaq	.23
MA Taylor (c) c & b Wasim	.0	(1)	c Rashid b Waqar	.0
DC Boon b Mushtaq	.19		not out	.114
ME Waugh c Zahid b Mushtaq	.20		b Waqar	.61
MG Bevan c Aamir b Mushtaq	.82		b Wasim	.0
SR Waugh b Waqar	.73		lbw Wasim	.0
IA Healy (+) c Rashid b Waqar	.57		c Rashid b Aamir	.8
SK Warne c Rashid b Aamir	.22		lbw Waqar	.0
J Angel b Wasim	.5		c Rashid b Wasim	.8
TBA May not out	.1		b Wasim	.1
GD McGrath b Waqar	.0		b Waqar	.1
EXTRAS (B 2, LB 12, NB 8)	.22		(B 7, LB 4, NB 5)	.16
TOTAL	.337			.232

FOW 1st Inns: 12 41 75 95 216 281 325 335 335 337
FOW 2nd Inns: 1 49 171 174 174 213 218 227 229 232

Bowling: *First Innings*: Wasim 25-4-75-3, Waqar 19.2-2-75-3, Mushtaq 24-2-97-3, Akram 14-1-50-0, Aamir 5-0-19-1, Salim 1-0-7-0. *Second Innings*: Wasim 22-3-63-5, Waqar 18-2-69-4, Mushtaq 21-3-51-1, Akram 10-1-19-0, Aamir 7-0-19-0.

PAKISTAN

Saeed Anwar c ME Waugh b May	.85		c & b Angel	.77
Aamir Sohail c Bevan b Warne	.36		run out	.34
Zahid Fazal b May	.27		c Boon b Warne	.3
Salim Malik (c) lbw Angel	.26		c Taylor b Angel	.43
Basit Ali c Bevan b McGrath	.0	(6)	lbw Warne	.12
Inzamam-ul-Haq c Taylor b Warne	.9	(8)	not out	.58
Rashid Latif (+) c Taylor b Warne	.2	(9)	lbw SR Waugh	.35
Wasim Akram c Healy b Angel	.39	(7)	c & b Warne	.4
Akram Raza b McGrath	.13	(5)	c Healy b Taylor	.2
Waqar Younis c Healy b Angel	.6		c Healy b Warne	.7
Mushtaq Ahmed not out	.2		not out	.20
EXTRAS (LB 7, NB 4)	.11		(B 4, LB 13, NB 3)	.20
TOTAL	.256			.9 for 315

FOW 1st Inns: 90 153 154 157 175 181 200 234 253 256
FOW 2nd Inns: 45 64 148 157 174 179 184 236 258

Bowling: *First Innings*: McGrath 25-6-70-2, Angel 13.1-0-54-3, May 20-5-55-2, Warne 27-10-61-3, SR Waugh 2-0-9-0. *Second Innings*: McGrath 6-2-18-0, Angel 28-8-92-2, SR Waugh 15-3-28-1, Warne 36.1-12-89-5, May 18-4-67-0, ME Waugh 3-1-4-0.

Umpires: HD Bird & Khizer Hayat (TV Umpire – Riazuddin)

SECOND TEST 1994–95 PAKISTAN v AUSTRALIA
Rawalpindi Cricket Stadium, Rawalpindi. October 5, 6, 7, 8, 9, 1994.
Toss: Pakistan. Match Drawn.

AUSTRALIA

MA Taylor (c) lbw Mohsin	.69	(2)	not out	.5
MJ Slater c Inzamam-ul-Haq b Mohsin	.110	(1)	b Waqar	.1
DC Boon b Mushtaq	.4		not out	.7
ME Waugh c Aamir b Mohsin	.68			
MG Bevan lbw Waqar	.70			
SR Waugh b Waqar	.98			
IA Healy (+) c Mohsin b Aamir	.58			
SK Warne c & b Aamir	.14			
J Angel b Wasim	.7			
CJ McDermott not out	.9			
DW Fleming				
EXTRAS (B 3, LB 3, W 3, NB 5)	.14		(LB 1)	.1
TOTAL	.9 dec 521			.1 for 14

FOW 1st Inns: 176 181 198 322 347 456 501 511 521
FOW 2nd Inns: 2

Bowling: *First Innings*: Wasim 23.5-3-62-1, Waqar 32-6-112-2, Mohsin 26-3-109-3, Mushtaq 36-2-145-1, Aamir 21-3-67-2, Aamir 5-2-16-0, Salim 1-0-4-0. *Second Innings*: Waqar 5-3-2-1, Rashid 2-0-10-0, Saeed 2-2-0-0, Mushtaq 1-0-1-0.

PAKISTAN

Saeed Anwar c SR Waugh b McDermott	.15		c Healy b ME Waugh	.75
Aamir Sohail b Fleming	.80		c Healy b McDermott	.72
Zahid Fazal b Fleming	.10		c Healy b ME Waugh	.1
Salim Malik (c) b McDermott	.33		c Healy b Fleming	.237
Aamir Malik lbw McDermott	.11		c Bevan b Fleming	.65
Inzamam-ul-Haq lbw Warne	.14		lbw Fleming	.0
Rashid Latif (+) c Slater b Fleming	.18		c Bevan b Taylor	.38
Wasim Akram not out	.45		c Healy b Angel	.5
Mushtaq Ahmed c Warne b McDermott	.0		c SR Waugh b McDermott	.0
Waqar Younis lbw Fleming	.13		lbw Slater	.10
Mohsin Kamal run out	.2		not out	.0
EXTRAS (B 10, LB 7, NB 2)	.19		(B 17, LB 13, W 1, NB 3)	.34
TOTAL	.260			.537

FOW 1st Inns: 28 90 119 152 155 189 189 198 253 260
FOW 2nd Inns: 79 227 336 469 469 478 495 496 537 537

Bowling: *First Innings*: McDermott 22-8-74-4, Fleming 22-3-75-4, Warne 21.4-8-58-1, Angel 11-2-36-0. *Second Innings*: McDermott 33-3-86-2, Fleming 26-2-86-3, Angel 28-1-124-1, ME Waugh 16-1-63-2, Warne 25-6-56-0, Bevan 4-0-27-0, SR Waugh 13-2-41-0, Slater 1.1-0-4-1, Boon 3-1-9-0, Taylor 3-1-11-1.

Umpires: KE Liebenberg & Mahboob Shah (TV Umpire – Javed Aktar)

THIRD TEST 1994–95 PAKISTAN v AUSTRALIA
Gaddafi Stadium, Lahore. November 1, 2, 3, 4, 5, 1994.
Toss: Pakistan. Match Drawn.

PAKISTAN

Saeed Anwar b Warne	.30	(2)	c Emery b McGrath	.32
Aamir Sohail c Emery b McGrath	.1	(7)	st Emery b Warne	.105
Inzamam-ul-Haq lbw May	.66		c Emery b McDermott	.3
Salim Malik (c) c Bevan b May	.75		b Bevan	.143
Ijaz Ahmed c Boon b Warne	.48		lbw McGrath	.6
Basit Ali c Waugh b Warne	.0	(1)	c Emery b McGrath	.2
Moin Khan (+) not out	.115	(6)	c McDermott b May	.16
Akram Raza b Warne	.0		lbw Warne	.32
Mushtaq Ahmed b May	.14		c Emery b McGrath	.27
Aaqib Javed c Waugh b Warne	.2		b Warne	.2
Mohsin Kamal lbw Warne	.4		not out	.0
EXTRAS (B 5, LB 7, NB 6)	.18		(B 8, LB 16, W 4, NB 8)	.36
TOTAL	.373			.404

FOW 1st Inns: 8 34 157 204 209 294 294 346 355 373
FOW 2nd Inns: 20 28 60 74 107 303 363 384 394 404

Bowling: *First Innings*: McDermott 24-4-87-0, McGrath 24-6-65-1, Warne 41.5-12-136-6, May 29-7-69-3, Waugh 2-0-4-0. *Second Innings*: McDermott 19-2-81-1, McGrath 25.1-1-92-4, Warne 30-2-104-3, May 25-4-60-1, Bevan 4-0-21-1, Waugh 6-0-22-0.

AUSTRALIA

MJ Slater c Moin b Mohsin	.74
MA Taylor (c) c Saeed b Mushtaq	.32
DC Boon c Moin b Akram	.5
PA Emery (+) not out	.8
ME Waugh c Moin b Mohsin	.71
MG Bevan c(S)Nadeem b Mushtaq	.91
JL Langer c Ijaz b Mohsin	.69
SK Warne c & b Mohsin	.33
CJ McDermott c & b Mushtaq	.29
TBA May c Moin b Akram	.10
GD McGrath b Mushtaq	.3
EXTRAS (B 3, LB 17, W 2, NB 8)	.30
TOTAL	.455

FOW 1st Inns: 97 106 126 248 318 402 406 443 450 455
Bowling: *First Innings*: Aaqib 31-9-75-0, Mohsin 28-3-116-4, Mushtaq 45.1-6-121-4, Akram 45-9-123-2.

Umpires: CJ Mitchley & Riazuddin (TV Umpire – Mian Mohammad Aslam)

Australian Averages

1994–95 PAKISTAN v AUSTRALIA

AUSTRALIA	M	Inn	NO	Runs	H.S	Avrge	Ct	St	Overs	Mds	Runs	Wkt	Avrge
Angel, J	2	3	-	20	8	6.67	1	-	80.1	11	306	6	51.00
Bevan, MG	3	4	-	243	91	60.75	5	-	8.0	-	48	1	48.00
Boon, DC	3	5	2	149	114*	49.67	3	-	3.0	1	9	-	-
Emery, PA	1	1	1	8	8*	-	5	1	-	-	-	-	-
Fleming, DW	1								48.0	5	161	7	23.00
Healy, IA	2	3	-	123	58	41.00	8	-	-	-	-	-	-
Langer, JL	1	1	-	69	69	69.00	-	-	-	-	-	-	-
May, TBA	2	3	1	12	10	6.00	-	-	92.0	20	251	6	41.83
McDermott, CJ	2	2	1	38	29	38.00	1	-	98.0	17	328	7	46.86
McGrath, GD	2	3	-	4	3	1.33	-	-	80.1	15	245	7	35.00
Slater, MJ	3	5	-	244	110	48.80	1	-	1.1	-	4	1	4.00
Taylor, MA	3	5	-	106	69	26.50	3	-	3.0	1	11	1	11.00
Warne, SK	3	4	-	69	33	17.25	2	-	181.4	50	504	18	28.00
Waugh, ME	3	4	-	220	71	55.00	2	-	27.0	2	93	2	46.50
Waugh, SR	2	3	-	171	98	57.00	2	-	30.0	5	78	1	78.00

Pakistani Averages

1994–95 PAKISTAN v AUSTRALIA

PAKISTAN	M	Inn	NO	Runs	H.S	Avrge	Ct	St	Overs	Mds	Runs	Wkt	Avrge
Aamir Malik	1	2	-	76	65	38.00	-	-	5.0	2	16	-	-
Aamir Sohail	3	6	-	328	105	54.67	3	-	33.0	3	105	3	35.00
Aaqib Javed	1	2	-	4	2	2.00	-	-	31.0	9	75	-	-
Akram Raza	2	4	-	47	32	11.75	-	-	69.0	11	192	2	96.00
Basit Ali	2	4	-	14	12	3.50	-	-	-	-	-	-	-
Ijaz Ahmed	1	2	-	54	48	27.00	1	-	-	-	-	-	-
Inzamam-ul-Haq	3	6	1	150	66	30.00	1	-	-	-	-	-	-
Mohsin Kamal	2	4	2	6	4	3.00	2	-	54.0	6	225	7	32.14
Moin Khan	1	2	1	131	115*	131.00	4	-	-	-	-	-	-
Mushtaq Ahmed	3	6	2	63	27	15.75	1	-	127.1	13	415	9	46.11
Rashid Latif	2	4	-	93	38	23.25	5	-	2.0	-	10	-	-
Saeed Anwar	3	6	-	314	85	52.33	1	-	2.0	2	0	-	-
Salim Malik	3	6	-	557	237	92.83	-	-	2.0	-	11	-	-
Waqar Younis	2	4	-	36	13	9.00	-	-	74.2	13	258	10	25.80
Wasim Akram	2	4	1	93	45*	31.00	-	-	70.5	10	200	9	22.22
Zahid Fazal	2	4	-	41	27	10.25	1	-	-	-	-	-	-

England embarks on mission impossible

Howzat? Craig McDermott traps Mike Gatting lbw for 10. That's how!

Sydney, Jan. 6. Michael Andrew Atherton. Your mission is to lead an England cricket side to Australia and return with a tiny urn filled with some ancient ashes.

To capture this prize, your side must win at least three of five Test matches played on Australian soil.

Sounds feasible?

But bear in mind that you will be hampered by back problems.

Opening batsman, Alec Stewart, will break his finger twice.

And your other star batsman, Graeme Hick, will head back to England with a prolapsed disc.

Your leading fast bowler, Devon Malcolm, will catch chicken pox.

And your great fast bowling hope, Darren Gough, will break a bone in his foot and return to England along with Shaun Udal, Martin McCague and Craig White.

You will get a replacement player, Neil Fairbrother. But he will dislocate his shoulder.

Sounds like mission impossible. What a pity Atherton didn't know that when he took on the job.

England lost the first Test at Brisbane by 184 runs, the second Test at Melbourne by 295 runs, and failed to capture the Ashes yesterday when the third Test was drawn at Sydney.

The first Test saw Australia's Mark Taylor score 176 runs and Mark Waugh 140 in Australia's first innings. Craig McDermott's 6/53 destroyed England's first innings and all those hours England spent studying videos of Shane Warne's spin came to nothing when Warne claimed 8/71.

Warne took his first hat-trick in the second Test. First, Phillip DeFreitas (0), lbw to a leg-break. Second, Darren Gough (0) caught at the wicket by Ian Healy. And third, Devon Malcolm (0) caught off his gloves after a brilliant dive at short leg from David Boon.

'I was going to have a go, but decided to bat properly,' Malcolm said on his way into the rooms.

Australia's David Boon did both. He never lost patience despite all sorts of time-wasting attempts by England. The little battler remained at the crease for 378 minutes to record his first Test century at the MCG and the twentieth of his career.

Yet in the rain-affected Sydney Test, Boon scored 3 and 17, and Warne bowled 52 overs for just one wicket. Atherton managed a valiant 88 runs in England's first innings, but alas, his mission is lost.

Shane Warne's hat-trick: 1. Phillip DeFreitas (lbw); 2. Darren Gough (c. Ian Healy); 3. Devon Malcolm (c. David Boon).

Brilliant Blewett 102 on Test debut

Adelaide, Jan. 30. The young South Australian batsman Greg Blewett joins an elite group of Australian cricketers by making a century in his debut Test appearance in the fourth Test against England at the Adelaide Oval.

Batting at no. 6, Blewett made an ice-cool 102 in Australia's first innings. He is the sixteenth Australian to make a century on his Test debut, and the fifth to do so at Adelaide.

He is a tall and stylish right-handed batsman and a capable right-arm medium-pace bowler. Since making his first class debut for South Australia against Queensland in 1992–93, Blewett has been a prolific run-getter in Shield games.

Recently he was Man of the Match with 113 runs when playing for Australia A against England at the SCG on January 12.

His Adelaide achievement was in front of a home-town crowd, on the ground where his father, Bob Blewett played as South Australian captain in the mid-1970s.

Zoe Goss batting for the Bradman XI in the charity match at the SCG. She also bowled Brian Lara.

England fight keeps series going

Mark Waugh made 140 elegant runs in Brisbane

Perth, Feb. 8. The Ashes series might have ended with a whimper had not England rallied to beat Australia by 106 runs in the fourth Test at Adelaide.

Mike Gatting, batting at number three, scored his first century for England since 1987.

Gatting was at the crease for 410 minutes to amass his 117 and was last out, caught by Steve Waugh at short third man off a leg-break from Peter McIntyre, making his Test debut. The other debutant, Greg Blewett, earned the distinction of a century in his maiden Test.

Mark Waugh snared 5/40 in England's second innings and took the vital wicket of Phillip DeFreitas (88), who smashed 22 runs (four fours and a six) off Craig McDermott's third over.

But bowling honours went to the England fast pair, Devon Malcolm (4/39) and Chris Lewis (4/24).

All out for 156 in its second innings at Adelaide, the Australians were desperate to make amends in the fifth Test here at Perth.

Australia won by 329 runs. Opener Michael Slater scored 124 runs, his third century of the series, and big totals were made by Mark Waugh (88), Steve Waugh (99 and 80) and Blewett (115).

Craig McDermott (6/38) and Glenn McGrath (3/40) destroyed England's second innings.

McDermott had the pleasure of the knockout punch when he sent the middle stump of last man Devon Malcolm catapulting through the air.

Australia A arrives

Adelaide, Dec. 12. It is called 'Australia A.' The A-team for short.

It is Australia's second eleven according to ACB chief executive Graham Halbish. And yesterday in the Benson and Hedges World Series, the A-team led by young Damien Martyn was only six runs away from beating Mark Taylor's Australia. Just what that kind of humiliation this might have been is one of many questions.

Is Australia A an experimental side?

Do Australian cricketers appreciate playing against their teammates?

How do they feel when Australian crowds naturally favour the underdog and support Australia A against the national side?

Is it an insult to England and Zimbabwe? Are they being used as match practice for two Australian sides? Too many questions…

The 30-odd diehards who have enlisted in England's 'Barmy Army' get to see the world and watch England get killed. Except in the fourth Test.

It's Queensland's Shield

Brisbane, March 28. After 69 long seasons, Queensland has finally won the Sheffield Shield.

The victors, led by Stuart Law, yesterday defeated Jamie Siddons' SA side by an innings and 101 runs in the Shield final at the 'Gabba.

Batting first, SA faltered to 4/30 after an hour's play. Middle-order men James Brayshaw (53) and Tim Nielsen (53) salvaged the innings (214), but Queensland grabbed the Shield with a huge 664-run reply. Centuries were made by Trevor Barsby (151) and Martin Love (146), while Allan Border went out on 98, possibly for the last time.

Paul Nobes' century and Darren Webber's 91 in SA's second innings were not enough to prevent Queensland's historic victory.

Trevor Barsby: 151 in Shield final.

Prize Bull in the Shield final is Carl Rackemann with five wickets.

Two G's gone

Perth, Feb. 7. Everyone knows there are three 'G's in cricket.

One is an historic ground in Melbourne. The others are a couple of old English cricketers.

But after today, only the Melbourne G remains. The English G's, Mike Gatting and Graham Gooch, are both retiring from Test cricket. Grey-bearded Gatting steps down at 37 after 79 Tests, 138 innings, 4409 runs and ten centuries (av. 35.56). His highest score was 207 against India at Madras in 1984–85.

Gooch, 41, debuted in 1975, and played 118 Tests – 215 innings, for 8900 runs and 20 centuries (av. 42.58). His highest score was 333 against India at Lord's in 1990.

Run-maker Jones

Brisbane, March 29. This year's Sheffield Shield Player of the Year is Victoria's Dean Jones, who topped the averages with 1216 runs and scored a career-best 324 runs against SA at the MCG in February.

Jones earned 25 votes from the umpires in his ten Shield matches.

He has also won the Player of the Year Award, which is sponsored by Lord's Taverner's and decided by votes from the players.

Over 30,000 people went to watch him in a 'testimonial' match at the MCG. But Jones has kept playing.

The people, the umpires and the players have voted for Jones. But for some reason, the votes that count most elude him – selectors'.

FIRST TEST 1994–95 AUSTRALIA v ENGLAND
Brisbane Cricket Ground, Brisbane. November 25, 26, 27, 28, 29, 1994.
Toss: Australia. Australia won by 184 runs.

AUSTRALIA

MJ Slater c Gatting b Gooch	176 (2)	lbw Gough	45
MA Taylor (c) run out	59 (1)	c Stewart b Tufnell	58
DC Boon b Gough	3	b Tufnell	28
ME Waugh c Stewart b Gough	140	b Tufnell	15
MG Bevan c Hick b Gough	7	c Rhodes b DeFreitas	21
SK Warne c Rhodes b Gough	2 (8)	c (S)C White b DeFreitas	0
SR Waugh c Hick b DeFreitas	19 (6)	c (S)C White b Tufnell	7
IA Healy (+) c Hick b DeFreitas	7 (7)	not out	45
CJ McDermott c Gough b McCague	2	c Rhodes b Gough	6
TBA May not out	3	not out	9
GD McGrath c Gough b McCague	0		
EXTRAS (B 5, LB 2, NB 1)	8	(B 2, LB 9, W 2, NB 1)	14
TOTAL	426	8 dec 248	

FOW 1st Inns: 99 126 308 326 352 379 407 419 425 426
FOW 2nd Inns: 109 117 139 174 183 190 191 201

Bowling: *First Innings:* DeFreitas 31-8-102-2, McCague 19.2-4-96-2, Gough 32-7-107-4, Tufnell 25-3-72-0, Hick 4-0-22-0, Gooch 9-2-20-1. *Second Innings:* DeFreitas 22-1-74-2, Gough 23-3-78-2, Tufnell 38-10-79-4, Gooch 3-2-5-0, Hick 2-1-1-0.

ENGLAND

MA Atherton (c) c Healy b McDermott	54	lbw Warne	23
AJ Stewart c Healy b McDermott	16	b Warne	33
GA Hick c Healy b McDermott	3	c Healy b Warne	80
GP Thorpe c & b Warne	28	b Warne	67
GA Gooch c Healy b May	20	c Healy b Warne	56
MW Gatting lbw McDermott	10	c Healy b McDermott	13
MJ McCague b McDermott	1 (10)	lbw Warne	0
SJ Rhodes (+) c Healy b McDermott	4 (7)	c Healy b McDermott	2
PAJ DeFreitas c Healy b Warne	7 (8)	b Warne	11
D Gough not out	17 (9)	c ME Waugh b Warne	10
PCR Tufnell c Taylor b Warne	0	not out	2
EXTRAS (LB 1, NB 6)	7	(B 9, LB 5, NB 12)	26
TOTAL	167	323	

FOW 1st Inns: 22 35 82 105 131 133 140 147 151 167
FOW 2nd Inns: 50 59 219 220 250 280 309 310 310 323

Bowling: *First Innings:* McDermott 19-3-53-6, McGrath 10-2-40-0, May 17-3-34-1, Warne 21.2-7-39-3. *Second Innings:* McDermott 23-4-90-2, McGrath 19-4-61-0, Warne 50.2-22-71-8, May 35-16-59-0, ME Waugh 7-1-17-0, Bevan 3-0-11-0.

Umpires: CJ Mitchley & SG Randell (TV Umpire – PD Parker)

SECOND TEST 1994–95 AUSTRALIA v ENGLAND
Melbourne Cricket Ground, Melbourne. December 24, 26, 27, 28, 29, 1994.
Toss: England. Australia won by 295 runs.

AUSTRALIA

MJ Slater run out	3 (2)	st Rhodes b Tufnell	44
MA Taylor (c) lbw DeFreitas	9 (1)	lbw Gough	19
DC Boon c Hick b Tufnell	41	lbw DeFreitas	131
ME Waugh c Thorpe b DeFreitas	71	c & b Gough	29
MG Bevan c Atherton b Gough	3	c (S)JP Crawley b Tufnell	35
SR Waugh not out	94	not out	26
IA Healy (+) c Rhodes b Tufnell	17	c Thorpe b Tufnell	17
SK Warne c Hick b Gough	6	c DeFreitas b Gough	0
TBA May lbw Gough	9		
CJ McDermott b Gough	0 (9)	not out	2
DW Fleming c Hick b Malcolm	16		
EXTRAS (LB 7, NB 3)	10	(B 1, LB 9, W 1, NB 6)	17
TOTAL	279	7 dec 320	

FOW 1st Inns: 10 39 91 100 171 208 220 242 242 279
FOW 2nd Inns: 61 81 157 269 275 316 317

Bowling: *First Innings:* Malcolm 28.3-4-78-1, DeFreitas 23-4-66-2, Gough 26-9-60-4, Tufnell 28-7-59-2, Hick 2-0-9-0. *Second Innings:* Malcolm 22-3-86-0, DeFreitas 26-2-70-1, Tufnell 48-8-90-3, Gough 25-6-59-3, Hick 3-2-5-0.

ENGLAND

MA Atherton (c) lbw Warne	44 (2)	c Healy b McDermott	25
AJ Stewart c & b Warne	16 (7)	not out	8
GA Hick c Healy b McDermott	23	b Fleming	2
GP Thorpe c ME Waugh b Warne	51	c Healy b McDermott	9
GA Gooch c & b McDermott	15 (1)	c Healy b Fleming	2
MW Gatting c SR Waugh b Warne	9 (5)	c Taylor b McDermott	25
D Gough c Healy b McDermott	20 (9)	c Healy b Warne	0
SJ Rhodes (+) c ME Waugh b Warne	0 (6)	c ME Waugh b McDermott	16
PAJ DeFreitas st Healy b Warne	14 (8)	lbw Warne	0
DE Malcolm not out	11	c Boon b Warne	0
PCR Tufnell run out	0	c Healy b McDermott	0
EXTRAS (LB 7, NB 2)	9	(LB 2, NB 3)	5
TOTAL	212	92	

FOW 1st Inns: 40 119 124 140 148 151 185 189 207 212
FOW 2nd Inns: 3 10 23 43 81 88 91 91 91 92

Bowling: *First Innings:* McDermott 24-6-72-3, Fleming 11-5-30-0, ME Waugh 3-0-11-0, Warne 27.4-8-64-6, May 18-5-28-0. *Second Innings:* McDermott 16.5-5-42-5, Fleming 9-1-24-2, Warne 13-6-16-3, May 4-1-8-0.

Umpires: SA Bucknor & SG Randell (TV Umpire - WP Sheahan)

THIRD TEST 1994–95 AUSTRALIA v ENGLAND
Sydney Cricket Ground, Sydney. January 1,2,3,4,5, 1995.
Toss: England. Match Drawn.

ENGLAND

GA Gooch c Healy b Fleming	1	lbw Fleming	29
MA Atherton (c) b McDermott	88	c Taylor b Fleming	67
GA Hick b McDermott	2	not out	98
GP Thorpe lbw McDermott	10	not out	47
JP Crawley c ME Waugh b Fleming	72		
MW Gatting c Healy b McDermott	0		
ARC Fraser c Healy b Fleming	27		
SJ Rhodes (+) run out	1		
D Gough c Fleming b McDermott	51		
DE Malcolm b Warne	29		
PCR Tufnell not out	4		
EXTRAS (B 8, LB 7, NB 9)	24	(LB 6, W 1, NB 7)	14
TOTAL	309	2 dec	255

FOW 1st Inns: 1 10 20 194 194 196 197 255 295 309
FOW 2nd Inns: 54 158

Bowling: *First Innings*: McDermott 30-7-101-5, Fleming 26.2-12-52-3, Warne 36-10-88-1, May 17-4-35-0, ME Waugh 6-1-10-0, Bevan 4-1-8-0. *Second Innings*: McDermott 24-2-76-0, Fleming 20-3-66-2, ME Waugh 2-1-4-0, Warne 16-2-48-0, May 10-1-55-0.

AUSTRALIA

MJ Slater b Malcolm	11 (2)	c Tufnell b Fraser	103
MA Taylor (c) c & b Gough	49 (1)	b Malcolm	113
DC Boon b Gough	3	c Hick b Gough	17
ME Waugh c Rhodes b Malcolm	3	lbw Fraser	25
MG Bevan c Thorpe b Fraser	8	c Rhodes b Fraser	7
SR Waugh b Gough	1	c Rhodes b Fraser	0
IA Healy (+) c Hick b Gough	10	c Rhodes b Fraser	5
SK Warne c Gatting b Fraser	0	not out	36
TBA May c Hick b Gough	0	not out	10
CJ McDermott not out	21		
DW Fleming b Gough	0		
EXTRAS (B 6, LB 1, NB 3)	10	(B 12, LB 3, W 1, NB 12)	28
TOTAL	116	7 for	344

FOW 1st Inns: 12 15 18 38 39 57 62 65 116 116
FOW 2nd Inns: 208 239 265 282 286 289 292

Bowling: *First Innings*: Malcolm 13-4-34-2, Gough 18.5-4-49-6, Fraser 11-1-26-2. *Second Innings*: Malcolm 21-4-75-1, Gough 28-4-72-1, Fraser 25-3-73-5, Tufnell 35.4-9-61-0, Hick 5-0-21-0, Gooch 7-1-27-0.

Umpires: SA Bucknor & DB Hair (TV Umpire – WA Cameron)

FIFTH TEST 1994–95 AUSTRALIA v ENGLAND
W.A.C.A. Ground, Perth. February 3,4,5,6,7, 1995.
Toss: Australia. Australia won by 329 runs.

AUSTRALIA

MJ Slater c Lewis b DeFreitas	124 (2)	c Atherton b Fraser	45
MA Taylor (c) c Rhodes b Lewis	9 (1)	b Fraser	52
DC Boon c Ramprakash b Lewis	1 (4)	c Rhodes b Malcolm	18
ME Waugh c DeFreitas b Lewis	88 (5)	c Rhodes b DeFreitas	1
SR Waugh not out	99 (6)	c Ramprakash b Lewis	80
GS Blewett c Rhodes b Fraser	20 (7)	c Malcolm b Lewis	115
IA Healy (+) c Lewis b DeFreitas	12 (8)	not out	11
SK Warne c Rhodes b DeFreitas	1 (9)	c Lewis b Malcolm	6
J Angel run out	11 (3)	run out	0
GD McGrath not out	0		
CJ McDermott run out	6		
EXTRAS (B 14, LB 4, W 4, NB 9)	31	(B 1, LB 9, NB 7)	17
TOTAL	402	8 dec	345

FOW 1st Inns: 47 55 238 247 287 320 328 386 388 402
FOW 2nd Inns: 75 79 102 115 123 326 333 345

Bowling: *First Innings*: Malcolm 31-6-93-0, DeFreitas 29-8-91-3, Fraser 32-11-84-1, Lewis 31.5-8-73-3, Gooch 1-1-0-0, Ramprakash 11-0-43-0. *Second Innings*: Malcolm 23.3-3-105-2, Fraser 21-3-74-2, Lewis 16-1-71-2, DeFreitas 22-10-54-1, Ramprakash 8-1-31-0.

ENGLAND

GA Gooch lbw ME Waugh	37	c & b McDermott	4
MA Atherton (c) c Healy b McGrath	4	c Healy b McGrath	8
MW Gatting b McGrath	0	b McDermott	8
GP Thorpe st Healy b Warne	123 (5)	c Taylor b McGrath	0
JP Crawley c Warne b ME Waugh	0 (6)	c ME Waugh b McDermott	0
MR Ramprakash b Warne	72 (7)	c SR Waugh b ME Waugh	42
SJ Rhodes (+) b Angel	2 (8)	not out	39
CC Lewis c Blewett b McGrath	40 (9)	lbw McDermott	11
PAJ DeFreitas b Angel	0 (10)	c Taylor b McDermott	0
ARC Fraser c Warne b Angel	9 (4)	lbw McGrath	5
DE Malcolm not out	0	b McDermott	0
EXTRAS (B 4, LB 1, NB 3)	8	(LB 1, W 1, NB 4)	6
TOTAL	295		123

FOW 1st Inns: 5 5 77 77 235 246 246 247 293 295
FOW 2nd Inns: 4 17 26 26 27 27 95 121 123 123

Bowling: *First Innings*: Angel 22.3-7-65-3, McGrath 25-6-88-3, Blewett 4-1-9-0, ME Waugh 9-2-29-2, Warne 23-8-58-2, McDermott 13.5-4-41-0. *Second Innings*: McDermott 15-4-38-6, McGrath 13-4-40-3, Angel 3-0-20-0, Warne 7-3-11-0, ME Waugh 3-0-13-1.

Umpires: KE Liebenberg & SG Randell (TV Umpire – TA Prue)

FOURTH TEST 1994–95 AUSTRALIA v ENGLAND
Adelaide Oval, Adelaide. January 26,27,28,29,30, 1995.
Toss: England. England won by 106 runs.

ENGLAND

GA Gooch c ME Waugh b Fleming	47	c Healy b McDermott	34
MA Atherton (c) c Boon b Fleming	80	lbw ME Waugh	14
MW Gatting c SR Waugh b McIntyre	117	b ME Waugh	0
GP Thorpe c Taylor b Warne	26	c Warne b McDermott	83
JP Crawley c Warne b Warne	28	c & b ME Waugh	71
SJ Rhodes (+) c Taylor b McDermott	6	c Fleming b Warne	2
CC Lewis c Blewett b McDermott	10	b Fleming	7
PAJ DeFreitas c Blewett b McIntyre	21	c Healy b ME Waugh	88
ARC Fraser run out	7	c McDermott b ME Waugh	5
DE Malcolm b McDermott	0	not out	10
PCR Tufnell not out	0	lbw Warne	0
EXTRAS (B 2, LB 5, W 2, NB 2)	11	(B 6, LB 8)	14
TOTAL	353		328

FOW 1st Inns: 93 175 211 286 293 307 334 353 353 353
FOW 2nd Inns: 26 30 83 154 169 181 270 317 317 328

Bowling: *First Innings*: McDermott 41-15-66-3, Fleming 25-6-65-2, Blewett 16-4-59-0, Warne 31-9-72-2, McIntyre 19.3-3-51-2, ME Waugh 9-1-33-0. *Second Innings*: McDermott 27-5-96-2, Fleming 11-3-37-1, Warne 30.5-9-82-2, ME Waugh 14-4-40-5, McIntyre 8-0-36-0, Blewett 4-0-23-0.

AUSTRALIA

MJ Slater c Atherton b DeFreitas	67 (2)	c Tufnell b Malcolm	5
MA Taylor (c) lbw Lewis	90 (1)	c Thorpe b Malcolm	13
DC Boon c Rhodes b DeFreitas	0	c Rhodes b Fraser	4
ME Waugh c Rhodes b Fraser	39	c Gatting b Tufnell	24
SR Waugh c Atherton b Lewis	19	b Malcolm	0
GS Blewett not out	102	c Rhodes b Lewis	12
IA Healy (+) c Rhodes b Malcolm	74	not out	51
SK Warne c Thorpe b Fraser	7	lbw Lewis	2
DW Fleming c Rhodes b Malcolm	0 (10)	lbw Lewis	24
PE McIntyre b Malcolm	0 (11)	lbw Malcolm	0
CJ McDermott c Crawley b Fraser	5 (9)	c Rhodes b Lewis	12
EXTRAS (B 2, LB 7, NB 7)	16	(B 3, LB 5, NB 13)	21
TOTAL	419		156

FOW 1st Inns: 128 130 202 207 232 396 405 406 414 419
FOW 2nd Inns: 17 22 22 23 64 75 83 83 152 156

Bowling: *First Innings*: Malcolm 26-5-78-3, Fraser 28.5-6-95-3, Tufnell 24-5-64-0, DeFreitas 20-3-70-2, Lewis 18-1-81-2, Gooch 5-0-22-0. *Second Innings*: Malcolm 16.1-3-39-4, Fraser 12-1-37-1, DeFreitas 11-3-31-0, Lewis 13-4-24-4, Tufnell 9-3-17-1.

Umpires: PD Parker & S Venkatagharavan (TV Umpire – SJ Davis)

Australian Averages

1994–95 AUSTRALIA v ENGLAND

AUSTRALIA	M	Inn	NO	Runs	H.S	Avrge	Ct	St	Overs	Mds	Runs	Wkt	Avrge
Angel, J	1	2	-	11	11	5.50	-	-	25.3	7	85	3	28.33
Bevan, MG	3	6	-	81	35	13.50	-	-	7.0	1	19	-	-
Blewett, GS	2	4	1	249	115	83.00	3	-	24.0	5	91	-	-
Boon, DC	5	10	-	246	131	24.60	2	-	-	-	-	-	-
Fleming, DW	3	4	-	40	24	10.00	2	-	102.2	30	274	10	27.40
Healy, IA	5	10	3	249	74	35.57	23	2	-	-	-	-	-
May, TBA	3	5	3	31	10*	15.50	-	-	101.0	30	219	1	219.00
McDermott, CJ	5	8	2	42	21*	7.00	3	-	232.5	56	675	32	21.09
McGrath, GD	2	2	-	0	0	0.00	-	-	67.0	16	229	6	38.17
McIntyre, PE	1	2	-	0	0	0.00	-	-	27.3	3	87	2	43.50
Slater, MJ	5	10	-	623	176	62.30	-	-	-	-	-	-	-
Taylor, MA	5	10	-	471	113	47.10	7	-	-	-	-	-	-
Warne, SK	5	10	1	60	36*	6.67	5	-	256.1	84	549	27	20.33
Waugh, ME	5	10	-	435	140	43.50	8	-	53.0	10	157	8	19.63
Waugh, SR	5	10	3	345	99*	49.29	3	-	-	-	-	-	-

English Averages

1994–95 AUSTRALIA v ENGLAND

ENGLAND	M	Inn	NO	Runs	H.S	Avrge	Ct	St	Overs	Mds	Runs	Wkt	Avrge
Atherton, MA	5	10	-	407	88	40.70	4	-	-	-	-	-	-
Crawley, JP	3	5	-	171	72	34.20	1	-	-	-	-	-	-
DeFreitas, PAJ	4	8	-	141	88	17.63	2	-	184.0	39	558	13	42.92
Fraser, ARC	3	5	-	53	27	10.60	-	-	129.5	25	389	14	27.79
Gatting, MW	5	9	-	182	117	20.22	3	-	-	-	-	-	-
Gooch, GA	5	10	-	245	56	24.50	4	-	25.0	6	74	1	74.00
Gough, D	3	5	1	98	51	24.50	4	-	152.5	33	425	20	21.25
Hick, GA	3	6	1	208	98*	41.60	9	-	16.0	3	58	-	-
Lewis, CC	2	4	-	68	40	17.00	3	-	78.5	14	249	11	22.64
Malcolm, DE	4	7	3	50	29	12.50	1	-	181.1	32	588	13	45.23
McCague, MJ	1	2	-	1	1	0.50	-	-	19.2	4	96	2	48.00
Ramprakash, MR	1	2	-	114	72	57.00	2	-	19.0	1	74	-	-
Rhodes, SJ	5	9	1	72	39*	9.00	20	1	-	-	-	-	-
Stewart, AJ	2	4	1	73	33	24.33	2	-	-	-	-	-	-
Thorpe, GP	5	10	-	444	123	49.33	5	-	-	-	-	-	-
Tufnell, PCR	4	7	3	6	4*	1.50	2	-	207.4	45	442	10	44.20

Shock Test win for Taylor's team

Bridgetown, April 2. Australia, beaten 2–0 at home by the West Indies in 1992–93, stunned the locals with an emphatic win in the first Test in only two-and-a-half days. And it was achieved without injured fast bowlers Craig McDermott (ankle) and Damien Fleming (shoulder).

A row marred the first day when Brian Lara, on 65, was given out caught by Steve Waugh off Brendon Julian. TV replays indicated the ball might have hit the ground. Waugh disagreed.

Ill-disciplined batting against Julian (4/36) and Glenn McGrath (3/46) saw the West Indies bowled out for 195 by tea.

With the stage set for the feared Curtly Ambrose to strike, a sore shoulder rendered him listless and Australia seized a lead of 151 with a score of 346 (Ian Healy 74 and Steve Waugh 65).

The real shock was the West Indies' lacklustre second innings. Wickets went down like rum and coke at nearby bars (Lara for nine), all 10 for 189. No one was comfortable against the pace of McGrath (5/68) and spin of Shane Warne (3/64).

Mark Taylor and Michael Slater wiped off the 39 runs needed for victory but they had to scamper from the field for fear of being set upon by unhappy fans. Slater lost his souvenir stump but the two batsmen survived to celebrate the 10-wicket win, a grand start for Taylor's men.

Glenn McGrath makes a strenuous appeal at Jamaica.

2nd Test up in air

St John's, April 13. Honours were shared in the rain-marred second Test at the Recreation Ground, St John's.

West Indies speedster Courtney Walsh, after a disappointing match at Bridgetown, was back to his best with 6/54 in Australia's lowly first innings of 216.

Mark Taylor (37) and Michael Slater (41) had put on 82 for the first wicket.

The West Indies replied with 260, Brian Lara cracking 88 in 154 minutes before falling to a brilliant one-handed catch at silly mid-on by David Boon off Steve Waugh. Waugh had also been Lara's nemesis in the first Test.

Boon and the Waughs hit half-centuries in Australia's second innnings of 7/300 declared, leaving the home side an unachievable target of 257 off 36 overs. Only 30 were bowled, the Windies ending on 2/80.

Glenn McGrath: Man of the Match.

Paul Reiffel and Shane Warne.

Skipper Taylor keeps boys honed for battle

In Mark Taylor, who hails from Wagga Wagga, Australia has a new captain with a rich vein of old-fashioned courtesy, a quality not easily sustained in the hurly-burly of non-stop play and persistent media scrutiny.

If he speaks a little too quickly, that is his style. Bradman had a high pitched voice and no one worried. Listen closely to Taylor and the word 'fairness' springs to mind. When he took over from Allan Border, Taylor laid down a few rules, firmly but politely. Cards (poor Doug Walters!) and cassette players were out. He wanted his men to watch the play, to become 'involved'. A 12th man who had been 'sleeping' on the job awoke.

There is no suggestion of the aloof about Taylor. He talks to his players as friend and confidante and they appreciate it. On the field, gum chewing seemingly his nerve-steadier, he is in control. He is prepared to take a punt – an unconventional bowling change or field placing.

Off the field Taylor, a surveyor, drew up a plan of attack for each West Indies player. Though he made only 153 Test runs at 25.5, players responded to his every call. He returned home with the Frank Worrell trophy, last won by Australia in 1975–76. He is a skipper Worrell would have liked: respected, calm in a crisis.

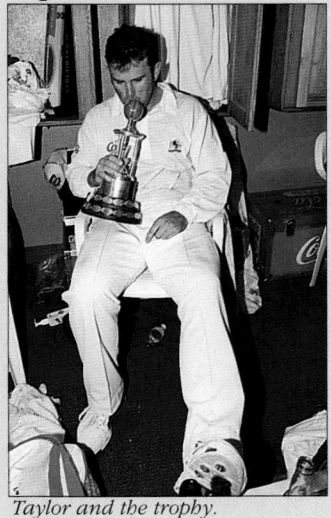

Taylor and the trophy.

Steve Waugh stands tall against Ambrose

Steve Waugh and Curtly Ambrose: eye to eye as Richie Richardson steps in.

Port-of-Spain, April 23. It was not his biggest score by a long haul, but Steve Waugh's unbeaten 63 against a fit and hostile Curtly Ambrose in the third Test was one of his finest innings. While all around him poked and fell on a spiteful pitch – wet and grassy – Waugh stood tall for 181 minutes in the most 'difficult' conditions he can remember in his 75 Tests.

He took no nonsense from Ambrose, who 'eyeballed' him at one stage and had to be pulled away by captain Richie Richardson. Referee Majid Khan later rebuked Ambrose mildly.

As for the wicket, Waugh said: 'It's the first time I've seen divots come up on the first day.'

When Australia's first innings ended at 128, Ambrose had 5/45 but not the wicket of Steve Waugh, a proud figure as he walked off Queen's Park Oval.

Having put Australia in, Richardson was hoping the pitch might behave more agreeably when the home side batted.

It wasn't to be. Glenn McGrath, with a career-best display of controlled fast bowling, upstaged even Ambrose and shot the home side out for 136 – a lead of only eight. McGrath claimed the wicket of Brian Lara (24) in his 6/47.

Australia made a better start in its second innings, Taylor (30) and Slater (15) putting on 26. But then Ambrose (4/20) and Courtney Walsh (3/35) struck. In a sensational collapse, Australia lost 5/2 to be all out for 105. This time Steve Waugh belted 21 in 36 minutes. The West Indies scored the 98 runs needed for victory for the loss of one wicket. With 9/65, Ambrose was clearly Man of the Match.

Jinx on Billy

Georgetown, March 22. Fast bowler Craig 'Billy' McDermott can't take a trick and is going home.

First, he injured his shoulder in the fourth one day game. Rested against Guyana, he watched play for a while then, to maintain his fitness, decided to run back to the team's hotel. On the way he jumped a cement wall while running along the beach and crashed over on his ankle, tearing the ligaments. He is to be replaced by his fellow Queenslander Carl Rackemann. Damien Fleming (shoulder) is also Australia-bound. Mark Waugh has a strained groin.

Despite adversity, Australia is playing with increasing confidence.

Coach Bob Simpson rests in hospital after being admitted with leg thrombosis.

The Waughs bring Australia home

Steve Waugh: number one.

Brothers-in-arms: Mark Waugh congratulates Steve on his first hundred.

Kingston, May 3. Sir Frank Worrell, who died in 1967, was one of cricket's most attractive stroke players and respected figures. Such was his love of the game, he would have rejoiced in the batting of the Waugh twins in the fourth Test at Sabina Park, even though they effectively wrested from the West Indies the trophy that bears his name.

Australia's victory by an innings and 53 runs in the 'decider', giving it the rubber 2–1, was an unlikely scenario on the first day when the West Indies were 1/102 after skipper Richie Richardson had won the toss.

Then in the space of four hours the home side was dismissed for 265, of which Richardson contributed a dogged 100, his 16th in Tests, and Brian Lara a characteristically breezy 65. The Australian bowlers toiled splendidly and shared the spoils, Paul Reiffel doing best with 3/48. Steve Waugh chipped in with two wickets at the end.

An Australian victory still looked far from a good thing when it lost 3/73 in its first innings, at which stage Steve Waugh joined younger brother Mark.

They batted together for 233 minutes, putting on 231 for the fourth wicket before Mark was out for a chanceless 126 in 276 min-

utes with 12 fours. An innings of polish and grace in the Worrell tradition. The disciplined Steve batted on and on, the surest way of answering those who felt him inadequate against genuine speed. He added 113 with Greg Blewett (69) and 73 with Reiffel before being last man out for 200 (555 minutes with 17 fours and a six) in a score of 531.

It was Steve Waugh's highest score in Tests. He had a stroke of luck at 42, being badly missed by 'keeper Browne. Had the chance been accepted, the game probably would have gone down to the wire.

For the Waugh twins, the day

was an excercise in brotherly love and contrasting styles. Both have now scored eight Test centuries.

With a lead of 276 to comfort them, the Australian bowlers got to work. Reiffel, bowling with the accuracy of a Lee Enfield .303, shot out the first three Windies batsmen for 46, including Lara lbw for 0.

The home side never recovered and was all out for 213 after lunch on the fourth day. Reiffel (4/47) and Shane Warne (4/70), a duo with a nice blend of cut and spinning thrust, shared the bowling honors.

Mark Taylor had the honor of holding the last catch at slip.

Trophy found

Kingston, May 3. The Frank Worrell trophy, first played for in 1964–65, was thought to have been lost, but has been gathering dust in the Caribbean since 1977–78. Its whereabouts were uncertain, but when Mark Taylor's Australians regained it at Sabina Park by a margin of 2–1, it came to light, was dusted off and presented to Taylor.

Australia had not won it since 1975–76 when Greg Chappell's side won 5–1 in Australia.

The trophy was struck after the highly successful West Indies tour of Australia in 1960–61. The teams were led by the popular Richie Benaud and Frank Worrell. Worrell was knighted in 1964.

Cricket bliss: Ian Healy and Mark Taylor with the elusive and long-awaited Frank Worrell Trophy.

FIRST TEST 1994–95 WEST INDIES v AUSTRALIA
Kensington Oval, Bridgetown. March 31, April 1, 2, 1995.
Toss: West Indies. Australia won by 10 wkts.

WEST INDIES

SC Williams c Taylor b Julian	1	c Healy b McGrath	10
SL Campbell c Healy b Reiffel	0	c SR Waugh b Warne	6
BC Lara c SR Waugh b Julian	65	c Healy b McGrath	9
RB Richardson (c) c Healy b Julian	0 (5)	b Reiffel	36
CL Hooper c Taylor b Julian	60 (4)	c Reiffel b Julian	16
JC Adams c Warne b McGrath	16	not out	39
JR Murray (+) c Taylor b McGrath	21	c SR Waugh b Warne	23
WKM Benjamin c Taylor b Warne	14	lbw McGrath	26
CEL Ambrose c Blewett b McGrath	7	c Blewett b McGrath	6
CA Walsh c SR Waugh b Warne	1	b McGrath	4
KCG Benjamin not out	0	b Warne	5
EXTRAS (B 3, W 1, NB 6)	10	(LB 1, NB 8)	9
TOTAL	195		189

FOW 1st Inns: 1 5 6 130 152 156 184 193 194 195
FOW 2nd Inns: 19 25 31 57 91 135 170 176 180 189

Bowling: *First Innings:* Reiffel 11-4-41-1, Julian 12-0-36-4, Warne 12-2-57-2, McGrath 12.1-1-46-3, ME Waugh 1-0-12-0. *Second Innings:* Reiffel 11-6-15-1, Julian 12-2-41-1, Warne 26.3-5-64-3, McGrath 22-6-68-5.

AUSTRALIA

MJ Slater c Williams b WKM Benjamin	18 (2)	not out	20
MA Taylor (c) c Hooper b KCG Benjamin	55 (1)	not out	16
DC Boon c WKM Benjamin b Walsh	20		
ME Waugh c Murray b Ambrose	40		
SR Waugh c Murray b KCG Benjamin	65		
GS Blewett c Murray b Ambrose	14		
IA Healy (+) not out	74		
BP Julian c KCG Benjamin b Hooper	31		
PR Reiffel b WKM Benjamin	1		
SK Warne c Adams b Walsh	6		
GD McGrath b WKM Benjamin	4		
EXTRAS (LB 13, NB 5)	18	(NB 3)	3
TOTAL	346		0 for 39

FOW 1st Inns: 27 72 121 166 194 230 290 291 331 346
FOW 2nd Inns:

Bowling: *First Innings:* Ambrose 20-7-41-2, Walsh 25-5-78-2, KCG Benjamin 20-1-84-2, WKM Benjamin 23.2-6-71-3, Hooper 12-0-59-1. *Second Innings:* Walsh 3-0-19-0, KCG Benjamin 2.5-1-14-0, Hooper 1-0-6-0.

Umpires: LH Barker & S Venkataraghavan (TV Umpire – H Moore)

SECOND TEST 1994–95 WEST INDIES v AUSTRALIA
Recreation Ground, St John's. April 8, 9, 10, 12, 13, 1995.
Toss: West Indies. Match Drawn.

AUSTRALIA

MJ Slater c Adams b Walsh	41 (2)	c Richardson b Walsh	18
MA Taylor (c) c Walsh b Ambrose	37 (1)	c Murray b Walsh	5
DC Boon b Walsh	21	lbw WKM Benjamin	67
ME Waugh c Hooper b Walsh	4	b WKM Benjamin	61
SR Waugh b KCG Benjamin	15	not out	65
GS Blewett c Murray b WKM Benjamin	11	c Williams b Hooper	19
IA Healy (+) c Walsh b WKM Benjamin	14	c Hooper b Walsh	26
BP Julian b Walsh	22	run out	6
PR Reiffel not out	22	not out	13
SK Warne c Arthurton b Walsh	11		
GD McGrath c Murray b Walsh	0		
EXTRAS (LB 12, NB 6)	18	(B 1, LB 9, NB 10)	20
TOTAL	216		7 dec 300

FOW 1st Inns: 82 84 89 126 126 150 168 188 204 216
FOW 2nd Inns: 22 43 149 162 196 254 273

Bowling: *First Innings:* Ambrose 14-5-34-1, Walsh 21.3-7-54-6, KCG Benjamin 16-3-58-1, WKM Benjamin 15-2-40-2, Hooper 2-0-18-0. *Second Innings:* Ambrose 19-3-42-0, Walsh 36-7-92-3, WKM Benjamin 24-2-72-2, KCG Benjamin 15-1-51-0, Arthurton 1-0-1-0, Hooper 9-3-16-1, Adams 4-0-16-0.

WEST INDIES

SC Williams c Boon b Warne	16	not out	31
RB Richardson (c) c SR Waugh b Julian	37	b Reiffel	2
BC Lara c Boon b SR Waugh	88	b Julian	43
JC Adams lbw Warne	22	not out	3
CL Hooper c Julian b SR Waugh	11		
KLT Arthurton c Taylor b Warne	26		
JR Murray (+) lbw Reiffel	26		
WKM Benjamin c Taylor b McGrath	4		
CEL Ambrose c Taylor b Reiffel	0		
CA Walsh b Reiffel	9		
KCG Benjamin not out	5		
EXTRAS (B 6, LB 3, W 1, NB 6)	16	(NB 1)	1
TOTAL	260		2 for 80

FOW 1st Inns: 34 106 168 186 187 240 240 240 254 260
FOW 2nd Inns: 11 69

Bowling: *First Innings:* Reiffel 17-3-53-3, Julian 10-5-36-1, Warne 28-9-83-3, McGrath 20.1-5-59-1, SR Waugh 6-1-20-2. *Second Innings:* Reiffel 6-2-12-1, Julian 5-2-15-1, Warne 7-0-18-0, McGrath 6-2-20-0, ME Waugh 6-2-15-0.

Umpires: SA Bucknor & DR Shepherd (TV Umpire – P White)

THIRD TEST 1994–95 WEST INDIES v AUSTRALIA
Queen's Park Oval, Port-of-Spain. April 21, 22, 23, 1995.
Toss: West Indies. West Indies won by 9 wkts.

AUSTRALIA

MA Taylor (c) c Adams b Ambrose	2 (2)	c Murray b KCG Benjamin	30
MJ Slater c Murray b Walsh	0 (1)	c Richardson b Walsh	15
DC Boon c Richardson b Ambrose	18	c (S)S Chanderpaul b Walsh	9
ME Waugh c Murray b Ambrose	2	lbw Ambrose	7
SR Waugh not out	63	c Hooper b KCG Benjamin	21
GS Blewett c Murray b WKM Benjamin	17	c Murray b KCG Benjamin	2
IA Healy (+) c Richardson b Walsh	8	b Ambrose	0
BP Julian c Adams b KCG Benjamin	0	b Ambrose	0
PR Reiffel c Lara b Walsh	11	c Hooper b Ambrose	6
SK Warne b Ambrose	0	c Hooper b Walsh	11
GD McGrath c Murray b Ambrose	0	not out	0
EXTRAS (LB 6, W 1)	7	(LB 3, NB 1)	4
TOTAL	128		105

FOW 1st Inns: 2 2 14 37 62 95 98 121 128 128
FOW 2nd Inns: 26 52 56 85 85 85 87 87 105 105

Bowling: *First Innings:* Ambrose 16-5-45-5, Walsh 17-4-50-3, WKM Benjamin 6-3-13-1, KCG Benjamin 8-2-14-1. *Second Innings:* Ambrose 10.1-1-20-4, Walsh 13-4-35-3, WKM Benjamin 5-0-15-0, KCG Benjamin 8-1-32-3.

WEST INDIES

SC Williams c Taylor b Reiffel	0	c Warne b ME Waugh	42
RB Richardson (c) c Healy b McGrath	2	not out	38
BC Lara c Taylor b McGrath	24	not out	14
JC Adams c ME Waugh b Reiffel	42		
CL Hooper c Reiffel b SR Waugh	21		
KLT Arthurton c ME Waugh b McGrath	5		
JR Murray (+) c Healy b McGrath	13		
WKM Benjamin c Slater b Warne	7		
CEL Ambrose c Slater b McGrath	1		
CA Walsh c Blewett b McGrath	14		
KCG Benjamin not out	1		
EXTRAS (LB 4, NB 2)	6	(B 4)	4
TOTAL	136		1 for 98

FOW 1st Inns: 1 6 42 87 95 106 113 114 129 136
FOW 2nd Inns: 81

Bowling: *First Innings:* McGrath 21.5-11-47-6, Reiffel 16-7-26-2, Julian 7-1-24-0, SR Waugh 3-1-19-1, Warne 12-5-16-1. *Second Innings:* McGrath 6-1-22-0, Reiffel 6-2-21-0, Julian 3-0-16-0, Warne 3.5-0-26-0, ME Waugh 2-0-9-1.

Umpires: CE Cumberbatch & DR Shepherd (TV Umpire – R Gosein)

FOURTH TEST 1994–95 WEST INDIES v AUSTRALIA
Sabina Park, Kingston. April 29, 30 May 1, 3, 1995.
Toss: West Indies. Australia won by an innings & 53 runs.

WEST INDIES

SC Williams c Blewett b Reiffel	0	b Reiffel	20
RB Richardson (c) lbw Reiffel	100	c & b Reiffel	14
BC Lara c Healy b Warne	65	lbw Reiffel	0
JC Adams c Slater b Julian	20	c SR Waugh b McGrath	18
CL Hooper c ME Waugh b Julian	23 (6)	run out	13
KLT Arthurton c Healy b McGrath	16 (7)	lbw Warne	14
CO Browne (+) c Boon b Warne	1 (8)	not out	31
WKM Benjamin lbw SR Waugh	7 (5)	lbw Reiffel	51
CEL Ambrose not out	6	st Healy b Warne	5
CA Walsh c Boon b SR Waugh	2	c Blewett b Warne	14
KCG Benjamin c Healy b Reiffel	5	c Taylor b Warne	6
EXTRAS (B 1, LB 9, W 1, NB 9)	20	(B 13, LB 8, NB 6)	27
TOTAL	265		213

FOW 1st Inns: 0 103 131 188 220 243 250 251 254 265
FOW 2nd Inns: 37 37 46 98 134 140 166 172 204 213

Bowling: *First Innings:* Reiffel 13.4-2-48-3, Julian 12-3-31-2, McGrath 20-4-79-1, Warne 25-6-72-2, SR Waugh 11-5-14-2, ME Waugh 4-1-11-0. *Second Innings:* Reiffel 18.5-5-47-4, Julian 10-2-37-0, Warne 23.4-8-70-4, ME Waugh 1-0-1-0, McGrath 13-2-28-1, SR Waugh 4-0-9-0.

AUSTRALIA

MA Taylor (c) c Adams b Walsh	8
MJ Slater c Lara b Walsh	27
DC Boon c Browne b Ambrose	17
ME Waugh c Adams b Hooper	126
SR Waugh c Lara b KCG Benjamin	200
GS Blewett c WKM Benjamin b Arthurton	69
IA Healy (+) c Lara b WKM Benjamin	6
BP Julian c Adams b Walsh	8
PR Reiffel b KCG Benjamin	23
SK Warne c Lara b KCG Benjamin	0
GD McGrath not out	3
EXTRAS (B 11, LB 6, W 1, NB 26)	44
TOTAL	531

FOW 1st Inns: 17 50 73 304 417 433 449 522 522 531

Bowling: *First Innings:* Ambrose 21-4-76-1, Walsh 33-6-103-3, KCG Benjamin 23.5-0-106-3, WKM Benjamin 24-3-80-1, Hooper 43-9-94-1, Adams 11-0-38-0, Arthurton 5-1-17-1.

Umpires: SA Bucknor & KE Liebenberg (TV Umpire – J Gayle)

Australian Averages

1994–95 WEST INDIES v AUSTRALIA

AUSTRALIA	M	Inn	NO	Runs	H.S	Avrge	Ct	St	Overs	Mds	Runs	Wkt	Avrge
Blewett, GS	4	6	-	132	69	22.00	5	-	-	-	-	-	-
Boon, DC	4	6	-	152	67	25.33	4	-	-	-	-	-	-
Healy, IA	4	6	1	128	74*	25.60	9	1	-	-	-	-	-
Julian, BP	4	6	-	67	31	11.17	1	-	71.0	15	236	9	26.22
McGrath, GD	4	5	2	7	4	2.33	-	-	121.1	32	369	17	21.71
Reiffel, PR	4	6	2	76	23	19.00	3	-	98.4	31	263	15	17.53
Slater, MJ	4	7	1	139	41	23.17	3	-	-	-	-	-	-
Taylor, MA	4	7	1	153	55	25.50	10	-	-	-	-	-	-
Warne, SK	4	5	-	28	11	5.60	2	-	138.0	35	406	15	27.07
Waugh, ME	4	6	-	240	126	40.00	3	-	14.0	3	48	1	48.00
Waugh, SR	4	6	2	429	200	107.25	6	-	24.0	7	62	5	12.40

West Indian Averages

1994–95 WEST INDIES v AUSTRALIA

WEST INDIES	M	Inn	NO	Runs	H.S	Avrge	Ct	St	Overs	Mds	Runs	Wkt	Avrge
Adams, JC	4	7	2	160	42	32.00	7	-	15.0	-	54	-	-
Ambrose, CEL	4	6	1	25	7	5.00	-	-	100.1	25	258	13	19.85
Arthurton, KLT	3	4	-	61	26	15.25	1	-	6.0	1	18	1	18.00
Benjamin, KCG	4	6	3	22	6	7.33	1	-	93.4	9	359	10	35.90
Benjamin, WKM	4	6	-	109	51	18.17	2	-	97.2	16	291	9	32.33
Browne, CO	1	2	1	32	31*	32.00	1	-	-	-	-	-	-
Campbell, SL	1	2	-	6	6	3.00	-	-	-	-	-	-	-
Hooper, CL	4	6	-	144	60	24.00	6	-	67.0	12	193	3	64.33
Lara, BC	4	8	1	308	88	44.00	5	-	-	-	-	-	-
Murray, JR	3	4	-	83	26	20.75	12	-	-	-	-	-	-
Richardson, RB	4	8	1	229	100	32.71	4	-	-	-	-	-	-
Walsh, CA	4	6	-	44	14	7.33	2	-	148.3	33	431	20	21.55
Williams, SC	4	8	1	120	42	17.14	2	-	-	-	-	-	-

Windies too good in one dayers

Georgetown, March 18. In the warm-up to the Tests, the West Indies asserted their superiority in the five one day internationals, winning 4–1 with Brian Lara making 256 in his only three innings.

Unfortunately for the 12,000 who rolled up for the last game here, Lara (hip) and Curtly Amrose (shoulder) could not play. Nor could Richie Richardson (jarred shoulder), on the sidelines since game one. Courtney Walsh has led the team in his absence.

Australia's lone success, by 26 runs, was in the second game in Port-of-Spain, Trinidad.

The series got away to an absorbing start in Bridgetown, Barbados with the home side winning by six runs. Batting first, the West Indies made 257 all out, Carl Hooper hitting 84 in 110 minutes and a relatively subdued Lara 55 in 101 minutes. Craig McDermott, in top form, took 3/25. Australia, in reply, was cruising at 1/94, at which stage Walsh removed Mark Taylor for 41 and Mark Waugh for 29. David Boon (85 not out) and Greg Blewett (33) tried hard to hit Australia to victory, but the tourists ran out of overs and ended on 6/251 – six short.

In its 26-run win in game two, Steve Waugh (58), Taylor (55) and Ian Healy (51) guided Australia to 8/260. McDermott and Paul Reiffel, three wickets apiece, kept the Windies to 234 after Lara (62) and Hooper (55) had threatened to bolt.

Lara's 139 in only 168 minutes off 125 balls spelt doom for Australia in game three. With support from Hooper (41) and Jimmy Adams (51 not out), the West Indies hammered their way to 5/282. Shane Warne's 10 overs cost 52 for no wickets. McDermott and Mark Waugh were out injured.

Australia, with Ricky Ponting making 43 and Steve Waugh 44, started well enough, reaching 3/118. It then lost six wickets for 31 to be all out for 149, hence defeat by a whopping 133 runs.

A noisy crowd of 10,000 weathered the rain for game four in Kingstown, St Vincent, where the West Indies clinched the series 3–1 on a faster run rate, 3/208 to Australia's 9/210. Rain halted play several times.

Despite the absence of Lara in the last game, the home side won with 16 balls to spare – 5/287 in reply to Australia's 286 (Mark Waugh 70 and Taylor 66).

Taylor makes it happen

When Mark Taylor succeeded Allan Border as Australian captain in 1994, he came to the job as a batsman with over 4000 Test runs on the board and centuries against seven countries. He knew the game, but his personal qualities were perhaps equally important.

He was a country boy. Not pushy or showy, but friendly, easygoing, honest and dependable. His team-mates respected him.

Taylor was born at Leeton, NSW in 1964. He spent his early years in the Riverina town of Wagga Wagga, which is also the birth-place of Australian cricketers Geoff Lawson and Michael Slater.

While still a teenager, his family moved to Sydney, where he was educated at Chatswood High School before studying surveying at the University of NSW.

On weekends, he played cricket for Northern District as an opening batsman. Here he caught the eye of former Northern District great, Neil Marks, who was a NSW selector.

Taylor scored 937 runs in his first class debut season for NSW (1985–86) and made his debut for Australia in the fourth Test against the West Indies in 1988–89.

It was not an auspicious start with scores in the fourth and fifth Tests of 25, 3, 3 and 36, but the young opener was invited to tour England in 1989. Here, he came of age, scoring 136 in the opening Test and 839 runs at 83.90 for the series. Only Don Bradman had better figures for an Ashes series.

A 329-run partnership between Taylor (219) and Geoff Marsh (138) in the fifth Test at Trent Bridge was a highlight of one of Australia's best Ashes campaigns. The pair became the first to bat for a full day's play in England and their 329 set a new first-wicket record for both Ashes Tests and all Tests in England. *Wisden* later named Taylor as one of its 'five cricketers of the year.'

He took some time to develop. Against England in 1990–91 he failed to make runs. And in 1991–92 he scored 94 in the first Test against India and 100 in the fourth, but did not reach 20 runs in four of his ten innings. Then he was back on track in the 1993 tour of England, with centuries in the first two Tests.

Taylor was a natural leader in many ways. He led sides as a schoolboy and, in the 1989–90 Sheffield Shield final, stepped into the job at 20 minutes notice

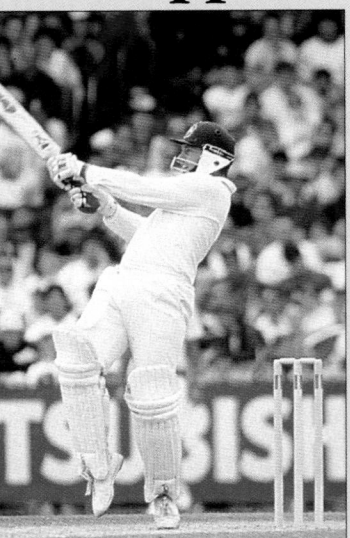

Mark Taylor - characteristic pull shot.

when Geoff Lawson was injured. The result: NSW won and Taylor scored centuries in both innings.

In his debut Test as Australian captain, Taylor made a pair against Pakistan at Karachi in October 1994, but the Ashes series later that summer was a brilliant personal and national success.

Under Taylor's leadership, in 1995 Australia brought the Frank Worrell Trophy back from the West Indies for the first time since 1973.

Taylor mistimed some hook shots and generally batted below his best in the Caribbean, but he had the pleasure of catching last man Kenny Benjamin at first slip in the final Test. Taylor's skills in slips are sometimes overlooked. In November 1995 he took seven catches for NSW in a Sheffield Shield match against Victoria.

When he was a young batsman playing for NSW his nickname was 'Stodge' because, he says: 'I used to just nick and nudge them around and play the odd pull shot and square cut.' That label perhaps hints at why the man now known as 'Tubby' has never been an outstanding limited overs batsman.

Poor batting form plagued some of his most recent seasons and during the 1997 South Africa tour he admitted he was mentally tired and his batting had suffered while captain. His old mentor, Neil Marks, reminded the media vultures that every batsman went through 'a bad trot,' with the possible exception of Bradman.

And it was testimony to Taylor's leadership that Australia did not also lose form in 1996–97.

Waughs top of the batting tree

The Waughs were the first twins to play Test cricket. But even though they bounced into the world on 2 June 1965, and became gifted batsmen, their arrival in the Test arena was in keeping with their appearance – non-identical.

Steve, as if by dint of his seniority – older than Mark by the time it takes to bowl an over of seamers, about four minutes — won his baggy green cap five years before his younger brother.

But Mark put to good use his inordinately long wait in the wings, scoring heavily and with flair at Sheffield Shield and English county level.

Australian cricket was at a low ebb, having surrendered in succession to the West Indies, England and New Zealand, when Steve, an aggressive batsman and accurate medium-pace bowler, stepped out as an all-rounder against India in the MCG Boxing Day Test in 1985.

It was an inauspicious Test debut – his 2/36 with deliveries that 'did a bit' attracting more notice than his 13 and five with the bat.

Bill O'Reilly applauded his selection, saying he had the instant appeal that Sid Barnes, Arthur Morris and Doug Walters possessed. O'Reilly accurately predicted that Waugh was 'custom-built to play one of the parts that our young men must adopt to restore the lost prestige of Australian cricket.'

Though in their formative years the Waughs followed parallel lines – first with Sydney club Bankstown, then with NSW and English county sides – Mark was in his 26th year before he got the nod from the Test selectors.

It came against England in the fourth Test in January 1991 and, as fate would have it, at the expense of Steve, dropped after a lean trot of 176 runs in 10 innings – in sharp contrast to his devastating form in England in 1989 when he plundered 506 runs at an average of 126.5 as Australia, under Allan Border, regained the Ashes.

Suddenly, after enduring a heavy workload in 42 Tests, scoring 2065 runs at 38.23 and taking 38 wickets, it was Steve's turn to watch Mark. And Steve was the first to congratulate his younger brother.

On his selection, Mark said he had 'mixed feelings because of Stephen. We were competitive when we were kids but we're not rivals now.'

The brothers Waugh celebrate their heroics in the West Indies 1995.

Unlike Steve who did not post his first century until his 27th Test – 177 not out at Leeds, which featured some brilliant square driving, followed by 152 not out at Lord's in that vintage English summer of '89 – Mark made haste, mindful that he had better get cracking to hold his place in such a strong Test batting line-up.

He had already done the groundwork, and then some, topping the 1989–90 Shield averages with 967 runs at 80.58 and, in 1990, helping the cause of Essex mightily with 2072 runs at 76.74. A dressing-room wit at Essex gave Waugh the nickname 'Afghan' – as in Afghanistan, the forgotten war.

For Mark, the pre-Test icing, so to speak, came five weeks before his initiation into Test ranks. The twins travelled to Perth with the NSW team and rewrote *Wisden* with an unbeaten partnership of 464, Mark scoring 229 not out and Steve 216 not out. It as the highest stand for any wicket by Australians.

Given the opportunity to play for Australia, Mark made his usual graceful entrance. In 126 balls at the Adelaide Oval he scored 100 runs as lovely as the ground itself. Coming in at 4/104, he sped from 21 to 116 after tea on the first day with flowing drives, off the back and front foot, neatly executed cuts and wristy deflections that raced to the on-side boundary.

He failed by only five runs to become the first player to score 100 runs in his first full batting session in Test cricket. When he went for 138 scored in 236 minutes he had become the 15th Australian to make a hundred on debut and the eighth to do so in the first innings of a Test against England.

If he sometimes looks casual, it is not a true reflection of his attitude. The nimble-footed Mark Edward Waugh makes batting look easy, as though the bowlers are his servants. *Wisden* observed: 'He is the type who can have 30 on the board without the bowlers realising he has his pads strapped on. Undemonstrative, compact and still at the crease, he works the ball rather than crashing it about. And being a high-quality cricketer he supplements his batting with useful medium-pace bowling and safe, adaptable fielding.'

The Waughs were born into a sporting family – one grandfather played rugby league for NSW country and their father Rodger beat Tony Roche in the final of the NSW under-14 tennis title. Their mother, Bev, was a top-class tennis and squash player.

The twins were naturals at soccer, tennis and cricket. Steve played cricket for NSW and soon for Somerset. Mark came into the NSW side at 20.

They played the first of their record 47 Tests together in the West Indies in April, 1991, nearly three months after Steve had been dropped. Playing at Port-of-Spain,

Mark made 64 and Steve 26.

It was in the West Indies four years later, in 1995, that the Waughs revealed their Test artistry in concert, combining for a stand of 231 that paved the way for Australia to win back the Frank Worrell trophy, locked away in the Caribbean since 1978.

They came together with Australia perilously placed at 3/73 in the fourth Test. When Mark departed for a chanceless 126 in 276 minutes, Australia was 4/304 and on its way to a total of 531 that enabled it to win by an innings.

Steve, a more disciplined player compared to earlier years when his flamboyant approach often led to his downfall, batted for 555 minutes for 200. His vulnerability against the rising ball, a trademark of the West Indian battery of fast bowlers, was mostly now a thing of the past. In the words of one observer, he was now a player of 'substance.'

Described as a 'cool, wary customer', Steve brooked no nonsense in the Caribbean. When Curtly Ambrose ran down the pitch to 'eyeball' him during the third Test, he gave as good as he got. West Indies skipper Richie Richardson pulled Ambrose away. And when Viv Richards criticised Waugh for claiming the gully catch that dismissed Brian Lara for 65 in the first Test, Waugh told him to mind his own business.

When the Waughs played their 45th Test together against South Africa in Port Elizabeth in March 1997, they beat the record of brothers Ian and Greg Chappell, with 44. Mark Waugh celebrated the occasion for them with 116.

Not known for their loquaciousness, the Waughs revealed their variety and wit in an interview with Greg Baum of the *Age* as they approached the record. When it came to talking about the record, Mark said: 'I'm glad you told us. We didn't have a clue.'

On tour, the Waughs have never roomed together. 'We had 20 years together in the same room,' said Mark, hinting that that was enough.

How do they get on? 'All right, yeah,' said Steve. 'But I don't want to mess your story up because everyone says we don't like each other and we don't talk. It's a pretty good story, leave it at that.'

And the best may be yet to come. Steve Waugh was appointed vice-captain of Australia – captain in waiting – for the 1997 Ashes tour.

1995-96

PAKISTAN IN AUSTRALIA

Salim Malik is not too welcome

Malik and Warne: controversial.

Brisbane, Nov. 8. On the eve of the first Test between Australia and Pakistan, the former Pakistani captain Salim Malik is attracting widespread media attention.

Malik was the focus of sensational allegations in February this year, when a newspaper reported that in October 1994 he had attempted to bribe Australian players Shane Warne, Mark Waugh and Tim May to throw the Karachi Test.

The Australians made statements to the ICC, and although Malik denied any involvement, he was later sacked as captain of Pakistan.

In an interesting decision, he has recently been cleared of any wrongdoing by a Pakistani judge.

The verdict has paved the way for his return to the Pakistan side.

Protests have greeted Malik's arrival in Australia, but he handles questions from the press as deftly as his footwork at the crease.

Shane Warne, however, is looking forward to taking his wicket.

Warne's 7/23 his second best

Brisbane, Nov. 13. Australian leg-spinner Shane Warne captured seven wickets for just 23 runs during the Pakistan innings in the first Test this week.

The return is his second best in Test cricket, behind his figures of 8/71 against England last year, which he also achieved at the 'Gabba ground.

Once known as a pace pitch, Warne's efforts suggest the 'Gabba is now becoming a slow man's turf.

Warne is the most exciting prospect in Australian cricket. He dominated Australia's victory over England in the 1993 Ashes series and claimed both Mike Gatting and Graham Gooch with stunning leg spin deliveries.

World title a non-event

Mark Taylor whacks one behind square leg at Bellerive.

Hobart, Nov. 21. It's all over. In the unofficial world championship of cricket the Australians are undisputed victors over the Pakistani pretenders.

Yesterday in the second Test Australia defeated Pakistan at Bellerive Oval by 155 runs. And it is only a week since Australia handed Pakistan a thrashing by more than an innings in the first Test in Brisbane.

It is strange that the public didn't seem to be captivated. Attendance at Brisbane was only 23,639 and at Hobart reached just 18,068.

Pakistan's Aamir Sohail hit fifteen fours in his second innings 99, but without a doubt Shane Warne's match aggregate of 11/77 was the highlight of the first Test. Warne took 4/54 in the second innings and an incredible 7/23 in the first, when Pakistan was all out for 97. Pakistan's controversial Salim Malik, who allegedly tried to bribe Warne last year, boasted that Warne was 'easy to read.' Australian captain Mark Taylor prevented Warne attempting a rising ball reprisal, but revenge was sweet when Malik was caught for a duck at mid-off when facing Warne's fourth spinning delivery.

All of the Australian top order batsmen scored solidly, especially Steve Waugh (112) and Mark Taylor (69). Taylor made 123 in the second Test, losing his wicket to a yorker from Waqar Younis.

Michael Slater, however, has had a modest series.

Savouring success: the 'sultan of spin,' Shane Warne.

'Mushy' saves face

Sydney, Dec. 4. Pakistan has struck back against Australia in the third Test at the SCG, which ended today in a Pakistan victory by 74 runs.

After convincing wins in Tests at Brisbane and Hobart, everyone was expecting this match to be a walkover for Australia, but the Pakistani leg-spinner Mushtaq Ahmed put an end to that.

Mushtaq captured nine wickets for the match, 5/95 in Australia's first innings and 4/91 in the second.

The ball he called his 'wrong one' generally proved to be the right one, but it was unsuccessful against Australia's Mark Waugh, who notched up a fine century.

Pakistan's Ijaz Ahmed was top-scorer in the match with 137.

FIRST TEST 1995–96 AUSTRALIA v PAKISTAN
Brisbane Cricket Ground, Brisbane. November 9, 10, 11, 13, 1995.
Toss: Australia. Australia won by an innings & 126 runs.

AUSTRALIA
MA Taylor (c) c Salim b Saqlain	.69
MJ Slater c Mohammad b Wasim	.42
DC Boon c Inzamam-ul-Haq b Wasim	.54
ME Waugh c Saleem b Saqlain	.59
SR Waugh not out	.112
GS Blewett lbw Waqar	.57
IA Healy (+) c(S)Mushtaq Ahmed b Mohammad	.18
PR Reiffel lbw Waqar	.9
SK Warne c Moin b Aamir	.5
CJ McDermott b Waqar	.8
GD McGrath st Moin b Aamir	.5
EXTRAS (B 2, LB 6, W 4, NB 13)	.25
TOTAL	.463

FOW 1st Inns: 107 119 213 250 385 411 434 441 452 463

Bowling: *First Innings*: Wasim 38-9-84-2, Waqar 29.5-7-101-3, Mohammad 33.1-4-97-1, Saqlain 44-12-130-2, Aamir 16.5-2-43-2.

PAKISTAN
Aamir Sohail st Healy b Warne	.32	b McGrath	.99
Saleem Elahi c Taylor b McDermott	.11	c Healy b McGrath	.2
Rameez Raja c Taylor b Warne	.8	c Healy b McGrath	.16
Saqlain Mushtaq lbw McGrath	.0 (9)	not out	.2
Inzamam-ul-Haq c SR Waugh b Warne	.5 (4)	c McDermott b ME Waugh	.62
Basit Ali c Taylor b Warne	.1 (5)	lbw McGrath	.26
Moin Khan (+) c McDermott b Warne	.4 (6)	c Healy b Reiffel	.9
Wasim Akram (c) c Boon b Warne	.1 (7)	c Slater b Warne	.6
Waqar Younis not out	.19 (10)	lbw Warne	.0
Mohammad Akram c Blewett b Warne	.1 (11)	lbw Warne	.0
Salim Malik	(8)	c McDermott b Warne	.0
EXTRAS (B 4, LB 5, NB 6)	.15	(B 7, NB 11)	.18
TOTAL	.9 dec 97		.240

FOW 1st Inns: 20 37 40 62 66 70 70 80 97
FOW 2nd Inns: 30 88 167 217 218 233 233 239 240 240

Bowling: *First Innings*: McDermott 11-4-32-1, McGrath 14-3-33-1, Warne 16.1-9-23-7.
Second Innings: McDermott 11-0-47-0, Reiffel 15-4-47-1, McGrath 25-7-76-4, Warne 27.5-10-54-4, SR Waugh 2-1-3-0, ME Waugh 5-2-6-1.

Umpires: KE Liebenberg & SG Randell (TV Umpire – AJ McQuillan)

THIRD TEST 1995–96 AUSTRALIA v PAKISTAN
Sydney Cricket Ground, Sydney. November 30, December 1, 2, 3, 4, 1995.
Toss: Pakistan. Pakistan won by 74 runs.

PAKISTAN
Aamir Sohail c ME Waugh b McDermott	.4	c Boon b McDermott	.9
Rameez Raja c Slater b Warne	.33	c ME Waugh b Warne	.39
Ijaz Ahmed c McGrath b Warne	.137	lbw Warne	.15
Inzamam-ul-Haq c Healy b Warne	.39 (6)	c Taylor b McDermott	.59
Salim Malik lbw McGrath	.36 (4)	lbw ME Waugh	.45
Basit Ali c Slater b McDermott	.17 (5)	b Warne	.14
Rashid Latif (+) c Healy b McDermott	.1 (8)	lbw Warne	.3
Wasim Akram (c) c & b McGrath	.21 (7)	lbw McDermott	.5
Saqlain Mushtaq run out	.0	c ME Waugh b McDermott	.2
Mushtaq Ahmed c McDermott b Warne	.0	lbw McDermott	.2
Waqar Younis not out	.0	not out	.1
EXTRAS (LB 3, W 2, NB 6)	.11	(B 1, LB 5, NB 4)	.10
TOTAL	.299		.204

FOW 1st Inns: 4 64 141 210 263 269 297 299 299 299
FOW 2nd Inns: 18 58 82 101 163 185 188 198 203 204

Bowling: *First Innings*: McDermott 21-6-62-3, McGrath 22.2-1-79-2, Reiffel 22-4-71-0, Warne 34-20-55-4, ME Waugh 10-4-23-0, Blewett 4-2-6-0. *Second Innings*: McDermott 15.3-0-49-5, McGrath 17-3-47-0, Warne 37-13-66-4, Reiffel 8.3-2-15-0, ME Waugh 14-4-21-1, Blewett 2-2-0-0.

AUSTRALIA
MJ Slater b Wasim	.1 (2)	lbw Mushtaq	.23
MA Taylor (c) c Rashid b Saqlain	.47 (1)	st Rashid b Mushtaq	.59
DC Boon c Rashid b Mushtaq	.16	c (S)Moin Khan b Saqlain	.6
ME Waugh c Mushtaq b Wasim	.116	c Rashid b Wasim	.34
SR Waugh st Rashid b Mushtaq	.38 (6)	b Mushtaq	.14
GS Blewett b Reiffel	.5 (7)	b Waqar	.14
IA Healy (+) c Rashid b Mushtaq	.6 (5)	c Rashid b Wasim	.7
PR Reiffel not out	.10 (10)	not out	.2
SK Warne c Rashid b Wasim	.2 (8)	c Saqlain b Mushtaq	.5
CJ McDermott b Wasim	.0 (9)	b Waqar	.0
GD McGrath c Wasim b Mushtaq	.0	b Waqar	.0
EXTRAS (LB 6, NB 10)	.16	(LB 5, NB 3)	.8
TOTAL	.257		.172

FOW 1st Inns: 2 44 91 174 182 226 240 249 249 257
FOW 2nd Inns: 42 69 117 126 146 153 170 170 172 172

Bowling: *First Innings*: Wasim 24-4-50-4, Waqar 11-4-26-0, Mushtaq 36.2-7-95-5, Saqlain 22-2-62-1, Aamir 5-0-18-0. *Second Innings*: Wasim 16-5-25-2, Waqar 6.1-2-15-3, Mushtaq 30-6-91-4, Saqlain 13-5-35-1, Aamir 1-0-1-0.

Umpires: HD Bird & SG Randell (TV Umpire – IS Thomas)

SECOND TEST 1995–96 AUSTRALIA v PAKISTAN
Bellerive Oval, Hobart. November 17, 18, 19, 20, 1995.
Toss: Australia. Australia won by 155 runs.

AUSTRALIA
MJ Slater lbw Wasim	.0 (2)	lbw Mushtaq	.73
MA Taylor (c) b Wasim	.40 (1)	b Waqar	.123
DC Boon run out	.34	c Waqar b Mushtaq	.0
ME Waugh c Rameez b Mushtaq	.88	b Wasim	.3
SR Waugh c Moin b Mushtaq	.7	c Moin b Mohammad	.29
GS Blewett b Mushtaq	.0	c Basit b Wasim	.11
IA Healy (+) c Basit b Mushtaq	.37	c Inzamam-ul-Haq b Wasim	.24
PR Reiffel c Mohammad b Mushtaq	.14	b Mushtaq	.0
SK Warne not out	.27		
CJ McDermott b Waqar	.0 (9)	c Wasim b Mushtaq	.20
GD McGrath b Wasim	.3 (10)	not out	.2
EXTRAS (B 3, LB 9, NB 5)	.17	(B 6, LB 5, W 1, NB 9)	.21
TOTAL	.267		.9 dec 306

FOW 1st Inns: 0 68 111 156 156 209 235 238 244 267
FOW 2nd Inns: 120 125 132 189 233 255 256 296 306

Bowling: *First Innings*: Wasim 18.3-7-42-3, Waqar 17-3-54-1, Mohammad 10-1-41-0, Mushtaq 30-5-115-5, Aamir 3-1-3-0. *Second Innings*: Wasim 26.1-7-72-3, Waqar 20-4-67-1, Mohammad 10-1-58-1, Mushtaq 38-8-83-4, Aamir 8-2-15-0.

PAKISTAN
Aamir Sohail c Healy b Reiffel	.32	c (S)BP Julian b Blewett	.57
Saleem Elahi b McGrath	.13	c Boon b McGrath	.17
Mushtaq Ahmed lbw McGrath	.0 (9)	b McGrath	.8
Rameez Raja c & b Reiffel	.59 (3)	lbw Reiffel	.25
Inzamam-ul-Haq c Healy b SR Waugh	.27 (4)	lbw Reiffel	.40
Ijaz Ahmed not out	.34 (5)	lbw Blewett	.4
Basit Ali lbw McGrath	.2 (6)	b Reiffel	.5
Moin Khan (+) b McDermott	.12 (7)	c ME Waugh b McGrath	.16
Wasim Akram (c) c Taylor b McDermott	.2 (8)	c Blewett b McGrath	.33
Waqar Younis c(S)BP Julian b Reiffel	.10	c Blewett b McGrath	.4
Mohammad Akram lbw McGrath	.0	not out	.0
EXTRAS (LB 1, NB 6)	.7	(LB 11)	.11
TOTAL	.198		.220

FOW 1st Inns: 24 24 79 126 150 155 173 183 198 198
FOW 2nd Inns: 27 62 132 142 152 157 205 210 220 220

Bowling: *First Innings*: McDermott 18-2-72-2, McGrath 19-4-46-3, Reiffel 15.5-5-38-4, ME Waugh 8-0-23-0, SR Waugh 6-0-18-1. *Second Innings*: McDermott 16-7-38-0, McGrath 24.3-7-61-5, Reiffel 14-6-42-3, ME Waugh 12-2-24-0, SR Waugh 8-1-19-0, Blewett 10-4-25-2.

Umpires: HD Bird & DB Hair (TV Umpire – SG Randell)

Australian Averages

1995–96 AUSTRALIA v PAKISTAN

AUSTRALIA	M	Inn	NO	Runs	H.S	Avrge	Ct	St	Overs	Mds	Runs	Wkt	Avrge
Blewett, GS	3	5	-	87	57	17.40	3	-	16.0	8	31	2	15.50
Boon, DC	3	5	-	110	54	22.00	3	-	-	-	-	-	-
Healy, IA	3	5	-	92	37	18.40	7	1	-	-	-	-	-
McDermott, CJ	3	5	-	28	20	5.60	2	-	92.3	19	300	11	27.27
McGrath, GD	3	5	1	10	5	2.50	2	-	121.5	25	342	15	22.80
Reiffel, PR	3	5	2	35	14	11.67	1	-	75.2	19	213	8	26.63
Slater, MJ	3	5	-	139	73	27.80	3	-	-	-	-	-	-
Taylor, MA	3	5	-	338	123	67.60	5	-	-	-	-	-	-
Warne, SK	3	4	1	39	27*	13.00	-	-	115.0	52	198	19	10.42
Waugh, ME	3	5	-	300	116	60.00	4	-	49.0	12	97	2	48.50
Waugh, SR	3	5	1	200	112*	50.00	1	-	16.0	2	40	1	40.00

Pakistani Averages

1995–96 AUSTRALIA v PAKISTAN

PAKISTAN	M	Inn	NO	Runs	H.S	Avrge	Ct	St	Overs	Mds	Runs	Wkt	Avrge
Aamir Sohail	3	6	-	233	99	38.83	-	-	33.5	5	80	2	40.00
Basit Ali	3	6	-	65	26	10.83	2	-	-	-	-	-	-
Ijaz Ahmed	2	4	1	190	137	63.33	-	-	-	-	-	-	-
Inzamam-ul-Haq	3	6	-	232	62	38.67	2	-	-	-	-	-	-
Mohammad Akram	2	4	1	1	1	0.33	-	-	53.1	6	196	2	98.00
Moin Khan	2	4	-	41	16	10.25	3	1	-	-	-	-	-
Mushtaq Ahmed	2	4	-	10	8	2.50	1	-	134.2	26	384	18	21.33
Rameez Raja	3	6	-	180	59	30.00	1	-	-	-	-	-	-
Rashid Latif	1	2	-	4	3	2.00	6	2	-	-	-	-	-
Saleem Elahi	2	4	-	43	17	10.75	1	-	-	-	-	-	-
Salim Malik	2	3	-	81	45	27.00	1	-	-	-	-	-	-
Saqlain Mushtaq	2	4	1	4	2*	1.33	1	-	79.0	19	227	4	56.75
Waqar Younis	3	6	3	34	19*	11.33	1	-	84.0	20	263	8	32.88
Wasim Akram	3	6	-	68	33	11.33	2	-	122.4	32	273	14	19.50

Chucking trouble

Bent arm? Muttiah Muralitharan.

Melbourne, Dec. 27. There's a stench of death at the MCG.

In the second Test yesterday, Australian umpire Darrell Hair seven times uttered 'no-ball' for throwing to Sri Lankan off-spinner Muttiah Muralitharan.

The Sri Lankan's action has previously been questioned at ICC level by umpires who say he illegally fails to straighten his arm during delivery. But his jerky, 'wristy' action is often hard to read.

Yesterday, Muralitharan was called when Hair was standing at the bowler's end, but not from square leg. New Zealand umpire Steve Dunne did not call him from either position, so Muralitharan was able to keep bowling from Dunne's end.

But Hair has now warned that he will call Muralitharan from either position unless his action changes.

Until yesterday, the young Sri Lankan was arguably the best off-spinner in the world.

What a difference a day makes.

A run-feast

Ricky Ponting: out for 96 on debut.

Adelaide, Jan. 30. Runs, runs and more runs have been the order of the day for Australia in three Test victories over Sri Lanka.

In each match, Australia was untroubled breaking the 500 run mark in an innings.

The pattern was set in the first Test at Perth, where Michael Slater (219) drew a leaf out of Victor Trumper's book, advancing down the pitch to smash several huge sixes off Sri Lankan spinner Muttiah Muralitharan. Other big scorers at Perth were Australia's Mark Taylor (96), Mark Waugh (111) and Ricky Ponting (96). Hashan Tillekaratne made 119 for Sri Lanka.

In the second Test at Melbourne, centuries were made by Australia's David Boon (110) and Steve Waugh (131), and for Sri Lanka by Asanka Gurisinha (143).

Both Waugh and Gurusinha also made centuries in the third Test at Adelaide.

Boonie bows out

No more victory chants for Boonie.

Adelaide, Jan. 29. After lapses in form and continued media pressure, Australian batsman David Boon anounced his retirement from international cricket on January 25. Boon made his 21st Test century just four weeks ago at Melbourne, and in his last pair of innings here in the third Test he scored 43 and 35, close to his average of 43.66. Delighted fans saw him run through the repertoire of strokes that made him one of the best of all time.

Boon is one of only two men to have scored more than 7000 runs for Australia. He has played over 100 Tests and taken 99 catches, many of these fielding in the dangerous short leg position.

Everyone cheered as an emotional 'Boonie' walked back to the rooms after his final innings. The Sri Lankan team stood and clapped.

But at the victory ceremony today, Boon did not take the dais. He stayed with his team-mates.

Australia 2–0 in testy but exciting one day finals

Sydney, Jan. 20. After rain interrupted play, Australia defeated Sri Lanka on run rate today in the second final of the Benson and Hedges World Series. The win gives Australia the series following its 18-run victory in the first final held in Melbourne two days ago.

Sri Lanka beat Australia twice in preliminary games. No love was lost between the sides following recent incidents involving ball tampering and throwing.

Australian bowler Glenn McGrath 'chested' Sri Lankan opener Sanath Jayasuriya in the final today. Craig McDermott had an altercation with Arjuna Ranatunga, and Sri Lankan captain Aravinda de Silva refused to shake the hand of Australia's Mark Taylor at the presentation.

Umpire Steve Randell initially refused to allow Sri Lankan captain Arjuna Ranatunga to use a runner in the second World Series final.

FIRST TEST 1995–96 AUSTRALIA v SRI LANKA
W.A.C.A. Ground, Perth. December 8, 9, 10, 11, 1995.
Toss: Sri Lanka. Australia won by an innings & 36 runs.

SRI LANKA

RS Mahanama c Warne b McDermott	15	b McGrath 48
UC Hathurusingha c Law b McGrath	14	c Healy b McGrath 11
AP Gurusinha b McGrath	46	c Healy b McDermott 7
PA De Silva c & b Warne	10	c Ponting b Warne 20
A Ranatunga (c) c Healy b McGrath	32	b McGrath 46
HP Tillakaratne lbw McDermott	6	c Ponting b Warne 119
RS Kaluwitharana (+) c Taylor b Warne	50	c Ponting b Julian 40
HDPK Dharmasena b McDermott	30	lbw McDermott 18
WPUJC Vaas c Healy b Warne	4	c Healy b Warne 4
GP Wickramasinghe c Julian b McGrath	28	c Warne b McDermott 0
M Muralidaran not out	0	not out 3
EXTRAS (B 4, LB 9, NB 3)	16	(LB 4, NB 10) 14
TOTAL	251	330

FOW 1st Inns: 25 38 54 129 132 172 193 205 251 251
FOW 2nd Inns: 35 56 87 105 193 258 310 318 319 330

Bowling: *First Innings*: McDermott 18.4-5-44-3, McGrath 24-3-81-4, Julian 17-8-32-0, Warne 27-7-75-3, Waugh 3-1-6-0. *Second Innings*: McGrath 24-7-86-3, McDermott 20-3-73-3, Warne 29.4-6-96-3, Julian 13-4-40-1, Waugh 4-0-22-0, Law 3-1-9-0.

AUSTRALIA

MJ Slater c & b Muralidaran	219
MA Taylor (c) lbw De Silva	96
DC Boon c Hathurusingha b Muralidaran	13
ME Waugh c Kaluwitharana b Vaas	111
RT Ponting lbw Vaas	96
SG Law not out	54
IA Healy (+)	
BP Julian	
SK Warne	
CJ McDermott	
GD McGrath	
EXTRAS (B 4, LB 6, NB 18)	28
TOTAL	5 dec 617

FOW 1st Inns: 228 266 422 496 617

Bowling: *First Innings*: Wickramasinghe 31-3-123-0, Vaas 31-5-103-2, Muralidaran 54-3-224-2, Hathurusingha 9-3-31-0, Dharmasena 31-5-84-0, De Silva 18-1-42-1.

Umpires: Khizer Hayat & PD Parker (TV Umpire – BT Rennie)

THIRD TEST 1995–96 AUSTRALIA v SRI LANKA
Adelaide Oval, Adelaide. January 25, 26, 27, 28, 29 1996.
Toss: Australia. Australia won by 148 runs.

AUSTRALIA

MA Taylor (c) c Kaluwitharana b Vaas	21 (2)	b Pushpakumara 10
MJ Slater c Kaluwitharana b Vaas	0 (1)	b Wickramasinghe 15
DC Boon b Pushpakumara	43	c Kaluwitharana b Vaas 35
ME Waugh c Pushpakumara b Wickramasinghe	71	c Tillakaratne b Vaas 12
SR Waugh b Pushpakumara	170	not out 61
RT Ponting c Kaluwitharana b Vaas	6	c Kaluwitharana b Vaas 20
IA Healy (+) c Pushpakumara b Dharmasena	70	c Hathurusingha b Pushpakumara .43
PR Reiffel c Gurusinha b Wickramasinghe	56	not out 14
SK Warne c Pushpakumara b Wickramasinghe	33	
CJ McDermott not out	15	
GD McGrath		
EXTRAS (B 5, LB 9, W 1, NB 2)	17	(B 1, LB 1, NB 3) 5
TOTAL	9 dec 502	.......6 dec 215

FOW 1st Inns: 1 36 96 181 196 326 443 467 502
FOW 2nd Inns: 22 36 70 75 122 186

Bowling: *First Innings*: Vaas 42-11-106-3, Pushpakumara 34-4-126-2, Wickramasinghe 39.3-7-120-3, Hathurusingha 4-0-15-0, Dharmasena 25-3-80-1, Jayasuriya 13-2-41-0. *Second Innings*: Vaas 21-6-44-3, Pushpakumara 17-2-63-2, Wickramasinghe 13-1-39-1, Dharmasena 22-1-67-0.

SRI LANKA

UC Hathurusingha c ME Waugh b Reiffel	28	c Healy b McGrath 14
ST Jayasuriya c Healy b Reiffel	48	c Healy b SR Waugh 112
AP Gurusinha c Reiffel b McGrath	17	b Reiffel 2
S Ranatunga c SR Waugh b McDermott	60	c Healy b SR Waugh 65
RS Kaluwitharana (+) lbw Reiffel	31	b SR Waugh 0
HP Tillakaratne c Healy b McGrath	65	c Healy b McGrath 3
PA De Silva (c) c Taylor b McGrath	19	c Taylor b ME Waugh 3
HDPK Dharmasena c Healy b McGrath	0	c Taylor b SR Waugh 2
WPUJC Vaas c ME Waugh b Reiffel	8	c Healy b McGrath 26
GP Wickramasinghe b Reiffel	10	b Warne 6
KR Pushpakumara not out	2	not out 3
EXTRAS (B 8, LB 13, W 1, NB 7)	29	(B 1, LB 6, NB 9) 16
TOTAL	317	252

FOW 1st Inns: 86 89 129 171 237 290 290 299 309 317
FOW 2nd Inns: 51 70 195 195 199 208 216 225 232 252

Bowling: *First Innings*: McDermott 20-5-81-1, McGrath 27-4-91-4, Warne 26-4-74-0, Reiffel 19.1-4-39-5, ME Waugh 5-2-11-0. *Second Innings*: McGrath 22.2-6-48-3, Reiffel 15-0-60-1, SR Waugh 19-8-34-4, Warne 27-11-68-1, McDermott 9-3-20-0, ME Waugh 4-1-15-1.

Umpires: LH Barker & SG Randell (TV Umpire – DJ Harper)

SECOND TEST 1995–96 AUSTRALIA v SRI LANKA
Melbourne Cricket Ground, Melbourne. December 26, 27, 28, 29, 30, 1995.
Toss: Sri Lanka. Australia won by 10 wkts.

AUSTRALIA

MJ Slater c Wickramasinghe b Vaas	62 (2)	not out 13
MA Taylor (c) b Wickramasinghe	7 (1)	not out 25
DC Boon c Muralidaran b Wickramasinghe	110	
ME Waugh b Muralidaran	61	
SR Waugh not out	131	
RT Ponting c Gurusinha b Silva	71	
IA Healy (+) c Muralidaran b De Silva	41	
PR Reiffel not out	4	
SK Warne		
CJ McDermott		
GD McGrath		
EXTRAS (LB 8, W 2, NB 3)	13	(LB 1, NB 2) 3
TOTAL	6 dec 500	.......0 for 41

FOW 1st Inns: 14 116 219 280 395 488
FOW 2nd Inns:

Bowling: *First Innings*: Wickramasinghe 30.2-9-77-2, Vaas 40.4-11-93-1, Hathurusingha 9-0-23-0, Gurusinha 2-0-8-0, Muralidaran 38-7-124-1, Silva 35-5-120-1, De Silva 10-0-47-1. *Second Innings*: Vaas 3-0-25-0, Gurusinha 3-1-6-0, De Silva 1-0-4-0, Tillakaratne 0.4-0-5-0.

SRI LANKA

RS Mahanama c Taylor b McGrath	3	c Warne b Reiffel 3
UC Hathurusingha lbw McGrath	23	lbw Warne 39
AP Gurusinha c Healy b Ponting	27	lbw Reiffel 143
PA De Silva c Reiffel b McGrath	18	c Healy b McDermott 28
A Ranatunga (c) c Warne b McDermott	51 (4)	not out 11
HP Tillakaratne c Taylor b Warne	14	c Ponting b ME Waugh 38
RS Kaluwitharana (+) c Boon b McDermott	50 (5)	st Healy b Warne 2
WPUJC Vaas c Healy b Reiffel	0	c Boon b McGrath 6
GP Wickramasinghe c Healy b McGrath	10	st Healy b Warne 17
M Muralidaran c Slater b McGrath	11	c Taylor b Warne 0
KJ Silva not out	7	b McGrath 0
EXTRAS (B 6, LB 7, NB 7)	20	(B 7, LB 5, W 8) 20
TOTAL	233	307

FOW 1st Inns: 3 64 68 128 140 182 183 213 221 233
FOW 2nd Inns: 11 97 168 172 255 273 285 306 306 307

Bowling: *First Innings*: McDermott 23-8-63-2, McGrath 23.4-9-40-5, Reiffel 20-5-60-1, Ponting 4-2-8-1, Warne 18-5-49-1. *Second Innings*: McGrath 33.5-6-92-2, McDermott 17-1-54-1, Reiffel 20-7-59-2, Warne 37-10-71-4, ME Waugh 9-1-19-1.

Umpires: RS Dunne & DB Hair (TV Umpire – WP Sheahan)

Australian Averages

1995–96 AUSTRALIA v SRI LANKA

AUSTRALIA	M	Inn	NO	Runs	H.S	Avrge	Ct	St	Overs	Mds	Runs	Wkt	Avrge
Boon, DC	3	4	-	201	110	50.25	2	-	-	-	-	-	-
Healy, IA	3	3	-	154	70	51.33	17	2	-	-	-	-	-
Julian, BP	1	-	-	-	-	-	1	-	30.0	12	72	1	72.00
Law, SG	1	1	1	54	54*	-	1	-	3.0	1	9	-	-
McDermott, CJ	3	1	1	15	15*	-	-	-	107.4	25	335	10	33.50
McGrath, GD	3	-	-	-	-	-	-	-	154.5	35	438	21	20.86
Ponting, RT	3	4	-	193	96	48.25	4	-	4.0	2	8	1	8.00
Reiffel, PR	2	3	2	74	56	74.00	2	-	74.1	16	218	9	24.22
Slater, MJ	3	5	1	309	219	77.25	1	-	-	-	-	-	-
Taylor, MA	3	5	1	159	96	39.75	7	-	-	-	-	-	-
Warne, SK	3	1	-	33	33	33.00	5	-	164.4	43	433	12	36.08
Waugh, ME	3	4	-	255	111	63.75	2	-	25.0	5	73	2	36.50
Waugh, SR	2	3	2	362	170	362.00	1	-	19.0	8	34	4	8.50

Sri Lankan Averages

1995–96 AUSTRALIA v SRI LANKA

SRI LANKA	M	Inn	NO	Runs	H.S	Avrge	Ct	St	Overs	Mds	Runs	Wkt	Avrge
De Silva, PA	3	6	-	98	28	16.33	-	-	29.0	1	93	2	46.50
Dharmasena, HDPK	2	4	-	50	30	12.50	-	-	78.0	9	231	1	231.00
Gurusinha, AP	3	6	-	242	143	40.33	2	-	5.0	1	14	-	-
Hathurusingha, UC	3	6	-	129	39	21.50	2	-	22.0	3	69	-	-
Jayasuriya, ST	1	2	-	160	112	80.00	-	-	13.0	2	41	-	-
Kaluwitharana, RS	3	6	-	173	50	28.83	6	-	-	-	-	-	-
Mahanama, RS	2	4	-	69	48	17.25	-	-	-	-	-	-	-
Muralidaran, M	2	4	2	14	11	7.00	3	-	92.0	10	348	3	116.00
Pushpakumara, KR	1	2	2	5	3*	-	3	-	51.0	6	189	4	47.25
Ranatunga, A	2	4	1	140	51	46.67	-	-	-	-	-	-	-
Ranatunga, S	1	2	-	125	65	62.50	-	-	-	-	-	-	-
Silva, KJ	1	2	1	6	6*	6.00	-	-	35.0	5	120	1	120.00
Tillakaratne, HP	3	6	-	245	119	40.83	1	-	0.4	-	5	-	-
Vaas, WPUJC	3	6	-	48	26	8.00	-	-	137.4	33	371	9	41.22
Wickramasinghe, GP	3	6	-	71	28	11.83	1	-	113.5	20	359	6	59.83

Australian surge, but Sri Lanka wins cup

Lahore, March 17. This is Sri Lankan cricket's finest hour. In a remarkable victory, Sri Lanka has defeated Australia by seven wickets in the final of the World Cup.

Amazingly, Sri Lanka won the toss but elected to field. For the first time, a team has batted second and won a World Cup final.

Mark Taylor scored 74 in Australia's innings and gave the Sri Lankans 241 runs to chase. Sri Lanka made a poor start, losing both openers for less than 15 runs.

Then Aravinda De Silva came to the crease. After bowling 3/42 that afternoon, De Silva was in fine form. He was unperturbed by the spin of Shane Warne (0/58) and survived two dropped catches to make an unbeaten 107 that set up the Sri Lankan victory. Asanka Gurusinghe (65) and Arjuna Ranatunga (47) also had a hand.

Naturally, the Australians were disappointed, but they deserve great credit just for making the final, especially in light of the terrorist bombing in Colombo which led both Australia and the West Indies to forfeit their early scheduled matches in the Sri Lankan city, despite exceptional safety assurances from local authorities.

The price of this decision was that Australia did not face Sri Lanka until the final. Along the way, Australia beat Kenya, India, Zimbabwe, New Zealand and the West Indies. Australia's sole loss was to the West Indies in a preliminary game.

The 1996 World Cup suggests that cricket's old order may be changing. Sri Lanka thrashed Australia for the Cup. England's only win was over the Netherlands, and Kenya thumped the West Indies by 73 runs. Is nothing sacred?

Australia's best World Cup moment: Courteney Walsh is out – we're in the final!

Coach 'Simmo' loses job, despite taking team to top

Melbourne, July 30. The last thing Bob Simpson needed was to be reminded of winter in Melbourne.

There he was, easing back into an armchair at his hotel in the south of Italy, when news came through that he had been replaced as coach of the Australian cricket team.

'Simmo' might be forgiven for having some difficulty in accepting the umpire's decision.

After all, his Australian side is widely ackowledged as the best Test cricket team in the world.

Since taking over in 1986, the 'drill sergeant' Simpson has taken what some critics called a rabble and moulded a unit that can fight with the best of them.

He led Australia through four triumphant Ashes campaigns, captured the 1987 World Cup, moulded a great general in Allan Border, and emerged victorious over the old West Indian enemy in 1995.

It is no wonder Simmo didn't see this one coming. But come it has. And this time, the veteran is out. Caught behind.

The 'powers that be' have decided that the time has come for a younger man with fresh ideas.

They have passed the bat to another former opener, the recently retired Geoff Marsh.

An era ends for coach Bob Simpson.

Disaster in Dismal Delhi

Delhi, Oct. 14. Australia had not played India in India for ten years – the series which Dean Jones made memorable with a double century in the tie at Madras. Four years since Australia played India in Australia – cricket relations have been mostly of the fleeting variety, one day stands, which like the one-night variety do not make for a satisfactory long-term relationship.

In the last four years India has played 96 one dayers and just 25 Tests, while Australia has played 94 one dayers and 45 Tests. The new president of the Indian cricket board murmurs that 'there is more money than runs' in Indian cricket and that Australian Test experience counts for little when the Australian team is without Shane Warne and Craig McDermott, let alone Allan Border and David Boon.

Australia went into this match with what some observers regarded as an unbalanced as well as inexperienced team – picking two wrist spinners with one Test between them – Peter McIntyre and Brad Hogg, and only two fast-medium bowlers, Glenn McGrath and Paul Reiffel.

The pitch at the Feroz Shah Ground was described by Greg Baum in the Melbourne *Age* as a 'paddy path of a pitch'. He quotes English umpire Peter Willey as saying it was the worst first-day pitch he had ever seen, and that he would take a piece of it home as proof.

That said, the Australians played the pitch like it was a dry version of a 'sticky' of old.

Steve Waugh, who had lasted just five balls in the first innings debacle of 182, fielded for a day and an hour watching Indian 'keeper and makeshift opener Nahan Mongia make 152 without taking risks.

Baum quotes Waugh as thinking that it 'was not the pitch that was unplayable, just that certain shots should not be played on it. If a batsman was disciplined enough to restrain himself to the one or two shots he knew were feasible, it would be impossible for an attack to dismiss him.'

The trouble for Australia was that from Michael Slater's attacking but fatally indiscreet slash outside the off stump and consequent duck, to Anil Kumble's teasing deceptions of Mark Waugh and Michael Bevan, there was no one else of like determination.

Waugh (67 not out) with help from tail-ender Peter McIntyre

Well Played. Mark Taylor congratulates Sourav Ganguly on India's win, as Steve Waugh shakes hands with Mohammad Azharuddin.

(who survived 73 balls to Waugh's 47 in their partnership) showed that Australia hadn't given up.

Mark Taylor agreed after India knocked off the 58 runs, saying the Australian batsmen took a day and a half to work out the pitch – by which time it was too late.

ONLY TEST 1996–97 INDIA v AUSTRALIA
Feroze Shah Kotla Ground, Delhi. October 10, 11, 12, 14, 1996.
Toss: Australia. India won by 7 wkts.

AUSTRALIA

MJ Slater c & b Kumble	44 (2)	c Azharuddin b Johnson ... 0
MA Taylor (c) lbw Prasad	27 (1)	c Rathore b Kapoor ... 37
RT Ponting b Kapoor	14	b Prasad ... 13
ME Waugh c Dravid b Joshi	26	c Mongia b Kumble ... 23
SR Waugh c Mongia b Kapoor	0	not out ... 67
MG Bevan lbw Joshi	26	c Azharuddin b Kumble ... 33
IA Healy (+) b Kumble	17	st Mongia b Kumble ... 12
GB Hogg c Rathore b Kumble	1	c Rathore b Kumble ... 4
PR Reiffel c Dravid b Kumble	7	lbw Kumble ... 6
PE McIntyre not out	6	lbw Prasad ... 16
GD McGrath run out	6	c Mongia b Prasad ... 0
EXTRAS (B 4, LB 3, NB 1)	8	(B 9, LB 6, W 1, NB 7) ... 23
TOTAL	182	... 234

FOW 1st Inns: 47 81 93 94 143 144 147 169 170 182
FOW 2nd Inns: 4 25 72 78 145 159 171 191 232 234

Bowling: *First Innings*: Prasad 12-4-34-1, Johnson 4-1-12-0, Joshi 23-7-36-2, Kumble 24-7-63-4, Kapoor 10-3-30-2. *Second Innings*: Prasad 13.3-7-18-3, Johnson 12-2-40-1, Kumble 41-12-67-5, Joshi 20-7-52-0, Kapoor 22-5-42-1.

INDIA

VS Rathore c Ponting b Reiffel	5	b Reiffel ... 14
NR Mongia (+) b Reiffel	152	lbw Reiffel ... 0
SC Ganguly c ME Waugh b Hogg	66	not out ... 21
SR Tendulkar (c) c ME Waugh b McIntyre	10	b McGrath ... 0
M Azharuddin b McGrath	17	not out ... 21
RS Dravid c Healy b SR Waugh	40	
SB Joshi c Ponting b McIntyre	23	
AR Kapoor c Ponting b ME Waugh	22	
AR Kumble lbw Reiffel	2	
D Johnson not out	0	
VBK Prasad b McIntyre	3	
EXTRAS (B 10, LB 1, NB 10)	21	(W 1, NB 1) ... 2
TOTAL	361	... 3 for 58

FOW 1st Inns: 13 144 169 199 260 303 341 353 354 361
FOW 2nd Inns: 1 25 26

Bowling: *First Innings*: McGrath 29-10-56-1, Reiffel 17-7-35-3, SR Waugh 13-5-25-1, McIntyre 37.4-7-103-3, Hogg 17-3-69-1, ME Waugh 18-0-62-1. *Second Innings*: McGrath 7-2-30-1, Reiffel 6-2-24-2, McIntyre 0.2-0-4-0.

Umpires: S Venkataraghavan & P Willey

Under new management

Brisbane, Nov. 20. New coach of the West Indies is fast bowling legend Malcolm Marshall, and new manager is batting and captaincy legend Clive Lloyd.

Both maintained in an interview with Greg Baum of the Melbourne *Age* that they will with new Australian coach Geoff Marsh 'try and make things a little bit better' between the teams.

Marshall said 'Let's put it this way: whatever happened in the past is past, and that's where I would like it to be.'

In the past are incidents such as the blow-up between Ian Healy and Desmond Haynes in 1991, and other incident involving Healy in 1992 – particularly the stumping of Brian Lara. After this Healy visited the West Indies rooms only to be asked by batsman Ken Arthurton 'Do you want your arse broken, man?'

On the subject of having a beer together after the game, Mark Taylor in the official program writes: 'That official line of getting together and having a beer was tried in '91 in the Caribbean as well. You can't fabricate feelings; they've got to be real. The feeling in the West Indies in '95 was good … I'd like to keep that going.'

New stars shine at Bellerive

Hobart, Nov. 18. Mark Ray in the *Sunday Age* wrote of the Australian XI first innings against a depleted West Indian attack: 'Watching Matthew Elliott and Matthew Hayden together was to see why the former will play plenty of Test matches and the latter, despite mountains of runs, might only play one.'

Elliott made 158 and Hayden 224 in an opening partnership of 323 which not only caused trouble for the West Indies and its lacklustre captain Brian Lara, but also for the following Australian XI batsmen – how were they to approach impressing the selectors?

Greg Blewett made steady 89 not out, captain Stuart Law a duck and Michael Bevan 29 – which may or may not have helped the selectors' dilemmas over Michael Slater, Ricky Ponting and Bevan.

As for the new bowlers on show, Jason Gillespie looked sharp and had no luck and Andy Bichel and Anthony Stuart took wickets.

The Australian XI won by ten wickets.

Innovative sponsorship: Test cricket sponsor, Ansett Australia, on the new MCG sight-screen, Mark Waugh and Shane Warne await their chances.

Healy and Ponting first-Test heroes

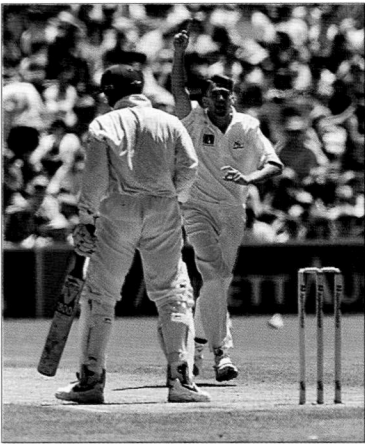

Glenn McGrath gets Carl Hooper.

Brisbane, Nov. 26. Ian Healy's third Test century, 161 not out, was also perhaps his best personal achievement in Test cricket. It set the tone for the first Test, and may have that effect on the series. He has bounced back from the dusty depression of Delhi, and seems to have been the spark that ignited the whole Australian team.

Ricky Ponting batted with aggression and some luck, both of which were necessary – and took a special catch to get rid of Carl Hooper for 102. Then, in one of those 'surprise' moves captain Mark Taylor has made predictable, brought him on to bowl, taking on an over Steve Waugh could not finish because of a groin strain. Ponting immediately trapped Jimmy Adams for a duck.

Matthew Elliott made a duck, as did Michael Bevan, but Bevan in Taylor's scheme of things can also bowl.

Bevan's 14 second-innings overs of fastish left-arm wrist-spinners conceded a miserly 46 runs, and snared the prize wickets of Sherwin Campbell (after a masterly 113 in a hopeless West Indies cause), Carl Hooper and also Ian Bishop.

The master wrist-spinner Shane Warne added 2/92 to his first innings 2/88 – from a total of 68 overs. His finger is better, but his confidence and attack is still on the mend.

Matchwinner Brian Lara looked out of sorts and out of form, but the West Indian captain says the West Indies are not cowed by Australia – and have comeback from one down before.

Ian Healy: 188 in first Test.

Mark Waugh at the 'Gabba.

Michael Bevan: Adelaide bag.

Mark Taylor: wins Worrell Trophy.

McGrath shines, Elliott crashes

Sydney Dec. 4. Glenn McGrath had the batting time of his life as he made 24 to help Australia from an insecure 288 to a competitive 331 in the first innings of the Test in Sydney. In Steve Waugh's absence (injured) Greg Blewett seized his chance on return to Test cricket with a fluent 69. Michael Bevan on the other hand was marooned and seemingly strokeless in making 16 in two hours.

The West Indies made 303 in reply. The supposed world's best batsman was again out, caught by Healy off Glenn McGrath, who has perfected a deceptive slower ball. It removed the dangerous Jimmy Adams.

Australia's second innings was marked, or marred, by an extraordinary mid-pitch collision between Matthew Elliott, sailing imperiously along to his first Test century, and Mark Waugh. Even more amazing than the crash which injured Elliott was that Carl Hooper, the bowler, failed to run out Mark Waugh.

The match was settled by Shane Warne on the last day with a fabulous in dipping leg-break that spun a mile outside left-hander Shivnarine Chanderpaul's off stump and hit middle. The West Indies' confidence, fragile in both Tests, was snapped, and they could not bat out the day. Australia is two up and on the way to retaining the Frank Worrell Trophy.

Australia crumbles in Melbourne

Melbourne, Dec. 29. The West Indies thudded back into contention with a six-wicket win at the MCG. The long-lethal form of injured fast bowler Curtly Ambrose was the inspiration, taking 4/17 in the second innings while captain Courtney Walsh and unsung Kenny Benjamin took three each in a batting debacle that threatened many scribes and fans' confidence in the batting of the Australian team.

Matthew Hayden was cruelly exposed letting one go, Justin Langer who looked compact in the first innings was not comfortable in the second and Greg Blewett was brave in the first but out of depth, it seemed, in the second innings. Of the experienced players, Mark Taylor's woes continued – he survived for 78 minutes and ten runs, Mark Waugh failed twice and only Steve Waugh looked like making runs. Aside from Waugh, Ian Healy is Australia's best batsman so far.

But as Taylor said: 'We're only one Test away from winning the series, they're two. … plus they had a wicket that was always going to suit their players. I can't remember an Australian cricket team playing well against the West Indies on an uneven wicket. They had four quick bowlers; we had two.' (Jason Gillespie only bowled three overs.)

The captains' course – steady as she goes.

Windies are Bev-boozled

Adelaide, Jan. 28. Peter Roebuck in the *Age* called the West Indies' batting performance in the first innings in the fourth Test 'staggeringly inept'. He said that 'Brian Lara in particular had particular reason to be ashamed.' He took an agricultural and contemptuous swipe at the first ball he faced from Shane Warne, and paid the price – caught at mid-on. For a team already hurt by the absence of Curtly Ambrose, ill-managed by his team in a vain attempt to win the one day series, Lara's action was desperately irresponsible.

Australia amassed 5/434 by the end of the second day. due as much to inept fielding and bowling as brilliant batting. Catches were taken off no-balls, dropped off good ones, lbw's thereabouts but not out.

In the end Australia progressed to 517. Lucky batsmen were Matthew Hayden who made 125 in his third Test and Mark Waugh an effortless 82. Unlucky Greg Blewett was out on 99. The only piece of luck for the West Indies was getting Steve Waugh off a long hop.

Michael Bevan took four wickets in the first innings, but even his best mate would not have predicted the devastation of the second innings when he bamboozled six West Indies batsmen.

Bevan's batting may have been laborious, but his bowling was glorious, securing the trophy.

Overheated in Perth

Perth, Feb. 3. Emotion in team sport is a strange phenomenon, and the balance changed the humiliation of Adelaide for the West Indies. Despite having lost the series, the return of Curtly Ambrose to the side in a game at the WACA where he had taken 17 wickets in two previous Tests charged up the West Indies – in conditions more fitting to roasting a chicken than playing cricket.

Australia, on the other hand, was off the boil, despite the heat, and struggled to 243, with only Mark Waugh (79) and Michael Bevan (that man again – 87 not out) looking at all comfortable. Courtney Walsh devised a plan to protect Ambrose and Ian Bishop from the heat by bowling them in one over alternating spells – which was effective.

Brian Lara, between bouts of mutual 'sledging' creaked toward his first century in 18 months – finding form at the end against Shane Warne whom he thumped for 22 in two overs. Lara complained about what was said to his partner Robert Samuels; the Australians contend that Lara is himself a provocateur.

Despite a 15-ball over from Ambrose, in his last over in Australia – Australia was bowled out for a paltry 194, with Hayden bravely battling to 47. The West Indies won the ill-humoured and overheated Test by ten wickets.

Bev's blow for lefties

Michael Bevan bowling at the SCG in the second Test.

Adelaide, Jan. 28. The rise and rise of Michael Bevan as a left-arm wrist-spinner has brought a few of his much maligned ancestors out of the woodwork.

Patron saint of all left-arm wrist spinners is 'Chuck' Fleetwood-Smith, whom Lindsay Kline told John McDonald in the *Australian* that Bill Ponsford told *him* was the only bowler who made the ball actually hum in the air.

Kline has one up on Bevan so far – he took a hat-trick against South Africa in 1960–61. 'The first ball was a flipper to Eddie Fuller that Richie Benaud caught at silly mid-on. The second was a quicker ball

to Hugh Tayfield which skidded on and got him lbw. I was going to bowl a leg-break to Neil Adcock, but changed my mind during my run-up. I bowled a wrong'un and Bobby Simpson took a terrific catch. I didn't realise how good it was until I saw it on the Movietone News.'

Other lefties include David Sincock, a prodigious spinner if somewhat erratic, David Hourn and Johnny Martin. Currently playing are David Freedman for NSW and Brad Hogg of WA. What Shane Warne has done for righties, Michael Bevan might do for lefties – if his batting holds up.

Barsby's farewell Shield

Perth, March 25. Queensland, and more particularly opening batsman Trevor Barsby won a second, stunning Sheffield Shield defeating WA by 160 runs.

Barsby, in his 100th and last game for Queensland, made 67 in the first innings. and 111 fighting sickness in the second innings, as well as a brilliant catch to get rid of the threatening Adam Gilchrist from the bowling of Michael Kasprowicz. Kasprowicz made a terrific return to wicket-taking form after his disappointing two Tests earlier in the summer, with 3/42 and 5/83. Tom Moody in a rearguard effort made 152.

Queensland captain Stuart Law, between singing verses of the adopted anthem 'Holy Grail', predicted 'more glory' for the young Queensland side.

World Rankings

Melbourne Dec. 16. Matthew Engel, editor of *Wisden*, published a proposal for a 'continuous world championship' of Test cricket, in Australian newspapers.

It takes the form of a continually updated table of results between the nine Test playing nations, who would all play a series, home and away, over a four-year period.

Series could be one, three or five Tests long – whatever the length, it would be two points for a winning series, one point for a draw and none for a loss. Series between particular countries would stay in the rankings until replaced by the same series in the next four–year cycle.

There are a number of problems with this simple model – the weighting of series, for example. Should Australia v South Africa in South Africa over three Tests have the same points as one Test against Zimbabwe at home?

FIRST TEST 1996–97 AUSTRALIA v WEST INDIES
Brisbane Cricket Ground, Brisbane. November 22, 23, 24, 25, 26, 1996.
Toss: West Indies. Australia won by 123 runs.

AUSTRALIA

MA Taylor (c) b Walsh	43	(2)	c Browne b Benjamin	36
MTG Elliott c Browne b Ambrose	0	(1)	b Bishop	21
RT Ponting c Walsh b Benjamin	88		c Browne b Bishop	9
ME Waugh c Browne b Walsh	38		c Browne b Bishop	57
SR Waugh c Lara b Bishop	66			
MG Bevan c Samuels b Walsh	0	(5)	c (S)AFG Griffith b Ambrose	20
IA Healy (+) not out	161	(6)	not out	45
PR Reiffel c & b Walsh	20	(7)	run out	11
SK Warne c & b Bishop	24			
MS Kasprowicz c Benjamin b Bishop	6			
GD McGrath b Benjamin	0			
EXTRAS (LB 8, W 3, NB 22)	33		(B 1, LB 3, NB 14)	18
TOTAL	479			6 dec 217

FOW 1st Inns: 4 130 146 196 196 338 407 468 477 479
FOW 2nd Inns: 55 74 82 137 189 217

Bowling: *First Innings*: Ambrose 34-4-93-1, Walsh 35-6-112-4, Benjamin 33-6-97-2, Bishop 30-2-105-3, Hooper 19-3-64-0. *Second Innings*: Ambrose 18-2-47-1, Walsh 17-1-58-0, Bishop 13-2-49-3, Benjamin 15-1-52-1, Hooper 2-0-7-0.

WEST INDIES

SL Campbell c Warne b Reiffel	18	lbw Bevan	113
RG Samuels c Healy b McGrath	10	c Taylor b Warne	29
BC Lara c ME Waugh b McGrath	26	c ME Waugh b Reiffel	44
CL Hooper c Ponting b SR Waugh	102	c Healy b Bevan	23
S Chanderpaul c ME Waugh b Reiffel	82	b McGrath	14
JC Adams lbw Ponting	0	lbw Warne	2
CO Browne (+) c Healy b Reiffel	4	c Healy b McGrath	20
IR Bishop lbw Warne	0	c Ponting b Bevan	24
CEL Ambrose c(S)JN Gillespie b Reiffel	0	c Warne b McGrath	7
KCG Benjamin lbw Warne	9	lbw McGrath	1
CA Walsh (c) not out	0	not out	1
EXTRAS (LB 8, W 1, NB 17)	26	(B 8, LB 3, NB 7)	18
TOTAL	277		296

FOW 1st Inns: 30 43 77 249 255 267 268 268 277 277
FOW 2nd Inns: 54 118 154 187 202 241 281 293 293 296

Bowling: *First Innings*: McGrath 21-7-32-2, Reiffel 24.1-6-58-4, Kasprowicz 22-5-60-0, Warne 27-3-88-2, SR Waugh 8.1-1-15-1, ME Waugh 4-1-16-0, Ponting 1.5-1-0-1. *Second Innings*: McGrath 29.5-12-60-4, Kasprowicz 13-2-29-0, Warne 41-16-92-2, Reiffel 9-0-58-1, Bevan 14-3-46-3.

Umpires: CJ Mitchley & SG Randell (TV Umpire – PD Parker)

SECOND TEST 1996–97 AUSTRALIA v WEST INDIES
Sydney Cricket Ground, Sydney. November 29, 30, December 1, 2, 3 1996.
Toss: Australia. Australia won by 124 runs.

AUSTRALIA

MA Taylor (c) c Chanderpaul b Bishop	27	(2)	c Lara b Bishop	16
MTG Elliott c Lara b Bishop	29	(1)	retired hurt	78
RT Ponting c Samuels b Walsh	9		c Browne b Bishop	4
ME Waugh c Lara b Walsh	19		c Browne b Ambrose	67
MG Bevan c Hooper b Benjamin	16		c Browne b Benjamin	52
GS Blewett c Adams b Walsh	69		not out	47
IA Healy (+) c Lara b Walsh	44		not out	22
SK Warne c Browne b Bishop	28			
MS Kasprowicz c Campbell b Walsh	21			
JN Gillespie not out	16			
GD McGrath lbw Adams	24			
EXTRAS (LB 10, W 1, NB 18)	29		(B 4, LB 10, W 3, NB 9)	26
TOTAL	331			4 dec 312

FOW 1st Inns: 54 68 73 94 131 224 245 283 288 331
FOW 2nd Inns: 51 67 209 274

Bowling: *First Innings*: Ambrose 25-5-73-0, Walsh 30-6-98-5, Benjamin 22-4-69-1, Hooper 14-6-15-0, Bishop 23-5-55-3, Adams 5.5-1-11-1. *Second Innings*: Ambrose 20-2-66-1, Walsh 19-6-36-0, Bishop 20-6-54-2, Benjamin 16-4-46-1, Adams 4-0-21-0, Hooper 27-7-75-0.

WEST INDIES

SL Campbell b Blewett	77	lbw McGrath	15
RG Samuels lbw McGrath	35	b Warne	16
BC Lara c Healy b McGrath	2	c Healy b McGrath	1
CL Hooper lbw McGrath	27	c Taylor b Warne	57
S Chanderpaul c & b Warne	48	b Warne	71
JC Adams c Bevan b McGrath	30	c Blewett b McGrath	5
CO Browne (+) c Blewett b McGrath	0	not out	25
IR Bishop c Elliott b Warne	48	run out	0
CEL Ambrose b Gillespie	9	b Bevan	0
KCG Benjamin b Gillespie	6	c Taylor b Warne	4
CA Walsh (c) not out	2	c McGrath b Warne	18
EXTRAS (B 4, LB 6, NB 10)	20	(LB 2, NB 1)	3
TOTAL	304		215

FOW 1st Inns: 92 108 136 166 229 229 243 286 298 304
FOW 2nd Inns: 33 33 35 152 157 176 176 176 183 215

Bowling: *First Innings*: McGrath 31-9-82-4, Kasprowicz 13-2-37-0, Warne 35.2-13-65-3, Gillespie 23-5-62-2, Bevan 11-0-35-0, Blewett 4-0-13-1. *Second Innings*: McGrath 17-7-36-3, Waugh 4-0-15-0, Gillespie 7-2-27-0, Warne 27.4-5-95-4, Bevan 14-2-40-2.

Umpires: DB Hair & DR Shepherd (TV Umpire – SJ Taufel)

THIRD TEST 1996–97 AUSTRALIA v WEST INDIES
Melbourne Cricket Ground, Melbourne. December 26, 27, 28, 1996.
Toss: Australia. West Indies won by 6 wkts.

AUSTRALIA
MA Taylor (c) b Ambrose	7 (2)	c Hooper b Walsh	10
ML Hayden c Hooper b Ambrose	5 (1)	b Ambrose	0
JL Langer run out	12	c Hooper b Ambrose	0
ME Waugh lbw Ambrose	0	lbw Walsh	19
SR Waugh c Murray b Bishop	58	b Benjamin	37
GS Blewett run out	62	c Murray b Walsh	7
IA Healy (+) c Hooper b Ambrose	36	b Benjamin	0
PR Reiffel c Samuels b Benjamin	0	lbw Benjamin	8
SK Warne c Campbell b Bishop	10	c Adams b Ambrose	18
JN Gillespie not out	4	lbw Ambrose	2
GD McGrath c Hooper b Ambrose	0	not out	5
EXTRAS (LB 8, NB 17)	25	(LB 4, W 1, NB 11)	16
TOTAL	219		122

FOW 1st Inns: 5 26 26 27 129 195 200 200 217 219
FOW 2nd Inns: 0 3 28 47 64 65 76 107 113 122

Bowling: *First Innings*: Ambrose 24.5-7-55-5, Bishop 11-1-31-2, Benjamin 19-2-64-1, Walsh 14-0-43-0, Adams 1-0-4-0, Hooper 5-1-14-0. *Second Innings*: Ambrose 12-4-17-4, Bishop 10-2-26-0, Benjamin 12.5-5-34-3, Walsh 11-4-41-3.

WEST INDIES
SL Campbell lbw McGrath	7	c Hayden b McGrath	0
RG Samuels c Taylor b Warne	17	lbw McGrath	13
S Chanderpaul c & b McGrath	58	b Reiffel	40
BC Lara c Warne b McGrath	2	c Hayden b McGrath	2
CL Hooper run out	7	not out	27
JC Adams not out	74	not out	1
JR Murray (+) c Reiffel b McGrath	53		
IR Bishop lbw McGrath	0		
CEL Ambrose b Warne	8		
KCG Benjamin b Reiffel	11		
CA Walsh (c) c ME Waugh b Warne	4		
EXTRAS (B 4, LB 7, NB 3)	14	(NB 4)	4
TOTAL	255		4 for 87

FOW 1st Inns: 12 62 71 86 107 197 197 215 230 255
FOW 2nd Inns: 0 25 32 82

Bowling: *First Innings*: McGrath 30-11-50-5, Reiffel 29-8-76-1, Warne 28.1-3-72-3, Gillespie 3-2-5-0, Blewett 9-3-19-0, SR Waugh 10-5-22-0. *Second Innings*: McGrath 9-1-41-3, Reiffel 9-2-16-1, Warne 3-0-17-0, Blewett 2.5-0-13-0.

Umpires: PD Parker & S Venkataraghavan (TV Umpire – WP Sheahan)

FIFTH TEST 1996–97 AUSTRALIA v WEST INDIES
W.A.C.A. Ground, Perth. February 1, 2, 3, 1997.
Toss: Australia. West Indies won by 10 wkts.

AUSTRALIA
ML Hayden c Lara b Ambrose	0 (2)	lbw Hooper	47
MA Taylor (c) run out	2 (1)	c Browne b Ambrose	1
GS Blewett c Browne b Simmons	17	b Ambrose	0
ME Waugh c Campbell b Ambrose	79	c Browne b Walsh	9
SR Waugh c Browne b Ambrose	1	c Hooper b Walsh	0
MG Bevan not out	87	c Simmons b Walsh	15
IA Healy (+) c Ambrose	7	c Chanderpaul b Walsh	29
PR Reiffel c Simmons b Ambrose	0	c Adams b Walsh	5
SK Warne c Browne b Bishop	9	c Simmons b Bishop	30
AJ Bichel c Browne b Bishop	15	c Samuels b Bishop	18
GD McGrath c Ambrose b Bishop	0	not out	2
EXTRAS (LB 10, W 2, NB 14)	26	(B 2, LB 8, W 6, NB 22)	38
TOTAL	243		194

FOW 1st Inns: 0 7 45 49 169 186 186 216 243 243
FOW 2nd Inns: 7 17 43 48 84 105 110 133 189 194

Bowling: *First Innings*: Ambrose 18-5-43-5, Bishop 18-5-54-3, Walsh 9-0-29-0, Simmons 20-5-58-1, Hooper 15-1-49-0. *Second Innings*: Ambrose 9-2-50-2, Bishop 12.3-1-44-2, Walsh 20-4-74-5, Simmons 3-0-9-0, Hooper 3-0-7-1.

WEST INDIES
SL Campbell c Healy b Reiffel	21	not out	16
RG Samuels c ME Waugh b Warne	76	not out	35
S Chanderpaul c Reiffel b McGrath	3		
BC Lara c Healy b Warne	132		
CL Hooper c Healy b Reiffel	57		
JC Adams c Healy b McGrath	18		
PV Simmons c ME Waugh b Reiffel	0		
CO Browne (+) c Warne b Reiffel	0		
IR Bishop c Taylor b Reiffel	13		
CEL Ambrose run out	15		
CA Walsh (c) not out	5		
EXTRAS (B 5, LB 10, W 1, NB 28)	44	(LB 2, W 1, NB 3)	6
TOTAL	384		0 for 57

FOW 1st Inns: 30 43 251 275 331 332 332 359 367 384
FOW 2nd Inns:

Bowling: *First Innings*: McGrath 30-5-86-2, Bichel 18-1-79-0, Reiffel 26-6-73-5, Warne 19-8-55-2, Blewett 6-2-19-0, Bevan 5-0-31-0, SR Waugh 7-1-26-0. *Second Innings*: McGrath 4-1-14-0, Reiffel 5-0-24-0, Bichel 1.3-0-17-0.

Umpires: DB Hair & P Willey (TV Umpire - TA Prue)

FOURTH TEST 1996–97 AUSTRALIA v WEST INDIES
Adelaide Oval, Adelaide. January 25, 26, 27, 28, 1997.
Toss: West Indies. Australia won by 183 runs.

WEST INDIES
SL Campbell c Healy b McGrath	0	c Taylor b Bevan	24
AFG Griffith lbw Bichel	13	c SR Waugh b McGrath	1
S Chanderpaul c Taylor b Warne	20	c Taylor b Bevan	8
BC Lara c Blewett b Warne	9	c Healy b Warne	78
CL Hooper c ME Waugh b McGrath	17	lbw Warne	45
JC Adams c & b Warne	10	c ME Waugh b Bevan	0
JR Murray (+) c Blewett b Bevan	34 (8)	c Taylor b Bevan	25
IR Bishop c Healy b Bevan	1 (7)	c Bevan b Warne	0
CA Walsh (c) c Healy b Bevan	0	c SR Waugh b Bevan	1
CE Cuffy c Healy b Bevan	2	not out	3
PIC Thompson not out	10	c Hayden b Bevan	6
EXTRAS (B 4, LB 1, NB 9)	14	(B 2, LB 5, NB 6)	13
TOTAL	130		204

FOW 1st Inns: 11 22 45 58 72 113 117 117 119 130
FOW 2nd Inns: 6 22 42 138 145 154 181 192 196 204

Bowling: *First Innings*: McGrath 12-4-21-2, Bichel 10-1-31-1, Bevan 9.5-2-31-4, Warne 16-4-42-3. *Second Innings*: McGrath 17-4-31-1, Bichel 8-4-16-0, Bevan 22.4-3-82-6, Warne 20-4-68-3, Blewett 2-2-0-0.

AUSTRALIA
MA Taylor (c) lbw Bishop	11
ML Hayden st Murray b Hooper	125
JL Langer c Murray b Cuffy	19
ME Waugh c Murray b Hooper	82
SR Waugh c Hooper b Chanderpaul	26
GS Blewett b Cuffy	99
MG Bevan not out	85
IA Healy (+) c Lara b Thompson	12
SK Warne c Hooper b Bishop	9
AJ Bichel c Lara b Walsh	7
GD McGrath b Walsh	1
EXTRAS (B 2, LB 15, W 4, NB 20)	41
TOTAL	517

FOW 1st Inns: 35 78 242 288 288 453 475 494 507 517

Bowling: *First Innings*: Walsh 37.3-6-101-2, Bishop 34-6-92-2, Cuffy 33-4-116-2, Thompson 16-0-80-1, Hooper 31-7-86-2, Adams 8-0-23-0, Chanderpaul 3-1-2-1.

Umpires: SG Randell & DR Shepherd (TV Umpire – DJ Harper)

Australian Averages

1996–97 AUSTRALIA v WEST INDIES												
AUSTRALIA	M	Inn	NO	Runs	H.S	Avrge	Ct	St	Overs	Mds	Runs	Wkt	Avrge
Bevan, MG	4	7	2	275	87*	55.00	2	-	76.3	10	265	15	17.67
Bichel, AJ	2	3	-	40	18	13.33	-	-	37.4	6	143	1	143.00
Blewett, GS	4	7	1	301	99	50.17	4	-	23.4	7	64	1	64.00
Elliott, MTG	2	4	1	128	78+	42.67	1	-	-	-	-	-	-
Gillespie, JN	2	3	2	22	16*	22.00	-	-	33.0	9	94	2	47.00
Hayden, ML	3	5	-	177	125	35.40	3	-	-	-	-	-	-
Healy, IA	5	9	3	356	161*	59.33	15	-	-	-	-	-	-
Kasprowicz, MS	2	2	-	27	21	13.50	-	-	48.0	9	126	-	-
Langer, JL	2	3	-	31	19	10.33	-	-	-	-	-	-	-
McGrath, GD	5	7	2	32	24	6.40	2	-	200.5	61	453	26	17.42
Ponting, RT	2	4	-	110	88	27.50	2	-	1.5	0	0	1	0.00
Reiffel, PR	3	6	-	44	20	7.33	-	-	102.1	22	305	12	25.42
Taylor, MA	5	9	-	153	43	17.00	9	-	-	-	-	-	-
Warne, SK	5	7	-	128	30	18.29	1	-	217.1	56	594	22	27.00
Waugh, ME	5	9	-	370	82	41.11	8	-	8.0	1	31	-	-
Waugh, SR	4	6	-	188	66	31.33	2	-	25.1	7	63	1	63.00

West Indian Averages

1996–97 AUSTRALIA v WEST INDIES												
WEST INDIES	M	Inn	NO	Runs	H.S	Avrge	Ct	St	Overs	Mds	Runs	Wkt	Avrge
Adams, JC	5	9	2	140	74*	20.00	3	-	18.5	1	59	1	59.00
Ambrose, CEL	4	6	-	39	15	6.50	1	-	160.5	31	444	19	23.36
Benjamin, KCG	3	5	-	31	11	6.20	1	-	117.5	22	362	9	40.22
Bishop, IR	5	8	-	86	48	10.75	1	-	171.3	30	510	20	25.50
Browne, CO	2	2	-	49	25*	12.25	15	-	-	-	-	-	-
Campbell, SL	5	10	1	291	113	32.33	3	-	-	-	-	-	-
Chanderpaul, S	5	9	-	344	82	38.22	2	-	3.0	1	2	1	2.00
Cuffy, CE	1	2	1	5	3*	5.00	-	-	33.0	4	116	2	58.00
Griffith, AFG	1	2	-	14	13	7.00	-	-	-	-	-	-	-
Hooper, CL	5	9	1	362	102	45.25	9	-	116.0	25	317	3	105.67
Lara, BC	5	9	-	296	132	32.89	8	-	-	-	-	-	-
Murray, JR	2	3	-	112	53	37.33	4	1	-	-	-	-	-
Samuels, RG	4	8	1	231	76	33.00	1	-	-	-	-	-	-
Simmons, PV	1	1	-	0	0	0.00	-	-	23.0	5	67	1	67.00
Thompson, PIC	1	2	1	16	10*	16.00	-	-	16.0	-	80	1	80.00
Walsh, CA	5	8	4	31	18	7.75	2	-	192.3	33	592	19	31.15

Australia on top of the world

Two Tests, three innings – Australia's batting heroes Greg Blewett, Steve Waugh and Mark Waugh scored 572 between them.

Pretoria, March 24. Australia lost the anticlimactic third Test but won the series and confirmed against the opinions of doubters that it is the best Test match side in the world. Except for a habit of losing 'dead' matches, Australia has shown that even with the captain completely out of form and a best opening partnership of 33, Australia has the resources of courage, skill and luck to beat the world. Surely after retaining the Frank Worrell trophy and now defeating South Africa, Australia is world champion at Test cricket.

Steve Waugh confirmed that he is the toughest batsman in the world. Ian Healy earned himself a two match suspension (to be served in the one day series) after disputing a caught behind decision (clearly off the pad) by umpire Cyril Mitchley. Umpiring standards in the Tests have been lamentable with bad decisions on no-balls and dismissals compounding a fiercely contested but friendly series.

How long before South Africa and Australia contest a full five-Test series

Australia's two wins were the result of three of the best innings ever seen in Test cricket – and that doesn't count Matthew Elliott's authoritative 85 in Australia's innings in the first Test. This match will go down in the Test annals as the day Steve Waugh (137 not out) and Greg Blewett (156 not out) batted all day, the 12th time in Test history.

Blewett went on to 214, the best by an Australian against South Africa, and Waugh to 160. Their stand of 385 was just 20 short of the record for the fifth wicket, and is the 12th highest partnership in Test cricket.

South Africa had made 302 batting first, thanks mainly to 'keeper Dave Richardson's 72 with the tail – but after Australia's 628 was always going to need a miracle to win. Commencing the last day already 4/99 and Shane Warne on song, one commentator quipped it was 'cruelty to dumb animals' to bring Michael Bevan on at the other end. Bevan took four wickets in 12 balls to end the match; Australia winning by an innings and 196 runs, the worst drubbing South Africa has received since returning to Test cricket.

The second Test was hardly a better result for South Africa, even though Australia was in mortal danger of losing at different stages. The game was won by Mark Waugh's best Test innings, 116, his 11th century. It was finished with an Ian Healy swipe for six.

Australia was set 270 to win and was a team renowned for an inability to chase runs, as well as one that loses close finishes.

Australia could thank Jason Gillespie, who has made great strides as a Test bowler, for the gettable total. He took 8/103 for the match.

But it was Mark Waugh's match – he rated it the best innings of his career, and Mark Taylor though a failure with the bat, said it was the greatest win in his career as a captain. That says something about this Australian side – the best in the world.

The torments of Tubby Taylor

Pretoria, March 24. With dignity and strength Australia's captain, Mark Taylor has been searching for that one innings that will turn the corner for him - as a batsman.

No one is questioning his ability as captain, but everyone - teammates and opponents as well, wishes he could make some runs.

His back injury is clearly contributing to his hesitant footwork - perhaps all he needs is a little time to rest in Australia's hectic schedule. Taylor is one of the most successful Australian captains – doing what Allan Border could not – wresting the Frank Worrell Trophy from the West Indies at home, and retaining it in Australia. And then also doing what Allan Border could not do – beating South Africa in a series on their paddocks.

This success has been a bit discomforting for Taylor's critics, most of whom have operated on a Test-by-Test basis – Australia is great because the West Indies are not what they used to be (after two Tests), Australia is no good (after three), the West Indies throw away another one (after four), the Windies are too good (after five).

It was the same in South Africa – South Africa hopeless (after two), Australia hopeless (after three).

The truth perhaps is that Australia only needs ten batsmen and bowlers plus Mark Taylor to win any series. Steve Waugh is vice captain for England, but he might have to wait. A Taylor ton could be just around the corner..

Ashes squad announced

Melbourne, April 17. The Australian selectors announced the squad to tour England would be led by Mark Taylor, despite rumour and poor form with the bat. But Ian Healy has been replaced by Steve Waugh as vice-captain. The selectors clearly prefer Waugh as a Test captain should injury or form mean Taylor misses a Test.

Michael Slater and Ricky Ponting return to favour, and join batsmen Matthew Elliott, Mark Waugh, Greg Blewett, Michael Bevan, and Justin Langer. Adam Gilchrist is the second 'keeper/batsman to Healy. Michael Kasprowicz and Brendon Julian also return, joining recent Test players Glenn McGrath, Jason Gillespie, Andy Bichel, and Shane Warne. Injury-prone Paul Reiffel is the unlucky bowler.

FIRST TEST 1996–97 SOUTH AFRICA v AUSTRALIA
Wanderers Stadium, Johannesburg. February 28, March 1, 2, 3, 4, 1997.
Toss: South Africa. Australia won by an innings & 196 runs.

SOUTH AFRICA
AC Hudson c Healy b McGrath	0	run out	31
G Kirsten c Healy b McGrath	9	b Warne	8
JH Kallis c ME Waugh b McGrath	6	b Warne	39
DJ Cullinan c Healy b McGrath	27	c Healy b Warne	0
WJ Cronje (c) c ME Waugh b Warne	76	c Healy b SR Waugh	22
JN Rhodes c Healy b Gillespie	22	lbw Warne	8
SM Pollock c SR Waugh b Bevan	35	not out	14
L Klusener c Taylor b Bevan	9	c Hayden b Bevan	0
DJ Richardson (+) not out	72	c Hayden b Bevan	2
AA Donald c Healy b Gillespie	21	b Bevan	0
PR Adams lbw Warne	15	b Bevan	0
EXTRAS (B 1, LB 3, W 3, NB 3)	10	(B 4, LB 2)	6
TOTAL	302		130

FOW 1st Inns: 0 15 25 78 115 165 183 195 253 302
FOW 2nd Inns: 36 41 46 90 108 127 128 130 130 130

Bowling: *First Innings*: McGrath 26-8-77-4, Gillespie 17-6-66-2, Warne 27.4-9-68-2, Bevan 17-1-64-2, Blewett 4-0-23-0. *Second Innings*: McGrath 10-5-17-0, Gillespie 11-4-24-0, Warne 28-15-43-4, Bevan 15-3-32-4, SR Waugh 4-1-4-1, ME Waugh 1-0-4-0.

AUSTRALIA
MA Taylor (c) b Pollock	16
ML Hayden c Cullinan b Pollock	40
MTG Elliott c Adams b Donald	85
ME Waugh c Richardson b Donald	26
SR Waugh c Richardson b Kallis	160
GS Blewett c Adams b LM Klusener	214
MG Bevan not out	37
IA Healy (+) c Kirsten b Adams	11
SK Warne b Cronje	9
JN Gillespie	
GD McGrath	
EXTRAS (B 1, LB 15, W 4, NB 10)	30
TOTAL	8 dec 628

FOW 1st Inns: 33 128 169 174 559 577 613 628

Bowling: *First Innings*: Donald 35-7-136-2, Pollock 32-3-105-2, Klusener 37-10-122-1, Kallis 21-4-54-1, Adams 52-7-163-1, Cronje 16.4-5-32-1.

Umpires: CJ Mitchley & S Venkataraghavan (TV Umpire – RE Koertzen)

SECOND TEST 1996–97 SOUTH AFRICA v AUSTRALIA
St George's Park, Port Elizabeth. March 14, 15, 16, 17, 1997.
Toss: Australia. Australia won by 2 wkts.

SOUTH AFRICA
G Kirsten c Hayden b Gillespie	0	b Gillespie	43
AM Bacher c Elliott b McGrath	11	c McGrath b Gillespie	49
JH Kallis c Blewett b Gillespie	0	run out	2
DJ Cullinan c Warne b Gillespie	34	lbw Gillespie	2
WJ Cronje (c) b McGrath	2	c Healy b Bevan	27
HH Gibbs b Gillespie	31	c ME Waugh b McGrath	7
BM McMillan c SR Waugh b Warne	55	lbw Bevan	2
SM Pollock lbw Gillespie	0	lbw Warne	17
DJ Richardson (+) c McGrath b Warne	47	not out	3
AA Donald c & b Warne	9	c Warne b Bevan	7
PR Adams not out	5	c Taylor b Warne	1
EXTRAS (B 8, LB 8, W 1)	17	(B 1, LB 5, NB 2)	8
TOTAL	209		168

FOW 1st Inns: 13 17 21 22 70 95 95 180 204 209
FOW 2nd Inns: 87 98 99 100 122 137 152 156 167 168

Bowling: *First Innings*: McGrath 22-7-66-2, Gillespie 23-10-54-5, Warne 23.4-5-62-3, Blewett 4-2-3-0, Bevan 2-0-8-0. *Second Innings*: McGrath 13-3-43-1, Gillespie 18-4-49-3, SR Waugh 4.3-0-16-0, Blewett 7.3-3-16-0, Warne 17.4-7-20-2, Bevan 13-3-18-3.

AUSTRALIA
ML Hayden c Cullinan b Pollock	0 (2)	run out	14
MA Taylor (c) c Richardson b Pollock	8 (1)	lbw McMillan	13
MTG Elliott run out	23	c & b Adams	44
ME Waugh lbw Cronje	20	b Kallis	116
SR Waugh c Richardson b McMillan	8	c Cronje b Kallis	18
GS Blewett b Donald	13	b Adams	7
MG Bevan c Richardson b McMillan	0	c Cullinan b Cronje	24
IA Healy (+) c Bacher b Cronje	5	not out	10
SK Warne lbw Adams	18	lbw Kallis	3
JN Gillespie not out	1	not out	0
GD McGrath c Richardson b Kallis	0		
EXTRAS (B 1, LB 7, W 2, NB 2)	12	(B 11, LB 8, W 3)	22
TOTAL	108		8 for 271

FOW 1st Inns: 1 13 48 64 66 70 85 86 106 108
FOW 2nd Inns: 23 30 113 167 192 258 258 265

Bowling: *First Innings*: Donald 23-13-18-1, Pollock 6-3-6-2, Adams 4-0-5-1, McMillan 14-2-32-2, Cronje 14-7-21-2, Kallis 9.4-2-18-1. *Second Innings*: Donald 26-6-75-0, McMillan 21-5-46-1, Cronje 9.3-1-36-1, Kallis 16-7-29-3, Adams 21-4-66-2.

Umpires: RE Koertzen & S Venkataraghavan (TV Umpire – DL Orchard)

THIRD TEST 1996–97 SOUTH AFRICA v AUSTRALIA
Centurion Park, Pretoria. March 21, 22, 23, 24, 1997.
Toss: South Africa. South Africa won by 8 wkts.

AUSTRALIA
MA Taylor (c) c Richardson b Klusener	38	c Richardson b Donald	5
ML Hayden b Schultz	10	lbw Schultz	0
MTG Elliott c Schultz b Donald	18	b Donald	12
ME Waugh b Donald	5	b Symcox	42
SR Waugh c Richardson b Schultz	67	not out	60
GS Blewett c Richardson b Symcox	37	b Donald	0
MG Bevan lbw Schultz	6	b Symcox	5
IA Healy (+) c Richardson b Donald	19	c Richardson b Schultz	12
SK Warne lbw Schultz	0	lbw Donald	12
JN Gillespie not out	6	b Donald	0
GD McGrath b Klusener	0	b Klusener	11
EXTRAS (B 1, LB 4, W 7, NB 9)	21	(B 2, LB 6, W 4, NB 14)	26
TOTAL	227		185

FOW 1st Inns: 23 60 72 110 190 197 212 212 226 227
FOW 2nd Inns: 5 10 28 94 99 108 131 164 164 185

Bowling: *First Innings*: Donald 20-5-60-3, Schultz 20-4-52-4, Cronje 5-3-5-0, Klusener 14.5-4-23-2, Symcox 23-4-62-1, Kallis 7-2-20-0. *Second Innings*: Donald 18-5-36-5, Schultz 17-4-39-2, Klusener 14.4-1-40-1, Symcox 19-5-49-2, Kallis 5-1-13-0.

SOUTH AFRICA
G Kirsten c Healy b McGrath	16	c Taylor b Blewett	6
AM Bacher lbw McGrath	96	c Elliott b Gillespie	5
BM McMillan c Hayden b ME Waugh	55	not out	7
DJ Cullinan b McGrath	47	not out	12
PL Symcox c Blewett b Gillespie	16		
JH Kallis c SR Waugh b McGrath	2		
WJ Cronje (c) not out	79		
DJ Richardson (+) b McGrath	0		
L Klusener b Gillespie	30		
AA Donald c Healy b Gillespie	8		
BN Schultz c Healy b McGrath	2		
EXTRAS (B 11, LB 16, W 1, NB 5)	33	(W 1, NB 1)	2
TOTAL	384		2 for 32

FOW 1st Inns: 26 128 229 252 255 262 262 330 367 384
FOW 2nd Inns: 11 15

Bowling: *First Innings*: McGrath 40.4-15-86-6, Gillespie 31-13-75-3, Blewett 5-0-19-0, Warne 36-11-89-0, Bevan 15-3-54-0, ME Waugh 7-1-34-1. *Second Innings*: Gillespie 3.4-0-19-1, Blewett 3-0-13-1.

Umpires: MJ Kitchen & CJ Mitchley (TV – RE Koertzen)

Australian Averages

1996–97 SOUTH AFRICA v AUSTRALIA
AUSTRALIA	M	Inn	NO	Runs	H.S	Avrge	Ct	St	Overs	Mdns	Runs	Wkts	Avrge
Bevan, MG	3	5	1	72	37*	18.00	-	-	62.0	10	176	9	19.56
Blewett, GS	3	5	-	271	214	54.20	2	-	23.3	5	74	1	74.00
Elliott, MTG	3	5	-	182	85	36.40	2	-	-	-	-	-	-
Gillespie, JN	3	4	3	7	6*	7.00	-	-	103.4	37	287	14	20.50
Hayden, ML	3	5	-	64	40	12.80	4	-	-	-	-	-	-
Healy, IA	3	5	1	57	19	14.25	11	-	-	-	-	-	-
McGrath, GD	3	3	-	11	11	3.67	2	-	111.4	38	289	13	22.23
Taylor, MA	3	5	-	80	38	16.00	3	-	-	-	-	-	-
Warne, SK	3	5	-	42	18	8.40	3	-	133.0	47	282	11	25.64
Waugh, ME	3	5	-	209	116	41.80	3	-	8.0	1	38	1	38.00
Waugh, SR	3	5	1	313	160	78.25	3	-	8.3	1	20	1	20.00

South African Averages

1996–97 SOUTH AFRICA v AUSTRALIA
SOUTH AFRICA	M	Inn	NO	Runs	H.S	Avrge	Ct	St	Overs	Mdns	Runs	Wkts	Avrge
Adams, PR	2	4	1	21	15	7.00	3	-	77.0	11	234	4	58.50
Bacher, AM	2	4	-	161	96	40.25	1	-	-	-	-	-	-
Cronje, WJ	3	5	1	204	79*	51.00	1	-	45.1	16	94	4	23.50
Cullinan, DJ	3	6	1	122	47	24.40	3	-	-	-	-	-	-
Donald, AA	3	5	-	45	21	9.00	-	-	122.0	36	325	11	29.55
Gibbs, HH	1	2	-	38	31	19.00	-	-	-	-	-	-	-
Hudson, AC	1	2	-	31	31	15.50	-	-	-	-	-	-	-
Kallis, JH	3	5	-	49	39	9.80	-	-	58.4	16	134	5	26.80
Kirsten, G	3	6	-	82	43	13.67	1	-	-	-	-	-	-
Klusener. L	2	3	-	39	30	13.00	-	-	66.3	15	185	4	46.25
McMillan. BM	2	4	1	119	55	39.67	-	-	35.0	7	78	3	26.00
Pollock, SM	2	4	1	66	35	22.00	-	-	38.0	6	111	4	27.75
Rhodes, JN	1	2	-	30	22	15.00	-	-	-	-	-	-	-
Richardson, DJ	3	5	2	124	72*	41.33	12	-	-	-	-	-	-
Schultz, BN	1	1	-	2	2	2.00	1	-	37.0	8	91	6	15.17
Symcox, PL	1	1	-	16	16	16.00	-	-	42.0	9	111	3	37.00

AUSTRALIAN TEST CRICKETERS

a'BECKETT, Edward Lambert
B : Aug 11, 1907.
D: June 2, 1989.
Bats: Right hand.
Bowls: Right arm.

First class debut:- 1927–28, 47 matches, 1636 runs, 7 50s, 2 100s, av. 29.21, 35 catches. 105 wkts at 29.16. HS: 152 BB: 6/119.
Test Debut:- 1928–29. 4 matches, 143 runs, av. 20.43, 4 catches. 3 wkts at 105.67. HS: 41 BB: 1/41.

ALDERMAN, Terrence Michael
B: June 12, 1956.
Bats: Right hand.
Bowls: Right arm.

First class debut:- 1974–75. 245 matches, 1307 runs, 1 50s, av. 8.32, 190 catches. 956 wkts at 23.74, 53 5-wkts, 8 10-wkts. HS: 52* BB: 8/46.
Test Debut:- 1981. 41 matches, 203 runs, av. 6.55, 27 catches. 170 wkts at 27.15, 14 5-wkts, 1 10-wkts. HS: 26* BB: 6/47.
Int. limited-overs debut:- 1981. 65 matches, 32 runs, av. 2.67, 28 catches. 88 wkts at 23.36, 2 5-wkts. HS: 9* BB: 5/17.

ALEXANDER, George
B: April 22, 1851.
D: Nov 6, 1930.
Bats: Right hand.
Bowls: Right arm.

First class debut:- 1875–76. 24 matches, 466 runs, 2 50s, av. 15.33, 16 catches. 33 wkts at 18.39, 1 5-wkts. HS: 75 BB: 6/57.
Test Debut:- 1880. 2 matches, 52 runs, av. 13.00, 2 catches. 2 wkts at 46.50. HS: 33 BB: 2/69.

ALEXANDER, Harry Houston
B: June 9, 1905.
D: April 15, 1993.
Bats: Right hand.
Bowls: Right arm.

First class debut:- 1928–29. 41 matches, 228 runs, av. 6.16, 17 catches. 95 wkts at 33.91, 2 5-wkts. HS: 23* BB: 7/95.
Test Debut:- 1932–33. 1 match, 17 runs, av. 17.00. 1 wkt at 154.00. HS: 17* BB: 1/129.

ALLAN, Francis Erskine
B: Dec 2, 1849.
D: Feb 9, 1917.
Bats: Left hand.
Bowls: Left arm.

First class debut:- 1867–68. 31 matches, 371 runs, av. 10.91, 14 catches. 124 wkts at 13.20, 11 5-wkts. HS: 35* BB: 8/20.
Test Debut:- 1878–79. 1 match, 5 runs, av. 5.00. 4 wkts at 20.00. HS: 5 BB: 2/30.

ALLAN, Peter John
B: Dec 31, 1935.
Bats: Right hand.
Bowls: Right arm.

First class debut:- 1959–60. 57 matches, 689 runs, av. 10.60, 23 catches. 206 wkts at 26.10, 12 5-wkts, 3 10-wkts. HS: 41 BB: 10/61.
Test Debut:- 1965–66. 1 match, 2 wkts at 41.50. HS: DNB BB: 2/58.

ALLEN, Reginald Charles
B: July 2, 1858.
D: May 2, 1952.
Bats: Right hand.

First class debut:- 1878–79. 17 matches, 382 runs, av. 12.32, 9 catches. 2 wkts at 58.50. HS: 41 BB: 1/14.
Test Debut:- 1886–87. 1 match, 44 runs, av. 22.00, 2 catches. HS: 30.

ANDREWS, Thomas James Edwin
B: Aug 26, 1890.
D: Jan 28, 1970.
Bats: Right hand.
Bowls: Right arm.

First class debut:- 1912–13. 151 matches, 8095 runs, 43 50s, 14 100s, av. 39.48, 85 catches. 95 wkts at 32.10, 3 5-wkts. HS: 247* BB: 6/109.
Test Debut:- 1921. 16 matches, 592 runs, 4 50s, av. 26.91, 12 catches. 1 wkt at 116.00. HS: 94 BB: 1/23.

ANGEL, Jo
B: April 22, 1968.
Bats: Left hand.
Bowls: Right arm.

First class debut:- 1991–92. 65 matches, 862 runs, 2 50s, av. 14.86, 20 catches. 271 wkts at 25.25, 11 5-wkts, 1 10-wkts. HS: 84* BB: 6/68.
Test debut:- 1992–93. 4 matches, 35 runs, av. 5.83, 1 catch. 10 wkts at 46.30. HS: 11 BB: 3/54.
Int. limited-overs debut:- 1994–95. 5 matches, 0 runs at 0.00. 3 wkts at 28.25. HS: 0 BB: 2/47.

ARCHER, Kenneth Alan
B: Jan 17, 1928.
Bats: Right hand.
Bowls: Right arm.

First class debut:- 1946–47. 82 matches, 3774 runs, 25 50s, 3 100s, av. 29.95, 56 catches, 1 stumping. 13 wkts at 53.69. HS: 134, BB: 2/16.
Test Debut:- 1950–51. 5 matches, 234 runs, av. 26.00. HS: 48.

ARCHER, Ronald Graham
B: Oct 25, 1933.
Bats: Right hand.
Bowls: Right arm.

First class debut:- 1951–52, Brisbane. 98 matches, 3768 runs, 21 50s, 4 100s, av. 31.93, 105 catches. 255 wkts at 23.36, 9 5-wkts, 1 10-wkts. HS: 148 BB: 7/56.
Test Debut:- 1952–53. 19 matches, 713 runs, 2 50s, 1 100s, av. 24.59, 20 catches. 48 wkts at 27.46, 1 5-wkts. HS: 128, BB: 5/53.

ARMSTRONG, Warwick Windridge
B: May 22, 1879.
D: July 13, 1947.
Bats: Right hand.
Bowls: Right arm.

First class debut:- 1898–99. 269 matches, 16158, 57 50s, 45 100s, av. 46.83, 274 catches. 832 wkts at 19.71, 50 5-wkts, 5 10-wkts. HS: 303* BB: 8/47.
Test Debut:- 1901–02. 50 matches, 2863 runs, 8 50s, 6 100s, av. 38.69, 44 catches. 87 wkts at 33.60, 3 5-wkts. HS: 159* BB: 6/35.

BADCOCK, Clayvel Lindsay
B: April 10, 1914.
D: Dec 13, 1982.
Bats: Right hand.

First class debut:- 1929–30. 97 matches, 7371 runs, 21 50s, 26 100s, av. 51.54, 41 catches. HS: 325.
Test Debut:- 1936–37. 7 matches, 160 runs, 1 100s, av. 14.55, 3 catches. HS: 118.

BANNERMAN, Alexander Chalmers
B: Mar 21, 1854.
D: Sep 19, 1924.
Bats: Right hand.
Bowls: Right arm.

First class debut:- 1876–77. 219 matches, 7816 runs, 30 50s, 1 100s, av. 22.14, 154 catches. 22 wkts at 29.81. HS: 134, BB: 3/12.
Test Debut:- 1878–79. 28 matches, 1108 runs, 8 50s, av. 23.08. 4 wkts at 40.75. HS: 94 BB: 3/111.

BANNERMAN, Charles
B: July 23, 1851.
D: Aug 20, 1930.
Bats: Right hand.

First class debut:- 1870–71. 44 matches, 1687 runs, 9 50s, 1 100s, av. 21.62, 20 catches. HS: 165+
Test Debut:- 1876–77. 3 matches, 239 runs, 1 100s, av. 59.75. HS: 165+

BARDSLEY, Warren
B: Dec 6, 1882.
D: Jan 20, 1954.
Bats: Left hand.

First class debut:- 1903–04. 250 matches, 17,025 runs, 73 50s, 53 100s, av. 49.92, 112 catches. HS: 264.
Test Debut:- 1909. 41 matches, 2469 runs, 14 50s, 6 100s, av. 40.48, 12 catches. HS: 193*

BARNES, Sidney George
B: June 5, 1916.
D: Dec 16, 1973.
Bats: Right hand.
Bowls: Right arm.

First class debut:- 1936–37. 110 matches, 8333 runs, 37 50s, 26 100s, av. 54.11, 80 catches, 4 stumpings. 57 wkts at 32.21. HS: 234 BB: 3/0.
Test Debut:- 1938. 13 matches, 1072 runs, 5 50s, 3 100s, av. 63.06, 14 catches. 4 wkts at 54.50. HS: 234 BB: 2/25.

BARNETT, Benjamin Arthur
B: Mar 23, 1908.
D: June 29, 1979.
Bats: Left hand batsman - Wicketkeeper.

First class debut:- 1929–30. 173 matches, 5531 runs, 31 50s, 4 100s, av. 27.51, 216 catches, 142 stumpings. 1 wkt at 20.00. HS: 131 BB: 1/3.
Test Debut:- 1938. 4 matches, 195 runs, 1 50s, av. 27.86, 3 catches, 2 stumpings. HS: 57.

BARRETT, John Edward
B: Oct 15, 1866.
D: Feb 6, 1916.
Bats: Left hand.
Bowls: Right arm.

First class debut:- 1884–85. 50 matches, 2039 runs, 13 50s, av. 25.81, 16 catches. 21 wkts at 16.00, 3 5-wkts, 1 10-wkts. HS: 97 BB: 6/49.
Test debut:- 1890. 2 matches, 80 runs, 1 50s, av. 26.67, 1 catch. HS: 67*

BEARD, Graeme Robert
B: Aug 19, 1950.
Bats: Right hand.
Bowls: Right arm.

First class debut:- 1975–76. 54 matches, 1441 runs, 11 50s, av. 23.62, 11 catches. 125 wkts at 28.19, 7 5-wkts, 1 10-wkts. HS: 75 BB: 5/33.
Test debut:- 1979–80. 3 matches, 114 runs, av. 22.80. 1 wkt at 109.00. HS: 49 BB: 1/26.
Int limited-overs debut:- 1980–81. 2 matches, 4 wkts at 17.50. HS: DNB BB: 2/20.

BENAUD, John
B: May 11, 1944.
Bats: Right hand.
Bowls: Right arm.

First class debut:- 1966–67. 47 matches, 2888 runs, 16 50s, 4 100s, av. 36.55, 30 catches. 5 wkts at 35.20. HS: 142 BB: 2/12.
Test debut:- 1972–73. 3 matches, 223 runs, 1 100s, av. 44.60. 2 wkts at 6.00. HS: 142 BB: 2/12.

BENAUD, Richie
B: Oct 6, 1930.
Bats: Right hand.
Bowls: Right arm.

First class debut:- 1948–49. 259 matches, 11719 runs, 61 50s, 23 100s, av. 36.50, 254 catches. 945 wkts at 24.73, 56 5-wkts, 9 10-wkts. HS: 187 BB: 7/18.
Test debut:- 1951–52. 63 matches, 2201 runs, 9 50s, 3 100s, av. 24.46, 65 catches. 248 wkts at 27.03, 16 5-wkts, 1 10-wkts. HS: 122 BB: 7/72.

BENNETT, Murray John
B: Nov 6, 1956.
Bats: Right hand.
Bowls: Left arm.

First class debut:- 1982–83. 62 matches, 1437 runs, 4 50s, av. 23.95, 49 catches. 157 wkts at 30.92, 5 5-wkts. HS: 59* BB: 6/32.
Test debut:- 1984–85. 3 matches, 71 runs, av. 23.67, 5 catches. 6 wkts at 54.17. HS: 23 BB: 3/79.
Int limited-overs debut:- 1984–85. 8 matches, 9 runs at 3.00. 4 wkts at 68.75. HS: 6* BB: 2/27.

BEVAN, Michael Gwyl
B: May 8, 1970
Bats: Left hand.
Bowls: Left arm.

First class debut:- 1989–90. 123 matches, 9287 runs, 48 50s, 30 100s, av. 53.07, 71 catches. 57 wkts at 42.05, 1 5-wkts, 1 10-wkts. HS: 203* BB: 6/82.
Test debut:- 1994–95. 14 matches, 730 runs, 6 50s, av. 34.76, 7 catches. 25 wkts at 20.32, 1 5-wkts, 1 10-wkts. HS: 91 BB: 6/82.
Int. limited-overs debut:- 1993–94. 56 matches, 1766 runs at 55.19. 17 wkts at 43.53. HS: 103 BB: 3/36.

BICHEL, Andrew John
B: Aug 27, 1970.
Bats: Right hand.
Bowls: Right arm.

First class debut:- 1992–93. 24 matches, 561 runs, 2 50s, av. 20.04, 15 catches. 103 wkts at 25.12, 7 5-wkts, 1 10-wkts. HS: 61* BB: 6/56.
Test debut:- 1996–97. 2 matches, 40 runs, av. 13.33. 1 wkt at 143.00. HS: 18 BB: 1/31.
Int. limited-overs debut:- 1996–97. 8 matches, 35 runs at 11.67. 12 wkts at 29.58. HS: 17 BB: 3/17.

BLACKHAM, John McCarthy
B: May 11, 1854
D: Dec 28, 1932.
Bats: Right hand - Wicketkeeper.

First class debut:- 1874–75. 275 matches, 6395 runs, 26 50s, 1 100s, av. 16.78, 273 catches, 180 stumpings. 2 wkts at 69.00. HS: 109 BB: 1/8.
Test debut:- 1876–77. 35 matches, 800 runs, 4 50s, av. 15.69, 37 catches, 24 stumpings. HS: 74.

BLACKIE, Donald Dearness
B: April 5, 1882.
D: April 18, 1955.
Bats: Left hand.
Bowls: Right arm.

First class debut:- 1924–25. 47 matches, 548 runs, 1 50s, av. 12.17. 213 wkts at 23.88, 12 5-wkts, 2 10-wkts. HS: 55 BB: 7/25.
Test debut:- 1928–29. 3 matches, 24 runs, av. 8.00, 2 catches. 14 wkts at 31.71, 1 5-wkts. HS: 11* BB: 6/94.

BLEWETT, Gregory Scott
B: Oct 29, 1971.
Bats: Right hand.
Bowls: Right arm.

First class debut:- 1991–92. 75 matches, 5752 runs, 29 50s, 16 100s, av. 47.54, 45 catches. 55 wkts at 39.45, 1 5-wkts. HS: 268. BB: 5/29.
Test debut:- 1994–95. 16 matches, 1040 runs, 5 50s, 3 100s, av. 41.60, 17 catches. 4 wkts at 65.00. HS: 214 BB: 2/25.
Int. limited-overs debut:- 1994–95. 23 matches, 431 runs at 22.68. 12 wkts at 44.92. HS: 57* BB: 2/34.

BONNOR, George John
B: Feb 25, 1855.
D: June 27, 1912.
Bats: Right hand.
Bowls: Right arm.

First class debut:- 1880. 148 matches, 4820 runs, 18 50s, 5 100s, av. 21.23, 127 catches, 1 stumping. 12 wkts at 39.16. HS: 128 BB: 3/34.
Test debut:- 1880. 17 matches, 512 runs, 2 50s, 1 100s, av. 17.07, 16 catches. 2 wkts at 42.00. HS: 128 BB: 1/5.

BOON, David Clarence
B: Dec 29, 1960.
Bats: Right hand.
Bowls: Right arm.

First class debut:- 1978–79. 278 matches, 19,439 runs, 87 50s, 60 100s, av. 45.74, 232 catches. 10 wkts at 53.00. HS: 227 BB: 1/0.
Test debut:- 1984–85. 107 matches, 7422 runs, 32 50s, 21 100s, av. 43.66, 99 catches. 0 wkts at –. HS: 200 BB: 0/00.
Int. limited-overs debut:- 1983–84. 181 matches, 5964 runs at 37.04.. HS: 122.

BOOTH, Brian Charles
B: Oct 19, 1933.
Bats: Right hand.
Bowls: Right arm.

First class debut:- 1954–55. 183 matches, 11,265 runs, 60 50s, 26 100s, av. 45.42, 119 catches. 16 wkts at 59.75. HS: 214* BB: 2/29.
Test debut:- 1961. 29 matches, 1773 runs, 1050s, 5 100s, av. 42.21, 17 catches. 3 wkts at 48.67. HS: 48.67 BB: 2/33.

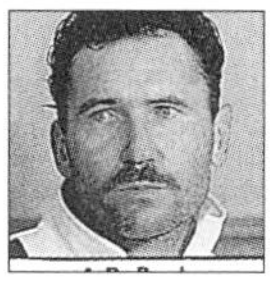

BORDER, Allan Robert
B: July 27, 1955.
Bats: Left hand.
Bowls: Left arm.

First class debut:- 1976–77. 385 matches, 27,131 runs, 142 50s, 70 100s, av. 51.38, 379 catches. 106 wkts at 39.25, 3 5-wkts, 1 10-wkts. HS: 205 BB:7/46.
Test debut:- 1978–79. 156 matches, 11,174 runs, 63 50s, 27 100s, av. 50.56, 156 catches. 39 wkts at 39.10, 2 5-wkts, 1 10-wkts. HS: 205 BB: 7/46.
Int limited-overs debut:- 1978–79. 273 matches, 6524 runs, 39 50s, 3 100s, av. 30.63, 127 catches. 73 wkts at 28.37. HS: 127* BB: 3/20.

BOYLE, Henry Frederick
B: Dec 10, 1847.
D: Nov 21, 1907.
Bats: Right hand.
Bowls: Right arm.

First class debut:- 1871–72. 140 matches, 1711 runs, 1 50s, 1 100s, av. 10.24, 125 catches. 370 wkts at 15.38, 26 5-wkts, 6 10-wkts. HS: 108 BB: 7/32.
Test debut:- 1878–79. 12 matches, 153 runs, av. 12.75, 10 catches. 32 wkts at 20.03, 1 5-wkts. HS: 36* BB: 6/42.

BRADMAN, Donald George
B: Aug 27, 1908.
Bats: Right hand.
Bowls: Right arm.

First class debut:- 1927–28. 234 matches, 28,067 runs, 69 50s, 117 100s, av. 95.14, 131 catches, 1 stumping. 36 wkts at 37.97. HS: 452* BB: 3/35.
Test debut:- 1928–29. 52 matches, 6996 runs, 13 50s, 29 100s, av. 99.94, 32 catches. 2 wkts at 36.00. HS: 334 BB: 1/8.

BRIGHT, Raymond James
B: July 13, 1954.
Bats: Right hand.
Bowls: Left arm.

First class debut:- 1972–73. 184 matches, 4130 runs, 12 50s, 2 100s, av. 21.07, 12 catches, 2 stumpings. 471 wkts at 32.08, 24 5-wkts, 2 10-wkts. HS: 108 BB: 7/87.
Test debut:- 1977. 25 matches, 445 runs, av. 14.35. 53 wkts at 41.13, 4 5-wkts, 1 10-wkts. HS: 33 BB: 7/87.
Int limited-overs debut:- 1973–74. 11 matches, 66 runs at 16.50. 3 wkts at 116.67. HS: 19* BB: 1/28.

BROMLEY, Ernest Harvey
B: Sep 2, 1912.
D: Feb 1, 1967.
Bats: Left hand.
Bowls: Left arm.

First class debut:- 1929–30. 52 matches, 2055 runs, 12 50s, 3 100s, av. 28.54, 43 catches. 39 wkts at 42.33. HS: 161 BB: 4/50.
Test debut:- 1932–33. 2 matches, 38 runs, av. 9.50, 2 catches. 0 wkts at –. HS: 26 BB: (Did not take a wicket).

BROWN, William Alfred
B: July 31, 1912.
Bats: Right hand.

First class debut:- 1932–33. 189 matches, 13,838 runs, 66 50s, 39 100s, av. 51.44, 110 catches, 1 stumping. 6 wkts at 18.33. HS: 265* BB: 4/16.
Test debut:- 1934. 22 matches, 1592 runs, 9 50s, 4 100s, av. 46.82, 14 catches. HS: 206*

BRUCE, William
B: May 22, 1864.
D: Aug 3, 1925.
Bats: Left hand.
Bowls: Left arm.

First class debut:- 1882–83. 145 matches, 5731 runs, 28 50s, 4 100s, av. 23.97, 103 catches. 143 wkts at 29.67, 5 5-wkts. HS: 191 BB: 7/72.
Test debut:- 1884–85. 14 matches, 702 runs, 5 50s, av. 29.25. 12 wkts at 36.67. HS: 80 BB: 3/88.

BURGE, Peter John Parnell
B: May 17, 1932.
Bats: Right hand.

First class debut:- 1952–53. 233 matches, 14640 runs, 68 50s, 38 100s, av. 47.33, 166 catches, 4 stumpings. 1 wkt at 129.00. HS: 283 BB: 1/0.
Test debut:- 1954–55. 42 matches, 2290 runs, 12 50s, 4 100s, av. 38.17, 23 catches. HS: 181.

BURKE, Jimmy Wallace
B: June 12, 1930.
D: Feb 2, 1979.
Bats: Right hand.
Bowls: Right arm.

First class debut:- 1948–49. 130 matches, 7563 runs, 35 50s, 21 100s, av. 45.01, 59 catches. 101 wkts at 29.11, 3 5-wkts. HS: 220 BB: 6/40.
Test debut:- 1950–51. 24 matches, 1280 runs, 5 50s, 3 100s, av. 34.59, 18 catches. 8 wkts at 28.75. HS: 189 BB: 4/37.

BURN, Edwin James Kenneth
B: Sep 17, 1862.
D: July 20, 1956.
Bats: Right hand.
Bowls: Right arm.

First class debut:- 1883–84. 48 matches, 1750 runs, 5 50s, 2 100s, av. 21.34, 31 catches. 14 wkts at 22.85. HS: 119 BB: 3/15.
Test debut:- 1890. 2 matches, 41 runs, av. 10.25. HS: 19.

BURTON, Frederick James
B: Nov 2, 1865.
D: Aug 25, 1929.
Bats: Right hand - Wicketkeeper.

First class debut:- 1885–86. 22 matches, 376 runs, av. 13.42, 25 catches, 7 stumpings. HS: 47.
Test debut:- 1886–87. 2 matches, 4 runs, av. 2.00, 1 catch, 1 stumping. HS: 2*.

CALLAWAY, Sydney Thomas
B: Feb 6, 1868.
D: Nov 25, 1923.
Bats: Right hand.
Bowls: Right arm.

First class debut:- 1888–89. 62 matches, 1747 runs, 10 50s, av. 16.79, 48 catches. 320 wkts at 17.06, 33 5-wkts, 12 10-wkts. HS: 86 BB: 8/33.
Test debut:- 1891–92. 3 matches, 87 runs, av. 17.40. 6 wkts at 23.67, 1 5-wkts. HS: 41 BB: 5/37.

CALLEN, Ian Wayne
B: May 2, 1955.
Bats: Left hand.
Bowls: Right arm.

First class debut:- 1976–77. 53 matches, 578 runs, av. 12.30, 19 catches. 197 wkts at 27.47, 7 5-wkts, 1 10-wkts. HS: 34 BB: 8/42.
Test debut:- 1977–78. 1 match, 26 runs, 1 catch. 6 wkts at 31.83. HS: 22* BB: 3/83.
Int. limited-overs debut:- 1977–78. 5 matches, 6 runs at 6.00. 5 wkts at 29.60. HS: 3* BB: 3/24.

CAMPBELL, Gregory Dale
B: Mar 10, 1964.
Bats: Right hand.
Bowls: Right arm.

First class debut:- 1986–87. 44 matches, 347 runs, av. 8.46, 10 catches. 120 wkts at 33.46, 5 5-wkts. HS: 41 BB: 6/80.
Test debut:- 1989. 4 matches, 10 runs, av. 2.50, 1 catch. 13 wkts at 38.69. HS: 6 BB: 3/79.
Int. limited-overs debut:- 1989–90. 12 matches, 6 runs at 3.00. 18 wkts at 22.44. HS: 4* BB: 3/17.

CARKEEK, William
B: Oct 17, 1878.
D: Feb 20, 1937.
Bats: Left hand - Wicketkeeper.

First class debut:- 1903–04. 95 matches, 1388 runs, 2 50s, av. 12.17, 114 catches, 45 stumpings. HS: 68.
Test debut:- 1912. 6 matches, 16 runs, av. 5.33, 6 catches. HS: 6*.

CARLSON, Phillip Henry B: Aug 8, 1951.
Bats: Right hand.
Bowls: Right arm.

First class debut:- 1969–70. 91 matches, 4167 runs, 19 50s, 5 100s, av. 28.34, 59 catches. 124 wkts at 24.96, 5 5-wkts, 1 10-wkts. HS: 110* BB: 7/42.
Test debut:- 1978–79. 2 matches, 23 runs, av. 5.75, 2 catches. 2 wkts at 49.50. HS: 21 BB: 2/41.
Int. limited-overs debut:- 1978–79. 4 matches, 11 runs, av. 5.50. 2 wkts at 35.00. HS: 11 BB: 1/21.

CARTER, Hanson
B: Mar 15, 1878.
D: June 8, 1948.
Bats: Right hand - Wicketkeeper.

First class debut:- 1897–98. 128 matches, 2897 runs,13 50s, 2 100s, av. 20.11, 182 catches, 89 stumpings. HS: 149.
Test debut:- 1907–08. 28 matches, 873 runs, 4 50s, av. 22.97, 44 catches, 21 stumpings. HS: 72.

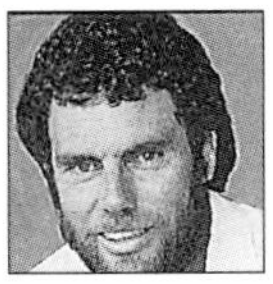

CHAPPELL, Gregory Stephen
B: Aug 7, 1948.
Bats: Right hand.
Bowls: Right arm.

First class debut:- 1966–67. 322 matches, 24,535 runs, 111 50s, 74 100s, av. 52.20, 377 catches. 291 wkts at 29.76, 5 5-wkts. HS: 247* BB: 7/40.
Test debut:- 1970–71. 88 matches, 7110 runs, 31 50s, 24 100s, av. 53.86, 122 catches. 47 wkts at 40.70, 1 5-wkts. HS: 247* BB: 5/61.
Int. limited-overs debut:- 1970–71. 74 matches, 2331 runs at 40.19. 72 wkts at 29.11. HS: 138* BB: 5/15.

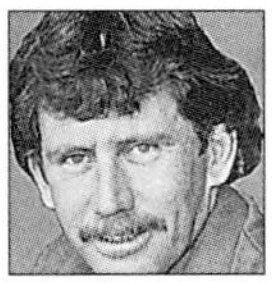

CHAPPELL, Ian Michael
B: Sep 26, 1943.
Bats: Right hand.
Bowls: Right arm.

First class debut:- 1961–62. 263 matches, 19,680 runs, 96 50s, 59 100s, av. 48.35, 312 catches, 1 stumping. 176 wkts at 37.57, 2 5-wkts. HS: 209 BB: 5/29.
Test debut:- 1964–65. 76 matches, 5345 runs, 26 50s, 14 100s, av. 42.42, 105 catches. 20 wkts at 65.80. HS: 196 BB: 2/21.
Int. limited-overs debut:- 1970–71. 16 matches, 673 runs at 48.07. 2 wkts at 11.50. HS: 86 BB: 2/14.

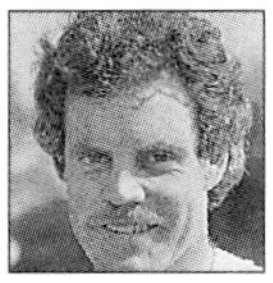

CHAPPELL, Trevor Michael
B: Oct 21, 1952.
Bats: Right hand.
Bowls: Right arm.

First class debut:- 1972–73. 88 matches, 4049 runs, 23 50s, 5 100s, av. 29.55, 47 catches. 59 wkts at 24.78. HS: 150 BB: 4/12.
Test debut:- 1981. 3 matches, 79 runs, av. 15.80. HS: 27.
Int. limited-overs debut:- 1980–81. 20 matches, 229 runs, 1 100s, av. 17.62, 8 catches. 19 wkts at 28.32. HS: 110 BB: 3/31.

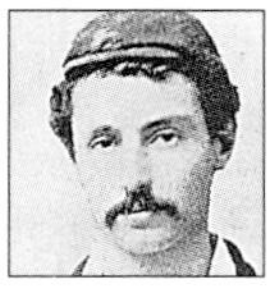

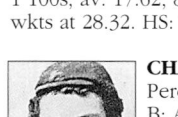

CHARLTON, Percie Chater
B: April 9, 1867.
D: Sep 30, 1954.
Bats: Right hand.
Bowls: Right arm.

First class debut:- 1888–89. 40 matches, 648 runs, 1 50s, av. 12.46, 38 catches. 97 wkts at 19.96, 6 5-wkts, 1 10-wkts. HS: 50 BB: 7/44.
Test debut:- 1890. 2 matches, 29 runs, av. 7.25. 3 wkts at 8.00. HS: 11 BB: 3/18.

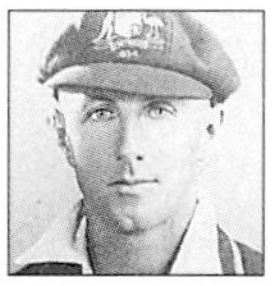

CHIPPERFIELD, Arthur Gordon
B: Nov 17, 1905.
D: July 29, 1987.
Bats: Right hand.
Bowls: Right arm.

First class debut:- 1933–34. 96 matches, 4295 runs, 22 50s, 9 100s, av. 38.34, 91 catches. 65 wkts at 39.72, 1 5-wkts. HS: 175 BB: 8/66.
Test debut:- 1934. 14 matches, 552 runs, 2 50s, 1 100s, av. 32.47, 15 catches. 5 wkts at 87.40. HS: 109 BB: 3/91.

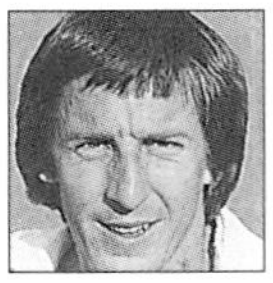

CLARK, Wayne Maxwell
B: Sep 19, 1953.
Bats: Right hand.
Bowls: Right arm.

First class debut:- 1974–75. 62 matches, 717 runs, av. 12.57, 23 catches. 210 wkts at 29.37, 6 5-wkts, 1 10-wkts. HS: 46* BB: 7/26.
Test debut:- 1977–78. 10 matches, 98 runs, av. 5.76, 6 catches. 44 wkts at 28.73. HS: 33 BB: 4/46.
Int. limited-overs debut:- 1977–78. 2 matches, 3 wkts at 20.33. HS: DNB. BB: 2/39.

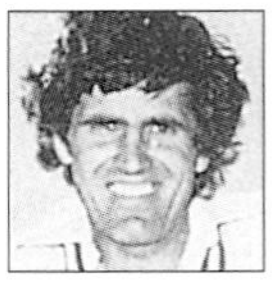

COLLEY, David John
B: Mar 15, 1947.
Bats: Right hand.
Bowls: Right arm.

First class debut:- 1969–70. 87 matches, 2374 runs, 13 50s, 1 100s, av. 23.74, 44 catches. 236 wkts at 31.60, 8 5-wkts. HS: 101 BB: 6/30.
Test debut:- 1972. 3 matches, 84 runs, 1 50s, av. 21.00, 1 catch. 6 wkts at 52.00. HS: 54 BB: 3/83.
Int. limited-overs debut:- 1972. 1 match, 0 wkts at –. BB: DNB. BB: 0/72.

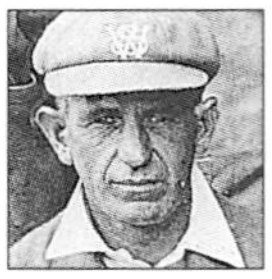

COLLINS, Herbert Leslie
B: Jan 21, 1888.
D: May 28, 1959.
Bats: Right hand.

First class debut:- 1909–10. 168 matches, 9924 runs, 40 50s, 32 100s, av. 40.01, 115 catches. 181 wkts at 21.38, 8 5-wkts, 2 10-wkts. HS: 282 BB: 8/31.
Test debut:- 1920–21. 19 matches, 1352 runs, 6 50s, 4 100s, av. 45.07, 13 catches. 4 wkts at 63.00. HS: 203 BB: 2/47.

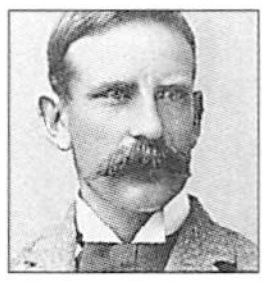

CONINGHAM, Arthur
B: July 14, 1863.
D: June 13, 1939.
Bats: Left hand.
Bowls: Left arm.

First class debut:- 1892–93. 35 matches, 896 runs, 2 50s, 1 100s, av. 15.71, 27 catches. 112 wkts at 23.24, 2 5-wkts. HS: 151 BB: 6/38.
Test debut:- 1894–95. 1 match, 13 runs, av. 6.50. 2 wkts at 38.00. HS: 10 BB: 2/17.

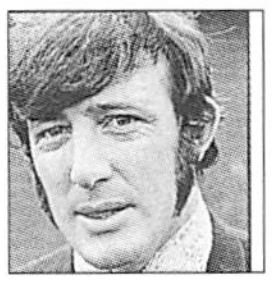

CONNOLLY, Alan Norman
B: June 29, 1939.
Bats: Right hand.
Bowls: Right arm.

First class debut:- 1959–60. 201 matches, 1073 runs, av. 8.79, 77 catches. 676 wkts at 26.58, 25 5-wkts, 4 10-wkts. HS: 40 BB: 9/67.
Test debut:- 1963–64. 30 matches, 260 runs, av. 10.40, 17 catches. 102 wkts at 29.23, 4 5-wkts. HS: 37 BB: 6/47.
Int. limited-overs debut:- 1970–71. 1 match, 0 wkts at –. HS: DNB BB: 0/62.

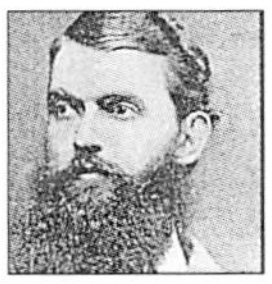

COOPER, Bransby Beauchamp
B: Mar 15, 1844.
D: Aug 7, 1914.
Bats: Right hand - Wicketkeeper.

First class debut:- 1863. 50 matches, 1600 runs, 7 50s, 1 100s, av. 20.51, 41 catches, 20 stumpings. HS: 101.
Test debut:- 1876–77. 1 match, 18 runs, av. 9.00, 2 catches. HS: 15.

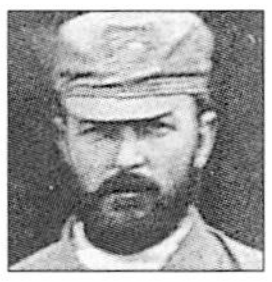

COOPER, William Henry
B: Sep 11, 1849.
D: April 5, 1939.
Bats: Right hand.
Bowls: Right arm.

First class debut:- 1878–79. 26 matches, 247 runs, av. 10.29, 16 catches. 71 wkts at 24.49, 5 5-wkts. HS: 46 BB: 7/37.
Test debut:- 1881–82. 2 matches, 13 runs, av. 6.50, 1 catch. 9 wkts at 25.11, 1 5-wkts. HS: 7 BB: 6/120.

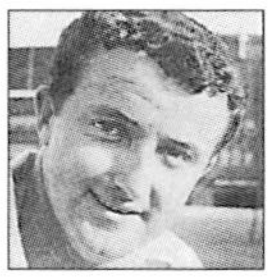

CORLING, Grahame Edward
B: July 13, 1941.
Bats: Right hand.
Bowls: Right arm.

First class debut:- 1963–64. 65 matches, 484 runs, av. 10.52, 11 catches. 173 wkts at 32.05, 6 5-wkts. HS: 42* BB: 5/44.
Test debut:- 1964. 5 matches, 5 runs, av. 1.67. 12 wkts at 37.25. HS: 3 BB: 4/60.

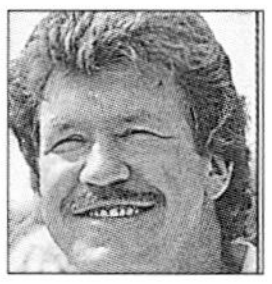

COSIER, Gary John
B: April 25, 1953.
Bats: Right Hand.
Bowls: Right arm.

First class debut:- 1971–72. 91 matches, 5005 runs, 27 50s, 7 100s, av. 32.92, 75 catches. 75 wkts at 30.68. HS: 168 BB: 3/20.
Test debut:- 1975–76. 18 matches, 897 runs, 3 50s, 2 100s, av. 28.94, 14 catches. 5 wkts at 68.20. HS: 168 BB: 2/26.
Int. limited-overs debut:- 1975–76. 9 matches, 154 runs, 1 50s, av. 30.80, 4 catches. 14 wkts at 17.71, 1 5-wkts. HS: 84 BB: 5/18.

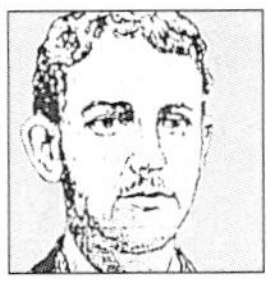

COTTAM, John Thomas
B: Sep 5, 1867.
D: Jan 30, 1897.
Bats: Right hand.
Bowls: Right arm.

First class debut:- 1886–87. 7 matches, 273 runs, 3 50s, av. 22.75, 4 catches. 3 wkts at 32.66. HS: 62 BB: 2/48.
Test debut:- 1886–87. 1 match, 4 runs, av. 2.00, 1 catch. HS: 3.

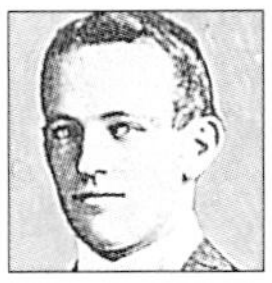

COTTER, Albert
B: Dec 3, 1884.
D: Oct 31, 1917.
Bats: Right hand.
Bowls: Right arm.

First class debut:- 1901–02. 113 matches, 2484 runs, 4 50s, av. 16.89, 63 catches. 442 wkts at 24.27, 31 5-wkts, 4 10-wkts. HS: 82 BB: 7/15.
Test debut:- 1903–04. 21 matches, 457 runs, av. 13.06, 8 catches. 89 wkts at 28.64, 7 5-wkts. HS: 45 BB: 7/148.

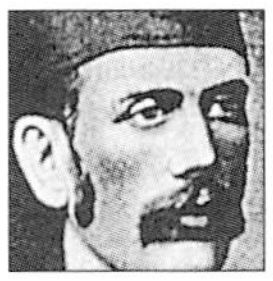

COULTHARD, George
B: Aug 1, 1856.
D: Oct 22, 1883.
Bats: Right hand.
Bowls: Right arm.

First class debut:- 1880–81. 6 matches, 92 runs, av. 11.50, 3 catches. 5 wkts at 25.00. HS: 31 BB: 3/29.
Test debut:- 1881–82. 1 match, 6 runs, av. –. HS: 6*.

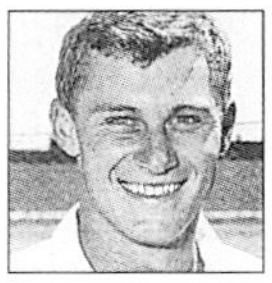

COWPER, Robert Maskew
B: Oct 5, 1940.
Bats: Left hand.
Bowls: Right arm.

First class debut:- 1959–60. 147 matches, 10,595 runs, 58 50s, 26 100s, av. 53.78, 151 catches. 183 wkts at 31.19, 1 5-wkts. HS: 307 BB: 7/42.
Test debut:- 1964. 27 matches, 2061 runs, 10 50s, 5 100s, av. 46.84, 21 catches. 36 wkts at 31.64. HS: 307 BB: 4/48.

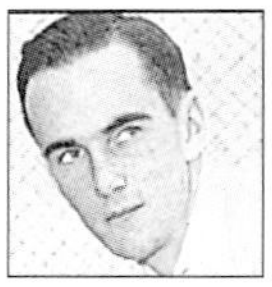

CRAIG, Ian David
B: June 12, 1935.
Bats: Right hand.

First class debut:- 1951–52. 144 matches, 7328 runs, 38 50s, 15 100s, av. 37.96, 70 catches. 1 wkt at 127.00. HS: 213* BB: 1/3.
Test debut:- 1952–53. 11 matches, 358 runs, 2 50s, av. 19.89, 2 catches. HS: 53.

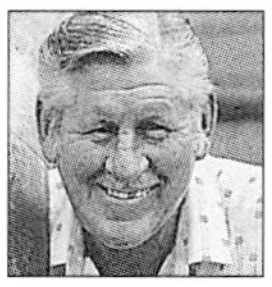

CRAWFORD, William Patrick Anthony
B: Aug 3, 1933.
Bats: Right hand.
Bowls: Right arm.

First class debut:- 1954–55. 37 matches, 424 runs, 1 50s, av. 19.27, 18 catches. 110 wkts at 21.02, 5 5-wkts, 1 10-wkts. HS: 86 BB: 6/55.
Test debut:- 1956. 4 matches, 53 runs, av. 17.67, 1 catch. 7 wkts at 15.29. HS: 34 BB: 3/28.

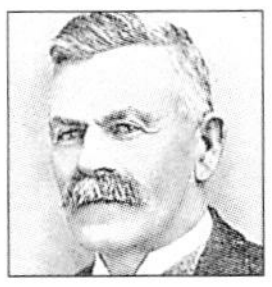

DARLING, Joseph
B: Nov 21, 1870.
D: Jan 2, 1946.
Bats: Left hand.

First class debut:- 1893–94. 202 matches, 10635 runs, 55 50s, 19 100s, av. 34.52, 148 catches. 1 wkt at 55.00. HS: 210 BB: 1/5.
Test debut:- 1894–95. 34 matches, 1657 runs, 8 50s, 3 100s, av. 28.57, 27 catches. HS: 178.

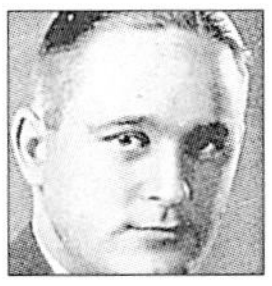

DARLING, Leonard Stuart
B: Aug 14, 1909.
D: June 24, 1992.
Bats: Left hand.
Bowls: Right arm.

First class debut:- 1926–27. 100 matches, 5780 runs, 26 50s, 16 100s, av. 42.50, 59 catches. 32 wkts at 47.00. HS: 188 BB: 3/57.
Test debut:- 1932–33. 12 matches, 474 runs, 3 50s, av. 27.88, 8 catches. 0 wkts at –. HS: 85 BB: 0/ .

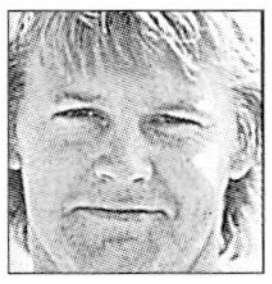

DARLING, Warrick Maxwell
B: April 1, 1957.
Bats: Right hand.

First class debut:- 1975–76. 98 matches, 5554 runs, 32 50s, 9 100s, av. 35.83, 30 catches. HS: 134.
Test debut:- 1977–78. 14 matches, 697 runs, 6 50s, av. 26.81, 5 catches. HS: 91.
Int. limited-overs debut:- 1977–78.18 matches, 363 runs, 1 50s, av. 21.35, 6 catches. HS: 74.

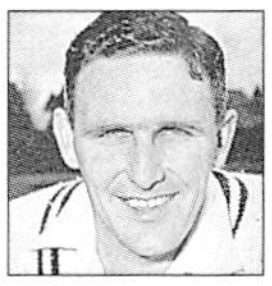

DAVIDSON, Alan Keith
B: June 14, 1929.
Bats: Left hand.
Bowls: Left arm.

First class debut:- 1949–50. 193 matches, 6804 runs, 36 50s, 9 100s, av. 32.86, 168 catches. 672 wkts at 20.90, 33 5-wkts, 2 10-wkts. HS: 129 BB: 7/31.
Test debut:- 1953. 44 matches, 1328 runs, 5 50s, av. 24.59, 42 catches. 186 wkts at 20.53, 14 5-wkts, 2 10-wkts. HS: 80 BB: 7/93.

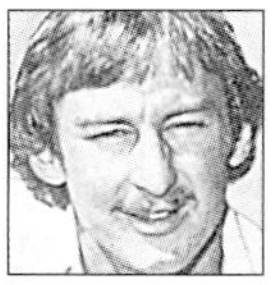

DAVIS, Ian Charles
B: June 25, 1953.
Bats: Right hand.

First class debut:- 1973–74. 76 matches, 3985 runs, 28 50s, 5 100s, av. 33.48, 36 catches. 0 wkts at –. HS: 156 BB: 0/7.

Test debut:- 1973–74. 15 matches, 692 runs, 4 50s, 1 100s, av. 26.62, 9 catches. HS: 105.
Int. limited-overs debut:- 1973–74. 3 matches, 12 runs at 6.00. HS: 11*.

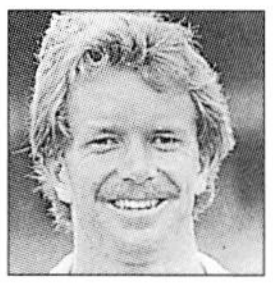

DAVIS, Simon Peter
B: Nov 8, 1959.
Bats: Right hand.
Bowls: Right arm.

First class debut:- 1983–84. 48 matches, 98 runs, av. 5.15, 13 catches. 124 wkts at 35.04, 5 5-wkts. HS: 15* BB: 7/104.
Test debut:- 1985–86. 1 match, 0 runs, av. 0.00. 0 wkts at –. HS: 0 BB: 0/70.
Int. limited-overs debut:- 1985–86. 39 matches, 20 runs at 5.00. 44 wkts at 25.75. HS: 6 BB: 3/10.

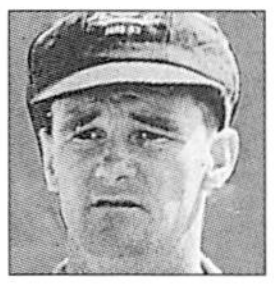

DE COURCY, James Harry
B: April 18, 1927.
Bats: Right hand.

First class debut:- 1947–48. 79 matches, 3778 runs, 23 50s, 6 100s, av. 37.03, 51 catches. HS: 204.
Test debut:- 1953. 3 matches, 81 runs at 16.20, 3 catches. HS: 41.

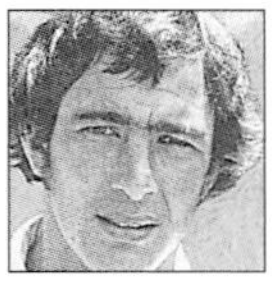

DELL, Anthony Ross
B: Aug 6, 1947.
Bats: Right hand.
Bowls: Left arm.

First class debut:- 1970–71. 41 matches, 169 runs, av. 5.63, 18 catches. 137 wkts at 26.70, 6 5-wkts, 1 10-wkts. HS: 13* BB: 6/17.
Test debut:- 1970–71. 2 matches, 6 runs. 6 wkts at 26.67. HS: 3* BB: 3/65.

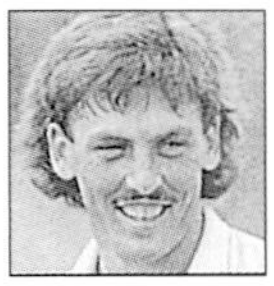

DODEMAIDE, Anthony Ian Christopher
B: Oct 5, 1963.
Bats: Right hand.
Bowls: Right arm.

First class debut:- 1983–84. 181 matches, 5957 runs, 27 50s, 5 100s, av. 28.92, 88 catches. 530 wkts at 31.83, 17 5-wkts. HS: 123 BB: 6/58.
Test debut:- 1987–88. 10 matches, 202 runs, 1 50s, av. 22.44, 6 catches. 34 wkts at 28.03, 1 5-wkts. HS: 50 BB: 6/58.
Int. limited-overs debut:- 1987–88. 24 matches, 124 runs at 13.78. 36 wkts at 20.92. HS: 30 BB: 5/21.

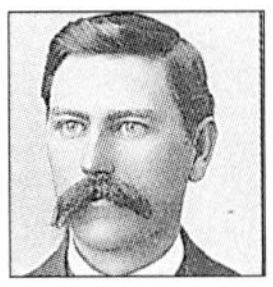

DONNAN, Henry
B: Nov 12, 1864.
D: Aug 13, 1956.
Bats: Right hand.
Bowls: Right arm.

First class debut:- 1887–88. 96 matches, 4262 runs, 22 50s, 6 100s, av. 29.19, 37 catches. 29 wkts at 41.06. HS: 167 BB: 3/14.
Test debut:- 1891–92. 5 matches, 75 runs, av. 8.33, 1 catch. 0 wkts at –. HS: 15 BB: 0/22.

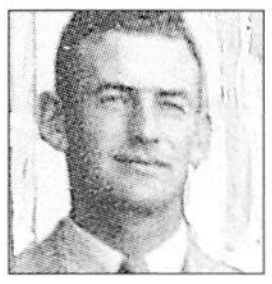

DOOLAND, Bruce
B: Nov 1, 1923.
D: Sep 8, 1980.
Bats: Right hand.
Bowls: Right arm.

First class debut:- 1945–46. 214 matches, 7141 runs, 41 50s, 4 100s, av. 24.37, 186 catches. 1016 wkts at 21.98, 84 5-wkts, 23 10-wkts. HS: 115* BB: 8/20.
Test debut:- 1946–47. 3 matches, 76 runs, av. 19.00, 3 catches. 9 wkts at 46.56. HS: 29 BB: 4/69.

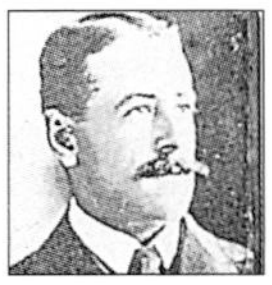

DUFF, Reginald Alexander
B: Aug 17, 1878.
D: Dec 13, 1911.
Bats: Right hand.
Bowls: Right arm.

First class debut:- 1898–99. 121 matches, 6589 runs, 33 50s, 10 100s, av. 35.04, 73 catches. 14 wkts at 34.14. HS: 271 BB: 2/17.
Test debut:- 1901–02. 22 matches, 1317 runs, 6 50s, 2 100s, av. 35.59, 14 catches. 4 wkts at 21.25. HS: 146 BB: 2/43.

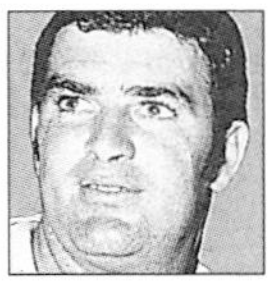

DUNCAN, John Ross Frederick
B: Mar 25, 1944.
Bats: Right hand.
Bowls: Right arm.

First class debut:- 1964–65. 71 matches, 649 runs, 1 50s, av. 8.42, 33 catches. 218 wkts at 31.19, 9 5-wkts, 1 10-wkts. HS: 52 BB: 8/55.
Test debut:- 1970–71. 1 match, 3 runs, av. 3.00. 0 wkts at –. HS: 3 BB: 0/30.

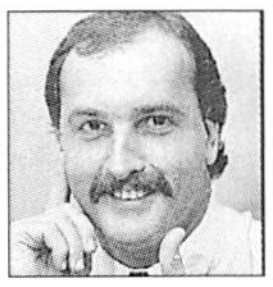

DYER, Gregory Charles
B: Mar 16, 1959.
Bats: Right hand - Wicketkeeper.

First class debut:- 1983–84. 51 matches, 1671 runs, 10 50s, 1 100s, av. 28.32, 123 catches, 18 stumpings. HS: 106.
Test debut:- 1986–87. 6 matches, 131 runs, 1 50s, av. 21.83, 22 catches, 2 stumpings. HS: 60.
Int. limited-overs debut:- 1986–87. 23 matches, 174 runs at 15.82. HS: 45*

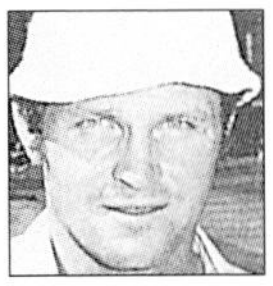

DYMOCK, Geoffrey
B: July 21, 1945.
Bats: Right hand.
Bowls: Left arm.

First class debut:- 1971–72. 126 matches, 1518 runs, 3 50s, 1 100s, av. 14.45, 41 catches. 425 wkts at 26.91, 13 5-wkts, 1 10-wkts. HS: 101* BB: 7/67.
Test debut:- 1973–74. 21 matches, 236 runs, av. 9.44, 1 catch. 78 wkts at 27.13, 5 5-wkts, 1 10-wkts. HS: 31* BB: 7/67.
Int. limited-overs debut:- 1973–74. 15 matches, 35 runs at 11.67. 15 wkts at 27.47. HS: 14* B: 2/21.

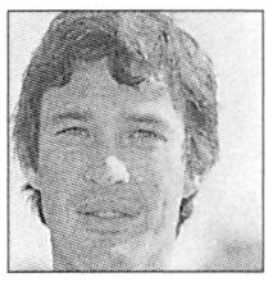

DYSON, John
B: June 11, 1954.
Bats: Right hand.

First class debut:- 1975–76. 156 matches, 9935 runs, 52 50s, 19 100s, av. 40.22, 99 catches. 2 wkts at 33.00. HS: 241 BB: 1/0.
Test debut:- 1977–78. 30 matches, 1359 runs, 5 50s, 2 100s, av. 26.65, 10 catches. HS: 127*.
Int. limited-overs debut:- 1980. 29 matches, 755 runs at 32.83. HS: 79.

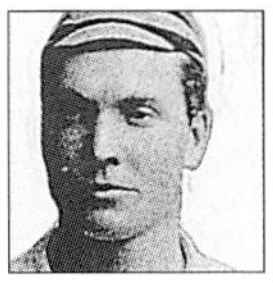

EADY, Charles John
B: Oct 29, 1870.
D: Dec 20, 1945.
Bats: Right hand.
Bowls: Right arm.

First class debut:- 1889–90. 42 matches, 1490 runs, 6 50s, 3 100s, av. 22.92, 45 catches. 136 wkts at 23.13, 12 5-wkts, 5 10-wkts. HS: 116 BB: 8/34.
Test debut:- 1896. 2 matches, 20 runs, av. 6.67, 2 catches. 7 wkts at 16.00. HS: 10* BB: 3/30.

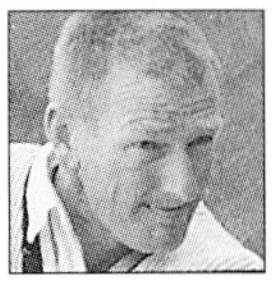

EASTWOOD, Kenneth Humphrey
B: Nov 23, 1935.
Bats: Left hand.
Bowls: Left arm.

First class debut:- 1959–60. 42 matches, 2722 runs, 8 50s, 9 100s, av. 41.87, 27 catches. 6 wkts at 63.83. HS: 221 BB: 1/10.
Test debut:- 1970–71. 1 match, 5 runs, av. 2.50. 1 wkt at 21.00. HS: 5 BB: 1/21.

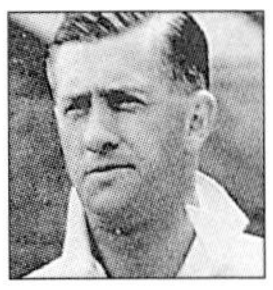

EBELING, Hans Irvine
B: Jan 1, 1905. D: Jan 12, 1980.
Bats: Right hand.
Bowls: Right arm.

First class debut:- 1923–24. 73 matches, 1005 runs, 3 50s, av. 14.15, 38 catches. 217 wkts at 26.58, 7 5-wkts, 2 10-wkts. HS: 76 BB: 7/33.
Test debut:- 1934. 1 match, 43 runs, av. 21.50. 3 wkts at 29.67. HS: 41 BB: 3/74.

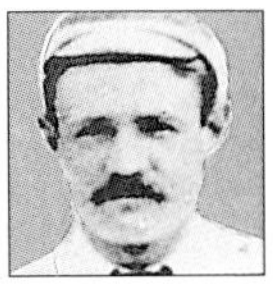

EDWARDS, John Dunlop
B: June 12, 1860.
D: July 31, 1911.
Bats: Right hand.
Bowls: Right arm.

First class debut:- 1880–81. 50 matches, 961 runs, 4 50s, av. 13.72, 19 catches. 7 wkts at 27.71. HS: 65 BB: 2/6.
Test debut:- 1888. 3 matches, 48 runs, av. 9.60, 1 catch. HS: 26.

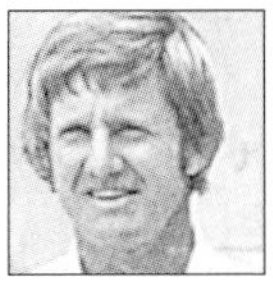

EDWARDS, Ross
B: Dec 1, 1942.
Bats: Right hand.

First class debut:- 1964–65. 126 matches, 7345 runs, 42 50s, 14 100s, av. 39.27, 111 catches, 11 stumpings. 1 wkt at 75.00. HS: 170* BB: 1/24.
Test debut:- 1972. 20 matches, 1171 runs, 9 50s, 2 100s, av. 40.38, 7 catches. 0 wkts at –. HS: 170* BB: 0/ .
Int. limited-overs debut:- 1972. 9 matches, 255 runs, 3 50s, av. 36.43. HS: 80*.

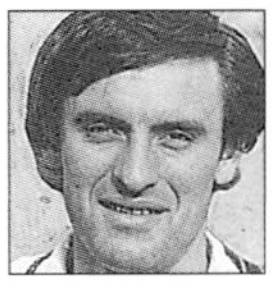

EDWARDS, Walter John
B: Dec 23, 1949.
Bats: Left hand.
Bowls: Right arm.

First class debut:- 1973–74. 25 matches, 1381 runs, 9 50s, 2 100s, av. 30.68, 16 catches. 2 wkts at 70.50. HS: 153 BB: 1/11.
Test debut:- 1974–75. 3 matches, 68 runs, av. 11.33. HS: 30.
Int. limited-overs debut:- 1974–75. 1 match, 2 runs at 2.00. 0 wkts at –. HS: 2 BB: 0/ .

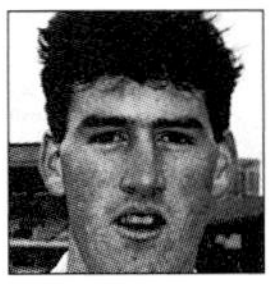

ELLIOTT, Matthew Thomas Gray
B: Sep 28, 1971.
Bats: Left hand.
Bowls: Left arm.

First class debut:- 1992–93. 50 matches, 4421 runs, 22 50s, 12 100s, av. 51.41, 60 catches. 3 wkts at 42.33. HS: 203 BB: 1/13.
Test debut:- 1996–97. 5 matches, 310 runs, 2 50s, av. 38.75, 3 catches. HS: 85.

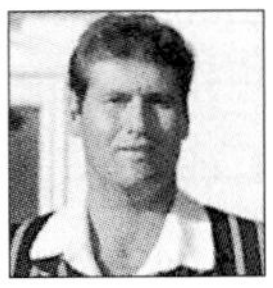

EMERY, Philip Allen
B: June 25, 1964.
Bats: Left hand - Wicketkeeper.

First class debut:- 1987–88. 101 matches, 2729 runs, 13 50s, 1 100s, av. 25.75, 297 catches, 35 stumpings. 0 wkts at –. HS: 100* BB: 0/ .
Test debut:- 1994–95. 1 match, 8 runs, av. –, 5 catches, 1 stumping. HS: 8*.
Int. limited-overs debut:- 1994–95. 1 match, 11 runs at –. HS: 11*.

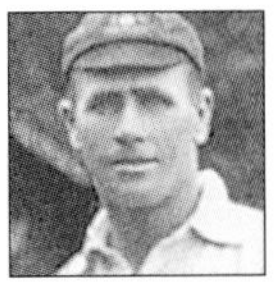

EMERY, Sidney Hand
B: Oct 16, 1885.
D: Jan 7, 1967.
Bats: Right hand.
Bowls: Right arm.

First class debut:- 1908–09. 58 matches, 1192 runs, 6 50s, av. 18.33, 30 catches. 183 wkts at 23.79, 11 5-wkts, 3 10-wkts. HS: 80* BB: 7/28.
Test debut:- 1912. 4 matches, 6 runs, av. 3.00, 2 catches. 5 wkts at 49.80. HS: 5 BB: 2/46.

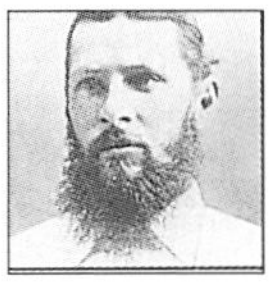

EVANS, Edwin
B: Mar 26, 1849.
D: July 2, 1921.
Bats: Right hand.
Bowls: Right arm.

First class debut:- 1874–75. 65 matches, 1006 runs, 2 50s, av. 12.26, 63 catches. 201 wkts at 16.69, 18 5-wkts, 4 10-wkts. HS: 74* BB: 7/16.
Test debut:- 1881–82. 6 matches, 82 runs, av. 10.25, 5 catches. 7 wkts at 47.43. HS: 33 BB: 3/64.

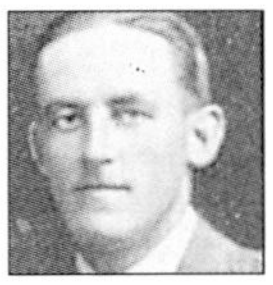

FAIRFAX, Alan George
B: June 16, 1906.
D: May 17, 1955.
Bats: Right hand.
Bowls: Right arm.

First class debut:- 1928–29. 55 matches, 1910 runs, 9 50s, 1 100s, av. 28.93, 41 catches. 134 wkts at 27.87, 2 5-wkts. HS: 104 BB: 6/54.
Test debut:- 1928–29. 10 matches, 410 runs, 4 50s, av. 51.25, 15 catches. 21 wkts at 30.71. HS: 65 BB: 4/31.

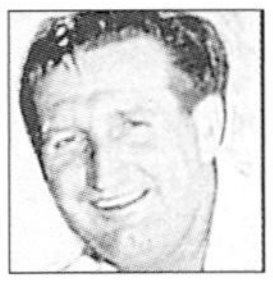

FAVELL, Leslie Ernest
B: Oct 6, 1929.
D: June 14, 1987.
Bats: Right hand.
Bowls: Right arm.

First class debut:- 1951–52. 202 matches, 12379 runs, 68 50s, 27 100s, av. 36.62, 110 catches. 5 wkts at 69.00. HS: 190 BB: 1/0.
Test debut:- 1954–55. 19 matches, 757 runs, 5 50s, 1 100s, v. 27.04, 9 catches. HS: 101.

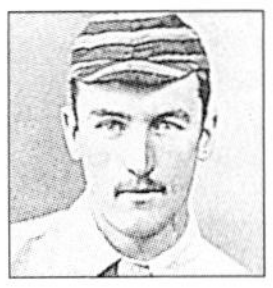

FERRIS, John James
B: May 21, 1867.
D: Nov 21, 1900.
Bats: Left hand.
Bowls: Left arm.

First class debut:- 1886–87. 198 matches, 4264 runs, 15 50s, 1 100s, av. 15.67, 90 catches. 813 wkts at 17.53, 63 5-wkts, 11 10-wkts. HS: 106 BB: 8/41.
Test debut:- 1886–87. 9 matches, 114 runs, av. 8.77, 4 catches. 61 wkts at 12.70, 6 5-wkts, 1 10-wkts. HS: 20* BB: 7/37.

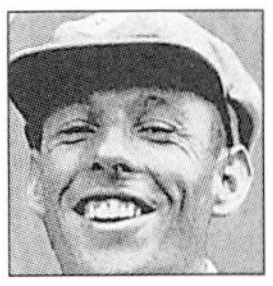

FINGLETON, John Henry Webb
B: April 28, 1908.
D: Nov 22, 1981.
Bats: Right hand.

First class debut:- 1928–29. 108 matches, 6816 runs, 31 50s, 22 100s, av. 44.54, 81 catches, 4 stumpings. 2 wkts at 27.00. HS: 167 BB: 1/6.
Test debut:- 1931–32. 18 matches, 1189 runs, 3 50s, 5 100s, av. 42.46, 13 catches. HS: 136.

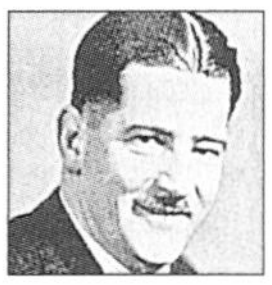

FLEETWOOD-SMITH, Leslie O'Brien
B: Mar 30, 1910.
D: Mar 16, 1971.
Bats: Right hand.
Bowls: Left arm.
First class debut:- 1931–32. 112 matches, 617 runs, 1 50s, av. 7.34, 42 catches. 597 wkts at 22.64, 57 5-wkts, 18 10-wkts. HS: 63 BB: 9/36.
Test debut:- 1935–36. 10 matches, 54 runs, av. 9.00. 42 wkts at 37.38, 2 5-wkts, 1 10-wkts. HS: 16* BB: 6/110.

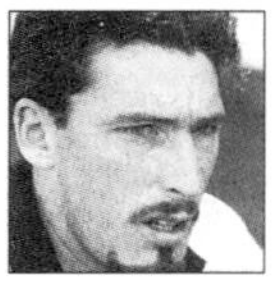

FLEMING, Damien William
B: April 24, 1970.
Bats: Right hand.
Bowls: Right arm.

First class debut:- 1989–90. 64 matches, 786 runs, 2 50s, av. 14.56, 33 catches. 211 wkts at 31.12, 6 5-wkts. HS: 63* BB: 7/90.
Test debut:- 1994–95. 4 matches, 40 runs, av. 10.00, 2 catches. 17 wkts at 25.59. HS: 24 BB: 4/75.
Int. limited-overs debut:- 1993–94. 27 matches, 19 runs at 6.33. 40 wkts at 24.88. HS: 5* BB: 5/36.

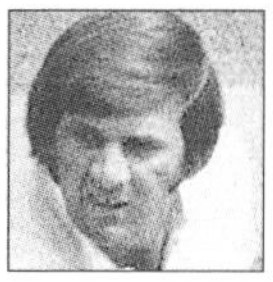

FRANCIS, Bruce Colin
B: Feb 18, 1948.
Bats: Right hand.

First class debut:- 1968–69. 109 matches, 6183 runs, 31 50s, 13 100s, av. 33.97, 42 catches. 1 wkt at 15.00. HS: 210 BB: 1/10.
Test debut:- 1972. 3 matches, 52 runs, av. 10.40, 1 catch. HS: 27.

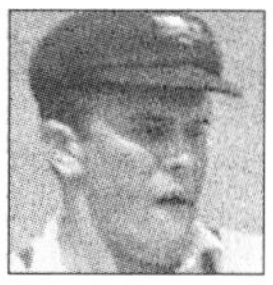

FREEMAN, Eric Walter
B: July 13, 1944.
Bats: Right hand.
Bowls: Right arm.

First class debut:- 1964–65. 83 matches, 2244 runs, 9 50s, 1 100s, av. 19.17, 60 catches. 241 wkts at 27.75, 7 5-wkts, 2 10-wkts. HS: 116 BB: 8/47.
Test debut:- 1967–68. 11 matches, 345 runs, 2 50s, av. 19.17, 5 catches. 34 wkts at 33.18. HS: 76 BB: 4/52.

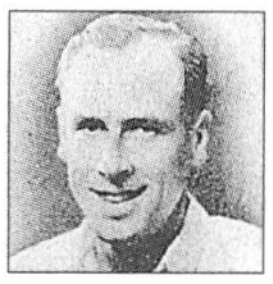

FREER, Frederick William
B: Dec 4, 1915.
Bats: Right hand.
Bowls: Right arm.
First class debut:- 1945–46. 40 matches, 1284 runs, 5 50s, 3 100s, av. 32.10, 25 catches. 104 wkts at 27.75, 4 5-wkts. HS: 132 BB: 7/29.
Test debut:- 1946–47. 1 match, 28 runs, av -. 3 wkts at 24.67. HS: 28* BB: 2/49.

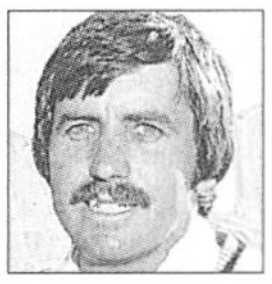

GANNON, John Bryant
B: Feb 8, 1947.
Bats: Right hand.
Bowls: Left arm.

First class debut:- 1966–67. 40 matches, 20 runs, av. 6.40, 19 catches. 117 wkts at 30.47, 2 5-wkts. HS: 20 BB: 6/107.
Test debut:- 1977–78. 3 matches, 3 runs, av. 3.00, 3 catches. 11 wkts at 32.82. HS: 3* BB: 4/77.

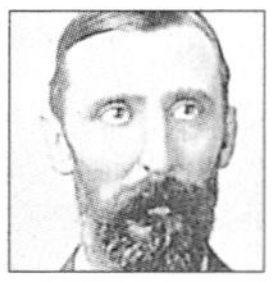

GARRETT, Thomas William
B: July 26, 1858.
D: Augt 6, 1943.
Bats: Right hand.
Bowls: Right arm.

First class debut:- 1876–77. 160 matches, 3673 runs, 10 50s, 2 100s, av. 16.18, 80 catches. 445 wkts at 18.77, 29 5-wkts, 5 10-wkts. HS: 163 BB: 7/38.
Test debut:- 1876–77. 19 matches, 339 runs, 1 50s, av. 12.56, 7 catches. 36 wkts at 26.94, 2 5-wkts. HS: 51* BB: 6/78.

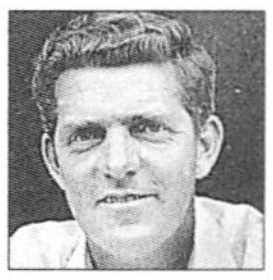

GAUNT, Ronald Arthur
B: Feb 26, 1934.
Bats: Left hand.
Bowls: Right arm.

First class debut:- 1955–56. 85 matches, 616 runs, av. 10.44, 31 catches. 266 wkts at 26.85, 10 5-wkts. HS: 32* BB: 7/104.
Test debut:- 1957–58. 3 matches, 6 runs, av. 3.00, 1 catch. 7 wkts at 44.29. HS: 3 BB: 3/53.

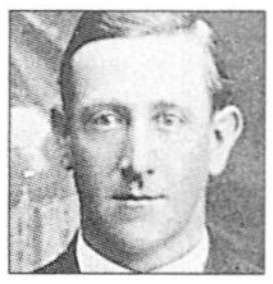

GEHRS, Donald Raeburn Algernon
B: Nov 29, 1880.
D: June 25, 1953.
Bats: Right hand - Wicketkeeper.
Bowls: Right arm.
First class debut:- 1902–03. 83 matches, 4377 runs, 16 50s, 13 100s, av. 33.66, 71 catches, 4 stumpings. 8 wkts at 52.00, HS: 170 BB: 2/9.
Test debut:- 1903–04. 6 matches, 221 runs, 2 50s, av. 20.09, 6 catches. 0 wkts at –. HS: 67 BB: 0/4.

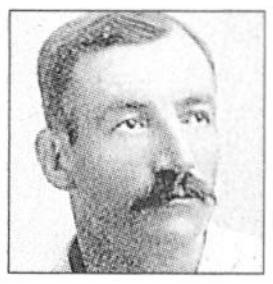

GIFFEN, George
B: Mar 27, 1859.
D: Nov 29, 1927.
Bats: Right hand.
Bowls: Right arm.

First class debut:- 1877–78. 251 matches, 11,758 runs, 54 50s, 18 100s, av. 29.54, 195 catches. 1023 wkts at 21.29, 95 5-wkts, 30 10-wkts. HS: 271 BB: 10/66.
Test debut:- 1881–82. 31 matches, 1238 runs, 6 50s, 1 100s, av. 23.36, 25 catches. 103 wkts at 27.10, 7 5-wkts, 1 10-wkts. HS: 161 BB: 7/117.

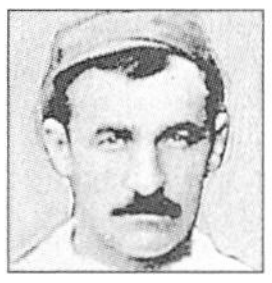

GIFFEN, Walter Frank
B: Sep 20, 1861.
D: June 28, 1949.
Bats: Right hand.

First class debut:- 1882–83. 47 matches, 1178 runs, 6 50s, av. 15.91, 23 catches. 0 wkts at –. HS: 89 BB: 0/15.
Test debut:- 1886–87. 3 matches, 11 runs, av. 1.83. HS: 3.

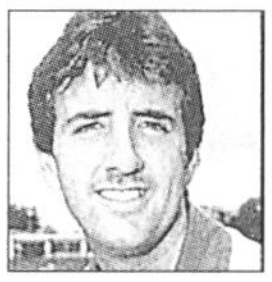

GILBERT, David Robert
B: Dec 29, 1960.
Bats: Right hand.
Bowls: Right arm.

First class debut:- 1983–84. 127 matches, 1374 runs, 1 50s, 1 100s, av. 14.31, 20 catches. 354 wkts at 32.40, 11 5-wkts, 1 10-wkts. HS: 117 BB: 8/55.
Test debut:- 1985. 9 matches, 57 runs, av. 7.13. 16 wkts at 52.69. HS: 15 BB: 3/48.
Int. limited-overs debut:- 1985–86. 14 matches, 39 runs at 7.80. 18 wkts at 30.67. HS: 8 BB: 5/46.

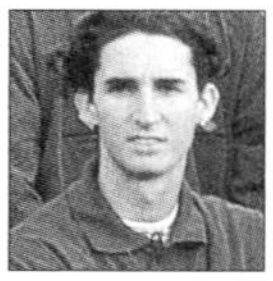

GILLESPIE, Jason Neil
B: April 19, 1975.
Bats: Right hand.
Bowls: Right arm.

First class debut:- 1994–95. 25 matches, 345 runs, 1 50s, av. 12.32, 10 catches. 99 wkts at 23.17, 4 5-wkts. HS: 58 BB: 7/34.
Test debut:- 1996–97. 5 matches, 29 runs, av. 14.50. 16 wkts at 23.81, 1 5-wkts. HS: 16* BB: 5/54.
Int. limited-overs debut:- 1996–97. 11 matches, 56 runs, av. 11.20. 12 wkts at 39.25. HS: 6 BB: 2/39.

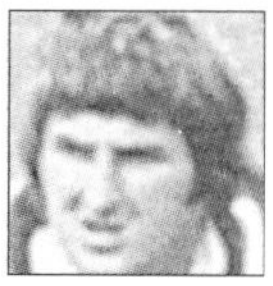

GILMOUR, Gary John
B: June 26, 1951.
Bats: Left hand.
Bowls: Left arm.

First class debut:- 1971–72. 75 matches, 3126 runs, 18 50s, 5 100s, av. 30.64, 68 catches. 233 wkts at 31.52, 6 5-wkts. HS: 122 BB: 6/85.
Test debut:- 1973–74. 15 matches, 483 runs, 3 50s, 1 100s, av. 23.00, 8 catches. 54 wkts at 26.04, 3 5-wkts. HS: 101 BB: 6/85.
Int. limited-overs debut:- 1973–74. 5 matches, 42 runs at 42.00. 16 wkts at 10.31. HS: 28* BB: 6/14.

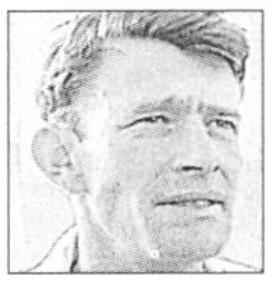

GLEESON, John William
B: Mar 14, 1938.
Bats: Right hand.
Bowls: Right arm.

First class debut:- 1966–67. 116 matches, 1095 runs, 1 50s, av. 11.06, 58 catches. 430 wkts at 24.95, 22 5-wkts, 2 10-wkts. HS: 59 BB: 7/52.
Test debut:- 1967–68. 30 matches, 395 runs, av. 10.39, 17 catches. 93 wkts at 36.20, 3 5-wkts. HS: 45 BB: 5/61.

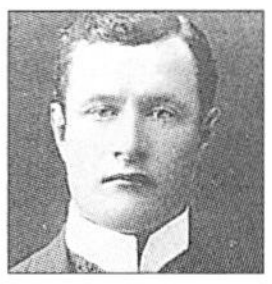

GRAHAM, Henry
B: Nov 22, 1870.
D: Feb 7, 1911.
Bats: Right hand.
Bowls: Right arm.

First class debut:- 1892–93. 114 matches, 5054 runs, 23 50s, 7 100s, av. 26.32, 87 catches. 6 wkts at 39.16. HS: 124 BB: 4/39.
Test debut:- 1893. 6 matches, 301 runs, 2 100s, av. 30.10, 3 catches. HS: 107.

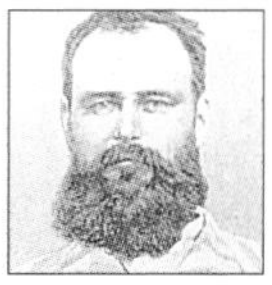

GREGORY, David William
B: April 15, 1845.
D: Aug 4, 1919.
Bats: Right hand.
Bowls: Right arm.

First class debut:- 1866–87. 41 matches, 889 runs, 5 50s, av. 14.57, 35 catches. 29 wkts at 19.06, 1 5-wkts. HS: 85 BB: 5/55.
Test debut:- 1876–77. 3 matches, 60 runs, av. 20.00. HS: 43.

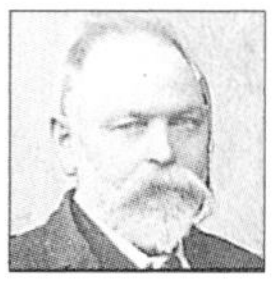

GREGORY, Edward James
B: May 29, 1839.
D: April 22, 1899.
Bats: Right hand.
Bowls: Right arm.

First class debut:- 1862–63. 16 matches, 470 runs, 2 50s, av. 17.40, 11 catches. 5 wkts at 21.20. HS: 65* BB: 2/14.
Test debut:- 1876–77. 1 match, 11 runs, av. 5.50, 1 catch. HS: 11.

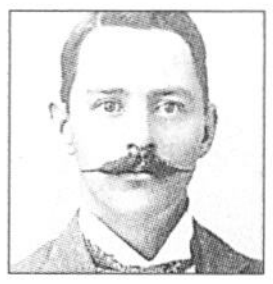

GREGORY, Edward Sydney
B: April 14, 1870.
D: Aug 1, 1929.
Bats: Right hand.

First class debut:- 1889–90. 368 matches, 15,192 runs, 65 50s, 25 100s, av. 28.55, 174 catches. 2 wkts at 197.00. HS: 201 BB: 1/8.
Test debut:- 1890. 58 matches, 2282 runs, 8 50s, 4 100s, av. 24.54, 25 catches. 0 wkts -. HS: 201. BB: 0/33.

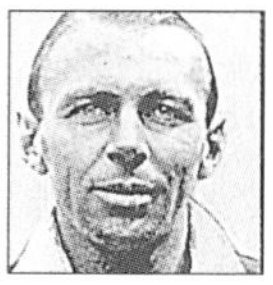

GREGORY, Jack Morrison
B: Aug 14, 1895.
D: Aug 7, 1973.
Bats: Left hand.
Bowls: Right arm.

First class debut:- 1919. 129 matches, 5561 runs, 27 50s, 13 100s, av. 36.52, 195 catches. 504 wkts at 20.99. 33 5-wkts, 8 10-wkts. HS: 152 BB: 9/32.
Test debut:- 1920–21. 24 matches, 1146 runs, 7 50s, 2 100s, av. 36.97, 37 catches. 85 wkts at 31.15, 4 5-wkts. HS: 119 BB: 7/69.

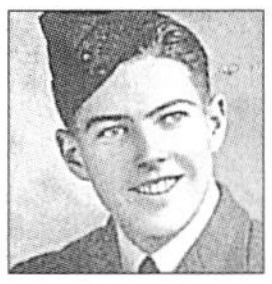

GREGORY, Ross Gerald
B: Feb 28, 1916.
D: June 10, 1942.
Bats: Right hand.
Bowls: Right arm.

First class debut:- 1933–34. 33 matches, 1874 runs, 17 50s, 1 100s, av. 38.24, 20 catches. 50 wkts at 35.34, 1 5-wkts. HS: 128 BB: 5/69.
Test debut:- 1936–37. 2 matches, 153 runs, 2 50s, av. 51.00, 1 catch. 0 wkts at –. HS: 80 BB: 0/14.

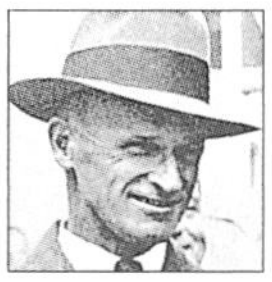

GRIMMETT, Clarence Victor
B: Dec 25, 1891.
D: May 2, 1980.
Bats: Right hand.
Bowls: Right arm.

First class debut:- 1911–12. 248 matches, 4720 runs, 12 50s, av. 17.67, 139 catches. 1424 wkts at 22.28, 127 5-wkts, 33 10-wkts. HS: 71* BB: 10/37.
Test debut:- 1924–25. 37 matches, 557 runs, 1 50s, av. 13.93, 17 catches. 216 wkts at 24.22, 21 5-wkts, 7 10-wkts. HS: 50 BB: 7/40.

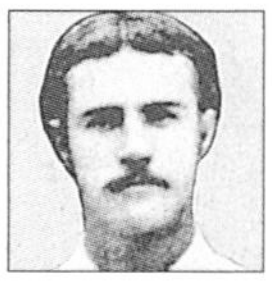

GROUBE, Thomas Underwood
B: Sep 2, 1857.
D: Aug 5, 1927.
Bats: Right hand.
Bowls: Right arm.
First class debut:- 1878–79. 13 matches, 179 runs, 1 50s, av. 8.52. HS: 61.
Test debut:- 1880. 1 match, 11 runs, av. 5.50. HS: 11.

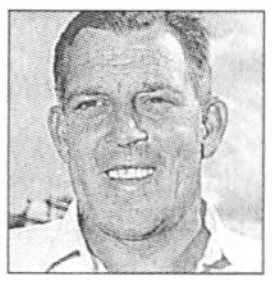

GROUT, Arthur Theodore Wallace
B: Mar 20, 1927.
D: Nov 9, 1968.
Bats: Right hand - Wicketkeeper.
First class debut:- 1946–47. 183 matches, 5168 runs, 25 50s, 4 100s, av. 22.56, 473 catches, 114 stumpings. 3 wkts at 38.33. HS: 119 BB: 1/22.
Test debut:- 1957–58. 51 matches, 890 runs, 3 50s, av. 15.08, 163 catches, 24 stumpings. HS: 74.

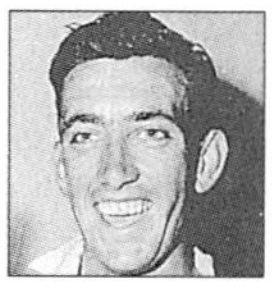

GUEST, Colin Ernest James
B: Oct 7, 1937.
Bats: Right hand.
Bowls: Right arm.

First class debut:- 1958–59. 36 matches, 922 runs, 3 50s, av. 19.20, 13 catches. 115 wkts at 27.13, 5 5-wkts, 1 10-wkts. HS: 74 BB: 7/95.
Test debut:- 1962–63. 1 match, 11 runs, av. 11.00. 0 wkts at –. HS: 11 BB: 0/8.

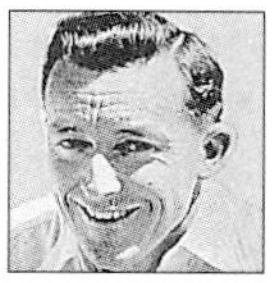

HAMENCE, Ronald Arthur
B: Nov 25, 1915.
Bats: Right hand.
Bowls: Right arm.

First class debut:- 1935–36. 99 matches, 5285 runs, 26 50s, 11 100s, av. 37.75, 34 catches. 8 wkts at 29.87. HS: 173 BB: 2/13.
Test debut:- 1946–47. 3 matches, 81 runs, av. 27.00, 1 catch. HS: 30*.

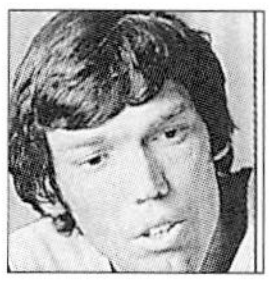

HAMMOND, Jeffrey Roy
B: April 19, 1950.
Bats: Right hand.
Bowls: Right arm.

First class debut:- 1969–70. 69 matches, 922 runs, 1 50s, av. 16.46, 36 catches. 184 wkts at 28.88, 8 5-wkts. HS: 53 BB: 6/15.
Test debut:- 1972–73. 5 matches, 28 runs, av. 9.33, 2 catches. 15 wkts at 32.53. HS: 19 BB: 4/38.
Int. limited-overs debut:- 1972. 1 match, 15 runs at –. 1 wkt at 41.00. HS: 15* BB: 1/41.

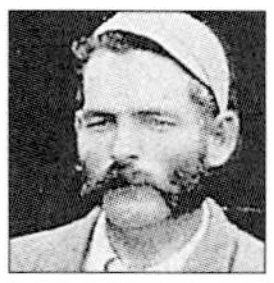

HARRY, John
B: Aug 1, 1857.
D: Oct 27, 1919.
Bats: Right hand - Wicketkeeper.
Bowls: Right arm.

First class debut:- 1883–84. 32 matches, 1466 runs, 9 50s, 2 100s, av. 25.71, 18 catches, 3 stumpings. 26 wkts at 26.76. HS: 114 BB: 4/15.
Test debut:- 1894–95. 1 match, 8 runs, av. 4.00, 1 catch. HS: 6.

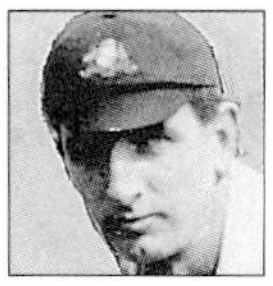

HARTIGAN, Roger Joseph
B: Dec 12, 1879.
D: June 7, 1958.
Bats: Right hand.

First class debut:- 1903–04. 45 matches, 1901 runs, 14 50s, 2 100s, av. 25.01, 36 catches. 9 wkts at 39.00. HS: 116 BB: 3/27.
Test debut:- 1907–08. 2 matches, 170 runs, 1 100s, av. 42.50, 1 catch. 0 wkts at –. HS: 116 BB: 0/7.

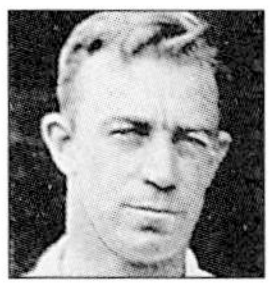

HARTKOPF, Albert Ernst Victor
B: Dec 28, 1889.
D: May 20, 1968.
Bats: Right hand.
Bowls: Right arm.
First class debut:- 1911–12. 41 matches, 1758 runs, 12 50s, 2 100s, av. 34.47, 36 catches. 121 wkts at 30.79, 7 5-wkts, 1 10-wkts. HS: 126 BB: 8/105.
Test debut:- 1924–25. 1 match, 80 runs, 1 50s, av. 40.00. 1 wkt at 134.00. HS: 80 BB: 1/120.

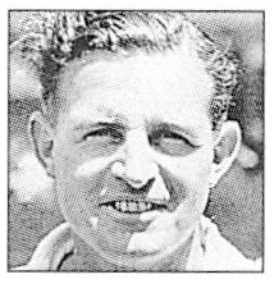

HARVEY, Mervyn Roye
B: April 29, 1918.
D: Mar 29, 1995.
Bats: Right hand.

First class debut:- 1940–41. 22 matches, 1147 runs, 3 50s, 3 100s, av. 38.23, 11 catches. HS: 163.
Test debut:- 1946–47. 1 match, 43 runs, av. 21.50. HS: 31.

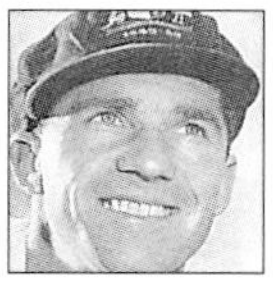

HARVEY, Robert Neil
B: Oct 8, 1928.
Bats: Left hand.
Bowls: Right arm.

First class debut:- 1946–47. 306 matches, 21,699 runs, 94 50s, 67 100s, av. 50.93, 229 catches. 30 wkts at 36.86. HS: 231* BB: 4/8.
Test debut:- 1947–48. 79 matches, 6149 runs, 24 50s, 21 100s, av. 48.42, 64 catches. 3 wkts at 40.00. HS: 205 BB: 1/8.

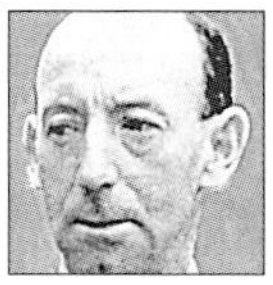

HASSETT, Arthur Lindsay
B: Aug 28, 1913.
D: June 16, 1993.
Bats: Right hand.
Bowls: Right arm.

First class debut:- 1932–33. 216 matches, 16,890 runs, 74 50s, 59 100s, av. 58.24, 170 catches. 18 wkts at 39.05. HS: 232 BB: 2/10.
Test debut:- 1938. 43 matches, 3073 runs, 11 50s, 10 100s, av. 46.56, 30 catches. 0 wkts at –. HS: 198* BB: 0/ .

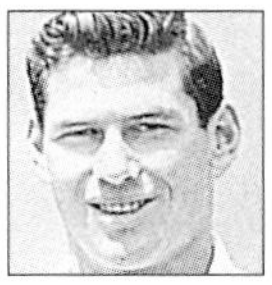

HAWKE, Neil James Napier
B: June 27, 1939.
Bats: Right hand.
Bowls: Right arm.

First class debut:- 1959–60. 145 matches, 3383 runs, 11 50s, 1 100s, av. 23.99, 85 catches. 458 wkts at 26.39, 23 5-wkts, 5 10-wkts. HS: 141* BB: 8/61.
Test debut:- 1962–63. 27 matches, 365 runs, av. 16.59, 9 catches. 91 wckts at 29.42, 6 5-wkts, 1 10-wkts. HS: 45* BB: 7/105.

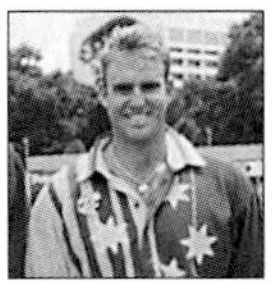

HAYDEN, Matthew Lawrence
B: Oct 29, 1971.
Bats: Left hand.
Bowls: Right arm.

First class debut:- 1991–92. 91 matches, 7834 runs, 32 50s, 24 100s, av. 54.40, 79 catches. 1 wkts at 116.00. HS: 234 BB: 1/24.
Test debut:- 1993–94. 7 matches, 261 runs, 1 100s, av. 21.75, 8 catches. HS: 125.
Int. limited-overs debut:- 1993. 13 matches, 286 runs at 26.00. HS: 67.

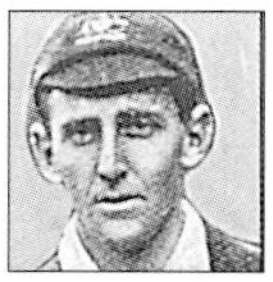

HAZLITT, Gervys Rignold
B: Sep 4, 1888.
D: Oct 30, 1915.
Bats: Right hand.
Bowls: Right arm.

First class debut:- 1905–06. 57 matches, 876 runs, 5 50s, av. 12.69, 31 catches. 188 wkts at 26.09, 8 5-wkts. HS: 82* BB: 7/25.
Test debut:- 1907–08. 9 matches, 89 runs, av. 11.13, 4 catches. 23 wkts at 27.09, 1 5-wkts. HS: 34* BB: 7/25.

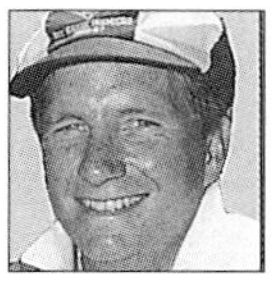

HEALY, Ian Andrew
B: April 30, 1964.
Bats: Right hand - Wicketkeeper.

First class debut:- 1986–87. 171 matches, 6310 runs, 31 50s, 3 100s, av. 31.87, 527 catches, 45 stumpings. HS: 161*.
Test debut:- 1988–89. 88 matches, 3245 runs, 17 50s, 3 100s, av. 28.22, 282 catches, 20 stumpings. HS: 161*.
Int. limited-overs debut:- 1988–89. 165 matches, 1713 runs at 21.15. HS: 56.

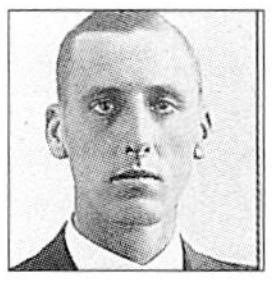

HENDRY, Hunter Scott Thomas Laurie
B: May 24, 1895.
D: Dec 16, 1988.
Bats: Right hand.
Bowls: Right arm.
First class debut:- 1918–19. 140 matches, 6799 runs, 34 50s, 14 100s, av. 37.56, 152 catches. 229 wkts at 29.02, 6 5-wkts, 1 10-wkts. HS: 325* BB: 8/33.
Test debut:- 1921. 11 matches, 335 runs, 1 100s, av. 20.94, 10 catches. 16 wkts at 40.00. HS: 112 BB: 3/36.

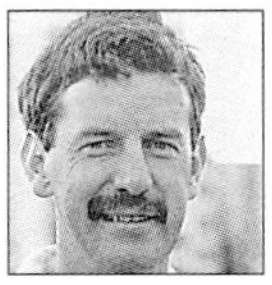

HIBBERT, Paul Anthony
B: July 23, 1952.
Bats: Left hand.
Bowls: Left arm.

First class debut:- 1974–75. 78 matches, 4790 runs, 25 50s, 9 100s, av. 38.62, 38 catches. 15 wkts at 19.00. HS: 163 BB: 4/28.
Test debut:- 1977–78. 1 match, 15 runs, av. 7.50, 1 catch. HS: 13.

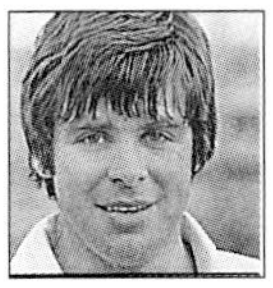

HIGGS, James Donald
B: July 11, 1950.
Bats: Right hand.
Bowls: Right arm.

First class debut:- 1970–71. 122 matches, 384 runs, av. 5.40, 43 catches. 399 wkts at 29.66, 19 5-wkts, 3 10-wkts. HS: 21 BB: 8/66.
Test debut:- 1977–78. 22 matches, 111 runs, av. 5.55, 3 catches. 66 wkts at 31.17, 2 5-wkts. HS: 16 BB: 7/143.

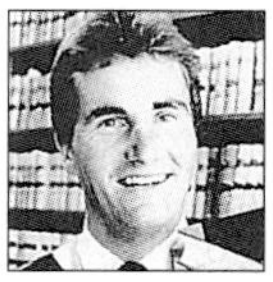

HILDITCH, Andrew Mark Jefferson
B: May 20, 1956.
Bats: Right hand.
Bowls: Right arm.

First class debut:- 1976–77. 156 matches, 9962 runs, 55 50s, 20 100s, av. 37.88, 101 catches. 4 wkts at 49.25. HS: 230 BB: 1/5.
Test debut:- 1978–79. 18 matches, 1073 runs, 6 50s, 2 100s, av. 31.56, 13 catches. HS: 119.
Int. limited-overs debut:- 1978–79. 8 matches, 226 runs at 28.25. HS: 72.

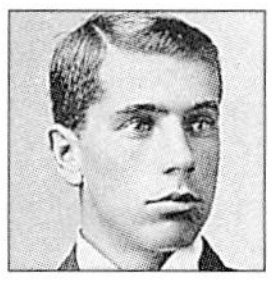

HILL, Clement
B: Mar 18, 1877.
D: Sep 5, 1945.
Bats: Left hand.

First class debut:- 1892–93. 252 matches, 17,213 runs, 83 50s, 45 100s, av. 43.57, 168 catches, 1 stumping. 10 wkts at 32.30. HS: 365* BB: 2/6.
Test debut:- 1896. 49 matches, 3412 runs, 19 50s, 7 100s, av. 39.22, 33 catches. HS: 191.

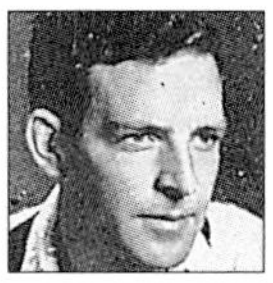

HILL, John Charles
B: June 25, 1923.
D: Aug 11, 1974.
Bats: Right hand.
Bowls: Right arm.

First class debut:- 1945–46. 69 matches, 867 runs, 1 50s, av. 16.05, 63 catches. 218 wkts at 23.11, 9 5-wkts, 1 10-wkts. HS: 51* BB: 7/51.
Test debut:- 1953. 3 matches, 21 runs, av. 7.00, 2 catches. 8 wkts at 34.13. HS: 8* BB: 3/35.

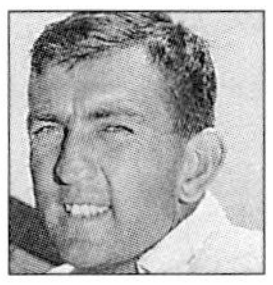

HOARE, Desmond Edward
B: Oct 19, 1934.
Bats: Right hand.
Bowls: Right arm.

First class debut:- 1955–56. 63 matches, 1276 runs, 3 50s, 1 100s, av. 18.49, 30 catches. 225 wkts at 26.91, 12 5-wkts, 1 10-wkts. HS: 133 BB: 8/98.
Test debut:- 1960–61. 1 match, 35 runs, av. 17.50, 2 catches. 2 wkts at 78.00. HS: 35 BB: 2/68.

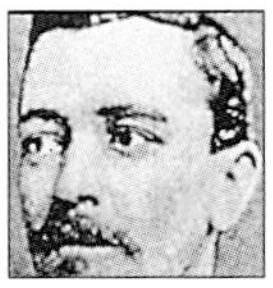

HODGES, John Robart
B: Aug 11, 1855.
D: Jan 17, 1933.
Bats: Left hand.
Bowls: Left arm.

First class debut:- 1876–77. 4 matches, 75 runs, av. 12.50, 1 catch. 12 wkts at 16.50. HS: 22 BB: 3/11.
Test debut:- 1876–77. 2 matches, 10 runs, av. 3.33. 6 wkts at 14.00. HS: 8 BB: 2/7.

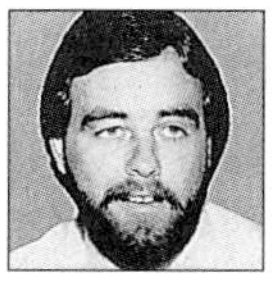

HOGAN, Tom George
B: Sep 23, 1956.
Bats: Right hand.
Bowls: Left arm.

First class debut:- 1981–82. 80 matches, 1756 runs, 6 50s, 1 100s, av. 20.18, 52 catches. 209 wkts at 35.87, 9 5-wkts. HS: 115* BB: 8/86.
Test debut:- 1982–83. 7 matches, 205 runs, av. 18.64, 2 catches. 15 wkts at 47.07, 1 5-wkts. HS: 42* BB: 5/66.
Int. limited-overs debut:- 1982–83. 16 matches, 72 runs, av. 9.00, 10 catches. 23 wkts at 24.96. HS: 27 BB: 4/33.

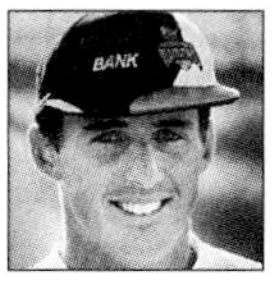

HOGG, George Bradley
B: Feb 6, 1971.
Bats: Left hand.
Bowls: Left arm.

First class debut:- 1993–94. 35 matches, 1093 runs, 6 50s, 2 100s, av. 26.02, 22 catches. 40 wkts at 49.83, 2 5-wkts. HS: 111* BB: 5/59.
Test debut:- 1996–97. 1 match, 5 runs, av. 2.50. 1 wkt at 69.00. HS: 4 BB: 1/69.
Int. limited-overs debut:- 1996–97. 7 matches, 38 runs at 12.67. 3 wkts at 72.67. HS: 11* BB: 1/23.

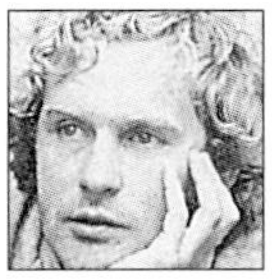

HOGG, Rodney Malcolm
B: Mar 5, 1951.
Bats: Right hand.
Bowls: Right arm.

First class debut:- 1975–76. 107 matches, 1185 runs, 1 50s, av. 10.48, 25 catches. 378 wkts at 24.36, 20 5-wkts, 4 10-wkts. HS: 52 BB: 7/53.
Test debut:- 1978–79. 38 matches, 439 runs, 1 50s, av. 9.76, 7 catches. 123 wkts at 28.48, 6 5-wkts, 2 10-wkts. HS: 52 BB: 6/74.
Int. limited-overs debut:- 1978–79. 71 matches, 137 runs, av. 9.13, 8 catches. 85 wkts at 28.45. HS: 22 BB: 4/29.

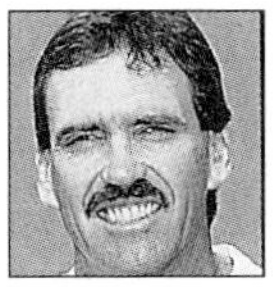

HOHNS, Trevor Victor
B: Jan 23, 1954.
Bats: Left hand.
Bowls: Right arm.

First class debut:- 1972–73. 152 matches, 5210 runs, 30 50s, 2 100s, av. 27.13, 86 catches. 288 wkts at 35.90, 11 5-wkts, 1 10-wkts. HS: 103 BB: 6/56.
Test debut:- 1988–89. 7 matches, 136 runs, av. 22.67, 3 catches. 17 wkts at 34.12. HS: 40 BB: 3/59.

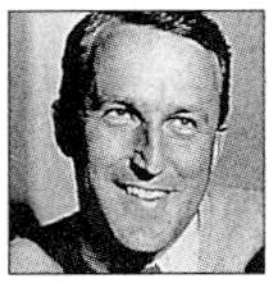

HOLE, Graeme Blake
B: Jan 6, 1931. D: Feb 14, 1990.
Bats: Right hand.
Bowls: Right arm.

First class debut:- 1949–50. 98 matches, 5647 runs, 31 50s, 11 100s, av. 36.66, 82 catches. 61 wkts at 44.03, 1 5-wkts. HS: 226 BB: 5/109.
Test debut:- 1950–51. 18 matches, 789 runs, 6 50s, av. 25.45, 21 catches. 3 wkts at 42.00. HS: 66 BB: 1/9.

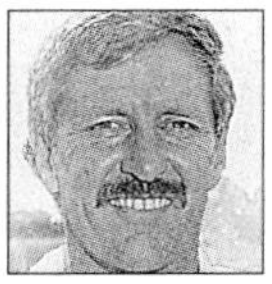

HOLLAND, Robert George
B: Oct 19, 1946
Bats: Right hand.
Bowls: Right arm.

First class debut:- 1978–79. 96 matches, 706 runs, 1 50s, av. 9.67, 55 catches.
316 wkts at 31.25, 14 5-wkts, 3 10-wkts. HS: 53 BB: 9/83.
Test Debut:- 1984–85.
11 matches, 35 runs, av. 3.18, 5 catches. 34 wkts at 39.76, 3 5-wkts, 2 10-wkts. HS: 10 BB: 6/54.
Int. limited-overs debut:- 1984–85. 2 matches, 2 wkts at 49.50. HS: DNB BB: 2/49.

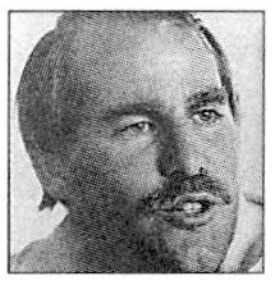

HOOKES, David William
B: May 3, 1955
Bats: Left hand.
Bowls: Left arm.

First class debut:- 1975–76.
156 matches, 9962 runs, 55 50s, 20 100s, av. 37.87, 101 catches.
18 wkts at 49.25. HS: 306* BB: 3/58.
Test Debut:- 1976–77.
23 matches, 1306 runs, 8 50s, 1 100s, av. 34.37, 12 catches.
1 wkt at 41.00. HS: 143* BB: 1/4.
Int. limited-overs debut:- 1977. 39 matches, 826 runs at 24.29, 1 wkt at 28.00. HS: 76 BB: 1/2.

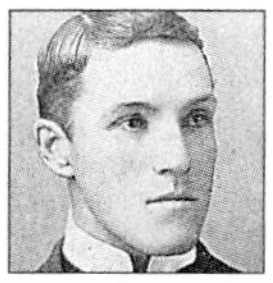

HOPKINS, Albert John Young
B: May 3, 1874.
D: April 25, 1931.
Bats: Right hand.
Bowls: Right arm.
First class debut:- 1896–97.
162 matches, 5563 runs, 22 50s, 8 100s, av. 25.40, 87 catches.
271 wkts at 24.40, 10 5-wkts. HS: 218 BB: 7/10.
Test Debut:- 1901–02.
20 matches, 509 runs, av. 16.42, 11 catches.
26 wkts at 26.77. HS: 43 BB: 4/81.

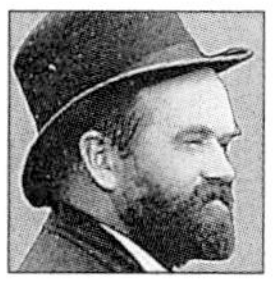

HORAN, Thomas Patrick
B: Mar 8, 1854.
D: April 16, 1916.
Bats: Right hand.
Bowls: Right arm.
First class debut:- 1874–75.
106 matches, 4027 runs, 12 50s, 8 100s, av. 23.27, 39 catches.
35 wkts at 23.68, 2 5-wkts. HS: 141* BB: 6/40.
Test Debut:- 1876–77.
15 matches, 471 runs, 1 50s, 1 100s, av. 18.84, 6 catches. 11 wkts at 13.00, 1 5-wkts. HS: 124 BB: 6/40.

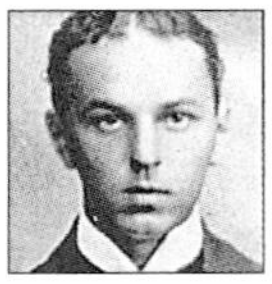

HORDERN, Herbert Vivian
B: Feb 10, 1883.
D: June 17, 1938.
Bats: Right hand.
Bowls: Right arm.

First class debut:- 1905–06.
33 matches, 721 runs, 3 50s, av. 16.38, 39 catches.
217 wkts at 16.79, 23 5-wkts, 9 10-wkts. HS: 64 BB: 8/31.
Test Debut:- 1910–11.
7 matches, 254 runs, 1 50s, av. 23.09, 6 catches. 46 wkts at 23.37, 5 5-wkts, 2 10-wkts. HS: 50 BB: 7/90.

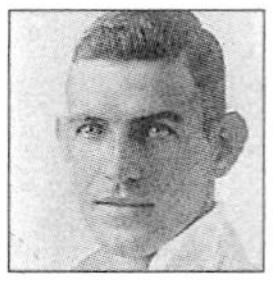

HORNIBROOK, Percival Mitchell
B: July 27, 1899.
D: Aug 25, 1976.
Bats: Left hand.
Bowls: Left arm.

First class debut:- 1919–20.
71 matches, 754 runs, 1 50s, av. 10.77, 66 catches. 279 wkts at 23.82, 17 5-wkts, 6 10-wkts. HS: 59* BB: 8/60.
Test Debut:- 1928–29.
6 matches, 60 runs, av. 10.00, 7 catches. 17 wkts at 39.06, 1 5-wkts. HS: 26 BB: 7/92.

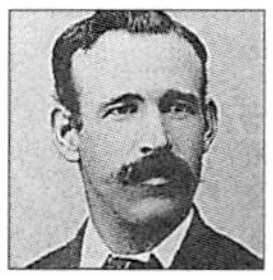

HOWELL, William Peter
B: Dec 29, 1869.
D: July 14, 1940.
Bats: Left hand.
Bowls: Right arm.

First class debut:- 1894–95.
141 matches, 2228 runs, 6 50s, 1 100s, av. 14.85, 124 catches.
520 wkts at 21.45, 30 5-wkts, 5 10-wkts. HS: 128 BB: 10/28.
Test Debut:- 1897–98.
18 matches, 158 runs, av. 7.52, 12 catches. 49 wkts at 28.71, 1 5-wkts. HS: 35 BB: 5/81.

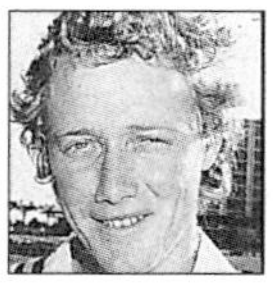

HUGHES, Kimberley John
B: Jan 26, 1954.
Bats: Right hand.

First class debut:- 1975–76.
216 matches, 12711 runs, 69 50s, 26 100s, av. 36.52, 155 catches. 3 wkts at 32.33. HS: 213 BB: 1/0.
Test Debut:- 1977.
70 matches, 4415 runs, 22 50s, 9 100s, 49 catches. HS: 213.
Int. limited-overs debut:- 1977. 97 matches, 1968 runs at 24.00. HS: 98.

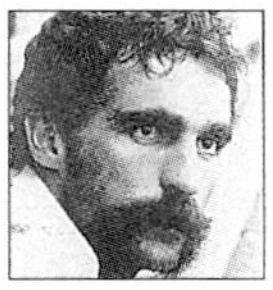

HUGHES, Mervyn Gregory
B: Nov 23, 1961.
Bats: Right hand.
Bowls: Right arm.

First class debut:- 1981–82.
165 matches, 2649 runs, 7 50s, av. 17.54, 56 catches. 593 wkts at 29.09, 21 5-wkts, 3 10-wkts. HS: 72* BB: 8/87.
Test Debut:- 1985–86.
53 matches, 1032 runs, 2 50s, av. 16.65, 23 catches. 212 wkts at 28.83, 7 5-wkts, 1 10-wkts. HS: 72* BB: 8/87.
Int. limited-overs debut:- 1988–89. 33 matches, 100 runs at 11.11, 38 wkts at 29.34. HS: 20 BB:4/44.

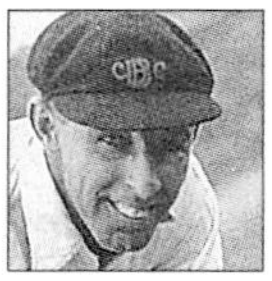

HUNT, William Alfred
B: Aug 26, 1908.
D: Dec 30, 1983.
Bats: Right hand.
Bowls: Left arm.

First class debut:- 1929–30.
18 matches, 301 runs, av. 14.33, 12 catches. 62 wkts at 23.00, 2 5-wkts. HS: 45 BB: 5/36.
Test Debut:- 1931–32. 1 match, 0 runs, av. 0.00, 1 catch. O wkts at –. HS: 0. BB: 0/14.

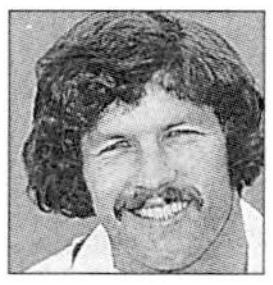

HURST, Alan George
B: July 15, 1950.
Bats: Right hand.
Bowls: Right arm.

First class debut:- 1972–73.
77 matches, 504 runs, av. 8.68, 26 catches. 280 wkts at 26.28, 11 5-wkts, 1 10-wkts. HS: 27* BB: 8/84
Test Debut:- 1973–74.
12 matches, 102 runs, av. 6.00, 4 catches. 43 wkts at 27.91, 2 5-wkts. HS: 26 BB: 5/28.
Int. limited-overs debut:- 1974–75. 8 matches, 7 runs at –, 12 wkts at 16.92. HS: 3* BB: 5/21.

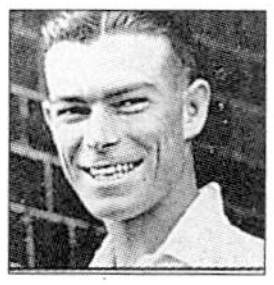

HURWOOD, Alexander
B: June 17, 1902.
D: Sep 26, 1982.
Bats: Right hand.
Bowls: Right arm.

First class debut:- 1925–26.
43 matches, 575 runs, 3 50s, av. 11.27, 29 catches.
113 wkts at 27.71, 5 5-wkts, 1 10-wkts. HS: 89 BB: 6/80.
Test Debut:- 1930–31.
2 matches, 5 runs, av. 2.50, 2 catches. 11 wkts at 15.45. HS: 5 BB: 4/22.

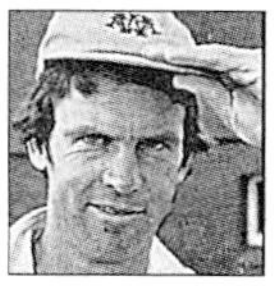

INVERARITY, Robert John
B: Jan 31, 1944.
Bats: Right hand.
Bowls: Left arm.

First class debut:- 1962–63.
223 matches, 11777 runs, 60 50s, 26 100s, av. 35.90, 250 catches. 221 wkts at 30.67, 7 5-wkts. HS: 187 BB: 7/86.
Test Debut:- 1968. 6 matches, 174 runs, 1 50s, av. 17.40, 4 catches. 4 wkts at 23.25. HS: 56 BB: 3/26.

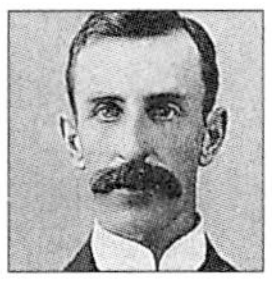

IREDALE, Francis Adams
B: June 19, 1867.
D: April 15, 1926.
Bats: Right hand.

First class debut:- 1888–89.
133 matches, 6794 runs, 36 50s, 12 100s, av. 33.63, 111 catches.
6 wkts at 35.16. HS: 196 BB: 3/1.
Test Debut:- 1894–95. 14 matches, 807 runs, 4 50s, 2 100s, av. 36.68, 16 catches. HS: 140.

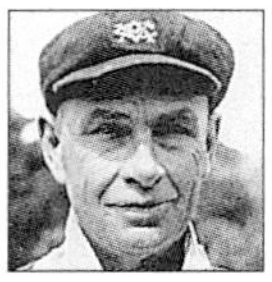

IRONMONGER, Herbert
B: April 7, 1882.
D: May 31, 1971.
Bats: Left hand.
Bowls: Left arm.

First class debut:- 1909–10.
96 matches, 476 runs, av. 5.95, 30 catches. 464 wkts at 21.50, 36 5-wkts, 10 10-wkts. HS: 36* BB: 8/31.
Test Debut:- 1928–29.
14 matches, 42 runs, av. 2.63, 3 catches. 74 wkts at 17.97, 4 5-wkts, 2 10-wkts. HS: 12 BB: 7/23.

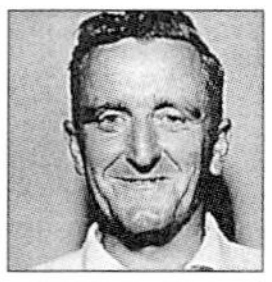

IVERSON, John Brian
B: July 27, 1915.
D: Oct 24, 1973.
Bats: Right hand.
Bowls: Right arm.

First class debut:- 1949–50.
34 matches, 277 runs, av. 14.57, 13 catches. 157 wkts at 19.22, 9 5-wkts, 1 10-wkts. HS: 31* BB: 7/77.
Test Debut:- 1950–51.
5 matches, 3 runs, av. 0.75, 2 catches. 21 wkts at 15.24, 1 5-wkts. HS: 1* BB: 6/27.

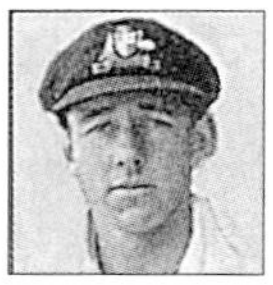

JACKSON, Archibald
B: Sep 5, 1909.
D: Feb 16, 1933.
Bats: Right hand.

First class debut:- 1926–27.
70 matches, 4383 runs, 23 50s, 11 100s, av. 45.65, 26 catches. HS: 182.
Test Debut:- 1928–29.
8 matches, 474 runs, 2 50s, 1 100s, av. 47.40, 7 catches. HS: 164.

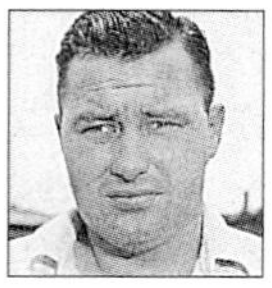

JARMAN, Barrington Noel
B: Feb 17, 1936.
Bats: Right hand - Wicketkeeper.

First class debut:- 1955–56.
191 matches, 5615 runs, 26 50s, 3 100s, av. 22.73, 431 catches, 129 stumpings. 3 wkts at 32.66. HS: 196 BB: 1/17.
Test debut:- 1959–60. 19 matches, 400 runs, 2 50s, av. 14.81, 50 catches, 4 stumpings. HS: 78.

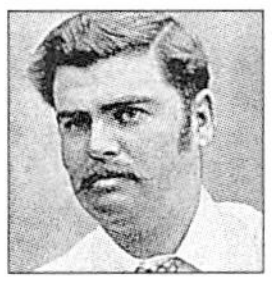

JARVIS, Arthur Harwood
B: Oct 19, 1860.
D: Nov 15, 1933.
Bats: Right hand - Wicketkeeper.

First class debut:- 1877–78.
141 matches, 3161 runs, 13 50s, av. 15.57, 114 catches, 82 stumpings. 1 wkt at 63.00. HS: 98* BB: 1/9.
Test debut:- 1884–85. 11 matches, 303 runs, 1 50s, av. 16.83, 9 catches, 9 stumpings. HS: 82.

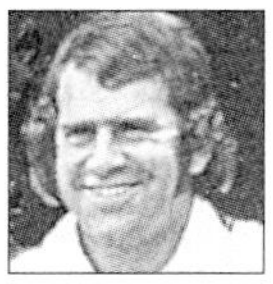

JENNER, Terrence James
B: Sep 8, 1944.
Bats: Right hand.
Bowls: Right arm.

First class debut:- 1963–64.
131 matches, 3580 runs, 10 50s, av. 22.23, 87 catches. 389 wkts at 32.18, 14 5-wkts, 1 10-wkts. HS: 86 BB: 7/84.
Test debut:- 1970–71. 9 matches, 208 runs, 1 50s, av. 23.11, 5 catches. 24 wkts at 31.21, 1 5-wkts. HS: 74 BB: 5/90.
Int. limited-overs debut:- 1974–75. 1 match, 12 runs, av. 12.00. O wkts at –. HS: 12 BB: 0/28.

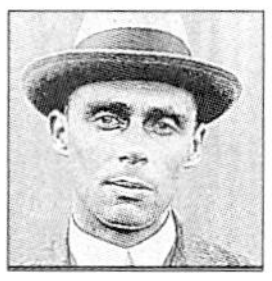

JENNINGS, Claude Burrows
B: June 5, 1884.
D: June 20, 1950.
Bats: Right hand

First class debut:- 1902–03. 60 matches, 2453 runs, 16 50s, 1 100s, av. 25.55, 38 catches, 3 stumpings. 0 wkts at –. HS: 123 BB: 0/ .
Test debut:- 1912. 6 matches, 107 runs, av. 17.83, 5 catches. HS: 32.

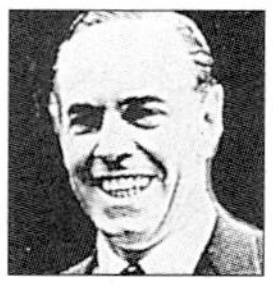

JOHNSON, Ian William
B: Dec 8, 1918.
Bats: Right hand.
Bowls: Right arm.

First class debut:- 1935–36.
189 matches, 4905 runs, 21 50s, 2 100s, av. 22.92, 137 catches.
619 wkts at 23.30, 27 5-wkts, 4 10-wkts. HS: 132* BB: 7/42.
Test debut:- 1945–46.
45 matches, 1000 runs, 6 50s, av. 18.52, 30 catches. 109 wkts at 29.19, 3 5-wkts. HS: 77 BB: 7/44.

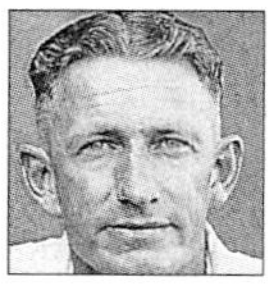

JOHNSON, Leonard Joseph
B: Mar 18, 1919.
D: April 20, 1977.
Bats: Right hand.
Bowls: Right arm.

First class debut:- 1946–47. 56 matches, 1139 runs, 3 50s, av. 16.75, 35 catches. 218 wkts at

23.17, 16 5-wkts, 1 10-wkts. HS: 75 BB: 7/43.
Test debut:- 1947–48. 1 match, 25 runs, av. –, 2 catches. 6 wkts at 12.33. HS: 25* BB: 3/8.

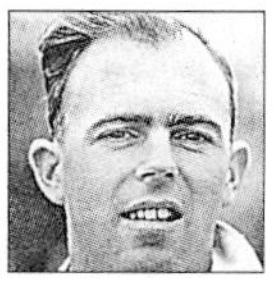

JOHNSTON, William Arras
B: Feb 26, 1922.
Bats: Left hand.
Bowls: Left arm.

First class debut:- 1945–46. 142 matches, 1129 runs, av. 12.68, 52 catches. 554 wkts at 23.39, 29 5-wkts, 6 10-wkts. HS: 38 BB: 8/52.
Test debut:- 1947–48. 40 matches, 273 runs, av. 11.38, 16 catches. 160 wkts at 23.91, 7 5-wkts. HS: 29 BB: 6/44.

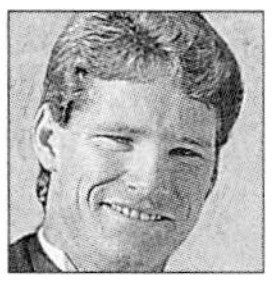

JONES, Dean Mervyn
B: Mar 24, 1961.
Bats: Right hand.
Bowls: Right arm.

First class debut:- 1981–82. 227 matches, 17,834 runs, 78 50s, 52 100s, av. 52.15, 175 catches. 27 wkts at 56.04, 1 5-wkts. HS: 324* BB: 5/112.
Test debut:- 1983–84. 52 matches, 3631 runs, 14 50s, 11 100s, av. 46.5, 34 catches. 1 wkt at 64.00. HS: 216 BB: 1/5.
Int. limited-overs debut:- 1983–84. 164 matches, 6068 runs at 44.62. 3 wkts at 27.00. HS: 145 BB: 2/34.

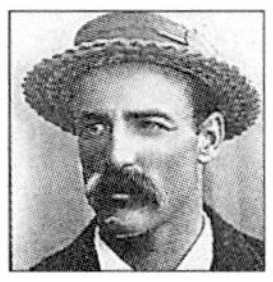

JONES, Ernest
B: Sep 30, 1869.
D: Nov 23, 1943.
Bats: Right hand.
Bowls: Right arm.

First class debut:- 1892–93. 144 matches, 2390 runs, 7 50s, av. 13.13, 107 catches. 641 wkts at 22.83, 47 5-wkts, 9 10-wkts. HS: 82 BB: 8/39.
Test debut:- 1894–95. 19 matches, 126 runs, av. 5.04, 21 catches. 64 wkts at 29.02, 3 5-wkts, 1 10-wkts. HS: 20 BB: 7/88.

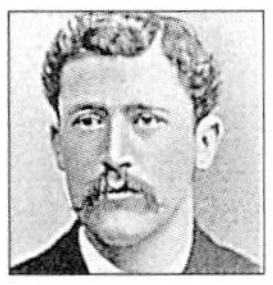

JONES, Samuel Percy
B: Aug 1, 1861.
D: July 14, 1951.
Bats: Right hand.
Bowls: Right arm.

First class debut:- 1880–81. 151 matches, 5193 runs, 24 50s, 5 100s, av. 21.10, 82 catches. 55 wkts at 33.52, 1 5-wkts. HS: 151 BB: 5/54.
Test debut:- 1881–82. 12 matches, 428 runs, 1 50s, av. 21.40, 12 catches. 6 wkts at 18.67. HS: 87 BB: 4/47.

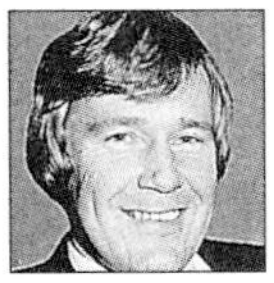

JOSLIN, Leslie Ronald
B: Dec 13, 1947.
Bats: Left hand.
Bowls: Left arm.

First class debut:- 1966–67. 44 matches, 1816 runs, 12 50s, 2 100s, av. 29.77, 27 catches. 1 wkt at 73.00. HS: 126 BB: 1/14.
Test debut:- 1967–68. 1 match, 9 runs, av. 4.50. HS: 7.

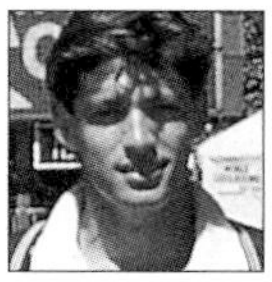

JULIAN, Brendon Paul
B: Aug 10, 1970.
Bats: Right hand.
Bowls: Left arm.

First class debut:- 1989–90. 100 matches, 2623 runs, 12 50s, 2 100s, av. 22.81, 61 catches. 321 wkts at 29.98, 19 5-wkts, 2 10-wkts. HS: 119 BB: 7/48.
Test debut:- 1993. 7 matches, 128 runs, 1 50s, av. 16.00. 15 wkts at 39.93. HS: 56* BB: 4/36.
Int. limited-overs debut:- 1993. 3 matches, 11 runs at 11.00. 5 wkts at 33.80. HS: 11 BB: 3/50.

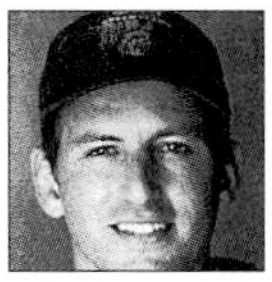

KASPROWICZ, Michael Scott
B: Feb 10, 1972.
Bats: Right hand.
Bowls: Right arm.

First class debut:- 1989–90. 78 matches, 1287 runs, av. 14.46, 28 catches. 305 wkts at 27.70, 21 5-wkts, 2 10-wkts. HS: 49 BB: 7/64.
Test debut:- 1996–97. 2 matches, 27 runs, av. 13.50. 0 wkts at –. HS: 21 BB: (Did not take a wicket).
Int. limited-overs debut:- 1995–96. 2 matches, - runs. 2 wkts at 41.50. HS: DNB. BB: 1/32.

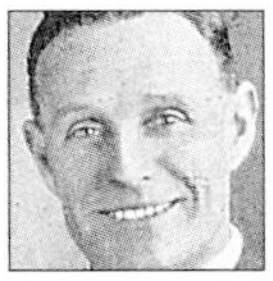

KELLEWAY, Charles
B: April 25, 1886.
D: Nov 16, 1944.
Bats: Right hand.
Bowls: Right arm.

First class debut:- 1907–08. 132 matches, 6389 runs, 28 50s, 15 100s, av. 35.10, 103 catches. 339 wkts at 26.32, 10 5-wkts, 1 10-wkts. HS: 168 (twice) BB: 7/35.
Test debut:- 1910–11. 26 matches, 1422 runs, 6 50s, 3 100s, av. 37.42, 24 catches. 52 wkts at 32.37, 1 5-wkts. HS: 147 BB: 5/33.

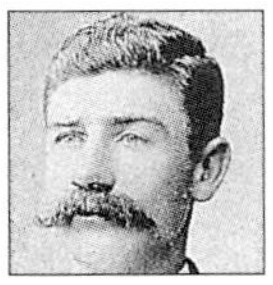

KELLY, James Joseph
B: May 10, 1867.
D: Aug 14, 1938.
Bats: Right hand
- Wicketkeeper.

First class debut:- 1894–95. 185 matches, 4108 runs, 16 50s, 3 100s, av. 19.94, 243 catches, 112 stumpings. HS: 108.
Test debut:- 1896. 36 matches, 664 runs, av. 17.03, 43 catches, 20 stumpings. HS: 46*.

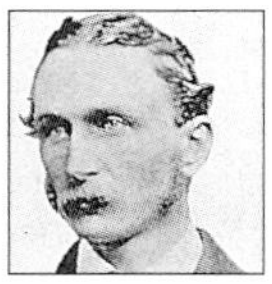

KELLY, Thomas Joseph Dart
B: May 3, 1844.
D: July 20, 1893.
Bats: Right hand
- Wicketkeeper.

First class debut:- 1865–66. 16 matches, 543 runs, 5 50s, av. 20.11, 20 catches. HS: 86
Test debut:- 1876–77. 2 matches, 64 runs at 21.33, 1 catch. HS: 35

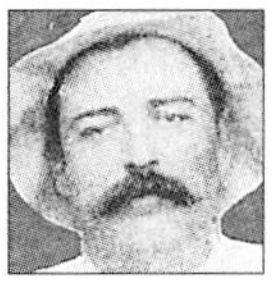

KENDALL, Thomas Kingston
B: Aug 24, 1851.
D: Aug 17, 1924.
Bats: Left hand.
Bowls: Left arm.

First class debut:- 1876–77. 8 matches, 141 runs, av. 12.81, 6 catches. 40 wkts at 16.65, 3 5-wkts. HS: 43 BB: 7/24.
Test debut:- 1876–77. 2 matches, 39 runs, av. 13.00, 2 catches. 14 wkts at 15.36, 1 5-wkts. HS: 17* BB: 7/55.

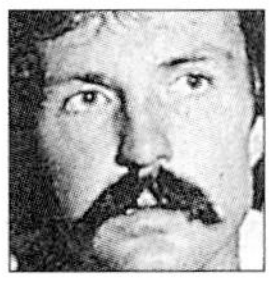

KENT, Martin Francis
B: Nov 23, 1953.
Bats: Right hand.

First class debut:- 1974–75. 64 matches, 3567 runs, 20 50s, 7 100s, av. 36.03, 60 catches. HS: 171.
Test debut:- 1981. 3 matches, 171 runs, 2 50s, av. 28.50, 6 catches. HS: 54.
Int. limited-overs debut:- 1980–81. 5 matches, 78 runs at 19.50. HS: 33.

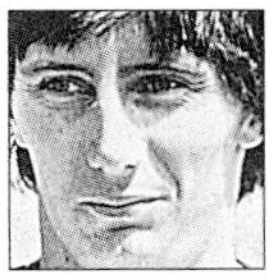

KERR, Robert Byers
B: June 16, 1961.
Bats: Right hand.
Bowls: Right arm.

First class debut:- 1981–82. 93 matches, 5709 runs, 28 50s, 16 100s, av. 37.31, 89 catches. 1 wkt at 16.00. HS: 201* BB: 1/12.
Test debut:- 1985–86. 2 matches, 31 runs, av. 7.75, 1 catch. HS: 17.
Int. limited-overs debut:- 1984–85. 4 matches, 97 runs at 32.33. HS: 87*. Highest Score: 87*.

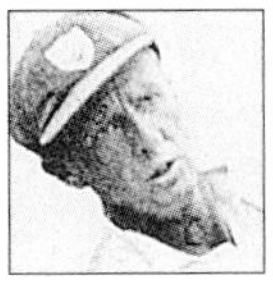

KIPPAX, Alan Falconer
B: May 25, 1897.
D: Sep 5, 1972.
Bats: Right hand.
Bowls: Right arm.

First class debut:- 1918–19. 175 matches, 12,762 runs, 45 50s, 43 100s, av. 57.22, 73 catches. 21 wkts at 52.33. HS: 315* BB: 4/66.
Test debut:- 1924–25. 22 matches, 1192 runs, 8 50s, 2 100s, av. 36.12, 13 catches. HS: 146

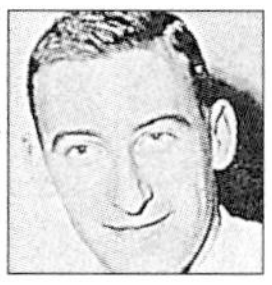

KLINE, Lindsay Francis
B: Sep 29, 1934.
Bats: Left hand.
Bowls: Left arm.

First class debut:- 1955–56. 88 matches, 559 runs, av. 8.60, 55 catches. 276 wkts at 27.39, 11 5-wkts. HS: 37* BB: 7/75.
Test debut:- 1957–58. 13 matches, 58 runs, av. 8.29, 9 catches. 34 wkts at 22.82, 1 5-wkts. HS: 15* BB: 7/75.

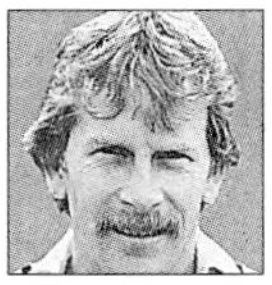

LAIRD, Bruce Malcolm
B: Nov 21, 1950.
Bats: Right hand.

First class debut:- 1972–73. 103 matches, 6085 runs, 41 50s, 8 100s, av. 35.37, 86 catches. HS: 171.
Test debut:- 1979–80. 21 matches, 1341 runs, 11 50s, av. 35.29, 16 catches. HS: 92.
Int. limited-overs debut:- 1979–80. 23 matches, 594 runs, 2 50s, 1 100s, av. 29.70, 5 catches. HS: 117*.

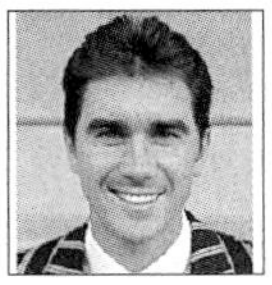

LANGER, Justin Lee
B: Nov 21, 1970.
Bats: Left hand.
Bowls: Right arm.

First class debut:- 1991–92. 71 matches, 5608 runs, 22 50s, 16 100s, av. 50.52, 54 catches. 0 wkts at –. HS: 274* BB: (Did not take a wicket).
Test debut:- 1992–93. 8 matches, 272 runs, 3 50s, av. 22.67, 2 catches. HS: 69.
Int. limited-overs debut:- 1993–94. 7 matches, 131 runs, av. 32.75, 1 catch, 1 stumping. HS: 36.

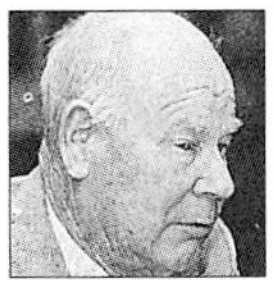

LANGLEY, Gilbert Roche Andrews
B: Sep 14, 1919.
Bats: Right hand
- Wicketkeeper.

First class debut:- 1945–46. 122 matches, 3236 runs, 12 50s, 4 100s, av. 25.68, 292 catches, 77 stumpings. HS: 160* BB:
Test debut:- 1951–52. 26 matches, 374 runs, 1 50s, av. 14.96, 83 catches, 15 stumpings. HS: 53.

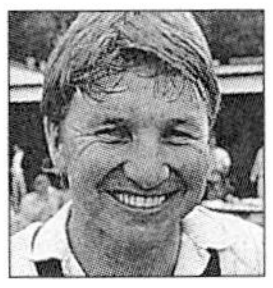

LAUGHLIN, Trevor John
B: Jan 30, 1951.
Bats: Left hand.
Bowls: Right arm.

First class debut:- 1974–75. 58 matches, 2770 runs, 19 50s, 1 100s, av. 32.58, 40 catches. 99 wkts at 31.92. 3 5-wkts. HS: 113 BB: 5/38.
Test debut:- 1977–78. 3 matches, 87 runs, av. 17.40, 3 catches. 6 wkts at 43.67, 1 5-wkts. HS: 35 BB: 5/101.
Int. limited-overs debut:- 1977–78. 6 matches, 105 runs at 26.25. 8 wkts at 28.00. HS: 74 BB: 3/54.

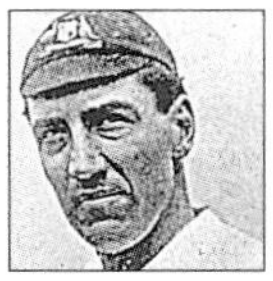

LAVER, Frank
B: Dec 7, 1869.
D: Sep 24, 1919.
Bats: Right hand.
Bowls: Right arm.

First class debut:- 1891–92. 163 matches, 5431 runs, 18 50s, 6 100s, av. 25.02, 148 catches. 404 wkts at 24.72, 19 5-wkts, 5 10-wkts. HS: 164 BB: 8/31.
Test debut:- 1899. 15 matches, 196 runs, av. 11.53, 8 catches. 37 wkts at 26.05, 2 5-wkts. HS: 45 BB: 8/31.

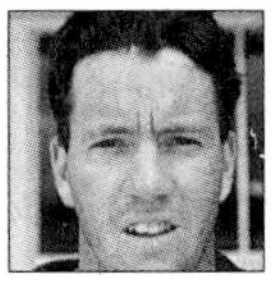

LAW, Stuart Grant
B: Oct 18, 1968.
Bats: Right hand.
Bowls: Right arm.

First class debut:- 1988–89. 116 matches, 8040 runs, 42 50s, 22 100s, av. 45.94, 116 catches. 59 wkts at 44.19, 1 5-wkts. HS: 179 BB: 5/39.
Test debut:- 1995–96. 1 match, 54 runs, 1 50s, av. –, 1 catch. 0 wkts at –. HS: 54* BB: 0/ .
Int. limited-overs debut:- 1994–95. 44 matches, 1145 runs, 6 50s, 1 100s, av. 29.36, 8 catches. 12 wkts at 47.67. HS: 110 BB: 2/22.

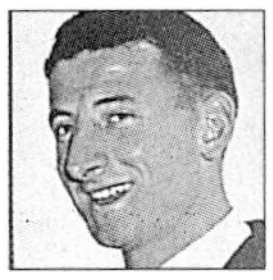

LAWRY, William Morris
B: Feb 11, 1937.
Bats: Left hand.

First class debut:- 1955–56. 250 matches, 18,734 runs, 100 50s, 50 100s, av. 50.90, 121 catches. 5 wkts at 37.60. HS: 266 BB: 1/3.
Test debut:- 1961. 68 matches, 5234 runs, 27 50s, 13 100s, av. 47.15, 30 catches. 0 wkts at –. HS: 210 BB: 0/6.
Int. limited-overs debut:- 1970–71. 1 match, 27 runs at 27.00. HS: 27.

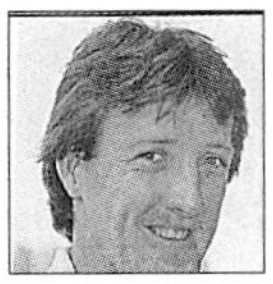

LAWSON, Geoffrey Francis
B: Dec 7, 1957.
Bats: Right hand.
Bowls: Right arm.

First class debut:- 1977–78. 191 matches, 2683 runs, 8 50s, av. 14.82, 75 catches. 666 wkta at 24.87, 28 5-wkts, 2 10-wkts. HS: 74 BB: 8/112.
Test debut:- 1980–81. 46 matches, 894 runs, 4 50s, av. 15.96, 10 catches. 180 wkts at 30.56, 11 5-wkts, 2 10-wkts. HS: 74 BB: 8/112.
Int. limited-overs debut:- 1980–81. 79 matches, 378 runs at 11.12. 88 wkts at 29.45. HS: 33* BB: 4/26.

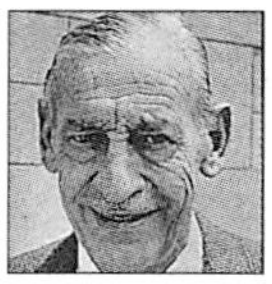

LEE, Philip Keith
B: Sep 15, 1904.
D: Aug 9, 1980.
Bats: Right hand.
Bowls: Right arm.

First class debut:- 1925–26. 55 matches, 1669 runs, 6 50s, 2 100s, av. 18.54, 23 catches. 152 wkts at 30.15, 6 5-wkts. HS: 106 BB: 5/23.
Test debut:- 1931–32. 2 matches, 57 runs, av. 19.00, 1 catch. 5 wkts at 42.40. HS: 42 BB: 4/111.

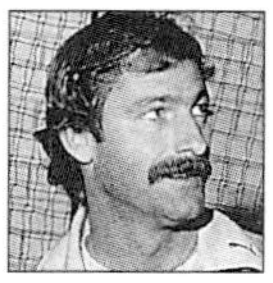

LILLEE, Dennis Keith
B: July 18, 1949.
Bats: Right hand.
Bowls: Right arm.

First class debut:- 1969–70. 198 matches, 2377 runs, 2 50s, av. 13.90, 67 catches. 882 wkts at 23.46, 50 5-wkts, 13 10-wkts. HS: 73* BB: 8/29.
Test debut:- 1970–71. 70 matches, 905 runs, 1 50s, av. 13.71, 23 catches. 355 wkts at 23.92, 23 5-wkts, 7 10-wkts. HS: 73* BB: 7/83.
Int. limited-overs debut:- 1972. 63 matches, 240 runs at 9.23. 103 wkt at 20.83. HS: 42* BB: 5/34.

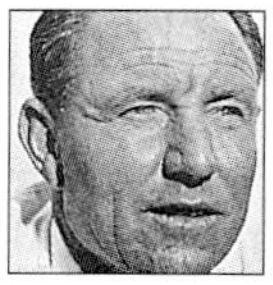

LINDWALL, Raymond Russell
B: Oct 3, 1921.
D: June 22, 1996.
Bats: Right hand.
Bowls: Right arm.

First class debut:- 1941–42. 228 matches, 5042 runs, 19 50s, 5 100s, av. 21.82, 123 catches. 794 wkts at 21.35, 34 5-wkts, 2 10-wkts. HS: 134* BB: 7/20.
Test debut:- 1945–46. 61 matches, 1502 runs, 5 50s, 2 100s, av. 21.15, 26 catches. 228 wkts at 23.03, 12 5-wkts. HS: 118 BB: 7/38.

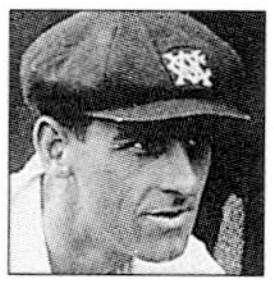

LOVE, Hampden Stanley Bray
B: Aug 10, 1895.
D: July 22, 1969.
Bats: Right hand - Wicketkeeper.

First class debut:- 1920–21. 54 matches, 2906 runs, 11 50s, 7 100s, av. 35.01, 73 catches, 29 stumpings. HS: 192.
Test debut:- 1932–33. 1 match, 8 runs, av. 4.00, 3 catches. HS: 5.

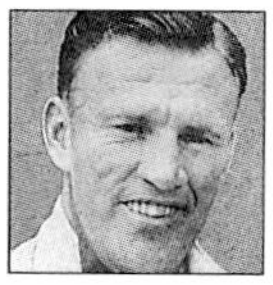

LOXTON, Samuel John Everett
B: Mar 29, 1921.
Bats: Right hand.
Bowls: Right arm.

First class debut:- 1946–47. 140 matches, 6249 runs, 32 50s, 13 100s, av. 36.97, 83 catches. 232 wkts at 25.73, 3 5-wkts. HS: 232* BB: 6/49.
Test debut:- 1947–48. 12 matches, 554 runs, 3 50s, 1 100s, av. 36.93, 7 catches. 8 wkts at 43.63. HS: 101 BB: 3/55.

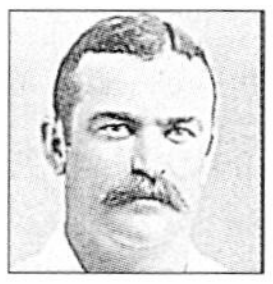

LYONS, John James
B: May 21, 1863.
D: July 21, 1927.
Bats: Right hand.
Bowls: Right arm.

First class debut:- 1884–85. 153 matches, 6752 runs, 28 50s, 11 100s, av. 25.57, 60 catches. 107 wkts at 30.14, 5 5-wkts. HS: 149 BB: 6/38.
Test debut:- 1886–87. 14 matches, 731 runs, 3 50s, 1 100s, av. 27.07, 3 catches. 6 wkts at 24.83, 1 5-wkts. HS: 134 BB: 5/30.

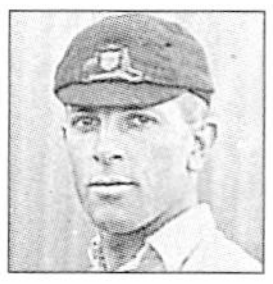

MACARTNEY, Charles George
B: June 27, 1886.
D: Sep 9, 1958.
Bats: Right hand.
Bowls: Left arm.

First class debut:- 1905–06. 249 matches, 15,019 runs, 53 50s, 49 100s, av. 45.78, 102 catches. 419 wkts at 20.95, 17 5-wkts, 1 10-wkts. HS: 345 BB: 7/58.
Test debut:- 1907–08. 35 matches, 2131 runs, 9 50s, 7 100s, av. 41.78, 17 catches. 45 wkts at 27.56, 2 5-wkts, 1 10-wkts. HS: 170 BB: 7/58.

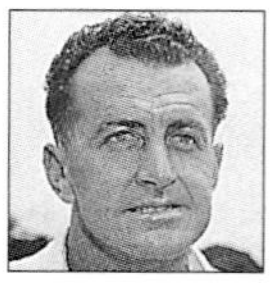

MACKAY, Kenneth Donald
B: Oct 24, 1925.
D: June 13, 1982.
Bats: Left hand.
Bowls: Right arm.

First class debut:- 1946–47. 201 matches, 10,823 runs, 59 50s, 23 100s, av. 43.64, 84 catches. 251 wkts at 33.31, 7 5-wkts. HS: 223 BB: 6/42.
Test debut:- 1956. 37 matches, 1507 runs, 13 50s, av. 33.49, 16 catches. 50 wkts at 34.42, 2 5-wkts. HS: 89 BB: 6/42.

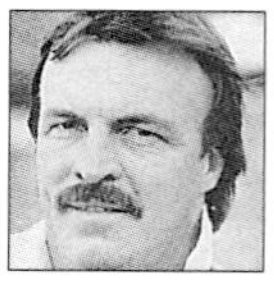

MACLEAN, John Alexander
B: April 27, 1946.
Bats: Right hand - Wicketkeeper.

First class debut:- 1968–69. 108 matches, 3888 runs, 14 50s, 2 100s, av. 24.45, 354 catches, 31 stumpings. HS: 156.
Test debut:- 1978–79. 4 matches, 79 runs, av. 11.29, 18 catches. HS: 33*.
Int. limited-overs debut:- 1978–79. 2 matches, 11 runs at 11.00. HS: 11.

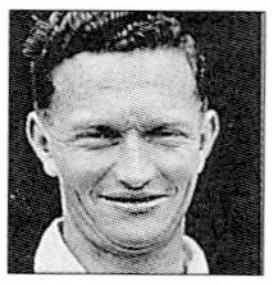

MADDOCKS, Leonard Victor
B: May 24, 1926.
Bats: Right hand - Wicketkeeper.

First class debut:- 1946–47. 112 matches, 4106 runs, 20 50s, 6 100s, av. 32.84, 209 catches, 68 stumpings. 1 wkt at 4.00. HS: 122* BB: 1/4.
Test debut:- 1954–55. 7 matches, 177 runs, 1 50s, av. 17.70, 18 catches, 1 stumping. HS: 69.

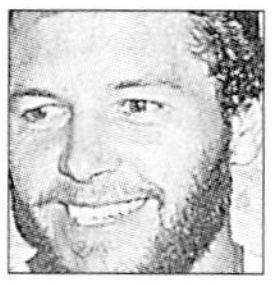

MAGUIRE, John Norman
B: Sep 15, 1956.
Bats: Right hand.
Bowls: Right arm.

First class debut:- 1977–78. 134 matches, 1162 runs, 2 50s, av. 10.96, 43 catches. 463 wkts at 27.75, 26 5-wkts, 3 10-wkts. HS: 65* BB: 7/46.
Test debut:- 1983–84. 3 matches, 28 runs, av. 7.00, 2 catches. 10 wkts at 32.30. HS: 15* BB: 4/57.
Int. limited-overs debut:- 1982–83. 23 matches, 42 runs at 7.00. 19 wkts at 40.47. HS: 14* BB: 3/61.

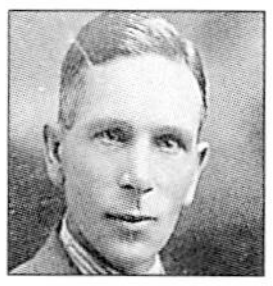

MAILEY, Arthur Alfred
B: Jan 3, 1886. D: Dec 31, 1967.
Bats: Right hand.
Bowls: Right arm.

First class debut:- 1912–13 158 matches, 1529 runs, 3 50s, av. 12.33, 157 catches. 779 wkts at 24.10, 61 5-wkts, 16 10-wkts. HS: 66 BB: 10/66.
Test debut:- 1920–21. 21 matches, 222 runs, av. 11.10, 14 catches. 99 wkts at 33.92, 6 5-wkts, 2 10-wkts. HS: 46* BB: 9/121.

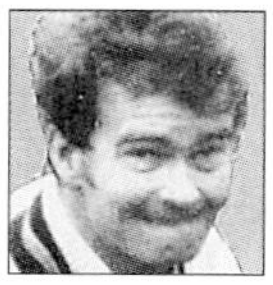

MALLETT, Ashley Alexander
B: July 13, 1945.
Bats: Right hand.
Bowls: Right arm.

First class debut:- 1967–68. 183 matches, 2326 runs, 2 50s, av. 13.60, 105 catches. 693 wkts at 26.27, 33 5-wkts, 5 10-wkts. HS: 92 BB: 8/59.
Test debut:- 1968. 39 matches, 430 runs, av. 11.62, 30 catches. 132 wkts at 29.85, 6 5-wkts, 1 10-wkts. HS: 43* BB: 8/59.
Int. limited-overs debut:- 1970–71. 9 matches, 14 runs at 7.00. 11 wkts at 31.00. HS: 8 BB: 3/34.

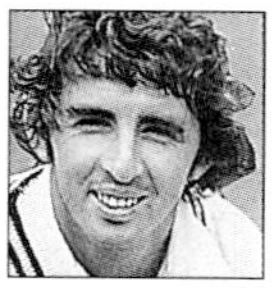

MALONE, Michael Francis
B: Oct 9, 1950.
Bats: Right hand.
Bowls: Right arm.

First class debut:- 1974–75. 73 matches, 914 runs, av. 16.03, 30 catches. 260 wkts at 24.77, 13 5-wkts, 1 10-wkts. HS: 46 BB: 7/88.
Test debut:- 1977. 1 match, 46 runs, av. 46.00. 6 wkts at 12.83, 1 5-wkts. HS: 46 BB: 5/63.
Int. limited-overs debut:- 1977. 10 matches, 36 runs at 9.00, 1 catch. 11 wkts at 28.64. HS: 15* BB: 2/9.

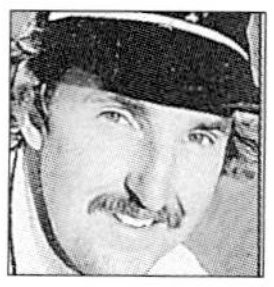

MANN, Anthony Longford
B: Nov 8, 1945.
Bats: Left hand.
Bowls: Right arm.

First class debut:- 1963–64. 80 matches, 2544 runs, 11 50s, 2 100s, av. 24.22, 47 catches. 200 wkts at 34.54, 5 5-wkts. HS: 110 BB: 6/94.
Test debut:- 1977–78. 4 matches, 189 runs, 1 100s, av. 23.63, 2 catches. 4 wkts at 79.00. HS: 105 BB: 3/12.

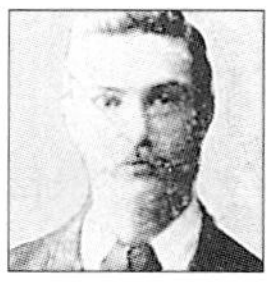

MARR, Alfred Percy
B: Mar 28, 1862.
D: Mar 15, 1940.
Bats: Right hand.
Bowls: Right arm.

First class debut:- 1882–83. 14 matches, 304 runs, 1 50s, av. 11.25, 8 catches. 14 wkts at 32.42. HS: 69 BB: 3/50.
Test debut:- 1884–85. 1 match, 5 runs, av. 2.50. HS: 5.

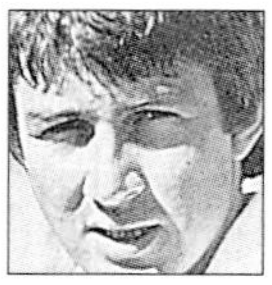

MARSH, Geoffrey Robert
B: Dec 31, 1958.
Bats: Right hand.

First class debut:- 1977–78. 184 matches, 11,760 runs, 46 50s, 33 100s, av. 39.46, 135 catches. 1 wkt at 9.00. HS: 355* BB: 1/1.
Test debut:- 1985–86. 50 matches, 2854 runs, 15 50s, 4 100s, av. 33.19, 38 catches. HS: 138.
Int. limited-overs debut:- 1985–86. 117 matches, 4357 runs, 22 50s, 2 100s, av. 39.97. HS: 126*.

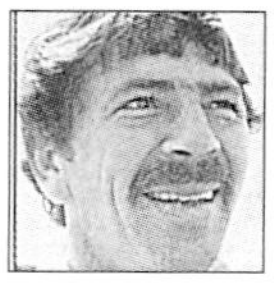

MARSH, Rodney William
B: Nov 11, 1947.
Bats: Left hand - Wicketkeeper.

First class debut:- 1968–69. 258 matches, 11,067 runs, 55 50s, 12 100s, av. 31.17, 805 catches, 65 stumpings. 1 wkt at 84.00. HS: 236 BB: 1/0.
Test debut:- 1970–71. 97 matches, 3633 runs, 16 50s, 3 100s, av. 26.52, 343 catches, 12 stumpings. HS: 132.
Int. limited-overs debut:- 1970–71. 92 matches, 1225 runs at 20.08. HS: 66.

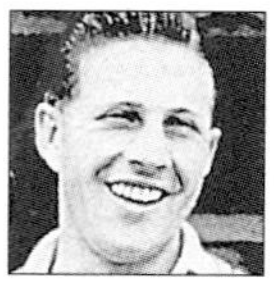

MARTIN, John Wesley
B: July 28, 1931.
D: July 16, 1992.
Bats: Left hand.
Bowls: Left hand.

First class debut:- 1956–57. 135 matches, 3970 runs, 21 50s, 1 100s, av. 23.77, 114 catches. 445 wkts at 31.17, 17 5-wkts, 1 10-wkts. HS: 101 BB: 8/97.
Test debut:- 1960–61. 8 matches, 214 runs, 1 50s, av. 16.46, 5 catches. 17 wkts at 48.94. HS: 55 BB: 3/56.

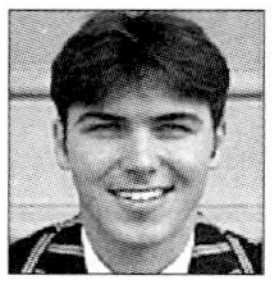

MARTYN, Damien Richard
B: Oct 21, 1971.
Bats: Right hand.
Bowls: Right arm.

First class debut:- 1990–91. 90 matches, 5959 runs, 29 50s, 17 100s, av. 44.47, 65 catches, 2 stumpings. 13 wkts at 55.38. HS: 203* BB: 3/29.
Test debut:- 1992–93. 7 matches, 317 runs, 3 50s, av. 28.82, 1 catch.. HS: 74
Int. limited-overs debut:- 1992–93. 11 matches, 166 runs at 18.44. HS: 51*

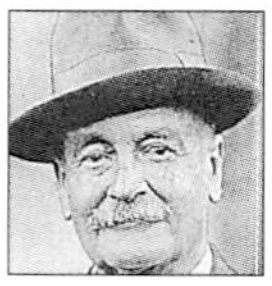

MASSIE, Hugh Hamon
B: April 11, 1854.
D: Oct 12, 1938.
Bats: Right hand.

First class debut:- 1877–78. 64 matches, 2485 runs, 13 50s, 1 100s, av. 23.00, 35 catches. 2 wkts at 30.00. HS: 206 BB: 2/39.
Test debut:- 1881–82. 9 matches, 249 runs, 1 50s, av. 15.56, 5 catches. HS: 55.

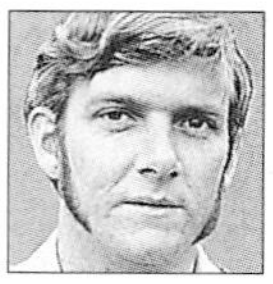

MASSIE, Robert Arnold Lockyer
B: April 14, 1947.
Bats: Left hand.
Bowls: Right arm.

First class debut:- 1965–66. 52 matches, 385 runs, av. 9.62, 8 catches. 179 wkts at 24.83, 6 5-wkts, 2 10-wkts. HS: 42 BB: 8/53.
Test debut:- 1972. 6 matches, 78 runs, av. 11.14, 1 catch. 31 wkts at 20.87, 2 5-wkts, 1 10-wkts. HS: 42 BB: 8/53.
Int. limited-overs debut:- 1972. 3 matches, 16 runs, 1 catch. 3 wkts at 43.00. HS: 16* BB: 2/35.

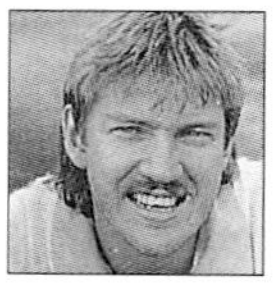

MATTHEWS, Christopher Darrell
B: Sep 22, 1962.
Bats: Left hand.
Bowls: Left arm.

First class debut:- 1984–85. 100 matches, 2146 runs, 9 50s, av. 20.25, 31 catches. 380 wkts at 28.11, 22 5-wkts. HS: 75 BB: 8/101.
Test debut:- 1986–87. 3 matches, 54 runs, av. 10.80, 1 catch. 6 wkts at 52.17. HS: 32 BB: 3/95.

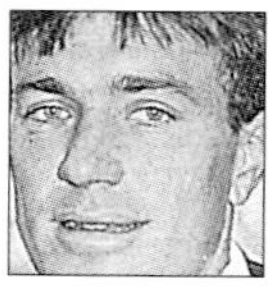

MATTHEWS, Gregory Richard John
B: Dec 15, 1959.
Bats: Left hand.
Bowls: Right arm.

First class debut:- 1982–83. 187 matches, 8766 runs, 48 50s, 13 100s, av. 38.62, 149 catches. 511 wkts at 31.45, 22 5-wkts, 6 10-wkts. HS: 184 BB: 8/52.
Test debut:- 1983–84. 33 matches, 1849 runs, 12 50s, 4 100s, av. 41.09, 17 catches. 61

wkts at 48.23, 2 5-wkts, 1 10-wkts. HS: 130 BB: 5/103.
Int. limited-overs debut:- 1983–84. 59 matches, 620 runs at 16.76. 57 wkts at 35.07. HS: 54 BB: 3/27.

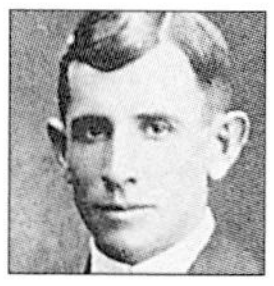

MATTHEWS, Thomas James
B: April 3, 1884.
D: Oct 14, 1943.
Bats: Right hand.
Bowls: Right arm.

First class debut:- 1906–07. 67 matches, 2149 runs, 14 50s, av. 24.98, 56 catches. 177 wkts at 25.46, 8 5-wkts, 1 10-wkts. HS: 93 BB: 7/46.
Test debut:- 1911–12. 8 matches, 153 runs, 1 50s, av. 17.00, 7 catches. 16 wkts at 26.19. HS: 53 BB: 4/29.

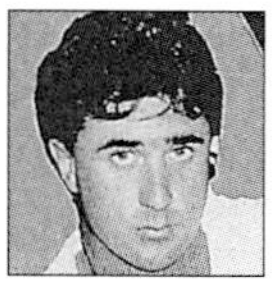

MAY, Timothy Brian Alexander
B: Jan 26, 1962.
Bats: Right hand.
Bowls: Right arm.

First class debut:- 1984–85. 142 matches, 1872 runs, 1 50s, 1 100s, av. 14.98, 42 catches. 439 wkts at 35.81, 19 5-wkts, 2 10-wkts. HS: 128 BB: 7/93.
Test debut:- 1987–88. 24 matches, 225 runs, av. 14.06, 6 catches. 75 wkts at 34.75, 3 5-wkts. HS: 42* BB: 5/9.
Int. limited-overs debut:- 1987–88. 47 matches, 39 runs at 9.75. 39 wkts at 45.44. HS: 15 BB: 3/19.

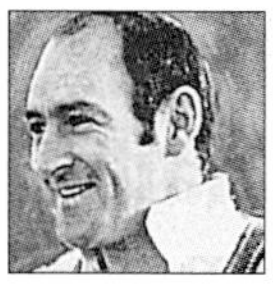

MAYNE, Lawrence Charles
B: Jan 23, 1942.
Bats: Left hand.
Bowls: Right arm.

First class debut:- 1961–62. 58 matches, 667 runs, 2 50s, av. 12.82, 21 catches. 203 wkts at 30.35, 6 5-wkts. HS: 72 BB: 7/75.
Test debut:- 1964–65. 6 matches, 76 runs, av. 9.50, 3 catches. 19 wkts at 33.05. HS: 13 BB: 4/43.

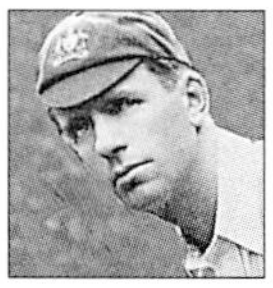

MAYNE, Richard Edgar
B: July 2, 1882 D: Oct 26, 1961.
Bats: Right hand.

First class debut:- 1906–07. 141 matches, 7620 runs, 39 50s, 14 100s, av. 32.70, 80 catches. 13 wkts at 33.84. HS: 209 BB: 3/6.
Test debut:- 1912. 4 matches, 64 runs, av. 21.33, 2 catches. HS: 25*.

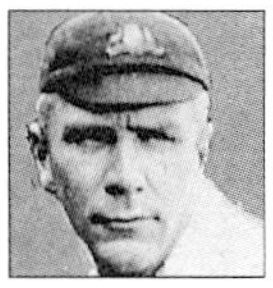

McALISTER, Peter Alexander
B: July 11, 1869.
D: May 10, 1938.
Bats: Right hand.

First class debut:- 1898–99. 85 matches, 4552 runs, 22 50s, 9 100s, av. 32.74, 91 catches. 3 wkts at 18.66. HS: 224 BB: 1/0.
Test debut:- 1903–04. 8 matches, 252 runs, av. 16.80, 10 catches. HS: 41.

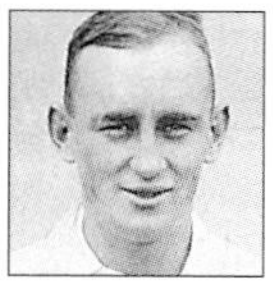

McCABE, Stanley Joseph
B: July 16, 1910.
D: Aug 25, 1968.
Bats: Right hand.
Bowls: Right arm.

First class debut:- 1928–29. 182 matches, 11,951 runs, 68 50s, 29 100s, av. 49.38, 139 catches. 159 wkts at 33.72, 1 5-wkts. HS: 240 BB: 5/36.
Test debut:- 1930. 39 matches, 2748 runs, 13 50s, 6 100s, av. 48.21, 41 catches. 36 wkts at 42.86. HS: 232 BB: 4/13.

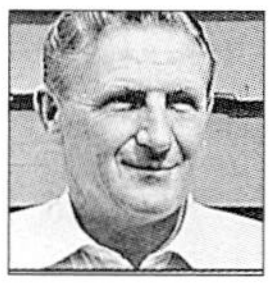

McCOOL, Colin Leslie
B: Dec 9, 1915
D: April 5, 1986.
Bats: Right hand.
Bowls: Right arm.

First class debut:- 1939-40. 251 matches, 12,420 runs, 66 50s, 18 100s, av. 32.85, 262 catches, 2 stumpings. 602 wkts at 27.47, 34 5-wkts, 2 10-wkts. HS: 172 BB: 8/74.
Test debut:- 1945–46. 14 matches, 459 runs, 1 50s, 1 100s, av. 35.31, 14 catches. 36 wkts at 26.61, 3 5-wkts. HS: 104* BB: 5/41.

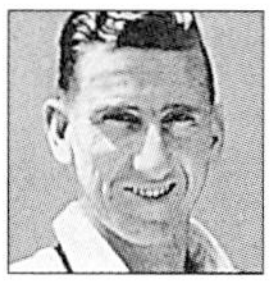

McCORMICK, Ernest Leslie
B: May 16, 1906.
D: June 28, 1991.
Bats: Left hand.
Bowls: Right arm.

First class debut:- 1929–30. 85 matches, 582 runs, 1 50s, av. 8.68, 46 catches. 231 wkts at 27.74, 6 5-wkts, 1 10-wkts. HS: 77* BB: 9/40.
Test debut:- 1935–36. 12 matches, 54 runs, av. 6.00, 8 catches. 36 wkts at 29.97. HS: 17* BB: 4/101.

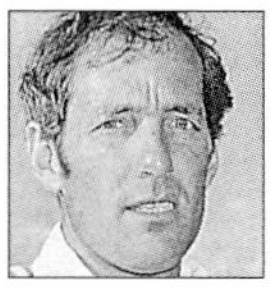

McCOSKER, Richard Bede
B: Dec 11, 1946.
Bats: Right hand.

First class debut:- 1973–74. 116 matches, 8260 runs, 43 50s, 26 100s, av. 44.64, 129 catches. 2 wkts at 59.50. HS: 168 BB: 2/28.
Test debut:- 1974–75. 25 matches, 1622 runs, 9 50s, 4 100s, av. 39.56, 21 catches. HS: 127.
Int. limited-overs debut:- 1975. 14 matches, 320 runs at 22.86. HS: 95.

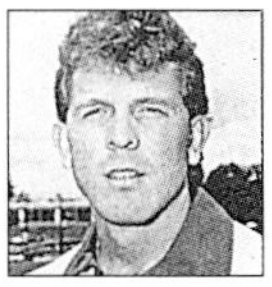

McDERMOTT, Craig John
B: April 14, 1965.
Bats: Right hand.
Bowls: Right arm.

First class debut:- 1983–84. 174 matches, 2856 runs, 7 50s, av. 16.32, 53 catches. 677 wkts at 28.10, 37 5-wkts, 4 10-wkts. HS: 74 BB: 8/44.
Test debut:- 1984–85. 71 matches, 940 runs, av. 12.21, 19 catches. 291 wkts at 28.63, 14 5-wkts, 2 10-wkts. HS: 42* BB: 8/97.
Int. limited-overs debut:- 1984–85. 138 matches, 432 runs at 7.08. 203 wkts at 24.73. HS: 37 BB: 5/44.

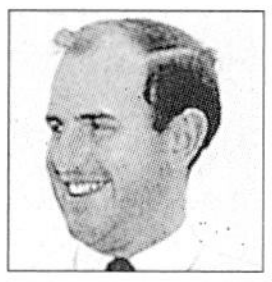

McDONALD, Colin Campbell
B: Nov 17, 1928.
Bats: Right hand.

First class debut:- 1947–48. 192 matches, 11,375 runs, 57 50s, 24 100s, av. 40.48, 53 catches, 2 stumpings. 3 wkts at 64.00. HS: 229 BB: 1/10.
Test debut:- 1951–52. 47 matches, 3107 runs, 17 50s, 5 100s, av. 39.33, 14 catches. HS: 170.

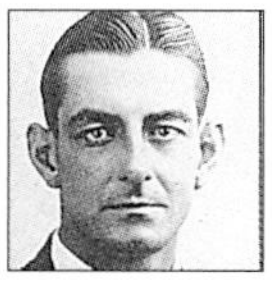

McDONALD, Edgar Arthur
B: Jan 6, 1891. D: July 22, 1937.
Bats: Right hand.
Bowls: Right arm.

First class debut:- 1909–10. 281 matches, 2663 runs, 2 50s, 1 100s, av. 10.44, 2 catches, 1 stumping. 1395 wkts at 20.76, 119 5-wkts, 31 10-wkts. HS: 100* BB: 8/41.
Test debut:- 1920–21. 11 matches, 116 runs, av. 16.57, 3 catches. 43 wkts at 33.28, 2 5-wkts. HS: 36 BB: 5/32.

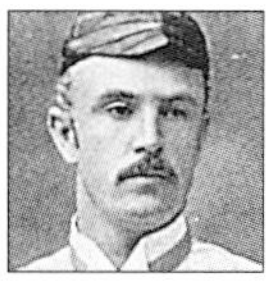

McDONNELL, Percy Stanislaus
B: Nov 13, 1858.
D: Sep 24, 1896.
Bats: Right hand.

First class debut:- 1877–78. 166 matches, 6470 runs, 24 50s, 7 100s, av. 23.52, 99 catches. 2 wkts at 123.50. HS: 239 BB: 1/7.
Test debut:- 1880. 19 matches, 955 runs, 2 50s, 3 100s, av. 28.94, 6 catches. HS: 147.

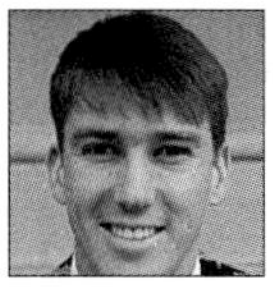

McGRATH, Glenn Donald
B: Feb 9, 1970.
Bats: Right hand.
Bowls: Right arm.

First class debut:- 1992–93. 54 matches, 156 runs, av. 4.11, 9 catches. 224 wkts at 23.84, 11 5-wkts, 1 10-wkts. HS: 24 BB: 6/47.
Test debut:- 1993–94. 28 matches, 81 runs, av. 3.24, 6 catches. 119 wkts at 24.66, 6 5-wkts. HS: 24 BB: 6/47.
Int. limited-overs debut:- 1993–94. 66 matches, 44 runs at 4.40. 82 wkts at 28.26. HS: 10 BB: 5/52.

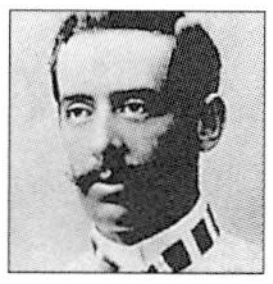

McILWRAITH, John
B: Sep 7, 1857.
D: July 5, 1938.
Bats: Right hand.

First class debut:- 1884–85. 44 matches, 1468 runs, 6 50s, 2 100s, av. 24.06, 24 catches. HS: 133.
Test debut:- 1886. 1 match, 9 runs, av. 4.50, 1 catch. HS: 7.

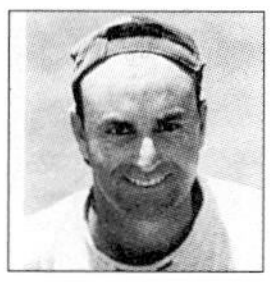

McINTYRE, Peter Edward
B: April 27, 1966.
Bats: Right hand.
Bowls: Right arm.

First class debut:- 1988–89. 72 matches, 475 runs, av. 6.99, 28 catches. 234 wkts at 40.24, 8 5-wkts, 2 10-wkts. HS: 32 BB: 6/43.
Test debut:- 1994–95. 2 matches, 22 runs, av. 7.33. 5 wkts at 38.80. HS: 16 BB: 3/103.

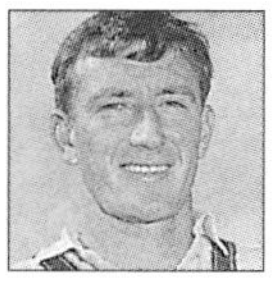

McKENZIE, Graham Douglas
B: June 24, 1941.
Bats: Right hand.
Bowls: Right arm.

First class debut:- 1959–60. 383 matches, 5662 runs, 18 50s, av. 15.64, 201 catches. 1219 wkts at 29.96, 49 5-wkts, 5 10-wkts. HS: 76 BB: 8/71.
Test debut:- 1961. 61 matches, 945 runs, 2 50s, av. 12.27, 34 catches. 246 wkts at 29.79, 16 5-wkts, 3 10-wkts. HS: 76 BB: 8/71.
Int. limited-overs debut:- 1970–71. 1 matches, 2 wkts at 11.00. HS: DNB. BB: 2/22.

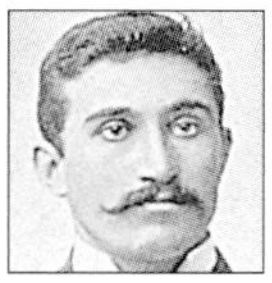

McKIBBIN, Thomas Robert
B: Dec 10, 1870.
D: Dec 15, 1939.
Bats: Right hand.
Bowls: Right arm.

First class debut:- 1894–95. 57 matches, 683 runs, 1 50s, av. 10.04, 46 catches. 319 wkts at 19.73, 28 5-wkts, 11 10-wkts. HS: 75 BB: 9/68.
Test debut:- 1894–95. 5 matches, 88 runs, av. 14.67, 4 catches. 17 wkts at 29.18. HS: 28* BB: 3/35.

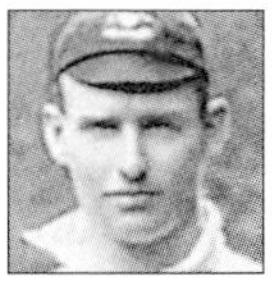

McLAREN, John William
B: Dec 22, 1886.
D: Nov 17, 1921.
Bats: Right hand.
Bowls: Right arm.

First class debut:- 1906–07. 34 matches, 564 runs, av. 12.53, 8 catches. 107 wkts at 26.74, 3 5-wkts. HS: 43* BB: 5/55.
Test debut:- 1911–12. 1 match, 0 runs, av. –. 1 wkt at 70.00. HS: 0* BB: 1/23.

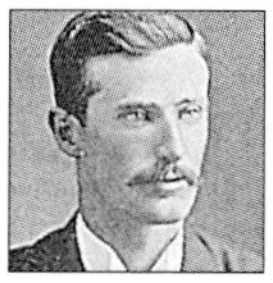

McLEOD, Charles Edwad
B: Oct 24, 1869.
D: Nov 26, 1918.
Bats: Right hand.
Bowls: Right arm.

First class debut:- 1893–94. 114 matches, 3321 runs, 17 50s, 2 100s, av. 21.15, 63 catches. 334 wkts at 24.32, 22 5-wkts, 4 10-wkts. HS: 112 BB: 7/34.
Test debut:- 1894–95. 17 matches, 573 runs, 4 50s, 1 100s, av. 23.88, 9 catches. 33 wkts at 40.15, 2 5-wkts. HS: 112 BB: 5/65.

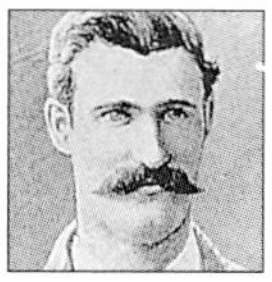

McLEOD, Robert William
B: Jan 19, 1868.
D: June 14, 1907.
Bats: Left hand.
Bowls: Right arm.

First class debut:- 1889–90. 57 matches, 1701 runs, 6 50s, 1 100s, av. 22.38, 39 catches. 141 wkts at 22.73, 7 5-wkts, 2 10-wkts. HS: 101 BB: 7/24.
Test debut:- 1891–92. 6 matches, 146 runs, av. 13.27, 3 catches. 12 wkts at 31.83, 1 5-wkts. HS: 31 BB: 5/53.

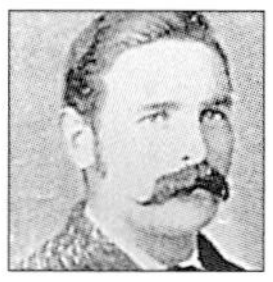

McSHANE, Frederick George
B: April 18, 1858.
D: Dec 11, 1903.
Bats: Left hand.
Bowls: Left arm.

First class debut:- 1880–81. 36 matches, 1117 runs, 5 50s, av. 18.31, 24 catches. 72 wkts at 25.37, 4 5-wkts, 1 10-wkts. HS: 88 BB: 9/45.
Test debut:- 1884–85. 3 matches, 26 runs, av. 5.20, 2 catches. 1 wkt at 48.00. HS: 12* BB: 1/39.

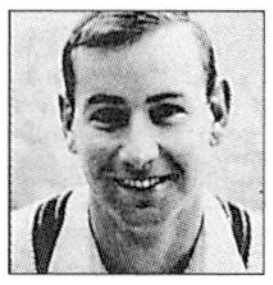

MECKIFF, Ian
B: Jan 6, 1935.
Bats: Right hand.
Bowls: Left arm.

First class debut:- 1956–57. 74 matches, 778 runs, 1 50s, av. 11.27, 37 catches. 269 wkts at 23.35, 12 5-wkts, 1 10-wkts. HS: 55 BB: 6/29.
Test debut:- 1957–58. 18 matches, 154 runs, av. 11.85, 9 catches. 45 wkts at 31.62, 2 5-wkts. HS: 45* BB: 6/38.

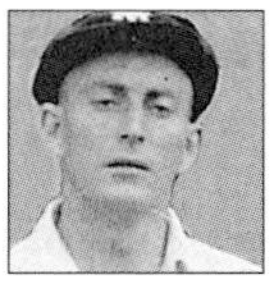

MEULEMAN, Kenneth Douglas
B: Sep 5, 1923.
Bats: Right Hand.
Bowls: Right arm.

First class debut:- 1945–46. 117 matches, 7855 runs, 41 50s, 22 100s, av. 47.60, 35 catches. 19 wkts at 50.31. HS: 234* BB: 3/7.
Test debut:- 1945–46. 1 match, 0 runs, av. 0.00, 1 catch. HS: 0.

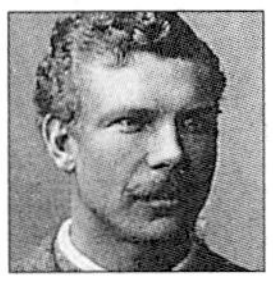

MIDWINTER, William Evans
B: June 19, 1851.
D: Dec 3, 1890.
Bats: Right hand.
Bowls: Right arm.

First class debut:- 1874–75 160 matches, 4497 runs, 12 50s, 3 100s, av. 18.97, 123 catches. 420 wkts at 17.35, 26 5-wkts, 3 10-wkts. HS: 137* BB: 7/27.
Test debut:- 1876–77. 12 matches, 269 runs, av. 13.45, 10 catches. 24 wkts at 25.21, 1 5-wkts. HS: 37 BB: 5/78.

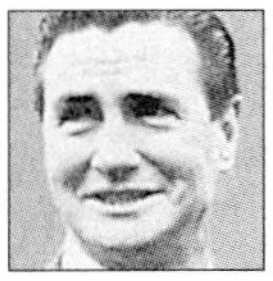

MILLER, Keith Ross
B: Nov 28, 1919.
Bats: Right hand.
Bowls: Right arm.

First class debut:- 1937–38. 226 matches, 14,183 runs, 63 50s, 41 100s, av. 48.90, 136 catches. 497 wkts at 22.30, 16 5-wkts, 1 10-wkts. HS: 281* BB: 7/12.
Test debut:- 1945–46. 55 matches, 2958 runs, 13 50s, 7 100s, av. 36.98, 38 catches. 170 wkts at 22.98, 7 5-wkts, 1 10-wkts. HS: 147 BB: 7/60.

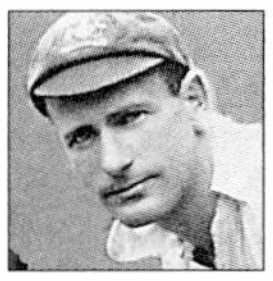

MINNETT, Roy Baldwin
B: June 13, 1888.
D: Oct 21, 1955.
Bats: Right hand.

First class debut:- 1906–07. 55 matches, 2203 runs, 12 50s, 2 100s, av. 28.98, 18 catches. 86 wkts at 25.02, 3 5-wkts, 1 10-wkts. HS: 216* BB: 8/50.
Test debut:- 1911–12. 9 matches, 391 runs, 3 50s, av. 26.07. 11 wkts at 26.36. HS: 90 BB: 4.34.

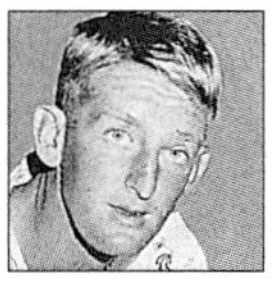

MISSON, Francis Michael
B: Nov 19, 1938.
Bats: Right hand.
Bowls: Right arm.

First class debut:- 1958–59. 71 matches, 1052 runs, 2 50s, av. 17.53, 58 catches. 177 wkts at 31.13, 1 5-wkts. HS: 51* BB: 6/75.
Test debut:- 1960–61. 5 matches, 38 runs, av. 19.00, 6 catches. 16 wkts at 38.50. HS: 25* BB: 4/58.

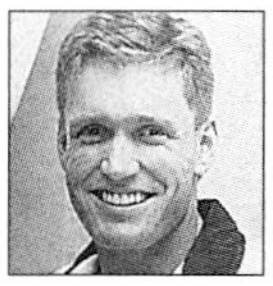

MOODY, Thomas Masson
B: Oct 2, 1965.
Bats: Right hand.
Bowls: Right arm.

First class debut:- 1985–86. 244 matches, 17,582 runs, 80 50s, 53 100s, av. 47.01, 244 catches. 250 wkts at 30.38, 6 5-wkts, 2 10-wkts. HS: 272 BB: 7/38.
Test debut:- 1989–90. 8 matches, 456 runs, 3 50s, 2 100s, av. 32.57, 9 catches. 2 wkts at 73.50. HS: 106 BB: 1/17.
Int. limited-overs debut:- 1987–88. 40 matches, 766 runs at 23.94. 21 wkts at 40.67. HS: 89 BB: 3/56.

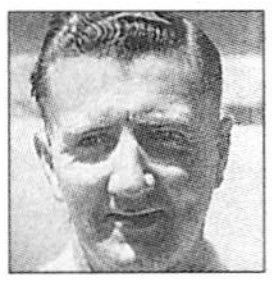

MORONEY, John
B: July 24, 1917.
Bats: Right hand.

First class debut:- 1945–46. 57 matches, 4023 runs, 22 50s, 12 100s, av. 52.24, 19 catches, 1 stumping. HS: 217.
Test debut:- 1949–50. 7 matches, 383 runs, 1 50s, 2 100s, av. 34.82. HS: 118.

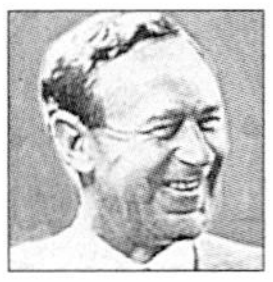

MORRIS, Arthur Robert
B: Jan 19, 1922.
Bats: Left hand.
Bowls: Left arm.

First class debut:- 1940–41. 162 matches, 12,614 runs, 46 50s, 46 100s, av. 53.67, 73 catches. 12 wkts at 49.33. HS: 290 BB: 3/36.
Test debut:- 1946–47. 46 matches, 3533 runs, 12 50s, 12 100s, av. 46.49, 15 catches. 2 wkts at 25.00. HS: 206 BB: 1/5.

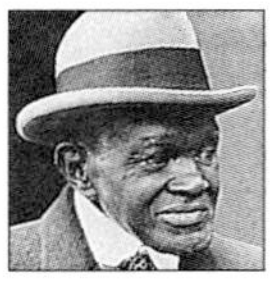

MORRIS, Samuel
B: June 22, 1855.
D: Sep 20, 1931.
Bats: Right hand.
Bowls: Right arm.

First class debut:- 1881–82. 21 matches, 623 runs, 5 50s, av. 18.32, 13 catches. 31 wkts at 26.09, 1 5-wkts. HS: 64* BB: 5/21.
Test debut:- 1884–85. 1 match, 14 runs, av. 14.00. 2 wkts at 36.50. HS: 10* BB: 2/73.

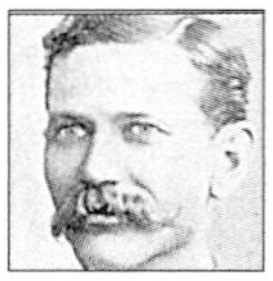

MOSES, Henry
B: Feb 13, 1858.
D: Dec 7, 1938.
Bats: Left hand.
Bowls: Right arm.

First class debut:- 1881–82. 48 matches, 2898 runs, 15 50s, 4 100s, av. 35.77, 25 catches. 1 wkt at 52.00. HS: 297* BB: 1/19.
Test debut:- 1886–87. 6 matches, 198 runs, av. 19.80, 1 catch. HS: 33.

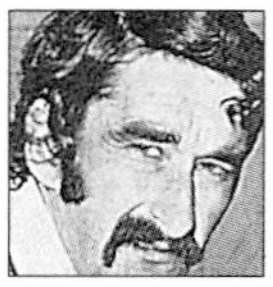

MOSS, Jeffrey Kenneth
B: June 29, 1947.
Bats: Left hand.

First class debut:- 1976–77. 51 matches, 3416 runs, 14 50s, 9 100s, av. 43.79, 33 catches. HS: 220.
Test debut:- 1978–79. 1 match, 60 runs, av. 60.00. HS: 38*
Int. limited-overs debut:- 1979. 1 match, 7 runs at 7.00. HS: 7.

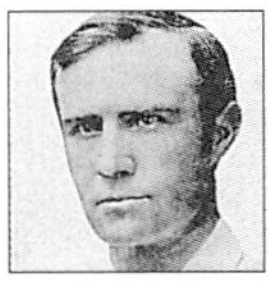

MOULE, William Henry
B: Jan 31, 1858.
D: Aug 24, 1939.
Bats: Right hand.
Bowls: Right arm.

First class debut:- 1878–79. 9 matches, 137 runs, av. 11.41, 7 catches. 5 wkts at 21.20. HS: 34 BB: 3/23.
Test debut:- 1880. 1 match, 40 runs, av. 20.00, 1 catch. 3 wkts at 7.67. HS: 34 BB: 3/23.

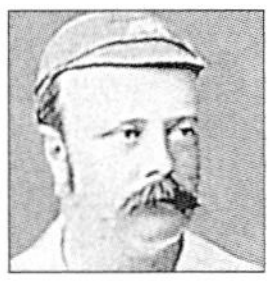

MURDOCH, William Lloyd
B: Oct 18, 1854.
D: Feb 18, 1911.
Bats: Right hand - Wicketkeeper.
Bowls: Right arm.

First class debut:- 1875–76. 391 matches, 16,953 runs, 85 50s, 19 100s, av. 26.86, 218 catches, 15 stumpings. 10 wkts at 43.00. HS: 321 BB: 2/11.
Test debut:- 1876–77. 19 matches, 908 runs, 1 50s, 2 100s, av. 31.311, 14 catches, 1 stumping. HS: 211.

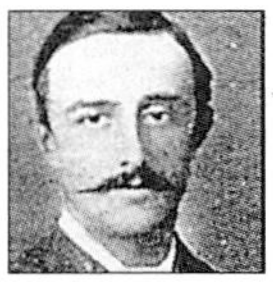

MUSGROVE, Henry Alfred
B: Nov 27, 1860.
D: Nov 2, 1931.
Bats: Right hand.

First class debut:- 1881–82. 7 matches, 99 runs, 1 50s, av. 8.25, 3 catches. HS: 62.
Test debut:- 1884–85. 1 match, 13 runs, av. 6.50. HS: 9.

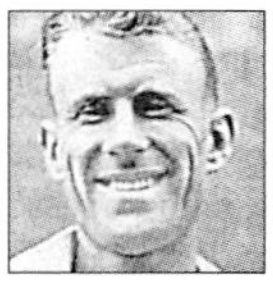

NAGEL, Leslie Ernest
B: Mar 6, 1905.
D: Nov 23, 1971.
Bats: Right hand.
Bowls: Right arm.

First class debut:- 1927–28. 26 matches, 407 runs, av. 12.33, 12 catches. 67 wkts at 28.35, 3 5-wkts. HS: 44 BB: 8/32.
Test debut:- 1932–33. 1 match, 21 runs, av. 21.00. 2 wkts at 55.00. HS: 21* BB: 2/110.

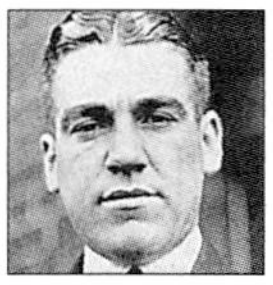

NASH, Laurence John
B: May 2, 1910.
D: July 24, 1986.
Bats: Right hand.
Bowls: Right arm.

First class debut:- 1929–30. 22 matches, 953 runs, 5 50s, 1 100s, av. 28.02, 19 catches. 69 wkts at 28.33, 3 5-wkts. HS: 110 BB: 7/50.
Test debut:- 1931–32. 2 matches, 30 runs, av. 15.00, 6 catches. 10 wkts at 12.60. HS: 17 BB: 4/18.

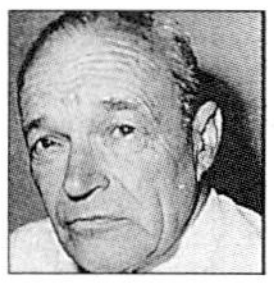

NITSCHKE, Holmesdale Carl
B: April 14, 1905.
D: Sep 29, 1982.
Bats: Left hand.

First class debut:- 1929–30. 45 matches, 3320 runs, 16 50s, 9 100s, av. 42.02, 22 catches. HS: 172.
Test debut:- 1931–32. 2 matches, 53 runs, av. 26.50, 3 catches. HS: 47.

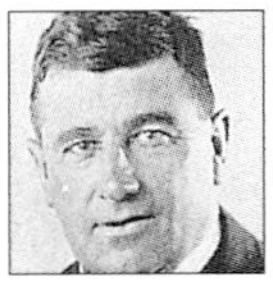

NOBLE, Montague Alfred
B: Jan 28, 1873.
D: June 22, 1940.
Bats: Right hand.
Bowls: Right arm.

First class debut:- 1893–94. 248 matches, 13,975 runs, 66 50s, 37 100s, av. 40.74, 191 catches. 625 wkts at 23.11, 33 5-wkts, 7 10-wkts. HS: 284 BB: 8/48.
Test debut:- 1897–98. 42 matches, 1997 runs, 16 50s, 1 100s, av. 30.26, 26 catches. 121 wkts at 25.00, 9 5-wkts, 2 10-wkts. HS: 133 BB: 7/17.

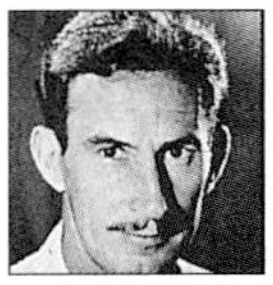

NOBLET, Geffery
B: Sep 14, 1916.
Bats: Right hand.
Bowls: Right arm.

First class debut:- 1945–46. 71 matches, 975 runs, 2 50s, av. 13.92, 44 catches. 282 wkts at 19.26, 13 5-wkts, 2 10-wkts. HS: 55* BB: 7/29.
Test debut:- 1949–50. 3 matches, 22 runs, av. 7.33, 1 catch. 7 wkts at 26.14. HS: 13* BB: 3/21.

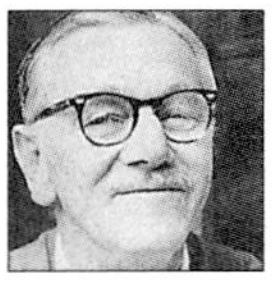

NOTHLING, Otto Ernst
B: Aug 1, 1900.
D: Sep 26, 1965.
Bats: Right hand.
Bowls: Right arm.

First class debut:- 1922–23. 21 matches, 882 runs, 6 50s, 1 100s, av. 24.50, 15 catches. 36 wkts at 41.05, 2 5-wkts. HS: 121 BB: 5/39.
Test debut:- 1928–29. 1 match, 52 runs, av. 26.00. 0 wkts at –. HS: 44 BB: 0/12.

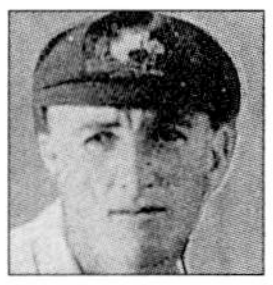

O'BRIEN, Leo Patrick Joseph
B: July 2, 1907.
D: Mar 13, 1997.
Bats: Left hand.
Bowls: Right arm.

First class debut:- 1929–30. 61 matches, 3303 runs, 16 50s, 7 100s, av. 36.70, 24 catches. 3 wkts at 42.33. HS: 173 BB: 1/3.
Test debut:- 1932–33. 5 matches, 211 runs, 2 50s, av. 26.38, 3 catches. HS: 61.

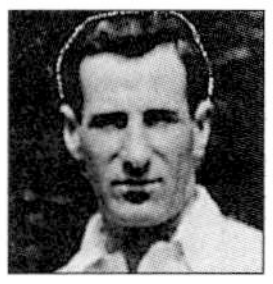

O'CONNOR, John Denis Alphonsus
B: Sep 9, 1875.
D: Aug 23, 1941.
Bats: Left hand.
Bowls: Right arm.

First class debut:- 1904–05. 50 matches, 695 runs, 2 50s, av. 11.77, 32 catches. 224 wkts at 23.45, 18 5-wkts, 5 10-wkts. HS: 54 BB: 7/36.
Test debut:- 1907–08. 4 matches, 86 runs, av. 12.29, 3 catches. 13 wkts at 26.15, 1 5-wkts. HS: 20 BB: 5/40.

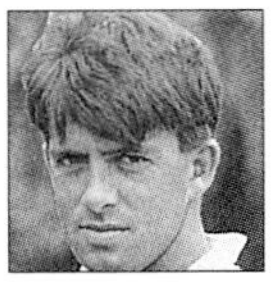

O'DONNELL, Simon Patrick
B: Jan 26, 1963.
Bats: Right hand.
Bowls: Right arm.

First class debut:- 1983–84. 83 matches, 4603 runs, 31 50s, 7 100s, av. 39.34, 60 catches. 151 wkts at 37.36, 2 5-wkts. HS: 130 BB: 6/54.
Test debut:- 1985. 6 matches, 206 runs, av. 29.43, 4 catches. 6 wkts at 84.00. HS: 48 BB: 3/37.
Int. limited-overs debut:- 1984–85. 87 matches, 1242 runs, 9 50s, av. 25.35, 22 catches. 108 wkts at 28.72, 1 5-wkts. HS: 74* BB: 5/13.

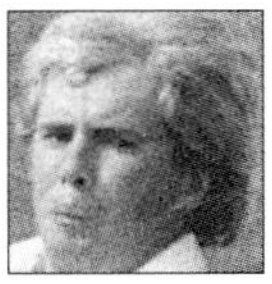

O'KEEFFE, Kerry James
B: Nov 25, 1949.
Bats: Right hand.
Bowls: Right arm.

First class debut:- 1968–69. 169 matches, 4169 runs, 13 50s, av. 26.05, 113 catches. 476 wkts at 28.11, 24 5-wkts, 5 10-wkts. HS: 99* BB: 7/38.
Test debut:- 1970–71. 24 matches, 644 runs, 1 50s, av. 25.76, 15 catches. 53 wkts at 38.08, 1 5-wkts. HS: 85 BB: 5/101.
Int. limited-overs debut:- 1977. 2 matches, 16 at 16.00. 2 wkts at 39.50. HS: 16* BB: 1/36.

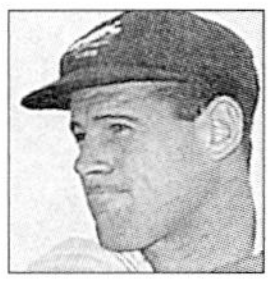

O'NEILL, Norman Clifford
B: Feb 19, 1937.
Bats: Right hand.
Bowls: Right arm.

First class debut:- 1955–56. 188 matches, 13,859 runs, 63 50s, 45 100s, av. 50.95, 104 catches. 99 wkts at 41.01. HS: 284 BB: 4/40.
Test debut:- 1958–59. 42 matches, 2779 runs, 15 50s, 6 100s, av. 45.56, 21 catches. 17 wkts at 39.24. HS: 181 BB: 4/41.

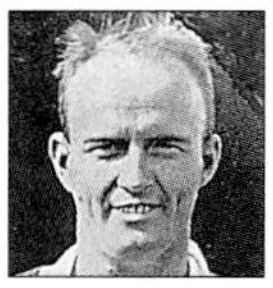

O'REILLY, William Joseph
B: Dec 20, 1905.
D: Oct 6, 1992.
Bats: Right hand.
Bowls: Right arm.

First class debut:- 1927–28. 135 matches, 1655 runs, 1 50s, av. 13.13, 65 catches. 774 wkts at 16.60, 63 5-wkts, 17 10-wkts. HS: 56* BB: 9/38.
Test debut:- 1931–32. 27 matches, 410 runs, 1 50s, av. 12.81, 7 catches. 144 wkts at 22.60, 11 5-wkts, 3 10-wkts. HS: 56* BB: 7/54.

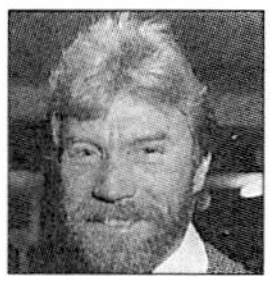

OGILVIE, Alan David
B: June 3, 1951.
Bats: Right hand.

First class debut:- 1974–75. 51 matches, 3006 runs, 10 50s, 8 100s, av. 34.15, 44 catches. HS: 194.
Test debut:- 1977–78. 5 matches, 178 runs, av. 17.80, 5 catches. HS: 47.

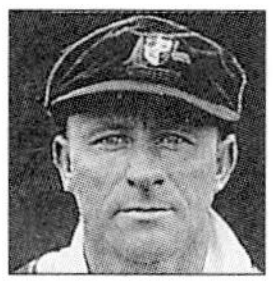

OLDFIELD, William Albert Stanley
B: Sep 9, 1894.
D: Aug 10, 1976.
Bats: Right hand - Wicketkeeper.

First class debut:- 1919. 245 matches, 6135 runs, 21 50s, 6 100s, av. 23.77, 399 catches, 262 stumpings. HS: 137.
Test debut:- 1920–21. 54 matches, 1427 runs, 4 50s, av. 22.65, 78 catches, 52 stumpings. HS: 65*.

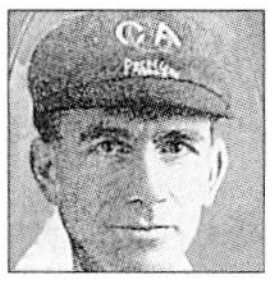

OXENHAM, Ronald Keven
B: July 28, 1891.
D: Aug 16, 1939.
Bats: Right hand.
Bowls: Right arm.

First class debut:- 1911–12. 97 matches, 3693 runs, 19 50s, 4 100s, av. 25.64, 45 catches. 369 wkts at 18.67, 22 5-wkts, 8 10-wkts. HS: 162* BB: 9/18.
Test debut:- 1928–29. 7 matches, 151 runs, av. 15.10, 4 catches. 14 wkts at 37.29. HS: 48 BB: 4/39.

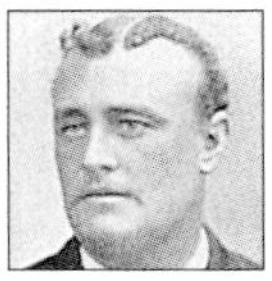

PALMER, George Eugene
B: Feb 22, 1860.
D: Aug 22, 1910.
Bats: Right hand.
Bowls: Right arm.

First class debut:- 1878–79. 133 matches, 2728 runs, 10 50s, 1 100s, av. 16.14, 108 catches. 594 wkts at 17.67, 54 5-wkts, 16 10-wkts. HS: 113 BB: 8/48.
Test debut:- 1880. 17 matches, 296 runs, av. 14.10, 13 catches. 78 wkts at 21.51, 6 5-wkts, 2 10-wkts. HS: 48 BB: 7/65.

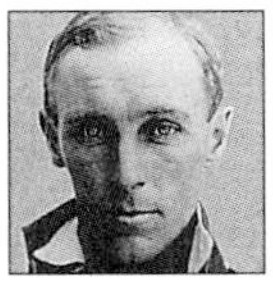

PARK, Roy Lindsay
B: July 30, 1892.
D: Jan 23, 1947.
Bats: Right hand.

First class debut:- 1912–13. 36 matches, 2514 runs, 10 50s, 9 100s, av. 39.28, 13 catches. 3 wkts at 46.33. HS: 228 BB: 1/15.
Test debut:- 1920–21. 1 match, 0 runs, av. 0.00. 0 wkts at –. HS: 0 BB: 0/9.

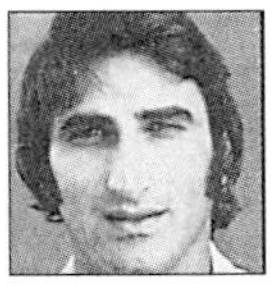

PASCOE, Leonard Stephen
B: Feb 13, 1950.
Bats: Right hand.
Bowls: Right arm.

First class debut:- 1974–75. 74 matches, 472 runs, 1 50s, av. 9.07, 22 catches. 289 wkts at 25.30, 10 5-wkts, 2 10-wkts. HS: 51* BB: 8/41.
Test debut:- 1977. 14 matches, 106 runs, av. 10.60, 2 catches. 64 wkts at 26.06, 1 5-wkts. HS: 30* BB: 5/59.
Int. limited-overs debut:- 1977. 29 matches, 39 runs, av. 9.75, 6 catches. 53 wkts at 20.11, 1 5-wkts. HS: 15* BB: 5/30.

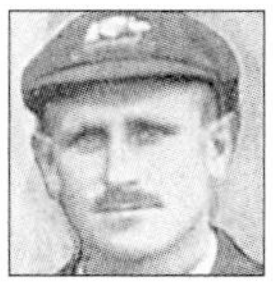

PELLEW, Clarence Everard
B: Sep 21, 1893.
D: May 9, 1981.
Bats: Right hand.
Bowls: Right arm.

First class debut:- 1913–14. 91 matches, 4536 runs, 21 50s, 9 100s, av. 33.60, 45 catches. 12 wkts at 70.75. HS: 271 BB: 3/119.
Test debut:- 1920–21. 10 matches, 484 runs, 1 50s, 2 100s, av. 37.23, 4 catches. 0 wkts at –. HS: 116 BB: 0/ .

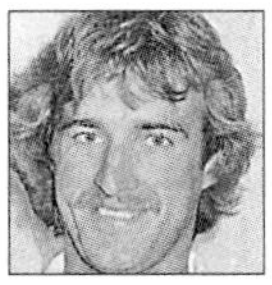

PHILLIPS, Wayne Bentley
B: Mar 1, 1958.
Bats: Left hand - Wicketkeeper.

First class debut:- 1977–78. 114 matches, 6907 runs, 33 50s, 13 100s, av. 37.74, 154 catches, 7 stumpings. HS: 260.
Test debut:- 1983–84. 27 matches, 1485 runs, 7 50s, 2 100s, av. 32.28, 52 catches. HS: 159.
Int. limited-overs debut:- 1982–83. 48 matches, 852 runs, 6 50s, av. 24.34, 42 catches, 7 stumpings. HS: 75*.

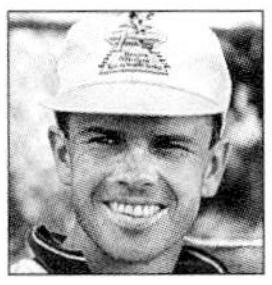

PHILLIPS, Wayne Norman
B: Nov 7, 1962.
Bats: Right hand.
Bowls: Right arm.

First class debut:- 1988–89. 60 matches, 3859 runs, 18 50s, 9 100s, av. 38.59, 24 catches. 1 wkt at 124.00. HS 205. BB 1/59.
Test debut:- 1991–92. 1 match, 22 runs, av. 11.00. HS: 14.

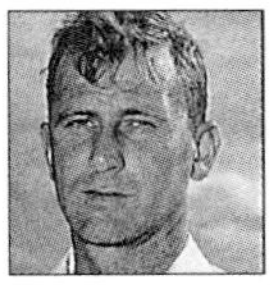

PHILPOTT, Peter Ian
B: Nov 21, 1934.
Bats: Right hand.
Bowls: Right arm.

First class debut:- 1954–55. 76 matches, 2886 runs, 15 50s, 4 100s, av. 31.36, 55 catches. 245 wkts at 30.31, 12 5-wkts, 2 10-wkts. HS: 156 BB: 7/53.
Test debut:- 1964–65. 8 matches, 93 runs, av. 10.33, 5 catches. 26 wkts at 38.46, 1 5-wkts. HS: 22 BB: 5/90.

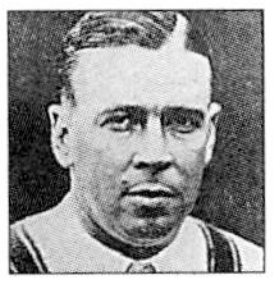

PONSFORD, William Harold
B: Oct 19, 1900.
D: April 6, 1991.
Bats: Right hand.

First class debut:- 1920–21. 162 matches, 13,819 runs, 43 50s, 47 100s, av. 65.18, 71 catches. HS: 437 .
Test debut:- 1924–25. 29 matches, 2122 runs, 6 50s, 7 100s, av. 48.23, 21 catches. HS: 266.

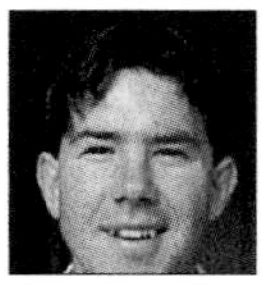

PONTING, Ricky Thomas
B: Dec 19, 1974.
Bats: Right hand.

First class debut:- 1992–93. 59 matches, 4795 runs, 22 50s, 16 100s, av. 52.69, 51 catches. 5 wkts at 67.20. HS: 211 BB: 1/0.
Test debut:- 1995–96. 6 matches, 330 runs, 3 50s, av. 33.00, 9 catches. 2 wkts at 4.00. HS: 96 BB: 1/0.
Int. limited-overs debut:- 1994–95. 33 matches, 929 runs at 30.97. HS: 123.

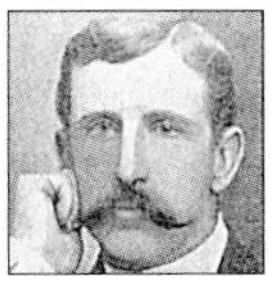

POPE, Roland James
B: Feb 18, 1864.
D: July 27, 1952.
Bats: Right hand.

First class debut:- 1884–85. 20 matches, 318 runs, av. 12.23, 13 catches. HS: 47.
Test debut:- 1884–85. 1 match, 3 runs, av. 1.50. HS: 3.

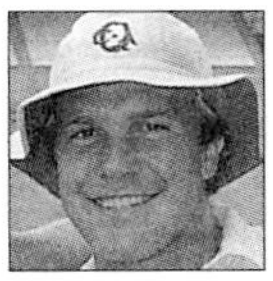

RACKEMANN, Carl Grey
B: June 3, 1960.
Bats: Right hand.
Bowls: Right arm.

First class debut:- 1979–80. 167 matches, 862 runs, av. 7.70, 41 catches. 616 wkts at 27.00, 22 5-wkts, 3 10-wkts. HS: 33 BB: 8/84.
Test debut:- 1982–83. 12 matches, 53 runs, av. 5.30, 2 catches. 39 wkts at 29.15, 3 5-wkts, 1 10-wkts. HS: 15* BB: 6/66.
Int. limited-overs debut:- 1982–83. 52 matches, 34 runs at 2.83. 82 wkts at 22.35. HS: 9* BB: 5/16.

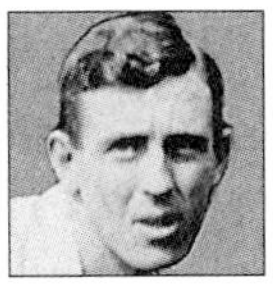

RANSFORD, Vernon Seymour
B: Mar 20, 1885.
D: Mar 19, 1958.
Bats: Left hand.

First class debut:- 1903–04. 142 matches, 8268 runs, 32 50s, 25 100s, av. 42.40, 74 catches. 29 wkts at 30.62, 1 5-wkts. HS: 190 BB: 6/38.
Test debut:- 1907–08. 20 matches, 1211 runs, 7 50s, 1 100s, av. 37.84, 10 catches. 1 wkt at 28.00. HS: 143* BB: 1/9.

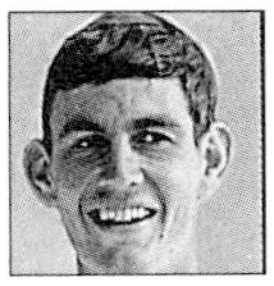

REDPATH, Ian Ritchie
B: May 11, 1941.
Bats: Right hand.
Bowls: Right arm.

First class debut:- 1961–62. 226 matches, 14,993 runs, 84 50s, 32 100s, av. 41.99, 211 catches. 13 wkts at 35.84. HS: 261 BB: 3/24.
Test debut:- 1963–64. 67 matches, 4737 runs, 31 50s, 8 100s, av. 43.46, 83 catches. HS: 171.
Int. limited-overs debut:- 1970–71. 5 matches, 46 runs at 9.20. HS: 24.

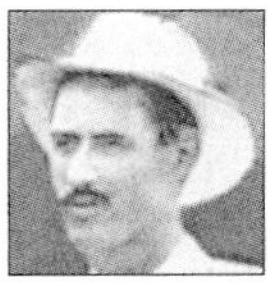

REEDMAN, John Cole
B: Oct 9, 1865.
D: Mar 23, 1924.
Bats: Right hand.
Bowls: Right arm.

First class debut:- 1887–88. 81 matches, 3338 runs, 15 50s, 2 100s, av. 23.34, 68 catches. 118 wkts at 32.09, 6 5-wkts, 1 10-wkts. HS: 113 BB: 7/54.
Test debut:- 1894–95. 1 match, 21 runs, av. 10.50, 1 catch. 1 wkt at 24.00. HS: 17 BB: 1/12.

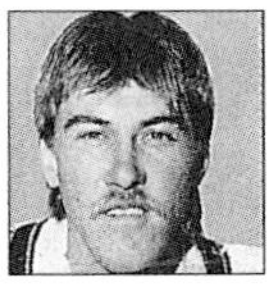

REID, Bruce Anthony
B: Mar 14, 1963.
Bats: Left hand.
Bowls: Left arm.

First class debut:- 1984–85. 96 matches, 503 runs, av. 7.86, 19 catches. 350 wkts at 26.64, 12 5-wkts, 3 10-wkts. HS: 30 BB: 7/51.
Test debut:- 1985–86. 27 matches, 93 runs, av. 4.65, 5 catches. 113 wkts at 24.64, 5 5-wkts, 2 10-wkts. HS: 13 BB: 7/51.
Int. limited-overs debut:- 1985–86. 61 matches, 49 runs at 3.77. 63 wkts at 34.94. HS: 10 BB: 5/53.

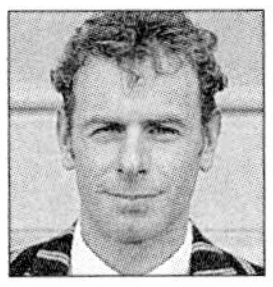

REIFFEL, Paul Ronald
B: April 19, 1966.
Bats: Right hand.
Bowls: Right arm.

First class debut:- 1987–88. 107 matches, 1895 runs, 6 50s, av. 21.06, 56 catches. 346 wkts at 28.41, 12 5-wkts, 2 10-wkts. HS: 86 BB: 6/57.
Test debut:- 1991–92. 25 matches, 469 runs, 2 50s, av. 18.04, 13 catches. 80 wkts at 26.35, 4 5-wkts. HS: 56 BB: 6/71.
Int. limited-overs debut:- 1991–92. 75 matches, 441 runs at 15.21. 90 wkts at 28.07. HS: 58 BB: 4/13.

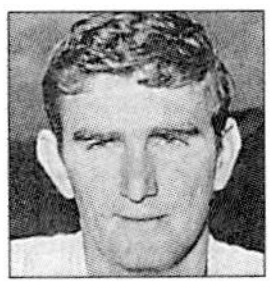

RENNEBERG, David Alexander
B: Sep 23, 1942.
Bats: Right hand.
Bowls: Right arm.

First class debut:- 1964–65. 90 matches, 466 runs, av. 7.06, 35 catches. 291 wkts at 29.30, 13 5-wkts, 1 10-wkts. HS: 26 BB: 8/72.
Test debut:- 1966–67. 8 matches, 22 runs, av. 3.67, 2 catches. 23 wkts at 36.09, 2 5-wkts. HS: 9 BB: 5/39.

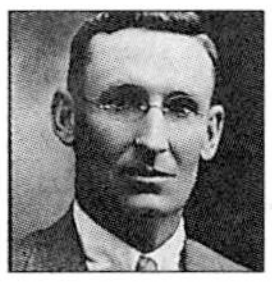

RICHARDSON, Arthur John
B: July 24, 1888.
D: Dec 23, 1973.
Bats: Right hand.
Bowls: Right arm.

First class debut:- 1918–19. 86 matches, 5238 runs, 16 50s, 13 100s, av. 41.57, 34 catches. 209 wkts at 31.36, 7 5-wkts, 1 10-wkts. HS: 280 BB: 6/28.
Test debut:- 1924–25. 9 matches, 403 runs, 2 50s, 1 100s, av. 31.00, 1 catch. 12 wkts at 43.42. HS: 100 BB: 2/20.

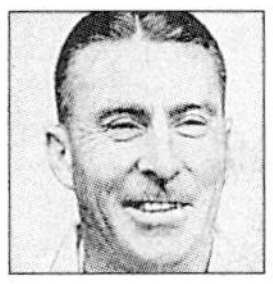

RICHARDSON, Victor York
B: Sep 7, 1894.
D: Oct 29, 1969.
Bats: Right hand.
Bowls: Right arm.

First class debut:- 1918–19. 184 matches, 10,727 runs, 47 50s, 27 100s, av. 37.63, 213 catches, 4 stumpings. 8 wkts at 68.12. HS: 231 BB: 3/22.
Test debut:- 1924–25. 19 matches, 706 runs, 1 50s, 1 100s, av. 23.53, 24 catches. HS: 138.

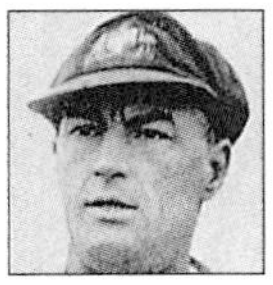

RIGG, Keith Edward
B: May 21, 1906.
D: Feb 28, 1995.
Bats: Right hand.

First class debut:- 1926–27. 87 matches, 5544 runs, 30 50s, 14 100s, av. 42.00, 56 catches. HS: 167*.
Test debut:- 1930–31. 8 matches, 401 runs, 1 50s, 1 100s, av. 33.42, 5 catches. HS: 127.

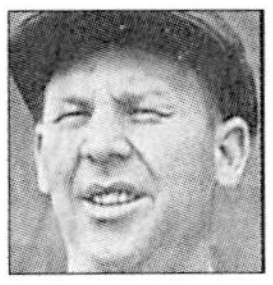

RING, Douglas Thomas
B: Oct 14, 1918.
Bats: Right hand.
Bowls: Right arm.

First class debut:- 1938–39. 129 matches, 3418 runs, 20 50s, 1 100s, av. 23.25, 93 catches. 451 wkts at 28.48, 21 5-wkts, 2 10-wkts. HS: 145 BB: 7/88.
Test debut:- 1947–48. 13 matches, 426 runs, 4 50s, av. 22.42, 5 catches. 35 wkts at 37.29, 2 5-wkts. HS: 67 BB: 6/72.

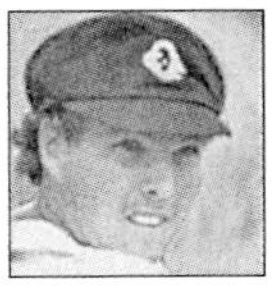

RITCHIE, Gregory Michael
B: Jan 23, 1960.
Bats: Right hand.
Bowls: Right arm.

First class debut:- 1980–81. 159 matches, 10,170 runs, 54 50s, 24 100s, av. 44.22, 115 catches. 5 wkts at 49.40. HS: 213* BB: 1/2.
Test debut:- 1982–83. 30 matches, 1690 runs, 7 50s, 3 100s, av. 35.21, 14 catches. HS: 146.
Int. limited-overs debut:- 1982–83. 44 matches, 959 runs, 6 50s, av. 27.40, 9 catches. HS: 84.

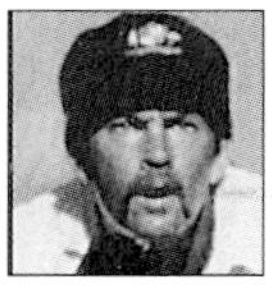

RIXON, Stephen John
B: Feb 25, 1954.
Bats: Right hand - Wicketkeeper.

First class debut:- 1974–75. 151 matches, 4303 runs, 14 50s, 6 100s, av. 23.13, 394 catches, 66 stumpings. HS: 128.
Test debut:- 1977–78. 13 matches, 394 runs, 2 50s, av. 18.76, 42 catches, 5 stumpings. HS: 54.
Int. limited-overs debut:- 1977–78. 6 matches, 40 runs, av. 13.33, 9 catches, 2 stumpings. HS: 20*

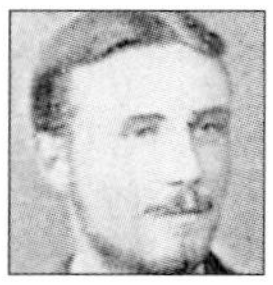

ROBERTSON, William Roderick
B: Oct 6, 1861.
D: June 24, 1938.
Bats: Right hand.
Bowls: Right arm.

First class debut:- 1884–85. 7 matches, 109 runs, av. 13.62, 3 catches. 15 wkts at 31.06, 1 5-wkts. HS: 33 BB: 5/46.
Test debut:- 1884–85. 1 match, 2 runs, av. 1.00. 0 wkts at –. HS: 2 BB: 0/24.

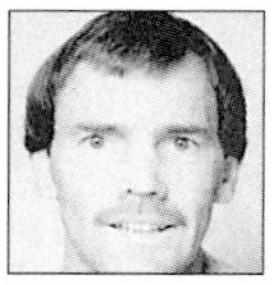

ROBINSON, Richard Daryl
B: June 8, 1946.
Bats: Right hand - Wicketkeeper.

First class debut:- 1971–72. 97 matches, 4776 runs, 22 50s, 7 100s, av. 39.80, 289 catches, 40 stumpings. HS: 185.
Test debut:- 1977. 3 matches, 100 runs, av. 16.67, 4 catches. HS: 34.
Int. limited-overs debut:- 1977. 2 matches, 82 runs, 1 50s, av. 41.00, 3 catches, 1 stumping. HS: 70.

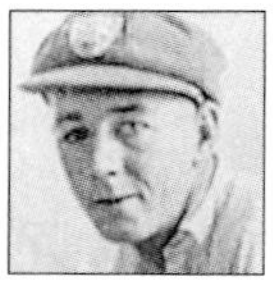

ROBINSON, Rayford Harold
B: Mar 26, 1914.
D: Aug 10, 1965.
Bats: Right hand.
Bowls: Right arm.

First class debut:- 1934–35. 46 matches, 2441 runs, 13 50s, 4 100s, av. 31.70, 24 catches. 44 wkts at 37.59. HS: 163 BB: 4/45.
Test debut:- 1936–37. 1 match, 5 runs, av. 2.50, 1 catch. HS: 3.

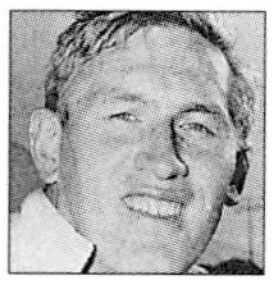

RORKE, Gordon Frederick
B: June 27, 1938.
Bats: Left hand.
Bowls: Right arm.

First class debut:- 1957–58. 36 matches, 248 runs, av. 10.78, 10 catches. 88 wkts at 24.60, 3 5-wkts. HS: 35 BB: 6/52.
Test debut:- 1958–59. 4 matches, 9 runs, av. 4.50, 1 catch. 10 wkts at 20.30. HS: 7 BB: 3/23.

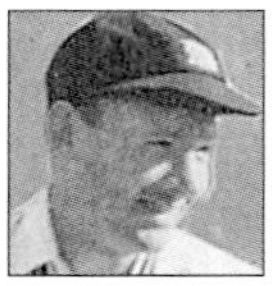

RUTHERFORD, John Walter
B: Sep 25, 1929.
Bats: Right hand.
Bowls: Right arm.

First class debut:- 1952–53. 67 matches, 3367 runs, 15 50s, 6 100s, av. 31.76, 53 catches. 29 wkts at 45.27. HS: 167 BB: 3/12.
Test debut:- 1956–57. 1 match, 30 runs, av. 30.00. 1 wkt at 15.00. HS: 30 BB: 1/11.

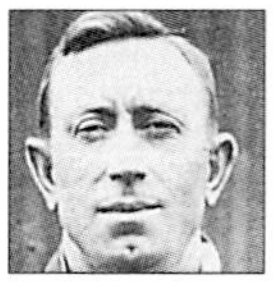

RYDER, John
B: Aug 8, 1889.
D: April 3, 1977.
Bats: Right hand.
Bowls: Right arm.

First class debut:- 1912–13. 177 matches, 10,499 runs, 55 50s, 24 100s, av. 44.29, 132 catches. 237 wkts at 29.80, 9 5-wkts, 1 10-wkts. HS: 295 BB: 7/53.
Test debut:- 1920–21. 20 matches, 1394 runs, 9 50s, 3 100s, av. 51.63, 17 catches. 17 wkts at 43.71. HS: 201* BB: 2/20.

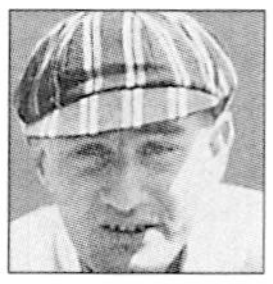

SAGGERS, Ronald Arthur
B: May 15, 1917.
D: Mar 31, 1987.
Bats: Right hand - Wicketkeeper.

First class debut:- 1939–40. 77 matches, 1888 runs, 8 50s, 1 100s, av. 23.89, 147 catches, 74 stumpings. HS: 104*.
Test debut:- 1948. 6 matches, 30 runs, av. 10.00, 16 catches, 8 stumpings. HS: 14.

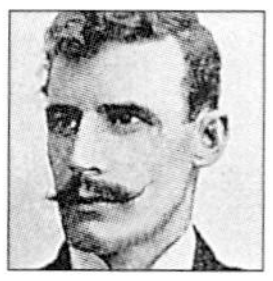

SAUNDERS, John Victor
B: Feb 3, 1876.
D: Dec 21, 1927.
Bats: Left hand.
Bowls: Left arm.

First class debut:- 1899–00. 107 matches, 586 runs, av. 4.76, 72 catches. 553 wkts at 21.81, 48 5-wkts, 9 10-wkts. HS: 29* BB: 8/106.
Test debut:- 1901–02. 14 matches, 39 runs, av. 2.29, 5 catches. 79 wkts at 22.73, 6 5-wkts. HS: 11* BB: 7/34.

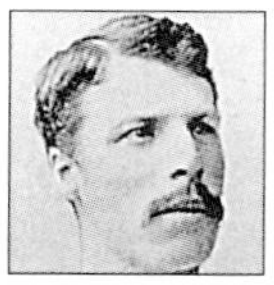

SCOTT, Henry James Herbert
B: Dec 26, 1858.
D: Sep 23, 1910.
Bats: Right hand.
Bowls: Right arm.

First class debut:- 1877–78. 85 matches, 2863 runs, 14 50s, 4 100s, av. 22.72, 57 catches. 18 wkts at 27.44, 1 5-wkts. HS: 123 BB: 6/33.
Test debut:- 1884. 8 matches, 359 runs, 1 50s, 1 100s, av. 27.62, 8 catches. HS: 102.

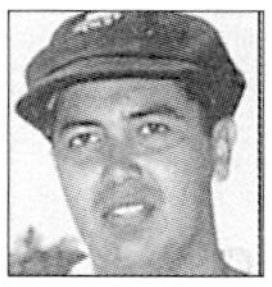

SELLERS, Reginald Hugh Durning
B: Aug 20, 1940.
Bats: Right hand.
Bowls: Right arm.

First class debut:- 1959–60. 53 matches, 1089 runs, 2 50s, av. 18.15, 41 catches. 121 wkts at 38.45, 4 5-wkts, 1 10-wkts. HS: 87 BB: 5/36.
Test debut:- 1964–65. 1 match, 0 runs, av. 0.00, 1 catch. 0 wkts at –. HS: 0 BB: 0/17.

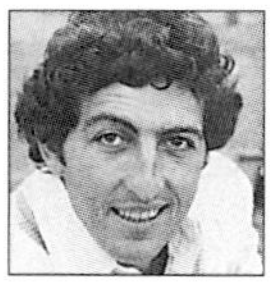

SERJEANT, Craig Stanton
B: Nov 1, 1951.
Bats: Right hand.

First class debut:- 1976–77. 80 matches, 4030 runs, 20 50s, 9 100s, av. 35.04, 90 catches. HS: 159.
Test debut:- 1977. 12 matches, 522 runs, 2 50s, 1 100s, av. 23.73, 13 catches. HS: 124.
Int. limited-overs debut:- 1977. 3 matches, 73 runs at 24.33. HS: 46.

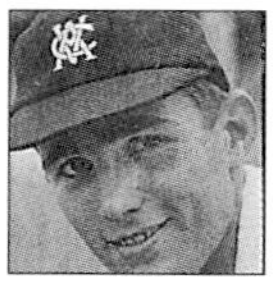

SHEAHAN, Andrew Paul
B: Sep 30, 1948.
Bats: Right hand.

First class debut:- 1965–66. 133 matches, 7987 runs, 38 50s, 19 100s, av. 46.16, 34 catches. 1 wkt at 66.00. HS: 202 BB: 1/19.
Test debut:- 1967–68. 31 matches, 1594 runs, 7 50s, 2 100s, av. 33.91, 17 catches. HS: 127.
Int. limited-overs debut:- 1972. 3 matches, 75 runs at 25.00. HS: 50.

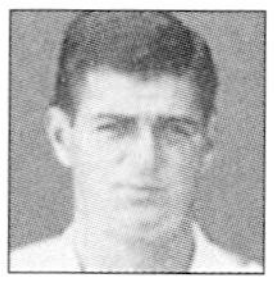

SHEPHERD, Barry Kenneth
B: April 23, 1937.
Bats: Left hand.
Bowls: Right arm.

First class debut:- 1955–56. 110 matches, 6834 runs, 36 50s, 13 100s, av. 41.16, 72 catches. 4 wkts at 85.75. HS: 219 BB: 1/1.
Test debut:- 1962–63. 9 matches, 502 runs, 5 50s, av. 41.83, 1 catch. 0 wkts at –. HS: 96 BB: 0/9.

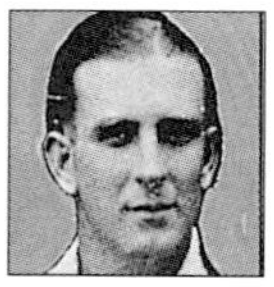

SIEVERS, Morris William
B: April 13, 1912.
D: May 10, 1968.
Bats: Right hand.
Bowls: Right arm.

First class debut:- 1933–34. 58 matches, 2075 runs, 14 50s, av. 29.64, 56 catches. 116 wkts at 33.36, 4 5-wkts. HS: 76 BB: 6/43.
Test debut:- 1936–37. 3 matches, 67 runs, av. 13.40, 4 catches. 9 wkts at 17.89, 1 5-wkts. HS: 25* BB: 5/21.

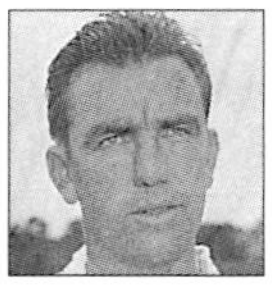

SIMPSON, Robert Baddeley
B: Feb 3, 1936.
Bats: Right hand.
Bowls: Right arm.

First class debut:- 1952–53. 257 matches, 21,029 runs, 100 50s, 60 100s, av. 56.22, 383 catches. 349 wkts at 38.07, 6 5-wkts. HS: 359 BB: 5/33.
Test debut:- 1957–58. 62 matches, 4869 runs, 27 50s, 10 100s, av. 46.82, 110 catches. 71 wkts at 42.27, 2 5-wkts. HS: 311 BB: 5/57.
Int. limited-overs debut:- 1977–78. 2 matches, 36 runs at 18.00. 2 wkts at 47.50. HS: 23 BB: 2/30.

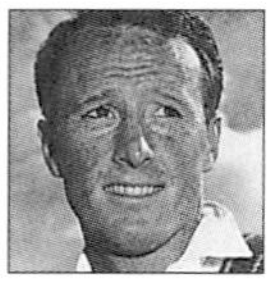

SINCOCK, David John
B: Feb 1, 1942.
Bats: Right hand.
Bowls: Left arm.

First class debut:- 1960–61. 46 matches, 838 runs, 4 50s, av. 17.45, 27 catches. 159 wkts at 36.87, 10 5-wkts, 1 10-wkts. HS: 61* BB: 7/48.
Test debut:- 1964–65. 3 matches, 80 runs, av. 26.67, 2 catches. 8 wkts at 51.25. HS: 29 BB: 3/67.

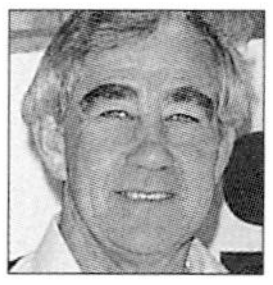

SLATER, Keith Nichol
B: Mar 12, 1936.
Bats: Right hand.
Bowls: Right arm.

First class debut:- 1955–56. 74 matches, 2198 runs, 13 50s, 1 100s, av. 21.13, 50 catches. 140 wkts at 42.30. HS: 154 BB: 4/33.
Test debut:- 1958–59. 1 match, 1 run, av. –. 2 wkts at 50.50. HS: 1* BB: 2/40.

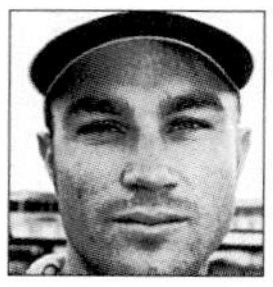

SLATER, Michael John
B: Feb 21, 1970.
Bats: Right hand.
Bowls: Right arm.

First class debut:- 1991–92. 90 matches, 6951 runs, 41 50s, 17 100s, av. 46.65, 44 catches. 1 wkt at 26.00. HS: 219 BB: 1/4.
Test debut:- 1993. 34 matches, 2655 runs, 10 50s, 7 100s, av. 47.41, 11 catches. 1 wkt at 4.00. HS: 219. BB: 1/4.
Int. limited-overs debut:- 1993–94. 40 matches, 969 runs at 24.85. HS: 73

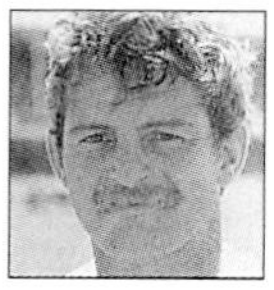

SLEEP, Peter Raymond
B: May 4, 1957.
Bats: Right hand.
Bowls: Right arm.

First class debut:- 1976–77. 174 matches, 8122 runs, 39 50s, 15 100s, av. 34.56, 103 catches, 1 stumping. 363 wkts at 39.36, 9 5-wkts. HS: 182 BB: 8/133.
Test debut:- 1978–79. 14 matches, 483 runs, 3 50s, av. 24.15, 4 catches. 31 wkts at 45.06, 1 5-wkts. HS: 90 BB: 5/72.

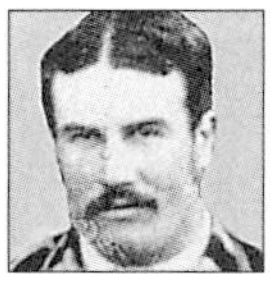

SLIGHT, James
B: Oct 20, 1855.
D: Dec 9, 1930.
Bats: Right hand.

First class debut:- 1874–75. 19 matches, 415 runs, 1 50s, av. 12.57, 4 catches. 3 wkts at 12.33. HS: 53 BB: 2/4.
Test debut:- 1880. 1 match, 11 runs, av. 5.50. HS: 11.

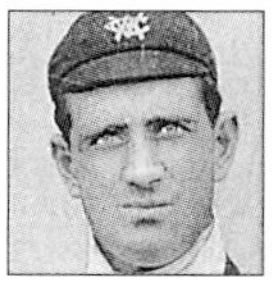

SMITH, David Betram Miller
B: Sep 14, 1884.
D: July 29, 1963.
Bats: Right hand.

First class debut:- 1908–09. 46 matches, 1764 runs, 6 50s, 3 100s, av. 23.83, 16 catches. 1 wkt at 22.00. HS: 146 BB: 1/22.
Test debut:- 1912. 2 matches, 30 runs, av. 15.00. HS: 24*

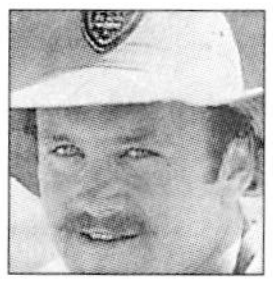

SMITH, Steven Barry
B: Oct 18, 1961.
Bats: Right hand.
Bowls: Right arm.

First class debut:- 1981–82. 90 matches, 5248 runs, 26 50s, 12 100s, av. 35.94, 66 catches. 1 wkt at 77.00. HS: 263 BB: 1/35.
Test debut:- 1983–84. 3 matches, 41 runs, av. 8.20, 1 catch. HS: 12.
Int. limited-overs debut:- 1982–83. 28 matches, 861 runs at 39.14. HS: 117

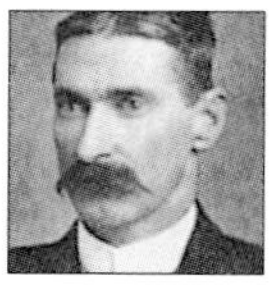

SPOFFORTH, Frederick Robert
B: Sep 9, 1853.
D: June 4, 1926.
Bats: Right hand.
Bowls: Right arm.

First class debut:- 1874–75. 155 matches, 1928 runs, 3 50s, av. 9.88, 83 catches. 853 wkts at 14.95, 84 5-wkts, 32 10-wkts. HS: 56 BB: 9/18.
Test debut:- 1876–77. 18 matches, 217 runs, 1 50s, av. 9.43, 11 catches. 94 wkts at 18.41, 7 5-wkts, 4 10-wkts. HS: 50 BB: 7/44.

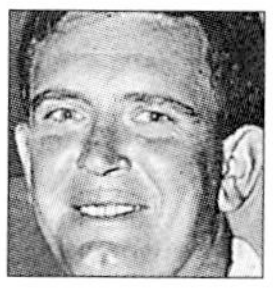

STACKPOLE, Keith Raymond
B: July 10, 1940.
Bats: Right hand.
Bowls: Right arm.

First class debut:- 1959–60. 167 matches, 10,100 runs, 50 50s, 22 100s, av. 39.29, 166 catches. 148 wkts at 39.28, 2 5-wkts. HS: 207 BB: 5/38.
Test debut:- 1965–66. 44 matches, 2807 runs, 14 50s, 7 100s, av. 37.43, 47 catches. 15 wkts at 66.73. HS: 207 BB: 2/33.

Int. limited-overs debut:- 1970–71. 6 matches, 224 runs at 37.33. 3 wkts at 18.00. HS: 61 BB: 3/40.

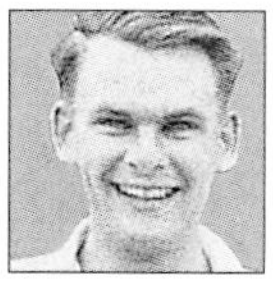

STEVENS, Gavin Byron
B: Feb 29, 1932.
Bats: Right hand.

First class debut:- 1952–53. 47 matches, 3061 runs, 11 50s, 7 100s, av. 38.26, 34 catches. 3 wkts at 41.00. HS: 259* BB: 2/16.
Test debut:- 1959–60. 4 matches, 112 runs, av. 16.00, 2 catches. HS: 28.

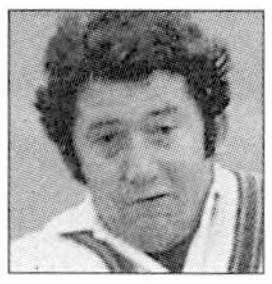

TABER, Hedley Brian
B: April 29, 1940.
Bats: Right hand - Wicketkeeper.

First class debut:- 1964–65. 129 matches, 2648 runs, 8 50s, 1 100s, av. 18.01, 345 catches, 50 stumpings. HS: 109.
Test debut:- 1966–67. 16 matches, 353 runs, av. 16.05, 56 catches, 4 stumpings. HS: 48.

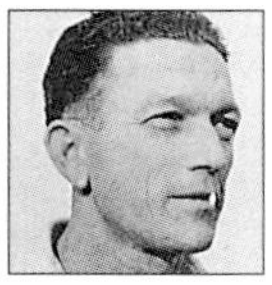

TALLON, Donald
B: Feb 17, 1916.
D: Sep 7, 1984.
Bats: Right hand - Wicketkeeper.

First class debut:- 1933–34. 150 matches, 6034 runs, 27 50s, 9 100s, av. 29.14, 303 catches, 129 stumpings. HS: 193.
Test debut:- 1945–46. 21 matches, 394 runs, 2 50s, av. 17.13, 50 catches, 8 stumpings. HS: 92.

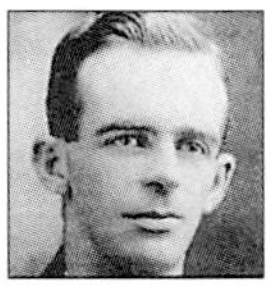

TAYLOR, John Morris
B: Oct 10, 1895.
D: May 12, 1971.
Bats: Right hand.

First class debut:- 1913–14. 135 matches, 6274 runs, 38 50s, 11 100s, av. 33.37, 68 catches. 1 wkt at 53.00. HS: 180 BB: 1/25.
Test debut:- 1920–21. 20 matches, 997 runs, 8 50s, 1 100s, av. 35.61, 11 catches. 1 wkt at 45.00. HS: 108 BB: 1/25.

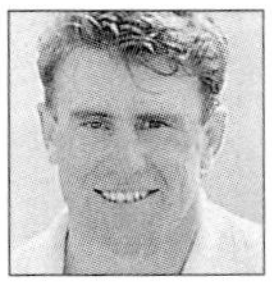

TAYLOR, Mark Anthony
B: Oct 27, 1964.
Bats: Left hand.
Bowls: Right arm.

First class debut:- 1985–86. 207 matches, 14,514 runs, 78 50s, 34 100s, av. 42.31, 292 catches. 2 wkts at 34.00. HS: 219 BB: 1/4.
Test debut:- 1988–89. 81 matches, 5799 runs, 33 50s, 14 100s, av. 42.64, 117 catches. 1 wkt at 26.00. HS: 219 BB: 1/11.
Int. limited-overs debut:- 1989–90. 111 matches, 3496 runs at 32.67. HS: 105.

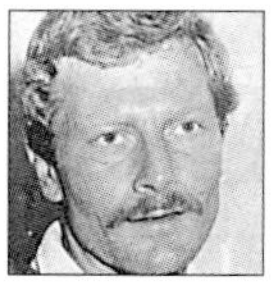

TAYLOR, Peter Laurence
B: Aug 22, 1956.
Bats: Right hand.
Bowls: Right arm.

First class debut:- 1985–86. 63 matches, 1919 runs, 10 50s, 1 100s, av. 30.95, 45 catches. 129 wkts at 37.36, 3 5-wkts. HS: 105* BB: 6/78.
Test debut:- 1986–87. 13 matches, 431 runs, 2 50s, av. 26.94, 10 catches. 27 wkts at 39.56, 1 5-wkts. HS: 87 BB: 6/78.
Int. limited-overs debut:- 1986–87. 83 matches, 437 runs at 19.86. 97 wkts at 28.25. HS: 54* BB: 4/38.

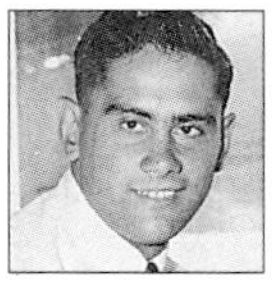

THOMAS, Grahame
B: Mar 21, 1938.
Bats: Right hand.

First class debut:- 1957–58. 100 matches, 5726 runs, 23 50s, 17 100s, av. 40.32, 92 catches, 2 stumpings. HS: 229.
Test debut:- 1964–65. 8 matches, 325 runs, 3 50s, av. 29.55, 3 catches. HS: 61.

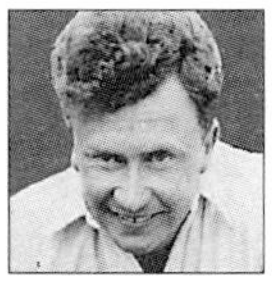

THOMS, George Ronald
B: Mar 22, 1927.
Bats: Right hand.

First class debut:- 1946–47. 19 matches, 1137 runs, 5 50s, 3 100s, av. 35.53, 10 catches. 1 wkt at 14.00. HS: 150 BB: 1/8.
Test debut:- 1951–52. 1 match, 44 runs, av. 22.00. HS: 28.

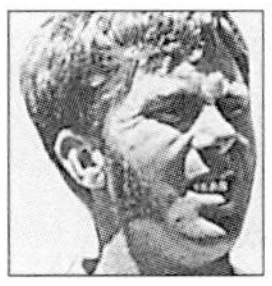

THOMSON, Alan Lloyd
B: Dec 2, 1945.
Bats: Right hand.
Bowls: Right arm.

First class debut:- 1968–69. 44 matches, 260 runs, av. 8.12, 12 catches. 184 wkts at 26.72, 12 5-wkts, 3 10-wkts. HS: 34* BB: 8/87.
Test debut:- 1970–71. 4 matches, 22 runs, av. 22.00. 12 wkts at 54.50. HS: 12* BB: 3/79.
Int. limited-overs debut:- 1970–71. 1 match, 1 wkt at 22.00. HS: DNB. BB: 1/22.

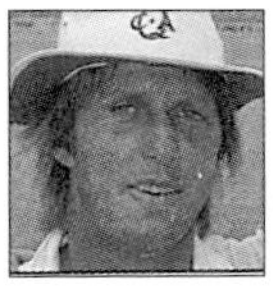

THOMSON, Jeffrey Robert
B: Aug 16, 1950.
Bats: Right hand.
Bowls: Right arm.

First class debut:- 1972–73. 187 matches, 2065 runs, 2 50s, av. 13.58, 63 catches. 675 wkts at 26.46, 28 5-wkts, 3 10-wkts. HS: 61 BB: 7/27.
Test debut:- 1972–73. 51 matches, 679 runs, av. 12.81, 20 catches. 200 wkts at 28.01, 8 5-wkts. HS: 49 BB: 6/46.
Int. limited-overs debut:- 1974–75. 50 matches, 181 runs at 7.54. 55 wkts at 35.31. HS: 21 BB: 4/67.

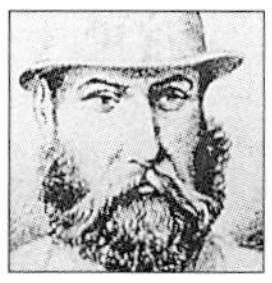

THOMSON, Nathaniel Frampton Davis
B: April 21, 1839.
D: Sep 2, 1896.
Bats: Right hand - Wicketkeeper.
Bowls: Right arm.

First class debut:- 1857–58. 27 matches, 705 runs, 3 50s, av. 14.10, 23 catches, 7 stumpings. 23 wkts at 22.26. HS: 73 BB: 3/13.
Test debut:- 1876–77. 2 matches, 67 runs, av. 16.75, 3 catches. 1 wkt at 31.00. HS: 41 BB: 1/14.

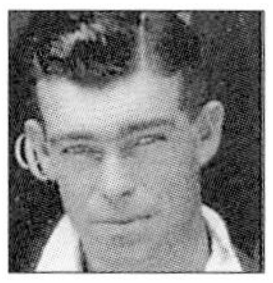

THURLOW, Hugh Mortley
B: Jan 10, 1903.
D: Dec 3, 1975.
Bats: Right hand.

First class debut:- 1928–29. 31 matches, 202 runs, av. 5.31, 10 catches. 80 wkts at 42.88, 5 5-wkts. HS: 23 BB: 6/59.
Test debut:- 1931–32. 1 match, 0 runs, av. 0.00. 0 wkts at –. HS: 0 BB: 0/33.

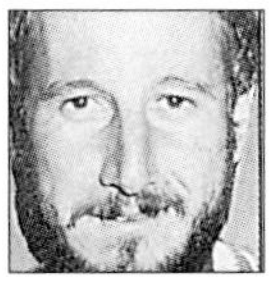

TOOHEY, Peter Michael
B: April 20, 1954.
Bats: Right hand.

First class debut:- 1974–75. 74 matches, 5735 runs, 31 50s, 12 100s, av. 37.98, 67 catches. HS: 158.
Test debut:- 1977–78. 15 matches, 893 runs, 7 50s, 1 100s, av. 31.89, 9 catches. HS: 122.
Int. limited-overs debut:- 1977–78. 5 matches, 105 runs at 52.50. HS: 54*

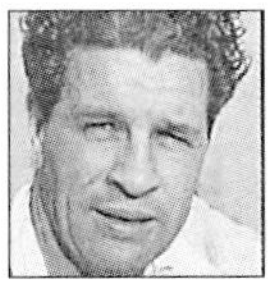

TOSHACK, Ernest Raymond Herbert
B: Dec 15, 1914.
Bats: Right hand.
Bowls: Left arm.

First class debut:- 1945–46. 48 matches, 185 runs, av. 5.78, 10 catches. 195 wkts at 20.37, 12 5-wkts, 1 10-wkts. HS: 20* BB: 7/81.
Test debut:- 1945–46. 12 matches, 73 runs, av. 14.60, 4 catches. 47 wkts at 21.04, 4 5-wkts, 1 10-wkts. HS: 20* BB: 6/29.

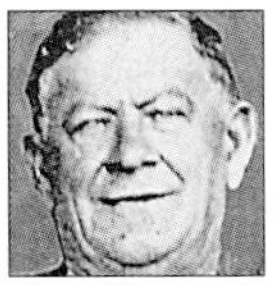

TRAVERS, Joseph Patrick Francis
B: Jan 10, 1871.
D: Sep 15, 1942.
Bats: Left hand.

First class debut:- 1895–96. 37 matches, 760 runs, 2 50s, av. 16.52, 25 catches. 117 wkts at 31.39, 6 5-wkts, 1 10-wkts. HS: 77 BB: 9/30.
Test debut:- 1901–02. 1 match, 10 runs, av. 5.00, 1 catch. 1 wkt at 14.00. HS: 9 BB: 1/14.

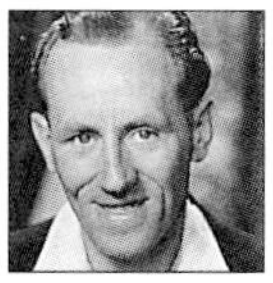

TRIBE, George Edward
B: Oct 4, 1920.
Bats: Left hand.
Bowls: Left arm.

First class debut:- 1945–46. 308 matches, 10,177 runs, 48 50s, 7 100s, av. 27.34, 243 catches. 1378 wkts at 20.55, 93 5-wkts, 23 10-wkts. HS: 136* BB: 9/43.
Test debut:- 1946–47. 3 matches, 35 runs, av. 17.50. 2 wkts at 165.00. HS: 25* BB: 2/48.

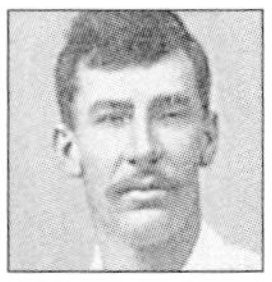

TROTT, Albert Edwin
B: Feb 6, 1873.
D: July 30, 1914.
Bats: Right hand.
Bowls: Right arm.

First class debut:- 1892–93. 375 matches, 10,696 runs, 44 50s, 8 100s, av. 19.48, 449 catches. 1674 wkts at 21.09, 132 5-wkts, 41 10-wkts. HS: 164 BB: 10/42.
Test debut:- 1894–95. 5 matches, 228 runs, av. 38.00, 4 catches. 26 wkts at 15.00, 2 5-wkts. HS: 85* BB: 8/43.

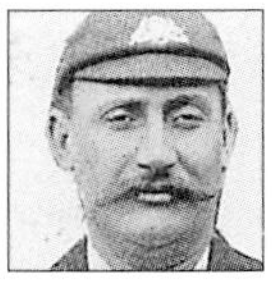

TROTT, George Henry Stevens
B: Aug 5, 1866.
D: Nov 10, 1917.
Bats: Right hand.
Bowls: Right arm.

First class debut:- 1885–86. 222 matches, 8797 runs, 40 50s, 9 100s, av. 23.52, 183 catches. 386 wkts at 25.12, 17 5-wkts, 2 10-wkts. HS: 186 BB: 8/63.
Test debut:- 1888. 24 matches, 921 runs, 4 50s, 1 100s, av. 21.93, 21 catches. 29 wkts at 35.14. HS: 143 BB: 4/71.

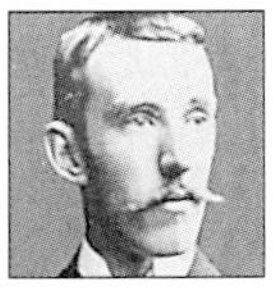

TRUMBLE, Hugh
B: May 12, 1867.
D: Aug 14, 1938.
Bats: Right hand.
Bowls: Right arm.

First class debut:- 1887–88. 213 matches, 5395 runs, 20 50s, 3 100s, av. 19.47, 329 catches. 929 wkts at 18.46, 69 5-wkts, 25 10-wkts. HS: 107 BB: 9/39.
Test debut:- 1890. 32 matches, 851 runs, 4 50s, av. 19.79, 45 catches. 141 wkts at 21.79, 9 5-wkts, 3 10-wkts. HS: 70 BB: 8/65.

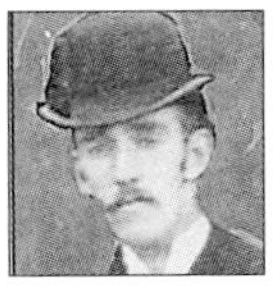

TRUMBLE, John William
B: Sep 16, 1863.
D: Aug 17, 1944.
Bats: Right hand.
Bowls: Right arm.

First class debut:- 1883–84. 63 matches, 1761 runs, 7 50s, av. 18.93, 33 catches. 109 wkts at 24.10, 5 5-wkts, 1 10-wkts. HS: 87 BB: 6/33.
Test debut:- 1884–85. 7 matches, 243 runs, 1 50s, av. 20.25, 3 catches. 10 wkts at 22.20. HS: 59 BB: 3/29.

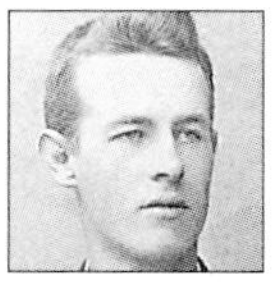

TRUMPER, Victor Thomas
B: Nov 2, 1877.
D: June 28, 1915.
Bats: Right hand.
Bowls: Right arm.

First class debut:- 1898–89. 255 matches, 16,939 runs, 87 50s, 42 100s, av. 44.57, 171 catches. 64 wkts at 31.73, 2 5-wkts. HS: 300* BB: 5/19.
Test debut:- 1899. 48 matches, 3163 runs, 13 50s, 8 100s, av. 39.05, 31 catches. 8 wkts at 39.63. HS: 214* BB: 3/60.

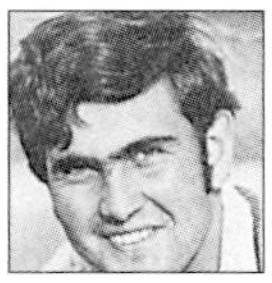

TURNER, Alan
B: July 23, 1950.
Bats: Left hand.

First class debut:- 1968–69. 105 matches, 5744 runs, 31 50s, 7 100s, av. 30.88, 80 catches. 1 wkt at 10.00. HS: 156 BB: 1/6.
Test debut:- 1975. 14 matches, 768 runs, 3 50s, 1 100s, av. 29.54, 15 catches. HS: 136.
Int. limited-overs debut:- 1975. 6 matches, 247 runs at 41.17. HS: 101.

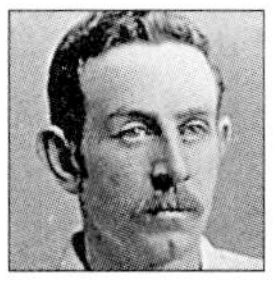

TURNER, Charles Thomas Biass
B: Nov 16, 1862.
D: Jan 1, 1944.
Bats: Right hand.
Bowls: Right arm.

First class debut:- 1882–83. 155 matches, 3856 runs, 11 50s, 2 100s, av. 15.54, 85 catches. 993 wkts at 14.24, 102 5-wkts, 35 10-wkts. HS: 103 BB: 9/15.
Test debut:- 1886–87. 17 matches, 323 runs, av. 11.54, 8 catches. 101 wkts at 16.53, 11 5-wkts, 2 10-wkts. HS: 29 BB: 7/43.

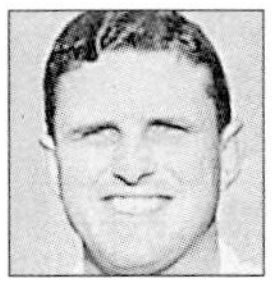

VEIVERS, Thomas Robert
B: April 6, 1937.
Bats: Left hand.
Bowls: Right arm.

First class debut:- 1958–59. 106 matches, 5100 runs, 37 50s, 4 100s, av. 36.95, 52 catches. 191 wkts at 38.70, 3 5-wkts. HS: 137 BB: 5/63.
Test debut:- 1963–64. 21 matches, 813 runs, 7 50s, av. 31.27, 7 catches. 33 wkts at 41.67. HS: 88 BB: 4/68.

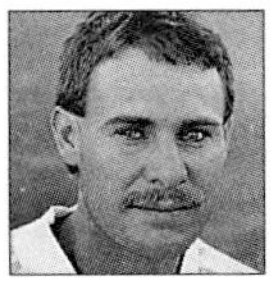

VELETTA, Michael Robert John
B: Oct 30, 1963.
Bats: Right hand.

First class debut:- 1983–84. 151 matches, 8802 runs, 48 50s, 20 100s, av. 39.12, 194 catches, 3 stumpings. HS: 262.

Test debut:- 1987–88. 8 matches, 207 runs, av. 18.82, 12 catches. HS: 39.
Int. limited-overs debut:- 1986–87. 20 matches, 484 runs, 2 50s, av. 32.27, 8 catches. HS: 68*.

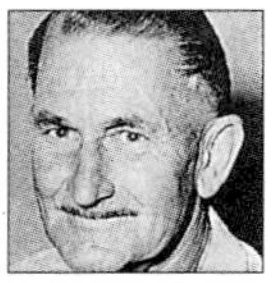

WAITE, Mervyn George
B: Jan 7, 1911. D: Dec 16, 1985.
Bats: Right hand.
Bowls: Right arm.

First class debut:- 1930–31. 103 matches, 3888 runs, 23 50s, 1 100s, av. 27.77, 66 catches. 192 wkts at 31.61, 5 5-wkts. HS: 137 BB: 7/101.
Test debut:- 1938. 2 matches, 11 runs, av. 3.67, 1 catch. 1 wkt at 190.00. HS: 8 BB: 1/150.

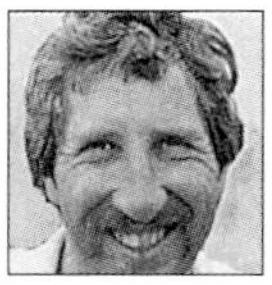

WALKER, Maxwell Henry Norman
B: Sep 12, 1948.
Bats: Right hand.
Bowls: Right arm.

First class debut:- 1968–69. 135 matches, 2014 runs, 3 50s, av. 15.49, 49 catches. 499 wkts at 26.47, 21 5-wkts. HS: 78* BB: 8/143.
Test debut:- 1972–73. 34 matches, 586 runs, 1 50s, av. 19.53 12 catches. 138 wkts at 27.48, 6 5-wkts. HS: 78* BB: 8/143.
Int. limited-overs debut:- 1973–74. 17 matches, 79 runs at 9.88. 20 wkts at 27.30. HS: 20 BB: 4/19.

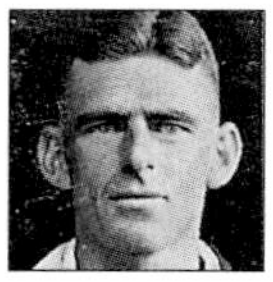

WALL, Thomas Welbourn
B: May 13, 1904.
D: Mar 26, 1981.
Bats: Right hand.
Bowls: Right arm.

First class debut:- 1924–25. 108 matches, 1071 runs, 1 50s, av. 10.50, 54 catches. 330 wkts at 29.93, 10 5-wkts, 2 10-wkts. HS: 53* BB: 10/36.
Test debut:- 1928–29. 18 matches, 121 runs, av. 6.37, 11 catches. 56 wkts at 35.89, 3 5-wkts. HS: 20 BB: 5/14.

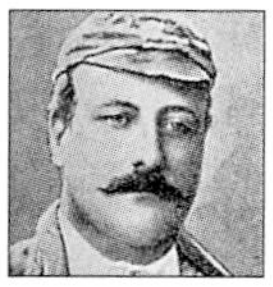

WALTERS, Francis Henry
B: Feb 9, 1860.
D: June 1, 1922.
Bats: Right hand.
Bowls: Right arm.

First class debut:- 1880–81. 56 matches, 1755 runs, 5 50s, 4 100s, av. 20.17, 31 catches. 1 wkt at 81.00. HS: 150 BB: 1/17.
Test debut:- 1884–85. 1 match, av. 6.00, 2 catches. HS: 7.

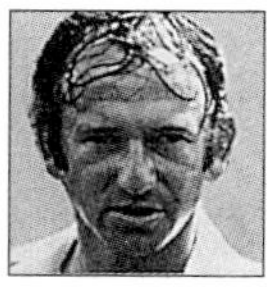

WALTERS, Kevin Douglas
B: Dec 21, 1945.
Bats: Right hand.
Bowls: Right arm.

First class debut:- 1962–63. 258 matches, 16,180 runs, 81 50s, 45 100s, av. 43.84, 149 catches. 190 wkts at 35.69, 6 5-wkts. HS: 253 BB: 7/63.
Test debut:- 1965–66. 75 matches, 5357 runs, 33 50s, 15 100s, av. 48.26, 43 catches. 49 wkts at 29.08, 1 5-wkts. HS: 250 BB: 5/66.
Int. limited-overs debut:- 1970–71. 28 matches, 513 runs at 28.50. 4 wkts at 68.25. HS: 59 BB: 2/24.

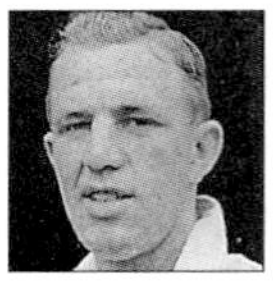

WARD, Francis Anthony
B: Feb 23, 1909.
D: May 25, 1974.
Bats: Right hand.
Bowls: Right arm.

First class debut:- 1935–36. 66 matches, 871 runs, 1 50s, av. 13.82, 42 catches. 320 wkts at 24.68, 24 5-wkts, 5 10-wkts. HS: 62 BB: 7/51.
Test debut:- 1936–37. 4 matches, 36 runs, av. 6.00, 1 catch, 11 wkts at 52.18, 1 5-wkts. HS: 18 BB: 6/102.

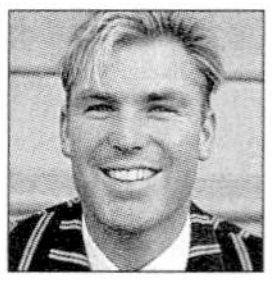

WARNE, Shane Keith
B: Sep 13, 1969.
Bats: Right hand.
Bowls: Right arm.

First class debut:- 1990–91. 97 matches, 1581 runs, 3 50s, av. 15.20, 62 catches. 414 wkts at 25.02, 17 5-wkts, 3 10-wkts. HS: 74* BB: 8/71.
Test debut:- 1991–92. 52 matches, 839 runs, 1 50s, av. 13.75, 39 catches. 240 wkts at 23.94, 10 5-wkts, 3 10-wkts. HS: 74* BB: 8/71.
Int. limited-overs debut:- 1992–93. 73 matches, 355 runs at 12.92. 128 wkts at 21.33. HS: 55 BB: 5/33.

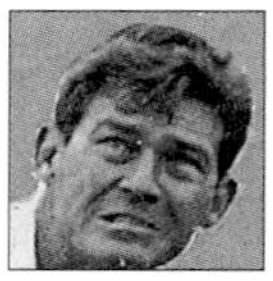

WATKINS, John Russell
B: April 16, 1943.
Bats: Right hand.
Bowls: Right arm.

First class debut:- 1971–72. 10 matches, 70 runs, av. 10.00, 10 catches. 20 wkts at 36.30. HS: 36 BB: 4/72.
Test debut:- 1972–73. 1 match, 39 runs, av. 39.00, 1 catch. 0 wkts at –. HS: 36. BB: 0/21.

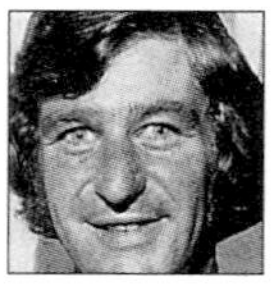

WATSON, Graeme Donald
B: Mar 8, 1945.
Bats: Right hand.
Bowls: Right arm.

First class debut:- 1964–65. 107 matches, 4764 runs, 25 50s, 7 100s, av. 32.68, 73 catches. 186 wkts at 25.31, 8 5-wkts. HS: 176 BB: 6/61.
Test debut:- 1966–67. 5 matches, 97 runs, 1 50s, av. 10.78, 1 catch. 6 wkts at 42.33. HS: 50 BB: 2/67.
Int. limited-overs debut:- 1972. 2 matches, 11 runs, av. 11.00. 2 wkts at 14.00. HS: 11* BB: 2/28.

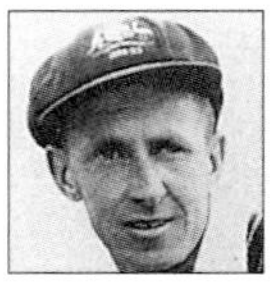

WATSON, William James
B: Jan 31, 1931.
Bats: Right hand.

First class debut:- 1953–54. 41 matches, 1958 runs, 5 50s, 6 100s, av. 32.09, 36 catches. HS: 206.
Test debut:- 1954–55. 4 matches, 106 runs, av. 17.67, 2 catches. HS: 30.

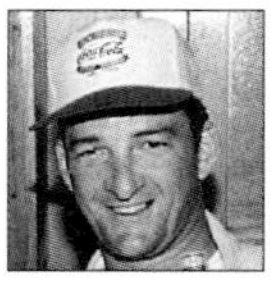

WAUGH, Mark Edward
B: June 2, 1965.
Bats: Right hand.
Bowls: Right arm.

First class debut:- 1985–86. 249 matches, 19,100 runs, 92 50s, 62 100s, av. 54.57, 293 catches. 180 wkts at 37.89, 3 5-wkts. HS: 229* BB: 6/68.
Test debut:- 1990–91. 63 matches, 4255 runs, 26 50s, 11 100s, av. 43.42, 81 catches. 40 wkts at 36.83, 1 5-wkts. HS: 140 BB: 5/40.
Int. limited-overs debut:- 1988–89. 132 matches, 4411 runs at 38.03. 70 wkts at 29.71. HS: 130 BB: 5/24.

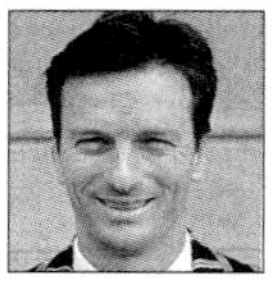

WAUGH, Stephen Rodger
B: June 2, 1965.
Bats: Right hand.
Bowls: Right arm.

First class debut:- 1984–85. 224 matches, 14,644 runs, 70 50s, 41 100s, av. 51.75, 193 catches. 233 wkts at 31.36, 5 5-wkts. HS: 216* BB: 6/51.
Test debut:- 1985–86. 89 matches, 5570 runs, 33 50s, 12 100s, av. 50.64, 66 catches. 80 wkts at 35.23, 3 5-wkts. HS: 200 BB: 5/28.
Int. limited-overs debut:- 1985–86. 218 matches, 5032 runs at 32.46. 172 wkts at 33.94. HS: 102* BB: 4/33.

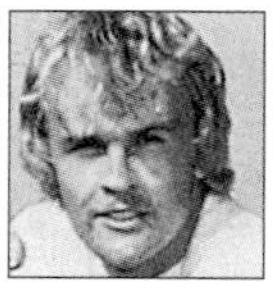

WELLHAM, Dirk McDonald
B: Mar 13, 1959.
Bats: Right hand.

First class debut:- 1980–81. 148 matches, 8662 runs, 53 50s, 16 100s, av. 42.25, 68 catches. 1 wkt at 25.00. HS: 167 BB: 1/11.
Test debut:- 1981. 6 matches, 257 runs, 1 100s, av. 13.36, 5 catches. HS: 103.
Int. limited-overs debut:- 1981–82. 17 matches, 379 runs, 1 50s, av. 25.27, 8 catches. HS: 97.

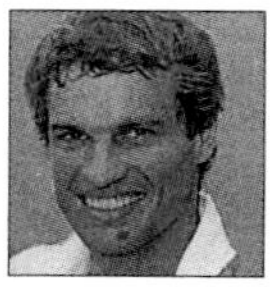

WESSELS, Kepler Christoffel
B: Sep 14, 1957.
Bats: Left hand.

First class debut:- 1979–80. 291 matches, 22,757 runs, 120 50s, 60 100s, av. 50.13, 43 catches. 12 wkts at 46.33. HS: 254 BB: 2/25.
Test debut:- 1982–83. 40 matches, 2788 runs, 15 50s, 6 100s, av. 41.00, 30 catches. HS: 179.
Int. limited-overs debut:- 1982–83. 109 matches, 3367 runs at 34.36. 18 wkts at 37.00. HS: 107 BB: 2/16.

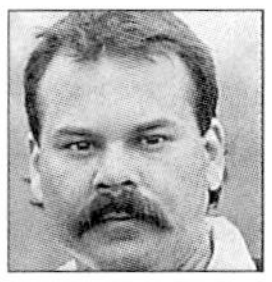

WHATMORE, Davenell Frederick
B: Mar 16, 1954.
Bats: Right hand.

First class debut:- 1975–76. 108 matches, 6116 runs, 35 50s, 10 100s, av. 33.97, 147 catches. 4 wkts at 27.25. HS: 170 BB: 1/0.
Test debut:- 1978–79. 7 matches, 293 runs, 2 50s, av. 22.54, 13 catches. HS: 77.
Int. limited-overs debut:- 1979–80. 1 match, 2 runs at 2.00. HS: 2.

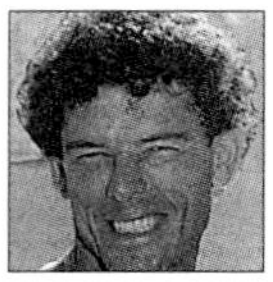

WHITNEY, Michael Roy
B: Feb 24, 1959.
Bats: Right hand.
Bowls: Left arm.

First class debut:- 1980–81. 118 matches, 415 runs, av. 5.61, 50 catches. 412 wkts at 26.75, 19 5-wkts, 1 10-wkts. HS: 28* BB: 7/27.
Test debut:- 1981. 12 matches, 68 runs, av. 6.18, 2 catches. 39 wkts at 33.97, 2 5-wkts, 1 10-wkts. HS: 13 BB: 7/27.
Int. limited-overs debut:- 1982–83. 38 matches, 40 runs, av. 6.67, 11 catches. 46 wkts at 27.15. HS: 9* BB: 4/34.

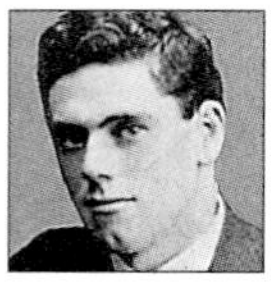

WHITTY, William James
B: Aug 15, 1886.
D: Jan 30, 1974.
Bats: Right hand.
Bowls: Left arm.

First class debut:- 1907–08. 119 matches, 1464 runs, 1 50s, av. 11.52, 35 catches. 491 wkts at 23.39, 26 5-wkts, 4 10-wkts. HS: 81 BB: 8/27.
Test debut:- 1909. 14 matches, 161 runs, av. 13.42, 4 catches. 65 wkts at 21.12, 3 5-wkts. HS: 39* BB: 6/17.

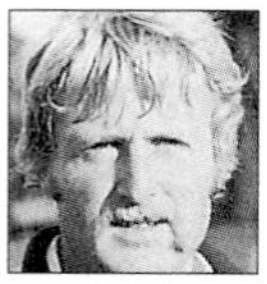

WIENER, Julien Mark
B: May 1, 1955.
Bats: Right hand.
Bowls: Right arm.

First class debut:- 1977–78. 66 matches, 3609 runs, 13 50s, 7 100s, av. 30.32, 49 catches. 17 wkts at 68.47. HS: 221* BB: 2/19.
Test debut:- 1979–80. 6 matches, 281 runs, 2 50s, av. 25.55, 4 catches. HS: 93.
Int. limited-overs debut:- 1979–80. 7 matches, 140 runs at 20.00. HS: 50.

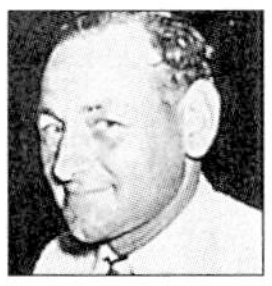

WILSON, John William
B: Aug 20, 1922.
D: Oct 13, 1985.
Bats: Right hand.
Bowls: left arm.

First class debut:- 1949–50. 78 matches, 287 runs, av. 5.74, 17 catches. 230 wkts at 30.51, 9 5-wkts, 1 10-wkts. HS: 19* BB: 7/11.
Test debut:- 1956–57. 1 match, 1 wkt at 64.00. HS: DNB. BB: 1/25.

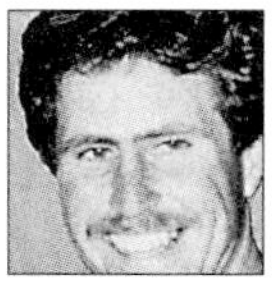

WOOD, Graeme Malcolm
B: Nov 6, 1956.
Bats: Left hand.
Bowls: Right arm.

First class debut:- 1976–77. 227 matches, 13,353 runs, 61 50s, 35 100s, av. 39.97, 155 catches. 6 wkts at 26.00. HS: 186* BB: 3/18.
Test debut:- 1977–78. 59 matches, 3374 runs, 13 50s, 9 100s, av. 31.83, 42 catches. HS: 172.
Int. limited-overs debut:- 1977–78. 83 matches, 2219 runs at 33.62. HS: 114*

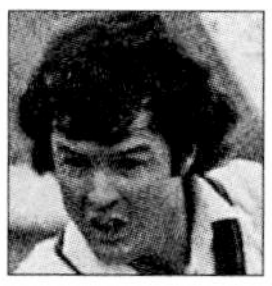

WOODCOCK, Ashley John
B: Feb 27, 1947.
Bats: Right hand.

First class debut:- 1967–68. 85 matches, 4550 runs, 31 50s, 5 100s, av. 30.95, 72 catches. HS: 141.
Test debut:- 1973–74. 1 match, 27 runs, av. 27.00, 1 catch. HS: 27.
Int. limited-overs debut:- 1973–74. 1 match, 53 runs at 53.00. HS: 53.

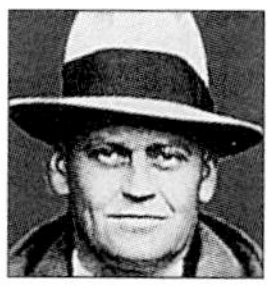

WOODFULL, William Maldon
B: Aug 22, 1897.
D: Aug 11, 1965.
Bats: Right hand.

First class debut:- 1921–22. 173 matches, 13,392 runs, 58 50s, 49 100s, av. 65.00, 77 catches. 1 wkt at 24.00. HS: 284 BB: 1/12.
Test debut:- 1926. 35 matches, 2300 runs, 13 50s, 7 100s, av. 46.00, 7 catches. HS: 161.

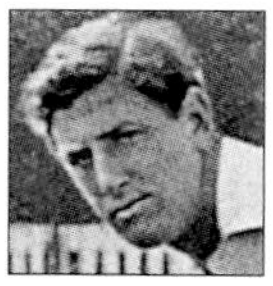

WOODS, Samuel Moses James
B: Aug 13, 1867.
D: April 30, 1931.
Bats: Right hand.
Bowls: Right arm.

First class debut:- 1886. 401 matches, 15345 runs, 62 50s, 19 100s, av. 23.42, 279 catches. 1040 wkts at 20.82, 77 5-wkts, 21 10-wkts. HS: 215 BB: 10/69.

Test debut:- 1888. 6 matches, 154 runs, 1 50s, av. 15.40, 5 catches. 10 wkts at 25.00. HS: 53 BB: 3/28.

WOOLLEY, Roger Douglas
B: Sep 16, 1954.
Bats: Right hand - Wicketkeeper.

First class debut:- 1977-78. 85 matches, 4781 runs, 30 50s, 7 100s, av. 40.17, 144 catches, 16 stumpings. HS: 144.
Test debut:- 1982-83. 2 matches, 21 runs, av. 10.50, 7 catches. HS: 13.
Int. limited-overs debut:- 1982-83. 4 matches, 31 runs, av. 31.00, 1 catch, 1 stumping. HS: 16.

WORRALL, John
B: June 21, 1861.
D: Nov 17, 1937.
Bats: Right hand.
Bowls: Right arm.

First class debut:- 1883-84. 142 matches, 4660 runs, 16 50s, 7 100s, av. 20.99, 101 catches. 105 wkts at 23.10, 4 5-wkts. HS: 128 BB: 5/20.
Test debut:- 1884-85. 11 matches, 478 runs, 5 50s, av. 25.16, 13 catches. 1 wkt at 127.00. HS: 76 BB: 1/97.

WRIGHT, Kevin John
B: Dec 27, 1953.
Bats: Right hand - Wicketkeeper.

First class debut:- 1974-75. 85 matches, 2551 runs, 10 50s, 2 100s, av. 26.85, 267 catches, 26 stumpings. HS: 105.
Test debut:- 1978-79. 10 matches, 219 runs, 1 50s, av. 16.85, 31 catches, 4 stumpings. HS: 55*.
Int. limited-overs debut:- 1978-79. 5 matches, 29 runs, av. 14.50, 8 catches. HS: 23.

YALLOP, Graham Neil
B: Oct 7, 1952.
Bats: Left hand.
Bowls: Left arm.

First class debut:- 1972-73. 164 matches, 11,615 runs, 56 50s, 30 100s, av. 45.90, 120 catches, 1 stumping. 14 wkts at 62.57. HS: 268 BB: 4/63.
Test debut:- 1975-76. 39 matches, 2756 runs, 9 50s, 8 100s, av. 41.13, 23 catches. 1 wkt at 116.00. HS: 268 BB: 1/21.
Int. limited-overs debut:- 1977-78. 30 matches, 823 runs, 7 50s, av. 39.19, 5 catches. 3 wkts at 39.67. HS: 66* BB: 2/28.

YARDLEY, Bruce
B: Sep 5, 1947.
Bats: Right hand.
Bowls: Right arm.

First class debut:- 1966-67. 104 matches, 2737 runs, 8 50s, av. 20.57, 63 catches. 342 wkts at 28.14, 20 5-wkts, 3 10-wkts. HS: 97* BB: 7/44.
Test debut:- 1977-78. 33 matches, 978 runs, 4 50s, av. 19.56, 31 catches. 126 wkts at 31.63, 6 5-wkts, 1 10-wkts. HS: 74 BB: 7/98.
Int. limited-overs debut:- 1977-78. 7 matches, 58 runs at 14.50, 1 catch. 7 wkts at 18.57. HS: 28 BB: 3/28.

ZOEHRER, Timothy Joseph
B: Sep 25, 1961.
Bats: Right hand - Wicketkeeper.
Bowls: Right arm.

First class debut:- 1980-81. 147 matches, 5348 runs, 27 50s, 7 100s, av. 29.55, 424 catches, 38 stumpings. 38 wkts at 46.53, 1 5-wkts. HS: 168 BB: 5/58.
Test debut:- 1985-86. 10 matches, 246 runs, 1 50s, av. 20.50, 18 catches, 1 stumping. HS: 52*.
Int. limited-overs debut:- 1985-86. 22 matches, 130 runs at 10.83. HS: 50.

Statistics by Ross Dundas. Current to 1 May 1997 (end of tour to South Africa).

Statistics include all Test matches and one day internationals played by Australian Test players – including matches played for England and South Africa. First class statistics include matches played by Australian Test players for English or South African teams.

KEY
HS: highest score.
BB: best bowling.
* : not out.
+ : retired hurt.
DNB: did not bat.

AUSTRALIAN TEST CAPTAINS

	No.	ENG	SAF	WI	NZ	IND	PAK	SR	Won	Lost	Drawn	Tied
DW GREGORY	3	3	–		–		–		2	1	–	–
WL MURDOCH	16	16	–		–		–		5	7	4	–
TP HORAN	2	2	–		–		–		–	2	–	–
HH MASSIE	1	1	–		–		–		1	–	–	–
JM BLACKHAM	8	8	–		–		–		3	3	2	–
HJH SCOTT	3	3	–		–		–		–	3	–	–
PS MCDONNELL	6	6	–		–		–		1	5	–	–
G GIFFEN	4	4	–		–		–		2	2	–	–
GHS TROTT	8	8	–		–		–		5	3	–	–
J DARLING	21	18	3		–		–		7	4	10	–
H TRUMBLE	2	2	–		–		–		2	–	–	–
MA NOBLE	15	15	–		–		–		8	5	2	–
C HILL	10	5	5		–		–		5	5	–	–
ES GREGORY	6	3	3		–		–		2	1	3	–
WW ARMSTRONG	10	10	–		–		–		8	–	2	–
HL COLLINS	11	8	3		–		–		5	2	4	–
W BARDSLEY	2	2	–		–		–		–	–	2	–
J RYDER	5	5	–		–		–		1	4	–	–
WM WOODFULL	25	15	5		–		–		14	7	4	–
VY RICHARDSON	5	–	5		–		–		4	–	1	–
DG BRADMAN	24	19	–	–	–	5	–	–	15	3	6	–
WA BROWN	1	–	–	–	1	–	–	–	1	–	–	–
AL HASSETT	24	10	10	4	–	–	–	–	14	4	6	–
AR MORRIS	2	1	–	1	–	–	–	–	–	2	–	–
IW JOHNSON	17	9	–	5	–	2	1	–	7	5	5	–
RR LINDWALL	1	–	–	–	1	–	–	–	1	–	–	–
ID CRAIG	5	–	5	–	–	–	–	–	3	2	–	–
R BENAUD	28	14	1	5	–	5	3	–	12	4	11	1
RN HARVEY	1	1	–	–	–	–	–	–	1	–	–	–
RB SIMPSON	39	8	9	10	–	10	2	–	12	12	15	–
BC BOOTH	2	2	–	–	–	–	–	–	–	1	1	–
WM LAWRY	26	10	4	5	–	7	–	–	9	8	9	–
BN JARMAN	1	1	–	–	–	–	–	–	–	–	1	–
IM CHAPPELL	30	16	–	5	6	–	3	–	15	5	10	–
GS CHAPPELL	48	15	–	12	8	3	9	1	21	13	14	–
GN YALLOP	7	6	–	–	–	–	1	–	1	6	–	–
KJ HUGHES	28	6	–	7	–	6	9	–	4	13	11	–
AR BORDER	93	29	6	18	17	11	6	6	32	22	38	1
MA TAYLOR	27	5	3	9	–	1	6	3	15	8	4	–

Photo Credit Index

KEY,
"t=top, m=middle, b=bottom, l=left, r=right.",
Detailed acknolwedgements on page 6.,
ACB,Australian Cricket Board pictures. Most were taken by Viv Jenkins.
AGE,"The Age Picture Library, Melbourne."
DF,David Frith
EAGAR,Patrick Eagar
JP,Jack Pollard
KWI,Kevin Weldon International
NSWCA,"New South Wales Cricket Association, especially the Bill O'Reilly Collection"

MCC,"Melbourne Cricket Club - Gallery of Sport, MCC Library."
OXLEY,"Oxley Library, Brisbane"
MCC,"Private collections, including John Chizmesta. John Dew, Garrie Hutchinson, John Ross, "
MULVANEY,John Mulvaney
NICHOLSON,Peter Nicholson
QCA,Queensland Cricket Association
RB,Richie Benaud
SLV,State Library of Victoria
SPOONER,John Spooner
VCA,Victorian Cricket Association

General Index

Page numbers in italics refer to illustrations. Page numbers in bold refer to major entries

Bibliography

Allan's Australian Cricket Annual, 1987-88 to 1995-96 - ed. & pub. Allan Miller, WA.

Arlott, John - *The Ashes 1972*, London, Pelham Books, 1972.

Armstrong, Geoff - *100 Years of Sheffield Shield Cricket*, Sydney, Ironbark Press, 1992.

Australian Cricket Almanac - ed. Phillip Derriman, pub. by ABC 1990 - 1994, The Age 1995, Ironbark 1996.

Australian Cricket Yearbook - ed. Eric Beecher, Phil Tressider 1970 - 1977 (pub. ACP Magazines).

Barnes, Sidney - *Eyes on the Ashes*, London, William Kimber, 1953.

- *It Isn't Cricket*, Sydney, Collins, 1953.

Beecher, Eric - *The cricket revolution: the inside story of the great cricket crisis of 1977-78*, Melbourne, Newspress, 1978.

Benaud, Richie - *A Tale of Two Tests with some thoughts on Captaincy*, London, Hodder & Stoughton, 1962.

- *Lights Camera Action: an illustrated history of the world series*, Melbourne, Hamlyn, 1990.

- *The New Champions, Australia in the West Indies 1965*, London, Hodder & Stoughton, 1965.

- *Spin me a Spinner*, Melbourne, Hodder & Stoughton, 1963

Boon, David - *Under the Southern Cross*, Sydney, HarperCollins, 1996.

Border, Allan - *Allan Border an autobiography*, Melbourne, Mandarin, 1990

- *Allan Border: beyond ten thousand, my life story*, Perth, Swan Publishing, 1993.

Bradman, Sir Donald - *The Bradman Albums, selections from Sir Donald Bradman's official collection*, two volumes, Sydney, Rigby, 1987.

- *Farewell to Cricket*, Sydney, Editions Tom Thompson, 1994.

Brown, Lionel H - *Victor Trumper and the 1902 Australians*, London, Secker & Warburg, 1981.

Boycott, Geoff - *In the Fast Lane*, London, Sphere, 1982.

Buzo Alex & Jamie Grant (eds), *The Longest Game: a collection of the best cricket writing from Alexander to Zavros, from the Gabba to the Yabba*, Melbourne, Mandarin, 1992.

Cardus, Neville - *Cardus on Cricket*, London, Souvenir Press, 1983.

- *Play Resumed With Cardus*, London, Souvenir Press, 1979.

Cardwell, Ronald - *The AIF Cricket Team*, Sydney, the author, 1980.

Cashman, Richard - *The 'Demon' Spofforth*, Sydney, New South Wales University Press, 1990.

- *'Ave a Go, yer Mug! Australian cricket crowds from larrikin to ocker*, Sydney, William Collins, 1984.

Cashman, Richard and Warwick Franks, Jim Maxwell, Brian Stoddart, Amanda Weaver, Ray Webster (eds) - *The Oxford Companion to Australian Cricket*, Melbourne, Oxford, 1997.

Cashman, Richard, David Headon and Graeme Kinross Smith (eds) - *The Oxford Book of Australian Sporting Anecdotes*, Oxford University Press, 1993.

Cashman, Richard and Amanda Weaver - *Wicket Women: cricket and women in Australia*, Sydney, NSW University Press, 1991.

Chappell, Greg - *The 100th Summer*, Melbourne, Garry Sparke, 1977.

Chappell, Ian - *Chappelli, the cutting edge*, Perth, Swan, 1992.

Chizmeysa, John - *Cricket Classics*, Sydney, Cassell, 1981

Cricketer Annual - ed. Eric Beecher, 1974 - 1977, pub. Cricketer Magazine/Newspress.

Cricket Digest / Cricket Year - ed. Ken Piesse, 1978 - 1982, pub. Peter Isaacson.

Cricket in Australia - annual 1981 - 1986, pub. by Garry Sparke.

Christen, Richard - *Some Grounds for Appeal: Australian venues for first class cricket*, Parramatta, the author, 1994.

Clarke, John - *The Australians in England 1964*, London, Stanley Paul, 1964.

Coleman, Robert - *Seasons in the Sun, the story of the Victorian Cricket Association*, Melbourne, Hargreen, 1993.

Coward, Mike - *Cricket Beyond the Bazaar*, Sydney, Allen & Unwin, 1990.

Coward, Mike and Michael Rayner - *Caribbean odyssey: Australia and cricket in the West Indies*, Sydney, Simon & Schuster, 1991.

- *Australia vs the new South Africa: cricket contact renewed*, Sydney Simon & Schuster, 1994.

Cricket Yearbook - ed. Richie Benaud, Sydney, Hamlyn, 1984-1996.

Davidson, Alan - *Fifteen Paces*, Melbourne, Marlin/Hutchinson, 1973.

Derriman, Phillip - *80 not out: a celebration of Test cricket at the Sydney Cricket Ground*, Sydney, Playbill, 1994.

- *The grand old ground: a history of the Sydney Cricket Ground*, Sydney, Cassell, 1981.

- *True to the blue, a history of the New South Wales Cricket Association*, Sydney, Richard Smart, 1985.

Fingleton, Jack - *Brightly Fades the Don*, London, Collins, 1949.

- *Cricket Crisis*, Melbourne, Cassell, 1946.

- *Four Chukkas to Australia, the 1958-59 MCC tour of Australia*, Melbourne, Heinemann, 1959.

- *The Immortal Victor Trumper*, London, Collins, 1978.

Dunstan, Keith - *The Paddock That Grew: the story of the Melbourne Cricket Club*, 3rd ed, Sydney Hutchinson, 1988.

Fishman, Roland - *Calypso cricket: the inside story of the 1991 Windies tour*, Sydney, Margaret Gee Publishing, 1991

Forsyth, Christopher - *The Great Cricket Hijack*, Melbourne, Widescope, 1978.

Frith, David - *Archie Jackson - the Keats of cricket* (rev ed), London, Pavilion-Michael Joseph, 1987.

- *Australia versus England: A pictorial history of every Test match since 1877*, 8th rev. edn., Sydney, Richard Smart Publishing, 1993.

- (ed) *Cricket Gallery, fifty profiles from the Cricketer*, Adelaide, Rigby, 1976.

- *Pageant of Cricket*, Melbourne, Macmillan, 1987.

Giffen, George - *With Bat & Ball*, London & Melbourne, Ward Lock, 1898.

Grace, Radcliffe - *Warwick Armstrong*, Melbourne, the author, 1975.

Griffiths, Edward - *Kepler the biography*, London, Pelham Books, 1994.

Haigh, Gideon (ed) - *Australian Cricket Anecdotes*, Melbourne, Oxford University Press, 1996.

- *The Border Years*, Melbourne, Text Publishing 1994.

- *One summer, every summer: an Ashes journal*, Melbourne, Text, 1995.

- *The cricket war: the inside story of Kerry Packer's World Series Cricket*, Melbourne, Text, 1993.

Harris, Bruce - *With England in Australia: The truth about the Tests*, London, Hutchinson, 1947.

Harte, Chris - *The history of Australian cricket*, London, Andre Deutsch, 1993.

- *The history of the Sheffield Shield*, Sydney, Allen & Unwin, 1987.

Harvey, Neil - *My World of Cricket*, London, Hodder & Stoughton, 1963.

Jaggard, Ed - *Garth: The story of Graham McKenzie*, Fremantle, Fremantle Arts Centre Press, 1993.

James, CLR - *Beyond a Boundary*, London, Stanley Paul, 1980.

Jenkins, Viv - *Fields of Glory*, Sydney, HarperCollins, 1995.

Jones, Dean - *My Call*, as told to Terry Brindle, Perth, Swan, 1994.

Johnson, Ian - intro, *Great Australian Cricket Pictures*, Melbourne, Sun Books, 1975.

Landsberg, Pat - *The Kangaroo Conquers, West Indies v Australia, 1955*, London, Museum Press, 1955.

Larwood, Harold (with Kevin Perkins) - *The Larwood Story*, Ringwood, Penguin, 1982.

Lawson, Geoff - *Geoff Lawson's Diary of the Ashes*, Sydney, Angus and Robertson, 1990.

- *Henry, The Geoff Lawson Story*, Sydney, Ironbark Press, 1993.

Lillee, Dennis - *My Life in Cricket*, Sydney, Methuen, 1982.

Mackay, Ken (Slasher) - *Quest for the Ashes*, London, Pelham Books, 1966.

Mailey, Arthur - *10 for 66 and all that*, London, Shakespeare Head, 1958.

Manley, Michael - *A History of West Indies Cricket*, rev ed, London, Andre Deutsch, 1990.

Marsh, Rod - *You'll Keep*, Melbourne, Hutchinson, 1976.

Martin-Jenkins, Christopher - *World Cricketers: a biographical dictionary*, Oxford, Oxford University Press, 1996.

Mason, Ronald - *Ashes in the Mouth, The story of the body-line tour 1932-33*, Harmondsworth, Penguin, 1984.

- *Warwick Armstrong's Australians*, London, Epworth Press, 1971.

Maxwell, Jim - *The ABC Cricket Book: the first 60 years*, Sydney ABC Books, 1994.

McDermott, Craig - *Strike Bowler*, Sydney, ABC Books, 1992.

McFarline, Peter - *A Game Divided*, Melbourne, Hutchinson, 1977.

- *A Testing Time*, Melbourne, Hutchinson, 1979.

McGregor, Adrian - *Greg Chappell*, Sydney, William Collins, 1985.

McGilvray, Alan - *The Game is Not the Same*, as told to Norman Tasker, Sydney, ABC Books, 1985.

McHarg, Jack - *Stan McCabe, the man and his cricket*, Sydney, William Collins, 1987.

- *Arthur Morris, an elegant genius*, Sydney, ABC Books, 1995.

Melbourne Cricket Club - *The MCG Story*, Melbourne, MCC, 1990.

Miller, Keith - *Cricket from the Grandstand*, London, Oldbourne, 1959.

Miller, Keith & R.S. Whitington - *Cricket Typhoon*, London, Macdonald, 1955.

- *Bumper!* London, Latimer House, n.d. (c.1950)

Moyes, A.G. (Johnnie) - *Australian Batsmen from Charles Bannerman to Neil Harvey*, Sydney, Angus & Robertson, 1954.

- *Australian Bowlers from Spofforth to Lindwall*, Sydney, Angus & Robertson, 1953.

- *Australian cricket - a history*, Sydney, Angus & Robertson, 1959.

- *Benaud & Co The story of the Tests 1958-59*, Sydney Angus & Robertson, 1959.

- *The Fight for the Ashes 1954-1955*, Sydney, Angus & Robertson, 1955.

- *With the West Indies in Australia 1951-52*, Sydney, Angus & Robertson, 1952.

- *With the West Indies in Australia, 1960-1961*, Sydney, Angus & Robertson, 1961.

Moyes, A.G. and Tom Goodman - *With the M.C.C. in Australia, 1962-3*, Sydney, Angus & Robertson, 1963.

Mullins, Pat and Phillip Derriman - *Bat & Pad, Writings on Australian cricket 1804 - 1984*, Melbourne, Oxford University Press, 1984.

Mulvaney, John and Rex Harcourt, *Cricket Walkabout, The Australian Aborigines in England*, rev. ed., Melbourne, Macmillan, 1988.

Nicholson, Rod and Tom Prior - *Ashes to Ashes: touring the West Indies with the 1991 Australian cricket team*, Sydney, Collins, 1991.

O'Reilly, Bill - *The Bradman Era* (compiled by Jack Egan) Sydney, ABC/William Collins, 1983.

- *Cricket Conquest*, London, Werner Laurie, 1948.

Philpott, Peter - *A Spinner's Yarn*, Sydney, ABC Books, 1990.

Piesse, Ken - (ed) *Cartoonists at the Cricket*, Melbourne, Currey O'Neil, 1983.

- (ed) *Great Australian Book of Cricket Stories*, Melbourne, Viking O'Neil, 1988.

- (ed) *Match Drawn!* Melbourne, Lothian, 1988.

- *Warne, Sultan of Spin an unauthorised biography*, Modern Publishing, 1995.

Pollard, Jack - *Australian cricket: The Game and the Players*, Sydney, Angus & Roberston, 1988.

- *The complete illustrated history of Australian cricket*, rev. edn., Melbourne, Viking, 1995.

- *The formative years of Australian cricket 1803 - 1893*, Sydney, Angus & Robertson, 1987.

- *The Glovemen, The world's best wicket keepers*, Sydney, Kangaroo Press, 1993.

- *Six and out: stories of Australia's cricketing heroes*, enlarged ed., Melbourne, Viking O'Neill, 1990.

Ray, Mark - *Border and beyond*, Sydney, ABC, 1995.

- *Cricket: the game behind the game*, Sydney, Pan Macmillan, 1984.

Ray, Mark and Alan Lee, *The Ashes: England in Australia 1990-91*, Melbourne, ConText, 1991.

Ranjitsinhji, Prince - *With Stoddart's Team in Australia*, (repr.1898 ed.) London, Constable, 1985.

Ringwood, John - *Ray Lindwall cricket legend*, Sydney, Kangaroo Press, 1995

Robinson, Ray - *Between Wickets*, Sydney, Collins, 1948.

- *From the Boundary*, Sydney, Collins, 1950.

- *Green Sprigs: Cricket's age of youth*, Sydney, Collins, 1955.

- *On Top Down Under: Australia's cricket captains*, enlarged ed. by Gideon Haigh, Adelaide, Wakefield Press, 1997.

Ross, Alan - *Australia '63*, London, Eyre & Spottiswoode, 1963.

Scott, Jas - *Early Cricket in Sydney*, ed. Richard Cashman & Stephen Gibbs, Sydney, NSWCA, 1991.

Selth, Don - *The Prime Minister's XI: the story of the Prime Minister's XI matches Menzies to Hawke*, Canberra, the author, 1990.

Simpson, Bobby - *The Australians in England 1968*, Melbourne, Hutchinson, 1968

- *Captain's Story*, Marlin/Hutchinson, 1977

Simpson, Bob - *The reasons why, A decade of coaching, a lifetime of cricket*, Sydney, HarperCollins, 1996.

Smith Rick - *Cricket Brawl, the 1912 dispute*, Launceston, Apple Books, 1995.

Smith, Rick & Ron Williams - *W.G. down under: Grace in Australia 1873-74 and 1891-92*, Launceston, Apple Books, 1994.

Sissons, Ric - *The Players, A social history of the professional cricketer*, Sydney, Pluto Press, 1988.

Swanton, E.W. - *Follow On*, London, Fontana, 1978.

- *Swanton in Australia with MCC 1946 - 1975*, London, Fontana, 1976.

Taylor, Mark, *Taylor Made, A year in the life of Australia's cricket captain*, Sydney, Ironbark, 1995.

Walters, Doug, *The Doug Walters Story*, Sydney, Rigby, 1985.

- *One for the road*, Perth, Swan, 1988.

Wat, Charlie - *Australian First Class Cricket*, Melbourne, Five Mile Press, 1993.

Waugh, Steve - *Steve Waugh's Ashes Diary*, Sydney, Ironbark, 1993.

- *Steve Waugh's South African Tour Diary*, Sydney, Ironbark, 1994.

- *Steve Waugh's West Indian Tour Diary*, Sydney HarperCollins, 1995.

Webster, Ray (comp.) & Allen Miller (ed.) - *First class cricket in Australia, Vol.1, 1850-51 - 1941-42*, Melb. the comp., 1991.

- *First class cricket in Australia, Vol 2 1945-46 - 1976-77* Melb., the comp. 1997.

Wellings, E.M. - *Simpson's Australians, the England tour 1964*, London, Robert Hale, 1964.

Whimpress, Bernard and Nigel Hart - *Test Eleven - great Ashes battles*, Adelaide, Wakefield Press, 1994.

Whitington, Richard S - *Australian Test Cricket 1877 - 1981*, Melbourne, Five Mile Press, 1981.

- *Australians Abroad: Australia's overseas Test tours*, Melbourne, Five Mile Press, 1983.

- *Fours Galore: The West Indies and their tour of Australia 1968-69*, Melbourne, Cassell, 1969.

- *An illustrated history of Australian cricket*, rev. edn., Melbourne, Currey O'Neil, 1987.

- *Keith Miller, the Golden Nugget*, Adelaide, Rigby, 1988.

- *Simpson's Safari, South African Test series 1966-67*, Melbourne, Heinemann, 1967.

Williams, Marcus (ed) - *Double Century, 200 Years of cricket in The Times*, London, Collins, 1985.

Wilmot, R.W.E. - *Defending the Ashes 1932-33*, Melbourne, Robertson & Mullens, 1933.

Wisden Cricketers' Almanack, ed. Matthew Engel, Guildford, John Wisden & Co, 1968 - 1997.

Wisden Anthology 1864 - 1900 ed. Benny Green, London, Queen Anne Press, 1979.

The Wisden Book of Test Cricket Vol 1 1877 - 1977, Vol II 1977 - 1994 comp. and ed. Bill Frindall, London, Headline, 1995.

Woodwood, Ian - *Cricket Not War, Australian Services XI and the Victory Tests of 1945*, Sydney, SMK, 1994.

Yallop, Graham - *Lambs to the Slaughter*, Melbourne, Outback Press, 1979.